June 12–16, 2011
Athens, Greece

Association for
Computing Machinery

Advancing Computing as a Science & Profession

SIGMOD'11

Proceedings of the 2011 International Conference on
Management of Data

Sponsored by:

ACM SIGMOD

Supported by:

EMC^2, Microsoft, Oracle, Google, IBM Research, SAP, Sybase, Yahoo! Labs, AsterData, HP, Intrasoft International, Kosmix, MarkLogic, Twitter, Virtualtrip, Greenplum, & NEC

Association for
Computing Machinery

Advancing Computing as a Science & Profession

The Association for Computing Machinery
2 Penn Plaza, Suite 701
New York, New York 10121-0701

ISBN: 978-1-4503-0934-9 (Digital)

ISBN: 978-1-4503-1259-2 (Print)

Additional copies may be ordered prepaid from:

ACM Order Department
PO Box 30777
New York, NY 10087-0777, USA

Phone: 1-800-342-6626 (USA and Canada)
+1-212-626-0500 (Global)
Fax: +1-212-944-1318
E-mail: acmhelp@acm.org
Hours of Operation: 8:30 am – 4:30 pm ET

Printed in the USA

SIGMOD 2011 Chairs' Welcome

Welcome to an exciting week in the city of Athens for the *2011 ACM SIGMOD Conference*. Athens is a metropolitan and cosmopolitan city, with so many things to do and to see. It is also known as the birth place of Democracy, the city with the world-renown "Acropolis and Parthenon", with the famous Theater of Herodes Atticus and the "marble stadium" where the first modern time Olympic Games took place in 1896, home of Socrates, Plato, Pericles (Golden Age), and home of the very successful 2004 Olympic Games. And now the home of the *2011 ACM SIGMOD Conference*! Athens is both an "ancient" and a "modern" city, in which visitors can walk safely and enjoy the rich — almost 5,000 year old — history it has to offer. The city offers a lot of sightseeing, museums, shopping and nightlife.

We have a program of several social events to complement an excellent technical program. The SIGMOD banquet is in the beautiful Island Restaurant by the sea, the SIGMOD reception on Monday at the Caravel Hotel (conference hotel) Roof Garden, and the PODS 30th Anniversary Colloquium and Reception on Sunday also at the hotel. Through the generous support from our sponsors (Platinum) EMC, Microsoft, and Oracle, (Gold) Google, IBM Research, SAP, Sybase, and Yahoo! Labs, (Silver) AsterData, HP, Intrasoft International, Kosmix, MarkLogic, Twitter, and VirtualTrip, and (Other Supporters) Greenplum and NEC, along with a contribution from ACM SIGMOD, we were able to keep the conference fees to a minimum with an extraordinarily low student registration that will allow many students to participate.

The scientific program was designed by over 150 dedicated volunteers. We would like to thank our chairs for all the time, knowledge, and insight they put into creating a very exciting program. In particular, we would like to thank our tutorial co-chairs Susan Davidson (University of Pennsylvania) and Tova Milo (Tel Aviv University), the keynote and panel chair Pat Selinger (IBM Research - Almaden), the industrial program co-chairs Richard Hull (IBM Research - Thomas J. Watson Research Ctr.) and Raghu Ramakrishnan (Yahoo! Research), the demonstration chair Chris Jermaine (Rice University), the workshop chair Christian S. Jensen (Aarhus University), and the undergraduate research program chair Irini Fundulaki (Institute of Computer Science - FORTH), along with our very wise advisory committee Laura Hass (IBM Research - Almaden) and Donald Kossmann (ETH Zurich). We also thank the SIGMOD Executive Committee for their guidance with special thanks to Lisa Singh for providing tremendously valuable history and advice.

We had 375 research papers submitted. A research program committee provided detailed reviews and extensive discussion following SIGMOD's double-blind reviewing policy. The program committee was led by nine group leaders: Sihem Amer-Yahia (Yahoo! Labs), Michael Böhlen (University of Zurich), Bettina Kemme (McGill University), Sam Madden (MIT), Jignesh Patel (University of Wisconsin), Dan Suciu (University of Washington), Wang-Chiew Tan (IBM Research - Almaden and UC Santa Cruz), Nesime Tatbul (ETH Zurich), and Min Wang (HP Labs China). The group leaders ensured that every paper had a champion and received thorough discussion. We accepted a record number of research papers. Nonetheless, it is clear there were still papers that were rejected that would have been valuable contributions to SIGMOD. The group leaders did a great job in keeping the discussions positive and reviewers focused on finding reasons to accept papers, rather than reasons to reject. We hope that SIGMOD continues the trend of accepting more papers to accommodate all the great ideas being produced by the community. All research papers have been invited to participate in SIGMOD's Experimental Repeatability effort, the goal of which is to help to enable SIGMOD papers to stand as reliable, archival work for future research.

A demonstration program committee of 35 people reviewed 81 proposals for system demonstrations and accepted 32. We will again be holding a Best Demonstration Award Competition to recognize the most innovative demonstrations. We encourage everyone to participate in the voting. An industrial program committee of 13 people reviewed 36 short presentation proposals, accepting 14. In addition, the industrial program will include two invited talks by Michael Abbot (Twitter) and Don Campbell (IBM). Rounding out the full program, we have a panel on data management issues in health and medical informatics, two invited talks by James Hamilton (Amazon) and Anastasia Ailamaki (EPFL), along with six tutorials on new applications of Datalog, flash memory, copy detection, data privacy, web data management, and statistical relational models.

SIGMOD continues its commitment to undergraduate research awarding eight scholarships to undergraduate researchers who will participate in the Undergraduate Research Poster session that will be co-located with a Graduate Research Poster session. In addition, we will host the Third Annual SIGMOD Programming Contest. Student teams from degree granting institutions were invited to compete in this annual contest. This year, the task is to implement a high-throughput main-memory index that is made durable using a flash-based SSD.

On behalf of the conference organization committee, we would like to thank you all for your submissions to SIGMOD 2011, your hard work serving on SIGMOD 2011 committees, and for participating in the conference. It is your ideas, interest and input that shaped the conference and that continue to make it such a valuable venue for our community.

Timos Sellis	**Renée J. Miller**	**Anastasios Kementsietsidis**	**Yannis Velegrakis**
General Chair	*Program Chair*	*Proceedings Co-Chair*	*Proceedings Co-Chair*

Table of Contents

Session 4: Data on the We

Session 5: Data Privacy and Security

Session 6: Data Consistency and Parallel DB

Session 7: Service Oriented Computing, Data Management in the Cloud

Session 8: Spatial and Temporal Data Management

Session 9: Shortest Paths and Sequence Data

Session 10: Data Provenance, Workflow and Cleaning

Session 11: Information Extraction

Session 20: Scalable Data Analytics

Session 21: Similarity Search and Queries

Keynote Addresses

Industrial Papers

Tutorials

Demo Session 1: Demonstrations on Systems and Performance

Demo Session 2: Demonstrations on Ranking, the Web, and Social Media

Demo Session 3: Demonstrations on Data Integration and Probabilistic Databases

Demo Session 4: Demonstrations on User Support and Development Environments

SIGMOD 2011 Conference Organization

General Chair: Timos Sellis *(IMIS/RC Athena)*

Program Chair: Renée J. Miller *(University of Toronto)*

Proceedings Chairs: Anastasios Kementsietsidis *(IBM T.J. Watson Research Center)*
Yannis Velegrakis *(University of Trento)*

Tutorials Chairs: Susan Davidson *(University of Pennsylvania)*
Tova Milo *(Tel Aviv University)*

Keynote and Panel Chair: Pat Selinger *(IBM Research - Almaden)*

Industrial Program Chairs: Richard Hull *(IBM T.J. Watson Research Center)*
Raghu Ramakrishnan *(Yahoo! Research)*

Advisory Committee: Laura Hass *(IBM Research - Almaden)*
Donald Kossmann *(ETH Zürich)*

Demo Chair: Chris Jermaine *(Rice University)*

New Researcher Symposium Chairs: Yanlei Diao *(University of Massachusetts)*
Christopher Ré *(University of Wisconsin-Madison)*

Workshop Chair: Christian S. Jensen *(Aarhus University)*

Undergraduate Research Program Chair: Irini Fundulaki *(Institute of Computer Science - FORTH)*

Finance Chair: Mike Hatzopoulos *(University of Athens)*

Publicity Chairs: Dieter Pfoser *(Inst. for the Mgmt. of Info. Systems)*
Ariel Fuxman *(Microsoft Research)*

Sponsorship Chairs: Mike Carey *(University of California - Irvine)*
Vasilis Vassalos *(Athens University of Economics & Business)*

Exhibits Chairs: Theodore Dalamagas *(IMIS/RC Athena)*
Flip Korn *(AT&T Labs - Research)*

Local Arrangements Chairs: Yannis Kotidis *(Athens U. of Economics & Business)*
Anastasios Patrikakos *(IMIS/RC Athena)*
Eva Paradissi (*IMIS/RC Athena*)

Registration Chair: Alex Delis *(University of Athens)*

Demonstration Chair: Maria Halkidi *(University of Piraeus)*

Web/Information Chair: Yannis Stavrakas *(IMIS/RC Athena)*

Graduate Poster Chairs:
Stefan Schoenauer *(University of Helsinki and HIIT)*
Mario A. Nascimento *(University of Alberta)*
Dirk Van Gucht *(Indiana University)*

Program Committee Group Leaders:
Sihem Amer-Yahia *(Yahoo! Labs)*
Michael Böhlen *(University of Zurich)*
Bettina Kemme *(McGill University)*
Sam Madden *(MIT)*
Jignesh Patel *(University of Wisconsin)*
Dan Suciu *(University of Washington)*
Wang-Chiew Tan *(IBM Research – Almaden & UC Santa Cruz)*
Nesime Tatbul *(ETH Zurich)*
Min Wang *(HP Labs China)*

Program Committee:
Daniel Abadi *(Yale University)*
Ashraf Aboulnaga *(University of Waterloo)*
Sihem Amer-Yahia *(Yahoo! Labs)*
Periklis Andritsos *(Ontario Cancer Institute)*
Marcelo Arenas *(PUC Chile)*
Denilson Barbosa *(University of Alberta)*
Zohra Bellahsene *(Université Montpellier)*
Michael Böhlen *(University of Zurich)*
Angela Bonifati *(CNR, Italy)*
Malu Castellanos *(HP)*
Tiziana Catarci *(Sapienza - Università di Roma)*
Ugur Cetintemel *(Brown University)*
Yi Chen *(Arizona State University)*
Lei Chen *(Hong Kong University of Science and Technology)*
Hong Cheng *(Chinese University of Hong Kong)*
Mitch Cherniak *(Brandeis University)*
Laura Chiticariu *(IBM Research - Almaden)*
Panos Chrysanthis *(University of Pittsburgh)*
Bobby Cochrane *(IBM)*
Isabel Cruz *(University of Illinois at Chicago)*
Theodore Dalamagas *(IMIS Institute/"Athena" R.C.)*
Nilesh Dalvi *(Yahoo! Research)*
Umesh Dayal *(HP)*
Amol Deshpande *(University of Maryland, College Park)*
Yanlei Diao *(University of Massachusetts, Amherst)*
Gill Dobbie *(University of Auckland)*
Luna Dong *(AT&T Labs - Research)*
Alan Fekete *(University of Sydney)*
Enrico Franconi *(Free University of Bolzano-Bozen)*
Christoph Freytag *(Humboldt-Universität zu Berlin)*

Program Committee (continued):

Ada Fu *(Chinese University of Hong Kong)*
Irini Fundulaki *(Institute of Computer Science - FORTH)*
Ariel Fuxman *(Microsoft Research)*
Johann Gamper *(Free University of Bolzano-Bozen)*
Floris Geerts *(University of Edinburgh)*
Boris Glavic *(University of Toronto)*
Lukasz Golab *(AT&T Labs - Research)*
Jonathan Goldstein *(Microsoft)*
Dimitrios Gounopoulos *(University of Athens)*
Todd J. Green *(University of California, Davis)*
Melanie Herschel *(University of Tubingen)*
Wynne Hsu *(National University of Singapore)*
Ihab Ilyas *(University of Waterloo)*
Zack Ives *(University of Pennsylvania)*
Ryan Johnson *(CMU)*
Jaewoo Kang *(Korea University)*
Verene Kantere *(Cyprus University of Technology)*
Anastasios Kementsietsidis *(IBM T.J. Watson Research Center)*
Bettina Kemme *(McGill University)*
Maurice van Keulen *(University of Twente)*
Masura Kitsuregawa *(The Univiversity of Tokyo)*
Solmaz Kolahi *(University of British Columbia)*
Georgia Koutrika *(Stanford University)*
Tim Kraska *(UC Berkeley)*
Alex Labrinidis *(University of Pittsburgh)*
Mong Li Lee *(National University of Singapore)*
Kristen Lefevre *(University of Michigan)*
Boon Thau Loo *(University of Pennsylvania)*
Qiong Luo *(Hong Kong University of Science and Technology)*
Sam Madden *(MIT)*
Volker Markl *(University of Berlin)*
Gianni Mecca *(Università della Basilicata)*
Alexandra Meliou *(University of Washington)*
Sergey Melnik *(Google)*
Mirella Moro *(Universidade Federal de Minas Gerais)*
Felix Naumann *(Hasso Plattner Institute)*
Raymond Ng *(University of British Columbia)*
Joann Ordille *(Avaya Labs)*
Fatma Ozcan *(IBM Research - Almaden)*
Meral Ozsoyoglu *(Case Western Reserve University)*
Themis Palpanas *(Univerity of Trento)*
Paolo Papotti *(Università Roma Tre)*
Jignesh M. Patel *(University of Wisconsin)*
Neoklis Polyzotis *(University of California, Santa Cruz)*
Rachel Pottinger *(University of British Columbia)*
Ken Pu *(UOIT)*
Vibhor Rastogi *(Yahoo! Research)*
Flavio Rizzolo *(Carleton University)*

Program Committee (continued):

Elke Rundensteiner *(Worcester Polytechnic Institute)*
Ana Carolina Salgado *(Federal University of Pernambucol)*
Eric Simon *(SAP)*
Lisa Singh *(Georgetown University)*
Radu Sion *(Stony Brook University)*
Dan Suciu *(University of Washington)*
Wang-Chiew Tan *(IBM Research - Almaden & UC Santa Cruz)*
Nesime Tatbul *(ETH Zurich)*
Evimaria Terzi *(Boston University)*
Patrick Valduriez *(INRIA, Montpellier)*
Yannis Velegrakis *(University of Trento)*
Stratis Viglas *(University of Edinburgh)*
Min Wang *(HP Labs China)*
Kyu-Young Whang *(Korea Adv. Inst. of Science & Technology)*
Melanie Wu *(Indiana University)*
Xifeng Yan *(University of California at Santa Barbara)*
Calisto Zuzarte *(IBM Canada)*

Additional reviewers:

Azza Abouzied
Kamil Bajda-Pawlikowski
Spyros Blanas
Chiranjeeb Buragohain
Ricardo Ciferri
Claudio Di Ciccio
Oktie Hassanzadeh
Jiewen Huang
Norio Katayama
Peer Kröger
Frank McSherry
Tadashi Ohmori
Christopher Olston
Aditya Parameswaran
Antonella Poggi
Rajeev Rastogi
Kunihiko Sadakane
Monica Scannapieco
Alexander Thomson
Valeria Times
Steven Whang
Diego Zardetto

SIGMOD 2011 Sponsor & Supporters

Sponsor: ACM SIGMOD

Platinum Supporters: EMC², ORACLE, Microsoft

Gold Supporters: Google, SAP, SYBASE An SAP Company, IBM Research, YAHOO! LABS

Silver Supporters: hp, aster data — more data. big insights. —, virtualtrip materializing innovation, MarkLogic, twitter, Kosmix, INTRASOFT INTERNATIONAL

Additional supporters: NEC, Greenplum

LazyFTL: A Page-level Flash Translation Layer Optimized for NAND Flash Memory

Dongzhe Ma Jianhua Feng Guoliang Li
Department of Computer Science and Technology
Tsinghua University, Beijing 100084, P.R. China
mdzf rst@yahoo.com.cn, {fengjh, liguoliang}@tsinghua.edu.cn

ABSTRACT

Flash is a type of electronically erasable programmable read-only memory (EEPROM), which has many advantages over traditional magnetic disks, such as lower access latency, lower power consumption, lack of noise, and shock resistance. However, due to its special characteristics, flash memory cannot be deployed directly in the place of traditional magnetic disks. The Flash Translation Layer (FTL) is a software layer built on raw flash memory that carries out garbage collection and wear leveling strategies and hides the special characteristics of flash memory from upper file systems by emulating a normal block device like magnetic disks. Most existing FTL schemes are optimized for some specific access patterns or bring about significant overhead of merge operations under certain circumstances. In this paper, we propose a novel FTL scheme named LazyFTL that exhibits low response latency and high scalability, and at the same time, eliminates the overhead of merge operations completely. Experimental results show that LazyFTL outperforms all the typical existing FTL schemes and is very close to the theoretically optimal solution. We also provide a basic design that assists LazyFTL to recover from system failures.

Categories and Subject Descriptors

D.4.2 [**Operating Systems**]: Storage Management—*Secondary storage*; B.7.1 [**Integrated Circuits**]: Types and Design Styles—*Memory technologies*; B.8.2 [**Performance and Reliability**]: Performance Analysis and Design Aids

General Terms

Design, Experimentation, Performance, Reliability

*This work is partly supported by the National Natural Science Foundation of China under Grant No. 60873065, the National Grand Fundamental Research 973 Program of China under Grant No. 2011CB302206, and the National S&T Major Project of China.

Keywords

Flash translation layer, LazyFTL, address translation, garbage collection

1. INTRODUCTION

Recent years have witnessed a rapid development of flash technologies. Advantages of flash memory, such as high density, low access latency, low power consumption, and shock resistance, greatly benefit database systems and other data-intensive applications. However, flash memory cannot be deployed directly in the place of traditional magnetic disks due to its special characteristics.

Like other EEPROM devices, if a page has been programmed, an erase operation needs to take place before new data can be written. To make things worse, the granularity of flash erase operations is much larger than that of read and write operations. If an in-place update is to be performed, we need to copy all valid pages in the corresponding block into the RAM, update the page in the RAM, erase the block, and write all valid pages back. This update method will not only degrade performance of the flash memory, but also reduce the life span of the chip and bring a potential consistency problem. To solve these problems, out-of-place updates are adopted. That is, when a page is to be overwritten, we allocate a new free or erased page, put the new data there, and use a software layer called FTL to indicate the physical location change of the page.

In addition, after about 10,000 $\sim$ 100,000 erase/write cycles, some blocks may become unstable and malfunction. Although a few blocks are reserved to replace broken ones, these extra blocks will eventually be exhausted. A technology named wear leveling is usually employed in the FTL to prolong the life span of flash memory by distributing erase cycles across the entire memory.

A lot of work from the database community focuses on designing efficient index structures, such as BFTL [29], μ-Tree [13], FlashDB [25], LA-Tree [2], and FD-Tree [22]. Some of these technologies are built upon the FTL while others work directly on raw flash memories, realizing functionalities of the FTL themselves, for example, address translation, garbage collection, and wear leveling. In all cases, the FTL is a crucial factor to all flash-based technologies.

Besides, since flash memories are purely electronic devices and have no moving parts, they have no seek or rotation latency like magnetic disks. Therefore, random access of flash memory can be as fast as sequential access and the latency of flash memory is almost linearly proportional to the amount of data being accessed, no matter where the data

Table 1: Magnetic Disk vs. NAND Flash [19]

	Read	Write	Erase
Magnetic Disk	12.7 ms	13.7 ms	N/A
NAND Flash	80 μs (2 KB)	200 μs (2 KB)	1.5 ms (128 KB)

is located. Another feature making flash memories different is that the write latency of flash memory is usually several times larger than the read latency as shown in Table 1 (we adopt the configuration described in [19]) since it takes longer to physically inject electrons into a storage cell than sense its status. Therefore, most flash technologies tend to focus on optimization of write performance, even if increase read operations sometimes.

Our study makes several contributions as follows.

- In this paper, we propose a novel FTL scheme named LazyFTL, which is optimized for NAND-type flash memories. To avoid the heavy overhead of merge operations in existing block-level and hybrid-mapping FTL schemes, LazyFTL employs a page-level mapping table. This makes LazyFTL a high performance FTL scheme compared with other existing ones. However, a page-level mapping scheme is hard to deploy on NAND-type flash memories since they can only be programmed in pages. If any part of the mapping table is immediately written in flash memory whenever it is modified, performance will be affected. If dirty data is kept in the SRAM and only written in flash memory when it is swapped out, we risk losing critical information and leaving the system in an inconsistent state. To solve this problem, LazyFTL keeps two small areas in flash memory and updates the page-level mapping table in a lazy manner.
- We implement a trace-driven simulator to help evaluate the performance of LazyFTL and six other typical FTL schemes, namely NFTL-1, NFTL-N, BAST, FAST, LAST, and A-SAST. Our empirical evaluation demonstrates that LazyFTL outperforms all typical FTL schemes while achieving consistency and reliability at the same time. Experimental results also show that LazyFTL successfully approaches the theoretically optimal solution.
- We test and measure the performance of LazyFTL when the ratio of the capacity of flash memory to that of the SRAM is increased. We discover that within a certain scope, LazyFTL can still achieve an excellent performance. This experiment indicates that the scalability of LazyFTL is high since it does not require that the capacity of the SRAM is enlarged as fast as flash memory. We also analyze the reliability of LazyFTL theoretically and present an algorithm that assists LazyFTL to recover from system failures efficiently.

The rest of this paper is organized as follows. In Section 2, we make a short introduction of flash memory and previous FTL designs. In Section 3, we provide an overview of the proposed LazyFTL scheme. A detailed description of the major functionalities of LazyFTL is given in Section 4 and Section 5 defines the states of pages and demonstrates the transition of states using a simple example. Experimental results are presented and analyzed in Section 6. We also analyze the scalability and reliability issues in Section 6. Finally, Section 7 draws some conclusions and directions for future work.

2. BACKGROUND

2.1 Introduction of Flash Memory

There are two types of flash memories, namely NOR and NAND. NOR provides independent address and data buses, allowing random access to any location of the memory, which makes NOR a perfect replacement of the traditional read-only memory (ROM), such as the BIOS chip of computers. On the other hand, address and data share the same I/O interface in NAND, which means that NAND can only be accessed in pages, though it has a higher density and lower cost per bit than NOR. NAND is usually used as a secondary storage device [1]. In the rest of this paper, we use the term flash to refer to NAND-type flash memory unless we explicitly indicate NOR-type flash memory.

Each flash chip consists of a constant number of blocks that are basic units of erase operations. And each block consists of a constant number of pages that are basic units of read and write operations. Most flash memories also provide a spare area for each page to store out-of-band (OOB) data, such as the error correction code (ECC), the logical page number, and the state flag for the page. As technology advances, different flash memory organizations have been developed as shown in Table 2.

Table 2: Organization of Flash Chips [23, 28, 13]

	Block Size	Page Size	OOB Size
Small-block SLC	16 KB	512 bytes	16 bytes
Large-block SLC	128 KB	2 KB	64 bytes
Large-block MLC[1]	512 KB	4 KB	128 bytes

2.2 Overview of FTL

According to the granularity of the mapping unit, existing FTL schemes can be divided into four categories: page-level, block-level, hybrid, and variable-length mappings.

Just as the name implies, in page-level FTLs, a logical page number (LPN) can be directly translated to a physical page number (PPN). In other words, page-level FTLs need to maintain a mapping entry for every logical page, which means that the mapping table of page-level FTLs is much larger than any other types. In fact, all page-level FTL schemes store the entire mapping table in flash memory and load the currently used parts into the SRAM dynamically using the LRU algorithm or some other strategy. However, since hot and cold data can be easily separated, page-level FTLs are quite efficient and flexible.

On the contrary, in block-level FTLs, an LPN is first divided into a logical block number (LBN) and an in-block offset. Then the LBN is translated to a physical block number (PBN) and finally some search algorithm is employed to find the target page. It is obvious that the mapping table of block-level FTLs is quite small and can be easily stored in the SRAM. Nevertheless, due to the mixture of hot and cold data and the overhead of moving valid pages during garbage collection, the performance of block-level FTL schemes is limited compared with other mapping methods.

Hybrid mapping schemes try to achieve the flexibility of page-level FTLs while keeping the mapping table relatively small and comparable to the block-level methods by dividing the flash memory into a data block area (DBA) and a log block area (LBA). Block-level mapping is applied to the

[1]An MLC device is capable of storing more than one bit of information in a single storage cell.

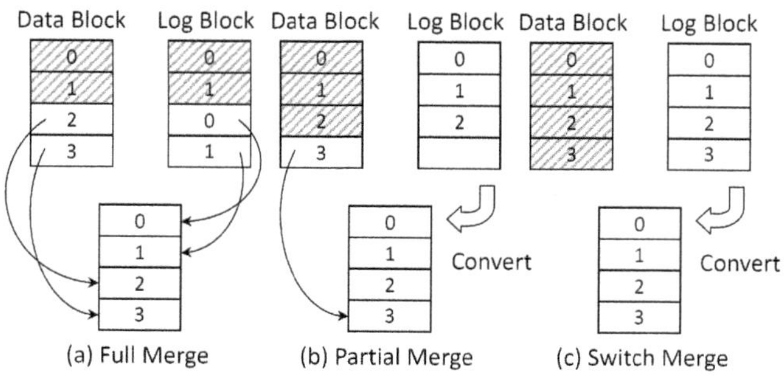

Figure 1: Three Types of Merge Operations

DBA which occupies most of the flash memory while each valid page in the LBA is traced by another page-level mapping. The LBA is very small and generally takes less than 5 percent of the entire flash memory. In hybrid FTLs (except HFTL [17]), the LBA is used to store overwriting data and different schemes adopt different strategies to merge data in the LBA to the DBA to generate new space for the LBA. There are three types of merge operations as illustrated in Figure 1. A full merge is a general but expensive operation in which all up-to-date pages need to be copied to a new allocated block and then old blocks are erased and put back into the free block pool. The partial and switch merges are efficient but can only be done in special cases since they can only be done when pages in the log block or the replacement block are all free or valid and each valid page is written in their own place. Although many hybrid FTL schemes try to do partial or switch merges whenever possible, full merges are difficult to avoid with different access patterns. This makes an insuperable bottleneck for all hybrid FTL schemes.

It is also possible to map variable-length continuous logical pages to continuous physical pages in flash memory. In this case, granularity can be adjusted dynamically when access pattern changes. However, since sizes of different mapping units are not identical and are changing, mapping entries can only be stored in some type of search tree, and as a result, the table look-up overhead of variable-length mappings is higher than other schemes of which the mapping table is nothing more than a simple address array.

2.3 Page-level FTL Schemes

The first FTL scheme was patented by Ban in 1995 [3] and was adopted by the PCMCIA as a standard for NOR-based flash memories several years later [12]. There is one issue that NOR-based FTLs should handle in the first place. When a page is overwritten, the relevant entry in flash memory needs to be updated to keep the operation atomic and reliable. (Remember that page-level FTL schemes keep an entire mirror of the mapping table in flash memory to reduce the SRAM overhead.) This presents no difficulty to the NOR-based FTL since NOR-type flash memories can be programmed in bytes. By assigning a replacement page list for the relevant mapping page when necessary, this mapping page can be updated (written in the first free entry of the same offset in the replacement page list) several times as long as the length of the list without rewriting the entire mapping page [12, 9].

DFTL (Demand-based FTL) [10], another page-level FTL scheme, makes the first attempt to transfer the former NOR-based FTL to NAND-type flash memories, omitting the replacement page part. This scheme, though efficient, faces a serious reliability problem since all modified information in the SRAM will be lost if a system failure occurs. In this case, spare areas of all data pages need to be scanned until the system recovers to a consistent state. Therefore, DFTL is not suitable, we believe, for circumstances where flash memory is regarded as a permanent and reliable storage device.

2.4 Block-level FTL Schemes

Ban patented two other FTL schemes in 1999 [4, 8, 9]. These schemes are designed for NAND-type flash memories and also known as the NFTLs. In this paper, they will be cited as NFTL-1 and NFTL-N. NFTL-1 is designed for flash memories that have a spare area for each page and NFTL-N is for devices without such storage.

When a page is overwritten, NFTL-1 first allocates a replacement block for the relevant logical block if there is none and writes overwriting pages one after another from the beginning of the replacement block. Since pages are written in an out-of-place manner in replacement blocks, NFTL-1 needs to scan all the spare areas in the replacement block in reversed order to find the most up-to-date version of a requested page. Fortunately, the spare areas in NAND-type flash memory are using a different addressing algorithm that is optimized for fast reference and the overhead of this search process is relatively low.

On the other hand, since some models of NAND flash memories have no spare areas to support fast search, NFTL-N keeps a replacement block list for some of the logical blocks when necessary and write requests for each logical page are first handled by the first block in the list and then the next one, keeping the in-block offset identical with that of the logical address. If all pages in the list with the request offset have been programmed, a new block is allocated and appended to the back of the list.

2.5 Hybrid FTL Schemes

BAST (Block-Associative Sector Translation) is the first hybrid FTL scheme proposed in 2002 [15], which is essentially an altered version of NFTL-1. As mentioned earlier, hybrid FTL schemes build a page-level mapping for the LBA. To keep this table small enough to reside in the SRAM, BAST limits the total number of replacement blocks (also known as log blocks). Obviously, the read performance of BAST is better than NFTL-1 because the SRAM is several orders of magnitude faster than flash memories. However, BAST does not work well with random overwrite patterns which may result in a block thrashing problem [20]. Since each replacement block can accommodate pages from only one logical block, BAST can easily run out of free replacement blocks and be forced to reclaim replacement blocks that have not been filled. Therefore, the utilization ratio of replacement blocks in BAST is low both theoretically and experimentally.

To solve the block thrashing problem, another hybrid FTL scheme named FAST (Fully Associative Sector Translation) was put forward [20]. FAST goes to the other extreme by allowing a log block to hold updates from any data block. Although FAST successfully delays garbage collections as much as possible, the system-wide latency for reclaiming a single log block may turn out to be longer than BAST, since the associativity of log blocks is only limited by the number of pages in a block. The associativity of a log block is defined as the number of different data blocks whose most up-to-date pages are located in the log block. The higher the associativity of a log block is, the more expensive it is to reclaim it. To increase the proportion of partial and switch merges, FAST reserves a sequential log block to perform sequential updates. This optimization is also limited since in modern multi-process environments, a sequential write is often interrupted by random writes and other sequential writes [18].

In the following years, researchers tried to find some intermediate proposals to balance between the log block utilization and the reclamation overhead. There are some typical representatives such as Superblock FTL [14], SAST (Set-Associative Sector Translation) [26], LAST (Locality-Aware Sector Translation) [18], and A-SAST (Adaptive SAST) [16].

Both Superblock FTL and SAST share (at most) K log blocks among N data blocks. The difference is that Superblock FTL keeps a page-level map in the spare areas of the superblock while SAST restricts the number of log blocks and maintains the page-level map in the SRAM. Due to the size limitation of spare areas, Superblock FTL needs to search at most three spare areas to find a requested page. And in SAST, different data block sets may compete for log blocks as a result of the small LBA. A common problem with these two schemes is that they both need to be tuned beforehand, which means that their performance may get worse if access pattern changes.

Unlike Superblock FTL and SAST, LAST divides the LBA into several functional segments to fully utilize the log blocks while keeping the reclamation overhead as low as possible. Longer requests are written in the sequential log buffer to perform partial or switch merges. Hot data that might be overwritten soon is written in the hot partition of the random log buffer and other write requests are served by the cold partition.

A-SAST is an optimized version of SAST which loosens the restriction of maximum number of log blocks shared within a data block set and can merge and split data block sets dynamically.

KAST (K-Associative Sector Translation) [6] is the same as FAST in essence but requires that the associativity of all log blocks should never exceed K. The scheme is designed for real-time systems since its reclamation latency is controllable. KAST can be considered as another tradeoff between the log block utilization and the reclamation overhead.

Unlike other hybrid schemes, HFTL (Hybrid FTL) [17] does not treat the page-mapping area as a buffer of updates. Instead, HFTL employs a hash-based hot data identification technique [11] and traces pages from hot blocks with the page-level mapping as long as they remain hot. However, when access pattern changes, some hot pages will need to be swapped out, which will introduce an extra overhead.

2.6 Other FTL Schemes

It is also possible to implement a variable-length mapping. One such scheme was proposed in 2004 [5] and in 2008 another one named μ-FTL, which adopts μ-Tree [13] as the mapping structure, was published [21]. The main disadvantage of these schemes is the address translation cost since variable-length mappings can only be implemented in search trees.

JFTL, proposed in 2009, is a technique to effectively deploy journal file systems on flash memory using the out-of-place characteristic [7], which can be built on any other FTL schemes. However, JFTL cannot do anything about the consistency problem of DFTL.

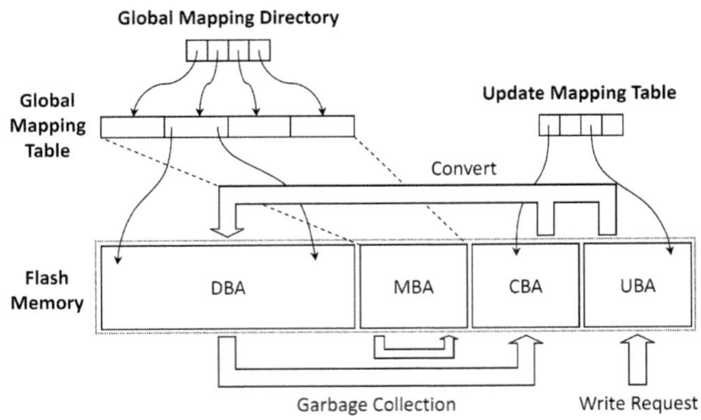

Figure 2: Architecture of LazyFTL

3. LAZYFTL OVERVIEW

3.1 Design Principles

After explaining the merits and demerits of different types of existing FTL schemes in Section 2, some design principles and considerations will be presented at the beginning of this section.

First of all, a storage system should guarantee the reliability of its operations, therefore dirty or altered data should be flushed into flash memory before an operation can return. DFTL violates this rule in order to obtain high performance. Although the system can recover by scanning the spare area of all pages, the resulting bootup delay is unacceptable along with the increase of the density and the capacity of flash memories.

To design a highly efficient FTL scheme, the mapping granularity should be decided in the first place. Among all the FTL schemes discussed in Section 2, the block-level mapping cannot distinguish cold data from hot ones and has to move cold data unnecessarily during the garbage collection procedure. The variable-length mapping can adjust its mapping granularity dynamically but the high complexity of address translation makes an inherent weakness. The hybrid mapping is feasible since costly full merge operations can be avoid as much as possible by partitioning the LBA or by sharing log blocks. However, no matter how subtly they are designed, hybrid mapping schemes can hardly eliminate full merge operations completely. The page-level mapping is the most efficient and effective mapping granularity but can hardly be applied to NAND flash without violating the first rule. This is not true however. The LazyFTL scheme proposed in this paper proves that by adopting an update buffer, like the LBA in hybrid mapping schemes, the page-level FTL can be transferred to NAND flash while keeping reliability and consistency at the same time.

3.2 LazyFTL Architecture

The architecture of the proposed LazyFTL scheme is presented in Figure 2. As illustrated, LazyFTL divides the entire flash memory into four parts: a data block area (DBA), a mapping block area (MBA), a cold block area (CBA), and an update block area (UBA). All these parts except the MBA are used to store user data.

Pages in the DBA are tracked by a page-level mapping table called the global mapping table (GMT). The GMT is organized in pages and stored in the MBA. A small cache adopting the LRU algorithm or similar is reserved in the SRAM to provide efficient reference of the most frequently accessed parts of the GMT. A secondary table named the global mapping directory (GMD) is stored in the SRAM and keeps physical locations of all valid mapping pages of the GMT. The CBA is used to accommodate cold blocks and the UBA is used to accommodate update blocks as the names indicate.

The main difference between LazyFTL and the original page-level FTL scheme [3, 12] is that LazyFTL reserves two small partitions, the CBA and the UBA, to delay modifications of the GMT caused by write requests or valid page movements. The total size of the CBA and the UBA is relatively small compared with the entire flash memory and, like the LBAs in hybrid FTL schemes, another page-level mapping table which is called the update mapping table (UMT) is built on these two areas. The UMT can be implemented as a hash table or a binary search tree to support efficient insertion, deletion, modification, and reference. The number of entries in the UMT is quite small, so these operations will not introduce too much overhead.

A block in the UBA called the current update block (CUB) is used to handle write operations. When the CUB overflows, another free block is allocated and becomes the new CUB. Similarly, there is a current cold block (CCB) in the CBA dealing with moved data pages. As a matter of fact, LazyFTL treats filled cold blocks in the CBA and filled update blocks in the UBA in the same way. In other words, the relative size of the CBA and the UBA can be adjusted dynamically. If the proportion of hot data rises, the convert cost (see 4.1) of blocks in the UBA will decrease more slowly and the UBA will expand. If space utilization increases, the CCB will be filled faster than the CUB and the CBA will be enlarged. In this way, LazyFTL can tune itself automatically for different access patterns.

It is necessary to mention that it is also feasible to divide the CBA and the UBA into smaller functional segments like LAST [18]. However, we decide to keep the design as simple as possible since the current design is quite efficient and there is no room for performance improvement.

We also maintain two bitmaps in the SRAM, the update flag and the invalidate flag. These two bitmaps help mark the states of all pages in the CBA and the UBA. Each bit in the update flag indicates whether the translation information of the corresponding page needs to be updated to the GMT. And each bit in the invalidate flag indicates whether the target page that the corresponding GMT entry points to needs to be invalidated.

4. MAJOR FUNCTIONALITIES

4.1 Convert Operation

Since the UMT is stored in the SRAM to support efficient reference, the CBA and the UBA cannot be too large and will eventually overflow, in which case, a convert operation is carried out. In hybrid FTL schemes, a merge operation needs to copy valid pages in the victim log block out of the LBA and reorganize relevant data blocks most of the time due to the in-place storage pattern in the DBA. However, LazyFTL only has to convert the victim block to a normal data block logically since pages in the DBA are also stored in an out-of-place manner. The only overhead of the convert operation is caused by the GMT updates which will be proved to be much cheaper than reorganizing data blocks.

A convert operation is achieved in four steps as illustrated in Algorithm 1. First, a filled block in the CBA or the UBA

Algorithm 1 Convert block **B**

Input: **B**: a victim block in the CBA or the UBA
Output: **B**: a normal data block

```
mapping_pages ← ∅
update_entries ← ∅
/* Gather relevant information */
for each valid page P in B do
  E ← <LPN_P, PPN_P>
  remove E from the UMT
  if the update flag of P is set then
    P' ← ⌊LPN_P / number_of_entries_per_page⌋
    mapping_pages ← mapping_pages ∪ {P'}
    update_entries ← update_entries ∪ {E}
  end if
end for
/* Gather entries that can also be updated */
for each entry E' in the UMT do
  if the relevant mapping page ∈ mapping_pages and
     the update flag of E' is set then
    update_entries ← update_entries ∪ {E'}
    the update flag of E' ← 0
  end if
end for
/* Make sure that each page is loaded only once */
sort update_entries by LPN
/* Update the GMT and invalidate old pages */
for each entry E'' ∈ update_entries do
  load the relevant mapping page P'' if necessary
  offset ← LPN_E'' mod number_of_entries_per_page
  if the invalidate flag of E'' is set then
    invalidate P''[offset]
    the invalidate flag of E'' ← 0
  end if
  P''[offset] ← PPN_E''
  if no more updates to P'' then
    write P'' to the MBA
    update the GMD
    invalidate the old page of P''
  end if
end for
```

with the lowest convert cost is selected as the victim. The convert cost of each candidate block is defined as the number of different mapping pages that valid pages in this block whose translation information need to be updated to the GMT belong to. Second, all relevant mapping pages are found and all mapping entries in the UMT that belong to these mapping pages are collected, including entries pointing to other blocks in the CBA and the UBA. Then modifications of the mapping pages are performed. Finally, mapping entries in the UMT that point to the victim block are removed and the victim block is converted to a normal data block logically.

One thing that should take our attention is that for the sake of efficiency an entry in the UMT is removed only when the block where the target page is located is converted, no matter whether this entry is updated in that operation. In other words, all valid pages in the CBA and the UBA are tracked by the UMT, even if some of them have already been updated when other blocks in the CBA or the UBA are converted.

As mentioned earlier, to help identify pages whose physical locations have not been updated to the GMT, an update

Algorithm 2 Reclaim block **B**

Input: **B**: a victim block in the DBA or the MBA
Output: **B**: a free block

```
if B is a mapping block then
    for each valid page P in B do
        move P to the MBA
    end for
else
    for each valid page P in B do
        if LPN_P can be found in the UMT then
            the invalidate flag of UMT[LPN_P] ← 0
        else
            if the CCB is filled up then
                if the UBA & CBA are filled up then
                    select a victim block and convert it
                end if
                allocate a new block for the CCB
            end if
            move P to the CBA
            add <LPN_P, PPN_P> to the UMT
            the update flag of P ← 1
            the invalidate flag of P ← 0
        end if
    end for
end if
erase B
put B into the free block pool
```

flag bitmap is maintained in the SRAM. Each bit in this bitmap is related to a page in the CBA or the UBA. If the update flag of a page is 1, we should modify the corresponding entry in the GMT whenever possible and at least before the block this page belongs to is converted. When a page is written to the UBA or moved to the CBA, its physical location changes which means that the initial update flag of all pages should be 1. And after the relevant GMT entry of a page in the CBA or the UBA is updated or if it is overwritten, its update flag should be cleared.

4.2 Garbage Collection

When the number of free blocks decreases to a predefined threshold, a victim block from the DBA or the MBA is selected to be erased. The cost to reclaim a certain block **B** can be defined as

$$(C_{read} + C_{write}) * N_B + C_{erase}$$

where C_{read}, C_{write}, and C_{erase} indicate the flash read, write, and erase operation latencies, respectively and N_B represents the number of valid pages in block **B**. Obviously, to reduce the overhead of garbage collection process, the block with the lowest reclaimation cost should be selected as the victim most of the time.

After the victim block is chosen, all pages of this block should be scanned and the valid ones should be moved to some other block. If the victim block stores mapping pages of the GMT, valid pages should be moved to a current mapping block (CMB) in the MBA that handles mapping page rewriting and the GMD is modified to track these changes. If the victim block stores user data, the valid pages should be moved to the CCB in the CBA. The philosophy is that these valid pages should be relatively colder than the invalid ones.

Note that there are two cases indicating a data page is invalid. If this page has been overwritten and the new version is still located in the UBA, the spare area of this page may have not been marked. However, if the new version has been converted, the old page in the DBA should have been invalidated. Therefore, when the state flag in the spare area indicates that a page is valid, we should further check whether its LPN can be found in the UMT. If this page has been overwritten, we should ignore it, and at the same time, we should clear the invalidate flag of the most up-to-date page since the target that the corresponding GMT entry points to has been erased and will be used to accommodate other data. It is seriously wrong to invalidate an empty page or an innocent one.

After all the valid pages have been moved, the victim block is erased and put into the free block pool again. An algorithmic description of garbage collection operations is presented in Algorithm 2.

Algorithm 3 Write page **P**

Input: **P**: new data to be written

```
if the CUB is filled up then
    if the UBA & CBA are filled up then
        select a victim block and convert it
    end if
    allocate a new block for the CUB
end if
write P in the UBA
/* Set the update flag */
the update flag of P ← 1
/* Inherit or set the invalidate flag */
if LPN_P can be found in the UMT then
    P' ← UMT[LPN_P]
    the invalidate flag of P ← the invalidate flag of P'
    invalidate P'
    the update flag of P' ← 0
    the invalidate flag of P' ← 0
else
    the invalidate flag of P ← 1
end if
add <LPN_P, PPN_P> to the UMT
```

4.3 Write Operation

The write operation of LazyFTL is much simpler than the convert operation and the garbage collection operation. We only need to write the new data in the UBA and do some bookkeeping. That is to say, we set the update flag, inherit or set the invalidate flag, invalidate the old page in the CBA or the UBA if there is one, and clear its two flags. The pseudo code of the write operation is given in Algorithm 3.

5. STATE TRANSITION

5.1 State Definition

As described earlier, the update and invalidate flags represent the state of the corresponding page in the CBA or the UBA. By taking pointers in the GMT and the UMT with the same LPN into consideration, we can figure out all possible states a page may have in LazyFTL.

To help readers understand the different page states and their transition paths and conditions, a state transition diagram is given in Figure 3. In this diagram, some states have a two-digit binary number on its upper right corner. The first digit stands for the update flag and the second one is the invalidate flag. Invalid pages are represented by a small

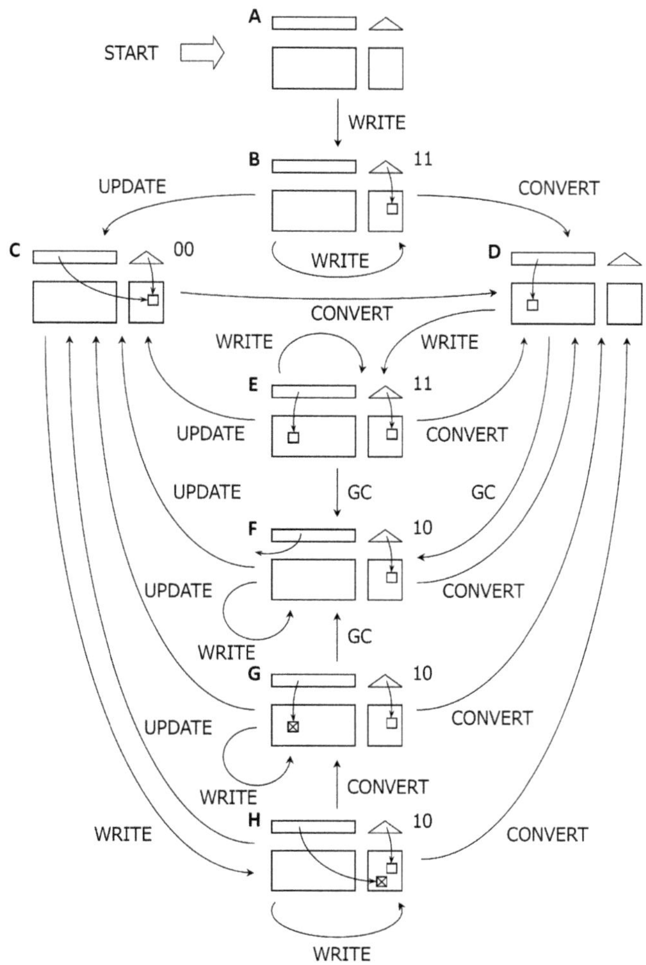

Figure 3: State Transition of Pages

square with a cross inside, such as in state **G** and **H**, and those that are pointed neither by the GMT nor by the UMT are omitted. In state **F**, a pointer in the GMT is pointing to nothing since its target has been moved to the CBA and the block has been erased. Transition conditions are labeled on the path. WRITE means a write operation. GC means the block this page is located in is reclaimed. CONVERT means the corresponding block is converted and UPDATE means that some other block is converted and the entry of this page in the UMT is updated.

Among the eight states in Figure 3, state **C** is the **updated state** since all update paths arrive at **C**. When a block is reclaimed, the relevant pages should be in **reclaimed state F**. All CONVERT paths except one point to **D** qualifies state **D** as the **converted state**. Between state **H** and state **G**, there is a path labeled as CONVERT which seems to violate the rule. This is a conversion of another block that contains a valid page which needs to be updated and shares the same mapping page with the one in our discussion, and therefore, this convert operation is different from others.

5.2 An Example of State Transition

In this section, we give an example to help readers understand how the update and invalidate flags are manipulated. We will start from a page that has never been written and follow its state transitions as illustrated in Figure 4.

- **A → B** As demonstrated in Algorithm 3, the update flag of each new written page is set as 1 and since no previous written page is found in the UBA or the CBA, the initial value of the invalidate flag is also set as 1.
- **B → D** When the corresponding block is selected as the convert victim, address translation information needs to be updated to the GMT since the update flag is set. However, no page needs to be invalidated though the invalidate flag is set since the relevant entry in the GMT has not been used.
- **D → E** This operation is similar to the first write request. The only thing we should pay attention to is that we do not try to alter the GMT entry or invalidate the old page at this time.
- **E → F** In this operation, a data block in the DBA where the old page is located is reclaimed. To tell whether a page is valid, we should first check the state flag in its spare area. If the flag indicates a valid page, we should further check whether this page has been overwritten in the UBA. In this case, the same LPN is found in the UMT, meaning that this page has been overwritten and thus should be discarded. Meanwhile, the invalidate flag of the up-to-date page is cleared since the old GMT entry is currently pointing to an erased page which should not be invalidated again.
- **F → C** This time, some other block is converted and the mapping information of this page is updated in passing. Do not forget to clear the update flag.
- **C → H** This page is overwritten again. Unlike the third operation, the old page is invalidated immediately after new data is written in. Note that invalidate flag of the new page is cleared not because the old page has just been invalidated but because its invalidate flag is not set. This is so-called the inheritance of invalidate flags in LazyFTL.
- **H → G** The block that holds the old page is converted and nothing needs to be done.
- **G → F** Another block related to the current page is reclaimed. This time, the old page is already invalidated and there is no need to check the UMT. The difference is in the first state **F** of Figure 4, the invalidate flag is cleared by the GC operation, while in the other state **F**, the flag is unchanged.
- **F → D** Finally, the block that holds the up-to-date page is converted and we need to modified the GMT entry but do not try to invalidate the page that the old entry points to just as the two flags indicate.

6. PERFORMANCE EVALUATION

To help evaluate the performance and understand other characteristics of the proposed LazyFTL scheme, we implement a trace-driven simulator for LazyFTL. For comparison, we also implement six other FTL schemes that are comparable with LazyFTL, namely NFTL-1, NFTL-N, BAST, FAST, LAST, and A-SAST.

6.1 Experimental Setup

The simulator is built on a large-block SLC flash (see Table 2) which is widely used in enterprise grade flash memories. The capacity is 1 GB and the access latencies are set as Table 1.

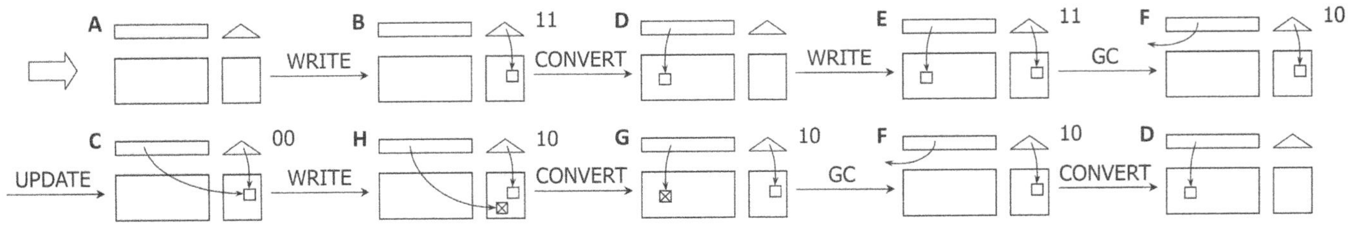

Figure 4: An Example of State Transition

We use the Microsoft Research Cambridge block I/O traces as described in [24]. These traces are collected from 13 enterprise servers for different applications, such as user home directories, print server, firewall/web proxy, source control, web/SQL server, and media server, which should cover all major access patterns. We have tested all the 36 traces in the package and obtained similar results. The space utilization of the adjusted traces varies from almost empty to 82.87%. And the relative standard deviation (RSD) of the numbers of accesses of all touched addresses ranges from 35.12% to 2526.16%. The larger the RSD value is, the more frequently hot data in the trace is accessed. It is necessary to point out that though our experiment touches no more than 82% of the address space, the relative performance of LazyFTL will not degrade if the device is filled up. In fact, we believe that the performance gap between LazyFTL and other existing schemes will expand because other FTLs do not fully utilize every page in a block and a higher space utilization means more frequent garbage collection calls for them.

The results presented in this paper were obtained by using trace *usr_2.csv*. The trace is scaled down to fit our 1 GB flash memory and 75.9% of the entire address space is touched, with an RSD of 193.60%. The largest request size is 256 pages, which are equivalent to 4 blocks or 0.5 MB. However, most requests involve less than 32 pages.

We also implement six comparative experiments, namely NFTL-1, NFTL-N, BAST, FAST, LAST, and A-SAST. All these schemes are typical block-level or hybrid-mapping FTL schemes that focus on optimization of average access performance and do not have to be tuned for specific access patterns. We do not try to compare LazyFTL with DFTL, another NAND-based page-level FTL scheme. On one hand, DFTL has a consistent disadvantage, and on the other, the performance of LazyFTL and DFTL should be similar since neither of them can overcome the theoretical barrier.

Suppose that 4 bytes are used to store a single page address or block address[2], then it takes $\lceil 1 \text{ GB} \div 128 \text{ KB} \times 4 \text{ bytes} \rceil = 32768$ bytes or 16 pages in the SRAM to store the block-level mapping table in comparative experiments. Another 32768 bytes are allocated in the SRAM to accommodate the page-level mapping table of hybrid FTL schemes, which means that $\lfloor 32768 \text{ bytes} \div 4 \text{ bytes} \rfloor = 8192$ pages or 128 blocks can be assigned to the LBA. These 128 blocks take only 1.56% of the entire flash memory. To keep the results comparable, the total size of the UBA and the CBA of LazyFTL is also limited to 128 blocks and at most 14 pages (another 2 pages are used to store the GMD) of the GMT can be cached in the LRU cache in the SRAM. Other data structures are either small or employed in all the schemes and therefore are not considered.

All implemented schemes adopt the greedy strategy to select garbage collection victims. NFTL-1 selects the block which has the most used pages in its replacement block. NFTL-N selects the block which has the longest replacement block list. All hybrid FTL schemes and LazyFTL select the block that has the least valid pages since these pages need to be moved and thus are considered as the overhead of the garbage collection. Some may argue that by taking the access pattern into consideration, we may figure out which free page is going to be used or which valid page is going to be invalidated. Garbage collection strategy is not within our discussion, however, and we only choose a block that has the least overhead or the most profit for a single operation as the victim.

In addition, wear leveling is omitted in all our implements because the wear leveling mechanism is relatively independent from other components. Wear leveling involves many issues, such as how to identify worn-out blocks, which blocks to reclaim and where to put valid data. Upper applications and the system architechture should also be taken into consideration. If multi-process is supported, garbage collection and wear leveling can be carried out in the background without interrupting other operations. However, in embedded environments or real-time systems these functions can only be done on demand, since the background way is either impossible or inacceptable, respectively. All in all, wear leveling is another interesting research topic and many existing works have studied this problem. It is unrealistic to permute all the combinations and difficult to find a representative strategy. Another reason why wear leveling is omitted is to provide a clear view of the performance comparison of different FTLs. For the sake of wear leveling, some data will need to be moved from cold blocks to worn-out ones on purpose, which will introduce many noise operations. Since our paper focuses on address translation and data organization, it is better not to be distracted from other components. We believe that an identical wear leveling strategy will similarly influence all the schemes and will not affect our simulation results.

To help evaluate the possibility of further improvement of the proposed LazyFTL, we also compare LazyFTL with the theoretically optimal solution. That is to say, each page read request causes a single page read operation, each page write request causes a single page write operation and a block erase operation is invoked every 64 page write operations.

When implementing NFTL-N, we discover that in the beginning, the response time for write requests decreases quickly when the length limit of replacement block lists is enlarged. However, after a certain point around 7, the write performance becomes stable and constant. Another issue that surprised us is that it seems that the search cost of read requests does not increase much when the limit is relaxed. This is probably because when a certain proportion of flash memory is used, the replacement block list has little

[2]The block address is shorter than the page address and may be stored in less than 4 bytes.

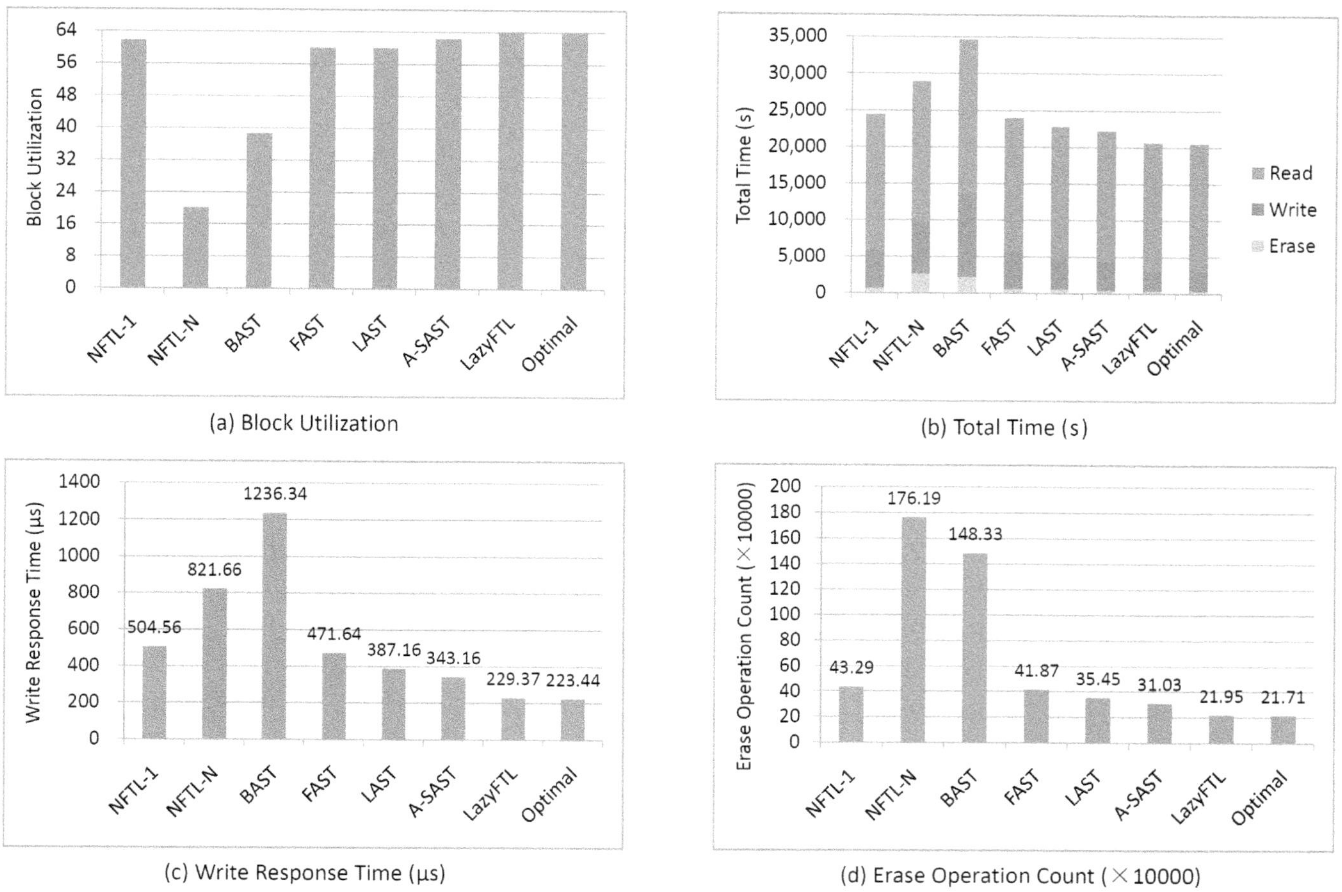

Figure 5: Comparison with Existing Schemes

chance to get longer before it is reclaimed, even though the limit has been enlarged. In our experiment, the maximum length of the replacement block lists is set to 16.

Tuning for LAST is relatively complex. In our experiments, 8 blocks are assigned to the sequential log block area and the other 120 blocks in the LBA are random log blocks. The threshold for the hot partition utility and that of the cold partition are set to 0.2 and 0.9 respectively.

Other schemes do not need special tuning and will not be presented in this section.

6.2 Comparison with Other Schemes

The results of our simulation are shown in Figure 5. We will focus on four parameters, the block utilization which indicates the average number of pages that have been used when a block is erased, the total time, the write response time, and the number of erase operations which will directly affect the life span of the flash memory.

Among all the implemented schemes, the performance of NFTL-1 is acceptable compared with NFTL-N and BAST and its simplicity makes a great selling point. However, the read performance is inferior to other schemes since it needs to search in the replacement block to find a certain page. In our experiment, 17.565 spare areas need to be scanned on average to serve a one-page read request.

NFTL-N is designed for NAND flash that does not have a spare area for each page. As a result, the block utilization ratio of NFTL-N is very low since pages can only be written in an in-place manner. This also implies that NFTL-N needs to perform more erase operations than other schemes as illustrated in Figure 5(d).

BAST is the first hybrid FTL scheme that tries to avoid the search overhead when reading a page. Due to the block thrashing problem, the block utilization ratio of BAST is also very low compared with other hybrid FTL schemes and the performance is worse than any other scheme including NFTL-N. That is because NFTL-N can always perform partial or switch merges while BAST needs to perform full merge almost all the time. In our experiment, we can hardly find any chance for BAST to perform a much cheaper partial or switch merge.

The simulation results of the other three hybrid FTLs are nearly the same. A-SAST is better than LAST, which is in turn better than FAST. We notice that the performance of FAST is very close to that of NFTL-1. Although FAST tries to delay merge operations as much as possible and reserves a sequential log block to perform partial and switch merges, the advantages gained are counteracted by the heavy overhead of full merges. LAST and A-SAST successfully make a tradeoff between the log block utilization and the reclamation overhead. Experimental results indicate that LAST and A-SAST achieve a much higher log block utilization than BAST and a much lower write response time than FAST at the same time.

As Figure 5 shows, the performance of LazyFTL is much better than those of other schemes and is very close to the optimal result. First of all, LazyFTL does not have to reclaim a block before it is filled. This implies that the block

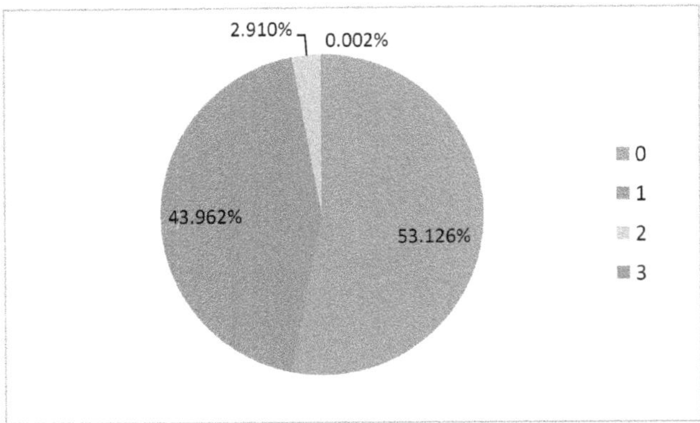

(a) Distrib. of Convert Cost (No. of mapping pages to be updated)

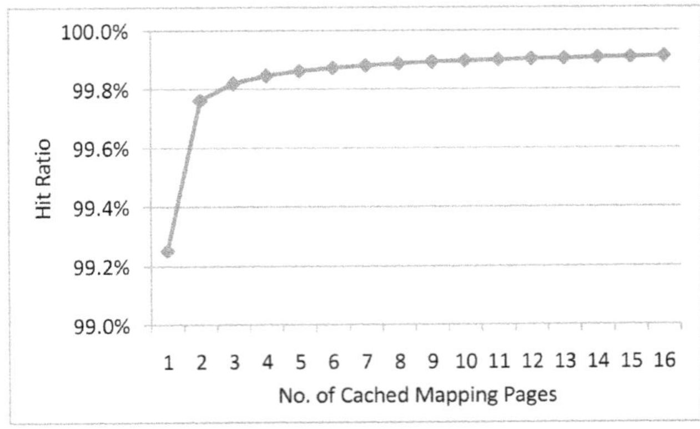

(b) No. of Cached Mapping Pages vs. Hit Ratio

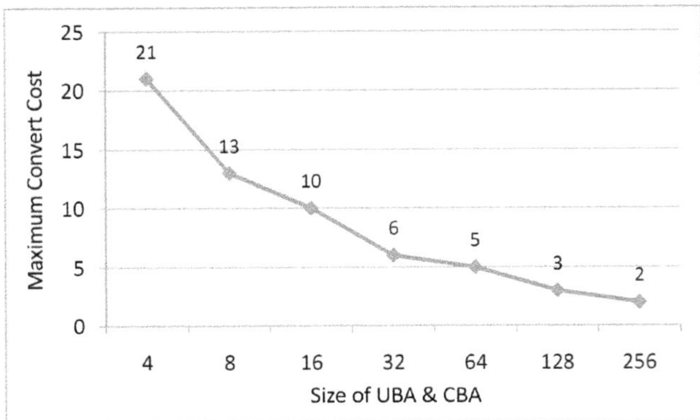

(c) Size of UBA & CBA vs. Maximum Convert Cost

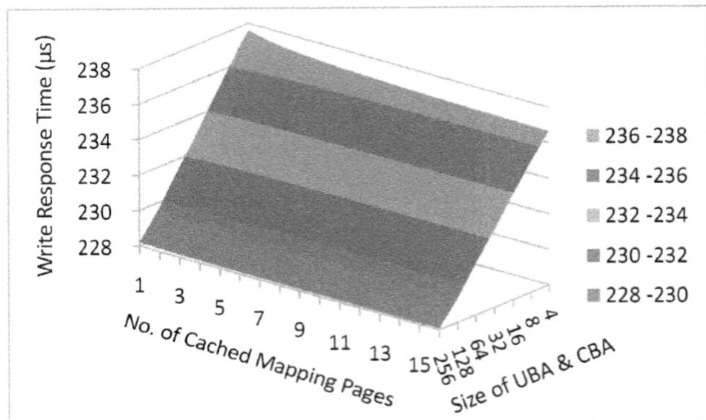

(d) Scalability of LazyFTL

Figure 6: Convert Cost and Scalability of LazyFTL

utilization of LazyFTL always equals the number of pages in a block, which also means that LazyFTL needs to perform fewer erase operations than other FTL schemes. If a proper wear leveling strategy is employed and the erase operations are distributed through the entire memory, LazyFTL will also prolong the life span of the flash chip.

One may argue that although LazyFTL successfully avoids merge operations, it has to convert a victim block in the UBA or the CBA when these two areas overflow. Nevertheless, Figure 6(a) indicates that in current configuration, LazyFTL needs to rewrite only a small number of mapping pages. We can also see from Figure 5(c) that LazyFTL has a much lower response latency for write requests than other schemes. This issue will be further discussed later.

The only disadvantage of LazyFTL is that when reading a page, LazyFTL sometimes has to load a mapping page before it knows the current location of the most up-to-date data. In hybrid FTL schemes, only one flash access is needed to serve a read request and block-level FTL schemes have to search the spare areas which is also very fast. However, for the trace we presented, LazyFTL has to read about 1.000727 pages on average to serve a one-page read request even though only 14 out of 1024 mapping pages can be cached in the SRAM.

6.3 Scalability of LazyFTL

When flash memory is organized in a larger array, designers may wish to control the size of the SRAM to reduce cost. Based on this assumption, we further examine the influence on the performance of LazyFTL when the size of the SRAM is reduced.

With other parameters unchanged, we first reduce the size of the LRU cache. This will increase the GMT access overhead since only a small part of the GMT is cached in the SRAM and only this small part can be read or modified. The GMT access overhead can be quantified by the cache miss ratio. As Figure 6(b) indicates, the cache hit ratio decreases very slowly at first until there are less than 5 pages cached in the SRAM. This trend means that the LRU cache can be reduced to save money or to save space for the UMT.

Then we diminish the size limit of the UBA and the CBA. Smaller UBA and CBA mean that convert operations have to be performed more frequently and some blocks may have to be converted before their convert costs have been lowered down. Similarly, other configurations are exactly the same as before. As Figure 6(c) shows, when this threshold is halved, the maximum convert cost increases slowly unless the threshold is under a certain level (around 32). Therefore, if LazyFTL is used in a real-time system which is strict with a single request latency, the total size of the UBA and the CBA should be kept above a certain level.

Figure 6(d) illustrates the combined influence on the performance of LazyFTL. One observation is that even though the SRAM size is greatly reduced, for example, 1 cached mapping page and at most 4 blocks in the UBA and the CBA, LazyFTL still outperforms other FTL schemes with an average latency of 237.613 μs for a write request. We can also see from Figure 6(d) that the size of the LRU cache also has a slight influence on the write response time especially when convert operations are more frequent and more expensive. This is because when converting a block, some mapping pages will need to be loaded from flash memory if they are not in the SRAM and if the LRU cache size is limited, it is more likely that these pages have been swapped out. A third observation can be made from this figure. In our original experiment, 32768 bytes in the SRAM is used to store the UMT and another 32768 bytes is used to store the cached part of the GMT and the GMD. Therefore, a tradeoff can be made between the UMT and the LRU cache of the GMT to further reduce the average write latency.

6.4 Reliability of LazyFTL

Among all the data structures used by LazyFTL, the GMD, the UMT, the update and invalidate flags are stored in the SRAM and will be lost when power is off (either due to a normal shutdown or a system failure). In this section, the reliability of LazyFTL will be presented and we will discuss how LazyFTL rebuilds these data structures during initialization.

Before the system is turned off, all blocks in the UBA and the CBA are converted to normal data blocks and each entry in the GMT is guaranteed to be correct. In this case, only the GMD needs to be built up during the next startup procedure.

When the system is initializing, spare areas of the first pages of all blocks in the flash memory are scanned and blocks that are holding mapping pages are found out. Then the spare areas of all pages in such blocks are scanned and valid mapping pages are identified. Based on this information, the GMD can be easily reconstructed.

After the GMD is ready, the system should be recovered to a consistent state if there is a failure. To this end, we should first identify blocks in the UBA or the CBA since address information of pages in these blocks may have not been updated to the GMT. Many methods can be adopted and we will list three of them.

- Researchers have discovered that by combining NOR-type and NAND-type flash memories together, complementary advantages can be achieved. If a small NOR-type chip is integrated in the flash memory, all this bookkeeping information can be easily preserved in NOR since NOR-type flash can be read and programmed in bytes. It is also possible for DFTL to use this method to keep a modification log in NOR to speed up the recover process. However, each time a page is rewritten, DFTL has to write a log record in NOR while LazyFTL only needs to write a record when a block in the UBA or the CBA is converted.
- The above method is not applicable everywhere since not all flash memories are equipped with a NOR facility. Another approach that is easy to implement is to keep the convert information in the MBA. When a block is converted, some mapping pages of the GMT may need to be updated. A small area of each mapping page can be reserved to store these information. If no mapping page is modified or if a checkpoint process is triggered to assist recovery procedures, a whole list of PBNs in the UBA and the CBA is written in the MBA in an independent page. This approach will slightly increase the overhead of convert operations but will improve the performance of recover procedures.
- Most manufacturers have reserved several bytes in the spare areas of their products. This provides us another chance. The technique is very simple. We can keep a counter in the spare area of the first page (or more) of each block that is wide enough and never overflows during the life span of flash memory. When a block is allocated to the UBA or the CBA, this counter is increased by one. And another age threshold is configured which is larger than the size limit of the UBA and the CBA. In our experiment, at most 128 blocks can be allocated to the UBA and the CBA. We may set the age threshold as 512, for example. This means that the largest difference between the counter of the newest block in the UBA or the CBA and the counters of other blocks in the UBA or the CBA can be 512 at most. When a block is getting too old, it is forced to be converted no matter how many mapping pages need to be updated. Following this protocol, we can assure that all blocks belong to the UBA or the CBA should be within the 512 most youngest blocks. Therefore, to find these blocks those have not been converted, a minimum heap is adopted and the 512 most youngest blocks are found and tried to be converted. Note that it should make no harm to convert a block that has been converted if a proper algorithm is adopted. We will not present this algorithm here due to space limitations.

When blocks in the UBA and the CBA are found and the UMT is built, the only remaining task is to recover the update flag and the invalidate flag for all entries in the UMT. We scan each entry of the UMT and find the relevant entry in the GMT since flags of an entry are determined by the states of the two tracked pages.

- If the relevant entry in the GMT has not been used, the two flags of the current entry should be '10' or '11' and this page is in state **B** as illustrated in Figure 3.
- If these two entries point to the same page, which means that the address translation information of this page has been updated to the GMT, the two flags should be set as '00' and the page is in state **C**.
- If the relevant entry in the GMT points to a free page or an invalid page or a valid page but has a different LPN, the two flags should be '10'. This scenario includes state **F**, **G**, and **H** in Figure 3.
- If the relevant entry in the GMT points to another valid page of this LPN, meaning that this page is in state **E**, we could set both flags of the page. We may also invalidate the old page in the DBA at once and set the two flags as '10' as what we do in state **G**.

When the GMD, the UMT and the two flag arrays are constructed, LazyFTL is ready to receive new requests. Note that there is no need to locate the two current blocks, the CUB and the CCB, since blocks that are not filled will make no difference. If, for some reason such as to save space, these two blocks are identified, there is also no need to distinguish them, since the concepts of cold data and hot data are not accurate themselves and a small quantity of misplacements will not be harmful.

Under some circumstances, we may find two different valid pages with the same LPN when scanning the MBA to rebuild the GMD or when scanning the UBA and the CBA to rebuild the UMT. This happens if the system fails after the new page is written and before the old one is invalidated. The solution has been introduced in [9]. By maintaining a 2-bit counter in the spare area of each page, we can easily tell the most up-to-date page from the old one.

7. CONCLUSION

Flash memory has emerged for tens of years and many efficient FTL schemes have been proposed. No matter whether the FTL is built as an independent software layer or it is built in the system software, technologies such as address translating, garbage collection, and wear leveling can be found in all flash-based applications.

To the best of our knowledge, the LazyFTL scheme proposed in this paper is the most efficient and effective FTL scheme ever invented, which is hard to surpass since we have successfully approached the theoretically optimal result. To overcome this theoretical barrier, knowledge of upper applications is critical. For example, to reduce flash traffic, IPL [19], BFTL [29], and FlashDB [25] try to pack the changed parts of a database system into fewer pages and reconstruct these pages when requested. These schemes are typical examples of making compromises between the read latency and the write performance.

Another research direction is presented in [27]. Unlike coaxial magnetic disks, different planes in a flash chip can operate in parallel sometimes, without competition for the flash channel. Therefore, garbage collections and merge operations in hybrid FTLs or convert operations in LazyFTL can be executed without interrupting current flash accesses if a proper strategy is adopted. Address translations can also be optimized to fit the parallel access feature. Some RAID techniques such as parallelization and load balancing have been intensively discussed. However, different characteristics of flash memory complicate matters.

8. ACKNOWLEDGEMENTS

We would like to thank all the anonymous reviewers for their professional dedication and their constructive comments on how to improve this paper.

9. REFERENCES

[1] Wikipedia: Flash memory, Sept. 2010. http://en.wikipedia.org/wiki/Flash_memory.

[2] D. Agrawal, D. Ganesan, R. Sitaraman, et al. Lazy-Adaptive Tree: An Optimized Index Structure for Flash Devices. In *VLDB'09*, Lyon, France, August 2009.

[3] A. Ban. Flash File System, Apr. 1995. United States Patent No. 5,404,485.

[4] A. Ban and R. Hasharon. Flash File System Optimized for Page-mode Flash Technologies, Aug. 1999. United States Patent No. 5,937,425.

[5] L.-P. Chang and T.-W. Kuo. An Efficient Management Scheme for Large-Scale Flash-Memory Storage Systems. In *SAC'04*, Nicosia, Cyprus, March 2004.

[6] H. Cho, D. Shin, and Y. I. Eom. KAST: K-Associative Sector Translation for NAND Flash Memory in Real-Time Systems. In *DATE'09*, April 2009.

[7] H. J. Choi, S.-H. Lim, and K. H. Park. JFTL: A Flash Translation Layer Based on a Journal Remapping for Flash Memory. *ACM Transactions on Storage*, 4(4), Jan. 2009.

[8] S. Choudhuri and T. Givargis. Performance Improvement of Block Based NAND Flash Translation Layer. In *CODES+ISSS'07*, Salzburg, Austria, 2007.

[9] E. Gal and S. Toledo. Algorithms and Data Structures for Flash Memories. *ACM Computing Surveys*, 37(2):138–163, June 2005.

[10] A. Gupta, Y. Kim, and B. Urgaonkar. DFTL: A Flash Translation Layer Employing Demand-based Selective Caching of Page-level Address Mappings. In *ASPLOS'09*, Washington, DC, USA, March 2009.

[11] J.-W. Hsieh, T.-W. Kuo, and L.-P. Chang. Efficient Identification of Hot Data for Flash Memory Storage Systems. *ACM Transactions on Storage*, 2(1):22–40, Feb. 2006.

[12] Intel. Understanding the Flash Translation Layer (FTL) Specification. Technical report, Intel Corporation, Dec. 1998.

[13] D. Kang, D. Jung, J.-U. Kang, and J.-S. Kim. μ-Tree: An Ordered Index Structure for NAND Flash Memory. In *EMSOFT'07*, Salzburg, Austria, 2007.

[14] J.-U. Kang, H. Jo, J.-S. Kim, and J. Lee. A Superblock-based Flash Translation Layer for NAND Flash Memory. In *EMSOFT'06*, Seoul, Korea, Oct. 2006.

[15] J. Kim, J. M. Kim, S. H. Noh, et al. A Space-efficient Flash Translation Layer for CompactFlash Systems. *IEEE Transactions on Consumer Electronics*, 48(2), May 2002.

[16] D. Koo and D. Shin. Adaptive Log Block Mapping Scheme for Log Buffer-based FTL (Flash Translation Layer). In *IWSSPS'09*, Grenoble, France, Oct. 2009.

[17] H.-S. Lee, H.-S. Yun, and D.-H. Lee. HFTL: Hybrid Flash Translation Layer based on Hot Data Identification for Flash Memory. *IEEE Transactions on Consumer Electronics*, 55(4), Nov. 2009.

[18] S. Lee, D. Shin, Y.-J. Kim, et al. LAST: Locality-Aware Sector Translation for NAND Flash Memory-Based Storage Systems. *ACM SIGOPS Operating Systems Review*, 42(6), Oct. 2008.

[19] S.-W. Lee and B. Moon. Design of Flash-Based DBMS: An In-Page Logging Approach. In *SIGMOD'07*, Beijing, China, June 2007.

[20] S.-W. Lee, D.-J. Park, T.-S. Chung, et al. A Log Buffer Based Flash Translation Layer using Fully Associative Sector Translation. *ACM Transactions on Embedded Computing Systems (TECS)*, 6(3), July 2007.

[21] Y.-G. Lee, D. Jung, D. Kang, et al. μ-FTL: A Memory-Efficient Flash Translation Layer Supporting Multiple Mapping Granularities. In *EMSOFT'08*, Atlanta, Georgia, USA, Oct. 2008.

[22] Y. Li, B. He, R. J. Yang, et al. Tree Indexing on Solid State Drives. In *Proceedings of the VLDB Endowment*, Singapore, Sept. 2010.

[23] Micron. Small-Block vs. Large-Block NAND Flash Devices. Technical report, Micron Technology, Inc., May 2007.

[24] D. Narayanan, A. Donnelly, and A. Rowstron. Write Off-Loading: Practical Power Management for Enterprise Storage. In *Proc. 6th USENIX Conference on File and Storage Technologies (FAST'08)*, 2008.

[25] S. Nath and A. Kansal. FlashDB: Dynamic Self-tuning Database for NAND Flash. In *IPSN'07*, Cambridge, Massachusetts, USA, April 2007.

[26] C. Park, W. Cheon, J. Kang, et al. A Reconfigurable FTL (Flash Translation Layer) Architecture for NAND Flash-Based Applications. *ACM Transactions on Embedded Computing Systems*, 7(4), July 2008.

[27] J.-Y. Shin, Z.-L. Xia, N.-Y. Xu, et al. FTL Design Exploration in Reconfigurable High-Performance SSD for Server Applications. In *ICS'09*, Yorktown Heights, New York, USA, June 2009.

[28] SuperTalent. SLC vs. MLC: An Analysis of Flash Memory. Technical report, Super Talent Technology, Inc., San Jose, CA, USA, 2008.

[29] C.-H. Wu, L.-P. Chang, and T.-W. Kuo. An Efficient B-Tree Layer for Flash-Memory Storage Systems. In *RTCSA'03*, Tainan, Taiwan, 2003.

Operation-Aware Buffer Management in Flash-based Systems

Yanfei Lv[1] Bin Cui[1] Bingsheng He[2] Xuexuan Chen[1]

[1] Department of Computer Science & Key Lab of High Confidence Software Technologies (Ministry of Education), Peking University
{lvyf,bin.cui,xuexuan}@pke.edu.cn

[2] Division of Computer Science School of Computer Engineering Nanyang Technological University
bshe@ntu.edu.sg

ABSTRACT

The inherent asymmetry of read and write speeds of flash memory poses great challenges for buffer management design. Most of existing flash-based buffer management policies adopt disk-oriented strategies by giving a specific priority to dirty pages, while not fully exploiting the characteristics of the flash memory. In this paper, we propose a novel buffer replacement algorithm named *FOR*, which stands for ***F***lash-based ***O***peration-aware buffer ***R***eplacement. The core idea of *FOR* is based on novel operation-aware page weight determination for buffer replacement. The weight metric not only measures the locality of read/write operations on a page, but also takes the cost difference of read/write operations into account. We further develop an efficient implementation FOR^{+} with the time complexity of $O(1)$ for each operation. Experiments on synthetic and benchmark traces demonstrate the efficiency of the proposed strategy, which yields better performance compared with some state-of-the-art flash-based buffer management policies.

Categories and Subject Descriptors

H.2.4 [**DATABASE MANAGEMENT**]: Systems—*Query processing*

General Terms

Algorithms, Design, Performance

Keywords

Flash memory, SSD, Buffer management, Operation aware

1. INTRODUCTION

Flash memory has dominated the storage for portable devices due to its advantages of light weight, power saving and shock resistance. With the increasing capacity and dropping price, flash-based solid state drive (SSD, or flash disks) has emerged as a popular storage for enterprise applications [7, 20]. Due to the characteristics of flash based storage, flash-based data structures and search algorithms [4, 14, 16, 18, 29, 30] on database systems have become a fruitful research field. Buffer manager is another core component in database systems, and the buffer replacement strategies need to be revisited on the flash-based storage.

The effectiveness of buffer management policies can heavily influence the performance of database systems. While flash disks have much better I/O performance than hard disks, they are still over two orders of magnitude slower than the main memory. An effective policy can reduce the number of costly disk accesses, and boost the overall performance of the database system. Thus there have been considerable interests in buffer management algorithms for database systems. Traditional disk-based policies [10, 8] mainly aim at reducing the rate of buffer misses that cause disk accesses. When a buffer page needs to be replaced, the victim is chosen based on the recency and/or frequency of the accesses on the page. However, minimizing the cache miss rate may achieve a sub-optimal I/O performance on flash-based systems. This is because, compared with hard disks, flash disks have an inherent feature, namely *read-write asymmetry*. The read-write asymmetry is that, write operations can be an order of magnitude slower than reads on the flash disk. Due to this asymmetry, buffer manager must distinguish read and write operations. For example, the benefit of keeping a write-intensive page tends to be higher than that of keeping a read-intensive one.

A number of buffer management policies [11, 12, 19, 21, 25] have been proposed to address the read-write asymmetry on the flash disk. Most of them adopt the disk-oriented buffer replacement strategies, such as LRU (Least Recently Used) and LIRS [8], but give a higher priority to the dirty pages to be kept in the buffer. The intuition is straightforward: replacement of a dirty page introduces a write on the flash disk, which is much more expensive than evicting a clean page. For example, CFLRU [25] maintains a window at the least used end of the LRU queue. Within the window, clean pages are preferred as victims and dirty pages are considered only when there is no clean page in the window. A series of WSR [11, 12] (Write Sequential Reorder) methods give another chance to a dirty page upon its eviction. While existing flash-based algorithms improve the performance of database systems on the flash disk, they simply improve the traditional disk-based buffer replacement policies with the consideration of current pages' states, and the temporal locality of the future *operations* is ignored. When multiple write operations perform on a dirty page, they result in at most one write operation, if the page is kept in the buffer. On the other hand, the dirty page that has no future write operations or has been inactive for long time should be evicted to free the precious buffer resource. Therefore, both the page state and the future operations are important for the buffer management.

In this paper, we argue for an integral combination between the future operations and the page state to define the *hotness* of a page in the buffer. The combination also takes the asymmetry of read and write speeds of the flash disk into account. The output of the combination is to assign a deliberate weight to each page in the buffer. The lower weight indicates that it is more likely to be a victim page. We start with quantifying the benefit of keeping a page in the buffer by distinguishing the page state (clean or dirty) and its next operation (read or write). For example, given a dirty page with a next operation (read), we can save a page read if we keep the page in the buffer. As for future operations, we introduce inter-operation distance (IOD) and the operation recency (OR) for a page operation to quantify its frequency and recency, respectively. Partial weights based on the metrics are finally combined into one.

We further design the algorithms of FOR, a ***F**lash-based **O**peration-aware buffer **R**eplacement policy*. The core component of FOR is the page weight calculation. A naive policy is to maintain the weight of each page upon each operation, and to choose the page with the lowest weight as the victim. However, this naive policy requires $O(n)$ time to handle a page operation, where n is the number of distinct pages that have been accessed. This is not efficient in real database systems. Therefore, we develop an approximated version of FOR, named FOR^+. The approximation adopts the metrics of the weight with binary representations to approximate the combination of operation type and page state. Additionally, FOR^+ embraces novel data structures to estimate the hotness of page operation and to select the victim page for buffer replacement. The proposed FOR^+ algorithm requires only $O(1)$ for each operation access in the buffer on average.

We evaluate the performance of the proposed buffer replacement approaches by comparing with the state-of-the-art flash-based algorithms. The experiments are conducted on both synthetic and real traces from public benchmarks including TPC-C, TPC-B, and TATP [3], and our experimental study shows that $FOR+$ approach is superior to the other buffer replacement methods.

The remainder of this paper is organized as follows. We review the related work in Section 2. We present the operation aware weight determination strategy in Section 3, followed by the implementation of our buffer algorithms in Section 4. Section 5 delivers the experimental results. Finally, we conclude the paper in Section 6.

2. PRELIMINARIES

In this section, we briefly introduce the background on flash memory, and review the related work on disk- and flash-based buffer management.

2.1 Flash Memory

Based on the characteristics of flash-based storage, we identify two following challenges for existing disk-based I/O systems. We refer readers to some recent studies [5, 6] for more details on flash memory.

- **Asymmetry of I/O:** Random write operations are much slower than reads, due to the costly erase operations. Note that, read latency and write latency of SSDs vary significantly for different brands. System components such as indexing and buffer management should be aware of this asymmetry.

- **Low access latency:** Flash disks are over an order of magnitude faster than hard disks. Such a low access latency prohibits complicated data structures and algorithms with high computational overhead. For example, selecting a victim in the buffer management should be simple to compensate the I/O benefit.

Flash-based databases have become a hot topic for several years. Detailed studies [5, 6] have been conducted to reveal the internal I/O feature of flash disks. Lee et al. [16] proposed an in-page logging strategy to reduce the number of writes. They [17] further performed extensive experiments on a commercial DBMS, which show that flash can improve the overall performance of DBMS especially in logging. A disk-flash mixed storage system [14] is proposed to adopt the merits of both hard disks and flashes. Flash-optimized data structures are developed to improve indexing performance in databases [30, 4, 18].

2.2 Buffer Management

Buffer management is a critical issue in database systems. There is a long stream of research on designing effective buffer replacement strategies, and many approaches have been proposed. LRU (Least Recently Used) and LFU (Least Frequently Used) are two classic buffer replacement policies for recency and frequency, respectively. Many approaches were proposed to combine the advantages of recency and frequency [22, 15, 28, 26]. Maximizing the buffer hit rate is the main goal of these disk-oriented buffer management strategies. This goal is no longer valid on the flash disk, due to the asymmetry of read and write speeds. This asymmetry calls for new buffer management policies on the flash disk.

A number of flash-based buffer management policies have recently been developed to improve the efficiency of traditional disk-based policies on the flash disk. FAB [9] and BPLRU [13] are two erase block-level buffer management strategies. They are both designed for embedded flash devices. Most existing buffer management policies on flash disk adopt existing disk-based policies by delaying dirty page eviction. CFLRU [25] defines a window in the least recently used end of the LRU queue. All the clean pages in the window are evicted first; dirty pages are evicted only when there is no clean page in the window. LIRS-WSR [12] and LRU-WSR [11] are adopted from LIRS and LRU, respectively. Both of them give higher priority to dirty pages, evicting a dirty page when it is selected as victim at the second time. CCF-LRU [19] improves LRU-WSR by dividing clean pages into hot and cold ones according to the access frequency. The eviction of a clean page is performed on the cold clean pages first and then on the hot clean pages. CASA [23] organizes the buffer as clean page list and dirty page list. Depending on the read/write cost ratio, it dynamically adjusts the size of the two lists. The decision of these flash-based algorithms (except CCF-LRU) is solely based on the current page state. However, the current page state itself is not sufficient to determine whether the page is a victim or not. Our approach remedies this by taking both the page state and the operation temporal locality into account.

By design, CCFLRU is inferior to FOR. CCFLRU fails to detect the hot clean page. When dirty pages fully occupy the entire buffer, it is very difficult for clean ones to get buffer back. This weakness is due to the design of CCFLRU. CCFLRU contains two lists: Cold Clean LRU (CCL) List and Mixed LRU (ML) List. Pages in the CCL list are evicted first. As a result, the CCL list decreases as the system goes, and the CCL list is likely to become empty. In this case, after a newly read page is inserted into the CCL list, this page is evicted immediately when a new page is required. Therefore, unless a page is read twice continuously, a clean page never has a chance to become hot. In comparison, FOR does not have this problem, because the read operation information is maintained even after the page is evicted. Therefore, a clean page has the opportunity to become hot when it is read again in FOR.

Write clustering has been considered as an effective technique in reducing the total cost [24, 27]. CFDC [24] enhances CFLRU by clustering dirty pages and evicting them as a batch. Similar techniques are used in recently-evicted-first algorithm [27]. Evicting dirty pages as a cluster is an orthogonal solution for buffer management, and it can be integrated into our policy easily to further improve the performance.

3. OPERATION AWARE WEIGHT DETERMINATION

In this section, we present our operation aware strategy to determine the weight of each page for buffer replacement. The weight determination takes the asymmetry of read and write speeds as well as operation-wise statistics such as frequency and recency into account. Table 1 facilitates fast checking on the notations used throughout this paper.

Table 1: Parameters Used in This Paper

Parameters	Description
W_p	Weight of page p
H_e	Hotness of a page operation e
IOD_r, IOD_w	Inter-operation distances of read and write respectively
OR_r, OR_w	Operation recency of read and write respectively
S_{buffer}	Buffer size (pages)
C_r, C_w	Time cost of reading and writing a page respectively
C_{tIO}	Total I/O cost of accessing flash device
C_{tb}	Total buffer cost
N_{df}	Total number of dirty pages flushed (when the system terminates or performs checkpoint)
L_{Upper}, L_{Lower}	Length of Upper queue and Lower queue in FOR^+ respectively
R_{cold}	Ratio of cold pages in the buffer

3.1 Effect of Page State

Read and write operations have similar costs in traditional disk-based database system. Thus, the primary target of buffer management for disk-based databases is to maximize the hit rate of buffer, ignoring what kind of operation is hit. Since the read/write characteristics of flash memory are different from those of hard disk, existing flash-based algorithms further consider cost difference of read/writes, and try to keep more dirty pages in the buffer to reduce the expensive cost of writes to the disk.

Most existing studies adopt total I/O cost to evaluate the performance of buffer replacement strategies. I/O cost may come in two ways. 1) At the run time, a buffer miss will incur a read from the disk device and may incur a write if the evicted page is dirty. 2) At the end of running or checkpointing, system will flush all the dirty pages in the buffer, where the number of writes performed is according to the number of dirty pages. Thus, by accumulating these two parts, we get the following formula for total I/O cost, where C_r and C_w stand for the time cost of performing a read and a write, respectively, and N_{df} stands for number of dirty pages which we need to flush at the end of running or checkpointing.

$$C_{tIO} = \sum_{all\ buffer\ misses} (C_r + evicted\ dirty?C_w : 0) + N_{df}C_w \quad (1)$$

The above formula is obtained by counting the I/O operations to the flash device. However, this is not convenient for buffer performance analysis, as it needs to know whether the evicted page is dirty and the number of dirty pages in the cache. Hence, we transfer the formula from the perspective of buffer operations. In the following analysis, we consider the operations to buffer instead of operations to flash device. We define *buffer cost* to be the cost of each operation to the buffer. Clearly, the buffer cost is subject to whether this operation is a hit or a miss as well as the operation type. We obtain buffer cost for each case in Table 2. The clean or dirty in the table refer to the page state before eviction if the operation is a miss.

Table 2: Buffer Cost for Different Operation Types

Operation	Clean		Dirty	
	miss	hit	miss	hit
read	C_r	0	C_r	0
write	$C_r + C_w$	C_w	$C_r + C_w$	0

It can be observed that a write operation causes a cost of $C_r + C_w$ for a buffer miss while a read causes C_r. A write hit on clean page also results in a cost of C_w. This is because the clean page turns dirty and needs to be written back in the future. For a trace, we can get cost from this table for each operation. Summing up these costs, we get the total buffer cost, recorded as C_{tb}. By comparing the number of read and write operation to flash device respectively, we have $C_{tb} = C_{tIO}$, i.e., the total buffer cost is the same as the total I/O cost.

We further derive the I/O time reduced by keeping a page in the buffer (defined as *buffer benefit*. By comparing miss and hit costs in Table 2, we obtain the buffer benefit of reads and writes in Table 3. Suppose a page is currently held by

Table 3: **Buffer Benefit on One Page Operation**

Future Operation	Clean	Dirty
Read	C_r	C_r
Write	C_r	C_r+C_w

the buffer waiting for some future operations. There are four cases in total according to the combination of future operations and page states, and each case is analyzed as follows.

1. **Read on clean page:** This means the current state of the page is clean and the next operation on this page is a read operation. If we keep the page in buffer, the page can be used directly without accessing the flash disk, i.e., no extra I/O time is needed. Otherwise, the page has to be loaded into buffer first, a flash read takes place. Thus, I/O time reduced is C_r in this case.
2. **Read on dirty page:** Similar analysis can be done as case 1. If the dirty page is kept in buffer, the operation cost is zero as we can access the buffered page directly. Otherwise, the cost is C_r. The I/O time of dirty page write back is not calculated because this write back will eventually happen afterwards.
3. **Write on clean page:** If the page is kept in the buffer, it will turn dirty. Otherwise, the page should be loaded into the buffer first which incurs read cost, then the page also turns dirty. Hence, the benefit of using buffer is C_r.
4. **Write on dirty page:** As the page is dirty, the write operation can be merged with the previous one if the page is reserved in the buffer, and hence the write cost is saved. On the contrary, a page write to the flash memory will be introduced if the page is evicted, and a page read is used to load it into the buffer. Consequently, the buffer benefit is C_r+C_w.

Only the immediately succeeding operation is enough for victim decision, because no matter whether a page is kept in the buffer, after the following operation, the page will certainly reside in buffer. Thus, the current victim decision can only affect the cost of the immediately following read and write operation. It can be observed from the table that the costs reduced by buffering a dirty page are totally different, which are affected by succeeding read/write operation on the dirty page. Therefore, not only the page state but also the future operation should be considered to determine an appropriate victim for buffer replacement.

3.2 Effect of Operation Locality

How to make full use of the information provided by operation sequence to estimate the hotness of a page is a key issue to solve in our operation-aware buffer management strategy. We denote a page operation as a pair $e=\langle p, m\rangle$, where p denotes the page to be accessed, and m is the access mode ($m \in \{\text{read, write}\}$). Thus $e_i=e_j$ means that $e_i.p=e_j.p$ and $e_i.m=e_j.m$. A reference sequence is a sequence of n page operations, $S = e_1, e_2, ..., e_n$, where e_i is a page operation. The latest operation is recorded as e_{latest}. We say $e_i \prec e_j$, if $i < j$ in the sequence, and $e_i \preceq e_j$, if $i \leq j$. And we define the previous same operation of e as $ps(e) = e_i$ if $(e_i = e) \wedge \neg\exists e_j((e_j = e) \wedge (e_i \prec e_j \prec e))$. Note that $ps(e)$ may be null.

Buffering the hot pages can generally increase the hit ratio of buffer replacement methods, and there are various metrics to evaluate the hotness of pages, among which frequency and recency are the commonly used metrics to reflect the hotness. In this study, we define two concepts Inter-Operation Distance (IOD) and Operation Recency (OR) to reflect the frequency and recency of a page operation, respectively.

DEFINITION 1. *Suppose the inter-operation set of a page operation e is*

$$IOS_e = \{e_j | ps(e) \preceq e_j \preceq e\} \tag{2}$$

Inter Operation Distance is defined as:

$$IOD_e = |IOS_e|, if\ ps(e) \neq null \tag{3}$$

IOD_e is the number of distinct operations performed between two consecutive "identical operations" on one page including the operation itself. IOD_e does not exist if $ps(e) = null$. Taking the operation sequence in Figure 1 as an example, the IOD of the last read on page B is 3, and the IOD of the last write on page A is 5. The smaller the IOD_e is, the hotter operation e is. Note that, the average frequency of an operation can be estimated by dividing the length of operation sequence by the number of the occurrences of the operation. However, such calculation is computationally expensive and infeasible in real applications. Therefore, we use IOD to represent the frequency in our study.

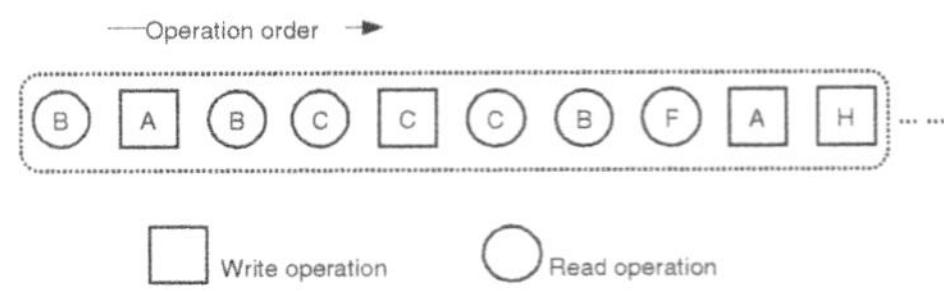

Figure 1: Illustration of inter operation distance

DEFINITION 2. *Operation Recency of a page operation e is defined as:*

$$OR_e = |\{e_j | e \preceq e_j \preceq e_{latest}\}| \tag{4}$$

The definition of OR_e denotes the number of distinct operations performed after e appeared. Note that recency is the potential IOD in the future. If only one e is in the operation sequence, the value of IOD_e does not exist. When the second e, i.e., the same operation on the same page, occurs, OR_e is equal to IOD_e. That means, the future IOD should be no less than the current operation recency.

The two metrics (IOD_e and OR_e) are complementary in measuring the hotness of the corresponding page accessed by e. The OR only reflects the freshness of the page operation, while ignoring the long-term workload pattern. On the other hand, only using IOD is problematic as the recency information is not included. For example, if an operation with low IOD never appears again in the operation sequence, the value of IOD will never change. Therefore, we design to integrate IOD and OR for page hotness determination.

DEFINITION 3. *Hotness of an operation e is reflected by weighted sum of IOD and OR.*

$$H_e = \alpha * IOD_e + (1 - \alpha) * OR_e \tag{5}$$

Where α is a tuning parameter to determine the importance of the two factors, and the experimental tuning evaluation will be presented in our performance study. If IOD_e does not exist, we use the value of OR_e as that of IOD_e in the above definition. H_e indicates the popularity of a page according to the operation statistics.

3.3 Operation-aware Page weight

In Sec 3.1 & 3.2, we have discussed the operation-wise page information which affects the buffer replacement strategy. According to our observation and analysis, we need to consider page state and page operation statistical information to determine the importance of a page for buffer management. We give the page weight in the Definition 4. In the formula, W_p distinguishes the I/O time reduced by buffering the page p as shown in Table 3, as well as the hotness of read/write operations on the page.

DEFINITION 4. *Suppose r and w are the latest read and write operations on page p, respectively. The weight of p (W_p) is defined as:*

$$W_p = \begin{cases} C_r/H_r + C_r/H_w, & p \text{ is clean} \\ C_r/H_r + (C_r + C_w)/H_w, & p \text{ is dirty} \end{cases} \quad (6)$$

Note that, if there is no previous read or write operation on a certain page, the corresponding item in above Formula 6 should be zero. Given the definition of W_p, we can calculate its value and choose the victim for buffer replacement using W_p. The page with the minimum weight is chosen as the victim. The algorithm will be presented in the next section.

4. THE IMPLEMENTATION OF *FOR*

In this section, we will introduce our algorithm for buffer management based on the concept of operation-aware page weight determination, named *FOR*, which stands for ***F***lash-based ***O***peration-aware buffer ***R***eplacement. Due to the computational complexity of *FOR*, we also design an approximated version of *FOR*, named FOR^+, which achieves $O(1)$ time complexity on handling a page operation.

4.1 The *FOR* algorithm

Based on the concept of page weight W_p, we develop a buffer replacement algorithm *FOR*, in which the page with the minimum weight is chosen as the victim. We use an LRU queue named *operation list* to facilitate computation of *IOD* and *OR*. As shown in Figure 2, the operation list stores the latest read and write operations for all the pages that have been accessed. Note that, we only use page ID in the list, and the pages may have already been evicted from the buffer. These operations are adjusted in the LRU manner. Thus the number of operations between the head and operation e is OR_e. When operation e comes again, OR_e at that time is IOD_e. On every operation performed, we can calculate its *IOD*. Thus, *OR* and *IOD* can be calculated for every operation in the operation list. Besides the data structure shown in Figure 2, all the control information including pointers to the node in operation list, pointer to the real data page, *IOD* and the state information of the page are integrated as a structure named *frame*. To accelerate page and information accesses, all the frames are indexed by an in-memory hash table according to page ID.

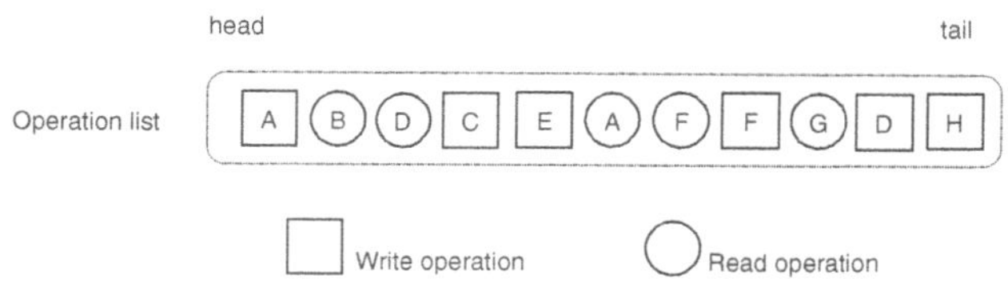

Figure 2: Data structure of *FOR*

The detailed algorithm of *FOR* is listed as Algorithm 1. If the buffer is full and thus an eviction is needed, we first calculate *OR*s and weights for all pages (Lines 2–5), and find a page with the minimum weight as victim (Lines 7-11). After the operation, we calculate IOD if the operation has already existed in the operation list (Line 16).

Algorithm 1: The FOR algorithm

```
    Input: an operation request e on page p
 1  if p is non-resident and buffer is full then
 2      foreach operation op in the operation list do
 3          calculate OR_op;
 4          calculate the weight of the corresponding
            page;
 5      end
 6      W_victim=inf;
 7      foreach page p_i in the buffer do
 8          if W_{p_i} < W_victim then
 9              update victim to p_i;
10          end
11      end
12      evict victim;
13  end
14  perform the operation;
15  if e exists on operation list then
16      adjust the operation list and calculate IOD_e;
17  else
18      add the operation to the head of operation list;
19  end
```

Upon each eviction, FOR calculates the weights for all accessed pages, and chooses the page with the lowest weight as the victim. Suppose the working set of the database system is n pages, and the buffer pool size is S_{buffer} pages. The loops in Lines 2–5 and 7–11 have the time complexity of $O(n)$ and $O(S_{buffer})$, respectively. Since in practice, $S_{buffer} \ll n$, the time complexity of handling a page operation in *FOR* is $O(n)$. The efficiency is unacceptable in a real database system. This motivates us to reduce the computational complexity while taking the weight concept into account.

4.2 An approximated version FOR^+

The dominant computational cost of *FOR* algorithm is the calculation of page weights in the buffer. To reduce the time complexity, we have to design an efficient metric to approximate the weight. In contrast to the numerical representation of weight, we adopt categorical weight states to approximate the weight of a page. That leads to an approximated algorithm FOR^+ with $O(1)$ time complexity.

In Equation 6, there are two adding factors for each weight state, including the page state and the operation hotness. So there are 4 high weight states in total. We can use 4 marks RCH (Read Clean page High), WCH (Write Clean page High), RDH (Read Dirty page High) and WDH (Write Dirty page High) to represent the high weights for C_r/H_r, C_r/H_w, C_r/H_r and $(C_r + C_w)/H_w$, respectively. Among these four marks, RCH and RDH are with same cost and similar semantic, so they can be combined to RH (Read page High). On the other hand, once a page is written, the state of page changes to dirty. So, WCH is volatile and we only reserve the WDH mark for a dirty page. Consequently, we utilize two weight status marks RH and WDH in our proposed FOR^+ approach.

For simplicity, FOR^+ sets the marks according to the value of IOD as the IOD reflects the access frequency, and cleans the marks according to the value of OR to discard the operation without reference for a long time. For example, for a read operation e, if C_r/IOD_e is relatively high among all the operations, we set e's RH.

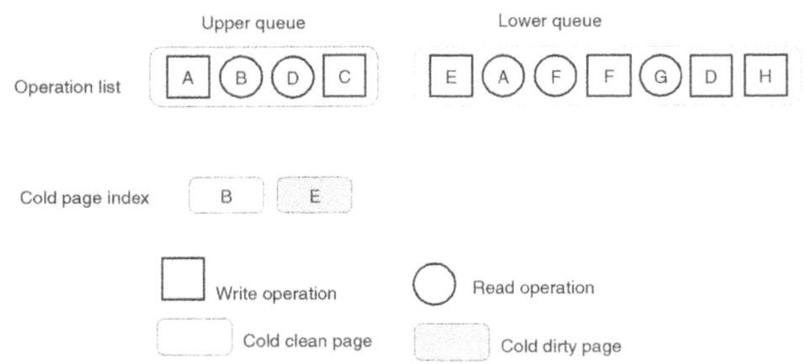

Figure 3: Data structure of FOR^+

FOR^+ extends the data structure shown in Figure 2 to facilitate the weight status mark determination. The operation list is divided into two virtual queues, i.e., Upper and Lower, as illustrated in Figure 3. Overall, these two queues work in the LRU manner as a whole, that is, the operation evicted from Upper queue is inserted into Lower queue as the head of Lower queue, while the operation hit on Lower queue or Upper queue is moved to the head of Upper queue. The most recent operation is inserted as the head of Upper queue. Thus, it can be observed easily that the number of operations from the head of Upper queue to an operation e is OR_e, and if an identical operation of e arrives, OR_e at that moment is IOD_e. For example, in Figure 3 the OR of operation write E is 5, and if a write E happens at this moment, IOD of write E is 5.

In FOR^+, we try to ensure $L_{Upper}/C_r = L_{Lower}/C_w$ during the buffer process, where L_{Upper} and L_{Lower} stand for length of Upper and Lower queues respectively. Thus, we can derive: $C_r/L_{Upper} = (C_r+C_w)/(L_{Lower}+L_{Upper})$, which is denoted as M_{bound}. We use the M_{bound} as the threshold to allocate the marks. Take the read operation e on B, in the Upper queue as an example, when another e comes, we have $IOD_e \leq L_{Upper}$, that is, $C_r/IOD_e \geq M_{bound}$. Thus, B's RH mark is set. Similarly, if a write hit on either Upper or Lower queue means $(C_r + C_w)/IOD_e \geq M_{bound}$, we set the WDH mark. Initially, we assume both marks of newly arrived pages are cleared.

The entire buffer pool in FOR^+ is virtually divided into two sub-pools, one for hot pages and the other for cold pages. A page is cold if it is a clean page without setting the RH mark, or it is a dirty page without setting RH or WDH. Otherwise, the page is hot. In FOR^+, only the cold pages can be selected as the victim for buffer replacement. FOR^+ ensures a certain ratio of cold pages (denoted as R_{cold}) in the buffer, which is a tuning parameter in our algorithm. If the corresponding marks of a page are set, the status of the page will be upgraded to hot. Meanwhile, if the ratio of cold pages in the buffer is lower than R_{cold}, we have to downgrade a page to the cold page pool, and this process is named as "Compensation". The byproduct of the compensation process is to maintain the ratio between L_{Upper} and L_{Lower}, and to shrink Upper queue or Lower queue to clear the marks of less important pages.

The process of compensation is realized by shrinking Upper queue and Lower queue in turn. If $L_{Upper}/C_r > L_{Lower}/C_w$, the Upper queue shrinks; otherwise, the Lower queue does. To shrink an operation queue, the tail operation of the queue is removed and the mark of that page is cleared. According to the operation types in different queues, we have following cases corresponding to the mark status: 1) If a read operation is removed from Upper queue, the RH mark of the corresponding page is cleared; 2) If a write operation is removed from Lower queue, the WDH mark is cleared. After that, a cold test is performed on the mark-cleared page, i.e., whether clean page with RH cleared, or a dirty page with RH and WDH cleared. If the page is changed to cold, the compensation process ends. Otherwise, the process above repeats until one hot page is changed to cold. The tail operation removed from lower queue will be deleted to save the space used, and this operation will be treated as new if the page is accessed again in the future.

Algorithm 2: The FOR$^+$ Algorithm

Input: an operation request, e
if *the frame does not exist in hash table* **then**
  create a new frame;
end
get the frame from hash table;
if *the frame is nonresident in buffer* **then**
  Allocate free slot(Algorithm 3);
end
perform the operation;
if *e is read* **and** *hit on Upper queue* **then**
  set e's RH mark;
end
if *e is write* **and** *(hit on Upper queue* **or** *on Lower queue)* **then**
  set e's WDH mark;
end
adjust the Upper queue and Lower queue in LRU manner as a whole;
if *the page operated is in cold page index* **then**
  if *the page operated is cold* **then**
    adjust the cold page index in the LRU manner;
  else
    remove the page from cold page index;
  end
end
L_{cold}= the number of cold pages in the buffer;
if $L_{cold} < R_{cold} * S_{buffer}$ **then**
  compensation (Algorithm 4);
end

Figure 4: An example of FOR^+

A cold page index is used to accelerate the eviction, as illustrated in Figure 3. The cold page pool works in the LRU manner. When a free slot is needed from the buffer, the cold page which is not referenced for the longest time is chosen as the victim. Page id instead of operation is stored in cold page index. Cold page index is a queue acting in the LRU manner. A new page is inserted at the head of cold page index. Every access hit on the index will cause the referenced page to be moved to the head, if the page is not upgraded to hot. Hence, the tail page is selected as the victim when a free slot is needed. With the help of cold page index, the victim can be determined quickly when an eviction takes place.

Algorithm 3: Allocate a free slot in FOR^+

```
if buffer is not full then
    return any free slot;
else
    get the tail from the cold page index;
    if the page is dirty then
        write back;
    end
    free and return the slot;
end
```

The overall process of FOR^+ algorithm is given in Algorithm 2. We extend a frame in FOR with the two weight status marks. The algorithm first gets the frame information and performs the operation (Lines 1-8). When a free page is requested, Algorithm 3 is called. After the operation is performed, the marks (Lines 9-14) and data structures (Lines

Algorithm 4: Compensation in FOR^+

```
repeat
    if L_Upper / C_r > L_Lower / C_w then    /* Shrink Upper queue */
        remove the tail operation from Upper queue;
        insert the operation into Lower queue;
        if the operation is read then
            clear the RH mark;
        end
    else                                     /* Shrink Lower queue */
        remove the tail operation from Lower queue;
        if the operation is write then
            clear the WDH mark;
        end
    end
    change = whether the clear marked page is changed from hot to cold;
    if change then
        add the page to the head of the cold page index;
    end
until a cold page is added ;
```

15-22) are updated. The queue adjustment process (Line 15) includes 1) inserting a new item into the head and 2) adjusting the queue in the LRU manner if one item is hit on the queue. The operation hit on Lower queue is also moved to the head of Upper queue. If the buffer pool is full, one page will be evicted from the buffer. Once a cold page is changed to hot, compensation may be called to change a hot page to a cold one (Lines 23-26) so that the number of cold page is constant in the buffer. Algorithm 4 illustrates the process of compensation. Compensation is done by shrinking Upper queue and Lower queue in turn, during which some marks are cleared, until a hot page is changed to cold.

An example is given in Figure 4 illustrating the process of FOR^+. Figure 4 (a) shows the initial state of the operation list and the cold page index. Suppose a write on the page C. According to FOR^+, the buffer state is shown in Figure 4 (b). Operation write C is moved to the head of Upper queue. Since this operation is a hit on the operation list, C's WDH is set. Similarly, we can handle a read on page B, and the buffer state is shown in Figure 4 (c). As reading B is a hit on Upper queue, B's RH is set, and B is removed from cold page index. The compensation process is invoked, because $L_{Upper}/C_r > L_{Lower}/C_w$. The operation at the end of Lower queue, operation H, is removed and inserted to the head of the cold page index. After that, reading F is performed, and a buffer miss occurs (Figure 4 (d)). To free a page slot, the end of the cold page index, E, is evicted from the buffer. As $L_{cold}<R_{cold} * S_{buffer}$, one page will be compensated. First, the write operation on D is removed from Lower queue, and its WDH mark is cleared. However, D is still not cold, so we continue the compensation process. As $L_{Upper}/C_r < L_{Lower}/C_w$, the read operation on D is moved from the tail of Upper queue to the head of Lower queue and RH operation of D is cleared. Thus, page D has no mark set, and it is inserted into the cold page index.

Since we simply record the page operation and page ID in the queue, our approach only introduces negligible space overhead compared with the buffered data. Each operation insertion and removal have the time complexity of $O(1)$. Note that, one operation is only removed once during the compensation process.

5. PERFORMANCE STUDY

In this section, we conduct a trace-driven simulation including benchmark and synthetic workloads to evaluate the effectiveness of our approach, and the experimental results are illustrated in comparison with some state-of-the-art flash-based buffer replacement algorithms, including CFLRU [25], LRUWSR [11], CCFLRU [19] and CASA [23]. The simulation is developed in Visual Studio 2010 using C#. All experiments are run on a Windows 7 PC with a 2.4 GHz Intel Quad CPU and 2 GB of physical memory.

5.1 Experimental setup

We use both real and synthetic traces for performance evaluation. Three benchmark traces on transactional processing are deployed, namely TATP [3], TPC-B, and TPC-C. To get the traces on buffer page accesses, we run the three benchmarks on PostgreSQL 8.3.5 with default settings, e.g., the page size is 8KB. For each benchmark, we run a sufficient period of time around 3 hours, including a 30-minute warm-up period. For all benchmarks, the number of clients is 20. Specification on the traces was given in Table 4. For the synthetic trace, we generate a operation sequence conforming to 80/20 distribution as those in the previous study [10], and an operation is randomly assigned as a read or a write such that the ratio of write operations ranges from 10% to 50%.

We consider two performance metrics: *Buffer Hit Ratio* which records the percentage of page hits in the buffer, and

Table 4: Specification on the Traces

	Page Number (thousands)	Reference Number (millions)	Write Ratio
TATP	50.6	2.5	4.6%
TPC-B	259	12.7	3.3%
TPC-C	95.7	16.8	16.3%
Synthetic	300	10	10%-50%

I/O cost per operation which is the result of *total I/O time* divided by *number of operations*. In our experiment, I/O cost per operation is used to evaluate the performance besides the traditional hit rate metric. The reason is that the read and write latency in flash-based systems are different, which actually motivates our work. We employ two types of settings for read and write asymmetry. One represents the NAND flash, i.e., C_r and C_w are $100\mu s$ and $800\mu s$ respectively for the 8K page [1]. We select one popular Samsung SSD [2] as the SSD representative, also used in [17, 18]. The parameters used in our experiments are listed in Table 5. Unless stated explicitly, the default parameter values, given in bold, are used.

Table 5: Experimental Parameters

Parameter	Value
$S_{buffer}(pages)$	32, 64, **128**, ..., 16384
$C_r, C_w(\mu s)$	**100, 800** (for flash chip) 245, 9663 (for Samsung SSD)
α	0, 0.1, 0.2, ..., 1
R_{cold}	0.01, **0.1**, 0.2, ..., 0.5

5.2 Parameter tuning of FOR approaches

We first evaluate the effect of the tuning parameter α in FOR and R_{cold} in FOR^+ on the buffer performance. α shown in *Definition* 3 is a tuning parameter for the importance of IOD and OR in page weight determination, and R_{cold} is the percentage of cold pages which can be selected as a victim for buffer replacement FOR^+. We use the synthetic trace in the default setting. As FOR is time consuming, we generate a trace with 1000 page operations.

As shown in Figure 5 (a), the performance curve is concave, meaning that there is an optimal α that should be used. When α is zero, only the recency information is considered; when $\alpha = 1$, the frequency is the only used information. The best performance is obtained when α is around 0.4 - 0.6, indicating that we should take both frequency and recency into account for optimal performance. Thus, IOD and OR are integrated to measure the hotness of the corresponding page in FOR. Figure 5 (b) shows the performance of FOR^+ by varying R_{cold}. If R_{cold} is too small, a recently used page may be evicted, because the page becomes hot only when it has been accessed more than twice. On the other hand, a larger R_{cold} decreases the buffer space used to store the frequently used pages. In our experiment, the optimal value for R_{cold} is 0.1.

Comparing the I/O cost per operation of FOR and FOR^+ in Figure 5, we found FOR^+ performs only slightly worse than FOR. This shows that the approximation in FOR^+ can effectively model the page hotness. However, it takes FOR over 120 times longer than FOR^+ to run this trace, due to the high time complexity of operation process in

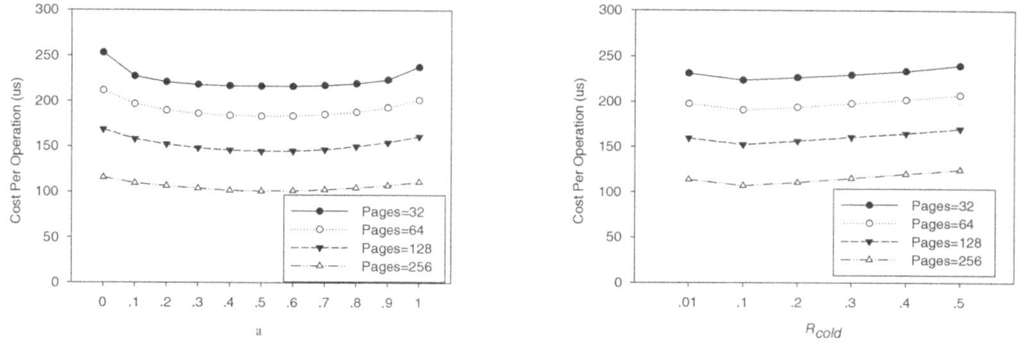

(a) α (b) R_{cold}

Figure 5: Parameters Tuning

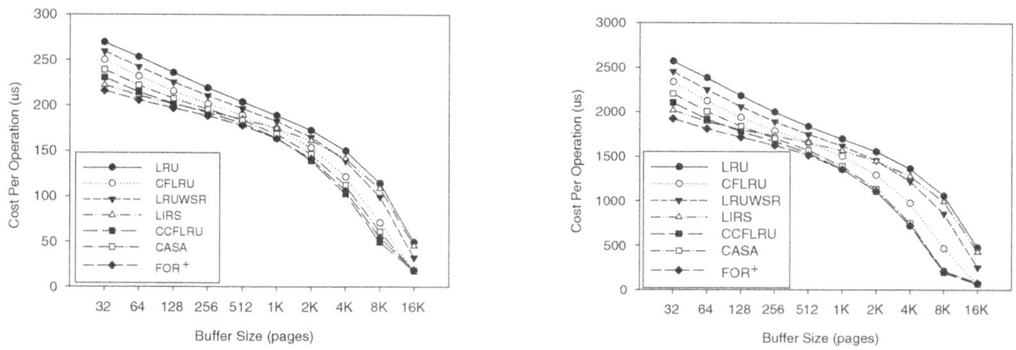

(a) I/O cost of synthetic trace on flash chip (b) I/O cost of synthetic trace on SSD

Figure 6: Buffer replacement performance on synthetic workload

FOR. Therefore, FOR^+ is a more promising choice for buffer replacement in real flash-based systems, and we only use FOR^+ in the following experiments.

5.3 Comparison with other techniques

We first demonstrate the results on synthetic workloads, followed by more experimental results on TATP, TPC-B and TPC-C.

5.3.1 Results on Synthetic Workloads

The experimental results on synthetic traces are shown in Figure 6. The write ratio is fixed to be 20%. The window size of CFLRU is set to 0.5, and the parameter of LIRS is set to 0.01. The buffer size ranges from 32 to 16384 pages. As the buffer size increases, the average operation cost of all the algorithms decreases rapidly. Overall, FOR^+ exceeds CASA by 5%-10%, has similar performance to CCFLRU, and significantly outperforms other algorithms by up to 100% on flash chip. As CCFLRU always allocates a rather high priority on dirty page, it can prevent the write operations as much as possible at the cost of more read operations. We can also see CCFLRU is more sensitive to traces in our later experiments on public benchmarks. LRUWSR, CFLRU and LRU have similar performance trends, as both LRUWSR and CFLRU are based on LRU. LIRS always outperforms LRU, but the difference becomes smaller as the buffer size increases. This is because LIRS keeps some historical information, which is more useful for a small buffer. The difference between FOR^+ and other algorithms is more significant on SSD, since the I/O asymmetry is larger on SSD.

Figure 7 shows the performance by varying the write ratio and with the buffer size fixed to 4096. The I/O costs per operation of all the algorithms increase, as the write ratio increases. The CCFLRU and FOR^+ perform similarly and better than others (e.g., up to 30% lower I/O cost than CFLRU), since both of them gives higher priority to dirty pages than other algorithms.

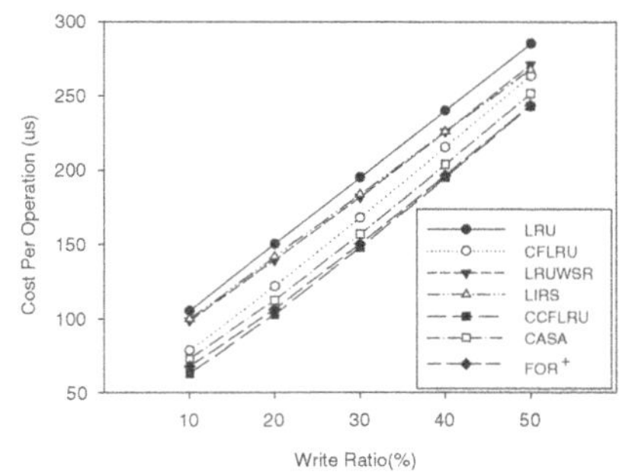

Figure 7: Performance effected by write ratio

5.3.2 Results on Benchmark Workloads

We first focus on comparing FOR^+ with other flash-based algorithms. Figures 8 (a), (b), (d) and (e) show I/O costs per

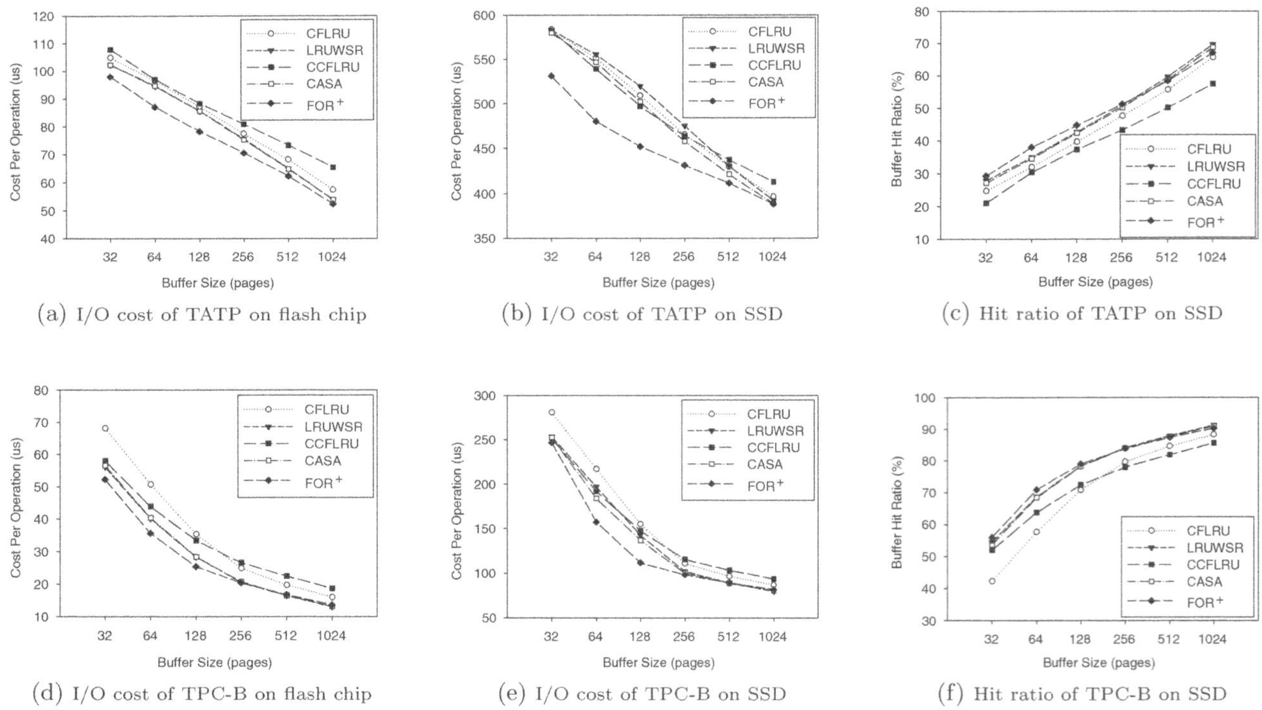

(a) I/O cost of TATP on flash chip
(b) I/O cost of TATP on SSD
(c) Hit ratio of TATP on SSD
(d) I/O cost of TPC-B on flash chip
(e) I/O cost of TPC-B on SSD
(f) Hit ratio of TPC-B on SSD

Figure 8: Comparison on buffer replacement performance

Table 6: Read and write counts to SSD on TATP for different algorithms

	CFLRU		LRUWSR		CCFLRU		CASA		FOR+	
Buffer Size(pages)	read	write	read	write	read	write	read	write	read	write
32	1766205	105547	1685335	107528	1861041	102910	1705125	106094	1664170	94693
64	1591511	101583	1512794	104724	1633644	97465	1526095	102114	1455070	86751
128	1406144	95445	1325756	100226	1469433	90757	1338712	95374	1291214	83650
256	1214153	88971	1130193	93707	1325149	85819	1149824	88693	1131086	82368
512	1017177	84863	914505	87668	1156174	83295	940055	84687	951406	81901
1024	770001	82629	669042	84077	975519	81596	693858	82548	736001	81410

operation of different approaches by varying the buffer size. FOR^+ is about 5–20% better than other algorithms averagely. The four competitors are based on LRU, which only takes recency and state of the page into consideration. However, The proposed FOR^+ algorithm exploits the read/write asymmetry and operation statistics for buffer replacement, thus it is more adaptive to system characteristics. The clean pages are much easier to be evicted in CFLRU than LRUWSR, because the cold clean page is evicted first, only if there is no cold clean page, victim will be selected on other pages as LRUWSR. Even though the buffer size is large, too many clean pages are evicted by CCFLRU which increases the number of read operation. This is why CCFLRU is worse than CFLRU and LRUWSR for large buffer size. CASA has very similar performance with LRUWSR. CASA only employs the access information of pages in the buffer which losses most of the historical information compared with FOR^+.

The I/O cost of each algorithm on SSD is illustrated in Figures 8 (b) & (e). FOR^+ yields more performance advantage over the competitors. Since the C_w/C_r of SSD is much larger than flash chip, the performance difference is more significant on SSD. CCFLRU performs relatively better on SSD compared with the case on flash chip, because the increment of C_w/C_r makes it more worthwhile to hold dirty pages in the buffer.

Figures 8 (c) and (f) show buffer hit ratios for SSD settings. The number of I/O read/write operations for TATP are also listed in Table 6. From the figures, we observe that the hit ratio of every algorithm increases with the enlargement of buffer size. All the flash-based algorithms aim to reduce some write operations at the expense of more read operations. The hit rate gain of our approach FOR^+ is not significant as that on I/O cost. From Table 6, we can see that the number of I/O write operations of FOR^+ is smaller than thoseof other algorithms, which means FOR^+ provides a better hit ratio of write operations. CFLRU always holds dirty pages in its window, while LRUWSR gives dirty pages only one more chance to be kept in the buffer. Consequently, the number of I/O write operations of CFLRU is smaller than that of LRUWSR. CFLRU decreases the effective buffer space for clean pages. The hit ratio of CFLRU is clearly lower than LRUWSR.

FOR^+ outperforms CCFLRU, because CCFLRU fails to detect hot clean pages. As Table 6 shows, CCFLRU often has a much larger number of read operations than FOR^+.

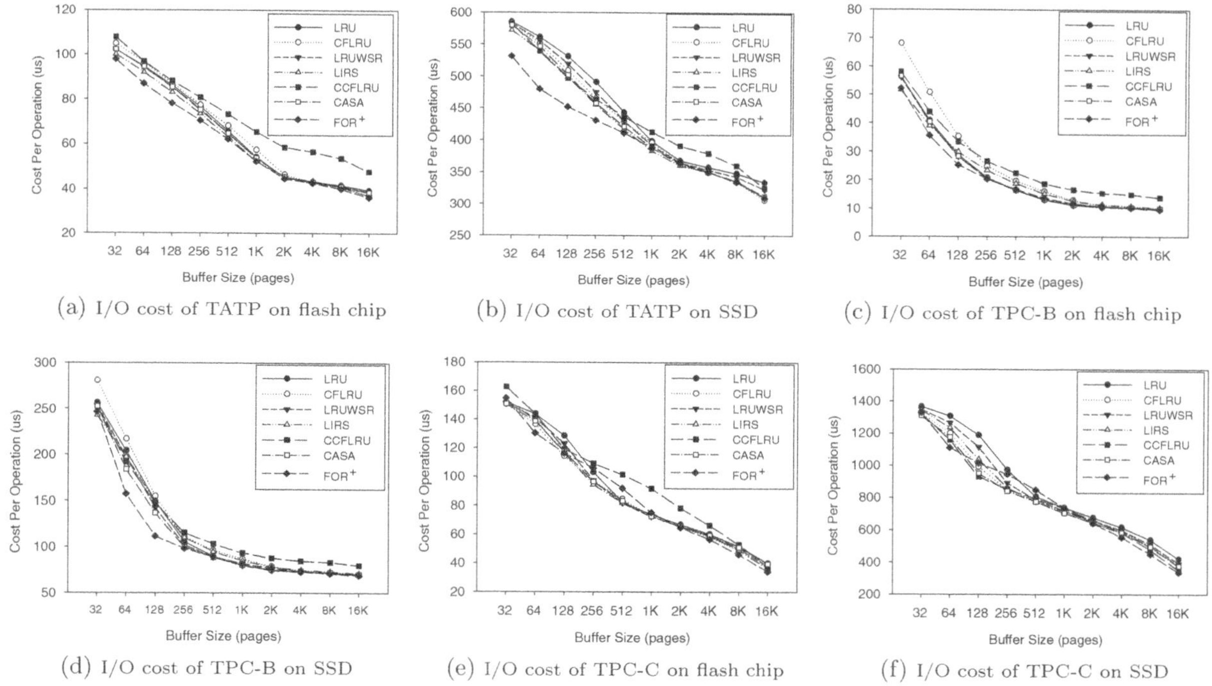

(a) I/O cost of TATP on flash chip (b) I/O cost of TATP on SSD (c) I/O cost of TPC-B on flash chip

(d) I/O cost of TPC-B on SSD (e) I/O cost of TPC-C on flash chip (f) I/O cost of TPC-C on SSD

Figure 9: More results on buffer replacement performance

Among these competitors, CCFLRU introduces most read operations in all cases.

More experimental comparisons are included in Figure 9. Besides the flash-based methods, we also include two traditional disk-based algorithms, i.e., LRU and LIRS [8]. We show the experimental results with larger range of buffer size from 32 to 16382 pages. The proposed FOR^+ is the best algorithm in most cases. The comparison on the hit ratio is similar to those in Figure 8, and we omit the results.

The performance gain decreases when the buffer size increases. This phenomena is reasonable and consistent with the findings in previous buffer management studies [11, 19]. As the buffer size increases, all the algorithms can hold more pages in the buffer. The hit ratio increases and the room for performance improvement becomes small.

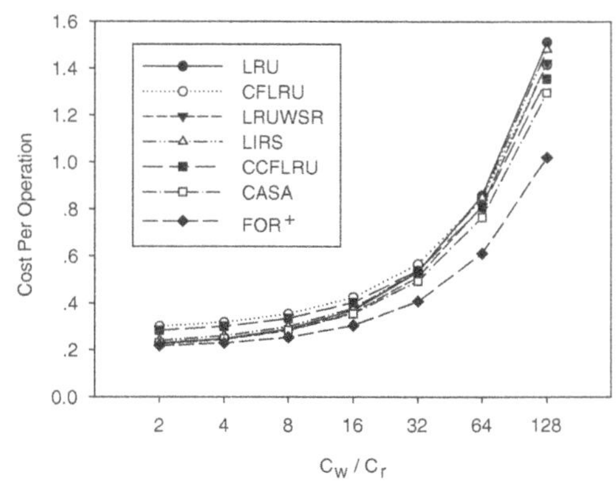

Figure 10: Performance effected by C_w/C_r

FOR^+ is able to adjust its policy according to flash characteristics in order to achieve better performance. The performance with varying C_w/C_r is given in Figure 10. We normalize C_r to be one, and range C_w from 2 to 128, so that the C_w/C_r cover the situations of most SSDs. The experiments are performed on TPC-B with buffer size 128 pages. As the ratio increases, the performance advantage of FOR^+ over other algorithm becomes larger. Our proposed approach well exploits the locality of read/write operation as well as the read/write asymmetry of the flash memory.

We further investigate the impact of different database sizes. Table 7 shows the I/O cost per operation for the TPC-C traces on 0.5GB to 4GB databases. We fix the buffer to 10% of total database size. FOR^+'s consistently outperforms other algorithms for different database sizes.

Table 7: Performance on TPC-C(μs) with 10% buffer/data ratio

Database Size(GB)	0.5	1	2	4
LRU	50.8	46.1	41.0	51.8
CFLRU	47.6	42.8	37.6	45.8
LRUWSR	48.7	43.9	38.7	48.0
LIRS	47.9	42.7	37.4	46.3
CCFLRU	49.5	44.4	39.1	44.8
CASA	49.4	45.4	40.4	48.7
FOR$^+$	45.0	39.8	35.0	42.7

Finally, we examine the average processing time for each operation as the computational overhead of buffer management. Table 8 shows the average processing time per operation when the buffer size is 128 pages. The results are similar for other buffer sizes. Since FOR$^+$ records more information and adopts additional lists compared with other

Table 8: Execution time(μs) for per operation

	TATP	TPC-B	TPC-C
LRU	3.9	3.9	4.3
CFLRU	4.1	4.0	4.4
LRUWSR	4.0	3.9	4.5
LIRS	4.5	4.1	4.7
CCFLRU	4.2	4.0	4.4
CASA	4.1	4.2	4.3
FOR$^+$	4.8	4.4	5.2

strategies, it has the largest average processing time per operation. Nevertheless, the time difference is less than 1 μs, which has negligible impact on the overall performance (compared with the I/O costs, shown in Figure 8).

6. CONCLUSION AND FUTURE WORK

The inherent features of flash memory pose great challenges for buffer management in flash-based systems. In this paper, we have presented a novel buffer replacement method named FOR to deal with the read/write asymmetry of flash memory. The proposed FOR algorithm exploits the read/write characteristics of flash memory and the operation-wise statistical information to determine the weight of buffered pages. Due to the computational complexity of FOR algorithm, we have developed an approximated version FOR^+ with novel data structure to reduce the computational complexity while preserving the key concepts in the weight determination of FOR. The experimental study on benchmark and synthetic traces demonstrates up to 20% improvements over some state-of-the-art flash-based buffer replacement strategies. As for future work, we plan to study write clustering on FOR^+, and to integrate the FOR^+ into a DBMS.

7. ACKNOWLEDGMENTS

This research was supported by the grants of Natural Science Foundation of China (No. 60873063) and MIIT grant 2010ZX01042-001-001-04.

8. REFERENCES

[1] http://samsung.com/global/business/semiconductor.

[2] http://uflip.inria.fr/ uFLIP.

[3] *Telecom Application Transaction Processing Benchmark.* http://tatpbenchmark.sourceforge.net/index.html.

[4] D. Agrawal, D. Ganesan, R. K. Sitaraman, Y. Diao, and S. Singh. Lazy-Adaptive Tree: An optimized index structure for flash devices. *PVLDB*, 2(1):361–372, 2009.

[5] L. Bouganim, B. T. Jónsson, and P. Bonnet. uFLIP: Understanding flash io patterns. In *CIDR*, 2009.

[6] F. Chen, D. A. Koufaty, and X. Zhang. Understanding intrinsic characteristics and system implications of flash memory based solid state drives. In *SIGMETRICS/Performance*, pages 181–192, 2009.

[7] J. Gray and B. Fitzgerald. Flash disk opportunity for server applications. *Queue*, 6(4), 2008.

[8] S. Jiang and X. Zhang. LIRS: an efficient low inter-reference recency set replacement policy to improve buffer cache performance. In *SIGMETRICS*, pages 31–42, 2002.

[9] H. Jo, J.-U. Kang, S.-Y. Park, J.-S. Kim, and J. Lee. FAB: Flash-aware buffer management policy for portable media players. *IEEE Transactions on Consumer Electronics*, 52(2):485–493, 7 2006.

[10] T. Johnson and D. Shasha. 2Q: A low overhead high performance buffer management replacement algorithm. In *VLDB*, pages 439–450, 1994.

[11] H. Jung, H. Shim, S. Park, S. Kang, and J. Cha. LRU-WSR: Integration of lru and writes sequence reordering for flash memory. *IEEE Transactions on Consumer Electronics*, 54(3):1215–1223, 10 2008.

[12] H. Jung, K. Yoon, H. Shim, S. Park, S. Kang, and J. Cha. LIRS-WSR: Integration of lirs and writes sequence reordering for flash memory. In *ICCSA (1)*, pages 224–237, 2007.

[13] H. Kim and S. Ahn. BPLRU: A buffer management scheme for improving random writes in flash storage. In M. Baker and E. Riedel, editors, *FAST*, pages 239–252. USENIX, 2008.

[14] I. Koltsidas and S. Viglas. Flashing up the storage layer. *PVLDB*, 1(1):514–525, 2008.

[15] D. Lee, J. Choi, J.-H. Kim, S. H. Noh, S. L. Min, Y. Cho, and C.-S. Kim. LRFU: A spectrum of policies that subsumes the least recently used and least frequently used policies. *IEEE Trans. Computers*, 50(12):1352–1361, 2001.

[16] S.-W. Lee and B. Moon. Design of flash-based DBMS: an in-page logging approach. In *SIGMOD Conference*, pages 55–66, 2007.

[17] S.-W. Lee, B. Moon, C. Park, J.-M. Kim, and S.-W. Kim. A case for flash memory ssd in enterprise database applications. In *SIGMOD Conference*, pages 1075–1086, 2008.

[18] Y. Li, B. He, Q. Luo, and K. Yi. Tree indexing on flash disks. In *ICDE*, pages 1303–1306, 2009.

[19] Z. Li, P. Jin, X. Su, K. Cui, and L. Yue. CCF-LRU: A new buffer replacement algorithm for flash memory. *IEEE Transactions on Consumer Electronics*, 55(3):1351–1359.

[20] D. Narayanan, E. Thereska, A. Donnelly, S. Elnikety, and A. Rowstron. Migrating server storage to SSDs: analysis of tradeoffs. In *ACM European conference on Computer systems*, 2009.

[21] S. T. On, Y. Li, B. He, M. Wu, Q. Luo, and J. Xu. FD-Buffer: A buffer manager for databases on flash disks. In *CIKM (short paper)*, 2010.

[22] E. J. O'Neil, P. E. O'Neil, and G. Weikum. The LRU-K page replacement algorithm for database disk buffering. In *SIGMOD Conference*, pages 297–306, 1993.

[23] Y. Ou and T. Härder. Clean first or dirty first?: a cost-aware self-adaptive buffer replacement policy. In *IDEAS*, pages 7–14, 2010.

[24] Y. Ou, T. Härder, and P. Jin. CFDC: a flash-aware replacement policy for database buffer management. In *DaMoN*, pages 15–20, 2009.

[25] S.-Y. Park, D. Jung, J.-U. Kang, J. Kim, and J. Lee. CFLRU: a replacement algorithm for flash memory. In *CASES*, pages 234–241, 2006.

[26] J. T. Robinson and M. V. Devarakonda. Data cache management using frequency-based replacement. In *SIGMETRICS*, pages 134–142, 1990.

[27] D. Seo and D. Shin. Recently-evicted-first buffer replacement policy for flash storage devices. *IEEE Transactions on Consumer Electronics*, 54(3):1228–1235, 10 2008.

[28] L. B. Sokolinsky. LFU-K: An effective buffer management replacement algorithm. In *DASFAA*, pages 670–681, 2004.

[29] D. Tsirogiannis, S. Harizopoulos, M. A. Shah, J. L. Wiener, and G. Graefe. Query processing techniques for solid state drives. In *SIGMOD conference*, 2009.

[30] D. Zeinalipour-Yazti, S. Lin, V. Kalogeraki, D. Gunopulos, and W. A. Najjar. MicroHash: An efficient index structure for flash-based sensor devices. In *FAST*, 2005.

SkimpyStash: RAM Space Skimpy Key-Value Store on Flash-based Storage

Biplob Debnath*,1 Sudipta Sengupta‡ Jin Li ‡
‡ Microsoft Research, Redmond, WA, USA
*EMC Corporation, Santa Clara, CA, USA

ABSTRACT

We present SkimpyStash, a RAM space skimpy key-value store on flas -based storage, designed for high throughput, low latency server applications. The distinguishing feature of SkimpyStash is the design goal of extremely low RAM footprint at about 1 ($\pm$ 0.5) byte per key-value pair, which is more aggressive than earlier designs. SkimpyStash uses a hash table directory in RAM to index key-value pairs stored in a log-structured manner on flash To break the barrier of a flas pointer (say, 4 bytes) worth of RAM overhead per key, it "moves" most of the pointers that locate each key-value pair from RAM to flas itself. This is realized by (i) resolving hash table collisions using linear chaining, where multiple keys that resolve (collide) to the same hash table bucket are chained in a linked list, and (ii) storing the linked lists on flas itself with a pointer in each hash table bucket in RAM pointing to the beginning record of the chain on flash hence incurring multiple flas reads per lookup. Two further techniques are used to improve performance: (iii) two-choice based load balancing to reduce wide variation in bucket sizes (hence, chain lengths and associated lookup times), and a bloom filte in each hash table directory slot in RAM to disambiguate the choice during lookup, and (iv) compaction procedure to pack bucket chain records contiguously onto flas pages so as to reduce flas reads during lookup. The average bucket size is the critical design parameter that serves as a powerful knob for making a continuum of tradeoffs between low RAM usage and low lookup latencies. Our evaluations on commodity server platforms with real-world data center applications show that SkimpyStash provides throughputs from few 10,000s to upwards of 100,000 `get-set` operations/sec.

Categories and Subject Descriptors

H.3 Information Storage and Retrieval [**H.3.1 Content Analysis and Indexing**]: Indexing Methods

General Terms

Algorithms, Design, Experimentation, Performance.

[1]Work done while Biplob Debnath was at Microsoft Research.

Keywords

Key-value store, Flash memory, Indexing, RAM space efficien index, Log-structured index.

1. INTRODUCTION

A broad range of server-side applications need an underlying, often persistent, key-value store to function. Examples include state maintenance in Internet applications like online multi-player gaming and inline storage deduplication (as described in Section 3). A high throughput persistent key-value store can help to improve the performance of such applications. Flash memory is a natural choice for such a store, providing persistency and 100-1000 times lower access times than hard disk. Compared to DRAM, flas access times are about 100 times higher. Flash stands in the middle between DRAM and disk also in terms of cost – it is 10x cheaper than DRAM, while 20x more expensive than disk – thus, making it an ideal gap fille between DRAM and disk.

It is only recently that flas memory, in the form of Solid State Drives (SSDs), is seeing widespread adoption in desktop and server applications. For example, MySpace.com recently switched from using hard disk drives in its servers to using PCI Express (PCIe) cards loaded with solid state flas chips as primary storage for its data center operations [5]. Also recently, Facebook released Flashcache, a simple write back persistent block cache designed to accelerate reads and writes from slower rotational media (hard disks) by caching data in SSDs [6]. These applications have different storage access patterns than typical consumer devices and pose new challenges to flas media to deliver sustained and high throughput (and low latency).

These challenges arising from new applications of flas are being addressed at different layers of the storage stack by flas device vendors and system builders, with the former focusing on techniques at the device driver software level and inside the device, and the latter driving innovation at the operating system and application layers. The work in this paper falls in the latter category. To get the maximum performance per dollar out of SSDs, it is necessary to use flas aware data structures and algorithms that work around constraints of flas media (e.g., avoid or reduce small random writes that not only have a higher latency but also reduce flas device lifetimes through increased page wearing). In the rest of the paper, we use NAND flas based SSDs as the architectural choice and simply refer to it as flas memory. We describe the internal architecture of SSDs in Section 2.

Recently, there are several interesting proposals to design key-value stores using flas memory [10, 11, 15, 16]. These designs use a combination RAM and flas memory – they store the full key-value pairs on flas memory and use a small amount of metadata per key-value pair in RAM to support faster insert and lookup operations. For example, FAWN [11], FlashStore [16], and ChunkStash [15] each require about six bytes of RAM space per key-value pair stored on flas memory. Thus, the amount of available RAM space limits the total number of key-value pairs that could be indexed on flas memory. As flas capacities are about an order of magnitude bigger than RAM and getting bigger, RAM size could well become the bottleneck for supporting large flash based key-value stores. By reducing the amount of RAM bytes needed per key-value pair stored on flas down to the extreme lows of about a byte, SkimpyStash can help to scale key-value stores on flas on a lean RAM size budget when existing current designs run out.

Our Contributions

In this paper, we present the design and evaluation of SkimpyStash, a RAM space skimpy key-value store on flas -based Storage, designed for high throughput server applications. *The distinguishing feature of SkimpyStash is the design goal of extremely low RAM footprint at about* 1 *byte per key-value pair*, which is more aggressive than earlier designs like FAWN [11], BufferHash [10], ChunkStash [15], and FlashStore [16]. Our base design uses less than 1 byte in RAM per key-value pair and our enhanced design takes slightly more than 1 byte per key-value pair. By being RAM space frugal, SkimpyStash can accommodate larger flas drive capacities for storing and indexing key-value pairs.

Design Innovations: SkimpyStash uses a hash table directory in RAM to index key-value pairs stored in a log-structure on flash To break the barrier of a flas pointer (say, 4 bytes) worth of RAM overhead per key, it "moves" most of the pointers that locate each key-value pair from RAM to flas itself. This is realized by

(i) Resolving hash table collisions using linear chaining, where multiple keys that resolve (collide) to the same hash table bucket are chained in a linked list, and

(ii) Storing the linked lists on flas itself with a pointer in each hash table bucket in RAM pointing to the beginning record of the chain on flash hence incurring multiple flas reads per lookup.

Two further techniques are used to improve performance:

(iii) Two-choice based load balancing [12] to reduce wide variation in bucket sizes (hence, chain lengths and associated lookup times), and a bloom filte [13] in each hash table directory slot in RAM for summarizing the records in that bucket so that at most one bucket chain on flas needs to be searched during a lookup, and

(iv) Compaction procedure to pack bucket chain records contiguously onto flas pages so as to reduce flas reads during lookup.

The average bucket size is the critical design parameter that serves as a powerful knob for making a continuum of tradeoffs between low RAM usage and low lookup latencies.

Evaluation on data center server applications: SkimpyStash can be used as a high throughput persistent key-value storage layer for a broad range of server class applications. We use real-world data traces from two data center applications, namely, Xbox LIVE Primetime online multi-player game and inline storage deduplication, to drive and evaluate the design of SkimpyStash on commodity server platforms. SkimpyStash provides throughputs from few 10,000s to upwards of 100,000 `get-set` operations/sec on the evaluated applications.

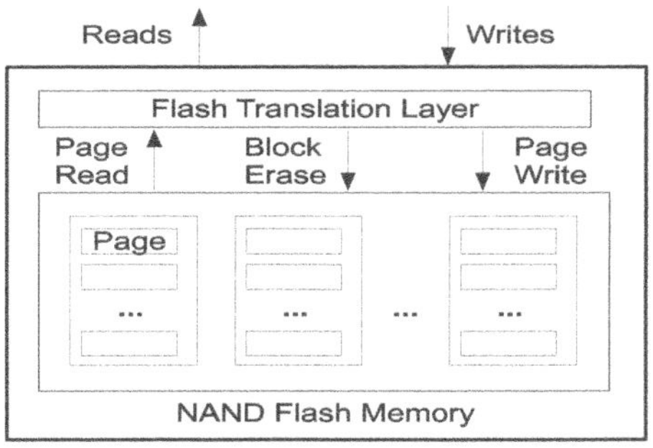

Figure 1: Internal architecture of a Solid State Drive (SSD)

The rest of the paper is organized as follows. We provide an overview of flas memory in Section 2. In Section 3, we describe two motivating real-world data center applications that can benefi from a high throughput key-value store and are used to evaluate SkimpyStash. We develop the design of SkimpyStash in Section 4. We evaluate SkimpyStash in Section 5. We review related work in Section 6. Finally, we conclude in Section 7.

2. FLASH MEMORY OVERVIEW

Figure 1 gives a block-diagram of an NAND flas based SSD. In flas memory, data is stored in an array of flas blocks. Each block spans 32-64 pages, where a page is the smallest unit of read and write operations. A distinguishing feature of flas memory is that read operations are very fast compared to magnetic disk drive. Moreover, unlike disks, random read operations are as fast as sequential read operations as there is no mechanical head movement. A major drawback of the flas memory is that it does not allow in-place updates (i.e., overwrite). Page write operations in a flas memory must be preceded by an erase operation and within a block, pages need be to written sequentially. The *in-place update* problem becomes complicated as write operations are performed in the page granularity, while erase operations are performed in the block granularity. The typical access latencies for read, write, and erase operations are 25 microseconds, 200 microseconds, and 1500 microseconds, respectively [9].

The Flash Translation layer (FTL) is an intermediate software layer inside SSD, which makes linear flas memory device act like a virtual disk. The FTL receives logical read and write commands from the applications and converts them to the internal flas memory commands. To emulate disk like in-place update operation for a logical page (L_p), the FTL writes data into a new physical page (P_p), maintains a mapping between logical pages and physical pages, and marks the previous physical location of L_p as invalid for future garbage collection. Although FTL allows current disk based application to use SSD without any modifications it needs to internally deal with flas physical constraint of erasing a block before overwriting a page in that block. Besides the *in-place update* problem, flas memory exhibits another limitation – a flas block can only be erased for limited number of times (e.g., 10K-100K) [9]. FTL uses various wear leveling techniques to even out the erase counts of different blocks in the flas memory to increase its overall longevity [17]. Recent studies show that current FTL schemes are very effective for the workloads with sequential access write patterns. However, for the workloads with random access patterns, these schemes show very poor performance [18, 20, 22]. One of the design goals of SkimpyStash is to use flas memory in FTL-friendly manner.

3. KEY-VALUE STORE APPLICATIONS

We describe two real-world applications that can use SkimpyStash as an underlying persistent key-value store. Data traces obtained from real-world instances of these applications are used to drive and evaluate the design of SkimpyStash.

3.1 Online Multi-player Gaming

Online multi-player gaming technology allows people from geographically diverse regions around the globe to participate in the same game. The number of concurrent players in such a game could range from tens to hundreds of thousands and the number of concurrent game instances offered by a single online service could range from tens to hundreds. An important challenge in online multi-player gaming is the requirement to scale the number of users per game and the number of simultaneous game instances. At the core of this is the need to maintain server-side state so as to track player actions on each client machine and update global game states to make them visible to other players as quickly as possible. These functionalities map to `set` and `get` key operations performed by clients on server-side state. The real-time responsiveness of the game is, thus, critically dependent on the response time and throughput of these operations.

There is also the requirement to store server-side game state in a persistent manner for (at least) the following reasons: (i) resume game from interrupted state if and when crashes occur, (ii) offlin analysis of game popularity, progression, and dynamics with the objective of improving the game, and (iii) verificatio of player actions for fairness when outcomes are associated with monetary rewards. We designed SkimpyStash to meet the high throughput and low latency requirement of such `get-set` key operations in online multi-player gaming.

3.2 Storage Deduplication

Deduplication is a recent trend in storage backup systems that eliminates redundancy of data across full and incremental backup data sets [28]. It works by splitting file into multiple chunks using a content-aware chunking algorithm like Rabin fingerprintin and using SHA-1 hash [24] signatures for each chunk to determine whether two chunks contain identical data [28]. In *inline* storage deduplication systems, the chunks (or their hashes) arrive one-at-a-time at the deduplication server from client systems. The server needs to lookup each chunk hash in an index it maintains for all chunk hashes seen so far for that backup location instance – if there is a match, the incoming chunk contains redundant data and can be deduplicated; if not, the (new) chunk hash needs to be inserted into the index.

Because storage systems currently need to scale to tens of terabytes to petabytes of data volume, the chunk hash index is too big to fi in RAM, hence it is stored on hard disk. Index operations are thus throughput limited by expensive disk seek operations. Since backups need to be completed over windows of half-a-day or so (e.g., nights and weekends), it is desirable to obtain high throughput in inline storage deduplication systems. RAM prefetching and bloom-filte based techniques used by Zhu et al. [28] can avoid disk I/Os on close to 99% of the index lookups. Even at this reduced rate, an index lookup going to disk contributes about 0.1msec to the *average* lookup time – this is about 10^3 times slower than a lookup hitting in RAM. SkimpyStash can be used as the chunk hash index for inline deduplication systems. By reducing the penalty of index lookup misses in RAM by orders of magnitude by serving such lookups from flas memory, SkimpyStash can help to increase deduplication throughput.

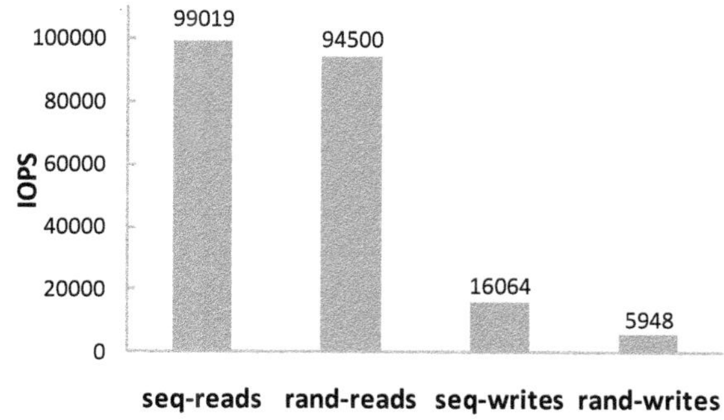

Figure 2: IOPS for sequential/random reads and writes using 4KB I/O request size on a 160GB fusionIO drive.

4. SkimpyStash DESIGN

We present the system architecture of SkimpyStash and the rationale behind some design choices in this section.

4.1 Coping with Flash Constraints

The design is driven by the need to work around two types of operations that are not efficien on flas media, namely:

1. **Random Writes:** Small random writes effectively need to update data portions within pages. Since a (physical) flas page cannot be updated in place, a new (physical) page will need to be allocated and the unmodifie portion of the data on the page needs to be relocated to the new page.

2. **Writes less than flash page size:** Since a page is the smallest unit of write on flash writing an amount less than a page renders the rest of the (physical) page wasted – any subsequent append to that partially written (logical) page will need copying of existing data and writing to a new (physical) page.

To validate the performance gap between sequential and random writes on flash we used Iometer [3], a widely used performance evaluation tool in the storage community, on a 160GB fusionIO SSD [2] attached over PCIe bus to an Intel Core 2 Duo E6850 3GHz CPU. The number of worker threads was fi ed at 8 and the number of outstanding I/Os for the drive at 64. The results for IOPS (I/O operations per sec) on 4KB I/O request sizes are summarized in Figure 2. Each test was run for 1 hour. The IOPS performance of sequential writes is about 3x that of random writes and worsens when the tests are run for longer durations (due to accumulating device garbage collection overheads). We also observe that the IOPS performance of (random/sequential) reads is about 6x that sequential writes. (The slight gap between IOPS performance of sequential and random reads is possibly due to prefetching inside the device.)

Given the above, the most efficien way to write flas is to simply use it as an append log, where an append operation involves a flas page worth of data, typically 2KB or 4KB. This is the main constraint that drives the rest of our key-value store design. Flash has been used in a log-structured manner and its benefit reported in earlier works [11, 14, 15, 16, 19, 23, 27].

4.2 Design Goals

The design of SkimpyStash is driven by the following guiding principles:

- **Support low-latency, high throughput operations.** This requirement is extracted from the needs of many server class applications that need an underlying key-value store to function. Two motivating applications that are used for evaluating SkimpyStash are described in Section 3.

- **Use flash aware data structures and algorithms.** This principle accommodates the constraints of the flas device so as to extract maximum performance out of it. Random writes and in-place updates are expensive on flas memory, hence must be reduced or avoided. Sequential writes should be used to the extent possible and the fast nature of random/sequential reads should be exploited.

- **Low RAM footprint per key independent of key-value size.** The goal here is to index all key-value pairs on flas in a RAM space efficien manner and make them accessible using a small number of flas reads per lookup. By being RAM space frugal, one can accommodate larger flas drive capacities and correspondingly larger number of key-value pairs stored in it. Key-value pairs can be arbitrarily large but the RAM footprint per key should be independent of it and small. We target a skimpy RAM usage of about 1 byte per key-value pair, a design point that is more aggressive than earlier designs like FAWN [11], BufferHash [10], ChunkStash [15], and FlashStore [16].

4.3 Architectural Components

SkimpyStash has the following main components. A base version of the design is shown in Figure 3 and an enhanced version in Figure 5. We will get to the details shortly.

RAM Write Buffer: This is a fi ed-size data structure maintained in RAM that buffers key-value writes so that a write to flas happens only after there is enough data to fil a flas page (which is typically 2KB or 4KB in size). To provide strict durability guarantees, writes can also happen to flas when a configurabl timeout interval (e.g., 1 msec) has expired (during which period multiple key-value pairs are collected in the buffer). The client call returns only after the write buffer is flushe to flash The RAM write buffer is sized to 2-3 times the flas page size so that key-value writes can still go through when part of the buffer is being written to flash

RAM Hash Table (HT) Directory: The directory structure, for key-value pairs stored on flash is maintained in RAM and is organized as a hash table with each slot containing a pointer to a chain of records on flash Each key-value pair record on flas contains, in addition to the key and value fields a pointer to the next record (in the order in its respective chain) on flash The chain of records on flas pointed to by each slot comprises the bucket of records corresponding to this slot in the HT directory. This is illustrated in Figure 3. The average number of records in a bucket, k, is a configurabl parameter. In summary, we resolve hash table directory collisions by linear chaining and store the chains in flash

In an enhancement of the design, we use two-choice based load balancing to reduce wide variation in bucket sizes (hence, chain lengths and associated lookup times), and introduce a bloom filte in each hash table directory slot in RAM for summarizing the records in that bucket so that at most one bucket chain on flas needs to be searched during a lookup. These enhancements form the the core of our design and are discussed in detail in Section 4.5.

Flash store: The flas store provides persistent storage for the key-value pairs and is organized as a *circular* append log. Key-value pairs are written to flas in units of a page size to the tail of the log. When the log accumulates garbage (consisting of deleted or

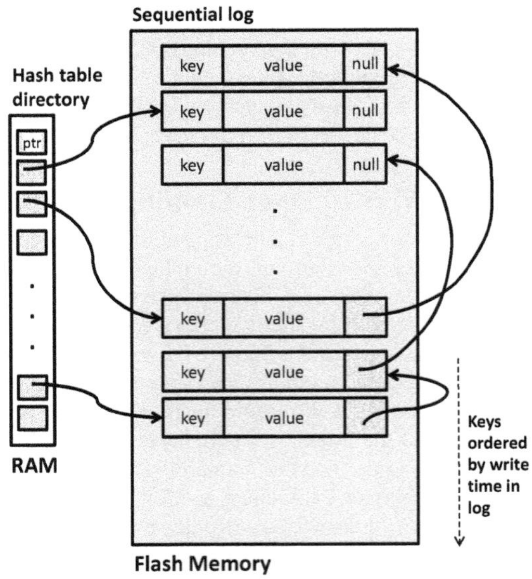

Figure 3: SkimpyStash architecture showing the sequential log organization of key-value pair records on flash and base design for the hash table directory in RAM. (RAM write buffer is not shown.)

older values of updated records) beyond a configurabl threshold, the pages on flas from the head of the log are recycled – valid entries from the head of the log are written back to the end of the log. This also helps to place the records in a given bucket contiguously on flas and improve read performance, as we elaborate shortly. Each key-value pair record on flas contains, in addition to the key and value fields a pointer to the next record (in the order in its HT bucket chain) on flash

4.4 Overview of Key Lookup and Insert Operations

To understand the relationship of the different storage areas in our design, it is helpful to follow the sequence of accesses in key insert and lookup operations performed by the client application.

A key ***lookup*** operation (`get`) firs looks up the RAM write buffer. Upon a miss there, it lookups up the HT directory in RAM and searches the chained key-value pair records on flas in the respective bucket.

A key ***insert*** (or, ***update***) operation (`set`) writes the key-value pair into the RAM write buffer. When there are enough key-value pairs in RAM write buffer to fil a flas page (or, a configurabl timeout interval since the client call has expired, say 1 msec), these entries are written to flas and inserted into the RAM HT directory and flash

A ***delete*** operation on a key is supported through insertion of a `null` value for that key. Eventually the *null* entry and earlier inserted values of the key on flas will be garbage collected.

When flas usage and fraction of garbage records in the flas log exceed a certain threshold, a garbage collection (and compaction) operation is initiated to reclaim storage on flas in a manner similar to that in log-structured fil systems [26]. This garbage collection operation starts scanning key-value pairs from the (current) head of the log – it discards garbage (invalid or orphaned, as define later) key-value pair records and moves valid key-value pair records from the head to the tail of the log. It stops when floo thresholds are reached for flas usage or fraction of garbage records remaining in the flas log.

The functionalities of (i) client key lookup/insert operations, (ii)

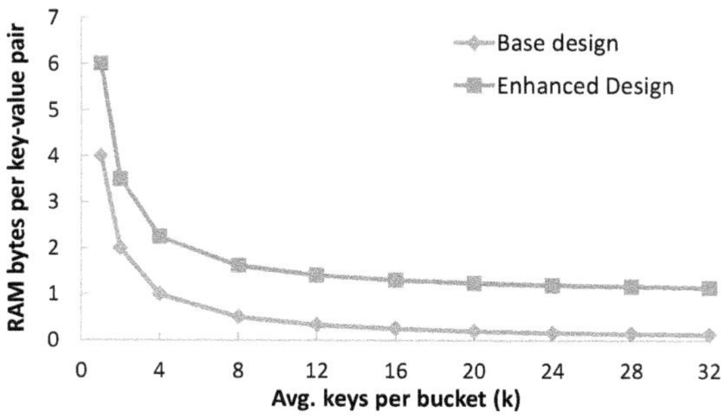

Figure 4: RAM space usage per key-value pair in SkimpyStash for the base and enhanced designs as the average number of keys per bucket (k) is varied.

writing key-value pairs to flas store and updating RAM HT directory, and (iii) reclaiming space on flas pages are handled by separate threads in a multi-threaded architecture. Concurrency issues with shared data structures arise in our multi-threaded design, which we address but do not describe here due to lack of space.

4.5 Hash Table Directory Design

At a high level, we use a hash table based index in RAM to index the key-value pairs on flash Earlier designs like FAWN [11] and ChunkStash [15] dedicate one entry of the hash table to point to a single key-value pair on flas together with a checksum that helps to avoid (with high probability) following the flas pointer to compare keys for every entry searched in the hash table during a lookup. The RAM overhead in FAWN and ChunkStash is 6 bytes per key-value pair stored on flash With such a design, we cannot get below the barrier of a flas pointer (say, 4 bytes) worth of RAM overhead per key-value pair (even if we ignore the other fields like checksums, in the hash table entry).

Our approach, at an intuitive level, is to move most of the pointers that locate each key-value pair from RAM to flas itself. We realize this by

- Resolving hash table collisions using *linear chaining*, where multiple keys that resolve (collide) to the same hash table bucket are chained in a linked list, and
- Storing the linked lists on flas itself with a pointer in each hash table bucket in RAM pointing to the beginning record of the chain on flash Each key-value pair record on flas contains, in addition to the key and value fields a pointer to the next record (in the order in its respective chain) on flash

Because we store the chain of key-value pairs in each bucket on flash we incur multiple flas reads upon lookup of a key in the store. This is the tradeoff that we need to make with lookup times in order to be able to skimp on RAM space overhead per key-value pair. We will see that the average number of keys in a bucket (k) is the critical parameter that allows us to make a continuum of tradeoffs between these two parameters – it serves as a powerful knob for reducing RAM space usage at the expense of increase in lookup times.

We firs begin with the base design of our hash table based index in RAM. Thereafter, we motivate and introduce some enhancements to the design to improve performance.

Base Design

The directory structure, for key-value pairs stored on flash is maintained in RAM and is organized as a hash table with each slot containing a pointer to a chain of records on flash as shown in Figure 3. Each key-value pair record on flas contains, in addition to the key and value fields a pointer to the next record (in the order in its respective chain) on flash The chain of records on flas pointed to by each slot comprises the bucket of records corresponding to this slot in the HT directory. A hash function h is used to map keys to slots in the HT directory. The average number of records in a bucket, k, is a configurabl parameter. Then, to accommodate up to some given number n key-value pairs, the number of slots required in the HT directory is about n/k. In summary, we resolve hash table directory collisions by linear chaining and store the chains in flash We next describe the *lookup*, *insert/update*, and *delete* operations on this data structure.

A ***lookup*** operation on a key uses the hash function h to obtain the HT directory bucket that this key belongs to. It uses the pointer stored in that slot to follow the chain of records on flas to search the key; upon findin the firs record in the chain whose key matches the search key, it returns the value. The number of flas reads for such a lookup is $k/2$ on the average, and at most the size of the bucket chain in the worst case.

An ***insert*** (or, ***update***) operation uses the hash function h to obtain the HT directory bucket that this key belongs to. Let a_1 be the address on flas of the firs record in this chain (i.e., what the pointer in this slot points to). Then a record is created corresponding to the inserted (or, updated) key-value pair with its next-pointer fiel equal to a_1. This record is appended to the log on flas and its address on flas now becomes the value of the pointer in the respective slot in RAM. Effectively, this new record is inserted at the beginning of the chain corresponding to this bucket. Thus, if this insert operation corresponds to an update operation on an earlier inserted key, the most recent value of the key will be (correctly) read during a lookup operation (the old value being further down the chain and accumulating as garbage in the log).

A ***delete*** operation is same as the ***insert*** (or, ***update***) with `null` value for that key. Eventually the *null* entry on flas and old values of the key will be garbage collected in the log.

RAM Space Overhead for Base Design: Let us say that the pointer to flas in each HT directory slot is 4 bytes. (This accommodates up to 4GB of byte-addressable log. If records are of a fi ed size, say 64 bytes, then this can accommodate up to 256GB of 64-byte granularity addressable log. Larger pointer sizes, up to 8 bytes, can be used according to application requirements.) Then, with a value of $k = 10$ average bucket size, the RAM space overhead is a mere $4/k = 0.4$ bytes $= 3.2$ bits per entry, independent of key-value size. At this sub-byte range, this design tests the extremes of low RAM space overhead per entry. The average number of flas reads per lookup is $k/2 = 5$; with current SSDs achieving flas read times in the range of 10μsec, this corresponds to a lookup latency of about 50 μsec. The parameter k provides a powerful knob for achieving tradeoffs between low RAM space usage and low lookup latencies. The RAM space usage per key-value pair for the base design as a function of k is shown in Figure 4.

Design Enhancements

We identify some performance inefficiencie in the base design and develop techniques to address them with only a slight increase in the RAM space overhead per key-value pair. The enhanced design is shown in Figure 5.

Load Balancing across Buckets

The hashing of keys to HT directory buckets may lead to skewed distributions in the number of keys in each bucket chain, thus creating variations in average lookup times across buckets. Thus, it

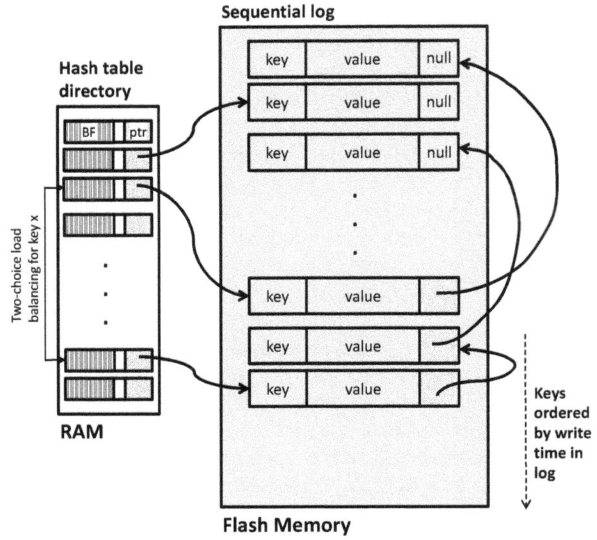

Figure 5: SkimpyStash architecture showing the sequential log organization of key-value pair records on flash and enhanced design for the hash table directory in RAM. (RAM write buffer is not shown.)

might be necessary to enforce fairly equal load balancing of keys across HT directory buckets in order to keep each bucket chain of about the same size. One simple way to achieve this is to use the *power of two choice idea* from [12] that has been applied to balance a distribution of balls thrown into bins. With a load balanced design for the HT directory, each key would be hashed to two candidate HT directory buckets, using two hash functions h_1 and h_2, and actually inserted into the one that has currently fewer elements. We investigate the impact of this design decision on balancing bucket sizes on our evaluation workloads in Section 5. To implement this load balancing idea, we add one byte of storage to each HT directory slot in RAM that holds the current number of keys in that bucket – this space allocation accommodates up to a maximum of $2^8 - 1 = 255$ keys per bucket.

Bloom Filter per Bucket

This design modification in its current form, will lead to an increase in the number of flas reads during lookup. Since each key will need to be looked up in both of its candidate buckets, the worst case number of flas reads (hence lookup times) would double. To remove this latency impact on the lookup pathway, we add a *bloom filter* [13] per HT directory slot that summarizes the keys that have been inserted in the respective bucket. Note that this bloom filte in each HT directory slot can be sized to contain about k keys, since load balancing ensures that when the hash table reaches its budgeted full capacity, each bucket will contain not many more than k keys with very high probability. A standard rule of thumb for dimensioning a bloom filte to use one byte per key (which gives a false positive probability of 2%), hence the bloom filte in each HT directory slot can be of size k bytes.

The introduction of bloom filter in each HT directory slot has another desirable side effect – lookups on non-existent keys will almost always *not* involve any flas reads since the bloom filter in both candidate slots of the key will indicate that the key is not present (module false positive probabilities). (Note that in the base design, lookups on non-existent keys also lead to flas reads and involve traversing the entire chain in the respective bucket.)

In an interesting reciprocity of benefits the bloom filter in each

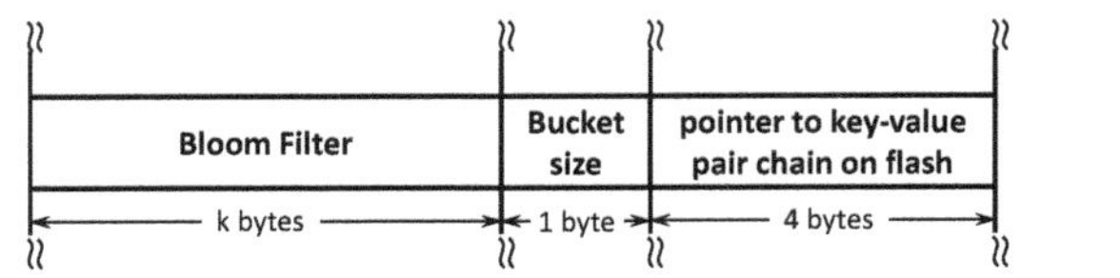

Figure 6: RAM hash table directory slot and sizes of component fields in the enhanced design of SkimpyStash. The parameter k is the average number of keys in a bucket.

bucket not only help in reducing lookup times when two-choice load balancing is used but also benefi from load balancing. Load balancing aims to keep the number of keys in each bucket upper bounded (roughly) by the parameter k. This helps to keep bloom filte false positive probabilities in that bucket bounded as per the dimensioned capacity of k keys. Without load balancing, many more than k keys could be inserted into a given bucket and this will increase the false positive rates of the respective bloom filte well beyond what it was dimensioned for.

The additional field added to each HT directory slot in RAM in the enhanced design are shown in Figure 6.

During a ***lookup*** operation, the key is hashed to its two candidate HT directory buckets and the chain on flas is searched only if the respective bloom filte indicates that the key may be there in that bucket. Thus, accounting for bloom filte false positives, the chain on flas will be searched with no success in less than 2% of the lookups.

When an ***insert*** operation corresponds to an ***update*** of an earlier inserted key, the record is always inserted in the same bucket as the earlier one, even if the choice determined by load balancing (out of two candidate buckets) is the other bucket. If we followed the choice given by load balancing, the key may be inserted in the bloom filter of both candidate slots – this would not preserve the design goal of traversing at most one bucket chain (with high probability) on flas during lookups. Moreover, the same problem would arise with version resolution during lookups if different versions of a key are allowed to be inserted in both candidate buckets. This rule also leads to efficiencie during garbage collection operations since all the obsolete values of a key appear in the same bucket chain on flash Note that this complication involving overriding of the load balancing based choice of insertion bucket can be avoided when the application does not perform updates to earlier inserted keys – one example of such an application is storage deduplication as described in Section 3.

In summary, in this enhancement of the base design, two-choice based load balancing strategy is used to reduce variations in the the number of keys assigned to each bucket (hence, chain lengths and associated lookup times). Each HT directory slot in RAM also contains a bloom filte summarizing the keys in the bucket and a size (count) fiel storing the current number of keys in that bucket.

RAM Space Overhead for Enhanced Design: With this design modification the RAM space overhead per bucket now has three components, namely,

- Pointer to chain on flas (4 bytes),
- Bucket size (1 byte), and
- Bloom filte (k bytes).

This space overhead per HT directory slot is amortized over an average of k keys (in that bucket), hence the RAM space overhead per entry can be computed as $(k + 1 + 4)/k = 1 + 5/k$ which is about 1.5 bytes for $k = 10$. The average number of flas reads per lookup is still $k/2 = 5$ (with high probability); with current SSDs achieving flas read times in the range of 10μsec, this corresponds to a lookup latency of about 50 μsec. Moreover, the variation across lookup latencies for different keys is better controlled in this design (compared to the base design) as bucket chains are about the same size due to two choice based load balancing of keys across buckets. The RAM space usage per key-value pair for the enhanced design as a function of k is shown in Figure 4.

Storing key-value pairs to flash: Key-value pairs are organized on flas in a log-structure in the order of the respective write operations coming into the system. Each slot in the HT directory contains a pointer to the beginning of the chain on flas that represents the keys in that bucket. Each key-value pair record on flas contains, in addition to the key and value fields a pointer to the next record (in the order in its respective chain) on flash We use a 4-byte pointer, which is a combination of a page pointer and a page offset. The all-zero pointer is reserved for the `null` pointer – in the HT directory slot, this represents an empty bucket, while on flas this indicates that the respective record has no successor in the chain.

RAM and Flash Capacity Considerations: We designed our RAM indexing scheme to use 1 byte in RAM per key-value pair so as to maximize the amount of indexable storage on flas for a given RAM usage size. Whether RAM or flas capacity becomes the bottleneck for storing key-value pairs on flas depends further on the key-value pair size. With 64-byte key-value pair records, 1GB of RAM can index about 1 billion key-value pairs on flas which occupy 64GB on flash This flas memory capacity is well within the capacity range of SSDs shipping in the market today (from 64GB to 640GB). On the other hand, with 1024-byte key-value pair records, the same 1GB of RAM can index 1 billion key-value pairs which now occupy 1TB on flas – at currently available SSD capacities, this will require multiple flas drives to store the dataset.

4.6 Flash Storage Management

Key-value pairs are organized on flas in a log-structure in the order of the respective write operations coming into the system. When there are enough key-value pairs in the RAM write buffer to fil a flas page (or, when a pre-specifie coalesce time interval is reached), they are written to flash The pages on flas are maintained *implicitly* as a circular log. Since the Flash Translation Layer (FTL) translates logical page numbers to physical ones, this circular log can be easily implemented as a contiguous block of logical page addresses with wraparound, realized by two page number variables, one for the firs valid page (oldest written) and the other for the last valid page (most recently written). We next describe two maintenance operations on flas in SkimpyStash, namely, *compaction* and *garbage collection*. Compaction is helpful in improving lookup latencies by reducing number of flas reads when searching bucket. Garbage collection is necessary to reclaim storage on flas and is a consequence of flas being used in a log-structured manner.

Compaction to Reduce Flash Reads during Lookups

In SkimpyStash , a lookup in a HT directory bucket involves following the chain of key-value records on flash For a chain length of c records in a bucket, this involves an average of $c/2$ flas reads. Over time, as keys are inserted into a bucket and earlier inserted keys are updated, the chain length on flas for this bucket keeps

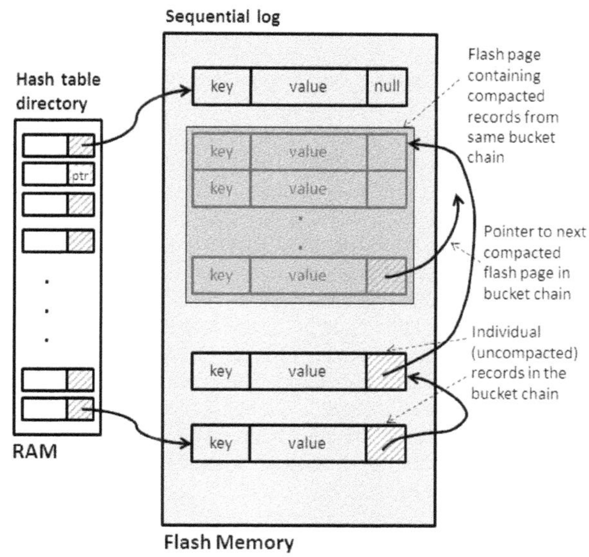

Figure 7: Diagram illustrating the effect of compaction procedure on the organization of a bucket chain on flash in SkimpyStash.

increasing and degrading lookup times. We address this by periodically *compacting* the chain on flas in a bucket by placing the valid keys in that chain contiguously on one or more flas pages that are appended to the tail of the log. Thus, if m key value pairs can be packed onto a single flas page (on the average), the number of flas reads required to search for a key in a bucket of k records is $k/(2m)$ on the average and at most $\lceil k/m \rceil$ in the worst case.

The compaction operations proceed over time in a bucket as follows. Initially, as key-value pairs are added at different times to a bucket, they appear on different flas pages and are chained together individually on flash When enough valid records accumulate in a bucket to fil a flas page (say, m of them), they are compacted and appended on a new flas page at the tail of the log – the chain is now of a single flas page size and requires one flas read (instead of m) to search fully. Thereafter, as further keys are appended to a bucket, they will be chained together individually and appear before the compacted group of keys in the chain. Over time, enough new records may accumulate in the bucket to allow them to be compacted to a second flas page, and so the process repeats. At any given time, the chain on flas for each bucket now begins with a chained sequence of individual records followed by groups of compacted records (each group appearing on the same flas page). This organization of a bucket chain as a result of compaction is illustrated in Figure 7.

When a key-value pair size is relatively small, say 64 bytes as in the storage deduplication application, there may not be enough records in a bucket to fil a flas page, since this number is (roughly) upper bounded by the parameter k. In this case, we may reap the same benefit of compaction by applying the procedure to groups of chains in multiple buckets at a time.

The compaction operation, as described above, will lead to *orphaned*) (or, garbage) records on the flas log. Moreover, garbage records also accumulate in the log as a result of key update and delete operations. These need to be garbage collected on flas as we describe next.

Garbage Collection

Garbage records (holes) accumulate in the log as a result of compaction and key update/delete operations. These operations create garbage records corresponding to all previous versions of respective keys.

When a certain configurabl fraction of garbage accumulates in the log (in terms of space occupied), a cleaning operation is performed to clean and compact the log. The cleaning operation considers currently used flas pages in *oldest first* order and deallocates them in a way similar to garbage collection in log-structured fil systems [26]. One each page, the sequence of key-value pairs are scanned to determine whether they are valid or not. The classificatio of a key-value pair record on flas follows from doing a lookup on the respective key starting from the HT directory – if this record is the same as that returned by the lookup, then it is *valid*; if it appears later in the chain than a valid record for that key, then this record is *invalid* and corresponds to an obsolete version of they key; otherwise, the record is *orphaned* and cannot be reached by following pointers from the HT directory (this may happen because of the compaction procedure, for example). When an orphaned record is encountered at the head of the log, it is skipped and the head position of the log is advanced to the next record.

From the description of the key insertion procedure in Section 4.5, it follows that the firs record in each bucket chain (the one pointed to from the HT directory slot) is the most recently inserted record, while the last record in the chain is the earliest inserted record in that bucket. Hence, the last record in a bucket chain will be encountered firs during the garbage collection process and it may be a valid or invalid (obsolete version of the respective key) record. A valid record needs to be reinserted at the tail of the log while an invalid record can be skipped. In either case, the next pointer in its predecessor record in the chain would need to be updated. Since we want to avoid in-place updates (random writes) on flash this requires relocating the predecessor record and so forth all the way to the firs record in the chain. *This effectively leads to the design decision of garbage collecting entire bucket chains on flash at a time.*

In summary, when the last record in a bucket chain is encountered in the log during garbage collection, all valid records in that chain are compacted and relocated to the tail of the log. This garbage collection strategy has two benefits

- First, the writing of an entire chain of records in a bucket to the tail of the log also allows them to be compacted and placed contiguously on one or more flas pages and helps to speed up the lookup operations on those keys, as explained above in the context of compaction operations, and
- Second, since garbage (orphaned) records are created further down the log between the (current) head and tail (corresponding to the locations of all records in the chain before relocation), this helps to speedup the garbage collection process for the respective pages when they are encountered later (since orphaned records can be simply discarded).

We investigate the impact of compaction and garbage collection on system throughput in Section 5.

4.7 Crash Recovery

SkimpyStash 's persistency guarantee enables it to recover from system crashes due to power failure or other reasons. Because the system logs all key-value write operations to flash it is straightforward to rebuild the HT directory in RAM by scanning all valid flas pages on flash Recovery using this method can take some time, however, depending on the total size of valid flas pages that need to be scanned and the read throughput of flas memory.

If crash recovery needs to be executed faster so as to support "near" real-time recovery, then it is necessary to checkpoint the RAM HT directory periodically into flas (in a separate area from the key-value pair logs). Then, recovery involves reading the last written HT directory checkpoint from flas and scanning key-value pair logged flas pages with timestamps after that and inserting them into the restored HT directory. During the operation of checkpointing the HT directory, all insert operations into it will need to be suspended (but the read operations can continue). We use a temporary, small in-RAM hash table to provide index for the interim items and log them to flash After the checkpointing operation completes, key-value pairs from the flas pages written in the interim are inserted into the HT directory. Key lookup operations, upon missing in the HT directory, will need to check in these flas pages (via the small additional hash table) until the later insertions into HT directory are complete. The flas garbage collection thread is suspended during the HT directory checkpointing operation, since the HT directory entries cannot be modifie during this time.

Trace	Total `get-set` ops	`get:set` ratio	Avg. size (bytes)	
			Key	Value
Xbox	5.5 millions	7.5:1	92	1200
Dedup	40 millions	2.2:1	20	44

Table 1: Properties of the two traces used in the performance evaluation of SkimpyStash.

5. EVALUATION

We evaluate SkimpyStash on real-world traces obtained from the two applications described in Section 3.

5.1 C# Implementation

We have prototyped SkimpyStash in approximately 3000 lines of C# code. MurmurHash [4] is used to realize the hash functions used in our implementation to compute hash table directory indices and bloom filte lookup positions; different seeds are used to generate different hash functions in this family. The metadata store on flas is maintained as a fil in the fil system and is created/opened in non-buffered mode so that *there are no buffering/caching/prefetching effects in RAM from within the operating system.* The `ReaderWriterLockSlim` and `Monitor` classes in .NET 3.0 framework [1] are used to implement the concurrency control solution for multi-threading.

5.2 Evaluation Platform and Datasets

We use a standard server configuratio to evaluate the performance of SkimpyStash. The server runs Windows Server 2008 R2 and uses an Intel Core2 Duo E6850 3GHz CPU, 4GB RAM, and fusionIO 160GB flas drive [2] attached over PCIe interface. We compare the throughput (`get-set` operations per sec) on the two traces described in Table 1.

We described two real-world applications in Section 3 that can use SkimpyStash as an underlying persistent key-value store. Data traces obtained from real-world instances of these applications are used to drive and evaluate the design of SkimpyStash.

Xbox LIVE Primetime trace

We evaluate the performance of SkimpyStash on a large trace of `get-set` key operations obtained from real-world instances of the Microsoft Xbox LIVE Primetime online multiplayer game [7]. In this application, the key is a dot-separated sequence of strings with total length averaging 94 characters and the value averages around 1200 bytes. The ratio of `get` operations to set `set` operations is about 7.5:1.

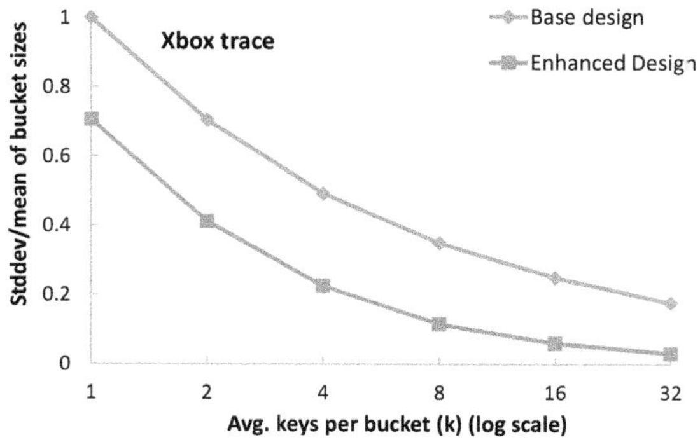

Figure 8: Xbox trace: Relative variation in bucket sizes (standard-deviation/mean) for different values of average bucket size (k) for the base and enhanced designs. (Behavior on dedup trace is similar.)

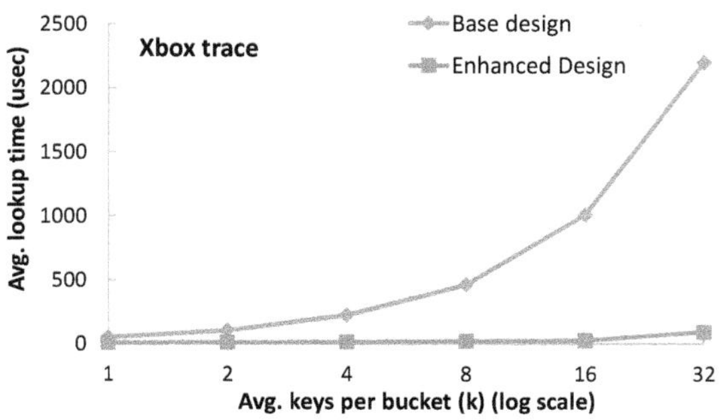

Figure 9: Xbox trace: Average lookup (get) time for different values of average bucket size (k) for the base and enhanced designs. The enhanced design reduces lookup times by factors of 6x-24x as k increases.

Storage Deduplication trace We have built a storage deduplication analysis tool that can crawl a root directory, generate the sequence of chunk hashes for a given average chunk hash size, and compute the number of deduplicated chunks and storage bytes. The enterprise data backup trace we use for evaluations in this paper was obtained by our storage deduplication analysis tool using 4KB chunk sizes. The trace contains 27,748,824 total chunks and 12,082,492 unique chunks. Using this, we obtain the ratio of `get` operations to `set` operations in the trace as 2.2:1. In this application, the key is a 20-byte SHA-1 hash of the corresponding chunk and the value is the meta-data for the chunk, with key-value pair total size upper bounded by 64 bytes.

The properties of the two traces are summarized in Table 1. Both traces include `get` operations on keys that have not been `set` earlier in the trace. (Such `get` operations will return `null`.) This is an inherent property of the nature of the application, hence we play the traces "as-is" to evaluate throughput in operations per second.

5.3 Performance Evaluation

We evaluate the performance impact of our design decisions and obtain ballpark ranges on lookup times and throughput (`get-set` operations/sec) for SkimpyStash on the Xbox LIVE Primetime online multi-player game and storage deduplication application traces (from Table 1). We disable the log compaction procedure for all but the last set of experiments. In the last set of experiments, we investigate the impact of garbage collection (which also does compaction) on system throughput.

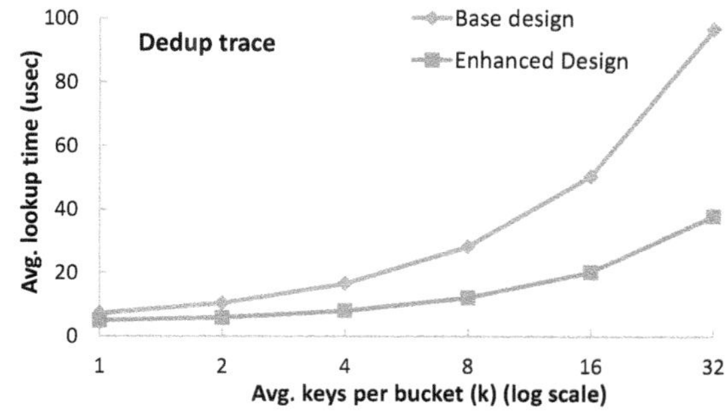

Figure 10: Dedup trace: Average lookup (get) time for different values of average bucket size (k) for the base and enhanced designs. The enhanced design reduces lookup times by factors of 1.5x-2.5x as k increases.

Impact of load balancing on bucket sizes: In the base design, hashing keys to single buckets can lead to wide variations in the chain length on flas in each bucket, and this translates to wide variations in lookup times. We investigate how two-choice based load balancing of keys to buckets can help reduce variance among bucket sizes. In Figure 8, we plot the relative variation in the bucket sizes (standard-deviation/mean of bucket sizes) for different values of $k = 1, 2, 4, 8, 16, 32$ on the Xbox trace (the behavior on dedup trace is similar). This metric is about 1.4x-6x times better for the enhanced design than for the based design on both traces. The gap starts at about 1.4x for the case $k = 1$ and increases to about 6x for the case $k = 32$. This provides conclusive evidence that two choice based load balancing is an effective strategy for reducing variations in bucket sizes.

Key lookup latencies: The two ideas of load balancing across buckets and using a bloom filte per bucket help to significantl reduce average key lookup times in the enhanced design, with the gains increasing as the average bucket size parameter k increases. At a value of $k = 8$, the average lookup time in the enhanced design is 20 μsec for the Xbox trace and 12 μsec for the dedup trace. In Figures 9 and 10, we plot the average lookup time for different values of $k = 1, 2, 4, 8, 16, 32$ on the two traces respectively. As the value of k increases, the gains in the enhanced design increase from 6x to 24x for the Xbox trace and from 1.5x to 2.5x for the dedup trace. The gains are more for the Xbox trace since that trace has many updates to earlier inserted keys (while the dedup trace has none), hence chains accumulate garbage records and get longer over time and bloom filter help even more to speedup lookups on non-existing keys (by avoiding searching the entire chain on flash)

Throughput (`get-set` operations/sec): The enhanced design achieves throughputs in the range of 10,000-69,000 ops/sec on the Xbox trace and 34,000-165,000 ops/sec on the dedup trace, with throughputs decreasing (as expected) with increasing values of k. This is shown in Figures 11 and 12. The throughput gains for the enhanced design over the base design are in the range of 3.5x-20x on the Xbox trace and 1.3x-2.5x on the dedup trace, with the gains increasing as the parameter k increases in value. These trends are in line with that of average lookup times.

The higher throughput of SkimpyStash on the dedup trace can be explained as follows. The write mix per unit operation (`get` or `set`) in the dedup trace is about 2.65 times that of the Xbox trace. However, since the key-value pair size is about 20 times smaller for the dedup trace, the number of syncs to stable storage per write

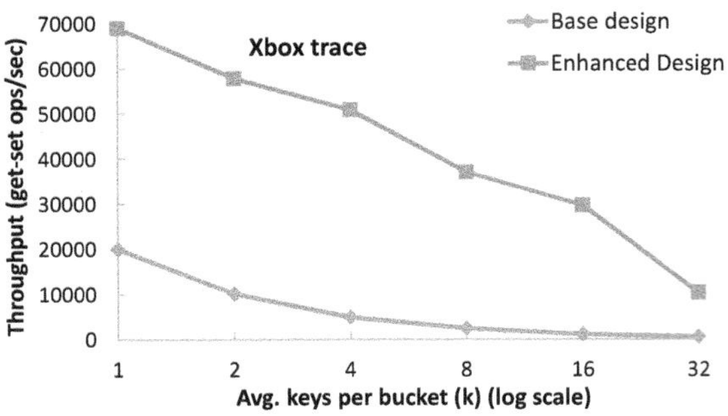

Figure 11: Xbox trace: Throughput (`get-set` ops/sec) for different values of average bucket size (k) for the base and enhanced designs. The enhanced design improves throughput by factors of 3.5x-20x as k increases.

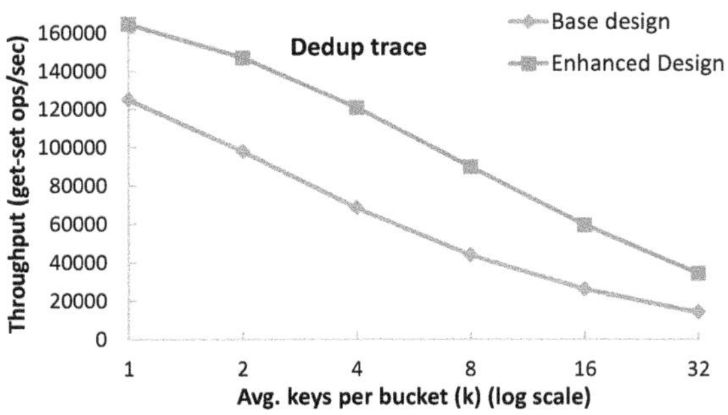

Figure 12: Dedup trace: Throughput (`get-set` ops/sec) for different values of average bucket size (k) for the base and enhanced designs. The enhanced design improves throughput by factors of 1.3x-2.5x as k increases.

operation is about 20 times less. Overall, the number of syncs to stable storage per unit operation is about 7.6 times less for the dedup trace. Moreover, bucket chains get longer in the Xbox trace due to invalid (garbage) records accumulating from key updates. For these reasons, SkimpyStash obtains higher throughputs on the dedup trace. In addition, since the dedup trace has no key update operations, the lookup operation can be avoided during key inserts for the dedup trace; this also contributes to the higher throughput of dedup trace over the Xbox trace. Garbage collection can help to improve performance on the Xbox trace, as we discuss next.

Impact of garbage collection activity: We study the impact of garbage collection (GC) activity on system throughput (ops/sec) and lookup times in SkimpyStash. The storage deduplication application does not involve updates to chunk metadata, hence we evaluate the impact of garbage collection on the Xbox trace. We fi an average bucket size of $k = 8$ for this set of experiments.

The aggressiveness of the garbage collection activity is controlled by a parameter g which is the interval of number of key *update* operations after which the garbage collector is invoked. Note that update operations are only those insert operations that update an earlier value of an already inserted key. Hence, the *garbage collector is invoked after every g key-value pair records worth of garbage accumulate in the log.* When the garbage collector is invoked, it starts scanning from the (current) head of the log and skips over orphaned records until it encounters the firs valid or invalid record (that is part of some bucket chain). Then, it garbage collects that entire bucket chain, compacts and writes the valid records in that chain to the tail of the log, and returns.

In Figure 13, we plot the throughput (ops/sec) obtained on the

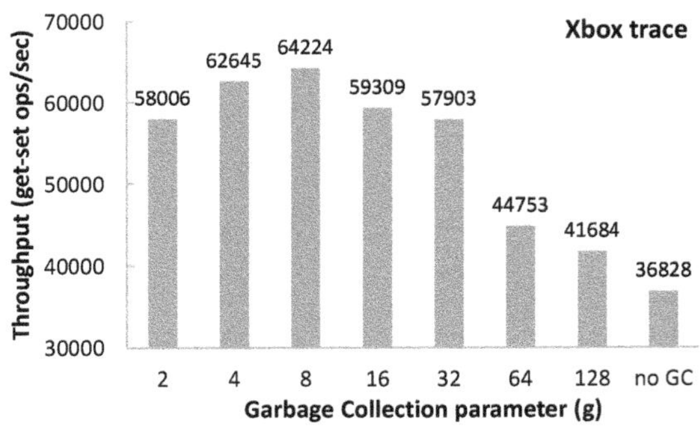

Figure 13: Xbox trace: Throughput (`get-set` ops/sec) for different values of the garbage collection parameter g. (The average bucket size parameter is fixed at $k = 8$.)

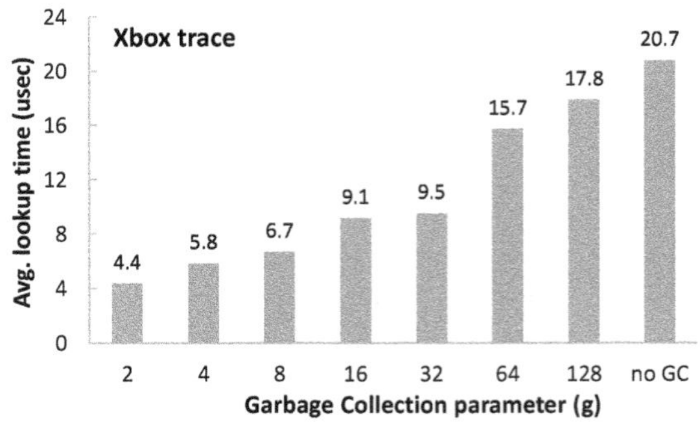

Figure 14: Xbox trace: Average lookup (`get`) time for different values of the garbage collection parameter g. (The average bucket size parameter is fixed at $k = 8$.)

Xbox trace as the garbage collection parameter g is varied. (The average bucket size parameter is fi ed at $k = 8$.) We see that as g is increased from $g = 2$ onwards, the throughput firs increases, peaks at $g = 8$, and then drops off all the the way to $g = 128$, at which point the throughput is close to that without garbage collection. This trend can be explained as follows. For small values of g, the high frequency of garbage collection is an overhead on system performance. As g is increased, the frequency of garbage collection activity decreases while lookup times continue to bene- fi (but less and less) from the compaction procedure involved in garbage collection (as explained in Section 4.6). Thus, the parameter g pulls system throughput in two different directions due to different effects, with the sweet spot for optimal performance occurring at $g_{opt} = 8$. We also reran the experiments for an average bucket size parameter of $k = 4$ and found the optimal value of g to be $g_{opt} = 8$ in that case also. It appears that the value of g_{opt} is a property of the trace and depends on the rate at which the application is generating garbage records.

Finally, we study the impact of the compaction procedure (as part of garbage collection activity) on average lookup times. As the compaction procedure helps to remove invalid records from bucket chains and reduce their lengths as well as place them contiguously on one or more flas pages, it helps to reduce search times in a bucket, as explained in Section 4.6. The impact can be seen in Figure 14, where lookup times steadily *decrease* as the aggressiveness of the garbage collection activity is *increased* (through *decrease* of the parameter g).

Comparison with earlier key-value store design: We compare SkimpyStash with FlashStore [16], a flash-base key-value store

Trace	FlashStore (ops/sec)	SkimpyStash ($k = 1$) (ops/sec)
Xbox	58,600	69,000
Dedup	75,100	165,000

Table 2: FlashStore [16] vs. SkimpyStash ($k = 1$).

which uses a variant of cuckoo hashing-based collision resolution policy [25] and compact key signatures to store metadata per key-value pair in the RAM. We use $n = 16$ hash functions to implement cuckoo hashing as suggested in [16]. Since FlashStore keeps metadata for only one key-value pair per hash table bucket, we compare it with the SkimpyStash design with the average bucket size parameter (k) set to 1, so as to keep the comparisons fair. Table 2 gives the summary of the throughput performance on Xbox and Dedup traces. SkimpyStash shows superior performance due to the fewer number of RAM accesses when non-existing keys are looked up – in such cases, SkimpyStash needs only two memory accesses, while FlashStore needs as many as 16. In addition, due to the nature of cuckoo hashing, FlashStore also needs to lookup an auxiliary hash table when items are not found in the main (cuckoo) hash table, which contributes to its reduced throughput. Since the ratio of the insert (set) to the lookup (get) operations on the Dedupe trace is higher than the Xbox trace (as explained in Section 5.2), SkimpyStash shows relatively better performance for the Dedupe trace as it has less overheads during the insertion of non-existing keys.

6. RELATED WORK

Flash memory has received lots of recent interest as a stable storage media that can overcome the access bottlenecks of hard disks. Researchers have considered modifying existing applications to improve performance on flas as well as providing operating system support for inserting flas as another layer in the storage hierarchy. In this section, we briefl review work that is related to SkimpyStash and point out its differentiating aspects.

MicroHash [27] designs a memory-constrained index structure for flash-base sensor devices with the goal of optimizing energy usage and minimizing memory footprint. Keys are assigned to buckets in a RAM directory based on range and flushe to flas when RAM buffer page is full. The directory needs to be repartitioned periodically based on bucket utilizations. SkimpyStash addresses this problem by hashing keys to hash table directory buckets and using two-choice load balancing across them, but gives up the ability to serve range queries. It also uses a bloom filte in each directory slot in RAM to disambiguate the two-choice during lookups. Moreover, MicroHash needs to write partially fille (index) pages to flas corresponding to keys in the same bucket, while the writes to flas in SkimpyStash always write full pages of key-value pair records.

FlashDB [23] is a self-tuning B^+-tree based index that dynamically adapts to the mix of reads and writes in the workload. Like MicroHash, it also targets memory and energy constrained sensor network devices. Because a B^+-tree needs to maintain partially fille leaf-level buckets on flash appending of new keys to these buckets involves random writes, which is not an efficien flas operation. Hence, an adaptive mechanism is also provided to switch between disk and log-based modes. The system leverages the fact that key values in sensor applications have a small range and that at any given time, a small number of these leaf-level buckets are active. Minimizing latency is not an explicit design goal.

Tree-based index structures optimized for the flas memory are proposed in [8, 21]. These works do not focus on the RAM space reduction. In contrast, here we are mainly focusing on the hash-based index structure with low RAM footprint.

The benefit of using flas in a log-like manner have been exploited in FlashLogging [14] for synchronous logging. This system uses multiple inexpensive USB drives and achieves performance comparable to flas SSDs but with much lower price. Flashlogging assumes sequential workloads. In contrast, SkimpyStash works with arbitrary key access workloads.

FAWN [11] uses an array of embedded processors equipped with small amounts of flas to build a power-efficien cluster architecture for data-intensive computing. The differentiating aspect of SkimpyStash includes the aggressive design goal of extremely low RAM usage – SkimpyStash incurs about 1 byte RAM overhead per key-value pair stored on flas while FAWN uses 6 bytes. This requires SkimpyStash to use some techniques that are different from FAWN. Moreover, we investigate the use of SkimpyStash in data center server-class applications that need to achieve high throughput on read-write mixed workloads.

BufferHash [10] builds a content addressable memory (CAM) system using flas storage for networking applications like WAN optimizers. It buffers key-value pairs in RAM, organized as a hash table, and flushe the hash table to flas when the buffer is full. Past copies of hash tables on flas are searched using a time series of Bloom filter maintained in RAM and searching keys on a given copy involve multiple flas reads. Thus, a key uses as many bytes in RAM (across all bloom filters as the number of times it is updated. Moreover, the storage of key-value pairs in hash tables on flas wastes space on flash since hash table load factors need to be well below 100% to keep lookup times bounded.

FlashStore [16] is a high throughput persistent key-value store that uses flas memory as a non-volatile *cache* between RAM and hard disk. It is designed to store the working set of key-value pairs on flas and use one flas read per key lookup. As the working set changes over time, space is made for the current working set by destaging recently unused key-value pairs to hard disk and recycling pages in the flas store. FlashStore organizes key-value pairs in a log-structure on flas to exploit faster sequential write performance. It uses an in-memory hash table to index them, with hash collisions resolved by a variant of cuckoo hashing [25]. The in-memory hash table stores compact key signatures instead of full keys so as to strike tradeoffs between RAM usage and false flas read operations. The RAM usage is 6 bytes per key-value stored on flash

ChunkStash [15] is a key-value store on flas that is designed for speeding up inline storage deduplication. It indexes data chunks (with SHA-1 hash as key) for identifying duplicate data. ChunkStash uses one flas read per chunk lookup and organizes chunk metadata in a log-structure on flas to exploit fast sequential writes. It builds an in-memory hash table to index them using techniques similar to FlashStore [16] to reduce RAM usage.

7. CONCLUSION

We designed SkimpyStash to be used as a high throughput persistent key-value storage layer for a broad range of server class applications. The distinguishing feature of SkimpyStash is the design goal of extremely low RAM footprint at about 1 byte per key-value pair, which is more aggressive than earlier designs. We used real-world data traces from two data center applications, namely, Xbox LIVE Primetime online multi-player game and inline storage deduplication, to drive and evaluate the design of SkimpyStash on commodity server platforms. SkimpyStash provides throughputs from few 10,000s to upwards of 100,000 `get-set` operations/sec on the evaluated applications.

8. REFERENCES

[1] C# System.Threading. http://msdn.microsoft.com/en-us/library/system.threading.aspx.

[2] Fusion-IO Drive Datasheet . http://www.fusionio.com/PDFs/Data_Sheet_ioDrive_2.pdf.

[3] Iometer. http://www.iometer.org/.

[4] MurmurHash Fuction. http://en.wikipedia.org/wiki/MurmurHash.

[5] MySpace Uses Fusion Powered I/O to Drive Greener and Better Data Centers. http://www.fusionio.com/case-studies/myspace-case-study.pdf.

[6] Releasing Flashcache. http://www.facebook.com/note.php?note_id=388112370932.

[7] Xbox LIVE Primetime game. http://www.xboxprimetime.com/.

[8] AGRAWAL, D., GANESAN, D., SITARAMAN, R., DIAO, Y., AND SINGH, S. Lazy-Adaptive Tree: An Optimized Index Structure for Flash Devices. In *VLDB* (2009).

[9] AGRAWAL, N., PRABHAKARAN, V., WOBBER, T., DAVIS, J., MANASSE, M., AND PANIGRAHY, R. Design Tradeoffs for SSD Performance. In *USENIX* (2008).

[10] ANAND, A., MUTHUKRISHNAN, C., KAPPES, S., AKELLA, A., AND NATH, S. Cheap and Large CAMs for High Performance Data-Intensive Networked Systems. In *NSDI* (2010).

[11] ANDERSEN, D., FRANKLIN, J., KAMINSKY, M., PHANISHAYEE, A., TAN, L., AND VASUDEVAN, V. FAWN: A Fast Array of Wimpy Nodes. In *SOSP* (2009).

[12] AZAR, Y., BRODER, A., KARLIN, A., AND UPFAL, E. Balanced Allocations. In *SIAM Journal on Computing* (1994).

[13] BRODER, A., AND MITZENMACHER, M. Network Applications of Bloom Filters: A Survey. In *Internet Mathematics* (2002).

[14] CHEN, S. FlashLogging: Exploiting Flash Devices for Synchronous Logging Performance. In *SIGMOD* (2009).

[15] DEBNATH, B., SENGUPTA, S., AND LI, J. ChunkStash: Speeding up Inline Storage Deduplication using Flash Memory. In *USENIX* (2010).

[16] DEBNATH, B., SENGUPTA, S., AND LI, J. FlashStore: High Throughput Persistent Key-Value Store. In *VLDB* (2010).

[17] GAL, E., AND TOLEDO, S. Algorithms and Data Structures for Flash Memories. In *ACM Computing Surveys* (2005), vol. 37.

[18] GUPTA, A., KIM, Y., AND URGAONKAR, B. DFTL: A Flash Translation Layer Employing Demand-Based Selective Caching of Page-Level Address Mappings. In *ASPLOS* (2009).

[19] KAWAGUCHI, A., NISHIOKA, S., AND MOTODA, H. A Flash-Memory Based File System. In *USENIX* (1995).

[20] KOLTSIDAS, I., AND VIGLAS, S. Flashing Up the Storage Layer. In *VLDB* (2008).

[21] LI, Y., HE, B., 0001, J. Y., LUO, Q., AND YI, K. Tree Indexing on Solid State Drives. *PVLDB 3*, 1 (2010).

[22] NATH, S., AND GIBBONS, P. Online Maintenance of Very Large Random Samples on Flash Storage. In *VLDB* (2008).

[23] NATH, S., AND KANSAL, A. FlashDB: Dynamic Self-tuning Database for NAND Flash. In *IPSN* (2007).

[24] NATIONAL INSTITUTE OF STANDARDS AND TECHNOLOGY, FIPS 180-1. Secure Hash Standard. U.S. Department of Commerce, 1995.

[25] PAGH, R., AND RODLER, F. F. Cuckoo hashing. *Journal of Algorithms 51*, 2 (May 2004).

[26] ROSENBLUM, M., AND OUSTERHOUT, J. The Design and Implementation of a Log-Structured File System. *ACM Transactions on Computer Systems 10* (1991).

[27] ZEINALIPOUR-YAZTI, D., LIN, S., KALOGERAKI, V., GUNOPULOS, D., AND NAJJAR, W. A. Microhash: An Efficien Index Structure for Flash-based Sensor Devices. In *FAST* (2005).

[28] ZHU, B., LI, K., AND PATTERSON, H. Avoiding the Disk Bottleneck in the Data Domain Deduplication File System. In *FAST* (2008).

Design and Evaluation of Main Memory Hash Join Algorithms for Multi-core CPUs

Spyros Blanas Yinan Li Jignesh M. Patel
University of Wisconsin–Madison
{sblanas, yinan, jignesh}@cs.wisc.edu

ABSTRACT

The focus of this paper is on investigating efficient hash join algorithms for modern multi-core processors in main memory environments. This paper dissects each internal phase of a typical hash join algorithm and considers different alternatives for implementing each phase, producing a family of hash join algorithms. Then, we implement these main memory algorithms on two radically different modern multiprocessor systems, and carefully examine the factors that impact the performance of each method.

Our analysis reveals some interesting results – a very simple hash join algorithm is very competitive to the other more complex methods. This simple join algorithm builds a shared hash table and does not partition the input relations. Its simplicity implies that it requires fewer parameter settings, thereby making it far easier for query optimizers and execution engines to use it in practice. Furthermore, the performance of this simple algorithm improves dramatically as the skew in the input data increases, and it quickly starts to outperform all other algorithms. Based on our results, we propose that database implementers consider adding this simple join algorithm to their repertoire of main memory join algorithms, or adapt their methods to mimic the strategy employed by this algorithm, especially when joining inputs with skewed data distributions.

Categories and Subject Descriptors

H.2.4. [**Database Management**]: Systems—*Query processing, Relational databases*

General Terms

Algorithms, Design, Performance

Keywords

hash join, multi-core, main memory

SIGMOD'11, June 12–16, 2011, Athens, Greece.

1. INTRODUCTION

Large scale multi-core processors are imminent. Modern processors today already have four or more cores, and for the past few years Intel has been introducing two more cores per processor roughly every 15 months. At this rate, it is not hard to imagine running database management systems (DBMSs) on processors with hundreds of cores in the near future. In addition, memory prices are continuing to drop. Today 1TB of memory costs as little as $25,000. Consequently, many databases now either fit entirely in main memory, or their working set is main memory resident. As a result, many DBMSs are becoming CPU bound.

In this evolving architectural landscape, DBMSs have the unique opportunity to leverage the inherent parallelism that is provided by the relational data model. Data is exposed by declarative query languages to user applications and the DBMS is free to choose its execution strategy. Coupled with the trend towards impending very large multi-cores, this implies that DBMSs must carefully rethink how they can exploit the parallelism that is provided by the modern multi-core processors, or DBMS performance will stall.

A natural question to ask then is whether there is anything new here. Beginning about three decades ago, at the inception of the field of parallel DBMSs, the database community thoroughly examined how a DBMS can use various forms of parallelism. These forms of parallelism include pure shared-nothing, shared-memory, and shared disk architectures [17]. If the modern multi-core architectures resemble any of these architectural templates, then we can simply adopt the methods that have already been designed.

In fact, to a large extent this is the approach that DBMSs have haven taken towards dealing with multi-core machines. Many commercial DBMSs simply treat a multi-core processor as a symmetric multi-processor (SMP) machine, leveraging previous work that was done by the DBMS vendors in reaction to the increasing popularity of SMP machines decades ago. These methods break up the task of a single operation, such as an equijoin, into disjoint parts and allow each processor (in an SMP box) to work on each part independently. At a high-level, these methods resemble variations of query processing techniques that were developed for parallel shared-nothing architectures [6], but adapted for SMP machines. In most commercial DBMSs, this approach is reflected across the entire design process, ranging from system internals (join processing, for example) to their pricing model, which is frequently done by scaling the SMP pricing model. On the other hand, open-source DBMSs have largely ignored multi-core processing and generally dedicate a single thread/process to each query.

The design space for modern high performance main memory join algorithms has two extremes. One extreme of this design space focuses on minimizing the number of processor cache misses. The radix-based hash join algorithm [2] is an example of a method in this design class. The other extreme is to focus on minimizing processor synchronization costs. In this paper we propose a "no partitioning" hash join algorithm that does not partition the input relations to embody an example of a method in this later design space.

A crucial question that we ask and answer in this paper is *what is the impact of these two extreme design points in modern multi-core processors for main memory hash join algorithms.* A perhaps surprising answer is that for modern multi-core architectures, in many cases the right approach is to focus on reducing the computation and synchronization costs, as modern processors are very effective in hiding cache miss latencies via simultaneous multi-threading. For example, in our experiments, the "no partitioning" hash join algorithm far outperforms the radix join algorithm when there is skew in the data (which is often the case in practice), even while it incurs many more processor cache and TLB misses. Even with uniform data, the radix join algorithm only outperforms the "no partitioning" algorithm on a modern Intel Xeon when the parameters for the radix join algorithm are set at or near their optimal setting. In contrast, the non-partitioned algorithm is "parameter-free", which is another important practical advantage.

Reflecting on the previous work in this area, one can observe that the database community has focused on optimizing query processing methods to reduce the number of processor cache and TLB misses. We hope that this paper opens up a new discussion on the entire design space for multi-core query processing techniques, and incites a similar examination of other aspects of query processing beyond the single hash join operation that we discuss in this paper.

This paper makes three main contributions. First, we systematically examine the design choices available for each internal phase of a canonical main memory hash join algorithm – namely, the partition, build, and probe phases – and enumerate a number of possible multi-core hash join algorithms based on different choices made in each of these phases. We then evaluate these join algorithms on two radically different architectures and show how the architectural differences can affect performance. Unlike previous work that has often focused on just one architecture, our use of two radically different architectures lets us gain deeper insights about hash join processing on multi-core processors. To the best of our knowledge, this is the first systematic exploration of multiple hash join techniques that spans multi-core architectures.

Second, we show that an algorithm that does not do any partitioning, but simply constructs a single shared hash table on the build relation often outperforms more complex algorithms. This simple "no-partitioning" hash join algorithm is robust to sub-optimal parameter choices by the optimizer, and does not require any knowledge of the characteristics of the input to work well. To the best of our knowledge, this simple hash join technique differs from what is currently implemented in existing DBMSs for multi-core hash join processing, and offers a tantalizingly simple, efficient, and robust technique for implementing the hash join operation.

Finally, we show that the simple "no-partitioning" hash join algorithm takes advantage of intrinsic hardware optimizations to handle skew. As a result, this simple hash join technique often benefits from skew and its relative performance increases as the skew increases! This property is a big advancement over the state-of-the-art methods, as it is important to have methods that can gracefully handle skew in practice [8].

The remainder of this paper is organized as follows: The next section covers background information. The hash join variants are presented in Section 3. Experimental results are described in Section 4, and related work is discussed in Section 5. Finally, Section 6 contains our concluding remarks.

2. THE MULTI-CORE LANDSCAPE

In the last few years alone, more than a dozen different multi-core CPU families have been introduced by CPU vendors. These new CPUs have ranged from powerful dual-CPU systems on the same die to prototype systems of hundreds of simple RISC cores.

This new level of integration has lead to architectural changes with deep impact on algorithm design. Although the first multi-core CPUs had dedicated caches for each core, we now see a shift towards more sharing at the lower levels of the cache hierarchy and consequently the need for access arbitration to shared caches within the chip. A shared cache means better single-threaded performance, as one core can utilize the whole cache, and more opportunities for sharing among cores. However, shared caches also increase conflict cache misses due to false sharing, and may increase capacity cache misses, if the cache sizes don't increase proportionally to the number of cores.

One idea that is employed to combat the diminishing returns of instruction-level parallelism is simultaneous multi-threading (SMT). Multi-threading attempts to find independent instructions across different threads of execution, instead of detecting independent instructions in the same thread. This way, the CPU will schedule instructions from each thread and achieve better overall utilization, increasing throughput at the expense of per-thread latency.

We briefly consider two modern architectures that we subsequently use for evaluation. At one end of the spectrum, the Intel Nehalem family is an instance of Intel's latest microarchitecture that offers high single-threaded performance because of its out-of-order execution and on-demand frequency scaling (TurboBoost). Multi-threaded performance is increased by using simultaneous multi-threading (HyperThreading). At the other end of the spectrum, the Sun UltraSPARC T2 has 8 simple cores that all share a single cache. This CPU can execute instructions from up to 8 threads per core, or a total of 64 threads for the entire chip, and extensively relies on simultaneous multi-threading to achieve maximum throughput.

3. HASH JOIN IMPLEMENTATION

In this section, we consider the anatomy of a canonical hash join algorithm, and carefully consider the design choices that are available in each internal phase of a hash join algorithm. Then using these design choices, we categorize various previous proposals for multi-core hash join processing. In the following discussion we also present information about some of the implementation details, as they often have a significant impact on the performance of the technique that is described.

A hash join operator works on two input relations, R and S. We assume that $|R| < |S|$. A typical hash join algorithm has three phases: partition, build, and probe. The partition phase is optional and divides tuples into distinct sets using a hash function on the join key attribute. The build phase scans the relation R and creates an in-memory hash table on the join key attribute. The probe phase scans the relation S, looks up the join key of each tuple in the hash table, and in the case of a match creates the output tuple(s).

Before we discuss the alternative techniques that are available in each phase of the join algorithm, we briefly digress to discuss the impact of the latch implementation on the join techniques. As a general comment, we have found that the latch implementation has a crucial impact on the overall join performance. In particular, when using the pthreads mutex implementation, several instructions are required to acquire and release an uncontended latch. If there are millions of buckets in a hash table, then the hash collision rate is small, and one can optimize for the expected case: latches being free. Furthermore, pthread mutexes have significant memory footprint as each requires approximately 40 bytes. If each bucket stores a few <key, record-id> pairs, then the size of the latch array may be greater than the size of the hash table itself. These characteristics make mutexes a prohibitively expensive synchronization primitive for buckets in a hash table. Hence, we implemented our own 1-byte latch for both the Intel and the Sun architectures, using the atomic primitives *xchgb* and *ldstub*, respectively. Protecting multiple hash buckets with a single latch to avoid cache thrashing did not result in significant performance improvements even when the number of partitions was high.

3.1 Partition phase

The partition phase is an optional step of a hash join algorithm, if the hash table for the relation R fits in main memory. If one partitions both the R and S relations such that each partition fits in the CPU cache, then the cache misses that are otherwise incurred during the subsequent build and probe phases are almost eliminated. The cost for partitioning both input relations is incurring additional memory writes for each tuple. Work by Shatdal et al. [16] has shown that the runtime cost of the additional memory writes during partitioning phase is less than the cost of missing in the cache – as a consequence partitioning improves overall performance. Recent work by Cieslewicz and Ross [4] has explored partitioning performance in detail. They introduce two algorithms that process the input once in a serial fashion and do not require any kind of global knowledge about the characteristics of the input. Another recent paper [11] describes a parallel implementation of radix partitioning [2] which gives impressive performance improvements on a modern multi-core system. This implementation requires that the entire input is available upfront and will not produce any output until the last input tuple has been seen. We experiment with all of these three partitioning algorithms, and we briefly summarize each implementation in Sections 3.1.1 and 3.1.2.

In our implementation, a partition is a linked list of output buffers. An output buffer is fully described by four elements: an integer specifying the size of the data block, a pointer to the start of the data block, a pointer to the free space inside the data block and a pointer to the next output buffer that is initially set to zero. If a buffer overflows, then we add an empty output buffer at the start of the list, and we make its next pointer point to the buffer that overflowed. Locating free space is a matter of checking the first buffer in the list.

Let p denote the desired number of partitions and n denote the number of threads that are processing the hash join operation. During the partitioning phase, all threads start reading tuples from the relation R, via a cursor. Each thread works on a large batch of tuples at a time, so as to minimize synchronization overheads on the input scan cursor. Each thread examines a tuple, then extracts the key k, and finally computes the partitioning hash function $h_p(k)$. Next, it then writes the tuple to partition $R_{h_p(k)}$ using one of the algorithms we describe below. When the R cursor runs out of tuples, the partitioning operation proceeds to process the tuples from the S relation. Again, each tuple is examined, the join key k is extracted and the tuple is written to the partition $S_{h_p(k)}$. The partitioning phase ends when all the S tuples have been partitioned.

Note that we classify the partitioning algorithms as "non-blocking" if they produce results on-the-fly and scan the input once, in contrast to a "blocking" algorithm that produces results after buffering the entire input and scanning it more than once. We acknowledge that the join operator overall is never truly non-blocking, as it will block during the build phase. The distinction is that the non-blocking algorithms only block for the time that is needed to scan and process the smaller input, and, as we will see in Section 4.3, this a very small fraction of the overall join time.

3.1.1 Non-blocking algorithms

The first partitioning algorithm creates p shared partitions among all the threads. The threads need to synchronize via a latch to make sure that the writes to a shared partition are isolated from each other.

The second partitioning algorithm creates $p * n$ partitions in total and each thread is assigned a private set of p partitions. Each thread then writes to its local partitions without any synchronization overhead. When the input relation is depleted, all threads synchronize at a barrier to consolidate the $p * n$ partitions into p partitions.

The benefit of creating private partitions is that there is no synchronization overhead on each access. The drawbacks, however, are (a) many partitions are created, possibly so many that the working set of the algorithm no longer fits in the data cache and the TLB; (b) at the end of the partition phase some thread has to chain n private partitions together to form a single partition, but this operation is quick and can be parallelized.

3.1.2 Blocking algorithm

Another partitioning technique is the parallel multi-pass radix partitioning algorithm described by Kim et al. [11]. The algorithm begins by having the entire input available in a contiguous block of memory. Each thread is responsible for a specific memory region in that contiguous block. A histogram with $p * n$ bins is allocated and the input is then scanned twice. During the first scan, each thread scans all the tuples in the memory region assigned to it, extracts the key k and then computes the exact histogram of the hash values $h_p(k)$ for this region. Thread $i \in [0, n-1]$ stores the number of tuples it encountered that will hash to partition $j \in [0, p-1]$ in histogram bin $j*n+i$. At the end of the scan, all the n threads compute the prefix sum on the histogram in parallel. The prefix sum can now be used to point to the beginning of each output partition for each thread in the single shared output buffer. Finally, each thread performs a second scan of its input region, and uses h_p to determine the output partition. This algorithm is recursively applied to each output partition for as many passes as requested.

The benefit of radix partitioning is that it makes few cache and TLB misses, as it bounds the number of output destinations in each pass. This particular implementation has the benefit that, by scanning the input twice for each pass, it computes exactly how much output space will be required for each partition, and hence avoids the synchronization overhead that is associated with sharing an output buffer. Apart from the drawbacks that are associated with any blocking algorithm when compared to a non-blocking counterpart, this implementation also places a burden on the previous operator in a query tree to produce the compact and contiguous output format that the radix partitioning requires as input. Efficiently producing a single shared output buffer is a problem that has been studied before [5].

3.2 Build phase

The build phase proceeds as follows: If the partition phase was omitted, then all the threads are assigned to work on the relation R. If partitioning was done, then each thread i is assigned to work on partitions $R_{i+0*n}, R_{i+1*n}, R_{i+2*n}$, etc. For example, a machine with four cores has $n = 4$, and thread 0 would work on partitions $R_0, R_4, R_8, ...$, thread 1 on $R_1, R_5, R_9, ...$, etc.

Next, an empty hash table is constructed for each partition of the input relation R. To reduce the number of cache misses that are incurred during the next (probe) phase, each bucket of this hash table is sized so that it fits on a few cache lines. Each thread scans every tuple t in its partition, extracts the join key k, and then hashes this key using a hash function $h(\cdot)$. Then, the tuple t is appended to the end of the hash bucket $h(k)$, creating a new hash bucket if necessary. If the partition phase was omitted, then all the threads share the hash table, and writes to each hash bucket have to be protected by a latch. The build phase is over when all the n threads have processed all the assigned partitions.

3.3 Probe phase

The probe phase schedules work to the n threads in a manner similar to the scheduling during the build phase, described above. Namely, if no partitioning has been done, then all the threads are assigned to S, and they synchronize before accessing the read cursor for S. Otherwise, the thread i is assigned to partitions S_{i+0*n}, S_{i+1*n}, S_{i+2*n}, etc.

During the probe phase, each thread reads every tuple s from its assigned partition and extracts the key k. It then checks if the key of each tuple r stored in hash bucket $h(k)$ matches k. This check is necessary to filter out possible hash collisions. If the keys match, then the tuples r and s are joined to form the output tuple. If the output is materialized, it is written to an output buffer that is private to the thread.

Notice that there is parallelism even inside the probe phase: looking up the key for each tuple r in a hash bucket and comparing it to k can be parallelized with the construction of the output tuple, which primarily involves shuffling bytes from tuples r and s. (See Section 4.10 for an experiment that explores this further.)

3.4 Hash Join Variants

The algorithms presented above outline an interesting design space for hash join algorithms. In this paper, we focus on the following four hash join variations:

1. **No partitioning join**: An implementation where partitioning is omitted. This implementation creates a shared hash table in the build phase.
2. **Shared partitioning join**: The first non-blocking partitioning algorithm of Section 3.1.1, where all the threads partition both input sources into shared partitions. Synchronization through a latch is necessary before writing to the shared partitions.
3. **Independent partitioning join**: The second non-blocking partitioning algorithm of Section 3.1.1, where all the threads partition both sources and create private partitions.
4. **Radix partitioning join**: An implementation where each input relation is stored in a single, contiguous memory region. Then, each thread participates in the radix partitioning, as described in Section 3.1.2.

4. EXPERIMENTAL EVALUATION

We have implemented the hash join algorithms described in Section 3.4 in a stand-alone C++ program. The program first loads data from the disk into main memory. Data is organized in memory using traditional slotted pages. The join algorithms are run after the data is loaded in memory. Since the focus of this work in on memory-resident datasets, we do not consider the time to load the data into main memory and only report join completion times.

For our workload, we wanted to simulate common and expensive join operations in decision support environments. The execution of a decision support query in a data warehouse typically involves multiple phases. First, one or more dimension relations are reduced based on the selection constraints. Then, these dimension relations are combined into an intermediate one, which is then joined with a much larger fact relation. Finally, aggregate statistics on the join output are computed and returned to the user. For example, in the TPC-H decision support benchmark, this execution pattern is encountered in at least 15 of the 22 queries.

We try to capture the essence of this operation by focusing on the most expensive component, namely the join operation between the intermediate relation R (the outcome of various operations on the dimension relations) with a much larger fact relation S. To allow us to focus on the core join performance, we initially do not consider the cost of materializing

	Intel Nehalem
CPU	Xeon X5650 @ 2.67GHz
Cores	6
Contexts per core	2
Cache size, sharing	12MB L3, shared
Memory	3x 4GB DDR3
	Sun UltraSPARC T2
CPU	UltraSPARC T2 @ 1.2GHz
Cores	8
Contexts per core	8
Cache size, sharing	4MB L2, shared
Memory	8x 2GB DDR2

Table 1: Platform characteristics.

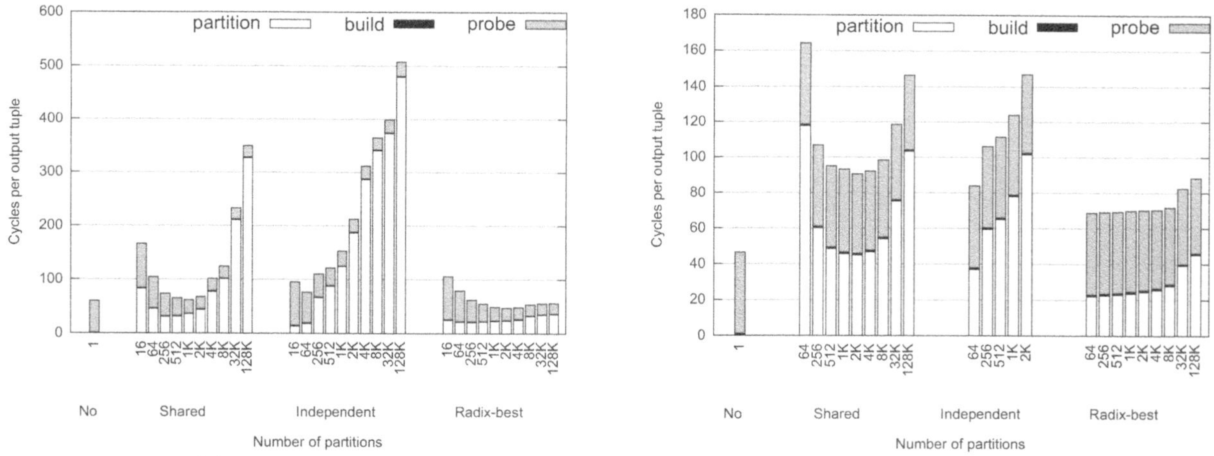

(a) Intel Nehalem (b) Sun UltraSPARC T2

Figure 1: Cycles per output tuple for the uniform dataset.

the output in memory, adopting a similar method as previous work [7, 11]. In later experiments (see Section 4.8), we consider the effect of materializing the join result – in these cases, the join result is created in main memory and not flushed to disk.

We describe the synthetic datasets that we used in the next section (Section 4.1). In Section 4.2 we give details about the hardware that we used for our experiments. We continue with a presentation of the results in Sections 4.3 and 4.4. We analyze the results further in Sections 4.5 through 4.7. We present results investigating the effect of output materialization, and the sensitivity to input sizes and selectivities in Sections 4.8 through 4.10.

4.1 Dataset

We experimented with three different datasets, which we denote as *uniform*, *low skew* and *high skew*, respectively. We assume that the relation R contains the primary key and the relation S contains a foreign key referencing tuples in R. In all the datasets we fix the cardinalities of R to 16M tuples and S to 256M tuples[1]. We picked the ratio of R to S to be 1:16 to mimic the common decision support settings. We experiment with different ratios in Section 4.9.

In our experiments both keys and payloads are eight bytes each. Each tuple is simply a <key, payload> pair, so tuples are 16 bytes long. Keys can either be the values themselves, if the key is numeric, or an 8-byte hash of the value in the case of strings. We chose to represent payloads as 8 bytes for two reasons: (a) Given that columnar storage is commonly used in data warehouses, we want to simulate storing <key, value> or <key, record-id> pairs in the hash table, and (b) make comparisons with existing work (i.e. [11, 4]) easier. Exploring alternative ways of constructing hash table entries is not a focus of this work, but has been explored before [15].

For the uniform dataset, we create tuples in the relation S such that each tuple matches every key in the relation R with equal probability. For the skewed datasets, we added skew to the distribution of the foreign keys in the relation S. (Adding skew to the relation R would violate the primary key constraint.) We created two skewed datasets, for two different s values of the Zipf distribution: low skew with $s = 1.05$ and high skew with $s = 1.25$. Intuitively, the most popular key appears in the low skew dataset 8% of the time, and the ten most popular keys account for 24% of the keys. In comparison, in the high skew dataset, the most popular key appears 22% of the time, and the ten most popular keys appear 52% of the time.

In all the experiments, the hash buckets that are created during the build phase have a fixed size: they always have 32 bytes of space for the payload, and 8 bytes are reserved for the pointer that points to the next hash bucket in case of overflow. These numbers were picked so that each bucket fits in a single, last-level cache line for both the architectures. We size the hash table appropriately so that no overflow occurs.

4.2 Platforms

We evaluated our methods on two different architectures: the Intel Nehalem and the Sun UltraSPARC T2. We describe the characteristics of each architecture in detail below, and we summarize key parameters in Table 1.

The Intel Nehalem microarchitecture is the successor of the Intel Core microarchitecture. All Nehalem-based CPUs are superscalar processors and exploit instruction-level parallelism by using out-of-order execution. The Nehalem family supports multi-threading, and allows two contexts to execute per core.

For our experiments, we use the six-core Intel Xeon X5650 that was released in Q1 of 2010. This CPU has a unified 12MB, 16-way associative L3 cache with a line size of 64 bytes. This L3 cache is shared by all twelve contexts executing on the six cores. Each core has a private 256KB, 8-way associative L2 cache, with a line size of 64 bytes. Finally, private 32KB instruction and data L1 caches connect to each core's load/store units.

The Sun UltraSPARC T2 was introduced in 2007 and relies heavily on multi-threading to achieve maximum throughput. An UltraSPARC T2 chip has eight cores and each core has hardware support for eight contexts. UltraSPARC T2 does not feature out-of-order execution. Each core has a single instruction fetch unit, a single floating point unit, a single memory unit and two arithmetic units. At every cycle, each core executes at most two instructions, each taken from two different contexts. Each context is scheduled in a round-robin fashion every cycle, unless the context has ini-

[1] Throughout the paper, $M=2^{20}$ and $K=2^{10}$.

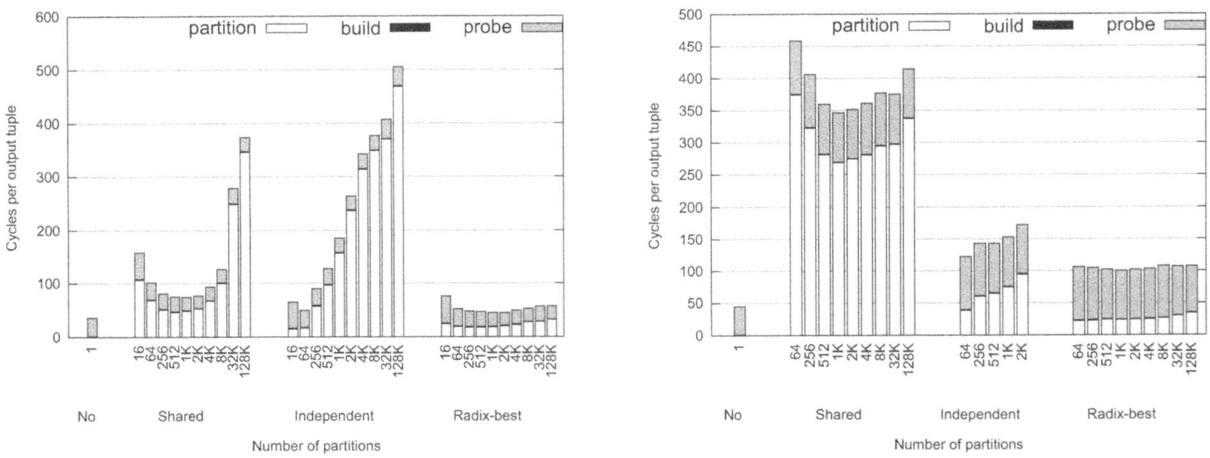

(a) Intel Nehalem (b) Sun UltraSPARC T2

Figure 2: Cycles per output tuple for the low skew dataset.

tiated a long-latency operation, such as a memory load that caused a cache miss, and has to wait for the outcome.

At the bottom of the cache hierarchy of the UltraSPARC T2 chip lies a shared 4MB, 16-way associative write-back L2 cache, with a line size of 64 bytes. To maximize throughput, the shared cache is physically split into eight banks. Therefore, up to eight cache requests can be handled concurrently, provided that each request hits a different bank. Each core connects to this shared cache through a non-blocking, pipelined crossbar. Finally, each core has a 8KB, 4-way associative write-through L1 data cache with 16 bytes per cache line that is shared by all the eight hardware contexts. Overall, in the absence of arbitration delays, the L2 cache hit latency is 20 cycles.

4.3 Results

We start with the uniform dataset. In Figure 1, we plot the average number of CPU cycles that it takes to produce one output tuple, without actually writing the output, for a varying number of partitions. (Note that to convert the CPU cycles to wall clock time, we simply divide the CPU cycles by the corresponding clock rate shown in Table 1). The horizontal axis shows the different join algorithms (bars "No", "Shared", "Independent"), corresponding to the first three hash join variants described in Section 3.4. For the radix join algorithm, we show the best result across any number of passes (bars marked "Radix-best"). Notice that we assume that the optimizer will always be correct and pick the optimal number of passes.

Overall, the build phase takes a very small fraction of the overall time, regardless of the partitioning strategy that is being used, across all architectures (see Figure 1). The reason for this behavior is two-fold. First and foremost, the smaller cardinality of the R relation translates into less work during the build phase. (We experiment with different cardinality ratios in Section 4.9.) Second, building a hash table is a really simple operation: it merely involves copying the input data into the appropriate hash bucket, which incurs a lot less computation than the other steps, such as the output tuple reconstruction that must take place in the probe phase. The performance of the join operation is therefore mostly determined by the time spent partitioning the input relations and probing the hash table.

As can be observed in Figure 1(a) for the Intel Nehalem architecture, the performance of the non-partitioned join algorithm is comparable to the optimal performance achieved by the partition-based algorithms. The shared partitioning algorithm performs best when sizing partitions so that they fit in the last level cache. This figure reveals a problem with the independent partitioning algorithm. For a high number of partitions, say 128K, each thread will create its own private buffer, for a total of 128K $*$ 12 $\approx$ 1.5 million output buffers. This high number of temporary buffers introduces two problems. First, it results in poor space utilization, as most of these buffers are filled with very few tuples. Second, the working set of the algorithm grows tremendously, and keeping track of 1.5 million cache lines requires a cache whose capacity is orders of magnitude larger than the 12MB L3 cache. The radix partitioning algorithm is not affected by this problem, because it operates in multiple passes and limits the number of partition output buffers in each pass.

Next, we experimented with the Sun UltraSPARC T2 architecture. In Figure 1(b) we see that doing no partitioning is at least 1.5X faster compared to all the other algorithms. The limited memory on this machine prevented us from running experiments with a high number of partitions for the independent partitioning algorithm because of the significant memory overhead discussed in the previous paragraph. As this machine supports nearly five times more hardware contexts than the Intel machine, the memory that is required for bookkeeping is five times higher as well.

To summarize our results with the uniform dataset, we see that on the Intel architecture the performance of the no partitioning join algorithm is comparable to the performance of all the other algorithms. For the Sun UltraSPARC T2, we see that the no partitioning join algorithm outperforms the other algorithms by at least 1.5X. Additionally, the no partitioning algorithm is more robust, as the performance of the other algorithms degrades if the query optimizer does not pick the optimal value for the number of partitions.

4.4 Effect of skew

We now consider the case when the distribution of foreign keys in the relation S is skewed. We again plot the average time to produce each tuple of the join (in machine cycles) in Figure 2 for the low skew dataset, and in Figure 3 for the high skew dataset.

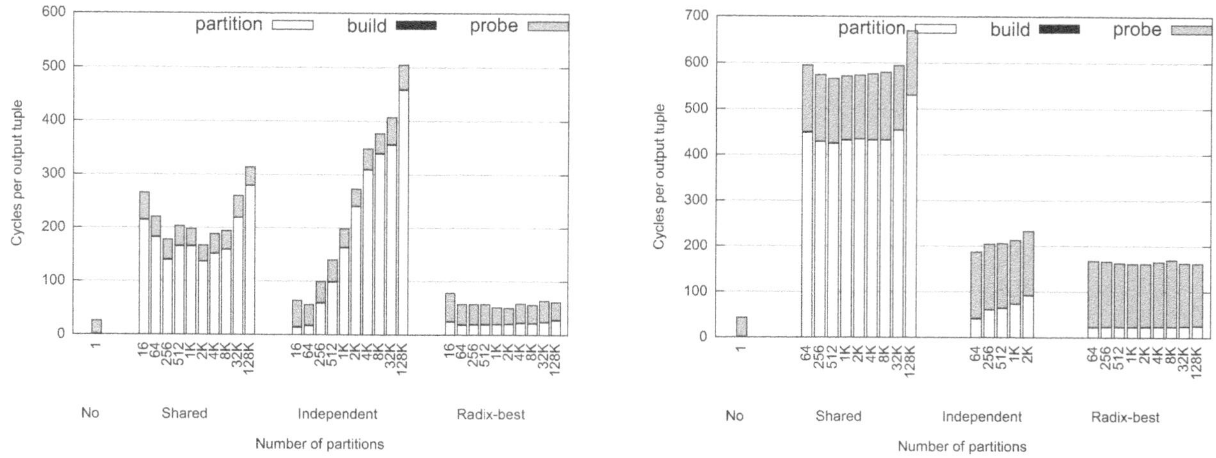

(a) Intel Nehalem

(b) Sun UltraSPARC T2

Figure 3: Cycles per output tuple for the high skew dataset.

	Intel Nehalem	Sun UltraSPARC T2
NO	No / 1	No / 1
SN	Indep. / 16	Indep. / 64
L2-S	Shared / 2048	Shared / 2048
L2-R	Radix / 2048	Radix / 2048

Table 2: Shorthand notation and corresponding partitioning strategy / number of partitions.

By comparing Figure 1 with Figure 2, we notice that, when using the shared hash table (bar "No" in all graphs), performance actually improves in the presence of skew! On the other hand, the performance of the shared partitioning algorithm degrades rapidly with increasing skew, while the performance of the independent partitioning and the radix partitioning algorithms shows little change on the Intel Nehalem and degrades on the Sun UltraSPARC T2. Moving to Figure 3, we see that the relative performance of the non-partitioned join algorithm increases rapidly under higher skew, compared to the other algorithms. The non-partitioned algorithm is generally 2X faster than the other algorithms on the Intel Nehalem, and more than 4X faster than the other algorithms on the Sun UltraSPARC T2.

To summarize these results, skew in the underlying join key values (data skew) manifests itself as partition size skew when using partitioning. For the shared partitioning algorithm, during the partition phase, skew causes latch contention on the partition with the most popular key(s). For all partitioning-based algorithms, during the probe phase, skew translates into a skewed work distribution per thread. Therefore, the overall join completion time is determined by the completion time of the partition with the most popular key. (We explore this behavior further in Section 4.7.1.) On the other hand, skew improves performance when sharing the hash table and not doing partitioning for two reasons. First, the no partitioning approach ensures an even work distribution per thread as all the threads are working concurrently on the single partition. This greedy scheduling strategy proves to be effective in hiding data skew. Second, performance increases because the hardware handles skew a lot more efficiently, as skewed memory access patterns cause significantly fewer cache misses.

		Cycles	L3 miss	Instruc-tions	TLB load miss	TLB store miss
NO	partition	0	0	0	0	0
	build	322	2	2,215	1	0
	probe	15,829	862	54,762	557	0
SN	partition	3,578	18	29,096	6	2
	build	328	8	2,064	0	0
	probe	21,717	866	54,761	505	0
L2-S	partition	11,778	103	31,117	167	257
	build	211	1	2,064	0	0
	probe	6,144	35	54,762	1	0
L2-R	partition	6,343	221	34,241	7	237
	build	210	1	2,064	0	0
	probe	6,152	36	54,761	1	0

Table 3: Performance counter averages for the uniform dataset (millions).

4.5 Performance counters

Due to space constraints, we focus on specific partitioning configurations from this section onward. We use "NO" to denote the no partitioning strategy where the hash table is shared by all threads, and we use "SN" to denote the case when we create as many partitions as hardware contexts (join threads), except we round the number of partitions up to the next power of two as is required for the radix partitioning algorithm. We use "L2" to denote the case when we create partitions to fit in the last level cache, appending "-S" when partitioning with shared output buffers, and "-R" for radix partitioning. We summarize this notation in Table 2. Notice that the L2 numbers correspond to the best performing configuration settings in the experiment with the uniform dataset (see Figure 1).

We now use the hardware performance counters to understand the characteristics of these join algorithms. In the interest of space, we only present our findings from a single architecture: the Intel Nehalem. We first show the results from the uniform dataset in Table 3. Each row indicates one particular partitioning algorithm and join phase, and each column shows a different architectural event. First, notice the code path length. It takes, on average, about 55 billion instructions to complete the probe phase and an additional 50% to 65% of that for partitioning, depending on the algorithm of choice. The NO algorithm pays a high cost in

		Cycles	L3 miss	Instruc- -tions	TLB load miss	TLB store miss
NO	partition	0	0	0	0	0
	build	323	3	2,215	1	0
	probe	6,433	98	54,762	201	0
SN	partition	3,577	17	29,096	6	1
	build	329	8	2,064	0	0
	probe	13,241	61	54,761	80	0
L2-S	partition	36,631	79	34,941	67	106
	build	210	5	2,064	0	0
	probe	8,024	13	54,762	1	0
L2-R	partition	5,344	178	34,241	5	72
	build	209	4	2,064	0	0
	probe	8,052	13	54,761	1	0

Table 4: Performance counter averages for the high skew dataset (millions).

terms of the L3 cache misses during the probe phase. The partitioning phase of the SN algorithm is fast but fails to contain the memory reference patterns that arise during the probe phase in the cache. The L2-S algorithm manages to minimize these memory references, but incurs a high L3 and TLB miss ratio during the partition phase compared to the NO and SN algorithms. The L2-R algorithm uses multiple passes to partition the input and carefully controls the L3 and TLB misses during these phases. Once the cache-sized partitions have been created, we see that both the L2-S and L2-R algorithms avoid incurring many L3 and TLB misses during the probe phase. In general, we see fewer cache and TLB misses across all algorithms when adding skew (in Table 4).

Unfortunately, interpreting performance counters is much more challenging with modern multi-core processors and will likely get worse. Processors have become a lot more complex over the last ten years, yet the events that counters capture have hardly changed. This trend causes a growing gap between the high-level algorithmic insights the user expects and the specific causes that trigger some processor state that the performance counters can capture. In a uniprocessor, for example, a cache miss is an indication that the working set exceeds the cache's capacity. The penalty is bringing the data from memory, an operation the costs hundreds of cycles. However, in a multi-core processor, a memory load might miss in the cache because the operation touches memory that some other core has just modified. The penalty in this case is looking in some other cache for the data. Although a neighboring cache lookup can be ten or a hundred times faster than bringing the data from memory, both scenarios will simply increment the cache miss counter and not record the cause of this event.

To illustrate this point, let's turn our attention to a case in Table 3 where the performance counter results can be misleading: The probe phase of the SN algorithm has slightly fewer L3 and TLB misses than the probe phase of the NO algorithm and equal path length, so the probe phase of the SN algorithm should be comparable or faster than probe phase of the NO algorithm. However, the probe phase of the NO algorithm is almost 25% faster! Another issue is latch contention, which causes neither L3 cache misses nor TLB misses, and therefore is not reported in the performance counters. For example, when comparing the uniform and high skew numbers for the L2-S algorithm, the number of the L3 cache misses during the high skew experiment is

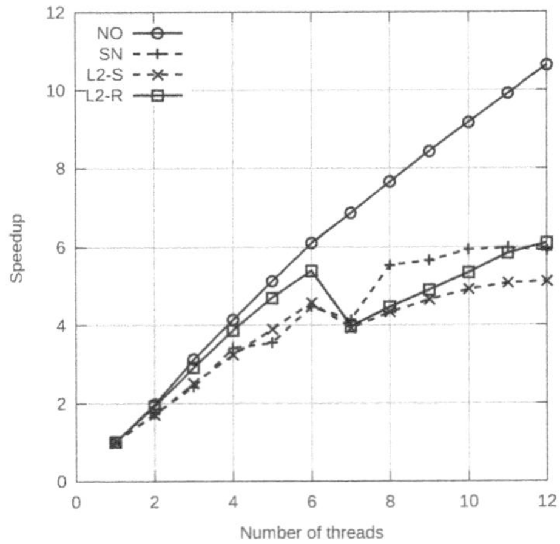

Figure 4: Speedup over single threaded execution, uniform dataset.

30% lower than the number of the cache misses observed during the uniform experiment. However, partitioning performance worsens by more than 3X when creating shared partitions under high skew!

The performance counters don't provide clean insights into why the non-partitioned algorithm exhibits similar or better performance than the other cache-efficient algorithms across all datasets. Although a cycle breakdown is still feasible at a macroscopic level where the assumption of no contention holds (for example as in Ailamaki et al. [1]), this experiment reveals that blindly assigning fixed cycle penalties to architectural events can lead to misleading conclusions.

4.6 Speedup from SMT

Modern processors improve the overall efficiency with hardware multithreading. Simultaneous multi-threading (SMT) permits multiple independent threads of execution to better utilize the resources provided by modern processor architectures. We now evaluate the impact of SMT on the hash join algorithms.

We first show a speedup experiment for the Intel Nehalem on the uniform dataset in Figure 4. We start by dedicating each thread to a core, and once we exceed the number of available physical cores (six for our Intel Nehalem), we then start assigning threads in a round-robin fashion to the available hardware contexts. We observe that the algorithms behave very differently when some cores are idle (fewer than six threads) versus in the SMT region (more than six threads). With fewer than six threads all the algorithms scale linearly, and the NO algorithm has optimal speedup. With more than six threads, the NO algorithm continues to scale, becoming almost 11X faster than the single-threaded version when using all available contexts. The partitioning-based algorithms SN, L2-S and L2-R, however, do not exhibit this behavior. The speedup curve for these three algorithms in the SMT region either flattens completely (SN algorithm), or increases at a reduced rate (L2-R algorithm) than the non-SMT region. In fact, performance drops for all partitioning algorithms for seven threads because of load imbalance: a single core has to do the work for two threads. (This imbalance can be ameliorated through load balancing, a technique that we explore in Section 4.7.1.)

	Uniform		
	6 threads	12 threads	Improvement
NO	28.23	16.15	1.75X
SN	34.04	25.62	1.33X
L2-S	19.27	18.13	1.06X
L2-R	14.46	12.71	1.14X
	High skew		
	6 threads	12 threads	Improvement
NO	9.34	6.76	1.38X
SN	19.50	17.15	1.14X
L2-S	38.37	44.87	0.86X
L2-R	15.04	13.61	1.11X

Table 5: Simultaneous multi-threading experiment on the Intel Nehalem, showing billions of cycles to join completion and relative improvement.

	Uniform		
	8 threads	64 threads	Improvement
NO	37.30	12.64	2.95X
SN	55.70	22.25	2.50X
L2-S	51.62	23.86	2.16X
L2-R	46.62	18.88	2.47X
	High skew		
	8 threads	64 threads	Improvement
NO	23.92	11.67	2.05X
SN	70.52	49.54	1.42X
L2-S	73.91	221.01	0.33X
L2-R	66.01	43.16	1.53X

Table 6: Simultaneous multi-threading experiment on the Sun UltraSPARC T2, showing billions of cycles to join completion and relative improvement.

We summarize the benefit of SMT in Table 5 for the Intel architecture, and in Table 6 for the Sun architecture. For the Intel Nehalem and the uniform dataset, the NO algorithm benefits significantly from SMT, becoming 1.75X faster. This algorithm is not optimized for cache performance, and as seen in Section 4.5, causes many cache misses. As a result, it provides more opportunities for SMT to efficiently overlap the memory accesses. On the other hand, the other three algorithms are optimized for cache performance to different degrees. Their computation is a large fraction of the total execution time, therefore they do not benefit significantly from using SMT. In addition, we notice that the NO algorithm is around 2X slower than the L2-R algorithm without SMT, but its performance increases to almost match the L2-R algorithm performance with SMT.

For the Sun UltraSPARC T2, the NO algorithm also benefits the most from SMT. In this architecture the code path length (i.e. instructions executed) has a direct impact on the join completion time, and therefore the NO algorithm performs best both with and without SMT. As the Sun machine cannot exploit instruction parallelism at all, we see increased benefits from SMT compared to the Intel architecture.

When comparing the high skew dataset with the uniform dataset across both architectures, we see that the improvement of SMT is reduced. The skewed key distribution incurs fewer cache misses, therefore SMT loses opportunities to hide processor pipeline stalls.

4.7 Synchronization

Synchronization is used in multithreaded programs to guarantee the consistency of shared data structures. In our join implementations, we use barrier synchronization when all the threads wait for tasks to be completed before they can proceed to the next task. (For example, at the end of each pass of the radix partition phase, each thread has to wait until all other threads complete before proceeding.) In this section, we study the effect of barrier synchronization on the performance of the hash join algorithm. In the interest of space, we only present results for the Intel Nehalem machine. Since the radix partitioning algorithm wins over the other partitioning algorithms across all datasets, our discussion only focuses on results for the non-partitioned algorithm (NO) and the radix partitioning algorithm (L2-R).

Synchronization has little impact on the non-partitioned (NO) algorithm for both the uniform and the high skew datasets, regardless of the number of threads that are running. The reason for this behavior is the simplicity of the NO algorithm. First, there is no partition phase at all, and each thread can proceed independently in the probe phase. Therefore synchronization is only necessary during the build phase, a phase that takes less than 2% of the total time (see Figure 1). Second, by dispensing with partitioning, this algorithm ensures an even distribution of work across the threads, as all the threads are working concurrently on the single shared hash table.

We now turn our attention to the radix partitioning algorithm, and break down the time spent by each thread. Unlike the non-partitioned algorithm, the radix partitioning algorithm is significantly impacted by synchronization on both the uniform and the high skew datasets. Figure 5(a) shows the time breakdown for the L2-R algorithm when running 12 threads on the Intel Nehalem machine with the high skew dataset. Each histogram in this figure represents the execution flow of a thread. The vertical axis can be viewed as a time axis (in machine cycles). White rectangles in these histograms represent tasks, the position of each rectangle indicates the beginning time of the task, and the height represents the completion time of this task for each thread. The gray rectangles represent the waiting time that is incurred by a thread that completes its task but needs to synchronize with the other threads before continuing. In the radix join algorithm, we can see five expensive operations that are synchronized through barriers: (1) computing the thread-private histogram, (2) computing the global histogram, (3) doing radix partitioning, (4) building a hash table for each partition of the relation R, and (5) probing each hash table with a partition from the relation S. The synchronization cost of the radix partitioning algorithm accounts for nearly half of the total join completion time for some threads.

The synchronization cost is so high under skew primarily because it is hard to statically divide work items into equally-sized subtasks. As a result, faster threads have to wait for slower threads. For example, if threads are statically assigned to work on partitions in the probe phase, the distribution of the work assigned to the threads will invariably also be skewed. Thus, the thread processing the partition with the most popular key becomes a bottleneck and the overall completion time is determined by the completion time of the partition with the most popular keys. In Figure 5(a), this is thread 3.

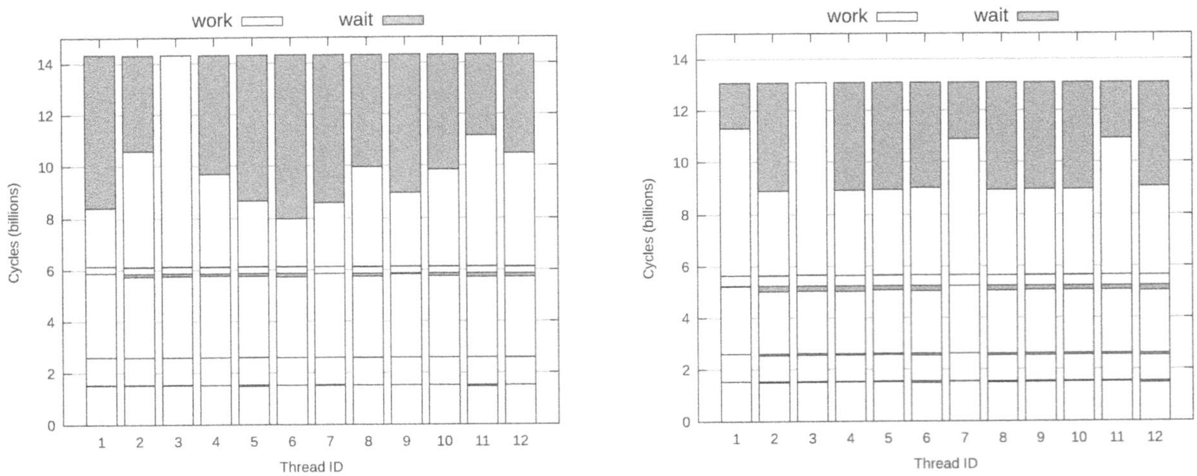

(a) High skew dataset (b) High skew dataset with work stealing

Figure 5: Time breakdown of the radix join.

4.7.1 Load balancing

If static work allocation is the problem, then how would the radix join algorithm perform under a dynamic work allocation policy and highly skewed input? To answer this question, we tweaked the join algorithm to allow the faster threads that have completed their probe phase to steal work from other slower threads. In our implementation, the unit of work is a single partition. In doing so, we slightly increase the synchronization cost because work queues need to now be protected with latches, but we balance the load better.

In Figure 5(b) we plot the breakdown of the radix partitioning algorithm (L2-R) using this work stealing policy when running on the Intel Nehalem machine with the high skew dataset. Although the work is now balanced almost perfectly for the smaller partitions, the partitions with the most popular keys are still a bottleneck. In the high skew dataset, the most popular key appears 22% of the time, and thread 3 in this case has been assigned only a single partition which happened to correspond to the most popular key. In comparison, for this particular experiment, the NO algorithm can complete the join in under 7 billion cycles (Table 4), and hence is 1.9X faster. An interesting area for future work is load balancing techniques that permit work stealing at a finer granularity than an entire partition with a reasonable synchronization cost.

To summarize, under skew, a load balancing technique improves the performance of the probe phase but does not address the inherent inefficiency of all the partitioning-based algorithms. In essence, there is a coordination cost to be paid for load balancing, as thread synchronization is necessary. Skew in this case causes contention, stressing the cache coherence protocol and increasing memory traffic. On the other hand, the no partitioning algorithm does skewed memory loads of read-only data, which is handled very efficiently by modern CPUs through caching.

4.8 Effect of output materialization

Early work in main memory join processing [7] did not take into account the cost of materialization. This decision was justified by pointing out that materialization comes at a fixed price for all algorithms and, therefore, a join algorithm will be faster regardless of the output being materialized or discarded. Recent work by Cieslewicz et al. [3] highlighted the trade-offs involved when materializing the output.

Machine	NO	SN	L2-S	L2-R
Intel Nehalem	23%	4%	7%	10%
Sun UltraSPARC T2	29%	21%	20%	23%

Table 7: Additional overhead of materialization with respect to total cycles without materialization on the uniform dataset.

	Scale 0.5	Scale 1	Scale 2
NO	7.65 (0.47X)	16.15 (1.00X)	62.27 (3.86X)
SN	11.76 (0.46X)	25.62 (1.00X)	98.82 (3.86X)
L2-S	8.47 (0.47X)	18.13 (1.00X)	68.48 (3.78X)
L2-R	5.82 (0.46X)	12.71 (1.00X)	DNF

Table 8: Join sensitivity with varying input cardinalities for the uniform dataset on Intel Nehalem. The table shows the cycles for computing the join (in billions) and the relative difference to scale 1.

In Table 7 we report the increase in the total join completion time when we materialize the output in memory for the uniform dataset and the partitioning strategies described in Table 2. If the join operator is part of a complex query plan, it is unlikely that the entire join output will ever need to be written in one big memory block, but, even in this extreme case, we see that no algorithm is being significantly impacted by materialization.

4.9 Cardinality experiments

We now explore how sensitive our findings are to variations in the cardinalities of the two input relations. Table 8 shows the results when running the join algorithms on the Intel Nehalem machine. The numbers obtained from the uniform dataset (described in detail in Section 4.1) are shown in the middle column. We first created one uniform dataset where both relations are half the size (scale 0.5). This means the relation R has 8M tuples and the relation S has 128M tuples. We also created a uniform dataset where both relations are twice the size (scale 2), i.e. the relation R has 32M tuples and the relation S has 512M tuples. The scale 2 dataset occupies 9GB out of the 12GB of memory our system has (Table 1) and leaves little working memory, but the serial

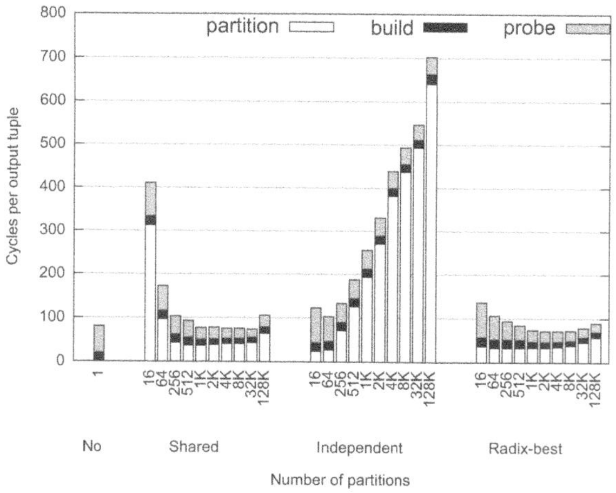

Figure 6: Experiment on Intel Nehalem with uniform dataset and |R|=|S|.

access pattern allows performance to degrade gracefully for all algorithms but the L2-R algorithm. The main memory optimizations of the L2-R algorithm cause many random accesses which hurt performance. We therefore mark the L2-R algorithm as not finished (DNF).

We now examine the impact of the relative size of the relations R and S. We fixed the cardinality of the relation S to be 16M tuples, making $|R| = |S|$, and we plot the cycles per output tuple for the uniform dataset when running on the Intel Nehalem in Figure 6. First, the partitioning time increases proportionally to $|R| + |S|$. Second, the build phase becomes significant, taking at least 25% of the total join completion time. The probe phase, however, is at most 30% slower, and less affected by the cardinality of the relation R. Overall, all the algorithms are slower when $|R| = |S|$ because they have to process more data, but the no partitioning algorithm is slightly favored because it avoids partitioning both input relations.

The results show that no join algorithm is particularly sensitive to our selection of input relation cardinalities, therefore our findings are expected to hold across a broader spectrum of cardinalities. The outcome of the experiments for the Sun UltraSPARC T2 is similar, and is omitted.

4.10 Selectivity experiment

We now turn our attention to how join selectivity affects performance. As all our original datasets are examples of joins between primary and foreign keys, all the experiments that have been presented so far have a selectivity of 100%. For this experiment we created two different S relations that have the same cardinality but only 50% and 12.5% of the tuples join with a tuple in the relation R. The key distribution is uniform.

Results for the Intel Nehalem are shown Figure 7(a). Decreasing join selectivity has a marginal benefit on the probe phase, but the other two phases are unaffected. The outcome of the same experiment on Sun UltraSPARC T2 is shown in Figure 7(b). In this architecture, the benefit of a small join selectivity on the probe phase is significant.

Inspecting the performance counters in this experiment revealed additional insights. Across all the architectures, the code path length (i.e. instructions executed) increases as join selectivity increases. The Intel Nehalem is practically insensitive to different join selectivities, because its out-of-order execution manages to overlap the data transfer with the byte shuffling that is required to assemble the output tuple. On the other hand, for the Sun UltraSPARC T2 machine, there is a strong linear correlation between the code path length and the cycles that are required for the probe phase to complete. The in-order Sun UltraSPARC T2 cannot automatically extract the instruction-level parallelism of the probe phase, unless the programmer explicitly expresses it by using multiple threads.

4.11 Implications

These results imply that DBMSs must reconsider their join algorithms for current and future multi-core processors. First, modern processors are very effective in hiding cache miss latencies through multi-threading (SMT), as it is shown in Tables 5 and 6. Second, optimizing for cache performance requires partitioning, and this has additional computation and synchronization overheads, and necessitates elaborate load balancing techniques to deal with skew. These costs of partitioning on a modern multi-core machine can be higher than the benefit of an increased cache hit rate, especially on skewed datasets (as shown in Figures 2 and 3.) To fully leverage the current and future CPUs, high performance main memory designs have to achieve good cache and TLB performance, while fully exploiting SMT, and minimizing synchronization costs.

5. RELATED WORK

There is a rich history of studying hash join performance for main memory database systems, starting with the early work of DeWitt et al. [7]. A decade later Shatdal et al. [16] studied cache-conscious algorithms for query execution and discovered that the probe phase dominates the overall hash join processing time. They also showed that hash join computation can be sped up if both the build and probe relations are partitioned so as to fit in the cache.

Ailamaki et al. [1] studied where DBMSs spend their time on modern processors, whereas Manegold et al. [12] inspected the time breakdown for a hash join operation. Both papers break down the query execution time by examining performance counters, and single out cache and TLB misses as the two primary culprits for suboptimal performance in main memory processing. A follow-up paper [13] presented a cost model on how to optimize the performance of the radix join algorithm on a uniprocessor [2].

Ross [15] presented a more efficient way to improve the performance of hash joins by using cuckoo hashing [14] and SIMD instructions. Garcia and Korth [9] have studied the benefits of using simultaneous multi-threading for hash join processing. Graefe et al. [10] described how hash-based algorithms can improve the performance of a commercial DBMS.

Finally, there has been prior work in handling skew during hash join processing. The experiments with a high number of partitions that we presented in Section 4.4 are an extension of an idea by DeWitt et al. [8] for a main memory, multi-core environment.

6. CONCLUSIONS AND FUTURE WORK

The rapidly evolving multi-core landscape requires that DBMSs carefully consider the interactions between query processing algorithms and the underlying hardware. In this

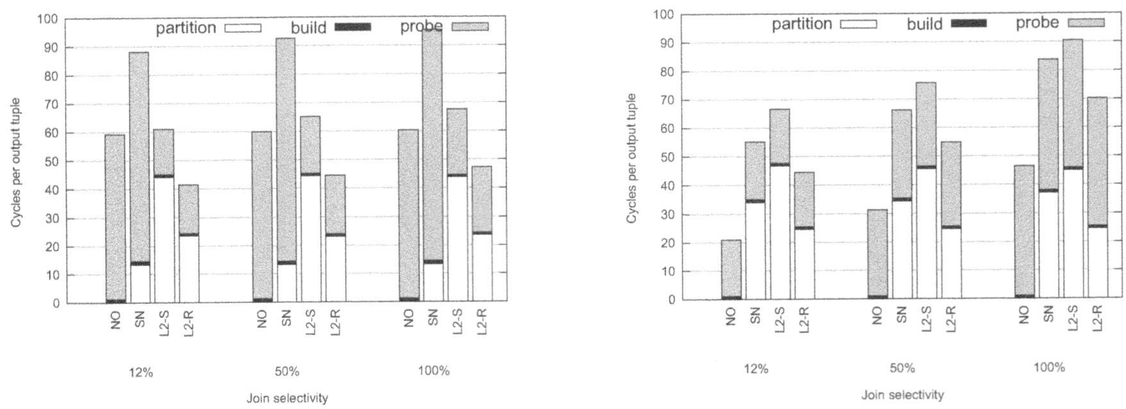

(a) Intel Nehalem (b) Sun UltraSPARC T2

Figure 7: Sensitivity to join selectivity. Increasing join selectivity impacts the critical path for the Sun UltraSPARC T2, while the out-of-order execution on Intel Nehalem overlaps computation with data transfer.

paper we examine these interactions when executing a hash join operation in a main memory DBMS. We implement a family of main memory hash join algorithms that vary in the way that they implement the partition, build, and probe phases of a canonical hash join algorithm.

We also evaluate our algorithms on two different multi-core processor architectures. Our results show that a simple hash join technique that does not do any partitioning of the input relations often outperforms the other more complex partitioning-based join alternatives. In addition, the relative performance of this simple hash join technique rapidly improves with increasing skew, and it outperforms every other algorithm in the presence of even small amounts of skew.

Minimizing cache misses requires additional computation, synchronization and load balancing to cope with skew. As our experiments show, these costs on a modern multi-core machine can be higher than the benefit of an increased cache hit rate. To fully leverage the current and future CPUs, high performance main memory designs have to consider how to minimize computation and synchronization costs, and fully exploit simultaneous multi-threading, in addition to maintaining good cache and TLB behavior. While a large part of the previous work in this area has mostly focused on minimizing cache and TLB misses for database query processing tasks, our work here suggests that paying attention to the computation and synchronization costs is also very important in modern processors. This work points to a rich direction for future work in exploring the design of more complex query processing techniques (beyond single joins) that consider the joint impact of computation, synchronization costs, load balancing, and cache behavior.

Acknowledgments

We thank David DeWitt for his deeply insightful comments on this paper. We also thank the reviewers of this paper and Willis Lang for their feedback on an earlier draft of this paper. David Wood and the Wisconsin Multifacet project were invaluable supporters of this project and gave us exclusive access to their hardware, and we thank them. This work was supported in part by a grant from the Microsoft Jim Gray Systems Lab, and in part by the National Science Foundation under grants IIS-0963993 and CNS-0551401.

7. REFERENCES

[1] A. Ailamaki, D. J. DeWitt, M. D. Hill, and D. A. Wood. DBMSs on a modern processor: Where does time go? In *VLDB*, pages 266–277, 1999.

[2] P. A. Boncz, S. Manegold, and M. L. Kersten. Database architecture optimized for the new bottleneck: Memory access. In *VLDB*, pages 54–65, 1999.

[3] J. Cieslewicz, W. Mee, and K. A. Ross. Cache-conscious buffering for database operators with state. In *DaMoN*, pages 43–51, 2009.

[4] J. Cieslewicz and K. A. Ross. Data partitioning on chip multiprocessors. In *DaMoN*, pages 25–34, 2008.

[5] J. Cieslewicz, K. A. Ross, and I. Giannakakis. Parallel buffers for chip multiprocessors. In *DaMoN*, 2007.

[6] D. J. DeWitt and J. Gray. Parallel database systems: The future of database processing or a passing fad? *SIGMOD Record*, 19(4):104–112, 1990.

[7] D. J. DeWitt, R. H. Katz, F. Olken, L. D. Shapiro, M. Stonebraker, and D. A. Wood. Implementation techniques for main memory database systems. In *SIGMOD Conference*, pages 1–8, 1984.

[8] D. J. DeWitt, J. F. Naughton, D. A. Schneider, and S. Seshadri. Practical skew handling in parallel joins. In *VLDB*, pages 27–40, 1992.

[9] P. Garcia and H. F. Korth. Database hash-join algorithms on multithreaded computer architectures. In *Conf. Computing Frontiers*, pages 241–252, 2006.

[10] G. Graefe, R. Bunker, and S. Cooper. Hash joins and hash teams in Microsoft SQL Server. In *VLDB*, pages 86–97, 1998.

[11] C. Kim, E. Sedlar, J. Chhugani, T. Kaldewey, A. D. Nguyen, A. D. Blas, V. W. Lee, N. Satish, and P. Dubey. Sort vs. hash revisited: Fast join implementation on modern multi-core CPUs. *PVLDB*, 2(2):1378–1389, 2009.

[12] S. Manegold, P. A. Boncz, and M. L. Kersten. What happens during a join? Dissecting CPU and memory optimization effects. In *VLDB*, pages 339–350, 2000.

[13] S. Manegold, P. A. Boncz, and M. L. Kersten. Optimizing main-memory join on modern hardware. *IEEE Trans. Knowl. Data Eng.*, 14(4):709–730, 2002.

[14] R. Pagh and F. F. Rodler. Cuckoo hashing. *J. Algorithms*, 51(2):122–144, 2004.

[15] K. A. Ross. Efficient hash probes on modern processors. In *ICDE*, pages 1297–1301, 2007.

[16] A. Shatdal, C. Kant, and J. F. Naughton. Cache conscious algorithms for relational query processing. In *VLDB*, pages 510–521, 1994.

[17] M. Stonebraker. The case for shared nothing. In *HPTS*, 1985.

Query Optimization Techniques for Partitioned Tables

Herodotos Herodotou
Duke University
Durham, North Carolina, USA
hero@cs.duke.edu

Nedyalko Borisov
Duke University
Durham, North Carolina, USA
nedyalko@cs.duke.edu

Shivnath Babu*
Duke University
Durham, North Carolina, USA
shivnath@cs.duke.edu

ABSTRACT

Table partitioning splits a table into smaller parts that can be accessed, stored, and maintained independent of one another. From their traditional use in improving query performance, partitioning strategies have evolved into a powerful mechanism to improve the overall manageability of database systems. Table partitioning simplifies administrative tasks like data loading, removal, backup, statistics maintenance, and storage provisioning. Query language extensions now enable applications and user queries to specify how their results should be partitioned for further use. However, query optimization techniques have not kept pace with the rapid advances in usage and user control of table partitioning. We address this gap by developing new techniques to generate efficient plans for SQL queries involving multiway joins over partitioned tables. Our techniques are designed for easy incorporation into bottom-up query optimizers that are in wide use today. We have prototyped these techniques in the PostgreSQL optimizer. An extensive evaluation shows that our partition-aware optimization techniques, with low optimization overhead, generate plans that can be an order of magnitude better than plans produced by current optimizers.

Categories and Subject Descriptors

H.2.4 [**Database Management**]: Systems—*query processing*

General Terms

Algorithms

Keywords

query optimization, partitioning

1. INTRODUCTION

Table partitioning is a standard feature in database systems today [13, 15, 20, 21]. For example, a sales records table may be partitioned *horizontally* based on value ranges of a date column. One partition may contain all sales records for the month of January, another partition may contain all sales records for February, and so on. A table can also be partitioned *vertically* with each partition containing a subset of columns in the table. Hierarchical combinations of horizontal and vertical partitioning may also be used.

Uses of Table Partitioning in Database Systems
Efficient pruning of unneeded data during query processing
Parallel data access (partitioned parallelism) during query processing
Reducing data contention during query processing and administrative tasks. Faster data loading, archival, and backup
Efficient statistics maintenance in response to insert, delete, and update rates. Better cardinality estimation for subplans that access few partitions
Prioritized data storage on faster/slower disks based on access patterns
Fine-grained control over physical design for database tuning
Efficient and online table and index defragmentation at the partition level

Table 1: Uses of table partitioning in database systems

The trend of rapidly growing data sizes has amplified the usage of partitioned tables in database systems. Table 1 lists various uses of table partitioning. Apart from giving major performance improvements, partitioning simplifies a number of common administrative tasks in database systems. In this paper, we focus on horizontal table partitioning in centralized row-store database systems such as those sold by major database vendors as well as popular open-source systems like MySQL and PostgreSQL. The uses of table partitioning in these systems have been studied [2, 24].

The growing usage of table partitioning has been accompanied by efforts to give applications and users the ability to specify partitioning conditions for tables that they derive from base data. SQL extensions from database vendors now enable queries to specify how derived tables are partitioned (e.g., [11]). Given such extensions, Database Administrators (DBAs) may not be able to control or restrict how tables accessed in a query are partitioned. Furthermore, multiple objectives—e.g., getting fast data loading along with good query performance—and constraints—e.g., on the maximum size or number of partitions per table—may need to be met while choosing how each table in the database is partitioned.

1.1 Query Optimization for Partitioned Tables

Query optimization technology has not kept pace with the growing usage and user control of table partitioning. Previously, query optimizers had to consider only the restricted partitioning schemes specified by the DBA on base tables. Today, the optimizer faces a diverse mix of partitioning schemes that expand on traditional schemes like hash and equi-range partitioning. *Hierarchical* (or *multidimensional*) partitioning is one such scheme to deal with multiple granularities or hierarchies in the data [4]. A table is first partitioned on one attribute. Each partition is further partitioned on a different attribute; and so on for two or more levels.

Figure 1 shows an example hierarchical partitioning for a table $S(a, b)$ where attribute a is an integer and attribute b is a date. S

*Supported by NSF grants 0964560 and 0917062

SIGMOD'11, June 12–16, 2011, Athens, Greece.

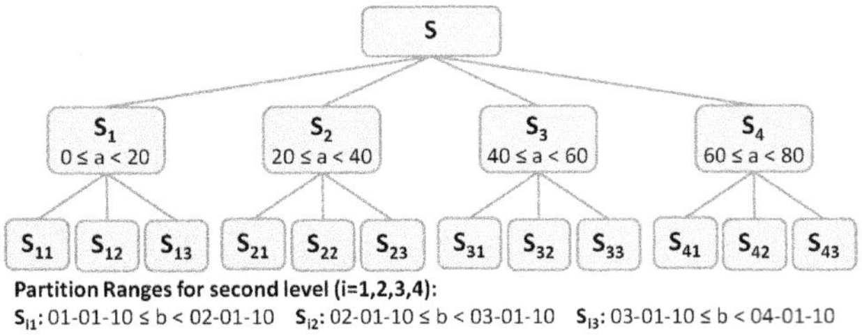

Figure 1: A hierarchical partitioning of table S

is equi-partitioned on ranges of a into four partitions S_1-S_4, each of which is further partitioned on ranges of b. Figure 2 shows how the hierarchical partitioning of table S can be interpreted as a two-dimensional partitioning. The figure also shows partitions for tables $R(a)$, $T(a)$, and $U(b)$. R, S, and T are all partitioned on a—typical for multiple related data sources or even star/snowflake schemas—but with different ranges due to data properties and storage considerations. For example, if the number of records with the same value of a is large in T (e.g., user clicks), then smaller ranges will give more manageable partitions.

Table U is partitioned using nonequi ranges on b for data loading and archival efficiency as well as workload performance. Daily partitions for daily loads are an attractive option since it is faster to load an entire partition at a time. However, maintenance overheads and database limitations on the maximum number of partitions can prevent the creation of daily partitions. Hence, 10-day ranges are used for recent partitions of U. Older data is accessed less frequently, so older 10-day partitions are merged into monthly ones to improve query performance and archival efficiency.

The flexible nature and rising complexity of partitioning schemes pose new challenges and opportunities during the optimization of queries over partitioned tables. Consider an example query Q_1 over the partitioned tables R, S, and T in Figure 2.

```
Q1: Select *
    From   R, S, T
    Where  R.a=S.a and S.a=T.a
           and S.b≥02-15-10 and T.a<25;
```

Use of filter conditions for partition pruning: An optimization that many current optimizers apply to Q_1 is to *prune* partitions T_4-T_8 and S_{11}, S_{21}, S_{31}, S_{41} from consideration because it is clear from the partitioning conditions that records in these partitions will not satisfy the filter conditions. Partition pruning can speed up query performance drastically by eliminating unnecessary table and index scans as well as reducing memory needs, disk spills, and contention-related overheads.

Use of join conditions for partition pruning: Based on a transitive closure of the filter and join conditions, partition pruning can also eliminate partitions S_{32}, S_{33}, S_{42}, S_{43}, R_3, R_4, and U_1.

Most current optimizers will stop here as far as exploiting partitions during the optimization of Q_1 is concerned; and generate a plan like Q_1P_1 shown in Figure 3. In a plan like Q_1P_1, the leaf operators logically append together (i.e., UNION ALL) the unpruned partitions for each table. Each unpruned partition is accessed using regular table or index scans. The appended partitions are joined using operators like hash, merge, and (index) nested-loop joins.

Partition-aware join path selection: Depending on the data properties, physical design, and storage characteristics in the database system, a plan like Q_1P_2 shown in Figure 3 can significantly outperform plan Q_1P_1. Q_1P_2 exploits a number of properties arising from partitioning in the given setting:

- Records in partition R_1 can join only with $S_{12} \cup S_{13}$ and $T_1 \cup T_2$. Similarly, records in partition R_2 can join only with $S_{22} \cup S_{23}$ and T_3. Thus, the full $R \bowtie S \bowtie T$ join can be broken up into smaller and more efficient *partition-wise joins*.
- The best join order for $R_1 \bowtie (S_{12} \cup S_{13}) \bowtie (T_1 \cup T_2)$ can be different from that for $R_2 \bowtie (S_{22} \cup S_{23}) \bowtie T_3$. One likely reason is change in the data properties of tables S and T over time, causing variations in statistics across partitions.[1]
- The best choice of join operators for $R_1 \bowtie (S_{12} \cup S_{13}) \bowtie (T_1 \cup T_2)$ may differ from that for $R_2 \bowtie (S_{22} \cup S_{23}) \bowtie T_3$, e.g., due to storage or physical design differences across partitions (e.g., index created on one partition but not on another).

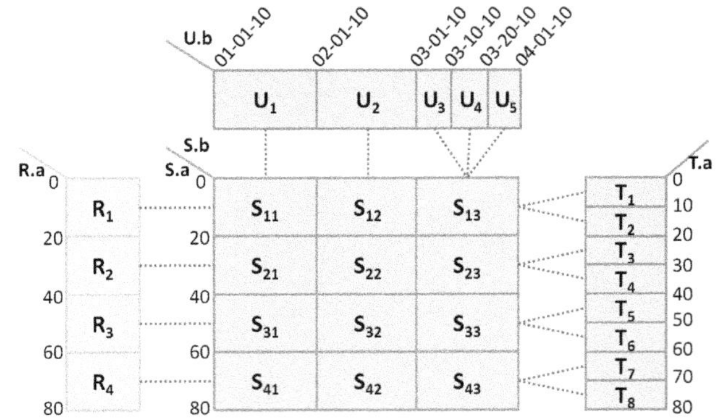

Figure 2: Partitioning of tables R, S, T, U. Dotted lines show partitions with potentially joining records

Let us now consider query Q_2 to further understand the challenges and opportunities arising while optimizing queries over partitioned tables. Q_2 is a typical query in traditional star schemas where a fact table is joined with several dimension tables on different attributes.

```
Q2: Select *
    From   R, S, U
    Where  R.a=S.a and S.b=U.b
           and U.b≥02-15-10 and R.a<25;
```

Plan Q_2P_1 from Figure 3 shows the plan that simply appends the unpruned partitions before performing the joins. Given the join and partitioning conditions for R and S, the optimizer has the option of creating the partition-wise joins $R_1 \bowtie (S_{12} \cup S_{13})$ and $R_2 \bowtie (S_{22} \cup S_{23})$. The output of these joins is logically partitioned on attribute a—which does not affect the later join with table U—leading to the plan Q_2P_2 in Figure 3. Alternatively, the optimizer has the option of creating partition-wise joins between S and U first, generating the plan Q_2P_3.

1.2 Challenges and Contributions

The above examples illustrate the optimization possibilities for SQL queries over partitioned tables, which enlarge the plan space drastically. To our knowledge, no current optimizer (commercial or research prototype) takes this space into account to find efficient plans with low optimization overhead. We address this limitation by developing a novel *partition-aware SQL query optimizer*:

Dealing with plan space explosion: A nontrivial challenge we have to address in a partition-aware optimizer is to keep the additional computational and memory overheads of the optimization process in check while enabling good plans to be found.

Incorporation into state-of-the-art optimizers: The new techniques we propose are designed for easy incorporation into bottom-up query optimizers (like the seminal System R optimizer [19]) that are in wide use today. With this design, we leverage decades of past investment as well as potential future enhancements to these optimizers (e.g., new rewrite rules, new join operators, and improvements in statistics and cardinality estimation).

[1] Most enterprises keep 6-24 months of historical data online.

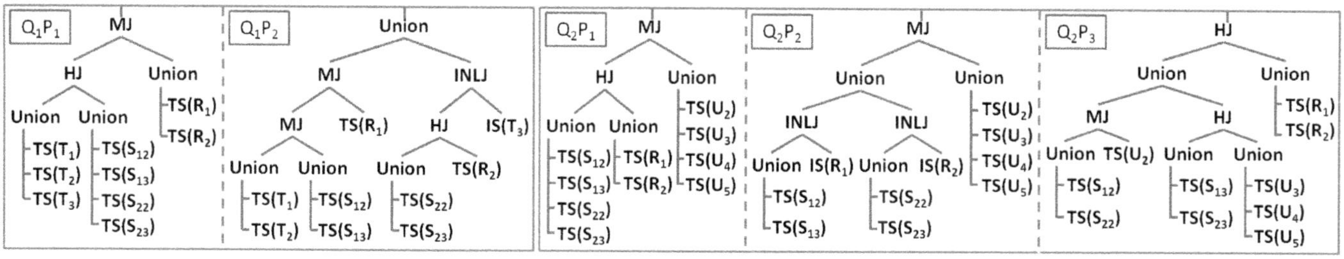

Figure 3: Q_1P_1 and Q_2P_1 are plans generated by current optimizers for our example queries Q_1 and Q_2 respectively. Q_1P_2, Q_2P_2, and Q_2P_3 are plans generated by our partition-aware optimizer. IS and TS are respectively index and table scan operators. HJ, MJ, and INLJ are respectively hash, merge, and index-nested-loop join operators. Union is a bag union operator

Partitions as physical or logical properties? The conventional wisdom in the database literature as well as implementation in commercial bottom-up query optimizers treat partitions as physical properties [18]. We show that treating partitions only as physical properties falls well short of making the best use of partitioned tables. Our optimizer considers partitions efficiently at both the logical and physical levels to get the best of two worlds: (a) generating plans like Q_1P_2, Q_2P_2, and Q_2P_3 in Figure 3, and (b) preserving *interesting partitions* [18] that may benefit operators (e.g., group-by) higher-up in the plan.

Supporting practical partitioning conditions: In addition to conventional DBA-specified partitioning conditions on base tables, our optimizer supports a wide range of user-specified partitioning conditions including multidimensional partitions, multi-level hierarchical partitions, and irregular ranges. The challenge here is to deal with complex join graphs arising at the partition level (like Figure 2) from the combination of the filter, join, and table-level partitioning conditions for a SQL query.

Improving cardinality estimates: A nonobvious effect arises from the fact that most database systems keep statistics (e.g., number of distinct values) at the level of individual partitions. Cardinality estimation for appended partitions necessitates combination of per-partition statistics. We have found that estimation errors from such combination are worse for a plan like Q_1P_1 compared to Q_1P_2.

Prototyping and evaluation: All our techniques have been prototyped in the PostgreSQL optimizer, and we report an extensive evaluation based on the popular TPC-H benchmark.

2. RELATED WORK

Various table partitioning schemes as well as techniques to find a good partitioning scheme automatically have been proposed as part of database physical design tuning (e.g., [2, 18]). In contrast, our goal is to fully exploit possible query optimization opportunities given the existing horizontal partitioning scheme in the database.

Partitioning in Centralized DBMSs: Commercial DBMS vendors (e.g., IBM, Microsoft, Oracle, and Sybase) provide support for different types of partitioning, including hash, range, and list partitioning, as well as support for hierarchical (multidimensional) partitioning. However, they implement different partition-aware optimization techniques. Most commercial optimizers have excellent support for per-table partition pruning. In addition to optimization-time pruning, systems like IBM DB2 support pruning of partitions at plan execution time, e.g., to account for join predicates in index-nested-loop joins [13]. Some optimizers generate plans containing n *one-to-one partition-wise joins* for any pair of tables R and S that are partitioned into the same number n of partitions with one-to-one correspondence between the partitions [15, 21]. For joins where only table R is partitioned, Oracle supports dynamic partitioning of S based on R's partitioning; effectively creating a one-to-one join between the partitions.

UNION ALL views are a useful construct that can be used to support table partitioning [27]. The techniques proposed in this paper are related closely to pushing joins down through UNION ALL views. For example, when a UNION ALL view representing a partitioned table $R = R_1 \cup \ldots \cup R_n$ is joined with a table S, IBM DB2's query optimizer considers pushing the join down to generate a UNION of base-table joins $(R_1 \bowtie S) \cup \ldots \cup (R_n \bowtie S)$ [27]. However, unlike our techniques, the join pushdown is considered in the query-rewrite phase. As the authors of [27] point out, this step can increase the time and memory overheads of optimization significantly because of the large number of joins generated (especially, if multiple UNION ALL views are joined like in our example queries in Figure 3). The techniques we propose are designed to keep these overheads in check—even in the presence of hundreds of partitions—while ensuring that good plans can be found.

Partitioning in Parallel/Distributed DBMSs: While we focus on centralized DBMSs, the partition-aware optimization techniques we propose are related closely to *data localization* in distributed DBMSs [16]. Data localization is a query-rewrite phase where heuristic rules like filter pushdown are used to prune partitions and their joins that will not contribute to the query result. A join graph is created for the partitions belonging to the joining tables, and inference rules are used to determine the empty joins [8]. While our work shares some goals with data localization, a number of differences exist. Instead of heuristic rewrite rules, we propose (provably optimal) cost-based optimization of partitioned tables. In particular, we address the accompanying nontrivial challenge of plan space explosion—especially in the presence of hundreds of partitions per table (e.g., daily partitions for a year)—and the need to incorporate the new optimization techniques into industry-strength cost-based SQL optimizers. Section 8.7 compares our techniques empirically with an adaptation of data localization to centralized DBMSs.

The cost-based optimization algorithms we present are independent of the physical join methods supported by the DBMS. Parallel DBMSs support several partition-aware join methods including collocated, directed, broadcast, and repartitioned joins [6]. SCOPE is a system for large-scale data analysis that uses cost-based optimization to select the repartitioning of tables and intermediate results [25]. Query optimizers in these systems attempt to minimize data transfer costs among nodes, which is orthogonal to our work.

Dynamic partitioning: *Selectivity-based partitioning* [17], *content-based routing* [7], and *conditional plans* [10] are techniques that enable different execution plans to be used for different subsets of the input data. Unlike our work, these techniques focus on dynamic partitioning of (unpartitioned) tables and data streams rather than exploiting the properties of existing partitions. Easy incorporation into widely-used SQL optimizers is not a focus of [7, 10, 17].

Predicate optimization: *Predicate move-around* [14] is a query transformation technique that moves predicates among different relations, and possibly query blocks, to generate potentially better plans. *Magic sets* [5] represent a complementary technique that can generate auxiliary tables to be used as early filters in a plan. Both techniques are applied in the rewrite phase of query optimization, thereby complementing our cost-based optimization techniques.

3. PROBLEM AND SOLUTION OVERVIEW

Our goal is to generate an efficient plan for a SQL query that contains joins of partitioned tables. In this paper, we focus on tables that are partitioned horizontally based on conditions specified on one or more *partitioning attributes* (columns). The condition that defines a partition of a table is an expression involving any number of binary subexpressions of the form *Attr Op Val*, connected by *AND* or *OR* logical operators. *Attr* is an attribute in the table, *Val* is a constant, and *Op* is one of $\{=, \neq, <, \leq, >, \geq\}$.

Joins in a SQL query can be equi or nonequi joins. The joined tables could have different numbers of partitions and could be partitioned on multiple attributes (like in Figure 2). Furthermore, the partitions between joined tables need not have one-on-one correspondence with each other. For example, a table may have one partition per month while another table has one partition per day.

Our approach for partition-aware query optimization is based on extending bottom-up query optimizers. We will give an overview of the well-known System R bottom-up query optimizer [19] on which a number of current optimizers are based, followed by an overview of the extensions we make.

A bottom-up optimizer starts by optimizing the smallest expressions in the query, and then uses this information to progressively optimize larger expressions until the optimal physical plan for the full query is found. First, the best *access path* (e.g., table or index scan) is found and retained for each table in the query. The best *join path* is then found and retained for each pair of joining tables R and S in the query. The join path consists of a physical join operator (e.g., hash or merge join) and the access paths found earlier for the tables. Next, the best join path is found and retained for all three-way joins in the query; and so on.

Bottom-up optimizers pay special attention to physical properties (e.g., sort order) that affect the ability to generate the optimal plan for an expression e by combining optimal plans for subexpressions of e. For example, for $R \bowtie S$, the System R optimizer stores the optimal join path for each *interesting sort order* [19] of $R \bowtie S$ that can potentially reduce the plan cost of any larger expression that contains $R \bowtie S$ (e.g., $R \bowtie S \bowtie U$).

Our extensions: Consider the join path selection in a bottom-up optimizer for two partitioned tables R and S. R and S can be base tables or the result of intermediate subexpressions. Let the respective partitions be R_1-R_r and S_1-S_s. For ease of exposition, we call R and S the *parent tables* in the join, and each R_i (S_j) a *child table*. By default, the optimizer will consider a join path corresponding to $(R_1 \cup \cdots \cup R_r) \bowtie (S_1 \cup \cdots \cup S_s)$, i.e., a physical join operator that takes the bag unions of the child tables as input. This approach leads to plans like Q_1P_1 and Q_2P_1 in Figure 3.

Partition-aware optimization must consider joins among the child tables in order to get efficient plans like Q_1P_2 in Figure 3; effectively, pushing the join below the union(s). Joins of the child tables are called *child joins*. When the bottom-up optimizer considers the join of partitioned tables R and S, we extend its search space to include plans consisting of the union of child joins. This process works in four phases: *applicability testing*, *matching*, *clustering*, and *path creation*.

Applicability testing: We first check whether the specified join condition between R and S match the partitioning conditions on R and S appropriately. Intuitively, efficient child joins can be utilized only when the partitioning columns are part of the join attributes. For example, the $R.a = S.a$ join condition makes it possible to utilize the $R_2 \bowtie (S_{22} \cup S_{23})$ child join in plan Q_1P_2 in Figure 3.

Matching: This phase uses the partitioning conditions to determine efficiently which joins between individual child tables of R and S can potentially generate output records, and to prune the empty child joins. For $R \bowtie S$ in our running example query Q_1, this phase outputs $\{(R_1, S_{12}),(R_1, S_{13}),(R_2, S_{22}), (R_2, S_{23})\}$.

Clustering: Production deployments can contain tables with many tens to hundreds of partitions that lead to a large number of joins between individual child tables.[2] To reduce the join path creation overhead, we carefully cluster the child tables; details are in Section 5. For $R \bowtie S$ in our running example, the matching phase's output is clustered such that only the two child joins $R_1 \bowtie (S_{12} \cup S_{13})$ and $R_2 \bowtie (S_{22} \cup S_{23})$ are considered during path creation.

Path Creation: This phase creates and costs join paths for all child joins output by the clustering phase, as well as the path that represents the union of the best child-join paths. This path will be chosen for $R \bowtie S$ if it costs lower than the one produced by the optimizer without our extensions.

The next three sections give the details of these phases. Section 6 will also discuss how our techniques can be incorporated into the bottom-up optimization process.

4. MATCHING PHASE

Suppose the bottom-up optimizer is in the process of selecting the join path for parent tables R and S with respective child tables R_1-R_r and S_1-S_s. The goal of the matching phase is to identify all *partition-wise join pairs* (R_i, S_j) such that $R_i \bowtie S_j$ can produce output tuples as per the given partitioning and join conditions. Equivalently, this algorithm prunes out (from all possible join pairs) partition-wise joins that cannot produce any results. An obvious matching algorithm would enumerate and check all the $r \times s$ possible child table pairs. In distributed query optimization, this algorithm is implemented by generating a join graph for the child tables [8]. The real inefficiency from this quadratic algorithm comes from the fact that it gets invoked from scratch for each distinct join of parent tables considered throughout the bottom-up optimization process. Note that R and S can be base tables or the result of intermediate subexpressions.

We developed an efficient matching algorithm that builds, probes, and reuses *Partition Index Trees (PITs)*. We will describe this new data structure, and then explain how the matching algorithm utilizes it to generate the partition-wise join pairs efficiently. PITs apply to range and list partitioning conditions. Section 7 describes how our techniques can be extended to handle hash partitioning.

4.1 Partition Index Trees

The core idea behind Partition Index Trees is to associate each child table with one or more *intervals* generated from the table's partitioning condition. An interval is specified as a *Low* to *High* range, which can be numeric (e.g., (0, 10]), date (e.g., [02-01-10, 03-01-10)), or a single numeric or categorical value (e.g., [5, 5], [*url,url*]). A PIT indexes all intervals of all child tables for one of the partitioning columns of a parent table. The PIT then enables efficient lookup of the intervals that overlap with a given probe interval from the other table. The use of PITs provides two main advantages:

- For most practical partitioning and join conditions, building and probing PITs has $O(r \log r)$ complexity (for r partitions in a table). The memory needs are $\theta(r)$.

[2] We are aware of such deployments in a leading social networking company and for a commercial parallel DBMS.

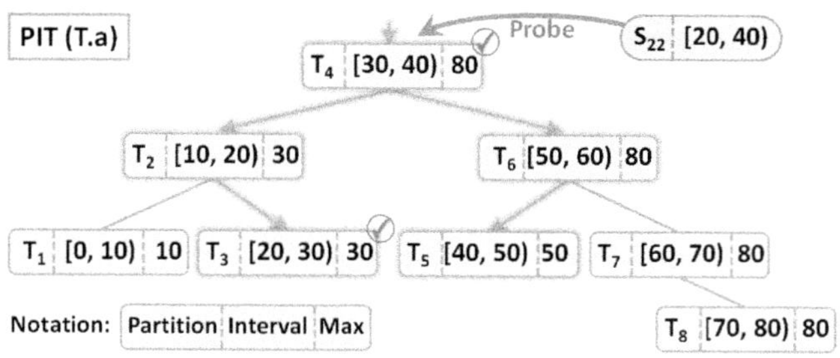

Figure 4: A partition index tree containing intervals for all child tables (partitions) of T from Figure 2

- Most PITs are built once and then reused many times over the course of the bottom-up optimization process (see Section 4.4).

Implementation: PIT, at a basic level, is an augmented *red-black* tree [9]. The tree is ordered by the *Low* values of the intervals, and an extra annotation is added to every node recording the maximum *High* value (denoted *Max*) across both its subtrees. Figure 4 shows the PIT created on attribute $T.a$ based on the partitioning conditions of all child tables of T (see Figure 2). The *Low* and *Max* values on each node are used during probing to efficiently guide the search for finding the overlapping intervals. When the interval $[20, 40)$ is used to probe the PIT, five intervals are checked (highlighted in Figure 4) and the two overlapping intervals $[20, 30)$ and $[30, 40)$ are returned.

A number of nontrivial enhancements to PITs were needed to support complex partitioning conditions that can arise in practice. First, PITs need support for multiple types of intervals: open, closed, partially closed, one sided, and single values (e.g., $(1, 5)$, $[1, 5]$, $[1, 5)$, $(-\infty, 5]$, and $[5, 5]$). In addition, supporting nonequi joins required support from PITs to efficiently find all intervals in the tree that are to the left or to the right of the probe interval.

Both partitioning and join conditions can be complex combinations of AND and OR subexpressions, as well as involve any operator in $\{=, \neq, <, \leq, >, \geq\}$. Our implementation handles all these cases by restricting PITs to unidimensional indexes and handling complex expressions appropriately in the matching algorithm.

4.2 Matching Algorithm

Figure 5 provides all the steps for the matching algorithm. The input consists of the two tables to be joined and the join condition. We will describe the algorithm using query Q_1 in our running example from Section 1. The join condition for $S \bowtie T$ in Q_1 is a simple equality expression: $S.a = T.a$. Later, we will discuss how the algorithm handles more complex conditions involving logical AND and OR operators, as well as nonequi join conditions. Since the matching phase is executed only if the Applicability Test passes (see Section 3), the attributes $S.a$ and $T.a$ must appear in the partitioning conditions for the partitions of S and T respectively.

The table with the smallest number of (unpruned) partitions is identified as the *build* relation and the other as the *probe* relation. In our example, T (with 3 partitions) will be the build relation and S (with 4 partitions) will be the probe one. Since partition pruning is performed before any joins are considered, only the unpruned child tables are used for building and probing the PIT. Then, the matching algorithm works as follows:

- *Build phase:* For each child table T_i of T, generate the interval for T_i's partitioning condition (explained in Section 4.3). Build a PIT that indexes all intervals from the child tables of T.
- *Probe phase:* For each child table S_j of S, generate the interval int for S_j's partitioning condition. Probe the PIT on $T.a$ to find intervals overlapping with int. Only T's child tables corresponding to these overlapping intervals can have tuples joining with S_j; output the identified join pairs.

Algorithm for performing the matching phase
Input: Relation R, Relation S, Join Condition
Output: All partition-wise join pairs (R_i,S_j) that can produce join results
For each (binary join expression in Join Condition) {
  Convert all partitioning conditions to intervals;
  Build PIT with intervals from partitions of R;
  Probe the PIT with intervals from partitions of S;
  Adjust matching result based on logical AND or OR semantics of the Join Condition;
}

Figure 5: Matching algorithm

For $S \bowtie T$ in our running example query, the PIT on $T.a$ will contain the intervals $[0, 10)$, $[10, 20)$ and $[20, 30)$, which are associated with partitions T_1, T_2, and T_3 respectively (Figure 2). When this PIT is probed with the interval $[20, 40)$ for child table S_{22}, the result will be the interval $[20, 30)$; indicating that only T_3 will join with S_{22}. Overall, this phase outputs $\{(S_{12}, T_1), (S_{12}, T_2), (S_{13}, T_1), (S_{13}, T_2), (S_{22}, T_3), (S_{23}, T_3)\}$; the remaining possible child joins are pruned.

4.3 Support for Complex Conditions

Before building and probing the PIT, we need to convert each partitioning condition into one or more intervals. A condition could be any expression involving logical ANDs, ORs, and binary expressions. Subexpressions that are ANDed together are used to build a single interval, whereas subexpressions that are ORed together will produce multiple intervals. For example, suppose the partitioning condition is ($R.a \geq 0$ AND $R.a < 20$). This condition will create the interval $[0, 20)$. The condition ($R.a > 0$ AND $R.b > 5$) will create the interval $(0, \infty)$, since only $R.a$ appears in the join conditions of query Q_1. The condition ($R.a < 0$ OR $R.a > 10$) will create the intervals $(-\infty, 0)$ and $(10, \infty)$. If the particular condition does not involve $R.a$, then the interval created is $(-\infty, \infty)$, as any value for $R.a$ is possible.

Our approach can also support nonequi joins, for example $R.a < S.a$. The PIT was adjusted in order to efficiently find all intervals in the PIT that are to the left or to the right of the provided interval. Suppose $A = (A1, A2)$ is an interval in the PIT and $B = (B1, B2)$ is the probing interval. The interval A is marked as an overlapping interval if $\exists \alpha \in A, \beta \in B$ such that $\alpha < \beta$. Note that this check is equivalent to finding all intervals in the PIT that overlap with the interval $(-\infty, B2)$.

Finally, we support complex join expressions involving logical ANDs and ORs. Suppose the join condition is ($R.a = S.a$ AND $R.b = S.b$). In this case, two PITs will be built; one for $R.a$ and one for $R.b$. After probing the two PITs, we will get two sets of join pairs. We then adjust the pairs based on whether the join conditions are ANDed or ORed together. In the example above, suppose that R_1 can join with S_1 based on $R.a$, and that R_1 can join with both S_1 and S_2 based on $R.b$. Since the two binary join expressions are ANDed together, we induce that R_1 can join only with S_1. However, if the join condition were ($R.a = S.a$ OR $R.b = S.b$), then we would induce that R_1 can join with both S_1 and S_2.

4.4 Complexity Analysis

Suppose N and M are the number of partitions for the build and probe relations respectively. Also suppose each partition condition is translated into a small, fixed number of intervals (which is usually the case). In fact, a simple range partitioning condition will generate exactly one interval. Then, building a PIT requires $O(N \times \log N)$ time. Probing a PIT with a single interval takes

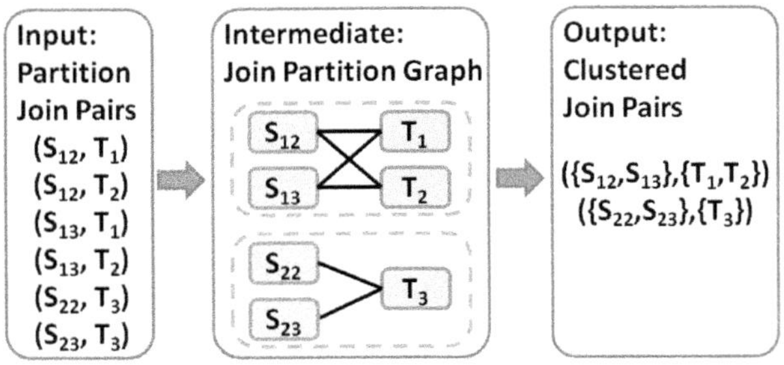

Figure 6: Clustering algorithm applied to example query Q_1

$O(min(N, k \times \log N))$ time, where k is the number of matching intervals. Hence, the overall time to identify all possible child join pairs is $O(M \times min(N, k \times \log N))$.

The space overhead introduced by a PIT is $\theta(N)$ since it is a binary tree. However, a PIT can be reused multiple times during the optimization process. Consider the join condition ($R.a$=$S.a$ AND $S.a$=$T.a$) for tables R, S, and T in Q_1. A PIT built for $S.a$ can be (re)used for performing the matching algorithm when considering the joins $R \bowtie S$, $S \bowtie T$, $(R \bowtie S) \bowtie T$, and $(S \bowtie T) \bowtie R$.

5. CLUSTERING PHASE

The number of join pairs output by the matching phase can be large, e.g., when each child table of R joins with multiple child tables of S. In such settings, it becomes important to reduce the number of join pairs that need to be considered during join path creation to avoid both optimization and execution inefficiencies. Join path creation introduces optimization-time overheads for enumerating join operators, accessing catalogs, and calculating cardinality estimates. During execution, if multiple child-join paths reference the same child table R_i, then R_i will be accessed multiple times; a situation we want to avoid.

The approach we use to reduce the number of join pairs is to cluster together multiple child tables of the same parent table. Figure 6 considers $S \bowtie T$ for query Q_1 from Section 1. The six partition-wise join pairs output by the matching phase are shown on the left. Notice that the join pairs (S_{22}, T_3) and (S_{23}, T_3) indicate that both S_{22} and S_{23} can join with T_3 to potentially generate output records. If S_{22} is clustered with S_{23}, then the single (clustered) join $(S_{22} \cup S_{23}) \bowtie T_3$ will be considered in the path creation phase instead of the two joins $S_{22} \bowtie T_3$ and $S_{23} \bowtie T_3$. Furthermore, because of the clustering, the child table T_3 will have only one access path (say, a table or index scan) in Q_1's plan.

Definition 1. **Clustering metric:** For an $R \bowtie S$ join, two (unpruned) child tables S_j and S_k of S will be clustered together iff there exists a (unpruned) child table R_i of R such that the matching phase outputs the join pairs (R_i, S_j) and (R_i, S_k). □

If S_j and S_k are clustered together when no such R_i exists, then the union of S_j and S_k will lead to unneeded joins with child tables of R; hurting plan performance during execution. In our running example in Figure 6, suppose we cluster S_{22} with S_{13}. Then, S_{22} will have to be considered unnecessarily in joins with T_1 and T_2.

On the other hand, failing to cluster S_j and S_k together when the matching phase outputs the join pairs (R_i, S_j) and (R_i, S_k) would result in considering join paths separately for $R_i \bowtie S_j$ and $R_i \bowtie S_k$. The result is higher optimization overhead as well as access of R_i in at least two separate paths during execution. In our example, if we consider separate join paths for $S_{22} \bowtie T_3$ and $S_{23} \bowtie T_3$, then partition T_3 will be accessed twice.

Clustering algorithm: Figure 7 shows the clustering algorithm that takes as input the join pairs output by the matching phase. The algorithm first constructs the *join partition graph* from the input

Algorithm for clustering the output of the matching phase
Input: Partition join pairs (output of matching phase)
Output: Clustered join pairs (which will be input to path creation phase)
Build a bipartite join graph from the input partition join pairs where:
  Child tables are the vertices, and
  Partition join pairs are the edges;
Use Breadth-First-Search to identify connected components in the graph;
Output a clustered join pair for each connected component;

Figure 7: Clustering algorithm

join pairs. Each child table is a vertex in this bipartite graph, and each join pair forms an edge between the corresponding vertices. Figure 6 shows the join partition graph for our example. Breadth-First-Search is used to identify all the connected components in the join partition graph. Each connected component will give a (possibly clustered) join pair. Following our example in Figure 6, S_{12} will be clustered with S_{13}, S_{22} with S_{23}, and T_1 with T_2, forming the output of the clustering phase consisting of the two (clustered) join pairs $(\{S_{12}, S_{13}\}, \{T_1, T_2\})$ and $(\{S_{22}, S_{23}\}, \{T_3\})$.

6. PATH CREATION AND SELECTION

We will now consider how to create and cost join paths for all the (clustered) child joins output by the clustering phase, as well as the union of the best child-join paths. Join path creation has to be coupled tightly with the physical join operators supported by the database system. As discussed in Section 1.2, we will leverage the functionality of a bottom-up query optimizer [19] to create join paths for the database system. The main challenge is how to extend the enumeration and path retention aspects of a bottom-up query optimizer in order to find the optimal plan in the new *extended plan space* efficiently.

Definition 2. **Optimal plan in the extended plan space:** In addition to the default plan space considered by the bottom-up optimizer for an n-way ($n \geq 2$) join of parent tables, the extended plan space includes the plans containing any possible join order and join path for joins of the child tables such that each child table (partition) is accessed at most once. The optimal plan is the plan with least estimated cost in the extended plan space. □

We will discuss three different approaches on how to extend the bottom-up optimizer to find the optimal plan in the extended plan space. Query Q_1 from Section 1 is used as an example throughout.

Note that Q_1 joins the three parent tables R, S, and T. For Q_1, a bottom-up optimizer will consider the three 2-way joins $R \bowtie S$, $R \bowtie T$, $S \bowtie T$, and the single 3-way join $R \bowtie S \bowtie T$. For each join considered, the optimizer will find and retain the best join path for each interesting order and the best "unordered" path. Sort orders on $R.a$, $S.a$, and $T.a$ are the candidate interesting orders for Q_1. When the optimizer is considering an n-way join, it only uses the best join paths retained for smaller joins.

6.1 Extended Enumeration

The first approach is to extend the existing path creation process that occurs during the enumeration of each possible join. The extended enumeration includes the path representing the union of the best child-join paths for the join. For instance, as part of the enumeration process for query Q_1, the optimizer will create and cost join paths for $S \bowtie T$. The conventional join paths include joining the union of S's partitions with the union of T's partitions using all applicable join operators (like hash join or merge join), leading to plans like Q_1P_1 in Figure 3. At this point, extended enumeration will also create join paths for $(S_{12} \cup S_{13}) \bowtie (T_1 \cup T_2)$ and $(S_{22} \cup S_{23}) \bowtie T_3$, find the corresponding best paths, and create the union of the best child-join paths. We will use the notation P_u in this section to denote the union of the best child-join paths.

As usual, the bottom-up optimizer will retain the best join path for each interesting order (a in this case) as well as the best (possibly unordered) overall path. If P_u is the best for one of these categories, then it will be retained. The paths retained will be the only paths considered later when the enumeration process moves on to larger joins. For example, when creating join paths for $(S \bowtie T) \bowtie R$, only the join paths retained for $S \bowtie T$ will be used (in addition to the access paths retained for R).

Property 1. Adding extended enumeration to a bottom-up optimizer will not always find the optimal plan in the extended plan space. □

We will prove Property 1 using our running example. Suppose plan P_u for $S \bowtie T$ is not retained because it is not a best path for any order. Without P_u for $S \bowtie T$, when the optimizer goes on to consider $(S \bowtie T) \bowtie R$, it will not be able to consider any 3-way child join. Thus, plans similar to Q_1P_2 from Figure 3 will never be considered; thereby losing the opportunity to find the optimal plan in the extended plan space.

6.2 Treating Partitions as a Physical Property

The next approach considers partitioning as a physical property of tables and the output of partition-wise joins. The parallel edition of DB2 follows this approach. The concept of *interesting partitions* (similar to interesting orders) can be used to incorporate partitioning as a physical property in the bottom-up optimizer. Interesting partitions are partitions on attributes referenced in equality join conditions and on grouping attributes [18]. In our example query Q_1, partitions on attributes $R.a$, $S.a$, and $T.a$ are interesting.

Paths with interesting partitions can make later joins and grouping operations less expensive when these operations can take advantage of the partitioning. For example, partitioning on $S.a$ for $S \bowtie T$ could lead to the creation of three-way child joins for $R \bowtie S \bowtie T$. Hence, the optimizer will retain the best path for each interesting partition, in addition to each interesting order. Overall, if there are n interesting orders and m interesting partitions, then the optimizer can retain up to $n \times m$ paths, one for each combination of interesting orders and interesting partitions.

Property 2. Treating partitioning as a physical property in a bottom-up optimizer will not always find the optimal plan in the extended plan space. □

Once again we will prove the above property using the example query Q_1. When the optimizer enumerates paths for $S \bowtie T$, it will consider P_u (the union of the best child-join paths). Unlike what happened in extended enumeration, P_u will now be retained since P_u has an interesting partition on $S.a$. Suppose the first and second child joins of P_u have the respective join paths $(S_{12} \cup S_{13})$ HJ $(T_1 \cup T_2)$ and $(S_{22} \cup S_{23})$ HJ T_3. (HJ and MJ denote hash and merge join operators respectively.) Also, the best join path for $S \bowtie T$ with an interesting order on $S.a$ is the union of the child-join paths $(S_{12} \cup S_{13})$ MJ $(T_1 \cup T_2)$ and $(S_{22} \cup S_{23})$ MJ T_3.

However, it can still be the case that the optimal plan for Q_1 is plan Q_1P_2 shown in Figure 3. Note that Q_1P_2 contains $(S_{12} \cup S_{13})$ MJ $(T_1 \cup T_2)$: the interesting order on $S.a$ in this child join led to a better overall plan. However, the interesting order on $S.a$ was not useful in the case of the second child join of $S \bowtie T$, so $(S_{22} \cup S_{23})$ MJ T_3 is not used in Q_1P_2. Simply adding interesting partitions alongside interesting orders to a bottom-up optimizer will not enable it to find the optimal plan Q_1P_2.

The optimizer was not able to generate plan Q_1P_2 in the above example because it did not consider interesting orders independently for each child join. Instead, the optimizer considered interesting orders and interesting partitions at the level of the parent tables (R, S, T) and joins of parent tables ($R \bowtie S$, $R \bowtie T$,

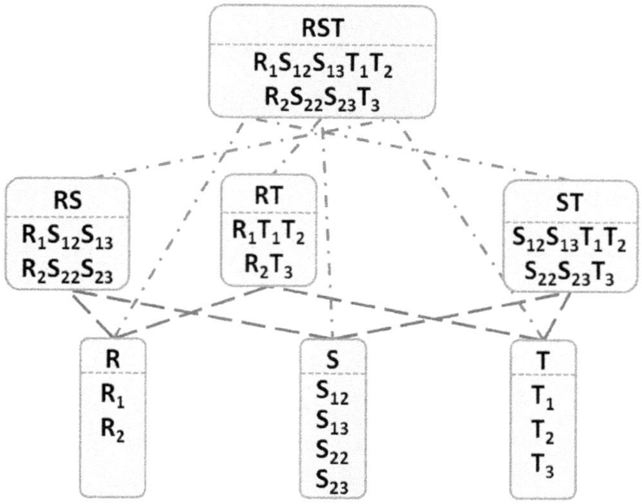

Figure 8: Logical relations (with child relations) enumerated for query Q_1 by our partition-aware bottom-up optimizer

$S \bowtie T$, $R \bowtie S \bowtie T$) only. An apparent solution would be for the optimizer to create union plans for all possible combinations of child-join paths with interesting orders. However, the number of such plans is exponential in the number of child joins per parent join, rendering this approach impractical.

6.3 Treating Partitions as a Logical Property

Our approach eliminates the aforementioned problems by treating partitioning as a property of the *logical relations* (tables or joins) that are enumerated during the bottom-up optimization process. A logical relation refers to the output produced by either accessing a table or joining multiple tables together. For example, the logical relation (join) RST represents the output produced when joining the tables R, S, and T, irrespective of the join order or the join operators used in the physical execution plan. Figure 8 shows all logical relations created during the enumeration process for our example query Q_1.

As illustrated in Figure 8, each logical relation maintains a list of logical child relations. A logical child table is created for each unpruned partition during partition pruning, whereas logical child joins are created based on the output of the clustering phase. For our example query Q_1, the child-join pairs $(\{S_{12}, S_{13}\}, \{T_1, T_2\})$ and $(\{S_{22}, S_{23}\}, \{T_3\})$ output by the clustering phase are used to create the respective logical child joins $S_{12}S_{13}T_1T_2$ and $S_{22}S_{23}T_3$. The logical child relations also maintain the partitioning conditions, which are propagated up when the child joins are created.

For each logical n-way join relation $J_n = J_{n-1} \bowtie J_1$, the logical child relations and partitioning conditions of J_{n-1} and J_1 form the input to J_n's matching phase (Section 4). The output of the matching phase forms the input to J_n's clustering phase (Section 5) which, in turn, outputs J_n's logical child joins. Note that both the matching and clustering phases work at the logical level, independent of physical plans (paths).

The logical relations are the entities for which the best paths found so far during the enumeration process are retained. The logical child joins behave in the same way as their parent joins, retaining the best paths for each interesting order and the best unordered path. Hence, the number of paths retained is *linear* in the number of child joins per parent join (instead of exponential as in the case when partitions are treated as physical properties). The optimizer considers all child-join paths with interesting orders during path creation for higher child joins, while ensuring the property:

Property 3. Paths with interesting orders for a single child join can be used later up the lattice, independent from all other child joins of the same parent relation. □

Suppose, the optimizer is considering joining ST with R to create paths for RST. The output of the clustering phase will produce the two child-join pairs $(S_{12}S_{13}T_1T_2, R_1)$ and $(S_{22}S_{23}T_3, R_2)$. Join paths for these two child joins will be created and costed independently from each other, using any paths with interesting orders and join operators that are available. The best join paths for $((S_{12} \cup S_{13}) \bowtie (T_1 \cup T_2)) \bowtie R_1$ and $((S_{22} \cup S_{23}) \bowtie T_3) \bowtie R_2)$ will be retained in the logical relations $R_1S_{12}S_{13}T_1T_2$ and $R_2S_{22}S_{23}T_3$ respectively (see Figure 8).

For each parent relation, the path representing the union of the best child-join paths is created only at the end of each enumeration level[3] and it is retained only if it is the best path. Hence, the optimizer will consider all join orders for each child join before creating the union, leading to the following property:

Property 4. The optimizer will consider plans where different child joins of the same parent relation can have different join orders and/or join operators. □

We have already seen how the optimizer created join paths $((S_{12} \cup S_{13}) \bowtie (T_1 \cup T_2)) \bowtie R_1$ and $((S_{22} \cup S_{23}) \bowtie T_3) \bowtie R_2$ when joining ST with R. Later, the optimizer will consider joining RS with T, creating join paths for $(R_1 \bowtie (S_{12} \cup S_{13})) \bowtie (T_1 \cup T_2)$ and $(R_2 \bowtie (S_{22} \cup S_{23})) \bowtie T_3$. It is possible that the best join path for $((S_{12} \cup S_{13}) \bowtie (T_1 \cup T_2)) \bowtie R_1$ is better than that for $(R_1 \bowtie (S_{12} \cup S_{13})) \bowtie (T_1 \cup T_2)$, while the opposite occurs between $((S_{22} \cup S_{23}) \bowtie T_3) \bowtie R_2$ and $(R_2 \bowtie (S_{22} \cup S_{23})) \bowtie T_3$; which leads to the plan Q_1P_2 in Figure 3.

Property 5. Optimality guarantee: By treating partitioning as a logical property, our bottom-up optimizer will find the optimal plan in the extended plan space. □

This property is a direct consequence of Properties 3 and 4. We have extended the plan space to include plans containing unions of child joins. Each child join is enumerated during the traditional bottom-up optimization process in the same way as its parent; the paths are built bottom-up, interesting orders are taken into consideration, and the best paths are retained. Since each child join is optimized independently, the topmost union of the best child-join paths is the optimal union of the child joins. Finally, recall that the union of the best child-join paths is created at the end of each enumeration level and retained only if it is the best plan for its parent join. Therefore, the full extended plan space is considered and the optimizer will be able to find the optimal plan (given the current database configuration, cost model, and physical design).

Traditionally, grouping (and aggregation) operators are added on top of the physical join trees produced by the bottom-up enumeration process [19]. In this case, interesting partitions are useful for pushing the grouping below the union of the child joins, in an attempt to create less expensive execution paths. With our approach, paths with interesting partitions on the grouping attributes can be constructed at the top node of the enumeration lattice, and used later on while considering the grouping operator.

Treating partitions as a property of the logical relations allows for a clean separation between the enumeration process of the logical relations and the construction of the physical plans. Hence, our algorithms are applicable to any database system that uses a bottom-up optimizer. Moreover, they can be adapted for non-database data processing systems like SCOPE and Hive that offer support for table partitioning and joins.

[3]Enumeration level n refers to the logical relations representing all possible n-way joins.

Name	Features
Basic	Per-table partition pruning only (like MySQL and PostgreSQL). Our evaluation uses the PostgreSQL 8.3.7 optimizer as the Basic optimizer
Intermediate	Per-table partition pruning and one-to-one partition-wise joins (like Oracle and SQLServer). The Intermediate optimizer is implemented as a variant of the Advanced optimizer that checks for and creates one-to-one partition-wise join pairs in place of the regular matching and clustering phases
Advanced	Per-table partition pruning and all the join optimizations for partitioned tables as described in the paper

Table 2: Optimizer categories considered in the evaluation

7. EXTENDING OUR TECHNIQUES TO PARALLEL DATABASE SYSTEMS

While this paper focuses on centralized DBMSs, our work is also useful in parallel DBMSs like Aster nCluster [3], Teradata [22], and HadoopDB [1] which try to partition tables such that most queries in the workload need intra-node processing only. A common data placement strategy in parallel DBMSs is to use hash partitioning to distribute tuples in a table among the nodes $N_1, \ldots, N_k$, and then use range/list partitioning of the tuples within each node. Our techniques extend to this setting: if two joining tables R and S have the same hash partitioning function and the same number of partitions, then a partition-wise join $R_i \bowtie S_i$ is created for each node N_i. If a secondary range/list partitioning has been used to further partition R_i and S_i at an individual node, then our techniques can be applied directly to produce child joins for $R_i \bowtie S_i$.

Another data placement strategy popular in data warehouses is to replicate the dimension tables on all nodes, while the fact table is partitioned across the nodes. The fact-table partition as well as the dimension tables may be further partitioned on each node, so our techniques can be used to create child joins at each node. In such settings, multi-dimensional partitioning of the fact table can improve query performance significantly as we show in Section 8.

8. EXPERIMENTAL EVALUATION

The purpose of this section is to evaluate the effectiveness and efficiency of our optimization techniques across a wide range of factors that affect table partitioning. We have prototyped all our techniques in the PostgreSQL 8.3.7 optimizer. All experiments were run on Amazon EC2 nodes of m1.large type. Each node has 7.5GB RAM, dual-core 2GHz CPU, and 850GB of storage. We used the TPC-H benchmark with scale factors ranging from 10 to 40, with 30 being the default scale. Following directions from the TPC-H Standard Specifications [23], we partitioned tables only on primary key, foreign key, and/or date columns. We present experimental results for a representative set of 10 out of the 22 TPC-H queries, ranging from 2-way up to the maximum possible 8-way joins. All results presented are averaged over three query executions.

8.1 Experimental Setup

The most important factor affecting query performance over partitioned tables is the partitioning scheme that determines which tables are partitioned and on which attribute. We identified two cases that arise in practice:

1. The DBA has full control in selecting and deploying the partitioning scheme to maximize query-processing efficiency.
2. The partitioning scheme is forced either partially or fully by practical reasons beyond query-processing efficiency.

For evaluation purposes, we categorized query optimizers into three categories—*Basic*, *Intermediate*, and *Advanced*—based on how they exploit partitioning information to perform optimization. Details

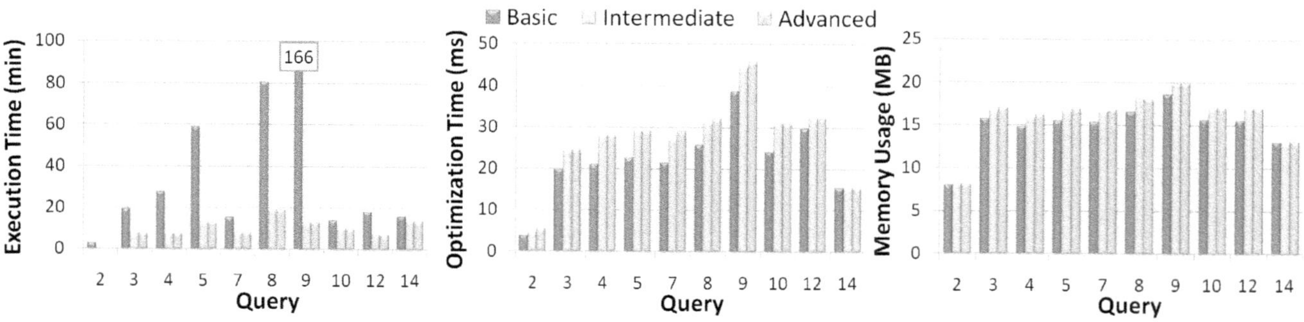

Figure 9: (a) Execution times, (b) Optimization times, (c) Memory usage for TPC-H queries over PS-J

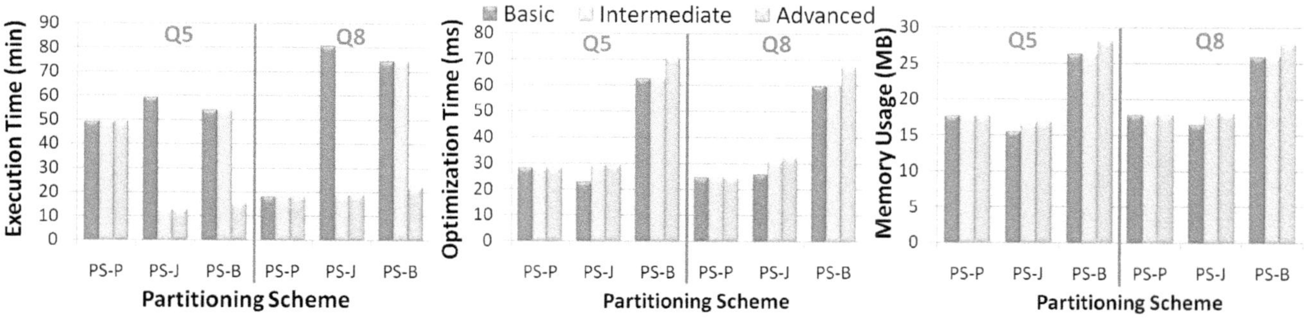

Figure 10: (a) Execution times, (b) Optimization times, (c) Memory usage for TPC-H queries 5 and 8 over three partitioning schemes

Partition Scheme	Table	Partitioning Attributes	Number of Partitions
PS-P	orders	o_orderdate	28
	lineitem	l_shipdate	85
PS-J	orders	o_orderkey	48
	lineitem	l_orderkey	48
	partsupp	ps_partkey	12
	part	p_partkey	12
PS-B	orders	o_orderkey, o_orderdate	72
	lineitem	l_orderkey, l_shipdate	120
	partsupp	ps_partkey	12
	part	p_partkey	6
PS-C	orders	o_orderkey, o_orderdate	36
	lineitem	l_orderkey, l_shipdate	168
	partsupp	ps_partkey	30
	part	p_partkey	6
	customer	c_custkey	6

Table 3: Partitioning schemes for TPC-H

are given in Table 2. We compare the optimizers on three metrics used to evaluate optimizers [12]: (i) query execution time, (ii) optimization time, and (iii) optimizer's memory usage.

8.2 Results from DBA-Controlled Schemes

Given the capabilities of the query optimizer, the DBA has a spectrum of choices regarding the partitioning scheme [26]. In one extreme, the DBA can partition tables based on attributes appearing in filter conditions in order to take maximum advantage of partition pruning. At the other extreme, the DBA can partition tables based on joining attributes in order to take maximum advantage of one-to-one partition-wise joins; assuming the optimizer supports such joins (like the Intermediate optimizer in Table 2). In addition, our techniques now enable the creation of multidimensional partitions to take advantage of both partition pruning and partition-wise joins. We will refer to the three above schemes as partitioning schemes respectively for pruning (PS-P), for joins (PS-J), and for both (PS-B). Table 3 lists all partitioning schemes used in our evaluation.

Figure 9(a) shows the execution times for the plans selected by the three query optimizers for the ten TPC-H queries running on the database with the PS-J scheme. The Intermediate and Advanced optimizers are able to generate a better plan than the Basic optimizer for all queries, providing up to an order of magnitude benefit for some of them. Note that the Intermediate and Advanced optimizers produce the same plan in all cases, since one-to-one partition-wise joins are the only join optimization option for both optimizers for the PS-J scheme.

Figure 9(b) presents the corresponding optimization times for the queries. The Intermediate optimizer introduces some overhead on optimization time—average of 17% and worst case of 21% due to the creation of child-join paths—compared to Basic. The additional overhead introduced by the Advanced optimizer over Intermediate is on average less than 3%. This overhead is due to the matching and clustering algorithms. Overall, the optimization overhead introduced by Advanced is low, and is most definitely gained back during execution as we can see by comparing the y-axes of Figures 9(a) and 9(b) (execution time is in minutes whereas optimization time is in milliseconds). The memory overheads shown in Figure 9(c) follow the same trend: average memory overhead of Advanced over Basic is around 7%, and the worst case is 10%.

Query performance is related directly to the optimizer capabilities and the partitioning scheme used in the database. Figure 10 shows the performance results for TPC-H queries 5 and 8 for the three optimizers over databases with different partitioning schemes. (Results for other queries are similar.) Since a database using the PS-P scheme only allows for partition pruning, all three optimizers behave in an identical manner. A PS-J scheme on the other hand, does not allow for any partition pruning since join attributes do not appear in filter conditions in the queries. Hence, the Basic optimizer performs poorly in many cases, whereas the Intermediate and Advanced optimizers take advantage of partition-wise joins to produce better plans with very low overhead.

The presence of multidimensional partitions in a PS-B scheme prevents the Intermediate optimizer from generating any one-to-one partition-wise joins, but it can still perform partition pruning

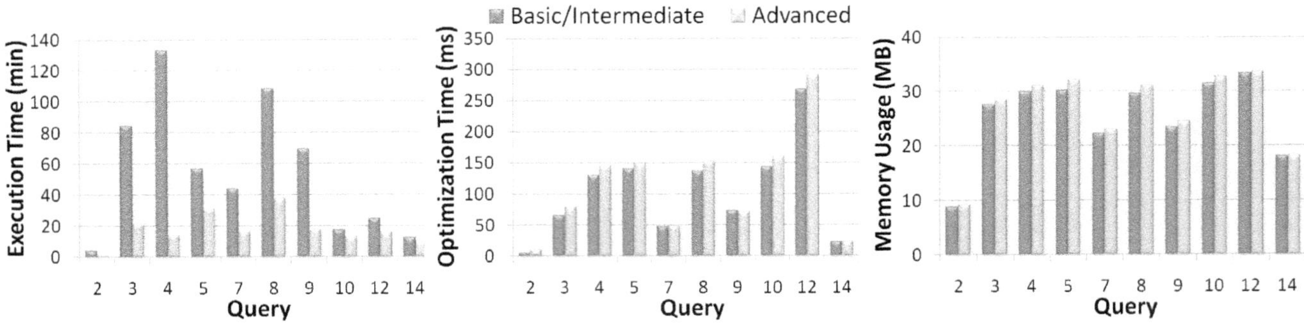

Figure 11: (a) Execution times, (b) Optimization times, (c) Memory usage for TPC-H queries over PS-C with partition size 128MB

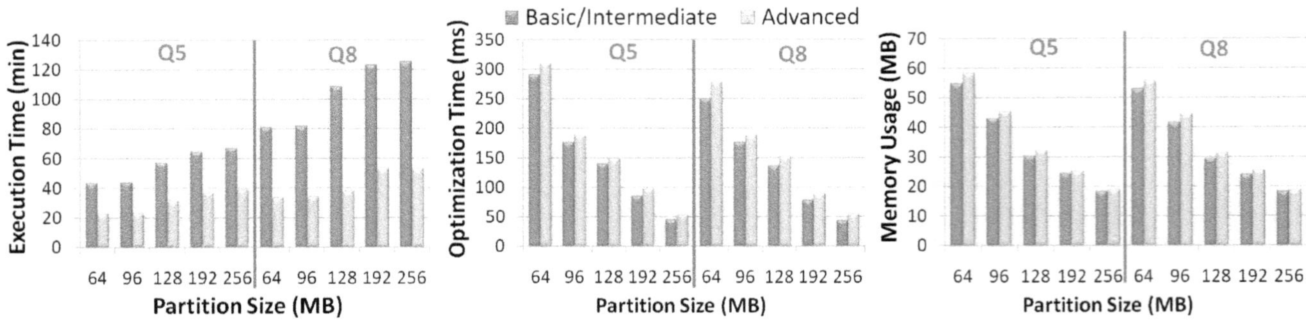

Figure 12: (a) Execution times, (b) Optimization times, (c) Memory usage as we vary the partition size for TPC-H queries 5 and 8

like the Basic optimizer. The Advanced optimizer utilizes both partition pruning and partition-wise joins to find better-performing plans. Consider the problem of picking the best partitioning scheme for a given query workload. The best query performance can be obtained either from (a) partition pruning (PS-P is best for query 8 in Figure 10), or (b) from partition-aware join processing (PS-J is best for query 5 in Figure 10), or (c) from a combination of both due to some workload or data properties. In all cases, the Advanced optimizer enables finding the plan with the best possible performance.

8.3 Results from Constrained Schemes

As discussed in Section 1, external constraints or objectives may limit the partitioning scheme that can be used. For instance, data arrival rates may require the creation of daily or weekly partitions; file-system properties may impose a maximum partition size to ensure that each partition is laid out contiguously; or optimizer limitations may impose a maximum number of partitions per table.

For a TPC-H scale factor of 30, biweekly partitions of the fact table lead to a 128MB partition size. We will impose a maximum partition size of 128MB to create the partitioning scheme PS-C used in this section (see Table 3). Figure 11 shows the results for the TPC-H queries executed over a database with the PS-C scheme. The constraint imposed on the partitioning scheme does not allow for any one-to-one partition-wise joins. Hence, the Intermediate optimizer produces the same plans as Basic, and is excluded from the figures for clarity. Once again, the Advanced optimizer was able to generate a better plan than the Basic optimizer for all queries, providing over $2x$ speedup for 50% of them. The average optimization time and memory overheads were just 7.9% and 3.6% respectively.

8.4 Effect of Size and Number of Partitions

In this section, we evaluate the performance of the optimizers as we vary the size (and thus the number) of partitions created for each table, using the PS-C scheme. As we vary the partition size from 64MB to 256MB, the number of partitions for the fact table vary from 336 to 84. Figure 12(b) shows the optimization times taken by the two optimizers for TPC-H queries 5 and 8. As the

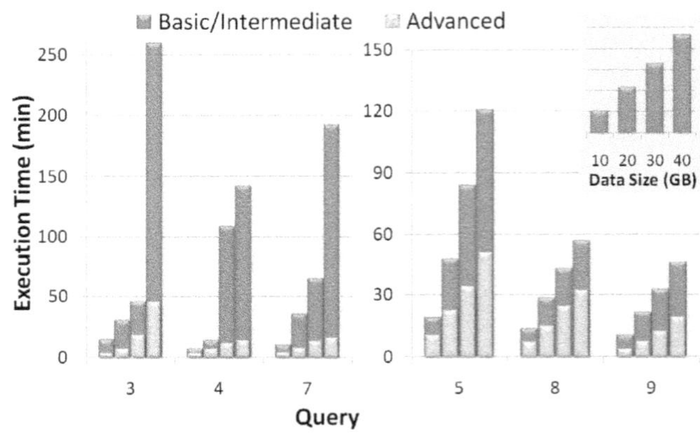

Figure 13: Execution times as we vary the total data size

partition size increases (and the number of partitions decreases), the optimization time decreases for both optimizers. We observe that (i) the optimization times for the Advanced optimizer scale in a similar way as for the Basic optimizer, and (ii) the overhead introduced by the creation of the partition-wise joins remains small (around 12%) in all cases.

The overhead added by our approach remains low due to two reasons. First, Clustering bounds the number of child joins for $R \bowtie S$ to *min(number of partitions in R,S)*; so we cause only a linear increase in paths enumerated per join. Second, optimizers have other overheads like parsing, rewrites, scan path enumeration, catalog and statistics access, and cardinality estimation. Let us consider Query 5 from Figure 12(b). Query 5 joins 5 tables, including *orders* and *lineitem* with 72 and 336 partitions respectively. In this case, Basic enumerated 2317 scan and join paths in total, while Advanced enumerated 2716 paths. The extra 17% paths are for the 72 partition-wise joins created by Advanced. The trends are similar for the memory consumption of the optimizers as seen in Figure 12(c).

Decreasing the partition size for the same total data size has a positive effect on plan execution times as seen in Figure 12: smaller

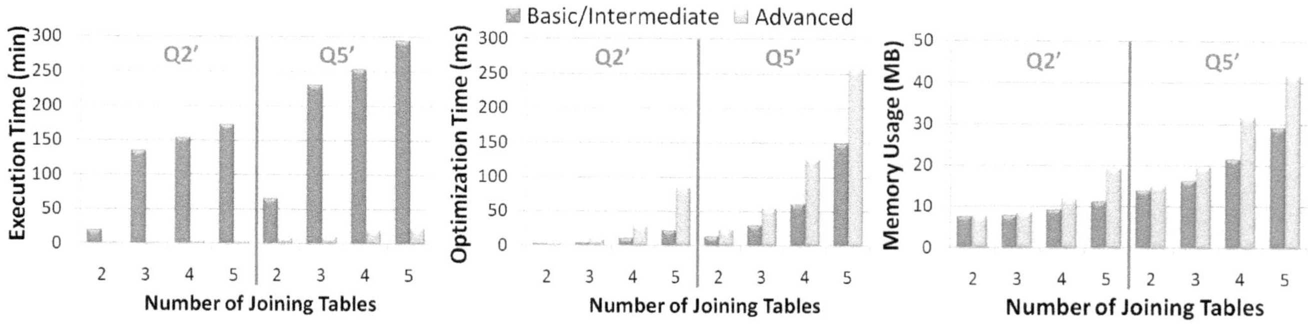

Figure 14: (a) Execution times, (b) Optimization times, (c) Memory usage as we vary the number of tables joined on the same attribute for a modified TPC-H schema and queries 2 and 5

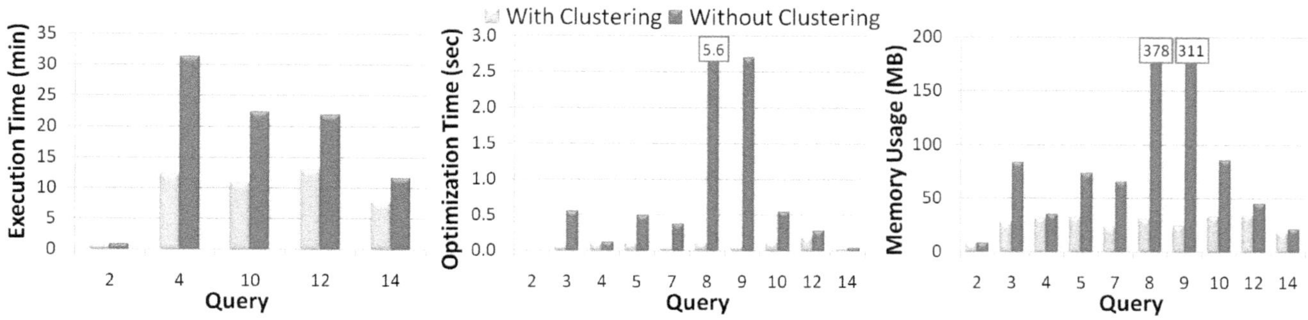

Figure 15: (a) Execution times, (b) Optimization times, (c) Memory usage for enabling and disabling clustering

partition sizes force finer-grained partition ranges, leading to better partition pruning and join execution. Looking into execution times at the subplan level, we observed that PostgreSQL was more effective in our experimental settings when it accessed partitions in the 64MB range. It is worth noting that current partitioning scheme recommenders [2, 18, 26] do not consider partition size tuning.

8.5 Effect of Data Size

We used the PS-C scheme with a partition size of 128 MB to study the effects of the overall data size on query performance. Figure 13 shows the query execution times as the amount of data stored in the database increases. For many queries, the plans selected by the Basic optimizer lead to a quadratic or exponential increase in execution time as data size increases linearly. We observed that joins for large data sizes cause the Basic optimizer to frequently resort to index nested loop joins (the system has 7.5GB RAM only).

On the other hand, the Advanced optimizer is able to generate smaller partition-wise joins that use more efficient join methods (like hash and merge joins); leading to the desired linear increase in execution time as data size increases linearly. For the queries where the Basic optimizer is also able to achieve a linear trend, the slope is much higher compared to the Advanced optimizer. Figure 13 shows that the benefits from our approach become more important for larger databases. Note that optimization times and memory consumption are independent of the data size.

8.6 Stress Testing on a Synthetic Benchmark

There exist practical scenarios where multiple tables may share a common joining key. In Web analytics, for example, customer data may reside in multiple tables—storing information such as page clicks, favorites, preferences, etc.—that have to be joined on the customer key. However, in traditional star and snowflake schemas, the fact tables join with the dimension tables on different attributes; so it is hard to create n-way child joins for $n \geq 3$. No TPC-H query plan, regardless of the partitioning schema, contains n-way child joins for $n \geq 4$. To evaluate our approach in non-star schemas, as well as to stress-test our approach, we came up with a synthetic partitioning schema where the tables *part* and *orders* from TPC-H are partitioned vertically into four tables each. Once again, we use the PS-C scheme with a partition size of 128 MB.

We modified TPC-H queries 2 and 5 to join all the vertical tables for *part* and *orders* respectively. Figure 14(a) shows the execution times for the two queries with increasing number of joining tables. We observe how the Advanced optimizer was again able to generate plans that are up to an order of magnitude better compared to the plans selected by the Basic optimizer. It is interesting to note that as the number of joining tables in the query increases, the execution times for the plans from the Advanced optimizer increase barely (due to efficient use of child joins); unlike the Basic optimizer's plans whose execution times increase drastically.

Figures 14(b) and 14(c) show the optimization times and memory consumption, respectively, as the number of "same-key-joining" tables in the query increases. Both metrics increase non-linearly for both optimizers; but the increase is more profound for the Advanced optimizer. The increasing optimization overhead comes from the non-linear complexity of the path selection process used by the regular PostgreSQL query optimizer (which we believe can be fixed through engineering effort unrelated to our work). With optimization times still in milliseconds, the additional overhead is certainly justified by the drastic reduction in execution times.

8.7 Effect of the Clustering Algorithm

Clustering (Section 5) is an essential phase in our overall partition-aware optimization approach that is missing from the data localization approach discussed in Section 2. When matching is applied without clustering, our optimizer implements a rough equivalent of the four-phase approach to distributed query optimization [16]. Figures 15(b) and 15(c) compare the optimization time and memory consumption of the optimizer when clustering is enabled and disabled in a database with the PS-C scheme. Disabling clustering causes high overhead—as seen in both figures—since the optimizer must now generate join paths for each child join produced by the matching phase. This issue shows why clustering is essential for

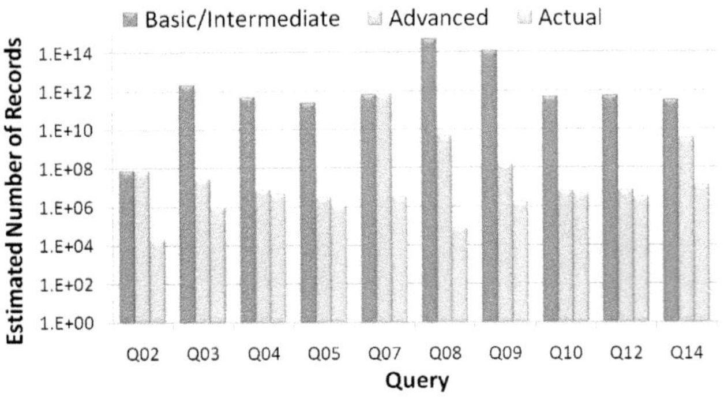

Figure 16: Estimated (and actual) number of records of TPC-H queries over PS-C

our optimizer to perform well in the presence of hundreds of partitions per table (e.g., daily partitions for a year).

Figure 15(a) shows the execution times for the plans generated when enabling and disabling clustering. In all cases shown, the plan generated without clustering is worse than the plan generated when clustering is used, since the generated plans scan the same partitions multiple times (in different joins). The queries that are not shown failed to complete because the system runs out of memory during plan execution. Note that with multidimensional partitioning and without clustering, literally thousands of child join paths are created, each requiring a small amount of memory during their initialization phase. We conclude that the use of clustering is crucial for finding good execution plans.

8.8 Impact on Cardinality Estimation

An additional benefit that child joins bring is better cardinality estimation for costing during path creation. Cardinality estimation for filter and join conditions is based on data-level statistics kept by the database system for each table (e.g., distribution histograms, minimum and maximum values, number of distinct values). For partitioned tables, databases like Oracle and PostgreSQL collect statistics for each individual partition. When the optimizer considers joining unions of partitions, the cardinality estimates needed are derived by aggregating statistics over partitions.

Figure 16 shows the estimated and actual number of records of TPC-H queries over the PS-C scheme. For the Basic Optimizer, we observe large cardinality errors. In contrast, partition-wise joins provide much more accurate cardinality estimation because these joins increase the chances of using partition-level statistics directly for costing. The same pattern was observed with all the partitioning schemes and queries used.

9. SUMMARY

Query optimization technology has not kept pace with the growing usage and user control of table partitioning. We addressed this gap by developing novel partition-aware optimization techniques to generate efficient plans for SQL queries over partitioned tables. We extended the search space to include plans with multiway partition-wise joins, and provided techniques to find the optimal plan efficiently. Our techniques are designed for easy incorporation into bottom-up query optimizers. An extensive experimental evaluation showed that our optimizer, with low optimization-time overhead, can generate plans that are an order of magnitude better than plans generated by current optimizers.

10. ACKNOWLEDGMENTS

We thank John Cieslewicz and Eric Friedman of Aster Data for introducing us to the problem and for many valuable discussions. We thank the anonymous reviewers and shepherd for helping us improve the paper in many ways.

11. REFERENCES

[1] A. Abouzeid, K. Bajda-Pawlikowski, D. Abadi, A. Rasin, and A. Silberschatz. HadoopDB: An Architectural Hybrid of MapReduce and DBMS Technologies for Analytical Workloads. In *VLDB*, 2009.

[2] S. Agrawal, V. Narasayya, and B. Yang. Integrating Vertical and Horizontal Partitioning into Automated Physical Database Design. In *ACM SIGMOD*, 2004.

[3] *Aster nCluster*. www.asterdata.com/product/ncluster_cloud.php.

[4] C. Baldwin, T. Eliassi-Rad, G. Abdulla, and T. Critchlow. The Evolution of a Hierarchical Partitioning Algorithm for Large-Scale Scientific Data: Three Steps of Increasing Complexity. *SSDB*, 2003.

[5] F. Bancilhon, D. Maier, Y. Sagiv, and J. D. Ullman. Magic Sets and Other Strange Ways to Implement Logic Programs. In *Proc. of the 5th ACM Symp. on Principles of Database Systems*, 1986.

[6] C. K. Baru, G. Fecteau, A. Goyal, H. Hsiao, A. Jhingran, S. Padmanabhan, G. P. Copeland, and W. G. Wilson. DB2 Parallel Edition. *IBM Systems Journal*, 34(2), 1995.

[7] P. Bizarro, S. Babu, D. J. DeWitt, and J. Widom. Content-based Routing: Different Plans for Different Data. In *VLDB*, 2005.

[8] S. Ceri and G. Gottlob. Optimizing Joins Between two Partitioned Relations in Distributed Databases. *Journal of Parallel and Distributed Computing*, 3, 1986.

[9] T. H. Cormen, C. E. Leiserson, R. L. Rivest, and C. Stein. *Introduction to Algorithms*. The MIT Press and McGraw-Hill Osborne Media, 2nd edition, 2003.

[10] A. Deshpande, C. Guestrin, W. Hong, and S. Madden. Exploiting Correlated Attributes in Acquisitional Query Processing. In *ICDE*, 2005.

[11] E. Friedman, P. Pawlowski, and J. Cieslewicz. SQL/MapReduce: A Practical Approach to Self-Describing, Polymorphic, and Parallelizable User-Defined Functions. In *VLDB*, 2009.

[12] L. Giakoumakis and C. Galindo-Legaria. Testing SQL Server's Query Optimizer: Challenges, Techniques and Experiences. In *IEEE Data Engineering Bulletin*. IEEE Computer Society, 2008.

[13] IBM DB2. *Partitioned tables*, 2007. http://publib.boulder.ibm.com/infocenter/db2luw/v9r7/topic/com.ibm.db2.luw.admin.partition.doc/doc/c0021560.html.

[14] A. Y. Levy, I. S. Mumick, and Y. Sagiv. Query Optimization by Predicate Move-Around. In *VLDB*, 1994.

[15] T. Morales. *Oracle(R) Database VLDB and Partitioning Guide 11g Release 1 (11.1)*. Oracle Corporation, 2007. http://download-uk.oracle.com/docs/cd/B28359_01/server.111/b32024/toc.htm.

[16] T. M. Ozsu and P. Valduriez. *Principles of Distributed Database Systems*. Prentice Hall, 1999.

[17] N. Polyzotis. Selectivity-based Partitioning: A Divide-and-union Paradigm for Effective Query Optimization. In *CIKM*, 2005.

[18] J. Rao, C. Zhang, N. Megiddo, and G. M. Lohman. Automating Physical Database Design in a Parallel Database. In *SIGMOD*, 2002.

[19] P. G. Selinger, M. M. Astrahan, D. D. Chamberlin, R. A. Lorie, and T. G. Price. Access Path Selection in a Relational Database Management System. In *ACM SIGMOD*, 1979.

[20] Sybase, Inc. *Performance and Tuning: Optimizer and Abstract Plans*, 2003. http://infocenter.sybase.com/help/topic/com.sybase.dc20023_1251/pdf/optimizer.pdf.

[21] R. Talmage. *Partitioned Table and Index Strategies Using SQL Server 2008*. Microsoft, 2009. http://msdn.microsoft.com/en-us/library/dd578580.aspx.

[22] *Teradata*. http://www.teradata.com.

[23] TPC. *TPC Benchmark H Standard Specification*, 2009. http://www.tpc.org/tpch/spec/tpch2.9.0.pdf.

[24] B. Zeller and A. Kemper. Experience Report: Exploiting Advanced Database Optimization Features for Large-Scale SAP R/3 Installations. In *VLDB*, 2002.

[25] J. Zhou, P.-Å. Larson, and R. Chaiken. Incorporating Partitioning and Parallel Plans into the SCOPE Optimizer. In *ICDE*, 2010.

[26] D. Zilio, A. Jhingran, and S. Padmanabhan. Partitioning Key Selection for a Shared-Nothing Parallel Database System. *IBM Research Report RC 19820*, 1994.

[27] C. Zuzarte, others Partitioning in DB2 Using the UNION ALL View. *IBM developerWorks*, 2002. http://www.ibm.com/developerworks/data/library/techarticle/0202zuzarte/0202zuzarte.pdf.

CrowdDB: Answering Queries with Crowdsourcing

Michael J. Franklin
AMPLab, UC Berkeley
franklin@cs.berkeley.edu

Donald Kossmann
Systems Group, ETH Zurich
donaldk@inf.ethz.ch

Tim Kraska
AMPLab, UC Berkeley
kraska@cs.berkeley.edu

Sukriti Ramesh
Systems Group, ETH Zurich
ramess@student.ethz.ch

Reynold Xin
AMPLab, UC Berkeley
rxin@cs.berkeley.edu

ABSTRACT

Some queries cannot be answered by machines only. Processing such queries requires human input for providing information that is missing from the database, for performing computationally difficult functions, and for matching, ranking, or aggregating results based on fuzzy criteria. CrowdDB uses human input via crowdsourcing to process queries that neither database systems nor search engines can adequately answer. It uses SQL both as a language for posing complex queries and as a way to model data. While CrowdDB leverages many aspects of traditional database systems, there are also important differences. Conceptually, a major change is that the traditional closed-world assumption for query processing does not hold for human input. From an implementation perspective, human-oriented query operators are needed to solicit, integrate and cleanse crowdsourced data. Furthermore, performance and cost depend on a number of new factors including worker affinity, training, fatigue, motivation and location. We describe the design of CrowdDB, report on an initial set of experiments using Amazon Mechanical Turk, and outline important avenues for future work in the development of crowdsourced query processing systems.

Categories and Subject Descriptors

H.2.4 [**Database Management**]: Systems

General Terms

Human Factors, Languages, Design, Performance

1. INTRODUCTION

Relational database systems have achieved widespread adoption, not only in the business environments for which they were originally envisioned, but also for many other types of structured data, such as personal, social, and even scientific information. Still, as data creation and use become increasingly democratized through web, mobile and other technologies, the limitations of the technology are becoming more apparent. RDBMSs make several key assumptions about the correctness, completeness and unambiguity of the data they store. When these assumptions fail to hold, relational systems will return incorrect or incomplete answers to user questions, if they return any answers at all.

SIGMOD'11, June 12–16, 2011, Athens, Greece.

1.1 Power to the People

One obvious situation where existing systems produce wrong answers is when they are missing information required for answering the question. For example, the query:

```
SELECT market_capitalization FROM company
WHERE name = "I.B.M.";
```

will return an empty answer if the company table instance in the database at that time does not contain a record for "I.B.M.". Of course, in reality, there are many reasons why such a record may be missing. For example, a data entry mistake may have omitted the I.B.M. record or the record may have been inadvertently deleted. Another possibility is that the record was entered incorrectly, say, as "I.B.N."

Traditional systems can erroneously return an empty result even when no errors are made. For example, if the record was entered correctly, but the name used was "International Business Machines" rather than "I.B.M." This latter "entity resolution" problem is not due to an error but is simply an artifact of having multiple ways to refer to the same real-world entity.

There are two fundamental problems at work here. First, relational database systems are based on the "Closed World Assumption": information that is not in the database is considered to be false or non-existent. Second, relational databases are extremely literal. They expect that data has been properly cleaned and validated before entry and do not natively tolerate inconsistencies in data or queries.

As another example, consider a query to find the best among a collection of images to use in a motivational slide show:

```
SELECT image FROM picture
WHERE topic = "Business Success"
ORDER BY relevance LIMIT 1;
```

In this case, unless the relevance of pictures to specific topics has been previously obtained and stored, there is simply no good way to ask this question of a standard RDBMS. The issue here is one of judgement: one cannot reliably answer the question simply by applying relational operators on the database.

All of the above queries, however, while unanswerable by today's relational database systems, could easily be answered by people, especially people who have access to the Internet.

1.2 CrowdDB

Recently, there has been substantial interest (e.g. [4, 6, 28]) in harnessing Human Computation for solving problems that are impossible or too expensive to answer correctly using computers. Microtask crowdsourcing platforms such as Amazon's Mechanical Turk (AMT)[3] provide the infrastructure, connectivity and payment mechanisms that enable hundreds of thousands of people to perform paid work on the Internet. AMT is used for many tasks that are easier for people than computers, from simple tasks such as labeling or segmenting images and tagging content to more complex tasks such as translating or even editing text.

It is natural, therefore, to explore how to leverage such human resources to extend the capabilities of database systems so that they can answer queries such as those posed above. The approach we take in CrowdDB is to exploit the extensibility of the iterator-based query processing paradigm to add crowd functionality into a DBMS. CrowdDB extends a traditonal query engine with a small number of operators that solicit human input by generating and submiting work requests to a microtask crowdsourcing platform.

As query processing elements, people and computers differ in fundamental ways. Obviously, the types of tasks at which each excel are quite different. Also, people exhibit wider variability, due to schedules such as nights, weekends and holidays, and the vast differences in expertise, diligence and temperament among people. Finally, as we discuss in the following sections, in a crowdsourcing system, the relationship between job requesters and workers extends beyond any one interaction and evolves over time. Care must be taken to properly maintain that relationship.

Crowdsourced operators must take into consideration the talents and limitations of human workers. For example, while it has been shown that crowds can be "programmed" to execute classical algorithms such as Quicksort on well-defined criteria [19], such a use of the crowd is neither performant nor cost-efficient.

Consider the example queries described in Section 1.1. Correctly answering these queries depends on two main capabilities of human computation compared to traditional query processing:

Finding new data - recall that a key limitation of relational technology stems from the Closed World Assumption. People, on the other hand, aided by tools such as search engines and reference sources, are quite capable of finding information that they do not have readily at hand.

Comparing data - people are skilled at making comparisons that are difficult or impossible to encode in a computer algorithm. For example, it is easy for a person to tell, if given the right context, if "I.B.M." and "International Business Machines" are names for the same entity. Likewise, people can easily compare items such as images along many dimensions, such as how well the image represents a particular concept.

Thus, for CrowdDB, we develop crowd-based implementations of query operators for finding and comparing data, while relying on the traditional relational query operators to do the heavy lifting for bulk data manipulation and processing. We also introduce some minimal extensions to the SQL data definition and query languages to enable the generation of queries that involve human computation.

1.3 Paper Overview

Our approach has four main benefits. First, by using SQL we create a declarative interface to the crowd. We strive to maintain SQL semantics so that developers are presented with a known computational model. Second, CrowdDB provides Physical Data Independence for the crowd. That is, application developers can write SQL queries without having to focus on which operations will be done in the database and which will be done by the crowd. Existing SQL queries can be run on CrowdDB, and in many cases will return more complete and correct answers than if run on a traditional DBMS. Third, as we discuss in subsequent sections, user interface design is a key factor in enabling questions to be answered by people. Our approach leverages schema information to support the automatic generation of effective user interfaces for crowdsourced tasks. Finally, because of its declarative programming environment and operator-based approach, CrowdDB presents the opportunity to implement cost-based optimizations to improve query cost, time, and accuracy — a facility that is lacking from most crowdsourcing platforms today.

Of course, there are many new challenges that must be addressed in the design of a crowd-enabled DBMS. The main ones stem from the fundamental differences in the way that people work compared to computers and from the inherent ambiguity in many of the human tasks, which often involve natural language understanding and matters of opinion. There are also technical challenges that arise due to the use of a specific crowdsourcing platform such as AMT. Such challenges include determining the most efficient organization of tasks submitted to the platform, quality control, incentives, payment mechanisms, etc.

In the following we explain these challenges and present initial solutions that address them. Our main contributions are:

- We propose simple SQL schema and query extensions that enable the integration of crowdsourced data and processing.
- We present the design of CrowdDB including new crowdsourced query operators and plan generation techniques that combine crowdsourced and traditional query operators.
- We describe methods for automatically generating effective user interfaces for crowdsourced tasks.
- We present the results of microbenchmarks of the performance of individual crowdsourced query operators on the AMT platform, and demonstrate that CrowdDB is indeed able to answer queries that traditional DBMSs cannot.

The remainder of this paper is organized as follows: Section 2 presents background on crowdsourcing and the AMT platform. Section 3 gives an overview of CrowdDB, followed by the CrowdSQL extension to SQL in Section 4, the user interface generation in Section 5, and query processing in Section 6. In Section 7 we present experimental results. Section 8 reviews related work. Section 9 presents conclusions and research challenges.

2. CROWDSOURCING

A crowdsourcing platform creates a marketplace on which requesters offer tasks and workers accept and work on the tasks. We chose to build CrowdDB using one of the leading platforms, Amazon Mechanical Turk (AMT). AMT provides an API for requesting and managing work, which enables us to directly connect it to the CrowdDB query processor. In this discussion, we focus on this particular platform and its interfaces.

AMT supports so-called microtasks. Microtasks usually do not require any special training and typically take no longer than one minute to complete; although in extreme cases, tasks can require up to one hour to finish [15]. In AMT, as part of specifying a task, a requester defines a price/reward (minimum $0.01) that the worker receives if the task is completed satisfactorily. In AMT currently, workers from anywhere in the world can participate but requesters must be holders of a US credit card. Amazon does not publish current statistics about the marketplace, but it contained over 200,000 workers (referred to as turkers) in 2006 [2], and by all estimates, the marketplace has grown dramatically since then [24].

2.1 Mechanical Turk Basics

AMT has established its own terminology. There are slight differences in terminology used by requesters and workers. For clarity in this paper, we use the requesters' terminology. Key terms are:

- **HIT**: A Human Intelligent Task, or HIT, is the smallest entity of work a worker can accept to do. HITs contain one or more jobs. For example, tagging 5 pictures could be one HIT. Note that "job" is not an official term used in AMT, but we use it in this paper where necessary.
- **Assignment**: Every HIT can be replicated into multiple assignments. AMT ensures that any particular worker processes at most a single assignment for each HIT, enabling the requester to obtain answers to the same HIT from multiple workers. Odd numbers of assignments per HIT enable majority voting for quality assurance, so it is typical to have 3 or 5 assignments per HIT. Requesters pay workers for each assignment completed satisfactorily.
- **HIT Group**: AMT automatically groups similar HITs together into HIT Groups based on the requester, the title of the HIT, the description, and the reward. For example, a HIT Group could contain 50 HITs, each HIT asking the worker to classify several pictures. As we discuss below, workers typically choose which work to perform based on HIT Groups.

The basic AMT workflow is as follows: A requester packages the jobs comprising his or her information needs into HITs, determines the number of assignments required for each HIT and posts the HITs. Requesters can optionally specify requirements that workers must meet in order to be able to accept the HIT. AMT Groups compatible HITs into HIT Groups and posts them so that they are searchable by workers. A worker accepts and processes assignments. Requesters then collect all the completed assignments for their HITs and apply whatever quality control methods they deem necessary.

Furthermore, requesters approve or reject each assignment completed by a worker: Approval is given at the discretion of the requester. Assignments are automatically deemed approved if not rejected within a time specified in the HIT configuration. For each approved assignment the requester pays the worker the pre-defined reward, an optional bonus, and a commission to Amazon.

Workers access AMT through their web browsers and deal with two kinds of user interfaces. One is the main AMT interface, which enables workers to search for HIT Groups, list the HITs in a HIT Group, and to accept assignments. The second interface is provided by the requester of the HIT and is used by the worker to actually complete the HIT's assignments. A good user interface can greatly improve result quality and worker productivity.

In AMT, requesters and workers have visible IDs so relationships and reputations can be established over time. For example, workers will often lean towards accepting assignments from requesters who are known to provide clearly-defined jobs with good user interfaces and who are known for having good payment practices. Information about requesters and HIT Groups are shared among workers via on-line forums.

2.2 Mechanical Turk APIs

A requester can automate his or her workflow of publishing HITs, etc. by using AMT's web service or REST APIs. The relevant (to CrowdDB) interfaces are:

- *createHIT(title, description, question, keywords, reward, duration, maxAssignments, lifetime)* $\rightarrow$ *HitID*: Calling this method creates a new HIT on the AMT marketplace. The *createHIT* method returns a *HitID* to the requester that is used to identify the HIT for all further communication. The *title, description,* and *reward* and other fields are used by AMT to combine HITs into HIT Groups. The *question* parameter encapsulates the user interface that workers use to process the HIT, including HTML pages. The *duration* parameter indicates how long the worker has to complete an assignment after accepting it. The *lifetime* attribute indicates an amount of time after which the HIT will no longer be available for workers to accept. Requesters can also constrain the set of workers that are allowed to process the HIT. CrowdDB, however, does not currently use this capability so the details of this and several other parameters are omitted for brevity.
- *getAssignmentsForHIT(HitID)* $\rightarrow$ *list(asnId, workerId, answer):* This method returns the results of all assignments of a HIT that have been provided by workers (at most, *maxAssignments* answers as specified when the requester created the HIT). Each answer of an assignment is given an *asnID* which is used by the requester to approve or reject that assignment (described next).
- *approveAssignment(asnID) / rejectAssignment(asnID)*: Approval triggers the payment of the reward to the worker and the commission to Amazon.
- *forceExpireHIT(HitID):* Expires a HIT immediately. Assignments that have already been accepted may be completed.

2.3 CrowdDB Design Considerations

The crowd can be seen as a set of specialized processors. Humans are good at certain tasks (e.g., image recognition) and relatively bad at others (e.g., number crunching). Likewise, machines are good and bad at certain tasks and it seems that people's and machines' capabilities complement each other nicely. It is this synergy that provides the opportunity to build a hybrid system such as CrowdDB. However, while the metaphor of humans as computing resources is powerful, it is important to understand when this metaphor works, and when it breaks down. In this section we highlight some key issues that have influenced the design of CrowdDB.

Performance and Variability: Obviously, people and machines differ greatly in the speed at which they work, the cost of that work, and the quality of the work they produce. More fundamentally, people show tremendous variability both from one individual to another and over time for a particular individual. Malicious behavior and "spamming" are also concerns. For CrowdDB these differences have implications for query planning, fault tolerance and answer quality.

Task Design and Ambiguity: Crowd-sourced tasks often have inherent ambiguities due to natural language and subjective requirements. The crowd requires a graphical user interface with human-readable instructions. Unlike programming language commands, such instructions can often be interpreted in different ways. Also, the layout and design of the interface can have a direct effect on the speed and accuracy with which people complete the tasks. The challenges here are that tasks must be carefully designed with the workers in mind and that quality-control mechanisms must be developed, even in cases where it is not possible to determine the absolute correctness of an answer.

Affinity and Learning: Unlike CPUs, which are largely fungible, crowd workers develop relationships with requesters and skills for certain HIT types. They learn over time how to optimize their revenue. Workers are hesitant to take on tasks for requesters who do not have a track record of providing well-defined tasks and paying appropriately and it is not uncommon for workers to specialize on specific HIT types (e.g., classifying pictures) or to favor HITs from certain requesters [16]. This behavior requires the CrowdDB design to take a longer-term view on task and worker community development.

Relatively Small Worker Pool: Despite the large and growing number of crowdsourcing workers, our experience, and that of others [18] is that the pool of workers available to work for any one requester is surprisingly small. This stems from a number of factors, some having to do with the specific design of the AMT web site, and others having to do with the affinity and learning issues discussed previously. For CrowdDB, this impacts design issues around parallelism and throughput.

Open vs. Closed World: Finally, as mentioned in the Introduction, a key difference between traditional data processing and crowd processing is that in the latter, there is an effectively unbounded amount of data available. Any one query operator could conceivably return an unlimited number of answers. This has profound implications for query planning, query execution costs and answer quality.

Having summarized the crowdsourcing platform, we now turn to the design and implementation of CrowdDB.

3. OVERVIEW OF CrowdDB

Figure 1 shows the general architecture of CrowdDB. An application issues requests using CrowdSQL, a moderate extension of standard SQL. Application programmers can build their applications in the traditional way; the complexities of dealing with the crowd are encapsulated by CrowdDB. CrowdDB answers queries using data stored in local tables when possible, and invokes the crowd otherwise. Results obtained from the crowd can be stored in the database for future use.

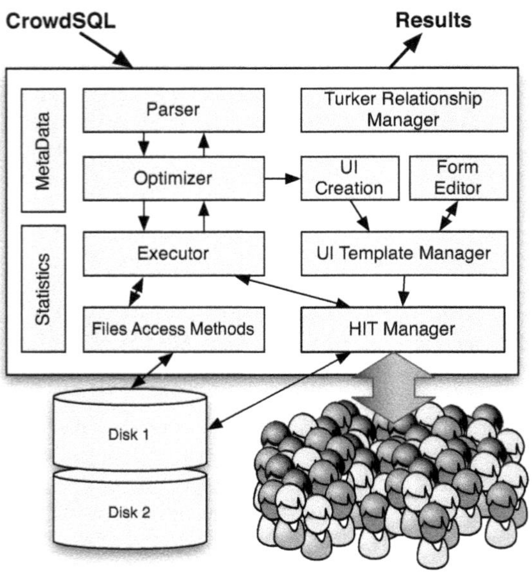

Figure 1: CrowdDB Architecture

As shown on the left side of the figure, CrowdDB incorporates the traditional query compilation, optimization and execution components. These components are extended to cope with human-generated input as described in subsequent sections. On the right side of the figure are new components that interact with the crowdsourcing platform. We briefly describe these from the top down.

Turker Relationship Management: As described in Section 2.3, the requester/worker relationship evolves over time and care must be taken to cultivate and maintain an effective worker pool. This module facilitates the most important duties of a requester, such as approving/rejecting assignments, paying and granting bonuses, etc. This way, CrowdDB helps to build communities for requesters which in the long run pays back in improved result quality, better response times, and lower cost.

User Interface Management: HITs require user interfaces and human-readable instructions. CrowdSQL extends SQL's data definition language to enable application developers to annotate tables with information that helps in user interface creation. At runtime, CrowdDB then automatically generates user interfaces for HITs based on these annotations as well as the standard type definitions and constraints that appear in the schema. Programmers can also create specific UI forms to override the standard UI generation in complex or exceptional cases.

The user interfaces generated for HITs are constrained where possible so that workers return only a pre-specified number of answers, and are designed to reduce errors by favoring simple tasks and limiting choices (i.e., adding dropdown lists or check boxes).

HIT Manager: This component manages the interactions between CrowdDB and the crowdsourcing platform (AMT in this case). It makes the API calls to post HITs, assess their status, and obtain the results of assignments. The HITs to be posted are determined by the query compiler and optimizer. The HIT manager also interacts with the storage engine in order to obtain values to preload into the HIT user interfaces and to store the results obtained from the crowd into the database.

The following sections explain the most important building blocks of CrowdDB in more detail: CrowdSQL, user interface generation, and query processing.

4. CrowdSQL

This section presents CrowdSQL, a SQL extension that supports crowdsourcing. We designed CrowdSQL to be a minimal extension to SQL to support use cases that involve missing data and subjective comparisons. This approach allows application programmers to write (Crowd) SQL code in the same way as they do for traditional databases. In most cases, developers are not aware that their code involves crowdsourcing. While this design results in a powerful language (CrowdSQL is a superset of SQL) with sound semantics, there are a number of practical considerations that such a powerful language entails. We discuss these issues and other extensions at the end of this section.

4.1 Incomplete Data

4.1.1 SQL DDL Extensions

Incomplete data can occur in two flavors: First, specific attributes of tuples could be crowdsourced. Second, entire tuples could be crowdsourced. We capture both cases by adding a special keyword, *CROWD*, to the SQL DDL, as shown in the following two examples.

EXAMPLE 1 (Crowdsourced Column) In the following *Department* table, the *url* is marked as crowdsourced. Such a model would be appropriate, say, if new departments are generated automatically (e.g., as part of an application program) and the *url* is often not provided but is likely available elsewhere.

```
CREATE TABLE Department (
  university STRING,
  name STRING,
  url  CROWD STRING,
```

```
  phone  STRING,
  PRIMARY KEY (university, name) );
```

EXAMPLE 2 (Crowdsourced Table) This example models a *Professor* table as a *crowdsourced table*. Such a crowdsourced table is appropriate if it is expected that the database typically only captures a subset of the professors of a department. In other words, CrowdDB will expect that additional professors may exist and possibly crowdsource more professors if required for processing specific queries.

```
CREATE CROWD TABLE Professor (
  name STRING PRIMARY KEY,
  email STRING UNIQUE,
  university STRING,
  department STRING,
  FOREIGN KEY (university, department)
     REF Department(university, name) );
```

CrowdDB allows any column and any table to be marked with the CROWD keyword. CrowdDB does not impose any limitations with regard to SQL types and integrity constraints; for instance, referential integrity constraints can be defined between two CROWD tables, two regular tables, and between a regular and a CROWD table in any direction. There is one exception: CROWD tables (e.g., *Professor*) must have a primary key so that CrowdDB can infer if two workers input the same new tuple (Section 4.3). Furthermore, CROWD columns and tables can be used in any SQL query and SQL DML statement, as shown in the following subsections.

4.1.2 SQL DML Semantics

In order to represent values in crowdsourced columns that have not yet been obtained, CrowdDB introduces a new value to each SQL type, referred to as *CNULL*. *CNULL* is the CROWD equivalent of the *NULL* value in standard SQL. *CNULL* indicates that a value should be crowdsourced when it is first used.

CNULL values are generated as a side-effect of `INSERT` statements. (The semantics of `DELETE` and `UPDATE` statements are unchanged in CrowdDB.) *CNULL* is the *default* value of any CROWD column. For instance,

```
INSERT INTO Department(university, name)
VALUES ("UC Berkeley", "EECS");
```

would create a new tuple. The *phone* field of the new department is initialized to *NULL*, as specified in standard SQL. The *url* field of the new department is initialized to *CNULL*, according to the special CrowdSQL semantics for CROWD columns. Both fields could be set later by an `UPDATE` statement. However, the *url* field could also be crowdsourced as a side-effect of queries, as described in the next subsection.

It is also possible to specify the value of a CROWD column as part of an `INSERT` statement; in this case, the value would not be crowdsourced (unless it is explicitly set to *CNULL* as part of an `UPDATE` statement); e.g.,

```
INSERT INTO Department(university, name, url)
VALUES ("ETH Zurich", "CS", "inf.ethz.ch");
```

It is also possible to initialize or set the value of a CROWD column to *NULL*; in such a case, crowdsourcing would not take effect. Furthermore, it is possible to explicitly initialize or set (as part of an `UPDATE` statement) the value of a CROWD column to *CNULL*.

CNULL is also important for CROWD tables, where *all* columns are implicitly crowdsourced. If an `INSERT` statement is executed on a CROWD table, then all non-key attributes would be initialized to *CNULL*, if not specified otherwise as part of the `INSERT` statement. However, the key of a CROWD table must be specified for the `INSERT` statement as the key is never allowed to contain *CNULL*. This rule is equivalent to the rule that keys must not be *NULL* enforced by most standard SQL database systems. However, new tuples of CROWD tables are typically crowdsourced entirely, as described in the next subsection.

In summary, CrowdSQL allows any kind of `INSERT`, `UPDATE`, and `DELETE` statements; all these statements can be applied to CROWD columns and tables. Furthermore, CrowdSQL supports all standard SQL types (including *NULL* values). A special *CNULL* value indicates data in CROWD columns that should be crowdsourced when needed as part of processing a query.

4.1.3 Query Semantics

CrowdDB supports any kind of SQL query on CROWD tables and columns; for instance, joins and sub-selects between two CROWD tables are allowed. Furthermore, the results of these queries are as expected according to the (standard) SQL semantics.

What makes CrowdSQL special is that it incorporates crowdsourced data as part of processing SQL queries. Specifically, CrowdDB asks the crowd to instantiate *CNULL* values if they are required to evaluate predicates of a query or if they are part of a query result. Furthermore, CrowdDB asks the crowd for new tuples of CROWD tables if such tuples are required to produce a query result. Crowdsourcing as a side-effect of query processing is best explained with the help of examples:

```
SELECT url FROM Department
WHERE name = "Math";
```

This query asks for the *url* of the Math department. If the *url* is *CNULL*, then the semantics of CrowdSQL require that the value be crowdsourced. The following query asks for all professors with Berkeley email addresses in the Math department:

```
SELECT * FROM Professor
WHERE email LIKE "%berkeley%" AND dept = "Math";
```

This query involves crowdsourcing the E-Mail address and department of all known professors (if their current value is *CNULL*) in order to evaluate the `WHERE` clause. Furthermore, processing this query involves asking the crowd for possibly additional Math professors that have not been crowdsourced yet.

CrowdSQL specifies that tables are updated as a side-effect of crowdsourcing. In the first query example above, for instance, the *url* column would be implicitly updated with the crowdsourced URL. Likewise, missing values in the *email* column would be implicitly populated and new professors would be implicitly inserted as a side-effect of processing the second query. Logically, these updates and inserts are carried out as part of the same transaction as the query and they are executed *before* the query; i.e., their effects are visible during query processing.

4.2 Subjective Comparisons

Recall that beyond finding missing data, the other main use of crowdsourcing in CrowdDB is subjective comparisons. In order to support this functionality, CrowdDB has two new built in functions: `CROWDEQUAL` and `CROWDORDER`.

`CROWDEQUAL` takes two parameters (an *lvalue* and an *rvalue*) and asks the crowd to decide whether the two values are equal. As syntactic sugar, we use the $\sim=$ symbol and an infix notation, as shown in the following example:

EXAMPLE 3 To ask for all "CS" departments, the following query could be posed. Here, the query writer asks the crowd to do entity resolution with the possibly different names given for Computer Science in the database:

```
SELECT profile FROM department
WHERE name ~= "CS";
```

CROWDORDER is used whenever the help of the crowd is needed to rank or order results. Again, this function is best illustrated with an example.

EXAMPLE 4 The following CrowdSQL query asks for a ranking of pictures with regard to how well these pictures depict the Golden Gate Bridge.

```
CREATE TABLE picture (
  p IMAGE,
  subject STRING
);
SELECT p FROM picture
WHERE subject = "Golden Gate Bridge"
ORDER BY CROWDORDER(p,
"Which picture visualizes better %subject");
```

As with missing data, CrowdDB stores the results of CROWDEQUAL and CROWDORDER calls so that the crowd is only asked once for each comparison. This *caching* is equivalent to the caching of expensive functions in traditional SQL databases, e.g., [13]. This cache can also be invalidated; the details of the syntax and API to control this cache are straightforward and omitted for brevity.

4.3 CrowdSQL in Practice

The current version of CrowdSQL was designed to be a minimal extension to SQL and address some of the use cases that involve incomplete data and subjective comparisons. This version was used in the first implementation of CrowdDB which was used as a platform for the experiments reported in Section 7. While this minimal extension is sound and powerful, there are a number of considerations that limit the usage of CrowdSQL in practice.

The first issue is that CrowdSQL changes the closed-world to an open-world assumption. Thus cost and response time of queries can be unbounded in CrowdSQL. If a query involves a CROWD table, then it is unclear how many tuples need to be crowdsourced in order to fully process the query. For queries that involve regular tables with CROWD columns or subjective comparisons, the amount of information that needs to be crowdsourced is bounded by the number of tuples and *CNULL* values stored in the database; nevertheless, the cost can be prohibitive. In order to be practical, CrowdSQL should provide a way to define a *budget* for a query. Depending on the use case, an application developer should be able to constrain the cost, the response time, and/or the result quality. For instance, in an emergency situation, response time may be critical whereas result quality should be given priority if a strategic decision of an organization depends on a query. In the current version of CrowdDB, we provide only one way to specify a budget — using a LIMIT clause [7]. The LIMIT clause constrains the number of tuples that are returned as a result of a query. This way, the LIMIT clause implicitly constrains the cost and response time of a query. A LIMIT clause (or similar syntax) is supported by most relational database systems and this clause has the same semantics in CrowdSQL as in (traditional) SQL. We used this mechanism because it was available and did not require any extensions to SQL syntax or semantics. It should be clear, however, that more sophisticated and explicit mechanisms to specify *budgets* are needed.

A second extension that we plan for the next version of CrowdSQL is *lineage*. In CrowdDB, data can be either crowdsourced as a side-effect of query processing or entered using SQL DML statements. In both cases, application developers may wish to query the lineage in order to take actions. For instance, it may become known that a certain worker is a spammer; in such a situation, it may be appropriate to reset all crowdsourced values to *CNULL* that were derived from input from that worker. Also, it may be important to know when data was entered in order to determine whether the data is outdated (i.e., time-to-live); the age of data may be relevant for both crowdsourced and machine-generated data.

A third practical issue involves the cleansing of crowdsourced data; in particular, entity resolution of crowdsourced data. As mentioned in Section 4.1, all CROWD tables must have a primary key. The current version of CrowdDB uses the primary key values in order to detect duplicate entries of CROWD tables. This approach works well if it can be assumed that two independent workers will enter exactly the same literals. In many cases, this assumption is not realistic. As part of future work, we plan to extend the DDL of CrowdSQL so that application developers can specify that data cleaning should be carried out on crowdsourced data (e.g., entity resolution). Of course, this feature comes at a cost so that developers should have control to use this feature depending on their budget.

5. USER INTERFACE GENERATION

Recall that a key to success in crowdsourcing is the provision of effective user interfaces. In this section we describe how CrowdDB automatically generates user interfaces for crowdsourcing incomplete information and subjective comparisons. As shown in Figure 1, the generation of user interfaces is a two-step process in CrowdDB. At compile-time, CrowdDB creates *templates* to crowdsource missing information from all CROWD tables and all regular tables which have CROWD columns. These user interfaces are HTML (and JavaScript) forms that are generated based on the CROWD annotations in the schema and optional free-text annotations of columns and tables that can also be found in the schema [21]. Furthermore, these templates can be edited by application developers to provide additional custom instructions. These templates are instantiated at runtime in order to provide a user interface for a concrete tuple or a set of tuples. The remainder of this section gives examples of user interfaces generated for the tables and subjective comparisons described in Section 4.

5.1 Basic Interfaces

Figure 2a shows an example user interface generated for crowdsourcing the *URL* of the "EECS" department of "UC Berkeley" (Example 1). The title of the HTML is the name of the Table (i.e., *Department* in this example) and the instructions ask the worker to input the missing information. In general, user interface templates are instantiated by copying the known field values from a tuple into the HTML form (e.g., "EECS" and "UC Berkeley" in this example). Furthermore, all fields of the tuple that have *CNULL* values become input fields of the HTML form (i.e., *URL* in this example).

In addition to HTML code, CrowdDB generates JavaScript code in order to check for the correct types of input provided by the workers. For instance, if the CrowdSQL involves a CHECK constraint that limits the domain of a crowdsourced attribute (e.g., "EUR", "USD", etc. for currencies), then a *select box* is generated that allows the worker to choose among the legal values for that attribute.

A possible optimization that is not shown in Figure 2a is to *batch*

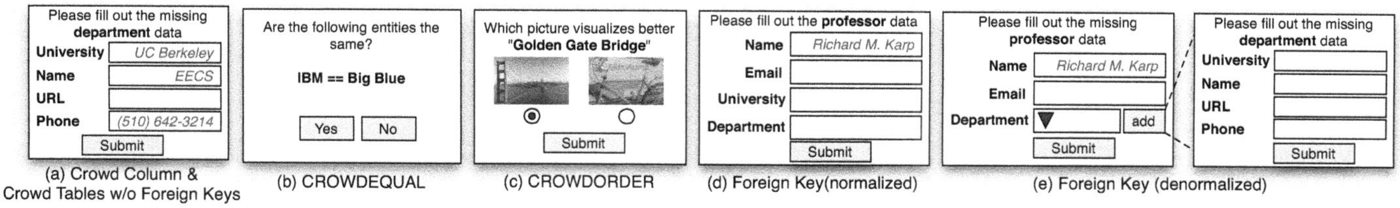

Figure 2: Example User Interfaces Generated by CrowdDB

several tuples. For instance, if the *URL* of several departments needs to be crowdsourced, then a single worker could be asked to provide the *URL* information of a set of department (e.g., EECS, Physics and Chemistry of UC Berkeley). The assumption is that it is cheaper to input two pieces of information of the same kind as part of a single form than twice as part of separate forms. CrowdDB supports this batching functionality.

Another optimization is *prefetching* of attributes for the same tuple. For instance, if both the *department* and *email* of a professor are unknown, but only the *email* of that professor is required to process a query, the question is whether the *department* should also be crowdsourced. The trade-offs are straight-forward: Prefetching may hurt the cost and response time of the current query, but it may help reduce the cost and response time of future queries. The current version of CrowdDB carries out prefetching, thereby assuming that the incremental cost of prefetching is lower than the return on the prefetching investment.

CrowdDB also creates user interfaces for the `CROWDEQUAL` and `CROWDORDER` functions. Figures 2b and 2c show example interfaces for comparing and ordering tuples. Both types of interfaces can also be batched as described earlier. However, for ordering tuples, our current implementation only supports binary comparisons. Multi-way comparisons remain future work.

5.2 Multi-Relation Interfaces

Crowdsourcing relations with foreign keys require special considerations. In the simplest case, the foreign key references a non-crowdsourced table. In this case, the generated user interface shows a drop-down box containing all the possible foriegn key values, or alternatively if the domain is too large for a drop-down box an Ajax-based "suggest" function is provided.

In contrast, if the referenced table is a CROWD table, the set of all possible foriegn key values is not known, and additional tuples of the referenced table may need to be crowdsourced. For the moment, let us assume that the *department* table is indeed a CROWD table (deviating from its definition in Example 1). In this case, a worker may wish to specify that a professor is member of a *new* department; i.e., a department that has not yet been obtained from the crowd.

CrowdDB supports two types of user interfaces for such situations. The first type is the *normalized* interface shown in Figure 2d. This interface requires the worker to enter values for the foreign key attributes, but does not allow him or her to enter any other fields of the referenced tuple. Here, as above, the "suggest" function can help to avoid entity resolution problems.

The second type is a *denormalized* interface, which allows a worker to enter missing values for non-key fields of the referenced table as part of the same task. To this end, the user interface provides an *add* button (in addition, the the drop down menu of *known* departments). Clicking on this *add* button brings up a *pop-up* window or new browser tab (depending on the browser configuration) that allows to enter the information of the new department as visualized in Figure 2e. How the optimizer chooses the interface for a particular query is explained in the next section.

Note that Figures 2d and 2e show the two types of user interfaces generated in the case where additional information is being crowdsourced for existing professor tuples. Similar user interfaces can be generated to crowdsource entirely *new* professor tuples. Such interfaces differ from these examples in the following ways: First, the key attribute(s) (i.e., the *name* of a professor in this case) becomes an input field. In order to restrict the set of possible new tuples, CrowdDB allows presetting the value of non-key attributes using the where clause, e.g. only considering professors from UC Berkeley. Second, JavaScript logic is generated that shows the names of professors that have already been recorded while typing in the name of a (potentially new) professor. Finally, an additional button is provided to allow workers to report if they cannot find any new professor records.

6. QUERY PROCESSING

Since CrowdDB is SQL-based, query plan generation and execution follows a largely traditional approach. In particular, as shown in Figure 1, CrowdDB has a parser, optimizer, and runtime system and these components play the same role in CrowdDB as in a traditional database system. The main differences are that the CrowdDB parser has been extended to parse CrowdSQL, CrowdDB has additional operators that effect crowdsourcing (in addition to the traditional relational algebra operators found in a traditional database system), and the CrowdDB optimizer includes special heuristics to generate plans with these additional Crowd operators. This section sketches these differences and discusses an example query plan.

6.1 Crowd Operators

CrowdDB implements all operators of the relational algebra, just like any traditional database system (e.g., join, group-by, index scans, etc.). In addition, CrowdDB implements a set of Crowd operators that encapsulate the instantiation of user interface templates at runtime and the collection of results obtained from crowdsourcing. This way, the implementation of traditional operators need not be changed. The next subsection describes how query plans are generated with such Crowd operators. This subsection describes the set of Crowd operators currently implemented in CrowdDB.

The basic functionality of all Crowd operators is the same. They are all initialized with a user interface template and the standard HIT parameters that are used for crowdsourcing as part of a particular Crowd operator. At runtime, they consume a set of tuples, e.g., *Professors*. Depending on the Crowd operator, crowdsourcing can be used to source missing values of a tuple (e.g., the *email* of a *Professor*) or to source new tuples. In both cases, each tuple represents one *job* (using the terminology from Section 2.1). Several tuples can be batched into a single *HIT* as described in Section 5.1; e.g., a user interface instance could be used to crowdsource the *email* of say, three, *Professors*. Furthermore, Crowd operators create *HIT Groups*. For instance, if the *email* of 300 professors needs to be sourced and each HIT involves three professors, then one HIT Group of 100 HITs could be generated. As shown in Section 7, when using AMT, the size of HIT Groups and how they are posted must be carefully tuned.

In addition to the creation of HITs and HIT Groups, each Crowd operator consumes results returned by the crowd and carries out

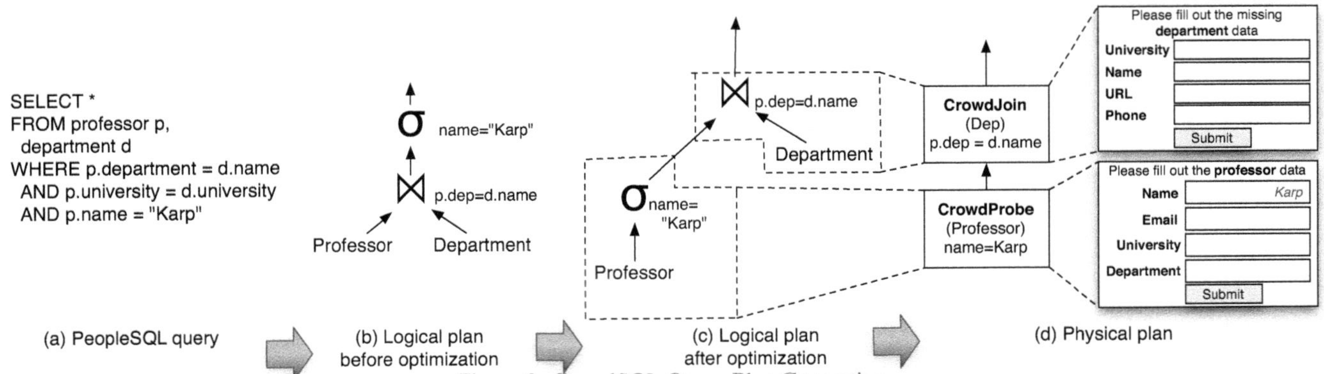

Figure 3: CrowdSQL Query Plan Generation

quality control. In the current CrowdDB prototype, quality control is carried out by a majority vote on the input provided by different workers for the same HIT. The number of workers assigned to each HIT is controlled by an *Assignments* parameter (Section 2.1). The initial number of *Assignments* is currently a static parameter of CrowdDB. As mentioned in Section 4.3, this parameter should be set by the CrowdDB optimizer based on budget constraints set via CrowdSQL.

The current version of CrowdDB has three Crowd operators:

- **CrowdProbe**: This operator crowdsources missing information of CROWD columns (i.e., *CNULL* values) and new tuples. It uses interfaces such as those shown in Figures 2a, 2d and 2e. The operator enforces quality control by selecting the majority answer for every attribute as the final value. That is, given the answers for a single tuple (i.e., entity with the same key), the majority of turkers have to enter the same value to make it the final value of the tuple. If no majority exists, more workers are asked until the majority agrees or a pre-set maximum of answers are collected. In the latter case, the final value is randomly selected from the values most workers had in common.

  In the case of newly created tuples it can happen that all workers enter tuples with different primary keys, making finding a majority impossible. In this case, the operator re-posts the tasks by leaving all non-confirmed attributes empty except the ones comprising the primary key. This allows CrowdDB to obtain more answers for every key in order to form a majority quorum.
- **CrowdJoin**: This operator implements an index nested-loop join over two tables, at least one of which is crowdsourced. For each tuple of the outer relation, this operator creates one or more HITs in order to crowdsource new tuples from the inner relation that matches the tuple of the outer relation. Correspondingly, the inner relation must be a CROWD table and the user interface to crowdsource new tuples from the inner relation is instantiated with the join column values of the tuple from the outer relation according to the join predicates. The quality control technique is the same as for CrowdProbe.
- **CrowdCompare**: This operator implements the *CROWDEQUAL* and *CROWDORDER* functions described in Section 4.2. It instantiates user interfaces such as those shown in Figures 2c and 2d. Note that CrowdCompare is typically used inside another traditional operator, such as sorting or predicate evaluation. For example, an operator that implements quick-sort might use CrowdCompare to perform the required binary comparisons. Quality control is based on the simple majority vote.

6.2 Physical Plan Generation

Figure 3 presents an end-to-end example that shows how CrowdDB creates a query plan for a simple CrowdSQL query. A query is first parsed; the result is a *logical plan*, as shown in Figure 3b. This *logical plan* is then optimized using traditional and crowd-specific optimizations. Figure 3c shows the optimized logical plan for this example. In this example, only predicate push-down was applied, a well-known traditional optimization technique. Some crowd-specific optimization heuristics used in CrowdDB are described in the next subsection. Finally, the *logical* plan is translated into a *physical plan* which can be executed by the CrowdDB runtime system. As part of this step, Crowd operators and traditional operators of the relational algebra are instantiated. In the example of Figure 3, the query is executed by a CrowdProbe operator in order to crowdsource missing information from the *Professor* table and a CrowdJoin operator in order to crowdsource missing information from the *Department* table. (In this example, it is assumed that the *Department* is a CROWD table; otherwise, the CrowdJoin operator would not be applicable.)

6.3 Heuristics

The current CrowdDB compiler is based on a simple rule-based optimizer. The optimizer implements several essential query rewriting rules such as predicate push-down, stopafter push-down [7], join-ordering and determining if the plan is bounded [5]. The last optimization deals with the open-world assumption by ensuring that the amount of data requested from the crowd is bounded. Thus, the heuristic first annotates the query plan with the cardinality predictions between the operators. Afterwards, the heuristic tries to re-order the operators to minimize the requests against the crowd and warns the user at compile-time if the number of requests cannot be bounded.

Furthermore, we also created a set of crowd-sourcing rules in order to set the basic crowdsourcing parameters (e.g., price, batching-size), select the user interface (e.g., normalized vs. denormalized) and several other simple cost-saving techniques. For example, a delete on a crowd-sourced table does not try to receive all tuples satisfying the expression in the delete statement before deleting them. Instead the optimizer rewrites the query to only look into existing tuples.

Nevertheless, in contrast to a cost-based optimizer, a rule-based optimizer is not able to exhaustively explore all parameters and thus, often produces a sub-optimal result. A cost-based optimizer for CrowdDB, which must also consider the changing conditions on AMT, remains future work.

7. EXPERIMENTS AND RESULTS

This section presents results from experiments run with CrowdDB and AMT. We ran over 25,000 HITs on AMT during October 2010, varying parameters such as price, jobs per HIT and time of day. We measured the response time and quality of the answers provided by the workers. Here, we report on Micro-benchmarks (Section 7.1), that use simple jobs involving finding new data or making subjective comparisons. The goals of these experiments are to ex-

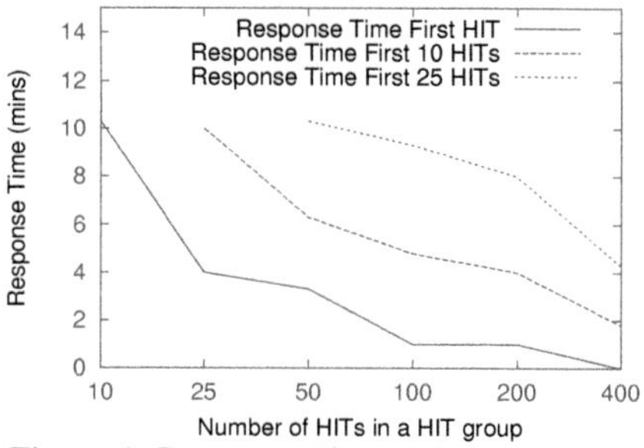

Figure 4: Response Time (min): Vary Hit Group *(1 Asgn/HIT, 1 cent Reward)*

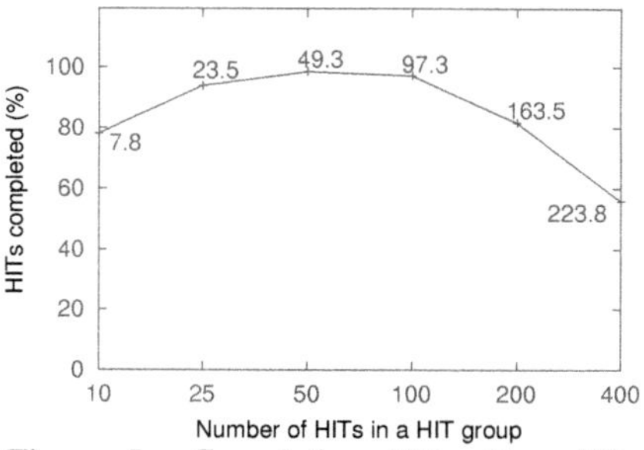

Figure 5: Completion (%): Vary Hit Group *(1 Asgn/HIT, 1 cent Reward)*

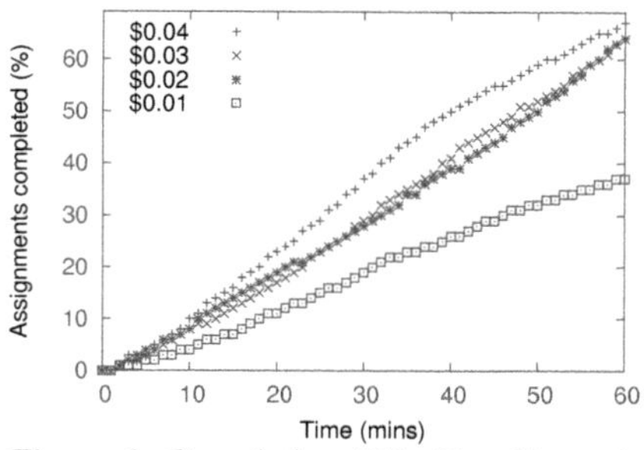

Figure 6: Completion (%): Vary Reward *(100 HITs/Group, 5 Asgn/HIT)*

amine the behavior of workers for the types of tasks required by CrowdDB, as well as to obtain insight that could be used in the development of cost models for query optimization. We also describe the results of experiments that demonstrate the execution of more complex queries (Section 7.2).

It is important to note that the results presented in this section are highly dependent on the properties of the AMT platform at a particular point in time (October 2010). AMT and other crowdsourcing platforms are evolving rapidly and it is quite likely that response time and quality properties will differ significantly between different platforms and even different versions of the same platform. Furthermore, our results are highly-dependent on the specific tasks we sent to the crowd. Nevertheless, we believe that a number of interesting and important observations can be made even from these initial experiments. We describe these below.

7.1 Micro Benchmarks

We begin by describing the results of experiments with simple tasks requiring workers to find and fill in missing data for a table with two crowdsourced columns:

```
CREATE TABLE businesses (
  name VARCHAR PRIMARY KEY,
  phone_number CROWD VARCHAR(32),
  address CROWD VARCHAR(256)
);
```

We populated this table with the names of 3607 businesses (restaurants, hotels, and shopping malls) in 40 USA cities. We studied the sourcing of the *phone_number* and *address* columns using the following query:

```
SELECT phone_number, address FROM businesses;
```

Since workers and skills are not evenly distributed across timezones, the time of day can impact both response time and answer quality [24]. While we ran tasks at many different times, in this paper we report only on experiments that were carried out between 0600 and 1500 PST, which reduces the variance in worker availability [14]. We repeated all experiments four times and provide the average values. Unless stated otherwise, groups of 100 HITs were posted and each HIT involved five assignments. By default the reward for each job was 1 cent and each HIT asked for the address and phone number of one business (i.e., 1 Job per HIT).

7.1.1 Experiment 1: Response Time, Vary HIT Groups

As mentioned in Section 2, AMT automatically groups HITs of the same kind into a HIT Group. In the first set of experiments we examined the response time of assignments as a function of the number of HITs in a HIT Group. For this experiment we varied the number of HITs per HIT Group from 10 to 400 and fixed the number of assignments per HIT to 1 (i.e., no replication). Figures 4 and 5 show the results of this experiment.

Figure 4 shows the time to completion of 1, 10, and 25 HITs as the HIT Group size is varied. The results show that response times decrease dramatically as the size of the HIT Groups is increased. For example, for a HIT Group of 25 HITs, the first result was obtained after approximately four minutes, while for a HIT Group containing 400 HITs, the first result was obtained in seconds.

Figure 5 provides a different view on the results of this experiment. In this case, we show the percentage of the HITs in a HIT Group completed within 30 minutes, for HIT Groups of different sizes. The points are annotated with the absolute number of HITs completed within 30 minutes. This graph shows that there is a tradeoff between throughput (in terms of HITs completed per unit time) and completion percent. That is, while the best throughput obtained was for the largest Group size (223.8 out of a Group of 400 HITs), the highest completion rates were obtained with Groups of 50 or 100 HITs. The implication is that performance for simple tasks can vary widely even when only a single parameter is changed. Thus, more work is required for understanding how to set the HIT Group size and other parameters — a prerequisite for the development of a true cost-based query optimizer for CrowdDB or any crowdsourced query answering system.

7.1.2 Experiment 2: Responsiveness, Vary Reward

While Experiment 1 showed that even a fairly technical parameter such as HIT Group size can greatly impact performance, there are other parameters that one would perhaps more obviously expect to influence the performance of a crowdbased system. High on this list would be the magnitude of the reward given to workers. Here, we report on a set of experiments that examine how the response time varies as a function of the reward. In these experiments, 100 HITs were posted per HIT Group and each HIT contained five assignments. The expectation is that the higher the reward for a HIT, the faster workers will engage into processing that HIT.

Figure 6 shows the fraction of HITs (i.e., all five assignments) that were completed as a function of time. The figure shows the results for HITs with a reward of (from the bottom up) 1, 2, 3, and 4 cents per assignment. Obviously, for all rewards, the longer we wait the more HITs are completed. The results show that for this particular task, paying 4 cents gives the best performance, while paying 1 cent gives the worst. Interestingly, there is very little difference between paying 2 cents and 3 cents per assignment.

Figure 7 shows the fraction of HITs that received at least one assignment as a function of time and reward. Comparing Figures 6 and 7, two observations can be made. First, within sixty minutes almost all HITs received at least one answer if a reward of 2, 3, or 4 cents was given (Figure 7), whereas only about 65% of the HITs

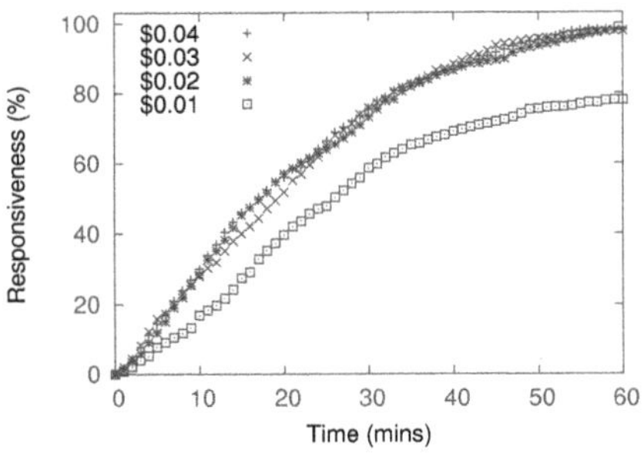

Figure 7: Completion (%): Vary Reward *(100 HITs/Group, 5 Asgn/HIT)*

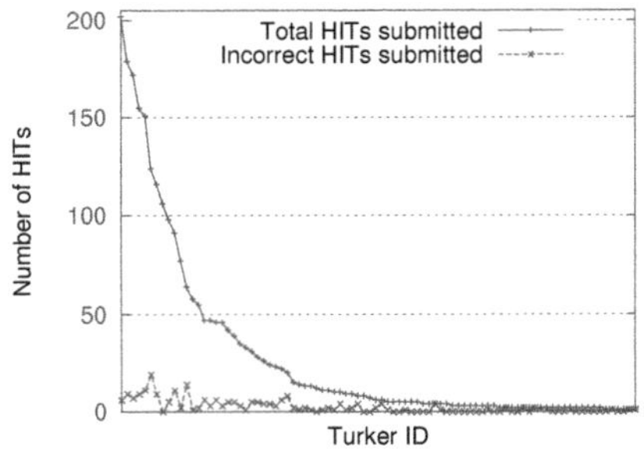

Figure 8: HITs/Quality by Worker *(Any HITs/Group, 5 Asgn/HIT, Any Reward)*

Non Uniform Name	Query Result	Votes
Bayerische Motoren Werke	BMW	3
International Business Machines	IBM	2
Company of Gillette	P&G	2
Big Blue	IBM	2

Figure 9: Entity Resolution on Company Names

were fully completed even for the highest reward of 4 cents (Figure 6). Second, if a single response to a HIT is acceptable, there is little incentive to pay more than 2 cents in this case.

As in Experiment 1, the results here show that parameters must be set carefully. In this case, of course, the parameter has a direct effect on the monetary cost of obtaining the data from the crowd, so setting it correctly for a given situation will be of significant importance, and tradeoffs between cost and response time will need to be exposed to users of the system.

7.1.3 Experiment 3: Worker Affinity and Quality

The previous experiments focused on the response time and throughput of the crowd. Here, we turn our attention to two other issues: distribution of work among workers and answer quality. In this experiment, every HIT had five assignments. We carried out majority votes among the five answers for phone numbers and computed the *ground truth* from this majority vote. Any answer that deviated from this ground truth (modulo formatting differences) was counted as an error.

Figure 8 shows the results. For each worker, Figure 8 shows the number of HITs computed by that worker and the number of errors made by that worker. In Figure 8, the workers are plotted along the x-axis in decreasing order of the number of HITs they processed. As can be seen, the distribution of workers performing HITs is highly skewed; this result confirms previous studies that have shown that requesters acquire communities of workers who specialize in processing their requests [15]. It seems that we were able to build a community of about a dozen fans.

We expected that one benefit of having such a community would be increased accuracy as workers gained experience with the task. However, we did not observe such an effect in our experiments. The lower curve in Figure 8 shows the number of errors made by each worker. In absolute numbers, heavy hitters, of course, have more errors. But in terms of error rate (Incorrect HITs / Total HITs, not shown) they were no more accurate than other workers, at least for the relatively simple task we examined here.

Note that the results shown in Figure 8 include HITs from the full reward range of 1 to 4 cents. In this range the reward had no noticeable impact on the error rate of the workers. We also observed that in our experiments the error rates did not depend on the HIT Group size.

7.2 Complex Queries

We now describe three experiments using CrowdSQL queries that cannot be asked of traditional database systems.

7.2.1 Entity Resolution on Companies

For this experiment, we used a simple company schema with two attributes, *company name* and *headquarter address*, and populated it with the Fortune 100 companies. We ran the following query to test entity resolution in CrowdDB:

```
SELECT name FROM company WHERE
  name~="[a non-uniform name of the company]"
```

In Figure 9 we show results for four different instances of this query. Each HIT involved comparing ten company names with one of the four "non-uniform names". Furthermore, each HIT had three assignments and the reward was 1 cent per HIT. Figure 9 shows that in all four cases, majority vote produced the correct answer. However, in only one of the cases (for BMW) was the vote unanimous. Note that the total time to complete the 40 HITs (i.e., 120 assignments) for these four queries was 39 minutes.

7.2.2 Ordering Pictures

For this experiment, we ran the query of Example 4 of Section 4; i.e., we asked for a ranking of pictures in different subject areas. Overall, we tested 30 subject areas having eight pictures for each subject area. Each HIT involved the comparison of four pairs of pictures. These rankings were conducted with 210 HITs, each with three assignments. It took 68 minutes to complete the experiment.

Figure 10 shows the ranking of the Top 8 pictures for the "Golden Gate" subject area. More concretely, Figure 10 shows the picture, the number of workers that voted for that picture, the ranking of that picture according to the majority vote, vs. the ranking according to a group of six experts who frequently visit the Golden Gate Bridge. In this case the CrowdDB results obtained via AMT match well with the ranks given by the experts.

7.2.3 Joining Professors and Departments

The last experiment we present compares the performance of two alternative plans for a join query. We populated the schema of Example 1 and 2 with 25 professors and 8 departments and asked the following SQL query:

```
SELECT p.name, p.email, d.name, d.phone
FROM   Professor p, Department d
WHERE  p.department = d.name AND
       p.university = d.university AND
       p.name = "[name of a professor]"
```

The first plan we executed for this query was the plan shown in Figure 3d (Section 6). That is, we first ask for the *Professor* information and the department the professor is associated with. Then in a second step, we ask for the remaining information (i.e., phone number) of the departments. The second plan was a *denormalized* variant that asked for the *Professor* and *Department* information in a single step, thereby creating only one type of HIT and the user interface of Figure 2e. For both plans, each HIT involved one job

(a) 15, 1, 1 (b) 15, 1, 2 (c) 14, 3, 4 (d) 13, 4, 5

(e) 10, 5, 6 (f) 9, 6, 3 (g) 4, 7, 7 (h) 4, 7, 8

Figure 10: Pictures of the Golden Gate Bridge [1] ordered by workers. The tuples in the sub-captions is in the following format: {the number of votes by the workers for this picture, rank of the picture ordered by the workers (based on votes), rank of the picture ordered by experts}.

(e.g., an entry form for a single professor) and three assignments. The reward per HIT was 1 cent.

The two plans were similar in execution time and cost but differed significantly in result quality. The first plan took 206 minutes and cost $0.99, while the second plan took 173 minutes and cost $0.75. In terms of quality, the second plan produced wrong results for all department telephone numbers. A close look at the data revealed that workers unanimously submitted the professors' phone numbers instead of the departments'. In contrast, only a single telephone number was incorrect when using the first plan.

7.3 Observations

In total, our experiments involved 25,817 assignments processed by 718 different workers. Overall, they confirm the basic hypothesis of our work: it is possible to employ human input via crowdsourcing to process queries that traditional systems cannot. The experiments also, however, pointed out some of the challenges that remain to be addressed, particularly in terms of understanding and controlling the factors that impact response time, cost and result quality. In this section, we outline several additional lessons we learned during our experimentation.

First, we observe that unlike computational resources, crowd resources involve long-term memory that can impact performance. Requesters can track workers' past performance and workers can track and discuss the past behavior of requesters. We found, for example, that to keep workers happy, it is wise to be less strict in approving HITs. In one case, when we rejected HITs that failed our quality controls, a worker posted the following on TurkOpticon [27]: "Of the 299 HITs I completed, 11 of them were rejected...I have attempted to contact the requester and will update...Until then be very wary of doing any work for this requester...". In another case, a bug in CrowdDB triggered false alarms in security warnings for browsers on the workers' computers, and within hours concerns about our jobs appeared on Turker Nation [26].

A second lesson is that user interface design and precise instructions matter. For our first experiments with AMT, we posted HITs with handcrafted user interfaces. In one HIT, we gave a list of company names and asked the workers to check the ones that matched "IBM". To our surprise, the quality of the answers was very low. The problem was that in some cases there were no good matches. We expected workers to simply not check any boxes in such cases, but this did not occur. Adding a checkbox for "None of the above" improved the quality dramatically.

Our experimental results, along with these anecdotes, demonstrate the complexity and new challenges that arise for crowdsourced query processing. They also show, we believe, the need to automate such decisions to shield query and application writers from these complexities and to enable robust behavior in the presence of environmental changes. Such a need should be familiar to database systems designers — it is essentially a requirement for a new form of *data independence*.

8. RELATED WORK

We discuss related work in two primary areas: database systems and the emerging crowdsourcing community.

CrowdDB leverages traditional techniques for relational query processing wherever possible. Furthermore, we found that some less-standard techniques developed for other scenarios were useful for crowdsourcing as well. For example, crowdsourced comparisons such *CROWDEQUAL*, can be seen as special instances of expensive predicates [13]. Top N optimizations [7] are a useful tool for dealing with the open-world nature of crowdsourcing, particularly when combined with operation-limiting techniques such as those developed for cloud scalability in [5]. Looking forward, we anticipate that the volatility of crowd performance will require the use of a range of adaptive query processing techniques [12].

An important feature of CrowdDB is the (semi-) automatic generation of user interfaces from meta-data (i.e., SQL schemas). As mentioned in Section 5, products such as Oracle Forms and MS Access have taken a similar approach. Model-driven architecture frameworks (MDA) enable similar functionality [17]. Finally, there are useful analogies between CrowdDB and federated database systems (e.g., [8, 11]): CrowdDB can be considered to be a mediator, the crowd can be seen as a data sources and the generated user interfaces can be regarded as wrappers for those sources.

As stated in the introduction, crowdsourcing has been gathering increasing attention in the research community. A recent survey of the area can be found in [10]. There have been a number of studies that analyze the behavior of microtask platforms such as Mechanical Turk. Ipeirotis, for instance, analyzed the AMT marketplace, gathering statistics about HITs, requesters, rewards, HIT completion rates, etc. [15]. Furthermore, the demographics of workers (e.g., age, gender, education, etc.) on AMT have been studied [24].

Systems making early attempts to automatically control quality and optimize response time include CrowdSearch [28] and Soylent [6]. TurKit is a set of tools that enables programming iterative algorithms over the crowd [19]. This toolkit has been used, for example, to decipher unreadable hand-writing. Finally, Usher is a research project that studies the design of data entry forms [9].

Independently of our work on CrowdDB, several groups in the

database research community have begun to explore the use of crowdsourcing in relational query processing. Two papers on the topic appeared in the recent CIDR 2011 conference [20, 23]. As with our work, both of these efforts suggest the use of a declarative query language in order to process queries involving human input. [20] proposes the use of user-defined functions in SQL to specify the user interfaces and the questions that should be crowdsourced as part of query processing. [23] suggests the use of Datalog for this purpose. However, neither of these early papers present details of the system design or experimental results. As these projects mature, it will be interesting to compare the design decisions made and implications with regard to usability and optimizability. Also related is recent work in the database community on graph searching using crowdsourcing [22]. Finally, there has also been work on defining workflow systems that involve machines and humans. Dustdar et al. describe in a recent vision paper how BPEL and web services technology could be used for this purpose [25].

9. CONCLUSION

This paper presented the design of CrowdDB, a relational query processing system that uses microtask-based crowdsourcing to answer queries that cannot otherwise be answered. We highlighted two cases where human input is needed: (a) unknown or incomplete data, and (b) subjective comparisons. CrowdDB extends SQL in order to address both of these cases and it extends the query compiler and runtime system with auto-generated user interfaces and new query operators that can obtain human input via these interfaces. Experiments with CrowdDB on Amazon Mechanical Turk demonstrated that human input can indeed be leveraged to dramatically extend the range of SQL-based query processing.

We described simple extensions to the SQL DDL and DML for crowdsourcing. These simple extensions, however, raise deep and fundamental issues for the design of crowd-enabled query languages and execution engines. Perhaps most importantly, they invalidate the closed-world assumption on which SQL semantics and processing strategies are based. We identified implementation challenges that arise as a result and outlined initial solutions.

Other important issues concern the assessment and preservation of answer quality. Quality is greatly impacted by the motivation and skills of the human workers as well as the structure and interfaces of the jobs they are asked to do. Performance, in terms of latency and cost, is also effected by the way in which CrowdDB interacts with workers. Through a series of micro-benchmarks we identified key design parameters such as the grouping of tasks, the rewards paid to workers, and the number of assignments per task. We also discussed the need to manage the long-term relationship with workers. It is important to build a community of workers and to provide them with timely and appropriate rewards and, if not, to give precise and understandable feedback.

Of course, there is future work to do. Answer quality is a pervasive issue that must be addressed. Clear semantics in the presence of the open-world assumption are needed for for both crowdsourced values and tables. While our existing approach preserves SQL semantics in principle, there are practical considerations due to cost and latency that can impact the answers that will be returned by any crowdsourced query processor.

There are also a host of exciting implementation challenges. Cost-based optimization for the crowd involves many new parameters and considerations. Time-of-day, pricing, worker fatigue, task user-interface design, etc. all impact performance and quality. Adaptive optimization techniques will clearly be needed. Caching and managing crowdsourced answers, if done properly, can greatly improve performance as well. Answer quality assessment and improvement will require the development of new techniques and operators.

The combination of human input with high-powered database processing not only extends the range of existing database systems, but also enables completely new applications and capabilities. For this reason, we expect this to be a fruitful area of research and development for many years.

Acknowledgements

This work was supported in part by AMPLab founding sponsors Google and SAP, and AMPLab sponsors Amazon Web Services, Cloudera, Huawei, IBM, Intel, Microsoft, NEC, NetApp, and VMWare.

10. REFERENCES

[1] Pictures of the Golden Gate Bridge retrieved from Flickr by akaporn, Dawn Endico, devinleedrew, di_the_huntress, Geoff Livingston, kevincole, Marc_Smith, and superstrikertwo under the Creative Commons Attribution 2.0 Generic license.

[2] Amazon. AWS Case Study: Smartsheet, 2006.

[3] Amazon Mechanical Turk. http://www.mturk.com, 2010.

[4] S. Amer-Yahia et al. Crowds, Clouds, and Algorithms: Exploring the Human Side of "Big Data" Applications. In *SIGMOD*, 2010.

[5] M. Armbrust et al. PIQL: A Performance Insightful Query Language. In *SIGMOD*, 2010.

[6] M. S. Bernstein et al. Soylent: A Word Processor with a Crowd Inside. In *ACM SUIST*, 2010.

[7] M. J. Carey and D. Kossmann. On saying "Enough already!" in SQL. *SIGMOD Rec.*, 26(2):219–230, 1997.

[8] S. S. Chawathe et al. The TSIMMIS Project: Integration of Heterogeneous Information Sources. In *IPSJ*, 1994.

[9] K. Chen et al. USHER: Improving Data Quality with Dynamic Forms. In *ICDE*, pages 321–332, 2010.

[10] A. Doan, R. Ramakrishnan, and A. Halevy. Crowdsourcing Systems on the World-Wide Web. *CACM*, 54:86–96, Apr. 2011.

[11] L. M. Haas et al. Optimizing Queries Across Diverse Data Sources. In *VLDB*, 1997.

[12] J. M. Hellerstein et al. Adaptive Query Processing: Technology in Evolution. *IEEE Data Eng. Bull.*, 2000.

[13] J. M. Hellerstein and J. F. Naughton. Query Execution Techniques for Caching Expensive Methods. In *SIGMOD*, pages 423–434, 1996.

[14] E. Huang et al. Toward Automatic Task Design: A Progress Report. In *HCOMP*, 2010.

[15] P. G. Ipeirotis. Analyzing the Amazon Mechanical Turk Marketplace. http://hdl.handle.net/2451/29801, 2010.

[16] P. G. Ipeirotis. Mechanical Turk, Low Wages, and the Market for Lemons. http://behind-the-enemy-lines.blogspot.com/2010/07/mechanical-turk-low-wages-and-market.html, 2010.

[17] A. G. Kleppe, J. Warmer, and W. Bast. *MDA Explained: The Model Driven Architecture: Practice and Promise*. Addison-Wesley, 2003.

[18] G. Little. How many turkers are there? http://groups.csail.mit.edu/uid/deneme/?p=502, 2009.

[19] G. Little et al. TurKit: Tools for Iterative Tasks on Mechanical Turk. In *HCOMP*, 2009.

[20] A. Marcus et al. Crowdsourced Databases: Query Processing with People. In *CIDR*, 2011.

[21] Microsoft. Table Column Properties (SQL Server), 2008.

[22] A. Parameswaran et al. Human-Assisted Graph Search: It's Okay to Ask Questions. In *VLDB*, 2011.

[23] A. Parameswaran and N. Polyzotis. Answering Queries using Humans, Algorithms and Databases. In *CIDR*, 2011.

[24] J. Ross et al. Who are the Crowdworkers? Shifting Demographics in Mechanical Turk. In *CHI EA*, 2010.

[25] D. Schall, S. Dustdar, and M. B. Blake. Programming Human and Software-Based Web Services. *Computer*, 43(7):82–85, 2010.

[26] Turker Nation. http://www.turkernation.com/, 2010.

[27] Turkopticon. http://turkopticon.differenceengines.com/, 2010.

[28] T. Yan, V. Kumar, and D. Ganesan. CrowdSearch: Exploiting Crowds for Accurate Real-time. Image Search on Mobile Phones. In *MobiSys*, 2010.

Skyline Query Processing over Joins

Akrivi Vlachou[1], Christos Doulkeridis[1], Neoklis Polyzotis[2]
[1]Norwegian University of Science and Technology (NTNU), Trondheim, Norway
[2]UC Santa Cruz, California, USA
{vlachou,cdoulk}@idi.ntnu.no, alkis@cs.ucsc.edu

ABSTRACT

This paper addresses the problem of efficiently computing the skyline set of a relational join. Existing techniques either require to access all tuples of the input relations or demand specialized multi-dimensional access methods to generate the skyline join result. To avoid these inefficiencies, we introduce the novel *SFSJ* algorithm that fuses the identification of skyline tuples with the computation of the join. *SFSJ* is able to compute the correct skyline set by accessing only a subset of the input tuples, i.e., it has the property of early termination. *SFSJ* employs standard access methods for reading the input tuples and is readily implementable in an existing database system. Moreover, it can be used in pipelined execution plans, as it generates the skyline tuples progressively. Additionally, we formally analyze the performance of *SFSJ* and propose a novel strategy for accessing the input tuples that is proven to be optimal for *SFSJ*. Finally, we present an extensive experimental study that validates the effectiveness of *SFSJ* and demonstrates its advantages over existing techniques.

Categories and Subject Descriptors

H.2.4 [**Database Management**]: Systems—*Query processing*

General Terms

Algorithms, Experimentation, Performance

Keywords

Skyline query, join operator

1. INTRODUCTION

In this paper, we propose a novel algorithm for efficiently computing the skyline set of a join $R_1 \bowtie R_2$ without generating all the join tuples and without accessing all tuples of R_1 and R_2. Our solution enables the progressive computation of the skyline join on large data sets or data derived from complex queries, and hence yields a very powerful tool for applications such as decision-making and complex data analysis (the typical use-cases for the skyline operator).

SIGMOD'11, June 12–16, 2011, Athens, Greece.

Hotels

HID	HName	Price	Rating	Location
h_1	Bridge Hotel	100	2	A
h_2	Tower Hotel	150	5	B
h_3	Hilton	200	10	A
h_4	Comfort Inn	400	8	A
h_5	Atlantis	300	3	C
h_6	Holiday Inn	350	7	B

Restaurants

RID	RName	Distance	Quality	Location
r_1	Egons	100	1	B
r_2	AB Bistro	250	3	C
r_3	Brewery	500	4	A
r_4	Joeys Bar	400	2	B
r_5	Cozy Lounge	200	1	C
r_6	DAlferno	500	1	A

SKYLINE(Hotels $\bowtie$ Restaurants)

HID	RID	HName	RName	Location	Price	Rating	Distance	Quality
h_1	r_3	Bridge Hotel	Brewery	A	100	2	500	4
h_2	r_1	Tower Hotel	Egons	B	150	5	100	1
h_3	r_3	Hilton	Brewery	A	200	10	500	4
h_2	r_4	Tower Hotel	Joeys Bar	B	150	5	400	2
h_5	r_2	Atlantis	AB Bistro	C	300	3	250	3
h_6	r_1	Holiday Inn	Egons	B	350	7	100	1
h_6	r_4	Holiday Inn	Joeys Bar	B	350	7	400	2

Figure 1: Example of skyline join.

Figure 1 illustrates an example of computing the skyline over the result of a join. Suppose that the database contains relations *Hotels* and *Restaurants* that store information about a specific city. A tourist may be interested in discovering the best combinations of hotels and restaurants in the same "Location", by minimizing the hotel's "Price", maximizing the hotel's "Rating", maximizing the restaurant's "Quality" and minimizing its "Distance" from a subway station. A sample SQL query that retrieves this information is the following[1]:

SELECT H.HID, R.RID, H.Hname, R.Rname, H.Location,
H.Price, H.Rating, R.Distance, R.Quality
FROM *Hotels* H,*Restaurants* R
WHERE H.Location = R.Location
SKYLINE OF H.Price MIN, H.Rating MAX,
R.Distance MIN, R.Quality MAX

The result of the query is depicted in Figure 1. As shown, the use of the skyline operator allows the retrieval of the most "important" join tuples according to the specified attributes.

The naive method of computing all join tuples first and then computing the skyline set leads to redundant processing, since the join is computed in its entirety (typically, an expensive operation) whereas the skyline set contains potentially only few tuples. Ideally, we would like to process and join only a subset of the input tuples in order to compute the skyline set of the join. This approach improves dramatically the performance of the naive method and makes the computation feasible in the context of large data sets. Unfortunately, it is non-trivial to decide which input tuples can be omitted without compromising the correctness of the computed skyline set. The reason is that the skyline set of the join depends both on the domination relationships in each input relation

[1]We assume that SQL is extended with a SKYLINE OF operator.

(e.g., which hotels have the best trade-off in rating and price, and which restaurants have the best trade-off in distance and quality), and on the join correlations across the two input relations (e.g., the existence of "good" hotels and restaurants in the same location). In general, the skyline set of the join is not necessarily identical to the join of the skyline sets of the input relations.

The majority of previous studies on skyline computation have focused on the case of a single relation [2, 4, 13]. The proposed techniques require the entire join result to be computed, and thus are prohibitively expensive as we explained earlier. Two recent studies have examined specifically the problem of computing the skyline over a join [7, 10]. However, we argue (and verify our claim experimentally) that these approaches are not effective. More specifically, the technique in [7] does not support early termination and hence it will always access all input tuples. The second technique, termed ProgXe [10], may terminate early under certain conditions, but it requires a specialized multi-dimensional access method whose parameters need to be tuned carefully. This requirement increases the overhead of integrating ProgXe in an existing system, and also precludes its usage in pipelined query plans where the inputs are generated by other physical operators. Moreover, ProgXe does not carry any theoretical guarantees on how early it can terminate, which may lead to unpredictable performance on certain inputs. This lack of robustness is particularly problematic in the context of ad-hoc data analysis, where good performance is critical.

Our Contributions. Motivated by the shortcomings of existing methods, we develop a novel algorithm, termed $SFSJ$, for computing the skyline set of a join $R_1 \bowtie R_2$. $SFSJ$ is the first skyline join algorithm that combines several salient properties: (a) it accesses only a subset of each input relation and computes the skyline set without generating all the join results, (b) it can be readily implemented in existing database systems, as it relies on common infrastructure and does not require any complicated data structures, (c) it generates the skyline progressively, which facilitates its incorporation in pipelined query execution plans, and (d) it carries optimality and instance-optimality guarantees for its performance, thus ensuring that it works robustly across a variety of inputs. More concretely, the technical contributions of our work can be summarized as follows:

- We develop a novel early-termination condition (Section 4) that allows an algorithm to compute the correct skyline join set after reading only a subset of the input tuples. The condition is applied on a simple model of sorted input access, which is readily supported in existing systems using either B-trees over base tables or a sort operator over complex expressions.
- We introduce the $SFSJ$ algorithm (Section 5) for computing the skyline over a join. $SFSJ$ alternates between its inputs and generates the skyline tuples progressively as it computes the join results. It relies on the early-termination condition in order to determine when it has accessed enough tuples to generate the complete skyline set.
- We formally analyze the performance of $SFSJ$ (Section 6) under different strategies that define the order in which the input relations are accessed. We introduce a new adaptive strategy that prioritizes access to the input relations and prove that it is optimal for $SFSJ$, i.e., it minimizes the total number of accessed tuples. Moreover, we provide a theoretical analysis that relies on techniques previously applied on the rank join problem [5, 11]. Specifically, we show that $SFSJ$ is instance-optimal with a ratio of two within all deterministic algorithms and the class of inputs with bounded repetitions. To the best of our knowledge, ours is the first work to provide strong optimality results for the specific problem.
- We conduct a detailed experimental study to evaluate the performance of $SFSJ$ (Section 7). Our results with synthetic and real-life data sets demonstrate that $SFSJ$ computes the skyline join result efficiently after accessing only a subset of the input tuples. $SFSJ$ outperforms two competitor techniques by a significant margin, thus validating its theoretical advantages over existing approaches.

2. RELATED WORK

Single-Relation Skyline. Previous studies have introduced a host of different techniques for computing the skyline of a single relation [1–4, 13]. Even though it is conceptually possible to apply these techniques on the results of a join operator, this solution is not likely to perform well in practice. Techniques that require an index over the input relation (e.g.,[13]) will need the join results to be computed in full and indexed before computing the skyline. Techniques that do not require an index (e.g.,[1, 2]) can be pipelined with the join operator, but they are decoupled from the semantics of the join and essentially examine the complete join stream before terminating. (We show this behavior analytically in Section 4.) In contrast, $SFSJ$ fuses the computation of the join and the skyline in order to terminate early, i.e., $SFSJ$ outputs the correct skyline without computing the full join or reading all the input tuples. Providing a condition for early termination in this setting is a key technical contribution of our work.

Join Skyline. Jin et al. [6] propose a multi-relational skyline operator that combines a sort-merge join algorithm with skyline processing. The operator involves a non-trivial processing cost, as it computes the skyline and group skyline tuples for all join values for each relation, then eliminates dominated tuples for each join value, and finally sorts the relations such that skyline tuples precede group skyline tuples. Clearly, the operator needs to access both relations multiple times to produce the correct result. Sun et al. [12] propose a distributed adaptation of SaLSa [1, 2] to compute the join skyline in a distributed setting. However, as will be shown in Section 4, this approach cannot lead to early termination. Moreover, the algorithms in [12] share the same restrictions with the approach proposed in [6]. In a follow-up study of [6], two non-blocking algorithms for skyline join are proposed [7]. The main idea is to interleave the join with the skyline computation, employing the nested-loop and sort-merge join algorithms. However, support for early termination is not provided. In contrast, our algorithm returns the correct result without accessing all input tuples.

In [10], the ProgXe framework is introduced for skyline join computation that supports progressive result generation. ProgXe partitions the input relations by using a multidimensional grid access method. This limits the framework to joins over base tables, whereas in practice the join may be also computed over complex relational expressions. Even in the case of base tables, the use of a multidimensional structure makes the performance of ProgXe sensitive to the number of dimensions, but most importantly to the resolution of the grid. ProgXe does not provide any method for optimizing its performance for two given relations (by setting the number of grid partitions to the most appropriate values), thus exhaustive testing is required. Further, as demonstrated in our experimental study, ProgXe does not terminate before exhausting both input relations in all common data distributions tested. Finally, the particular access method is not part of conventional database systems and hence requires an additional implementation effort. The techniques that we develop rely simply on sorted access, which is implementable with existing relational operators, and do not require tuning. Moreover, we are able to prove strong optimality properties about the early termination of our algorithms.

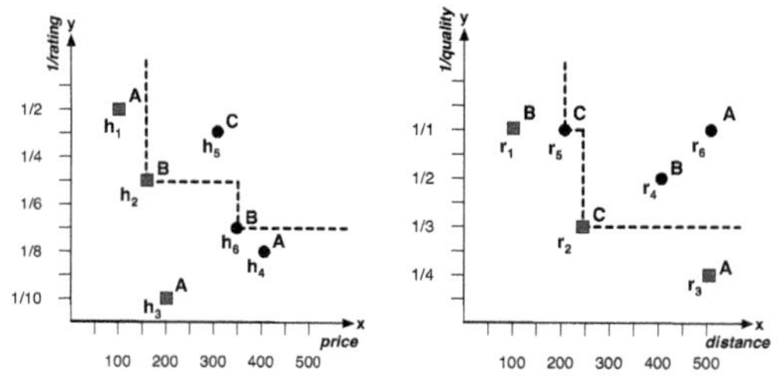

(a) *Hotels* relation (b) *Restaurants* relation

Figure 2: Relations *Hotels* and *Restaurants* from Figure 1.

Other works have also considered the issue of skyline join computation. The first work that implicitly deals with skyline join is from Koudas et al. [8]. Nevertheless, the proposed algorithms either do not support early termination or require multiple indexes over each input relation. In [9], a framework is proposed for preference evaluation inside the query processor, however their approach for skyline joins relies on [6]. Computing the skyline over a cartesian product of relations has been studied in [14], but the main focus is on identifying tuples of the individual relations that produce skyline join results, and not on the efficient computation of the skyline join.

3. PRELIMINARIES

Let R denote a relation and $\mathcal{B}$ denote a set of numerical attributes in the schema of R. Let τ and τ' represent tuples in R. We say that tuple τ' is *dominated by* τ with respect to $\mathcal{B}$, denoted as $\tau \prec_{\mathcal{B}} \tau'$, if and only if $\pi_{\mathcal{B}}(\tau') \neq \pi_{\mathcal{B}}(\tau)$ and $\pi_{\beta}(\tau') \geq \pi_{\beta}(\tau)$ for all $\beta \in \mathcal{B}$. Accordingly, we define the *skyline set* of R with respect to $\mathcal{B}$, denoted $SKY_{\mathcal{B}}(R)$, as the minimal subset of R that dominates every other tuple in R, that is, $\forall \tau' \in (R - SKY_{\mathcal{B}}(R))\ \exists \tau \in SKY_{\mathcal{B}}(R)$ such that $(\tau \prec_{\mathcal{B}} \tau')$. We can extend our definitions based on maximizing values or a hybrid of the two models. We now introduce the *skyline join problem* that we address in this paper.

DEFINITION 1. *(Skyline Join Problem) An instance I of the Skyline Join Problem is a tuple $(R_1 \bowtie_{\text{eq}} R_2, \mathcal{B}_1, \mathcal{B}_2)$, where $R_1 \bowtie_{\text{eq}} R_2$ is an equi-join expression and $\mathcal{B}_i$ is a set of numerical attributes from R_i, $i = 1, 2$. The solution to an instance I is the set $SKY_{\mathcal{B}_1 \cup \mathcal{B}_2}(R_1 \bowtie_{\text{eq}} R_2)$.*

As an example, the SQL query in Section 1 specifies an instance of the skyline join problem over relations Hotels and Restaurants and attribute-sets $\mathcal{B}_1 = \{\text{Price}, \text{Rating}\}$ and $\mathcal{B}_2 = \{\text{Distance}, \text{Quality}\}$ respectively.

The problem definition does not place any constraints on relations R_1 and R_2. Indeed, they may result from complex relational expressions or simply be base tables. To facilitate exposition, we make two simplifying assumptions that are not crucial for our techniques. First, we assume that the join expression is a natural join on a single common attribute α, and henceforth write $R_1 \bowtie R_2$. We use $\tau_i.\alpha$ to denote the value of the join attribute for a tuple $\tau_i \in R_i$, $i = 1, 2$. Second, we assume that the domain of any attribute in $\mathcal{B}_1 \cup \mathcal{B}_2$ is the interval $[0, 1]$, and use the term skyline or scoring attribute to refer to any $\beta \in \mathcal{B}_i$. We also simplify our notation by omitting the attribute-set from the skyline notation. Hence, for an instance $I = (R_1, R_2, \mathcal{B}_1, \mathcal{B}_2)$, the skyline set $SKY(R_1 \bowtie R_2)$ is taken with respect to $\mathcal{B}_1 \cup \mathcal{B}_2$. Similarly, the skyline set $SKY(R_i)$ is taken with respect to $\mathcal{B}_i$. We extend this simplification to the notation for tuple dominance.

On a final note, we introduce the auxiliary concept of *group skyline* which is used in the development of our techniques.

DEFINITION 2. *(Group Skyline) Given an instance I of the skyline join problem, the group skyline of R_i with respect to value x of the joining attribute is defined as $SKY(R_i, x) = SKY(\sigma_{\alpha=x}(R_i))$.*

A consequence of this definition is that if a tuple $\tau_i \in R_i$ appears in $SKY(R_i)$ then it also appears in $SKY(R_i, x)$ for $x = \tau_i.\alpha$. For example, Figure 2(a) depicts the tuples of relation Hotels (see Figure 1) with respect to the set $\mathcal{B} = \{\text{Price}, \text{Rating}\}$. Each tuple is mapped to a point in the 2-dimensional space defined by the value of the price and the rating of the hotel. The point is annotated with the tuple id and the corresponding value of the join attribute. Skyline tuples are depicted with squares. We also use a dashed line to connect the group skyline tuples for join value B. Notice that the skyline tuple h_2 is also a group skyline tuple for B. Figure 2(b) shows a similar visualization for relation Restaurants. Group skylines enable the formulation of a very useful property.

PROPERTY 1. *Let $\tau \equiv \tau_1 \bowtie \tau_2$ be a tuple in $R_1 \bowtie R_2$. It holds that $\tau \notin SKY(R_1 \bowtie R_2)$ if $\exists i : \tau_i \notin SKY(R_i, \tau_i.\alpha)$*

Essentially, tuples $\tau_i \in R_i$ that are not group skyline tuples cannot contribute to the join skyline. The reason is that the produced join tuples are guaranteed to be dominated. Returning to the example of Figure 2(a), h_4 cannot produce a skyline join result, since $h_3 \prec h_4$ and $h_3 \in SKY(\textit{Hotels}, A)$, and hence any join result $h_4 \bowtie r$ (e.g., for $r = r_6$) will be dominated by the result $h_3 \bowtie r$. Furthermore, the joined tuple that consists of a skyline tuple (e.g., r_1) joined with a group skyline tuple (e.g., h_6) is always a skyline join result. Notice that we cannot ascertain whether the combination of group skyline tuples produces skyline join results beforehand.

4. EARLY TERMINATION

Given an instance I of the skyline join problem, it is always possible to compute the set $SKY(R_1 \bowtie R_2)$ by first generating all tuples of $R_1 \bowtie R_2$ and then applying a conventional single-relation skyline algorithm [3, 4]. Obviously, this method leads to redundant processing, and hence bad performance, since it requires accessing all tuples of both relations and generate all join results, in order to return the potentially few skyline tuples.

In contrast, the high-level idea of our approach is to compute the $SKY(R_1 \bowtie R_2)$ by *accessing only a prefix of R_1 and R_2*, assuming that their tuples are accessed in a sorted order defined by the skyline attributes. We refer to this feature of a skyline join algorithm as *early termination* to differentiate from algorithms that need to access all tuples of both relations R_i to compute the skyline join result. Early termination is desirable because it results in savings in I/O (fewer tuples are accessed) and computation (fewer join results are generated and fewer dominance tests are required), and can thus improve substantially on the performance of techniques that exhaust their inputs.

More specifically, we assume that each relation R_i is accessed one tuple at a time, in an ascending order according to the following function:

$$fmin(\tau_i) = \min_{\beta \in \mathcal{B}_i} \{\pi_\beta(\tau_i)\}, \tag{1}$$

for $i = 1, 2$. Figure 3 shows an illustration of this sorted access model. Essentially, the tuples are organized in "bands" of increasing *fmin* value. Hence, an algorithm will need to exhaust all the tuples in the current band before observing an increase in the *fmin* value. Moreover, the corner point of each band dominates all the tuples in higher bands. This observation plays a central role in the development of our techniques.

A key advantage of this access model is that it can be implemented easily in an existing system, using common infrastructure

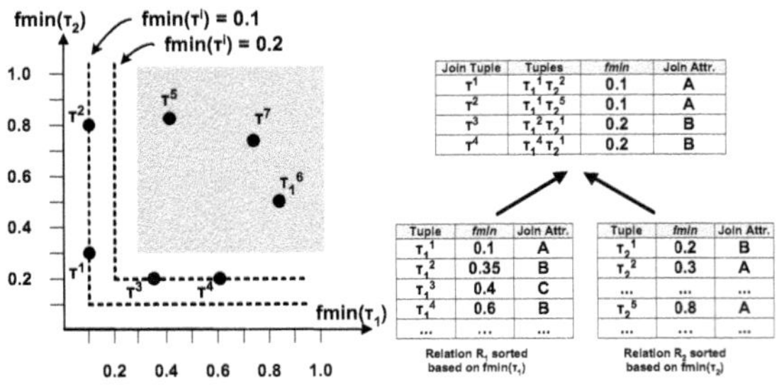

Figure 3: Example of SaLSa on relation $R_1 \bowtie R_2$.

such as secondary B-tree indexes. We discuss the details at the end of the section, but for the time being we note that the overhead is much smaller compared to the specialized access methods required by other techniques [10].

In this section, we formalize a condition that allows an algorithm to check whether $SKY(R_1 \bowtie R_2) = SKY(S_1 \bowtie S_2)$, where S_i denotes a prefix of R_i according to the sorted order. Clearly, this is the crucial prerequisite in order to support early termination. The condition that we introduce is novel in that it takes into account the semantics of both the join and the skyline operator, and thus differs from previous works that consider solely the skyline operator.

4.1 Inadequacy of Existing Techniques

Before presenting the details of the new early-termination condition, we examine if the algorithms that employ sorted access to solve the single-relation skyline problem [1, 2, 13] can be adapted to the skyline join problem. Our analysis yields a negative answer: existing algorithms employ a stopping condition that is oblivious to the semantics of the join operator, and hence fails to effectively support early termination.

The analysis that we present is based on the state-of-the-art SaLSa algorithm of Bartolini et al. [1, 2]. SaLSa receives as input a single stream of tuples that are sorted based on $fmin$, and outputs the skyline set of the input tuples. The algorithm accesses its input one-tuple-at-a-time, and maintains the current skyline set and an associated threshold x. The current skyline set is returned as the output once the next input tuple has an $fmin$ value that is not smaller than x.

In the context of the skyline join problem, we must couple SaLSa with a join algorithm, say A, that reads R_1 and R_2 in sorted order of $fmin$ and progressively computes $R_1 \bowtie R_2$ also in sorted order of $fmin$. For instance, A can be a rank join algorithm that employs $fmin$ as the scoring function. Algorithm A returns the next join tuple as requested by SaLSa, and terminates when SaLSa satisfies the aforementioned termination condition.

Unfortunately, the previous scheme is not effective. We prove that any correct algorithm A will have to exhaust at least R_1 or R_2 if $SKY(R_1 \bowtie R_2)$ is a *non-trivial* skyline set. Formally speaking, a trivial skyline set satisfies the following property: $\tau.\beta = \rho.\beta$ for all $\beta \in \mathcal{B}_1 \cup \mathcal{B}_2$ and for all τ and ρ in $SKY(R_1 \bowtie R_2)$. Essentially, all the skyline join tuples are identical and correspond to a single point that dominates every other join tuple. In practice we expect to see non-trivial skylines, in which case A will have to exhaust at least one input.

THEOREM 1. *Let A be a correct deterministic algorithm that computes $R_1 \bowtie R_2$ in ascending order of $fmin$ (using some arbitrary tie breaking rule), assuming that R_1 and R_2 are also accessed in sorted order of $fmin$. Suppose that SaLSa reads the output of A and let τ^{last} be the last tuple that SaLSa reads before it returns the skyline $SKY(R_1 \bowtie R_2)$. If $SKY(R_1 \bowtie R_2)$ is non-trivial, then A has to exhaust at least one of its inputs in order to generate the results up to τ^{last}.*

PROOF. Let $\tau^{\text{first}} \equiv \tau_1 \bowtie \tau_2$ be the first tuple accessed by SaLSa. Clearly, $fmin(\tau^{\text{first}}) \leq fmin(\tau^{\text{last}})$. Without loss of generality, assume that $fmin(\tau) = fmin(\tau_1)$. The proof is symmetric if $fmin(\tau) = fmin(\tau_2)$.

We prove first an auxiliary result, namely that $fmin(\tau^{\text{first}}) < fmin(\tau^{\text{last}})$. Suppose that this is false, i.e., $fmin(\tau^{\text{first}}) = fmin(\tau^{\text{last}})$. Since SaLSa terminates after reading τ^{last}, it holds that $fmin(\tau^{\text{last}}) \geq x$, where x is the threshold maintained by SaLSa. By definition, $x = \max\{\rho.\beta | \beta \in \mathcal{B}_1 \cup \mathcal{B}_2\}$, where ρ is the tuple in the current skyline set that has the minimum maximum coordinate, i.e., $\rho = \arg\min\{\max\{\tau.\beta | \beta \in \mathcal{B}_1 \cup \mathcal{B}_2\} | \tau \text{ is a skyline tuple}\}$. From our hypothesis, it holds that $x = \max\{\rho.\beta | \beta \in \mathcal{B}_1 \cup \mathcal{B}_2\} \leq fmin(\tau^{\text{first}})$, and since $x \geq fmin(\rho) \geq fmin(\tau^{\text{first}})$, it follows that $x = \max\{\rho.\beta | \beta \in \mathcal{B}_1 \cup \mathcal{B}_2\} = fmin(\tau^{\text{first}}) = fmin(\rho)$. This means that ρ corresponds to the corner-point $(fmin(\tau^{\text{first}}), \ldots, fmin(\tau^{\text{first}}))$ and hence it dominates every other tuple in $R_1 \bowtie R_2$. This is a contradiction, as we assumed that $SKY(R_1 \bowtie R_2)$ is non-trivial. Hence, it must be that $fmin(\tau^{\text{first}}) < fmin(\tau^{\text{last}})$.

We proceed to show that A will exhaust R_2. Suppose otherwise. Since $fmin(\tau^{\text{last}}) > fmin(\tau^{\text{first}})$, this means that A has generated all the join results whose $fmin$ value is equal to $fmin(\tau^{\text{first}})$ without having accessed the last tuple of R_2. It is straightforward to show that A commits a mistake if that last tuple joins with τ_1, which contradicts our assumption that A is a correct algorithm. □

Figure 3 shows an example of applying SaLSa for computing the skyline join set[2]. The x-axis and y-axis represent the $fmin(\tau_i)$ values with respect to R_1 and R_2 respectively. R_i is sorted based on $fmin(\tau_i)$, $i = 1, 2$, but the join tuples are accessed by SaLSa with respect to $fmin(\tau)$. Henceforth, we use the superscript of a tuple to denote its rank in the corresponding sorted relation. SaLSa would first process tuple τ^1 with $fmin(\tau^1) = 0.1$ and set a threshold $x = \max_{\beta \in \mathcal{B}_1 \cup \mathcal{B}_2}\{\pi_\beta(\tau^1)\} = 0.3$. Based on the termination condition of SaLSa, tuples τ^i are accessed until $fmin(\tau^i) \geq x$. Thus, in Figure 3, all tuples enclosed in the shadowed rectangle are pruned. On the other hand, all join tuples that fall on a dashed line have the same $fmin$ value. For example, tuples τ^1 and τ^2 have the same $fmin$ value, and they are produced by the first tuple τ_1^1 of R_1 and tuples τ_2^2 and τ_2^5 of R_2. In general, the first tuple of R_1 can be combined with the last tuple of R_2, as long as they have the same join value and the generated join tuple will have the minimum $fmin$ score. Thus, SaLSa needs to access all tuples of R_2 in order to ensure that no other tuple τ_2^i can be joined with τ_1^1.

The behavior of SaLSa is clearly problematic. Performance is impacted negatively, particularly if the exhausted input corresponds to a large relation. Moreover, the trigger for this bad performance is a high-level property (non-trivial skyline sets) that is quite likely to appear in practice. The proof reveals that the problem lies with the design of SaLSa's termination condition, which is tailored to the single-relation problem and is thus oblivious of the underlying join operation. In contrast, we develop an early termination condition that directly takes into account the semantics of the join operation, and hence avoids the pitfalls of SaLSa's termination condition.

4.2 Condition for Early Termination

We develop a condition that asserts the following: $SKY(R_1 \bowtie R_2)$ is equal to $SKY(S_1 \bowtie S_2)$, where each S_i denotes a prefix of R_i according to the sorted access model. We first provide a

[2]Recall that the subscript of a tuple denotes the relation the tuple belongs to, whereas the absence of subscript denotes a join tuple.

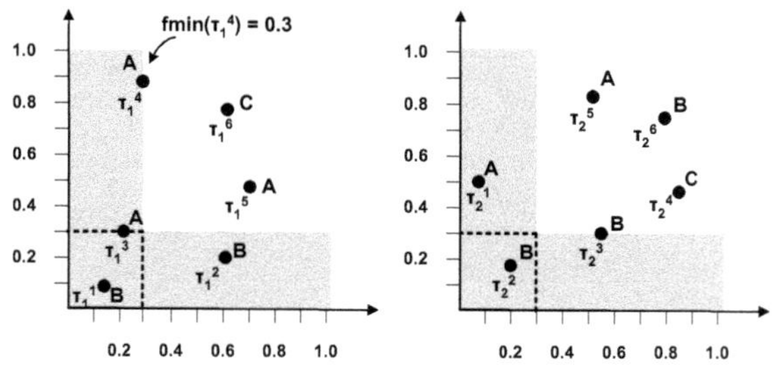

(a) Relation R_1 (b) Relation R_2

Figure 4: Example relations R_1 and R_2.

precise definition of the prefix that is considered in the termination condition.

DEFINITION 3. *(Closed Prefix of Relation R_i) Let S_i be a non-empty prefix of relation R_i, and define $t(S_i) = \max\{fmin(\rho_i) \mid \rho_i \in S_i\}$. S_i is called a closed prefix of R_i iff $fmin(\tau_i) > t(S_i)$ for all $\tau_i \in R_i - S_i$.*

Essentially, the tuples in $R_i - S_i$ correspond to bands with strictly higher *fmin* values than all tuples in the closed prefix S_i. An example is shown in Figure 4 for two sample relations R_1 and R_2. We assume that each relation has two skyline attributes. We can assert that $S_1 = \{\tau_1^1, \tau_1^2, \tau_1^3, \tau_1^4\}$ forms a closed prefix for R_1 according to the previous definition, since every other tuple in R_1 has a *fmin* value that is *higher than* $t(S_1) = \max\{fmin(\tau_1^1), fmin(\tau_1^2), fmin(\tau_1^3), fmin(\tau_1^4)\}$. A similar observation can be made for $S_2 = \{\tau_2^1, \tau_2^2, \tau_2^3\}$.

The significance of the closed prefix S_i is that it defines a point, namely the corner of the last accessed band, that dominates all tuples in $R_i - S_i$. Indeed, the point $(t(S_i), t(S_i), \ldots, t(S_i))$ dominates all tuples in $R_i - S_i$. In turn, any tuple that dominates this corner also dominates $R_i - S_i$. We capture this property through the *minimum anti-dominance region* $MAD(S_i)$.

DEFINITION 4. *(Minimum Anti-Dominance Region) The minimum anti-dominance region of a closed prefix S_i is defined as $MAD(S_i) = \{\rho_i \mid \rho_i \in S_i \wedge \rho_i.\beta \leq t(S_i) \forall \beta \in \mathcal{B}_i\}$.*

The dashed rectangles in Figure 4 depict $MAD(S_i)$, assuming that S_i contains the tuples in the corresponding shaded region.

Assuming that $MAD(S_i) \neq \emptyset$, none of the tuples in $R_i - S_i$ can appear in $SKY(R_i)$, and hence we can assert that $SKY(R_i) = SKY(S_i)$. This can be verified on the example of Figure 4. Nevertheless, this condition is not sufficient for stopping accessing tuples of R_i, because group skyline tuples (which may not appear in $SKY(R_i)$) may also contribute to $SKY(R_1 \bowtie R_2)$ (see the properties of the skyline join discussed in Section 3). A correct alternative would be to stop accessing R_i only if S_i contains all the group skyline tuples. However, this approach is not viable in practice, because the number of distinct join values may not be known. In this case, all the tuples in R_i have to be accessed in order to ensure that no other group skyline tuple exists. Moreover, the cost of computing all group skyline tuples can be prohibitively high (if the domain of join values is of high cardinality), while some group skyline tuples may not contribute to the skyline join result at all (for example, this is case for join value C in Figure 4). Therefore, the main challenge is to find an early-termination condition that does not require computing the group skyline sets for all join values. We achieve this goal by taking advantage of the properties of $MAD(S_i)$, that lead to the formulation of a sufficient condition for when a tuple in $R_i - S_i$ can generate a skyline join result.

LEMMA 1. *If $MAD(S_j) \neq \emptyset$ and $\pi_\alpha(SKY(S_j)) - \pi_\alpha(MAD(S_i)) = \emptyset$ for $i \neq j$ then there exists no tuple in $R_i - S_i$ that can generate a skyline join result, i.e., $SKY(R_i \bowtie R_j) \cap ((R_i - S_i) \bowtie R_j) = \emptyset$.*

PROOF. By contradiction. Suppose that there exists a $\tau \equiv \tau_i \bowtie \tau_j$ that belongs to $SKY(R_i \bowtie R_j) \cap ((R_i - S_i) \bowtie R_j)$.

The fact that $MAD(S_j) \neq \emptyset$ implies that $SKY(S_j) = SKY(R_j)$. It follows that $MAD(S_i) \neq \emptyset$, because $SKY(S_j) \neq \emptyset$ and otherwise the condition would not be true. We consider two cases for τ_i.

Case 1: $\tau_i.\alpha \in \pi_\alpha(MAD(S_i))$. It follows that there exists $\rho_i \in MAD(S_i)$ such that $\tau_i.\alpha = \rho_i.\alpha$. Clearly, $\rho_i \bowtie \tau_j$ is a valid join result, and it also holds that that $\rho_i \prec \tau_i$ due to the dominance property of $MAD(S_i)$. Hence, $\rho_i \bowtie \tau_j \prec \tau_i \bowtie \tau_j$.

Case 2: $\tau_i.\alpha \notin \pi_\alpha(MAD(S_i))$. Since $\tau_j.\alpha = \tau_i.\alpha$ and $\pi_\alpha(SKY(S_j)) \subseteq \pi_\alpha(MAD(S_i))$, it follows that $\tau_j.\alpha \notin \pi_\alpha(SKY(S_j))$ and hence $\tau_j \notin SKY(S_j)$. Given that $SKY(S_j) = SKY(R_j)$, there exists $\tau_j' \in SKY(S_j)$ such that $\tau_j' \prec \tau_j$. The condition ensures that $MAD(S_i)$ contains a tuple τ_i' such that $\tau_i'.\alpha = \tau_j'.\alpha$. Since $\tau_i' \prec \tau_i$ (by the dominance property of $MAD(S_i)$), it holds that $\tau_i' \bowtie \tau_j' \prec \tau_i \bowtie \tau_j$.

In both cases, we identify a join tuple that dominates $\tau_i \bowtie \tau_j$, which contradicts our assumption that $\tau_i \bowtie \tau_j \in SKY(R_i \bowtie R_j)$. □

Lemma 1 states that if for every skyline tuple in $SKY(S_1)$ ($j = 1$) there exists a tuple in $MAD(S_2)$ ($i = 2$) with same join value, then the tuples in $R_2 - S_2$ do not contribute to the skyline join result. We illustrate the basic intuition with a simple example.

Assume two group skyline tuples $\rho_1 \in SKY(R_1, \beta)$, $\rho_2 \in SKY(R_2, \beta)$ of R_1 and R_2 respectively, such that $\rho_2 \in R_2 - S_2$. Let us first assume that ρ_1 is also a skyline tuple ($\rho_1 \in SKY(R_1)$). Since $MAD(S_1) \neq \emptyset$, it holds that $\rho_1 \in SKY(S_1)$ and that there exists a tuple $\tau_2 \in MAD(S_2)$ such that $\rho_1.\alpha = \tau_2.\alpha = \beta$. This leads to a contradiction, since τ_2 dominates ρ_2 and therefore ρ_2 is not a group skyline tuple and does not contribute to the skyline join result. On the other hand, if $\rho_1 \notin SKY(R_1)$, then there exists a tuple $\tau_1 \in SKY(S_1) = SKY(R_1)$ such that τ_1 dominates ρ_1. Based on the condition of Lemma 1, there exists also a tuple $\tau_2 \in MAD(S_2)$ such that $\tau_1.\alpha = \tau_2.\alpha = \beta$. Furthermore, τ_2 dominates ρ_2, since it dominates all tuples in $R_2 - S_2$. We can thus verify that $\tau_1 \bowtie \tau_2 \prec \rho_1 \bowtie \rho_2$, since $\tau_1 \prec \rho_1$ and $\tau_2 \prec \rho_2$. Hence, any tuple in $R_2 - S_2$ is not relevant for the computation of $SKY(R_1 \bowtie R_2)$, and this is independent of whether $R_2 - S_2$ contains additional group skyline tuples $SKY(R_2, \beta)$.

Overall, the join values that appear in $MAD(S_i)$ and $SKY(S_i)$ ($i = 1, 2$) are sufficient for deciding whether it holds that $SKY(S_1 \bowtie S_2) = SKY(R_1 \bowtie R_2)$. Building on Lemma 1, it is straightforward to define our early-termination condition.

THEOREM 2. *(Early Termination Condition) It holds that $SKY(R_1 \bowtie R_2) = SKY(S_1 \bowtie S_2)$ if the following holds:*

$$\pi_\alpha(SKY(S_1)) - \pi_\alpha(MAD(S_2)) = \emptyset \wedge$$
$$\pi_\alpha(SKY(S_2)) - \pi_\alpha(MAD(S_1)) = \emptyset$$

PROOF. Follows directly by applying Lemma 1 for each conjunct. □

We further illustrate Theorem 2 using the example of Figure 4. We first verify that the condition for early termination holds in this example, and then we explain why no combination of any group skyline tuple can produce additional skyline join results. The early termination condition demands that for every join value of any tuple in $SKY(S_i)$, there exists a tuple in $MAD(S_j)$ with the same join value. Indeed, looking at Figure 4, for $\tau_1^1 \in SKY(R_1)$ there exists the tuple $\tau_2^1 \in MAD(S_2)$, and for $\tau_2^1, \tau_2^2 \in SKY(R_2)$ the tuples $\tau_1^3, \tau_1^1 \in MAD(S_1)$ respectively. Based on the early termination condition, no skyline results can be generated by tuples in $R_1 - S_1$ and $R_2 - S_2$.

Now, let us consider group skyline tuples. Since $MAD(S_i) \neq \emptyset$ (for $i = 1, 2$), all join results produced by the skyline tuples of R_1 and R_2 have been generated. Skyline tuples of R_i can be also combined with group skyline tuples of R_j to produce skyline join results. Given a tuple $\tau_i \in SKY(R_i)$ with join value β, there exists a tuple in $MAD(S_j)$ with the same join value. Therefore, no group skyline tuple $SKY(R_j, \beta)$ can be found in $R_j - S_j$, if there exists a tuple $\tau_i \in SKY(R_i)$ with join value β. For example, in Figure 4, the tuple $\tau_1^1 \in SKY(R_1)$ has the join value B, which is the join value of tuple $\tau_2^2 \in MAD(S_2)$. Then, no group skyline tuple for B can be found in $R_2 - S_2$, since any such tuple is dominated by τ_2^2. Finally, group skyline tuples of R_1, R_2 that have a join value different than those that appear in the tuples of $SKY(R_1)$ and $SKY(R_2)$ may produce skyline join results. A group skyline tuple of R_1, in our example τ_1^6, has a dominating tuple $\tau_1^1 \in SKY(R_1)$. Clearly, the join result $\tau_1^6 \bowtie \tau_2^4$ is dominated by $\tau_1^1 \bowtie \tau_2^2$ and hence cannot appear in $SKY(R_1 \bowtie R_2)$. Thus, our early termination condition does not require to retrieve all group skyline tuples for all join values.

4.3 Implementing Sorted Access

This subsection examines the implementation of the sorted access model. First, we consider the case where R_i is a base table. One obvious solution is to maintain a B-tree index on R_i for each possible choice of B_i, using the result of *fmin* as the key of the index. This approach is feasible if there are relatively few choices for B_i and the relation is not updated frequently.

An alternative approach is to realize the sorted access through several B-tree indices. More specifically, let $\mathcal{B}$ be the set of attributes of R_i that can be potentially used as scoring attributes. For each $\beta \in \mathcal{B}$, we maintain a separate index that uses β as its key and the remaining attributes in $\mathcal{B}$ as "follow" attributes. Hence, a tuple τ_i is mapped to an index entry that records all the attributes of $\mathcal{B}$ and the corresponding record identifier (RID), and the index entries are sorted based on β. This means that the index can provide a stream of RIDs sorted on β. Given a specific choice for $\mathcal{B}_i \subseteq \mathcal{B}$, we open cursors to the corresponding indices and essentially perform a merge of the RID streams in a single RID stream, which can then be transformed to a sorted tuple stream. To avoid the generation of duplicates, an RID is returned from an index scan only if the key value is the minimum of all attributes in $\mathcal{B}_i$ for the corresponding tuple. This check can be performed efficiently, since all attributes in $\mathcal{B}_i$ can be found in the follow attributes of the index entry. Even though this scheme is not as efficient as accessing R_i through a single index, the advantage is that the number of indices is small, equal to the number of attributes in $\mathcal{B}$.

Next, let us examine the case where R_i is generated by a relational expression. One obvious solution is to sort R_i based on $\mathcal{B}_i$, but this would require scanning all of R_i. Another choice is to evaluate the expression using a physical plan that generates R_i in the correct order. For instance, assume that R_i is the result of applying a selection predicate on a base table T. If T is accessed based on one of the previous schemes, then R_i can be generated by applying the predicate on-the-fly on the tuples accessed from T.

5. THE *SFSJ* ALGORITHM

In this section, we introduce a novel skyline join algorithm termed

```
Function SFSJ(I)
Input: An instance I = (R1, R2, B1, B2) of the skyline join problem
       such that I ∈ 𝓘.
Output: The skyline SKY(R1 ⋈ R2).
Data: Tuple-sets S1 and S2 for R1 and R2 respectively initialized to
      ∅; Current groups B1 and B2; Tuple-sets M1 and M2
      initialized to ∅; Current bounds t1 and t2 initialized to −∞.
Parameters: Deterministic pulling strategy P.
1  halt ← false;
2  while !halt do
3      i ← next input index from P ;
4      j ← {1, 2} − {i} ;
5      τi ← next tuple from Ri ;
6      if fmin(τi) = ti then
7          Bi ← Bi ∪ {τi} ;
8      else
9          for ρi ∈ Bi do
10             if ∄ρ'i ∈ Si ∪ Bi: ρ'i ≺ ρi and ρ'i.α = ρi.α then
11                 add ρi to Si ;
12                 H ← H ∪ {ρi} ⋈ Sj ;
13         for (τ ∈ H) do
14             if ∄τ' ∈ H ∪ O : τ' ≺ τ then add τ to O;
15         for τ'i ∈ Si: πβ(τ'i) ≤ fmin(τi) for all β ∈ 𝓑i do
16             add τ'i to Mi;
17         halt ← Evaluate condition of Theorem 2 using Mi for
           MAD(Si) ;
18         Bi ← {τi}, ti ← fmin(τi) ;
19 return O;
```

Figure 5: The *SFSJ* algorithm.

SFSJ (short for *Sort-First-Skyline-Join*). At a high-level, *SFSJ* alternates between relations R_1 and R_2 and employs Theorem 2 to check whether the accessed tuples are sufficient to compute the correct skyline join result. An important feature is that it generates skyline tuples as soon as possible, even before the early termination condition is satisfied. Moreover, it prunes input tuples if they cannot contribute to the join skyline, thus reducing the number of generated join results and dominance tests.

Algorithm Description. Figure 5 presents the pseudocode for *SFSJ*. We first describe the data structures used by the algorithm. For each input R_i, *SFSJ* maintains a tuple-set S_i that is conceptually equivalent to a closed prefix of the input. Accordingly, a tuple-set M_i is used to record the current anti-dominance region based on S_i. Finally, the algorithm maintains a tuple-set B_i that maintains all the recently accessed tuples with the same *fmin* value, which is recorded in variable t_i. This tuple-set enables *SFSJ* to process for each relation R_i groups of tuples with the same *fmin* value.

Moreover, the algorithm is parameterized by a deterministic pulling strategy P that determines the order in which *SFSJ* accesses its inputs. One obvious choice is to employ simple round-robin access, but it is also possible to favor one input over the other (e.g., pull from R_1 twice as much as from R_2), or determine the next input to pull adaptively based on the observed data values. We analyze possible pulling strategies in the next section. We do not make any further assumptions about P, except that it always returns an index i such that R_i is not yet exhausted.

SFSJ works in iterations, where in each iteration it accesses a new tuple from a relation R_i that is determined by the strategy P (line 3). If the newly accessed tuple τ_i satisfies $fmin(\tau_i) = t_i$ (line 6), then τ_i is added to the current batch B_i and the algorithm continues with the next iteration. Otherwise, τ_i signals the start of a new group, and the tuples in B_i are integrated in S_i and new join tuples are produced (lines 9–12). The batch-update of S_i ensures that S_i is always a valid closed prefix of R_i, as defined by Definition 3. Furthermore, as an optimization, *SFSJ* adds to S_i only group skyline tuples (line 10), since otherwise they cannot contribute to the skyline join result (Property 1). Subsequently, each tuple ρ_i that is added to S_i is joined with the tuples in S_j ($j \neq i$), and any join results are kept in set H (line 12).

After all tuples in B_i have been processed, the generated tuples in H are tested for dominance against the tuples in $H \cup O$, and the non-dominated tuples are added to O (lines 13–14). $SFSJ$ can report the skyline join tuples progressively, as soon as they are added to O (line 14). Any tuple in $R_i - S_i$ has an *fmin* value greater than t_i, and therefore (as we will prove in Lemma 2) cannot produce join tuples that dominate any of the existing tuples in O. The next and final step is to update the anti-dominance region M_i based on the updated S_i (lines 15–16). Once M_i has been updated, the algorithm checks the stopping condition (line 17) to determine whether it is safe to terminate early.

Correctness. As already mentioned, $SFSJ$ relies on the condition of Theorem 2 in order to terminate early with a correct solution. However, it deviates from a naive application of the condition in two important ways: it reports skyline join results progressively, and it prunes tuples that are not group skyline tuples. We show that these features do not affect correctness.

First, we prove a key lemma for progressive result generation.

LEMMA 2. *Let* $\tau = \tau_1 \bowtie \tau_2$ *and* $\tau' = \tau_1' \bowtie \tau_2'$ *that appear in* $R_1 \bowtie R_2$. *It holds that* $\tau_i' \nprec \tau_i$ *if* $\exists i$ *such that* $fmin(\tau_i) < fmin(\tau_i')$.

PROOF. It holds that $fmin(\tau_i) < fmin(\tau_i')$ and therefore there exists at least one skyline attribute β for which $\tau_i.\beta < \tau_i'.\beta$. It follows that τ' cannot dominate τ. □

The above lemma guarantees that if every relation R_i is accessed in ascending order of the *fmin* values and all tuples with the same *fmin* value are processed in a batch, then the join results of a tuple τ_i' cannot dominate those of tuple τ_i, if τ_i is in a batch that precedes the batch of τ_i'. This enables the progressiveness of our algorithm.

Our second result states the overall correctness of $SFSJ$.

THEOREM 3. *When the stopping condition holds, SFSJ has obtained the correct skyline join result.*

PROOF. Theorem 2 proves that the stopping condition always guarantees that the complete and correct skyline join result set is computed, if S_1 and S_2 are closed prefixes of R_1 and R_2 respectively. Lemma 2 proves that only skyline join tuples are added to the result set (lines 13–14). Finally, the correctness of $SFSJ$ is not violated by discarding tuples that are not group skyline tuples (line 10). Property 1 guarantees that all tuples of S_1 and S_2 that may produce skyline join tuples have been processed, since only tuples that do not belong to any group skyline set are discarded. Furthermore, the stopping condition cannot be satisfied earlier due to discarding of tuples of S_i, since (a) the skyline set $SKY(S_i)$ does not change by discarding dominated tuples, and (b) the distinct values of the joining attribute in M_i are not influenced by discarding tuples that are not group skyline tuples (a tuple τ_i is added to M_i, unless there exists a tuple $\tau_i' \in M_i$ such that $\tau_i.\alpha = \tau_i'.\alpha$ and $\tau_i' \prec \tau_i$). Therefore, we conclude that $SFSJ$ can safely stop processing tuples when the stopping condition holds, even though only group skyline tuples are maintained in the sets S_i. □

Implementation Details. We discuss next some important details about the efficient maintenance of the tuple-sets used by $SFSJ$, namely S_i, M_i, and $SKY(S_i)$. The key observation is that we can efficiently maintain these tuple-sets by taking advantage of the property that they are append-only. This property stems from the fact that each relation R_i is accessed in ascending order of *fmin*.

In more detail, the set of tuples S_i of relation R_i is implemented as a sorted list of tuples sorted by $fmax(\tau_i) = \max_{\beta \in \mathcal{B}_i}\{\pi_\beta(\tau_i)\}$. For any two tuples $\tau_i, \tau_i' \in S_i$, if $fmax(\tau_i) < fmax(\tau_i')$, then τ_i precedes τ_i' in the list S_i. This technique allows efficient implementation of M_i, namely as a pointer to a tuple $\hat{\tau}_i \in S_i$. Given the last processed tuple τ_i, M_i is updated by examining the tuples starting from $\hat{\tau}_i$ and stopping at the first tuple τ_i' for which $fmax(\tau_i') < fmin(\tau_i)$. The tuple $\hat{\tau}_i$ preceding τ_i' is the new position for the pointer that delineates M_i. Then, M_i is a subset of the tuple-set S_i containing all tuples starting from the first tuple of S_i up to the tuple $\hat{\tau}_i$. For example, consider the relation R_2 depicted in Figure 4(b), where τ_2^3 is the last processed tuple and $S_2 = \{\tau_2^2, \tau_2^3, \tau_2^1\}$. Only the value of $fmax(\tau_2^2) = 0.2$ is smaller than $fmin(\tau_2^3) = 0.3$. Therefore, M_2 is defined by a pointer to τ_2^2 indicating that only τ_2^2 belongs to M_2.

The set of skyline tuples $SKY(S_i)$ can also be maintained efficiently in order to speed-up the evaluation of the stopping condition. Again, due to the sorted access model, $SFSJ$ will always append tuples in $SKY(S_i)$. Therefore, we only need to check whether a newly processed tuple τ_i is dominated by a tuple $\tau_i' \in SKY(S_i)$. If this is not the case, τ_i is inserted in $SKY(S_i)$.

Finally, to improve even further the performance of $SFSJ$, the tuple-set S_i can be maintained as the union of two sets of tuples namely $SKY(S_i)$ and $X_i = S_i - SKY(S_i)$. A tuple τ_i of S_i is only inserted in the set X_i if it is dominated by a tuple $\tau_i' \in SKY(S_i) \cup B_i$. In this way, the domination tests between join tuples are reduced, since the join results of a newly accessed tuple τ_i with the tuples $\tau_j \in SKY(S_j)$ can be added immediately to the skyline join result without any domination tests. Furthermore, if the newly accessed tuple τ_i is a skyline tuple ($\tau_i \in SKY(S_i)$), also the join tuples produced by joining τ_i with tuples of X_j can be added immediately to the skyline join result without any domination tests. Both sets $SKY(S_i)$ and X_i are implemented as sorted lists. Maintenance of tuple-set M_i is achieved by means of two pointers (for the sets $SKY(S_i)$ and X_i respectively), which are managed as described previously.

6. ANALYSIS OF PULLING STRATEGIES

As mentioned in the previous section, $SFSJ$ employs a pulling strategy to determine the order in which the two inputs are accessed. The choice of the strategy clearly affects how "deep" $SFSJ$ reaches in its inputs, and hence it is interesting to investigate the existence of optimal strategies that minimize the number of accessed tuples, or equivalently, the amount of I/O performed by the algorithm. In what follows, we present a theoretical analysis of this problem and identify two provably good strategies: simple round-robin, and a novel adaptive strategy that we introduce below. The proofs of all theoretical results can be found in the Appendix.

Adaptive Pulling. The adaptive pulling strategy prioritizes access among the two relations based on the observed data. The main idea is to read tuples from a relation only if there is evidence that the new tuples will help satisfy the termination condition. Intuitively, this prioritization helps the algorithm terminate sooner, thus improving its performance.

Recall that the early termination condition requires each join value present in $SKY(S_i)$ to be also present in $MAD(S_j)$ ($j \neq i$). Let us assume that the early termination condition does not hold, because there exists a tuple $\tau_i \in SKY(S_i)$ for which $\nexists \rho_j \in MAD(S_j)$ such that $\tau_i.\alpha = \rho_j.\alpha$. Note that $SKY(S_i)$ can only grow as more tuples are accessed from S_i. Hence, the algorithm can satisfy the early termination condition with respect to $\tau_i.\alpha$ only by enlarging $MAD(S_j)$, i.e., by pulling more tuples from R_j. Based on this property, we define the priority of R_j as the number of distinct mismatched join values. Formally:

DEFINITION 5. *The priority of a relation R_j is defined as $priority_{SC}(R_j) = |\pi_\alpha(SKY(S_i)) - \pi_\alpha(MAD(S_j))|$.*

The computation of $priority_{SC}(R_j)$ can be folded in the evaluation of the termination condition (see Theorem 2). The adaptive pulling strategy always pulls from the relation with the highest priority. Ties are broken based on least current depth. The pulling strategy has two interesting properties. First, $priority_{SC}(R_1) = priority_{SC}(R_2) = 0$ when the termination condition is satisfied. Second, the strategy will freeze access to an input if it cannot contribute to skyline results currently. As an example, consider again the two relations depicted in Figure 4. For all join values of the tuples in $SKY(S_1)$, there exists a tuple in $MAD(S_2)$ with the same join value. Thus, tuples in $R_2 - S_2$ combined with tuples of S_1 cannot produce any skyline join result. The proposed pulling strategy will freeze access to relation R_2 (since $priority_{SC}(R_2) = 0$) and pull from R_1. No further tuples of R_2 will be accessed, unless new join values are added to $SKY(S_1)$.

Optimality Analysis. We first describe the performance metrics that we consider and the associated notions of optimality. We write $\mathcal{I}$ to denote the set of skyline join problem instances. We use $\mathcal{SJA}$ to denote the class of deterministic algorithms that solve correctly any problem instance $I \in \mathcal{I}$, and write $\mathcal{SFSJ}$ to denote the set of all instantiations of *SFSJ* with a different pulling strategy ($\mathcal{SFSJ} \subseteq \mathcal{SJA}$). Given $I \in \mathcal{I}$ and $A \in \mathcal{SJA}$, we define $depth(A, I, i)$ as the number of tuples accessed from relation R_i when A terminates. We also define a total depth metric $totDepth(A, I) = depth(A, I, 1) + depth(A, I, 2)$. This metric is indicative of the total I/O performed by A, and hence it has a direct correspondence to the efficiency of the algorithm.

We employ two notions of optimality. Let $\mathbb{A}$ be a class of skyline join algorithms. We say that an algorithm $A \in \mathbb{A}$ is optimal if $totDepth(A, I) \leq totDepth(B, I)$ for any instance $I \in \mathcal{I}$ and algorithm $B \in \mathbb{A}$. We say that A is instance-optimal if there exist constants c and c' such that $totDepth(A, I) \leq c \cdot totDepth(B, I) + c'$ for any instance $I \in \mathcal{I}$ and algorithm $B \in \mathbb{A}$. Intuitively, A always performs within a factor of c of the optimal algorithm for any instance I. Constant c is termed the instance-optimality ratio of A.

In the first part of our analysis, we set $\mathbb{A} = \mathcal{SFSJ}$ in order to identify optimal strategies for the *SFSJ* algorithm. We begin with an examination of the round-robin strategy. In what follows, we use *SFSJ-RR* to denote the corresponding instantiation of *SFSJ*. Our first result states that *SFSJ-RR* is instance optimal with a ratio of two. The significance of this finding is that *SFSJ-RR* will never perform arbitrarily bad for any problem instance, and thus carries a property of robustness.

THEOREM 4. *SFSJ-RR is instance-optimal within $\mathcal{SFSJ}$ and $\mathcal{I}$ with a ratio of 2.*

A natural question is whether we can identify an optimal pulling strategy. We answer this positively, showing that the *SC* pulling strategy (see Definition 5) is optimal. Formally, let *SFSJ-SC* be the instantiation of *SFSJ* with the *SC* strategy.

THEOREM 5. *SFSJ-SC is optimal within $\mathcal{SFSJ}$ and $\mathcal{I}$.*

In fact, we can show an even stronger result: no other instantiation of *SFSJ* will outperform *SFSJ-SC* on *any input relation*. Thus, *SFSJ-SC* is optimal in a stronger sense than implied with the *totDepth* metric.

The next part of our analysis considers the performance of pulling strategies within the larger class $\mathcal{SJA}$. The goal is now different: instead of comparing pulling strategies to each other, we basically want to compare *SFSJ* (with appropriate strategies) against other deterministic algorithms.

We develop our first result for a specific class of problem instances. We define $\mathcal{I}^K$ as the class of problem instances such that at most K tuples in each input have the same *fmin* value. The reason we target this class is due to the access logic of *SFSJ*, which examines tuples in groups of the same *fmin* value. Class $\mathcal{I}^K$ essentially bounds the size of these groups, and hence the amount of data that *SFSJ* must read before termination. In this case, we prove that *SFSJ-RR* and *SFSJ-SC* are instance optimal with a ratio of two.

THEOREM 6. *Both SFSJ-RR and SFSJ-SC are instance optimal within $\mathcal{SJA}$ and $\mathcal{I}^K$ with a ratio of 2.*

Up to this point, our results provide strong evidence for the choice of *SFSJ-SC* as the de jure instantiation of *SFSJ*. *SFSJ-SC* employs the optimal access strategy within the instantiations of *SFSJ*, and hence has the optimal I/O "footprint" in this family. Within the larger context of deterministic algorithms, *SFSJ-SC* may not be optimal but it maintains the important property of instance optimality when *fmin* values have bounded repetitions.

A favorable case can also be made for *SFSJ-RR*. The round-robin strategy is instance optimal in all examined cases, and is certainly more efficient than the adaptive pulling strategy which requires the manipulation of sets. Indeed, it is important to point out that all optimality results are with respect to the *totDepth* metric that reflects I/O performance, but the total running time of the algorithm also includes the computational overhead of the pulling strategy.

Can we show similar optimality results for the general class of inputs $\mathcal{I}$? Unfortunately, the following theorem gives a negative answer.

THEOREM 7. *There exists no algorithm $A \in SFSJ$ such that A is instance-optimal within $\mathcal{SJA}$ and $\mathcal{I}$.*

The problem is that *SFSJ* accesses tuples from each input in groups of the same *fmin* value, and the size of these groups can be unbounded in the general case. In turn, this precludes any performance guarantees. The investigation of an instance-optimal skyline join algorithm within $\mathcal{SJA}$ and $\mathcal{I}$ remains an interesting direction for future work.

7. EXPERIMENTAL EVALUATION

In this section, we perform an experimental evaluation of the *SFSJ* algorithm and we report our main findings. All algorithms are implemented in Java and the experiments run on a machine with an Intel Core2 Quad 2.33GHz processor and 4GB of RAM.

7.1 Experimental Setup

The basic experimental setup employs an instance of the skyline join problem where $R_1 \bowtie R_2$ is a many-to-many join. The cardinality of each relation is denoted as $|R_i|$, $i = 1, 2$. Each relation has m_i ($i = 1, 2$) scoring attributes (i.e., $|\mathcal{B}_i| = m_i$).

Data sets and Queries. We generated synthetic data sets in order to study the effect of different data characteristics on the performance of skyline join algorithms. As common in skyline research,

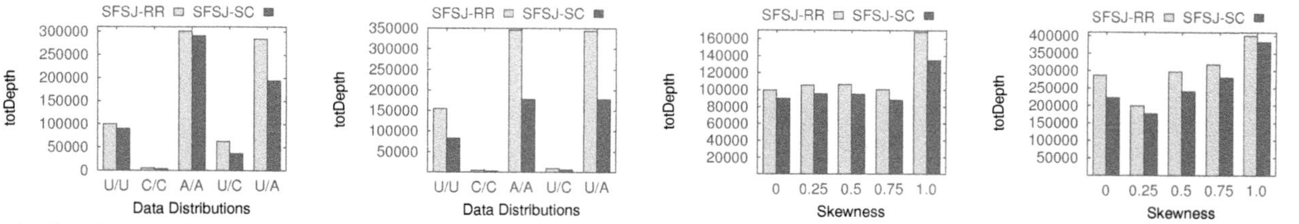

(a) Depths (m_1=2, m_2=2). (b) Depths (m_1=1, m_2=3). (c) Varying skewness of α (U). (d) Varying skewness of α (CL).

Figure 6: Comparison of pulling strategies for different data distributions.

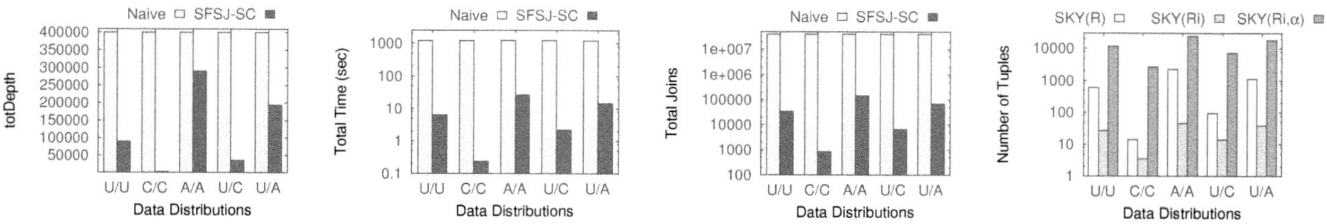

(a) Depths. (b) Total time. (c) Total joins. (d) Statistics.

Figure 7: Comparison of $SFSJ$-SC to Naive for different data distributions.

we used uniform (U), correlated (C) and anti-correlated (A) data distribution for the scoring attributes. In addition, we used a clustered (CL) data distribution, where 5 cluster centroids are generated at random and the value of each scoring attribute follows a normal distribution with variance 0.05 and mean equal to the corresponding coordinate of the centroid. We also vary the distribution of join values using a zipfian distribution with parameter ranging from 0 (uniform) to 1 (skewed). Our default setup is: $|R_i|$=200K, $|m_i|$=2, the join selectivity is 10^{-3}, the zipf parameter is set to 0, and the data distribution is uniform. Notice that we conducted experiments with different join selectivities and obtained similar results.

In order to test the performance of $SFSJ$ with real data, we used the NBA data set[3], which contains statistics of NBA players from 1946 to 2008. We created two data sets termed *NBA-1* and *NBA-2*. In *NBA-1*, the relations R_1 and R_2 record performance statistics for players during the regular season on a yearly basis. Relation R_1 records the field goals made and free throws, and relation R_2 records the number of points and assists. Each relation contains 21384 tuples. The skyline join is performed on attributes {player,year}, and the query tries to identify the best pairs of players on a yearly basis. In *NBA-2*, R_2 is the same as *NBA-1*, while R_1 contains 1307 tuples and records the number of wins and the number of points made by each team in each season. The skyline join is performed on attributes {team,year} and its purpose is to retrieve the best teams and corresponding players on a yearly basis.

Algorithms. We implemented $SFSJ$ with the round-robin ($SFSJ$-RR) and the adaptive pulling strategies ($SFSJ$-SC). We also implemented three competitor skyline join techniques. The first is an algorithm (denoted as *Naive*) that takes as input the initial relations and performs the complete join, while discarding dominated join tuples during processing. The second competitor is the approach of Jin et al. [6], denoted as $SMSJ$ (sort-merge skyline join). We implemented the most efficient of the $SMSJ$ variants, as reported in [6]. This variant first computes the skyline set and the group skylines of each relation (R_i) and then processes each relation sorted (R'_i) with skyline tuples preceding the group skyline tuples after having discarded the remaining tuples. For the necessary skyline computation, we employ the SFS algorithm [4]. $SFSJ$ and $SMSJ$ (through its usage of SFS) require their input to be sorted by $fmin$ and entropy value respectively. The third competitor is the $ProgXe$ algorithm [10]. We implemented the version of $ProgXe$ that employs progressive driven ordering, as reported in [10]. To ensure a fair comparison, the cost of preprocessing is discounted for all algorithms. Qualitatively, $ProgXe$ has the highest overhead, due to the construction of a customized index structure. Both $SFSJ$ and $SMSJ$ have lower overhead, as they merely require sorting of the inputs. The Naive algorithm requires no preprocessing, but on the other hand it requires a full computation of the join results.

[3]Available from: http://databasebasketball.com.

Metrics. Given a problem instance, we employ the following metrics: a) $totDepth$ which is the sum of depths of accessed tuples for both relations, b) the total execution time, c) the number of dominance tests, and d) the total number of generated join results that each algorithm performed for producing the skyline join result.

For our experiments on synthetic data, we report the average of each metric over 10 different instances of the data set. We generate the different instances by keeping the parameters fixed and changing the seeds of the random number generator. We adopt this approach in order to factor out the effects of randomization.

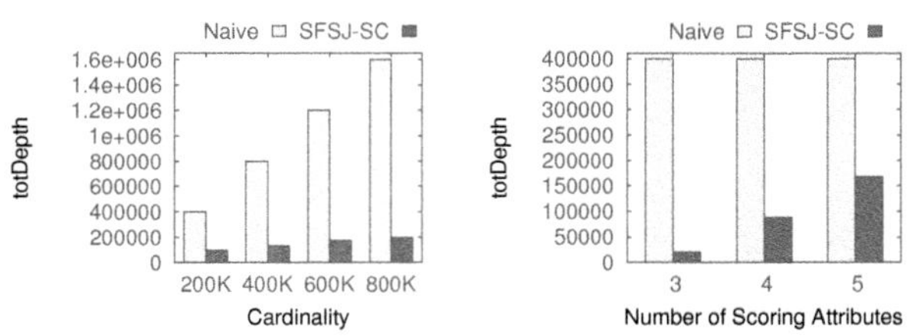

(a) Varying cardinality. (b) Varying scoring attributes.

Figure 8: Sensitivity analysis of algorithm $SFSJ$-SC.

7.2 Experimental Results

Evaluation of Pulling Strategies. In Figure 6, we perform an experiment that aims to quantify the gain of $SFSJ$-SC compared to $SFSJ$-RR. Our goal is to gather empirical evidence to complement our theoretical analysis that $SFSJ$-SC always terminates earlier than any other pulling strategy.

In Figure 6(a), we use the default setup of two scoring attributes per relation (m_1=2 and m_2=2). In all cases, $SFSJ$-SC performs better than its competitor and stops at a lower depth. We performed the same experiment for m_1=1 and m_2=3 in order to examine the

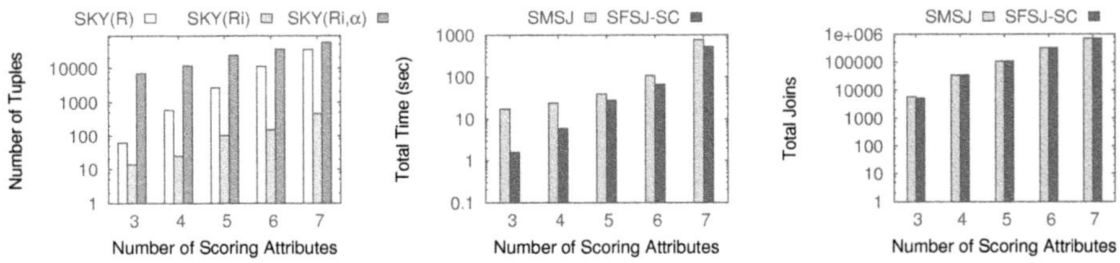

(a) Statistics. (b) Total time. (c) Total joins.

Figure 9: Comparison of $SFSJ$ to $SMSJ$ algorithm.

effect of different number of scoring attributes per relation. Figure 6(b) shows the results. Again, $SFSJ$-SC performs much better than $SFSJ$-RR in all setups. It is noteworthy that the increased number of scoring attributes in R_2 for A/A and U/A data distributions makes $SFSJ$-RR read more tuples in total. In contrast, $SFSJ$-SC is more robust and is not affected by this setup. We also provide in Figure 6(c) an experiment for evaluating the effect of varying the skewness in the join values. So far, we examined the case that the join values are uniformly distributed (skewness 0). We gradually increase the skewness using a zipf distribution with parameter up to 1. The chart shows that $SFSJ$-SC consistently outperforms the round-robin pulling strategy, irrespective of skewness in the join values. The measurements for the total time metric followed the same trends as the $totDepth$ metric, and are omitted in the interest of space. Similar results are obtained in Figure 6(d) for the clustered data set, only the absolute values are higher, because any algorithm needs to examine more tuples to compute the skyline join result.

Comparison to Naive. Next, we study the performance of $SFSJ$-SC compared to the Naive algorithm for all tested data distributions. Figure 7 depicts the results of our comparison. With respect to the $totDepth$ metric (Figure 7(a)), notice that the Naive algorithm always needs to access the complete inputs, therefore its $totDepth$ equals to $|R_1| + |R_2|$. $SFSJ$-SC always terminates much earlier than Naive, and in the best case (C/C) only accesses less than 1% of the $totDepth$ of Naive. For the demanding A/A data distribution, where any algorithm is prone to go deep to ensure safe termination, $SFSJ$-SC needs to access more tuples, but still improves Naive by more than 25%. In terms of total time, $SFSJ$-SC is notably more efficient than Naive, as shown in Figure 7(b). Even in the case of A/A data set, $SFSJ$-SC is almost two orders of magnitude faster than Naive. The reason is clearly depicted in Figure 7(c) that shows the number of computed join results for each algorithm. $SFSJ$-SC performs significantly fewer join operations than Naive, because $SFSJ$-SC a) avoids many unnecessary join operations by eagerly pruning tuples that cannot produce skyline join results, and b) exploits the early termination condition to stop accessing the input relations as soon as the complete skyline join result is computed.

In Figure 7(d), we provide some interesting statistics that are relevant to the previous performance results. Specifically, we report the number of: skyline join results ($SKY(R)$), skyline tuples per relation ($SKY(R_i)$), and group skyline tuples per relation ($SKY(R_i, \alpha)$). Notice that the performance of $SFSJ$-SC in terms of total time and total joins relates directly to the cardinality of $SKY(R)$. Except for the U/C and C/C data sets, we note that the cardinality of $SKY(R)$ is high (close to 1000), with highest values for data set A/A. Also, we observe that $SKY(R_i, \alpha)$ is at least one order of magnitude larger than $SKY(R)$.

Sensitivity Analysis. The next set of experiments considers the sensitivity of $SFSJ$ with respect to several interesting parameters. We also include *Naive* as a baseline. In the interest of space, we only show the results for the $totDepth$ metric, and report on the trends of the other two metrics.

We first consider the effect of input cardinality as it increases from 200K to 800K tuples. The results for the two algorithms are shown in Figure 8(a). $SFSJ$-SC always terminates at an earlier depth than Naive. In terms of total time, $SFSJ$-SC is consistently more than two orders of magnitude faster than Naive and scales gracefully even when the cardinality increases by a factor of 4. The same result is obtained for the number of total join operations performed by each algorithm to produce the skyline join result. $SFSJ$-SC is highly efficient and is practically unaffected by the increased cardinality, whereas Naive scales poorly. Figure 8(b) studies the effect of increasing the number of scoring attributes. $SFSJ$-SC terminates earlier than Naive in all setups. An increased number of scoring attributes causes $SFSJ$-SC to scan more tuples, which is expected as the skyline and group skyline tuples increase rapidly with increasing dimensionality.

Comparative Study to $SMSJ$. Figure 9 presents the results of a comparative study between $SFSJ$-SC and the $SMSJ$ algorithm [6]. We study the scalability of both algorithms for increased number of scoring attributes, from 3 to 7. We do not report results on the $totDepth$ metric, since $SMSJ$ computes the skyline over relations that result from a transformation of the original relations.

Figure 9(a) shows the number of skyline join results, skyline and group skyline tuples in the data set, in order to aid the interpretation of the experimental results. All values increase with the number of scoring attributes. Notice that the number of skyline join results increases significantly as the number of scoring attributes grows. In Figure 9(b), we measure the total time of $SFSJ$-SC versus $SMSJ$. Our algorithm is faster than $SMSJ$, due to the non-negligible processing cost of $SMSJ$ for computing the skyline and group skyline tuples. This is clearly demonstrated in Figure 9(c), where the number of total join operations that each algorithm performs is shown. Notice that $SFSJ$-SC requires slightly fewer join operations than $SMSJ$, although $SMSJ$ operates only on the skyline and group skyline tuples of each relation. This is a strong argument in favor of a) the online pruning achieved by $SFSJ$ due to sorted access, and b) the efficiency of the stopping condition that avoids redundant accesses on the input relations.

Comparative Study to $ProgXe$. In Figure 10, we compare the performance of $SFSJ$ to $ProgXe$ [10] for different data distributions. We use 20K tuples per relation and m_1=m_2=2 scoring attributes. We set the number of input and output partitions per dimension to 10 and 20 respectively. We note that there is no way to tune these parameters, unless one evaluates all possible values. Figure 10(a) shows that in all tested data distributions $ProgXe$ needs to exhaust both inputs to ensure that the complete and correct result set is reported. Although $ProgXe$ avoids processing all possible combinations of input partitions, it still accesses each input partition at least once, hence it cannot terminate early (in contrast to $SFSJ$). Figure 10(b) depicts the number of dominance tests employed by each algorithm. Clearly, $ProgXe$ performs significantly more dom-

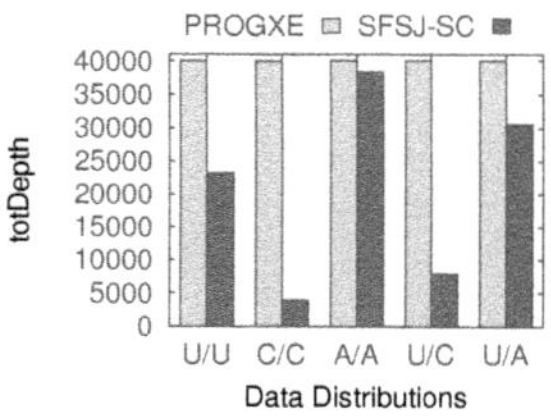

(a) Depths.

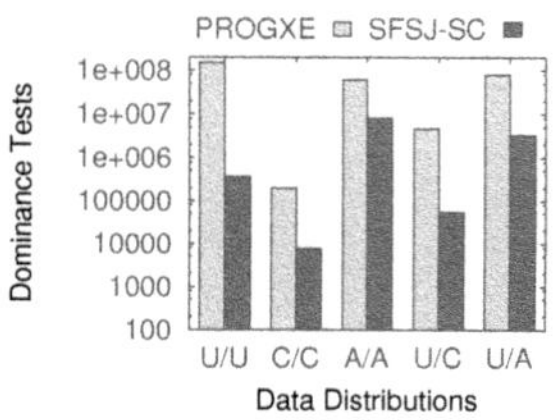

(b) Dominance tests.

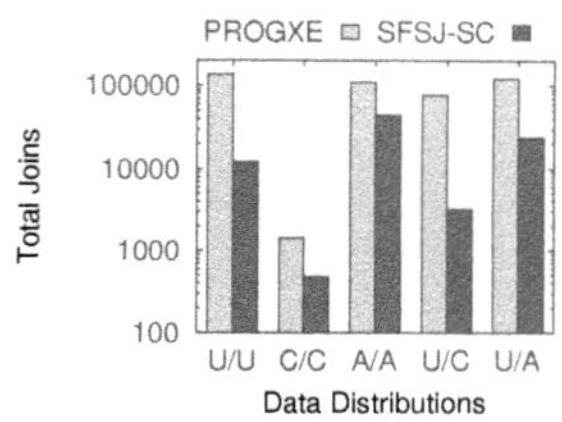

(c) Total joins.

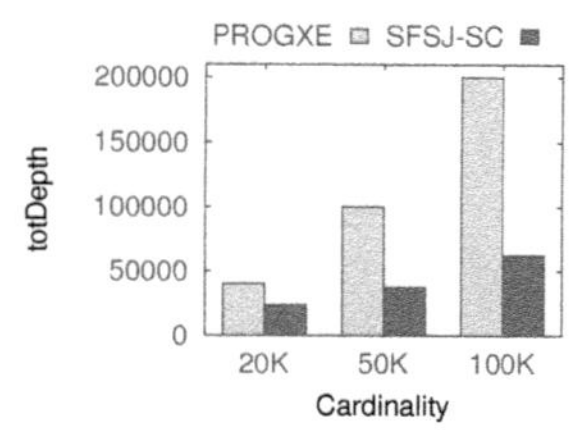

(d) Depths.

Figure 10: Comparison of $SFSJ$ to $ProgXe$ algorithm.

inance tests than $SFSJ$, because $ProgXe$ uses dominance tests not only between tuples but also between partitions. Also, as shown in Figure 10(c), $ProgXe$ needs to perform more join operations of tuples to produce the skyline join result. Then, in Figure 10(d), we increase the cardinality of the input relations. The results show that the relative gain of $SFSJ$ to $ProgXe$ increases with the cardinality of the relations, demonstrating the scalability of our approach.

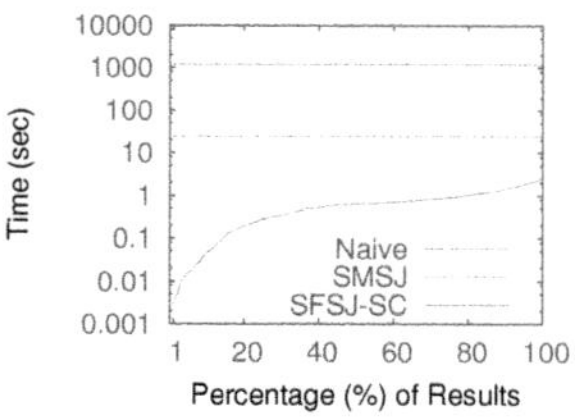

(a) Progressiveness (U/U).

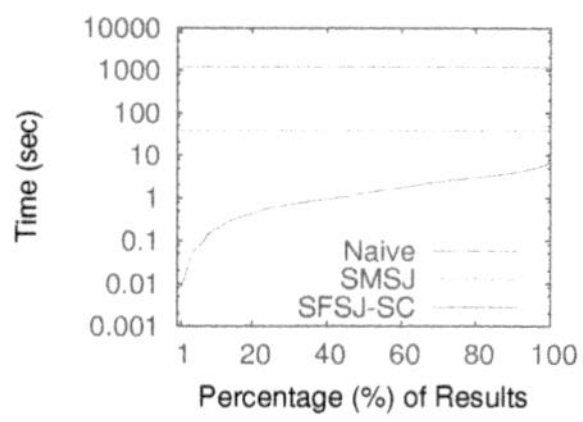

(b) Progressiveness (U/A).

Figure 11: Progressiveness.

Progressiveness. Furthermore, in the next set of experiments in Figures 11(a) and 11(b), we evaluate the progressive property of $SFSJ$ algorithm. The charts correspond to the data distributions U/U and U/A respectively, in order to examine our default setup and a hard setup for any algorithm, while the U/C and C/C setups are trivial. The y-axis shows the time at which a percentage (shown on the x-axis) of the total skyline join result set is reported. In all cases, $SFSJ\text{-}SC$ reports a significant percentage of the result set in a fraction of a second. The charts clearly demonstrate the advantages of $SFSJ\text{-}SC$, in contrast to $SMSJ$ and Naive which need to complete processing, before reporting the skyline join result.

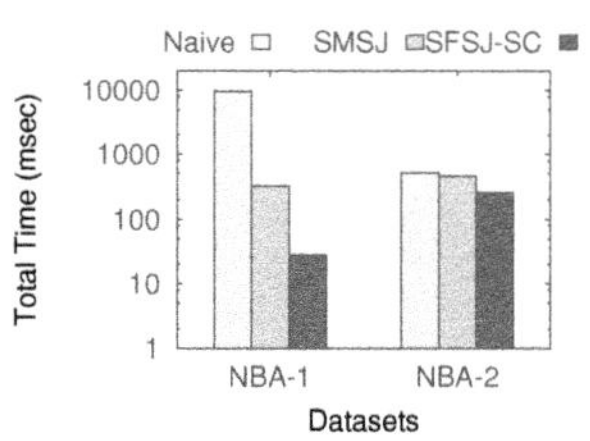

(a) Total time.

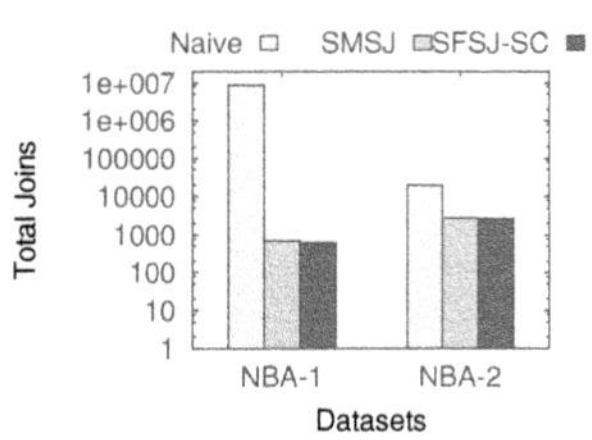

(b) Total joins.

Figure 12: Real data sets (NBA-1 and NBA-2).

Experiments with Real Data. In Figure 12, we report the experimental results on the real data sets. The general trends are in accordance with the study of the synthetic data sets. Notice that the absolute measured values are smaller than in the case of the synthetic data, because the real data set is smaller than the synthetic ones. The total time for both data sets (NBA-1 and NBA-2) is shown in Figure 12(a), where $SFSJ\text{-}SC$ outperforms the other algorithms in both cases. Also, in Figure 12(b), we depict the number of join operations performed, and $SFSJ\text{-}SC$ requires marginally fewer operations than $SMSJ$ and significantly fewer than Naive. In all cases, $SFSJ\text{-}SC$ outperforms its competitors for both data sets.

8. CONCLUSIONS

In this paper, we study the problem of computing the skyline set of a join assuming that the join inputs are accessed in sorted order. We introduced the $SFSJ$ algorithm that combines several nice properties: it avoids useless join computation; it generates the results progressively; it can terminate early; and, it has strong optimality guarantees for its performance. The experimental results validated the effectiveness of $SFSJ$ and demonstrated its numerous advantages over competitor techniques.

Acknowledgments. This work was supported in part by the National Science Foundation under Grant No. IIS-0447966.

References

[1] I. Bartolini, P. Ciaccia, and M. Patella. SaLSa: computing the skyline without scanning the whole sky. In *Proceedings of CIKM*, 2006.

[2] I. Bartolini, P. Ciaccia, and M. Patella. Efficient sort-based skyline evaluation. *ACM Trans. Database Syst.*, 33(4), 2008.

[3] S. Börzsönyi, D. Kossmann, and K. Stocker. The skyline operator. In *Proceedings of ICDE*, pages 421–430, 2001.

[4] J. Chomicki, P. Godfrey, J. Gryz, and D. Liang. Skyline with presorting. In *Proceedings of ICDE*, pages 717–816, 2003.

[5] R. Fagin, A. Lotem, and M. Naor. Optimal aggregation algorithms for middleware. In *Proceedings of PODS*, 2001.

[6] W. Jin, M. Ester, Z. Hu, and J. Han. The multi-relational skyline operator. In *Proceedings of ICDE*, 2007.

[7] W. Jin, M. Morse, J. Patel, M. Ester, and Z. Hu. Evaluating skylines in the presence of equi-joins. In *Proceedings of ICDE*, 2010.

[8] N. Koudas, C. Li, A. K. H. Tung, and R. Vernica. Relaxing join and selection queries. In *Proceedings of VLDB*, 2006.

[9] J. Levandoski, M. F. Mokbel, and M. Khalefa. FlexPref: A framework for extensible preference evaluation in database systems. In *Proceedings of ICDE*, 2010.

[10] V. Raghavan and E. Rundensteiner. Progressive result generation for multi-criteria decision support queries. In *Proceedings of ICDE*, 2010.

[11] K. Schnaitter and N. Polyzotis. Evaluating rank joins with optimal cost. In *Proceedings of PODS*, 2008.

[12] D. Sun, S. Wu, J. Li, and A. K. H. Tung. Skyline-join in distributed databases. In *ICDE Workshops*, 2008.

[13] Y. Tao, X. Xiao, and J. Pei. Subsky: Efficient computation of skylines in subspaces. In *Proceedings of ICDE*, 2006.

[14] Q. Wan, R. C.-W. Wong, I. F. Ilyas, M. T. Özsu, and Y. Peng. Creating competitive products. *PVLDB*, 2(1):898–909, 2009.

APPENDIX

A. PROOFS OF RESULTS IN SECTION 6

Our proofs make use of the following implications that are trivial to prove: $\tau_i \in MAD(S_i) \Rightarrow \forall \rho_i \in R_i - S_i(\tau_i \prec \rho_i)$ and $MAD(S_i) \neq \emptyset \Rightarrow SKY(S_i) = SKY(R_i)$. We also employ the notation $\hat{\imath}$ to denote the input index $\{1,2\} - \{i\}$ for $i \in \{1,2\}$.

We begin by proving three auxiliary lemmata.

LEMMA 3. $\max_{j=1,2} depth(SFSJ\text{-}RR, I, j) \leq \max_{j=1,2} depth(A, I, j)$ *for all* $I \in \mathcal{I}$ *and* $A \in \mathcal{SFSJ}$.

PROOF. By contradiction. Define $d_k^A = \max_{j=1,2} depth(A, I, j)$ and assume that $d_k < \max_{j=1,2} depth(SFSJ\text{-}RR, I, j)$. It follows that *SFSJ-RR* pulls at depth $d_k^A + 1$ on one input i. Let p_1, p_2 be the depths of *SFSJ-RR* just before this happens (hence, $p_i = d_k^A$), and let S_1, S_2 denote the corresponding tuple-sets. Define S_1^A, S_2^A as the tuple-sets that A has examined when it terminates. It holds that $d_{\hat{k}}^A \leq d_k^A = p_i \leq p_{\hat{i}}$, where the last inequality follows from the round-robin strategy. We conclude that A has examined a subset of tuples observed by *SFSJ-RR*.

We know that A satisfies the stopping condition and hence $MAD(S_j^A) \neq \emptyset$. Given that $S_j \supseteq S_j^A \Rightarrow MAD(S_j) \supseteq MAD(S_j^A) \neq \emptyset$, we can assert that $SKY(S_j) = SKY(R_j) = SKY(S_j^A)$. The following implication follows immediately:

$$\pi_\alpha(SKY(S_j^A)) - \pi_\alpha(MAD(S_{\hat{j}}^A)) = \emptyset \Rightarrow$$
$$\pi_\alpha(SKY(S_j)) - \pi_\alpha(MAD(S_{\hat{j}})) = \emptyset$$

We can thus assert that the stopping condition must also be true for S_1 and S_2, which contradicts our assumption that *SFSJ-RR* pulls past p_i. □

LEMMA 4. *$depth(SFSJ\text{-}SC, I, j) \leq depth(A, I, j)$ for all $I \in \mathcal{I}$, $A \in \mathcal{SFSJ}$ and $j = 1, 2$.*

PROOF. By contradiction. Let us assume that A stops earlier on input k. Define $d_j^A = depth(A, I, j)$, and let S_1^A, S_2^A be the observed tuple-sets when A terminates. Clearly, the stopping condition is true for S_1^A and S_2^A.

Let S_1, S_2 be the observed tuples for *SFSJ-SC* just before it pulls at depth $d_k^A + 1$. We have that $S_k = S_k^A$, and it must also hold that $S_{\hat{k}} \subset S_{\hat{k}}^A$, otherwise the stopping condition would be true for *SFSJ-SC* as well. Hence, $SKY(S_{\hat{k}}) \subseteq SKY(S_{\hat{k}}^A)$.

Since the stopping condition is satisfied when A terminates, it follows that $\pi_\alpha(SKY(S_j^A)) - \pi_\alpha(MAD(S_{\hat{j}}^A)) = \emptyset$, for $j = 1, 2$. Given that $SKY(S_{\hat{k}}^A) \supseteq SKY(S_{\hat{k}})$ and $MAD(S_k) = MAD(S_k^A)$, we conclude that $\pi_a(SKY(S_{\hat{k}})) - \pi_\alpha(MAD(S_k)) = \emptyset$. This implies that $priority_{SC}(R_k) = 0$. However, since $priority_{SC}(R_k) \geq priority_{SC}(R_{\hat{k}}) \geq 0$ (*SFSJ-SC* pulls from relation R_k next), it must hold that $priority_{SC}(R_{\hat{k}}) = 0$, which in turn means that the stopping condition is satisfied with S_1 and S_2. This contradicts our assumption that A pulls past depth $d^k + 1$. □

LEMMA 5. *$\max_{j=1,2} depth(SFSJ\text{-}RR, I, j) \leq \max_{j=1,2} depth(A, I, j) + K$ for all $I \in \mathcal{I}^K$ and $A \in \mathcal{SJA}$.*

PROOF. Let k be the input index on which A pulls the most tuples. Let m be defined similarly for *SFSJ-RR*. We will assume that $depth(SFSJ\text{-}RR, I, m) > depth(A, I, k) + K$ and show that this leads to a contradiction.

Let p_1 and p_2 be the depths of *SFSJ-RR* right before it pulls past depth $depth(A, I, k) + K$ on input m. Let S_1 and S_2 denote the corresponding sets of seen tuples. Define d_1^A, d_2^A as the termination depths of A. The following is true: $p_m = d_k^A + K \geq d_{\hat{m}}^A + K$, and $p_{\hat{m}} \geq p_m$, due to the round-robin strategy. We conclude that $p_{\hat{m}} \geq d_{\hat{m}}^A + K$. Since both p_1 and p_2 exceed K, it means that *SFSJ-RR* has witnessed a change of *fmin* value in both inputs, and hence $S_1 \neq \emptyset$ and $S_2 \neq \emptyset$.

Sets S_1 and S_2 do not satisfy the stopping condition, since *SFSJ-RR* pulls another tuple. This gives rise to two cases. In each case, we will construct a new instance I' on which A commits a mistake. This yields the contradiction that completes the proof, as we have assumed that A is a correct algorithm.

Case 1: $\pi_\alpha(SKY(S_{\hat{m}})) - \pi_\alpha(MAD(S_m)) \neq \emptyset$ Since $SKY(S_{\hat{m}}) \neq \emptyset$, there exists a tuple $\tau_{\hat{m}} \in SKY(S_{\hat{m}})$ such that $\tau_{\hat{m}}.\alpha \equiv y \notin \pi_\alpha(MAD(S_m))$. Let τ_m denote the $(d_k^A) + 1$-th tuple of R_m. We construct the new instance I' from I by substituting τ_m with a new tuple τ_m' such that: $\tau_m'.\alpha = y$, and all skyline coordinates of τ_m' are set equal to $fmin(\tau_m)$. It is straightforward to verify that τ_m' appears in $SKY(R_m', y)$, otherwise the tuple that dominates it would be contained in $MAD(S_m)$ and hence the value y would appear in $\pi_\alpha(MAD(S_m))$. We conclude that $\tau_{\hat{m}} \bowtie \tau_m'$ must appear in the solution for I', since $\tau_{\hat{m}}$ appears in the global skyline and τ_m' in a group skyline.

Case 2: $\pi_\alpha(SKY(S_m)) - \pi_\alpha(MAD(S_{\hat{m}})) \neq \emptyset$ Following the same reasoning as before, we construct I' by altering the $(d_k^A + 1)$-th tuple in $R_{\hat{m}}$.

In both cases, I' changes the tuple at depth $d_k^A + 1$ in one of the two inputs. This tuple is never accessed by A and also leads to the generation of a new result. It follows that A will compute the wrong solution. □

We now proceed with the proofs of the main theorems.

Proof of Theorem 4 We use Lemma 3. Let d_1, d_2 be the termination depths of *SFSJ-RR* and define d_1^A and d_2^A similarly for A.

$$totDepth(SFSJ\text{-}RR, I) = d_1 + d_2 \leq 2 \cdot \max\{d_1, d_2\} \leq$$
$$2 \cdot \max\{d_1^A, d_2^A\} \leq 2 \cdot (d_1^A + d_2^A) = 2 \cdot totDepth(A, I)$$

□

Proof of Theorem 5 The proof follows directly from Lemma 4.□

Proof of Theorem 6 We use Lemma 5. Let d_1 and d_2 denote the termination depths of *SFSJ-RR*, and define d_1^A and d_2^A similarly for A.

$$\begin{aligned} totDepth(SFSJ\text{-}RR, I) &= d_1 + d_2 \leq 2\max\{d_1, d_2\} \\ &\leq 2\max\{d_1^A, d_2^A\} + 2K \\ &\leq 2 \cdot totDepth(A, I) + 2K \end{aligned}$$

This proves that *SFSJ-RR* is instance optimal, since $2K$ can be treated as a constant that does not depend on A or I. The instance optimality of *SFSJ-SC* follows directly by Lemma 4□

Proof of Theorem 7 Consider the following instance in $\mathcal{I}$.

R_1

	α	β_1	β_2
τ_1^1	a	.2	.1
τ_1^2	a	.1	.2
τ_1^3	b	.3	.3
...			
τ_1^{n+3}	b	.3	.3
τ_1^{n+4}	b	.5	.5

R_2

	α	β_3
τ_2^1	a	.1
τ_2^2	b	.2

Suppose that an algorithm $B \in \mathcal{SJA}$ accesses the following prefixes: $S_1' = \{\tau_1^1, \tau_1^2, \tau_1^3\}$ from R_1 and $S_2' = \{\tau_2^1, \tau_2^2\}$ from R_2. Based on the sorted access model, B can reason that $SKY(R_1) = \{\tau_1^1, \tau_1^2\}$, since τ_1^3 will dominate any other tuple in $R_1 - S_1'$. Similarly, it is straightforward to verify that $SKY(R_2) = \{\tau_2^1\}$. Since $SKY(R_1) \bowtie SKY(R_2) \equiv SKY(R_1) \times SKY(R_2)$ for this case, B can safely terminate since there are no more skyline results.

Consider an algorithm $A \in \mathcal{SJA}$. In order to make $MAD(S_1) \neq \emptyset$, and thus have a chance to satisfy the stopping condition, the algorithm has to access at least until τ_1^{4+n}. Hence, $totDepth(A, I)$ can become arbitrarily worse compared to $totDepth(B, I) = 5$, which in turn implies that A cannot be instance-optimal.□

Efficient Parallel Skyline Processing using Hyperplane Projections

Henning Köhler[1] henning@itee.uq.edu.au
Jing Yang[2] jingyang@ruc.edu.cn
Xiaofang Zhou[1,2] zxf@uq.edu.au

[1] School of Information Technology and Electrical Engineering, The University of Queensland, Australia
[2] School of Information, Renmin University of China
Key Labs of Data Engineering and Knowledge Engineering, Ministry of Education, China

ABSTRACT

The skyline of a set of multi-dimensional points (tuples) consists of those points for which no clearly better point exists in the given set, using component-wise comparison on domains of interest. Skyline queries, i.e., queries that involve computation of a skyline, can be computationally expensive, so it is natural to consider parallelized approaches which make good use of multiple processors. We approach this problem by using hyperplane projections to obtain useful partitions of the data set for parallel processing. These partitions not only ensure small local skyline sets, but enable efficient merging of results as well. Our experiments show that our method consistently outperforms similar approaches for parallel skyline computation, regardless of data distribution, and provides insights on the impacts of different optimization strategies.

Categories and Subject Descriptors

H.2.8 [**Information Systems**]: Database Management—*Database Applications*

General Terms

Algorithms, Performance

Keywords

Skyline Query, Parallel Processing, Data Partitioning, Hyperplane Projection

1. INTRODUCTION

There are many applications where a user is interested in viewing the 'best' objects chosen from a large collection, based on multiple criteria, e.g. price and mileage for used cars. There are multiple ways to approach this problem. Top-k queries [5] require a user to define a ranking function over the object collection, and return the k top-ranked objects. In contrast, skyline queries, first introduced by [4], only require users to express their preferences for each domain of interest, e.g. price and mileage should both be low. They then return all objects for which no clearly better object exists, i.e., an object which is at least as good on every domain and strictly better in at least one. Figure 1 shows such a skyline (containing four points) for used cars. Shaded areas indicate values for which strictly better points exists.

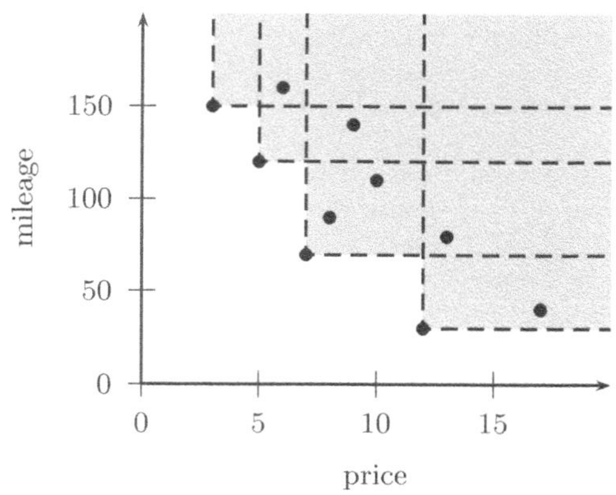

Figure 1: Skyline of used cars

The resulting skyline can provide a user with a better understanding of the trade-offs involved, without requiring any precise ranking functions to be specified. This flexibility makes skylines preferable to top-k approaches for many scenarios, and has caused them to receive much attention in recent years.

As data sets used for skyline processing are often huge, computation can be expensive, and efficient algorithms are vital for applications requiring fast response times. With the advance of multi-core architectures and other parallel computing platforms, parallel skyline algorithms offer a new way to boost performance. In this paper we will develop such a parallel algorithm, with focus on the initial data partitioning. The key idea here is to group points based on their direction from the origin, thus increasing the likelihood of dominance between them. This is achieved by projecting points onto a hyperplane, and ensures that local skyline sets are small. At the same time, merging of result sets can be done efficiently.

Our approach is closest to the angle-based partitioning approach of [23], which also generates small local skylines, but is consistently faster (by up to one order of magnitude), especially for anti-correlated data sets. The improvement hails from a more sophisticated merge step, as well as faster initial partitioning. In addition, we investigate the impact of an approximate skyline pre-processing step, which is generally applicable, and has already proven helpful for sequential skyline computation [12].

The rest of this paper is organized as follows. In Section 2 we give a brief overview of existing work on distributed and parallel skyline computation. The most closely related approach of [23] is discussed in more detail in Section 3, where we develop our plane-project-parallel-skyline (PPPS) algorithm. Experimental evaluation of our and related approaches can be found in Section 4. Section 5 concludes.

2. RELATED WORK

The skyline operation is useful for extracting interesting information from multidimensional databases. It originates from the maximal vector problem in computational geometry [15]. Those early algorithms, including [2, 16], are in-memory algorithms which are only suitable for small datasets. In the original database-oriented paper by Borzsonyi et al. [4] where the concept of the skyline operator is introduced for large databases, a number of efficient external memory algorithms are also proposed, including the block-nested-loop (BNL) algorithm that scans the dataset while employing a bounded buffer for tracking the points that cannot be dominated by other points in the buffer, and the divide-and-conquer (DC) algorithm that recursively partitions the dataset until each partition is small enough to fit in memory to compute the local skyline for each partition followed by a merge step to form the global skyline. There exist numerous efficient skyline query processing approaches, such as the bitmap-based progressive algorithm [22], the sorting-and-filtering approach [6, 12], the nearest neighbor based approach [14], and the I/O optimal R-tree based branch-and-bound algorithm [17, 18].

Due to its high processing cost, there has been a growing interest lately in distributed and parallel skyline query processing. Deviating from centralized skyline query processing approaches, a new approach for computing skyline objects over distributed sources is first presented by Balke et al. [1]. It supports skyline operations over web databases where data is vertically partitioned and each site provides one attribute of the data object. Skyline points are calculated per site and reported to the user at a central point. The algorithm first retrieves values in every dimension from remote data sites using sorted access in round-robin fashion on all dimensions until all dimension values of an object, called the terminating object, have been retrieved. Then those non-skyline objects will be filtered from all those objects with at least one dimension value retrieved. The problem setting for this work is specialized, and the use of a central point can limit the scale of distribution.

There are several data partitioning based approaches for skyline computation in peer-to-peer environment. Wang et al. [24] developed the Skyline Space Partitioning (SSP) approach to compute skylines on a tree-structured P2P platform. That approach uses the z-curve method to partition the multidimensional data space into linearly ordered regions which can be mapped to different peer nodes according to the underlying P2P protocols. As in most partition-based parallel processing schemes, load-balancing is a critical issue. Under the SSP approach, a small number of peers (those that are allocated with partitions close to the origin of the axes) can often take much heavier workload than other peers, while many peers do not contribute to the final skyline results.

Wu et al. [25] are among the first to address the problem of parallel skyline query execution over a large number of machines by leveraging on content-based data partitioning. By using the query range to recursively partition the data region on every data site involved, and encoding each involved sub-region dynamically, their method avoids accessing sites not containing potential skyline points and can report correct skyline points progressively. The proposed algorithm named DSL [25] horizontally partitions data across different machines, i.e. each machine stores a subset of the entire data record set. One advantage of this approach is that it provides incremental scalability, where its performance can be improved by adding additional machines to the cluster. Their system can automatically balance the load by distributing objects to the new nodes. This work, however, requires each node to start the skyline computation on its data after receiving the results of other nodes based on the partial order. Therefore, its parallelism is limited to the pipeline fashion. Differing from the previous work, Cui et al. [8] approach parallel skyline computing without the assumption of any overlay availability on top of the original network. They tackle constrained skyline queries in large-scale distributed environments with horizontally partitioned data distribution. The problem of parallel skyline computing is also considered in an environment of one-processor-multiple-disk architecture to enable disk access parallelism and effective pruning using the parallel R-tree [11].

Dehne et al. [10] propose an optimal coarse-grained parallel algorithm for computing skylines in three dimensions; but their approach does not seem to lead to practical algorithms for higher-dimensional point sets. Random data partitioning is used in [7] which uses the divide-and-conquer algorithm by Kung et al. [15] and the branch-and-bound algorithm by Papadias et al. [18] as building blocks. This can ensure a similar data distribution in each partition to the original dataset. Then each machine processes the skyline over its local data using the branch-and-bound algorithm. The main drawback of this random partitioning approach is that the size of the local result sets is not minimized and many points that belong to the local skyline sets do not belong in the final skyline result set.

In contrast to those parallel skyline algorithms designed for a shared-nothing distributed environment where the participating nodes can only communicate only by exchanging messages [13, 21, 25], [19] focuses on exploiting properties specific to multi-core architectures in which participating cores inside a processor share everything and communicate simply by updating the main memory. They proposed two parallel skyline algorithms: a parallel version of the branch-and-bound algorithm [18] and a new parallel algorithm based on skeletal parallel programming, which is already in use by such database programming models as MapReduce [9, 20] and Map-Reduce-Merge [26].

Grid-based data space partitioning has been commonly used in distributed and parallel skyline processing. For example, in [25], the space is partitioned based on CAN [21], whereas in [24] a tree-structured overlay is used to partition the data space. Such grid-based partitioning, however, is not suitable for skyline queries when all partitions are to be examined at different machines in parallel, since many data partitions do not contribute to the final skyline set (you can think that many partitions are actually dominated by other partitions). This can result in significant redundant processing at some nodes as well as higher overall costs for data communication and merger after location skylines are computed. In [23], a novel angle-based space partitioning scheme is proposed to use the hyperspherical coordinates of the data points to alleviate most of the problems found in traditional random and grid partitioning techniques. It first maps the entire dataset from the Cartesian coordinate space into a hyperspherical space, in which the data space is partitioned based on the angular coordinates. While this type of partitioning has some attractive features, it employs a centralized step to transform the coordinates of each and every point of the dataset to hyperspherical coordinates. We will discuss more details of this approach in the next section when we introduce our ideas.

3. PARALLEL SKYLINE PROCESSING

We will now describe our approach to parallel skyline processing. For parallel algorithms, there is typically a tradeoff. If we spend time to pre-process the data before allocating tasks to different processors, the processing itself and/or the final merge phase may become cheaper. On the other hand, the time used for pre-processing contributes to the overall running time. Finding a good balance which minimizes overall running time is vital.

Computationally, there is a significant difference between cases where the skyline set is small and cases where it is large. For small skyline sets, skyline computation is I/O bound, but it becomes CPU-bound for large skyline sets as the number of dominance-checks between skyline points grows (quadratically in the worst case). To ensure that our algorithm is efficient for both small and large skyline sets, we must combine a number of processing techniques. By focusing on preprocessing steps which can be performed as part of a single scan of the data set for data partitioning, we remain efficient for small skyline sets.

As a first step we attempt to reduce the number of points to consider for further computation. Here we employ fast algorithms for approximating the skyline. That is, we filter out points which we can quickly identify as not being part of the skyline. An approach for approximate skyline computation is discussed in Section 3.1.

Next we must partition our data set. Each partition will then be transferred to one of the available processors for local skyline computation. Here it is vital to partition in such a manner that non-skyline points can be eliminated during local skyline computation as much as possible, i.e., we would like to group points which are likely to dominate each other into the same partition. The angle-based approach for skyline partitioning proposed in [23] achieves this, but requires rather complex and costly conversion of points into hypersphere coordinates, and does not cater for efficient merging. We will show that equally good partitions can be found through hyper-plane projection (which is much simpler and cheaper to compute), and that such projections allow for efficient merge steps. Our partitioning approach is detailed in Section 3.2, while efficient merging of local skylines is discussed in Section 3.3.

Note that the computation of the approximate skyline of P (see Section 3.1) and its partition into $P_1, \ldots, P_n$ can be done together in a single parse of P, thereby minimizing I/O costs for large data sets.

3.1 Approximate Skyline

Computing the exact skyline of a set P can be expensive, as each point may be compared to many other points. However, it is often possible to eliminate the majority of non-skyline points with few comparisons, especially in cases where the skyline set is small. The idea for this is the following: We pick a small set $B \subset P$ of comparison points, then test for every point in P whether it is dominated by a point in B. Those that are dominated can safely be discarded, so that the resulting approximate skyline set is guaranteed to contain all skyline points, but likely some non-skyline points as well. Importantly, for fixed size B (we found $|B| \approx 10$ to work well), computing the approximate skyline can be done in linear time with a single pass over the data set. For details on strategies for selecting B see [12], which employs similar techniques for optimizing sort-based skyline computation. As we want to avoid scanning the data set multiple times, we select B based on a small sample subset of P.

In addition to reducing transport and computation costs, early elimination of non-skyline points has another positive side-effect. As we partition P such that *input* sets are of similar size for each processor, it can easily happen that the respective local skylines differ significantly in size. As the skyline size impacts on computation time, this can cause unbalanced workloads. Removal of non-skyline points tends to strengthen the relationship between input and output (skyline) size, thus reducing the chance for and/or severity of imbalanced loads.

3.2 Partitioning via Hyperplane Projection

For partitioning the data space, we will employ techniques similar to the angle-based partitioning approach from [23]. The central idea in [23] is to transform each point (treated as a vector in some euclidian space) into hypersphere coordinates. Partitioning is then done based on the transformed values, ignoring the distance from the origin. As a result, points which lie in similar direction from the origin, but possibly at different distances, are likely to be assigned to the same partition. Hence points that can dominate a given non-skyline point are likely to lie in the same partition, thus allowing it to be eliminated during local skyline computation. Figure 2 illustrates this approach - on the left the partition in the original space is shown, on the right the same partition after projection and transformation into hypersphere coordinates.

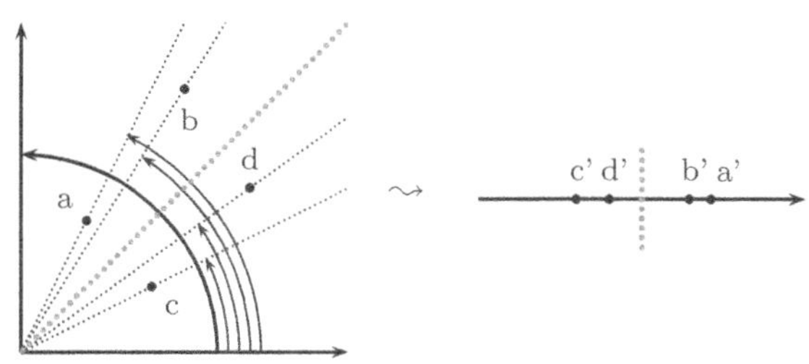

Figure 2: Angle-based Partitioning

Unfortunately, transformation into hypersphere coordinates is time-consuming. This is less noticeable in cases where the skyline is large, but can become a bottleneck if the skyline set is small (and thus computation fast), as these transformations are performed centrally. In our approach, we avoid costly transformation of coordinates into hypersphere coordinates. Instead, we use projection onto the hyperplane $x_1 + \ldots + x_d = 1$. Note that we do not project orthogonally, but by intersecting the line through the origin with the hyperplane. Afterwards, points are allocated to partitions based on their projections. This is illustrated in Figure 3 - the partition of the original space is shown on the left and its hyperplane projection on the right, where it is possible to decide which partition a point belongs to based on a single projected coordinate.

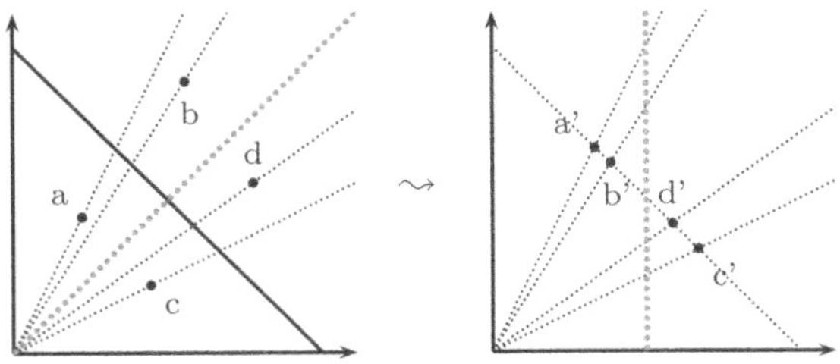

Figure 3: Hyperplane-projection-based Partitioning

In 2-dimensional space, every angle-based partition is also a hyperplane-based partition and vice versa, although this fails to hold for dimension higher than 2. Note that unlike the angle-based coordinate transformation, our projection does not affect the dimensionality of the data set. While all projected points lie in a hyperplane, these projections are still represented in the original euclidian space. Importantly, points that are in a dominance relationship are likely to have similar hyperplane projections, and thus are likely allocated to the same partition for local skyline computation. This realizes the driving goals behind the angle-based partitioning approach [23], but unlike transformations into hypersphere coordinates, hyperplane projections are simple and cheap to compute:

$$\begin{pmatrix} x_1 \\ \vdots \\ x_d \end{pmatrix} \mapsto \begin{pmatrix} x_1 \\ \vdots \\ x_d \end{pmatrix} \cdot \frac{1}{x_1 + \ldots + x_d}$$

While grid-based partitioning methods, which define a space partition by partitioning each dimension, are not directly applicable to the resulting hyperplane, as the positive section of the hyperplane is not a hypercube, recursive partitioning methods are well suited. Here we split a given dataset into two partitions, based on a single coordinate. Each partition is then split again (using a different coordinate), until the desired number of partitions (=number of processors) is reached. The split conditions (e.g. $x_2 \leq 0.2$) should be chosen such that each partition contains roughly the same number of points for a randomly selected sample set. This can be done efficiently by using one of the well-known selection algorithms such as quick-select, which find the kth smallest element in (worst-case or expected) linear time [3].

Of course, the number of parallel processors available need not be a power of 2 in general. In such a case, whenever we perform a split, we also split the set of processors into two groups of nearly equal size (e.g. 3 and 4 if 7 processors are available), and then select the split point such that the point partitions contain points in the same ratio (e.g. 3:4), and assign each partition to their respective set of processors. A similar approach can be used to deal with processors of different computational power.

Compared to the dynamic space partitioning approach suggested in [23], which repeatedly splits the largest partition into two until the desired number of partitions is reached, our method has two advantages. First, it allows partitioning of the entire data set in a single pass, which reduces I/O costs for large data sets. Second, partitions are very similar in size, whereas the partitions obtained by the method in [23] differ by up to factor two.

Example 1. *Consider the set of 3D points P given below:*

$$P = \left\{ \begin{pmatrix} 9 \\ 6 \\ 15 \end{pmatrix}, \begin{pmatrix} 13 \\ 3 \\ 4 \end{pmatrix}, \begin{pmatrix} 15 \\ 5 \\ 5 \end{pmatrix}, \begin{pmatrix} 12 \\ 8 \\ 20 \end{pmatrix} \right\}$$

Projection on the hyperplane $x + y + z = 1$ results in the following projected points:

$$\mathcal{H}(P) = \left\{ \begin{pmatrix} 0.3 \\ 0.2 \\ 0.5 \end{pmatrix}, \begin{pmatrix} 0.65 \\ 0.15 \\ 0.2 \end{pmatrix}, \begin{pmatrix} 0.6 \\ 0.2 \\ 0.2 \end{pmatrix}, \begin{pmatrix} 0.3 \\ 0.2 \\ 0.5 \end{pmatrix} \right\}$$

Imposing a split condition $x_1 \leq 0.4$ partitions P into

$$P_1 = \left\{ \begin{pmatrix} 9 \\ 6 \\ 15 \end{pmatrix}, \begin{pmatrix} 12 \\ 8 \\ 20 \end{pmatrix} \right\} \quad \text{and} \quad P_2 = \left\{ \begin{pmatrix} 13 \\ 3 \\ 4 \end{pmatrix}, \begin{pmatrix} 15 \\ 5 \\ 5 \end{pmatrix} \right\}$$

Note that rotating dimensions for splitting helps to ensure that the projections of points within a partition are similar in all dimensions, thus increasing the probability that points within the same partition dominate each other.

Finally, the choice of hyperplane $x_1 + \ldots + x_d = 1$ works best if all coordinates have roughly the same range of values. If this is not the case, we can scale dimensions, e.g. by their (estimated) average value $Ave(X_i)$, giving us the transformation

$$\begin{pmatrix} x_1 \\ \vdots \\ x_d \end{pmatrix} \mapsto \begin{pmatrix} \frac{x_1}{Ave(X_1)} \\ \vdots \\ \frac{x_d}{Ave(X_d)} \end{pmatrix} \cdot \frac{1}{\frac{x_1}{Ave(X_1)} + \ldots + \frac{x_d}{Ave(X_d)}}$$

3.3 Merging Skylines

When merging the partial skyline sets to obtain the final skyline results, we focus on two objectives. First, the merging process should make good use of all processors, i.e. the workload should be shared. Second, we want to make merging efficient by reducing the number of comparisons between partial skyline points.

Our basic approach for addressing the first objective is rather straight forward. We perform a bottom-up merge, using the recursively constructed space partitioning tree (Algorithm 1). This is clearly advantageous to a centralized merge, as the workload is shared. It also ensures that partial skyline sets merged still have similar projections, so non-skyline points are eliminated early.

We must note though that this basic approach still requires pairwise comparison of all skyline points, which can be expensive if the final skyline set is large. To reduce this cost, which is our second objective, space-partitioning schemes commonly utilize the following two observations:

Proposition 1. *If there exists a coordinate x such that all $p_1 \in P_1$ have lower x-value than all $p_2 \in P_2$, then*

1. *no point in P_2 can dominate a point in P_1, and*
2. *a point in P_1 dominates a point in P_2 iff it dominates it (or is equal to) in the $(d-1)$-dimensional subspace excluding the x-coordinate.*

While the pre-condition of Proposition 1 only holds for the projected points, and points in P_2 can still dominate points in P_1, not all is lost. When comparing partial skyline points $p_1 \in P_1$ and $p_2 \in P_2$, it is still likely (just not certain) that p_1 has a smaller x-value than p_2. Hence, we will sort partial skyline points in P_2 by their x-value, which enables us to only compare those points in p_1, p_2 where $p_1.x \leq p_2.x$ holds, which likely are few. In our experiments we found that this heuristic works extremely well.

It is also possible to employ this heuristic when filtering out non-skyline points in P_2. Here we sort points in P_1 by the sum of their values *other than* x. We found this heuristic to be beneficial here as well, albeit to a lesser degree, and mainly for cases of low dimensionality.

Furthermore, the second conclusion remains valid, i.e., dominance of points in P_2 by points in P_1 on the $(d-1)$-dimensional subspace implies actual dominance.

Theorem 2. *Let S_1, S_2 be the subspaces of $\mathbb{R}^d$ defined by*

$$S_1 : \frac{x_1}{x_1 + \ldots + x_d} \leq c$$

$$S_2 : \frac{x_1}{x_1 + \ldots + x_d} > c$$

for some constant c, $p \in S_1$ and $s \in S_2$. Then p dominates s iff p dominates or equals s on $X_2, \ldots, X_d$.

Proof. The 'only if' direction is trivial, so consider the 'if' direction. By definition of S_1, S_2 we have

$$\frac{p_1}{p_1 + p_2 + \ldots + p_d} \leq c < \frac{s_1}{s_1 + s_2 + \ldots + s_d}$$

$$\Rightarrow \quad p_1 \cdot (s_1 + s_2 + \ldots + s_d) < s_1 \cdot (p_1 + p_2 + \ldots + p_d)$$

$$\Rightarrow \quad p_1 \cdot (s_2 + \ldots + s_d) < s_1 \cdot (p_2 + \ldots + p_d) \leq s_1 \cdot (s_2 + \ldots + s_d)$$

$$\Rightarrow \quad p_1 < s_1$$

which shows that p dominates s. □

Hence we can first compute the skyline (approximate or exact) of P_1 w.r.t. $X_2, \ldots, X_d$ before using it to eliminate points in P_2. During our experiments we found that this strategy is useful for up to about 5 dimensions. For more dimensions the number of skyline points in P_1 eliminated becomes too small to compensate for the additional cost in computing the skyline on $X_2, \ldots, X_d$.

A detailed description of our recursive split and merge approach is given in Algorithm 1. Here we use the notations $[p]$ to denote the hyperplane-projection of p, and $p.d$ to denote the d-th coordinate of p. For a set of points P we use the notation

$$[P] := \{[p] \mid p \in P\}$$

$$P.d := \{p.d \mid p \in P\}$$

We note that direct application of Algorithm 1 is only efficient if the entire data set fits into memory. In order to avoid multiple passes for large data sets, we first apply the splitting phase of Algorithm 1 to a small sample set, storing the *split_values* found in a *space partition tree* (an annotated binary tree describing how the data space is to be partitioned). Afterwards we can use our space partition tree to assign each data point to its partition in a single pass.

Algorithm 1 Split-Skyline-Merge (SSM)

Input: P = points, n = #processors, d = split dimension
Output: skyline of P

if $n = 1$ **then**
    $S := skyline(P)$
    return S
else
    $n_1 := n\ div\ 2$; $n_2 := n - n_1$
    $P_1, P_2 := SPLIT(P, n_1, n_2, d)$
    $next\_d := d + 1\ mod\ \#dimensions$
    $S_1 := SSM(P_1, n_1, next\_d)$
    $S_2 := SSM(P_2, n_2, next\_d)$
    return $MERGE(S_1, S_2, d)$

Subroutine SPLIT(P, n_1, n_2, d)
Output: P_1, P_2 with $P_1 \cup P_2 = P$, $[P_1].d < [P_2].d$, $\frac{|P_1|}{|P_2|} \approx \frac{n_1}{n_2}$

$split\_index := |P| \cdot \frac{n_1}{n1+n2}$
$split\_value := quick\_select([P].d, split\_index)$
$P_1 := \{p \in P \mid [p].d \leq split\_value\}$
$P_2 := \{p \in P \mid [p].d > split\_value\}$
return P_1, P_2

Subroutine MERGE(S_1, S_2, d)
Input: local skylines S_1, S_2 with $[S_1].d < [S_2].d$
Output: $skyline(S_1 \cup S_2)$

sort S_1, S_2 by d-th coordinate
for all $p_1 \in S_1$ **do**
    for all $p_2 \in S_2$ with $p_2.d \leq p_1.d$ **do**
        if p_2 dominates p_1 **then**
            $S_1 := S_1 \setminus \{p_1\}$
if #dimensions ≤ 5 **then**
    $S_1' := skyline(S_1)$ on dimensions other than d
else
    $S_1' := S_1$
for all $p_2 \in S_2$ **do**
    if $\exists p_1 \in S_1'$ with p_1 dominates p_2 **then**
        $S_2 := S_2 \setminus \{p_2\}$
return $S_1 \cup S_2$

3.4 Local Skyline Size

We conclude this section with a brief qualitative analysis regarding the size of local skylines under different partitioning strategies, in order to give the reader a better intuition about them. The central idea is that a "good" partitioning will ensure that many points which dominate each other are assigned to the same partition, so that local skylines are small. In turn, having small local skylines ensures fast response times. In [23] the notion of *pruning power* was introduced, measuring the percentage of space a point p dominates within its partition under some partitioning $\mathcal{X}$. For uniform data distribution, this equates to the probability that it dominates another random point within its partition:

$$\text{Pow}(\mathcal{X}, p) := P\big(p \leq q \mid \mathcal{X}(p) = \mathcal{X}(q)\big)$$

where $\mathcal{X}(p)$ denotes the partition w.r.t. $\mathcal{X}$ in which p lies. A large (average) pruning power typically translates into small local skylines, although the exact relationship between these two measures is complex, even for uniform distributions, and not explored further.

However, it appears that pruning power is ill-suited for qualitative comparison of partitionings, requiring complex analysis even for uniform data distribution [23], thereby providing little intuition. We will thus use the following alternative measure:

DEFINITION 3 (LOCAL MATCH RATIO). *The* local match ratio *of a partitioning* $\mathcal{X}$ *is*

$$LMR(\mathcal{X}) := P(\mathcal{X}(p) = \mathcal{X}(q) \mid p \leq q) = P(\mathcal{X}(p) = \mathcal{X}(q) \mid p \leq q \vee q \leq p)$$

For a fixed point p *the local match ratio w.r.t.* $\mathcal{X}$ *is*

$$LMR(p, \mathcal{X}) := P(\mathcal{X}(p) = \mathcal{X}(q) \mid p \leq q \vee q \leq p)$$

Note that the average pruning power and the local match ratio of a partition are closely related:

$$\mathrm{LMR}(\mathcal{X}) = \mathrm{Pow}(\mathcal{X}) \cdot \frac{P(\mathcal{X}(p) = \mathcal{X}(q))}{P(p \leq q)}$$

Figure 4 illustrates the difference between plane-projection and grid-based partitions for uniform data distribution. Shades areas indicate points comparable to p.

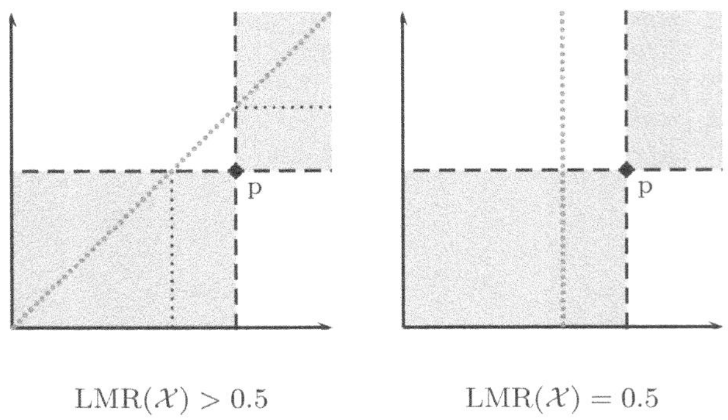

Figure 4: Local match ratio for plane-project and grid-based partitioning

From the left graph in Figure 4, it is clear that the LMR for plane-projection based partitioning is at least 0.5 for every point p, resulting in a global LMR value strictly larger than 0.5 (approximately 0.56), i.e., at least half of the shaded area lies in the same partition as p. For grid-based partitioning (right graph in Figure 4), the LMR value is precisely 0.5. An interesting case which highlights the benefits of the LMR measure is random partitioning. Its LMR value is always 0.5 (for 2 equally probable partitions), regardless of dimensionality and data distribution, thus serving as a good baseline for comparison.

While we omit a quantitative analysis (see [23] for details of how pruning power can be calculated - LMR is similar), it should by now be clear that plane-projection based partitioning leads to smaller local skylines than grid-based or random partitioning, at least for uniform data distributions. For anti-correlated data we would expect grid-based partitions to work relatively well. A quantitative comparison for different data distributions and dimensions can be found in the following Section 4.

4. EXPERIMENTS

In order to test the efficiency of our approach for parallel skyline computation, we ran it over randomly generated data sets, and compared it to alternative approaches. Here we considered uniform, correlated and anti-correlated data distributions, under different parameter settings. The experiments were run on a PC with 2.6GHz AMD Athlon 64 X2 dual core processor and 3GB RAM. The default parameter settings are shown in Table 1.

Table 1: Default Parameter Settings

parameter	value	range
nr. of points	100k	10k–1M
dimensions	5	2–8
nr. of processors	8	2–64
network speed	1GBit/s	10MBit/s–∞

For each parameter, we ran one set of experiments (on uniform, correlated and anti-correlated data), where we varied that parameter while keeping the other ones at their default setting. While our implementation is actually sequential, we track time as if computation was performed in parallel, and simulate costs for transporting data between processors (here an infinite network speed means no extra cost, which may be realistic e.g. for multi-core processors, where each core takes the role of a processor).

The different skyline algorithms we considered are

- Plane-Project-Parallel-Skyline (PPPS)
- Angle-based-Parallel-Skyline (APS)
- Grid-based-Parallel-Skyline (GPS)
- Random-Parallel-Skyline (RPS)
- Sort-Filter-Skyline (SFS)

Our algorithm PPPS is described in detail in Section 3. Algorithm APS refers to the Angle-based-space-partitioning approach described in [23], using dynamic space partitioning. The GPS algorithm (Grid-based Parallel skyline) partitions the data set without projecting first, but unlike APS makes use of (a simplified version of) the merge strategy described in Section 3.3. RPS partitions the data set randomly, thus reducing pre-processing costs, at the price of not being able employ efficient merge strategies. The only non-parallel algorithm is SFS [6], which sorts the data set before making dominance checks. SFS is used as basic algorithm for local skyline computation and merging, and for baseline comparison. All skyline algorithms employ the approximate skyline computation pre-processing step described in Section 3.1, as it reduces transport and partitioning costs (this actually makes our SFS implementation more similar to the advanced LESS algorithm [12]).

A direct comparison of computation speed for hypersphere- and hyperplane projection under varying dimensionality is given in Figure 5. As predicted, hyperplane projection is significantly faster, with the difference increasing for growing dimensionality.

Figure 6 shows computation time of the different algorithms for different randomly generated data sets, with varying pairwise correlation. Note that possible correlation values are limited from below by $1/(1-n)$, where n is the

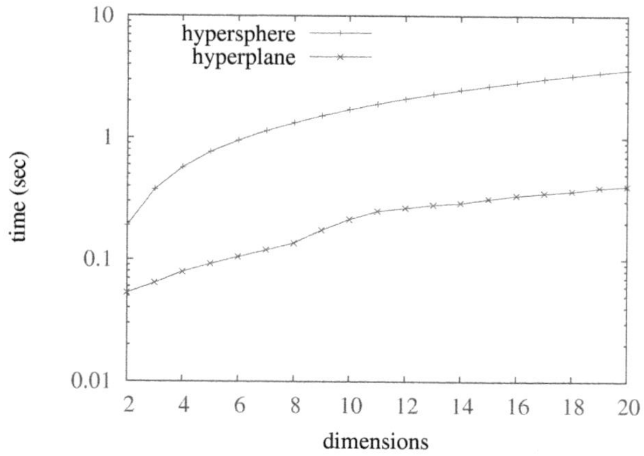

Figure 5: Projection speed comparison

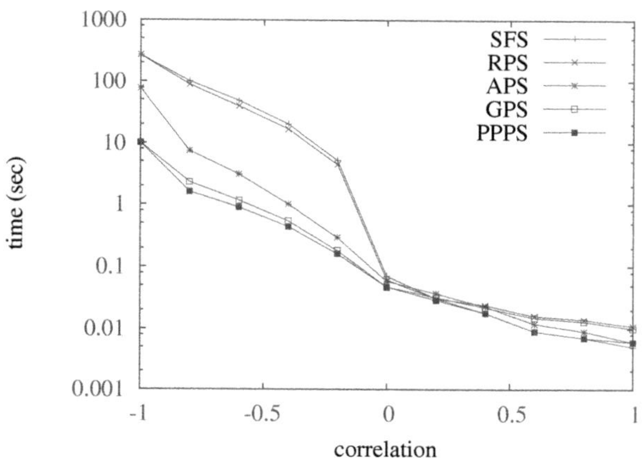

Figure 6: Varying correlation

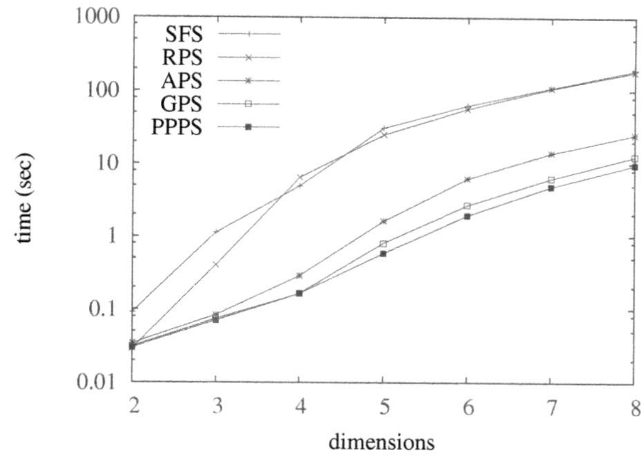

Figure 7: Varying dimensions (anti-correlated)

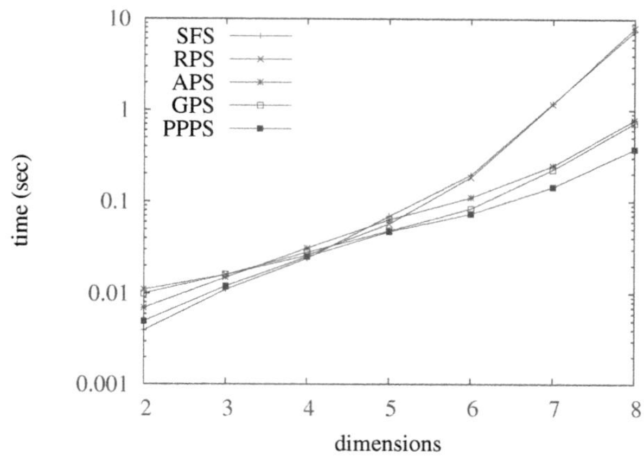

Figure 8: Varying dimensions (uniform)

number of dimensions (5 here), so for negative correlation the given values are linearly scaled accordingly (-1 indicates pairwise correlation of $-\frac{1}{4}$, $-\frac{1}{2}$ corresponds to pairwise correlation of $-\frac{1}{8}$, etc).

The running times seem to indicate that the benefit of applying parallel algorithms is smaller for uniform or positively correlated data sets. The reason here is that the actual skyline is small, so that a large percentage of the time is just spent on pre-processing steps and data transport. However, larger skylines can also occur for uniform and positively correlated data when the dimensionality is high. Figures 7, 8 and 9 show results for varying number of dimensions and anti-correlated (corr=-0.5), uniform and correlated (corr=0.5) data, respectively.

Once again we see that parallel skyline computation is only effective in cases where the actual skyline is reasonably large, this time due to high dimensionality. In all such cases, our PPPS algorithm is considerably faster (note that time is in log-scale) than the alternatives considered. It is worth noting that the difference to the angle-based partitioning approach (APS) is not just due to the faster projection method, but mainly caused by the efficient merge algorithm. GPS outperforms APS for the same reason.

In order to judge the impact of the different optimization applied, namely

1. approximate skyline pre-processing, and
2. efficient merging

we compare our PPPS algorithm with variants employing none or only one of the above optimization. Figure 10 shows the behavior of the different algorithms for varying correlations. PPPS(A+M) denotes the PPPS algorithm with both approximate skyline pre-processing and efficient merge, PPPS(M) is PPPS without approximate skyline, etc.

We find that approximate skyline pre-processing is helpful for uniform or correlated data sets, as it reduces transport costs as well as sorting costs for SFS. For anti-correlated data is has virtually no impact, as other costs dominate and the approximate skyline grows in size. Efficient merging on the other hand is extremely beneficial for anti-correlated data, but actually increases processing costs for uniform and correlated data sets, due to overheads exceeding costs for simple "brute-force" skyline merge.

Figures 11, 12 and 13 show how the different algorithms scale with data set size. The dimensionality used is 5, 10 and 15 for the anti-correlated, uniform and correlated case respectively, to ensure that the skyline is large enough to necessitate parallel skyline algorithms.

As is to be expected, the increase in time is more than linear but slightly less than quadratic in the size increase,

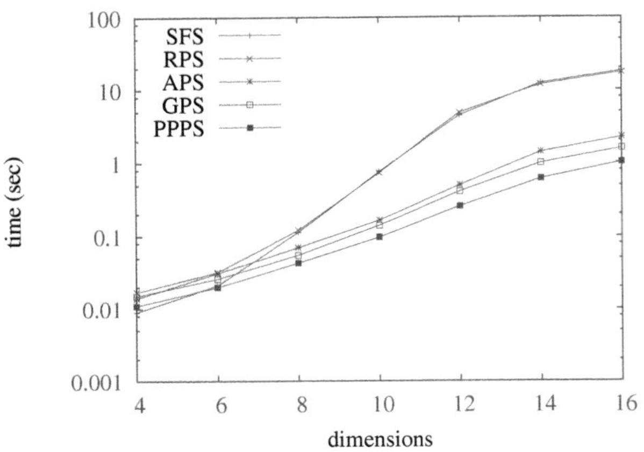

Figure 9: Varying dimensions (correlated)

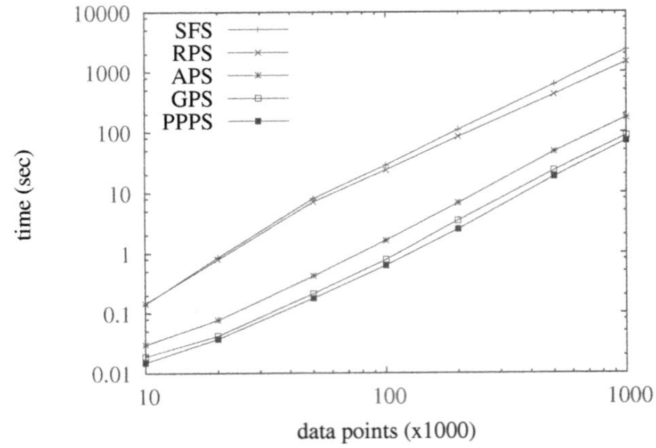

Figure 11: Varying size (anti-correlated)

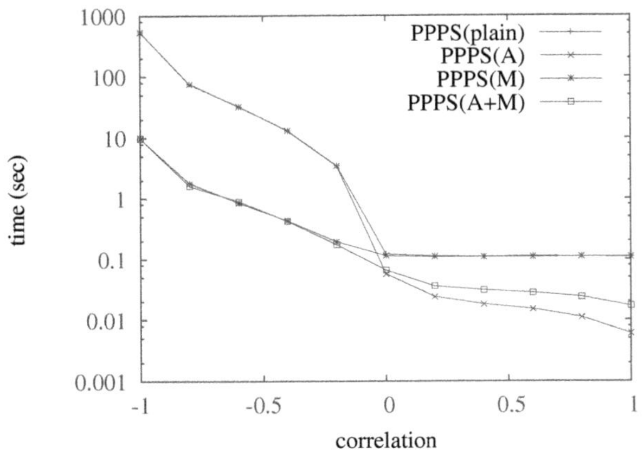

Figure 10: Varying correlation (by optimization)

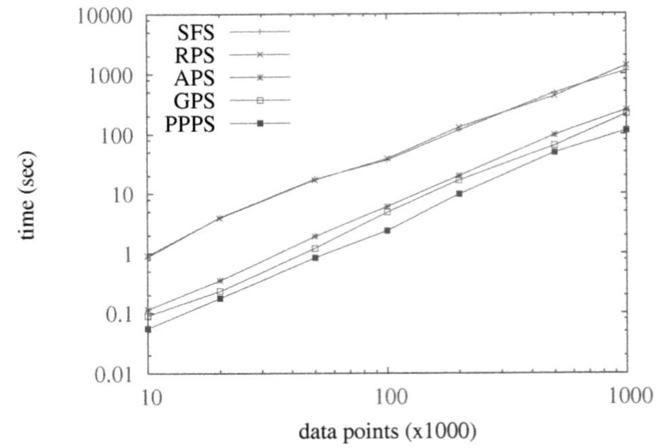

Figure 12: Varying size (uniform)

similar to the underlying SFS algorithm used for local skyline computation. The difference in speed between the algorithms grows slightly with increasing data set size, up to about 50,000, from which point on it remains fairly constant. This is due to the preprocessing costs (approximate skyline computation, partitioning, transport costs) becoming less significant, as they grow only linearly in the data size. Our PPPS algorithm is consistently the fastest, by more than one order of magnitude compared to SFS. This is interesting in so far as the speed factor exceeds the number of processors (8 here). The explanation is that the efficient merge step helps greatly in reducing skyline point comparisons, making our approach superior to SFS/LESS even when run sequentially.

The effect that the number of processors has on processing time is shown in Figures 14, 15 and 16.

For PPPS, computation time drops quickly with rising number of processors, up to about 32 for our anti-correlated data set, at which point preprocessing and merge costs become dominant and further increases in the number of processors bring no significant benefit. For APS this point is reached earlier at about 8 processors, and later for GPS, while the random partitioning approach (RPS) hardly profits from parallel processing power at all. Again, the reason is an inefficient merge step, which becomes more costly as the partitions become finer. We conclude that random partitioning is not suitable for parallel skyline computation, regardless of the number of processors available. We found that the point at which further increases in the number of processors does not improve performance of PPPS (respectively APS) increases slowly with growing data set size.

Table 2: Local-Approximate Skyline Sizes

dimensions	5	10	15
correlation	anti-corr	uniform	correlated
skyline size	17668	26442	13812
plane-project	18378 (+4%)	34366 (+30%)	17646 (+28%)
angle-based	18363 (+4%)	34884 (+32%)	17962 (+30%)
grid-based	19578 (+11%)	46568 (+76%)	20910 (+51%)
random	26783 (+52%)	47584 (+80%)	20618 (+49%)

It is worth noting that in cases where the skyline set is large, merging of local skylines can be quite expensive. On the other hand, this step often eliminates only a very small fraction of points. Thus, if a good approximation of the actual skyline set is sufficient for the application scenario, one may want to omit this final merge step. This is particularly profitable if the application requires further parallel processing of the skyline set, as this may eliminate the need for synchronization and merge completely. Table 2 shows

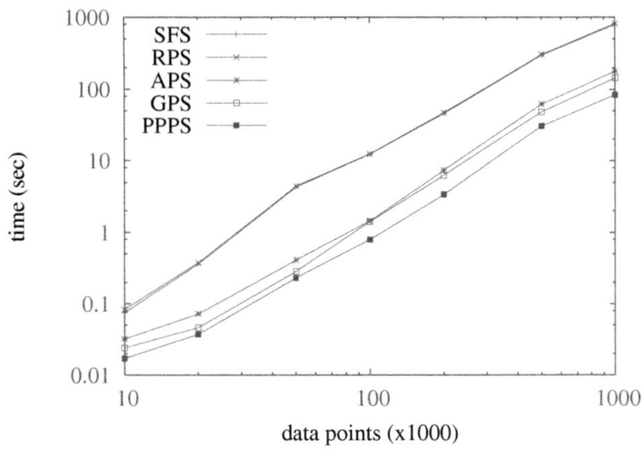

Figure 13: Varying size (correlated)

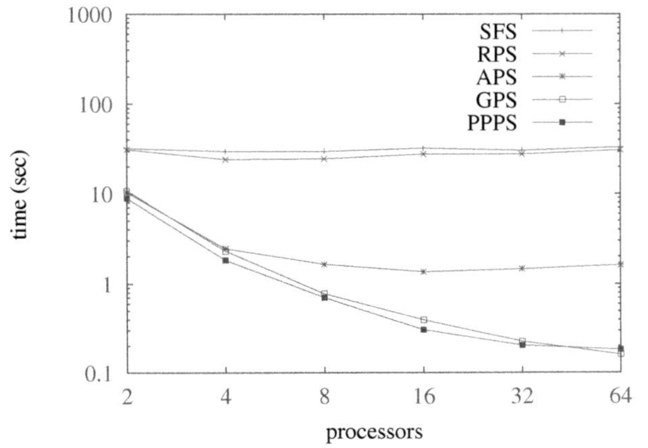

Figure 14: Number of processors (anti-correlated)

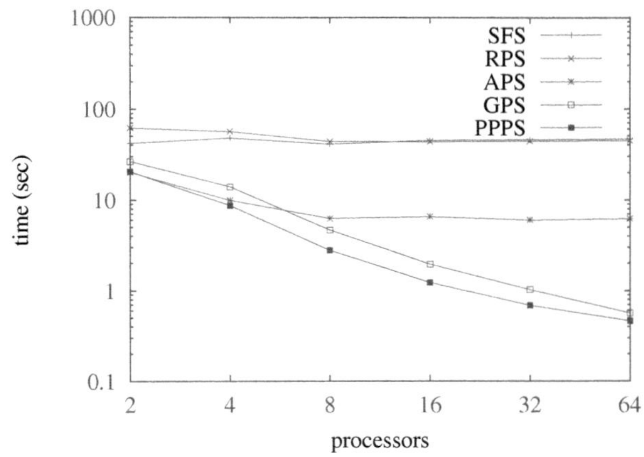

Figure 15: Number of processors (uniform)

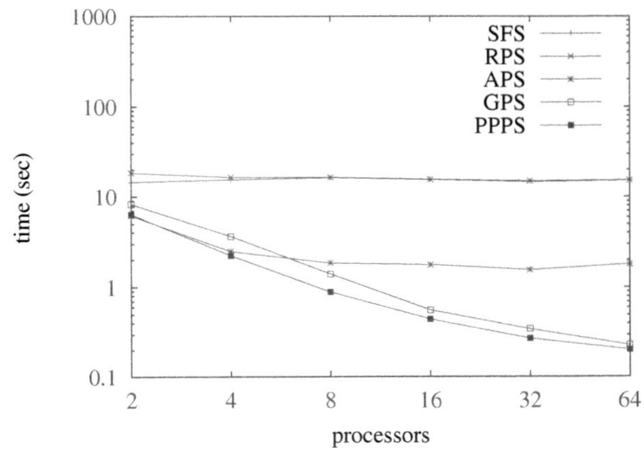

Figure 16: Number of processors (correlated)

the size of the actual skyline and of the (union of) local skyline sets resulting from the different partitioning approaches, for different data sets.

We find that random partitioning leads to large local skylines in all cases. Grid-based partitioning provides small local skylines for anti-correlated data in few dimensions, albeit still larger than for plane-project or angle-based projection, but fails for uniform or correlated ones with high dimensionality. This confirms the quantitative results of Section 3.4. Plane-projection and angle-based partitioning approaches perform best in all cases, but the difference between local skyline and global skyline is still significant for high-dimensional data.

5. CONCLUSION

We have investigated a novel approach to parallel skyline computation, based on a data partitioning strategy which uses projection of points onto a hyperplane. It combines the benefits of small local skylines, as achieved by angle-based partitioning [23], with an effective merge strategy, as used in various grid-based partitioning schemes, and outperforms both. In addition, we investigated the benefits of initial approximate skyline pre-computation, and the impact of various optimizations under different data distributions.

For future work, we will to investigate a combination of our partitioning strategy with the recursive merge-approach devised in [15].

Acknowledgement: The work reported in this paper is supported by the Australian Research Council research grants DP0987557 and LP0882957. Yang's research is also partially supported by the National Science Foundation of China (grant number: 61070056, 61033010) and National High Technology Research and Development Program 863 of China (grant number: 2008AA01Z120).

6. REFERENCES

[1] W.-T. Balke, U. Güntzer, and J. X. Zheng. Efficient distributed skylining for web information systems. In *EDBT*, pages 256–273, 2004.

[2] J. L. Bentley, H. T. Kung, M. Schkolnick, and C. D. Thompson. On the average number of maxima in a set of vectors and applications. *J. ACM*, 25(4):536–543, 1978.

[3] M. Blum, R. W. Floyd, V. R. Pratt, R. L. Rivest, and R. E. Tarjan. Time bounds for selection. *J. Comput. Syst. Sci.*, 7(4):448–461, 1973.

[4] S. Börzsönyi, D. Kossmann, and K. Stocker. The skyline operator. In *ICDE*, pages 421–430, 2001.

[5] M. J. Carey and D. Kossmann. On saying 'Enough Already!' in SQL. In *SIGMOD*, pages 219–230, 1997.

[6] J. Chomicki, P. Godfrey, J. Gryz, and D. Liang. Skyline with presorting. In *ICDE*, pages 717–719, 2003.

[7] A. Cosgaya-Lozano, A. Rau-Chaplin, and N. Zeh. Parallel computation of skyline queries. In *21st International Symposium on High Performance Computing Systems and Applications (HPCS)*, page 12, 2007.

[8] B. Cui, H. Lu, Q. Xu, L. Chen, Y. Dai, and Y. Zhou. Parallel distributed processing of constrained skyline queries by filtering. In *ICDE*, pages 546–555, 2008.

[9] J. Dean and S. Ghemawat. Mapreduce: simplified data processing on large clusters. In *6th Symposium on Operating System Design and Implementation (OSDI)*, pages 137–150, 2004.

[10] F. Dehne, A. Fabri, and A. Rau-Chaplin. Scalable parallel geometric algorithms for coarse grained multicomputers. In *9th Annual Symposium on Computational Geometry (SCG)*, pages 298–307, 1993.

[11] Y. Gao, G. Chen, L. Chen, and C. Chen. Parallelizing progressive computation for skyline queries in multi-disk environment. In *DEXA*, pages 697–706, 2006.

[12] P. Godfrey, R. Shipley, and J. Gryz. Maximal vector computation in large data sets. In *VLDB*, pages 229–240, 2005.

[13] Z. Huang, C. S. Jensen, H. Lu, and B. C. Ooi. Skyline queries against mobile lightweight devices in manets. In *ICDE*, page 66, 2006.

[14] D. Kossmann, F. Ramsak, and S. Rost. Shooting stars in the sky: an online algorithm for skyline queries. In *VLDB*, pages 275–286, 2002.

[15] H. T. Kung, F. Luccio, and F. P. Preparata. On finding the maxima of a set of vectors. *J. ACM*, 22(4):469–476, 1975.

[16] J. Matoušek. Computing dominances in e^n (short communication). *Information Processing Letters*, 38(5):277–278, 1991.

[17] D. Papadias, Y. Tao, G. Fu, and B. Seeger. An optimal and progressive algorithm for skyline queries. In *SIGMOD*, pages 467–478, 2003.

[18] D. Papadias, Y. Tao, G. Fu, and B. Seeger. Progressive skyline computation in database systems. *TODS*, 30(1):41–82, 2005.

[19] S. Park, T. Kim, J. Park, J. Kim, and H. Im. Parallel skyline computation on multicore architectures. In *ICDE*, pages 760–771, 2009.

[20] C. Ranger, R. Raghuraman, A. Penmetsa, G. Bradski, and C. Kozyrakis. Evaluating mapreduce for multi-core and multiprocessor systems. In *IEEE 13th International Symposium on High Performance Computer Architecture (HPCA)*, pages 13–24, 2007.

[21] S. Ratnasamy, P. Francis, M. Handley, R. Karp, and S. Shenker. A scalable content-addressable network. In *SIGCOMM*, pages 161–172, 2001.

[22] K.-L. Tan, P.-K. Eng, and B. C. Ooi. Efficient progressive skyline computation. In *VLDB*, pages 301–310, 2001.

[23] A. Vlachou, C. Doulkeridis, and Y. Kotidis. Angle-based space partitioning for efficient parallel skyline computation. In *SIGMOD*, pages 227–238, 2008.

[24] S. Wang, B. C. Ooi, and A. K. H. Tung. Efficient skyline query processing on peer-to-peer networks. In *ICDE*, pages 1126–1135, 2007.

[25] P. Wu, C. Zhang, Y. Feng, B. Y. Zhao, D. Agrawal, and A. E. Abbadi. Parallelizing skyline queries for scalable distribution. In *EDBT*, pages 112–130, 2006.

[26] H. Yang, A. Dasdan, R.-L. Hsiao, and D. S. Parker. Map-reduce-merge: simplified relational data processing on large clusters. In *SIGMOD*, pages 1029–1040, 2007.

Scalable Query Rewriting: A Graph-Based Approach

George Konstantinidis
Information Sciences Institute
University of Southern California
Marina Del Rey, CA 90292
konstant@usc.edu

José Luis Ambite
Information Sciences Institute
University of Southern California
Marina Del Rey, CA 90292
ambite@isi.edu

ABSTRACT

In this paper we consider the problem of answering queries using views, which is important for data integration, query optimization, and data warehouses. We consider its simplest form, conjunctive queries and views, which already is NP-complete. Our context is data integration, so we search for maximally-contained rewritings. By looking at the problem from a graph perspective we are able to gain a better insight and develop an algorithm which compactly represents common patterns in the source descriptions, and (optionally) pushes some computation offline. This together with other optimizations result in an experimental performance about two orders of magnitude faster than current state-of-the-art algorithms, rewriting queries using over 10000 views within seconds.

Categories and Subject Descriptors

H.2.4 [**Database Management**]: Systems—*Query processing*; H.2.5 [**Database Management**]: Heterogeneous Databases; G.2.2 [**Discrete Mathematics**]: Graph Theory—*Hypergraphs*

General Terms

Algorithms, Performance, Experimentation

1. INTRODUCTION

Given a conjunctive query Q, over a database schema D and a set of view definitions $V_1, ..., V_n$ over the same schema, the problem that we study is to find answers to Q using only $V_1, ..., V_n$.

This is an important problem extensively studied in the contexts of query optimization, data integration and other areas [13, 15]. From the query optimization perspective, views are previous queries who have been already evaluated and their answers have been materialized. In this context, systems rewrite subsequent queries substituting *a part* of the original query with some of the views, so as to come up with an *equivalent* optimized query.

In our context, of data integration, multiple heterogenous sources (as web sites, databases, peer data etc.) are integrated under a global query interface. These sources are usually presented as relational schemas and the system offers a virtual mediated schema to the user for posing queries. Then, the system needs to rewrite user queries as queries over the sources' schemas *only*. Moreover, some sources might be incomplete; hence the system needs to produce query rewritings that instead of equivalent are *maximally-contained*.

Mappings between the sources' schemas and the mediator schema are usually given in the form of logical formulas, which we call *source descriptions*. One approach for describing the sources, known as *global-as-view* (GAV) [11], is to have the mediated relations expressed as views over the schema that the sources' relations constitute. An alternative approach is using *local-as-view* (LAV) mappings [16, 10], where each source relation is expressed as a view over the mediator schema.

In this paper, we address the problem of rewriting a conjunctive query using LAV descriptions, to a maximally-contained union of conjunctive rewritings; this is fundamental to data integration and related areas. To align the problem with the recent frontier of data integration research we should mention current works that build and extend on LAV rewriting algorithms (e.g., [18, 2, 14]) or use their intuitions [20, 6]). There are also recent works that build on LAV rewriting foundations (e.g., in composition of schema mappings [6, 4] or in uncertain data integration [3]) or assume the off-the-self usage of a LAV rewriting algorithm (e.g., [6, 5]). It is critical for all data integration systems to be able to support a large number of sources, so our solution focuses on *scalability* to the number of views.

Generally, the number of rewritings that a single input query can reformulate to, can grow exponentially to the number of views, as the problem (which is NP-complete [16]) involves checking containment mappings[1] from subgoals of the query to candidate rewritings in the cross-product of the views. Previous algorithms (as MiniCon [19] and MCDSAT [7]) have exploited the join conditions of the variables within a query and the views, so as to prune the number of unnecessary mappings to irrelevant views while searching for rewritings.

We pursue this intuition further. The key idea behind our algorithm (called Graph-based Query Rewriting or GQR) is to compactly represent common subexpressions in the views; at the same time we treat each subgoal atomically (as the bucket algorithm [17]) while taking into account (as MiniCon does) the way each of the query variables interacts with the available view patterns, and the way these view patterns interact with each other. Contrary to previous algorithms however, we don't try to a priori map entire "chunks" of the query to (each one of) the views; rather this mapping comes out naturally as we incrementally combine (relevant to the query) atomic view subgoals to larger ones. Consequently, the second

[1]Not to be confused with source descriptions which are mappings from the sources' schema to that of the mediator.

SIGMOD'11, June 12–16, 2011, Athens, Greece.

phase of our algorithm needs to combine much fewer and really relevant view patterns, building a whole batch of rewritings right away. Our specific contributions are the following:

- We present an approach which decomposes the query and the views to simple atomic subgoals and depicts them as graphs; we so abstract from the variable names by having only two types of variable nodes: distinguished and existential.
- That makes it easier to identify the same graph patterns across sources and compactly represent them. This can be done offline, as a view preprocessing phase which is independent of the user query and can be done at any time the sources become available to the system, thereby speeding up system's online performance.
- Subsequently we devise a query reformulation phase where query graph patterns are mapped (through much fewer containment mappings) to our compact representation of view patterns. By bookkeeping some information on our variable nodes (regarding their join conditions) we can combine the different view subgraphs to larger ones, progressively covering larger parts of the query.
- During the above phase each graph "carries" a part of the rewriting, so we incrementally build up the rewriting as we combine graphs; we conclude with a maximally-contained rewriting that uses only view relations, while at the same time we try to minimize its size.
- Our compact form of representing the pieces of the views allows us to also reject an entire batch of irrelevant views (and candidate rewritings), by "failing" to map on a view pattern. This also allows the algorithm to "fail-fast" as soon as a query subgoal cannot map to any of the (few) view patterns.
- These characteristics make our algorithm perform close to two orders of magnitude faster than the current state-of-the-art algorithm, MCDSAT [7]. We exhibit our performance by reformulating queries using up to 10000 views.

In Sect. 2 we present some preliminary notions about queries and containment and introduce the necessary definitions for the problem. Our graph representation of queries and sources is presented in Sect. 3 and our algorithm for scalable query rewriting in Sect. 4. Our experimental results against MCDSAT are given in Sect. 5. In Sect. 6 we compare against related work. We conclude in Sect. 7 where we also state our plans for future work.

2. THE QUERY REWRITING PROBLEM

This section will formally define our problem after going through some necessary preliminary definitions. We use the well-known notions of constants, variables, predicates, terms, and atoms of first-order logic. We use safe conjunctive queries; these are rules of the form $Q(\vec{x}) \leftarrow P_1(\vec{y_1}), ..., P_n(\vec{y_n})$ where $Q, P_1, ..., P_n$ are predicates of some finite arity and $\vec{x}, \vec{y_1}, ..., \vec{y_n}$ are tuples of variables. In the scope of the current paper (and similarly to [7]) we have not considered constant symbols or built-in predicates. We believe however, that our results can be extended to these cases (in the spirit of [19]). We define the body of the query to be $body(Q) = \{P_1(\vec{y_1}), ..., P_n(\vec{y_n})\}$. Any non-empty subset of $body(Q)$ is called a *subgoal* of Q. A singleton subgoal is an *atomic subgoal*. $Q(\vec{x})$ is the *head* of the query.

Predicates appearing in the body stand for relations of a database D, while the head represents the answer relation of the query over D. The query being "safe" means that $\vec{x} \subseteq \bigcup_{i=1}^{n} \vec{y_i}$. All variables in the head are called *head*, *distinguished*, or *returning* variables, while the variables appearing only in the body (i.e., those in $\bigcup_{i=1}^{n} \vec{y_i} \setminus \vec{x}$) are called *existential* variables. We will call *type* of a variable its property of being distinguished or existential. For all sets of atoms S, $vars(S)$ is the set of variables appearing in all the atoms in S (e.g., $vars(Q)$[2] is the set of all query variables). $Q(D)$ refers to the result of evaluating the query Q over the database D.

A *view* V is a named query. The result set of a view is called the *extension* of the view. In the context of data integration a view could be incomplete, in the sense that its extension could only be a subset of the relation $V(D)$. Users pose conjunctive queries over D and the system needs to *rewrite* or *reformulate* these queries into a union of conjunctive queries (UCQ) that only use the views' head predicates so as to obtain all of the tuples in $Q(D)$ that are available in the sources. We will refer to this UCQ as the query *rewriting* while an individual conjunctive query in a rewriting will be called a *conjunctive* rewriting [7]. Query rewriting is closely related to the problem of query containment [16].

We say that Q_2 is *contained* in Q_1, denoted by $Q_2 \subseteq Q_1$, iff for all databases D, $Q_2(D) \subseteq Q_1(D)$. If additionally there exists one database D' such that $Q_2(D') \subset Q_1(D')$, we say that Q_2 is *strictly* contained in Q_1 (denoted $Q_2 \subset Q_1$). If queries Q_1, Q_2 are both contained in each other then they are *equivalent* ($Q_1 \cong Q_2$) and produce the same answers for any database. For all Q_1, Q_2 over the same schema, $Q_2 \subseteq Q_1$ iff there is a containment mapping from Q_1 to Q_2 [8]. Given two queries Q_1, Q_2, a *containment mapping* from Q_1 to Q_2 is a homomorphism h:$vars(Q_1) \rightarrow vars(Q_2)$ (h is extended over atoms, sets of atoms, and queries in the obvious manner), such that: (1) for all atoms $A \in body(Q_1)$, it holds that $h(A) \in body(Q_2)$, and (2)$h(head(Q_1)) = head(Q_2)$ (modulo the names of Q_1, Q_2). Deciding query containment for two conjunctive queries is an NP-complete problem [8].

Data integration systems operate with the open-world assumption; they assume that extensions of views might miss some tuples or that the exact information needed by the query cannot be provided by the views. In that case we would like to provide the maximal available subset of the needed information given the views we have. Note that we demand *complete* rewritings in the sense that they contain only view head predicates [15].

DEF. 1. ***Maximally-contained, complete rewriting:*** *For all databases D, for all sets of views over D, $V = \{V_1, ..., V_n\}$, for all queries R, Q: R is a maximally-contained and complete rewriting of Q using V, iff*

- *Q is a conjunctive query over D and R is a UCQ using only head predicates of V, and*
- *for all (possibly incomplete) extensions of the views $u_1, ..., u_n$, where $u_i \subseteq V_i(D)$ it is the case that $R(u_1, ..., u_n) \subseteq Q(D)$, and*
- *there does not exist a query R' such that $R(u_1, ..., u_n) \subset R'(u_1, ..., u_n)$ and $R'(u_1, ..., u_n) \subseteq Q(D)$*

Our algorithm finds a maximally-contained and complete rewriting R, for the problem of answering a conjunctive query Q with a set of conjunctive views. Taking notice at the containment mapping definition we see that in order to check query containment between R and Q, we need them to be over the same schema. This is done by taking the expansions of the conjunctive rewritings in R. Given $r \in R$, we define the *expansion* or r, $exp(r)$, to be the conjunctive query we obtain if we unfold the views, i.e., substitute the view heads in the body of r with their descriptions (i.e, the bodies of those view definitions). Note that, when the views get unfolded,

[2]When clear from the context we'll use Q or V to refer to either the datalog rule, the set of atoms of the rule, or just the head.

the existential variables in the view definitions are renamed so as to get *fresh* variables.

For speeding up the actual query evaluation on the sources, query rewriting algorithms pay attention to finding minimal conjunctive rewritings inside R. More formally we can define a "minimization" ordering $\leq_m$ as follows:

DEF. 2. ***Minimal conjunctive rewriting:*** *For all conjunctive queries R_1, R_2: $R_1 \leq_m R_2$ iff*

- *$R_1 \cong R_2$, and*
- *there exists a set $U \subseteq vars(body(R_2))$ and there exists an isomorphism $i : vars(body(R_1)) \rightarrow U$ (i is extended in the obvious manner to atoms) such that (1) for all atoms $A \in body(R_1)$ it holds that $i(A) \in body(R_2)$, and (2) $i(head(R_1)) = head(R_2)$.*

The problem of minimizing a rewriting is NP-complete [16] and therefore most algorithms produce a number of non-minimal conjunctive rewritings in their solutions. An additional problem related to minimality is that of *redundant* rewritings, when more than one equivalent conjunctions exist in the same UCQ rewriting. Our algorithm produces fewer conjunctive rewritings than the current state-of-the-art algorithm, but we also suffer from redundant and non-minimal ones. A containment mapping from a query Q to a rewriting R is also seen as the *covering* of Q by (the views in) R. Similarly we can define:

DEF. 3. ***Covering:*** *For all queries Q, for all views V, for all subgoals $g_q \in body(Q)$, for all subgoals $g_v \in body(V)$, for all partial homomorphisms $\varphi : vars(Q) \rightarrow vars(V)$, we say that a view subgoal g_v covers a subgoal g_q of Q with φ iff:*

- *$\varphi(g_q) = g_v$, and*
- *for all $x \in vars(g_q)$ if x is distinguished then $\varphi(x) \in vars(g_v)$ is distinguished.*

The intuition behind the second part of the definition is that whenever a part of a query *needs* a value, you can not cover that part with a view that does not explicitly provide this value. On occasion, we might abuse the above definition to say that a greater subgoal, or even V itself, covers g_q with φ (since these coverings involve trivial extensions of φ). For all variables $x \in g_q$ and $y \in g_v$ we say that x *maps* on y (or y covers x) iff for a covering involving φ, $\varphi(x) = y$.

To ground these definitions consider the following example. Assume that we have two sources, S_1 and S_2, that provide information about road traffic and routes (identified by a unique id). S_1 contains ids of routes one should avoid; i.e., routes for which there is at least one alternative route with less traffic. S_2 contains points of intersection between two routes. The contents of these sources are modeled respectively by the two following LAV rules (or views):

$S_1(r_1) \rightarrow$ AltRoutes(r_1,r_2), LessTraffic(r_2, r_1)

$S_2(r_3, r_4, p_1) \rightarrow$ ConnectingRoutes(r_3, r_4, p_1)

Assume the user asks for all avoidable routes and all exit points from these routes:

$q(x,p) \rightarrow$ AltRoutes(x,y), LessTraffic(y,x), ConnectingRoutes(x,z,p)

The rewriting of q is: $q'(x,p) \leftarrow S_1(x), S_2(x,f,p)$

In this example, the selection of relevant views to answer the user query and the reformulation process was quite simple since there were only two views. We just built a conjunctive query q' using the two views and tested that exp(q')$\subseteq q$, where exp(q') is:

$q''(x,p) \rightarrow$ AltRoutes(x,f_1),LessTraffic(f_1, x),ConnectingRoutes(x, f, p)

However, in general, there could be many more conjunctive rewritings in the rewriting than q', and as mentioned checking containment is an expensive procedure. Notice that in order to construct a conjunctive rewriting contained in the query, we select views that have relevant predicates, i.e., that there is a mapping (covering) from a query atom to the view atom. Coverings are essentially components of the final containment mapping from the query to the (expansion of the) combination of views that forms a conjunctive rewriting. Paying close attention to how we construct coverings and select views can help us avoid building conjunctive rewritings which are not contained in the query. The second part of Def. 3 states that coverings should map distinguished query variables to distinguished view ones, as the containment definition demands. In our example, had one of S_1 or S_2 the first attribute (i.e., r_1 or r_3) missing from their head, they would be useless. In effect, we want the variable x of q to map onto a distinguished variable in a relevant view. Additionally to their definition coverings should adhere to one more constraint. Consider q_1 which asks for avoidable routes and all exit points from these routes to *some alternative route with less traffic*:

$q_1(x,p) \rightarrow$ AltRoutes(x,y), LessTraffic(y,x), ConnectingRoutes(x,y,p)

Now the query demands that the second argument of *ConnectingRoutes* is joined with one of x's alternative routes. This is impossible to answer, given S_1 and S_2, as S_1 does not provide x's alternative routes (i.e., r_2 in its definition). The property revealed here is that *whenever an existential variable y in the query maps on an existential variable in a view, this view can be used for a rewriting only if it covers all predicates that mention y in the query.* This property is referred to as (clause $C2$ in) *Property 1* in MiniCon[19]. This is also the basic idea of the MiniCon algorithm: trying to map all query predicates of q_1 to all possible views, it will notice that the existential query variable y in the query maps on r_2 in S_1; since r_2 is existential it needs to go back to the query and check wether all predicates mentioning y can be covered by S_1. Here *ConnectingRoutes(x,y,p)* cannot. We notice that there is duplicate work being done in this process. First, MiniCon does this procedure *for every query predicate*, this means that if q_1 had multiple occurrences of $AltRoutes$ it would try to use S_1 multiple times and fail (although as the authors of [19] say *certain* repeated predicates can be ruled out of consideration). Second, MiniCon would try to do this for *every possible view*, even for those that contain the same pattern of S_1, as S_3 below which offers avoidable routes where also an accident has recently occurred:

$S_3(r_1) \rightarrow$ AltRoutes(r_1,r_2), LessTraffic(r_2, r_1), RoutesWithAccidents(r_1)

S_3 cannot be used for q_1 as it violates MiniCon's Property1, again due to its second variable, r_2, being existential and *ConnectingRoutes* not covered. Our idea is to avoid this redundant work by compactly representing all occurrences of the same view pattern. To this end we use a graph representation of queries and views presented subsequently.

3. QUERIES AND VIEWS AS GRAPHS

Our graph representation of conjunctive queries is inspired by previous graph-based knowledge representation approaches (see conceptual graphs in [9]). Predicates and their arguments correspond to graph nodes. Predicate nodes are labeled with the name of the predicate and they are connected through edges to their arguments. Shared variables between atoms result in shared variable nodes, directly connected to predicate nodes.

We need to keep track of the arguments' order inside an atom. Therefore, we equip our edges with integer labels that stand for the variables' positions within the atom's parentheses. In effect,

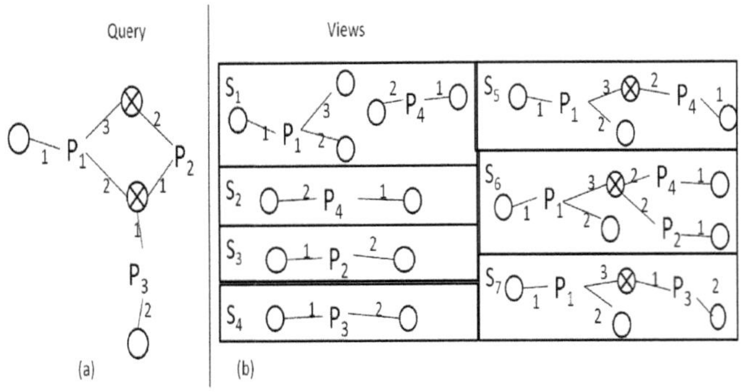

Figure 1: Query Q, and sources S_1-S_7 as a graphs.

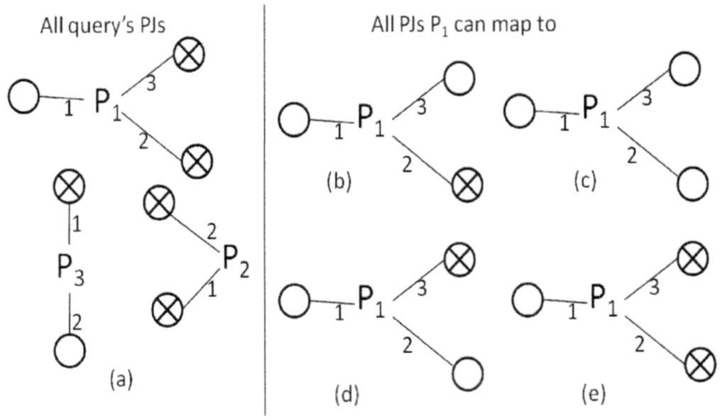

Figure 2: Predicate Join Patterns.

an edge labeled with "1" will be attached to the node representing the leftmost variable within an atom's parentheses, e.t.c. Thus we can discard variables' names; from our perspective we only need to remember a variable's type (i.e., whether the ith variable of a specific atom is distinguished or not within the query or the view). This choice can be justified upon examination of Def. 3; the only knowledge we require for deciding on a covering is the types of the variables involved. Distinguished variable nodes are depicted with a circle, while for existential ones we use the symbol $\otimes$. Using these constructs the query:

$$Q(x_1, x_2) \leftarrow P_1(x_1, y, z), P_2(y, z), P_3(y, x_2)$$

corresponds to the graph seen in Fig. 1(a). Fig. 1(b) shows the graph alterego of the following 7 LAV source descriptions:

$$S_1(x, y, z, g, f) \rightarrow P_1(x, y, z), P_4(g, f)$$
$$S_2(a, b) \rightarrow P_4(b, a)$$
$$S_3(c, d) \rightarrow P_2(c, d)$$
$$S_4(e, h) \rightarrow P_3(e, h)$$
$$S_5(i, k, j) \rightarrow P_1(i, k, x), P_4(j, x)$$
$$S_6(l, m, n, o) \rightarrow P_1(l, n, x), P_4(m, x), P_2(o, x)$$
$$S_7(t, w, u) \rightarrow P_1(t, u, x), P_3(x, w)$$

3.1 Predicate Join Patterns

Our algorithm consists of mapping subgraphs of the query to subgraphs of the sources, and to this end the smallest subgraphs we consider represent one atom's "pattern": they consist of one central predicate node and its (existential or distinguished) variable nodes. These primitive graphs are called *predicate join patterns* (or PJs) for the predicate they contain. Fig. 2(a) shows all predicate joins that the query Q contains, (i.e., all the *query PJs*). We will refer to greater subgoals than simple PJs as *compound predicate join patterns* or CPJs (PJs are also CPJs, although atomic ones). We can now restate Def. 3 using our graph terminology: A view CPJ *covers* a query CPJ if there is a graph homomorphism h, from the query graph to the view one, such that (1) h is the identity on predicate nodes and labeled edges and (2) if a query variable node u is distinguished then $h(u)$ is also distinguished. For the query PJ for P_1 in Fig. 2(a), all PJs that can potentially cover it, appear in Fig. 2(b)-(e). Notice that under this perspective:

- Given two specific PJs A an B, we can check whether A covers B in linear time[3].
- Given a specific query PJ A, there is an exponential number of PJs that can cover it (in effect, their number is 2^d with d being the number of existential variables in A).

A critical feature that boosts our algorithm's performance is that the patterns of subgoals as graphs repeat themselves across different source descriptions. Therefore we choose to compactly represent each such different view subgoal with the same CPJ. This has a tremendous advantage (as also discussed in Sect. 6); mappings from a query PJ (or CPJ) to a view are computed just once instead of every time this subgoal is met in a source description (with the exception of repeated predicates which are addressed in Sect. 4.2.4). Nevertheless, the "join conditions", for a particular PJ within each view, are different; more "bookkeeping" is needed to capture this. In Sect. 3.2 we describe a conceptual data structure that takes care of all the "bookkeeping". At this point, we should notice that our graph constructs resemble some relevant and well study concepts from the literature, namely hypergraphs and hyperedges [1] discussed in Sect. 6.

3.2 Information Boxes

Each variable node of a PJ holds within it information about other PJs this variable (directly) connects to within a query or view. To retain this information we use a conceptual data structure called *information box* (or infobox). Each infobox is attached to a variable v. Fig. 3 shows an example infobox for a variable node. A view (or source) PJ represents a specific subgoal pattern found in multiple sources. Therefore we want to document all the joins a variable participates in, for every view. Hence, our infobox contains a list of views that this PJ appears in; for each of these views, we maintain a structure that we call *sourcebox* (also seen in Fig. 3), where we record information about the other PJs, that v is connected to. In effect we need to mark which PJ and on which edge of this PJ, v is attached to in that particular view. We call this information a *join description* of a variable within a sourcebox (inside an infobox, attached to a PJ's variable). For ease of representation we will denote each join description of a variable v in a sourcebox, with the name of the other predicate where we superscript the number of the edge v is attached to, on this other predicate (Sect. 4.2.4 clarifies this in the face of repeated predicates).

Fig. 4 shows for all predicates of Q, all the different PJs that appear in sources $S_1 - S_7$ with their infoboxes. Note that the infoboxes belonging to a query PJ contain only one sourcebox (that of the query), which in turn contains the join descriptions of the variables in the query. We omit to present the infoboxes of Q as its joins can be easily seen from Fig. 1(a).

[3]Since the edges of the two PJs are labeled, we can write them down as strings, hash and compare them (modulo the type of variable nodes).

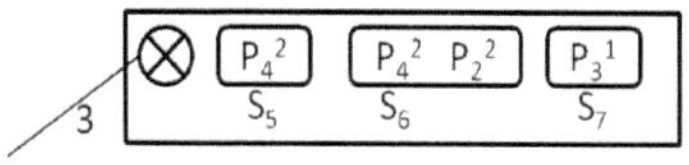

Figure 3: Infobox for a variable node. The node is existential and is attached on its predicate node on edge with label 3 (this variable is the third argument of the corresponding atom). We can find this specific PJ in three views, so there are three source-boxes in the infobox. The two join descriptions in the sourcebox S_6 tell us that this variable, in view S_6, joins with the second argument of P_4 and the second argument of P_2.

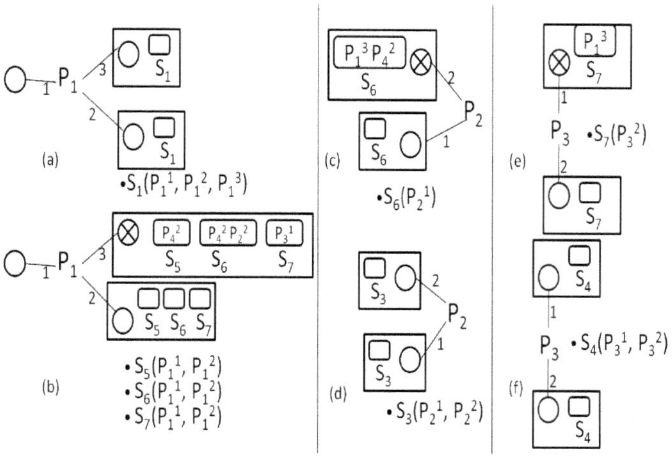

Figure 4: All existing source PJs for the predicates of the query Q. For presentation purposes the infoboxes of the first variable of P_1 are omitted. The partial conjunctive rewritings (view heads) each PJ maintains, are "descriptions" of the current PJ and are candidate parts of the final conjunctive rewritings. During our preprocessing phase, PJs for P_4 (which also exists in the sources) would also be constructed but are omitted from being presented here (as they are dropped by our later phase). Using these constructs we can compactly represent all the 8 occurrences of P_1 P_2 and P_3 in the sources $S1$-$S7$, with the 6 PJs presented here.

3.3 Partial conjunctive rewritings

Our compact representation of patterns allows us another major improvement. Previous algorithms would first finish with a view-query mapping discovery phase and then go on to gather up all "relevant" view subgoals to form a (conjunctive) rewriting. Our approach exploits the insight an algorithm gains during this phase so as to start building the correct rewriting right away. At different steps of our algorithm, each source CPJ covers a certain part of the query and within this source CPJ (and only in source CPJs) we maintain a list of conjunctions of atoms, which are candidate parts of the final conjunctive rewritings that will cover this part of the query. We call these *partial* conjunctive rewritings. These conjunctions maintain information about which view variables out of the views' head are used and which of them are equated, i.e., joined (if at all). For example, the PJ in Fig. 4(a) contains the partial rewriting $S_1(P_1{}^1, P_1{}^2, P_1{}^3)$.

4. GRAPH-BASED QUERY REWRITING

Our solution is divided in two phases. Initially, we process all view descriptions and construct all source PJs. In our second phase, we start by matching each atomic query subgoal (i.e., PJ) to the source PJs and we go on by combining the relevant source PJs to form larger subgraphs (CPJs) that cover larger "underlying" query subgoals. We continue combining source CPJS and during this bottom-up combination, we also combine their partial rewritings by taking their cross-product and either merge some of their atoms or equate some of their variables. Note that we might also need to "drop" some rewritings on the way, if they are no longer feasible (see Sect. 4.2.3). We continue until we cover the entire query graph, whereby we have incrementally built the maximally-contained and complete rewriting.

4.1 Source Preprocessing

Given the set of view descriptions and considering them as graphs, we break them down to atomic PJs, by splitting each graph on the shared variable nodes. On top of the PJ generation we construct infoboxes for every variable node in those PJs. Moreover, for every PJ we generate a list of partial conjunctive rewritings, each containing the head of a different view this PJ can be found in.

Fig. 4 shows all the source PJs as constructed by the preprocessing phase. For presentation purposes, in the partial conjunctive rewritings, the view heads include only the arguments that we are actually using at this phase. Similarly to the naming scheme of the join descriptions, we use a positional scheme for uniquely naming variables in a partial conjunctive rewriting. For instance, $S_7.P_3{}^2$ is the 2nd argument of PJ P_3 in source S_7 (Sect. 4.2.4 explains how we disambiguate occurrences of the same predicate in a given view). This naming policy is beneficial as it allows us to save valuable variable substitution time.

An advantage of our approach is that our preprocessing phase does not need any information from the query, as it was designed to involve only views. Typically, a data integration system has access to all sources and view descriptions a priori (before any query). In such a case, the views can be preprocessed off-line and the PJs can be stored until a query appears. The details of this algorithm are rather obvious and omitted, but it can be easily verified that this preprocessing phase has a polynomial complexity to the number and length of the views.

Nonetheless, one can create more sophisticated indices on the sources. As seen in Fig. 2 there are 2^d potential query PJs that a source PJ can cover, with d being the number of distinguished variable nodes in the source PJ. For our implementation we chose to generate those indices; for every source PJ we construct all the (exponentially many) potential query PJs that the former could cover. Consequently given a query PJ will are able to efficiently retrieve the source PJs that cover it. The payoff for all indexing choices depends on the actual data integration application (e.g., whether the preprocessing is an off-line procedure or how large does d grow per atom etc.). Nevertheless, any offline cost is amortized over the system's live usage. Moreover, the experiments of Sect. 5 show a good performance of our algorithm even when taking the preprocessing time into account.

4.2 Query Reformulation

Our main procedure, called GQR (Graph-based Query Rewriting) and shown in Algorithm 1, retrieves all the alternative source PJs for each query PJ and stores them (as a set of CPJs) in S which is a set of sets of CPJs initially empty (lines 1-6). As we go on (line 7 and below) we remove any two CPJ sets[4] from S, combine all their elements in pairs (as Algorithm 2 shows), construct a set containing larger CPJs (which cover the union of the underlying query PJs) and put it back in S. This procedure goes on until we cover the entire query (combine all sets of CPJs) or until we fail to combine

[4]Our choice is arbitrary; nevertheless a heuristic order of combination of CPJ sets could be imposed for more efficiency.

Algorithm 1 GQR

Input: A query Q
Output: A set of rewritings for the query
1: **for all** predicate join patterns PJ_q in the query **do**
2: $SetP \leftarrow RetrievePJSet(PJ_q)$
3: **if** $SetP$ empty **then**
4: **FAIL**
5: **else**
6: add $SetP$ to S //S is the set of all CPJ sets
7: **repeat**
8: *select and remove* $A, B \in S$
9: $C \leftarrow combineSets(A, B)$
10: **if** C is empty **then**
11: **FAIL**
12: add C to S
13: **until** all elements in S are chosen
14: **return** rewritings in S

Algorithm 2 combineSets

Input: sets of CPJs A, B
Output: a set of CPJs combinations of A, B
for all pairs (a,b) $\in A \times B$ **do**
$c \leftarrow combineCPJs(a, b)$
if c is not empty **then**
add c to C
return C

two sets of CPJs which means there is no combination of views to cover the underlying query subgoals. If none of the pairs in Alg. 2 has a "legitimate" combination as explained subsequently, the sets of CPJs fail to be combined (line 11 of Alg. 1). Fig. 5(c),(g) shows the combination of PJs for P_1 with PJs for P_2, and in turn their combination with the PJ for P_3 (Fig. 5(h),(i)) to cover the whole query.

4.2.1 *Join preservation*

While we combine graphs we concatenate the partial conjunctive rewritings that they contain. When these rewritings contain the same view, the newly formed rewriting either uses this view twice, or only once; depending on whether the query joins are preserved across the mapping to this source.

DEF. 4. ***Join preservation:*** *For all PJ_A, PJ_B source PJs, for all Q_A, Q_B query PJs where PJ_A covers Q_A and PJ_B covers Q_B, for all views V that contain both PJ_A and PJ_B, we say that V preserves the joins of Q_A and Q_B w.r.t PJ_A and PJ_B iff for all join variables u between Q_A and Q_B:*

- *if a is the variable node u maps onto in PJ_A and b is the variable node u maps onto in PJ_B, then a and b are of the same type, and both a and b's infoboxes contain a sourcebox for V in which a has a join description for b, and b has a join description for a, and*
- *there exists a u such that a and b are existential, or (1) a and b are essentially the same variable of V (in the same position) and (2) for all variables of PJ_A, a', and of PJ_B, b', such that no join variables of the query map on a' or b', either a' and b' are don't care variables (they are distinguished (in V) but no distinguished variable of the query maps on them) or (without loss of generality): a' covers a distinguished query variable and b' is a don't care variable.*

Intuitively when a view preserves the query joins with respect to two PJs, our rewriting can use the view head only once (using both the source PJs) to cover the two underlying query subgoals; this is actually necessary when the PJs cover an existential join variable with an existential view one (as in Property 1 of MiniCon [19]). S_6 for example, preserves the query join between $P_1{}^3$,$P_2{}^2$ with respect to the PJs of Fig. 4(b) and (c). If on the other hand all view variables that cover join variables are distinguished, Def. 4 states the conditions[5] under which using the view head two times, would be correct but not minimal according to Def. 2. For example consider the following query and view:

$$q(x, y, z) \rightarrow p_1(x,y,z), p_2(y,z,w)$$

$$v(a, b, c, d) \rightarrow p_1(a,b,c), p_2(b,c,d)$$

A naive covering of p_1 and p_2 would use v two times, coming up with the conjunctive rewriting:

$$r(x, y, z) \rightarrow v(x,y,z,f'), v(f'',y,z,f''')$$

If we enforce Def. 4 when combining the view patterns for $p_1(a,b,c)$ and $p_2(b,c,d)$ we'll notice that b and c do fall on the same positions in v, and while the first pattern (p_1) covers more query variables (uses a to cover x) the second one has don't cares (d in p_2 is a don't care as rewritten as f'''). In this case we can merge the two occurrences of v (using their most general unifier) and come up with a more minimal rewriting: $r(x, y, z) \rightarrow v(x,y,z,f''')$.

This optimization is discussed in Sect. 4 of [16]. It is important to notice the dual function of Def. 4. On one hand, given two source PJs that cover an existential join with existential variables, a view *must* preserve the join in order to be used. If, on the other hand, all source variables that cover query joins are distinguished, the view *can* preserve the join, and be used a minimal number of times.

Algorithm 3 retrievePJSet

Input: a predicate join pattern PJ_q in the query
Output: The set of source PJs that cover PJ_q.
1: **for all** PJ_s, source PJs that covers PJ_q **do**
2: $OkToAdd \leftarrow$ **true**
3: **for all** u variable nodes in PJ_q **do**
4: $v \leftarrow$ variable of PJ_s that u maps on to
5: **if** v is existential **then**
6: **if** u is existential **then**
7: **for all** sourceboxes S in v's infobox **do**
8: **if** joins in $u \not\subseteq$ joins in S **then**
9: drop S from PJ_s
10: **if** some of PJs infoboxes became empty **then**
11: $OkToAdd \leftarrow$ **false**
12: **break**
13: **if** $OkToAdd$ **then**
14: link PJ_s to PJ_q
15: add PJ_s to C
16: Prime members of C returned in the past
17: **return** C

4.2.2 *Retrieving source PJs*

After the source indexing phase, our first job when a query is given to the system is to construct PJs and information boxes for all its predicates. We then retrieve, with the use of Alg. 3, all the relevant source PJs that cover each query PJ (i.e., the output of the algorithm is a set of PJs). For an input query PJ, line 1 of Alg. 3 iterates over all (existing) view PJs that cover the input. Moreover, as already discussed, if both a query variable and its mapped view variable (u and v correspondingly) are existential, we won't be able to use this view PJ if the view cannot preserve the join patterns of the query, under any circumstances. Therefore if view variable v is existential, we have to inspect every sourcebox of v's infobox

[5]These are relaxed constraints; we are investigating more cases under which a rewriting could be minimized.

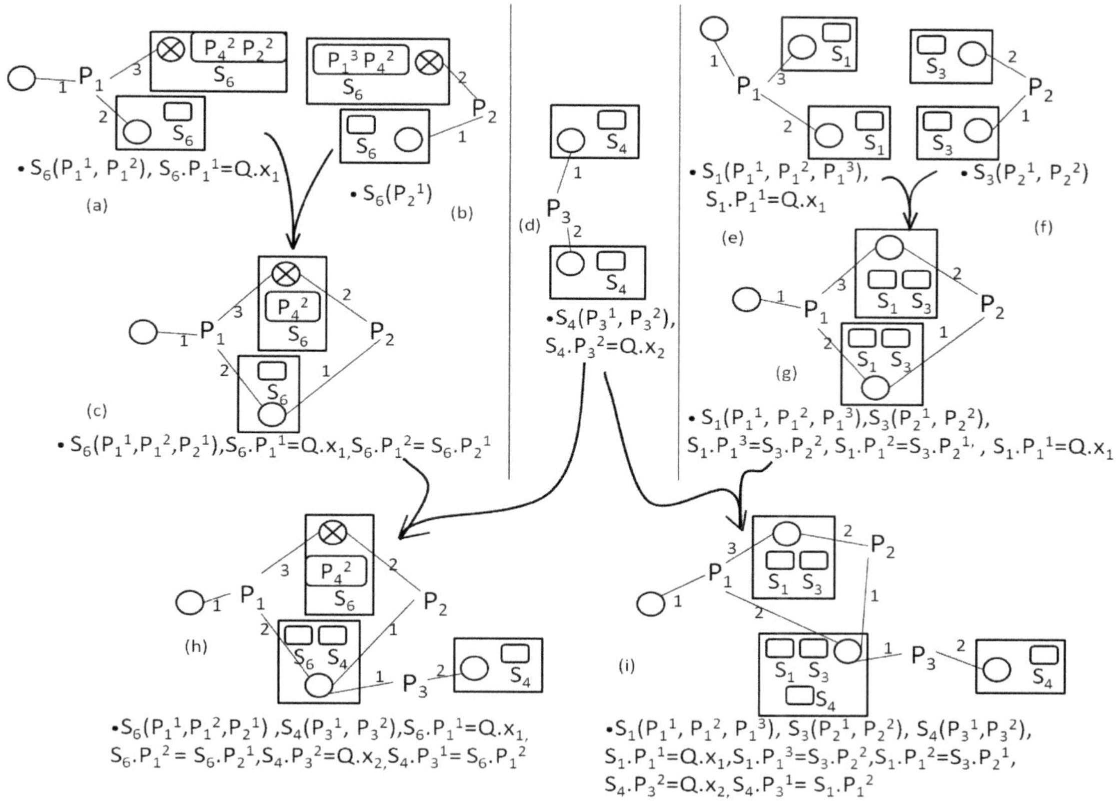

Figure 5: All source PJs that cover P_1 are combined with all PJs that cover P_2. As Alg. 2 suggests, we try all combinations of CPJs that cover the query. The figure does not show the un-combinable pairs (as e.g., the PJ in (a) with the PJ in (f)). Note that combining two nodes we eliminate the join descriptions we just satisfied. In the current example, PJ (d) is combined with both (c) and (g) which alternatively cover the same part of the query. The union of the resulting rewritings of (h) and (i) is our solution.

(lines 7-9) and verify that all join descriptions of u are included in there. If we find a sourcebox that breaks this requirement we drop this sourcebox from every infobox of this view PJ and we delete the partial conjunctive rewriting that mentions the corresponding view as well (line 9). We do all that as if this source PJ pattern never appeared in that view (for the specific subgoal of the query, the specific view subgoal that this source PJ represents is useless).

For example, when the query PJ for P_1, shown in Fig. 2(a), is given to $retrievePJSet$ the latter will consider the preconstructed PJs shown in Fig. 4(a),(b); for the one in Fig. 4(b) line 9 will drop the sourceboxes and the partial conjunctive rewritings related to S_5 and S_7 since only the infobox of S_6 is describing the query joins.

This fail-fast behavior allows us to keep only the necessary view's references in a PJ (which, in the above example is S_6). Moreover, if none of the views can cover a query subgoal, the PJ itself is ignored, leading to a huge time saving as (1) a dropped view PJ means that a significant number of source pieces/partial rewritings are ignored and (2) if we ignore all source PJs that could cover a specific query PJ, the algorithm fails instantly. For example, consider the query PJ for P_3, in Fig. 2(a), which joins existentially with P_1 and P_2 on its 1st argument. In order to use the view PJ of Fig. 4(e) (which also has its first node existential) to cover it, we need to make sure that the PJ of Fig. 4(e) includes at least one sourcebox (attached to its 1st variable) which contains all the query join descriptions.

However the only sourcebox in that infobox is for S_7 and it does not describe the query join with P_2. Therefore sourcebox S_7 is dropped, and as the view PJ remains empty, it is never returned by Alg. 3. On the other hand if some PJs go through this procedure and get returned, these are really relevant and have a high possibility of generating rewritings. For our query of Fig. 1, $retrievePJset$ will be called three times (each time it will iterate over one column of Fig. 4): for P_1 it will return the PJs in Fig. 5(a) and (e), for P_2 gives Fig. 5(b) and (f) and for P_3 it returns the PJ shown in Fig. 5(d).

Note that Alg. 3 also marks (line 14) which variables correspond to returning variables of the query[6]. This is done by equating some of the partial conjunctive rewritings' variables to distinguished query variables (as seen in Fig. 5(a), (d) and (e), we include some "equating" predicates in the rewriting). Also, notice that since our example query Q does not contain P_4 none of the PJs for P_4 is retrieved. Line 16 of the algorithm is explained in Sect. 4.2.4. Notice that Alg. 3 returns a set of PJs which alternatively cover the same query PJ. Furthermore the different sets that Alg. 3 returns, cover different (and all) subgoals of the query. That makes it easier to straightforwardly combine these sets to cover larger parts of the query. We treat the element of each set as a CPJ (initially they are atomic CPJs, i.e., PJs), and we pairwise combine all the elements (CPJs) of two sets that cover two query subgoals; we construct a resulting set containing larger combined CPJs. The latter alternatively cover the larger underlying query subgoal. Next section describes how we combine two CPJs to a greater one.

4.2.3 Combination of CPJs

Algorithm 4 takes two CPJs a and b and returns their combination CPJ. If the underlying query subgoals that these CPJs cover do

[6]In an effort to be user-friendly we are maintaining the original names of the query variables.

not join with each other our algorithm just cross products the partial conjunctive rewritings these CPJs contain and returns a greater CPJ containing all PJs in both CPJs. If on the other hand underlying joins exist, procedure $lookupJoins$ in line 1 returns all pairs of variables (v_a,v_b), where v_a in a and v_b in b, that cover the join variables. For example, for the PJs of Fig. 5(a) and (b), $lookupJoins$ will return the two pairs of variables (for the two joins in the query between P_1 and P_2): ($S_6.P_1{}^3$,$S_6.P_2{}^2$) and ($S_6.P_1{}^2$,$S_6.P_2{}^1$). Next we want to enforce Def. 4 and "merge" the view heads in the partial conjunctive rewritings that preserve the join (lines 9 and 17) or equate some of them so as to satisfy the join (line 19). By *merging* two atoms of the same predicate, we keep the predicate (i.e., the view head) only once and merge their arguments. Otherwise we consider their conjunction and *equate* the variables that cover the query join variable.

Algorithm 4 combineCPJs

Input: two CPJS a,b
Output: a CPJ, combination of a, b
1: **for all** join J in $lookupJoins(a, b)$ **do**
2: $v_a \leftarrow$ get from J variable in a
3: $v_b \leftarrow$ get from J variable in b
4: **if** type of $v_a \neq$ type of v_b **then**
5: **return** $\emptyset$ //$\emptyset$ means un-combinable
6: **else if** type of $v_a = \otimes$ **then**
7: **for all** sourceboxes S in v_a's infobox **do**
8: **if** S contains a join description for v_b **then**
9: $markForMerge(S, v_a, v_b)$
10: **else**
11: drop S from a and b
12: **if** v_a infobox $= \emptyset$ **then**
13: **return** $\emptyset$
14: **else**
15: **for all** pairs of sourceboxes $(s_a, s_b) \in$ (infobox of v_a) $\times$ (infobox of v_b) **do**
16: **if** s_a preserves the joins of the query w.r.t. v_a and v_b **then**
17: $markForMerge(s_a, v_a, v_b)$ //preserves implies that $s_a = s_b$
18: **else**
19: $markForEquate(s_a, v_a, s_b, v_b)$
20: $crw \leftarrow crossproductRewritings(a, b)$
21: $enforceMergeAndEquations(crw)$
22: $c \leftarrow mergeGraphsUpdateInfoboxes()$
23: **return** c

Notice that we only can enforce joins on view variables of the same type (line 4); we either join existential variables within the same source or join/equate distinguished variables across sources. If the view variables that cover the join are existential "merging" is our only option; if v_a contains sourceboxes for different sources as v_b does, or if their common sourceboxes regard views that don't preserve the join, we drop these sourceboxes (line 11) and the corresponding partial conjunctive rewritings. If by this dropping we "empty" a PJ of source references, this is no longer useful to us and so a and b are *un-combinable* (line 13). This "pruning" is similar to the one in Alg. 3 and can happen often.

On the other hand, if the view variables that cover the query join are distinguished, we either merge the partial conjunctive rewritings on the corresponding view head (in case that the view satisfies Def. 4) or we equate v_a and v_b in the two view heads (line 19). Finally, we consider the cross product of the remaining partial conjunctive rewritings creating larger ones, and we iterate over them to enforce all merging and equating we just noted down. For example, in Fig. 5 when our algorithm examines the existential join between the PJs shown in (a) and (b), it marks S_6 for merging since S_6 preserves the join. At another iteration of line 1, regarding the same PJs but for the distinguished join this time, we need to equate two variables of S_6 (namely, $P_1{}^2$ with $P_2{}^1$). At the end both these decisions are enforced as seen in the partial conjunctive rewriting of Fig. 5(c). As we go on, algorithm 1 combines all elements of S and produces C, the set containing the CPJs seen in 5(h) and (i). Their conjunctive rewritings are the conjunctive rewritings of the solution and their union is the maximally-contained and complete rewriting:

$$Q(x_1, x_2) \leftarrow S_6(x_1, \_, y, y), S_4(y, x_2)$$

$$Q(x_1, x_2) \leftarrow S_1(x_1, y, z, \_, \_), S_3(y, z), S_4(y, x_2)$$

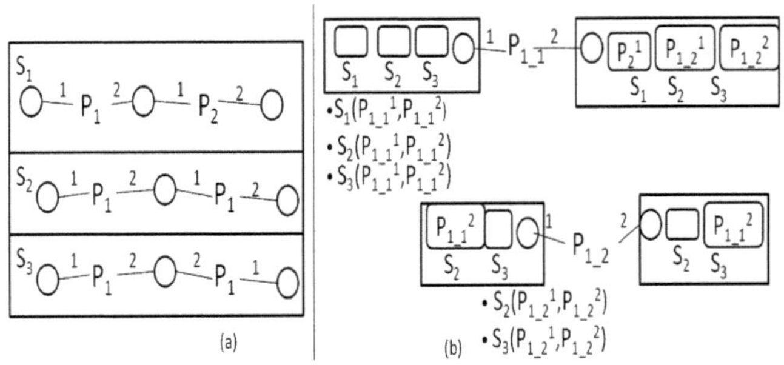

Figure 6: Repeated Predicates. In (b) only the PJs for P_1 are shown; these "capture" all five occurrences of P_1 in the sources S_1,S_2 and S_3 of (a).

4.2.4 *Repeated Predicates*

In general repeated predicates in the view descriptions should be treated separately; we create multiple PJs per predicate per source and name these PJs differently. We then can create and use infoboxes as described so far. For a query containing the corresponding predicate the algorithm would try to use all these alternative PJs and combine them with PJs that cover other parts of the query so as to capture the multiplicity of the predicate in the sources. An important notice is that we only need to maintain different PJs for predicates within the same source, but not across sources; hence the maximum number of different source PJs for the same predicate is the maximum number a predicate repeats itself within any source. Fig. 6(b) shows how we can use two different PJs to hold the information needed for all the five occurrences of P_1 in Fig. 6(a).

In the face of multiple occurrences of the same predicate in the query, it is suitable to imagine all PJs discussed so far as classes of PJs: we instantiate the set of PJs that cover a specific predicate as many times as the predicate appears in the query. Each time we instantiate the same PJ we "prime" the sources appearing in the partial rewritings so as to know that we are calling the same source but a second, different time (and as our argument names are positional, "priming" the sources allows us to differentiate among two instances of the same variable in the same source). Line 16 of algorithm 3 does exactly that. Having said the above, Fig. 7 shows all the PJs for the sources of Fig. 6 created for query Q of Fig. 7. Rewritings for this query will come out of the 4 possible combinations of these 4 instantiations of the two PJs (of Fig. 6).

4.2.5 *GQR Correctness*

Below we give a sketch proof that our algorithm is correct; for soundness we show that any conjunctive rewriting in our output is contained in the query, and for completeness that for any possible conjunctive rewriting of the query, we always produce a conjunctive rewriting which contains it.

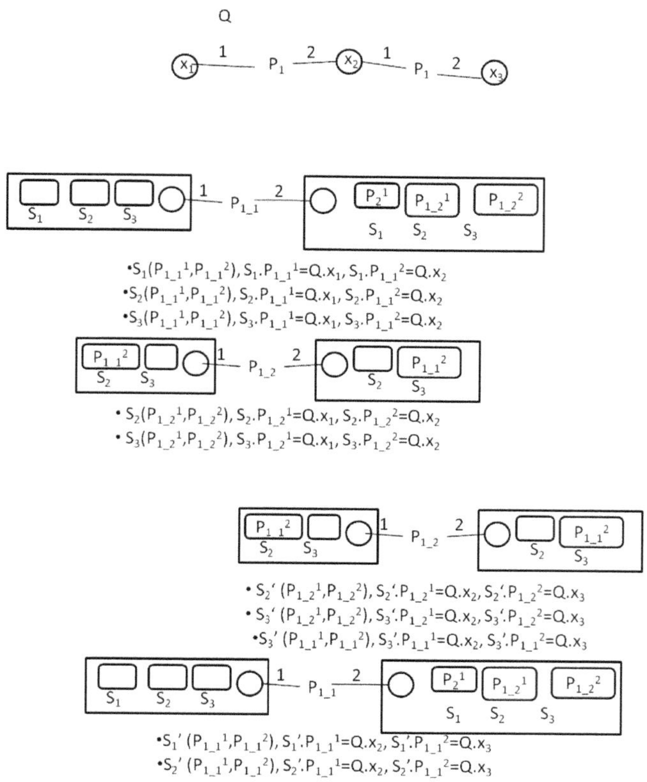

Figure 7: Repeated predicates in the query (returning variable names are shown in Q's graph for convenience). For the sources of Fig. 6(a), the algorithm "instantiates" the matching PJs (Fig. 6(b)) for every occurrence of the same query predicate.

THEOREM 1. *Given a conjunctive query Q and conjunctive views $V_1, ..., V_n$, the GQR algorithm produces a UCQ that is a maximally-contained and complete rewriting of Q using $V_1, ..., V_n$.*

PROOF. *Soundness.* Consider an output conjunctive rewriting r of our algorithm. We need to show that $exp(r) = r' \subseteq Q$. This means that there is a containment mapping from Q to r'. Keep in mind that the atoms in r' however exist in different views (not in the same as the containment mapping definition demands). It is not difficult to see that our approach "constructs" the containment mapping through coverings; each covering is a mapping from a subpart of the query to a part of r'. Considering multiple such coverings will give us our containment mapping from Q to our combination of views (that r contains).

Completeness. Consider a conjunctive rewriting p element of a problem's maximally-contained and complete rewriting. There is a containment mapping from Q to $exp(p)$. This means that depicted as graphs, there is a graph homomorphism h_1 from the query to some of the PJs for the predicates that constitute $exp(p)$. Breaking up the homomorphism per individual target PJ means that there are coverings from parts of the query to these PJs (these coverings do not get affected if we compactly represent these PJs, gathering them up in patterns as in section 4.1). It is not hard to verify that if such coverings exist our algorithm will consider them when looking at different view PJs; hence it will produce a rewriting r for the crossproduct of the views these PJs belong in, for which it will hold that there exists a containment mapping (and a graph homomorphism) $h_2 : vars(Q) \rightarrow vars(exp(r))$. Moreover for all variables q_v of Q which map on distinguished variables d in those view PJs of r (i.e., $h_2(q_v) = d$), it holds also that h_1 maps q_v on the same node d in the PJs of $exp(p)$. Hence whenever r (which is written over view head predicates) has a distinguished variable in some view in its body, p has the same variable on the same position on the same view (modulo renaming). Hence, there is a containment mapping from r to p, which means that $p \subseteq r$. □

5. EXPERIMENTAL EVALUATION

For evaluating our approach we compared with the most efficient (to the best of our knowledge) state-of-the-art algortihm, MCDSAT [7] (which outperformed MiniCon [19]). We show our performance in two kinds of queries/views: star and chain queries. In all cases GQR outperforms MCDSAT even by close to two orders of magnitude. For producing our queries and views we used a random query generator[7].

5.1 Star queries

We generated 100 star queries and a dataset of 140 views for each query. We created a space with 8 predicate names out of which each query or view chooses randomly 5 to populate its body and it can choose the same one up to 5 times (for instantiating repeated predicates). Each atom has 4 randomly generated variables and each query and view have 4 distinguished variables. We measured the performance of each of the queries scaling from 0 to 140 views. We run our experiments on a cluster of 2GHz processors each with 1Gb of memory; each processor was allocated all the 140 runs for one query, and we enforced 24 hours wall time for that job to be finished. Fig. 8(a) shows the average query reformulation time for 99 queries which met the time and memory bounds. On this set of experiments we perform 32 times faster than MCDSAT. Fig. 8(a) also shows how the average number of conjunctive rewritings grows with respect to the number of views.

5.2 Chain queries

For the chain queries we generated again 100 queries and a dataset of 140 views for each query. Our generator could now choose 8 body predicates (on a chain), for any rule, out of a pool of 20 predicates of length 4. Up to 5 predicates in each rule can be the same. Input queries have 10 distinguished variables. With this experiment, we would like to avoid measuring exponential response times simply because the size of the rewriting grows exponentially. Hence, trying to create a "phase transition point", we generated the first 80 views for all our view sets containing 10 distinguished variables and each additional view (up to 140) with only 3 distinguished variables. This causes the number of conjunctive rewritings to grow exponentially up to 80 views, but this rate becomes much slower from there and after. This trend in the number of rewritings can be seen in Fig. 8(b).

As seen in Fig. 8(b), GQR runs 75 times faster than MCDSAT and it is much more scalable, as it "fails" very fast (7 chain queries did not meet our experimental bounds, either for GQR or MCDSAT). This can be seen when there are no rewritings at all, as well as after the point of 80 views; the time of reformulation clearly depends more on the size of the output than that of the problem. As also seen in Fig. 8(b), GQR produces fewer conjunctive rewritings than MCDSAT. An example query where MCDSAT produced a redundant rewriting was the following. Given the query and view:

$q(x_1, x_2, x_3) \rightarrow p_1(x_0, x_1, x_2, x_3), p_2(x_1)$

$v(y_1, y_2, y_3, y_4, y_5, y_6, y_7) \rightarrow p_1(y_2, y_3, y_9, y_{10}), p_1(y_4, y_5, y_6, y_7), p_2(y_1)$

MCDSAT produces both rewritings below, while GQR produces only the second (which contains the first):

[7]The generator was kindly provided to us by R. Pottinger, and it is the same one that she used for the original experimental evaluation of MiniCon.

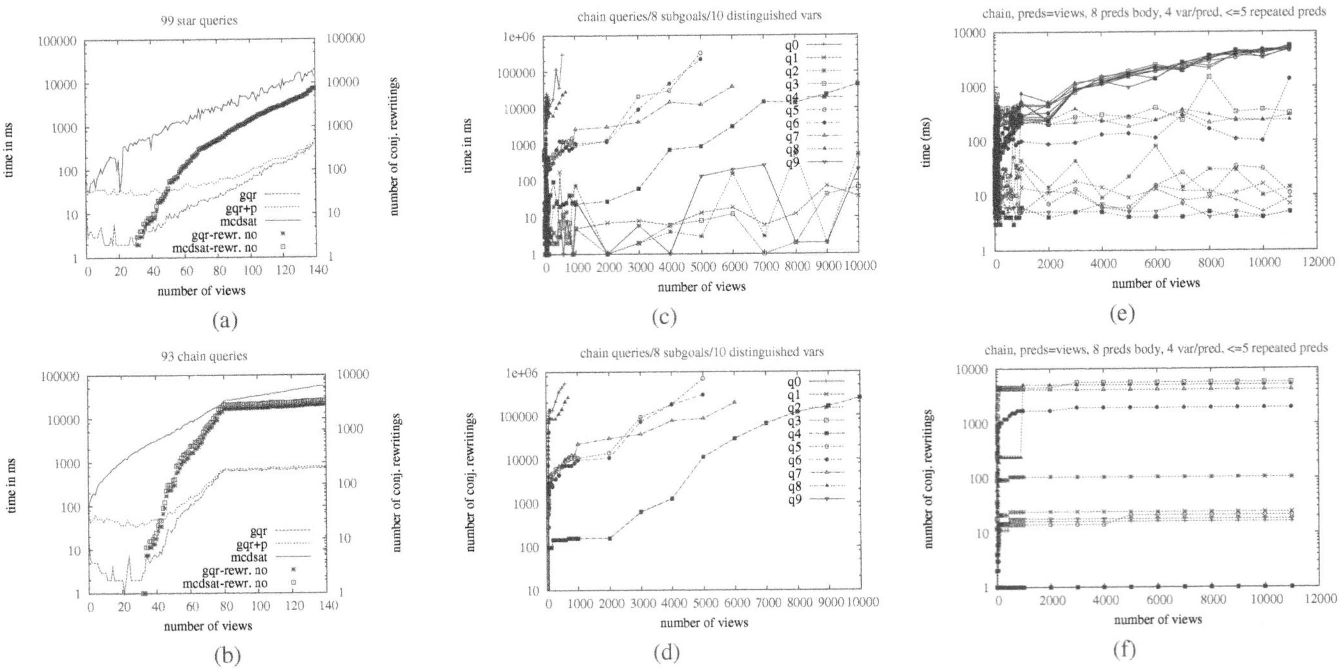

Figure 8: (a) Average time and size of rewritings for star queries. GQR time does not take into account the source preprocessing time while gqr+p does. As we can see the preprocessing phase (for this small set of views) does not add much to our algorithm; the query reformulation phase is dominating the time as the number of views increases. (b) Average time and size of rewritings for chain queries. After the point of 80 views, while the problem size continues to grow linearly, the output (number of rewritings) grows very slowly. (c) Average reformulation time for 10 chain queries. Preprocessing time is not included in the plot. (d) Average size of rewriting for chain queries of (c). Queries $q1$,$q2$,$q3$ and $q9$ don't produce any rewritings. (e) Ten chain queries on views constructed from an increasing predicate space. The upper bunch of straight lines gives the total time for the queries, while the lower dotted part gives only the reformulation time. (f) Number of rewritings for (e).

$q(x_1, x_2, x_3) \rightarrow \mathrm{v}(x_1, f_1, f_2, x_0, x_1, x_2, x_3)$

$q(x_1, x_2, x_3) \rightarrow \mathrm{v}(f_0, f_1, f_2, x_0, x_1, x_2, x_3),$
$\mathrm{v}(x_1, f_8, f_9, f_{10}, f_{11}, f_{12}, f_{13})$

5.3 Chain queries using 10000 views

In Fig. 8(c) we expose the times for 10 chain queries with the very same experimental setting of the previous subsection, using 10000 views. As previously the first 80 views for each query have 10 distinguished variables, and the rest only 3. However, as the figure shows, our "transition phase point" did not work well for the queries that had already produced some rewritings within the first 80 views (namely, $q0$,$q4$,$q5$,$q6$,$q7$ and $q8$). The number of conjunctive rewritings for these queries grows exponentially to the number of views. On the other hand 4 queries did not produce rewritings up to 80 views; and they also did not produce any from that point and on (as the number of distinguished variables for all views after 80 is too constraining to, e.g, cover an atom that has 4 distinguished variables). Nevertheless this figure serves our point. The unfinished queries have crashed on a number of views that caused too many conjunctive rewritings, as Fig. 8(d) shows. In this setting, our algorithm runs in less than a second for queries that don't produce rewritings for 10000 views, while it produces 250.000 conjunctive rewritings for 10000 views in 44 seconds (for $q4$).

Lastly, in an effort to keep the number of conjunctive rewritings low, we decided to set the predicate space (out of which we populate our rules) to equal the number of views at each point. Fig. 8(e), shows how ten chain queries performed with and without the preprocessing times. As seen from the graph the exponential burden of solving the problem lies on the preprocessing phase, while the online reformulation time is less than second for all queries, even the ones producing thousands of rewritings (Fig. 8(f) shows the number of rewritings for these queries).

6. COMPARISON WITH RELATED WORK

Early approaches dealing with query rewriting involve algorithms as the *bucket* [17] and the *inverse rules* [10]. A more efficient approach was proposed in 2001, by the MiniCon [19] algorithm. Similar to our notion of CPJs, MiniCon devises MCDs (MiniCon Descriptions), which are coverings as defined in Def. 3 (they are defined per distinct query and view subgoals) having the additional property that they always consider as a whole the existentially chained pieces of the query whenever one existential query variable is mapped to an existential one on the view (Property 1 as discussed in Sect. 2). Minimal MCDs are MCDs which don't contain anything more than these existential chained pieces. In the following, we briefly describe the two phases of the MiniCon algorithm and give our algorithm's advantages against each one of its steps. It is important to notice that MCDSAT which exhibited a better performance than MiniCon [7], is essentially the MiniCon algorithm casted as a satisfiability problem, and comparing our algorithm against MiniCon, reveals our advantages against the foundations of MCDSAT also.

6.1 MiniCon Phase One

Before considering a covering of an atomic query subgoal g_q with a view V, MiniCon uses a head homomorphism $h{:}vars(\{head(V$ $\rightarrow vars(\{head(V)\})$ to possibly equate some variables in the head of V (for all variables x, if x is existential $h(x) = x$ and if it is distinguished, then $h(x)$ is distinguished and $h(h(x)) = h(x)$). It then can look for a homomorphism φ so as to cover g_q with an atomic subgoal $h(g_v) \in h(V)$. Note in that the original MiniCon algorithm the authors suggest a search over the entire space of all *least-restrictive* head homomorphisms h, and mappings φ so that $\varphi(g_q) = h(g_v) \in h(V)$ ($STEP1$).

Subsequently, for each g_q,g_v and pair of functions h,φ that come out of $STEP1$, the algorithm produces a minimal MCD ($STEP2$). Formally, an MCD M is a tuple $< V, \varphi, h, G_q >$ where (a) $h(V)$ covers $G_q \subseteq body(Q)$ (containing g_q) with φ and (b) for all x, if $\varphi(x)$ is an existential variable, then all atomic subgoals $g_i \in body(Q)$ that mention x are in G_q. An MCD M is minimal if (c) it covers[8] g_v together with the minimum additional subset of $body(Q)$ so as to satisfy (a) and (b). A minimal MCD intuitively covers only one *connected* subgraph of the query graph which adheres to property (b) above (clause $C2$ of Property 1 in [19]).

6.2 MiniCon Phase Two

In its second phase the MiniCon algorithm, needs to choose sets of MCDs which cover *mutually exclusive* parts of the query, and their union covers the entire query ($STEP3$). It then follows a lightweight generation of a conjunctive rewriting for each MCD combination ($STEP4$). For each conjunctive rewriting that it produces, the analogous of our Def. 4 is employed in order to "minimize" some of the rewritings ($STEP5$).

6.3 MCDSAT

In MCDSAT, the authors cast MiniCon's first phase (the MCDs generation problem) into a propositional theory whose models constitute the MCDs. This theory is then compiled into a normal form called d-DNNF that implements model enumeration in polynomial time in the size of the compiled theory. $STEP1$, and properties (a), (b) and (c) of $STEP2$ result in clauses of that theory, which is further extended with more optimization clauses. The result is an efficient algorithm for generating MCDs. Nevertheless, as we discuss below we believe that we have a better encoding of the problem than MiniCon's steps 1 and 2, that MCDSAT also employs.

For the second phase, that of MCD combination and rewriting generation, MCDSAT considers either a traditional implementation of MiniCon's second phase or yet another satisfiability approach: some additional clauses are devised in order to present an extended logical theory whose models are in correspondence with the rewritings. Note, that although the authors present an experimental performance of the compilation times of these extended theories, for our own evaluation we consider (and exhibit much better performance on) the times to get the actual rewritings themselves. Nonetheless, a contribution of these compiled extended theories is that they serve as compact repositories of rewritings; once compiled one can get the rewritings in polynomial time to the size of the compiled theory.

6.4 GQR vs MiniCon and MCDSAT

Our encoding of the problem exhibits several advantages against steps $STEP1$-$STEP5$. Firstly, we don't need to explicitly deal with finding h in $STEP1$, since we abstract from variable names. Returning variables are equated implicitly as we build up our CPJs. Moreover, MiniCon iterates over every input subgoals g_q and g_v. In combination with $STEP2$(b) this implies that some query subgoals will be considered more than once. In effect, while in $STEP2$ the query subgoals g_i are included in an MCD for input g_q (that came out of $STEP1$), subsequent iterations will result them forming the same MCD (among others) when they are themselves considered as the input subgoals of $STEP1$[9]. GQR on the other hand considers each query subgoal exactly once and thus avoids these redundant mappings.

A major advantage of our encoding is that while $STEP2$ is considered for every distinct atomic view subgoal of every view, we consider PJs; being compact representations of view patterns they are dramatically fewer than the distinct view subgoals. Nevertheless this does not mean "more work" for a subsequent phase. On the contrary, during our iteration of this less number of constructs we avoid the heavy computation of $STEP2$. We essentially avoid "tracking" each individual existentially chained piece in a view, for every query subgoal we map onto a part of it (as $STEP2$(b) suggests). Same piece patterns are consider just once for all sources, at the time we combine their individual parts (PJs and CPJs).

This design also benefits our performance in the face of repeated predicates in a view. Consider the view $V_1(x, g, f) \to P_1(x, y)$, $P_2(y, z)$, $P_3(z, g)$, $P_3(z, f)$ and the query $Q(a, b) \to P_1(a, y)$, $P_2(y, z)$, $P_3(z, b)$. Here MiniCon will most probably (to the best of our knowledge) create two MCDs for P_3, each time recomputing the mapping of $P_1(a, y)$, $P_2(y, z)$ to the view. On the other hand, we will consider this mapping just once. Moreover as our previous argument exposed, this join pattern of P_1 and P_2 will be at the same time detected in every source it appears in (at the same step we also rule out of future consideration all the non combinable sources that contain these patterns).

We would like to point out that we do consider the whole set of mappings from every atomic query subgoal to all the atomic view subgoals per view, in a way very similar to $STEP1$. We do this however in our preprocessing phase where we additionally compute the PJ infoboxes. As a result we are left with both drastically less constructs to deal with and in a more straightforward and less costly manner than $STEP2$.

Moreover our algorithm exhibits additional advantages in that its second phase (the CPJ combination) already encapsulates the entire second phase of MiniCon and MCDSAT. And it does so even more efficiently; the $STEP3$ of the related algorithms needs to explicitly choose "mutually exclusive" MCDs in order to provide non redundant rewritings; in our case all sets of CPJs (as seen in Sect. 4) are mutually exclusive. Yet, we do need to combine all their elements pairwise, however we can fail-fast in the case one such pair is un-combinable as the reader can also see from Sect. 4. The formulation of the actual rewritings ($STEP4$ for MiniCon) is embodied in our second phase and is done incrementally (through the partial rewritings) during the combination of the CPJs to larger graphs. $STEP5$ is also smoothly incorporated with this incremental building of a rewriting through the implementation of Def. 4. In conclusion, PJs (and CPJs) seem to be better constructs than MCDs in encoding the problem. This is also why we believe our solution performs better than the other algorithms.

6.5 Hypergraphs and Hypertree Decompositions

As already mentioned, our graphs and PJs resemble some relevant and well study concepts from the literature, namely hypergraphs and hyperedges [1] accordingly. Nevertheless we find our own notation more suitable for focusing on the type of the query's variables as well as making their join descriptions explicit. Since hypergraphs were developed for representing single queries, it is less convenient (although entirely symmetrical to our approach) to attach infoboxes on them, or have hyperedges represent information across multiple views. In [12], hypertree decompositions were

[8]Since MCDs are essentially descriptions of coverings, we'll abuse terminology to say that an MCD covers a subgoal.

[9]Although the algorithm suggests such a brute force approach, it is indeed possible that the original MiniCon implementation did prune out some redundant MCDs. The MCDSAT satisfiability perspective most probably also avoids this redundancy.

devised; these were hierarchical join patterns which combined hyperedges bottom-up into ever larger query fragments. Nevertheless the focus of this representation is different; each vertex of these constructs can represent a whole a set of atoms and/or variables and each variable and atom induces a connected subtree. On the other hand, looking at our own incremental build-up of the view CPJs as a tree of combinations, we differentiate; we keep some compact "hyperedges" per vertex and each parent vertex contains all and exactly its children. Again it possible that our CPJ combination could be translated to a variation of hypertree decompositions and we plan to further investigate this perspective in the future.

7. DISCUSSION AND FUTURE WORK

We presented GQR, a scalable query rewriting algorithm that computes the rewritings in an incremental, bottom up fashion. Using a graph perspective of queries and views, it finds and indexes common patterns in the views making rewriting more efficient. Optionally, this view preprocessing/indexing can be done offline thereby speeding up online performance even more. The bottom-up rewriting process also has a fail-fast behavior. In our experiments, GQR is about 2 orders of magnitude faster than the state of the art and scales up to 10000 views.

GQR opens several areas of future work. First, the current algorithm picks an arbitrary order for the bottom up combination of CPJs. However, we plan to investage heuristic orderings that could speed the process even further, by failing faster and/or computing a smaller number of intermediate partial rewritings. Second, we will like to explore the phase transitions in the space of rewritings. Third, we plan to investigate the nature of minimal rewritings and encode additional minimizations. Fourth, we plan to extend the algorithm with constants and interpreted predicates, such as comparisons. Fifth, we will like to use the insights of our graph-based representation to define a novel SAT encoding that may lead to an even faster algortihm, given the significant optimization effort invested in state-of-the-art SAT solvers. Finally, we want to extend our algorithm to richer interschema axioms such as GLAV (source to target rules that have conjunctive antecedents and consequents) and to rewrite in the presence of constraints, particularly from more expressive languages such as Description Logics.

8. ACKNOWLEDGMENTS

We thank Rachel Pottinger and Maria Esther Vidal for graciously sharing their code. This work was supported in part by the NIH through the NCRR grant: the Biomedical Informatics Research Network (1 U24 RR025736-01), and in part through the NIMH grant: Collaborative Center for Genetic Studies of Mental Disorders (2U24MH068457-06).

9. REFERENCES

[1] S. Abiteboul, R. Hull, and V. Vianu. *Foundations of databases*. Citeseer, 1995.

[2] F. Afrati and N. Kiourtis. Query answering using views in the presence of dependencies. *New Trends in Information Integration (NTII)*, pages 8—-11, 2008.

[3] P. Agrawal, A. D. Sarma, J. Ullman, and J. Widom. Foundations of Uncertain-Data Integration. *Proceedings of the VLDB Endowment*, 3(1):1–24, 2010.

[4] M. Arenas, J. Pérez, J. Reutter, and C. Riveros. Composition and inversion of schema mappings. *ACM SIGMOD Record*, 38(3):17, Dec. 2010.

[5] M. Arenas, J. Pérez, J. L. Reutter, and C. Riveros. Foundations of schema mapping management. In *PODS '10: Proceedings of the twenty-ninth ACM SIGMOD-SIGACT-SIGART symposium on Principles of database systems of data*, pages 227–238, New York, NY, USA, 2010. ACM.

[6] P. C. Arocena, A. Fuxman, and R. J. Miller. Composing local-as-view mappings: closure and applications. In *Proceedings of the 13th International Conference on Database Theory*, pages 209–218. ACM, 2010.

[7] Y. Arvelo, B. Bonet, and M. E. Vidal. Compilation of query-rewriting problems into tractable fragments of propositional logic. In *AAAI'06: Proceedings of the 21st national conference on Artificial intelligence*, pages 225–230. AAAI Press, 2006.

[8] A. Chandra and P. Merlin. Optimal implementation of conjunctive queries in relational data bases. In *Proceedings of the ninth annual ACM symposium on Theory of computing*, pages 77–90. ACM, 1977.

[9] M. Chein and M.-L. Mugnier. *Graph-based Knowledge Representation: Computational Foundations of Conceptual Graphs*. Springer Publishing Company, Incorporated, 2008.

[10] O. M. Duschka and M. R. Genesereth. Answering recursive queries using views. In *PODS '97: Proceedings of the sixteenth ACM SIGACT-SIGMOD-SIGART symposium on Principles of database systems*, pages 109–116, New York, NY, USA, 1997. ACM.

[11] H. Garcia-Molina, J. Hammer, K. Ireland, Y. Papakonstantinou, J. Ullman, and J. Widom. Integrating and accessing heterogeneous information sources in tsimmis. In *Proceedings of the AAAI Symposium on Information Gathering, pp. 61-64*, March 1995.

[12] G. Gottlob, N. Leone, and F. Scarcello. Hypertree decompositions and tractable queries. In *Proceedings of the eighteenth ACM SIGMOD-SIGACT-SIGART symposium on Principles of database systems*, pages 21–32. ACM, 1999.

[13] A. Halevy. Answering queries using views: A survey. *The VLDB Journal*, 10(4):270–294, Dec. 2001.

[14] H. Kondylakis and D. Plexousakis. Enabling ontology evolution in data integration. In *Proceedings of the 2010 EDBT Workshops*, pages 1–7. ACM, 2010.

[15] M. Lenzerini. Data integration: A theoretical perspective. In *PODS*, pages 233–246, 2002.

[16] A. Levy, A. Mendelzon, Y. Sagiv, and D. Srivastava. Answering queries using views (extended abstract). In *Proceedings of the fourteenth ACM SIGACT-SIGMOD-SIGART symposium on Principles of database systems*, pages 95–104. ACM, 1995.

[17] A. Levy, A. Rajaraman, and J. Ordille. Querying heterogeneous information sources using source descriptions. pages 251–262, 1996.

[18] V. Lín, V. Vassalos, and P. Malakasiotis. MiniCount: Efficient Rewriting of COUNT-Queries Using Views. *22nd International Conference on Data Engineering (ICDE'06)*, pages 1–1, 2006.

[19] R. Pottinger and A. Halevy. MiniCon: A scalable algorithm for answering queries using views. *The VLDB Journal*, 10(2):182–198, 2001.

[20] L. Zhou, H. Chen, Y. Zhang, and C. Zhou. A Semantic Mapping System for Bridging the Gap between Relational Database and Semantic Web. *American Association for Artificial Intelligence (www. aaai. org)*, 2008.

Automatic Discovery of Attributes in Relational Databases

Meihui Zhang
National University of Singapore
mhzhang@comp.nus.edu.sg

Marios Hadjieleftheriou
AT&T Labs - Research
marioh@research.att.com

Beng Chin Ooi
National University of Singapore
ooibc@comp.nus.edu.sg

Cecilia M. Procopiuc
AT&T Labs - Research
magda@research.att.com

Divesh Srivastava
AT&T Labs - Research
divesh@research.att.com

ABSTRACT

In this work we design algorithms for clustering relational columns into *attributes*, i.e., for identifying strong relationships between columns based on the common properties and characteristics of the values they contain. For example, identifying whether a certain set of columns refers to *telephone* numbers versus *social security* numbers, or names of *customers* versus names of *nations*. Traditional relational database schema languages use very limited primitive data types and simple foreign key constraints to express relationships between columns. Object oriented schema languages allow the definition of custom data types; still, certain relationships between columns might be unknown at design time or they might appear only in a particular database instance. Nevertheless, these relationships are an invaluable tool for schema matching, and generally for better understanding and working with the data. Here, we introduce data oriented solutions (we do not consider solutions that assume the existence of any external knowledge) that use statistical measures to identify strong relationships between the values of a set of columns. Interpreting the database as a graph where nodes correspond to database columns and edges correspond to column relationships, we decompose the graph into connected components and cluster sets of columns into attributes. To test the quality of our solution, we also provide a comprehensive experimental evaluation using real and synthetic datasets.

Categories and Subject Descriptors

H.m [**Information Systems**]: Miscellaneous

General Terms

Algorithms

Keywords

Attribute discovery, Schema matching

1. INTRODUCTION

Relational databases are described using a strict formal language in the form of a relational schema. A relational schema specifies various properties of tables and columns within tables, the most important of which is the type of data contained in each column. There is a well defined set of possible primitive data types, ranging from numerical values and strings, to sets and large binary objects. The relational schema also allows one to define relationships between columns of different tables in the form of foreign key constraints. Even though the relational schema is a powerful description of the data, it has certain limitations in practice. In particular, it cannot accurately describe relationships between columns in the form of *attributes*, i.e., *strongly connected sets of values that appear to have the same or similar meaning within the context of a particular database instance*.

For example, consider a database instance that contains columns about telephone numbers and social security numbers. All such columns can be declared using the same primitive data type (e.g., decimal), but in reality there is never a case where these two types of columns need to be joined with each other: semantically, there is no reason why these columns should belong to the same type. Even though this fact might be known to users (or easy to deduce), it is nowhere explicitly specified within the schema. As another example, consider a database instance that contains a table of customer names and defines two views, one with European and one with Asian customers. Ostensibly, the customer name columns in the European and Asian views will not have any (or very few) values in common. Nevertheless, all three customer name columns belong to the same attribute. Moreover, suppose that there exists a fourth column that contains nation names. Clearly, nation names should not be classified in the same attribute as customer names even though these columns contain the same types of values (i.e., strings). Differentiating between these fundamentally different attributes can be an invaluable tool for data integration and schema matching applications, and, generally speaking, for better understanding and working with the data.

Existing schema matching techniques for identifying relationships between columns use simple statistics and string-based comparisons, e.g., prefix/suffix tests, edit distance, value ranges, min/max similarity, and mutual information based on q-gram distributions [11, 7, 8, 12, 13]. Other approaches use external information like thesauri, standard schemas, and past mappings. Our work on discovering attributes can be used as a valuable addition to all of the above, for designing automated schema mapping tools.

It is important to note here that attribute relationships are not always known in advance to database designers, so it is not always possible to encode them a priori (for example, by using constraints or object oriented schema languages). Certain relationships might hold solely for a particular database instance, others develop over time as the structure of the database evolves, yet others are obvious in hindsight only. Furthermore, there exists a large number of legacy databases (sometimes with sizes in the order of hundreds of tables and thousands of columns) for which schema definitions or

SIGMOD'11, June 12–16, 2011, Athens, Greece.

folklore knowledge of column meanings might have been lost. To make matters worse, in many practical situations users have access only to a keyhole view of the database (due to access privileges). In such cases users access the data through materialized views, without any information about the underlying schema, or even about the view definitions. In other words, as far as the user is concerned, all schema information has been lost.

Our approach for discovering attributes is purely data oriented. We do not examine solutions that depend on external knowledge about the data. We compute various statistical measures between all pairs of columns within the database, and derive positive and negative relationships between certain pairs of columns. Viewing the database instance as a graph where every column is a node and every positive/negative relationship is an edge, we decompose the graph into connected components. Then, we further decompose each component into a set of attributes.

In particular, in order to discern the type of relationship between any pair of columns, we use Earth Mover's Distance to find the similarity between the distributions of the values contained in the columns. We introduce two types of connections, one based on the *overall distribution* of values and one based on the *intersection distribution* (distribution with respect to the common values only). Low distribution similarity strongly suggests no attribute ties. High intersection distribution similarity suggests very strong attribute ties. We also propose the notion of a *witness column* for introducing relationships by indirect association (i.e., for columns that have no values in common directly, but share a lot of values with the witness column).

Our main contribution is to provide a robust, unsupervised solution that reports a clustering of columns into attributes. In addition, we perform a comprehensive empirical study using real and synthetic datasets to validate our solution, and show that it has very high precision in practice.

Section 2 gives some necessary background and definitions. Section 3 presents our solution. Section 4 discusses performance issues. Section 5 presents a comprehensive experimental evaluation of the proposed technique. Section 6 discusses related work. Finally, Section 7 concludes this paper.

2. DEFINITIONS AND BACKGROUND

Conventionally, in relational database terminology the term attribute is a synonym for a column. In this work, we use the term attribute to refer to a much stronger notion, based on the *actual meaning* of the values contained in a column. Formally:

DEFINITION 1 (ATTRIBUTE). *An* attribute *is a set of relational columns, such that columns in the same attribute are semantically equivalent to each other.*

In other words, an attribute is a logical notion based on common properties and characteristics of the values contained in the columns comprising that attribute.

For example, Figure 1 shows an excerpt of the schema of the TPC-H benchmark [16], which models a business environment and contains information about products, suppliers, customers, orders, etc. The figure shows three tables, CUSTOMER, NATION and ORDERS, and foreign-primary key relationships between some columns of these tables. A customer is associated with six columns in this example: CUSTKEY, NAME, ADDRESS, NATIONKEY, PHONE and COMMENT. Since CUSTOMER.NATIONKEY is a foreign key of NATION.NATIONKEY, the two NATIONKEY columns are by definition semantically equal and hence they belong to the same attribute. The same is true for ORDERS.CUSTKEY and CUSTOMER.CUSTKEY. Another example appears in Figure 2 which shows a slightly more

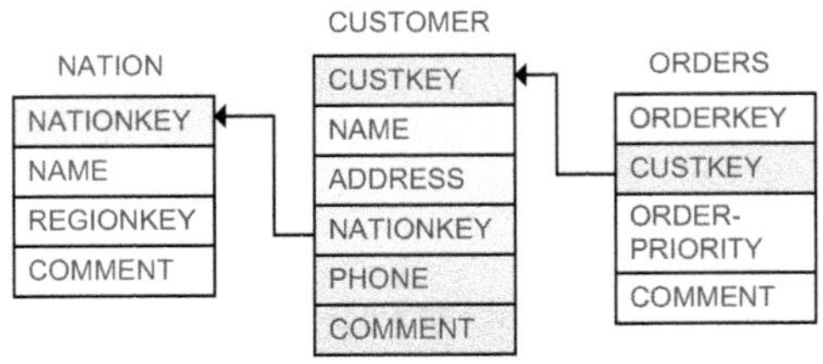

Figure 1: Excerpt of the TPC-H schema.

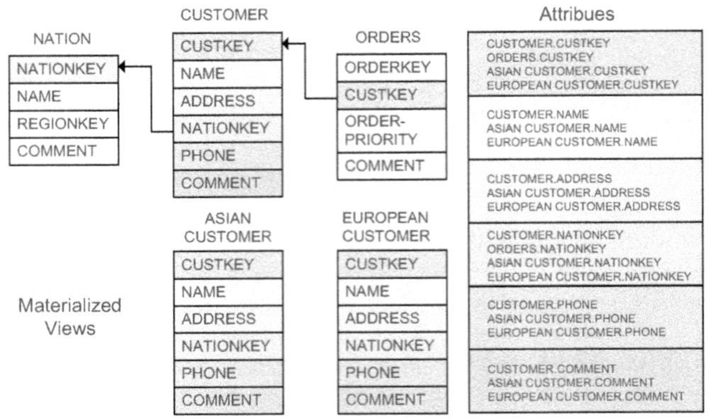

Figure 2: Attributes in TPC-H example, which contains three base tables and two materialized views of CUSTOMER table.

complex scenario that considers the existence of materialized views, i.e., ASIAN CUSTOMER and EUROPEAN CUSTOMER created from the CUSTOMER table based on NATIONKEY. The ideal clustering of the six columns contained in the CUSTOMER table is shown on the right side of the figure. Clearly, all columns from the three related tables belong to the same attribute, even if there is no direct association specified in the schema (e.g., in the form of primary/foreign keys) and despite the fact that, probably, EUROPEAN CUSTOMER and ASIAN CUSTOMER have no values in common.

We now formalize the problem of attribute discovery as follows:

DEFINITION 2 (ATTRIBUTE DISCOVERY). *Given a collection of relational tables, denoted* $\mathbf{T}$, *let* $\mathbf{C}$ *be the set of all columns in* $\mathbf{T}$. Attribute Discovery *is the process of partitioning* $\mathbf{C}$ *into* m *clusters* $\mathbf{A} = \{A_1, A_2, \ldots, A_m\}$ *such that each* $A_k = \{C_1^k, C_2^k, \ldots, C_{n_k}^k\}$ *is an attribute with respect to the set of tables* $\mathbf{T}$.

According to Definition 1, two columns C and C' are part of the same attribute if and only if semantically they behave the same. The semantics of two columns can be inferred by the type of relationship these columns have within a database instance. We define the following relationship types:

1. A primary/foreign key;
2. Two foreign keys referring to the same primary key;
3. A column in a view and the corresponding column in the base table;
4. Two columns in two views but from the same column in the base table;
5. No explicit relationship but semantically equivalent (e.g., non-key, customer name columns from different tables).

The first four relationship types are, by definition, indicators of strong attribute ties. The fifth relationship type encompasses all columns that are semantically equivalent where this information cannot be inferred from the database schema, but only from the actual values contained in the columns. Only relationship type 1 has been studied in the past. To the best of our knowledge no previous work has studied relationship types 2-5. Nevertheless, existing work can easily be adapted to identify types 2-4. In what follows, we list a set of existing techniques that can be used to identify pairs of columns belonging to these relationship types. In each case, we point out why they are insufficient for identifying *all* relationship types - particularly type 5.

2.1 Name Similarity

It is natural to consider using the similarity of column names to infer column semantics, since, to a certain extent, names reflect the meaning of the values within a column. Indeed, previous work, especially in the area of schema matching, has applied this technique to identify associations between columns [14]. However, this is not always a robust solution for three reasons. First, a given database might not use strict naming conventions. Second, columns with no meaningful associations oftentimes have similar or even identical names. For instance, a column called NAME appears in both the NATION and CUSTOMER tables of TPC-H, even though the two columns refer to two semantically unrelated concepts. Third, two semantically related columns may happen to have very different names. For example, the columns in a view might have completely different names from the source columns in the base table. This happens when views are generated automatically, or when long, representative column names have to be abbreviated due to length constraints (e.g., the 30 characters limit in Oracle). Hence, simply relying on column name similarity can lead to both false positives and false negatives, for the purpose of discovering attributes.

2.2 Value Similarity

Another straightforward technique is to consider the similarity of the data values contained in a set of columns. The Jaccard coefficient $J(C_1, C_2) = \frac{|C_1 \cap C_2|}{|C_1 \cup C_2|}$ (or any other set similarity measure) can be used for this purpose, which can be efficiently estimated in practice [6]. However, this idea has its own drawbacks. For example, in our TPC-H database instance, column CUSTOMER.CUSTKEY contains values from 1 to 150,000, while column PART.PARTKEY contains all integers from 1 to 200,000. The overlap of the values in these two columns is very high: their Jaccard coefficient is 0.75. Nevertheless, the columns are not semantically related. Conversely, two columns can have a strong semantic relationship but no common values at all, e.g., EUROPEAN CUSTOMER and ASIAN CUSTOMER. Of course, one could argue that in this case the two columns belong to two different attributes. However, in our solution we would like to cluster these columns primarily as customer names (as opposed to, for example, nation names) and, optionally, also partition them into sub-attributes. In this case, using data value similarity alone would lead to a false dismissal.

2.3 Distribution Similarity

Data distribution similarity has been used before for finding associations between columns, for example, using Earth Mover's Distance (EMD) to discover meaningful primary/foreign key constraints [17]. Earth Mover's Distance is a measure of similarity between two data distributions on an underlying metric space. In the context of primary/foreign key relationships, it can be used based on the observation that, for the majority of cases, the distinct values in a foreign key column are selected at random from the values of the primary key column, and hence have similar underlying distributions. (This might not always be true, for example, when the foreign key column is produced in a way that some correlations are preserved, as is the case with locations and telephone number prefixes; a foreign key column containing telephone numbers from a specific geographical region would result in a well defined range of numbers and would not be random with respect to a primary key column containing numbers from all regions.) Notice that in the case of primary/foreign keys there is also an implicit *containment* assumption, i.e., that the values in the foreign key are a subset (or approximately a subset) of the values in the primary key.

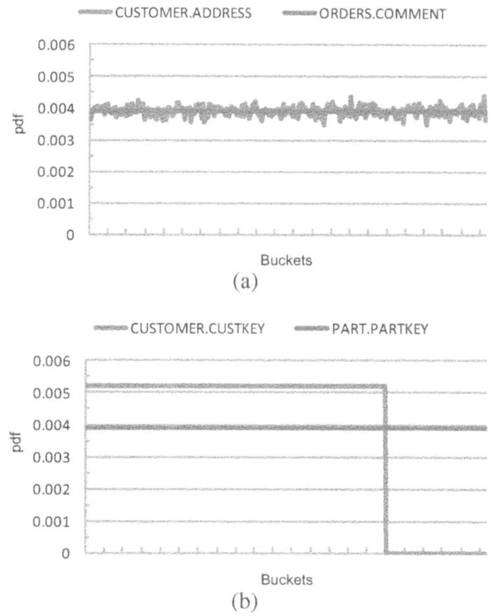

Figure 3: Data distribution histograms of two examples from TPC-H.

Earth Mover's Distance is defined as follows:

DEFINITION 3. *Given probability density functions (pdfs) C and C' on an underlying metric space, let a unit amount of work be equal to moving a unit of probability mass for a unit distance. Then, $EMD(C, C')$ is equal to the minimum amount of work needed to convert pdf C into pdf C'.*

The smaller the EMD value between two distributions is, the more similar these distributions are considered to be. In the context of sets of values, EMD is defined as the minimum amount of work needed to convert one set of values into another, where a unit of work is defined according to the *rank* of the values in the sorted order of the union of the two sets. For example, consider two sets of strings. First, we take the union of strings, sort them lexicographically and assign to each string its rank in the lexicographic order. Then, the amount of work needed to convert one string into another is equal to the distance of their ranks. For numerical values the only difference is that we sort the values in numeric instead of lexicographic order. See [17] for more details. Notice that we consider rank distributions for EMD computation purposes. Thus, the type of sorting affects the ranks of values and hence the distributions.

Computing distribution similarity is a necessary step in our setting, since we can use it to discover primary/foreign key constraints (one of the core relationship types we are interested in). However, it is not sufficient for our purposes. Consider for example the values in CUSTOMER.ADDRESS and ORDERS.COMMENT. If we sort them in lexicographic order for the purpose of computing EMD, they follow very similar distributions. The proportion of strings from one column that fall within a given range of strings from the other column in lexicographic order is very similar. To illustrate this point, we plot the two distributions in Figure 3(a). The buckets are constructed using an equi-depth histogram based on the quantiles of column ORDERS.COMMENT. Then, we simply tally the number of strings from column CUSTOMER.ADDRESS that fall within each bucket. The plot clearly shows that the values in CUSTOMER.ADDRESS also follow a nearly uniform distribution across buckets. Indeed, the EMD between the two columns is only 0.0004. Still, computing distribution similarity does eliminate a large number of other column pairs: for example, the histograms for columns CUSTOMER.CUSTKEY and PART.PARTKEY, whose EMD is 0.125, are shown in Figure 3(b). We conclude that EMD values are a useful but insufficient filter. The main reason why EMD works for discovering primary/foreign key relationships, but not for discovering attributes, is the fact that for primary/foreign keys a containment relationship needs to hold: By definition, most, if not all, values from the foreign key must belong to the primary key. Thus, we would never consider ORDERS.COMMENT and CUSTOMER.ADDRESS as a valid primary/foreign key candidate in the first place, since they are not expected to have many strings in common. By contrast, for columns belonging to the same attribute no containment relationship needs to hold (e.g., EUROPEAN CUSTOMER and ASIAN CUSTOMER).

3. ATTRIBUTE DISCOVERY

It is clear that simply applying the aforementioned methods for discovering attributes will not yield accurate results. In this section we present a novel two-step approach. Intuitively, most of the time columns that belong to the same attribute tend to contain values that are drawn from the same underlying distribution. Conversely, if the values of two columns have different distributions, they more likely belong to different attributes. Therefore, here we advocate an algorithm that uses data distribution similarity, based on EMD, for partitioning columns into *distribution clusters*. This first step is used to separate columns into major categories, for example clusters that contain strings and clusters that contain only numerical columns. Furthermore, this step will also separate numerical columns with widely differing distributions, based for example on the range of values within the columns.

The use of EMD to create distribution clusters has some limitations. First and foremost, as can be seen from the example in Figure 3(a), not all the columns in one distribution cluster belong to the same attribute, especially when it comes to columns containing strings. String columns tend to have very similar distributions irrespective of the attribute these strings are derived from (e.g., addresses and comments). Second, using EMD might place some columns that belong to the same attribute into different clusters. This will happen for example if several views are defined on a table containing regions and telephone numbers, and the views select telephone numbers only from particular regions. Clearly, the telephone numbers in each view will start with a particular prefix. These correlations result in significantly different distribution of values between columns of the same attribute, rendering distribution based measures ineffective.

To solve the first problem, we use a subsequent, refinement phase that relies on computing the similarity of the distribution based on the intersection of two columns. We also use indirect associations through witness columns for cases where two columns have no values in common. We leave the solution of the second problem as future work, and identify this scenario as a limitation of our algorithm. From our experience, columns that have been generated based on indirect correlations do exist, but are rare in practice.

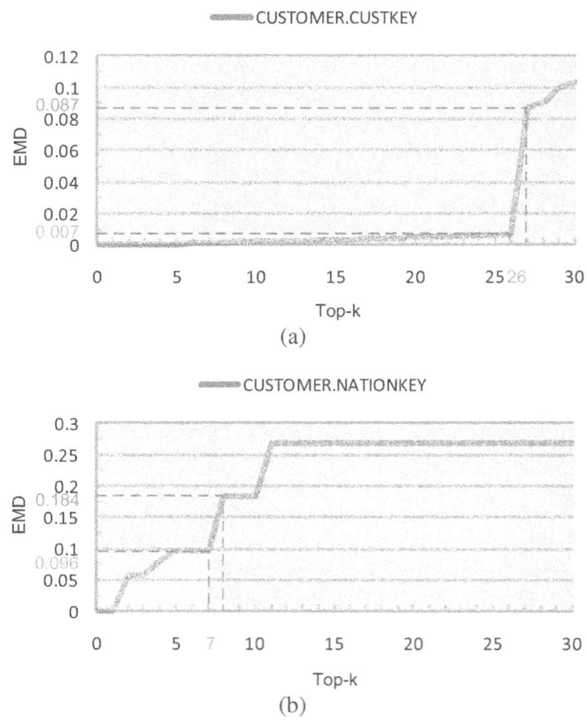

Figure 4: EMD plot of two examples in TPC-H.

3.1 Phase One: Computing Distribution Clusters

Given a set of columns $\mathbf{C}$, we form distribution clusters by computing the EMD between all pairs of columns in $\mathbf{C}$. Since EMD is a symmetric measure, this step requires $\frac{|\mathbf{C}|(|\mathbf{C}|-1)}{2}$ EMD computations. Then, given all pairwise EMDs we need to decide how to partition columns into clusters. The main idea here is to derive for every column a set of neighboring columns with small EMD, such that no two columns that intuitively belong to the same attribute are ultimately split into separate clusters. For every column C, we sort its EMD values to every other column in increasing order. Now we have to choose a cutoff EMD threshold that will determine the neighborhood $\mathbf{N}_C$ of C. After all neighborhoods have been determined, we will form a graph G_D, where nodes correspond to columns and undirected edges are created between a column C and all other columns in $\mathbf{N}_C$. Finally, the distribution clusters are formed by computing all connected components in G_D.

In practice, a small EMD value is not only subjective, but also attribute dependent. From our experience, different types of attributes exhibit significantly different behavior in terms of the similarity of the distribution of values across columns of that attribute, even when they are of the same primitive data type. We illustrate this with an example from TPC-H in Figure 4. For columns CUSTOMER.CUSTKEY and NATION.NATIONKEY, we sort their EMD values to all other columns in the database in increasing order of EMD, and plot the top-30 results. From careful, manual analysis of the data, we have determined that the columns belonging to the same attribute as CUSTKEY and NATIONKEY fall in the green region of the plots. We can clearly see that both the cutoff EMD value and the value of k that bound the green regions in the plots, differ significantly for these two attributes. For our purposes we would like to be able to identify the EMD cutoff threshold for each column automatically (and not by choosing a global EMD threshold or value k), and clearly this means that we have to resort to heuristics.

We observe an interesting property that holds for most columns, in all test cases that we have examined. Given a column C and all pairwise EMD values, it appears that there usually exists a big gap in the magnitude of EMD values, in the sorted order. For example, in both Figures 4(a) and 4(b) we observe a big gap in the sorted EMD order, after the cutoff region (the dotted red lines in the plots). Intuitively, the gap signifies a cutoff point below which other columns seem to have similar distributions with C, and above which columns seem to be completely unrelated to C (recall that small EMD means *similar* and large EMD means *different*). This is expected for most column types in realistic scenarios. For example, numerical columns are more similar to each other than string columns (hence, a big gap exists in the EMD values where numerical columns end and string columns begin); even among numerical columns, smaller gaps occur because of the different ranges of values in the columns (e.g., salaries vs. zip codes). Conservatively choosing this gap to be the cutoff EMD threshold that defines the neighborhood $\mathbf{N}_C$ guarantees that most false cluster splits are avoided in practice (in other words we do not end up with too many clusters). In addition, we can also use a conservative global EMD cutoff threshold θ (a value large enough to signal that two distributions are significantly different) to make sure that the opposite problem does not occur either, i.e., we do not end up with too few distribution clusters.

Algorithmically identifying the cutoff EMD threshold for a column C is straightforward. Let θ be the global threshold, and $L(C)$ be the sorted list of EMD values for C, i.e., $L(C)$ contains all values $e = EMD(C, C'), \forall C' \in \mathbf{C}$, in increasing order. We truncate $L(C)$ to values smaller than θ and identify the largest difference between two consecutive EMD values in the truncated list. The pseudo code appears in Algorithm 1. In the algorithm we also add θ in the list of EMD values to capture the special case were the largest gap between two values happens to involve θ.

Algorithm 1 ComputeCutoffThreshold $(L(C), \theta)$

$L(C)$: list of EMD/column-name pairs (e, C'), $e = EMD(C, C')$
$L = L \cup (\theta, \emptyset)$
Sort L in increasing order of EMD values
$\phi_C = 0, i = 0, gap = 0$
while $L[i+1] \leq \theta$ **do**
  if $gap < L[i+1].e - L[i].e$ **then**
    $gap = L[i+1].e - L[i].e$
    $\phi_C = L[i].e$
  $i = i + 1$
Return ϕ_C

Once the cutoff value ϕ_C for each column C has been computed we can define the neighborhood of a column as follows:

DEFINITION 4 (NEIGHBORHOOD). *The neighborhood* $\mathbf{N}_C$ *of column* C *consists of all columns* C' *with* $EMD(C, C') \leq \phi_C$.

Then, we build the *distribution graph*, which is defined as follows:

DEFINITION 5 (DISTRIBUTION GRAPH). *A* Distribution Graph $G_D = (V_D, E_D)$ *is an undirected graph where each column* $C \in \mathbf{C}$ *corresponds to a node* $C \in V_D$*, and an edge between nodes* C *and* C' *exists iff* $C \in \mathbf{N}_{C'} \vee C' \in \mathbf{N}_C$.

Alternatively, we can define the edges as $C \in \mathbf{N}_{C'} \wedge C' \in \mathbf{N}_C$, but our experimental evaluation shows that in practice this does not affect precision.

The distribution clusters are obtained by computing the connected components in the resulting distribution graph:

Algorithm 2 ComputeDistributionClusters $(\mathbf{C}, \theta)$

1: $G_D = \emptyset$
2: A is a hash table of lists of EMD/column-name pairs (e, C)
3: **for** $i \leftarrow 1$ to $|\mathbf{C}|$ **do**
4:   **for** $j \leftarrow i + 1$ to $|\mathbf{C}|$ **do**
5:     $e = EMD(C_i, C_j)$
6:     $A[C_i].insert(e, C_j)$
7:     $A[C_j].insert(e, C_i)$
8:   $G_D.AddNode(C_i)$
9: **for** $i \leftarrow 1$ to $|\mathbf{C}|$ **do**
10:   $\phi_{C_i} = ComputeCutoffThreshold(A[C_i], \theta)$
11:   **for all** $C_j \in \mathbf{N}_{C_i}$ **do**
12:     $G_D.AddEdge(C_i, C_j)$
13: Return connected components of G_D

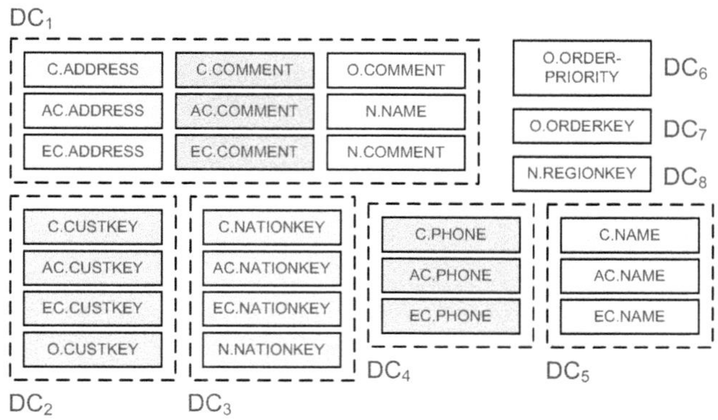

Figure 5: Distribution clusters of TPC-H example.

DEFINITION 6 (DISTRIBUTION CLUSTER). *Let* $G_i = (V_D^i, E_D^i), V_D^i \subset V_D, E_D^i \subset E_D, 1 \leq i \leq n$ *be the set of* n *connected components in distribution graph* G_D. *The set of columns corresponding to the nodes in* V_D^i *determines distribution cluster* $\mathbf{DC}_i$.

The pseudo code for computing distribution clusters is shown in Algorithm 2. We can compute the connected components of graph G_D (line 13 of Algorithm 2) using either depth-first or breadth-first search.

Figure 5 shows the distribution clusters of the TPC-H example in Figure 2, which contains three base tables and two materialized views (table names EUROPEAN CUSTOMER and ASIAN CUSTOMER are shortened to EC and AC). Using the distribution graph, twenty six columns are partitioned into eight clusters. Columns from distinctly different domains are immediately separated (e.g., numeric values and strings). The numeric columns with different ranges of values are also correctly clustered (e.g., key columns like CUSTKEY, NATIONKEY, ORDERKEY and REGIONKEY), as well as columns that contain specially formatted values (e.g., PHONE which contains numerals and dashes). However, distribution clusters cannot always differentiate between different string columns (e.g., ADDRESS and COMMENT).

3.2 Phase two: Computing Attributes

We now describe in detail how to further decompose distribution clusters into attributes, specifically for identifying columns that have very similar distributions overall but do not belong to the same attributes, as is the case for many string columns. We use an intersection distribution metric and witness columns, to construct one attribute graph per distribution cluster and then correlation clustering to decompose the cluster into attributes.

3.2.1 *The Attribute Graph*

In order to decompose clusters into attributes we create one *attribute graph* G_A per cluster. Given that all columns within the same distribution cluster have similar distributions of values, we need to differentiate between attributes by also taking into account the values these columns have in common. Clearly, columns with large intersection of values are highly related and should belong to the same attribute (this is similar to automatically identifying whether two columns have a primary/foreign key relationship, as in [17]). On the other hand, columns that have very few or no values in common, might or might not belong to the same attribute (e.g., as is the case of EUROPEAN CUSTOMER and ASIAN CUSTOMER, and conversely, ADDRESS and COMMENT).

We make here the following key observation. We can determine whether two columns with empty intersection come from the same attribute by using a *witness* column, i.e., a third column that is highly related to both columns. In other words, we introduce *relationships by indirect association*. For example, we know for a fact that both EUROPEAN CUSTOMER and ASIAN CUSTOMER have a large number of values in common with CUSTOMER, but not with each other. After identifying that CUSTOMER is related with EUROPEAN CUSTOMER and ASIAN CUSTOMER, we can deduce with high confidence that EUROPEAN CUSTOMER and ASIAN CUSTOMER are also related. Formally:

DEFINITION 7 (WITNESS COLUMN). *Consider three distinct columns C, C', C''. Column C'' is a witness for C and C' if and only if both conditions hold:*

1. *C'' and C are in the same attribute.*
2. *C'' and C' are in the same attribute.*

Clearly, if two columns belong to the same attribute, have no values in common, and no witness column, then we will not be able to identify these columns. This is one more limitation of our approach, but in practice, such cases might either be identifiable using orthogonal techniques (e.g., column name similarity), or in other cases might be hard to identify using any unsupervised solution.

Based on these observations, we create the *attribute graph* of each cluster $\mathbf{DC}$, similarly to the distribution graph of $\mathbf{C}$. Here, a node corresponds to a column of $\mathbf{DC}$ and an edge corresponds to an intersection relationship between two columns.

We also have to define a measure over these edges, which we call Intersection EMD. Intersection EMD measures the likelihood that a pair of columns are part of the same attribute, taking into account the distribution of the values within each column with respect to the *common* values. In general, for an edge (C, C'), $EMD(C, C\cap C') \neq EMD(C', C\cap C')$. Since the edge is undirected, we define its weight as the arithmetic mean of these two values. Formally:

DEFINITION 8 (INTERSECTION EMD). *Given columns C, C', the* Intersection EMD *is defined as:*

$$EMD_\cap(C, C') = \frac{1}{2}(EMD(C, C\cap C') + EMD(C', C\cap C')).$$

Let $EMD_\cap(C, C') = \infty$, if $C \cap C' = \emptyset$.

Clearly, Intersection EMD can differentiate between columns like ADDRESS and COMMENT, since their intersection is empty. Even if they did have a small number of values in common, their Intersection EMD would be very large.

Similar to the case of computing distribution clusters, we need to decide whether the Intersection EMD between two clusters is small enough to place the columns into the same attribute. We are trying to balance the number of attributes to create (small thresholds will result in too many attributes and large thresholds in too few). For each individual column, we compute a cutoff threshold as before (see Algorithm 1), but instead of using EMD we use Intersection EMD. Similarly, we define the neighborhood $\mathbf{N}_C$ of a column C, this time with respect to Intersection EMD.

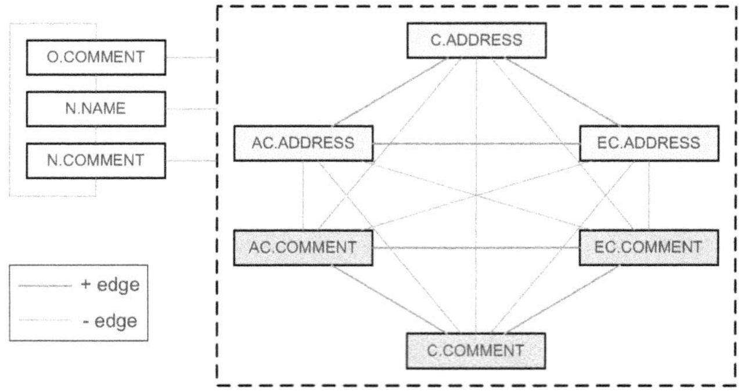

Figure 6: A possible attribute graph of distribution cluster $\mathbf{DC}_1$.

We now give the formal definition of the attribute graph corresponding to a distribution cluster:

DEFINITION 9 (ATTRIBUTE GRAPH). *The attribute graph $G_A = (V_A, E_A)$ of a distribution cluster $\mathbf{DC}$ is a* complete graph *over the set of vertices of $\mathbf{DC}$, such that the weights of edges in E_A are either 1 (positive edges) or -1 (negative edges). Let E_A^+, E_A^- denote the set of positive, resp. negative, edges in G_A. To define them, consider an arbitrary pair of vertices $C, C' \in V_A$.*

1. *Neighborhood: If $C \in \mathbf{N}_{C'} \vee C' \in \mathbf{N}_C$, then $e_{CC'} \in E_{A1}^+$.*
2. *Witness: If $\exists C'' \in V_A$ s.t. $e_{CC''} \in E_{A1}^+ \wedge e_{C'C''} \in E_{A1}^+$, then $e_{CC'} \in E_{A2}^+$.*

We define $E_A^+ = E_{A1}^+ \cup E_{A2}^+$, and $E_A^- = E_A \setminus E_A^+$.

Figure 6 shows the attribute graph of distribution cluster $\mathbf{DC}_1$ from Figure 5. The green lines in the figure denote positive edges while the red lines are negative edges. The edges between the three nodes outside the dashed box to all other nodes are negative. Using Intersection EMD we are able to separate columns like ADDRESS and COMMENT, while AC.ADDRESS and EC.ADDRESS are connected through the witness column C.ADDRESS. The same holds for AC.COMMENT and EC.COMMENT.

The next step is to decompose the graph into attributes. Clearly, we could decompose the graph into connected components (by simply ignoring negative edges) similarly to phase one. Nevertheless, due to the nature of Intersection EMD and the fact that after phase one, attribute graphs consist of a small number of nodes, in practice attribute graphs tend to comprise of a single (or very few) connected components. A better approach here is to use the negative weights productively to find an optimal clustering of nodes into attributes that minimizes the number of conflicting nodes that end up into the same cluster and the number of related nodes that end up in different clusters. As it turns out, this is exactly the goal of *correlation clustering*.

3.2.2 *Correlation Clustering*

Let $G = (V, E)$ be an undirected graph with edge weights 1 or -1. Let E^+ be the set of positive edges, and E^- be the set of negative edges; $E = E^+ \cup E^-$. Intuitively, edge $e_{uv} \in E^+$ if u and v are similar; and $e_{uv} \in E^-$ if u and v are dissimilar. The correlation clustering problem [3] on G is defined as follows:

DEFINITION 10 (CORRELATION CLUSTERING). *Compute disjoint clusters covering V, such that the following cost function is minimized:*

$$\begin{aligned} cost &= |\{e_{uv} \in E^+ \mid Cl(u) \neq Cl(v)\}| + \\ &\quad |\{e_{uv} \in E^- \mid Cl(u) = Cl(v)\}|, \end{aligned}$$

where $Cl(v)$ denotes the cluster node v is assigned to.

This definition minimizes the total number of disagreements, i.e., the number of positive edges whose endpoints are in different clusters, plus the number of negative edges whose endpoints are in the same cluster. Alternatively, one can define the dual problem of maximizing the total agreement. More general versions of the problem exist, e.g., when weights are arbitrary real values. However, this version is sufficient for our purposes.

Correlation clustering can be written as an integer program, as follows. For any pair of vertices u and v, let $X_{uv} = 0$ if $Cl(u) = Cl(v)$, and 1 otherwise. The integer program is

Minimize:

$$\sum_{e_{uv} \in E^+} X_{uv} + \sum_{e_{uv} \in E^-} (1 - X_{uv})$$

s.t.

$$\forall u, v, w : X_{uw} \leq X_{uv} + X_{vw}$$

$$\forall u, v : X_{uv} \in \{0, 1\}$$

The condition $X_{uw} \leq X_{uv} + X_{vw}$ ensures that the following transitivity property is satisfied: if $X_{uv} = 0$ and $X_{vw} = 0$, then $X_{uw} = 0$ (note that this is equivalent to: if $Cl(u) = Cl(v)$ and $Cl(v) = Cl(w)$, then $Cl(u) = Cl(w)$). Therefore X defines an equivalence relationship, and the clusters are its equivalence classes. Correlation clustering is NP-Complete [3]. Nevertheless, the above integer program can be solved exactly by IP solvers (e.g., CPLEX [10]) for sufficiently small graphs. For larger graphs, one can use polynomial time approximation algorithms [2].

Going back to the example of Figure 6, correlation clustering on this graph will further decompose nine columns into five attributes, as shown in Figure 7. If all the edges in the attribute graph are correctly labeled, such as the simple example in Figure 6, then the graph results in perfect clustering, meaning that there are no disagreements. (When this is the case, simply removing all the negative edges and computing the connected components in the remaining graph also returns the correct attributes.) However, if a few edges are assigned conflicting labels, there is no perfect clustering. For example, Figure 8 shows a different attribute graph for distribution cluster DC_1, obtained by setting a higher threshold θ in Algorithm 1. The edge between AC.ADDRESS and AC.COMMENT is now labeled positive. In addition, two other positive edges are created, since AC.ADDRESS and AC.COMMENT act as witnesses for C.ADDRESS and C.COMMENT. As it turns out, in this case correlation clustering is still able to separate the columns correctly, by finding a partition that agrees as much as possible with the edge labels. Of course, in some cases correlation clustering will result in mistakes, but in the end our solution will decompose the graph into attributes that can be manually inspected much more easily than having to look at the complete distribution graph.

We now summarize phase two. The pseudo code is shown in Algorithm 3. For each distribution cluster computed in phase one, compute the Intersection EMD between each pair of columns in the cluster and store the resulting values in a hash table I in increasing order of Intersection EMD. Then compute the cutoff threshold for each column. Construct the attribute graph G_A according to Definition 9. Creating positive edges based on witness columns is implemented by creating positive edges between nodes with path of length two. This is accomplished by first computing the adjacency matrix E of graph $G_{A1} = (V_A, E^+_{A1})$, where $E[C_i][C_j] = 1$ means the edge between node C_i and C_j is positive. The adjacency matrix of graph $G_A = (V_A, E^+_{A2})$ can be computed by multiplying E by itself. The sum of the two matrices is the final adjacency matrix M of attribute graph $G_A = (V_A, E_A)$. Finally, we compute attributes using correlation clustering on graph G_A.

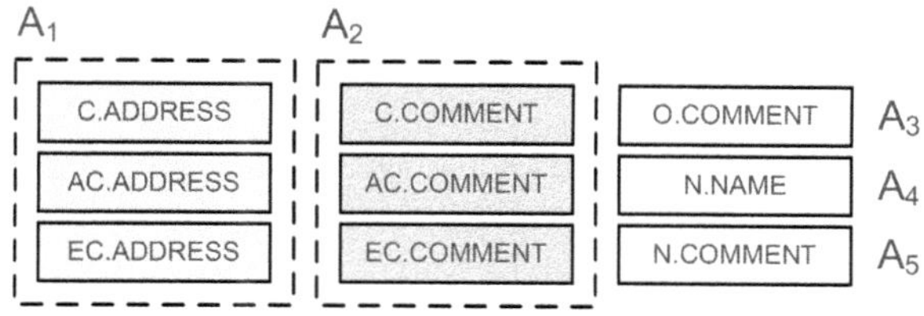

Figure 7: Attributes discovered in the attribute graph of distribution cluster $\mathbf{DC}_1$.

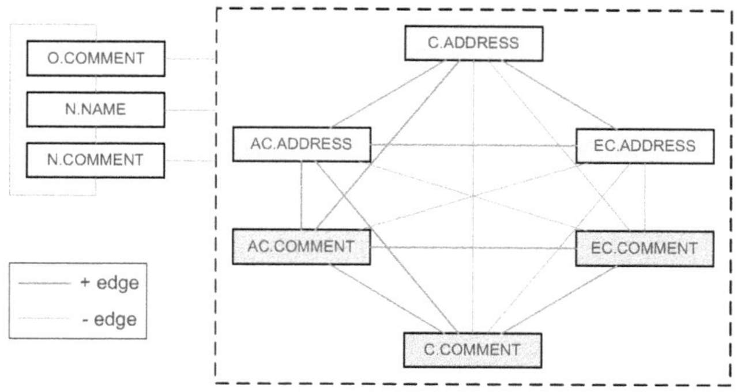

Figure 8: Another possible attribute graph of distribution cluster $\mathbf{DC}_1$.

Algorithm 3 ComputeAttributes ($\mathbf{DC}$, θ)

```
G_A = ∅, E[][] = 0, M[][] = 0
I is a hash table of lists of Intersection-EMD/column-name pairs (e, C)
for i ← 1 to |DC| do
    for j ← i + 1 to |DC| do
        e = EMD_∩(C_i, C_j)
        I[C_i].insert(e, C_j)
        I[C_j].insert(e, C_i)
    φ_{C_i} = ComputeCutoffThreshold(I[C_i], θ)
    for all C_j ∈ N_{C_i} do
        E[C_i][C_j] = 1
    G_A.AddNode(C_i)
M = E + E × E
for i ← 1 to |DC| do
    for j ← 1 to |DC| do
        if M[i][j] == 0 then
            G_A.AddNegativeEdge(C_i, C_j)
        else
            G_A.AddPositiveEdge(C_i, C_j)
Return correlation clustering of G_A
```

4. PERFORMANCE CONSIDERATIONS

Clearly, due to the difficult and subjective nature of this problem, no unsupervised solution will lead to 100% precision 100% of the time. The solution provided here can be used in conjunction with other techniques for improving quality. Notice that the two phases of our algorithm are quite similar. We create a graph based on some similarity measure and decompose the graph based on connected components or correlation clustering. The heuristic nature of the algorithm raises a number of questions about possible alternative strategies. For example, we could reverse the two steps, or use Intersection EMD instead of EMD first. We can also use correlation clustering in the first phase of the algorithm.

We use EMD first simply because it is a weaker notion of similarity than Intersection EMD. EMD acts upon all values of two columns, while Intersection EMD acts upon the common values. EMD is used to roughly decompose the instance graph into smaller problems, by separating columns that clearly belong to different attributes; strings from numerical columns and columns with significantly different ranges and distributions of values. The graph based on EMD edges alone (without any Intersection EMD edges) is sparse and easy to partition into smaller instances. Of course, we could combine both phases into one by creating a graph with EMD, Intersection EMD and witness edges, but we use a two phase approach here for efficiency. For the same reason we do not use correlation clustering in the first phase. Running correlation clustering on the distribution graph G_D can be very expensive due to the large number of nodes. On the other hand, running correlation clustering independently on the much smaller connected components is manageable.

Notice that the cost of computing EMD and Intersection EMD depends on the size of the columns involved. Clearly, for columns containing a very large number of distinct values the cost of computing all pairwise EMD and Intersection EMD values can be prohibitive.

For that reason we can approximate both measures by using a technique introduced in [17], which is based on quantiles. Essentially the technique computes a fixed number of quantiles from all columns (e.g., 256 quantiles) and then computes EMD between two columns by using the quantile histograms. In particular, given two columns C and C', $EMD(C, C')$ is computed by taking the quantile histogram of C and performing a linear scan of C' to find the number of values in C' falling into each bucket of the histogram of C (notice that we cannot compute EMD between two quantile histograms directly, since the bucket boundaries might not coincide, in which case EMD is undefined). Then $EMD(C, C')$ is approximated as the EMD between the two resulting histograms. The intuition here is that quantile summaries are a good approximation of the distribution of values in the first place, hence the EMD between two quantile summaries is a good approximation of the EMD between the actual columns. Moreover, this approach has a proven bounded error of approximation, as shown in [17].

Computing Intersection EMD entails computing the intersection between all pairs of columns, which of course is a very expensive operation, especially if no index exists on either column. In order to improve performance we build Bloom filters [4] and use the Bloom filters to compute an approximate intersection between sets. Given two columns C and C', we first perform a linear scan of column C, probe the Bloom filter of C', and if the answer is positive, use the existing quantile histograms of C and C' to (approximately) compute both $EMD(C, C \cap C')$ and $EMD(C', C \cap C')$. Optionally, we can improve the approximation of the intersection by also scanning column C' and probing the Bloom filter of C. Given that Bloom filters introduce false positives, this approach can result in cases where two columns have an empty intersection, but their approximate Intersection EMD is finite. Nevertheless, for columns of very large cardinality (especially in the absence of indexes), using Bloom filters results in significant performance improvement. One can further balance accuracy and performance, by using exact intersection computations for small columns, and Bloom filters for large columns.

As discussed above, correlation clustering is NP-Complete. Nevertheless, we solve it exactly, by running CPLEX [10] on its corresponding integer program. In our experiments, CPLEX was able to find solutions for large graph instances very fast. The largest graph instance we tried contained 170 nodes, 14365 variables, and 2.5 million constraints and took 62 seconds to complete using four Intel IA-64 1.5GHz CPUs and four threads. Alternatively, one can use polynomial time approximation algorithms [2] if faster solutions are required for larger graphs.

5. EXPERIMENTS

We conducted extensive experiments to evaluate our approach on three datasets based on the TPC-H[1] benchmark (with scale factor 1), and the IMDb[2] and DBLP[3] databases. For each dataset, we created a large set of materialized views to simulate a more complex scenario. The detailed statistics of all datasets are given in Table 1. The views are created from a selection of rows based on the values of a specific column (mostly columns that contain categorical data) and each of the views represents a semantically meaningful subset of the data in the base table. Table 2 summarizes the views generated in each dataset. The experiments were run on an Intel Core2 Duo 2.33 GHz CPU Windows XP box and CPLEX was run on a four Intel IA-64 1.5GHz CPU Linux box.

	Base tables	Views	Columns	Rows
TPC-H	8	110	785	12,680,058
IMDb	9	118	254	12,048,155
DBLP	6	66	285	8,647,713

Table 1: Datasets statistics.

We use two standard metrics, *precision* and *recall*, to measure the quality of discovered attributes. The gold standard was manually identified from a careful analysis of each dataset. Given the nature of the problem, we define precision as a measure of purity of a discovered attribute (how similar is the set of columns contained in the attribute with respect to the gold standard), and recall as a measure of completeness. Let the set of discovered attributes be $\mathbf{A} = \{A_1, A_2, \ldots, A_m\}$ and the gold standard be $\mathbf{T} = \{T_1, T_2, \ldots, T_{m'}\}$. We first define the precision and recall of a discovered attribute A_i. Each column in A_i belongs to an attribute in $\mathbf{T}$. Let A_i correspond to T_j if and only if the majority of columns in A_i also belong in T_j. Then, the precision and recall of A_i are defined as:

$$Precision(A_i) = \frac{|A_i \cap T_j|}{|A_i|}, Recall(A_i) = \frac{|A_i \cap T_j|}{|T_j|}.$$

We then define the precision and recall of the final result $\mathbf{A}$ as the average over all attributes:

$$Precision(\mathbf{A}) = \frac{\sum_{i=1}^{m} Precision(A_i)}{m},$$

$$Recall(\mathbf{A}) = \frac{\sum_{i=1}^{m} Recall(A_i)}{m}.$$

[1]http://www.tpc.org/tpch

[2]http://www.imdb.com/interfaces

[3]http://dblp.uni-trier.de/xml/

Dataset	Base Table	View No.	Selection	Description
TPC-H	CUSTOMER	1-2	ACCTBAL	Customers with positive/negative account balance.
		3-7	MKTSEGMENT	Customers in each market segment.
		8-37	NATIONKEY	Customers from each nation/region.
	NATION	38-42	REGIONKEY	Nations in each region.
	PART	43-67	BRAND	Parts of each brand.
		68-72	MFGR	Parts by each manufacture.
	SUPPLIER	73-102	NATIONKEY	Suppliers from each nation/region.
	ORDERS	103-105	ORDERSTATUS	Orders in each status.
		106-110	ORDERPRIORITY	Orders with each priority.
IMDb	MOVIE	1-28	COUNTRY	Movies released in each country.
		29-118	YEAR	Movies released in each year.
DBLP	ARTICLES	1-20	YEAR	Journal papers published in each year.
	INPROCEEDINGS	21-38	YEAR	Conference papers published in each year.
	BOOKS	39-66	YEAR	Books published in each year.

Table 2: Description of materialized views.

5.1 Distribution Similarity

As already discussed, in most cases columns that belong to the same attribute tend to have similar distributions, and columns that have different distributions more likely belong to different attributes. First, we run experiments to verify this intuition. For each dataset, we examine the EMD values between all pairs of columns in the same attribute, based on the gold standard, and plot the distribution histograms (for efficiency we approximate all EMD computations using quantile histograms). Figure 9 shows the results for TPC-H and DBLP. For TPC-H 87.3% EMD values between columns of the same attribute are smaller than 0.05. For DBLP 62.5% are below 0.05 and only 2.8% are above 0.2. This verifies our intuition that EMD is a robust measure for phase one of the algorithm.

Notice that a few pairs of columns in TPC-H have very large EMD. This is caused by the four attributes shown in Table 3. View1 and View2 select customers with positive and negative balance (see Table 2), which results in a horizontal partition of the base table and very different distributions in each partition. The same happens for attributes phone number and order date. Since View8-37 and View73-102 select customers and suppliers from a particular nation/region, the phone numbers in each view start with the same prefixes. View103-105 are the orders in each particular status and order status is correlated to the date when the order is placed. Distribution similarity fails to discover the associations between columns if such correlations exist, and this is a limitation of our approach. However, we can see here that distribution similarity between columns of the same attribute holds for the large majority of columns. After removing the horizontal partitions mentioned above from TPC-H (65 columns in total), the EMD values between all pairs of columns within the same attribute are below 0.2 and for up to 99.5% of the pairs, EMD is below 0.05.

Attribute	Columns
Customer account balance	ACCTBAL in CUSTOMER and View1-2
Customer phone number	PHONE in CUSTOMER and View8-37
Supplier phone number	PHONE in SUPPLIER and View73-102
Order date	DATE in ORDERS and View103-105

Table 3: Attributes that contain horizontally partitioned columns in TPC-H.

To illustrate the point that columns of the same attribute do not necessarily have too many values in common, in Figure 10 we plot a histogram of the pairwise Jaccard similarity of columns within the same attribute, based on the golden standard. Recall that a high

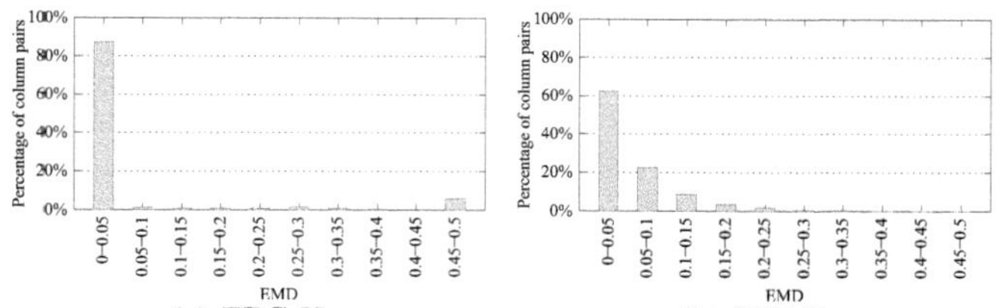

(a) TPC-H (b) DBLP

Figure 9: Distribution histograms of EMD values between all pairs of columns in the same attribute for TPC-H and DBLP.

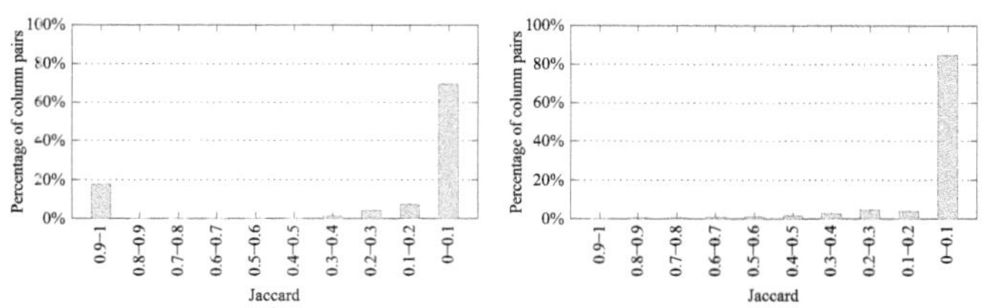

(a) TPC-H (b) DBLP

Figure 10: Distribution histograms of Jaccard values between all pairs of columns in the same attribute for TPC-H and DBLP.

Jaccard value implies a large number of common values and vice versa. We observe that for TPC-H 70% of column pairs have Jaccard similarity smaller than 0.1, and only 19% have Jaccard above 0.9. The results for DBLP are even more striking, with more than 80% of column pairs having Jaccard similarity smaller than 0.1. It is thus clear that Jaccard similarity is a poor measure for clustering columns into attributes. In particular, a naive approach for discovering attributes would be to create a column similarity graph with edges weighted according to pairwise Jaccard similarity, then remove edges with Jaccard similarity smaller than some threshold, and finally compute the connected components. Figure 10 clearly shows that dropping edges with reasonably small Jaccard similarity would result in a very sparse graph, separating columns into atomic attributes. On the other hand, retaining all edges would tend to separate columns into two attributes, one for numerical attributes and one for strings.

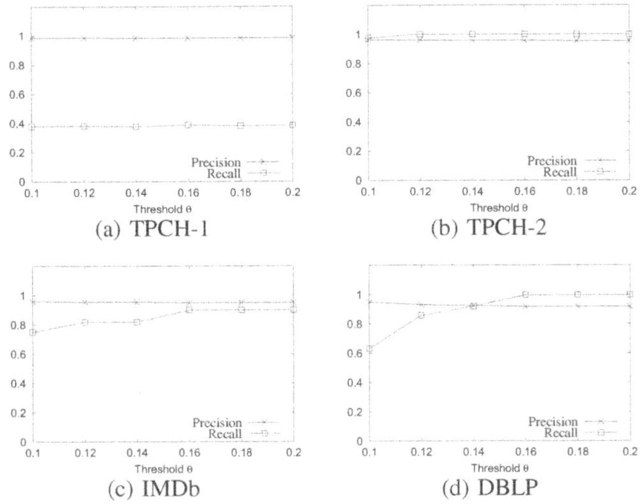

(a) TPCH-1 (b) TPCH-2 (c) IMDb (d) DBLP

Figure 11: Accuracy results on TPC-H, IMDb and DBLP for varying thresholds θ.

5.2 Attribute Discovery

Here we measure the accuracy of our technique for discovering attributes. We use a single global threshold θ for computing the distribution clusters in Phase one as well as building the attribute graph in Phase two. Furthermore, we use Bloom filter for all columns, across the board, to approximate Intersection EMD. In the experiments, we vary θ from 0.1 to 0.2. Table 4 shows the accuracy results for all datasets. For TPC-H, we report two sets of results. TPCH-1 refers to the results with respect to the original dataset. TPCH-2 refers to the results with respect to a reduced dataset, obtained by removing the horizontally partitioned columns. For readability, we also plot the precision and recall in Figure 11. We can see that for large ranges of thresholds θ (0.16-0.2) we achieve high precision and recall for all datasets, which makes our approach easy to use in practice.

Threshold θ		0.1	0.12	0.14	0.16	0.18	0.2
TPCH-1	m'	46					
	m	108	107	106	103	102	101
	P	0.986	0.985	0.984	0.984	0.983	0.983
	R	0.379	0.383	0.377	0.388	0.382	0.385
TPCH-2	m'	45					
	m	41	40	39	39	38	38
	P	0.962	0.961	0.957	0.957	0.953	0.953
	R	0.976	1	1	1	0.999	0.998
IMDb	m'	10					
	m	12	11	11	10	10	10
	P	0.958	0.955	0.955	0.95	0.95	0.95
	R	0.75	0.818	0.818	0.9	0.9	0.9
DBLP	m'	14					
	m	19	14	13	12	12	12
	P	0.949	0.93	0.924	0.918	0.918	0.918
	R	0.632	0.857	0.92	0.997	0.997	0.997

Table 4: Accuracy results on TPC-H, IMDb and DBLP for different thresholds θ; m' true number of attributes; m attributes in our solution; P is precision; R is recall.

For the TPC-H dataset, as already explained, 65 columns (belonging to only 4 attributes out of 45) are from horizontal partitions of the base tables due to indirect correlations between columns. Here, distribution similarity fails to cluster such columns together, more precisely each view becomes its own cluster, resulting in more than 100 attributes overall. However, as shown in TPCH-2, by drilling down we can see that our approach achieves high precision and recall for discovering attributes in the remaining set of columns. It should be noted here that columns that form unit clusters can be singled out and treated separately during post-processing. For future work, we are investigating whether it is possible to identify if unit clusters belonging to horizontally partitioned columns can be concatenated as a subsequent step.

Our approach discovers fewer attributes than the gold standard. Table 5 shows the attributes that cause the errors for $\theta = 0.12$. As shown, nine distinct attributes are clustered into four attributes by our algorithm (one attribute per row), and that accounts for the five missing attributes. Here, 9997 out of 10000 values in SUPPLIER.ADDRESS are identical to the values in CUSTOMER.ADDRESS (due to the way addresses are generated in TPC-H), making these two columns indistinguishable; DISCOUNT contains all values in TAX; the same is true for SUPPKEY and AVAILQTY; 12.8% of values in SUPPLIER.ACCTBAL appear in CUSTOMER.ACCTBAL. Finally, LINEITEM.COMMENT has no intersection with ADDRESS, but the false clustering here occurs due to false positives produced by the Bloom filter in phase two.

Correlation clustering proves to be a robust way of separating attributes in the attribute graph. Figure 12 shows an attribute subgraph of TPC-H, for varying θ from 0.14 to 0.2 (negative edges are removed for readability). For $\theta = 0.14$, the four clusters are totally disconnected (there are no positive edges between different attributes). Correlation clustering (or even connected components) in this case would separate the graph into four attributes. Our method is able to separate CUSTOMER.COMMENT views from PART.COMMENT views, while, for example, the method of comparing column names will fail in this case. On the other hand, CUSTOMER.ADDRESS and SUPPLIER.ADDRESS are clustered together, but this is clearly because 9997 out of 10000 addresses are the same. As θ increases, the number of positive edges across attributes increases as well. This is evident in Figure 12(d). However, after running correlation clustering we are still able to separate the graph into four attributes once again, with very few errors. For $\theta = 0.16$, the result is exactly the same as for $\theta = 0.14$. For $\theta = 0.18$, correlation clustering will place one view of PART.NAME in the attribute of CUSTOMER.COMMENT. For $\theta = 0.2$, one view of PART.COMMENT will be placed in the attribute for ADDRESS.

For IMDb we achieve 0.95 precision and 0.9 recall for θ ranging from 0.16 to 0.2. In our result, ACTOR.NAME and DIRECTOR.NAME are clustered together due to very large overlap of values. Since most directors are also actors, in this case choosing whether directors and actors should be treated differently depends on application context. In this case of course, a simple solution based on column names can provide an answer. Another problem is column MEXICO.MOVIENAME which is not included in the movie names attribute. Some simple data analysis here shows that 14.0% of movie names in MEXICO.MOVIENAME start with *la/las/los* and 11.5% names start with *el*, making the distribution of this column significantly different from movie names in other views. Decreasing θ to 0.14 and 0.12 results in splitting SPAIN.MOVIENAME out as well, for the same reason. When using threshold $\theta = 0.1$, HONGKONG.MOVIENAME and TAIWAN.MOVIENAME are also separated. This is not surprising, since both mainly contain names in Chinese and have small overlap with the movie names in other views.

Finally, for the DBLP dataset we also achieve precision above 0.9 and recall above 0.997, for θ ranging from 0.16 to 0.2. The errors occur in four attributes. Here, AUTHOR.NAME and EDITOR.NAME are clustered together given that 596 out of 621 editors

1	DISCOUNT	TAX	
2	SUPPKEY	AVAILQTY	
3	CUSTOMER.ACCTBAL	SUPPLIER.ACCTBAL	
4	CUSTOMER.ADDRESS	SUPPLIER.ADDRESS	LINEITEM.COMMENT

Table 5: Attributes that are incorrectly clustered together in TPC-H for $\theta = 0.12$.

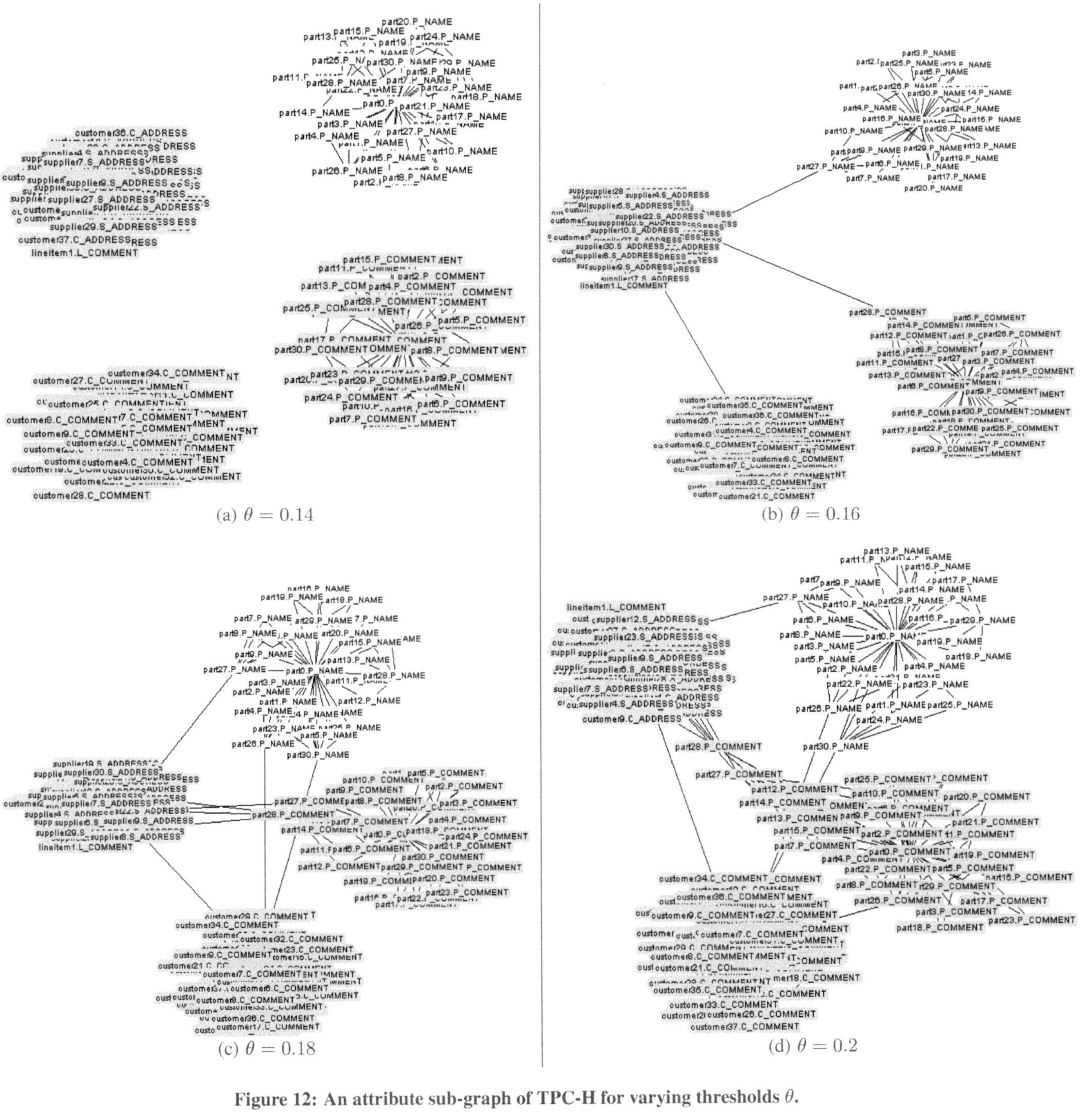

(a) $\theta = 0.14$

(b) $\theta = 0.16$

(c) $\theta = 0.18$

(d) $\theta = 0.2$

Figure 12: An attribute sub-graph of TPC-H for varying thresholds θ.

appear in the AUTHOR table as well. The same is true for ARTICLES.TITLE and INPROCEEDINGS.TITLE, since it seems that the majority of papers submitted to journal publications have the exact same title as the conference versions of the papers.

Overall, clearly it is in some cases difficult even for humans to decide what constitutes an attribute, without additional application dependent context. Our technique is able to separate major attributes very well, and make only minor mistakes that can either be corrected by supervision and simple statistical analysis, or by using orthogonal approaches (e.g., column name matching, if meaningful schema information exists).

6. RELATED WORK

The work of Zhang et al. [17] was the main impetus behind our approach, since they introduced the usage of EMD for correlating columns based on the distribution of their values. Zhang et al. introduced the quantile approximation of EMD that we also use here and laid the foundation of using EMD to express primary/foreign key relationships that are one of our main relationship types. Nevertheless, here we extend this work by building distribution and attribute graphs based on EMD and Intersection EMD, which is a novel statistical measure of the relationship between two columns.

In the context of relational databases there has been little work that concentrates on classifying columns into attributes. The only previous work that we are aware of is by Ahmadi et al. [1], that utilizes q-gram based signatures to capture column type information based on formatting characteristics of data values (for example the presence of '@' in email addresses). The technique builds signatures based on the most popular q-grams within each column and clusters columns according to basic data types, like email addresses, telephone numbers, etc. In that respect, the goal of this work is orthogonal to ours: It tries to categorize columns into generic data types. Our work takes into account the distribution of values, the distribution with respect to common values, and indirect associations through witnesses, as opposed to only using the distribution of q-grams.

Related work from the field of schema matching has concentrated on three major themes. The first is semantic schema matching that uses information provided only by the schema and not from particular data instances. The second is syntactic schema matching that uses the actual data instances. The third uses external information, like thesauri, standard schemas, and past mappings. Most solutions use hybrid approaches that cover all three themes. Our work falls purely under the second category. Existing data driven approaches have not used any distributional information to discover relationships between columns, apart from simple statistics. Current approaches use string-based comparisons (prefix/suffix tests, edit distance, etc.), value ranges, min/max similarity, and mutual information based on q-gram distributions [11, 7, 8, 12, 13]. Rahm and Bernstein [15] conducted a survey on schema matching techniques.

Previous work tangentially related to discovering attributes is that on discovering columns that contain similar values. A number of statistical summaries have been developed for that purpose, including min-hash signatures [5], and locality sensitive hashing [9]. These techniques cannot be used for discovering attributes, since they only capture intersection relationships between columns and no distributional information.

7. CONCLUSION

We argued that discovering attributes in relational databases is an important step in better understanding and working with the data. Toward this goal, we proposed an efficient solution, based on statistical measures between pairs of columns, to identify such attributes given a database instance. Our solution was able to correctly identify attributes in real and synthetic databases with very high accuracy. In the future, we plan to investigate whether the techniques proposed here can be extended to discover multi-column attributes (for example when customer names are expressed as separate first/last name columns) and also explore whether information theoretic techniques can be used to solve the problem of horizontally partitioned attributes (like telephone numbers based on locations).

8. ACKNOWLEDGEMENT

The work of Meihui Zhang and Beng Chin Ooi were in part supported by Singapore MDA grant R-252-000-376-279.

9. REFERENCES

[1] B. Ahmadi, M. Hadjieleftheriou, T. Seidl, D. Srivastava, and S. Venkatasubramanian. Type-based categorization of relational attributes. In *EDBT*, pages 84–95, 2009.

[2] N. Ailon, M. Charikar, and A. Newman. Aggregating inconsistent information: Ranking and clustering. *Journal of the ACM*, 55(5), 2008.

[3] N. Bansal, A. Blum, and S. Chawla. Correlation clustering. *Machine Learning*, 56:89–113, June 2004.

[4] B. H. Bloom. Space/time trade-offs in hash coding with allowable errors. *CACM*, 13(7):422–426, 1970.

[5] A. Z. Broder, M. Charikar, A. M. Frieze, and M. Mitzenmacher. Min-wise independent permutations. *Journal of Computer and System Sciences*, 60(3):630–659, 2000.

[6] S. Chaudhuri, V. Ganti, and R. Kaushik. A primitive operator for similarity joins in data cleaning. In *ICDE*, page 5, 2006.

[7] R. Dhamankar, Y. Lee, A. Doan, A. Y. Halevy, and P. Domingos. iMAP: Discovering complex mappings between database schemas. In *SIGMOD*, pages 383–394, 2004.

[8] H. H. Do and E. Rahm. COMA - a system for flexible combination of schema matching approaches. In *VLDB*, pages 610–621, 2002.

[9] A. Gionis, P. Indyk, and R. Motwani. Similarity search in high dimensions via hashing. In *VLDB*, pages 518–529, 1999.

[10] IBM. CPLEX optimizer. http://www.ibm.com/software/integration/optimization/cplex-optimizer.

[11] J. Kang and J. F. Naughton. On schema matching with opaque column names and data values. In *SIGMOD*, pages 205–216, 2003.

[12] J. Madhavan, P. A. Bernstein, and E. Rahm. Generic schema matching with cupid. In *VLDB*, pages 49–58, 2001.

[13] S. Melnik, E. Rahm, and P. A. Bernstein. Rondo: A programming platform for generic model management. In *SIGMOD*, pages 193–204, 2003.

[14] T. Milo and S. Zohar. Using schema matching to simplify heterogeneous data translation. In *VLDB*, pages 122–133, 1998.

[15] E. Rahm and P. A. Bernstein. A survey of approaches to automatic schema matching. *The VLDB Journal*, 10(4):334–350, 2001.

[16] T. P. P. C. (TPC). TPC benchmarks. http://www.tpc.org/.

[17] M. Zhang, M. Hadjieleftheriou, B. C. Ooi, C. M. Procopiuc, and D. Srivastava. On multi-column foreign key discovery. *PVLDB*, 3(1):805–814, 2010.

Leveraging Query Logs for Schema Mapping Generation in U-MAP*

Hazem Elmeleegy
AT&T Labs - Research
hazem@research.att.com

Ahmed Elmagarmid
Qatar Computing Research Institute
Qatar Foundation
aelmagarmid@qf.org.qa

Jaewoo Lee
Purdue University
lee748@cs.purdue.edu

ABSTRACT

In this paper, we introduce U-MAP, a new system for schema mapping generation. U-MAP builds upon and extends existing schema mapping techniques. However, it mitigates some key problems in this area, which have not been previously addressed. The key tenet of U-MAP is to exploit the *usage* information extracted from the *query logs* associated with the schemas being mapped. We describe our experience in applying our proposed system to realistic datasets from the retail and life sciences domains. Our results demonstrate the effectiveness and efficiency of U-MAP compared to traditional approaches.

Categories and Subject Descriptors

H.2.5 [**Database Management**]: Heterogeneous Databases

General Terms

Algorithms, Design

Keywords

schema mapping, query logs, usage, data exchange, data integration

1. INTRODUCTION

One of the most common data management tasks is the transformation of data residing in one data source according to a given schema into the schema of another source. The problem of automatically discovering the necessary transformation rules to carry out this task is known as *schema mapping*, and the discovered rules are usually referred to as *mappings*.

There are multiple scenarios in which schema mapping is necessary. The first scenario is *data exchange* (e.g., [23]), where the data needs to be physically moved from one source to another, perhaps for data migration purposes. The second scenario is *data integration* (e.g., [29]) where it is required to answer queries expressed based on some mediated schema, while the result is obtained from some underlying sources, usually with different schemas. The query result, in this case, needs to be transformed to conform to the mediated schema before returning it to the user. Other application scenarios include schema evolution (e.g., [30]), peer data management systems (e.g., [15]), and model management [5].

It is evident, however, that the quality, and hence usefulness, of the transformed data hinges on the quality of the mappings used for the transformation. Therefore, it is crucial for the mapping generation process to be as accurate as possible, especially that any following data cleaning operations are generally quite expensive.

To this end, several systems (e.g., [3, 7, 11, 16, 22]) have been proposed in the literature for the generation of schema mappings. Over the last decade, these research efforts, and in particular the Clio project [11], played a great role in making the schema mapping field reach higher levels of maturity. Nevertheless, there are still several issues with the existing schema mapping tools, as their generated mappings do not take into consideration specific cases, which are very common in real-world schemas.

These issues include: (1) the unawareness of those tables representing special case entities, which have an *IS-A* relationship with higher-level entity types; (2) the inability to generate meaningful mappings, which involve joining tables with certain *many-to-many* relationships; and (3) the inability to resolve attribute correspondence conflicts which can arise during mapping generation. All of these issues will be explained in detail later in the paper.

The semantic approach for schema mapping [3] attempts to address some of these issues. However, it is only applicable when the schemas' *conceptual models* are available – a hard requirement to satisfy in many real-world scenarios. Moreover, we will also show that even when the conceptual models are available, there are many common cases, in which the method proposed in [3] will not be able to accurately generate the desired mappings.

In this paper, we introduce the U-MAP system, which mitigates the above problems by leveraging the *usage* information available in the query logs of the data sources being mapped. We show that this new resource, while not exploited before in the context of schema mapping, can be very valuable in generating significantly higher quality mappings. We summarize our contributions as follows.

- We describe a new mechanism for handling tables having *IS-A relationships*. The mechanism takes into account how to detect those tables, how to learn from the query log whether they are overlapping or not, and finally how to *merge* them appropriately in the generated mappings.
- We describe a new version of the chase algorithm [17] (commonly used for mapping generation). The new version, called the *aggressive chase*, enables the generation of mappings spanning all types of *many-to-many relationships*, as long as such mappings are deemed "semantically meaningful" based on the analysis of the query log.
- We describe a novel *conflict resolution* technique, which identifies the most likely mapping to resolve the attribute correspondence conflicts across the *logical relations* of the two schemas. At the core of this technique are two new methods: one for *context-based matching* of attributes between logical relations and queries from the log; and another for *context-based grouping* of attributes to limit the search space of possible mappings.
- We describe an experimental study on a working prototype for U-MAP using databases from the retail and life sciences domains. Our results demonstrate the effectiveness of U-MAP in dealing with the issues we raise in this paper as opposed to previous approaches.

The rest of the paper is organized as follows. Section 2 presents our running example and also some necessary background on the schema

*This research was supported by QCRI and by NSF-IIS 0916614. The work was mostly done while the first author was at Purdue University.

mapping problem and the existing solutions for it. Section 3 illustrates some key outstanding issues with those existing solutions. The U-MAP approach is explained in detail in Section 4. Our experimental evaluation is given in Section 5. Section 6 describes the related work, and Section 7 finally concludes the paper.

2. RUNNING EXAMPLE AND BACKGROUND

2.1 Running Example

In this subsection, we describe our running example, which we will be referring to throughout the paper. The example shown in Figure 1 is from the retail domain. In particular, it represents the schemas of two bookstores. Each schema covers information on customers, books, authors, and orders – but using two different schema structures. Although not shown in the figure, it is assumed that attribute correspondences are also given. They could have either been generated manually or using an automatic schema matching tool (e.g., [24]). Any two attributes with the same name in both schemas correspond to each other (e.g., X_Customer.c_uname and Y_Customer.c_uname). There are also correspondences between pairs of attributes on both sides which do not have the exact same name (e.g., X_Distributor.d_uname and Y_Customer.c_uname). Finally, only non-key attributes are included in correspondences (e.g., there is no correspondence for c_id).

2.2 The Schema Mapping Problem

Consider the situation where we have two database systems, each with its own schema. It is required to develop declarative rules that specify how data records can be transformed from one schema (the source) to another (the target). The generated rules are generally called *schema mappings*.

We consider the most common formalism for schema mappings, which is *source-to-target tuple-generating dependencies*, or simply *s-t tgds*. Each mapping specifies how one or more records (with each record coming from a different table) from the source schema should be used to generate one or more records in the target schema. The mapping should clearly indicate how the multiple records (if more than one) at each schema are related (i.e., their join predicates), and additionally how the data values should be copied from the source attributes to the target attributes.

We use a "query-like" representation for the mappings, which will be illustrated in the following example.

Example 1: In our bookstores example, the following mapping specifies how a book record along with its corresponding author record in the X-Schema are transformed into three records in the Y-Schema, particularly, in the Y_Book, Y_Book_Author, and Y_Author tables.

m_1
```
for a in X_Author, b in X_Book
where (a.a_id = b.b_a_id)
⇒ exists a' in Y_Author, b' in Y_Book, ba' in Y_Book_Author
where (a'.a_id = ba'.ba_a_id ∧ b'.b_id = ba'.ba_b_id)
with (a'.a_fname = a.a_fname ∧ a'.a_lname = a.a_lname
∧ b'.b_title = b.b_title ∧ b'.b_pub_date = b.b_pub_date)
```

The for clause specifies the tables from which the source records are collected. The following where clause specifies the predicates for joining these records. Moreover, the exists clause indicates the tables of the generated records in the target schema. Similar to the first where clause, the second where clause also provides the join predicates for the target records. However, in addition, it also shows how the target attributes are populated using the values of the source attributes, as shown in the last two lines of m_1. □

More formally, the schema mapping problem can be defined by the tuple $(S, T, \Sigma_S, \Sigma_T, V, \Sigma_{ST})$, where S, T, Σ_S, Σ_T, and V are inputs, while Σ_{ST} is the desired output. S and T are the source and target schemas respectively. Σ_S and Σ_T are the constraints (typically referential integrity constraints) defined on each of S and T respectively. V is the set of attribute correspondences between S and T, which can be either automatically computed in a preceding schema matching step, or directly provided by the user. Σ_{ST} is the set of s-t tgds representing the desired schema mappings.

2.3 Existing Solutions

The commonly used approach for schema mapping is the one adopted in the Clio system [11], which is based on analyzing the referential integrity constraints in the source and target schemas. We will refer to this approach as the *RIC-based approach*. A more recent approach relies on using additional semantic information about both schemas, which can be found in their associated conceptual models (e.g., ER diagrams, UML). This approach will be referred to as the *semantic approach*. In what follows, we overview the two approaches (with a little more emphasis on the RIC-based approach since our proposed techniques will be building on it).

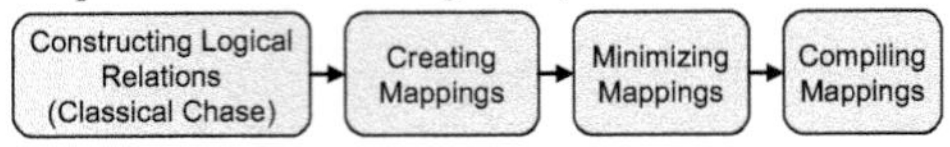

Figure 2: The RIC-based schema mapping process.

2.3.1 RIC-Based Approach

This approach proceeds in four main steps as shown in Figure 2.

Step 1 (Constructing Logical Relations): At first, we construct what is referred to as the *logical relations*, separately for each schema. A logical relation is meant to group together all the *related* concepts (or attributes) in a schema, even if these concepts do not reside in the same table in the schema. In other words, a logical relation can be the result of joining multiple tables together.

Since there is typically a large number of possible joins to be done in a schema, where most of them is not semantically meaningful, the goal in this step is to limit the generation of logical relations to the meaningful ones only. For this purpose, the RIC-based technique "expands" each table, A, in the schema into its corresponding logical relation by joining A with all the tables it references to get some intermediate logical relation. Then, the just-generated intermediate logical relation is, in turn, joined with all the tables it references, and so on. The final logical relation corresponding to A is the one which does not contain any more foreign keys.

The process we just described is essentially applying the chase algorithm [17] on each table, where the set of constraints applied during the chase are the referential integrity constraints in each of the schemas (i.e., Σ_S and Σ_T for S and T respectively).

Step 2 (Creating Mappings): Once the logical relations are identified for both schemas, the second step is to find all the pairs of logical relations (one from each schema), which cover one or more attribute correspondences from V. Each such pair will constitute a mapping.

Example 2: Considering the mapping m_1 from Example 1, we find that it *maps* a logical relation from S, specified in the for and first where clauses, to a logical relation from T, specified in the exists and second where clauses. The attribute correspondences between the two logical relations are specified in the with clause, in order to show how values should be copied from the source attributes to the target attributes. □

When a target attribute does not have a corresponding source attribute, we cannot simply have it populated by nulls, because it may be a required attribute, where nulls are not allowed. Moreover, it may not have a default value, which makes it necessary to synthesize new values for its population. These synthetic values, usually referred to as *labeled nulls*, are generated using *Skolem functions*.

Skolem functions ensure that their outputs are different whenever their inputs are different. One of their essential uses is to maintain the referential integrity in the target database. So for example a book record in T will only be linked to the record of its own author, and not any other author records. In this case, the Skolem functions used to generate the book id and author id in the Y_Book and Y_Author records, respectively, should be identical to the ones used to generate the foreign keys in the corresponding Y_Book_Author record.

Step 3 (Minimizing Mappings): The third step is an optimization step, which has been introduced in [13]. In this step, the set of generated mappings can be *minimized* by discarding all the mappings *subsumed* or *implied* by other mappings. The criteria for when a mapping is considered to subsume or imply another mapping are given in [13].

Step 4 (Compiling Mappings): The final step is to compile the minimal set of mappings into an executable script, e.g. SQL queries.

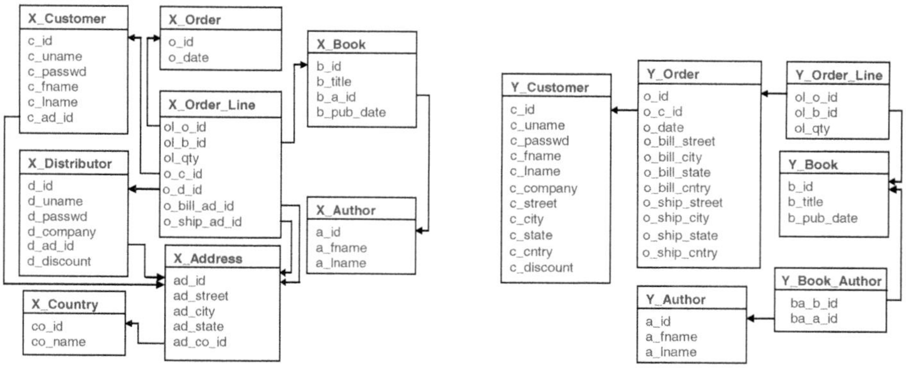

(a) X-Schema (b) Y-Schema

Figure 1: Schemas of two bookstores.

Running this script should actually move the data from the source to the target while making the necessary transformations, which would still respect the constraints of both the source and the target.

2.3.2 Semantic Approach

The semantic approach for schema mapping [3] does not only rely on the source and target schemas, as is the case with the typical RIC-based approach. Instead, it takes the *conceptual models* for both the source and the target into account as well. Examples for information that can be found in conceptual models, but not in schemas, include the *cardinalities* of the relationships between entities, and also special types of relationships like the *IS-A* relationship.

In many cases, this additional information helps in distinguishing the more meaningful mappings from the less meaningful ones. If only the RIC-based approach is used, then such mappings will all seem to be equally meaningful to the mapping tool. The details of how the semantic approach exploits this information can be found in [3].

3. ISSUES WITH EXISTING SOLUTIONS

In this section, we describe in more detail the issues involved when relying on the RIC-based approach. At the same time, we point out the situations in which the semantic approach can address some of these issues, and those situations in which some issues remain unresolved. Most clearly, the semantic approach will not be helpful whenever the conceptual models are missing, which needless to say, is a common scenario in the real world. We now explain each of such issues.

3.1 Unawareness of IS-A Relationships

In many schemas, multiple tables can represent different specializations of a higher-level abstract concept or *superclass* (e.g., *student* and *instructor* tables would both store information about *persons*). In other words, they have an *IS-A* relationship with the superclass (which may not itself have have a separate table in the schema). Such tables will thereby have common attributes pertaining to their superclass, in addition to other attributes specific to each of them.

A key question is whether these tables are disjoint or not. In other words, can the same real-world entity have a record in each of these tables? The answer to this question determines how the tables should be correctly *merged*. Merging the tables will be needed if they are to be mapped from the source schema to a single table in the target schema. If they are disjoint, then the merger can be achieved using a simple union. Otherwise, they will need to be *outer-joined* to guarantee that no data duplication occurs in the target database. This can be illustrated by the following example.

Example 3: In our bookstore example, the tables X_Customer and X_Distributor can both be thought of as having an IS-A relationship with some abstract concept, *Buyer*. Hence, if we blindly apply the RIC-based method, we will generate the two mappings m_2 and m_3 given below.

m_2 for c in X_Customer, ad in X_Address, co in X_Country
where (c.c_ad_id = ad.ad_id ∧ ad.ad_co_id = co.co_id)
⇒ exists c' in Y_Customer
with (c'.c_uname = c.c_uname ∧ c'.c_passwd = c.c_passwd
∧ c'.c_fname = c.c_fname ∧ c'.c_lname = c.c_lname
∧ c'.c_street = ad.ad_street ∧ c'.c_city = ad.ad_city
∧ c'.c_state = ad.ad_state ∧ c'.c_cntry = co.co_name)

m_3 for d in X_Distributor, ad in X_Address, co in X_Country
where (d.d_ad_id = ad.ad_id ∧ ad.ad_co_id = co.co_id)
⇒ exists c' in Y_Customer
with (c'.c_uname = d.d_uname ∧ c'.c_passwd = d.d_passwd
∧ c'.c_company = d.d_company
∧ c'.c_street = ad.ad_street ∧ c'.c_city = ad.ad_city
∧ c'.c_state = ad.ad_state ∧ c'.c_cntry = co.co_name)

These two mappings separately map the records of each of X_Customer and X_Distributor in the X-Schema to the Y_Customer table in the Y-Schema. However, we may be able to determine that X_Customer and X_Distributor are overlapping; i.e., some distributors also have records in X_Customer (perhaps to maintain the contact person information for the distributor). In this case, the best mapping to populate Y_Customer should look as follows.

m_4 for (c in X_Customer outerjoin d in X_Distributor),
ad in X_Address, co in X_Country
where (ad.ad_id = ifnull(c.c_ad_id,d.d_ad_id)
∧ ad.ad_co_id = co.co_id)
⇒ exists c' in Y_Customer
with (c'.c_uname = ifnull(c.c_uname,d.d_uname)
∧ c'.c_passwd = ifnull(c.c_passwd,d.d_passwd)
∧ c'.c_fname = c.c_fname ∧ c'.c_lname = c.c_lname
∧ c'.c_company = d.d_company
∧ c'.c_street = ad.ad_street ∧ c'.c_city = ad.ad_city
∧ c'.c_state = ad.ad_state ∧ c'.c_cntry = co.co_name)

Note that the mapping m_4 first computes the *outer join* of X_Customer and X_Distributor to ensure that records belonging to the same real world entity from both tables are merged first. (The ifnull function is used to merge common attributes in X_Customer and X_Distributor into a single attribute in Y_Customer. It returns the first parameter, or the second in case the first was null.) Then, the records of the resulting outer join are used to populate the Y_Customer table. This approach guarantees that a given real world entity (e.g., a distributor) will only have one record in Y_Customer. If X_Customer and X_Distributor were disjoint, then just using m_2 and m_3 would be sufficient to populate Y_Customer with the union of the two source tables, and hence no special treatment is needed in this case. □

Of course, beyond our running example, many other examples exist in the real world for tables with overlapping sets of entities. Consider for instance singers and actors, graduate students and instructors, mobile phones and digital cameras – to name just a few.

Using the semantic approach to detect IS-A relationships, as well as the disjointness of the involved tables, can only be possible if the conceptual model for each schema is available and if the disjointness constraints are specified in them. Unfortunately, the RIC-based approach, which is more commonly used does not recognize IS-A relationships or disjointness constraints.

It is worth mentioning that a newly introduced technique [18] can handle a special case of this problem. In particular, [18] presents a post-processing mapping re-writing algorithm, which focuses on maintaining the key constraints (equality generating dependencies, or egds) on the target. This technique works well when the key attributes in the source tables (with an IS-A relationship) are mapped to the key attribute in the target table. The re-written mappings will ensure that records for the same entity in the source tables will be not be mapped to different records in the target table, since they all have the same key in the source, and that key will be mapped to the target as well.

However, it is quite common that keys are just serial numbers and are not included in the correspondences because they do not have any semantic meaning (as in Example 3). Instead, new keys are generated at the target for each newly inserted record. In this scenario, the technique in [18] cannot prevent duplicate records in the target because even if they refer to the same real-world entity, each will be assigned a separate key, and hence no key constraint violations will occur.

3.2 Incomplete Coverage of Logical Relations

As we explained in Section 2.3.1, the RIC-based approach relies on the chase algorithm to generate the logical relations. This algorithm chases foreign keys in the forward direction only; i.e., it follows the edges in the schema going from the foreign key in one table to the primary key in the other table, but it never chases them in the opposite direction. The joins resulting from this chase will always be *lossless*; i.e., at least one of the relations participating in the join can be reconstructed just by applying projection on the join result. The fact that the generated logical relation is a result of a lossless join guarantees that all the records in that relation are semantically meaningful.

In contrast, if the join involved edges going in opposite directions, then the join will be considered a *lossy join*; i.e., it is not guaranteed that any of the participating relations can be reconstructed just by applying projection on the join result. In this case, some of the records in the output relation may not even be meaningful. Moreover, the number of possible lossy joins in a schema can be overwhelming. For these reasons, the RIC-based approach does not consider lossy joins when generating the logical relations.

However, we argue that some lossy joins may in fact be meaningful, and hence it is essential to include them in the finally generated mappings.

The following two examples will illustrate the concepts of lossy and lossless joins, as well as when they result in meaningful records and when they do not.

Example 4: Consider the case when the RIC-based technique generates the target logical relation starting from the Y_Order_Line table. It will chase the foreign keys referencing the Y_Book and Y_Order tables, and then it will chase the foreign key in Y_Order, which references Y_Customer. At this point, no more foreign keys will be left to chase, and the algorithm stops.

Note that this chase does not relate the order line information to the book's author information, although it is quite logical to have them related. The reason is that in the Y-Schema, Y_Book and Y_Author have a many-to-many relationship. Thus, each book is not directly referencing its author(s), but rather they are connected through an intermediate table which references both of them. Since the chase algorithm only goes in one direction, it stops at the Y_Book table.

Ideally, we would like the mapping responsible for populating the Y_Order_Line table to connect each order line record with its corresponding author record as shown in the mapping m_5 below. However, the RIC-based approach will never generate m_5.

```
m5   for ol in X_Order_Line, b in X_Book, a in X_Author, ···
     where (ol.ol_b_id = b.b_id ∧ b.b_a_id = a.a_id ∧ ··· )
     ⇒ exists ol' in Y_Order_Line, b' in Y_Book,
     ba' in Y_Book_Author, a' in Y_Author, ···
     where (ol'.ol_b_id = b'.b_id ∧ b'.b_id = ba'.ba_b_id
     ∧ a'.a_id = ba'.ba_a_id ∧ ··· )
     with (a'.a_fname = a.a_fname ∧ a'.a_lname = a.a_lname
     ∧ b'.b_title = b.b_title ∧ b'.b_pub_date = b.b_pub_date
     ∧ ol'.ol_qty = ol.ol_qty ∧ ··· ) □
```

To make our point even clearer regarding the need for considering lossy joins in certain situations, we present the following example.

Example 5: Consider that we have a third schema, Z-Schema, containing a single table called Z_Reader_Author, which tracks the readers for each author. Hence, Z-Schema will simply look as follows.

Z_Reader_Author(r_fname, r_lname, a_fname, a_lname)

When we generate mappings from the Y-Schema (source) to the Z-Schema (target), there must be a logical relation in the Y-Schema which connects the authors to the customers through the book orders made by the customers. As explained in Example 3, the RIC-based approach will not generate this logical relation. Instead, it will populate the target table using the two logical relations for X_Customer and X_Author. In other words, some records will contain the customer (reader) names only and others will contain the author names only, with no linkage between them – which defeats the whole purpose of building the target table. □

We will now show a scenario where chasing foreign keys in opposite directions can indeed result in semantically meaningless logical relations, and hence the need for a mechanism to distinguish between the situations in which lossy joins should be considered and those in which they should not.

Example 6: In the X-Schema, consider that the table X_Author has an extra attribute a_nationality, which references X_Country. Clearly, there is no meaning in creating a logical relation connecting authors to customers through the X_Country table just because a customer resides in the same country where an author is a citizen(!). □

It is worth noting that the semantic approach attempts to identify some of the situations where a lossy join is meaningful by considering the cardinality constraints for the relationships between entities, as indicated in the conceptual model. If for example two entities in the source have a many-to-many relationship and two corresponding entities in the target also have a many-to-many relationship, then a mapping is generated from the join of the two corresponding source tables to the join of the two corresponding target tables. The mapping is generated even if the joins are lossy, because in this case, the semantic approach considers the compatibility of the cardinality constraints as an indication that the mapping is semantically meaningful.

Even if we assume that the source and target conceptual models are available, this strategy of the semantic approach would still have two main drawbacks. First, a mapping involving lossy joins may be semantically meaningful even if the cardinality constraints for the relationships in both schemas are not compatible. For example, the relationship between order lines and authors is one-to-many in the X-Schema and many-to-many in the Y-Schema, yet the mapping m_5 (from Example 4), which maps the two relationships is semantically meaningful. The semantic approach will not generate m_5.

Second, if relationships between corresponding entities in both the source and the target have compatible cardinality constraints, then still a mapping between the joins of their participating tables can be semantically meaningless. This was shown in Example 6, where the composite relationship between X_Author and X_Customer (going through X_Country) is many-to-many, and similarly the composite relationship between Y_Author and Y_Customer (going through Y_Book_Author, Y_Book, Y_Order_Line, and Y_Order) is also many-to-many. Still, however, generating a mapping between the two relationships is meaningless, primarily because the first relationship (in the X-Schema) is itself not semantically meaningful.

Moreover, some of the recent works [8, 19] proposed that users can provide certain "joins", which are deemed important to consider during the construction of logical relations, to compensate for those missed by the chase algorithm. However, no automatic method for discovering such important joins have been presented.

3.3 Unresolved Correspondences

During the construction of mappings, sometimes it is not clear how to populate the target attributes using the source attribute values. This situation occurs when the correspondences between the attributes of the two logical relations being mapped are conflicting. Such conflicts may exist even if the original set of correspondences, V, is conflict-free. To see why, note that constructing a logical relation typically involves joining tables together. Sometimes the same table is included in the logical relation *more than once*. In this case, the attributes of such a table will appear multiple times in the logical relation (certainly with different semantics, or contexts, depending on the join predicates used each time the table is joined).

Now, if a repeated attribute in a source logical relation corresponds to some target attribute, populating that target attribute becomes unresolved since its values can be obtained from more than one source attribute.

Example 7: In the X-Schema, the X_Order_Line table has two foreign keys referencing X_Address, representing the shipping and billing addresses associated with the order line. Clearly, the logical relation for X_Order_Line will include the address attributes (i.e., street, city, ···, etc) more than once.

Similarly, the target logical relation for Y_Order_Line also contains more than one set of address attributes (to capture the billing, shipping, and customer addresses). The mapping m_6 given below is the one which correctly resolves all the conflicts in the attribute correspondences between the source and target logical relations.

```
m6 for o in X_Order, ol in X_Order_Line, ad1 in X_Address,
     ad2 in X_Address, co1 in X_Country, co2 in X_Country, ···
     where (ol.ol_o_id = o.o_id ∧ ol.ol_bill_ad_id = ad1.ad_id
     ∧ ol.ol_ship_ad_id = ad2.ad_id ∧ ad1.ad_co_id = co1.co_id
     ∧ ad2.ad_co_id = co2.co_id ∧ ··· )
     ⇒ exists o' in Y_Order, ol' in Y_Order_Line, ···
     where (ol'.ol_o_id = o'.o_id ∧ ···
     with ∧ o'.o_date = o.o_date ∧ ol'.ol_qty = ol.ol_qty
     ∧ o'.o_bill_street = ad1.ad_street ∧ o'.o_bill_city = ad1.ad_city
     ∧ o'.o_bill_state = ad1.ad_state ∧ o'.o_bill_cntry = co1.co_name)
     ∧ o'.o_ship_street = ad2.ad_street ∧ o'.o_ship_city = ad2.ad_city
     ∧ o'.o_ship_state = ad2.ad_state ∧ o'.o_ship_cntry = co2.co_name)
     ∧ ··· ) □
```

The existing RIC-based approach cannot independently determine that m_6 from Example 7 is the correct mapping. Hence, it generates a number of mappings equal to the number of all possible ways to resolve the correspondence conflicts. It then becomes the user's duty to select the correct mapping, which is both time-consuming and error-prone. Using the semantic approach will not help in this case either, because the conceptual model (if available) does not contain the necessary information to recognize that m_6 is the correct mapping.

Some recent extensions to the RIC-based approach attempt to reduce the amount of effort needed to resolve the correspondence conflicts. In particular, [1] proposed to assist the user in resolving the ambiguity among mappings using data instances. Given a real data instance from the source for a given mapping, the user is asked to choose the correct values for the target attributes involved in that mapping. The user choices will then determine which of the ambiguous mappings is correct. Also, [20] describes a GUI which allows the user to duplicate certain tables in the schema, and then specify the correspondences for each one of the duplicates separately. Such duplications can help in resolving correspondence conflicts.

However, the above two approaches still require a lot of human time and effort, especially for large and complex schemas. This becomes evident in Section 5.2, where we found that after the construction of logical relations for a moderate-sized schema, more than one thousand attributes in those logical relations were involved in correspondence conflicts.

4. THE U-MAP APPROACH

In this section, we describe our approach in the U-MAP system. We show how we can boost the schema mapping quality when we take query logs into account to address all of the aforementioned issues. In particular, we enrich the schema mapping process as illustrated in Figure 3, where the **boldfaced** steps are either newly introduced or significantly modified. Each one of the introduced/modified steps addresses one of the issues raised in Section 3, mainly by exploiting information present in the query log.

The "merging sibling relations" step is introduced as a pre-processing step to merge groups of tables, which seem to be a specialization of the same parent abstract concept (and overalapping), into a single unified relation. Then, during the "constructing logical relations" step, the classical chase algorithm is replaced by a more aggressive version, which is able to discover additional semantically meaningful logical relations. Moreover, the core "creating mappings" step is extended to enable conflict resolution for attribute correspondences, which may arise in situations similar to those described in Section 3.3. The minimization step remains unchanged in U-MAP. However, a post-processing "re-writing mappings" step is introduced to ensure that the generated mappings only refer to original relations in the input schemas and not to any derived relations that could have been added during the initial merging step. Finally, the "compiling mappings" step is not shown in the figure because U-MAP currently focuses only on the generation process itself for the mappings.

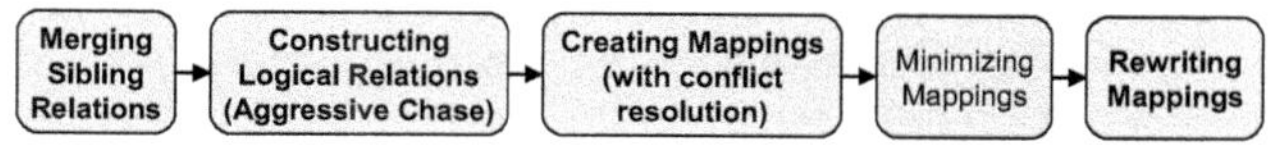

Figure 3: The schema mapping process used in U-MAP. Boldfaced steps are either newly introduced or modified, compared to classical RIC-based schema mapping.

4.1 Managing Sibling Relations

To properly handle the issue of *overlapping sibling relations* (tables having an IS-A relationship with an abstract superclass, and whose records overlap), we need to introduce a pre-processing step and a post-processing step. The goal of the pre-processing step is to first *discover* all the overlapping sibling relations in the schemas, and then to *merge* and replace them with some derived *super relations*. This way, the schema mapping problem will appear to the next steps in the pipeline to be free of any issues related to overlapping sibling relations. In the post-processing step, however, all the output mappings will need to be *re-written* to replace any reference to the super relations with the original sibling relations they represent.

For the pre-processing step, we initially use a simple scheme to discover candidate sibling relations. We consider that two tables are siblings if they have one or more *shared* attributes. Two attributes are considered to be shared across two tables if they both correspond to the same attribute in the other schema. Although simple, this scheme is effective enough to discover sibling relations with a high recall. In our running example, both X_Customer and X_Distributor will be considered siblings because their attributes c_uname and d_uname both correspond to c_uname in Y_Customer for instance.

Since we are only interested in *overlapping* sibling relations, we now need to filter out all the disjoint sibling relations, and the non-sibling relations which might have been erroneously returned by the initial discovery scheme. This is where we rely on the query logs.

The key idea is to determine if there were already specific queries looking for that overlap. In particular, we scan the query log, and for each pair of tables we find to be joined on their primary keys, we check this pair against the discovered pairs of sibling relations. If found, then we mark the pair as overlapping. All pairs which were not found to be joined on their primary keys are filtered out. Note that if the two tables were disjoint, or not siblings in the first place, then their primary keys will be unrelated and it would be pointless to join them using their primary keys.

Each pair of overlapping sibling relations will then be merged into a new super relation, which is the outer join (on the primary keys) of the two sibling relations. The attributes of the super relation will be the union of the attributes of both relations, as shown in the following example.

Example 8: Consider that the two relations X_Customer and X_Distributor in the X-Schema are found to be overlapping sibling relations. Then, their super relation (call it X_Buyer) will be defined using the following query.

```
X_Buyer = select ifnull(c.c_id,d.d_id) bu_id,
          ifnull(c.c_uname,d.d_uname) bu_uname,
          ifnull(c.c_passwd,d.d_passwd) bu_passwd,
          c.c_fname bu_fname, c.c_lname bu_lname,
          d.d_company bu_company, d.d_discount bu_discount,
          ifnull(c.c_ad_id,d.d_ad_id) bu_ad_id
          from X_Customer c outerjoin X_Distributor d
          on c.c_id=d.d_id
```

Note that each pair of common attributes in X_Customer and X_Distributor are mapped to a single attribute in X_Buyer using the ifnull function. For example, c_uname in X_Customer and d_uname in X_Distributor are mapped to bu_uname in X_Buyer using the function ifnull(c_uname,d_uname). □

To complete the merging process, both the schema and the query log need to be updated such that the newly created super relations properly replace the sibling relations they represent. For the schema, any foreign keys referencing the sibling relations should be updated to reference the new super relation instead. For the query log, it should also be updated to be consistent with the schema. In particular, each reference to a sibling relation in a query is replaced by its corresponding super relation. This query re-writing process is fairly straightforward because each of the sibling relations can be regarded as a projection over the super relation, and hence query re-writing will proceed based on the well-understood view-unfolding mechanism [25].

In case more than one pair of overlapping sibling relations were discovered, then the process described above will be repeated for each pair iteratively, until all the pairs have been merged.

As a result of this merging process, the output mappings will still be referring to the super relations, which were not part of the original input schemas. Therefore, in the post-processing step, all the mappings will be re-written – also using the view-unfolding mechanism. But this time, the views defining the super relations in terms of their underlying sibling relations will be used instead (See Example 8). During rewriting, every reference to an attribute in a super relation representing the merger of two attributes, a and b, is replaced by ifnull(a,b) (with the order being currently arbitrary in U-MAP), leading to mappings similar to m_4 in Example 3. Note that the use of the ifnull function in the final output mappings is comparable to the use of skolemization/concat functions in [26] for instance.

4.2 Aggressive Chase

Now that we are confident that the updated input schemas will not have any overlapping sibling relations, we can proceed with the "constructing logical relations" step. We have seen in Section 3.2 that relying on the classical chase algorithm in this step can result in missing some meaningful logical relations. In this section, we describe how we can exploit the information in the query logs to extend the classical chase algorithm into a more aggressive version, where even when no foreign keys are left to chase in the forward direction, the algorithm may still decide to chase a foreign key in the reverse direction.

We start by formally analyzing the situations where the classical chase will either discover or miss interesting logical relations. Let us first note that a logical relation can essentially be represented by a *directed tree*, with the root being the table where the chase starts. The other nodes represent the other tables visited during the chase, and the edges indicate the direction in which the chase occurred. With classical chase, the directed tree is always an *arborescence* (i.e., all edges point away from the root). If the chase is permitted to occur in the reverse direction (as we will explain shortly), then the directed tree will be a general one, where edges can either point to or away from the root.

Moreover, we can classify the types of associations between attributes in a logical relation as follows. Given two attributes a and b in the same logical relation, which originally belong to tables A and B respectively, the relationship between A and B can either be 1-1, 1-m, m-1, or m-m. Without loss of generality, we will only focus on the m-1 and m-m relationships (since 1-m is identical to m-1 given that the two tables are switched, and 1-1 is a special case of m-1).

In the directed tree representation of a logical relation, an m-1 relationship occurs between A and B if A is the ancestor of B, as shown in Figure 4(a). For m-m relationships, we can actually further classify them into two types: *common-ancestor many-to-many* and *common-ancestor-free many-to-many* according to the definitions below.

Definition 1: Common-Ancestor Many-to-Many (CA-m-m) Relationships: *Two relations A and B, which are both used in constructing the same logical relation, $\mathbb{A}$, are said to have a common-ancestor many-to-many (CA-m-m) relationship if there exists a third relation C also used in constructing $\mathbb{A}$, such that the relationships between C and A is many-to-one and between C and B is also many-to-one (i.e., C is the common ancestor of both A and B in the directed tree representation of $\mathbb{A}$).*

Definition 2: Common-Ancestor-Free Many-to-Many (CAF-m-m) Relationships: *Two relations A and B, which are both used in constructing the same logical relation, $\mathbb{A}$, are said to have a common-ancestor-free many-to-many (CAF-m-m) relationship if (1) there does NOT exist a third relation C also used in constructing $\mathbb{A}$, such that the relationships between C and A is many-to-one and between C and B is also many-to-one; and (2) the relationship between A and B is neither m-1 nor 1-m (i.e., there is NO common ancestor for both A and B in the directed tree representation of $\mathbb{A}$).*

The two types of relationships, CA-m-m and CAF-m-m, are illustrated in Figures 4(b) and 4(c) respectively. The classical chase can construct logical relations capturing m-1 and CA-m-m relationships, because starting from the common ancestor the chase can proceed in the forward direction to include both A and B. However, it cannot capture CAF-m-m relationships (for the absence of a common ancestor), although such relationships can be interesting as was shown in Examples 4 and 5 in Section 3.2. We show next how we discover interesting CAF-m-m relationships with the help of query logs.

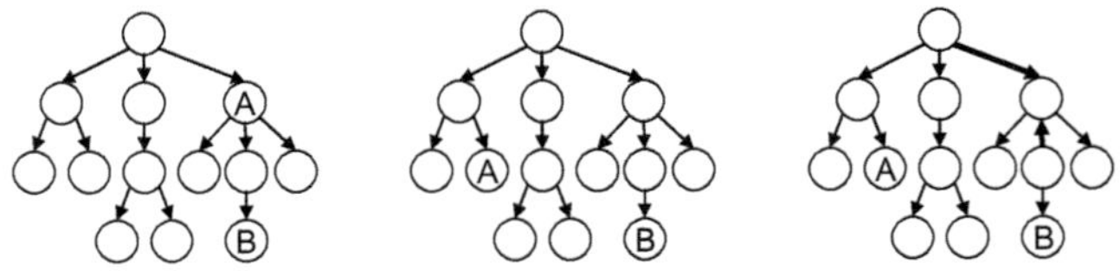

(a) m-1 (b) CA-m-m (c) CAF-m-m

Figure 4: Possible relationships between two tables, A and B, in a logical relation.

Building the FR-Index: In U-MAP, prior to executing the chase algorithm, we first analyze the query log and build an index structure, which we refer to as the *FR-Index* (short for Forward-Reverse Index). Each entry in the FR-Index contains a pair of opposing references; i.e. two different foreign keys referencing the same primary key (see Figure 5(b) for an example). The first reference is considered the forward reference, and the second one is considered the reverse reference. What characterizes the specific pairs maintained in the FR-Index is that joining the referenced table with the two referencing tables using such pairs of foreign keys should result in a semantically meaningful output.

The FR-Index is constructed as follows. Each query encountered in the query log is modeled as a graph, where nodes represent the tables involved in the query, and edges represent the join predicates used to join each pair of tables. If the same table is used more than once in the query, then it will be represented by multiple nodes in the graph.

For a node with n incoming edges, the $\binom{n}{2}$ possible pairs of such edges are stored in the FR-Index. Since each edge in a given pair can either be considered as a forward or a reverse reference (depending on which edge is traversed first), a pair of edges (e,e') is stored twice in the FR-Index: as (e,e') and as (e',e) to account for both cases.

The following example illustrates how a single query is analyzed, and how the FR-Index is populated as a result of this analysis.

Example 9: Consider a query posed on the Y-Schema that requests for customer "John Smith" all the pairs of books written by the same author that John has ordered within less than 30 days. The query will look as follows.

Q_1
```
select b1.b_title, b2.b_title, a1.a_fname, a1.a_lname
from Y_Customer c1, Y_Order o1, Y_Order_Line ol1,
Y_Book b1, Y_Book_Author ba1, Y_Author a1, Y_Order o2,
Y_Order_Line ol2, Y_Book b2, Y_Book_Author ba2
where c1.c_id=o1.o_c_id and o1.o_id=ol1.ol_o_id
and ol1.ol_b_id=b1.b_id and b1.b_id=ba1.ba_b_id
and ba1.ba_a_id=a1.a_id and c2.c_id=o2.o_c_id
and o2.o_id=ol2.ol_o_id and ol2.ol_b_id=b2.b_id
and b2.b_id=ba2.ba_b_id and ba2.ba_a_id=a2.a_id
and ba1.ba_a_id=ba2.ba_a_id and b1.b_title<>b2.b_title
and abs(o1.o_date-o2.o_date)<30 and o1.o_c_id=o2.o_c_id
and c1.c_fname='John' and c1.c_lname='Smith'
```

The graph constructed for Q_1 is shown in Figure 5(a), and Figure 5(b) shows how the FR-Index is finally populated as a result of analyzing Q_1. The **bold** edges are the ones corresponding to the opposing references, which get stored in the FR-Index. Note that in this case, Y_Order_Line and Y_Book_Author give an example of an interesting CAF-m-m relationship. □

Aggressive Chase Algorithm: Given the FR-Index, the chase algorithm can now be modified as shown in Algorithm 1. Starting from a given table A, the algorithm will execute a series of alternating *rounds of chase*: (forward chase, reverse chase, forward chase, ... etc). The first round is a regular forward chase where A is joined with all the tables it references to create the first intermediate logical relation. The

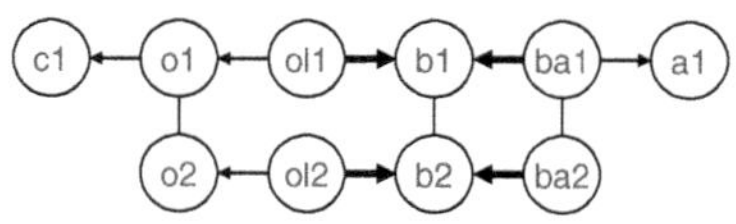

(a) Query Graph

FR-Index

Forward	Reverse
(Y_Book_Author.ia_b_id, Y_Book.b_id)	(Y_Order_Line.ol_b_id, Y_Book.b_id)
(Y_Order_Line.ol_b_id, Y_Book.b_id)	(Y_Book_Author.ia_b_id, Y_Book.b_id)

(b) FR-Index

Figure 5: Q_1's query graph and the corresponding entries in the FR-Index for Example 9.

second round is a reverse chase, where the algorithm will check each forward reference it used in the previous round against the FR-Index. If one or more lookups for the forward references return corresponding reverse references, then the algorithm will proceed by joining the current intermediate logical relation to all the referencing tables covered by the reverse references returned from the FR-Index. The alternation between forward and reverse chase rounds will then continue, until a forward chase round is reached, where there are no further foreign keys to chase. The aggressive chase algorithm will then stop.

Algorithm 1 AggressiveChase(A: input table, FR-Index)

```
𝔸 = A {initialize logical relation 𝔸 with input table A}
F = set of forward references outgoing from 𝔸
R = set of reverse references incoming to 𝔸
while F is not empty do
  {forward chase}
  for f in F (where f is a forward reference of the form: 𝔸.a_i → B.b_j) do
    𝔸 = output of joining 𝔸 with B
  end for
  {reverse chase}
  for f in F do
    if an entry (f, r) exists in the FR-Index (where r is a reverse reference of the form: 𝔸.a_i ← C.c_k then
      𝔸 = output of joining 𝔸 with C
    end if
  end for
  {update forward and reverse references}
  F = set of forward references outgoing from 𝔸
  R = set of reverse references incoming to 𝔸
end while
return 𝔸
```

Note that with the above algorithm, the path from one table to another in the directed tree of the generated logical relation can contain one or more reverse edges, and hence the two tables may not have a common ancestor. Therefore, the aggressive chase indeed captures the CAF-m-m relationships as long as they are deemed interesting according to the query log.

4.3 Resolving Correspondence Conflicts

Once we have constructed all the logical relations in both schemas, the next step is to construct the mappings between them. However, we explained in Section 3.3 that the correspondences between the attributes of the two logical relations may not be conflict-free. In this section, we explain the process we follow in U-MAP to resolve these conflicts, and hence find the most meaningful mapping in such situations. This is in contrast to simply generating mappings for all the possible resolutions of the correspondence conflicts.

Problem Formulation: We will now formulate the problem of conflict resolution as follows. Given two logical relations $\mathbb{A}$ and $\mathbb{B}$ with attributes $\{a_1, a_2, \ldots, a_I\}$ and $\{b_1, b_2, \ldots, b_J\}$ respectively, and a set of correspondences in the form of $(a_i, b_j), i \in [1, I], j \in [1, J]$, a pair of correspondences are said to be *conflicting* if they were in the form of $\langle(a_i, b_{j_1}), (a_i, b_{j_2})\rangle$ or $\langle(a_{i_1}, b_j), (a_{i_2}, b_j)\rangle$. In these two cases, the attributes b_{j_1}, b_{j_2}, a_{i_1}, and a_{i_2} are said to be *conflicting attributes*.

Moreover, unlike the attributes of regular schema tables, each attribute in a logical relation is associated with what we refer to as a *logical attribute path*, which specifies how this attribute was reached when constructing the logical relation. Hence, the same attribute from the same table may appear multiple times in the logical relation, but each time with a different associated path. It can be formally defined as follows.

Definition 3: Logical Attribute Path ($LAP(a)$): *A logical attribute path is a sequence of K join predicates connecting an initial table A_0 to an attribute a in some table A_K, where $K \geq 0$.*

Consider that a_{i_k} denotes the primary key of a table A_k, and that $a_{i'_k}$ denotes a foreign key in $A_k, k \in [0, K]$. Thus, if all the join predicates in $LAP(a)$ represent forward references, then $LAP(a)$ is given as follows.

$LAP(a) =$ "$(A_0.a_{i'_0} = A_1.a_{i_1}), (A_1.a_{i'_1} = A_2.a_{i_2}), \ldots,$ $(A_{K-1}.a_{i'_{K-1}} = A_K.a_{i_K}), A_K.a$".

Otherwise, if the join predicates in $LAP(a)$ include opposing references, then $LAP(a)$ is given as follows.

$LAP(a) =$ "$(A_0.a_{i'_0} = A_1.a_{i_1}), \ldots, (A_{k-1}.a_{i'_{k-1}} = A_k.a_{i_k}),$ $(A_k.a_{i_k} = A_{k+1}.a_{i'_{k+1}}), \ldots, A_K.a$".

In view of the above discussion, the conflict resolution problem is to search the space of all possible *conflict-free* mappings between the attributes of $\mathbb{A}$ and $\mathbb{B}$, and find the mapping that is most semantically meaningful in terms of how the attributes (with their associated paths) are matched on both sides.

Example 10: Figure 6 shows some conflicting correspondences between the attributes of the X_Order_Line and Y_Order_Line logical relations. In particular, it focuses on those conflicts between the "city" attributes on both sides. Each attribute is shown along with its path in the figure. (Note that the table names in the paths are abbreviated for space limitation.) □

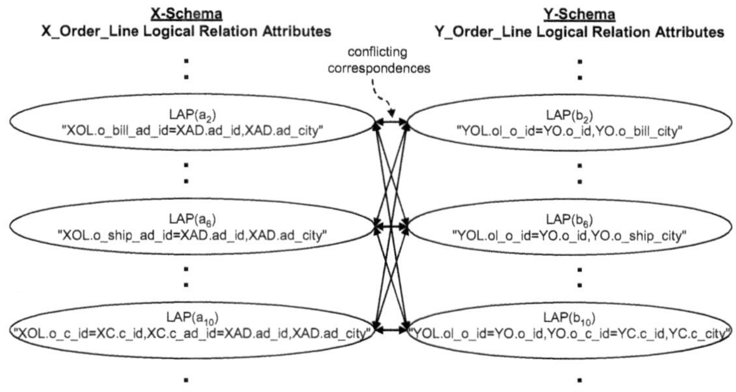

Figure 6: Correspondence conflicts for all "city" attributes when mapping the logical relations for X_Order_Line and Y_Order_Line.

Solution Overview: Our proposed solution is centered around two ideas, which translate into two consecutive stages.

- *Attribute Grouping:* The purpose of the first stage is to reduce the size of the search space by excluding as many illogical mappings as possible, and hence ensure that they will not be erroneously selected in the following stage. This is achieved by first dividing the attribute sets of each of $\mathbb{A}$ and $\mathbb{B}$ into groups of semantically-related attributes. Then, the only mappings considered are those where no two attributes in the same group on one side are mapped to two attributes in different groups on the other side.

- *Usage-based Conflict Resolution:* The second stage actually selects the most meaningful mapping. Its main idea is to match a pair of attributes from $\mathbb{A}$ and $\mathbb{B}$ only when their *usage patterns* (as reflected in their respective query logs) seem more compatible compared to other alternative matches.

4.3.1 Attribute Grouping

The intuition behind this stage is based on the observation that conflicting attributes in a logical relation result from using the same *concepts* in different *contexts*. For example, as mentioned in Example 7, the logical relations for X_Order_Line and Y_Order_Line both contain multiple versions of address attributes (i.e., street, city, state, . . . , etc), where each version corresponds to a different context (e.g., billing address, shipping address, customer address, . . . , etc).

Formally speaking, the full context of an attribute a in a logical relation is given by $LAP(a)$. Consequently, an attribute a is said to have a more similar context to attribute b compared to attribute c if $LAP(a)$ and $LAP(b)$ share a longer prefix compared to $LAP(a)$ and $LAP(c)$.

The idea of grouping is to ensure that attributes having similar contexts are grouped together. This way, we can match whole groups of attributes across the source and target logical relations. This approach is in contrast to matching individual attributes, which may lead to matching two attributes in the same context on one side to two attributes in two different contexts on the other side, which would clearly result in a wrong mapping.

Goal: Our goal is to generate attribute groups that satisfy the following properties: (1) All attributes in the same group must be non-conflicting with one another; (2) Given any two attributes a and b in two different groups G_1 and G_2 respectively, the common prefix of $LAP(a)$ and $LAP(b)$ cannot be longer than the common prefix of $LAP(a)$ and $LAP(c)$, for any other attribute c in G_1; and (3) The number of generated groups must be minimal given that they satisfy the above two properties.

The first property ensures that matching attributes from one group on one side to another group on the other side will not involve any further conflict resolution. The second property ensures that attributes within the same group are closer to each other, in terms of their contexts, compared to attributes in other groups. Finally, the third property ensures that groups satisfying the first two properties are not unnecessarily split into smaller subgroups, which in turn ensures that the space of possible mappings to be explored is kept to a minimum.

Attribute Grouping Algorithm: The input to our grouping algorithm is the list of all conflicting attributes in the logical relation, along with their paths. The output is a list of groups of attributes satisfying the properties described above. The algorithm operates as follows. For each conflicting attribute a, $LAP(a)$ is inserted into a *trie*, or a prefix tree. Briefly, a trie is a tree structure for efficiently storing strings (logical attribute paths in our case). Each leaf node stores one of the inserted paths. Internal nodes store the common prefix for all the paths stored in its descendant nodes. Each node also maintains pointers to the set of attributes represented by its descendants (and hence are considered to be represented by that node as well).

The populated trie is then used to partition the attributes into groups as follows. We perform a depth first search starting from the root node. For each visited node, if some attributes in the set it represents conflict with one another, then this set cannot be considered as a group, and its descendant nodes are visited in the standard depth first search order (i.e., the set of attributes must be further split). Conversely, if the set of attributes in the visited node are not conflicting with one another, then the set will be considered as one of the output groups, and none of node's descendants will be visited (i.e., no further splitting is performed). The pseudocode for this algorithm has been omitted for space limitations.

Example 11: Figure 7 shows how the conflicting attributes are grouped in the Y_Order_Line logical relation. The list of such conflicting attributes, along with their paths, is given in Figure 7(a). After all the paths are inserted into a trie, the populated trie will then look as shown in Figure 7(b). The output groups in this case are the sets of attributes associated with each one of the second-level nodes (highlighted nodes). This is because they are all conflict-free, as opposed to the set of attributes associated with the root node (e.g., b_2, b_6, and b_{10} in the root node are all "city" attributes, and hence they conflict with one another).□

Note that the attribute grouping stage is optional, in the sense that conflict resolution (described next) can occur even if the attributes were not grouped. However, we found in our experiments that the grouping constraints introduced in this stage indeed help in protecting the next stage from making wrong decisions, and hence improve the overall quality of the generated mappings.

4.3.2 Usage-based Conflict Resolution

The goal of this stage is to match the groups generated during the attribute grouping stage between the source and target logical relations. (If no grouping was performed, then each individual attribute will be considered as a group.) The straightforward approach would be to match the common path prefixes defining the shared context among the attributes in each group.

For example, the common path prefixes for the attributes in the two groups representing the billing and shipping addresses in the logical relation of X_Order_Line are "(X_Order_Line.ol_bill_ad_id = X_Address.ad_id)," and "(X_Order_Line.ol_ship_ad_id = X_Address.ad_id)," respectively. Similarly, for the logical relation of Y_Order, the common prefixes for the attributes in the two corresponding groups are "Y_Order.o_bill_" and "Y_Order.o_ship_" respectively.

Clearly, in this case, measuring the textual similarity between the prefixes on each side can lead us to the correct matching. For instance, we can break up each prefix into a set of text fragments and then measure the Jaccard similarity coefficient between the resulting sets. However, this approach will not be useful if the attribute naming was not similar in both schemas – for example, if o_bill_city and o_ship_city are instead named o_city1 and o_city2. An even more extreme example is when the two schemas are in two different languages.

For this reason, we do not assume that textual similarity between the prefixes always exists, and instead we rely on a different source of information. In particular, we assume that a group of attributes representing certain concepts in a given context are expected to exhibit different *usage patterns* compared to another group of attributes representing the same concepts but in a different context. For example, the usage of the billing address attributes can be different from the usage of the shipping address attributes as reflected in the query log.

Usage-Based Schema Matching: The idea of relying on the usage information for matching attributes has already been proposed in [10]. However, the focus in [10] was on full-fledged schema matching. In our case, we need to match the attributes of two logical relations rather than two schemas. Moreover, the fact that the same schema attribute may occur multiple times in a logical relation poses new challenges which were not addressed in [10].

The technique proposed in [10] can be summarized as follows. It relies on collecting statistical information from the query logs for each attribute, or each pair of attributes (e.g., their co-occurrence frequency in the select clause, or in the select and where clauses respectively, and so on). Then those collected statistics are compared across the two schemas. The set of attribute correspondences, which result in the highest similarity for the collected statistics in both schemas (based on a scoring function described in [10]), is returned as the schema matching output.

A New Matching Problem: In our problem setting, however, we found that before we can match the attributes of logical relations as described above, a totally separate *matching problem* needs to be solved first – one that requires a new strategy too. In particular, the statistics collected from the query logs for those attributes which appear multiple times in the logical relation must now be split across the different versions of each such attribute. For this purpose, each occurrence of this attribute in the query log must be *matched* to one of the versions in the logical relation. This way we can correctly account for the statistics pertaining to each individual version.

Matching in this scenario will be *context-based* – if an attribute occurs in a query in a *context* similar to that of a given version of the same attribute in the logical relation, then they are matched together. We call this problem *attribute context matching*. To understand how we address this problem, we will explain next how we specify attribute contexts when they occur in logical relations and in queries, and how we actually match them.

Attribute Contexts in Logical Relations: As we mentioned earlier, the context of an attribute a is generally determined based on its path, $LAP(a)$. This path, however, can sometimes be too long, and hence represents a very specific context, which will unlikely match with the contexts found in the query log. In principle, we only need the context

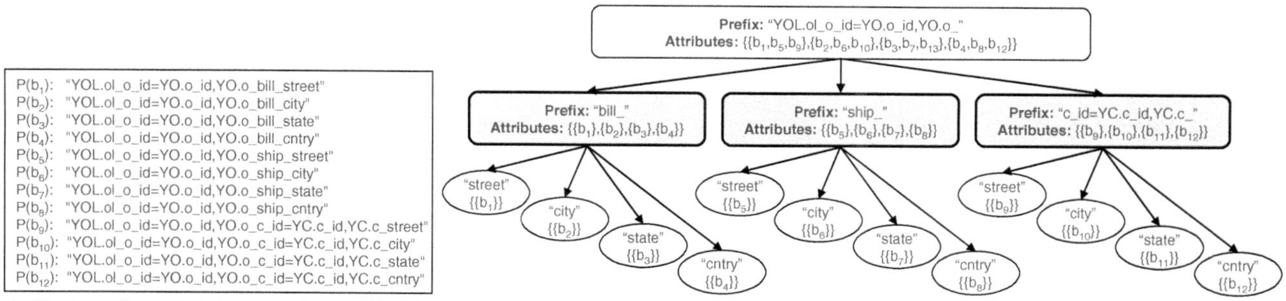

(a) Paths of conflicting attributes in the X_Order_Line logical relation

(b) The trie built for all the paths in (a)

Figure 7: Attribute grouping for the Y_Order_Line logical relation. The output groups of attributes are highlighted.

of an attribute to be specific enough to *distinguish* it from the contexts of the other versions of the same attribute in the logical relation.

Let us consider that attributes $\{a_1, a_2, \ldots, a_n\}$ in a logical relation $\mathbb{A}$ are different versions of the same attribute a in some table A. The paths of all attributes $a_i, i \in [1, n]$, will have the same beginning (the root of the logical relation) and ending (attribute a). Only the internal components in these paths are what distinguish them from one another. Hence, the least specific path for an attribute in a logical relation which can still distinguish it from all other attributes in the same logical relation is given by the following definition.

Definition 4: Minimal Distinguishing Logical Attribute Path ($MDLAP(a)$): *Given an attribute a in a logical relation $\mathbb{A}$, the minimal distinguishing logical attribute path of a, or $MDLAP(a)$, is defined as the minimal* suffix *of $LAP(a)$, such that there does not exist an attribute b in $\mathbb{A}$, where $MDLAP(a)$ is also a suffix of $LAP(b)$.*

In conclusion, for the purpose of attribute context matching across logical relations and queries, the context of an attribute a in a logical relation is given by $MDLAP(a)$.

Attribute Contexts in Queries: In order to identify the context of the attributes appearing in a query, we first need to build its query graph as described in Section 4.2. Then, using this graph, we can compute the path of join predicates leading to the table instance where each attribute belongs. This is achieved by starting form the node in the graph representing the attribute's table instance, and then visiting the chain of its ancestor nodes in the graph. The format of this path for an attribute a will be identical to that of $LAP(a)$ given in Definition 3. However, we will denote the path extracted from a query by $QAP(a)$ – short for *query attribute path*.

The main difference between a query and a logical relation is that the former is represented by a general directed graph, while the latter is represented by a rooted directed tree. As a result, each attribute in a logical relation will only have one path starting from the root. But in theory, an attribute in a query may have multiple paths. (In our running example, for instance, a query may request all addresses which were used both as billing and shipping addresses for the same order. In this case, each address attribute will have two paths corresponding to its billing and shipping roles.) Therefore, for the sake of generality, an attribute in a query is allowed to have multiple contexts depending on how many paths are discovered for it in the query.

Context Matching: To decide whether an attribute a_q appearing in a query is actually an occurrence of an attribute a_l appearing in a logical relation, we need to first match their recognized contexts (or paths). For this purpose, we use the following strategy. For each path $QAP_i(a_q)$ associated with a_q, if $MDLAP(a_l)$ is a *suffix* of $QAP(a_q)$, then a_q is considered to be an occurrence of a_l in the query.

This criterion guarantees that given the context of a_q in the query, a_q will be unambiguously matched to a single attribute, a_l, in the logical relation. This is because the context of a_l is already known to be unique in the logical relation. And since the context for a_q must be *as specific as, or even more specific than,* that of a_l, then a_q cannot be matched to any other attribute in the logical relation given that context. In case a_q has more than one context (as discussed earlier), then it may be matched to more than one attribute in the logical relation – one for each such context.

By solving the context matching problem as described above, we can then directly apply the usage-based matching technique described in [10] to resolve the correspondence conflicts across the two logical relations, and thereby find the most meaningful conflict-free mapping.

5. EVALUATION

To evaluate our approach, we have conducted experiments in two main scenarios: the bookstores scenario, and the life sciences scenario, as will be described next. Unfortunately, research benchmarks such as STBenchmark [2] were not suitable for our experiments because they did not include query log information, which is needed for the operation of U-MAP.

5.1 Bookstores Scenario

In this section, we describe an experimental study whose goal is to measure the effect of each of the new features introduced in the U-MAP system on the quality of the generated mappings, in comparison with the classical RIC-based approach. We also study the performance of the mapping generation process.

Dataset: We have considered schemas from the bookstores domain, based on the industry-standard TPC-W benchmark [27]. TPC-W gives the specifications for building an online bookstore, including the database schema, the data stored in it, and the system workload. In order to simulate the presence of two different bookstore systems, we created two perturbed versions of the specified schema, very similar to those shown in Figure 1. The schemas used in the experiments, however, contain more tables (e.g. related to the shopping cart information), and more attributes (e.g., book subjects and stock levels). In summary, the two schemas used in our experiments contain a total of 18 tables and 82 attributes, covering 30 different correspondences.

In order to generate the query logs, we used the Wisconsin implementation of TPC-W [28], and ran the bookstore system under the different workload mixes specified by the benchmark. In particular, there are three such mixes: a browsing mix, a shopping mix, and an ordering mix, where the read-only Web interactions constitute 95%, 80%, and 50% respectively. By running the system under each mix, we could generate two corresponding query logs for the source and target schemas. The query logs were generated by re-writing the original queries so that they conform to each of the two schemas. To ensure heterogeneity, we assumed that the two schemas were associated with the two most different query logs (browsing for the source, and ordering for the target). A single run of each workload mix was performed by running 30 emulated browsers, which simultaneously submit requests to the bookstore system for about 3 hours. These runs resulted in query logs containing 5,231 and 11,424 queries for the source and target schemas respectively.

It is worth noting that TPC-W is focused on a single use case for the bookstore database, namely that of the bookstore's online customers. Hence, it does not account for other typical use cases of the same database, such as the queries made by the shipping department, the accounting department, etc. In the query logs we used, we tried to account for those use cases as well, while making the smallest possible changes to the original query logs. In particular, we assumed that queries requesting the information of specific orders are not only coming from the online customers. But they might also be coming from the shipping department (which will normally be interested in the order's shipping address), and the accounting department (which, in contrast, will be interested in the billing address). We also assumed that the requests of the accounting department are generally more frequent than those of the shipping department. The rationale is that, unlike the accounting department, the shipping department is only concerned with an order until it gets shipped.

Methodology: We implemented the U-MAP system such that all of its new features can either be enabled or disabled. In particular, we refer to the following four features: merging sibling relations (MSR), aggressive chase (AC), attribute grouping (AG), and usage-based conflict resolution (UCR). To indicate that a given feature is disabled, we prefix it with "!" (e.g., "!AC" implies that aggressive chase is not used). Clearly, if all four features are disabled, then U-MAP will behave similar to a classical RIC-based mapping system.

In the experiments, we run U-MAP using its 16 possible configurations. For each run, we measure the precision and recall by comparing the generated mappings against a set of manually-created ground truth mappings. Both the generated and ground truth mappings represent the set of *minimized* mappings (i.e., they are the outcome of step 3 described in Section 2.3.1). For our experimental setting, we found the total number of ground truth mappings to be 15. Moreover, we also measured the processing time given the different configurations of U-MAP, averaged over 20 independent runs each. The experiments were conducted on a 4-core Windows 7 machine with 2.66 GHz core speed and 6GB of RAM.

Unlike the RIC-based approach, we did not directly compare U-MAP to the semantic approach in our experiments. Beside the fact that no implementation for the semantic approach was available to us, we were also more interested in the general case, where a conceptual model does not necessarily exist. (In fact, no conceptual models were available for the bookstore schemas we used.) Moreover, we could show in Section 3, that even in the presence of the conceptual models, the semantic approach will neither help in discovering some of the meaningful logical relations, nor will it help in resolving correspondence conflicts.

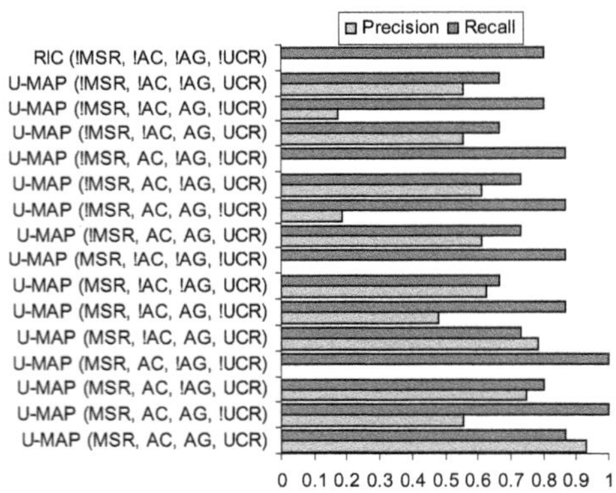

Figure 8: Precision and recall for the different U-MAP configurations, including the classical RIC configuration.

5.1.1 *Quality Study*

Overview: Figure 8 shows the precision and recall measurements for each of the 16 configurations of U-MAP. Figure 8 shows that the best configuration is where all the new features are enabled. This configuration resulted in a precision and recall of 0.93 and 0.87 respectively. In particular, exactly 14 mappings were generated with one false positive and two false negatives.

The false positive is because of generating an incorrect mapping between the logical relations of X_Buyer (the super relation of X_Customer and X_Distributer) and Y_Order, which incorrectly maps the customer address attributes in X_Buyer to the shipping address attributes in Y_Order.

The reason for this glitch is that the highest-score mapping (based on the scoring function described in [10]) between the two logical relations is discarded during the minimization step despite being the correct mapping. However, we have set our implementation such that if the highest-score mapping is discarded, it gets *replaced* with the second highest-score mapping, and so on. We found that this replacement strategy generally leads to better results, compared to no-replacement. In some cases however (as in this case), it results in generating incorrect mappings. The choice of replacement versus no-replacement is controlled by a configurable parameter in U-MAP.

The two false negatives are because we assumed that there are *two* ground truth mappings between the logical relations of X_Address and Y_Order, and similarly between those of X_Country and Y_Order. These mappings correspond to mapping the address information once to the billing address in Y_Order, and once to the shipping address. In U-MAP, however, we only generate the highest-score mapping between each pair of logical relations, and hence the second ground truth mapping (which scored less) was missed.

Another observation from Figure 8 is that the precision is almost zero whenever both AG and UCR are both disabled (including the RIC configuration). The reason is that in all of these cases, the number of incorrectly generated mappings is exponentially large, because all the possible mappings for all possible conflict resolutions are generated without any grouping constraints.

It is also worth mentioning that in all of our experiments, executing each of MSR, AC, and AG has always been accurate; i.e., overlapping sibling relations were correctly detected and merged whenever MSR was enabled, meaningful reverse references were correctly detected and chased whenever AC was enabled, and the attributes were correctly grouped whenever AG was enabled. In what follows, we study the impact of each individual new feature on the quality of the generated mappings.

Effect of Merging Sibling Relations: To assess the impact of MSR, we will compare the best configuration, where all new features are enabled, to that where all are enabled except for MSR. The precision and recall dropped from 0.93 and 0.87 for the former configuration to 0.56 and 0.67 respectively for the latter configuration. In particular, in the latter configuration, 18 mappings are generated with 8 false positives and 5 false negatives (compared to 1 and 2 respectively for the former).

Clearly, the false positives in this case are mostly because of generating mappings involving X_Customer and X_Distributor, while the false negatives are because of *not* generating the mappings involving X_Buyer.

Effect of Aggressive Chase: The configuration where all new features are enabled except for AC results in a precision and recall of 0.79 and 0.73 respectively. In this case, exactly 14 mappings are generated, similar to the best configuration. However, unlike the best configuration, 3 false positives and 4 false negatives occur. As expected, the additional false positives are due to the generation of mappings involving the chase of Y_Order_Line without including the author information. Also, the additional false negatives are attributed to *not* generating the mappings involving the chase of Y_Order_Line with the author information included.

Effect of Attribute Grouping: When using the configuration where all the new features are enabled except for AG, we find that the precision and recall drop to 0.75 and 0.8 compared to 0.93 and 0.87 respectively, when all features are enabled, including AG. These figures correspond to 16 generated mappings, with 4 false positives and 3 false negatives.

In the absence of grouping constraints, the conflict resolution step will have to search for the best mapping within a large number of possible conflict resolutions. For this reason, it becomes more prone to errors. And indeed, this is what we observed in this experiment. Both the false positives and false negatives occurred, precisely, because some of the generated mappings incorrectly mapped address attributes from the same group in the X-Schema to address attributes in two different groups in the Y-Schema. For example, the mapping between the logical relations of X_Address and Y_Order mapped the street, city, and country attributes in the X-Schema to their corresponding *customer* address attributes in the Y-Schema. Conversely, however, the city attribute in the X-Schema was mapped to the *shipping* city in the Y-Schema.

Effect of Conflict Resolution: Figure 8 shows that the configuration where all the new features are enabled except for UCR, achieves a recall of 1. This is expected because with no conflict resolution, the mappings corresponding to all possible resolutions are generated, including all the desirable ones. The precision however drops from 0.93 to 0.55, compared to the best configuration. Clearly, the reason is that many incorrect mappings are also generated in this case. In particular, 27 mappings are generated for this configuration. This number goes up to 2763 generated mappings for the configuration where both AG and UCR are disabled (i.e., with no grouping constraints).

5.1.2 *Performance Study*

Although the mapping generation process is typically a one-time offline process, and hence the computational efficiency comes at a lower priority compared to the quality of the generated mappings – we still, however, report here the performance results in our experiments to demonstrate the practicality of U-MAP.

In terms of the processing time, the configuration where all the new features were enabled took about 12.5 seconds to generate all the mappings. The remaining configurations ranged from 0.3 to 16 seconds, except for the four configurations where both MSR and AG were disabled, which took several hours each. These four cases required trying all the possible ways to match 16 address attributes on the source side with 12 address attributes on the target side. Additionally, the two target attributes c_uname and c_passwd had 4 different ways to be matched to the source attributes: c_uname, c_passwd, d_uname, and d_passwd. This striking difference in the processing time underscores the value of the "merging sibling relations" and "attribute grouping" features in U-MAP.

5.2 Life Sciences Scenario

To further assess the validity of our approach, we report in this section our experience with a larger-scale real-world data set from the life sciences domain. In this scenario, we only focus on one system (as opposed to two parallel systems serving as the source and the target). This is primarily because it is the one where information on both its schema and its queries were available to us. While measuring the accuracy and performance of the complete mapping process is not possible in this case, studying this particular system was still quite helpful in showing that: (1) the issues U-MAP is addressing are indeed likely to occur in real-world schemas, and (2) the usage information can help us better understand the semantics of a database schema, and hence perform a better job in mapping it to other schemas.

In particular, we could obtain the schema of a functional genomics database [4] from its authors. The database keeps track of millions of biological measurements collected for over 60,000 tissue samples of the Arabidopsis plant, including both mutant and normal samples. It has been in operation for over four years serving biologists worldwide, who are interested in this particular plant.

The schema, whose layout is shown on the right side of Figure 9, contains 35 tables and 273 attributes. We could not get access to the full-fledged query log for this database. However, we could obtain a list of 73 *query templates* (or parameterized queries), which are embedded in the source code of the application that runs on top of it. Although the frequency information for these queries was missing, they were still an excellent source of information for the usage patterns of the different tables and attributes in the schema. Table 1 summarizes some statistics, which characterize the schema and queries we consider in this scenario. We now discuss how such characteristics can highlight the value of our newly introduced features in U-MAP.

Sibling Relations: While this schema does contain 6 sibling relations (two groups of three relations each), none of them is overlapping. However, the people table (magnified in the left side of Figure 9) in fact represents different types of people: customers requesting the analysis, providers of the samples, specialists who plant and harvest the samples, and analysts who collect and analyze the measurements. Therefore, a very likely alternative design would have a separate table assigned to each type of people. Moreover, the roles of these people often overlap, causing such tables to become overlapping sibling relations. For example, the analyst can also be the person who plants and harvests the sample, and so on. In this case, we can only avoid having duplicate records in the target database, if we appropriately merge those overlapping sibling relations prior to mapping generation.

Table 1: Statistics from the life sciences scenario.

Schema and Queries	
# tables	35
# attributes	273
# query templates	73
Sibling Relations	
# sibling relations	6
# overlapping sibling relations	0
Aggressive Chase	
# pairs of opposite edges	106
# interesting pairs of opposing references	3
# logical relations using opposing references	7
Conflict Resolution	
# logical relations with conflicting attributes	16
# conflicting attributes in all logical relations	1267

Aggressive Chase: We analyzed all the referential integrity constraints in the schema and found that the overall number of pairs of opposing references is 106. Moreover, by analyzing the queries associated with the schema, we discovered that 3 out of those 106 pairs are interesting. An interesting pair is one that is used to join three tables in some query, and hence suggests that their attributes should be associated. When applying the aggressive chase, the discovered interesting pairs are used in constructing 7 different logical relations. To appreciate the significance of this finding on the quality of the generated mappings (between this schema and any other schema), we note that all mappings involving any of the 7 aforementioned logical relations will be missing important associations, and hence considered incorrect, unless the aggressive chase is applied.

Conflict Resolution: The schema in Figure 9 contains numerous cases where one table refers to another table multiple times, and for a different purpose each time (similar to the billing and shipping addresses in the bookstores scenario). For example, the table called trayinfo (shown in the left side of Figure 9, and which covers information about each experiment for planting sample tissues) references the people table three times to track the persons who planted, harvested, and analyzed the results for the tissue sample. It also references a table called typedet (not magnified in the figure, however, it is a general-purpose table used to maintain the possible *types* of different concepts in the schema) twice – once to track the type of the tissue being planted, and another for the growing medium type.

As a result of these and many other similar cases in the schema, 16 of the constructed logical relations were found to contain a total of 1267 conflicting attributes(!). Considering the number of mappings these logical relations will be involved in, and the number of correspondence conflicts they will generate, we can immediately realize how impractical it is to leave the conflict resolution task for the user to perform manually in complex real-world scenarios.

6. RELATED WORK

The problem of mapping generation has received a lot of attention, especially in the last decade(e.g., [3, 6, 9, 11, 13, 21, 23]). In the context of the Clio project, several techniques were proposed for mapping discovery, first for relational data sources [21], and then for XML data sources [23]. Later, the notion of "nested mappings" was introduced in [13], which showed how we can combine multiple mappings together into a single nested mapping.

Besides Clio, other research efforts were made for the discovery of complex mappings beyond the simple attribute correspondences. The semantic approach [3] described in Section 2 is an example. As we already mentioned, a key drawback in this approach is that the conceptual models, which it relies upon, are not often present in real-world scenarios. iMap [9] focuses on finding complex relations between attributes in both schemas such as price=rate*(1+tax). Bohannon et al. [6] introduced *contextual schema matching*, in which a match between a pair of attributes is valid only when certain conditions are met in the data instances.

None of the above techniques, however, relied on query logs. Only

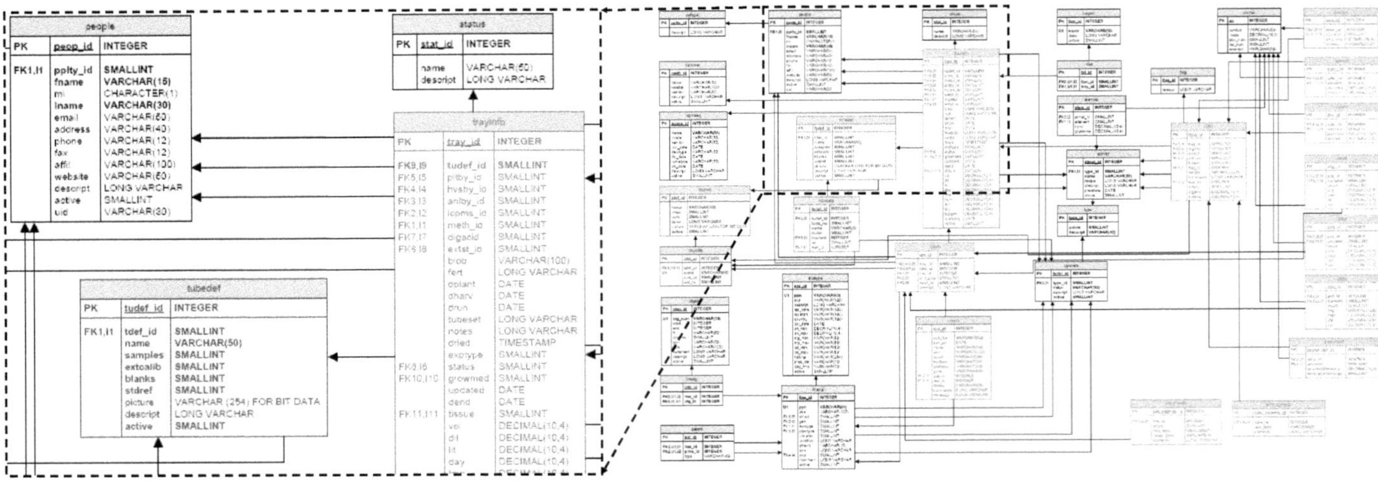

Figure 9: The life sciences schema (right side) with the dashed rectangle containing the people and trayinfo tables magnified (left side).

in a recent overview paper on the Clio project [11], it was briefly mentioned that query logs can be used to find associations between attributes. The paper essentially refers to non-RIC-based associations like having the first two letters in the course ID for instance equal to the department ID. This idea is complementary to the techniques we propose in this paper.

More recently, several works have focused on the post mapping generation phase, where the generated mappings are re-written to obtain a new set of mappings with desirable properties. For example, [26, 19] are two independent approaches for re-writing mappings to generate SQL scripts capable of computing what is known as the *core solution* for a data exchange problem [12]. Also, [14] shows how schema mappings can be normalized in the same spirit in which relational schemas are normalized. The technique proposed in [18] addresses the situation where key constraints and functional dependencies (egds) hold on the target. Given a mapping scenario with s-t tgds along with target egds, a best-effort algorithm is given to re-write this scenario into one with no egds, which can be efficiently executed. However, we explained in Section 3.1 that this technique can handle the problem of merging sibling relations, but not when the key attributes are not mapped across the source and the target. Hence, the above works either do not consider the same problems we address in this paper, or only handle special cases for some of them. It would be useful, however, to have them incorporated into the "minimization step" in Figure 3.

As described in Section 3.3, Muse [1] and +Spicy [20] attempt to solve the problem of unresolved correspondences. However, their solutions involve substantial manual labor and can be tedious for large and complex schemas. Our work is also related to the usage-based schema matching technique presented in [10] in the sense that they both exploit the query logs. However, as we explained in Section 4.3, this work is only focused on the generation of simple attribute correspondences across two schemas.

7. CONCLUSION

We have presented U-MAP, a schema mapping system, which emphasizes the value of the usage information in the query logs to address several unresolved problems in the schema mapping area. We also verified the effectiveness and efficiency of U-MAP by running it on realistic databases from the retail and life sciences domains. Our results suggest that the best quality for the generated mappings is obtained when all the new features in U-MAP are turned on.

8. REFERENCES

[1] B. Alexe, L. Chiticariu, R. J. Miller, and W. C. Tan. Muse: Mapping understanding and design by example. In *ICDE*, 2008.

[2] B. Alexe, W. C. Tan, and Y. Velegrakis. Stbenchmark: towards a benchmark for mapping systems. *PVLDB*, 1(1):230–244, 2008.

[3] Y. An, A. Borgida, R. J. Miller, and J. Mylopoulos. A semantic approach to discovering schema mapping expressions. In *ICDE*, 2007.

[4] I. Baxter et al. PIIMS: An Integrated Functional Genomics Platform. *Plant Physiology*, 143:600–611, 2007.

[5] P. Bernstein, A. Halevy, and R. Pottinger. A vision for management of complex models. *SIGMOD Record*, 29(4):55–63, 2000.

[6] P. Bohannon, E. Elnahrawy, W. Fan, and M. Flaster. Putting context into schema matching. In *VLDB*, 2006.

[7] A. Bonifati et al. Heptox: Marrying xml and hetergeneity in your p2p databases. In *VLDB*, 2005.

[8] L. Cabibbo. On keys, foreign keys and nullable attributes in relational mapping systems. In *EDBT*, pages 263–274, 2009.

[9] R. Dhamankar et al. imap: Discovering complex mappings between database schemas. In *SIGMOD*, 2004.

[10] H. Elmeleegy, M. Ouzzani, and A. Elmagarmid. Usage-based schema matching. In *ICDE*, 2008.

[11] R. Fagin et al. Clio: Schema mapping creation and data exchange. *Conceptual Modeling: Foundations and Applications*, pages 198–236, 2009.

[12] R. Fagin, P. G. Kolaitis, and L. Popa. Data exchange: Getting to the core. *ACM TODS*, 30(1):174–210, 2005.

[13] A. Fuxman, M. A. Hernandez, H. Ho, R. J. Miller, P. Papotti, and L. Popa. Netsed mappings: Schema mapping reloaded. In *VLDB*, 2006.

[14] G. Gottlob, R. Pichler, and V. Savenkov. Normalization and optimization of schema mappings. *PVLDB*, 2(1):1102–1113, 2009.

[15] A. Halevy, Z. G. Ives, J. Madhavan, P. Mork, D. Suciu, and I. Tatarinov. The piazza peer data management system. *TKDE*, 16(7):787–798, 2004.

[16] Z. Kedad and M. Bouzeghoub. Discovering view expressions from a multi-source information system. In *CoopIS*, 1999.

[17] D. Maier and A. Mendelzon. Testing implications of data dependencies. *ACM TODS*, 4:455–469, 1979.

[18] B. Marnette, G. Mecca, and P. Papotti. Scalable data exchange with functional dependencies. *PVLDB*, 3(1):105–116, 2010.

[19] G. Mecca, P. Papotti, and S. Raunich. Core schema mappings. In *SIGMOD*, 2009.

[20] G. Mecca, P. Papotti, S. Raunich, and M. Buoncristiano. Concise and expressive mappings with +spicy. *PVLDB*, 2(2):1582–1585, 2009.

[21] R. J. Miller, L. M. Haas, and M. A. Hernández. Schema mapping as query discovery. In *VLDB*, 2000.

[22] T. Milo and S. Zohar. Using schema matching to simplify heterogeneous data translation. In *VLDB*, 1998.

[23] L. Popa, Y. Velegrakis, R. J. Miller, M. A. Hernandez, and R. Fagin. Translating web data. In *VLDB*, 2002.

[24] E. Rahm and P. A. Bernstein. A survey of approaches to automatic schema matching. *VLDB J.*, 10(4):334–350, 2001.

[25] M. Stonebraker. Implementation of integrity constraints and views by query modification. In *SIGMOD*, 1975.

[26] B. ten Cate et al. Laconic schema mappings: Computing the core with sql queries. *PVLDB*, 2(1):1006–1017, 2009.

[27] The TPC-W benchmark. http://tpc.org/tpcw.

[28] http://www.ece.wisc.edu/ pharm/tpcw.shtml.

[29] C. Yu and L. Popa. Constraint-based xml rewriting for data integration. In *SIGMOD*, 2004.

[30] C. Yu and L. Popa. Semantic adaptation of schema mappings when schemas evolve. In *VLDB*, 2005.

Designing and Refining Schema Mappings via Data Examples*

Bogdan Alexe
UCSC
abogdan@cs.ucsc.edu

Balder ten Cate
UCSC
balder.tencate@gmail.com

Phokion G. Kolaitis
UCSC & IBM Research - Almaden
kolaitis@cs.ucsc.edu

Wang-Chiew Tan
IBM Research - Almaden & UCSC
wangchiew@us.ibm.com

ABSTRACT

A schema mapping is a specification of the relationship between a source schema and a target schema. Schema mappings are fundamental building blocks in data integration and data exchange and, as such, obtaining the right schema mapping constitutes a major step towards the integration or exchange of data. Up to now, schema mappings have typically been specified manually or have been derived using mapping-design systems that automatically generate a schema mapping from a visual specification of the relationship between two schemas.

We present a novel paradigm and develop a system for the interactive design of schema mappings via data examples. Each data example represents a partial specification of the semantics of the desired schema mapping. At the core of our system lies a sound and complete algorithm that, given a finite set of data examples, decides whether or not there exists a GLAV schema mapping (i.e., a schema mapping specified by Global-and-Local-As-View constraints) that "fits" these data examples. If such a fitting GLAV schema mapping exists, then our system constructs the "most general" one.

We give a rigorous computational complexity analysis of the underlying decision problem concerning the existence of a fitting GLAV schema mapping, given a set of data examples. Specifically, we prove that this problem is complete for the second level of the polynomial hierarchy, hence, in a precise sense, harder than NP-complete. This worst-case complexity analysis notwithstanding, we conduct an experimental evaluation of our prototype implementation that demonstrates the feasibility of interactively designing schema mappings using data examples. In particular, our experiments show that our system achieves very good performance in real-life scenarios.

Categories and Subject Descriptors: H.2.5 [Database Management]: Heterogeneous Databases; H.2.4 [Database Management]: Systems - *relational databases*

General Terms: Algorithms, Design, Languages

Keywords: schema mappings, data examples, data exchange, data integration

*Research on this paper was supported by NSF grant IIS-0905276 and NSF Career Award IIS-0347065.

1. INTRODUCTION

A schema mapping is a high-level, declarative specification of the relationship between two database schemas, usually called the source schema and the target schema. By now, schema mappings are regarded as the fundamental building blocks in data exchange and data integration (see the surveys [5, 16, 17]). A crucial first step in these and other major data inter-operability tasks is the design and derivation of schema mappings between two database schemas.

Due to the complexity and scale of many real-world schemas, designing the "right" schema mapping can be a daunting task. This is further exacerbated by the fact that the formal specification of a schema mapping between such real-world schemas is typically long and difficult to grasp. For this reason, several different mapping-design systems have been developed to facilitate the process of designing schema mappings. These systems include Clio [15], HePToX [7], Microsoft's mapping composer [6], Altova Mapforce[1], and Stylus Studio[2]. The latter two systems directly produce transformations in the form of executable code, but can be viewed as implicitly constructing a schema mapping. Declarative specifications of schema mappings, as opposed to executable code, are more amenable to reasoning and analysis of data inter-operability tasks; furthermore, such specifications can be compiled into executable code for data exchange.

All mapping-design systems mentioned above adhere to the same general methodology for facilitating the process of designing schema mappings. Specifically, first a visual specification of the relationship between elements of the source and target schemas is solicited from the user (perhaps with the help of a schema matching module) and then a schema mapping is derived from the visual specification. However, several pairwise logically inequivalent schema mappings may be consistent with a visual specification, and, as noted in [4], differing schema mappings may be produced from the same visual specification, depending on which system is used. Thus, the user is still required to understand the formal specification in order to understand the semantics of the derived schema mapping.

In this paper, we present an alternative paradigm and develop a novel system for designing and refining schema mappings interactively via data examples. The intended users of our system are mapping designers who wish to design a schema mapping over a pair of source and target relational schemas. Furthermore, our system is tailored for schema mappings specified by *GLAV (Global-and-Local-As-View) constraints* (also known as *source-to-target tuple generating dependencies*, or *s-t tgds*). We call such schema mappings *GLAV schema mappings*. GLAV constraints have been extensively studied in the context of data exchange and data integration [16, 17]. The GLAV schema mappings contain, as important spe-

[1] http://www.altova.com/mapforce.html

[2] http://www.stylusstudio.com/xml_mapper.html

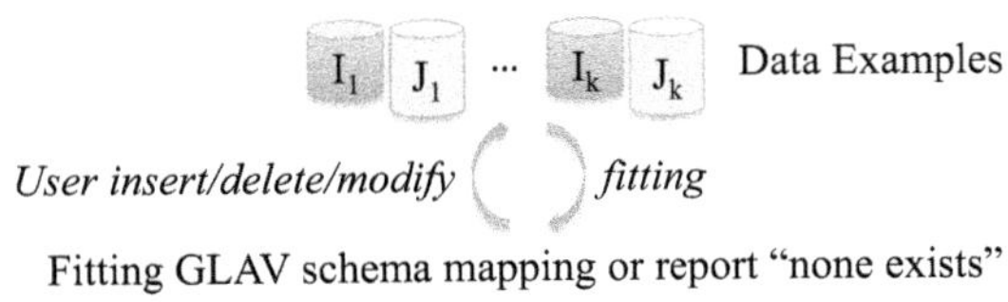

Figure 1: Workflow for interactive design and refinement of schema mappings via data examples.

cial cases, *Local-As-View (LAV)* schema mappings and *Global-As-View (GAV)* schema mappings. They are also used in such systems as Clio [15] and HePToX [7].

An important property of every GLAV schema mapping $\mathcal{M}$, first identified in [9], is that for every source instance I, there is a target instance J that is a *universal solution for I w.r.t. $\mathcal{M}$*. Intuitively, a universal solution of I w.r.t. $\mathcal{M}$ is a "most general" target instance of I that, together with I, satisfies the specifications of $\mathcal{M}$. Furthermore, a universal solution for I represents, in a precise technical sense, the entire space of solutions for I. As a result, universal solutions have become the preferred solutions and the standard semantics of data exchange. Our system makes systematic use of universal solutions, as we explain next.

The interaction between the user and our system begins with the user providing an initial finite set $\mathcal{E}$ of data examples, where a data example is a pair (I, J) consisting of a source instance and a target instance that conform to a source and target relational schema. Intuitively, each data example in $\mathcal{E}$ provides a partial specification of the semantics of the desired schema mapping. Furthermore, the user stipulates that, for each data example (I, J), the target instance J is a *universal solution for I* w.r.t. the desired schema mapping. The system responds by generating a GLAV schema mapping that *fits* the data examples in $\mathcal{E}$ or by reporting that no such GLAV schema mapping exists. Here, we say that a schema mapping $\mathcal{M}$ *fits a set $\mathcal{E}$* of data examples if for every data example $(I, J) \in \mathcal{E}$, the target instance J is a universal solution of the source instance I w.r.t. $\mathcal{M}$. The user is then allowed to modify the data examples in $\mathcal{E}$ and provide the system with another finite set $\mathcal{E}'$ of data examples. After this, the system tests whether or not there is a GLAV schema mapping that fits $\mathcal{E}'$ and, as before, returns such a GLAV schema mapping, if one exists, or reports that none exists, otherwise. The cycle of generating schema mappings and modifying data examples can be repeated until the user is satisfied with the schema mapping obtained in this way. We call this process the *interactive refinement* of a schema mapping via data examples. The workflow of our system is depicted in Figure 1.

The GLAV Fitting Algorithm At the core of our system lies a sound and complete algorithm for determining the existence of a fitting GLAV schema mapping, given a finite set of data examples. This GLAV fitting algorithm has several desirable properties. To begin with, if a fitting GLAV schema mapping exists, then the algorithm returns the *most general* fitting GLAV schema mapping. In other words, it returns a fitting GLAV schema mapping $\mathcal{M}$ such that for every alternative (non-equivalent) fitting GLAV schema mapping $\mathcal{M}'$, we have that $\mathcal{M}'$ logically implies $\mathcal{M}$. This is clearly the most natural choice among all the fitting GLAV schema mappings. The correctness of our algorithm is based on the following key technical result: the existence of a GLAV schema mapping that fits a given set $\mathcal{E}$ of data examples can be determined using a *homomorphism extension test*, which is an effective procedure that checks whether every homomorphism from the source instance of a data example $E_1 \in \mathcal{E}$ to that of another data example $E_2 \in \mathcal{E}$ can be extended to a homomorphism from the target instance of E_1 to the target instance of E_2. Actually, this homomorphism extension condition not only is a necessary and sufficient condition for the existence of a fitting GLAV schema mapping, but also implies the existence of a most general fitting GLAV schema mapping; furthermore, once the homomorphism extension test has been completed, the most general fitting GLAV schema mapping can be computed from the data examples $\mathcal{E}$ in linear time. The second and perhaps even more important feature of our algorithm is that our paradigm of designing schema mappings via data examples is complete, in the sense that every GLAV schema mapping can be produced by our algorithm. More precisely, for every GLAV schema mapping $\mathcal{M}$, there is a finite set of data examples $\mathcal{E}$ such that, when $\mathcal{E}$ is given as input, our GLAV fitting algorithm will produce a GLAV schema mapping that is logically equivalent to the desired one.

Complexity analysis The GLAV fitting algorithm that we described above runs in exponential time in the worst case. This is so because the homomorphism extension test entails examining, in the worst case, exponentially many homomorphisms. We show that, unless P = NP, this worst-case behavior is unavoidable. Indeed, we show that the underlying *GLAV fitting decision problem* (i.e., the problem of deciding whether, given a finite set of data examples, there is a fitting GLAV schema mapping) is Π_2^p-complete, where Π_2^p is the second level of the polynomial hierarchy. In particular, this means that, in all likelihood, the GLAV fitting decision problem is harder than NP-complete. Furthermore, we show that the *GLAV fitting verification problem* (i.e., the problem of deciding whether a given GLAV schema mapping fits a given set of data examples) is Π_2^p-complete as well.

Experimental Evaluation We built a prototype system and conducted an extensive experimental evaluation. In this evaluation, our system achieved very good performance on sets of data examples based on real-life scenarios, and thus confirmed the feasibility of interactively designing and refining schema mappings via data examples. The experimental results supporting this finding, as well as other observations regarding the behavior of our system on a variety of real-life and synthetic scenarios are discussed in Section 5.

1.1 An Illustration of Our System

Next, we will describe our system with a hypothetical execution of the workflow for Figure 1.

Suppose a user wishes to design a schema mapping between the source schema and target schema shown in the top-left corner of Figure 2. The source schema has two relations: Patient and Doctor, and the target schema has two relations: History and Physician. As a first step, the user specifies a single data example, shown in the first box, which essentially states that `Anna` is the doctor of patient `Joe`, whose health plan is `Plus`, and date-of-visit is `Jan`. In the target relation, there is a single fact that consolidates this information, omitting the name of the patient.

Based on this single data example, our system will infer that the desired schema mapping is the one shown on the right of the box. This schema mapping states that whenever a Patient tuple and Doctor tuple agree on the `pid` value (i.e., a natural join between Patient and Doctor), create a target tuple with the `pid`, `healthplan`, `date`, and `docid` values from Patient and Doctor. The user may choose to refine the data example further. (It may be because she realized that there was a typographical error in the specified data example, or she may have examined the schema mapping returned by the system and decide that further refinements are needed.)

After refinement, the data example shown in the second box is obtained. For this data example, the source instance remains unchanged, but the user has now modified the target instance to consist of two tuples: a History tuple and a Physician tuple which are "connected" through the value `N1`. Observe that the values `N1`

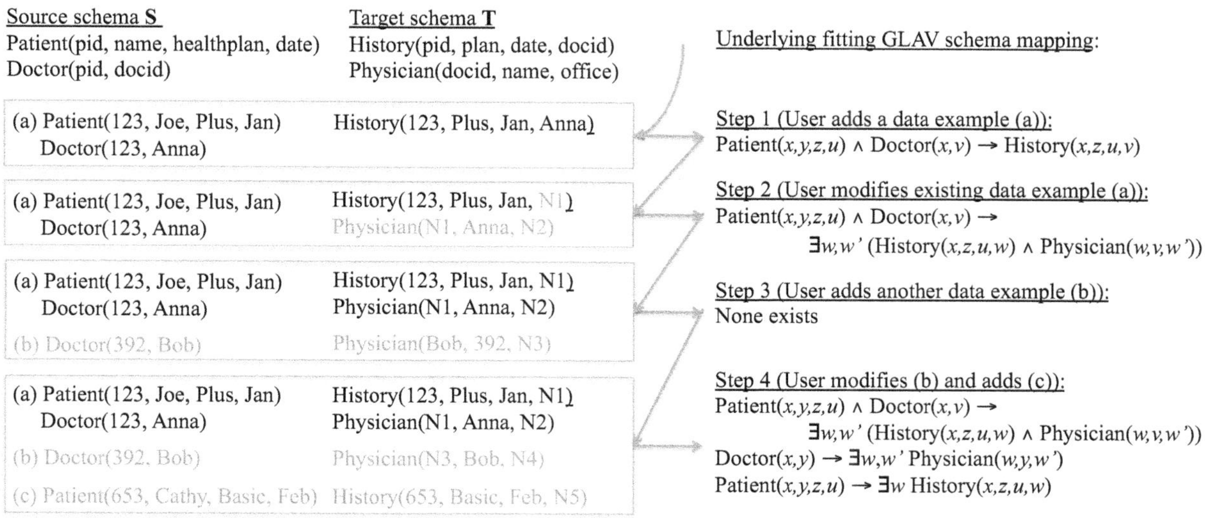

Figure 2: An example of Figure 1. Left: Each box is an input set of data examples. Right: Derived schema mapping, or none exists.

and N2 in the target instance do not occur among the values of the source instance and they, intuitively, represent unknown and possibly different values. Based on this single data example, our system infers the desired schema mapping shown on the right (i.e., under Step 2). Intuitively, this schema mapping states that information from the inner join of Patient and Doctor should be migrated to the target History and Physician relations, with appropriate nulls to represent unknown and possibly different values.

Further refinement steps can occur on the data examples. In the third box of Figure 2, the user adds a second data example (b) to the existing data example, and our system now reports that no schema mapping can "fit". This is because data example (b) describes a pattern of data migration that is inconsistent with data example (a): According to (b), every Doctor(pid,docid) fact in the source must have a corresponding Physician(docid,pid,office) fact in the target. Observe that the `pid` value is copied to the second column of the corresponding Physician fact. However, this is inconsistent with what (a) states, where a Doctor(pid, docid) has a corresponding Physician(_,docid,_) fact in the target, and `docid` gets copied to the second column of the corresponding Physician fact instead.

Finally, in the fourth box, the user modifies data example (b) and adds a third data example (c). Based on these data examples, our system reports the schema mapping shown under Step 4 on the right. Essentially, the schema mapping migrates information from the outer join of Doctor and Patient to the corresponding relations in the target.

1.2 Related Work

Data examples have already been used to illustrate different syntactic objects such as relational queries [18], dataflow programs [19], and schema mappings [2, 23]. These papers assume the existence of a syntactic object, and the goal is to produce informative examples that highlight particular features of the syntactic object under consideration. In addition, the systems of [2, 23] support the selection of a schema mapping among competing alternatives by offering the user a choice of examples, each of which illustrates one of the alternative schema mappings.

More recent work [3, 22] investigated whether or not a schema mapping can be uniquely characterized via a finite set of data examples of different types. Universal examples turned out to be the most robust and useful type of data example for capturing schema mappings, where a universal example is a data example (I, J) such that J is a universal solution for I w.r.t. a schema mapping. In particular, in [3] it was shown that for every LAV schema mapping, there is a finite set of universal examples that uniquely characterizes it among all LAV schema mappings. Furthermore, in [22], a necessary and sufficient condition was given for the unique characterizability of GAV schema mappings. The robustness and usefulness of universal examples are the reasons why we assume that for every input data example (I, J) to our system, the user intends that J is a universal solution for I w.r.t. the schema mapping that she has in mind.

Finally, there is a body of work on deriving a relational query or a schema mapping from one or more data examples [12, 13, 14, 21]. The work of [14] gave a theoretical framework and complexity results for the problem of deriving a schema mapping from a single data example. Even though a cost model is proposed to choose among schema mappings that can be used to describe a data example, they do not provide a direct algorithm for deriving a schema mapping from the data example. In [12], the goal is to heuristically derive a syntactic expression whose semantics coincide with a (possibly infinite) set of data examples. The papers [13, 21] are closer to our work, but both consider unirelational schemas only. The problem studied in [13] takes as input a finite set of pairs consisting of a single source relation and a single target relation, and asks whether or not there is a relational algebra expression that produces each of the target relations when evaluated on the corresponding source relation. In [21], a problem similar to the preceding one is studied, except that only a rather restricted class of relational algebra expressions (essentially unions of selections) is considered. In addition, the authors consider variations of the problem that take into account the size of the syntactic descriptions and notions of approximation.

2. PRELIMINARIES

Schemas and Instances A *relational schema* $\mathbf{R}$ is a finite sequence $(P_1, \ldots, P_k)$ of relation symbols, each of a fixed arity. An *instance* K over $\mathbf{R}$ is a sequence $(P_1^K, \ldots, P_k^K)$, where each P_i^K is a relation of the same arity as P_i. We shall often write P_i to denote both the relation symbol and the relation P_i^K that interprets it. Here, we assume that all values occurring in relations belong to some fixed infinite set dom of values. A *fact* of an instance K over a schema $\mathbf{R}$ is an expression $P(a_1, \ldots, a_m)$ such that P is a relation symbol of $\mathbf{R}$ and $(a_1, \ldots, a_m) \in P^K$. We denote by

$\mathrm{adom}(K)$ the *active domain* of an instance K, that is to say, the set of all values from dom occurring in facts of K.

Schema Mappings In what follows, we will typically consider two relational schemas, a *source schema* $\mathbf{S}$ and a *target schema* $\mathbf{T}$. We will often use I to denote an instance of $\mathbf{S}$ and J to denote an instance of $\mathbf{T}$, and we will refer to I as a *source instance* and to J as a *target instance*. A *schema mapping* is a triple $\mathcal{M} = (\mathbf{S}, \mathbf{T}, \Sigma)$ consisting of a source schema $\mathbf{S}$, a target schema $\mathbf{T}$, and a set Σ of constraints that are usually expressed as formulas in some logical formalism. In this paper, we focus on schema mappings specified by GLAV constraints. By definition, a *GLAV (Global-Local-As-View) constraint* is a first-order sentence φ of the form

$$\forall \mathbf{x}(\varphi(\mathbf{x}) \rightarrow \exists \mathbf{y}\psi(\mathbf{x}, \mathbf{y})),$$

where $\varphi(\mathbf{x})$ is a conjunction of atoms over $\mathbf{S}$, each variable in $\mathbf{x}$ occurs in at least one atom in $\varphi(\mathbf{x})$, and $\psi(\mathbf{x}, \mathbf{y})$ is a conjunction of atoms over $\mathbf{T}$ with variables from $\mathbf{x}$ and $\mathbf{y}$. By an *atom* over a schema $\mathbf{R}$, we mean a formula $P(x_1, \ldots, x_m)$, where $P \in \mathbf{R}$ and $x_1, \ldots, x_m$ are variables, not necessarily distinct. For notational simplicity, we will often drop the universal quantifiers $\forall \mathbf{x}$ in the front of GLAV constraints.

GLAV constraints contain both GAV constraints and LAV constraints as important special cases. A *GAV (Global-As-View)* constraint is a GLAV constraint in which the right-hand side is a single atom, i.e., it is of the form

$$\forall \mathbf{x}(\varphi(\mathbf{x}) \rightarrow P(\mathbf{x})) \ ,$$

while a *LAV (Local-As-View)* constraint is a GLAV constraint in which the left-hand side is a single atom, i.e., it is of the form

$$\forall \mathbf{x}(Q(\mathbf{x}) \rightarrow \exists \mathbf{y}\psi(\mathbf{x}, \mathbf{y})) \ .$$

As an illustration of these notions, the constraint

$$\mathrm{Patient}(x, y, z, u) \wedge \mathrm{Doctor}(x, v) \rightarrow$$
$$\exists w, w'(\mathrm{History}(x, z, u, w) \wedge \mathrm{Physician}(w, v, w'))$$

is a GLAV constraint that is neither a GAV nor a LAV constraint. The constraint

$$\mathrm{Patient}(x, y, z, u) \wedge \mathrm{Doctor}(x, v) \rightarrow \mathrm{History}(x, z, u, v)$$

is a GAV constraint that is not a LAV constraint, while

$$\mathrm{Doctor}(x, y) \rightarrow \exists w, w'\mathrm{Physician}(w, y, w')$$

is a LAV constraint that is not a GAV constraint.

A *GLAV schema mapping* is a schema mapping $\mathcal{M} = (\mathbf{S}, \mathbf{T}, \Sigma)$ such that Σ is a finite set of GLAV constraints. Similarly, *GAV schema mappings* and *LAV schema mappings* are schema mappings in which Σ is a finite set of GAV constraints or, respectively, a finite set of LAV constraints.

Let $\mathcal{M} = (\mathbf{S}, \mathbf{T}, \Sigma)$ be a schema mapping, I a source instance, and J a target instance. We say that J is a *solution of I w.r.t. $\mathcal{M}$* if $(I, J) \models \Sigma$, i.e., if (I, J) satisfies every constraint in Σ.

As a concrete example, suppose the source schema consists of the relation symbol Patient, the target schema consists of the relation symbol Physician, and the schema mapping $\mathcal{M}$ is specified by the LAV constraint $\mathrm{Doctor}(x, y) \rightarrow \exists w, w'\mathrm{Physician}(w, y, w')$. Consider the source instance

$$I = \{\mathrm{Doctor}(123, \mathrm{Anna}), \mathrm{Doctor}(392, \mathrm{Bob})\}$$

and the target instances

$$J_1 = \{\mathrm{Physician}(N1, \mathrm{Anna}, N2), \mathrm{Physician}(N3, \mathrm{Bob}, N4)\}$$
$$J_2 = \{\mathrm{Physician}(N1, \mathrm{Anna}, N2), \mathrm{Physician}(392, \mathrm{Bob}, N4)\}$$
$$J_3 = \{\mathrm{Physician}(N1, \mathrm{Anna}, N2)\}.$$

Both J_1 and J_2 are solutions for I w.r.t. $\mathcal{M}$, but J_3 is not. Observe that the solutions J_1 and J_2 contains values (namely, $N1$, $N2$, $N3$, $N4$) that do not occur in the active domain of the source instance I. Intuitively, these values can be thought of as labeled nulls.

Data Exchange, Homomorphisms, and Universal Solutions *Data exchange* is the following problem: given a schema mapping $\mathcal{M}$ and a source instance I, construct a solution J for I w.r.t. $\mathcal{M}$. As we just saw, a source instance may have more than one solution with respect to a given GLAV schema mapping. We will be interested expressly in *universal solutions*, which were identified in [9] as the preferred solutions for data exchange purposes. Universal solutions are defined in terms of *homomorphisms*, as follows.

Let I_1 and I_2 be two instances over the same relational schema $\mathbf{R}$. A *homomorphism* $h : I_1 \rightarrow I_2$ is a function from $\mathrm{adom}(I_1)$ to $\mathrm{adom}(I_2)$ such that for every fact $P(a_1, \ldots, a_m)$ of I_1, we have that $P(h(a_1), \ldots, h(a_m))$ is a fact of I_2. We write $I_1 \rightarrow I_2$ to denote the existence of a homomorphism $h : I_1 \rightarrow I_2$.

Let $\mathcal{M} = (\mathbf{S}, \mathbf{T}, \Sigma)$ be a schema mapping and let I be a source instance. A target instance J is a *universal solution* for I w.r.t. $\mathcal{M}$ if the following hold:

1. J is a solution for I w.r.t. $\mathcal{M}$.
2. For every solution J' of I w.r.t. $\mathcal{M}$, there is a homomorphism $h : J \rightarrow J'$ that is constant on $\mathrm{adom}(I) \cap \mathrm{adom}(J)$, that is to say, $h(a) = a$, for every value $a \in \mathrm{adom}(I) \cap \mathrm{adom}(J)$.

Intuitively, universal solutions are the "most general" solutions. Furthermore, in a precise sense, they represent the entire space of solutions (see [9]). For this reason, universal solutions have become the standard semantics for data exchange. Going back to our previous example, note that J_1 is a universal solution for I w.r.t the schema mapping $\mathcal{M}$ specified by the LAV constraint $\mathrm{Doctor}(x, y) \rightarrow \exists w, w'\mathrm{Physician}(w, y, w')$. In contrast, J_2 is not a universal solution for I w.r.t. $\mathcal{M}$, since there is no homomorphism from J_2 to J_1 that is constant on $\mathrm{adom}(I) \cap \mathrm{adom}(J_2)$.

For GLAV schema mappings $\mathcal{M}$ (and in fact for a much wider class of schema mappings), a variant of the *chase procedure* can be used to compute, given a source instance I, a *canonical* universal solution for I w.r.t. $\mathcal{M}$ in time bounded by a polynomial in the size of I (see [9]).

3. THE FITTING PROBLEM

In this section, we describe our algorithms for the fitting problem and its variants, prove the correctness of the algorithms, and obtain sharp complexity results for the fitting problem and its variants.

DEFINITION 3.1. Let $\mathbf{S}$ be a source schema and $\mathbf{T}$ be a target schema. A *data example* is a pair (I, J) such that I is a source instance and J is a target instance.

We say that a schema mapping $\mathcal{M} = (\mathbf{S}, \mathbf{T}, \Sigma)$ *fits a data example* (I, J) if J is a universal solution for I w.r.t. $\mathcal{M}$.

We say that $\mathcal{M}$ *fits a set $\mathcal{E}$ of data examples* if $\mathcal{M}$ fits every data example $(I, J) \in \mathcal{E}$.

Returning to the example of Section 2, the schema mapping specified by $\mathrm{Doctor}(x, y) \rightarrow \exists w, w'\mathrm{Physician}(w, y, w')$ fits the data example (I, J_1), but does not fit (I, J_2).

Data examples were considered in [3] as a means to illustrate and understand schema mappings. Several different notions of "fitting" were explored, including the just defined notion of fitting in terms of universal examples. This notion was shown in [3, 22] to be the most robust and useful one for capturing schema mappings via data examples.

One could also consider an alternative notion of "fitting" in which a schema mapping $\mathcal{M}$ fits a data example (I, J) if J is a solution (not necessarily a universal solution) for I w.r.t. $\mathcal{M}$. The main reason we chose to use universal solutions in the notion of fitting is that universal solutions, being the most general solutions, are natural as data examples. Universal solutions contain just the information needed to represent the desired outcome of migrating data from source to target. In particular, they contain no extraneous or overspecified facts, unlike arbitrary solutions in general.

We now introduce two variants of the fitting problem, namely, the *fitting generation problem*, which is a function problem, and the *fitting decision problem*, which is the underlying decision problem. We begin with the latter.

DEFINITION 3.2. (GLAV Fitting Decision Problem) Given a source schema $\mathbf{S}$, a target schema $\mathbf{T}$, and a finite set $\mathcal{E}$ of data examples that conform to the schemas, the *GLAV Fitting Decision Problem* asks to tell whether or not there is a GLAV schema mapping $\mathcal{M}$ that fits $\mathcal{E}$.

DEFINITION 3.3. (GLAV Fitting Generation Problem) Given a source schema $\mathbf{S}$, a target schema $\mathbf{T}$, and a set $\mathcal{E}$ of data examples that conform to the schemas, the *GLAV Fitting Generation Problem* asks to construct a GLAV schema mapping $\mathcal{M}$ that fits $\mathcal{E}$, if such a schema mapping exists, or to report that "None exists", otherwise.

In a similar manner, we can define analogous fitting problems for GAV schema mappings and for LAV schema mappings. These problems will be briefly considered towards the end of this section. Our main focus, however, will be on the fitting problems for GLAV schema mappings.

Note that the alternative notion of "fitting" with solutions in place of universal solutions gives rise to trivial fitting decision and fitting generation problems since, in this case, the schema mapping with an empty set of constraints would "fit" every data example (I, J) (in fact, it would be the most general "fitting" schema mapping).

3.1 The GLAV Fitting Algorithm

In this section, we present our algorithm for the GLAV Fitting Generation Problem and establish its properties. The algorithm is given in Figure 3. We begin by discussing the main steps of the algorithm in detail.

As seen in Figure 3, our algorithm has two main steps. Given a finite set $\mathcal{E}$ of data examples, the first step of the algorithm tests for the existence of a GLAV schema mapping fitting $\mathcal{E}$. If no such fitting GLAV schema mapping exists, then the algorithm simply reports that none exists. Otherwise, the second step of the algorithm proceeds to construct a GLAV schema mapping that fits the set $\mathcal{E}$. Actually, the GLAV schema mapping constructed by our algorithm will turn out to have a number of additional desirable properties that we will document in what follows.

Homomorphism Extension Test Let (I, J) and (I', J') be two data examples. We say that a homomorphism $h : I \to I'$ *extends to a homomorphism* $\widehat{h} : J \to J'$ if for all $a \in adom(I) \cap adom(J)$, we have that $\widehat{h}(a) = h(a)$. The first step of the algorithm consists of the *homomorphism extension test*. Specifically, for every pair of data examples from the given set $\mathcal{E}$, the algorithm tests whether every homomorphism between the source instances of the two examples extends to a homomorphism between the corresponding target instances. If this homomorphism extension test fails, the algorithm reports that no GLAV schema mapping fitting the set $\mathcal{E}$ exists. Otherwise, it proceeds to the next step.

Constructing a Fitting Canonical GLAV Schema Mapping In the second step of the algorithm, we make crucial use of the notion of

---

Algorithm: GLAV Fitting
Input: A source schema $\mathbf{S}$ and a target schema $\mathbf{T}$
A finite set $\mathcal{E}$ of data examples $(I_1, J_1) \ldots (I_n, J_n)$ over $\mathbf{S}, \mathbf{T}$
Output: Either a fitting GLAV schema mapping or 'None exists'

// Homomorphism Extension Test:
// Test for existence of a fitting GLAV schema mapping
for all $i, j \le n$ **do**
  for all homomorphisms $h : I_i \to I_j$ **do**
    if not(h extends to a homomorphism $\widehat{h} : J_i \to J_j$) **then**
      fail('None exists')
    end if
  end for
end for;
// Construct a fitting canonical GLAV schema mapping
$\Sigma := \emptyset$;
for all $i \le n$ **do**
  add to Σ the canonical GLAV constraint of (I_i, J_i)
end for;
return $(\mathbf{S}, \mathbf{T}, \Sigma)$

Figure 3: The GLAV Fitting Generation Algorithm

a *canonical GLAV schema mapping* associated with a set of data examples. Intuitively, this is analogous to the familiar notion of a *canonical conjunctive query* associated with a database instance. If (I, J) is a data example, then the *canonical GLAV constraint of* (I, J) is the GLAV constraint $\forall \mathbf{x}(q_I(\mathbf{x}) \to \exists \mathbf{y} q_J(\mathbf{x}, \mathbf{y}))$, where $q_I(\mathbf{x})$ is the conjunction of all facts of I (with each value from the active domain of I replaced by a universally quantified variable from $\mathbf{x}$) and $q_J(\mathbf{x}, \mathbf{y})$ is the conjunction of all facts of J (with each value from $\text{adom}(J) \setminus \text{adom}(I)$ replaced by an existentially quantified variable from $\mathbf{y}$). If $\mathcal{E}$ is a finite set of data examples over a source schema $\mathbf{S}$ and a target schema $\mathbf{T}$, then the *canonical GLAV schema mapping of* $\mathcal{E}$ is the schema mapping $\mathcal{M} = (\mathbf{S}, \mathbf{T}, \Sigma)$, where Σ consists of the canonical GLAV constraints of the data examples in $\mathcal{E}$. The second step of the algorithm amounts simply to computing the canonical GLAV schema mapping of the given set of data examples. Notice that this step takes time linear in the size of the given set $\mathcal{E}$ of data examples.

It is important to point out that the canonical GLAV schema mapping of a given set of data examples need *not* fit this set of examples; as a matter of fact, this is what makes the GLAV fitting generation problem interesting and nontrivial. To illustrate this, consider the set $\mathcal{E}$ consisting of the data examples $(\{S(a, b)\}, \{T(a)\})$ and $(\{S(c, c)\}, \{U(c, d)\})$. The canonical GLAV schema mapping of $\mathcal{E}$ is specified by the GLAV constraints $\forall xy(S(x, y) \to T(x))$ and $\forall x(S(x, x) \to \exists z U(x, z))$. This schema mapping does not fit $\mathcal{E}$, as the second data example violates the first constraint. Note also that our homomorphism extension test in the first step of the algorithm would detect this: the homomorphism h that maps $S(a, b)$ to $S(c, c)$ does not extend to any target homomorphism from $T(a)$ to $U(c, d)$. Hence, in this case, our algorithm will terminate after the first step and report that "None exists".

Correctness The following result establishes the correctness of the GLAV fitting generation algorithm in Figure 3.

THEOREM 3.4. *Let $\mathcal{E}$ be a finite set of data examples. The following statements are equivalent:*

1. *The canonical GLAV schema mapping of $\mathcal{E}$ fits $\mathcal{E}$.*
2. *There is a GLAV schema mapping that fits $\mathcal{E}$.*
3. *For all $(I, J), (I', J') \in \mathcal{E}$, every homomorphism $h : I \to I'$ extends to a homomorphism $\widehat{h} : J \to J'$.*

PROOF HINT. The proof proceeds in a round-robin fashion. The implication $1 \Rightarrow 2$ is immediate. The implication $2 \Rightarrow 3$ is proved using a monotonicity property of the chase. Finally, the implication $3 \Rightarrow 1$ follows from the construction of the canonical GLAV schema mapping. The basic idea is that, if (I, J) and (I', J') are data examples and $\forall \mathbf{x}(\phi(\mathbf{x}) \rightarrow \exists \mathbf{y}\ \psi(\mathbf{x}, \mathbf{y}))$ is the canonical GLAV constraint of (I, J), then each homomorphisms $h : I \rightarrow I'$ corresponds to an assignment for $\mathbf{x}$ under which $\phi(\mathbf{x})$ is true in I', and each extension $\widehat{h} : J \rightarrow J'$ of h corresponds to an assignment for $\mathbf{x}, \mathbf{y}$ under which $\psi(\mathbf{x}, \mathbf{y})$ is true in J'. □

The last condition in Theorem 3.4 is the homomorphism extension test used in the first step of the algorithm. Theorem 3.4 shows that this is a necessary and sufficient condition for determining whether GLAV schema mapping fitting $\mathcal{E}$ exists. Furthermore, this condition is also a necessary and sufficient condition for determining whether the canonical GLAV schema mapping of $\mathcal{E}$ fits $\mathcal{E}$. Hence, the algorithm is correct in that it reports that no fitting GLAV schema mapping exists, if there is none, and it returns a fitting GLAV schema mapping, whenever there is one.

Most General Fitting GLAV Schema Mapping Given a finite set $\mathcal{E}$ of data examples, there may be a multitude of GLAV schema mappings that fit it. For example, both $R(x, y) \rightarrow P(x, y)$ and $R(x, x) \rightarrow P(x, x)$ fit the data example $(\{R(a, a)\}, \{P(a, a)\})$. In this case, the GLAV fitting algorithm will return the latter mapping $R(x, x) \rightarrow P(x, x)$. We will see that our GLAV fitting algorithm does this for a very good reason. Specifically, if a fitting GLAV schema mapping exists, then our algorithm returns *the most general* fitting GLAV schema mapping.

Let $\mathcal{M} = (\mathbf{S}, \mathbf{T}, \Sigma)$ and $\mathcal{M}' = (\mathbf{S}, \mathbf{T}, \Sigma)$ be two schema mappings over the same source and target schemas. We say that $\mathcal{M}$ is *more general than* $\mathcal{M}'$ if Σ' logically implies Σ, i.e., if for every data example (I, J) such that (I, J) satisfies Σ', we have that (I, J) also satisfies Σ.

THEOREM 3.5. *Let $\mathcal{E}$ be a finite set of data examples. If there is a GLAV schema mapping that fits $\mathcal{E}$, then the canonical GLAV schema mapping of $\mathcal{E}$ is the most general GLAV schema mapping that fits $\mathcal{E}$. In other words, the canonical GLAV schema mapping is more general than any GLAV schema mapping that fits $\mathcal{E}$.*

Theorems 3.4 and 3.5 imply that if a fitting GLAV schema mapping exists for a given set $\mathcal{E}$ of data examples, then our GLAV fitting algorithm returns the most general GLAV schema mapping that fits $\mathcal{E}$. Note that this most general schema mapping is unique up to logical equivalence.

The most general schema mapping produced by our GLAV fitting generation algorithm has size linear in the size of the input set of data examples. This linear bound on the size of the most general schema mapping cannot be improved in general. To see this, for every integer $n > 2$, consider the data example (I_n, J_n), where $I_n = \{E(1,2), E(2,3), \ldots, E(n-1, n)\}$ and $J_n = \{F(1, n)\}$. Then, for every n, the most general schema mapping fitting (I_n, J_n) is the schema mapping $\mathcal{M}_n$ specified by the single s-t tgd $E(x_1, x_2) \wedge E(x_2, x_3) \wedge \ldots \wedge E(x_{n-1}, x_n) \rightarrow F(x_1, x_n)$. It is not hard to see that no schema mapping logically equivalent to $\mathcal{M}_n$ has size less than that of $\mathcal{M}_n$. This is so because, intuitively, a schema mapping $\mathcal{M}$ that is logically equivalent to $\mathcal{M}_n$ must contain an s-t tgd where the left-hand-side has at least $n - 1$ atoms.

The most general GLAV schema mapping $\mathcal{M}$ enjoys a robustness property in that $\mathcal{M}$ can be used to derive the "certain certain answers", as we describe next. Let $\mathcal{M} = (\mathbf{S}, \mathbf{T}, \Sigma)$ be a schema mapping and let q be a query over the target schema $\mathbf{T}$. If I is a source instance, then the *certain answers of q on I w.r.t. $\mathcal{M}$*, denoted by $\text{certain}_{\mathcal{M}}(q, I)$, are defined by

$$\text{certain}_{\mathcal{M}}(\text{q, I}) = \bigcap\{\text{q(J)} : J \text{ is a solution for } I \text{ w.r.t. } \mathcal{M}\}.$$

The certain answers are the standard semantics of target queries in data exchange [9]. Now, it is not hard to show that if $\mathcal{M} = (\mathbf{S}, \mathbf{T}, \Sigma)$ and $\mathcal{M}' = (\mathbf{S}, \mathbf{T}, \Sigma')$ are two GLAV schema mappings such that $\mathcal{M}$ is more general than $\mathcal{M}'$, then for every source instance I and for every target conjunctive query q, we have that $\text{certain}_{\mathcal{M}}(q, I) \subseteq \text{certain}_{\mathcal{M}'}(q, I)$. In turn, this observation implies the following result.

COROLLARY 3.6. *Let $\mathcal{E}$ be a finite set of data examples for which there exists a GLAV schema mapping that fits it. Let $\mathcal{G}$ be the set of all GLAV schema mappings that fit $\mathcal{E}$ and let $\mathcal{M} \in \mathcal{G}$ be the canonical GLAV schema mapping of $\mathcal{E}$. Then, for every source instance I and every target conjunctive query q, we have that* $\text{certain}_{\mathcal{M}}(q, I) = \bigcap_{\mathcal{M}' \in \mathcal{G}} \text{certain}_{\mathcal{M}'}(q, I)$.

Informally, Corollary 3.6 asserts that if $\mathcal{E}$ is a finite set of data examples, then the certain answers of a target conjunctive query w.r.t. to the canonical GLAV schema mapping of $\mathcal{E}$ are the "certain certain answers" over all GLAV schema mappings that fit $\mathcal{E}$.

Completeness for GLAV-Schema-Mapping Design A more important beneficial feature of the GLAV fitting algorithm that we wish to highlight here is that it is *complete for GLAV-schema-mapping design*, in the sense expressed by the next result.

THEOREM 3.7. *For every GLAV schema mapping $\mathcal{M}$, there is a finite set of data examples $\mathcal{E}_{\mathcal{M}}$, such that, when given $\mathcal{E}_{\mathcal{M}}$ as input, the GLAV fitting algorithm returns a schema mapping that is logically equivalent to $\mathcal{M}$.*

In other words, every GLAV schema mapping can be produced (up to logical equivalence) by our GLAV fitting algorithm. The proof of Theorem 3.7 is based on the notion of a *canonical set of examples for a GLAV schema mapping* (cf. also Section 5). Let $\mathcal{M} = (\mathbf{S}, \mathbf{T}, \Sigma)$ be a GLAV schema mapping. For every GLAV constraint $\sigma \in \Sigma$ of the form $\forall \mathbf{x}(\phi(\mathbf{x}) \rightarrow \exists \mathbf{y} \psi(\mathbf{x}, \mathbf{y}))$, let I_σ be the canonical instance of $\phi(\mathbf{x})$ and let J_σ be the universal solution of I_σ w.r.t. $\mathcal{M}$ obtained by chasing I_σ with Σ. We define the *canonical set of examples of* $\mathcal{M}$ to be the set of all examples (I_σ, J_σ) such that $\sigma \in \Sigma$. Now, it can be verified that, for every GLAV schema mapping $\mathcal{M}$, the canonical schema mapping of the canonical set of examples of $\mathcal{M}$ is logically equivalent to $\mathcal{M}$; consequently, Theorem 3.7 holds.

Complexity Analysis As mentioned earlier, the second step of the GLAV fitting algorithm is linear in the size of the input set of data examples. In contrast, the first step of the GLAV fitting algorithm can be exponential, since the number of homomorphisms between two database instances can be exponential; thus, the GLAV fitting algorithm runs in exponential time in the worst case. Furthermore, this worst-case behavior is realized on every input for which a fitting GLAV schema mapping exists, since, in such cases, it is not possible to terminate early the task of verifying that every homomorphism between the source instances of every pair of data examples indeed extends to a homomorphism on the respective target instances. However, the GLAV fitting algorithm needs a polynomial amount of memory only; this is so because the size of each particular homomorphism is polynomial, and it is possible to enumerate all homomorphisms between two instances using only a polynomial amount of memory.

Assuming that P $\neq$ NP, this exponential worst-case running time is unavoidable. Indeed, every algorithm that solves the GLAV

Fitting Generation Problem also solves the GLAV Fitting Decision Problem, which is NP-hard. In fact, our next result shows that the GLAV Fitting Decision Problem is complete for the second level Π_2^p of the polynomial hierarchy **PH**, hence, in all likelihood, it is harder than NP-complete. Recall that Π_2^p (also known as coNP^{NP}) is the class of all decision problems that can be solved by a coNP-algorithm using an NP-complete problem as an oracle. Furthermore, $\text{NP} \cup \text{coNP} \subseteq \Pi_2^p \subseteq \text{PSPACE}$ (see [20]).

THEOREM 3.8. *The GLAV Fitting Decision Problem is Π_2^p-complete.*

The GLAV fitting algorithm in Figure 3 actually shows that the GLAV fitting decision problem is in the class Π_2^p. Indeed, the homomorphism extension test in the first step involves a universal quantification over homomorphisms followed by an existential quantification over homomorphisms; this is a Π_2^p-computation. The Π_2^p-hardness of the GLAV fitting decision problem is proved via a reduction from the evaluation problem for quantified Boolean formulas of the form $\forall \mathbf{x} \exists \mathbf{y} \psi(\mathbf{x}, \mathbf{y})$, where $\psi(\mathbf{x}, \mathbf{y})$ is a 3CNF Boolean formula. Perhaps surprisingly, the lower bound holds even for inputs consisting of a single data example over fixed schemas; roughly speaking, for a given quantified Boolean formula of the form $\forall \mathbf{x} \exists \mathbf{y} \psi(\mathbf{x}, \mathbf{y})$, an example (I, J) is constructed in such a way that each nontrivial endomorphism of I corresponds to a valuation for $\mathbf{x}$, and J has facts describing the clauses of $\psi(\mathbf{x}, \mathbf{y})$.

We conclude the complexity analysis by mentioning in passing a consequence that Theorem 3.8 has for another variant of the fitting problem.

DEFINITION 3.9. (GLAV Fitting Verification Problem) Given a GLAV schema mapping $\mathcal{M} = (\mathbf{S}, \mathbf{T}, \Sigma)$ and a finite set $\mathcal{E}$ of data examples, the *GLAV Fitting Verification Problem* asks to tell whether or not $\mathcal{M}$ fits $\mathcal{E}$.

COROLLARY 3.10. *The GLAV Fitting Verification Problem is Π_2^p-complete.*

In other words, testing for the existence of a fitting GLAV schema mapping is no harder than testing whether a given GLAV schema mapping fits a given set of data examples. The lower bound follows directly from Theorems 3.4 and 3.8. The proof of the upper bound uses (among other things) the fact that GLAV constraints belong to the universal-existential fragment of first-order logic.

3.2 GAV and LAV Schema Mappings

GAV schema mappings and LAV schema mappings are syntactically simpler types of GLAV schema mappings that enjoy several additional good properties and are supported by many data-exchange and data-integration systems. In this section, we consider the GAV fitting generation problem and the LAV fitting generation problem, i.e., the problem that asks, given a finite set $\mathcal{E}$ of data examples, to generate a GAV (or a LAV) schema mapping that fits $\mathcal{E}$. Note that even if, for a given set of data examples, there exists a fitting GAV or fitting LAV schema mapping, there is no guarantee that a GLAV fitting generation algorithm (and, in particular, our GLAV fitting algorithm) will produce such a GAV or a LAV schema mapping. In what follows, we discuss how our GLAV fitting generation algorithm can be adapted in order to solve the GAV fitting generation problem and the LAV fitting generation problem.

GAV schema mappings It is known from [22] that the GAV fitting decision problem is DP-complete, and that it is NP-complete for inputs consisting of ground data examples. We say a data example (I, J) is *ground* if $adom(J) \subseteq adom(I)$. In other words, the instance J consists entirely of values from I.

THEOREM 3.11 ([22]). *The GAV fitting decision problem is DP-complete. It is coNP-complete if the input consists of ground data examples.*

As in the GLAV case, the lower bounds hold already for inputs consisting of a single example, over a fixed source schema and target schema. Recall that DP is the class of problems that can be defined as the conjunction of an NP-problem and a coNP-problem. It is known that $\text{NP} \cup \text{coNP} \subseteq \text{DP} \subseteq \Pi_2^p$, and it is widely believed that both containments are proper. In particular, just as in the GLAV case, we cannot hope for a polynomial-time algorithm that solves the GAV fitting generation problem.

We present here a concrete algorithm for solving the GAV fitting generation problem. The algorithm is given in Figure 4. It is a variation of the algorithm for the GLAV fitting generation problem given in Figure 3. Comparing the two algorithms, one can see that there are three essential differences.

The first difference is that the algorithm checks that each data example is essentially ground. Recall that we say a data example is *ground* if $adom(J) \subseteq adom(I)$. A data example is *essentially ground* if there is a homomorphism $h : J \to J$ such that $h(a) = a$ for all $a \in adom(I)$, and such that $rng(h) \subseteq adom(I)$. This is equivalent to saying that the core of J (as defined in [11], where the values from $adom(I)$ are viewed as constants, and the values from $adom(J) \setminus adom(I)$ are viewed as labeled nulls) contains only values from $adom(I)$.

The second difference is that the homomorphism extension test is now simplified. The test simply checks whether every homomorphism between the source instances of two examples is also a partial homomorphism (i.e., a partial function that preserves facts) between the corresponding target instances. Another way to say the same thing is that for every pair of examples $(I, J), (I', J')$, every homomorphism $h : I \to I'$ is a homomorphism from $J_\downarrow$ to $J'_\downarrow$, where $J_\downarrow$ is the subinstance of J containing only values from $\text{adom}(I)$, and $J'_\downarrow$ is the subinstance of J' containing only values from $\text{adom}(I')$.

Third, instead of constructing the *canonical GLAV schema mapping*, the algorithm constructs the *canonical GAV schema mapping*. For any set $\mathcal{E}$ of examples, the *canonical GAV schema mapping of* $\mathcal{E}$ is defined in the same way as the canonical GLAV schema mapping of $\mathcal{E}$, but ignoring all target facts containing nulls. In other words, the canonical GAV schema mapping of $\mathcal{E}$ is the canonical GLAV schema mapping of $\{(I, J_\downarrow) \mid (I, J) \in \mathcal{E}\}$), where $J_\downarrow$ consists of all facts of J that contain only values from $\text{adom}(I)$. Note that this is indeed a GAV schema mapping.

The correctness of our algorithm is given by the following result.

THEOREM 3.12. *Let $\mathcal{E}$ be a finite set of data examples. The following are equivalent:*

- *The canonical GAV schema mapping of $\mathcal{E}$ fits $\mathcal{E}$.*
- *There is a GAV schema mapping that $\mathcal{E}$.*
- *Each data example $(I, J) \in \mathcal{E}$ is essentially ground, and for all $(I, J), (I', J') \in \mathcal{E}$, every homomorphism $h : I \to I'$ is a partial homomorphism $h : J \to J'$.*

The proof of Theorem 3.12 is along the same lines as the one of Theorem 3.4, but using also the fact that, for GAV schema mappings, every source instance has a ground universal solution.

As in the GLAV case, the GAV schema mapping produced by our algorithm is the most general fitting GAV schema mapping.

THEOREM 3.13. *Let $\mathcal{E}$ be a finite set of data examples for which there exists a fitting GAV schema mapping. Then the canonical GAV schema mapping of $\mathcal{E}$ is the most general fitting GAV schema mapping of $\mathcal{E}$.*

Algorithm: GAV fitting
Input: A source schema **S** *and a target schema* **T**
A finite set of data examples $(I_1, J_1) \ldots (I_n, J_n)$ *over* **S**, **T**
Output: either a fitting GAV schema mapping or 'None exists'

// Test that each data example is essentially ground
for all $i \leq n$ **do**
  if not(there is a homomorphism $h : J_i \rightarrow J_i$ such that
    $h(a) = a$ for all $a \in adom(I)$ and $rng(h) \subseteq adom(I)$) **then**
    fail('None exists');
  end if
end for;
// Simplified Homomorphism Extension Test:
// test for the existence of a fitting GAV schema mapping
for all $i, j \leq n$ **do**
  for all homomorphisms $h : I_i \rightarrow I_j$ **do**
    if not(h is a partial homomorphism $h : J_i \rightarrow J_j$) **then**
      fail('None exists')
    end if
  end for
end for;
// Construct fitting canonical GAV schema mapping
$\Sigma := \emptyset$;
for all $i \leq n$ **do**
  add to Σ the canonical GAV constraint of (I_i, J_i)
end for;
return (**S**, **T**, Σ)

Figure 4: The GAV Fitting Generation Algorithm

Theorem 3.13 is implicit in [22], even though the notion of a canonical GAV schema mapping was not introduced there.

Furthermore, just as the GLAV fitting generation algorithm is complete for GLAV-schema-mapping design (cf. Theorem 3.7), in the same way the GAV fitting generation algorithm can be shown to be complete for GAV-schema-mapping design.

THEOREM 3.14. *For every GAV schema mapping $\mathcal{M}$, there is a finite set of data examples $\mathcal{E}_{\mathcal{M}}$, such that, when given $\mathcal{E}_{\mathcal{M}}$ as input, the GAV fitting algorithm returns a schema mapping that is logically equivalent to $\mathcal{M}$.*

LAV schema mappings For LAV schema mappings, the situation is a bit different. Unlike in the case of GLAV schema mappings or GAV schema mappings, there is no natural notion of a *canonical LAV* schema mapping, for a given set of examples. Furthermore, a set of examples for which there are fitting LAV schema mappings may not have a most general fitting LAV schema mapping. Indeed, consider the single example (I, J) where $I = \{P(a), Q(a)\}$ and $J = \{R(a)\}$. It is not hard to see that there are two incomparable maximally general fitting LAV schema mappings, specified by the LAV constraints $\forall x(P(x) \rightarrow R(x))$ and $\forall x(Q(x) \rightarrow R(x))$ respectively. Nevertheless, the LAV fitting generation problem can be solved in exponential time. For lack of space, we omit a detailed description of the algorithm, and state only the following result:

THEOREM 3.15. *The LAV fitting decision problem is NP-complete.*

The upper bound is proved by giving a non-deterministic polynomial-time algorithm that has an accepting run if and only if there is a LAV fitting decision problem, and that, moreover, computes a fitting LAV schema mapping if it exists. The algorithm builds on results from [10, 11] concerning core solutions, retracts, and fact blocks. Roughly speaking, it starts by guessing a retract of the target instance of each data example. It then computes the fact blocks of the retracted target instances. Next, it guesses for each fact block a single source tuple that can intuitively be seen as being responsible for the creation of this fact block. Based on these guesses, a candidate LAV schema mapping is constructed, and finally, the algorithm tests in non-deterministic polynomial time if this LAV schema mapping fits the original data examples.

The lower bound is proved by a reduction from the NP-complete problem of whether two graphs are homomorphically equivalent. The lower bound holds even for a single example over a fixed schema, containing only two source tuples, or for two examples, each containing a single source tuple.

4. IMPLEMENTATION

We describe briefly our approach for the implementation of the GLAV fitting generation algorithm, presented in pseudocode in Figure 3. We will focus on the homomorphism extension test (also known henceforth simply as the *fitting test*), since constructing the canonical GLAV schema mapping is straightforward: it basically requires a linear pass over the set of data examples.

Let $\mathcal{E}$ be a set of data examples for the pair of schemas $(\mathbf{S}, \mathbf{T})$. Our system stores these data examples in the IBM DB2 database system. The logical design being used follows closely the schemas $(\mathbf{S}, \mathbf{T})$, with the addition of an extra attribute exid in each relation that identifies the data example to which a particular tuple belongs. To illustrate, reconsider the set of two data examples in step 3 of Figure 2, which we will denote by (I_1, J_1) and (I_2, J_2). These examples are stored in the database as in Figure 5.

Patient

exid	pid	name	healthplan	date
1	123	Joe	Plus	Jan

Doctor

exid	pid	docid
1	123	Anna
2	392	Bob

History

exid	pid	plan	date	docid
1	123	Plus	Jan	N1

Physician

exid	docid	name	office
1	N1	Anna	N2
2	Bob	392	N3

I_1 (rows with exid 1 of Patient and Doctor), I_2 (row with exid 2 of Doctor); J_1 (rows with exid 1 of History and Physician), J_2 (row with exid 2 of Physician)

Figure 5: Database instance used to store the set of data examples in step 3 of Figure 2

The fitting test over $\mathcal{E}$ is implemented as a set of DB2 user-defined functions, one for each data example in $\mathcal{E}$. Intuitively, the function associated to an example $E_1 = (I_1, J_1) \in \mathcal{E}$ tries to find a witness to the failure of the fitting test: whether for some example $E_2 = (I_2, J_2) \in \mathcal{E}$, there exists a homomorphism from I_1 to I_2 which does not extend to a homomorphism from J_1 to J_2. In effect, if such a homomorphism exists, then there is no fitting GLAV schema mapping for the set $\mathcal{E}$ of data examples.

From the Chandra-Merlin theorem for conjunctive queries [8], we know that computing homomorphisms from an instance I_1 to an instance I_2 is equivalent to executing the canonical query of I_1 on I_2. The results of executing the canonical query of I_1 on I_2, hence the valuations for the variables in the canonical query of I_1, provide the homomorphisms from I_1 to I_2. Returning to the data examples above, the canonical query of I_1 has the following form:

$$Q^{I_1} : \text{Patient}(x, y, z, t) \land \text{Doctor}(x, u)$$

This query contains one relational atom for each tuple in I_1, and it employs repeated variables for multiple occurrences of a value in I_1 (e.g., the variable x for the value 123). Executing Q^{I_1} on I_1 returns the identity homomorphism from I_1 to itself. However, executing Q^{I_1} on I_2 returns an empty answer, since there are no homomorphisms from I_1 to I_2, as there are no Patient tuples in I_2.

In our implementation, the function associated to each example $E \in \mathcal{E}$ essentially executes a nested SQL query, where the outer and inner blocks are (correlated) canonical queries of the source and target instances of E, respectively. More concretely, the nested SQL query has the following form:

$$\underline{\text{select}}\ s_1.\text{exid}\ \underline{\text{from}}\ S_1\ s_1, \ldots, S_p\ s_p$$
$$\underline{\text{where}}\ s_2.\text{exid} = s_1.\text{exid}\ \underline{\text{and}} \ldots \underline{\text{and}}\ s_p.\text{exid} = s_1.\text{exid}$$
$$\underline{\text{and}}\ C_1\ \underline{\text{and}} \ldots \underline{\text{and}}\ C_k$$
$$\underline{\text{and not exists}}$$
$$(\ \underline{\text{select}}\ T_1.\text{exid}\ \underline{\text{from}}\ T_1\ t_1, \ldots, T_q\ t_q$$
$$\underline{\text{where}}\ t_1.\text{exid} = s_1.\text{exid}\ \underline{\text{and}} \ldots \underline{\text{and}}\ t_q.\text{exid} = s_1.\text{exid}$$
$$\underline{\text{and}}\ C'_1\ \underline{\text{and}} \ldots \underline{\text{and}}\ C'_m\ )$$

In the query above, the from clauses contain one variable for each tuple of the source instance, and the target instance, respectively (in other words, one variable for each relational atom in the source and target canonical queries). The first set of equality conditions in the where clauses ensure that all tuples in the result belong to the same data example, identified by the same exid value. Furthermore, the conditions $C_i, 1 \leq i \leq k$ are equalities corresponding to multiple appearances of the same value in the source instance. Similarly, $C'_j, 1 \leq j \leq m$ correspond to multiple appearances of the same value in the target instance, or to a source value appearing in the target instance.

Continuing our illustration, the instantiation of the template above for the example (I_1, J_1) has the form shown at the end of this paragraph. It will return an empty result since there are no homomorphisms from I_1 to I_2. However, the corresponding query for (I_2, J_2) will return a non-empty result. The homomorphism $\{392 \rightarrow 123, \text{Bob} \rightarrow \text{Anna}\}$ from I_2 to I_1 cannot be consistently extended to a homomorphism from J_2 to J_1, hence it represents a witness to the failure of the fitting test.

$$\underline{\text{select}}\ p.\text{exid}\ \underline{\text{from}}\ \text{Patient}\ p, \text{Doctor}\ d$$
$$\underline{\text{where}}\ d.\text{exid} = p.\text{exid}$$
$$\underline{\text{and}}\ p.\text{pid} = d.\text{pid}$$
$$\underline{\text{and not exists}}$$
$$(\ \underline{\text{select}}\ h.\text{exid}\ \underline{\text{from}}\ \text{History}\ h, \text{Physician}\ y$$
$$\underline{\text{where}}\ h.\text{exid} = p.\text{exid}\ \underline{\text{and}}\ y.\text{exid} = p.\text{exid}$$
$$\underline{\text{and}}\ h.\text{pid} = p.\text{pid}\ \underline{\text{and}}\ h.\text{plan} = p.\text{healthplan}$$
$$\underline{\text{and}}\ h.\text{date} = p.\text{date}\ \underline{\text{and}}\ h.\text{docid} = y.\text{docid}$$
$$\underline{\text{and}}\ y.\text{name} = d.\text{docid}\ )$$

The fitting test succeeds if the functions corresponding to all the data examples return empty answers.

4.1 An Optimization

The number of tuple variables in the from clauses of the nested SQL queries described above is equal to the number of tuples in the source and target instances of the data examples. For arbitrary sets of data examples, this can lead to very large joins which translate to very long execution times for the fitting test. However, in our experience, such very large data examples proved to be uncommon in user-interactive schema mapping design scenarios.

The following theorem provides an optimization for the fitting test because it allows the test to be decomposed into tests that apply to disconnected components. By a *connected component* of a data example (I, J) we mean a set of elements from $adom(I) \cup adom(J)$ that forms a connected component of the Gaifman graph of (I, J) (i.e., the graph that contains an edge between two values if they co-occur in a fact of I or J).

THEOREM 4.1. *For all source instances I_1, I_2 and target instances J_1, J_2, the following are equivalent:*

- *Every homomorphism $h : I_1 \rightarrow I_2$ extends to a homomorphism $\widehat{h} : J_1 \rightarrow J_2$*
- *Either there is no homomorphism $h : I_1 \rightarrow I_2$, or for every connected component C of $I_1 \cup J_1$, every homomorphism $h : I_1 \cap C \rightarrow I_2$ extends to a homomorphism $\widehat{h} : J_1 \cap C \rightarrow J_2$.*

This result justifies the decomposition of the queries that implement the fitting test into simpler uncorrelated queries which can be evaluated independently. Intuitively, each simpler nested SQL statement executes the canonical queries of a data example subinstance corresponding to a connected component. As a consequence, the number of tuple variables in the from clauses decreases. Our experiments confirm the intuition that such decrease leads to an improvement in fitting test execution times.

As an important particular case, the fitting test function we generate becomes much simpler for a data example whose target instance contains only nulls. Intuitively, the nested SQL statement generated for such a data example is replaced by a sequence of two independent SQL statements without nesting, each implementing the canonical query of the source and the target instance, respectively. We will examine the effects of this optimization in the experimental analysis of Section 5.2.

5. EVALUATION

In the following, we present an experimental evaluation of our framework for designing schema mappings via data examples. We implemented our approach as a prototype in Java 6, with IBM DB2 Express-C v9.7 as the underlying database engine, running on a Dual Intel Xeon 3.4GHz Linux workstation with 4GB RAM.

We begin by giving an overview of the datasets used in our experiments. Then we present results concerning the efficiency of our implementation of the GLAV fitting algorithm, as well as some observations on the behavior of the fitting test when the structural characteristics of the underlying dataset change. Finally, we test our approach in a dynamic setting that simulates an interactive schema mapping refinement process.

The worst-case complexity of the GLAV fitting problem notwithstanding, the experimental results that we have obtained demonstrate the feasibility of interactively designing schema mappings using data examples. In particular, our experiments show that our system achieves very good performance in real-life scenarios.

5.1 Datasets

For our experimental evaluation, we use sets of data examples based on real-life schema mapping scenarios, as well as synthetically generated datasets.

Data examples based on real-life scenarios. We consider three real-life mapping scenarios. The first two involve scientific bibliographies (DBLP: `dblp.uni-trier.de/db` and Amalgam: `dblab.cs.toronto.edu/~miller/amalgam`, with mappings inspired by the Clio benchmarks[3]), and the third is from the biological domain (on fragments of the GUS:`www.gusdb.org` and BioSQL: `www.biosql.org` schemas). Some statistics on these scenarios are presented in the left half of Table 1. For instance, in the DBLP-Amalgam scenario, the source schema consists of 7 relations of average arity 6.5, and the target schema consists of 9 relations of the same average arity 6.5. Moreover, the schema mapping in this scenario is specified by 10 GLAV constraints, averaging 1.4 atoms in the left-hand-side and 2.2 atoms in the right-hand-side.

We use the *canonical sets of data examples*, introduced in Section 3.1, for each of the real-life mapping scenarios as input to our fitting algorithm. In the canonical set of data examples for a schema mapping, the source instances are the canonical instances of the

[3] queens.db.toronto.edu/project/clio/index.php#testschemas

	# of source relations	Avg. source arity	# of target relations	Avg. target arity	# of GLAV constraints	Avg. # of LHS atoms	Avg. # of RHS atoms	# of canonical examples	Time to generate canonical examples (s)	Avg. # of nonempty source relations	Avg. # of tuples per source relation	Avg. # of nonempty target relations	Avg. # of tuples per target relation
DBLP - Amalgam	7	6.5	9	6.5	10	1.4	2.2	10	4.8	1.4	1.0	2.2	1.1
Amalgam S1 - S2	15	6.7	27	2.0	71	1.2	2.1	15	9	1.9	1.0	10.7	1.1
GUS - BioSQL	7	6.4	6	5.5	8	1.6	1.9	7	2.3	1.6	1.1	2.1	2.3

Table 1: Statistics on real-life mapping scenarios and their canonical examples

left-hand-sides for each GLAV constraint in the mapping specification (pruned for isomorphic copies), and the target instances are the results of *chasing* each source instance with the schema mapping. We consider here a variant of the *chase procedure* (see [1]), called the *naive* chase. Given a source instance I, the naive chase produces a universal solution [9] for I, denoted by $chase_{\mathcal{M}}(I)$, as follows. For every GLAV constraint

$$\forall \mathbf{x}(\varphi(\mathbf{x}) \rightarrow \exists \mathbf{y}\psi(\mathbf{x},\mathbf{y}))$$

in the specification of $\mathcal{M}$ and for every tuple $\mathbf{a}$ of source values from $\text{adom}(I)$ such that $I \models \varphi(\mathbf{a})$, we add to $chase_{\mathcal{M}}(I)$ all facts in $\psi(\mathbf{a},\mathbf{b})$, where $\mathbf{b}$ is a tuple of new nulls interpreting the existentially quantified variables $\mathbf{y}$.

Through the construction of the canonical sets of examples, the GLAV fitting algorithm will always return a positive answer on such sets of examples, since the chase procedure generates universal solutions. The canonical examples make a good test case to stress our implementation of the fitting test, because the guaranteed positive fitting result means the system indeed iterates over all source homomorphisms and checks for target extensions, since a failure witness is not encountered. In addition, by Theorem 3.7, the execution of the fitting algorithm on the set of canonical examples for a schema mapping $\mathcal{M}$ will produce a schema mapping that is logically equivalent to $\mathcal{M}$. Hence, the canonical examples are a natural choice as the starting point in an example driven refinement of an initial mapping specification.

Statistics on the canonical data examples of the real-life scenarios we used are presented in the right half of Table 1. For instance, the set of canonical data examples for the DBLP-Amalgam scenario consists of 10 data examples, and took 4.8 seconds to generate. Each canonical data example has on the average 1.4 nonempty source relations with one tuple each, and 2.2 nonempty target relations with 1.1 tuples each.

Synthetic data examples. To stress test the performance of the fitting test, we use synthetic sets of data examples for the schemas of the real-life mapping scenarios. The generation of the synthetic datasets is controlled via four parameters (n, t, d, f), as follows:

- n is the number of data examples in the dataset
- t is the number of tuples for each relation in the schemas
- d, called *diversity*, controls the number of occurrences of distinct values, hence determines the size of the domains for the source and target instances of a data example
- f, called *source value fraction*, determines how the domain of a target instance is split between source values and nulls.

More precisely, consider a pair of schemas $(\mathbf{S},\mathbf{T})$. In our experiments, these schemas originate in the real-life mapping scenarios considered above. Given a parameter tuple (n,t,d,f), a set $\mathcal{E}$ of n data examples is generated as follows. Every example $E = (I,J) \in \mathcal{E}$ contains, for each $R \in (\mathbf{S},\mathbf{T})$, an R relation consisting of t tuples. The domain of the source instance I is $D = \{a_1,\ldots,a_m\}$, where $m = d \times t \times \sum_{R \in \mathbf{S}} \text{arity}(R)$. Each value in I is chosen through a uniform random pick from D. The domain of the target instance J is $D' = \{a_1,\ldots,a_k,b_{k+1},\ldots,b_{m'}\}$, where $m' = d \times t \times \sum_{R \in \mathbf{T}} \text{arity}(R)$, and $k = \min(|\text{adom}(I)|, f \times m')$. The values $\{a_1,\ldots,a_k\}$ are among the source values appearing in I, while the rest of the values in D' are fresh nulls. Each value in J is picked through a uniform random choice from D'.

5.2 Fitting Test Efficiency

We now describe the experiments we conducted to determine the efficiency of the fitting test on the canonical sets of examples for the real-life scenarios. The results for this first set of experiments are presented in Table 2 (the rightmost column will be discussed in Section 5.3), and are averaged over 50 experimental runs.

We remark that performing the GLAV fitting test on the canonical examples for the real-life scenarios takes only a few seconds (1.6, 3.6, 1.2), showing this is a promising first step in designing schema mapping via examples, following the workflow in Figure 1. Data examples of size comparable to the canonical examples are common in a user-interactive schema design environment.

	Number of examples	Size of each example (# of source + target tuples)	Initial fitting test (s)	Fitting test per user change (s)
DBLP - Amalgam	10	3.8	1.6	0.2
Amalgam S1 - S2	15	13.7	3.6	0.3
GUS - BioSQL	7	6.6	1.2	0.2

Table 2: Experimental results on canonical data examples of real-life scenarios

We conducted additional experimental analysis to determine the performance of the fitting test on different types of synthetic sets of data examples on the schemas of the real-life scenarios. The synthetic data examples are generated following the procedure in Section 5.1. We used sets of $n = 10$ data examples, where in each example, each source and each target relation was populated with $t = 3$ tuples. In the GUS-BioSQL scenario, this translates to 21 source tuples and 18 target tuples in each data example, for a total of 210 source tuples and 180 target tuples over the entire set of data examples. The experimental results for the synthetic data examples based on the GUS-BioSQL scenario are presented in Figure 6. The trends exhibited by the sets of synthetic data examples based on the remaining two scenarios, as well as for other values of the synthetic data generation parameters are not shown here, but are similar. The results we present are averaged over 200 experimental runs.

For the first experiment, in **Figure 6(a)**, we kept the source value fraction parameter f constant at 0.7, and we varied the diversity parameter d from 0.1 to 1.2 in increments of 0.1. The decrease in the fitting test execution times as the diversity increases is justified by the progressive simplification of the queries our system generates (see Section 4). When the diversity of an instance increases, repeated occurrences of a given value become less frequent, hence the canonical queries that are executed for the GLAV fitting test contain where clauses with fewer conditions, the rest being equal. This, combined with the fact that our implementation cannot make use of indexes (since we do not possess apriori knowledge on the

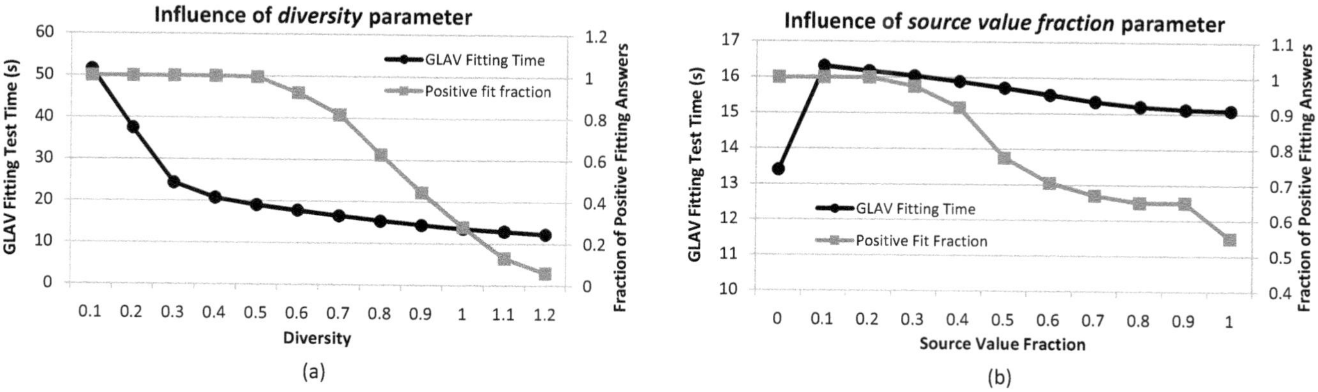

Figure 6: Experimental results for the fitting test on synthetic sets of data examples based on the GUS - BioSQL scenario: 10 data examples, each consisting of 39 tuples (21 in the source and 18 in the target) (a) Influence of the *diversity* parameter, when the *source value fraction* is 0.7; (b) Influence of the *source value fraction* parameter, when the *diversity* is 0.8.

values used in the data examples), explains the decrease in execution times. We also remark the decrease in the fraction of positive answers to the GLAV fitting test as the diversity parameter increases. Intuitively, the number of source homomorphisms increases as diversity increases (the canonical queries of the source instances become less constrained). Since the majority of values in the target instances are source values, it becomes increasingly difficult to find, for each source homomorphism h, a target homomorphism $\widehat{h}$ that is in fact an extension of h.

In the second experiment, we varied the source value fraction parameter between 0 and 1, while maintaining the diversity parameter constant at 0.8. As shown in **Figure 6(b)**, we observe an initial increase in the GLAV fitting time, followed by a decreasing trend. The increase occurs when the source value fraction increases above 0. For the source value fraction equal to 0, the target instances contain only nulls. As we mentioned in Section 4.1, the queries executed for the fitting test in this case can be simplified, leading to reduced execution times. When the source value fraction is greater than 0, the fitting test implementation executes the more involved nested and correlated SQL statements which take longer times to execute. However, as the source value fraction increases beyond 0.1, there is a slight decrease in the fitting test times. This happens because while the fraction of source values in the target instances increases, target homomorphisms become more pre-determined by the source homomorphisms. In other words, the space of target homomorphisms to be explored becomes smaller. In particular, when the source value fraction is 1, the target instances consist exclusively of source values, hence the fitting tests essentially perform only consistency checks. However, these are still more complex and require longer time than the simpler uncorrelated queries executed at source value fraction equal to 0. Finally, we remark the decrease in the fraction of positive answers to the fitting test as the source value fraction increases. This follows the intuition that as the source value fraction increases, the ratio of source values to nulls in the target instances increases, and thus it becomes more difficult to find consistent extensions of source homomorphisms to target homomorphisms.

Although the fitting test behaves well in terms of execution time on sets of data examples of practical size, the underlying high complexity of the decision procedure resurfaces in handcrafted scenarios like the following. Consider a source schema $\mathbf{S} = \{P\}$ and a target schema $\mathbf{T} = \{R\}$, where P and R are binary relations, and a set $\mathcal{E}$ consisting of the single data example (I, J), where $I = \{P(a, b_1), \ldots, P(a, b_n)\}$ and $J = \{R(c, b_1), \ldots, R(c, b_n)\}$. Even for relatively modest sizes of the data example above, such as for $n = 10$, the fitting test requires very long execution times. However, this is not entirely unexpected, since the fitting test was shown to be Π_2^{P}-complete (Theorem 3.8). In fact, in the scenario above, the number of source homomorphisms from I to itself is of the order n^n. We remark that encoding our fitting tests as quantified boolean formulas (QBF), followed by testing the satisfiability of such formulas using some of the leading QBF solvers[4] leads to similar very long execution times.

5.3 Interactive Mapping Refinement

To further investigate the practicality of our techniques, we simulate an interactive mapping refinement process via data examples, and study the behavior of the fitting test.

The simulation starts from a set of canonical examples for a real-life mapping scenario, or from a set of synthetic examples based on the schemas of a real-life scenario, and consists of a sequence of changes that a user might apply to the data examples to align them to the intended mapping semantics. The types of user changes we consider here are insertions and deletions of tuples in the target instances of data examples. In our experiments, each run consisted of a sequence of 20 changes, with equal probability tuple insertions or deletions. For a deletion change, the tuple to be deleted was chosen through a uniform random choice over the tuples in the target instances. For an insertion change, the target relation to be updated was chosen uniformly at random. Each value of the tuple to be inserted was chosen to be either a source value (with probability 0.4), or a null. If a null was inserted, it was either a fresh value (with probability 0.6), or one of the pre-existing nulls in the target instance. Furthermore, after the failure of a fitting test, the previous user change is undone with probability 0.75. This improves the realism of our simulation, by modeling situations in which the user decides to take back a change once the fitting test fails.

The results obtained following the simulations are presented in Table 2 for canonical sets of examples of the real-life scenarios, and in Table 3 for synthetic sets of examples based on the same scenarios. The synthetic examples were generated using the configuration tuple $(n = 10, t = 3, d = 0.6, f = 0.7)$, which was chosen here for illustration purposes, as the results obtained with other configuration parameters were similar. The numbers are averaged over 50 experimental runs. The times required for the fitting test scale as expected from the canonical data examples to the syn-

[4]http://www.qbflib.org/qbfeval

	Number of examples	Size of each example (# of source + target tuples)	Initial fitting test (s)	Fitting test per user change (s)
DBLP - Amalgam	10	48	17.7	1.8
Amalgam S1 - S2	10	126	222.4	23.1
GUS - BioSQL	10	39	14.2	1.5

Table 3: Interactive mapping refinement on synthetic sets of data examples ($n = 10, t = 3, d = 0.6, f = 0.7$) based on real-life scenarios

thetic data examples, given the significant increase in the size of each data example.

We remark a sharp decrease in the time needed for the fitting test after each of the user changes (column 5), from the initial test before the first user change (column 4). For instance, on the canonical sets of examples for the real-life scenarios, the decrease is from 1.6s to 0.2s, from 3.6s to 0.3s, and from 1.2s to 0.2s. This is a consequence of our implementation technique. In our experiments, the example sets were small enough to fit entirely in the DB2 buffer pool in main memory. Moreover, there were no other concurrent workloads on the database. Thus, the user changes updated data in main memory. Since there are no other workloads competing for buffer space, the updated examples are still in main memory when the next fitting test is performed. Hence these fitting tests execute much faster than the initial test, which needs to read the data from disk. In addition, after each user change on a data example E, only the definition of the function associated to E (see Section 4) has to be altered, redeployed to DB2 and recompiled.

Another consequence of our implementation approach is that a negative result for a fitting test is obtained faster than a positive result. In our experiments, positive fitting results represent a minority, which is not surprising, since intuitively it is difficult to maintain the existence of a fitting mapping through random changes. However, we observed that the times required for positive and negative fitting tests do not differ significantly. Hence, the sharp decrease in execution times during the interactive design simulation we discussed above is not significantly affected by this phenomenon.

6. CONCLUDING REMARKS

We developed a principled framework for the interactive design and refinement of schema mappings using data examples. A fundamental component of our framework is the GLAV fitting generation problem, which we brought into center stage and investigated in depth. We presented an algorithm that, given a finite set of data examples, either produces a GLAV schema mapping that fits these examples, or reports that none exists. We showed that the fitting schema mapping produced by the algorithm, if one such schema mapping exists, possesses several desirable properties. In particular, it is guaranteed to be the most general GLAV schema mapping that fits the given data examples, and also to have length linear in the total size of the input data examples. Furthermore, our GLAV fitting algorithm is complete for GLAV-schema-mapping design, in the sense that (up to logical equivalence) every GLAV schema mapping can be obtained by our algorithm when given the right set of data examples. In the worst-case, our GLAV fitting algorithm runs in exponential time, which is an inevitable consequence of the NP-hardness of the underlying GLAV fitting decision problem (in fact, we showed that this problem is complete for Π_2^p, hence harder than NP-complete). In spite of this worst-case complexity, extensive experimental evaluation of our prototype implementation established the viability of the example-driven approach to schema mapping design. In particular, interactive response times were achieved for real-life scenarios.

We believe that the example-driven approach to schema mapping design proposed here can be fruitfully combined with other extant approaches. Concretely, our approach may be used as a module within other schema-mapping-design systems, such as those described in the Introduction. After an initial candidate schema mapping is derived (for instance, on the basis of a visual specification), an initial set of data examples could be generated from this candidate schema mapping and presented to a user, who may either accept or modify the examples. By running our GLAV fitting generation algorithm on the updated set of data examples, a new schema mapping can then be generated, and this interactive process can be iterated until the user is satisfied with the result.

7. REFERENCES

[1] S. Abiteboul, R. Hull, and V. Vianu. *Foundations of Databases*. Addison-Wesley, 1995.

[2] B. Alexe, L. Chiticariu, R. J. Miller, and W. C. Tan. Muse: Mapping Understanding and deSign by Example. In *ICDE*, pages 10–19, 2008.

[3] B. Alexe, P. G. Kolaitis, and W. C. Tan. Characterizing schema mappings via data examples. In *ACM PODS*, pages 261–272, 2010.

[4] B. Alexe, W. C. Tan, and Y. Velegrakis. STBenchmark: Towards a Benchmark for Mapping Systems. *PVLDB*, 1(1):230–244, 2008.

[5] P. Barceló. Logical foundations of relational data exchange. *SIGMOD Record*, 38(1):49–58, 2009.

[6] P. A. Bernstein, T. J. Green, S. Melnik, and A. Nash. Implementing Mapping Composition. *VLDB Journal*, 17(2):333–353, 2008.

[7] A. Bonifati, E. Q. Chang, T. Ho, V. S. Lakshmanan, and R. Pottinger. HePToX: Marrying XML and Heterogeneity in Your P2P Databases. In *VLDB*, pages 1267–1270, 2005.

[8] A. K. Chandra and P. M. Merlin. Optimal implementation of conjunctive queries in relational data bases. In *STOC*, pages 77–90, 1977.

[9] R. Fagin, P. G. Kolaitis, R. J. Miller, and L. Popa. Data Exchange: Semantics and Query Answering. *TCS*, 336(1):89–124, 2005.

[10] R. Fagin, P. G. Kolaitis, A. Nash, and L. Popa. Towards a Theory of Schema-Mapping Optimization. In *ACM PODS*, pages 33–42, 2008.

[11] R. Fagin, P. G. Kolaitis, and L. Popa. Data Exchange: Getting to the Core. *ACM TODS*, 30(1):174–210, 2005.

[12] G. H. Fletcher and C. M. Wyss. Towards a general framework for effective solutions to the data mapping problem. *Journal on Data Semantics*, XIV, 2009.

[13] G. H. L. Fletcher, M. Gyssens, J. Paredaens, and D. V. Gucht. On the expressive power of the relational algebra on finite sets of relation pairs. *TKDE*, 21(6):939–942, 2009.

[14] G. Gottlob and P. Senellart. Schema mapping discovery from data instances. *JACM*, 57(2), 2010.

[15] L. M. Haas, M. A. Hernández, H. Ho, L. Popa, and M. Roth. Clio Grows Up: From Research Prototype to Industrial Tool. In *ACM SIGMOD*, pages 805–810, 2005.

[16] P. G. Kolaitis. Schema Mappings, Data Exchange, and Metadata Management. In *ACM PODS*, pages 61–75, 2005.

[17] M. Lenzerini. Data Integration: A Theoretical Perspective. In *ACM PODS*, pages 233–246, 2002.

[18] H. Mannila and K.-J. Räihä. Automatic generation of test data for relational queries. *JCSS*, 38(2):240–258, 1989.

[19] C. Olston, S. Chopra, and U. Srivastava. Generating example data for dataflow programs. In *ACM SIGMOD*, pages 245–256, 2009.

[20] C. H. Papadimitriou. *Computational Complexity*. Addison-Wesley, 1994.

[21] A. D. Sarma, A. G. Parameswaran, H. Garcia-Molina, and J. Widom. Synthesizing view definitions from data. In *ICDT*, pages 89–103, 2010.

[22] B. ten Cate, P. G. Kolaitis, and W. C. Tan. Database constraints and homomorphism dualities. In *CP*, 2010.

[23] L. Yan, R. J. Miller, L. M. Haas, and R. Fagin. Data-Driven Understanding and Refinement of Schema Mappings. In *ACM SIGMOD*, pages 485–496, 2001.

Apples and Oranges: A Comparison of RDF Benchmarks and Real RDF Datasets

Songyun Duan Anastasios Kementsietsidis Kavitha Srinivas Octavian Udrea
IBM Research - Thomas J. Watson Research Ctr.
19 Skyline Dr
Hawthorne, New York
{sduan, akement, ksrinivs, oudrea}@us.ibm.com

ABSTRACT

The widespread adoption of the Resource Description Framework (RDF) for the representation of both open web and enterprise data is the driving force behind the increasing research interest in RDF data management. As RDF data management systems proliferate, so are benchmarks to test the scalability and performance of these systems under data and workloads with various characteristics.

In this paper, we compare data generated with existing RDF benchmarks and data found in widely used real RDF datasets. The results of our comparison illustrate that existing benchmark data have little in common with real data. Therefore any conclusions drawn from existing benchmark tests might not actually translate to expected behaviours in real settings. In terms of the comparison itself, we show that simple primitive data metrics are inadequate to flesh out the fundamental differences between real and benchmark data. We make two contributions in this paper: (1) To address the limitations of the primitive metrics, we introduce intuitive and novel metrics that can indeed highlight the key differences between distinct datasets; (2) To address the limitations of existing benchmarks, we introduce a new benchmark generator with the following novel characteristics: (a) the generator can use any (real or synthetic) dataset and convert it into a benchmark dataset; (b) the generator can generate data that mimic the characteristics of real datasets with user-specified data properties. On the technical side, we formulate the benchmark generation problem as an integer programming problem whose solution provides us with the desired benchmark datasets. To our knowledge, this is the first methodological study of RDF benchmarks, as well as the first attempt on generating RDF benchmarks in a principled way.

Categories and Subject Descriptors

H.2 **[Systems]**; K.6.2 **[Management Of Computing And Information Systems]**: Installation Management—*Benchmarks*

General Terms

Measurement

SIGMOD'11, June 12–16, 2011, Athens, Greece.

1. INTRODUCTION

The RDF (Resource Description Framework) [24] is quickly becoming the *de-facto* standard for the representation and exchange of information. This is nowhere more evident than in the recent Linked Open Data (LOD) [7] initiative where data from varying domains like geographic locations, people, companies, books, films, scientific data (genes, proteins, drugs), statistical data, and the like, are interlinked to provide one large data cloud. As of October 2010, this cloud consists of around 200 data sources contributing a total of 25 billion RDF triples. The acceptance of RDF is not limited, however, to open data that are available on the web. Governments (most notably from US [13] and UK [14]) are adopting RDF. Many large companies and organizations are using RDF as the *business* data representation format, either for semantic data integration (*e.g.*, Pfizer [19]), search engine optimization and better product search (*e.g.*, Best Buy [6]), or for representation of data from information extraction (*e.g.*, BBC [5]). Indeed, with Google and Yahoo promoting the use of RDF for search engine optimization, there is clearly incentive for its growth on the web.

One of the main reasons for the widespread acceptance of RDF is its inherent flexibility: A *diverse* set of data, ranging from structured data (*e.g.*, DBLP [18]) to unstructured data (*e.g.*, Wikipedia/DBpedia [8]), can all be represented in RDF. Traditionally, the *structuredness* of a dataset is one of the key considerations while deciding an appropriate data representation format (*e.g.*, relational for structured and XML for semi-structured data). The choice, in turn, largely determines how we organize data (*e.g.*, dependency theory and normal forms for the relational model [2], and XML [4]). It is of central importance when deciding how to index it (*e.g.*, B+-tree indexes for relational and numbering scheme-based indexes for XML [25]). Structuredness also influences how we query the data (*e.g.*, using SQL for the relational and XPath/XQuery for XML). In other words, data structuredness permeates every aspect of data management, and accordingly the performance of data management systems is commonly measured against data with the expected level of structuredness (*e.g.*, the TPC-H [29] benchmark for relational and the XMark [31] benchmark for XML data). The main strength of RDF is precisely that it can be used to represent data across the full spectrum of structuredness, from unstructured to structured. This flexibility of RDF, however, comes at a cost. By blurring the structuredness lines, RDF data management becomes a challenge since no assumptions can be made *a-priori* by an RDF DBMS as to what type(s) of data it is going to manage. Unlike the relational and XML case, an RDF DBMS has the onerous requirement that its performance should be tested against very diverse data sets (in terms of structuredness).

A number of RDF data management systems (a.k.a. RDF stores) are currently available, with Sesame [11], Virtuoso [15],

3Store [17], and Jena [20], being some of the most notable ones. There are also research prototypes, with RDF-3X [22] and SW-Store [1] being the most notable representatives. To test the performance of these RDF stores, a number of RDF benchmarks have also been developed, namely, BSBM [10], LUBM [16], and SP^2Bench [26]. For the same purposes of testing RDF stores, the use of certain real datasets has been popularized (*e.g.*, the MIT Barton Library dataset [28]). While the focus of existing benchmarks is mainly on the performance of the RDF stores in terms of scalability (*i.e.*, the number of triples in the tested RDF data), a natural question to ask is *which types of RDF data these RDF stores are actually tested against*. That is, we want to investigate: (a) whether existing performance tests are limited to certain areas of the structuredness spectrum; and (b) what are these tested areas in the spectrum. The results of this investigation constitute one of our key contributions. Specifically, we show that (i) the structuredness of each benchmark dataset is practically *fixed*; (ii) even if a store is tested against the full set of available benchmark data, these tests cover only a small portion of the structuredness spectrum. However, we show that many real RDF datasets lie in currently untested parts of the spectrum.

These two points provide the motivation for our next contribution. To expand benchmarks to cover the structuredness spectrum, we introduce a novel benchmark data generator with the following unique characteristics: Our generator accepts as input any dataset (*e.g.*, a dataset generated from any of the existing benchmarks, or any real data set) along with a desired level of structuredness and size, and uses the input dataset as a *seed* to produce a dataset with the indicated size and structuredness. Our data generator has several advantages over existing ones. The first obvious advantage is that our generator offers complete control over both the structuredness and the size of the generated data. Unlike existing benchmark generators whose data domain and accompanying queries are *fixed* (*e.g.*, LUBM considers a schema which includes Professors, Students and Courses, and the like, along with 14 fixed queries over the generated data), our generator allows users to pick their dataset and queries of choice and methodically create a benchmark out of them. By fixing an input dataset and output size, and by changing the value of structuredness, a user can test the performance of a system across any desired level of structuredness. At the same time, by considering alternative dataset sizes, the user can perform scalability tests similar to the ones performed by the current benchmarks. By offering the ability to perform all the above using a variety of input datasets (and therefore a variety of data and value distributions, as well as query workloads), our benchmark generator can be used for extensive system testing of a system's performance along multiple independent dimensions.

Aside from the practical contributions in the domain of RDF benchmarking, there is a clear technical side to our work. In more detail, the notion of structuredness has been presented up to this point in a rather intuitive manner. In Section 3, we offer a formal definition of structuredness and we show how the structuredness of a particular set can be measured. The generation of datasets with varying sizes and levels of structuredness poses its own challenges. As we show, one of the main challenges is due to the fact that *there is an interaction between data size and structuredness: altering the size of a dataset can affect its structuredness, and correspondingly altering the structuredness of a dataset can affect its size*. So, given an input dataset, a desired size and structuredness for an output dataset, we cannot just randomly add/remove triples in the input dataset until we reach the desired output size. Such an approach provides no guarantees as to the structuredness of the output dataset and is almost guaranteed to result in an output dataset with structuredness which is different from the one desired. Similarly, we cannot just adjust the structuredness of the input dataset until we reach the desired level, since this process again is almost guaranteed to result in a dataset with incorrect size. In Section 4, we show that the solution to our benchmark generation problem comes in the form of two objective functions, one for structuredness and one for size, and in a formulation of our problem as an integer programming problem.

To summarize, our main contributions are as follows:

• To our knowledge, this is the *first* study of the characteristics of real and benchmark RDF datasets. Our study provides a first glimpse on the wide spectrum of RDF data, and can be used as the basis for the design, development and evaluation of RDF data management systems.

• We introduce the formal definition of structuredness and propose its use as one of the main metrics for the characterization of RDF data. Through an extensive set of experiments, we show that more primitive metrics, although useful, are inadequate for differentiating datasets in terms of their structuredness. Using our structuredness metrics, we show that existing benchmarks cover only a small range of the structuredness spectrum, which has little overlap with the spectrum covered by real RDF data.

• We develop a principled, generic technique to generate an RDF benchmark dataset that varies independently along the dimensions of structuredness and size. We show that unlike existing benchmarks, our benchmark generator can output datasets that resemble real datasets not only in terms of structuredness, but also in terms of content. This is feasible since our generator can use any dataset as input (real or synthetic) and generate a benchmark out of it.

The rest of the paper is organized as follows: In the next section, we review the datasets used in our study, and present an extensive list of primitive metrics over them. Then, in Section 3 we introduce our own structuredness metrics, and we compute the structuredness for all our datasets and contrasts our metrics with the primitive ones. In Section 4, we present our own benchmark generator, and the paper concludes in Section 5 with a summary of our results and a discussion of the future directions.

2. DATASETS

In this section, we present briefly each dataset used in our benchmark study. For each dataset, we only considered their RDF representation, without any RDFS inferencing, both for real and benchmark datasets. At the end of the section, we also offer an initial set of primitive metrics that we computed for the selected datasets. Since the RDF data model is closer to the object oriented data model and not the relational data model (by nature), the list of primitive metrics considered is sufficient and comprehensive for our needs. These metrics will illustrate the need for a more systematic set of structuredness metrics.

2.1 Real datasets

• **DBpedia:** DBpedia [8] extracts structured information from Wikipedia. The dataset consists of approximately 150 million triples (22 GB). The entities stored in the triples come from a wide range of data types, including Person, Film, (Music) Album, Place, Organization, etc. In terms of properties, the generic wikilink property is the one with the most instantiations. Given the variety of entities stored in the dataset, a wide range of queries can be evaluated over it, but there is no clear set of *representative* queries.

DBpedia comes with many different type systems. One commonly used type system is a subset of the YAGO [32] ontology, and uses approximately 5000 types from YAGO. We report this dataset as DBpedia-Y. The other is a broader type system that includes types from the DBpedia ontology, with approximately 150,000 types. We refer to this as DBpedia-B (for Base). Later on, while reporting metrics, some will depend on the type system (*e.g.*, instances per type), whereas others will be type system-independent (*e.g.*, the number of triples in the dataset). For the latter set of metrics, we will just refer to DBpedia (without a type system qualifier).

• **UniProt:** The UniProt dataset [3] contains information about proteins and the representation of the dataset in RDF consists of approximately 1.6 billion triples (280 GB). The dataset consists of instances mainly from type Resource (for a life science resource) and Sequence (for amino acid sequences), as well as instances of type Cluster (for clusters of proteins with similar sequences) and of course type Protein. The most instantiated properties, namely properties created and modified, record the creation and modification dates of resources. The UniProt datasets contained a number of reified RDF statements which can give us an inaccurate picture of the actual statistics on the data. We therefore consider only the non-reified statements in our analysis (as with all our datasets).

• **YAGO:** The YAGO ontology [27,32] brings together knowledge from both Wikipedia and Wordnet, and currently the dataset consists of 19 million triples (2.4GB). Types like WordNet_Person and WordNet_Village are some of the most instantiated, as are properties like describes. In terms of a query load, Neumann and Weikum [21] provide 8 queries over the YAGO dataset that they use to benchmark the RDF-3X system.

• **Barton Library Dataset:** The Barton library dataset [28] consists of approximately 45 million RDF triples (5.5 GB) that are generated by converting the Machine Readable Catalog (MARC) data of the MIT Libraries Barton catalog to RDF. Some of the most instantiated data types in the dataset are Record and Item, the latter being associated with instances of type Person and with instances of Description. The more *primitive* Title and Date type are the most instantiated, while in terms of properties, the generic value property is the one appearing in most entities. In terms of queries, the work of Abadi et al. [1] considers 7 queries as a representative load for the dataset, all of which involve grouping and aggregation.

• **WordNet:** The RDF representation [30] of the well-known WordNet dataset was also used in our study, which currently consists of 1.9 million triples (300MB). In the dataset, the NounWordSense, NounSynset and Word types are among the ones with the most instances, while the tagCount and word properties are some of the most commonly used.

• **Linked Sensor Dataset:** The Linked Sensor dataset [23] contains expressive descriptions of approximately 20,000 weather stations in the United States. The dataset is divided up into multiple subsets, which reflect weather data for specific hurricanes or blizzards from the past. We report our analyses on the dataset about hurricane Ike, under the assumption that the other subsets of data will contain the same characteristics. The Ike hurricane dataset contains approximately 500 million triples (101 GB), but only about 16 types. Most of the instances are from the MeasureData type, which is natural since most instances provided various weather measurements.

2.2 Benchmark datasets

• **TPC-H:** The TPC Benchmark H (TPC-H) [29] is a well-known decision support benchmark in relational databases. We use the TPC-H benchmark in this study as our *baseline*. In more detail, notice that the structuredness of the TPC-H dataset should be almost *perfect*, since these are relational data that are converted to RDF. Therefore, the are two obvious reasons to use TPC-H as our baseline: First, the dataset can be used to check the correctness of our introduced structuredness metrics since any metrics that we devise

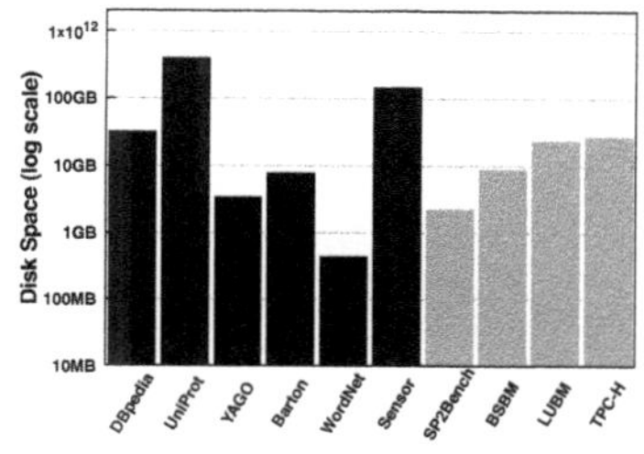

Figure 1: Disk space

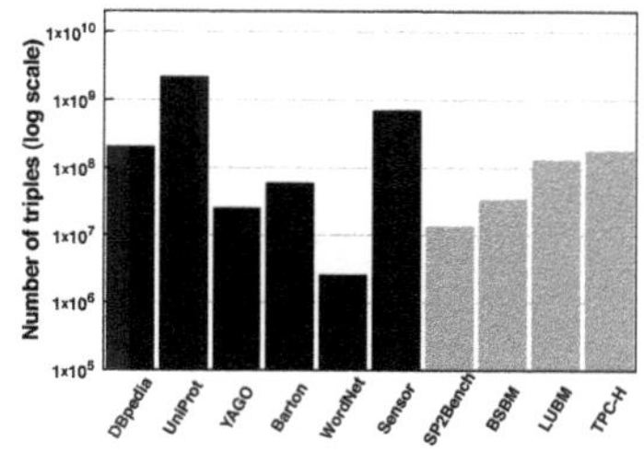

Figure 2: Number of triples

must indeed confirm the high structuredness of TPC-H. Second, the dataset can be used as a baseline to which we can compare all the other datasets in the study. If a dataset has close, or similar, structuredness to TPC-H, then we expect that this dataset can also be classified as being a relational dataset with an RDF representation.

To represent TPC-H in RDF, we use the DBGEN TPC-H generator to generate a TPC-H relational dataset of approximately 10 million tuples with 6 million LINEITEM, 1.5 million ORDER, 800,000 PARTSUP, 200,000 PART and 150,000 CUSTOMER. Then, we use the widely used D2R tool [12] to convert the relational dataset to the equivalent RDF one. This process results in an RDF dataset with 130 million triples (19 GB).

• **BSBM Dataset:** The Berlin SPARQL Benchmark (BSBM) [10] considers an e-commerce domain where types Product, Offer and Vendor are used to model the relationships between products and the vendors offering them, while types Person and Review are used to model the relationship between users and product reviews these users write. We use the BSBM data generator and create a dataset with 25M triples (6.1 GB). In BSBM, type Offer is the most instantiated one, as is the case for the properties of this type. The benchmark also comes with 12 queries and 2 query mixes (sequences of the 12 queries) for the purposes of testing RDF store performance.

• **LUBM Dataset:** The Lehigh University Benchmark (LUBM) [16] considers a University domain, with types like UndergraduateStudent, Publication, GraduateCourse, AssistantProfessor, to name a few. Using the LUBM generator, we create a dataset of 100 million triples (17 GB). In the LUBM dataset, Publication is the most instantiated type, while properties like name and takesCourse are some of the most instantiated. The LUBM benchmark also provides 14 test queries for the purposes of testing the performance of RDF stores.

• **SP^{2}Bench Dataset:** The SP^{2}Bench benchmark [26] uses the DBLP as a domain for the dataset. Therefore, the types encountered include Person, Inproceedings, Article and the like. Using the SP^{2}Bench generator we create a dataset with approximately 10 million triples (1.6 GB). The Person type is the most instantiated in the dataset, as is the case for the name and homepage properties. The SP^{2}Bench benchmark is accompanied by 12 queries.

2.3 Basic metrics

In this section, we present an initial set of metrics collected from the datasets presented in the previous section.

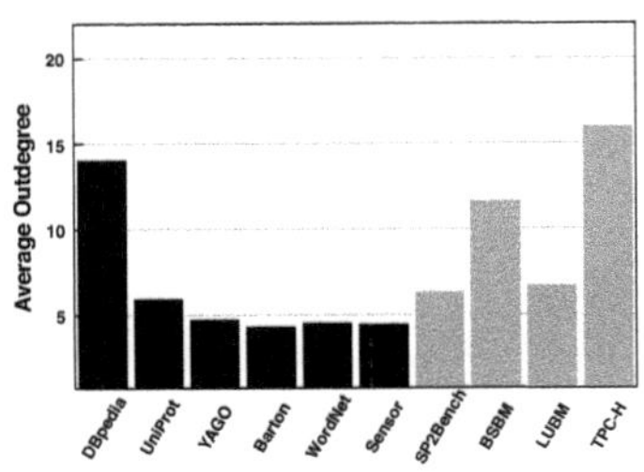

Figure 3: Average Outdegree

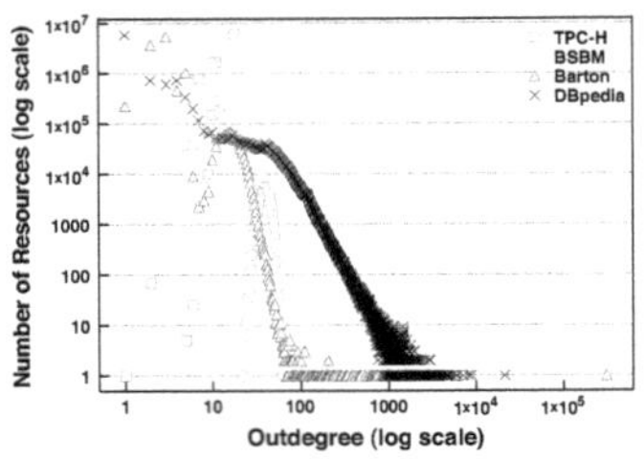

Figure 4: Outdegree distribution

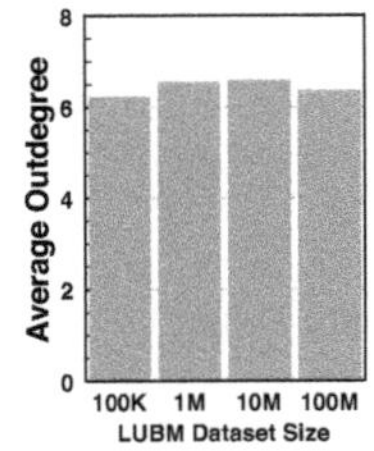

Figure 5: LUBM

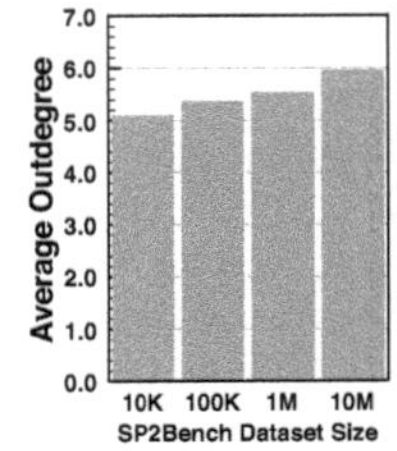

Figure 6: SP^{2}Bench

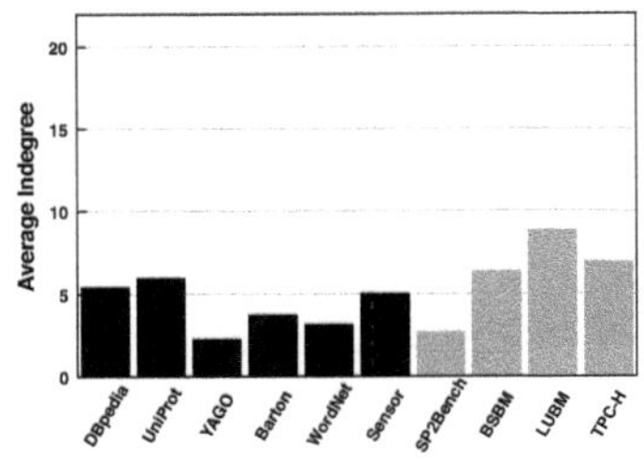

Figure 7: Average Indegree

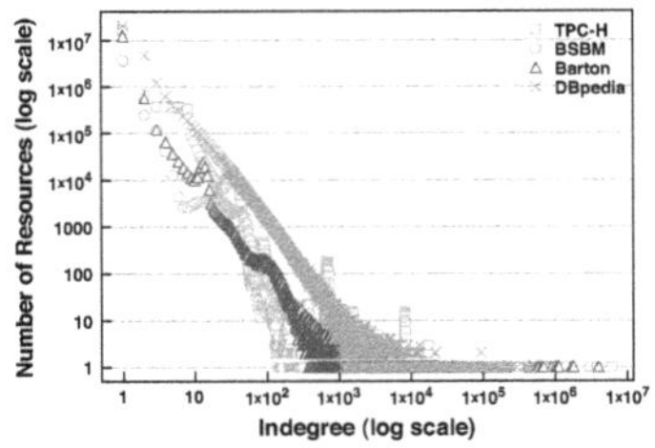

Figure 8: Indegree distribution

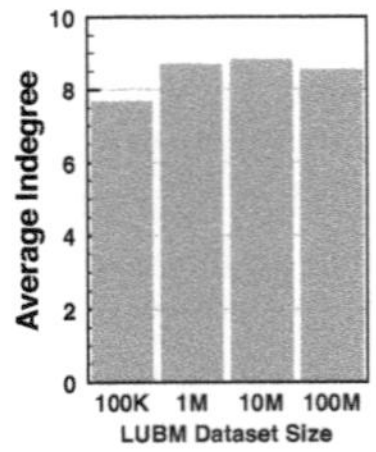

Figure 9: LUBM

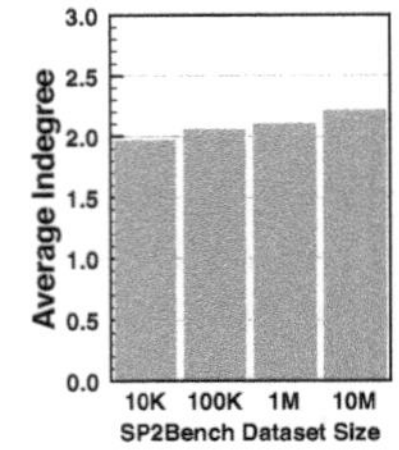

Figure 10: SP^{2}Bench

2.3.1 *Collecting the metrics*

To collect these metrics, the following procedure was followed:

■ **Step 1:** For some of the datasets (*e.g.,* LUBM), the dataset triples were distributed over a (large) number of files. Therefore, the first step in our procedure is to assemble all the triples into a single file. Hereafter, we use the dataset-independent file name SDF.rdf (Single Dataset File) to refer to this file.

■ **Step 2:** We also perform some *data cleaning* and *normalization*. In more detail, some of the real datasets contain a small percentage of triples that are syntactically incorrect. In this stage, we identify such triples, and we either correct the syntax, if the fix is obvious (*e.g.,* missing quote or angle bracket symbols), or we drop the triple from consideration, when the information in the triple is incomplete. We also drop triples in a reified form (*e.g.,* as in UniProt) and normalize all the datasets by converting all of them in the N-Triples format, which is a plain text RDF format, where each line in the text corresponds to a triple, and each triple is represented by the subject, property and object separated by space and the line terminates with a full stop symbol. We refer to SDF.nt as the file with the N-Triples representation of file SDF.rdf.

■ **Step 3:** We generate three new files, namely SDF_subj.nt, SDF_prop.nt, and SDF_obj.nt, by independently sorting the file SDF.nt by the subjects, properties and objects of the triples in SDF.nt. Each sorted output file is useful for different types of collected metrics, and the advantage of sorting is that the corresponding metrics can be collected by making a *single pass* of the sorted file. Although the sorting simplifies the computation cost of metrics, there is an initial considerable overhead since sorting files with billions of triples that occupy many GBs on disk requires large amounts of memory and processing power (for some datasets, each individual sort took more than two days in a dual processor server with 24GB of memory and 6TB of disk space). However, the advantage of this approach is that the sorting need only be done *once*. After sorting is done, metrics can be collected efficiently and new metrics can be developed that take advantage of the sort order. Another important advantage of sorting the SDF.nt file is that this way duplicate triples are eliminated during the sorting process. Such duplicate triples occur especially when the input dataset is originally split into multiple files.

■ **Step 4:** We select the SDF_subj.nt file generated in the previous step, and use it to extract the type system of the current dataset. The reason for extracting the type system will become clear in the next section where we introduce the structuredness metrics.

■ **Step 5:** We use file SDF_subj.nt to collect metrics such as counting the *number of subjects* and *triples* in the input dataset, as well as detailed statistics about the *outdegree* of the subjects (*i.e.,* the number of properties associated with the subject); we use file SDF_prop.nt to collect metrics such as the *number of properties* in the dataset as well as detailed statistics about the occurrences of each property; and we use file SDF_obj.nt to collect metrics such as the *number of objects* in the dataset as well as detailed statistics about the *indegree* of the objects (*i.e.,* the number of properties associated with the object).

Overall, to collect metrics we had to process over 2.5 billion triples from our input datasets, and we generated approximately 2TB of intermediate and output files. In the next section, we present an analysis of the collected metrics.

2.3.2 *Analysis of metrics*

Figures 1 to 18 show the collected primitive metrics for all our datasets. In the figures, we cluster the real and benchmark data sets together, and we use black bars for the former and gray bars for the latter datasets.

Figure 1 shows (in logarithmic scale) the space required for each dataset on disk, while Figure 2 shows in logarithmic scale the number of triples per dataset. Notice that there is a clear correlation between the two numbers, and the majority of datasets have between 10^7 to 10^8 triples, with the exception of UniProt which has in the order of 10^9 triples.

In terms of the indegree and outdegree, we note that some of the datasets have a power law-like distribution of indegree/outdegree, as shown in Figures 4 and 8, for only four of our input datasets (two benchmark and two real). In both figures, we see that there is a large concentration of entities around the 1 to 10 range (*i.e.,* the average number of properties of a subject or to an object is between 1 and 10) while a small number of entities have very large numbers of indegree and outdegree. In Figures 3 and 7 we plot the average outdegree and indegree for all our datasets. In terms of the standard deviation of the average outdegree, for most datasets this is

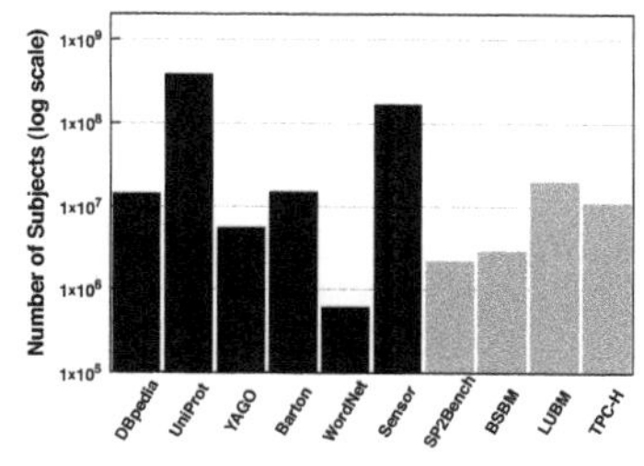

Figure 11: Dataset subjects

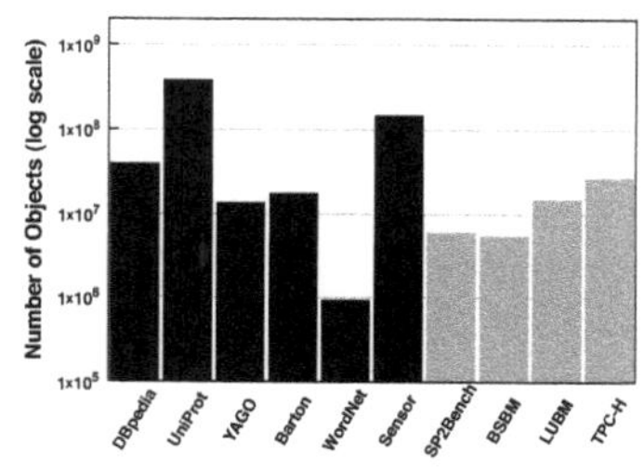

Figure 12: Dataset objects

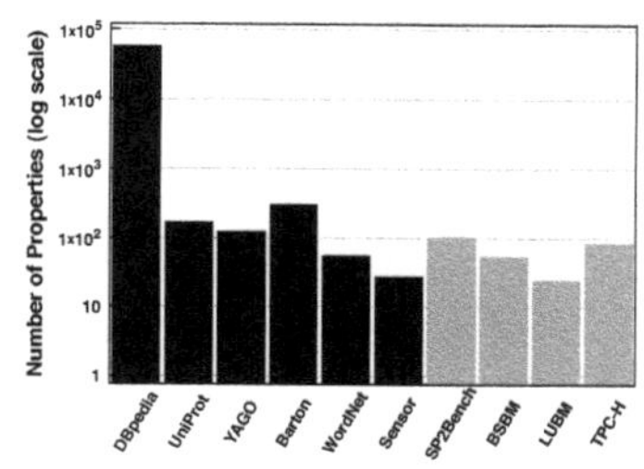

Figure 13: Dataset properties

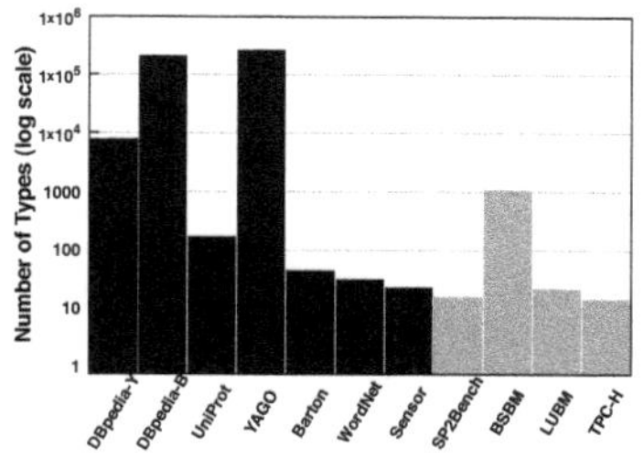

Figure 14: Number of Types

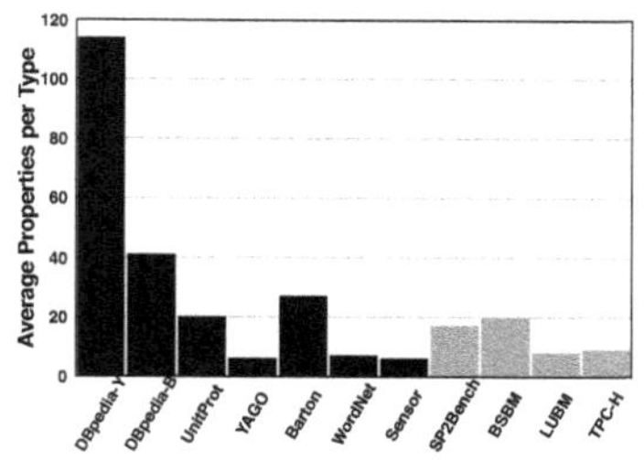

Figure 15: Average type properties

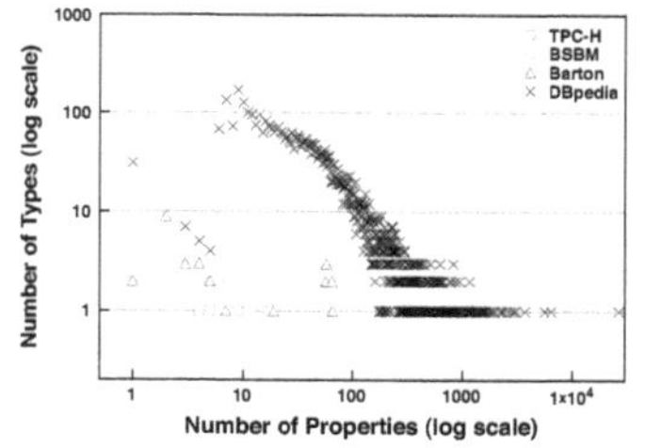

Figure 16: Type properties distribution for 4 datasets

relatively small (between 3 and 6) with the exception of DBpedia, Sensor, and Barton datasets. For these three datasets the deviation is in the order of 40, 60 and 80, respectively. In terms of the standard deviation of the average indegree, for almost all datasets this is relatively large (in the order of many hundreds). Finally, in Figures 5 and 6 we plot the average outdegrees for two of our benchmark datasets, namely, for LUBM and SP^{2}Bench, for various dataset sizes. The figures clearly illustrate that outdegrees are not a function of dataset sizes, since the average outdegree remains almost constant across datasets whose sizes span across four orders of magnitude. Figures 9 and 10 show that the same is true for indegrees.

For the next set of figures, we consider the number of subjects, objects and properties per dataset, shown (in log scale) in Figures 11, 12 and 13, respectively. The first two figures show that each dataset has subjects and objects in the same order of magnitude. However, looking at the raw data reveals that the TPC-H, BSBM, SP^{2}Bench, WordNet, Barton, YAGO and DBpedia datasets have more objects than subjects, whereas the opposite holds for the LUBM, UniProt and Sensor datasets. In terms of properties, most datasets have around 100 distinct properties, with the exception of DBpedia which has almost 3 orders of magnitude more properties.

Figure 14 shows the number of types in the type system of each dataset. Most datasets have only a few types (less than 100), with the exception of DBpedia-Y, DBpedia-B and the YAGO datasets. DBpedia-Y has approximately 5,000 types, while both DBpedia-B and YAGO have more than 140,000 types. Figure 15 shows the average number of properties per type. Notice that most datasets have less than 20 properties per type (on average) with the exception of DBpedia-Y which has approximately 111 properties per type, and DBpedia-B which has 38 properties per type. We must note that to compute the average number of properties per type we cannot just divide the distinct number of properties (shown in Figure 13) by the number of types (shown in Figure 14) since the former number counts properties irrespectively of the types these properties belong to. Such a division would incorrectly state that DBpedia has only 8 properties per type on average. This is also verified by Figure 16 which shows the actual distribution of properties per type for 4 datasets. In the x-axis we plot the number of properties and in the y-axis we plot how many types in the dataset have this number of properties.

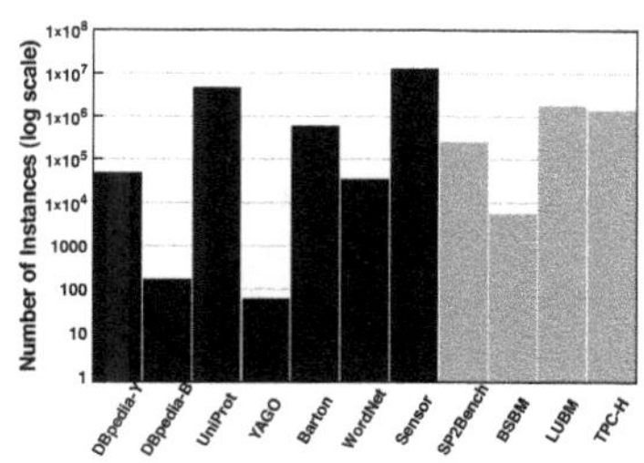

Figure 17: Average number of instances per type

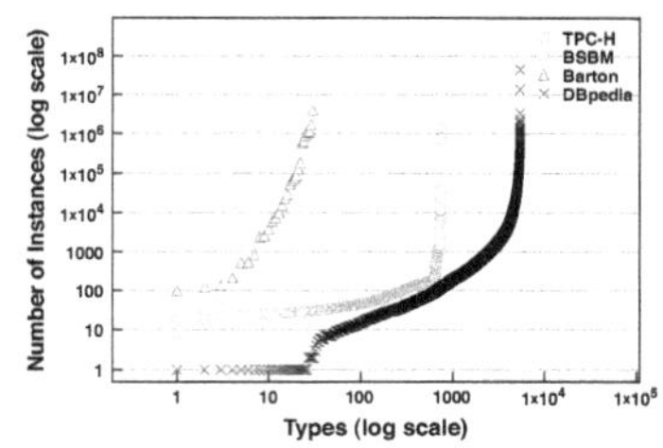

Figure 18: Instance distribution for 4 datasets

In terms of the number of instances for these types, Figure 17 shows that on average in most datasets a type has approximately 10^5 instances. A notable exception to this is the YAGO dataset. Since YAGO is essentially an ontology, there are only a few instances in the dataset (and a lot of types, as we already mentioned). It is interesting to notice the difference between DBpedia-B and DBpedia-Y in this metric. Since the type system in DBpedia-B is more *fine-grained*, there are only a few instances for each type (approximately, on average, 100 instances for each of the 150,000 DBpedia-B types). On the other hand, DBpedia-Y has a more *coarse-grained* type system, with only 5,000 types and these types are bound to aggregate a larger number of instances. Indeed, in DBpedia-Y there are approximately, on average, 30,000 instances per type. In terms of more concrete distributions of instances per type, Figure 18 shows how instances are distributed in various types, for 4 of our datasets. In the x-axis of the figure, we plot the types by assigning a unique id to each type of each dataset. In the y-axis, we plot the exact number of instances for each type.

2.3.3 Discussion

What can we say about the structure and nature of these datasets? Not much, apparently, if all we have are these metrics. UniProt is the dataset with the most triples, TPC-H is the dataset with the biggest average outdegree, and LUBM the dataset with the largest average indegree. DBpedia has the most properties, and YAGO has the most types. Different datasets have different characteristics for different primitive metrics. Can we say that YAGO is more structured than UniProt? Or can the metrics capture the intuition that TPC-H is more structured than DBpedia? *It is really hard from the above primitive metrics to say anything concrete about the structure of the datasets under consideration, and how they compare to each other.* Even more importantly, it is impossible to compare a new dataset with the analyzed datasets.

Each primitive metric quantifies some specific aspect of each dataset. Each metric in isolation offers no clues about the dataset as a whole. Clearly, what is required here is some intuitive way to combine all these metrics into a single composite metric that can characterize each dataset by itself, and by comparison to other datasets. In the next section, we introduce such a composite metric.

3. COVERAGE AND COHERENCE

In what follows, we formally define the notion of structuredness (through the coverage and coherence metrics) and show the values of these metrics for the datasets introduced in the previous section.

3.1 The metrics

Intuitively, the level of structuredness of a dataset D with respect to a type T is determined by how well the instance data in D *conform* to type T. Consider for example the dataset D of RDF triples in Figure 19(a). For simplicity, assume that the type T of these triples has properties name, office and ext. If each entity (subject) in D sets values for most (if not all) of the properties of T, then all the entities in D have a fairly similar structure that conforms to T. In this case, we can say that D has *high structuredness* with respect to T. This is indeed the case for the dataset D in Figure 19(a). Consider now a dataset D_M that consists of the union $D \cup D'$ of triples in Figures 19(a) and (b). For illustration purposes, consider a type T_M with properties major and GPA, in addition to the properties of T. Dataset D_M has low structuredness with respect to T_M. To see why this is the case, notice that type T_M *bundles* together entities with overlapping properties. So, while all entities in D_M have a value for the name property, the first three entities (those belonging to dataset D) set values only for the office and ext properties, while the last three entities (those belonging to dataset D') only set values for the major and GPA properties. The objective of our work is to measure the level of structuredness of a dataset (whatever it is), and to generate datasets with a desired (high or low) structuredness level for the purpose of benchmarking. In what follows, we formally define structuredness and show how it can be measured.

The first step in the computation of structuredness is clearly the determination of the type system $\mathcal{T}$. Conceivably, one might infer the type system $\mathcal{T}$ of a dataset D *intensionally*, through an RDFS or OWL specification associated with D. In practice, however, many datasets do not come with such specifications. Morever, when OWL or RDFS specifications exist, they often do not specify the schema or the type system; as an example in DBpedia the instances of a given type have many properties that are not defined in any of its multiple type systems [9]. This is because RDFS and OWL are mechanisms to infer new facts in the dataset rather than schema specifications. RDFS domain and range for example, are not constraints that the data needs to adhere to, but rather they are inference rules for a reasoner to apply to add new facts into the dataset D using open world semantics.

To address the fact that there is no schema available in RDF datasets to apply an intensional approach, we determine the type system $\mathcal{T}$ of D *extensionally* through the dataset itself, and thus do not need any *schema*-level information. Specifically, we scan D looking for triples whose property is <http://www.w3.org/1999/02/22-rdf-syntax-ns#type> (hereafter abbreviated to w3type), and for these triples we extract the type T that appears as the object of the triple. That is,

DEFINITION 1. *The type system $\mathcal{T}$ of* D *is*

$$\mathcal{T} = \{ \mathsf{T} \mid \exists(\mathsf{s}, \mathsf{w3type}, \mathsf{T}) \in \mathsf{D} \} \tag{1}$$

Now, consider a particular type $\mathsf{T} \in \mathcal{T}$. Then,

DEFINITION 2. *The set* $\mathsf{I}(\mathsf{T}, \mathsf{D})$ *of instances of* T *in* D *is*

$$\mathsf{I}(\mathsf{T}, \mathsf{D}) = \{ \mathsf{s} \mid \exists(\mathsf{s}, \mathsf{w3type}, \mathsf{T}) \in \mathsf{D}\} \tag{2}$$

We then determine the properties of a type T through the union of all the properties that the instances of type T have. In more detail,

DEFINITION 3. *The set* $\mathsf{P}(\mathsf{T})$ *of properties of* T *is*

$$\mathsf{P}(\mathsf{T}) = \{ \mathsf{p} \mid \mathsf{s} \in \mathsf{I}(\mathsf{T}, \mathsf{D}) \textit{ and } \exists(\mathsf{s}, \mathsf{p}, \mathsf{o}) \in \mathsf{D} \} \tag{3}$$

Notice that we are not interested in the number of times a property p is set for an instance of T. Intuitively, this is because the structuredness of T is affected by the sparsity (presence) of its properties across instances, rather than the number of occurrences of the properties. Since an entity might belong to more than one types, the properties of this entity contribute to P(T), for each such type T.

DEFINITION 4. *The number of occurrences* $\mathsf{OC}(\mathsf{p}, \mathsf{I}(\mathsf{T}, \mathsf{D}))$ *of a property* p *in* $\mathsf{I}(\mathsf{T}, \mathsf{D})$ *is*

$$\mathsf{OC}(\mathsf{p}, \mathsf{I}(\mathsf{T}, \mathsf{D})) = | \{ \mathsf{s} \mid (\mathsf{s} \in \mathsf{I}(\mathsf{T}, \mathsf{D}) \textit{ and } \exists(\mathsf{s}, \mathsf{p}, \mathsf{o}) \in \mathsf{D}\} | \tag{4}$$

The last definition counts the number of entities for which property p has its value set in the instances $\mathsf{I}(\mathsf{T}, \mathsf{D})$ of T. In this manner, we count essentially the number of times p is set in $\mathsf{I}(\mathsf{T}, \mathsf{D})$. Similar to the definition of P(T), we are only interested in whether a property is present or not for a particular entity instead of how many times the property is set for this entity. Going back to Figure 19(a), for the type and dataset defined there, $\mathsf{P}(\mathsf{T}) = \{\mathsf{name}, \mathsf{office}, \mathsf{ext}\}$, $\mathsf{I}(\mathsf{T}, \mathsf{D})$ is equal to $\{\mathsf{person0}, \mathsf{person1}, \mathsf{person2}\}$, while $\mathsf{OC}(\mathsf{office}, \mathsf{T})$ is equal to 2 (since property office is set for the first two entities, not the third entity in dataset D).

DEFINITION 5. *The coverage* $\mathsf{CV}(\mathsf{T}, \mathsf{D})$ *of* T *on a dataset* D *is*

$$\mathsf{CV}(\mathsf{T}, \mathsf{D}) = \frac{\sum_{\forall \mathsf{p} \in \mathsf{P}(\mathsf{T})} \mathsf{OC}(\mathsf{p}, \mathsf{I}(\mathsf{T}, \mathsf{D}))}{|\mathsf{P}(\mathsf{T})| \times |\mathsf{I}(\mathsf{T}, \mathsf{D})|} \tag{5}$$

To understand the intuition behind coverage, consider Figure 20. The figure considers the type T_M and dataset D_M, as defined by Figure 19 earlier. Note that $|\mathsf{P}(\mathsf{T})_M| = 5$, since there are five properties in the combined type system, and $|\mathsf{I}(\mathsf{T}_M, \mathsf{D}_M)| = 6$ for the six person instances. For each property p, the figure plots $\mathsf{OC}(\mathsf{p}, \mathsf{I}(\mathsf{T}_M, \mathsf{D}_M))$. So, for example, for property name $\mathsf{OC}(\mathsf{name}, \mathsf{I}(\mathsf{T}_M, \mathsf{D}_M))$ is equal to 6, while for property major $\mathsf{OC}(\mathsf{major}, \mathsf{I}(\mathsf{T}_M, \mathsf{D}_M))$ is equal to 1. Now, as mentioned above, the structuredness of a type depends on whether the instances of the type set a value for all its properties. So, for a dataset D_M of T_M with *perfect* structuredness, every instance of the type in D_M sets all its properties, that

(person0, name, Eric)
(person0, office, BA7430)
(person0, ext, x4402)
(person1, name, Kenny)
(person1, office, BA7349)
(person1, office, BA7350)
(person1, ext, x5304)
(person2, name, Kyle)
(person2, ext, x6282)

(a) Dataset D

(person3, name, Timmy)
(person3, major, C.S.)
(person3, GPA, 3.4)
(person4, name, Stan)
(person4, GPA, 3.8)
(person5, name, Jimmy)
(person5, GPA, 3.7)

(b) Dataset D'

Figure 19: RDF sample triples

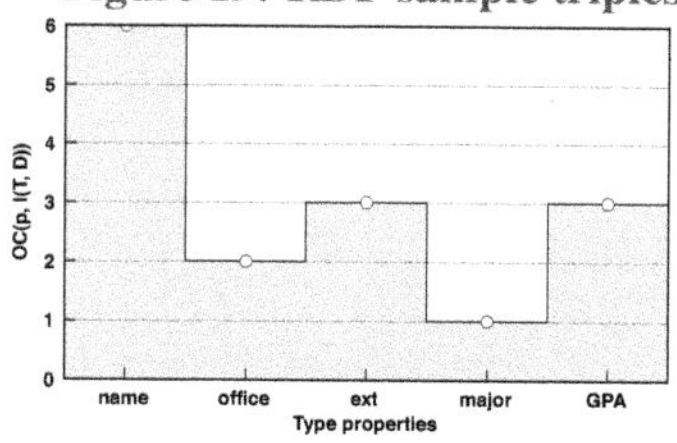

Figure 20: OC(p, T) **for each property** p **of** T

is, $OC(p, I(T_M, D_M))$ is equal to $|I(T_M, D_M)|$, for every property $p \in P(T_M)$. Then, in the figure perfect structuredness translates to the area covered by $|P(T_M)| \times |I(T_M, D_M)|$, *i.e.,* the area corresponding to the rectangle of the whole Figure 20 (this is also the denominator in the computation of $CV(T_M, D_M)$). In general, however, not all properties are set for every instance. Then, the shaded area in Figure 20 (computed by the numerator in the computation of $CV(T_M, D_M)$) corresponds to the current level of structuredness of D_M with respect to T_M. Given the above, the formula of the coverage $CV(T_M, D_M)$ above is essentially an indication of the structuredness of D_M with respect to T_M normalized in the [0, 1] interval (with values close to 0 corresponding to low structuredness, and 1 corresponding to perfect structuredness). In our specific example, the value of the computed coverage for $CV(T_M, D_M)$ is equal to $\frac{6+2+3+1+3}{30} = 0.5$ which intuitively states that each instance of type T_M in dataset D_M only sets half of its properties.

Formula 5 considers the structuredness of a dataset with respect to a *single* type. Obviously, a dataset D has entities from multiple types, with each entity belonging to at least one of these types (if multiple instantiation is supported). It is possible that dataset D might have a high structuredness for a type T, say $CV(T, D) = 0.8$, and a low structuredness for another type T', say $CV(T', D) = 0.15$. But then, what is the structuredness of the whole dataset with respect to our type system (set of all types) $\mathcal{T}$? We propose a mechanism to compute this, by considering the weighted sum of the coverage $CV(T, D)$ of individual types. In more detail, for each type T, we weight its coverage using the following formula:

$$WT(CV(T, D)) = \frac{|P(T)| + |I(T, D)|}{\sum_{\forall T' \in \mathcal{T}}(|P(T')| + |I(T', D)|)} \quad (6)$$

where $|P(T)|$ is the number of properties for a type T, $|I(T, D)|$ is the number of entities in D of type T, and the denominator sums up these numbers for all the types in the type system $\mathcal{T}$. The weight formula has a number of desirable properties: It is easy to see that if the coverage $CV(T, D)$ is equal to 1, for every type T in $\mathcal{T}$, then the weighted sum of the coverage for all types T in $\mathcal{T}$ is equal to 1. The formula also gives higher weight to types with more instances. So, the coverage of a type with, say a single instance, has a lower influence in the computation of structuredness of the whole dataset, than the coverage of a type with hundreds of instances. This also matches our intuition that types with a small number of instances are usually more structured than types with larger number of instances. Finally, the formula gives higher weight to types with a larger number of properties. Again, this matches our intuition that one expects to find less variance in the instances of a type with, say only two properties, than the variance that one encounters in the instances of a type with hundreds of properties. The latter type is expected to have a larger number of *optional* properties, and therefore if the type has high coverage, this should carry more weight than a type with high coverage which only has two properties.

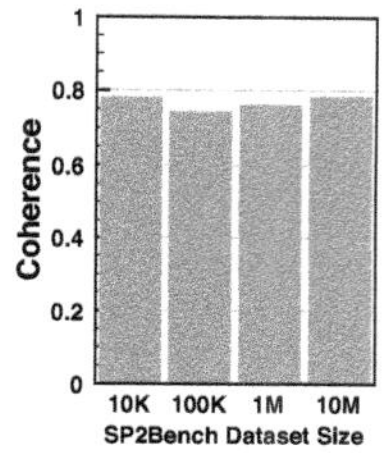

Figure 21: SP²Bench coherence

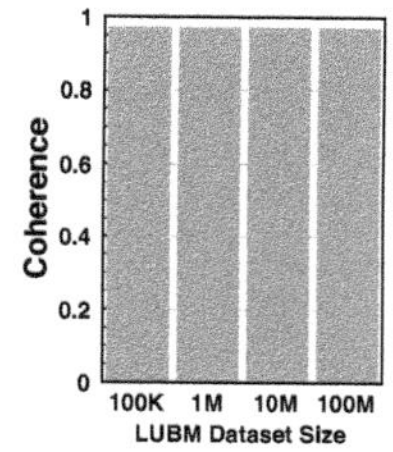

Figure 22: LUBM coherence

We are now ready to compute the structuredness, hereafter termed as *coherence*, of a whole dataset D with respect to a type system $\mathcal{T}$ (to avoid confusion with the term coverage which is used to describe the structuredness of a single type).

DEFINITION 6. *We define the coherence* $CH(\mathcal{T}, D)$ *of a dataset* D *with respect to a type system* $\mathcal{T}$ *as*

$$CH(\mathcal{T}, D) = \sum_{\forall T \ in \ \mathcal{T}} WT(CV(T, D)) \times CV(T, D) \quad (7)$$

3.2 Computing coherence

To compute the coherence of an input dataset, we consider file SDF_subj.nt (see Section 2.3.1). Remember that the file contains all the triples in the dataset (after cleaning, normalization and duplicate elimination) expressed in the N-Triples format. We proceed by *annotating* each triple in SDF_subj.nt with the type of triple's subject and object. This process converts each triple to a quintuple. We call the resulted file SDF_WT.nt (for Single Dataset File With Types). One more pass of the SDF_WT.nt file suffices to collect for each type T of the dataset the value of $OC(p, I(T, D))$, for each property p of T. At the same time, we compute the values for $P(T)$ and $I(T, D)$, and at the end of processing the file we are in a position to compute $CV(T, D)$, $WT(CV(T, D))$ and finally $CH(\mathcal{T}, D)$.

In the introduction, we claim that coherence (structuredness) is relatively fixed in existing benchmarks. Figures 21 and 22 verify our claim. In more detail, Figure 21 shows the coherence of SP²Bench datasets, as we scale the size of the generated data in the benchmark. The figure shows that coherence does not change for the different sizes, and more importantly that even the minor fluctuations are outside the user's control. Figure 22 shows the trend for the LUBM benchmark where coherence is practically constant (the situation is similar for the other benchmarks as well).

Figure 23 shows the computed coherence values for all our datasets. A few important observations are necessary here. Remember our choice of the TPC-H dataset as our baseline over which to compare all the other datasets. Since TPC-H is a relational dataset, we expect that it will have high structuredness. Indeed, *our coherence metric verifies this since TPC-H has a computed coherence equal to 1.* Contrast this result with Figures 1 to 18 which show the collected primitive metrics. None of the primitives metrics could have been used to identify and highlight the structuredness of TPC-H.

The second important observation we make is *the striking distinction between benchmark datasets and real datasets.* Indeed,

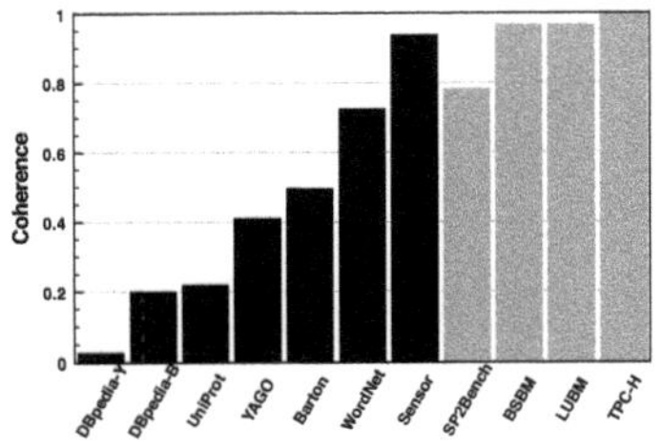

Figure 23: Coherence metric for all input datasets

there is a clear divide between the two sets of datasets, with the former datasets being fairly structured and relational-like (given the proximity of their coherence value to the one of TPC-H), while the latter datasets cover the whole spectrum of structuredness. DBpedia, a fairly popular and well-known dataset, is extremely unstructured with a coherence value of 0.002 for DBpedia-Y and 0.175 for DBpedia-B. Intuitively, this low coherence compared to a dataset like TPC-H can be interpreted as follows: If one considers two instances of the same type in DBpedia, with high probability, the properties set by the two instances are expected to be non-overlapping. Given that the instances belong to the same type, this is a rather surprising and interesting characteristic of the dataset (the situation is actually worse in DBpedia-Y since it *aggregates* more diverse instances under the same type, when compared to DBpedia-B). Conversely, for TPC-H one expects that for any two instances of the same type, the instances have exactly the same properties. Such a difference in the characteristics of the data is bound to have consequences on the storage of the data (TPC-H RDF data fit comfortably in a relational database, while DBpedia data will probably result in relational tables with lots of NULL values, if a relational representation of RDF data is chosen), and it also has effects on how the data are indexed, and queried (a simple SPARQL query returning all resources to a specified property always has the same selectivity for TPC-H, but the selectivity is different for each property in DBpedia). But these are some key dimensions existing RDF stores are tested and compared against each other. Remember in the introduction that we posed a simple question, namely, which types of RDF data existing RDF stores are tested against. *Figure 23 is the answer to this question: Existing RDF stores are tested and compared against each other with respect to datasets that are not representative of most real RDF data.* Again, we refer the reader to Figures 1 to 18 which show the collected primitive metrics. Nowhere in these figures is this distinction as clear cut and visible as in Figure 23. Yet, in a sense our coverage and coherence formulas incorporate the underlying metrics shown in these figures, since the formulas use the number of types, properties, properties per type, instance entities per type (distinct subjects for a type), and instance properties for these entities for the computation of our introduced metrics.

Since RDF benchmarks are distinct from real RDF datasets, the key question is whether we can design a benchmark that generates data which more accurately represent real RDF data, in terms of structuredness. We investigate this next, and present a benchmark generator that can convert any existing dataset (even datasets generated with existing benchmarks) into a series of datasets with varying characteristics in terms of size and structuredness.

4. BENCHMARK GENERATION

There are two overall methods to be considered in generating benchmarks with structuredness that better represent real datasets. The first method, similar to the approach taken by the developers of LUBM, SP^{2}Bench and BSBM is to generate a dataset with a given coherence and size from scratch. The main issue with this approach is that the generated benchmark is domain specific. In all the aforementioned benchmark datasets, the relationships and relative cardinalities between different types come from knowledge of the target domain, and are hard-coded into the generation algorithms and thus not controllable by the user. For instance, the relative cardinalities of professors and students or students and courses in LUBM are a feature of the generation algorithm and not available to the user generating the benchmark.

The second method, which applies to any domain for which there already is a benchmark or real dataset, involves taking a given dataset, *and producing a dataset with a specified smaller size and coherence.* Ideally, we would like to take an existing benchmark or real dataset D and produce a dataset D' with a specified size $|D'| < |D|$ and a specified coherence $CH(\mathcal{T}, D') < CH(\mathcal{T}, D)$. We believe the latter method has a larger impact in practice, since it can be used on top of any already existing benchmark or real-world dataset.

The central idea behind our approach is that under certain circumstances we can estimate the impact that removing a set of triples with the same subject and property can have on coherence. Let *(s, p, o)* be a triple from D and let $\mathcal{T}$ (s) = $\{T_s^1, \ldots, T_s^n\}$ be the set of types[1] of instance s. We are going to compute the impact on coherence of removing all triples with subject s and property p from D, under the following two assumptions:

- (A1) We do not completely remove property p from any of the types $\{T_s^1, \ldots, T_s^n\}$. That is, after the removal, for each type there will exist instances that have property p.

- (A2) We do not completely remove instance s from the dataset. This can be very easily enforced by keeping the triples $\{s, \text{rdf:type}, T_s^i\}$ in the dataset.

Under these two assumptions, the weights WT(CV(T, D)) for the coverage of any type $T \in \mathcal{T}(s)$ do not change since we keep the same number of properties and instances for each such type. For each type $T \in \mathcal{T}(s)$, we can compute the new coverage as

$$CV(T, D)' = \frac{\sum_{\forall q \in P(T)-\{p\}} OC(q, I(T, D)) + OC(p, I(T, D) - 1)}{|P(T)| \times |I(T, D)|} \qquad (8)$$

Note that there is one less instance (specifically, s) that has property p for type T. It is evident from this formula that removing all triples with subject s and property p will decrease the coverage of all types $T \in \mathcal{T}(s)$ by CV(T, D) - CV(T, D)'. Consequently, we can also compute the coherence $CH(\mathcal{T}, D)'$ of D after removing these triples by simply replacing CV(T, D) with CV(T, D)' for all types T in $\mathcal{T}$ (s). Finally, we compute the impact on the coherence of D of the removal as:

$$coin(\mathcal{T}(s), p) = CH(\mathcal{T}, D) - CH(\mathcal{T}, D)'$$

Let us illustrate this process with an example. Consider the dataset D_M introduced in Figure 19, and assume we would like to remove the triple (person1, ext, x5304) from D_M. Then the new coverage for the type person in this dataset becomes $\frac{6+2+2+1+3}{30} \approx 0.467$, hence the impact on the coverage of person is approximately $0.5 - 0.467 = 0.033$. In this example, D_M contains a single type, therefore the coherence of the dataset is the same as the coverage for person, which brings us to coin({person },ext) ≈ 0.033.

[1]We remind the reader that a single instance s can have multiple types, for example a GraduateStudent can also be a ResearchAssistant.

4.1 Benchmark generation algorithm

In this section we outline our algorithm to generate benchmark datasets of desired coherence and size by taking a dataset D and producing a dataset D' ⊂ D such that $\mathsf{CH}(\mathcal{T}, \mathsf{D'}) = \gamma$ and $|\mathsf{D'}| = \sigma$, where γ and σ are specified by the user. To do this, we need to determine which triples need to be removed from D to obtain D'. We will formulate this as an integer programming problem and solve it using an existing integer programming solver.

Previously in this section, for a set of types $\mathcal{S} \subseteq \mathcal{T}$ and a property p, we have shown how to compute coin($\mathcal{S}$,p), which represents the impact on coherence of removing all triples with subjects that are instances of the types in $\mathcal{S}$ and properties equal to p. For simplification, we will overload notation and use $|\mathsf{coin}(\mathcal{S}, \mathsf{p})|$ to denote the number of subjects that are instances of all the types in $\mathcal{S}$ and have at least one triple with property p, *i.e.,*

$$|\mathsf{coin}(\mathcal{S}, \mathsf{p})| = |\{s \in \bigcap_{T \in \mathcal{S}} \mathsf{I}(\mathsf{T}, \mathsf{D}) | \exists (s, p, v) \in \mathsf{D}\}|$$

Our objective is to formulate an integer programming problem whose solutions will tell us how many "coins" (triples with subjects that are instances of certain types and with a given property) to remove to achieve the desired coherence γ and size σ. Although we could use the same integer programming approach (with a different objective function and different constraints) for adding triples to the dataset, we did not explore this option because adding triples means we would have to "invent" new values/URIs/blank nodes, which is effectively what most benchmark generators do already. The challenge here is to have a systematic way to invent meaningful nodes that can have an impact on query evaluation (for instance, the invented nodes are returned as part of query answers) over various datasets; otherwise, the invented nodes have little value for the benchmarking purpose. We therefore took the approach of removing triples in existing datasets to create versions that reflect varying degrees of coherence and data size. This approach has an additional advantage that it can be applied to multiple different benchmark datasets with different primitive metrics (such as number of types, number of properties, and average indegree) and is still be able to generate a dataset with desired size and coherence.

In our benchmark generation algorithm, we will use X($\mathcal{S}$,p) to denote the integer programming variable representing the number of coins to remove for each type of coin. In the worst case, the number of such variables (and the corresponding coin types) for D can be $2^{\tau}\pi$, where τ is the number of types and π is the number of properties in the dataset. However, in practice, many type combinations will not have any instances. For instance, in LUBM, we will not find instances of UndergraduateStudent that are also instance of Course or Department. For LUBM, we found that although there are 15 types and 18 properties, we only have 73 valid combinations (sets of types and property with at least one coin available).

To achieve the desired coherence, we formulate the following constraint and maximization criteria for the integer programming problem.

$$\sum_{\mathcal{S} \subseteq \mathcal{T}, p} \mathsf{coin}(\mathcal{S}, \mathsf{p}) \times \mathsf{X}(\mathcal{S}, \mathsf{p}) \leq \mathsf{CH}(\mathcal{T}, \mathsf{D}) - \gamma \qquad \text{(C1)}$$

$$MAXIMIZE \sum_{\mathcal{S} \subseteq \mathcal{D}, p} \mathsf{coin}(\mathcal{S}, \mathsf{p}) \times \mathsf{X}(\mathcal{S}, \mathsf{p}) \qquad \text{(M)}$$

Inequality C1 states that the amount by which we decrease coherence (by removing coins) should be less than or equal than the amount we need to remove to get from $\mathsf{CH}(\mathcal{T}, \mathsf{D})$ (the coherence of the original dataset) to γ (the desired coherence). The objective function M states that the amount by which we decrease coherence should be maximized. The two elements together ensure that we decrease the coherence of D by as much as possible, while not going below γ.

We will also put lower and upper bounds on the number of coins that can be removed. Remember that assumption (A1) required us not to completely remove any properties from any types, so we will ensure that at least one coin of each type remains. Furthermore, we will enforce assumption (A2) about not removing instances from the dataset by always keeping triples with the rdf:type property.

$$\forall \mathcal{S} \subseteq \mathcal{T}, p \;\; 0 \leq \mathsf{X}(\mathcal{S}, \mathsf{p}) \leq |\mathsf{coin}(\mathcal{S}, \mathsf{p})| - 1 \qquad \text{(C2)}$$

Achieving the desired size σ is similar, but requires an approximation. Under the simplifying assumption that all properties are single-valued (*i.e.,* there is only one triple with a given subject and a given property in D), we could write the following constraint:

$$\sum_{\mathcal{S} \subseteq \mathcal{T}, p} |\mathsf{X}(\mathcal{S}, \mathsf{p})| = |\mathsf{D}| - \sigma$$

This equation would ensure that we remove exactly the right number of coins to obtain size σ assuming that all properties are single-valued (meaning one coin represents exactly one triple). However, this assumption does not hold for any of the datasets we have seen. In particular, for LUBM, many properties are multi-valued. As an example, a student can be enrolled in multiple courses, a paper has many authors, etc. We will address this by computing an average number of triples per coin type, which we denote by ct($\mathcal{S}$,p), and relaxing the size constraint as follows:

$$(1 - \rho) \times (|\mathsf{D}| - \sigma) \leq \sum_{\mathcal{S} \subseteq \mathcal{T}, p} \mathsf{X}(\mathcal{S}, \mathsf{p}) \times \mathsf{ct}(\mathcal{S}, \mathsf{p}) \qquad \text{(C3)}$$

$$\sum_{\mathcal{S} \subseteq \mathcal{T}, p} \mathsf{X}(\mathcal{S}, \mathsf{p}) \times \mathsf{ct}(\mathcal{S}, \mathsf{p}) \leq (1 + \rho) \times (|\mathsf{D}| - \sigma) \qquad \text{(C4)}$$

In these two constraints, ρ is a relaxation parameter. The presence of ρ is required because of the approximation we introduced by using the average number of triples per coin. In practice, setting ρ helped us tune the result of our algorithm closer to the target coherence and size.

We can now outline the algorithm that generates a benchmark dataset of desired coherence γ and size σ from an input dataset D:

(Step 1) Compute the coherence $\mathsf{CH}(\mathcal{T}, \mathsf{D})$ and the coin values coin($\mathcal{S}$,p) and average triples per coin ct($\mathcal{S}$,p) for all sets of types $\mathcal{S} \subseteq \mathcal{T}$ and all properties p.

(Step 2) Formulate the integer programming problem by writing constraints C1, C2, C3, C4 and objective function M. Solve the integer programming problem.

(Step 3) If the problem did not have a solution, then try to make the dataset smaller by removing a percentage of instances and continue from Step 1.

(Step 4) If the problem had a solution, then for each coin given by $\mathcal{S}$ and p, remove triples with X($\mathcal{S}$,p) subjects that are instances of types in $\mathcal{S}$ and have property p.

(Step 5) If the resulting dataset size is larger than σ, perform post-processing by attempting to remove from triples with the same subject and property.

We have previously explained in detail how steps (1) and (2) can be executed. Step (3) is an adjustment in case there is no solution to the linear programming problem. Remember that assumption (A2) required us not to remove entire instances from the dataset if the integer programming formulation is to produce the correct number of coins to remove. In practice we found that for certain combinations of γ and σ the integer programming problem does not have solutions – in particular for cases where the desired coherence γ is high, but the desired size σ is low (*i.e.,* we have to remove many coins, but we should not decrease coherence much). For these cases, we found that we can remove entire instances from D first to bring down its size, then reformulate the integer programming problem and find a solution. The intuition behind this approach is that when starting with original datasets of very high coherence (e.g., LUBM, TPC-H, etc.), removing instances uniformly at random will not decrease coherence much (if at all), since the coverage for all types is high, but it can decrease dataset size to a point where our integer programming approach finds a solution.

To perform this removal of instances effectively, we needed to understand how many instances to remove from the original dataset to have a high probability of finding a solution on the new dataset. In our experiments, the integer programming problem always had a solution for $\frac{\sigma}{|\mathsf{D}|} \approx \frac{\gamma}{\mathsf{CH}(\mathcal{T},\mathsf{D})}$. Therefore, we want to remove enough instances as to have the size of our new dataset approximately $\frac{\mathsf{CH}(\mathcal{T},\mathsf{D})}{\gamma} \times \sigma$. Assuming that the dataset size is proportional to the number of instances[2], then we should remove uniformly at random a proportion of $1 - \frac{\mathsf{CH}(\mathcal{T},\mathsf{D})}{\gamma} \times \frac{\sigma}{|\mathsf{D}|}$ instances to arrive at a dataset for which we have a good chance of solving the integer programming problem. After this process, we must restart the algorithm since the coherence and the numbers of coins for the dataset after the instance removal may be different than those of the original dataset.

In Step (4), we perform the actual removal of triples according to the solutions to the integer programming problem. Step (5) is a post-processing step that attempts to compensate for the approximation introduced by constraints C3 and C4 of the integer programming problem. Specifically, if the solution we obtain after Step (4) has a size higher than σ, then we can compensate by looking at triples with the same subject and property. Note that based on the way we have defined coverage for types, the formula measures whether instances have *at least one value* for each property of that type. Therefore, if a property is multi-valued, we can safely remove the triples containing extra values (ensuring that we keep at least one value), and therefore reduce the size of the dataset. While this step is optional, it can improve the match between σ and the actual size of the resulting dataset.

Note that the algorithm presented in this section performs at least two passes through the original dataset D. The first pass is performed in Step (1) to compute coherence and coin values and the average number of triples per coin. The second pass is performed in Step (4), where coins are removed from D to generate the desired dataset. If the integer programming problem does not have a solution, then at least four passes are required: one pass in Step (1), one pass in Step (3) to remove instances, a third pass in Step (1) to compute coherence and coin values after instance removal and finally a fourth pass in Step (4) to remove coins from the dataset. In addition, in either case there may be an additional pass over the resulting dataset to adjust for size (Step 5).

Our discussion of future work in Section 5 includes a query evaluation study that looks at how coherence of a dataset affects query performance. To perform such a study, we will need datasets with the same size but varying coherence and a set of queries that return the same results for each dataset. In our implementation, we added an additional option of specifying a list of triples that should not be removed from a dataset. This option impacts Step (2) where we need impose different upper bounds on the $\mathsf{X}(\mathcal{S},\mathsf{p})$ (to account for coins that cannot be removed) and in Step (4), to avoid removing the "forbidden" triples. The following process helps obtain the necessary datasets for a query evaluation study:

1. Start with a dataset D of high coherence and size.
2. Generate a first dataset D_0 with the desired size σ and the same coherence as D by removing entire instances uniformly at random.
3. Issue queries over D_0 and record *all triples required to produce answers* to these queries.
4. Generate datasets $\mathsf{D}_1, \ldots, \mathsf{D}_n$ of different coherence and the same size σ using the benchmark generation algorithm presented here. Use the set of triples computed in the previous step as "forbidden" triples during the generation to ensure that all datasets yield the same answers to all queries.

By experimenting with the option of avoiding triples, we found that it works well for queries of medium to high selectivity. Queries of low selectivity require many triples to answer, thus greatly diminishing the set of useful coins that can reduce coherence of a dataset.

4.2 Experimental results and discussion

We implemented our benchmark generation algorithm in Java and performed experiments on multiple original datasets, both benchmark and real-world. We used lpsolve 5.5[3] as our integer programming solver with a timeout of 100 seconds per problem. We report results from running the benchmark generation on four servers with identical configuration: 2 dual-core 3GHz processors, 24GB of memory and 12 TB of shared disk space. We used these machines to run experiments in parallel, but we also performed similar experiments (one at a time) on a standard T7700 2.4 Ghz 3GB of RAM laptop machine.

We started with the LUBM dataset in different sizes (100K triples, 1, 10 and 100 million triples). For each, we executed benchmark generation with nine sets of parameters, $\gamma \in \{0.25, 0.5, 0.75\}$ and $\sigma \in \{0.25, 0.5, 0.75\} \times |\mathsf{D}|$. The results are shown in Figures 24–27. In each figure, the x axis represents the percentage of the original dataset size desired and the y axis represents the coherence desired (as an absolute value, not as a percentage of original coherence). The square markers in each figure represent the ideal output and the *X* markers represent the achieved size/coherence combination. We can easily see that with the exception of the 75% size, 0.25 coherence combination the algorithm achieves almost perfect matches. The relaxation parameter ρ was set to a default of 0.1 for all LUBM runs.

The 75% size, 0.25 coherence combination essentially requires that we lower coherence by a large margin (remember that the original coherence of LUBM is above 0.9), while maintaining most of the triples in the dataset. In this case, the integer programming solver maximizes the amount of coherence that can be removed (as instructed by the objective function), but cannot achieve perfect coherence. This is caused by the fact that we have an upper bound on the amount by which coherence should decrease (constraint C1), but no lower bound like we do for size. However, we noticed that by introducing a lower bound for the amount by which coherence can decrease has two downsides: (i) it introduces a new control parameter (in addition to ρ) and (ii) without adjustment of this parameter, the integer programming solver either times out or cannot solve the problem in many cases. As a result, we decided that the algorithm is more useful without the lower bound on coherence reduction (which means an upperbound on resulting coherence). As

[2]We found this to be true for all datasets we examined.

[3]http://lpsolve.sourceforge.net/5.5/

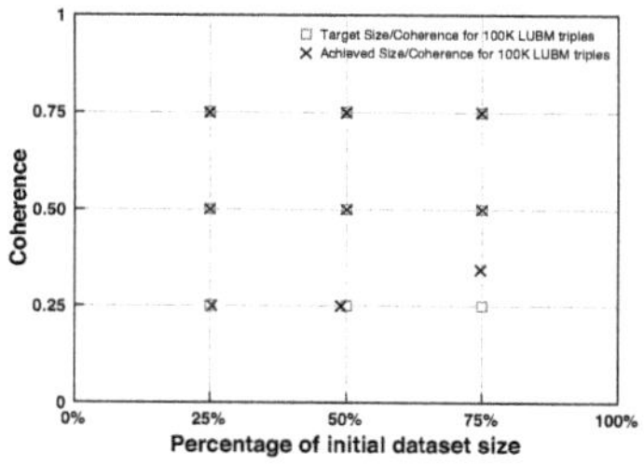

Figure 24: LUBM 100K

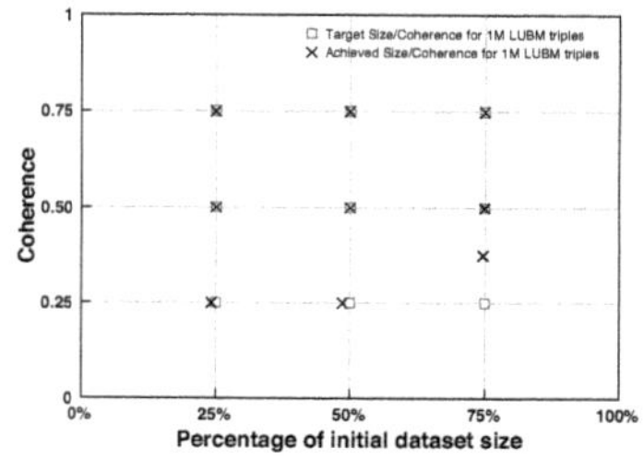

Figure 25: LUBM 1M

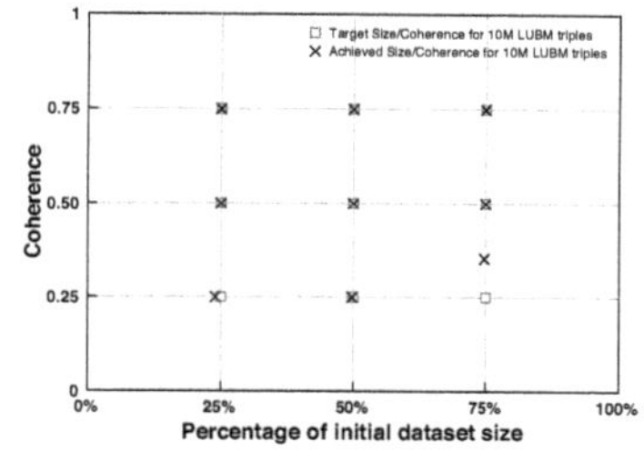

Figure 26: LUBM 10M

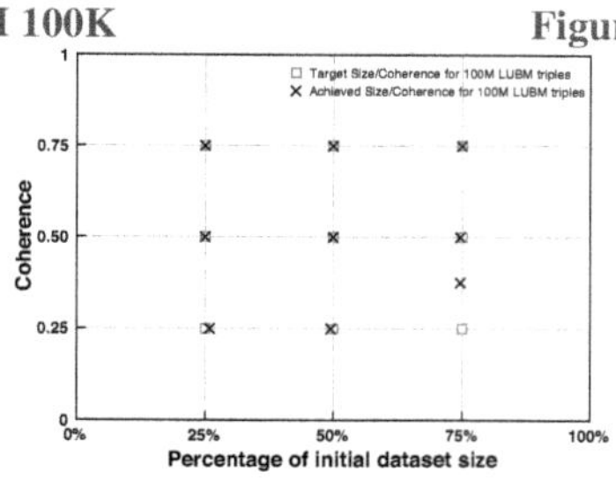

Figure 27: LUBM 100M

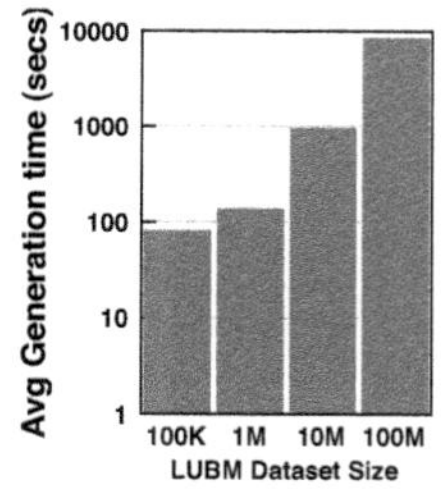

Figure 28: Running time: LUBM

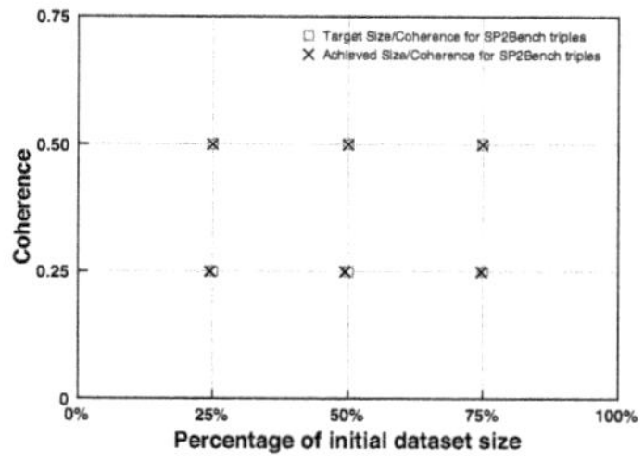

Figure 29: SP²Bench

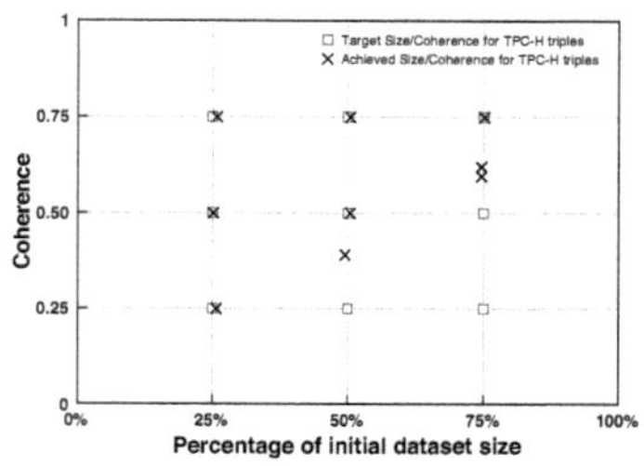

Figure 30: TPC-H

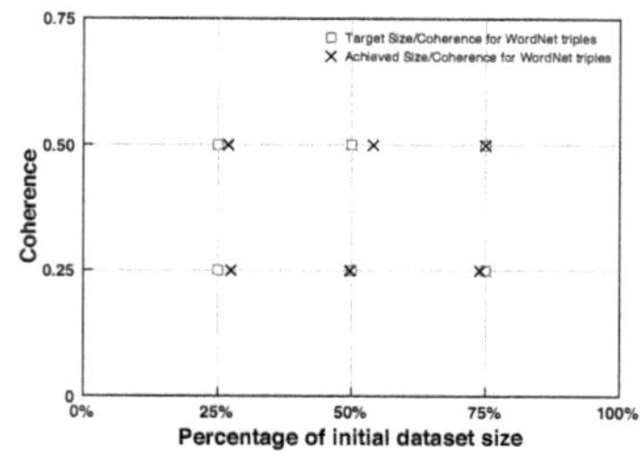

Figure 31: Wordnet

an alternative, in cases where such combinations are desired, the user can start with a larger dataset size – for instance, instead of starting with a 1 million triple dataset requiring 75% size and 0.25 coherence, the user can start with a 3 million triple dataset and request 25% size and 0.25 coherence.

The average running time for the benchmark generation over LUBM is shown in Figure 28 and is linear in the size of the dataset (in the figure, both axes are on a logarithmic scale), since the algorithm requires between 2 and 4 passes over the original dataset.

Next, we ran our algorithm with SP^{2}Bench, TPC-H and Wordnet as the original dataset. The results are shown in Figures 29 – 31. Note that for Wordnet and SP^{2}Bench, the maximal achievable coherence is 0.5 (given the original coherence of these datasets). SP^{2}Bench contains a number of RDF container objects, which contain elements in no particular order. In its n-triples format, each container had *numbered* predicate edges to each of the contained elements (e.g., the container was connected to value $v1$ by $p1$, value $v2$ by $p2$, and so on). Because this numbering of containment relationships is arbitrary, and it can skew any measurement of type coherence for the container type, we replaced all numbered predicate labels with a single containment relationship before generation. For TPC-H, the relaxation parameter ρ is 0.01 for all 9 points. Notice that as in the case of LUBM, the integer programming solver finds a sub-optimal solution for some points. So the solver finds a solution that has the right size but misses coherence. For SP^{2}Bench, the relaxation is 0.01 for the points with size 25% and 0.05 for the points with size 50%. For Wordnet, ρ varies between 0.01 and 0.05. We observed the following in practice about setting the relaxation parameter ρ. Low values of ρ mean that the bounds on the size of the generated dataset are tighter, therefore we are more likely to achieve the desired size. However, remember that there is a lower and an upper bound on size reduction (depending on ρ), whereas there is a single upper bound on coherence reduction. This means that if size bounds are tight, the integer programming solver will attempt to find the optimal coherence reduction within the given size bounds, which may not be very close to the desired coherence γ. On the other hand, if the size bounds are loose (higher ρ), that means that the integer programming solver may find a better optimal value for the coherence reduction, and our algorithm can still approach the desired size using the compensation in Step (5). Generally, choosing ρ depends on the original dataset size and the desired dataset size. For small initial datasets, having "loose" bounds (*i.e.,* $\rho = 0.1$) is a good option because it gives the integer programming solver a larger solution space to work for. For larger datasets, we do not want too much flexibility in the size, hence we can choose low relaxation values (*i.e.,* 0.01 in TPC-H). However, if the target dataset size is also large (75% of the original), we can again have higher values of the relaxation parameter because we still achieve a good match.

5. CONCLUSIONS

We presented an extensive study of the characteristics of real and benchmark RDF data. Through this study, we illustrated that primitive metrics, although useful, offer little insight about the inherent characteristics of datasets and how these compare to each other. We introduced a *macroscopic* metric, called coherence, that essentially combines many of these primitive metrics and is used to measure the structuredness of different datasets. We showed that while real datasets cover the whole structuredness spectrum, benchmark datasets are very limited in their structuredness and are mostly relational-like. Since structuredness plays an important role on how we store, index and query data, the above result indicates that existing benchmarks do not accurately predict the behaviour of RDF stores in realistic scenarios. In response to this limitation, we also introduced a benchmark generator which can be used to generate benchmark datasets that actually resemble real datasets in terms of structuredness, size, and content. This is feasible since our generator can use any dataset as input (real or synthetic) and generate a benchmark out of it. On the technical side, we formally introduced structuredness through the coherence metric, and we showed how the challenge of benchmark generation can be solved by formulating it as an integer programming problem.

Using this work as a starting point, there are several avenues we are investigating next. Specifically, one important topic is the effects of structuredness on RDF storage strategies. Our preliminary investigation shows that while relational column stores are considered a popular and effective storage strategy for RDF data, this assumption holds true mainly for data with high structuredness. Such data often exhibit a small number of types in their type system, and each type has a small number of properties. Then, a column store approach to RDF requires only a few tens of tables in the RDBMS. However, data with low structuredness, like DBpedia or Yago, have large number of types and properties (in the thousands). For such datasets, a column store solution would require thousands of tables in RDBMS and is thus not expected to scale.

Another avenue we are investigating relates to the indexing and querying of RDF data. Structuredness influences both the type and the density of the indexes used. At the same time, it influences the selectivity of queries and therefore the overall query performance. We plan to investigate the concrete effects of structuredness on query performance and contrast the performance of equivalent queries over datasets with varying structuredness. Ideally, for this comparison to be meaningful, the queries should return identical results across all varying structuredness datasets. We have done some preliminary work, and included an exclusion list in our integer programming formulation so as to exclude certain triples (those that participate in the query result) from removal, as we compute a new dataset with smaller structuredness. It turns out however, that trying to maintain such triples for low-selectivity queries often leads to a linear programming problem that is impossible to solve. Therefore, we are considering other alternatives to meaningfully compare low-selectivity queries across the different datasets.

6. REFERENCES

[1] D. J. Abadi, A. Marcus, S. R. Madden, and K. Hollenbach. Scalable semantic web data management using vertical partitioning. In *VLDB*, pages 411–422, 2007.

[2] S. Abiteboul, R. Hull, and V. Vianu. *Foundations of Databases*. Addison-Wesley, 1995.

[3] R. Apweiler, A. Bairoch, C. H. Wu, W. C. Barker, B. Boeckmann, S. Ferro, E. Gasteiger, H. Huang, R. Lopez, M. Magrane, M. J. Martin, D. A. Natale, C. O'Donovan, N. Redaschi, and L. S. Yeh. Uniprot: the universal protein knowledgebase. *Nucleic Acids Res.*, 32:D115–D119, 2004.

[4] M. Arenas and L. Libkin. A normal form for xml documents. In *PODS*, pages 85–96, 2002.

[5] BBC World Cup 2010 dynamic semantic publishing. `http://www.bbc.co.uk/blogs/bbcinternet/2010/07/bbc_world_cup_2010_dynamic_sem.html`.

[6] Best Buy jump starts data web marketing. `http://www.chiefmartec.com/2009/12/best-buy-jump-starts-data-web-marketing.html`.

[7] C. Bizer, T. Heath, and T. Berners-Lee. Linked data - the story so far. *Int. J. Semantic Web Inf. Syst.*, 5(3):1–22, 2009.

[8] C. Bizer, J. Lehmann, G. Kobilarov, S. Auer, C. Becker, R. Cyganiak, and S. Hellmann. DBpedia—a crystallization point for the web of data. *Web Semantics*, 7(3):154–165, 2009.

[9] C. Bizer, J. Lehmann, G. Kobilarov, S. Auer, C. Becker, R. Cyganiak, and S. Hellmann. Dbpedia - a crystallization point for the web of data. *Web Semant.*, 7:154–165, September 2009.

[10] C. Bizer and A. Schultz. The berlin sparql benchmark. *Int. J. Semantic Web Inf. Syst.*, 5(2):1–24, 2009.

[11] J. Broekstra, A. Kampman, and F. van Harmelen. Sesame: A generic architecture for storing and querying rdf and rdf schema. In *ISWC*, pages 54–68, 2002.

[12] D2R Server: Publishing Relational Databases on the Semantic Web. `http://www4.wiwiss.fu-berlin.de/bizer/d2r-server/`.

[13] Data.gov. `http://www.data.gov/`.

[14] Data.gov.uk. `http://www.data.gov.uk/`.

[15] O. Erling and I. Mikhailov. Rdf support in the virtuoso dbms. In *CSSW*, pages 59–68, 2007.

[16] Y. Guo, Z. Pan, and J. Heflin. Lubm: A benchmark for owl knowledge base systems. *J. Web Semantics*, 3(2-3):158–182, 2005.

[17] S. Harris and N. Gibbins. 3store: Efficient bulk rdf storage. In *PSSS*, 2003.

[18] L3S Research Center D2R Server publishing the DBLP Bibliography Database. `http://dblp.l3s.de/d2r/`.

[19] Making a Semantic Web Business Case at Pfizer. `http://www.semanticweb.com/news/making_a_semantic_web_business_case_at_pfizer_161731.asp`.

[20] B. McBride. Jena: Implementing the rdf model and syntax specification. In *SemWeb*, 2001.

[21] T. Neumann and G. Weikum. Rdf-3x: a risc-style engine for rdf. *PVLDB*, 1(1):647–659, 2008.

[22] T. Neumann and G. Weikum. The rdf-3x engine for scalable management of rdf data. *VLDB J.*, 19(1):91–113, 2010.

[23] H. Patni, C. Henson, and A. Sheth. Linked sensor data. 2010.

[24] Resource Description Framework (RDF). `http://www.w3.org/RDF/`.

[25] V. Sans and D. Laurent. Prefix based numbering schemes for xml: techniques, applications and performances. *Proc. VLDB Endow.*, 1(2):1564–1573, 2008.

[26] M. Schmidt, T. Hornung, G. Lausen, and C. Pinkel. Sp2bench: A sparql performance benchmark. In *ICDE*, pages 222–233, 2009.

[27] F. M. Suchanek, G. Kasneci, and G. Weikum. Yago: A large ontology from wikipedia and wordnet. *J. Web Sem.*, 6(3):203–217, 2008.

[28] The MIT Barton Library dataset. `http://simile.mit.edu/rdf-test-data/`.

[29] The TPC Benchmark H. `http://www.tpc.org/tpch`.

[30] WordNet: A lexical database for English. `http://www.w3.org/2006/03/wn/wn20/`.

[31] XMark: An XML Benchmark Project. `http://www.xml-benchmark.org/`.

[32] YAGO: Yet Another Great Ontology. `http://www.mpi-inf.mpg.de/yago-naga/yago/`.

Efficient Query Answering in Probabilistic RDF Graphs

Xiang Lian and Lei Chen
Department of Computer Science and Engineering
The Hong Kong University of Science and Technology
Hong Kong, China
{xlian, leichen}@cse.ust.hk

ABSTRACT

In this paper, we tackle the problem of efficiently answering queries on probabilistic RDF data graphs. Specifically, we model RDF data by probabilistic graphs, and an RDF query is equivalent to a search over subgraphs of probabilistic graphs that have high probabilities to match with a given query graph. To efficiently process queries on probabilistic RDF graphs, we propose effective pruning mechanisms, structural and probabilistic pruning. For the structural pruning, we carefully design synopses for vertex/edge labels by considering their distributions and other structural information, in order to improve the pruning power. For the probabilistic pruning, we derive a cost model to guide the pre-computation of probability upper bounds such that the query cost is expected to be low. We construct an index structure that integrates synopses/statistics for structural and probabilistic pruning, and propose an efficient approach to answer queries on probabilistic RDF graph data. The efficiency of our solutions has been verified through extensive experiments.

Categories and Subject Descriptors

H.2.4 [**Database Management**]: Systems—*Query processing*; H.3.3 [**Information Systems**]: Information Storage and retrieval—*Information search and retrieval, Search process*

General Terms

Algorithms, Design, Experimentation, Performance, Theory

Keywords

probabilistic RDF graph, probabilistic data, RDF

1. INTRODUCTION

The RDF (Resource Description Framework) data model is a W3C standard to describe resources on the Web and capture their relationships. RDF has been proposed for a decade, and nowadays it has been widely used in many real applications such as the Semantic Web [1]. In RDF, data items are represented in the form of triples, (*subject*, *predicate*, *object*), also known as (*subject*, *property*, *object*) triples. As an example, information about two persons with identities (IDs), pid_1 and pid_2, could include the triples as shown in Figure 1 (note: not all triples are depicted).

SIGMOD'11, June 12–16, 2011, Athens, Greece.

RDF triples from data source A:
(1) ("Zoe", <givenNameOf>, pid_1);
(2) ("Panos", <familyNameOf>, pid_1);
(3) (pid_1, <type>, "scientist");
(4) (pid_1, <bornInLocation>,"Athens");
(5) (pid_1, <studyIn>,"Athens");
(6) ("Athens", <bornStudyRel.>, "Athens");
(7) ("Athens", <locationIn>, "Greece");
(8) (pid_1, <hasDoctoralAdvisor> pid_2);
...
(9) (pid_2, <bornInLocation>, "Athens");
(10) ("Athens", <locationIn>, "Greece");
...

Figure 1: RDF triple data.

From the triples, the first person with ID pid_1 is a scientist (observed from triple (3)) called "Zoe Panos" (from triples (1) and (2)), born and studying in Athens, Greece (triples (5)-(7)), and her PhD advisor is the person with ID pid_2 (triple (8)). Similarly, the second person with ID pid_2 was also born in Athens, Greece (obtained from triples (9) and (10)).

RDF triples can be equivalently viewed from a graph perspective [3]. That is, for each RDF triple (S, P, O), *subject*, S, and *object*, O, can be considered as labels of two adjacent vertices in a graph, and *predicate*, P, is treated as the label of a directed edge from S to O. Figure 2(a) presents the equivalent graph representation of RDF triples above. In the previous example, the top-left vertex in Figure 2(a) has label "Zoe", connecting with a vertex pid_1 through the directed edge labeled "givenNameOf", and it exactly corresponds to the subject of triple (1), ("Zoe", <givenNameOf>, pid_1).

In practice, RDF data can be highly unreliable [13, 15] for reasons such as data errors or expirations. For example, in the application of information extraction (IE) [28] from unstructured Web data, IE methods will naturally infer top-k possible (uncertain) data, associated with extraction accuracies, in the probabilistic RDF form.

Similarly, during the data integration [11, 12], we need to incorporate RDF data from various data sources into a database. Here, the uncertainty/inconsistency in the integrated data can result from either the extraction accuracy or the reliability of sources [11, 12]. For example, assume that another data source, B, has collected the same set of information about the two persons, pid_1 and pid_2, however, with a few different triples from data source, A, listed below.

Different RDF triples in data source B from that in data source A:
(4') (pid_1, <bornInLocation>, "Aarau");
(5') (pid_1, <studyIn>,"Aarau");
(6') ("Aarau", <bornStudyRel.>, "Aarau");
(9') (pid_2, <bornInLocation>, "Berlin");
(10') ("Berlin", <locatedIn>, "Germany");
(11') ("Aarau", <locationIn.>, "Switzerland");

Taking triples (4) and (4') as an example, the two data sources A and B report inconsistent places where person pid_1 was born, that is, "Athens" and "Aarau", respectively.

In order to model/resolve such inconsistencies [6, 10], we can assign each possible birthplace with a probability to indicate its

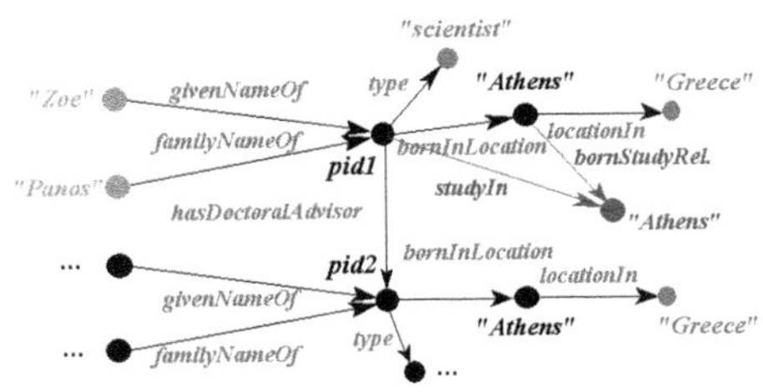

(a)

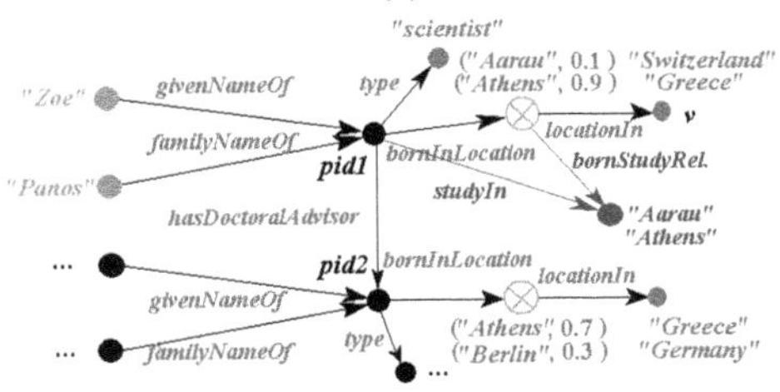

(b)

Figure 2: Graph representation of certain and probabilistic RDF data. (a) Certain RDF data graph. (b) Probabilistic RDF data graph.

confidence to be true. Accordingly, in the graph of Figure 2(b) for such integrated RDF data, the top vertex "⊗" is associated with a probability table containing labels for possible birthplaces, that is, "Athens" with probability 0.9 and "Aarau" with probability 0.1. Here, probabilities can be inferred from the reliability of data from different sources [11]. Similarly, the vertex v adjacent to top vertex "⊗" via an out-going edge labeled "locationIn" is associated with a (conditional) probability table, containing entries for labels "Switzerland" and "Greece". That is, since "Aarau" is a city of "Switzerland", rather than "Greece", vertex v takes label "Switzerland" with probability 1, given that vertex "⊗" takes label "Aarau"; moreover, v takes value "Greece" with probability 1, given that "⊗" takes "Athens". Therefore, this graph representation (via conditional probability tables in vertices) is generic enough to capture the correlations/constraints among labels of vertices [20].

The SPARQL query is a standard language for querying RDF data, and supports conjunctions (disjunctions as well) of triple patterns. However, it usually assumes that RDF data are certain and accurate. To give an example, the SPARQL query below retrieves the given name and family name of a scientist, who was born in Greece, and whose doctoral supervisor was also born in Greece.

```
select ?gn ?fn
where { ?gn <givenNameOf> ?p. ?fn <familyNameOf> ?p.
        ?p <type> "scientist". ?p <bornInLocation> ?city.
        ?city <locatedIn> "Greece".
        ?p <hasDoctoralAdvisor> ?a.
        ?a <bornInLocation> ?city2. ?city2 <locatedIn> "Greece"}
```

Note that, within the "where" clause of this SPARQL query, triple patterns contain either variables or literals, and they are concatenated by dots (indicating conjunctions). The SPARQL query is to find bindings of variables (e.g., $?gn$ and $?fn$) that satisfy the conjunctions in the "where" clause.

Each SPARQL query can be also represented by a graph [3], which contains directed edges corresponding to triple patterns. Figure 3 shows the query graph of our SPARQL example mentioned above. As a result, any SPARQL query can be considered as a subgraph pattern matching problem, which identifies subgraphs in RDF data graph matching with structures/labels of the query graph.

In the case of data integration, RDF data graph integrated from different data sources can be considered as a probabilistic graph. Thus, in this paper, our goal is to efficiently and effectively conduct a SPARQL query over probabilistic RDF data graphs.

In order to guarantee the confidence of the returned query answer, we re-define the matching probability between a subgraph

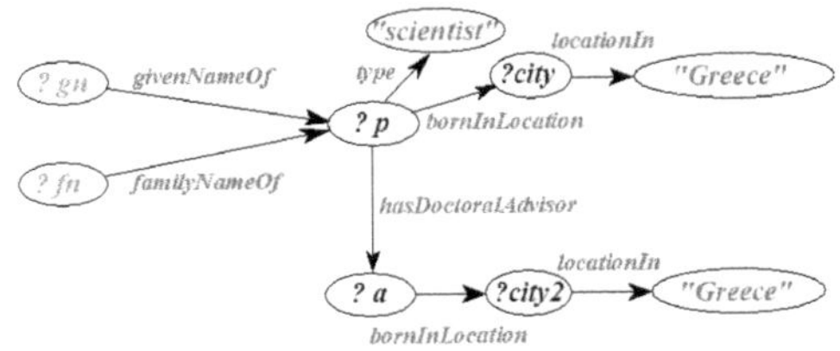

Figure 3: A SPARQL query on (probabilistic) RDF data.

and a query graph in probabilistic RDF graphs. However, the query answering in such probabilistic RDF graph is challenging, in terms of the query efficiency. First, the subgraph matching probabilities need to consider uncertainties and correlations of labels for vertices, which is costly to compute. That is, the computation of subgraph matching probabilities requires to take into account the *possible worlds* semantics [10] for probabilistic RDF graph, where each possible world is a materialized instance of the data graph. However, since the number of possible worlds can be exponential, it is not time- and space- efficient to materialize and query on all possible worlds. Thus, existing solutions to querying certain RDF data do not easily apply to probabilistic RDF data well, in terms of query efficiency. Second, RDF data graphs have their own properties, for example, some vertices in the graph have very large (mega-scale) degrees, or labels with skewed distributions. Therefore, such properties may incur low query efficiency, if we use indexes for usual probabilistic graphs that do not have these properties.

To tackle the challenging problems mentioned above, in this paper, we first formalize the problem of answering SPARQL queries over probabilistic RDF data, in the presence of label correlations. Then, we propose effective pruning techniques for RDF queries, with respect to both structural and probabilistic pruning. For the structural pruning, we design novel filtering synopses that are adaptive to label distributions, in order to improve the pruning power. The rationale behind our synopses is due to an observation, that highly frequent labels are less likely to help prune false alarms. Our synopses take into account this observation, and assign less frequent labels with higher weights. This way, we can reduce the chances of hashing confliction in synopses, and the pruning power is expected to be higher. We derive a cost model to decide the parameter settings in our hashing functions for synopses. For the probabilistic pruning, we propose another cost model to formalize the query cost, and adaptively store pre-computed probability upper bounds to facilitate the pruning such that the query cost is minimized in light of our cost model.

To summarize, we make the following contributions.

- We give a general framework for answering RDF queries in the probabilistic RDF data graph.
- For the structural pruning, we propose effective methods to increase the pruning ability of graph synopses w.r.t. labels and graph structures, by adaptively considering the distribution of hashed labels based on our proposed cost model.
- For the probabilistic pruning, we design a cost model to formalize the query cost w.r.t. probability upper bounds. Then, we adaptively determine the number of pre-computed bounds that we store for the pruning, so as to achieve low query cost.
- We propose an effective index to summarize/store the pre-computed data in synopses, and present an efficient approach for query answering over probabilistic RDF data graph.

Section 5 shows through extensive experiments the efficiency and effectiveness of our approaches. Section 6 reviews previous works on query answering in certain RDF databases, as well as that in probabilistic databases. Finally, Section 7 concludes this paper.

2. PROBLEM DEFINITION

2.1 Probabilistic RDF Data Graph

Probabilistic RDF Graph Databases: First, we define a probabilistic RDF graph database $\mathcal{G}$ that contains probabilistic graphs G, modeled by *Bayesian networks* [29] in the probability theory.

DEFINITION 2.1. *(Probabilistic RDF Data Graph) A probabilistic RDF data graph $G \in \mathcal{G}$ is represented by a triple ($V(G)$, $E(G)$, $S(G)$). Here, we have:*

- *$V(G)$ is a finite set of vertices v_i with possible labels $l(v_i)$;*
- *$E(G)$ is a finite set of directed edges e_{ij} with labels $l(e_{ij})$;*
- *$S(G)$ is a finite set of conditional probability tables (CPTs), $T(v_i|pa(v_i))$, associated with vertices $v_i \in G$, which describe probabilities that v_i take labels $l(v_i)$, given that vertices $v_j \in pa(v_i)$ take some labels $l(v_j)$, where $pa(v_i)$ contains parent vertices that point to v_i via directed edges.*

In Definition 2.1, each vertex $v_i \in V(G)$ of graph G has one or multiple possible labels, $l(v_i)$, corresponding to either *subjects* or *objects* in RDF triples collected from data sources. Moreover, $e_{ij} \in E(G)$ is a directed edge from vertex v_i to vertex v_j, with a deterministic edge label $l(e_{ij})$ that corresponds to the *predicate* in RDF triples.

Furthermore, any CPT, $T(v_i|pa(v_i))$, in $S(G)$ stores the correlations of possible labels for vertex v_i and its parents in $pa(v_i)$. In particular, a CPT contains 3 types of attributes: labels $l(v_i)$, $l(v_j)$, and conditional probabilities $Pr\{l(v_i)|l(v_j)\}$, where v_j is the parent of v_i (i.e., $v_j \in pa(v_i)$).

In our previous example of Figure 2(b), the top vertex "$\otimes$" in the probabilistic RDF data graph is associated with a CPT, which contains 2 entries: $Pr\{$"Aarau"$|\ pid_1\} = 0.1$ and $Pr\{$"Athens" $|\ pid_1\} = 0.9$. Intuitively, this CPT stores the probability that top vertex "$\otimes$" takes a possible birthplace (e.g., "Aarau" or "Athens"), conditioned on its parent, that is, a particular person ID pid_1.

Remarks: Different from certain RDF graphs where every vertex has a deterministic label, the probabilistic RDF data graph in Definition 2.1 contains vertices with uncertain labels. In particular, set $V(G)$ includes vertices that can take different possible labels with some confidences, whereas set $S(G)$ has CPTs that store correlations of uncertain labels assigned to vertices. Note that, by storing different conditional probabilities among variables in CPTs, we can capture arbitrary correlations (including, but not limited to, mutually exclusive or independent relationship) for labels in vertices.

Moreover, in our model, each vertex of probabilistic RDF graphs is associated with uncertain labels, which is quite different from the model assumption in [15] that considers the existence probabilities of edges to appear in reality (with certain vertex labels).

Possible Worlds of Probabilistic RDF Data Graphs: In the literature of probabilistic databases [10], we usually consider the *possible worlds* semantics, where each possible world is a materialized instance of the database that can appear in the real world. Similarly, we also consider the possible worlds semantics in a probabilistic RDF data graph. As will be described later in Section 2.2, RDF queries are defined over such possible worlds.

DEFINITION 2.2. *(Possible Worlds of a Probabilistic RDF Data Graph, $pw(G)$) The possible world, $pw(G)$, of a probabilistic RDF graph $G \in \mathcal{G}$ is an instance of probabilistic graph G such that each vertex $v_i \in V(G)$ is assigned with a deterministic label $l(v_i)$.*

The certain RDF data graph shown in Figure 2(a) is exactly one possible world of the probabilistic RDF data graph in Figure 2(b), where each vertex is associated with a deterministic label (e.g., both vertices "$\otimes$" in Figure 2(b) take labels "Athens" in Figure 2(a)).

Each possible world $pw(G)$ of a probabilistic RDF graph G has its own appearance probabilities given below.

DEFINITION 2.3. *(The Appearance Probability of a Possible World, $Pr\{pw(G)\}$) Given a probabilistic RDF graph $G \in \mathcal{G}$, the appearance probability, $Pr\{pw(G)\}$, of possible world $pw(G)$ is:*

$$Pr\{pw(G)\} = \prod_{\forall v_i \in V(pw(G))} Pr\{l(v_i) \mid l(v_j), \forall v_j \in pa(v_i)\}, \quad (1)$$

where $pa(v_j)$ is a set of parent vertices of v_j.

Intuitively, Eq. (1) calculates the (joint) probability of one possible label binding (i.e., $l(v_i)$) for all vertices v_i in the probabilistic graph G, which can be obtained by multiplying conditional probabilities, $Pr\{l(v_i) \mid l(v_j), \forall v_j \in pa(v_i)\}$, in CPTs of $S(G)$.

In the previous example of Figure 2(b), assume that all vertices except for two "$\otimes$" have CPTs with conditional probabilities equal to 1. Then, one of its possible worlds, $pw(G)$, shown in Figure 2(a) has the appearance probability $Pr\{pw(G)\} = Pr\{$"Athens"$|pid_1\}$ $\cdot Pr\{$"Athens" $|\ pid_2\} = 0.9 \times 0.7 = 0.63$.

2.2 Subgraph Matching on Probabilistic RDF Data Graph

Queries Over Probabilistic RDF Graph Databases: As mentioned earlier, we can transform any SPARQL query to a query graph q (containing vertices with or without labels specified by the query issuer), and then retrieve those subgraphs, g, in probabilistic RDF data graphs G that match with q. In the probabilistic RDF graph database, we formally define RDF queries below.

DEFINITION 2.4. *(RDF Queries in the Probabilistic RDF Graph Database) Given a probabilistic RDF graph $G \in \mathcal{G}$, a query graph q, and a user-specified probabilistic threshold $\alpha \in [0, 1)$, a subgraph matching query obtains those subgraphs $g \in G$ and their label bindings $l(g_i)$ for vertices $g_i \in V(g)$, such that (1) g is isomorphic to q, and (2) $Pr\{g\} > \alpha$ holds.*

In Definition 2.4, a subgraph g in G matches with query graph q, if and only if two conditions are satisfied. The first condition indicates that subgraph g and query graph q should be isomorphic to each other. Note that, similar to SPARQL queries on certain RDF graph where it is rare to let predicates (edge labels) be variables (unspecified), we assume that all edge labels are specified in query graph q, and variables only appear in vertex labels of q[1]. Thus, g and q are isomorphic, if and only if they structurally match with each other, have the exact matching of edge labels, and have the same vertex labels in g as that specified in q. Finally, the second condition adds a probabilistic constraint to guarantee high confidences of query answers, and only returns those subgraphs g that appear in reality with probabilities $Pr\{g\}$ greater than α.

2.3 Major Challenges

According to the definition of subgraph matching on probabilistic RDF data graph, one straightforward method is to compare every possible subgraph g and its label bindings with the query graph q, and return those subgraphs that satisfy the two conditions given in Definition 2.4. Clearly, this method is not efficient, since there are exponential number of subgraphs $g \in G$, the cost of checking the isomorphism is high, and the computation of matching probabilities $Pr\{g\}$ (in the second condition) is also costly by considering exponential number of possible worlds $pw(g)$ of g. Therefore, this raises a serious problem about the query efficiency. Most importantly, a probabilistic RDF data graph has its own features, for example, its labels/degrees of vertices can be highly skewed, which may lead to low pruning power of query answering through indexes, and moreover, the correlated label information may cause the appearance probabilities difficult to compute.

[1] The case where an edge has a label variable can be easily handled by treating this edge as a special vertex with a label variable, connecting to its two adjacent vertices.

Symbol	Description
$\mathcal{G}$	a probabilistic RDF graph database
$V(G)$ $(E(G))$	a set of vertices (edges) in probabilistic RDF graphs G
$S(G)$	a set of conditional probability tables (CPTs) in probabilistic RDF graphs G
$pw(G)$	a possible world of probabilistic RDF graphs G
$Pr\{pw(G)\}$	the appearance probability of a possible world of G
q	an RDF query graph containing $\|q\|$ vertices
v_i, q_i, or g_i	the name of a vertex
$pa(v_i)$	a set of parent vertices of vertex v_i
e_{ij} (or e_g)	the name of a directed edge $\overrightarrow{v_iv_j}$ (or that in graph g)
$l(v_i)$ (or $l(e_{ij})$)	the label of a vertex v_i (or a directed edge e_{ij})
α	a probabilistic threshold for RDF subgraph matching

Table 1: Symbols and descriptions.

Observing the challenges above, in this paper, we follow a filter-and-refine framework to first filter out those false alarms of subgraph candidates and then refine the remaining candidates. The detailed steps will be discussed in Section 3.1. Table 1 summarizes the commonly used symbols.

3. SUBGRAPH MATCHING OVER PROBABILISTIC RDF GRAPHS

3.1 Framework

Figure 4 illustrates the pseudo-code of the general framework for answering queries in a probabilistic RDF graph database, namely Prob_RDF_QA_Framework. In particular, this framework consists of 4 phases, *indexing*, *query pre-processing*, *pruning*, and *refinement phases*. The first indexing phase builds a tree index, $\mathcal{I}$, for synopses of subgraphs g in a probabilistic RDF graph database $\mathcal{G}$ (line 1). Next, for any RDF query with a query graph q, we access index $\mathcal{I}$ and obtain those matching subgraphs g (lines 2-5).

Specifically, upon the query request, the query pre-processing phase evaluates query graph q via estimations and chooses a good query plan that can achieve the expected low query cost (line 3). Then, we traverse index $\mathcal{I}$ in the pruning phase by applying the structural and probabilistic pruning on nodes/subgraphs in $\mathcal{I}$ (line 4). After the index traversal, we can combine and refine the remaining candidate subgraphs based on Definition 2.4 (line 5). Finally, we return actual RDF query answers to the query issuer (line 6).

3.2 RDF Query Pre-Processing

As illustrated in procedure Prob_RDF_QA_Framework (Figure 4), the query pre-processing phase needs to identify a good query plan to traverse the index $\mathcal{I}$ with low query cost.

In fact, our query procedure (discussed later in Section 4) first starts with vertices $q_i \in V(q)$ in the query graph q that have the user-specified labels $l(q_i)$, and then traverses index $\mathcal{I}$ to find their matching vertex candidates v_i in G in parallel, satisfying $l(v_i) = l(q_i)$ (filtering with other information, if possible). Meanwhile, we combine candidates v_i to obtain subgraphs g that match with q. To enable the pruning of candidate subgraphs, we can utilize the information such as the shortest path distances between two matching candidates v_i and v_j (w.r.t. q_i and q_j, respectively).

In particular, as will be illustrated in Section 3.3, we will check whether or not neighbors within several hops from the two candidates share any common labels, in order to prune with the graph distance. Thus, with a larger graph distance from q_i to q_j, we will consider more neighbor hops, and thus neighbors of candidates v_i and v_j are more likely to share common labels, which incurs lower pruning power and produces more intermediate results. Therefore, in order to enhance the pruning power, our query plan selection aims to find a number of close vertex pairs (q_i, q_j) in q (note: both $l(q_i)$ and $l(q_j)$ are specified by q), such that only a small number of false candidates (in intermediate results) are kept for further processing (join), and low query cost can be achieved.

Based on the intuition above, we aim to online obtain a set, *QPlan*, containing pairs of labeled vertices (q_i, q_j) $(i \neq j)$ in q

Procedure Prob_RDF_QA_Framework {
Input: a probabilistic RDF graph database $\mathcal{G}$, a query graph q, and a probabilistic threshold α
Output: subgraphs g from $\mathcal{G}$ that match with q with probability $Pr\{g\} > \alpha$
(1) construct an index $\mathcal{I}$ for synopses of subgraphs g in $\mathcal{G}$
// *indexing phase*
(2) for any RDF query with query graph q
(3) obtain a good query plan via estimations on q
// *query pre-processing phase*
(4) perform structural and probabilistic pruning while traversing index $\mathcal{I}$
// *pruning phase*
(5) combine and refine candidate subgraphs
// *refinement phase*
(6) return the matching subgraphs g
}

Figure 4: Framework for probabilistic RDF query answering.

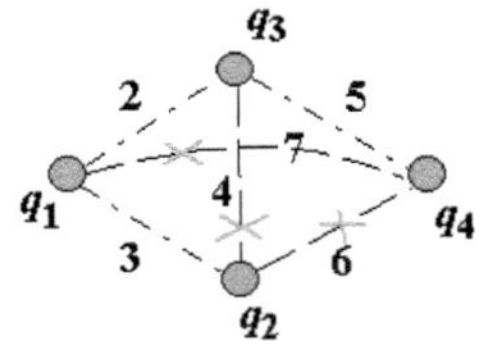

Figure 5: Example of obtaining query plan (*QPlan* $=\{(q_1, q_3), (q_1, q_2), (q_3, q_4)\}$).

with small graph distances, such that we can use the graph distance pruning to filter out false alarms of candidates during the index traversal. In particular, we conceptually view each labeled vertex $q_i \in V(q)$ in q as a node in a conceptual graph K, and the shortest path length between pairwise labeled vertices, q_i and q_j, as the weight of their connecting edge in K. This way, we can obtain such a set *QPlan* by finding a *minimum spanning tree*, T, in the graph K, and storing their edges $E(T)$ in *QPlan*. Intuitively, the minimum spanning tree has edges with small weights (i.e., with small number of intermediate candidates) and has the minimum number of edges (i.e., $|V(T)|-1$) to connect all nodes in $V(T)$.

Algorithm of Obtaining a Query Plan: We illustrate the procedure of obtaining such a minimum spanning tree T (equivalent to a query plan), by using an example in Figure 5, where 4 vertices q_i $(1 \leq i \leq 4)$ in query graph q have user-specified labels (note: $|V(q)| > 4$). We first construct a conceptual graph K from the query graph q. In particular, graph K contains 4 labeled vertices q_i $(1 \leq i \leq 4)$ in q. Between any vertex pair (q_i, q_j) in K, there is a virtual edge, whose distance weight equals to the shortest path distance between q_i and q_j (computed by classical Dijkstra's algorithm). Note that, here we only obtain the weight without considering the path direction, which can facilitate the graph distance pruning discussed later. In Figure 5, (q_1, q_3) has distance weight 2, and in K we draw a dashed line between q_1 and q_3 to indicate the virtual edge.

To obtain a minimum spanning tree T from K, our algorithm starts from a virtual edge that has the smallest distance weight in K, and add it to *QPlan*. Then, the algorithm keeps adding edges to *QPlan* in non-descending order of weights and without introducing loops, until all edges in K are added/discarded. In the example of Figure 5, the initial edge in *QPlan* is (q_1, q_3) with the minimum weight 2. Next, we include edge (q_1, q_2) with the second smallest weight 3 in *QPlan*. Since the third shortest edge, (q_2, q_3), introduces a loop in *QPlan*, we discard it, and instead add the fourth shortest one (q_3, q_4). This way, we can obtain a final query plan *QPlan*, containing 3 virtual edges (q_1, q_3), (q_1, q_2), and (q_3, q_4).

3.3 Structural Pruning

In the sequel, we will illustrate the essential idea of our structural pruning, which uses properties of the graph structure to filter out false alarms that do not match with query graph q. Note that, the structural pruning has been extensively studied in the literature of certain graph databases [34]. Our problem can simply adopt the pruning techniques proposed in these works. Nevertheless, due to

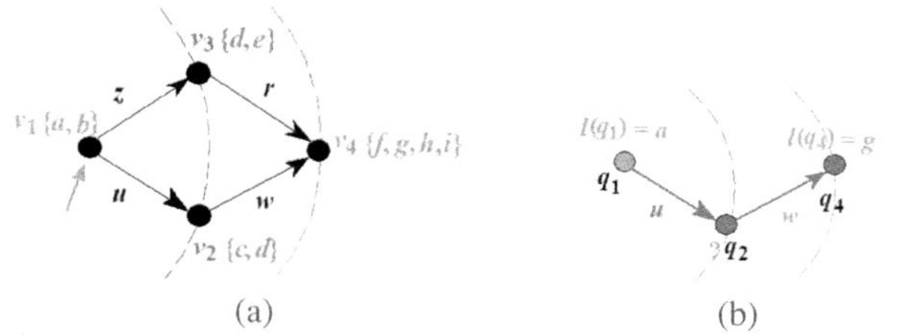

Figure 6: An example of structural pruning. (a) Probabilistic RDF data graph g. (b) RDF query graph q.

special features of probabilistic RDF graphs, these techniques may incur low filtering power. For example, the distribution of label frequencies in probabilistic RDF graphs can be quite skewed, which may produce many conflictions in synopses, leading to low query efficiency. Thus, after introducing our synopses to facilitate the structural pruning, we will propose adaptive synopses that consider label distributions in the probabilistic RDF graph.

3.3.1 Synopsis Design

Basically, since an RDF query specifies all edge labels and partial vertex labels, our synopses should be able to encode these edge and vertex labels for probabilistic RDF data graphs.

Synopses for Vertex Labels: Specifically, for each vertex $v_i \in V(G)$ and each of its possible labels $l(v_i)$, we perform a breadth-first search through out-going and in-coming edges separately[2]. For each direction, we can obtain labels within k-hop neighbors of v_i, for all $1 \leq k \leq d_{max}$, where d_{max} is the maximum possible diameter of query graph q.

Then, for each k value, we maintain a bit vector $BV_{\leq k}(v_i)$, in which all bits are initialized to 0. For simplicity, in this paper, we use bit vectors of the same size B, and we would like to leave the topic of using different vector sizes that are adaptive to k as our future work. We use a hash function, $H(z)$, to map the label of each v_i's neighbor with hop-counter not greater than k to a position in $BV_{\leq k}(v_i)$, and set its $H(l(v_i))$-th position to 1. Note that, to facilitate the pruning, we can select m (≥ 1) hash functions, denoted as $H^{(m')}(z)$ (for $1 \leq m' \leq m$).

Figure 6(a) shows an example of probabilistic RDF data graph, where possible (uncertain) labels of each vertex v_i are given in brackets. Starting from vertex v_1, 1-hop neighbors of v_1 include v_2 and v_3; similarly, the 2-hop neighbor of v_1 is v_4. As a result, for vertex v_1, we maintain two bit vectors, $BV_{\leq 1}(v_1)$ encoding labels $a \sim e$, and $BV_{\leq 2}(v_1)$ encoding labels $a \sim i$.

Synopses for Edge Labels: Similar to vertex labels, we can also construct synopses for edge labels. That is, for each vertex $v_i \in V(g)$, we traverse the graph from v_i in a breadth-first manner, and obtain edge labels within k hops from v_i, where $1 \leq k \leq d_{max}$. Then, for each k value, we construct a bit vector $BV^e_{\leq k}(v_i)$ of size B by hashing ($\leq k$)-hop edge labels to some positions in $BV^e_{\leq k}(v_i)$ via hash function $H(z)$.

In the example of Figure 6(a), bit vector $BV^e_{\leq 1}(v_1)$ encodes labels z and u, whereas $BV^e_{\leq 2}(v_1)$ contains hashed labels $\{z, u, r, w\}$.

3.3.2 Pruning With Synopses

We now illustrate how to utilize synopses designed above to prune false alarms for probabilistic RDF subgraph matching (in Definition 2.4). In brief, for any online query graph q, we can also construct synopses for vertex/edge labels (e.g., $BV_{\leq k}(q_i)$ or $BV^e_{\leq k}(q_i)$). Then, by comparing synopses and statistics between data and query graphs, we can obtain three pruning methods below, label pruning, graph distance pruning, and degree/counter pruning.

[2]Note that, to distinguish directions of edges will increase the pruning power. In the following discussions, however, to keep the notation simple, we will not explicitly mark distinct directions in symbols, if the context is clear.

Label Pruning: The label pruning method checks the existence of vertex/edge labels in data and query graphs, and prunes those candidate subgraphs g that do not correctly contain labels in query graph q. We first give the rationale of label pruning for vertices.

Pruning with Vertex Labels: Similar to the data graph, for any labeled vertex q_i in query graph q, we can obtain a bit vector $BV_{\leq k}(q_i)$. Then, intuitively, assuming that q matches with a subgraph $g \in G$ with $l(q_i) = l(v_i)$, it must hold that: for any position $1 \leq j \leq B$, if $BV_{\leq k}(q_i)[j] = 1$ holds, we have $BV_{\leq k}(v_i)[j] = 1$. We rewrite this matching property via bit-AND operation in the lemma below.

LEMMA 3.1. *Given a query graph q and a subgraph candidate g, if q structurally matches with g, then there must exist two vertices $q_i \in V(q)$ and $v_i \in V(g)$ with the same label (i.e., $l(q_i) = l(v_i)$), such that for any $1 \leq k \leq d_{max}$, we have:*

$$BV_{\leq k}(v_i) \wedge BV_{\leq k}(q_i) = BV_{\leq k}(q_i). \quad (2)$$

In the example of Figure 6, since query graph q in Figure 6(b) is subgraph matching to that in Figure 6(a), bit vector $BV_{\leq 1}(v_1)$ encodes labels $\{a \sim e\}$, which is a superset of that encoded by $BV_{\leq 1}(q_1)$ (i.e., $\{a\}$). The case where $k = 2$ is the same.

From Lemma 3.1, we can immediately have the following corollary to prune a subgraph g that does not structurally match with query graph q.

COROLLARY 3.1. (*Label Pruning*) *If for any vertex $v_i \in V(g)$ satisfying $l(v_i) = l(q_i)$, Eq. (2) does not hold for some $k \in [1, d_{max}]$, then subgraph g can be safely pruned.*

Intuitively, if Eq. (2) does not hold for some k value, then it indicates that there exists a label, $l(q_i)$, of some vertex within k hops from q_i, such that $l(q_i)$ does not appear in k-hop neighbors of v_i in subgraph g. This implies that at least v_i should not be matched to q_i. Thus, if this case happens for all vertices $v_i \in V(g)$ with the same label as q_i, then it is guaranteed that q does not match with g.

Pruning with Edge Labels: For the pruning with edge labels, we can simply replace the bit vector, $BV_k(v_i)$, for vertex labels in Corollary 3.1 with $BV^e_{\leq k}(v_i)$ for edge labels.

Graph Distance Pruning: The synopses in Section 3.3.1 can be also used to prune false alarms by considering the graph distance of vertex pair (v_i, v_j).

LEMMA 3.2. (*Graph Distance Pruning*) *Assume that we have $(q_i, q_j) \in QPlan$ ($i \neq j$), and it holds that $dist(q_i, q_j) = len$, where $dist(x, y)$ is the shortest path distance between vertices x and y in the graph. For vertices $v_i, v_j \in V(g)$, if it holds for some $k \in [1, len)$ that:*

$$BV_{\leq k}(v_i) \wedge BV_{\leq len-k}(v_j) = O, \quad (3)$$

then the candidate pair (v_i, v_j) can be safely pruned, where all bits in bit vector O equal to 0.

Intuitively, if a vertex pair (v_i, v_j) in G matches with (q_i, q_j) in q, then the shortest path distance $dist(v_i, v_j)$ from v_i to v_j in G should not be greater than that from q_i to q_j in q (i.e., $dist(q_i, q_j) = len$). In other words, there must exist some common labels between ($\leq k$)-hop neighbors of v_i and ($\leq len-k$)-hop neighbors of v_j. Thus, when we have bit-AND on their corresponding bit vectors (as given on the LHS of Eq. (3)), $BV_{\leq k}(v_i)$ and $BV_{\leq len-k}(v_j)$, there should exist some nonzero position.

For example, in Figure 6, since we have $dist(q_1, q_4) = len = 2$, (≤ 1)-hop neighbor of v_1 ($k = 1$) and (≤ 1)-hop neighbor of v_4 ($len - k = 1$) have common vertices v_2 and v_3 (labels as well).

In the case where Eq. (3) in Lemma 3.2 holds, it indicates that vertices v_i and v_j have their shortest path distance longer than len. Thus, candidate pair (v_i, v_j) does not match with (q_i, q_j), and can be safely pruned.

To further enhance the pruning power, we can take into account the directions of edges. That is, we construct bit vectors, denoted as $BV^{+}_{\le k}(v_i)$ and $BV^{-}_{\le k}(v_i)$, for ($\le k$)-hop vertices that can reach v_i or that v_i can reach (i.e., considering incoming and out-going edges), respectively. Assume that $dist(v_i, v_j) = len_1$ and $dist(v_j, v_i) = len_2$. The pruning condition in Eq. (3) can be rewritten as:

$$BV^{-}_{\le k}(v_i) \wedge BV^{+}_{\le len_1 - k}(v_j) = O,$$

or

$$BV^{-}_{\le k}(v_j) \wedge BV^{+}_{\le len_2 - k}(v_i) = O.$$

Degree/Counter Pruning: Apart from the pruning with labels and graph distances, there are some other structural metrics to facilitate the pruning. For example, we can record the degree, $deg(v_i)$ of each vertex v_i, the total number, $cnt_k(v_i)$ (or $cnt^e_k(v_i)$), of vertices (or edges) within ($\le k$)-hop neighbors of v_i, where $1 \le k \le d_{max}$. Correspondingly , for query graph q, we also have statistics such as $deg(q_i)$, $cnt_k(q_i)$, and $cnt^e_k(q_i)$ for vertex $q_i \in V(q)$. We use these metrics to prune false alarms in the following lemma.

LEMMA 3.3. *(Degree/Counter Pruning) For a query graph q and a subgraph candidate g with $l(v_i) = l(q_i)$, g can be safely pruned, if either of the following conditions holds: $deg(v_i) < deg(q_i), cnt_k(v_i) < cnt_k(q_i), or\ cnt^e_k(v_i) < cnt^e_k(q_i)$.*

The reason that we use degree/counter pruning is that probabilistic RDF data graphs can sometimes be very sparse. That is, they may contain vertices of low degrees and a small number of vertices/edges within k hops of a vertex v_i. Thus, such structural statistics can be used as an effective means to filter out false alarms in probabilistic RDF data.

3.3.3 Adaptive Hashing for Synopses

The label pruning and graph distance pruning discussed in Section 3.3.2 utilize synopses, which are bit vectors summarizing labels via some hashing functions $H(z)$. Below, we will discuss how to choose good hash functions $H(z)$ that can achieve high filtering effect of our structural pruning.

Uniform Hashing Function, $H_{uni}(z)$: We first consider a straightforward uniform hashing function $H_{uni}(z)$. That is, for each label $l(v_i)$, we map $l(v_i)$ to a bit vector $BV(\cdot)$ such that each position between 1 and B has equal probability to be selected. With this uniform hashing function, although the resulting synopses can work correctly, the pruning power may not be high. This is because uncertain vertex/edge labels in RDF graphs can be quite skewed. While our structural pruning is essentially to check the existence of a label in a synopsis, those frequently appearing labels may have lower pruning power than those infrequently appearing ones. The hashing function $H_{uni}(z)$, however, maps them to positions with equal chance, regardless of their high or low frequencies. As a consequence, those infrequent labels may have confliction with frequent ones, that is, they are hashed to the same position in the bit vector, which makes infrequent labels unable to prune false alarms.

Adaptive Hashing Function, $H_{ada}(z)$: Based on heuristics above, we design an adaptive hashing function $H_{ada}(z)$, which takes into account label frequencies. Our basic idea is to hash those labels of low (high) frequencies to a position in the bit vector $BV(\cdot)$ with higher (lower) probabilities (inversely proportional to frequencies). This way, an infrequent label in a query graph q is more likely to prune a subgraph candidate g that does not contain this label (due to the lower confliction probability with frequent ones).

Let l_1, l_2, ..., and l_L be L labels with frequencies $w(l_1)$, $w(l_2)$, ..., and $w(l_L)$, respectively. We next aim to obtain m hashing functions $H^{(m')}_{ada}(z)$ that map these L labels l_i to some positions in $BV(\cdot)$ with probability inversely proportional to their frequencies, $w(l_i)$. In particular, each hashing function takes a random order of labels, denoted as $l^{(m')}_1$, $l^{(m')}_2$, ..., and $l^{(m')}_L$, as input. For brevity, we omit superscripts (m') below, when the context is clear.

Denote $W = \sum_{i=1}^{L} w(l_i)$. For each label l_i, we first randomly generate a real number, ran_i, within $[0, w(l_i))$. Then, our adaptive hashing function $H_{ada}(z)$ will map label l_i to a position:

$$H_{ada}(l_i) = \left\lfloor B \cdot \frac{\sum_{j=1}^{i-1} w(l_j) + ran_i}{W} \right\rfloor$$

in a bit vector $BV(\cdot)$ of size B. Intuitively, $H_{ada}(z)$ maps label l_i to a random position within $\left[\lfloor B \cdot \sum_{j=1}^{i-1} w(l_j)/W \rfloor, \lfloor B \cdot \sum_{j=1}^{i} w(l_j)/W \rfloor\right)$, in which each position contains this label with a probability proportional to $1/w(l_i)$. This way, a label with large $w(l_i)$ would have lower chance to conflict with an infrequent one at a position, which can achieve high pruning power.

For m different hashing functions $H^{(m')}_{ada}(l_i)$ (for $1 \le m' \le m$), we record m hashed positions for each label l_i, respectively, in a label dictionary, which is used for online look-up.

Analysis of Adaptive Hashing Function: The only remaining issue to address now is how to decide parameters in adaptive hashing functions, including the number, m, of hashing functions and the size, B, of bit vectors. In brief, we design a cost model which computes the maximum confliction probability, and then select good parameters (m, B) to achieve low confliction probability according to the cost model. Specifically, the confliction probability, $CP(l_i)$, that label l_i is expected to conflict with others is given by:

$$CP(l_i) = \frac{1}{L-1} \sum_{j \ne i \wedge j = 1 \sim L} CP(l_i, l_j)$$

where $CP(l_i, l_j)$ is the confliction probability that labels l_i and l_j are mapped to the same position in $BV(\cdot)$.

Moreover, let X_r be a real random number independently and identically drawn from a variable following a probability density function $pdf(l_i) = w(l_i)/W$ $(1 \le i \le L)$, with mean μ and variance σ^2. We can derive the maximum confliction probability, that is, the upper bound of $CP(l_i, l_j)$, as follows.

$$\begin{aligned} & CP(l_i, l_j) \\ = & Pr\left\{ \lfloor B \cdot (\sum_{r=1}^{i-1} X_r + ran_i/W) \rfloor = \lfloor B \cdot (\sum_{r'=1}^{j-1} X_{r'} + ran_j/W) \rfloor \right\} \\ \le & Pr\left\{ \left| B \cdot (\sum_{r=1}^{i-1} X_r + ran_i/W) - B \cdot (\sum_{r'=1}^{j-1} X_{r'} + ran_j/W) \right| < 1 \right\}. \end{aligned} \quad (4)$$

Intuitively, the hashed position of a label l_i is given by $\lfloor B \cdot (\sum_{r=1}^{i-1} X_r + ran_i/W) \rfloor$. Eq. (4) derives an upper bound of probability $CP(l_i, l_j)$ that l_i and l_j are mapped to the same position, which can be obtained by applying central limit theory (CLT) [31].

Next, we consider our problem of using m hashing functions (w.r.t. m random orders of labels) in synopses. Let $kHop(v)$ be a set of labels for k-hop neighbors of vertex v. The confliction probability, $U(q_i, m, B)$, that a label $l(q_i)$ in query graph q is conflicting with labels of v_i's k-hop neighbors can be given by:

$$\begin{aligned} U(q_i, m, B) &= [1 - (1 - CP(l(q_i))^{|kHop(v)|}]^m \\ &\approx (1 - e^{-|kHop(v)| \cdot CP(l(q_i))})^m, \end{aligned} \quad (5)$$

where $|kHop(v)|$ is the average number of labels in set $kHop(v)$.

Therefore, from Eq. (5), if we require that the confliction probability should be smaller than or equal to a threshold ε. Then, we can have the inequality: $U(q_i, m, B) \le \varepsilon$, that is,

$$(1 - e^{-|kHop(v)| \cdot CP(l(q_i))})^m \le \varepsilon, \quad (6)$$

or equivalently,

$$m \ge \frac{ln(\varepsilon)}{ln(1 - e^{-|kHop(v)| \cdot CP(l(q_i))})}. \quad (7)$$

As a result, we can take different possible values of B, and obtain the smallest value of m that satisfy Eq. (7). Our goal is to consider

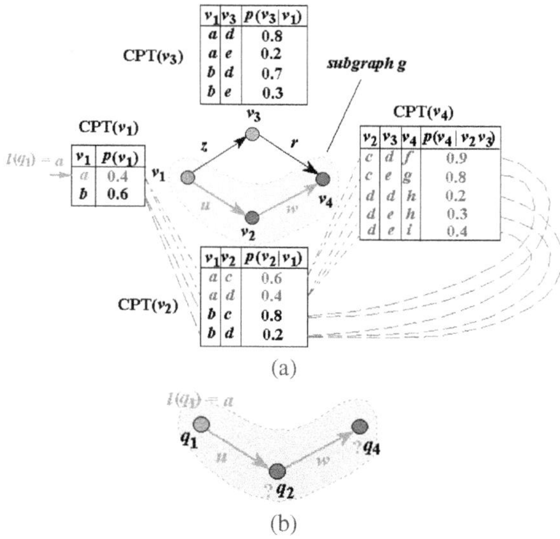

Figure 7: An example of probabilistic pruning. (a) Probabilistic RDF data graph G containing a subgraph g. (b) RDF query graph q.

different combinations of value pair (m, B), and then select one such that the required space $(m \cdot B)$ is minimized.

3.4 Probabilistic Pruning

In this subsection, we will consider unique probabilistic information in probabilistic RDF graphs, and propose an effective probabilistic pruning methods to filter out false alarms. From Definition 2.4, if a subgraph g matches with a query graph q, then it holds that its appearance probability, $Pr\{g\}$, should be above a probabilistic threshold α. However, the computation of $Pr\{g\}$ (in Eq. (1)) is costly, due to label correlations in an exponential number of possible worlds in probabilistic RDF data graphs.

Figure 7 illustrates an example of subgraph matching in a probabilistic RDF graph G, where a subgraph $g \in G$ and a query graph q are shown in Figures 7(a) and 7(b), respectively. In G, each vertex v_i (for $1 \leq i \leq 4$) is associated with a conditional probability table (CPT), CPT(v_i), which records correlations between vertex label $l(v_i)$ and that of its parent vertices $pa(v_i)$. One straightforward method to compute the appearance probability $Pr\{g\}$ of subgraph g is as follows. We first join all the CPTs, CPT(v_1) $\sim$ CPT(v_4), and meanwhile multiply conditional probabilities of joining tuples in CPTs, where (partial) join relationships of tuples between CPTs are represented by edges. Then, in the join result, we project on vertex labels needed in q, and eliminate duplicates by summing up their existence probabilities. Finally, we return those joining tuples with probabilities greater than α. However, this method is clearly time inefficient for the sake of join, duplicate elimination, and probability multiplication.

In order to efficiently answer RDF queries, in the sequel, we will propose an effective probabilistic pruning method to reduce the search space of finding matching subgraphs g. Specifically, our basic idea is to derive an upper bound, $UB\_P(g)$, for the appearance probability $Pr\{g\}$ of probabilistic subgraph g at a low cost. Then, if the probability upper bound is already smaller than or equal to threshold α, we can safely prune subgraph g. We summarize this pruning method in the following lemma.

LEMMA 3.4. *(Probabilistic Pruning) Given a subgraph g, let $UB\_P(g)$ be an upper bound of the appearance probability $Pr\{g\}$ (i.e., $UB\_P(g) \geq Pr\{g\}$). Then, for a given threshold $\alpha \in [0, 1)$, if it holds that $UB\_P(g) < \alpha$, we can safely filter out subgraph g.*

Intuitively, in Lemma 3.4, if $UB\_P(g) < \alpha$ holds, then we can infer that $Pr\{g\} < \alpha$, and safely discard g from the candidate list.

v_1	v_2	v_4	$Pr\{g\}$
a	c	f	$0.4 \times 0.6 \times 0.9$
a	c	g	$0.4 \times 0.6 \times 0.8$
a	d	h	$0.4 \times 0.4 \times (0.2 + 0.3)$
a	d	i	$0.4 \times 0.4 \times 0.4$

Table 2: Join results for subgraph g in the example of Figure 7.

Derivation of Probability Upper Bound $UB\_P(g, v_i)$: We now address the issue of deriving the upper bound, $UB\_P(g, v_i)$ of appearance probability $Pr\{g\}$. Our idea is based on the process of computing probability $Pr\{g\}$ among CPTs. In the sequel, we will use an example in Figure 7 to illustrate how to derive this upper bound from our observation.

As shown in Figure 7(b), query graph q contains a vertex q_1 with the user-specified label "a". Thus, in probabilistic RDF graph G (depicted in Figure 7(a)), we can first find vertex $v_1 \in V(g)$, which also has label "a". Then, we start from the first entry in CPT(v_1) (i.e., with label "a"), and join it with CPT(v_2), followed by CPT(v_4), through dash-dot lines (in Figure 7(a)) among CPTs.

In particular, when v_1 takes label "a", v_2 can take label "c" or "d" with conditional probability 0.6 or 0.4, respectively. If $l(v_2)$ ="c" holds, vertex v_4 has labels "f" and "g" with probabilities 0.9 and 0.8, respectively; otherwise, if $l(v_2)$ ="d" holds, then v_4 can take label "h" or "i" with probability 0.5 (=0.2+0.3) or 0.4, respectively. The final join results for $(v_1, v_2, v_4, Pr\{g\})$ are listed in Table 2, where the appearance probability, $Pr\{g\}$, of each possible subgraph g is given by multiplications of probabilities in CPTs.

Based on this observation, our rationale to obtain an upper bound of $Pr\{g\}$ is to overestimate the conditional probability in each CPT that participates in the calculation of $Pr\{g\}$ (as depicted in Table 2). In our example, when we start from label "a" of vertex v_1, we take probability 0.4 associated with "a" in CPT(v_1). Then, for CPT(v_2), we take the maximum probability 0.6 (instead of 0.4) for entries that can join with label "a" in CPT(v_1). Next, for CPT(v_3), we will take the largest probability 0.9 (among 4 possible probabilities in Table 2). This way, we can obtain a probability upper bound $UB\_P(g, v_1) = 0.4 \times 0.6 \times 0.9$ for subgraph g.

Formally, within each CPT(v_i), we project on each variable, $v_j \in pa(v_i)$, and v_i, and remove duplicate (label) tuples by summing up their existence probabilities. Then, for each label $l(v_j)$ of variable v_j, we can obtain a maximum existence probability $p_{max}(l(v_j))$, which can be used as a multiplicative factor to compute the probability upper bound for a subgraph g.

Our basic idea of calculating this upper bound in a probabilistic RDF data graph $G \in \mathcal{G}$ is as follows. For each entry in a CPT of vertex $v_i \in V(G)$, we aim to pre-compute a probability upper bound $UB\_P(g, v_i)$ for any subgraph $g \in G$ that contains (the entry in) vertex v_i, where the size of g can vary from 1 to n_{max}. Here, n_{max} is the maximum possible size of query graph q (i.e., the number of vertices, $|V(q)|$). Specifically, we follow the same procedure as joining the initial entry in CPT(v_i) with other CPTs in a breadth-first manner, but use upper bounds w.r.t. $p_{max}(l(v_j))$ (rather than exact existence probabilities in CPTs) in order to compute $UB\_P(g, v_i)$.

Let a function $P_{max}(n, i)$ represent the probability upper bound for any subgraph g (containing the initial entry in CPT(v_i)) of size n (i.e., $|V(g)| = n$), when we have accessed the i-th level of CPTs, denoted as S_i (note: "level" is the breadth-first search level). Then, we can obtain a recursive function for $P_{max}(n, i)$ below:

$$\begin{aligned} & P_{max}(n, i) \\ = \; & \max\left\{ \max_{\forall v_l \in S_i}\left\{ P_{max}(n-1, i-1) \cdot \max_{\forall v_j}\{p_{max}(l(v_j))\}\right\},\right. \\ & \left. P_{max}(n, i-1)\right\}. \end{aligned} \quad (8)$$

Intuitively, within the outer $\max\{\cdot\}$ of Eq. (8), the first term computes a probability upper bound such that subgraph g contains

$(n-1)$ vertices within $(i-1)$ levels of CPTs (i.e., $S_1 \cup ... \cup S_{i-1}$), and moreover one vertex from the i-level CPTs (i.e., S_i); the second term, $P_{max}(n, i-1)$, is the probability upper bound that all n vertices are from $S_1 \cup ... \cup S_{i-1}$.

This way, by the recursive function in Eq. (8), we can offline pre-compute the probability upper bound $P_{max}(n, d_{max})$ for each possible n value, where $1 \leq n \leq n_{max}$ and d_{max} is the largest diameter of the query graph q. For any RDF query with a query graph of size n, to compare with a candidate subgraph g w.r.t. an entry in CPT(v_i), we only need to check whether or not $P_{max}(n, d_{max}) \leq \alpha$ holds for this entry (from the probabilistic pruning in Lemma 3.4). If the answer is yes, then we can safely prune this subgraph g.

Note that, although the above methods can pre-compute probability upper bounds for any query size n from 1 to n_{max}, it requires $O(n_{max})$ space cost for each entry in CPTs, which incurs much I/O cost. We observe that, when n becomes larger, the probability upper bound would decrease dramatically. Thus, it is not necessary to store all the n_{max} pre-computed bounds, so as to save the I/O cost. Inspired by this, in the sequel, we will first formalize the pruning power (I/O cost as well) for probabilistic pruning by a cost model, and then propose a novel approach to adaptively decide how many pre-computed values are necessary to guarantee low query cost.

Analysis of Probabilistic Pruning: To evaluate the effectiveness of our probabilistic pruning method (as mentioned in Lemma 3.4), below we provide a cost model to measure the probability that the pre-computed probability upper bounds can be used for pruning (i.e., $\leq \alpha$).

Specifically, assume that for each vertex $v_i \in G$, we offline pre-compute probability upper bounds $P_{max}(\cdot, d_{max})$ for subgraphs g with size from 1 to n_i. In the case where the actual query size $n > n_i$, we will simply use the pre-computed value w.r.t. n_i as the upper bound, since $P_{max}(n, d_{max}) \leq P_{max}(n_i, d_{max})$ holds for $n > n_i$. Furthermore, we assume that two parameters in users' RDF queries, the query size n and the probabilistic threshold $\alpha_n \in [\alpha_{min}, \alpha_{max}]$, follow a probability density function $pdf(n, \alpha_n)$ (which can be inferred from historical queries).

Then, we have the formula of pruning power as follows:

$$PP = \sum_{i=1}^{N} \left(\sum_{n=1}^{n_{max}} \int_{\alpha_{min}}^{\alpha_{max}} pdf(n, \alpha_n) \cdot \chi(F(n, n_i) < \alpha_n) d\alpha_n \right) \quad (9)$$

where $\chi(true) = 1$, $\chi(false) = 0$, and

$$F(n, n_i) = \begin{cases} P_{max}(n, d_{max}) & \text{if } n \leq n_i; \\ P_{max}(n_i, d_{max}) & \text{otherwise.} \end{cases} \quad (10)$$

In Eq. (9), the pruning power of each vertex v_i is given by:

$$PP_i = \sum_{n=1}^{n_{max}} \int_{\alpha_{min}}^{\alpha_{max}} pdf(n, \alpha_n) \cdot \chi(F(n, n_i) < \alpha_n) d\alpha_n$$

When we increase the number of pre-computed probability upper bounds n_i for vertex v_i, the pruning power is also expected to increase (due to the tighter bound); on the other hand, however, more bounds need to be stored on the disk, which incurs higher I/O costs to access them. Therefore, in the sequel, we will model such I/O cost for each vertex v_i, with which we can later select an optimal n_i value to achieve low query cost.

In particular, we denote the I/O cost of accessing v_i's pre-computed probability bounds as $G(v_i)$. We also assume that if v_i is a false alarm, then it can be quickly filtered out by probabilistic pruning via the index (discussed in Section 4)) without accessing the data, and thus its cost can be ignored. Therefore, we have:

$$G(v_i) = (1 - PP_i) \cdot (C_{IO} \cdot n_i) \quad (11)$$

where C_{IO} is a unit I/O cost for a pre-computed probability upper bound. In Eq. (11), the first term for $G(v_i)$ is the probability that v_i cannot be pruned by our probabilistic pruning, and the second term is the I/O cost that we have to access the pre-computed probability upper bounds.

Adaptive Pre-Computations Based on Cost Model: From our derived cost model $G(v_i)$ in Eq. (11) for the query cost of a vertex v_i, our goal is to adaptively obtain an optimal value of n_i (i.e., the number of pre-computed bounds we maintain for v_i), such that the query cost is the smallest. In fact, this goal can be achieved, when n_i satisfies the equality below:

$$\frac{\partial G(v_i)}{\partial n_i} = \frac{\partial((1 - PP_i) \cdot (C_{IO} \cdot n_i))}{\partial n_i} = 0, \quad (12)$$

which, by letting $J = 1 - PP_i$, can be rewritten as:

$$C_{IO} \cdot J + C_{IO} \cdot n_i \cdot \frac{\partial J}{\partial n_i} = 0. \quad (13)$$

As a result, for each vertex v_i, we will select an optimal value for n_i, such that by Eq. (13), $J + n_i \cdot \frac{\partial J}{\partial n_i} = 0$ holds, where J and $\frac{\partial J}{\partial n_i}$ are given in Appendix A.

4. PROBABILISTIC RDF QUERY ANSWERING

4.1 Index Construction

In this subsection, we illustrate the details of constructing a tree index, $\mathcal{I}$, for synopses of probabilistic RDF data graphs. As mentioned earlier in Section 3.3.1, we present the structural pruning methods that use structural information such as synopses for vertex/edge labels, degrees, and the number of edges/vertices to facilitate the pruning. Moreover, in Section 3.4, we provide the pre-computed probabilistic upper bound to enable probabilistic pruning. Therefore, we will integrate these synopses/parameters for our proposed pruning techniques into the index $\mathcal{I}$.

Data Format: In the index $\mathcal{I}$, we store possible labels of each vertex v_i in probabilistic RDF graphs G, as well as their surrounding structural/probabilistic information. In particular, for each label $l(v_i)$ of vertex v_i, we collect its synopses $BV_{\leq k}(v_i)$ and $BV^e_{\leq k}(v_i)$, degrees/counters $deg(v_i)$, $cnt_k(v_i)$, $cnt^e_k(v_i)$, and probabilistic upper bounds $F(n, n_i)$, where $1 \leq k \leq d_{max}$ and $1 \leq n \leq n_i$ for adaptive choice of n_i.

Index Structure: To index the probabilistic RDF data mentioned above, we will build a B$^+$-tree-like data structure, $\mathcal{I}$, whose primary sorting keys are (possible) labels of vertices in probabilistic RDF graphs. In leaf nodes, we store structural/probabilistic information of vertices in the aforementioned data format. On the other hand, each intermediate node N_a stores a summarization of synopses and parameters for all data under N_a. Specifically, for synopses, we have:

$BV_{\leq k}(N_a) = \bigvee_{\forall v_i \in N_a} BV_{\leq k}(v_i)$ and
$BV^e_{\leq k}(N_a) = \bigvee_{\forall v_i \in N_a} BV^e_{\leq k}(v_i)$.

For degree/counters, we have:

$deg(N_a) = \max_{\forall v_i \in N_a} deg(v_i)$,
$cnt_k(N_a) = \max_{\forall v_i \in N_a} cnt_k(v_i)$, and
$cnt^e_k(N_a) = \max_{\forall v_i \in N_a} cnt^e_k(v_i)$.

For probabilistic upper bound, we have:

$F(n, n_a) = \max_{\forall v_i \in N_a} \{F(n, n_i)\}$,

where $n_a = \max_{\forall v_i \in N_a} \{n_i\}$.

Note that, the pruning techniques for intermediate nodes are similar to that for vertex v_i, as described in Section 3. We only need to replace synopses/parameters for vertices with that for nodes .

Insert: We insert the label $l(v_i)$ of a vertex into $\mathcal{I}$ by a variant of "insert" operator in the B$^+$-tree. That is, we start with the tree root, $root(\mathcal{I})$, and always descend to subtrees that contain the label $l(v_i)$. When multiple subtrees contain the same label $l(v_i)$, we will choose one branch to descend, which is determined by bit vector

Procedure Prob_RDF_Processing {
Input: a probabilistic RDF graph database $\mathcal{G}$, a tree index $\mathcal{I}$ over $\mathcal{G}$, a query graph q with some , and a probabilistic threshold α
Output: subgraphs g that match with q with confidence α

(1) pre-process q to obtain the query plan, *QPlan* // pre-processing phase
(2) let *QS* be a set of vertices in q with user-specified labels
(3) obtain synopses and parameters for each $q_i \in QS$, and initialize an empty candidate list $cand(q_i)$ for each q_i
(4) for each entry N_a in $root(\mathcal{I})$
(5) for each $q_i \in QS$
(6) if N_a cannot be pruned by q via label/degree/counter/probabilistic pruning
(7) add N_a to $cand(q_i)$
(8) for $(q_i, q_j) \in QPlan$
(9) apply graph distance pruning to filter out false alarms of pairwise nodes between $cand(q_i)$ and $cand(q_j)$, and obtain candidate set $cand(q_i q_j)$
(10) while $(cand(\cdot)$ contains nodes)
(11) obtain children nodes/vertices via index $\mathcal{I}$ for each $N_i \in \bigcup_{\forall i} cand(q_i)$
(12) for each $(N_i, N_j) \in cand(q_i q_j)$
(13) use structural/probabilistic pruning to prune (N_a, N_b) for $N_a \in N_i$ and $N_b \in N_j$
(14) add (N_a, N_b) to $cand^{new}(q_i q_j)$ if it is not pruned
(15) $cand(q_i q_j) = cand^{new}(q_i q_j)$
(16) join candidate lists among $cand(q_i q_j)$ for (q_i, q_j) in *QPlan*
(17) refine candidate subgraphs in the join results and return the actual answers
}

Figure 8: Query answering in the probabilistic RDF graph database.

synopses, probabilistic upper bounds, degrees, and counters. For synopses $BV_{\leq k}(N_a)$, we consider the hamming distance between bit vectors before and after including new data of v_i; the case of $BV^e_{\leq k}(N_a)$ is similar. This way, we will select a branch with the minimum hamming distance to descend. In the case of tie, we consider the smallest increase of probability upper bounds, degrees, and counters in order.

Split: When a tree node N_a is full (i.e., overflows), we will split it into two new nodes N_{a1} and N_{a2}, which are of approximately equal size. The criteria of splitting are similar to the insertion. That is, the splitting should follow the order of vertex labels, $l(N_{a1}) \leq l(N_{a2})$. Moreover, with the same vertex label, two split groups should have small (summed) hamming distances between pairwise bit vectors, and small increases of probability upper bounds, degrees, or counters.

Delete: Since we assume static probabilistic RDF graphs without any deletions, we will not discuss it in detail. Nevertheless, it can be easily handled by removing the corresponding vertex labels from the index, and merging synopses/parameters of two nodes into one in the case of underflow.

4.2 Query Procedure

We next illustrate the pseudo code of our query procedure, namely Prob_RDF_Processing, for answering RDF queries through the tree index in Figure 8. Specifically, given a query graph q, we first pre-process g by obtaining a query plan, *QPlan*, for using graph distance pruning and joining pairs of candidate vertices during the index traversal (line 1). Moreover, for each vertex $q_i \in QS$ that has a user-specified label, we obtain its synopses and parameters used later for pruning methods, and also initialize an empty candidate list $cand(q_i)$ for candidate vertices v_i in RDF data (lines 2-3).

To start the index traversal, we first insert into candidate list $cand(q_i)$ those entries N_a in the root, $root(\mathcal{I})$, of index $\mathcal{I}$ that cannot be pruned by label/degree/counter/probabilistic pruning methods w.r.t. vertex $q_i \in QS$ (lines 4-7). Moreover, for pair (q_i, q_j) in *QPlan*, we obtain a set, $cand(q_i q_j)$, of candidate pairs via graph distance pruning (lines 8-9). Then, each time we access children nodes/vertices of nodes that appear in candidate lists $cand(\cdot)$, and apply our proposed structural/probabilistic pruning methods to obtain candidate pairs $cand(q_i q_j)$ for nodes/vertices on lower level of the index (lines 10-15). The iteration stops when the leaf nodes are visited (line 10). After that, we join candidate lists $cand(q_i q_j)$ for (q_i, q_j) in *QPlan*, and obtain a set of candidate subgraphs g (line

Parameters	Settings
α	$0.1, 0.2, \mathbf{0.5}, 0.8, 0.9$
$deg(v_i)$	$\mathbf{2}, 3, 5, 8, 10$
n_{max}	$2, 3, \mathbf{5}, 8, 10$
N	$10K, 20K, \mathbf{50K}, 80K, 100K$

Table 3: The experimental settings.

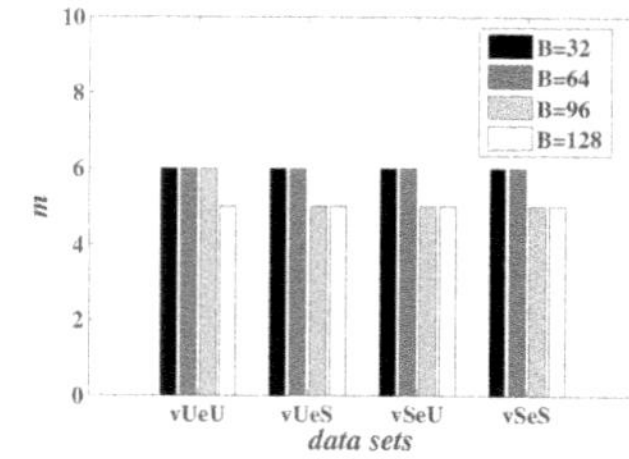

Figure 9: Choosing (B, m) parameter pairs with our cost model.

16). Finally, we refine candidate subgraphs g by checking their structures and appearance probabilities, and return the actual RDF query answers (line 17).

5. EXPERIMENTAL STUDY

In this section, we evaluate the query performance of our proposed approaches for answering queries in probabilistic RDF graphs. Specifically, we use both real and synthetic data sets. For synthetic data, we generate an RDF graph by randomly connecting each vertex v_i with others in the graph with average in- and out-degrees $deg(v_i)$, and then for each vertex v_i (or edge e_{ij}), generating $L \in [L_{min}, L_{max}]$ possible labels, $l(v_i)$ (or one label $l(e_{ij})$ for e_{ij}), following either Uniform or Skew distribution. By considering Uniform/Skew (denoted as U and S) distributions of vertex/edge (v and e for short) labels, we can obtain 4 types of data sets, $vUeU$, $vUeS$, $vSeU$, and $vSeS$. In addition, for each vertex v_i, we construct a conditional probability table (CPT), CPT(v_i), which contains probabilities (randomly generated) that v_i has label $l(v_i)$, given the labels of its parent vertices. For real data, we used "directed_CheckedFactExtractor" in the YAGO [26] data set, which contains RDF data associated with the confidence among facts (i.e., subjects/objects). We construct data graphs from such real RDF data such that each triple corresponds to an edge (with predicate as the label) that connects two vertices (i.e., subject/object). Then, for each vertex, we assume 2 possible labels, one (i.e., object/subject name) is specified in data (with a confidence), and the other one is randomly produced from existing vertex labels. Similarly, we create a CPT for vertex v_i, such that in CPT the summed probability for each label of $v_j \in pa(v_i)$ (specified in the data) follows its own confidence. For other data sets with different parameter settings, the results are similar and thus omitted.

To evaluate the performance of RDF queries, we extract 50 query graphs q from probabilistic RDF data graphs G, by starting from any random vertex in G and then traversing the graph through connecting incoming / outgoing random edges, where the maximum number, n_{max}, of vertices in query graph q is 5 by default, and the diameter, d_{max}, of q is also set to 5. This way, for each vertex v_i we encounter, we obtain a corresponding vertex q_i in q, and set

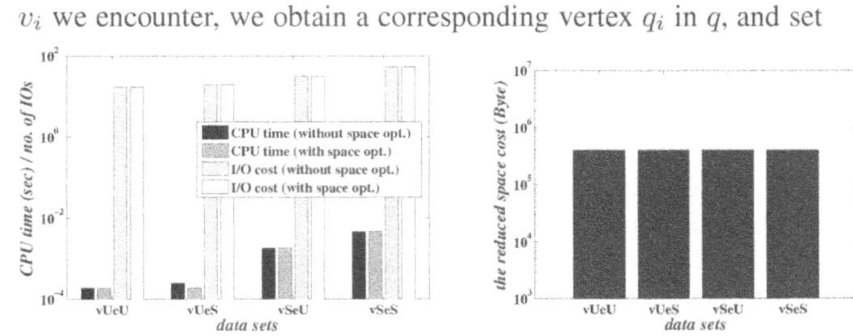

(a) (b)

Figure 10: Performance with and without space optimization.

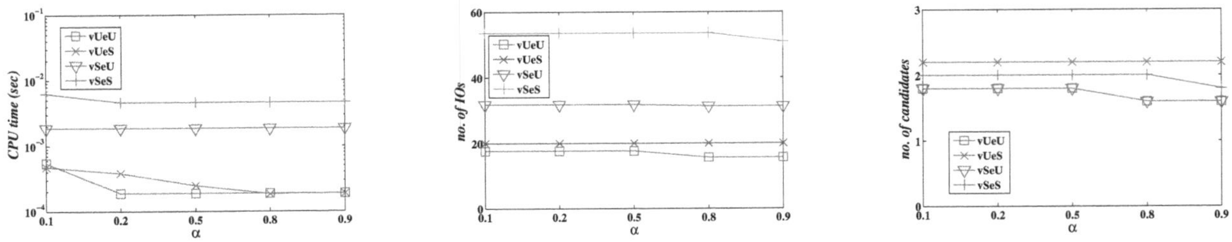

(a) CPU time (b) No. of I/Os (c) No. of candidates

Figure 13: Probabilistic RDF query performance vs. α.

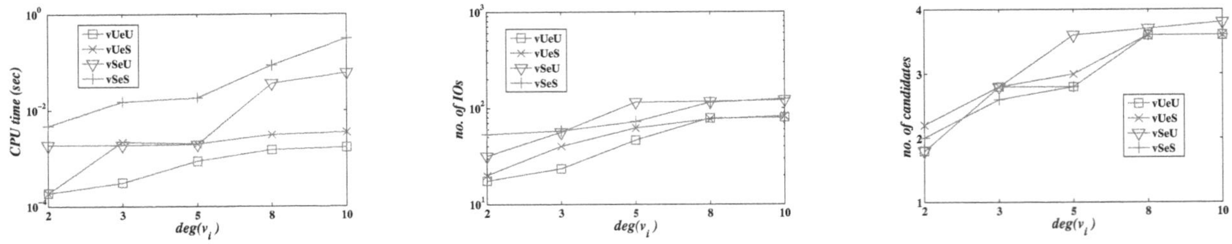

(a) CPU time (b) No. of I/Os (c) No. of candidates

Figure 14: Probabilistic RDF query performance vs. $deg(v_i)$.

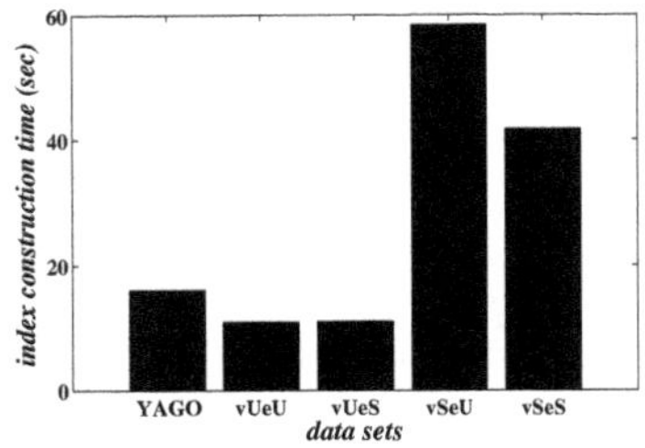

Figure 11: Index construction time for both real/synthetic data.

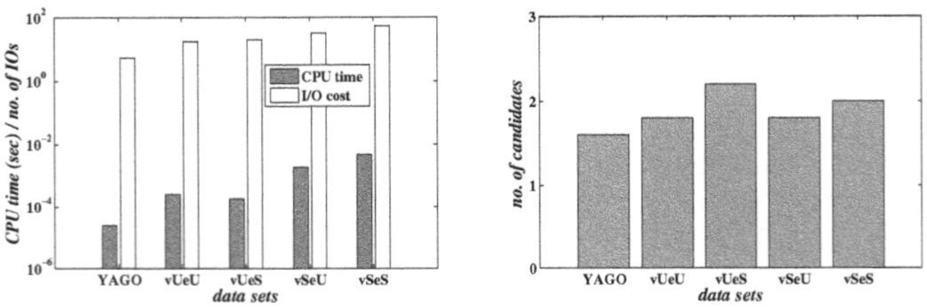

(a) (b)

Figure 12: Probabilistic RDF query efficiency on real/synthetic data.

label $l(q_i)$ to one random label of v_i. Note that, a straightforward baseline method to process RDF queries is to compare query graph q with at least N subgraphs of G, where $N = |V(G)|$. Clearly, since this baseline does not use any pruning methods, our proposed approach outperforms the baseline by orders of magnitude. Thus, we would not report comparison results with the baseline approach. Moreover, the work in [15] assumes the RDF model of with (independent) edge existence probabilities, whereas our problem considers a different one with correlated uncertainties in RDF labels. We thus do not compare with this work either, since our problem cannot be solved using techniques in [15].

We measure the performance of RDF queries in terms of the number of remaining subgraph candidates, CPU time (filtering via the index), and the number of I/Os. Table 3 summarizes experimental settings in our experiments, where the numbers in bold font are default values. In subsequent experiments, each time we vary one parameter, while setting others to default values.

Effect of Adaptive Hashing Function: In the first set of experiments, we first decide 2 parameters B and m for the adaptive hash function H_{ada}, where B is the size of a bit vector, and m is the number of bit vectors for each synopsis (Section 3.3). We assume that the smallest synopsis unit is an integer of 4 Bytes (i.e., 32 bits). Thus, we will select a B value that is a multiple of 32. In our experiments, we test B values from 32 to 128, and set a smallest m value such that Inequality (7) holds, where we require the confliction probability be below 0.1 (i.e., $\varepsilon = 0.1$). Figure 9 shows the plot of possible (B, m) pairs by Inequality (7). When B increases in each data set, the change of m is not large (only decreases from 6 to 5). To achieve small synopsis size ($B \cdot m$)) yet guarantee good pruning power, below we will select the pair $(B, m) = (32, 6)$ with the minimum space consumption in experiments.

Effect of Adaptive Pre-Computations for Probabilistic Pruning: Figure 10(a) shows the time and I/O costs for using and without using adaptive pre-computations mentioned in Section 3.4. In the figure, the performance of using our adaptive pre-computations does not degrade much (in some cases, it performs even better due to less I/O cost with the reduced space). In Figure 10(b), we report the benefit from our adaptive pre-computations. That is, with a probabilistic RDF graph data containing $50K$ vertices, we can reduce the space cost of about $400K$ Bytes from index synopses.

Index Construction Time: Figure 11 reports the time cost of index construction over real/synthetic data sets, where default parameters are used for synthetic data sets. Here, the index construction time not only includes the time cost of building the tree index, but also include that of pre-computing synopses/statistics for indexing probabilistic RDF data graphs. In the figure, the required time is small, that is, from several seconds up to a minute.

Performance vs. Data Sets: We now show the performance of subgraph matching on probabilistic RDF graph data sets in Figure 12. From the figure, we can see that our filtering time through the index for real/synthetic data sets is low (i.e., below 0.01 second), and the number of page accesses is similar (only 5.4 and 15-54 for real and synthetic data, respectively). After filtering, the number of candidate graphs is small (i.e., 1-3), which can greatly save the refinement time (i.e., the isomorphism checking and computation of matching probabilities). In the sequel, we will report the robustness of our approach on synthetic data with different parameter settings.

Performance vs. Probabilistic Threshold α: Figure 13 varies the probabilistic threshold α from 0.1 to 0.9, under the default parameter settings. From figures, when α increases, the I/O cost and the number of candidates are non-increasing. This is because larger α threshold can possibly remove more false alarms with low confidences, which confirms the effect of our probabilistic pruning w.r.t. α (via probability upper bounds). Thus, larger α will reduce the I/O cost and lead to fewer candidates for refinement. Note

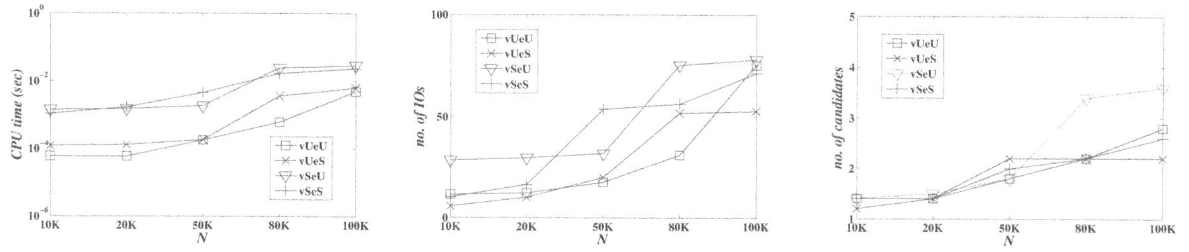

Figure 15: Probabilistic RDF query performance vs. N.

that, the curves in figures are somewhat flat, for example, when $\alpha = 0.1, 0.2$, and 0.5, because probability upper bounds of most candidates are above the thresholds. Moreover, the time cost of our approach is small (i.e., below 0.1 second).

Performance vs. Degree $deg(v_i)$: In Figure 14, we vary the average degree of vertices for probabilistic RDF graphs from 2 to 10. From figures, higher degrees of vertices in probabilistic RDF graphs lead to the increase of both time and I/O costs. This is because RDF graphs with higher degrees would have more possible candidates when pruning with synopses. Further, the pre-computed probability upper bound is less tighter w.r.t. higher degrees, which incurs lower pruning power. Nonetheless, in figures, the CPU and I/O costs for probabilistic RDF data with different degrees are low, and the number of remaining candidates is small (i.e., around 2-4).

The performance trends w.r.t. parameter n_{max} values (i.e., the number of vertices in the query graph q) are similar to that of $deg(v_i)$ in Figure 14. Thus, we omit it due to the space limitation.

Scalability vs. Data Size N: Finally, Figure 15 reports the scalability of our approach against data size N varying from $10K$ to $100K$, with default values of other parameters. In figures, the time and I/O costs of our proposed approach smoothly increase with the increase of data size N. This is expected, since in a larger RDF graph, more subgraphs would match with query graph q. Nonetheless, the number of candidates is small, and the time cost for all data sizes remains low (i.e., below 0.1 second). This confirms the efficiency and effectiveness of our query answering approach in probabilistic RDF graph databases.

6. RELATED WORK

RDF is a W3C standard to represent information, which has nowadays gained much attention in real applications such as the Semantic Web. RDF data have several equivalent formats, for example, triple store [30, 19, 5], column store [25, 2, 23], property tables [33, 32], or graphs [3, 27]. Many existing works focus on improving the performance of answering SPARQL join queries in systems such as C-Store [2], RDF-3X [18], MonetDB [23], and Hexastore [30]. These works usually utilize indexes or join plans to speed up the RDF query efficiency. Tran et al. [27] explored the keyword search problem in a large RDF data graph, which retrieves combinations of keywords contained in subgraphs with the highest scores. This is different from our work in that the structure of the query graph is known in our problem. Thus, the direct usage of keyword search techniques to tackle our problem would incur many candidates (due to the unspecified structure among keywords).

In certain graph databases, Zhao and Han [34] designed a neighborhood signature to directly store labels within k hops from each vertex. In contrast, our work uses synopses to compactly store uncertain labels, which can efficiently filter out false alarms by the structural pruning via bit operators (e.g., bit-AND). Most importantly, our synopses can be also used to enable the graph distance pruning, and the synopsis design is based on an adaptive hashing (instead of uniform one) to increase the pruning power.

In XML databases, XSKETCH [21] and DescribeX [9] use summary subgraphs or paths in trees to represent XML features. Thus, they differ from synopses which encode uncertain labels of k-hop neighbors, and are specifically designed by considering probabilistic RDF features. Moreover, Gutierrez et al. [14] considered certain RDF data with additional temporal information, whereas our work studies RDF with uncertainty which involves label correlations and joint probabilities in possible worlds, and is thus more challenging.

All the aforementioned works assume that the underlying (RDF) graph data are reliable and precise. However, as mentioned in Section 1, during the data integration [11, 12], the integrated RDF data from different sources may often contain inconsistent or imprecise information. Therefore, they can be modeled as probabilistic RDF data. Due to the uncertainty in probabilistic RDF data, previous techniques for answering queries on certain RDF cannot guarantee high probabilistic confidence of query answers, and they are thus not directly applicable to our probabilistic RDF problem.

Some previous works [15, 13] in the Semantic Web considered the uncertainty in the RDF data. Huang and Liu [15] modeled such RDF data by a probabilistic database. However, this model assumes that RDF triples (corresponding to edges in RDF graphs) have independent existence probabilities to appear in reality. Based on this assumption, their query processing method is to decompose the query graph into triple patterns (edges), compute probabilities of candidates for each triple pattern, and finally join candidates by calculating their actual probabilities. In contrast, our problem involves a different model of probabilistic RDF graphs, which have correlated and uncertain vertex labels (but certain edge labels), rather than uncertain edges (certain labels). Therefore, techniques in [15] (proposed for RDF data with the edge independence and edge existence uncertainty) cannot be applied to solve our problem. Furthermore, Fukushige [13] extended the RDF vocabulary to allow the probabilistic confidence existing in RDF data (via a graphical model). However, it more focused on how to represent probabilistic RDF data, rather than how to efficiently answer probabilistic RDF queries, which is the focus of our problem in this paper.

In the literature of probabilistic databases [10], there are many existing systems that manage probabilistic and uncertain data, for example, MystiQ [7], Orion [8], TRIO [6], MayBMS [4], MCDB [16], and BayesStore [29]. The query evaluation usually considers possible worlds semantics, where each possible world is a possible instance of the probabilistic database in reality. That is, the query can be answered by obtaining query answers in each possible world, and then aggregating the returned answers. By using different aggregation methods, we can have distinct definitions of query semantics in probabilistic databases, for example, probabilistic top-k query [24, 17]. Potamias et al. [22] considered approximate approaches to obtain k-nearest neighbors of a query point in a probabilistic graph (considering the shortest path) by sampling possible worlds. In contrast, our work takes into account special features of probabilistic RDF graphs (w.r.t., label frequency/distributions and probabilistic correlations), and designs efficient approaches to improve the efficiency of RDF queries on probabilistic graph data.

7. CONCLUSION

Probabilistic RDF graphs pervasively exist in real applications such as data integration, where data often exhibit uncertainties. In this paper, we study the problem of retrieving subgraphs from probabilistic RDF graph databases that match with a given query graph with high confidence. To efficiently tackle this problem, we propose effective structural pruning methods with the help of synopses that are adaptively designed according to label distributions in RDF graphs. Further, we also utilize the probabilistic information in RDF graphs to enable the pruning, which is also adaptively designed according to a formal cost model, minimizing the query cost. We build a tree index structure that incorporates synopses and pre-computed data to facilitate online structural/probabilistic pruning. Extensive experiments have been conducted to demonstrate the efficiency and effectiveness of our approaches.

Acknowledgments

Funding for this work was provided by RGC NSFC JOINT Grant under Project No. N_HKUST61 2/09, HKUST RPC10EG13, and NSFC Grant No. 60736013, 60803105, 60873022, and 60903053.

8. REFERENCES

[1] W3C: Resource description framework (RDF). In *http://www.w3.org/RDF/*.

[2] D. J. Abadi, A. Marcus, S. R. Madden, and K. Hollenbach. Scalable semantic web data management using vertical partitioning. In *VLDB*, 2007.

[3] R. Angles and C. Gutierrez. Querying RDF data from a graph database perspective. In *The Semantic Web: Research and Applications*, 2005.

[4] L. Antova, C. Koch, and D. Olteanu. MayBMS: Managing incomplete information with probabilistic world-set decompositions. In *ICDE*, 2007.

[5] M. Atre, V. Chaoji, M. J. Zaki, and J. A. Hendler. Matrix "bit" loaded: a scalable lightweight join query processor for rdf data. In *WWW*, 2010.

[6] O. Benjelloun, A. Das Sarma, A. Y. Halevy, and J. Widom. ULDBs: Databases with uncertainty and lineage. In *VLDB*, 2006.

[7] J. Boulos, N. N. Dalvi, B. Mandhani, S. Mathur, C. Ré, and D. Suciu. Mystiq: a system for finding more answers by using probabilities. In *SIGMOD*, 2005.

[8] R. Cheng, S. Singh, and S. Prabhakar. U-DBMS: A database system for managing constantly-evolving data. In *VLDB*, 2005.

[9] Mariano P. Consens, Renée J. Miller, Flavio Rizzolo, and Alejandro A. Vaisman. Exploring XML web collections with describex. *TWEB*, 4(3), 2010.

[10] N. N. Dalvi and D. Suciu. Efficient query evaluation on probabilistic databases. *The VLDB Journal*, 16(4), 2007.

[11] X. L. Dong, L. Berti-Equille, and D. Srivastava. Integrating conflicting data: The role of source dependence. *PVLDB*, 2(1), 2009.

[12] X. L. Dong, A. Halevy, and C. Yu. Data integration with uncertainty. *VLDBJ*, 18(2), 2009.

[13] Y. Fukushige. Representing probabilistic relations in RDF, 2005.

[14] C. Gutierrez, C. A. Hurtado, and A. Vaisman. Introducing time into RDF. *TKDE*, 19(2), 2007.

[15] H. Huang and C. Liu. Query evaluation on probabilistic RDF databases. In *WISE*, 2009.

[16] R. Jampani, F. Xu, M. Wu, L. L. Perez, C. Jermaine, and P. J. Haas. Mcdb: a monte carlo approach to managing uncertain data. In *SIGMOD*, 2008.

[17] J. Li, B. Saha, and A. Deshpande. A unified approach to ranking in probabilistic databases. *PVLDB*, 2(1), 2009.

[18] T. Neumann, M. Bender, S. Michel, R. Schenkel, P. Triantafillou, and G. Weikum. Distributed top-k aggregation queries at large. *Distributed and Parallel Databases*, 26(1), 2009.

[19] T. Neumann and G. Weikum. RDF-3X: a risc-style engine for RDF. *PVLDB*, 1(1), 2008.

[20] A. Nierman and H. V. Jagadish. Protdb: Probabilistic data in XML. In *VLDB*, 2002.

[21] N. Polyzotis and M. Garofalakis. XSKETCH synopses for XML data graphs. *TODS*, 31(3), 2006.

[22] M. Potamias, F. Bonchi, A. Gionis, and G. Kollios. k-nearest neighbors in uncertain graphs. *PVLDB*, 3(1), 2010.

[23] L. Sidirourgos, R. Goncalves, M. Kersten, N. Nes, and S. Manegold. Column-store support for RDF data management: not all swans are white. *PVLDB*, 1(2), 2008.

[24] M. A. Soliman, I. F. Ilyas, and K. C. Chang. Top-k query processing in uncertain databases. In *ICDE*, 2007.

[25] M. Stonebraker, D. J. Abadi, A. Batkin, X.Chen, M. Cherniack, M. Ferreira, E. Lau, A. Lin, S. Madden, E. O'Neil, P. O'Neil, A. Rasin, N. Tran, and S. Zdonik. C-store: a column-oriented dbms. In *VLDB*, 2005.

[26] F. M. Suchanek, G. Kasneci, and G. Weikum. Yago: A large ontology from wikipedia and wordnet. *Web Semant.*, 6(3), 2008.

[27] T. Tran, H. Wang, S. Rudolph, and P. Cimiano. Top-k exploration of query candidates for efficient keyword search on graph-shaped (RDF) data. In *ICDE*, 2009.

[28] D. Z. Wang, M. J. Franklin, M. Garofalakis, and J. M. Hellerstein. Querying probabilistic information extraction. *PVLDB*, 3(1), 2010.

[29] D. Z. Wang, E. Michelakis, M. Garofalakis, and J. Hellerstein. Bayestore: Managing large, uncertain data repositories with probabilistic graphical models. In *VLDB*, 2008.

[30] C. Weiss, P. Karras, and A. Bernstein. Hexastore: sextuple indexing for semantic web data management. *PVLDB*, 1(1), 2008.

[31] E. W. Weisstein. Central Limit Theorem. *http://mathworld.wolfram.com/CentralLimitTheorem.html*.

[32] K. Wilkinson. Jena property table implementation. In *SSWS*, 2006.

[33] K. Wilkinson, C. Sayers, H. Kuno, D. Reynolds, and J. Database. Efficient RDF storage and retrieval in Jena2. In *ESWDB*, 2003.

[34] P. Zhao and J. Han. On graph query optimization in large networks. *PVLDB*, 3(1), 2010.

Appendix

A. Derivation of J and $\partial J/\partial n_i$ in Eq. (13).

We expand formulae of J and $\partial J/\partial n_i$ as follows.

$$\begin{aligned} J = & \ 1 - PP_i \qquad (14) \\ = & \int_{\alpha_{min}}^{\alpha_{max}} \sum_{n=1}^{n_{max}} pdf(n, \alpha_n) \cdot \chi(F(n, n_i) \geq \alpha_n) d\alpha_n \\ = & \int_{\alpha_{min}}^{F(n_i, n_i)} \sum_{n=1}^{n_{max}} pdf(n, \alpha_n) \cdot 1 \, d\alpha_n \\ & + \int_{F(n_i, n_i)}^{\alpha_{max}} \left(\left(\sum_{n=1}^{n_\alpha : F(n_\alpha, n_i) = \alpha_n} pdf(n, \alpha_n) \cdot 1 \right) \right. \\ & + \left. \left(\sum_{n=n_\alpha}^{\alpha_{max}} pdf(n, \alpha_n) \cdot 0 \right) \right) d\alpha_n \\ = & \int_{\alpha_{min}}^{\alpha_{max}} \sum_{n=1}^{n_\alpha} pdf(n, \alpha_n) d\alpha_n + \int_{\alpha_{min}}^{F(n_i, n_i)} \sum_{n=n_\alpha+1}^{n_{max}} pdf(n, \alpha_n) d\alpha_n \end{aligned}$$

For probability upper bound function $f(n_\alpha) = P_{max}(n_\alpha, d_{max}) = \alpha$, we denote its inverse function $n_\alpha = f^{-1}(\alpha)$. Then, from Eq. (14), while the first term in J is not with respect to n_i, we have:

$$\begin{aligned} \frac{\partial J}{\partial n_i} &= \frac{d}{dn_i} \int_{\alpha_{min}}^{F(n_i, n_i)} \sum_{n=n_\alpha+1}^{n_{max}} pdf(n, \alpha) d\alpha \\ &= \frac{d}{dn_i} \int_{\alpha_{min}}^{f(n_i)} \sum_{n=n_\alpha+1}^{n_{max}} pdf(n, n_\alpha) \cdot df(n_\alpha) \\ &= \frac{d}{dn_i} \int_{f^{-1}(\alpha_{min})}^{n_i} \sum_{n=t+1}^{n_{max}} pdf(n, t) \cdot f'(t) dt \\ &= \sum_{n=t+1}^{n_{max}} pdf(n, t) \cdot f'(t) \, |_{f^{-1}(\alpha_{min})}^{n_i} \qquad (15) \end{aligned}$$

where $f'(\cdot)$ is the derivation of function $f(\cdot)$.

Facet Discovery for Structured Web Search: A Query-log Mining Approach

Jeffrey Pound*
University of Waterloo
Waterloo, Canada
jpound@cs.uwaterloo.ca

Stelios Paparizos
Microsoft Research
Mountain View, CA, USA
steliosp@microsoft.com

Panayiotis Tsaparas
Microsoft Research
Mountain View, CA, USA
panats@microsoft.com

ABSTRACT

In recent years, there has been a strong trend of incorporating results from structured data sources into keyword-based web search systems such as Bing or Amazon. When presenting structured data, facets are a powerful tool for navigating, refining, and grouping the results. For a given structured data source, a fundamental problem in supporting faceted search is finding an ordered selection of attributes and values that will populate the facets. This creates two sets of challenges. First, because of the limited screen real-estate, it is important that the top facets best match the anticipated user intent. Second, the huge scale of available data to such engines demands an automated unsupervised solution.

In this paper, we model the user faceted-search behavior using the intersection of web query-logs with existing structured data. Since web queries are formulated as free-text queries, a challenge in our approach is the inherent ambiguity in mapping keywords to the different possible attributes of a given entity type. We present an automated solution that elicits user preferences on attributes and values, employing different disambiguation techniques ranging from simple keyword matching, to more sophisticated probabilistic models. We demonstrate experimentally the scalability of our solution by running it on over a thousand categories of diverse entity types and measure the facet quality with a real-user study.

Categories and Subject Descriptors: H.2.8 [Database Management]: Data Mining

General Terms: Algorithms, Experimentation, Human Factors.

Keywords: Facets, Faceted search, Structured web-search.

1. INTRODUCTION

In recent years, search engines like Google or Bing have evolved to include in their results information from structured data sources along with text documents. Furthermore, there are specialized search verticals like Amazon that rely on an even greater variety of structured data sources for their results. Structured data have the advantage of having rich meta-data, allowing for an improved search experience compared to just keyword search.

Faceted search is a common interaction paradigm that utilizes structured information to provide a user-friendly alternative to keyword search. In this paradigm, facets are used as summarized data axes that allow the users to pivot on the information shown and create a different or more selective result set. If we abstract the structured data as typed entities grouped together into logical tables, one per entity type. A table *facet* corresponds to a table attribute and underlying attribute values. Faceted search is enabled via a *facet system* which exposes an ordered list of attributes and an ordered list of attribute values.

For example, for a table of digital cameras, a facet could be a popular attribute such as *brand* and prominent values such as '*Canon*', '*Nikon*', and '*Sony*'. Other facets could be *megapixel resolution*, *color*, *size* and corresponding values per attribute. Exposing them into a facet system, allows the user to quickly zoom into the appropriate camera subset by selecting characteristics of interest. Similar examples exist in other domains with structured data, such as automobiles or movies.

It is clear that the user experience for structured web-search can benefit from facets. However for an engine to support facets effectively it needs to address two groups of challenges: (a) Given the limited screen real estate and the large number of possible facets to consider, we need to select the top-k most important facets, where k is usually a small number. Facet importance in this case can be measured by the *utility* of a facet towards a user's anticipated action like a pivot or refinement. Since an entity-type can have over one hundred attributes, the challenge becomes finding the few most important attributes, and attribute values with the maximum anticipated utility. (b) There is a huge number of structured data sources currently available to engines like Google or Amazon. If we abstract the data as de-normalized entity-type tables, there are thousands of such tables to consider. So a solution that finds facets from these tables must be fully automated to scale appropriately.

The best method to learn the utility of attributes for users would be to consume user-produced signals. Such an ideal signal would be produced if all possible attributes for all possible entity-type tables are shown and then the system observes and records which ones are being selected by an extensive user study. Unfortunately, this is not feasible due to the scale of data and the number of required users for statistical significance. Instead, common practice [8, 10] has been to show attributes selected manually by experts with values populated from sampling the results. It is debatable how well a domain expert can match the average user intent, but regardless, the scale of structured data available to web engines makes it impossible to go this route with consistently good quality across all tables. As a result, existing approaches [3, 22] rely on automatically learning

*Work done while at Microsoft Research.

SIGMOD'11, June 12–16, 2011, Athens, Greece.

facets from the structured data. However, such approaches do not capture the true user intent since they focus on the structured data without incorporating user signals.

In this work we use web query logs intersected with the structured data to model the facet utility. Our intuition is that query logs act as a proxy for the exploration process of the users when navigating through a structured domain. We assume that users issue queries to refine or alter their results into an appropriate consideration set in a similar manner they would have used facets if there were available. The attributes that appear frequently in the query logs are the ones that users would use to narrow down their search, and thus they are appropriate for facets. The values of these attributes that appear frequently in the queries are good values to populate the facets. This formulation has the advantage that it can lead to a scalable automated solution that captures the real user needs better than the opinion of an expert, or the just the statistics of the structured data. Additionally, it adapts to the needs and preferences of the users as they change over time. It is worth mentioning that trying to match the user intent for attribute importance has been studied in the past, see [7, 21], with the application domain being either attribute ranking or product visibility. Although the high-level principle is similar, the underlying models and corresponding solutions are different from those for discovering the facet utility.

Using the web query logs to find frequently queried values and attributes would be easy if the attribute-value pairs were clearly specified in the queries as in SQL statements. However, although the data is structured, web queries are free-text keywords. Finding the frequent attributes poses two hard challenges due to the inherent ambiguity of translating the keywords to attribute-value pairs. (a) Mapping the query to the appropriate structured source – e.g., map the keyword '*apple*' to either mp3 players, computers, or fruit; and (b) identifying and disambiguating the occurrence of attributes in the query amongst attributes of the same entity-type – e.g., for the table televisions, disambiguate the keyword '*30inch*' between the *diagonal screen size*, *height* or *width* of a television; or for the table watches, map the keyword '*gold*' to the *color* or *material* of a watch.

In this paper, we assume that the first problem, understanding if a query targets a source of structured data and which source in particular, has been addressed from existing literature, such as [13, 19, 24]. We use the existing work to find the appropriate target data source. We focus on the second problem, disambiguating between attributes within an entity-type domain. Using appropriate disambiguation, we learn the most suitable facet attributes and values. Furthermore, we also discuss how data statistics can be used to help with the disambiguation process by being tolerant to data noise and imperfections, and also which data statistics indicate good facets.

Our contributions are summarized as follows: (i) We formulate the problem of query-log based facet attribute and value selection, presented in Section 2. (ii) We introduce different attribute-value identification and disambiguation techniques in Section 3, which we extend for computing facet values, including context-dependent ones, in Section 4. (iii) We explore the effect of appropriate data statistics in facet selection, presented in Section 5. And (iv), we perform a detailed experimental study on a large scale data set with a thorough evaluation on the quality of the results from real users, presented in Section 6, where we discuss the qualitative difference between our techniques as well as show our best approach outperforming state-of-the-industry systems. We conclude with related work in Section 7 and final thoughts in Section 8.

2. FACET SELECTION

In this section we formulate our problem, and provide the necessary definitions for the remainder of the paper.

2.1 Problem Formulation

We assume that structured data are organized as a collection of *tables* $\mathcal{T} = \{T_1, T_2, \ldots, T_\tau\}$[1]. A table T is a set of related *entities* defined over a set of *attributes*, $T.\mathcal{A} = \{T.A_1, T.A_2, \ldots, T.A_\alpha\}$. We use $T.A.\mathcal{V}$ to denote the domain of the attribute $T.A$. We omit the prefix T and use A, whenever the table is unambiguous.

Given a table T we define a *facet system* $\mathcal{F} = \langle F_1, ..., F_k \rangle$ for table T as an ordered list of k *facets*, where k is is the facet budget. A facet $F_i = \{A_i, \langle A_i.v_1, ..., A_i.v_{m_i} \rangle\}$ consists of an attribute A_i and an ordered list of m_i values, where m_i is the value budget for attribute A_i. For the following we use $\mathcal{A}_\mathcal{F}$ (or $\mathcal{F}.\mathcal{A}$) to denote the set of attributes of $\mathcal{F}$, and $A.\mathcal{V}_\mathcal{F}$ to denote the set of values for attribute $A \in \mathcal{A}_\mathcal{F}$ in facet system $\mathcal{F}$. We say that a facet system *supports* an attribute A if $A \in \mathcal{A}_\mathcal{F}$, and we define the attribute-support function as follows:

$$\text{ASUP}(\mathcal{F}, A) = \begin{cases} 1, & \text{if } \mathcal{F} \text{ supports } A \\ 0, & \text{otherwise} \end{cases} \quad (1)$$

We also say that a facet attribute $A_f \in \mathcal{A}_\mathcal{F}$ supports value v if $v \in A_f.\mathcal{V}_\mathcal{F}$, and we define the attribute-value support function as follows:

$$\text{VSUP}(A_f, v) = \begin{cases} 1, & \text{if } A_f \text{ supports } v \\ 0, & \text{otherwise} \end{cases} \quad (2)$$

A facet system is exposed through the user interface, and it enables the user to navigate through the data in the table T by selecting values for the different attributes. The design and analysis of faceted user interfaces is an active research area in the HCI community [10]. In any faceted search system, the facet selection is paramount to the success of the system. The order of facets is also important since it determines how the facets will be displayed, with more important facets being displayed more prominently. The goal is to maximize the user engagement and satisfaction, and the i-th facet corresponds to the i-th best attribute for this task. A similar reasoning applies also to the ordering of the facet values within a facet. However, for a selected facet attribute there is usually a greater flexibility in the presentation of values (drop-down menus, slider bars, text boxes) making the value selection and ordering less critical. We thus consider the *facet attribute ordering* problem and the *facet attribute value ordering* problem separately, with the former being more important than the latter.

In this work we are interested in constructing a facet system using web search queries. We assume that we have a query log $\mathcal{Q} = \{q_1, ..., q_n\}$, consisting of queries posed to a generic web search engine. For each query q_i we also have a weight w_i denoting the importance of the query, e.g., the number of times that the query appears in the query log.

Although queries are posed to the search engine, it is common that users make queries that are targeted to structured data. For example, the query "*canon powershot*" can be interpreted as targeting a table with structured data about digital cameras. For a given table T let $\mathcal{Q}_T \subseteq \mathcal{Q}$ denote the subset of queries that target table T. We will drop the subscript T whenever the table is unambiguous. We assume that each query $q \in \mathcal{Q}_T$ specifies a set of attribute-value pairs $\mathcal{AV}_q = \{AV_i\}$ of the form $AV_i = (A_i, A_i.v_j)$. For example, the query "*canon powershot*" specifies the value '*canon*' for attribute *brand*, and the value '*powershot*' for attribute *product line*. We can thus map the query q ="*canon powershot*" to the set $\mathcal{A}_q$ ={(*brand*,'*canon*'),(*product line*,'*powershot*')}. We use $\mathcal{A}_q$

[1]The organization of data into tables is purely conceptual and orthogonal to the underlying storage layer: the data can be physically stored in XML files, relational tables, retrieved from remote web services, etc. Our assumption is that a mapping between the storage layer and the "schema" of table collection $\mathcal{T}$ has been defined.

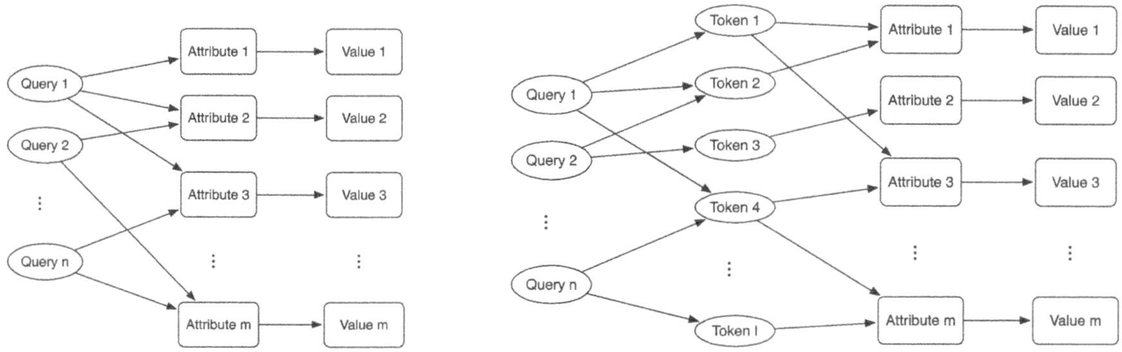

(a) Queries to discrete attribute-value pairs (b) Queries to attribute-value pairs through tagged tokens

Figure 1: Query to Attribute-Value Pairs Mappings

to denote the set of attributes specified in the query. Figure 1(a) depicts graphically an example. Note that we only assume that such a mapping exists; obtaining it from the web log is a challenging problem as we elaborate below.

We now define the *attribute utility* of a facet system $\mathcal{F}$, making use of the attribute support function defined in Equation 1.

DEFINITION 1 (ATTRIBUTE UTILITY). *Given a facet system $\mathcal{F}$, and a query q, we define the* attribute utility *of $\mathcal{F}$ for q as*

$$U_a(\mathcal{F}, q) = \sum_{A \in \mathcal{A}_q} \text{ASUP}(\mathcal{F}, A)$$

the number of attributes in $\mathcal{A}_q$ supported by $\mathcal{F}$. The attribute utility of $\mathcal{F}$ for query log $\mathcal{Q}$ is defined as

$$U_a(\mathcal{F}, \mathcal{Q}) = \sum_{q \in \mathcal{Q}} w_q U_a(\mathcal{F}, q)$$

where w_q denotes the weight of query q.

We can similarly define the *attribute-value utility* of a facet attribute A_f, making use of the attribute-value support function defined in Equation 2.

DEFINITION 2 (ATTRIBUTE-VALUE UTILITY). *Given a facet attribute A_f and a query q, we define the* attribute-value utility *of A_f for q as*

$$U_v(A_f, q) = \sum_{(A,v) \in \mathcal{AV}_q : A = A_f} \text{VSUP}(A_f, v)$$

the number of values in $\mathcal{AV}_q$ supported by A_f. The attribute-value utility of A_f for query log $\mathcal{Q}$ is defined as

$$U_v(A_f, \mathcal{Q}) = \sum_{q \in \mathcal{Q}} w_q U_v(A_f, q)$$

where w_q denotes the weight of query q.

As we have already argued, queries act as a proxy for the exploration process of the users over the structured data. Users include in their queries attributes over which they want to dissect the table. A good faceted system should anticipate the information need of the user and select attributes (and values) that maximize the utility to the users. We thus have the following definition of the *query-based* facet selection problems.

PROBLEM 1 (QUERY-BASED FACET ATTRIBUTE SELECTION). *Given a table T, and a query log $\mathcal{Q}_T$ over table T, create an ordering $\mathcal{L}(T.\mathcal{A})$ of the attributes $T.\mathcal{A}$ such that for any $k \geq 1$, a facet system $\mathcal{F}$ with attribute set $\mathcal{F}.\mathcal{A} = \mathcal{L}_k(T.\mathcal{A})$ — the top-k attributes according to ordering $\mathcal{L}$ — has maximum attribute utility $U_a(\mathcal{F}, \mathcal{Q}_T)$ over all facet systems with attribute set of size k.*

PROBLEM 2 (QUERY-BASED FACET VALUE SELECTION). *Given a table T, an attribute $A \in T.\mathcal{A}$, and a query log $\mathcal{Q}_T$ over table T, create an ordering $\mathcal{L}(A.\mathcal{V})$ of the values in $A.\mathcal{V}$ such that for any $m \geq 1$, a facet system $\mathcal{F}$ that contains A with attribute value set $A.\mathcal{V}_{\mathcal{F}} = \mathcal{L}_m(A.\mathcal{V})$ — the top-m attributes according to ordering $\mathcal{L}$ — has maximum attribute-value utility $U_v(A, \mathcal{Q}_T)$ over all facet systems that contain A with attribute-value set of size m.*

If we are given the mapping $\mathcal{AV}_q$ from queries to attribute value pairs, as in Figure 1(a) then the facet selection problems we defined above are easy to solve. This is the case for example with structured query logs (e.g. SQL), where the user specifies explicitly the attributes and values they are interested in. Then, it is straightforward to see that the optimal solution for Problem 1 is to order the attributes according to their *popularity* in the query log. The popularity $F_{\mathcal{Q}}(A_i)$ of attribute A_i over query log $\mathcal{Q}$ is computed as

$$F_{\mathcal{Q}}(A_i) = \sum_{q \in \mathcal{Q}} \sum_{(A_i, v) \in \mathcal{AV}_q} w_q \tag{3}$$

The popularity $F_{\mathcal{Q}}(A_i)$ is thus the number of attribute-value pairs in $\mathcal{Q}$ that contain attribute A_i weighted by the weight of the query in which they appear.

Similarly, the optimal solution for Problem 2 is to order the values within attribute A_i according to their popularity in the query log. The popularity of a value v_j of attribute A_i is computed as

$$F_{\mathcal{Q}}(A_i.v_j) = \sum_{q \in \mathcal{Q}} \sum_{(A_i, v_j) \in \mathcal{AV}_q} w_q \tag{4}$$

the number of attribute value pairs in the query log, where A_i is the attribute and v_j is the value.

Unfortunately, in the case of web query logs this mapping is not given to us and we need to discover it from the data. We elaborate on this challenge in the following section.

2.2 Mapping Web Queries to Structured Data

In order to extract attribute value pairs from the queries in the unstructured web query log, we need to address two issues: (a) for every table T, identify the queries in $\mathcal{Q}$ that target table T, i.e., determine the set $\mathcal{Q}_T$, and (b) identify and disambiguate the attribute occurrences in the queries. As previously discussed, we use existing work [13, 24] to solve (a) and instead focus on the latter problem.

Given a query $q \in \mathcal{Q}_T$ we now need to identify the occurrences of the attributes in $T.\mathcal{A}$ in the query q. We assume a *tagging* process TAGGER that performs this task. Define a *token* to be a string consisting of one or more contiguous words, and let L_q denote the set of all tokens in q. The TAGGER produces all tokens $t \in L_q$, and matches them with attributes in $T.\mathcal{A}$, producing attribute-token

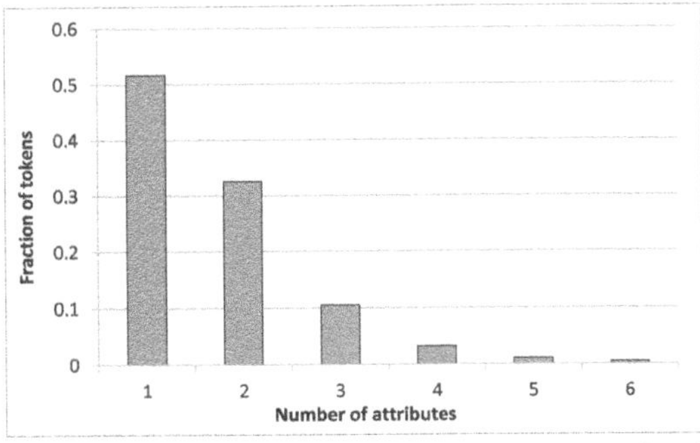

Figure 2: Fraction of tokens mapped to varying num of attributes.

pairs, $AT = (\mathcal{A}, t)$. For a categorical attribute $A_c \in T.\mathcal{A}$, the TAGGER outputs an attribute-token pair $AT = (A_c, t)$, if the token t appears in $A_c.\mathcal{V}$. Approximate, or synonymous matching is also possible as an extension of the same process, although discussing it in detail is outside the scope of this paper. For a numerical attribute A_n with unit u (e.g., inches, Kg, or x zoom), the TAGGER produces an attribute-token pair $AT = (A_n, t)$ for every token t that consists of a number followed by a unit u. For example, the tagger output for the query "*5x nikon*" over the digital cameras table is {(*digital zoom*, '*5x*'), (*optical zoom*, '*5x*'), (*brand*, '*nikon*')}.

For a query q we use $\mathcal{AT}_q = \{(A, t)\} \subseteq T.\mathcal{A} \times L_q$ to denote the set of attribute-token pairs output by the TAGGER . Note that attribute-token pairs are different from attribute-value pairs, since a token may not be a value in the table T. This is the case with synonyms and approximate matches, as well as with numeric attributes. For example, in the query "*30 inch lcd TV*", the token '*TV*' can match the data value '*Television,*' and the token '*30 inch*' can be mapped to *diagonal screen size* even though we may only have televisions with 27 and 32 inch diagonals.

Given the query log $\mathcal{Q}$ the TAGGER outputs a set of attribute-token pairs $\mathcal{AT}_{\mathcal{Q}}$. It would appear that our job is now done, since we can compute the popularity of attributes and values as before, simply by interchanging tokens with values, and attribute-value pairs with attribute-token pairs. However, this is not the case due to *ambiguity* in the token interpretation. The domains of attributes in a table often overlap, and as a result a token t can map to more than one attribute. For example, in the query "*30 inch lcd TV*", the token '*30 inch*' is potentially mapped to the *diagonal*, *width*, *height*, and *depth* attributes, since all these attributes are numeric with the same unit; similarly in the query "*camera with 3x zoom*", '*3x*' can be either *optical zoom* or *digital zoom*. Such confusion is not limited to just numeric attributes. For example in the query "*gold watch*", the token '*gold*' can specify either the *material*, or the *color* attribute; similarly for "*leather dress shoes*" the token '*leather*' can map to either the *top shoe material* or the *shoe sole*. There are many such examples that appear in web queries. We computed the number of attributes of the same table that a token matches on average, over all queries. As we can see from Figure 2, approximately half the tokens are confused over at least two or more attributes. So ambiguity is a real problem that needs to be addressed.

Estimating attribute popularity in the presence of ambiguity becomes problematic. Our data no longer looks like Figure 1(a), but instead like Figure 1(b). Computing the attribute popularity over attribute-token pairs using Equation 3 will lead to misleading results: TV *height* will incorrectly be deemed equally important to TV *diagonal*, and camera *digital zoom* the same as *optical zoom*. In order to obtain correct estimates for the true popularity of an attribute, we need to *disambiguate* the ambiguous tokens.

Let $\tilde{t}$ denote a token in a query q. We say that token $\tilde{t}$ is ambiguous for a table T, if there are at least two attribute-token pairs $(A_i, \tilde{t})$ involving $\tilde{t}$. We use $\mathcal{A}_{\tilde{t}}$ to denote the set of candidate attributes to which the token $\tilde{t}$ is mapped. Our goal is to disambiguate between the attributes in $\mathcal{A}_{\tilde{t}}$. We do this by estimating the probability of an attribute given the ambiguous token. We thus have the following problem definition.

PROBLEM 3 (ATTRIBUTE DISAMBIGUATION). *Given a table T, a query log $\mathcal{Q}$ over T, and an ambiguous token $\tilde{t} \in L_{\mathcal{Q}}$ that maps to the set of attributes $\mathcal{A}_{\tilde{t}} \subseteq T.\mathcal{A}$, compute the* disambiguation probability distribution, *denoted $P(A|\tilde{t})$, over the set of candidate attributes $A \in \mathcal{A}_{\tilde{t}}$.*

Given $P(A|\tilde{t})$ we now have a measure of likelihood for the mapping of token $\tilde{t}$ to attribute A. We can use this probability to perform either hard or soft disambiguation. In hard disambiguation, we map token $\tilde{t}$ to the most likely attribute $A_{\tilde{t}} = \arg\max_{A \in \mathcal{A}_{\tilde{t}}} P(A|\tilde{t})$. In hard disambiguation our data will take the form of Figure 1(a), and we can apply directly Equation 3 to estimate the attribute popularity. In soft disambiguation, we modify Equation 3 such that each occurrence of attribute A with the ambiguous token $\tilde{t}$ is weighted by the probability $P(A|\tilde{t})$. We thus have

$$\tilde{F}_{\mathcal{Q}}(A_i) = \sum_{q \in \mathcal{Q}} \sum_{(A_i, t) \in \mathcal{AT}_q} w_q P(A_i|t) \tag{5}$$

We have $P(A|t) = 1$ if token t maps unambiguously to attribute A.

3. ATTRIBUTE DISAMBIGUATION

In this section we describe four different approaches for attribute disambiguation. The first three rely on the principle that the best solution is the one that better *explains* the attribute-token pairs we observe. If we assume that the attributes in the table are generating queries and tokens, we identify the attribute that is most likely to have generated the tokens we are observing. The three different algorithms differ in the granularity at which they try to explain the data, becoming progressively more complex. The last approach relies on user feedback from a click-log to disambiguate between different interpretations of a token.

3.1 Token-level Disambiguation

The first algorithm we consider treats each token independently and tries to find the attribute that is most likely to have generated this specific token. Let $\tilde{t}$ denote an ambiguous token and let $\mathcal{A}_{\tilde{t}}$ the set of candidate attributes for $\tilde{t}$. We want to estimate $P(A|\tilde{t})$ for all $A \in \mathcal{A}_{\tilde{t}}$. Using Bayes rule we have

$$P(A|\tilde{t}) = \frac{P(\tilde{t}|A)P(A)}{\sum_{A_i \in \mathcal{A}_{\tilde{t}}} P(\tilde{t}|A_i)P(A_i)}$$

We will estimate the right-hand side using the data in T. Assuming that all attributes are equally likely in the table (i.e., $P(A)$ is the same for all attributes in the table), then $P(A|\tilde{t})$ is proportional to $P_T(\tilde{t}|A)$, the probability that the token $\tilde{t}$ is generated from the distribution of A in the table. We have that

$$P_T(\tilde{t}|A_i) = \frac{|T(A, \tilde{t})|}{|A|}$$

where $T(A, \tilde{t})$ denotes the set of entries in the table where the attribute A takes the value $\tilde{t}$, and $|A|$ is the number of table entries with some value for attribute A. Numeric attributes are similarly described using histograms to deal with the continuity of numbers.

Therefore, according to this algorithm, the most likely attribute is the one that is most likely to have generated token $\tilde{t}$. From an information theoretic point-of-view, this is the attribute who's value distribution can encode token $\tilde{t}$ with the fewest number of bits, i.e., the one that reduces the uncertainty the most for $\tilde{t}$.

3.2 Cluster-level Disambiguation

The token-level disambiguation approach considers the probability of each token independently mapping to a candidate attribute. A natural extension to this model is to consider the ambiguity among a cluster of tokens confused with the same set of attributes. In this cluster-based approach, we aggregate over all tokens in the query-log to find clusters of ambiguous attribute-token pairs. We then resolve which attributes in the cluster are better candidates to model the distribution of confused tokens over the *full* cluster.

Consider the bipartite graph formed by the set of attribute-token pairs in $\mathcal{AT}_\mathcal{Q}$ (e.g., see Figure 3 (a)). Each time a token is mapped to a set of attributes, it *supports* the ambiguity of these attributes. For example, if the token '*8x*' is mapped to both *digital zoom* and *optical zoom*, it supports the ambiguity of these two attributes. If the token '*2x*' is mapped to *digital zoom*, *optical zoom*, and *model* it supports the ambiguity of all three of these attributes. By aggregating over all tokens in the query log, we can find the groups of attributes most commonly confused. In particular, if we consider the set of all tokens that form a bi-clique with a set of attributes, then these attributes are all pairwise ambiguous over the same set of tokens, and the support for the ambiguity of this cluster is proportional to the number of tokens in the bi-clique. It is these strongly supported bi-cliques that we aim to find.

To find clusters of ambiguous attributes, we first construct an *attribute ambiguity graph* per table. For a table T, consider a graph $G = (V, E, w)$ where there exists a vertex $v_a \in V$ for every attribute $a \in \mathcal{T}.\mathcal{A}$. We create an edge $e = \langle v_{A_1}, v_{A_2}\rangle$ between two vertices v_{A_1} and v_{A_2} if some token in the query log is mapped to both A_1 and A_2 over all interpretations of queries. The weight function $w(e)$ assigns a weight to the edge e equal to the number of tokens confused between (the attributes denoted by) v_{A_1} and v_{A_2}. We then enumerate all cliques in the attribute ambiguity graph, with the support being the minimum edge weight in the clique. For example, in Figure 3 (b), the support of the 2-clique containing *digital zoom* and *optical zoom* is ten, while the support of the 3-clique containing *digital zoom*, *optical zoom*, and *model* is two.

After identifying the clusters of ambiguous attributes, we want to compute how likely each attribute is to model the set of confused tokens. We do this by computing the KL-divergence (Kullback-Leibler divergence) between the value distribution of the attribute and the set of confused tokens. Let $C = (\mathcal{A}_C, L_C)$ denote an attribute-token cluster. We compute the disambiguation probability of an attribute $A \in \mathcal{A}_C$ given the cluster C as follows.

$$P(A|C) = \frac{KL(A||C)}{\sum_{Ai \in C} KL(Ai||C)}$$

where the KL-divergence between two distributions P and Q is defined as follows.

$$KL(P||Q) = \sum_x p(x) \log \frac{p(x)}{q(x)}$$

For every ambiguous attribute-token pair $(A, \tilde{t}) \in L_C$, we set the disambiguation probability $P(A|\tilde{t}) = P(A|C)$.

The intuition in this kind of disambiguation is that the attribute which forms a better model for the query token distribution is more likely to be the correct attribute users had in mind when formulating these queries. For example, if a collection of tokens around measurements are confused among television *height* and *diagonal*, we would expect to find the distribution of values in the *diagonal* attribute to be a better model for the set of confused query tokens.

As an example, consider Figure 3. There are eight tokens with the same connectivity of the token labeled '*8x*', two tokens with the same connectivity as '*2x*', and five tokens with the same connectivity as '*Pix*.' The ambiguous attribute clusters correspond to the 2-clique {*Digital Zoom*, *Optical Zoom*} with support 10, the 2-clique {*Product Name*, *Model*} with support five, and lastly the 3-clique {*Digital Zoom*, *Optical Zoom*, *Model*} with a support of two. The 3-clique will be used to disambiguate among tokens confused with all three attributes, while the sub-clique will be used to disambiguate between tokens confused among only those two attributes. We may also find the remaining two 2-cliques {*Digital Zoom*, *Model*} and {*Optical Zoom*, *Model*} however in our implementation we are not concerned with these as there are no tokens that confuse *Model* with one of the other attributes and not the third (i.e., all tokens confused with *Model* and *Optical Zoom* are also confused with *Digital Zoom*, and all tokens confused with *Model* and *Digital Zoom* are also confused with *Optical Zoom*).

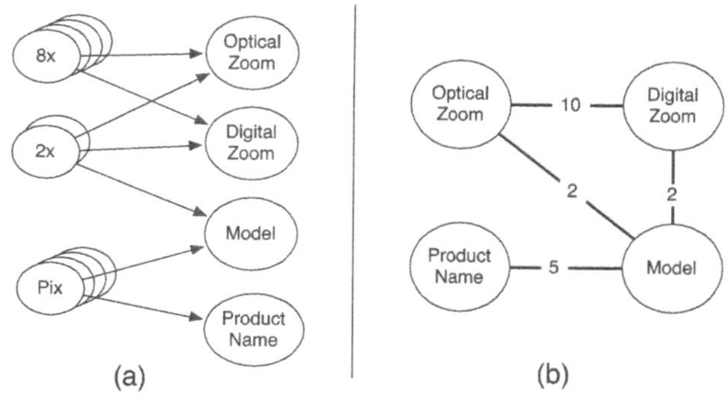

Figure 3: (a) a bipartite token-attribute graph and (b) the resulting attribute ambiguity graph.

3.3 Query-log-level Disambiguation

We now present an approach that considers the tokens in the full query log, and estimates the probability $P(A|\tilde{t})$ for ambiguous tokens $\tilde{t}$, such that the likelihood of the full observed query log is maximized. Let $\mathcal{Q}$ be a query log over table T. Let $L_\mathcal{Q}$ denote the set of all tokens generated by the TAGGER that appear in the attribute-token pairs $\mathcal{AT}_\mathcal{Q}$. Each token t is assigned a weight

$$w_t = \sum_{q \in \mathcal{Q}} \sum_{(A_i, t) \in \mathcal{AT}_q} w_q,$$

the total weight of queries in which token t appears. For simplicity we can consider w_t to be the frequency of the token t in $\mathcal{AT}_\mathcal{Q}$.

We assume that the tokens in $L_\mathcal{Q}$ were generated according to a generative model, which generates tokens as follows: an attribute A_i is selected with probability $P(A_i)$, and then a token t is drawn from the data distribution $P_T(t|A_i)$. Thus token t is generated with a probability given by the following.

$$P(t) = \sum_{A_i \in T.\mathcal{A}} P_T(t|A_i) P(A_i)$$

The probability of observing the full set of tokens $L_\mathcal{Q}$ is then

$$P(L_\mathcal{Q}) = \prod_{t \in \mathcal{Q}} P(t)^{w_t}$$

The generative model we have described has α parameters $\pi_i = P(A_i)$, one for each attribute A_i in the table T. Parameter π_i is the probability that attribute A_i is activated for the generation of a given token, and we have that $\sum_{i=1}^{\alpha} \pi_i = 1$. Let π denote the vector of parameters $\pi_1, ..., \pi_\alpha$. We perform Maximum Likelihood

Estimation of π, and we look for the value of π that maximizes the probability that we observe the tokens in $L_{\mathcal{Q}}$. Using log-likelihood notation we want to minimize the following.

$$\mathcal{L}(L_{\mathcal{Q}}) = -\log P(L_{\mathcal{Q}}) = -\sum_{t \in \mathcal{Q}} w_t \log P(t)$$

We use an iterative EM algorithm for finding the Maximum Likelihood Estimate for π. The algorithm initializes the values of the parameters π_i to an arbitrary distribution, in our implementation uniform. Then it alternates between the following two steps.

In the E-step given an estimation for the parameters π, for each attribute-token pair (A_i, t_j) in $L_{\mathcal{Q}}$ we compute the posterior probability of the attribute A_i given token t_j

$$P(A_i|t_j) = \frac{P(t_j|A_i)\pi_i}{\sum_{A_\ell \in \mathcal{AT}.\mathcal{A}} P(t_j|A_\ell)\pi_\ell} \quad (6)$$

In the M-step, we can now estimate new values for the parameters in π as follows,

$$\pi_i = \sum_{(A_i,t) \in \mathcal{AT}_{\mathcal{Q}}} P(A_i|t)P(t) = \frac{w_t}{W} \sum_{(A_i,t) \in \mathcal{AT}_{\mathcal{Q}}} P(A_i|t) \quad (7)$$

where $W = \sum_{t \in L_{\mathcal{Q}}} w_t$ is the total weight of all tokens.

We repeat these two steps until the algorithm converges. Given that the optimization function is convex we know that it will reach a global maximum. After the algorithm has converged, for an ambiguous token $\tilde{t}$ we can now compute $P(A|\tilde{t})$ using Equation 6.

The Maximum Likelihood Estimation of the probabilities $P(A_i)$ finds a set of values that best explains the full query log we observe. Intuitively what this means is that when observing a token t, even though attribute A_1 may have the highest probability $P(t|A_1)$, the token t may be attributed to another attribute A_2 since this is overall more likely to occur in the log. For example, consider a query-log with queries over the televisions table, and let L_{inch} denote the set of all tokens of the form number followed by the unit "inch". If the overall distribution of these tokens agrees better with the attribute *diagonal* than *height* then for a token like '*30 inch*' in L_{inch} the attribute *diagonal* will have higher probability $P(A|t)$ even though the value is more likely in the *height* attribute. This agrees well with our intuition that '*30 inch*' is more likely to refer to the *diagonal* rather than the *height*, since it is typical for users to query for *diagonal* when querying for televisions. The iterative algorithm captures nicely this intuition.

3.4 Clicks-based Disambiguation

The ambiguity problem is essentially an intent issue. Given an ambiguous token, and multiple interpretations of the token in the data table we have no indication which interpretation was intended by the user. In an online environment, a strong indication of intent is the user click behavior.

A query-click log $\mathcal{QC} = \{(q_1, e_1), ..., (q_n, e_n)\}$ over a table T is a set of query-entity pairs, where q is a query posed in a commercial search engine, and e is an entity in table T that was shown to the user as a result of the query and the user chose to click on it to obtain further information about it. An entity e is an entry in table T. We represent it as a set of attribute-value pairs $e = \{(A_i, A_i.v_j)\}$ for every attribute A_i in table T. Given a query-click pair (q, e), we make the assumption that the user who posed the query intended to access the attributes of clicked entity e.

Since we now have an indication for the intent of the user, the disambiguation problem becomes significantly easier to tackle. Given an ambiguous token $\tilde{t}$ that maps to attributes $\mathcal{A}_{\tilde{t}} = \{A_{i_1}, ..., A_{i_k}\}$ we disambiguate by selecting from entity e the attribute $A^* \in \mathcal{A}_{\tilde{t}}$ that has value $A^*.v$ that best *matches* token $\tilde{t}$.

The notion of a match depends on the type of token that we consider. In the case of categorical tokens we require that $A^*.v = \tilde{t}$. In such cases we have that $P(A^*|\tilde{t}) = 1$, since we assume complete certainty in our mapping. If there is more than one attribute that match token $\tilde{t}$ then we assume that $\tilde{t}$ maps to all of them, and we assign equal probability to all. It is worth noting that, although possible, this event is not very probable. In our experiments, we did not observe any case where multiple categorical attributes match on the same token for the same clicked entity. In the case of numerical tokens, we map token $\tilde{t}$ to the attribute A^* that has the closest value, i.e., it minimizes the difference $|\tilde{t} - A^*.v|$. we compute the disambiguation probability as

$$P(A^*|\tilde{t}) = \frac{\exp(-|\tilde{t} - A^*.v|)}{\sum_{A \in \mathcal{A}_{\tilde{t}}} \exp(-|\tilde{t} - A^*.v|)}$$

favoring the attributes with smallest distance.

Clicks have been used extensively in web search for eliciting the preferences of users [14, 19]. It is well known that they contain a very strong signal for the intent of the user, but they also come with different caveats, such as presentation bias (users click only on what they are shown), ranking bias (users tend to click on the top positions), and noise. We discuss some of these issues in the experimental evaluation (see Section 6).

4. ATTRIBUTE VALUE SELECTION

Equally important to finding important attributes, is the problem of finding important values to populate the facets. We apply the same philosophy for values as we do for attributes; popular values in a query log will be strong facet values that are important to users. In the following section, we discuss two types of facet value selection: category-dependent facet value selection, and dynamic context-dependent facet value selection.

4.1 Table Dependent Value Selection

To compute the value score, we consider Equation 4 and modify it such that each occurrence of attribute A and value v with the ambiguous token $\tilde{t}$ is weighted by the probability $P(A.v|\tilde{t})$. We then have the popularity of a value as the following.

$$\tilde{F}_{\mathcal{Q}}(A_i.v_j) = \sum_{q \in \mathcal{Q}} \sum_{(A_i,\tilde{t}) \in \mathcal{AT}_q} w_q P(A_i.v_j|\tilde{t}) \quad (8)$$

In the case that value v_j does not map to the token $\tilde{t}$, the probability will be zero. Also, for all attributes A_i of the same table we have $P(A_i.v_j|t) = P(A_i|t)$ since the token to value mapping is part of the attribute based disambiguation. Hence each of the attribute disambiguation methods from Section 3 are directly applicable. For numeric attributes, we can compute weights for buckets of values via the usage of a histogram. This method allows for each table attribute to display a set of values based on user popularity. For example, for the golf clubs table and *brand* attribute, the top 3 facet values would be '*Nike*', '*Ping*', and '*TaylorMade*'.

4.2 Context Dependent Value Selection

We described how to use query log popularity to find good facet values given the table and an attribute. However, we still have the problem that certain combination of values across attributes will return empty results. For example, consider a faceted search engine which includes *brand* and *golf club type* among its facets for the golf clubs table. There exist some specialized brands that only produce very few types of golf clubs, i.e. '*Odyssey*' or '*Scotty Cameron*' only produce '*putters*'. So now when a user selects '*Odyssey*', then *golf club type* values such as '*drivers*' or '*wedges*' are not good facet choices since selecting them would produce empty results. Showing '*putters*' would be a much better choice.

Also consider the flip side of this example that exposes another interesting problem. When the first user action is to select '*putters*' as *golf club type*, then popular choices such as '*Nike*' or '*TaylorMade*' for *brand* will produce valid results, albeit not necessarily the most desirable ones. Golf aficionados may prefer '*Odyssey*' or '*Scotty Cameron*' putters. Although it is not that dramatic to put the generally popular '*Nike*' on top, it is arguably a better user experience to be able to show '*Odyssey*' given the '*putters*' selection. The example output from our implementation can be seen in Figure 4. In summary, it is preferable for a facet system to take into consideration the existing user context, in the form of pre-selected attribute-value pairs from a facet selection or a user query (via [20, 24]), and dynamically adjust the shown facet values.

One way to achieve this task would be to consider the data and pre-compute the correlation between all possible value combinations across attributes. This information is then stored for online processing and use the context to filter the possible choices. However, such computation is very expensive for the scale of data sets available in a web search engine. Even after this expensive computation, supporting the retrieval of such information for real-time search is a non-negligible investment that will have an overall impact in resource usage and result response time. Besides the computational cost, it is also not clear whether data-correlation frequency corresponds well with the user intent.

To limit the computational cost while still trying to best satisfy the user, we turn again to query logs. We compute co-occurrence for value pairs across different attributes that appear frequently together in the same query. We then validate the co-occurring values against the database to ensure a non-zero entity count in the results. By going to the query logs we significantly reduce the space of possible data value pairs to consider when compared to all attributes and all values of a table. As a result, we effectively address the issue of empty results without significantly affecting the response time, resource usage and off-line computation cost. More importantly, we further optimize the user experience by dynamically placing the most relevant facet values at the top of the list for a given selection.

To compute the co-occurrence, we define the conditional score of a value for a given attribute by the probability that the value represents the attribute in a query that co-occurs with a given attribute value pair. Let $A_c.v_c$ denote conditional value v_c bound to attribute A_c, $A.v$ denote value v bound to attribute A, and $\tilde{t}$ be a token. We want to estimate $P(A.v|\tilde{t}, A_c.v_c)$, the probability of value v bound to attribute A given the observed token and conditional attribute-value binding. Since tokens are tagged independent of one another, this simplifies to $P(A.v|\tilde{t})$ which we can compute using Equation 8. The difference is in which queries are used from the query-log when computing the popularity. Given a query log $\mathcal{Q}$ and attribute-value pair $AV = (A_c, A_c.v_c)$, let $\mathcal{Q}_{AV}$ denote the subset of queries $\{q \mid q \in \mathcal{Q} \wedge (A_c, A_c.v_c) \in \mathcal{AV}_q\}$. We then estimate the popularity of a value over all queries satisfying the given attribute-value condition.

$$\tilde{F}_{\mathcal{Q}_{AV}}(A.v) = \sum_{q \in \mathcal{Q}_{\mathcal{AV}}} \sum_{(A,v) \in \mathcal{AV}_q} w_q P(A.v|\tilde{t})$$

The last consideration for context-dependent facet values is the case where there are multiple selection conditions specified in the query. This may occur either as multiple recognized attribute values in a keyword query, or as multiple facet selections. Supporting n-way conditionals with exact information is impractical. The data-driven approach suffers the combinatorial explosion of an already large data set, and the query log driven approach suffers from the sparseness of queries. After filtering by multiple selection conditions, the number of queries from which to compute popularity frequencies becomes too small. For this scenario, we adopt a simple approach of intersecting value lists and aggregating popularity counts by addition. This will find values relevant to multiple selections, and score them proportionally to how relevant they are to their respective conditional selections. Handling an empty intersection is more of a user interface design decision. One could eliminate the facet entirely, or default to the category-dependent values.

Input	Table: Golf Clubs	Query: "golf putters"
Facet Values	Nike Ping TaylorMade	Odyssey Ping Scotty Cameron

Figure 4: Example top-3 facet values for golf club brand.

5. FACETS AND DATA STATISTICS

The query logs can reveal which attributes in the table are popular among the users. However, just because an attribute is popular does not necessarily mean that it is good to be used as a facet. In this section we discuss how to use some signals from the data to discover which attributes make better facets.

Information Content: Recall that the goal of facets is to enable the users to quickly zoom into a smaller subset of products that are of interest to them. Therefore, in order for an attribute A to be a good candidate for a facet, it should have high information content, that is, the value selection v for the attribute A should give information about the tuples of interest to the user. This property is naturally captured in the *entropy* of the attribute A. For an attribute A defined over the domain $A.\mathcal{V}$, the entropy of A is defined as

$$H(A) = -\sum_{v \in \mathcal{V}} P_A(v) \log P_A(v)$$

where $P_A(v)$ is the fraction of entries in the table where attribute A takes value v, over the number of entries in the table where the attribute A takes any value (i.e., is non-null).

Attributes with low entropy do not make good facets. For such attributes the distribution of values is highly skewed, and the knowledge of the value gives very little information for the subset of entities of interest to the user. This is clear in the extreme example when the entropy is zero, meaning that all entities take the same value. In this case, the attribute is useless for navigation, since it gives no information about which entities the user is interested in. For example, the attribute *color* in the televisions table conveys no useful information as a facet if all televisions are '*black*'.

An alternative interpretation of $H(A)$ is that it captures the decrease in the uncertainty for the preference of the user for the entities (rows) in table T. When no facet attribute has been selected, any entity $e \in E$ is equally likely to be of interest to the user, therefore, if N is the number of entities in the table, each entity has probability $P(e) = 1/N$. The uncertainty is captured in the entropy of the random variable E, which in this case is maximum, $H(E) = \log N$. Now assume that the user is allowed to use attribute A to zoom in on a smaller subset of entries. The uncertainty for E decreased given the knowledge of the value in A is measured as $H(E) - H(E|A)$, where $H(E|A)$ is the conditional entropy of E given A. It is well known that $H(E|A) = H(E, A) - H(A)$. Since each entity is distinct from the rest, and assuming that A takes a value for all entities, we have that $H(E, A) = H(E) = \log N$. Therefore, $H(E|A) = H(E) - H(A)$. Thus the entropy $H(A)$ captures how much our uncertainty for the entities that the user is interested in will decrease when we have the knowledge for attribute A. If $H(A) = 0$, then the knowledge of A gives no extra information for E and thus it is redundant. It follows naturally, that attributes with low entropy should not be used as facets.

Sparsity: Real-world data is often noisy with missing or incomplete information. As a result there are often cases where some attributes are only sparsely populated. If such an attribute is selected for faceted navigation, then selecting any value will immediately discard most of the entities since they do not have a values for the sparse attribute. This could be ok if this corresponded to a rare feature, in which case missing information corresponds to negative information for the existence of the feature. However, it is often the case that sparsity is due to noise in the data collection, in which case, the entities that are eliminated are valid for the selected facet, yet will never be visible to users. Furthermore, noisy attributes are often likely to contain incorrect values, confusing the tagging process of the queries and the corresponding probabilities.

Therefore, we exclude from the candidate attributes the ones that are very sparse. The sparsity of attribute A is defined as

$$R(A) = \frac{|T(A)|}{|T|}$$

where $T(A)$ is the set of entries in which the attribute has a non-null value, and $|T|$ is the total number of entries in the table. Similarly to entropy, sparse attributes are usually not good facet candidates.

6. EXPERIMENTAL EVALUATION

We abstract the structured data as tables, each containing entities of the same type. For our experiments we have 1164 such tables that we crawled using the MSN shopping XML API[2]. The tables correspond to products used to answer shopping queries and are similar to the data used by sites like Amazon or Google Product Search. We consider each category of products to be a table of entities of the same type. The available range covers entities from electronics like digital cameras or televisions to golf clubs and soft goods like shoes and shirts. In total, there were around 10 million structured distinct product entities occupying approximately 300GB on disk when stored in our database. Besides the structured data, we also use a web query log and a vertical click log.

The *web query log* contains queries posed on a major search engine on a period of five months from July to November 2009. The web queries are approximately 31 million distinct queries all in the English language. As query weight we use the aggregated impressions count – each time a query is asked it increments its impression count. We limit ourselves to queries with at least 10 impressions to reduce noise in the queries. The total aggregate impression weight of the log is approximately 4.2 billion impressions. The average query length is 3.42 words and 22.04 characters.

The *click log* is available via toolbar usage logs collected from users that have explicitly opted-in to install the toolbar browser add-on of a major search engine. It contains queries and clicks on Amazon products over a period of one year from March 2009 to February 2010. Since our structured data set is in the shopping domain, we were able to map the Amazon click log to our product entities using unique identifier references like UPC and EIN codes. The format of the log is query, entity-id and number of clicks as the query weight. The total number of distinct queries is in the order of 2.2 million with average length of 3.67 and 24.1 characters. It is worth noting that the click log is smaller although the period used is longer. This is attributed to two reasons: there are more queries on a search engine than on Amazon, and the toolbar, as an add-on, means that it can only capture a fraction of the click activity since it is opt-in only and many users do not install such add-ons. However both logs provide very valuable information.

[2]See http://shopping.msn.com/xml/v1/getresults.aspx?text=digital+cameras for for a table of digital cameras and http://shopping.msn.com/xml/v1/getspecs.aspx?itemid=25236859 for an example of a camera entity with its attributes.

For our experiments, we implemented our work as part of [23] and exploit the query annotator described in [24] to map queries to tables in our collection and provide the token to attribute-value mapping. We run the annotator on our web query log and kept only the interpretation to tables that are above the threshold of $\theta = 1$. Since a query can map to more than one table, we took all the plausible tables and normalized their probabilities to fractions summing to 1. Then we used each fraction to map the query to the table while appropriately adjusting the query weight. Thus we produced a subset of the query log for each table, with each query having a weight that is the corresponding fraction of its impressions multiplied by the normalized table probability.

We tested the various techniques we proposed in the paper and we present the results below. The naming scheme is as follows: *DataProb* is the probabilistic disambiguation from Section 3.1, *ClusterProb* the cluster-based approach from Section 3.2, *Iterative* is the approach described in Section 3.3, and *Clicks* utilizes the click log as described in Section 3.4.

In addition to these techniques, we use a simpler one, shown as *NoProb*, that computes the score using for each query mapped to a table T, all the plausible token-attribute pairs from the table T, while assigning to all of them equally the query weight multiplied by the normalized table weight produced by the annotator. *NoProb* is not blind counting because it does consider the query weight and annotation probability, from [24], that we used in assigning the queries to tables. Thus we consider *NoProb* as a state-of-art baseline. The main difference with our proposed disambiguation techniques is that it does not use an explicit probabilistic disambiguation on the possible token-attribute mappings within each table.

6.1 Relevance Judgments

To measure the effectiveness of our results we conducted an extensive study using Amazon Mechanical Turk. Assessing the entire dataset of all possible tables and all possible attributes would have been prohibitively expensive. Instead we chose a diverse subset of our tables covering a variety of different areas representing as much as possible the entire data spectrum. The tables used in our evaluation were televisions, microwave ovens, cell phones, golf clubs, mp3 players, shoes, laptop computers, printers, watches, video games, engagement rings, digital cameras, skin cleansers, and camera bags and cases.

We ran all our approaches on the full set of tables and produced a set of facet attributes for each table and each algorithm. Then we took the results for the evaluation tables and created a single pool of attributes for judging by merging the results of all algorithms. We posted Mechanical Turk HITs (Human Intelligence Tasks) to obtain user judged relevance for the quality of attributes for search. Users were asked to judge how important a given attribute was for searching within a given category (with the example of faceted search explained) on a three-point scale. The scale items were labeled "highly important", "somewhat important", and "not important."

Producing high quality judgments in a crowd-sourced environment like Mechanical Turk is a challenging problem on its own. We employed a number of methods to ensure quality judgments. First, we created HITs of ten judgments from our result set and we added an extra honey-pot judgment used for spam detection. The additional honey-pot judgment was drawn from a pool of judgments we performed manually, and for which we felt there was a clear "highly

judgements		mturk		
		1	2	3
manual judgments	1	6	15	3
	2	6	34	4
	3	2	17	50

Figure 5: Confusion matrix between mturk and manual judgments.

important" or "not important" answer. The deviation of workers from our gold standard tasks was often a clear indication of spam. However, to ensure fair judgment, we manually inspected the results of any candidate spammer for consistency. The average completion time of a worker was also used as an aid in detecting unreliable workers. Lastly, each task was repeated by nine unique workers. This allowed us to find majority decisions for roughly two-thirds of all attribute judgments. For the remaining third without a majority, we took the average score. The result is a single valuation of the importance of each attribute.

Using these graded judgments we computed the normalized discounted cumulative gain (NDCG) for the ranked output of each approach. Given a list of results L, DCG was computed using linear gain and a logarithmic rank discount as follows.

$$\text{DCG}(L) = \sum_{i=1}^{k} \frac{rel(L_i)}{log_2(i+1)}$$

Where $rel(L_i)$ denotes the judged relevance of result L_i. Relevance scores where assigned from zero to two for the three judgment levels. Let I denote the ideal result ordering (the list of all possible results ordered by judged relevance), then NDCG is defined as follows.

$$\text{NDCG}(L) = \frac{\text{DCG}(L)}{\text{DCG}(I)}$$

We report on various values of k, the number of attributes returned. If a system returned less than k attributes it was penalized with a relevance score of 0 for each missing value.

While we were confident in our quality assurance techniques, we further validated the collection for significant outliers, by manually judging five categories for which we have personal knowledge of the domain through shopping experience. The table in Figure 5 shows the confusion matrix for the judgments. Across the top are the Mechanical Turk judgments, and on the left are the manual judgments. Entry (i, j) is the number of times the manual judgment was i, and the Mechanical Turk was j. We round averaged Mechanical Turk valuations to the nearest integer for this computation. We can see from this that the Mechanical Turk workers often favor the "safe" middle valuation. The effect of averaging judgements that do not reach a majority may also push valuations to the middle. The manual judgments tend to distribute more judgments to the "highly important" and "not important" valuations. Overall, we see exact agreement on 66% of judgments, with opposing 1 vs 3 valuations on only 4%. The Mechanical Turk valuations are therefore somewhat more coarse grained than our careful manual evaluations, but are still similar in overall trend. We have also run all of our experiments over the manual judgments and found the results to be equivalent in terms of trend and rank order of the systems. We omit these graphs for brevity of presentation.

6.2 Attribute Pre-selection with Data Filters

We start with an experiment that measures the effect of data statistics on the produced facets such as selectivity and entropy as described in Section 5. The results are summarized in Figure 6.

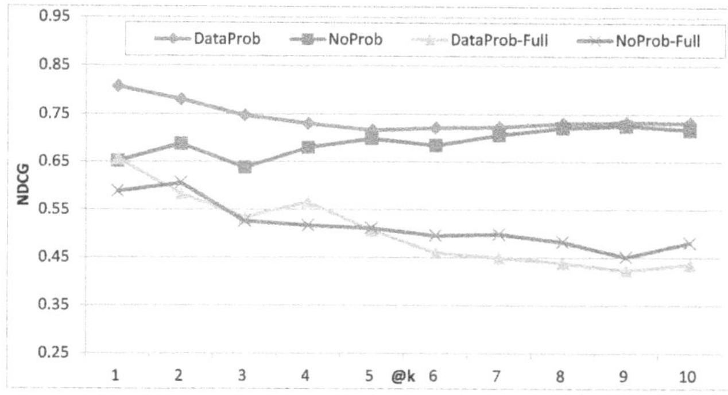

Figure 6: Attribute pre-selection using data filters.

The first step was to take all attributes for each table[3] and perform a run on our two simpler algorithms, shown as *NoProb-Full* and *DataProb-Full* in Figure 6. Surprisingly, *DataProb-Full* does not improve much over *NoProb-Full*. In fact it actually performs worse at higher values of k. Upon further investigation, this is understandable due to how certain attributes affect the computed probabilities. For example, there is an attribute called *video input type* for digital cameras where the value is almost always '*digital camera*'. The probability $P(t|A)$ for the token '*digital camera*' was very high, affecting the disambiguation process whenever it was recognized in a query. As a result the *DataProb-Full* got skewed in counting the proper attribute importance incorrectly. There were other such attributes with similar characteristics that produced a skewed behavior. We observed that such attributes had in common certain data statistics such as low value entropy and low attribute sparsity.

We did a second run where we removed attributes that appear in less than 10% ($R(A) < 0.1$) of the entities and have entropy less than 0.1 ($H(A) < 0.1$). Using this data set we run again the same two algorithms, shown as *NoProb* and *DataProb* in Figure 6. The pre-selection step reduced noise in the data significantly and also removed attributes that have little information content (low entropy) and are not appropriate for facets. As a result the same algorithm with the pre-selected data set perform much better. Now the actual data probabilities used for intra-table attribute disambiguation are more meaningful and *DataProb* performs better than *NoProb*.

Entropy and sparsity can be seen as continuous discount values. We saw in practice that using them as parameterized filters is easier and produces good results. The specific values we used capture the problems with our particular data set and might not be optimal for all data sets. But the point we wish to make is that one has to consider such data filters to pre-select good attribute candidates in the mining algorithms. The full attribute set triggers bad results even on the more complex algorithms. It is not shown here for presentation simplicity. The remainder of the experimental section uses the same pre-selected set of attributes for all our techniques.

6.3 Explicit Disambiguation

Using the above mentioned preselected attribute set we ran all of our disambiguation algorithms. The results are shown in Figure 7. As we discussed in Section 6.2, *DataProb* has clear advantages over *NoProb*. However *DataProb* has the problem of treating attributes independently. For example, in the query "*30 inch television,*" *DataProb* will incorrectly determine the *height* attribute to be most probable over *diagonal screen size*. The confusion happens because televisions in that range generally have diagonals of 32 or 27 inches, whereas large 50 inch televisions tend to have a *height* around 30

[3]We exclude metadata and boolean attributes with values like 'yes/no', 'true/false'

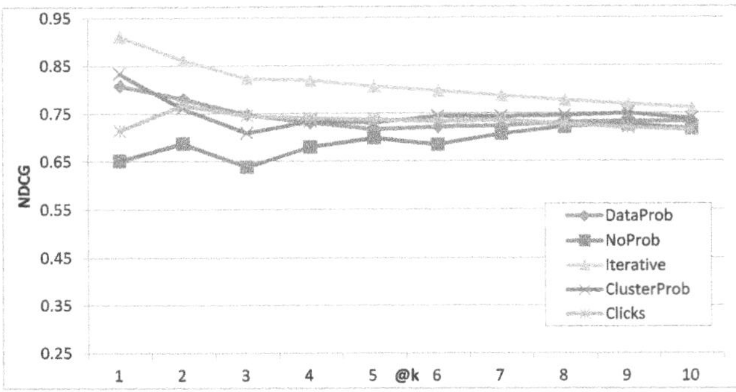

Figure 7: Token-attribute disambiguation comparison

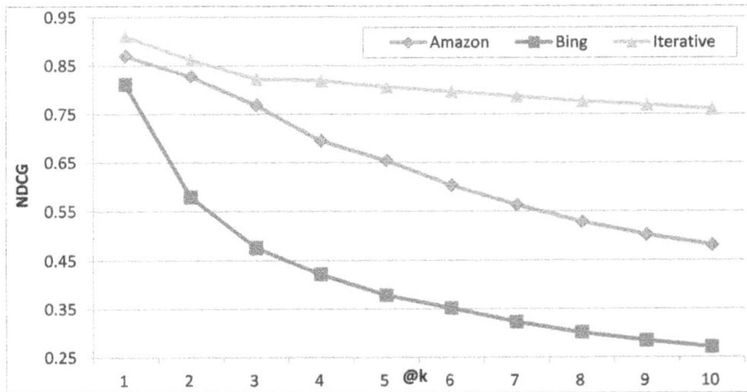

Figure 8: Comparing with Amazon and Bing.

inches. Since there are many 50 inch televisions in the data, *height* is assigned a higher probability for the token '*30 inch*.'

While *ClusterProb* appeared to be an intuitive solution to this issue, we see in practice that it performs no better than *DataProb*. *ClusterProb* works well for categorical attributes, but it actually does even worse on numerical ones for a couple of reasons. First, since user queries do not always reflect the exact values of numeric attributes it tries to map the continuous domain into discrete buckets. That discretization process makes the issue of the query token '*30 inch*' matching the *diagonal* data values 27 or 32 inch even worse than *DataProb*. Because the actual data values vary from the query tokens, the values of the user-intended attribute do not form a good model for the query tokens. Furthermore, KL-divergence is only well defined for distributions that have non-zero probability over the entire value domain, meaning even depth with actual small numeric values is assigned a small probability for large values like 50 inches, thus further enhancing the confusion of numeric attributes.

Iterative tries to detect correlations between data and queries and it exploits the overall bias of users towards the correct attributes. Intuitively, the reason it disambiguates the best is due to how users enter queries. Although the system can be confused with multiple interpretations, users actually know which attributes they are looking for when they enter their values. When examined across the full query log, the user behavior tends to match the intended attribute. For example, although token '*30 inch*' can be consider closer to a TV *height* than *diagonal screen size* for many modern televisions, users query much more frequently for *diagonal screen size* including other values like '*50inch*' or '*55inch*'. This creates a bias for *inch* tokens towards the attribute diagonal, which *Iterative* applies to the '*30 inch*' token. This causes diagonal size to be preferred over height even for that particular value.

One surprise in the disambiguation methods is that *Clicks* do more or less similarly to *DataProb*. At first, one would think that clicks offer the perfect disambiguation method. A user click on a particular entity id allows us to select only the attributes that closely match that entity id disambiguating attributes almost perfectly. However, clicks have problems in the way they were produced that make them less than optimal for learning good facets. First, a user can only click on results shown to them, so clicks incorporate the engine bias and do not represent the true popularity of how many times all possible queries are asked. Hence some attributes are under-represented in a click log due to the engine bias of what results were shown. Second, there are far fewer queries with clicked results than generally asked, meaning many categories have very few queries. This means the mined facets do not have much support and are somewhat erratic. Finally, the queries that tend to trigger clicks are very specific queries looking for one or few products, e.g. "*canon eos 50d digital camera.*" More general category based queries tend to have few clicks and commonly followed by a refinement since they return a large result set that users cannot easily consider, e.g. "*12 megapixel digital camera.*" This creates a skew of the importance learned towards attributes that act as unique keys. However these attributes are not well-suited for facets. If a user already knows the unique key they are looking for (like camera model), they can simply select it from the results and do not need a facet for it. Instead such attributes are better suited for entity snippets, that is summarized views that help users differentiate amongst entities.

6.4 Commercial Faceted Search

Commercial web engines are already supporting faceted search. Although we do not know the technical details of industrial implementations, we felt the best way to test the real world effectiveness of our solution is by comparing against state of the industry engines. Since our data is shopping based, we considered Amazon as the world's most popular shopping engine. Furthermore, since our data comes from the public MSN Shopping API, we considered Bing Shopping (redirects from MSN Shopping) as a shopping engine that is using the same data set as our experiments. Both Amazon and Bing Shopping show facets. To test them, we crawled the attributes shown on Amazon and Bing for our test categories and submitted them in the same pool of attributes that we labeled with mturk judges. To remove any bias, we dropped any affiliation information on the web site. Furthermore, we did not consider the handful of generic shopping attributes shown on both Amazon and Bing, like *price* or *shipping options*. Although very valuable facets there is no need for an automated technique to discover them, as such attributes can easily be added to all categories. Instead we limited our comparison to only *category specific* attributes from each solution. The results are summarized in Figure 8.

Our best solution performs better than Amazon and significantly better than Bing Shopping. For many categories Amazon shows very few attributes and Bing shows even less. As a result, both Amazon and Bing drop dramatically as the size k increases in our experiments. It is important to note that Amazon does show up to 12 category-dependent facets in some cases (e.g., watches) so screen real-estate is not a limiting factor. For small values of k ($k \leq 3$) we still do better but the difference, particularly with Amazon, is smaller. We are not familiar with the details of their facet selection approach and so their techniques cannot be contrasted to ours. However, since they are a popular site with lots of query traffic and domain knowledge, we expect their facet selection to be of the highest caliber. Having our best solution perform even better than Amazon, demonstrates the true value of a pure query-based automated solution and how well it approximates the desired facet

Judgment	Context-depndt	Table-depndt	Equivalent
Preferred	46.3%	23.96%	29.74%

Figure 9: Comparison of facet values for context-dependent vs. category-dependent approach.

utility. Furthermore, it shows that our best method deals more than adequately with ambiguity amongst attributes within each table.

6.5 Values

Our approach populates facets with the most popular values found in the query-log. This is done in a query-independent way, by looking at all values for all attributes as described in Section 4. We report on results using token-level disambiguation, though we find the resulting value orders to be similar with the other techniques as well. So for every category, for the top facets we have computed the top values in a category-dependent list. It would be very expensive to perform an NDCG experiment on values, as the potential judgements needed to capture the value relevancy, in a statistically significant way, is very large. Furthermore, given how we find the popular values, we believe that the quality of those values will correlate with the results of our disambiguation techniques and such NDCG experiments would be moot. However, we wanted to validate the benefit of showing the context-dependent conditional values, which were computed off-line as described in Section 4.2.

We created a synthetic online experiment by generating queries using the top values for the top facets for our test categories. For example, using the *brand* for golf clubs, we generated *"odyssey golf clubs"* or *"callaway golf clubs"* as test queries. For each query, we judged the quality of the context-dependent conditional value list vs. the table-dependent value list for the top facets. The judgement favored one or the other list for each facet, based on the relevance of the values shown given the query. If the values seemed equally relevant, they were judged to be equal. In many cases, the query itself may dictate whether the values are correct or not based on what is present in the data. For example, if the condition specifies the brand *'taylormade'*, then a value specific to a *'nike'* product is simply incorrect. Other times, results require specialized knowledge of the domain, for example, that the brand *'odyssey'* is well known for putters or that *'callaway'* is famous for drivers. The results are summarized in Figure 9.

As expected, context-dependent values are preferred more than table-dependent ones. However, at first look, it is surprising to see the table-dependent values gaining so much preference. This happens because context-independent attributes are quite often a super set of the context-dependent ones. The nature of conditional computation has smaller support thus eliminating some values. For example, the conditional list may show values {*'mens'*, *'womens'*} while the table-dependent list shows {*'mens'*, *'womens'*, *'juniors'*} which is perceived as better or more complete. A solution to this is to take the cases where the context-dependent is a subset of the table-dependent list, show the superset but force the conditional ones to the top. We performed the same experiment after we applied this simple heuristic and found that only 1.98% of the queries went to table-dependent whereas the context-dependent jumped to 65.58%. There was no significant change in the equivalent cases, as they are generally similar value sets with small order differences.

7. RELATED WORK

Our problem of discovering important facets in a query-log is related to a number of research areas, including faceted search, attribute ordering, query understanding, and search over structured data. We survey a sample of the relevant work in each of these areas.

Faceted Search The problem of automatically discovering facets (or facet hierarchies) from text has been studied in the past in [5, 6, 18, 25]. The principle challenges in this domain are in finding the terms which can be used to describe (sub)categories, and in building the hierarchy of categories. This is in contrast to our setting, where the actual facets have a direct correspondence to the structured data attributes. The process of extracting facets from text often makes use of structured resources like WordNet [5, 25] or semi-structured sources like Wikipedia [5], but only for categorization and hierarchy extraction, rather than the extraction of attributes. In these works, the facet selection is achieved by ranking based on a navigation cost [6, 18], or by frequency-based metrics [5].

Recently, there is also work on facet selection for structured data [3, 16, 17, 22], which looks for structured data attributes as potential facets. Facet ranking is generally done by estimating the user cost to identify a result when searching with the facets [3], or by ordering the facets according to some property in the data, such as the partitioning balance, cardinality, or attribute frequency [22]. This does not have the benefit of approximating the true user intent as in our query-log based approach. The use of data properties however, is similar to our application of data statistics. In [17] facets are ranked based on a history of user preference for documents. However the facet-value pairs are given explicitly for each document so there are no challenges in resolving ambiguity. In [16], a cost model driven by user actions is approximated using user relevance judgements over attributes. This is in contrast to our scenario, where user relevance is not explicit and must be extracted from query-logs.

Attribute Ordering The problem of ordering or ranking attributes of structured data repositories is a related problem to facet discovery. The goals of attribute ordering problems however, often differ to that of ranking facets. In [7, 15], the aim was to choose a subset attributes that are most "useful" to display to a user when rendering structured search results with limited screen space. Usefulness was formalized as the attributes most influential in the search systems ranking function. A related problem is product visibility, in which attributes are chosen that will distinguish one's product from others in the database. In [21] the product visibility problem was approached by finding the k attributes that cause a product to appear in the maximum number of results over a given query log.

The idea of using a query-log as a source of important attributes has also be studied in previous work. Miah et al. proposed to compute the frequency of the the attribute names in a query log as a signal of importance for the product visibility problem [21]. However, they assume binary attributes, such that each attribute is essentially an attribute/value pair in our data model (e.g., the attribute *four door* describes the boolean property of a car having four doors or not, as opposed to an attribute like *doors* having values *'two'*, *'three'*, *'four'*, or *'five'*). This is different from our approach in that we mine attribute instances from the query-log, and thus have to deal with the ambiguity in mapping instances to their correct attributes. Chaudhuri et al. have also used query-log mining to rank attributes based on their probability of being correlated with a query, with the intention of ranking structured results [4]. However, their work considered structured queries, and thus a structured query-log which does not suffer from ambiguity in query tokens.

Query Understanding A number of recent works have looked at query understanding using structured data [9, 20, 24]. Because our approach rests on having query interpretations, this field is particularly relevant. As part of our experiments we implemented the work in [24] and benefit from it in finding plausible query interpretations and assigning queries to tables. However, the facet discovery problem poses more strenuous requirements than previous query understanding work in disambiguating amongst multiple query to attribute mappings within the same table. In other words, it is not enough to just find the plausible interpretations of a query on a table. For facet discovery we have to actually be able to distinguish amongst them with high confidence. An approximation of this effect is the results of *NoProb* vs. all the other disambiguation techniques we discussed – *NoProb* can be viewed as using the annotation score by [24] to disambiguate. As we can see, such deep query understanding provides a very good baseline, however our work is different and can be considered an extension to previous work. In fact, we have observed that the attribute importance score learned by our intra-table disambiguation can be used as a signal to further improve the quality of structured annotations described in [24], however further discussion on this is outside the scope of this paper.

A related problem to query understanding is search over structured data, a field that has received a lot of attention in recent years. Search over structured data is also the core motivation for our work of supporting faceted search over structured collections. In this context, each unique mapping of a keyword query into a structured database represents an understanding of the query. Early work focused on how to assemble search results, with ranking based on candidate network size [2, 12], graph-based weight propagation [1], or integrating IR style ranking functions [11]. However, no particular effort has been made in this field to disambiguate among possible mappings of query tokens to attributes.

8. CONCLUSIONS

Structured web search in the form of a unified ecosystem like Google or Bing, or in the form of a specialized vertical like Amazon can take advantage of rich meta-data to produce a better user experience with the appropriate facets. An important problem in this setting is that of selecting the attributes and values for the facet system. Discovering facets must also deal with the scale of data and the restricted screen real estate that only allows for the ones best matching the anticipated user intent.

In this paper we proposed a model that exploits the intersection of web query-logs and structured data to find the facet utility. We showed a variety of techniques that dealt with disambiguating amongst different overlapping attribute-value pairs per query. We extended them to capture values and conditional values that give a dynamic context-dependent facet experience, and we also discussed how data statistics play a role in producing better facets. Finally, we showed experimentally that our approach is scalable, it works well in practice, and even outperforms popular commercial systems that offer facet functionality.

9. REFERENCES

[1] B. Aditya, G. Bhalotia, S. Chakrabarti, A. Hulgeri, C. Nakhe, P. Parag, and S. Sudarshan. Banks: browsing and keyword searching in relational databases. In *Proc. VLDB Conf.*, pages 1083–1086. VLDB Endowment, 2002.

[2] S. Agrawal, S. Chaudhuri, and G. Das. Dbxplorer: A system for keyword-based search over relational databases. In *Proc. ICDE Conf.*, page 5, Washington, DC, USA, 2002. IEEE Computer Society.

[3] S. Basu Roy, H. Wang, G. Das, U. Nambiar, and M. Mohania. Minimum-effort driven dynamic faceted search in structured databases. In *Proc. CIKM*, pages 13–22, 2008.

[4] S. Chaudhuri, G. Das, V. Hristidis, and G. Weikum. Probabilistic information retrieval approach for ranking of database query results. *ACM Trans. Database Syst.*, 31(3):1134–1168, 2006.

[5] W. Dakka and P. G. Ipeirotis. Automatic extraction of useful facet hierarchies from text databases. In *Proc. ICDE Conf.*, pages 466–475, Washington, DC, USA, 2008. IEEE Computer Society.

[6] W. Dakka, P. G. Ipeirotis, and K. R. Wood. Automatic construction of multifaceted browsing interfaces. In *Proc. CIKM*, pages 768–775, New York, NY, USA, 2005. ACM.

[7] G. Das, V. Hristidis, N. Kapoor, and S. Sudarshan. Ordering the attributes of query results. In *Proc. SIGMOD Conf.*, pages 395–406, New York, NY, USA, 2006. ACM.

[8] P. Dmitriev, P. Serdyukov, and S. Chernov. Enterprise and desktop search. In *Proc. WWW Conf.*, pages 1345–1346, April 2010.

[9] R. Fagin, B. Kimelfeld, Y. Li, S. Raghavan, and S. Vaithyanathan. Understanding queries in a search database system. In *Proc. PODS Conf.*, pages 273–284, 2010.

[10] M. A. Hearst. *Search User Interfaces*. Cambridge University Press, 2009.

[11] V. Hristidis, L. Gravano, and Y. Papakonstantinou. Efficient ir-style keyword search over relational databases. In *Proc. VLDB Conf.*, pages 850–861. VLDB Endowment, 2003.

[12] V. Hristidis and Y. Papakonstantinou. Discover: keyword search in relational databases. In *Proc. VLDB Conf.*, pages 670–681. VLDB Endowment, 2002.

[13] P. Ipeirotis and L. Gravano. Distributed search over the hidden web: Hierarchical database sampling and selection. In *Proc. VLDB Conf.*, August 2002.

[14] T. Joachims and F. Radlinski. Search engines that learn from implicit feedback. *IEEE Computer*, 40(8):34–40, 2007.

[15] N. Kapoor, G. Das, V. Hristidis, S. Sudarshan, and G. Weikum. Star: A system for tuple and attribute ranking of query answers. In *Proc. ICDE Conf.*, 2007.

[16] A. Kashyap, V. Hristidis, and M. Petropoulos. Facetor: cost-driven exploration of faceted query results. In *Proc. CIKM Conf.*, 2010.

[17] J. Koren, Y. Zhang, and X. Liu. Personalized interactive faceted search. In *Proc. WWW Conf.*, pages 477–486, 2008.

[18] C. Li, N. Yan, S. B. Roy, L. Lisham, and G. Das. Facetedpedia: dynamic generation of query-dependent faceted interfaces for wikipedia. In *Proc. WWW Conf.*, pages 651–660, 2010.

[19] X. Li, Y.-Y. Wang, and A. Acero. Learning query intent from regularized click graphs. In *Proc. SIGIR Conf.*, pages 339–346, 2008.

[20] X. Li, Y.-Y. Wang, and A. Acero. Extracting Structured Information from User Queries with Semi-supervised Conditional Random Fields. In *Proc. SIGIR Conf.*, pages 572–579, 2009.

[21] M. Miah, G. Das, V. Hristidis, and H. Mannila. Standing out in a crowd: Selecting attributes for maximum visibility. In *Proc. ICDE Conf.*, pages 356–365, 2008.

[22] E. Oren, R. Delbru, and S. Decker. Extending faceted navigation for RDF data. *The Semantic Web-ISWC 2006*, pages 559–572, 2006.

[23] S. Paparizos, A. Ntoulas, J. Shafer, and R. Agrawal. Answering web queries using structured data sources. In *Proc. SIGMOD Conf.*, 2009.

[24] N. Sarkas, S. Paparizos, and P. Tsaparas. Structured annotations of web queries. In *Proc. SIGMOD Conf.*, June 2010.

[25] E. Stoica, M. A. Hearst, and M. Richardson. Automating creation of hierarchical faceted metadata structures. *In Proc. Human Language Technology Conf. (NAACL HLT*, 2007.

Schema-As-You-Go: On Probabilistic Tagging and Querying of Wide Tables

Meiyu Lu‡ Divyakant Agrawal§ Bing Tian Dai‡ Anthony K. H. Tung‡

‡School of Computing
National University of Singapore
{lumeiyu, daibingt, atung}@comp.nus.edu.sg

§Department of Computer Science
University of California, Santa Barbara
agrawal@cs.ucsb.edu

ABSTRACT

The emergence of Web 2.0 has resulted in a huge amount of heterogeneous data that are contributed by a large number of users, engendering new challenges for data management and query processing. Given that the data are unified from various sources and accessed by numerous users, providing users with a unified mediated schema as data integration is insufficient. On one hand, a deterministic mediated schema restricts users' freedom to express queries in their preferred vocabulary; on the other hand, it is not realistic for users to remember the numerous attribute names that arise from integrating various data sources. As such, a user-oriented data management and query interface is required.

In this paper, we propose an out-of-the-box approach that separates users' actions from database operations. This separating layer deals with the challenges from a semantic perspective. It interprets the semantics of each data value through tags that are provided by users, and then inserts the value into the database together with these tags. When querying the database, this layer also serves as a platform for retrieving data by interpreting the semantics of the queried tags from the users. Experiments are conducted to illustrate both the effectiveness and efficiency of our approach.

Categories and Subject Descriptors

H.2.8 [**Database Management**]: Database applications

General Terms

Management, Measurement, Performance

Keywords

Probabilistic Tagging, Wide Table, Dynamic Instantiation

1. INTRODUCTION

The rapid growth of Web 2.0 technologies and social networks has provided us with new opportunities for sharing data and collaborating with others. Within a community, users may like to contribute their own data, share the data with friends, and meanwhile explore the shared data at the community scale. Effectively and efficiently managing and exploring these data at a web-scale level is an interesting and important problem.

In this paper, we focus on the management of shared structured tables (e.g. Google fusion table [16]) which is an important type of data in Web 2.0. Such data have some inherent properties that make their management challenging.

Heterogeneity. Data provided by different users may be widely heterogeneous, containing different attribute names that describe semantically similar values or same attribute name with different semantics. For example, in Figure 1(a), user A chooses attribute `make` to describe the car manufacturer in his/her private data, while user B uses `manufacturer` to represent the same meaning. Similarly, the semantics of `car` in (b) is model but in (c) it contains both make and model information.

Numerosity. As all users can publish their data into the community as shown in Figure 1(a), (b) and (c), the number of distinct attributes will grow drastically as more users participate. This results in a *wide table* [7] as Figure 1(d) which is essentially a structured table with a large number of attributes and many empty cells. Given such a wide table, most existing data integration approaches [23] create a global mediated schema that usually contains a huge number of attributes. Such huge mediated schema is difficult to query as users cannot remember all the attributes. Therefore, a more flexible and user-oriented query interface is required. This interface should allow users to choose different attribute names to represent the same semantics in different queries, and have the power to express their confidence over the attribute semantic heterogeneity in posed queries.

Personalized Attributes. Since attributes are contributed by users, there could be many personalized attributes, which cannot be captured by existing ontology or taxonomy, such as DBpedia[1] and WordNet[2]. Examples of such personalized attributes include `myear` in Figure 1(c), which represents the production year of a car, and `eadd`, the abbreviation for email address. Due to this, existing techniques that rely on ontology for schema mapping [26, 30] will not be suitable any more. A better system should be able to infer more popular attributes for such personalized ones, so that these data can be explored by the other users asides from its owner.

[1]DBpedia, http://dbpedia.org/About
[2]WordNet, http://wordnet.princeton.edu

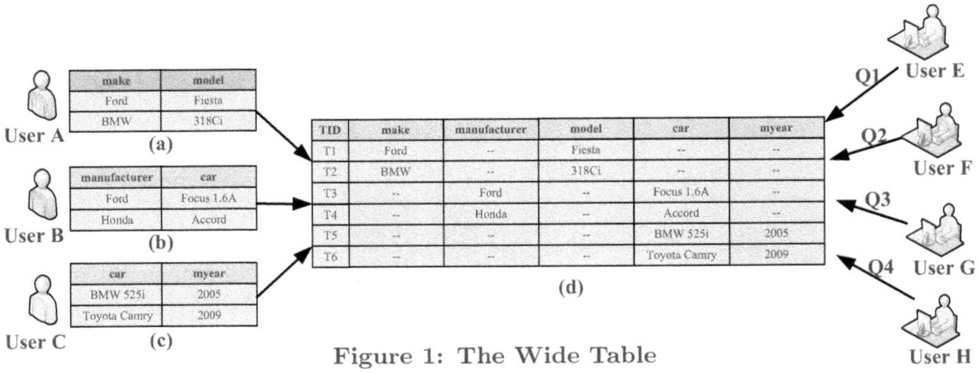

Figure 1: The Wide Table

Tag1	Tag2	Similarity
make	manufacturer	0.95
make	car	0.5
manufacturer	car	0.52
model	car	0.65

Figure 2: Tag Similarity

Due to the inherent semantic heterogeneity of the attributes in user contributed data, we will no longer refer to them as "attribute". Instead, we borrow the term *tag* from the multimedia domain [1, 2], and view these attribute names as just a way to annotate the values that are provided by users[3]. In this paper, we describe a query system which enables users to effectively query a large quantity of user contributed data. Our system provides the following functionalities.

- Users can contribute and share data by inserting them into a single wide table together with their tags, as shown in Figure 1(d).
- Our system is able to automatically discover the semantic relationships between users' tags, which is handled by our tag inference approach in Section 3. Figure 2 illustrates the semantic similarities between each pair of tags produced by our approach for the example data in Figure 1[4].
- Users can use their own preferred tags to query the database, and the system then dynamically determines the semantics of these tags at query time.

Combining the data from Figure 1(d) with the tag similarities in Figure 2, we can easily obtain the virtual probabilistic tagged data, as shown in Figure 3, where each value is associated with a list of $\langle tag, probability \rangle$ pairs. The probability indicates the semantic association strength between the value and tag pair. The generation of such semantic association probabilities is called *probabilistic tagging*, and its formal definition will be given in Section 2.

We next present an example to illustrate several characteristics of our query interface via a set of queries.

EXAMPLE 1. *Figure 1 shows a scenario where four users, A, B, C and D contribute and share their datasets. The wide table is used to store the shared data. User E, F, G and H then submit four different queries which are Q1, Q2, Q3 and Q4, respectively. The queries are shown in Table 1 in an extended SQL format. The delimiter '@' in the query is for users to explicitly specify their confidence over tag semantics. Its formal definition is presented in Section 2. Here we can interpret* `make@0.9` *as a set of tags in Figure 2 which are similar to* `make` *with confidence no less than 90%. The table name* `CAR` *refers to the probabilistic tagging table in Figure 3. Values in the result tuples have the same order as the tags in the* `SELECT` *clause.*

From the query result in Table 1, we observe that ***i)*** *different users can choose different tags to express the same semantics, such as Q1 and Q2;* ***ii)*** *explicit confidence specification gives users control over the search scope. For instance, with lower confidence Q3 retrieves two more tuples than Q1;* ***iii)*** *schema for users' query is dynamically determined at query time, which is user-oriented rather than predefined. Take Q4 as an example, where a user would like to retrieve values that are associated with* `car` *and* `model` *from* `CAR`*. From the data perspective, for T3 and T4, tag* `car` *in the query should be aligned with* `car` *in the source table. But from the users' perspective, intuitively the best schema alignment for T3 and T4 should be (car, model). This is what our system retrieves given Q4.*

To further see the benefit of our approach, Figure 4 shows the result of Q4 over tuples T3 and T4 using our approach and the one proposed by Dong and Halevy in [12, 25][5]. Both records returned by our approach are correct and ranked in the right order. However, the top two ranked tuples retrieved by probabilistic integration are not correct although their score is much higher than the correct ones. The result differs because we are dynamically determining the semantics for user posed tags at query time. The reasons for such differences will be explained in Section 2.2.

Besides the functionalities discussed above, our work also makes the following contributions:

- We proposed the concept of *probabilistic tagging* to represent the associations between values and tags.
- We presented an effective distance function to measure the semantic distance between a pair of tags. Based on this, we are able to automatically infer semantically similar tags for each value.

[3]In this case, users might even choose to annotate the same value with multiple tags.

[4]As our similarity measure is symmetric, we only show unidirectional tag similarity in Figure 2.

[5]Please refer to Appendix A for the detailed score computation for probabilistic integration.

Table 1: Example Queries

QID	Query	Result
Q1	`SELECT make@0.9 FROM CAR;`	T1(Ford),T2(BMW),T3(Ford),T4(Honda)
Q2	`SELECT manufacturer@0.85 FROM CAR;`	T1(Ford),T2(BMW),T3(Ford),T4(Honda)
Q3	`SELECT make@0.5 FROM CAR;`	T1(Ford),T2(BMW),T3(Ford),T4(Honda), T5(BMW 525i),T6(Toyota Camry)
Q4	`SELECT car, model FROM CAR;`	T1(Ford,Fiesta),T2(BMW,318Ci), T3(Ford,Focus 1.6A),T4(Honda, Accord)

TID	Value	Probabilistic Tagging
T1	Ford	<make,1.0>,<manufacturer,0.95>,<car,0.5>
T1	Fiesta	<model,1.0>,<car,0.65>
T2	BMW	<make,1.0>,<manufacturer,0.95>,<car,0.5>
T2	318Ci	<model,1.0>,<car,0.65>
T3	Ford	<manufacturer,1.0>,<make,0.95>,<car,0.52>
T3	Focus 1.6A	<car,1.0>,<model,0.65>,<manufacturer,0.52>,<make,0.5>
T4	Honda	<manufacturer,1.0>,<make,0.95>,<car,0.52>
T4	Accord	<car,1.0>,<model,0.65>,<manufacturer,0.52>,<make,0.5>
T5	BMW	<car,1.0>,<model,0.65>,<manufacturer,0.52>,<make,0.5>
T5	2005	<myear,1.0>
T6	Toyota	<car,1.0>,<model,0.65>,<manufacturer,0.52>,<make,0.5>
T6	2009	<myear,1.0>

Figure 3: Probabilistic Tagging

QID	Q4
Query	SELECT car, model FROM CAR

Our Result

TID	car	model	rank
T3	Ford	Focus 1.6A	1
T4	Honda	Accord	2

Data Integration Result

TID	car	model	rank
T3	Focus 1.6A	Focus 1.6A	1
T4	Accord	Accord	2
T3	Ford	Focus 1.6A	3
T4	Honda	Accord	4

Figure 4: Query Result Comparison

- We proposed an efficient dynamic instantiation approach to associate the queried tags and data values during query processing.
- A complete and extensive experimental study is conducted to validate our approach.

2. PROBLEM DEFINITION

2.1 Probabilistic Tagging

As discussed earlier, one of our main objectives is to provide a flexible interface, which allows users to query the underlying database with any tag they like. The very first challenge is to discover which tags are similar in semantics. However, this is insufficient since some tags are more similar to each other in semantics while others are not. Taking T1 in Figure 3 as an example, it is intuitive that the semantics of 'Ford' is better reflected by `manufacturer` than `car` since the semantics of `manufacturer` is quite specific, while `car` is a relatively more general term. Therefore, the second issue is that the semantic association strength between a value and tag should be well quantified, as shown in Figure 3.

In this paper, for a given value v in the wide table, we interpret its semantic association with a tag t as the likelihood/belief that v is tagged by t.

DEFINITION 1 (PROBABILISTIC TAGGING). *Let T be a set of tags, for a value v in Wide Table and a tag $t \in T$, probabilistic tagging refers to the process of associating a probability $\zeta_{v,t}$ for v and t, such that value v is tagged by tag t with probability $\zeta_{v,t}$.*

The probability $\zeta_{v,t}$ is called the associated probability or association probability. If the semantic association between value v and tag t is stronger, then their associated probability $\zeta_{v,t}$ will be higher and vice versa. As shown by T1 in Figure 3, for the value 'Ford', its associated probability with its original tag `make` is 1.0 while its associated probability with inferred tags `manufacturer` and `car` are 0.95 and 0.5, showing difference in the strength of semantic association.

We note here that unlike previous works [12, 25, 17] in data integration, the probabilities for all tags being associated with a value v do not sum up to 1. This is because there is no assumption of mutual exclusion between tags at this stage of data processing. We avoid doing so to prevent a label bias problem in which a value v will have much lower associated probability with each tag if it can be semantically described by many different tags. For example, a value associated with 5 or more tags will have much lower probability than value with 2 or less tags. Instead, we choose to introduce the assumption of mutual exclusion during query time where the semantic meaning of the tags are clearer.

2.2 Query Semantics

After discovering and quantifying the tag semantic relationships during probabilistic tagging, the resulting probabilistic table is shown as in Figure 3. In this table, each value is associated with a $\langle tag, probability \rangle$ pair list. Query over such probabilistic table is much more challenging than with a predefined schema. We will now look into the query relevant issues over a probabilistically tagged table.

2.2.1 Extended SQL Query

In this paper we adopted a SQL like query syntax to support our tag based queries. Specifically, we extended SQL query to allow users to express their semantic confidence for each tag using the delimiter '@'. We show some examples in Table 1. Below is a more complex extended SQL query.

```
SELECT     car, year@0.9, price@0.3
FROM       CAR
WHERE      make@0.5 = 'Ford'
      AND  price ≥ 10,000
      AND  price ≤ 20,000
```

When a user provides a tag with high confidence, it means that he is very sure about the semantics of the tag, and does not want our system to do much tag inference. In contrast, if the user is unsure of the semantics and he likes to use more tags that are similar to the queried tag, then he can provide a lower confidence threshold.

Definition 2 (Tag Expansion). *Given a tag t_q and its semantic confidence δ in query q, $t_q@\delta$ refers to the expanded tag set $T_e = \{t_{e_i} | i = 1, \ldots, n\}$, where for each tag $t_{e_i} \in T_e$, $Semsim(t_q, t_{e_i}) \geq \delta$. We call T_e as the expanded tag set for t_q.*

In the above definition, $Semsim(t_q, t_{e_i})$ is the semantic similarity between tag t_q and t_{e_i}, which is formally defined by Equation 6 in Section 3. When processing query q, t_q will be expanded to a tag set T_e, a set of tags that are semantically similar to t_q based on a threshold δ. All values that are originally associated with any of the tags in T_e are valid for this tag expansion condition, and should be taken into consideration when answering the query. If no semantic confidence is explicitly specified for t_q, we will expand it to all our inferred tags.

Take the queries in Table 1 as example, `make@0.5` will be expanded to all the tags that are similar to `make` in semantics inferred by our system, that is {`manufacturer`,`car`}, but `make@0.9` will only be expanded to {`manufacturer`}.

2.2.2 Query Answering

Before explaining the semantics of query answering, we first look at the intuitions behind our query answering techniques. Intuitively, syntactically equivalent tags in user posed queries should be instantiated with the same value, no matter how many places it appears in the query. For example, although `price` occurs three times in the example query in Section 2.2.1, once in the `SELECT` clause and twice in the `WHERE` clause, it is obvious that all the occurrences of `price` refer to exactly the same semantics, i.e. price of a car. Thus, in the resulting record, all these three instances of `price` should be instantiated with the same value. Based on this, we proposed the following **Consolidation Rule** for our query answering.

Rule 1 (Consolidation Rule). *Let set $T_q = \{t_i | i = 1, \ldots, n\}$ be the set of tags in query q, for two tags $t_i, t_j \in T_q$, if $t_i = t_j$, then t_i and t_j should be instantiated with the same value from the underlying record.*

Consider the query in Section 2.2.1, although we know tag `car` and `make` are similar in semantics from Figure 2, in this query they actually represent different attributes because the user specifies them as different. In other words, `car` and `make` are mutually exclusive from each other in this query, and should be instantiated with different values in the resultant record. We proposed our **Mutual Exclusion Rule** as below.

Rule 2 (Mutual Exclusion Rule). *Let $T_q = \{t_i | i = 1, \ldots, n\}$ be the set of tags in query q, for two tags $t_i, t_j \in T_q$, if $t_i \neq t_j$, then t_i and t_j should be instantiated with different values from the underlying record.*

We have discussed the impact of our mutual exclusion rule using Q4 earlier (in Example 1). There for T3, we argued that `car` in the query should be aligned with `manufacturer` in the source table. Here we look at the query in Section 2.2.1, where a user would like to retrieve the value associated with `car` from a record whose value 'Ford' is associated with `make` (for simplicity, we skipped the other constraints). Now for T3, it is more reasonable for `car` in the query to be aligned with `car` in the source table. Comparing these two queries, we can see that with our mutual exclusion rule, the same tag (`car`) can be aligned with different semantics in different queries even for the same record (T3). As explained earlier, applying the mutual exclusion rule during query answering time allows us to avoid the label bias problem. Moreover, our mutual exclusion rule cannot be trivially introduced in [12, 25, 17] since they enforced the fact that two attributes/tags are either semantically equivalent (associated with the same value) or not in each possible world. As such, the problem illustrated by Figure 4 in Example 1 is inherent for [12, 25, 17].

For a given tuple/record, we aim to find its possible best alignment to the queried tags. As the semantics of queried tags are determined dynamically on the fly, our query answering is referred to as **Dynamic Instantiation**.

Definition 3 (Dynamic Instantiation). *Let set $T_q = \{t_i | i = 1, \ldots, n\}$ be the set of tags in query q, and $V_r = \{v_j | j = 1, \ldots, m\}$ be the set of values from a record r, we refer to a mapping $f : T_q \to V_r$ as the dynamic instantiation of V_r with respect to T_q. Based on f, the instantiated score $Score(r)$ for r with respect to q is defined as the multiplication of associated probabilities for edges in f, i.e. $Score(r) = \prod_{i=1}^{n} \zeta_{f(t_i),t_i}$. In addition, all the following conditions must be satisfied in f:*

1. *f satisfies all the value constraints in the `WHERE` clause.*
2. *f satisfies both Consolidation Rule and Mutual Exclusion Rule;*
3. *The associated probability for each edge in f, i.e. $\zeta_{f(t_i),t_i}$, must satisfy its corresponding tag expansion;*
4. *Among the mappings in which all the above three conditions hold, dynamic instantiation refers to f whose score is maximized, i.e. $f = \arg\max_f Score(r)$.*

The first condition states that if tag t has value constraints in the `WHERE` clause, then its mapped value $f(t)$ should satisfy all the value constraints over t in query q. The second condition is for us to better capture the users' intention as discussed earlier. The third condition is used to meet the tag semantic specifications. Finally, the last condition is to find the best possible instantiation between tags set T_q and values set V_r, i.e. the one with maximum instantiation score $Score(r)$. Our instantiated score is defined as the multiplication of associated probabilities in the instantiation f, that is because in our case the associations between tag and value pairs are independent, and based on our mutual exclusion rule, all the edges falling outside of f are invalid.

Due to the semantic uncertainty of tags, answering a query q can result in a large number of records with score larger than 0. In view of this, we mainly focus on top-k query processing to find the best k answers based on our query answering semantics.

Definition 4 (Top-k Query Answering). *Given a query q, a user specified positive integer k, and a set of records $R = \{r_i | i = 1, \ldots, |R|\}$, the problem of top-k query* *answering is to retrieve a record set RS, such that $RS \subseteq R$, $|RS|$ is maximized with the condition $|RS| \leq k$, $\forall r \in RS$ and $\forall r' \in \overline{RS}$, which is the complementary set of RS, $Score(r) \geq Score(r')$.*

From the above definition, it is possible that less than k results are retrieved. We however feel that it is a worthy cost to pay for freeing users from a fixed mediated schema and providing relaxation over the tag specifications.

3. TAG INFERENCE

We next describe our tag inference process which is essential for discovering the semantic relationships between tags, and computing the associated probabilities between tag and value pairs. We use $T = \{t_i | i = 1, \ldots, n\}$ to denote all the tags in our database, and $V = \{v_j | j = 1, \ldots, m\}$ to denote all the values. For a tag $t \in T$, we use $V_t \subseteq V$ to represent the set of values that fall under the tag t in the wide table.

Effectively discovering the semantic similarities between user contributed tags however is challenging. Although several approaches have been proposed in the literature [23, 26, 30], none of them is suitable for our case. First, string similarity over tag names could not convey all cases [26, 23]. With such approaches, `model` and `model_year` will be treated as similar but `make` and `manufacturer` will be treated as dissimilar. Second, ontology and taxonomy based methods [26, 30] are not applicable, as there are many personalized tags like `myear` and `eadd`, which cannot be captured by any existing ontology and taxonomy. Finally, similarity function based on values overlap [23] works only for categorical values, not for string and numerical values. For example, given two set of emails that are contributed by different users using two different tags, it is unlikely that there is much overlap between the two set of emails.

Our approach to discovering the semantic similarities in this paper can generally be described in two steps. First, soft clustering [28] is applied to the values in the wide table to separate them probabilistically into K clusters, i.e. each value can belong to each of the K clusters with different probabilities. Since each tag is associated with a set of values with different probabilities, we can thus indirectly compute the probability of these tags being associated with the K clusters. In the second step, we measure the distance between tags by comparing the probability distribution of their associated membership to each of the K clusters using KL-divergence [8, 9]. KL-divergence is a function for measuring the relative entropy between two distributions. Specifically, if the probabilistic cluster membership distributions for two tags are p and q respectively, their relative entropy is $KL(p\|q) = \sum_{i=1..K} p_i \log \frac{p_i}{q_i}$, where p_i is the probability of the first tag being associated to cluster i and q_i is the probability of the second tag being associated to cluster i.

3.1 Tag Semantic Distance Discovery

To perform the soft clustering, our approach first extracts a set of features $\mathcal{F}$ from the underlying data V. Depending on the type of values in t, different approaches are adopted to generate the features for t. If values in t are string values, we extract a set of frequent q-grams called *sigrams* as its features. If values in t are numerical values, bins of the distribution histogram over V_t are extracted as its features. After extracting the features $\mathcal{F}$ for all values V, soft clustering [28, 8] is performed over $\mathcal{F}$. In soft clustering, the membership of a value in a cluster is probabilistic. Suppose there are K clusters $\mathcal{C} = \{c_1, \ldots, c_K\}$, for a value v, its membership probabilities in each cluster form a vector $\tau(v) = \langle p_1, \ldots, p_K \rangle$, where $\sum_{i=1}^{K} p_i = 1$, and p_i is the probability that v belongs to cluster c_i. We call $\tau(v)$ the cluster probability distribution for value v over $\mathcal{C}$. Based on [8], our soft clustering based tag inference is robust when $K>100$. We set K to be 200 in this paper.

Since a tag t can be associated with different values which have different cluster probability distributions on the K clusters, we can indirectly compute a cluster probability distribution for a tag t (denoted as $\tau(t)$) by taking the average cluster probability distributions of all its associated values V_t:

$$\tau(t) = \sum_{v_t \in V_t} \frac{1}{|V_t|} \cdot \tau(v_t)$$

To measure the semantic relationship between two tags, t_1 and t_2, one important factor that needs to be considered first is the semantic scope of each of these tags. Intuitively, if the semantics of a tag t is more general, the values associated with it will be more diverse. For instance, both make and model information of a car can be tagged by `car`, while only the make information can be tagged by `make`. Thus, the semantic scope $Scope(t)$ for tag t can be captured by the average KL-divergence between $\tau(v_t)$ and $\tau(t)$:

$$Scope(t) = \sum_{v_t \in V_t} \frac{1}{|V_t|} \cdot KL(\tau(v_t)\|\tau(t)) \qquad (1)$$

Another important factor we need to consider is the distance between tag t_1 and the *values* of tag t_2. If t_1 is similar to t_2, then $\tau(v_{t_1})$ should be close to $\tau(t_2)$. For clarity, we define the distance between the value set V_{t_1} of tag t_1 and another tag t_2 as $D_V(V_{t_1}, t_2)$:

$$D_V(V_{t_1}, t_2) = \sum_{v_{t_1} \in V_{t_1}} \frac{1}{|V_{t_1}|} \cdot KL(\tau(v_{t_1})\|\tau(t_2)) \qquad (2)$$

Based on the above discussion, if two tags t_1 and t_2 are similar in semantics, they should *i)* have similar semantic scopes; and *ii)* close to the value set of each other. Now we consider one extreme case: the distance between two semantically equivalent tags t_1 and t_1. We can easily find that $D_V(V_{t_1}, t_1) = Scope(t_1)$. From this we can see that if tag t_1 is more similar to t_2, the ratio of $D_V(V_{t_1}, t_2)$ over $Scope(t_1)$ will be closer to 1, and vise versa. Thus, the dissimilarity between two tags t_1 and t_2 is defined by such ratios:

$$Dis(t_1, t_2) = \frac{D_V(V_{t_1}, t_2)}{Scope(t_1)} + \frac{D_V(V_{t_2}, t_1)}{Scope(t_2)} \qquad (3)$$

However, it is costly to compute such tag dissimilarity for each tag pairs based on Equation 3 since we need to enumerate all values in V_{t_1} and compute their KL-divergence to t_2 to obtain $D_V(V_{t_1}, t_2)$ and vice versa. Assuming there are n tags in T, and each tag t being associated with m values, the complexity for computing all tag-pair dissimilarity using Equation 3 is $O(C_n^2 \cdot m + nm)$.

Fortunately, we are able to use the following proposition to reduce the computational complexity.

PROPOSITION 1 (BREGMAN INFORMATION EQUALITY). *Let X be a random variable that takes values in $\mathcal{X} = \{x_i\}_{i=1}^{n} \subseteq$*

$\mathbb{R}^d$ *following the probability measure* $\pi = \{\pi(x_i)\}_{i=1}^n$, *given a Bregman divergence* ϕ [6] *and another point* y,

$$\mathbb{E}_\pi[d_\phi(\mathcal{X}, y)] = \mathbb{E}_\pi[d_\phi(\mathcal{X}, \mu)] + d_\phi(\mu, y)$$

where $\mu = \mathbb{E}_\pi[\mathcal{X}]$.

PROOF. $\mathbb{E}_\pi[d_\phi(\mathcal{X}, y)] = \sum_{i=1}^n \pi(x_i) d_\phi(x_i, y)$
$= \sum_{i=1}^n \pi(x_i)\{\phi(x_i) - \phi(y) - \langle x_i - y, \nabla\phi(y)\rangle\}$
$= \sum_{i=1}^n \pi(x_i)\{\phi(x_i) - \phi(\mu) - \langle x_i - \mu, \nabla\phi(\mu)\rangle$
$+\langle x_i - \mu, \nabla\phi(\mu)\rangle + \phi(\mu) - \phi(y) - \langle x_i - \mu + \mu - y, \nabla\phi(y)\rangle\}$
$= \sum_{i=1}^n \pi(x_i)\{\phi(x_i) - \phi(\mu) - \langle x_i - \mu, \nabla\phi(\mu)\rangle\}$
$+ \sum_{i=1}^n \pi(x_i)\{\phi(\mu) - \phi(y) - \langle \mu - y, \nabla\phi(y)\rangle\}$
$= \mathbb{E}_\pi[d_\phi(\mathcal{X}, \mu)] + d_\phi(\mu, y)$

As $\sum_{i=1}^n \pi(x_i)(x_i - \mu) = 0$, and both $\sum_{i=1}^n \pi(x_i)\langle x_i - \mu, \nabla\phi(\mu)\rangle = \sum_{i=1}^n \pi(x_i)\langle x_i - \mu, \nabla\phi(y)\rangle = 0$, that is how the second last equation comes from. □

Intuitively, our proposition simply states that the expected KL-divergence between a random variable $\mathcal{X}$ following the probability distribution π and a point y is equivalent to the sum of the KL-divergence between $\mathcal{X}$ and its means μ plus the KL-divergence between μ and y. By this proposition and [3], we can show that the distance between the set of values associated with tag t_1 (i.e. V_{t_1}) and the tag t_2 can in fact be computed simply by using $Scope(t_1)$ and the KL-divergence between $\tau(t_1)$ and $\tau(t_2)$.

$$\begin{aligned} D_V(V_{t_1}, t_2) &= \sum_{v_{t_1} \in V_{t_1}} \frac{1}{|V_{t_1}|} \cdot KL(\tau(v_{t_1}) \| \tau(t_2)) \\ &= \sum_{v_{t_1} \in V_{t_1}} \frac{1}{|V_{t_1}|} \cdot KL(\tau(v_{t_1}) \| \tau(t_1)) \\ &\quad + KL(\tau(t_1) \| \tau(t_2)) \\ &= Scope(t_1) + KL(\tau(t_1) \| \tau(t_2)) \end{aligned} \quad (4)$$

By applying Equation 4 over Equation 3, we can now define our semantic distance between t_1 and t_2 as:

$$D(t_1, t_2) = \frac{KL(\tau(t_1) \| \tau(t_2))}{Scope(t_1)} + \frac{KL(\tau(t_2) \| \tau(t_1))}{Scope(t_2)} \quad (5)$$

$D(t_1, t_2)$ is symmetric, however, it does not satisfy triangle inequality. This coincides with the intuition that two tags cannot be inferred as similar via a third tag. For example, we cannot say `model` and `make` are similar although both are semantically similar to `car`.

Note that unlike Equation 3, the computation of the new distance function only involves the semantic scope, and pairwise KL-divergence between tags. The computational complexity for all tag pair distances is thus reduced from $O(C_n^2 \cdot m + nm)$ to $O(C_n^2 + nm)$.

3.2 Tag Inference

With the tag distance defined above, now we give our semantic similarity between two tags by taking the power of the negative distance, i.e.

$$SemSim(t_1, t_2) = e^{-\alpha \cdot D(t_1, t_2)} \quad (6)$$

where α is a parameter which controls the power of inference. When α is set to be 0, every value will be associated with every tag; when α is set to be infinity, there will be no inference among tags. In the experiments, we set α at 0.5. An example tag similarity table is shown in Figure 2.

[6]Note that KL-divergence is a special instance of Bregman divergence [32] and thus the derivation here immediately applies to KL-divergence.

Table 2: TagTable for `make`

TID	LID	Value	Probability
1	1	Ford	1.0
2	1	BMW	1.0
3	1	Ford	0.95
4	1	Honda	0.95
5	1	BMW 525i	0.5
6	1	Toyota Camry	0.5

Suppose value v is originally associated with tag t in user contributed data, then the associated probability of v with respect to other tags $t_i \in T$ is defined as follows.

$$\zeta_{v,t_i} = \zeta_{v,t} \cdot Semsim(t, t_i) = Semsim(t, t_i) \quad (7)$$

associated probability $\zeta_{v,t} = 1$ as v is originally associated with t. After applying the above tag inference equation, each value in the database will be associated with a set of semantically similar tags with proper probabilities. One example probabilistic tagged data is shown in Figure 3.

4. TOP-k QUERY PROCESSING

Next we will look at our top-k query processing approaches.

4.1 Data Organization

To facilitate top-k query processing, we partition the probabilistic tagged table according to tags. For a specific tag t, all its associated values are stored into one relational table, and this table is named by the tag name, i.e. t. We call such a table **TagTable**. Table 2 shows the TagTable for `make`.

Each TagTable has four attributes: `TID` (tuple id), `LID` (location offset in the source tuple), `Value` (data value) and `Probability` (associated probability). Note that the majority of ζ is approximately 0 and only values with associated probability above a cutoff threshold are stored. On the other hand, value v may be associated with multiple tags, so there is a copy of v in each of its associated TagTable. For each TagTable, a B^+-tree index is built over the attributes $\langle Value, Probability\rangle$, which will be used for the sorted list retrieval in top-k query processing.

4.2 Dynamic Instantiation

Given a query q and record r, let T_q be the set of tags in q, and V_r be the set of values from r. We can build a weighted bipartite graph $G = (U, V, E)$ as follows. Let $U = V_r$, $V = T_q$, and for each $v_r \in V_r$, each $t_q \in T_q$, if v_r satisfies the value constraints over t_q and ζ_{v_r,t_q} meets the tag expansion condition, we add an edge $e\langle v_r, t_q\rangle$ to E, with weight $\ln \zeta_{v_r,t_q}$. For simplicity, we denote this bipartite graph as $G = (V_r, T_q, \ln \zeta_{V_r,T_q})$.

After taking logarithm over the associated probabilities ζ_{V_r,T_q}, it is easy for us to apply Hungarian algorithm [18] on $G = (V_r, T_q, \ln \zeta_{V_r,T_q})$ to find the best one to one matching between V_r and T_q, where the total sum of cost/weight is maximized. We denote the maximum score found by Hungarian algorithm for record r as $Score_H(r)$. Based on Definition 3, we can see that the mapping found by Hungarian algorithm is exactly the dynamic instantiation. The first and third statements in Definition 3 are met by our edge

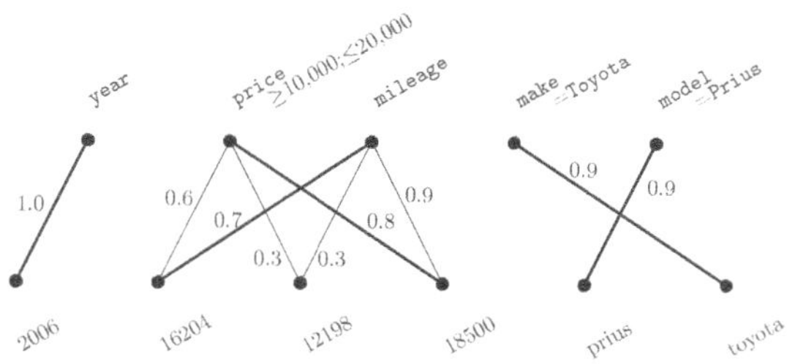

Figure 5: Dynamic Instantiation Illustration

insertion constraints discussed above; one to one mapping guarantees the second statement; and the last statement is fulfilled as the solution found by Hungarian algorithm is optimal. From the above discussion, it can be easily proven that

$$Score(r) = e^{Score_H(r)}$$

Take the following extended SQL query as an example. The values associated with tags `year`, `price` and `mileage` are to be retrieved, with constraints issued over tags `make`, `model` and `price`.

```
SELECT      year@0.9, price@0.3, mileage
FROM        CAR
WHERE       make@0.8 = 'Toyota'
       AND  model = 'Prius'
       AND  price ≥ 10,000
       AND  price ≤ 20,000
```

The corresponding bipartite graph is shown in Figure 5. For clarity, edge weights in the figure are original associated probabilities without logarithm. As illustrated by Figure 5, if `mileage` is instantiated with `16204` and `price` is instantiated with `18500` as the darker lines indicate, it gives the best instantiation as the multiplication of the associated probabilities is maximized.

4.3 Top-k Query Answering

Next we will discuss the retrieval of top-k answers. For ease of illustration, we refer to tags in the `SELECT` clause as **QTags**, and tags in the `WHERE` clause as **VTags**. Tag set in query q is denoted as T_q.

4.3.1 Sorted List Retrieval

For each queried tag $t_q \in T_q$, we aim to retrieve a list of valid values from its TagTable, sorted over associated probability from high to low. For a tag that appears in both VTags and QTags, we merge its constraints from `SELECT` and `WHERE` clauses, and retrieve one sorted list.

We first study the situation where a user-specified semantic confidence δ is issued over t_q, i.e. $t_q@\delta$. Based on Definition 2, t_q will be expanded to a tag set $T_e = \{t_{e_i} | Semsim(t_q, t_{e_i}) \geq \delta\}$. Next we will look at the associated probabilities with t_q for valid and invalid values, respectively. **Valid case**: Given a valid value v, suppose it is originally associated with tag $t_{e_i} \in T_e$. The associated probability between v and t_q is $\zeta_{v,t_q} = Semsim(t_q, t_{e_i}) \geq \delta$. This means that for each valid value, its associated probability in TagTable t_q is not less than δ. **Invalid case**: Given an invalid value v', we know that its original tag falls outside of T_e. Assume its original tag is $t_{v'}$. From Definition 2, we know that $Semsim(t_q, t_{v'}) < \delta$. Therefore, the associated probability between v' and t_q, i.e. $\zeta_{v',t_q} = Semsim(t_q, t_{v'}) < \delta$. In other words, for each invalid value, its associated probability in TagTable t_q is less than δ. In conclusion, associated probability with valid value is not less than δ, while with invalid value is. Hence, the sorted list for $t_q@\delta$ can be retrieved by the following SQL statement issued over the TagTable for t_q:

```
SELECT * FROM t_q WHERE Probability ≥ δ
                  ORDER BY Probability DESC;
```

We then look at the complex situation where there is value constraint over t_q besides the tag expansion, i.e. $t_q@\delta$ `op` v_q. Here `op` is a comparison operator and v_q is a specific value. Its sorted list can be resolved by adding one `WHERE` condition "`Value op` v_q" into the above SQL statement. For the simple cases where there is no tag expansion or value constraint over t_q, their sorted lists can be easily retrieved by removing the corresponding `WHERE` condition from the SQL statement. Benefiting from the B^+-tree index built over attributes $\langle Value, Probability \rangle$ for each TagTable, most sorted lists can be done by an index-only scan.

After retrieving the sorted list for each tag t_q, Threshold Algorithm (TA) [13] can be applied to fetch the top-k results, using Hungarian algorithm to find the best instantiation. We proposed two TA-based approaches for top-k query processing: **Eager** and **Lazy**.

4.3.2 Eager Top-k Query Answering

In eager query answering, for each tag t_q in query q, its sorted list is retrieved and maintained. TA [13] is then performed over all the retrieved sorted lists. The main idea is shown in Algorithm 1.

A priority queue RS is maintained to store the best k records that have been processed so far. All the scanned records are inserted into S_r to avoid accessing the same record more times. Each time, we scan the top unseen records from all the sorted lists, and pop the record r with the highest logarithmic probability (MP) from its sorted list (line 14). If there are more than one sorted lists whose top probability is equal to MP, our algorithm randomly chooses one from them. The popped record r is then retrieved and Hungarian algorithm is applied to get its score $Score_H(r)$ (line 15). Finally, priority queue RS is updated accordingly (line 16-19), and r is inserted into the scanned record set S_r (line 20).

For all the unseen records, their scores are upper bounded by the summation of the top probabilities from each sorted list, i.e. UBS. This is because our sorted list is ranked over probability, so the probability for each unseen record in SL_{t_q} is not greater than $SL_{t_q}.top.prob$. Algorithm 1 can be terminated when the kth score in the result set RS is not less than the upper bound score UBS (line 23), or any sorted list is exhausted (line 21).

Eager query processing searches through the sorted lists for all queried tags, including all QTags and VTags. However, this is not efficient enough. Generally, the sorted lists for QTags are much longer than those for VTags, because VTags have value constraints in the `WHERE` clause, while most QTags do not, especially for those that only exist in QTags. Due to the low selectivity of QTags, their sorted lists usually contain lots of invalid items. Based on this, we proposed another approach, namely lazy top-k query answering, which only focuses on the sorted lists of VTags.

Algorithm 1: Eager top-k Query Processing

```
Input  : A query q in extended SQL
         A positive integer k
Output: Result set RS
1  T_q ← tags in query q;
2  RS ← ∅; // top-k result set
3  S_r ← ∅; // scanned records
4  foreach tag t_q ∈ T_q do
5      SL_{t_q} ← sorted list of t_q;
6  Let SL_{t_q}.top be the most top unseen item in SL_{t_q};
7  Let SL_{t_q}.top.prob be the probability of item SL_{t_q}.top;
8  while true do
9      UBS ← 0; // upper bound score for unseen records
10     MP ← −∞; // maximum in all SL_{t_q}.top.prob
11     foreach tag t_q ∈ T_q do
12         UBS ← UBS + SL_{t_q}.top.prob;
13         MP ← max(MP, SL_{t_q}.top.prob);
14     Pop record r from SL_t where SL_t.top.prob = MP;
15     Let score = Score_H(r); // computed by Hungarian
16     if |RS| < k or score > the k^th score in RS then
17         if |RS| = k then
18             pop one item from RS;
19         insert (score, r) into RS;
20     insert record r into S_r;
21     if SL_t has reached its end then
22         break; // while loop is terminated
23     if |RS| = k and UBS ≤ the k^th score in RS then
24         break; // while loop is terminated
25 return RS;
```

4.3.3 Lazy Top-k Query Answering

Unlike the eager approach, our lazy approach only retrieves and maintains sorted lists for VTags in query q. For a record, any values that are not related to Vtags are only accessed when computing its Hungarian score (line 15). For queried tags falling outside of Vtags, we assume their associated probabilities to be 1 (the largest associated probability) when computing the upper bound score (UBS). Compared to the eager approach, our lazy approach does not need to probe the long sorted lists which include many invalid records, making it more I/O efficient.

In both eager and lazy approaches, the score for each unseen record is upper bounded by the summation of all the top item scores. Hence, the correctness of our algorithms can be guaranteed.

5. EXPERIMENTAL STUDIES

We now present the experiments to validate the performance of our system. We have two main goals in this section: 1) to examine the effectiveness of our tag inference approach, 2) to show that our top-k query processing is capable of retrieving top-k results with high precision and low cost.

5.1 Experimental Setup

We implement our system on top of MySQL. The tag inference and query answering algorithms are written in C++. The system is set up on a PC with Intel(R) Core(TM)2 Duo CPU at speed 2.33GHz and 3.5GB memory. Through all the experiments, we randomly select 2% samples for soft clustering.

1. Car Datasets (CAR Domain). The first datasets we deal with are datasets in the car domain. We insert 101 different tables from different sources into a wide table to simulate the scenario where different users share their data. Among the 101 tables, one is obtained from Google Base, and has 24 thousand tuples and 15 columns, while the others are downloaded from *Many Eyes*[7]. These tables have different sizes, with number of tuples ranging from dozens to thousands, and the number of columns ranging from 5 to 31. In total, there are 94,854 rows, 284 distinct tags and 850,215 distinct values after combining the data into one wide table.

2. Directory Datasets (DIR Domain). We extract three directory datasets from three websites that provide directory services[8]. The directory data sets consist of information about companies, such as company name, address, telephone, fax, email and so on. In total, there are 139,022 tuples, 31 distinct tags and 495,908 distinct values.

5.2 Tag Inference Validation

We verify the effectiveness of our tag inference approach first on real datasets, and compare it with the matching results from Open II. We then further validate it over the semi-real Google Base car datasets.

5.2.1 Validation over Real Datasets

To evaluate our tag inference approach, we first compare it with Open II [26] based on the *golden standard*. Open II is an open source data integration toolkit that has implemented several schema matching methods[9]. In this experiment, for Open II, we choose all the matching methods it implemented to produce its matching result. These matchers include "Name Similarity Matcher", "Documentation Matcher", "Mapping Matcher", "Exact Matcher", "Quick Matcher" and "WordNet Matcher". The *golden standard* is identified by manually scanning through all the columns in each domain.

In car domain, totally there are 160 semantically equivalent tag pairs in the golden standard. Both the output format of Open II and our system are a list of tag pairs, each associated with a similarity score. For car domain, Figure 6 shows the precision for the top-k similar tag pairs in Open II and our approach, with k varying from 20 to 200. The result clearly demonstrates that our approach achieves better precision than Open II when we are looking at the same number of top-k similar tag pairs. The reason is that we define the tag semantic similarity based on soft clustering and KL-divergence, rather than directly over attributes. Hence, we are able to discover similar tags that have different syntaxes, such as `make` and `manufacturer`, while they cannot be found by Open II. At the same time, Open II makes many

[7]http://manyeyes.alphaworks.ibm.com/manyeyes/

[8]They are thegreenbook.com, streetdirectory.com and yellowpages.com.sg respectively.

[9]Note that Open II is a schema level mapper while our approach is an instance-based approach [23]. As such, Open II takes only one second for all its attribute mappings while our approach takes on average 2.5 hours to perform high dimensional clustering. These operations are however preprocessing which do not affect the query answering efficiency of our approach.

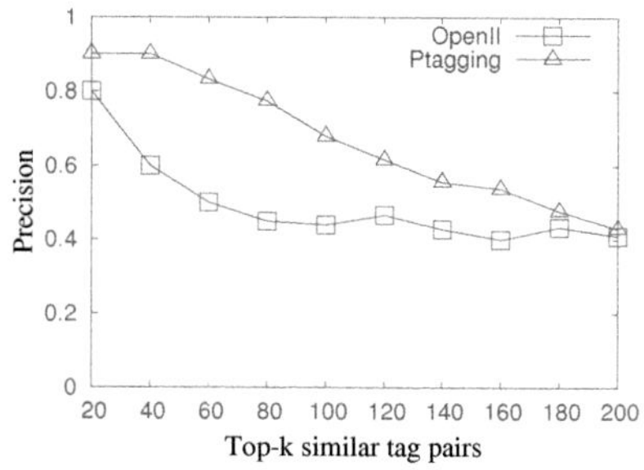

Figure 6: Comparison with Open II

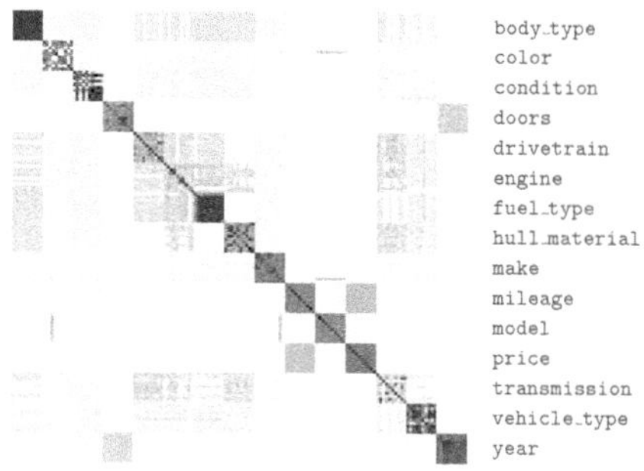

Figure 7: Tag Similarity Bitmap

wrong predictions on tag pairs which are similar in names but different in semantics. Examples include `fuel_type` and `body_type`, `model` and `model_year` etc.

Figure 6 also indicates that our precision decreases when k increases. This is because there are some semantically different tags whose value distributions are so similar that our approach cannot tell them apart, such tags include `price` and `mileage` in car domain, `telephone` and `fax` in directory domain. For such tag pairs, it might not even be possible for human being to distinguish them if no extra information is provided. The result in directory domain is similar, due to limited space, we do not list it here.

5.2.2 *Validation over Semi-real Datasets*

We further validate our tag inference by artificially introducing semantically similar tags. The large Google Base, which contains 15 different columns and about 2 million records, is pre-processed as follows[10]. For each attribute, we create 9 different attributes from the original one, with shared prefix. For example, we create another 9 attributes `make_a`, `make_b`, ..., `make_i` from attribute `make`. These attribute names are then used to simulate the scenario where different tags with same semantics come from heterogeneous data sources.

In addition, with the observation that there are many small datasets but few large ones, we take this into account in our data generation. The 10 semantically similar tags are divided into four groups with different probabilities. The first group contains 4 attributes, `make`, `make_a`, `make_b` and `make_c`, each with probability 5%; the second group contains 3 attributes, `make_d`, `make_e` and `make_f`, each with probability 10%; the third group has only two attributes, `make_g` and `make_h`, each having probability 15%; the last group, with the sole attribute `make_i`, is assigned with probability 20%. We then assign every value to a tag according to this probability distribution. In the experiment, we consider each attribute as a tag, and run our soft clustering 3 times with different initializations on a 2% sample (~40 thousand data values).

Figure 7 shows the pairwise similarity between tags. Each row and column represents a tag. The similarity between the row and column tag at a given pixel is related to the darkness of the pixel. The darker the square is, more similar the tag pairs are. Note that the tags are arranged in the same order in both row and column orientations, and tags generated from the same original tags are grouped together. From Figure 7 we can see that the squares on the diagonal are much darker than the other squares. This coincides with the fact that tags generated from the same attribute are much more similar with each other than the other tags. However, the only outlier is the fourth last attribute `price` and the sixth last attribute `mileage`. Their diagonal intersections only give a moderate grey scale. This is because `mileage` and `price` share very similar value distributions, as explained earlier.

[10]We used the entire Google Base data in data generation, but only 10% samples in tag inference to avoid dominance.

5.3 Top-k Query Processing Validation

We evaluate the performance of our top-k query processing over both car domain datasets and directory domain datasets. For car domain data, we vary the number of distinct tags in a query from 1 to 5, and denote them as $T1$ to $T5$. For each $Ti, i \in \{1, \dots, 5\}$, we choose 5 different queries with approximately equal number of tags in `SELECT` clause and `WHERE` clause. When selecting queries, we randomly vary the selectivity for predicates in the `WHERE` clause. The process is similar for directory domain data, except that we vary the distinct number of tags from 2 to 4, as directory domain has less number of tags.

To get the precision and recall for query result, we build the *golden standard* as follows. We manually check the extended SQL query to determine its semantics, then translate it to a set of traditional SQL queries over each source data set, and finally merge the results retrieved by SQL queries. For instance, if tags in {`make`, `manufacturer`, `g_make`} are semantically equivalent to each other, then an extended SQL query containing `make` will be broadcasted to each data source that includes any equivalent tag of `make`. On average, a tag-based query can be translated to 4 to 6 SQL queries.

Based on golden standard, we define *precision* and *recall* as follows: let P be the set of answers retrieved by the query processor, and GS be the set of answers in *golden standard*, then $Precision = \frac{|P \cap GS|}{|P|}$, and $Recall = \frac{|P \cap GS|}{|GS|}$.

5.3.1 *Effectiveness*

Figure 8(a) shows the precision over car datasets, with top-k% varying from 20% to 100%. For each k%, it also illustrates the precision for each Ti, with i (i.e., the number of distinct tags) ranging from 1 to 5. Note that our top-k% query is a little different from the traditional top-k query. In top-k query, the number of returned answers is k. However, in top-k% query it is $|GS| * k\%$. The reason we choose top-k% query is that we would like to see how recall changes with different number of distinct tags. As golden standard size for different queries may differ a lot, setting the same absolute k for all queries will make recall bias the performance

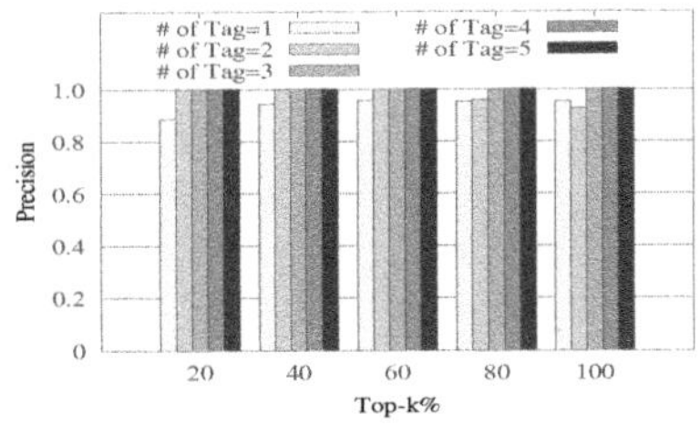

(a) Precision in CAR domain

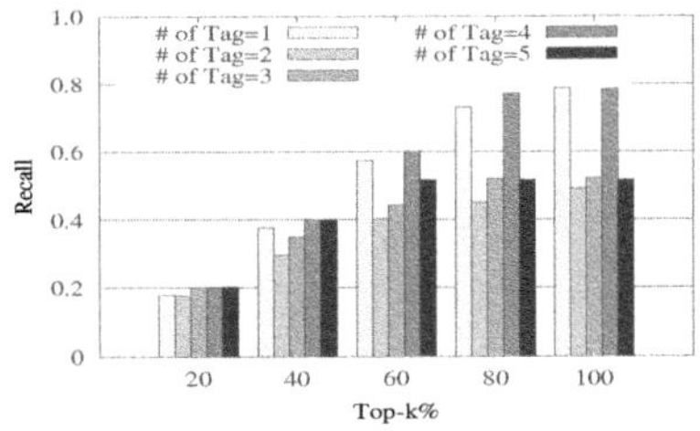

(b) Recall in CAR domain

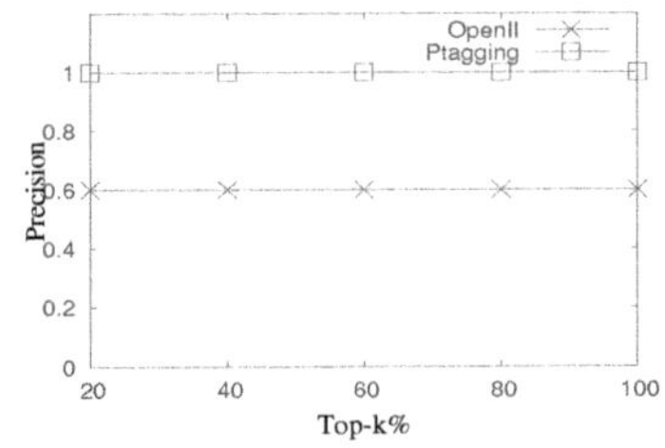

(c) Precision Comparison

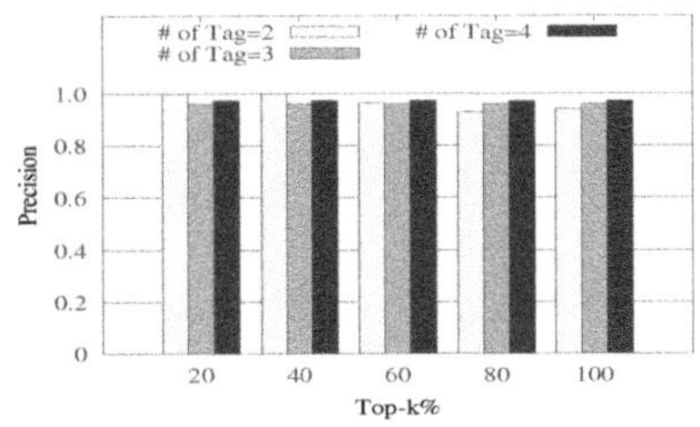

(d) Precision in DIR domain

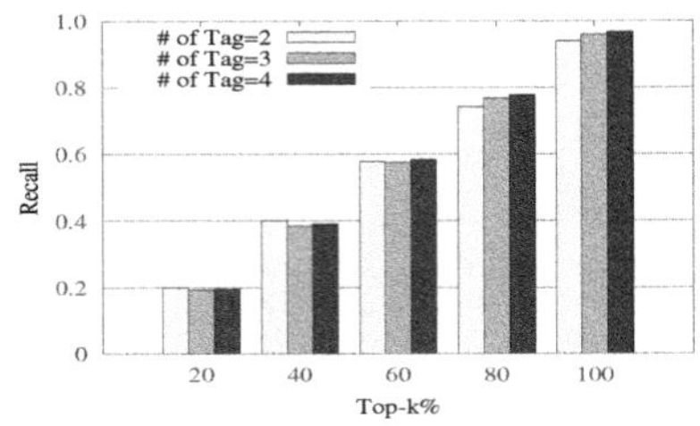

(e) Recall in DIR domain

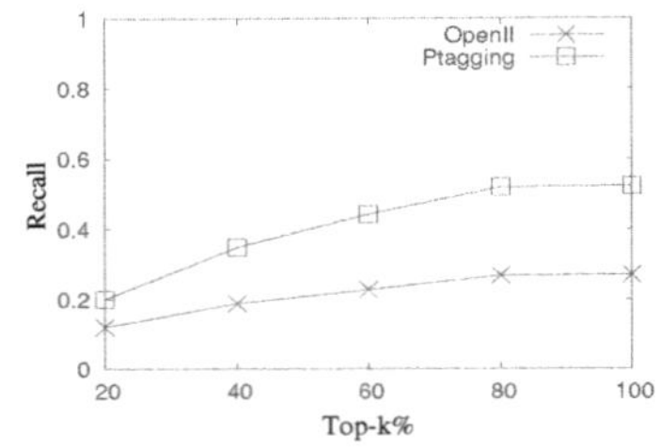

(f) Recall Comparison

Figure 8: Precision and Recall by Varying k%

towards queries with small answer set. Top-k% query avoids this problem since no matter how much the golden standard differs, recall for top-k% query is upper bounded by k%.

Figure 8(a) shows that our approach achieves high precision in all the cases, and is not sensitive to k%. It also indicates that for $T1$, precision increases slightly with larger k% while $T2$ has a slight decrement. The reason is that our tag inference approach is unable to distinguish tag pairs with similar value distributions (e.g. `price` and `mileage`). Such false positives are ranked higher in $T1$ than in $T2$. However, this problem can be eliminated by our dynamic instantiation when `price` and `mileage` are queried together, as our query processor always attempts to find the best instantiation.

Figure 8(b) shows the corresponding recall for car domain datasets. We can see that when k% increases, there is a steady increase for recall. As mentioned before, recall in k% case is upper bounded by k%. However, since we missed some true similar tag pairs in tag inference, we cannot grantee 100% recall. Such missed tags are those which are semantically similar but have heterogeneous values. For example, it is difficult to associate `year` which has format "yyyy" with `model_year` which has format "yy". This problem will become severer if there are more tags in query, because the possibility of including missed tags also increases, as shown in case $T5$. However, for queries containing less distinct tags, our approach is still able to achieve good recall. Consider the first 4 cases $T1$ to $T4$, at the point where k% equals to 100%, our approach can achieve 0.7 recall in average. Together with the high precision we provide, our proposed approach is quite effective.

We also get precision and recall on the directory data, shown in Figure 8(d) and Figure 8(e) respectively. As there are less number of tags than the car dataset, we vary its distinct number of tags from 2 to 4. We observe similar behavior as over car datasets. Since the number of tags in the directory datasets is less, and most are well-formatted, its recall is much better than the car datasets.

Finally, we compare our work with Open II for the query processing. Comparisons over precision and recall are shown in Figure 8(c) and Figure 8(f), respectively. In particular, we only list the results for $T3$ case over car datasets. The reason is that Open II makes many wrong inferences, as such, precision in most cases is really low. Here we choose its best case, i.e. $T3$, for comparison. It is indicated that our approach provides better precision and recall than Open II. Specifically, among the 5 queries in $T3$, Open II produces 0% precision for two of them because they contain wrong matched tags, and 100% precision for the rest three. In average, Open II has 60% precision across all k% cases. With less correct records returned, Open II has lower recall than ours.

5.3.2 *Efficiency*

We validate the efficiency of our top-k query processing over $T3$ on car datasets. For the directory data sets and the other queries, the overall trend is similar.

We first compare the running time of our approaches with the translated SQL queries, as shown in Figure 9. Note that when k% is set to 100%, our approaches retrieve almost the same number of tuples as the translated SQLs. As illustrated, the running time of the translated SQL queries is quite stable with respect to different top-k%, because they always retrieve the golden standard (i.e. all the true answers), no matter how k% changes. In contrast, the running time of our approaches, i.e., lazy retrieval and eager retrieval, increases linearly when top-k% increases. However, eager retrieval takes longer time than lazy retrieval by almost 1.5 times since eager retrieval maintains and probes the sorted lists for QTags, but most tuples in them are invalid. The running time that lazy retrieval takes is almost k% of translated SQLs, which clearly shows the efficiency of our lazy retrieval approach.

We next look at how the number of random and sequential accesses vary as we vary k. Figure 10(a) shows the number of random accesses for eager and lazy retrieval when varying k from 20 to 120. The corresponding graphs for sequential I/Os are in Figure 10(b). Note that in both figures, we adopt top-k rather than top-k%, as the number of tuples

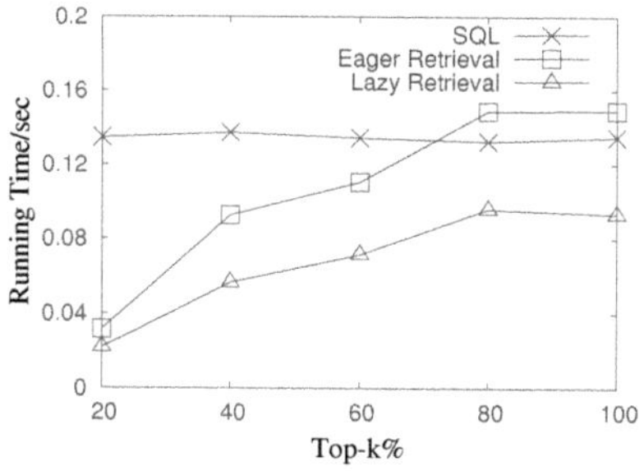

Figure 9: Running Time by Varying $k\%$

returned by top-$k\%$ varies proportionally to query's answer set. Consistent with earlier observation that eager retrieval takes almost 1.5 times longer than lazy retrieval, the same conclusion holds for both the number of sequential accesses and random accesses.

6. RELATED WORK

Query Relaxation. In the recent decade, there are several efforts to provide users a more friendly query interface that requires minimal or no user knowledge of the database schema. Such effort includes the extensive studies about keyword searches over RDBMS [19, 31]. However, keyword query confines users from issuing structural constraints, and it is not applicable for range queries. Moreover, it does not allow users to express semantic confidence over tags. In [15, 21], it was illustrated that tags on multimedia objects are prevalent over Web 2.0 application [1, 2], to facilitate searching over multimedia objects. Our use of tags here serves the same purpose.

Database Relaxation. There is also some effort to relax the strict schema defined in RDBMS, including researches on malleable schemas [11, 33], Bigtable [6], Wide-table [7], WebTable [5], and RDF tables [22]. These approaches provide some flexibility for users to interact with the schema without the strict constraints of a RDBMS. However, most of them only provide a flexible interface to store data, but the columns or attributes in their system play the same role as in RDBMS. While [33] did look at issues involving query relaxation, they only do so for string attributes and have to generate many alternate relaxed queries in order to retrieve relevant data. Users are also not given the control over which attributes to relax.

Probabilistic Database. There also exist a large body of work over probabilistic databases, dealing with row existence and value existence uncertainty [14, 27], or lineages [24, 29]. However, the uncertainties they aim to handle are different with ours. Our uncertainties on one hand, come from the semantic heterogeneities of the attributes and on the other hand, also come from the semantic uncertainties of user's queries. In other words, our uncertainties are in schemas. As far as we know, none of the existing approaches over probabilistic databases have considered schema uncertainties.

Data Integration and Schema Matching. Data integration aims to create a unified mediated schema. One main drawback of most data integration approaches [23] is that when the number of data sources becomes large, the global mediated schema will be too huge for users to query. Our work discovers semantic relationships among different tags so that users can choose preferred tag/attribute to query the database, rather than over the mediated schema. Among them, probabilistic data integration proposed by Dong and Halevy [12, 25] is closest to our work. However, their mutual exclusion rule is issued prior to the query answering, and our query-time mutual exclusion rule cannot be trivially applied to them. Consequently, they are not able to dynamically determine the tag semantics as ours. Moreover, we do not need to enumerate two levels of probability (i.e. mediated schema level and schema mapping level) in query answering as they do, so our work is more efficient.

Our tag inference approach also differs from the existing instance-based schema matching approaches [20, 10, 4]. They assume the existence of a database with a "correct" schema which data from other sources will be mapped to. Data from this database is used as training data in supervised learning (i.e. classification) to map attributes from other sources to the "correct" schema. Our problem in this paper however assumes no existence of a "correct" schema. Instead we need to derive the semantic similarity for many different sets of tags provided by different users. As such, we adopt unsupervised learning (i.e. clustering) as a way to find the similarity between tags. Our emphasis is on not confining the users to a single mediated schema and allowing them to query the data freely with different tags. The clustering-based tag inference method is essential towards this aim.

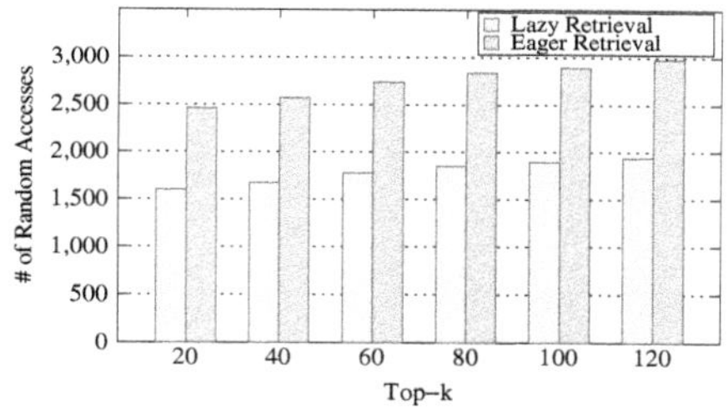

(a) Random I/O Comparison

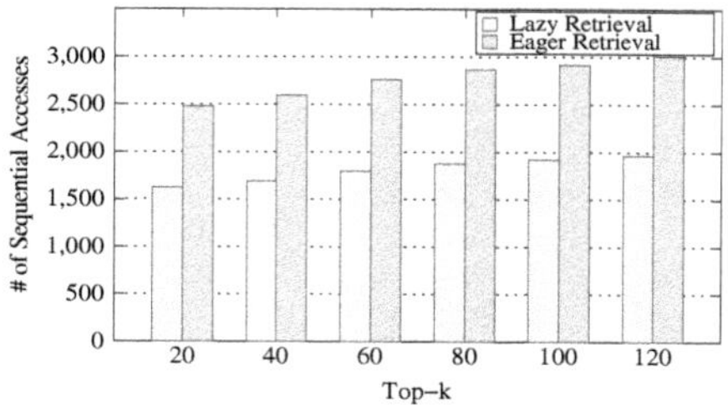

(b) Sequential I/O Comparison

Figure 10: Random I/O and Sequential I/O

7. CONCLUSION

We proposed a framework of tagging data values with probabilities on top of the wide table. Under this framework, we introduced our model of probabilistic tagging, approach of performing tag inference for all values based on their relative entropy, and the efficient and effective dynamic instantiation for query processing. We believe our approach is able to grant more privileges to non-expert database users and to better maintain the database quality.

8. ACKNOWLEDGEMENT

The work of Meiyu Lu, Bing Tian Dai and Anthony K. H. Tung were in part supported by Singapore MDA grant R-252-000-376-279.

9. REFERENCES

[1] Flickr - photo sharing, http://www.flickr.com.
[2] Youtube - broadcast yourself, http://www.youtube.com.
[3] A. Banerjee, S. Merugu, I. S. Dhillon, and J. Ghosh. Clustering with bregman divergences. *Journal of Machine Learning Research*, 6:1705–1749, 2005.
[4] J. Berlin and A. Motro. Database schema matching using machine learning with feature selection. In *CAiSE*, pages 452–466, 2002.
[5] M. J. Cafarella, A. Y. Halevy, D. Z. Wang, E. Wu, and Y. Zhang. Webtables: exploring the power of tables on the web. *PVLDB*, 1(1):538–549, 2008.
[6] F. Chang, J. Dean, S. Ghemawat, W. C. Hsieh, D. A. Wallach, M. Burrows, T. Chandra, A. Fikes, and R. Gruber. Bigtable: A distributed storage system for structured data. In *OSDI*, pages 205–218, 2006.
[7] E. Chu, J. L. Beckmann, and J. F. Naughton. The case for a wide-table approach to manage sparse relational data sets. In *SIGMOD Conference*, pages 821–832, 2007.
[8] B. T. Dai, N. Koudas, B. C. Ooi, D. Srivastava, and S. Venkatasubramanian. Rapid identification of column heterogeneity. In *ICDM*, pages 159–170, 2006.
[9] B. T. Dai, N. Koudas, D. Srivastava, A. K. H. Tung, and S. Venkatasubramanian. Validating multi-column schema matchings by type. In *ICDE*, pages 120–129, 2008.
[10] A. Doan, P. Domingos, and A. Y. Halevy. Reconciling schemas of disparate data sources: A machine-learning approach. In *SIGMOD Conference*, pages 509–520, 2001.
[11] X. Dong and A. Y. Halevy. Malleable schemas: A preliminary report. In *WebDB*, pages 139–144, 2005.
[12] X. L. Dong, A. Y. Halevy, and C. Yu. Data integration with uncertainty. In *VLDB*, pages 687–698, 2007.
[13] R. Fagin, A. Lotem, and M. Naor. Optimal aggregation algorithms for middleware. In *PODS*, 2001.
[14] T. Ge, S. B. Zdonik, and S. Madden. Top-k queries on uncertain data: on score distribution and typical answers. In *SIGMOD Conference*, pages 375–388, 2009.
[15] S. A. Golder and B. A. Huberman. The structure of collaborative tagging systems. *CoRR*, 2005.
[16] H. Gonzalez, A. Halevy, C. Jensen, A. Langen, J. Madhavan, R. Shapley, and W. Shen. Google fusion tables: data management, integration and collaboration in the cloud. In *Proceedings of the 1st ACM symposium on Cloud computing*, pages 175–180. ACM, 2010.
[17] E. Ioannou, W. Nejdl, C. Niederée, and Y. Velegrakis. On-the-fly entity-aware query processing in the presence of linkage. *PVLDB*, 3(1):429–438, 2010.
[18] E. L. Lawler. *Combinatorial Optimization: Networks and Matroids*. Dover Publications, 2001.
[19] G. Li, B. C. Ooi, J. Feng, J. Wang, and L. Zhou. Ease: an effective 3-in-1 keyword search method for unstructured, semi-structured and structured data. In *SIGMOD Conference*, pages 903–914, 2008.
[20] W.-S. Li and C. Clifton. Semantic integration in heterogeneous databases using neural networks. In *VLDB*, pages 1–12, 1994.
[21] B. Markines, C. Cattuto, F. Menczer, D. Benz, A. Hotho, and G. Stumme. Evaluating similarity measures for emergent semantics of social tagging. In *WWW*, pages 641–650, 2009.
[22] T. Neumann and G. Weikum. Rdf-3x: a risc-style engine for rdf. *PVLDB*, 1(1):647–659, 2008.
[23] E. Rahm and P. A. Bernstein. A survey of approaches to automatic schema matching. *The VLDB Journal*, 10(4):334–350, 2001.
[24] C. Ré and D. Suciu. Approximate lineage for probabilistic databases. *PVLDB*, 1(1):797–808, 2008.
[25] A. D. Sarma, X. Dong, and A. Y. Halevy. Bootstrapping pay-as-you-go data integration systems. In *SIGMOD Conference*, pages 861–874, 2008.
[26] L. Seligman, P. Mork, A. Halevy, K. Smith, M. J. Carey, K. Chen, C. Wolf, J. Madhavan, A. Kannan, and D. Burdick. Openii: an open source information integration toolkit. In *SIGMOD '10*, pages 1057–1060, 2010.
[27] M. A. Soliman, I. F. Ilyas, and K. C.-C. Chang. Top-k query processing in uncertain databases. In *ICDE*, pages 896–905, 2007.
[28] N. Tishby, F. C. Pereira, and W. Bialek. The information bottleneck method. *CoRR*, 2000.
[29] J. Widom. Trio: A system for integrated management of data, accuracy, and lineage. In *CIDR*, pages 262–276, 2005.
[30] D. Xin and H. Alon. Indexing dataspaces. In *ACM SIGMOD*, pages 43–54, 2007.
[31] B. Yu, G. Li, K. R. Sollins, and A. K. H. Tung. Effective keyword-based selection of relational databases. In *SIGMOD Conference*, pages 139–150, 2007.
[32] Z. Zhang, B. Ooi, S. Parthasarathy, and A. Tung. Similarity search on bregman divergence: Towards non-metric indexing. *Proceedings of the VLDB Endowment*, 2(1):13–24, 2009.
[33] X. Zhou, J. Gaugaz, W.-T. Balke, and W. Nejdl. Query relaxation using malleable schemas. In *SIGMOD Conference*, pages 545–556, 2007.

APPENDIX

A. PROBABILISTIC DATA INTEGRATION

Score computation for tuple T3 and T4 over query Q4 using approaches from [25] is discussed below. As assumed in [25] that different data sources are independent, now we only consider the data source that T3 and T4 come from (i.e. Figure 1(b)) and denote it as S. For clarity, We denote `manufacturer` in S as B_1, `car` as B_2, and $p(M)$ is used to represent the probability of M. The attribute set in mediated schema is {`manufacturer`, `car`, `model`}. Due to the semantic heterogeneity of `car` (semantics of `manufacturer` and `model` are specific), probabilistic mediated schema $\mathbf{M}$ has two possible schemas, i.e. $\mathbf{M} = \{M_1, M_2\}$. Specifically, attributes in M_1 are $A_1 = \{manufacturer, car\}$ and $A_2 = \{model\}$, and attributes in M_2 are $A_3 = \{manufacturer\}$ and $A_4 = \{car, model\}$. According to [25], $p(M_1) + p(M_2) = 1$, and $p(M_1) < p(M_2)$ because `manufacturer` and `car` co-occur in S. Thus, $p(M_1) < 0.5$ and $p(M_2) > 0.5$.

Next we consider probabilistic schema mappings. As the actual semantics of B_1 is manufacturer, and B_2 is model, we firstly drop the wrong correspondences such as (B_1, A_2), (B_2, A_1), (B_1, A_4) and (B_2, A_3). Based on the tag similarities from Figure 2, the attribute correspondences between S and M_1 are $p(B_1, A_1) = (1+0.52)/(1+0.52) = 1$ and $p(B_2, A_2) = 0.65/(1+0.52) = 0.43$; and correspondences between S and M_2 are $p(B_1, A_3) = 1/(1+0.65) = 0.61$ and $p(B_2, A_4) = (1+0.65)/(1+0.65) = 1$. According to [25], we list all the possible schema mappings as follows, each followed by the probability.

Schema mappings between S and M_1 are:
m1: (B_1, A_1), (B_2, A_2) : 0.43
m2: (B_1, A_1) : 0.57

Schema mappings between S and M_2 are:
m3: (B_1, A_3), (B_2, A_4) : 0.61
m4: (B_2, A_4) : 0.39

Scores for the result tuples produced by [25] are as follows.
$p(\text{Focus 1.6A}, \text{Focus 1.6A}) = (0.39+0.61) * p(M_2) = p(M_2) > 0.5$
$p(\text{Accord}, \text{Accord}) = (0.39 + 0.61) * p(M_2) = p(M_2) > 0.5$
$p(\text{Ford}, \text{Focus 1.6A}) = 0.43 * p(M_1) < 0.215$
$p(\text{Honda}, \text{Accord}) = 0.43 * p(M_1) < 0.215$

No Free Lunch in Data Privacy

Daniel Kifer
Penn State University
dan+sigmod11@cse.psu.edu

Ashwin Machanavajjhala
Yahoo! Research
mvnak@yahoo-inc.com

ABSTRACT

Differential privacy is a powerful tool for providing privacy-preserving noisy query answers over statistical databases. It guarantees that the distribution of noisy query answers changes very little with the addition or deletion of any tuple. It is frequently accompanied by popularized claims that it provides privacy without any assumptions about the data and that it protects against attackers who know all but one record. In this paper we critically analyze the privacy protections offered by differential privacy.

First, we use a no-free-lunch theorem, which defines non-privacy as a game, to argue that it is not possible to provide privacy and utility without making assumptions about how the data are generated. Then we explain where assumptions are needed. We argue that privacy of an individual is preserved when it is possible to limit the inference of an attacker about the *participation* of the individual in the data generating process. This is different from limiting the inference about the presence of a tuple (for example, Bob's participation in a social network may cause edges to form between pairs of his friends, so that it affects more than just the tuple labeled as "Bob"). The definition of evidence of participation, in turn, depends on how the data are generated – this is how assumptions enter the picture. We explain these ideas using examples from social network research as well as tabular data for which deterministic statistics have been previously released. In both cases the notion of participation varies, the use of differential privacy can lead to privacy breaches, and differential privacy does not always adequately limit inference about participation.

Categories and Subject Descriptors

H.2.8 [**Database Applications**]: Statistical Databases; K.4.1 [**Computers and Society**]: Privacy

General Terms

Security

SIGMOD'11, June12–16, 2011, Athens, Greece.

1. INTRODUCTION

Data privacy is an expanding sub-field of data management whose goal is to answer queries over sensitive datasets without compromising the privacy of the individuals whose records are contained in these databases.

One recent breakthrough in this field is a privacy definition called *differential privacy* [10, 8]. Query answering algorithms that satisfy differential privacy must produce noisy query answers such that the distribution of query answers changes very little with the addition, deletion, or modification of any tuple. Recent work has shown that the resulting query answers can enable very accurate privacy-preserving statistical analyses of sensitive datasets [25, 13, 5, 18]. There are two flavors of differential privacy, which we call *unbounded* and *bounded*. The formal definitions are:

DEFINITION 1.1. (Unbounded Differential Privacy [8]). *A randomized algorithm $\mathcal{A}$ satisfies unbounded ϵ-differential privacy if $P(\mathcal{A}(D_1) \in S) \leq e^{\epsilon} P(\mathcal{A}(D_2) \in S)$ for any set S and any pairs of databases D_1, D_2 where D_1 can be obtained from D_2 by either adding or removing one tuple.*

DEFINITION 1.2. (Bounded Differential Privacy [10]). *A randomized algorithm $\mathcal{A}$ satisfies bounded ϵ-differential privacy if $P(\mathcal{A}(D_1) \in S) \leq e^{\epsilon} P(\mathcal{A}(D_2) \in S)$ for any set S and any pairs of databases D_1, D_2 where D_1 can be obtained from D_2 by changing the value of exactly one tuple.*

Bounded differential privacy derives its name from the fact that all of the datasets D_1, D_2 have a fixed size n, while unbounded differential privacy has no such restriction.

Additional *popularized* claims have been made about the privacy guarantees of differential privacy. These include:

- It makes no assumptions about how data are generated.
- It protects an individual's information (even) if an attacker knows about all other individuals in the data.
- It is robust to arbitrary background knowledge.

These are loose, though popular, interpretations of formal guarantees provided by differential privacy. In this paper, we critically analyze the guarantees of differential privacy.

We start with a no-free-lunch theorem, which defines non-privacy as a game, and which states that it is impossible to provide privacy and utility without making assumptions about the data. This is a reformulation, simplification, and re-interpretation of an impossibility result of Dwork and Naor [8, 11] (by removing dependence on cryptographic techniques and related complications, the result is accessible to a wider audience). This shows that assumptions about the data are needed for differential privacy to avoid this game-theoretic notion of non-privacy. For comparison, we present a variation of differential privacy which does guarantees privacy without assumptions but which provides very little utility.

Then we argue that a major criterion for a privacy definition is the following: can it hide the evidence of an individual's participation in the data generating process? That is, can it limit the ability of an attacker to infer that an individual has participated? The notion of *evidence of participation* depends on how the data are generated and is different from the presence or absence of a tuple - for example, Bob's participation in a social network can cause links to form between pairs of Bob's friends and so the participation affects more than just the tuple marked "Bob". Formalizing the notion of participation is extremely difficult, but as with non-privacy, it is easier to identify cases where evidence of participation is not protected from inference. We do this with social networks (Section 3) and tabular data for which deterministic statistics have been previously released (Section 4). In each case, the notion of participation is different: in social networks, an individual can influence other people's data; for tabular data, the released query answers already provide some evidence of participation. We believe that under any reasonable formalization of *evidence of participation*, such evidence can be encapsulated by exactly one tuple only when all tuples are independent (but not necessarily generated from the same distribution). We believe this independence assumption is a good rule of thumb when considering the applicability of differential privacy.

Relying on the principle that the privacy of an individual is preserved whenever we can prevent inference about the individual's participation, we see that the main guarantee of differential privacy (i.e. the distribution of noisy query answers changes very little with the addition, deletion, or modification of a tuple) does not always guarantee privacy since deletion of a tuple is not the same as removal of evidence of participation. Since evidence of participation requires additional assumptions about the data (as we demonstrate in detail in Sections 3 and 4), this addresses the first popularized claim – that differential privacy requires no assumptions about the data.

The second popularized claim is better interpreted as stating that differential privacy limits (up to a multiplicative factor) the probabilistic inference of an attacker who knows all but one record in a dataset. This claim implicitly assumes that the more an attacker knows, the greater the privacy risks. We show that this latter assumption is flawed by (1) creating variations of differential privacy where the corresponding attackers have more knowledge yet less noise is added to query answers and (2) showing that this leaks more private information to attackers with less prior knowledge. Thus when choosing privacy definitions based on resistance to certain classes of attackers, the right choice of attackers is crucial for meaningful privacy guarantees, but the right choice is by no means obvious. We argue that the attackers to consider are those from whom it is possible to hide (i.e., limit inference about) the participation of an individual in the data generating process. This is different from limiting inference about the presence or absence of a tuple t in a dataset, especially when other tuples are correlated with t; those other tuples may provide evidence about the participation of t and this evidence must be hidden as well. With this interpretation, we should not simply assume that an attacker already has this evidence since more knowledgeable attackers are not always the biggest threats.

The third claim, that differential privacy is robust to arbitrary background knowledge, has been formalized and studied by [19]. More accurately, differential privacy is robust when certain subsets of the tuples are known by an attacker. However, many reasonable types of background knowledge can cause privacy breaches when combined with differential privacy (in other words, differential privacy composes well with itself [14] but not necessarily with other privacy definitions or data release mechanisms). Such background knowledge includes previously released exact query answers. We demonstrate a privacy breach using this background knowledge in Section 4 and we propose solutions that account for those previously released query answers.

The goal of this paper is to clear up misconceptions about differential privacy and to provide guidelines for determining its applicability. In particular our contributions are that we (1) simplify a result of Dwork and Naor [8, 11] in order to show how privacy relies on assumptions about data generation, (2) propose a participation-based guideline – "does deleting an individual's tuple erase all evidence of that individual's participation in the data-generating process?" – for determining whether differential privacy is suitable for a given application, (3) demonstrate that differential privacy does not meet this guideline when applied to arbitrary social networks and show how this can result in a privacy breach, (4) demonstrate that differential privacy does not meet this guideline when applied to tabular data when an attacker has aggregate-level background knowledge (and show a potential privacy breach), and (5) propose a modification of differential privacy that avoids privacy breaches for tabular data with aggregate-level background knowledge.

The outline of this paper is as follows. We discuss the no-free-lunch theorem and the game-theoretic definition of non-privacy in Section 2, where we also show that more knowledgeable attackers do not necessarily present the greatest risks to privacy. We specialize this discussion to social networks in Section 3, where experiments with several popular social network models show that differential privacy does not adequately limit inference about the participation of an edge in the network. We then consider tabular data, with a side release of global statistics, in Section 4. The notion of participation is very different here because some evidence of participation is already provided by the released statistics. We propose a generalization differential privacy to take into account those statistics to limit further privacy breaches, and algorithms that satisfy our generalizations.

2. ANALYSIS OF ATTACKERS

2.1 The No-Free-Lunch Theorem

In this section we argue that it is not possible to guarantee privacy and utility without making assumptions about the data-generating mechanism.

2.1.1 Utility

To capture the notion of utility, we define a *lower bound* on utility called the *discriminant*. It measures whether there exists *any* query that can be answered reasonably accurately.

DEFINITION 2.1. (Discriminant ω). *Given an integer $k > 1$, a privacy-infusing query processor $\mathcal{A}$, and some constant c, we say that the discriminant $\omega(k, \mathcal{A}) \geq c$ if there exist k possible database instances $D_1, \ldots, D_k$ and disjoint sets $S_1, \ldots, S_k$ such that $P(\mathcal{A}(D_i) \in S_i) \geq c$ for $i = 1, \ldots, k$ (the randomness only depends on $\mathcal{A}$).*

We illustrate this definition with an example. Suppose we are asking a query about how many cancer patients are in the data. If the privacy-infusing query processor $\mathcal{A}$ can answer this query with reasonable accuracy, then the discriminant $\omega(k, \mathcal{A})$ is close to 1. To see this, we set $k = 3$ (for example) and D_1 to be any database with 0 cancer patients, D_2 to be any database with 10,000 cancer patients and D_3 to be any database with 20,000 cancer patients. Suppose $\mathcal{A}$ works as follows: if there are 0 cancer patients, it outputs some number in the range $[0, 1000]$ with probability 0.95; if there are 10,000 cancer patients, it outputs some number in the range $[9000, 11000]$ with probability 0.95; if there are 20,000 cancer patients it outputs a number in the range $[19000, \infty]$ with probability 0.95. Then we set $S_1 = [0, 1000]$ (in Definition 2.1), $S_2 = [9000, 11000]$ and $S_3 = [19000, \infty]$. Since $P(\mathcal{A}(D_i) \in S_i) \geq 0.95$ and the S_i are pairwise disjoint we must have $\omega(k, \mathcal{A}) \geq 0.95$.

From this example we see that if $\omega(k, \mathcal{A})$ is close to one, then we may get a reasonably useful answer to some query (or we may not, this is only a lower bound). On the other hand, if $\omega(k, \mathcal{A})$ is close to $1/k$ (which can happen when the output of $\mathcal{A}$ is uniformly distributed and does not depend on the data), then we *cannot* get useful answers to *any* query.

Since the goal of modern privacy definitions is to answer queries relatively accurately, they all allow the use of algorithms with discriminants close to 1. For example, the discriminant of proposed k-anonymity algorithms [31] is 1.

Proposed differentially private algorithms also have discriminants close to or equal to 1. For example, the Laplace Mechanism [8] is an algorithm satisfying differential privacy that answers a count query by adding noise from the Laplace distribution with density function $\frac{\epsilon}{2}e^{-|x|\epsilon}$.

PROPOSITION 2.1. *The discriminant $\omega(k, \mathcal{A})$ of the Laplace Mechanism for unbounded differential privacy is 1 for any k. For bounded differential privacy, the discriminant of the Laplace Mechanism becomes arbitrarily close to 1 as the data size increases.*

PROOF. Fix k and $\delta > 0$ and let X be a random variable with density function $\frac{\epsilon}{2}e^{-|x|\epsilon}$. Choose n large enough so that $P(X > 2n/3k) < \delta$. For $i = 1, \ldots, k$ let D_i be a database with in/k cancer patients and define $S_i = [in/k - n/3k,\ in/k + n/3k]$ (an interval centered around in/k with width $2n/3k$). Note that all the S_i are disjoint. We will use the Laplace Mechanism $\mathcal{A}$ to answer the query "how many cancer patients are there". By construction, for any r, $P(\mathcal{A}(D_i) \in S_i) > 1 - \delta$. Thus $\omega(k, \mathcal{A}) \geq 1 - \delta$. Since δ is arbitrary, we get $\omega(k, \mathcal{A}) = 1$ for unbounded differential privacy. The result for bounded differential privacy follows since we can make δ arbitrarily small by making n large. □

2.1.2 Non-privacy

Motivated by Dwork and Naor's proof [8, 11] on the impossibility of Dalenius' vision of statistical privacy [6], we define a game between an attacker and a data curator. Let $\mathcal{D}$ be a database schema and let q be a *sensitive query*, with k possible outputs, such that $q(D)$ is considered sensitive for any database instance D. For example, $q(D)$ may return the first record in D. Let $\mathcal{P}$ be a data-generating mechanism. The game proceeds as follows.

DEFINITION 2.2. (Non-Privacy Game). *The data curator obtains a database instance D from the data-generating mechanism $\mathcal{P}$. The data curator provides the attacker with the output $\mathcal{A}(D)$ of a privacy-infusing query processor $\mathcal{A}$. The attacker then guesses the value of $q(D)$. If the guess is correct, the attacker wins and non-privacy is achieved.*

The following no-free-lunch theorem states that if there are no restrictions on the data-generating mechanism and if the privacy-infusing query processor $\mathcal{A}$ has sufficient utility (discriminant close to 1) then there exists a data-generating mechanism $\mathcal{P}$ such that the attacker's guess, without access to $\mathcal{A}(D)$, is correct with probability $1/k$ (k is the number of possible outputs of the query).[1] However, with access to $\mathcal{A}(D)$, the attacker wins with probability close to 1.

THEOREM 2.1 (NO FREE LUNCH). *Let q be a sensitive query with k possible outcomes. Let $\mathcal{A}$ be a privacy-infusing query processor with discriminant $\omega(k, \mathcal{A}) > 1 - \epsilon$ (for some $\epsilon > 0$). Then there exists a probability distribution $\mathcal{P}$ over database instances D such that $q(D)$ is uniformly distributed but the attacker wins with probability at least $1 - \epsilon$ when given $\mathcal{A}(D)$.*

PROOF. Choose database instances $D_1, \ldots, D_k$ such that $\forall i, q(D_i) = i$. Choose sets $S_1, \ldots, S_k$ as in Definition 2.1 (discriminant) so that $\omega(k, \mathcal{A}) \geq \min_i P(\mathcal{A}(D_i) \in S_i) > 1 - \epsilon$, with the probability depending only on the randomness in $\mathcal{A}$. Let $\mathcal{P}$ be the uniform distribution over $D_1, \ldots, D_k$. The attacker's strategy is to guess $q(D) = i$ if $\mathcal{A}(D) \in S_i$ and to guess randomly if $\mathcal{A}(D)$ is not in any of the S_i. Clearly the attacker wins with probability at least $1 - \epsilon$. □

This theorem can be viewed as a weaker reformulation and significant simplification of Dwork and Naor's result [8, 11]: we eliminated the use of auxiliary side information, introduced a more natural notion of utility, and gave a shorter and transparent proof. It is now clear why assumptions are needed: without restrictions on $\mathcal{P}$, we cannot guarantee that the privacy-infusing query processor $\mathcal{A}$ avoids non-privacy.

2.1.3 No-Free-Lunch and Differential Privacy

We now explain how the no-free-lunch theorem relates to differential privacy and evidence of participation and how an assumption that $\mathcal{P}$ generates records independently can prevent an attacker from winning against a differentially private algorithm. Suppose Bob's sensitive attribute R can take one of the values $1, \ldots, k$. Consider a $\mathcal{P}$ which generates data where Bob's record always appears and when Bob's sensitive attribute $R = j$ then there are $j \times 10,000$ cancer patients in the data. An attacker can ask "how many cancer patients are there?" and to satisfy 0.1-differential privacy, the query processor $\mathcal{A}$ can add Laplace(10) noise to the true answer (with variance 200). The attacker then can divide the noisy answer by 10,000, round to the nearest integer j, and, with high probability, this will be the correct value of Bob's sensitive attribute R (since $200 << 10,000$). In this case,

[1]The theorem easily extends to probabilities other than $1/k$.

the number of cancer patients provide evidence about Bob's participation.

This example relies on a correlation between Bob's sensitive attribute and the other records in the database to provide evidence of participation. In this particular case, such a correlation seems artificial and so we are likely to *assume* that there is no such dependence between records, so that the number of cancer patients can no longer provide evidence about Bob. If we assume that $\mathcal{P}$ generates records independently (and if the assumption is correct), the attacker would not be able to guess Bob's sensitive attribute from the number of cancer patients. Thus under the assumption of independence of records, differential privacy would be safe from this attack. In Sections 3 and 4 we will see examples of correlations which are not artificial and for which the use of differential privacy can lead to privacy breaches.

Before concluding this section, note that there do exist privacy definitions which make no assumptions about the data. One example is:

Definition 2.3. (Free-Lunch Privacy). *A randomized algorithm $\mathcal{A}$ satisfies ϵ-free-lunch privacy if for* any *pair of database instances D_1, D_2 (not just those differing in one tuple) and for any set S, $P(\mathcal{A}(D_1) \in S) \leq e^\epsilon P(\mathcal{A}(D_2) \in S)$.*

It is not hard to see that the discriminant $\omega(k, \mathcal{A})$ of any algorithm $\mathcal{A}$ satisfying ϵ-free-lunch privacy is bounded by $\frac{e^\epsilon}{k-1+e^\epsilon}$. Notice that this is bounded away from 1 whether we restrict the size of the database or not. In contrast, virtually all noise-infusing privacy definitions (such as bounded differential privacy, randomized response [32], etc.) have discriminants that become arbitrarily close to 1 as the data size increases. Thus with free-lunch privacy, we would have difficulty distinguishing between small and large databases (let alone finer details such as answers to range queries). This lack of utility is also clear from its definition; this is the price we must pay for making no assumptions about the data-generating mechanism.

2.2 Knowledge vs. Privacy Risk

Before discussing privacy breaches in social networks and tabular data (with pre-released exact query answers) in Sections 3 and 4, we present in this section a general guideline for determining whether a privacy definition is suitable for a given application. This guideline is based on "hiding evidence of participation" of an individual from an attacker. In many cases this guideline calls for limiting the inferences made by attackers that are *less* knowledgeable than those considered by differential privacy (i.e. attackers who know about all but one tuple in a database). Somewhat counterintuitively, this can actually *decrease* the probability of disclosing sensitive information. Thus we first show that privacy definitions that limit the inference of more knowledgeable attackers can sometimes leak more sensitive information than privacy definitions that protect against less knowledgeable attackers. Then we present our "evidence of participation" guideline.

Let us start with two more forms of differential privacy – attribute and bit differential privacy.

Definition 2.4. (Attribute Differential Privacy). *An algorithm $\mathcal{A}$ satisfies ϵ-attribute differential privacy if for every pair D_1, D_2 of databases such that D_2 is obtained by changing <u>one attribute value</u> of one tuple in D_1, we must have $P(\mathcal{A}(D_1) \in S) \leq e^\epsilon P(\mathcal{A}(D_2) \in S)$ (for any set S).*

Definition 2.5. (Bit Differential Privacy). *An algorithm $\mathcal{A}$ satisfies ϵ-attribute differential privacy if for every pair D_1, D_2 of databases such that D_2 is obtained by changing <u>one bit</u> of one attribute value of one tuple in D_1, we must have $P(\mathcal{A}(D_1) \in S) \leq e^\epsilon P(\mathcal{A}(D_2) \in S)$ (for any set S).*

Attribute differential privacy corresponds to an attacker who has full information about the database except for one attribute of one record. Bit differential privacy corresponds to an attacker who knows everything except one bit in the database encoding. Both definitions limit the attacker's inference about the remainder of the data. Clearly the attacker for bit-differential privacy knows more than the attacker for attribute-differential privacy who knows more than the corresponding attacker for bounded-differential privacy (Definition 1.2) who only knows all records but one.

It is easy to see that an algorithm $\mathcal{A}$ that satisfies bounded-differential privacy also satisfies attribute-differential privacy and an algorithm that satisfies attribute-differential privacy also satisfies bit-differential privacy. In these cases, an algorithm that protects against (i.e. limits the inference of) a less knowledgeable attacker also protects against the more knowledgeable attacker. However, we now show that an algorithm that limits the inference of a more knowledgeable attacker can leak private information to a less knowledgeable attacker.

Consider the following table with 1 tuple (Bob) and two 2-bit attributes R_1 and R_2:

	R₁	**R₂**
Bob	00	10

There are 16 possible databases instances with 1 tuple. Bounded-differential privacy allows an algorithm $\mathcal{A}_1$ to output Bob's tuple with probability $\frac{e^\epsilon}{15+e^\epsilon}$ and any other tuple with probability $\frac{1}{15+e^\epsilon}$. Attribute-differential privacy allows an algorithm $\mathcal{A}_2$ to output Bob's record with probability $\frac{e^{2\epsilon}}{9+6e^\epsilon+e^{2\epsilon}}$ (each of the 6 records where only one attribute differs from Bob can be output with probability $\frac{e^\epsilon}{9+6e^\epsilon+e^{2\epsilon}}$, and each of the 9 remaining records can be output with probability $\frac{1}{9+6e^\epsilon+e^{2\epsilon}}$). The allowable distribution for bit-differential privacy is more complicated, but Bob's record can be output with probability $\frac{e^{4\epsilon}}{e^{4\epsilon}+4e^{3\epsilon}+6e^{2\epsilon}+4e^\epsilon+1}$. Figure 1 plots the different probabilities of outputting Bob's record as ϵ ranges from 0 to 1. We clearly see that bit-differential privacy, with which we associate the most knowledgeable attacker, outputs Bob's record with the highest probability, followed by attribute-differential privacy and followed by bounded-differential privacy (which we associate with the least knowledgeable attacker).

The intuition about why bit-differential privacy leaked the most amount of private information is that, since the attacker already knows so much about Bob's record, there is little need to output a record drastically different from it. There is very little left for the attacker to learn and so we can concentrate *most* of the randomness on this area of the attacker's uncertainty, which would be the set of records that differ from Bob's by 1 bit. Another example is an attacker who knows everything: we can release the entire database without the attacker learning anything new.

We can extend these ideas to correlated data. Consider the following example:

Example 2.1. *Bob or one of his 9 immediate family members may have contracted a highly contagious disease, in which case the entire family would have been infected. An*

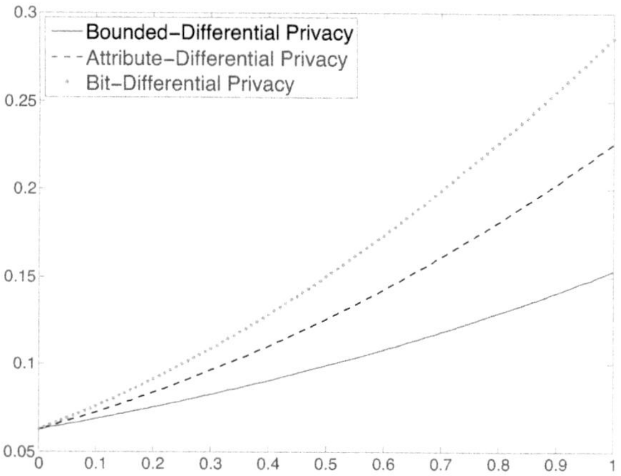

Figure 1: Probability (y-axis) of outputting Bob's record as ϵ (x-axis) varies for bit-differential privacy (top line), attribute-differential privacy (middle line), bounded-differential privacy (bottom line)

attacker who knows all 9 family members have this disease already has strong evidence that Bob is infected. A weaker attacker who knows nothing about the family's health can ask the query "how many in Bob's family have this disease?". The true answer is almost certainly going to be either 0 *or* 10. *Suppose Laplace*$(1/\epsilon)$ *noise is added to the true answer and that the resulting differentially private query answer was* 12. *The answer* 12 *is* $e^{10\epsilon}$ *times more likely when the true answer is* 10 *(and hence Bob is sick) than when the true answer is* 0 *(and Bob is healthy). Thus data correlation and a differentially private answer produced a result where a weaker attacker's probability estimate (of Bob being sick) can change by a (large) factor of* $e^{10\epsilon}$. *In contrast, differential privacy guarantees that the stronger attacker (who already knows 9 family members are sick) can change his probability estimate by a factor of at most* e^{ϵ}.

Other types of correlations are also possible. In Section 3 we show how correlations between edges in a social network can lead to a privacy breach, and in Section 4 we show that prior release of deterministic aggregate statistics can cause tuples to become correlated and that this can also lead to a privacy breach.

2.2.1 Participation-based guidelines

The key feature of Example 2.1 was that Bob's tuple had influence over other tuples in the data. Deleting Bob's tuple would not remove Bob's *influence* on the data and so the rest of the data provides *evidence* about Bob and his health. This evidence comes from Bob's participation in the data generating mechanism: Bob's interaction with family members (i.e. participation) and the mechanisms governing infection and growth of pathogens (i.e. other relevant aspects of data generation).

Thus if privacy guarantees are based on limiting the inference of a class of attackers, this class must be chosen wisely. We argue that an important consideration when evaluating a privacy definition is the following question: how well can it hide the *evidence of participation* of an individual from an attacker who has little prior evidence of this individual's participation? When data records are independent, then deleting one record eliminates all evidence of its participation. In such as case, differential privacy is appropriate since it guarantees that differentially private query answers are barely affected by record deletion. On the other hand, when records are not assumed to be independent, record deletion may not hide evidence of participation (in which case differential privacy may not be suitable). In general, it is the data-generating mechanism which determines what properties of the data provide evidence of participation (as we show in Sections 3 and 4). Thus the definition of participation and hence the suitability of various privacy definitions actually depends on how the data are generated.

It is difficult to create a general definition of "participation" that applies to all data-generating mechanisms. One of the difficulties is that if aggregate statistics about the data have already been released, then those statistics already provide *some* evidence of Bob's participation; protecting the *rest* of this evidence seems to entail some concept of *degree* of participation. Thus instead of a general definition, we consider special cases. In Section 3, where we show that differential privacy does not always hide the participation of an *edge* in a social network, we show that the presence or absence of one edge can have a dramatic effect on the subsequent growth of a network. In Section 4, where we discuss prior release of statistics, we show that a number of other records need to be modified in order to alter evidence about an individual without an attacker realizing it (thus providing a notion of plausible deniability).

3. SOCIAL NETWORKS

In this section we investigate how well differential privacy can hide (limit inference about) the participation of entities in social networks. There are two natural choices for such entities: nodes and edges. A standard application of differential privacy would try to prevent inference about whether or not a node (or edge) has been subsequently removed from the data. For nodes, a differentially private algorithm $\mathcal{A}_{node}$ must satisfy $P(\mathcal{A}_{node}(D_1) \in S) \le e^{\epsilon}P(\mathcal{A}_{node}(D_2) \in S)$ for all sets S and for all pairs of databases D_1 and D_2 such that one can be constructed from the other by removing a node and all of its incident edges. For edges, a differentially private algorithm $\mathcal{A}_{edge}$ must satisfy $P(\mathcal{A}_{edge}(D_1) \in S) \le e^{\epsilon}P(\mathcal{A}_{edge}(D_2) \in S)$ for all sets S and for all pairs of databases D_1 and D_2 such that one can be constructed from the other by removing an edge.

It is widely believed that differentially private algorithms $\mathcal{A}_{node}$ that try to limit inference about nodes can only return query answers that are too noisy for practical applications [17], and so it is common to sacrifice privacy for more utility by using differentially private algorithms $\mathcal{A}_{edge}$ for edges [12]. Thus in this section we will examine whether limiting inference about whether an edge has been subsequently removed is the same as limiting inference about the participation of that edge in the social network.

It is difficult to formulate a general and formal definition for what *evidence of participation* means, but it is very easy to identify special cases where this evidence is clearly not protected from inference. One such example is the following. Suppose a social network starts with two distinct communities that do not interact (they share at most one edge); one reason is that they may be unaware of each other. The attacker knows this, and also knows that if there is an edge between the two communities, then it is between Bob, a member of Community 1, and someone else in Community 2. Let us define a privacy breach to be the event that the attacker can determine (with high probability) whether or not Bob had an edge to someone in the second community. We will let these communities grow, using three different social network models [22, 21, 24], after which the attacker will ask the query "how many edges are there between the two communities". We now consider (1) how deleting Bob's edge from the database affects the query answer and (2) how the answer would have been affected if Bob's had not existed. Deleting Bob's edge simply changes the answer by 1. Differential privacy would guarantee that if the true answer were either X or $X - 1$, the noisy answer would be the same, with high probability, in either case. Now let us consider the effect of the participation of Bob's edge in the network. Suppose that Bob's edge was incident to Charlie (from Community 2). Because of their friendship, Bob introduces Alice (from Community 1) to Charlie. Alice then introduces her friends (from Community 1) to Charlie, and so on. Thus Bob's initial edge could have caused many additional edges to form (and most of them would not even be incident to Bob). If Bob did not have that initial edge, it is possible that those additional edges would not have formed and so the query answer could have been significantly different. To check how different, we use several popular social network models [22, 21, 24] to simulate this "what if" scenario.

For each model and parameter setting, we ran the model starting from a network where there is an edge between Bob and a member of a different community and also in the case where no such edge exists. In each case we run the model $1,000,000$ times to get an accurate estimate of the expected number of edges between the two communities (with and without that initial edge) after the network has being growing for a while. The difference Y, between the expected number of edges when Bob had a link to another community and when he did not, is a measure of the degradation of the differential privacy guarantees. It is also a measure of the causal influence of Bob's edge. A naïve application of ϵ-differential privacy would add Laplace($1/\epsilon$) noise (with variance $2/\epsilon^2$) to the query "how many edges are there between the two communities". However, to prevent inference about the participation of Bob's edge, at least Laplace(Y/ϵ) noise (with variance $2Y^2/\epsilon^2$) would have to be added (more noise could be needed, since Y is only the difference in expectation, and there could be more revealing queries). Furthermore, we would not know Y a priori unless we knew the model parameters (i.e. made assumptions about how the data were generated). Otherwise, we would have no guidance on how much noise to add.

Forest Fire Model [22]. The first model we use is the forest fire model [22]. We modify it slightly to make it more fair to differential privacy (in the original version, if there was no edge between two communities, no such edge would ever form). When using this model, our initial network has 10 nodes (5 per community) with three random within-community outlinks per node. We grow this network until it has 50 nodes as follows. When a new node enters the network, it picks an ambassador node uniformly at random. The new node then joins the same community as the ambassador and forms an edge to the ambassador. The new node picks a number k from a geometric distribution with mean $p/(1-p)$ and forms an edge with k of the ambassador's outlinks. The new node uses the same process to form an edge with some of the ambassador's inlinks. Now the new node repeats the link generation process with its new neighbors (duplicate edges between nodes are not allowed). Finally, with probability q (which we set to 0.1) the new node adds a link to a randomly chosen node (this modification allows for new edges to form between communities that had no edges before). We used the parameters investigated by Leskovec et al. [22] where the parameter for the geometric distribution for outlinks is 0.37 and for inlinks it is 0.32. When Bob had no edge to another community, the expected number of cross-community edges (after the network grew to a size of 50) is ≈ 119. However, when Bob did initially have an edge to another community, the expected number of cross-community edges was ≈ 240. This is a significant difference, and ϵ-differential privacy would need an extremely small ϵ value to hide the participation of Bob's initial edge (thereby adding a large amount of noise); ϵ should be at least $240 - 119 = 121$ times smaller than a naïve application of differential privacy would suggest. In addition, this difference in number of cross-community edges depends on the model parameters, and so we cannot set ϵ reliably *unless we know the parameters of the network-generating distribution.* Even for the particular parameters we chose, considering the small size of the network (50 nodes), such a value of ϵ would add large amounts of noise to any query, thus providing virtually no information about the social network. Thus, in order to use differential privacy to provide meaningful information about social networks, we would have to assume that the network was *not* generated by a forest fire model. Alternatively, a naïve application of differential privacy which did not take into account possible large effects of causality would let our attacker infer the participation of Bob's edge.

Copying Model [21]. The second model we use is the copying model [21]. This model does not grow as fast as the forest fire model because the out-degree of each node is bounded. The network again starts with 10 nodes (5 per community) and set we the out-degree of each node to be 3. The network grows as follows. When a new node enters the network, it chooses a prototype node uniformly at random and joins the same community as the prototype. For each outlink neighbor of the prototype, the new node links to that neighbor with probability $1 - p$ and links to a random node with probability p. We ran two sets of experiments. In the first set, we fixed the final network size to be 50 and varied the random link probability p. The results are shown in Figure 2. In the second set, we fixed the random link probability p to 0.05 and varied the final network size. The results are shown in Figure 3.

When the random link probability increases (Figure 2), the copying model begins to degenerate into a random graph model where edges are chosen randomly and so the effect of causality decreases. However, as the network size grows for a fixed p, so does the difference in the expected value of cross-community edges (Figure 3). The growth is modest compared to the forest fire model, but makes it difficult for differential privacy to limit inference about Bob's initial edge. The reason is that the effect of causality grows with time and so the noise parameter ϵ would depend on the size of the final network (and other parameters). Again, it is not possible to set ϵ reliably unless we know or make assumptions about the actual parameters of the data generating

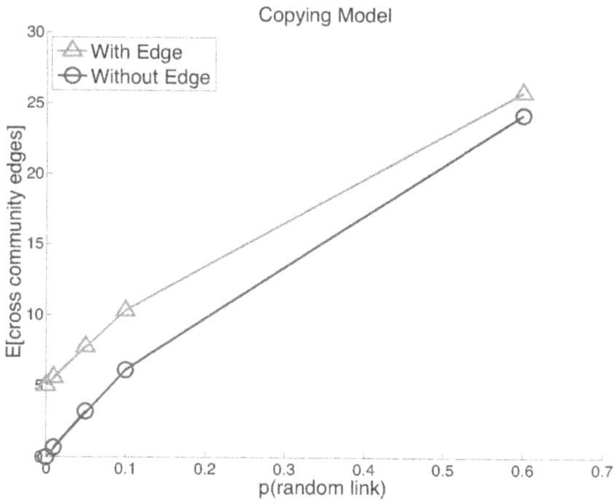

Figure 2: Causal effects in the Copying Model as a function of the random link probability.

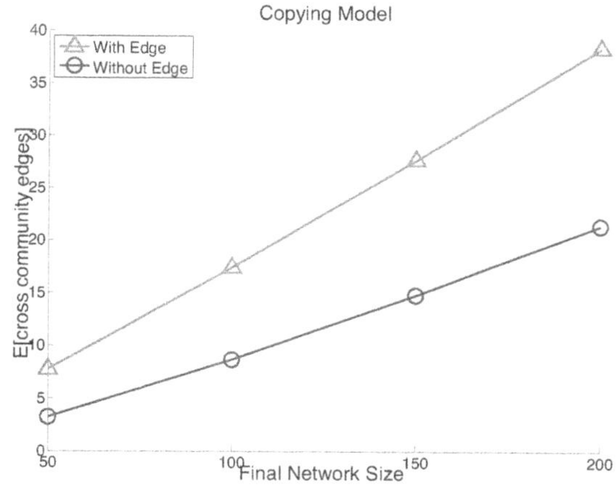

Figure 3: Causal effects in the Copying Model as a function of the final network size

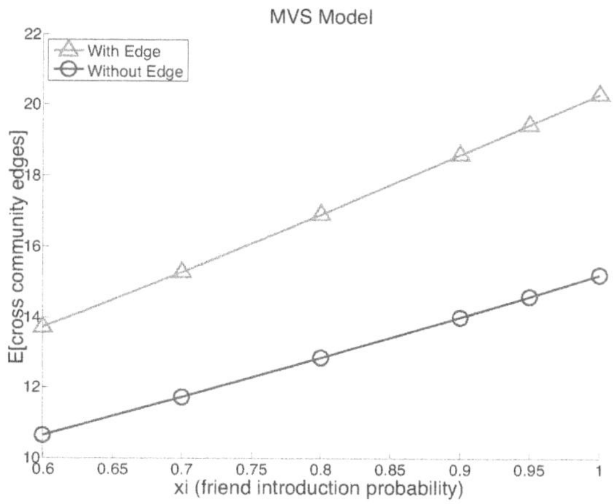

Figure 4: Causal effects in the MVS Model as a function of ξ, the friend-introduction probability.

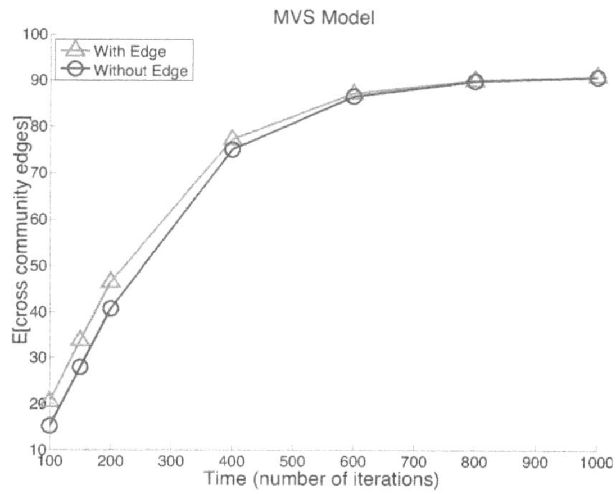

Figure 5: Causal effects in the MVS Model as a function of time (nearness to steady state).

distribution. The alternatives are to set ϵ very small (thus destroying utility), or to ignore causality (i.e. naïve apply differential privacy) and possibly reveal the participation of Bob's edge.

MVS Model [24]. Our final model is the MVS model [24]. In contrast to the forest fire and copying models, this model is actually an ergodic Markov chain (whose state space consists of graphs) and has a steady state distribution. Thus the number of edges does not have a tendency to increase over time as with the other two models. The original MVS model is a continuous time process, which we discretize in a way similar to [24]. In this model, the number of nodes remains constant. At each timestep, with probability η, a link is added between two random nodes. With probability ξ, a randomly selected node selects one of its neighbors at random and asks for an introduction to one of its neighbors. Finally k edges are deleted, where k is a random variable drawn from a Poisson(λ) distribution. Initially both communities have an equal number of nodes and community membership does not change. Initially each node has 2 within community links. We perform two sets of experiments. In the first set of experiments, the network has 20 nodes and we vary ξ, the friend-introduction probability. We compute the number of cross-community edges after 100 time steps (before the network has reached a steady state). This is shown in Figure 4. In the second set of experiments, we set the network size to be 20, we set $\xi = 1$, and we vary the number of iterations to let the network achieve its steady state. This is shown in Figure 5. Note that once the process achieves steady state, the initial conditions (or, more generally, network configurations in the distant past) are irrelevant and the evidence that other edges provide about the participation of Bob's initial link is automatically destroyed by the network model itself. However, there can still be evidence about edges formed in the not-so-distant past.

We see from Figure 4, that depending on network parameters, the expected difference in cross-community edges can be moderately large, but we see that this difference disappears as the network is allowed to reach its steady state (Figure 5). Thus differential privacy may be a reasonable choice for limiting inference about the participation of Bob's edge in such a scenario. However, applying differential privacy here still requires the assumption that the data were generated by such a favorable model (as opposed to a forest fire model, for example).

4. CONTINGENCY TABLES

In this section we consider privacy-preserving query answering over a table for which some deterministic statistics have already been released. In addition to motivating this problem, we show that applications of differential privacy in this setting can lead to a privacy breach beyond the possible breach caused by the initial release of those statistics. We then propose a solution by modifying differential privacy to take into account such prior deterministic data releases.

The U.S. Census Bureau is one of the largest consumers of privacy technology. It both collects and disseminates data about the U.S. population. Privacy is an important issue so many of the datasets released to the public have been perturbed, masked, or otherwise modified to protect the confidentiality of individuals in the data.

In some cases, utility is more important than privacy. One example is in the release of population counts which are used for apportionment (allocating seats in the House of Representatives to the states). Since this is a highly-charged political issue with significant consequences, these counts must be as accurate as possible so that sampling (which can be broadly interpreted to include noise infusion and complicated statistical data editing) is prohibited. Of particular significance is the 2002 Supreme Court case Utah v. Evans (our short discussion here is based on [3]). This case concerned the year 2000 Decennial Census and the way in which it dealt with missing and inconsistent data. The Census Bureau used statistical imputation to adjust counts for households for which data were not reported. This adjustment was enough to add one seat in the House of Representatives to North Carolina at the expense of Utah. In the Supreme Court case, the State of Utah unsuccessfully argued that statistical imputation should have been considered a form of sampling and therefore disallowed. Even though Utah lost this case illustrates the contentiousness of even a small perturbation of the data.

This case illustrates an interesting application for privacy technology. In some cases utility is so important that some *exact* statistics about the data must be released. After this initial data release, additional queries can be answered, with degraded accuracy, as long as they do not introduce an additional privacy breach (note that this is a special case of the dual privacy problem where the goal is to provide as much privacy subject to utility constraints [15]). For example:

EXAMPLE 4.1. *Due to overriding utility concerns, a university releases the number of male and female employees, a histogram of employee salaries, and a separate histogram for each additional attribute in its employees table. An economist may later seek to determine if salary and gender are independent of each other at this institution. This question cannot be answered from the released statistics but could be answered from the original data by using the chi-squared test (for example). Thus the university would like to provide a privacy-preserving estimate of the chi-squared value on the original data. The release of this approximate chi-squared value should not lead to additional leakage of privacy (when combined with the previously released histograms).*

Differential privacy does not allow for any deterministic release of statistics, so the initial data release in Example 4.1 falls outside of this framework. However, differential privacy might later be used to release a perturbed version of the chi-squared statistic. In cases like these, privacy guarantees may degrade. We provide a simple demonstration in Section 4.1.

4.1 A Privacy Leak

We now show that when deterministic statistics have been previously released, applying differential privacy to subsequent data releases is not enough to prevent *additional* privacy breaches (beyond the possible breaches caused by the initial release of statistics). The reason is that those statistics could add correlations into the data and into future queries that otherwise would be unrelated.

Consider a table T with one attribute R that can take values $r_1, \dots, r_k$. Suppose that due to overriding utility concerns, the following $k-1$ queries have been answered exactly:

SELECT COUNT(*) FROM T WHERE R=r_1 OR R=r_2

$\vdots$

SELECT COUNT(*) FROM T WHERE R=r_{j-1} OR R=r_j

$\vdots$

SELECT COUNT(*) FROM T WHERE R=r_{k-1} OR R=r_k

This does not provide enough information to always reconstruct the original table (there are k unknowns but $k-1$ linear equations). However, if we knew the answer to "SELECT COUNT(*) FROM T WHERE R=r_i" for any r_i, then we would be able to exactly reconstruct the table T. In this way the tuples are correlated and we are one exact query answer away from a complete privacy breach (i.e. reconstruction of the table).

Now, differential privacy would allow us to answer the following k queries by adding independent Laplace($1/\epsilon$) noise (with variance $2/\epsilon^2$) to each query [8]:

SELECT COUNT(*)+noise FROM T WHERE R=r_1

$\vdots$

SELECT COUNT(*)+noise FROM T WHERE R=r_j

$\vdots$

SELECT COUNT(*)+noise FROM T WHERE R=r_k

By themselves, without use of the previously released exact queries, these noisy query answers are innocuous and have little dependence on the value of Bob's tuple. In fact, the only query that would have even a slight dependence on Bob is the query where r_i matched Bob's attribute value.

However, because of the previous release of exact query answers, *each* noisy query now leaks some small amount of information about *every tuple*. To see this, note that simple linear algebra and a noisy answer to "number of people with $R = r_i$", with noise variance $2/\epsilon^2$, allows us to compute a noisy estimate for "number of people with $R = r_1$" also with variance $2/\epsilon^2$. Thus for each of these k noisy queries we can estimate the number of tuples with $R = r_1$ (with variance $2/\epsilon^2$). By averaging over all of these estimates, we get a better estimate for the number of tuples with $R = r_1$ with variance $2/(k\epsilon^2)$, and in fact we can estimate of the number of tuples with $R = r_i$ (for any i) with variance $2/(k\epsilon^2)$.

When k is large (for example R is a d-bit attribute with 2^d possible values), the variance is small so that the table T is reconstructed with very high probability, thus causing a complete privacy breach. This was only possible because additional noisy queries were answered without taking into account prior release of information.

Thus the guarantee that the distribution of future noisy query answers changes very little if one deletes or arbitrarily modifies one tuple is not sufficient to prevent a privacy breach when exact query answers had been previously released – those exact answers add correlations between the noisy answers that otherwise might not exist.

4.2 A Plausible Deniability

The result of Section 4.1 shows that once deterministic query answers have been released released, Bob (if his information is in the data) can no longer opt out of the data or opt to change his tuple arbitrarily – opting out would have only been meaningful *before* any query answers were released – so the differential privacy guarantees for future query answers would not be as compelling to Bob. Bob can still try to limit *further* damage by opting to modify his tuple in a way that maintains consistency with the previously answered exact queries. If the distributions of future noisy query answers before and after such modifications are guaranteed to be similar, then Bob can limit further damage[2] – this is a form of plausible deniability.

One simple example of this idea is the relationship between bounded and unbounded differential privacy. Unbounded differential privacy (Definition 1.1) guarantees that the distribution of noisy query answers will change only slightly if Bob removed his tuple from the data. However, if the query "how many tuples are in the data" had been previously answered exactly, then Bob can maintain consistency with this query answer by modifying his tuple arbitrarily (but not deleting it) since the number of tuples would then stay the same. This is the approach taken by *bounded* differential privacy (Definition 1.2), which guarantees that the distribution of future noisy query answers changes only slightly if Bob arbitrarily alters (but not deletes) his tuple.

In the general case, there may be no modification that Bob can make to his tuple that would leave the data consistent with previous query answers. For example, if, for every attribute X, the queries "SELECT X, COUNT(*) GROUP BY X" were exactly answered, then no modification of Bob's tuple alone can leave the data consistent with those query answers (several tuples must be modified simultaneously). However, Bob may collaborate with Alice to jointly change their tuples to maintain consistency. For example, if the number of males and females in the data were released, Bob can change the gender attribute of his tuple to female and Alice can change the gender attribute of her tuple to male to maintain consistency.

Our extension to differential privacy, which accounts for previously released exact query answers, follows these ideas by providing the guarantee that the distribution of future noisy query answers changes only slightly if a small set of tuples were modified in any way that is still consistent with previously answered queries.

4.3 Differential Privacy Subject to Background Knowledge

In this section we modify differential privacy to account for previously released exact query answers. In Section 4.4 we discuss algorithms for privacy-preserving query answering. First, we need the following definitions:

DEFINITION 4.1. (Contingency Table, Cell, Cell count). *Given a table T with attributes $R_1, \ldots, R_d$, a* contingency table *is the (exact) answer to the query:*

```
SELECT R_1, ..., R_d,COUNT(*) FROM T
GROUP BY R_1, ..., R_d
```

A cell *is a specific assignment of values to the attributes (e.g. $R_1 = r_1, \ldots, R_d = r_d$), and a* cell count *is the number of tuples in that cell.*

A contingency table is essentially a table of counts (or a fine-grained histogram).

DEFINITION 4.2. (Move). *Given a contingency table T, a* move *m is a process that adds or deletes a tuple from T, resulting in a contingency table $m(T)$. Thus the value of exactly one cell count changes – it either increases by 1, or decreases by 1 (as long as the result is nonnegative).*

Using this notion of a move, we can define several notions of *neighboring tables.* These different notions will be used with the following definition to allow us to instantiate different versions of differential privacy.

DEFINITION 4.3 (GENERIC DIFFERENTIAL PRIVACY). *A randomized algorithm $\mathcal{A}$ satisfies ϵ-differential privacy if for any set S, $P(\mathcal{A}(T_i)) \leq e^\epsilon P(\mathcal{A}(T_j))$ whenever contingency tables T_i and T_j are* **neighbors**.

This definition can be specialized into bounded and unbounded differential privacy (Definitions 1.2 and 1.1) through the following choice of neighbors.

- **Unbounded Neighbors $\mathcal{N}_1$**: Contingency tables T_i and T_j are *unbounded neighbors* if one can transform T_i to T_j using only one move. Define the relation $\mathcal{N}_1(T_i, T_j)$ to be true if and only if T_i and T_j are unbounded neighbors.
- **Bounded Neighbors $\mathcal{N}_2$**: Contingency tables T_i and T_j are *bounded neighbors* if the sum of cells of both tables are equal (i.e. T_i and T_j have the same number of tuples) and T_i can be transformed into T_j using exactly 2 moves. Define the relation $\mathcal{N}_2(T_i, T_j)$ to be true if and only if T_i and T_j are neighbors.

Clearly, the use of unbounded neighbors $\mathcal{N}_1$ in Definition 4.3 results in unbounded differential privacy. The use of bounded neighbors $\mathcal{N}_2$ in Definition 4.3 results in bounded differential privacy (compare to Definition 1.2) because changing the value of one tuple from t_1 to t_2 is equivalent to first removing that tuple t_1 (the first move) and then adding t_2 (the second move).

In terms of moves, it is natural to ask why the definition of bounded neighbors $\mathcal{N}_2$ required exactly 2 moves. The reason is that this is the smallest amount of moves that is needed to transform T_i into another table that is consistent with previously released statistics (i.e. the number of tuples in the table, which is assumed to be known in the case of bounded differential privacy).

Another way to think about bounded neighbors $\mathcal{N}_2$ in the context of differential privacy is that T_i and T_j are neighbors if and only if they are as similar as possible, subject to constraints imposed by previously released exact query

[2]Under suitable further assumptions, such as initial independence of records before the release of query answers (See Sections 2 and 3).

answers. Bounded differential privacy then guarantees that an attacker who knows that the true table is either T_i or T_j will have great difficulty distinguishing between these two tables. Note that knowing the true table is either T_i or T_j is the same as knowing $n-1$ tuples in the true database and being unsure about whether the remaining tuple is t_1 or t_2.

4.3.1 Neighbors induced by prior statistics.

Now let us generalize this reasoning to a case where additional exact query answers have been previously released.

EXAMPLE 4.2. *Let T be a contingency table with attributes $R_1, \ldots, R_k$. Due to overriding utility concerns, the following query has already been answered exactly:*

```
SELECT GENDER, COUNT(*) FROM T GROUP BY GENDER
```

Suppose n is the number of individuals in the table T (i.e. the total cell count), n_F is the number of females and n_M is the number of males. The quantities n_M, n_F, and $n = n_F + n_M$ are now known.

Suppose Drew is in this table. Some limited information about Drew has been disclosed by this query, and now Drew would like a variant of differential privacy to limit any possible damage due to future (noisy) query answers. We seek some form of plausible deniability: the attacker should have difficulty distinguishing between tables T_i and T_j that both have n_F females and n_M males and are otherwise similar except that Drew's tuple takes different values in T_i and T_j.

Thus we need a good choice of neighbors of T (the original table) which should be difficult to distinguish from each other. Unbounded neighbors $\mathcal{N}_1$, used in the definition of unbounded differential privacy (see Definitions 1.1 and 4.3), do not work here; removing or adding a tuple to T changes the number of males and females – thus it is not clear what kind of plausible deniability this would provide. Bounded neighbors $\mathcal{N}_2$, used in the definition of bounded differential privacy (see Definitions 1.1 and 4.3), also do not work; we cannot arbitrarily modify a single tuple and hope to be consistent with the previously released query answers. However, we can make limited changes to 1 or 2 tuples to maintain consistency. For example, we can choose one tuple and modify the attributes other than gender arbitrarily. We can also choose 2 tuples, 1 male and 1 female, swap their gender attributes, and modify the rest of their attributes arbitrarily. Both transformations keep the number of males and females constant. Thus we can provide some level of plausible deniability by making it difficult for an attacker to detect whether one of these transformations has been performed.

This example illustrates 3 important points. First, in the absence of additional correlations (as discussed in Sections 2 and 3), privacy is guaranteed by ensuring that an attacker has difficulty distinguishing between the original table T and a set of neighboring tables that are similar to T. Each neighboring table T' differs from T by a small set of changes (for example, by modifying the value of Drew's tuple and possibly a few others), thus the attacker would have difficulty in detecting these changes (i.e. the attacker would be uncertain about the value of Drew's tuple). Second, each neighboring table T' of T must be consistent with the previously released exact query answers; the reason is that if T' were not consistent, then it would be easy to distinguish between T and T' (since an attacker would know that T' could not possibly be the original table). The third point is that differential

	Cell A	Cell B	Cell C	Cell D
Table T_a	4	5	7	3

	Cell A	Cell B	Cell C	Cell D
Table T_b	5	4	6	4

	Cell A	Cell B	Cell C	Cell D
Table T_c	5	4	7	3

Figure 6: Three Contingency Tables

privacy can be made aware of prior data release simply by choosing the appropriate notion of neighbors in Definition 4.3 (such modifications have also been suggested by [20]).

Based on this discussion, we can formally define the concept of neighbors induced by exact query answers (Definition 4.4). Plugging this into generic differential privacy (Definition 4.3), we arrive at the version of differential privacy that takes into account previously released exact query answers.

Before presenting Definition 4.4, first note that if T_a and T_b are contingency tables, then the smallest number of moves needed to transform T_a into T_b is the sum of the absolute difference in cell counts. For example, in Figure 6, this smallest number of moves is 4: first +1 for cell A, then +1 for cell D, then −1 for cell C, and finally −1 for cell B. Note that any permutation of these moves also transforms T_a into T_b, and these permutations account for all of the shortest sequence of moves (i.e. of length 4) for turning T_a into T_b.

DEFINITION 4.4. (Induced Neighbors $\mathcal{N}_Q$). *Given a set $Q = \{Q_1, \ldots, Q_k\}$ of constraints, let $\mathcal{T}_Q$ be the set of contingency tables satisfying those constraints. Let T_a and T_b be two contingency tables. Let n_{ab} be the smallest number of moves necessary to transform T_a into T_b and let $m_1, \ldots, m_{n_{ab}}$ be one such sequence of moves.*[3] *We say that T_a and T_b are* neighbors induced by Q, *denoted as $\mathcal{N}_Q(T_a, T_b)$ =true, if the following holds.*

- *$T_a \in \mathcal{T}_Q$ and $T_b \in \mathcal{T}_Q$.*
- *No subset of $\{m_1, \ldots, m_{n_{ab}}\}$ can transform T_a into some $T_c \in \mathcal{T}_Q$.*

We illustrate this notion of induced neighbors $\mathcal{N}_Q$ (which can now be plugged into generic differential privacy in Definition 4.3) with the following example. Consider contingency table T_a and T_b from Figure 6. Suppose the constraints Q are imposed by our knowledge that the sum of cells A and B is 9 and the sum of cells C and D is 10. We can transform T_a into T_b using the following move sequence: first +1 for cell A, then +1 for cell D, then −1 for cell C, and finally −1 for cell B. However, using only a subset of these moves, namely +1 for cell A and −1 for cell B, we can transform T_a into T_c. Since T_a, T_b and T_c satisfy all of our constraints, T_a and T_b are not neighbors.

Continuing this example, it is easy to see that T_a and T_c are neighbors and T_b and T_c are neighbors (even though T_a and T_b are not). Thus T_a and T_c are as similar as possible while still satisfying constraints imposed by previously released exact query answers (and similarly for T_b and T_c). Thus using this definition of neighbors in generic differential privacy (Definition 4.3), we would be guaranteeing that an

[3]Note that all other such sequences of moves are simply permutations of this sequence.

attacker has difficulty distinguishing between T_a and T_c and also between T_b and T_c.

4.4 Neighbor-based Algorithms for Differential Privacy

In this section we adapt two algorithms for (generic) differential privacy that use the concept of induced neighbors $\mathcal{N}_Q$ (Definition 4.4) to guarantee privacy. We also show that in general this problem (i.e. accounting for previously released exact query answers) is computationally hard.

The first algorithm is an application of the exponential mechanism [26]. To use it, we first need to define a distance function $d(T_a, T_b)$ between two contingency tables. We define the distance function $d(T_a, T_b)$ as follows. Let $\mathcal{T}_Q$ be the set of all contingency tables consistent with previously released query answers. Create a graph where the tables in $\mathcal{T}_Q$ are the nodes, and where there is an edge between tables T_a and T_b if and only if T_a and T_b are induced neighbors. Define $d(T_a, T_b)$ to be the length of the shortest path from T_a to T_b in this graph. The exponential mechanism now works as follows. If T is the true table, we output a table T' with probability proportional to $e^{-\epsilon d(T,T')}$. Following the proof in [26], we can show that this will guarantee 2ϵ-generic differential privacy (Definition 4.3, using $\mathcal{N}_Q$ as the definition of neighbors).

The exponential mechanism [26] generally does not lead to efficient algorithms, even without the complication of induced neighbors $\mathcal{N}_Q$. However, we can modify the Laplace mechanism [8] to suit our purposes. To do this, we first need the concept of *sensitivity*.

Definition 4.5 (Sensitivity). *Let $Q = \{Q_1, \ldots, Q_k\}$ be a set of constraints, let $\mathcal{T}_Q$ be the set of contingency tables satisfying those constraints, and let $\mathcal{N}_Q$ be the associated induced neighbors relation. The sensitivity $S_Q(q)$ of a query q over $\mathcal{T}_Q$ is defined as:*

$$S_Q(q) = \max_{\mathcal{N}_Q(T_1,T_2)=true} |q(T_1) - q(T_2)| \qquad (1)$$

The Laplace mechanism adds Laplace$(S_Q(q)/\epsilon)$ noise (the probability density function is $f(x) = \frac{\epsilon}{2S_Q(q)} e^{-\epsilon x / S_Q(q)}$) to the query answer. The proof of correctness is similar to [8]. Thus we need to be able to compute (an upper bound on) the sensitivity of queries. In some cases (which we describe below) this leads to efficient algorithms, but in general the constraints Q imposed by previously released exact query answers will make the data release problem computationally intractable, as the following results show. We omit detailed proofs due to space constraints.

Proposition 4.1. *Let $Q = \{Q_1, \ldots, Q_k\}$ be a set of constraints. Let S be a table with 3 attributes and let T be the associated contingency table. The following two decision problems are NP-hard in the number of possible attribute values.*

- *Checking whether T has at least one neighbor.*
- *Checking whether two tables T_a, T_b that are consistent with the constraints in Q are* not *neighbors.*

Proposition 4.2. *Given a set $Q = \{Q_1, \ldots, Q_k\}$ of constraints, let $\mathcal{T}_Q$ be the set of contingency tables satisfying those constraints. For any count query q, deciding whether $S_Q(q) > 0$ is NP-hard.*

+	−	
−		+
	+	−

+	−		
−		+	
	+		−
		−	+

+	−			
−		+		
	+		−	
		−		+
			+	−

Figure 7:

The above propositions show that the general problem of finding an upper bound on the sensitivity of a query ($S_Q(q) < d$) is at least co-NP-hard, and we suspect that the problem is Π_2^p-complete.

In certain cases, efficient algorithms do exist. For example, consider a 2-dimensional table with attributes R_1 and R_2, and suppose all the row and columns sums are fixed. Let the query q_{all} be defined as:

```
SELECT R_1, R_2, COUNT(*) FROM T GROUP BY R_1, R_2.
```

The following theorem computes the sensitivity of q_{all}, which can then be answered using the Laplace mechanism.

Lemma 4.1. *Let Q be the row and column sums for a 2-dimensional $r \times c$ table. The sensitivity $S_Q(q_{all})$ is given by* $\min(2r, 2c)$.

Proof. (sketch) The key insight is that for a set of moves corresponding to the shortest path from table T_1 to T_2, there can only be exactly 1 tuple added and 1 tuple deleted from cells in the same row or same column. Suppose the contrary: i.e., without loss of generality, there is a designated row where more than 1 tuple is added. Since the row sums are constant, if m tuples are added in a row, then m tuples must have been deleted from cells in the same row. Now suppose we mark every addition to a cell with '+' and a deletion with '-'. Also, if '+' and '-' appear in the same row or column, then draw an edge from the '+' cell to the '-' cell. It is easy to see that if the row and column sums are fixed, then either all or a subset of the marked cells are part of a Hamiltonian cycle alternating in '+' and '-'. If a subset of the marked cells forms the Hamiltonian cycle then we can remove them to get a shorter path from T_1 to T_2 (the cells in the cycle have row and column sums equal to 0, by construction, so their removal preserves the row and column sums). Thus after finitely many such removals we may assume that all of the cells containing a '+' or '-' are part of a Hamiltonian cycle alternating in '+' and '-'. A sequential walk on this loop is a valid set of alternating tuple addition and deletion moves to change T_1 to T_2. This loop enters the designated row for the first time at cell c_1 and exits the designated row for the last time at cell c_2. Cells c_1 and c_2 must have distinct signs. If we drop the part of the loop from c_1 to c_2 and replace it with an edge from c_1 to c_2, we get a new valid cycle from T_1 to T_2. The new cycle is shorter and thus gives a smaller set of moves to change T_1 to T_2; contradicting the fact that the original set of moves was the smallest set of moves. Therefore, each row and column has either no marked cells or exactly one cell marked '+' and one cell marked '-'. Thus the maximum number of moves between any pair of neighbors is at most $\min(2r, 2c)$.

To show that the sensitivity can achieve $\min(2r, 2c)$, we consider pairs of $\ell \times \ell$ tables that differ in the counts as shown (for $\ell = 3, 4, 5$) in Figure 7. It is easy to show pairs of tables for which the smallest set of moves is as described in Figure 7. □

5. RELATED WORK

Differential privacy was developed in a series of papers [1, 10, 8] following the impossibility results of Dinur and Nissim [7] that showed that answering many queries with bounded noise can allow an attacker to reproduce the original database almost exactly. Since then, many additional variations of differential privacy have been proposed [9, 4, 29, 2, 23, 20, 28].

With the success of differentially private algorithms for tabular data [16, 8, 1, 25, 26, 13, 18, 5], there has been interest in developing differentially private mechanisms for other domains, such as social networks [12]. For social networks, examples include [17, 27, 30]. Rastogi et al. [30] proposed a relaxation of differential privacy for social networks by proving an equivalence to adversarial privacy (which makes assumptions about the data), and then adding further constraints on the data-generating mechanism. By the no-free-lunch theorem, the other applications also require assumptions about the data to avoid non-privacy.

Dwork and Naor [8, 11] have several results stating that any privacy definition which provides minimal utility guarantees cannot even safeguard the privacy of an individual whose records are *not collected* by the data curator (because there always exists some auxiliary information that can be combined with query answers to create a threat to privacy). Thus Dwork proposed the principle that privacy definitions should only guarantee privacy for individuals in the data. Kasiviswanathan and Smith [19] formalized the notion of resistance to various attackers including those who know about all but one record in a table and showed an equivalence to differential privacy.

6. CONCLUSIONS

In this paper we addressed several popular misconceptions about differential privacy. We showed that, without further assumptions about the data, its privacy guarantees can degrade when applied to social networks or when deterministic statistics have been previously released. We proposed a principle for evaluating the suitability of a privacy definition to an application: can it hide evidence of an individual's participation in the data generating process from an attacker? When tuples are believed to be independent, deleting one tuple is equivalent to hiding evidence of participation, in which case differential privacy is a suitable definition to use. Providing privacy for correlated data is an interesting direction for future work.

7. REFERENCES

[1] A. Blum, C. Dwork, F. McSherry, and K. Nissim. Practical privacy: the SuLQ framework. In *PODS*, 2005.

[2] A. Blum, K. Ligett, and A. Roth. A learning theory approach to non-interactive database privacy. In *STOC*, 2008.

[3] P. J. Cantwell, H. Hogan, and K. M. Styles. The use of statistical methods in the u.s. census: ütah v. evans. *The American Statistician*, 58(3):203–212, 2004.

[4] K. Chaudhuri and N. Mishra. When random sampling preserves privacy. In *CRYPTO*, 2006.

[5] K. Chaudhuri, C. Monteleoni, and A. D. Sarwate. Differentially private empirical risk minimization. http://arxiv.org/abs/0912.0071.

[6] T. Dalenius. Towards a methodology for statistical disclosure control. *Statistik Tidskrift 15*, 1977.

[7] I. Dinur and K. Nissim. Revealing information while preserving privacy. In *PODS*, 2003.

[8] C. Dwork. Differential privacy. In *ICALP*, 2006.

[9] C. Dwork, K. Kenthapadi, F. McSherry, and I. Mironov. Our data, ourselves: Privacy via distributed noise generation. In *EUROCRYPT*, 2006.

[10] C. Dwork, F. McSherry, K. Nissim, and A. Smith. Calibrating noise to sensitivity in private data analysis. In *TCC*, pages 265–284, 2006.

[11] C. Dwork and M. Naor. On the difficulties of disclosure prevention in statistical databases or the case for differential privacy. *JPC*, 2(1), 2010.

[12] C. Dwork and A. Smith. Differential privacy for statistics: What we know and what we want to learn. *JPC*, 1(2), 2009.

[13] A. Friedman and A. Schuster. Data mining with differential privacy. In *KDD*, 2010.

[14] S. R. Ganta, S. P. Kasiviswanathan, and A. Smith. Composition attacks and auxiliary information in data privacy. In *KDD*, 2008.

[15] G. Ghinita, P. Karras, P. Kalnis, and N. Mamoulis. A framework for efficient data anonymization under privacy and accuracy constraints. *ACM TODS*, 34(2), 2009.

[16] M. Hardt and K. Talwar. On the geometry of differential privacy. In *STOC*, 2010.

[17] M. Hay, C. Li, G. Miklau, and D. Jensen. Accurate estimation of the degree distribution of private networks. In *ICDM*, 2009.

[18] G. Jagannathan, K. Pillaipakkamnatt, and R. N. Wright. A practical differentially private random decision tree classifier. In *ICDM Workshops*, 2009.

[19] S. P. Kasiviswanathan and A. Smith. A note on differential privacy: Defining resistance to arbitrary side information. http://arxiv.org/abs/0803.3946, 2008.

[20] D. Kifer and B.-R. Lin. Towards an axiomatization of statistical privacy and utility. In *PODS*, 2010.

[21] R. Kumar, P. Raghavan, S. Rajagopalan, D. Sivakumar, A. Tomkins, and E. Upfal. Stochastic models for the web graph. In *FOCS*, 2000.

[22] J. Leskovec, J. Kleinberg, and C. Faloutsos. Graph evolution: Densification and shrinking diameters. *TKDD*, 1(1), 2007.

[23] A. Machanavajjhala, D. Kifer, J. Abowd, J. Gehrke, and L. Vihuber. Privacy: From theory to practice on the map. In *ICDE*, 2008.

[24] M. Marsili, F. Vega-Redondo, and F. Slanina. The rise and fall of a networked society: A formal model. *PNAS*, 101(6), 2004.

[25] F. McSherry and I. Mironov. Differentially private recommender systems: building privacy into the net. In *KDD*, 2009.

[26] F. McSherry and K. Talwar. Mechanism design via differential privacy. In *FOCS*, 2007.

[27] D. J. Mir and R. N. Wright. A differentially private graph estimator. In *ICDM Workshops*, 2009.

[28] I. Mironov, O. Pandey, O. Reingold, and S. Vadhan. Computational differential privacy. In *CRYPTO*, 2009.

[29] K. Nissim, S. Raskhodnikova, and A. Smith. Smooth sensitivity and sampling in private data analysis. In *STOC*, 2007.

[30] V. Rastogi, M. Hay, G. Miklau, and D. Suciu. Relationship privacy: Output perturbation for queries with joins. In *PODS*, 2009.

[31] P. Samarati. Protecting respondents' identities in microdata release. *TKDE*, pages 1010 – 1027, 2001.

[32] S. L. Warner. Randomized response: A survey technique for eliminating evasive answer bias. *Journal of the American Statistical Association*, 1965.

TrustedDB: A Trusted Hardware based Database with Privacy and Data Confidentiality

Sumeet Bajaj
Stony Brook Computer Science
Stony Brook, New York, USA
sbajaj@cs.stonybrook.edu

Radu Sion
Stony Brook Computer Science
Stony Brook, New York, USA
sion@cs.stonybrook.edu

ABSTRACT

TrustedDB is an outsourced database prototype that allows clients to execute SQL queries with privacy and under regulatory compliance constraints without having to trust the service provider. TrustedDB achieves this by leveraging server-hosted tamper-proof trusted hardware in critical query processing stages.

TrustedDB does not limit the query expressiveness of supported queries. And, despite the cost overhead and performance limitations of trusted hardware, the costs per query are orders of magnitude lower than any (existing or) potential future software-only mechanisms. TrustedDB is built and runs on actual hardware, and its performance and costs are evaluated here.

Categories and Subject Descriptors

H.2.0 [**DATABASE MANAGEMENT**]: General—*Security, integrity, and protection*; H.2.4 [**DATABASE MANAGEMENT**]: Systems—*Query Processing*

General Terms

Security

Keywords

Database, Trusted Hardware

1. INTRODUCTION

Outsourcing has finally arrived, due in no small part to the availability of cheap high speed networks, storage and CPUs. Clients can now minimize their management overheads and virtually eliminate infrastructure costs[1].

Virtually all major "cloud" providers today offer a database service of some kind as part of their overall solution. Numerous startups also feature more targeted data management and/or database platforms.

Yet, significant challenges lie in the path of large-scale adoption. Such services often require their customers to inherently trust the provider with full access to the outsourced datasets. But numerous instances of illicit insider behavior or data leaks have left clients reluctant to place sensitive data under the control of a remote, third-party provider, without practical assurances of *privacy* and *confidentiality* – especially in business, healthcare and government frameworks. And today's privacy guarantees of such services are at best declarative and subject customers to unreasonable fine-print clauses – e.g., allowing the server operator (or malicious attackers gaining access to its systems) to use customer behavior and content for commercial, profiling, or governmental surveillance purposes [15, 16].

Existing research addresses several such outsourcing security aspects, including access privacy, searches on encrypted data, range queries, and aggregate queries. To achieve privacy, in most of these efforts data is encrypted before outsourcing. Once encrypted however, inherent limitations in the types of primitive operations that can be performed on encrypted data lead to fundamental expressiveness and practicality constraints.

Recent theoretical cryptography results provide hope by proving the existence of universal homomorphisms, i.e., encryption mechanisms that allow computation of arbitrary functions without decrypting the inputs [43]. Unfortunately actual instances of such mechanisms seem to be decades away from being practical [19].

Ideas have also been proposed to leverage tamper-proof hardware to privately process data server-side, ranging from smartcard deployment [29] in healthcare, to more general database operations [8, 28, 31].

Yet, common wisdom so far has been that trusted hardware is generally impractical due to its performance limitations and higher acquisition costs. As a result, with very few exceptions [29], these efforts have stopped short of proposing or building full - fledged database processing engines.

However, *recent insights* [14] *into the cost-performance trade-off seem to suggest that things stand somewhat differently.* Specifically, at scale, in outsourced contexts, *computation inside secure processors is orders of magnitude cheaper than any equivalent cryptographic operation performed on the provider's unsecured common server hardware*[2], despite the overall greater acquisition cost of secure hardware.

[1]Discussing the merits or faults of outsourcing and "clouds" is beyond the scope of this paper. Others have done and continue to do so [7, 40, 41].

[2]e.g., it is much cheaper to add numbers privately inside expensive cryptographic coprocessors than to perform the ex-

SIGMOD'11, June 12–16, 2011, Athens, Greece.

This is so because cryptographic overheads (for cryptography that allows some processing by the server) are extremely high even for simple operations, a fact rooted not in cipher implementation inefficiencies but rather in fundamental cryptographic hardness assumptions and constructs (such as trapdoor functions – the cheapest we have so far being at least as expensive as modular multiplication [35]). This is unlikely to change anytime soon (none of the current primitives have, in the past half-century). New mathematical hardness problems (e.g., elliptic curve cryptography – which unfortunately is only a bit more efficient) will need to be discovered to allow hope of more efficient cryptography.

As a result, we posit that a full-fledged strong-privacy enabling secure database leveraging server-side trusted hardware can be built and run at a fraction of the cost of any (existing or future) cryptography-enabled private data processing on common hardware. We validate by designing and implementing TrustedDB, an SQL database processing engine that makes use of IBM 4764/5 [5, 6] cryptographic coprocessors programmed to run custom components securely.

Tamper resistant designs however are significantly constrained in both computational ability and memory capacity which makes implementing fully featured database solutions using secure coprocessors (SCPUs) very challenging. TrustedDB achieves this by utilizing common unsecured server resources to the maximum extent possible. For example TrustedDB enables the SCPU to transparently access external storage while preserving data confidentiality with on-the-fly encryption. This eliminates the limitations on the size of databases that can be supported. Moreover, client queries are pre-processed to identify sensitive components to be run inside the SCPU. Non-sensitive operations are off-loaded to the untrusted host server. This greatly improves performance and reduces the cost of transactions.

Overall, despite the overheads and performance limitations of trusted hardware, the costs of running TrustedDB are orders of magnitude lower than any (existing or) potential future cryptography-only mechanisms. The TrustedDB design provides strong data confidentiality assurances. Moreover, it does not limit query expressiveness.

The contributions of this paper are two-fold: (i) the introduction of new cost models and insights that explain and quantify the advantages of deploying trusted hardware for data processing, and (ii) the design, development, and evaluation of TrustedDB, a trusted hardware based relational database with full data confidentiality.

2. MODEL AND TOOLS

Deployment. We will consider the following concise yet representative deployment model. Sensitive data is placed by a client with a remote (untrusted) *service provider*. For confidentiality, parts of the data are encrypted before outsourcing. Later, the client or an authorized third party queries the outsourced datasets through an interface exposed by the server. It is imperative for the client that certain sensitive portions of the database are never revealed. Queries will need to be performed by the outsourcing server with full computational privacy. Moreover, the client prefers to not be restricted in the nature of queries. Network layer confidentiality is assured by mechanisms such as SSL/IPSec. Other security issues such as authentication and authorization have been extensively addressed in existing research and therefore are not the main focus here.

Adversary. For strong assurances, we consider the server to be untrusted and curious. Given the possibility to get away undetected, it will attempt to compromise data confidentiality. Overt denial of service attacks are not of interest.

Trusted Hardware. TrustedDB leverages the existence of trusted hardware such as the IBM 4758 PCI [4] and the newer IBM 4764 PCI-X [5] cryptographic coprocessors (SCPUs) in close data proximity. The 4764 is a PowerPC 405 based board, runs embedded Linux and can be custom programmed. Both SCPUs feature tamper resistant and responsive designs [27] and thus provide a secure execution environment. In the eventuality of illicit physical handling, the devices destroy their internal state and shut down.

However, tamper resistant designs face major challenges in heat dissipation and as a result, SCPUs are significantly constrained in both computation ability and memory capacity. This requires careful consideration in achieving efficient protocols. Efficient solutions can be achieved by balancing a trade-off in which cheap untrusted main CPUs perform unsensitive query components while operations on private sensitive data are performed inside the SCPUs.

Cryptography. The deployed SCPUs offer several cryptographic primitives including symmetric key encryption (AES, 3DES), public key encryption on key lengths up to 4096 bits (RSA), pseudo random number generation and cryptographic hash functions (e.g., in the SHA-family).

We will denote by $E(M, K)$ the encryption of message M with key K. PK_{ALICE} denotes a public key that belongs to Alice while SK_{ALICE} represents her private key. Digital signatures are written as $S(M, K)$ – a signature of message M with private key K. The cryptographic hash of message M is denoted by $H(M)$. $||$ represents concatenation. $\oplus$ denotes the bit-XOR operation.

3. THE REAL COSTS OF SECURITY

Traditional wisdom suggests that deploying trusted hardware is generally feasible only in niche-markets such as banking and ATM security while generally impractical due to performance limitations and high acquisition costs.

This idea has propagated also to the secure outsourcing realm mainly due to the belief that practical data confidentiality and protection against curious and malicious insiders can be achieved on untrusted common hardware in "software" only, e.g., by wisely applied combinations of cryptography and data security protocols.

Further, confirmation has been achieved, for *correctness* assurances (no data confidentiality) where this seems to be indeed the case at least for simple types of queries. Several results provide relatively efficient mechanisms that guarantee query correctness e.g., for range queries [25, 30].

Yet, as soon as confidentiality becomes a concern, data needs to be encrypted before outsourcing. Once encrypted, solutions can be envisioned that: (A) straightforwardly transfer data back to the client where it can be decrypted and queried, (B) deploy cryptographic constructs server-side to process encrypted data directly or indirectly, and (C) process the encrypted data server-side inside tamper-proof enclosures of trusted hardware (which the client trusts).

In the remainder of this section we will compare the per-transaction costs of each of these cases. This is possible

pensive cryptography needed to add the numbers encrypted on plain server hardware with privacy.

	H, S	M	L
monthly	\$44.90	\$95	\$13
bandwidth (d/u)	15/5 Mbps	per 1Mbps	per 1Mbps
dedicated	No	Yes	Yes
picocent/bit	115/345	3665	500

Figure 1: Network service costs [12–14].

in view of novel results of Chen et al. [12–14] that allow such quantification. We will show that, at scale, in outsourced contexts, (C) *computation inside secure hardware processors is orders of magnitude cheaper than any equivalent cryptographic operation performed on the provider's unsecured common server hardware* (B). Moreover, due to the extremely high cost of networking when compared with computation, the overhead of transferring (even a small subset of the data) back to the client (for decryption and processing) in (A) is overall significantly more expensive than (C).

The main intuition behind this has to do with the amortized cost of CPU cycles in both trusted and common hardware, as well as the cost of transferring network bits. Due to economies of scale, provider-hosted CPU cycles are 1-2 orders of magnitude cheaper than that of clients, for CPU cycles in traditional hardware but most importantly also for *trusted* hardware. The cost of a CPU cycle in trusted hardware (56+ picocents[3], discussed below) becomes thus of the same order as the cost of a traditional CPU cycle at client sites (e.g., 14-27 picocents for small businesses). These include both acquisition and running components.

Additionally, when data is hosted far from its accessing clients, the extremely expensive network traffic often dominates; transferring *a single bit* of data over a network costs upwards of 3500 picocents!

Finally, cryptography that would allow processing on encrypted data demands extremely large numbers of cycles even for very simple operations such as addition. And, this limitation is rooted in fundamental cryptographic hardness assumptions and constructs (such as cryptographic trapdoors – the cheapest we have so far being at least as expensive as modular multiplication [35] – which comes at a pricetag of upwards of *tens of thousands of picocents per operation* [14]) and is unlikely to change anytime soon (none of the current primitives have, in the past half-century).

The above insights lead to (C) being a significantly more cost-efficient solution than (A) and (B). We now detail.

3.1 Cost of Primitives

Compute Cycles and Networks. In [12–14] Chen et al. derived the cost of compute cycles for a set of environments ranging from individual homes with a few PCs (H) to large enterprises and compute clouds running upwards of tens of thousands of CPUs (L) (M,L=medium,large sized business). These costs include a number of factors, such as hardware (server, networking), building (floor space leasing), energy (electricity), service (personnel, maintenance, administration) etc.

Their main thesis is that, because of the economies of scale and associated favorable operating parameters, per-cycle costs decrease dramatically when run in large compute providers' infrastructures (Figure 2). The resulting costs range from 27 picocents for a small business environment to less than half of a picocent for large cloud computing providers with infrastructures of tens of thousands of servers.

[3] 1 US picocent = 10^{-14} USD

Parameters	H	S	M	L
Scale	<10	<1000	<10k	>10k
CPU utilization	5-8%	10-12%	15-20%	40-56%
server:admin ratio	N.A.	100-140	140-200	800-1000
Space (\$/sqft/month)	N.A.	0.5	0.5	0.25
PUE	N.A.	2-2.5	1.6-2	1.2-1.5
Hardware (\$/CPU)	750	500	500	350
Electricity (\$/KW)	0.09	0.07	0.07	0.06
CPU Cycle (picocent)	5	14-27	2	<0.5

Figure 2: Summarized costs and key parameters for different computing environments [12–14].

Network service costs (Figure 1) range from a few hundred picocents per bit for *non-dedicated* service to thousands of picocents in the case of medium sized businesses.

Validation. We chose to validate these analytical numbers by exploring today's offerings and their pricing points. Results are surprisingly close. Amazon for e.g., charges 1-2.5 picocents per cycle (this price includes their markup as well as additional resources such as local storage and some networking traffic), whereas rackspace.com's CPU cycles range from 0.3-2.4 picocents. Similarly, amazon.com's network service can be had at price points ranging from 800 to 2500 picocents per bit, depending on source and destination region.

Trusted Hardware. We now evaluate the cost of SCPU cycles. Two main cost-impacting differences between general purpose trusted hardware SCPUs and traditional hardware are: reduced computation speeds and increased pricing points. The considered IBM 4764/5 SCPUs are connected to the world through PCI-X/PCIe buses and motherboards controlled by traditional CPUs. The main CPUs act only as a communication conduit for the SCPUs and do not need to spend time to service the SCPU otherwise.

For simplicity we consider only one SCPU per main CPU. For tighter packing of multiple SCPUs per motherboard (up to 4), the overall efficiency of the system is even higher.

SCPU energy consumption peaks by design at only 25W, yet, we conservatively estimate the deployment of SCPUs effectively doubles energy and service costs i.e., to defend against any critique claiming that in effect the main CPU will need to be dedicated as a communication conduit. In reality message forwarding takes only a few percentage points of the main CPU's compute capacity.

SCPUs are expensive (roughly one order of magnitude higher than traditional server hardware. At the time of writing the IBM 4764 could be purchased for around \$8,000 at retail which is the number we will deploy in our estimation (unofficial bulk pricing is around \$5,000 excluding support services). Finally, the 4764 runs a Motorola PowerPC 405 RISC CPU at 233 MHz. For consistency, we would like to normalize this to CISC x86 cycles. We performed extensive benchmarking (detailed results are out of scope here) and have identified that branching, integer ops and memory access performance (essential for DBMS query processing) is almost identical to an x86 AMD K6 model 6 at 200 MHz with 512 KB L2-cache – which in turn performs equivalently to a Pentium II core at 166 MHz [2].

Considering these numbers in equation (1) in [12–14] we derive the cost of (x86-equivalent) CPU cycles inside cloud-hosted SCPUs to be approximately 56 picocents. We note that while this is indeed much higher than the < 0.5 picocent cost of a cycle on cloud commodity hardware, it is comparable to the cost of cycles in CPUs hosted in small sized enterprises (14-27 picocents).

We validated these costs also by different avenues, e.g., by considering the core SCPU power consumption, acquisition costs, mean time between failure etc. For 56% utilization we arrived at the more favorable estimate of 48 picocents per cycle. Nevertheless, for consistency, in the following we use the above conservative 56 picocents value.

3.2 Comparison

Given these data points we now compare the (A), (B) and (C) alternatives discussed above. We consider the following simple scenario: a client outsources a dataset composed of integers encrypted to a service provider. The encrypted data is then subjected to a simple aggregation (SUM) query in which the server is to add all the integers and return the result to the client. We chose this mechanism not only for its illustrative simplicity but also because SUM aggregation is one of the very few types of queries for which non-hardware solutions have been proposed in existing research. This allows us to directly compare with existing work. Later we also generalize for arbitrary queries. Figure 3 summarizes the cost analysis that follows.

Querying un-encrypted data. No confidentiality. As a baseline consider the most prevalent scenario today, in which the client's data is stored unencrypted with the service provider. Client queries are executed entirely on the provider's side and only the results are transferred back. Although this is the most cost - effective solution it offers no data confidentiality. The lower bound cost of query execution in this case is as follows[4]:

$Cost_{unencrypted}$ = Cost of addition operations on server + Cost of transmitting results.

$$Cost_{unencrypted} = 2 \cdot D \cdot C_{bit\_transmit} + \left(\frac{N}{D} - 1\right) \cdot C_{cycle\_server} \cdot \eta_{addition} \tag{1}$$

where N is the size of the entire database in bits, $D = 32$ (32 bit integers), C_{cycle_server} is the cost of one CPU cycle on server hardware, $\eta_{addition} = 1$ is the average number of CPU cycles required for an addition operation [26]. $C_{bit\_transmit}$ is the cost of transmitting 1 bit of data from the service provider to the client (discussed above).

(A) Transferring encrypted data to client. The first baseline solution that provides data confidentiality works by transferring the entire database to the client. The client then decrypts the database and performs the aggregation. The cost of this alternative becomes

$Cost_{transfer}$ = Cost of data transmission + Cost of decryption on client + Cost of addition operations on client.

$$Cost_{transfer} = N \cdot (C_{bit\_transmit} + C_{bit\_decryption}) + \left(\frac{N}{D} - 1\right) \cdot C_{cycle\_client} \cdot \eta_{addition} \tag{2}$$

Where $C_{bit\_decryption} = 8$ picocents is the (normalized) cost of decrypting one bit with AES-128 in a medium-sized (M) enterprise and $C_{cycle\_client} = 2$ picocents is the cost of a single client CPU cycle in medium sized enterprises. Naturally we observe that here the cost of transferring the database to the client dominates.

(B) Cryptography. Traditional additive homomorphisms [33, 34, 37] have been used in existing work [22, 42] to allow servers to run aggregation queries over encrypted data. Additive homomorphic encryption allows the computation of the encryption of the sum of a set of encrypted values without requiring their decryption in the process.

Existing homomorphisms require the equivalent work of at least a modular multiplication in performing their corresponding operation (e.g., addition). Moreover, for security, this modular multiplication needs to be performed in fields with a large modulus. For efficiency [42] goes one step further and proposes to perform aggregation in "parallel" by simultaneously adding multiple 32-bit integer values (in fact exactly 32 integer pairs – 32 integers in each 1024 bit chunk). They achieve this by adding two 1024-bit chunks of data (encrypted by the client before outsourcing) at a time. Due to the properties of the Paillier cryptosystem, each such addition involves one 2048-bit modular multiplication[5].

The server then computes the encrypted sum of all such large integers (achieved by a single modular multiplication of the 2048-bit encrypted values – this multiplication happens modulo 2048) and returns the result to the client. The client decrypts the (2048 bit) result into a 1024 bit plaintext, splits this into 32 integers of 32 bits each, and computes their sum. The cost of this scheme is given by

$Cost_{homomorphic}$ = Cost of Modular Multiplications on server + Cost of data transmission + Cost of decryption on client + Cost of addition operations on client

$$Cost_{homomorphic} = \frac{B_h}{D} \cdot \left(\left(\frac{N}{B_h} - 1\right) \cdot C_{modular\_mul} + 2 \cdot B_h \cdot C_{bit\_transmit} + C_{homomorphic\_dec} + \left(\frac{B_h}{D} - 1\right) \cdot C_{cycle\_client} \cdot \eta_{addition} \right) \tag{3}$$

where $B_h = 1024$ is the plaintext block size and $C_{modular\_mul}$ is the cost of performing a single modular multiplication modulo 2048 on the server. $C_{homomorphic\_dec}$ is the cost of performing the single decryption on client and involves modular multiplication and exponentiation.

(C) SCPUs. A possible use of a SCPU in the execution of the aggregation query is to perform the aggregation fully inside the SCPU. The result can then be re-encrypted and transmitted back to the client.

In addition to the core CPU processing costs (which can be computed directly from the cost of SCPU cycles), data transfer overheads are incurred i.e., to bring encrypted data into the SCPU and then transfer the encrypted results back to the host server. The total cost of the solution becomes

$Cost_{scpu}$ = Cost of data transmission between the host server and SCPU + Cost of decryption inside SCPU + Cost of addition operations inside SCPU + Cost of data transmission from server to client + Cost of decryption at client

$$Cost_{scpu} = \left\lceil \frac{N}{B_s} \right\rceil \cdot (\delta_{srv} \cdot C_{cycle\_srv} + \delta_{scpu} \cdot C_{cycle\_scpu}) + N \cdot C_{bit\_decryption\_scpu} + \left(\frac{N}{D} - 1\right) \cdot C_{cycle\_scpu} \cdot \eta_{addition\_scpu} + B_c \cdot C_{bit\_encryption\_scpu} + B_c \cdot C_{bit\_transmit} + B_c \cdot C_{bit\_decyption\_client} \tag{4}$$

[4]The cost of reading data from storage into main memory is a common factor in all solutions and thus not included here

[5]To process n-bit plaintexts, Paillier operates in $n^2 = 2048$ bit fields for 1024 bit plaintexts. Ciphertexts are 2048 bit.

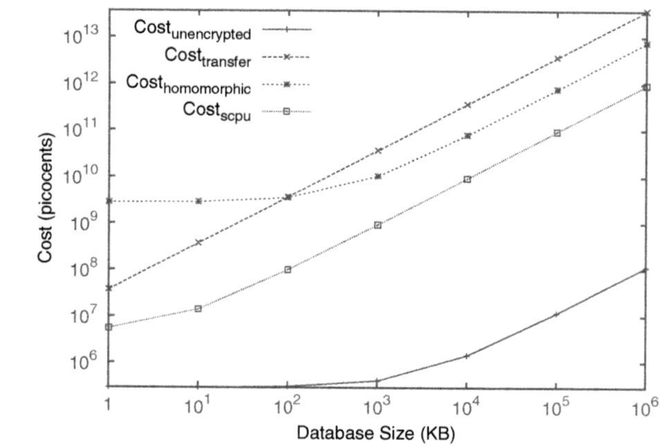

Figure 3: Comparison of outsourced aggregation query solutions (logarithmic)

Where δ_{srv} and δ_{scpu} are the server and SCPU cycles used to setup data transfer and include the cost of setting up and handling DMA interrupts. C_{cycle_scpu} is the cost of a SCPU cycle. $B_s = 64KB$ is the block size of data transmitted between the server and the SCPU in one round and B_c is the cipher block size (128 bits for AES). $\eta_{addition\_scpu} = 2$ is the number of cycles per addition operation in the SCPU for 64 bit addition (on a 32 bit architecture).

Figure 3 shows the cost relationship between the solutions. It can be seen that for any data set sizes $Cost_{scpu} < Cost_{homomorphic}$ and $Cost_{scpu} < Cost_{transfer}$. We also note that for data sets of size $< 100KB$, the cost of client-side homomorphic decryptions (which involves modular exponentiation) dominates and exceeds the data transmission cost in $Cost_{transfer}$. Overall, the use of SCPUs is the most efficient from a cost-centric point of view, by more than an order of magnitude when compared with cryptographic alternatives.

3.3 Generalized Argument

Yet, the use of a specific cryptographic mechanism in the analysis above seems to leave doubts regarding the generality of the conclusion. The fact that this holds today does not seem to imply its validity tomorrow. Thus, it would be important to provide a generalized argument as to why this conclusion should hold in general. We do so here.

Recall that current cryptographic constructs that guarantee confidentiality are based on trapdoor functions [21]. Currently viable trapdoors are based on modular exponentiation in large fields (e.g., 2048 bit modular operations) and viable homomorphisms involve a trapdoor for computing the ciphertexts (the encrypted data on which computations are performed). Additionally, the homomorphic operation itself involves processing these encrypted values at the server in large fields, while respecting the underlying encryption trapdoor. This involves at least the cost of a modular multiplication in large fields (e.g., 2048 or 4096 bits) [33, 34, 37]. This fundamental cryptography has not improved in efficiency in decades and would require the invention of new mathematical tools before such improvements are possible.

Thus, overall, for large scale, efficient deployments (e.g., clouds) where CPU cycles are extremely cheap (e.g., 0.45 picocents/cycle), performing (the cheapest, least secure) homomorphic operations (modular multiplication) comes at a pricetag of at least 30,000 picocents [14] even for values as small as 32-bit (e.g., salaries, zipcodes).

Thus, even if we assume that in future developments homomorphisms will be invented that can allow full Turing Machine languages to be "run" under the encryption envelope (today we can just add or multiply numbers), unless new trapdoor math is discovered (none was in the past 3+ decades), each operation will cost at least 30,000 picocents when run on efficient servers. By comparison, SCPUs process data at a cost of 56 picocents/cycle. This is a difference of several orders of magnitude in cost!. We also note that, while ECC signatures (e.g., even the weak ECC-192) may be faster, ECC-based trapdoors would be even more expensive, as they would require two point multiplications, coming at a price-tag of least 780,000 cycles ([17] page 402).

Yet, this is not entirely accurate, as we also need to account for the fact that SCPUs need to read data in before processing. The SCPUs considered here feature a decryption throughput of about 10-14 MBytes/second for AES decryption [5], confirmed also by our benchmarks. This limits the ability to process data and the real costs of e.g., comparing (in a JOIN operation) two 32-bit integers becomes dominated not by the single-cycle conditional JUMP CPU operation but by the cost of decryption. At 166-200 megacycles/second (recall the 4764 was benchmarked as 166-200MHz x86 equivalent), this results in the SCPU having to idly wait anywhere between 47 and 80 cycles for decryption to happen (in the crypto engine module) before it can process the data. This in effect results in an amortized SCPU cost of between 2632 and 4480 picocents (3556 picocents on average) for each operation which reduces the above 3 orders of magnitude difference to only one order of magnitude, yet still in favor of SCPUs [6].

The above holds even for the case when the SCPU has only enough memory for the two compared values. Further, in the presence of significantly higher, realistic amounts of SCPU memory (e.g., M = 32MBytes for 4764-001), optimizations can be achieved for certain types of queries such as relational JOINs. The SCPU can read in and decrypt data pages (instead of single data items) and run the (partial) JOIN query over as many of the decrypted data pages as would fit in memory at one time. This results in significant savings. To illustrate, consider a page size of P (32-bit words) and a simple JOIN algorithm for two tables of size N 32-bit integers each (we're just concerned with the join attribute). Then the SCPU will perform a number of $(N/P)^2 + (N/P)$ page fetches each involving also a page data decryption at a cost of $P \cdot 3556$ picocents[7]. Thus we get a total cost (decryption + operations) of $(\frac{N^2}{P} + N) \cdot 3556 + N^2 \cdot 56$. For reasonable sizes (e.g., $P = M/2/4 = 4$ million 32-bit words can be accommodated) this cost becomes 3+ orders of magnitude lower than the $N^2 \cdot 30000$ picocent cost incurred in the cryptography-based case!

Cost vs. Performance. Given these 3+ orders of magnitude cost advantages of the SCPU over cryptography-based mechanisms, we expect that for the above discussed aggregation query mechanism [42], the SCPU's overall *performance* will also be at least comparable if not better despite the CPU speed handicap. We experimentally evaluated this hy-

[6]The cost can be reduced further by up to 50% if instead of AES, a cipher is built using a faster cryptographic hash as a pseudo-random function [10].

[7]Recall that decrypting 32-bits incurs an amortized cost of around 3556 picocents.

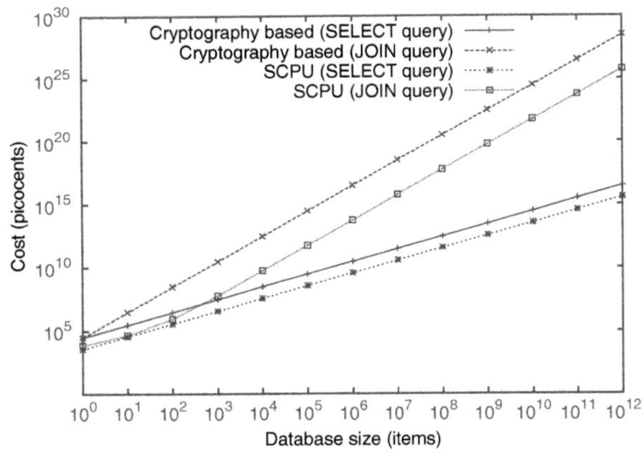

Figure 4: The SCPU is 1-5 orders of magnitude cheaper than deploying cryptography. (logarithmic)

pothesis and achieved a throughput of about 1.07 million tuples/second for the SCPU. By contrast, in [42] best-case scenario throughputs range between 0.58 and 0.92 million tuples/second (and at much higher overall cost).

Why Cost and Not Performance? Overall, we believe – despite being tightly related through the energy factor, *cost per transaction* constitutes an often more appropriate and practical metric of performance than overall *asymptotic runtime complexity* – which is neither meant to capture constants nor any other cost-driven performance factors. Moreover, transaction cost provides increased versatility in system design, allowing fine-tuning of a desired overall cost/performance ratio. This is especially true in scenarios involving highly-parallelizable processing, e.g., relational queries that can often be rewritten to target different data segments in parallel. In such cases, a straightforward strategy for maximizing performance while minimizing cost can be applied: pick the lowest per-transaction cost solution and allocate enough hardware resources to it to achieve a desired transaction throughput. We believe such cost-centric computing paradigms have the potential to fundamentally change the way systems and algorithms are designed.

Conclusion Summary. As Figure 4 illustrates, for linear processing queries (e.g., SELECT) the SCPU is roughly one+ order of magnitude cheaper than any cryptography based mechanisms. For JOIN queries, the SCPU costs drop even further even when assuming no available memory. Finally, in the presence of realistic amounts of memory, due to increased overhead amortization, the SCPU is *multiple* orders of magnitude cheaper than software-only cryptographic solutions on legacy hardware.

Cheaper Niches. We note that the above conclusion *may not* apply to targeted niche scenarios. E.g., it is entirely possible that by maintaining client pre-computed metadata server-side, processing of a pre-defined expected set of queries can be aided. To protect data confidentiality, this metadata requires the use of cryptography (by definition) – but due to the pre-computation step it *may* result in fewer such operations and a lower cost; all this while balancing a storage – expressivity – query arrival rate trade-off. This is a bit counter-intuitive – after all it seems that the access to the encrypted metadata brings us back to square one – but we should not pessimistically discount it yet. Depending on

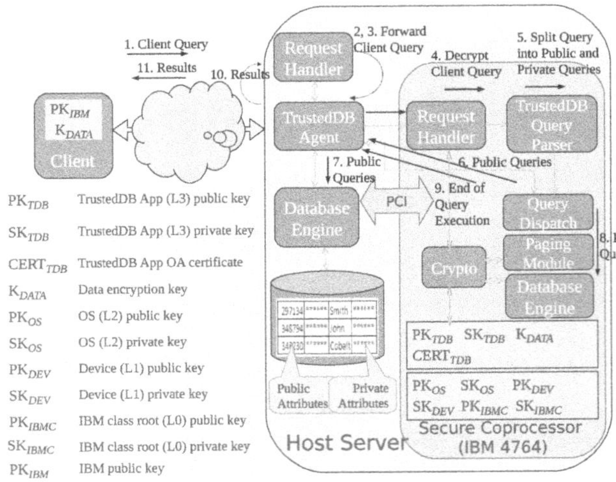

Figure 5: TrustedDB architecture

the cost of the additional required data storage at the time[8] and incoming query patterns, such query-targeted, niche solutions may turn out to be cheaper than general-purpose full-fledged SCPU-backed databases like TrustedDB.

4. ARCHITECTURE

TrustedDB is built around a set of core components (Figure 5) including a *request handler*, a *processing agent and communication conduit*, a *query parser*, a *paging module*, a *query dispatch module*, a *cryptography library*, and two *database engines*. While presenting a detailed architectural blueprint is not possible in this space, in the following we discuss some of the key elements and challenges faced in designing and building TrustedDB.

4.1 Outline

Challenges. The IBM 4764 SCPU presents significant challenges in designing and deploying custom code to be run within its enclosure. For strong security, the underlying hardware code as well as the OS are embedded and no hooks are possible e.g., to augment virtual memory and paging mechanisms. We were faced with the choice of having to provide virtual memory and paging in user land, specifically inside the query processor as well as all the support software. The embedded Linux OS is a Motorola PowerPC 405 port with stripped down libraries required to support the IBM cryptography codebase and nothing else. This constituted a significant hurdle, as cross-compilation became a complex task of mixing native logic with custom-ported functionality. The SCPU communicates with the outside world synchronously through fixed sized messages exchanged over the PCI-X bus in exact sequences. Interfacing such a synchronous channel with the communication model of the query processors and associated paging components required the development of the TrustedDB Paging Module. The SCPU's cryptographic hardware engine features a set of latencies that effectively crippled the ability to run for highly interactive mechanisms manipulating small amounts of data (e.g., 32 bit integers). To handle this we ported several cryptographic primitives to be run on the SCPU's

[8]Which will be a function of both the number of supported queries and the data size. Storing one bit for one year currently costs 100+ picocents [12–14].

Figure 6: Database Schema

main processor instead, and thus eliminate the hardware latencies for small data items. Space constraints prevent the discussion of the numerous other encountered challenges.

Overview. To remove SCPU-related storage limitations, the outsourced data is stored at the host provider's site. Query processing engines are run on both the server and in the SCPU. Attributes in the database are classified as being either public or private. Private attributes are encrypted and can only be decrypted by the client or by the SCPU.

Since the entire database resides outside the SCPU, its size is not bound by SCPU memory limitations. Pages that need to be accessed by the SCPU-side query processing engine are pulled in on demand by the Paging Module.

Query execution entails a set of stages. (0) In the first stage a client defines a database schema (and partially populates it). Sensitive attributes are marked, i.e., by deploying the "SENSITIVE" keyword that the client layer transparently processes by encrypting the corresponding attributes:

```
CREATE TABLE customer(ID integer primary key,
Name char(72) SENSITIVE, Address char(120) SENSITIVE);
```

(1) Later, a client sends a query request to the host server through a standard SQL interface. The query is transparently encrypted at the client site using the public key of the SCPU. The host server thus cannot decrypt the query. (2) The host server forwards the encrypted query to the Request Handler inside the SCPU. (3) The Request Handler decrypts the query and forwards it to the Query Parser. The query is parsed and rewritten as a set of sub-queries, and, according to their target data set classification, each query is identified as being either public or private. (4) The Query Dispatcher forwards the public queries to the host server and the private queries to the SCPU database engine while handling dependencies. The net result is that the maximum possible work is run on the host server's cheap cycles. (5) The final query result is assembled, encrypted (and digitally signed if correctness assurances are desired) by the SCPU database and the Query Dispatcher and sent back to the client.

4.2 Query Parsing

Outline. Sensitive attributes can occur anywhere within a query (e.g., in SELECT, WHERE or GROUP-BY clauses, in aggregation operators, or within sub-queries). The Query Parser's job is then:

- To ensure that any processing involving private attributes is done within the SCPU. All private attributes are encrypted using a shared data encryption keys between the client and the SCPU (Section 4.4), hence the host server cannot decipher these attributes.
- To optimize the rewrite of the client query such that most of the work is performed on the host server. This significantly increases performance.

To exemplify how public and private queries are generated from the original client query we use examples from the TPC-H benchmark [3]. TPC-H does not specify any classification of attributes based on security. Therefore, we define a attribute set classification into private (encrypted) and public (non-encrypted). The resultant schema is listed in Figure 6. In brief, all attributes that convey identifying information about Customers, Suppliers and Parts are considered private. The resulting query plans (including rewrites into main CPU and SCPU components) for TPC-H queries Q3, Q4, and Q6 are illustrated in Figure 7.

Aggregation Example. For queries that have WHERE clause conditions on public attributes, the server can first SELECT all the tuples that meet the criteria. The private attributes' queries are then performed inside the SCPU on these intermediate results, to yield the final result. For e.g., query *Q6* of the TPC-H benchmark is processed as shown in Figure 7 (a) [9]. The host server first executes a public query that filters all tuples which fall within the desired *ship date* and *quantity* range, both of these being public attributes. The result from this public query is then used by the SCPU to perform the aggregation on the private attributes *extended price* and *discount*. While performing the aggregation the private attributes are decrypted inside the SCPU. Since the aggregation operation results in a new attribute composing of private attributes it is re-encrypted before sending to the client. This encryption is also done within the SCPU.

Note that the execution of private queries depends on the results from the execution of public queries and vice-a-versa even though they execute in separate database engines. This is made possible by the TrustedDB Query Dispatcher in conjunction with the Paging Module.

Grouping Example. If the client query specifies a GROUP or ORDER BY on public attributes but the selection includes an aggregation of the private attributes, the grouping or sort operation is performed inside the SCPU. Figure 7 (b) illustrates this for the TPC-H query *Q3*. If the aggregation did not involve any private attributes then the host server performs all the GROUP BY and sorting operations.

Nested Queries. The case of nested queries is similar, yet additional care should be taken when computing execution plans to limit the amount of data transfer between the host server and the SCPU which may result in suboptimal performance. One such example is query *Q4* of the TPC-H benchmark which includes a sub-query on a private attribute. The query plan illustrated in Figure 7 (c) runs the removal of duplicates on attribute *order key* within the SCPU. An alternative would be to perform this operation on the host server. The choice to do this in the SCPU is made to reduce the traffic over the PCI interface. Efficient handling of nested queries is subject to ongoing work.

[9] More efficient query plans for these queries exist and constitute the subject of ongoing work.

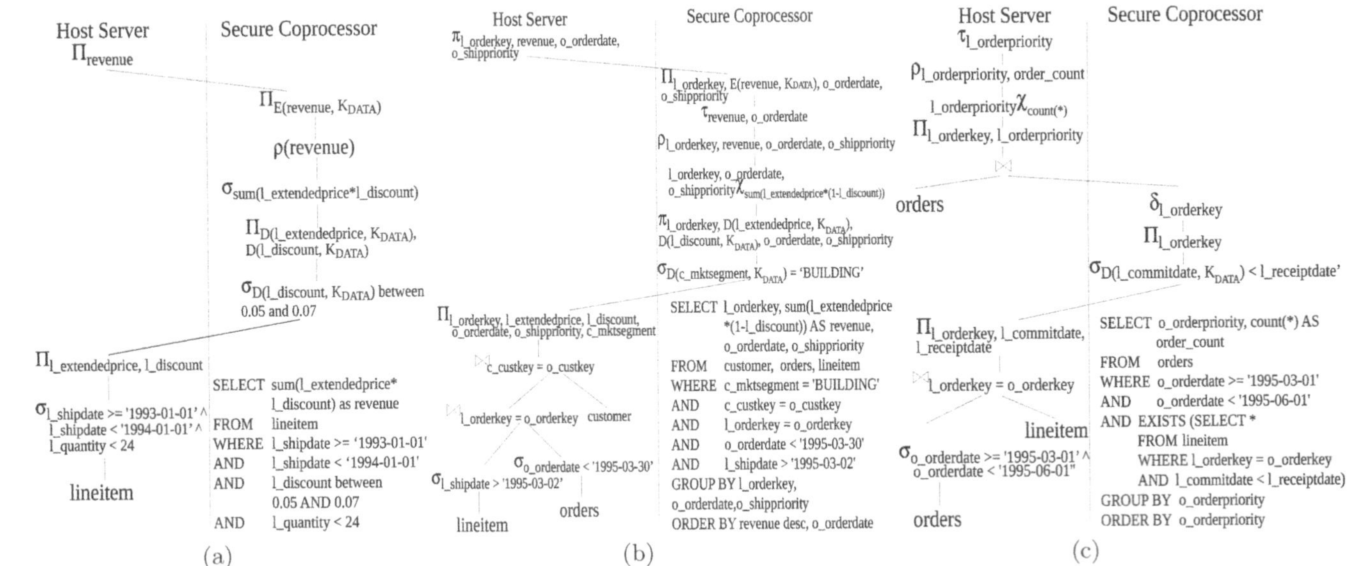

Figure 7: TrustedDB query plans for TPC-H queries (a) Q6, (b) Q3, and (c) Q4.

4.3 Dispatching. Paging. DBMS Engines.

The TrustedDB stack inside the SCPU includes a Query Dispatcher, a Paging Module and a DBMS Engine as well as a general communication conduit library running on top of the PCI-X bus. These components connect to the world through the server/host-side TrustedDB Agent running on the main server CPU.

As discussed above, the Query Dispatcher is in charge of forwarding public sub-queries to the host server and private queries to the SCPU DBMS Engine while handling all dependencies between the sub-queries. The main goal is to maximize the utilization of cheap cycles on the host server.

The SCPU DBMS Engine (a heavily modified PowerPC ported SQLite core) interfaces with the Paging Module to extend its database pages buffer pool with storage outsourced transparently on demand to the server. To achieve this, the TrustedDB Paging Module traps I/O requests made by the SCPU DBMS engine. It then interacts with the external TrustedDB Agent and (en)decrypts (e)ingres pages on demand. This paging mechanism is key in enabling support for large databases.

The main CPU DBMS is an unmodified MySQL 14.12 Distrib 5.0.45 engine. As the TrustedDB stack makes no assumptions about this engine, it can be substituted with any other SQL engine with minimal effort (SQL syntax related).

4.4 Security

Data Encryption is only one of the links in a chain of trust that ensures the security of TrustedDB. Several other assurances are required. Clients need to be confident that (i) the remote SCPU was not tampered with and (ii) runs the correct TrustedDB code stack (including the correct user-land TrustedDB modules as well as the underlying OS and SCPU hardware logic). Finally, clients need to have the means to (iii) communicate secretly with the TrustedDB modules running inside the SCPU.

(i) is assured by the tamper-resistant construction of the SCPU which meets the FIPS 140-2 level 4 [1] physical security requirements. In the event of SCPU tamper detection, sensitive memory areas containing critical secrets are automatically erased. (ii) can be ensured by deploying the SCPU *Outbound Authentication* [39] mechanisms discussed below. (iii) is achieved by deploying public-private key cryptography in key messaging stages. Both, client and the SCPU possess a public-private key pair (Figure 5). Not unlike HTTPS/SSL communication between a web-browser and server, messages sent between the client and the SCPU are encrypted [10]. The client's public key certificate and key PK_{CLIENT} is provided to the SCPU on demand. The SCPU public key is available via Outbound Authentication (OA). While full details are significantly more complex and out of scope [39], we now discuss the main OA insights.

Outbound Authentication. The main idea behind outbound authentication is to provide ways for clients to ascertain the security state of a remote secure processing unit that allows running of arbitrary code. This is achieved by bootstrapping a chain of trust rooted in the clients' trust in known basic pieces of logic running on the SCPU.

The SCPU is divided into four layers running software of differing levels of trust: Layer 0 (Miniboot 0 software), Layer 1 (Miniboot 1 software), Layer 2 (OS), and Layer 3 (application software). The layers can be loaded in increasing order of their number. Once loaded, each layer is issued a public key pair (Figure 5) certified by the layer below. The Layer 0 public key (PK_{IBMC}) is certified by the manufacturer using its private key. The Layer 1 public key (PK_{DEVICE}) is certified by the layer 0 private key (SK_{IBMC}). The Layer 2 public key (PK_{OS}) is certified by the layer 1 private key (SK_{DEVICE}) and finally the Layer 3 public key (PK_{TDB}) is certified by the layer 2 private key (SK_{OS}). This effectively builds a chain of trust rooted in the manufacturer's public key (PK_{IBM}). The chain of all these public key certificates constitutes the *Outbound Authentication certificate*. It can be used to provably assert to remote parties *what software* currently runs inside the SCPU as shown in Figure 8(a). The OA certificate guarantees that the public key PK_{TDB} indeed belongs to an application running inside a SCPU.

Moreover, the OA certificate chain also contains the signed crypto hash of the software installed in each Layer. By veri-

[10]And thus, despite acting as a communication conduit between the client and the SCPU, the server cannot perform man-in-the-middle attacks and gain access to sensitive data.

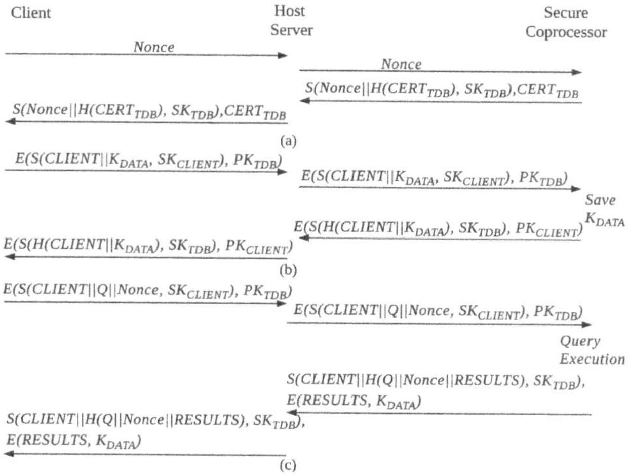

Figure 8: (a) Acquiring Outbound Authentication certificate. (b) Setup of Data Encryption Key. (c) Secure Transmission of query results

fying this software hash against an expected published value (e.g., for the TrustedDB stack) the client can trust the software executing in all the layers. If the software in any layer is updated then the key pairs for that layer and all layers above it will be re-generated and re-attested. The updated software hashes will be available the next time client requests an OA certificate. This satisfies requirement (ii).

The TrustedDB application running within the SCPU generates its own public-private key pair (PK_{TDB}, SK_{TDB}). Any request made by the client to the SCPU is encrypted using the public key PK_{TDB} (or a symmetric key generated out of a Diffie-Hellman key exchange). The client trusts the SCPU public key as it is attested to using the OA certificate.

Data Encryption. While communication security has been discussed above, data confidentiality still remains to be guarded. The client database consists of public (non-encrypted) and private (encrypted) attributes. The private attributes are transparently encrypted by the client layer before the database is uploaded to the host server or as part of any insert/update queries. The encryption is performed using the data encryption key K_{DATA} generated by the client (of at least 160 bits [10]). The TrustedDB stack within the SCPU gains access to this key as shown in Figure 8(b).

Conversely, when query execution generates new *private* attributes they are encrypted inside the SCPU before sending them back to the client. E.g., consider the query `SELECT avg(SALARY) FROM EMPLOYEES`. The result of `avg(SALARY)` is an aggregation over an existing private attribute. In this case the result is encrypted inside the SCPU using the key K_{DATA} (Figure 8(c) - and signed if needed for authenticity) before transmitting back to the client[11].

For increased efficiency, different avenues for data encryption are available. (I) In the simplest case, the entire database is encrypted at page level and TrustedDB is fetching and decrypting *pages* on demand. This features the highest throughput, but limits the ability to use the main CPU's cycles in the process (as the data set is first decrypted inside the SCPU before anything). This case is suitable for queries on data sets that feature ONLY sensitive attributes. (II) For more complex queries, a straightforward application of a symmetric encryption mechanism such as AES can be envisioned. Each tuple is encrypted separately with K_{DATA} and some randomness added to ensure indistinguishability. This mechanism is viable for BLOBS and large-sized attribute values (e.g., hundreds of KBytes+) but less so for small data items such as integers due to encryption latencies and ciphertext blow-up factors. (III) Finally, for fine-grained encryption of data, each individual attribute value within each tuple is encrypted separately with random keys generated by a cryptographic hash function based cipher initialized with K_{DATA} and per-tuple additional data that guarantees its uniqueness across the entire database. Extensive details and cryptographic proofs are out of scope. The result is based on a NMAC construction [10, 21]:

$$\begin{aligned} E(tbl.attr.val) &= ctr_{attr} \mid\mid tbl.pri\_key \mid\mid idx_K \mid\mid (tbl.attr.val \oplus k) \\ k &= F(K_{DATA}[idx_K] \mid\mid ctr_{attr} \mid\mid tbl.pri\_key \mid\mid F(K_{DATA}[idx_K])) \end{aligned} \quad (5)$$

where *tbl* is the table name, *tbl.attr* is the attribute to be considered, *tbl.attr.val* is the plaintext value of the current tuple, *tbl.pri_key* is the primary key of the current tuple in table *tbl*, ctr_{attr} is a unique identifying number associated with *tbl.attr*[12], idx_K is an index in a table of K_{DATA} keys which allows multiple such keys to exist simultaneously (and be refreshed periodically) for increased security, and $F(\cdot)$ is a cryptographic hash function (SHA,MD5) [10][13].

5. DISCUSSION

Handling Database Updates. Data manipulation queries (INSERT, UPDATE) also undergo a rewrite. Moreover, any new generated attribute values are re-encrypted within the SCPU before updating the database. For illustration, consider the query `UPDATE EMPLOYEES SET SALARY = SALARY + 2000 WHERE ZIP = 98239`. If `SALARY` is a private attribute then the query works by first decrypting the `SALARY` attribute, performing the addition and then re-encrypting the updated values and is executed within the SCPU. On the other hand if `SALARY` is a public attribute then the query will be executed entirely by the host server.

Limitations of the current query parser. The current query parser does not provide efficient support for query nesting, specifically for queries with large intermediate results. In ongoing work we try to understand whether something can be done to alleviate the costs associated with such large intermediate results that need to be transfered synchronously through the SCPU. A key element in future work will involve designing query parsers to generate efficient query plans while optimizing trade-offs between multiple metrics such as overall dollar cost of execution or performance, in addition to data confidentiality constraints.

Access Patterns. The current implementation reveals access patterns to the externally stored data pages. While this may not be an issue in many applications, it would be interesting to explore the deployment of efficient private information retrieval mechanisms to prevent the server from learning these patterns.

Caching. TrustedDB query execution can result in intermediary results which can often be cached and re-used for

[11]We note that in this case, also correctness guarantees – against an actively malicious server – can be achieved for free, but only for queries involving solely private attributes.

[12]For storage efficiency we don't want to use the entire *tbl.attr* value in the result.

[13]Note that the known MD5 *collision - resistance* related vulnerabilities are not a problem here where it is used as a source of randomness only.

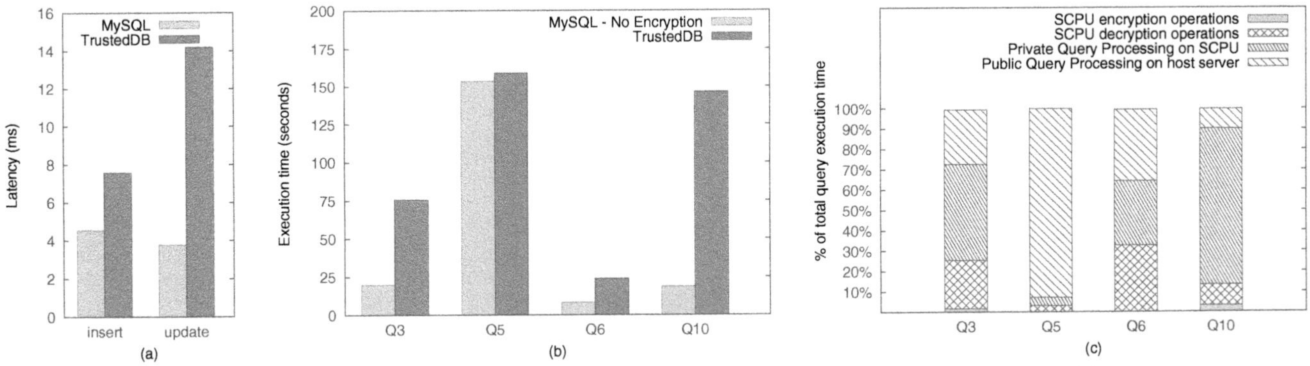

Figure 9: (a) Query latencies. (b) Execution times. (c) Query time profile.

efficiency. Similarly, the query plan decisions need not be repeated, but rather previously devised plans can be cached, e.g., for hot queries. The plans can be encrypted and stored on external storage with the aid of the Paging Module.

Parallelism. The current prototype runs on a single SCPU. An extension to multiple SCPUs is straightforward and would allow better scaling to target desired throughputs.

Compliance. TrustedDB can also be easily augmented with a Compliance Module to support regulatory compliance. Policies that regulate data can be communicated to and enforced by the SCPU securely at runtime. Since sensitive attributes are only accessed within the SCPU the enforcement of policies is guaranteed at very little additional cost. An example of such a compliance policy would be to enforce tuple-level mandatory retention times as well as additional lifecycle management enablers.

6. EXPERIMENTS

Setup. The SCPU of choice is the IBM 4764-001 PCI-X with the 3.30.05 release toolkit featuring 32MBytes of RAM and a PowerPC 405GPr at 233 MHz. The SCPU sits on the PCI-X bus of an Intel Xeon 3.4 GHz, 4GB RAM Linux box (kernel 2.6.18). The server DBMS is a standard MySQL 14.12 Distrib 5.0.45 engine. The SCPU DBMS is a heavily modified SQLite custom port to the PowerPC. The TrustedDB stack (including Communication Conduit, Query Parser, Query Dispatcher, Paging Module, Crypto Engine, TrustedDB Agent etc.) is written in C.

Throughput and Latency. In Section 3 we discussed a benchmarked throughput of 10-14 MB/second for page-level AES encryption. We have also discussed how to achieve a 1+ million tuples/second throughput in an aggregation query on relational data that does not involve public attributes.

While the above numbers are impressive, they only hold for niche cases such as aggregation. For *general* queries, the data needs to be provided encrypted per-tuple with additional fields that allow the SCPU DBMS to reconstruct the individual tuple decryption key (equation (5), Section 4.4).

In such cases, fewer optimizations are possible, and the resulting queries have higher execution times. For example for $F(\cdot)$=MD5 in equation (5), TrustedDB can achieve sustained I/O decryption throughputs of over 80,000 sensitive attribute values per second, and does not limit the non-sensitive data related throughput (processed by the server).

A comparison of MySQL and TrustedDB latencies of INSERT and UPDATE queries are illustrated in Figure 9 (a) and are likely dominated by I/O elements in both cases.

TPC-H Query Load. To evaluate the runtime of generalized queries, instead of concocting our own, we chose several non-nested[14] queries ($Q3$, $Q5$, $Q6$ and $Q10$) from the TPC-H set [3] of varying degrees of difficulty and privacy. These queries all target the standard TPC-H schema in Figure 6 augmented with SENSITIVE attributes. The TPC-H scale factor was 1 (database size of $1GB$).

These queries were selected as they require operations on private attributes and are sufficiently complex. Figure 9 (b) shows the execution times compared to a simple unencrypted MySQL setup.

Figure 9 (c) also depicts the breakdown of times spent in execution of the public (executed on host server) and private (executed on the SCPU) sub-queries. The execution times of private queries include the time required for encryption and decryption operations inside the SCPU. The public queries executed on the host server also include the processing times to interface the TrustedDB stack with the server database engine and output the final results.

As can be seen, when compared with the completely unsecured baseline, security does not come cheap – the execution times are higher by factors between 1.03 and 7.8. These factors benefit from the TrustedDB leveraging of the untrusted server's CPU for non-sensitive query portions. However, recall from Section 3 that the actual costs are orders of magnitude lower than any solution based on software-only cryptography on legacy server hardware.

7. RELATED WORK

Trusted Hardware in Data Management. In [9] SCPUs are used to retrieve X509 certificates from a database.

[38] uses multiple SCPUs to provide key based search. The entire database is scanned by the SCPUs to return matching records. [36, 44] implement arbitrary joins by reading the entire database through the SCPU.

Chip-Secured Data Access [29] uses a smart card for query processing and for enforcing access rights. The client query is split into three parts - server, client and a terminal query. The idea is that the server query performs majority of the computation. The solution is limited by the fact that the client query executing within the smart cannot generate any

[14]Recall that the TrustedDB query parser does not yet efficiently support query nesting, especially when it results in large intermediary results.

intermediate results since there is no storage available on the card. In follow-up work, GhostDB [32] proposes to embed a database inside an USB key equipped with a CPU. It "allows linking [of] private data carried on the USB Key and public data available on a public server. GhostDB ensures that the only information revealed to a potential spy is the query issued and the public data accessed."

[28, 31] explore the use and limitations of SCPUs for outsourced databases and "sketch how a practical system meeting the definition could be built and proven secure".

[8] discusses the use of a SCPU-based service in a secure multi-party setting in which " participating data providers send encrypted relations to the service that sends the encrypted results to the recipients".

In [11] a database engine is proposed inside a SCPU for data sharing and mining. The SCPU fetches data from external sources using secure jdbc connections. The entire data is treated as private which means that queries must be completely executed inside the coprocessor and the host server resources are not utilized. The overhead of jdbc connections is between 20% and 70% of the total query processing time.

Queries on Encrypted Data. Hacigumus et al. [23] propose a method to execute SQL queries over partly obfuscated outsourced data. The data is divided into secret partitions and queries over the original data can be rewritten in terms of the resulting partition identifiers; the server then performs queries over the partitions. The information leaked to the server is claimed to be 1-out-of-s where s is the partition size. This balances a trade-off between client-side and server-side processing, as a function of the data segment size. At one extreme, privacy is completely compromised (small segment sizes) but client processing is minimal. At the other extreme, a high level of privacy can be attained at the expense of the client processing the queries in their entirety after retrieving the entire dataset.

In [24] the authors explore optimal bucket sizes for certain range queries. Similarly, data partitioning is deployed in building "almost"-private indexes on attributes considered sensitive. An untrusted server is then able to execute "obfuscated range queries with minimal information leakage". An associated privacy-utility trade-off for the index is discussed. The main drawbacks of these solutions lies in the fact that the cost-security trade-off is linear. The increase in security is linear in the increase in the cost of the solution, not unlike case (A) in Section 3.

Aggregation queries over relational databases is provided in [22] by making use of homomorphic encryption based on Privacy Homomorphism [37]. The authors in [18] have suggested that this scheme is vulnerable to a cipher text only attack. Instead [18] proposes an alternative scheme to perform aggregation queries based on bucketization [23]. Here the data owner precomputes aggregate values such as SUM and COUNT for partitions and stores them encrypted at the server. Although this makes processing of certain queries faster it does not significantly reduce client side processing.

Query Correctness. Numerous query correctness solutions for outsourced frameworks have been proposed. Due to space constraints we direct the reader to [20].

8. CONCLUSIONS

This paper's contributions are two-fold: (i) the introduction of new cost models and insights that explain and quantify the advantages of deploying trusted hardware for data processing, and (ii) the design and development of TrustedDB, a trusted hardware based relational database with full data confidentiality and no limitations on query expressiveness.

This work's inherent thesis is that, at scale, in outsourced contexts, computation inside secure hardware processors is orders of magnitude cheaper than any equivalent cryptography performed on a provider's unsecured common server hardware, despite the overall greater acquisition cost of secure hardware. We thus propose to make trusted hardware a first-class citizen in the secure data management arena. Moreover, we hope that cost-centric insights and architectural paradigms will fundamentally change the way systems and algorithms are designed.

9. ACKNOWLEDGMENTS

We would like to thank Sumeet Dash and Nilesh Mahajan for their help with implementing TrustedDB, as well as our sponsors, NSF (0937833, 0845192, 0803197), CA Technologies, NGC, Xerox, IBM, and Microsoft.

10. REFERENCES

[1] FIPS PUB 140-2, Security Requirements for Cryptographic Modules. Online at http://csrc.nist.gov/groups/STM/cmvp/standards.html#02.

[2] The UBENCH Toolkit. Online at http://www.phystech.com/download/ubench.html.

[3] TPC-H Benchmark. Online at http://www.tpc.org/tpch/.

[4] IBM 4758 PCI Cryptographic Coprocessor. Online at http://www-03.ibm.com/security/cryptocards/pcicc/overview.shtml, 2006.

[5] IBM 4764 PCI-X Cryptographic Coprocessor. Online at http://www-03.ibm.com/security/cryptocards/pcixcc/overview.shtml, 2007.

[6] IBM 4765 PCIe Cryptographic Coprocessor. Online at http://www-03.ibm.com/security/cryptocards/pciecc/overview.shtml, 2010.

[7] Daniel Abadi, Michael J. Carey, Surajit Chaudhuri, Hector Garcia-Molina, Jignesh M. Patel, and Raghu Ramakrishnan. Cloud databases: What's new? *PVLDB*, 3(2):1657, 2010.

[8] Rakesh Agrawal, Dmitri Asonov, Murat Kantarcioglu, and Yaping Li. Sovereign joins. In Ling Liu, Andreas Reuter, Kyu-Young Whang, and Jianjun Zhang, editors, *ICDE*, page 26. IEEE Computer Society, 2006.

[9] Alexander Iliev and Sean W Smith. Protecting Client Privacy with Trusted Computing at the Server. *IEEE, Security and Privacy*, 3(2), Apr 2005.

[10] Mihir Bellare. New proofs for nmac and hmac: Security without collision-resistance. pages 602–619. Springer-Verlag, 2006.

[11] Bishwaranjan Bhattacharjee, Naoki Abe, Kenneth Goldman, Bianca Zadrozny, Chid Apte, Vamsavardhana R. Chillakuru and Marysabel del Carpio. Using secure coprocessors for privacy preserving collaborative data mining and analysis. In *Proceedings of the 2nd international workshop on Data management on new hardware*, 2006.

[12] Yao Chen and Radu Sion. On the (Im)Practicality of Securing Untrusted Computing Clouds with

Cryptography. Online at `http://www.cs.sunysb.edu/~sion/research/`.

[13] Yao Chen and Radu Sion. To Cloud or Not To. Online at `http://www.cs.sunysb.edu/~sion/research/`.

[14] Yao Chen and Radu Sion. On securing untrusted clouds with cryptography. In *WPES '10: Proceedings of the 9th annual ACM workshop on Privacy in the electronic society*, pages 109–114, New York, NY, USA, 2010. ACM.

[15] CNN. Feds seek Google records in porn probe. Online at `http://www.cnn.com`, January 2006.

[16] CNN. YouTube ordered to reveal its viewers. Online at `http://www.cnn.com`, July 2008.

[17] Tom Denis. *Cryptography for Developers*. Syngress.

[18] Einar Mykletun and Gene Tsudik. Aggregation Queries in the Database-As-a-Service Model. *Data and Applications Security*, 4127, 2006.

[19] Rosario Gennaro, Craig Gentry, and Bryan Parno. Non-interactive verifiable computing: Outsourcing computation to untrusted workers. In Tal Rabin, editor, *CRYPTO*, volume 6223 of *Lecture Notes in Computer Science*, pages 465–482. Springer, 2010.

[20] Michael Gertz and Sushil Jajodia. *Handbook of Database Security: Applications and Trends*. Springer.

[21] O. Goldreich. *Foundations of Cryptography I*. Cambridge University Press, 2001.

[22] Bala Iyer Hakan Hacigumus and Sharad Mehrotra. Efficient execution of aggregation queries over encrypted relational databases. In *Database Systems for Advanced Applications*, volume 2973, pages 633–650, 2004.

[23] Hakan Hacigumus, Bala Iyer, Chen Li and Sharad Mehrotra. Executing SQL over Encrypted Data in the Database-Service-Provider Model. In *Proceedings of the 2002 ACM SIGMOD international conference on Management of data*, pages 216–227, 2002.

[24] B. Hore, S. Mehrotra, and G. Tsudik. A privacy-preserving index for range queries. In *Proceedings of ACM SIGMOD*, 2004.

[25] HweeHwa Pang and Arpit Jain and Krithi Ramamritham and Kian-Lee Tan. Verifying Completeness of Relational Query Results in Data Publishing. In *Proceedings of ACM SIGMOD*, 2005.

[26] Intel. *Intel 64 and IA-32 Architectures Optimization Reference Manual*, 2008.

[27] Joan G. Dyer, Mark Lindemann, Ronald Perez, Reiner Sailer and Leendert van Doorn. Building the IBM 4758 Secure Coprocessor. *IEEE*, 34(10), 2001.

[28] Murat Kantarcioglu and Chris Clifton. Security issues in querying encrypted data. In Sushil Jajodia and Duminda Wijesekera, editors, *DBSec*, volume 3654 of *Lecture Notes in Computer Science*, pages 325–337. Springer, 2005.

[29] Luc Bouganim and Philippe Pucheral. Chip-secured data access: confidential data on untrusted server. In *Proceedings of the 28th international conference on Very Large Data Bases*, pages 131–141. VLDB Endowment, 2002.

[30] Maithili Narasimha and Gene Tsudik. DSAC: integrity for outsourced databases with signature aggregation and chaining. In *Proceedings of the 14th ACM international conference on Information and knowledge management*, pages 235–236, 2005.

[31] Einar Mykletun and Gene Tsudik. Incorporating a secure coprocessor in the database-as-a-service model. In *IWIA '05: Proceedings of the Innovative Architecture on Future Generation High-Performance Processors and Systems*, pages 38–44, Washington, DC, USA, 2005. IEEE Computer Society.

[32] Nicolas Anciaux, Mehdi Benzine, Luc Bouganim, Philippe Pucheral and Dennis Shasha. GhostDB: Querying Visible and Hidden Data Without Leaks. In *Proceedings of the ACM SIGMOD international conference on Management of data*, 2007.

[33] P. Paillier. Public-key cryptosystems based on composite degree residuosity classes. In *Proceedings of EuroCrypt*, 1999.

[34] Pascal Paillier. A trapdoor permutation equivalent to factoring. In *PKC '99: Proceedings of the Second International Workshop on Practice and Theory in Public Key Cryptography*, pages 219–222, London, UK, 1999. Springer-Verlag.

[35] M. O. Rabin. Digitalized signatures and public-key functions as intractable as factorization. Technical report, Cambridge, MA, USA, 1979.

[36] Rakesh Agrawal, Dmitri Asonov, Murat Kantarcioglu, Yaping Li. Sovereign Joins. In *Proceedings of the 22nd International Conference on Data Engineering*, page 26. IEEE Computer Society, 2006.

[37] Ronald Rivest, Len Adleman and Michael Dertouzos. On data banks and privacy homomorphisms. *Foundations of Secure Computation*, 1978.

[38] S. W. Smith and D. Safford. Practical server privacy with secure coprocessors. *IBM SYSTEMS JOURNAL*, 40(3), 2001.

[39] Sean W. Smith. Outbound authentication for programmable secure coprocessors. Online at `http://citeseerx.ist.psu.edu/viewdoc/summary?doi=10.1.1.58.4066`.

[40] Michael Stonebraker, Daniel J. Abadi, David J. DeWitt, Samuel Madden, Erik Paulson, Andrew Pavlo, and Alexander Rasin. Mapreduce and parallel dbmss: friends or foes? *Commun. ACM*, 53(1):64–71, 2010.

[41] Alexander Thomson and Daniel J. Abadi. The case for determinism in database systems. *PVLDB*, 3(1):70–80, 2010.

[42] Tingjian Ge and Stan Zdonik. Answering Aggregation Queries in a Secure System Model. In *Proceedings of the 33rd international conference on Very large data bases*, pages 519–530. VLDB Endowment, 2007.

[43] Marten van Dijk, Craig Gentry, Shai Halevi, and Vinod Vaikuntanathan. Fully homomorphic encryption over the integers. In Henri Gilbert, editor, *EUROCRYPT*, volume 6110 of *Lecture Notes in Computer Science*, pages 24–43. Springer, 2010.

[44] Yaping Li. Privacy Preserving Joins on Secure Coprocessors. Technical Report UCB/EECS-2008-158, EECS Department, University of California Berkeley, Dec 2008. `http://www.eecs.berkeley.edu/Pubs/TechRpts/2008/EECS-2008-158.html`.

Differentially Private Data Cubes: Optimizing Noise Sources and Consistency

Bolin Ding[1] Marianne Winslett[2,1] Jiawei Han[1] Zhenhui Li[1]
[1]Department of Computer Science, University of Illinois at Urbana-Champaign, IL, USA
[2]Advanced Digital Sciences Center, Singapore
{bding3, winslett, hanj, zli28}@uiuc.edu

ABSTRACT

Data cubes play an essential role in data analysis and decision support. In a data cube, data from a *fact table* is aggregated on subsets of the table's dimensions, forming a collection of smaller tables called *cuboids*. When the fact table includes sensitive data such as salary or diagnosis, publishing even a subset of its cuboids may compromise individuals' privacy. In this paper, we address this problem using *differential privacy* (DP), which provides provable privacy guarantees for individuals by adding noise to query answers. We choose an initial subset of cuboids to compute directly from the fact table, injecting DP noise as usual; and then compute the remaining cuboids from the initial set. Given a fixed privacy guarantee, we show that it is NP-hard to choose the initial set of cuboids so that the maximal noise over all published cuboids is minimized, or so that the number of cuboids with noise below a given threshold (*precise cuboids*) is maximized. We provide an efficient procedure with running time polynomial in the number of cuboids to select the initial set of cuboids, such that the maximal noise in all published cuboids will be within a factor $(\ln|\mathcal{L}| + 1)^2$ of the optimal, where $|\mathcal{L}|$ is the number of cuboids to be published, or the number of precise cuboids will be within a factor $(1 - 1/e)$ of the optimal. We also show how to enforce consistency in the published cuboids while simultaneously improving their utility (reducing error). In an empirical evaluation on real and synthetic data, we report the amounts of error of different publishing algorithms, and show that our approaches outperform baselines significantly.

Categories and Subject Descriptors

H.2.8 [**DATABASE MANAGEMENT**]: Database Applications—*Data mining*; H.2.7 [**DATABASE MANAGEMENT**]: Database Administration—*Security, integrity, and protection*

General Terms

Algorithms, Security, Theory

Keywords

OLAP, data cube, differential privacy, private data analysis

1. INTRODUCTION

Data cubes play an essential role in multidimensional data analysis and fast OLAP operations. Often the underlying data is sensitive, and publishing all or part of the cube may endanger the privacy of individuals. For example, privacy concerns prevent Singapore's Ministry of Health (MOH) from performing wide-scale monitoring for adverse drug reactions among Singapore's three main ethnic groups, none of which are typically included in pharmaceutical companies' drug trials. Privacy concerns also limit MOH's published health summary tables to extremely coarse categories, reducing their utility for policy planning. Institutional Review Board (IRB) approval is now required for access to most high-level summary tables from studies funded by the US National Institutes of Health, making it very hard to leverage results from past studies to plan new studies. In these and many other scenarios, society can greatly benefit from the publication of detailed, high-utility data cubes that also preserve individuals' privacy.

The data cube of a fact table consists of *cells* and *cuboids*. A cell aggregates the rows in the fact table that match on certain dimensions. The fact table in Figure 1(a) has three dimensions, to be aggregated with count measure. As in Figures 1(b)-1(d), a cuboid can be viewed as the projection of a fact table on a subset of dimensions, producing a set of cells with associated aggregate measures.

With background knowledge, an adversary can infer sensitive information about an individual from a published cube [16, 21, 35]. For example, in the data cube in Figure 1, if we know that Alice is aged 31-40 and is in the table, the count in cuboid {Age, Salary} tells us her salary is 50-200k. If we know Bob is in the table and is aged 21-30, we learn there is a 75% chance that his salary is 10-50k and a 25% chance it is 50-200k. If we also know that Carl, aged 21-30 and with salary 50-200k, is in the table, then the values of count in cuboid {Age, Salary} tell us Bob's salary is 10-50k.

Even publishing large actual aggregate counts is still not safe, if an adversary has enough background knowledge. For example, suppose there are 100 individuals in a fact table (Sex, Age, Salary), and we publish two cells ($*$, $*$, 10-50k) and ($*$, $*$, 50-200k), both with count equal to 50. Suppose the adversary knows everyone's salary except Bob's: if 49 people have salary 10-50k and 50 have 50-200k, then s/he can infer that Bob's salary is 10-50k.

We apply the notion of *ϵ-differential privacy* [10] (DP or ϵ-DP for short in the rest of this paper) in data cube publishing. Compared to previous techniques for privacy-preserving data publishing (see [2, 15] for surveys), DP makes very conservative assumptions about the adversary's background knowledge. The privacy guarantee it provides is independent of any background knowledge the adversary may have about the database. In particular, a publishing algorithm satisfying DP protects the privacy of any individual row in the database even if the adversary knows every other row [10].

Sex	Age	Salary
F	21-30	10-50k
F	21-30	10-50k
F	31-40	50-200k
F	41-50	500k+
M	21-30	10-50k
M	21-30	50-200k
M	31-40	50-200k
M	60+	500k+

(a) Fact Table T

Sex	Age	Salary	c
*	*	0-10k	0
*	*	10-50k	3
*	*	50-200k	3
*	*	...	...

(b) Cuboid {Salary}

Sex	Age	Salary	c
F	21-30	0-10k	0
F	21-30	10-50k	2
...	...	...	...

(c) Cuboid {Sex, Age, Salary}

Sex	Age	Salary	c
*	21-30	0-10k	0
*	21-30	10-50k	3
*	21-30	50-200k	1
*	21-30	200-500k	0
*	21-30	500k+	0
*	31-40	0-10k	0
*	31-40	10-50k	0
*	31-40	50-200k	2
*	31-40	200-500k	0
*	31-40	500k+	0
*	...	...	...

(d) Cuboid {Age, Salary}

Figure 1: Fact Table and count Data Cube

Informally, DP guarantees that the presence/absence or specific value of any particular individual's record has a negligible impact on the likelihood that a particular result is returned to a query. Thus an adversary cannot make meaningful inferences about any one individual's record values, or even whether the record was present.

One way to achieve DP is to add random noise to query results [10]. The noise is carefully calibrated to the query's *sensitivity*, which measures the total change of the query output under a small change of the input. As the variance of the noise increases, the privacy guarantee becomes stronger, but the utility of the result drops.

To publish an ϵ-DP data cube over d dimensions, there are two baselines. (i) We can compute the count measure for each cuboid from the fact table, and then add noise to each cell. As changing one row in the table affects 2^d cells, according to [12], each cell needs Laplace noise $\text{Lap}(2^d/\epsilon)$, which destroys the utility of the cube unless d is small. The same idea is applied in [4] to publish a set of marginals of a contingency table. (ii) If we only compute count for the *base cuboid* ({Sex, Age, Salary} in Figure 1(c)) from the fact table, $\text{Lap}(1/\epsilon)$ suffices. We compute the other cuboids from the noisy base cuboid to ensure DP. However, noise in high-level cuboids, such as {Salary}, will be magnified significantly, and utility will be low. This idea can be applied to universal histograms, but noise accumulation also makes them ineffective there [19].

Another possible way is to treat each cell in a cuboid as a query, and apply methods in [23] to answer a workload of count queries while ensuring DP. But this approach is not practical in our context, as its running time/space is at least quadratic in the number of cells.

If we roll up measures across DP cuboids, the sums may not match the totals recorded in other cuboids. According to a Microsoft user study [1], users are likely to accept these kinds of small inconsistencies if they trust the original data and understand why the inconsistencies are present. However, if the users do not trust the original data, they may interpret the inconsistencies as evidence of bad data. So it is desirable to enforce a requirement for correct roll-up totals across dimensions in the DP cuboids to be published. Consistency also boosts accuracy of DP data publishing in some cases, e.g., in answering one-dimensional range queries [19].

Contributions. We study how to *publish all or part of a data cube for a given fact table, while ensuring ϵ-differential privacy and limiting the variance of the noise added to the cube.* We propose a general noise control framework in which a subset $\mathcal{L}_{\text{pre}}$ of cuboids is computed from the fact table, plus random noise. The remaining cuboids are computed directly from those in $\mathcal{L}_{\text{pre}}$, which is the "source of noise". When $\mathcal{L}_{\text{pre}}$ is larger, each of its members requires more noise, but the cuboids computed from $\mathcal{L}_{\text{pre}}$ accumulate less noise. So a clever selection of $\mathcal{L}_{\text{pre}}$ can reduce the overall noise.

We define two publishing scenarios that fit the needs of the Ministry of Health. In the first scenario, MOH identifies a set of cuboids which must be released, and the goal is to minimize the max noise in the cuboids. In the second scenario, MOH has a large body of cross-tabulations that can be useful for urban planners and the medical community. A weighting function indicates the importance of releasing each cuboid. The question is, which of these cuboids can be released in a DP manner, while respecting a given noise variance bound for each cell (called *precise cuboids*)–the goal is to maximize the sum of the weights of the released precise cuboids.

We formalize these two optimization problems for the selection of $\mathcal{L}_{\text{pre}}$, prove that they are NP-hard, and give efficient algorithms with provable approximation guarantees. For the first problem, the max noise variance in all published cuboids will be within a factor $(\ln|\mathcal{L}|+1)^2$ of optimal, where $|\mathcal{L}|$ is the number of cuboids to be published; and for the second, the number/weight of precise cuboids will be within a factor $(1-1/e)$ of optimal.

We also show how to enforce consistency over a DP data cube by computing a *consistent measure* from the *noisy measure* released by a DP algorithm. We minimize the L^p distance between the consistent measure and the noisy measure. The revised data cube is still DP, as we do not revisit the fact table when enforcing consistency. The consistency-enforcing techniques in [4] are similar to our L^∞ version, but our L^1 version yields a much better theoretical bound on error than the L^∞ version. We show that in the L^2 version, the consistent measure can be computed efficiently, and provide better utility than the original inconsistent noisy measure.

Organization. Section 2 provides background for data cubes and DP, plus our noise-control goals. Section 3 gives our noise-control publishing framework and formalizes the optimization problems for noise control. Section 4 gives approximation algorithms for these problems. Section 5 shows how to enforce consistency across cuboids. Experimental results are reported in Section 6, followed by discussion and extension of our techniques in Section 7, and related work in Section 8. Proofs of all theorems are in the Appendix.

2. BACKGROUND AND PROBLEM

Data Cubes

Consider a *fact table* T with d *nominal dimensions* $\mathcal{A}=\{A_1, A_2, \ldots, A_d\}$. We also use A_i to denote the set of all possible values for the ith dimension, and $|A_i|$ to denote the number of distinct values (i.e., *cardinality*). For a row $r \in T$, $r[i]$ is r's value for A_i.

The *data cube* of T consists of *cells* and *cuboids*. A cell a takes the form $(a[1], a[2], \ldots, a[d])$, where $a[i] \in (A_i \cup \{*\})$ denotes the ith dimension's value for this cell. A cell is associated with certain aggregate measure of interest. In this paper, we first focus on the count *measure* $\mathsf{c}(a)$ and discuss how to handle other measures in Section 7.3. $\mathsf{c}(a)$ is the number of rows r in T that are aggregated in cell a (with the same values on non-$*$ dimensions of a): $\mathsf{c}(a) = |\{r \in T \mid \forall 1 \le i \le d,\ r[i] = a[i] \vee a[i] = *\}|$.

Cell a is an *m-dim cell* if exactly m of $a[1], a[2], \ldots, a[d]$ are *not* $*$. An *m-dim cuboid* C is specified by m dimensions $[C] = \{A_{i_1}, A_{i_2}, \ldots, A_{i_m}\}$. The cuboid C consists of all m-dim cells a such that $\forall 1 \le k \le m$, $a[i_k] \in A_{i_k}$, and C can be interpreted as the projection of T on the set of dimensions $[C]$. The d-dim cuboid is called the *base cuboid* and the cells in it are *base cells*.

For two cuboids C_1 and C_2, if $[C_1] \subseteq [C_2]$ (denoted as $C_1 \preceq C_2$), then (measures of cells in) C_1 can be computed from C_2. C_1 is said to be an *ancestor* of C_2, and C_2 is a *descendant* of C_1. Let $\mathcal{L}_{\text{all}}$ denote the set of all cuboids. Clearly, $(\mathcal{L}_{\text{all}}, \preceq)$ forms a *lattice*.

EXAMPLE 2.1. *Fact table T in Table 1 has three dimensions:* Sex = {M, F}*;* Age = {0-10, 11-20, 21-30, 31-40, 41-50, 51-60, 60+}*; and* Salary = {0-10k, 10-50k, 50-200k, 200-500k, 500k+}*. Figure 2(a) shows the lattice of cuboids of T. As* {Salary} $\subseteq$ {Age, Salary}*, cuboid* {Salary} *can be computed from cuboid* {Age, Salary}*. For example, to compute cell* ($*$, $*$, 10-50k)*, we aggregate cells* ($*$, 0-10, 10-50k)*, ..., * ($*$, 60+, 10-50k).

ϵ-Differential Privacy

Differential privacy (*DP* for short in the rest of this paper) is based on the concept of *neighbors*. Two tables T_1 and T_2 are neighbors if they differ by at most one row, i.e., $|(T_1 - T_2) \cup (T_2 - T_1)| = 1$.[1] Let $\text{nbrs}(T)$ be the neighbors of T, and $\mathbb{TB}$ be the set of all possible table instances with dimensions $A_1, \ldots, A_d$. Let $F : \mathbb{TB} \rightarrow \mathbb{R}^n$ be a function that produces a vector of length n from a table instance. In our context, F computes the set of cuboids we select.

Definition 1. (*Differential Privacy* [10]) A randomized algorithm $\mathcal{K}$ is ϵ-differentially private if for any two neighboring tables T_1 and T_2 and any subset S of the output of $\mathcal{K}$,

$$\Pr[\mathcal{K}(T_1) \in S] \leq \exp(\epsilon) \times \Pr[\mathcal{K}(T_2) \in S],$$

where the probability is taken over the randomness of $\mathcal{K}$.

Consider an individual's concern about the privacy of her/his record r. When the publisher specifies a small ϵ, Definition 1 ensures that the inclusion or exclusion of r in the fact table makes a negligible difference in the chances of $\mathcal{K}$ returning any particular answer.

Definition 2. (*Sensitivity* [10]) The L_1 sensitivity of F is:

$$S(F) = \max_{\forall T_1, T_2 \in \mathbb{TB}\,:\, T_1 \in \text{nbrs}(T_2)} ||F(T_1) - F(T_2)||_1,$$

where $||x - y||_1 = \sum_{1 \leq i \leq n} |x_i - y_i|$ is the L^1 distance between two n-dimensional vectors $x = \langle x_1, \ldots, x_n \rangle$ and $y = \langle y_1, \ldots, y_n \rangle$.

Let $\text{Lap}(\lambda)$ denote a sample Y taken from a zero-mean Laplace distribution with probability density function $f(x) = \frac{1}{2\lambda} e^{-|x|/\lambda}$. Here, $\text{E}[Y] = 0$ and variance $\text{Var}[Y] = 2\lambda^2$. We write $\langle \text{Lap}(\lambda) \rangle^n$ to denote a vector of n independent random samples $\text{Lap}(\lambda)$.

THEOREM 1. ([12]) *Let F be a query sequence of length n. The randomized algorithm that takes as input database T and output $\tilde{F}(T) = F(T) + \langle \text{Lap}(S(F)/\epsilon) \rangle^n$ is ϵ-differentially private.*

Problem Description

Given a d-dimensional fact table T, we aim to publish a subset $\mathcal{L}$ of all T's cuboids $\mathcal{L}_{\text{all}}$ with measure $\tilde{\mathsf{c}}(\cdot)$, a noisy version of the count measure $\mathsf{c}(\cdot)$, using an algorithm $\mathcal{K}$ that ensures ϵ-differential privacy. In particular, for any cell a in a cuboid in $\mathcal{L}$, we want to publish a noisy count measure $\tilde{\mathsf{c}}(a)$ using the DP algorithm $\mathcal{K}$.

Measuring Noise. We *measure the utility of an algorithm by the variance of the noisy measure it publishes.* As we apply Laplace mechanism in Theorem 1, we will show noisy measure $\tilde{\mathsf{c}}(\cdot)$ published by our algorithms is unbiased, i.e., the expectation $\text{E}[\tilde{\mathsf{c}}(a)] = \mathsf{c}(a)$. So for one cell, the variance $\text{Var}[\tilde{\mathsf{c}}(a)]$ is equal to the *expected squared error*, i.e., $\text{Var}[\tilde{\mathsf{c}}(a)] = \text{E}\left[(\tilde{\mathsf{c}}(a) - \mathsf{c}(a))^2\right]$, and we use it to measure the noise/error in $\tilde{\mathsf{c}}(a)$. Similarly, for any set P of cells, we use $\text{Var}\left[\sum_{a \in P} \tilde{\mathsf{c}}(a)\right]$ to measure the noise/error.

[1] Some DP papers use a slightly different definition: T_1 and T_2 are neighbors if they have the same cardinality and T_1 can be obtained from T_2 by replacing one row (ϵ-indistinguishable [12]). Our algorithms also work with this definition, if we double the noise.

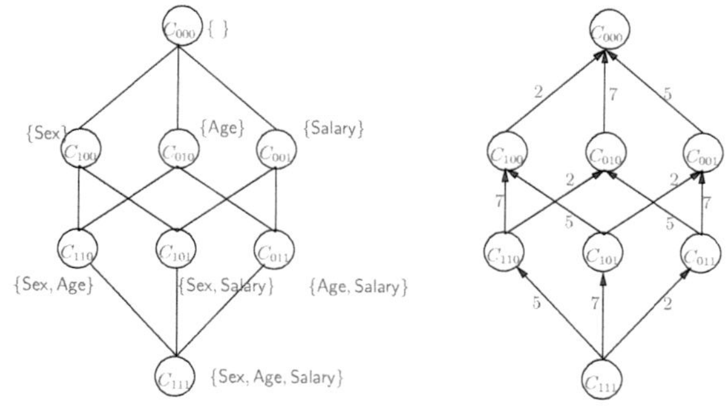

(a) Lattice Structure of Cuboids (b) Variance Magnification

Figure 2: Lattice of cuboids, Variance magnification of noise

Noise-Control Objectives. We aim to control the noise in the published cuboids in one of the following two ways:

(i) (*Bounding max noise*) Minimize the maximal variance over all cells, $\max_a \text{Var}[\tilde{\mathsf{c}}(a)]$, in the published cuboids.

(ii) (*Publishing as many as possible*) Given a threshold θ_0, a cuboid C is said to be *precise* if $\text{Var}[\tilde{\mathsf{c}}(a)] \leq \theta_0$ for all cells a in C. Maximize the number of precise cuboids in all published ones.

Enforcing Consistency. When the consistency is required, we show how to take noisy measure $\tilde{\mathsf{c}}(\cdot)$ as input and alter it into measure $\hat{\mathsf{c}}(\cdot)$ to fit *consistency constraints* that the cuboids should sum up correctly. Our consistency-enforcing algorithm takes only $\tilde{\mathsf{c}}(\cdot)$ as input (not touching the fact table T), and thus from the composition property of differential privacy [28], it is also ϵ-DP. The output consistent measure $\hat{\mathsf{c}}(\cdot)$ should be as close to $\tilde{\mathsf{c}}(\cdot)$ and $\mathsf{c}(\cdot)$ as possible. The consistency constraints will be formulated in Section 5.

3. NOISE CONTROL FRAMEWORK

We first present two straw man approaches, $\mathcal{K}_{\text{all}}$ and $\mathcal{K}_{\text{base}}$, followed by our noise-optimizing approach $\mathcal{K}_{\text{part}}$.

Straw Man Release Algorithms $\mathcal{K}_{\text{all}}$ and $\mathcal{K}_{\text{base}}$

One option, $\mathcal{K}_{\text{all}}$, is to compute the exact measure $\mathsf{c}(a)$ for each cell a in each cuboid in $\mathcal{L}$, and add noise to each cell independently, including empty cells. Formally, let $F_{\text{all}}(T)$ be the vector containing measure $\mathsf{c}(a)$ for each cell a of each cuboid in $\mathcal{L}$. F_{all} has sensitivity $|\mathcal{L}|$ (Definition 2), since a row in T contributes 1 to exactly one cell in each cuboid in $\mathcal{L}$. $\mathcal{K}_{\text{all}}$ adds noise drawn from $\text{Lap}(|\mathcal{L}|/\epsilon)$ to each cell–$\tilde{\mathsf{c}}(a) = \mathsf{c}(a) + \text{Lap}(|\mathcal{L}|/\epsilon)$–and publishes the resulting vector. The noise variance in $\mathcal{K}_{\text{all}}$ is high. With 8 dimensions, $|\mathcal{L}|$ can reach 2^8, making $\text{Var}[\tilde{\mathsf{c}}(a)] = 2 \cdot 2^{16}/\epsilon^2$. We will discuss the relationship between $\mathcal{K}_{\text{all}}$ and related work [4, 36] in Section 8.

THEOREM 2. *$\mathcal{K}_{\text{all}}$ is ϵ-differentially private. For any cell a to be published,* $\text{E}[\tilde{\mathsf{c}}(a)] = \mathsf{c}(a)$ *and* $\text{Var}[\tilde{\mathsf{c}}(a)] = 2|\mathcal{L}|^2/\epsilon^2$.

Another option, $\mathcal{K}_{\text{base}}$, computes only the cells in the d-dim cuboid, i.e., the base cuboid, directly from T, and adds noise into them. $\mathcal{K}_{\text{base}}$ computes the measures of the remaining cells to be released by aggregating the noisy measures of the base cells. The vector $F_{\text{base}}(T)$ has each entry as the measure $\mathsf{c}(a)$ of a cell in the base cuboid, and thus its sensitivity is 1; therefore, publishing $\tilde{\mathsf{c}}(a) = \mathsf{c}(a) + \text{Lap}(1/\epsilon)$ for each base cell preserves ϵ-differential privacy. When $\mathcal{K}_{\text{base}}$ computes higher-level cuboids from $F_{\text{base}}(T)$, we do not touch T, so ϵ-DP is preserved. However, the noise variance grows as we aggregate more base cells for cells in higher levels.

THEOREM 3. *$\mathcal{K}_{\text{base}}$ is ϵ-differentially private. For any published cell a,* $\text{E}[\tilde{\mathsf{c}}(a)] = \mathsf{c}(a)$*. If a is in a cuboid with dimensions $[C]$, then $\tilde{\mathsf{c}}(a)$ has noise variance* $\text{Var}[\tilde{\mathsf{c}}(a)] = 2\prod_{A_j \notin [C]} |A_j|/\epsilon^2$.

EXAMPLE 3.1. *For the fact table T in Figure 1(a), Figure 2(a) shows the lattice of cuboids under the relationship $\preceq$. Three dimensions* Sex, Age, *and* Salary *have cardinality 2, 7, and 5, respectively. Each cuboid is labeled as $C_{x_1x_2x_3}$, where $x_i = 1$ iff the ith dimension is in this cuboid. For example, C_{011} is the cuboid* {Age, Salary}. *The label on an edge from C to C' in Figure 2(b) is the* variance magnification *ratio when cells in cuboid C are aggregated to compute the cells in C'. For example, if C_{011} is computed from C_{111}, the noise variance doubles, since the dimension* Sex *has 2 distinct values–each cell in C_{011} is the aggregation of 2 cells in C_{111}. If C_{001} is computed from C_{111}, the noise variance is magnified $2 \times 7 = 14$ times, since 14 cells in C_{111} form one in C_{001}.*

Suppose we want to publish all the cuboids in Figure 2(a). Using $\mathcal{K}_{\text{all}}$, we add Laplace noise $\text{Lap}(8/\epsilon)$ to each cell, giving noise variance $2 \times 64/\epsilon^2 = 128/\epsilon^2$ for one cell. Using $\mathcal{K}_{\text{base}}$, we add Laplace noise $\text{Lap}(1/\epsilon)$ to each cell in C_{111} and then aggregate its cells. Each cell in C_{100} is built from 7×5 cells in C_{111}, with noise variance $35 \times 2/\epsilon^2 = 70/\epsilon^2$. A cell in C_{000} is built from $7 \times 5 \times 2$ cells in C_{111}, with noise variance $70 \times 2/\epsilon^2 = 140/\epsilon^2$.

A better approach is to compute cuboids $C_{111}, C_{110}, C_{101}$, and C_{100} from T, adding Laplace noise $\text{Lap}(4/\epsilon)$ to each (the sensitivity is 4). We compute the other cuboids from these. Then the noise variance in C_{100} is $32/\epsilon^2$ and in C_{000} is $2 \times 32/\epsilon^2 = 64/\epsilon^2$ (aggregating 2 cells of C_{100}).

As shown in Example 3.1, the more cuboids we compute directly from the table T, the higher their sensitivity is, and so the more noise they require, but the less noise is accumulated when other cuboids are computed from them. $\mathcal{K}_{\text{all}}$ and $\mathcal{K}_{\text{base}}$ represent the extremes of computing as many or as few cuboids as possible directly from T. There must be a strategy between $\mathcal{K}_{\text{all}}$ and $\mathcal{K}_{\text{base}}$ that gives better bounds for the noise variance of released cuboids.

A Better Algorithm $\mathcal{K}_{\text{part}}$

To publish a set $\mathcal{L} \subseteq \mathcal{L}_{\text{all}}$ of cuboids, $\mathcal{K}_{\text{part}}$ chooses which cuboids, denoted as $\mathcal{L}_{\text{pre}}$, to compute directly from the fact table T, in a manner that reduces the overall noise. $\mathcal{L}_{\text{post}} = \mathcal{L} - \mathcal{L}_{\text{pre}}$ includes all the other cuboids in $\mathcal{L}$. We do *not* require $\mathcal{L}_{\text{pre}} \subseteq \mathcal{L}$.

1. (*Noise Sources*) For each cell a of cuboids in $\mathcal{L}_{\text{pre}}$, $\mathcal{K}_{\text{part}}$ computes $\mathsf{c}(a)$ from T and releases $\tilde{\mathsf{c}}(a) = \mathsf{c}(a) + \text{Lap}(s/\epsilon)$, where the sensitivity $s = |\mathcal{L}_{\text{pre}}|$. Note that $\mathcal{L}_{\text{pre}}$ is selected by our algorithms in Section 4.1 s.t. all cuboids in $\mathcal{L}$ can be computed from $\mathcal{L}_{\text{pre}}$.

2. (*Aggregation*) For each cuboid $C \in \mathcal{L}_{\text{post}}$, $\mathcal{K}_{\text{part}}$ selects a descendant cuboid C^* from $\mathcal{L}_{\text{pre}}$ s.t. $C^* \succeq C$, and computes $\tilde{\mathsf{c}}(a)$ for each cell $a \in C$ by aggregating the noisy measure of cells in C^*. We discuss how to pick C^* as follows.

The measure $\tilde{\mathsf{c}}(a)$ output by $\mathcal{K}_{\text{part}}$ is an unbiased estimator of $\mathsf{c}(a)$ for every cell a, i.e., $\text{E}[\tilde{\mathsf{c}}(a)] = \mathsf{c}(a)$. For a cell a in cuboid $C' \in \mathcal{L}_{\text{pre}}$, $\text{Var}[\tilde{\mathsf{c}}(a)] = 2s^2/\epsilon^2$ ($s = |\mathcal{L}_{\text{pre}}|$). Suppose cell a in $C \in \mathcal{L}_{\text{post}}$ is computed from $C' \in \mathcal{L}_{\text{pre}}$ by aggregating on dimensions $[C'] - [C] = \{A_{k_1}, \ldots, A_{k_q}\}$, the *variance magnification* is defined as $\text{mag}(C, C') = \prod_{1 \le i \le q} |A_{k_i}|$. So the noise variance is

$$\text{Var}[\tilde{\mathsf{c}}(a)] = \text{mag}(C, C') \cdot 2s^2/\epsilon^2. \tag{1}$$

Let $\text{mag}(C, C) = 1$. If C cannot be computed from C' ($C \not\preceq C'$), let $\text{mag}(C, C') = \infty$. We should compute the cells in $C \in \mathcal{L}_{\text{post}}$ from the cuboid $C^* \in \mathcal{L}_{\text{pre}}$ for which $\text{mag}(C, C^*)$ is minimal, i.e., $\text{mag}(C, C^*) = \min_{C' \in \mathcal{L}_{\text{pre}}} \text{mag}(C, C')$. Let

$$\text{noise}(C, \mathcal{L}_{\text{pre}}) = \min_{C' \in \mathcal{L}_{\text{pre}}} \text{mag}(C, C') \cdot 2s^2/\epsilon^2 \tag{2}$$

be the smallest possible noise variance when computing C from a single cuboid in $\mathcal{L}_{\text{pre}}$. For $C' \in \mathcal{L}_{\text{pre}}$, $\text{noise}(C', \mathcal{L}_{\text{pre}}) = 2s^2/\epsilon^2$.

THEOREM 4. *Algorithm $\mathcal{K}_{\text{part}}$ is ϵ-differentially private. For any cuboid cell a to be released,* $\text{E}[\tilde{\mathsf{c}}(a)] = \mathsf{c}(a)$.

EXAMPLE 3.2. *Consider the data cube in Example 2.1 and release algorithm $\mathcal{K}_{\text{part}}$ with $\mathcal{L}_{\text{pre}} = \{C_{111}, C_{110}, C_{101}, C_{100}\}$. C_{000} can be computed from C_{100} with noise variance $2 \times 32/\epsilon^2$, since* $\text{mag}(C_{000}, C_{100}) = 2$; *or from C_{110} with noise variance $14 \times 32/\epsilon^2 = 448/\epsilon^2$, since* $\text{mag}(C_{000}, C_{110}) = 2 \times 7 = 14$. *So $\mathcal{K}_{\text{part}}$ computes C_{000} from C_{100}, and* $\text{noise}(C_{000}, \mathcal{L}_{\text{pre}}) = 64/\epsilon^2$.

$\mathcal{K}_{\text{part}}$ shares some similarities to the *matrix mechanism* in [23]. $\mathcal{K}_{\text{part}}$ chooses cuboids $\mathcal{L}_{\text{pre}}$ to compute $\mathcal{L}$, while [23] chooses a set of queries to answer a given workload of count queries. If we adapt the matrix mechanism for our problem by treating a cell as a count query, we need to manipulate matrices of sizes equal to the number of cells (e.g., matrices with $10^6 \times 10^6$ entries for a moderate data cube with 10^6 cells). So [23] is not applicable in our context.

Efficient Implementation of $\mathcal{K}_{\text{part}}$. Suppose $\mathcal{L}_{\text{pre}}$ is given. A naive way to compute DP cuboids in $\mathcal{L}$ is to first inject noise into each cuboid in $\mathcal{L}_{\text{pre}}$. Then for each $C \in \mathcal{L}$, query its descendant $C^* \in \mathcal{L}_{\text{pre}}$ ($C \preceq C^*$), and aggregate cells in C^* to compute cells in C.

We can compute DP cuboids in $\mathcal{L}$ more efficiently with fewer cell queries. Suppose $C \preceq C'' \preceq C^*$, noise is injected into $C^* \in \mathcal{L}_{\text{pre}}$ for ensuring DP, and C'' is computed from C^*. Then computing C from C^* is equivalent to computing it from C'', with DP ensured. So after noise is injected into all cuboids in $\mathcal{L}_{\text{pre}}$, DP cuboids in $\mathcal{L}$ can be computed in a level-by-level way, i.e., computing i-dim cuboids from $(i+1)$-dim cuboids. The total running time is $O(Nd^2)$, where $N = \Pi_j(|A_j| + 1)$ is the total number of cells.

Problems of Optimizing Noise Source: Choosing $\mathcal{L}_{\text{pre}}$

We formalize two versions of the problem of choosing $\mathcal{L}_{\text{pre}}$ with different goals, given table T and set $\mathcal{L}$ of cuboids to be published.

Problem 1. (BOUND MAX VARIANCE) Choose a set $\mathcal{L}_{\text{pre}}$ of cuboids s.t. all cuboids in $\mathcal{L}$ can be computed from $\mathcal{L}_{\text{pre}}$ and the max noise $\text{noise}(\mathcal{L}_{\text{pre}}) = \max_{C \in \mathcal{L}} \text{noise}(C, \mathcal{L}_{\text{pre}})$ is minimized.

Problem 2. (PUBLISH MOST) Given threshold θ_0 and cuboid weighting $w(\cdot)$, choose $\mathcal{L}_{\text{pre}}$ s.t. $\sum_{C \in \mathcal{L}:\ \text{noise}(C, \mathcal{L}_{\text{pre}}) \le \theta_0} w(C)$ is maximized. In other words, maximize the weight of the cuboids computed from $\mathcal{L}_{\text{pre}}$ with noise variance no more than θ_0.

THEOREM 5. BOUND MAX VARIANCE *and* PUBLISH MOST *are both NP-hard, where $|\mathcal{L}|$ is the input size.*

The proof uses a *non-trivial* reduction from the VERTEX COVER problem in degree-3 graphs. Details are in the appendix.

Note that $\mathcal{K}_{\text{all}}$ and $\mathcal{K}_{\text{base}}$ are special cases of $\mathcal{K}_{\text{part}}$ by letting $\mathcal{L}_{\text{pre}} = \mathcal{L}$ and $\mathcal{L}_{\text{pre}} = \{\text{the base cuboid}\}$, respectively. We will introduce two algorithms that choose $\mathcal{L}_{\text{pre}}$ carefully so that $\mathcal{K}_{\text{part}}$ is better than $\mathcal{K}_{\text{all}}$ and $\mathcal{K}_{\text{base}}$ w.r.t. objectives in Problems 1 and 2.

4. OPTIMIZING THE SOURCE OF NOISE

A brute force approach for Problems 1 and 2–enumerating all possible choices of $\mathcal{L}_{\text{pre}}$ (all possible cuboid subsets)–takes $O(2^{2^d})$ time, which is *not* practical even for $d = 5$. Due to the hardness result in Theorem 5, we introduce approximation algorithms for these two problems, with running time polynomial in 2^d.

4.1 Bounding the Maximum Variance

We now present a $(\ln(|\mathcal{L}|)+1)^2$-approximation algorithm for the BOUND MAX VARIANCE problem, with running time polynomial in $|\mathcal{L}|$ and 2^d. First, suppose we have an efficient algorithm FEASIBLE for subproblem FEASIBILITY($\mathcal{L}$,θ, s): for a fixed θ and s, is there a set of s cuboids $\mathcal{L}_{\text{pre}}$ s.t. for all $C \in \mathcal{L}$, $\text{noise}(C, \mathcal{L}_{\text{pre}}) \leq \theta$? Let FEASIBLE($\mathcal{L}$,$\theta$, s) return $\mathcal{L}_{\text{pre}}$ if a solution exists, and "NO" otherwise. Then to solve Problem 1, we can find the minimum θ such that for some s, FEASIBLE($\mathcal{L}$,θ, s) returns a feasible solution. This θ can be found using binary search instead of guessing all possible values. Algorithm 1 provides the details.

1: $\theta_L \leftarrow 0$, $\theta_R \leftarrow 2|\mathcal{L}|^2/\epsilon^2$ (or $\theta_R \leftarrow 2 \cdot 4^d/\epsilon^2$ if $|\mathcal{L}| = 2^d$);
2: **while** $|\theta_L - \theta_R| > 1/\epsilon^2$ **do**
3: $\quad\theta \leftarrow (\theta_L + \theta_R)/2$;
4: $\quad$**if** FEASIBLE($\mathcal{L}$,θ, s) = NO for all $s = 1, \ldots, |\mathcal{L}|$ **then** $\theta_L \leftarrow \theta$;
$\quad$**else** $\theta_R \leftarrow \theta$;
5: **return** $\theta^* = \theta_R$ and the solution found by FEASIBLE($\mathcal{L}$,θ^*, s).
FEASIBLE($\mathcal{L}$,θ, s)
6: Compute coverage $\text{cov}(C)$ for each cuboid based on θ and s;
7: $\mathcal{R} \leftarrow \varnothing$, $\mathcal{COV} \leftarrow \varnothing$;
8: **repeat** the following two steps s times
9: $\quad$Select a cuboid C' such that $|\text{cov}(C') - \mathcal{COV}|$ is maximized
10: $\quad\mathcal{R} \leftarrow \mathcal{R} \cup \{C'\}$, $\mathcal{COV} \leftarrow \mathcal{COV} \cup \text{cov}(C')$;
11: **if** $\mathcal{COV} = \mathcal{L}$ **then return** $\mathcal{R}$ as $\mathcal{L}_{\text{pre}}$;
12: **else return** NO.

Algorithm 1: Algorithm for BOUND MAX VARIANCE problem

Theorem 5 says that BOUND MAX VARIANCE is NP-hard, so there cannot be an efficient exact algorithm for the subproblem FEASIBILITY. We provide a greedy algorithm (analogous to that for SET COVER) that achieves the promised approximation guarantee $(\ln|\mathcal{L}| + 1)^2$ for the BOUND MAX VARIANCE problem.

Using (2), we rewrite FEASIBILITY's noise constraint as:

$$\text{noise}(C, \mathcal{L}_{\text{pre}}) \leq \theta \Leftrightarrow \min_{C' \in \mathcal{L}_{\text{pre}}} \text{mag}(C, C') \leq \tfrac{\theta\epsilon^2}{2s^2}. \quad (3)$$

For fixed θ, ϵ, and s, cuboid C' *covers* cuboid C if $C \preceq C'$ and $\text{mag}(C, C') \leq \frac{\theta\epsilon^2}{2s^2}$. Define C''s *coverage* to be:

$$\text{cov}(C', \theta, \epsilon, s) = \{C \in \mathcal{L} \mid C \preceq C',\ \text{mag}(C, C') \leq \tfrac{\theta\epsilon^2}{2s^2}\}. \quad (4)$$

For simplicity, we write $\text{cov}(C')$ for $\text{cov}(C', \theta, \epsilon, s)$ when θ, ϵ, and s are fixed. The following lemma is from (3) and (4).

LEMMA 1. $\text{noise}(C, \mathcal{L}_{\text{pre}}) \leq \theta$ *if and only if there exists* $C' \in \mathcal{L}_{\text{pre}}$ *such that* $C \in \text{cov}(C', \theta, \epsilon, |\mathcal{L}_{\text{pre}}|)$.

By Lemma 1, FEASIBILITY($\mathcal{L}$,θ, s) reduces to finding s cuboids that cover all cuboids in $\mathcal{L}$. To solve this problem, we employ the greedy algorithm for the SET COVER problem: in each of s iterations, we add to $\mathcal{L}_{\text{pre}}$ the cuboid that covers the maximum number of not-yet-covered members of $\mathcal{L}$. The greedy algorithm can find at most $(\ln|\mathcal{L}| + 1)s^*$ cuboids to cover all cuboids in $\mathcal{L}$ if the minimum covering set has size at least s^*. This algorithm, denoted as FEASIBLE($\mathcal{L}$,θ, s), appears in lines 6-12 of Algorithm 1.

THEOREM 6. *Algorithm 1 finds an* $(\ln|\mathcal{L}|+1)^2$*-approximation to Problem 1 in* $O(\min\{3^d,\ 2^d|\mathcal{L}|\}|\mathcal{L}|\log|\mathcal{L}|)$ *time. Moreover, using the solution* $\mathcal{L}_{\text{pre}}$ *produced by Algorithm 1,* $\mathcal{K}_{\text{part}}$ *is at least as good as* $\mathcal{K}_{\text{all}}$ *and* $\mathcal{K}_{\text{base}}$*, in terms of the objective in Problem 1.*

Algorithm 1's running time is polynomial in 2^d and $|\mathcal{L}|$, and it provides a logarithmic approximation. Note that parameter d is not very large in most applications, but $|\mathcal{L}|$ can be as large as 2^d.

EXAMPLE 4.1. *Suppose we want to publish all cuboids in Figure 2(a)* ($\mathcal{L} = \mathcal{L}_{\text{all}}$)*. When* FEASIBLE($\cdot$) *is called with* $\theta = 80/\epsilon^2$ *and* $s = 2$*, from (4),* C' *covers* C *iff* $C \preceq C'$ *and* $\text{mag}(C, C') \leq 10$. $\text{mag}(C, C')$ *can be computed from Figure 2(b) by multiplying the edge weights on the path from* C' *to* C*. In the first iteration of lines 8-10, Algorithm 1 chooses* C_{111} *for* $\text{cov}(C_{111}) = \{C_{111}, C_{110}, C_{010}, C_{101}, C_{011}\}$ *covers the most cuboids in* $\mathcal{L}$*, and puts* C_{111} *into* $\mathcal{R}$*. In the second iteration, Algorithm 1 chooses* C_{101} *because* $\text{cov}(C_{101}) = \{C_{101}, C_{100}, C_{001}, C_{000}\}$ *which covers three (the most) cuboids not covered by* C_{111} *yet.* C_{111} *and* C_{101} *cover all the cuboids, so* FEASIBLE($\cdot$) *returns* $\mathcal{L}_{\text{pre}} = \{C_{111}, C_{101}\}$.

The binary search in Algorithm 1 determines that $64/\epsilon^2$ *is the smallest value of* θ *for which* FEASIBLE *finds a feasible* $\mathcal{L}_{\text{pre}}$ *for some* s*. In that iteration, for* $s = 4$*,* FEASIBLE *returns* $\mathcal{L}_{\text{pre}} = \{C_{111}, C_{110}, C_{101}, C_{100}\}$*. There, we have* $\text{cov}(C_{111}) = \{C_{111}, C_{011}\}$, $\text{cov}(C_{110}) = \{C_{110}, C_{010}\}$, $\text{cov}(C_{101}) = \{C_{101}, C_{001}\}$*, and* $\text{cov}(C_{100}) = \{C_{100}, C_{000}\}$.

4.2 Publishing as Many as Possible

We now present a $(1 - 1/e)$-approximation algorithm for the PUBLISH MOST problem, with running time polynomial in $|\mathcal{L}|$ and 2^d. Given threshold θ_0, assuming the optimal solution has s cuboids, from Lemma 1, PUBLISH MOST is equivalent to finding a set of s cuboids $\mathcal{L}_{\text{pre}}$ s.t. the weighted sum of the cuboids in $\mathcal{L}$ that they cover (with $\theta = \theta_0$ and the fixed s) is as high as possible. We will consider values up to $|\mathcal{L}|$ for s, and apply the greedy algorithm for the MAXIMUM COVERAGE problem for each choice of s.

As outlined in Algorithm 2, initially $\mathcal{R}$ and $\mathcal{COV}$ are empty. In each iteration, we find the cuboid for which the total weight of the not-previously-covered cuboids it covers in $\mathcal{L}$ is maximal. We put this cuboid into $\mathcal{R}$ and put the newly covered cuboids into $\mathcal{COV}$. After repeating this s times, $|\mathcal{R}| = s$ and $\mathcal{COV}$ is the set of cuboids with noise variance no more than θ_0 if computed from $\mathcal{R}$. At the end, pick the best $\mathcal{R}$ over all choices of s as $\mathcal{L}_{\text{pre}}$. If some cuboids in $\mathcal{L}$ cannot be computed from $\mathcal{L}_{\text{pre}}$ but we desire to publish them, we can simply add one more cuboid, the base cuboid, into $\mathcal{L}_{\text{pre}}$.

1: **for** $s = 1, 2, \ldots, |\mathcal{L}|$ **do** $\mathcal{R}_s \leftarrow$ GREEDYCOVER($\mathcal{L}$,θ_0, s);
2: **return** the best $\mathcal{R}_s$ as $\mathcal{L}_{\text{pre}}$;
GREEDYCOVER($\mathcal{L}$,θ_0, s)
3: Compute coverage $\text{cov}(C)$ for each cuboid based on θ_0 and s;
4: $\mathcal{R} \leftarrow \varnothing$, $\mathcal{COV} \leftarrow \varnothing$;
5: **repeat** the following steps s times
6: $\quad$Select a cuboid C' such that $|\text{cov}(C') - \mathcal{COV}|$ is maximized
$\quad\quad$(or $\sum_{C \in \text{cov}(C') - \mathcal{COV}} w(C)$ is maximized)
7: $\quad\mathcal{R} \leftarrow \mathcal{R} \cup \{C'\}$, $\mathcal{COV} \leftarrow \mathcal{COV} \cup \text{cov}(C')$;
8: **return** $\mathcal{R}$.

Algorithm 2: Algorithm for PUBLISH MOST

THEOREM 7. *Algorithm 2 finds a* $(1 - 1/e)$*-approximation to Problem 2 in* $O(\min\{3^d,\ 2^d|\mathcal{L}|\}d|\mathcal{L}|)$ *time. Moreover, using the solution* $\mathcal{L}_{\text{pre}}$ *produced by Algorithm 2,* $\mathcal{K}_{\text{part}}$ *is as least as good as* $\mathcal{K}_{\text{all}}$ *and* $\mathcal{K}_{\text{base}}$*, in terms of the objective in Problem 2.*

EXAMPLE 4.2. *Consider the effect of Algorithm 2 on Example 4.1, with* $\theta_0 = 40/\epsilon^2$ *and all cuboids to be published with equal weights. For* $s = 2$*, when we call* GREEDYCOVER($\mathcal{L}$, $40/\epsilon^2$, 2), $\{C_{111}, C_{101}\}$ *is returned as* $\mathcal{R}$ *in line 8. Since no other value of* s *covers more cuboids,* $\{C_{111}, C_{101}\}$ *is finally returned as* $\mathcal{L}_{\text{pre}}$.

5. ENFORCING CONSISTENCY

Suppose $\mathcal{L}_{\text{pre}} = \{C_1, C_2\}$, where $[C_1] = \{A_1, A_2, A_3\}$ and $[C_2] = \{A_1, A_2, A_4\}$. Consider cuboid $[C] = \{A_1, A_2\}$ to be published. C can be computed from either C_1 or C_2. Since we add noise to C_1 and C_2 independently, the two computations of C will probably yield different results. If we revise $\mathcal{K}_{\text{part}}$ by letting C be the weighted (based on variance) average of the two results, then C will not be an exact roll-up of either C_1 or C_2, though it will be unbiased. Such inconsistency occurs in data cubes released by both $\mathcal{K}_{\text{all}}$ and $\mathcal{K}_{\text{part}}$, as long as $\mathcal{L}_{\text{pre}}$ contains more than one cuboid.

In this section, we introduce systematic approaches to enforce consistency across released cuboids. The basic idea is as follows. Consider the noisy measures $\tilde{c}(\cdot)$ of cells in each cuboid $C \in \mathcal{L}_{\text{pre}}$ released by $\mathcal{K}_{\text{part}}$, where $\mathcal{L}_{\text{pre}}$ is selected by either Algorithm 1 or Algorithm 2. Recall that, in $\mathcal{K}_{\text{all}}$, $\mathcal{L}_{\text{pre}}$ is the set of all cuboids to be published. We construct *consistent measure* $\hat{c}(\cdot)$ from $\tilde{c}(\cdot)$ so that the consistency constraints are enforced and the distance between $\hat{c}(\cdot)$ and $\tilde{c}(\cdot)$ is minimized. Since the algorithm takes only $\tilde{c}(\cdot)$ as the input and does not touch the real count measure $c(\cdot)$ or the fact table T, ϵ-DP is automatically preserved.

Consistency Constraints and Distance Measures

Clearly, there is no inconsistency if we compute measures of all cells from the base cells (i.e., d-dim cells). For a cell a, let $\text{Base}(a)$ be the set of all base cells, each of which aggregates a disjoint subset of rows that are contained in a. Formally, $a' \in \text{Base}(a)$ if and only if for any dimension A_i, $a[i] \neq *$ implies $a[i] = a'[i]$. So we enforce *consistency constraints* for measure $\hat{c}(\cdot)$ as follows.

$$\sum_{a' \in \text{Base}(a)} \hat{c}(a') = \hat{c}(a), \quad \forall \text{ cells } a. \tag{5}$$

We seek the choice of $\hat{c}(\cdot)$ that satisfies consistency constraints in (5) and is as close as possible to $\tilde{c}(\cdot)$, but can be computed without reexamining $c(\cdot)$. We use L^p *distance* ($p \geq 1$) to measure how close $\hat{c}(\cdot)$ and $\tilde{c}(\cdot)$ are. Let $\mathcal{E}_{\text{pre}}$ be the set of cells in cuboids belonging to $\mathcal{L}_{\text{pre}}$. Treat $\hat{c}(\cdot)$ and $\tilde{c}(\cdot)$ as vectors in $\mathbb{R}^{\mathcal{E}_{\text{pre}}}$, and the L^p distance between is $||\hat{c}(\cdot) - \tilde{c}(\cdot)||_p = \sum_{a \in \mathcal{E}_{\text{pre}}} (|\hat{c}(a) - \tilde{c}(a)|^p)^{1/p}$.

Finding $\hat{c}(\cdot)$ to minimize $||\hat{c}(\cdot) - \tilde{c}(\cdot)||_p$ subject to (5) can be viewed as a *least-norm problem*. From classic results from convex optimization [7], it can be solved efficiently, at least in theory. We will prove that the utility of optimal solutions for L^1, L^2, and L^∞ distances satisfies certain statistical guarantees. More importantly, classic algorithms do not work in our context because the number of variables involved in (5) is equal to the number of cells, which is huge. We provide a practical and theoretically sound algorithm that minimizes the L^2 distance in time linear in the number of cells.

5.1 Minimizing L^∞ and L^1 Distance

We first consider minimizing the L^∞ distance, which is essentially minimizing the maximal difference between $\tilde{c}(a)$ and $\hat{c}(a)$ for any cell in $\mathcal{E}_{\text{pre}}$, i.e., $||\hat{c}(\cdot) - \tilde{c}(\cdot)||_\infty = \max_{a \in \mathcal{E}_{\text{pre}}} |\hat{c}(a) - \tilde{c}(a)|$. Equivalently, we solve for $\hat{c}(\cdot)$ in the following linear program.

$$\begin{aligned} &\text{minimize } z \\ &\text{s.t. } |\hat{c}(a) - \tilde{c}(a)| \leq z, \ \forall \text{ cells } a \in \mathcal{E}_{\text{pre}}; \\ &\sum_{a' \in \text{Base}(a)} \hat{c}(a') = \hat{c}(a), \ \forall \text{ cells } a \in \mathcal{E}_{\text{pre}}. \end{aligned} \tag{6}$$

[4] considers a similar consistency enforcing scheme, but injects noise into all cuboids instead of the carefully-selected subset of cuboids $\mathcal{L}_{\text{pre}}$. We can bound the error of $\hat{c}(\cdot)$ as follows.

THEOREM 8. (Generalized Theorem 8 in [4]) *For $\hat{c}(\cdot)$ obtained by solving (6), with probability at least $1 - \delta$, where $\delta = \frac{|\mathcal{E}_{\text{pre}}|}{e^{\eta/2}}$,*

$$\sum_{a \in \mathcal{E}_{\text{pre}}} |\hat{c}(a) - c(a)| \leq \frac{|\mathcal{E}_{\text{pre}}||\mathcal{L}_{\text{pre}}|}{\epsilon} 2 \log \frac{|\mathcal{E}_{\text{pre}}|}{\delta} = \frac{|\mathcal{E}_{\text{pre}}||\mathcal{L}_{\text{pre}}|}{\epsilon} \eta.$$

A linear program can also be used to minimize the L^1 distance. As $||\hat{c}(\cdot) - \tilde{c}(\cdot)||_1 = \sum_a |\hat{c}(a) - \tilde{c}(a)|$, by introducing an auxiliary variable z_a for each cell a with constraint $-z_a \leq \hat{c}(a) - \tilde{c}(a) \leq z_a$, minimizing $||\hat{c}(\cdot) - \tilde{c}(\cdot)||_1$ while enforcing consistency in $\hat{c}(\cdot)$ is equivalent to the following linear program.

$$\begin{aligned} &\text{minimize } \sum_{a \in \mathcal{E}_{\text{pre}}} z_a \\ &\text{s.t. } |\hat{c}(a) - \tilde{c}(a)| \leq z_a, \ \forall \text{ cell } a \in \mathcal{E}_{\text{pre}}; \\ &\sum_{a' \in \text{Base}(a)} \hat{c}(a') = \hat{c}(a), \ \forall \text{ cell } a \in \mathcal{E}_{\text{pre}}. \end{aligned} \tag{7}$$

THEOREM 9. *For $\hat{c}(\cdot)$ obtained by solving (7), if $\epsilon \leq 1$, with probability at least $1 - \delta$, where $\delta = (\frac{\eta}{2e^{\eta/2-1}})^{|\mathcal{E}_{\text{pre}}|}$ ($\eta > 2$),*

$$\sum_{a \in \mathcal{E}_{\text{pre}}} |\hat{c}(a) - c(a)| \leq \frac{|\mathcal{E}_{\text{pre}}||\mathcal{L}_{\text{pre}}|}{\epsilon} \eta.$$

For a data cube where the cardinality of every dimension is two, Theorem 8 in [4] yields a bound similar to that of our Theorem 8, by discarding the integrality constraint (i.e., counts are integers).

Theorem 9 mirrors Theorem 8, but replaces the upper tail $\delta = \frac{|\mathcal{E}_{\text{pre}}|}{e^\eta}$ with $(\frac{\eta}{2e^{\eta/2-1}})^{|\mathcal{E}_{\text{pre}}|}$. As $|\mathcal{E}_{\text{pre}}|$ is usually large, linear program (7) and Theorem 9 give a much better bound on the average error in $\hat{c}(\cdot)$ than linear program (6) and Theorem 8.

To enforce the integrality constraint for $\hat{c}(\cdot)$ obtained from linear program (6) or (7), we can simply round $\hat{c}(a)$ for each cell to the nearest integer, which will replace the error bound $\frac{|\mathcal{E}_{\text{pre}}||\mathcal{L}_{\text{pre}}|}{\epsilon}\eta$ with $\frac{|\mathcal{E}_{\text{pre}}||\mathcal{L}_{\text{pre}}|}{\epsilon}\eta + |\mathcal{E}_{\text{pre}}|$ in both Theorems 8 and 9.

5.2 Minimizing L^2 Distance

Now let's focus on minimizing the L^2 distance, i.e., the sum of squared differences between $\tilde{c}(a)$ and $\hat{c}(a)$ for all cells. This problem has a very efficient solution with good statistical guarantees.

$$\begin{aligned} &\text{minimize } \sum_{a \in \mathcal{E}_{\text{pre}}} (\hat{c}(a) - \tilde{c}(a))^2 \\ &\text{s.t. } \sum_{a' \in \text{Base}(a)} \hat{c}(a') = \hat{c}(a), \ \forall \text{ cell } a \in \mathcal{L}_{\text{pre}}. \end{aligned} \tag{8}$$

Program (8) can be viewed as a *least L^2-norm problem*. Its unique solution $\hat{c}(\cdot)$, called *the least square solution*, can be found using linear algebra [7]. The classical method needs to compute multiplication/inversion of $M \times M$-matrices, where $M = \Pi_j |A_j|$ is the total number of *base cells*. Since M is typically larger than 10^6, the classical method is inefficient in our context. Fortunately, we can derive the optimal solution $\hat{c}(\cdot)$ much more efficiently by utilizing the structure of data cubes, as follows.

We define $\text{Ancs}(a')$ to be the set of *ancestor cells* of cell a': $a \in \text{Ancs}(a')$ if and only if a is in an ancestor of the cuboid containing a' and has the same value as a' on all non-$*$ dimensions; formally, $a \in \text{Ancs}(a')$ if and only if for any dimension A_i, $a[i] \neq *$ implies $a[i] = a'[i]$. If a' is a base cell, $a \in \text{Ancs}(a') \Leftrightarrow a' \in \text{Base}(a)$.

For a cell a and a cuboid C, let $a[C]$ be a's values on dimensions of $[C]$. Suppose $[C] = \{A_{i_1}, \ldots, A_{i_k}\}$, $a[C] = \langle a[i_1], \ldots, a[i_k] \rangle$.

For two cuboids C_1 and C_2, let $C_1 \vee C_2$ be the cuboid with dimensions $[C_1] \cup [C_2]$ and $C_1 \wedge C_2$ with dimensions $[C_1] \cap [C_2]$.

We provide the following two-stage algorithm to compute the consistent measure $\hat{c}(\cdot)$ that is the optimal solution to program (8):
1. Bottom-up stage: We first compute $\text{obs}(a'')$ for every cell a'' in a cuboid C'' that can be computed from $\mathcal{L}_{\text{pre}}$. Let

$$\text{obs}(a'') = \sum_{a' \in \text{Base}(a'')} \sum_{a \in \mathcal{E}_{\text{pre}} \cap \text{Ancs}(a')} \tilde{c}(a). \tag{9}$$

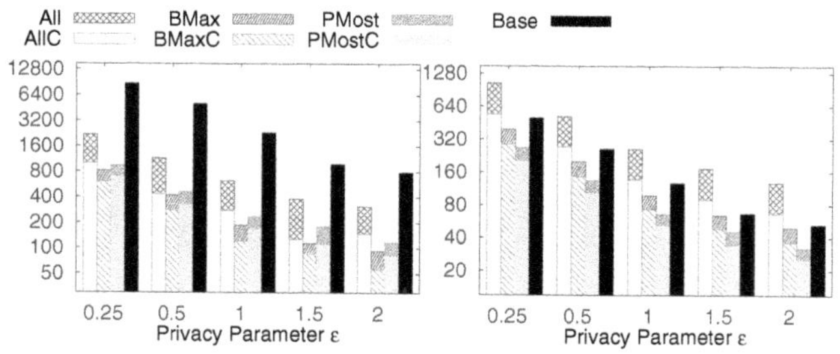

(a) Max Cuboid Error (b) Average Cuboid Error

Figure 3: Varying privacy parameter ϵ

A cuboid $C \in \mathcal{L}_{\text{pre}}$ is *maximal in* $\mathcal{L}_{\text{pre}}$ if there is no $C' \in \mathcal{L}_{\text{pre}}$ s.t. $C \prec C'$. In all maximal cuboids C'' in $\mathcal{L}_{\text{pre}}$, $\text{obs}(a'')$ can be computed as in Formula (9). In all the other cuboids that can be computed from $\mathcal{L}_{\text{pre}}$, $\text{obs}(a'')$ can be computed recursively as follows: suppose $a'' \in C''$ and C'' can be computed from $\mathcal{L}_{\text{pre}}$, there must be some cuboid C with dimensionality $\dim(C'') + 1$ s.t. either $C \in \mathcal{L}_{\text{pre}}$ or C can be computed from $\mathcal{L}_{\text{pre}}$; then,

$$\text{obs}(a'') = \sum_{\substack{a:\, a \in C \\ a[C''] = a''[C'']}} \text{obs}(a). \tag{10}$$

2. Top-down stage: After $\text{obs}(a'')$ is computed for every possible cell a'', consider another quantity $\text{est}(a'')$ for each cell $a'' \in C''$:

$$\text{est}(a'') = \sum_{C \in \mathcal{L}_{\text{pre}}} \sum_{\substack{b:\, b \in (C \wedge C''), \\ b[C \wedge C''] = a''[C \wedge C'']}} \deg(C \vee C'')\hat{\mathsf{c}}(b). \tag{11}$$

where $\deg(C) = \prod_{A_i \in \mathcal{A} - [C]} |A_i|$ and $\mathcal{A}$ is the set of all dimensions and $|A_i|$ is the cardinality of dimension A_i. Suppose $\text{obs}(\cdot)$'s are computed in the first stage as constants and $\hat{\mathsf{c}}(\cdot)$'s are variables. Solving the equations $\text{est}(a'') = \text{obs}(a'')$, we can compute $\hat{\mathsf{c}}(\cdot)$'s in a top-down manner (from ancestors to descendants) as follows:

$$\text{ratio}(C'') = \sum_{\substack{C:\, C \in \mathcal{L}_{\text{pre}}, \\ C'' \preceq C}} \deg(C \vee C''), \tag{12}$$

$$\text{aux}(a'') = \sum_{\substack{C:\, C \in \mathcal{L}_{\text{pre}}, \\ C'' \npreceq C}} \sum_{\substack{b:\, b \in (C \wedge C''), \\ b[C \wedge C''] = a''[C \wedge C'']}} \deg(C \vee C'')\hat{\mathsf{c}}(b), \tag{13}$$

$$\hat{\mathsf{c}}(a'') = \frac{1}{\text{ratio}(C'')} \left(\text{obs}(a'') - \text{aux}(a'')\right). \tag{14}$$

The above approach can be also applied to $\mathcal{K}_{\text{all}}$ because $\mathcal{K}_{\text{all}}$ is a special case of $\mathcal{K}_{\text{part}}$ obtained by setting $\mathcal{L}_{\text{pre}} = \mathcal{L}$.

Note that this approach generalizes the consistency-enforcing scheme in [19] from a tree-like structure (hierarchy of intervals) to a lattice. The method in [19] cannot be directly applied here.

Optimality. We can prove $\hat{\mathsf{c}}(\cdot)$ obtained above is not only consistent but also an unbiased estimator of $\mathsf{c}(\cdot)$. Also, $\hat{\mathsf{c}}(\cdot)$ is optimal in the sense that no other linear unbiased estimator of $\mathsf{c}(\cdot)$ obtained from $\tilde{\mathsf{c}}(\cdot)$ has smaller variance, i.e., smaller expected squared error.

THEOREM 10. *(i) The above algorithm correctly computes a value for $\hat{\mathsf{c}}(\cdot)$ that is consistent and solves the L^2 minimization problem* (8). *(ii) The above algorithm requires $O(N(d^2 + d|\mathcal{L}_{\text{pre}}|))$ time to compute $\hat{\mathsf{c}}(\cdot)$ for all N cells. (iii) For any cell of cuboids in $\mathcal{L}_{\text{pre}}$, $\hat{\mathsf{c}}(a)$ is an unbiased estimator of $\mathsf{c}(a)$, i.e., $\mathrm{E}[\hat{\mathsf{c}}(a)] = \mathsf{c}(a)$. (iv) For any cell a, $\hat{\mathsf{c}}(a)$ has the smallest variance among any linear unbiased estimator (e.g., $\tilde{\mathsf{c}}(a)$) of $\mathsf{c}(a)$ obtained from $\tilde{\mathsf{c}}(\cdot)$. (v) For any set P of cells, $\sum_{a \in P} \hat{\mathsf{c}}(a)$ has the smallest variance among any linear unbiased estimator of $\sum_{a \in P} \mathsf{c}(a)$ obtained from $\tilde{\mathsf{c}}(\cdot)$.*

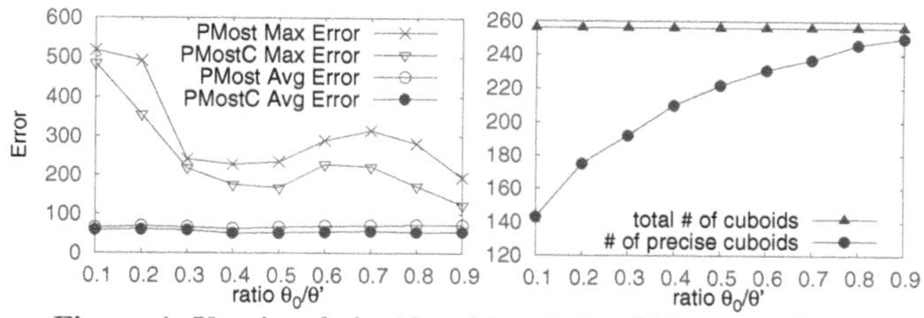

Figure 4: Varying θ_0 in Algorithm 2 (for PMost and PMostC)

6. EXPERIMENTS

We evaluate and compare seven proposed techniques on both real and synthetic datasets. The first two techniques are $\mathcal{K}_{\text{all}}$ and $\mathcal{K}_{\text{base}}$, which were defined at the beginning of Section 3. We denote them as All and Base, respectively, in this section. Another two are based on our generalized framework $\mathcal{K}_{\text{part}}$. One of these has the objective of bounding the max noise variance (Problem 1) and is denoted by BMax ($\mathcal{K}_{\text{part}}$ + Algorithm 1). The other one has the objective of maximizing the number of cuboids with noise variance no more than a given variance threshold θ_0 (Problem 2) and is denoted by PMost ($\mathcal{K}_{\text{part}}$ + Algorithm 2). The last three techniques involve applying the methods in Section 5.2 to enforce consistency in the data cubes published by All ($\mathcal{L}_{\text{pre}} = \mathcal{L}$), BMax, and PMost. The resulting three techniques are denoted AllC, BMaxC, and PMostC, respectively. The LP-based techniques in Section 5.1 are not practical for large tables. All seven algorithms are coded in C++ and evaluated on an 8GB 64-bit 2.40GHz PC.

Real dataset: We use the Adult dataset from the UCI Machine Learning Repository (http://archive.ics.uci.edu/ml/) with census information. It contains 32,561 rows with 8 categorical dimensions: workclass (cardinality 9), education (16), marital-status (7), occupation (15), relationship (6), race (5), sex (2), and salary (2).

Synthetic dataset: To generate the fact table, we first fix the number of dimensions and the dimension cardinalities. Then we generate each row independently, with each of its column values drawn uniformly and independently from the domain of its dimension.

Error measurement: We compute the error as the absolute difference between the real count measure computed directly from the fact table and the noisy measure released by one of the seven ϵ-DP algorithms. The *cuboid error* is the average error for all cells in this cuboid. We report both the *max cuboid error* and the *average cuboid error* among all published cuboids.

We release $\mathcal{L}$ = all cuboids and evaluate all algorithms on the same set of published cuboids. This is the hardest test for all algorithms, as less noise will be needed if $\mathcal{L}$ omits some cuboids.

Exp-I: Varying privacy parameter ϵ. Using the Adult dataset, we vary privacy parameter ϵ from 0.25 to 2. Smaller ϵ implies more privacy and thus more noise. Recall Algorithm 2 (for PMost) takes a variance threshold θ_0 in the input; here, we set $\theta_0 = 0.5\theta'$, where θ' is the variance bound found by Algorithm 1 (for BMax).

Figure 3 uses a logarithmic scale to show the max/average error in the released cuboids. As the inconsistent version of an approach always has at least as much error as the consistent version, the two versions (All/AllC, BMax/BMaxC, and PMost/PMostC) are stacked together on a single bar in each histogram in Section 6.

BMax and PMost always incur much less error than the two baselines Base and All. BMax is better than PMost for bounding the max error, while PMost is better than BMax for bounding the average error. Base performs the worst in terms of the max error, because only the base cuboid is computed from the table, and the noise is magnified significantly when cuboids at higher levels are computed by aggregating cells in the base cuboid. All is the worst

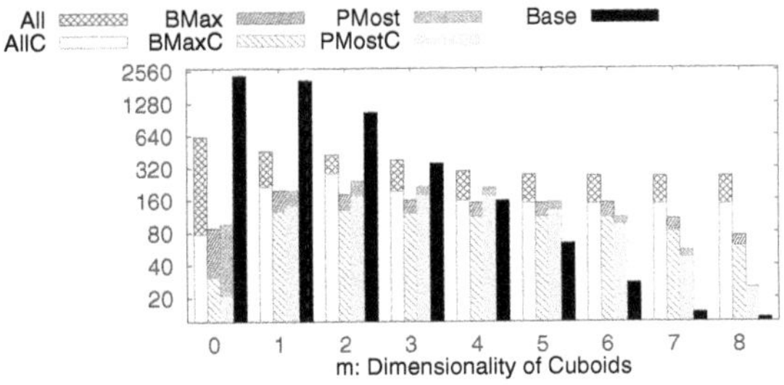

Figure 5: Max cuboid error in different cuboids as dimensionality varies, when all cuboids must be released

in terms of the average error, for the large amount of noise initially injected in each cuboid. Error decreases as ϵ increases.

As suggested by Theorem 10 (iv)-(v), our consistency enforcing techniques tend to reduce error, since the variance of the consistent measure $\hat{c}(\cdot)$ is no larger than that of the inconsistent $\tilde{c}(\cdot)$. So AllC/BMaxC/PMostC reduces error by 30%-50%, compared to All/BMax/PMost, while providing the same privacy guarantee.

Exp-II: Varying variance threshold θ_0. Note that performance of PMost and PMostC depends on the input threshold θ_0 in Problem 2, as θ_0 determines $\mathcal{L}_{\text{pre}}$. Fix $\epsilon = 1$. Given the variance bound θ' found by Algorithm 1, we vary θ_0 from $0.1\theta'$ to $0.9\theta'$. Figure 4 shows how θ_0 affects Algorithm 2 on the Adult dataset. As θ_0 increases, we have more precise cuboids, i.e., the released cuboids with noise variance no more than θ_0. When $\theta_0 = \theta'$, all $2^8 = 256$ cuboids are precise, and PMost/PMostC is equivalent to BMax/BMaxC, as the same $\mathcal{L}_{\text{pre}}$ is used. But the max/average error of PMost and PMostC does not increase monotonically with θ_0: both $\theta_0 = \theta'$ and $\theta_0 = 0.5\theta'$ are local optimums for minimizing errors. In the remaining experiments, we set $\theta_0 = 0.5\theta'$.

Exp-III: Noise in different cuboids. Figure 5 shows the max error in cuboids of different dimensionality on Adult, for $\epsilon = 1$. Recall in an m-dim cuboid, a cell has non-$*$ values on exactly m dimensions. As m decreases, a cell in an m-dim cuboid aggregates more base cells. So Base aggregates more noise from base cells as m drops, and performs the worst for $m < 3$. BMaxC is the best when $0 < m < 5$, and its max error changes little for $0 < m < 7$. The consistency-enforcing techniques, AllC/BMaxC/PMostC, are very effective for small m, reducing error by up to 70%.

Exp-IV: Varying number of dimensions. We create two more dimensions, each of which has cardinality 4, on the Adult dataset, and generate their values randomly for each row. We consider the fact table with the first 6 to all the 10 dimensions. Fix $\epsilon = 1$. We report the max/average error of the seven approaches in Figure 6. As the number of dimensions increases, BMaxC and PMostC are always the best two, and the error in both All and Base is much larger and increases faster than the error in others.

Exp-V: Varying cardinality of dimensions. We generate synthetic tables with 7 dimensions, each of which has the same cardinality. We vary the cardinality from 2 to 10, and generate a table with 10^8 rows randomly for each. We report the error of each approach in Figure 7, for $\epsilon = 1$. The performance of Base deteriorates quickly as the cardinality increases, because more cells in the base cuboid need to be aggregated. The performance of All does not change much, for its performance is mainly determined by the number of dimensions, which determines the total number of cuboids. Again, BMaxC and PMostC perform best in most cases.

Exp-VI: Efficiency. Consider a data cube with 5-10 dimensions on the Adult dataset (with two more synthetic dimensions as in Exp-IV). The overall DP data cube publishing time is reported in Figure 8, which can be decomposed as follows. Recall Algorithms 1-2

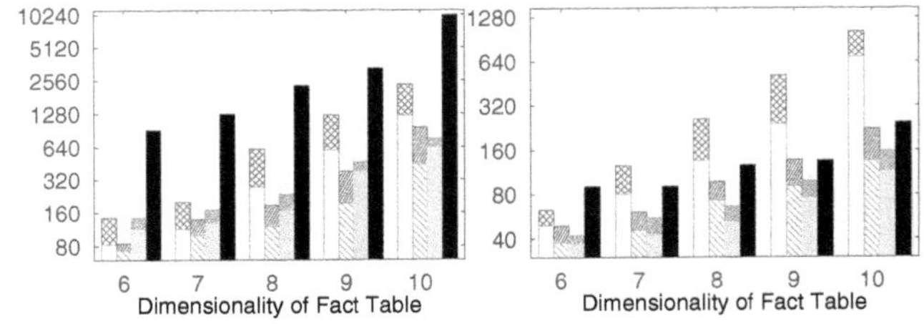

(a) Max cuboid error (b) Average cuboid error

Figure 6: Varying dimensionality of fact table

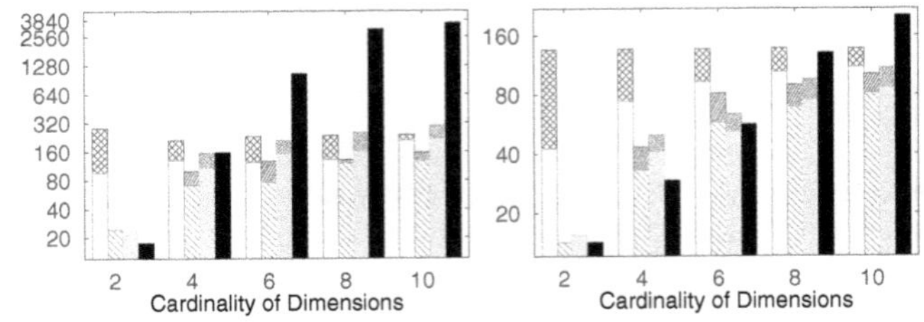

(a) Max Cuboid Error (b) Average Cuboid Error

Figure 7: Varying cardinality of dimensions (7 dimensions)

select $\mathcal{L}_{\text{pre}}$ for BMax/BMaxC and PMost/PMostC, respectively. The running time of Algorithms 1-2 is reported in Figure 9(a). For different choices of $\mathcal{L}_{\text{pre}}$ on the 8-dim table, the time needed for noise injection ($\mathcal{K}_{\text{part}}$) and consistency enforcement (the method in Section 5.2) in all cuboids is reported in Figure 9(b).

From Figure 9(a), although the running time of Algorithms 1-2 is polynomial in 2^d, they are not the bottleneck. Their running time is always a very small portion of the overall DP data cube publishing.

From Figure 9(b), it is shown that the consistency-enforcement time increases linearly with $|\mathcal{L}_{\text{pre}}|$, as predicted by Theorem 10 (ii). The time for noise injection decreases as $|\mathcal{L}_{\text{pre}}|$ increases. This is because when more cuboids are initially injected with noise, less aggregation of noise occurs later on.

From Figure 8, using consistency enforcement, AllC is especially expensive, because $|\mathcal{L}_{\text{pre}}| = 2^d$ in AllC. BMaxC and PMostC, although using consistency enforcement, usually only need 3%-10% time of AllC, for they use smaller $\mathcal{L}_{\text{pre}}$'s. For all approaches, the publishing time increases exponentially with the dimensionality, mainly because the total number of cells increases exponentially.

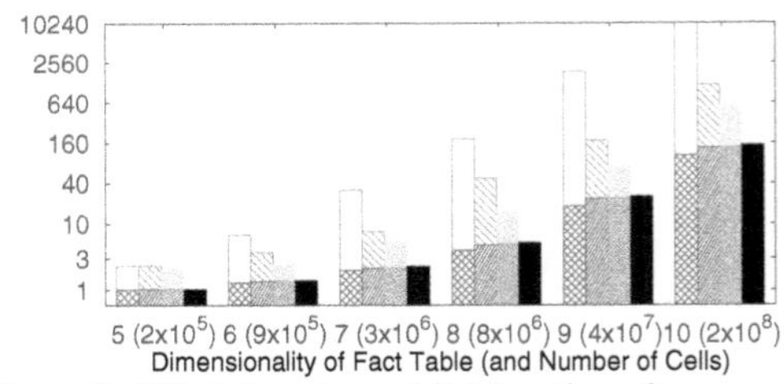

Figure 8: DP data cube publishing time (in seconds)

Summary. Both All and Base are sensitive to the dimensionality of the fact table, and Base is also sensitive to cardinalities of dimensions. All usually has a large average error, as a large amount of noise is injected into all cuboids. Base has a large max error, because noise is aggregated from the base cells; and that is why Base incurs small average errors in the cuboids close to the base cuboid. BMaxC and PMostC are the best most of the time.

All/BMax/PMost run much faster than AllC/BMaxC/PMostC. But with our consistency enforcement, AllC/BMaxC/PMostC reduce error in All/BMax/PMost, respectively, by typically 30%-70% or more, and ensure that the published data is consistent.

The error of BMaxC and PMostC is usually only 5%-30% of

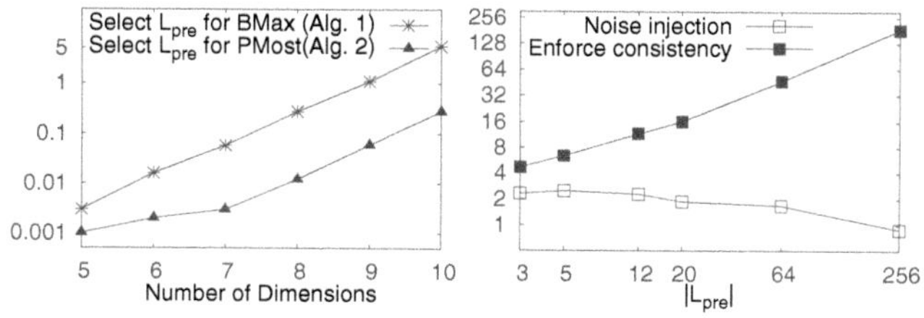

(a) Time (in seconds) (b) Time (in seconds)

Figure 9: Efficiency of different algorithms

the error incurred by All, and 20%-50% of the error of AllC. Note that the y-axis in our figures is always in logarithmic scale.

Because of our consistency-enforcing method, the error of AllC is sometimes comparable to BMax/BMaxC and PMost/PMostC, when the dimensionality of the fact table is low. However, AllC is very expensive because $|\mathcal{L}_{\text{pre}}|$ in AllC is equal to 2^d (recall Theorem 10 for the running time of our consistency enforcement). When there are more than five dimensions, AllC's publishing time is 6-10 times larger than BMaxC's ($>$ 10 times for ten dimensions), and 10-40 times larger than PMostC's ($>$ 40 times for ten dimensions).

7. DISCUSSION AND EXTENSIONS

7.1 Relative Error vs. Absolute Error

The amount of noise $\mathcal{K}_{\text{part}}$ adds to DP cuboids is independent of the number of rows and specific data in the fact table. Instead, the selection of $\mathcal{L}_{\text{pre}}$ and the amount of noise depend only on which cuboids are to be published, the number of dimensions, and their cardinalities. So our expected absolute error is fixed if the structure of the fact table is fixed, no matter how many rows there are. This feature of our approaches is also true in DP-based frameworks for different publishing tasks [4, 19, 23, 36]. The implication is that the expected relative error cannot be bounded in general. Because, with the expected absolute error fixed, some cells may have very small values of the count measure (e.g., 1), while some have very large values (e.g., 10^3). That is also why we report absolute error in Section 6. On the other hand, the advantage is, for a particular cell, it has less relative error if it aggregates more rows.

7.2 Further Reduction of Noise

We can generalize our noise-control framework $\mathcal{K}_{\text{part}}$ by adding different amounts of noise to different cuboids in $\mathcal{L}_{\text{pre}}$ to further reduce noise. Suppose $\mathcal{L}_{\text{pre}} = \{C_1, \ldots, C_s\}$ and noise $\text{Lap}(\lambda_i)$ is injected into each cell in C_i. By the composition property of DP [28], we claim that if $\sum_{i=1}^{s} 1/\lambda_i = \epsilon$, then publishing $\mathcal{L}_{\text{pre}}$ is ϵ-DP. Finding the optimal $\mathcal{L}_{\text{pre}}$ and parameters $\langle\lambda_i\rangle$ to achieve the goals in Problems 1 and 2 is hard, but Algorithms 1 and 2 can be modified to provide approximate solutions. Here, privacy parameter ϵ can be interpreted as the cost budget in WEIGHTED SET COVER.

To enforce consistency and yield an optimality result similar to Theorem 10, we can solve a weighted version of the least squares problem in Section 5.2. Our experiments show this reduces absolute error in BMaxC/PMostC by 10%. We omit the details here.

7.3 Extension to Other Measures

Our techniques for the count measure can be extended to other two basic measures sum and avg. sum can be considered as a generalized count measure, where each row in the fact table is associated with a value instead of just 0-1. Compared to count, the sensitivity of a publishing function for sum is magnified Δ times, where Δ is the range of possible values for any individual fact table tuple. Thus our techniques for count can be applied to sum, with the noise variance magnified Δ^2 times. To handle the average measure avg, we can compute two DP data cubes (partitioning the privacy budget across them), one with sum measure and one with count measure, from the same fact table. The avg measure of a cell can be computed from the two cubes, without violating DP.

7.4 Handling Larger Data Cubes

Our approaches introduced so far are applicable for mid-size data cubes, e.g., with $\leq$ 12 dimensions or $\leq 10^9$ cells. Since the current framework needs to store all cells for consistency enforcement, it cannot handle data cubes with too many cells.

For even larger data cubes (e.g., with $\geq$ 20 dimensions and $\geq 2^{20}$ cuboids), it is unnecessary to publish all cuboids at one time, as typical users are likely to query only a very small portion of them. Also, it is impossible to publish all cuboids while ensuring DP, as the huge amount of noise will make the result meaningless. So we outline an online version of our approach as follows.

Initially, $\mathcal{L}_{\text{pre}} = \varnothing$ and we have certain amount ϵ of privacy budget. When a cuboid query C comes, if $C \notin \mathcal{L}_{\text{pre}}$ and C can be computed from some DP cuboid $C^* \in \mathcal{L}_{\text{pre}}$, there are two choices: a) compute C from C^*, with error in C^* magnified in C; or b) compute real cuboid C using high-dimensional OLAP techniques like [25], inject noise into C to obtain a DP cuboid, insert C into $\mathcal{L}_{\text{pre}}$, and deduct a certain amount of privacy budget from ϵ. If $C \notin \mathcal{L}_{\text{pre}}$ but C cannot be computed from any DP cuboid $C^* \in \mathcal{L}_{\text{pre}}$, we have to follow b) above. If $C \in \mathcal{L}_{\text{pre}}$ or C used to be queried, we can directly output the old DP cuboid C. After we run out of privacy budget ϵ, to ensure ϵ-DP, we cannot create new DP cuboids in $\mathcal{L}_{\text{pre}}$ any more and may be unable to answer new queries. How to distribute the privacy budget online so that more queries can be answered with less error is interesting future work.

8. RELATED WORK

Since ϵ-differential privacy (DP) [12] was introduced, many techniques have been proposed for different data publishing and analysis tasks (refer to [10, 11] for a comprehensive review). For example, the notion of DP has been applied to releasing query and click histograms from search logs [18, 22], recommender systems [29], publishing commuting patterns [27], publishing results of machine learning [6, 8, 20], clustering [13, 30], decision tree [14], mining frequent patterns [5], and aggregating distributed time-series [31]. For a single counting query, one method to ensure DP [12] has been shown to be optimal under a certain utility model [17].

Recent works [36, 19, 23] on differentially private count queries over histograms are related to our work. Xiao *et al.* [36] propose to use the Haar wavelet for range count queries. Hay *et al.* [19] propose an approach based on a hierarchy of intervals. Li *et al.* [23] propose a general framework which supports answering a given workload of count queries, and consider the problem of finding optimal strategies for a workload. While [36] and [19] can be unified in the framework in [23], the specific algorithms given in [36, 19] are more efficient than the matrix multiplication used in [23].

Xiao *et al.* extend their wavelet approach to nominal attributes and multidimensional count queries. Their extended approach can be applied in our problem to achieve the same noise bounds as our $\mathcal{K}_{\text{all}}$ (refer to Theorem 3 in [36] and Theorem 2 in this work). In general, our $\mathcal{K}_{\text{part}}$ will add less noise, as shown in Theorems 6-7.

Barak *et al.* [4] show how to publish a set of marginals of a contingency table while ensuring DP. One of their two approaches is similar to $\mathcal{K}_{\text{all}}$: add noise to all the marginals to be published. Their LP-rounding method minimizes the L^∞ distance while enforcing consistency and integrality and removing negative numbers in the publishing. Our Theorem 9 shows that minimizing the L^1 distance yields a much better theoretical bound on error. The other approach in [4] is similar, but moves to the Fourier domain at first. Unlike our work, they do not optimize the publishing strategy (i.e., the selection of $\mathcal{L}_{\text{pre}}$). Moreover, the number of variables in the LP equals the number of cells (often $> 10^6$ in our experiments). So LP-based methods can only handle data cubes with small numbers of cells.

Agrawal *et al.* [3] study how to support OLAP queries while ensuring a limited form of (ρ_1, ρ_2)-privacy, by randomizing each entry in the fact table with a constant probability. An OLAP query on the fact table can be answered from the perturbed table within roughly $\sqrt{|\text{dataset}|}$ [4]. (ρ_1, ρ_2)-privacy is in general not as strong as ϵ-differential privacy. Also, the error incurred by this method [3] depends on the dataset size; in our framework, the amount of noise to be added is data-independent, only determined by the number of cuboids to be published and the structure of the fact table.

Differential privacy provides much stronger privacy guarantees than other privacy concepts based on deterministic algorithms do, such as k-anonymity [32] and its extension l-diversity [26] and t-closeness [24]. [34] studies how to specify authorization and control inferences for OLAP queries in the data cube.

9. CONCLUSIONS

We have introduced a general noise-control framework to release all or part of a data cube in an ϵ-differentially private way. To reduce the noise in the released cuboids, we choose certain cuboids $\mathcal{L}_{\text{pre}}$ to compute directly from the fact table, and add noise to make them differentially private. All the other cuboids are computed directly from the cuboids in $\mathcal{L}_{\text{pre}}$, without adding additional noise or revisiting the fact table. We modeled the selection of $\mathcal{L}_{\text{pre}}$ as two optimization problems, proved them NP-hard, and proposed approximation algorithms. To ensure consistency across different rollups of released cuboids, we proposed consistency-enforcing techniques that have the side benefit of reducing noise.

10. ACKNOWLEDGMENTS

We thank the reviewers for their insightful suggestions that immensely improved the paper. This work was supported in part by NSF IIS-09-05215, U.S. Air Force Office of Scientific Research MURI award FA9550-08-1-0265, the U.S. Army Research Laboratory under Cooperative Agreement Number W911NF-09-2-0053 (NS-CTA), A*STAR SERC grant 1021580074, and a grant from Boeing. The views and conclusions contained in this document are those of the authors and should not be interpreted as representing the official policies, either expressed or implied, of the Army Research Laboratory or the U.S. Government. The U.S. Government is authorized to reproduce and distribute reprints for Government purposes notwithstanding any copyright notation hereon.

11. REFERENCES

[1] www.cs.cmu.edu/ compthink/mindswaps/oct07/difpriv.ppt. 2007.

[2] N. R. Adam and J. C. Wortmann. Security-control methods for statistical databases: A comparative study. *ACM Comput. Surv.*, 21(4):515–556, 1989.

[3] R. Agrawal, R. Srikant, and D. Thomas. Privacy preserving OLAP. In *SIGMOD*, pages 251–262, 2005.

[4] B. Barak, K. Chaudhuri, C. Dwork, S. Kale, F. McSherry, and K. Talwar. Privacy, accuracy, and consistency too: a holistic solution to contingency table release. In *PODS*, pages 273–282, 2007.

[5] R. Bhaskar, S. Laxman, A. Smith, and A. Thakurta. Discovering frequent patterns in sensitive data. In *KDD*, pages 503–512, 2010.

[6] A. Blum, K. Ligett, and A. Roth. A learning theory approach to non-interactive database privacy. In *STOC*, pages 609–618, 2008.

[7] S. Boyd and L. Vandenberghe. *Convex Optimization*. Cambridge Univ. Press, 2004.

[8] K. Chaudhuri and C. Monteleoni. Privacy-preserving logistic regression. In *NIPS*, pages 289–296, 2008.

[9] D. P. Dubhashi and A. Panconesi. *Concentration of Measure for the Analysis of Randomized Algorithms*. Cambridge Univ. Press, 2009.

[10] C. Dwork. Differential privacy: A survey of results. In *TAMC*, pages 1–19, 2008.

[11] C. Dwork. The differential privacy frontier (extended abstract). In *TCC*, pages 496–502, 2009.

[12] C. Dwork, F. McSherry, K. Nissim, and A. Smith. Calibrating noise to sensitivity in private data analysis. In *TCC*, pages 265–284, 2006.

[13] D. Feldman, A. Fiat, H. Kaplan, and K. Nissim. Private coresets. In *STOC*, pages 361–370, 2009.

[14] A. Friedman and A. Schuster. Data mining with differential privacy. In *KDD*, pages 493–502, 2010.

[15] B. C. M. Fung, K. Wang, R. Chen, and P. S. Yu. Privacy-preserving data publishing: A survey on recent developments. *ACM Comput. Surv.*, 42(4), 2010.

[16] S. R. Ganta, S. P. Kasiviswanathan, and A. Smith. Composition attacks and auxiliary information in data privacy. In *KDD*, pages 265–273, 2008.

[17] A. Ghosh, T. Roughgarden, and M. Sundararajan. Universally utility-maximizing privacy mechanisms. In *STOC*, pages 351–360, 2009.

[18] M. Götz, A. Machanavajjhala, G. Wang, X. Xiao, and J. Gehrke. Publishing search logs - a comparative study of privacy guarantees. *TKDE*, 2011.

[19] M. Hay, V. Rastogi, G. Miklau, and D. Suciu. Boosting the accuracy of differentially-private queries through consistency. In *PVLDB*, pages 1021–1032, 2010.

[20] S. P. Kasiviswanathan, H. K. Lee, K. Nissim, S. Raskhodnikova, and A. Smith. What can we learn privately? In *FOCS*, pages 531–540, 2008.

[21] D. Kifer. Attacks on privacy and deFinetti's theorem. In *SIGMOD*, pages 127–138, 2009.

[22] A. Korolova, K. Kenthapadi, N. Mishra, and A. Ntoulas. Releasing search queries and clicks privately. In *WWW*, pages 171–180, 2009.

[23] C. Li, M. Hay, V. Rastogi, G. Miklau, and A. McGregor. Optimizing histogram queries under differential privacy. In *PODS*, pages 123–134, 2010.

[24] N. Li, T. Li, and S. Venkatasubramanian. t-closeness: Privacy beyond k-anonymity and l-diversity. In *ICDE*, pages 106–115, 2007.

[25] X. Li, J. Han, and H. Gonzalez. High-dimensional OLAP: A minimal cubing approach. In *VLDB*, pages 528–539, 2004.

[26] A. Machanavajjhala, J. Gehrke, D. Kifer, and M. Venkitasubramaniam. l-diversity: Privacy beyond k-anonymity. In *ICDE*, page 24, 2006.

[27] A. Machanavajjhala, D. Kifer, J. M. Abowd, J. Gehrke, and L. Vilhuber. Privacy: Theory meets practice on the map. In *ICDE*, pages 277–286, 2008.

[28] F. McSherry. Privacy integrated queries: an extensible platform for privacy-preserving data analysis. In *SIGMOD*, pages 19–30, 2009.

[29] F. McSherry and I. Mironov. Differentially private recommender systems: building privacy into the Netflix prize contenders. In *KDD*, pages 627–636, 2009.

[30] K. Nissim, S. Raskhodnikova, and A. Smith. Smooth sensitivity and sampling in private data analysis. In *STOC*, pages 75–84, 2007.

[31] V. Rastogi and S. Nath. Differentially private aggregation of distributed time-series with transformation and encryption. In *SIGMOD*, pages 735–746, 2010.

[32] P. Samarati and L. Sweeney. Generalizing data to provide anonymity when disclosing information (abstract). In *PODS*, page 188, 1998.

[33] S. D. Silvey. *Statistical Inference*. Chapman-Hall, 1975.

[34] L. Wang, S. Jajodia, and D. Wijesekera. Preserving privacy in on-line analytical processing data cubes. In *Secure Data Management in Decentralized Systems*, pages 355–380. 2007.

[35] R. C.-W. Wong, A. W.-C. Fu, K. Wang, and J. Pei. Minimality attack in privacy preserving data publishing. In *VLDB*, pages 543–554, 2007.

[36] X. Xiao, G. Wang, and J. Gehrke. Differential privacy via wavelet transforms. In *ICDE*, pages 225–236, 2010.

APPENDIX: Proofs

Proof of Theorem 2. The vector $F_{\text{all}}(T)$ has sensitivity $S(F_{\text{all}}) = |\mathcal{L}|$. So from Theorem 1, $\mathcal{K}_{\text{all}}$ is ϵ-DP. As the noise is $\text{Lap}(|\mathcal{L}|/\epsilon)$, we have $\text{E}[\tilde{c}(a)] = c(a)$ and $\text{Var}[\tilde{c}(a)] = 2|\mathcal{L}|/\epsilon^2$. □

Proof of Theorem 3. The sensitivity $S(F_{\text{base}}) = 1$. So from Theorem 1, publishing $F_{\text{base}}(T)+\langle\text{Lap}(1/\epsilon)\rangle$ is ϵ-DP. For any other cell a not in the base cuboid, the computation of $\tilde{c}(a)$ takes the released base cuboid as input, so from the composition property [28], is ϵ-DP. For a cell a in a cuboid C, it aggregates $\Pi_{A_j\notin[C]}|A_j|$ cells $\{a'\}$ in the base cuboid. Then $\text{E}[\tilde{c}(a)] = \Sigma_{a'}\text{E}[\tilde{c}(a')] = \Sigma_{a'}c(a') = c(a)$. And since noise is generated independently, we have the variance $\text{Var}[\tilde{c}(a)] = \Sigma_{a'}\text{Var}[\tilde{c}(a')] = \left(\Pi_{A_j\notin[C]}|A_j|\right)\cdot 2/\epsilon^2$. □

Proof of Theorem 4.

Consider measures $\langle c(a)\rangle$ for all cells in the s selected cuboids in $\mathcal{L}_{\text{pre}}$, the sensitivity of publishing $\mathcal{L}_{\text{pre}}$ is $s = |\mathcal{L}_{\text{pre}}|$. So by Theorem 1 and the composition property of DP, adding a noise $\text{Lap}(s/\epsilon)$ to each cell in $\mathcal{L}_{\text{pre}}$ and computing $\mathcal{L}$ from $\mathcal{L}_{\text{pre}}$ is ϵ-DP.

$\text{E}[\tilde{c}(a)] = c(a)$ is also from the linearity of expectation. □

Proof of Theorem 5.

To complete the proof, we reduce the problem VERTEX COVER IN DEGREE-3 GRAPHS to the BOUND MAX VARIANCE problem. Then the hardness of the PUBLISH MOST problem follows.

Following is an instance of the VERTEX COVER problem in a degree-3 graph (where the degree of a vertex is bounded by 3). Given a degree-3 (undirected) graph $G(V, E)$ where $|V| = n$, decide if G has a vertex cover $V' \subseteq V$ with at most m ($< n$) vertices. $V' \subseteq V$ is said to be a vertex cover of G iff for any edge $uv \in E$, we have either $u \in V'$ or $v \in V'$. Abusing the notations a bit, let $\text{cov}(v)$ be the edges incident on a vertex v, then we want to decide if there is $V' \subseteq V$ such that $\cup_{v\in V'}\text{cov}(v) = E$ and $|V'| \leq m$.

We can assume the degree of any vertex in V is larger than 1, since a degree-1 vertex will be never chosen into a minimum vertex cover. And since there is at least one vertex with degree 3 (otherwise G can be decomposed into cycles which are the trivial case for the VERTEX COVER problem), we have $|E| > 2n/2 = n$.

Construct an instance of the BOUND MAX VARIANCE problem from the above instance of VERTEX COVER problem, accordingly:

(i) For each edge $e \in E$, create a dimension A_e with cardinality $|A_e| = 2$, and a 1-dim cuboid $[C_e^1] = \{A_e\}$.

(ii) Create $3n$ distinct dimensions $B_1, \ldots, B_{3n}$, each of cardinality 2. For each of them, create a 1-dim cuboid $[C_i^1] = \{B_i\}$.

(iii) For each vertex $v \in V$, create a 3-dim cuboid $[C_v^3] = \{A_{e_1}, A_{e_2}, A_{e_3}\}$ for each edge e_i incident on v. Note that a vertex may have less than 3 edges incident on it; in this case, we create one or two new distinct dimensions with cardinality 2, and include them in $[C_v^3]$. So we create n 3-dim cuboids here.

(iv) Create another n 3-dim cuboids C_x^3's: each cuboid $[C_x^3] = \{B_{x_1}, B_{x_2}, B_{x_3}\}$, where each B_{x_i}'s are distinct dimensions with cardinality 2 created in (ii).

(v) For each 3-dim cuboid, $[C_v^3] = \{A_{e_1}, A_{e_2}, A_{e_3}\}$ or $[C_x^3] = \{B_{x_1}, B_{x_2}, B_{x_3}\}$, create a new dimension D_v or D_x, respectively, with cardinality 4, and a 4-dim cuboid $[C_v^4] = \{A_{e_1}, A_{e_2}, A_{e_3}, D_v\}$ or $[C_x^4] = \{B_{x_1}, B_{x_2}, B_{x_3}, D_x\}$, respectively. So in total, we have $2n$ 4-dim cuboids created here.

In this instance of the BOUND MAX VARIANCE problem, we want to publish all the 1-dim, 3-dim, and 4-dim cuboids in (i)-(v), denoted by $\mathcal{L}$, and to decide if we can select a set of cuboids $\mathcal{L}_{\text{pre}}$ such that the max noise variance in releasing $\mathcal{L}$ from $\mathcal{L}_{\text{pre}}$ using $\mathcal{K}_{\text{part}}$ is at most $8(3n+m)^2/\epsilon^2$ ($\text{noise}(\mathcal{L}_{\text{pre}}) \leq 8(3n+m)^2/\epsilon^2$).

We prove the VERTEX COVER instance is YES if and only if the BOUND MAX VARIANCE instance is YES, to complete our proof. Due to the space limit, details are deferred to the full version. □

Remark. The main difficulty in the reduction is the lattice structure of cuboids. And, how to prove/disprove the NP-hardness when the number of dimensions d is bounded ($d = O(\log|\mathcal{L}|)$) and how to prove the hardness of approximation are interesting open questions.

Proof of Lemma 1. The proof is from the definition: Let $s = |\mathcal{L}_{\text{pre}}|$. If $\text{noise}(C, \mathcal{L}_{\text{pre}}) \leq \theta$, from Equation (2), there is a $C' \in \mathcal{L}_{\text{pre}}$ s.t. $\text{mag}(C, C') \leq \frac{\theta\epsilon^2}{2s^2}$. Thus from Equation (4), $C \in \text{cov}(C', \theta, \epsilon, s)$. The converse direction is similar. □

Proof of Theorem 6.

Approximation Ratio. Suppose the optimal solution is θ^*, i.e., there are s^* cuboids $\mathcal{L}_{\text{pre}}$ s.t. for any $C \in \mathcal{L}$, $\text{noise}(C, \mathcal{L}_{\text{pre}}) \leq \theta^*$. From Lemma 1, equivalently, there are s^* cuboids $C_1^*, \ldots, C_{s^*}^*$ s.t. $\bigcup_{i=1}^{s^*}\text{cov}(C_i^*, \theta^*, \epsilon, s^*) = \mathcal{L}$. And, from Equation (4), for any cuboid C and $\alpha > 0$, $\text{cov}(C, \alpha^2\theta^*, \epsilon, \alpha s^*) = \text{cov}(C, \theta^*, \epsilon, s^*)$.

Suppose in line 4 of Algorithm 1, we have $\theta = \alpha^2\theta^*$ and $s = \alpha s^*$. In the following part, we will prove when $\alpha = \ln|\mathcal{L}| + 1$, the algorithm FEASIBLE($\mathcal{L}$,θ, s) can find s cuboids $C_1', \ldots, C_s'$, s.t. $\bigcup_{i=1}^{s}\text{cov}(C_i', \theta, \epsilon, s) = \mathcal{L}$, which implies that, with $\mathcal{L}_{\text{pre}} = \{C_1', \ldots, C_s'\}$, $\max_{C\in\mathcal{L}}\text{noise}(C, \mathcal{L}_{\text{pre}}) \leq \theta = \alpha^2\theta^*$. So we can conclude that Algorithm 1 finds an $(\ln|\mathcal{L}| + 1)^2$-approximation.

Since for any cuboid C, $\text{cov}(C, \theta, \epsilon, s) = \text{cov}(C, \theta^*, \epsilon, s^*)$ for the selection of θ and p above, we write both of them as $\text{cov}(C)$. Now we only need to prove: if there exists s^* cuboids $C_1^*, \ldots, C_{s^*}^*$ such that $\bigcup_{i=1}^{s^*}\text{cov}(C_i^*) = \mathcal{L}$, the algorithm FEASIBLE finds $s = \alpha s^*$ cuboids $C_1', \ldots, C_s'$ (in this order) s.t. $\bigcup_{i=1}^{s}\text{cov}(C_i') = \mathcal{L}$.

We apply the analysis of the greedy SET COVER algorithm here. Let l_i be the number of cuboids in $\mathcal{L}$ uncovered by $\{C_1', C_2', \ldots, C_i'\}$. Define $l_0 = |\mathcal{L}|$. It is easy to see $l_i \leq (1 - 1/s^*)l_{i-1}$, since every iteration we choose C', which covers the most uncovered cuboids in $\mathcal{L}$ ($\{C_1^*, \ldots, C_{s^*}^*\}$ also cover these uncovered cuboids, so the selected C' covers no less than any of them). So $l_i \leq (1 - 1/s^*)^i|\mathcal{L}|$. When $i \geq (\ln|\mathcal{L}| + 1)s^*$, $l_i < 1$. So, FEASIBLE finds at most $s = (\ln|\mathcal{L}| + 1)s^*$ cuboids covering $\mathcal{L}$.

Comparison to $\mathcal{K}_{\text{all}}$ and $\mathcal{K}_{\text{base}}$. $\mathcal{K}_{\text{all}}$ and $\mathcal{K}_{\text{base}}$ are two special cases of $\mathcal{K}_{\text{part}}$ with $\mathcal{L}_{\text{pre}} = \mathcal{L}$ and $\mathcal{L}_{\text{pre}} = \{\text{the base cuboid}\}$, respectively. Let θ_{all} and θ_{base} be the max noise in $\mathcal{L}$ for these two choices of $\mathcal{L}_{\text{pre}}$ respectively. It is not hard to see, both when $\theta = \theta_{\text{all}}$ and $s = |\mathcal{L}|$, and when $\theta = \theta_{\text{base}}$ and $s = 1$, FEASIBLE will return a solution. So the one found by Algorithm 1 is at least as good.

Time Complexity. If for some θ, the algorithm FEASIBLE returns a feasible solution for some s, then for any $\theta' \geq \theta$, it also returns a feasible solution for some s'. So from the above comparison to $\mathcal{K}_{\text{all}}$, we can use $\theta_R = \theta_{\text{all}} = 2|\mathcal{L}|^2/\epsilon^2$ as upper bound and apply binary search to find the minimum "feasible" θ. Also, it is not hard to see for any two different cuboid sets $\mathcal{L}_{\text{pre}}$ and $\mathcal{L}_{\text{pre}}'$, we have either $\text{noise}(\mathcal{L}_{\text{pre}}) = \text{noise}(\mathcal{L}_{\text{pre}}')$ or $|\text{noise}(\mathcal{L}_{\text{pre}}) - \text{noise}(\mathcal{L}_{\text{pre}}')| \geq 1/\epsilon^2$, for $\text{mag}(C, C')$ is always an integer for any two cuboids C and C'. So we can stop when $|\theta_L - \theta_R| \leq 1/\epsilon^2$. Therefore, overall, lines 2-4 in Algorithm 1 repeats at most $O(\log(|\mathcal{L}|))$ times.

In each iteration of lines 2-4, the algorithm FEASIBLE is called $|\mathcal{L}|$ times. Similar to the SET COVER greedy algorithm, a standard implementation of FEASIBLE needs $O(\sum_{\text{all cuboids } C}|\text{cov}(C)|)$ time (using a linked list of cuboids ordered by their coverage).

$\sum_C|\text{cov}(C)|$ is bounded in two ways: i) There are a total of 2^d cuboids C and each $|\text{cov}(C)| \leq |\mathcal{L}|$. ii) For a k-dim cuboid C, $|\text{cov}(C)| \leq 2^k$; so $\sum_C|\text{cov}(C)| \leq \sum_{k=0}^{d}\binom{d}{k}2^k = 3^d$. So we have $\sum_C|\text{cov}(C)| \leq \min\{3^d, 2^d|\mathcal{L}|\}$. So the overall running time of Algorithm 1 is $O(\min\{3^d, 2^d|\mathcal{L}|\}|\mathcal{L}|\log|\mathcal{L}|)$. □

Proof of Theorem 7.

Approximation Ratio. Suppose the optimal solution is to select s^* cuboids $C_1^*, C_2^*, \ldots, C_{s^*}^*$ as $\mathcal{L}_{\text{pre}}$ such that the number of covered cuboids $|\bigcup_{i=1}^{s^*} \text{cov}(C_i^*, \theta_0, \epsilon, s^*)| = \text{OPT}$ is maximized. Of course, $s^* \leq |\mathcal{L}|$. When $s = s^*$ in line 1 of Algorithm 2, GREEDYCOVER($\mathcal{L}, \theta_0, s^*$) is called. To prove the promised approximation ratio, we only need to prove GREEDYCOVER will select s^* cuboids $C_1', C_2', \ldots, C_{s^*}'$ (in this order) as $\mathcal{L}_{\text{pre}}$ such that $|\bigcup_{i=1}^{s^*} \text{cov}(C_i', \theta_0, \epsilon, s^*)| \geq (1 - 1/e)\text{OPT}$. The proof for this is similar to the one in the proof of Theorem 6. So for the space limit, we omit it here. The weight version (maximize the weight of cuboids covered by $\mathcal{L}_{\text{pre}}$) is very similar to the above.

Comparison to $\mathcal{K}_{\text{all}}$ and $\mathcal{K}_{\text{base}}$. The solution offered by $\mathcal{K}_{\text{all}}$ and $\mathcal{K}_{\text{base}}$ is achieved by Algorithm 2 when $s = |\mathcal{L}|$ and 1, respectively. So the final solution output by Algorithm 2 is at least as good.

Time Complexity. Selecting more than $|\mathcal{L}|$ cuboids into $\mathcal{L}_{\text{pre}}$ does not help, since selecting $\mathcal{L}_{\text{pre}} = \mathcal{L}$ is a better solution than that. So we only consider s from 1 up to $|\mathcal{L}|$. Similar to FEASIBLE, GREEDYCOVER can be implemented in $O(\min\{3^d, 2^d|\mathcal{L}|\})$ time. For the weighted version, an additional factor $O(\log(2^d)) = O(d)$ is needed since we need to maintain a priority queue for all cuboids. So the overall running time is $O(\min\{3^d, 2^d|\mathcal{L}|\}d|\mathcal{L}|)$. □

Proof of Theorem 8.

Independent Laplace noise $\text{Lap}(|\mathcal{L}_{\text{pre}}|/\epsilon)$ is injected to each cell measure $\text{c}(a)$ to publish $\tilde{\text{c}}(a)$. There are a total of $|\mathcal{E}_{\text{pre}}|$ cells; so from the CDF of Laplace distribution and union bound, with probability $1 - \delta$, none of the cells has the absolute noise $|\tilde{\text{c}}(a) - \text{c}(a)|$ larger than $(|\mathcal{L}_{\text{pre}}|/\epsilon) \log(|\mathcal{E}_{\text{pre}}|/\delta)$. $\text{c}(\cdot)$ is a feasible solution to (6) and $\hat{\text{c}}(\cdot)$ is the optimal. So $\forall a \in \mathcal{E}_{\text{pre}}: |\hat{\text{c}}(a) - \text{c}(a)| \leq |\hat{\text{c}}(a) - \tilde{\text{c}}(a)| + |\text{c}(a) - \tilde{\text{c}}(a)| \leq 2|\tilde{\text{c}}(a) - \text{c}(a)| \leq (2|\mathcal{L}_{\text{pre}}|/\epsilon) \log(|\mathcal{E}_{\text{pre}}|/\delta)$. The conclusion follows by summing the above inequalities up. □

Proof of Theorem 9.

LEMMA 2. (Problem 1.10 in [9]) *Let $X = X_1 + X_2 + \ldots + X_n$ where X_i's are independent and identically distributed with the exponential distribution with parameter $\alpha \in (0, 1)$. With probability at least $1 - \delta$, where $\delta = \left(\frac{\eta}{e^{\eta - 1}}\right)^n$, we have $X \leq \eta \text{E}[X]$ ($\eta > 1$).*

The above lemma can be proved by considering the moment generating function. We utilize it to prove Theorem 9 as follows:

For each cell $a \in \mathcal{E}_{\text{pre}}$, since $Y_a = \tilde{\text{c}}(a) - \text{c}(a)$ is a Laplace noise $\text{Lap}(|\mathcal{L}_{\text{pre}}|/\epsilon)$, we have $X_a = |Y_a|$ is distributed with the exponential distribution with parameter $\epsilon/|\mathcal{L}_{\text{pre}}| \in (0, 1)$ if $\epsilon \leq |\mathcal{L}_{\text{pre}}|$. Let $X = \sum_{a \in \mathcal{E}_{\text{pre}}} X_a$. We have $\text{E}[X] = |\mathcal{E}_{\text{pre}}||\mathcal{L}_{\text{pre}}|/\epsilon$. From Lemma 2, we have, with probability at least $1 - \delta$, where $\delta = (\frac{\eta}{e^{\eta-1}})^{|\mathcal{E}_{\text{pre}}|}$, $\sum_{a \in \mathcal{E}_{\text{pre}}} |\tilde{\text{c}}(a) - \text{c}(a)| \leq \frac{|\mathcal{E}_{\text{pre}}||\mathcal{L}_{\text{pre}}|}{\epsilon}\eta$. So $\sum_{a \in \mathcal{E}_{\text{pre}}} |\hat{\text{c}}(a) - \text{c}(a)| \leq \sum_{a \in \mathcal{E}_{\text{pre}}} |\hat{\text{c}}(a) - \tilde{\text{c}}(a)| + \sum_{a \in \mathcal{E}_{\text{pre}}} |\tilde{\text{c}}(a) - \text{c}(a)| \leq \sum_{a \in \mathcal{E}_{\text{pre}}} |\text{c}(a) - \tilde{\text{c}}(a)| + \sum_{a \in \mathcal{E}_{\text{pre}}} |\tilde{\text{c}}(a) - \text{c}(a)| \leq \frac{|\mathcal{E}_{\text{pre}}||\mathcal{L}_{\text{pre}}|}{\epsilon} 2\eta$. The second inequality above is because $\text{c}(\cdot)$ is a feasible solution to (7) but $\hat{\text{c}}(\cdot)$ is the optimal. Set $\eta = \eta/2$ to complete the proof. □

Proof of Theorem 10.

(i) Correctness. We rewrite (8) as an unconstrained version:

$$\text{minimize } f(\hat{\text{c}}(\cdot)) = \sum_{a \in \mathcal{E}_{\text{pre}}} \left[\left(\sum_{a' \in \text{Base}(a)} \hat{\text{c}}(a') \right) - \tilde{\text{c}}(a) \right]^2.$$

To obtain the optimal solution, setting the gradient of $f(\hat{\text{c}}(\cdot))$ w.r.t. $\hat{\text{c}}(a')$ for each base cell a' to be zero. For each base cell a',

$$\frac{\partial f}{\partial \hat{\text{c}}(a')} = 2 \sum_{a:\, a \in \mathcal{E}_{\text{pre}},\, a' \in \text{Base}(a)} \left[\left(\sum_{a' \in \text{Base}(a)} \hat{\text{c}}(a') \right) - \tilde{\text{c}}(a) \right]$$
$$= 2 \sum_{a \in \mathcal{E}_{\text{pre}} \cap \text{Ancs}(a')} (\hat{\text{c}}(a) - \tilde{\text{c}}(a)) = 0,$$

which is equivalent to
$$\sum_{a \in \mathcal{E}_{\text{pre}} \cap \text{Ancs}(a')} \hat{\text{c}}(a) = \sum_{a \in \mathcal{E}_{\text{pre}} \cap \text{Ancs}(a')} \tilde{\text{c}}(a). \quad (15)$$

For any cell a'' in a cuboid C'', sum up Equation (15) for all base cells $a' \in \text{Base}(a'')$. On the left-hand side, we have (let Base denote the set of all base cells)

$$\begin{aligned}
\text{est}(a'') &= \sum_{a' \in \text{Base}(a'')} \sum_{a \in \mathcal{E}_{\text{pre}} \cap \text{Ancs}(a')} \hat{\text{c}}(a) \\
&= \sum_{C \in \mathcal{L}_{\text{pre}}} \sum_{a' \in \text{Base}(a'')} \sum_{a \in C \cap \text{Ancs}(a')} \hat{\text{c}}(a) \\
&= \sum_{C \in \mathcal{L}_{\text{pre}}} \sum_{\substack{a':\, a' \in \text{Base}, \\ a'[C''] = a''[C'']}} \sum_{\substack{a:\, a \in C, \\ a[C] = a'[C]}} \hat{\text{c}}(a) \\
&= \sum_{C \in \mathcal{L}_{\text{pre}}} \sum_{a \in C} \sum_{\substack{a':\, a' \in \text{Base},\, a[C] = a'[C] \\ a'[C''] = a''[C'']}} \hat{\text{c}}(a) \\
&= \sum_{C \in \mathcal{L}_{\text{pre}}} \sum_{\substack{a:\, a \in C, \\ a[C \wedge C''] = a''[C \wedge C'']}} \sum_{\substack{a':\, a' \in \text{Base},\, a[C] = a'[C] \\ a'[C''] = a''[C'']}} \hat{\text{c}}(a) \\
&= \sum_{C \in \mathcal{L}_{\text{pre}}} \sum_{\substack{a:\, a \in C, \\ a[C \wedge C''] = a''[C \wedge C'']}} \left(\hat{\text{c}}(a) \prod_{A_i \in \mathcal{A} - [C] - [C'']} |A_i| \right) \\
&= \sum_{C \in \mathcal{L}_{\text{pre}}} \sum_{\substack{b:\, b \in (C \wedge C''), \\ b[C \wedge C''] = a''[C \wedge C'']}} \left(\hat{\text{c}}(b) \prod_{A_i \in \mathcal{A} - [C] - [C'']} |A_i| \right) \\
&= \sum_{C \in \mathcal{L}_{\text{pre}}} \sum_{\substack{b:\, b \in (C \wedge C''), \\ b[C \wedge C''] = a''[C \wedge C'']}} \deg(C \vee C'') \hat{\text{c}}(b),
\end{aligned} \quad (16)$$

where $\deg(C) = \prod_{A_i \in \mathcal{A} - [C]} |A_i|$ and $\mathcal{A}$ is the set of all dimensions and $|A_i|$ is the cardinality of dimension A_i.

On the right-hand side, we have

$$\text{obs}(a'') = \sum_{a' \in \text{Base}(a'')} \sum_{a \in \mathcal{E}_{\text{pre}} \cap \text{Ancs}(a')} \tilde{\text{c}}(a) = \sum_{\substack{a:\, a \in C \\ a[C''] = a''[C'']}} \text{obs}(a), \quad (17)$$

where C could be any cuboid that is a descendant of C'' and can be computed from $\mathcal{L}_{\text{pre}}$. So $\text{obs}(a'')$ can be computed recursively.

From Equation (15), we know $\text{est}(a'') = \text{obs}(a'')$. Solving a system of linear equations, we can obtain $\hat{\text{c}}(\cdot)$ as in (9)-(14).

(ii) Time Complexity. We consider how to compute $\hat{\text{c}}(a)$ for all cells here (of course including the ones in $\mathcal{L}$). For each base cell a', we compute $\text{obs}(a')$ as in (9) (recall $\text{Base}(a') = \{a'\}$ for a base cell a'), for all base cells using $O(M|\mathcal{L}_{\text{pre}}|)$ time. For other cells a'' in the data cube, we compute $\text{obs}(a'')$ as in (10), from d-dim cuboids to the 0-dim cuboid, using $O(Nd^2)$ time in total.

Now we compute $\hat{\text{c}}(a)$ from the 0-dim cuboid to d-dim cuboids as in (12)-(14): assuming $\deg(\cdot)$ and $\text{ratio}(\cdot)$ have been precomputed, $\text{aux}(a'')$ (and thus $\hat{\text{c}}(a'')$) can be computed in $O(d|\mathcal{L}_{\text{pre}}|)$ time as for each $C \in \mathcal{L}_{\text{pre}}$, there is only one cell b satisfying the summing-up condition in (13). So in total, we need $O(N(d^2 + d|\mathcal{L}_{\text{pre}}|))$ time to compute $\hat{\text{c}}(a)$ for all cells in the data cube.

(iii) Unbiased. We can prove $\text{E}[\hat{\text{c}}(a)] = \text{c}(a)$ by induction on the dimensionality of a. Recall $\text{E}[\tilde{\text{c}}(a)] = \text{c}(a)$. For the 0-dim cell a_0, we have $\text{aux}(a_0) = 0$, and thus from (9) and (14), $\hat{\text{c}}(a_0)$ is nothing but the weighted average of "different ways to obtain it from cuboids in $\mathcal{L}_{\text{pre}}$". We can show $\text{E}[\hat{\text{c}}(a_0)] = \text{c}(a_0)$ using the linearity of expectation. For an i-dim cell, we first take expectation on both sides of (14), and then use the linearity of expectation and the induction assumption to draw the conclusion.

(iv)-(v) Optimality. For (i) and (iii), $\hat{\text{c}}(\cdot)$ is the *ordinary least squares estimator* (minimizing L^2 norm (8)) and unbiased. Independent noise with identical variance is injected. So the promised properties follow from the Gauss-Markov theorem [33]. □

iReduct: Differential Privacy with Reduced Relative Errors

Xiaokui Xiao†, Gabriel Bender‡, Michael Hay‡, Johannes Gehrke‡

† School of Computer Engineering
Nanyang Technological University
Singapore
xkxiao@ntu.edu.sg

‡Department of Computer Science
Cornell University
Ithaca, NY, USA
{gbender,mhay,johannes}@cs.cornell.edu

ABSTRACT

Prior work in differential privacy has produced techniques for answering aggregate queries over sensitive data in a privacy-preserving way. These techniques achieve privacy by adding noise to the query answers. Their objective is typically to minimize *absolute* errors while satisfying differential privacy. Thus, query answers are injected with noise whose scale is *independent of whether the answers are large or small*. The noisy results for queries whose true answers are small therefore tend to be dominated by noise, which leads to inferior data utility.

This paper introduces *iReduct*, a differentially private algorithm for computing answers with reduced *relative* errors. The basic idea of *iReduct* is to inject different amounts of noise to different query results, so that smaller (larger) values are more likely to be injected with less (more) noise. The algorithm is based on a novel resampling technique that employs *correlated* noise to improve data utility. Performance is evaluated on an instantiation of *iReduct* that generates *marginals*, i.e., projections of multi-dimensional histograms onto subsets of their attributes. Experiments on real data demonstrate the effectiveness of our solution.

Categories and Subject Descriptors

H.2.0 [**DATABASE MANAGEMENT**]: Security, integrity, and protection

General Terms

Algorithms, Security

Keywords

Privacy, Differential Privacy

1. INTRODUCTION

Disseminating aggregate statistics of private data has much benefit to the public. For example, census bureaus already publish aggregate information about census data to improve decisions about the allocation of funding; hospitals could release aggregate information about their patients for medical research. However, since those datasets contain private information, it is important to ensure that the published statistics do not leak sensitive information about any individual who contributed data. Methods for protecting against such information leakage have been the subject of research for decades.

The current state-of-the-art paradigm for privacy-preserving data publishing is *differential privacy*. Differential privacy requires that the aggregate statistics reported by a data publisher should be perturbed by a randomized algorithm $\mathcal{G}$, so that the output of $\mathcal{G}$ remains roughly the same even if any single tuple in the input data is arbitrarily modified. This ensures that given the output of $\mathcal{G}$, an adversary will not be able to infer much about any single tuple in the input, and thus privacy is protected.

In this paper, we consider the setting in which the goal is to publish answers to a batch set of queries, each of which maps the input dataset to a real number [4,8,16,17,21,23,32]. The pioneering work by Dwork et al. [8] showed that it is possible to achieve differential privacy by adding i.i.d. random noise to each query answer if the noise is sampled from a Laplace distribution where the scale of the noise is appropriately calibrated to the query set. In recent years, there has been much research on developing new differentially private methods with improved accuracy [4,16,17,21,32]. Such work has generally focused on reducing the *absolute* error of the queries, and thus the amount of noise injected into a query is *independent of the actual magnitude of the query answer*.

In many applications, however, the error that can be tolerated is *relative* to the magnitude of the query answer: larger answers can tolerate more noise. For example, suppose that a hospital performs queries q_1 and q_2 on a patient record database in order to obtain counts of two different but potentially overlapping medical conditions. Suppose the first condition is relatively rare, so that the exact answer for q_1 is 10, while the second is common, so that the exact answer for q_2 is 10000. In that case, the noisy answer to q_1 might be dominated by noise, even though the result of q_2 would be quite accurate. Other applications where *relative* errors are important include learning classification models [12], selectivity estimation [13], and approximate query processing [29].

Our Contributions. This paper introduces several techniques that automatically adjust the scale of the noise to reduce *relative* errors while still ensuring differential privacy. Our main contribution is the *iReduct* algorithm (Section 4). In a nutshell, *iReduct* initially obtains very rough estimates of the query answers and subsequently uses this information to iteratively refine its estimates with the goal of minimizing relative errors. Ordinarily, iterative resampling would incur a considerable privacy "cost" because each noisy answer to the same query leaks additional information. We avoid this cost by using an innovative resampling function we call *NoiseDown*. The key to *NoiseDown* is that it resamples conditioned on previous samples, generating a sequence of correlated estimates of successively reduced noise magnitude. We prove that the privacy cost of the sequence is equivalent to the cost of sampling a *single* Laplace random variable having the same noise magnitude as the last estimate in the sequence produced by *NoiseDown*.

To demonstrate the application of *iReduct*, we present an instantiation of *iReduct* for generating *marginals*, i.e., the projections of a multi-dimensional histogram onto various subsets of its attributes (Section 5). With extensive experiments on real data (Section 6), we show that *iReduct* has lower relative errors than existing solutions and other baseline techniques introduced in this paper. In addition, we demonstrate the practical utility of optimizing for relative errors, showing that it yields more accurate machine learning classifiers.

2. PRELIMINARIES

2.1 Problem Formulation

Let T be a dataset, and $Q = [q_1, \dots, q_m]$ be a sequence of m queries on T, each of which maps T to a real number. We aim to publish the results of all queries in Q on T using an algorithm that satisfies *ϵ-differential privacy*, a notion of privacy defined based on the concept of *neighboring datasets*.

DEFINITION 1 (NEIGHBORING DATASETS). *Two datasets T_1 and T_2 are* ***neighboring datasets*** *if they have the same cardinality but differ in one tuple.* □

DEFINITION 2 (ϵ-DIFFERENTIAL PRIVACY [9]). *A randomized algorithm $\mathcal{G}$ satisfies* ***ϵ-differential privacy****, if for any output O of $\mathcal{G}$ and any neighboring datasets T_1 and T_2,*

$$Pr\left[\mathcal{G}(T_1) = O\right] \le e^{\epsilon} \cdot Pr\left[\mathcal{G}(T_2) = O\right]. \ \square$$

We measure the quality of the published query results by their *relative errors*. In particular, the relative error of a published numerical answer r^* with respect to the original answer r is defined as

$$err(r^*) = \frac{|r^* - r|}{\max\{r, \delta\}}, \tag{1}$$

where δ is a user-specified constant (referred to as the *sanity bound*) used to mitigate the effect of excessively small query results. This definition of relative error follows from previous work [13,29]. For ease of exposition, we assume that all queries in Q have the same sanity bound, but our techniques can be easily extended to the case when the sanity bound varies from query to query. Table 1 summarizes the notations that will be frequently used in this paper.

Symbol	Description
$q(T)$	the result of a query q on a dataset T
Q	a given sequence of m queries $[q_1, \dots, q_m]$
Λ	a sequence of m noise scales $[\lambda_1, \dots, \lambda_m]$
δ	the sanity bound for the queries in Q
$S(Q)$	the sensitivity of Q
$GS(Q, \Lambda)$	the generalized sensitivity of Q with respect to Λ
x	an arbitrary real number
y_i	a random variable such that $y_i - x$ follows a Laplace distribution
ξ	$\xi = \min\{x, y - 1\}$
f	the conditional probability density function of y' given x, y, λ, and λ', as defined in Equation 6

Table 1: Frequently Used Notations

2.2 Differential Privacy via Laplace Noise

Dwork et al. [9] show that ϵ-differential privacy can be achieved by adding i.i.d. noise to the result of each query in Q. Specifically, the noise is sampled from the *Laplace distribution* which has the following probability density function (p.d.f.)

$$Pr[\eta = x] = \frac{1}{2\lambda} e^{-|x-\mu|/\lambda}, \tag{2}$$

where μ is the mean of the distribution (we assume $\mu = 0$ unless stated otherwise) and λ (referred to as the *noise scale*) is a parameter that controls the degree of privacy protection. A random variable that follows the Laplace distribution has a standard deviation of $\sqrt{2} \cdot \lambda$ and an expected absolute deviation of λ (ie. $E|\eta - \mu| = \lambda$).

The resulting privacy depends both on the scale of the noise and the *sensitivity* of Q. Informally, sensitivity measures the maximum change in query answers due to changing a single tuple in the database.

DEFINITION 3 (SENSITIVITY [9]). *The* ***sensitivity*** *of a sequence Q of queries is defined as*

$$S(Q) = \max_{T_1, T_2} \sum_{i=1}^{m} |q_i(T_1) - q_i(T_2)| \tag{3}$$

where T_1 and T_2 are any neighboring datasets. □

Dwork et al. prove that adding Laplace noise of scale λ leads to $(S(Q)/\lambda)$-differential privacy.

PROPOSITION 1 (PRIVACY FROM LAPLACE NOISE [9]). *Let Q be a sequence of queries and $\mathcal{G}$ be an algorithm that adds i.i.d. noise to the result of each query in Q, such that the noise follows a Laplace distribution of scale λ. Then, $\mathcal{G}$ satisfies $(S(Q)/\lambda)$-differential privacy.* □

3. FIRST-CUT SOLUTIONS

Dwork et al.'s method, described above, may have high relative errors because it adds noise of fixed scale to every query answer *regardless of whether the answer is large or small*. Thus, queries with small answers have much higher expected relative errors than queries with large answers. In this paper, we propose several techniques that calibrate the noise scale to reduce relative errors. This section describes two approaches. The first is a simple idea that achieves uniform expected relative errors but fails to satisfy differential privacy, while the second is a first attempt at a differentially private solution.

Before presenting the strategies, we introduce an extension to Dwork et al.'s method that adds unequal noise to query answers (adapted from [32]). Let $\Lambda = [\lambda_1, \dots, \lambda_m]$ be a sequence of positive real numbers such that q_i will be answered with noise scale λ_i for $i \in [1, m]$. We extend the notion of sensitivity to a sequence of queries Q and a corresponding sequence of noise scales Λ.

DEFINITION 4 (GENERALIZED SENSITIVITY [32]). *Let Q be a sequence of m queries $[q_1, \dots, q_m]$, and Λ be a sequence of m positive constants $[\lambda_1, \dots, \lambda_m]$. The* ***generalized sensitivity*** *of Q with respect to Λ is defined as*

$$GS(Q, \Lambda) = \max_{T_1, T_2} \sum_{i=1}^{m} \left(\frac{1}{\lambda_i} \cdot |q_i(T_1) - q_i(T_2)| \right), \tag{4}$$

where T_1 and T_2 are any neighboring datasets. □

The following proposition states that adding Laplace noise with unequal scale leads to $GS(Q, \Lambda)$-differential privacy.

PROPOSITION 2 (PRIVACY FROM UNEQUAL NOISE [32]). *Let $Q = [q_1, \ldots, q_m]$ be a sequence of m queries and $\Lambda = [\lambda_1, \ldots, \lambda_m]$ be a sequence of m positive real numbers. Let $\mathcal{G}$ be an algorithm that adds independent noise to the result of each query q_i in Q ($i \in [1, m]$), such that the noise follows a Laplace distribution of scale λ_i. Then, $\mathcal{G}$ satisfies $GS(Q, \Lambda)$-differential privacy.* □

For convenience, we use *LaplaceNoise*(T, Q, Λ) to denote the above algorithm. On input T, Q, Λ, it returns a sequence of noisy answers $Y = [y_1, \ldots, y_m]$, where $y_i = q_i(T) + \eta_i$ and η_i is a sample from a Laplace distribution of scale λ_i for $i \in [1, m]$.

3.1 Proportional Laplace Noise

To reduce relative errors, a natural but ultimately flawed approach is to set the scale of the noise to be proportional to the actual query answer. (Extremely small answers are problematic, so we can set the noise scale to be the maximum of $q_i(T)$ and the sanity bound δ.) We refer to this strategy as *Proportional*. The expected relative error for query q_i is $\lambda_i / \max\{q_i(T), \delta\}$, and so setting $\lambda_i = c \max\{q_i(T), \delta\}$ for some constant c ensures that all query answers have equal expected relative errors, thereby minimizing the *worst-case relative error*.

Unfortunately *Proportional* is flawed because it violates differential privacy. This is because the scale of the noise depends on the input. As a consequence, two neighboring datasets may have different noise scales for the same query, and hence, some outputs may become considerably more likely on one dataset than the other. The following example illustrates the privacy defect of *Proportional*.

EXAMPLE 1. Let $\delta = 1$ and $\epsilon = 1$. Suppose that we have a census dataset that reports the ages of a population consisting of 5 individuals: $T_1 = \{42, 17, 35, 19, 55\}$. We have two queries: q_1 asks for the number of teenagers (ages $13 - 19$), and q_2 asks for the number of people under the age of retirement (ages under 65). Since we have $q_1(T_1) = 2$ and $q_2(T_2) = 5$, the *Proportional* algorithm would set $\Lambda = [\lambda_1, \lambda_2]$ such that $\lambda_1 = 2c$ and $\lambda_2 = 5c$ for some constant c. It can be verified that $c = 7/10$ achieves $GS(Q, \Lambda) = \epsilon$. Thus, we set $\lambda_1 = 2c = 1.4$ and $\lambda_2 = 5c = 3.5$.

Now consider a neighboring dataset T_2 in which one of the teenagers has been replaced with a 20-year old: $T_2 = \{42, 17, 35, \underline{20}, 55\}$. Compared to T_1, the answer on T_2 for q_1 is smaller by 1 and q_2 is unchanged, and accordingly *Proportional* sets the scales so that $\lambda_1 = c$ and $\lambda_2 = 5c$. It can be verified that $c = 6/5$ achieves $GS(Q, \Lambda) = \epsilon$ and so $\lambda_1 = 1.2$ and $\lambda_2 = 6$. Thus, the expected error of q_1 is *higher* on T_1 than on T_2.

If we consider the probability of an output that gives a highly inaccurate answer for the first query, such as $y_1 = 102$ and $y_2 = 5$, we can see it is much more likely on T_1 than T_2:

$$\begin{aligned}
&\frac{Pr[\textit{Proportional} \text{ outputs } y_1, y_2 \text{ given } T_1]}{Pr[\textit{Proportional} \text{ outputs } y_1, y_2 \text{ given } T_2]} \\
&= \frac{\exp(-|y_1 - q_1(T_1)|/1.4) \cdot \exp(-|y_2 - q_2(T_1)|/3.5)}{\exp(-|y_1 - q_1(T_2)|/1.2) \cdot \exp(-|y_2 - q_2(T_2)|/6)} \\
&= \exp(-100/1.4 + 101/1.2) \\
&= \exp(535/42) > \exp(\epsilon).
\end{aligned}$$

This demonstrates that *Proportional* violates differential privacy. □

Algorithm *TwoPhase* $(T, Q, \delta, \epsilon_1, \epsilon_2)$
1. let $m = |Q|$ and q_i be the i-th ($i \in [1, m]$) query in Q
2. initialize $\Lambda = [\lambda_1, \ldots, \lambda_m]$ such that $\lambda_i = S(Q)/\epsilon_1$
3. $Y =$ *LaplaceNoise*(T, Q, Λ)
4. $\Lambda' =$ *Rescale*$(Y, \Lambda, \delta, \epsilon_2)$
5. if $GS(Q, \Lambda') \leq \epsilon_2$
6. $\quad Y' =$ *LaplaceNoise*(T, Q, Λ')
7. $\quad$ for any $i \in [1, m]$
8. $\quad\quad y_i = (\lambda_i'^2 \cdot y_i + \lambda_i^2 \cdot y_i')/(\lambda_i^2 + \lambda_i'^2)$
9. return Y

Figure 1: The *TwoPhase* Algorithm

3.2 Two-Phase Noise Injection

To overcome the drawback of *Proportional*, a natural idea is to ensure that the scale of the noise is decided in a differentially private manner. Towards this end, we may first apply *LaplaceNoise* to compute a noisy answer for each query in Q, and then use the noisy answers (instead of the exact answers) to determine the noise scale. This motivates the *TwoPhase* algorithm illustrated in Figure 1.

TwoPhase takes as input five parameters: a dataset T, a sequence Q of queries, a sanity bound δ, and two positive real numbers ϵ_1 and ϵ_2. Its output is a sequence $Y = [y_1, \ldots, y_m]$ such that y_i is a noisy answer for each query q_i. The algorithm is called *TwoPhase* because it interacts with the private data twice. In the first phase (Lines 1-3), it uses *LaplaceNoise* to compute noisy query answers, such that the scale of noise for all queries is equal to $S(Q)/\epsilon_1$.

In the second phase (Lines 4-8), the noise scales are adjusted (based on the output of the first phase) and a second sequence of noisy answers is obtained. Intuitively, we would like to rescale the noise so that it is reduced for queries that had small noisy answers in the first phase. This could be done in a manner similar to *Proportional* where the noisy answer y_i is used instead of the private answer $q_i(T)$—i.e., set λ_i' proportional to $\max\{y_i, \delta\}$. However, it is possible to get even lower relative errors by exploiting the structure of the query sequence Q. For now, we will treat this as a "black box" (referred to as *Rescale* on Line 4) and we will instantiate it when we consider specific applications in Section 5. Using the adjusted noise scales Λ', *TwoPhase* regenerates a noisy result y_i' for each query q_i (Line 6), and then estimates the final answer as a weighted average between the two noisy answers for each query (Line 7). Specifically, the final answer for q_i equals $(\lambda_i'^2 \cdot y_i + \lambda_i^2 \cdot y_i')/(\lambda_i^2 + \lambda_i'^2)$, which is an estimate of $q_i(T)$ with the minimum variance among all unbiased estimators of $q_i(T)$ given y_i and y_i' (this can be proved using a Lagrange multiplier and the fact that y_i and y_i' have variance $2\lambda_i^2$ and $2\lambda_i'^2$, respectively).

The following proposition states that *TwoPhase* ensures ϵ-differential privacy.

PROPOSITION 3 (PRIVACY OF *TwoPhase*). *TwoPhase ensures ϵ-differential privacy when its input parameters ϵ_1 and ϵ_2 satisfy $\epsilon_1 + \epsilon_2 \leq \epsilon$.* □

PROOF. *TwoPhase* only interacts with the private data T through two invocations of the *LaplaceNoise* mechanism. The first invocation satisfies ϵ_1-differential privacy, which follows from Proposition 1 and the fact that $\lambda_i = S(Q)/\epsilon_1$ for $i \in [1, m]$. Before the second invocation, the algorithm checks that the generalized sensitivity is at most ϵ_2, therefore by Proposition 2 it satisfies ϵ_2-differential privacy. Finally, differentially private algorithms compose: the sequential application of algorithms $\{G_i\}$, each satisfying ϵ_i-differential privacy, yields $(\sum_i \epsilon_i)$-differential privacy [24]. Therefore *TwoPhase* satisfies $(\epsilon_1 + \epsilon_2)$-differential privacy. □

TwoPhase differs from *Proportional* in that the noise scale is decided based on noisy answers rather than the correct (but private!) answers. While this is an improvement over *Proportional* from a privacy perspective, *TwoPhase* has two principal limitations in terms of utility. The first obvious issue is that errors in the first phase can lead to mis-calibrated noise in the second phase. For example, if we have two queries q_1 and q_2 with $q_1(T) < q_2(T)$, the first phase may generate y_1 and y_2 such that $y_1 > y_2$. In that case, the second phase of *TwoPhase* would incorrectly reduce the noise for q_2.

The second, more subtle issue is that given the requirement that $\epsilon_1 + \epsilon_2 \leq \epsilon$ for a fixed ϵ, it is unclear how to set ϵ_1 and ϵ_2 so that the expected relative error is minimized. There is a tradeoff: If ϵ_1 is too small, the answers in the first phase will be inaccurate and the noise will be mis-calibrated in the second phase, possibly leading to high relative errors for some queries. Although increasing ϵ_1 makes it more likely that the noise scale in the second phase will be appropriately calibrated, the answers in the second phase will be less accurate overall as the noise scale of all queries increases with decreasing ϵ_2. In general, ϵ_1 and ϵ_2 must be chosen to strive a balance between the effectiveness of the first and second phases, which may be challenging without prior knowledge of the data distribution. In the next section, we will remedy this deficiency with a method that does not require user inputs on the allocation of privacy budgets.

4. ITERATIVE NOISE REDUCTION

This section presents *iReduct* (iterative noise reduction), an improvement over the *TwoPhase* algorithm discussed in Section 3. The core of *iReduct* is an iterative process that adaptively adjusts the amount of noise injected into each query answer. *iReduct* begins by producing a noisy answer y_i for each query $q_i \in Q$ by adding Laplace noise of relatively large scale. In each subsequent iteration, *iReduct* first identifies a set Q_Δ of queries whose noisy answers are small and may therefore have high relative error. Next, *iReduct* resamples a noisy answer for each query in Q_Δ, reducing the noise scale of each query by a constant. This iterative process is repeated until *iReduct* cannot decrease the noise scale of any answer without violating differential privacy. Intuitively, *iReduct* optimizes the relative errors of the queries because it gives queries with smaller answers more opportunities for noise reduction.

The aforementioned iterative process is built upon an algorithm called *NoiseDown* which takes as input a noisy result y_i and outputs a new version of y_i with reduced noise scale. We will introduce *NoiseDown* in Sections 4.1 and 4.2 below and present the details of *iReduct* in Section 4.3.

4.1 Rationale of *NoiseDown*

At a high level, given a query q and a dataset T, *iReduct* estimates $q(T)$ by iteratively invoking *NoiseDown* to generate noisy answers to q with reduced noise scales. The properties of the *NoiseDown* function ensure that an adversary who sees the entire sequence of noisy answers can infer no more about the dataset T than an adversary who sees only the last answer in the sequence. For ease of exposition, we focus on executing a single invocation of *NoiseDown*. Let Y (Y') be a Laplace random variable with mean value $q(T)$ and scale λ (λ'), such that $\lambda' < \lambda$. Intuitively, Y represents the noisy answer to q obtained in one iteration, and Y' corresponds to the noisy estimate generated in the next iteration.

Given Y, the simplest approach to generating Y' is to add to the true answer $q(T)$ fresh Laplace noise that is independent of Y and has scale λ'. This approach, however, incurs considerable privacy cost. For example, let q be a count query, such that for any two neighboring datasets T_1 and T_2, we have $q(T_1) - q(T_2) \in \{-1, 0, 1\}$. We will show that an algorithm that publishes independent samples Y' and Y in this scenario can satisfy ϵ-differential privacy only if $\epsilon \geq \frac{1}{\lambda'} + \frac{1}{\lambda}$. In other words, the privacy "cost" of publishing independent estimates of Y' and Y is $\frac{1}{\lambda'} + \frac{1}{\lambda}$.

For any neighboring datasets T_1 and T_2, let q be a count query such that $q(T_1) = c$ and $q(T_2) = c + 1$ for some integer constant c. Then for any noisy answers $y, y' < c$, we have

$$\begin{aligned}
&\frac{Pr\left[Y' = y', Y = y \mid T = T_1\right]}{Pr\left[Y' = y', Y = y \mid T = T_2\right]} \\
&= \frac{Pr\left[Y' = y', Y = y \mid q(T) = c\right]}{Pr\left[Y' = y', Y = y \mid q(T) = c+1\right]} \\
&= \frac{\frac{1}{2\lambda'} \exp\left(-|c - y'|/\lambda'\right) \cdot \frac{1}{2\lambda} \exp\left(-|c - y|/\lambda\right)}{\frac{1}{2\lambda'} \exp\left(-|c + 1 - y'|/\lambda'\right) \cdot \frac{1}{2\lambda} \exp\left(-|c + 1 - y|/\lambda\right)} \\
&= \exp\left(\frac{1}{\lambda'}\left(|c + 1 - y'| - |c - y'|\right) + \frac{1}{\lambda}\left(|c + 1 - y| - |c - y|\right)\right) \\
&= \exp\left(1/\lambda' + 1/\lambda\right).
\end{aligned}$$

In contrast, the privacy cost of publishing Y' alone is $1/\lambda'$. That is, we pay an extra cost of $1/\lambda$ for sampling Y, even though the sample is discarded once we generate Y'[1].

Intuitively, the reason for this excess privacy cost is that both Y and Y' leak information about the state of the dataset T. Even though Y is less accurate than Y', an adversary who knows Y in addition to Y' has more information than an adversary that knows only Y', because the two samples are *independent*. The problem, then, is that the sampling process for Y' does not depend on the previously sampled value of Y. Therefore, instead of sampling Y' from a fresh Laplace distribution, we want to sample Y' from a distribution that depends on Y. Our aim is to do so in a way such that Y provides no new information about the dataset once the value of Y' is known. We can formalize this objective as follows. From an adversary's perspective, the dataset T is unknown and can be modeled as a random variable. The adversary tries to infer the contents of the dataset by looking at Y' and Y. For any possible dataset T_1, we want the following property to hold:

$$Pr\left[T = T_1 \mid Y = y, Y' = y'\right] = Pr[T = T_1 \mid Y' = y'] \quad (5)$$

To see how this restriction allows us to use the privacy budget more efficiently, let us again consider any two neighboring datasets T_1 and T_2. Observe that when Equation 5 is satisfied, we can apply Bayes' rule (twice) to show that:

$$\begin{aligned}
&Pr[Y' = y', Y = y \mid T = T_i] \\
&= Pr[T = T_i \mid Y' = y', Y = y] \cdot \frac{Pr[Y' = y', Y = y]}{Pr[T = T_i]} \\
&= Pr[T = T_i \mid Y' = y'] \cdot \frac{Pr[Y' = y', Y = y]}{Pr[T = T_i]} \\
&= \frac{Pr[Y' = y' \mid T = T_i] Pr[T = T_i]}{Pr[Y' = y']} \cdot \frac{Pr[Y' = y', Y = y]}{Pr[T = T_i]} \\
&= Pr[Y' = y' \mid T = T_i] \cdot Pr[Y = y \mid Y' = y']
\end{aligned}$$

where the term $Pr[Y = y \mid Y' = y']$ does not depend on the value of T.

[1]Rather than discarding Y, one could combine Y and Y' to derive an estimate of $q(T)$, as done in the *TwoPhase* algorithm (see Line 8 in Figure 1). This does reduce the expected error, but it still has excess privacy cost compared to *NoiseDown*, as explained in Appendix A.

This allows us to derive an upper bound on the privacy cost of an algorithm that outputs Y followed by Y'. Let us again consider a count query q such that $q(T_1) - q(T_2) \in \{-1, 0, 1\}$. Let Y' be a random variable that (i) follows a Laplace distribution with mean $q(T)$ and scale λ' but (ii) is generated in a way that *depends* on the observed value for Y. If these criteria are satisfied and Equation 5 holds, it follows that:

$$\begin{aligned}&\frac{Pr[Y'=y', Y=y \mid T=T_1]}{Pr[Y'=y', Y=y \mid T=T_2]}\\ =&\frac{Pr[Y'=y' \mid T=T_1]\cdot Pr[Y=y \mid Y'=y']}{Pr[Y'=y' \mid T=T_2]\cdot Pr[Y=y \mid Y'=y']}\\ =&\frac{Pr[Y'=y' \mid T=T_1]}{Pr[Y'=y' \mid T=T_2]} \le \exp(1/\lambda')\end{aligned}$$

The last step works because of our assumption that Y' follows a Laplace distribution with scale λ'. The above inequality implies that obtaining *correlated* samples Y' and Y now incurs a total privacy cost of just $1/\lambda'$, i.e., no privacy budget is wasted on Y.

In summary, if Y' follows a Laplace distribution but is sampled from a distribution that depends on Y, and if Equation 5 is satisfied, then we can perform the desired resampling procedure without incurring any loss in the privacy budget. We now define the conditional probability distribution of Y'.

DEFINITION 5 (NOISE DOWN DISTRIBUTION). *The* Noise Down distribution *is a conditional probability distribution on Y' given that $Y = y$. It is defined by the following conditional probability distribution function (p.d.f.). Let μ, λ, λ' be fixed parameters. The conditional p.d.f. of Y' given that $Y = y$ is defined as:*

$$f_{\mu,\lambda,\lambda'}(y'|Y=y) = \frac{\lambda}{\lambda'}\cdot\frac{\exp\left(-\frac{|y'-\mu|}{\lambda'}\right)}{\exp\left(-\frac{|y-\mu|}{\lambda}\right)}\cdot\gamma(\lambda',\lambda,y',y) \quad (6)$$

where $\gamma(\lambda', \lambda, y', y)$

$$\begin{aligned}=&\frac{1}{4\lambda}\cdot\frac{1}{\cosh\left(\frac{1}{\lambda'}\right)-1}\cdot\left(2\cosh\left(\tfrac{1}{\lambda'}\right)\cdot\exp\left(-\tfrac{|y-y'|}{\lambda}\right)\right.\\ &\left.-\exp\left(-\tfrac{|y-y'-1|}{\lambda}\right)-\exp\left(-\tfrac{|y-y'+1|}{\lambda}\right)\right). \quad (7)\end{aligned}$$

and $\cosh(\cdot)$ *denotes the hyperbolic cosine function, i.e.,* $\cosh(z) = (e^z + e^{-z})/2$ *for any* z.

Theorem 1 shows that this conditional distribution has the desired properties, namely, (i) Y' follows a Laplace distribution and (ii) releasing Y in addition to Y' leaks no additional information.

THEOREM 1 (PROPERTIES OF NOISE DOWN). *Let Y be a random variable that follows a Laplace distribution with mean $q(T)$ and scale λ. Let Y' be a random variable drawn from a Noise Down distribution conditioned on the value of Y with parameters μ, λ, λ' such that $\mu = q(T)$ and $\lambda' < \lambda$. Then, Y' follows a Laplace distribution with mean $q(T)$ and scale λ'. Further, Y' and Y satisfy Equation 5 for any values of y', y, and T_1.*

Theorem 1 provides the theoretical basis for the iterative resampling that is key to *iReduct*. The next section describes an algorithm for sampling from the Noise Down distribution.

4.2 Implementing *NoiseDown*

To describe an algorithm for sampling from the Noise Down distribution (Equation 6), it is sufficient to fix $Y = y$ for some real constant y and fix parameters μ, λ, and λ'. Let $f : \mathbb{R} \to [0, 1]$ be defined by $f(y') = f_{\mu,\lambda,\lambda'}(y' \mid Y = y)$, i.e., the conditional p.d.f. from Equation 6. We now describe an algorithm for sampling from the probability distribution defined by f. In the following derivation, we focus on the case where $\mu \le y$; we will describe later the modifications that are necessary to handle the case where $\mu > y$.

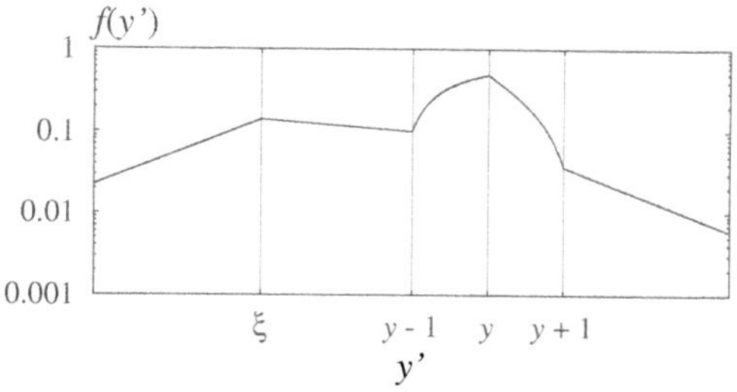

Figure 2: Illustration of f

Let $\xi = \min\{\mu, y-1\}$. By Equation 6, for any $y' \le \xi$,

$$f(y') = e^{y'/\lambda'}\cdot\gamma(\lambda',\lambda,y',y)\cdot\frac{\lambda}{\lambda'}\cdot\exp\left(\frac{-\mu}{\lambda'}+\frac{y-\mu}{\lambda}\right),$$

where

$$\begin{aligned}\gamma(\lambda',\lambda,y',y) =& e^{y'/\lambda}\cdot\frac{1}{4\lambda}\cdot\frac{1}{\cosh\left(\frac{1}{\lambda'}\right)-1}\\ &\cdot\left(2\cosh\left(\tfrac{1}{\lambda'}\right)\cdot\exp\left(\tfrac{-y}{\lambda}\right)-\exp\left(\tfrac{1-y}{\lambda}\right)-\exp\left(\tfrac{-1-y}{\lambda}\right)\right).\end{aligned}$$

(Note that the function γ above is as defined in Equation 7 but takes a simplified form given $y' < \xi$). As μ, y, λ, and λ' are all given, $f(y') \propto \exp(y'/\lambda' + y'/\lambda)$ holds. Similarly, it can be verified that

1. $\forall y' \in (\xi, y-1]$, $f(y') \propto \exp(y'/\lambda - y'/\lambda')$;
2. $\forall y' \in [y+1, +\infty)$, $f(y') \propto \exp(-y'/\lambda' - y'/\lambda)$.

For example, Figure 2 illustrates f with the y-axis in log-scale.

In summary, f conforms to an exponential distribution on each of the following intervals: $(-\infty, \xi]$, $(\xi, y-1]$, and $[y+1, +\infty)$. When the probability mass of f on each of the three intervals is known, it is straightforward to generate random variables that follow f on those intervals. Let $\theta_1 = \int_{-\infty}^{\xi} f(y')dy'$, $\theta_2 = \int_{\xi}^{y-1} f(y')dy'$, and $\theta_3 = \int_{y+1}^{+\infty} f(y')dy'$. It can be shown that

$$\theta_1 = \frac{\lambda\cdot\left(\cosh(\frac{1}{\lambda'})-\cosh(\frac{1}{\lambda})\right)\cdot\exp\left((\frac{1}{\lambda'}+\frac{1}{\lambda})\cdot(\xi-\mu)\right)}{2(\lambda'+\lambda)\cdot\left(\cosh(\frac{1}{\lambda'})-1\right)}, \quad (8)$$

$$\begin{aligned}\theta_2 =& \frac{\lambda\cdot\cosh(\frac{1}{\lambda'})\cdot\left(e^{1/\lambda'}-e^{1/\lambda}\right)\cdot(1-e^{-1/\lambda'-1/\lambda})}{4(\lambda-\lambda')\cdot\left(\cosh(\frac{1}{\lambda'})-1\right)}\\ &\cdot\left(1-\exp\left((\frac{1}{\lambda'}-\frac{1}{\lambda})\cdot(\xi-y+1)\right)\right), \quad (9)\end{aligned}$$

$$\theta_3 = \frac{\lambda\cdot\left(\cosh(\frac{1}{\lambda'})-\cosh(\frac{1}{\lambda})\right)\cdot\exp\left(\frac{\mu-y-1}{\lambda'}-\frac{\mu-y+1}{\lambda}\right)}{2(\lambda'+\lambda)\cdot\left(\cosh(\frac{1}{\lambda'})-1\right)}. \quad (10)$$

For the remaining interval $(y-1, y+1)$ on which f has a complex form, we resort to a standard importance sampling approach. Specifically, we first generate a random sample y' that is uniformly distributed in $(y-1, y+1)$. After that, we toss a coin that comes

Algorithm *NoiseDown* (μ, y, λ, λ')

initialize a boolean variable *invert* = true
if $\mu > y$
  set $\mu = -\mu$, $y = -y$, and *invert* = false
$\xi = \min\{\mu, y - 1\}$
let θ_1, θ_2, θ_3, and φ be as defined in Eqn. 8, 9, 10, and 11
generate a random variable u uniformly distributed in $[0, 1]$
if $u \in [0, \theta_1)$
  generate a random variable $y' \in (-\infty, \xi]$ such that $Pr[y' = y'] \propto \exp(y'/\lambda' + y'/\lambda)$
else if $u \in [\theta_1, \theta_1 + \theta_2]$
  generate a random variable $y' \in (\xi, y - 1]$ such that $Pr[y' = y'] \propto \exp(y'/\lambda - y'/\lambda')$
else if $u \in [1 - \theta_3, 1]$
  generate a random variable $y' \in [y + 1, +\infty)$ such that $Pr[y' = y'] \propto \exp(-y'/\lambda' - y'/\lambda)$
else
  while true
    generate a random variable y' uniformly distributed in $(y - 1, y + 1)$
    generate a random variable u' uniformly distributed in $[0, 1]$
    if $u' \leq f(y')/\varphi$ then break
if *invert* = true then return y'; otherwise, return $-y'$

Figure 3: The *NoiseDown* Algorithm

up heads with a probability $f(y')/\varphi$, where

$$\varphi = \frac{1}{2\lambda'} \cdot \frac{\cosh\left(\frac{1}{\lambda'}\right) - \exp\left(-\frac{1}{\lambda}\right)}{\cosh\left(\frac{1}{\lambda'}\right) - 1} \cdot \exp\left(\frac{y - \mu}{\lambda} - \frac{\max\{0, y - \mu - 1\}}{\lambda'}\right). \quad (11)$$

If the coin shows a tail, we resample y' from a uniform distribution on $(y - 1, y + 1)$, and we toss the coin again. This process is repeated until the coin shows a head, at which time we return y' as a sample from f. The following proposition proves the correctness of our sampling approach.

PROPOSITION 4 (NOISE DOWN SAMPLING). *Given $\mu \leq y$, we have $f(y') < \varphi$ for any $y' \in (y - 1, y + 1)$.* □

So far, we have focused on the case where $\mu \leq y$. For the case when $\mu > y$, we first set $\mu = -\mu$, $y = -y$, and then generate y' using the method described above. After that, we set $y' = -y'$ before returning it as a sample from f. The correctness of this method follows from the following property of the Noise Down distribution $f_{\mu,\lambda,\lambda'}(y'|Y = y)$ (as defined Equation 6):

$$f_{\mu,\lambda,\lambda'}(y'|Y = y) = f_{-\mu,\lambda,\lambda'}(-y'|Y = -y)$$

for any $\mu, \lambda, \lambda', y', y$. As a summary, Figure 3 shows the pseudo-code of the *NoiseDown* function that takes as input $\mu, y, \lambda, \lambda'$ and returns a sample from the distribution defined in Equation 6.

4.3 The *iReduct* Algorithm

We are now ready to present the *iReduct* algorithm, as illustrated in Figure 4. It takes as input a dataset T, a sequence Q of queries on T, a sanity bound δ, and three positive real numbers ϵ, λ_{max}, and λ_Δ. *iReduct* starts by initializing a variable λ_i for each query $q_i \in Q$ ($i \in [1, m]$), setting $\lambda_i = \lambda_{max}$ (Lines 1-2). The user-specified parameter λ_{max} is a large constant that corresponds to the greatest amount of Laplace noise that a user is willing to accept in any query answer returned by *iReduct*. For example, if Q is a sequence of count queries on T then a user may set λ_{max} to 10% of the number of tuples in the dataset T.

Algorithm *iReduct* (T, Q, δ, ϵ, λ_{max}, λ_Δ)

1. let $m = |Q|$ and q_i be the i-th ($i \in [1, m]$) query in Q
2. initialize $\Lambda = [\lambda_1, \ldots, \lambda_m]$, such that $\lambda_i = \lambda_{max}$
3. if $GS(Q, \Lambda) > \epsilon$ then return $\emptyset$
4. $Y = $ *LaplaceNoise*(T, Q, Λ)
5. let $Q' = Q$
6. while $Q' \neq \emptyset$
7. $Q_\Delta = $ *PickQueries*(Q', Y, Λ, δ)
8.   for each $i \in [1, m]$
9.   if $q_i \in Q_\Delta$ then $\lambda_i = \lambda_i - \lambda_\Delta$
10.   if $GS(Q, \Lambda) \leq \epsilon$
11.   for each $i \in [1, m]$
12.   if $q_i \in Q_\Delta$ then $y_i = $ *NoiseDown*$(q_i(T), y_i, \lambda_i + \lambda_\Delta, \lambda_i)$
13.   else
14.   for each $i \in [1, m]$
15.   if $q_i \in Q_\Delta$ then $\lambda_i = \lambda_i + \lambda_\Delta$
16. $Q' = Q' \setminus Q_\Delta$
17. return Y

Figure 4: The *iReduct* Algorithm

As a second step, *iReduct* checks whether the conservative setting of the noise scale guarantees ϵ-differential privacy (Line 3). This is done by measuring the generalized sensitivity of the query sequence given noise scales Λ. If the generalized sensitivity exceeds ϵ, *iReduct* returns an empty set to indicate that the results of Q cannot be released without adding excessive amounts of noise to the queries. Otherwise, *iReduct* generates a noisy result y_i for each query $q_i \in Q$ by applying Laplace noise of scale λ_i (Line 4).

Given Y, *iReduct* iteratively applies *NoiseDown* to adjust the noise in y_i so that noise magnitude is reduced for queries that appear to have high relative errors (Lines 5-16). In each iteration, *iReduct* first identifies a set Q_Δ of queries (Line 7) and then tries to decrease the noise scales of the queries in Q_Δ by a constant λ_Δ (Lines 8-16). The selection of Q_Δ is performed by an application-specific function that we refer to as *PickQueries*. An instantiation of *PickQueries* is given in Section 5.3, but in general, any algorithm can be applied, so long as the algorithm utilizes only the sanity bound δ, the noisy queries answers seen so far, and the queries' noise scales, and does not rely on the true answer $q_i(T)$ of any query q_i. This requirement ensures that the selection of Q_Δ does not reveal any private information beyond what has been disclosed by the noisy results generated so far. For example, if we aim to minimize the maximum relative error of the query results, we may implement *PickQueries* as a function that returns the query q_i that maximizes $\lambda_i / \max\{y_i, \delta\}$, i.e., the query whose noise scale is likely to be large with respect to its actual result.

Once Q_Δ is selected and the scales λ_i have been adjusted accordingly, *iReduct* checks whether the revised scales are permissible given the privacy budget. This is done by measuring the generalized sensitivity given the revised scales (Line 10). If the revised scales are permissible, *iReduct* applies *NoiseDown* to reduce the noise scale of each q_i in Q_Δ by λ_Δ (Lines 11-12). Otherwise, *iReduct* reverts the changes in Λ and removes the queries in Q_Δ from its working set (Line 13-16). This iterative process is repeated until no more queries remain in the working set, which indicates that *iReduct* cannot find a subset of queries whose noise can be reduced without violating the privacy constraint. At this point, it outputs the noisy answers Y.

THEOREM 2 (PRIVACY OF *iReduct*). *iReduct ensures ϵ'-differential privacy whenever its input parameter ϵ satisfies $\epsilon \leq \epsilon'$.* □

5. CASE STUDY: PRIVATE MARGINALS

In this section, we present an instantiation of the *TwoPhase* and *iReduct* algorithms for generating privacy-preserving *marginals*. Section 5.1 describes the problem and discusses existing solutions and Sections 5.2 and 5.3 describe the instantiations of *TwoPhase* and *iReduct*.

5.1 Motivation and Existing Solution

A marginal is a table of counts that summarize a dataset along some dimensions. Marginals are widely used by the U.S. Census Bureau and other federal agencies to release statistics about the U.S. population. More formally, a marginal M of a dataset T is a table of counts that corresponds to a subset $\mathcal{A}$ of the attributes in T. If $\mathcal{A}$ contains k attributes $A_1, A_2, \ldots, A_k$, then M comprises $\prod_{i=1}^{k} |A_i|$ counts, where $|A_i|$ denotes the number of values in the domain of A_i. Each count in M pertains to a point $\langle v_1, v_2, \ldots, v_k \rangle$ in the k-dimensional space $A_1 \times A_2 \times \cdots \times A_k$, and the count equals the number of tuples whose value on A_i is v_i ($i \in [1, k]$). For example, Table 2 illustrates a dataset T that contains three attributes: Age, (Marital) Status, and Gender. Table 3 shows a marginal of T on {Status, Gender}. In general, a marginal defined over a set of k attributes is referred to as a *k-dimensional marginal*.

While a dataset with k attributes can be equivalently represented as a single k-dimensional marginal, such a marginal is likely very sparse (i.e., all counts near zero), and thus will not be able to tolerate the random noise added for privacy. Instead, we therefore publish a set $\mathcal{M}$ of low dimensional marginals, each of which is a projection onto j dimensions for some small $j < k$. This is common practice at statistical agencies, and is consistent with prior work on differentially private marginal release [1].

We can publish $\mathcal{M}$ in a ϵ-differentially private manner as long as we add Laplace noise of scale $2 \cdot |\mathcal{M}|/\epsilon$ to each count in every marginal. This is because changing a record affects only two counts in each marginal (each count would be offset by one), thus the sensitivity of the marginals is $2 \cdot |\mathcal{M}|$, i.e., Laplace noise of scale $2 \cdot |\mathcal{M}|/\epsilon$ suffices for privacy, as shown in Proposition 1. However, adding an equal amount of noise to each marginal in $\mathcal{M}$ may lead to sub-optimal results. For example, suppose that $\mathcal{M}$ contains two marginals M_1 and M_2, such that M_1 (M_2) has a large (small) number of counts, all of which are small (large). If identical amount of noise is injected to M_1 and M_2, then the noisy counts in M_1 would have much higher relative errors than the noisy counts in M_2. Intuitively, a better solution is to apply smaller (larger) amount of noise to M_1 (M_2), so as to balance the quality of M_1 and M_2 without degrading their overall privacy guarantee.

We measure the utility of a set of noisy marginals in terms of minimizing *overall error*, as defined next. Each marginal $M_i \in \mathcal{M}$ is represented as a sequence of queries $[q_{i1}, \ldots, q_{i|M_i|}]$ where q_{ij} denotes the jth query in M_i for $i \in [1, |\mathcal{M}|]$ and $j \in [1, |M_i|]$. Let M_i^* denote a noisy version of marginal M_i and let y_{ij} denote to the noisy answer to q_{ij} for $i \in [1, |\mathcal{M}|]$ and $j \in [1, |M_i|]$.

DEFINITION 6 (OVERALL ERROR OF MARGINALS). *The* overall error *of a set of noisy marginals* $\{M_1^*, \ldots, M_{|\mathcal{M}|}^*\}$ *is defined as*

$$\frac{1}{|\mathcal{M}|} \cdot \sum_{i=1}^{|\mathcal{M}|} \frac{1}{|M_i^*|} \cdot \sum_{j=1}^{|M_i^*|} \frac{|y_{ij} - q_{ij}(T)|}{\max\{\delta, q_{ij}(T)\}}$$

□

We next describe how we instantiate *TwoPhase* and *iReduct* with this utility goal in mind. The query sequence input to both algorithms is simply the concatenation of the individual query sequences for each marginal; i.e., $Q = [q_{11}, \ldots, q_{1|M_1|}, \ldots, q_{|\mathcal{M}|1}, \ldots, q_{|\mathcal{M}||M_{|\mathcal{M}|}|}]$.

Age	Status	Gender
23	Single	M
25	Single	F
35	Married	F
37	Married	F
85	Widowed	F

Table 2: A dataset T

Status	Gender: M	Gender: F
Single	1	1
Married	0	2
Divorced	0	0
Widowed	0	1

Table 3: A marginal of T

5.2 Instantiation of *TwoPhase*

To instantiate *TwoPhase*, we must describe the implementation of the *Rescale* subroutine that was treated as a "black box" in Section 3.2.

Let us first consider an ideal scenario where the first phase of *TwoPhase* returns the exact count of every query q_{ij}. In this case, we know that if we added Laplace noise of scale λ_i to every count in a marginal M_i, then each count $q_{ij}(T)$ in M_i would have an expected relative error of $\lambda_i / \max\{\delta, q_{ij}(T)\}$. (Recall that the expected absolute deviation of a Laplace variable equals its scale.) The expected average relative error in M_i would therefore be $\lambda_i/|M_i| \cdot \left(\sum_{j=1}^{|M_i|} 1/\max\{\delta, q_{ij}(T)\}\right)$. Consequently, to minimize the expected overall error of the marginals, it suffices to ensure that $\sum_{M_i} \left(\lambda_i/|M_i| \cdot \sum_{j=1}^{|M_i|} 1/\max\{\delta, q_{ij}(T)\}\right)$ is minimized, subject to the privacy constraint that the marginals should ensure ϵ-differential privacy, i.e., $\sum_{i=1}^{|\mathcal{M}|} 2/\lambda_i \le \epsilon$. Using a Lagrange multiplier, it can be shown that λ_i should be proportional to $\sqrt{|M_i|/(\sum_{j=1}^{|M_i|} 1/\max\{\delta, q_{ij}(T)\})}$. We refer to this optimal strategy for deciding noise scale as the *Oracle* method. *Oracle* is similar to the *Proportional* algorithm described in Section 3.1, but sets its λ_i values to minimize average rather than worst-case relative error.

Rescale sets the noise scale similarly to how it is set by *Oracle* except that it uses the noisy counts to approximate the exact counts. To be precise, λ_i is proportional to $\sqrt{|M_i|/\sum_{j=1}^{|M_i|} \max\{\delta, y_{ij}\}}$, where y_{ij} denotes the noisy answer produced by the first phase of *TwoPhase*.

5.3 Instantiation of *iReduct*

Before we can use *iReduct* to publish marginals, we need to instantiate two of its subroutines: (i) a method for computing the generalized sensitivity of a set of weighted marginal queries and (ii) an implementation of the *PickQueries* black box (discussed in Section 4.3) that chooses a set Q_Δ of marginal queries for noise reduction. In practice, the sensitivity of a set of marginals depends only on the smallest noise scale in each marginal, and so we gain the best tradeoff between low sensitivity and high utility by always selecting the same noise scale for every count in a given marginal. We maintain the invariant by (i) initially setting all marginal counts to have the same noise scale λ_{max} and (ii) having *PickQueries* always pass to *NoiseDown* the queries corresponding to a single marginal M_i^* in which the noise scale for each cell in M_i^* is reduced by the same constant λ_Δ.

As the counts in the same marginal always have identical noise scale, we can easily derive the generalized sensitivity of the marginal queries as follows. Assume that, in the beginning of a certain iteration, the counts in M_i^* ($i \in [1, |\mathcal{M}|]$) have noise scale λ_i.

	Age	Gender	Marital Status	State	Birth Place	Race	Education	Occupation	Class of Worker
Brazil	101	2	4	26	29	5	5	512	4
US	92	2	4	51	52	14	5	477	4

Table 4: Sizes of Attribute Domains

It can be verified that the generalized sensitivity of the marginals is

$$g_\alpha = \sum_{i \in [1, |\mathcal{M}|]} \frac{2}{\lambda_i} \tag{12}$$

Consider that we apply *NoiseDown* on a noisy marginal M_j^* ($j \in [1, |\mathcal{M}|]$). The noise scale of the queries in M_j^* would become $\lambda_j - \lambda_\Delta$, in which case the generalized sensitivity would become:

$$g_\beta = \frac{2}{\lambda_j - \lambda_\Delta} + \sum_{i \in [1, |\mathcal{M}|] \wedge i \neq j} \frac{2}{\lambda_i}. \tag{13}$$

Recall that, in each iteration of *iReduct*, we aim to ensure that the generalized sensitivity of the queries does not exceed ϵ. Therefore, we can apply *NoiseDown* on a marginal M_j^* only if $g_\beta \leq \epsilon$.

We now discuss our implementation of the *PickQueries* function. Notice that when we apply *NoiseDown* to a noisy marginal M_j^* ($j \in [1, |\mathcal{M}|]$), the expected errors of the estimated counts for that marginal decrease (due to the decrease in the noise scale of M_j^*) but the privacy guarantee degrades. Ideally, running *NoiseDown* on the selected marginal should lead to a large drop in the overall error and a small increase in the privacy overhead. To identify good candidates, we adopt the following methods to quantify the changes in the overall error and privacy overhead that are incurred by invoking *NoiseDown* on a marginal M_j^*.

First, recall that when we employ *NoiseDown* to reduce the noise scale λ_j of M_j^* by a constant λ_Δ, the generalized sensitivity of the noisy marginals increases from g_α to g_β, where g_α and g_β are as defined in Equations 12 and 13. In light of this, we quantify the cost of privacy entailed by applying *NoiseDown* on M_j^* as

$$g_\beta - g_\alpha = \frac{2}{\lambda_j - \lambda_\Delta} - \frac{2}{\lambda_j}. \tag{14}$$

Second, for each noisy count y in M_j^*, we estimate its relative error as $\lambda_j / \max\{y, \delta\}$, where δ is the sanity bound. In other words, we use y to approximate the true count, and we estimate the absolute error of y as the expected absolute deviation λ_j of the Laplace noise added in y. Accordingly, the average relative error of M_j^* is estimated as $\lambda_j \cdot \sum_{y \in M_j^*} 1/\max\{y, \delta\}$. Following the same rationale, we estimate the average relative error of M_j^* after the application of *NoiseDown* as $(\lambda_j - \lambda_\Delta) \cdot \sum_{y \in M_j^*} 1/\max\{y, \delta\}$. Naturally, the decrease in the overall error of the marginals (resulted from invoking *NoiseDown* on M_j^*) is quantified as

$$\frac{1}{|\mathcal{M}|} \cdot \Big(\lambda_j \cdot \sum_{y \in M_j^*} \frac{1}{\max\{y, \delta\}} - (\lambda_j - \lambda_\Delta) \cdot \sum_{y \in M_j^*} \frac{1}{\max\{y, \delta\}}\Big)$$
$$= \frac{\lambda_\Delta}{|\mathcal{M}|} \cdot \sum_{y \in M_j^*} \frac{1}{\max\{y, \delta\}} \tag{15}$$

Given Equations 14 and 15, in each iteration of *iReduct*, we heuristically choose the marginal M_j^* that maximizes

$$\Big(\frac{\lambda_\Delta}{|\mathcal{M}|} \cdot \sum_{y \in M_j^*} \frac{1}{\max\{y, \delta\}}\Big) \Big/ \Big(\frac{2}{\lambda_j - \lambda_\Delta} - \frac{2}{\lambda_j}\Big).$$

That is, we select the marginal that maximizes the ratio between the estimated decrease in overall error and the estimated increase in privacy cost.

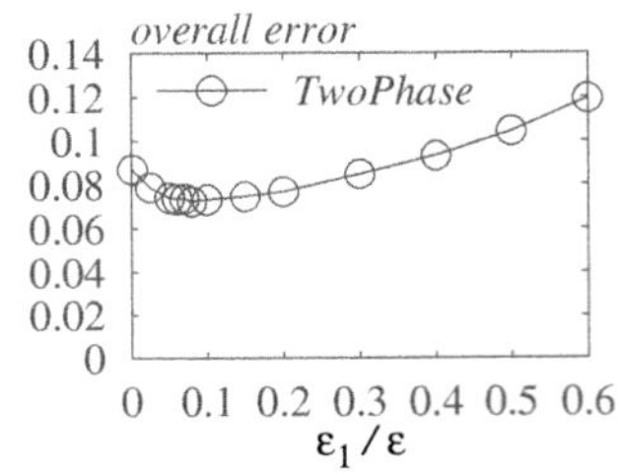

(a) Brazil

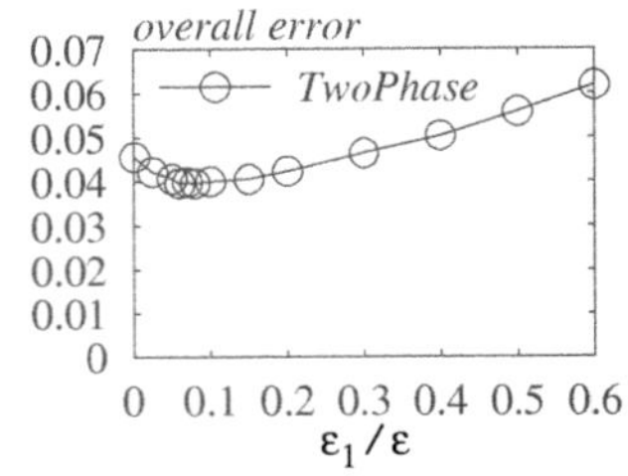

(b) USA

Figure 5: Overall Error vs. ϵ_1/ϵ (1D Marginals)

6. EXPERIMENTS

We evaluate the accuracy of the proposed algorithms on three tasks: estimating all one-way marginals (Section 6.3), estimating all two-way marginals (Section 6.4), and learning a Naive Bayes classifier (Section 6.5).

6.1 Experimental Settings

We use two datasets[2] that are composed of census records collected from Brazil and the US respectively. Each dataset contains nine attributes, whose domain sizes are as illustrated in Table 4. The Brazil dataset consists of nearly 10 million tuples, while the US dataset has around 14 million records.

We use *iReduct* to generate noisy marginals from each dataset, and we compare the performance of *iReduct* against four alternate methods. The first method is the *Oracle* algorithm presented in Section 5.2, which utilizes the exact counts in the marginals to decide the noise scale of each marginal in a manner that minimizes the expected overall error. Although *Oracle* does not conform to ϵ-differential privacy, it provides a lower bound on the error incurred by any member of a large class of ϵ-differential privacy algorithms. The second and third methods are the *TwoPhase* and *iResamp* algorithms presented in Section 3 and Appendix A respectively. The final technique, henceforth referred to as *Dwork*, is Dwork et al.'s method (Section 2.2), which adds an equal amount of noise to each marginal.

We measure the quality of noisy marginals by their overall errors, as defined in Section 5.1. In every experiment, we run each algorithm 10 times, and we report the mean of the overall errors incurred by the algorithm. Among the input parameters of *iReduct*, we fix $\lambda_{max} = |T|/10$ and $\lambda_\Delta = |T|/10^6$, where $|T|$ denotes the number of tuples in the dataset. That is, *iReduct* starts by adding Laplace noise of scale $|T|/10$ to each marginal and, in each iteration, it reduces the noise scale of a selected marginal by $|T|/10^6$. All of our experiments are run on a computer with a 2.66GHz CPU and 24GB memory.

6.2 Calibrating *TwoPhase*

As was discussed in Section 3.2, the performance of the *TwoPhase* algorithm depends on how the fixed privacy budget is allocated across its two phases. This means that before we can use

[2]Both datasets are available online as part of the *Integrated Public Use Microdata Series* [25].

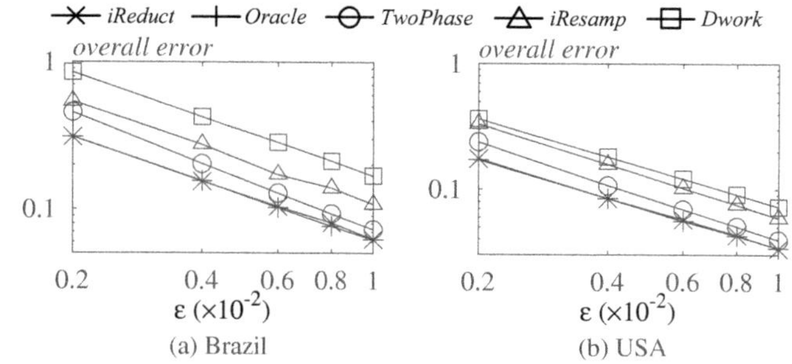

Figure 6: Overall Error vs. ϵ (1D Marginals)

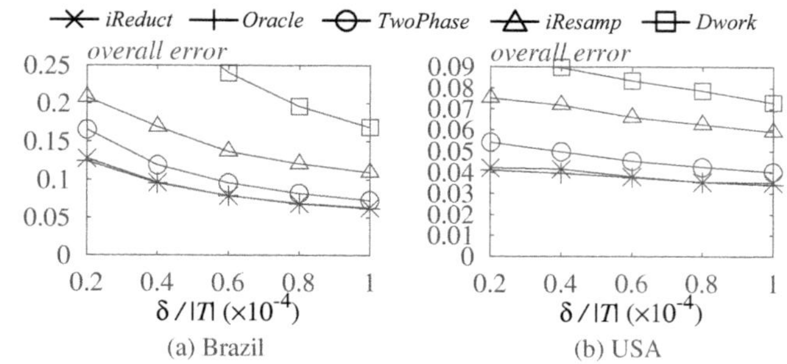

Figure 7: Overall Error vs. δ (1D Marginals)

the *TwoPhase* algorithm, we must decide how to set the values of ϵ_1 and ϵ_2 to optimize the quality of the noisy marginals.

To determine the appropriate setting, we fix $\epsilon = 0.01$ and measure the overall error of *TwoPhase* when ϵ_1 varies and $\epsilon_2 = \epsilon - \epsilon_1$. Figure 5 illustrates the overall error on the set of one-dimensional marginals as a function of ϵ_1/ϵ. As ϵ_1/ϵ increases, the overall error of *TwoPhase* decreases until it reaches a minimum and then increases monotonically. When ϵ_1 is too small, the first step of *TwoPhase* is unable to generate accurate estimates of the marginal counts. This renders the second step of *TwoPhase* less effective, since it relies on the estimates from the first step to determine the noise scale for each marginal. On the other hand, making ϵ_1 too large causes ϵ_2 to becomes small and forces the second step to inject large amounts of noise into all of the marginal counts. The utility of the noisy marginals is optimized only when ϵ_1/ϵ strikes a good balance between the effectiveness of the first and second steps. As shown in Figure 5, the overall error of *TwoPhase* hits a sweet spot when $\epsilon_1 \in [0.06\epsilon, 0.08\epsilon]$. We set $\epsilon_1 = 0.07\epsilon$ in the experiments that follow.

6.3 Results on 1D Marginals

We compare the overall error incurred when each of the five algorithms described above is used to produce differentially private estimates of the one-dimensional marginals of the Brazil and USA census data. We vary both ϵ and δ. Figure 6 shows the overall error of each algorithm as a function of ϵ, with δ fixed to $10^{-4} \cdot |T|$. *iReduct* yields error values that are almost equal to those of *Oracle*, which indicates that its performance is close to optimal. *TwoPhase* performs worse than *iReduct* in all cases, but it still consistently outperforms the other methods. The overall error of *iResamp* is comparable to that of *Dwork*.

Figure 7 illustrates the overall error of each method as a function of the sanity bound δ when $\epsilon = 0.01$. The relative performance of each method is the same as in Figure 6. The overall errors of all algorithms decrease as δ increases, since a larger δ leads to lower relative errors for marginal counts smaller than δ (see Equation 1).

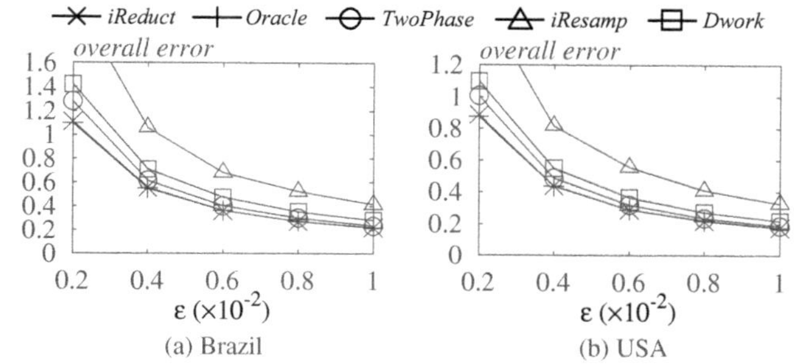

Figure 8: Overall Error vs. ϵ (2D Marginals)

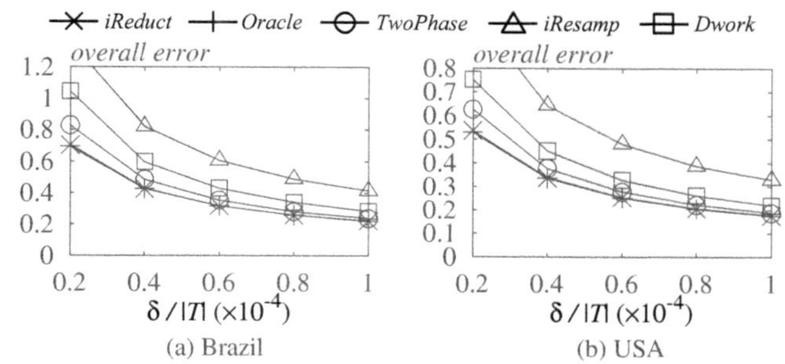

Figure 9: Overall Error vs. δ (2D Marginals)

In the aforementioned experiments, every method but *iReduct* needs only a few linear scans of the marginal counts to generate its output, and therefore incurs negligible computation cost. In contrast, the inner loop of *iReduct* is executed $O(\lambda_{max}/\lambda_\Delta)$ times, and the *iReduct* takes around 5 seconds to output a set of marginal counts. The relative high computational overhead of *iReduct* is justified by the fact that it provides improved data utility over the other methods.

6.4 Results on 2D Marginals

In the second sets of experiments, we consider the task of generating all two-dimensional marginals of the datasets. For the input parameters of *TwoPhase*, we set $\epsilon_1/\epsilon = 0.025$ based on an experiment similar to that described in Section 6.2. Figure 8 shows the overall error of each method when $\delta = 10^{-4} \cdot |T|$ and ϵ varies. The overall error of *iReduct* is almost the same as that of *Oracle*. *TwoPhase* is outperformed by *iReduct*, but its overall error is consistently lower than that of *iResamp* or *Dwork*. Interestingly, the performance gaps among *iReduct*, *TwoPhase*, and *Dwork* are not as substantial as the case for one-dimensional marginals. The reason is that a large fraction of the two-dimensional marginals are sparse. As a consequence, *iReduct* and *TwoPhase* apply roughly equal amounts of noise to those marginals in order to reduce overall error. The noise scale of the marginals is therefore relatively uniform: the allocation of noise scale selected by *iReduct* or *TwoPhase* does not differ too much from the allocation used by *Dwork*. This explains why the improvement of *iReduct* and *TwoPhase* over *Dwork* is less significant. Figure 9 illustrates the overall error of each algorithm as a function of δ, with $\epsilon = 0.1$. The relative performance of each technique remains the same as in Figure 8.

Regarding computation cost, *iReduct* requires around 15 minutes to generate each set of two-dimensional marginals. This running time is considerably longer than for one-dimensional marginals because *iReduct* must handle more marginal counts in the two-dimensional case.

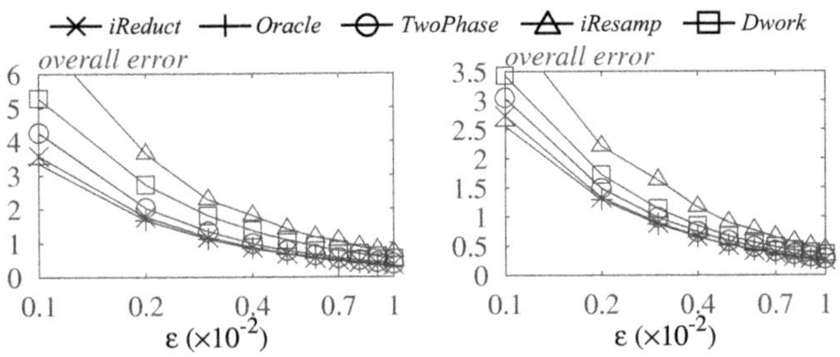

(a) Brazil (b) USA

Figure 10: Overall Error vs. ϵ (Marginals for Classifier)

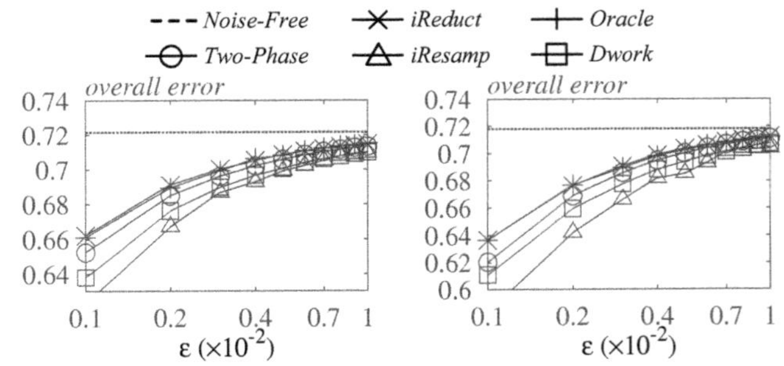

(a) Brazil (b) USA

Figure 11: Accuracy of Classifier vs. ϵ

6.5 Results on Naive Bayes Classifier

Our last set of experiments demonstrates that relative error is an important metric for real-world analytic tasks. In these experiments, we consider the task of constructing a Naive Bayes classifier from each dataset. We use *Education* as the class variable and the remaining attributes as feature variables. The construction of such a classifier requires 9 marginals: a one-dimensional marginal on *Education* and 8 two-dimensional marginals, each of which contains *Education* along with another attribute. We apply each algorithm to generate noisy versions of the 9 marginals, and we measure the accuracy of the classifier built from the noisy data[3].

For robustness of measurements, we adopt 10-fold cross-validation in evaluating the accuracy of classification. That is, we first randomly divide the dataset into 10 equal-size subsets. Next, we take the union of 9 subsets as the training set and use the remaining subset for validation. This process is repeated 10 times in total, using each subset for validation exactly once. We report (i) the average overall error of the 10 sets of noisy marginals generated from the 10 training datasets and (ii) the average accuracy of the classifiers built from the 10 sets of noisy marginals.

Figure 10 illustrates the overall error incurred by each algorithm when $\delta = 10^{-4} \cdot |T|$ and ϵ varies. (The input parameter ϵ_1 of *TwoPhase* is set to 0.03 based on an experiment similar to that described in Section 6.2.) Again, *iReduct* and *Oracle* entail the smallest errors in all cases, followed by *TwoPhase*. In addition, *iResamp* consistently incurs higher error than *Dwork* does. Figure 11 shows the accuracy of the classifiers built upon the output of each algorithm. The dashed line in the figure illustrates the accuracy of a classifier constructed from a set of marginals without any injected noise. Observe that methods that incur lower relative errors lead to more accurate classifiers.

7. RELATED WORK

There is a plethora of techniques [1–5, 5, 9–12, 14, 15, 17–20, 22, 26–28, 32] for enforcing ϵ-differential privacy in the publication of various types of data, such as relational tables [9, 17, 21, 32], search logs [15, 20], data mining results [12, 23], and so on. None of these techniques optimizes the relative errors of the published data; instead, they optimize either (i) the variance of the noisy results or (ii) some application-specific metric such as the accuracy of classification [12]. Below, we will discuss several pieces of work that are closely related to (but different from) ours.

Barak et al. [1] devise a technique for publishing marginals of a given dataset. Their objective, however, is not to improve the accuracy of the released marginal counts. Instead, their technique is designed to make the noisy marginals more user-friendly by ensuring that (i) every marginal count is non-negative and (ii) all marginals are *consistent*, i.e. the sum of the counts in one marginal should equal the sum in any other marginal. Kasiviswanathan et al. [19] present a theoretical study on marginal publishing, and they prove several lower bounds on the absolute errors of the noisy marginal counts. Nevertheless, they do not propose any concrete algorithm for releasing marginals.

Blum et al. [4] present a method for releasing one-dimensional data that provides a worst-case guarantee on the absolute errors of range count query results. Hay et al. [17] propose a algorithm that improves the performance bound of Blum et al.'s method, while Xiao et al. [32] devise an approach for multi-dimensional data that achieves a bound similar to Hay et al.'s. Li et al. [21] generalize both Hay et al.'s and Xiao et al.'s approaches, and propose an optimal technique that minimizes the absolute errors of any given set of range count queries. In principle, the techniques above can also be adapted for marginal publishing, since each marginal count can be regarded as the answer to a range count query. However, since those techniques optimize only the absolute errors of the marginal counts, they would incur large relative errors for small counts in the marginals, as is the case for Dwork et al's method.

Besides the aforementioned work on ϵ-differential privacy, there is also a technique by Xiao et al. [31] that is worth mentioning. Given a dataset T, Xiao et al.'s technique generates a collection of noisy datasets $\{T_1^*, T_2^*, \ldots, T_m^*\}$ that satisfies two conditions. First, for any $j < i$, T_j^* contains more noise than T_i^*. Second, $Pr[T \mid T_1^*, \ldots, T_m^*] = Pr[T \mid T_m^*]$, i.e., the combination of all noisy data reveals no more information than the least noisy version T_m^* of T. Our *NoiseDown* algorithm provides a very similar guarantee. Nevertheless, Xiao et al.'s method cannot be used to implement *NoiseDown*, since their method is applicable only when the noisy data is computed using an approach called *randomized response* [30]. In contrast, *NoiseDown* requires that the the noise injected into query outputs follow a Laplace distribution.

8. CONCLUSIONS

Existing techniques for differentially private query publishing optimize only the absolute error of the published query results, which may lead to large relative errors for queries with small answers. This paper remedies the problem with *iReduct*, a novel algorithm for generating differentially private results with reduced relative errors. We present an instantiation of *iReduct* for generating marginals, and we demonstrate its effectiveness through extensive experiments with real data. *iReduct* outperforms several other candidate approaches and, unlike *TwoPhase*, it does not require parameter tuning.

Our technique for generating marginals could be used as a ba-

[3]Following previous work [6], we postprocess each noisy marginal cell y by setting $y = \max\{y + 1, 1\}$ before constructing the classifier from the marginals.

sis for releasing a table of "synthetic" records. Since our computations are differentially private, the table would satisfy a much stronger guarantee than approaches based on anonymity. Furthermore, many counting queries executed on the synthetic records would have low relative errors relative to the original data. There is a tight connection between marginals and log-linear statistical models, as well as algorithms for sampling [7]. However, a challenge remains: the noise introduced for privacy may produce marginals that are *infeasible*, meaning that it is impossible to construct a table that is consistent with the marginals.

Finally, note that the *iReduct* algorithm introduces subtle correlations between the answers that it outputs. This is because the magnitude of the noise injected into each query answer depends not only on the true answer for that query but also on noisy answers to the other queries under consideration. We believe that such correlations may be necessary to minimize relative error. In fact, differentially private techniques that produce correlated answers are not uncommon [1, 4, 15, 17, 21, 29]. Further investigation into the implications of such correlations is left as future work.

9. ACKNOWLEDGMENTS

This work was supported by Nanyang Technological University under SUG Grant M58020016 and AcRF Tier 1 Grant RG 35/09, by the Agency for Science, Technology and Research (Singapore) under SERG Grant 1021580074, by the Computing Innovation Fellows Project (`http://cifellows.org/`), funded by the Computing Research Association/Computing Community Consortium through NSF Grant 1019343, by the NSF under Grants IIS-0627680 and IIS-1012593, and by the New York State Foundation for Science, Technology, and Innovation under Agreement C050061. Any opinions, findings, conclusions or recommendations expressed are those of the authors and do not necessarily reflect the views of the sponsors.

10. REFERENCES

[1] B. Barak, K. Chaudhuri, C. Dwork, S. Kale, F. McSherry, and K. Talwar. Privacy, accuracy, and consistency too: a holistic solution to contingency table release. In *Proc. of ACM Symposium on Principles of Database Systems (PODS)*, pages 273–282, 2007.

[2] A. Beimel, S. P. Kasiviswanathan, and K. Nissim. Bounds on the sample complexity for private learning and private data release. In *Theory of Cryptography Conference (TCC)*, pages 437–454, 2010.

[3] R. Bhaskar, S. Laxman, A. Smith, and A. Thakurta. Discovering frequent patterns in sensitive data. In *Proc. of ACM Knowledge Discovery and Data Mining (SIGKDD)*, pages 503–512, 2010.

[4] A. Blum, K. Ligett, and A. Roth. A learning theory approach to non-interactive database privacy. In *Proc. of ACM Symposium on Theory of Computing (STOC)*, pages 609–618, 2008.

[5] K. Chaudhuri and C. Monteleoni. Privacy-preserving logistic regression. In *Proc. of the Neural Information Processing Systems (NIPS)*, pages 289–296, 2008.

[6] G. Cormode. Individual privacy vs population privacy: Learning to attack anonymization. *Computing Research Repository (CoRR)*, abs/1011.2511, 2010.

[7] P. Diaconis and B. Sturmfels. Algebraic algorithms for sampling from conditional distributions. *Annals of Statistics*, 1998.

[8] C. Dwork. Differential privacy. In *International Colloquium on Automata, Languages and Programming (ICALP)*, pages 1–12, 2006.

[9] C. Dwork, F. McSherry, K. Nissim, and A. Smith. Calibrating noise to sensitivity in private data analysis. In *Theory of Cryptography Conference (TCC)*, pages 265–284, 2006.

[10] C. Dwork, M. Naor, T. Pitassi, and G. N. Rothblum. Differential privacy under continual observation. In *Proc. of ACM Symposium on Theory of Computing (STOC)*, pages 715–724, 2010.

[11] D. Feldman, A. Fiat, H. Kaplan, and K. Nissim. Private coresets. In *Proc. of ACM Symposium on Theory of Computing (STOC)*, pages 361–370, 2009.

[12] A. Friedman and A. Schuster. Data mining with differential privacy. In *Proc. of ACM Knowledge Discovery and Data Mining (SIGKDD)*, pages 493–502, 2010.

[13] M. N. Garofalakis and A. Kumar. Wavelet synopses for general error metrics. *ACM Transactions on Database Systems (TODS)*, 30(4):888–928, 2005.

[14] A. Ghosh, T. Roughgarden, and M. Sundararajan. Universally utility-maximizing privacy mechanisms. In *Proc. of ACM Symposium on Theory of Computing (STOC)*, pages 351–360, 2009.

[15] M. Götz, A. Machanavajjhala, G. Wang, X. Xiao, and J. Gehrke. Publishing search logs - a comparative study of privacy guarantees. *IEEE Transactions on Knowledge and Data Engineering (TKDE)*, 99, 2011.

[16] M. Hardt and K. Talwar. On the geometry of differential privacy. In *Proc. of ACM Symposium on Theory of Computing (STOC)*, 2010.

[17] M. Hay, V. Rastogi, G. Miklau, and D. Suciu. Boosting the accuracy of differentially private histograms through consistency. *Proc. of Very Large Data Bases (VLDB) Endowment*, 3(1):1021–1032, 2010.

[18] S. P. Kasiviswanathan, H. K. Lee, K. Nissim, S. Raskhodnikova, and A. Smith. What can we learn privately? In *Symposium on Foundations of Computer Science (FOCS)*, pages 531–540, 2008.

[19] S. P. Kasiviswanathan, M. Rudelson, A. Smith, and J. Ullman. The price of privately releasing contingency tables and the spectra of random matrices with correlated rows. In *Proc. of ACM Symposium on Theory of Computing (STOC)*, pages 775–784, 2010.

[20] A. Korolova, K. Kenthapadi, N. Mishra, and A. Ntoulas. Releasing search queries and clicks privately. In *International World Wide Web Conference (WWW)*, pages 171–180, 2009.

[21] C. Li, M. Hay, V. Rastogi, G. Miklau, and A. McGregor. Optimizing linear counting queries under differential privacy. In *Proc. of ACM Symposium on Principles of Database Systems (PODS)*, pages 123–134, 2010.

[22] A. Machanavajjhala, D. Kifer, J. M. Abowd, J. Gehrke, and L. Vilhuber. Privacy: Theory meets practice on the map. In *Proc. of International Conference on Data Engineering (ICDE)*, pages 277–286, 2008.

[23] F. McSherry and I. Mironov. Differentially private recommender systems: Building privacy into the netflix prize contenders. In *Proc. of ACM Knowledge Discovery and Data Mining (SIGKDD)*, pages 627–636, 2009.

[24] F. McSherry and K. Talwar. Mechanism design via

differential privacy. In *Symposium on Foundations of Computer Science (FOCS)*, pages 94–103, 2007.

[25] Minnesota Population Center. Integrated public use microdata series – international: Version 5.0. 2009. `https://international.ipums.org`.

[26] K. Nissim, S. Raskhodnikova, and A. Smith. Smooth sensitivity and sampling in private data analysis. In *Proc. of ACM Symposium on Theory of Computing (STOC)*, pages 75–84, 2007.

[27] V. Rastogi and S. Nath. Differentially private aggregation of distributed time-series with transformation and encryption. In *Proc. of ACM Management of Data (SIGMOD)*, pages 735–746, 2010.

[28] A. Roth and T. Roughgarden. Interactive privacy via the median mechanism. In *Proc. of ACM Symposium on Theory of Computing (STOC)*, pages 765–774, 2010.

[29] J. S. Vitter and M. Wang. Approximate computation of multidimensional aggregates of sparse data using wavelets. In *Proc. of ACM Management of Data (SIGMOD)*, pages 193–204, 1999.

[30] S. L. Warner. Randomized response: A survey technique for eliminating evasive answer bias. *J. of the American Statistical Association*, 60(309):63–69, 1965.

[31] X. Xiao, Y. Tao, and M. Chen. Optimal random perturbation at multiple privacy levels. *Proc. of Very Large Data Bases (VLDB) Endowment*, 2(1):814–825, 2009.

[32] X. Xiao, G. Wang, and J. Gehrke. Differential privacy via wavelet transforms. In *Proc. of International Conference on Data Engineering (ICDE)*, pages 225–236, 2010.

APPENDIX

A. ALTERNATE METHOD FOR NOISE REDUCTION

Let q_i be a query, and let y'_i (resp. y_i) be a noisy version of $q_i(T)$ injected with Laplace noise of scale λ'_i (resp. λ_i), such that (i) $\lambda'_i < \lambda_i$, and (ii) y'_i and y_i are generated independently. As discussed in Section 3, we can combine y'_i and y_i to obtain an estimate of $q_i(T)$ that is more accurate than either y'_i or y_i alone. In particular, let $y^*_i = (\lambda_i^2 \cdot y'_i + \lambda_i'^2 \cdot y_i)/(\lambda_i'^2 + \lambda_i^2)$. It can be verified that y^*_i has a variance $2\lambda_i'^2\lambda_i^2/(\lambda_i'^2 + \lambda_i^2)$, which is smaller than the variances of both y'_i and y_i. Furthermore, the variance of y^*_i is the minimum among all unbiased estimators of $q(T)$ given y'_i and y_i.

Nevertheless, generating y^*_i is not cost-effective since, intuitively, it incurs a privacy overhead of $1/\lambda'_i + 1/\lambda_i$ (i.e., the combined cost of producing y'_i and y_i). In contrast, with the same privacy cost, we could have first generated y_i and then applied *NoiseDown* on y_i to obtain a noisy version of $q_i(T)$ with a variance $2\lambda_i'^2\lambda_i^2/(\lambda'_i + \lambda_i)^2$, which is smaller than the variance of y^*_i. This indicates that generating and combining independent noisy versions leads to lower data utility than *NoiseDown* does. To further illustrate this point, we present *iResamp* (iterative resampling), an alternative to *iReduct* that iteratively samples independent noisy query answers instead of using *NoiseDown*. We compare the performance of ***iResamp*** with that of *iReduct* in the experiments in Section 6.

Figure 12 shows the pseudo-code of *iResamp*. Like *iReduct*, *iResamp* generates initial estimates of query values by adding a large amount of Laplace noise to the true values (Lines 1-5 in Figure 12) and then iteratively refines the noisy query results (Lines 6-21). In each iteration, it also invokes the *PickQueries* black box function to select a set Q_Δ queries for noise reduction. The reduction pro-

Algorithm *iResamp* $(T, Q, \delta, \epsilon, \lambda_{max})$
1. let $m = |Q|$ and q_i be the i-th ($i \in [1, m]$) query in Q
2. initialize $\Lambda = [\lambda_1, \ldots, \lambda_m]$, such that $\lambda_i = \lambda_{max}$
3. if $GS(Q, \Lambda) > \epsilon$ then return $\emptyset$
4. Y = *LaplaceNoise*(T, Q, Λ)
5. let $Q' = Q$
6. while $Q' \neq \emptyset$
7. $\quad Q_\Delta$ = *PickQueries*(Q', Y, Λ, δ)
8. $\quad$ for each $i \in [1, m]$
9. $\quad\quad$ if $q_i \in Q_\Delta$ then $\lambda_i = \lambda_i/2$
10. $\quad$ let $\Lambda' = [\lambda'_1, \ldots, \lambda'_m]$, such that $\lambda'_i = 1/(2/\lambda_i - 1/\lambda_{max})$
11. $\quad$ if $GS(Q, \Lambda') \le \epsilon$
12. $\quad\quad$ for each $i \in [1, m]$
13. $\quad\quad\quad$ if $q_i \in Q_\Delta$
14. $\quad\quad\quad\quad$ let $y_i^{(1)}, \ldots y_i^{(k-1)}$ be the noisy versions of $q_i(T)$ that have been generated in the previous iterations
15. $\quad\quad\quad\quad$ $y_i^{(k)}$ = *LaplaceNoise*(T, q_i, λ_i)
16. $\quad\quad\quad\quad$ calculate y^*_i based on $y_i^{(1)}, \ldots y_i^{(k)}$ according to Eqn. 16
17. $\quad\quad\quad\quad$ $y_i = y^*_i$
18. $\quad$ else
19. $\quad\quad$ for each $i \in [1, m]$
20. $\quad\quad\quad$ if $q_i \in Q_\Delta$ then $\lambda_i = 2\lambda_i$
21. $\quad\quad$ $Q' = Q' \setminus Q_\Delta$
22. return Y

Figure 12: The *iResamp* Algorithm

cess, however, is not performed by applying *NoiseDown*, but by generating new noisy answers that are independent of the noisy estimates obtained in previous iterations (Line 15). Specifically, if the most recent noisy answer generated for a query $q_i \in Q_\Delta$ has noise scale λ_i then the new noisy result will have noise scale $\lambda_i/2$, i.e. the amount of noise is reduced by half each time a value is resampled (Lines 8-9). After the new noisy estimate is generated, *iResamp* takes a weighted average of all the noisy results that have been obtained for q_i so far (Line 16) in order to derive a variance-minimized estimate of $q_i(T)$. In particular, if there are k independent noisy samples $y_i^{(j)}$ ($j \in [1, n]$) of $q_i(T)$ such that $y_i^{(j)}$ has noise scale $\lambda_i^{(j)}$, then the variance-minimized unbiased estimate of $q_i(T)$ is:

$$y^*_i = \frac{\sum_{j=1}^{k} y_i^{(j)} / \left(\lambda_i^{(j)} \cdot \lambda_i^{(j)}\right)}{\sum_{j=1}^{k} 1 / \left(\lambda_i^{(j)} \cdot \lambda_i^{(j)}\right)}. \tag{16}$$

The new estimates are then used by the *PickQueries* function for query selections in the next iteration (Line 17).

To show that the algorithm guarantees ϵ-differential privacy, it suffices to show that the set of all noisy query estimates (generated in all iterations) of all the marginals is ϵ-differentially private. Notice that for any query q_i, the k-th noisy answer $y_i^{(k)}$ for q_i (generated by *iResamp*) has noise scale $\lambda_{max}/2^{k-1}$. This is true because the first noisy answer $y_i^{(1)}$ has noise scale λ_{max} and the noise scale of $y_i^{(j)}$ equals half of the noise scale of $y_i^{(j-1)}$ ($j > 1$). By summing the terms of the resulting geometric series, it can be verified that the privacy cost of producing $y_i^{(1)}, \ldots, y_i^{(k)}$ is bounded above by the cost of generating a noisy answer for q_i with Laplace noise of scale $2/\lambda_i - 1/\lambda_{max}$, where λ_i denotes the noise scale of $y_i^{(k)}$. Therefore, to ensure that all noisy results produced by ***iResamp*** are ϵ-differentially private, it suffices to guarantee that the sequence Q of input queries has generalized sensitivity at most ϵ with respect to $\Lambda' = [\lambda'_1, \ldots, \lambda'_m]$, where $\lambda'_i = 1/(2/\lambda_i - 1/\lambda_{max})$. This explains the rationale of Lines 10 and 11 in Figure 12. The above argument concludes our proof of the following theorem:

THEOREM 3 (PRIVACY OF *iResamp*). *iResamp ensures ϵ'-differential privacy whenever its input parameter ϵ satisfies $\epsilon \le \epsilon'$.* □

A Latency and Fault-Tolerance Optimizer for Online Parallel Query Plans

Prasang Upadhyaya
University of Washington
prasang@cs.uw.edu

YongChul Kwon
University of Washington
yongchul@cs.uw.edu

Magdalena Balazinska
University of Washington
magda@cs.uw.edu

ABSTRACT

We address the problem of making online, parallel query plans fault-tolerant: *i.e.*, provide *intra-query fault-tolerance without blocking*. We develop an approach that not only achieves this goal but does so through the use of *different fault-tolerance techniques at different operators within a query plan*. Enabling each operator to use a different fault-tolerance strategy leads to a space of fault-tolerance plans amenable to cost-based optimization. We develop FTOpt, a cost-based fault-tolerance optimizer that automatically selects the best strategy for *each* operator in a query plan in a manner that minimizes the expected processing time with failures for the entire query. We implement our approach in a prototype parallel query-processing engine. Our experiments demonstrate that (1) there is no single best fault-tolerance strategy for all query plans, (2) often hybrid strategies that mix-and-match recovery techniques outperform any uniform strategy, and (3) our optimizer correctly identifies winning fault-tolerance configurations.

Categories and Subject Descriptors

C.4 [**Performance of Systems**]: *Fault tolerance, modeling techniques*; H.2.4 [**Database Management**]: Systems—*Parallel databases, Query processing*

General Terms

Performance

1. INTRODUCTION

The ability to analyze large-scale datasets has become a critical requirement for modern business and science. To carry out their analyses, users are increasingly turning toward parallel database management systems (DBMSs) [14, 39, 43] and other parallel data processing engines [10, 15, 20] deployed in shared-nothing clusters of commodity servers.

In many systems, users can express their data processing needs using SQL or other specialized languages (*e.g.*, Pig Latin [30], DryadLINQ [45]). The resulting queries or scripts are then translated into a directed acyclic graph (DAG) of operators (*e.g.*, relational operators, maps, reduces, or other [20]) that execute in the cluster.

An important challenge faced by these systems is fault-tolerance. When running a parallel query at large scale, some form of failure is likely to occur during execution [9]. Existing systems take two radically different strategies to handle failures: parallel DBMSs restart queries if failures occur during their execution. The limitation of this approach is that a single failure can cause the system to reprocess a query in its entirety. While this is not a problem for queries running across a small number of servers and for a short period of time, it becomes undesirable for long queries using large numbers of servers. In contrast, MapReduce [10] and similar systems [15] materialize the output of each operator and restart individual operators when failures occur. This approach limits the amount of work repeated in the face of failures, but comes at the cost of materializing all intermediate data, which adds significant overhead even in the absence of failures. Furthermore, because MapReduce materializes data in a blocking fashion, this approach prevents users from seeing results incrementally. Partial results are a desirable feature during interactive data analysis now commonly performed with these systems [41].

In this paper, we study the problem of providing users both the ability to see early results as motivated by online query processing [17, 18] and achieve a low expected total runtime. We thus seek to *enable intra-query fault-tolerance without blocking* and we want to do so in a manner that *minimizes the expected total runtime in the presence of failures*. Other objective functions could also be useful (*e.g.*, minimize runtime without failures subject to a constraint on recovery time.) We choose to minimize the sum of time under normal processing and time in failure recovery. This function combines high-performance at runtime with fast failure recovery into a single objective. We want to minimize this function while preserving pipelining.

Recent work [41] has also looked at the problem of combining pipelining and fault-tolerance: they developed techniques for increased data pipelining in MapReduce. This system *both* pipelines and materializes data between operators. We observe, however, that data materialization is only one of several strategies for achieving fault-tolerance in a pipelined query plan. Other strategies are possible including restarting a query or operator but skipping over previously processed data [21, 24] or checkpointing operator states and restarting from these checkpoints [11, 21]. Additionally, the

SIGMOD'11, June 12–16, 2011, Athens, Greece.

most appropriate fault-tolerance method may depend on the available resources, failure rates, and query plan properties. For example, an expensive join operator may need to checkpoint its state while an inexpensive filter may simply skip over previously processed data after a failure.

Given these observations, we develop (1) a framework that enables *mixing-and-matching of fault-tolerance techniques in a single, pipelined query plan* and (2) *FTOpt, a cost-based fault-tolerance optimizer* for this framework. Our framework enables intra-query fault-tolerance *without blocking*, thus preserving pipelining. Given a query plan and information about the cluster and expected failure rates, FTOpt automatically selects the fault-tolerance strategy for each operator in a query plan such that the overall query runtime with failures is minimized. We call the resulting configuration a *fault-tolerance plan*. In our fault-tolerance plans, each operator can individually recover after failure and it can recover using a different strategy than other operators in the same plan. In summary, we make the following contributions:

1. *Extensible, heterogeneous fault-tolerance framework.* We propose a framework that enables the mixing and matching of different fault-tolerance techniques in a single distributed, parallel, and pipelined query plan. Our framework is extensible in that it is agnostic of the specific operators and fault-tolerance strategies used. We also describe how three well-known strategies can be integrated into our framework (Section 4).
2. *Fault-tolerance optimizer.* We develop a cost-based fault-tolerance optimizer. Given a query plan and a failure model, the optimizer selects the fault-tolerance strategy *for each operator* that minimizes the total time to complete the query given an expected number of failures (Section 5).
3. *Operator models for pipelined plans.* We model the processing and recovery times for a small set of representative operators. Our models capture operator performance *within a pipelined query plan* rather than in isolation. They are sufficiently accurate for the fault-tolerance optimizer to select good plans yet sufficiently simple for global optimization using a Geometric Program Solver [3]. We also develop an approach that simplifies the modeling of other operators within our framework thus simplifying extensibility (Section 5.3).

We implemented our approach in a prototype parallel query processing engine. The implementation includes our new fault-tolerance framework, specific per-operator fault-tolerance strategies for a small set of representative operators (select, join, and aggregate[1]), and a MATLAB module for the FTOpt optimizer. Our experiments demonstrate that different fault-tolerance strategies, often hybrid ones, lead to the best performance in different settings: for the configurations tested, total runtimes with as little as *one* failure differed by up to 70% depending on the fault-tolerance method selected. These results show that fault-tolerance can significantly affect performance. Additionally, our optimizer is able to correctly identify the winning fault-tolerance strategy for a given query plan. Overall, FTOpt

[1]As in online aggregation [18], aggregates can occur at top of plans. Our prototype uses a standard aggregate operator but it could be replaced with an online one.

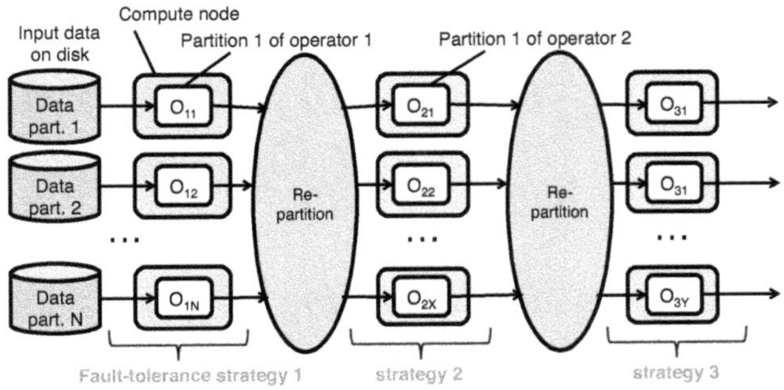

Figure 1: Parallel query plan comprising three operators (O_1, O_2, O_3) and one input from disk. Each operator is partitioned across a possibly different number of nodes. Data can be re-partitioned between operators. Fault-tolerance strategies are selected at the granularity of operators.

is thus an important component of parallel data processing, enabling performance gains similar in magnitude to several other recently proposed MapReduce optimizations [22, 26].

2. MODEL AND ASSUMPTIONS

Query Model and Resource Allocation. In parallel data processing systems, queries take the form of directed acyclic graphs (DAGs) of operators that are distributed across servers in a cluster as illustrated in Figure 1. Servers are also referred to as *nodes*. Each operator can be partitioned and these partitions then execute in parallel on the same or on different nodes. Multiple operators can also share the same nodes. In this paper, we focus on *non-blocking query plans*, which take the form of trees (rather than DAGs), where operators are scheduled and executed at the same time, and where data is pipelined from one operator to the next, *producing results incrementally*. We assume that aggregation operators, if any, appear only at the top of a plan. Since input data comes from disk, it can be read and consumed at a steady pace (there are no unexpected bursts as in a streaming system for example). If a query plan is too large for all operators to run simultaneously, our approach will optimize fault-tolerance for pipelined subsets of the plan, materializing results at the end.

Fault-tolerance choices and resource allocation are intertwined: an operator can perform more complex fault-tolerance if it is allocated a greater fraction of the compute resources. In addition to fault-tolerance strategies, our optimizer computes the appropriate allocation of resources to operators. Due to space constraints, however, in this paper, we assume that each operator is partitioned across a given number of compute nodes and is allocated its own core(s) and disk on that node. For the resource allocation details, we refer the reader to the technical report [42].

Failure Model. In a shared-nothing cluster, different types of failures occur. Our approach handles a variety of failures from process failures to network failures. To simplify the presentation, we first focus on *process failures*: *i.e.*, we assume that each operator partition runs in its own process and that these processes crash and are then restarted (with an empty state) independently of one another. We come back to more complex failures in Section 5.5.

To make fault-tolerance choices, our optimizer must know the likelihood for different types of failures. If n_i is the total number of processes allocated to operator i, we assume that the expected number of failures during query execution for that operator is given by: $z_i = \frac{n_i}{n} Z$ where $n = \sum_{j \in \mathcal{O}} n_j$, $\mathcal{O}$ is the set of all operators in the plan, and Z is the expected number of process failures for the query. Z can be estimated from the observed failure rates for previous queries and administrators typically know this number [9]. We assume Z to be independent of the chosen fault-tolerance plan. Z depends on the query runtime, whose order of magnitude can be estimated by FTOpt as the total runtime without fault-tolerance and without failures (we show that results are robust to small errors in Z's value in Section 6.6).

Operator Determinism. We assume that individual operator partitions are deterministic, *i.e.*, an operator partition produces an identical output when it processes the same input tuples in the same order. This is a common assumption [20, 44, 36, 2, 35, 23] and most relational operators are deterministic. In a distributed system, however, the order in which input tuples reach an operator partition may not be deterministic. Our approach handles this scenario.

3. RELATED WORK

Fault-Tolerance in Relational DBMSs. Commercial relational DBMSs provide fault-tolerance through replication [6, 33, 38]. Similarly, parallel DBMSs [14, 39, 43] use replication to handle various types of failures. Neither, however, provides intra-query fault-tolerance [32].

Main-memory DBMSs [25, 34, 28] use a variety of checkpointing strategies to preserve the in-memory state of their databases. In contrast, our approach preserves and recovers the state of ongoing computations.

Fault-Tolerance in MapReduce-type systems. The MapReduce framework [10] provides intra-query fault-tolerance by materializing results between operators and re-processing these results upon operator failures. This approach, however, imposes a high runtime overhead and prevents users from seeing any output until the job completes. In Dryad [20], data between operators can either be pipelined or materialized. In contrast, we strive to achieve both pipelining and fault-tolerance at the same time. We also study how to decide when to materialize or checkpoint data. Recent work [44] applies MapReduce-style fault-tolerance to distributed databases by breaking long-running queries into small ones that execute and can be restarted independently. This approach, however, supports only a specific type of queries over a star schema. In contrast, we explore techniques that are more generally applicable. Recent work also introduced the ability to partly pipeline data in Hadoop [41], a MapReduce-type platform. This work is complementary to ours as it retains the use of materialization throughout the query plan for fault-tolerance purposes.

Other Fault-Tolerance Strategies. In the distributed systems and stream processing literatures, several additional fault-tolerance strategies have been proposed [11, 21, 36]. All these strategies involve replication. One set of techniques is based on the *state-machine* approach. Here, the same computation is performed in parallel by two processing nodes [2, 35, 36]. We do not consider such techniques in this paper because of their overhead: to tolerate even a single failure, they require twice the resources. The second set of techniques uses *rollback recovery* methods [11, 21], where the system takes periodic snapshots of its state that it copies onto stable storage (*i.e.*, into memory of other nodes or onto disk). We show how to integrate the latter techniques into our fault-tolerance optimization framework (Section 4.2).

Recently, Simitsis et. al. [37] studied the problem of selecting fault-tolerance strategies and recovery points for ETL flows. Similar to us they consider using different fault-tolerance strategies within a single flow. In contrast to our work, they do not propose a general heterogeneous fault-tolerance framework, do not have individually recoverable operators, and do not optimize for overall latency nor show how fault-tolerance choices affect processing latencies.

Additional Related Work. Hwang *et al.* [19] studied self-configuring high-availability methods. Their approach is orthogonal to our work as it is based on a uniform checkpointing strategy and optimizes the time when checkpoints are taken and the backup nodes where they are saved.

Techniques for query suspend and resume [4, 5] use rollback recovery but are otherwise orthogonal to our work.

Phoenix/App [27] explores the problem of heterogeneous fault-tolerance in the context of web enterprise applications. This approach identifies three types of software components: Persistent, Transactional, and External depending on the fault-tolerance strategy that each uses (message logging with checkpointing, transactions, or nothing respectively). Phoenix/App then defines different "interaction contracts" for each combination of component types. Each contract implements a different protocol with different guarantees. Thus in Phoenix/App, the protocol depends on the fault-tolerance capabilities of the communicating components. In contrast, our approach enables the mixing-and-matching of fault-tolerance strategies without changes to the protocol.

4. FRAMEWORK FOR HETEROGENEOUS FAULT-TOLERANCE

We present a framework for mixing and matching fault-tolerance techniques. Our framework relies on concepts from the literature including logging, acknowledging, and replaying tuples as previously done in uniform fault-tolerance settings [21, 36] and "contract-based" methods for query suspend-resume [4]. Our contribution lies in *articulating how these strategies can be used to enable fault-tolerance heterogeneity.* We also discuss how three fault-tolerance techniques from the literature can be used within our framework.

4.1 Protocol

To enable heterogeneous fault-tolerance between consecutive operators in a query plan, we isolate these operators by fixing the semantics of their interactions through a set of four rules. These rules enable each operator to be *individually restartable* without requiring any blocking materialization as in MapReduce and also without requiring that all operators use the same fault-tolerance strategy.

In our framework, as in any parallel data processing system, operators receive input tuples from their upstream neighbors; they process these tuples and send results downstream. For example, in Figure 1, each partition of operator O_2 receives data from each O_1 partition and sends data to all O_3 partitions. If an operator partition such as O_{21} fails, a new instance of the operator partition is started with an empty state. To recover the failed state, in our framework, the new instance can read any state persistently captured by the operator's fault-tolerance strategy. It can also ask upstream operators to resend (a subset) of their data. To enable such replays, tuples must have unique identifiers, which may or may not be visible to applications, and operators must remember the output they produced. For this, we define the following two rules:

RULE 4.1. *Each relation must have a key.*

RULE 4.2. Producer replay guarantee. *Upon request, an operator, must regenerate and resend* in order *and* without duplicates *any subset of unacknowledged output tuples.*

Acknowledgments mentioned in this rule help reduce the potential overhead of storing old output tuples by bounding how much history must be retained [21, 36]. In our framework, acknowledgments are optional and are sent from downstream operators to upstream ones. For example, once all operator partitions O_{21} through O_{2X} that have received an input tuple t from operator partition O_{11} acknowledge this tuple, the tuple need no longer be retained by O_{11}. Upon sending an acknowledgment, an operator promises never to ask for the corresponding tuple again. Formally,

RULE 4.3. Consumer progress guarantee. *If an operator acknowledges a tuple r_x, it guarantees that, even in case of failure, it will never ask for r_x again.*

Most parallel data processing systems use in-order communication (*e.g.*, TCP) between operators. In that case, an operator can send a single message with the identifier of a tuple r_x to acknowledge all tuples up to and including r_x.

When a failure occurs and an operator restarts with an empty state, most fault-tolerance techniques will cause the operator to produce duplicate tuples during recovery. To ensure that an operator can eliminate duplicates before sending them downstream, we add a last requirement:

RULE 4.4. Consumer Durability Guarantee. *Upon request, an operator O_d must produce the identifier of the most recent input tuple that it has received from an upstream neighbor O_u.*

Together, these four rules enable a parallel system to ensure that it produces the same output tuples in the same order with and without failure (the tuples may still be delayed due to failure recovery.) They also enable operators to be individually restartable and the query plan to be both pipelined and fault-tolerant, since data can be transmitted at anytime between operators. Finally, the framework is agnostic of the fault-tolerance method used as long as the method works within the pre-defined types of interactions.

From the above four rules, only the "Producer replay guarantee" rule potentially adds a visible overhead to the system since it requires that a producer be able to re-generate (part of) its output.[2] A no-cost solution to satisfy this rule is for an operator to restart itself upon receiving a replay request. With this strategy, an operator failure can cause a cascading rollback effect, where all preceding operators in the plan get also restarted. This approach is equivalent to restarting a subset of the query plan after a failure occurs and is no worse than what parallel DBMSs do today. Alternatively, an operator could write its output to disk. Finally, some operators, such as joins, can also easily re-generate their output from their state without the need to log their output. Each of these solutions leads to different expected query runtimes with and without failures. Our optimizer is precisely designed to select the correct strategy for each operator (from a pre-defined set of strategies) in a way that minimizes the total runtime with failures for a given query plan as we discuss further below.

[2]Our framework also requires unique identifiers for tuples. In our implementation, we create unique identifiers consisting of 3 integers [42]; for the 512 byte tuples used in our experiments the space overhead is less than 2.5%.

4.2 Concrete Framework Instance

We now discuss how three fault-tolerance strategies from the literature can be integrated into our framework.

Even though the operators in our framework are deterministic (see Section 2), in a distributed setting tuples may arrive in different interleaved order on different inputs. We develop a low-overhead method –based on lightweight logging of information about input tuple processing order– to ensure determinism in this case, but we omit it due to space constraints and refer the reader to the technical report [42].

Strategy NONE. Within our framework, an operator can choose to do nothing to make itself fault-tolerant. We call this strategy NONE. To ensure that it can recover from a failure, such an operator can simply avoid sending any acknowledgments upstream. Upon a failure, that operator can then request that its upstream neighbors replay their entire output. This strategy is analogous to the *upstream backup* approach developed for stream processing engines [21].

As in upstream backup, operators such as select or project that do not maintain state between consecutive tuples (*i.e.*, "stateless operators") can send acknowledgments in some cases: *e.g.*, if an input tuple r makes it through a selection to generate the output q and is acknowledged by all operators downstream, then r can be acknowledged. Unlike upstream backup, which uses different types of acknowledgments [21], our approach uses only one type of acknowledgments facilitating heterogeneous fault-tolerance. This approach of skipping over input data during recovery has also been used for resumptions of interrupted warehouse loads [24].

To handle a request for output tuples, a stateless operator can fail and restart itself to reproduce the requested data. For stateful operators (*i.e.*, operators such as joins that maintain state between consecutive tuples), a more efficient strategy is to maintain an output queue and replay the requested data [21]. Such a queue, however, can still impose a significant memory overhead and an I/O overhead if the queue is written to disk. We observe, however, that stateful relational operators *need not keep such output queue* but, instead, can re-generate the data from their state. We implement this strategy and use it in our evaluation.

Strategy MATERIALIZE. An alternate rollback recovery approach consists in logging intermediate results between operators as in MapReduce [10]. While CHCKPT speeds-up recovery for the checkpointed operator itself, MATERIALIZE potentially speeds-up recovery for downstream operators: to satisfy a replay request, an operator can simply re-read the materialized data. Since materialized output tuples need never be generated again, an operator can use the same acknowledgement and recovery policy as in NONE.

Strategy CHCKPT. This strategy is a type of *rollback recovery* strategy where operators' state is periodically saved to stable storage. Because our framework recovers operators individually, it requires what is called *uncoordinated checkpointing with logging* [11]. One approach that can directly be applied is *passive standby* [21], where operators take periodic checkpoints of their state, independently of other operators.

Our framework requires that an operator save sufficient information to guarantee the consumer progress, consumer durability, and producer replay guarantees. For this, the operator must log its state (*e.g.*, partial aggregates, join hash tables) and, when applicable, its output queue. The operator can acknowledge checkpointed input tuples. Upon failures, the operator restarts from the last checkpoint. As an optimization, operators can checkpoint only delta-changes of their state [11]. Other optimizations are also possible [11, 19, 23] and can be used with our framework.

Unlike NONE and MATERIALIZE, with CHCKPT blocking operators also benefit from fault-tolerance provisioning as they can checkpoint their state periodically and restart from the latest checkpoint after a failure.[3]

In summary, while our framework imposes constraints on operator interactions, all three of these common fault-tolerance strategies can easily be incorporated into it.

5. FTOpt

FTOpt is an optimizer for our heterogeneous fault-tolerance framework. FTOpt runs as a post-processing step: it takes as input (a) a query plan selected by the query optimizer and annotates it with the fault-tolerance strategies to use. The optimizer also takes as input (b) information about the cluster resources and cluster failure model, and (c) models for the operators in the plan under different fault-tolerance strategies. FTOpt produces as output a fault-tolerance plan that minimizes an objective function (*i.e.*, the expected runtime with failures) given a set of constraints (that model the plan).

FTOpt's fault-tolerance plans have three parts: (1) a fault-tolerance strategy for each operator, (2) checkpoint frequencies for all operators that should checkpoint their states, and (3) an allocation of resources to operators. As indicated in Section 2, however, we do not discuss resource allocation in this paper due to space constraints. We assume a given resource allocation to operators.

For a given query plan, the optimizer's search space thus consists of all combinations of fault-tolerance strategies. In this paper, we use a brute-force technique to enumerate through that search space and leave more efficient enumeration algorithms for future work. For each such combination, FTOpt estimates the expected total runtime with failures, the optimal checkpoint frequencies and, optionally, an allocation of resources to operators [42]. It then chooses the plan with the minimum total runtime with failures.

5.1 Geometric Model

As it enumerates through the search-space, given a potential fault-tolerance plan, in order to select optimal checkpoint frequencies and estimate the total runtime with failures for the plan, FTOpt uses a geometric programming (GP) framework. GP allows expressions that model resource scaling (for resource allocation) and non-linear operator behavior, but still finds a global minima for the model [3].

In a geometric optimization problem, the goal is to minimize a function $f_0(\vec{x})$, where $\vec{x}$ is the optimization variable vector. The optimization is subject to constraints on other functions $f_i(\vec{x})$ and $g_i(\vec{x})$. All of $\vec{x}$, $g(\vec{x})$, and $f(\vec{x})$ are constrained to take the following specific forms:

- $\vec{x} = (x_1, \ldots, x_n)$ such that $\forall i \;\; x_i > 0, x_i \in \mathbb{R}$.
- $g(\vec{x})$ must be a monomial of the form $cx_1^{a_1}x_2^{a_2}\ldots x_n^{a_n}$ with $c > 0$ and $a_i \in \mathbb{R}$.
- $f(\vec{x})$ must be a posynomial defined as a sum of one or more monomials. Specifically, with $c_k > 0$ and $a_{ik} \in \mathbb{R}$: $f(\vec{x}) = \sum_{k=1}^{k=K} c_k x_1^{a_{1k}} x_2^{a_{2k}} \ldots x_n^{a_{nk}}$.

The optimization is then expressed as follows:

$$\begin{aligned} \text{minimize} \quad & f_0(\vec{x}) \\ \text{subject to} \quad & f_i(\vec{x}) \leq 1, \quad i = 1, \ldots, m \\ & g_i(\vec{x}) = 1, \quad i = 1, \ldots, p \end{aligned}$$

In our case, $\vec{x} = \cup_{i \in \mathcal{O}}(c_i, N_i, x_i^N, x_i^{RD}, x_i^{RS})$ where $\mathcal{O}$ is the set of all operators in the query plan and $\cup$ denotes concatenation. Each operator has a vector of variables that includes: c_i, its checkpoint frequency, N_i, the number of nodes assigned to it (we assume that it is fixed in this paper), and x_i^N, x_i^{RD}, and x_i^{RS}, which capture the average time between two consecutive output tuples, requested replay tuples, and "units of recovery" (a measure of recovery speed), respectively. Tables 1 and 2 summarize these parameters (we come back to the tables shortly).

Our objective function, $f_0(\vec{x}) = T_{total}$, is the total time to execute the query including time spent recovering from failures. We define it more precisely in Sections 5.2 and 5.3.

Our constraints comprise framework and operator constraints. The former constrain how operator models are composed: (a) the average input and output rates of consecutive operators must be equal since the query plan is pipelined, (b) aggregate input and output rates for operators cannot exceed the network and processing limits, and (c) if an operator uses an output queue, it must either checkpoint its output queue to disk frequently enough, or must receive acknowledgements from downstream operators frequently enough to never run out of memory. Individual operators can add further constraints (see Section 5.3).

5.2 Objective Function

FTOpt minimizes the following cost function, that captures the expected runtime of a query plan:

$$T_{total} = \max_{p \in \mathcal{P}} \left(\mathbf{T_{p_d}} + \sum_{i=1}^{i=d-1} \mathbf{D_{p_i}} \right) + \sum_{i \in \mathcal{O}} z_i \cdot \mathbf{R_i} \qquad (1)$$

The first term is the total time needed to completely process the query including the overhead of fault-tolerance if no failures occur The second term is the expected time spent in recovery from failures. Failure recovery can be added on top of normal processing because, with our approach, when a failure occurs, it blocks the entire pipeline. Indeed, even if one operator partition fails, operators upstream from that partition stop executing normally and take part in the recovery. A side-effect of this approach is that recovering a single operator partition or recovering all partitions yield approximately the same recovery time.

In more detail, for the first term, $\mathcal{P}$ is the set of all paths from the root of the query tree to the leaves. For a given path $p \in P$ of length d, the root is labeled with p_1 and the leaf with p_d; D_{p_i} is the delay introduced by operator p_i

[3]FTOpt works irrespective of a blocking operator's placement in a query plan. We focus on online query processing since FTOpt is especially useful for such plans: it enables fault-tolerance without creating unnecessary blocking.

Table 1: **Functions capturing operator behavior.**

Delay to produce the first tuple	
$D^N(\Theta)$	Average delay to output first tuple during normal processing (with fault-tolerance overheads).
$D^{RD}(\Theta)$	Average delay to produce first tuple requested by a downstream operator during a replay.
$D^{RS}(\Theta)$	Average delay to the start of state recovery on failure.
Average processing time	
$x^N(\Theta)$	Average time interval between successive output tuples during normal runtime (with fault-tolerance overheads).
$x^{RD}(\Theta)$	Average time interval between successive output tuples requested by a downstream operator.
$x^{RS}(\Theta)$	Average time-interval between strategy-specific "units of recovery" (*e.g.*, checkpointed tuples read from disk).
Acknowledgement interval, $a(\Theta)$, sent to upstream nodes.	

Table 2: **Operator behavior parameters(Θ).**

Query parameters	
$\lvert I_u \rvert$	Number of input tuples received from upstream operator u.
$\lvert I \rvert$	Number of tuples produced by current operator.
Operator parameters	
t^{cpu}	Operator cost in terms of time to process one tuple.
t^{io}	The time taken to write a tuple to disk.
Runtime parameters	
x_u^N	Average inter-tuple arrival time from upstream operator u in normal processing.
F	Fault-tolerance strategy.
c	Number of tuples processed between consecutive checkpoints.
N	The number of nodes assigned to the operator.
Surrounding fault-tolerance context	
a_d	Maximum number of unacknowledged output tuples.
x_u^{RD}	Average inter-tuple arrival time from upstream operator u during a replay.

where the delay is defined as the time taken to produce its first output tuple from the moment it receives its first input tuple; and, T_{p_d} is the time taken by the leaf operator to complete all processing after receiving its first input tuple. $T_{p_d} = D_{p_d} + x_{p_d}^N |I|$, where $|I|$ is the number of output tuples produced by the leaf operator. D_{p_i} and T_{p_d} depend on the input tuple arrival rate at an operator, which depend on how fast previous operators are in the pipeline. We capture these dependencies with constraints as mentioned in Section 5.1.

For the second term, $\mathcal{O}$ is the set of all operators in the tree. For operator $i \in \mathcal{O}$, z_i is the expected number of failures during query execution, and $\mathbf{R}_i$ is the *expected* recovery time from a failure. We estimate z_i using an administrator-provided failure model as described in Section 2.

To adapt T_{total} to be a posynomial, we need to eliminate the *max* operator. For this, we introduce a variable T for T_{total} and decompose the objective to be "minimize T with a constraint for each path such that: $(T)^{-1} \times$ [expected total time for the path] $<= 1$". Since the expected total time (for a single path) is a posynomial, the constraints are posynomials, and the entire program is a GP.

5.3 Operator Modeling

To compute the objective function, FTOpt thus requires that each operator provide expressions that characterize its delay and processing time during normal operation and when failures occur. These expressions must be provided for each fault-tolerance strategy that the operator supports. Formally, FTOpt needs to be given the functions in Table 1 expressed in terms of the parameters, represented by Θ in Table 2 (these parameters capture the inter-dependencies between operators). FTOpt combines these functions together to derive the overall processing time T_{total}.

In this section, we show how to express such functions in our framework. We proceed through an example: we derive the constraint equations for join (symmetric hash-join). The models for select and aggregate are similarly derived [42].

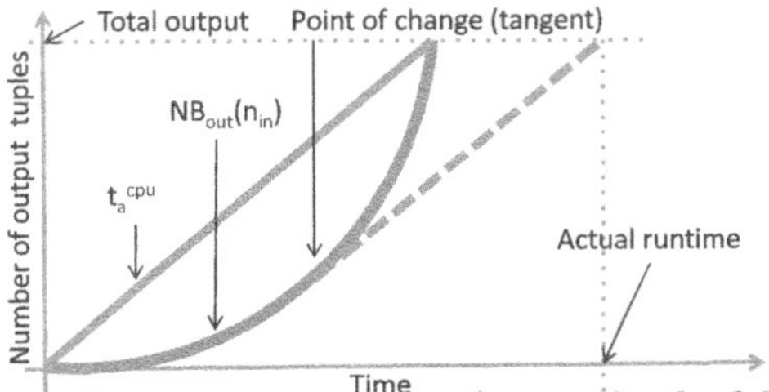

Figure 2: Data output curve (comprised of $NB_{out}(\cdot)$ curve till the "Point of change" and the dashed line after it) for a symmetric-hash join operator.

5.3.1 Modeling Basic Operator Runtime

To model our problem as a GP, we must (a) derive the operator output rate (given by the inter-output-tuple delay, x^N) in the absence of failures, and (b) derive the delay, D^N. The delay, however, is simply either negligible for selects and the symmetric hash-join that we model or equal to the total processing time for aggregates.[4]

The challenge in expressing an operator's output rate is that x^N can follow a complex curve for some operators such as certain non-blocking join algorithms as illustrated in Figure 2. The figure shows the data output curve for a symmetric hash-join operator. For this operator, the more tuples that it has already processed, the more likely the join is to find matching tuples, and thus it outputs tuples at an increasingly faster rate. As a result, at the beginning of the computation, the bottleneck is the input data rate (the $\mathrm{NB_{out}(n_{in})}$ curve) and the operator produces increasingly more output tuples for each input tuple. Eventually, the CPU at the join becomes the bottleneck (t_a^{cpu} curve) and the output rate flattens.

We found that ignoring such effects and assuming a constant output significantly underestimated the total runtime for the operator. Alternatively, modeling these effects and exposing them to downstream operators significantly complicated the overall optimization problem. We thus opted for the following middle-ground: we model the non-uniform output rate of an operator to derive its total runtime. Given the total runtime, we compute the equivalent average output rate that we use as a constant input arrival rate for the next operator. The GP framework is helpful here to express these non-linear behaviors.

Interestingly, we find that we can automatically derive the above curve from the following operator properties:

- t_a^{cpu}: Average time to generate one output tuple if all input is available with no delay.
- $NB_{out}(n_{in})$: This function provides the total number of output tuples produced for a given number of tuples (n_{in}) received across all input streams.

The above functions can easily be derived (hence simplifying optimizer extensibility). Both these functions are extensions of parameters of standard query optimizers: (a) t_a^{cpu} corresponds to the standard query optimizer function for computing an operator's cost, except that we then divide this cost by the operator output cardinality, and (b)

[4]To compute total query times, we ignore any partial results that an online aggregate may produce.

$NB_{out}(n_{in})$ is similar to computing the cardinality of an operator output, except that it also captures how that output is produced as the input data arrives. Simple operators like select or merge join have $NB_{out} = \sigma n_{in}$, where σ is the operator selectivity. For blocking operators such as aggregates, after the delay $D^N(\Theta)$ all the output tuples are produced at once and hence $NB_{out} = |I|$. For other non-blocking operators the relationship can be more complex as we discuss next using our symmetric hash-join as example.

For the symmetric hash-join operator, define I_{utot} to be the set of all tuples received from both upstream input channels. Hence, $|I_{utot}| = |I_1| + |I_2|$. For this operator:

$$t_a^{cpu} = |I|^{-1} \left(|I_{utot}| + |I|\right) t^{cpu}$$

The expression is a product of the average time taken to process either an input or output tuple (t^{cpu}, obtained through micro-benchmarks) and the total number of tuples seen by the operator, including the input tuples (I_{utot}) and the output join tuples (I). This number is then divided by the total number of output tuples ($|I|$) to get the average time per output tuple.

To get the NB_{out} function for a symmetric hash-join we assume that the input tuples from the two input channels can arrive in any order, each order being equally likely. Let $\hat{\sigma}$ (a function of the join selectivity σ, $|I_1|$ and $|I_2|$ [42]) be the probability that two tuples from different channels join and p_i be the probability that a tuple belongs to the ith*channel*. In this case, the function $NB_{out}(n_{in})$ is defined as follows:

$$\mathrm{NB_{out}(n_{in})} = \hat{\sigma} p_1 p_2 n_{in}(n_{in} - 1) \approx \hat{\sigma} p_1 p_2 n_{in}^2$$

Intuitively, $n_{in}(n_{in} - 1)$ is the count of pairs of distinct tuples to join, $p_1 p_2$ is the probability that they come from different channels, and $\hat{\sigma}$ is the probability that they join.

We now show how our optimizer translates these functions into a set of inequalities that characterize the average time interval between successive output tuples produced by an operator. For this, we require that the $NB_{out}(n_{in})$ function take the form: $NB_{out}(n_{in}) = \gamma n_{in}^k$, in order to fit into the GP framework. Thus, for our join operator: $\gamma = \hat{\sigma} p_1 p_2$ and $k = 2$. Informally, as the operator sees more input tuples, the number of the output tuples produced after processing a single new input tuple should never decrease.

Given the above, the average time interval between consecutive output tuples, x^N, is given by the following inequalities:

$$\begin{aligned} m_e &= \gamma (x^{IN})^{-k} k t_f^{k-1} \\ m_e &\leq (t_a^{cpu})^{-1} \\ m_e &\leq \gamma^{\frac{1}{k}} (x^{IN})^{-1} k |I|^{1-\frac{1}{k}} \\ (1 - k^{-1}) t_f + |I| m_e^{-1} &\leq x^N |I| \end{aligned}$$

The above inequalities take x^{IN} as input, which is the time interval at which input tuples are arriving. x^{IN} depends on the current execution context. If we are operating normally, it is the average time interval between tuples produced by the upstream operators; if we are recovering from a failure, we might read the input tuples from disk at the maximum bandwidth possible for the disk.

For the exact derivation of this mode, we refer the reader to the technical report [42]. Here, we only provide the intuition behind it.

In the above equations, $|I|$ is the output cardinality; γ and k come from the $NB_{out}(n_{in})$ function; m_e is the number of output tuples produced per second at the instant the processing ends and t_f is the *first* time at which the output produces tuples at the rate m_e. The first equation realizes this relationship between m_e and t_f. The following inequality states that the operator can not take less than t_a^{cpu} time to produce an output tuple, since this is the least amount of time the processor needs per tuple, given the resources it has. For the second inequality, its right hand side is the maximum rate at which output could be produced if the only bottleneck was the rate of arrival of input tuples. Note that, since we require the $NB_{out}(\cdot)$ function to have a non-negative rate of change, the fastest output production rate will be at the end of the computation and the derivative of the function $NB_{out}(\cdot)$, with respect to x^{IN}, at the end gives us this value. Since, in a real computation the processing cost is positive, the actual observed rate has to be less than the derivative (the right hand side in the second inequality). The third inequality states that the total time to process all tuples (which is equal to the average output rate times the number of output produced) must be higher than the actual processing time, which is its left hand side.

To model a different operator, the functions for t_a^{cpu} and $NB_{out}(n_{in})$ would change, while the form of the inequalities and equalities used by the optimizer would remain the same. They simply use the above as parameters.

We model a partitioned operator as a single operator that scales linearly with allocated resources. This approach suffices to show the feasibility and impact of fault-tolerance optimization. We leave extensions to more complex models, including data skew between partitions, for future work.

5.3.2 Modeling Overhead of Fault-tolerance

Fault-tolerance overhead only affects t_a^{cpu}, the time an operator needs to produce an output. The model depends on the operator implementation. For MATERIALIZE, our join writes all output tuples to disk. For CHCKPT, it logs the incoming tuples to disk incrementally[5]. The join does not maintain any output queue.

For brevity, we use the notation that $\mathbb{I}^N$, $\mathbb{I}^M$ and $\mathbb{I}^C$ are 1 if NONE, MATERIALIZE or CHCKPT is the chosen fault tolerance option, respectively, and are 0 otherwise. Although we need one equation per fault-tolerance strategy we represent them as a single one.

$$t_a^{cpu} = |I|^{-1} \left(t^{cpu}(|I_{utot}| + |I|) + \mathbb{I}^C t^{io} |I_{utot}| + \mathbb{I}^M t^{io} |I| \right)$$

Here t^{io} is the time to write a tuple to disk and is also obtained through micro-benchmarks.

5.3.3 Modeling Replay Request Times

FTOpt also needs to know the average rate at which output tuples are produced to satisfy a replay request and the delay in generating the first requested tuple. The replay rate may depend on when, during the course of the query, the downstream fails. For example, if the replay behaves as during normal operations for the symmetric hash-join, it might be slower if the downstream fails early on and be faster later. To approximate the recovery rate we find the time it takes to replay all output tuples and divide that number by

[5] Out of simplicity, our join checkpoints input tuples as they arrive rather than checkpointing the hash table. When it rebuilds the hash table from a checkpoint, the operator does not redo the join.

the total number of output tuples. During this replay phase, the operator has no fault-tolerance overheads.

As before, the exact model depends on the implementation details. Our join implementation uses its in-memory hash table to regenerate outputs and hence the delay is negligible. But it could be significant for a join that can not use either its state or its output to answer tuple requests.

To get the average output rate, we reuse the framework we developed in the previous section. Thus we only need to specify t_a^{cpu} and $NB_{out}(n_{in})$ for the replay mode.

Since, during replay, we only reprocess the inputs without any fault tolerance overhead: $t_a^{cpu} = |I|^{-1}(|I_{utot}| + |I|)\,t^{cpu}$.

The form of the $NB_{out}(\cdot)$ remains the same as for the normal processing. Also, during reprocessing the input tuples are already in memory, hence the inter-tuple arrival time of inputs x^{IN} is at least t^{cpu} and we take $x^{IN} = t^{cpu}$.

5.3.4 *Modeling Recovery Time*

To compute the total time to recover from a failure, we need to know the average rate at which recovery proceeds.

As before, the exact recovery model depends on the implementation. For our join, upon failure the MATERIALIZE and the NONE options have to request all the input from the upstream nodes and rebuild the hash table exactly as it was before (using Rule 4.2 and operator determinism [42]), while CHCKPT rebuilds it from the input tuples logged to disk.

In all cases, during recovery, no output is produced when the input tuples are processed to remake the hash table. Thus, $t_a^{cpu} = t^{cpu}$ since we look at each input tuple once.

To define the function $NB_{out}(n_{in})$ we think of the hash table being rebuilt as the desired "output" and the input tuples as the inputs. Since all the input tuples are used to generate the "output" hash table: $NB_{out}(n_{in}) = n_{in}$. For MATERIALIZE and NONE, x^{IN} is the average time interval in which requested tuples from the upstream nodes arrive. For CHCKPT, since we directly read tuples from the disk: $x^{IN} = t^{io}$.

The delay in getting the first input is negligible if we use CHCKPT and is equal to the delay of the upstream tuples in the case of NONE and MATERIALIZE.

We approximate the expected hash table size to recover to be $\frac{1}{2}|I_{utot}|$. Thus, the expected time to recover is the sum of (1) the delay to receive the first input tuple, and (2) the product of the expected hash table size and the average time per tuple spent in adding a tuple to that hash table.

In summary, compared to existing cost models for parallel query runtime estimation [13, 12] and fault-tolerance in streaming engines [21], our models capture the dynamic operator interactions in pipelined queries, which we observed to affect runtime predictions and fault-tolerance optimization. For example, a fast operator following a slow one in a pipeline will produce its output slowly. At the same time, we do not require that an operator's output tuples be uniformly spread across the entire execution time of the operator [16, 46]. Indeed, because we use a GP framework, we support simple types of non-uniform outputs such as that of asymmetric hash-join. Of course, our GP framework may not cover all cases. In particular, for multi-phase operators (*e.g.*, a symmetric hash-join that spills state to disk), we may still need to split the operator into multiple sub-operators for more accurate modeling of each phase.

5.4 Approach Implementability

Our approach consists of (1) a protocol that enables heterogeneous fault-tolerance in a parallel query plan and (2) an optimizer that automatically selects the fault-tolerance strategy that each operator should use. We now discuss the difficulty of implementing this approach in a parallel data processing system.

To implement our approach, developers need to (a) implement desired fault-tolerance strategies for their operators in a manner that follows our protocol. In Section 4.2, however, we showed, how to efficiently implement three well-known fault-tolerance strategies for generic stateless and stateful operators. Existing libraries can also help with such implementation (*e.g.*, [23]). Developers must also (b) model their operator costs within a pipelined query plan. To simplify this latter task, we develop an approach that requires only that developers specify well-known functions under different fault-tolerance strategies and during recovery: an operator cost function and a function that computes how the output size of an operator grows with the input size. Our optimizer derives the resulting operator dynamics automatically. For parallel database systems [39, 14] and MapReduce-type systems such as Hive [1] or Pig [30], which come with predefined operators, the above overhead needs only be paid once and we thus posit that it is a reasonable requirement.

For user-defined operators (UDOs), the above may still be too much to ask. In that case, the simplest strategy is to treat UDOs as if they could only support the NONE or MATERIALIZE strategies (depending on the underlying platform) without ever producing acknowledgments. With this approach, UDO writers need not do any extra work at all, yet the overall query plan can still be optimized and achieve higher performance than without fault-tolerance optimization as we show in Section 6.4.

Finally, our approach relies on a set of parameters including IO cost (expressed as the time t^{io} spent in a byte sized disk IO), per-operator CPU cost (expressed as the time t^{cpu} spent processing each tuple), and total network bandwidth. Commercial database systems already automate the collection of such statistics (*e.g.*, [31]), though t^{cpu} is typically expanded into a more detailed formula.

Other necessary information includes the expected number of failures for the query (see Section 2), operator selectivities (standard optimizer-provided metric), and an estimate of the total checkpointable state. As shown in Section 6.6, our optimizer is insensitive to small errors in these estimates.

Overall, the requirements of our fault-tolerance optimization framework are thus similar to those of existing cost-based query optimizers.

5.5 Handling Complex Failure Scenarios

So far, we have focused on process failures. However, our approach also handles other types of failures.

Our approach still works when entire physical machines fail (*e.g.*, due to a disk failure, a power failure, or a network failure). To support such failures, checkpoints must be written to remote nodes instead of locally [19], which adds network and CPU costs that must be taken into account by the optimizer. Given that the optimizer knows the size of these checkpoints, it can take that cost into account. Second, when a physical machine fails or becomes disconnected, the number of nodes in the cluster is reduced by one, which must also be taken into account by the optimizer.

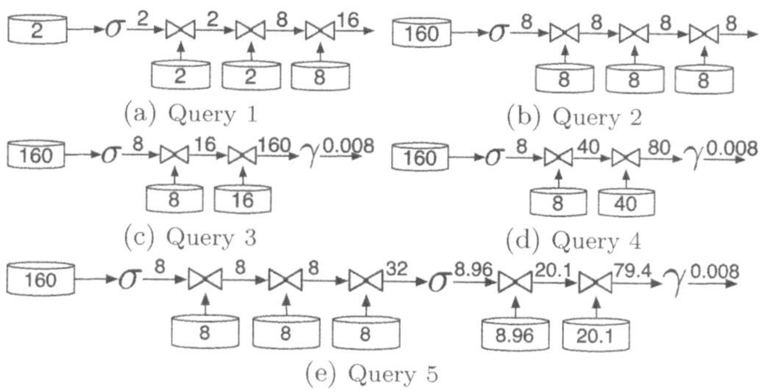

Figure 3: Query plans used in experiments. σ, $\bowtie$, γ denote Select, Join, and Aggregation, respectively. All numbers are in millions.

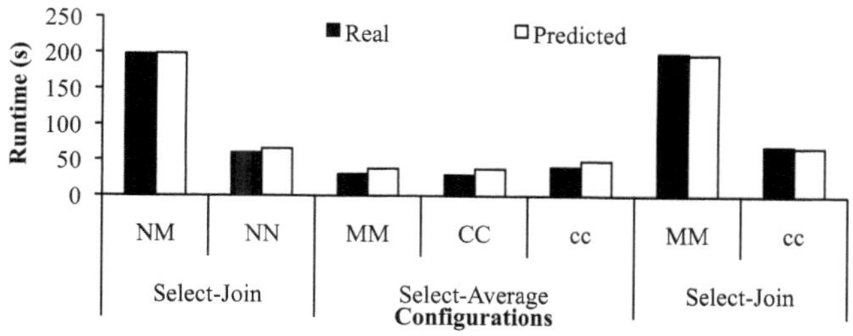

Figure 4: Runtime without failures for various two-operator queries. X-axis labels show the fault-tolerance strategy chosen: N for NONE, M for MATERIALIZE, C for CHCKPT with a total of 10 checkpoints, and c for CHCKPT with 1K checkpoints.

Our approach does not currently handle failures that affect a large number of machines. Indeed, such failures can cause the temporary loss of input data or checkpointed data. In such cases, the query needs to be restarted in its entirety once the input data becomes available again. In general, however, large-scale rack and network failures are infrequent, while single machine failures are common. For example, Google reports 5 average worker deaths per MapReduce job in March 2006 [9], but only approximately 20 rack failures per year (and similarly few network failures) [8].

Even though our approach does not handle large-scale failures that cause the loss of input or checkpointed data, it does handle multiple operators failing at the same time. The only requirement in such cases is that operators be restarted from downstream to upstream, ensuring that each operator knows where to start recovering from before asking upstream neighbors to replay data.

6. EVALUATION

We evaluate FTOpt by answering the following questions: (1) Does the choice of fault-tolerance strategy for a parallel query matter? (2) Are there configurations where a *hybrid* plan, where different operators use different fault-tolerance techniques, outperforms uniform plans? (3) Is our optimizer able to find good fault-tolerance plans automatically? (4) How do user-defined operators affect FTOpt? (5) What is the scalability of our approach? (6) How sensitive is FTOpt to estimation errors in its various parameters?

We answer these questions through experiments with a variety of queries in a 17-node cluster. Each node has dual 2.5 GHz Quad Core E5420 processors and 16 GB RAM running Linux kernel 2.6.18 with two 7.2K RPM 750 GB SATA hard disks. The cluster runs a simple parallel data processing engine that we wrote in Java. The implementation includes our new fault-tolerance framework and specific per-operator fault-tolerance strategies for a small set of representative operators. All fault-tolerance strategies were moderately optimized (see Section 4.2). We implemented the optimizer in MATLAB using the *cvx* package [7].

The query plans that we use in the experiments are shown in Figure 3. They include an SJJJ and SJJA query (we also test a more complex query later in this section). For both queries we have 8 partitions per operator with 2 cores and 1 disk per partition. Partitions of the same operator run on different machines. The input data is synthetic and without skew. Tuples are 0.5 KB in size. The schema consists of 4 attributes used to hash-partition tuples for each operator, a 5th attribute for grouping the aggregates, and a 6th one for the join predicates. A separate producer process generates input tuples. For a given plan, we get the expected recovery time by injecting a failure midway through the time the plan takes to execute with no failures. We inject *exactly one* failure per run and show the recovery time averaged over all distinct operators in the plan.

6.1 Model Validation Experiments

FTOpt requires the t^{cpu} and the t^{io} values for each operator. It also requires the network bandwidth for each machine in the cluster. Through micro-benchmarks, we find that the average time to read a tuple from disk (sequential read) is $t^{io} = 13.0\ \mu s$ for a 0.5 KB tuple. This number is equivalent to a disk throughput of 37 MBps. For select and aggregate operators, we measure t^{cpu} to be $1.82\mu s$. The join operator, internally, works in two parts: (1) hashing the input tuple and storing it in one of the tables for a cost of $t_1 = 8\mu s$ and (2) joining the hashed input tuple to the corresponding tuples from the other table for a cost of $t_2 = 1\mu s$. We use t_1, t_2, and the operator's selectivity to estimate its t^{cpu}. Finally, we measure the network I/O time per 0.5 KB tuple to be $4.7\mu s$, which is equivalent to a network bandwidth of 109.4 MBps and is close to the theoretical maximum of 1 Gbps network bandwidth for each machine in the cluster.

These parameters along with our operator models enable FTOpt to predict the runtime for an entire query plan. Figure 4 shows the runtime without failure for a few two-operator queries. While the median percentage difference between real and predicted runtime is 9.5%, this error is small given the overall differences in runtime between various configurations. We measure the sensitivity of our approach to the benchmarked parameter values in Section 6.6.

6.2 Impact of Fault-Tolerance Strategy

The first question that we ask is whether a fault-tolerance optimizer is useful: how much does it really matter what fault-tolerance strategy is used for a query plan?

Figures 5 through 7 show the actual and predicted runtimes for Queries 1 through 3 from Figure 3 with 8 partitions per operator. Note that, each join receives input from *two* sources: its upstream operator in the plan and a producer process. In all our experiments, an equal number of tuples was received from each source. Whenever FTOpt selects CHCKPT as a strategy, it also chooses the checkpoint frequency (Query 3). In other cases, we use 100 checkpoints, a

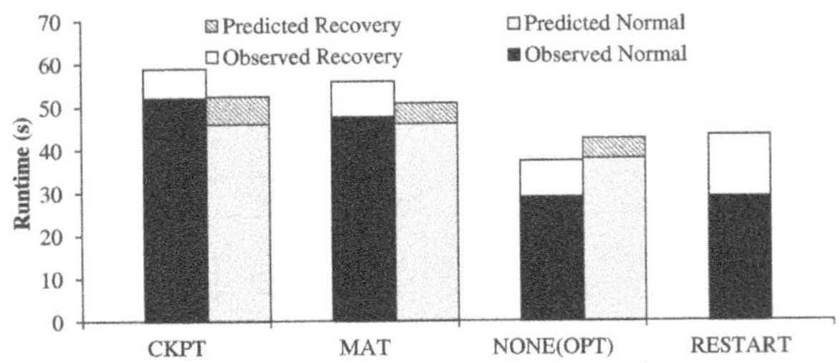

Figure 5: Query 1 (SJJJ)

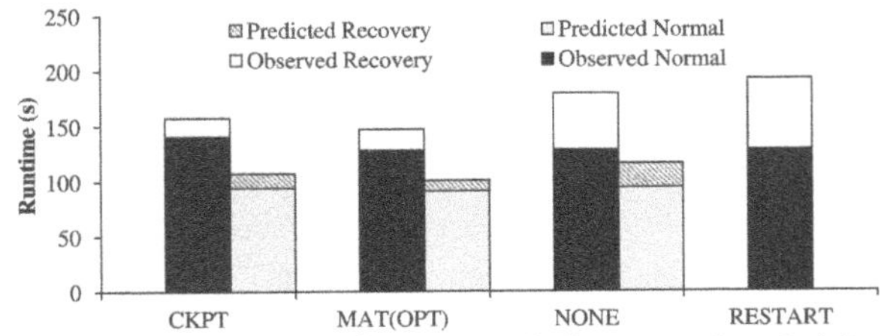

Figure 6: Query 2 (SJJJ with lower selectivities)

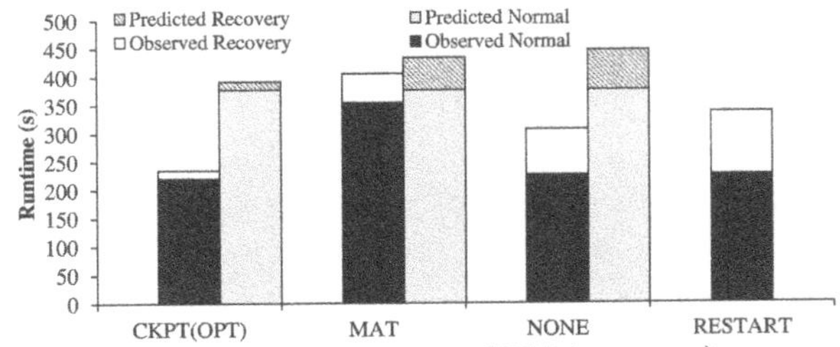

Figure 7: Query 3 (SJJA query)

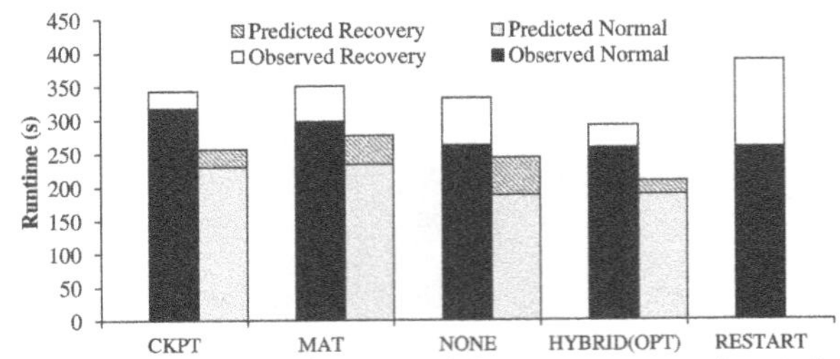

Figure 8: Query 4 (SJJA with more expensive joins). The hybrid strategy is to materialize after select, do nothing for joins, and checkpoint the aggregate

manually selected value that we found to give high performance in these experiments.

The most important result from these experiments is that, while these queries are all similar to each other, *each one requires a different fault-tolerance plan to achieve best performance.* For Query 1, a uniform NONE strategy is best. For Query 2, uniform MATERIALIZE wins. Finally, for Query 3, uniform CHCKPT outperforms the other options.

Second, restarting a query is at most 50% slower than a strategy with more fine-grained fault-tolerance. The fine-grained strategy gains the most when it reduces recovery times with minimal impact on runtime without failures. For some queries, the appropriate choice of fault-tolerance gets close to this theoretical upper bound. For Query 2, RESTART is 31% worse than the best strategy while for Query 3, restarting is 44% slower than the best strategy. Achieving such gains, however, requires fault-tolerance optimization. Indeed, different strategies win for different queries and a wrong fault-tolerance strategy choice leads to much worse performance than restarting a query. Overall, the differences between the best and worst plan are high: 58% for Query 1, 31% for Query 2, and 72% for Query 3.

Finally, in all cases, *FTOpt is able to identify the winning strategy!* Predicted runtimes do not always match the observed ones exactly. Most of the difference is attributable to our simple model for the network and FTOpt's predictions are thus more accurate when either CPU or disk IO is the bottleneck in a query plan and less accurate when it is the network. While we could further refine our models, to pick the optimal strategy, we only need to have correct relative order of predicted runtimes for different plans. As shown in Figures 4 through 8, FTOpt preserves that order when runtime differences are large. When two configurations lead to very similar runtimes, FTOpt may not find the best of these plans but the choice of plan matters less in such a case and FTOpt always suggests one of the good plans.

In summary, the correct choice of fault-tolerance strategy can significantly impact query runtime and that choice is not obvious as similar query plans may require very different strategies. FTOpt can automatically select a good plan.

6.3 Benefits of Hybrid Configurations

We now consider a query (Query 4), similar to Query 3, but with the joins processing and producing much more data, making checkpointing expensive. Figure 8 shows that a hybrid strategy that materializes the select's output, does nothing for the joins, and checkpoints the aggregate's state for a total of 40 checkpoints (value selected by the optimizer), yields the best performance. The uniform strategies are 15% slower at best and 21% slower at worst while RESTART is 35% slower.

We observe similar gains for a longer query (Query 5) with *eight* operators. Figure 9 shows that the hybrid plan (chosen by the optimizer) materializes both selects' outputs, does nothing for joins and takes 20 checkpoints of the aggregate. The best and worst uniform strategies and RESTART are 16%, 23% and 36% slower, respectively. Manually, we found that checkpointing the first two joins in the hybrid plan led to another hybrid plan that was 2% faster. While the optimizer did not choose this better plan, the plan it chose performs similarly. Further, both the observed and predicted best plans are hybrid.

The experiments thus show that hybrid fault-tolerance strategies can be advantageous and the best strategy for an operator depends not only on the operator but on the whole query plan: the same operator can use different strategies in different query plans: *e.g.*, select in Queries 3 and 4.

Note that we inject only one failure per experiment. Thus, our graphs show the minimum guaranteed gains. Additional failures amplify differences between strategies.

6.4 Performance in Presence of UDOs

We look at the applicability of heterogeneous fault-tolerance when an operator is a user-defined function with limited fault-tolerance capabilities. We experiment with Query 3, but treat its last operator, the aggregate, as a UDO that can only restart from scratch if it fails. Note that Rule 4.2 and operator determinism [42] allow restarting a UDO in isolation without restarting the entire query.

Figure 10 shows the results. Previously, the best fault-tolerance strategy, with a single failure, was to checkpoint every operator ("With CKPT") and checkpointing aggregate provided significant savings in recovery time. Now that the aggregate can use NONE as sole strategy, we find that ma-

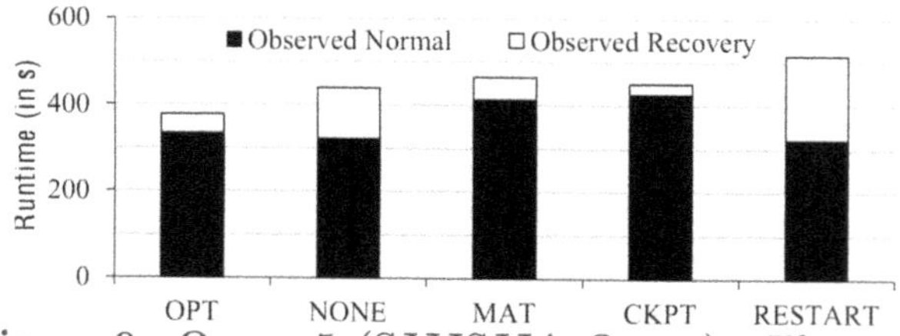

Figure 9: Query 5 (SJJJSJJA Query). The optimal hybrid strategy is MNNNMNNC where M denotes MATERIALIZE and N denotes NONE and C denotes CHCKPT. In the optimal configuration 20 checkpoints are taken.

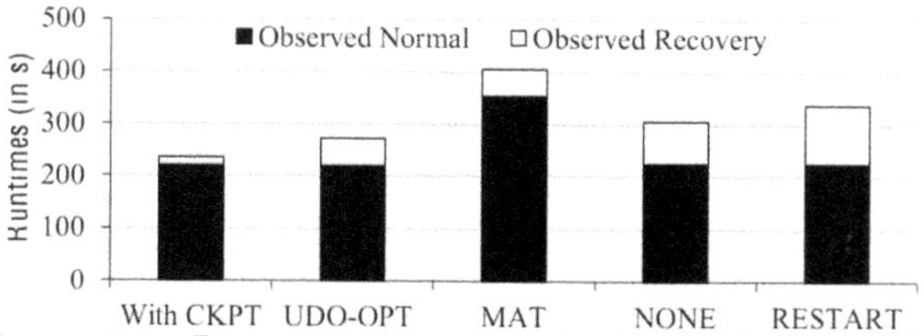

Figure 10: Impact of aggregate becoming a UDOs without fault-tolerance capabilities on Query 3. The optimal strategy is to materialize after select and do nothing elsewhere.

terializing the first operator's output and using NONE for the remaining operators outperforms uniformly materializing, none and RESTART by 48%, 12%, and 24%, respectively. The hybrid strategy is itself 16% slower than the optimal strategy for Query 3 ("With CKPT").

Hence even in the presence of fault-tolerance agnostic UDOs, FTOpt can generate significant runtime savings.

6.5 Scalability

FTOpt currently uses a brute force search algorithm, but we find that simple heuristics can significantly prune the search space. Indeed, we observe that the best hybrid plans use the NONE strategy for many operators and using another strategy in place of NONE will always increase the runtime *without failures*. Thus, if the runtime without failure for a plan exceeds the runtime with failures for another plan, we can prune the former plan. Hence, evaluating plans in the decreasing order of the number of operators that use the NONE strategy can prune significant fractions of the search space. For example, with this heuristic, the optimizer examines only 28 out of 81 configurations for Query 4. In addition, the search essentially computes the least costly of a set of independent optimization problems and all of these problems can be optimized in parallel.

FTOpt's MATLAB implementation uses the cvx package, which offers a *successive approximation* solver using SDPT3 [40]. In our prototype, the average time to solve the optimization problem per plan is around 25s for the 4 operator plans in the previous sections. However, an optimized solver can solve a larger problem in *a sub millisecond* [29]. The behavior of an operator for a fault-tolerance strategy is modeled using at most 12 inequality and 4 equality constraints of 11 variables. Thus, a query with n operators can be modeled using $11n$ variables, $13n + 1$ inequality and $4n$ equality constraints. Further, all but one of the constraints are sparse: they depend on just a few variables independent of n. For example, with 4 operators, our models use 44 variables, 16 equalities, and 53 inequalities. The existing

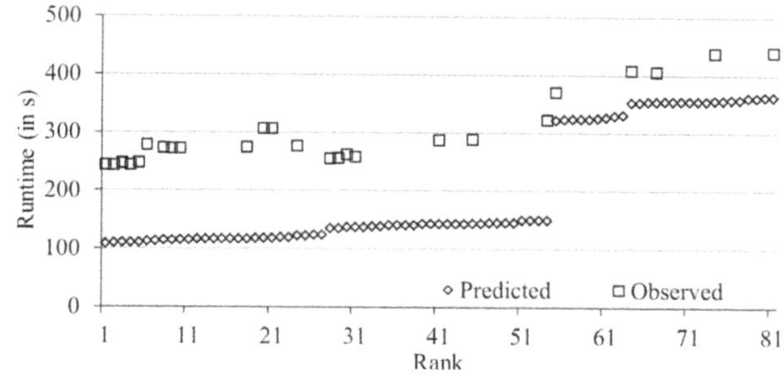

Figure 11: Observed and predicted runtimes for Query 3, sorted on the predicted runtime, for all 81 fault-tolerance plans for the query.

Table 3: Real rankings of top 5 plans from perturbed configurations.

Perturbation	Rankings				
Failing thrice instead of once	1	2	3	4	5
IO cost 2.0x of true value	1	6	8	9	18
IO cost 0.5x of true value	2	1	3	4	5
IO cost 10x of true value	6	18	20	21	24
IO cost 0.1x of true value	2	28	31	30	29
Selectivity of all operators 1.1x	1	2	3	4	5
Selectivity of all operators 0.9x	1	2	3	4	5
Selectivity of all operators 2.0x	1	2	3	4	5
Selectivity of all operators 0.5x	56	1	66	67	10

optimized solvers can solve a problem of 140 variables, 120 equalities, and 60 inequalities in 0.425 ms on average [29].

To sum up, with an optimized solver, and a parallelized heuristic search algorithm, FTOpt could be scalable enough to handle larger query plans within a few seconds.

6.6 Optimizer Sensitivity

We evaluate FTOpt's sensitivity to inaccuracies in parameter estimates. We experiment with Query 3 since it is most sensitive to wrong choices: Figure 11 shows that runtimes vary from about 250s to 400s depending on the chosen plan.

To evaluate the sensitivity for a given parameter, we rerun FTOpt, feeding it a perturbed parameter value. We only perturb a single parameter at a time while keeping the other parameters at their true values. We then compute the top 5 plans with the perturbed value and report the ranks of these plans in FTOpt's original ranking (Figure 11). Table 3 shows the results. As an example, in this table, when IO cost increases to 2X its true value, the second best plan identified by FTOpt was ranked 6th with the real IO costs.

Table 3 shows that FTOpt is very robust to small errors in the number of failures and it is fairly robust to even large errors in IO cost: a 10x change still leads to a good plan (with true rank 6) being chosen, though the subsequent plans have poor true rankings. FTOpt is least robust to cardinality estimation errors. In our experiments, we varied the selectivities of all the operators in tandem (and with the join always processing the same number of tuples from both streams). In this scenario, our predictions were unchanged for changes of 1.1x, 2x and 0.9x in selectivity but for a 0.5x change, the top choice's true rank was 56 with an observed runtime about 70% worse than that of the best configuration possible.

The robustness to I/O cost errors and failure errors can be explained by the fact that the effect of these errors is mostly linear on the optimizer. However, imprecise selectivity estimates have an exponential effect (the further an operator is from the beginning, the less data it processes and it produces even less output) on FTOpt. Thus, the optimizer is more sensitive to perturbations in selectivity estimates.

7. CONCLUSION

In this paper, we presented a framework for heterogeneous fault-tolerance, a concrete instance of that framework, and FTOpt, a latency and fault-tolerance optimizer for parallel data processing systems. Given a pipelined query plan, a shared-nothing cluster, and a failure model, FTOpt selects the fault-tolerance strategy for *each* operator in a query plan to minimize the time to complete the query with failures. We implemented our approach in a prototype parallel query processing engine. Our experimental results show that different fault-tolerance strategies, often hybrid ones, lead to the best performance in different settings and that our optimizer is able to correctly identify a winning strategy.

Acknowledgments

We thank Phil Bernstein, Bill Howe, Julie Letchner, Dan Suciu, and the anonymous reviewers for helpful comments on the paper's early drafts. This work is supported in part by the National Science Foundation grants NSF CAREER IIS-0845397 and IIS-0713123, gifts from Microsoft Research, and Balazinska's Microsoft Research Faculty Fellowship.

8. REFERENCES

[1] Ashish Thusoo et. al. Hive - a petabyte scale data warehouse using hadoop. In *Proc. of the 26th ICDE Conf.*, 2010.
[2] M. Balazinska, H. Balakrishnan, S. Madden, and M. Stonebraker. Fault-tolerance in the Borealis distributed stream processing system. In *Proc. of the SIGMOD Conf.*, June 2005.
[3] S. P. Boyd, S. J. Kim, L. Vandenberghe, and A. Hassibi. A tutorial on geometric programming. Technical report, Stanford University, Info. Systems Laboratory, Dept. Elect. Eng., 2004.
[4] B. Chandramouli, C. N. Bond, S. Babu, and J. Yang. Query suspend and resume. In *Proc. of the SIGMOD Conf.*, 2007.
[5] S. Chaudhuri, R. Kaushik, A. Pol, and R. Ramamurthy. Stop-and-restart style execution for long running decision support queries. In *Proc. of the 33rd VLDB Conf.*, 2007.
[6] Chen et. al. High availability and scalability guide for DB2 on linux, unix, and windows. IBM Redbooks `http://www.redbooks.ibm.com/redbooks/pdfs/sg247363.pdf`, Sept. 2007.
[7] Cvx. `http://www.stanford.edu/~boyd/cvx/`.
[8] J. Dean. Software engineering advice from building large-scale distributed systems. `http://research.google.com/people/jeff/stanford-295-talk.pdf`.
[9] J. Dean. Experiences with MapReduce, an abstraction for large-scale computation. Keynote I: PACT, 2006.
[10] J. Dean and S. Ghemawat. MapReduce: simplified data processing on large clusters. In *Proc. of the 6th OSDI Symp.*, 2004.
[11] E. N. M. Elnozahy, L. Alvisi, Y.-M. Wang, and D. B. Johnson. A survey of rollback-recovery protocols in message-passing systems. *ACM Computing Surveys*, 34(3), 2002.
[12] S. Ganguly, A. Goel, and A. Silberschatz. Efficient and accurate cost models for parallel query optimization (extended abstract). In *Proc. of the 15rd PODS Symp.*, 1996.
[13] S. Ganguly, W. Hasan, and R. Krishnamurthy. Query optimization for parallel execution. In *Proc. of the SIGMOD Conf.*, pages 9–18, 1992.
[14] Greenplum database. `http://www.greenplum.com/`.
[15] Hadoop. `http://hadoop.apache.org/`.
[16] W. Hasan and R. Motwani. Optimization algorithms for exploiting the parallelism-communication tradeoff in pipelined parallelism. In *Proc. of the 20th VLDB Conf.*, 1994.
[17] J. M. Hellerstein, R. Avnur, and V. Raman. Informix under CONTROL: Online query processing. *Data Mining and Knowledge Discovery*, 4(4):281–314, 2000.
[18] J. M. Hellerstein, P. J. Haas, and H. J. Wang. Online aggregation. In *Proc. of the SIGMOD Conf.*, 1997.
[19] J.-H. Hwang, Y. Xing, U. Çetintemel, and S. Zdonik. A cooperative, self-configuring high-availability solution for stream processing. In *Proc. of ICDE Conf.*, Apr. 2007.
[20] M. Isard, M. Budiu, Y. Yu, A. Birrell, and D. Fetterly. Dryad: Distributed data-parallel programs from sequential building blocks. In *Proc. of the EuroSys Conf.*, pages 59–72, 2007.
[21] Jeong-Hyon Hwang et. al. High-availability algorithms for distributed stream processing. In *Proc. of the 21st ICDE Conf.*, Apr. 2005.
[22] S. Y. Ko, I. Hoque, B. Cho, and I. Gupta. Making cloud intermediate data fault-tolerant. In *Proc. of the 1st ACM symposium on Cloud computing (SOCC)*, pages 181–192, 2010.
[23] Y. Kwon, M. Balazinska, and A. Greenberg. Fault-tolerant stream processing using a distributed, replicated file system. In *Proc. of the 34th VLDB Conf.*, 2008.
[24] W. J. Labio, J. L. Wiener, H. Garcia-Molina, and V. Gorelik. Efficient resumption of interrupted warehouse loads. *SIGMOD Record*, 29(2):46–57, 2000.
[25] A.-P. Liedes and A. Wolski. Siren: A memory-conserving, snapshot-consistent checkpoint algorithm for in-memory databases. In *Proc. of the 22nd ICDE Conf.*, page 99, 2006.
[26] D. Logothetis, C. Olston, B. Reed, K. C. Webb, and K. Yocum. Stateful bulk processing for incremental analytics. In *Proc. of the 1st ACM symposium on Cloud computing (SOCC)*, 2010.
[27] D. Lomet. Dependability, abstraction, and programming. In *DASFAA '09: Proc. of the 14th Int. Conf. on Database Systems for Advanced Applications*, pages 1–21, 2009.
[28] Marcos Vaz Salles et. al. An evaluation of checkpoint recovery for massively multiplayer online games. In *Proc. of the 35th VLDB Conf.*, 2009.
[29] J. Mattingley and S. Boyd. Automatic code generation for real-time convex optimization. In *Convex Optimization in Signal Processing Optimization*. Cambridge U. Press, 2009.
[30] C. Olston, B. Reed, U. Srivastava, R. Kumar, and A. Tomkins. Pig latin: a not-so-foreign language for data processing. In *Proc. of the SIGMOD Conf.*, pages 1099–1110, 2008.
[31] Oracle database. `http://www.oracle.com/`.
[32] A. Pavlo et. al. A comparison of approaches to large-scale data analysis. In *Proc. of the SIGMOD Conf.*, 2009.
[33] A. Ray. Oracle data guard: Ensuring disaster recovery for the enterprise. An Oracle white paper, Mar. 2002.
[34] K. Salem and H. Garcia-Molina. Checkpointing memory-resident databases. In *Proc. of the 5th ICDE Conf.*, pages 452–462, 1989.
[35] F. B. Schneider. Implementing fault-tolerant services using the state machine approach: a tutorial. *ACM Computing Surveys*, 22(4):299–319, 1990.
[36] M. Shah, J. Hellerstein, and E. Brewer. Highly-available, fault-tolerant, parallel dataflows. In *Proc. of the SIGMOD Conf.*, June 2004.
[37] A. Simitsis, K. Wilkinson, U. Dayal, and M. Castellanos. Optimizing etl workflows for fault-tolerance. In *Proc. of the 26th ICDE Conf.*, 2010.
[38] R. Talmage. Database mirroring in SQL Server 2005. `http://www.microsoft.com/technet/prodtechnol/sql/2005/dbmirror.mspx`, Apr. 2005.
[39] Teradata. `http://www.teradata.com/`.
[40] R. H. Tütüncü, K. C. Toh, and M. J. Todd. Solving semidefinite-quadratic-linear programs using SDPT3. *Mathematical programming*, 95(2):189–217, 2003.
[41] Tyson Condie et. al. MapReduce online. In *Proc. of the 7th NSDI Symp.*, 2010.
[42] P. Upadhyaya, Y. Kwon, and M. Balazinska. A latency and fault-tolerance optimizer for online parallel query plans. Technical report, Department of Computer Science and Engineering, Univ. of Washington, 2010.
[43] Vertica, inc. `http://www.vertica.com/`.
[44] C. Yang, C. Yen, C. Tan, and S. R. Madden. Osprey: Implementing MapReduce-style fault tolerance in a shared-nothing distributed database. In *Proc. of the 26th ICDE Conf.*, 2010.
[45] Yuan Yu et. al. DryadLINQ: A system for general-purpose distributed data-parallel computing using a high-level language. In *Proc. of the 8th OSDI Symp.*, 2008.
[46] M. Zaït, D. Florescu, and P. Valduriez. Benchmarking the DBS3 parallel query optimizer. *IEEE Parallel Distrib. Technol.*, 4(2):26–40, 1996.

ArrayStore: A Storage Manager for Complex Parallel Array Processing

Emad Soroush, Magdalena Balazinska
Computer Science Department
University of Washington
Seattle, USA
{soroush, magda}@cs.washington.edu

Daniel Wang
SLAC National Accelerator Laboratory
Menlo Park, CA
danielw@slac.stanford.edu

ABSTRACT

We present the design, implementation, and evaluation of ArrayStore, a new storage manager for complex, parallel array processing. ArrayStore builds on prior work in the area of multidimensional data storage, but considers the new problem of supporting a *parallel* and more *varied* workload comprising not only range-queries, but also binary operations such as joins and complex user-defined functions.

This paper makes two key contributions. First, it examines several existing single-site storage management strategies and array partitioning strategies to identify which combination is best suited for the array-processing workload above. Second, it develops a new and efficient storage-management mechanism that enables parallel processing of operations that must access data from adjacent partitions.

We evaluate ArrayStore on over 80GB of real data from two scientific domains and real operators used in these domains. We show that ArrayStore outperforms previously proposed storage management strategies in the context of its diverse target workload.

Categories and Subject Descriptors

H.2.4 [**Information Systems**]: Database Management—Systems; H.2.8 [**Information Systems**]: Database Management—Database applications

General Terms

Algorithms, Design, Performance

1. INTRODUCTION

Scientists today are able to generate data at unprecedented scale and rate [18, 23]. To support these growing data management needs many advocate that one should move away from the relational model and adopt a multidimensional array data model [14, 40]. The main reason is that scientists typically work with array data and simulating arrays on top of relations can be highly inefficient [40]. Scientists also need to perform array-specific operations such as feature extraction [19], smoothing [35], and cross-matching [26], which are not built-in operations in relational DBMSs. As a result, many engines are being built today to support multidimensional arrays [4, 14, 35, 42]. To handle today's large-scale datasets, arrays must also be partitioned and processed in a shared-nothing cluster [35].

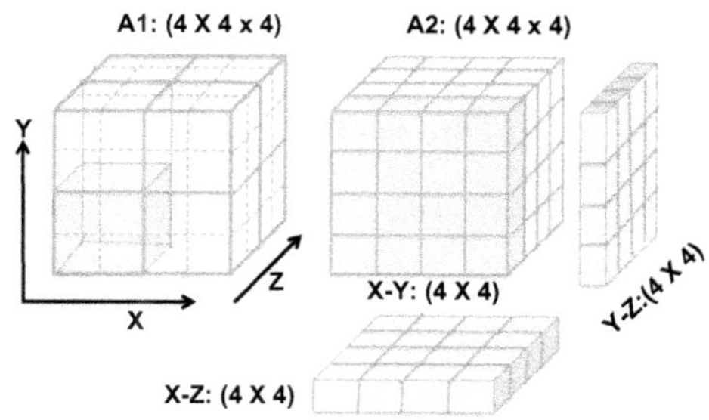

Figure 1: (1) The 4x4x4 array A1 is divided into eight 2x2x2 chunks. Each chunk is a unit of I/O (a disk block or larger). Each X-Y, X-Z, or Y-Z slice needs to load 4 I/O units. (2) Array A2 is laid out linearly through nested traversal of its axes without chunking. X-Y needs to load only one I/O unit, while X-Z and Y-Z need to load the entire array.

In this paper, we address the following key question: *what is the appropriate storage management strategy for a parallel array processing system?* Unlike most other array-processing systems being built today [4, 11, 14, 42], we are not interested in building an array engine on top of a relational DBMS, but rather building a specialized storage manager from scratch. In this paper, we consider read-only arrays and do not address the problem of updating arrays.

There is a long line of work on storing and indexing multidimensional data (see Section 6). A standard approach to storing an array is to partition it into sub-arrays called chunks [36] as illustrated in Figure 1. Each chunk is typically the size of a storage block. Chunking an array helps alleviate "dimension dependency" [38], where the number of blocks read from disk depends on the dimensions involved in a range-selection query rather than just the range size.

Requirements. The design of a parallel array storage manager must thus answer the following questions (1) what is the most efficient array chunking strategy for a given workload, (2) how should the storage manager partition chunks across machines in a shared-nothing cluster to support parallel pro-

SIGMOD'11, June 12–16, 2011, Athens, Greece.

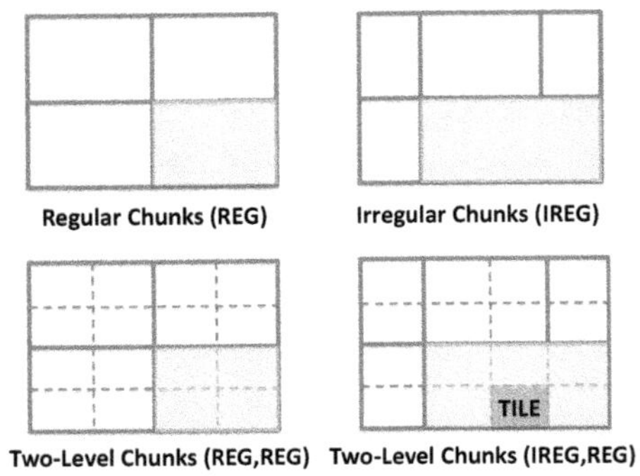

Figure 2: Four different chunking strategies applied to the same rectangular array. Solid lines shows chunk boundaries of the logical array (sample chunks shaded). Inner-level tiles are represented by dashed lines (one tile is textured).

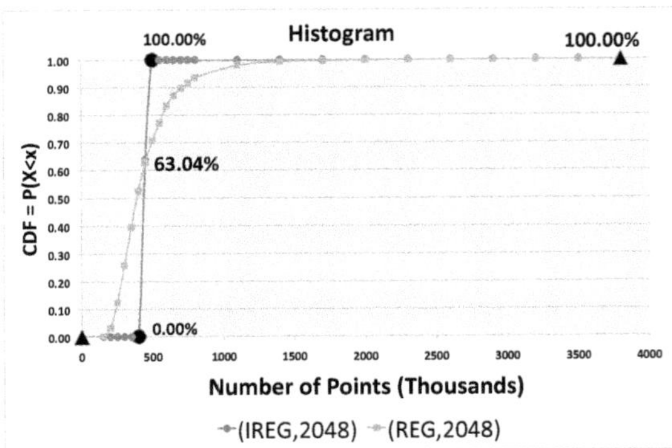

Figure 3: Cumulative distribution function of number of points (*i.e.*, non-null cells) per chunk for regular (REG) and irregular (IREG) chunking in astronomy simulation snapshot S92. Both strategies use 2048 chunks. Large circles for IREG and large triangles for REG mark the 0% and 100% points in each distribution.

cessing, and (3) how to efficiently support array operations that need to access data in adjacent chunks possibly located on other machines during parallel processing? Prior work examined some of these questions but only in the context of array scans and range-selection, nearest-neighbors, and other "lookup-style" operations [7, 8, 16, 24, 25, 28, 29, 34, 36, 38]. In contrast, our goal is to support a more varied workload as required by the science community [40]. In particular, we aim at supporting a workload comprising the following types of operations: (1) array slicing and dicing (*i.e.*, operations that extract a subset of an array [8, 9, 35]), (2) array scans (*e.g.*, filters, regrids [40], and other operations that process an entire array), (3) binary array operations (*e.g.*, joins, cross-match [26]), and (4) operations that need to access data from adjacent partitions during parallel processing (*e.g.*, canopy clustering [1]). We want to support both single-site and parallel versions of these operations.

Challenges. The above types of operations impose *very different, even contradictory, requirements* on the storage manager. Indeed, array dicing can benefit from small, finely tuned chunks [16]. In contrast, user-defined functions may incur overhead when chunks are too small and processed in parallel [19] and they may need to efficiently access data in adjacent chunks. Different yet, joins need to simultaneously access corresponding pieces of two arrays, and they need a chunking method that facilitates this task. When processed in parallel, all these operations may also suffer from skew, where some groups of chunks take much longer to process than others [12, 19, 20], slowing down the entire operation. Binary operations also require that matching chunks from different arrays be co-located possibly causing data shuffling and thus imposing I/O overhead.

These requirements are especially hard to satisfy for sparse arrays (*i.e.*, an array is said to be sparse when most of its cells do not contain any data) because data in a sparse array is unevenly distributed, which can worsen skew (*e.g.*, in one of our datasets, when splitting an array into 2048 chunks, we found a 25X difference between the chunk with the most and least amount of data). Common representations of sparse arrays in the form of an unordered list of coordinates and values also slow down access to subsets of an array chunk, because all data points must be scanned. In this paper, we thus focus on sparse arrays. We assume there are no value indexes on these arrays.

Contributions. We present the design, implementation, and evaluation of ArrayStore, a storage manager for parallel array processing. ArrayStore is designed to support *complex and varied* operations on arrays and parallel processing of these operations in a shared-nothing cluster. ArrayStore builds on techniques from the literature and introduces new techniques. The key contribution of this paper is to answer the following two questions:

(1) *What combination of chunking and array partitioning strategies lead to highest performance under a varied parallel array processing workload?* (Sections 3.1 through 3.3). As in prior work, ArrayStore breaks arrays into multidimensional chunks, although we consider much larger chunks than prior work (hundreds of KBs to hundreds of MBs rather than a single disk block). We study four different array chunking techniques as summarized in Figure 2: regular chunks (REG), irregular chunks (IREG), and two-level chunks (IREG-REG and REG-REG).[1] In the case of regular chunks, the domain of each array index is divided into uniform partitions. For irregular chunks, we create chunk boundaries such that each chunk contains the *same amount of data* (in bytes), thus reducing possible skew when processing data chunks in parallel. Figure 3 illustrates the per-chunk data distribution differences when applying either the REG or IREG strategies. Finally, the basic idea behind the two-level approaches is to split an array into regular or irregular chunks, and then further divide each chunk into smaller regular fragments that we call *tiles*.

(2) *How to enable an operator to efficiently access data in neighboring array chunks during parallel processing?* (Section 3.4) We develop two new techniques to enable an operator to efficiently access a variable-amount of data in neighboring chunks during parallel processing. The first technique leverages directly our two-level REG-REG storage layout to

[1]In this paper, we do not study indexing data within chunks, which is a complementary technique and could further speed-up some operations, nor data compression on disk.

enable an operator to efficiently read and process as much overlap data as needed. The second technique stores separate materialized views of increasingly distant overlapping data for each chunk.

We wrap the above techniques with a simple, yet flexible access method that we present in Section 4.

We implement ArrayStore and a set of representative operators in a standalone C++ system and evaluate the system on two real datasets from the science domain. The first one is a 74 GB dataset comprising two snapshots from an astronomy simulation [22] (3D data). The second dataset is the output of a flow cytometer from the oceanography domain [3] (6D data). For the first question, we show that a two-level REG-REG strategy leads to the best overall performance under a varied workload and requires the least tuning. Indeed, it provides high-performance for single-site processing of all operations in our workload and can be organized to avoid both skew and data shuffling during parallel processing. None of the other techniques simultaneously achieves all these goals. For the second question, we show that ArrayStore's techniques outperform by a factor of 2X more naïve techniques where either overlap data is not explicitly supported or a pre-defined amount of overlap data is stored within or even separately from each chunk.

2. PROBLEM STATEMENT

We start with a more formal problem statement. We define an array similarly to Furtado and Baumann [16]: Given a discrete coordinate set $S = S_1 \times \ldots \times S_d$, where each $S_i, i \in [1, d]$ is a finite totally ordered discrete set, an array is defined by a d-dimensional domain $D = [I_1, \ldots, I_d]$, where each I_i is a subinterval of the corresponding S_i. Each combination of dimension values in D defines a *cell*. All cells in a given array have the same type T, which is a tuple as in a relational DBMS.

ArrayStore must efficiently support the types of array operations outlined in Section 1, which we formalize by presenting one or more representative operators for each type of operations. We use these operators throughout the paper.

Array Scan (e.g., *filter*). Many operators process all chunks of an array such that each chunk can be processed independently of other chunks. Filter, $A' =$ FILTER(A,P), is representative of this type of operators (assuming no value-based indexes). Here, A is an input array and P is a predicate over cell values. The output array A' has the same dimensions as A such that if v is a vector of dimension values, A' contains $A(v)$ if $P(A(v))$ returns true, otherwise it contains *null*. A parallel filter, $A' =$ P_FILTER(A,P), can be computed by partitioning A into N sets of non-overlapping chunks, with a partitioning strategy R. Second, FILTER(n_i,P) is applied independently to each partition $n_i \in N$. A' is the union of the results.

Array Dicing (e.g., *subsample*). We also want to support unary range-selection (or dicing) operators. *Subsample* [40], $A' =$ SUBSAMPLE(A,P), is representative of this type of operators. Here A is an array and P is a predicate over A's dimensions. SUBSAMPLE returns an array A' that has the same number of dimensions as A, but a smaller number of dimension values. In this paper, we study subsample operators, where P takes the form of a d-dimensional subinterval $d = [i_1, \ldots, i_d]$, and selects all cells that fall within this subinterval. Similar to filter, subsample can process an array's chunks independently of one another and is thus trivial to parallelize.

Binary Array Operation (e.g., *join*). In addition to unary operators, we need to support binary operators such as *JOIN*. As representative operator, we consider a simple version of a structural join [35], $B =$ JOIN(A,A'), where A, A', and B are defined over the same d-dimensional domain D and each cell in B is the concatenation of cells in A and A'. As a concrete example, such a join operator can correlate an array of temperature values with an array of pressure values, outputting tuples that comprise both values for each combination of dimension values. In practice, joins can get more complex. For example, a cross-match [26] compares cell values that are near each other in two input arrays rather than being at the exact same location. However, the key requirement of bringing together and processing corresponding array chunks remains. It is the key type of operation that we want to support. To execute a join in parallel, the strategy that we adopt is to re-partition array A' such that all cells corresponding to cells in A get physically co-located. Each pair of array partitions can then be processed independently and the results can be unioned.

Overlap Operations (e.g., *clustering and volume-density*). Many array operations cannot be computed by simply partitioning an array, processing its partitions independently, and unioning the result. Instead, processing each array fragment requires access to data in adjacent fragments. We consider two types of such *overlap-based* operators: (1) operators that need to see a fixed amount of adjacent data and (2) operators that need to see a bounded, though not fixed, amount of adjacent data. We use canopy clustering as representative of the former type of operators and a volume-density application as representative of the latter. We describe them further in Sections 3.4 and 4.

Non-requirements. Due to space constraints, in this paper, we do not include in our workload iterative operations nor operations that examine a large number of input cells stretching across the array to compute the value of an output cell: *e.g.*, data clustering operations where a cluster can span a large fraction of the array. We discuss the latter elsewhere [39].

3. ArrayStore STORAGE MANAGER

In this section, we present the design of ArrayStore.

3.1 Basic Array Chunking

As in prior work on storage management for multidimensional data (see Section 6), ArrayStore takes the approach of breaking an array into fragments called *chunks* and storing these chunks on disk. We now present two types of chunking schemes studied in the literature and the two-level strategy that we develop in ArrayStore.

Regular Chunks (REG). The first approach of breaking an array into chunks is to use what are called *regular chunks* [13, 16], where all chunks have the same size in terms of the coordinate space. For example, consider a $3D$ astronomy simulation snapshot with dimensions (X, Y, Z) such that X=[−0.5:0.5],Y=[−0.5:0.5], and Z=[−0.5:0.5]. We can break the array into 256 regular chunks, by splitting each X, Y, and Z dimension into 8, 8, and 4 respectively. Each chunk in the array will then have size $0.125 * 0.125 * 0.25$. Regular chunks are commonly used for storing arrays on disk [8, 15, 29, 36]. Figure 2 illustrates this approach.

Irregular Chunks (IREG). Several schemes have also been proposed where an array is fragmented in a less regular fashion [16, 9]. In this paper, we call all such strategies *irregular* chunking schemes and illustrate them in Figure 2. Irregular chunking can speed-up range-selection queries when the chunk size and shape is tuned to the workload [16]. While our goal is not to tune storage for such specific queries, we consider irregular chunking, because it may help reduce skew in parallel array processing. The key idea is to chunk the array such that each chunk covers a different volume of the logical coordinate space but holds the same amount of data [20] as shown in Figure 3.[2] One approach that has been proposed for creating such chunks [20] is to use a kd-tree [6], which splits a multidimensional space into increasingly small partitions considering the data distribution to ensure load balance between partitions. If chunks are irregular, they must be indexed to support efficient access to subsets of an array. In our implementation, we index chunks using an R-tree. Other indexes are possible, but we do not find that the index lookup time is a bottleneck in our experiments.

Two-level Chunks (REG-REG or IREG-REG). For either of the above strategies a question that arises is that of appropriate chunk size. Large chunks help amortize seek times when reading data from disk. They also help amortize any potential fixed-costs associated with processing a data chunk by an operator. However, for arrays containing sparse data, large chunks increase the amount of processing required if an operator only needs a subset of a chunk (*e.g.*, subsample or an operator accessing data from adjacent chunks) because the lack of internal chunk structure forces the operator to examine all data points within the chunk.

To address these contradictory requirements, an alternate approach is to create *two-level chunks*. The basic idea is to split an array into small, regular chunks but then combine them together to form larger chunks that are either regular (*REG-REG*) or irregular (*IREG-REG*) as illustrated in Figure 2. With this approach, the larger chunks are the unit of disk I/O, while the smaller *tiles* can be the unit of array processing. Regular chunks and tiles efficiently support binary operators on a single-node and across nodes because they facilitates the co-location and co-processing of matching cells across two arrays. In contrast, irregular chunks can help smooth-out data skew during parallel processing.

Two-level chunking has been studied before [33, 38], but only as a container to place multiple chunks on a single disk block. This approach is a form of IREG-REG, since regular tiles are grouped into irregular chunks. We push the idea further by not only using bigger chunks to amortize seek time overhead (unit of I/O) and operator overhead, but also by enabling operators to process different granularity of chunks as needed (see Section 4), by leveraging the two-level structure to efficiently support overlap processing (see Section 3.4), and by exploring the regular-regular (*REG-REG*) approach as an alternative to IREG-REG. Through experiments (see Section 5), we show that REG-REG is not only the simpler of the two strategies but also leads to highest performance under a varied workload.

[2]For dense arrays, this approach is identical to regular chunks.

3.2 Organizing Chunks on Disk

Each array in ArrayStore is represented with one data file and one metadata file. The data file contains the actual array values. The metadata file contains array meta information such as number of dimensions, total number of chunks, and in the case of regular chunking the number of chunks along each dimension. The metadata file also contains overlap information (see Section 3.4). For irregular chunking, a chunk index is stored in a separate file. In this paper, we do not study how chunk layout on disk affects performance as it mostly matters for dicing queries [38]. For sparse arrays, only non-null cells are stored inside chunks and their order is arbitrary. The only way to access a particular cell in a chunk is thus to sequentially scan the cells inside the chunk. This approach avoids the overhead of creating an index within each chunk and we show that the two-level REG-REG storage management enables high performance even without such index.

3.3 Organizing Chunks across Disks

To support parallel array processing, ArrayStore can spread array chunks across multiple independent processing units or *nodes* (*i.e.*, physical machines, processes on the same machine, or other). For this, ArrayStore partitions an array into N *segments*, each holding a subset of the array chunks, not necessarily contiguous, and distributes each segment to a node.

We study the performance of several array partitioning strategies including (1) random (assign each chunk to a randomly selected segment), (2) round-robin (iterate over chunks in some order and assign them to each segment in turn), (3) range (split the array into N disjoint ranges of chunks and assign all chunks within a range to a segment), or (5) block-cyclic (split the array into M regular *blocks* of N chunks each. Iterate over the chunks of a block in some pre-defined order and assign them to each of the N segments in turn). Block-cyclic is thus similar to round-robin but it helps spread dense array regions across more nodes (along all dimensions). For example, consider a 2D array $A_{4\times4}$ which consists of 16 chunks labeled 1 to 16 in row-major order (first row holds chunks $\{1, 2, 3, 4\}$, second row holds $\{5, 6, 7, 8\}$, etc). Block-cyclic partitions chunks in array $A_{4\times4}$ on 4 nodes such that chunks labeled {1,3,9,11} are assigned to the first node, while in round-robin, that node contains {1,5,9,13}, all the chunks in the first array column. We do not study hash-partitioning, because it is equivalent to either random or a form of block-cyclic partitioning.

3.4 Overlap Data Support

When processing an array in parallel, ideally, one would like to process each array segment (or even chunk or tile) independently of the others and simply union the results. Many scientific array operations, however, cannot be parallelized using this simple strategy. Indeed, operations such as regression or clustering require that an operator considers data from a range of neighboring cells in order to produce each output cell. To illustrate the problem and our approach to addressing it, we use canopy clustering [1] as running example. In this section, we assume that the unit of parallel processing is an array chunk. We come back to tile-based and segment-based processing in Section 4

Canopy clustering is a fast clustering method typically used to create preliminary clusters that are then further processed by more sophisticated algorithms [1]. Canopy clustering can serve to cluster data points in a sparse array, such as the 3D astronomy or 6D flow-cytometer datasets. In fact, data clustering is commonly used in both domains [19].

The canopy clustering algorithm takes as input a distance metric and two distance thresholds $T1 > T2$. To cluster data points stored in a sparse array, the algorithm proceeds iteratively: it first removes a point at random from the array and uses it to form a new cluster. The algorithm then iterates over the remaining points. If the distance between a remaining point and the original point is less than $T1$, the algorithm adds the point to the new cluster. If the distance is also less than $T2$, the algorithm eliminates the point from the set. Once the iteration completes, the algorithm selects one of the remaining points (*i.e.*, those not eliminated by the $T2$ threshold rule) as a new cluster and repeats the above procedure. The algorithm continues until the original set of points is empty. The algorithm outputs a set of canopies each of them with one or more data points.

Problems with Ignoring Overlap Needs. To run canopy clustering in parallel, one approach is to partition the array into chunks and process chunks independently of one another. The problem is that points at chunk boundary may need to be added to clusters in adjacent chunks and two points (even from different chunks) within $T2$ of each other should not both yield a new canopy. A common approach to these problems is to perform a post-processing step [1, 19, 20]. For canopy clustering, this second step clusters canopy centers found in individual partitions and assigns points to these final canopies [1]. Such a post-processing phase, however, can add significant overhead as we show in Section 5.

Single-Layer Overlap. To avoid a post-processing phase, some have suggested to extract, for each array chunk, an overlap area ϵ from neighboring chunks, store the overlap together with the original chunk [35, 37], and provide both to the operator during processing. In the case of canopy clustering, an overlap of size $T1$ can help reconcile canopies at partition boundary. The key insight is that the overlap area needed for many algorithms is typically small compared to the chunk size. A key challenge with this approach, however, is that even small overlap can impose significant overhead for multidimensional arrays. For example, if chunks become 10% larger along each dimension (only 5% on each side) to cover the overlapping area, the total I/O and CPU overhead is 33% for a 3D chunk and over 75% for a 6D one!

A simple optimization is to store overlap data separately from the core array and provide it to operators on demand. This optimization helps operators that do not use overlap data. However, operators that need the overlap still face the problem of having access to a single overlap region, which must be large-enough to satisfy all queries.

Multi-Layer Overlap Leveraging Two-level Storage. In ArrayStore, we propose a more efficient approach to supporting overlap data processing. We present our core approach here and an important optimization below.

Algorithm 1 Multi-Layer Overlap over Two-level Storage

Multi-Layer Overlap over Two-level Storage
Input: chunk *core_chunk* and predicate *overlap_region*.
Output: chunk *result_chunk* containing all overlap tiles.
ochunkSet ← all chunks overlapping *overlap_region*.
tileSet ← ∅
for all Chunk $ochunk_i$ in *ochunkSet* − *core_chunk* **do**
  Load $ochunk_i$ into memory.
  tis ← all tiles in $ochunk_i$ overlapping *overlap_region*.
  tileSet ← *tileset* ∪ *tis*
end for
Combine *tilesSet* into one chunk *result_chunk*.
return *result_chunk*.

ArrayStore enables an operator to request an *arbitrary amount of overlap data* for a chunk. No maximum overlap area needs to be configured ahead of time. Each operator can use a different amount of overlap data. In fact, an operator can use a different amount of overlap data *for each chunk*. We show in Section 5, that this approach yields significant performance gains over all strategies described above.

To support this strategy, ArrayStore leverages its two-level array layout. When an operator requests overlap data, it specifies a desired range around its current chunk. In the case of canopy clustering, given a chunk that covers the interval $[a_i, b_i]$ along each dimension i, the operator can ask for overlap in the region $[a_i - T_1, b_i + T_1]$. To serve the request, ArrayStore looks-up all chunks overlapping the desired area (omitting the chunk that the operator already has). It loads them into memory, but cuts out only those tiles that fall within the desired range. It combines all tiles into one chunk and passes it to the operator. Algorithm 1 shows the corresponding pseudo-code.

As an optimization, an operator can specify the desired overlap as a a hypercube with a hole in the middle. For example, in Figure 4, canopy clustering first requests all data that falls within range L_1 and later requests L_2. For other chunks, it may also need L_3.

When partitioning array data into segments (for parallel processing across different nodes), ArrayStore replicates chunks necessary to provide a pre-defined amount of overlap data. Requests for additional overlap data can be accommodated but require data transfers between nodes.

Multi-Layer Overlap through Materialized Overlap Views. While superior to single-layer overlap, the above approach suffers from two inefficiencies: First, when an operator requests overlap data within a neighboring chunk, the entire chunk must be read from disk. Second, overlap layers are defined at the granularity of tiles.

To address both inefficiencies, ArrayStore also supports *materialized overlap views*. A materialized overlap view is defined like a set of onion-skin layers around chunks: *e.g.*, layers L_1 through L_3 in Figure 4. A view definition takes the form $(n, w_1, \ldots, w_d)$, where n is the number of layers requested and each w_i is the thickness of a layer along dimension i. Multiple views can exist for a single array.

To serve a request for overlap data, ArrayStore first chooses the materialized view that covers the entire range of requested data and will result in the least amount of extra data read and processed. From that view, ArrayStore loads only those layers that cover the requested region, combines

Algorithm 2 Multi-Layer Overlap using Overlap Views

```
Multi-Layer Overlap using Overlap Views
Input: chunk core_chunk and predicate overlap_region.
Output: chunk result_chunk containing requested overlap data.
Identify materialized view M to use.
L ← layers l_i ∈ M that overlap overlap_region.
Initialize an empty result_chunk
for all Layer l_i ∈ L do
    Load layer l_i into memory.
    Add l_i to result_chunk.
end for
return result_chunk.
```

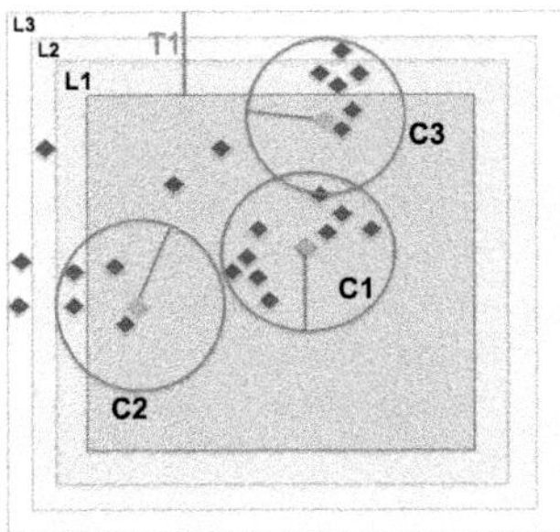

Figure 4: Example of multi-layer overlap used during canopy clustering. $C2$ necessitates that the operator loads a small amount of overlap data denoted with $L1$. $C3$, however, requires an additional overlap layer. So $L2$ is also loaded.

them into a chunk and passes the chunk to the operator. Algorithm 2 shows the pseudo-code.

Materialized overlap views impose storage overhead. As above, a 10% overlap along each dimension adds 33% total storage for a 3D array. With 20% overlap, the overhead grows to 75%. In a 6D array, the same overlaps add 75% and 3X, respectively. Because storage is cheap, however, we argue that such overheads are reasonable. We further discuss materialized overlap views selection in Secion 5.3.

4. ACCESS METHOD

ArrayStore provides a single access method that supports the various operator types presented in Section 2, including overlap data access. The basic access method enables an operator to iterate over array chunks, but how that iteration is performed is highly configurable.

Array Iterator API. The array iterator provides the five methods shown in Table 4. This API is exposed to operator developers not end-users. Our API assumes a chunk-based model for programming operators, which helps the system deliver high-performance.

Method `open` opens an iterator over an array (or array segment). This method takes two *optional* parameters as input: a range predicate (`Range r`) over array dimensions, which limits the iteration to those array chunks that overlap with r; the second parameter is, what we call the *packing ratio* (`PackRatio p`). It enables an operator to set the granularity of the iteration to either "tiles" (default), "chunks", or "combined". Tiles are perfect for operators that benefit from finely-structured data such as subsample. For this packing ratio, the iterator returns individual tiles as chunks on each call to `getNext()`. In contrast, the "chunks" packing ratio works best for operators that incur overhead with each unit of processing, such as operators that work with overlap data. Finally, the "combined" packing ratio combines into a single chunk all tiles that overlap with r. If r is "null", "combined" returns all chunks of the underlying array (or array segment) as one chunk. If an array segment comprises chunks that are not connected or will not all fit in memory, "combined" iterates over chunks without combining them. In the next section, we show how a binary operator such as join greatly benefits from the option to "combine" chunks.

Array Iterator Methods
open(Range r, PackRatio p)
boolean hasNext()
Chunk getNext() throws NoSuchElementException
Chunk getOverlap(Range r) throws NoSuchElementException
close()

Table 1: Access Method API

Methods `hasNext()`, `getNext()`, and `close()` have the standard semantics.

Method `getOverlap(Range r)` returns as a single chunk all cells that overlap with the given region and surround the current element (tile, chunk, or combined). Because overlap data is only retrieved at the granularity of tiles or overlap layers specified in the materialized views, extra cells may be returned. Overlap data can be requested for a tile, a chunk, or a group of tiles/chunks. However, ArrayStore supports materialized overlap views only at the granularity of chunks or groups of chunks. The intuition behind this design decision is that, in most cases, operators that need to process overlap data would incur too much overhead doing so for individual tiles and ArrayStore thus optimizes for the case where overlap is requested for entire chunks or larger.

Example Operator Algorithms. We illustrate ArrayStore's access method by showing how several representative operators (from Section 2) can be implemented.

Filter processes array cells independently of one another. Given an array segment, a filter operator can thus call `open()` without any arguments followed by `getNext()` until all tiles have been processed. Each input tile serves to produce one output tile.

Subsample. Given an array segment, a subsample operator can call `open(r)`, where r is the requested range over the array, followed by a series of `getNext()` calls. Each call to `getNext()` will return a tile. If the tile is completely inside r, it can be copied to the output unchanged, which is very efficient. If the tile partially overlaps the range, it must be processed to remove all cells outside r.

Join. As described in Section 2, we consider a structural join [35] that works as follows: For each pair of cells at matching positions in the input arrays, compute the output cell tuple based on the two input cell tuples. This join can be implemented as a type of nested-loop join (Algorithm 3). The join iterates over chunks of the outer array, $array_1$ (it could also process an entire outer array segment at once), preferably the one with the larger chunks. For each chunk, it looks-up the corresponding tiles in the inner array, $array_2$, retrieves them all as a single chunk (*i.e.*, option "combined"), and joins the two chunks. In our experiments, we found that combining inner tiles could reduce cache misses by half, leading to a similar decrease in runtime.

All three operators above can directly execute in parallel using the same algorithms. The only requirement is that chunks of two arrays that need to be joined be physically

Algorithm 3 Join algorithm.

```
JoinArray
input: array1 and array2, iterators over arrays to join
output: result_array, set of result array chunks
array1.open(null, "chunk")
while array1.hasNext() do
    Chunk chunk1 = array1.getNext()
    Range r = rectangular boundary of chunk1
    array2.open(r,"combined")
    if array2.hasNext() then
        Chunk chunk2 = array2.getNext()
        result_chunk = JOIN(chunk1, chunk2)
        result_array = result_array ∪ result_chunk
    end if
end while
return result_array
```

co-located. As a result different array partitioning strategies yield different performance results for join (see Section 5).

Canopy Clustering. We described the canopy clustering algorithm in Section 3.4. Here we present its implementation on top of ArrayStore. The pseudo-code of the algorithm is omitted due to the space constraints. The algorithm iterates over array chunks. Each chunk is processed independently of the others and the results are unioned. For each chunk, when needed, the algorithm incrementally grows the region under consideration (through successive calls to `getOverlap()`) to ensure that, every time a point x_i starts a new cluster, all points within $T1$ of x_i are added to the cluster just as in the centralized version of the algorithm. The maximum overlap area used for any chunk is thus $T1$. Points within $T2 < T1$ of each other should not both yield new canopies. In our implementation, to avoid double-reporting canopies that cross partition boundaries, only canopies whose centroids are inside the original chunk are returned.

Volume-Density algorithm. The Volume-Density algorithm is most commonly used to find what is called a *virial radius* in astronomy [21]. It further demonstrates the benefit of multi-layer overlap. Given a set of points in a multidimensional space (*i.e.*, a sparse array) and a set of cluster centroids, the volume-density algorithm finds the size of the sphere around each centroid such that the density of the sphere is just below some threshold T. In the astronomy simulation domain, data points are particles and the sphere density is given by: $d = \frac{\Sigma mass(p_i)}{volume(r)}$, where each p_i is a point inside the sphere of radius r. This algorithm can benefit from overlap: Given a centroid c inside a chunk, the algorithm can grow the sphere around c incrementally, requesting increasingly further overlap data if the sphere exceeds chunk boundary.

5. EVALUATION

In this section, we evaluate ArrayStore's performance on two real datasets and on eight dual quad-core 2.66GHz Intel/AMD OpteronPentium-based machines with 16GB of RAM running RHEL5.

The first dataset comprises two snapshots, $S43$ and $S92$, from a large-scale astronomy simulation [22] for a total of 74GB of data. The simulation models the evolution of cosmic structure from about 100K years after the Big Bang to the present day. Each snapshot represents the universe as a set of particles in a 3D space, which naturally leads to the following schema: `Array Simulation {id,vx,vy,vz,mass,phi} [X,Y,Z]`, where X, Y, and Z are the array dimensions and `id, vx, vy, vz, mass, phi` are the attributes of each array cell. `id` is a signed 8 byte integer while all other attributes a 4 byte floats. We store each snapshot in a separate array. Since the universe is becoming increasingly structured over time, data in snapshot $S92$ is more skewed than in $S43$. In Figure 3, the largest regular chunk has 25X more data points than the smallest one. The ratio is only 7 in $S43$ for the same number of chunks.

The second dataset is the output of a flow cytometer [3]. A flow cytometer measures scattered and fluoresced light from a stream of water particles. Similar microorganisms exhibit similar intensities of scattered light. In this dataset, the data takes the form of points in a 6-dimensional space, where each point represents a particle or organism in the water and the dimensions are the measured properties. We thus use the following schema for this dataset: `Array Cytometer {day, filenumber, row, pulseWidth, D1, D2} [FSCsmall, FSCperp, FSCbig, PE, CHLsmall, CHLbig]`, where all attributes are 2-byte unsigned integers. Each array is approximately 7 GB in size. Join queries thus run on 14 GB of 6D data.

Table 2 shows the naming convention for the experimental setups. ArrayStore's best-performing strategy is highlighted

5.1 Basic Performance of Two-Level Storage

First, we demonstrate the benefits of ArrayStore's two-level REG-REG storage manager compared with IREG-REG, REG, and IREG when running on a single node (single-threaded processing). We compare the performance of these different strategies for the subsample and join operators, which are the only operators in our representative set that are affected by the chunk shape. We show that REG-REG yields the highest performance and requires the least tuning. Figures 5 and 6 show the results. In both figures, the y-axis is the total query processing time.

Array dicing query. Figure 5(a) shows the results of a range selection query, when the selected region is a 3D rectangular slice of $S92$ (we observe the same trend in $S43$). Each bar shows the average of 10 runs. The error bars show the minimum and maximum runtimes. In each run, we randomly select the region of interest. All the randomly selected, rectangular regions are 1% of the array volume. Selecting 0.1% and 10% region sizes yielded the same trends. We compare the results for REG, IREG, REG-REG, and IREG-REG.

For both single-level techniques (REG and IREG), larger chunks yield worse performance than smaller ones because more unnecessary data must be processed (chunks are *misaligned* compared with the selected region). When chunk sizes become too small (at 262144 chunks in this experiment), however, disk seek times start to visibly hurt performance. In this experiment, the best performance is achieved for 65536 chunks (approximately 0.56 MB per chunk).

The disk seek time effect is more pronounced for REG than IREG simply because we used a different chunk layout for REG than IREG (row-major order *v.s.* z-order [38]) and our range-selection queries were worst-case for the REG layout. Otherwise, the two techniques perform similarly. Indeed, the key performance trade-off is disk I/O overhead for small chunks *v.s.* CPU overhead for large chunks. IREG

Notation	Description
(REG,N)	One-level, regular chunks. Array split into N chunks total.
(IREG,N)	One-level, irregular chunks. Array split into N chunks total.
(REG-REG, N1-N2)	Two-level chunks. Array split into N1 regular chunks and N2 regular tiles.
(IREG-REG,N1-N2)	Two-level chunks. Array split into N1 irregular chunks and N2 regular tiles.

Table 2: Naming convention used in experiments.

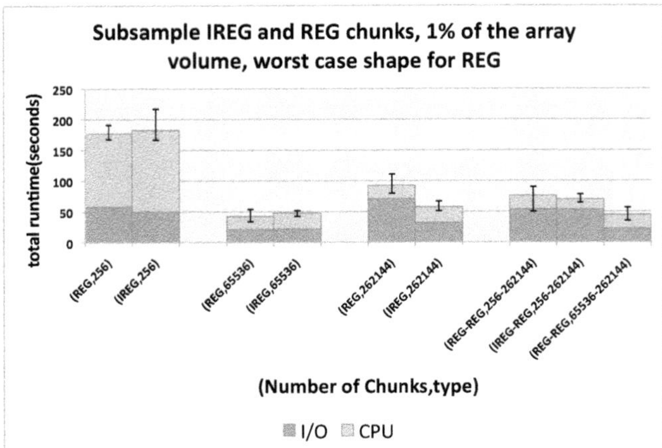

(a) Performance of array dicing query on 3D slices that are 1% of the array volume on S92. Two-level storage strategy yields the best overall performance and also the most consistent performance for different parameter choices.

Type	I/O time (Sec)	Proc. time (Sec)
(REG,4096)	28	115
(REG,262144)	46	51
(REG,2097152)	90	66
(REG-REG,4096-2097152)	28	64

(b) Same experiment as above but on 6D dataset. The two-level strategy dominates the one-level approach again.

Figure 5: Array dicing query on 3D and 6D datasets.

only keeps the variance low between experiments since all chunks contain the same amount of data.

The overhead of disk seek times rapidly grows with the number of dimensions: for the 6D flow cytometer dataset (Figure 5(b)), disk I/O increases by a factor of 3X as we increase the number of chunks from 4096 to 2097152 while processing times decreases by a factor of 2X. Processing times do not improve for the smallest chunk size (2097152) because our range-selection queries pick up the same amount of data, just spread across a larger number of chunks.

Most importantly, for these types of queries, the two-level storage management strategies are clear winners: they can achieve the low I/O times of small but not too small chunk sizes and the processing times of the smallest chunk sizes. The effect can be seen for both the 3D and 6D datasets. Additionally, the two-level storage strategies are significantly more resilient to suboptimal parameter choices, leading to consistently good performance. The two-level storage thus requires much less tuning to achieve high performance compared with a single-level storage strategy.

Join query. Figure 6(a) shows the total query runtime results when joining two 3D arrays (two different snapshots or same snapshot as indicated). Figure 6(c) shows the results for a self-join on the 6D array.

We first consider the first three bars in Figure 6(a). The first bar shows the performance of joining two arrays, each using the IREG storage strategy. The second bar shows what happens when REG is used but the array chunks are misaligned: That is, each chunk in the finer-chunked array overlaps with multiple chunks in the coarser-chunked array. In both cases, the total time to complete the join is high such that it becomes worth to re-chunk one of the arrays to match the layout of the other as shown in the third bar. For each chunk in the outer array, the overhead of the chunk misalignment comes from scanning points in partly overlapping tiles in the inner array before doing the join only on subsets of these points.

The following two bars (A4 and A5) show the results of joining two arrays with different chunk sizes but with aligned regular chunks. That is, each chunk in the finer-chunked array overlaps with exactly one chunk in the coarser-chunked array. In that case, independent of how the arrays are chunked, performance is high and consistent. We tried other configurations, which all yielded similar results.

Interestingly, the overhead of chunk misalignment (always occurring with IREG and occurring in some REG configurations as discussed above) can rapidly grow with array dimensionality. The processing time of non-aligned 3D arrays is $3.5X$ that of aligned ones, while the factor is $6X$ for 6D arrays (Figure 6(c)).

Finally, the last three bars in Figure 6(a) show the results of joining two arrays with either one-level REG or two-level IREG-REG or REG-REG strategies. In all cases, we selected configurations where tiles were aligned. The alignment of inner tiles is the key factor to achieving high performance and thus all configurations result in similar runtimes.

Summary The above experiments show that IREG array chunking does not outperform REG on array dicing queries and can significantly worsen performance in the case of joins. In contrast, a two-level chunking strategy, even with regular chunks at both levels can improve performance for some operators (dicing queries) without hurting others (selection queries and joins). The latter thus appears as the winning strategy for single-node array processing.

5.2 Skew-Tolerance of Regular Chunks

While regular chunking yields high performance for single-threaded array processing, an important reason for considering irregular chunks is skew. Indeed, in the latter case, all chunks contain the same amount of information and thus have a better chance of taking the same amount of time to process. In this section, we study skew during parallel query processing for different types of queries and different storage management strategies. We use a real distributed setup with 8 physical machines (1 node = 1 machine). To run parallel experiments, we first run the data shuffling phase and then run ArrayStore locally at each node. During shuffling, all nodes exchange data simultaneously using TCP. Note that in the study of data skew over multiple nodes, REG-REG and IREG-REG converge to REG and IREG storage strategies, respectively because we always partition data based on chunks rather than tiles.

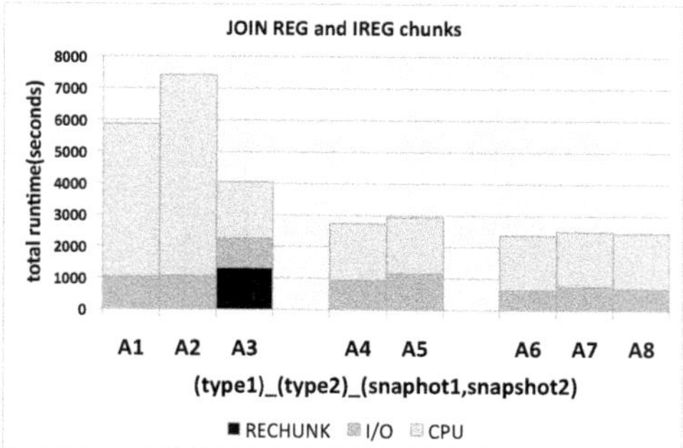

(a) Join query performance on 3D array. Tile alignment is the key factor for the performance gain.

A1	(IREG,512)_(IREG,2048)_(92,43)
A2	(REG,512)_(REG,400)_(92,92)
A3	Rechunk(A2) + (REG,512)_(REG,2048)_(92,92)
A4	(REG,512)_(REG,2048)_(92,92)
A5	(REG,65536)_(REG,262144)_(92,92)
A6	(IREG-REG,256-262144)_(REG,2048)_(92,43)
A7	(REG-REG,256-262144)_(REG-REG,2048-262144)_(92,43)
A8	(REG,256)_(REG,2048)_(92,43)

(b) Notation.

Type	I/O time	Proc. time
(REG,REG)_NONALIGNED_6D	205	6227
(REG,REG)_ALIGNED_6D	221	988
(REG-REG,REG-REG)_ALIGNED_6D	222	993

(c) Join query performance on 6D array. Processing time of non-aligned configuration is 6X that of the aligned one.

Figure 6: Join query on 3D and 6D arrays.

Parallel Selection. Figure 7 shows the total runtime of a parallel selection query on 8 nodes with random, range, block-cyclic, and round-robin partitioning strategies. All these scenarios use regular chunks. The experiment shows results for the S92 dataset (our most highly skewed dataset). The figure also shows results for IREG and random partitioning, one of the ideal configurations to avoid data skew. On the y-axis, each bar shows the ratio between the maximum and minimum runtime across all eight nodes in the cluster (*i.e.*, $MAX/MIN = \frac{max(r_i)}{min(r_j)}$ where $i, j \in [1, N]$ and r_i is equal to the total runtime of the selection query on node i). Error bars show results for different chunk sizes from 140 MB to 140 KB.

For REG, block-cyclic data partitioning exhibits almost no skew with results similar to those of IREG and random partitioning. Runtimes stay within 9% of each other for all chunk sizes. Runtimes in round-robin also stays within 14% for all chunk sizes. Performance is a bit worse than block-cyclic as the latter better spreads dense regions along *all* dimensions. For random data partitioning, skew can be eliminated with sufficiently small chunk sizes. The only strategy that heavily suffers from skew is range partitioning.

Parallel Dicing. Similarly to selection queries in parallel DBMSs, parallel array dicing queries can incur significant skew when only some nodes hold the desired array fragments as shown in Figure 8. In this case, the problem comes from the way data is partitioned and is not alleviated by using an IREG chunking strategy. Instead, distributing chunks using the block-cyclic data partitioning strategy with small chunks can spread the load much more evenly across nodes.

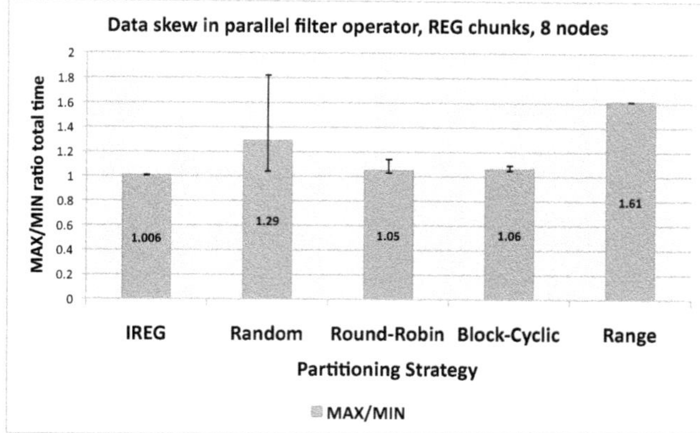

Figure 7: Parallel selection on 8 nodes with different partitioning strategies on REG chunks. We vary chunk sizes from 140 MB to 140 KB. Error bars show the variation of MAX/MIN runtime ratios in that range of chunk sizes. Round-Robin and Block-Cyclic have the lowest skew and variance. Results for these strategies are similar to those of IREG.

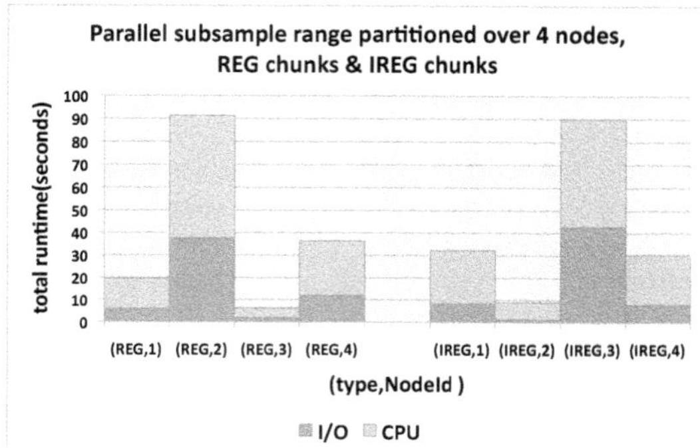

Figure 8: Parallel subsample with REG or IREG chunks distributed using range partitioning across 4 nodes. Subsample runs only on a few nodes causing skew, independent of the chunking scheme chosen.

We measure a MAX/MIN ratio of just 1.11 with 4 nodes and 65536 chunks with a std deviation of 0.036 (figure not shown due to space constraints).

Parallel Join. Array joins can be performed in parallel using a two-phase strategy. First, data from one of the arrays is shuffled such that chunks that need to be joined together become co-located. During shuffling, all nodes exchange data simultaneously using TCP. In our experiments, we shuffle the array with the smaller chunks. Second, each node can perform a local join operation between overlapping chunks.

Table 3 shows the percent data shuffled in an 8-node configuration. Shuffling can be completely avoided when arrays follow the same REG chunking scheme and chunks are partitioned deterministically. When arrays use different REG chunks, the same number of chunks are shuffled for all strategies. The shuffling time, however, is lowest for range and block-cyclic thanks to lower network contention. With range partitioning, each node only sends data to nodes with neighboring chunks. Block-cyclic spreads dense chunks better across nodes than round-robin and assigns the same number of chunks to each node unlike random. Range par-

Partitioning Strategy	Type	Shuffling
Same chunking strategy, chunks are co-located, no shuffling.		
Block-Cyclic	(REG-2048,REG-2048)	(00.0%,0)
Round-Robin	(REG-2048,REG-2048)	(00.0%,0)
Range (same dim)	(REG-2048,REG-2048)	(00.0%,0)
Different chunking strategies for two arrays, shuffling required.		
Round-robin	(REG-2048,REG-65536)	(87.5%,1498)
Random	(REG-2048,REG-65536)	(87.6%,1416)
Block-Cyclic	(REG-2048,REG-65536)	(87.5%,1326)
Range (same dim)	(REG-2048,REG-65536)	(00.0%,0)
Range (different dim)	(REG-2048,REG-65536)	(87.5%,1313)
IREG-REG chunks, shuffling required.		
Random	(TYPE1,TYPE2)	(62.0%,895)
Round-Robin	(TYPE1,TYPE2)	(73.0%,836)
Range (same dim)	(TYPE1,TYPE2)	(11.0%,210)
Block-Cyclic	(TYPE1,TYPE2)	N/A

Table 3: Parallel join (shuffling phase) for different types of chunk partitioning strategies across 8 nodes. TYPE1=(IREG-REG,2048-262144) in S43 and TYPE2= (IREG-REG,2048-262144) in S92. Each value in "Shuffling" column is a pair of (Cost,Time(sec.)).

Technique:	Random	Round-robin	Range	Block-cyclic
Avg	1.24	1.08	1.18	1.06
Max - Min	1.56-1.16	1.08-1.08	1.18-1.18	1.06-1.06

Table 4: "Local join phase" with regular chunks partitioned across 8 nodes. The values in the table are the ratios of total runtime between the slowest and fastest parallel nodes. The table shows the Avg, Min, and Max ratios across 10 experiments. Block-cyclic has the least skew, (6%) compared to other techniques.

titioning, however, exhibits skew in the "local join phase" (Table 4), leaving block-cyclic as the winning approach.

Table 3 also shows the shuffling cost with IREG-REG chunks. Irregular chunks always suffer from at least some shuffling overhead. The best strategy, range partitioning, still shuffles 11% of data even when both arrays are ranged partition along the same dimension.

Summary. The above experiments show block-cyclic with REG chunks as the winning strategy: For parallel selection, block-cyclic has less than 9% skew for all regular chunk sizes. For parallel dicing, it also effectively distributes the workload across nodes. Finally, for parallel join block-cyclic can avoid data shuffling and offers the best performance for the local join phase. Irregular chunks can smooth out skew for some operations such as selections, but they hurt join performance both in the local join and data shuffling phases.

5.3 Performance of Overlap Storage

We present the performance of ArrayStore's overlap processing strategy. We compare four options: ArrayStore's multi-layered overlap implemented on top of the two-level storage manager, ArrayStore's materialized multi-layer overlap, single-layer overlap, and no-overlap.

In all experiments, we use (REG-REG,2048-262144) for the 3D arrays and (REG-REG,4096-2097152) for the 6D arrays. In ArrayStore, we assume that the user knows how much overlap his queries need (*e.g.*, canopy threshold T1) and he creates sufficiently large materialized overlap views to satisfy most queries within storage space constraints. The width of overlap layers is tunable, but we find its effect to be less significant. Hence, we expect that a single view with thin layers should suffice for most arrays. In our experiments, we materialize 20 thin layers of overlap data for each chunk, which cover a total of 0.5 and 0.2 of each dimension length in 3D and 6D, respectively. The choice of 20 layers is arbitrary. The single-layer overlap is the concatenation of these 20 layers. Experiments are on a single node.

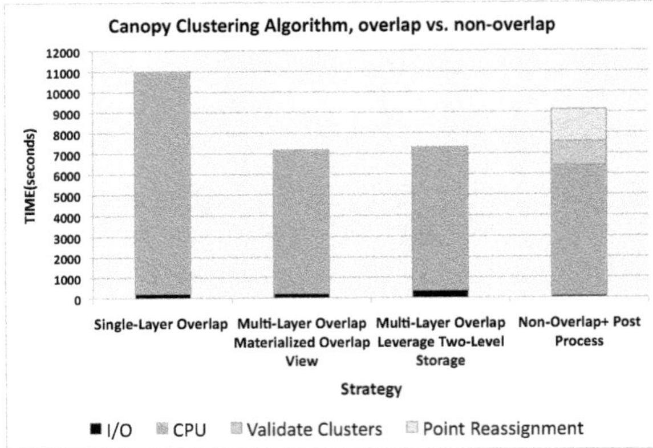

Figure 9: Canopy Clustering algorithm with or without overlap on the 3D dataset. Single-layer overlap does not perform well because of a large maximum overlap-size chosen. Both multi-layer overlap techniques outperforms no-overlap by 25%.

Figure 9 presents the performance results for the canopy clustering algorithm. $T1$ is set to 0.0125 (20% of the dimension length). We set $T2 = (0.75)T1$. Note that in the no-overlap case, a post processing phase is required to combine locally found canopies into global ones [1]. As the figure shows, both multi-layer overlap strategies outperform no-overlap and single-layer overlap by 25% and 35% respectively. The performance of single-layer overlap varies significantly depending on the overlap size chosen. In this experiment, the single-layer overlap is large to emphasize the drawback of inaccurate settings for this approach. In contrast, with multi-layered overlap, we can choose fine grained overlap layers (using views or small-size tiles), and get high-performance without tuning the total overlap size. Additionally, different applications can use different overlap sizes without hurting each other's performance, which is not the case for the single-layer overlap approach. We ran the canopy application on the 6D dataset with the same $T1$ and $T2$ settings as in the 3D experiment and observed 16% improvement in total runtime for multi-layer overlap using materialized view compared with no-overlap. When leveraging the two-level storage, the improvement was 11%, mainly because of I/O overhead due to loading entire chunks.

Figure 10 shows the results from the volume-density application described in Section 4 on the 3D dataset. As shown in the figure, the multi-layer overlap strategy through materialized overlap views outperforms no-overlap by a factor of almost two! Indeed, in order to compute the volume-density of the points close to the boundary, without overlap, we may need to load and process up to $3^N - 1$ neighboring chunks, where N is the number of dimensions (*e.g.*, 26 chunks for the 3D dataset). In contrast, the multi-layer strategy loads and processes only thin layers of overlap data as needed. We observe the same trend on the 6D dataset which is not shown due to space constraints.

In this experiment, materialized views also outperform multi-layer using the two-level storage because views can

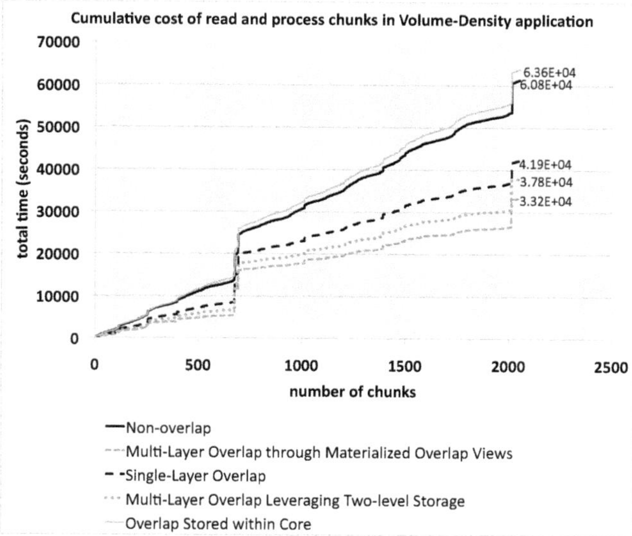

Figure 10: Volume-density application on 3D dataset with and without overlap. Multi-layer overlap outperforms no-overlap by almost $2X$.

load overlap layers thinner than tiles. Similarly, single-layer overlap loses because it does not have this flexibility in choosing the overlap granularity to load and process. For completeness, in this experiment, we also show the performance when overlap data is stored directly inside chunks as suggested in related work [35, 37]. The performance in this case is even worse than no-overlap. The reason is that the no-overlap case loads and processes neighboring chunks only when required, but when overlap data is stored inside the chunk, we are forced to process unnecessary overlap data.

Multi-layer overlap can outperform single-layer overlap even when overlap size is perfectly tuned. Indeed, in the volume-density application, we find that 90% of chunks only need 3 out of the 20 layers of overlap, but the maximum number of layers required is 10. This large difference between the average and maximum amount of overlap required is the key reason why multi-layer overlap can outperform single-layer overlap even for a single application (even if we ignore varying overlap needs of different operators).

6. RELATED WORK

MOLAP systems store data in multidimensional arrays [31, 41], but they focus on unary aggregation and selection queries, while we consider a broader set of operations. Today's business intelligence (BI) suites utilize closed source, proprietary MOLAP engine solutions such as Oracle Database OLAP Option [27], Cognos PowerPlay [10], and others to analyze large datasets. To the best of our knowledge, Palo [30] is the only open source memory-based MOLAP engine, which is specifically developed for spreadsheet data storage and analysis. However, Palo is not designed for large databases.

Many existing array-processing systems [8, 13, 15, 35] use regular tiling for data storage. Others support user-defined irregular tiles [9]. None of these systems, however, studies the impact of different tiling strategies on query processing performance, although they do consider different tile layouts on disk [8] and across disks [8, 25] for range-selection queries.

RasDaMan [14] is a multidimensional array DBMS implemented on top of a relational DBMS. Furtado and Baumann [16] studied the performance of different tiling strategies in RasDaMan (including regular and irregular tiles). Their study, however, was limited to scans and different types of array dicing operations. Their conclusions are thus different from ours since they find that arbitrary tiling tuned to a specific workload outperforms regular tiling. Reiner *et al.* [33] studied hierarchical storage support for large-scale multi-dimensional arrays in RasDaMan. Their approach is analogous to the two-level, IREG-REG, chunking strategy. However, their study is constrained to range-selection queries.

Shimada *et al.* [38] propose a chunking scheme for sparse arrays, where multiple chunks are compressed and stored in a single physical page. This approach is analogous to the two-level, IREG-REG, storage system that we study. Shimada *et al.*, also introduce "extended chunks", which are similar to IREG. Again, however, this earlier study was limited to range-selection queries.

Prior work studied the tuning of chunk shape, size, and layout on disk for a given workload and for regular chunking [29, 36]. This work is orthogonal to ours since we comparatively study regular *v.s.* irregular *v.s.* two-level chunking schemes and support for overlap data.

Seamons and Winslett [37] examine different storage management strategies for regularly-tiled arrays. In particular, they propose that data from multiple arrays be either stored separately or be interleaved on disk. This strategy is orthogonal to those we study in this paper. They also consider storage strategies for overlap data mentioning both the option to store overlap data together with or separately from the core data. Their implementation and evaluation, however, only examine the co-located scenario, similarly to SciDB [35].

There exist many data structures for indexing multi-dimensional data including the R-Tree [17] and its variants [2, 5], the KD-Tree [6], the KDB-Tree [34], the GammaSLK [24], the Pyramid technique [7], the Gamma strategy [28], RPST [32], and more. All these indexes organize a raw dataset into a multi-dimensional data structure to speed-up range-, containment-, and nearest-neighbor queries. In contrast, we study storage management techniques for more varied array operations.

7. CONCLUSION

We presented the design, implementation, and evaluation of ArrayStore, a storage manager for complex, parallel array processing. For efficient processing, ArrayStore partitions an array into chunks and we showed that a two-level chunking strategy with regular chunks and regular tiles (REG-REG) leads to the best and most consistent performance for a varied set of operations both on a single node and in a shared-nothing cluster. ArrayStore also enables operators to access data from adjacent array fragments during parallel processing. We presented two new techniques to support this need: one leverages ArrayStore's two-level storage layout and the other one uses additional materialized views. Both techniques significantly outperform approaches that do not provide overlap or provide only a pre-defined single overlap layer. The overall performance gain was up to 2X on real queries and real data from two science domains.

ArrayStore's design focuses on the workload from Section 2. It does not consider iterative operations nor array updates, which may be poorly served by our regular-tiled, read-only store. It also does not consider operations that examine input cells across the array to compute the value of an output cell. Such operations do not benefit from overlap and some of them may be difficult to code with a chunk-based API. Finally, we did not study the impact of indexing data inside chunks, which could further accelerate some operations. All these considerations are interesting future work.

8. ACKNOWLEDGEMENTS

The astronomy simulation dataset was graciously supplied by T. Quinn and F. Governato of the UW Dept. of Astronomy. We thank T. Quinn, J. P. Garner and Y. Kwon for their help with the data, user-defined functions, and comments on drafts of this paper. We thank the SciDB team for insightful discussions and the anonymous reviewers for their comments. This work is partially supported by NSF CDI grant OIA-1028195, gifts from Microsoft Research, and Balazinska's Microsoft Research Faculty Fellowship.

9. REFERENCES

[1] `http://mahout.apache.org/`.

[2] Arge et. al. The priority r-tree: a practically efficient and worst-case optimal r-tree. In *Proc. of the SIGMOD Conf.*, pages 347–358, 2004.

[3] SeaFlow cytometer. `http://armbrustlab.ocean.washington.edu/resources/sea_flow`.

[4] Ballegooij et. al. Distribution rules for array database queries. In *16th. DEXA Conf.*, pages 55–64, 2005.

[5] Beckmann et. al. The r*-tree: an efficient and robust access method for points and rectangles. *SIGMOD Record*, 19(2):322–331, 1990.

[6] J. L. Bentley. Multidimensional binary search trees used for associative searching. *Communications of the ACM*, 18(9):509–517, 1975.

[7] Berchtold et. al. The pyramid-technique: towards breaking the curse of dimensionality. In *Proc. of the SIGMOD Conf.*, pages 142–153, 1998.

[8] Chang et. al. Titan: A high-performance remote sensing database. In *Proc. of the 13th ICDE Conf.*, pages 375–384, 1997.

[9] Chang et. al. T2: a customizable parallel database for multi-dimensional data. *SIGMOD Record*, 27(1):58–66, 1998.

[10] Cognos PowerPlay. `http://www-01.ibm.com/software/data/cognos/products/series7/powerplay/`.

[11] Cohen et. al. MAD skills: new analysis practices for big data. *PVLDB*, 2(2):1481–1492, 2009.

[12] DeWitt et. al. Parallel database systems: the future of high performance database systems. *Communications of the ACM*, 35(6):85–98, 1992.

[13] DeWitt et. al. Client-server paradise. In *Proc. of the 20th Int. Conf. on Very Large DataBases (VLDB)*, pages 558–569, 1994.

[14] Baumann et. al. The multidimensional database system RasDaMan. In *Proc. of the SIGMOD Conf.*, pages 575–577, 1998.

[15] Marathe et. al. Query processing techniques for arrays. *The VLDB Journal*, 11(1):68–91, 2002.

[16] Furtado et. al. Storage of multidimensional arrays based on arbitrary tiling. In *Proc. of the 15th ICDE Conf.*, page 480, 1999.

[17] A. Guttman. R-trees: a dynamic index structure for spatial searching. In *Proc. of the SIGMOD Conf.*, pages 47–57, 1984.

[18] Hey et. al., editor. *The Fourth Paradigm: Data-Intensive Scientific Discovery.* Microsoft Research, 2009.

[19] Y. Kwon, M. Balazinska, B. Howe, and J. Rolia. Skew-resistant parallel processing of feature-extracting scientific user-defined functions. In *Proc. of SOCC Symp.*, June 2010.

[20] Y. Kwon, D. Nunley, J.P. Gardner, M. Balazinska, B. Howe, and S. Loebman. Scalable clustering algorithm for N-body simulations in a shared-nothing cluster. In *Proc of 22nd SSDBM*, 2010.

[21] Lacey et. al. Merger rates in hierarchical models of galaxy formation - part two - comparison with n-body simulations. *Monthly Notices of the Royal Astronomical Society (mnras)*, 271:676–+, December 1994.

[22] Loebman et. al. Analyzing massive astrophysical datasets: Can Pig/Hadoop or a relational DBMS help? In *Proceedings of the Workshop on Interfaces and Architectures for Scientific Data Storage (IASDS)*, 2009.

[23] Large Synoptic Survey Telescope. `http://www.lsst.org/`.

[24] Lukaszuk et. al. Efficient high-dimensional indexing by superimposing space-partitioning schemes. In *Proc. of the 8th IDEAS Symp.*, pages 257–264, 2004.

[25] Moon et. al. Scalability analysis of declustering methods for multidimensional range queries. *IEEE TKDE*, 10(2):310–327, 1998.

[26] Nieto-santisteban et. al. Cross-matching very large datasets. In *National Science and Technology Council(NSTC) NASA Conference*, 2006.

[27] Oracle OLAP. `http://www.oracle.com/technetwork/database/options/olap/index.html`.

[28] Orlandic et. al. The design of a retrieval technique for high-dimensional data on tertiary storage. *SIGMOD Record*, 31(2):15–21, 2002.

[29] Otoo et. al. Optimal chunking of large multidimensional arrays for data warehousing. In *Proc. of the 10th DOLAP Conf.*, pages 25–32, 2007.

[30] Palo. `http://www.palo.net/`.

[31] Pedersen et. al. Multidimensional database technology. *IEEE Computer*, 34(12):40–46, 2001.

[32] Ratko et. al. A class of region-preserving space transformations for indexing high-dimensional data. *Journal of Computer Science*, 1:89–97, 2005.

[33] Reiner et. al. Hierarchical storage support and management for large-scale multidimensional array database management systems. In *13th. DEXA Conf.*, pages 689–700, 2002.

[34] John T. Robinson. The K-D-B-tree: a search structure for large multidimensional dynamic indexes. In *Proc. of the SIGMOD Conf.*, pages 10–18, 1981.

[35] Rogers et. al. Overview of SciDB: Large scale array storage, processing and analysis. In *Proc. of the SIGMOD Conf.*, 2010.

[36] Sarawagi et. al. Efficient organization of large multidimensional arrays. In *Proc. of the 10th ICDE Conf.*, pages 328–336, 1994.

[37] Seamons et. al. Physical schemas for large multidimensional arrays in scientific computing applications. In *Proc of 7th SSDBM*, pages 218–227, 1994.

[38] Shimada et. al. A storage scheme for multidimensional data alleviating dimension dependency. In *Proc. of the 3rd ICDIM Conf.*, pages 662–668, 2008.

[39] E. Soroush and M. Balazinska. Hybrid merge/overlap execution technique for parallel array processing. In *1st Workshop on Array Databases (AD2011)*, 2011.

[40] Stonebraker et. al. Requirements for science data bases and SciDB. In *Fourth CIDR Conf. (perspectives)*, 2009.

[41] Tsuji et. al. An extendible multidimensional array system for MOLAP. In *Proc. of the 21st SAC Symp.*, pages 503–510, 2006.

[42] Zhang et. al. RIOT: I/O-efficient numerical computing without SQL. In *Proc. of the Fourth CIDR Conf.*, 2009.

Fast Checkpoint Recovery Algorithms for Frequently Consistent Applications

Tuan Cao, Marcos Vaz Salles, Benjamin Sowell, Yao Yue,
Alan Demers, Johannes Gehrke, Walker White
Cornell University
Ithaca, NY 14853, USA
{tuancao,vmarcos,sowell,yaoyue,ademers,johannes,wmwhite}@cs.cornell.edu

ABSTRACT

Advances in hardware have enabled many long-running applications to execute entirely in main memory. As a result, these applications have increasingly turned to database techniques to ensure durability in the event of a crash. However, many of these applications, such as massively multiplayer online games and main-memory OLTP systems, must sustain extremely high update rates – often hundreds of thousands of updates per second. Providing durability for these applications without introducing excessive overhead or latency spikes remains a challenge for application developers.

In this paper, we take advantage of frequent *points of consistency* in many of these applications to develop novel checkpoint recovery algorithms that trade additional space in main memory for significantly lower overhead and latency. Compared to previous work, our new algorithms do not require any locking or bulk copies of the application state. Our experimental evaluation shows that one of our new algorithms attains nearly constant latency and reduces overhead by more than an order of magnitude for low to medium update rates. Additionally, in a heavily loaded main-memory transaction processing system, it still reduces overhead by more than a factor of two.

Categories and Subject Descriptors

H.2.2 [**Information Systems**]: Database Management—*Recovery and restart*

General Terms

Algorithms, Performance, Reliability

1. INTRODUCTION

An increasing number of data-intensive applications are being executed entirely in main memory and eschewing traditional database concurrency control mechanisms in order to achieve high throughput. Examples include applications as diverse as massively multiplayer online games (MMOs) and scientific simulations, as well as certain classes of main-memory OLTP systems and search engines. Many of these systems either serialize operations and execute them sequentially [36, 28] or develop application-specific ways to avoid locking and prevent costly conflicts and rollbacks [34, 35, 29]. These approaches lead to applications with *frequent points of consistency*, which we call *frequently consistent* or FC applications. Unlike traditional database applications, which may never reach a point of consistency without quiescing the system, FC applications reach natural points of consistency very frequently (typically at least once a second) during normal operation.

Since FC applications store data in main memory, durability is an important and challenging property to ensure, particularly given the strict performance requirements of many FC applications. In this paper we leverage frequent points of consistency to develop checkpoint recovery algorithms with extremely low overhead. We start by describing several important use cases.

MMOs are an important class of FC applications that have recently received attention in the database community [27, 11]. MMOs are large persistent games that allow users to socialize and compete in a virtual world. Most MMOs use a time-stepped processing model where character behavior is divided into atomic time steps or *ticks* that are executed many times per second and update the entire state of the game [35]. The game state is guaranteed to be consistent at tick boundaries. Behavioral and agent-based simulations, which are often used by scientists to model phenomena such as traffic congestion and animal motion, also use a time-stepped model and have similar points of consistency [34].

Though we use MMOs as a running example throughout this paper, our techniques can be applied to any application with frequent points of consistency. For example, certain classes of main-memory OLTP systems also have frequent points of consistency. Traditional OLTP systems are heavily mutli-threaded to mask the huge differences between access times to main memory and disk, but the tradeoffs change when all data is stored in memory. New OLTP systems like H-Store [28] (and its commercial version VoltDB [33]) serialize all transactions so that each machine can execute them using a single thread in order to avoid the overhead of concurrency control and increase throughput. In these applications the end of each transaction marks a point of consistency [32]. Other examples of FC applications include new data-parallel systems to program the cloud, such as BOOM [2], deterministic transaction processing systems [30, 36], and in-memory search engines [29].

Many frequently consistent applications must handle very high update rates, which can complicate recovery. For example, popular MMO servers may have to process hundreds of thousands of updates per second, including behaviors such as character movement. Many traditional database recovery algorithms that rely on physical logging simply cannot sustain this update rate without resorting to expensive special-purpose hardware [20, 24]. Another common

SIGMOD'11, June 12–16, 2011, Athens, Greece.

recovery approach, used by some OLTP systems such as H-Store, is to replicate state on several machines and apply updates to all replicas [28]. While this provides high availability, replication is usually still combined with additional mechanisms such as regular checkpointing to protect against large scale failures such as power outages. Checkpointing can also be used to transfer state between nodes during recovery or when a new replica is added to the system.

We can take advantage of frequent points of consistency to take periodic *consistent checkpoints* of the entire application state and use *logical logging* to provide durability between checkpoints. Since we have frequent points of consistency, there is no need to quiesce the system in order to take a checkpoint, and we benefit from not having to maintain a costly physical log. Furthermore, we can avoid the primary disadvantage of logical logging, namely the cost of replaying the log during recovery. Since there are many points of consistency, we can take checkpoints very frequently (every few seconds), so the log can be replayed very fast.

Of course, taking very frequent checkpoints can increase the overhead associated with providing durability. To make this feasible, we need high performance checkpointing algorithms. In particular, we have identified several important requirements. First, the algorithm should have low overhead during normal operation. Ideally, taking a checkpoint should have very little impact on the throughput of the system. Second, the algorithm should distribute its overhead uniformly and not introduce performance spikes or highly variable response times. This is particularly important in applications such as MMOs where high latency may create "hiccups" in the immersive virtual experience. Finally, it should be possible to take checkpoints very frequently so that the logical log can be replayed quickly in the event of a failure. In a recent experimental study, Vaz Salles et al. evaluated existing main-memory checkpointing algorithms for use in MMOs [27], however these algorithms either use locks or large synchronous copy operations, which hurt throughput and latency, respectively.

In this paper we propose and evaluate two new checkpointing algorithms, called Wait-Free Zigzag and Wait-Free Ping-Pong, which avoid the use of locks and are designed to distribute overhead smoothly. Wait-Free Ping-Pong also makes use of additional main memory to further reduce overhead. We evaluate these algorithms using a high-performance implementation of TPC-C running in the cloud as well a synthetic workload with a wide variety of update rates. Our experiments show that both algorithms are successful in greatly reducing the latency spikes associated with checkpointing and that Wait-Free Ping-Pong also has considerably lower overhead: up to an order of magnitude less for low to medium update rates and more than a factor of two in our TPC-C experiments.

In Section 2 of this paper, we review several existing checkpointing algorithms [27]. We then make the following contributions:

1. We analyze the performance bottlenecks in prior work, and propose two new algorithms to address them (Section 3).
2. We explore the impact of data layout in main memory on cache performance and do a careful cache-aware implementation of all of our algorithms, as well as the best previous algorithms [27]. We find that our algorithms are particularly amenable to these low level optimizations (Section 4).
3. We perform a thorough evaluation of our new algorithms and compare them to existing methods. We find that Wait-Free Ping-Pong exhibits lower overhead than all other algorithms by up to an of magnitude over a wide range of update rates. It also completely eliminates the latency spikes that plagued previous consistent checkpointing algorithms (Section 5).

We review related work in Section 6 and conclude in Section 7.

2. BACKGROUND

A *frequently consistent* (FC) application is a distributed application in which the state of each node frequently reaches a point of consistency. A point of consistency is simply a time at which the state of the node is valid according to the semantics of the application. The definition of frequently depends on the application, but we expect it to be less than a second. For example, MMO servers execute approximately 10 ticks/sec, while modern OLTP systems may be able to execute a small transaction in tens of microseconds [28, 17].

Throughout the paper, we use *application state* to refer to the *dynamic, memory-resident state* of an FC application. FC applications may have additional read-only or read-mostly state that can simply be written to stable storage when it is created. For example, in an MMO, each character will have some attributes such as position, health, or experience that are frequently updated and thus part of the dynamic state, but it will also have other attributes such as name, race, or class (the type or job of the character) that are unlikely to change. Additionally, some applications include secondary data structures such as indices that can be rebuilt during recovery. We will focus exclusively on making the primary dynamic state durable.

In this paper, we use *coordinated checkpointing* to provide durability for distributed FC applications at low cost [6]. Many applications already use replication to increase availability and provide some fault tolerance [28], but checkpointing can still be used to copy state during recovery and provide durability to protect against power outages and other widespread failures.

Furthermore, we will focus exclusively on developing robust *single-node* checkpointing algorithms, as these form the core of most distributed checkpointing schemes. There is a large distributed systems literature that explores how to generalize efficient single-node checkpointing algorithms to multiple nodes. Tightly synchronized FC applications that reach global points of consistency during normal operation are particularly easy to checkpoint, as they can reuse their existing synchronization mechanisms to decide on a global point of consistency at which each node can take a local checkpoint. More general distributed applications may need to use techniques such as message logging to create a consistent checkpoint. These distributed approaches are discussed at length in a recent survey by Elnozahy et al [9].

In the remainder of this section we discuss requirements for checkpoint-recovery algorithms targeted at FC applications (Section 2.1) and we present existing checkpoint-recovery methods for these applications (Sections 2.2 and 2.3).

2.1 Requirements for Checkpoint Recovery Algorithms

We can summarize the requirements for a checkpointing algorithm for FC applications as follows:

1. The method must have *low overhead*. During normal operation, FC applications must process very high update rates, and the cost of checkpointing state for recovery should not greatly reduce the throughput.
2. The method should *distribute overhead uniformly*, so that application performance is consistent. Even when the total overhead is low, many applications depend on predictable performance. For example, fluctuations in overhead affect MMOs by interfering with time-synchronized subsystems like the physics engine [16]. This problem is made even worse when the checkpointing algorithm must pause the system in order to perform a synchronous operation like a bulk

Interface 1: Algorithmic Framework

Mutator::PrepareForNextCheckpoint()
Mutator::PointOfConsistency()
Mutator::HandleRead(index)
Mutator::HandleWrite(index, update)

AsynchronousWriter::WriteToStableStorage()

copy. Such *latency spikes* can also be a problem for distributed applications. If a node sending a message experiences a latency spike, the receiver may block, spreading the effect of the latency spike throughout the system and reducing overall throughput.

3. The method should have *fast recovery* in the event of failure. Ideally, the recovery time should be on the order of a few seconds to avoid significant disruption. We will accomplish this primarily by increasing the frequency of checkpoints.

Traditional approaches to database recovery such as ARIES-style physiological logging [21] and fuzzy checkpointing [12, 26], which uses physical logging, cannot keep up with the extremely high update rates of FC applications without resorting to extremely expensive special-purpose hardware such as battery backed RAM [10, 20, 24]. As the dollar cost per gigabyte of battery-backed RAM exceeds the cost of traditional RAM by over an order of magnitude, it is unlikely that cloud infrastructures or large enterprise clusters will package this technology for use by FC applications.

In the following subsections, we review the framework we previously proposed for checkpointing MMOs on commodity hardware and discuss how it can be extended to support FC applications [27].

2.2 Algorithmic Framework

In this section we discuss the basic algorithmic framework we use for checkpointing. During normal operation, the application takes *periodic checkpoints* of its entire dynamic state and maintains a *logical log* of all actions. For example, in an MMO we would log all user actions sent to the server; in a system like H-Store, we would log all stored procedure calls. Because each logical update may translate into many physical updates, we expect the overhead of maintaining this log to be quite small, and we will focus primarily on the overhead associated with checkpointing. In order to compare with existing algorithms for games, we will use the same algorithmic framework for checkpointing originally introduced by Vaz Salles et al. [27]. Interface 1 lists the key methods in this API.

We model main-memory checkpointing algorithms using a single *Mutator* thread that executes the application logic and synchronously updates the application state. Our techniques can be naturally extended to support applications with multithreaded mutators as long as we include enough information in the logical log to enable deterministic replay. For OLTP applications, for instance, this might include transaction commit order so that transactions can be serialized during replay. This may lengthen the recovery time somewhat, but in practice we have observed that many FC applications are already deterministic or can be made deterministic using existing methods [30].

In addition to the Mutator, we use two threads to write data to disk. The *Logical Logger* thread synchronously flushes logical log entries to disk. This could be done directly in the Mutator thread, but we implement it as a separate thread so that we can overlap computation and process additional actions while we are waiting for the disk write to complete. Note that we must wait for all disk writes to finish before proceeding to the next point of consistency (e.g. reporting a transaction as committed).

The final thread, the *Asynchronous Writer*, writes some or all of the main-memory state to disk. Note that this thread can be run in the background while the Mutator concurrently updates the state. Since the performance of the Asynchronous Writer thread is primarily determined by disk bandwidth, we will focus on the synchronous overhead introduced in the Mutator thread. However, it is important to note that some existing checkpointing algorithms require that the Asynchronous Writer acquire locks on portions of the application state, which can impact the performance of all of the threads [27].

The Mutator thread makes function calls before starting a new checkpoint (`PrepareForNextCheckpoint`), when a point of consistency is reached (`PointOfConsistency`), and during each read and write of the application state (`HandleRead` and `HandleWrite`). The `PointOfConsistency` method must be executed at a point of consistency, but it need not be executed at every point of consistency. If points of consistency are very frequent (e.g., every few microseconds), we can wait for several of them to pass before calling the method.

Different algorithms will implement these methods differently depending on how they manage the application state. Most algorithms will maintain one or more *shadow copies* of the state in main memory. The Mutator may use this *shadow state* during the checkpoint before it is written to stable storage by the Asynchronous Writer. In the rest of the paper, we will refer to the time between successive calls to `PrepareForNextCheckpoint` as a *checkpoint period*. Note that this must be long enough for the Asynchronous Writer to finish creating a checkpoint on disk. These checkpoints may be organized on disk in several different ways. In our implementation, we use a double-backup organization for all of the algorithms, as it was reported in previous work to consistently outperform a log-based implementation [27].

The recovery procedure is the same for all algorithms that implement this framework. First, the most recent consistent checkpoint is read from disk and materialized as the new application state. Then, the logical log is replayed from the time of the last checkpoint until the state is up-to-date. Since we take checkpoints very frequently, the time to replay the logical log is quite small.

2.3 Existing Algorithms

Based on their experimental evaluation for MMOs, Vaz Salles et al. concluded that there was no single checkpointing algorithm that outperformed all the others over the entire range of update rates [27]. Their evaluation included a number of synthetic experiments, and we believe they provide a reasonable model for many FC applications. They concluded that two algorithms, *Copy-on-Update* and *Naive-Snapshot*, performed best for low and high update rates, respectively.

Naive-Snapshot synchronously copies the entire state of the application to the shadow copy at a point of consistency and then writes it out asynchronously to disk. Naive-Snapshot is among the best algorithms when the update rate is very high since it does not perform any checkpoint-specific work in the `HandleRead` or `HandleWrite` functions.

Copy-on-Update groups application objects into blocks and copies each block to the shadow state the first time it is updated during a checkpoint period. During a checkpoint, the Asynchronous writer either reads state from the application state or the shadow copy based on whether the corresponding block has been updated. Since the Mutator is concurrently updating the application state, it must acquire locks on the blocks it references. This may introduce considerable overhead. By varying the memory block size, Copy-on-Update can trade off between copying and locking overhead.

Method	Overhead Factor			
	Bulk Copying	Locking	Bulk Bit-Array Reset	Memory Usage
Naive-Snapshot	Yes	No	No	×2
Copy-on-Update	No	Yes	Yes	×2
Wait-Free Zigzag	No	No	Yes	×2
Wait-Free Ping-Pong	No	No	No	×3

Table 1: Overhead factors of checkpoint-recovery algorithms.

3. NEW ALGORITHMS

In this section, we present two novel checkpoint recovery algorithms for FC applications. We first discuss important design tradeoffs that differentiate our algorithms from state-of-the-art methods (Section 3.1) and then introduce each algorithm in turn (Sections 3.2 and 3.3).

3.1 Design Overview

We have identified four primary factors that affect the performance of checkpoint recovery algorithms:

1. **Bulk State Copying:** The method may need to pause the application to take a snapshot of the whole application state, as in Naive-Snapshot.
2. **Locking:** The method may need to use locking to isolate the Mutator from the Asynchronous Writer, if they work on shared regions of the application state.
3. **Bulk Bit-Array Reset:** If the method uses metadata bits to flag dirty portions of the state, it may need to pause the application and perform a bulk clean-up of this metadata before the start of a new checkpoint period.
4. **Memory Usage:** In order to avoid synchronous writes to disk, the method may need to allocate additional main memory to hold copies of the application state.

Table 1 shows how the factors above apply to both Naive-Snapshot and Copy-on-Update. Naive-Snapshot eliminates all locking and bulk bit-array resetting overhead, but must perform a bulk copy of the whole application state. This introduces a latency spike in the application since it must block during the copy. Copy-on-Update avoids this problem since it does not perform synchronous bulk copies, but incurs both locking and bulk bit-array resetting overhead. This extra overhead is small for moderate update rates, but is significant for higher update rates [27]. Both methods require additional main memory of roughly the size of the entire application state. So the memory usage for the dynamic application state increases to about twice its original size.

Our new algorithms, Wait-Free Zigzag and Wait-Free Ping-Pong, are designed to eliminate all overhead associated with bulk state copying and locking. Unlike Naive-Snapshot, they spread their overhead over time instead of concentrating it at a single point of consistency. Unlike Copy-on-Update, they only require synchronization between the Mutator and Asynchronous Writer at the end of a checkpoint period. This eliminates all locking overhead during state updates. Additionally, the Mutator and Asynchronous Writer are each guaranteed to make progress even if the other is preempted within a checkpoint period. As a consequence, both algorithms are wait-free within a checkpoint period [13]. Table 1 also summarizes the overhead factors our algorithms incur.

To eliminate overhead factors, both of our new algorithms strictly separate the state being updated by the Mutator from the state being read by the Asynchronous Writer. In addition, both track updates at very fine, word-level granularity. However, the algorithms use different amounts of main memory. Wait-Free Zigzag, like Naive-Snapshot and Copy-On-Update, uses additional main memory on the order of the size of the application state. Wait-Free Ping-Pong, however, requires twice that amount. We believe that this is a reasonable tradeoff for most MMOs and OLTP applications, as the size of the dynamically updated state is generally quite small – usually only a small fraction of the whole state.

3.2 Wait-Free Zigzag

The main intuition behind Wait-Free Zigzag is to maintain an untouched copy of every word in the application state for the duration of a checkpoint period. These copies form the consistent image that is written to disk by the Asynchronous Writer. As these copies are never changed during the checkpoint period, the Asynchronous Writer is free to read them without acquiring locks.

The algorithm starts with two identical copies of the application state: AS_0 and AS_1 (Figure 1(a)). For each word i in the application state, we maintain two bits: $MR[i]$ and $MW[i]$. The first bit, $MR[i]$, indicates which application state should be used for Mutator reads from word i, while the second bit, $MW[i]$, indicates which should be used for Mutator writes. The bit array MR is initialized with zeros and MW with ones.

The bits in MW are never updated during a checkpoint period. This ensures that for every word i, $AS_{\neg MW[i]}[i]$ is also never updated by the Mutator during a checkpoint period. The Asynchronous Writer flushes exactly these words to disk in order to take a checkpoint. To avoid blocking the Mutator, however, we must also apply updates to the application state. Whenever a new update comes to word i, we write that update to position $AS_{MW[i]}[i]$ and set $MR[i]$ to $MW[i]$. Before any read of a word i, the Mutator inspects $MR[i]$ and directs the read to the most recently updated word $AS_{MR[i]}[i]$. Figure 1(b) shows the situation after updates are applied to the shaded words. For example, the value written for the third word by the Asynchronous Writer resides in AS_0 and remains unchanged during the first checkpoint. Any reads by the Mutator after the first update return the value in AS_1.

At the end of the checkpoint period, the Mutator assigns the negation of MR to MW, i.e., $\forall i, MW[i] := \neg MR[i]$. This is done so that the current state of the application is not updated by the Mutator during the next checkpoint period and can be written to disk by the Asynchronous Writer. Figure 1(c) shows the state right after the Mutator performs this assignment in our example. Again, updates during the next checkpoint period follow the same procedure outlined above. Figure 1(d) shows the application state after two updates during the second checkpoint period. Note that the current application state, as well as the state being checkpointed to disk, is now distributed between AS_0 and AS_1.

Algorithm 1 summarizes Wait-Free Zigzag. While most of this algorithm is a straightforward translation of the explanation above, one further observation applies to the `PointOfConsistency` procedure. This Mutator procedure checks whether the Asynchronous Writer has finished writing the current checkpoint to disk. Though the threads communicate, this does not violate the wait-free property of the algorithm, as it can be implemented using store and load barriers instead of locks. Heavier synchronization methods are only necessary at the end of every checkpoint period.

Wait-Free Zigzag does not require any lock synchronization during a checkpoint period. In addition, there is no need to copy memory blocks in response to an update from the Mutator. This eliminates some of the largest overheads of Copy-on-Update. In addition, Wait-Free Zigzag distributes its overhead smoothly and avoids the latency spikes of Naive-Snapshot. On the other hand, Wait-Free Zigzag adds bit checking and setting overhead to both reads and writes issued by the Mutator. It also exhibits a small

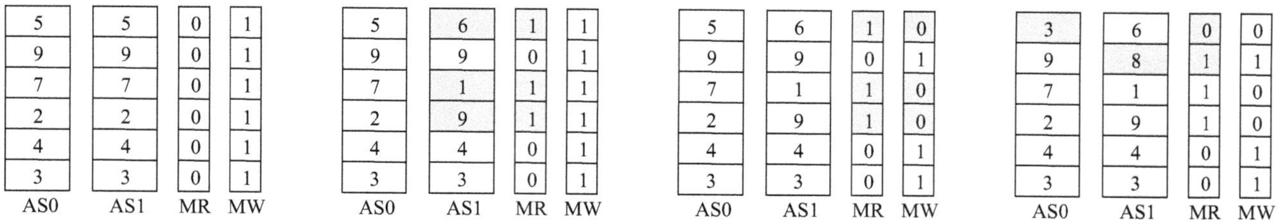

(a) At the beginning of time, AS_0 and AS_1 contain the same information

(b) During the first checkpoint period, some updates from the Mutator are applied

(c) The state right after switching to the second checkpoint period

(d) In the second checkpoint period, the Mutator applies additional updates

Figure 1: Wait-Free Zigzag Example

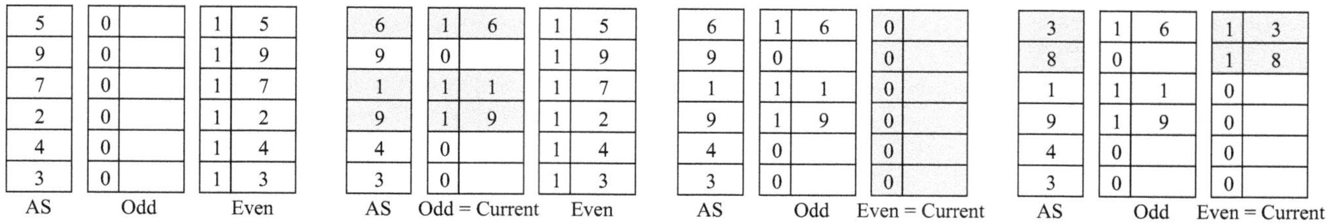

(a) At the beginning of time, *AS* and *Even* contain the same information

(b) During the first checkpoint period, *Odd* collects updates, while *Even* is flushed to disk

(c) The state right after switching to the second checkpoint period

(d) In the second checkpoint period, *Odd* and *Even* invert roles

Figure 2: Wait-Free Ping-Pong Example

Algorithm 1: Wait-Free Zigzag

```
input:
/* ApplicationState is a vector containing words */
ApplicationState AS_0 ← initial application state
ApplicationState AS_1 ← initial application state
/* size of application state in words */
sizeWords ← |AS_0|
/* reads from the Mutator reference AS_MR[k] */
BitArray MR ← {0,0,...,0}
/* writes from the Mutator affect AS_MW[k] */
BitArray MW ← {1,1,...,1}

Mutator::PrepareForNextCheckpoint()
  for i = 0 to sizeWords do
    MW[i] ← ¬MR[i]
  end for

Mutator::PointOfConsistency()
  if Asynchronous Writer done then
    PrepareForNextCheckpoint()
    NotifyAsynchronousWriter()
  end if

Mutator::HandleRead(index)
  return AS_MR[index][index]

Mutator::HandleWrite(index, newValue)
  AS_MW[index][index] ← newValue
  MR[index] ← MW[index]

AsynchronousWriter::WriteToStableStorage()
  loop
    WaitForMutatorNotification()
    for k = 0 to sizeWords do
      write-to-disk AS_¬MW[k][k]
    end for
  end loop
```

latency peak associated with negating the bit array at checkpoint boundaries.

3.3 Wait-Free Ping-Pong

All algorithms we have analyzed so far may introduce latency spikes at the end of a checkpoint period due to either synchronous copying or bulk bit-array reset. In this section, we present Wait-Free Ping-Pong, an algorithm that invests extra main memory and extra work per update to avoid these peaks. Wait-Free Ping-Pong uses a total of three versions of the application state. Two of these are used to ensure that the Mutator and Asynchronous Writer always access separate versions of the state and never have to acquire locks. The final copy allows Wait-Free Ping-Pong to do only a constant amount of work at checkpoint boundaries. Rather than performing a large copy or linear time bit-array reset, it only needs to swap two pointers before starting the next checkpoint.

The three copies of the state maintained by Wait-Free Ping-Pong are called *AS*, *Odd*, and *Even*. The Mutator thread reads from *AS* and applies each update to both *AS* and one of the other copies (either *Odd* or *Even*). The Asynchronous Writer uses the other copy to construct a consistent checkpoint that it writes to disk in the background. At the end of the checkpoint period the roles of *Odd* and *Even* are switched so that new updates can be flushed to disk. In order to avoid unnecessary disk writes, each word in *Odd* and *Even* has an associated mark bit that indicates whether it has been updated during the current checkpoint period. The Asynchronous Writer merges those words that have their mark bits set with the previous checkpoint in order to create a new consistent checkpoint.

We show the initial state of Wait-Free Ping-Pong in Figure 2(a). *AS* contains the application state, *Odd* is empty, and *Even* contains a copy of *AS*. The Asynchronous Writer will process *Even* and flush to disk all of the words that have a mark bit set. During the first checkpoint period, this corresponds to the whole state. In the meantime, the Mutator applies updates to *AS*. For every such update, the Mutator must guarantee that the corresponding mark bit for the updated word is set on *Odd* and that the update is also applied to *Odd*. The situation after a few mutator updates is shown in

Algorithm 2: Wait-Free Ping-Pong

```
input:
/* ApplicationState is vector containing words */
ApplicationState AS ← initial application state
ApplicationState currentAS
ApplicationState previousAS ← initial application state
/* size of application state in words */
sizeWords ← |AS|
/* dirty words in the current checkpoint */
BitArray currentBA ← {0,0,...,0}
/* dirty words from the last checkpoint */
BitArray previousBA ← {1,1,...,1}

Mutator::PrepareForNextCheckpoint()
 1: /* pointer swapping */
    swap (previousAS, currentAS)
    swap (previousBA, currentBA)

Mutator::PointOfConsistency()
 1: if Asynchronous Writer done then
 2:     PrepareForNextCheckpoint()
 3:     NotifyAsynchronousWriter()
 4: end if

Mutator::HandleWrite(index, newValue)
 1: AS[index] ← newValue
 2: currentAS[index] ← newValue
 3: currenBA[index] ← 1

AsynchronousWriter::WriteToStableStorage()
 1: loop
 2:     WaitForMutatorNotification()
 3:     for k = 0 to sizeWords do
 4:         if previousBA[k] then
 5:             write-to-disk previousAS[k]
 6:             previousBA[k] ← 0
 7:             previousAS[k] ← empty
 8:         else
 9:             write-to-disk word k from previous checkpoint
10:         end if
11:     end for
12: end loop
```

Figure 2(b). Updated words are shaded in the figure – their most recent values are present in both *AS* and *Odd*.

At the end of the first checkpoint period, the Asynchronous Writer will have written all of the marked words in *Even* out to disk. In addition, it will have reset their mark bits. For clarity of presentation, we assume that not only the mark bits but also the contents of those words are reset by the Asynchronous Writer. In an implementation, however, this latter action may be skipped for performance. Note that the Mutator is still applying updates to *Odd* up to this point. Now, the Asynchronous Writer is done with this checkpoint period. The next checkpoint period proceeds similarly with the roles of *Odd* and *Even* inverted. This is shown in Figure 2(c). During the next checkpoint period, the algorithm applies updates to *Even* and the words marked in *Odd* are flushed to disk by the Asynchronous Writer. Figure 2(d) displays the situation after a few updates from the Mutator in the second checkpoint period.

Algorithm 2 presents the logic of Wait-Free Ping-Pong. Note that *currentAS* and *currentBA* point to the copy of the application state collecting updates for the current checkpoint period (either *Odd* or *Even*). From a high-level perspective, *currentAS* and *currentBA* may be seen as an in-memory, compressed implementation of a log of updates for this checkpoint period.

Note that as part of the `WriteToStableStorage` method, the Asynchronous Writer must merge the words updated during the most recent checkpoint (*previousAS*[*k*]) with the last consistent checkpoint in order to construct a new consistent checkpoint that can be written to disk (lines 5 and 9). This merge can be done in one of two ways. In the first method, which we call **Copy**, the Asynchronous Writer maintains an extra copy of the application state which it "rolls forward" by applying the new updates before flushing the full checkpoint to disk. In the second method, called **Merge**, the Asynchronous Writer reads the most recent checkpoint from disk and applies the new updates before streaming the new checkpoint to disk. Note that the updates can be applied as the checkpoint is read, so it is not necessary to maintain an additional copy of the state in main memory. We compare these alternatives in Section 5.5

Wait-Free Ping-Pong introduces negligible overhead to the Mutator at the end of a checkpoint period; only simple pointer swaps are needed. Thus, there is no single point in time at which the algorithm introduces a latency peak. On the other hand, this algorithm doubles the number of updates, as each update is applied both to the application state and to a copy.

4. IMPLEMENTATION

Since all of the algorithms we evaluate make frequent access to multiple copies of the application state in main memory, cache and TLB performance are important considerations to reduce overhead. In this section, we describe the important features of our cache-optimized implementations.

4.1 Existing Algorithms

We start by describing our implementations of the two existing algorithms: Naive-Snapshot and Copy-on-Update.

Naive Snapshot (NS). As this algorithm is relatively straightforward, we focused on making the memory copy at the beginning of a new checkpoint period as efficient as possible. With microbenchmarks, we observed that a `memcpy` of a memory-aligned application state was better than our attempts to manually unroll the copy loop.

Bit-Array Packed Copy-on-Update (BACOU). The main data structures used by Copy-on-Update include the primary and shadow states maintained by the algorithm, bit arrays with metadata on dirty memory blocks, and lock information for these blocks. In order to minimize the overhead of bulk bit-array resetting, we packed the bits into (64 byte) cache lines and used long word instructions for all operations. Furthermore, we interleaved blocks of the primary and shadow copies of the application state into one cache line, so that they will be fetched together. This optimized implementation gave us a factor of five improvement over a naive implementation of the algorithm.

4.2 Wait-Free Zigzag

The Wait-Free Zigzag algorithm has two major sources of overhead: the bit array lookups in the `handleRead` and `handleWrite` routines, and the bulk negation in the `prepareForNextCheckpoint` routine. To address these sources of overhead, we devised the following data layout variations.

Naive Wait-Free Zigzag (NZZ). This is the naive translation of the algorithm presented in Section 3.2. We represented each of AS_0, AS_1, MR, and MW as a separate array in main memory and encoded each bit of MR and MW as one byte for efficient access.

Interleaved Wait-Free Zigzag (IZZ). In this variant, we interleaved the main-memory layout of AS_0, AS_1, MR, and MW. Each cache line holds a fixed number of *interleaved records*, containing a word from each data structure, stored in order. Placing all of the words necessary for `handleRead` and `handleWrite` in the same cache line reduces memory stalls on read and write instructions.

Packed Wait-Free Zigzag (PZZ). This variant is similar to IZZ, but organizes data inside of a cache line differently. Instead of laying out interleaved records row-at-a-time, we laid them out column-at-a-time, in a style reminiscent of PAX [1]. This maintains the benefits for `handleRead` and `handleWrite`, while allowing `prepareForNextCheckpoint` to be implemented more efficiently with long word negation instructions.

Bit-Array Packed Wait-Free Zigzag (BAZZ). We observed experimentally that negating the MR bits at the end of each checkpoint period was the major source of overhead in Wait-Free Zigzag (Section 5.2). As with BACOU, we optimized this bulk negation by combining the representation of MR and MW into a single bit-packed array. We divided each cache line in the array in half, and used the first half for the bits of MR and the second half for bits of MW. In a system with a cache line size of 64 bytes, each cache line encodes 256 bits from each array. We negated the bits of MR efficiently with long word instructions.

4.3 Wait-Free Ping-Pong

Unlike Wait-Free Zigzag, Wait-Free Ping-Pong has a very inexpensive `prepareForNextCheckpoint` routine. On the other hand, it must write to two copies of the application state during each update. With this in mind, we investigate the following two variants of Wait-Free Ping-Pong.

Naive Wait-Free Ping-Pong (NPP). In this variant, we allocated *AS*, *Odd*, *Even*, and their respective bit arrays as independent arrays in main memory. Additionally, we also represented each bit using one byte in order to avoid bit encoding overhead on writes.

Interleaved Wait-Free Ping-Pong (IPP). As in the corresponding variant for Wait-Free Zigzag, we interleaved the memory layout of *AS*, *Odd*, *Even*, and their respective bit arrays. Each cache line contains a set of interleaved records with one word from each data structure in sequence. In this way, the additional writes of `handleWrite` fall on the same cache line as the original write to the application state. We thus expect to eliminate any DTLB or cache miss overheads associated with the additional writes of Wait-Free Ping-Pong using this organization.

We also applied a number of other optimizations, including using different page sizes, eliminating conditionals, and aggressively inlining code. Using large pages resulted in a considerable performance improvement, which we report in Section 5.6.

5. EXPERIMENTS

In this section we compare the performance of Wait-Free Zigzag and Wait-Free Ping-Pong with existing algorithms. We consider several metrics in our evaluation. First, we look at the synchronous overhead per checkpoint. This added overhead indicates the total amount of work done by the checkpointing algorithm during a checkpoint period. We also measure how the overhead is distributed over time in order to see whether the checkpointing algorithms introduce any unacceptable latency peaks.

5.1 Setup and Datasets

We compare Wait-Free Zigzag and Wait-Free Ping-Pong with Naive-Snapshot and Copy-on-Update using two different synthetic workloads and a main-memory TPC-C application.

Synthetic Workloads. For the synthetic workloads, we produced trace files containing the sequence of physical updates to apply to the application. We make these traces sufficiently large to avoid transient effects and keep them in main memory to avoid I/O effects. Updates are applied as fast as possible by our benchmark, but to normalize results for presentation, we group updates into intervals that correspond to 0.1 seconds of simulated application logic. In addition, to meaningfully compare the overhead of checkpointing algorithms, we ensure that the checkpointing interval is the same for all algorithms.

In the first workload, we model the application state as a set of 8 KB objects. Different FC applications may have different data models or schemas, but this is a reasonable general model that allows us to vary the state size by changing the number of objects. We use 25,000 rows as a default, which yields approximately 200 MB of dynamic state. In this workload, we distribute updates by selecting an object and then selecting one of the 2,000 four-byte words of the object using identical Zipf-distributions with parameter α. Using this skewed distribution allows us to model applications in which part of the state is "hot" and is frequently updated. We have found that our results remain consistent across a range of α values, so for space reasons we present all results with $\alpha = 0.5$.

We also experimented with a synthetic MMO workload. Accurately modeling an MMO is challenging as games vary widely, but we have attempted to capture the salient features using a Markov model. Each agent in the game is represented as an object and modeled with a set of five semi-independent probabilistic state machines associated with common gameplay behaviors. We tuned the transition probabilities for each state machine by looking at update rates produced for each type of action. We then adjusted the state-transition probabilities until these update rates corresponded to those we have observed in specific MMOs. For our experiments, we used 2,000 players and a total of 531,530 updates per second. Each player object contains roughly 100 KB of state corresponding to a wide variety of character attributes.

We ran all synthetic experiments on a local Intel Xeon 5500 2.66 GHz with 12 GB RAM and four cores running CentOS. Its Nehalem-based CPU has 32 KB L1 cache, 256 KB L2 cache for each core and a shared L3 cache of 8 MB. We measured disk bandwidth in this server to be roughly 60 MB/s. For the experiments with synthetic workloads, we first ensured that the checkpoint interval was large enough for any of the algorithms to finish writing the entire checkpoint to disk. Then, we normalized checkpoint interval at roughly 4 seconds, so as to provide for short estimated recovery time. Once we established this, we turned off both the Asynchronous Writer and logical logging. These mechanisms perform the same amount of work independently of checkpointing method, and disabling them enabled us to measure the synchronous overhead introduced by different algorithms more accurately.

TPC-C Application. We implemented a single-threaded transaction processing system in main memory. Following the methodology from [28], we implemented the TPC-C workload by writing stored procedures in C++. We drive this application with a memory-resident trace containing transaction procedure calls respecting the transaction mix dictated by the TPC-C specification. As in [28], we do not model think times in order to stress our implementation. As usual, we report the number of new order transactions per second.

Unlike in the synthetic benchmark experiments, we checkpoint as frequently as possible in order to understand the maximum impact of our algorithms in a realistic application. This yields the minimum possible recovery time, as the length of the log since the last checkpoint is minimized. We ran our TPC-C application on an Amazon Cluster Compute Quadruple Extra Large instance with 23 GB RAM, and computing power equivalent to two Intel Xeon X5570 quad-core Nehalem-based processors. We write checkpoints and the log to two separate RAID-0 devices, which we configured with ten Amazon Elastic Block Storage (Amazon EBS) volumes. We observed that the aggregate bandwidth of these RAID-0 devices depended on the size of the I/O request, ranging from under 10 MB/s for small requests to over 150 MB/s for large requests exceeding 1 GB. In order to completely utilize disk bandwidth, we scale the checkpoint interval with the size of the dynamic application state, so that the Asynchronous Writer always writes data to disk as fast as possible. This differs from our synthetic experiments where we set the checkpoint interval to a constant for all measurements. Nevertheless, to fairly compare the overhead of different algorithms, we set the length of the checkpoint interval to be the same for all methods at each database size.

Since each EC2 instance communicates with EBS over the network, there is a CPU cost to writing out state in the Asynchronous Writer. To limit this effect, we set the thread affinity so that the Asynchronous Writer always runs on a separate core from the Mutator thread. As the number of cores per machine continues to increase, we believe that it will become increasingly feasible to devote a core to durability in this way. A thorough evaluation of these methods on a single core remains future work.

In addition to turning on the Asynchronous Writer, we also enable logging for these experiments. To minimize synchronous I/O effects, we configured the Logger thread to perform group commit in batches of 500 transactions. We also overlap computation with IO operations so that when the Logger is writing the actions of one batch of transactions, the Mutator is processing the next batch.

In standard OLTP systems, it is common to use the ARIES recovery algorithm [21]. As a baseline for our TPC-C experiments, we have implemented an optimized version of ARIES for main-memory databases. As FC applications do not have transactions in flight at points of consistency, checkpointing does not need to be aware of transaction aborts. This eliminates the need to maintain undo information. In addition, since the database is entirely resident in main memory, there is no need to keep a dirty page table. So in our scenario, ARIES reduces to physical redo logging with periodic fuzzy checkpoints. To optimize it as much as possible, we compressed the format of physical log records by exploiting schema information instead of recording explicit offsets and lengths whenever profitable.

In the remainder of this section, we first compare the different implementation options from Section 4 for our algorithms (Section 5.2). After selecting the alternatives with the best performance, we observe how our new algorithms compare to existing methods using both the Zipf and MMO workloads (Sections 5.3 and 5.4). Then, we report on how our methods affect application throughput in our TPC-C application (Section 5.5). Finally, we investigate the impact of a further optimization, using large pages, on the relative performance of all algorithms (Section 5.6).

5.2 Comparison of Implementation Variants

In this section we compare the performance of the different implementations of our algorithms on the Zipf workload. To get a deeper understanding of the runtime characteristics, we profiled our implementation with the Intel VTune Performance Analyzer [15]. Table 2 shows a subset of the statistics we collected from VTune. It includes cycles per instruction (CPI) as well as various measures to characterize the behavior of cache, DTLB, and page walks. For reference, we display these statistics not only for all algorithms, but also for the raw Mutator program without checkpointing.

5.2.1 *Wait-Free Zigzag*

Figure 3 shows the average overhead per checkpoint period of the different variants. Both IZZ and PZZ are less efficient than NZZ, except for extremely high update rates. With NZZ and PZZ, the use of long word instructions during negation brings benefits over IZZ, which negates single bytes at a time. However, the benefits are much smaller for PZZ, given that it still interleaves state information between small bit blocks. BAZZ, a variant that focuses on optimizing bulk bit-array negation, dominates all other variants.

Algorithm[a]	CPI	L1D Misses / Update	L1D Miss Rate	L2 Miss Rate	DTLB Miss % (STORE)	# Page Walks / Update
NS	1.79	2.1	6.6%	10.8%	7.1%	0.50
COU	2.91	1.2	8.5%	9.2%	23.5%	0.53
BACOU	2.51	1.1	4.5%	4.5%	6.5%	0.41
NZZ-UP	13.6	0.8	22.3%	24.6%	95.2%	0.78
NZZ-NE	0.7	0.2	3.1%	3.1%	0.8%	-
IZZ-UP	11.1	0.2	7.7%	7.2%	49.2%	0.29
IZZ-NE	0.7	1.0	3.0%	3.4%	1.6%	0.02
PZZ-UP	7.1	0.3	5.0%	5.2%	48.7%	0.37
PZZ-NE	5.0	0.8	22.8%	25.4%	3.3%	0.02
BAZZ-UP	1.5	0.04	6.9%	7.2%	0.03%	-
BAZZ-NE	1.6	0.03	6.9%	8.0%	-	-
NPP	7.1	1.9	23.6%	24.0%	97.4%	0.96
IPP	2.5	1.7	7.4%	7.8%	98.3%	.85
Raw Mutator	2.4	2.0	9.4%	8.0%	96.0%	1.00

[a] -UP: update handling phase; -NE: bulk negation phase

Table 2: Profiling on synthetic workload, 320K updates/sec

In general, there is a tension between accelerating bulk bit-array negation and reducing per-update overhead. Table 2 shows profiling results for 320,000 updates per second. NZZ's update handling phase has an L1D cache miss rate of 22.3% and an L2 cache miss rate of 24.6%. In addition, every update incurs 0.78 page walks on average, given NZZ's independent allocation of data structures. Bulk negation, on the other hand, benefits from prefetching on these data structures. The cache miss rate is about 3% for both the L1D and the L2 cache; the DTLB miss rate is also low. IZZ trades bulk negation performance for better update performance. Its DTLB miss rate is much lower than that of NZZ. The ratio of cache misses to updates for IZZ is much higher during the bulk negation phase, however. PZZ pays more on cache misses and page walks at the update phase, but less during the bulk negation phase. Meanwhile, BAZZ focuses solely on making negation more compact, and dramatically improves performance despite a higher cache miss rate. As Figure 3 shows, this is an important effect at most update rates.

Overall, we have observed that negation is the most significant source of overhead for Wait-Free Zigzag unless the update rate is extremely high. Thus, BAZZ is the best variant for this algorithm under typical workloads. For example, at 320,000 updates per second, BAZZ exhibits about half as much overhead as NZZ and one third the overhead of IZZ.

5.2.2 *Wait-Free Ping-Pong*

Figure 4 shows the overhead of the two variants of Wait-Free Ping-Pong. NPP's overhead is roughly six times higher than IPP's over all update rates. Like NZZ, NPP runs into similar problems with DTLB and cache performance. Table 2 shows observation. that NPP's cycle-per-instruction ratio (CPI) is 2.8 times higher.

IPP, on the other hand, potentially incurs a cache miss on the write to the application state, but then is guaranteed to find the other words to be written on the same cache line. This has a positive effect in the L1D LOAD hit rate and eliminates most of the stalls on LOAD. IPP pays only a 43% performance overhead on top of the raw Mutator, a great improvement compared to the 258% of NPP. These numbers are very consistent across update rates.

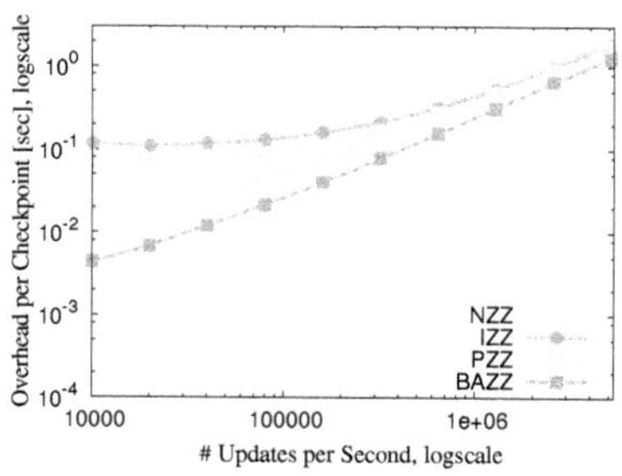

Figure 3: Wait-Free Zigzag Overhead

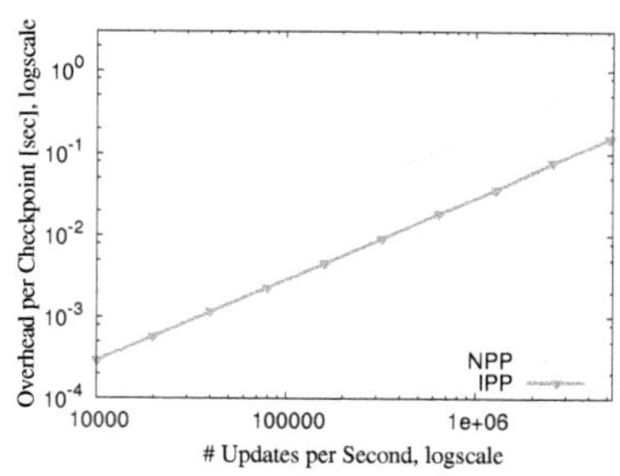

Figure 4: Wait-Free Ping-Pong Overhead

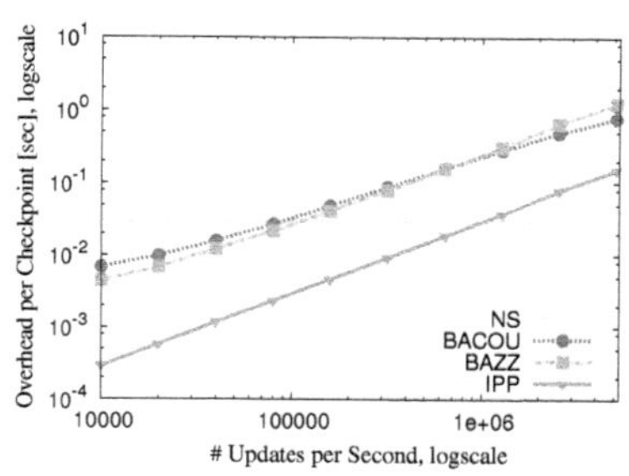

Figure 5: Zipf workload: Overhead

In short, this experiment shows that IPP comfortably dominates NPP over the whole spectrum of update rates evaluated.

5.3 Synthetic Zipf Workload

In this section, we compare the performance of our new algorithms with the best cache-aware variants of Naive Snapshot (NS) and Copy-on-Update (BACOU). We report numbers for the optimized variants described in Section 4. For both BACOU and BAZZ, the overhead numbers we report are lower bounds. Since we turned off the Asynchronous Writer, there is no lock contention between the Mutator and the Asynchronous Writer in BACOU. We also do not model reads, which discounts the small amount of per-read overhead for BAZZ. As shown below, IPP significantly dominates all these algorithms, so we do not explore these effects further.

Checkpointing Overhead. Figure 5 shows the overhead of the algorithms for update rates between 10,000 and 5,120,000 updates per second. As expected, NS is essentially constant regardless of the number of updates, since it always copies the entire state. This is the worst strategy for very low update rates since many unchanged cells get copied, but it dominates the other algorithms, with the notable exception of IPP, for more than 160,000 updates per second. This agrees with the results of [27] – when a large fraction of the words gets updated, taking a checkpoint requires copying most of the state anyway, and NS does this very efficiently.

Among the existing algorithms, BACOU is the best strategy for low update rates [27], and it is four times faster than NS for 10,000 updates per second. Its overhead increases steadily with the update rate, however, since it must lock and copy a memory block the first time the block is updated. As we increase the update rate, more blocks get updated, leading to higher locking and copying overheads. Even though updates are distributed using a Zipf distribution, we have observed only a minor effect from the fact that updates have higher likelihood to hit hot words that fall into the same memory block. This measurement corroborates prior simulation results [27]. We observe that BACOU is never the best algorithm for any update rate. It is always dominated by IPP, and it is also dominated by NS for high update rates.

IPP displays the best performance of any of the algorithms for all but the highest update rates. At 80,000 updates per second, it is nine times better than BAZZ and over an order of magnitude better than NS and BACOU. At 320,000 updates per second, the gap is still a factor of 8.4 with respect to BAZZ, 9.6 with respect to BACOU and three with respect to NS. IPP scales linearly with the number of updates over the entire range of update rates, since the predominant cost is updating each of two copies of the application state. The absolute overhead of the extra updates performed by IPP is extremely low, however, due to its cache-aware data layout and its wait-free operation. Unlike in BAZZ, in IPP the Mutator does not do any bit negations, and the beginning of a checkpoint consists only of swapping pointers.

This experiment shows that, for our default application state size of 200MB, IPP is the method with the lowest overhead for all but the highest update rates. Next, we validate that this trend is robust for a wide range of state sizes.

Scaling the State Size. To understand how our algorithms perform for applications with larger state sizes, we scale the application state from 100 MB to 1.6 GB by adding more objects to the state. Figures 6 and 7 show the overhead per checkpoint period for two different update rates. In each case, we scale the update rate with the state size, so in Figure 6, for every second, we update a number of words equal to 0.08% of the state size. This corresponds to 40,000 updates per second for 200 MB of state. In Figure 7 the update rate corresponds to 2.56%, which is 1,280,000 updates per second for 200 MB of state.

From these graphs we confirm that the trends we described above for 200 MB of application state continue to hold for larger state sizes. When the update rate is fairly low (Figure 6), IPP has roughly an order of magnitude lower overhead than NS regardless of the state size. On the other hand, when the update rate is very high (Figure 7), NS dominates all other algorithms, as it is insensitive to the number of updates. IPP continues to dominate BACOU and BAZZ for larger state sizes regardless of the update rate.

Overhead Distribution. The above experiments already show that IPP dominates BACOU and is preferable to NS for all but the highest update rates, but the overhead does not tell the whole story. As discussed in Section 2.1, we also want the overhead to be uniformly distributed over time. Figures 8 and 9 show the cost of the Mutator thread for 320,000 and 1,280,000 updates per second, respectively. Points on the x-axis correspond to time intervals of 0.1 sec, or alternatively the time it takes to execute 32,000 or 128,000 updates. Each point in the graphs indicates the total time taken by the Mutator thread during one such interval. The graphs thus give us an indication of how work is distributed over time.

From these graphs, we see that NS has the worst overhead distribution of any of the algorithms. At 320,000 updates per second (Figure 8) it has a latency peak of 29 ms during intervals when the state is copied. BAZZ and BACOU have much smaller peaks, at 4 ms and 6 ms, respectively. These results indicate that there is a tradeoff between the absolute overhead per checkpoint and the overhead distribution. Recall from Figure 5 that NS has lower overhead than BACOU at 320,000 updates per second, but the latter has a much lower spike. Fortunately, this tradeoff is not present for IPP, which has a nearly constant overhead of 0.8 ms per 0.1 second interval at 320,000 updates per second. This is because IPP only has to swap pointers at the beginning of each checkpoint, and most of the work is distributed evenly among the updates.

Figure 9 tells a slightly different story. The number of updates executed during each point of the graph has increased to 128,000, and this increases the baseline overhead for all of the strategies that do some work per update. BAZZ shows the most dramatic increase with a nearly constant overhead of 10 ms. BACOU and IPP also show modest overhead increases. Additionally, we can see the finer

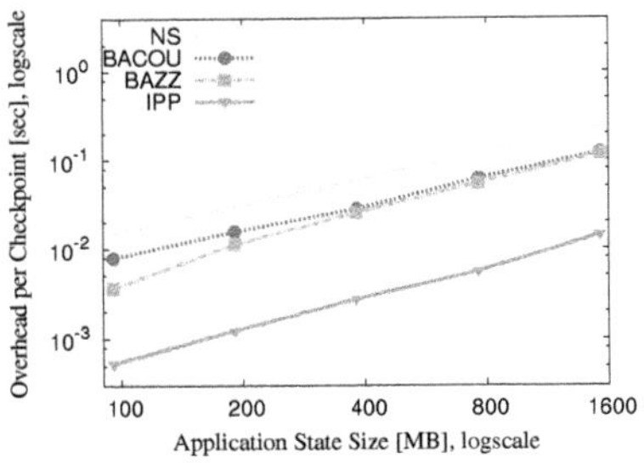

Figure 6: Scaleup: 0.08% updates/sec

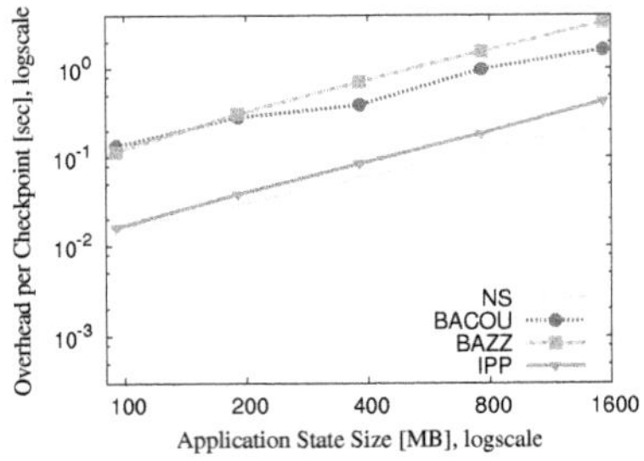

Figure 7: Scaleup: 2.56% updates/sec

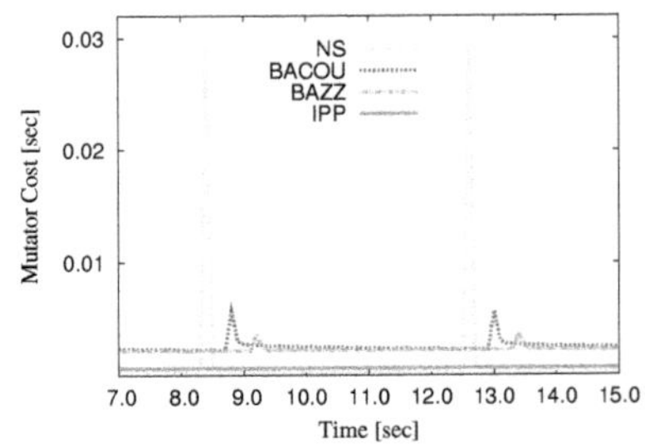

Figure 8: Latency: 320K updates/sec

structure of BACOU. There is a spike in the overhead at the end of each checkpoint period, and then the overhead gradually decreases during the checkpoint. This is because BACOU only has to copy a block the first time it is updated. As the checkpoint progresses, more blocks are already dirty and do not need to be copied.

Significantly, the behavior of NS changes very little at the higher update rate. This is because all of the work done by NS is done at the end of a checkpoint period. The small increase in the figure is due to the time necessary to apply the updates. This indicates a distinction between the overhead incurred by NS and the overhead incurred by the other algorithms. Aside from the small spikes for BAZZ and BACOU, the other algorithms incur most of their cost for work they do at each update. Thus as we increase the number of updates per unit of time, we expect their overhead to increase. Furthermore, the cost shown in each point of Figures 8 and 9 is distributed across all of the updates in the 0.1 second increment. On the other hand, the entire cost of NS occurs between two updates at the end of each checkpoint period. Thus NS is insensitive to the update rate, but it may force the system to block for a considerable amount of time during the synchronous copy. As the height of NS's latency spike is proportional to the application state size, this problem becomes worse when we scale the state size.

Overall, IPP has the most consistent overhead of any tested algorithm, and its total overhead is also lowest for all but the highest update rates. Thus we believe that it best satisfies the requirements for FC applications described in Section 2.1.

5.4 Synthetic MMO Workload

We also ran our experiments on a trace produced using our MMO workload. Figure 10 shows the checkpoint overhead. In this case, both wait-free strategies outperform BACOU. As expected, IPP performs the best, with nearly seven times less overhead than NS. BAZZ is comparable to NS, even though it had higher overhead than NS for 500,000 updates per second in the Zipf experiments. Part of the reason our new algorithms do so well in this case is that many attributes were almost never updated. About 80 percent of the attributes are only updated in response to player actions, which are human initiated and thus occur infrequently. This type of workload is bad for NS, as it has to copy many cells that are never updated.

Figure 11 shows the performance of each algorithm in the MMO simulation over time. The Mutator cost is quite variable compared to Figure 8, due to the more realistic workload, but the trends are the same. NS shows peaks of up to 29 ms, while IPP has a very low, almost uniform latency of at most 0.9 ms. These results suggest that Wait-Free Ping-Pong offers real advantages for MMO workloads.

Finally, we measured the recovery time for the MMO workload. We expected this to be the same for all of the algorithms, as they all store complete checkpoints on disk. In addition, this time is the same as for the synthetic workload, given that the application state size for both scenarios is the same. To measure this time, we observed the time to reread the checkpoint from disk after a crash simulated by server reboot, obtaining an average of 3.9 seconds out of five measurements. To simulate replaying the logical log, we can reapply the updates from the MMO trace file that occurred since the last checkpoint. The maximum time to reapply those updates is equal to our checkpointing interval of 4.2 seconds, resulting in a worst-case recovery time of only 8.1 seconds. Given that current MMO players regularly tolerate downtime [7], we think this is very reasonable for real systems.

In short, the above experiments show that IPP is the method with the lowest overhead and the best overhead distribution for a realistic application with hundreds of thousands of updates per second. In addition, IPP exhibits short recovery times in this scenario.

5.5 TPC-C Application

To validate the usefulness of our techniques in realistic FC applications with logging and checkpoint writing enabled, we compare the total overhead introduced by different checkpointing techniques in our main-memory implementation of the TPC-C benchmark [31]. We stress our implementation by processing as many transactions per second as possible and show results for the two best methods for high update rates: Naive Snapshot (NS) and Wait-Free Ping-Pong (IPP). In addition, we show the performance of our optimized version of ARIES (OPT. ARIES) as a baseline method.

Figure 12 shows throughput as we increase the number of warehouses in TPC-C. Recall that in this measurement we keep the ratio of application state size to checkpoint interval fixed. In other words, we checkpoint as fast as possible to achieve short recovery times while ensuring that the checkpoint interval is equal for all methods so as to allow for direct overhead comparison. Thus the checkpoint sizes grow and so do the costs per checkpoint. The maximum attainable performance is displayed by running the application with checkpointing disabled. Maximum throughput declines as we scale the number of warehouses given that we must operate over a larger database in main memory.

We observe that the relative performance of all methods remains roughly unchanged as we scale the number of warehouses. The variants of IPP using the Copy and Merge methods described in Section3.3 for merging the new updates with the previous checkpoint perform similarly. IPP-Copy always slightly outperforms IPP-Merge at the cost of maintaining an additional copy of the application state. Both IPP variants dominate NS, which in turn dominates OPT. ARIES. At 60 warehouses, application throughput decreases by 10.11% when using IPP-Copy, by 27.92% when using NS, and by 34.21% when using OPT. ARIES.

In order to understand the distribution of overhead in the TPC-C experiment, we also measured the response time of each of the algorithms. Figure 13 reports these results, where each point corresponds to a batch of 500 transactions that are committed together. The response time is measured as the time between the start of one batch of transactions and the start of the next. The large peaks in the response time of NS are due to the synchronous copy time at the

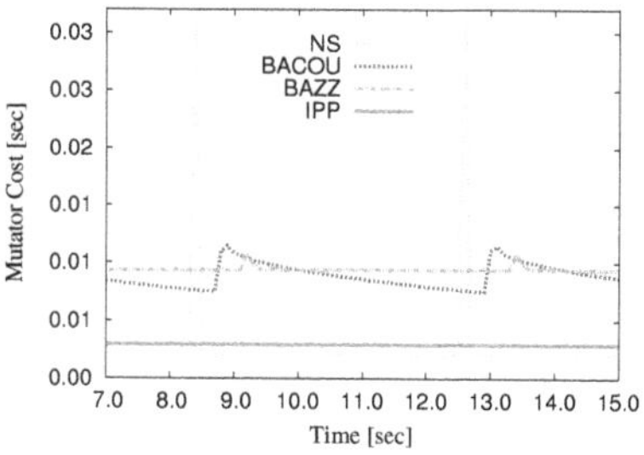

Figure 9: Latency: 1,280K updates/sec

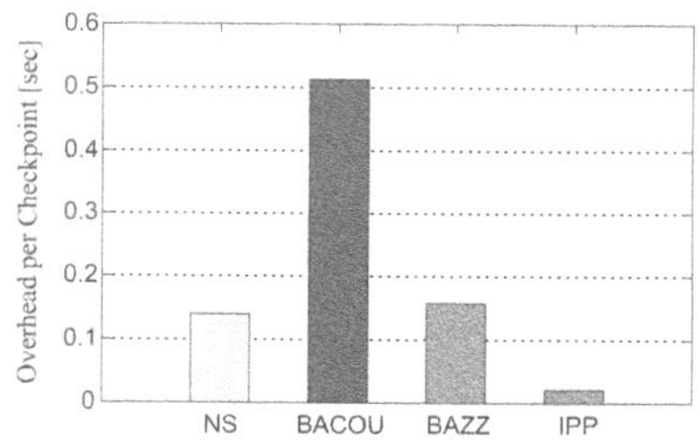

Figure 10: MMO: Overhead

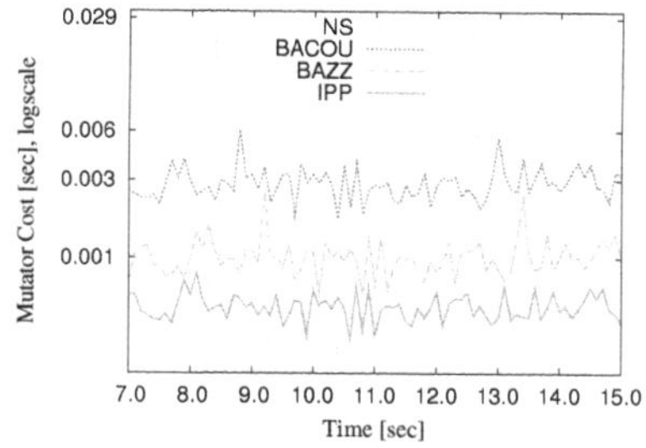

Figure 11: MMO: Latency

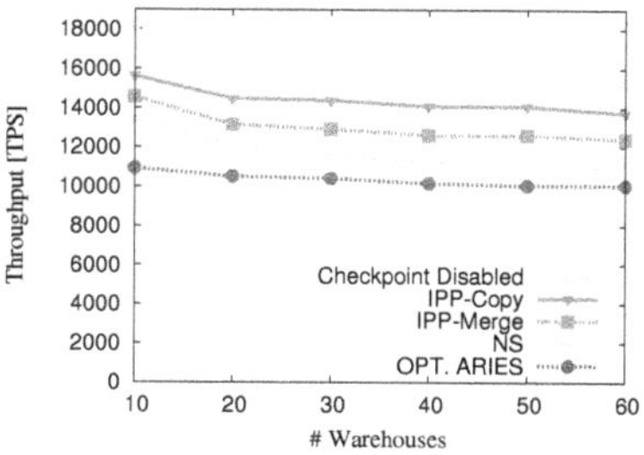

Figure 12: TPC-C Throughput

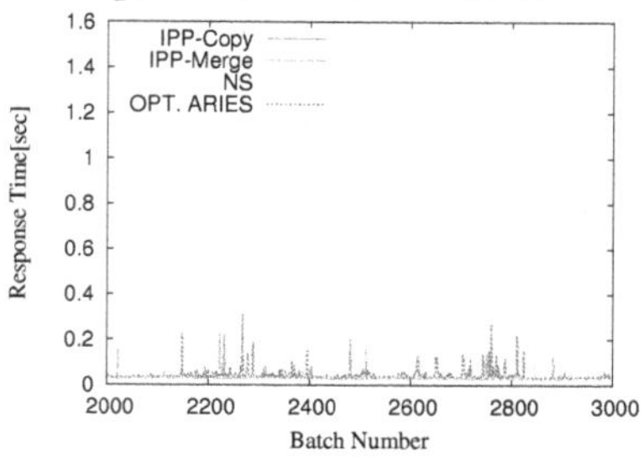

Figure 13: TPC-C Latency

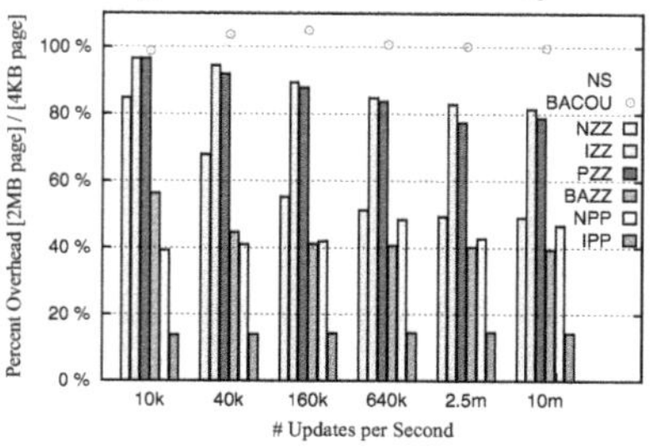

Figure 14: Large Page Overhead

end of each checkpoint period. The remaining peaks in all of the algorithms are due to the cost of logging to EBS. Recall that while the Logger is writing to EBS, the Mutator executes the next batch of transactions. This hides some of the disk latency, but the Mutator still blocks if it finishes the next batch before the Logger. Thus the response time is still quite erratic due to variability in transaction lengths and EBS latency. Since OPT. ARIES uses physical logging, it must write more data to disk, and thus the peaks for OPT. ARIES are both larger and more frequent than the other methods.

Based on these results, we find that IPP allows for frequent checkpointing with significantly lower overhead than the best existing methods. Further, it distributes overhead more evenly than either Naive Snapshot or ARIES, and thus is more suitable for latency-sensitive applications. As the memory capacity and number of cores in a single node continue to increase, we will be able to process even more warehouses within a single machine. Thus, the absolute difference in throughput between using IPP and existing methods will become even more dramatic in the future. Therefore, our experiments suggest that IPP should be the checkpointing method of choice for FC applications.

5.6 Further Optimizations: Large Pages

In order to further increase update rates and stress the limits of all methods, we investigate the effect of an additional optimization. As discussed above, page walks resulting from TLB misses are a significant bottleneck for the Mutator in most algorithms we examined. Large pages may reduce TLB misses because they cover the same region of physical memory with a smaller number of TLB entries. In our scenario, the whole application state and auxiliary data structures are implemented as a few large objects in memory, so using large pages causes very little internal fragmentation.

Figure 14 shows the reduction in overhead when we use different page sizes in the Synthetic Zipf workload. Large pages have little impact on NS and BACOU, since these two methods do not put much stress on TLB (Table 2). In constrast, all variants of Wait-Free Zigzag and Wait-Free Ping-Pong benefit noticeably from large pages. In BAZZ, using large pages yields a 40% to 60% cut in overhead. In IPP, a consistent 80% overhead cut is obtained. These two algorithms benefit the most from using large pages, and remain the best candidates from their respective family of variants. We also increased the update rates to an extremely high value to compare the overhead of IPP and NS when using large pages. Over a range up to ten million updates per second, IPP outperforms NS by up to three orders of magnitude and maintains nearly constant latency.

6. RELATED WORK

There has been extensive work in checkpointing algorithms for main-memory DBMSs [8, 23, 25, 26, 36]. Recently, Vaz Salles et al. evaluated the performance of these algorithms for MMO workloads [27]. Naive-Snapshot and Copy-on-Update came out as the most appropriate algorithms for checkpointing these FC applications. As we have seen in our experiments, Wait-Free Ping-Pong dominates those methods over a wide range of update rates. In contrast to Naive-Snapshot, Wait-Free Ping-Pong distributes overhead better over time, eliminating latency peaks. In contrast to Copy-on-Update, Wait-Free Ping-Pong completely eliminates locking overheads, as it is wait-free within checkpoint periods.

There have been different approaches to integrating checkpoint-recovery systems with applications. One consideration is whether to integrate checkpointing at the system [19, 22] or application level [4, 5]. Additionally, checkpointing may be offered to applications embedded in a language runtime [37], through a library [22], or via compiler support [5]. Our work performs application-level checkpointing and integrates with the application logic through a library API (Section 2.2). Thus we are able to checkpoint only the relevant state of the application, something not achieved by system-level checkpointing schemes. We are also able to exploit application semantics, such as frequent points of consistency, to determine when a consistent image of the state is present in main memory.

In classic relational DBMSs, ARIES is the gold standard for recovery [21]. As we have seen in Section 5.5, approaches that necessitate physical logging, such as ARIES or fuzzy checkpointing [12, 26], exhibit unacceptable logging overheads for the stream of updates produced by FC applications in main memory.

Hot standby architectures have been commonly used to provide fault tolerance on multiple database nodes [3, 14]. Recently, Lau and Madden [18] and Stonebraker et al. [28] propose implementing active standbys by keeping up to *K* replicas of the state. Systems using this approach can survive up to *K* failures, and they can also use those replicas to speed up query processing. Our checkpointing algorithms can be used in tandem with these approaches to bulk-copy state during recovery or when the set of replicas changes. Many replicated systems (such as VoltDB [33]) also include checkpointing in order to ensure durability in the event that all replicas fail (e.g., due to a power outage).

7. CONCLUSIONS

In this paper, we have proposed two novel checkpoint recovery algorithms optimized for frequently-consistent applications. Both methods implement highly granular tracking of updates to eliminate latency spikes due to bulk state copying. Moreover, the wait-free properties of our methods within a checkpoint period allow them to benefit significantly from cache-aware data layout optimizations, dramatically reducing overhead. Wait-Free Zigzag eliminates locking overhead by keeping an untouched copy of the state during a checkpoint period. Wait-Free Ping-Pong improves both overhead and latency even more by using additional main memory space. Our thorough experimental evaluation shows that Wait-Free Ping-Pong outperforms the state of the art in terms of overhead as well as maximum latency by over an order of magnitude. In fact, given that Wait-Free Ping-Pong dominates Copy-on-Update and may have significantly lower overhead than Naive-Snapshot over a wide range of update rates, our new algorithm should be considered as an alternative wherever copy on write methods have been used in the past.

Acknowledgments. We would like to thank our shepherd, Daniel Abadi, for his detailed and insightful comments as well as the anonymous reviewers for their feedback. This material is based upon work supported by the New York State Foundation for Science, Technology, and Innovation under Agreement C050061, by the National Science Foundation under Grants 0725260 and 0534404, by the iAd Project funded by the Research Council of Norway, by the AFOSR under Award FA9550-10-1-0202, and by Microsoft. Any opinions, findings and conclusions or recommendations expressed in this material are those of the authors and do not necessarily reflect the views of the funding agencies.

8. REFERENCES

[1] A. Ailamaki, D. DeWitt, M. Hill, and M. Skounakis. Weaving Relations for Cache Performance. In *Proc. VLDB*, 2001.

[2] P. Alvaro, T. Condie, N. Conway, K. Elmeleegy, J. M. Hellerstein, and R. C. Sears. BOOM: Data-centric programming in the datacenter. Technical Report UCB/EECS-2009-113, EECS Department, University of California, Berkeley, 2009.

[3] J. Bartlett, J. Gray, and B. Horst. Fault tolerance in tandem computer systems. Technical Report 86.2, PN87616, Tandem Computers, 1986.

[4] A. Beguelin, E. Seligman, and P. Stephan. Application Level Fault Tolerance in Heterogeneous Networks of Workstations. *Journal of Parallel and Distributed Computing*, 43(2):147–155, 1997.

[5] G. Bronevetsky, M. Schulz, P. Szwed, D. Marques, and K. Pingali. Application-level Checkpointing for Shared Memory Programs. In *Proc. ASPLOS*, 2004.

[6] K. M. Chandy and L. Lamport. Distributed Snapshots: Determining Global States of Distributed Systems. *ACM TOCS*, 3(1):63–75, 1985.

[7] R. Cortez. World Class Networking Infrastructure. In *Proc. Austin GDC*, 2007.

[8] D. J. DeWitt, R. Katz, F. Olken, L. Shapiro, M. Stonebraker, and D. Wood. Implementation Techniques for Main Memory Database Systems. In *Proc. SIGMOD*, 1984.

[9] M. Elnozahy, L. Alvisi, Y.-M. Wang, and D. B. Johnson. A Survey of Rollback-Recovery Protocols in Message-Passing Systems. *ACM Computing Surveys*, 34(3):375–408, 2002.

[10] H. F. Guðjónsson. The Server Technology of EVE Online: How to Cope With 300,000 Players on One Server. In *Proc. Austin GDC*, 2008.

[11] N. Gupta, A. J. Demers, J. Gehrke, P. Unterbrunner, and W. M. White. Scalability for virtual worlds. In *ICDE*, 2009.

[12] R. Hagmann. A Crash Recovery Scheme for a Memory-Resident Database System. *IEEE Transactions on Computers*, 35(9):839–843, 1986.

[13] M. Herlihy. Wait-free Synchronization. *ACM TOPLAS*, 13(1):124–149, 1991.

[14] S.-O. Hvasshovd, O. Torbjornsen, S. Bratsberg, and P. Holager. The ClustRa Telecom Database: High Availability, High Throughput, and Real-Time Response. In *Proc. VLDB*, 1995.

[15] Intel VTune Performance Analyzer. http://software.intel.com/en-us/intel-vtune.

[16] Jason Gregory. *Game Engine Architecture (Section 7.5)*. A K Peters, 2009.

[17] E. P. C. Jones, D. J. Abadi, and S. Madden. Low overhead concurrency control for partitioned main memory databases. In *Proc. SIGMOD*, 2010.

[18] E. Lau and S. Madden. An Integrated Approach to Recovery and High Availability in an Updatable, Distributed Data Warehouse. In *Proc. VLDB*, 2006.

[19] M. Litzkow, T. Tannenbaum, J. Basney, and M. Livny. Checkpoint and Migration of Unix Processes in the Condor Distributed Processing System. Technical Report 1346, University of Winsconsin-Madison, 1997.

[20] T. MacDonald. Solid-state Storage Not Just a Flash in the Pan. *Storage Magazine*, 2007. http://searchStorage.techtarget.com/magazineFeature/0,296894,sid5_gci1276095,00.html .

[21] C. Mohan, D. Haderle, B. Lindsay, H. Pirahesh, and P. Schwarz. ARIES: A Transaction Recovery Method Supporting Fine-Granularity Locking and Partial Rollbacks Using Write-Ahead Logging. *ACM TODS*, 17(1):94–162, 1992.

[22] J. S. Plank, M. Beck, G. Kingsley, and K. Li. Libckpt: Transparent Checkpointing under UNIX. In *Proc. USENIX Winter Technical Conference*, 1995.

[23] C. Pu. On-the-Fly, Incremental, Consistent Reading of Entire Databases. *Algorithmica*, 1:271–287, 1986.

[24] RamSan-400 Specifications. http://www.ramsan.com/products/ramsan-400.htm .

[25] D. Rosenkrantz. Dynamic Database Dumping. In *Proc. SIGMOD*, 1978.

[26] K. Salem and H. Garcia-Molina. Checkpointing Memory-Resident Databases. In *Proc. ICDE*, 1989.

[27] M. V. Salles, T. Cao, B. Sowell, A. Demers, J. Gehrke, C. Koch, and W. White. An evaluation of checkpoint recovery for massively multiplayer online games. In *Proc. VLDB*, 2009.

[28] M. Stonebraker, S. Madden, D. Abadi, S. Harizopoulos, N. Hachem, and P. Helland. The End of an Architectural Era (It's Time for a Complete Rewrite). In *Proc. VLDB*, 2007.

[29] T. Strohman and W. B. Croft. Efficient Document Retrieval in Main Memory. In *Proc. SIGIR*, 2007.

[30] A. Thomson and D. Abadi. The case for determinism in database systems. In *Proc. VLDB*, 2010.

[31] Transaction Processing Council. TPC Benchmark(TM) C, 2010. http://www.tpc.org/tpcc/spec/tpcc_current.pdf.

[32] P. Unterbrunner, G. Giannikis, G. Alonso, D. Fauser, and D. Kossmann. Predictable performance for unpredictable workloads. *PVLDB*, 2(1):706–717, 2009.

[33] VoltDB. http://voltdb.com/product.

[34] G. Wang, M. V. Salles, B. Sowell, X. Wang, T. Cao, A. Demers, J. Gehrke, and W. White. Behavioral simulations in mapreduce. In *Proc. VLDB*, 2010.

[35] W. White, A. Demers, C. Koch, J. Gehrke, and R. Rajagopalan. Scaling Games to Epic Proportions. In *Proc. SIGMOD*, 2007.

[36] A. Whitney, D. Shasha, and S. Apter. High Volume Transaction Processing Without Concurrency Control, Two Phase Commit, SQL, or C++. In *Proc. HPTS*, 1997.

[37] G. Zheng, L. Shi, and L. V. Kale. FTC-Charm++: an In-Memory Checkpoint-Based Fault Tolerant Runtime for Charm++ and MPI. In *Proc. CLUSTER*, 2004.

Warding off the Dangers of Data Corruption with Amulet

Nedyalko Borisov
Duke University
nedyalko@cs.duke.edu

Shivnath Babu*
Duke University
shivnath@cs.duke.edu

Nagapramod Mandagere
IBM Almaden Research
nmandage@us.ibm.com

Sandeep Uttamchandani
IBM Almaden Research
sandeepu@us.ibm.com

ABSTRACT

Occasional corruption of stored data is an unfortunate byproduct of the complexity of modern systems. Hardware errors, software bugs, and mistakes by human administrators can corrupt important sources of data. The dominant practice to deal with data corruption today involves administrators writing ad hoc scripts that run data-integrity tests at the application, database, file-system, and storage levels. This manual approach is tedious, error-prone, and provides no understanding of the potential system unavailability and data loss if a corruption were to occur. We introduce the *Amulet* system that addresses the problem of verifying the correctness of stored data proactively and continuously. To our knowledge, Amulet is the first system that: (i) gives administrators a declarative language to specify their objectives regarding the detection and repair of data corruption; (ii) contains optimization and execution algorithms to ensure that the administrator's objectives are met robustly and with least cost, e.g., using pay-as-you cloud resources; and (iii) provides timely notification when corruption is detected, allowing proactive repair of corruption before it impacts users and applications. We describe the implementation and a comprehensive evaluation of Amulet for a database software stack deployed on an infrastructure-as-a-service cloud provider.

Categories and Subject Descriptors

H.2.0 [**Datbase Management**]: Data Protection

General Terms

Management, Reliability, Verification

1. INTRODUCTION

Data corruption—where bits of data in persistent storage differ from what they are supposed to be—is an ugly reality that database and storage administrators have to deal with occasionally; often when they are least prepared [6, 11, 14, 17, 25, 30]. Hardware problems such as errors in magnetic media (*bit rot*), erratic disk-arm movements or power supplies, and bit flips in CPU or RAM due to alpha particles can cause data corruption. Bugs in software or firmware as well as mistakes by human administrators are more worrisome. Bugs in the hundreds of thousands of lines of disk firmware code have caused corruption due to *misdirected writes*, *partial writes*, and *lost writes* [14]. Bugs in storage software [11], OS device drivers, and higher-level layers like load balancers [21] and database software [6] have caused corruption and data loss. Recent trends make data corruption more likely to occur than ever:

- Production use of fairly new data management systems: A bug in the CouchDB NoSQL system caused data loss because writes were not being committed to disk [6]. A recent bug triggered by a storage software update caused 0.02% of Gmail users to lose their email data (which had to be restored from tape) [11].
- Use of large numbers of commodity "white-box" systems in datacenters instead of more expensive servers. The lower price comes from the use of less reliable hardware components that are more prone to corruption and failures [3, 22].
- More software layers due to virtualization and cloud services: Customers of the Amazon Simple Storage Service (S3) have experienced data corruption where the data they got back on reads was different from the data they had stored originally [21].

Data loss can have serious consequences. It took only one unfortunate instance of file-system corruption (which spread to data backups), and the consequent loss of data stored by users, to put the social-bookmarking site Ma.gnolia.com out of business [15].

Most systems have a first line of defense to corruption in the form of detection and repair mechanisms. Storing checksums, both at the software and hardware levels, is a common mechanism used to detect corruption [18]. Storing redundant data—e.g., in the form of error correcting codes (ECC) or replicas—as well as duplication of work—e.g., writing to two separate hosts—lowers the chances of data loss due to corruption from bit flips, partial writes, and lost writes. Despite these mechanisms, recent literature [14] as well as plenty of anecdotal evidence show that problems due to corruption happen, and more frequently than expected [3, 22]. A particularly dangerous scenario that the authors as well as others (e.g., [15, 17]) have come across involves the propagation of corruption from the production system to critical backups.

Thus, systems have developed a second line of defense in the form of data-integrity tests (hereafter, *tests*). A test: (a) performs checks in order to detect specific types of data corruption, and/or (b) repairs specific types of data corruption. Table 1 lists popular tests for detecting and repairing corruption that occur in different system layers Tests have the following characteristics:

- Tests perform more sophisticated detection and repair of corruption than is possible automatically during regular system operation through mechanisms like checksums and RAID [25].
- Barring few exceptions, tests have been developed to be run offline when the system is not serving a workload. If a workload

*Supported by NSF grants 0964560 and 0917062

Test	System	Description	Does Repair	Runs Online
		Application Level		
Eseutil, Isinteg	Exchange Server	Uses checksums and structure rules (knowledge of logical schema and physical properties) to check the mailbox database for errors in messages, folders, or attachments; checks whether all data pages are correct and match their checksums [9]	Yes	No
Tripwire	Any file	Creates a database with the hash and attributes of the content of all files in the system. Checks for mismatch between the current state of the files and the information stored in the database [26]	No	No
par, par2	Any file	Uses an error correcting code to create parity data. Checks whether the given file's content matches its stored parity data [20]	Yes	No
		Database Level		
myisamchk	MySQL	Uses checksums and structure rules (flags, table metadata) to check whether data pages and records are correct and indexes point to correct records. This suite contains 5 distinct tests that do increasingly rigorous and time-consuming checks [16, 25]	Yes	No
DBVerify	Oracle	Uses checksums and structure rules (head & tail info) to check the database content and data pages. Can check backups [19]	No	No
db2dart	DB2	Uses checksums and structure rules (page headers, properties of records) to check the database, data pages, and records [7]	Yes	No
Checkdb, Checktable	SQL Server	Uses structure rules (page headers, properties of indexes) to check whether data pages are stored correctly and index entries point to the correct records [24]	Yes	No
		File-System Level		
xfs_check, xfs_repair	XFS	Uses the file-system's journal (log of operations done) and verifies the integrity of the inode hierarchy and that the content of the inodes is in sync with the stored file-system data. Checks superblock, free-space, and inode maps [28]	Yes	No
fsck	ext3, ext4	Uses the journal (in ext4) and file structures (in ext3) to check the superblock, file pathnames, data block connectivity, and the file and inode reference counts [10]	Yes	No
ScanDisk, Chkdsk	FAT*, NTFS	Uses file structures to check the disk headers, file content, file attributes, lost disk space, and file crosslinks [5]	Yes	No
zpool scrub	ZFS	Uses built-in block checksums and block replication mechanisms in the ZFS file-system to check file content for errors [29, 30]	Yes	Yes
		Storage Level		
Scrubbing	Disks	Uses checksums stored at the level of disk media blocks to verify that each block's content matches its checksum [23]	No	No
Scrubbing	RAID	Uses stored parity information or replicas at the RAID level (instead of per disk) to verify the content of each data block [14]	Yes	Yes

Table 1: Data integrity tests to detect and possibly repair data corruption at different levels of the database software stack

	Description of Example Objectives in English
1	If the *myisamchk* test detects corruption in the *lineitem* table in my MySQL OLTP DBMS, then I want to have immediate access to an older corruption-free version of the table that is less than 1 hour old.
2	(A security vulnerability patch was applied in the ext4 file-system that my production DBMS is using. I am afraid that the patch may inadvertently cause data corruption.) Run the *fsck* file-system test at least once every hour. Notify me immediately of any corruption detected.
3	My production DBMS runs on an Amazon EC2 m1.large host. I have the same objectives as in 1, but I am willing to spend up to 12 dollars per day for additional resources on the Amazon cloud to meet these objectives. How recent of a corruption-free version of the data can I have immediate access to if a corruption were to be detected?
4	My objectives are a combination of 1 and 2, but I want the time intervals to be 30 minutes instead of 60. I am cost conscious. What minimum number of m1.small EC2 hosts should I rent to run tests?

Table 2: Examples of objectives that an administrator may have regarding timely detection and repair of data corruption

changes the data concurrently with a test execution, the test may detect (and worse, fix) spurious corruptions. The workload could also return incorrect results because of modifications made by the test. As one example, it is recommended that the file-system be unmounted while running the *fsck* test.

- Most of the tests are very resource-intensive.

Because of the above characteristics of tests, database and storage administrators often struggle with questions on when and where to run tests. If the administrator is not proactive in running tests, then, when corruption strikes eventually, high system downtime and data loss (and possibly, loss of the administrator's job) will result.

Administrators usually have specific objectives in mind for proactive detection and repair of data corruption. Table 2 gives examples of such objectives. To our knowledge, no system today helps administrators specify objectives like these easily, and automates the nontrivial task of running tests to meet these objectives. The result is usually a convoluted mix of ad hoc scripts and testing practices with nobody having a clear idea of the downtime and data loss a potential corruption can cause.

1.1 Amulet: Challenges and Overview

A typical *database software stack* that production systems use is shown in Figure 1. Different levels of the software stack maintain different sources of data. All these data sources have to be kept corruption-free to guarantee correct behavior, good performance, and availability of applications running on the software stack.

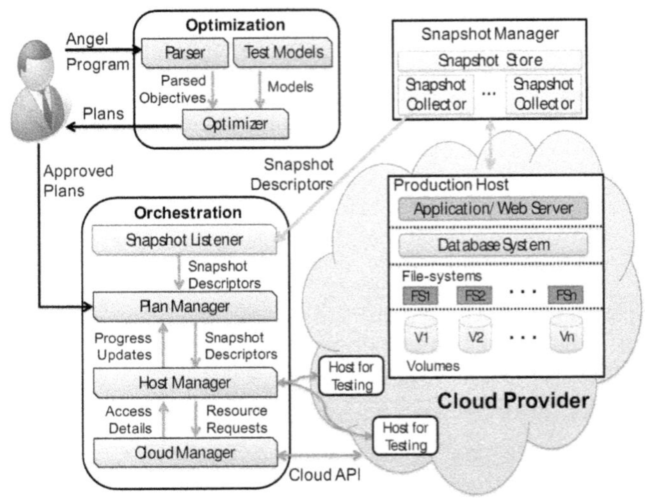

Figure 1: Overview of Amulet's optimization and orchestration

The database level has data in tables as well as plenty of metadata such as indexes, materialized views, and information in the database catalog. Databases store their data and metadata as files and directories in a file-system or directly as blocks on *volumes*. The file-system level has files containing data stored by the database level, as well as metadata such as the directory structure, *inodes* (indexes storing file-to-block mappings) and *journals* (log of operations done). A file-system, in turn, stores its own data and metadata on a volume. A volume provides an interface to read and write blocks of data. Beneath this interface, the volume may be a physical block device (e.g., a hard disk or solid state drive) or a logical entity (e.g., representing storage on a networked server or a combination of partitions from multiple hard disks).

Proactive Testing for Data Corruption: Tests are run to verify the correctness of data. Table 1 lists commonly-used tests at each level of the database software stack. For example, MySQL's *myisamchk* suite contains five different tests invoked through distinct invoca-

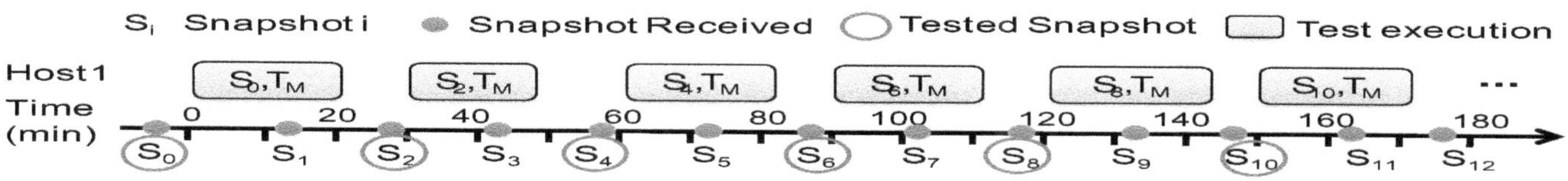

Figure 2: Actual execution timeline, in minutes, of a testing plan in Amulet for Example 1 from Table 2. Each box denotes a run of the myisamchk (T_M) test on the respective snapshot S_i. The horizontal width of each box corresponds to the test execution time.

tion options: fast, check-only-changed, check (default), medium-check, and extended-check. These tests apply checks of increasing sophistication and thoroughness to verify the correctness of tables and indexes in the database. The checks include verifying page-level and record-level checksums as well as verifying that each index entry points to a valid record in the corresponding table, and vice versa. The fsck and xfs_check tests verify the correctness of metadata and data in the ext3 and XFS file-systems respectively. For example, they ensure consistency between the file-system journal and the data blocks, and verify that all the data block pointers in the inodes are correct.

The first challenge that Amulet faces is how to run a test automatically. Most of the tests in Table 1 cannot be run concurrently with the regular workload on the production system because of performance and correctness problems. The tests can consume significant CPU or I/O resources. The tests may also have to lock large amounts of data, making response times for the production workload slow and unpredictable. Amulet addresses these problems using the following three-step approach to run tests automatically:

1. *Create snapshot:* A *snapshot* is a persistent copy of a point-in-time version of the data needed for a test. Snapshots can be taken at the database, file-system, or volume levels. In this paper, we focus on volume-level snapshots because they capture the data needed for any test in the software stack. While the time to create the first snapshot will depend on the volume size, later snapshots only need to copy the changes since the last snapshot (similar to incremental backups).[1]
2. *Run tests:* A snapshot is loaded on to one or more *testing hosts* where tests are run. As shown in Figure 1, testing hosts are different from the production host to avoid performance problems.
3. *Apply changes:* If tests detect and repair corruption in a snapshot, then the administrator can choose to apply these changes or load the repaired snapshot on the production system.

Amulet's Declarative Language: Making it easy and intuitive for administrators to declare objectives like those in Table 2 poses a nontrivial language design problem. A dissection of the examples in Table 2 reveals the important features that are needed:

- Specification of one or more tests t, and associating t with the data and type of resources on which it should be run.
- Specification of *tested recovery points* to be maintained over a recent window of time. These points enable quick system recovery in case serious corruption is detected.
- Ability to declare different objectives such as the minimum number of test runs per time window or a cost budget for provisioning pay-as-you-go resources to run tests.
- Ability to combine multiple objectives as well as to specify an optimization objective.

Angel, Amulet's declarative language, is designed to support such features. The semantics and simplified syntax of Angel are described in Section 4 and Table 4.

Amulet's Optimization Phase: Amulet can run a comprehensive suite of tests, including new user-defined ones, to detect and possibly repair data corruption anywhere in the software stack. To use Amulet, as shown in Figure 1, a user or application submits a declarative Angel program that references one or more volumes on the production system. For each volume V, the program specifies: (a) the tests to be run on data contained in V, and (b) the objectives to be met. For volume V, Amulet's *Optimizer* will generate an efficient execution strategy—called a *testing plan*—using an optimization algorithm that maximizes or minimizes one objective subject to satisfying all other objectives. Amulet's *Orchestrator* will execute the testing plan automatically and continuously by provisioning testing hosts and scheduling tests on a resource provider.

Figure 2 shows an actual execution timeline of a testing plan P for an Angel program corresponding to Example 1 from Table 2. Plan P uses one testing host that runs the myisamchk test on snapshots taken from the production host. One snapshot is tested every 30 minutes, and each test takes around 20 minutes to complete. As we will see in Section 7, this plan minimizes execution cost while meeting the objective of continuously maintaining a tested recovery point for a past 1-hour window. This testing plan, while simple, illustrates a number of challenges facing Amulet.

Characterizing the testing plan space: A testing plan has multiple aspects. First, there is a provisioning aspect that determines how many testing hosts are used to meet the specified objectives. Second, there is a scheduling aspect that determines the rate at which snapshots are tested and how test runs are scheduled on the provisioned hosts. Third, there is a sustainability aspect that determines whether the plan will continuously meet the specified objectives as time progresses. Section 5 gives a formal characterization of a testing plan in Amulet, thereby defining the space of testing plans.

Developing a cost model for tests: To find whether a plan enumerated from the testing plan space will meet the objectives specified in an Angel program, the Optimizer needs models to estimate the execution times of tests scheduled by the plan. A novel component of Amulet is a library of models to estimate test execution times. The library currently covers tests for the MySQL database and the ext3 and XFS file-systems; discussed further in Section 3.

Finding a good testing plan: For each volume referenced in an Angel program, the Optimizer has to find a good plan from a huge plan space. We propose a novel algorithm for this optimization problem that considers all three aspects of testing plans: provisioning testing hosts, scheduling tests on snapshots and hosts, and ensuring plan sustainability over time. While our algorithm is not guaranteed to find the optimal plan, we show empirically—based on comparisons with an exhaustive search algorithm—that our algorithm is very efficient and finds the optimal plan most of the time.

Amulet's Orchestration Phase: After submitting an Angel program, the administrator can view the testing plans generated, and when satisfied, submit the plans to Amulet's Orchestrator for execution. The Orchestrator executes testing plans continuously by working in conjunction with a Snapshot Manager and a resource provider, both of which are external to Amulet. The Snapshot Manager notifies the Orchestrator when a new snapshot of a volume on the production system is available for testing. The Orchestrator allocates testing hosts from the resource provider which, cur-

[1]Production deployments that need near-real-time disaster recovery take snapshots regularly and store them on cloud storage [27].

rently, can be any infrastructure-as-a-service cloud provider. A major challenge faced by the Orchestrator is in dealing with unpredictable events arising during plan execution:

- *Repairs:* It is impossible to predict when a corruption will be detected and a repair action needs to be taken.
- *Straggler hosts:* A host used to run tests on the cloud may become slow temporarily, causing the test execution schedule to lag behind the optimizer-planned schedule.
- *Wrong estimates:* Lags in the testing schedule can also be caused by inaccurate estimates of test execution times from the models.

Rather than complicating the Optimizer or making unrealistic assumptions, Amulet's solution is to reserve a cost budget in each testing plan that the Orchestrator can use to provision additional hosts on demand to deal with unpredictable events; discussed in Section 6. The novel effect is that a testing plan has a statically-planned component generated by the Optimizer as well as an adaptive component managed by the Orchestrator. Section 7 will present comprehensive experimental results from a prototype of Amulet running on the Amazon cloud.

2. RELATED WORK

A number of recent empirical studies show that corruption of critical data is a reality and occurs much more commonly than assumed previously. It is perhaps surprising that the database research community has paid little attention to this problem.

2.1 The Dangers of Data Corruption

The authors of [3] analyzed corruption instances recorded in more than 10,000 production and development storage systems. Their main focus was on studying *silent data corruption* which is corruption undetected by the disk drive or by any other hardware component. Among corruption instances logged over a 41-month period among a total of 1.53 million disk drives of various types, the authors found more than 400,000 instances of checksum mismatches. The study also showed that cheaper nearline SATA disks (and their adapters) develop checksum mismatches an order of magnitude more often than the more expensive and carefully-engineered SCSI disks. However, corruption can also occur in the latter which are enterprise-class drives.

The authors of [22] analyzed memory errors collected over a period of 2.5 years in the majority of servers used by Google. The authors found that the rate of data corruption in DRAM is orders of magnitude higher than previously reported, with more than 8% of dual in-line memory modules (DIMMs) affected by errors per year. Memory errors can be classified into soft errors, that corrupt bits randomly but do not leave physical damage; and hard errors, that corrupt bits in a repeatable manner because of a physical defect. Memory errors found in the study were dominated by hard errors, rather than soft errors as assumed previously.

Injecting faults into the database software stack provide insights into system behavior and data loss under different types of corruption. A recent study used fault injections into a popular open-source DBMS (MySQL) to show that certain types of data corruption can harm the system, e.g., causing system crashes, data loss, and incorrect results [25]. The authors also point out that concurrency control and recovery features of database systems are not designed to detect or repair corrupted data or metadata resulting from hardware, software, or human errors. A similar study has been done for the ZFS file-system that, compared to popular Linux file-systems like ext3 and XFS, has novel features like *end-to-end checksums* for corruption detection [30]. The authors show that while ZFS is very resilient to disk-level corruption, memory-level corruption can lead to crashes and incorrect results.

2.2 Dealing with Data Corruption

The techniques categorized as the first line of defense in Section 1 check for data correctness during reads and writes in the production workload; usually based on additional stored information like parity bits and checksums. These techniques are not sufficient to prevent or detect corruption caused by complex issues such as lost and misdirected writes due to bugs in the software stack [3]. For example, the authors of [14] show the inability of techniques like parity-based RAID to avoid data corruption. The authors also show how common techniques used in RAID can spread data corruption across multiple disks and cause data loss. The first line of defense adds performance overheads during workload execution. Enterprise systems have historically preferred performance over the (wrongly assumed) rare chance of data corruption. Amulet addresses these problems by enabling complex and resource-intensive tests like those in Table 1 to be run in a timely fashion. To our knowledge, Amulet is the first system of its kind that works across different point-in-time copies of data to detect and repair data corruption efficiently in the end-to-end software stack.

Modeling the performance of tests or improving their efficiency has received little attention. For example, most tests still use single-threaded execution and cannot exploit multicore CPUs. Currently, every test t is an opaque execution script to Amulet apart from the model used to estimate t's execution time. With more visibility into tests, Amulet can do a better job of optimizing t's execution. A promising development in this regard is the writing of tests in declarative languages like SQL as done in [12].

Amulet's goal of early detection and repair of data corruption forms a crucial part of disaster recovery planning. The authors of [27] argue that cloud computing platforms are well suited for offering disaster recovery as a service due to (a) the cloud's pay-as-you-go pricing model that can lower costs, and (b) the cloud's use of elastic virtual platforms. Amulet is a proof-of-concept system for this argument applied to the problem of data corruption.

The concept of declarative system management is gaining currency. Chef, Puppet, and Microsoft SQL Server's policy-driven manager are now popular tools that take declarative specifications as input, and then configure and maintain systems automatically [13]. However, unlike Amulet, these tools do not support objectives that are specified declaratively and optimized automatically.

3. MODELING OF TESTS

For each test t, Amulet's Optimizer needs a model to estimate t's run-time behavior—e.g., execution time, usage of CPU, memory, and I/O resources—when t is run on given data and system resources. We divide the input parameters for a test model into three categories: (i) data-dependent attributes, (ii) resource-dependent attributes, and (iii) attributes to capture transient effects. In this section, we discuss attributes in the test model and their impact for the myisamchk, fsck, and xfs_check tests from Table 1. Our focus is on models for estimating test execution time. Note that we generate separate models for the same test when invoked with significantly different options. For example, fsck has separate models based on whether it is invoked to check file-system metadata compared to data. The fsck metadata test involves verifying the superblock, inodes, and free block list, while the data test does a full scan to find all bad blocks.

3.1 Data-dependent Attributes

Data-dependent attributes have a first-order impact on test execution times. Fortunately, this impact can be captured fully based on properties that correspond to the size of the data and are easily measurable. Different data-dependent attributes are relevant depending

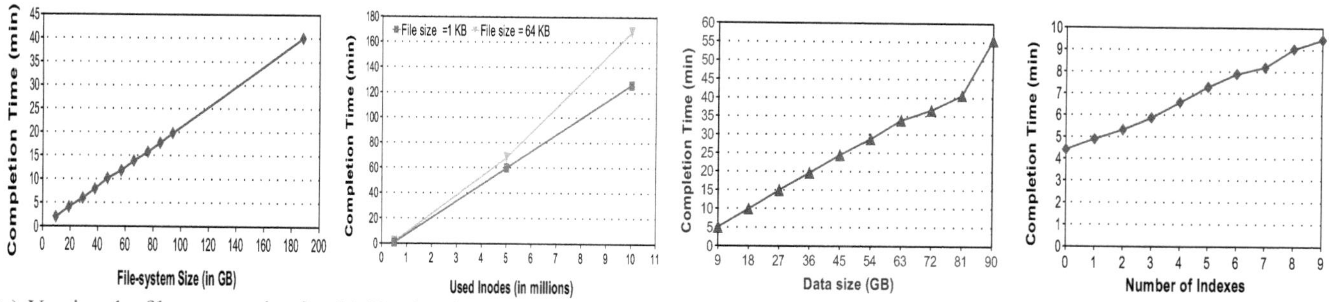

(a) Varying the file-system size for fsck test on ext3 (b) Varying the number of used inodes for xfs_check on XFS (c) Varying the input data size for myisamchk medium test (d) Varying number of indexes for myisamchk medium test

Figure 3: Effect of data-dependent attributes on the completion time of the fsck, xfs_check, and myisamchk tests

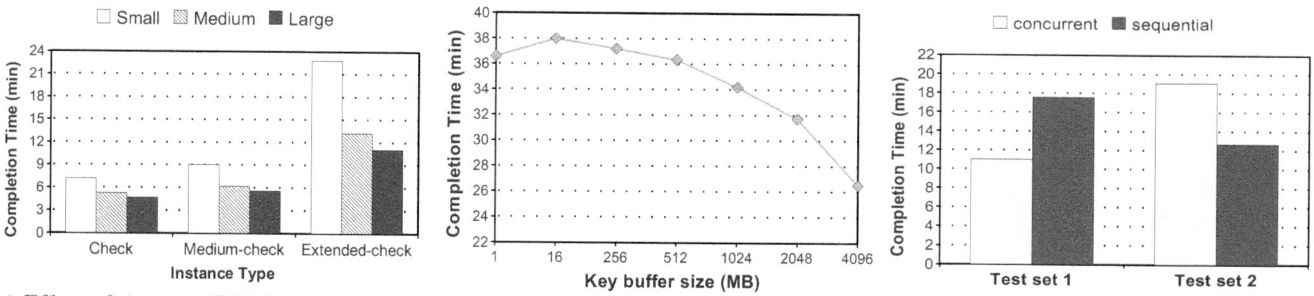

(a) Effect of Amazon EC2 instance type on myisamchk tests for a 14GB database (b) Effect of MySQL's key_buffer_size parameter for myisamchk extended test (c) Concurrent vs sequential execution of myisamchk tests w/ diff. invocation options

Figure 4: Effect of resource-dependent attributes and concurrent test execution on the execution time of myisamchk tests

on whether the test is at the application, database, file-system, or storage levels. For fsck and xfs_check, we explored a wide range of attributes to capture the file-system data: size of the file-system, total number of inodes, number of used inodes, average file size, files per directory, and size of inodes and data blocks. Based on a comprehensive empirical analysis, we found that there are three attributes with the most impact: total inodes, used inodes, and average file size. Total inodes represents the total available capacity of the file-system, while used inodes are indicative of the used space.

The block check version of fsck on the ext3 file-system verifies the correctness of the used portion of the file-system as well as that of the unused inodes and free blocks. Thus, as shown in Figure 3(a), the execution time of the fsck data test depends on the file-system size. In contrast, the optimized xfs_check test for the XFS file-system verifies only the used portion of the file-system. Thus, the execution time of xfs_check depends on the number of used inodes as shown in Figure 3(b), and is independent of the total file-system size.

For the myisamchk tests, the total input data size to the test is the primary data-dependent attribute. Figure 3(c) shows the linear effect of the input data size on test execution time. In addition to the data size, the number of indexes present on table columns affects the execution time of certain myisamchk tests. Once again, the effect is linear as shown in Figure 3(d).

3.2 Resource-dependent Attributes

The execution time of a test is expected to vary with the hardware and software resources allocated to run the test. The trend among infrastructure-as-a-service cloud providers is to provide hardware resources such as CPU, memory, and storage in terms of a small number of discrete choices. For example, the hardware resource space is discretized into micro, small, medium, and large node configurations on the Amazon cloud. Such discretization vastly simplifies Amulet's task of modeling test execution times for varying resource properties.

Figure 4(a) shows the execution times of myisamchk tests for different Amazon EC2 host types for a total database size of 14 GB. We observe a 100% speedup for the myisamchk extended test between a small host (1.7 GB memory with 1 EC2 compute unit) and a large host (7.5 GB memory with 4 EC2 compute units). In general, we observed that the more thorough myisamchk tests are both compute- and memory-intensive. Execution times of fsck did not vary significantly across the different Amazon EC2 host types. fsck is I/O-intensive and does not exploit the increased CPU or memory resources when going from the small to the large hosts.

Software-level resources like caches can also impact test execution times. For example, the myisamchk tests use a cache called the *key buffer*. The size of this cache, given by the key_buffer_size input parameter, affects the execution time of certain myisamchk tests. Figure 4(b) shows the variation in the execution time of the myisamchk extended test for input data of size 12 GB.

3.3 Transient Effects

Test execution times can vary due to transient effects like warm versus cold caches or resource contention when tests are run concurrently. A major advantage Amulet enjoys in this context is that Amulet's Orchestrator can ensure that tests are run in configurations similar to the ones used during test modeling. Furthermore, as we discuss next, Amulet's Optimizer prioritizes predictable behavior (i.e., *robust testing plans*) over potential optimality since the former is more important in proactive testing.

Warm Vs. cold caches: Data caching for the memory/disk interface within a host does not benefit tests such as fsck and xfs_check that access data directly at the block level. However, as mentioned before, such caching benefits higher-level tests such as myisamchk. Data caching at the host/network interface while using networked storage benefits most tests. We have observed up to 2x differences in test execution times for warm Vs. cold caches in this context. The test models have been enhanced to account for these effects.

Name	Description
O_1-O_n	SSO, RPO, SIO, TCO, or CO objectives specified per volume in an Angel program (Table 4 gives a summary)
O_{opt}	Optimization objective for a volume in an Angel program
t, s, h, τ, x, and d	Used to denote respectively tests, volume snapshots, hosts, time intervals, numeric constants, and currency values
τ_{rpo}	The time interval in an RPO (see Table 4)
d_{co}	The maximum cost budget in a CO (see Table 4)
P	Testing plan for a volume in an Angel program
P_W	Plan P's window. The plan repeats every P_W time units
P_I	Time interval between successive snapshots in plan P
P_M	Test-to-snapshot mapping in plan P
P_S	Schedule of test execution in plan P
P_R	P's cost budget reserved to handle unpredictable events
$ExecTime(t)$	Execution time of test t
$Time(s_i)$	Time when i^{th} snapshot s_i, $1 \leq i \leq \frac{P_W}{P_I}$, is available in plan P relative to the start of the plan window P_W
$start(h)$	Time when host h is first used in the plan window
$end(h)$	Time when host h will finish its last scheduled test for the plan window ($end(h)$ can be $> P_W$)
$cost(P_S)$, $cost(h)$	Cost incurred for the plan schedule P_S or a host h for one plan window

Table 3: Notation used in the paper

Concurrent execution of tests on the same host: Concurrent execution makes test execution times difficult to estimate. Figure 4(c) illustrates this complexity. Test sets 1 and 2 are runs of two myisamchk tests on two different tables. The tests in each set lead to different outcomes when run in concurrent versus sequential fashion. The tests in set 2 cause memory thrashing when run concurrently. Since the number of distinct tests is not large,[2] we can train models to estimate execution times for tests run concurrently in pairs. As such, if Amulet's Optimizer does not have a model to estimate the running time of concurrent tests, it will simply choose not to consider testing plans with concurrent tests. The goal of the Optimizer is to find a robust testing plan, where a robust plan is one whose performance is almost never much worse than promised.

4. ANGEL DECLARATIVE LANGUAGE

Recall from Section 1.1 that an Angel program specifies tests and the objectives to be met while running the tests. We now discuss the main statements in Angel. Table 4 provides a summary.

Tests: Angel's `Test` statement defines a test t by specifying the command to run t as well as references to t's input data (specified by a `Data` statement) and the type of host on which to run t (specified by a `Host` statement). Angel's `Repair` statement enables a repair action to be associated with a test t for invocation if t detects a corruption (as indicated by a specific return code from t).

Data: Angel's `Data` and related statements define the input data for a test, including the volume that the data belongs to, the data type (from a set of supported types), and the data properties. The properties, which are specific to the type of data, form inputs to the models that the Optimizer uses to estimate test execution times. The Optimizer does semantic checks to ensure that the Angel program specifies values for all input parameters required by the model for each test in the program. While helper tools are available to extract these values from the corresponding input data, the administrator can also specify values based on their domain knowledge.

Hosts: The primary use of Angel's `Host` statement is to define a host type (from a set of supported types) for a test t so that the Orchestrator will always run t on testing hosts of that type.

[2]From our experience, most administrators prefer to use standard tests that come with each system, rather than writing new tests.

Name	Simplified Specification Syntax
Test	`Test(Data:` *data*, `Host:` *host*, exec scripts, ...)
Input data for test	`Data(Volume:` V, type, properties, ...)
Host to run test	`Host`(type, setup scripts, ...)
Volume	`Volume(Host:` production host where V is located, path on host, volume id, properties, ...)
Repair action	`Repair(Test:` t, t's return code, exec scripts, ...)
SSO: Safe Snapshot Objective	List of tests $\{t_1, t_2, \ldots, t_k\}$, for volume V
RPO: Recovery Point Objective	`Recovery_point` $\leq \tau$, for volume V
SIO: Snapshot Interval Objective	`Snapshot_interval` *Op* τ, for volume V
TCO: Test Count Objective	`Test_count`(t) *Op* x, in time interval τ, for volume V
CO: Cost Objective	`Cost` $\leq d$, in time interval τ, with reservation $x\%$, for volume V
O_{opt}: Optimization Objective	`Maximize` (when *Op* is $\geq$ in an SIO or TCO), `Minimize` (when *Op* is $\leq$ in an RPO, SIO, or CO)
Notification	SQL triggers on event tables in log database

Table 4: Summary of important Angel statements. ***Op*** $\in \{\leq, \geq\}$**.** t**,** τ**,** x**, and** d **are constants of respective types test, time interval, numeric, and currency**

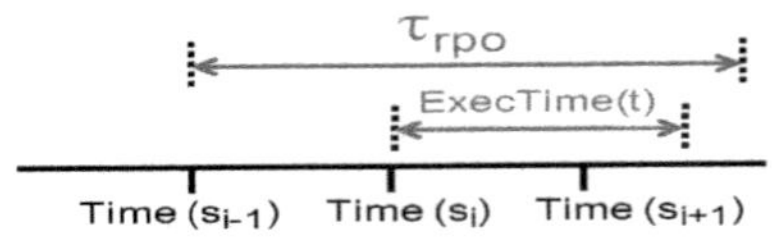

Figure 5: Illustration of RPO

4.1 Objectives

An Angel program can specify one of five types of objectives. These objectives can be used independently or combined together to specify a variety of requirements for running tests. Each objective O references a unique volume. The Optimizer will partition the objectives in an Angel program based on the volumes referenced, and generate one testing plan per volume.

Safe Snapshot Objective (SSO): An SSO for a volume V specifies the full list of tests $t_1, \ldots, t_k$ to be run on a given snapshot s for V before s can be labeled *corruption-free*. If none of the tests $t_1, \ldots, t_k$ find corruption in s, then s is labeled corruption-free. If a test t_i detects a corruption in s, then s is labeled *corrupted* and any repair action associated with t_i will be run on s.

Recovery Point Objective (RPO): When corruption is detected in the data in a volume V, it is useful to have immediate access to a tested recovery point for V from the recent past. A recovery point is a corruption-free snapshot of V from which the database software stack can be brought back online quickly. Recovery points are an essential part of disaster recovery planning strategies [27].

Figure 5 shows two successive snapshots s_{i-1} and s_i for a volume on which a test t is run. If a corruption were to be detected when t runs on s_i, then the administrator wants s_{i-1} to be a recovery point. An RPO expresses this requirement. RPO specifies the maximum (sliding) time interval τ_{rpo} into the past within which a recovery point must exist for a volume if corruption were to be detected on a snapshot. Amulet should ensure that the sum of test t's expected running time and the snapshot interval between s_{i-1} and s_i is not greater than τ_{rpo} (as illustrated in Figure 5). Using notation from Table 3, the RPO mandates:

$$ExecTime(t) + Time(s_i) - Time(s_{i-1}) \leq \tau_{rpo} \quad (1)$$

An RPO together with an SSO with a list of tests $t_1, \ldots, t_k$ is a powerful combination to express recovery points. Now Amulet should ensure that all of $t_1, \ldots, t_k$ will finish on s_i in time $\leq \tau_{rpo}$

Find the Least-Cost Plan P=$\langle P_W$,P_I,P_M,P_S,$P_R\rangle$ that Satisfies the n Objectives O_1-O_n (without O_{opt}) for a Volume V in an Angel Program
1. Use Fig. 7 to pick the snapshot interval P_I for O_1-O_n;
2. Select the plan window P_W, and scale O_1-O_n to P_W (Section 5.3);
3. Use Fig. 8 to pick the test-to-snapshot mapping P_M for O_1-O_n,P_W,P_I;
4. Pick test execution schedule P_S for P_W,P_I,P_M (details given in [4]);
5. P_R is available from the CO in O_1-O_n, or a default is used;

Figure 6: Finding the least-cost plan for given objectives O_1-O_n

$-$ ($Time(s_i)$ $-$ $Time(s_{i-1})$). If any of these tests were to detect a corruption in s_i, then s_{i-1} will serve as a recovery point that is not more than τ_{rpo} into the past. At this point, the administrator or the Snapshot Manager can decide how to proceed regarding the production system: restart the system with snapshot s_{i-1}, ignore the corruption for now, etc. Amulet does not interfere here.

Snapshot Interval Objective (SIO): For a volume V, an SIO has the form: `Snapshot_interval` *Op* τ, for time interval τ and *Op* in $\{\geq, \leq\}$. `Snapshot_interval` refers to the expected time interval between two successive snapshots of V. Note that Amulet does not control the Snapshot Manager which collects snapshots from the production system. SIOs express the feasible snapshot intervals that Amulet should consider during plan selection.

Test Count Objective (TCO): For a volume V, a TCO has the form: `Test_count(`t`)` *Op* x, in a time interval τ for a test t. Here, `Test_count` specifies the number of unique snapshots of V in the interval τ on which Amulet should run test t. The typical use of TCOs are to express requirements of the form: "Run t at least four times every day." A plan chosen by the Optimizer for this TCO will do the intuitive thing of spacing out the four test runs uniformly in the specified time interval of 1 day.

Cost Objective (CO): A CO for a volume V has the form: `Cost` $\leq d$, in a time interval τ, with (optional) reservation x. Here, d is a cost measure for the resource provider from which the Orchestrator will allocate resources to run tests. The CO applies to the entire testing plan that the Optimizer generates for V. A CO can be specified only if the *pricing model* that the resource provider uses to charge for resource usage is input to Amulet. Section 7 describes the pricing model that we use in our evaluation.

The CO also specifies a fraction of the overall cost budget that is reserved for the Orchestrator to respond to three types of unpredictable events that can occur during the execution of the testing plan: repairs, straggler hosts, and inaccurate estimates of test execution times by the models used in the Optimizer. Section 6 will discuss how the Orchestrator uses the reserved cost budget to provision hosts on demand to handle these unpredictable events. By default, the reservation is set to the cost of using one testing host.

Optimization Objective (O_{opt}): An appropriate `Maximize` or `Minimize` optimization objective (O_{opt}) can be specified along with an RPO, SIO, TCO, or CO for a volume V in an Angel program. `Maximize` can be used when *Op* in the objective is $\geq$, and `Minimize` can be used when *Op* is $\leq$. Specifically, applying `Maximize` to an SIO or TCO of the form `value` $\geq$ *const* asks to make *const* as high as possible. Applying `Minimize` to an RPO, SIO, or CO of the form `value` $\leq$ *const* asks to make *const* as low as possible. One and only one O_{opt} is allowed per volume. The default is `Minimize` CO if no O_{opt} is specified in the program.

5. OPTIMIZER

In this section, we will discuss the algorithm used by Amulet's Optimizer. Given an Angel program, the Optimizer first partitions the objectives in the program based on the volumes referenced, and then selects one testing plan per volume. The selection of the testing plan is treated as the following optimization problem:

Testing-plan Selection Problem for Volume V: *Given n objectives O_1-O_n (each of type SSO, RPO, SIO, TCO, or CO) and an optimization objective O_{opt} (of type* `Maximize` *or* `Minimize` *on one of O_1-O_n) for a volume V, find the testing plan (if any) that meets all of O_1-O_n while giving the best (maximum or minimum, as appropriate) value for O_{opt}.*

5.1 Testing Plans in Amulet for a Volume V

Formally, a testing plan P contains five components:

1. *Snapshot interval* P_I is the uniformly-spaced minimum time interval between consecutive snapshots that the plan needs to test to meet all the objectives specified.
2. *Window* P_W is a time interval such that the plan repeats every P_W time units. The plan processes $\frac{P_W}{P_I}$ snapshots per window.
3. *Test-to-snapshot mapping* P_M specifies, for each snapshot s in the plan window, the set of tests that need to be run on s.
4. *Test execution schedule* P_S specifies the number and respective types of testing hosts to use, and when to run each test from P_M on these hosts.
5. *Reserved cost budget* P_R is the part of the plan's total cost budget that is reserved for the Orchestrator to deal with unpredictable events that can arise during plan execution.

The core of Amulet's Optimizer is a *cost-optimal* planning algorithm that can find the minimum-cost plan (if valid plans exist) to meet a given set of objectives. We will begin in Sections 5.3–5.5 by describing the stages in which the cost-optimal planning algorithm works. As illustrated in Figure 6, each stage selects one of the five components of the minimum-cost plan, going in the order P_I, P_W, P_M, P_S, and P_R. Section 6 will describe how the Orchestrator uses the reserved cost budget P_R.

If the Angel program's optimization objective is not cost minimization, then Amulet uses a higher-level planning algorithm. This algorithm, discussed in Section 5.6, repeatedly invokes the cost-optimal planning algorithm with a series of increasingly stricter objectives until no valid plan can be found. The optimal plan can be identified at that point.

5.2 Selecting the Snapshot Interval

The Optimizer's goal in this stage is to pick the maximum value that P_I can have while meeting all the RPO, SIO, and TCO objectives specified. Maximizing P_I translates into minimizing the number of snapshots that need to be processed. Consequently, the cost of the plan is minimized—which is our goal—since more snapshots mean higher test execution and host requirements.

Figure 7 shows the steps involved in this stage. The algorithm goes through the objectives one by one, while maintaining an upper (P_I^{max}) and lower (P_I^{min}) bound on feasible values of P_I. Finally, the largest feasible value of P_I, if any, is selected.

5.3 Selecting the Plan Window

Recall from Section 4 and Table 4 that the objectives RPO, TCO, and CO for a volume V in an Angel program specify time intervals. The plan window P_W serves as a mechanism for the Optimizer to consider the intervals in all objectives in a uniform fashion. P_W is picked as the least multiple of P_I ($P_W = n \times P_I$, $n \in \mathbb{N}$) such that P_W is greater than or equal to the maximum among: (a) the time intervals in RPO, TCO, and CO objectives, and (b) *ExecTime*(t) for each test t specified in an SSO or TCO objective. Picking $P_W >$ *ExecTime*(t) for all tests (i.e., Case (b) above) is needed to ensure the *sustainability* of schedules as we will explain in Section 5.5.

Once P_W has been determined, the corresponding parameters in

Selecting the Plan Snapshot Interval P_I in a Testing Plan

Inputs: Objectives O_1-O_n (with syntax from Table 4)

P_I^{min} = Snapshot interval from the Snapshot Manager;
$P_I^{max} = \infty$; $\tau_{rpo} = \infty$;
if ($O_1, \ldots, O_n$ contains RPO: `Recovery_point` $\leq \tau$) {
  $\tau_{rpo}=\tau$; $P_I^{max} = \frac{\tau_{rpo}}{2}$; /* test $\geq$2 snapshots in τ_{rpo} to meet RPO */}
for (every Objective O in $O_1, \ldots, O_n$) {
  if (O is SSO: List of tests $\{t_1, \ldots, t_k\}$) {
    for (Test t in $t_1, \ldots, t_k$)
      P_I^{max} = Min[P_I^{max}, τ_{rpo} - *ExecTime*(t)]; } /* Equation 1 */
  if (O is TCO: `Test_count`$(t) \geq x$, in time interval τ)
    P_I^{max} = Min[P_I^{max}, τ_{rpo} - *ExecTime*(t), $\frac{\tau}{x}$]; /* Equation 1 */
  if (O is SIO: `Snapshot_interval` $\geq \tau$)
    P_I^{min} = Max[P_I^{min}, τ];
  if (O is SIO: `Snapshot_interval` $\leq \tau$)
    P_I^{max} = Min[P_I^{max}, τ];
}
if ($P_I^{max} < P_I^{min}$) return "No feasible P_I exists for O_1-O_n";
else set $P_I = P_I^{max}$;

Figure 7: Selection of P_I (notation used from Tables 3 and 4)

all TCO and CO objectives are scaled proportionately to P_W. For example, a CO that specifies a cost budget (d_{co}) of U.S. \$10 in 1 hour, will be scaled to a cost budget of U.S. \$15 for $P_W = 1.5$ hours. Note that the time interval in an RPO (τ_{rpo}) is independent of P_W, and should not be scaled.

5.4 Selecting the Test-to-Snapshot Mapping

For the $\frac{P_W}{P_I}$ snapshots in a plan window, this stage decides which tests need to be run on which snapshots. Figure 8 shows the steps involved. For each test t specified in an SSO or TCO, the algorithm in Figure 8 maintains upper ($COUNT_t^{max}$) and lower ($COUNT_t^{min}$) bounds on how many snapshots t should be run on. Test t is mapped at uniformly-spaced intervals to the minimum number of snapshots that t needs to be run on. Note that the tests in an SSO should be run on all $\frac{P_W}{P_I}$ snapshots (Lines 4-6 in Figure 8).

5.5 Selecting the Schedule of Test Execution

After the test-to-snapshot mapping P_M has been generated, the Optimizer selects the test execution schedule as well as the minimum number of hosts needed for running these tests. This stage is by far the most complex one in the Optimizer. Note that the Optimizer is only identifying a good schedule. The schedule will be executed—including actual allocation of testing hosts and running of the tests on the resource provider—only after the selected testing plan is submitted to the Orchestrator.

The complete details of the algorithm used in this stage are given in the online technical report [4]. This greedy algorithm goes through the snapshots s_i in one plan window in order from i=1 to i=$\frac{P_W}{P_I}$, as well as the tests t_{ij} that have been mapped to s_i. A host h_k is identified to run t_{ij} on s_i in one of three ways as discussed next.

The first way is by means of *test grouping*, where t_{ij} will be run concurrently with another test or group of tests on a host that has already been allocated to the plan. Recall that Amulet strives to generate a robust testing plan, i.e., a plan whose chances of performing worse than estimated is low [2]. If there is no model to estimate how the concurrent execution of a set of tests will perform, then the Optimizer will take the low-risk route of avoiding such executions.

While selecting the test execution schedule, the algorithm also addresses the important issue of *schedule sustainability* which ensures that the plan generated for one window can be run continuously for any number of windows that come one after the other. Using notation from Table 3, let *start*(h) denote the time (relative

Selecting the Test-to-Snapshot Mapping P_M in a Testing Plan

Inputs: Scaled objectives O_1-O_n, Plan Window P_W, Snapshot Interval P_I

1. for (every test t referenced in an SSO or TCO in $O_1, \ldots, O_n$) {
2. $COUNT_t^{min}$ = 0; $COUNT_t^{max}$ = $\frac{P_W}{P_I}$; }
3. for (every Objective O in $O_1, \ldots, O_n$) {
4.   if (O is SSO: List of tests $\{t_1, \ldots, t_k\}$) {
5.   for (Test t in $t_1, \ldots, t_k$) /* t has to run on all $\frac{P_W}{P_I}$ snapshots */
6. $COUNT_t^{min}$ = Max[$COUNT_t^{min}$, $\frac{P_W}{P_I}$]; }
7.   if (O is TCO: `Test_count`$(t) \geq x$, in time interval P_W)
8. $COUNT_t^{min}$ = Max[$COUNT_t^{min}$, x];
9.   if (O is TCO: `Test_count`$(t) \leq x$, in time interval P_W)
10. $COUNT_t^{max}$ = Min[$COUNT_t^{max}$, x];
11. }
12. $P_M = \emptyset$;
13. for (every test t referenced in an SSO or TCO in $O_1, \ldots, O_n$) {
14.   if ($COUNT_t^{max} < COUNT_t^{min}$) return "No feasible P_M exists";
15.   else {
16.   Map test t to $COUNT_t^{min}$ snapshots spread uniformly across the $\frac{P_W}{P_I}$ snapshots in the plan window. Add the mappings to P_M; }
17. }

Figure 8: Selection of P_M (notation used from Tables 3 and 4)

to the start of the plan window) when a host h is first used to run a test in the window. *end*(h) denotes the corresponding time when host h will finish its last scheduled test for the window. (*end*(h) can be greater than P_W.) For the schedule to be sustainable across multiple successive windows, we need:

$$P_W + start(h) > end(h) \qquad (2)$$

This condition ensures that by the time host h is needed to run tests for a plan window, all tests scheduled on h for the previous plan window will have completed. In fact, tests scheduled on h for all past windows will have completed because our technique from Section 5.3 to select the window size P_W ensures that no test run will span more than two consecutive windows.

The second way to schedule test t_{ij} is to run t_{ij} on a host h_k after all tests currently scheduled on h_k complete. Apart from the standard checks for RPO violation and sustainability, the algorithm also checks whether t_{ij} can be started over s_i on h_k before the next snapshot s_{i+1} arrives. The aim here is to achieve a balanced test execution workload (to the extent possible) throughout the window.

If it is not feasible to schedule t_{ij} on a testing host that is already allocated in the plan, then the third way is to schedule t_{ij} on a new testing host added to the plan. This step will use the resource provider's pricing model to ensure that the addition of a new testing host will not overshoot the cost budget specified in the Angel program. Note that the allocation of a new testing host to run t_{ij} will not violate schedule sustainability because $ExecTime(t_{ij}) \leq P_W$ (from Section 5.3).

5.6 Handling Non-cost Optimization Objectives

So far we focused on finding a testing plan that minimizes cost while meeting all the given objectives. Amulet's Optimizer can handle non-cost optimization objectives as well, and does so by repeatedly invoking the cost-optimal planning algorithm with increasingly stricter objectives until no valid plan can be found. The complete details of two algorithms that we have developed for non-cost optimization are given in the online technical report [4]. These algorithms differ in how the stricter objectives are generated: one algorithm does so in *linear* increments while the second algorithm uses a *binary-search* technique to improve efficiency.

Consider the objective of minimizing the interval τ_{rpo} in an RPO. (Example 3 from Table 2 has this optimization objective.) It emerges

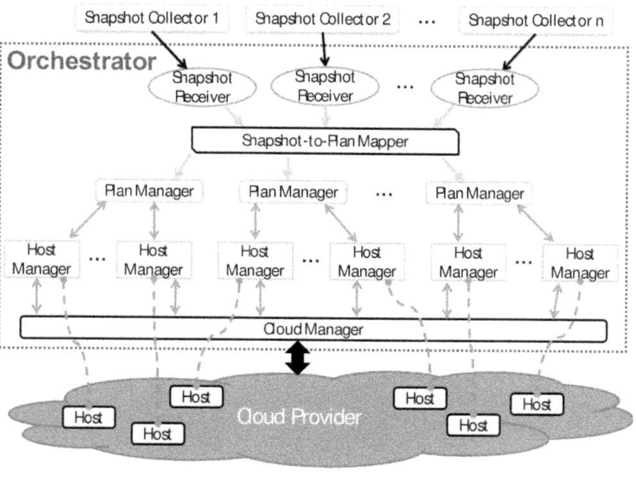

Figure 9: Amulet's Orchestrator

from Equation 1 that the way to achieve lower values of τ_{rpo} is by reducing the snapshot interval $P_I = Time(s_i) - Time(s_{i-1})$. ($ExecTime(t)$ cannot be changed for the host type specified by the Angel program to run test t.) Given a current valid plan P, this rationale can be used to check whether lowering the snapshot interval in P to add one or more snapshots to the plan window will still give a valid testing plan P^{new}. This process of adding stricter objectives continues until no valid plan can be found; at that point, the minimum feasible τ_{rpo} is known, namely, it is the RPO interval in the valid plan found for the previous set of objectives.

6. ORCHESTRATOR

Recall from Section 1 and Figure 1 that testing plans are submitted to Amulet's Orchestrator for execution. The Orchestrator will execute each submitted plan continuously by working in conjunction with the Snapshot Manager and resource provider. Figure 9 shows the multi-threaded design of the Orchestrator which has three concurrent execution paths—snapshot management, host management, and plan management—that we will discuss next.

Snapshot Management: The external Snapshot Manager (see Figure 1) informs the Orchestrator about the availability of a new snapshot s by sending a descriptor for s. Snapshots are never copied to the Orchestrator. Since s is at the level of a volume V, the *Plan Manager* in charge of the testing plan for V is notified. In turn, the *Host Managers* responsible for hosts allocated to this plan from the external resource provider get notified. Recall that the plan generated by the Optimizer was based on $\frac{P_W}{P_I}$ uniformly-spaced snapshots per plan window. The Plan and Host Managers determine which snapshot in the window, if any, s should be mapped to.

Host Management: A Host Manager is responsible for using and monitoring a host allocated to a testing plan from the resource provider. Amulet's implementation supports any infrastructure-as-a-service cloud provider (e.g., Amazon Web Services, Joyent, Rackspace) as the resource provider by using an appropriate *Cloud Manager* (Figure 9). The Host Manager uses the API provided by the Cloud Manager to allocate, establish connections with, and terminate hosts as well as to load snapshots on to allocated hosts.

Plan Management: A Plan Manager is responsible for shepherding the execution of a testing plan P through one or more plan windows until P is terminated. The Plan Manager's role is straightforward at the conceptual level if P behaves as the Optimizer estimated when P was generated. The challenge is when the Plan Manager has to deal with unpredictable lags in the actual schedule of execution from the Optimizer-estimated schedule, and with repair actions that need to be run when corruption is detected.

Dealing with Lags: This process involves two steps: (i) identifying *straggler hosts* on which the lag is observed; and (ii) allocating one or more *helper hosts* for each straggler host subject to the reserved cost budget P_R earmarked for the Orchestrator to deal with unpredictable events. A testing host h is marked as a straggler when two conditions hold:

1. The actual execution time of tests for a snapshot s on h has overshot the corresponding estimated time by more than an allowed slack. (The slack is used to prevent overreaction.) Straggler hosts are prioritized based on the age of s.
2. The next snapshot s' on which host h is scheduled to run tests has become available.

Each helper host h' for a straggler host h will take a share of h's workload adaptively. The helper host h' will be terminated if, on completing the execution of tests on a snapshot, it is found that the corresponding testing host h is no longer a straggler.

Handling Repairs: This process also involves two steps:

1. The first test t that detects a corruption on a snapshot s, and has an associated repair action, will cause a *repair host* to be allocated to run the repair. Repairs for any future tests that detect corruption on s will be run on the same host in order to generate a single fully-repaired snapshot. Note that applying repairs offers much less scope for parallel execution compared to running tests to detect different types of corruption.
2. Once the repairs complete, a snapshot is taken to preserve the repaired version of s, and the repair host is terminated.

When a new helper or repair host is needed, the Plan Manager checks whether it has enough remaining budget from P_R to allocate a new host. If not, the Plan Manager will repeat the check at frequent intervals. In the worst case—e.g., if estimates of test execution times from models were significantly lower than actual execution times—an RPO or TCO objective will eventually get violated before a host can be allocated. In that case, the Orchestrator will terminate the plan and send a notification to the administrator.

7. EXPERIMENTAL EVALUATION

7.1 Experimental Methodology and Setup

Methodology: We have implemented Amulet with all the components and algorithms as described in the previous sections. We now present a comprehensive evaluation of Amulet when run using the Amazon Web Services platform [1] as the infrastructure-as-a-service cloud provider. Section 7.2 considers the end-to-end execution, with both optimization and orchestration, of Angel programs in Amulet. For ease of exposition, we consider four scenarios that are simple in terms of Amulet's functionality, but illustrate the challenges that Amulet has to deal with. Amulet's power will become more clear in Section 7.3 where we consider both the efficiency (how fast?) and effectiveness (how good is the selected plan?) of the Optimizer while generating testing plans for huge plan spaces.

Database software stack and tests: For the production system, we choose a popular database software stack composed of MySQL as the database system, XFS or ext3 as the file-system, and Amazon's *Elastic Block Storage (EBS)* volumes for persistent storage (we used 50GB volumes) [8]. For each layer of the stack, we chose a representative test from Table 1: myisamchk for MySQL database integrity checking, and fsck and xfs_check for file-system integrity checking. Execution-time estimation models for these tests were trained and validated on the Amazon cloud (see Section 3).

Snapshots and storage: We implemented a Snapshot Manager that automates periodic volume-level snapshots (currently, the only type supported by the Amazon cloud). When the XFS file-system is used, the Snapshot Manager freezes the MySQL database as well as the XFS file-system (all caches are flushed to the disk) before a volume-level snapshot is taken [8]. This process finishes within seconds. For the ext3 file-system, only the database is frozen since ext3 does not support the freeze feature of XFS.

Amazon provides two persistent storage services: Simple Storage Service (S3) and Elastic Block Storage (EBS). EBS provides much faster data access rates than S3, but has lower redundancy. Amazon supports snapshots of EBS volumes with the caveat that these snapshots are stored in S3. Specifically, when the Snapshot Manager initiates a snapshot, Amazon copies the EBS volume data to S3. All but the first snapshot request to the same EBS volume will copy to S3 only the changed data since the last snapshot.

Amazon does not provide direct access to data in a snapshot s. Instead, Amulet can create an EBS volume from s, and attach this volume to a testing host h that needs to run tests on s. This process copies data in a background fashion from the snapshot stored in S3 to h—prioritizing block read/write requests from h—making the volume accessible in h before the data movement is complete. Snapshot creation and restore times depend on bandwidth constraints and the amount of data that needs to be copied from S3 to EBS or EBS to S3. In our experiments, we observed an average bandwidth of 20 MB/s in both directions. This process can be made much faster by removing the intermediate copy to S3, which is part of our future work.

Plan costs: Recall from Section 4.1 that a pricing model for the resource provider has to be input to Amulet in order to specify cost objectives in Angel programs. For evaluation purposes, we used a pricing model motivated by how resource usage is charged in a pay-as-you-go fashion on the Amazon cloud [1]. Table 5 outlines this pricing model in terms of how the four main types of resources used in a testing plan are charged. Given a testing plan P, Amulet's Optimizer will use the pricing model to find how much P's use of each resource will cost in one plan window; and add all the per-resource costs to estimate P's total cost per plan window. The total number of block I/O requests to persistent storage is computed based on the total input data size for each test and the file-system's block size. This strategy was chosen based on our empirical observations. Enhancing each test model to estimate the number of I/O requests that the test will make is part of our future work.

7.2 End-to-end Processing of Angel Programs

7.2.1 Case 1: Maintaining a Tested Recovery Point

Angel program: We first submit to Amulet the Angel program corresponding to Example 1 from Table 2. The program specifies two objectives, an RPO and an SSO, for a single volume. The time interval τ_{rpo} in the RPO is 60 minutes. The SSO specifies a single test: a myisamchk medium test (denoted T_M) on a database table of size approximately 10 GB with no indexes. The test has to be run on hosts of type *Small* (m1.small on the Amazon cloud). The Snapshot Manager sends snapshot descriptors announcing new snapshots to Amulet every 15 minutes on average.

Testing Plan from the Optimizer: The model for estimating T_M's execution time returns an estimate of 20 minutes when invoked by the Optimizer for this setting. The minimum-cost plan P generated by the Optimizer's algorithm in Figure 6 for this setting has:

- P_I = 30 minutes
- P_W = 60 minutes ($\frac{P_W}{P_I}$ = 2 snapshots s_1 and s_2 per window)
- P_M consists of test T_M mapped to both snapshots in P_W
- P_S assigns one Small host to run T_M on s_1 and s_2

Resource Used	Pay-as-you-go Pricing Method
Testing hosts	Hosts of the Small type (see Figure 4(a)) cost \$0.085 per hour. Medium / Large types cost \$0.17 / \$0.34 per hour respectively
Storage	\$0.10 per month per 1 GB of persistent storage used
I/O to storage	\$0.10 per 1 million block I/O requests to persistent storage
Snapshot access	\$0.05 per 1000 store or load requests for snapshots

Table 5: Pricing model used in our evaluation

- Since no CO is specified, P_R takes the default value which in this case is the cost of one Small host (see Section 4.1)

Orchestration Timeline: Figure 2 shows the actual execution timeline of plan P when it is submitted to and run by the Orchestrator on the Amazon cloud. The meaning of each important symbol used in the figure is described at the top. The execution of P is shown for three plan windows, i.e., a total of 3 hours. When P is submitted, the Orchestrator starts by requesting the needed testing host from the cloud provider. When the host is available, the Orchestrator starts the plan execution (0 minutes in the timeline in Figure 2).

The Orchestrator is continuously executing the schedule P_S given by the Optimizer for each plan window. As part of this process, the Orchestrator (actually the Plan and Host Managers from Section 6) has to map the snapshots s_i, $1 \leq i \leq \frac{P_W}{P_I}$, identified by the Optimizer in the plan window to actual snapshots S_j collected by the Snapshot Manager. Notice from Figure 2 that the Snapshot Manager is submitting snapshot descriptors every 15 minutes on average, while the snapshot interval P_I in the plan is 30 minutes.

At *Time*(s_i), $1 \leq i \leq \frac{P_W}{P_I}$, in the plan window, the Orchestrator checks whether a snapshot S is available from the Snapshot Manager; if so, S will be tested. Otherwise, the Orchestrator waits for a slack interval to see whether a new snapshot is submitted. If no new snapshot arrives, then the last submitted snapshot will be tested. If this snapshot has already been tested, then an error notification is generated. The Host Manager uses P_S to find out whether it has to load a submitted snapshot (and if so, which tests it needs to run on the snapshot and how). Notice from Figure 2 that every other snapshot submitted is tested. The boxes with notation S_jT_M in Figure 2 denote the actual run of test T_M on snapshot S_j submitted by the Snapshot Manager. The width of each box is the actual execution time of the test. These times are in the 18-22 minutes range which matches the estimated execution time of 20 minutes.

7.2.2 Case 2: Multiple Tests and Multiple Objectives

Angel program: We now consider a more complex Angel program with more tests as well as more and stricter objectives. The program specifies an RPO, an SSO, and an SIO for a single volume. The time interval τ_{rpo} in the RPO is reduced to 30 minutes from before. The SSO specifies three tests: two myisamchk medium tests respectively on a 2.4 GB lineitem table and a 1 GB orders table (with no index on either table), and an fsck metadata test. All tests have to be run on Small hosts. The SIO specifies `Snapshot_interval` $\leq$ 10 minutes. The Snapshot Manager sends snapshot descriptors announcing new snapshots to Amulet every 10 minutes on average.

Testing Plan from the Optimizer: The minimum-cost plan P generated by the Optimizer is more complex than before:

- P_I = 10 minutes
- P_W = 30 minutes ($\frac{P_W}{P_I}$ = 3 snapshots s_1, s_2, s_3 per window)
- P_M has all three tests mapped to all three snapshots in P_W
- P_S assigns one host to run the fsck test (estimated to run in 6 minutes). The two myisamchk tests are run concurrently on a second Small host, with estimated times of 9 and 7 minutes.
- P_R takes the default value as in Case 1

Orchestration Timeline: Figure 10 shows the actual execution timeline of the above plan P. Note that P_I = 10 minutes causes

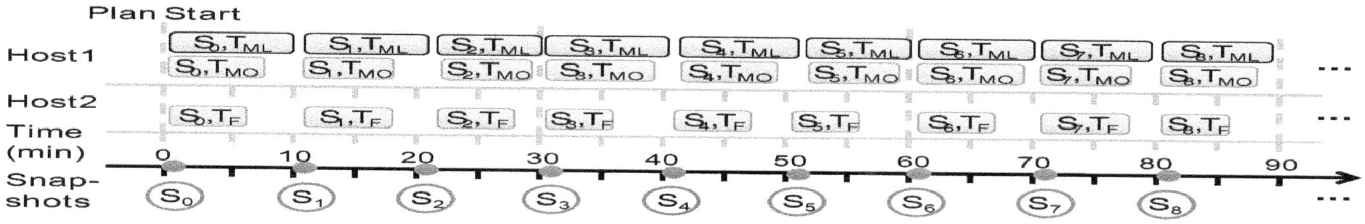

Figure 10: Actual execution timeline on the Amazon Cloud for Case 2 in our evaluation

all submitted snapshots to be tested. T_{ML} denotes the myisamchk test on lineitem, T_{MO} denotes the myisamchk test on orders, and T_F denotes the fsck test. While there is some variance in the actual execution times of the grouped test (1-2 minutes deviation from the estimates), the plan works as the optimizer estimated.

7.2.3 Case 3: Dealing with Unpredictable Lags

Here we run the same Angel program as in Case 2. Thus, the same plan P is picked and run as in Section 7.2.2. However, in this case, we cause a problem on $Host_1$ which causes the T_{ML} test on the host to run almost $2x$ slower than expected. Figure 11 shows the actual execution timeline.

Notice that test T_{ML} on snapshot S_4 now takes around 16 minutes to run compared to the estimated time of 9 minutes. The Plan Manager will mark $Host_1$ as a straggler because the two conditions for stragglers from Section 6 get satisfied at around 52 minutes in the timeline. $Host_1$ has overshot the estimated time, and the next snapshot S_5 on which $Host_1$ has to run tests is ready. (A slack interval of 2 minutes is used.) The Plan Manager will use the reserved cost budget P_R to request a helper host at time 52 minutes. The helper host is available at time 54 minutes, and takes over the running of the T_{ML} and T_{MO} tests on snapshot S_5 from $Host_1$. These tests complete at time 63. At that point, a check reveals that $Host_1$ is no longer a straggler host; thus, the helper host is released back to the resource provider. Intuitively, the helper host was pulled in adaptively to help the plan tide over a transient problem.

7.2.4 Case 4: Corruption Detection and Repair

In this case, we cause a data corruption in the production system that manifests itself in two snapshots. We create a scenario where a corruption happens due to a software bug that does a misdirected write on the production system. We run the Angel program from Case 2 with one change. The modified program associates repair actions with the myisamchk tests on the lineitem and orders tables. The repair actions invoke myisamchk with the "-r" option.

Figure 12 shows the actual execution timeline in this case. We inject the misdirected write in the interval between 30 and 40 minutes in the timeline, which corrupts the data in the lineitem table. Snapshots S_4 and S_5 submitted by the Snapshot Manager contain this corruption. The corruption will be detected by T_{ML} when executed on S_4 (S_4, T_{ML} in Figure 12). The corruption is reported to the Plan Manager which uses the reserved cost budget P_R to request a repair host. The repair action is run on the repair host. When the repair finishes around time 60, a snapshot of the repaired data is taken and the Snapshot Manager is notified. Around that time, the Plan manager gets notified of the corruption detected in S_5. The repair on S_5 is run on the same repair host, and the repaired snapshot is available at time 66. Since no pending repairs exist at this point, the repair host is released.

7.3 Evaluation of Amulet's Optimizer

To understand the space of testing plans and to evaluate the quality and efficiency of Amulet's Optimizer, we developed an *Exhaustive Optimizer (EOpt)*. EOpt works by enumerating the (nearly) full space of possible testing plans per volume as follows:

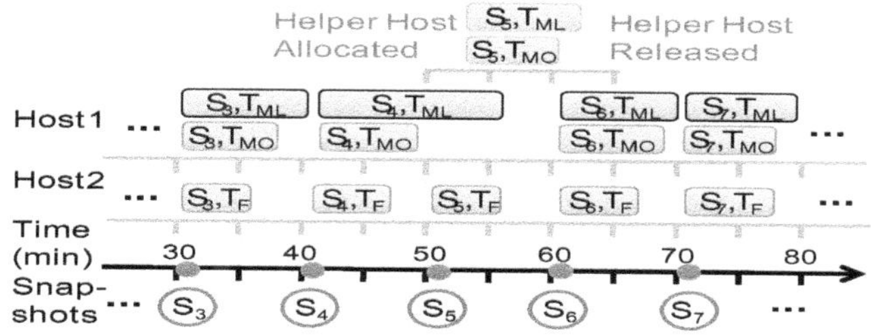

Figure 11: Actual execution timeline for Case 3

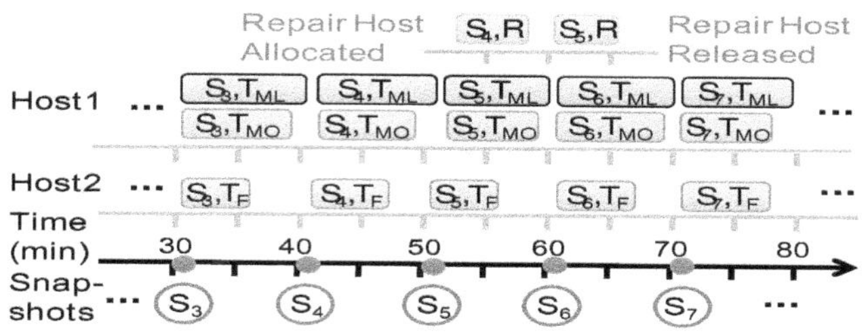

Figure 12: Actual execution timeline for Case 4

- P_W is set to the maximum among intervals in all objectives.
- The number of uniformly-spaced snapshots in P_W is varied from 1 to $\frac{P_W}{P_I^{min}}$, where we set the minimum snapshot interval P_I^{min} to 5 minutes.
- For each number of snapshots in P_W, EOpt enumerates all possible test scheduling combinations starting from all tests running on a single host (if all tests specify the same host type, otherwise, the minimum distinct host types), and finishing at a separate host per test.

Plan space size: We consider the Angel program with an RPO and an SSO from Case 1 in Section 7.2.1, and add more tests to the SSO. For each distinct number of tests in the SSO, we varied the τ_{rpo} in the RPO. For each unique Angel program generated in this manner, Figure 13(a) shows the total number of plans obtained by running EOpt. Note the $\log_{10}$ scale in Figure 13(a) on the z-axis which shows the total size of the plan space. The plan space increases drastically as the number of tests increase because the size of the space is exponential in the number of tests.

Cost distribution of valid plans: More than 99% of the plans in the space enumerated by EOpt were invalid for most Angel programs, i.e., their test schedules (P_S) violate one of the specified objectives or are unsustainable (see Equation 2). Figure 13(b) shows the distribution of valid plans according to their respective total cost for an Angel program with $\tau_{rpo} = 60$ minutes and an SSO with 4 tests. The figure shows that there is more than one optimal (in this case, minimum cost) plan. In this case—as well as in all cases where we could run EOpt in a reasonable time frame—Amulet's Optimizer generated one of the optimal plans.

Scalability: Given the large plan space per volume and the speed at which it grows (Figure 13(a)), we measured the time that each optimizer takes to find a testing plan per volume. We fixed τ_{rpo}

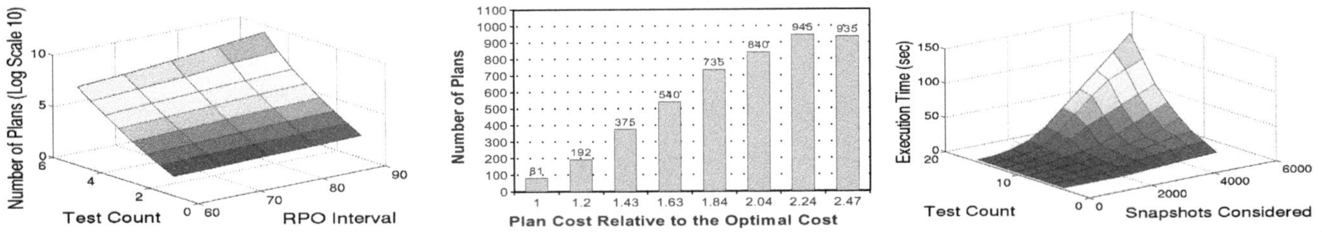

(a) Number of plans in the testing plan space (b) Number of valid plans per price bucket (c) Amulet Optimizer's running time for cost optimization

Figure 13: Characteristics of the testing plan space and the performance of Amulet's Optimizer

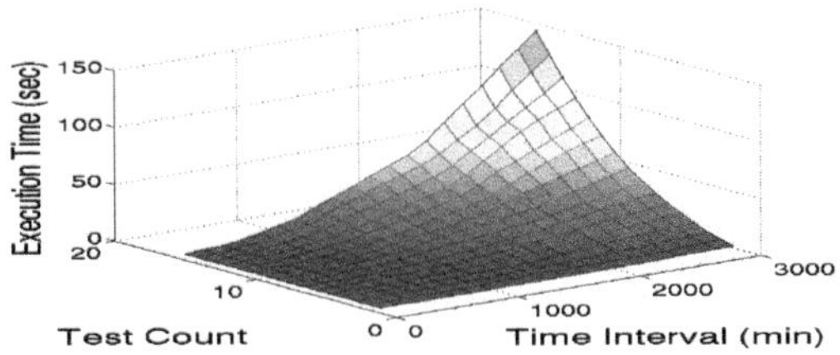

Figure 14: Amulet Optimizer's running time for non-cost optimization

to 60 minutes in the RPO, and varied the number of tests in the SSO from 1 to 6. EOpt's times increased rapidly from 0.5 seconds to 30+ minutes. (With 6 tests, we killed EOpt after 35 minutes.) Amulet's Optimizer ran in under 0.5 seconds in all these cases. We further increased the number of tests up to 16 (which would be a high-end number for tests on a single volume). Our Optimizer's running time remained under 0.5 seconds.

Next, we increased the τ_{rpo} interval in the RPO, and specified an SIO with a maximum snapshot interval of 1 minute to force our Optimizer to come up with a plan where a snapshot is tested every minute. Figure 13(c) summarizes the results. Planning for 3000 snapshots on each of which 16 tests should be run on average, gave an Optimizer running time under 1 minute. We can see this result as: If the snapshot interval P_I is 5 minutes, then Amulet's optimizer needs less than a minute to produce a plan with a window P_W spanning 10 days (3000 snapshots at P_I=5 minutes per snapshot). We conclude that Amulet's Optimizer is efficient for today's needs.

Finally, Figure 14 shows how Amulet's Optimizer continues to remain efficient even under non-cost optimization objectives. The binary-search algorithm from Section 5.6 was used. We defined a TCO and varied the time interval and the number of tests that are part of the TCO. No cost objective was specified. The goal was to maximize the number of tests in the plan. While non-cost optimization is more expensive, the trend in Figure 14 is similar to what we observed for the cost optimization objective in Figure 13(c).

8. CONCLUSIONS AND FUTURE WORK

Hardware errors, software bugs, and mistakes by human administrators can corrupt important sources of data. Current approaches to deal with data corruption are ad hoc and labor-intensive. We introduced the Amulet system that gives administrators a declarative language to specify their objectives regarding the detection and repair of data corruption. Amulet automatically finds and orchestrates efficient testing plans that run integrity tests to meet the specified objectives in cost-effective ways. We believe that Amulet provides a general framework for administrators to analyze cost versus risk tradeoffs regarding data protection. Although we prototyped Amulet on a cloud platform, Amulet can be applied to conventional enterprise environments with minor modifications. We intend to build on the current framework in future, and explore several directions including adaptive techniques for plan optimization.

9. ACKNOWLEDGMENTS

We thank the anonymous reviewers and shepherd for helping us improve the paper in many ways.

10. REFERENCES

[1] *Amazon Web Services*. aws.amazon.com.

[2] B. Babcock and S. Chaudhuri. Towards a Robust Query Optimizer: A Principled and Practical Approach. In *SIGMOD*, 2005.

[3] L. N. Bairavasundaram, G. R. Goodson, B. Schroeder, A. C. Arpaci-Dusseau, and R. H. Arpaci-Dusseau. An Analysis of Data Corruption in the Storage Stack. In *FAST*, 2008.

[4] N. Borisov, S. Babu, N. Mandagere, and S. Uttamchandani. Warding off the Dangers of Data Corruption with Amulet. Technical report, 2011.

[5] How to Use Chkdsk. http://bit.ly/vyyZL.

[6] *Data corruption in CouchDB*. couchdb.apache.org/notice/1.0.1.html.

[7] Comparison of INSPECT and db2dart. http://bit.ly/hPYpq5.

[8] *Running MySQL on Amazon EC2 with EBS*. http://bit.ly/b7SWwg.

[9] Eseutil tutorial. http://bit.ly/f0iPY1.

[10] *Checking and Repairing Unix File system with fsck*. http://adminschoice.com/repairing-unix-file-system-fsck.

[11] Storage software update causes 0.02% of Gmail users to lose their emails. http://bit.ly/e5Xn18.

[12] H. S. Gunawi, A. Rajimwale, A. C. Arpaci-Dusseau, and R. H. Arpaci-Susseau. SQCK: A Declarative File System Checker. In *OSDI*, 2008.

[13] H. Guo, D. Jones, J. L. Beckmann, and P. Seshadri. Declarative Database Management in SQLServer. *PVLDB*, 2(2), 2009.

[14] A. Krioukov, L. N. Bairavasundaram, G. R. Goodson, K. Srinivasan, R. Thelen, A. C. Arpaci-Dusseau, and R. H. Arpaci-Dusseau. Parity Lost and Parity Regained. In *FAST*, 2008.

[15] *Data corruption at Ma.gnolia.com*. en.wikipedia.org/wiki/Gnolia.

[16] MySQL myisamchk command. http://bit.ly/gGFRUP.

[17] *Corrupted backups*. http://bit.ly/iffTC8.

[18] Oracle HARD Initiative. http://bit.ly/eTxiqa.

[19] Detecting and Recovering from Database Corruption. http://bit.ly/eKXMAi.

[20] Parchive. http://parchive.sourceforge.net/.

[21] *Data corruption in Amazon S3*. http://bit.ly/foWIul.

[22] B. Schroeder, E. Pinheiro, and W. D. Weber. DRAM Errors in the Wild: A Large-Scale Field Study. In *SIGMETRICS*, 2009.

[23] T. Schwarz, Q. Xin, E. Miller, D. Long, A. Hospodor, and S. Ng. Disk Scrubbing in Large Archival Storage Systems. In *MASCOTS*, 2004.

[24] Microsoft SQL Server checkDB command. http://bit.ly/gawaHF.

[25] S. Subramanian, Y. Zhang, R. Vaidyanathan, H. S. Gunawi, A. C. Arpaci-Dusseau, R. H. Arpaci-Dusseau, and J. F. Naughton. Impact of Disk Corruption on Open-Source DBMS. In *ICDE*, 2010.

[26] *Tripwire Tutorial*. http://bit.ly/csCvmr.

[27] T. Wood, E. Cecchet, K. Ramakrishnan, P. Shenoy, J. van der Merwe, and A. Venkataramani. Disaster Recovery as a Cloud Service: Economic Benefits and Deployment Challenges. In *HotCloud*, 2010.

[28] Fixing XFS. http://bit.ly/1XRuDy.

[29] *Solaris ZFS Administration Guide*. http://bit.ly/cw1EZY.

[30] Y. Zhang, A. Rajimwale, A. C. Arpaci-Dusseau, and R. H. Arpaci-Dusseau. End-to-end Data Integrity for File Systems: A ZFS Case Study. In *FAST*, 2010.

Schedule Optimization for Data Processing Flows on the Cloud

Herald Kllapi
herald@di.uoa.gr

Eva Sitaridi *
evas@di.uoa.gr

Manolis M. Tsangaris
mmt@di.uoa.gr

Yannis Ioannidis
yannis@di.uoa.gr

MaDgIK Lab, Dept. of Informatics and Telecommunications
University of Athens, Ilissia GR15784, Greece.

ABSTRACT

Scheduling data processing workflows (dataflows) on the cloud is a very complex and challenging task. It is essentially an optimization problem, very similar to query optimization, that is characteristically different from traditional problems in two aspects: Its space of alternative schedules is very rich, due to various optimization opportunities that cloud computing offers; its optimization criterion is at least two-dimensional, with monetary cost of using the cloud being at least as important as query completion time. In this paper, we study scheduling of dataflows that involve arbitrary data processing operators in the context of three different problems: 1) minimize completion time given a fixed budget, 2) minimize monetary cost given a deadline, and 3) find trade-offs between completion time and monetary cost without any a-priori constraints. We formulate these problems and present an approximate optimization framework to address them that uses resource elasticity in the cloud. To investigate the effectiveness of our approach, we incorporate the devised framework into a prototype system for dataflow evaluation and instantiate it with several greedy, probabilistic, and exhaustive search algorithms. Finally, through several experiments that we have conducted with the prototype elastic optimizer on numerous scientific and synthetic dataflows, we identify several interesting general characteristics of the space of alternative schedules as well as the advantages and disadvantages of the various search algorithms. The overall results are quite promising and indicate the effectiveness of our approach.

Categories and Subject Descriptors

G.1.6 [**Mathematics of Computing**]: Optimization—*Constrained optimization, Simulated annealing*; H.2.4 [**Database Management**]: Systems—*Distributed databases, Query processing*; H.2.8 [**Database Management**]: Database Applications; H.4 [**Database Management**]: Information Systems Applications

*Present address: Columbia University, New York, NY 10027.

General Terms

Algorithms, Design, Economics, Experimentation, Performance

Keywords

Cloud computing, Dataflows, Query optimization, Scheduling

1. INTRODUCTION

Complex on-demand data retrieval and processing is a characteristic of several applications and combines the notions of querying & search, information filtering & retrieval, data transformation & analysis, and other data manipulations. Such rich tasks are typically represented by data processing graphs, having arbitrary data operators as nodes and their producer-consumer interactions as edges. Suppose a user wants to find the names and images of authors of ACM publications. This could be expressed in SQL as follows:

```
SELECT UNIQUE auth.name, img.image
FROM AuthorDB auth, ImageBD img
WHERE auth.pub="ACM" AND auth.name=face(img.image)
```

Function `face()` detects the face of the person in a particular image and returns her name. The SQL query is optimized [18] and transformed into an execution plan, represented as a dataflow graph. In a distributed environment, the optimizer must decide, among others, where each node of the plan will be executed. This level of optimization is called scheduling. Scheduling the processing nodes of a dataflow graph onto a set of available machines is a well-known NP-complete problem, even in its simplest form [13] [25]. Traditionally, the only criterion to optimize is the completion time or makespan of the dataflow and many heuristic scheduling algorithms have been proposed for that problem [19].

Recently, *cloud computing* has attracted much attention from the research community [1]. Thanks to virtualization, it has evolved over the years from a paradigm of basic IT infrastructures used for a specific purpose (Ad-Hoc Clusters), to Grid computing [10], and finally to several paradigms of resource provisioning services: depending on the particular needs, infrastructures (IaaS), platforms (PaaS), and software (SaaS) can be provided as services [12].

One of the differences between Ad-Hoc Clusters and Clouds under the Infrastructure as a Service (IaaS) paradigm, is the cost model of resources. Ad-Hoc Clusters represent a fixed capital investment made up-front and relatively small operational cost paid over time. On the other hand, Clouds are characterized by elasticity and offer their users the ability to lease resources only for as long as needed, based on a per quantum pricing scheme, e.g. one hour [2]. Together with the lack of any up-front cost, this represents a major benefit of Clouds over Ad-Hoc Clusters. The ability to use computational resources that are available on demand challenges the way we implement algorithms and systems. Execution of dataflows can now be *elastic*, providing several choices of price-to-performance ratio and making the optimization problem of dataflow scheduling at least two dimensional.

To illustrate the complexity of this task, we use the example of dataflow graph in Fig. 1. Nodes represent data processing operations (operators) and edges represent producer-consumer relationships. Assume that the execution time of A and C is 1 hour and the execution time of each B is 10 minutes. Also assume that a pricing scheme of charging the use of a machine per hour is employed by the Cloud. Consider two possible schedules for this dataflow: *Schedule 1*: execute all operators in one virtual host.

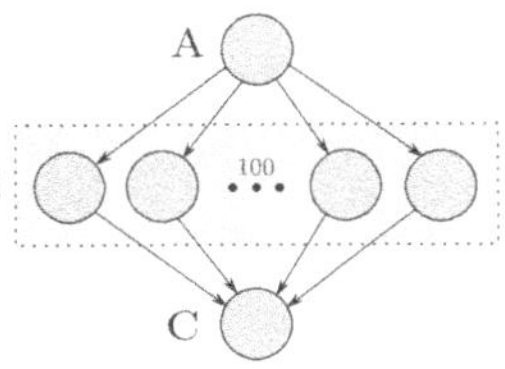

Figure 1: A split (A), compute(B), and merge(C) dataflow.

First A is executed, then 100 Bs, and finally C. The time required for the dataflow to complete is the sum of the execution times of all operators: $60 + 10 \cdot 100 + 60 = 1120$ minutes or 18.6 hours. Since there is only one host involved, the cost for this schedule corresponds to 19 hours of use. *Schedule 2*: execute each operator in a different virtual host. First, A is executed and the data produced is transferred to the hosts that execute B. All Bs are executed in parallel and their data is transferred to one host, which executes C. Assuming that the data transfer time is negligible, the completion time is only $60+10+60 = 130$ minutes or 2 hours and 10 minutes. However, the cost for this schedule is huge and corresponds to 102 hours of resource usage. All hours will be charged for all virtual hosts. *Schedule 2* will run about 9 times faster than *Schedule 1* but will cost 5 times more.□

The number, nature, and temporal & monetary costs of available schedules depend on many parameters, such as the dataflow characteristics (execution time of operators, amount of data generated, etc.), the cloud pricing scheme (quantum length and price), the network bandwidth, and more. The choice of how much parallelism to use or, equivalently, the optimal trade-off between completion time and money spent, depends on the needs of the particular user concerned. For example, a user may have budget constraints but be relaxed about completion time; another user may have a strict deadline but no concern about money; finally, a third user may have no a-priori constraints but wants to choose herself the best trade-off after having been shown all choices.

In this work, we make the following contributions:

- We model the scheduling of dataflows on the cloud as a 2D optimization problem between time and money, which is mostly ignored until now.
- We study the space of alternative schedules that arise from that model and investigate the time-money trade-off these provide for different types of dataflows and cloud environments.
- We propose several greedy, probabilistic, and exhaustive optimization algorithms to explore the space of alternative schedules.
- We present the results of several experiments and draw various interesting insights on the trade-offs available and the effectiveness of all algorithms in exploring these trade-offs.

The remainder of the paper is organized as follows. In Section 2, 3, 4, and 5, we formulate the problem of dataflow scheduling in the context of ADP [30], a prototype dataflow evaluation system, which has served as our experimental testbed in this work. In Section 6, we present our approach along with different optimization algorithms that we use. In Section 7, we present the results of the experimental evaluation. In Section 8, we present an overview of the related work and finally, in Section 9, we conclude and present some future directions.

2. PROBLEM FORMULATION

User requests take the form of queries in some high-level language (e.g. SQL, Hive [28], etc.). In principle, optimization could proceed in one giant step, examining all execution plans that could answer the original query and choosing the one that is optimal and satisfies the required constraints. Alternatively, given the size of the alternatives space, optimization could proceed in multiple smaller steps, each one operating at some level and making assumptions about the levels below. This is in analogy to query optimization and execution in traditional databases but with the following differences: operators may represent arbitrary operations on data with unknown semantics, algebraic properties, and performance characteristics, and are not restricted to come from a well-known fixed set of operators (e.g., those of relational algebra); optimality may be subject to QoS or other constraints and may be based on multiple diverse relevant criteria, e.g., monetary cost of resources, staleness of data, etc., and not just solely on performance; the resources available for the execution of a data processing graph are flexible and reservable on demand and are not fixed a-priori. These differences make dataflow optimization essentially a new challenging problem; they also generate the need for run-time mechanisms that are not usually available. Our optimization process introduced in [30] has three different layers of abstractions described below.

Operator Graphs: Their nodes are data operators and their (directed) edges are operator interactions in the form of producing and consuming data. Operators encapsulate data processing algorithms and may be custom-made by end users. At this abstraction layer, of great importance are algebraic equivalences that operators satisfy. These include typical algebraic transformations, e.g., associativity, commutativity, or distributivity, (de)compositions, i.e., operators being abstractions of whole operator graphs that involve compositions, aggregations, and other interactions of more specific operators, and partitions, i.e., operators being amenable to replication and parallel processing by each replica of part of the original input, in conjunction with some pre- and post-processing operators.

Concrete Operator Graphs: These are similar to operator graphs but their nodes are concrete operators, i.e., software components that implement operators in a particular way and carry all necessary details for their execution. At this layer, capturing an operator's available implementation(s) is the critical information. In general, there may be multiple concrete operators implementing an operator, e.g., a low-memory but expensive version and a high-memory but fast one; a multi-threaded version and a single-threaded one; or two totally different but logically equivalent implementations of the same operator. An example from databases is the $join$ operator, which has multiple implementations: $nested - loops$ join has low memory consumption but long execution time; $hash$-join uses more memory but has short execution time.

Execution Plans: These are similar to concrete operator graphs, but their nodes are concrete operators that have been allocated resources for execution and have all their parameters set. At this layer, the assignment of concrete operators to containers is performed. The crucial information here is the resources needed to execute the operators, e.g., CPU and memory. This paper presents the modeling and a methodology for this stage of optimization. The statistics needed are assumed to be known, calculated either by mathematical formulas or by historical data.

A **dataflow** is represented as a directed acyclic graph (DAG) $graph(ops, flows)$. Nodes (ops) correspond to arbitrary concrete operators and edges ($flows$) correspond to data transferred between them. An **operator** in ops is modeled as $op(time, cpu, memory, behavior)$ where $time$ is the execution time of the operator & cpu is its average CPU utilization measured as a percentage of the host CPU power when executed in isolation (without the presence of other operators), $memory$ is the maximum memory required for the effective execution of the operator, and $behavior$ is a flag that is equal to either *pipeline* (PL) or *store-and-forward* (S&F). If behavior is equal to S&F, all inputs to the operator must be available before execution; if it is equal to PL, execution can start as soon as some input is available. Two typical examples from databases are $sort$ and $select$ operators: $sort$ is S&F and $select$ is PL. We assume that each operator has a uniform resource consumption during its execution (cpu, $memory$, and $behavior$ do not change). A **flow** between two operators, producer and consumer, is modeled as $flow(producer, consumer, data)$, where $data$ is the size of the data transferred.

The **container** is the abstraction of the host, virtual or physical, encapsulating the resources provided by the underlying infrastructure. Containers are responsible for supervising operators and providing the necessary context for executing them. A container is described by its CPU, its available memory, and its network bandwidth: $cont(cpu, memory, network)$.

A **schedule** S_G of a dataflow graph G is an assignment of its operators into containers $schedule(assigns)$. An individual operator **assignment** is modeled as: $assign(op, cont, start, end)$ where $start$ and end are the start and end time of the operator correspondingly, executed in the presence of other operators.

Time $t(S_G)$ and **money** $m(S_G)$ costs are the completion time and the monetary cost of a schedule S_G of a dataflow graph G. The following two sections define the way we model and calculate the time and money costs of a schedule.

The **cloud** is a provider of virtual hosts (containers). We model only the compute service of the cloud and not the storage service. Assuming that the storage service is not used as temporary space, a particular dataflow G will read and write the same amount of data for any schedule S_G of operators into containers. So the cost of reading the input and writing the output is the same.

In the rest of the paper, we use the "." notation to denote a property, e.g., the running time of an operator A is denoted as $A.time$. Indifferent values are denoted by "$-$", e.g., $assign(op, cont, -, -)$.

3. TIME MODELING

To calculate the completion time of a schedule executed over a set of containers, several aspects of operator execution must be modeled. This is an issue for any distributed system and our particular approaches do not depend on having a Cloud underneath or any other architecture. In this section we present the approach adapted in our work, inspired by or taken from earlier works.

There are two types of temporal constraints, those implied by the dataflow graph and those imposed by the execution environment. The dataflow graph implies constraints based on the inter-operator dependencies captured by its edges, but also by the nature of the operators themselves. An S&F operator cannot be executed until all its inputs are available, while a PL operator must wait for all inputs produced by S&F operators. This raises an important issue especially when the two operators are in different containers and introduce network costs. We describe our approach to model the various cases in Section 3.1.

The execution environment constraints are due to resource limitations when multiple operators use them concurrently. In that respect, we categorize container resources as time-shared and space-shared [11]. Time-shared resources can be used by multiple operators concurrently at very low overhead. Concurrent use of space-shared resources, however, implies high overheads beyond container limits of resources. We consider memory as the only space-shared resource, whereas CPU and network as time-shared resources. Constraints are imposed only by space-shared resources: in every container, at any given moment, memory must be sufficient for the execution of the running operators. On the other hand, CPU requires particular treatment. We describe our approach to model CPU overloading in Section 3.2.

3.1 Network Cost

Two issues must be addressed regarding network cost: handling of S&F and handling of PL operators. The network communication is modeled with special operators that perform data transferring (dt). These operators are injected between the operators of a flow $flow(producer, consumer, data)$, if $producer$ and $consumer$ are assigned to different containers. Always two dt operators are injected, one attached after the producer and one attached before the consumer. If the operator is S&F (Fig. 2), the dt operator creates a new node in the dataflow graph. On the other

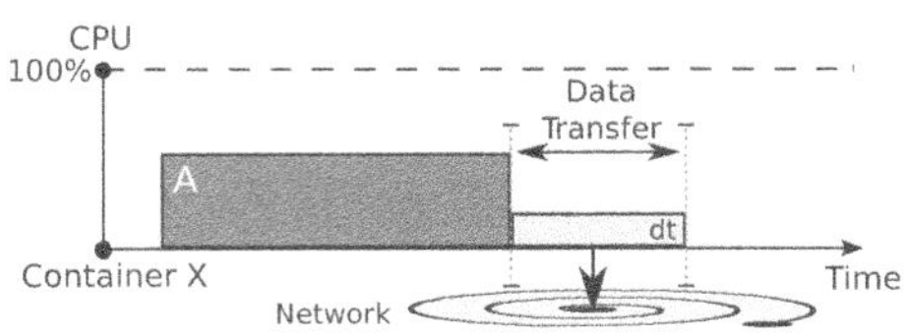

Figure 2: An S&F operator with a data transfer operator attached.

hand, if the operator is PL (Fig. 3), the functionality of the dt operator is injected into the operator itself without changing the dataflow graph. Fig. 3A illustrates the actual execution of the pipeline op-

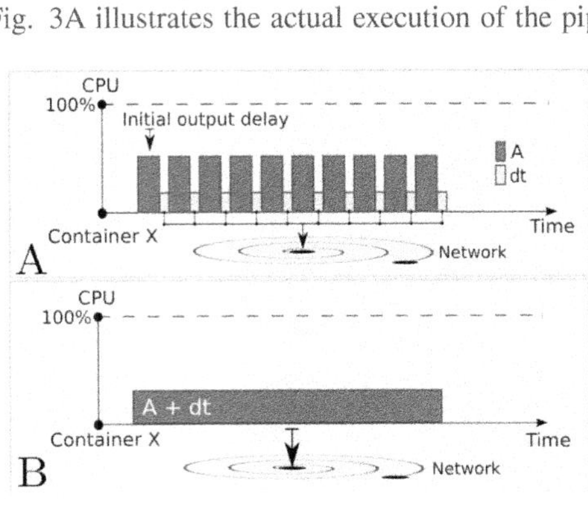

Figure 3: PL operator A intermixed with data transfer operator dt (A) and the modeling of the operator (B)

erator A intermixed with the dt operator and Fig. 3B illustrates the modeling of A. The execution time is increased and the CPU utilization is decreased. For simplicity, we assume that the initial output delay is 0. In the transformed graph, all network communication is performed by PL operators, no matter what the initial nodes were.

Store-and-Forward: Let A be an S&F operator that belongs to dataflow G defined as $A(-,-,-,S\&F)$ with $assign(A,X,-,-)$. For every operator B with $flow(A,B,D_{A\to B})$ and $assign(B,Y,-,-)$, if $X \neq Y$ insert in G a data transfer operator node dt between A and B as follows: remove $flow(A,B,D_{A\to B})$, insert $flow(A,dt,D_{A\to B})$, $flow(dt,B,D_{A\to B})$, and $assign(dt,X,-,-)$. The execution time of dt is as follows:

$$dt.time = \frac{D_{A\to B}}{\min(X.network, Y.network)} \tag{1}$$

$$dt(time, DT_{CPU}, DT_{MEM}, PL)$$

with DT_{CPU} and DT_{MEM} being fixed system-wide values for the CPU utilization and memory requirements of data transfer operators. The same method is followed for all operators C $flow(C,A,D_{C\to A})$, whose outputs are consumed by A.

Pipeline: Consider two connected PL operators A and B (Fig. 3). We assume that the execution time of both operators is fully overlapped. Let A and B be two connected pipeline operators that belong to dataflow graph G with $flow(A,B,D_{A\to B})$. Let the assignments of A and B be $assign(A,X,-,-)$ and $assign(B,Y,-,-)$ correspondingly, with $X \neq Y$. Using Eq. 1, the running time is:

$$T = \max(A.time + dt.time, B.time + dt.time)$$

The new properties of operator A will be:

$$A(T, \frac{A.time * A.cpu + dt.time * DT_{CPU}}{T}, -, -)$$

The *memory* and *behavior* of A will not change. The new properties of B are calculated in a similar way. The same technique is applied on all connected PL operators.

3.2 Operator Overlap

Two or more operators assigned to the same container share container resources. A particular problem arises with the CPU when overlapping operators require at some point more than 100% utilization together. For example consider Fig. 4 with the three overlapping operators A, B, and C. Given the assumption of uniform resource consumption by operators, the regions between those thresholds have uniform CPU utilization. There is a problem in region X, where the total CPU requirements are higher than the container's capacity. This is addressed by uniformly extending the

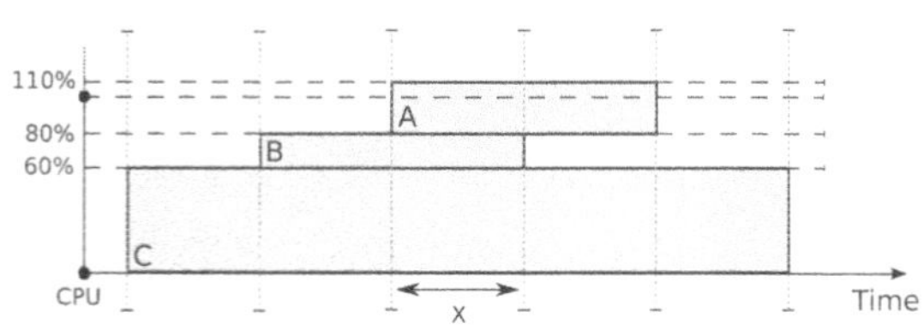

Figure 4: Operator A, B, and C executing in the same container. At region X the overall CPU utilization exceeds 100% and as a result the operators will get a fraction of the processor and their duration will stretch by 10% during that region.

length of region X and, therefore, the overall execution time of all operators by reducing their CPU utilization within X.

More specifically, let G be a dataflow graph and C a container. Let $OP = \{op_j\}$ the set of operators assigned to C and $R = \{r_i\}$ the set of time regions formed by the beginning and endings of operators (in order of i). Let $time(r_i)$ and $cpu(r_i)$ be the duration and CPU utilization of region r_i. Based on the above, the following holds:

$$cpu(r_i) = \sum_{j=1}^{|OP|} (op_j).cpu * \delta(op_j, r_i, C)$$

with

$$\delta(op_j, r_i, C) = \begin{cases} 1, & \text{if } op_j \text{ active in } r_i \text{ in } C \\ 0, & \text{otherwise} \end{cases}$$

The duration of r_i is calculated as follows:

$$time(r_i) = \begin{cases} time(t_i), & \text{if } cpu(t_i) \leq 1 \\ time(t_i) * cpu(t_i), & \text{otherwise} \end{cases}$$

The scaling of region r_i affects the duration of all operators in OP that are active in r_i. The same technique used for CPU sharing is applied for network sharing as well.

4. MONEY MODELING

Cloud providers lease computing resources that are typically charged based on a per time quantum pricing scheme. This quantum is typically one hour although recently other alternatives seem to appear as well [2]. The minimum monetary cost $m(S_G)_{min}$ of executing a dataflow graph G in a cloud environment given a schedule S_G and the cloud pricing scheme (quantum time Q_t and cost Q_m of leasing a container for Q_t) is a challenging task. In this work we employ an approximation. On each container, we slice time into windows of length Q_t starting from the first operator of the schedule. The financial cost is then a simple count of the time-windows that have at least one operator running, multiplied by Q_m.

$$m(S_G) = Q_m * (\sum_{i=1}^{|C|}\sum_{j=1}^{|W|} \epsilon(c_i, w_j))$$

with $C = \{c_i\}$ being the set of containers, $W = \{w_j\}$ being the set of time-windows, and

$$\epsilon(c_i, w_j) = \begin{cases} 1, & \text{if at least one operator is active in } w_j \text{ in } c_i \\ 0, & \text{otherwise} \end{cases}$$

The fragmentation $f(S_G)$ of a schedule S_G is the time during which the resources are not being used but are charged for.

$$f(S_G) = Q_t * \sum_{i=1}^{|C|}\sum_{j=1}^{|W|} (\epsilon(c_i, w_j) - \tau(c_i, w_j))$$

with $\tau(c, w)$ being the fraction of time that operators are active in the container c_i during time window w_j. It is easily proved that $\lim_{Q_t \to 0} f(S_G) = 0$ for any given dataflow. That is that if cloud resources are charged for exactly the time being used, there is no fragmentation overhead. In Fig. 5 we show a plan with four operators. The monetary cost is $5 * Q_m$. There are three quanta not fully used. The fragmentation of the schedule is $5 * Q_t - (1 + \frac{1}{4} + \frac{1}{4} + 1 + \frac{1}{2}) * Q_t = 2 * Q_t$. □

5. SCHEDULING PROBLEMS

As mentioned earlier, the space of solutions is two dimensional. The solutions that belong to the skyline (Pareto curve) [24] represent trade-offs between time and money. We define two types

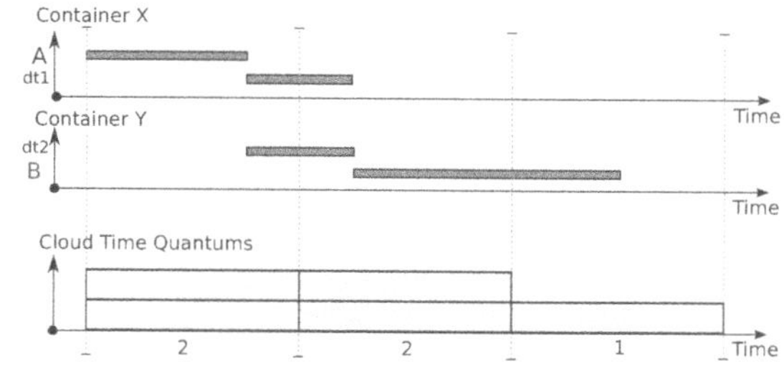

Figure 5: Financial cost of a scheduling plan. Operators A and B are assigned to different containers. The time is sliced into 3 time-windows and 5 quanta are leased during the execution.

of optimization problems: constrained and skyline. All problems are illustrated in Fig. 6. The **constrained** problems are (C1) *find the fastest plan within a pre-specified financial budget* (Fig. 6A) and (C2) *find the cheapest plan within a pre-specified deadline*(Fig. 6B). Those problems are symmetric and are essentially

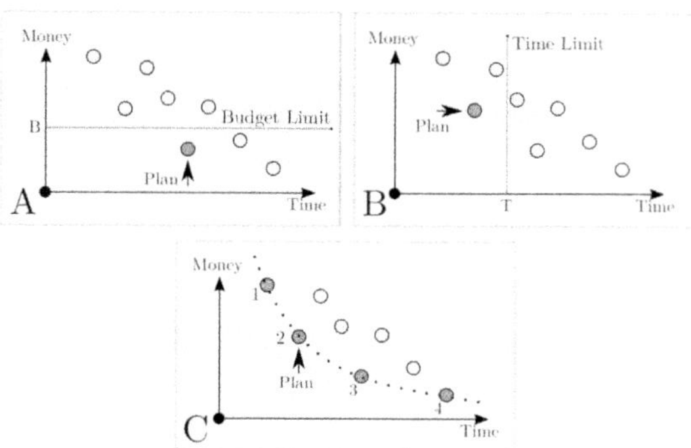

Figure 6: The three optimization problems: constraints (A and B) and skyline (C). The chosen plans are shown with an arrow.

one-dimensional optimization problems, only under constraints on the other dimension. In the **skyline** problem (SK), no constraints are specified a-priori. Several solutions are proposed that are on the skyline of the time/money space and the one with the best trade-off between time and money is chosen after optimization. In Fig. 6C, skyline optimization will return all the Pareto optimal solutions, and the relevant user will choose the one the user thinks best.

The above skyline shape can be captured by a metric called *Dataflow Elasticity* as follows:

$$E = \frac{(T_{max} - T_{min})/T_{max}}{(M_{max} - M_{min})/M_{max}}$$

with T_{min} and T_{max} being the min and max values in the time dimension of the skyline of schedules. Likewise, M_{min} and M_{max} are the min and max values in the money dimension. This metric expresses the acceleration of the completion time when paying more money [31]. For dataflows with high elasticity, a small amount of money makes a great difference in time (i.e. is worth paying for completion time). On the other hand, paying more does not have a significant impact on completion time for low elasticity dataflows. For them, it is worth paying, say, 50% less to lose only 10% in completion time!

6. SCHEDULING ALGORITHMS

Independent of the particular type of optimization problem solved, essentially the same algorithms can be used to search the space of alternatives and find the optimal one(s). We propose a family of algorithms that follow a nested loop approach. The outer loop calls the inner optimizer several times, with different upper bounds on the number of parallel containers to be used in the schedule and stops when the optimality criterion doesn't improve much after a particular number of consecutive iterations.

The degree of parallelism P_G of a dataflow G is an important predictor of performance. It captures the maximum number of concurrent running operators, when the computation has infinite resources. Assume the number of containers and the network bandwidth to be infinite. Satisfying only the constraints implied by the dataflow, an approximation of P_G is the maximum number of operators whose execution overlap.

The inner loop, optimizes on either time or money under a constraint on the other. We use a suite of greedy and probabilistic local search algorithms for the inner loop that are presented in the following subsections.

6.1 Outer Loop Algorithm

We have implemented one generic nested loop optimizer (Alg. 1) that solves any of the constrained or skyline problems, depending on the values of its parameters. The parameters of Alg. 1 are:

Algorithm 1 Nested Loop Optimizer

Input:
G: The dataflow graph
CONST: Solution constraints
FILTER: Solution space filter
LIMIT: Container limit sequence generator
STOP: Stopping condition
OPT: Lower level optimizer

Output:
$space$: The space of solutions

```
space ← ∅
while LIMIT.hasNext() and STOP.continue() do
    limit ← LIMIT.getNext()
    next ← OPT(G, limit, CONST)
    space ← FILTER(space ∪ {next})
    STOP.addFeedback(next)
    LIMIT.addFeedback(next)
end while
return space
```

1) The dataflow graph G as defined in Section 2. 2) $CONST$ is a boolean routine returning whether or not a schedule is satisfying the constraints. If $CONST$ returns always true ($time < \infty$ & $money < \infty$) is enough to express the lack of constraints used in the skyline problem. 3) $FILTER$ is a routine that is applied on a set of schedules and returns a reduced set, removing the schedules that are dominated by others, according to time, money, or both (skyline). 4) $LIMIT$ is a generator of container limits. In its simplest form, it just has to generate limits up to the total number of operators in the dataflow. However, in most cases, this is a very loose upper bound. 5) $STOP$ is a boolean routine determining whether or not to stop the exploration based on some of many possible criteria. The simplest way is to call the lower level sequentially for all limits generated by $LIMIT$. Another possibility is to end the exploration when the difference between the values of the OPT parameter for a specified number of consecutive schedules is below a particular threshold. Finally, OPT is a single-objective optimizer that tries to optimally assign the operators to containers, minimizing either the time or the money related to the schedule. Below we outline how some of the parameters of Alg. 1 are instantiated for each of the three optimization problems defined above.

Problem C1: $CONST$ checks whether or not a schedule is covered by the given financial budget. $FILTER$ returns only the fastest schedule. $LIMIT$ generates at most 20 container limits splitting equally the $[1, P_G]$ range. Condition $STOP$ is the last five schedules to not differ significantly with respect to completion time. Using linear regression, we compute the line in the time/iteration space using the five last iterations. If the slope of that line is less than 0.1 the exploration stops. OPT minimizes completion time having a budget limitation as constraint.

Problem C2: $CONST$ checks whether or not a schedule is within the given time limit. $FILTER$ return only the cheapest schedule. $LIMIT$ is the same as in Problem C1. $STOP$ is calculated in the same way as in C1 but the line is computed on the money/iteration space. OPT minimizes money having the time limitation as constraint.

Problem SK: $CONST$ accepts any schedule. $FILTER$ returns the skyline of solutions. $LIMIT$ is the same as C1 and the $STOP$ condition is always false. OPT can be any algorithm described in the following subsections. The size of the skyline is at most the number of container limits produced by $LIMIT$.

In the following subsections we define the various algorithms we have explored with respect to OPT.

6.2 Greedy Scheduling Algorithms

We have implemented several greedy scheduling algorithms [17] using different heuristics. In Alg. 2, we present the generic greedy algorithm. Only two routines have to be defined: $NEXT$ returns the next operator to be assigned choosing from a set of operators ready for that and $ASSIGN$ returns the container where the next operator will be assigned to. An operator is a candidate for assignment as soon as it has no dependencies to other operators as follows: By default, operators that have no inputs, have no dependencies. An S&F operator is a candidate as soon as all of its inputs are available. A PL operator is a candidate as soon as all of its inputs come from PL or from terminated S&F operators.

Algorithm 2 Generic Greedy (GG)

Input:
G: The dataflow graph
C: The maximum number of parallel containers to use
CONST: Solution constraints
NEXT: Next operator to assign
ASSIGN: Container the next operator is assigned to
Output:
S_G: The schedule of G with at most C containers

$S_G.assigns \leftarrow \oslash$
$ready \leftarrow$ {operators in G that has no dependencies}
while $ready \neq \oslash$ **do**
  $n \leftarrow$ NEXT($ready$)
  $candidates \leftarrow$ {containers that assignment of n satisfy CONST}
  if $candidates = \oslash$ **then**
    return $ERROR$
  end if
  $c \leftarrow$ ASSIGN($n, candidates$)
  $ready \leftarrow ready - \{n\}$
  $ready \leftarrow ready +$ {operators in G that constraints no longer exist}
  $S_G.assigns \leftarrow S_G.assigns + \{assign(n, c, -, -)\}$
end while
return S_G

We define four greedy algorithms: **G-BRT** balances container utilization, **G-MNT** minimizes network traffic, **G-MPT** minimizes completion time, and **G-MPM** minimizes monetary cost. In particular, at every step, G-BRT assigns the operator with maximum running time to the container that will minimize the standard deviation of the utilization of the containers in the schedule. The latter is the summation of the execution time of the operators assigned to the container. G-MNT assigns the operator with the maximum output size to the container that minimizes the data transferred through the network. G-MPT assigns the operator with the maximum execution time to the container that minimizes completion time. Finally, G-MPM assigns the operator with the maximum output size to the container that minimizes monetary cost.

6.3 Local Search Scheduling Algorithms

The local search method we use is simulated annealing [14]. We implemented a generic simulated annealing that requires the definition of only three routines: $INIT$ specifies the initial schedule from which the search begin, $COST$ returns the value of the optimization parameter for a particular schedule, and $NEIGHBOR$ returns a neighbor of a particular schedule. We do not accept neighbors that do not satisfy the constraints.

We define the following algorithms: **SA-MPT** begins with a random assignment and the $COST$ routine returns the completion time of a particular schedule, **SA-MPT2** begins with the output of G-MPT as its initial state and has the same $COST$ routine as SA-MPT, **SA-MPM** begins with a random assignment and the $COST$ routine returns the money of a particular schedule, and **SA-MPM2** begins with the output of G-MPM as its initial state and has the same $COST$ routine as SA-MPM. All algorithms produce a random neighbor by assigning a random operator to another container also chosen randomly. More sophisticated methods of choosing neighbors are left for future work.

6.4 Schedule Duration Estimation

Alg. 3 is in the heart of all algorithms described. Given any (partial) schedule of operators, this algorithm estimates when and for how long every operator will run. Thus, the completion time and monetary cost is estimated for the whole schedule.

Algorithm 3 Schedule Duration Estimation (SDE)

Input:
G: The dataflow graph
S_G: A (partial) $schedule(assigns)$
Output:
S_G: The schedule with calculated $start$ and end for all ops in S_G

$ready \leftarrow \oslash$
$time \leftarrow 0$
$G \leftarrow G +$ {data transfer ops before & after S&F operators if needed}
$queued \leftarrow$ {ops in G that have no dependencies}
for all operators A in $queued$ that satisfy memory constraints **do**
  $ready \leftarrow ready + \{assign(A, -, time, -)\}$
end for
while $ready \neq \oslash$ **do**
  $next\_event \leftarrow$ find_next_event($ready$)
  $terminated \leftarrow$ forward_in_time($next\_event, ready$)
  $time \leftarrow next\_event$
  for all operators A in $terminated$ **do**
    $S_G \leftarrow S_G + \{assign(A, -, -, time)\}$
  end for
  $ready \leftarrow ready - terminated$
  $queued \leftarrow queued +$ {ops in G that constraints no longer exist}
  for all ops A in $queued$ that satisfy memory constraints **do**
    $ready \leftarrow ready + \{assign(A, -, time, -)\}$
  end for
end while
return S_G

Routine find_next_event returns the time-stamp when first termination of operator occurs assuming uniform behavior. The

Table 1: Lattice Dataflows

H-B:	500-1	11-3	9-4	7-7	5-21	3-498
Size:	500	485	426	457	485	500

`forward_in_time` routine simulates the execution of all operators in *ready* until the time-stamp computed by `find_next_event`, and returns the ones that have terminated.

7. EXPERIMENTAL EVALUATION

In this section, we describe the overall setup of our experimentation effort and the results we have obtained from it. Although we have experimented with all three optimization problems, we only present the results of the one on skyline optimization, i.e., with no budget or deadline constraints, as it is the most challenging. Similar things hold for all parameters influencing our experiments, where only the most interesting or characteristic results are discussed, the rest offering not much additional insight.

7.1 Experimental Setup

The experiments conducted are characterized by four elements:

Execution Environment: In our experiments, we have realistically assumed that all containers are identical, i.e., they have the same resources (cpu, memory, and network). In particular, we have assumed containers with one CPU and total memory and maximum network bandwidth equal to 1.0.

Dataflow Graph Structure: We examine four families of dataflows: Montage [16] (Fig. 7A), Ligo [8] (Fig. 7B), Cybershake [7] (Fig. 7C), and Lattice (Fig. 8A). The first three are abstractions of actual dataflows that are used in real applications: Montage is used by NASA to generate custom mosaics of the sky, Ligo is used by the Laser Interferometer Gravitational-wave Observatory to analyze galactic binary systems, and Cybershake is used by the Southern California Earthquake Center to characterize earthquakes.

If we observe the time behavior of the workloads, we can identify phases of high and low parallelism. Parallelism is reduced when operators collect or distribute data from a lot of other operators (bottlenecks) or when an increased amount of data is to be transferred. Montage experiences a phase with the highest amount of parallelism, while it has several bottleneck operators. Ligo has more evenly distributed phases of parallelism and moderate number of bottleneck operators. Cybershake has two high parallelism phases and just four bottleneck operators, while it transfers large data volumes. Lattice, by design, provides us with a choice of parallelism and bottlenecks. Lattice is a purely synthetic dataflow family that we have designed generalizing the typical Map-Reduce dataflow (such as that of Fig. 1). Specific Lattice dataflows have a certain height (H) and branching factor (B) and are denoted as H-B Lattice. For example, Fig. 8B shows the 5-2 Lattice.

We have experimented with several sizes of dataflow graphs, from 5 to approximately 500 operators. Here we present the results of the largest graphs (500 operators) as they are the most challenging. The nature of the results for smaller graphs has been similar. Montage, Ligo, and Cybershake dataflows have been produced by the Pegasus dataflow generator [4]. Lattice dataflows have been handcrafted in several forms according to the H-B parameters and are shown in Table 1.

Operator Types: In our experiments, we have indicated the values of operator properties as percentages of the corresponding parameters of container resources. For example, an operator having memory needs equal to 0.4 uses 40% of a container's memory. Furthermore, execution times are given as percentages of the cloud's time quantum and so are data sizes (inputs/outputs of operators),

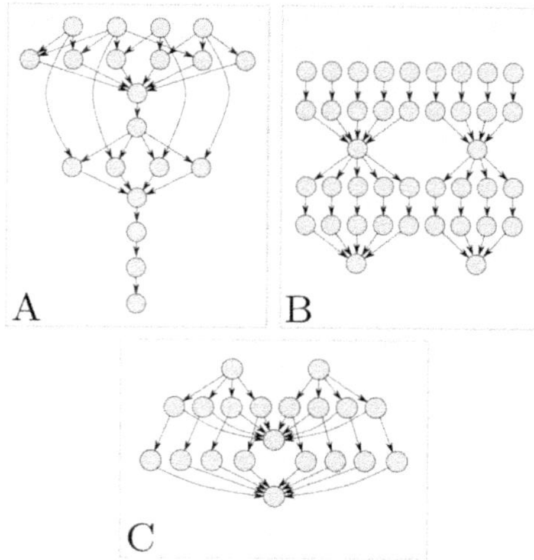

Figure 7: Montage(A), Ligo(B), and Cybershake(C) dataflows.

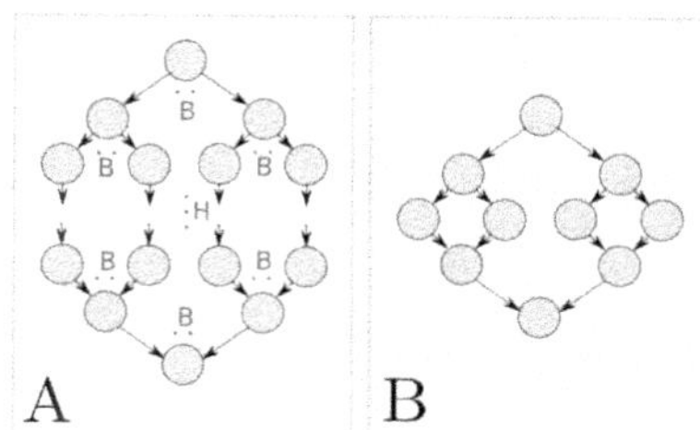

Figure 8: Lattice - general dataflow graph (A) and an example with $H = 5$ and $B = 2$ (B).

Table 2: Lattice Operator Properties

Property	Values
time	0.2, 0.4, 0.6, 0.8, 1.0
cpu	0.4, 0.45, 0.5, 0.55, 0.6
memory	0.05, 0.1, 0.15, 0.2, 0.25
data	0.2, 0.4, 0.6, 0.8, 1.0

taking into account the network speed. For example, an execution time of 0.5 indicates that the operator requires half of a time quantum to complete its execution (say, 30 minutes according to the predominant Amazon cost model). Likewise, an output of size 0.2 requires one fifth of a time quantum to be transferred through the network if needed. This way, the output data size is in inverse correlation with network speed. Money is measured as described in Section 4.

We have used synthetic workloads based on Montage, Ligo, and Cybershake dataflows as defined in [4]. Since our intention was to study data intensive workloads, we scaled up the specified run times and operator output sizes by a factor of 50 and 1000 respectively; run time to output size ratio was increased by 20. We also set operator memory to 10% of the container capacity, since they were not specified by the original benchmarks. The properties of operators in Lattice are chosen with uniform probability from the corresponding sets of values shown in Table 2.

Data transfer CPU utilization is $DT_{CPU} = 0.05$ and memory needs $DT_{MEM} = 0.001$ (defined in Section 2). We experimented with changing the output by a factor of $\frac{1}{0.64}$, $\frac{1}{2.56}$, $\frac{1}{40.96}$, and $\frac{1}{10485.76}$. We have used dataflows with all operators being S&F and all being PL.

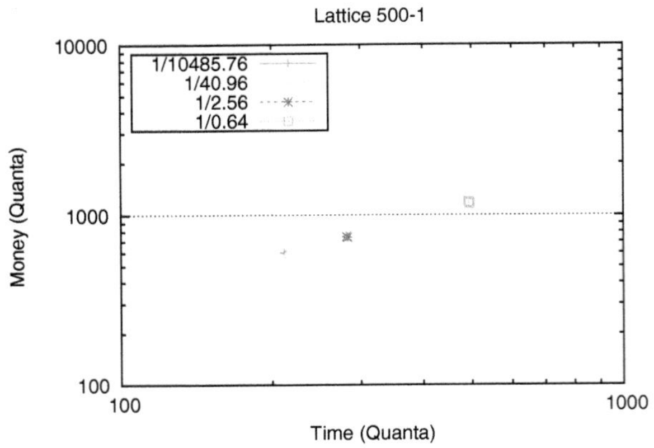

Figure 10: Time/Money skylines of S&F 500-1 Lattice with different output sizes (log-log scale).

Schedule Optimization Algorithms: For the outer loop of our Nested Loops Optimizer (Alg. 1), the numbers of available containers examined have been 10, 30, 50, 70, 90, 110, 130, and 150.

For the inner loop, we have experimented with all algorithms described in Section 6: greedy (G-BRT, G-MNT, G-MPT, G-MPM) and simulated annealing (SA-MPT, SA-MPT2, SA-MPM, SA-MPM2). In addition, we have also run experiments with a random schedule generator to explore the time/money space of solutions and gain insights into the nature of the optimization problem at hand. The next subsection presents the findings of exactly that experiment, whereas the following one those with the actual optimization algorithms.

7.2 Time/Money Space Exploration

The random schedule generator used for this experiment produces 10,000 (almost) random schedules for each dataflow studied. The details of the algorithm are omitted due to lack of space. Below we analyze how the time/money space is affected by various characteristics of the dataflow optimized or the execution environment.

Output Data Size: In Fig. 9, we show the skylines for various output data sizes of two Lattice dataflows (3-498 and 7-7) and in Fig. 12 we show the skylines of Ligo, Montage, and Cybershake. The key observation is that, for a particular dataflow graph G, in general, the elasticity metric E^G increases as the output size decreases. Also, for small output, elasticity is greater for high degree of parallelism ($E^{3-498}_{small} > E^{7-7}_{small}$). In some cases the output size does not affect the elasticity too much (Lattice 7-7 in Fig. 9 and Ligo in Fig. 12).

The elasticity metric is almost undefined ($E^{3-498}_{small} \approx \frac{0}{0}$) for 3-498 Lattice dataflow with large output. This is also the case for all outputs in 500-1 Lattice dataflow shown in Fig. 10. This means that there is no time/money trade-off, consequently, the fastest schedule is also the cheapest one.

In Fig. 11, we plot entire solution spaces (not just the skylines), for the same dataflow graphs but only for the smallest ($\frac{1}{10485.76}$) and largest ($\frac{1}{0.64}$) outputs. For small outputs, the more containers we use, the faster the schedules run in general, i.e., time and money are anti-correlated and true elasticity is present. For large outputs, in the extreme case, they are correlated and the fastest schedule is also the cheapest. We also observe that, for large outputs, sometimes the solution space is not continuous. This happens because when the memory is not sufficient, the operator execution is delayed. For large outputs, the data transfer operators are long running, so their delay adds significant delay in the whole dataflow.

In Fig. 12, we show the skylines of Ligo, Montage, and Cybershake. We observe that $E^{Ligo}_{small} > E^{Montage}_{small} > E^{Cybershake}_{small}$, i.e., elasticity is analogous to the amount of parallelism exhibited by the dataflow structure, where Ligo has more parallelism than Montage, which has more than Cybershake.

Multi-processing vs. Uni-processing: Our model allows multiple operators to run concurrently in the same container. The skylines of Lattice dataflows produced with multi- and uni-processing are shown in Fig. 13. Schedules produced under uni-processing are slower and more expensive than those produced under multi-processing for small output sizes while not differing much for large output sizes. The main reason for this is under-utilization of the container when running one operator at a time. Domination of the network usage time over the processing time for large outputs explains the fact that the skylines do not differ much.

Cloud Time Quantum: We have also experimented with the cloud time quantum size. In Fig. 14, we show the skyline of Lattice dataflows for quantum size 0 and 1 using multi- and uni-processing. We observe that the cloud quantum time affects the fastest schedules (many containers) more than the slowest (few containers). This was expected since, in general, the more containers we use, the higher fragmentation we have. In Fig. 14, we also observe that, under uni-processing, elasticity is very high ($E^{7-7}_{small} \approx \frac{T_{max}-T_{min}}{0}$) so, the fastest and slowest schedule cost the same. Hence, for these specific cases, the optimization problem becomes one dimensional.

Pipeline vs. Store-&-Forward: In Fig. 15, we observe that the 500-1 Lattice dataflow with PL operators has some elasticity, while that with S&F operators does not. Furthermore, the schedules of the former are faster and some of them cheaper. On the other hand, the schedules for the 7-7 Lattice dataflow with PL operators are in general slower and more expensive than for that with S&F operators. This has two explanations: 1) due to PL operator execution overlapping, all are stretched in time to reach the one with the maximum execution time and 2) due to data transfer overlapping with processing, the space-shared resources (memory) consumed by PL operators are occupied for a longer period of time. This also explains the fact that for large number of containers, the 7-7 Lattice dataflows schedules are faster than S&F because more memory is available. Two connected PL operators assigned to the same container will be executed faster than two S&F with the same functionality, but when are assigned to different containers, this may not be the case.

General conclusions: Based on the above discussion, one can draw the following interesting conclusions regarding the time/money space of alternative schedules:

1. There is correlation between an operator's completion time and the time spent on data transfer. For large values of $\frac{time}{data}$ completion time is anti-correlated with monetary cost and the level of elasticity is high. On the other hand, for small values, time is correlated to money and there is limited elasticity, so solving a one-dimensional optimization problem is enough. For example, linear dataflows with S&F operators are not elastic while those with PL are.

2. Multi-processing, in general, produces faster and cheaper plans than uni-processing.

3. Pipelining should be used with caution, since it can add a significant overhead in both completion time and money.

4. Fragmentation of resources causes significant increases in monetary costs, especially when using many containers.

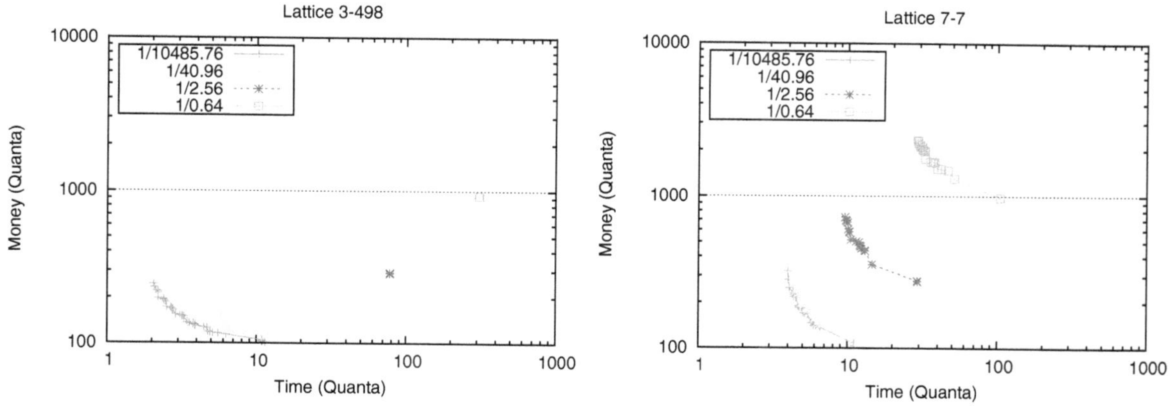

Figure 9: Time/Money skylines of S&F Lattice dataflows with different output sizes (log-log scale).

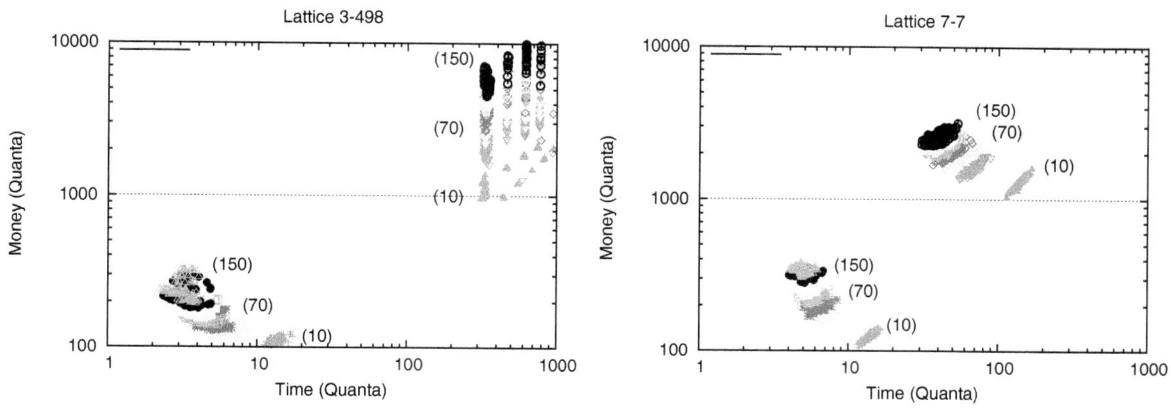

Figure 11: Time/Money of S&F Lattice dataflows with small ($\frac{1}{10485.76}$) and large ($\frac{1}{0.64}$) output size using different numbers of available containers.

5. Different types of elasticity exist for different types of dataflows. Some dataflows are more elastic than others, and some are not elastic at all.

7.3 Schedule Optimization

In Fig. 16, we present the schedules produced by the subsequent invocations of the algorithms against Montage with S&F operators and small output. We see that there is elasticity between time and money. It is clear that the time decreases when the number of parallel containers increases. Money tends to increase with the number of containers but not strictly. There are two different reasons for this: First, availability of a number of containers does not imply use of all of them in the schedule obtained; the schedule's actual maximum parallelism may be less than the number of available containers or the schedule identified by the optimization algorithms as optimal may have not used all the available parallelism. The number of available containers is just an upper limit. Second, due to the quantized pricing policy, the average usage of quanta is better and the produced schedule more compact.

In Fig. 17, we show the time/money space of Montage and the skylines produced by various algorithms. Interestingly, when these skylines are merged together, the overall skyline has schedules from different algorithms. Schedules given by SA-MPM give cheap schedules, SA-MPT give solutions faster than SA-MPM but more expensive, and G-BRT give the fastest and most expensive solutions. It appears that one size does not fit all. We also observe

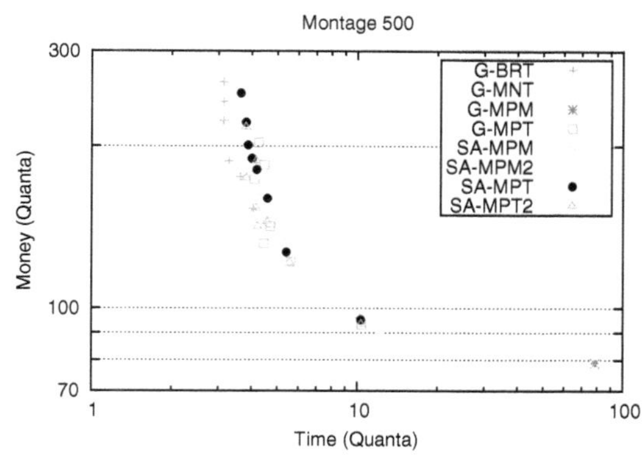

Figure 17: Time/Money by different algorithms for Montage dataflow with small output (log-log scale).

that G-MNT (minimize network traffic) gives solutions similar to G-MPM using only a small number of containers. Algorithm SA-MPT starts with a random assignment and the solution it finds is very close to the one produced by the greedy G-MPT. Algorithms G-MPM and SA-MPM2 do not provide trade-offs. This happens because all operators are S&F and thus, the cheapest schedule is always the one using a single container. On the other hand, SA-MPM, starting with a random schedule, give elasticity.

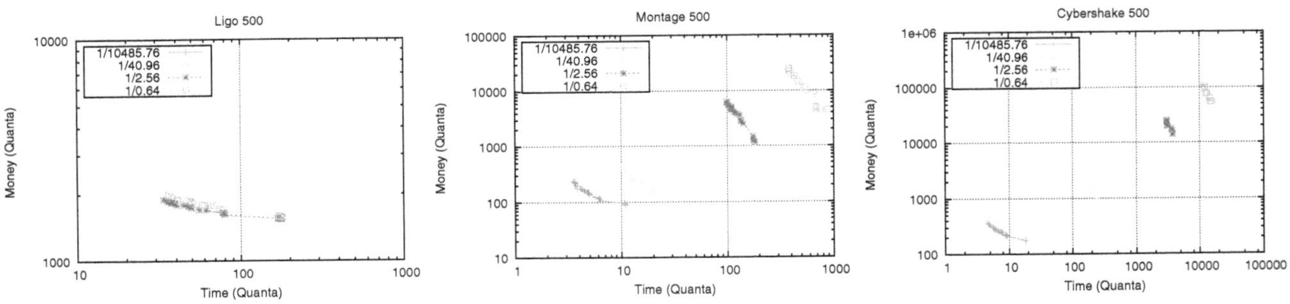

Figure 12: Time/Money skylines of Ligo, Montage, and Cybershake dataflows using different output sizes (log-log scale).

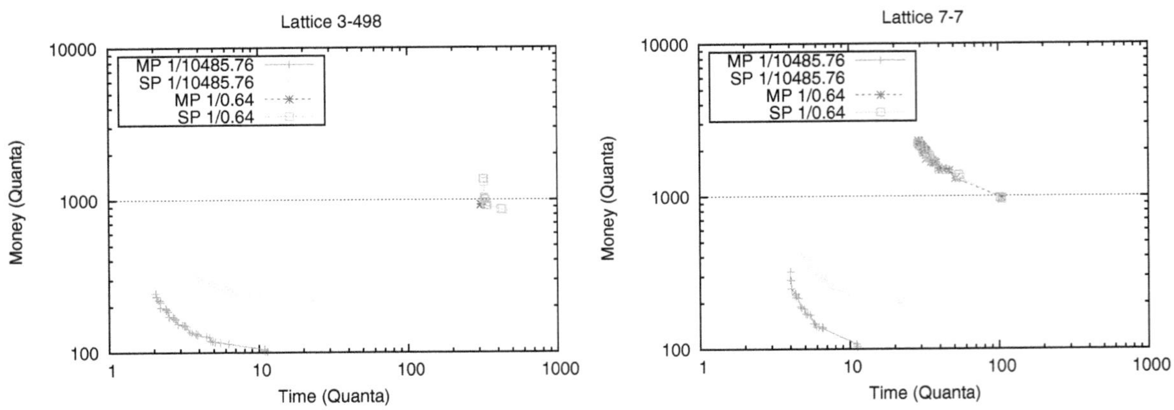

Figure 13: Uni-processing vs. multi-processing skylines of S&F Lattice dataflows (log-log scale).

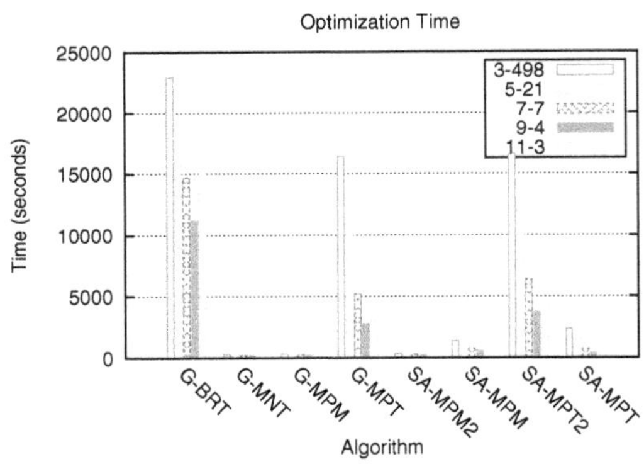

Figure 18: Optimization time of all algorithms against the Lattice dataflows.

In Fig. 18, we show the running time of the different algorithms for several types of S&F Lattice dataflows with small output. Clearly, the level of parallelism afforded by the dataflow graph affects the running time of the algorithms, some more (e.g., G-MPT, SA-MPT2) than others (e.g., G-BRT, SA-MPT). Since, G-BRT uniformly distributes the operators into containers, the expected number of containers used is near to those available. Naturally, this algorithm is near the worst case among all greedy algorithms.

General conclusions: In summary, the following are the key observations on the behavior of the various optimization algorithms:

1. Different optimization algorithms tend to explore different areas of the time/money space, some of them generating skyline schedules that exhibit interesting trade-offs that no other algorithm does. This raises a meta question of choosing the optimal optimization algorithm depending on the user needs, which is left for future work.

2. Sophisticated search methods, such as simulated annealing, do not seem to improve significantly the schedules produced by greedy algorithms, while they require much more time to execute. The space of alternatives is huge and more study need to be done in finding ways of exploring the solution space efficiently. For large dataflows, greedy algorithms appear to be the right choice.

8. RELATED WORK

Typically, some middleware is used to execute user-defined code in distributed environments. The Condor/DAGMan/Stork [20] set is the state-of-the-art technology of High Performance Computing. Nevertheless, Condor was designed to harvest CPU cycles on idle machines; running data intensive workflows with DAGMan is very inefficient [26]. Many systems use DAGMan as middleware, like Pegasus [6] and GridDB [21]. Proposals for extensions of Condor to deal with data intensive scientific workflows do exist [26], but to the best of our knowledge, they have not been materialized yet. In [9] is presented a case study of executing the Montage dataflow on the cloud examining the trade-offs of different dataflow execution modes and provisioning plans for cloud resources.

Hadoop is a platform that follows the Map-Reduce [5] paradigm to achieve fault tolerance and massive parallelism. Several high-lever query languages have been developed on top of Hadoop, e.g., PigLatin [22] and Hive [28] (used by Facebook), and the same holds for several applications, e.g., Mahout [3], a platform for large-scale machine learning. The dataflow graphs used in Map-Reduce

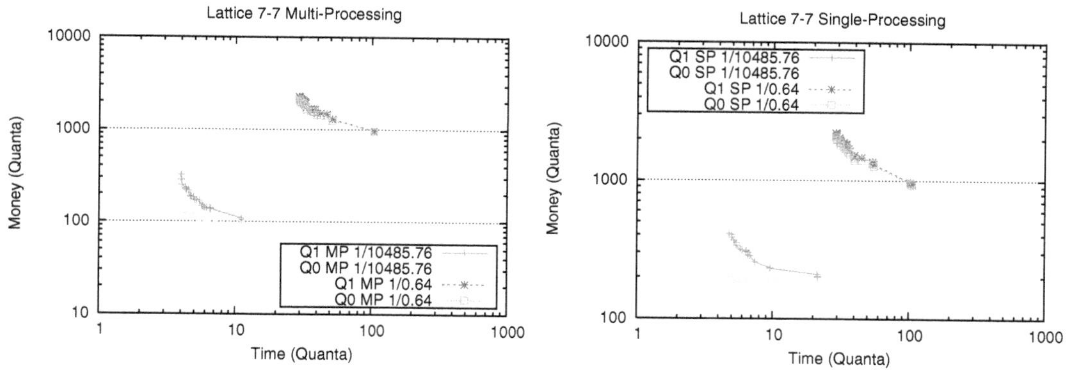

Figure 14: Time/Money skylines of S&F Lattice dataflows with quantum size equal to 0 and 1 (log-log scale).

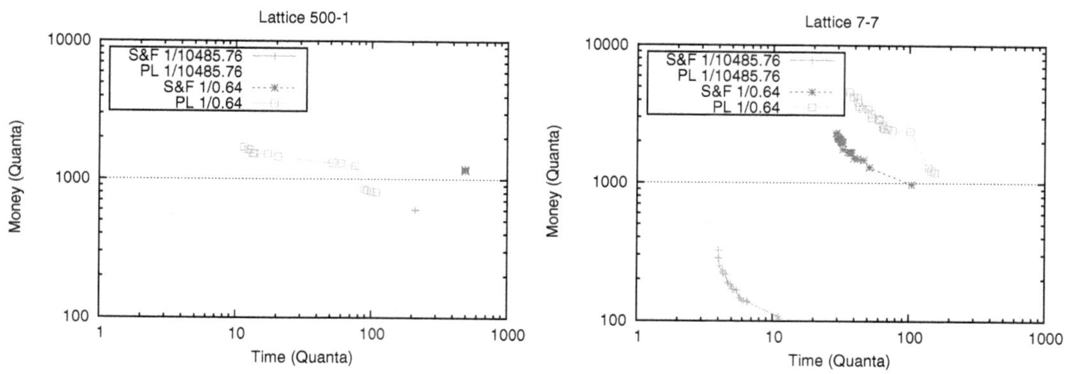

Figure 15: Time/Money store and forward vs. pipeline for different dataflows and outputs (log-log scale).

are relatively restricted, as they are mostly Lattice 3-N dataflows, for some N, and this reduces opportunities for optimization.

Dryad [15] is a commercial middleware by Microsoft that has a more general architecture than Map-Reduce since it can parallelize any dataflow. Its schedule optimization, however, relies heavily on hints requiring knowledge of node proximity, which are generally not available in a cloud environment. It also deals with job migration by instantiating another copy of a job and not by moving the job to another machine. This might be acceptable when optimizing solely time but not when the financial cost of allocating additional containers matters.

Nefeli [29] is a cloud gateway that uses hints for efficient execution of workloads. It uses the cloud at a lower level than our work, being aware of the physical resources and the actual locations of the virtual machines. This information may not be generally available, however, especially in commercial clouds.

There are also several efforts that move in the same direction as our work but try to solve simpler versions of the problem. Examples include a particle swarm optimization of general dataflows having a single-dimensional weighted average parameter of several metrics as the optimization criterion [23] and a heuristic optimization of independent tasks (no dependencies) having the number of machines that should be allocated to maximize speedup as the optimization crieterion given a predefined budget[27].

Finally, at the foundational level, we have followed a parallelism and resource-sharing model for optimal scheduling of relational operators of query execution plans with time and space-shared resources [11] and have generalized it to arbitrary operators.

In summary, we capitalize on the elasticity of clouds and produce multiple schedules, enabling the user to select the desired tradeoff. To the best of our knowledge, no dataflow processing system deals with the concept of elasticity or two-dimensional time/space optimization, which constitute our key novelties.

9. CONCLUSIONS & FUTURE WORK

We have presented a framework for three different problems of dataflow schedule optimization on the Cloud, for a two-dimensional optimality criterion of time and money, and a methodology to solve these problems. Experimental results have revealed interesting insights on the space of alternatives that needs to be explored, on the different levels of elasticity offered by different cases of dataflow structures, operator characteristics, and other parameters, and on the effectiveness and efficiency of several optimization algorithms.

The methodology proposed is used in the final step of the optimization of the ADP system and all the parameters are instantiated automatically using functions or statistics collected during previous executions. It can also be used separately, however, helping cloud service providers in advising consumers on choosing the appropriate time/money trade-offs.

Our plans for future work move in several directions. We intend to study the concept of elasticity further and identify its sensitivity to different workloads and environment characteristics, as well as the ability of optimization algorithms to exploit it. We also plan to evaluate the model itself on how good is in predicting the real workload. Furthermore, we plan to investigate the problem of scalability using adaptive and incremental schedule generation techniques. Finally, we intend to compare our approach with the optimization methods of other distributed computing systems such as Hadoop.

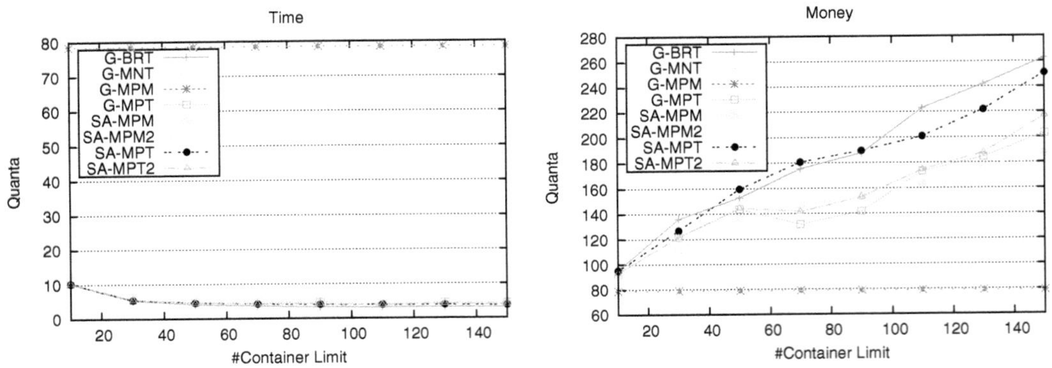

Figure 16: Time & Money as a function of the number of containers for different algorithms on the Montage dataflow for small output.

10. REFERENCES

[1] R. Agrawal et al. "The Claremont report on database research". *SIGMOD Record*, 37(3):9–19, 2008.

[2] Amazon. "Amazon Elastic Compute Cloud (EC2), http://aws.amazon.com/ec2/", 2010.

[3] Apache. "Mahout : Scalable machine-learning and data-mining library, http://mahout.apache.org/", 2010.

[4] S. Bharathi, A. Chervenak, E. Deelman, G. Mehta, M.-H. Su, and K. Vahi. Characterization of scientific workflows. pp. 1 –10, nov. 2008.

[5] J. Dean and S. Ghemawat. "MapReduce: Simplified Data Processing on Large Clusters". In *6th Symposium on Operating System Design and Implementation*, pp. 137–150, 2004.

[6] E. Deelman and e. al. "Pegasus: Mapping Large Scale Workflows to Distributed Resources in Workflows in e-Science". *Springer*, 2006.

[7] E. Deelman et al. Managing large-scale workflow execution from resource provisioning to provenance tracking: The cybershake example. In *IEEE e-Science*, pp. 14, 2006.

[8] E. Deelman, C. Kesselman, and more. "GriPhyN and LIGO, Building a Virtual Data Grid for Gravitational Wave Scientists". In *IEEE HPDC*, pp. 225–, 2002.

[9] E. Deelman, G. Singh, M. Livny, G. B. Berriman, and J. Good. The cost of doing science on the cloud: the montage example. In *IEEE/ACM SC*, pp. 50, 2008.

[10] I. T. Foster. "The Anatomy of the Grid: Enabling Scalable Virtual Organizations". In *CCGRID*, pp. 6–7, 2001.

[11] M. N. Garofalakis and Y. E. Ioannidis. "Parallel Query Scheduling and Optimization with Time- and Space-Shared Resources". In *VLDB*, pp. 296–305, 1997.

[12] L. M. V. Gonzalez, L. R. Merino, J. Caceres, and M. Lindner. "A break in the clouds: towards a cloud definition". *Computer Communication Review*, 39(1):50–55, 2009.

[13] R. L. Graham. "Bounds on Multiprocessing Timing Anomalies". *SIAM Journal of Applied Mathematics*, 17(2):416–429, 1969.

[14] Y. E. Ioannidis and E. Wong. "Query Optimization by Simulated Annealing". In *SIGMOD Conference*, pp. 9–22, 1987.

[15] M. Isard, M. Budiu, Y. Yu, A. Birrell, and D. Fetterly. "Dryad: distributed data-parallel programs from sequential building blocks". In *EuroSys*, pp. 59–72, 2007.

[16] J. C. Jacob et al. "Montage: a grid portal and software toolkit for science, grade astronomical image mosaicking". *Int. J. Comput. Sci. Eng.*, 4(2):73–87, 2009.

[17] J. Kleinberg and E. Tardos. *"Algorithm Design"*. Addison-Wesley Longman Publishing Co., Inc., Boston, MA, USA, 2005.

[18] D. Kossmann. "The state of the art in distributed query processing". *ACM Comput. Surv.*, 32(4):422–469, 2000.

[19] Y.-K. Kwok and I. Ahmad. "Benchmarking and Comparison of the Task Graph Scheduling Algorithms". *J. Parallel Distrib. Comput.*, 59(3):381–422, 1999.

[20] M. J. Litzkow, M. Livny, and M. W. Mutka. "Condor - A Hunter of Idle Workstations". In *ICDCS*, pp. 104–111, 1988.

[21] D. T. Liu and M. J. Franklin. "The Design of GridDB: A Data-Centric Overlay for the Scientific Grid". In *VLDB*, pp. 600–611, 2004.

[22] C. Olston et al. "Pig latin: a not-so-foreign language for data processing". In *SIGMOD Conference*, pp. 1099–1110, 2008.

[23] S. Pandey, L. Wu, S. M. Guru, and R. Buyya. A particle swarm optimization-based heuristic for scheduling workflow applications in cloud computing environments. In *IEEE AINA*, pp. 400–407, 2010.

[24] C. H. Papadimitriou and M. Yannakakis. "Multiobjective Query Optimization". In *PODS*, 2001.

[25] G. M. R., J. D. S., and S. Ravi. "The Complexity of Flowshop and Jobshop Scheduling". *Mathematics of operations research*, 1(2):117–129, 1976.

[26] S. Shankar and D. J. DeWitt. "Data driven workflow planning in cluster management systems". In *HPDC*, pp. 127–136, 2007.

[27] J. N. Silva, L. Veiga, and P. Ferreira. Heuristic for resources allocation on utility computing infrastructures. In B. Schulze and G. Fox, editors, *MGC*, pp. 9. ACM, 2008.

[28] A. Thusoo et al. "Hive - a petabyte scale data warehouse using Hadoop". In *ICDE*, pp. 996–1005, 2010.

[29] K. Tsakalozos, M. Roussopoulos, V. Floros, and A. Delis. Nefeli: Hint-based execution of workloads in clouds. In *IEEE ICDCS*, pp. 74–85, 2010.

[30] M. M. Tsangaris and more. Dataflow processing and optimization on grid and cloud infrastructures. *IEEE Data Eng. Bull.*, 32(1):67–74, 2009.

[31] H. R. Varian. *"Intermediate Microeconomics : A Modern Approach"*, chapter 15, Market Demand. W. W. Norton and Company, 7th edition, Dec. 2005.

Zephyr: Live Migration in Shared Nothing Databases for Elastic Cloud Platforms

Aaron J. Elmore Sudipto Das Divyakant Agrawal Amr El Abbadi
Department of Computer Science
University of California, Santa Barbara
Santa Barbara, CA 93106-5110, USA
{aelmore, sudipto, agrawal, amr}@cs.ucsb.edu

ABSTRACT

Multitenant data infrastructures for large cloud platforms hosting hundreds of thousands of applications face the challenge of serving applications characterized by small data footprint and unpredictable load patterns. When such a platform is built on an elastic pay-per-use infrastructure, an added challenge is to minimize the system's operating cost while guaranteeing the tenants' service level agreements (SLA). *Elastic load balancing* is therefore an important feature to enable scale-up during high load while scaling down when the load is low. *Live migration*, a technique to migrate tenants with minimal service interruption and no downtime, is critical to allow lightweight elastic scaling. We focus on the problem of live migration in the database layer. We propose **Zephyr**, a technique to efficiently migrate a live database in a shared nothing transactional database architecture. Zephyr uses phases of on-demand pull and asynchronous push of data, requires minimal synchronization, results no service unavailability and few or no aborted transactions, minimizes the data transfer overhead, provides ACID guarantees during migration, and ensures correctness in the presence of failures. We outline a prototype implementation using an open source relational database engine and an present a thorough evaluation using various transactional workloads. Zephyr's efficiency is evident from the few tens of failed operations, 10-20% change in average transaction latency, minimal messaging, and no overhead during normal operation when migrating a live database.

Categories and Subject Descriptors

H.2.4 [**Database Management**]: Systems—*Relational databases, Transaction processing*; H.3.4 [**Information Storage and Retrieval**]: Systems and Software—*Distributed systems*

General Terms

Design, Experimentation, Performance, Reliability

Keywords

Cloud computing, multitenancy, elastic data management, database migration, shared nothing architectures

SIGMOD'11, June 12–16, 2011, Athens, Greece.

1. INTRODUCTION

The increasing popularity of service oriented computing has seen hundreds of thousands of applications being deployed on various cloud platforms [15]. The sheer scale of the number of application databases, or **tenants**, and their small footprint (both in terms of size and load) mandate a shared infrastructure to minimize the operating cost [11, 19, 25, 26]. These applications often have unpredictable load patterns, such as flash crowds originating from a sudden and viral popularity, resulting in the tenants' resource requirements changing with little notice. Load balancing is therefore an important feature to minimize the impact of a heavily loaded tenant on the other co-located tenants. Furthermore, a platform deployed on a pay-per-use infrastructure (like Amazon EC2) provides the potential to minimize the system's operating cost. *Elasticity*, i.e. the ability to scale up to deal with high load while scaling down in periods of low load, is a critical feature to minimize the operating cost. **Elastic load balancing** is therefore a first class feature in the design of modern database management systems for the cloud [11, 12], and requires a low cost technique to migrate tenants between hosts, a feature referred to as **live migration** [8, 20].[1]

Our focus is the problem of live migration in the database layer supporting a multitenant cloud platform where the service provider manages the applications' databases. Force.com, Microsoft Azure, and Google AppEngine are examples of such multitenant cloud platforms. Even though a number of techniques are prevalent to scale the DBMS layer, elasticity is often ignored primarily due to static infrastructure provisioning. In a multitenant platform built on an infrastructure as a service (IaaS) abstraction, elastic scaling allows minimizing the system's operating cost leveraging the pay-per-use pricing. Most current DBMSs, however, only support heavyweight techniques for elastic scale-up where adding new nodes requires manual intervention or long service disruption to migrate a tenant's database to these newly added nodes. Therefore, to enable lightweight elasticity as a first class notion, live migration is a critical functionality.

We present **Zephyr**,[2] a technique for live migration in a shared nothing transactional database. Das et al. [13] proposed a solution for live database migration in a shared storage architecture while Curino et al. [10] outlined a possible solution for live migration in a shared nothing architecture. Zephyr is the first complete solution for live migration in a shared nothing database architecture.

Zephyr minimizes service interruption for the tenant being migrated by introducing a synchronized *dual mode* that allows both the source and destination to simultaneously execute transactions

[1]Our use of the term migration is different from migration between different database versions or different schema.

[2]Zephyr, meaning a gentle breeze, is symbolic of the lightweight nature of the proposed technique.

for the tenant. Migration starts with the transfer of the tenant's metadata to the destination which can then start serving new transactions, while the source completes the transactions that were active when migration started. Read/write access (called **ownership**) on database pages of the tenant is partitioned between the two nodes with the source node owning all pages at the start and the destination acquiring page ownership on-demand as transactions at the destination access those pages. The index structures are replicated at the source and destination and are immutable during migration. Lightweight synchronization between the source and the destination, only during the short dual mode, guarantees serializability, while obviating the need for two phase commit [16]. Once the source node completes execution of all active transactions, migration completes with the ownership transfer of all database pages owned by the source to the destination node. Zephyr thus allows migration of individual tenant databases that share a database process at a node and where live VM migration [8] cannot be used.

Zephyr guarantees no service disruption for other tenants, no system downtime, minimizes data transferred between the nodes, guarantees *safe* migration in the presence of failures, and ensures the strongest level of transaction isolation. Zephyr uses standard tree based indices and lock based concurrency control, thus allowing it to be used in a variety of DBMS implementations. Zephyr does not rely on replication in the database layer, thus providing greater flexibility in selecting the destination for migration, which might or might not have the tenant's replica. However, considerable performance improvement is possible in the presence of replication when a tenant is migrated to one of the replicas.

We implemented Zephyr in an open source RDBMS. Our evaluation using a variety of transactional workloads shows that Zephyr results in only a few tens of failed operations, compared to hundreds to thousands of failed transactions when using a simple heavyweight migration technique. Zephyr results in no operational overhead during normal operation, minimal messaging overhead during migration, and between 10-20% increase in average transaction latency compared to an execution where no migration was performed. These results demonstrate the lightweight nature of Zephyr allowing live migration with minimal service interruption.

The main contributions of this paper are as follows:

- We present Zephyr, the first complete end-to-end solution for live migration in a shared nothing database architecture.
- We present a detailed analysis of the guarantees provided by Zephyr, analyze the associated trade-offs, and prove safety and liveness guarantees in the presence of failures.
- We provide a detailed evaluation of our prototype evaluation using a variety of workloads that demonstrate interesting trade-offs in performance.

The rest of the paper is organized as: Section 2 provides background on multitenancy models, the system model used, migration cost measures, and describes some straightforward migration techniques. Section 3 describes Zephyr, Section 4 proves transaction correctness, and Section 5 discusses some extensions and optimizations. Section 6 describes the details of a prototype implementation and Section 7 provides a detailed evaluation. Section 8 provides a survey of related literature and Section 9 concludes the paper.

2. BACKGROUND

2.1 Multitenancy Models

The three most common multitenancy models are: *shared table*, *shared process*, and *shared machine*. The shared table model is used primarily in the context of Software as a Service (SaaS) such

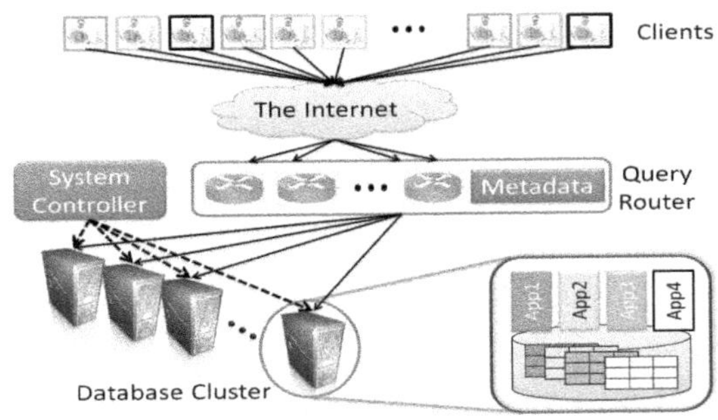

Figure 1: A shared nothing multitenant DBMS architecture.

as in Saleforce.com [25]. It allows efficient resource sharing while providing row level isolation between tenants. All tenants' data is stored in a few big tables, with additional access structures or tables for metadata management and query processing. For instance, in the Saleforce.com architecture [25], a centralized table (called the *heap*) stores all tenants' data, while additional tables (called *pivot tables*) are used to access data in the heap. To allow schema flexibility, the heap table cannot use native types and hence custom query processing and indexing layers are needed. Such a design is suitable when most of the tenants have almost similar schema with minor customizations per tenant. However, this model leads to various challenges when application schemas differ considerably. Moreover, row level isolation between tenants complicates on-demand tenant migration.

The shared machine model [24] uses different virtual machines (VM) or database processes per tenant, thus allowing for stronger VM or OS level isolation. Using a VM per tenant can leverage VM migration techniques [8, 20] for elastic load balancing. However, experimental studies have shown that this stronger isolation comes at the cost of increased overhead during normal operation resulting in inefficient resource sharing between tenants [10]. This overhead due to redundant components can be significantly reduced by the shared process model.

The shared process model allows independent schemas for tenants while sharing the database process amongst multiple tenants [3, 10, 11, 26]. This model provides better isolation compared to the shared table model while allowing effective sharing and consolidation of multiple tenants in the same database process [10]. However, such a model cannot leverage VM migration to move individual tenants from a shared database process. This calls for efficient and low cost live database migration techniques, such as Zephyr, to provide a good mix of effective sharing and ease of migration.

2.2 System Architecture

We use a standard shared nothing database model for transaction processing (OLTP) systems executing short running transactions, with a two phase locking [14] based scheduler, and a page based model with a B+ tree index [4]. Figure 1 provides an overview of the architecture. Following are the salient features of the system. First, clients connect to the database through **query routers** that handle client connections and hide the physical location of the tenant's database. Routers store this mapping as metadata which is updated whenever there is a migration. Second, we use the **shared process** multitenancy model which strikes a balance between isolation and scale. Conceptually, each tenant has its own transaction manager and buffer pool. However, since most current systems do not support this, we use a design where co-located tenants share all resources within a database instance, but is shared nothing across nodes. Finally, there exists a **system controller** that determines the tenant to be migrated, the initiation time, and the destination of migration. The system controller gathers usage statistics and builds a model to optimize the system's operating cost while guaranteeing the tenant's SLAs. The detailed design and implementation of the controller is orthogonal to the problem considered in this paper and is left for future work.

2.3 Migration Cost

The goal of any migration technique is to minimize migration cost. Das et al. [13] discuss some measures to quantify the cost of migration. Low migration cost allows the system controller to effectively use it for elastic load balancing.

- **Service interruption:** Live migration must ensure minimal service interruption for the tenant being migrated and should not result in downtime.[3] We use *downtime* for an entire system outage and *service interruption* for small interruption in service for some tenants. The number of transactions or operations aborted during migration is a measure of service interruption and is used to determine the impact of migration on the tenant's SLA.
- **Migration Overhead:** Migration overhead is the additional work done or resources consumed to enable and perform migration. This cost also includes performance impact as a result of migration, such as increase in transaction latency or reduction in throughput. This comprises of:
  - *Overhead during normal operation:* Additional work done during normal database operation to enable migration.
  - *Overhead during migration:* Performance impact on the tenant being migrated as well as other tenants co-located at the source or destination of migration.
  - *Overhead after migration:* Performance impact on transactions executing at the destination node after migration.
- **Additional data transferred:** Since the source and destination of migration do not share storage, the persistent image of the database must be moved from the source to the destination. This measure accounts for any data transfer that migration incurs, in addition to transferring the persistent database image.

2.4 Known Migration Techniques

Most enterprise database infrastructures are statically provisioned for the peak capacity. Migrating tenants on-demand for elasticity is therefore not a common operation. As a result, live migration is not a feature supported off-the-shelf by most database systems, resulting in the use of heavyweight techniques. We now discuss two known techniques for database migration.

Stop and copy: This is the simplest and arguably most heavy-handed approach to migrate a database. In this technique, the system stops serving updates for the tenant, checkpoints the state, moves the persistent image, and restarts the tenant at the destination. This technique incurs a long service interruption and a high post migration penalty to warm up the cache at the destination. The advantage is its simplicity and efficiency in terms of minimizing the amount of data transferred. However inefficient this technique might be, this is the only technique available in many current database systems (including RDBMSs like MySQL and *Key-Value* stores such as HBase) to migrate a tenant to a node which is not already running a replica.

Iterative State Replication: The long unavailability of *stop and copy* arises due to the time taken to create the checkpoint and to copy it to the destination. An optimization, Iterative State Replication (**ISR**), is to use an iterative approach, similar to [13], where the checkpoint is created and iteratively copied. The source checkpoints the tenant's database and starts migrating the checkpoint to the destination, while it continues serving requests. While the destination loads the checkpoint, the source maintains the differential changes which are iteratively copied until the amount of change to be transferred is small enough or a maximum iteration count is reached. At this point, a final stop and copy is performed. The iterative copy can be performed using either page level copying or shipping the transaction log and replaying it at the destination.

Consider applications such as shopping cart management or online games such as Farmville that represent workloads with a high percentage of reads followed by updates, and that require high availability for continued customer satisfaction. In ISR, the tenant's database is unavailable to updates during the final stop phase. Even though the system can potentially serve read-only transactions during this window, *all* transactions with at least one update will be aborted during this *small* window. On the other hand, Zephyr does not render the tenant unavailable by allowing concurrent transaction execution at both the source and the destination. However, during migration, Zephyr will abort a transaction in two cases: (i) if at the source it accesses an already migrated page, or (ii) if at either node, it issues an update operation that modifies the index structures. Hence, Zephyr may abort a fraction of update transactions during migration. The exact impact of either technique on transaction execution will depend on the workload and other tenant characteristics, and needs to be evaluated experimentally.

The iterative copying of differential updates in ISR can lead to more data being transferred during migration, especially for update heavy workloads that result in more changes to the database state. Zephyr, on the other hand, migrates a database page only once and hence is expected to have lower data transfer overhead.

Since ISR creates multiple checkpoints during migration, it will result in higher disk I/O at the source. Therefore, when migrating a tenant from a heavily loaded source node, this additional disk I/O can result in significant impact on co-located tenants which are potentially already disk I/O limited due to increased load. However, due to the log replay, the destination will start with a warm cache and hence will minimize the post migration overhead. On the other hand, Zephyr does not incur additional disk I/O at the source due to checkpointing, but the cold start at the destination results in higher post migration overhead and more I/O at the destination. Therefore, Zephyr results in less overhead at the source and is suitable for scale-out scenarios where the source is already heavily loaded, while ISR is attractive for consolidation during scale-down where it will result in lower impact on tenants co-located at the destination.

Finally, since ISR creates a replica of the tenant's state at another node, it can iteratively copy the updates to multiple nodes, thus creating replicas on the fly during migration. Zephyr however does not allow for this easy extension.

It is therefore evident that ISR and Zephyr are both viable techniques for live database migration; a detailed experimental comparison between the two is left for future work. This paper focusses on Zephyr since it is expected to have minimal service interruption which is critical to ensure high tenant availability.

3. ZEPHYR DESIGN

In this section, we provide an overview of Zephyr using some simplifying assumptions to ease presentation. We assume *no failures*, *small tenants* limited to a single node in the system, and *no replication*. Furthermore, the *index structures* are made *immutable* during migration. Failure handling and correctness is discussed in

[3]A longer interruption might result in a penalty. For instance, in platforms like Windows Azure, service availability below 99.9% results in a penalty. http://www.microsoft.com/windowsazure/sla/

Notation	Description
$\mathbb{D}_M$	The tenant database being migrated
$\mathbb{N}_S$	Source node for $\mathbb{D}_M$
$\mathbb{N}_D$	Destination node for $\mathbb{D}_M$
T_{Si}, T_{Di}	Transaction executing at nodes $\mathbb{N}_S$ and $\mathbb{N}_D$ respectively
P_k	Database page k

Table 1: Notational Conventions.

Section 4, while an extended design relaxing these assumptions is described in Section 5. The notational conventions used are summarized in Table 1.

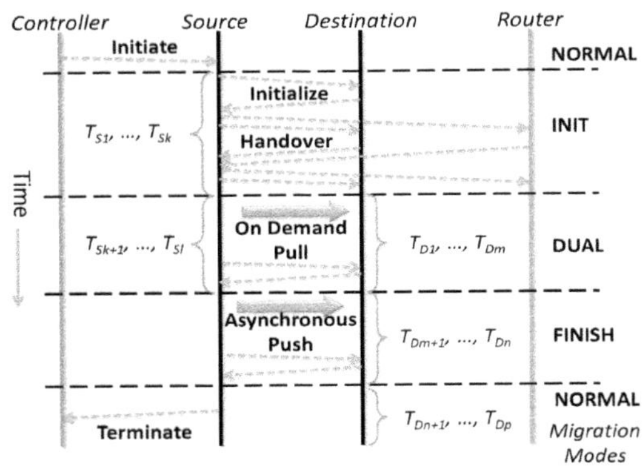

Figure 2: Timeline for different phases during migration. Vertical lines correspond to the nodes, the broken arrows represent control messages and the thick solid arrows represent data transfer. Time progresses from top towards the bottom.

3.1 Design Overview

Zephyr's main design goal is to minimize the service interruption resulting from migrating a tenant's database ($\mathbb{D}_M$). Zephyr does not incur a stop phase where $\mathbb{D}_M$ is unavailable for executing updates; it uses a sequence of three modes to allow the migration of $\mathbb{D}_M$ while transactions are executing on it. During normal operation (called the **Normal Mode**), $\mathbb{N}_S$ is the node serving $\mathbb{D}_M$ and executing all transactions $T_{S1}, \ldots, T_{Sk}$ on $\mathbb{D}_M$. A node that has the rights to execute update transactions on $\mathbb{D}_M$ is called an **owner** of $\mathbb{D}_M$. Once the system controller determines the destination for migration ($\mathbb{N}_D$), it notifies $\mathbb{N}_S$ which initiates migration to $\mathbb{N}_D$. Figure 2 shows the timeline of this migration algorithm and the control and data messages exchanged between the nodes. As time progresses from the top to the bottom, Figure 2 shows the progress of the different migration modes, starting from the **Init Mode** which initiates migration, the **Dual Mode** where both $\mathbb{N}_S$ and $\mathbb{N}_D$ share the ownership of $\mathbb{D}_M$ and simultaneously execute transactions on $\mathbb{D}_M$, and the **Finish Mode** which is the last step of migration before $\mathbb{N}_D$ assumes full ownership of $\mathbb{D}_M$. Figure 3 shows the transition of $\mathbb{D}_M$'s data through the three migration modes, depicted using ownership of database pages and executing transactions.

Init Mode: In the Init Mode, $\mathbb{N}_S$ bootstraps $\mathbb{N}_D$ by sending the minimal information (the **wireframe** of $\mathbb{D}_M$) such that $\mathbb{N}_D$ can execute transactions on $\mathbb{D}_M$. The wireframe consists of the schema and data definitions of $\mathbb{D}_M$, index structures, and user authentication information. Indices migrated include the internal nodes of the clustered index storing the database and all secondary indices. Non-indexed attributes are accessed through the clustered index. In this mode, $\mathbb{N}_S$ is still the unique owner of $\mathbb{D}_M$ and executes transactions ($T_{S1}, \ldots, T_{Sk}$) without synchronizing with any other node. Therefore, there is no service interruption for $\mathbb{D}_M$ while $\mathbb{N}_D$ initializes the necessary resources for $\mathbb{D}_M$. We assume a B+ tree index, where the internal nodes of the index contain only the keys while the actual data pages are in the leaves. The wireframe therefore only includes these internal nodes of the indices for the database tables. Figure 4 illustrates this, where the part of the tree enclosed in a rectangular box is the *index wireframe*. At $\mathbb{N}_S$, the wireframe is constructed with minimal impact on concurrent operations using shared multi-granularity intention locks on the indices. When $\mathbb{N}_D$ receives the wireframe, it has $\mathbb{D}_M$'s metadata, but the data is still owned by $\mathbb{N}_S$. Since migration involves a gradual transfer of page level ownership, both $\mathbb{N}_S$ and $\mathbb{N}_D$ must maintain a list of owned pages. We use the B+ tree index for tracking page ownership. A valid pointer to a database page implies unique page ownership, while a sentinel value (NULL) indicates a missing page. In the init mode, $\mathbb{N}_D$ therefore initializes all the pointers to the leaf nodes of the index to the sentinel value. Once $\mathbb{N}_D$ completes initialization of $\mathbb{D}_M$, it notifies $\mathbb{N}_S$, which then initiates the transition to the dual mode. $\mathbb{N}_S$ then executes the **Atomic Handover** protocol which notifies the *query router* to direct all new transactions to $\mathbb{N}_D$.

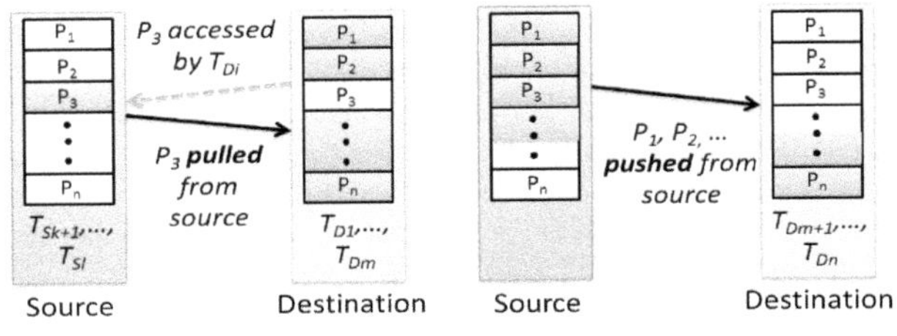

(a) Dual Mode. (b) Finish Mode.

Figure 3: Ownership transfer of the database pages during migration. P_i represents a database page and a white box around P_i represents that the node currently *owns* the page.

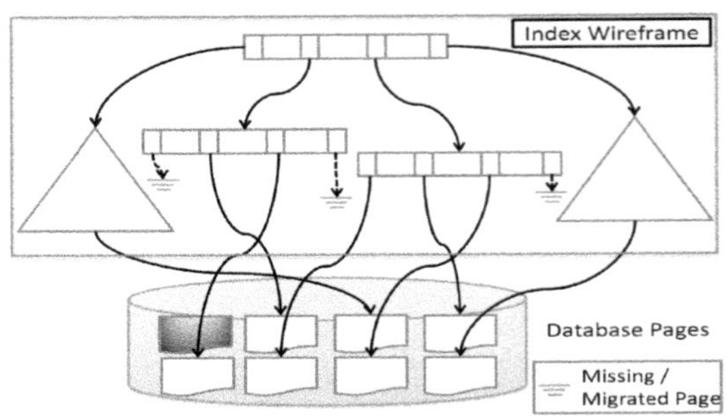

Figure 4: B+ tree index structure with page ownership information. A sentinel marks missing pages. An allocated database page without ownership is represented as a grayed page.

Dual Mode: In the dual mode, both $\mathbb{N}_S$ and $\mathbb{N}_D$ execute transactions on $\mathbb{D}_M$, and database pages are migrated to $\mathbb{N}_D$ *on-demand*. All new transactions ($T_{D1}, \ldots, T_{Dm}$) arrive at $\mathbb{N}_D$, while $\mathbb{N}_S$ continues executing transactions that were active at the start of this mode ($T_{Sk+1}, \ldots, T_{Sl}$). Since $\mathbb{N}_S$ and $\mathbb{N}_D$ share ownership of $\mathbb{D}_M$, they synchronize to ensure transaction correctness. Zephyr however requires minimal synchronization between these nodes.

At $\mathbb{N}_S$, transactions execute normally using local index and page level locking, until a transaction T_{Sj} accesses a page P_j which has already been migrated. In our simplistic design, a database page is migrated only once. Therefore, such an access fails and the transaction is aborted. When a transaction T_{Di} executing at $\mathbb{N}_D$ accesses a page P_i that is not owned by $\mathbb{N}_D$, it **pulls** P_i from $\mathbb{N}_S$ *on demand* (pull phase as shown in Figure 3(a)); this pull request is serviced only if P_i is not locked at $\mathbb{N}_S$, in which case the request is blocked. As the pages are migrated, both $\mathbb{N}_S$ and $\mathbb{N}_D$ update their ownership mapping. Once $\mathbb{N}_D$ receives P_i, it proceeds to execute T_{Di}. Apart from fetching missing pages from $\mathbb{N}_S$, transactions at $\mathbb{N}_S$ and $\mathbb{N}_D$ do not need to synchronize. Due to our assumption that the index structure cannot change at $\mathbb{N}_S$, local locking of the index structure and pages is enough. This ensures minimal synchronization between $\mathbb{N}_S$ and $\mathbb{N}_D$ only during this short dual mode, while ensuring serializable transaction execution.

When $\mathbb{N}_S$ has finished executing all transactions $T_{Sk+1}, \ldots, T_{Sl}$ that were active at the start of dual mode (i.e. $\mathbb{T}(\mathbb{N}_S) = \phi$), it initiates transfer of exclusive ownership to $\mathbb{N}_D$. This transfer is achieved through a handshake between $\mathbb{N}_S$ and $\mathbb{N}_D$ after which both nodes enter the finish mode for $\mathbb{D}_M$.

Finish Mode: In the finish mode, $\mathbb{N}_D$ is the only node executing transactions on $\mathbb{D}_M$ ($T_{Dm+1}, \ldots, T_{Dn}$), but does not yet have ownership of all the database pages (Figure 3(b)). In this phase, $\mathbb{N}_S$ **pushes** the remaining database pages to $\mathbb{N}_D$. While the pages are migrated from $\mathbb{N}_S$, if a transaction T_{Di} accesses a page that is not yet owned by $\mathbb{N}_D$, the page is requested as a *pull* from $\mathbb{N}_S$ in a way similar to that in the dual mode. Ideally, $\mathbb{N}_S$ must migrate the pages at the highest possible transfer rate such that the delays resulting from $\mathbb{N}_D$ fetching missing pages is minimized. However, such a high throughput push can impact other tenants co-located at $\mathbb{N}_S$ and $\mathbb{N}_D$. Therefore, the rate of transfer is a trade-off between the tenant SLAs and migration overhead. The page ownership information is also updated during this bulk transfer. When all the database pages have been moved to $\mathbb{N}_D$, $\mathbb{N}_S$ initiates the termination of migration so that operation switches back to the normal mode. This again involves a handshake between $\mathbb{N}_S$ and $\mathbb{N}_D$. On successful completion of this handshake, it is guaranteed that $\mathbb{N}_D$ has a persistent image of $\mathbb{D}_M$, and so $\mathbb{N}_S$ can safely release all of $\mathbb{D}_M$'s resources. $\mathbb{N}_D$ executes transactions on $\mathbb{D}_M$ without any interaction with $\mathbb{N}_S$. Once migration terminates, $\mathbb{N}_S$ notifies the system controller.

3.2 Migration Cost Analysis

Migration cost in Zephyr results from copying the initial wireframe, operation overhead during migration, and transactions or operations aborted during migration. In the wireframe transferred, the schema and authentication information is typically small. The indices for the tables however have a non-trivial size. A simple analysis provides an estimate of index sizes. Assuming 4KB pages, 8 byte keys (integers or double precision floating point numbers), and 4 byte pointers, each internal node in the tree can hold about $4096/12 \approx 340$ keys. Therefore, a three-level B+ tree can have up to $340^2 = 115600$ leaf nodes, which can index a $(115600 \times 4096 \times 0.8)/10^6 \approx 400$ MB database, assuming 80% page utilization. Similarly, a four-level tree can index a 125 GB database. For a three level tree, the size of the wireframe is a mere $340 \times 4096/10^6 \approx 1.4$ MB while for a 4-level tree, it is about 400 MB. For most multitenant databases whose representative sizes are in the range of hundreds of megabytes to a few gigabytes, an index size of the order of tens of megabytes is a realistic conservative estimate [25,26]. These index sizes add up for the multiple tables and indices maintained for the database.

Overhead during migration stems from creating the wireframe and fetching pages over the network. $\mathbb{N}_S$ uses standard *multi-granularity* locking [17] of the index to construct the index wireframe. This scan to create the wireframe needs intention read locks at the internal nodes which only conflict with write locks [4] on the internal node. Therefore, this scan can execute in parallel with any transaction T_{Si} executing at $\mathbb{N}_S$, only blocking update transactions that result in an update in the index structure that requires a conflicting write lock on an internal node. On the other hand, on-demand pull of a page from $\mathbb{N}_S$ over the network is also not very expensive compared to fetches from the disk – disks have an access latency of about a millisecond while most data center networks have round trip latencies of less than a millisecond. The cost incurred by this remote pull is therefore of the same order as a cache miss during normal operation resulting in a disk access. Assuming an OLTP workload with predominantly small transactions, the period for which $\mathbb{D}_M$ remains in the dual mode is expected to be small. Therefore, the cost incurred in this short period in the dual mode is expected to be small.

Another contributor to the migration cost is failed transactions at $\mathbb{N}_S$ resulting from accesses to pages that have been migrated. In its simplest form as described, Zephyr does not guarantee zero transaction failure; this however can be guaranteed by an extended design as shown later in Section 5.

4. CORRECTNESS AND FAULT TOLERANCE

Any migration technique should guarantee transaction correctness and migration safety in the presence of arbitrary failures. We first prove that Zephyr guarantees serializable isolation even during migration. We then prove the atomicity and durability properties of both transaction execution as well the migration protocol.

4.1 Isolation guarantees

Transactions executing with serializable isolation, use two phase locking (2PL) [14] with multi-granularity [17]. In the init mode and finish mode, only one of $\mathbb{N}_S$ and $\mathbb{N}_D$ is executing transactions on $\mathbb{D}_M$. The init mode is equivalent to normal operation while in finish mode, $\mathbb{N}_S$ acts as the storage node for the database serving pages on demand. Guaranteeing serializability is straightforward in these modes. We only need to prove correctness in the dual mode where both $\mathbb{N}_S$ and $\mathbb{N}_D$ are executing transactions on $\mathbb{D}_M$. In the dual mode, $\mathbb{N}_S$ and $\mathbb{N}_D$ share the internal nodes of the index which are immutable in our design, while the leaf nodes (i.e. the data pages) are still uniquely owned by one of the two nodes. To guarantee serializability, we first prove that the phantom problem [14] is impossible, and then prove general serializability of transactions executing in the dual mode. The phantom problem arises from predicate based accesses where a transaction inserts or deletes an item that matches the predicate of a concurrently executing transaction.

LEMMA 1. ***Phantom problem:*** *Local predicate locking at the internal index nodes and exclusive page level locking between nodes is enough to ensure impossibility of phantoms.*

PROOF. **Proof by contradiction:** Assume for contradiction that a phantom is possible resulting in predicate instability. Let T_1 and T_2 be two transactions such that T_1 has a predicate and T_2 is inserting (or deleting) at least one element that matches T_1's predicate. T_1 and T_2 cannot be executing at the same node, since local predicate locking would prevent such a behavior. Therefore, these transactions must be executing on different nodes. Without loss of generality, assume that T_1 is executing at $\mathbb{N}_S$ and T_2 is executing at $\mathbb{N}_D$. Let T_1's predicate match pages $P_i, P_{i+1}, \ldots, P_j$ representing a range of keys. Since Zephyr does not allow an update that changes the index during migration, therefore, T_2 cannot insert to a newly created page at $\mathbb{N}_D$. Therefore, if T_2 was inserting to (or deleting from) one of the pages $P_i, P_{i+1}, \ldots, P_j$ while T_1 was executing, then it implies that both $\mathbb{N}_S$ and $\mathbb{N}_D$ have ownership of the page. This results in a contradiction. Hence the proof. □

LEMMA 2. ***Serializability at a node:*** *Transactions executing at the same node (either $\mathbb{N}_S$ or $\mathbb{N}_D$) cannot have a cycle in the conflict graph involving these transactions.*

The proof of Lemma 2 follows directly from the correctness of 2PL [14], since all transactions executing at the same node use 2PL for concurrency control.

LEMMA 3. *Let T_{Sj} be a transaction executing at $\mathbb{N}_S$ and T_{Di} be a transaction executing at $\mathbb{N}_D$, it is impossible to have a conflict dependency $T_{Di} \rightarrow T_{Sj}$.*

PROOF. **Proof by contradiction:** Assume for contradiction that there exists a dependency of the form $T_{Di} \rightarrow T_{Sj}$. This implies that T_{Sj} makes a conflicting access to an item in page P_i after T_{Di} accessed P_i. Due to the two phase locking rule, the conflict $T_{Di} \rightarrow T_{Sj}$ implies that commit of T_{Di} precedes the conflicting access by T_{Sj}, which in turn implies that T_{Sj} accesses P_i after it was migrated to $\mathbb{N}_D$ as a result of an access by T_{Di}. This leads to a contradiction since in Zephyr, once P_i is migrated from $\mathbb{N}_S$ to $\mathbb{N}_D$, all subsequent accesses to P_i at $\mathbb{N}_S$ fail. Hence the proof. □

Corollary 4 follows by applying induction on Lemma 3.

COROLLARY 4. *It is impossible to have a path $T_{Di} \rightarrow \ldots \rightarrow T_{Sj}$ in the conflict graph.*

THEOREM 5. ***Serializability in dual mode.*** *It is impossible to have a cycle in the conflict graph of transactions executing in the dual mode.*

PROOF. **Proof by contradiction:** Assume for contradiction that there exists a set of transactions $T_1, T_2, \ldots, T_k$ such that there is a cycle $T_1 \rightarrow T_2 \rightarrow \ldots \rightarrow T_k \rightarrow T_1$ in the conflict graph. If all transactions are executing at the same node, then this is a contradiction to Lemma 2. Consider the case where some transactions are executing at $\mathbb{N}_S$ and some at $\mathbb{N}_D$. Let us first assume that T_1 executed at $\mathbb{N}_S$. Let T_i be the first transaction in the sequence which executed at $\mathbb{N}_D$. The above cycle implies that there exists a path of the form $T_i \rightarrow \ldots \rightarrow T_1$ where T_i executed at $\mathbb{N}_D$ and T_1 executed at $\mathbb{N}_S$. This is a contradiction to Corollary 4. Similarly, if T_1 executed at $\mathbb{N}_D$, then there exists at least one transaction T_j which executed at $\mathbb{N}_S$, which implies a path of the form $T_1 \rightarrow \ldots \rightarrow T_j$, again a contradiction to Corollary 4. Hence the proof. □

Snapshot Isolation (SI) [2], arguably the most commonly used isolation level, can also be guaranteed in Zephyr. A transaction T_i writing to a page P_i must have unique ownership of P_i, while a read can be performed from a snapshot shared by both nodes. This condition of unique page ownership is sufficient to ensure that during validation of transactions in SI, the transaction manager can detect two concurrent transactions writing to the same page and abort one. Zephyr therefore guarantees transactional isolation with minimal synchronization and without much migration overhead.

4.2 Fault tolerance

Our failure model assumes that all message transfers use reliable communication channels that guarantee in-order, at most once delivery. We consider node crash failures and network partitions; we however do not consider malicious node behavior. We assume that a node failure does not lead to loss of the persistent disk image. In case of a failure during migration, our design first recovers state of the committed transactions and then recovers the state of migration.

4.2.1 Transaction State Recovery

Transactions executing during migration use write ahead logging for transaction state recovery [4,23]. Updates made by a transaction are *forced* to the log before it commits, thus resulting in a total order on transactions executing at the node. After a crash, a node recovers its transaction state using standard log replay techniques, ARIES [23] being an example.

In the dual mode, $\mathbb{N}_S$ and $\mathbb{N}_D$ append transactions to their respective node's local transaction log. Log entries in a single log file have a local order. However, since the log for $\mathbb{D}_M$ is spread over $\mathbb{N}_S$ and $\mathbb{N}_D$, a logical global order of transactions on $\mathbb{D}_M$ is needed to ensure that the transactions from the two logs are applied in the correct order to recover from a failure during migration. The ordering of transactions is important only when there is a conflict between two transactions. If two transactions, T_S and T_D, executing on $\mathbb{N}_S$ and $\mathbb{N}_D$, conflict on item i, they must access the same database page P_i. Since at any instant of time only one of $\mathbb{N}_S$ and $\mathbb{N}_D$ is the owner of P_i, the two nodes must synchronize to arbitrate on P_i. This synchronization forms the basis for establishing a total order between the transactions. During migration, a **commit sequence number** (CSN) is assigned to every transaction at commit time, and is appended along with the commit record of the transaction. This CSN is a monotonically increasing sequence number maintained locally at the nodes and determines the order in which transactions commit. If P_i was owned by $\mathbb{N}_S$ and T_S was the last committed transaction before the migration request for P_i was made, then $CSN(T_S)$ is piggy-backed with P_i. On receipt of a page P_i, $\mathbb{N}_D$ sets its CSN as the maximum of its local CSN and that received with P_i such that at $\mathbb{N}_D$, $CSN(T_D) > CSN(T_S)$. This causal conflict ordering creates a global order per database page, where all transactions at $\mathbb{N}_S$ accessing P_i are ordered before all transactions at $\mathbb{N}_D$ that access P_i. We formally state this property as Theorem 6:

THEOREM 6. *The transaction recovery and the conflict ordering protocol ensures that for every database page, conflicting transactions are replayed in the same order in which they committed.*

4.2.2 Migration State Recovery

Migration progress is logged to guarantee atomicity and consistency in the presence of failures. Migration safety is ensured by using rigorous recovery protocols. A failure of either $\mathbb{N}_S$ or $\mathbb{N}_D$ in the dual mode or the finish mode requires coordinated recovery between the two nodes. We first discuss recovering from a failure during transition of migration modes and discuss recovery after failure in different migration modes.

Transitions of Migration Modes: During migration, a transition from one state to another is logged. Except for the transition from the init mode to dual mode, which involves the query router metadata in addition to $\mathbb{N}_S$ and $\mathbb{N}_D$, all other transitions involve only $\mathbb{N}_S$ and $\mathbb{N}_D$. Such transitions occur through a one-phase handshake between $\mathbb{N}_S$ and $\mathbb{N}_D$ (as shown in Figure 2). At the occurrence of an event triggering a state transition, $\mathbb{N}_S$ initiates the transition by sending a message to $\mathbb{N}_D$. On receipt of the message, $\mathbb{N}_D$ moves to the next migration mode, forces a log entry for this change, and sends an acknowledgment to $\mathbb{N}_S$. Receipt of this acknowledgment completes this transition and $\mathbb{N}_S$ forces another entry to its log.

If $\mathbb{N}_S$ fails before sending the message to $\mathbb{N}_D$, the mode remains unchanged when $\mathbb{N}_S$ recovers, and $\mathbb{N}_S$ re-initiates the transition. If $\mathbb{N}_S$ fails after sending the message, then it knows about the message after it recovers and establishes contact with $\mathbb{N}_D$. Therefore, a state transition results in two messages and two writes to the log. Logging of messages at $\mathbb{N}_S$ and $\mathbb{N}_D$ provides message idempotence, detects and rejects duplicate messages resulting from failure of $\mathbb{N}_S$ or $\mathbb{N}_D$, and guarantees safety with repeating failures.

Atomic Handover: A transition from the init mode to the dual mode involves three participants ($\mathbb{N}_S$, $\mathbb{N}_D$, and the query router metadata) that must together change the state. A one-phase handshake is therefore not enough. We use the two-phase commit (2PC) [16] protocol, a standard protocol for atomic commitment over multiple sites. Once $\mathbb{N}_D$ has acknowledged the initialization of $\mathbb{D}_M$, $\mathbb{N}_S$ initiates the transition and sends a message to the router to direct all future transactions accessing $\mathbb{D}_M$ to $\mathbb{N}_D$, and a message to $\mathbb{N}_D$ to start accepting new transactions for $\mathbb{D}_M$ whose ownership is shared with $\mathbb{N}_S$. On receipt of the messages, both $\mathbb{N}_D$ and the router log their messages and reply back to $\mathbb{N}_S$. Once $\mathbb{N}_S$ has received messages from both $\mathbb{N}_D$ and the router, it logs the successful handover in its own log, changes its state to dual mode and sends acknowledgments to $\mathbb{N}_D$ and the router which update their respective states. Atomicity of this handover process follows directly from the atomicity proof of 2PC [16]. This protocol also exhibits the blocking behavior of 2PC when $\mathbb{N}_S$ (the coordinator) fails. This blocking however only affects $\mathbb{D}_M$ which is anyways unavailable as a result of $\mathbb{N}_S$'s failure. Atomic handover therefore does not introduce any additional blocking when compared to traditional 2PC where a coordinator failure blocks any other conflicting transaction.

Recovering Migration Progress: The page ownership information is critical for migration progress as well as safety. A simple fault-tolerant design is to make this ownership information durable – any page (P_i) transferred from $\mathbb{N}_S$ is immediately flushed to the disk at $\mathbb{N}_D$. $\mathbb{N}_S$ also makes this transfer persistent, either by logging the transfer or by updating P_i's parent page in the index, and flushing it to the disk. This simple solution will guarantee resilience to failure but introduces a lot of disk I/O which considerably increases migration cost and impacts other co-located tenants.

An optimized solution uses the semantics of the operation that resulted in P_i's on-demand migration. When P_i is migrated, $\mathbb{N}_S$ has its persistent (or at least recoverable) image. After the migration of P_i, if a committed transaction at $\mathbb{N}_D$ updated P_i, then the update will be in $\mathbb{N}_D$'s transaction log. Therefore, after a failure, $\mathbb{N}_D$ recovers P_i from its log and the persistent image at $\mathbb{N}_S$. The presence of a log entry accessing P_i at $\mathbb{N}_D$ implies that $\mathbb{N}_D$ owns P_i, thus preserving the ownership information after recovery. In case P_i was migrated only for a read operation or if an update transaction at $\mathbb{N}_D$ did not commit, then this migration is not persistent at $\mathbb{N}_D$. When $\mathbb{N}_D$ recovers, it synchronizes its knowledge of page ownership with that of $\mathbb{N}_S$, any missing page P_i is detected during this synchronization. For these missing pages, either $\mathbb{N}_S$ or $\mathbb{N}_D$ can be assigned P_i's ownership; assigning it to $\mathbb{N}_D$ will need copying P_i to $\mathbb{N}_D$ yet again.

On the other hand, if $\mathbb{N}_S$ fails after migrating P_i, it recovers and synchronizes its page ownership information with $\mathbb{N}_D$ when the missing P_i is detected, and $\mathbb{N}_S$ updates its ownership mapping. Failure of both $\mathbb{N}_S$ and $\mathbb{N}_D$ immediately following P_i's transfer is equivalent to the failure of $\mathbb{N}_D$ without P_i making it to the disk at $\mathbb{N}_D$, and all undecided pages can be assigned ownership as described earlier. Logging the pages at $\mathbb{N}_D$ guarantees idempotence of page transfers, thus allowing migration to deal with repeated failures and prevent lost updates at $\mathbb{N}_D$. These optimizations considerably reduces the disk I/O during the dual mode. However, in the finish mode, since pages are transferred in bulk, the pages transferred can be immediately flushed to the disk; the large number of pages per flush amortizes the disk I/O.

Since the transfer of pages to $\mathbb{N}_D$ does not force an immediate flush, after migration terminates, $\mathbb{N}_D$ must ensure a flush before the state of $\mathbb{D}_M$ can be purged at $\mathbb{N}_S$. This is achieved through a fuzzy checkpoint [4] at $\mathbb{N}_D$. A fuzzy checkpoint is used by a DBMS during normal operation to reduce the recovery time after a failure. It causes minimal disruption to transaction processing, as a background thread scans through the database cache and flushes modified pages, while the database can continue to process updates. As part of the final state transition, $\mathbb{N}_D$ initiates a fuzzy checkpoint and acknowledges $\mathbb{N}_S$ only after the checkpoint completes. After the checkpoint, $\mathbb{N}_D$ can independently recover and $\mathbb{N}_S$ can safely purge $\mathbb{D}_M$'s state. This recovery protocol guarantees that in the presence of a failure, migration recovers to a consistent point before the crash. Theorem 7 formalizes this recovery guarantee.

THEOREM 7. ***Migration recovery:*** *At any instant during migration, its progress is recoverable, i.e. after transaction state recovery is complete, database page ownership information is restored to a consistent state and every page has exactly one owner.*

Failure and Availability: A failure in any migration mode results in partial or complete unavailability. In the init mode, $\mathbb{N}_S$ is still the exclusive owner of $\mathbb{D}_M$. If $\mathbb{N}_D$ fails, $\mathbb{N}_S$ can single-handedly abort the migration or continue processing new transactions until $\mathbb{N}_D$ recovers and migration is resumed. In case this migration is aborted in the init mode, $\mathbb{N}_S$ notifies the controller which might select a new destination. A failure of $\mathbb{N}_S$ however makes $\mathbb{D}_M$ unavailable and is equivalent to $\mathbb{N}_S$'s failure during normal operation. In this case, $\mathbb{N}_D$ can abort migration at its discretion. If $\mathbb{N}_S$ fails in the dual mode or the finish mode, then $\mathbb{N}_D$ can only process transactions that access pages whose ownership was migrated to $\mathbb{N}_D$ before $\mathbb{N}_S$ failed. This is equivalent to a disk failing, making parts of the database unavailable. When $\mathbb{N}_D$ fails, $\mathbb{N}_S$ can only process transactions that do not access the migrated pages. A failure of $\mathbb{N}_D$ in the finish mode however makes $\mathbb{D}_M$ unavailable since $\mathbb{N}_D$ is now the exclusive owner of $\mathbb{D}_M$. This failure is equivalent to $\mathbb{N}_D$'s failure during normal operation.

4.3 Migration Safety and Liveness

Migration safety ensures correctness in the presence of a failure, while liveness ensures that 'something good' will eventually happen. We first establish formal definitions for safety and liveness, and then show how Zephyr guarantees these properties.

DEFINITION 1. ***Safety*** *of migration requires the following conditions: (i)* Transactional correctness: *serializability is guaranteed for transactions executing during migration; (ii)* Transaction durability: *updates from committed transactions are never lost; and (iii)* Migration consistency: *a failure during migration does not leave the system's state and data inconsistent.*

DEFINITION 2. ***Liveness*** *of migration requires the following conditions to be met: (i)* Termination: *if $\mathbb{N}_S$ and $\mathbb{N}_D$ are not faulty and can communicate with each other for a sufficiently long period during migration, this process will terminate; and (ii)* Starvation Freedom: *in the presence of one or more failures, $\mathbb{D}_M$ will eventually have at least one node that can execute its transactions.*

Transaction correctness follows from Theorem 5. We now prove transaction durability and migration consistency.

THEOREM 8. ***Transaction durability:*** *Changes made by a committed transaction are never lost, even in the presence of an arbitrary sequence of failure.*

PROOF. The proof follows from the following two conditions: *(i)* during normal operation, transactions force their updates to the log before commit, making them durable; and *(ii)* on successful termination of migration, $\mathbb{N}_S$ purges its transaction log and the database image only after the fuzzy checkpoint at $\mathbb{N}_D$ completes, ensuring that changes at $\mathbb{N}_S$ and $\mathbb{N}_D$ during migration are durable. □

THEOREM 9. ***Migration consistency:*** *In the presence of arbitrary or repeated failures, Zephyr ensures: (i) updates made to data pages are consistent even in the presence of failures; (ii) a failure does not leave a page P_i of $\mathbb{D}_M$ without an owner; and (iii) both $\mathbb{N}_S$ and $\mathbb{N}_D$ are in the same migration mode.*

The condition for exclusive page ownership along with Theorem 5 and 6 ensures that updates to the database pages are always consistent, both during normal operation and after a failure. Theorem 7 guarantees that no database page is without an owner, while the atomicity of the atomic handover and other state transition protocols discussed in Section 4.2.2 guarantee that both $\mathbb{N}_S$ and $\mathbb{N}_D$ are in the same migration mode. Theorem 5, 8, and 9 therefore guarantee migration safety.

THEOREM 10. ***Migration termination:*** *If $\mathbb{N}_S$ and $\mathbb{N}_D$ are not faulty and can communicate for a long enough period, Zephyr guarantees progress and termination.*

PROOF. Zephyr successfully terminates if: (*i*) the set of active transactions ($\mathbb{T}$) at $\mathbb{N}_S$ at the start of the dual mode have completed, i.e. $\mathbb{T} = \phi$; and (*ii*) the persistent image of $\mathbb{D}_M$ is migrated to $\mathbb{N}_D$ and is recoverable. If $\mathbb{N}_S$ is not faulty in the dual mode, all transactions in $\mathbb{T}$ will eventually complete, irrespective of whether $\mathbb{N}_D$ has failed or not. If there is a failure of $\mathbb{N}_S$ at any point during migration, after recovery, it is guaranteed that $\mathbb{T} = \phi$. Therefore, the first condition is guaranteed to be satisfied eventually. After the condition $\mathbb{T} = \phi$, if $\mathbb{N}_S$ and $\mathbb{N}_D$ can communicate long enough, all the pages of $\mathbb{D}_M$ at $\mathbb{N}_S$ will be migrated and recoverable at $\mathbb{N}_D$. □

THEOREM 11. ***Starvation freedom:*** *Even after an arbitrary sequence of failures, there will be at least one node that can execute transactions on $\mathbb{D}_M$.*

The proof of Theorem 11 follows from Theorem 9 which ensures that $\mathbb{N}_S$ and $\mathbb{N}_D$ are in the same migration mode, and hence have a consistent view of $\mathbb{D}_M$'s ownership.

Theorem 10 and 11 together guarantee liveness. Zephyr guarantees safety in the presence of repeated failures or a network partition between $\mathbb{N}_S$ and $\mathbb{N}_D$, though progress is not guaranteed. Even though such failures are rare, proven guarantees in such scenarios improves the users' reliance on the system.

5. OPTIMIZATIONS AND EXTENSIONS

We now discuss some extensions that relax some of the assumptions made to simplify our initial description of Zephyr.

5.1 Replicated Tenants

In our discussion so far, we assume that the destination of migration does not have any prior information about $\mathbb{D}_M$. Many production database installations however use some form of replication for fault-tolerance and availability. In such a scenario, $\mathbb{D}_M$ can be migrated to a node which already has its replica. Since most DBMS implementations use lazy replication techniques to circumvent the high cost of synchronous replication [4], replicas often lag behind the master. Zephyr can be adapted to leverage this form of replication. Since $\mathbb{N}_D$ already has a replica, there is no need for the init mode. When $\mathbb{N}_S$ is notified to initiate migration, it executes the atomic handover protocol to enter the dual mode. Since $\mathbb{N}_D$'s copy of the database is potentially stale, when a transaction T_{Di} accesses a page P_i, similar to the original design, $\mathbb{N}_D$ synchronizes with $\mathbb{N}_S$ to transfer ownership. $\mathbb{N}_D$ sends the sequence number associated with its version of P_i to determine if it has the latest version of P_i; P_i is transferred only if $\mathbb{N}_D$'s version is stale. Furthermore, in the finish mode, $\mathbb{N}_S$ only needs to send a small number of pages that were not replicated to $\mathbb{N}_D$ due to a lag in replication. Replication can therefore considerably improve the performance of Zephyr.

5.2 Sharded Tenants

Our initial description assumes that a tenant is small and is served from a single node, i.e. a single partition tenant. However, Zephyr can also handle a large tenant that is sharded across multiple nodes, primarily due to the fact that $\mathbb{N}_S$ completes the execution of all transactions that were active when migration was initiated. Let $\mathbb{D}_M$ consist of partitions $\mathbb{D}_{M1}, \ldots, \mathbb{D}_{Mp}$ and assume that we are migrating $\mathbb{D}_{Mi}$ from $\mathbb{N}_S$ to $\mathbb{N}_D$. Transactions accessing only $\mathbb{D}_{Mi}$ are handled similar to the case of a single partition tenant. Let T_i be a multi-partition transaction where $\mathbb{D}_{Mi}$ is a participant. If T_i was active at the start of migration, then $\mathbb{N}_S$ is the node that executes T_i, and $\mathbb{D}_{Mi}$ will transition to finish mode only when all such T_i's have completed. On the other hand, if T_i started after $\mathbb{D}_{Mi}$ had transitioned to the dual mode, then $\mathbb{N}_D$ is the node executing T_i. At any given node, T_i is executed in the same way as in a small single partition tenant.

5.3 Data Sharing in Dual Mode

In Dual Mode, both $\mathbb{N}_S$ and $\mathbb{N}_D$ are executing update transactions on $\mathbb{D}_M$. This design is reminiscent of data sharing systems [7], the difference being that our design does not use a shared lock manager. However, our design can be augmented to use a shared lock manager to support a larger set of operations during migration, including arbitrary updates and minimizing transaction aborts at $\mathbb{N}_S$.

In the modified design, we replace the concept of page ownership with page level locking, allowing the locks to be shared when both $\mathbb{N}_S$ and $\mathbb{N}_D$ are reading a page. Every node in the system has a **Local Lock Manager (LLM)** and a **Global Lock Manager (GLM)**. The LLM is responsible for the local locking of pages while the GLM is responsible for arbitrating locks for remote pages. In all migration modes except dual mode, locks are local and hence serviced by the LLM. However, in the dual mode, $\mathbb{N}_S$ and $\mathbb{N}_D$ must synchronize through the GLMs. The only change needed is in the page ownership transfer, with the rest of the algorithm remains unchanged. Note that scalability limitations of a shared lock manager is not significant in our case since any instance of the lock manager is shared only between two nodes. We now describe how this extended design can remove some limitations of the original design. Details have been omitted due to space constraints.

In the original design of Zephyr, when a transaction T_{Di} requests access for a page P_i, $\mathbb{N}_D$ transfers ownership from $\mathbb{N}_S$. Therefore, future accesses to P_i (even reads) must fail to ensure serializable isolation. In this extended design, if $\mathbb{N}_D$ only needs a shared lock on P_i to service reads, then $\mathbb{N}_S$ can also continue processing reads from $T_{Sk+1}, \ldots, T_{Sl}$ that access P_i. Furthermore, even if $\mathbb{N}_D$ had acquired an exclusive lock, $\mathbb{N}_S$ can request a lock to $\mathbb{N}_D$'s GLM for the desired lock on P_i. This allows processing transactions at $\mathbb{N}_S$ that access a migrated page; the request to migrate the page back to $\mathbb{N}_S$ might be blocked in case it is locked at $\mathbb{N}_D$. The trade-off associated with this flexibility is the cost of additional synchronization between $\mathbb{N}_S$ and $\mathbb{N}_D$ to arbitrate shared locks, and the higher network overhead arising from the need to potentially copy P_i multiple times, while in the initial design, P_i was migrated exactly once. The original design made the index structure at both $\mathbb{N}_S$ and $\mathbb{N}_D$

immutable during migration and did not allow insertions or deletions that required a change in the index structure. The shared lock manager in the modified design circumvents this limitation by sharing locks at the index level as well, such that normal index traversal will use shared intention locks while an update to the index will acquire an exclusive lock on the index nodes being updated.

Zephyr, adapted to the data sharing architecture, allows more flexibility by allowing arbitrary updates and minimizing transactions or operations aborted due to migration. The implication on the correctness is straightforward. Since page ownership can be transferred back to $\mathbb{N}_S$, Lemma 3 does not hold any longer. However, Theorem 5 still holds since page level locking is done in a two phase manner using the shared lock managers, which ensures that a cycle in the conflict graph is impossible. The detailed proof is omitted for space limitations. Similarly, the proof for Lemma 1 has to be augmented with the case for index changes. However, since index changes will need the transaction inserting an item (T_2 in Lemma 1) to acquire an exclusive on the index page being modified, it will be blocked by the predicate lock acquired by the transaction with the predicate (T_1 in Lemma 1) on the index pages. Therefore, transactional correctness is still satisfied in the modified design; the other correctness arguments remain unchanged.

In summary, all these optimizations provide interesting tradeoffs between minimizing the service disruption resulting from migration and the additional migration overhead manifested as higher network traffic and increased synchronization between $\mathbb{N}_S$ and $\mathbb{N}_D$. A detailed analysis and evaluation is left for future work.

6. IMPLEMENTATION DETAILS

Our prototype implementation of Zephyr extends an open source OLTP database H2 [18]. H2 is a lightweight relational database with a small footprint built entirely in Java supporting both embedded and server mode operation. Though primarily designed for embedded operation, one of the major applications of H2 is as a replacement of commercial RDBMS servers for development and testing. It supports a standard SQL/JDBC API, serializable and repeatable reads isolation levels [2], tree indices, and a relational data model with foreign keys and referential integrity constraints.

H2's architecture resembles the shared process multitenancy model where an H2 instance can have multiple independent databases with different schemas. Each database maintains its independent database cache, transaction manager, transaction log, and recovery manager. In H2, a database is stored as a file on disk which is internally organized as a collection of fixed size database pages. The first four pages store the database's metadata. The data definitions and user authentication information is stored as a metadata table (called `INFORMATION_SCHEMA`) which is part of the database. Every table in H2 is organized as a tree index. If a table is defined with a primary key which is of type integer or real number, then the primary key index stores data for the table. In case the primary key has other types (such as varchar) or if the primary key was not specified at table creation, the table's data are stored in a tree index whose key is auto-generated by the system. A table can have multiple indices which are maintained separate from the primary key index. The fourth page in the database file stores a pointer to the root of the `INFORMATION_SCHEMA` table, which in turn stores pointers to the other user tables. H2 supports classic multi-step transactions with serializable and read committed isolation level.

We use SQL Router[4], an open source package, to implement the query router. It is a JDBC wrapper that transparently migrates JDBC connections from $\mathbb{N}_S$ to $\mathbb{N}_D$. This SQL router runs a server listener that is notified when $\mathbb{D}_M$'s location changes. When migration is initiated, $\mathbb{N}_S$ spawns a migration thread T. In *init mode*, T transfers the database metadata pages, the entire `INFORMATION_SCHEMA` table of H2, and the internal nodes of the indices. Conceptually, this wireframe can be constructed by traversing the index trees to determine the internal index nodes. This however might incur a large number of random disk accesses for infrequently accessed parts of the index, which can considerably increase the migration overhead. We therefore use an optimization in the implementation where T sequentially scans through the database file and transfers only the internal nodes of the indices. When processing a database index page, it synchronizes with any concurrent transactions and obtains the latest version from the cache, if needed. Since the index structure is frozen during migration, this scan uses shared locking, allowing other update transactions to proceed. T notifies $\mathbb{N}_D$ of the number of pages skipped, which is used to update page ownership information at $\mathbb{N}_D$.

In the *dual mode*, $\mathbb{N}_D$ pulls pages from $\mathbb{N}_S$ on-demand while $\mathbb{N}_S$ continues transaction execution. Before a page is migrated, $\mathbb{N}_S$ obtains an exclusive lock on the page, updates the ownership mapping, and then sends it to $\mathbb{N}_D$. This ensures that the page is migrated only if it is not locked by any concurrent transaction. In the *finish mode*, $\mathbb{N}_S$ pushes all remaining pages that were not migrated in the dual mode, while serving any page fetch request from $\mathbb{N}_D$; pages transferred twice as a result of both the push from $\mathbb{N}_S$ and pull from $\mathbb{N}_D$ are detected at $\mathbb{N}_D$ and duplicate pages are rejected. Since $\mathbb{N}_S$ does not execute any transactions in finish mode, this push does not require any synchronization at $\mathbb{N}_S$.

7. EXPERIMENTAL EVALUATION

We now present a thorough experimental evaluation of Zephyr for live database migration using our prototype implementation. We compare Zephyr with the off-the-shelf **stop and copy** technique that stops the database at $\mathbb{N}_S$, flushes all changes, copies over the persistent image, and restarts the database at $\mathbb{N}_D$. Our evaluation uses two server nodes that run the database instances and a separate set of client machines that generate load on the database. Each server node has a 2.40GHz Intel Core 2 Quad processor, 8 GB RAM, a 7200 RPM SATA hard drive with 32MB Cache, and runs a 64-bit Ubuntu Server Edition with Java 1.6. The nodes are connected via a gigabit switch. Workload is generated from a different set of client machines. Since migration only involves $\mathbb{N}_S$ and $\mathbb{N}_D$, our evaluation focusses only on these two nodes and is oblivious of other nodes. We measure the migration cost as the number of failed operations, the amount of data transferred during migration, and the impact on transaction latency during and after migration.

7.1 Benchmark Description

We use the Yahoo! cloud serving benchmark (YCSB) [9] in our evaluation. YCSB emulates a synthetic workload generator that can be parameterized to vary the read/write ratio, access distributions, etc. Since the underlying database layer is multitenant, we run one benchmark instance for each tenant database. YCSB was originally designed to evaluate *Key-Value* stores, and hence primarily designed for single key operations or scans. We augmented this workload model and added multi-step transactions, where each transaction consists of multiple operations, the number of operations in a transaction (called **transaction size**) is another workload parameter. The number of read operations in a transaction is another parameter and so is the access distribution to select the rows accessed by a transaction. These parameters allow us to evaluate the behavior of the migration cost for different workloads and access patterns. We use the cost measures discussed in Section 2.3.

[4]`http://www.continuent.com/community/tungsten-sql-router`

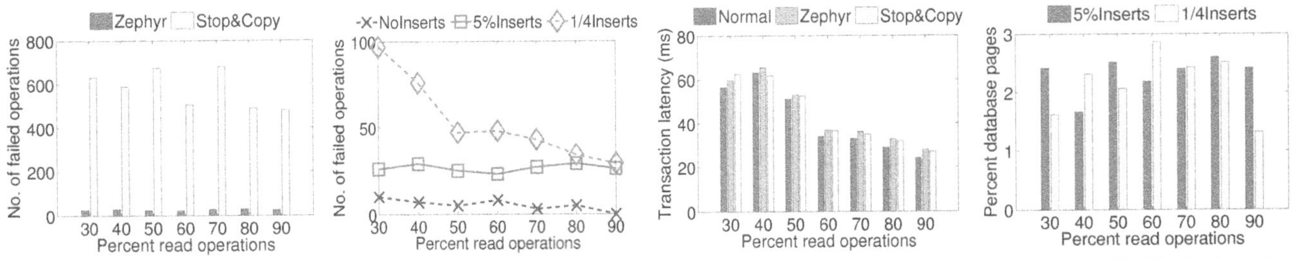

(a) Failed operations (b) Different insert ratios (c) Average latency (d) Pages pulled in dual mode

Figure 5: Impact of the distribution of reads, updates, and inserts on migration cost; default configurations used for rest of the parameters. We also vary the different insert ratios – 5% inserts correspond to a fixed percentage of inserts, while $1/4$ inserts correspond to a distribution where a fourth of the write operations are inserts. The benchmark executes 60,000 operations.

The workload emulates multiple user sessions where a user connects to a tenant's database, executes hundred transactions and then disconnects. A workload consists of sixty such sessions, i.e. a total of $6,000$ transactions. The default configurations use transactions with ten operations, 80% being read operations, 15% update operations and 5% new rows inserted. Each tenant's database consists of a single table with an integer primary key and ten columns of type varchar. Keys accessed by a transaction are chosen from a Zipfian distribution over a database with $100,000$ rows ($\sim$ 250 MB on disk); the Zipfian co-efficient is set to 1.0. The workload generator is multi-threaded with target throughput of 50 transactions per second (TPS). The default database page size is set to 16 KB and the cache size is set to 32 MB. These default configurations are representative of medium sized tenants [25, 26]. We vary these parameters, one at a time, to analyze their impact on migration cost.

7.2 Migration Cost

Our first experiment analyzes the impact on migration cost when varying the percentage read operations in a transaction. Figure 5(a) plots the number of failed operations during migration; clients continue issuing operations on the tenant even during migration. A client thread sequentially issues the operations of a transaction. All operations are well-formed, and any error reported by the database server after an operation has been issued account for a failed operation. As is evident from Figure 5(a), the number of failed operations in Zephyr is one to two orders of magnitude lesser when compared to stop and copy. Two reasons contribute to more failed operations in stop and copy: (i) abortion of all transactions active at the start of migration, and (ii) abortion of all new transactions that access the tenant when it is unavailable during migration. Zephyr does not incur any unavailability; operations fail only when they result in a change to the index structure during migration.

Figure 5(b) plots the number of failed operations when using Zephyr for workloads with different insert ratios. Zephyr results in only few tens of failed operations when the workload does not have a high percentage of inserts, even for cases with a high update proportion. As the workload becomes predominantly read-only, the probability of an operation resulting in a change in the index structure decreases. This results in a decrease in the number of failed operations in Zephyr. Stop and copy also results in fewer failed operations for higher values of read percentages, the reason being the smaller unavailability window resulting from fewer updates that need to be flushed before migration.

Figure 5(c) plots the average transaction latency as observed by a client during normal operation (i.e. when no migration is performed) and that with a migration occurring midway; the two bars correspond to the two migration techniques used. We report latency averaged over all the $6,000$ transactions that constitute the workload. We only report latency of committed transactions; aborted transactions are ignored. When compared to normal operation, the increased latency in stop and copy results from the cost of warming up the cache at $\mathbb{N}_D$ and the cost of clients re-establishing the database connections after migration. In addition to the aforementioned costs, Zephyr fetches pages from $\mathbb{N}_S$ on-demand during migration; the page can be fetched from $\mathbb{N}_S$'s cache or from its disk. This results in additional latency overhead in Zephyr when compared to stop and copy.

Figure 5(d) shows the percentage of database pages pulled during the dual mode of Zephyr. Since the dual mode runs for a very short period, only a small fraction of pages are pulled on demand.

In our experiments, stop and copy took 3 to 8 seconds to migrate a tenant. Since all transactions in the workload have at least one update operation, when using stop and copy, all transactions issued during migration are aborted. On the other hand, even though Zephyr requires about 10 to 18 seconds to migrate the tenant, there is no downtime. As a result, the tenants observe few failed operations. Zephyr also incurs minimal messaging overhead beyond that needed to migrate the persistent database image. Every page transferred is preceded with its unique identifier; a pull request in the dual mode requires one round trip of messaging to fetch the page from $\mathbb{N}_S$. Stop and copy only requires the persistent image of the database to be migrated and does not incur any additional data transfer/messaging overhead.

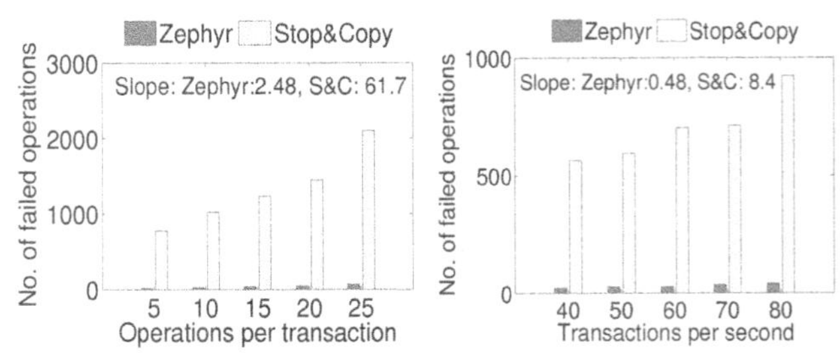

(a) Transaction size (b) Load

Figure 6: Impact of varying the transaction size and load on number of failed transactions. We also report the slope of an approximate linear fit of the points in a series.

We now evaluate the impact of transaction sizes and load (see Figure 6). Varying the transaction size implies varying the number of operations in a transaction. Since the load is kept constant at 50 TPS, a higher number of operations per transaction implies more operations issued per unit time. Varying the load implies varying

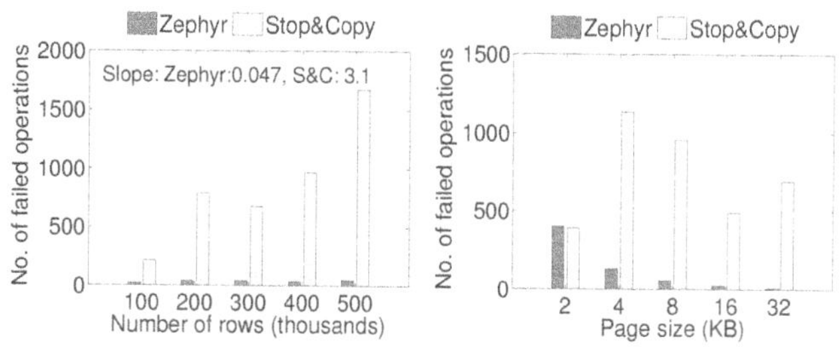

(a) Database size (b) Database page size

Figure 7: Impact of the database page size and database size on number of failed operations.

the number of transactions issued. Therefore, higher load also implies more operations issued per unit time. Moreover, since the percentage of updates is kept constant, more operations result in more updates. For stop and copy, more updates result in more data to be flushed before migration. This results in a longer unavailability window which in turn results in more operations failing. On the other hand, for Zephyr, more updates imply a higher probability of changes to the index structure during migration, resulting in more failed operations. However, the rate of increase in failed operations is lower in Zephyr when compared to stop and copy. This is evident from the slope of an approximate linear fit of the data points in Figure 6; the linear fit for Zephyr has a considerably smaller slope than that for stop and copy. This shows that Zephyr is more robust to the use for a variety of workloads. The effect on transaction latency is similar and hence is omitted. We also varied the cache size allocated to the tenants, however, the impact of cache size on service interruption was not significant. Even though a large cache size will result in potentially more changes to be flushed to the disk, the Zipfian access distribution coupled with a high percentage of read operations result in very few changed objects in the cache.

Figure 7(a) plots the impact of the database size on failed operations. In this experiment, we increase the database size up to 500K rows in the database (about 1.3 GB). As the database size increases, more time is needed to copy the database's persistent image, resulting in a longer unavailability window for stop and copy. On the other hand, for Zephyr, a larger database implies a longer finish mode. However, since Zephyr does not result in any unavailability, the database size has almost no impact on the number of failed operations. This is again evident from the slope of the linear fit of the data points; the slope is considerably higher for stop and copy, while that of Zephyr is negligible. Therefore, Zephyr is more robust for larger databases when compared to stop and copy.

Figure 7(b) shows an interesting interplay of the database page size on the number of operations failing. As the database page size increases, the number of failed operations decreases considerably for Zephyr, while that of stop and copy remains almost un-affected. When the page size is small, each page could fit only a few rows. For instance, in our setting, each row is close to a kilobyte, and a 2K page is already full with two rows. As a result, a majority of inserts result in structural changes to the index, which result in a lot of these inserts failing during migration. If we consider the experiment with 2K page size, more than 95% of the failed operations were inserts. However, as the page size increases, the leaf pages have more unused capacity. Therefore, only a few inserts result in a change to the index structure. Since stop and copy is oblivious of the page size and transfers the raw bytes of the database file, its performance is almost unchanged as a result of a change in the page size. However, when the page size is increased beyond the block size of the underlying filesystem, reading a page from the disk becomes more expensive resulting in an increase in the transaction latency when the page size is larger than the file system block size.

In summary, Zephyr results in minimal service interruption. In a cloud platform, high availability is extremely critical for customer satisfaction, thus making Zephyr more attractive. In spite of Zephyr not allowing changes to the index structure during migration, it resulted in very few operations failing. A significant failure rate was observed only with a high row size to page size ratio. Zephyr is therefore more robust to variances in read-write ratios, database sizes, and transaction sizes when compared to stop and copy, thus making it suitable for a variety of workloads and applications.

8. RELATED WORK

Multitenant database systems have been used for many years in large enterprises. Traditionally, multitenancy in the database layer has been in the form of the shared table model with major proponents including Force.com [25], Google AppEngine [1] etc. A detailed analysis of the different models, associated trade-offs, and representative designs was presented in Section 2.1. *Key-Value* stores, such as Bigtable, PNUTS, Dynamo etc., have also been used for multitenant application deployment. They provide a unified namespace over a cluster of machines and multiple tenants store their databases in this shared namespace. The data store however manages data placement and co-location of tenants. Hence this sharing cannot be directly mapped to any of the common multitenancy models. On the other hand, a large number of database systems have been designed and proposed for the cloud [6, 10, 22], but the focus for most of them have been to scale-out using the cloud infrastructure.

Elasticity is a crucial factor to the success of a system in the cloud, and live migration is important for lightweight elasticity. The history of live migration can be traced back to more than two decades and relates to migration of live processes [27]. These process migration techniques have been extended in the context of virtual machine (VM) migration, and a number of techniques have been proposed for Live VM migration [8, 20], which is now a standard feature supported by most VMs. These techniques use a combination of stop-and-copy, pull, and push phases to migrate memory pages and process states, but rely on a shared persistent storage abstraction between the source and the destination. Bradford et al. [5] propose a technique to consistently migrate a VM image and persistent local state across a WAN. The authors use a technique based on disk checkpointing followed by checkpoint migration and copying over the differential changes. Our technique differs from the VM migration techniques in that we use the semantics of the DBMS such as database pages, locking during transaction execution, and proven database and distributed systems recovery protocols to migrate a live database while guaranteeing correctness in the presence of arbitrary failures.

Recently, techniques for live migration in the database layer have also been proposed. Most of these techniques draw inspiration from VM migration techniques and use database operation semantics. Das et al. [13] propose a technique, called *Iterative Copy* (IC), for a shared storage database architecture. Since the storage is shared, the authors focus on copying the cache during migration such that the destination starts with a hot cache. Our technique, on the other hand, focuses on the shared nothing architecture and involves transfer of the entire persistent image of the database. Our goal, therefore, is to minimize service interruption. In another closely related work, Curino et al. [10] also identify the need for live migration in a shared nothing database architecture. Our technique is similar in spirit to that of Curino et al. where they suggest starting execution of transactions at the destination and the destination fetching pages on demand.

Lomet [21] proposes the use of replicated and partitioned indices for scaling out a database. Zephyr uses a similar concept where the index wireframe is replicated at the source and the destination nodes while page ownership is partitioned between them. However, Zephyr maintains the same structure of the index at both nodes while [21] allows the indices to have different structures while propagating updates asynchronously.

9. CONCLUSION

Live migration is an important feature to enable elasticity as a first class feature in multitenant databases for cloud platforms. We presented Zephyr, a technique to efficiently migrate a tenant's live database in a shared nothing architecture. Our technique uses a combination of on-demand pull and asynchronous push to migrate a tenant with minimal service interruption. Using light weight synchronization, we minimize the number of failed operations during migration, while also reducing the amount of data transferred during migration. We also provided a detailed analysis of the guarantees provided and proved the safety and liveness of Zephyr. Our technique relies on generic structures such as lock managers, standard B+ tree indices, and minimal changes to write ahead logging, thus making it suitable to be used in a variety of standard database engines with minimal changes to the existing code base. Our implementation in a standard lightweight open source RDBMS implementation shows that Zephyr allows lightweight migration of a live tenant database with minimal service interruption, thus allowing migration to be effectively used for elastic load balancing.

In the future, we plan to augment this technique with the control logic that determines which tenant to migrate and where to migrate. This control logic along with the ability to migrate live tenants, together form the basis for autonomous elasticity in multitenant databases for cloud platforms.

Acknowledgments

The authors would like to thank Shoji Nishimura, the anonymous reviewers, and our anonymous shepherd for providing useful feedback to improve this paper. This work is partly funded by NSF grants III 1018637 and CNS 1053594, and NEC Labs America.

10. REFERENCES

[1] J. Baker, C. Bond, J. Corbett, J. Furman, A. Khorlin, J. Larson, J.-M. Leon, Y. Li, A. Lloyd, and V. Yushprakh. Megastore: Providing Scalable, Highly Available Storage for Interactive Services. In *CIDR*, pages 223–234, 2011.

[2] H. Berenson, P. Bernstein, J. Gray, J. Melton, E. O'Neil, and P. O'Neil. A critique of ANSI SQL isolation levels. In *SIGMOD*, pages 1–10, 1995.

[3] P. A. Bernstein, I. Cseri, N. Dani, N. Ellis, A. Kalhan, G. Kakivaya, D. B. Lomet, R. Manner, L. Novik, and T. Talius. Adapting Microsoft SQL Server for Cloud Computing. In *ICDE*, 2011.

[4] P. A. Bernstein and E. Newcomer. *Principles of Transaction Processing*. Morgan Kaufmann Publishers Inc., second edition, 2009.

[5] R. Bradford, E. Kotsovinos, A. Feldmann, and H. Schiöberg. Live wide-area migration of virtual machines including local persistent state. In *VEE*, pages 169–179, 2007.

[6] M. Brantner, D. Florescu, D. Graf, D. Kossmann, and T. Kraska. Building a database on S3. In *SIGMOD*, pages 251–264, 2008.

[7] S. Chandrasekaran and R. Bamford. Shared cache - the future of parallel databases. In *ICDE*, pages 840–850, 2003.

[8] C. Clark, K. Fraser, S. Hand, J. G. Hansen, E. Jul, C. Limpach, I. Pratt, and A. Warfield. Live migration of virtual machines. In *NSDI*, pages 273–286, 2005.

[9] B. F. Cooper, A. Silberstein, E. Tam, R. Ramakrishnan, and R. Sears. Benchmarking Cloud Serving Systems with YCSB. In *ACM SoCC*, pages 143–154, 2010.

[10] C. Curino, E. Jones, R. Popa, N. Malviya, E. Wu, S. Madden, H. Balakrishnan, and N. Zeldovich. Relational Cloud: A Database Service for the Cloud. In *CIDR*, pages 235–240, 2011.

[11] S. Das, S. Agarwal, D. Agrawal, and A. El Abbadi. ElasTraS: An Elastic, Scalable, and Self Managing Transactional Database for the Cloud. Technical Report 2010-04, CS, UCSB, 2010.

[12] S. Das, D. Agrawal, and A. El Abbadi. ElasTraS: An Elastic Transactional Data Store in the Cloud. In *USENIX HotCloud*, 2009.

[13] S. Das, S. Nishimura, D. Agrawal, and A. El Abbadi. Live Database Migration for Elasticity in a Multitenant Database for Cloud Platforms. Technical Report 2010-09, CS, UCSB, 2010.

[14] K. P. Eswaran, J. N. Gray, R. A. Lorie, and I. L. Traiger. The notions of consistency and predicate locks in a database system. *Commun. ACM*, 19(11):624–633, 1976.

[15] Facebook Statistics. `http://www.facebook.com/press/info.php?statistics`, Retreived March 18, 2010.

[16] J. Gray. Notes on data base operating systems. In *Operating Systems, An Advanced Course*, pages 393–481, London, UK, 1978. Springer-Verlag.

[17] J. N. Gray, R. A. Lorie, and G. R. Putzolu. Granularity of locks in a shared data base. In *VLDB*, pages 428–451, 1975.

[18] H2 Database Engine. `http://www.h2database.com/html/main.html`, 2011.

[19] D. Jacobs and S. Aulbach. Ruminations on multi-tenant databases. In *BTW*, pages 514–521, 2007.

[20] H. Liu, H. Jin, X. Liao, L. Hu, and C. Yu. Live migration of virtual machine based on full system trace and replay. In *HPDC*, pages 101–110, 2009.

[21] D. B. Lomet. Replicated indexes for distributed data. In *PDIS*, pages 108–119. IEEE Computer Society, 1996.

[22] D. B. Lomet, A. Fekete, G. Weikum, and M. J. Zwilling. Unbundling transaction services in the cloud. In *CIDR*, 2009.

[23] C. Mohan, D. Haderle, B. Lindsay, H. Pirahesh, and P. Schwarz. Aries: a transaction recovery method supporting fine-granularity locking and partial rollbacks using write-ahead logging. *ACM TODS*, 17(1):94–162, 1992.

[24] A. A. Soror, U. F. Minhas, A. Aboulnaga, K. Salem, P. Kokosielis, and S. Kamath. Automatic virtual machine configuration for database workloads. In *SIGMOD*, pages 953–966, 2008.

[25] C. D. Weissman and S. Bobrowski. The design of the force.com multitenant internet application development platform. In *SIGMOD*, pages 889–896, 2009.

[26] F. Yang, J. Shanmugasundaram, and R. Yerneni. A scalable data platform for a large number of small applications. In *CIDR*, 2009.

[27] E. Zayas. Attacking the process migration bottleneck. *SIGOPS Oper. Syst. Rev.*, 21(5):13–24, 1987.

Workload-Aware Database Monitoring and Consolidation

Carlo Curino
curino@mit.edu

Evan P. C. Jones
evanj@mit.edu

Samuel Madden
madden@csail.mit.edu

Hari Balakrishnan
hari@csail.mit.edu

ABSTRACT

In most enterprises, databases are deployed on dedicated database servers. Often, these servers are underutilized much of the time. For example, in traces from almost 200 production servers from different organizations, we see an average CPU utilization of less than 4%. This unused capacity can be potentially harnessed to consolidate multiple databases on fewer machines, reducing hardware and operational costs. Virtual machine (VM) technology is one popular way to approach this problem. However, as we demonstrate in this paper, VMs fail to adequately support database consolidation, because databases place a unique and challenging set of demands on hardware resources, which are not well-suited to the assumptions made by VM-based consolidation.

Instead, our system for database consolidation, named Kairos, uses novel techniques to measure the hardware requirements of database workloads, as well as models to predict the combined resource utilization of those workloads. We formalize the consolidation problem as a non-linear optimization program, aiming to minimize the number of servers and balance load, while achieving near-zero performance degradation. We compare Kairos against virtual machines, showing up to a factor of 12× higher throughput on a TPC-C-like benchmark. We also tested the effectiveness of our approach on real-world data collected from production servers at Wikia.com, Wikipedia, Second Life, and MIT CSAIL, showing absolute consolidation ratios ranging between 5.5:1 and 17:1.

Categories and Subject Descriptors

H.2.4 [**Systems**]: Relational databases; Distributed databases; H.2.7 [**Database Administration**]: Metrics

General Terms

Experimentation, Measurement, Performance

Keywords

consolidation, multi-tenant databases

1. INTRODUCTION

With the advent of outsourced computing and storage in the form of public clouds, as well as the rapid rise in the number of web, mobile, and enterprise database applications, it is now common for a single data center within an organization to deploy hundreds or thousands of individual relational database management systems (DBMSs). For example, one large telecommunications company with which we are familiar has more than 20,000 DBMS instances deployed in its internal infrastructure. Oftentimes, each database is deployed on a dedicated server, with the machine provisioned for the peak load that is expected to be placed on the database. However, it is unlikely that all the DBMS instances in a data center will be hit by peak loads at the same time. In practice, most databases have natural ebbs and flows, occasional unexpected events, and a certain degree of statistical correlation (or lack of correlation) with other databases in the same data center. Over-provisioning and uncorrelated loads provide the opportunity to consolidate servers onto fewer physical machines. For example, by analyzing data we gathered from production database systems run by Wikia.com, Wikipedia, Second Life, and MIT CSAIL we found that a 5.5× to 17× reduction in the number of database servers is possible. This kind of savings can reduce hardware expenses, lower the administrative burden, and consume less energy [10].

The process of consolidation involves analyzing the load characteristics of multiple dedicated database servers and packing their workloads into fewer physical machines, reducing the resources consumed without changing the application performance. Of course, consolidating servers is not new a new idea, and has been the driver for widespread deployment of virtual machines (VMs) in data centers. VMs have been particularly successful at consolidating services that are not data-intensive, as well as testing/development environments. However, as we will show in this paper, consolidating databases is harder because DBMSs make strong assumptions regarding the characteristics and performance of the underlying physical system (e.g., that the buffer pool will always be located in RAM) and are designed to use all the resources they are given. This makes it hard for existing VMs or administrators to estimate the true resource requirements of complex DBMS software when trying to identify opportunities for consolidation. Furthermore, the use of a VM per database leads to significant redundancy (e.g., multiple independent disk operations for log and data writes, multiple copies of the OS and DBMS, etc.). For these reasons, we believe that VM-based consolidation is appropriate only when hard isolation between databases is more important than cost or performance.

We have identified two key challenges that need to be tackled when building a database consolidation system. First, tools are needed to accurately monitor the resource utilization of each database and to estimate the utilization of a combined set of databases. Second, algorithms are needed to choose which databases should be combined and placed on which hardware, given hundreds of databases and physical resources to choose from. This second challenge is difficult because, unlike many other software systems, data-intensive computations are not easy to migrate between physical machines[1], thus, common load balancing strategies that perform migration in reaction to change in load cannot be applied. As a result, stable assignments of databases to physical machines that can run unchanged for days are more suitable.

This paper presents the design, implementation, and experimental evaluation of *Kairos*,[2] a system that consolidates multiple OLTP and Web database workloads on to a shared hardware infrastructure. These workloads are amongst the most common and profligate in enterprises, and are amenable to consolidation; handling large, scan-intensive OLAP workloads requires different modeling techniques, which are not discussed here.

Kairos begins with a set of independent database workloads running on dedicated servers. The output is a consolidation strategy mapping workloads to physical nodes. After consolidation, each physical node runs a *single* DBMS instance that processes transactions on behalf of multiple databases, while meeting the application's performance requirements. In particular, in this paper, we use the throughput of a database before consolidation as an implicit service level agreement (SLA) on the performance the system should provide after consolidation. Extending the system to support latency-based SLAs would make an interesting future extension of our work.[3]

In this paper, we concentrate on scenarios where each logical database places a moderate but non-trivial load on the underlying system, which is what enables consolidation. We envision tens to hundreds of databases being consolidated onto a single server—for this reason we ignore the schema scalability problems that arise in extreme multi-tenancy scenarios where thousands of almost inactive database workloads with very similar schemas are consolidated onto a single physical server. Such problems have been been investigated in depth by others [15, 3, 14].

This paper makes three principal contributions:

1. Techniques to estimate resource requirements, particularly CPU, RAM and disk I/O, and models to estimate resource needs for combined workloads.

2. A method to analyze the resource consumption for each database over time in order to produce an assignment of databases to physical machines. Using the resource models mentioned above, we apply mixed-integer non-linear optimization to minimize the number of required machines and balance their load, without changing the perceived performance of the databases. The technique can be used to find the best assignment of databases to machines at time-scales ranging from hours to months.

3. Experiments on real-world load statistics from almost 200 production servers provided by Wikia.com, Wikipedia, Second Life and our lab. We find consolidation ratios (i.e., the ratio of machines used before and after consolidation) ranging from 5.5:1 to 17:1. We compare our approach of one database instance per machine with one virtual machine per workload, as well as one database process per workload. We show up to 12× greater throughput and consolidation ratios up to 3.3× higher when running TPC-C.

2. SYSTEM OVERVIEW

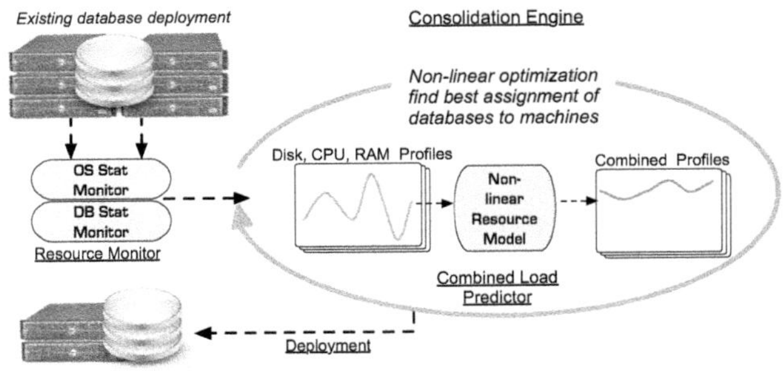

Figure 1: The architecture of the Kairos system.

Kairos takes as input an existing (non-consolidated) collection of database workloads, and a set of target physical machines on which to consolidate those workloads. The source and target hardware resources are allowed to overlap.

As shown in Figure 1 the key components are:

1. *Resource Monitor*: Kairos includes an automated statistics collection tool that captures data from the DBMS and OS to estimate the resource consumption of individual databases while running. This monitoring must be done without introducing any overhead. Estimating the RAM required by a database is particularly challenging and important; Kairos uses a simple, novel technique to gauge the working set size of a database—see Section 3.

2. *Combined Load Estimator:* Given the hardware resource consumption of individual databases running on dedicated hardware is a starting point, the next step is to predict how they interact when consolidated onto a single database server. Modeling the interaction is especially challenging for disk I/O because disk throughput is a complicated nonlinear function of the load, unlike with CPU or RAM which basically combine linearly. To solve this problem for the disk, we built a tool that creates a hardware-specific model of a given DBMS configuration, allowing us to predict how arbitrary workload mixes will perform on that configuration—see Section 4.

3. *Consolidation Engine:* Kairos uses nonlinear optimization techniques to find assignments of databases onto physical resources that: (i) minimize the number of machines required to support a user's workloads (ii) maximize load balance across the consolidated servers, and (iii) guarantee that every workload is assigned to a server without over-committing any server. Replication and other requirements on workload placement are naturally handled as additional constraints. The consolidation engine is described in Section 5, with implementation details in Section 6.

One way to think of Kairos is as a "consolidation advisor," which produces a static placement that database administrators (DBAs) can use to manually optimize their infrastructure. This procedure can be repeated periodically. Ideally, this process should be automated. We are in the process of working on a system to seamlessly migrate databases to handle this, as part of our Relational Cloud project [7]. For experiments in this paper, we manually implemented the consolidation strategies recommended by Kairos.

We note two important caveats about Kairos:

1. Our implementation is primarily for MySQL, though we believe the ideas we present generalize to other DBMS servers. The consolidation algorithm itself is more widely applicable, but the resource models used are based principally on observations and workload profiles from MySQL. In some cases, we have run additional experiments with PostgreSQL, demonstrating a slightly wider range of applicability of the ideas. To the extent possible, we point out where other database systems might differ from what we observed or where amendments to our techniques are required.

[1]This is particularly true for direct-attached storage, but remains valid for storage-area networks (SANs). In fact, even with a SAN, there are limits to the available I/O and to the number of physical machines that can be connected.

[2]The Greek god of opportunity, which seems an apt name for a system that relies on opportunism.

[3]One reason explicit SLAs were not our initial focus was that we gathered from interviews with a few consultants and administrators that database-level SLAs were rarely used, compared to application-level SLAs.

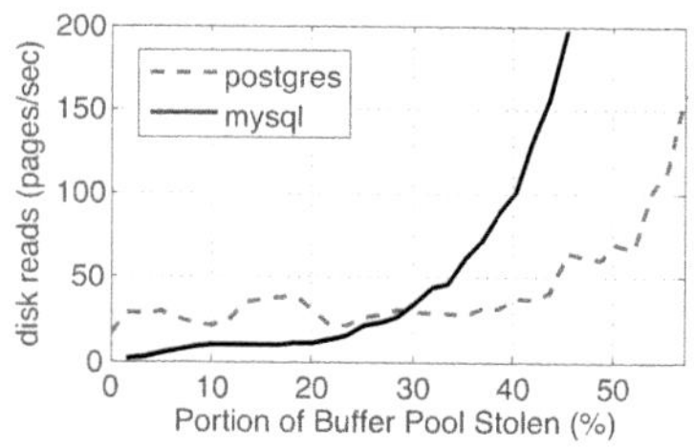

Figure 2: Buffer Pool Gauging

2. Consolidation is likely to increase latency and recovery time, because both are proportional to the load on the database system. Database consolidation, regardless of the specific consolidation approach, may not be appropriate for applications that are very sensitive to these effects.

3. RESOURCE MONITOR

The resource monitor queries the OS and DBMS running on each machine for statistics about CPU, RAM, and disk I/O, buffer pool utilization, and log flushes. This data is then used to predict the resource consumption of workloads if they are combined. For CPU, this task is straightforward because the CPU utilization of a consolidated workload is the sum of the CPU loads of its each of its constituent workloads, minus some small savings from reducing the number of OS and DBMS instances.

For RAM, the statistics provided by the OS tend to overestimate the actual resources required, as they can only report the total memory allocated to the database process, rather than the memory actually in use. This gap between the apparent and actual resource utilization is one of the primary reasons why VM-based consolidation does not work well with databases. This overestimate occurs because DBMSs have traditionally been designed to be the primary service on a machine, and thus attempt to use all available resources, even if they do not *need* those resources to sustain the same transactional throughput. For example, most databases will fill the buffer pool with pages from disk, even if the working set for the application is smaller than the buffer pool.

Thus, unless the application is actively accessing the entire buffer pool at maximum throughput, most DBMSs can deliver identical performance using less RAM. The challenge is accurately estimating the required RAM.

For disk, OS tools like `iostat` provide an easy way to estimate the disk I/Os of a single DBMS. The challenge is that databases often use unused disk bandwidth to proactively complete tasks—for example, when idle, MySQL/InnoDB aggressively flushes dirty pages from the buffer pool to reduce recovery time. Under most conditions, this flushing has no effect on transaction throughput, and the degree of flushing or I/O will change when multiple databases are combined together. We address the problem of estimating the I/O requirements of combined database workloads in the next section.

3.1 Buffer Pool Gauging for RAM Estimation

To operate efficiently, an OLTP DBMS needs to keep the *working set* of the application it is serving in main memory. Because it is difficult to estimate the working set size, it is common for administrators to devote nearly all the available RAM on the machine to the DBMS. Typical configurations include a very large buffer pool and no OS file cache (suggested configuration for most DBMSs including MySQL/InnoDB), or a combination of buffer pool and OS file cache (suggested configuration for PostgreSQL). In both configurations, after running for some time, all the memory accessible to the DBMS, i.e., the entire buffer pool and potentially the OS file cache, will be full of data pages. However, for many applications on modern servers with large amounts of RAM, the total amount of memory far exceeds the actual working set at any point in time—such over-provisioned applications are exactly those that are amenable to aggressive consolidation. Thus the challenge is to develop techniques that estimate the working set size of a database to determine if two or more databases can be consolidated together.

```
function bufferGauge(db, probeTable):
  tableLength = 0
  if db.tableExists(probeTable):
    tableLength = db.execute("SELECT COUNT(*) from ?", probeTable)
  else:
    db.execute("CREATE TABLE ? (id int, dummy char(?))",
      probeTable, PAGE_SIZE)

  scanLength = INITIAL_SCAN_ROWS
  while scanLength < MAX_SCAN_ROWS:
    if tableLength < scanLength:
      appendRows(db, probeTable, scanLength - tableLength)
      tableLength = scanLength

    for i in range(0, SCANS_PER_INSERT):
      db.execute("SELECT COUNT(*) FROM ? WHERE id < ?",
          probeTable, scanLength)
      sleep(READ_WAIT_SECONDS)
    scanLength += SCAN_INCREASE_COUNT
```

Figure 3: Probing Procedure

The first step in our gauging process is to determine if the system is over-provisioned. To do so we collect statistics about *OS-level disk reads*, and *DBMS-level buffer pool miss ratios*. This information tells us whether: (i) the working set fits in the buffer pool (the miss ratio of the buffer pool is close to zero), (ii) the working set does not fit in the buffer pool, but fits in the OS file cache (high buffer pool miss ratio is but very few physical disk reads), or (iii) the working set size exceeds the memory accessible to the DBMS, causing it to serve data from disk (high buffer pool miss ratio and many physical disk reads). Case (iii) indicates that memory is not over-provisioned, and that the total RAM accessible to the DBMS is actively used. n cases (i) and (ii), we need some facility to measure how much memory the database is actively using, either in the OS file cache, as in case (ii), or in the buffer pool, as in case (i).

We have discussed this subject with a number of database administrators who agree that it is common for OLTP/web databases to be over-provisioned in real-world installations. This motivated the design of a new technique, *buffer pool gauging*, to measure the working set size of an application.

Our technique issues SQL queries to an unmodified DBMS and observes internal statistics to estimate the database working set size. Pseudocode for our gauging procedure is shown in Figure 3. It works by creating an empty *probe table* in the database and growing it slowly, or reusing an existing probe table if we have performed gauging on this DBMS before. While adding to the probe table, we force the DBMS to keep its pages in the buffer pool by querying it several times for every round of inserts. The contents of the probe table and its query workload were chosen to force the data to be memory-resident without introducing additional logging or much CPU load: (i) the probe table has only a few large tuples that fit exactly into the page size, (ii) the queries are simple COUNT(*) aggregates over non-indexed fields, and (iii) there are no updates. While growing this table, we monitor disk reads that the DBMS performs using the statistics provided by the DBMS and the OS. By slowly "stealing" buffer pool/file cache space and monitoring the number of pages the DBMS reads back from disk, we are able to detect when we start to push *useful* pages out of the buffer pool/file cache. This is because queries from the legitimate user's workload cause evicted pages to be read back from disk.

Determining how quickly to grow the probe table (the `SCANS_PER_INSERT` parameter in Figure 3) is an interesting

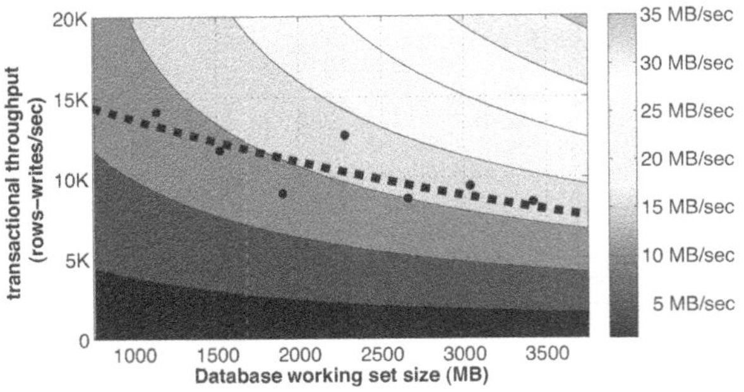

Figure 4: Disk Model for Our Experimental Configuration

question. On one hand, we want to to avoid affecting the overall query throughput of the system with our probing. On the other hand, if we grow the probe table very slowly it may take a long time to complete the gauging. In our current implementation, we used a simple adaptive strategy that accelerates the speed at which we inflate the probe table if there is no increase in the physical reads, while slowing down when we see even a small increase in the average number of physical reads per seconds over a short time window (the default in our tests is 10 seconds). In our tests the probe table growth speed can be as high as several MB/sec or as low as tens of KB/sec depending on the user workload. This allows us to avoid degrading the throughput of the database while maximizing the rate at which we can probe.

The frequency at which we query the probe table (`READ_WAIT_SECONDS` in Figure 3) also requires a careful balance: we need to guarantee that the probe table is queried frequently enough for the buffer manager to keep data in RAM, but we also want to avoid frequent queries that will only add to the CPU overhead. In our experiments, querying the probe table once every 1–10 seconds forces the DBMS to keep the probe data in RAM, while keeping the CPU overhead to under 5%.

We implemented this technique on MySQL and PostgreSQL and tested it using: (i) TPC-C, (ii) synthetic micro-benchmarks, and (iii) a benchmark we derived from Wikipedia. In the following discussion, we use TPC-C to discuss the effectiveness of our approach; in Section 7 we report a more thorough evaluation of the technique's effectiveness and impact on user performance.

Figure 2 shows the number of physical page reads/sec issued by the DBMS as we grow the probe table for TPC-C, scaled to 5 warehouses. The two lines present: (i) MySQL with 953 MB of buffer pool configured using O_DIRECT writes to bypass the OS file cache and (ii) PostgreSQL, configured with 953 MB of shared buffer, and using the OS file cache—filling the remaining 1GB of RAM. In both cases, the working set fits in the buffer pool, and we can "steal" up to 30%-40% of the buffer pool with a negligible increase in buffer pool misses (and thus of disk I/O). This matches our expected TPC-C working set size, which is around 120-150MB per warehouse. This allows us to detect that identical performance can be achieved by using a significantly smaller amount of RAM. To verify that this could not be done properly by the OS, we looked at Linux's reported "active" pages, which and found that all of the database buffer pool was shown to be active (1.7GB.) Thus, compared to OS metrics, we reduced the memory requirement estimate by almost a factor 2.8×. In Section 7, we report factors up to 7.2× in tests using the Wikipedia benchmark.

Our current prototype performed well in our experiments using MySQL and PostgreSQL on several workloads, and we thus believe this technique to be widely applicable. However, adapting it to a wide range of production environments requires significant engineering effort to deal with: (i) systems operating with multiple buffer pools (e.g., DB2), (ii) DBMSs which dynamically adapting buffer pool resources, (iii) cold databases with empty buffer pools, or (iv) quickly changing working set sizes.

4. COMBINED LOAD ESTIMATOR

In this section, we address the problem of estimating the resource requirements of a combination of several database workloads. For CPU and RAM, this problem is straightforward (once we have properly gauged the RAM requirements of each database): for each time instant we can simply *sum* the CPU and RAM of individual workloads being co-located. For disk, the problem is much more challenging.

4.1 Combined Disk I/O Performance

Predicting the disk performance of a set of database workloads is a hard problem, for a number of reasons:

1. DBMSs typically exploit unused disk bandwidth to flush dirty buffer pool pages back to disk whenever the disk is underutilized. Although this flushing is not required for correctness, it reduces recovery times, and may avoid mandatory writes due to future buffer pool misses or log reclamation. While using idle resources is in general a good strategy, it makes it very hard to estimate the minimum I/O resources required to achieve certain performance.
2. We have observed that disk I/O throughput grows sub-linearly with the workload size and the speed at which the DBMS is driven by user requests: more update operations will hit the same page at higher rates. Thus, each page that is written back includes writes from many transactions. Additionally, for larger data-set sizes, the ratio of log-writes to page flushes also changes.
3. Complex interactions between the DBMS, OS, and disk controller make it hard to predict how sequential or random the combination of a set of workloads will be.
4. There are a number of hardware and software configuration parameters that influence the I/O throughput a system can achieve, including group-commit timeouts, log-file sizes, workload speed and size, dirty page flushing policies, the number and types of disks, and caching in the OS and disk controller.

We can simplify the modeling problem because we are only concerned with modeling several consolidated databases inside a single DBMS instance, rather than the more complex problem of modeling several independent DBMSs running in one or more OSes.

A DBMS, regardless of the number of databases it hosts, coordinates I/O between those databases by: i) combining log writes from different workloads into a single sequential stream of log writes, which also leverages group-commit[4], and ii) delaying write-back operations of dirty pages for all databases and performing them in sorted order to reduce disk seeks. The result is a more efficient and predictable estimate of I/O throughput.

However, the complex behavior of disk subsystems still makes modeling the I/O requirements of a combined workload difficult. There are two ways one might attempt to address this problem: i) by building an analytical model of each component and algorithm affecting disk performance in the DBMS, or ii) by treating the system as a black box and experimentally deriving its transfer function.

In our experience the first strategy has two major drawbacks; first, it requires a detailed understanding of many DBMS internals, which are often not available for commercial products. Second,

[4]Some DBMSs support a separate log per database. This is useful when there is a separate disk per log, in which case our model can be applied to each disk independently. However, the general argument remains valid: the DBMS, even when writing multiple logs, controls the scheduling of log writes, and thus produces more sequential disk access patterns than a general purpose I/O scheduler.

any change in the algorithms or parameters, OS settings, or hardware requires modifying the model. We initially set out to build such an analytical model, but found that it only applied to very specific configurations. For these reasons, we adopted the second approach. We built a tool that automates the process of collecting experimental data from a live system and builds an *empirical model* that captures disk behavior.

Given a DBMS/OS/hardware configuration, our tool tests the disk subsystem with a controlled synthetic workload that sweeps through a range of database working set sizes and user request rates—this testing can be done as on offline process on a similar configuration, and does not need to interfere with the production database. The workload we use for this test is based on TPC-C, and represents a general OLTP workload. Our workload generator allows us to control both the working set size and rate at which rows are updated. At each step, the tool records the rows updated per second, the working set size in bytes, and the overall disk throughput in bytes per second. The result is a map of the system response to various degrees of load and working set sizes.

For the experiments in this section we collected over 7,000 data points on a test machines equipped with two quad-core Xeon 2.66 GHz CPUs, 32 GB of RAM and a single 7200 RPM SATA drive, running MySQL. The working set for the workload always fits in RAM, since this is the common configuration for the OLTP environments we are targeting.

Figure 4 shows a two-dimensional polynomial fit of this data—the actual data points are not shown for the sake of clarity. The X-axis shows the working-set size, the Y-axis shows the throughput in updated tuples per second, and the contours indicates the bytes written per second[5]. Increasing the rate at which rows are updated results in a non-linear increase in the aggregate I/O. Somewhat surprisingly, a larger working set also results in more I/O, again with a non-linear relationship. This is because when updates are spread throughout a larger working set, they are more likely to touch clean pages, resulting in more total dirty pages per unit of time and causing more pages to be written back. The thick dashed line shows a quadratic curve fit to the maximum disk throughput for each dataset size (the maximum throughput points are plotted as black circles). This is the point of disk-I/O saturation for our single disk configuration. Larger working set sizes yield lower throughput because they require in average more pages to be written back to achieve the same transaction throughput, and this experiment is disk bound.

This map is used to predict how multiple workloads will behave when combined. After a large number of exploratory experiments we observed (and later validated) that the combined throughput of several workloads respects the following property when the working set of the consolidated databases fits into memory:

Running multiple databases, with aggregate working set size X, at an aggregate row modification throughput (i.e., update, insert, or delete rate) Y produces the same disk I/O request rate as running a single workload with working set size X at update throughput Y.

This property holds for two reasons. First, in the steady state, no data needs to be read from disk since we assume that all working sets fit in memory. Second, the disk I/O is composed of: i) log writes, whose throughput depends only on the update rate Y and transaction log record size, which is roughly constant and small for typical OLTP workloads, and ii) dirty pages being written back to disk, which results in a similar mix of sorted random writes for either the single or multiple database case.

Therefore, to predict the amount of disk I/O that will be used when multiple workloads run inside a single DBMS, we monitor each workload for a period of time, collecting the working set size and the row update rate. By summing these parameters from all workloads, and using a profile like that shown in Figure 4 for the target host machine and database, we can predict how much disk I/O the combined workload will need. To the purpose of consolidation, it is only relevant to obtain a precise estimate for the high-load portion of the curve, as this is the part required to verify that the combined workload will not saturate the disk. Precision for very low disk load is not nearly as important, since it will not influence consolidation decisions anyway. As we show in Section 7, this model is significantly more accurate than the simple approach of summing the disk I/O of a set of consolidated workloads, especially for high-load situations where it reduces the estimation error by up to a factor of 32×.

In Section 7.5 we present experimental evidence that, for a broad range of workloads, the profile is independent of number of databases, database size and transaction types, and that it only depends on: (i) row update rates, (ii) the working set size, and (iii) the DBMS/OS/hardware configuration. This allows us to reuse profiles across a broad spectrum of workloads.

In our implementation we profile a machine by scanning the space of throughputs and working set sizes, testing each possible combination, this takes about two hours. We are investigating ways to speed up this process, including sampling fewer points, and building models incrementally. If a similar configuration has already been profiled, a small number of data points should be sufficient to adapt an existing profile.

5. CONSOLIDATION ENGINE

We now turn to the problem of determining which workloads should be combined together. The goal is to find an assignment that minimizes the number of machines, and that balances load across those machines as evenly as possible, while avoiding resource overcommitment. We model the problem of assigning workloads to servers as a mixed-integer non-linear optimization problem. The inputs to this problem are a list of machines with disk, memory, and CPU capacities, and a collection of workload profiles specifying the resource utilization of each resource as a time series sampled at regular intervals. We also allow the user to specify replication requirements for each workload, as well as pin individual workloads to specific machines. Machine capacities and resource utilizations are scaled appropriately to account for heterogeneous hardware.

Formally, we state the optimization problem as follows (these functions have been simplified for the sake of presentation; additional details are in Section 6):

$$\min_{x} \quad \sum_{tj}(e^{(\sum_i C_{ti}*x_{ij})} * signum(\sum_i x_{ij}));$$

$$\text{subject to} \quad \forall i \sum_j x_{ij} = R_i;$$

$$\forall j\; max_t(\sum_i CPU_{ti} * x_{ij}) < MaxCPU_j;$$

$$\forall j\; max_t(\sum_i MEM_{ti} * x_{ij}) < MaxMEM_j;$$

$$\forall j\; diskModel(DISK_{ti}, x_{ij}) < MaxDISK_j;$$

$$\ldots$$

$$additional\; placement\; constraints$$

$$\forall i, j x_{ij} \in N; 0 \leq x_{ij} \leq 1$$

[5]We use a Least Absolute Residuals (LAR) second-order, polynomial fit of the disk I/O to build the disk model shown by the contour of Figure 4. We chose this model because it was accurate enough in our experiment to accurately predict disk I/O rates and in our consolidated workloads.

where $x_{ij} = 1$ if workload i is assigned to server j and 0 otherwise, and R_i is the number of replicas desired for workload i. $MaxCPU_j, MaxMEM_j, MaxDISK_j$, are the maximum amount of CPU, RAM and, disk I/O available at server j (these can be $< 100\%$ to allow for some headroom), and C_{ti} is the time series describing the utilization of resource C (CPU, RAM, disk) for workload i at time t.

Objective function: The primary goal of the objective function is to minimize the number of servers used for the consolidated workloads; our formulation achieves this by using the $signum$ function, which is equal to 1 when its input is > 0 and 0 when its input is 0 ($signum$ of a vector v is a vector v' where $v'_i = signum(v_i)$).

This model guarantees that any solution using $k-1$ servers will have a lower objective function value than any k server solution—if no workloads are assigned to a server the $signum$ function is zero, and the entire cost associated with that server is discarded. When at least one workload is assigned to a server, we evaluate the server's contribution by weighting its resource utilization over time C_{ti} using an exponential function[6]. This penalizes solutions that are unbalanced. In fact, for any given number of servers, our objective function has a minimum when the load is balanced. This corresponds to solutions for which the risk of saturation is minimized. The global minimum of our objective function is the most balanced solution among those using the smallest number of servers. Figure 5 shows a rendering of our objective function as a projection on a 2D plane, for a hypothetical scenario in which a 4-server solution is the optimum. The figure also shows that the solver we use increases the value of the objective function by a large factor when constraints are violated, as shown by the spike on the left side for less than 4 servers.

Constraints: The constraints guarantee the feasibility of the solution. Because each x_{ij} can only be 0 or 1, and because the sum of the x_{ij} values for a given i must equal R_i, we guarantee that each workload i has R_i replicas assigned to *different* servers. The CPU, RAM, and disk constraints guarantee that the combined load imposed on each server will not exceed the available resources at any moment in time—thus avoiding saturation and overcommitment of the servers. Notice that extending the set of constraints to include other resources (e.g., network, disk space) is straightforward. In this paper, we focus on CPU, RAM and disk I/O since these were the most constrained in the real-world datasets we obtained. In particular, for CPU and RAM the constraints are a simple maximum of the sum (matrix product) over time t, while for disk we use a non-linear function based on the disk model discussed in Section 4.

Since we compute the combination of resources over time, we introduce more non-linearities. However, this allows us to leverage time-dependent utilization patterns to achieve greater consolidation. To this end, we assume that the future resource utilization of a workload is strongly correlated with the past resource utilization. We validate this assumption using real-world data in Section 7.5.

Replication: Our model also allows us to handle replication and other workload placement issues by introducing additional constraints. The R_i parameter allows us to control many replicas of each workload need to be placed; we operate under the conservative assumption that the replica will consume the same amount of resources as the primary. However, if the input workloads are already replicated, we can use the actual load of the replicas.

In either case we need to guarantee that the consolidation engine will not place replicas on the same physical node. This requirement is achieved by adding constraints of the form: $\forall j \; x_{i'j} + x_{i''j} \leq 1$,

[6]We can use any linear combination of the resources, to favor balancing one resource over the other.

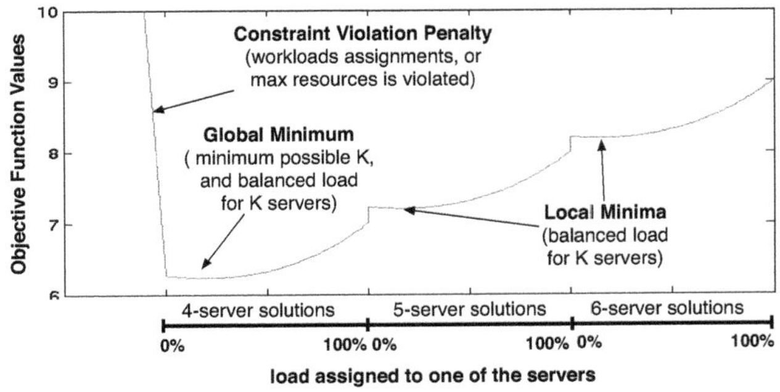

Figure 5: Simplified rendering of the objective function

which enforces that at most one of the two workloads i' or i'' are placed on a given target server j. Similarly we can support user requirements that pin a certain workload i' to a specific node j', by forcing $x_{i'j'} = 1$.

The cost of optimization: Since both our objective function and some of the functions characterizing resource constraints are non-linear, and because the overall optimization problem has several local minima, we employ a general-purpose global optimization algorithm called DIRECT [16] to find a solution. This makes the search expensive, motivating us to find ways to improve the performance of the consolidation engine by exploiting the characteristics of our problem, as discussed in Section 6. We report the performance of our solver in Section 7.5.

6. IMPLEMENTATION & OPTIMIZATION

We implemented the monitoring tools discussed in the earlier sections in Java. They connect to the databases to be consolidated via JDBC, and use SSH to collect OS-level statistics. The consolidation engine is based on the implementation of the DIRECT algorithm provided by the Tomlab [12] solver library for Matlab. The data collection tools and output consolidation schemes have been tested against various combinations of MySQL and PostgreSQL, and various versions of Linux, running on x86 servers. We chose these configurations because they are popular in production systems; in particular, MySQL+Linux is used in all the real-world datasets we obtained.

Speeding up the consolidation engine: In the previous section, we described the non-linear programming approach we took to assign workloads to machines. The search for the global minimum is hard due to: i) the presence of local minima, ii) the non-linearity of the problem (forcing us to use a less efficient general-purpose global solver), and iii) the large number of variables and constraints. The key problem is the time spent by the solver considering solutions around local minima. This situation can be partially improved by controlling a parameter of DIRECT that determines the ratio of time spent in local versus global search. However, this risks compromising the quality of the load assignment solution, since not enough time is spent "polishing" the final solution around the global minimum. To address this problem, we developed an optimization that leverages our domain-specific knowledge.

The optimization attempts to reduce the number of variables by bounding the number of servers K that the optimizer has to consider. Suppose we can compute the minimum number of servers K' for which a valid solution exists. Then the solver can simply discard any solution using more than K' servers. While the value of K' is unknown, we can estimate reasonable lower and upper bounds for it. The lower bound is provided by a single-resource fractional solution that optimistically assumes that the workloads can be assigned fractionally to machines, and that each resource can be considered independently. With these assumptions, the lower bound $\underline{K}$ can be computed as the maximum of the sum of each resource over time divided by the total available resources. A loose upper-bound $\overline{K}$ is the number of machines currently in use; better upper-bounds can be found by running cheap, greedy workload allocation strategies.

Since upper and lower bounds are typically not too far apart, we can binary search to determine the lowest value K' of K that leads to a viable solution. We start with our upper and lower bounds, and run the optimizer with the midpoint number of servers. We either terminate it as soon as it finds a valid solution, or consider K to not be feasible if it runs longer than a configured time limit. We then repeat on the upper or lower range, as appropriate, until we determine K'. We then re-run the solver, giving it a maximum of K' servers to allocate to the workloads and we do not stop until the optimal solution is found or a maximum optimization time is reached. Limiting the number of possible servers reduces the number of variables, and thus explores a much smaller solution space where many local minima have been discarded. This allows us to parametrize the DIRECT algorithm in favor of local searches to increase the quality of the final solution. In all the cases we tested, this approach leads to significantly lower running times than a direct application of the solver to the entire solution space—up to a 45× reduction in running time. Near-optimal solutions are found in less than 8 minutes for problems with up to 100 workloads and 20 output servers.

Normalization and preprocessing of data: The above description simplifies the objective and constraint functions used in our non-linear optimizer for the sake of presentation. There are several additional details that we describe here for completeness. The first additional complication is that we limit the argument of the exponential objective function shown in Figure 5 to the $[0, 1]$ interval through normalization. This provides a function with a concave shape, and with reasonable numeric limits for the optimizer. Also we introduce weighting constants on each term in the linear combination of resources inside the objective function. These weights allow us to indicate that certain resources are more important to be balanced, while still preferring solutions with more servers over those with less less servers.

The CPU utilization reported by the Linux kernel is expressed as a percentage of one CPU core. Thus a value of 250 means that the system is using 2.5 cores. We first convert the percentages from heterogeneous machines to a "standard" core by scaling based on clock speed (ideally we would also scale based on CPU architecture). Then we convert the utilization to a fraction of a "target" machine. In our case, we assume the target machine has 12 cores. Thus, a CPU utilization of 250% would become $\frac{2.5}{12} = 0.208$.

When aggregating CPU and RAM from multiple workloads, we applied several other techniques:

CPU: Operating systems and databases each introduce some CPU overhead. When consolidating multiple workloads, simply summing the CPU utilization will double-count this portion of the load, since each machine we measure is running a separate OS and DBMS, while our consolidated solution has only one OS and one DBMS. To address this, the function that sums CPU usage in our consolidation engine removes a small, experimentally determined, fraction of CPU-load for each consolidated workload.

RAM: Our RAM model allows users to input a user-defined "scaling" factor that linearly scales down the measured RAM values. This can be used when buffer pool gauging techniques are not applicable. This is the case for the historical statistics we obtained from some of the organizations for this paper (Wikipedia, Second Life). For these workloads, we estimated an approximate 30% savings would be possible, based on manually examining a few production databases. Precisely determining this parameter requires significant domain/application knowledge.

7. PERFORMANCE EVALUATION

In this section, we begin by demonstrating the accuracy of our combined resource consumption models for CPU, RAM and disk, and testing our consolidation engine on a small-scale deployment in our lab. We then study the effectiveness of our consolidation algorithm on resource utilization profiles from almost 200 production servers from four organizations. Finally, we compare our approach to VM-based consolidation and validate that past load is a good predictor for future load.

7.1 Datasets and Experimental Setup

We experimented with two kinds of datasets: (i) *Database Workloads*, a series of synthetic and real workloads used to run fully controlled experiments, and (ii) *Real-World Load Statistics*, a set of historical statistics from production databases, used to verify the applicability of our consolidation engine. We could not test our entire suite of load profiling tools for these production databases, because we were not given access to the machines, but only the statistics that these organizations already collect.

Database Workloads: We used three main database workloads: (i) a synthetic micro-benchmark, (ii) TPC-C, and (iii) a benchmark derived from Wikipedia .

The synthetic micro-benchmark is used to verify that our resource models and consolidation engine function as expected. This benchmark contains five independent workloads that each operate on a single table, issuing a mix of updates and CPU-intensive selects (using expensive cryptographic functions). These workloads are designed so we can precisely control the amount of RAM, CPU and disk I/O consumed. To achieve this, we vary the working set size, the rate of selects, and the rate of updates. By adjusting these parameters, we generated five different workloads. Each workload has different time-varying patterns (e.g., sinusoidal, sawtooth, flat with different amplitude and period). The goal was to validate that Kairos properly predicts resource utilization for a very different set of workloads very than the one used to devise the resource models (based on TPC-C). It also tests the ability of the consolidation engine to detect opportunity for consolidation when multiple resource constraints make it challenging.

The second workload is based on TPC-C. We control the request rate and the working set size (by changing the number of warehouses clients access). TPC-C represents a typical OLTP workload, and we use it to validate the impact of consolidation on throughput and latency.

The third workload is based on Wikipedia. This benchmark models the actual workload on Wikipedia's database servers. We used the publicly available source code and data, along with a trace containing 10% of 4 months of actual HTTP requests served by Wikipedia's data centers, obtained from the Wikimedia Foundation. By combining this information with published statistics about the effectiveness of the many caching layers in the application [23], as well as private communication with Wikipedia engineers, we built a simulator that generates a workload similar to that observed by the backend MySQL database servers. We can scale this benchmark from a few tens of megabytes to the full 4 TB of the Wikipedia database by sampling an appropriate subset. This workload is transactional with 4 types of transactions, and models reads and edits of articles, watch list management, user logins, IP blocks, and a number of other features. On average 92% of the queries are reads and

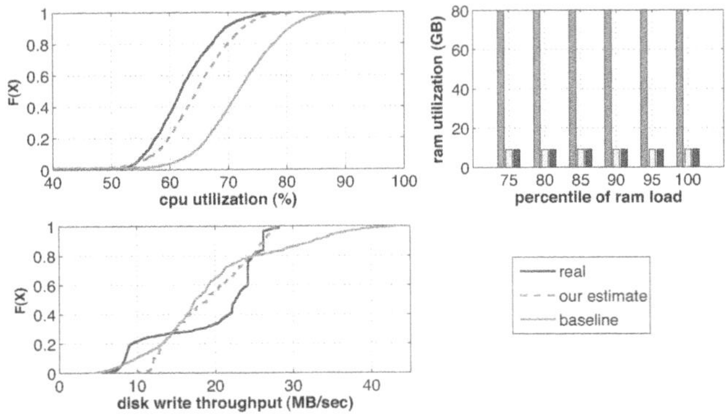

Figure 6: Validating resource models and consolidation engine

about 8% are writes. Tuple sizes range from 70 bytes to 3.6 MB (due to article text).

Real-World Load Statistics: We also validated our approach using real data obtained data from four organization:

- *Internal*: data from 25 servers that support general purpose computing from our lab's IT staff. This workload is a combination of production systems as well as test and development servers.
- *Wikia.com*: a collaborative publishing platform with over 34 database servers.
- *Wikipedia*: the popular free on-line encyclopedia. We obtained monitoring data from their Tampa, Florida database cluster, containing 40 database servers.
- *Second Life*: the data from 97 database servers powering the on-line virtual world.

The statistics were stored in the `rrdtool` format, used by open source monitoring tools such as Cacti, Ganglia, and Munin, and as recorded by the respective organizations, and thus they do not include our buffer pool gauging technique for accurately measuring RAM utilization. The data includes CPU, RAM, and (for some machines) disk I/O numbers as reported by Linux, averaged over different time intervals—ranging from every 15 seconds for the last hour to every 24 hours for the last year.

In our experiments, we use a 24 hour time window with samples every 5 minutes—this was the best compromise between length of observation and sampling rates (we obtained similar results on weekly and monthly data). We normalized the CPU data by considering the number of cores per machine and the CPU-speed where available. We have detailed CPU and RAM statistics for all machines, but we have disk I/O statistics for only a small subset. We used the available data to estimate the disk utilization on other nodes. All of the database servers in these datasets are running MySQL, with the exception of 1 machine in the Internal dataset running Postgres.

Hardware: The database servers used for our experiments have: *Server 1:* two quad-core Intel Xeon 2.66 GHz E5430 CPUs, 32 GB of RAM, and a single 7200 RPM SATA disk, and *Server 2:* two Intel Xeon 3.2 GHz, 2GB of RAM, and a single 7200 RPM SATA disk. Both machines run Linux 2.6.31 and MySQL 5.5.5-m3. Our target machine for consolidation of the real-world dataset is a server with 12 cores and 96 GB of RAM, which represents a higher-end class of machines used by two of our data providers. This type of server costs between USD $6,000–$10,000 at the time of writing, depending on exact the configuration.

7.2 Resource Models and Consolidation

To test the accuracy of our monitoring techniques (Section 3) and models for combined resource utilization (Section 4), as well as the ability of our consolidation engine (Section 5) to discover consolidation opportunities even in difficult scenarios, we set up a controlled experiment based on the five synthetic workloads described above. We varied several parameters to generate workloads with differing request rates, read/writes ratios, CPU/RAM/disk load, and request patterns.

The workloads used in this test were chosen to *barely fit* within a single physical machine, with individual resource utilization patterns that make it hard to detect the opportunity for consolidation due to the combination of constraints induced by multiple resources. We first use our monitoring tools to collect load statistics for individual workloads in isolation, then predict their combined load and compute a consolidation strategy with our engine.

Kairos successfully predicts that the workloads can be allocated together on a single server. We further validate the proposed consolidation strategy by physically co-locating the workloads and running them, while monitoring the consolidated system's latency and throughput. As expected, the workloads fit within a single physical server, yielding *identical* throughput and 95th percentile latency increases of less than 1 ms.

For each resource (CPU, RAM, and disk), we recorded the estimated and measured load over time. In Figure 6 we show the fraction of the total resource used by the combined workload in each time window estimated using our models ("our estimate"), measured on our server ("real"), and estimated using a straight sum of the operating system metrics ("baseline"). The baseline represents the simple approach to estimating the combined utilization. We plot the Cumulative Distribution Function (CDF) for CPU and disk and percentiles for RAM in Figure 6 (since the working set sizes are constant and the CDF would be a simple vertical line). The estimates for most heavily loaded windows are the most important because, as discussed in Section 3, we need accurate estimates when a resource is nearing 100% utilization.

This experiment shows the need for sophisticated resource models, and the accuracy of the models we proposed. In particular:

RAM: For these synthetic data sets, we control the actual working set sizes, which range between 512 MB and 2.5 GB, and are constant over time. The figure shows that buffer pool gauging (Section 3.1) accurately measures these working set sizes, while summing the OS statistics grossly overestimates the memory utilization as almost 9× the actual value of 9 GB.

Disk I/O: the CDF of disk I/O shown in Figure 6 shows that our disk model (Section 4.1) is very accurate at estimating the 75th-100th percentile of load, as in this range, the "estimate" CDF is very close to the "real" CDF. We have a maximum error of 800 KB/sec, while the baseline overestimates by 26MB/sec. However, our approach is only marginally better than the baseline for the central portion, and even worse than baseline in the bottom 30%. As noted above, we are primarily concerned with estimating the load on servers nearing 100% utilization—which is where the accuracy might affect consolidation decisions. Although it is not important to accurately estimate lower load percentiles in our application, if doing so was valuable, one could create a hybrid model that uses the baseline for percentiles below 30%.

CPU: our resource estimate factors out the fraction of CPU load introduced by additional copies of the OS and DBMS that are not needed when consolidated, and is thus able to reduce the estimation error to about 6%, compared to over 15% for the baseline.

Consolidation effectiveness: We now validate the claim that the consolidation strategies produced by our system are able to maintain the same performance as in the unconsolidated case. In Table 1 we show experiments in which we ran different workloads using TPC-C scaled to 2 and 10-warehouses and Wikipedia scaled to 100K pages. We vary the intensity of the workloads by changing

Table 1: Impact of consolidation on Performance

Test id (DBMS)	Dataset	Throughput w/o cons.	Throughput w/ cons.	AVG Latency w/o cons.	AVG Latency w/ cons.
Consolidation recommended					
1 (MySQL)	TPC-C (10w) Wikipedia (100K p)	50 tps 100 tps	50 tps 100 tps	76 ms 12.7 ms	98 ms 16 ms
2 (MySQL)	TPC-C (10w) Wikipedia (100K p)	250 tps 500 tps	250 tps 500 tps	113 ms 43 ms	180 ms 49 ms
3 (MySQL)	5× TPC-C (10w)	5×100 tps	5×100 tps	77 ms	110 ms
4 (MySQL)	8× TPC-C (10w) Wikipedia (100K p)	8× 50 tps 50 tps	8× 50 tps 50 tps	76 ms 12.7 ms	125.8 ms 19 ms
Consolidation not recommended					
5 (MySQL)	5× TPC-C (10w)	5×400 tps	5× 177 tps	77 ms	426 ms
6 (MySQL)	8× TPC-C (10w) Wikipedia (100K p)	8× 100 tps 100 tps	8×87 tps 86.2 tps	77 ms 12.7 ms	1180 ms 1047 ms

the rate at which user requests are generated. For experiments 1–4 our consolidation engine predicts that consolidation of the input workloads is possible since: (i) the combined size of the measured working sets fits in the buffer pool of our test machines, (ii) the estimated CPU and Disk I/O are well within the 90% max utilization. The results presented in the table show that the throughput is unaffected, and that while there is some increase in latency, it is only a few milliseconds. This is small compared to some normal fluctuations that occur. For example, when MySQL performs a checkpoint in order to garbage collect log files, the average latency can increase by as much as 150 ms. Experiments 5–6 show cases in which our consolidation engine suggested that the workloads can not be consolidated, due to memory or disk I/O limits. If we attempt to consolidate anyway the result is significantly decreased performance. Additionally, these experiments showed that the loss in latency and throughput is approximately uniform across the consolidated databases, suggesting that MySQL does a reasonable job of dividing resources amongst a number of databases.

7.3 Consolidation with Real-World Data

In this set of experiments, we measure the consolidation ratios and the load balance that our consolidation algorithm can achieve on the Internal, Wikia.com, Wikipedia, and Second Life datasets.

Figure 7 shows the consolidation ratios that our system finds for these four datasets, as well as for the combination of all workloads merged together, named ALL. We compare with three alternative strategies. The first is the current deployment without consolidation (*reference solution*).

The second is a single-resource greedy bin-packing approach (*greedy*). This algorithm considers only a single resource, and places each workload in the most loaded server where it will fit using a first-fit bin packer. We then discard final solutions that violate the constraints on the other resources. We repeat this packing once for each resource, then take the solution that requires the fewest servers.

The third is an idealized lower bound, in which we assume both that workloads can be assigned as fractions of their load, *and* that we can decouple usage of multiple resources (*frac./idealized*). As shown in Figure 7, our approach matches the idealized lower bound in almost every scenario. It consistently outperforms the greedy approach, achieving consolidation factors ranging from 5.5:1 to 17:1. The greedy algorithm cannot be applied in all scenarios, because it finds solutions that violate constraints on the other resources; in these cases, no result is shown. It also tends to find highly imbalanced configurations, while Kairos finds well balanced workloads.

Since the consolidation ratios depend on the configuration of machines being consolidated onto, we also confirmed that our engine substantially reduces the total resource requirements; for example,

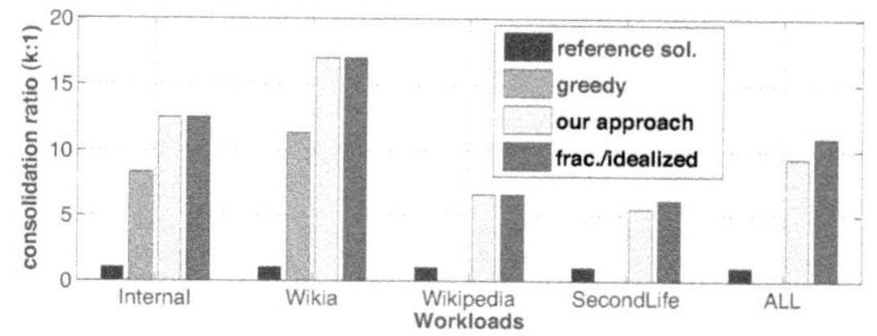

Figure 7: Consolidation Ratios for real-world datasets

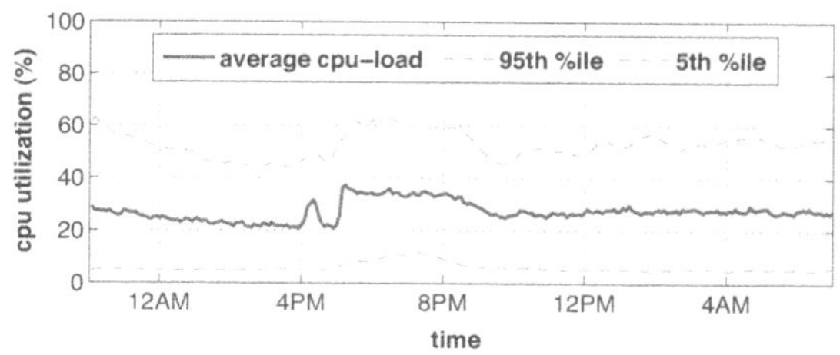

Figure 8: Aggregate CPU-load for 197 consolidated workloads.

in the ALL case, the original 197 servers has a total of 1419 cores versus 252 cores in the consolidated configuration.

We also measured the balance of resource utilization across servers. Figure 8 shows the average, 95th and 5th percentile of CPU-utilization for the 21 consolidated servers in the "ALL" experiments of Figure 7. The figure shows that the high and low utilizations are close, suggesting we have achieved good balance, and that the 95th percentile is far from the maximum utilization, suggesting low risk of saturation. Note that perfect balance, where all servers are close to the average load, is not achievable because: i) load cannot be assigned fractionally, and ii) there are multiple-resource constraints, thus, the most balanced solution for one resource might not be viable for other resources. Greedy solutions like the one we tested lead to much higher imbalance with 95th percentile load close to saturation on some machines.

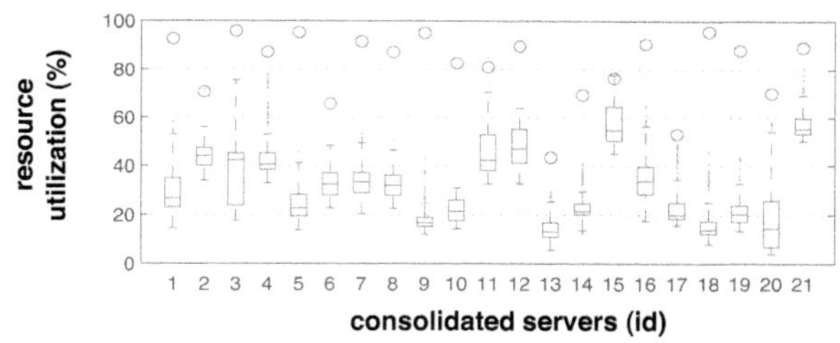

Figure 9: CPU load (error-bars) and RAM load (circles) for 197 real-world workloads consolidated on 21 servers.

Figure 9 shows the RAM and CPU utilization for these same 21 servers, showing the load across all time for each of the servers (rather than the aggregate load across all servers.) The values for each server are computed as the sum of the estimates of RAM and CPU of each workload consolidated on that server. The circles show the maximum RAM consumption on each server, while the CPU utilization is shown as a box plot. The top and bottom of the boxes represent the 25th and 75th percentile, while the line in the box indicates the median. The whiskers show the minimal and maximal values, and any outliers are plotted as points. Outliers are defined as points that are outside the interval $[q_1 - \frac{3}{2}(q_3 - q_1), q_3 + \frac{3}{2}(q_3 - q_1)]$, where q_1 and q_3 are the 25th and 75th percentiles, respectively. This figure shows that there is no easy way to further consolidate this load, since either RAM or CPU prevents combining any two servers. The figure also shows that the load is approximately balanced across the machines, and

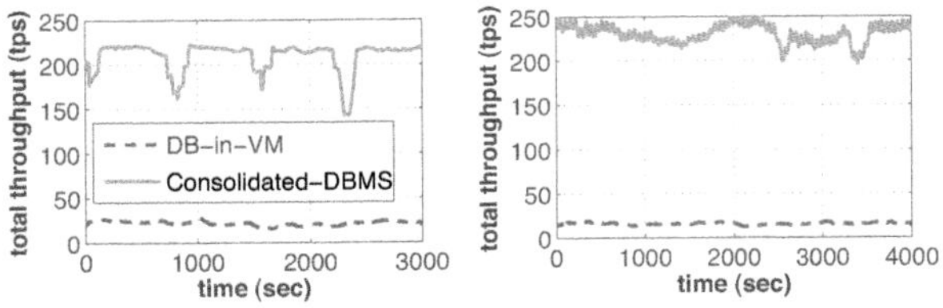

Figure 10: Hardware virtualization (fixed 20:1 consolidation)

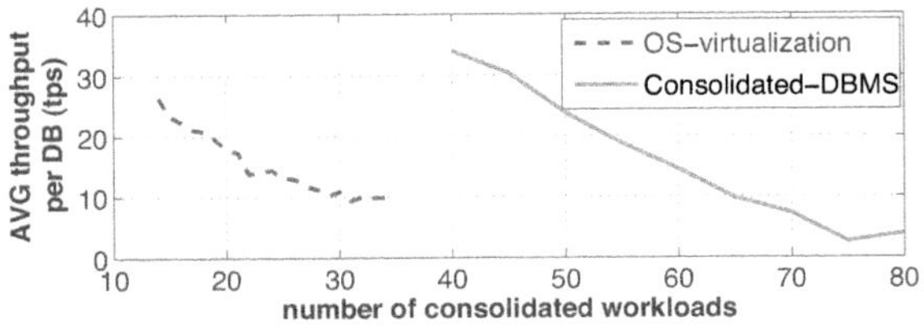

Figure 11: OS virtualization with varying consolidation levels

that we maintain a "margin of error" (set to 5% in this experiment) even for the most heavily loaded servers—this accounts for potential workload changes. Note that 5% of the machine's capacity represents close to 50% of the load of a single database, due to the nearly 10:1 consolidation ratio.

7.4 Comparing against DB-in-VM

In this section, we compare our database-aware consolidation to: i) hardware virtualization, where each database is running on top of its own operating system and virtual machine, using VMware ESXi, and ii) OS virtualization, where multiple MySQL instances run on a single Linux kernel, avoiding virtualization overhead (in this case, we do not use any additional virtualization software, and simply run each instance as a separate process.) We use multiple TPC-C instances to simulate users' workloads.

In order to investigate the performance of hardware virtualization using VMware ESXi, we show the throughput for a fixed consolidation level of 20 TPC-C instances in Figure 10. For this experiment, we found that VMware's RAM overcommitment feature made no difference, so we show results without overcommitment. The left-hand figure shows the throughput when all 20 workloads have the same request rate. The right-hand figure shows a skewed workload where 19 databases are throttled to one request per second, and 1 database runs at maximum speed. This shows that database consolidation can handle both uniform and skewed workloads, and yields better performance than hardware virtualization. Here, our approach provides between 6× and 12× higher throughput.

There are many reasons for this large performance difference:

- Running the workloads in separate database servers incurs a significant amount of redundant work for operations like log writes and log reclamations. Our approach more effectively exploits group-commit and coordinates disk requests across all databases, rather than each database making independent decisions. This allows our approach to achieve higher efficiency when using the disk.
- Our approach avoids allocating RAM for multiple copies of DBMS (MySQL ≈190 MB) and the OS (≈64 MB). VMware's "transparent page sharing" feature is intended to reduce this problem, however, it only reclaimed small amount of duplicated RAM.
- The virtual machine approach leads to more frequent and more expensive context switches, due to a higher number of processes.
- More effective utilization of CPU caches because more code and data is shared between workloads.

To remove virtualization overhead, we switched to OS virtualization, which is similar to container-based virtualization like Linux Containers or Solaris Zones. We then re-ran the experiment

Table 2: Impact of Probing on User's Perceived Performance

Target request rate	Throughput w/o gauging	Throughput w/ gauging	Latency w/o gauging	Latency w/ gauging
200 tps	200 tps	200 tps	8.57 ms	11.4 ms
600 tps	600 tps	600 tps	15.0 ms	19.1 ms
1000 tps	1000 tps	1000 tps	19.5 ms	23.9 ms
MAX	1923 tps	1689 tps	28.3 ms	32.1 ms

with a wide range of consolidation ratios. Figure 11 compares the throughput of OS virtualization and the Kairos consolidation system. In this experiment, we vary the number of consolidated workloads running on one machine, then measure the maximum average throughput achievable for each database, when the load is uniform across all databases. Given a specific target throughput, our approach yields consolidation levels 1.9× to 3.3× higher than OS virtualization. This translates to a significant reduction in hardware costs. The limitations of the VM approach remain when considering OS-level virtualization.

Finally we note that our approach and a VM- or OS-based approaches are not totally orthogonal. It is possible to combine the two approaches, running our consolidation inside a VM, to provide both benefits of virtualization and the performance of our approach.

7.5 Additional Experiments

In this section, we show the results of additional experiments that measure the overhead of our techniques, the independence of our disk model from database size and workload type, and test our assumptions regarding workload predictability.

Impact of buffer pool gauging on performance: In Section 3.1 we showed that Kairos can accurately estimate the size of the working set of a system on both MySQL and PostgreSQL. The case we reported used a benchmark running at *maximum speed* on a database with a 953 MB buffer pool, growing our probe rate by 136KB/sec on average. This allowed us to limit the impact on performance to less than a 5% decrease in throughput and about 1ms additional latency, even though the machine was running at saturation. However, in typical scenarios we are going to face multi-gigabyte buffer pools and less busy machines.

To test that our approach can quickly measure large buffer pools without affecting performance, we tested a MySQL node with a 16 GB buffer pool. We ran the Wikipedia benchmark scaled to 100K pages (67 GB of data and a 2.2 GB working set). We forced the system to aggressively grow the probe table at an average rate of about 6.4 MB/sec. This allowed us to determine the working set size in about 37 minutes. Table 2 reports throughput and latency achieved by the system with and without the gauging for different user target request rates—we control user target requests rates by throttling the generation of requests on the machines simulating the Wikipedia clients.

The values reported correspond to the phase of gauging before we start stealing valuable user pages, at which point we quickly stop the probing and report the measured working set size. The MAX experiment is a control case, in which we test the impact of an aggressive gauging on a server that is already operating at saturation—and is thus not likely to be of any interest for consolidation.

Solver Performance: We also used the real world load statistics to test the efficiency of the optimization discussed in Section 6. The results vary with the dataset, but it consistently decreases the runtime of the solver, with the maximum reduction occurring with the Wikia.com dataset, where the runtime reduces by a factor of 45×—an equally consolidated and balanced solution is found in 44 sec instead of over 33 min in the unoptimized case. Running times for all individual consolidations were *below* 8 minutes, with

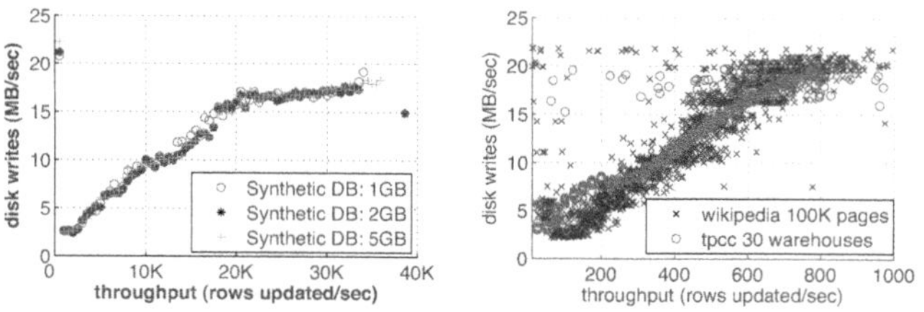

Figure 12: a) Database size does not matter, b) transaction type does not matter

the exception of the ALL workload, for which lack of RAM in our test machine prevented a proper measure (run-time heavily affected by swapping). A possible way to scale our solutions to handle tens of thousands of databases, consists in pre-grouping the input workloads, and solve the multiple consolidation problems independently. This might miss some small opportunity of consolidation (workloads across groups will not be considered for co-location), but it can be proven to scale indefinitely.

Disk Model Generality: In order to further validate our disk model, we need to show that: (i) the database size does not significantly affect disk I/O throughput (i.e., that a model learned on a dataset of size X still applies if that dataset grows to something much larger than X), and that (ii) the model is independent of the specific transaction being run, and thus that we can build a single disk model for a given DBMS/OS/hardware configuration without regard to the specific database workload.

In Figure 12a, we experimentally validate our hypothesis that the total database size does not influence the disk I/O throughput, but that only the working set size matters. For this experiment, we designed a synthetic test with a database of increasing size, and a workload that only accesses a random 512 MB portion of the database. The figure shows that the I/O throughput patterns for different database sizes are nearly identical, thus confirming the hypothesis that database size does not influence disk I/O.

In order to validated the hypothesis that the disk write throughput does not depend on the specific set of transactions being executed, but only on the overall number of rows updated per unit of time, and the overall working set size, we pick two very different workloads: TPC-C with 30 warehouses and Wikipedia with 100K pages; these databases have comparable working set sizes of about 2.2GB. Figure 12b shows the disk write throughput in MB/sec for a wide range of rows updated per second. It is clear that the two workloads, despite their major differences, impose almost identical pressure on the disk subsystem. Interestingly, while the average disk I/O rate for each rows-updated/throughput point is quite similar, Wikipedia has a significantly higher variance, due to the wider range of tuple sizes (from 70 bytes up to 3.68 MB). Note that the TPC-C database size is about 4.8GB while the Wikipedia one is over 67GB; this large difference further confirms the hypothesis tested above: database size has no noticeable impact disk I/O.

Past Performance as a Predictor of Future: Our final experiment tests whether past workload behavior is a good predictor of its future behavior. This is crucial to ensure that our computed strategy will satisfy the transaction throughput requirements over time.

We used our Wikipedia and Second Life largest real world load datasets to validate our hypothesis that workloads are predictable. We examine the total CPU utilization across all servers, as this is typically the most volatile measure. We divided the data into weekly periods, and used the average load of each time interval in the first two weeks to predict the third week. Figure 13 shows that this average is a good predictor, as errors in both experiments are low with root mean squared error (RMSE) of about 25. This means

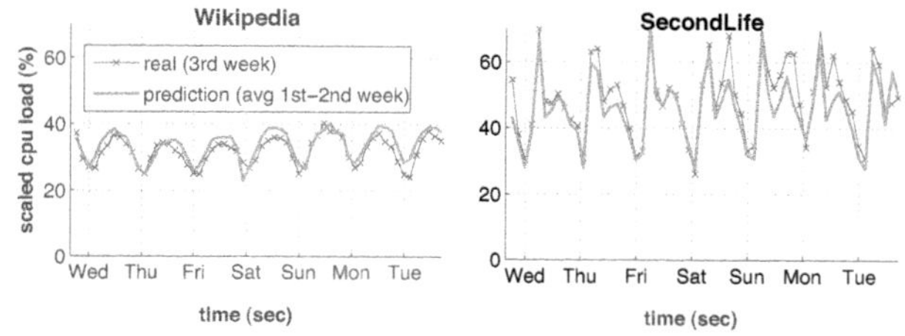

Figure 13: Predicting CPU utilization

our predictions are 7-8% off from the actual load. This is a tolerable error that can be accounted for by adding a small safety margin and slightly over-provisioning the servers, as we did in our experiments. Note that the Second Life data shows a combination of natural user utilization cycles and scheduled jobs—the late-night peaks are due to a pool of 27 database machines performing snapshot operations. This shows that prediction works any time of workload that repeats over time. This indicates that, even for front facing applications, it is not uncommon for the database machines to experience relatively stable workloads. For such applications, Kairos consolidation strategies are likely to remain valid for long.

8. RELATED WORK

Significant research has been devoted to improve multi-tenancy and support for mixed-workloads inside a single DBMS [5, 11]. These advances allows us to rely on the design of modern DBMSs to deal with multiple workloads/tenants. In our experiments MySQL and PostgreSQL divided resources fairly among multiple databases, as long as the DBMS had sufficient hardware resources.

Database consolidation using virtual machines has been discussed as a way to reduce operational costs [17]. Soror et al. look at configuring multiple VMs running on the same hardware to support multiple database workloads [20]. Their work is suited to consolidating small number of workloads rather than the large numbers we consider, or when other requirements (e.g., security) call for a VM-based approach. Similarly, Soundararajan et al. presented a system for determining how to partition VM resources between multiple virtual machines on a single physical machine [21]. Their work is complementary to ours, as it could be used to optimize the assignment that is found by our system.

There have been several efforts to provide extreme levels of multi-tenancy [15, 3, 14], aiming to consolidate tens of thousands of nearly inactive databases onto a single server, especially when those databases have identical or similar schemas. The key challenge of this prior work has been on overcoming DBMSs' limitations at dealing with extremely large numbers of tables and/or columns. This is complementary to our work, as our approach can run into similar internal DBMS limitations. However, our workloads do not typically share any data or schemas.

Another relevant area of research is dynamic resource allocation in data centers [6, 4, 24]. Such work shares some of our goals, but is aimed at consolidating unpredictable stateless web workloads, with a focus on quick response to load changes and latency guarantees. This work combines sophisticated predictive models and dynamic reactive components, but ignores the issues that arise when migrating and consolidating data-intensive services like databases.

Gulati et al. analyze disk I/O for several types of workloads, presenting results on combining random and sequential I/O patterns that are consistent with our observations [9]. They also present a disk model that is not database specific, although more complex than ours [8]. Their evaluation only tests synthetic workloads. Ozmen et al. present a model that predicts the disk I/O created by a given database workload, without needing to measure the production system [19]. Such a system is complementary to our work, as it reduces the need for detailed runtime statistics. There has been significant work on modeling of disk performance, usually from a non-database specific perspective. For example, Lee and Katz [18] present an analytical model for estimating the throughput of a combined load (consisting of a mixture of sequential and random I/Os) on a disk array; Varki et al [25] address a similar problem but build a model that includes caching and other effects.

Our use of a growing database table to put pressure on the buffer pool is somewhat similar VMware's "balloon driver" [26], which add memory pressure to force a guest OS to free unused or infrequently used pages. VMWare, however, doesn't use this technique to estimate RAM usage, but rather to force the OS to evict pages to make room for a new virtual machine. Furthermore, this the balloon driver runs inside of a guest OS, rather than inside of the DBMS. Such an OS-level technique is unlikely to work well, since the OS has no good way to choose which buffer pool pages to swap to disk, and may often choose pages containing data actively used.

Finally in the area of distributed database systems, substantial research has looked at the problem of allocating data to servers to optimize response-time or throughput [2, 22]. This work has different goals, since it aims at obtaining performance and scalability from a fixed set of machines, rather than consolidating them into the minimal number of physical nodes while meeting user performance expectations. Similarly, Aboulnaga et al. tackled the problem of "packing" map-reduce tasks on a cluster of machines, but the batch-oriented nature of the problem makes it significantly different from our scenario, leading to scheduling-oriented solutions [1].

Existing commercial systems [13] provide mechanisms for consolidation, but leave to the administrator the costly and error-prone task of devising a consolidation strategy. Our work automates the decision process, enabling larger scale and better consolidation.

9. CONCLUSION

In this paper, we presented a consolidation scheme for over-provisioned database servers; our approach allows enterprises to dramatically reduce the number of physical servers required to run their database infrastructure. We developed new monitoring techniques and resource models, as well as a non-linear mixed-integer programming approach to workload allocation, that analyze a database deployment and consolidate it. Our results, which show consolidation factors between 5.5:1 and 17:1, are based on experiments with synthetic and real-world data-sets from production servers running at MIT CSAIL, Wikia.com, Wikipedia, and Second Life. In addition to achieving high consolidation factors, our algorithms balance load across servers without affecting the throughput of the consolidated workloads. Additionally, we show that existing virtual machine technologies are not nearly as effective as our techniques at consolidating database workloads.

10. ACKNOWLEDGEMENTS

We thank A. Bergman of Wikia.net, D. Mituzas of Wikimedia.org, B. O'Connor of Linden Labs, and the The Infrastructure Group (TIG) at MIT CSAIL for providing the data sets used in the paper. This work was supported in part by Quanta Computer as a part of the T-Party Project.

11. REFERENCES

[1] A. Aboulnaga, Z. Wang, and Z. Y. Zhang. Packing the most onto your cloud. In *CloudDB*, 2009.

[2] P. Apers. Data allocation in distributed database systems. *ACM Transactions on Database Systems (TODS)*, 13(3):263–304, 1988.

[3] S. Aulbach, T. Grust, D. Jacobs, A. Kemper, and J. Rittinger. Multi-tenant databases for software as a service: schema-mapping techniques. In *SIGMOD*, 2008.

[4] M. Bennani and D. Menasce. Resource allocation for autonomic data centers using analytic performance models. In *ICAC*, 2005.

[5] K. Brown, M. Carey, D. DeWitt, M. Mehta, and J. Naughton. Resource allocation and scheduling for mixed database workloads. Technical Report TR1095, University of Wisconsin - Madison CS Department, July 1992.

[6] A. Chandra, W. Gong, and P. Shenoy. Dynamic resource allocation for shared data centers using online measurements. In *IWQoS*, 2003.

[7] C. Curino, E. P. C. Jones, R. A. Popa, N. Malviya, E. Wu, S. Madden, H. Balakrishnan, and N. Zeldovich. Relationalcloud: a database service for the cloud. In *CIDR*, 2011.

[8] A. Gulati, C. Kumar, and I. Ahmad. Modeling workloads and devices for IO load balancing in virtualized environments. *SIGMETRICS Perform. Eval. Rev.*, 37(3):61–66, 2009.

[9] A. Gulati, C. Kumar, and I. Ahmad. Storage workload characterization and consolidation in virtualized environments. In *VPACT*, 2009.

[10] S. Harizopoulos, M. Shah, J. Meza, and P. Ranganathan. Energy efficiency: The new holy grail of data management systems research. In *CIDR*, pages 4–7, 2009.

[11] M. Heaton. Hosting Nirvana—The Future of Shared Hosting! [Online] `http://mattheaton.com/?p=185`, April 2009.

[12] K. Holmström. The TOMLAB optimization environment in Matlab. *Advanced Modeling and Optimization*, 1(1):47–69, 1999.

[13] HP. Polyserve: Product Overview. [Online] `http://bit.ly/azE3kA`, February 2009.

[14] M. Hui, D. Jiang, G. Li, and Y. Zhou. Supporting database applications as a service. In *ICDE*, pages 832–843, 2009.

[15] D. Jacobs and S. Aulbach. Ruminations on multi-tenant databases. *BTW Proceedings*, 2007.

[16] D. R. Jones. DIRECT global optimization algorithm. In *Encyclopedia of Optimization*, pages 725–735. 2009.

[17] D. Jonker. Combining database clustering and virtualization to consolidate mission-critical servers. Jan. 2009.

[18] E. K. Lee and R. H. Katz. An analytic performance model of disk arrays. *SIGMETRICS*, 21(1):98–109, 1993.

[19] O. Ozmen, K. Salem, M. Uysal, and H. S. Attar. Storage workload estimation for database management systems. In *SIGMOD*, 2007.

[20] A. A. Soror, U. F. Minhas, A. Aboulnaga, K. Salem, P. Kokosielis, and S. Kamath. Automatic virtual machine configuration for database workloads. *ACM Trans. Database Syst.*, 35(1), 2010.

[21] G. Soundararajan, D. Lupei, S. Ghanbari, A. D. Popescu, J. Chen, and C. Amza. Dynamic resource allocation for database servers running on virtual storage. In *FAST*, 2009.

[22] T. Stöhr, H. Martens, and E. Rahm. Multi-dimensional database allocation for parallel data warehouses. In *VLDB*, 2000.

[23] G. Urdaneta, G. Pierre, and M. van Steen. Wikipedia workload analysis for decentralized hosting. *Elsevier Computer Networks*, 53(11), 2009.

[24] B. Urgaonkar, P. Shenoy, A. Chandra, P. Goyal, and T. Wood. Agile dynamic provisioning of multi-tier internet applications. *ACM Trans. Auton. Adapt. Syst.*, 3(1), 2008.

[25] E. Varki, A. Merchant, J. Xu, and X. Qiu. Issues and challenges in the performance analysis of real disk arrays. *IEEE TPDS*, 15(6):559–574, 2004.

[26] C. A. Waldspurger. Memory resource management in VMware ESX server. In *OSDI'02*, pages 181–194, 2002.

Predicting Cost Amortization for Query Services

Verena Kantere*
Cyprus University of Technology
A. Kyprianos 31, P.O. Box 50329, 3603 Lemesos, Cyprus
verena.kantere@cut.ac.cy

Debabrata Dash*
ArcSight, an HP Company
Avenue de Florissant 22
Renens, 1020, Switlzerland
debabrata.dash@hp.com

Georgios Gratsias*
ELCA Informatique SA
Av. de la Harpe 22-24 C.P. 519, 1001 Lausanne, Switzerland
georgios.gratsias@elca.ch

Anastasia Ailamaki
École Polytechnique Fédérale de Lausanne
1015 Lausanne, Switzerland
anastasia.ailamaki@epfl.ch

ABSTRACT

Emerging providers of online services offer access to data collections. Such data service providers need to build data structures, e.g. materialized views and indexes, in order to offer better performance for user query execution. The cost of such structures is charged to the user as part of the overall query service cost. In order to ensure the economic viability of the provider, the building and maintenance cost of new structures has to be amortized to a set of prospective query services that will use them. This work proposes a novel stochastic model that predicts the extent of cost amortization in time and number of services. The model is completed with a novel method that regresses query traffic statistics and provides input to the prediction model. In order to demonstrate the effectiveness of the prediction model, we study its application on an extension of an existing economy model for the management of a cloud DBMS. A thorough experimental study shows that the prediction model ensures the economic viability of the cloud DBMS while enabling the offer of fast and cheap query services.

Categories and Subject Descriptors

H.2 [**Database Management**]: Database Applications

General Terms

Theory, Performance, Experimentation

1. INTRODUCTION

In the new world of computing it is more and more common to share information through the web. Producers and consumers of data scattered all over the globe meet through online services. Such services provide users with remote access to data sources and may offer possibilities for expedition of query execution. This is achieved through building data structures, such as materialized views and indexes. The provider trades query performance for the building and maintenance cost of such structures. The workload evolution prohibits the uncontrolled building and maintenance of data structures, because the cost outweighs the benefit on query performance.

As a business, the data provider aims at assuring its economic viability, without overcharging the user. The goal of the provider is twofold. First, keep the price of individual services low, in order to remain competitive. Therefore, it is very important to amortize the cost of data structures, such as views and indexes, to all prospective user queries that will benefit from its usage. Second, limit the risk of investment loss due to building and maintaining structures that are not reused. The extent of cost amortization both in time and number of user queries has to be decided beforehand, at the building time of a data structure. Hence, it is necessary to develop a technique that predicts the utilization of a new structure in the future and decides the appropriate extent of cost amortization.

In this work we predict the value of new data structures to the execution of future queries using a novel generic stochastic model. Given the building cost of a structure, the model outputs the extent in time and number of prospective queries for cost amortization. In case the structure has to be evicted from the server for some reason, (data update or storage cost exceeding the building cost), the provider is considered to suffer the loss of the remaining non-amortized cost.

The model predictions are based on the observation of past workload. We present a novel method that regresses the observed workload and provides input for the prediction model. The goal of the regression is to transform existing statistics on query traffic into estimations for the lifetime of potential data structures from the time they are built to the time they are evicted.

We demonstrate the effectiveness of the prediction model on the economy management of a cloud DBMS. An existing economic model for a cloud DBMS [6] is extended so that it takes into account user preferences and budget requirements for query execution in order to decide which data structures to build. The building and maintenance cost of the new structures is amortized to future queries that use them based on the presented prediction model. Without amortization, the cost of a new data structure has to be charged on a single potential query service, which leads to a high cost of this service. High cost makes the potential service non-competitive with existing ones in the cloud, and, therefore, not worth of investing. Hence, the cloud cannot improve the query services, unless it over-charges

*This research was conducted while the first, second and third author were working at the École Polytechnique Fédérale de Lausanne.

SIGMOD'11, June 12–16, 2011, Athens, Greece.

the user. Yet, over-charging a potential service usually exceeds the user's budget. The employment of the prediction model balances offer and demand: hot structures useful to many users are offered at a low cost, whereas specialized structures useful to few users are offered at higher cost, such that the cloud economy is viable.

A thorough experimental study on the cloud DBMS shows the effectiveness of cost amortization using the prediction model for both cheap and expensive data structures. Furthermore, cost amortization benefits simple and, especially, complex queries, the response time of which is decreased due to the earlier building of expensive data structures. Cost amortization leads to offering fast query plans at low prices. Overall, cost amortization achieves the economic viability, and, moreover, the profitability of the cloud DBMS, while gradually improving query services with respect to both response time and cost. The results show that the model achieves effective cost amortization in presence of data updates as well as in absence of data access locality.

In the rest of this paper Section 2 summarizes the related work. Section 3 describes the prediction model for cost amortization and Section 4 the data regression method. Section 5 summarizes the cloud DBMS description, presents the extended cloud economy and discusses the overhead for query execution cost. Section 6 presents the experimental study and Section 7 concludes the paper.

2. RELATED WORK

A big share of research on workload prediction is related to cost assessment of query execution and online index selection. The work in [19] proposes techniques that estimate the correlation of pairs of attributes. The correlation statistics are used in order to improve selectivity estimation for query optimization. The more recent work in [21] proposes algorithms for the discovery of soft multi-attribute functional dependencies that can be employed in query execution and a model that estimates query execution cost. These works focus on the mining of data value correlations and are related to the prediction of the utility of primary and secondary indexes in the presence of query predicates. Similarly, the works in [23] and [10] focus on the estimation of query execution cost using indexes on high-dimensional data and [10] proposes a technique for online index recommendations based on data statistics and query patterns. All the above works contribute in the prediction of query execution cost based on the availability of indexes. Starting from there: our model takes the indexes as input and can output a payment schedule for the amortization of the building and maintenance cost of these indexes.

The recent work in [36] deals with the problem of guaranteeing a predictable performance for any workload and proposes a solution based on a novel implementation of the relational table. This work is orthogonal to ours, since it focuses on implementation decisions that support similar performance irrespective to workload behavior.

There has been notable work on workload prediction in grid and super-computer environments [26, 8, 30, 24]. These works deal with the problem of workload modeling for the production of synthetic workloads employed for the evaluation of real systems. They focus on the site execution locality [8] or the temporal locality [26] of workload characteristics such as runtime, memory and CPU usage etc [24]. These works are orthogonal to ours, which focuses on workload characteristics of the data level. Specific works on modeling job arrivals [29, 25] are complementary to ours, since they can provide the workload distribution for special grid environments.

Structure usage prediction has been studied in other areas, such as the processor cache-line access and survivability prediction [3]. One proposal is a trace-based mechanism that predicts when a cache-line has been last accessed [22]. Another is a time-based mechanism that predicts the death of a block after a specific timeout period [18]. A third one is a counting-based predictor [20] that predicts the line to be dead after a fixed number of accesses. Our approach is closest to the last one; yet, we propose a sophisticated prediction model to utilize the computing and storage power available to full processors compared to the limited power on a cache.

Database as a service has been proposed by many researchers, starting with NetDB2 [11]. The authors identify security, remote access, and user interface as the main challenges. Recently, it has been argued that scalability and privacy still remain the unsolved challenges [1]. While these issues have been addressed in the literature, pricing the service has been generally ignored. In industry, salesforce.com was the first company to successfully commercialize the database as service paradigm [16]. Recently, Amazon's EC2 service [12], Google's AppEngine [13], and Microsoft's Azure service [15] have expanded the commercial application of the paradigm.

3. PREDICTION MODEL

A query service provider offers the possibility to users to query data collections. A query service is the execution of a user query employing a specific query plan. The provider builds data structures, such as indexes and materialized views, at a certain cost, in order to improve query performance. As soon as a structure is built, it is maintained, incurring a maintenance cost. The maintenance cost is the cost of storing the structure in the provider; building cost is expected to be orders of magnitude bigger than maintenance cost[1].

The user pays for each query service. The query service cost is $c_1 + c_2$, where c_1 is the cost of query execution and c_2 is some part of the building cost of data structures employed in this query service. The building cost $Build_S(.)$ of a new structure S has to be amortized to future user query services that employ this structure. In order to choose the value for the smaller number n of query services to which the cost of a structure S should be amortized, we have to estimate the number of prospective queries n' that will benefit from S. The overall gain of the provider is: $n' \cdot (Build_S(S)/n)$. Ideally, we would like $n' > n$. Two opposite factors should be considered to estimate n correctly: (i) As n increases, the initial cost of S is disseminated to more query services, making their overall (individual) cost smaller (ii) As n increases, the risk of a false estimation of n' increases, too; A false estimation $n' < n$ will damage the economy of the provider. Therefore the goal is to predict the value of n so that it is smaller but close to n'.

We present a generic stochastic model for the amortization of the building cost of new data structures. The model estimates n based on provider statistics on query traffic, data update and execution of query plans. This approach focuses on constant amortization CA of the building cost, i.e.:

$$CA(n, Build_S(S)) = Build_S(S)/n \tag{1}$$

Selecting n is a challenging problem, as it depends on the provider's risk aversion as well as the query arrival pattern. First, the model estimates the maximal time extent t_e until which amortization should be completed. Second, the model estimates the number of prospective queries n until the time point t_e that will use the structure.

3.1 Cost Amortization in Time

The model proposes the extent of cost amortization in time, t_e, based on an estimation of the lifetime of the new structure S in the data provider. The lifetime of S ends if one of the following occurs: (i) S is not used in the prospective queries, (ii) the data related to S

[1]Based on the pricing scheme of Amazon EC2 [12] for I/O operations, disk space, CPU time and network bandwidth, the cost of building an index or caching a table column is on average 7 orders of magnitude bigger than the cost of maintaining it thereafter.

is updated. We define respectively the notions of (i) *usefulness* of S and (ii) *stability* of S, in time, which give the probability of $failure$ of S in time. If S is not useful or stable at some time point, it fails, and therefore its lifetime ends. As long as S has not failed yet, it is considered a *reliable* structure, and cost amortization can still be performed. As time moves on from the building point, the reliability of S decreases and the probability of failure increases. The model proposes as the extent of cost amortization in time, t_e, the crossing point after which S is more probable to fail than to remain reliable.

DEFINITION 1. *The usefulness of a structure S, $d_S = d_S(t)$, is the probability that the structure S is useful to the provider cache, i.e. prospective selected query plans will employ S.*

The usefulness of S is the conditional probability of the observed fact that S is useful to a selected query plan, on the grounds that a query has arrived.

DEFINITION 2. *The probability that the data related to a structure S is stable, i.e. not updated, is $st_S = st_S(t)$.*

DEFINITION 3. *The failure $f_S = f_S(t)$ of a structure S is the probability distribution of the occurrences that S is not employed in selected query plans. The cumulative probability of failure of S is denoted as F_S.*

Based on survival analysis [5], $F_S(t)$ represents the fact that the structure S will fail in the time period $[t_0, t]$, where t_0 is the time that S is built in the cache. For simplicity we set $t_0 = 0$.

PROPOSITION 1. *The cumulative failure probability of a structure S, (at a time point t), is the the probability that S is not useful any more to selected query plans or it has become obsolete due to the support of data that has been updated, (at time t).*

JUSTIFICATION It is assumed that a query occurrence is not the result of another query occurrence, and thus a query occurrence does not depend on the results of other queries. Generally, the query workload is not dependent on the data, and therefore, on the update (or, equally, the stability) of data. Thus, the probability of data stability, $st_S(t)$, is independent from the probability of usefulness of S, $d_S(t)$. The joint probability $st_S(t) \cdot d_S(t)$ denotes the fact that S is not obsolete and still useful at time t. In order for this to be true, S must have not failed in the time period $[0, t]$ because of any of these two reasons. Therefore:

$$F_S(t) = 1 - st_S(t) \cdot d_S(t) \tag{2}$$

The failure f_S is easily computed from the cumulative failure F_S as: $f_S(t) = -st_S(t) \cdot \frac{d(d_s)}{dt} - d_S(t) \cdot \frac{d(st_s)}{dt}$. Observe that for the building time $t = 0$, for which the probability that the data is stable and the structure is useful is the highest, (i.e. $st_S(0) = d_S(0) = 1$), the failure depends directly on the rate of change of data stability and structure usefulness: $f_S(t) = -(\frac{d(d_s)}{dt} + \frac{d(st_s)}{dt})$.

PROPOSITION 2. *The extension in time of building cost amortization of a new structure S to n individual payments balances the opposite tends of (a) minimizing the individual payment for the usage of S in a query plan and (b) minimizing the risk of failure of S, i.e. the risk that some of the building cost of S is not amortized.*

JUSTIFICATION The data that the incoming queries request change with time. Data changes cause the necessity to update existing structures (e.g. indexes) that involve the changed data, or even drop, and, possibly, reconstruct them from scratch (e.g.materialized views). We call the incidents of need to change existing structures (update, or dropping and reconstruction) 'failures'. Failures of a structure S incur additional building cost. Frequent failures of S may increase the

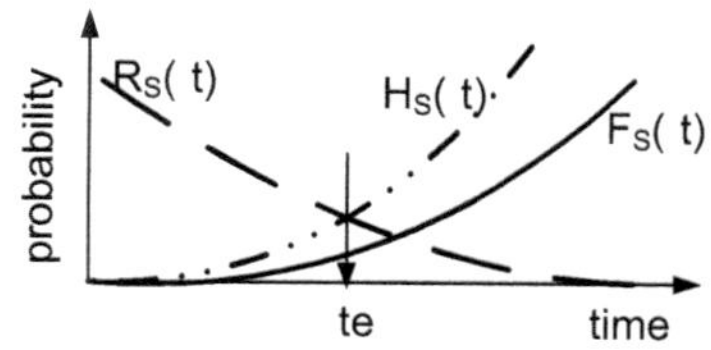

Figure 1: The maximal time of amortization is defined by the reliability and the hazard of failure.

accumulated building cost of S substantially, such that it is never completely amortized to prospective user queries. Therefore, amortizing $Builds_S(S)$ to a small number of prospective queries reduces the risk that the completion of amortization fails. Yet, extending amortization to a big number of prospective queries, the selected plan of which will benefit from the employment of S, reduces the individual amortization payment, and therefore the overall cost of each query service.

DEFINITION 4. *The reliability $R_S(t)$ of a structure S is the quality of S that indicates that the non-amortized building cost of S at time t will be amortized in the future, (t, ∞).*

From survival analysis, the reliability of a structure is related to the failure of a structure as follows:

$$R_S(t) = 1 - F_S(t) \tag{3}$$

Intuitively, the reliability of a structure depends on the usefulness of it to prospective queries, as well as on the stability of data[2]. Indeed, the combination of equations 2 and 3 shows that: $R_S(t) = st_S(t) \cdot d_S(t)$. The rate of reliability change r_S at time t depends directly on the probability of failure at this time: $r_S(t) = -f_S(t)$.

PROPOSITION 3. *Since a structure S is reliable at building time $t = 0$, the cumulative probability that S will fail in a future time t is:*

$$H_S(t) = \int_0^t \frac{f_S(t)}{R_S(t)} dt \tag{4}$$

JUSTIFICATION The hazard rate, denoted by $h_S(t)$ represents the instantaneous conditional failure of a structure S and by definition it is calculated as: $h(t) = \frac{f(t)}{R(t)}$ [5]. Qualitatively, there is a fine difference between the hazard rate and failure. The hazard rate evaluates the probability that the system is operational on time t, on the condition that it has not failed in $[0, t)$, whereas failure evaluates the probability that the system fails at time t, no matter if it has failed before. The usage of structure S is a 'repairable' process, i.e. structure failures of usage in selected query plans may be followed by success of structure usage in prospective selected query plans. For such a system, the hazard rate provides a safer estimation of future failure, taking into account the degradation of the structure reliability with time. Therefore, since a structure S is reliable at building time $t = 0$, the cumulative probability that S will fail in a future time t is given by the cumulative probability of hazard, $H_S(t)$.

A trade-off between the hazard H_S and the reliability R_S of a structure S can indicate the maximal time limit t_e up to which the cost amortization should extend.

DEFINITION 5. *The balancing rate b_S at time t for a structure S is the difference of the reliability R_S and hazard H_S at this time:*

$$b_S(t) = R_S(t) - H_S(t) \tag{5}$$

[2]The compound reliability of a set of table columns (w.r.t. either caching or indexing) is calculated as $R(t) = R_1(t) \cdots R_k(j)$. Dealing with the problem of dependent reliabilities of j table columns is future work.

b_S indicates the time that amortization should terminate.

PROPOSITION 4. *The amortization of $Builds$ for a new structure S should extend until the time point t_e, such that the cumulative balance between the respective reliability and hazard is maximized. Therefore, the cumulative balance between benefit and hazard is:*

$$B_S(t) = \int_0^t R_S(t) - H_S(t)dt \tag{6}$$

and the extention time for amortization of $Builds_S(S)$ is:

$$B_S(t_i, k) < B_S(t_e, k), \forall t_i, 0 \leq t_i, t_e \tag{7}$$

JUSTIFICATION The balancing rate b_S represents the instant balance between the opposite tends of reliability and hazard. The integral of b_S in a time interval $[t_1, t_2]$ represents the cumulative balance of this pair of tends in this interval. Fixing this interval from the beginning of amortization, i.e. $t = t_0$ until this balance is maximized, $t = t_e$ guarantees the maximal cumulative probability that full amortization of the cost of S will be achieved.

Since both the reliability and hazard are monotonic and continuous [5], the maximization of their cumulative balance occurs at t_e, s.t. $R(t_e) = H(t_e)$, as shown in Figure 1.

3.2 Cost Amortization in Number of Queries

Given the maximal extent of cost amortization in time, t_e, we can estimate the (smaller) number of prospective queries on which the cost will be amortized, n. Taking into account the query arrival pattern and the reliability of S we define the notion of *usage* of S that denotes the number of queries that use S at a time point. Based on the usage of S in time we define the probability of *gain* which gives an estimation of how the cost is amortized in time. We select n based on a fixed cumulative probability of gain related to the *influence* of S to the economy management of the data provider. As explained in Section 5, the influence of a structure S in the economy of a cloud DBMS represents the financial loss of the cloud before building S incurred by not being able to service queries using S.

For a general purpose prediction, we model the arrival of queries in the provider as a stochastic process $N = \{N_t : t \in T\}$, where T represents time, i.e. $T \equiv [0, \infty)$. The collection N of random variables N_t (or else $N(t)$) takes values from the state space $[1, 2, \ldots, \infty)$ and represents the number of queries that have arrived to the provider in the period $[0, t]$. We assume that the number of users of the provider is big and that queries for service arrive to the provider independently. Therefore, we assume that query arrival follows the Poisson distribution with parameter λ. Thus, the probability that at time t the number of arrived queries is k is given as: $P(N_t = k) = \frac{(\lambda \cdot t)^k}{k!} e^{-\lambda \cdot t}$. Based on the law of large numbers, the parameter can be calculated as $\lambda = N(t_o)/t_o$ for some t_o that can give a general picture about the service traffic of the provider. Thus, λ can be calculated based on traffic statistics (see Section 4).

PROPOSITION 5. *The number of incoming queries to the provider for a time period that statistics of query arrivals do not vary significantly constitute a homogeneous Poisson process.*

JUSTIFICATION Since no assumption is made for the provider and the users, structure usage and query arrivals are independent, and queries arrive on random time points. Since $N(t)$ follows a Poisson distribution the number of query arrivals in any time interval $[t_1, t_2]$, $t_1 < t_2$ is still a Poisson distribution (based on the respective property of the Poisson distribution). Moreover, since individual query arrivals are independent, sets of non-overlapping query arrivals are also independent, i.e. $N(t_2 - t_1)$ is probabilistically independent to $N(t_4 - t_3)$, for any $0 \leq t_1 < t_2 < t_3 < t_4$. Finally, the rate λ of query arrival for a given time period with non-fluctuating statistics $[0, t_o]$, has a constant value, i.e. $\lambda(t) = c, c \in \Re^+$ for $t \in [0, t_o]$. These three facts are by definition [34] necessary and sufficient to infer that the query arrival N in $T = [0, t_o]$ is a homogeneous Poisson process.

The prediction model can accomodate query arrival patterns other than the homogeneous Poisson process, as long as these are known; such input can be offered by recent works [29, 25] that propose query arrival modeling of non-independent query arrival patterns.

DEFINITION 6. *The usage of a structure S, u_S, is the probability of occurrences of the fact that S is employed in a selected query plan.*

PROPOSITION 6. *For a new structure S that is built in the provider, the usage of it in selected query plans, u_S, is a function of time t and query arrivals k, i.e. $u_S = u_S(t, k)$. This function is a correlation of the query arrival probability and the reliability of S.*

JUSTIFICATION It is straightforward that query arrival, $p_N(k, \lambda) = P(N_t = k)$ is independent from the usefulness of S, $d_S(t)$, and the data stability, $st_S(t)$. Therefore, it is safe to assume that R_S is *uncorrelated* to p_N, since there is no evidence that in general the usefulness of S, d_S or the stability of data related to S, st_S are linearly dependent on query arrival [3]. Thus, the usage of S is the joint distribution of the its reliability R_S and the distribution of query arrivals p_N. Therefore, the following form of u_S is adopted:

$$u_S(k, t) = R_S(t) \cdot p_N(k, \lambda) \tag{8}$$

where k is the number of query arrivals at each time point. The above form of $u_S(k, t)$ reflects the following intuitive requirements: (i) if the reliability of S is not degraded with time, i.e. $d_S(t) = st_S(t) = 1$, then S is used in all selected query plans, and therefore $u_S(k, t) = p_N$; (ii) if S is not reliable (for example, S is obsolete: $st_S(t) = 0$ or not useful: $d_S(t) = 0$), then S is not used in any selected query plans, regardless of the query arrival, i.e. $u_S(k, t) = 0$.

Let us assume that G_t is a random variable that represents the amortization of $Builds_S(S)$. Since G depends deterministically on the variable that represents the usage of structure S, S_t, we create the following gain probability distribution, $g(t, k)$ w.r.t. time and query arrival.

$$g_S(k, t) = P(G_t = k\frac{Builds_S(S)}{n}) = \frac{u_S(t, k)}{\int_0^\infty R_S(t)dt}, k \leq n. \tag{9}$$

The cumulative gain probability is denoted as G_S. The amortization of $Builds_S(S)$ to a number of selected query plans that use S, n, is based on G_S. We assume that the influence of the cost of a new structure S, denoted as $Inf(S)$, is a relative measure that indicates the importance of S in the economy of the data service provider w.r.t. the importance of the rest of the structures:

DEFINITION 7. *Assume a vector $w_S[.]$, where each element $w_S[S]$ corresponds $1 - 1$ to the S element of the set of structures offered by the provider and represents a quantification of the importance of S to the economy of the provider. The influence of the cost of a new structure S to the economy is the importance of S, $w_S[S]$ normalized by the importance of all structures in w_S:*

$$Inf(S) = \frac{w_S[S]}{\sum_{i=0}^{|w_S|} w_S[S]} \tag{10}$$

[3]Of course, R_S may be dependent with some other way on p_N, for example R_S may be dependent on p_N^2

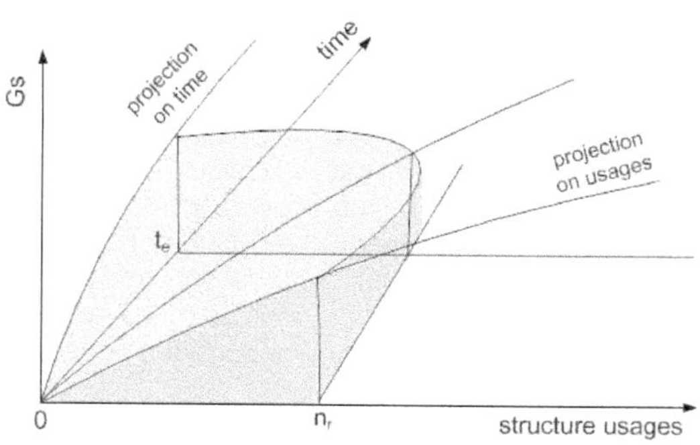

Figure 2: The shaded space is selected to be equal $Inf(S)$.

PROPOSITION 7. *The number n of amortization payments for $Builds_S(S)$ is selected such that the gain probability of at most n payments of $Builds_S(S)$ in the interval $[0, t_e]$ is equal to the influence of $Builds_S(S)$ to the provider economy, $Inf(S)$:*

$$G_S(k \leq n_r, t \leq t_e) = Inf(S) \tag{11}$$

Where n_r is the average rate of usage occurrences of S. The number of payments is calculated as $n = n_r \cdot \int_0^{t_e} R_S(t)dt$.

JUSTIFICATION The probability that at most n_r queries per time unit for an overall time $[0, t_e]$ arrive and $Builds_S(S)$ is amortized to them is given by: $G_S(k \leq n_r, t \leq t_e) = \int_0^{n_r} \int_0^{t_e} g_S(k,t)dtdk = \frac{\int_0^{t_e} R_S(t)dt}{\int_0^{\infty} R_S(t)dt} \cdot \int_0^{n_r} p_N dk = P(k \leq n_r) \cdot \frac{\int_0^{t_e} R_S(t)dt}{\int_0^{\infty} R_S(t)dt}$. Therefore $G_S(n_r < k, t \leq t_e) = 1 - G_S(t_e < t) - G_S(k \leq n_r, t \leq t_e) = 1 - G_S(t_e < t) - P(k \leq n_r) \cdot \frac{\int_0^{t_e} R_S(t)dt}{\int_0^{\infty} R_S(t)dt}$. We choose the value of $G_S(k \leq n_r, t \leq t_e)$ to be equal to the influence of S to the provider economy, $Inf(S)$. Intuitively, if S has been influential to the provider economy, i.e. possibly a lot of queries would have benefited from it in the past, it is most likely that this will be the case in the future, too. The opposite holds, too. Thus, the bigger $Inf(S)$ is, the bigger $G_S(k \leq n_r, t \leq t_e)$ is, the bigger n_r and n is, and, of course, the more risk we take in amortization, since, $G_S(n_r < k, t \leq t_e)$ becomes smaller. Figure 2 depicts the the probability $G_S(k \leq n_r, t \leq t_e)$. The constraint on $G_S(k \leq n_r, t \leq t_e)$ is actually a constraint on $P(k \leq n_r)$, which gives the value of n_r. The latter is the selected expected value of query arrival rate. Based on equation 8, we estimate the total number of payments n by weighting n_r with the reliability of the structure and integrating for the whole time interval $[0, t_e]$, i.e. $n = n_r \cdot \int_0^{t_e} R_S(t)dt$. This n is conservative w.r.t. the limit, $Inf(S)$, providing full amortization, (even independently of the importance condition) with success probability $> 1 - Inf(S)$.

4. DATA REGRESSION METHOD

To fit the real workload and selected query plans of the provider to the prediction model, we follow a regression procedure based on an observation period T_{obs} of provider service. The observation data consists of the: (i) query arrivals, (ii) structures employed in selected query plans, (iii) usage occurrences of each structure in the plans, and (iv) the update of data that are related to already built structures.

The time series of query arrivals T_{obs}, $\mathcal{Q} = \{Q_t, t \in T_{obs}\}$ is fit into a Poisson distribution, $p_N(k, \lambda)$, (i.e. the λ parameter is estimated) using the Poisson regression method [7]. Each element Q_t represents the number of queries that arrived at time t. Experimentally, T_{obs} is an ordered set of equal time slots t, and, therefore, Q_t is the number of queries that occurred in time slot t.

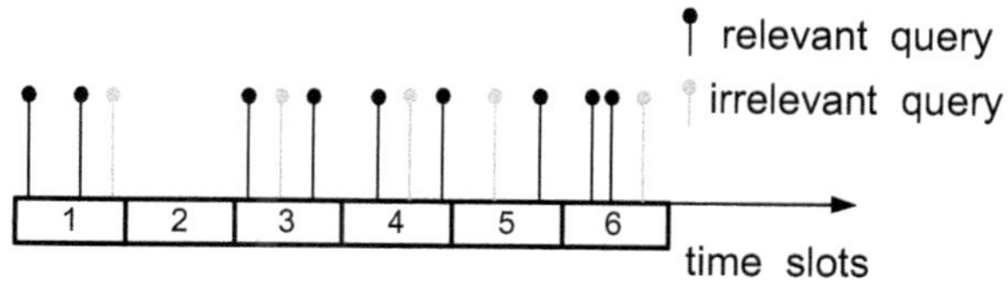

Figure 3: The maximal time of amortization is defined by the reliability and the hazard of failure.

Beyond fitting the query arrival, it is necessary to regress the observation data in order to fit the probability of usefulness, $d_S(t)$, and the probability of data stability, $st_S(t)$, for each newly built structure S. In the following, we describe how the observation data is processed in order to fit the probability of usefulness, $d_S(t)$.

The time series of usefulness w.r.t. a built structure S is $\mathcal{D}_S = \{D_{S_t}, t \in T'_{obs}\}$, where $D_{S_t} \leq Q_t$ and $T'_{obs} \subseteq T_{obs}$, s.t. $t \in T_{obs} \wedge t \in T'_{obs}$ iff $Q_t \neq 0$. Informally, the series $\mathcal{D}_S$ includes only the times (experimentally, time slots) for which there are query arrivals; for each time t, D_{S_t} is the number of arrived queries that employed S in their selected plan.

We process the series $\mathcal{D}_S$ in order to extract a series of sets of consecutive usages of S in selected query plans: Let us assume that the time series of query arrivals that corresponds to the filtered set of times T'_{obs}, is denoted as $\mathcal{Q}'$; it holds that $\mathcal{Q}' \subseteq \mathcal{Q}$. Two or more consecutive events in $\mathcal{D}_S$ are merged according to the *grace period* parameter v, defined as follows:

DEFINITION 8. *The grace period parameter, denoted as v is the sensitivity of the regression process to the observed failures of structure usage. The regression procedure is by v sensitive to $\mathcal{D}_S$ iff two or more consecutive events $D_{S_i}, \cdots, D_{S_{i+m}}$, $i = 1, \cdots, |T'_{obs} - m|$, $m \geq 1$ can be merged in one, s.t. $\forall j, k, i \leq j < k \leq i + m \wedge \forall p \in [j, k]$ it holds that $Q'_p - D_{S_p} \neq 0$ and $\sum_{p=j}^{p=k} Q'_j - D_{S_j} \leq v$.*

The value of v is equal to the maximal number of consecutively occurring selected query plans that did not use the structure S and that are ignored by the regression process. The merging procedure w.r.t. v results into:

$$\mathcal{L}_S = \{L_{S_t} \in P_S\}, |P_S| \leq T'_{obs} \tag{12}$$

$\mathcal{L}_S$ is a new time series and can be employed to perform survival analysis [5] in order to find the overall lifetime probability distribution of the usefulness of a structure S. Specifically, each time $t \in P_S$ is a member of the population P_S, with size $|P_S|$. Each member $t \in P_S$ has a lifetime equal to L_{S_t}. Intuitively, P_S is the set of occurrences of extended usage of the structure S in selected query plans in the observed time period T_{obs}. The lifetime of each such occurrence is the usage of S in terms of query arrivals.

EXAMPLE 1. *Figure 3 shows an example where the observation time is divided into 6 slots and queries relevant or irrelevant to the structure S are shown in black or gray, respectively. The regression ignores slot 2 since there are no queries. If the grace period is $v = 1$, all the gray queries are ignored and S is considered to have survived through all five slots. If $v = 0$, the lifetime of S is considered to end when a gray query occurs and begins again on the arrival of a black one. This results in 5 short lifetime instances of S.*

The regression process fits the lifetimes $\mathcal{L}_S$ of the population P_S to a Weibull distribution [7]. Weibull is employed as the failure [5] w.r.t. the usefulness of the structure S, $d_S(t)$, for $t \in [0, \infty)$, where $t = 0$ is the building time of S.

The regression process calculates the distribution of data stability w.r.t. a structure S, st_S, in a similar way. In this case, the regression is performed on the whole time interval T_{obs} and not on T'_{obs}. At each time $t \in T_{obs}$ the occurrence of unchanged data is modeled as a *success* and the occurrence of data update is modeled as a *failure*. A time series $\mathcal{ST}_S = \{ST_{S_t}, t \in T_{obs}\}$ is created, s.t. ST_{S_t} is the sum of successes decreased by the sum of failures in time t. $\mathcal{ST}$ is regressed to a Weibull distribution using the methodology described for the regression of the time series $\mathcal{D}_S$.

5. A CLOUD DBMS

We demonstrate the effectiveness of cost amortization using the proposed prediction model through its application to the economy management of a cloud that provides data services. Such a cloud DBMS is described in [6].

Briefly, data are permanently stored in a cloud of databases and data structures, i.e. indexes, materialized views and cached columns, as well as multiple processors in the cloud DBMS expedite query execution. Users queries are charged in order to be served. Queries are either executed in the cloud DBMS or on the cloud databases. The goal of the cloud is to hold an economy self-tuned along the lines of the following policies: (i) individual user satisfaction with the query services they receive w.r.t. the money they are charged, (ii) increasing overall quality of query services, and (iii) cloud profitability at all times. Query performance is measured in terms of execution time. The faster the execution, the more expensive the service. Quality increment of services is achieved with money investment on new data structures. The user defines her preferences concerning the service of her query by indicating the budget she is willing to spend on a specific query, according to the respective execution time that the cloud can provide. Also, the user can provide a preference for faster or cheaper query services. The cloud receives the query and the user preferences and produces respective alternative query plans. The price of these query plans is estimated and juxtaposed to the preferences of the user. If there are query plans that the user can afford, according to her budget, then the cloud chooses the most appropriate one of them, w.r.t. the policies.

The cloud's intention is to receive repay for these investments. However, without cost amortization the cloud does not actually arrive at the point of making new investments: If the cost of a new structure is repaid by a single or a few prospective users that use it, then the cost of the respective services can be so high that it most probably exceeds the users' budgets. In this case, the new structure will not be used in prospective query executions and, therefore, the cloud will never decide to build it. Overall, without cost amortization the quality of the services remains static, since the cloud will never decide to invest on new data structures. Employing the prediction model, however, the cost of new structures can be amortized to numerous prospective queries that will be executed using them. Cost amortization reduces the individual user payments to an amount that is covered by the users' budgets. This leads the cloud to improve the services by investing on new structures. We choose to guide cost amortization of a new structure S based on the *regret* of the cloud for not having already invested in S. Therefore the importance of a structure S, $w_S[S]$ (see definition 7) is identified as the respective regret $regret_S[S]$, which is calculated as described in Section 5.1.

Section 5.1 summarizes the operation of a cloud DBMS that provides data services and Section 5.2 extends the economy presented in [6]. The extended economy takes into account user preferences as well as budget requirements for query execution and assigns normalized values to the regret of possible new structures. Section 5.3 discusses the overhead of cost estimation for query execution plans.

5.1 Cloud Operation

The cloud has an account where the user payments for the services they receive are deposited. Also, money from this account are used for new inventory, i.e. new cache structures that can be used to execute queries in the cache, faster and cheaper. The overall credit in this account is denoted as CR. It is not the intension of the cloud to make profit from its investments. Some profit, however, is made in cases that the user is willing to pay more for the provided services than they really cost, without taking advantage of the difference of offered compensation and real cost for services. Moreover, the cloud aims at total amortization of investment cost.

The investment on a new structure is decided based on the notion of *regret*, inspired by [35]. Essentially, the cloud is not able to offer services that employ structures that are not yet built. In case that a structure is available, it is possible that the execution of some queries could benefit by employing it, either in terms of time or cost. The regret for not being able to offer a service because a structure is not built is accumulated and monitored; if the regret for the absence of a structure becomes substantial, then the cloud decides to invest in the construction of this structure.

DEFINITION 9. *The regret for a structure S, which is possible new inventory of the cloud, is a quantification of the accumulated value of the missed chances to provide better quality query services that comprise S.*

The regret is the incentive for the improvement of the query services. The cost of new inventory is paid from the cloud's account. The cost is amortized to prospective users that receive services which include the new inventory. The aim of amortization is to reduce the individual cost of the services. Cost reduction increases the potential that the user's budget covers the price of the offered services. In such a case, the cloud benefits from the difference of actual cost and offered user compensation; therefore, the cloud increases its profit, and thus, CR, which gives the opportunity for more investments directed by regret, leading to even more quality services.

The cloud maintains a pool of structures relevant to the queries in the recent past. Cache structures considered by the cloud are CPU nodes, table columns and indexes. In the current infrastructure the columns of the tables in the back-end databases are cached, in order to facilitate a comparison with [27]. Moreover, indexes constructed in the cache, accelerate the queries. Future work includes the expansion of the infrastructure with caching of materialized views, similar to [37], or partial columns, similar to [33]. The columns are determined by the definition of the queries, and the indexes are subsets of *per-query-optimal* candidate index sets [4]. These indexes typically contain many attributes relevant to a query and indexes which provide useful ordering columns to benefit join and aggregation processing. Since disk is the least expensive, the cloud tends to prefer such large candidate indexes. Additional CPUs are employed to speed up the parallelizable queries. Summarizing, the cache decides on building and maintaining three different types of structures: 1) CPU nodes N, 2) table columns T, and 3) indexes I.

These structures are garbage-collected using LRU policy, so that the structure cache can be searched and processed efficiently for each incoming query plan. Upon receiving an incoming query Q, the cloud considers a set of plans, $\mathcal{P}_Q$. This set consists of two non-overlapping subsets: the set of plans that include only existing cache structures, $\mathcal{P}_{Q_{exist}}$, and the set of plans that include also possible new cache structures, $\mathcal{P}_{Q_{pos}}$. The cloud determines the most optimal execution plan in $\mathcal{P}_{Q_{exist}}$[4] and considers the plans in $\mathcal{P}_{Q_{pos}}$ for possible investment in new cache structures.

[4]The optimal plan can be determined by querying the optimizer or by looking up a set of plans cached from earlier queries.

The cloud produces a set of alternative query plans for the input query Q, $\mathcal{P}_Q$, which holds only the two skylines of query plans (w.r.t. execution time and overall cost) in $\mathcal{P}_{Q_{pos}}$ and $\mathcal{P}_{Q_{exist}}$. From the implementation point of view, the cloud finds the structures it can use to execute an incoming query. First, it requires the column information for all the tables to be included in the query. Second, it determines the set of indexes that are possibly beneficial to the query by analyzing the query structure. Many of the queries can be parallelized using a bushy plan and most of the database vendors support parallelizing such queries. The queries can also be parallalized in a domain-specific way, as shown in [31].

EXAMPLE 2. *Consider the query select* `Q = max(A) from T where B = 0.1`. *The cloud needs columns "A", and "B" to execute the query. The latter can be sped up by using indexes on (A), (B), or (B,A). The query can be parallelized easily using multiple CPUs to scan the index and find the maximum value of A.*

The cost of each query plan $P_Q \in \mathcal{P}_Q$ is estimated according to the cost model described in [6], and produces a discrete budget function $B_{P_Q}(t) : t_{\mathcal{P}_Q} \mapsto \Re^+$, where $t_{\mathcal{P}_Q}$ is the set of execution time values for all plans in $\mathcal{P}_Q$. $B_{P_Q}(t)$ is typically a monotonically decreasing function, i.e. $B_{P_Q}(t_1) \geq B_{P_Q}(t_2), \forall t_1, t_2 \in t_{\mathcal{P}_Q}$ $s.t.$ $t_1 < t_2$.

The cloud maintains the array $regrets_{\mathcal{S}}$, which stores the accumulated regret values for each physical structure or set of cached data $S \in \mathcal{S}$ that is employed by any plan $P_Q \in \mathcal{P}_Q$, for any input user query Q. Specifically, the regret for a non-chosen query plan P_Q is added to the positions in $regrets_{\mathcal{S}}$ that correspond to the $S \in \mathcal{S}$ that are employed by P_Q. The accumulated regret value for each S shows the overall regret of the cloud for not employing it in executed query plans. A high regret value indicates that S could have been employed in either numerous or expensive, or both, query plans. When the regret for S, $regrets_{\mathcal{S}}[S]$ reaches a high value, then the cloud makes an investment and constructs S. Assuming that the overall credit in the cloud account is CR, then the $regrets_{\mathcal{S}}[S]$ must rise to a fraction a of CR, in order for S to be considered for imminent investment:

$$InvestIn(S) = round(\frac{regrets_{\mathcal{S}}[S]}{a \cdot CR}) \tag{13}$$

5.2 Cloud Economy

In the following we extend the economy model presented in [6]. The user input to the cloud is a query Q and the elements:

- a preference between short execution time or small cost
- a budget function

It is straightforward that the user always wants her query to be executed in minimum time with minimum cost. By default these two are conflicting directions for query plan selection; therefore, the user is given the choice to express a preference between the two. Moreover, the user is given the choice to input a budget function $B_Q(t)$ that indicates the price she is willing to pay according to the execution time of the query. There are no limitations for the structure of B_Q, while the user is expected to input a function that is descending with time. Specifically, the user inputs a set of possibly non-null elements in the following form:

$$UI = (preference, B_Q(t)), preference = \text{"time"}, \text{"cost"} \tag{14}$$

The form of UI enables a flexible user input for query execution directions. For example, the user is allowed to not give any preference or budget function[5], just input a query execution time limit with a preference on faster plans, Figure 4(a), or cheaper plans Figure 4(b), or define a specific budget function without any preferenece on time or cost, Figure 4(c).

A query plan that conforms to the user's budget, but also supports the three policies defined earlier is chosen, depending on B_{P_Q} and UI as follows: The cloud budget, B_{P_Q}, is compared with the user's budget, B_Q. The part of B_{P_Q} that is *covered* by B_Q, is stored in $B^a_{P_Q}$, i.e. $P_Q \in B^a_{P_Q}$ iff $P_Q \in B_{P_Q} \wedge B_{P_Q}(t_{P_Q}) \leq B_Q(t_{P_Q})$. The cloud selects from $B^a_{P_Q}$ an existing query plan to be executed, $P_{Q_{sel}} \in \mathcal{P}_{Q_{exist}}$ and a subset of the possible query plans, $\mathcal{P}_{Q_{regret}} \subseteq \mathcal{P}_{Q_{pos}}$ for which the regret is calculated. $P_{Q_{sel}}$ and $\mathcal{P}_{Q_{regret}}$ are selected depending on combinations of the following:

- the set $B^a_{P_Q}$
- the value of $UI.preference$

The possible combinations are:

1: The user budget does not cover the cloud budget, i.e. $B^a_{P_Q} = \emptyset$[6].

The user is presented with all the query plans in $\mathcal{P}_{Q_{exist}}$ accompanied with their cost and the execution time. The user can pick and pay for one plan $P_{Q_{sel}} \in \mathcal{P}_{Q_{exist}}$ or none. The cloud selects the subset of the possible query plans, $\mathcal{P}_{Q_{regret}} \subseteq \mathcal{P}_{Q_{pos}}$, for which the regret is calculated, depending on the preference value:
1a: If $UI.preference = null$ the regret is not calculated for any possible query plans, i.e. $\mathcal{P}_{Q_{regret}} = \emptyset$[7].
1b: If $UI.preference$ = "cost", the regret is calculated for all possible plans that are cheaper, i.e. $P_Q \in \mathcal{P}_{Q_{regret}}$ iff $P_Q \in \mathcal{P}_{Q_{pos}} \wedge B^a_{P_Q}(t_{P_Q}) \leq B^a_{P_Q}(t_{P_{Q_{sel}}})$.
1c: If $UI.preference$ = "time", the regret is calculated for all possible plans that are faster, i.e. $P_Q \in \mathcal{P}_{Q_{regret}}$ iff $P_Q \in \mathcal{P}_{Q_{pos}} \wedge t_{P_Q} \leq t_{P_{Q_{sel}}}$.

2: The user budget covers the cloud budget, i.e. $B^a_{P_Q} \neq \emptyset$.

A query plan is selected based on the preference value:
2a: If $UI.preference = null$, the cloud chooses the plan $P_{Q_{sel}}$ that minimizes the gain from the user's payment diminished by the actual cost of the plan, i.e. the plan $P_{Q_{sel}}$ is picked, $s.t.$ $B_Q(t_{P_{Q_{sel}}}) - B^a_{P_Q}(t_{P_{Q_{sel}}}) \leq B_Q(t_{P_{Q_j}}) - B^a_{P_Q}(t_{P_{Q_j}}), sel \neq j, P_{Q_j} \in \mathcal{P}_{Q_{exist}}$. The regret is calculated for all possible plans that are less profitable for the cloud, i.e. $P_Q \in \mathcal{P}_{Q_{regret}}$ iff $P_Q \in \mathcal{P}_{Q_{pos}} \wedge B_Q(t_{P_{Q_{sel}}}) - B^a_{P_Q}(t_{P_{Q_{sel}}}) \geq B_Q(t_{P_Q}) - B^a_{P_Q}(t_{P_Q})$
2b: If $UI.preference$ = "cost", the cloud chooses the query plan $P_{Q_{sel}}$ that is cheaper, i.e. $\forall P_Q \in \mathcal{P}_{Q_{exist}}, B^a_{P_Q}(t_{P_{Q_{sel}}}) \leq B^a_{P_Q}(t_{P_Q})$. The regret is calculated for all possible plans that are cheaper, i.e. $P_Q \in \mathcal{P}_{Q_{regret}}$ iff $P_Q \in \mathcal{P}_{Q_{pos}} \wedge B^a_{P_Q}(t_{P_Q}) \leq B^a_{P_Q}(t_{P_{Q_{sel}}})$.
2c: If $UI.preference$ = "time", the cloud chooses the query plan $P_{Q_{sel}}$ that is faster, i.e. $\forall P_Q \in \mathcal{P}_{Q_{exist}}, t_{P_{Q_{sel}}} \leq t_{P_Q}$. The regret is calculated for all possible plans that are faster, i.e. $P_Q \in \mathcal{P}_{Q_{regret}}$ iff $P_Q \in \mathcal{P}_{Q_{pos}} \wedge t_{P_Q} \leq t_{P_{Q_{sel}}}$.

In case 2 the profit $B_Q(t_{P_{Q_{sel}}}) - B_{P_Q}(t_{P_{Q_{sel}}})$ is credited to the cloud account, and can be invested on new cache structures.

The cloud calculates the regret for not investing in the alternative plans $\mathcal{P}_{Q_{regret}}$, as a weighted difference between the cost of the chosen and the alternative plan:

$$regret(P_Q) = \frac{|B^a_{P_Q}(t_{P_{Q_{sel}}}) - B^a_{P_Q}(t_{P_Q})|}{B^a_{P_Q}(t_{P_Q})}, \forall P_Q \in \mathcal{P}_{Q_{regret}} \tag{15}$$

[5]By convention, a $B_Q(t) = 0$ represents a non-defined user budget.

[6]Note that $B^a_{P_Q} = \emptyset$ also holds in the case that B_Q does not exist.

[7]In practice, if all the users define no preferences, the cloud may choose as default preference = "time".

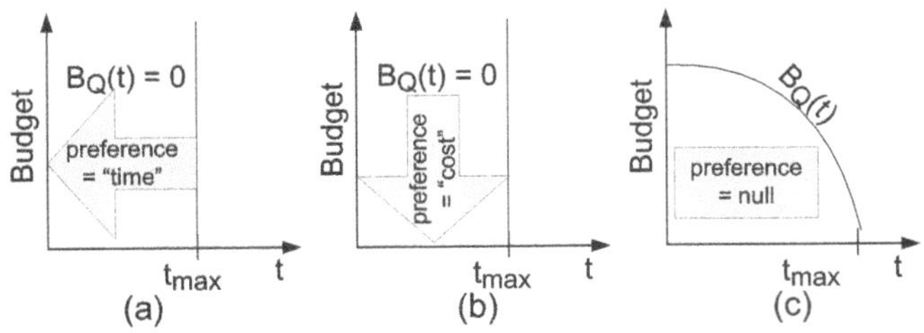

Figure 4: Examples of user preferences and budgets: (a) time-limited budget and preference on time, (b) time-limited budget and preference on cost, (c) budget function without preference.

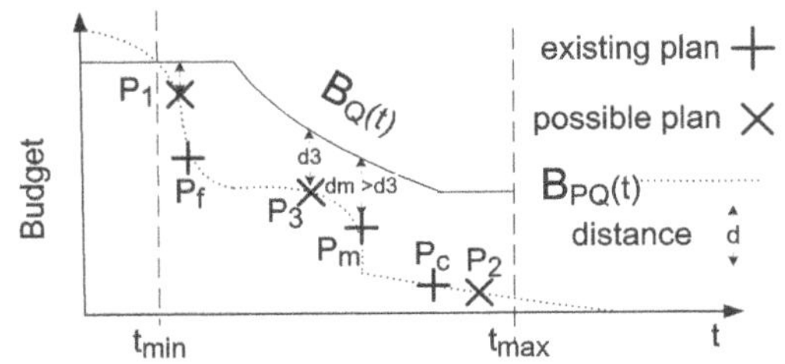

Figure 5: Comparison of the user's and the cloud budget and selection of plans for execution and regret calculation.

The role of the denominator in formula 15 is to decrease the influence of expensive plans in the regret assigned in the involved cache structures. The following example illustrates the service of a user query according to her input directions and the calculation of regret.

EXAMPLE 3. *Assume that the user sends the query Q and the input* $UI = (preference, B_Q)$ *where* B_Q *is a piecewise function limited in time, as shown in Figure 5. The skylines of the possible and existing query plans form the cloud budget* B_{P_Q}*. The cloud budget* $B^a_{P_Q} = B_{P_Q} \wedge t \in [t_{min}, t_{max}]$*, which is covered by* B_Q*, is considered for the plan selection. If the user prefers faster over cheaper plans, the cloud selects* $P_{Q_{sel}} = P_f$ *and calculates the regret for the possible plan covered by* B_Q *that is faster than* P_f*, i.e.* P_1*. If she prefers cheaper over faster queries, the cloud selects* $P_{Q_{sel}} = P_c$ *and calculates the regret for the possible plan covered by* B_Q*, that is cheaper, i.e.* P_2*. If the user does not define any preference, the cloud selects* $P_{Q_{sel}} = P_m$*, i.e. the plan with the cost closer to the user's budget. The regret is calculated for the possible plans* P_1*,* P_3 *with cost even closer to the user's budget.*

The cloud aims at maximizing the probability that the cloud budget is covered by the user's budget, i.e. $B^a_{P_Q} \rightarrow B_Q$. This is achieved by amortizing the cost of new structures to numerous prospective selected query plans.

5.3 Cost of Query Execution

The model that estimates the building and maintenance cost for new data structures can be found in [6]. To determine the structure to be used in the optimizer, the cache needs to find the minimal query cost for the existing structures and the plans for the potential structures. If the regret is assigned only to one plan, then the cache can invoke the optimizer twice, once with existing indexes and once with "what-if" indexes [4]. These simulate statistics for the real indexes, without actually building one. They can be maintained without the overhead of full indexes. Since each optimizer invocation takes in the order of hundreds of milliseconds, for expensive queries the overhead is small.

In case the regret is assigned to all possible query plans, the cache needs to invoke the optimizer many times to estimate costs for all possible index combinations. The overhead can be substantial. To reduce the overhead we use the configuration parametric query optimization techniques, such as INUM [32] and C-PQO [2]. In the the time to estimate costs of many index combinations are reduced by orders of magnitude. Since INUM works outside of the optimizer and C-PQO requires access to the optimizer internals, we prefer to employ INUM for the cloud. INUM caches some "key" plans for each query to determine plans for every possible index combinations. The number of plans cached for each query depends on the join and the ordering query columns. Typically, for TPCH-like complex queries, caching 100 plans on average for each query is required. INUM allows an approximation method [32] that caches only two plans per query to provide a reasonably close upper bound on the query cost. This approximation is used to determine the query cost. This technique provides the upper bound and the cache behaves conservatively, while estimating which structures to materialize.

To further reduce the cost estimation overhead, query similarity can be exploited. Typically, the queries are generated by applications, with limited free form query generation. The cloud extracts the query templates and caches the plans only for the respective queries, using techniques proposed by Ghosh et al. [9]. This drastically reduces the overhead of cost estimation. The costs estimated based on templates are upper bounds on the actual query costs. If higher accuracy is desired, the cache can monitor the actual plan used for each query and adjust the cost based on templates. Modern databases provide simple techniques to retrieve the actually used query plans [14]. Using the above techniques, the cloud reduces the overhead of cost estimation and make the query service realistic.

6. EXPERIMENTS

We present the experimental study for the cost amortization of data structures used in query services of a cloud DBMS that employs the proposed prediction and economy models.

6.1 Experimental Setup and Methodology

Setup. The cloud DBMS is set up with one back-end database. This is the best possible scenario for the back-end database as it eliminates the inter-database communication to answer the queries. The cloud DBMS is operated under a TPC-H-based workload first used in [28]. It consists of 7 TPC-H query templates and simulates the query evolution of a million real SDSS [17] queries against a 2.5TB back-end database. The workload mainly simulates the evolution of column usage seen in SDSS workloads. The authors first plot the column co-occurence matrix, and temporal locality of the columns in the SDSS workload. Then they select 7 queries and change the query composition over time to simulate similar column co-occurence and locality. We select this workload, as it is more portable across different DBMS, and the queries are tunable by using the query generation mechanism of the TPC-H benchmark. The reason that we employ a simulation of the workload rather than run the real 1 million SDSS queries, is that (i) it would take months to run the real workload, and (i) the real queries were posed by the astronomers in a period of one year, and, in order to test the prediction model in a realistic situation of data services, we needed to simulate accurately all the workload features, including time. Furthermore, in order to prove the effectiveness of the prediction model we need a big workload, for which the model could observe and regress a substantial part of it that is able to give enough information for the prediction of the rest. We copy the detailed experimental setup, including the cost model parameters from [6]. The building and maintenance cost of structures is calculated using the prices on I/O operations, disk space, CPU time and network bandwidth of Amazon EC2 [12]. Computations show that the building cost is on average 7

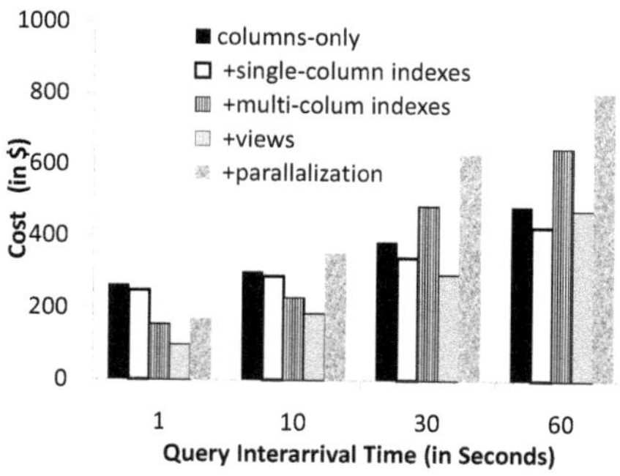

Figure 6: Sensitivity of provider cost w.r.t. availability of database features.

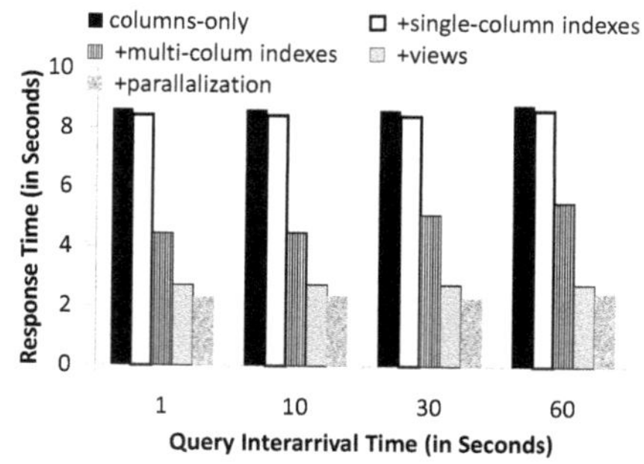

Figure 7: Sensitivity of response times w.r.t. availability of database features.

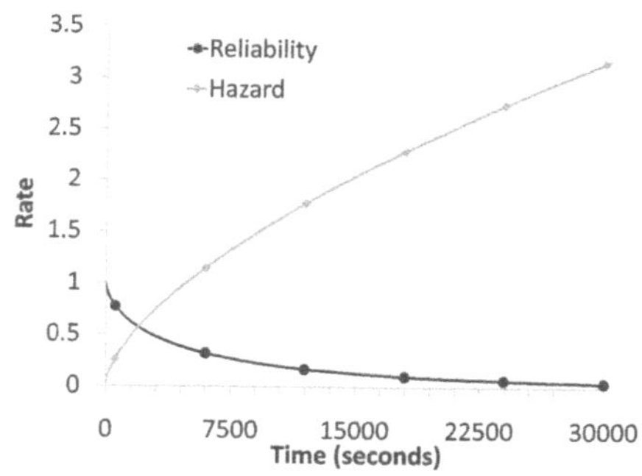

Figure 8: Balance between reliability R and cumulative hazard H.

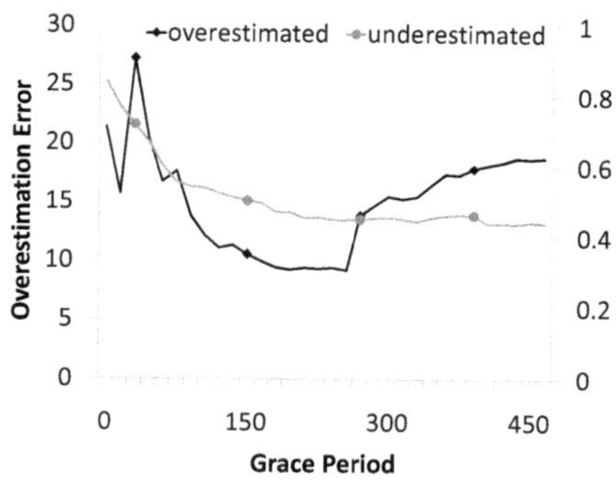

Figure 9: Avg. over- and under-estimation error w.r.t. grace period.

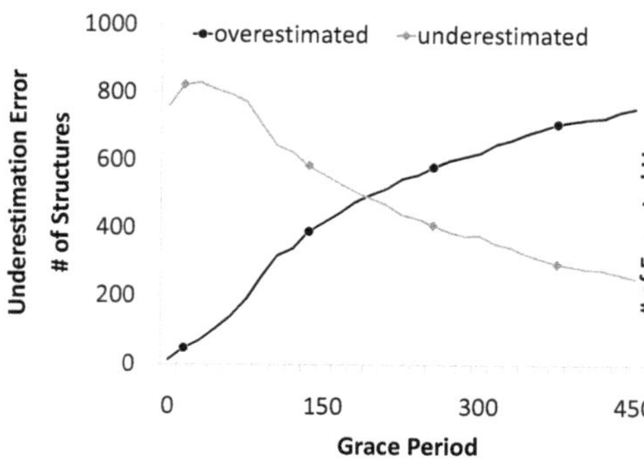

Figure 10: Avg. # of over- and under-estimated structures w.r.t. grace period.

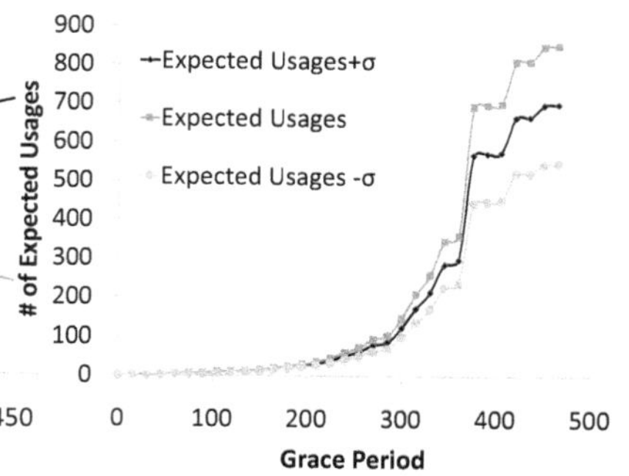

Figure 11: Avg. # of expected structure usages w.r.t. grace period.

orders of magnitude bigger than the maintenance cost. Nevertheless, the fitting of the prediction model is performed with the real SDSS workload.

Methodology. Six sets of experiments cover the major aspects of the proposed cost amortization for data services.

The first set of experiments assumes that the cloud is read-only, thoroughly altruistic, and does not charge anything for building the cache structures. The goal of these experiments is to show the variation of the cloud performance w.r.t. availability of different database features, such as indexes, materialized views, and parallelization. The second set of experiments presents results on fitting the prediction model of Section 3 based on regression of the dataset. The third set of experiments present the results on building cost amortization, as described in Section 3. The fourth set presents results w.r.t. the economy sensitivity to the two most influential workload features, the frequency of data update and the locality of data access. The fifth set of experiments presents results w.r.t. the complexity of queries, which results in long-running query execution. The sixth set of experiments presents results w.r.t. the overhead of constructing the query plans. In the first set of experiments we set the user preference equal to "time" (i.e. the economy selects fast query plans) whereas in all the rest we set preference equal to "cost".

6.2 Experimental Results

This section presents the experimental results.

6.2.1 Comparison of different database features

Figures 6 and 7 show the operating cost of a read-only cloud cache and the average query response time for different database features using different inter-query time intervals. We start the cloud database with only database columns, then each of the next columns in the chart adds a database feature to the one on left. We add single-column indexes, then multi-column indexes, then materialized views, and finally multiple CPUs to parallelize the query processing. We observe that the operating cost of the cloud is reasonable in presence of all the features. Hence, the caching service for SDSS-like workload is viable. We also observe that the materialized views provide the most improvement in response time and operating cost. This is especially true, since we do not consider cost of updating the materialized views, and each of the materialized view is optimal for the templates selected in the workload. Hence, the results using materialized views represent the upper bound on the cloud performance. In the absence of materialized views, the cloud should build multi-column indexes even though due to the sizes they become expensive to maintain in large query arrival intervals.

6.2.2 Fit of the prediction model

The SDSS-like workload contains data for the period of T = 95 days (specifically 8,214,506 seconds). The regression procedure on the workload showed that it fits the proposed prediction model. Specifically, the query arrivals are regressed w.r.t. the Poisson distribution. The mean value of the standard deviance of the residuals of the Poisson regression is $\approx -0,31$ and the respective standard deviation is $2,82{\cdot}10^{-6}$, which shows a very good fit. Moreover, this conclusion is reinforced by the R-squared value, which is close to 1 [7]. The mean of the Poisson distribution is estimated as $\lambda \approx 0,0273$ (every 1 second). The observed data is regressed using the method in Section 4 in order to calculate the failure and, therefore, the reliability of each structure. The entire workload period, T, is divided in three parts and two of them are used as the observation time T_{obs}, whereas the third one has been used for testing. The cross-validation of the regression and test sets gives the results presented in Figures 9, 10 and 11. Each time slot $t \in T_{obs}$ is set to 15 seconds. Both the observed and predicted data refer to 2054 cached columns. The sensitivity of the regression method, v is varied on the x-axis of the

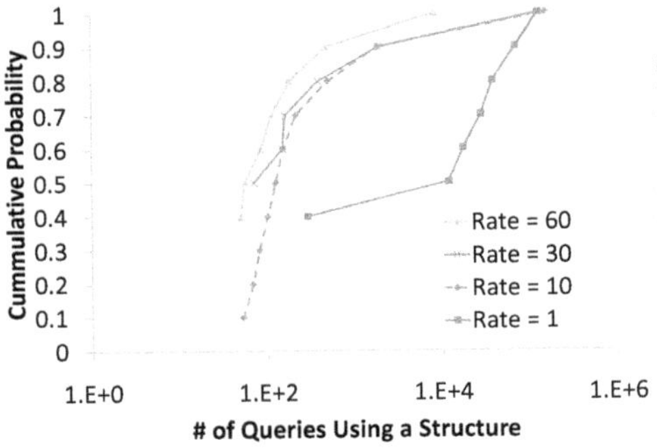

Figure 12: Cumulative probability for the number of queries that use a structure.

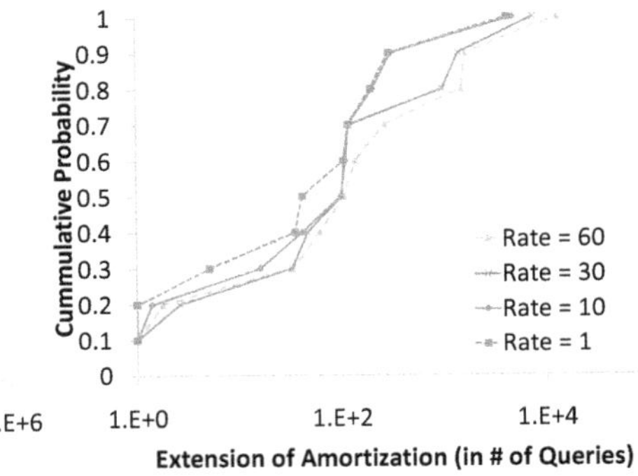

Figure 13: Cumulative probability for total cost amortization.

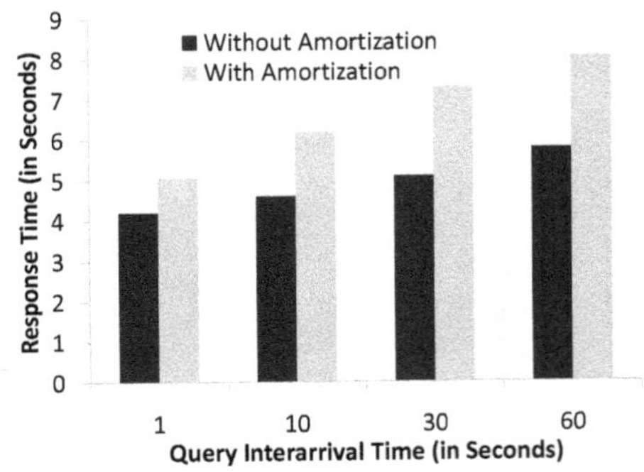

Figure 14: Response times using amortization.

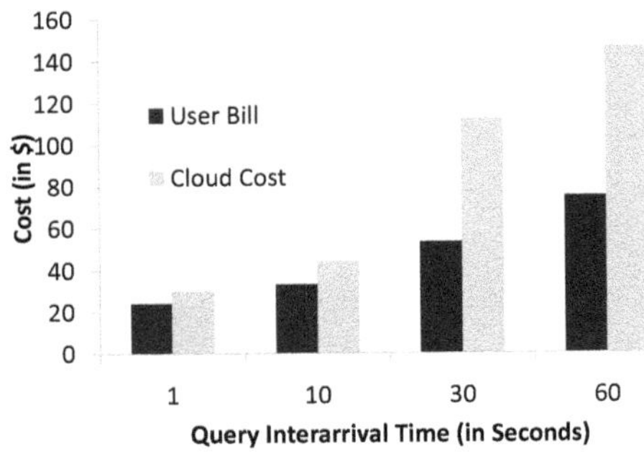

Figure 15: Building and maintenance cost recovery.

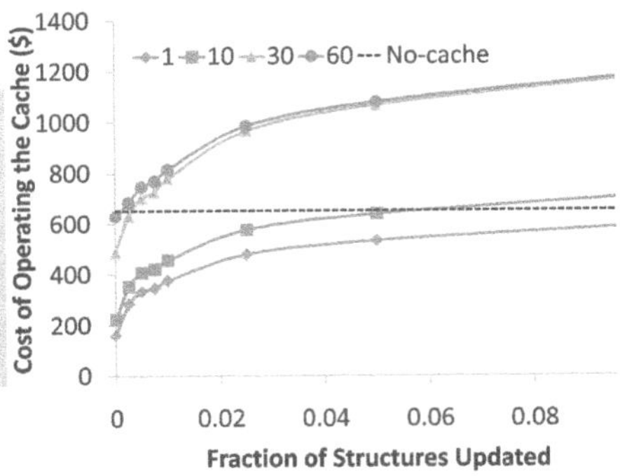

Figure 16: Sensitivity to the frequency of data update.

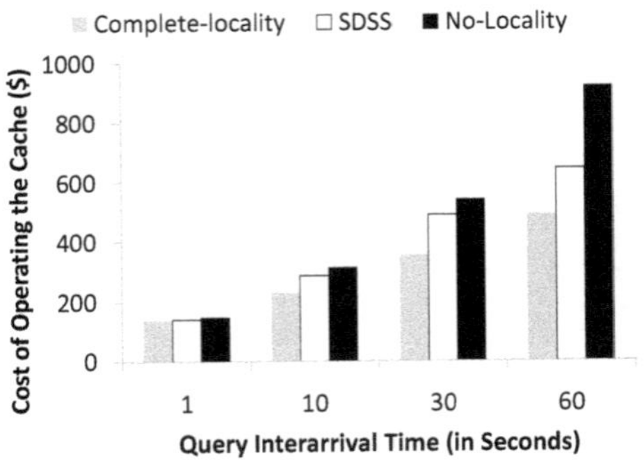

Figure 17: Sensitivity to the locality of data access

respective graphs, so that $0 - 450$ consecutive usage failures are ignored in the cache lifetime of a column. The results show the average error in over- and under-estimation w.r.t. the expected usage of the column in prospective selected query plans. Specifically, the error for each column is computed as:

$$error = \frac{\sum(expected\_\#usages - actual\_\#usages)}{\sum actual\_\#usages} \quad (16)$$

over the entire test period. Naturally, the range of the over- and under-estimation error are not comparable, and therefore they are presented separately. The lowest the errors are, the better the prediction is. Figure 9 shows that under-estimation error is monotonically decreasing, while the over-estimation error has a *bathtub* curve: For small sensitivity values, the error is big because it averages only big errors originating on columns used for long in the train set but not used at all in the test set. Inevitably, as regression becomes less sensitive to the observed usage failures, the predicted column lifetimes are longer and the model is more prone to overestimation. These two tends are balanced for $v = 150, \cdots, 300$ and the over-estimation error is minimized. Moreover, Figure 10 shows that for $v \approx 225$ there is the maximum compensation of over- and under-estimation in terms of number of columns. Naturally, there is a point of sensitivity of the regression to the survival analysis, which balances the influence of sparse and dense occurrences of column usage w.r.t. the predicted lifetime. Figure 11 shows the range (using the standard deviation σ) and the average expected number of occurrences of column usage. Naturally, the average and range of expected usages increases as the regression becomes less sensitive. Employing the regression for $v = 225$, we use survival analysis to predict the reliability of the columns. The mean μ and standard deviation σ values of the predicted failure distributions, i.e. Weibull [5], are $\mu = 291.35$, $\sigma = 1772$ for the shape parameter, and $\mu = 1.21$, $\sigma = 1.004$, for the scale parameter. This means that the failure rate f_S is increasing with time for all columns, but the increment rate df_S/dt varies a lot depending on the column. Figure 8 shows the reliability and the cumulative hazard for the mean predicted failure distribution. The maximum amortization time t_e varies in $[0, 188830]$ sec. and $t_e = 1816$ sec. on average for $v = 225$. 524 columns are predicted with zero lifetime; this is a good prediction since these columns are actually used by 2 queries on average and by 14 queries at most.

6.2.3 *Effect of cost amortization*

This set of experiments examines the effect of cost amortization to the cloud economy. The cloud remains altruistic but, unlike in the case of Section 6.2.1, the building cost of a structure is amortized to the queries for which a plan that uses this structure is selected. Figure 12 shows the computed cumulative distributions for the number of queries that use each cache structure in the workload, while varying the inter-arrival time. Apparently, all structures are used at least by 80 queries even if the queries arrive every 60 seconds. As expected, if the query arrivals are very frequent, i.e. every 1 second, then the number of queries that use a structure increases exponentially and reaches the number of at least 10000 queries with 0.5 probability. Figure 13 shows the computed cumulative distributions for the recovery of the total cost through its amortization on prospective queries. The results show that the success of total cost recovery is sensitive to the arrival rate of queries. The reason is that as the inter-arrival time increases, the maintenance cost increases, too. In order to keep the total cost of the query plans low, the structure cost has to be amortized on more queries to be fully recovered.

The next experiment shows the results for response time and actual cost recovery if the cost is amortized to 100 queries. We run this experiment using column caching and multi-column indexes while

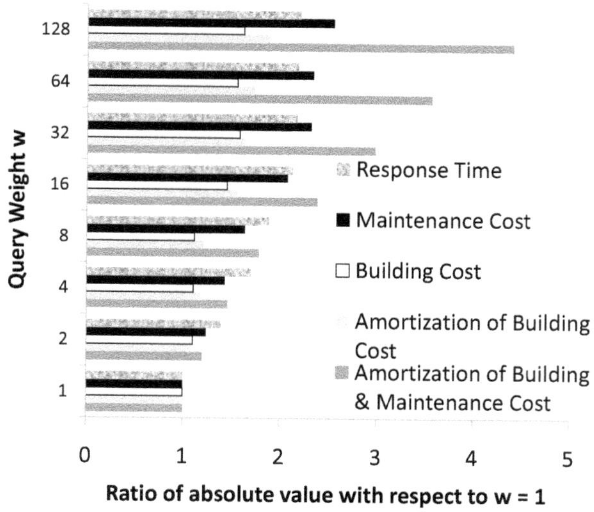

Figure 18: Cost and response time w.r.t. query complexity.

varying query inter-arrival time. Figure 14 shows the response time in the case that the cloud targets to the maximization of cost recovery from the user. Naturally, the cloud is conservative in building new structures and the response time is bigger than in the case of Section 6.2.1. However, as shown in Figure 15, the cloud recovers most of the cost for high to average arrival rates (every 1-10 seconds). In case of sparse arrivals (every 60 seconds), the maintenance cost increases substantially, reducing the competitiveness of the plans, and their chances to be selected to serve query execution. Note that, the cloud does not charge anything after the entire cost of a structure has been recovered.

Overall, the experiments prove the viability of the altruistic cloud, which reconciles the following policies: (i) moderately charging the users for the built structures, giving priority to their satisfaction in terms of cost (i.e. offering them the cheapest plan) (ii) recovering the operational cost with a big guarantee, and (iii) enhancing the offered query services by building new structures. These are the policies that tune an altruistic cloud, as denoted in Section 5.1. Therefore, the proposed cloud achieves its purpose.

6.2.4 Sensitivity to workload changes

Figure 16 shows the sensitivity of the cost for operating the cloud cache to the update frequency in the workload. The results correspond to the scenario that the structures are evicted upon any change to related data. The x-axis shows the fraction of structures that are evicted because of updates and the y-axis shows the the cost of query execution. The cache uses Amazon's cost model, with indexes. For comparison, the graph includes the results for query execution performed thoroughly in the back-end database. For small (= 1 sec.) or moderate (= 10 sec.) query inter-arrival interval, the cloud cache remains beneficial to the user even for high-frequency data update. For big inter-arrival intervals the cached structures are evicted because of data update before they are used to answer the queries. Therefore, the cache is beneficial to the user only for small update frequency.

Figure 17 shows the sensitivity of the cache to the data-access locality. The SDSS workload is compared with two artificial ones. The first is a workload with zero locality, i.e. the query data access is generated randomly. The second is a workload with high locality, i.e. each query is issued about 150,000 times before switching over to a new one. The graph shows that the cost of operating the cache with the SDSS workload is very close to the workload with high locality. Even with the random workload, the cache performs well compared to the SDSS workload, especially for small to moderate query inter-arrival intervals.

6.2.5 Sensitivity to complex queries

Figure 18 shows the effect of complex queries, i.e. long-running queries, on the cloud DBMS. To observe the economy behavior on complex queries, for each possible query plan, we scale the intended running time by a factor w, as shown on the y-axis. The x-axis shows the (i) the average response time, (ii) the maintenance cost, (iii) the building cost of all structures (iv) the amortized building cost for all structures over the entire workload and (v) the amortized of both building and maintenance cost. Concerning the results of trend (v), the maintenance cost was amortized by charging the cheapest (and therefore selected for execution query plan) more but not exceeding the cost of the second cheapest plan. Instead of showing the absolute values, we show the ratio of these values over the respective values corresponding to $w = 1$. In this way we save space by presenting all the trends in the same graph. These results refer to query inter-arrival rate equal to 10 seconds. All values increase as the query weight (w) is increased. The increment, however, is sub-linear. As w increases, the regret increases proportionally to the cost of the possible plans, but the cost to build the structures remains the same. This allows the cloud to build structures much earlier and turn 'possible' plans to 'existing' ones. These new plans are faster but cheaper than old plans, and, thus, they are selected for execution. Therefore, as times goes query services improve, as they are both faster and cheaper. Therefore the response time remains small, even for very complex queries; e.g., for the query plans that are assumed to run $w = 128$ slower than they actually do, the average response time of queries increases only by a factor of 2, because of faster availability of expensive structures. Since the cloud builds more structures, the building and maintenance cost increases. The amortization of the building cost remunerates all of it for $w = 1$ and more than the actual cost as w increases. This increment is much bigger in case the maintenance cost is amortized, too. Therefore, cost amortization not only ensures the economic viability of the cloud, but also its profitability.

6.2.6 Query cost estimation overhead

As discussed in Section 5.3, cost estimation is the biggest overhead in query execution in the cloud. This experiment compares the overhead of different cost estimation methods and their accuracies. The first column of Table 1 shows the total number of optimizer calls that the cloud performs to estimate the query costs. The *Query* method calls the optimizer for each query and each potential combination of indexes; the *INUM* method uses INUM to reduce the combinations needed investigation; the *INUM Approx* method approximates INUM's cost estimation by calling the optimizer only once for each query; *Template* identifies the templates from the queries and uses the templates to estimate the costs for every index combination. The next two techniques, i.e., *Template + INUM* and *Template + INUM Approx* use the INUM and approximation methods. The results show the expected number of optimizer calls for each of these techniques. The *Query* method is the most expensive and it invokes the optimizer about 150 million times. *INUM* improves on that by reducing the number of calls by an order of magnitude, but is still quite expensive. Overheads of *INUM Approx* and *Template* methods are very similar, and using *INUM + Template* reduces the overhead by another factor of 9. Finally, Template + INUM Approx achieves the lowest overhead (about 1803 optimizer calls). The second column of Table 1 shows the cost estimation error for the techniques. The table presents the percentage of average extra cost assigned to the query w.r.t. *Query*. *Template* achieves the smallest estimation error, and *Template + INUM Approx* incurs the highest estimation

Estimation Technique	Estimated Optimizer Calls	Percentage Over Estimation
Query	147396994	0
INUM	18255591	9.051037
INUM Approx	676133	25.22721
Template	387960	4.657116
Template+INUM	48681	13.79859
Template+INUM Approx	1803	32.06346

Table 1: Comparison of query-plan estimation techniques.

error. Comparing the number of optimizer calls with the respective estimation error, we suggest that the cloud uses *Template + INUM* for a balance between the accuracy and overhead of cost estimation.

7. CONCLUSION

In this paper we propose the cost amortization of data structures employed in data services in order to ensure the economic viability of the data provider. We present a novel generic stochastic model that predicts the appropriate amortization in time and number of prospective queries. A novel data regression model processes query statistics and gives input to the prediction model. In order to study the effectiveness of cost amortization we extend an existing economy model for the management of a cloud DBMS. A thorough experimental study demonstrates that cost amortization of data structures can achieve the economic viability of the cloud DBMS, and, moreover, its profitability, while improving the offered query services in terms of both cost and response time.

8. REFERENCES

[1] D. Agrawal, A. E. Abbadi, F. Emekci, and A. Metwally. Database management as a service: Challenges and opportunities. In *ICDE '09*, pages 1709–1716, 2009.

[2] N. Bruno and R. V. Nehme. Configuration-parametric query optimization for physical design tuning. In *SIGMOD*, 2008.

[3] B. Calder and D. Grunwald. Next cache line and set prediction. In *ISCA*, pages 287–296, 1995.

[4] S. Chaudhuri and V. R. Narasayya. An efficient cost-driven index selection tool for Microsoft SQL server. In *VLDB*, 1997.

[5] D. R. Cox and D. Oakes. *Analysis of Survival Data*. CRC Press, 1984.

[6] D. Dash, V. Kantere, and A. Ailamaki. An economic model for self-tuned cloud caching. In *ICDE*, pages 1687–1693, 2009.

[7] J. J. Faraway. *Extending the linear model with R: generalized linear, mixed effects and nonparametric regression models*. CRC Press, 2006.

[8] D. G. Feitelson. Locality of sampling and diversity in parallel system workloads. In *Intl. Conf. Supercomputing*, 2007.

[9] A. Ghosh, J. Parikh, V. S. Sengar, and J. R. Haritsa. Plan selection based on query clustering. In *VLDB*, 2002.

[10] M. Gibas, G. Canahuate, and H. Ferhatosmanoglu. Online index recommendations for high-dimensional databases using query workloads. *IEEE TKDE*, 20(2):246–260, 2008.

[11] H. Hacigumus, B. Iyer, and S. Mehrotra. Providing database as a service. In *ICDE '02: Proceedings of the 18th International Conference on Data Engineering*, page 29, Washington, DC, USA, 2002. IEEE Computer Society.

[12] http://aws.amazon.com/ec2/.

[13] http://code.google.com/appengine/.

[14] http://msdn.microsoft.com/en us/library/ms189747.aspx.

[15] http://www.microsoft.com/azure/.

[16] http://www.salesforce.com/.

[17] http://www.sdss.org/.

[18] Z. Hu, S. Kaxiras, and M. Martonosi. Timekeeping in the memory system: predicting and optimizing memory behavior. *SIGARCH Comput. Archit. News*, 30(2):209–220, 2002.

[19] I. F. Ilyas, V. Markl, P. Haas, P. Brown, and A. Aboulnaga. Cords: Automatic discovery of correlations and soft functional dependencies. In *In SIGMOD*, pages 647–658, 2004.

[20] M. Kharbutli and Y. Solihin. Counter-based cache replacement and bypassing algorithms. *IEEE Trans. Comput.*, 57(4):433–447, 2008.

[21] H. Kimura, G. Huo, A. Rasin, S. Madden, and S. B. Zdonik. Correlation maps: A compressed access method for exploiting soft functional dependencies. In *VLDB*, 2009.

[22] A.-C. Lai, C. Fide, and B. Falsafi. Dead-block prediction & dead-block correlating prefetchers. *SIGARCH Comput. Archit. News*, 29(2):144–154, 2001.

[23] C. A. Lang and A. K. Singh. Modeling high-dimensional index structures using sampling. *SIGMOD Rec.*, 30(2):389–400, 2001.

[24] H. Li, D. Groep, and L. Wolters. Workload characteristics of a multi-cluster supercomputer. In *Workshop on Job Scheduling Strategies for Parallel Processing*, 2004.

[25] H. Li, M. Muskulus, and L. Wolters. Modeling job arrivals in a data-intensive grid. In *Workshop on Job Scheduling Strategies for Parallel Processing*, 2006.

[26] H. Li, M. Muskulus, and L. Wolters. Modeling correlated workloads by combining model based clustering and a localized sampling algorithm. In *ICS*, pages 64–72. ACM, 2007.

[27] T. Malik, R. C. Burns, and A. Chaudhary. Bypass caching: Making scientific databases good network citizens. In *ICDE*, 2005.

[28] T. Malik, X. Wang, R. Burns, D. Dash, and A. Ailamaki. Automated physical design in database caches. In *SMDB*, 2008.

[29] T. N. Minh and L. Wolters. Modeling job arrival process with long range dependence and burstiness characteristics. In *CCGRID*, pages 324–330. IEEE, 2009.

[30] T. N. Minh and L. Wolters. Modeling parallel system workloads with temporal locality. In *Workshop on Job Scheduling Strategies for Parallel Processing*, 2009.

[31] M. A. Nieto-Santisteban, J. Gray, A. S. Szalay, J. Annis, A. R. Thakar, and W. J. OÕmullane. When database systems meet the grid. In *CIDR*, 2005.

[32] S. Papadomanolakis, D. Dash, and A. Ailamaki. Efficient use of the query optimizer for automated database design. In *VLDB*, pages 1093–1104, 2007.

[33] M. Stonebraker, P. M. Aoki, W. Litwin, A. Pfeffer, A. Sah, J. Sidell, C. Staelin, and A. Yu. Mariposa: A wide-area distributed database system. *VLDB J.*, 5(1):48–63, 1996.

[34] H. Taylor and S. Karlin. *An Introduction to Stochastic Modeling*. Academic Press, third edition, 1998.

[35] A. Tewari and P. Bartlett. Optimistic linear programming gives logarithmic regret for irreducible mdps. In *Advances in Neural Information Processing Systems 20*.

[36] P. Unterbrunner, G. Giannikis, G. Alonso, D. Fauser, and D. Kossmann. Predictable performance for unpredictable workloads. In *VLDB*, 2009.

[37] X. Wang, T. Malik, R. C. Burns, S. Papadomanolakis, and A. Ailamaki. A workload-driven unit of cache replacement for mid-tier database caching. In *DASFAA*, pages 374–385, 2007.

Performance Prediction for Concurrent Database Workloads

Jennie Duggan
Brown University

Ugur Cetintemel
Brown University

Olga Papaemmanouil
Brandeis University

Eli Upfal
Brown University

ABSTRACT

Current trends in data management systems, such as cloud and multi-tenant databases, are leading to data processing environments that concurrently execute heterogeneous query workloads. At the same time, these systems need to satisfy diverse performance expectations. In these newly-emerging settings, avoiding potential Quality-of-Service (QoS) violations heavily relies on performance predictability, i.e., the ability to estimate the impact of concurrent query execution on the performance of individual queries in a continuously evolving workload.

This paper presents a modeling approach to estimate the impact of concurrency on query performance for analytical workloads. Our solution relies on the analysis of query behavior in isolation, pairwise query interactions and sampling techniques to predict resource contention under various query mixes and concurrency levels. We introduce a simple yet powerful metric that accurately captures the joint effects of disk and memory contention on query performance in a single value. We also discuss predicting the execution behavior of a time-varying query workload through query-interaction timelines, i.e., a fine-grained estimation of the time segments during which discrete mixes will be executed concurrently. Our experimental evaluation on top of PostgreSQL/TPC-H demonstrates that our models can provide query latency predictions within approximately 20% of the actual values in the average case.

Categories and Subject Descriptors

C.4 [**Computer Systems Organization**]: Performance of Systems Modeling Techniques

General Terms

Measurement, Performance

1. INTRODUCTION

Concurrent query execution facilitates improved resource utilization and aggregate throughput, while making it a challenge to accurately predict individual query performance. Modeling the performance impact of complex interactions that arise when multiple queries share computing resources and data is difficult albeit critical for a number of tasks such as Quality of Service (QoS) management in the emerging cloud-based database platforms, effective resource allocation for time-sensitive processing tasks, and user experience management for interactive database systems.

SIGMOD'11, June 12–16, 2011, Athens, Greece.

Consider a cloud-based database-as-a-service platform for data analytics. The service provider would negotiate service level agreements (SLAs) with its users. Such SLAs are often expressed in terms of QoS (e.g., latency, throughput) requirements for various query classes, as well as penalties applied if the QoS targets are violated. The service provider has to allocate sufficient resources to user queries to avoid such violations, or else face consequences in the form of lost revenue and damaged reputation. Thus, it is important to be able to accurately predict the runtime of an incoming query on the available machines, as well as its impact on the existing queries, so that the scheduling of the query does not lead to any QoS violations. The service provider may have to scale up and allocate more cloud resources if it deems that existing resources are insufficient to accommodate the incoming query.

This paper addresses the performance prediction problem for analytical concurrent query workloads. Specifically, we study the following problem: "Given a collection of queries $q_1, q_2, q_3, ..., q_n$, concurrently executing on the same machine at arbitrary stages of their execution, predict when each query will finish its execution."

To predict QoS, we target time elapsed rather than metrics such as throughput or resource utilization. We elected execution latency because in practice it has the greatest impact on user experience. Users are generally more concerned about when a query returns its output, rather than how many are sharing a host or the number of physical I/Os required.

We propose a two-phase solution for this problem.

- **Model Building** We build a composite, multivariate regression model that captures the execution behavior of queries under concurrency. We use this model to predict the logical I/O latency for each query in a given workload mix.

- **Timeline Analysis** We analyze the execution timeline of the workload to predict the termination points for individual queries. This timeline analysis starts by predicting the first query to complete and then repeatedly performs prediction for the remaining queries.

One of our key ideas is to use a *logical* I/O-based metric, called BAL, to quantify the performance impact of concurrently executing queries. This simple yet highly-predictive metric gives us an aggregate level cost without having to model the more complex underlying physical systems individually.

Furthermore, we extend our modeling framework to support time-changing workloads by calculating incremental predictions of the execution latency for discrete mixes as they occur. When an incoming query is added to a mix, we project how it will impact the currently running queries as well as estimate the execution latency for the new addition. We extend this system to allow for longer-term resource planning by modeling a queue of queries.

This paper makes the following novel contributions:

- We argue and experimentally demonstrate that BAL, a simple metric that captures the latency of a logical I/O, is a robust indicator for query performance even in the presence of concurrency. BAL facilitates the modeling of the joint effects of physical I/O delay and memory contention with a single value, normalized over the execution of the query.
- We develop a multivariate regression model that predicts the impact of higher-degree concurrent query interactions derived primarily from isolated (degree-1) and pairwise (degree-2) concurrent execution samples.
- We show experimental results obtained from a PostgreSQL / TPC-H study that supports our claims and verifies the effectiveness of our predictive models. Our predictions are on the average within nearly 20% of the actual values, while timeline analysis leads to additional improvements, reducing our average error to an average of 9% with periodic prediction re-evaluation.

The rest of the paper is organized as follows. Section 2 looks at model building for query interactions by examining changes in logical I/O latency. After that we consider how to predict the logical I/O latency metric in Section 3. Next we examine training techniques for these models in Section 4. Immediately following in Section 5 we leverage these models to produce end-to-end latency estimates by simulating the lifetime of the query. Section 6 provides experimental evaluation of this work. In Section 7 we examine related work, and finally we conclude in Section 8.

2. QUERY LATENCY INDICATORS

The goal of our framework is to predict the response latency of concurrently running queries. Query latency is directly affected by resource contention in the underlying hardware. As the number of queries that are presently executing goes up their query latency increases as they share access to disk, CPU time as well as memory. Therefore our first step was to identify effective *query latency indicators*, i.e., metrics that can capture the resource contention in the underlying hardware and can be used to predict the latency of concurrent queries. In this section we discuss the various query latency indicators we examined. We also explore in more detail our most effective indicator, the *Buffer Access Latency (BAL)* metric. We continue with a brief description of our workload.

2.1 Analytical Workload

In this work we target analytical workloads. We assume that all queries are derived from a set of known query classes (e.g., TPC-H templates) and that they are primarily I/O-bound. We target medium-weight queries. For the context of this work, we define medium-weight queries as the 10 classes in TPC-H with latency on and around the median latency of all of query classes.

The query classes in our workload stress different parts of our system and the impact of concurrency on their latencies fluctuates at varying magnitudes. In Table 1, we study the variance of the 10 medium-weight TPC-H query classes. The tables shows the variance of query latency (and their average latency) when queries are executed in different multiprogramming levels (i.e., number of queries executing concurrently). We note that a multiprogramming level of x means that x queries run concurrently. For all queries,

Query Class	MPL 2	MPL 3	MPL 4	MPL 5
3	456 (141)	2663 (178)	2596 (214)	10750 (279)
4	398 (156)	1883 (199)	3564 (223)	5638 (279)
5	56 (129)	2219 (160)	3539 (198)	10424 (257)
6	345 (114)	160 (126)	1115 (160)	1666 (185)
7	343 (155)	2547 (197)	4595 (222)	9050 (307)
8	218 (136)	1231 (151)	7771 (225)	5236 (253)
10	126 (141)	2139 (203)	2699 (214)	6667 (270)
14	408 (117)	430 (126)	909 (159)	1681 (183)
18	98 (141)	2630 (186)	2044 (206)	18821 (312)
19	488 (119)	694 (147)	1637 (177)	1354 (192)

Table 1: Variance in observed latencies (in seconds) for different multiprogramming levels (MPLs). In parentheses are the average latencies under the same conditions.

their average latency increases as we increase the degree of concurrency. Moreover, the variance of latencies also increases. Some query classes, such as 7 and 18 exhibit much more uncertainty in their latency under concurrency. These queries are very I/O-bound and require complex data access patterns of cascading joins and aggregation. This causes them to be more sensitive to the queries they are running with because it causes them to speed up or slow down based on the amount of sharing that goes on among their working set. In contrast, query class 6 has a simple execution plan (consisting of a table scan and a light aggregate). In this work we formulate predictions for individual queries based on their template and the query mix(es) they are a part of.

2.2 I/O-Based Indicators

Our framework addresses concurrent query performance predictions for analytical queries. These workloads include mostly read-only operations and typically involve high number of I/O operations. Our first goal was to identify a metric that is strongly correlated with query latency of OLAP queries and can capture the impact of concurrency on the query performance. Since I/O operations are the dominant factor of query latency we aimed to identify query latency indicators that quantify how the cost of I/O operations changed due to concurrently running queries.

We can think of an I/O operation as a sequence of access methods. When fetching a page for a query, a request is first sent to the buffer pool which is the fastest way to access data. If the requested page is not found, the lookup is passed on to the OS-level cache, which is the second fastest option. Finally, if this fails, the request is enqueued for disk access to retrieve the block containing the requested data. This disk access may be a seek or a sequential read, causing the cost to access a data block to vary dramatically. Given this sequence of access methods, concurrency affects the number of I/O operations required by a query as multiple queries need to share the buffer pool and OS-level cache and the physical disk.

We hypothesized that *block reads* from disk, *buffer pool hits* and a *multivariate model* of the two would be well-correlated with latency. We experimented with using linear regression models for predicting query latency based on these metrics for different multiprogramming levels. Our results are shown in Table 2. Our experimental setup is detailed in Section 6.1. The table shows the prediction error for each of these metrics. In general, we found that these metrics were all disrupted from performing well by inherent variance in the latency of a block from disk. In the next paragraphs we discuss the limitations of each of these metrics.

I/O Block Reads. The first metric we considered was counting the number of physical blocks read by a query. If a query's execution speed is highly tied to how fast it can complete I/Os (since

Query	I/O Blocks	BP Hits	Both	BAL
Avg	25%	25%	24%	5%
3	29%	29%	28%	5%
4	24%	25%	24%	6%
5	30%	30%	29%	3%
6	17%	17%	15%	3%
7	26%	27%	25%	4%
8	26%	27%	24%	3%
10	28%	29%	28%	6%
14	21%	21%	17%	3%
18	27%	26%	30%	12%
19	22%	22%	20%	3%

Table 2: Mean relative error ($\frac{|observed-prediction|}{observed}$) of I/O-based latency indicators trained at MPL 1-5.

reads from memory have low impact on the latency), then the number of blocks read could give us an indicator of how much query progress has been accomplished over time and how much time it requires to complete.

Table 2 shows that the latency prediction based on blocks read has an error less than 29% in most cases. This implies that there is a correlation between number of blocks read in a query's execution time and the query's latency. However, for certain query classes, such as 3 and 5, this prediction is weaker. The prediction is less strongly correlated because these queries spent considerable time on their CPUs, and during that time they relinquish control over the I/O bandwidth. These CPU-intensive query plans cause the queries to be more sensitive to the degree of overlap between their working set and that of the queries that they are executing alongside of. This is because the queries frequently make short data accesses punctuated by longer periods of CPU usage. Thus if the disk arm remains roughly in the same region that they are executing from, the cost of an I/O will remain relatively uniform. But if the data access patterns are more random, this uncertainty will be reflected in the cost of an I/O operation.

Buffer Pool Hits. We also studied if the buffer pool hits could be used as query latency indicator. Our assumption was that the latency overhead of disk access may be relatively fixed and that we could subtract the I/O operations saved by each buffer pool hit from this base overhead to estimate the query latency. We found that this metric was correlated with latency, but the prediction errors were similar to those of the I/O block reads indicator. There were a number of factors contributed to this, including the fact that the overall system has multiple layers of in-memory storage (i.e., buffer pool, OS cache) and so it was difficult to infer the savings due to memory. Also, these savings did not adequately capture the changing behavior of I/O operations, i.e., the physical blocks read and written. The mix of seeks and sequential reads was not fixed, making it harder to obtain consistently good predictions.

I/O Block Reads & Buffer Pool Hits. Finally, we experimented with multivariate regression on both of these metrics. Our assumption in this case was that these two metrics would complement each other since buffer pool hits replace disk reads (i.e., a hit to the buffer pool allows us to skip a disk access). Table 2 show that this model did not significantly improve our prediction errors.

The results in Table 2 demonstrate that the number of physical I/O blocks read and buffer pool hits are moderately correlated with query latency. This is primarily because there is a high degree of variance with regard to how long it takes to bring an individual block in from disk. If the block is a part of a sequential read, then it may occur quickly. However seeks are highly variable in their cost. Physical I/O latency per block is proportional to the distance that

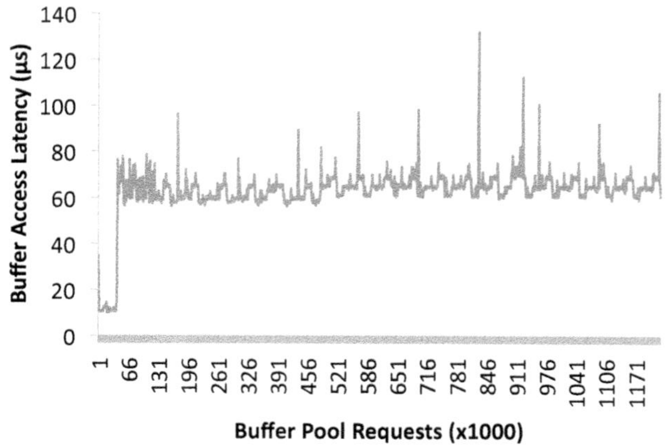

Figure 1: BAL as it changes over time for TPC-H Query 14. Averaged over 5 examples of the template in isolation.

the disk arm moves to fetch a target block. Thus in practice, the speed of reading an individual block of data can vary by up to an order of magnitude. This causes both the I/O count and buffer pool hits to have distorted latency predictions as they model the average I/O latency, when the quantity has an unknown (and routinely changing) distribution.

2.3 Buffer Access Latency (BAL) as an Indicator

We found that handling each of block access methods individually had limited utility because the interactions were too complex. To simplify the problem, we identified the initial request to the buffer pool as a gateway that all queries must go through to receive their data. When a query requests a block of data, it submits its request to the buffer pool manager. When the buffer pool receives a request it queries its levels of storage one after another until it acquires the needed disk block. The time that elapses on average between when a request is issued and when the necessary block is returned constitutes the average delay for a *logical I/O request*.

Therefore, rather than modeling each the steps of a buffer pool request independently, we use the average latency of a logical I/O operation as our query latency indicator. We call this metric *buffer access latency* or *BAL*. Averaging this metric over the duration of a query allows us to capture the interactions of disk seeks, sequential reads, OS cache hits and buffer pool hits in a normalized manner.

Each average BAL is typically an aggregate of more than a million logical I/O requests, so this allows us to infer changes in the mix of I/O types (sequential reads, seeks, etc.) for individual queries. A low average BAL when the query runs in isolation implies that we have a lightweight query that reads most of its data from memory. In contrast, high BAL readings mean that a query is requesting diverse data that is not memory-resident such as a fact table scan or an index scan, necessitating expensive seeks.

To measure the BAL metric we modified the database engine we used (PostgreSQL 8.4.3). Specifically, we intercepted the point in the buffer pool manager where the query executor issues page requests. A timer starts when the request is issued to the buffer pool. If the page is not found, then the process refers the request to the storage manager, which interfaces with the disk and operating system. The timer stops when the requisite page is returned to the query executor, regardless of its source. To generate the BAL metric, we sum up the time elapsed for each page request and divide it by the logical number of pages accessed by our query plan. In Table 2 we examine the quality of BAL in comparison to the other

I/O-based indicators we studied to predict latency. Our prediction errors drop to around 3%-6% in most cases.

One of the reasons that BAL is a good indicator for latency is because it is averaged over many samples over the lifetime of a query. Thus, even when a query goes through very complex interactions with the OS as well as other queries, it will still converge to an accurate prediction of the overall latency.

In Figure 1 we display how the typical values of BAL vary through the lifetime of a query when run in isolation. All of our BAL measurements are averages of 1000 buffer pool requests. This particular query (of TPC-H template 14) goes through a brief period of low latency in BAL while the query is warming up (i.e., it is loading all of the database binaries). It then reaches a relatively stable state where it is continuously reading blocks and joining tuples. The BAL periodically fluctuates as the query cycles through seeks and sequential reads in the course of a join. When we consider all of the queries in our workload the average standard deviation was around 33% of the query's BAL average. This variance can be attributed to the inherent noisiness of the metrics BAL is capturing (i..e, a mixture of buffer pool reads, seeks and sequential physical I/Os). BAL is a robust metric because it captures the aggregate of these complex interactions over many logical page requests, converging on a stable average behavior.

2.4 Predicting Query Latency using BAL (B2L)

We used a linear regression model to predict the end-to-end query latency using the BAL metric. The intuition is that an I/O-bound query will have latency directly proportional to how long it waits for a logical I/O on average plus some relatively fixed overhead for CPU time and fixed database support. So if the average BAL for a query α is B_α and O_α is its fixed CPU overhead then the latency of the query α L is given by the equation:

$$L = O_\alpha + P_\alpha \times B_\alpha \quad (1)$$

Our system finds the fixed overhead of each query class and this comprises the y-intercept (O_α) of the model. The P_α coefficient allows us to model the number of logical page requests required by the query plan. Therefore, if the average latency of a logical I/O (i.e., the BAL metric) of a query running in a query mix is known, we can predict its latency using the above model. We call this end-to-end latency prediction model *BAL to Latency* or *B2L*.

We use the coefficient of determination (R^2) to assess the goodness of fit of the model to the data. R^2 is a normalized measure that relates the error of the model to the overall variance of the data set. It ranges from 0 to 1, with higher values denoting a better fit. It captures the error of the model, SS_{err}, by calculating the sum-squared errors of each data point in the training set, normalized by the total variability of the data, SS_{tot}, calculated by taking the sum of squared deviations of the individual data points from the mean. R^2 is calculated as $1 - SS_{err}/SS_{tot}$.

The strength of this above model is demonstrated in its R^2 values for each query class in our training set. We train on an average 259 examples of each template. The R^2 coefficients varied from 0.83-0.99 for the 10 queries in our TPC-H workload; all of our queries were very well-fitted by this model.

We found that TPC-H templates conform well to this model. Queries within the same class rarely change their query execution plan. We capture this consistency with the slope of our linear model. In practice, we found that our query templates did not have their I/O request count vary by greater than 5%, despite operating with range predicates and indices. In some cases, such as a skewed data distribution or a highly varying range predicate, we would need to create multiple models per query template. In that case, we would subdivide our templates into predicate ranges as described in [1].

More details of our experiments are shown in Section 6. In summary, BAL was our strongest query performance indicator. In the next section, we discuss how this metric can be predicted for concurrent workloads.

3. BUFFER ACCESS LATENCY PREDICTION

As we explored in the previous section, the average buffer access latency of a query is a consistent indicator of its latency throughout changing query mixes and concurrency levels. In this section, we propose a technique for predicting this metric by modeling the interactions of query templates based on observations among pairs. At a high level, we aim to quantify how a query's performance changes as it shares resources with competing processes. To capture this effect, we first characterize how a query class runs in isolation. We then extrapolate how interacting with other query classes impacts its performance.

3.1 Modeling Query Interactions

To predict the concurrent performance for a query class, we need to quantify its average BAL metric under contention. In this section we create a prediction model for BAL for light-to-moderate levels of query contention. We start by examining (a) the resource utilization of a query class under optimal conditions (i.e., queries running in isolation), and (b) the resources that concurrent queries will expect to consume. For our purposes, resource needs refer primarily to the I/O bandwidth and memory used, whose joint effects are captured by the BAL of each query. We estimate how much these queries will contend with each other on a template-by-template basis, by examining how their BAL is affected when they are interacting in pairs.

For example, when TPC-H Query 6 is run with Query 14, both enjoy a speedup of about 10 seconds on average. This is because both of their query execution plans are dominated by sequential scans on the fact table. In contrast, when Q19 is run with Q7, they slow down by approximately 50% and 30% respectively. In this case, the two queries share less overlap in their working sets and both require significant memory to do expensive joins.

To better characterize how queries interact, we first looked at all pairwise interactions. For a workload of n queries, we executed all unique combinations (a total of 55 pairwise combinations in our case of 10 query classes). These pairings allowed us to characterize the magnitude and sign (positive or negative to denote slow down or speed up respectively) of how each query affects others in the workload. We also studied the incremental utility of building our model on multiple, higher-degree interactions, which did not yield any consistent or notable improvements while being more expensive. Hence, we concluded that models based on pairwise interactions, enhanced with additional statistics, strike a good balance between practicality and accuracy.

Specifically, by analyzing how pairs affect each other, we model the BAL at higher degrees of concurrency. We do this by building a composite of the BAL based on a base cost of the individual BALs of the queries in isolation. We then incorporate the cost of interactions indicated by the change in BAL due to direct and indirect interactions among the queries. We use this pairwise interaction rate and isolated runs to build our multivariate regression model. We call this BAL estimation model *BALs to concurrent BAL* or *B2cB*, which we describe in detail next.

Variables	R^2
I	0.167
I & C	0.169
I & C & D	0.219
I & C & D & G	0.358

Table 3: R^2 values for different BAL prediction models (variables: Isolated (I), Complement Sum (C), Direct (D), Indirect (G)) Training on multiprogramming level 3.

3.1.1 *Predicting BAL Under Concurrency*

In our model for predicting the concurrent BAL we distinguish between *primary* and *complement* queries. When we predict the concurrent BAL of a query, we call it the *primary*. Queries that are running concurrently with the primary are its *complements*. The intuition behind our model is that when we are dealing with a non-overloaded state, the cost of contention increases linearly and is a function of fixed costs for each query in the mix as well as variable costs for each pairwise interaction among the queries (divided into direct and indirect interaction with the primary query). For example, if we assume round-robin scheduling, then the cost (i.e., delay) to obtain a data block with concurrency (i.e., its concurrent BAL) equals to the cost to obtain a data block when no concurrent queries exist, plus the cost of one average page read of each of the complement concurrent queries, plus any observed interaction cost among all of the queries in the workload.

Our BAL prediction model has the following four independent variables provided from training data:

- *Isolated*: This variable represents the BAL of the primary query when it is run in isolation. Examining isolated BAL creates a baseline to assess the concurrent BAL. It provides us the default page access time for the primary query under optimal circumstances. We denote the isolated BAL of a query i as T_i.

- *Complement*: Similarly, we need to consider the resource requirements of the complement queries in our mix. The complement variable is the sum of complement queries' isolated BALs. Summing the BAL of the complements allows us to build an estimate of the rate at which they consume I/O bandwidth given fair scheduling. This is a rough estimate of the "cost" of complement queries.

- *Direct*: This variable is the sum of the change in BAL for the primary when paired with each of its complements. The direct variable captures the change in the primary's BAL from direct query interactions. We quantify a direct query interaction $T_{i/j}$ as the average BAL of query i measured while running concurrently with query j. The change in this measurement is $\Delta T_{i/j} = T_{i/j} - T_i$. If this quantity is positive, we are experiencing slowdown. If it is negative, then we have a beneficial interaction between queries.

- *Indirect*: Finally we examine the change in BAL between the complement queries. This gives us a glimpse into how much contention they are creating and how much their interaction will affect the primary query. Note that their interactions may not be symmetrical ($\Delta T_{i/j} \neq \Delta T_{j/i}$). For example, an equi-join requires dedicated memory to complete its comparisons efficiently. If it is run concurrently with a table scan, the table scan will not be as affected by the join because it uses each tuple only once. The scanning query disproportionately affects the latency of the joining query due to it having access to less memory. We define the indirect variable as the sum of the change in BAL for each complement when run with each other complement.

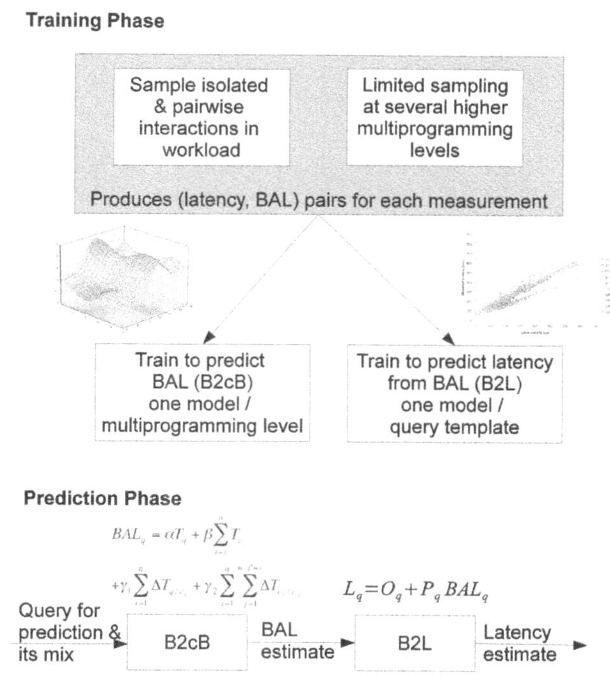

Figure 2: System model for query latency predictions of arbitrary mixes.

We found that all of these independent variables were necessary to build a complete model. As Table 3 demonstrates, the quality of our prediction model, as measured by the R^2 coefficient, improves significantly once we start considering isolated costs with interactions. Moreover, the sum-squared error is improved by greater than 50% when solving for four variables rather than relying solely on the isolated BAL.

We predict average concurrent BAL for query q while running concurrently with its complement $c_1..c_n$ as:

$$B = \alpha T_q + \beta \sum_{i=1}^{n} T_{c_i} + \gamma_1 \sum_{i=1}^{n} \Delta T_{q/c_i} + \gamma_2 \sum_{i=1}^{n} \sum_{j=1}^{n,j!=i} \Delta T_{c_i/c_j} \tag{2}$$

We solve for the coefficients α, β, γ_1 and γ_2 using linear multivariate regression for all queries in our training set, once per each multiprogramming level. We elect to do this regression at this granularity to model several degrees of contention. The regression derives our coefficients using the least sum-squared error method.

Predicting end-to-end latency. The lower portion of Figure 2 demonstrates the steps of our predicting end-to-end query latency for varying concurrency levels. Given a query and its mix of complements, we can rapidly create an average concurrent BAL estimate using the B2cB model. The concurrent B2cB is the input to our B2L model which provides the final latency estimate.

To provide a more concrete example, if we are predicting the BAL of query a and it is being run with queries b and c, we start out with the following inputs:

- T_a, T_b, T_c - the average isolated BAL of a, b and c.
- $\Delta T_{a/b}, \Delta T_{a/c}$, etc. - change in BAL of a when run with b or c ($\Delta T_{a/b} = T_{a/b} - T_a$)

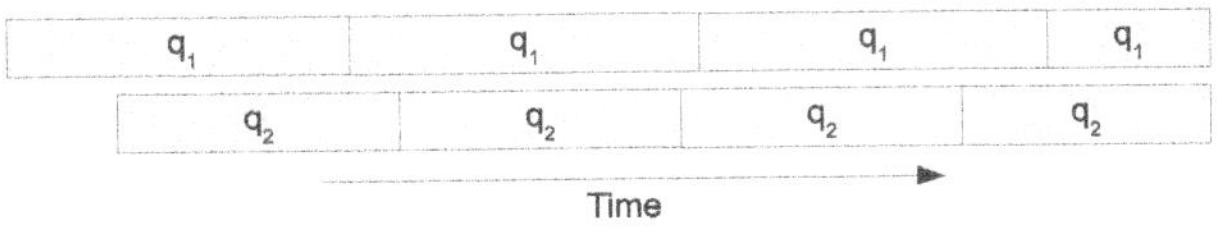

Figure 3: An example of steady state sampling for queries q_1 and q_2.

We predict the average BAL B_a of query a using Equation 2:

$$B_a = \alpha T_a + \beta(T_b + T_c) + \gamma_1(\Delta T_{a/b} + \Delta T_{a/c}) + \gamma_2(\Delta T_{b/c} + \Delta T_{c/b})$$

Then, we can predict the end-to-end query latency using Equation 1. We would apply the coefficient P_a, or the logical page coefficient for this query class and O_a, the fixed overhead for a. We would then predict our end-to-end latency by calculating:

$$L = O_a + P_a \times B_a$$

4. TRAINING THE PREDICTION MODELS

To obtain performance estimates, we need to train our prediction models. The training phase consists of running our workload in isolation, pairs as well as at several higher multiprogramming levels. This provides the coefficients for evaluating our B2L and B2cB prediction models. All of our samples are used to train both prediction systems.

To model query interactions flexibly, we must summarize their effects in a way that is agnostic to the offsets of individual query start times and representative of the variations within a query template. We model this by temporarily fixing the mix in which a query is participating and randomizing the offset at which each query starts. We call this measurement *steady state*. Steady state sampling allows us to reason about how a query will react to a continuous level of contention and a fixed set of complements. An example of steady state is shown in Figure 3

Furthermore, in order to obtain measurements that capture only interactions, our experiments are based on *warm cache*. i.e., we omit the first few samples. This allows us ignore to the overhead of the initial query set up and caching of small supporting structures This approach also allows us to sample the changing interactions from queries overlapping at different phases in their execution.

In the next paragraphs, we describe how we obtain our training set for the two prediction models (B2L and B2cB) which we described in the previous sections.

4.1 Sampling-Based Training Sets

In our framework we build our prediction model by sampling a subset of the configurations for which we are creating predictions. Experiment-driven modeling allows us to approximate the landscape of how queries in a workload interact. Our model samples queries in isolation, pairwise and higher degrees of concurrency for training. The use of our training runs are displayed in Figure 2.

First we characterize the workload that we have in terms of how each query behaves in isolation. This baseline allows us to get an estimate of what constitutes normal, unimpeded progress for a query class and how much we are speeding up or slowing down as new queries are added to the mix. In our experiments we average over many examples of each query class running in isolation with a warm cache and we record both the latency and BAL metric for each query class. The BAL-latency pair is used in the training of the B2L latency prediction model as well as as input for the first two terms of the B2cB model.

Next, we build a matrix of interactions by running all unique pairwise combinations, 55 in our case. This allows us to succinctly estimate the degree of contention that each query class in a workload puts on every potential complement. As with our isolated measurements, we get both end-to-end latency as well as average BAL measurements for all of these combinations. These BAL-latency pairs are used for training the B2L model. In addition, they are used as inputs by the B2cB model to estimate BAL.

Query	1	2	3	4	5
1		X			
2					X
3	X				
4			X		
5				X	

Figure 4: An example of 2-D Latin hypercube sampling.

This moderate number of samples is necessary for both our BAL and latency predictions. The pairwise interactions provide us with inputs for the independent variables of B2cB. They also give us our input for our B2L model. B2L builds upon many concurrency levels in order to plot how latency grows as contention increases. Each multiprogramming level helps us complete the model.

Next, we build our model coefficients for interactions of degree greater than two. We sample at this level using Latin hypercube sampling (LHS). LHS uniformly distributes our sample selection throughout our prediction space. This is done by creating a hypercube with the same dimensionality as our multiprogramming level. We then select our samples such that every value on every plane gets intersected exactly once. Each sampling run of this technique produces at most n combinations, where n is the number of unique queries in our workload. A simple example of Latin hypercube sampling is shown in Figure 4. These sample runs are used to create the coefficients for B2cB at each multiprogramming level. We do multivariate B2cB linear regression on a set of Latin hypercube sampled data points.

LHS is a general sampling technique and is not a perfect fit for exploring this space of all possible query combinations. LHS does not take into account the difference between combinations and permutations when exploring our sampling space. For example, to the sampler, the combination of (3, 4) and (4, 3) would both be considered distinct samples. From the database's point of view they are both simply one instance of Q3 and one instance of Q4 running concurrently. We eliminated LHS in which the same combination appears more than once from our training set because each run produces data for all queries involved (i.e., when we execute mix (3,4), we record data for both Q3 and Q4).

For our training phase we used this sampling technique three times for each concurrency level. Experimentally we found that as more samples were taken we naturally get a more comprehensive picture of the cost of contention in our system. On the other hand, more sampling takes more time. We found that three LHS runs for each multiprogramming level was a good trade off between these competing objectives. Acquiring more samples did not improve our prediction accuracy.

Each LHS run consists of ten steady state combinations, resulting in 30 training combinations sampled for each multiprogramming level. Initially this may seem like many samples, but it is not that many in comparison to all possible combinations. This is especially true for higher multiprogramming levels where our set of combinations grows exponentially every time we add a query. The complexity of our training space does grow significantly as our workload becomes more complex. If we are training on a set of n queries, we must first execute it in isolation, incorporate it into all pairs and higher level sampling. For pairs, we sample all combinations with replacement, producing $(n^2 + n)/2$ steady state runs.

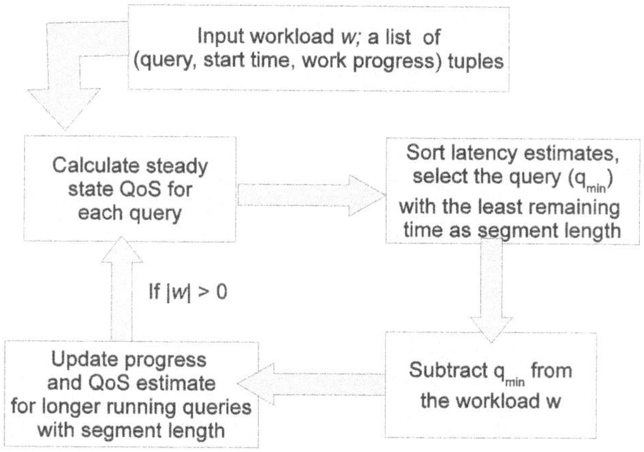

Figure 5: Just-in-Time evaluation flowchart

If we sample m multiprogramming levels greater than two and we run l LHS samples, our number of required training runs can be calculated as $n + (n^2 + n)/2 + lmn$. In our case, this comes to 155 sampled combinations.

In practice, the total training period took approximately two days in our modest setup. This may seem like considerable time, but we are only required to train once and can then use the results for any arbitrary mixes indefinitely. It is also worth noting that this up-front training period is what allows our model to be extremely lightweight once it reaches the evaluation phase (i.e., when it is producing query latency estimates). The cost of creating an estimate is negligible once the model is trained. It is only the cost of applying the B2cB model (summing the primary, complement, direct and indirect I/O contributions) and providing the output to a B2L model ($L = O_\alpha + P_\alpha * B_\alpha$).

5. TIMELINE ANALYSIS: PERFORMANCE PREDICTION FOR CHANGING MIXES

Using the B2cB and B2L methods we can predict the latency of individual queries being executed if the mix does not change during a query's execution. This system is useful for simple cases, where we only want an estimate for how long a query will run in a very homogeneous mix. However, in most circumstances the query mix over which we are evaluating is constantly changing as new queries are submitted by users and pre-existing ones terminate at varying intervals. For example, in a production system, managers and other decision-makers submit queries when they are at work and would benefit from an estimated time of arrival for the results. With modeling we can give them real time feedback of how long a new query will run and how much it will affect their currently executing workload using "what-if"-style analysis.

This type of system necessitates an incremental evaluation of a larger set of circumstances. We need to consider all of the mixes that will happen during a query's execution as the number and/or type of complement queries varies. This system must quantify the slowdown (or speedup) caused by these mixes, and estimate what percentage of the query's work will be accomplished in each mix.

We propose two formulations for evaluating our predictions. In the first scenario new queries are being submitted for immediate execution. We refer to this as *just-in-time (JIT) modeling (JIT)*. In JIT the number of queries monotonically decreases as members of the currently executing batch completes. In the second scenario we consider a queue-based approach, where our system is given a fixed multiprogramming level and an ordered list of queries to run. In this case we also model the mixes that will occur, by projecting when queries from the queue will start during the query's execution. Next, we describe these modeling scenarios.

5.1 Just-in-Time Modeling

Just-in-Time modeling allows us to ask the questions: "If I schedule a query now, how long will it take? How will it affect the presently running queries' completion times?" JIT estimates are more flexible in that they support more than one multiprogramming level in our estimate and model real-time changes in the workload.

Also, this more incremental approach allows us to refine our estimates as time progresses. As we predict latency every time a query is added we can correct past estimates by examining how the query has progressed since we last forecasted its end-to-end latency. In the context of an SLA, this may allow us to prevent QoS violations from happening by giving us the ability to intervene and load balance as time passes. Experimentally we saw an average approximately 10% error in our QoS estimates with this approach.

This JIT modeling requires estimates of the latency for each query in each mix and the percentage of its execution time each mix will occupy. The JIT algorithm is charted in Figure 5. In our timeline-based QoS estimator, first we look at the progress of all the n queries that are presently executing in a mix. We create a list of the time that has elapsed since each presently executing query began and initialize our performance estimate with this quantity. We also record the number of logical I/O requests that have been serviced for each query. This second metric gives us an estimate of what percentage of the query's work has been completed.

Next we must look at the estimated QoS for each query in the proposed mix, operating under the temporary assumption that the mix does not change. We can use the techniques in the previous section to create end-to-end latency estimates for each query in the workload under these steady state conditions. This first estimates BAL using the B2cB prediction model, which we then translate into latency using B2L model. We multiply the steady state estimate by the percentage of the query that we project remains based on the number of logical I/Os serviced.

After this we sort the steady state estimates and pick the query with the minimum remaining time as our first *segment* of evaluation. This defines the period over which we evaluate our first discrete mix. We select this query q_{min} and its estimated latency l_{min} as the time when our mix state will change next. We subtract q_{min} from the mix and we update the progress of each query q that is not equal to q_{min} by taking the ratio of l_{min}/l_q and multiplying it by the logical I/O requests remaining. We also add l_{min} to our estimate for each query in the workload that is not terminating. Finally, we subtract q_{min} from our workload because we project that it will have ended at this prediction point. We keep iteratively predicting and eliminating the query with the least time remaining until we have completed our estimates for all queries in the workload.

To summarize, we start with n queries and project a completion time for each in n segments. Each segment contains one less query than the previous segment as we subtract the query that we forecast will terminate next. At each concurrency level greater than two, we use our B2cB and B2L models to create QoS estimates. For isolated and pairwise cases we use the latencies recorded during the training phase.

5.2 Queue Modeler

Another scenario under which this system is be useful is for estimating how long a query will take if we have a fixed multiprogramming level. In [14] the authors discussed how multiprogramming level is a common "knob" for optimizing DBMS performance while scheduling concurrent resources. In this formulation,

Algorithm 1 Queue modeling algorithm where q_p is the primary query, p_i is the progress of query i, R_i is the number of logical page requests for i. Iterating over all queries in workload w

```
q_min = ∅, t = 0
while q_min ≠ q_p do
    for each q_i in w do
        l_i = EstimateTimeRemaining(q_i, p_r, w)
    end for
    w = sort(l, q) // sort to find the query with the lowest remaining time estimate
    t+ = l_0 // add minimum time to primary's estimate
    for i = 1; i ≤ |w|; ++i do
        p_i+ = (l_0/l_i) * (R_i − p_i)
    end for
    w_0 = get_queue_next() // replace the query with the least remaining time with the next one in the queue
end while
return t;
```

we model our changing mix by looking ahead in the queue when we project that our current mix will end. We refer to this scenario as a *Queue Modeler (QM)*.

The Queue Modeler requires access to a queue of queries submitted. QM works very similarly to JIT predictions, except it examines the currently executing workload and models the addition of the next query in the queue as a replacement when a current query will terminate. This system allows us to give an end-to-end estimate of progress without starting the execution of some of the queries that are included in our prediction.

The Queue Modeler is shown in Algorithm 1. Queue modeling starts with a list of status information for each presently executing query, much like JIT. This too is a pair of the query execution time and the progress the query has made in terms of logical I/O requests. We add the new query to the list (q_p) with its progress and current latency at zero. Next we model the steady state latency of each query in the mix and sort the resulting estimates of latency remaining. The query with the least projected time remaining, q_{min}, is estimated to continue running for l_{min} time. Next we update the progress of the remaining queries by taking the ratio of l_{min} to their projected time remaining. We update their latency estimate by adding q_{min}'s projected completion time to model the amount of time that the query will remain in this mix. Finally we replace q_{min} with the next one on the queue. We continue this cycle until the query for which where are creating a prediction is q_{min}.

6. EXPERIMENTAL EVALUATION

In this section we set out to verify the accuracy and utility of the four modules in our framework. First we look at the accuracy of B2L, or how well our experiment-driven model can use buffer access latency to predict end-to-end query latency under varying concurrency levels and query mixes. Next, we examine how well our B2cB model can predict BAL for use with B2L. After that we explore the accuracy of combining these two techniques to produce end-to-end latency estimates. Finally, we experiment with creating prediction on random, dynamically generated workloads at a fixed multiprogramming level using our JIT and queue modeler timeline analysis techniques.

We gathered data in two phases for our steady state experiments. Initially, we create our training data consisting of several steady state mixes. Our training set draws from samples at multiprogramming levels 1-5. Using the training data set we build our prediction models for the concurrent buffer access latency (B2cB) and the end-to-end latency (B2L). The details of this training process are in Section 4. B2cB produces coefficients for the multivariate prediction model for each multiprogramming level. B2L produces its simple linear model for each query class.

Next we looked at a test data set, consisting of randomly selected mixes that are disjoint from the training data. Our test data set is drawn from two Latin hypercube sample sets per multiprogramming level, producing 20 steady state measurements. Each steady state measurement is comprised of at least 5 queries per template in the mix.

Finally, we experimented with completely arbitrary mixes, relaxing our steady state assumption. This allowed us to evaluate our timeline analysis. Here we looked at both incremental re-evaluation of our predictions (JIT) as well as creating only one prediction when each query started (queue modeler).

6.1 Setup

We experimented with a TPC-H query workload consisting of moderate weight queries that exert strain on different parts of the database system. We targeted OLAP because the queries are longer running, giving us a more time to characterize their interactions. Analytical queries tend to be more highly I/O-bound, allowing us to focus on this element for our interaction modeling rather than a more complex multidimensional model that would have to take into account CPU slicing and other resource sharing.

We worked with a mix of ten moderate weight queries. Specifically, our workload is comprised of TPC-H queries 3, 4, 5, 6, 7, 8, 10, 14, 18 and 19 on an instance of TPC-H, scale factor 10. We selected the ten queries on and around the median execution time for all of the TPC-H templates. We focus on medium-weight queries because they are long running enough such that we can make useful inferences about their behavior. They are also light enough to allow for us to experiment with meaningful multiprogramming levels.

Furthermore, we wanted to predict realistic workloads. We study concurrent query mixes of different multiprogramming levels, however we do not address predictions for cases of very high contention. Therefore, we do not consider cases where it is likely that a mix of queries could complete all of their executions in isolation faster than running its queries concurrently.

We also elected to focus on moderate-weight queries because modeling across multiple query weights adds another layer to the problem as demonstrated in [8]. In this work they classified their queries according to a relative weight and built models for each group. In future work, we may extend our framework with a similar labeling strategy.

In our experimental configuration we added the primary key indexes provided by the standard TPC-H implementation. The benchmark was deployed on a modified version of PostgreSQL 8.4.3. The source code was instrumented to measure BAL. All of our trials were run on a machine with an Intel i7 2.8 GHz processors and 8 GB of RAM. The machine ran on Ubuntu 9.04 on Linux 2.6.28-11.

6.2 Predicting Query Contention

In this section we will look at how well our B2cB and B2L system can predict BAL and end-to-end latency. All of the results below are evaluated on our test data, disjoint from the training samples.

6.2.1 B2L

First we examine the effectiveness of B2L for estimating latency based on a provided BAL. We built our linear models for each query class on our training set at multiprogramming levels 1-5. Our train-

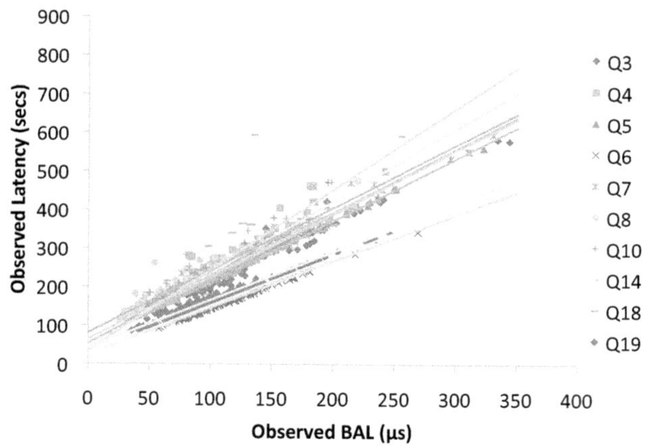

Figure 6: Fit of B2L to steady state data at multiprogramming levels 3-5. Error rates for this data are in Table 2

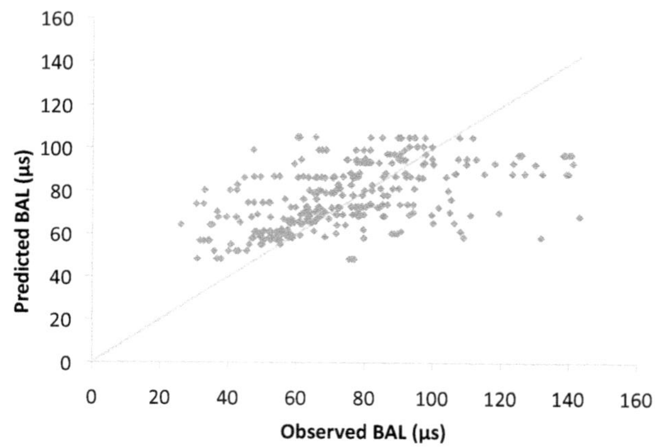

Figure 7: B2cB predictions on steady state data, multiprogramming level 3

ing phase produces simple equations of the form $L = O_\alpha + P_\alpha * B_\alpha$ for each query class in our workload.

We demonstrate the fit of our model with Figure 6. The points on this graph are all from individual queries of our test data set with concurrency levels 3-5. The lines denote the slope of an individual B2L model. Each query class fits very well with its regression model. Our evaluation data produced an average error of just 5%. This tight fit is because queries generally will have latency proportional to the rate at which they can access physical pages. This shows that despite relatively few mixes sampled and varying concurrency levels, buffer access latency is an efficient and robust estimator of query latency. To reiterate, none of the points evaluated here were a part of the training phase.

It is clear that our B2L models fall into two main trajectories. These different slopes are a consequence of our query templates having different query execution plan layouts. Query plans can be divided into processing pipelines. These pipelines delineate points in the query execution where results from the previous pipeline must be completed before the next phase of a query may start. For example, sorts require access to all of the tuples in their operation and thus require that executor start a new pipeline for them (separate from the operators that provided tuples to the sort). In future work, we may consider breaking our predictions down to the granularity of pipelines as was done for progress estimators in [7].

The queries with smaller latency growth (queries 6, 14 and 19) had a single pipeline (i.e., no materialization points such as sorts or group-by aggregates). The remaining query classes which demonstrated a faster latency increase in proportion to their BAL generally had greater than one pipeline in their query plans. This means that the overall growth rate for each BAL is higher, due to the overhead of the tuples having to traverse multiple pipelines and typically be evaluated by more operators in the query plan.

6.2.2 *B2cB*

Now that we have established that average BAL is a good predictor of latency in the case of varying resource contention, we turn to evaluating how well we can predict this metric. We examine the accuracy of the B2cB approach for predicting average BAL on the test data set.

The fit of B2cB predictions to measured BAL at multiprogramming level 3 in is displayed in Figure 7. This charts all of the queries in the test mixes in steady state. There were a total of 20 steady state mixes sampled for this experiment.

Our samples create a uniform fit around the trend line, denoting that the model can make reasonable "ballpark estimates" of BAL. There is some variance within queries of the same class and mix. Much of this can attributed to buffer pool contents and changing predicates for each example of a query template.

Another cause of variance is temporal shifts (i.e., queries in the same mix start at different times in relation to their complements). These shifts are displays as horizontal lines of points on this graph. We have experimented with breaking our queries into sections and evaluating our predictions on this finer-grained basis. Experimentally we did not find significant improvements by evaluating these queries on a section-by-section basis. We also found that sampling to quantify all pairs at this granularity caused our training time to grow significantly.

Also, our model works best at low–to moderate–levels of contention. As contention increases (denoted by a higher observed BAL), our estimates have reduced accuracy. This is because as we get closer to a state of overload, our growth pattern gradually shifts from linear to exponential. Modeling overload and the shift in our distribution of BAL is left to future work.

In summary, our B2cB estimates had an average error of 24-35%. As we increased our multiprogramming level, our estimates became slightly less accurate as we neared a state of overload.

6.3 Steady State Predictions

Next we examine our ability to predict end-to-end latency under steady state conditions by composing our BAL estimates with B2L. For each query in a steady state run we first predict the BAL using B2cB. Then we translate this predicted BAL to latency using the B2L models depicted in Figure 6. We hold the mix constant to allow us to model discrete mixes despite the underlying queries having different execution latencies. We will later quantify the additional challenges posed by continuously changing query mixes.

In Figure 8 we assess our model's accuracy on the test data. We divide our findings into query classes and also averaged overall. We tested this system for multiprogramming levels 3-5. The figure shows our relative error, calculated as: $\frac{|recordedQoS - prediction|}{recordedQoS}$.

For reference, we include the standard deviation for each query in each mix. This is normalized to the average latency of the sample that it came from. This is to quantify the variance-inducing conditions caused by temporal offsets and changes in our template predicates. It is averaged over multiprogramming levels 3-5.

At multiprogramming level 3, our error rate roughly equals to the average standard deviation. Our error averages to 15%, which is well-fitted considering the variety of cases handled (20 discrete

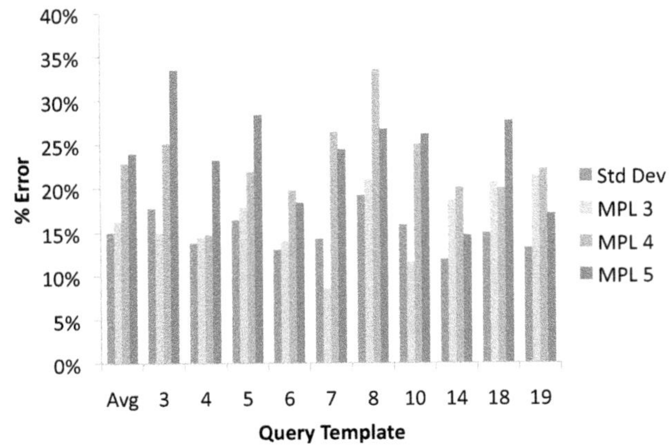

Figure 8: Steady state relative prediction errors for query latency at multiprogramming levels 3-5

mixes times 3 queries per mix). Queries that have relatively simple, highly I/O dominated plans such as Q6 are modeled well. Queries that have more complex aggregation are more reliant on prefetching and consequently are sensitive to the temporal offsets of their complements. Examples of this phenomenon include Q3 and Q5. Later we will discuss the effects of relaxing this steady state assumption.

6.4 Timeline Evaluation

Next we evaluate how well our timeline approaches estimates individual query latency. Once again, we experimented with three multiprogramming levels. We ran 250 randomly generated queries (both the template and predicates were selected in this manner). These measurements excluded a warmup and cool down period for each run to allow our multiprogramming level to remain constant. All of these results are from the same set of query executions, processed for both JIT and queue modeling timeline analysis.

JIT predictions produce a latency estimate for all queries currently executing when a new query is started. We use this technique to simulate the scenario where users are submitting queries that are run immediately. This system will enable the user to estimate how long a new query will take and its projected impact on currently running queries' latencies. In this context, we work from the scenario where the user has no way of predicting the incoming workload. Thus we re-evaluate our latency predictions every time a new query is introduced into the mix.

This technique also allows us to do real-time "course corrections" for our estimates. We can see how our prediction errors converge as time passes for the JIT technique in Figure 9. Our predictions naturally follow a half-cone shaped distribution. The closer a query is to completion, the better our predictions are. We could improve our readings further by evaluating more frequently, perhaps at regular intervals rather than when we are scheduling a new query. This would be useful if we are (for example) updating a real-time progress indicator for users who are awaiting query results or running real-time load balancing.

With the JIT estimator our average error is around 10%. This is a combination of having good latency estimates paired with corrections from the re-evaluations. This is the reason that the higher multiprogramming levels generally perform better; they re-evaluate more frequently as they schedule queries at a faster rate.

This outcome demonstrates that we can (a) give users real-time guidance about how scheduling decisions will affect currently running queries as well as ones that they are considering scheduling; and (b) we can make predictions with arbitrary mixes. Thus we are not limited by our initial steady state configuration. The ability to

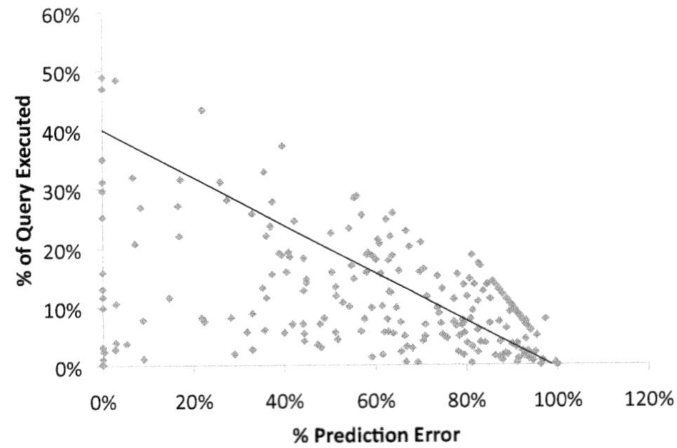

Figure 9: JIT prediction errors as we re-evaluate queries periodically at multiprogramming level 3.

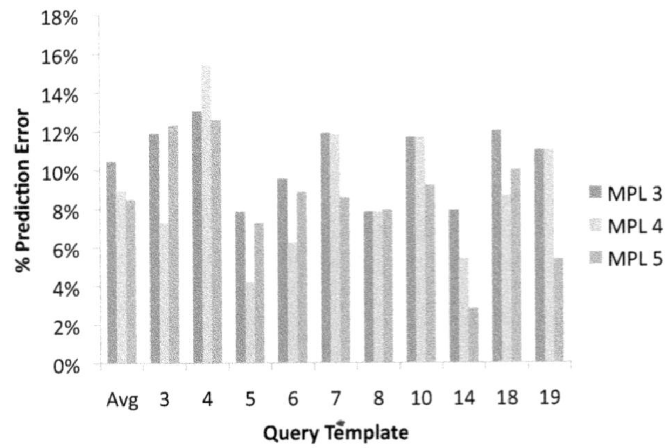

Figure 10: JIT relative latency estimation errors at various multiprogramming levels.

depart from steady state estimates and still produce similar error rates is caused by the database being so large that most of it cannot fit in memory at any given time. Thus, our estimates adapt to the RAM changing its contents regularly, negating the necessity of discretely modeling buffer pool state.

Finally in Figure 11, we examine how well our predictor can handle arbitrary mixes paired with more uncertainty about the duration and content of the individual mixes. Using the queue modeler technique, we build a latency estimate from predicting both when the primary query and its complements will terminate. We model for a continuous multiprogramming level by adding new queries from a provided queue when complement queries are projected to terminate. The simulation ends when our primary query is projected to be the next query replaced by an element of the queue.

Overall, this brings our accuracy levels to an average of 21%. This is close to our estimation accuracy in steady state. This accuracy demonstrates that our framework can make predictions under realistic scenarios of queries starting and stopping at intervals offset from each other. This allows a user to make straightforward "what-if" analysis when they are considering scheduling a batch of queries. This framework could potentially enable a user to formulate different orderings of their queries and submit them for evaluation to our system. This would search for time-saving orderings of submitted queries.

These results also demonstrate that our system can tolerate some

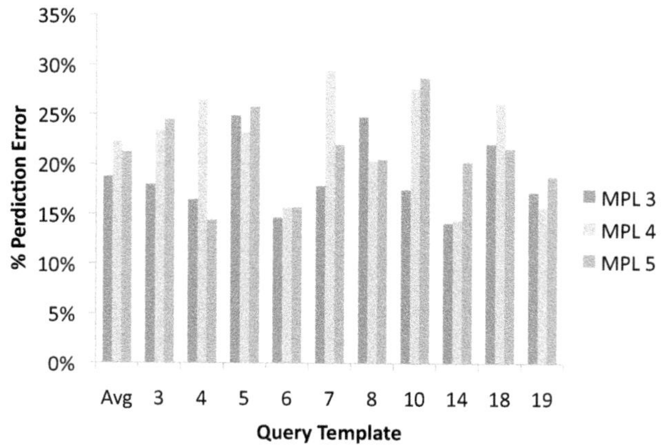

Figure 11: Queue modeling relative latency estimation errors at various multiprogramming levels.

uncertainty about the mixes being executed. Despite our steady state estimates having limited inherent errors, this does not unduly affect our mixed workload case. In many cases the timeline errors are not significant because as we are transitioning between mixes, we do this one query at a time. Thus the subsequent mixes are only slightly different from each other in terms of how they affect the primary query.

7. RELATED WORK

The topic of performance prediction for database workloads has recently gained significant interest in the research community. There have been many studies regarding how to characterize workloads, plot query progress and predict query performance. In this section we explore each of these topics in turn.

Workload Characterization Prior work characterizing database performance [11, 17] study utilization of individual resources (such as CPU time) for a database workload and how to profile queries. In our research we target a higher level metric: query latency.

In [5] the authors analyzed how to classify workloads. Work has been done to characterize the usage of specific resources in databases including [4] and [10]. Here the authors examined memory and CPU usage under various workloads respectively.

Query Progress Indicators There has also been significant work on query progress indicators [7, 13, 12, 6]. In [7], the authors reason about the percent of the query completed, however their solution does not address direct latency predictions for database queries and does not apply on concurrent workloads. In [12], the authors estimate the remaining execution time for multiple, concurrent running queries and their approach relies on previous work on single-query progress indicators. Therefore, they rely on semantic information of the SQL queries. Our solution is simpler as it uses statistics collected through experimental sampling and we predict the total response time of the queries with similar accuracy. [6] provides a survey of existing progress indicators and recommends the best ones for use in practice.

In [13] the authors propose a single query progress indicator that can be applied on a large subset of database query types. Their solution uses semantic segmentation of the query plans and strongly relies on the optimizer's (often inaccurate) estimates for cardinality and result sizes. Although their progress estimator takes into account the system load, their work does not specifically estimate progress of concurrent queries and includes limited experiments on resource contention. In the contrary, our work primary focuses on concurrent workloads and does not rely on the optimizer's estimates. Moreover, our timeline analysis identifies the overlap between concurrent queries to continuously improve the prediction error and thus can effectively address resource contention for concurrent queries. Finally, progress estimators have been researched for MapReduce queries [15]. This work assumes a different workload model from the one we have developed for analytical queries.

Query Performance Prediction In [8] the authors use machine learning techniques to predict multiple performance metrics of analytical queries. Although their predictions include our QoS metric (query latency), their system does not address concurrent workloads. Moreover, their solution relies on statistics based on the SQL text as well as ones obtained from the query execution plan.

In [9] the authors also use machine learning to predict query performance. They predict a range for their query execution latency. Like us, their work considers concurrency, but only models based on the multiprogramming level rather than individual query mixes. In contrast, we provide a direct latency estimate and consider system strain at a higher granularity.

Furthermore, [12] examines predicting query latency with concurrency. The authors make predictions including remaining latency on queries that are executing concurrently. Like this work, the authors consider the addition and removal of queries during the time for which they are creating a prediction. In contrast to this work, it does not consider multiple, diverse query classes.

Query interactions have also been addressed and greatly advanced in [1] and [2]. In this work the authors create these concurrency-aware models to build schedules for batches of OLAP queries. Their solutions create regression models based on sampling techniques similar to the ones that we use. These systems created schedules for a list of OLAP queries to minimize end-to-end latency for a large set of queries. Our experiment-driven approach predicts the response time of *individual* queries, and presumes that the order of execution of the queries is fixed for a real-time environment.

[3] models the mixes of concurrent queries over time from a provided workload, but does not target individual query latencies, instead optimizing for end-to-end workload latencies. This approach uses an incremental evaluation approach, which our timeline analysis is inspired by. Our timeline modeling uses a very different framework to project latency.

Finally, [14] explores how to schedule OLAP mixes by varying the multiprogramming level and priority assigned to individual queries. They use this priority-based control mechanism to prevent overload and under-load, allowing the database to maintain a good throughput rate. Like this work, our model experiments for many multiprogramming levels, but our focus in this work is in predicting execution latency rather than prioritizing queries effectively.

8. CONCLUSIONS AND FUTURE WORK

This work proposes a lightweight estimator for concurrent query execution performance for analytical workloads. To the best of our knowledge it is the first to predict execution latency for individual queries for real-time reporting without using semantic information.

Our system starts with studying the relationship between BAL and quality of service as measured by query execution latency. We have demonstrated that there is a strong linear relationship between these two metrics, which we model with our system B2L. This relationship is based on the observation that as long as there is contention for a resource and we can instrument its bottleneck, then we can accurately predict latency. We produce very accurate estimates of latency given the average BAL despite this metric exhibiting moderate variance. We accomplish this because our queries are sufficiently long that we collect enough samples to produce a representative average. This naturally is proportional to the latency because the queries are primarily I/O-bound. We predict the BAL by extrapolating higher degree interactions using pairwise BALs in a system we call B2cB.

We then adapt this baseline system to a dynamically changing workload using timeline analysis. We predict the steady state latency of each query in a workload and determine which will terminate first. We then estimate the progress of each query after the first terminates and conjecture about which will end next. We continue this cycle in two formulations: just-in-time and queue-modeler. In the former, we build our prediction based on the currently executing batch. The latter fixes our multiprogramming level and predicts when new queries will be started as old ones end.

There are several open directions for future work in the area of concurrent query performance prediction. In the short term, we plan to experiment with more advance machine learning techniques for predicting the query latency. One approach we are considering is extending the Kernel Canonical Correlation Analysis that was used in [8] to predicting single query latency in the context of concurrent execution. We can apply this technique to mapping mixes to latencies by mapping features to performance. We could also benefit from using a richer feature set including query execution plan data to refine our predictions.

We also plan to capture our BAL distribution under varying conditions using a Gaussian process model [16]. This would enable us to smooth the surface of our predictions by developing a piecewise model for predicting BAL. It may enable us to serve a wider workload range.

Another direction we plan to research in the future is incrementally tuning our estimates to workloads as they change over time. We would have to incrementally update our B2L model to handle changing table cardinalities from inserts and deletes. This would also require us to identify when the query execution plan changes in response to growing or shrinking data and how this impacts our indicator metrics.

Finally, this paper performs modeling at the granularity of query templates. We would like to generalize our solution for cases in which such templates are not available. To this end, we are interested in automatically identifying clusters of queries that exhibit similar concurrent interaction behavior and use these as the basis for predictive modeling.

9. ACKNOWLEDGEMENTS

This work was funded by in part by NSF under Grants IIS-0905553 and IIS-0916691.

10. REFERENCES

[1] M. Ahmad, A. Aboulnaga, S. Babu, and K. Munagala. Modeling and exploiting query interactions in database systems. In *Proceeding of the 17th ACM conference on Information and knowledge management*, CIKM '08, pages 183–192, New York, NY, USA, 2008. ACM.

[2] M. Ahmad, A. Aboulnaga, S. Babu, and K. Munagala. Qshuffler: Getting the query mix right. *Data Engineering, International Conference on*, 0:1415–1417, 2008.

[3] M. Ahmad, S. Duan, A. Aboulnaga, and S. Babu. Interaction-aware prediction of business intelligence workload completion times. *Data Engineering, International Conference on*, 0:413–416, 2010.

[4] L. A. Barroso, K. Gharachorloo, and E. Bugnion. Memory system characterization of commercial workloads. In *Proceedings of the 25th annual international symposium on Computer architecture*, ISCA '98, pages 3–14, Washington, DC, USA, 1998. IEEE Computer Society.

[5] M. Calzarossa and G. Serazzi. Workload characterization: A survey. In *Proceedings of the IEEE*, pages 1136–1150, 1993.

[6] S. Chaudhuri, R. Kaushik, and R. Ramamurthy. When can we trust progress estimators for SQL queries? In *Proceedings of the 2005 ACM SIGMOD international conference on Management of data*, SIGMOD '05, pages 575–586, New York, NY, USA, 2005. ACM.

[7] S. Chaudhuri, V. Narasayya, and R. Ramamurthy. Estimating progress of execution for sql queries. In *Proceedings of the 2004 ACM SIGMOD international conference on Management of data*, SIGMOD '04, pages 803–814, New York, NY, USA, 2004. ACM.

[8] A. Ganapathi, H. Kuno, U. Dayal, J. L. Wiener, A. Fox, M. Jordan, and D. Patterson. Predicting multiple metrics for queries: Better decisions enabled by machine learning. In *ICDE '09: Proceedings of the 2009 IEEE International Conference on Data Engineering*, pages 592–603, Washington, DC, USA, 2009. IEEE Computer Society.

[9] C. Gupta, A. Mehta, and U. Dayal. PQR: Predicting Query Execution Times for Autonomous Workload Management. *Autonomic Computing, International Conference on*, 0:13–22, 2008.

[10] K. Keeton, D. A. Patterson, Y. Q. He, R. C. Raphael, and W. E. Baker. Performance characterization of a Quad Pentium Pro SMP using OLTP workloads. volume 26, pages 15–26, New York, NY, USA, April 1998. ACM.

[11] J. L. Lo, L. A. Barroso, S. J. Eggers, K. Gharachorloo, H. M. Levy, and S. S. Parekh. An analysis of database workload performance on simultaneous multithreaded processors. *SIGARCH. News*, 26(3):39–50, 1998.

[12] G. Luo, J. Naughton, and P. Yu. Multi-query sql progress indicators. In Y. Ioannidis, M. Scholl, J. Schmidt, F. Matthes, M. Hatzopoulos, K. Boehm, A. Kemper, T. Grust, and C. Boehm, editors, *Advances in Database Technology - EDBT 2006*, volume 3896 of *Lecture Notes in Computer Science*, pages 921–941. Springer Berlin / Heidelberg, 2006.

[13] G. Luo, J. F. Naughton, C. J. Ellmann, and M. W. Watzke. Toward a progress indicator for database queries. In *Proceedings of the 2004 ACM SIGMOD international conference on Management of data*, SIGMOD '04, pages 791–802, New York, NY, USA, 2004. ACM.

[14] A. Mehta, C. Gupta, and U. Dayal. BI batch manager: a system for managing batch workloads on enterprise data-warehouses. In *Proceedings of the 11th international conference on Extending database technology: Advances in database technology*, EDBT '08, pages 640–651, New York, NY, USA, 2008. ACM.

[15] K. Morton, M. Balazinska, and D. Grossman. ParaTimer: a progress indicator for MapReduce DAGs. In *Proceedings of the 2010 international conference on Management of data*, SIGMOD '10, pages 507–518, New York, NY, USA, 2010. ACM.

[16] C. Rasmussen. Gaussian processes in machine learning. In *Advanced Lectures on Machine Learning*, volume 3176, pages 63–71. Springer Berlin / Heidelberg, 2004.

[17] P. Yu, M.-S. Chen, H.-U. Heiss, and S. Lee. On workload characterization of relational database environments. *IEEE Transactions on Software Engineering*, 18:347–355, 1992.

Reverse Spatial and Textual k Nearest Neighbor Search

Jiaheng Lu   Ying Lu
DEKE, MOE and School of Information
Renmin University of China
{jiahenglu, yinglu}@ruc.edu.cn

Gao Cong
School of Computer Engineering
Nanyang Technological University, Singapore
gaocong@ntu.edu.sg

ABSTRACT

Geographic objects associated with descriptive texts are becoming prevalent. This gives prominence to spatial keyword queries that take into account both the locations and textual descriptions of content. Specifically, the relevance of an object to a query is measured by *spatial-textual similarity* that is based on both spatial proximity and textual similarity. In this paper, we define Reverse Spatial Textual k Nearest Neighbor (RSTkNN) query, i.e., finding objects that take the query object as one of their k most spatial-textual similar objects. Existing works on reverse kNN queries focus solely on spatial locations but ignore text relevance.

To answer RSTkNN queries efficiently, we propose a hybrid index tree called IUR-tree (Intersection-Union R-Tree) that effectively combines location proximity with textual similarity. Based on the IUR-tree, we design a branch-and-bound search algorithm. To further accelerate the query processing, we propose an enhanced variant of the IUR-tree called clustered IUR-tree and two corresponding optimization algorithms. Empirical studies show that the proposed algorithms offer scalability and are capable of excellent performance.

Categories and Subject Descriptors

H.2.8 [**Database Management**]: Database Applications—*Spatial databases and GIS*

General Terms

Algorithms, Design, Experimentation, Performance

Keywords

Reverse k nearest neighbor, Spatial-keyword query

1. INTRODUCTION

Reverse k Nearest Neighbor (RkNN) [10] query, which is to find objects whose k nearest neighbors (kNN) include the query point, has received considerable attention. Among many applications, it is used to discover the influence sets, *i.e.*, objects in a dataset highly influenced by the query object [10]. In the literature [2, 3, 7, 10, 19, 20, 22, 25], spatial distance is usually considered as the sole influence factor. However, in real applications, distance alone is not sufficient to characterize the influence between two objects. For example, two objects, *e.g.*, restaurant, are more likely to influence each other if their textual descriptions (*e.g.*, seafood buffet lunch including crab and shrimp) are similar.

In contrast, we take into account textual similarity in RkNN, and study a new kind of RkNN problem that is called **Reverse Spatial and Textual k Nearest Neighbor (RSTkNN)** queries that consider both spatial distance and textual similarity. An RSTkNN query is to find the objects that have the query object as one of their k most spatial-textual similar objects. This new type of query is different from RkNN (e.g., [10]), and spatial-keyword queries (*e.g.*, LkT [6]). (See Section 8 for a detailed comparison).

Figure 1 gives an example to illustrate the RSTkNN query we proposed and the conventional RkNN query. Points $p_1 \cdots p_9$ in Fig.1(a) are existing branch stores in a region, and q is a new store which will open. (N1$\cdots$N7 in Fig.1(a) are MBRs to be explained in Section 4). Products of each branch store are given in Fig.1(b), where the weight of each item can be calculated by TF-IDF [18]. Then an RSTkNN query with q as query object finds the existing stores that will be influenced most by q considering both the locations of the stores and the stuffs that the stores sell. Assume k=2, the results of traditional RkNN query are $\{p_4, p_5, p_9\}$, while the results of our *RSTkNN* query will be $\{p_1, p_4, p_5, p_9\}$. Note p_1 is one of answers since the textual description of p_1 is quite similar with that of q, though q is not a 2NN of p_1 in terms of spatial distance alone.

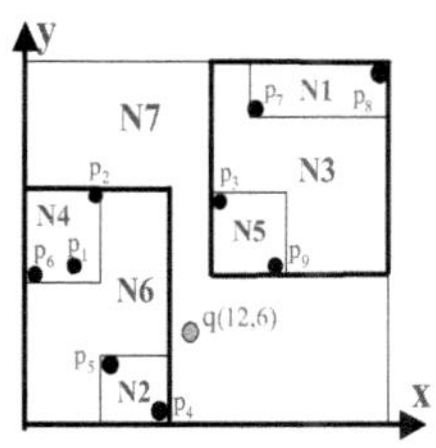

(a) Distribution of branch stores

	x	y	vectors	stationery	sportswear	pan	diaper	camera	laptop
p_1	3	12	ObjVct1	8	8	0	0	0	0
p_2	4	16	ObjVct2	1	1	8	8	4	4
p_3	14	15	ObjVct3	1	1	4	4	1	1
p_4	11	0	ObjVct4	7	7	1	1	0	0
p_5	6	5	ObjVct5	4	4	1	1	0	0
p_6	0	11	ObjVct6	1	1	7	7	0	0
p_7	18	20	ObjVct7	0	0	0	0	8	8
p_8	25	22	ObjVct8	1	1	0	0	7	7
p_9	19	10	ObjVct9	0	0	1	1	4	4
q	12	6	ObjVctQ	8	8	0	0	0	0

(b) Locations and products of branch stores in (a)

Figure 1: An example of RSTkNN queries

RSTkNN queries have many applications ranging from map-based Web search to GIS decision support. For example, a shopping mall can use an RSTkNN query to find potential customers whose profiles are relevant to the products of the shopping mall and whose locations are close to this shopping mall. As another example, a person who want to buy/rent a house would describe her/his desired house with both location and textual description that specifies the amenities (s)he wants. RSTkNN query can help landlords find the potential buyers/renters who may be interested in their houses based on the location and description of the houses.

Unfortunately, taking into account the textual relevance in RSTkNN will pose great challenges to the existing techniques for processing conventional RkNN (without considering textual relevance), and render them inapplicable to process RSTkNN queries (see Section 3.1 for the detailed analysis).

To process the RSTkNN queries efficiently, we propose a hybrid indexing structures and an efficient approach that take into account the fusion of location proximity and document similarity. The contributions and the organization of this paper are summarized as follows.

1. We propose and analyze the problem of Reverse Spatial and Textual k Nearest Neighbor (RSTkNN) search. To the best of our knowledge, this is the first work on RSTkNN queries (Section 2, 3).

2. We propose an efficient algorithm to process RSTkNN queries. The algorithm is based on an effective hybrid indexing structure called Intersection-Union-R tree (IUR-tree) that stores spatial and textual information for the database objects (Section 4). By effectively computing spatial-textual similarities between index nodes, we exploit a branch-and-bound algorithm to prune the irrelevant subtrees (Section 5). We also theoretically analyze the performance of the algorithm based on IUR-tree.

3. IUR-trees organize the data points by considering only spatial distance, which may damp the pruning power due to the diversity of textual contents in one node. we propose an enhanced hybrid index, called Clustered IUR-tree (CIUR-tree) incorporating textual clusters and two optimization algorithms based on CIUR-tree (Section 6).

4. Results of empirical studies with implementations of the proposed techniques demonstrate the scalability and efficiency of proposed indexes and algorithms (Section 7).

2. PROBLEM DEFINITION

In this work, the document of an object is treated as a bag of weighted words using vector space model [14]. Formally, a document is defined as $\{<d_i, w_i>\}$, $i = 1 \cdots m$, where w_i is the weight of word d_i. The weight could be computed by the well-known TF-IDF scheme [18].

Let P be a universal spatial object set. Each spatial object $p \in P$ is defined as a pair $(p.loc, p.vct)$, where $p.loc$ represents the spatial location information and $p.vct$ is the associated text represented in vector space model. We define RSTkNN query as follows. Given a set of objects P and a query point q (loc, vct), RSTkNN(q, k, P) finds all objects in the database that have the query point q as one of the k most "similar" neighbors among all points in P, where the similarity metric combines the spatial distance and textual similarity. Following the previous work [6, 12], we define a similarity metric, called **spatial-textual similarity**[1], in Eqn(1), where parameter $\alpha \in [0, 1]$ is used to adjust the importance of spatial proximity factor and the textual similarity factor. Note that in our setting, we allow users to adjust the parameter α at the query time.

$$SimST(p_1, p_2) = \alpha * SimS(p_1.loc, p_2.loc) + (1 - \alpha) * SimT(p_1.vct, p_2.vct) \quad (1)$$

$$SimS(p_1.loc, p_2.loc) = 1 - \frac{dist(p_1.loc, p_2.loc) - \varphi_s}{\psi_s - \varphi_s} \quad (2)$$

$$SimT(p_1.vct, p_2.vct) = \frac{EJ(p_1.vct, p_2.vct) - \varphi_t}{\psi_t - \varphi_t} \quad (3)$$

As shown in Eqn(2), the spatial distance $SimS(.,.)$ of objects p_1, $p_2 \in P$ is the Euclidean distance denoted as $dist(p_1.loc,\ p_2.loc)$. In Eqn(2), φ_s and ψ_s denote the minimum and maximum distance of pairs of distinct objects in P. They are used to normalize the spatial distance to the range $[0, 1]$. The textual similarity $SimT(.,.)$ of objects $p_1, p_2 \in P$ is shown in Eqn(3). Similarly, φ_t and ψ_t are the minimum and maximum textual similarity of pairs of distinct objects in the dataset, respectively. Specifically, $EJ(p_1.vct, p_2.vct)$ is the Extended Jaccard [21], which is widely used in textual similarity computing, as shown in Eqn(4).

$$EJ(\vec{v}, \vec{v'}) = \frac{\sum_{j=1}^{n} w_j \times w'_j}{\sum_{j=1}^{n} w_j^2 + \sum_{j=1}^{n} {w'_j}^2 - \sum_{j=1}^{n} w_j \times w'_j}, \quad (4)$$
$$where\ \vec{v} =< w_1, \cdots, w_n >,\ \vec{v'} =< w'_1, \cdots, w'_n >$$

Formally, given a query object q=$(loc,\ vct)$, an object $p \in P$ is one of k most similar objects with q, denoted by $p \in STkNN(q, k, P)$ if and only if it satisfies the condition:

$$|\{o \in P | SimST(o, q) \geq SimST(p, q)\}| < k$$

Given a query q, RSTkNN query retrieves objects whose k most similar objects include q. It is formally defined as:

$$RSTkNN(q, k, P) = \{p \in P | q \in STkNN(p, k, P)\} \quad (5)$$

For example, in Fig.1, given a query $q(12, 6)$ whose textual vector is <($stationery$,8),($sportwear$,8)>, and k=2, α=0.6, then $RSTkNN(q, k, P)$=$\{p_1, p_4, p_5, p_9\}$. Note that p_1 is an answer due to the high textual similarity between p_1 and q.

3. PROBLEM ANALYSIS AND BASELINE METHODS

We first analyze the main technical challenges of processing RSTkNN queries and then present the baseline solutions.

3.1 Problem Analysis

Recall that our similarity metric combines both text and location information, and to the best of our knowledge, the previous methods for RkNN queries cannot be employed to handle the RSTkNN queries due to the new challenges.

Existing approaches for processing RkNN can be grouped into four categories. First, typical solutions (e.g. [3, 13, 15, 22, 25]) are based on ℓp norm metric space. For example, hyperplanes [15, 22, 25] and Voronoi cells [13] technologies are employed to exploit the Euclidean geometry properties; and [3] makes use of the properties of ℓp norm metric to develop a branch-and-bound algorithm to answer RkNN queries. Despite their significant contributions, the ℓp norm metric space is not suitable for computing the similarity

[1]Hereafter, "spatial-textual similarity" is also called "similarity" for short.

between textual descriptions as they are sparse and high-dimensional vectors [21], and hence the techniques based on the Euclidean geometry are not applicable to RSTkNN queries. Second, the approach to prune the objects using the hyper-Voronoi diagram and 60-degree-pruning method [20] is infeasible to process RSTkNN due to the high dimensions of text. Third, the existing methods based on pre-processing [2,7,10] do *not* suffice the requirement of RSTkNN that the importance of text relevance verse spatial proximity (controlled by parameter α) may vary at query time. In addition, they cannot handle dynamic parameter k, which may vary at querying time too. Fourth, the works [1,19] focus on only approximate results while they are successful to handle high dimensional and general metric spaces.

3.2 Baseline methods

No baseline algorithm exists for *RSTkNN* queries. Readers might be tempted to answer *RSTkNN* queries by separately computing the reverse spatial k nearest neighbors (*RSkNN*) and the reverse textual k nearest neighbors(*RTkNN*), and then finding a way to combine the two results. This idea has two serious problems: 1) existing methods cannot be used to compute RkNN queries in terms of text similarity, and more importantly 2) there is no sensible way to combine the two results to get the answers since the result of an $RSTkNN$ query may even not belong to the set of the union of the results from its corresponding $RSkNN$ query and $RTkNN$ query.

We develop a non-trivial baseline algorithm to correctly find *all* answers. The idea is that: for each object p, we first pre-compute the location proximity and textual similarity respectively with *all* the other objects to obtain two sorted lists. At query time, we find top-k objects that have the highest overall grades of the function in Eqn(1) combining the two lists using the threshold algorithm (TA) [9]. Thus if the spatial-textual similarity of the k-th object is smaller than the similarity between p and query q, then p is added to the result. This method can handle dynamic parameters k and α. However, it is expensive as it demands computing the $STkNN$ for *all* the objects in the dataset.

We also explore other baselines using existing techniques. However, they are much slower than the above baseline in our experiments, and are ignored. For example, we tried a baseline method without pre-computation. The idea is that, for each object p, find its top-k most similar objects using the existing spatial-and-textual *kNN* query techniques (*e.g.*, [6]), and if the kth result is smaller than the similarity between p and query q, then p is added to the result.

4. A HYBRID INDEX: IUR-TREE

To answer the RSTkNN queries efficiently, we propose an effective hybrid index called IUR-tree (Intersection-Union R-tree), which is a combination of textual vectors and R-tree [11] We can also use other R-tree-based indexes to build IUR-tree. In particular, each node of an IUR-tree contains both spatial location and textual information. The former is represented with a minimum bounding rectangle(MBR), and the latter is represented with two textual vectors: an intersection vector and a union vector. The two vectors are used to compute the similarity approximations (Section 5.1.1 shows the formulas later).

Leaf nodes contain entries[2] in the form of ($ObjPtr$, $ObjLoc$, $ObjVct$), where $ObjPtr$ refers to an object in the database; $ObjLoc$ represents the coordinates of the object; and $ObjVct$ is the textual vector of the object.

A non-leaf node R of IUR-tree contains entries in the form of (Ptr, mbr, $IntUniVct$, cnt), where 1)Ptr is the pointer to a child node of R; 2)mbr is the MBR of the child node of R; 3)$IntUniVct$ is the pointer to the intersection and union textual vectors that intersect and union all textual vectors in the entries of the child node, respectively. The weight of each item in the intersection (resp. union) textual vector is the minimum (resp. maximum) weight of the items in the documents contained in the subtree rooted at Ptr. Note that the two vectors are stored in a separate storage region; and 4)cnt is the number of objects (in the leaf nodes) in the subtree rooted at Ptr.

Figure 2 illustrates the IUR-tree for the objects in Figure 1. The intersection and union textual vectors are presented in Fig.3. For example, the weights of item *camera* in the intersection and union vectors ($IntUniVct2$) of an entry in node $N3$ are 7 and 8, respectively, which are the minimum and maximum weights of the item in the two text vectors $ObjVct7$ and $ObjVct8$ (shown in Fig.1) in node $N1$.

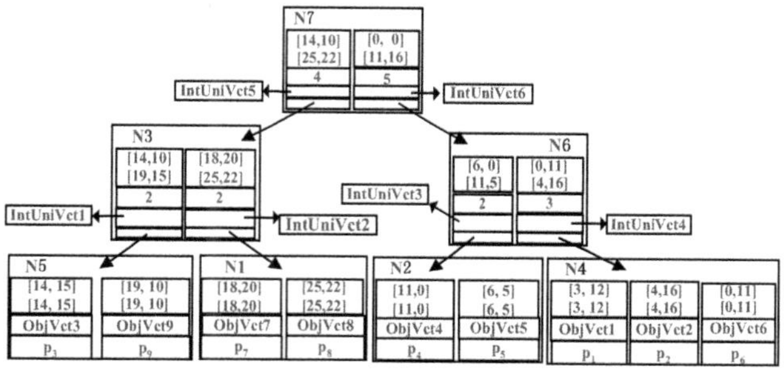

Figure 2: The IUR-tree of Figure 1

		stationery	sportswear	pan	diaper	camera	laptop		stationery	sportswear	pan	diaper	camera	laptop
IntUniVct1 →	IntVct1	0	0	1	1	1	1	UniVct1	1	1	4	4	4	4
IntUniVct2 →	IntVct2	0	0	0	0	7	7	UniVct2	1	1	0	0	8	8
IntUniVct3 →	IntVct3	4	4	1	1	0	0	UniVct3	7	7	1	1	0	0
IntUniVct4 →	IntVct4	1	1	0	0	0	0	UniVct4	8	8	8	8	4	4
IntUniVct5 →	IntVct5	0	0	0	0	1	1	UniVct5	1	1	4	4	8	8
IntUniVct6 →	IntVct6	1	1	0	0	0	0	UniVct6	8	8	8	8	4	4

Figure 3: Text vectors for IUR-tree in Figure 2

Algorithm 1 is presented to construct the IUR-tree, which is using an insert operation that is adapted from the corresponding R-tree operation [11]. To update an IUR-tree incrementally, we use *order preserving minimal perfect hashing function* (*OPMPHF*) [4] to store keywords contained in the subtree of the index node N in the form of ($d_i.p$, $d_i.w$) $i \in [0, m]$, where m is the total number of words contained in the document of N, $d_i.p$ is an integer (position in the words collection) hashed from word d_i using *OPMPHF*, and $d_i.w$ is the weight of word d_i. In particular, in Algorithm 1, Function $Convert()$ in Line 1 is to convert a document to a vector in the form of ($d_i.p$, $d_i.w$). Line 2∽14 use an R-tree based implementation of $ChooseLeaf$ and node split and append with text vectors. We modify the standard $AdjustTree$ method to maintain the text description (Line 15 and 19): if a pair ($d_i.p$, $d_i.w$) is inserted to entry E, then the intersection and union vectors of each E's ancestor should be updated recursively.

[2]For brevity, objects in the dataset and index nodes in the hybrid tree are collectively referred as entries.

Algorithm 1 Insert (*MBR*, *document*)

```
TextVct←Convert(document);   //Covert document into text vector in form of (d_i.p, d_i.w).
N ← ChooseLeaf(MBR);
add TextVct and MBR to node N;
if N needs to be split then
    {O, P} ← N.split();
    if N.isroot() then
        initialize a new node M;
        M.append(O.MBR, O.TextVct);
        M.append(P.MBR, P.TextVct);
        StoreNode(M);
        StoreNode(O);
        StoreNode(P);
        R.RootNode ← M;
    else
        AdjustTree(N.ParentNode, O, P);
else
    StoreNode(N);
    if ¬N.isroot() then
        AdjustTree(N.ParentNode, N, null);
```

5. RSTKNN QUERY ALGORITHM

We present a novel approach to compute the lower and upper bounds of similarity between a node in the IUR-tree and its kth most similar objects in Section 5.1. Based on the bounds, we present a branch-and-bound algorithm to answer RSTkNN queries in Section 5.2.

5.1 Computing Lower and Upper Bounds

For each entry E in an IUR-tree, we need compute the lower and upper bounds of similarity between E and its kth most similar objects, denoted by $kNN^L(E)$ and $kNN^U(E)$, respectively.

5.1.1 Similarity Approximations

To efficiently compute $kNN^L(E)$ and $kNN^U(E)$ during IUR-tree traversal, we make full use of each entry traveled by approximating the similarities among entries, and by defining minimal and maximal similarity functions. Since the spatial distance approximation is thoroughly studied in several publications concerning spatial indexing (*e.g.*, [3, 17]), here we do not repeat their detailed definitions. Rather, we concentrate on the more specialized textual part. The proofs of lemmas in this section can be found in Appendix A.

Let the intersection and union textual vectors of an entry E in IUR-tree be $<E.i_1,\cdots,E.i_n>$ and $<E.u_1,\cdots,E.u_n>$, respectively, where n is the total number of words.

DEFINITION 1 ($MinST$). *The minimal spatial-textual similarity between two entries E and E' in IUR-tree, denoted by $MinST(E, E')$, is defined as:*

$$MinST(E,E') = \alpha(1 - \frac{MaxS(E,E') - \varphi_s}{\psi_s - \varphi_s}) + (1-\alpha)\frac{MinT(E,E') - \varphi_t}{\psi_t - \varphi_t} \quad (6)$$

where $MaxS(E, E')$ is the maximal Euclidian distance between two MBRs of E and E', and

$$MinT(E,E') = \frac{\sum_{j=1}^{n} E.w_j \times E'.w_j}{\sum_{j=1}^{n} E.w_j^2 + \sum_{j=1}^{n} E'.w_j{}^2 - \sum_{j=1}^{n} E.w_j \times E'.w_j},$$

$$\begin{cases} E.w_j = E.u_j, E'.w_j = E'.i_j & \text{if } E.i_j * E.u_j \geq E'.i_j * E'.u_j \\ E.w_j = E.i_j, E'.w_j = E'.u_j & \text{otherwise} \end{cases} \quad (7)$$

LEMMA 1. *$MinST(E, E')$ satisfies the property that $\forall o \in E$, $\forall\, o' \in E'$, $SimST(o, o') \geq MinST(E, E')$.*

Lemma 1 suggests that there are at least $|E'|$ objects o' in E' s.t. $\forall o \in E$, $SimST(o, o') \geq MinST(E, E')$. Therefore, we can use $MinST(E, E')$ to estimate the lower bound $kNN^L(E)$ that should be greater than $MinST(E, E')$.

We next propose another similarity definition which is larger than $MinST(E, E')$ and thus may be used as a tighter bound estimation.

DEFINITION 2 ($TightMinST$). *A tight minimal spatial-textual similarity between two entries E and E' in IUR-tree, denoted as $TightMinST(E, E')$, is defined as:*

$$TightMinST(E,E') = max\Big\{ \alpha(1 - \frac{MinMaxS(E,E') - \varphi_s}{\psi_s - \varphi_s}) + (1-\alpha)\frac{MinT(E,E') - \varphi_t}{\psi_t - \varphi_t}, \alpha(1 - \frac{MaxS(E,E') - \varphi_s}{\psi_s - \varphi_s}) + (1-\alpha)\frac{TightMinT(E,E') - \varphi_t}{\psi_t - \varphi_t} \Big\} \quad (8)$$

where, $MinMaxS(E, E')$ [3] is a tighter Euclidian distance function than $MaxS(E, E')$ holding the property that there is at least one object o' in E' such that the distances between o' and all the objects in E are smaller or equal to $MinMaxS(E, E')$. $TightMinT(E, E') =$

$$\max_{1 \leq r \leq n} \frac{E.w_r \times E'.w_r + \sum_{j=1, j \neq r}^{n} E.w_j \times E'.w_j}{E.w_r^2 + E'.w_r^2 - E.w_r \times E'.w_r + \sum_{j=1, j \neq r}^{n} (E.w_j^2 + E'.w_j^2 - E.w_j \times E'.w_j)}$$

$$E'.w_r = \begin{cases} E'.u_r & \text{if } E.i_r * E.u_r > E'.i_r * E'.u_r \\ E'.i_r & \text{otherwise} \end{cases} \quad (9)$$

$$E.w_r = \begin{cases} E.i_r & \text{if } \sqrt{E.i_r * E.u_r} < E'.w_r; \\ E.u_r & \text{otherwise;} \end{cases} \quad (10)$$

and $E.w_j$ and $E'.w_j$ are assigned as Eqn(7).

LEMMA 2. *$TightMinST(E, E')$ has the property that $\exists\, o' \in E'$ s.t. $\forall o \in E$, $SimST(o, o') \geq TightMinST(o, o')$.*

As suggested from Lemma 2, there is at least one object o' in E' s.t. $\forall o \in E$, $SimST(o, o') \geq TightMinST(E, E')$. Hence, unlike $MinST$ which can contribute $|E|$ objects, $TightMinST$ can contribute only one object to be the kNNs of E', but $TightMinST$ is much tighter than $MinST$.

DEFINITION 3 ($MaxST$). *The maximal spatial-textual similarity between two entries E and E' in IUR-tree, denoted as $MaxST(E, E')$, is defined as:*

$$MaxST(E,E') = \alpha(1 - \frac{MinS(E,E') - \varphi_s}{\psi_s - \varphi_s}) + (1-\alpha)\frac{MaxT(E,E') - \varphi_t}{\psi_t - \varphi_t} \quad (11)$$

where $MinS(E, E')$ is the minimal Euclidian distance between two MBRs of E and E'; maximal textual similarity between E and E' $MaxT(E,E') = \frac{\sum_{j=1}^{n} E.w_j \times E'.w_j}{\sum_{j=1}^{n} E.w_j^2 + \sum_{j=1}^{n} E'.w_j{}^2 - \sum_{j=1}^{n} E.w_j \times E'.w_j}$,

$$\begin{cases} E.w_j = E.i_j,\ E'.w_j = E'.u_j & \text{if } E.i_j > E'.u_j \\ E.w_j = E.u_j,\ E'.w_j = E'.i_j & \text{if } E.u_j < E'.i_j \\ E.w_j = E'.w_j = E.u_j & \text{if } E'.i_j \leq E.u_j \leq E'.u_j \\ E.w_j = E'.w_j = E'.u_j & \text{otherwise.} \end{cases} \quad (12)$$

LEMMA 3. *$MaxST(E, E')$ has the property that $\forall\, o' \in E'$, $\forall o \in E$, $SimST(o, o') \leq MaxST(E, E')$.*

COROLLARY 1. *There is at most one object o' in E' s.t. $\forall o \in E$, $SimST(o, o') = MaxST(E, E')$.*

5.1.2 Lower and Upper Bound Contribution Lists

We are ready to explore the similarity approximations defined above to identify the lower and upper bounds $kNN^L(E)$, $kNN^U(E)$ of the most similar k objects for each entry E.

DEFINITION 4 (LOWER BOUND CONTRIBUTION LIST). *Let $\mathcal{T}$ be a set of entries in the IUR-tree that do not have ancestor-descendant relationship. Given an entry $E \in \mathcal{T}$, a lower bound contribution list of E, denoted as $E.^L CL$, is a sequence of t ($1 \leq t \leq k$) triples $<s_i, E'_i, num_i>$ sorted in descending order of s_i, where $E'_i \neq E$, $E' \in \mathcal{T}$, s_i is $MinST(E, E')$ or $TightMinST(E, E')$, and*

$$num_i = \begin{cases} |E'| - 1 & \text{if } s_i = MinST(E, E') \\ 1 & \text{otherwise.} \end{cases}$$

such that t is the minimal number fulfilling $\sum_{i=1}^{t} num_i \geq k$.

For $s_i = MinST(E, E')$, the rationale for subtracting one from $|E'|$ is due to the potential presence of one object in E' with more precise approximation by $TightMinST$. Following the notations in Definition 4, we have the following Lemma.

LEMMA 4. *If the t-th element (i.e., $E.^L CL.s_t$) is larger than or equal to the maximal similarity between E and q (denoted by $MaxST(E, q)$), no answer exists in subtree(E), the subtree rooted at E, and thus we can safely prune subtree(E).*

The proof of Lemma 4 is obvious: when the condition holds, there are at least k distinct objects whose similarities with any object $o \in E$ are larger than or equal to $MaxST(E, q)$. Hence we can safely prune away *subtree*(E), avoiding the traverse of *subtree*(E) during query processing. Thus we let the lower bound $kNN^L(E)$ be $E.^L CL.s_t$. That is we can prune E if $kNN^L(E) \geq MaxST(E, q)$.

DEFINITION 5 (UPPER BOUND CONTRIBUTION LIST). *Let $\mathcal{T}$ be a set of entries in the IUR-tree that do not have ancestor-descendant relationships. An upper bound contribution list of an entry E in IUR-tree, denoted as $E.^U CL$, is a sequence of t pairs $<s_i, E'_i>$, $i \in [1, \cdots, t]$, sorted in descending order of s_i where $E'_i \neq E$, $E' \in \mathcal{T}$, $s_i = MaxST(E, E')$, and t is the maximal number fulfilling $1 + \sum_{i=1}^{t-1} |E'_i| \leq k$.*

Following the notations in Definition 5, we have the following Lemma.

LEMMA 5. *If the t-th element (i.e., $E.^U CL.s_t$) is smaller than the minimal similarity between E and q (denoted by $MinST(E, q)$), then q must be one of the top-k most similar objects for all objects in E, and objects in E are included as results.*

The proof of Lemma 5 is obvious: there are at most k-1 distinct objects whose similarities with any object $o \in E$ are equal to or larger than $MinST(E, q)$, and thus all objects in E will be reported as part of the answer. Thus we let the upper bound $kNN^U(E)$ be $E.^U CL.s_t$. That is we can report E to be a result entry if $kNN^U(E) < MinST(E, q)$.

Figure 4 illustrates the strategies of using $kNN^L(E)$ and $kNN^U(E)$ to determine whether entry E is a result. The similarity approximations in $E.^L CL$ (resp. $E.^U CL$) are within the shaded ring "L" (resp. "U"). Specially, the dashed line in "L" (resp. "U") is $kNN^L(E)$ (resp. $kNN^U(E)$). Note that the circle that is farther away from E indicates the similarity between object on the circle and entry E is smaller. If $q3$ is the query object, we can prune E since the similarity $MaxST(E, q)$ between E and $q3$ is within the dashed ring $kNN^L(E)$ (*i.e.*, is equal to or larger than $kNN^L(E)$). If $q1$ is the query, we report E as a result entry since the similarity $MinST(E, q)$ between E and $q1$ is within the ring $kNN^U(E)$. If query is $q2$, we cannot determine whether E belongs to results based on $kNN^L(E)$ and $kNN^U(E)$.

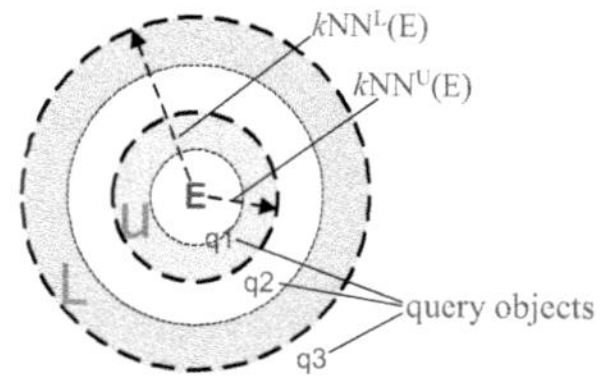

Figure 4: Illustration of pruning and reporting results using $kNN^L(E)$ and $kNN^U(E)$

5.2 Search algorithm

We proceed to develop an efficient algorithm to answer RST*k*NN queries (see Algorithm 2). At high-level, the algorithm descends the IUR-tree in the branch and bound manner, progressively computing the thresholds $kNN^L(E)$ and $kNN^U(E)$ for each entry E by inheriting and updating the lower and upper contribution list; based on the thresholds, the algorithm then decides whether to prune an entry E, to report all objects in E as results, or to consider objects of E as candidates.

The algorithm uses the following data structures: a max-priority queue U, which stores nodes E associated with the priority $MaxST(E, q)$, a candidate object list *COL* that needs to be checked, a pruned entry list *PEL* that will not be results, and a result object *ROL*.

The algorithm begins with initialization and then enqueues the root of the IUR-tree into U (Line 1–2). When U is not empty (Line 3), we dequeue the entry P from U with the highest priority (Line 4). For each child entry E of P, E first *inherits* the upper/lower bound lists of P (which is discussed in more details later)(Line 6), based on which, we determine whether E is a result entry ("*hit*") or can be pruned ("*drop*") by invoking procedure IsHitOrDrop (Line 7). If E can be pruned (Line 29), E is added to *PEL*, and if E is reported as a result entry (Line 33), E is added to *ROL*; Otherwise, we use E to "*mutual-effect*" $E' \in COL \cup ROL \cup U$ to update the upper/lower bound contribution lists to mutually tighten their upper/lower bounds (Line 9 and 12). If E' is pruned or reported as a result entry then remove E' from its original data structure U or *COL* (Line 13–14). If E is determined as a hit or drop, then consider next child entry of P (Line 10). If E still cannot be determined whether to be a result entry after effected by all the entries in *COL*, *ROL* and U, then add E to the corresponding list or queue (Line 15–17). Finally, when the priority queue U is empty, we still need to process objects in the candidate list *COL* to decide if they belong to answers by invoking Procedure FinalVerification (Line 18).

Note that here we adopt a tricky idea called "*lazy travel-down*" for each entry E' in the pruned list *PEL* to save I/O cost. That is, in Line 8, we do not access the subtree of $\forall E' \in PEL$ to affect entry E that is processed currently until we reach the final verification phase. In this way, as shown in the experimental section, "*lazy travel-down*" accelerates the query processing by avoiding the scan of many portions of the IUR-tree.

Algorithm 2 RSTkNN (R: IUR-tree root, q: query)

Output: All objects o, s.t. $o \in RSTkNN(q, k, R)$.

1: Initialize a priority queue U, and lists COL, ROL, PEL;
2: EnQueue(U, R);
3: **while** U is not empty **do**
4:   $P \leftarrow$ DeQueue(U);//Priority of U is $MaxST(P, q)$
5:   **for** each child entry E of P **do**
6:     Inherit($E.CLs$, $P.CLs$);
7:     **if** (IsHitOrDrop(E, q)=**false**) **then**
8:       **for** each entry E' in COL, ROL, U **do**
9:         UpdateCL(E,E');//update contribution lists of E.
10:         **if** (IsHitOrDrop(E, q)=**true**) **then break;**
11:         **if** $E' \in U \cup COL$ **then**
12:           UpdateCL(E',E);//update contribution lists of E' using E.
13:           **if** (IsHitOrDrop(E', q)=**true**) **then**
14:             Remove E' from U or COL;
15:       **if** (E is not a hit or drop) **then**
16:         **if** E is an index node **then**
17:           EnQueue(U, E);
18:         **else** COL.append(E); //a database object
19: FinalVerification(COL, PEL, ROL);

Procedure FinalVerification(COL, PEL, q)

20: **while** ($COL \neq \emptyset$) **do**
21:   Let E be an entry in PEL with the lowest level;
22:   PEL=PEL-$\{E\}$;
23:   **for** each object o in COL **do**
24:     UpdateCL(o,E);//*update contribution lists of o.*
25:     **if** (IsHitOrDrop(o, q)=**true**) **then**
26:       COL=COL-$\{o\}$;
27:   **for** each child entry E' of E **do**
28:     PEL=$PEL \cup \{E'\}$; //*access the children of* E'

Procedure IsHitOrDrop(E: entry, q: query)

29: **if** $kNN^L(E) \geq MaxST(E, q)$ **then**
30:   PEL.append(E); //Lemma 4
31:   return **true**;
32: **else**
33:   **if** $kNN^U(E) < MinST(E, q)$ and E is the rightest child entry **then**
34:     ROL.append($subtree(E)$); //Lemma 5
35:     return **true**;
36:   **else** return **false**;

Procedure UpdateCL(E: entry, E': entry)

37: **for** each tuple $<s_i, E'_i, num_i> \in E.^LCL$ **do**
38:   **if** E'_i=E or E'_i=Parent(E) **then**
39:     remove $<s_i, E'_i, num_i>$ from $E.^LCL$; //Clean Conflicts
40: **if** $kNN^U(E) < MaxST(E, E')$ **then**
41:   $E.^UCL \leftarrow$TopkMax($E.^UCL$, $MaxST(E, E')$, 1);
42: **if** $kNN^L(E) < TightMinST(E, E')$ **then**
43:   $E.^LCL \leftarrow$TopkMax($E.^LCL$, $TightMinST(E, E')$, 1);
44: **if** $kNN^L(E) < MinST(E, E')$ **then**
45:   $E.^LCL \leftarrow$TopkMax($E.^LCL$, $MinST(E, E')$, $|E'|$-1);

SubProcedure TopkMax(L,$f(E, E')$,C)

46: Return the t-th triple in contribution list L, where t is the minimal number fulfilling $\sum_{i=1}^{t} L.num_i \geq k$.

Procedure FinalVerification: it is to determine if the candidate objects in COL are "*hits*" or "*drops*". The main idea is to check the effect of the entries in PEL on each candidate in COL. Specifically, we update the contribution lists for candidate in COL until we can correctly determine if each candidate object belongs to an answer or not. In particular, Line 20 selects the entry E in PEL which has the lowest level in the IUR-tree. This is because the entries in the lower level often have the tighter bounds than those in the higher level and thus they are more likely to identify whether the candidates are results. Line 23 uses the entry E to update the contribution list of each candidate o in COL and Line 24 checks if o can be removed from the candidate list. Finally, we add children of E into PEL since they may also affect the candidates in COL (Line 26–27). This process continues until COL becomes empty.

In particular, Line 6 in Algorithm 2 introduces an efficient technology called **Inherit**, *i.e.*, a child entry inherits (copies) the contribution lists from its parent entry. Inherit makes use of the parent nodes to avoid computing contribution lists from the scratch, and thus reducing runtime (to be shown in our experimental results). However, inherit will lead to a problem called *object conflict*: the same object in the contribution lists of a child entry may be counted twice (one from the inheritance of parent entry and the other one from itself after other entries' affecting), resulting in wrong upper or lower bounds of the child entry. In order to avoid such a problem, Line 37–38 in Algorithm 2 guarantee that there is no object in contribution lists which is double counted, as illustrated in the following example.

Table 1: Trace of *RSTkNN* algorithm in Example 1

Steps	Actions	U	COL	ROL	PEL
1	Dequeue N7; Enqueue N3,N6	N6,N3	$\emptyset$	$\emptyset$	$\emptyset$
2	Dequeue N6; Enqueue N2,N4	N2,N3,N4	$\emptyset$	$\emptyset$	$\emptyset$
3	Dequeue N2;	N3, N4	p5	p4	$\emptyset$
4	Dequeue N3; Enqueue N5	N5, N4	p5	p4	N1
5	Dequeue N5	N4	p5,p9	p4	N1,p3
6	Dequeue N4	$\emptyset$	p9	p4,p1,p5	N1,p3
7	Verify p9	$\emptyset$	$\emptyset$	p4,p1,p5,p9	N1,p3

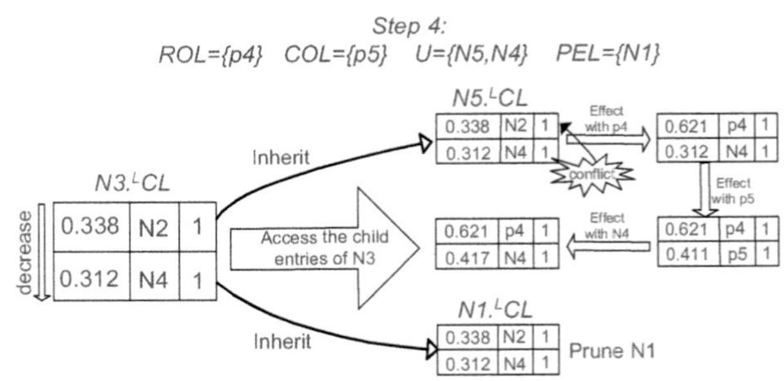

Figure 5: Illustration to *RSTkNN* algorithm

Example 1: *We use this example to illustrate RSTkNN algorithm. Consider the dataset in Figure 1 and a query object* $q(12, 6)$, $q.vct = <(stationary, 8), (sportswear, 8)>$, *and let* k=2, α=0.6. *The algorithm starts by enqueueing N7 into a priority queue U, and the trace of the algorithm is shown in Table 1. The query answers have four objects: p1, p4, p5 and p9, as shown in Step 7 of Table 1.*

Here we focus on Step 4 of Table 1 to illustrate the mutual-effect strategy and inherit technology (See Fig. 4). After N3 is dequeued from U in Step 4, we access its child entries N5 and N1.

1) N5 also inherits the contribution list from N3 (Line 6 in Algorithm 2). However, it can neither be pruned nor be determined to be results (Line 7). Thus it will "mutual-effect" with p4, p5, and N4 (Line 8–17). When we consider *the effect of p4 on the contribution list ($N5.^LCL$) of N5 (Line 9), N2 (inherited from $N3.^LCL$) in $N5.^LCL$ conflicts with p4 since p4 is a child of N2 and N2 may contribute the same object p4 for $N5.^LCL$. To solve the conflict, we remove N2 from $N5.^LCL$ (Line 38), and add p4 to $N5.^LCL$ with a more accurate estimation (0.621) of similarity with N5 than N2. The triple <0.621, p4, 1> is added in $N5.^LCL$. Next in a similar way, we use p5 and N4 to effect with N5, respectively. Finally N5 still cannot be determined to be a hit or drop and it is enqueued to U (Line 16).*

2) N1 inherits the contribution list from N3 (Line 6) and is pruned immediately according to Lemma 4 (Line 29) without having effect on any other entries, which illustrates the benefit of inherit technology. This is because $MaxST(N1,q)=0.308$ is smaller than $N3.^LCL.s_2=0.312$, thus $MaxST(N1,q) \leq TightMinST(N1, N4) \leq TightMinST(N1, N2)$, i.e., there are at least two objects o′ in N4 and N2, s.t. $\forall o \in N1$, $SimST(o,o') \geq TightMinST(N1,q)$, therefore we can prune N1 according to Lemma 4. □

Theorem 1. *Given an integer k, a query q and an index tree R, Algorithm 2 correctly returns all RSTkNN points.*

The proof of Theorem 1 is given in Appendix A.4.

Performance Analysis: We propose an analytical model to estimate the cost of *RSTkNN* queries and theoretically analyze the performance of the *RSTkNN* algorithm based on IUR-tree, *i.e.*. We estimate the number of expected disk accesses *DA* of IUR-tree index nodes by the *RSTkNN* algorithm as follows.

LEMMA 6. *Suppose that N objects are uniformly distributed in 2-dimension space [23], and M distinct words are randomly distributed on the N objects such that the average number of words per object is m ($m \leq M$). The number of expected disk accesses DA is $\mathcal{O}(k\sqrt{k}+\sqrt{k}N)$, where f is the average capacity (fanout) of the IUR-tree, k is the parameter specified by the RSTkNN query.*

The details for the analysis model and the proof of Lemma 6 can be found in [16].

6. REFINEMENTS FOR HYBRID INDEX

Like the R-tree, the IUR-tree is built based on the heuristics of minimizing the area of MBR of nodes. However, the associated texts of the spatial objects in the same MBR can be very different, because the near spatial objects often belong to different specific categories, such as retail, accommodations, restaurants, and tourist attractions.

To compute tighter *k*NN bounds of the entries, we enhance the IUR-tree with text cluster, yielding an index tree called CIUR-tree given in Section 6.1. We present two optimization methods to improve the search performance based on CIUR-tree in Section 6.2 and Section 6.3, respectively.

6.1 Cluster IUR-tree: CIUR-tree

We propose to use text clustering to enhance IUR-tree. In the pre-processing stage, we group all the database objects into clusters $C_1, \cdots C_n$ according to their text similarities. We extend each IUR-tree node by the cluster information to generate a hybrid tree called Cluster IUR-tree(CIUR-tree). The CIUR-tree is built based on the spatial proximity as does the IUR-tee. However, each node of the CIUR-tree includes a new entry *ClusterList* in the form of $(ID{:}N)$, where ID is the cluster id and N is the number of objects of cluster ID in the subtree of the node. The *ClusterList* on the upper layer *CParent* is the superimposing of that on lower layer *CChild*. That is, $CParent.N = \sum_{j=1}^{M} CChild_j.N$, where M is the number of children of the node.

The intersection and union vectors at each node of the IUR-tree is also extended with cluster information. For each cluster C_i, $CIntVct_i$ and $CUniVct_i$ include the minimal and maximal weights of each word in C_i, respectively. For example, suppose all the objects in Fig.1 are clustered into three clusters: $C_1=\{p_1, p_4, p_5\}$, $C_2=\{p_2, p_3, p_6\}$ and $C_3=\{p_7, p_8, p_9\}$, the intersection and union text vectors of which are shown in Fig 6(a). The CIUR-tree is shown in Fig 6(b).

		stationery	sportswear	pan	diaper	camera	laptop		stationery	sportswear	pan	diaper	camera	laptop
C1	CIntVct1	4	4	0	0	0	0	CUniVct1	8	8	1	1	0	0
C2	CIntVct2	1	1	4	4	0	0	CUniVct2	1	1	8	8	4	4
C3	CIntVct3	0	0	0	0	4	4	CUniVct3	1	1	1	1	8	8

(a) Intersection and union text vectors of each cluster

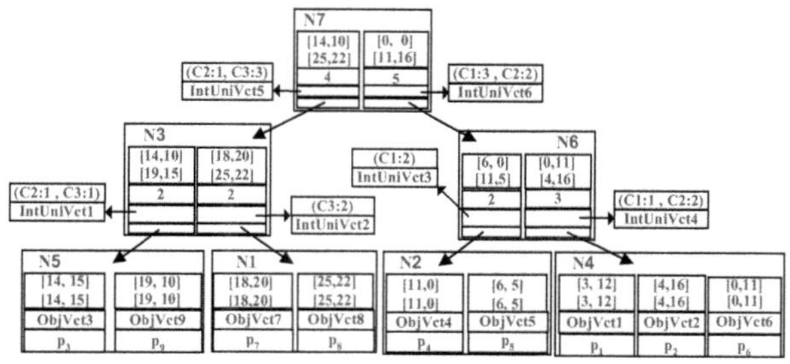

(b) CIUR-tree

Figure 6: The Cluster IUR-tree of Figure 1

6.2 Outlier Detection and Extraction

To give a tighter bound during CIUR-tree traversal, we need to purify the textual description in the index nodes by extracting outliers from the documents based on cluster IDs. We take the outliers into special account and calculate their bounds separately so that the bounds of the original entry can be tighter. We identify the index node E containing outlier clusters in the following two cases:

Case *I*: Most objects in $subtree(E)$ can be pruned, but there exit few objects in $subtree(E)$ that cannot be pruned, and are called "outliers", thus making the whole E non-prunable. More precisely, given a query q, we say one entry E belongs to Case I if 1) $MinST(E,q) < kNN^L(E)$, 2) $MaxST(E,q) > kNN^L(E)$, and 3) there exits a subset of clusters in E, denoted by S_I, such that $\sum_{C_i \in S_I} C_i.N \geq \lambda|E|$, where parameter λ is a threshold close to 1, and $\forall C_i \in S_I$ s.t. $\alpha(1-\frac{MinS(E,q)-\varphi_s}{\psi_s-\varphi_s})+(1-\alpha)MaxT(C_i,q) < kNN^L(E)$. The objects that are in E but not in S_I are outliers.

Case *II*: Most objects in $subtree(E)$ can be reported as answers, but there exit few objects that are not answers and thus the whole E cannot be reported as a result entry. More precisely, given a query q, an entry E belongs to case II if 1) $MinST(E,q) < kNN^U(E)$, 2) $MaxST(E,q) > kNN^U(E)$, and 3) there exits a subset of clusters in E, denoted by S_{II}, such that $\sum_{C_i \in S_{II}} C_i.N \geq \mu|E|$, where parameter μ is a threshold close to 1, and $\forall C_i \in S_{II}$ s.t. $\alpha(1-\frac{MaxS(E,q)-\varphi_s}{\psi_s-\varphi_s})+(1-\alpha)MinT(C_i,q) > kNN^U(E)$.

Having identified entries in Case *I* or Case *II*, we decompose them and identify if their subtree entries can be pruned or added as results. To implement the optimization of outlier detection and extraction for *RSTkNN* queries, the only change is to replace Line 17 in Algorithm 2 with the following pseudocodes. First, we determine whether the index node E is in Case *I* or *II*: if not, then enter E into priority queue U; if yes, then we check whether E's subtree entries e is a result according to the corresponding relationship between the set C_e of clusters in e and cluster set S_I, S_{II}.

Replace Line 17 in Algorithm 2

```
if (E is in Case I or II) then
  for each entry e ∈ subtree(E)
    if Ce⊂SI then prune e;//Ce is the set of clusters in e
    else if Ce⊂SII then report e as a result entry;
         else if (e is an index node) then EnQueue(U,e);
              else COL.append(e);
else EnQueue(U, E);
```

6.3 Text-entropy based optimization

We proceed to propose the second optimization based on CIUR-tree to improve performance. In particular, we use *TextEntropy* to depict the distribution of text clusters in an entry of CIUR-tree. Intuitively, the more diverse the clusters are, the larger the *TextEntropy* of the entry is. The following formula calculates *TextEntropy* for the leaf and inner nodes in CIUR-tree recursively.

$$H(E) = \begin{cases} -\sum_{i=1}^{n} \frac{cnum_i}{|E|} log \frac{cnum_i}{|E|} & \text{if } E \text{ is a leaf node;} \\ \sum_{j=1}^{M} \frac{|E.child_j|}{|E|} H(E.child_j) & \text{otherwise.} \end{cases}$$

where $cnum_i$ is the number of objects of Cluster i in entry E, and $|E|$ is the number of objects in E. If E is a leaf node, the *TextEntropy* describes the distribution of textual cluster in E. If E is an intermediate node, *TextEntropy* of E is a weighted combination of the *TextEntropy* of its child entries $E.child_i$.

We use *TextEntropy* as the priority (key) for the max-priority queue U. If an entry is more diverse in its text description, it has a higher priority to be visited first. By doing so, we expect that decomposing entries/nodes with diverse textual description into sub-entries would reduce the diversity of the entries, and thus would be more likely to enable to quickly tighten the estimation of the lower/upper bounds of similarity between each entry and its kth most similar object through "mutually effect" among entries. In addition, since *TextEntropy* can be computed offline during the indexing construction, we do not need to access the *ClusterLists* from disk during the query time. Therefore, *TextEntropy* based method needs less I/O cost compared to the outlier-detection based optimization

A salient feature of the two optimizations in Section 6.2 and Section 6.3 is that they are orthogonal and can be combined, as implemented in our experiments.

7. EXPERIMENTAL STUDIES

We present an experimental study to evaluate the efficiency and scalability of our methods to answer *RSTkNN* queries.

Implemented algorithms. We implemented the proposed algorithm based on IUR-tree, the two optimizations based on CIUR-tree: outlier-detection-extraction optimization (ODE-CIUR) and text-entropy optimization (TE-CIUR), and the combination of two optimizations (ODE-TE). In addition, we also implemented the baseline method (Section 3.2). The other baseline discussed in Section 3.2 performs much worse and is ignored here.

Table 2: Datasets for the experiments

Statistics	Shop	CD	GN
total # of objects	304,008	1,555,209	1,868,821
total unique words in dataset	3933	21,578	222,409
average # words per object	45	47	4

Datasets and Queries. The algorithms were evaluated using three datasets: ShopBranches (Shop), GeographicNames (GN), and CaliforniaDBpedia (CD). These datasets differ from each other in terms of data-size, spatial-distribution, word-cardinality and text-size. Our goal in choosing these diverse sources is to understand the usefulness and efficiency of our algorithms in different environments. The statistics of each dataset are shown in Table 2. In particular, the GeographicNames dataset (geonames.usgs.gov) is a real-life dataset from the U.S. Board on geographic names with a large number of words to describe the information about each geographic location. The CaliforniaDBpedia dataset combines a real spatial data at California (www.usgs.gov) and a real document collection of abstracts about California in DBpedia (wiki.dbpedia.org/Downloads351). Finally, the ShopBranches are extended from a small real data describing 955 shop branches and their products by generating new spatial objects while maintaining the distribution of the real location and textual information of the objects.

For each dataset, we generated 7 sets of query sets, in which the number of words is 2, 4, 8, 16, 32, 64 and 128, respectively. Each query set comprises 100 queries that are randomly selected from the respective dataset. We report the average running time of 100 queries for each query set.

Setup and metrics. We implemented all the algorithms with VC++6.0, and an Intel(R) Core(TM)2 Quad CPU Q8200 @2.33GHz with 4GB of RAM. We implemented algorithms based on both disk-resident and memory-resident for the proposed index structures, namely the IUR-tree and the CIUR-tree. The page size is 4KB and the branch number of each index node is 102. Both parameters λ and μ in ODE-CIUR are set at 0.9 by default. In CIUR-tree, we clustered the textual vectors of objects into different number of clusters using the *DBSCAN* [8] cluster algorithm.

We compared varied algorithms with different experimental settings as follows:

parameter k: $1 \sim 9$, default 3
parameter α: $0 \sim 1$, default 0.7
number of query words qw: 1~128, default 16
number of clusters: 18~14337, default 187

Space requirement. The space requirement for the structures used by the algorithms is shown in Table 3. Obviously, the baseline method needs the largest disk space as it needs to store the two lists of objects ranked by location proximity and textual similarity respectively for each object. The disk requirement of the baseline on CD and GN is beyond the capacity of our computer (800G). As for the disk storage requirement of IUR-tree, compared with the original R-tree [11], the number of non-leaf nodes are comparable with that of the R-tree and the size of text vectors in the entries

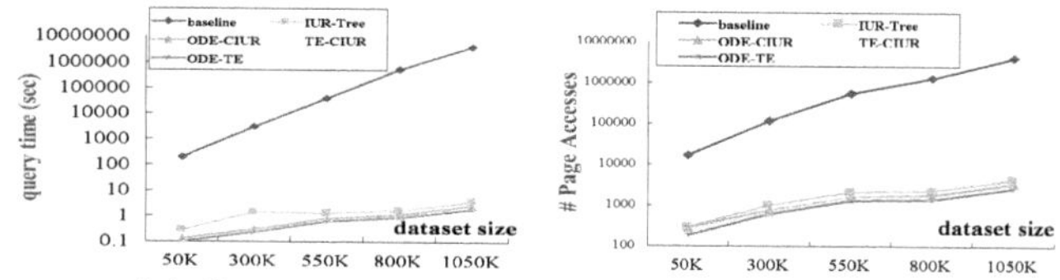

(a) Query time (b) Page access

Figure 7: Varying dataset sizes for Shop (log-scale)

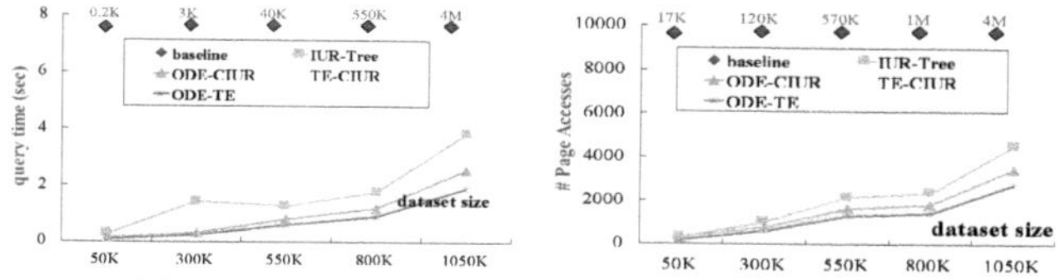

(a) Query time (b) Page access

Figure 8: Varying dataset sizes for Shop

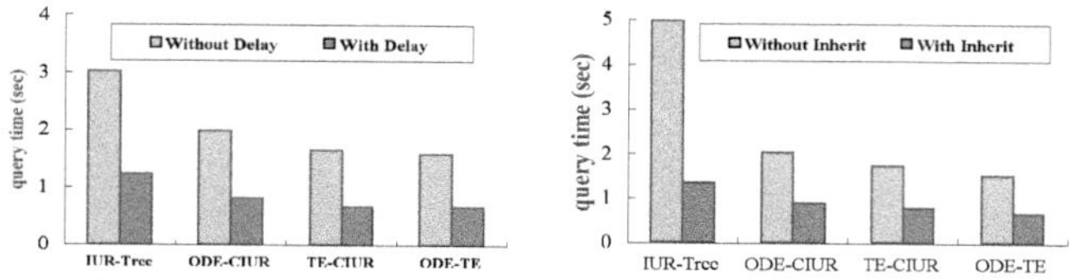

(a) Lazy Travel Down (b) Inherit

Figure 9: Study on the Proposed Algorithm

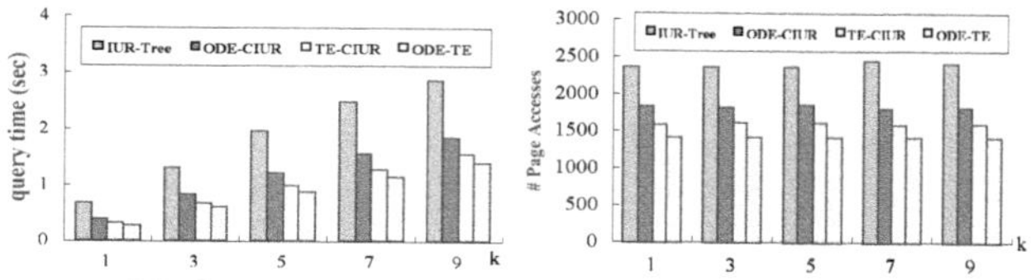

(a) Query time (b) Page access

Figure 10: Varying k for Shop

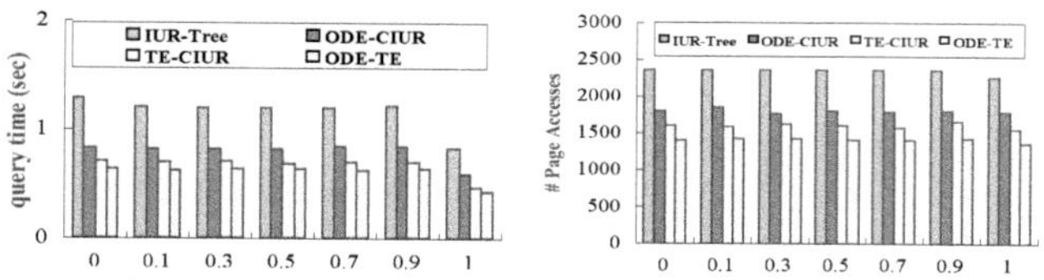

(a) Query time (b) Page access

Figure 11: Varying α for Shop

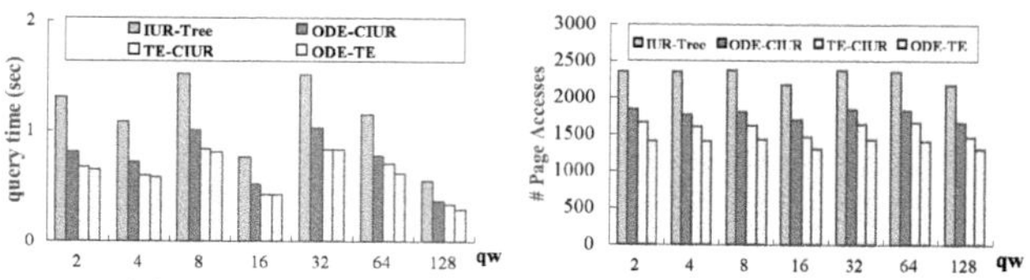

(a) Query time (b) Page access

Figure 12: Varying the number of query words

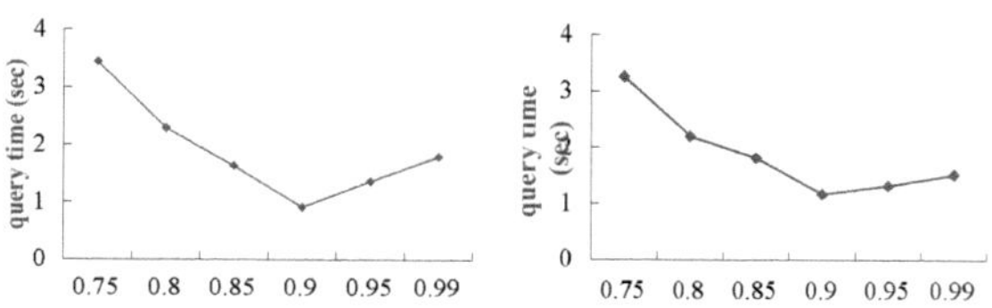

(a) λ (b) μ

Figure 13: Effect of λ and μ for ODE-CIUR

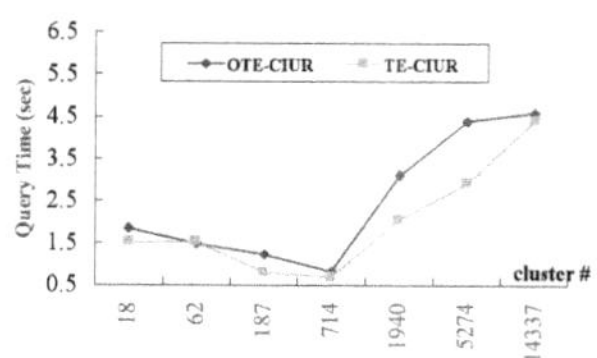

Figure 14: Effect of textual cluster number

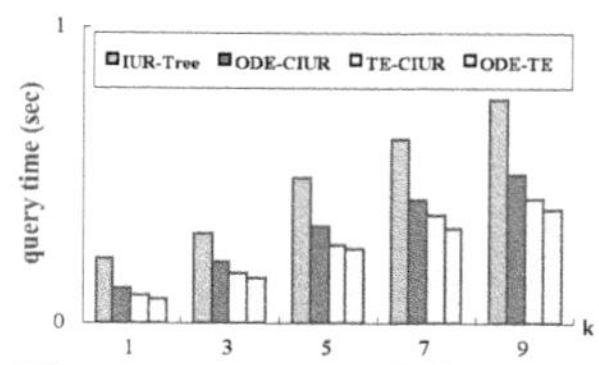

Figure 15: Memory Resident for Shop

of leaf nodes of IUR-tree is comparable with the size of the text components of the dataset. Thus the additional disk requirement for IUR-tree is the text vectors in the entries of non-leaf nodes. For each entry, the size of its intersection vector in an index node is at most the maximal number of words in an object, and the size of its union vector is at most the number of distinct words in the dataset. The space of CIUR-tree is a bit larger than IUR-tree since it needs extra space to store the intersection and union vectors for each cluster.

Table 3: Sizes of indexing structures for Shop

Data	Two lists for Baseline	IUR-tree	CIUR-tree
Shop	224GB	40MB	47MB
CD	-	218MB	237MB
GN	-	264MB	306MB

Performance of different algorithms and scalability In the first set of experiments, we evaluated the performances and the scalability of various algorithms using the ShopBranches dataset. As shown in Fig. 7 (note the log-scale), our proposed algorithms significantly outperform the baseline method for datasets of different sizes in terms of query time and the number of node accesses by orders of magnitude. This is primarily because the baseline method computes the *STkNN* for *all* the objects in the dataset (Note that the *SkNN* and *TkNN* of each object has been pre-computed and stored in disk).

In Fig. 8, we replotted the same data as Fig. 7 using linear scale to see the differences of various optimizations clearly. We observed that the *CIUR*-tree-based algorithms outperform *IUR*-tree-based approaches, which indicates that the two optimizations enhance the filtering power and reduce the number of index nodes visited. Note that the *ODE-TE* algorithm that combines two optimized approaches is the fastest algorithm in our experiments and scales well with the sizes of data sets.

To demonstrate the usefulness of the techniques used in our *RSTkNN* algorithm: "*lazy travel-down*" and "*inherit*", we made experiments and plotted Fig. 9(a) and 9(b). (1) The "*lazy travel-down*" approach speeds up all four algorithms by over 50%. This is because it can avoid visiting some irrelevant entries. (2) Fig.9(b) shows the benefit of *inherit* technology for all the algorithms. We can see that *inherit* can significantly improve the performance since it could avoid the computation of contribution lists from the scratch.

Effect of parameters k, α and qw. In the second set of experiments, we sought to analyze how system performance is impacted by three parameters: the number of returned top results k, the combination ratio of the similarity function α and the number of words in queries qw. The results are reported in Figures 10~ 12.

(1) Figure 10 shows the runtime and number of page accesses *w.r.t* k; we fix α=0.7 and qw=16, and vary k from 1

to 9. The results show that the runtime and required I/O of our algorithms increase slightly with the increase of k.

(2) To evaluate the impact of α, we vary α from 0 to 1, thus adjusting the importance between textual similarity and spatial proximity. From Fig. 11, we can see that our algorithm is not sensitive to α. When α=1 meaning that text documents are totally ignored, the runtime is obviously shorter, as expected.

(3) Figure 12 shows the results when we vary the number of query words qw. We can see that algorithms run faster with the increase of qw. In particular, while qw is varied from 2 to 32, the more the query words, the faster the algorithms run. A deep analysis indicates that more query words may improve the pruning power by decreasing the average textual similarity between query words and data points.

Effect of parameters λ and μ for ODE-CIUR. This experiment is to study the effects of parameters λ and μ for ODE-CIUR. As shown in Fig.13(a), with the increase of λ, the runtime first decreases then increases since most entries would be treated as Case I to be traveled down if λ is too small and most entries cannot identified as Case I to lose the benefits of the optimization of ODE-CIUR if λ is too large. An appropriate setting of λ is about 0.9 in our experiment. The effect of parameter μ shown in Fig.13(b). When μ is about 0.9, the performance is the best in our experiment.

Effect of cluster number. As shown in Fig.14, the performance of both ODE-CIUR and TE-CIUR is not sensitive to the number of clusters, and they achieve the best performance when the number of cluster is around 200-1000. We can see that runtime decreases from 18 clusters to 187 clusters, but then increases from 1,940 clusters to 14,337 clusters. This behavior occurs because the time needed for processing clusters counteracts the time saved by text cluster enhancement.

Memory-resident implementation. This experiment is to evaluate the performance of algorithms on memory-resident. Since the baseline method cannot be fit in memory due to the large size of two ranking lists, we evaluated the performance of the other four algorithms in memory using the dataset ShopBranches. As shown in Fig. 15, when varying the parameter k, the performance of all the algorithms speed up at least 50% since there is no I/O cost for the indexes comparing Fig. 10 for disk resident.

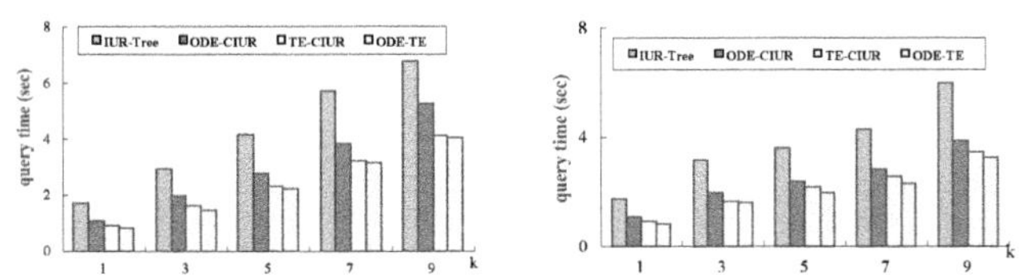

(a) Varying k for CD (b) Varying k for GN

Figure 16: Results of varying k for data CD and GN

Experiments on other datasets. All the above experimental results are reported based on ShopBranches data set. We also conducted extensive experiments on the other two datasets GeographicNames and CaliforniaDBpedia. Due to the space limitation, we only give their results for varying the parameter k in RSTkNN in Fig.16(a) and Fig.16(b) respectively. Both of the experimental results are consistent with those on dataset ShopBranches. The baseline method does not work on the two datasets since the disk space required by preprocessing is beyond the limitation of disk capacity.

To summarize, our experimental results show that our proposed hybrid indexes and search algorithms outperform the baseline method. We also show that the two optimizations with text-entropy and outline-detection indeed improve the performance of the *RSTkNN* queries.

8. RELATED WORK

Our *RSTkNN* queries combine reverse k nearest neighbor (RkNN) queries and textual similarity searches. Existing works [7, 10, 15, 22, 25] on RkNN queries mainly focus on spatial proximity. As discussed in Section 3.1, the existing approaches are not applicable to answer RSTkNN queries. Recent work *Reverse top-k queries* [24] retrieves RkNN objects in a weighted feature space, which, however, does not consider spatial proximity. Therefore existing technologies on RkNN queries cannot be applied on *RSTkNN* queries.

Recently, queries on spatial objects associated with textual information have received significant attentions. *Top*-k *spatial keyword queries* [12], *Location-aware top-k text retrieval(LkT) query* [6], *m-closest keywords (mCK) query* [26], and *prestige-based spatial-keyword query* [5], combine keyword queries with spatial queries. However, none of them considers reverse kNN query. Additionally, the hybrid index structures in this paper is different from the hybrid index structures used in the existing work on spatial-keyword query. One main difference is that we augment R-tree with intersection and union text vectors to represent the text component so that we can compute/estimate the textual similarity between objects/entries, while the existing hybrid indexes usually augment R-tree nodes with inverted file or signature file to compute the relevance between objects/entries and query. In particular, the IR^2-tree [12] integrating the R-tree and signature, and the bR*-tree [26] combining the R*-tree with bitmap are used for Boolean keyword query, but not IR-style ranking queries. They are quite different from the IUR-tree. The IR-tree [6] augments a node with inverted lists, which are suitable for keyword queries that just concern about the query keywords; while in the IUR-tree a node is augmented with text vector, which is suitable for similarity search. Moreover, IR-tree keeps only union information of text while the IUR-tree contain union and intersection information, which are required to compute the similarity approximations between entries. Clustering is also used to optimize query processing in the IR-tree [6], where the clustering is used in a different manner. Hence, the proposed algorithms in this paper are very different from the algorithms for answering spatial-keyword query.

9. CONCLUSIONS AND FUTURE WORK

This paper addressed the new problem *RSTkNN* query, which is the extension of *RkNN* query with the fusion of spatial information and textual description, making it much richer and more complex for the construction and traverse of the index. This paper presented the IUR-tree to represent and index the hybrid information and proposed *RSTkNN* algorithms to quickly compute contribution lists, and adjust the thresholds to prune unrelated points and identify true hits as early as possible. As for the future works, this paper opens to a number of promising directions. First, it is necessary to extend our algorithms to bichromatic version, considering the semantical relevancy for documents of two types of objects. Second, it would be interesting to consider some variants of *RSTkNN* queries, such as skyline *RSTkNN* queries. Third, it is of interest to develop algorithms if the spatial objects are moving objects, fuzzy objects, or are constrained to a road network.

10. ACKNOWLEDGEMENTS

This paper benefitted tremendously from many insightful comments from Tok Wang Ling, Wei Wu, and Xiaofang Zhou as well as the anonymous reviewers. Jiaheng Lu was sponsored partially by the NSF China (60903056) and Beijing Municipal Natural Science Foundation (4112030).

11. REFERENCES

[1] E. Achtert, C. Böhm, P. Kröger, and P. Kunath. Approximate reverse k-nearest neighbor search in general metric spaces. In *CIKM*, pages 788–789, 2006.

[2] E. Achtert, C. Böhm, P. Kröger, and P. Kunath. Efficient reverse k-nearest neighbor search in arbitrary metric spaces. In *SIGMOD*, pages 515–526, 2006.

[3] E. Achtert, H.-P. Kriegel, P. Kröger, M. Renz, and A. Züfle. Reverse k-nearest neighbor search in dynamic and general metric databases. In *EDBT*, pages 886–897, 2009.

[4] E. A.Fox, Q. F. Chen, A. M.Daoud, and L. S.Heath. Order-preserving minimal perfect hash functions and information retrieval. In *TOIS*, pages 281–308, 1991.

[5] X. Cao, G. Cong, and C. S. Jensen. Retrieving top-k prestige-based relevant spatial web objects. *PVLDB*, 3(1):373–384, 2010.

[6] G. Cong, C. S.Jensen, and D. Wu. Efficient retrieval of the top-k most relevant spatial web objects. In *PVLDB*, pages 337–348, 2009.

[7] C.Yang and K.I.Lin. An index structure for efficient reverse nearest neighbor queries. In *ICDE*, pages 485–492, 2001.

[8] M. Ester, H.-P. Kriegel, J. Sander, and X. Xu. A density-based algorithm for discovering clusters in large spatial databases with noise. In *KDD*, pages 226–231, 1996.

[9] R. Fagin, A. Lotem, and M. Naor. Optimal aggregation algorithms for middleware. In *J.Comput. Syst. Sci.*, pages 614–656, 2003.

[10] F.Korn and S.Muthukrishnan. Influenced sets based on reverse nearest neighbor queries. In *SIGMOD*, pages 201–212, 2000.

[11] A. Guttman. R-trees: a dynamic index structure for spatial searching. In *SIGMOD*, pages 47–57, 1984.

[12] I.D.Felipe, V.Hristidis, and N.Rishe. Keyword search on spatial databases. In *ICDE*, pages 656–665, 2008.

[13] I.Stanoi, M.Riedewald, D.Agrawal, and A.E.Abbadi. Discovery of influence sets in frequently updated databases. In *VLDB*, pages 99–108, 2001.

[14] K.Nigam, A.K.McCallum, S.Thrun, and T.M.Mitchel. Text classification from labeled and unlabeled documents using em. In *Machine Learning*, pages 103–134, 2000.

[15] H. P. Kriegel, P. Kröger, M. Renz, A. Züfle, and A. Katzdobler. Incremental reverse nearest neighbor ranking. In *ICDE*, pages 1560–1567, 2009.

[16] J. Lu, Y. Lu, and G. Cong. Technical report, renmin university of china. 2011.

[17] N.Roussopoulos, S.Kelley, and F.Vincent. Nearest neighbor queries. In *SIGMOD*, pages 71–79, 1995.

[18] Salton. Term-weighting approaches in automatic text retrieval. In *Information Processing and Management*, pages 513–523, 1988.

[19] A. Singh, H. Ferhatosmanoglu, and A. S. Tosun. High dimensional reverse nearest neighbor queries. In *CIKM*, pages 91–98, 2003.

[20] I. Stanoi, D. Agrawal, and A. E. Abbadi. Reverse nearest neighbor queries for dynamic databases. In *ACM SIGMOD Workshop on Research Issues in Data Mining and Knowledge Discovery*, pages 44–53, 2000.

[21] P.-N. Tan, M. Steinbach, and V. Kumar. *Introduction to Data Mining*. Addison-Wesley, 2005.

[22] Y. Tao, D. Papadias, and X. Lian. Reverse knn search in arbitrary dimensionality. In *VLDB*, pages 744–755, 2004.

[23] Y. Theodoridis and T. Sellis. A model for the prediction of r-tree performance. In *PODS*, pages 161–171, 1996.

[24] A. Vlachou, C. Doulkeridis, Y. Kotidis, and K. Nørvåg. Reverse top-k queries. In *ICDE*, pages 365–376, 2010.

[25] W. Wu, F. Yang, C.-Y. Chan, and K.-L. Tan. Finch:evaluating reverse k-nearest-neighbor queries on location data. In *PVLDB*, pages 1056–1067, 2008.

[26] D. Zhang, Y. M. Chee, A. Mondal, A. K. H. Tung, and M. Kitsuregawa. Keyword search in spatial databases: Towards searching by document. In *ICDE*, pages 688–699, 2009.

APPENDIX

A. PROOFS

A.1 Proof of Lemma 1

PROOF. To prove the property of $MinST$ in Lemma 1, we first give a definition called *similarity preserving* function.

DEFINITION 6 (SIMILARITY PRESERVING FUNCTION). *Given two functions* $fsim$: $V \times V \rightarrow R$ *and* $fdim$: $R \times R \rightarrow R$, *where* V *denotes the domain of* n*-element vectors and* R *the real numbers. We call* $fsim$ *a similarity preserving function w.r.t* $fdim$, *such that for any three vectors* $\overrightarrow{p}=<x_1, \cdots, x_n>$, $\overrightarrow{p'}=<x'_1, \cdots, x'_n>$, $\overrightarrow{p''}=<x''_1, \cdots, x''_n>$, *if* $\forall i \in [1,n]$, $fdim(x_i, x'_i) \geq fdim(x_i, x''_i)$, *then we have* $fsim(\overrightarrow{p}, \overrightarrow{p'}) \geq fsim(\overrightarrow{p}, \overrightarrow{p''})$.

CLAIM 2. *Euclidian distance function is a similarity preserving function, w.r.t function* $fdim(x, x') = |x - x'|$.

Given the Euclidian function $dist(\overrightarrow{X}, \overrightarrow{X'}) = \sqrt{\sum_{i=1}^{n}(x_i - x'_i)^2}$, obviously, we have that if each dimension i, $|x_i - x'_i| \geq |x_i - x''_i|$, then $dist(\overrightarrow{X}, \overrightarrow{X'}) \geq dist(\overrightarrow{X}, \overrightarrow{X''})$. Thus Claim 2 is true.

CLAIM 3. *Extended Jaccard is a similarity preserving function, w.r.t function* $fdim(x, x') = \frac{min\{x,x'\}}{max\{x,x'\}}$, $x, x' > 0$.

Given x_i, x'_i, x''_i, where $i \in [1,n]$, such that $fdim(x_i, x'_i) \geq fdim(x_i, x''_i)$ and x'_i ,x_i, $x''_i > 0$, we can prove that $\frac{2x_i x'_i}{x_i^2 + x_i'^2} \geq \frac{2x_i x''_i}{x_i^2 + x_i''^2}$, then we can derive inequality (13) is true by means of mathematical induction. Thus extend Jaccard is a similarity preserving function, *i.e.*, if $\forall i \in [1,n]$, $x_i \leq \sqrt{x'_i x''_i}$, and $x'_i \leq x''_i$, then $EJ(\vec{p}, \vec{p'}) \geq EJ(\vec{p}, \vec{p''})$. Therefore Claim 3 holds.

$$\frac{\sum_{i=1}^{n} x_i x'_i}{\sum_{i=1}^{n} \frac{x_i^2 + x_i'^2}{2}} \geq \frac{\sum_{i=1}^{n} x_i x''_i}{\sum_{i=1}^{n} \frac{x_i^2 + x_i''^2}{2}} \tag{13}$$

$$\Rightarrow \frac{\sum_{i=1}^{n} x_i x'_i}{\sum_{i=1}^{n} x_i^2 + \sum_{i=1}^{n} x_i'^2 - \sum_{i=1}^{n} x_i x'_i} \geq \frac{\sum_{i=1}^{n} x_i x''_i}{\sum_{i=1}^{n} x_i^2 + \sum_{i=1}^{n} x_i''^2 - \sum_{i=1}^{n} x_i x''_i}$$

$$\Rightarrow \quad EJ(\overrightarrow{p}, \overrightarrow{p'}) \geq EJ(\overrightarrow{p}, \overrightarrow{p''})$$

Based on Claim 3, we proceed to prove the property of $MinST$, which is the fusion of $MaxS$ and $MinT$.

$MinT$ in Eqn(7): For each dimension j, as shown in Fig.17(a), when $\sqrt{E.i_j \cdot E.u_j} \geq \sqrt{E'.i_j \cdot E'.u_j}$ (Case 1), *i.e.*,

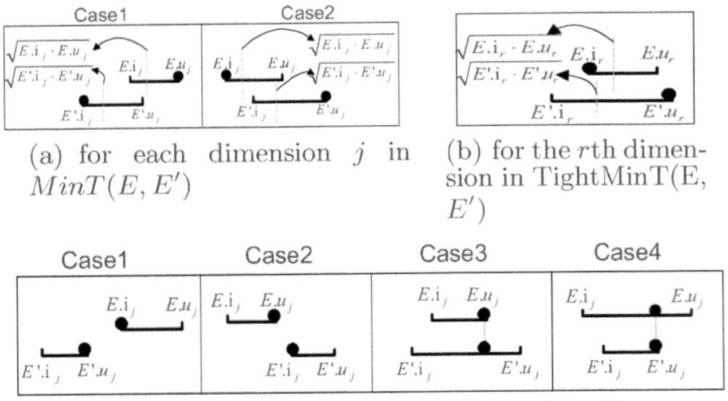

(a) for each dimension j in $MinT(E, E')$

(b) for the rth dimension in TightMinT(E, E')

(c) for each dimension j in $MaxT(E, E')$

Figure 17: Assignments of approximations

$\frac{E'.i_j}{E.u_j} \leq \frac{E.i_j}{E'.u_j}$, then for $\forall E.w \in [E.i_j, E.u_j]$ and $\forall E'.w \in [E'.i_j, E'.u_j]$, we have $\frac{E'.i_j}{E.u_j} \leq \frac{min\{E.w_j, E'.w_j\}}{max\{E.w_j, E'.w_j\}}$. Thus according to Claim 3, the assignments $E.w_j = E.u_j$, $E'.w_j = E'.i_j$ can guarantee that $MinST(E, E')$ is the minimum similarity between two entries E and E', *i.e.*, $\forall\ o \in subtree(E)$, $\forall o' \in subtree(E')$, $MinT(E, E') \leq SimT(o, o')$. And for Case 2, the property of $MinST$ can be similarly proved.

For $MinST$ in Eqn(6), since $\forall o \in E$, $\forall o' \in E'$ are enclosed in the MBRs of index nodes E and E' respectively, the maximum Euclidian distance between E and E' $MaxS(E, E')$ is no less than the Euclidian distance between o and o', *i.e.*, $MaxS(E, E') \geq dist(o, o')$, thus $\alpha(1 - \frac{MaxS(E,E') - \varphi_s}{\psi_s - \varphi_s}) \leq \alpha(1 - \frac{dist(o,o') - \varphi_s}{\psi_s - \varphi_s})$, where φ_s, ψ_s are constants and $\alpha \in [0, 1]$. And as proved above that $\forall o \in E$, $\forall o' \in E'$, $MinT(E, E') \leq SimT(o, o')$. Thus Eqn(6) can guarantee that $\forall o \in E$, $\forall o' \in E'$, $MinST(E, E') \leq SimST(o, o')$, *i.e.*, Lemma 1 is true. □

A.2 Proof of Lemma 2

PROOF. Eqn(8) suggests that $TightMinST$ is composed of $MinMaxS$, $MinT$, $MaxS$ and $TightMinT$, which have the following properties respectively.

$MinMaxS$: According to the work [3], $MinMaxS$ has the property that there exists an object $o \in E'$, so that $\forall o' \in E$, $dist(o, o') \leq MinMaxS(E, E')$.

$MaxT$ in Eqn(12): As shown in Fig.17(c), for each dimension j, if $E.i_j > E'.u_j$ (Case 1), then $\forall E.w \in [E.i_j, E.u_j]$ and $\forall E'.w \in [E'.i_j, E'.u_j]$, we have $\frac{E'.u_j}{E.i_j} \geq \frac{min\{E.w, E'.w\}}{max\{E.w, E'.w\}}$, thus based on Claim 3, the assignment $E.w_j = E.i_j$, $E'.w_j = E'.u_j$ can guarantee that $\forall\ o \in\ subtree(E)$, $\forall o' \in subtree(E')$, $MaxT(E, E') \geq SimT(o, o')$. It is similar if $E.u_j < E'.i_j$ (Case 2). For other cases, *i.e.*, the intervals $[E.i_j, E.u_j]$ and $[E'.i_j, E'.u_j]$ overlap, so obviously, $E.w_j$ and $E'.w_j$ should be assigned as the same value according to the preserving function. Further, both of $E.w_j$ and $E'.w_j$ should be assigned the largest value in the intersection between $[E.i_j, E.u_j]$ and $[E'.i_j, E'.u_j]$ shown in Case 3 and Case 4 since Extended Jaccard function is an increasing function as the increase of the values. Thus the assignment in Eqn(12) satisfies the property of $MaxT(E, E')$.

$TightMinT$ in Eqn(10): As shown the assignment of one dimension r in Fig.17(b), when $\sqrt{E'.i_r \cdot E'.u_r} < \sqrt{E.i_r \cdot E.u_r}$, let $E'.w_r = E'.u_r$, then $\exists E'.w_r \in [E'.i_r, E'.u_r]$, $\frac{min\{E.w_r, E'.w_r\}}{max\{E.w_r, E'.w_r\}} \leq \frac{min\{E.w_r, E'.u_r\}}{max\{E.w_r, E'.u_r\}}$. Then given $E'.w_r > \sqrt{E.i_r \cdot E.u_r}$, let $E.w_r = E.i_r$ so that $\forall\ E.w_r \in [E.i_r, E.u_r]$, $\frac{min\{E.w_r, E'.w_r\}}{max\{E.w_r, E'.w_r\}} \geq \frac{min\{E.i_r, E'.w_r\}}{max\{E.i_r, E'.w_r\}}$. Additionally, the rest dimension weights $E.w_j$ and $E'.w_j$ are assigned as Fig.17(a). Therefore, according to Claim 3, there exists an object $o' \in E'$, the rth dimension of which is $E'.u_r$, so that $\forall o \in E$, $SimT(o, o') \geq TightMinT(E, E')$. Finally, to make the approximation accurate, we take the maximum as the final approximation for $TightMinT$.

$TightMinST(E, E')$ in Eqn(8): Since $\exists\ o' \in E'$, $\forall\ o \in E$, $dist(o, o') \leq MinMaxS(E, E')$, moreover, since $\forall o'' \in E$, $\forall o \in E$, $EJ(o, o'') \geq MinT(E, E')$, so for $o' \in E'$, it is also true that $EJ(o, o') \geq MinT(E, E')$. Thus $\exists o' \in E'$, $\forall o \in E$, $SimST(o, o') = \alpha(1 - \frac{dist(o,o') - \varphi_s}{\psi_s - \varphi_s}) + (1 - \alpha)\frac{EJ(o,o') - \varphi_t}{\psi_t - \varphi_t} \geq \alpha(1 - \frac{MinMaxS(E,E') - \varphi_s}{\psi_s - \varphi_s}) + (1 - \alpha)\frac{MinT(E,E') - \varphi_t}{\psi_t - \varphi_t}$. Similarly, $\exists o' \in E'$, $\forall o \in E$ $SimST(o, o') \geq \alpha(1 - \frac{MaxS(E,E') - \varphi_s}{\psi_s - \varphi_s}) + (1 - \alpha)\frac{TightMinT(E,E') - \varphi_t}{\psi_t - \varphi_t}$. To make the approximation accurate, the final approximation of $TightMinST(E, E')$ is the maximum one with the guarantee of satisfying the corresponding property. □

A.3 Proof of Lemma 3

The proof is similar to that in Lemma 1 and omitted here due to space limitation.

A.4 Proof of Theorem 1

PROOF. (Sketch) We prove that (1) Algorithm *RSTkNN* is correct, that is all returned objects are desired answers; and that (2) the returned results are complete.

Correctness: The search strategy in *RSTkNN* algorithm is to prune entries E in the tree using the lower bound of spatial-textual *kNN* of E: $kNN^L(E)$ (Line 29) and to report entries E using the upper bound $kNN^U(E)$ (Line 33). $kNN^L(E)$ is calculated by means of $MinST$ and $TightMinST$ in the lower-bound contribution list of E. According to the properties of $MinST$ and $TightMinST$ in Lemma 1 and Lemma 2, entry E can be safely pruned if $MaxST(E, q) \leq kNN^L(E)$ since it can guarantee that there are at least k objects whose similarities are larger than or equal to the maximum similarity between E and query object q. Analogously, based on Lemma 3, entry E can be safely reported as a result entry if $MinST(E, q) > kNN^U(E)$ with the condition that there are at most k objects (among all the objects) whose similarities are smaller than $MinST(E, q)$. Furthermore, we can prove the correctness of the technique of "inherit" (Line 6) and "lazy travel-down" (Line 8) based on the observation that the similarity approximations of ancestor entries are more conservative than that of descendant entries.

Completeness: All objects which can not be safely pruned or reported as results, are appended to the candidate object list *COL* (Line 17). In the $FinalVerification$ procedure, all the candidate objects can be determined whether they are results through traveling down the pruned entries. It is because that even in the worst case, we can access all the objects in the subtree of the pruned entries to determine each candidate object if it is an answer in $IsHitOrDrop$ (Line 24) while $MinST$ and $MaxST$ between two database objects are equal. Thus our algorithm is complete, *i.e.*, it can return all the *RSTkNN* data points.

Hence, Theorem 1 is true. □

Location-Aware Type Ahead Search on Spatial Databases : Semantics and Efficiency

Senjuti Basu Roy*
University of Texas at Arlington
senjuti.basuroy@mavs.uta.edu

Kaushik Chakrabarti
Microsoft Research
kaushik@microsoft.com

ABSTRACT

Users often search spatial databases like yellow page data using keywords to find businesses near their current location. Such searches are increasingly being performed from mobile devices. Typing the entire query is cumbersome and prone to errors, especially from mobile phones. We address this problem by introducing type-ahead search functionality on spatial databases. Like keyword search on spatial data, type-ahead search needs to be *location-aware*, i.e., with every letter being typed, it needs to return spatial objects whose names (or descriptions) are valid completions of the query string typed so far, and which rank highest in terms of proximity to the user's location and other static scores. Existing solutions for type-ahead search cannot be used directly as they are not location-aware. We show that a straight-forward combination of existing techniques for performing type-ahead search with those for performing proximity search perform poorly. We propose a formal model for query processing cost and develop novel techniques that optimize that cost. Our empirical evaluations on real and synthetic datasets demonstrate the effectiveness of our techniques. To the best of our knowledge, this is the first work on location-aware type-ahead search.

Categories and Subject Descriptors

H.4 [**Information Systems Applications**]: Information Storage and Retrieval—*Information Search and Retrieval*[Search Process]

General Terms

Algorithms, Performance

1. INTRODUCTION

Spatial databases like yellow page data are often searched using keywords. For example, users use local search engines to find businesses, products or services *near their current location*. Hence, local search engines need to be *"location aware"*, i.e., the businesses are ranked not only by relevance to the keyword query but also by their proximity to user's location. Other factors like the popularity and ratings of businesses are also required to be taken into account [10, 6].

While many such searches are conducted from personal computers, users are increasingly using their mobile devices to perform such searches [1]. For example, users often need to find a nearby Starbucks or gas station on-the-go; they conduct such searches from their mobile devices like smart phones, where typing is cumbersome and susceptible to errors. We wish to reduce the amount of typing and clicking required before the user gets to see the final results.

In this paper, we propose to *progressively return relevant businesses as the user is typing in her query*. Consider a user looking for a nearby Starbucks. Suppose she has typed in the letters "star" on her mobile device. Note that the user's location can be obtained via a GPS-equipped mobile device. Based on that, it will be immensely useful to return the address and phone number of the nearest Starbucks, as it saves her from typing in the rest of the query. Furthermore, unlike in the case of autocompletion which returns likely query completions and requires the user to select the desired query, *no clicking is required* to see the final results here. This functionality is referred to as *type ahead search (TAS)* [14, 3]. In this paper, *we introduce the problem of supporting TAS on spatial databases.*

While TAS has been studied in the context of text documents and relational databases, to the best of our knowledge, ours is the first effort to solve TAS for spatial databases [14, 3]. What distinguishes TAS over spatial data from general TAS is that, like keyword search over spatial data, it needs to be *location-aware*. With every letter being typed, TAS should return k spatial objects whose names (or descriptions) are valid completions of the query string typed so far *and* which are closest to the user's location.

Semantics of Location-aware TAS: We define the semantics of TAS on spatial databases. Consider a spatial database containing names and locations of businesses shown in Table 1; locations are represented as points in 2-D space. We ignore the static score column for the time being. Suppose a user has typed in "star" so far from location (36, 0). O_7 and O_{10} are valid completions of the query. Suppose the user is interested in the top-1 result. TAS should return O_{10} as it is much closer to the user's location compared to O_7.

Note that it is crucial to consider spatial proximity *at a fine granularity*. Being proximity-oblivious for all objects inside a city might result in undesirable answers. For example, if we assume all the objects in Table 1 are located in the same city, a proximity-oblivious search might fail to distinguish between the nearest Starbucks O_{10} (for the previous query), and a much farther one O_7.

Furthermore, other factors like the popularity and ratings of the objects should also be considered; we model all these factors as a *single static score* associated with each object. Consider the query "shan" from location (37,3), and the corresponding valid completions (O_5 and O_6). Ignoring static score, we will get object O_6 as the top-1 result. But intu-

*Work done while visiting Microsoft Research

SIGMOD'11, June 12–16, 2011, Athens, Greece.

ID	String	Location	Static Score
O_1	Target	(3,9)	200
O_2	Thai Basil Leaf Restaurant	(50,30)	5
O_3	Sushi Rock	(9,50)	7
O_4	Sushi at Plano	(0,9)	25
O_5	Shanghai Cafe	(41,2)	500
O_6	Shanghai Garden	(38,5)	10
O_7	Starbucks	(32,8)	100
O_8	Super China Buffet	(42,5)	100
O_9	Staples	(45,12)	300
O_{10}	Starbucks	(35,0)	100

Table 1: Spatial Database $\mathcal{D}$ with 10 Objects

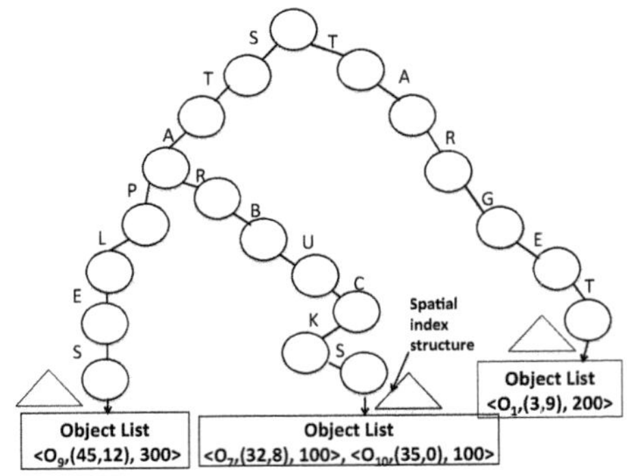

Figure 1: Integrated Architecture for Location-Aware TAS

itively O_5 is a better answer, since it is a much more popular restaurant and is only slightly farther from the user's current location compared to O_6. In Section 2, we define semantics that takes both proximity and static scores into account.

Architecture: One may think that location-aware TAS can be supported by simply partitioning the entire geographical space into a set of spatial regions and using the location-unaware TAS solution (i.e., build a trie) for the objects in each region. In Section 3.1, we argue the limitations of that solution. We propose a novel architecture that *integrates the trie with a spatial data structure to enable location-aware TAS.* The basic idea is to maintain a single trie for the entire database, and augment it with spatial information of the objects. Such a trie for a subset of database in Table 1 (consisting of O_1, O_7, O_9, O_{10}) is shown in Figure 1. Benefits of such an architecture is discussed in Section 3.2. A simple baseline algorithm to support location aware TAS in this architecture is to first identify the trie node that matches with the query string, then traverse the entire subtree below it, compute the scores of the objects in that subtree, and finally return the top k objects based on the ranking function.

Improving Response Time: A TAS system has to be responsive – it must look instantaneous to the user. Prior work has shown that this implies a maximum response time of 100ms. In a client-server setting, this 100ms bound includes not only the trie search time but also network overhead. Hence, it is desirable to keep the trie search time minimal. The above baseline algorithm fails to meet that requirements, as it traverses too many links in the trie and scores too many objects. An efficient algorithm must avoid such unnecessary traversals and score computations.

One option is to materialize the top-k answers for each query prefix and for each query location; this is clearly infeasible due to the space overhead. A variant that maintains the top-k answers at the granularity of "regions" is also infeasible: the regions need to be granular enough to support the desirable semantics which results in high space overhead.

We propose to materialize *score bounds* at trie nodes: these are upper bounds of the scores of any object under that node. At query time, these bounds are used to *prune*, i.e., avoid traversal in parts of the trie that cannot contribute to the top-k results. Observe that the actual scores depend on the query location; therefore a single score bound per trie node is *not tight enough* for effective pruning – we need score bounds at a fine spatial granularity for effective pruning.

Since the trie needs to be memory resident, and the amount of main memory is limited, storing score-bounds at a fine spatial granularity at each trie node is not possible. We argue that we can materialize bounds only in a subset of trie nodes. Furthermore, we observe that *not all such subsets are equally beneficial* in saving *query processing cost.* For example, materializing at a parent and its child node in a trie with similar score bounds is less beneficial compared with choosing two nodes with significantly different upper bounds. Hence, it is important to select the subset *judiciously.* In addition, *the benefit of storing score bounds at a fine spatial granularity in much higher in some regions than in others.* For example, where the score-bounds exhibit high spatial locality, we do not need to store fine granularity score-bounds. Therefore, we need to be *adaptive* in our choice of granularity, i.e., store coarse-granularity bounds over regions that have high locality, and fine-granularity bounds elsewhere.

Summary of Contributions: The main technical challenge we address in this paper is: *how to distribute available memory among the nodes in the trie in order to minimize the expected query processing cost?* We refer to this as the *memory distribution problem.* We address this challenge by proposing a novel, rigorous modeling of query processing cost for TAS queries, and formalizing it as an optimization problem. Our contributions can be summarized as follows:

- We introduce the problem of location-aware TAS on spatial databases, define its semantics, and propose an integrated architecture for it (Section 3.2).
- We propose a novel analytical model for TAS query processing cost (Section 4.1)
- We formalize the memory distribution problem as an optimization problem (Section 4.4). Unfortunately, this problem is extremely hard as it is exponential in two factors: (i) number of trie nodes, and (ii) available space budget. As a reasonable alternative, we propose a slightly restricted problem: how to select a subset of M trie nodes and store R bounds in each of them such that expected query processing cost can be minimized? We refer to this as the $\{M, R\}$*-Memory Distribution Problem.* We show that the above problem can be split into two independent optimization problems:

(i) **M-node selection problem**: The problem is to select a set of M nodes where bound materialization would minimize the query processing cost. Based on that, we introduce the notion of "benefit" of materializing bounds at a set of nodes, and formalize the M-node selection as an optimization problem. We prove that the problem is NP-complete, and design a hill-climbing based algorithm as an efficient alternative (Section 5.1).

(ii) **R-cover computation problem**: The problem is to create a partitioning of size R of the entire geographic region such that the query processing cost is minimized. We formalize the problem as an optimization problem based on the popular maximum-error metric. We show the problem is NP-hard. We consider a novel, restricted version of the problem, where the rectangles are restricted to the regions of a quadtree [11], and provide an optimal algorithm for it (Section 5.2).

- We propose a novel query processing algorithm. We prove its optimality in query processing cost (Section 6).
- Finally, we perform extensive experiments using real and synthetic dataset (Section 7). Our experiments show that our algorithms leveraging score bounds are *3-4 times faster* than the baseline algorithm that does not use score bounds.

2. SEMANTICS OF LOCATION-AWARE TAS

We start by introducing our data model, query model, proposed ranking framework, and finally define the location-aware TAS problem.

2.1 Data model

Let $\mathcal{D}$ be a spatial database. Each spatial object O is defined as the tuple $\langle O.id, O.str, O.loc, O.sscore\rangle$ where, $O.id$ is the unique id of that object, $O.str$ is the description string of O, $O.loc$ is the location descriptor in multidimensional space, and $O.sscore$ is the static score. In this work, we assume two dimensional space, i.e., $O.loc = (x, y)$ and describes x and y co-ordinates respectively. These coordinates can be derived from longitude and latitude information. Type ahead search is performed over $O.str$.

Consider a Yellow Page database containing names and locations of all businesses. There, $O.str$ denotes name of the object (this enables TAS over name), $O.loc$ is its geographical location, and $O.sscore$ is the overall score computed using a number of factors like the popularity, number of reviews, and ratings of the business.

Note that sometimes users search by the type of business instead of the name of the business. For example, users might type in "coffee shop" while looking for coffee shops. We would like the TAS system to return the nearest Starbucks, Tully's Coffee, and other coffee shops. Observe that these results will not be returned if $O.str$ is the name of the business (because the above names do not start with "coffee"). We can address this problem by associating, in addition to the name, strings that describe the type of business to the objects, and performing search over those strings.

We use the spatial database in Table 1 as a running example. In this example, we assume the business name is only description string associated with the $O.str$. Note that the same string can be associated with multiple objects (e.g., string "Starbucks" associated to all Starbucks stores).

2.2 Query Model

The TAS query interface is as follows: As the user types in the query, with every key stroke, the string typed so far is sent to the TAS system along with the user's location. In response, the TAS system returns the set of most *relevant* k spatial objects. The query Q therefore has two components: (i) the string typed so far; we denote it by $Q.str$, and (ii) the location $Q.loc$ of the user during query.

Furthermore, without loss of generality, we assume that the database $\mathcal{D}$ induces a global rectangular region $Global = \{ll, ur\}$ such that all objects in $\mathcal{D}$ are spatially contained in it. $Global.ll$ and $Global.ur$ denote the lower left and upper right corner respectively of $Global$. Furthermore, we assume $Q.loc$ is contained inside $Global$.

Note that the above query model corresponds to a stateless TAS system. In reality, the TAS system can be stateful: such a system can compute answers incrementally by using results of earlier queries, as the user types in more characters. For simplicity, we present our techniques in the context of a stateless TAS system. The general technique of materializing score bounds and using them to prune trie traversal applies to a stateful system as well. However, our query processing algorithm needs to be adapted to exploit cached results from earlier queries; we wish to explore that direction in future work.

2.3 Ranking Framework

Given a query Q and a spatial database $\mathcal{D}$, TAS should only return objects from $\mathcal{D}$ that are valid completions of $Q.str$. Any type-ahead search system must satisfy this basic property. We denote the set of such objects as $MatchSet(Q, \mathcal{D})$. Since $\mathcal{D}$ is fixed, for simplicity, we henceforth omit $\mathcal{D}$ from our notation. Formally,
$MatchSet(Q) = \{O | O \in \mathcal{D} \wedge Q.str \text{ is a prefix of } O.str\}$.

Among these objects, we want to return the k objects that are in *close proximity to the query location* and have high *static score*. We next describe such a ranking function.

Combination Model: Let $Dist(Q.loc, O.loc)$ denote the distance between the location of the query Q and object O. In this paper, we use the Euclidean distance function but any function that is monotone with respect to the distance along each dimension (i.e., x, y) can be used. In fact, all L_p distance functions satisfy this property.

The overall score of an object $O \in MatchSet(Q)$ for query Q is defined as $\mathcal{F}(Dist(Q.loc, O.loc), O.sscore)$, where $\mathcal{F}$ is a function monotone with respect to the two components. Although our techniques apply to the above class of scoring function, for simplicity, we describe our techniques in the context of the linear interpolation function proposed in [6, 10].

Specifically, the final score is a linear interpolation of the individual normalized scores of the two components:

$$\mathcal{F}(Q, O) = w_d \times (1 - \frac{Dist(Q.loc.O.loc)}{maxDist}) + w_s \times \frac{O.sscore}{maxSScore} \quad (1)$$

where w_d, w_s are the two parameters, s.t.$w_d + w_s = 1$. They allow the system designer to control the relative importance of the two components in the overall score. $maxDist$ is the maximum distance between any object and query and $maxSScore$ is the maximum static score of any object in the database. We compute $maxDist$ as $Dist(G.ll, G.ur)$. $maxDist$ (similarly $maxSScore$) is used to normalize the distance score (static score).

Note that our study focuses on efficient techniques for type-ahead search; hence, we adapt existing distance functions instead of developing new ones.

2.4 Problem Statement

Given a query $Q = (str, loc)$, a spatial database $\mathcal{D}$, and an integer k, identify the result set $Res(Q, k)$ of objects, such that,
(i) $|\text{Res(Q,k)}| = k$
(ii) $\forall O \in Res(Q, k), O \in MatchSet(Q)$, and
(iii) the objects in $Res(Q, k)$ have the highest scores among all objects in $MatchSet(Q)$, i.e.,for any object $O \in Res(Q, k)$ and any object $O' \in MatchSet(Q) - Res(Q, k)$, $\mathcal{F}(Q, O) \geq \mathcal{F}(Q, O')$.

3. ARCHITECTURES FOR LOCATION AWARE TAS

Standard (i.e., non location-aware) TAS systems require ordered tree data structure such as *trie*. Type ahead search is enabled by inserting all search strings into a trie $\mathcal{T}$. Let

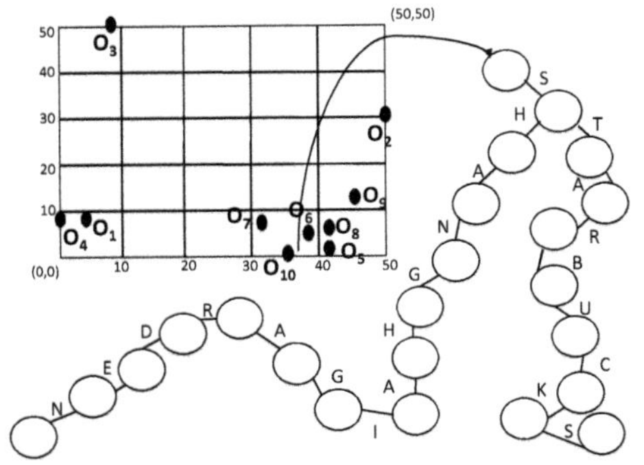

Figure 2: Partition Space Build Trie for Location-Aware TAS

$n_{\mathcal{T}}$ be a node in $\mathcal{T}$, and Subtree($n_{\mathcal{T}}$) is the entire subtree under it.

Note that each trie node $n_{\mathcal{T}}$ can be uniquely identified by a string (denoted by $str(n_{\mathcal{T}})$); that string corresponds to the labeled path from the root node to $n_{\mathcal{T}}$. For example, in the trie in Figure 1, the string identifying the left child of the root is "s", the one identifying its (only) child is "st", and so on. Searching is performed by first identifying the node $n_{\mathcal{T}}$ that matches the query string, i.e., $str(n_{\mathcal{T}}) = Q.str$. This node is henceforth referred to as the *query matched node*, denoted by QMN(Q). Subsequently, Subtree(QMN(Q)) is searched to obtain the results. Existing work offers several optimized version of trie, such as Patricia Tree [7], and we adopt those optimized versions. Now, to make the search location aware, these are the two possibilities.

3.1 Partition Space then Build Trie

One possibility is to first partition the global space *Global* into a set of spatial regions. Maintain a trie containing description strings of the objects inside each region. Given a query Q, the system first identifies the region that contains the query location. It then performs a standard trie search operation inside that region to identify $Res(Q,k)$. $Res(Q,k)$ is determined solely based on static scores of the objects, ignoring distance. Figure 2 corresponds to this architecture, where 25 spatial regions of $\mathcal{D}$ are created (each of dimension 10×10), and the trie corresponding to the region $\{(30,0),(40,10)\}$ is shown.

Although simple and similar in principle to standard TAS architecture, this architecture suffers from several potential demerits:

Missing cross-boundary objects: Recall the example "shan" in Section 1. This architecture first determines the $Q.loc$ specific spatial region $\{(30,0),(40,10)\}$, then performs trie search and returns O_6 as the top-1 completion. A more desirable result O_5 will be missed as it fails to consider cross-boundary objects.

Inability to support desired semantics: The ranking of an object inside a spatial region is oblivious to distance. Recall example "star" in Section 1; the above architecture fails to distinguish between farther Starbucks O_7 and the nearer one O_{10}, and may return either of them. Observe that, a very fine-granularity partition (e.g., one partition per zip code) may mitigate such effects to some extent. However, such partitions are extremely space redundant as they require to replicate the same string numerous times (in each spatial region specific trie). Limited availability of main memory makes this possibility unrealistic in practice.

3.2 Integrate Trie with Spatial Data Structure

An alternative possibility is to maintain a single trie over all description strings of objects in $\mathcal{D}$. Each trie leaf contains a list of objects (denoted as *object list*). Each object is described by $\langle O.id, O.loc, O.sscore\rangle$. Observe that, any object whose description string is the string identifying the node $l_{\mathcal{T}}$, is in the object list of $l_{\mathcal{T}}$. Figure 1 shows this architecture over a subset of objects O_1, O_7, O_9, and O_{10} from the database in Table 1.

Given a query Q, the search begins in $\mathcal{T}$ by identifying QMN(Q). $Res(Q,k)$ is computed by visiting each leaf $l_{\mathcal{T}}$ in Subtree(QMN(Q)) and resolving complete scores of all objects encountered there, and finally selecting k objects that contain the overall k-highest scores. The algorithm uses a global priority queue `ResultsPQ` to maintain the k-objects with highest scores encountered thus far. `ResultsPQ` is updated as the score of an object in a leaf node is computed (denoted as `LeafNodeSearch`). The pseudocode is listed in Algorithm 1.

Algorithm 1 Baseline-TAS -Baseline Algorithm for location-aware TAS

Require: Trie $\mathcal{T}$, Query Q, an integer k

`ResultsPQ` $= \phi$
Perform lookup in Trie $\mathcal{T}$ to determine QMN(Q)
for each leaf $l_{\mathcal{T}} \in Subtree(QMN(Q))$ **do**
    Execute LeafNodeSearch($l_{\mathcal{T}}$) and update `ResultsPQ`
return $Res(Q,k)$ from `ResultsPQ`

The benefit of this integrated architecture is various: first, this architecture is able to support any ranking function. Note that, for both example queries, it will be able to return the desired semantics. Second, this architecture is optimum in space requirement. Hence we adopt this integrated architecture.

Efficient Implementation of `LeafNodeSearch`: The above implementation of `LeafNodeSearch` scans the entire object list in the leaf node, and computes scores of all the objects. This can be expensive if the object list is large. This can be avoided by using the threshold family of algorithms [9]. NRA can be used if only sorted accesses on each individual ranking component (a getNext() interface on static score and distance[1]) is provided. A TA [9] based solution can be used and may terminate even earlier if random access is also available on static score table. The k-th largest score in `ResultsPQ` is used to determine the termination condition of TA. Baseline-TAS is used as our baseline algorithm with TA like implementation for `LeafNodeSearch`.

Limitations: Algorithm `Baseline-TAS` still visits each leaf in QMN(Q), and performs several score computations in each leaf.

4. QUERY PROCESSING USING INTEGRATE ARCHITECTURE

Given a query Q, the goal is to return the k best objects ($Res(Q,k)$) in $MatchSet(Q)$ according to a ranking function $\mathcal{F}$, as stated in Subsection 2.4.

4.1 Query Processing Cost Model

We begin our discussion by formally defining processing cost to determine $Res(Q,k)$ using integrated architecture. Recall that, in order to determine $Res(Q,k)$, node QMN(Q)

[1] main memory based spatial data structures like KD-tree, quad tree can enable efficient getNext() interface on distance

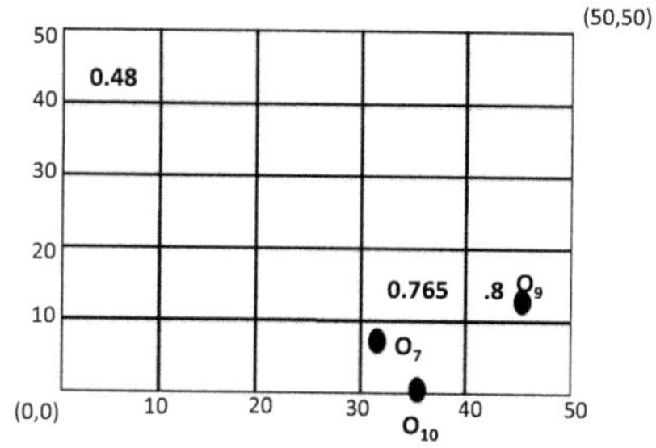

Figure 3: SGB at node "STA" of $\mathcal{T}$

needs to be determined first. The next task is to visit the leaf nodes following the links of Subtree(QMN(Q)), and finally compute scores of the objects encountered there.

Let, $\mathcal{L}_{\{Q,k\}}$ be the total number of links traversed, and $Sc_{\{Q,k\}}$ be the total number of objects for which score is computed during query processing.

DEFINITION 1. **(Query Processing Cost Model)** $\texttt{QPCost(Q,k)} = \texttt{Cost(QMN(Q))} + c_l \times \mathcal{L}_{\{Q,k\}} + c_{sc} \times Sc_{\{Q,k\}}$, *where c_l and c_{sc} are two constants, that denote unit link traversal, and score computation costs respectively.*

Observe that, any algorithm has to incur Cost(QMN(Q)) and is negligible compared to other two costs. Hence, we ignore Cost(QMN(Q)), and focus only upon the improvement of link traversal and score computation cost.

4.1.1 Query Processing Cost of `Baseline-TAS`

One may notice that during computation of the $Res(Q,k)$, Algorithm 1 needs to traverse entire Subtree(QMN(Q)). Let, $|Subtree(QMN(Q))|$ be the subtree size, and $Obj_{l_\mathcal{T}}$ be the number of objects processed at leaf $l_\mathcal{T}$ during leaf node search.

QPCost(Q,k) $= (c_l \times |Subtree(QMN(Q))|)$
$+ \Sigma_{\forall l_\mathcal{T} \in Subtree(QMN(Q))}(c_{sc} \times Obj_{l_\mathcal{T}})$.

We argue that returning top-k valid completions are most useful to a user during few initial query key strokes, especially in the case of mobile applications, where typing is cumbersome and error-prone. Unfortunately, the size of the Subtree(QMN(Q)) is prohibitively large in the beginning. `Baseline-TAS` must traverse that entire subtree, and hence incurs substantial query processing cost. Moreover, many of the link traversal and score computation get wasted as only a very small fraction of the leaf nodes of Subtree(QMN(Q)) eventually contributes to the set $Res(Q,k)$. We note that an efficient query processing technique must intelligently select those paths of Subtree(QMN(Q)) for traversal such that they eventually contributes to the final $Res(Q,k)$. Next, we discuss these possibilities in detail.

4.2 Techniques to Reduce Query Processing Cost

Note that, link traversal and score computation cost can be significantly reduced, if the actual $Res(Q,k)$ is pre-computed and materialized for each intermediate node of $\mathcal{T}$. Unfortunately, such techniques *immediately fail* in our case, since, i) $Res(Q,k)$ varies based on query location according to our ranking framework, and ii) Materializing $Res(Q,k)$ for every possible location at every intermediate node is impossible to follow in practice. An alternative possibility is to materialize at a very fine spatial granularity to support desirable ranking semantics. However, such granularity requires humongous space that our main memory based integrated architecture fails to support.

We therefore propose materialization of *score-bound* at a trie node, that denotes the *maximum-score* any object under that subtree may get, when a query matches that node. Note that, the challenge is to ensure that *score-bound* is correct *irrespective of query location.*

EXAMPLE 1. **(Single Score Bound)** *Consider the spatial database in Table 1, and the corresponding partial trie in Figure 1. Observe that, the object list under the trie node "STA" contains O_7, O_9, and O_{10}. The object with highest static score (O_9) determines the score-bound of that node. Note that, score-bound of an object needs to be computed considering the maximum-score for the distance component that occurs when $Q.loc = O.loc$. The score-bound of static score component of O_9 after normalization becomes 0.3, whereas, that of distance component is 0.5, with an overall score-bound of 0.8 after addition (assuming $w_d = w_s = 0.5$ in Equation 1).*

Query processing algorithm benefits from pre-computed score-bound in the following way: if the score-bound of a node in Subtree(QMN(Q)) is not larger than the k-th largest object score (computed thus far during query processing), the entire subtree under that node can be pruned, i.e., can be saved from traversal. Therefore, score-bound at a node needs to be *tight* for effective pruning.

However, the actual score of an object under a node may be significantly smaller than the pre-computed score-bound of that node. In fact, in the previous example, actual score of O_9 will never reach 0.8, unless $Q.loc = O_9.loc$. For any other $Q.loc$, the distance component score will be smaller than 0.5. Therefore, we argue that storing *only one* score-bound per trie node may not be *enough* since that may fail to generate sufficiently *tight* score-bounds. But also, storing score-bounds at the finest granularity is an impossible task, especially because the entire data structure needs to reside in the main memory during query processing.

In this work, we take up an intermediate approach by partitioning *Global* into a set of spatial regions and storing score-bounds for them.

The set of regions together must satisfy the *cover* property over *Global*, i.e., each point location in *Global* must be contained in one of the regions. We begin by considering a special case of cover at a node, where the regions are non-overlapping, equal size rectangles. Such a cover at node $n_\mathcal{T}$ with bounds is referred to as the *spatial grid of bounds* (henceforth denoted as SGB($n_\mathcal{T}$)). Each region of a spatial grid ($\mathcal{G}$) is referred to as a *grid cell* or simply a *cell* (g). The granularity of a spatial grid is determined by a domain expert, and we assign score-bounds for them. Next we define *Score-bound* of a grid cell g.

DEFINITION 2. **(Score-bound of a grid cell)** *It is the maximum-score of any object under $n_\mathcal{T}$ (for any $Q.loc$ inside g).*
Score-bound$(g, n_\mathcal{T}) = max_{\forall O_i \in Subtree(n_\mathcal{T})}$ *Max-Score*(O_i), *s.t.* $g.ll.x \le Q.loc.x \le g.ur.x$ *and* $g.ll.y \le Q.loc.y \le g.ur.y$

EXAMPLE 2. **(SGB)** *Consider Figure 3 that shows an SGB of the node "STA" with granularity 10×10. Observe that only the grid cell $\{(40,10),(50,20)\}$ has score-bound 0.8, whereas the grid-cell*

$\{(0,40),(10,50)\}$ *contains a much smaller score-bound of* 0.48. *A query that is contained in the latter cell thus acquires tighter score-bound (as compared to a single score-bound) by the SGB.*

4.3 Main Insights

• **Judicious Node Selection:** It is *not possible* to materialize SGB at every trie node. Only a subset of trie nodes can be materialized. Different subset of nodes offers different *benefit* towards query processing. For example, materializing a parent and child node in a trie with similar score bounds is less beneficial compared to choosing two nodes with significantly different score bounds. Therefore, judicious node selection is important.

•**Adaptive Cover Computation:** Consider an example trie node that contains only one object with very high static score (all other objects have very low static scores), and assume $w_s \gg w_d$ in the ranking function. Most likely that object will influence the score-bounds of such a node for most *Q.loc*. Therefore, the score-bounds will exhibit very high spatial locality. Creating partitions of finer granularity is not useful for such nodes. However fine granularity partitions may be beneficial for a case, that shows substantial variation in score-bounds at different *Q.loc*. Therefore, cover computation needs to be adaptive.

4.4 Memory Distribution

Intuitively, our objective is to minimize the expected cost of top-k query processing on any query, using the materialized trie.

Let $\mathcal{N}_\mathcal{T}$ be the set of intermediate nodes in a trie $\mathcal{T}$, and S be the space available for materialization. Let $p(Q)$ denote the probability or likelihood of Q being issued [2]. The formal problem is stated as follows.

Generalized Memory Distribution Problem:
Minimize $\Sigma_{\forall Q} p(Q) \times QPCost(Q)$
such that $(0 \leq s_{n_\mathcal{T}} \leq S)$, and $\forall_{n_\mathcal{T} \in \mathcal{N}_\mathcal{T}} (\Sigma s_{n_\mathcal{T}} \leq S)$,
where $s_{n_\mathcal{T}}$ is the allocated space for materialization at the intermediate trie node $n_\mathcal{T} \in \mathcal{N}_\mathcal{T}$.

Although clearly very important, this problem is unfortunately quite challenging to solve optimally, since it is exponential in both S and $\mathcal{N}_\mathcal{T}$. As a first step toward addressing these challenges, we consider a restricted version, where the possible assignments for $s_{n_\mathcal{T}}$'s are either 0 (no materialization) or R (a predefined number designed by the domain expert), and our task is to select the set of M nodes such that each of them has R space allocation, s.t., $S = M \times R$. With this simplified assumption, we define the $\{M, R\}$ Memory Distribution Problem as follows.

DEFINITION 3. **($\{M, R\}$ Memory Distribution Problem)**
Minimize $\Sigma_{\forall Q} p(Q) \times QPCost(Q)$
s.t., $s_{n_\mathcal{T}} = 0$ *or* R*, and* $|\{n_\mathcal{T}|(s_{n_\mathcal{T}=R})\}| = M$*, where* $s_{n_\mathcal{T}}$ *is the allocated space at the trie node* $n_\mathcal{T} \in \mathcal{N}_\mathcal{T}$*.*

5. $\{M, R\}$ DISTRIBUTION PROBLEM SOLUTION

Note that, the optimal cover of size R (R cover in short) can be computed independently at a trie node, while the M node selection process needs to use R-cover to determine the set $\mathcal{M}$ (s.t., $|\mathcal{M}| = M$). A trie with M materialized nodes, where each materialized node has R-cover is known as bound materialized trie $\mathcal{T}_{\mathcal{BM}}$.

[2]can be derived from query log

We begin our discussion by illustrating the M Node Selection problem, then discuss R cover computation problem.

5.1 M Node Selection

We aim at modeling the *benefit* of a set $\mathcal{M}$ of materialized trie nodes for reducing *QPCost*, and then pose the optimization problem.

We begin by analyzing the *benefit* of a single materialized node $n_\mathcal{T}$ in a set of materialized nodes for a query Q. Materialization at a node $n_\mathcal{T}$ benefits only those queries whose QMN(Q) is an ancestor of $n_\mathcal{T}$. *Benefit* of materializing at $n_\mathcal{T}$[3] for an ancestor $n'_\mathcal{T}$ is modeled by considering the following two aspects.

Likelihood of Pruning - Suppose *Q.loc* is known. Let, g and g' be the cells in SGB($n_\mathcal{T}$) and SGB($n'_\mathcal{T}$) respectively that contains *Q.loc*. Therefore, akin to actual pruning, $\frac{score-bound(g', n'_\mathcal{T})}{score-bound(g, n_\mathcal{T})}$ approximates the relative value of actual k-th largest score at $n'_\mathcal{T}$, and the score-bound at $n_\mathcal{T}$; a larger ratio increases the *likelihood* of pruning. Observe that, in this model, we are required to capture this *likelihood* for any *Q.loc*. Therefore, the likelihood of pruning is measured by considering the ratio of Expected-Score-bound($n'_\mathcal{T}$), and Expected-Score-bound($n_\mathcal{T}$), by leveraging location distribution information of past $n'_\mathcal{T}$ queries from query logs.[4]

Cost Save if Pruned - Next, we capture how much *QPCost* node $n_\mathcal{T}$ *saves* upon materialization (irrespective of its ancestors), considering rest of the materialized nodes in set $\mathcal{M}$ that are $n_\mathcal{T}$'s descendants. We define the *materialized frontier* of a node $n_\mathcal{T}$ in that context.

DEFINITION 4. **(Materialized Frontier)**
MFr($n_\mathcal{T}$) - The nearest *set of materialized descendant nodes of* $n_\mathcal{T}$ *together creates a materialized frontier.*

Figure 4 shows a materialized frontier of $\mathcal{T}$ root, and a materialized frontier of node "STA".

Note that, without $n_\mathcal{T}$ being materialized, query processing algorithm must proceed further down and traverse the entire Subtree($n_\mathcal{T}$), except the subtree of $n_\mathcal{T}$'s materialized frontier. We argue that $n_\mathcal{T}$ saves higher *QPCost* upon materialization, if $QPCost(n_\mathcal{T})$ is much larger than the query processing cost of its materialized frontier[5].Therefore,

DEFINITION 5. **(Cost-save)**
$CostSave(n_\mathcal{T}) = QPCost(n_\mathcal{T}) - \Sigma_{\forall n''_\mathcal{T} \in MFr(n_\mathcal{T})} QPCost(n''_\mathcal{T})$

As an example, in Figure 4 for node "STA" $QPCost(n_\mathcal{T})$ is 13 and $\Sigma_{\forall MFr(n_\mathcal{T})} QPCost(MFr(n_\mathcal{T}))$ is 9 (assuming $c_l = 1$ and $c_{sc} = 1$). A larger CostSave denotes higher worth of $n_\mathcal{T}$'s benefit.

Finally, given an ancestor $n'_\mathcal{T}$, likelihood of pruning at $n_\mathcal{T}$ and CostSave($n_\mathcal{T}$) are multiplied to denote $n_\mathcal{T}$'s *benefit* towards $QPCost(n'_\mathcal{T})$. Then, we sum it over each ancestor of $n_\mathcal{T}$ to compute $n_\mathcal{T}$'s total *benefit.*

Similarly, the *benefit* of a set of nodes is the sum of *benefit* of each node in that set.

DEFINITION 6. **(Benefit)**
$Benefit(\mathcal{M}) = \Sigma_{\forall n_\mathcal{T} \in \mathcal{M}} Benefit(n_\mathcal{T}, \mathcal{M})$*, and*
$Benefit(n_\mathcal{T}, \mathcal{M}) = \Sigma_{\forall_{n'_\mathcal{T}}} \frac{Expected-Score-bound(n'_\mathcal{T})}{Expected-Score-bound(n_\mathcal{T})} \times CostSave($
s.t., $n'_\mathcal{T}$ *is an ancestor of node* $n_\mathcal{T}$*.*

[3]$n'_\mathcal{T}$ and Q will be used interchangeably in this discussion.
[4]We compute Average-Score-bound in the absence of a query log.
[5]Note that, Subtree $n_\mathcal{T}$ may not even have any materialized frontier.

Algorithm 2 Randomized M Node Selection : Algorithm to compute the best set of M nodes

Require:
$\mathcal{N}_\mathcal{T}$ - set of intermediate trie nodes, `NumReStart` - number of random restart, M - the number of selected nodes

$\mathcal{M} = \{\}$, $PrevSet = \{\}$, $PrevBenefit = 0$, and $i = 1$
repeat
  $\mathcal{M} = \{$a randomly chosen set of M trie nodes$\}$
  while $AllNeighborSet(\mathcal{M})$ are *not* visited **do**
    $\mathcal{M}'$ = Remove one node from $\mathcal{M}$ uniform randomly, and replace that with a node chosen uniform randomly from $\{\mathcal{N}_\mathcal{T}\} - \{\mathcal{M}\}$.
    $\mathcal{M} = \mathcal{M}'$ if $Benefit(\mathcal{M}') > Benefit(\mathcal{M})$
  if $PrevBenefit < Benefit(\mathcal{M})$ **then**
    $PrevSet = \mathcal{M}$
    $PrevBenefit = Benefit(\mathcal{M})$
  $i = i + 1$
until $\{i > NumReStart\}$
$\mathcal{M} = PrevSet$
return $\mathcal{M}$

Optimization Problem - M Node Selection:
Given a set of $\mathcal{N}_\mathcal{T}$ trie nodes, select a set $\mathcal{M}$ ($|\mathcal{M}| = M$), s.t. $Benefit(\mathcal{M})$ is maximized.
Next, we argue that identifying the best set $\mathcal{M}$ according to the optimization problem is provably challenging, since this requires to solve an NP-complete problem.

THEOREM 1. **(Hardness Result)**
Finding the set $\mathcal{M}$ which maximizes $Benefit(\mathcal{M})$ is NP-Complete.

NP-completeness is proved using a reduction from the set cover problem [12], using a very simple benefit function. Due to lack of space, we omit the details of that proof from this version of the paper. Unfortunately, an approximation algorithm for set cover does not lend to our problem easily, since the actual benefit of a node is much complicated in reality.

Efficient Algorithm
As a reasonably efficient alternative of this hard problem, we propose a *randomized hill climbing* algorithm to search for a local optima, starting from a random $\mathcal{M}$ set and computing its associated benefit. At each step, the algorithm goes to a "neighboring set" of $\mathcal{M}$, by swapping one random node from the existing $\mathcal{M}$ set that results in higher $Benefit(\mathcal{M})$. One complete hill climbing process terminates when all swapping possibilities of a set $\mathcal{M}$ are explored. We design a random-restart approach (with a predefined number, `NumReStart`) on top of the hill-climbing method, that iteratively performs hill-climbing search, each time with a random initial set $\mathcal{M}$. The hill climbing results $\mathcal{M}$ that corresponds to the highest $Benefit(\mathcal{M})$ is retained after all iterations. Note that, random-restart enhances the chances of obtaining the global optima. The pseudo-code of this algorithm is listed in Algorithm 2.

5.2 R Cover Computation

We discuss the R cover computation problem at a trie node. We perform the following two tasks:
- Compute SGB of grid $\mathcal{G}$.
- If the number of cells in SGB is more than R, we compute an R cover on that.

5.2.1 SGB Computation

Recall that, score-bound of a grid cell at a trie node is the maximum *Max-Score* of each satisfying object under that

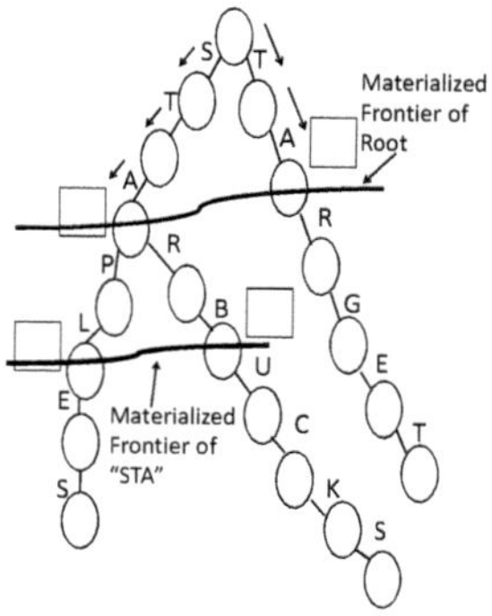

Figure 4: Query Processing Using Bound-Materialized Trie

node for any $Q.loc$ in that cell. Max-Score of an object can be efficiently computed considering MINDIST [19][6].

$$\text{Max-Score}(O, g) = w_d \times \left(1 - \frac{MINDIST(O.loc, g)}{maxDist}\right) + w_s \frac{O.sscore}{maxSScore}$$

DEFINITION 7. **(MINDIST)**
$MINDIST(O, g) = |O.x - g_{r.x}|^2 + |O.y - g_{r.y}|^2$, where, $g_{r.x}$ ($g_{r.y}$)
$= g.ll.x$ ($g.ll.y$) if $O.loc.x$ ($O.loc.y$) $< g.ll.x$ ($g.ll.y$)
$= g.ur.x$ ($g.ur.y$) if $O.loc.x$ ($O.loc.y$) $> g.ur.x$ ($g.ur.y$)
$= O.loc.x$ ($O.loc.y$) otherwise.

Given a cell g at $n_\mathcal{T}$, Max-score needs to be computed for each object under $n_\mathcal{T}$ to compute Score-bound$(g, n_\mathcal{T})$. Then, score-bound needs to be computed for every g in the grid $\mathcal{G}$. Observe that, a naive computation is quadratic in the number of objects, and the number of cells. Although done in preprocessing, repeating this quadratic computation at every trie node is impractical.

We propose a novel solution at this juncture. Given a cell g under $n_\mathcal{T}$, the Score-bound$(g, n_\mathcal{T})$ is the *highest* (top-1) *Max-Score* of an object under $n_\mathcal{T}$. Observe that, the overall score of an object is a monotonic combination of distance score and static score, where distance score is again monotonic along x and y dimensions. Therefore, Threshold algorithm [9] (TA) style computation can be enabled, and Score-bound$(g, n_\mathcal{T})$ may be computed without computing Max-score of all objects under $n_\mathcal{T}$. Three lists are to be used for the objects under $n_\mathcal{T}$ during TA - `List.x` (sorted in increasing x-coordinate distance), `List.y` (sorted in increasing y-coordinate distance), `List.sscore` (sorted in decreasing static score). As in TA, each entry in the list is an object id, its complete score can be resolved using the object database $\mathcal{D}$.

To compute the score-bound of a cell g, we perform region specific TA, by identifying *interesting regions* of g, that we define next.

DEFINITION 8. **(Interesting Regions)**
interesting regions(g) = Partitions of Global (Global.ll, Global.ur) wrt g($g.ll$, $g.ur$).

Consider Figure 5, that shows interesting regions of a cell g for the root node of the trie $\mathcal{T}$.

First of all, the score-bounds of the internal regions of all cells in a grid can be computed efficiently - a single scan over $\mathcal{D}$ is sufficient to assign a score-bound in internal region of each cell in $\mathcal{G}$.

[6]Although, MINDIST is defined using Euclidean distance here, our solution framework can be generalized to any L_p distance metric

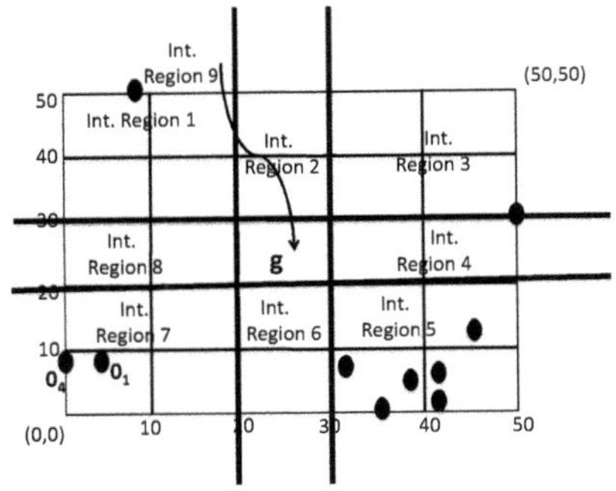

Figure 5: Computing Score-bound(g) at $\mathcal{T}$ root

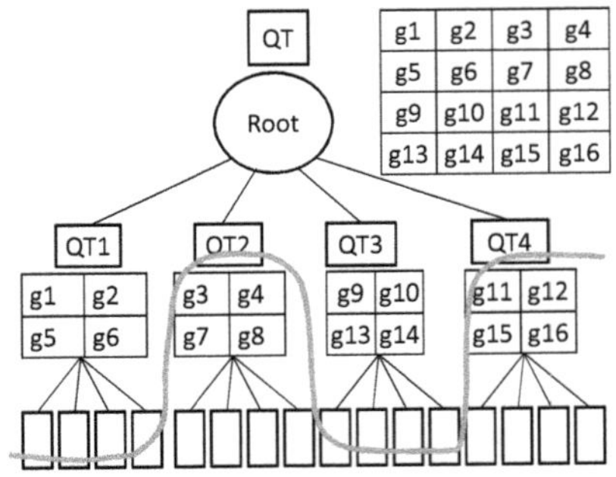

Figure 7: Quad-Tree of a SGB($n_{\mathcal{T}}$)

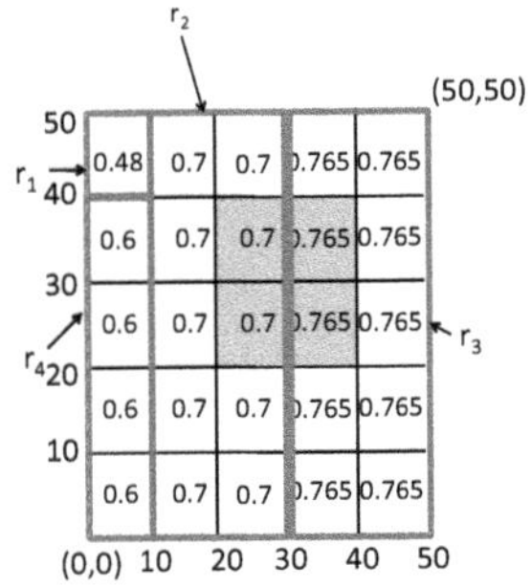

Figure 6: R Cover Creation

We explain the score-bound computation of g that has 9 interesting regions (8 external, 1 internal) next. For each external region of g, we perform region specific TA. We now describe how score-bound of region specific TA at Int.Region 7 can be computed. Note that, only objects O_1 and O_4 are to be considered during `RegionTA` computation of Int.Region 7, and *MINDIST* needs to be computed considering the closest boundary point of g (which happens to be $g.ll$), and location of the objects inside Int.Region 7 (O_1, O_4). `RegionTA` in other interesting regions will follow similar argument. Finally, Score-bound(g) is the maximum of these 9 interesting region specific Max-Score.

5.2.2 *R Cover Creation*

Given an SGB($n_{\mathcal{T}}$), the task is to create a cover with R regions. A natural approach of creating R cover is by merging cells of SGB($n_{\mathcal{T}}$). An R cover must satisfy the following conditions: the score-bound of every region $r \in R$ (Score-bound($r, n_{\mathcal{T}}$)) is correct.

Observe that, in order to satisfy this condition, Score-bound($r, n_{\mathcal{T}}$) must be the *maximum* of the score-bounds of the cells inside it, as Lemma 1 suggests.

LEMMA 1. **(Score-bound of a region)** *Score-bound*$(r, n_{\mathcal{T}}) = max_{\forall g \in r}$ *Score-bound*$(g, n_{\mathcal{T}})$.

Due to lack of space, we omit the details of the proof from this version of the paper.

As an example, consider the SGB in Figure 6 (the bound values are imaginary numbers here). The correct score-bound of the region (grey filled) is 0.765 - hence, the original grid cells with 0.7 bounds now get a higher score bound of 0.765. In other words, merging introduces *looseness* in the score-bound and is detrimental to effective pruning. But note that, different merging induces different looseness. For example, if the cell with score-bound 0.48 is merged with the cell with bound 0.7, that induces more looseness for the former cell, as compared to merging 0.6 score-bound cell with 0.7.

We define *error* in that context. For a given g, that is merged inside a region r, the difference in score-bound between these two is denoted as g's *error*. Note that, error captures looseness in bounds, hence may affect the effectiveness of pruning, but not the correctness of results.

While it is mandatory to maintain the correct score-bound in r, it is also important to preserve *tight* bounds for effective pruning. Therefore, a cover creation algorithm must adaptively form R regions. Our next optimization problem intends to create R cover such that it minimizes the *maximum-error* of the regions in the cover.

DEFINITION 9. **(Maximum-Error of a region)** *Maximum-error*$(r, n_{\mathcal{T}}) = max_{\forall g \in r}$ *Score-bound*$(g, n_{\mathcal{T}})$ - $min_{\forall g'}$ *Score-bound*$(g', n_{\mathcal{T}})$

Optimization Problem - R Cover Creation : Given an SGB($n_{\mathcal{T}}$), create R cover such that,

$max_{\forall_{r \in R}}$Maximum-error$(r, n_{\mathcal{T}})$ is minimized.

Although seemingly practical and important, optimally solving R Cover Creation problem is unfortunately very challenging - since it requires us to solve an NP-complete problem. A direct mapping exists between this known NP-hard [15] problem and our problem. Furthermore, any reasonable approximation algorithm is also unknown. The difficulty comes from the fact that it needs to consider exponential number of possible region formations to compute optimal cover. Figure 6 shows an optimal cover of size 4 (r_1, r_2, r_3, r_4), where each cell has 0 error.

THEOREM 2. **(Hardness Result)** *Computing optimal cover of size R based on the maximum-error metric is NP-complete.*

We consider a viable alternative of this hard problem by restricting the choice of possible regions to the nodes of a quad tree `QT` of SGB. The benefit of quad-tree [11] is, it allows us to design an *optimal algorithm* to select R cover. In a nutshell, the basic idea is to create a `QT` of SGB($n_{\mathcal{T}}$) (the leaf nodes of `QT` are the actual cells), and select a R-size frontier of it that optimizes the maximum-error metric. Figure 7 depicts a quad-tree with 16 cells, and a size 10 frontier (with the wriggly line) of it.

Algorithm to Select R-size Frontier of `QT`: Algorithm 3 selects R-size Frontier - initially the cover (referred to as `Cover` in the pseudo-code) consists of the leaf nodes of `QT`, therefore has 0 error. The algorithm begins by sorting the intermediate nodes of `QT` in the increasing order of maximum-error. At a certain point, if the size of the current cover is larger than R, the algorithm selects the

Algorithm 3 `Select`R`Frontier` : Algorithm to Select R-size Frontier of `QT`

Require:
`QT` - a quad tree of SGB($n_{\mathcal{T}}$), R - an integer
`Cover` = { leaf nodes of `QT`}
$\mathcal{I}$ = { set of intermediate `QT` nodes, sorted in increasing order of *error* }
while |`Cover`| $\neq (R \pm 3)$ **do**
  Consider the first node $\mathcal{I}_1 \in \mathcal{I}$
  $\mathcal{I} = \{\mathcal{I}\} - \{\mathcal{I}_1\}$
  `Cover` = {`Cover`} + $\{\mathcal{I}_1\}$ − {`Children`$_{\mathcal{I}_1}$}
return `Cover`

"best" (with lowest maximum-error) available intermediate node, and add that to the existing cover. Each time a new node is added in the cover, all its immediate children nodes are removed from there; thus this operation overall reduces the size of the cover by 3. Also, the maximum-error of the cover at that point is the maximum-error of that newly-added node. The algorithm terminates when cover has R regions[7].

It can be shown that Algorithm `Select`R`Frontier` is an optimal algorithm, as the Lemma 2 suggests.

LEMMA 2. **(Optimality)**
Algorithm `Select`R`Frontier` *is optimal for maximum-error metric.*

6. EFFICIENT QUERY PROCESSING

Finally, we discuss algorithm (`BMT-TAS`) that leverages T_{BM} to compute $Res(Q, k)$. The pseudo-code is written in Algorithm 4.

Consider the case, where each node in the trie contains materialized bounds. In such cases, the algorithm `BMT-TAS` can follow the best-first search [7] like execution fashion of nearest-neighbor queries in multi-dimensional index structure, that has been shown to be optimal [19].

However, T_{BM} is unique, since only a judiciously selected set of M nodes in the trie contains materialized information. Therefore, we employ a *hybrid-approach*, that performs *depth-first search* [7] traversal in a subtree rooted at a materialized node (SRM), but performs best-first like traversal across SRMs. Lines 7-15 in the pseudocode perform these two operations.

Algorithm `BMT-TAS` maintains two data-structures in this process - a stack for depth-first search, and a *priority queue* for best-first search. The current best-k results are maintained in a global priority queue `ResultsPQ`. During depth-first search (inner loop), if the algorithm encounters a materialized node, that node is pushed into the priority quere, with the priority as its score-bound [8]. Best-first search is performed in the outer loop across SRMs. During best-first search, the algorithm first obtains the top item in the priority queue, i.e., the unexplored SRM with the highest score bound. Next it determines if the termination condition (if the k-th largest object score is not smaller than the score bound of the top unexplored SRM) is satisfied. If satisfied, it terminates, otherwise, it continues with exploring the top unexplored SRM. This process terminates automatically when the entire $Subtree(QMN(Q))$ is traversed.

It can be proved that algorithm `BMT-TAS` is optimal in query processing cost.

[7]We note that for certain cases, the resultant frontier size may vary by ±3 from R - this happens due to the restricted quad-tree structure and we allow such a negligible deviation

[8]Note that, the depth first search may encounter even leaf nodes in that process if there is no materialization.

LEMMA 3. **(Optimality)**
`BMT-TAS` is an optimal algorithm in query processing cost.

Algorithm 4 `BMT-TAS` - Efficient Algorithm for location-aware TAS using T_{BM}

Require: Trie T_{BM}, Query Q, an integer k
1: `ResultsPQ` = ϕ, `stackForDFS` = ϕ, `pqforBFS` = ϕ
2: Perform lookup in Trie T_{BM} to determine QMN(Q)
3: stackForDFS.Push(QMN(Q))
4: **while** *true* **do**
5:   **while** (*!stackForDFS.empty()*) **do**
6:     *nextNodeToTraverse* = *stackForDFS.Pop()*
7:     **if** (*nextNodeToTraverse* == LeafNode) **then**
8:       `resultsPQ` = `LeafNodeSearch`(*nextNodeToTraverse*);
9:     **else**
10:       **for all** *childNode* ∈ *nextNodeToTraverse.children* **do**
11:         **if** (*childNode.IsMaterialized*) **then**
12:           *bound* = *GetBound(childNode.RCover, Q.loc)*
13:           `pqForBFS`.*Enqueue(ChildNode, bound)*
14:         **else**
15:           `stackForDFS`.*Push(ChildNode)*
16:   **if** (`pqForBFS`.*IsEmpty()*) **then**
17:     break
18:   *rootOfNextSubtreeToTraverse* = `pqForBFS`.*Dequeue()*
19:   **if** (k-th largest score in `resultsPQ` ≥ *rootOfNextSubtreeToTraverse.Priority*) **then**
20:     break
21:   **else**
22:     *stackForDFS.Push(topItemFromPQ.Value)*
23: **return** *Res*(Q, k) from `ResultsPQ`

7. EXPERIMENTAL EVALUATION

We present an experimental evaluation of the techniques proposed in the paper. The goals of our study are:

- To measure the benefit of materializing score bounds using the $\{M, R\}$ distribution technique to query performance
- To evaluate the benefit of judicious node selection and adaptive cover creation using the $\{M, R\}$ distribution technique over arbitrary node and cover selection
- To study the sensitivity of query performance of `BMT-TAS` algorithm to M and R
- To study the scalability of `BMT-TAS` to database size
- To study the sensitivity of query performance of `BMT-TAS` to k
- To study the sensitivity of query performance of `BMT-TAS` to the ranking function, specifically the weights w_d and w_s of the two components.

7.1 Experimental Setting

Implementation: We implemented two algorithms: (i) the baseline algorithm `Baseline-TAS` and (ii) the proposed algorithm `BMT-TAS` using the bound materialized trie. For `Baseline-TAS`, we modify the standard trie as follows. For each leaf node $l_{\mathcal{T}}$, we store two pointers:
(i) **Pointer to a** *kd***-tree**: We store the spatial locations of the objects in the object list of $l_{\mathcal{T}}$ (along with the object ids) in a *kd*-tree and store a pointer to the root of that *kd*-tree in $l_{\mathcal{T}}$.
(ii) **Pointer to static score list**: We store the ids, static stores and locations of those objects in a list sorted in decreasing order of static scores. We store a pointer to that list in $l_{\mathcal{T}}$ as well.
By exploiting the getNext() interface of *kd*-tree, getNext() interface of static score list as well as random access interface to the static score list, we implemented the `LeafNodeSearch` subroutine using the TA algorithm as discussed in Section

3.2. This implementation of `LeafNodeSearch` is used by both `Baseline-TAS` and `BMT-TAS`. The remaining implementation of `Baseline-TAS` follows the pseudocode of Algorithm 1.

For `BMT-TAS`, we further modify the trie as follows. We first execute the node and cover selection process. Subsequently, for each trie node $n_{\mathcal{T}}$ selected, we store the regions in R-cover and the score bound for each region in $n_{\mathcal{T}}$. Since each region is a node in the quad-tree over the basic grid $\mathcal{G}$ of $n_{\mathcal{T}}$, we store a single number that encodes the quad-tree node [18]. At query time, we can use the encoding to determine the region that contains the query location efficiently.

Datasets: We report results over a real-world dataset and a synthetic dataset.

Yellow Page dataset: This dataset contains names, locations (in latitude and longtitude) and popularities of 100,000 business entities in the state of Washington, USA. We use the popularities of the businesses as their static scores. Each business name has an average of 20 characters.

Synthetic dataset: We synthetically generated spatial datasets that emulate real-life spatial data for scalability experiments. We make three observations about real-world spatial data: (i) the number of objects having the same description string follows the Zipf distribution, i.e., there are a few strings associated with many objects (e.g., "Starbucks", "Bank of America", "Mcdonald's") while most strings are associated with very few objects (ii) the popularities of objects also follow the Zipf distribution: some objects are extremely popular while most are modestly popular and (iii) locations of objects follow a clustered distribution. Based on these observations, we generate a synthetic dataset as follows. We have a large set of business names (but not their locations and popularities) from the customer database of a Fortune 500 company: we randomly select a string from that set. We then generate a number z (scaled by the desired size of the database) from a Zipf distribution and generate z objects associated with the string. We generate the locations of the objects following the clustered distribution and the popularities following the Zipf distribution. We iterate the process till we obtain the desired number of objects.

Queries: For each dataset, we generated 100 queries as follows. We randomly select 100 prefixes of object strings (of length 1, 2 and 3 characters) whose selectivities are between 1% and 10%. We associate the location of a randomly selected object from the database with each prefix. An example of a query for Yellow Page dataset is ("ma", (47.60, -122.33)). All our results are averaged over 100 such queries. We use a $k = 10$ unless otherwise specified. We use $w_d = 0.5$ and $w_s = 0.5$ unless otherwise specified.

All experiments were conducted on an Intel x64 machine with two 2.66GHz Intel Xeon processor and 8GB RAM, running Windows 2008 Server (R2 Enterprise x64 edition). In all experiments, the trie resides completely in main memory.

7.2 Experimental Results: Synthetic Dataset

Benefit of bound materialization: We first evaluate the benefit of materializing the bounds computed by the $\{M, R\}$-technique on a synthetic database of 1 million objects. We compare the query processing cost of `BMT-TAS` algorithm with that of `Baseline-TAS`. We measure the query processing cost not only by execution time but also the two main components: (i) number of score computations, and (ii) number of links traversed. Figure 8 shows the number of score computations for `Baseline-TAS` and `BMT-TAS`. The leftmost point in each chart shows the number for `Baseline-TAS` (labeled Baseline in all charts) while the remaining points show the number for `BMT-TAS` for various values of M and R. For all values of M and R, `BMT-TAS` performs fewer score computations compared to baseline. `BMT-TAS` is most beneficial when bounds are materialized in 100,000 or more nodes and the number of regions is at 100 or more. For example, for $M = 100,000$ and $R = 100$, `BMT-TAS` *performs 3 times fewer score computations* compared with `Baseline-TAS`. For $M = 200,000$ and $R = 200$, `BMT-TAS` outperforms `Baseline-TAS` *by a factor of 5.* [9] This implies that the bounds help in avoiding most score computations.

We next compare the performance of the two algorithms in terms of the second component of the cost: the number of links traversed. Figure 9 plots the results. The results are quite similar to the case of score computations: `BMT-TAS` performs fewer score computations compared to `Baseline-TAS` for all values of M and R. Again, `BMT-TAS` is most beneficial for $M \geq 100000$ and $R \geq 100$. For example, for $M = 100,000$ and $R = 100$, `BMT-TAS` *traverses 2.5 times fewer links* compared with `Baseline-TAS`. For $M = 200,000$ and $R = 200$, `BMT-TAS` outperforms `Baseline-TAS` *by a factor of 4.5.* This implies that the bounds help in avoiding traversing most of the links.

Finally, we compare the two algorithms in terms of the execution time. Figure 10 shows the results. The results follow the same pattern as the previous two figures. First, this validates our model of query processing cost: the execution time is a weighted combination of the above two costs. Second, `BMT-TAS` outperforms `Baseline-TAS` for all values of M and R, For $M = 100,000$ and $R = 100$, `BMT-TAS` is *2 times faster* than `Baseline-TAS`. For $M = 200,000$ and $R = 200$, `BMT-TAS` is *4 times faster* than `Baseline-TAS`. As discussed in Section 1, it is crucial to keep the trie search time well below 100 ms: `BMT-TAS` achieves the above goal. While `Baseline-TAS` takes an average of 212 ms, `BMT-TAS` with $M = 200,000$ and $R = 200$ takes an average of only 54ms. In summary, our techniques make location-aware TAS feasible.

Comparison with Random Node Selection: The above charts show that bound materialization saves the query processing cost. However, do we really need judicious node selection and adaptive cover creation using the $\{M, R\}$ distribution technique? Or would randomly selecting M nodes and an uniform grid of R cells in each of those nodes would have been equally beneficial (referred to as *Rand-Uni* materialization)? We conducted experiments to answer the above questions. We selected the nodes and the covers using the Rand-Uni technique and augmented the trie with it. We then executed queries using `BMT-TAS` on such a trie. Figures 11 shows the performance in terms execution time for various values of M and R. Rand-Uni materialization do have some benefit over `Baseline-TAS` but our $\{M, R\}$ distribution technique yields much more benefit for the same space overhead (i.e., $M \times R$). For example, for $M = 200,000$ and $R = 200$, the number of score computations, number of links traversed and execution time for Rand-Uni materialization are $31k$, $424k$ and 162ms respectively; for the $\{M, R\}$ technique, these numbers are $11k$, $149k$ and $53ms$. This implies that the benefit modeling and node selection based

[9] Assuming average object size of 36 bytes (20 bytes for string, 4 bytes for id, 8 bytes for location and 4 bytes for static score), the trie along with the objects have a size of 36MB. With $M = 100,000$ and $R = 100$, the space to materialize the bounds is roughly $100000 \times 100 \times 8 = 80MB$ (assuming 8 bytes per region) Hence, $M = 100,000$ and $R = 100$ or even $M = 200,000$ and $R = 200$ is feasible in modern hardware.

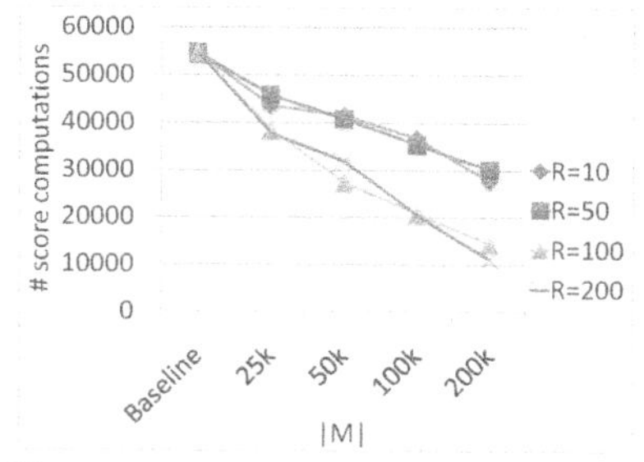

Figure 8: Num score computations w.r.t. M and R

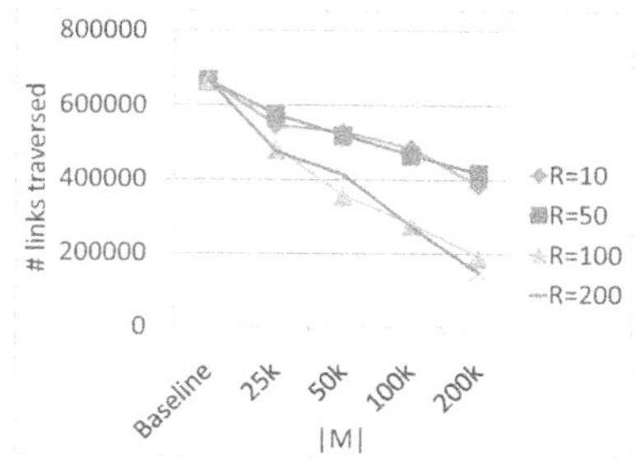

Figure 9: Num links traversed w.r.t. M and R

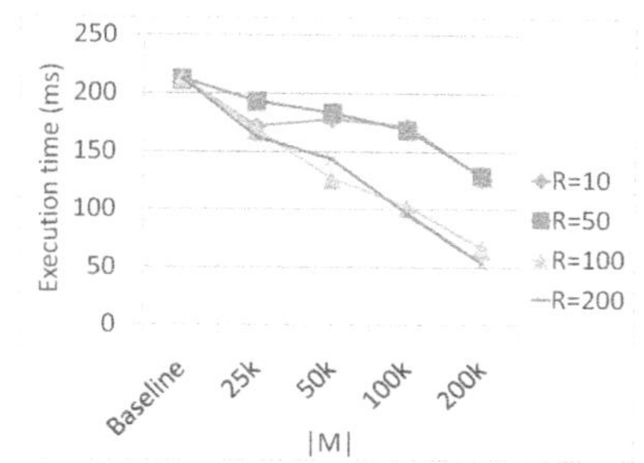

Figure 10: Execution time w.r.t. M and R

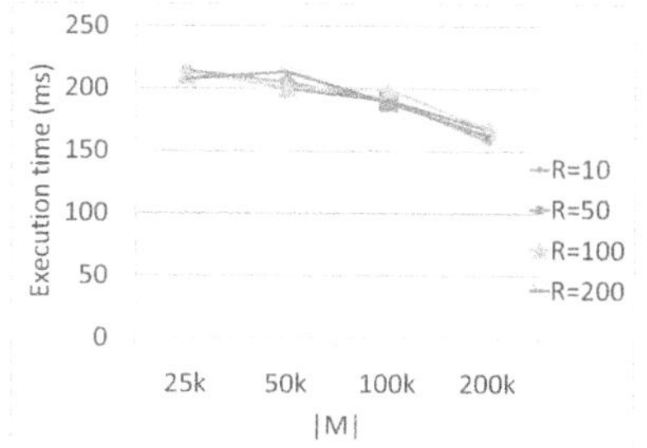

Figure 11: Execution time for Rand-Uni materialization

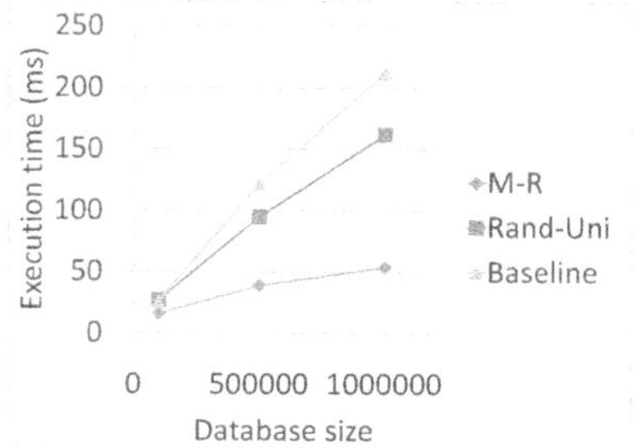

Figure 12: Scalability to database size

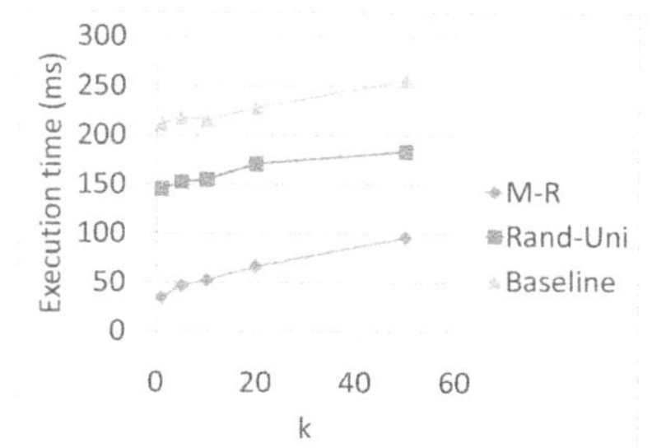

Figure 13: Execution time w.r.t. k

on benefit are important; similarly, the adaptive choice of regions is also important.

Scalability to database size: We evaluate the scalability of `Baseline-TAS` and `BMT-TAS` using $\{M, R\}$-based materialization and Rand-Uni materialization. We generated synthetic databases of size 100k, 500k and 1 million. For the materialization approaches, we chose M to be 20% of the database size (i.e., 20k, 100k and 200k respectively) and $R = 200$. Figure 12 the performance in terms of execution time. $\{M, R\}$ technique significantly outperforms `Baseline-TAS` and Rand-Uni for all database sizes. The gap increases with increase in database size. We observed similar behavior for the two components of the cost; we omit those charts to avoid repetition.

Sensitivity to k: We evaluate the sensitivity of the algorithms to the number k of results desired. Figure 13 plots the execution time of the 3 techniques for various values of k. For all values of k, $\{M, R\}$ technique significantly outperforms the other two techniques.

7.3 Experimental Results: Real Dataset

Benefit of bound materialization: We first evaluate the benefit of bound materialization for the real world dataset. Figure 14 shows the average execution time for `Baseline-TAS` (Baseline) and `BMT-TAS`. As in the synthetic dataset, `BMT-TAS` is most beneficial when the bounds are materialized in enough nodes. In this case, that number is 10000. For $M = 20000$ and $R = 10$, `BMT-TAS` outperforms `Baseline-TAS` *by a factor of 3*. We observe that covers consisting a few regions (e.g., 10) suffices for this dataset; further increasing R does not provide additional benefit. We investigated this behavior in depth. A highly popular business (that is a valid completion) typically has the highest overall score for queries originating from the area surrounding it, i.e., it dominates over less popular businesses in the surrounding area. Since the real dataset is spatially sparser compared with the synthetic dataset (10 times fewer objects distributed over the same geographical space), the highly popular businesses are spread farther apart and each of them dominates in even larger surrounding areas. Hence, many regions around it will have the same upper bound score, i.e., the bounds will have more spatial locality. In such cases, our adaptive R cover algorithm can cover the geographic space with a small number of regions without introducing much error.

Sensitivity to ranking function: Finally, we evaluate the sensitivity of the $\{M, R\}$ technique to the ranking function. Specifically, we study how sensitive is the query performance to the weights w_d and w_s. All previous experiments used $w_d = 0.5$ and $w_s = 0.5$. Figures 15 and 16 show the execution times for $w_d = 0.25, w_s = 0.75$ and $w_d = 0.75, w_s = 0.25$. `BMT-TAS` outperforms `Baseline-TAS` for these values of weights as well. Note that when the weight on spatial proximity increases to 0.75, the domination of highly popular businesses in surrounding areas reduces. This reduces the spatial locality of the bounds. Hence, increasing R does provide additional benefit.

8. RELATED WORK

To the best of our knowledge, this is the first work on TAS over spatial databases. Our semantics and architecture build upon prior works on keyword search on spatial databases, standard TAS, and autocompletion. However, our principal technical contributions remain in the novel formulations and solutions of the memory distribution problem.

Keyword search on spatial databases: Keyword search on spatial data has been recently studied in [10, 6]. Existing work proposes ranking metric that considers both proximity and relevance of the object with the query. Our ranking framework uses similar intuition by combining distance and static score in location-aware TAS. However, location-aware TAS is required to return top-k valid completions with every key stroke, making our problem and solution tangentially different from [10, 6].

Autocompletion and TAS: The TAS problem is related to autocompletion [8, 16, 5]. In autocompletion, as the user types in her query, the system displays the set of likely completions of the query. While autocompletion reduces the amount of typing, it still requires a large amount of clicking before the user gets to see the final results.

Our work differs from prior work on TAS as prior approaches are *not location-aware* [14, 3]. TAS on spatial data needs to be location-aware; hence, prior semantics, architecture, and algorithms are inadequate. Another example of TAS is the recently released *Google Instant (GI)*. With a

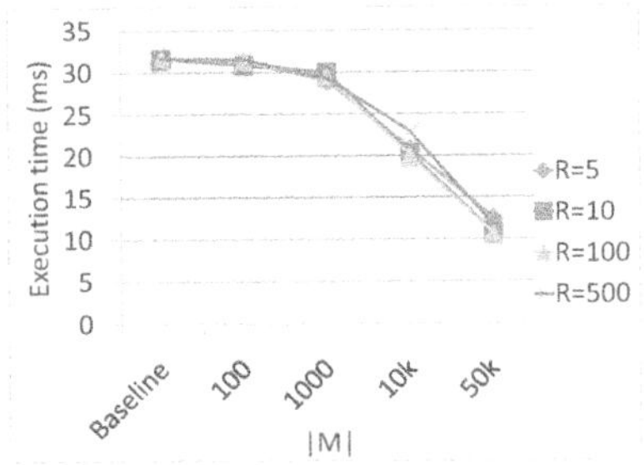

Figure 14: Execution time for real dataset, $w_d = 0.5, w_s = 0.5$

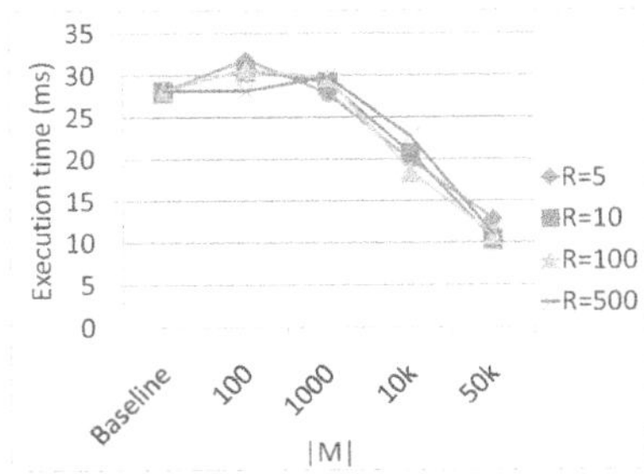

Figure 15: Execution time for real dataset, $w_d = 0.25, w_s = 0.75$

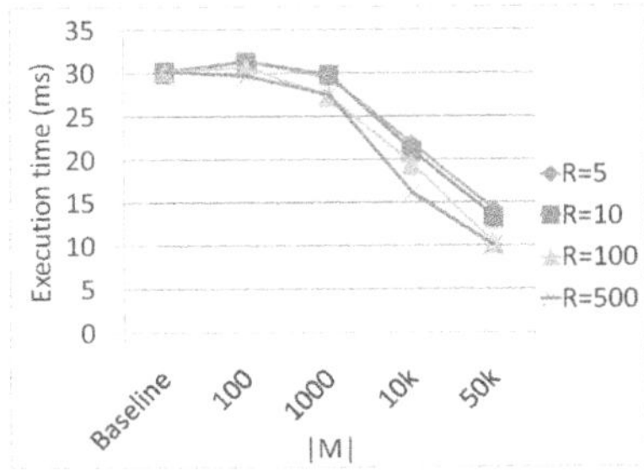

Figure 16: Execution time for real dataset, $w_d = 0.75, w_s = 0.25$

query being typed, GI selects the most popular completion and returns the results for it. However, in the cases where the most popular completion is not the intended query, the results will be undesirable. We, on the other hand, return the *"best" set of results among all the likely completions of the query* and use location as a strong signal to select the "best" results. Due to the diversity of the results, our results are much more likely to include the desired result even with just a few letters typed.

Spatial index structures and other data structures: We use spatial data structures as components of our location aware TAS system [4, 11]. In the integrated architecture proposed in this paper, we index the spatial locations of the objects in each leaf node using a main memory spatial index structure (e.g., kdtree). Subsequently, we can use the threshold algorithm to efficiently implement `LeafNodeSearch`. Spatial grids have been used for indexing spatial objects [2, 17]. In this paper, we use grids for storing the bounds instead of indexing objects. Furthermore, our main contribution is the adaptive cover computed using the spatial grid of bounds. Our R-cover selection algorithm uses a quad-tree as a basis [11]; our main contribution here is the optimal cover selection algorithm. Furthermore, `BMT-TAS` employs a best-first search [7] approach to search in T_{BM}, leveraging priority queue [7] data structure.

Optimization problems: We formalize two optimization problems to pre-compute T_{BM}. Unfortunately, both of them are computationally hard. We show the NP-Completeness of M Node Selection problem by reducing classical set cover [12] problem to it, even for a much simpler benefit function. In the absence of a reasonable approximation algorithm, applicable for our actual benefit function, we design a hill climbing based heuristic solution.

Our R Cover Creation problem aims to optimize maximum-error [13] of individual grid cells, and is also NP-hard. It directly maps to the existing work [15], that shows the hardness of rectangular partitioning in two-dimensional space. Although efficient approximation algorithm is designed for cases where the objective is to minimize the number of regions that is required to satisfy an error bound, those results do not extend to our case where the number of regions(R) is given and the task is to determine the partitioning that minimizes the error.

9. CONCLUSION

In this work, we introduce the problem of location-aware TAS on spatial databases. We show that standard TAS techniques can not be adapted effectively on spatial data. We propose an integrated architecture for location-aware TAS. Furthermore, we suggest novel techniques to augment that architecture with materialized information for efficient query processing. The challenges mainly surfaces due to the limited availability of main memory. We formalize two optimization problems in that contexts by modeling query processing cost. We demonstrate the hardness of both problems, and design efficient algorithmic solutions. Finally, we devise an optimal query processing algorithm that uses that augmented architecture for efficient query processing. We perform extensive experiments on real and synthetic data that corroborate the efficiency of our proposed solution.

10. REFERENCES

[1] *http://www.marketwire.com/press-release/Study-Shows-Double-Digit-Growth-Local-Mobile-Usage-Unlocking-Access-Younger-Wealthier-1297436.htm.*

[2] *Spatial databases with application to GIS.* Morgan Kaufmann Publishers Inc., 2002.

[3] H. Bast and I. Weber. Type less, find more: fast autocompletion search with a succinct index. In *SIGIR*, pages 364–371, 2006.

[4] J. L. Bentley. Multidimensional binary search trees in database applications. *IEEE Trans. Software Eng.*, 5(4):333–340, 1979.

[5] S. Chaudhuri and R. Kaushik. Extending autocompletion to tolerate errors. In *SIGMOD Conference*, pages 707–718, 2009.

[6] G. Cong, C. S. Jensen, and D. Wu. Efficient retrieval of the top-k most relevant spatial web objects. *PVLDB*, 2(1):337–348, 2009.

[7] T. H. Cormen, C. E. Leiserson, R. L. Rivest, and C. Stein. *Introduction to Algorithms, Second Edition.* The MIT Press and McGraw-Hill Book Company, 2001.

[8] J. J. Darragh and I. H. Witten. Adaptive predictive text generation and the reactive keyboard. *Interacting with Computers*, 3(1):27–50, 1991.

[9] R. Fagin and et. al. Optimal Aggregation Algorithms for Middleware. In *PODS*, 2001.

[10] I. D. Felipe, V. Hristidis, and N. Rishe. Keyword search on spatial databases. In *ICDE*, pages 656–665, 2008.

[11] R. A. Finkel and J. L. Bentley. Quad trees: A data structure for retrieval on composite keys. *Acta Inf.*, 4:1–9, 1974.

[12] M. R. Garey and D. S. Johnson. *Computers and Intractability: A Guide to the Theory of NP-Completeness.* W.H. Freeman and Company, 1979.

[13] M. N. Garofalakis and A. Kumar. Deterministic wavelet thresholding for maximum-error metrics. In *PODS*, pages 166–176, 2004.

[14] G. Li, S. Ji, C. Li, and J. Feng. Efficient type-ahead search on relational data: a tastier approach. In *SIGMOD Conference*, pages 695–706, 2009.

[15] S. Muthukrishnan, V. Poosala, and T. Suel. On rectangular partitionings in two dimensions: Algorithms, complexity, and applications. In *ICDT*, pages 236–256, 1999.

[16] A. Nandi and H. V. Jagadish. Assisted querying using instant-response interfaces. In *SIGMOD Conference*, pages 1156–1158, 2007.

[17] J. Nievergelt, H. Hinterberger, and K. C. Sevcik. The grid file: An adaptable, symmetric multikey file structure. *ACM Transactions on Database Systems*, 1984.

[18] M. Prez, X. Benavent, and R. Olanda. Efficient coding of quadtree nodes. In *Computational Science ICCS 2006.* 2006.

[19] N. Roussopoulos, S. Kelley, and F. Vincent. Nearest neighbor queries. In *SIGMOD Conference*, 1995.

Collective Spatial Keyword Querying

Xin Cao[1], Gao Cong[1], Christian S. Jensen[2], Beng Chin Ooi[3]
[1]School of Computer Engineering, Nanyang Technological University, Singapore
[2]Department of Computer Science, Aarhus University, Denmark
[3]School of Computing, National University of Singapore, Singapore
xcao1@e.ntu.edu.sg, gaocong@ntu.edu.sg, csj@cs.au.dk, ooibc@comp.nus.edu.sg

ABSTRACT

With the proliferation of geo-positioning and geo-tagging, spatial web objects that possess both a geographical location and a textual description are gaining in prevalence, and spatial keyword queries that exploit both location and textual description are gaining in prominence. However, the queries studied so far generally focus on finding individual objects that each satisfy a query rather than finding groups of objects where the objects in a group collectively satisfy a query.

We define the problem of retrieving a group of spatial web objects such that the group's keywords cover the query's keywords and such that objects are nearest to the query location and have the lowest inter-object distances. Specifically, we study two variants of this problem, both of which are NP-complete. We devise exact solutions as well as approximate solutions with provable approximation bounds to the problems. We present empirical studies that offer insight into the efficiency and accuracy of the solutions.

Categories and Subject Descriptors

H.2.8 [**Database Management**]: Database Applications—*Spatial databases and GIS*

General Terms

Algorithms, Experimentation, Performance

Keywords

Spatial keyword query, Spatial group keyword query

1. INTRODUCTION

With the proliferation of geo-positioning, e.g., by means of GPS or systems that exploit the wireless communication infrastructure, accurate user location is increasingly available. Similarly, increasing numbers of objects are available on the web that have an associated geographical location and textual description. Such *spatial web objects* include stores, tourist attractions, restaurants, hotels, and businesses.

This development gives prominence to *spatial keyword queries* [5, 6, 8, 10]. A typical such query takes a location and a set of keywords as arguments and returns the single spatial web object that best matches these arguments.

We observe that user needs may exist that are not easily satisfied by a single object, but where groups of objects may combine to meet the user needs. Put differently, the objects in a group collectively meet the user needs. For example, a tourist may have particular shopping, dining, and accommodation needs that may best be met by several spatial web objects. As another example, a user may wish to set up a project consortium of partners within a certain spatial proximity that combine to offer the capabilities required for the successful execution of the project.

To address the need for such collective answers to spatial keyword queries, we assume a database of spatial web objects and then consider the problem of how to retrieve a group of spatial objects that collectively meet the user's needs given as location and a set of keywords: 1) the textual description of the group of objects must cover the query keywords, 2) the objects are close to the query point, and 3) the objects in the group are close to each other.

Specifically, given a set of spatial web objects D, and a query $q = (\lambda, \psi)$, where λ is a location and ψ is a set of keywords, we consider two instantiations of the *spatial group keyword query*.

1. We aim to find a group of objects χ that cover the keywords in q such that the sum of their spatial distances to the query is minimized.
2. We aim to find a group of objects χ that cover the keywords in q such that the sum of the maximum distance between an object in χ and query q and the maximum distance between two objects in χ is minimized.

It turns out that the subproblems corresponding to these two instantiations are both NP-complete. The first subproblem can be reduced from the weighted set cover problem. We propose a greedy algorithm that provides an approximate solution to the problem. This algorithm utilizes a spatial-keyword index such as the IR-tree [8] to prune the search space. The algorithm has a provable approximation bound. Based on the assumption that in some applications, the number of keywords in a query q may not be large, we also propose an exact algorithm that exploits dynamic programming and a spatial-keyword index. The exact algorithm avoids enumerating the combinations of data objects in the database. Rather, it enumerates the query keywords and exploits a series of pruning strategies to reduce the search space.

For the second subproblem, we develop two approximation algorithms based on a spatial-keyword index with provable approximation bounds. The first approximation algorithm has a 3-approximation ratio, while the second algorithm has a 2-approximation ratio. We also develop an exact algorithm that exploits a spatial-keyword index and the geometric property and branch-and-bound search to prune the search space.

SIGMOD'11, June 12–16, 2011, Athens, Greece.

In summary, our contribution is threefold. First, we propose a new type of queries, called *spatial group keyword queries*, that find groups of objects that collectively satisfy a query. We consider two instantiations of the problem and show that both are NP-complete.

Second, we propose algorithms that offer approximate solutions to the two subproblems with provable approximation bounds. We also present exact algorithms for the two subproblems. All algorithms exploit a spatial keyword index to prune the search space.

Third, we study the properties of the paper's proposals empirically based on prototype implementations of the proposals. The results demonstrate that the proposals offer scalability and are capable of excellent performance.

The rest of the paper is organized as follows. Section 2 formally defines the problem and establishes the computational complexities of the problem. Section 3 presents an approximate algorithm and an exact algorithm for the first subproblem. Section 4 presents two approximate algorithms and an exact algorithm for the second subproblem. We report on the empirical studies in Section 5. Finally, we cover related work in Section 6 and offer conclusions and research directions in Section 7.

2. PROBLEM STATEMENT

Let S be a set of keywords. The keywords may capture user preferences or required project partner capabilities, depending on the application. Let D be a database consisting of m spatial web objects. Each object o in D is associated with a location $o.\lambda$ and a set of keywords $o.\psi$, $o.\psi \subset S$, that describe the object (e.g., the menu of restaurant or the skills of a possible project partner).

Consider a spatial group keyword query $q = \langle q.\lambda, q.\psi \rangle$, where $q.\lambda$ is a location and $q.\psi$ represents a set of keywords. The *spatial group keyword query* finds a group of objects χ, $\chi \subseteq D$, such that $\cup_{r \in \chi} r.\psi \supseteq q.\psi$ and such that the cost $\mathsf{Cost}(\chi)$ is minimized.

We proceed to present cost functions. Given a set of objects χ, the cost function has two weighted components:

$$\mathsf{Cost}(q, \chi) = \alpha C_1(q, \chi) + (1 - \alpha) C_2(\chi),$$

where $C_1(\cdot)$ is dependent on the distance of the objects in χ to the query object and $C_2(\cdot)$ characterizes the inter-object distances among the objects in χ.

This type of cost function is capable of expressing that result object should be near the query location ($C_1(\cdot)$), that the result objects should be near to each other ($C_2(\cdot)$, and that these two aspects are given different weights (α). We consider two instantiations of the cost function $\mathsf{Cost}(q, \chi)$ that we believe match the intended applications well.

TYPE1 cost function:

$$\mathsf{Cost}(q, \chi) = \sum_{r \in \chi} (\mathsf{Dist}(r, q)) \tag{1}$$

The cost function is the sum of the distance between each object in χ and the query location. This may fit with applications where the objects need to meet at the query location, such as incident handling or the finding of project partners.

TYPE2 cost function:

$$\begin{aligned} \mathsf{Cost}(q, \chi) &= \alpha \max_{r \in \chi}(\mathsf{Dist}(r, q)) + \\ &\quad (1 - \alpha) \max_{r_1, r_2 \in \chi} (\mathsf{Dist}(r_1, r_2)) \end{aligned} \tag{2}$$

The first part of this cost function is the maximal distance between any object in χ and the query location q, and the second part is the maximum distance between two objects in χ (this can be understood as the diameter of the result). When there are multiple optimal groups of objects, we choose one group randomly. This second cost function may fit with applications such as tourists planning visits to several points of interest.

For ease of presentation, we disregard parameter α in the rest of this paper. But the proposed algorithms remain applicable when α is enabled.

Lemma 2.1: *The decision version of spatial group keyword query problem using either a* TYPE1 *or a* TYPE2 *cost function is NP-complete.*

Proof: *We first consider the* TYPE1 *cost function. We prove the lemma by reduction from the weighted set cover problem. An instance of the weighted cover problem consists of a universe U = { 1, 2, ..., n} of n elements and a family of sets $\mathcal{S} = \{S_1, S_2, ..., S_m\}$, where $S_i \subseteq U$ and each S_i is associated with a positive cost C_{S_i}. The decision problem is to decide if we can find a subset $\mathcal{F}$ of $\mathcal{S}$ such that $\cup_{S_i \in \mathcal{F}} S_i = U$ and such that its cost $\sum_{S_i \in \mathcal{F}} (C_{S_i})$ is minimized.*

To reduce this problem to the TYPE1 *spatial group keyword query problem, we observe thateach element in U corresponds to a keyword in $q.\phi$, that each S_i corresponds to a spatial object containing a set of keywords, and that the weight of S_i is $dist(q, S_i)$. It is easy to show that there exists a solution to the weighted set cover problem if and only if there exits a solution to query q.*

Considering next the TYPE2 *cost function, we prove the lemma by reduction from the 3-SAT problem. An instance of the 3-SAT problem consists of $\Phi = C_1 \wedge C_2, ..., \wedge C_l$, where each clause $C_j = x_j \vee y_j \vee z_j$, and $\{x_j, y_j, z_j\} \in \{e_1, \bar{e_1}, e_2, \bar{e_2}, ..., e_n, \bar{e_n}\}$. The decision problem is to determine whether we can assign a truth value to each of the literals (e_1 through e_n) such that Φ is* true.

Next, we reduce this problem to an instance of the TYPE2 *spatial group keyword query problem. The reduction is inspired by the proof for the hardness of the Multiple-Choice cover problem [2] (that is different from our problem). Consider a circle with diameter d and with the query point q as its center, and let each variable e_i correspond to a point in the circle, while its negation $\bar{e_i}$ corresponds to the diametrically opposite on the circle. The distance between e_i and $\bar{e_i}$ is d. We choose d such that $d > d_1$ is sufficiently close to d_1; thus, the distance between any two points corresponding to different variables are smaller than d_1.*

Each set S_i ($i \in [1, n]$) contains a pair of points e_i and $\bar{e_i}$, and the two points contain a distinct keyword in $q.\psi$. Each set S_j ($j \in [n+1, n+l]$) contains each triple of points corresponding to a cause C_{j-n}, and they contain a distinct keyword in $q.\psi$. Thus, to cover all keywords in $q.\psi$, a query result of q must contain one point from each S_i (i.e., e_i and $\bar{e_i}$), and it must contain at least one point from each S_j (corresponding to clause C_{j-n}).

Given this mapping, we can see that if there exits a truth assignment for Φ, all the keywords in q are covered, and $max_{r \in \chi}\mathsf{dist}(q, r) + max_{i,j \in \chi}\mathsf{dist}(i, j) = \frac{d}{2} + max\mathsf{dist}(i, j), i, j \in \chi$ is minimized, i.e., a feasible solution χ with at most $\frac{d}{2} + d_1$ exists. On the other hand, if there exists a subset of points on the circle whose diameter is at most d_1, there exists a truth assignment for the instance Φ. This completes the proof. □

3. PROCESSING OF TYPE1 SPATIAL GROUP KEYWORD QUERIES

3.1 Preliminaries: The IR-Tree

We briefly review the IR-tree [8], which we use as an index structure in the algorithms to be presented. We note that other spatial-keyword indexes (e.g., [10]) may be used in its place.

The IR-tree [8] is essentially an R-tree [12] extended with inverted files [16]. Each leaf node in the IR-tree contains entries of the form $(o, o.\lambda, o.di)$, where o refers to an object in dataset D, $o.\lambda$ is the bounding rectangle of o, and $o.di$ is an identifier of the description of o. Each leaf node also contains a pointer to an inverted file with the keywords of the objects stored in the node.

An inverted file index has two main components.

- A vocabulary of all distinct words appearing in the description of an object.
- A posting list for each word t that is a sequence of identifiers of the objects whose descriptions contain t.

Each non-leaf node R in the IR-tree contains a number of entries of the form $(cp, rect, cp.di)$, where cp is the address of a child node of R, $rect$ is the minimum bounding rectangle (MBR) of all rectangles in entries of the child node, and $cp.di$ is an identifier of a pseudo text description that is the union of all text descriptions in the entries of the child node.

As an example, Figure 1(a) contains eight spatial objects $o_1, o_2, \ldots, o_8$, and Figure 1(b) shows the words appearing in the description of each object. Figure 2 illustrates the corresponding IR-tree, and Table 1 shows the content of the inverted files associated with the nodes.

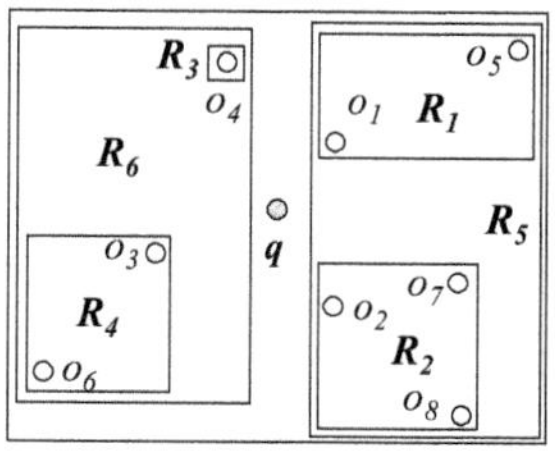

(a) object locations

object	words
o_1	t_1, t_2
o_2	t_2, t_3
o_3	t_1, t_3
o_4	t_1, t_5
o_5	t_2, t_4
o_6	t_4, t_6
o_7	t_4, t_5
o_8	t_1, t_5

(b) object descriptions

Figure 1: A Dataset of Spatial Keyword Objects

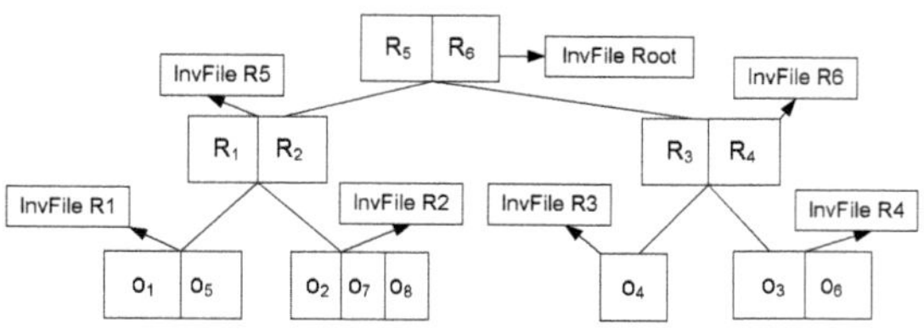

Figure 2: Example IR-Tree

Table 1: Content of Inverted Files of the IR-Tree

$Root$	R_5	R_6	R_1	R_2	R_3	R_4
t_1: R_5, R_6	t_1: R_1, R_2	t_1: R_3, R_4	t_1: o_1	t_1: o_8	t_1: o_4	t_1: o_3
t_2: R_5	t_2: R_1, R_2	t_3: R_4	t_2: o_1, o_5	t_2: o_2	t_5: o_4	t_3: o_3
t_3: R_5, R_6	t_3: R_2	t_4: R_4	t_4: o_5	t_3: o_2		t_4: o_6
t_4: R_5, R_6	t_4: R_1, R_2	t_5: R_3		t_4: o_7		t_6: o_6
t_5: R_5, R_6	t_5: R_2	t_6: R_4		t_5: o_7, o_8		
t_6: R_6						

3.2 Approximation Algorithm

We show that the first subproblem is NP-complete by a reduction from the Weighted Set Cover (WSC) problem in Lemma 2.1. The reduction in the proof is approximation preserving. Thus, the approximation properties of the WSC problem carry over to our problem.

For the WSC problem, it is known (see [7]) that a greedy algorithm is an H_k-approximation algorithm for the weighted k-set cover, where $H_k = \sum_{i=1}^{k} \frac{1}{i}$ is the k-th harmonic number. In our problem, k is the number of query keywords. Thus, we can adapt the greedy algorithm to process the TYPE1 spatial group keyword query.

A straightforward method of adapting the greedy algorithm is to decompose the given user query q dynamically into a sequence of partial queries, each containing a different set of keywords depending on the preceding partial queries, and then to evaluate these partial queries. Specifically, we start with the user query q, which can be regarded as the first partial query, and we find the object with the lowest cost that covers part or all of the keywords in q. The object is added to the result set. The uncovered keywords in q form a new partial query with the same spatial location as q. We then find an object with the lowest cost that covers part or all of the keywords in the new partial query. This process continues until all keywords are covered or some keyword cannot be covered by any object. This method needs to scan the dataset multiple times, once for each partial query.

To avoid multiple scans, we propose a greedy algorithm on top of the IR-tree. We proceed to focus on two aspects of the idea that are important to the performance: (1) how to find the object with the lowest cost for each partial query using the IR-tree, and (2) whether we can reuse the computation for the preceding partial query when computing the next partial query.

Given a partial query q_s, we adopt the best-first strategy to traverse the IR-tree. We use a min-priority queue to maintain the intermediate results. The key of the queue is the cost of each element. The cost of an object o is computed by $\frac{\mathsf{Dist}(q,o)}{|o.\psi \cap q_s.\psi|}$; the cost of a node entry e is computed by $\frac{\mathsf{minDist}(q,e)}{|e.\psi \cap q_s.\psi|}$, where $\mathsf{minDist}$ (q, e) represents the minimum distance between q and e.

Lemma 3.1: *Given a partial query q_s and an IR-tree, the cost of a node is a lower bound of the cost of any of its child nodes.*

Proof: *Given a node e and any of its child nodes e', we have* $\mathsf{minDist}$ $(q, e) \leq \mathsf{minDist}$ (q, e'), *and* $|e.\psi \cap q_s.\psi| \geq |e'.\psi \cap q_s.\psi|$. □

Lemma 3.1 says that the cost of a node is a lower bound of the costs of all objects in the subtree rooted at the node. Thus, if the cost exceeds that of some object that has been visited, we can disregard all objects in the subtree for q_s. This guarantees the correctness of the best-first strategy for finding an object with the lowest cost for a partial query q_s.

We next discuss whether we can reuse the computation for preceding partial queries. An obvious method is to process each partial query from scratch. However, this incurs repeated computation when a node or an object is visited for multiple times. To avoid this, we divide the entries (corresponding to leaf and non-leaf nodes) in the priority queue into two parts: (1) the entries that have already been visited when processing previous partial queries, and (2) the entries that have not yet been visited.

Lemma 3.2: *The elements in the priority queue that have been visited when processing previous partial queries can be disregarded when processing a new partial query.*

Proof: *The keyword set of a previous partial query is a superset of the keyword set of a new partial query. For a visited node, all its entries containing keywords of the new partial query have been enqueued into the priority queue; thus, we can disregard the elements that have been visited.* □

The pseudocode is outlined in Algorithm 1. The algorithm uses a min-priority queue for the best-first search with the cost as the key. Variable $mSet$ keeps the keyword set of the current partial query, and $pSet$ keeps the keyword set of the preceding partial query. For each partial query, we use the best-first search to find an object that overlaps with the query keyword $mSet$ and has the lowest cost.

Algorithm 1: Type1Greedy(q, $irTree$)

```
1  U ← new min-priority queue;
2  U.Enqueue(irTree.root, 0);
3  V ← ∅; Cost ← 0;
4  mSet ← q.ψ; pSet ← q.ψ;
5  while mSet ≠ ∅ do
6      while U is not empty do
7          e ← U.Dequeue();
8          Cost ← Cost + e.Key;
9          if e is an object then
10             V ← V ∪ e;
11             pSet ← mSet ;
12             mSet ← mSet \ e.ψ;
13             for each entry e' in U do
14                 if e'.λ ∩ e.λ ≠ ∅ then
15                     e'.key = e'.key*|e'.λ∩mSet| / |e'.λ∩pSet| ;
16                 else remove e from U;
17             reorganize priority queue U using new key values;
18             break;
19         else
20             read the posting lists of e for keywords in mSet;
21             for each entry e' in node e do
22                 if mSet ∩ e'.ψ ≠ ∅ then
23                     if e is a non-leaf node then
24                         U.Enqueue(e', minDist(q,e') / |mSet∩e'.ψ| );
25                     else
26                         U.Enqueue(e', Dist(q,o) / |mSet∩o.ψ|);
27 return Cost and V ;                                    // results
```

The algorithm computes the cost for a non-object node (line 23) and the cost for an object (line 25).

Whenever the algorithm pops an object from U, it is guaranteed that the text description of the object overlaps with $mSet$ (the keyword set of the current partial query), and that the object has the lowest cost. Thus, it becomes part of the result. The algorithm proceeds with the next partial query by changing the keyword component (line 12). Based on Lemma 3.2, we do not need to scan all objects to process the new partial query. Rather, we only have to update the unvisited elements in the priority queue with the new cost based on the new partial query (lines 13–16). We then use the best-first search to process the new partial query.

3.3 Exact Algorithm

The number of keywords of a query may be small in some applications. This motivates us to develop an exact algorithm for processing the TYPE1 spatial keyword group query.

We present a dynamic programming algorithm that does not use an index in Section 3.3.1, and we present a version of the algorithm that uses an index to prune the search space in Section 3.3.2.

3.3.1 Exact Algorithm Without an Index

An obvious exact algorithm enumerates every subset of spatial objects whose text descriptions overlap with the query keyword set in D.For each such subset, the algorithm then checks whether the subset covers all query keywords and computes its cost. This yields an exponential running time in terms of the number of objects, which is very expensive if D is large.

A better method is to perform the exhaustive search on a smaller set of objects. We proceed to introduce a lemma that lays the foundation for the algorithm to be proposed.

Lemma 3.3: *Consider a query q and two objects o_i and o_j, each of which contains a subset of the query keywords. Let $ws_i = q.\psi \cap o_i.\psi$ and $ws_j = q.\psi \cap o_j.\psi$. If $\mathsf{Dist}(q, o_i) < \mathsf{Dist}(q, o_j)$, $\{o_i\}$ is a better group than $\{o_j\}$ for any keyword subset of $ws_i \cap ws_j$.*

Proof: *Obvious since o_i always incurs lower cost than does o_j for any keyword subset $ws_i \cap ws_j$.* □

According to the lemma, given a subset of query keywords ws, among the objects covering ws, the one that is the closest to the query contributes the lowest cost to ws.

Example 3.1: Consider a query q with keywords $q.\psi = \{t_1, t_2, t_3\}$ and the four objects in Table 2. We know that $\mathsf{Dist}(q, o_1) < \mathsf{Dist}(q, o_2)$ and $o_1 \cap o_2 = \{t_2\}$. According to lemma 3.3, $\{o_1\}$ is a better result set for the query with keyword set $\{t_2\}$. □

	o_1	o_2	o_3	o_4
Distance to the query	1	2	2.5	4
Keywords	t_1,t_2	t_2,t_3	t_1,t_3	t_1

Table 2: Example data set

Since the set of query keywords is small, the number of its subsets is not large although it is exponential to the number of query keywords. For each subset of query keywords, we find the object that covers the subset of query keywords and has the lowest costs according to Lemma 3.3. Then an exhaustive search on these objects can find the best group. However, this method is time-consuming since it runs exponentially in terms of the number of objects, which can be exponential in the number of query keywords.

Instead, we develop a dynamic programming algorithm with exponential running time in terms of the number of query keywords. The idea of the algorithm is summarized as follows: Given a query q with n $(= |q.\psi|)$ keywords, we process the subsets of $q.\psi$ in breadth-first order, i.e., we process subsets in ascending order of their length. For each subset X of $q.\psi$, we find the best set of covering objects, i.e., a set of objects that cover X and have the lowest cost, by utilizing the best covering sets of the subsets of X.

Existing WSC algorithms are mostly approximation algorithms. Several recent proposals [4, 9] have good (e.g., constant) approximation guarantees with moderately exponential running time. Björklund et al. [3] propose an exact algorithm for the unweighted set cover problem using the inclusion-exclusion principle, which is not directly applicable to the WSC problem.

Formally, let F be the set of all subsets of $q.\psi$. For each subset $X \subseteq q.\psi$, we denote the set of objects that cover X and has the lowest cost by $\mathsf{Group}(X)$ and the cost of covering set X by $\mathsf{Cost}(X)$.

Our dynamic programming algorithm avoids enumerating all the set partitions. Equation 3 shows the approach to computing the lowest cost for each subset X. If X is not covered by any object o, its cost is initialized to ∞; otherwise, its cost is initialized to the cost of the best covering object, as shown in Equation 3. Then the dynamic programming idea is adopted to find the lowest cost of each subset X in ascending order of the length of X. Specifically, for each X, we check each pair of component subsets (whose optimal costs are already known) to find a pair with the lowest cost. Note that the optimal set of two subsets may share some objects whose costs are computed by oCost.

$$\mathsf{Cost}(X) = \begin{cases} \min_{o \in D \wedge X \subseteq o.\psi} \{\mathsf{Dist}(q, o)\}, & \exists o (X \subseteq o.\psi) \\ \infty, & \text{otherwise} \end{cases} \quad (3)$$

$$\mathsf{Cost}(X) = \min_{S \in F \wedge S \subseteq X} \{\mathsf{Cost}(X \setminus S) + \mathsf{Cost}(S) - \mathsf{oCost}(S, X \setminus S)\}$$

$$\mathsf{oCost}(S, X \setminus S) = \sum_{o \in \mathsf{Group}(X \setminus S) \cap \mathsf{Group}(S)} \mathsf{Dist}(o, q) \quad (4)$$

Algorithm 2: Type1ExactNoIndex (q, D)

```
1  n ← |q.ψ|;
2  for i from 1 to 2^n − 1 do Cost[i] ← ∞, Group[i] ← ∅;
3  for each object o_i in D do
4      if o_i.ψ ∩ q.ψ ≠ ∅ then
5          Dist[o_i] ← Dist (o_i, q);
6          for each subset s_i in o_i.ψ ∩ q.ψ do
7              i ← MapToInteger(s_i);
8              if Cost[i] > Dist [o_i] then
9                  Cost[i] ← Dist [o_i];
10                 Group[i] ← {o_i};

11 for i from 1 to 2^n − 1 do
12     minValue ← ∞, bestSplit ← 0;
13     for j from 1 to i/2 do
14         if j & i = j then
15             S ← Group[j] ∩ Group[i − j];
16             oDist ← 0;
17             for each object o in S do
18                 oDist ← oDist + Dist [o];
19             cost ← Cost[j] + Cost[i − j] − oDist;
20             if cost < minValue then
21                 minValue ← cost;
22                 bestSplit ← j;

23     if Cost[i] > minValue then
24         Cost[i] ← minValue;
25         Group[i] ← Group[bestSplit] ∪ Group[i − bestSplit];
26 return Cost[2^n − 1] and Group[2^n − 1]
```

$$\mathsf{Group}(X) = \begin{cases} \arg\min_{o \in D \wedge X \subseteq o.\psi}\{\mathsf{Dist}(q, o)\}, & \exists o(X \subseteq o.\psi) \\ \emptyset, & \text{otherwise} \end{cases}$$
$$S* = \underset{S \in F \wedge S \subseteq X}{\arg\min}\ \{\mathsf{Cost}(X \setminus S) + \mathsf{Cost}(S) - \mathsf{oCost}(S, X \setminus S)\}$$
$$\mathsf{Group}(X) = \mathsf{Group}(S*) \cup \mathsf{Group}(X \setminus S*) \tag{5}$$

To implement the algorithm efficiently, we encode the subsets. A query q with n keywords $q.\psi = \{t_1, t_2, \ldots, t_n\}$ has $(2^n - 1)$ non-empty subsets of keywords. We encode each subset X by an integer i of n bits, where each bit corresponds to a keyword in q. If the jth keyword is contained in X, the jth bit in the binary format of i is set to 1; otherwise, it is set to 0. For example, for $q.\psi$=$\{t_1, t_2, t_3\}$, we can encode subset $\{t_1\}$ by 1, $\{t_2\}$ by 2, and $\{t_1, t_2\}$ by 3.

We maintain two arrays: $\mathsf{Cost}[i]$ records the lowest cost of the subset that is encoded by integer i, and $\mathsf{Group}[i]$ records the group of objects that contribute to the lowest cost. Equations 4 and 5 can be rewritten as the following equation:

$$\mathsf{Cost}[i] = \min_{j, i\&j=j}\{\mathsf{Cost}[j] + \mathsf{Cost}[i-j] - \mathsf{oCost}(i, j)\}$$
$$\mathsf{oCost}(i, j) = \sum_{o \in \mathsf{Group}[i] \cap \mathsf{Group}[i-j]} \mathsf{Dist}(o, q) \tag{6}$$
$$opt = \arg\min_{j, i\&j=j}\{\mathsf{Cost}[j] + \mathsf{Cost}[i-j] - \mathsf{oCost}(i, j)\}$$
$$\mathsf{Group}[i] = \mathsf{Group}[opt] \cup \mathsf{Group}[i - opt]$$

Here, & is the bit-wise AND operator, and $i\&j = j$ states that the set represented by j is a subset of the set represented by i.

The pseudocode is outlined in Algorithm 2. We progressively compute $\mathsf{Cost}[i]$ and $\mathsf{Group}[i]$ from $i = 1$ to $(2^n - 1)$. When i = $(2^n - 1)$, we get the results with the lowest cost, $\mathsf{Cost}[2^n - 1]$, and the best group, $\mathsf{Group}[2^n - 1]$. We scan the dataset D. For each single object that overlaps with query keyword set $q.\psi$, we check whether the object contributes to the lowest cost for a keyword subset (lines 3–10). If a keyword subset is not contained by any single object, its cost is initialized to ∞.

The algorithm proceeds to use Equation 6 to compute the lowest cost for each subset (lines 11–25). We check each subset, represented by j, of the current keyword subset, represented by i, to see whether the subset represented by j and the subset represented by $(i - j)$ contribute a lower cost (lines 13–22). The lowest cost from combining two subsets is kept in $minValue$, and the integer that represents the corresponding subset is kept in $bestSplit$. If the $minValue$ contributed by aggregating two subsets is smaller than the current lowest cost of the keyword subset represented by i, we update its cost $\mathsf{Cost}[i]$ and update the group of objects $\mathsf{Group}[i]$ that covers it (lines 23–25). Finally, we return the lowest cost and the best group (line 26).

The algorithm scans the whole dataset D in lines 3–10, and it finds the best group according to Equation 6 in lines 11–22. Therefore, it runs exponentially in terms of the number of query keywords and linearly in terms of the size of the dataset.

Example 3.2: We proceed to illustrate Algorithm 2. Given a query q with the keywords set $q.\psi = \{t_1, t_2, t_3\}$ and three objects o_1, o_2, and o_3 with description: $o_1.\psi = \{t_1, t_2\}$ and Dist $(q, o_1) = 1$; $o_2.\psi$ =$\{t_2, t_3\}$ and Dist $(q, o_2) = 2$; $o_3.\psi = \{t_1, t_2, t_3\}$ and Dist (q, o_3) = 4. Lines 3–10 return the following results:

i	1	2	3	4	5	6	7
Cost	1	1	1	2	4	2	4
Group	o_1	o_1	o_1	o_2	o_3	o_2	o_3

We subsequently utilize these values to compute the final results. For example, when computing Cost[5], we determine that $\{o_1, o_2\}$(Cost[1]+Cost[4]) is better than $\{o_3\}$, and we update its value. Finally, we have the following results:

i	1	2	3	4	5	6	7
Cost	1	1	1	2	3	2	3
Group	o_1	o_1	o_1	o_2	o_1, o_2	o_2	o_1, o_2

□

3.3.2 *Exact Algorithm Using an Index*

The dynamic programming algorithm presented above needs to scan the whole dataset. This has two drawbacks: (1) it wastes computation when checking many unnecessary objects that do not contain any query keyword, and (2) all the objects whose text descriptions overlap with the query keywords are scanned to obtain the lowest costs for the query keyword subsets.

To overcome the first drawback, we utilize the IR-tree that enables us to retrieve only the objects that contain some query keywords while avoiding checking the objects containing no query keywords. For the second drawback, we show that it is not always necessary to scan all the objects covering part of the query keywords.

We propose the following principle for our algorithm: we process objects in ascending order of their distances to a query q. By following that order, we know that the lowest cost of a subset is always contributed by a single or a group of closer objects based on Lemma 3.3.

Lemma 3.4: *Consider a query q. If we process objects in ascending order of their distances to q, when we reach an object o_i containing a query keyword subset ws, all subsets of ws will get their lowest costs.*

Proof: *Obvious since all objects to be visited after o_i have larger cost for any subset of ws; thus, its lowest cost is either contributed by o_i or by objects visited earlier.* □

Example 3.3: Recall the query in Example 3.1. We first process object o_1, and we know 1 is the lowest costs of subsets $\{t_1, t_2\}$, $\{t_1\}$, and $\{t_2\}$. Then we reach o_2, and we know 2 is the lowest costs of subsets $\{t_2, t_3\}$ and $\{t_3\}$ ($\{t_2\}$ already has lowest cost 1). □

Based on Lemma 3.4, we can derive a stopping condition for our algorithm—we reach an object that contains all the query keywords. However, if no such object exists in the dataset, the algorithm is still required to scan to the furthest object containing some query keywords before it can stop. In the example in Table 2, we need to read all the four objects. But if the third furthest object o_3 covers $\{t_1, t_2, t_3\}$, we need not read o_4.

We proceed to present an additional stopping condition.

Lemma 3.5: *Given two query keyword subsets ws_i and ws_j, and with union $ws_u = ws_i \cup ws_j$, we have* $\mathsf{Cost}(ws_u) \leq \mathsf{Cost}(ws_i) + \mathsf{Cost}(ws_j)$.

Proof: *Obvious from Equations 3–5.* □

Based on Lemma 3.5, for any two keyword subsets whose lowest costs are known, we can obtain an upper bound of the lowest cost value for the keyword subset that is the union of the two keyword subsets. We denote the upper bound by $Cost_u$.

In our algorithm, we keep track of the upper bounds for the subsets whose costs are still unknown. Whenever we reach an object from which some keyword subset gets its lowest cost (according to Lemma 3.4), the subset, together with each of the subsets that have either lowest costs or upper bounds of cost (i.e., the keyword subsets that are covered by visited objects), are used to update the upper bound cost values of the corresponding union keyword subsets.

Example 3.4: Recall Example 3.1. After the object o_2 is scanned, $\{t_3\}$ gets its lowest cost 2. We can compute an upper bound for $\{t_1, t_3\}$ using the costs of $\{t_1\}$ and $\{t_3\}$, i.e., $Cost_u(\{t_1, t_3\}) = \mathsf{Cost}(\{t_1\}) + \mathsf{Cost}(\{t_3\}) = 3$ (covered by o_1 and o_2). Similarly, we can also compute an upper bound value 3 for $\{t_1, t_2, t_3\}$ using the costs of $\{t_1, t_2\}$ and $\{t_3\}$, and the set is also covered by o_1 and o_2.

When we reach o_3, we get a lower cost of 2.5 for $\{t_1, t_3\}$(the previous upper bound of 3 is updated). Then $\{t_1, t_3\}$ are combined with $\{t_2\}$ to form $\{t_1, t_2, t_3\}$ with a cost of 3.5. Since this value exceeds its current upper bound, no update is needed. □

We are ready to introduce a lemma that provides an early stopping condition for our algorithm.

Lemma 3.6: *Suppose that we scan objects in ascending order of their distances to q. Given a keyword subset ws, when we reach object o_i, and if* $\mathsf{Dist}(q, o_i) \geq Cost_u(ws)$, *then* $\mathsf{Cost}(ws) = Cost_u(ws)$, *where $Cost_u(ws)$ is the current upper bound of ws.*

Proof: *We prove this by contradiction. If any object o_j further to q than o_i is a member of the best group then it must have*

$$\mathsf{Cost}(ws) \geq \mathsf{Dist}(q, o_j) \geq \mathsf{Dist}(q, o_i) \geq Cost_u(ws)$$

Since $Cost_u(ws)$ cannot be smaller than $\mathsf{Cost}(ws)$, *no further object will be contained in the best group. In addition, $Cost_u(ws)$ is the current minimum cost value, and thus it becomes the lowest cost of ws.* □

Example 3.5: Recall again Example 3.1. By following ascending order of distances, when the algorithm reaches o_4 (Dist $(q, o_4) = 4$), we can conclude that $Cost_u(\{t_1, t_2, t_3\}) = 3$ is the lowest cost and that the best group is (o_1, o_2). □

The pseudocode is described in Algorithm 3. All the keyword subsets whose lowest costs are already known are stored in the variable *markedSet*, and the subsets that have upper bounds are

Algorithm 3: Type1ExactWIndex(q, $irTree$)

```
1  markedSet ← ∅, valuedSet ← ∅;
2  n ← |q.ψ|;
3  for i from 1 to 2^n − 1 do Cost[i] ← ∞, Group[i] ← ∅;
4  U ← new min-priority queue;
5  U.Enqueue(irTree.root, 0);
6  while U is not empty do
7      e ← U.Dequeue();
8      ks ← q.ψ ∩ e.ψ ;
9      if ks ∉ markedSet then
10         if e is a non-leaf node then
11             foreach entry e' in node e do
12                 if q.ψ ∩ e'.ψ ≠ ∅ and q.ψ ∩ e'.ψ ∉ markedSet
                   then U.Enqueue(e', minDist(q, e'));
13         else if e is a leaf node then
14             foreach object o in leaf node e do
15                 if q.ψ ∩ o.ψ ≠ ∅ and q.ψ ∩ o.ψ ∉ markedSet
                   then U.Enqueue(o, Dist(q, o));
16         else                                  // e is an object
17             foreach set S ∈ valuedSet do
18                 i ← MapToInteger(S);
19                 if Cost[i] < Dist (q, e) then
20                     if i = 2^n − 1 then                // Lemma 3.6
21                         return Cost[2^n − 1] and Group[2^n − 1];
22                     valuedSet ← valuedSet \ S;
23                     markedSet ← markedSet ∪ S;
24             tempSet ← ∅;
25             foreach subset ss ⊆ ks do // Lemma 3.4
26                 if ss ∉ markedSet then
27                     i ← MapToInteger(ss);
28                     markedSet ← markedSet ∪ ss;
29                     tempSet ← tempSet ∪ ss;
30                     if ss ∈ valuedSet then
31                         valuedSet ← valuedSet \ ss;
32                     Cost[i] ← Dist (e, q);
33                     Group[i] ← {e};
34                     if j = 2^n − 1 then              // Lemma 3.4
35                         return Cost[2^n − 1] and Group[2^n − 1];
36             foreach set ts ∈ tempSet do
37                 j ← MapToInteger(ts);
38                 for i from 1 to 2^n − 1 do
39                     if Cost[i] = ∞ then continue;
40                     unionKey ← i|j;
41                     if unionKey = i ∧ unionKey = j then
42                         continue;
43                     D ← Cost[i] + Dist (e, q);
44                     if Cost[unionKey] > D then
45                         Cost[unionKey] ← D;
46                         Group[unionKey] ← Group[i] ∩ {e};
47 return Cost[2^n − 1] and Group[2^n − 1];
```

stored in the variable *valuedSet*. The IR-tree is used for retrieving the next nearest object that covers some query keywords. We use a min-priority queue U to store the IR-tree nodes and objects, where their distances to the query are the keys.

The priority queue U is initialized to the root node of the IR-tree (line 4). We dequeue an element e from U, and we compute the keyword intersection ks between e and q (lines 7–8). If the keyword subset ks is contained in *markedSet* (whose lowest costs are known), we do not need to process e according to Lemma 3.3 (line 9). Otherwise, we process e according to its type: 1) If e is a non-leaf index node, we check each of its child nodes, denoted by e', to see whether e' contains a keyword subset of q that is not contained in $markedSet$. If so, e' is inserted into U with its minimum distance to query q as its priority key (lines 10–12). 2) If e is a leaf node, we handle each object in e similarly to how we handle each child node in 1) (lines 13–15). 3) If e is an object, we first utilize its distance to q to move some keyword subsets from $valuedSet$ to $markedSet$. The subsets whose upper bounds are smaller than Dist(q, e) get their lowest costs (lines 17–23) according to Lemma 3.6. If the query keyword set $q.\psi$ is confirmed to get its lowest cost, the algorithm terminates (line 21). Then for each subset ss of $q.\psi \cap e.\psi$, if its lowest cost is unknown (line 26), the object e constitutes the best group (Lemma 3.4) for ss. Since ss may already be covered by previously visited objects and have an upper bound of its lowest cost, we remove ss from $valuedSet$ (lines 30–31). Once $q.\psi$ gets its lowest cost, the algorithm terminates (lines 34–35). In lines 36–46, we combine each subset ts that newly obtained its lowest cost with the subsets that already have cost values (Lemma 3.5). In line 40, "|" is the bit-wise OR operator. If one is the subset of the other (line 41), we do not combine the two subsets; otherwise, we update the cost value for the union of the two subsets (lines 44–46).

This algorithm runs faster than Type1ExactNoIndex due to two reasons: first, using the IR-tree avoids scanning the whole dataset; second, based on Lemma 3.6, we are able to find the best group without scanning objects whose distances exceed the cost of the current group.

Example 3.6: Recall Table 2 in Example 3.1. The algorithm works as follows. 1) After processing o_1, the result is shown in Table 3, in which i is the integer representing a keyword subset and status "M" means that the subset is contained in $markedSet$. Table 3 shows that $\{t_1\}$ $(i = 1)$, $\{t_2\}$ $(i = 2)$, and $\{t_1, t_2\}$ $(i = 3)$ get their lowest costs and best groups. 2) After processing o_2, the result is shown in Table 4. Except for $\{t_1, t_3\}$ and $\{t_1, t_2, t_3\}$, all the subsets obtain their lowest costs. The cost values of the two subsets are obtained by combining other subsets with known lowest cost. The status value "V" means that the subset is stored in $valuedSet$. 3) After processing o_3, we have the result shown in Table 5. Here, $\{t_1, t_3\}$ gets its lowest cost since it is covered by o_3. 4) When we reach o_4, since its distance to the query is already larger than the currently lowest cost of $\{t_1, t_2, t_3\}$ (the only element in $valuedSet$), we do not need to process it. Set $\{t_1, t_2, t_3\}$ gets the lowest cost value 3 and is moved to $markedSet$. We now find the best group and the lowest cost.

i	1	2	3	4	5	6	7
Cost	1	1	1	∞	∞	∞	∞
Group	o_1	o_1	o_1	null	null	null	null
Status	M	M	M	null	null	null	null

Table 3: Results after processing o_1

i	1	2	3	4	5	6	7
Cost	1	1	1	2	3	2	3
Group	o_1	o_1	o_1	o_2	o_1,o_2	o_2	o_1,o_2
Status	M	M	M	M	V	M	V

Table 4: Results after processing o_2

i	1	2	3	4	5	6	7
Cost	1	1	1	2	2.5	2	3
Group	o_1	o_1	o_1	o_2	o_3	o_2	o_1,o_2
Status	M	M	M	M	M	M	V

Table 5: Results after processing o_3 □

4. PROCESSING TYPE2 SPATIAL GROUP KEYWORD QUERIES

We present two approximation algorithms in Sections 4.1 and 4.2 and an exact algorithm in Section 4.3.

Algorithm 4: Type2Appro1(q, $irTree$)

```
1  U ← new min-priority queue;
2  U.Enqueue(irTree.root, 0);
3  V ← ∅;
4  uSkiSet ← q.ψ ;                          // uncovered keywords
5  while U is not empty do
6      e ← U.Dequeue();
7      if e is an object then
8          V ← V ∪ e;                       // add e to result
9          uSkiSet ← uSkiSet \ e.ψ;
10         if uSkiSet=∅ then break;
11     else
12         read the posting lists of e for keywords in uSkiSet;
13         foreach entry e' in node e do
14             if uSkiSet ∩ e'.ψ ≠ ∅ then
15                 if e is a non-leaf node then
16                     U.Enqueue(e', minDist(q, e'));
17                 else U.Enqueue(o, Dist(q, o));
18 return V;                                // results
```

4.1 Approximation Algorithm 1

Given a query q, the idea of the algorithm, called Type2Appro1, is to find the nearest object for each keyword t_i in $q.\psi$. The set of all such nearest objects make up the result set. The pseudocode, which assumes that the dataset is indexed using the IR-tree, is outlined in Algorithm 4. The algorithm uses a min-priority queue U for the best-first search. In each iteration, we dequeue an element e from U. If e is an object, we push it into the result set and update the uncovered keyword subset (lines 7–10); if e is a node in the IR-tree, we insert all its child nodes that contain some uncovered keywords into U (lines 12–17). The runtime of this algorithm is linear in the number of query keywords.

Example 4.1: Consider a query $q.\psi = \{t_1, t_3, t_5\}$ and the objects shown in Figure 1. The object o_1 covering t_1 is first added to the result. Then o_2 containing t_3 is added, and when o_4 containing t_5 is retrieved, we obtain a group. Object o_4 has the maximum distance to query, which is 4. The maximum diameter is 6, which is the distance between o_2 and o_4. Hence, the cost of this group is 10. □

We proceed to show that Type2Appro1 is within an approximation factor of 3.

Theorem 4.1: *The cost of the solution V, returned by* Type2Appro1 *for a given query q, is at most three times the cost of the optimal solution OPT:* Cost$(V) \leq 3 \cdot$ Cost(OPT).

Proof: *Let $d = max_{o_i \in V}\{$Dist$(o_i, q)\}$, where V is the solution returned by* Type2Appro1. *Obviously, the optimal solution OPT satisfies* Cost$(OPT) \geq d$.

For the solution V, the largest possible distance between two objects in V is $2d$. Thus, we have the following cost: Cost$(V) \leq d + 2d \leq 3 \cdot$ Cost(OPT). □

4.2 Approximation Algorithm 2

Based on Type2Appro1, we present an algorithm with a better approximation bound.

Let o_f be the furthest object returned by Type2Appro1, and let t_s be the keyword covered by o_f, but not by nearer objects in the result set. We create a new query q_{o_f} using the position of o_f and the keywords of the original query q, i.e., $q_{o_f}.\lambda = o_f.\lambda$ and $q_{o_f}.\psi = q.\psi$. We invoke Type2Appro1 to find a group of objects for q_{o_f}. We compute the cost of this group with respect to q, and this cost serves as the initial lowest cost.

Algorithm 5: Type2Appro2(q, $irTree$)

```
1  U ← new min-priority queue;
2  U.Enqueue(irTree.root, 0);
3  V ← Type2Appro1(q, irTree);
4  Cost_V ← the cost of V;
5  t_s ← the word only covered by the furthest object in V;
6  while U is not empty do
7      e ← U.Dequeue();
8      if e is not an object then
9          if minDist(q, e) ≥ Cost_V then break;
10         foreach entry e' in node e do
11             if t_s ∈ e'.ψ then
12                 if e is a non-leaf node then
13                     U.Enqueue(e', minDist(q, e'));
14                 else U.Enqueue(e', Dist(q, e'));
15     else
16         if Dist(q, e) ≥ Cost_V then break;
17         q_e.λ ← e.λ; q_e.ψ ← q.ψ;
18         V' ← Type2Appro1(q_e, irTree);
19         Cost_V' ← the cost of V';
20         if Cost_V' < Cost_V then
21             Cost_V ← Cost_V';
22             V ← V';
23 return V
```

Then we incrementally find the next nearest objects containing keyword t_s. For each such object o_{t_s}, we create a query for o_{t_s} in the same way as for o_f. Similarly, Type2Appro1 is used to find a group of objects for the query. If the cost of this group is smaller than $Cost_V$, we update $Cost_V$, and this group becomes the current best group. This process is repeated until we reach an object whose distance to q is larger than $Cost_V$, or until we have considered all objects containing keyword t_s.

The pseudocode is given in Algorithm 5. In lines 3–4, we find a group V that satisfies the query using Type2Appro1, and we compute its cost $Cost_V$. Then we find the word t_s that is only contained in the furthest object in V (line 5). In lines 6–22, we incrementally search for the next nearest objects containing t_s within the range of $Cost_V$ to q. We dequeue an element e from U. If it is an IR-tree node, we check if its minimum distance exceeds $Cost_V$ (line 9). If so, the algorithm terminates since all further-away objects have a higher cost than the current best solution and will not be contained in the result group. Otherwise, we read all its child nodes and insert the nodes that contain t_s into U according to their minimum distances to q (lines 10–14). If e is a spatial object, we also compare its distance to q with $Cost_V$ to determine whether the algorithm terminates (line 16). In lines 17–19, we create a new query q_e with the position of e and the texts of q, and we then find a group using q_e as the query and compute its cost. If this new cost is smaller than $Cost_V$, we update $Cost_V$ and the current best group (lines 20–22). Finally, we return V as the result group.

Since we invoke algorithm Type2Appro1 on each object containing t_s, in the worst case, this algorithm runs linearly in terms of both the number of query keywords and the size of the dataset. However, in practice, only a fraction of the dataset needs to be considered.

Example 4.2: Recall query q and the dataset in Example 4.1. Algorithm Type2Appro1 is invoked to return a group $\{o_1, o_2, o_4\}$, in which o_4 is the furthest and contains t_5. We search for a group near o_4, that is $\{o_1, o_3, o_4\}$ with cost 9 ($\text{Dist}(q, o_4)$ + $\text{Dist}(o_3, o_4)$ = 4 + 5). The next nearest object containing t_5 is o_7. For o_7, we find a group $\{o_2, o_7, o_8\}$ with cost 8 ($\text{Dist}(q, o_8)$ + $\text{Dist}(o_7, o_8)$ = 6 + 2), which is better than that of the previous one. Therefore $\{o_2, o_7, o_8\}$ is the result. Note that the optimal group is $\{o_1, o_2, o_7\}$ with cost 7.5 (($\text{Dist}(q, o_7)$ + $\text{Dist}(o_7, o_1)$ = 5 + 2.5). □

We proceed to study the approximation ratio of the algorithm.

Lemma 4.2: *Given an object o_j containing t_s, the cost of the group found at the position of o_j, denoted by $Cost_V(o_j)$, is in the following range: $\text{Dist}(q, o_j) + \text{Dist}(o_j, o_{max}) \leq Cost_V(o_j) \leq \text{Dist}(q, o_j) + 3\text{Dist}(o_j, o_{max})$, in which o_{max} is the furthest object from o_j in the group.*

Proof: *1) $\text{Dist}(q, o_j)$ is a lower bound on the distance of this group to q, and $\text{Dist}(o_j, o_{max})$ is a lower bound on the diameter of this group. As a result, the minimum cost of this group is $\text{Dist}(q, o_j) + \text{Dist}(o_j, o_{max})$.*

2) $\text{Dist}(q, o_j) + \text{Dist}(o_j, o_{max})$ is the maximum possible distance to q of this group. Further, the diameter will not exceed $2\text{Dist}(o_j, o_{max})$ since every object of this group is in the circle with center o_j and radius $\text{Dist}(o_j, o_{max})$. Therefore, the cost of this group is upper bounded by $\text{Dist}(q, o_j) + 3\text{Dist}(o_j, o_{max})$. □

Lemma 4.3: *Let OPT denote the optimal group, and let o_j denote the object containing word t_s in OPT, and let o_{max} denote the furthest object to o_j in group V found by* Type2Appro1. *It holds that: $Cost_{OPT} \geq \text{Dist}(q, o_j) + \text{Dist}(o_j, o_{max})$.*

Proof: *Object o_{max} must contain some keyword, denoted by t, which is not covered by the other objects in V. Among objects containing t, o_{max} is the closest to o_j. Therefore, in OPT, the object covering t cannot be closer to o_j than o_{max}. As a result, $\text{Dist}(o_j, o_{max})$ is a lower bound on the diameter of OPT. $\text{Dist}(q, o_j)$ is a lower bound on the distance between q and OPT. Therefore, $Cost_{OPT} \geq \text{Dist}(q, o_j) + \text{Dist}(o_j, o_{max})$.* □

Lemma 4.4: *The approximation ratio of algorithm Type2Appro2 is not larger than 2.*

Proof: *Let o_j denote the object containing word t_s in the optimal group OPT. Let $Cost_{APPR}$ be the cost returned by Algorithm* Type2Appro2. *We know that $Cost_{APPR} \leq Cost_V(o_j)$, because $Cost_{APPR}$ is the smallest among all cost values of groups found at each object containing t_s. Let o_i be the nearest object containing t_s. We get $Cost_{APPR} \leq Cost_V(o_i) \leq 3\text{Dist}(q, o_i)$ according to Theorem 4.1. Therefore,*

$$\frac{Cost_{APPR}}{Cost_{OPT}} \leq \frac{3\text{Dist}(q, o_i)}{Cost_{OPT}} \leq \frac{3\text{Dist}(q, o_i)}{\text{Dist}(q, o_j) + \text{Dist}(o_j, o_{max})}$$

$$= 2 + \frac{3\text{Dist}(q, o_i) - 2(\text{Dist}(q, o_j) + \text{Dist}(o_j, o_{max}))}{\text{Dist}(q, o_j) + \text{Dist}(o_j, o_{max})}$$

a) If $\text{Dist}(q, o_j) + \text{Dist}(o_j, o_{max}) \geq 1.5\text{Dist}(q, o_i)$ then $Cost_{APPR} Cost_{OPT} \leq 2$.
b) If $\text{Dist}(q, o_j) + \text{Dist}(o_j, o_{max}) < 1.5\text{Dist}(q, o_i)$, because $\text{Dist}(q, o_j) \geq \text{Dist}(q, o_i)$, then $\text{Dist}(o_j, o_{max}) \leq 0.5\text{Dist}(q, o_j)$. Since $Cost_{APPR} \leq Cost_V(o_j)$, we have:

$$\frac{Cost_{APPR}}{Cost_{OPT}} \leq \frac{Cost_V(o_j)}{Cost_{OPT}}$$

$$\leq \frac{\text{Dist}(q, o_j) + 3\text{Dist}(o_j, o_{max})}{\text{Dist}(q, o_j) + \text{Dist}(o_j, o_{max})}$$

$$= 2 + \frac{\text{Dist}(o_j, o_{max}) - \text{Dist}(q, o_j)}{\text{Dist}(q, o_j) + \text{Dist}(o_j, o_{max})}$$

$$\leq 2 - 0.5\frac{\text{Dist}(o_j, o_{max})}{\text{Dist}(q, o_j) + \text{Dist}(o_j, o_{max})} \leq 2$$

Thus, we complete the proof. □

4.3 Exact Algorithm

It is challenging to develop an exact algorithm for TYPE2 spatial group keyword queries, as it appears that an exact algorithm cannot avoid an exhaustive search of the object space.

We utilize the Type2Appro2 algorithm to first derive an upper bound cost for the best group and then use this cost to bound the exhaustive search in the object space. Specifically, we develop several pruning strategies to prune the enumeration space. With these efforts, we expect the exact algorithm to be reasonably efficient when the dataset contains at most tens of thousands of objects and the number of query keywords is small.

Before presenting the idea underlying the algorithm, we define the concept of *covering node set* and the lower bound cost of such a set.

DEFINITION 1 (COVERING NODE SET). *Given a query q, a covering node set is a set of nodes that cover the query keywords, with each node contributing at least one object to the final result.*

DEFINITION 2. *Given a query q and a covering node set N,*
1) if N contains only one node e, its lower bound cost is:

$$minCost(N) = \mathsf{minDist}(q, e)$$

2) if N contains multiple nodes, its lower bound cost is:

$$minCost(N) = max_{e_i \in N} \mathsf{minDist}(q, e_i) + max_{e_j, e_k \in N} \mathsf{minDist}(e_j, e_k),$$

where $max_{e_i \in N}\mathsf{minDist}(q, e_i)$ *is the minimum distance from q to a group from N, and* $max_{e_j,e_k \in N}\mathsf{minDist}(e_j, e_k)$ *is the minimum diameter of a group from N. Therefore,* $minCost(N)$ *is the lower bound of the cost of the best group from N.*

The algorithm's idea is to perform a best-first search on the IR-tree to find the covering node sets, with some objects from these nodes constituting a group satisfying the keywords requirement of a query. We process the covering node set with the lowest cost to find covering node sets from their child nodes. When we reach a covering node set consisting of leaf nodes, we find a group of objects with the lowest cost by performing an exhaustive search.

The pseudocode is given in Algorithm 6. A priority queue U stores the covering node sets. Algorithm 4 (Type2Appro1) is invoked to find a group, and its cost serves as the current lowest cost (lines 3–4). We next search from the root node, enumerating all its child node sets to find covering node sets. If a node set covers the query keywords, we estimate its lower bound cost by Definition 2 and insert it into U with the estimated cost as the key. After we finish enumerating the covering node sets of a covering node set, we dequeue a covering node set N from U, and we find its lower level covering node sets that cover the query keywords. The covering node sets whose lower bounds are smaller than the current lowest cost are inserted into U (lines 14–17). Once we reach a leaf node, we do an exhaustive search to get the best group in the covering node set, and we update the lowest cost stored in $Cost_V$ with the cost of this group (lines 10–12).

The algorithm terminates when the lower bound of the covering node set at the top position of U is larger than the current lowest cost (line 7) because the remaining covering node sets in U have larger costs than the current lowest cost, and because covering node sets at their lower levels do not contain better groups according to Lemma 4.5.

Lemma 4.5: *For any lower level covering node set L enumerated from covering node set N, we have* $minCost(L) \geq minCost(N)$.

Algorithm 6: Top-Down Search $(q, irTree)$

1 $U \leftarrow$ new min-priority queue;
2 U.Enqueue($irTree.root$,0);
3 $V \leftarrow$ Type2App2(q, $irTree$);
4 $Cost_V \leftarrow$ the cost of V;
5 **while** *U is not empty* **do**
6     $N \leftarrow U$.Dequeue();
7   **if** *minCost(N)* $\geq Cost_V$ **then break**;
8   **if** *N contains leaf nodes* **then**
9         $V' \leftarrow$ ExhaustiveSearch(N);
10         $Cost_{V'} \leftarrow$ the cost of V';
11   **if** $Cost_{V'} < Cost_V$ **then**
12             $Cost_V \leftarrow Cost_{V'}$; $V \leftarrow V'$;
13   **else**
14         $S \leftarrow$ EnumerateNodeSets(N, $Cost_V$, q);
15   **foreach** *node set ns in S* **do**
16   **if** $q.\psi \subseteq ns.\psi$ **then**
17   U.Enqueue(ns, minCost(ns));
18 **return** V and $Cost_V$

Proof: *a) Denote by* l_a *the child node of the node* n_i *that is the furthest from Q in N. We have:* $\mathsf{minDist}(q, l_a) \geq \mathsf{minDist}(q, n_i)$. *b) Denote by* l_b *and* l_c *the child nodes of* n_j *and* n_k *that have the largest distance among all pairs of child nodes from* n_j *and* n_k*. We then have:* $\mathsf{minDist}(l_b, l_c) \geq \mathsf{minDist}(n_j, n_k)$*. In addition, as* l_a, l_b, *and* $l_c \in L$, *it is true that* $max_{l_i \in L}\mathsf{minDist}(q, l_i) \geq \mathsf{minDist}(q, l_a)$, *and* $max_{l_j,l_k \in L}\mathsf{minDist}(l_j, l_k) \geq \mathsf{minDist}(l_b, l_c)$. *We then obtain* $minCost(L) \geq \mathsf{minDist}(q, l_a) + \mathsf{minDist}(l_b, l_c) \geq minCost(N)$. □

Algorithm 7: EnumerateNodeSets (N, $Cost$, q)

$setList \leftarrow \emptyset$;
foreach *node* n_i *in* N **do**
    $cList_i \leftarrow \emptyset$;
    $L_i^1 \leftarrow \emptyset$;
    foreach *child node* c_i *of* n_i **do**
        if *minCost(*c_i*)* $\geq Cost$ **then** $L_i^1 \leftarrow L_i^1 \bigcup c_i$;
    for m *from* 2 *to* $(|q.\psi| - |N| + 1)$ **do**
        $L_i^m \leftarrow \emptyset$;
        foreach *node set* $NS_1 \in L_i^{m-1}$ **do**
            foreach *node set* $NS_2 \in L_i^{m-1}$ **do**
                if NS_1 *and* NS_2 *share the first* $(m-1)$ *nodes* **then**
                    $NS \leftarrow$ Merge(NS_1, NS_2);
                    if *minCost(NS)* $< Cost$ **then**
                        $L_i^m \leftarrow L_i^m \bigcup NS$;
        $cList_i \leftarrow cList_i \bigcup L_i^m$;
foreach *node set ns formed by node sets selected from each of* $cList_1 ... cList_n$ **do**
    if $minCost(ns) < Cost$ **then**
        $setList \leftarrow setList \bigcup ns$;
return $setList$;

We proceed to describe EnumerateNodeSets called in line 14, which enumerates all possible lower level covering node sets from an upper level covering node set. First, we consider the simple case where the covering node set N only contains one node. We use a bottom-up method to find all the covering node sets. Let $n = |q.\psi|$ be the number of keywords in query q. The size of a covering node set is at most n based on the pigeon-hole principle.

We first enumerate the covering node sets that consist of a single node. Then these covering node sets are combined to form covering node sets with two members. In general, all the covering node sets of size m can be combined by two covering node sets of size $(m-1)$. If two covering node sets with size $(m-1)$ share the first $(m-2)$ nodes and the lower bound cost of the new combined node set is smaller than that of the current lowest cost, this new set is a candidate covering node set.

Next, we move to the case where a covering node set N contains more than one node. For each node, we follow the previous method to get a list of candidate node sets. However, we do not need to enumerate all combinations. Rather, we only need to enumerate its child nodes up to size $(|q.\psi|-|N|+1)$ according to the pigeon-hole principle (each node in N must contribute at least one child node). After we get a list of child node sets from each node, we select a node set from each list and merge them to determine whether they are a covering node set and to learn whether the merged node set has a lower bound cost that is smaller than the current lowest cost. The details of EnumerateNodeSets are covered in Algorithm 7.

5. EXPERIMENTAL STUDY

5.1 Experimental Settings

Algorithms. For the TYPE1 spatial group keyword query, we consider the approximation algorithm from Section 3.1 (denoted by T1A1), the exact algorithm without index from Section 3.2 (denoted by T1E1), and the exact algorithm utilizing the IR-tree from Section 3.3 (denoted by T1E2). For the TYPE2 spatial group keyword query, we study the two approximation algorithms in Sections 4.1 and 4.2 (denoted by T2A1 and T2A2, respectively) and the exact algorithm from Section 4.3 (denoted by T2E1).

Dataset and queries. We use three datasets. Table 6 shows some properties of these datasets. Dataset GN is extracted from the U.S. Board on Geographic Names (geonames.usgs.gov), in which each object is a location with a geographic name (e.g., valley). Dataset Web is generated from two real datasets. One is WEBSPAM-UK2007[1] that consists of a large number of web documents; the other is a spatial dataset containing the tiger Census blocks in Iowa, Kansas, Missouri, and Nebraska (www. rtreeportal.org). We randomly combine web documents and spatial objects to get the Web dataset. Dataset Hotel contains spatial objects that represent some hotels in the U.S. (www.allstays.com). Each object has a location and a set of words that describe the hotel (e.g., restaurant, pool).

Hotel is small and is used to evaluate the performance of our algorithms when the dataset and index are memory resident, and the other two large datasets are used to evaluate our algorithms when the dataset and index are disk-based.

Property	Web	GN	Hotel
Number of objects	579,727	1,868,821	20,790
Number of unique words	2,899,175	222,409	602
Number of words	249,132,883	18,374,228	80,845

Table 6: Dataset properties

We generate 5 query sets in the space of GN, in which the number of keywords is 3, 6, 9, 12, and 15, respectively. We also generate 5 similar query sets in the space of both Web and Hotel. Each set comprises 50 queries. We rank words in descending order of their frequencies in each dataset. The keywords of each query are randomly generated from the words in the percentile range of 10–40, and the location is randomly generated in the whole region of the dataset. Such queries would need similar processing time, and we report the average cost of queries in each query set. We also conduct experiments on queries generated in other ways, and a summary of experimental results is presented in Section 5.2.3.

Setup. The IR-tree index structure is disk resident, and the page size is 4KB. The number of children of a node in the IR-tree is computed given the fact that each node occupies a page. This translates to 100 children per node in our implementation.

All algorithms were implemented in VC++ and run on an Intel(R) Core(TM)2 Duo CPU E6550 @2.66GHz with 4GB RAM.

5.2 Experimental Results

5.2.1 *Type 1 Spatial Group Keyword Query*

Efficiency of different algorithms. The objective of this set of experiments is to study the efficiency of the three algorithms when we vary the number of query keywords. Figure 3 shows the runtime of the three algorithms on the dataset GN. As expected, the approximation algorithm T1A1 runs much faster than the two exact algorithms, i.e., T1E1 and T1E2. The runtime of the approximation algorithm T1A1 increases almost linearly with the number of query keywords. It is understandable that its running time is in proportion to the number of query keywords: T1A1 keeps searching for the object with the lowest cost that covers part or all of the query keywords, and it terminates when a group of objects that covers the query keywords has been found.

For the two exact algorithms, T1E1 runs slower than T1E2. T1E1 needs to scan the whole dataset and process all the objects that overlap with the query keywords. In contrast, T1E2 avoids scanning objects that do not contain query keywords by utilizing the IR-tree and can avoid accessing the objects whose distances to the query are larger than the cost of the discovered group, thus pruning the search space significantly. The experimental results demonstrate the usefulness of the IR-tree based pruning strategies. It can also be observed that the runtimes of T1E1 and T1E2 increase with the number of keywords; however, the increase is not exponential. The reason is that computing the costs of objects dominates the running time over the dynamic programming component (with an exponential complexity in terms of the number of keywords).

The runtime is consistent with I/O costs, and we do not report I/O costs due to the space limitation.

Accuracy of the approximation algorithm. Figure 4 shows the accuracy of T1A1 on GN. The approximation algorithm is capable of achieving very accurate results.

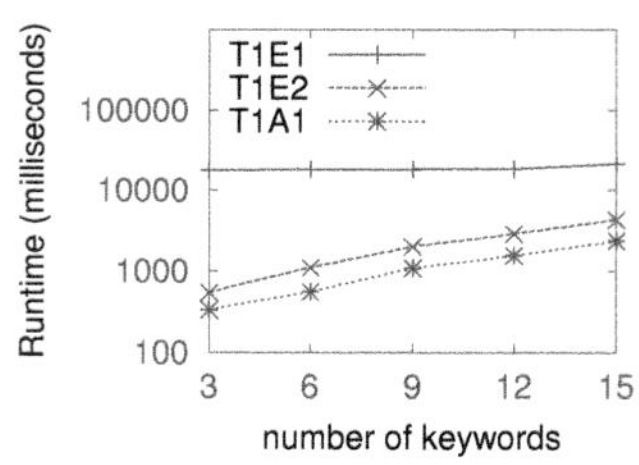

Figure 3: Runtime (GN)

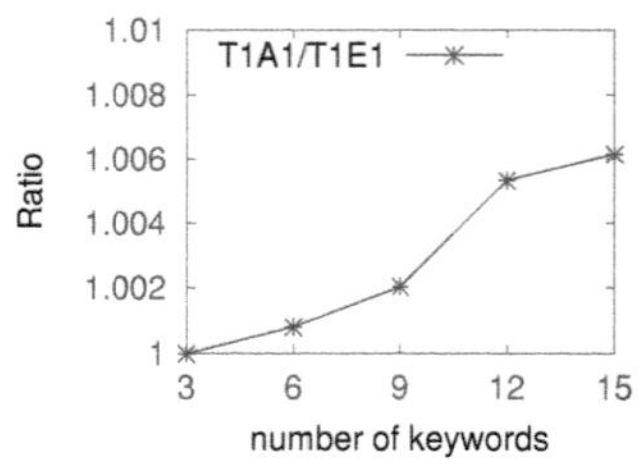

Figure 4: Appro. Ratio (GN)

Experiments on Web. This experiment studies the efficiency and accuracy on the dataset Web in which each object is associated with a large set of keywords. Figure 5 shows the runtime of the algorithms T1A1 and T1E2, and Figure 6 shows the accuracy of T1E2. To ensure readability of the figures, we omit T1E1 since it is inferior to T1E2 (in orders of magnitude). We observe qualitatively similar results on Web as we do on GN.

Experiments on the memory-resident dataset Hotel. This experiment studies the performance of our algorithms when the dataset

[1] http://barcelona.research.yahoo.net/webspam/datasets/uk2007

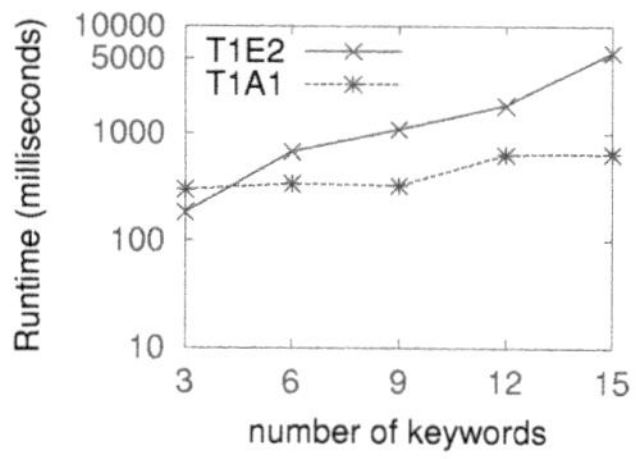

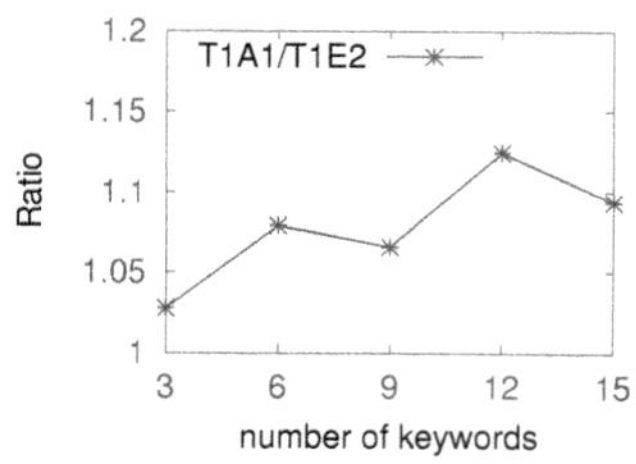

Figure 5: Runtime (Web) **Figure 6: Appro. Ratio (Web)**

and index are in memory. Figure 7 shows the runtime and Figure 8 shows the accuracy of T1A1. We observe qualitatively similar results as we do on the two disk-resident datasets. T1E2 takes only slightly more time than T1A1 when the number of keywords is smaller than 12, while T1E1 performs much slower. We also conduct experiments on Hotel when the data and index are disk-based, and we observe qualitatively similar results.

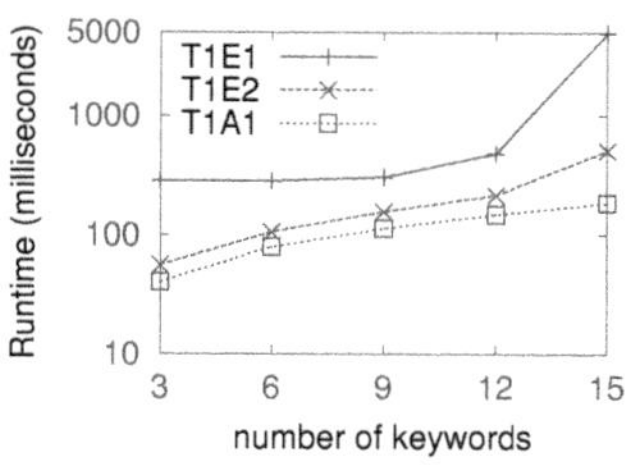

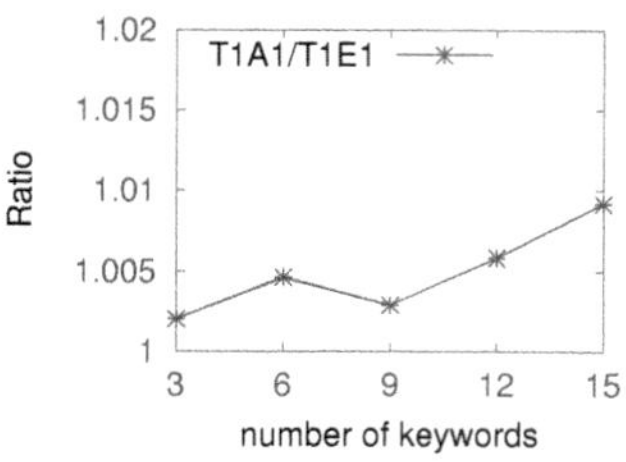

Figure 7: Runtime (Hotel) **Figure 8: Appro. Ratio(Hotel)**

Scalability. To evaluate scalability, we generate 5 datasets containing from 2 to 10 million objects: we generate new locations by copying the locations in GN to nearby locations while maintaining the real distribution of the objects; for each new location, a document is selected randomly from the text descriptions of the objects in GN. Figure 9 shows the runtime of T1A1 and T1E2 (the number of query keywords is 6). T1A1 scales well with the size of the dataset. The exact algorithm T1E2 also scales well. The accuracy changes only slightly; we omit the details due to the space limitation. T1E1 runs much slower than T1A1 and T1E2 and is omitted.

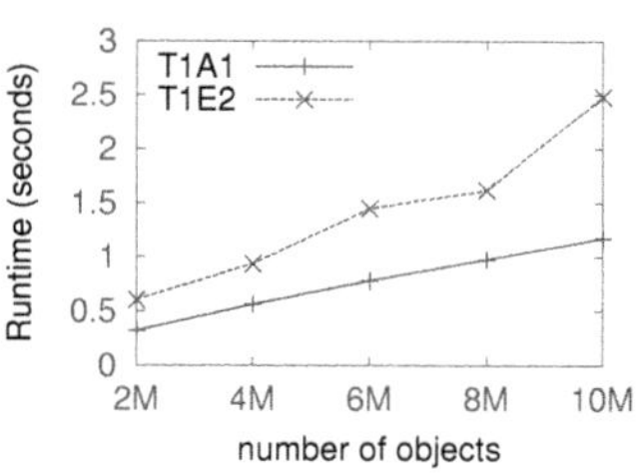

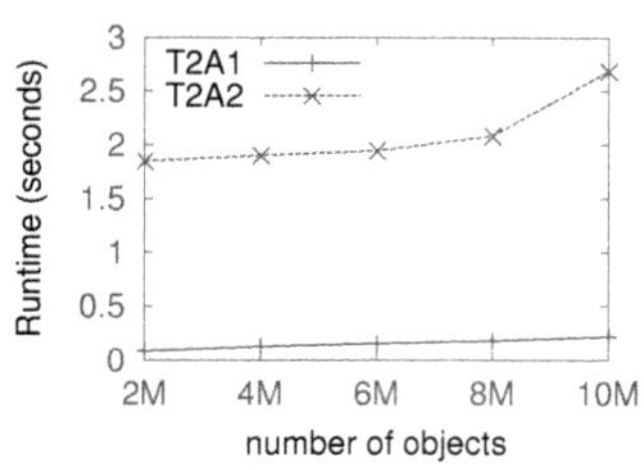

Figure 9: Scalability (Type1) **Figure 10: Scalability (Type2)**

5.2.2 Type 2 Spatial Group Keyword Query

Efficiency of the algorithms and accuracy of the approximation algorithms. The objective of this set of experiments is to evaluate the efficiency of the two approximation algorithms T2A1 and T2A2 and the exact algorithm T2E1, and to evaluate the accuracy of the two approximation algorithms, when we vary the number of query keywords. Figure 11 shows the runtime of the three algorithms, and Figure 12 shows the accuracy of T2A1 and T2A2 on GN.

As can be seen, T2A1 outperforms T2A2 in terms of runtime, and the accuracy of T2A1 is worse than that of T2A2. This is because T2A1 terminates once a group of nearest objects covering query keywords is found. In contrast, T2A2 may invoke T2A1 multiple times. Both T2A1 and T2A2 achieve good accuracy compared with the optimal group returned by T2E1. T2E1 is able to find the optimal group. However, it is much slower than the two approximation algorithms. As expected, with the increase in the number of keywords, the runtime of T2E1 increases exponentially due to its enumerating the covering node sets and performing exhaustive search. When the number of keywords is small, its runtime would be reasonable for applications without a high demand on query time, e.g., finding research partners. However, approximation algorithms represent a better option when the query time is essential.

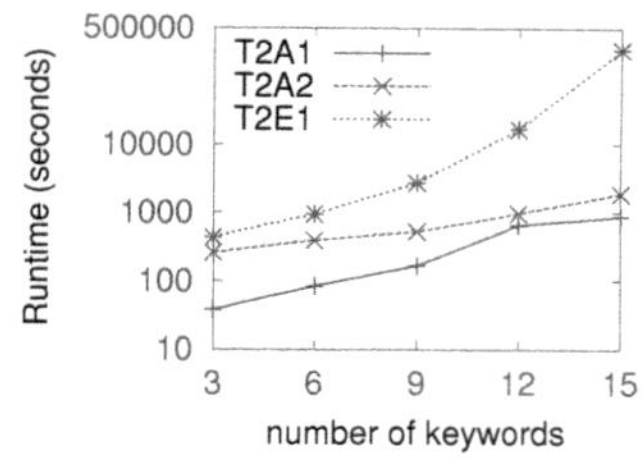

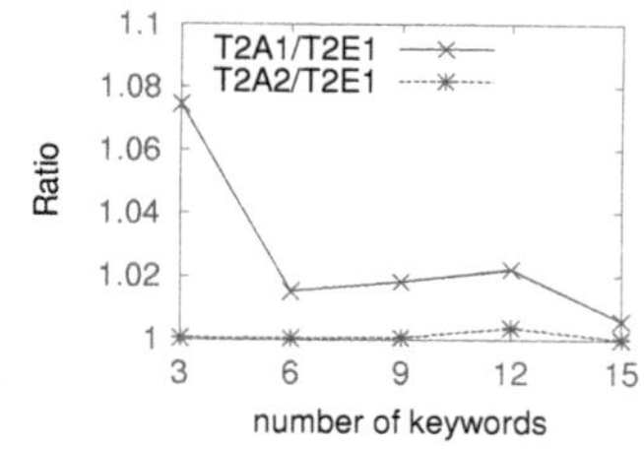

Figure 11: Runtime (GN) **Figure 12: Appro. Ratio (GN)**

Experiments on Web. Figure 13 shows the runtimes of T2A1, T2A2, and T2E1. Figure 14 shows the accuracy of T2A1 and T2A2. We observe qualitatively similar results on Web as we do on GN.

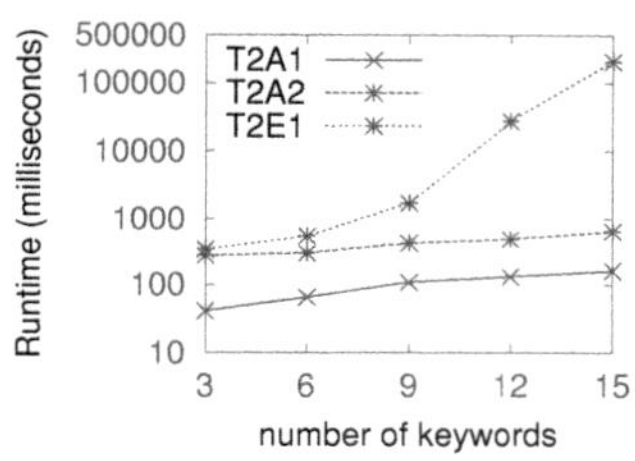

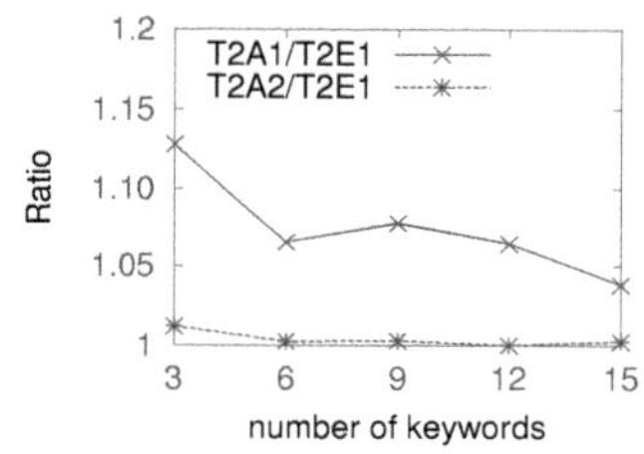

Figure 13: Runtime (Web) **Figure 14: Appro. Ratio(Web)**

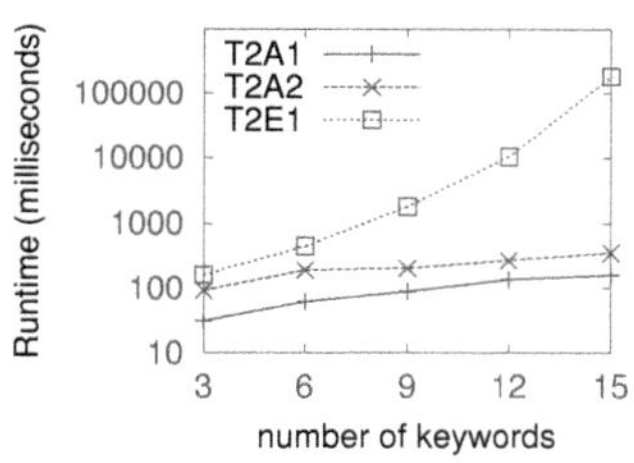

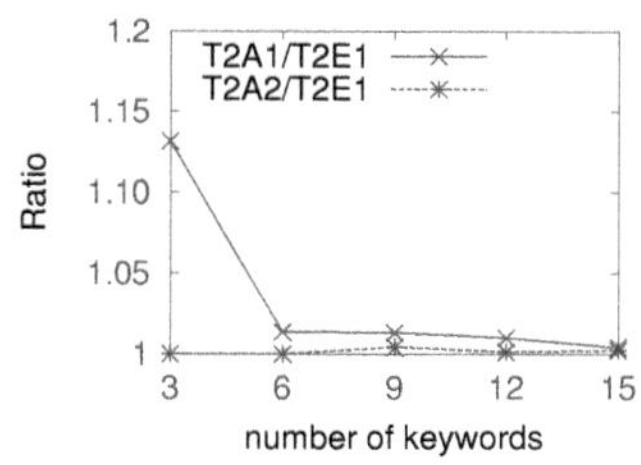

Figure 15: Runtime (Hotel) **Figure 16: Appro. Ratio(Hotel)**

Experiments on memory-resident dataset Hotel. We evaluate performance when the dataset and index are in memory using Hotel. Figure 15 shows the runtime of the three algorithms on Hotel, and Figure 16 shows the accuracy of T2A1 and T2A2. The results are consistent with those obtained for disk-resident datasets. T2A2 runs slower than T2A1 while it has better accuracy. The runtime of T2E1 increases exponentially with the number of keywords. When the dataset Hotel and index are disk-based, we observe qualitatively similar results.

Scalability. We use the same settings as those used in the scalability experiment for TYPE1 query. Figure 10 shows the runtime of T2A1 and T2A2. Both approximation algorithms scale well with the size of the dataset. The runtime of T2E1 increases exponentially with the dataset size. Thus, to ensure readability of the figure, we omit T2E1, which is orders of magnitudes slower than the approximation algorithms.

5.2.3 Additional Experiments

We also generate queries using the keywords beyond the percentile range of 10–40, and we report a summary of experimental results. From the perspective of efficiency, the approximation algorithms perform similarly on all the queries, irrespective of the frequencies of the query keywords. However, on queries containing frequent words, the runtime of exact algorithm T1E2 is slightly slower than the runtime reported in Section 5.2.1, and T2E1 performs much worse than the results reported in Section 5.2.2. If we use infrequent words as query keywords, the exact algorithms run faster, but are still much slower than the approximate algorithms.

In terms of accuracy, the approximation algorithms have better approximation ratio on queries containing many infrequent words. In the extreme case, when all query keywords occur once in the dataset, the approximation algorithms return the correct results. Generally, the approximation ratio becomes worse when frequent words are used, e.g., around 1.2–1.5 for T1E1.

6. RELATED WORK

Spatial web objects are gaining in prevalence, and numerous works on geographical retrieval study the problem of extracting geographic information from web pages (e.g., [1, 11, 13]), which yields spatial web objects that can subsequently be queried.

Commercial services such as Google and Yahoo! offer local-search functionality. Given a spatial keyword query, they return spatial web objects, e.g., stores and restaurants, near the query location. The results consist of single objects that each satisfy the query in isolation. In contrast, we aim to find groups of objects such that the objects in a group collectively satisfy a query.

Several recently proposed hybrid indexes [5, 8, 10, 14, 15] that tightly integrate spatial indexing (e.g., the R-tree) and text indexing (e.g., inverted lists). In these indexes, each entry e in a tree node stores a *keyword summary field* that concisely summarizes the keywords in the subtree rooted at e. This enables irrelevant entries to be pruned during query processing.

The *IR^2-tree* and the *bR*-tree* [14] augment the R-tree with signatures and bitmaps, respectively. We use the IR-tree [8], covered in Section 3.1, as our index structure due to two features of the IR-tree. First, the fanout of the tree is independent of the number of words of objects in the dataset. Second, during query processing, only (a few) posting lists relevant to the query keywords need to be fetched. However, we note that our proposed algorithms are not tied to the IR-tree, but can be used also with the other tightly combined index.

Most existing works on spatial keyword queries retrieve single objects that are close to the query point and are relevant to the query keywords. In contrast, we retrieve groups of objects that are close to the query point and collectively meet the keywords requirement.

To the best of our knowledge, the only work that retrieves groups of spatial keyword objects relates to the mCK query [14, 15] that takes a set of m keyword as argument. It returns m objects of minimum diameter that match the m keywords. It is assumed that each object in the result corresponds to a unique query keyword. In contrast, our query takes both a spatial location and a set of keywords as arguments, and its semantics are quite different from those of the mCK query.

7. CONCLUSIONS AND FUTURE WORK

We present the new problem of retrieving a group of spatial objects, each associated with a set of keywords, such that the group covers the query's keywords and has the lowest cost measured by their distance to the query point, and the distances between the objects in the group. We study two particular instances of the problem, both of which are NP-complete. We develop approximation algorithms with provable approximation bounds and exact algorithms to solve the two problems. Results of experimental evaluation offer insight into the efficiency and the accuracy of the approximation algorithms, and the efficiency of the exact algorithms.

This work opens to a number of promising directions for future work. First, it is worth extending the algorithm to find top-k groups. An open problem here is to what extent we should allow the overlap among top-k groups. The top-k groups would provide users more options. It might not be useful to return groups sharing lots of members, while it seems to be reasonable to allow a certain degree of overlap groups. Second, it is of interest to develop algorithms for alternative cost functions, such as SUM for both $C_1(\cdot)$ and $C_2(\cdot)$. For the top-k groups problem, one meaningful research issue is to determine which types of cost function are most amenable to efficient processing. Third, it is of interest to consider the problem of partial coverage of query keywords. Finally, treating all query keywords equally may not be suitable in some application scenarios. It is of interest to consider an information retrieval ranking model, such as the vector space model, when computing the text relevance for the spatial group query problem.

8. ACKNOWLEDGEMENTS

We thank the anonymous reviewers for their insightful comments. C. S. Jensen is an adjunct professor at University of Agder, Norway. This research was supported in part by the Geocrowd project.

9. REFERENCES

[1] E. Amitay, N. Har'El, R. Sivan, and A. Soffer. Web-a-where: geotagging web content. In *SIGIR*, pp. 273–280, 2004.

[2] E. M. Arkin and R. Hassin. Minimum-diameter covering problems. *Networks*, 36(3):147–155, 2000.

[3] A. Björklund, T. Husfeldt, and M. Koivisto. Set partitioning via inclusion-exclusion. *SIAM J. Comput.*, 39(2):546–563, 2009.

[4] N. Bourgeois, B. Escoffier, and V. T. Paschos. Efficient approximation of min set cover by moderately exponential algorithms. *Theor. Comput. Sci.*, 410(21-23):2184–2195, 2009.

[5] X. Cao, G. Cong, and C. S. Jensen. Retrieving top-k prestige-based relevant spatial web objects. *PVLDB*, 3(1):373–384, 2010.

[6] Y.-Y. Chen, T. Suel, and A. Markowetz. Efficient query processing in geographic web search engines. In *SIGMOD*, pp. 277–288, 2006.

[7] V. Chvatal. A greedy heuristic for the set-covering problem. *Mathematics of Operations Research*, 4:233–235, 1979.

[8] G. Cong, C. S. Jensen, and D. Wu. Efficient retrieval of the top-k most relevant spatial web objects. *PVLDB*, 2(1):337–348, 2009.

[9] M. Cygan, L. Kowalik, and M. Wykurz. Exponential-time approximation of weighted set cover. *Inf. Process. Lett.*, 109(16):957–961, 2009.

[10] I. De Felipe, V. Hristidis, and N. Rishe. Keyword search on spatial databases. In *ICDE*, pp. 656–665, 2008.

[11] J. Ding, L. Gravano, and N. Shivakumar. Computing geographical scopes of web resources. In *VLDB*, 2000.

[12] A. Guttman. R-trees: A dynamic index structure for spatial searching. In B. Yormark, editor, *SIGMOD'84, Proceedings of Annual Meeting, Boston, Massachusetts, June 18-21, 1984*, pp. 47–57. ACM Press, 1984.

[13] K. S. McCurley. Geospatial mapping and navigation of the web. In *WWW*, pp. 221–229, 2001.

[14] D. Zhang, Y. M. Chee, A. Mondal, A. K. H. Tung, and M. Kitsuregawa. Keyword search in spatial databases: Towards searching by document. In *ICDE*, pp. 688–699, 2009.

[15] D. Zhang, B. C. Ooi, and A. K. H. Tung. Locating mapped resources in web 2.0. In *ICDE*, pp. 521–532, 2010.

[16] J. Zobel and A. Moffat. Inverted files for text search engines. *ACM Comput. Surv.*, 38(2):6, 2006.

Finding Semantics in Time Series

Peng Wang [1,2]* Haixun Wang [2] Wei Wang [1]
[1]Fudan University, Shanghai, China
{pengwang5, weiwang1}@fudan.edu.cn
[2]Microsoft Research Asia, Beijing, China
haixunw@microsoft.com

ABSTRACT

In order to understand a complex system, we analyze its output or its log data. For example, we track a system's resource consumption (CPU, memory, message queues of different types, etc) to help avert system failures; we examine economic indicators to assess the severity of a recession; we monitor a patient's heart rate or EEG for disease diagnosis. Time series data is involved in many such applications. Much work has been devoted to pattern discovery from time series data, but not much has attempted to use the time series data to unveil a system's internal dynamics. In this paper, we go beyond learning patterns from time series data. We focus on obtaining a better understanding of its data generating mechanism, and we regard patterns and their temporal relations as organic components of the hidden mechanism. Specifically, we propose to model time series data using a novel pattern-based hidden Markov model (pHMM), which aims at revealing a global picture of the system that generates the time series data. We propose an iterative approach to refine pHMMs learned from the data. In each iteration, we use the current pHMM to guide time series segmentation and clustering, which enables us to learn a more accurate pHMM. Furthermore, we propose three pruning strategies to speed up the refinement process. Empirical results on real datasets demonstrate the feasibility and effectiveness of the proposed approach.

Categories and Subject Descriptors

H.2.8 [**Database Management**]: Database Applications—*Data Mining*

General Terms

Algorithms, Performance

Keywords

Time Series, Hidden Markov Model, Pattern

*This work was done at Microsoft Research Asia

SIGMOD'11, June 12–16, 2011, Athens, Greece.

1. INTRODUCTION

Time series data is being generated at an unprecedented speed and volume in a wide range of applications in almost every domain. For example, daily fluctuations of the stock market, traces produced by a computer cluster, medical and biological experimental observations, readings obtained from sensor networks, position updates of moving objects in location-based services, etc, are all represented in time series. Consequently, there is an enormous interest in analyzing (including query processing and mining) time series data, which has resulted in a large number of works on new methodologies for indexing, classifying, clustering, and summarizing time series data [8, 28, 13].

In this paper, we propose to study time series from a new angle. Our goal is to understand the complex system that produces the time series. Thus, instead of finding isolated historic patterns, or predicting the next time series value based on the pattern in the most recent time window, we focus on explaining the relationships between the patterns, in particular, how they fit into a big, holistic picture that describes the underlying system.

1.1 State of the art

Much work has been done on time series analysis, including time series prediction [1, 6, 13, 9, 21], time series segmentation and symbolization [12, 14], time series representation [7, 25], and similar time series matching [8, 18]. However, not much attempt has been made to use the time series data to explain how the underlying system works.

Well known time series models such as ARIMA and Linear Regression models, have been used for time series forecasting, which is concerned with the problem of predicting time series values X_t given observations $X_1, X_2, \cdots, X_{t-1}$. One frequently used assumption in time series forecasting is that the time series has a short memory, which means current values are only related to values in a recent time window. In other words, these approaches focus on local characteristics in the time series, and do not attempt to explain observations using the internal dynamics of the system.

Approaches such as Discrete Fourier Transform [8], Discrete Wavelet Transform [2], Piecewise Linear Representation [11], and Symbolic Aggregate Approximation [14], try to model the whole time series. Their goal lies in representing the original time series in a more concise way so that we can summarize the time series or index the time series for fast pattern matching or pattern discovery. These methods cannot reveal the internal dynamics of the system, though. In DFT [8], for example, a time series is described by a set of coefficients in the frequency domain. However, the coefficients are not interpretable, that is, knowing the coefficients in the frequency domain does not necessarily enable us to understand how the system works. Similarly, in PLR [11], a time series is segmented into disjoint intervals, each of which is represented by a line segment. However, the line segments are isolated. For instance, we do not know whether the similarity between the line segments at time t_1 and t_2 means the system is in the same internal state at t_1 and t_2.

Much work has been done on discovering frequent patterns (also called motifs) in time series [17, 16]. However, frequent patterns may not necessarily be important patterns, in terms of whether they can inform us how the system works. Many mining algorithms discover a large number of patterns that are hard to interpret, which adds to the complexity of understanding the system instead of helping reduce it.

1.2 Revealing system dynamics

Our goal is to obtain a better understanding of the system that generates the time series. We assume the system that generates the time series operates under a number of latent states [23, 24, 9, 21, 5, 4]. Many systems fall into this category. Our approach is based on two important observations we made about such systems. The first observation is that once a system is in a latent state, it will stay in the state for a period of time until a certain event occurs which leads the system to another latent state. For example, when memory usage is below the physical memory capacity, the system behaves in a certain way. The system exhibits stable patterns until memory usage exceeds the physical memory capacity, when the system starts paging. The second observation is that the system goes through the same states over and over again. For example, once memory usage recedes, the system will return to its old state (without paging).

To have a better understanding of the system means to reveal the latent states of the system, and how they alternate among themselves. In this paper, we regard the time series as the output generated by a state transition machine. Time series produced in each state demonstrates a certain pattern of fluctuation, and transitions between states reflect system dynamics. That is, the information of once the system ending a certain state, what's the most likely state the system will enter.

The next question is what constitutes a state, or what constitutes a unit of observation? This is the most challenging question when using a state transition machine (e.g., an HMM) on time series data, since it is not trivial to align an observation sequence with a state sequence. A naïve and straightforward choice is to consider a single observed value as an output token of a state. However, in time series data, a single value contains very little semantics. We illustrate this by an example in Figure 1. Although A and B have the same value, the underlying system is likely to be in two different states when it outputs A and B, because A is in an upward trend and B is in a downward trend. If our goal is to predict the next time series value, then knowing the system in that value state has no predictive power. As a consequence, with single values as states, the obtained machine will be full of uncertainty, which is not we want.

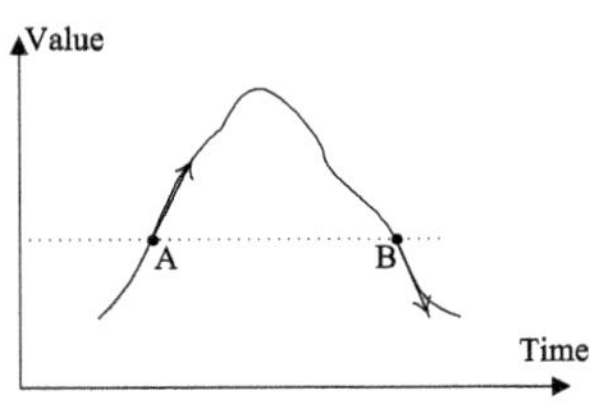

Figure 1: Single value as state

A better choice is to group neighboring values into a pattern, and regard a pattern as a unit of observation (an observation token). A good choice for a pattern is a line segment or a polynomial curve. If line segments are used, the time series in Figure 1 will be represented by two line segments with different shapes, indicating that the underlying system is in two different states. There are several benefits of using line segments: 1) lines have simple shapes and the trends they represent are easy to understand; 2) in many applications, a time series can be represented well by a sequence of line segments.

Thus, our task is to: i) define a set of observation tokens, each being a representative line segment in the time series; ii) convert the time series to an observation sequence such that each observation token aligns with a state in the unknown state sequence; iii) learn an HMM from the observation sequence. However, the task of obtaining the observation sequence, or more specifically, the task of segmenting a time series and then clustering the segments to obtain representative line segments, is not trivial. The objective of many time series segmentation and clustering approaches is to minimize the difference between the time series and the resulting line segment sequence. However, this objective is not necessarily aligned with that of finding the best state transition machine.

To see this, consider a toy example in Figure 2. Suppose we have 4 line segments $A_1, \cdots, A_4$, and the question is whether we should consider A_1 and A_2 as the same observation (i.e., representing A_1 and A_2 using the same observation token), or consider A_3 and A_4 as the same observation. It is clear that A_1 and A_2 are more similar to each other in shape. Thus, traditional clustering approaches, which aim at minimizing approximation error, will group A_1 and A_2 together.

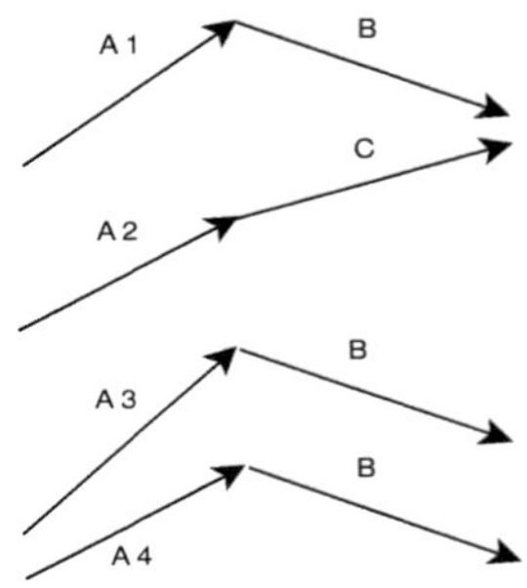

Figure 2: Segmenting

However, clustering line segments as if they are a set of disconnected elements is problematic. For instance, the line segments following A_3 and A_4 have exactly the same shape, which suggests that A_3 and A_4 may be generated by the system in the same state. On the other hand, the line segments following A_1 and A_2 are totally different, which suggests that the slight difference between A_1 and A_2 may indicate that they actually belong to two different states. To understand the internal dynamics of the system requires us to pay attention to these temporal constraints instead of just minimizing the approximation error.

1.3 A Two Phase, Iterative Approach

To achieve the goal of revealing internal system dynamics, we propose a pattern-based Hidden Markov model (pHMM) for time series data. We discover patterns in the time series, and we ensure that the discovered patterns are not disconnected or isolated, but rather, they are organic components of a state transition machine, which produces the original time series. Then, the challenges are the following: i) in order to segment the time series and discover patterns we should know the state transition machine first, because it tells us the likelihood of one pattern being followed by another pattern, otherwise we run into problems demonstrated by the example in Figure 2; and ii) to build the state transition machine we must know the patterns first, as patterns are the sole components of the state transition machine.

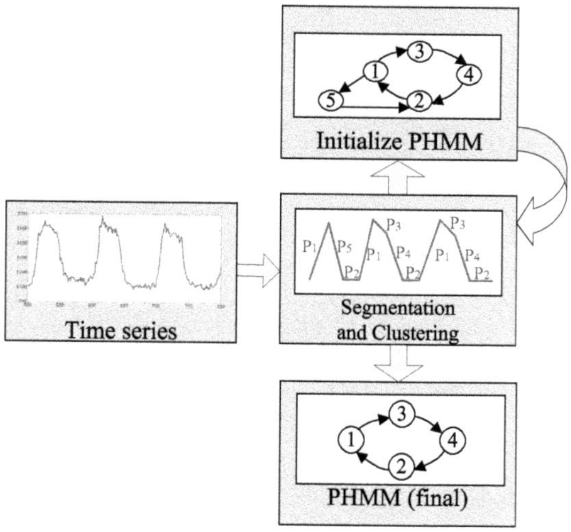

Figure 3: Overview of our approach

To solve this dilemma, we propose a two phase approach. In phase one, we first segment the time series using traditional optimization techniques. Because we do not have any knowledge about the underlying state transition machine, the best thing we can do is to use a standard approach [11] to convert the time series into a piecewise linear representation. In other words, we approximate the time series using line segments that minimize the approximation error. Then, we cluster the resulting segments using a greedy clustering method (considering both the similarity and the temporal constraints). Finally, from the segmented time series, we learn a hidden Markov model.

In phase two, we use an iterative process to refine the model. Specifically, in each round, we first segment and cluster the time series based on the learned pHMM. The pHMM provides important guidance for segmenting and clustering, resulting in higher quality patterns. Then we update the pHMM based on learned patterns. We prove that the iteration process always improves the quality of the model. The whole framework is illustrated in Figure 3.

1.4 Applications and Contributions

Our goal is to reveal the system beneath the time series data it produces. With the knowledge of the underlying system, we will be able to perform a large variety of challenging tasks. A representative list of tasks include the following:

- Trend prediction. With the knowledge of the state transition machine, we can derive the temporal relations between patterns. This enables us to answer queries such as: What the trend of the time series is in 10 minutes; or when will the time series end the current downward trend and enter an upward trend?
- Accurate multi-step value prediction. Predicting time series values long into the future is a challenging and important task. Specifically, given time series before time point t, we want to predict the values at time $t + \delta$, where δ is much bigger than 1.
- Pattern based correlation detection. In traditional approaches, in order to compute correlation between two time series, we map the time series into a vector space (e.g. using DFT or DWT), and use a distance measure (e.g. Euclidean distance or Dynamic Time Warping [7]) to calculate their similarity. Now we can compute correlation based on patterns. Furthermore, we can correlate the time series by rules such as: whenever pattern P_1 occurs in time series S_1, P_2 will occur in time series S_2.

In summary, the contributions we make in this paper are the following:

- We introduce a pattern-based hidden Markov model (pHMM) for time series data. It focuses on revealing the internal dynamics of the system that produces the time series.
- We propose an iterative approach to refine the model. Furthermore, we propose several pruning strategies to speed up the refinement process.
- We propose algorithms that use pHMM to perform multi-step value prediction, trend prediction and pattern based correlation detection.
- We conduct extensive experiments to verify the effectiveness and efficiency of the proposed approach.

1.5 Paper Organization

The rest of the paper is organized as follows. Section 2 discusses the problem and the challenges. Section 3 introduces the algorithm in the initial phase. Section 4 describes the method to refine pHMM. Section 5 shows how to utilize the learned model. Section 6 shows experimental results. In Section 7, we discuss related work, and we conclude in Section 8.

2. PRELIMINARY AND APPROACH

In this paper, we propose using the pattern-based hidden Markov model (pHMM) to reveal system dynamics from time series data.

2.1 Background of HMM

A hidden Markov model (HMM) is a statistical model in which the system being modeled is assumed to be a Markov process. It includes a finite set of states, each of which is associated with a probability distribution over all possible output tokens. Transitions among the states are governed by a set of probabilities. The states are not visible, but outputs produced by the states are. Given a sequence of observations, we learn an HMM and derive a sequence of hidden states that correspond to the sequence of observations.

Formally, an HMM, denoted by $\lambda = \{S, A, B, \pi\}$, is described with the following parameters:

- A set of states $S = \{1, 2, \cdots, K\}$.
- State transition probabilities $A = \{a_{ij}\}$, $1 \leq i, j \leq K$, i.e., a_{ij} is the probability of state i transiting to state j.
- Output probabilities $B = \{b_i(o)\}$, $1 \leq i \leq K$. o is an observation with a continuous or discrete value (or value vector). $b_i(o)$ is the probability of state i generating observation o.
- Initial probabilities $\pi = \{\pi_i\}$, $1 \leq i \leq K$. π_i is the probability of the time series beginning with state i.

When we learn an HMM, the basic assumption is that the observation sequence and the hidden state sequence is aligned. In our case, however, one big challenge is to derive the alignment.

One fundamental problem associated with HMMs is the *decoding problem*: given a model, λ, and a sequence of observations,

O, find the optimal state sequence that produces the observations. Another problem is the *learning problem*: how to estimate the parameter λ of the HMM, so that the probability of the observation sequence generated by the optimal state sequence is maximized. In both cases, an important measurement is the *production probability*. Given an HMM λ, and a sequence of observations O, the production probability is the probability of HMM λ generating O along a state sequence $\mathbf{s} = (s_1, \cdots, s_m)$, and it is computed as:

$$P(O, \mathbf{s}|\lambda) = \pi_{s_1} b_{s_1}(o_1) \prod_{j=2}^{m} a_{s_{j-1},s_j} b_{s_j}(o_j) \quad (1)$$

The larger the production probability, the better λ and the state sequence $\mathbf{s}$ describe O.

2.2 Problem Statement

Given a time series $X = x_1, x_2, \cdots, x_n$, we aim at learning a pattern-based Hidden Markov Model (pHMM), which reveals the dynamics of the system that generates the time series.

Formally, we want to solve the following problem:

- Convert the time series X into a sequence of line segments, $\mathbf{L} = (L_1, L_2, \cdots, L_m)$;
- Learn a hidden Markov model from observation sequence $\mathbf{L}$.

so that production probability

$$P(\mathbf{L}, \mathbf{s}^*|\lambda) = \pi_{s_1} b_{s_1}(L_1) \prod_{j=2}^{m} a_{s_{j-1},s_j} b_{s_j}(L_j) \quad (2)$$

is maximized, where $\mathbf{s}^* = (s_1, s_2, \cdots, s_m)$ is the optimal state sequence, where s_j generates line L_j with probability $b_{s_j}(L_j)$.

2.3 Challenges and Overview of Our Approach

Although much research has been done on HMMs, and HMMs have been successfully applied in many applications, it is a non-trivial challenge to learn a pattern based HMM for the time series data.

As we know, a traditional HMM is learned from an observation sequence. We can estimate the parameters of an HMM using the classic Baum-Welch algorithm. However, the premise is that we have the observation sequence. In our case, the observation sequence is essentially unknown, since it needs to be learned from the time series itself. Moreover, in the time series, the number of possible patterns is infinite. For example, in our case, we represent a pattern by a line segment, whose slope and duration are all continuous values.

Furthermore, the process of learning an observation sequence from the time series cannot be decoupled from the process of learning a hidden Markov model from the observation sequence. Intuitively, producing an observation sequence from a time series is done by time series segmentation. Existing approaches segment time series by solving an optimization problem where the objective is to minimize the difference between the time series and the line segment sequence. However, these approaches consider segments as independent and isolated, and ignore the temporal relations between them, but such temporal relations are critical in learning HMM. In our work, we learn the observation sequence and the HMM simultaneously.

We solve the above problem using a two-phase approach. In the first phase, we initialize the pHMM using a cluster-based approach. The observation sequence used to learn the initial pHMM is learned from the time series without any knowledge of the pHMM. In the second phase, we refine the model with an iterative process. In each round, we first segment the time series and cluster the line segments under the guidance of a previously learned pHMM, then the pHMM is updated based on the new segmentation.

3. THE INITIAL PHMM

We introduce our approach to build the initial pHMM in 3 steps. First, we segment the time series. Second, we cluster line segments. Third, based on the clusters, we learn the first pHMM.

3.1 From Time Series to Line Segments

In phase one, information about latent states is not available, so we perform a traditional segmentation. We use a bottom-up approach to convert the time series X into a piecewise linear representation [12]. Initially, we approximate X with $\lfloor \frac{n}{2} \rfloor$ line segments. The i-th line, L_i, connects x_{2i-1} and x_{2i}. Next, we iteratively merge the neighboring lines. In each iteration, we merge the two neighboring segments into one new line segment that has the minimal approximation error. The merging process repeats until every possible merge leads to a line whose error exceeds a user specified threshold, denoted by ε_r. Clearly, without knowledge of the latent states, it is very likely that the initial segmentation is not optimal for our goal (see Section 4.1).

3.2 From Line Segments to Clusters

After obtaining the line segments, we group them into clusters $\{C_1, C_2, \cdots, C_K\}$. A key issue is to define the similarity between line segments. Had our goal been to summarize or compress the time series, we could have used the approximation error or minimal description length as the objective function. However, as our goal is to learn a pattern-based HMM, such an approach is not always optimal.

We consider two clustering criteria:

- The similarity criterion. This is the same criterion for traditional clustering. In our case, the line segments in the same cluster should have similar shapes (slopes and lengths), and the line segments in different clusters have different shapes.
- The temporal criterion. If L_i and L_j belong to the same cluster, then L_{i+1} and L_{j+1}, which follow L_i and L_j respectively, should have the same distribution (in terms of which cluster they belong to); more often than not they belong to the same cluster.

We now formalize these two criteria. For the similarity criterion, we measure the variance of the line segments in each cluster. For cluster C_i, the relative error is computed as:

$$R(i) = \frac{1}{|C_i|} \sum_{(l_j,\theta_j) \in C_i} \{(\frac{l_j - \bar{l}_i}{\bar{l}_i})^2 + (\frac{\theta_j - \bar{\theta}_i}{\bar{\theta}_i})^2\}$$

where $|C_i|$ is the number of lines in cluster C_i, $\bar{l}_i$ and $\bar{\theta}_i$ are the average length and the average slope of lines in C_i. Clearly, the smaller $R(i)$ is, the more similar the line segments in C_i are.

For the second criterion, we use entropy to measure the uncertainty of the clusters following the lines of cluster C_i:

$$I(i) = \sum_{j=1}^{K} -p(j|i) \log p(j|i) \quad (3)$$

where $p(j|i)$ denotes the probability that a line in C_i is followed by a line in C_j. Intuitively, the smaller the $I(i)$, the more certain we are about the clusters that follow lines in C_i.

A straightforward way of clustering is to construct an objective function based on these two criteria as:

$$F = \alpha \cdot R + (1 - \alpha) \cdot I \quad (4)$$

where $R = \sum_{i=1}^{K} |C_i|R(i)$ is the overall relative error of all clusters, $I = \sum_{i=1}^{K} p(i)I(i)$ is the overall entropy of all clusters, and $\alpha \in [0, 1]$ is a user-provided parameter. Then we cluster the segment lines to minimize the objective function F. However, it is hard to set a reasonable α. We illustrate it with an example. Assume we want to cluster three lines, L_1, L_2 and L_3. They have the same length, and their slopes satisfy: $\theta_1 < \theta_2 < \theta_3$. Moreover, L_1 and L_3 are followed by lines in the same cluster while L_2 is followed by a line in another cluster, and the lines in these two clusters have very different shapes. If we set a very large α, the similarity criterion is dominant. It is likely that all three lines are clustered into one cluster. On the other hand, if we set a small α, the temporal criterion will dominate. A possible result is that L_1 and L_3 are put into the same cluster C while L_2 is not. However, this is unreasonable, as L_2 is "enveloped" by L_1 and L_3.

In this paper, instead of optimizing Eq. 4 directly, we adopt a greedy approach. Initially, each line is considered as a cluster on its own. Then at each iteration, we merge two clusters by considering two criteria in turn. The approach includes three steps:

Step 1. (Similarity Criterion) For each cluster C_i, find its most similar cluster, called C_i's candidate cluster.

DEFINITION 1 (CANDIDATE CLUSTER). *For each cluster C_i, its candidate cluster, denoted as T_i, is the cluster that satisfies:*

1. *$R(T_i \cup C_i) \leq R(C \cup C_i)$ holds for any $C \neq T_i$, where $T_i \cup C_i$ is the new cluster generated by merging T_i and C_i, and $R(T_i \cup C_i)$ is its relative error.*

2. *$R(T_i \cup C_i) \leq \varepsilon_c$, where ε_c is a user-specified threshold, called the relative error threshold.*

Step 2. (Temporal Criterion) For any cluster pair (C_i, T_i), compute the entropy of new cluster $C_i \cup T_i$.

Step 3. Merge a pair with minimal entropy to a new cluster.

This process continues until every possible merge results in a relative error that exceeds the threshold ε_c.

Connection between the two measurements. In clustering, we use the similarity and the temporal criteria to measure the quality of clusters. In the problem statement, we use the production probability to measure the quality of the learned model. In fact, we can build a connection between these two measurements.

We decompose production probability into P' and P''.

$$\begin{aligned} P(\mathbf{L}, \mathbf{s}^*|\lambda) &= \pi_{s_1} b_{s_1}(L_1) \prod_{j=2}^{m} a_{s_{j-1},s_j} b_{s_j}(L_j) \\ &= \prod_{j=1}^{m} b_{s_j}(L_j) \cdot \pi_{s_1} \prod_{j=2}^{m} a_{s_{j-1},s_j} \\ &= P' \cdot P'' \end{aligned} \quad (5)$$

P' measures how well the states match the occurrences of the line segments, and it corresponds to the similarity criterion. P'' measures the certainty of transitions between states, and it corresponds to the temporal criterion. So they are consistent with each other.

3.3 From Clusters to HMM

Based on the obtained clusters, we initialize the hidden Markov model λ as follows. Assume the clusters are $\{C_1, C_2, \cdots, C_K\}$, we initialize an HMM with K states, $\{1, 2, \cdots, K\}$, in which state i corresponds to cluster C_i. In other words, we assume lines in each cluster represent the typical fluctuation of time series when the system stays in the same state.

Before discussing how to initialize the output probabilities, we first define the output probability in terms of segment lines as observations. We assume slopes and lengths are independent to each other. For line $L = (l, \theta)$, the output probability is defined as a product of two probabilities:

$$b_i(L) = p_l(l|i)p_s(\theta|i)$$

in which $p_l(l|i)$ is the probability of state i generating the line with length l, and $p_s(\theta|i)$ is the probability of i generating the line with slope θ.

In many real life applications, the system operates in different states; and in each state, the system exhibits stable behavior. Each observation of one state can be regarded as the stable behavior plus some slight fluctuations, or errors. Since the observational error in an experiment is often described by Gaussian Distribution, we use it here to describe the distribution of segment lines. Formally, we assume $p_l(\cdot|i)$ and $p_s(\cdot|i)$ follow 1-dimension Gaussian Distributions, $\mathcal{N}(\mu_{il}, \sigma_{il}^2)$, and $\mathcal{N}(\mu_{is}, \sigma_{is}^2)$ respectively.

Some experiments are conducted to verify the assumption and results are shown in Figure 4. For both the Spot and Power datasets, we select one big cluster randomly, since the big cluster contains more lines that can demonstrate the distribution more clearly. It can be seen that both length and slope can be approximated by Gaussian distribution.

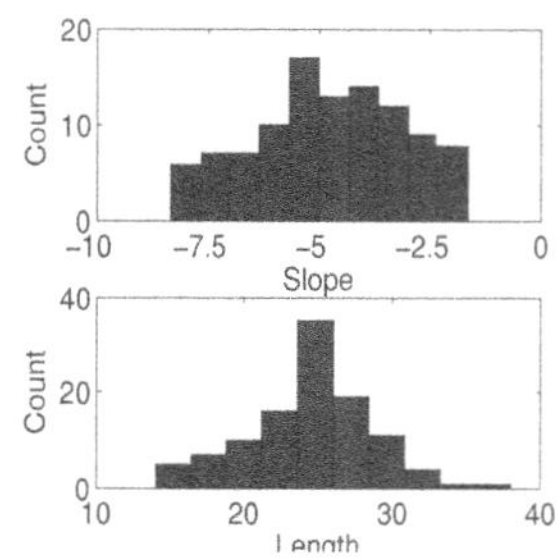

(a) Spot Dataset

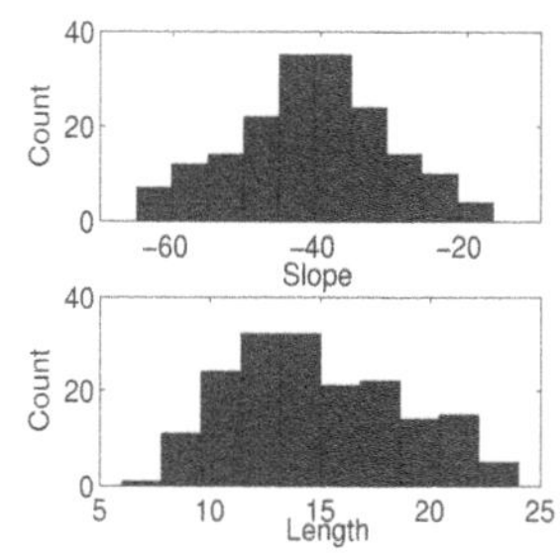

(b) Power Dataset

Figure 4: Slope and length distribution

To initialize output probabilities of state i, we need to initialize 4 parameters: $\mu_{il}, \sigma_{il}^2, \mu_{is}, \sigma_{is}^2$. We estimate μ_{il} and σ_{il}^2 as the mean and variance of lines' lengths in C_i, and estimate μ_{is} and σ_{is}^2 as the mean and variance of lines' slopes in C_i.

We build a state sequence to initialize transition probabilities and initial probabilities. In line sequence $(L_1, L_2, \cdots, L_m)$, we replace each line with the cluster it belongs to. Since cluster C_i corresponds to state i $(1 \leq i \leq K)$, a state sequence is obtained. Then based on this, we estimate transition probabilities and initial probabilities as in the traditional HMM.

4. ITERATIVE PHMM REFINEMENT

We iteratively refine the pHMM learned in the previous round. Each iteration has two steps. In step one, based on the current pHMM, we use an extended Viterbi algorithm to segment the time series and learn the optimal state sequence. In step two, based on the new line segment sequence and the state sequence, we update the pHMM. The iteration stops until the pHMM does not change.

4.1 Motivation of Iterative Refinement

We illustrate the benefit of refining with an example in Figure 5. Assume in the initial phase, the time series is segmented into S_1, as shown in Figure 5(a). Consider intervals $[a, b]$, $[c, d]$ and $[e, f]$. It can be seen that subsequences in all of them have similar shapes.

Moreover, the lines before and after them are all similar. However, in S_1, $[a, b]$ is represented by line L_2, while $[c, d]$ is represented by two lines L_6 and L_7. Since the shape of L_2 is apparently different to L_6 or L_7 respectively, they cannot be clustered into a group. So, S_1 misses the information that L_2 is similar to the connection of L_6 and L_7. Moreover, according to the cluster approach, three clusters, as well as three states, will be generated: $C_1 = (L_6, L_{10})$, $C_2 = (L_7, L_{11})$ and $C_3 = (L_2)$. While the first two are meaningful states, C_3 is very likely to be a noise state. Note that such issues cannot be solved by frequent pattern mining, as such patterns may not necessarily be frequent in the entire time series.

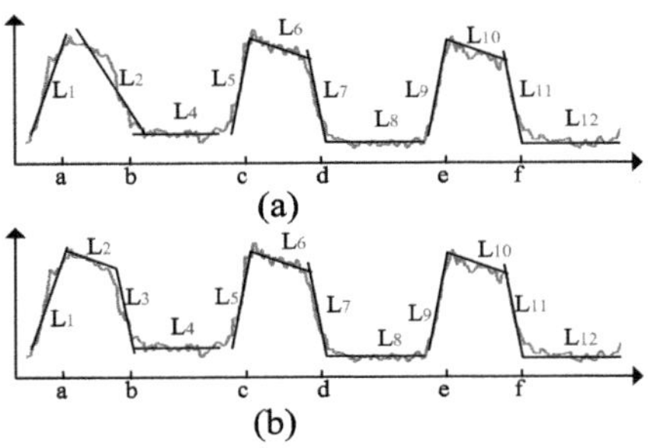

Figure 5: Segmentation with/without Refinement

In the refinement process, the time series will be re-segmented with the guidance of the current pHMM. Intuitively, the new segmentation will identify the lines that can be generated by certain states with a high probability. So $[a, b]$ will be split into L_2 and L_3, as shown in Figure 5(b). Obviously, it achieves a better pHMM.

4.2 pHMM-based Segmentation

Given an observation sequence, the Viterbi algorithm can find the optimal state sequence. However, it only works if the observation sequence is known. In our case, we only have the raw time series, instead of the observation sequence (a sequence of line segments). In this work, we extend the Viterbi algorithm to learn the line segment and the state sequence simultaneously.

4.2.1 *The Traditional Viterbi Algorithm*

The Viterbi algorithm is an efficient method of learning the optimal state sequence $\mathbf{s}^*$, given the HMM λ and the observation sequence O. It has a recursive procedure, and it works in parallel for all states in a strictly time synchronous manner.

The key component in the Viterbi algorithm is the *optimal probability*, denoted as $\delta_t(i)$, which is the maximal probability of HMM generating the observation segment $o_1, \cdots, o_t$, along the optimal state sequence $s_1, \cdots, s_t$, in which $s_t = i$. That is,

$$\begin{aligned}\delta_t(i) &= \max_{s_1,\cdots,s_{t-1}} P(o_1, \cdots, o_t, s_1, \cdots, s_{t-1}, s_t = i|\lambda) \\ &= \max_{s_1,\cdots,s_{t-1}} \pi_{s_1} b_{s_1}(o_1) \prod_{j=2}^{t} (a_{s_{j-1},s_j} b_{s_j}(o_j))\end{aligned}$$

The algorithm scans the observation sequence from $t = 1$, at which point the optimal probability for state i is initiated as

$$\delta_1(i) = \pi_i b_i(o_1)$$

Assume all $\delta_{t-1}(j), 1 \leq j \leq K$, are already obtained. The algorithm computes $\delta_t(i)$ as:

$$\delta_t(i) = \max_j(\delta_{t-1}(j)a_{ji})b_i(o_t)$$

When the algorithm reaches the last time point n, we obtain all optimal probabilities: $\delta_n(i), 1 \leq i \leq K$. By comparing all of them, and backtracking the largest one, this algorithm obtains the optimal state sequence.

4.2.2 *Extending the Viterbi Algorithm*

As analyzed before, we need to learn the line sequence and the state sequence simultaneously. We implement it with a modified optimal probability, $\delta_t(i)$. In other words, in the traditional Viterbi algorithm, we only learn the optimal state sequence when computing $\delta_t(i)$, while in our algorithm, we not only learn the optimal state sequence, but also find the optimal line sequence.

In our case, an observation token, or the unit of observation, is a line segment. Therefore, we define $\delta_t(i)$ as the maximal probability of the current HMM generating any line sequence up to t along the optimal state sequence ending with state i. Formally,

$$\delta_t(i) = \max_{L_1,\cdots,L_k} \max_{s_1,\cdots,s_{k-1}} P(L_1, \cdots, L_k, s_1, \cdots, s_k = i|\lambda)$$

where $\{L_1, \cdots, L_k\}$ is a line sequence, in which the last line segment L_k ends at time point t, and its corresponding state is i. state s_k corresponds to the k-th line. Note that k can be any value not exceeding $\lfloor \frac{t}{2} \rfloor$.

Intuitively, in the Viterbi algorithm, when $\delta_t(i)$ is computed from $\delta_{t-1}(j)$, it implies that the observation at time t is added to the observation sequence. Similarly, in our algorithm, when $\delta_t(i)$ is computed, it implies a "new observation" is added to the observation sequence. However, here the observation is a line segment ending at t, instead of a single value.

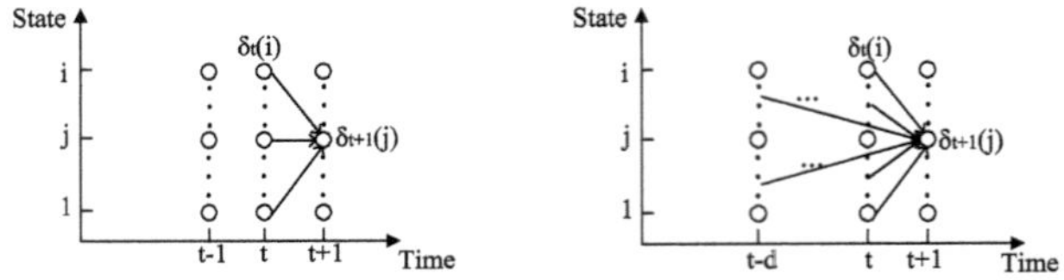

(a) Traditional (b) Extended

Figure 6: Computing optimal probability

To be specific, we compute a possible $\delta'_t(i)$ based on any previous optimal probability $\delta_{t-d}(j)$ as

$$\delta'_t(i) = \delta_{t-d}(j)a_{ji}b_i(L)$$

where L is the new observed line, which begins at $t-d+1$ and ends at t, and its corresponding state is i. The new line L is determined by t and d. The only limitation of d is that the approximation error of L on the interval $[t - d + 1, t]$ cannot exceed ε_r.

Since we do not know the optimal line sequence, we cannot determine the value of d beforehand. We compute $\delta_t(i)$ by checking all possible previous optimal probabilities, and choose the largest result as the final $\delta_t(i)$:

$$\delta_t(i) = \max_{d,j}(\delta_{t-d}(j)a_{ji})b_i(L)$$

where line L is a variable for different previous optimal probabilities. Figure 6 illustrates the difference between our approach with the traditional Viterbi algorithm.

When the algorithm reaches time n, we obtain the maximal optimal probability $\max_i \delta_n(i)$. Through backtracking it, we obtain the optimal observation sequence and the corresponding state sequence. The detailed algorithm is shown in Algorithm 1.

In Algorithm 1, function $BestLine(x, y)$ (line 7) learns the best-fit line beginning from x and ending at y, which has the minimal

Algorithm 1 Detect_state_sequence

Input ε_r:maximal error threshold of line approximation
Initialize $\delta_1(i) = 0\ (1 \le i \le K)$
for $t \leftarrow 2, n$ **do**
  for $i \leftarrow 1, K$ **do**
    $\delta_t(i) = 0$
    for $d \leftarrow 2, t$ **do**
      $L = BestLine(t-d+1, t)$
      if $Err(L) > \varepsilon_r$ **then**
        Break
      else
        if $t == d$ **then**
          $temp = \pi_i b_i(L)$
        else
          $temp = \max_j(\delta_{t-d}(j) \cdot a_{ji}) b_i(L)$
        end if
        if $temp > \delta_t(i)$ **then**
          $\delta_t(i) = temp$
          $prev_d(t) = t - d$
          $prev_s(t) = j$
        end if
      end if
    end for
  end for
end for
Obtain maximal optimal probability $\delta_n(i)$, which holds

$$\delta_n(i) \ge \delta_n(j), j \neq i$$

Obtain state sequence by backtracking sequence of $prev_s$
Obtain line sequence by backtracking sequence of $prev_d$

approximation error. Function $Err(L)$ computes the approximation error of L.

Performance analysis. In the traditional Viterbi algorithm, at each time point, it computes K probabilities: $\delta_t(i), i = 1, \cdots, K$. To compute each $\delta_t(i)$, it checks K probabilities $\delta_{t-1}(j)$, $j = 1, 2, \cdots, K$. So the time complexity is $O(nK^2)$ in each round.

In our task, at each time point, we also compute K probabilities: $\delta_t(i)$,$i = 1, 2, \cdots, K$. However, to compute each $\delta_t(i)$, we need to check $(t-1)*K$ possible probabilities $\delta_{t-d}(j)$, $(j = 1, 2, \cdots, K$, $1 \le d < t)$ at most. Thus, the time complexity is $O(n^2K^2)$ in each round. Clearly, for long sequences, it is not feasible. Next, we introduce three pruning strategies to improve the efficiency.

4.2.3 Three Pruning Strategies

We propose three pruning strategies, two of which are lossless and the third is lossy (with respect to whether the final result is the same as that of the exact approach discussed before).

Strategy 1: Prune with threshold ε_r. The first one is based on the requirement that the approximation error of each line cannot exceed threshold ε_r. So we use ε_r to filter state transitions which need not be checked. Assume the current time point is t, and we compute $\delta_t(i)$. We check optimal probabilities of previous time points from $t-1$ to 1. If we find a time point t', which satisfies

$$Err(BestLine(t'-1, t)) > \varepsilon_r \text{ and } Err(BestLine(t', t)) < \varepsilon_r$$

it means the approximation error of the line covering interval $[t'-1, t]$ must exceed ε_r. So later we need not check the optimal probabilities before t'. Note that while the process continues, t' will move forward gradually.

Strategy 2: Prune with optimal possibility. The second pruning strategy uses obtained candidates of optimal probabilities to filter useless optimal probabilities. In algorithm 1, to compute $\delta_t(i)$, we need to check lots of previous optimal probabilities. Each time a previous optimal probability is checked, we get a candidate of $\delta_t(i)$. Since computing optimal probability finds the maximal one, we can make pruning based on the obtained candidates.

We maintain all previous optimal probabilities in a list, denoted as LT, in which all probabilities are sorted in descending order. The optimal probability will be deleted from LT once the approximation error of the line L generated by it exceeds ε_r. We use LT_i to indicate the i-th optimal probability in LT. To compute $\delta_t(i)$, we check the entries in LT from top to bottom. Assume after we check the top-j entries in LT, the obtained maximal candidate is δ'. Then we check the $(j+1)$-th entry, LT_{j+1}, in LT. We compute whether the following inequality holds:

$$LT_{j+1} \cdot a_{max}(i) \cdot b_{max}(i) < \delta'$$

where $b_{max}(i)$ is the maximal output probability generated by state i and $a_{max}(i)$ is the highest transition probability from any state to state i.

If it holds, it indicates that from LT_{j+1}, as well as all entries after it, we cannot obtain a candidate of $\delta_t(i)$ larger than δ'. So δ' is the final $\delta_t(i)$. We add it into LT for later computing.

Strategy 3: Prune with boundary points. Although the first two strategies reduce the unit cost of computing an optimal probability, the process may still be time consuming since it needs to compute optimal probabilities for each time point. In this strategy, we reduce the number of points where we need to compute optimal probabilities, which can greatly speed up the process.

In fact, the goal of the extended Viterbi algorithm is to find the optimal line sequence, which is determined by boundary points of lines. If we only compute optimal probabilities on these points, instead of all time points, we can speed up the process greatly, while the accuracy doesn't suffer too much. An important question is: *which points are more likely to be boundaries in the optimal segmentation?* We answer this question with the following observation:

OBSERVATION 1. *If two neighboring lines before and after t have apparently different slopes, t is more likely to be a boundary.*

The reason is that if the two neighboring lines have similar slopes, it is more likely that they are merged into a line, and consequently t is a point in the middle of this line, instead of being a boundary. We illustrate the observation in Figure 7. It is obvious that points A and C should be boundaries. For D and E, the lines before and after them have similar slopes, so they are less possible to be the boundaries than A and C.

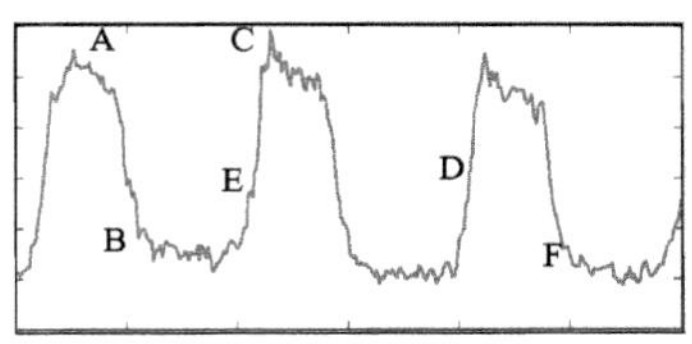

Figure 7: Boundary points

We choose points based on the above observation. Remember that in the initial phase, we segment the time series in a bottom-up way. At each step, two neighboring lines are merged and the point connecting them changes from a boundary to a middle point.

The sooner a boundary point is changed, the less likely that it is a boundary. So we sort all the time points according to the order they become middle points, and select the last N time points to form a boundary candidate list, where N is a user-specified parameter. Then, we execute Algorithm 1 only on these points. Continuing the example in Figure 7, assume we only consider these six points. They should be sorted as:

$$\cdots, D, E, B, F, A, C$$

If we just select 4 points from them to run Algorithm 1, C, A, F and B will be selected.

Strategies 1 and 2 are lossless ones and don't affect the accuracy, while the third one is a lossy strategy, since it may cause some points, which should be optimal segmentation boundaries, to be missed. However, our method of choosing points guarantees that we choose the points which are most likely to be the boundaries. Experimental results verify that this strategy can reduce the time consumption dynamically, while keeping the accuracy similar to the exact model.

4.3 Updating pHMM

Assume in round k, the current pHMM is λ^{k-1}. The obtained optimal line sequence and state sequence are denoted as $\mathbf{L}^k$ and $\mathbf{s}^k$ respectively. We update the current pHMM, so that it can generate $\mathbf{L}^k$ and $\mathbf{s}^k$ with the largest probability. Let $\mathbf{L}^k = (L_1, L_2, \cdots, L_m)$ and $\mathbf{s}^k = (s_1, s_2, \cdots, s_m)$. Note that the number of lines in $\mathbf{L}^k$, m, is possible to vary over different rounds.

Transition probabilities and initial probabilities are updated according to state sequence $\mathbf{s}^k$. To update output probabilities, we cluster the lines in $\mathbf{L}^k$ according to the corresponding states. Specifically,

$$C_i = \{L_j | s_j = i\}, i = 1, 2, \cdots, K$$

Then we update the mean and the variance of slopes and lengths with the method in the initial phase. After that, we obtain the pHMM in this round, denoted as λ^k. It happens that certain states in λ^{k-1} disappear from λ^k, if these states don't occur in state sequence $\mathbf{s}^k$.

Finally, we prove the correctness of the refinement approach, that is, the new production probability in the current round is not less than that in the last round.

THEOREM 1. *The production probability of round k is not less than that of round $k-1$, that is:*

$$P(\mathbf{L}^k, \mathbf{s}^k | \lambda^k) \geq P(\mathbf{L}^{k-1}, \mathbf{s}^{k-1} | \lambda^{k-1})$$

PROOF. Since $\mathbf{L}^k$ and $\mathbf{s}^k$ are the optimal observation sequence and state sequence which has maximal probability based on the pHMM in last round, it holds:

$$P(\mathbf{L}^k, \mathbf{s}^k | \lambda^{k-1}) \geq P(\mathbf{L}^{k-1}, \mathbf{s}^{k-1} | \lambda^{k-1}) \quad (6)$$

Next, since the parameters in λ^k are the results of maximum likelihood estimation. So it holds

$$P(\mathbf{L}^k, \mathbf{s}^k | \lambda^k) \geq P(\mathbf{L}^k, \mathbf{s}^k | \lambda^{k-1}) \quad (7)$$

Combining Eq. 6 and Eq. 7, we can obtain

$$P(\mathbf{L}^k, \mathbf{s}^k | \lambda^k) \geq P(\mathbf{L}^{k-1}, \mathbf{s}^{k-1} | \lambda^{k-1}) \quad (8)$$

□

5. APPLICATIONS OF THE MODEL

The pHMM reveals the system dynamics from the time series it produces. With knowledge of the underlying system, we can deal with some advanced tasks. In this section, we introduce how to use pHMM to perform these tasks.

5.1 Multi-step Value Prediction

Different from traditional prediction models, which make predictions based on previous values, the pHMM makes predictions based on patterns. To be specific, assume we already learn a pHMM from the training time series. Now, we go through a testing time series and predict the values based on the learned pHMM. Let t be the current time point, we first detect the current state. Then based on the current state, we predict the values of $t+1, t+2, \cdots$. Multi-step value prediction is very useful in the application of system monitoring, in which earlier detection of the anomaly value is critical.

Assume we already obtain a pHMM, and $Y = \{y_1, y_2, \cdots\}$ is the time series we monitor to make predictions. We first detect the current state, with the extended Viterbi algorithm in Section 4. Pruning strategies 1 and 2 can both be used here, but the third one is not, since it requires that we already have the segmentation of the whole time series, which is not available in online monitoring.

To speed up the process, we utilize another pruning strategy introduced in [18], which can be executed on the fly. It aims at reducing the number of points, at which we checked the previous optimal probabilities to compute the current optimal probability. Specifically, if we find that a past point is not likely to be a boundary, we delete all the optimal probabilities at this point from LT.

We do it as follows. Given a minimal distance D and a minimal percentage P, we dynamically remove points y_t and $y_{t'}$ if they hold

$$|t - t'| < D \text{ and } \frac{|y_t - y_{t'}|}{|y_t + y_{t'}|/2} < P$$

If these two inequalities hold, it means that these two points are near and there is no large fluctuation between their values. By this strategy, we only need to maintain a small number of optimal probabilities, by which we can compute current optimal probability efficiently.

Assume the new arrival value is y_t, we compute $\delta_t(i), 1 \leq i \leq K$, and obtain the optimal line sequence and state sequence up to t. Then we make predictions of future values based on the current state.

5.2 Trend Prediction

In many applications, users are not interested in forecasting specific values. Instead, they are interested in the evolving of trends. With pHMM, we can predict the future trends easily. For example, we can answer queries like: *what is the trend of time series after 10 minutes*; or *when will the time series end the current downward trend and enter an upward trend.*

The approach is similar with that of multi-step value prediction. When monitoring a time series, we first detect the current state online, and then make prediction based on this. For example, to estimate how long the system will stay in the current state, we compute the difference between the mean duration of the current state, and its current duration; A more useful case is to estimate the trend in a future period, such as predicting the temperature trend tomorrow between 9:00-10:00am. To answer this query, we first predict the time span of the next state based on transition probability. If it covers the period in question, we use the mean of the slope in the next state as the estimated trend; if not, we predict the state after the next state. We continue this process until the period in question is covered.

5.3 Pattern-based Correlation Detection

Correlation detection is an important operation in time series mining. Measurements, like the correlation coefficient, can tell whether similar subsequences exist between two time series. However, it is advantageous to detect a more general correlation between two time series based on patterns. Consider the example shown in Figure 8. When a burst, P_1, occurs in time series X, a more stable upward trend, P_2, will occur in time series Y with probability 80%. Note that P_1 and P_2 can be two totally different patterns. Moreover, they can have different lengths and not align. For example, occurrences of P_2 are always 5 seconds later than those of P_1. In general, we learn the correlations based on patterns, instead of values. We call this type of correlation the pattern-based correlation.

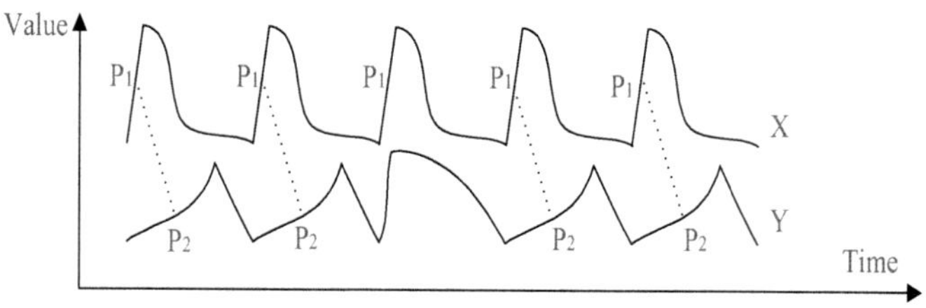

Figure 8: General correlation

pHMM can be used to find the pattern-based correlation effectively. Given two time series X and Y, we learn two pHMMs for them respectively. Then we compute the correlations between patterns in these two pHMMs. We use two criteria to measure the general correlation. The first one is frequency, which measures whether these two patterns have a similar number of occurrences. Assume we measure the correlation between pattern P_1 in X and P_2 in Y. Let P_1 occur m_1 times and P_2 occur m_2 times ($m_1 \leq m_2$). The first criterion is computed as

$$f(P_1, P_2) = \frac{m_1}{m_2}$$

The second criterion is about how well their occurrences align. It is better if most of their occurrences have similar gaps, or delays. To measure the second criterion, we compute the minimal average of their gaps' square. Since there exist many possible matchings, we choose the one with minimal gap-square-average. In the example shown in Figure 8, the best matching of P_1 and P_2 is illustrated by dotted lines.

If $m_1 \leq m_2$, we pick out m_1 occurrences of P_2, which can best match occurrences of P_1. Let $\{c_j\}$, $1 \leq j \leq m_1$, be the central time points of occurrences of P_1, and $\{c_{i_j}\}$, $1 \leq i_j \leq m_2$, be central points of m_1 occurrences of P_2. We measure the second criterion as follows:

$$g(P_1, P_2) = \min\left\{\frac{1}{m_1}\sum_{j=1}^{m_1}(c_j - c_{i_j})^2\right\}$$

which can be efficiently computed with a dynamic programming approach. We combine these two criteria to measure the general correlation between patterns P_1 and P_2 as:

$$GC(P_1, P_2) = \frac{g(P_1, P_2)}{f(P_1, P_2)}$$

The smaller $GC(P_1, P_2)$, the more correlated patterns P_1 and P_2.

6. EXPERIMENT

We conducted extensive performance tests for our approach. All algorithms are implemented in Matlab 7.0, and are tested on a PC with Intel Pentium IV 2.4GHz CPU and 2GB RAM.

6.1 Experiment Setup

We choose two types of real-life time series, the first is a relatively regular time series, and the second is less regular. We normalize values of both datasets into interval [0,1].

1. Power demand time series [27]. It is the 15 minutes of averaged values of power demand for research facility (ECN) in the full year 1997 and it contains 35,050 data points. The training subsequence and testing subsequence both contain 2,000 time points. Since the fluctuation of power demand in each day is similar, it is more regular.

2. Spot prices time series. It contain the spot prices for daily exchange rates of 12 kinds of currencies relative to the US dollar. For each currency, there are 2,567 (work-)daily spot prices over the period 10/9/86 to 8/9/96. In each experiment, we randomly select one currency.

We conducted three groups of experiments. In the first group of experiments, we test the efficiency of the proposed approach, especially of the three pruning strategies. In the second group of experiments, we analyze the impact of parameters ε_r and ε_c. Finally, we test the effectiveness of pHMM for answering three types of queries introduced in Section 5.

6.2 Experiment Results

Efficiency. We conduct the experiments on the Power dataset. We train the model in three scenarios: no pruning, pruning with strategy 1, pruning with both strategies 1 and 2. In each scenario, we compare the runtime under different N, the selection ratio of boundary points. For example, 0.05 means we choose $0.05{*}2000 = 100$ time points to train the model. The results are shown in Table 1. It can be seen that pruning reduces runtime significantly, especially pruning with both strategies 1 and 2.

N	0.05	0.1	0.5	1
No-Prune	96	381	9265	-
Prune 1	41	93	689	1921
Prune 1&2	29	70	425	934

Table 1: Runtime Comparison(s)

Since pruning loses information, we test its influence on the quality of learned pHMM. As a larger N leads to longer training time, it is desirable that a relatively small N can still build a high-quality model. We directly measure the quality of the model with the whole production probability. We test it on both the Power dataset and the Spot dataset. The production probability is replaced by the value of negative logarithm, $-\log(P(\mathbf{L}, \mathbf{s}|\lambda))$. The results are shown in Figure 9.

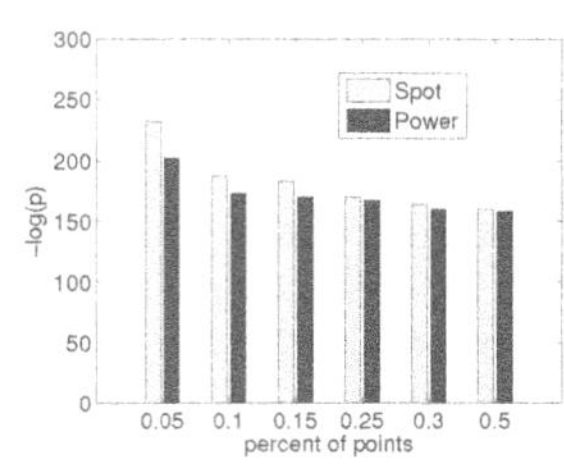

Figure 9: Influence of N

We can see that in both datasets, when the percentage is equal to or larger than 0.1, the production probability is not affected much, which verifies the effectiveness of this pruning strategy. In other words, we can still learn high quality models by looking at a small number of time points. In our experiments, we set N as 0.1.

The influence of ε_r *and* ε_c. In this group of experiments, we test the influence of two parameters, ε_r, approximation error threshold in time series segmentation, and ε_c, relative error threshold in line clustering. The experiments are conducted on the Spot dataset and the Power dataset. The following two measurements are used to measure the quality of the learned pHMM:

- Residual error per time point. It measures how accurately pHMM represents the original time series by segment lines. It is computed as follows. After obtaining the model and the optimal segmentation, $\mathbf{L}$, for each interval L_i, we use the 'central' line of state s_i to approximate the subsequence. The errors are summarized and then divided by the length of the whole time series. A smaller residual error means the learned model represents the time series more accurately.

- Entropy. It is the second criterion used in clustering segment lines in the initial phase, I in Eq. 4. It measures the certainty of the states about the next state. The smaller the entropy, the more certain the states are about the following state.

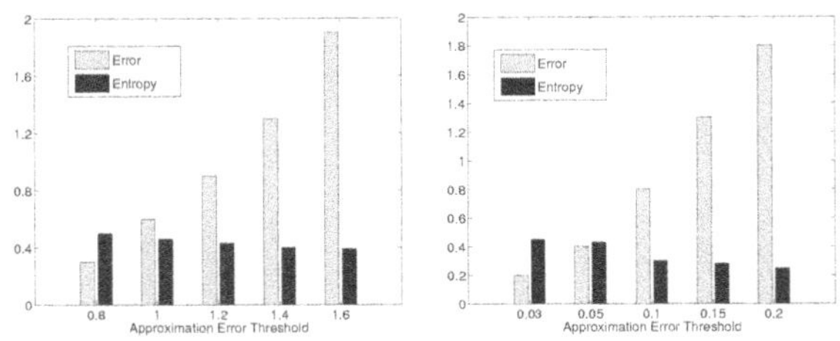

(a) Spot Dataset (b) Power Dataset

Figure 10: Residual Error and Entropy Vs. ε_r

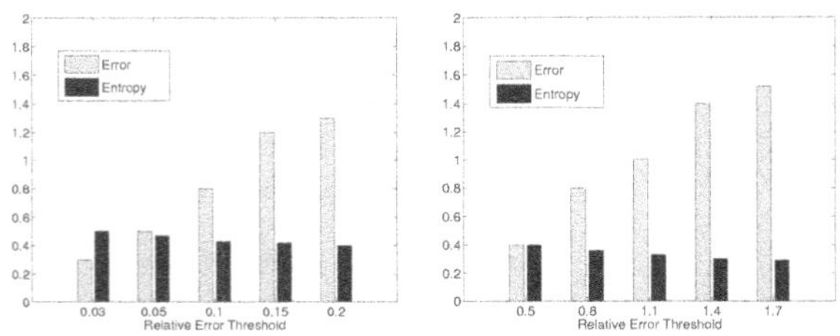

(a) Spot dataset (b) Power dataset

Figure 11: Residual Error and Entropy Vs. ε_c

Figure 10 shows the results with varying ε_r. To make the comparison of two measurements clearer, we scale residual error by a factor of 0.002. It can be seen that in both datasets, when ε_r increases, the residual error also increases. It means larger ε_r will reduce the accuracy of the learned model to approximate the time series. In contrast, when ε_r increases, the entropy decreases. So in different applications, users can set ε_r according to the following requirement: To represent the time series more accurately, users should choose a smaller ε_r; to be more certain about states, users should choose a larger ε_r.

The results of varying ε_c are shown in Figure 11. The same scale is used as in the experiment of the residual error. It can be seen that ε_c has the same characteristics with ε_r. When it increases, since the relative error of the lines in a cluster is larger, more residual error is generated. On the contrary, entropy decreases when ε_c increases.

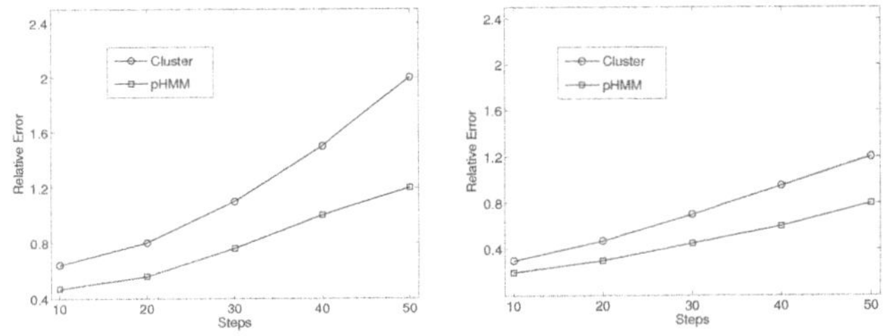

(a) Spot dataset (b) Power dataset

Figure 12: Accuracy of Trend Prediction

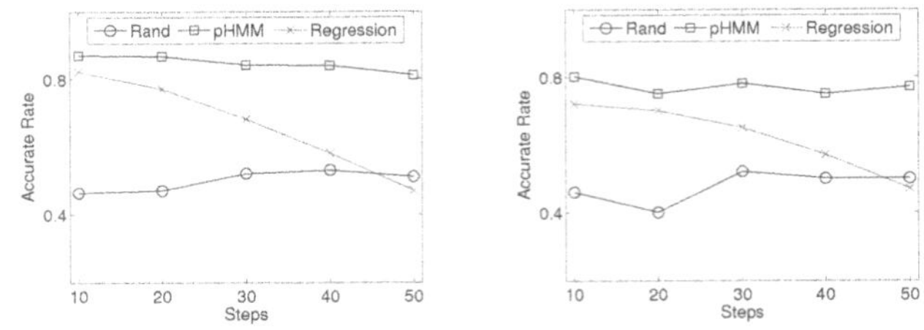

(a) Spot dataset (b) Power dataset

Figure 13: Accuracy of binary trend prediction

Trend Prediction. The major advantage of pHMM is that it can be used to perform the tasks discussed in Section 5. In this experiment, we first test the effectiveness of the proposed approach for trend prediction.

The experiments are conducted on both the Spot dataset and the Power dataset respectively. We compute the prediction accuracy as follows. In the testing time series, we randomly select 50 time points. At each time point, we make the trend predictions after 5 different gaps, 10, 20, 30, 40, 50. Assume the current time point is t. For each gap d, we predict the trend of 20-length subsequence $[t+d+1, t+d+20]$. The trend is represented by a segment line. We compare the true trend with the estimated trend by our approach. For example, at time point 100, we predict the trend of $[111, 130]$, $[121, 140] \cdots$. We compute the relative error as $\frac{e(l)-b(l)}{b(l)}$, where $e(l)$ is the slope of the estimated line, and $b(l)$ is that of the best-fit line. The accuracy of two models are compared. The first one is the pHMM model obtained by only clustering, the second by both clustering and refinement. Through this experiment, we test the effectiveness of both the cluster algorithm and the refinement process. The results are shown in Figure 12. It can be seen that in the cluster-based model, the relative error does not increase dramatically as the gap increases, which verifies the effectiveness of our clustering approach. For both datasets, especially the Spot dataset, which is less regular than the Power dataset, pHMM is more accurate. This result clearly demonstrates the effectiveness of the refinement process.

We also conduct experiments for binary trend prediction. For each testing time series, we make a binary trend prediction: up or down. Three approaches are compared: Rand, Regression and pHMM. The Rand approach makes random guesses. The Regression approach predicts by first computing the linear regression of the time series in the current time window, and then making predictions with it. For each dataset, we also pick 50 time points to predict the trend of the next 10, 20, 30, 40 and 50 steps. Figure 13 shows the average accuracy of all 50 time points. It can be seen that pHMM is more accurate than other approaches.

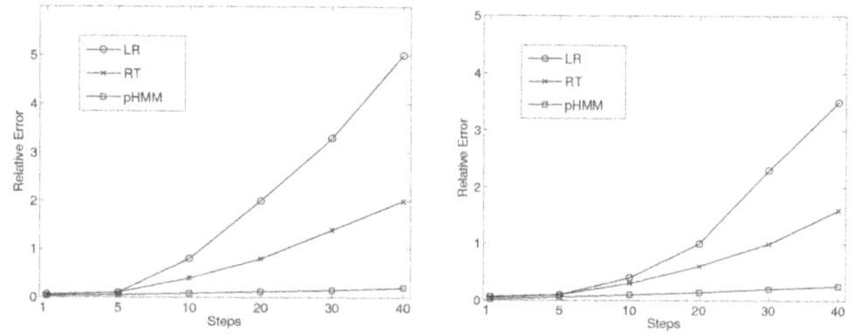

(a) Spot dataset (b) Power dataset

Figure 14: Accuracy of Multi-step Value Prediction

Multi-step Value Prediction. In this experiment, we test the accuracy of pHMM for multi-step value prediction. The experiments are conducted for both Spot and Power datasets. We select 50 points randomly. For each selected point, we predict the values after 1, 5, 10, 20 ,30 and 40 steps respectively. The pHMM is compared with two classic approaches: a linear regression model (denoted by LR) and a regression tree (denoted by RT) [1]. Both approaches are trained based on values of the previous 20 time points. For the linear regression model, we learn the model in the online way. That is, at each selected time point, the model is learned based on the previous 20 values. Then all 5 predictions are made based on this model. For the regression tree, we train the model before making predictions. First, we build a training dataset from the original time series, where each row contains 20 input values and 1 output value. Then a regression tree is learned from this dataset. We make predictions as follows. Assume the current time point is t. First we predict the value at $t+1$ based on values at $t-19, t-18, \cdots, t$. Then we consider the estimated value at $t+1$ as an input value, and estimate the value at $t+2$. This process continues until all 5 values at $t+1, t+10, t+20, t+30, t+40$ are estimated.

We use relative error as the measurement. The results are shown in Figure 14. It can be seen that on both datasets, pHMM is more accurate than the other two approaches. In LR, the values are predicted based on the current line, which obviously cannot accurately predict the values after a large gap. Unlike LR, RT contains multiple prediction rules, so when the step increases, it still can find the fittest model to make predictions. However, since it has no knowledge whether the estimated value is appropriate, it cannot adjust the next predictions, even if the previous estimated value has a large error. Hence when the step increases, its accuracy drops. The results show that these two models are applicable for predicting the next value, but not for multi-step prediction. To increase the accuracy for these approaches, an alternative way is to train a specific model for the prediction with a specific step, but it needs to learn a lot of models, which is infeasible in practice. In contrast, pHMM can make predictions accurately, even when the step increases. It verifies the advantage of the pattern-based model.

Pattern-based Correlation Detection. Finally, we test the effectiveness of pHMM for pattern-based correlation detection. We conduct this experiment on the Spot dataset. Since all time series are over the same time period, we hope to find correlations between price trends of different currencies. We use time series for "French Franc" as the reference time series, and compute correlations between it and 5 other currencies (including "Australian Dollar", "Belgian Franc", "Canadian Dollar" and so on). For each time series, we train the pHMM model. Then, for each state of "French Franc", we compute its pattern-based correlation(GC) with any state in the 5 other time series. Table 2 shows both minimal GC and average GC. For example, in the first row, Minimal GC means the minimal GC computed between any state pair in which one is from "French Franc" and the other is from "Australian Dollar". Average GC is the average of all GCs between all state pairs from two currencies.

	Minimal GC	Average GC
Australian Dollar	88.33	130.45
Belgian Franc	**41.25**	**50.62**
Canadian Dollar	120.41	160.37
German Mark	60.57	120.46
Japanese Yenr	130.59	170.96

Table 2: Pattern-based Correlation

It can be seen that 5 target currencies demonstrate different correlations. The fluctuation of "Belgian Franc" is most similar to that of "French Franc", so both the minimal and average GC are minimal compared to all other currencies. "German Mark" also has a similar state with "French Franc", although its average GC is still high. For all the 3 other currencies, their states are more different with those of "French Franc". This experiment shows that with pattern-based correlation, we can compare time series in the higher level.

7. RELATED WORK

Time series representation and forecasting. A number of techniques have been proposed in the literature to represent time series with patterns. In [7], authors give an extensive performance comparison of popular time series representation approaches. They can be categorized into two groups. Those in the first group split the whole time series into disjoint segmentations and represent each segment with the mean value or a regression line, such as PLA [11] and PAA [10]. These techniques can provide an approximate shape of the time series. However, they don't exploit the relationships between segments. Those in the second category represent time series with a few dominant coefficients of certain transformations, such as DFT [8] and DWT [2]. However, the coefficients are not interpretable, that is, knowing the coefficients in the frequency domain does not necessarily enable us to understand how the system works.

Time series motifs are approximately repeated subsequences of a longer time series stream. Motifs are defined and categorized using their support, distance, cardinality, length, dimension, underlying similarity measure, etc. Many researchers have introduced techniques to find them efficiently in the case of a large database or streams [16]. But still, the set of motifs cannot provide us with the whole picture of the time series.

Recently, some works dealing with relations between patterns has been proposed. Pattern Growth Graph (PGG) [22] detects and manages variations over pseudo periodical streams. It first splits time series into segments, each of which is an occurrence of the pseudo period, and then describes time series by several connected lines. However, this work can only deal with pseudo periodical time series, and is not applied to the general time series. In [19], a multi-scale schema is proposed to compress time series. It uses techniques such as FFT and random projection to represent the original time series. However, patterns are still isolated, and hence cannot be used to make predictions.

Time series forecasting has been a topic of extensive research [1, 3]. In particular, many tools for forecasting and processing time series appear in statistics and signal processing fields. The traditional method includes ARIMA [1]. Other well-known machine learning approaches include Bayesian Network, Regression Tree,

CART and Random Forests [28]. These methods try to capture relationships between the predicted value, y_t, with observed values $y_{t-1}, \cdots, y_{t-n}$. Our approach is different to them, since our goal is to build a model based on patterns instead of single values.

Markov model and the related extension models. The hidden Markov model (HMM) assumes that the states are unobservable and the observation symbols are emitted by the states according to the output probability. A well-known problem of HMM is that the first-order assumption restricts it from accurately modeling the time series data with highly varied dynamics, as it is often that the future state not only depends on the present state, but also the past states. To increase the accuracy of modeling, the n-gram model was presented [15], but the complexity and the learning cost increase exponentially when n increases.

In contrast with n-gram, variable length Markov model (VLMM) learns a minimum set of contexts with variable lengths to model the high-order Markovian process [20]. VLMM aims to extend the states to variable length contexts, which is composed of several connected states. It reduces the number and complexity of contexts by allowing the context to have variable lengths. However, VLMM is limited as an observable Markov model and not a hidden Markov model. In other words, all states are observable, and no output probability is needed.

Another Markov model related to our work is Variable length hidden Markov model (VLHMM) combines the advantages of both HMM and VLMM [26]. Instead of generating observations using single states, VLHMM extends states to contexts, which are composed of variable of states. An EM algorithm is used to learn the parameters of the model, which aims to maximize the likelihood of generating time series by the model. The difference between these models and the proposed pHMM is that they take the value of each time point as an observation, while in pHMM, the observations are patterns.

8. CONCLUSION

In this paper, we reveal the dynamics of a complex system by learning a pattern-based hidden Markov model from the time series data generated by this system. The biggest difference between a pHMM and a traditional HMM is that in pHMM, observations are not given, but learned from the data as well. We propose an approach to learn patterns (observations) and the model simultaneously. Furthermore, three pruning strategies are proposed to speed up the learning process. With pHMM, we are able to perform pattern based tasks, such as trend prediction and pattern-based correlation detection. Empirical results on real datasets demonstrate the feasibility and effectiveness of the proposed approach.

9. REFERENCES

[1] G. Box, G. Jenkins, and G. Reinsel. *Time series analysis: forecasting and control.* Prentice Hall, 1994.

[2] K. Chan and W. Fu. Efficient time series matching by wavelets. In *ICDE*, 1999.

[3] C. Chatfield. *The analysis of time series: an introduction.* Chapman & Hall/CRC, 2004.

[4] S. Chen, H. Wang, and S. Zhou. Concept clustering of evolving data. In *ICDE*, 2009.

[5] S. Chen, H. Wang, S. Zhou, and P. Yu. Stop chasing trends: Discovering high order models in evolving data. In *ICDE*, 2008.

[6] G. Dangelmayr, S. Gadaleta, D. Hundley, and M. Kirby. Time series prediction by estimating markov probabilities through topology preserving maps. In *SPIE*, 1999.

[7] H. Ding, G. Trajcevski, P. Scheuermann, X. Wang, and E. Keogh. Querying and mining of time series data: Experimental comparison of representations and distance measures. In *VLDB*, 2008.

[8] C. Faloutsos, M. Ranganathan, and Y. Manolopoulos. Fast subsequence matching in time-series databases. In *SIGMOD*, 1994.

[9] X. Gu and H. Wang. Online anomaly prediction for robust cluster systems. In *ICDE*, 2009.

[10] E. Keogh, K. Chakrabarti, M. Pazzani, and S. Mehrotra. Dimensionality reduction for fast similarity search in large time series databases. *KAIS*, 2000.

[11] E. Keogh and M. Pazzani. An enhanced representation of time series which allows fast and accurate classification, clustering and relevance feedback. In *SIGKDD*, 1998.

[12] E. Keogh, S.Chu, D. Hart, and M. Pazzani. An online algorithm for segmenting time series. In *ICDM*, 2001.

[13] E. J. Keogh. A decade of progress in indexing and mining large time series databases. In *VLDB*, 2006.

[14] J. Lin, E. J. Keogh, L. Wei, and S. Lonardi. Experiencing sax: a novel symbolic representation of time series. In *DMKD*, 2007.

[15] J. F. Mari, D. Fohr, and J. C. Junqira. A second-order hmm for high performance word and phoneme-based continuous speech recognition. In *ICASSP*, 1996.

[16] A. Mueen and E. Keogh. Online discovery and maintenance of time series motifs. In *SIGKDD*, 2010.

[17] A. Mueen, E. Keogh, and N. Bigdely-Shamlo. Finding time series motifs in disk-resident data. In *ICDM*, 2009.

[18] C. Perng, H. Wang, S. R. Zhang, and D. Parker. Landmarks: A new model for similarity-based pattern querying in time series databases. In *ICDE*, 2000.

[19] G. Reeves, J. Liu, S. Nath, and F. Zhao. Managing massive time series streams with multiscale compressed trickles. In *VLDB*, 2009.

[20] D. Ron, Y. Singer, and N. Tishby. The power of amnesia: Learning probabilistic automata with variable memory length. *Machine Learning*, pages 117–149, 1996.

[21] Y. Tan, X. Gu, and H. Wang. Adaptive system anomaly prediction for large-scale hosting infrastructures. In *PODC*, 2010.

[22] L. Tang, B. Cui, H. Li, G. Miao, D. Yang, and X. Zhou. Effective variation management for pseudo periodical streams. In *SIGMOD*, 2007.

[23] H. Wang, W. Fan, P. S. Yu, and J. Han. Mining concept-drifting data streams using ensemble classifiers. In *SIGKDD*, 2003.

[24] H. Wang, J. Yin, J. Pei, P. S. Yu, and J. X. Yu. Suppressing model overfitting in mining concept-drifting data streams. In *SIGKDD*, 2006.

[25] P. Wang, H. Wang, M. Liu, and W. Wang. An algorithmic approach to event summarization. In *SIGMOD*, 2010.

[26] Y. Wang and L. Zhou. Mining complex time-series data by learning the temporal structure using bayesian techniques and markovian models. In *ICDM*, 2006.

[27] J. J. Wiik and E. R. Selow. Cluster and calendar based visualization of time series data. In *INFOVIS*, 1999.

[28] I. H. Witten and E. Frank. *Data mining: practical machine learning tools and techniques.* Morgan Kaufmann, 2005.

Querying Contract Databases Based on Temporal Behavior

Elio Damaggio
UC San Diego
elio@cs.ucsd.edu

Alin Deutsch
UC San Diego
deutsch@cs.ucsd.edu

Dayou Zhou
UC San Diego
dzhou@cs.ucsd.edu

ABSTRACT

Considering a broad definition for service contracts (beyond web services and software, e.g. airline tickets and insurance policies), we tackle the challenges of building a high performance broker in which contracts are both specified and queried through their temporal behavior. The temporal dimension, in conjunction with traditional relational attributes, enables our system to better address difficulties arising from the great deal of information regarding the temporal interaction of the various events cited in contracts (e.g. "No refunds are allowed *after* a reschedule of the flight, which can be requested only *before* any flight leg has been used"). On the other hand, querying large repositories of temporal specifications poses an interesting indexing challenge. In this paper, we introduce two distinct and complementary indexing techniques that enable our system to scale the evaluation of a novel and theoretically sound notion of *permission* of a temporal query by a service contract. Our notion of permission is inspired by previous work on model checking but, given the specific characteristic of our problem, does not reduce to it. We evaluate experimentally our implementation, showing that it scales well with both the number and the complexity of the contracts.

Categories and Subject Descriptors

H.2.1 [**Database Management**]: Logical Design—*Data Model*; J.1 [**Computer Applications**]: Administraitive Data Processing—*Business, Law*

General Terms

Algorithms, Perfomance, Theory

Keywords

temporal behavior, contracts, Linear Temporal Logic, LTL, indexing, Büchi automata

1. INTRODUCTION

Service contracts are seldom completely represented by a set of predefined attributes and as such are usually modeled only partially in IT systems. As an example, consider the market of airfares. Every plane ticket is actually a complex contract with dozens of conditions regarding validity, refundability and changeability, among others. Some fixed categories exist (e.g. economy tickets, business, first class), but they do not express all the subtleties of the contracts that the customers are required to sign. Any non-standard travel arrangement requires sifting through the full text of the contracts of the fares returned by such brokers as Expedia, Orbitz and Travelocity, or asking an expert travel agent. Generally, analogous characteristics are found in service markets where there is no negotiation of the contracts, but that present many possible choices in direct competition (e.g. airfares, insurances, warranties).

EXAMPLE 1. *Over 100 airlines operate in the US market [26], each of them offering around 20 different fares [27], [24]. Fare rules specify a great deal of temporal conditions such as (from the United Airlines Fare Contract [1]): '1) Passenger may change the routing and/or the ultimate destination [...] provided that, after transportation has commenced, a one-way ticket will not be converted into a round-trip, circle-trip, or openjaw trip ticket.' Note, also, that voluntary rerouting might be possible only by reissuing a ticket with a different 'booking code' which in turn has to abide to additional restrictions such as minimum stays and advanced purchase requirements [24].*

In this work, we envision a contract brokering system that, in addition to standard relational attributes, allows contracts to be specified and queried by their temporal behavior. For illustration purposes, we introduce now a running example in the airfares scenario. Airlines, as contract providers, register all their fares on our brokering system. Each airfare specifies its temporal aspects, in addition to the usual relational attributes (e.g. baggage conditions, prices). These aspects involve how tickets are changed (if and when it is possible), how the customers can be refunded and so on. A possible query could look for: *the cheapest fare on 10/19/2010 from San Diego to New York, that allows a partial ticket refund or a date change after the first leg has been missed.* In order to answer this query, our broker would first retrieve the list of fares available from San Diego to New York, along with their prices, using a standard DBMS. It would then use the temporal specifications to filter the fares that do not satisfy the temporal portion of the query (e.g. '... that allows a date change even in the case of a missed flight'). In this work, we focus on the temporal aspect of our system.

EXAMPLE 2. *Assume that all the airfares* 'from San Diego to New York on 10/19/2010' *returned by the DBMS fall into three categories of tickets (e.g. United Business, AA Economy for Platinum Clients) that differ in their policies regarding refunds and changeability. Their contract restrictions are the following:*

Ticket A *1. No refunds are allowed after date changes*
2. *Unlimited date changes*

Ticket B *1. Refunds always allowed*
2. *Date changes only before the scheduled departure*

SIGMOD'11, June 12–16, 2011, Athens, Greece.

Ticket C *1. No refunds are allowed*
2. Only one date change is allowed
3. Date changes only before the scheduled departure

Our system has to identify which of these contracts satisfy the temporal portion of the query: 'allows a partial ticket refund or a date change after the first leg has been missed'. *Intuitively, the system should return **Ticket A** (because it would allow a reschedule) and **Ticket B** (that would allow a refund). It should not return **Ticket C** because it does not allow any refund nor rescheduling after a missed flight.*

Our design is guided by the following requirements:
i) Specifications and queries need to be expressive enough to capture realistic temporal behavior,
ii) The interface between customers and providers should be compact and reasonably stable,
iii) Published contract specifications should not require revisions if a contract with a different policy is published,
iv) Our representation for contracts and queries should declare a set of declarative clauses, in order to loosely follow natural language specifications.

Modeling complex temporal behavior with relational attributes is tempting but falls short in all stated requirements for the following reasons. Let us consider a customer's specific requirement regarding the refundability options of a partially used ticket (as in Example 2). It would be easy to add an attribute 'refundable' with a set of predefined values that code the various situations: 'no refunds', 'only full refunds', 'partial refunds allowed'. The problem lies in the interaction of these categories with other ticket features like changeability, e.g. a refund might not be available for a ticket that was changed. Moreover, both aspects interact with the various phases of the trip (e.g. before or after the first flight leg was completed or missed). In principle, every new aspect can interact with all the others, leading to an exponential blow up of the number of possible interaction 'categories' (e.g. 'partial refunds allowed only if requested before the date of the first flight leg', 'partial refunds allowed even if the first leg is missed'). These categories then become too numerous to specify as schema attributes. They are hard to define and specify for the contract providers and, even more importantly, hard for the consumer to understand, leading either to a lack of expressiveness (violating requirement *i*) or a bloated interface (*ii*). Moreover, publishing contracts with policies that differ from the existing ones might change the relational schema, adding and/or modifying attributes. This would force the revision of previously published contracts (*iii*). Lastly, the relational schema resulting from such a modeling would be very far from the original informal description (*iv*).

Our proposal considers a common vocabulary of events (e.g. 'ticket refunded', 'flight used', 'flight missed', 'date changed') that is small enough to overview and will act as the interface between providers of contracts and customers that query them. Analogously to the real world, the temporal behavior of contracts is specified as a set of declarative clauses referring to the common vocabulary, as are the temporal properties required by the customer. The vocabulary refers to a set of familiar events pertaining to the application domain, and is much more compact than the rich family of temporal behaviors usually expressed as declarative clauses in contracts (e.g. 'allowing a partial refund after the first leg is used'). Intuitively, a contract allows only certain temporal *sequences* of events. The allowed sequences have to simultaneously satisfy all the clauses in the contract. When interested in a particular property of a contract (e.g. 'allowing a partial refund after the first leg is used'), customers formulate an ad-hoc query against the vocabulary, detailing the property of a desired temporal sequence of events. The query simply returns all contracts that allow a sequence satisfying the desired property. We say that such contracts *permit* the query.

EXAMPLE 3. *We use the following event vocabulary to crudely model single-trip flights:* purchase *(ticket purchased),* use *(ticket used),* missedFlight *(customer missed the flight),* refund *(customer is refunded for the ticket),* dateChange *(the flight is rescheduled).*

*The temporal behavior of an airfare that allows flight reschedulings (e.g. **Ticket A** of Example 2) is described by clauses satisfied by temporal sequences in which this happens, but also sequences in which the ticket is used in the originally scheduled date:*

1. (purchase) --→ (use) --→ ...
2. (purchase) --→ (dateChange) --→ (use) --→ ...
3. ...

A customer looking for a ticket that allows reschedules even after a missed flight, would look for sequences with the form:
(purchase) --→ (missedFlight) --→ (dateChange) --→ ...

We believe that representing contracts' temporal behavior and user queries with declarative clauses leads to a system that satisfies the aforementioned requirements. The use of a common vocabulary along with ad hoc declarative clauses satisfies both the need of expressiveness and the requirement of a compact and stable interface (*i* and *ii*). In §2.1 we will show how with our notion of permission, we avoid unnecessary revisions of contracts specifications (*iii*). Finally, we show in §2.2 that our system representation is reasonably close to the natural language specification of Example 2 (*iv*).

Summarizing our problem setting:
a. We focus on the temporal aspect of querying contracts, so we assume a traditional DBMS takes care of the features modeled as relational attributes.
b. The temporal behavior of a *contract* is *specified with declarative clauses* that represent a *set of allowed temporal sequences of events*.
d. A contract *permits* a temporal query (also specified as a declarative clause) if it allows a sequence satisfying the query property.
e. Our system stores the temporal specification of all contracts and has to provide a scalable and high performance way to retrieve all contracts that permit an online temporal query.

Solving this problem involved the following contributions:
1. We model an intuitive notion of permission with respect to contracts and queries, which captures the temporal behavior aspects that are not handled currently by state-of-the-art systems. Our notion gracefully handles the fact that contracts might not specify the behavior of all events mentioned in a query, finding the best design tradeoff between two extremes. Indeed, returning contracts that do not *explicitly* allow the requested behavior for a particular event would incentivize publishing underspecified contracts, making the system useless to consumers. While forcing full specification would dramatically increase publishing costs.
2. Aiming to represent and reason about temporal aspects, we picked a standard and well established formalism, namely Linear Temporal Logic. Checking permission does not reduce to any of the many decision problems studied for LTL, so we developed a novel algorithm. Note that we do not expect end users to utilize LTL directly. Analogously to SQL in database-powered e-commerce systems, LTL will be used in our system only by application developers. User-friendly GUIs for LTL have previously been studied [5], but they are not the focus of this paper.
3. We develop a novel indexing scheme for large scale databases of contracts that allows our system to quickly identify a set of candidate contracts for a given temporal query. This eliminates the need to execute the complex permission algorithm on every single contract temporal specification in the repository and is extremely effective for highly selective complex queries.

4. We develop a novel way to automatically simplify temporal specifications of contracts based on the events cited in a query. This allows our system to execute the permission algorithm on smaller contract specifications and provides the best results for simple queries that mention few events.
5. Finally, we provide an experimental evaluation of our techniques to prove the feasibility of our approach. Exploiting both our indexing techniques, we show an optimized average query evaluation time of 6sec over databases of 3000 contracts, improving by more than an order of magnitude over the unoptimized average time of 98sec. Note that our prototype ran on a standard desktop pc and did not take advantage of multiple cores, as we focused on the benefits of the indexing techniques and not of a particular hardware platform. The size of the tested databases is adequate for most applications as a complete implementation would use relational attributes (e.g. travel date and destination) to pre-select contracts from a potentially much larger database.

The rest of the paper is organized as follows. Section 2 informally introduces the temporal search problem, Section 3 presents a high level unoptimized system architecture along with our novel permission algorithm, Section 4 describes our indexing scheme, Section 5 describes our automatic simplification technique, Section 6 details the formal foundations of our work, Section 7 presents our experimental results, Section 8 discusses some related work, and Section 9 concludes the paper.

2. QUERYING CONTRACTS

To ease the presentation of our contributions we provide an intuitive description of our work in the first sections of the paper and we relegate the formal foundations of our results to §6.

Following §1, we refine the intuition of 'sequence of events' by adding the notion of *snapshot*. At every moment in the temporal sequence, many events could be happening, a *snapshot* captures all the information regarding the events in a particular moment (i.e. a truth assignment for every event in the vocabulary). A temporal *sequence* is then just a list of snapshots. Intuitively, we are able to define declaratively properties of these temporal sequences using *clauses*. We define a *contract* as a set of clauses that identify the set of allowed temporal sequences of snapshots, and a *query* as a clause that specifies the required property of a temporal sequence.

2.1 Designing the Permission Semantics

Usually, customers are interested in knowing if a certain sequence will be possible if they subscribe to a contract. More precisely, they are interested in a particular property of that sequence (e.g. the fact that a ticket is partially refundable), which they specify using the query clause. A natural first-cut semantics would be that a contract is returned as a result of a query q, if at least one of its allowed sequences satisfies q. This semantics, however, has a subtle problem.

EXAMPLE 4. *Let us consider **Ticket A** of Example 2, but with a common vocabulary that contains also the event* 'class upgrade'. *The airfare policy is still that no refund is allowed after a date change and that date changes are unlimited. Let us assume that a customer issues the following query:*

Q2 *An airfare that allows a class upgrade after a date change.*

*If we think of a sequence of events in which the customer obtains a date change and then obtains a class upgrade, we can easily see that it satisfies all clauses of **Ticket A** (since they impose no restriction of class upgrades, which are not mentioned). It follows that under this semantics **Ticket A** will be returned as part of the result.*

In Example 4, using the first-cut semantics, a contract, which did not say anything about class upgrades, is returned as part of the result of a query regarding class upgrades. Clearly, the contract is not fully specified with respect to **Q2**. We contend that returning contracts that are underspecified w.r.t. a query (as in Example 4) would not serve customers well for two reasons. First, customers would be required to read all returned contracts in order to know which contracts explicitly permit the query and which ones were underspecified. Second, in order to gain visibility, publishers would be incentivized to publish underspecied contracts, that would be selected by more queries. This would exacerbate the first problem and make our system useless. However, we cannot solve the problem of underspecified contracts by forcing full specification on the part of contract publishers, as it would raise the publishing cost considerably. It would also prevent a simple introduction of new events in the common vocabulary, as a modified vocabulary would force a revision of all contract specifications in the system.

For these reasons we refine the first-cut semantics in order to exclude contracts that do not explicitly allow some events. Our refined semantics takes into account only the events cited in each contract, and assumes that the contract makes no commitment on events not explicitly cited in its clauses. In Example 4, **Ticket A** would not be returned because it never cites events regarding class upgrades. This discussion motivates the following final semantics for permission, stated formally in §6.1 and informally as:

Definition 1. A contract *permits* a query if and only if there exists a sequence that **(a)** is allowed by the contract, **(b)** consists only of the events mentioned in the contract, and **(c)** satisfies the query.

Note that the restriction to the events cited in the contract does not result simply in the immediate conclusion that a contract that does not mention all events in a query q does not permit q. Considering **Ticket B** of Example 2 (i.e. all refunds, date changes only before scheduled departure), it is easy to see that it should be returned if the customer is interested in the following contracts:

Q3 After a date change, airfare allows a class upgrade or a refund.

This is because, even though **Ticket B** does not specify a class upgrade policy, it explicitly allows refunds after date changes.

2.2 Declarative language

During the modeling of both synthetic and real-world contracts and queries, we found that temporal logic resulted expressive enough to capture the temporal behaviors at hand and also very close to the informal specification. Moreover, many other domains deal with temporal behavior of systems, most notably model checking and verification ([25]). In all these domains, temporal logic has become the accepted standard formalism for declaration of properties over temporal sequences, and many techniques based on this kind of logic are successfully applied to industrial level implementations of tools [14], [4], [17].

We use the simplest form of temporal logic (Linear Temporal Logic, LTL [20]) as the formalism to capture declarative clauses, informally introduced in §1. For the formal treatment of the use of LTL refer to §6.1. As an example, we report here the LTL specification of **Ticket C** from Example 2:

Ticket C
1. $\mathbf{G}(\neg refund)$
2. $\mathbf{G}(dateChange \to \mathbf{X}(\neg \mathbf{F} dateChange))$
3. $\mathbf{G}(missedFlight \to \neg \mathbf{F} dateChange)$

Clause 1 is read 'globally not *refund*', *globally* (**G**) means that a certain formula has to be true in all the snapshots of a sequence. Clause 2 reads 'globally, if a date change occurs, then in the next instant (**X**) it is not the case that eventually another date change occurs', *eventually* (**F**) means that a certain formula will be true in some future instant. Clause 3 reads 'globally, if a flight is missed, it is never the case that eventually a date chage occurs'. Note how these formulas are close to the informal description of Example 2.

In our LTL specifications, we consider a common vocabulary of propositional variables $\mathcal{V}$. A variable is intuitively associated to an event and it is $true$ in a snapshot where its associated event happens. LTL is essentially a propositional logic which, in addition to the usual boolean operators, uses some temporal operators with the following intuitive meaning:

- $\mathbf{X}p$, p is true on the *next* instant
- $\mathbf{F}p$, *eventually* p is true
- $p\mathbf{U}q$, q is eventually true and p is true *until* q is true
- $\mathbf{G}p$, *globally* (i.e. in every instant) p is true
- $p\mathbf{B}q$, p is true *before* q is true
- $p\mathbf{W}q$, *weak until*: p is always true or p is true *until* q is true

EXAMPLE 5. *Let us see how the clauses of the contracts in Example 2 can be expressed in LTL. We assume a vocabulary $\mathcal{V}$ containing the event variables* {purchase, use, missedFlight, refund, dateChange}.*First, we need to model the intuitive meaning of the events in the vocabulary with some additional clauses that are common to all three airfares. Informally:*

C1 *The ticket is purchased once.*

C2 *The ticket has to be purchased before any of the following events: it is used, the flight missed or rescheduled, or the customer is refunded.*

C3 *If the flight is missed, the ticket is unusable unless rescheduled*

C4 *If a refund is issued, then no other event can happen*

C5 *If the ticket is used, then no other event can happen*

The full LTL specification is then:

C0 *In this case, we force the fact that only one event happens in each instant,*
$\mathbf{G}(purchase \rightarrow \neg use \wedge \neg missedFlight \wedge \neg refund \wedge \neg dateChange)$,
$\mathbf{G}(use \rightarrow \neg purchase \wedge \neg missedFlight \wedge \neg refund \wedge \neg dateChange)$,
...,

C1 $\mathbf{G}(purchase \rightarrow \mathbf{X}(\neg \mathbf{F} purchase))$

C2 $\mathbf{G}(purchase\ \mathbf{B}\ (use \vee missedFlight \vee refund \vee dateChange))$

C3 $\mathbf{G}((missedFlight \rightarrow \neg \mathbf{F} use)\ \mathbf{W}\ dateChange)$

C4 $\mathbf{G}(refund \rightarrow \neg \mathbf{F}(use \vee missedFlight \vee refund \vee dateChange))$

C5 $\mathbf{G}(use \rightarrow \neg \mathbf{F}(use \vee missedFlight \vee refund \vee dateChange))$

Ticket A *1.* $\mathbf{G}(dateChange \rightarrow \neg \mathbf{F} refund)$
2. no clause necessary

Ticket B *1.* no clause necessary
2. $\mathbf{G}(missedFlight \rightarrow \neg \mathbf{F} dateChange)$

Ticket C *1.* $\mathbf{G}(\neg refund)$
2. $\mathbf{G}(dateChange \rightarrow \mathbf{X}(\neg \mathbf{F} dateChange))$
3. $\mathbf{G}(missedFlight \rightarrow \neg \mathbf{F} dateChange)$

*Note that the specifications of the contracts will be the conjunction of all common clauses along with the specific ones (e.g. for **Ticket A**: C0,C1,C2,C3,C4,C5,TicketA). Also, note that some natural language clauses (e.g. 'Unlimited date changes') did not require any additional LTL clause, as they are implicit in the LTL semantics. This is because they did not add any additional constraints to what was already specified in the common clauses (e.g. for date changes: C0,C2,C3,C4,C5).*

LTL as a developer language We want to stress the fact that the usage of LTL in our scenario is similar to the use of SQL in database powered e-commerce applications: LTL will be used by the application developers. User-friendly GUIs for LTL have been studied [5] and they are not the focus of the present paper.

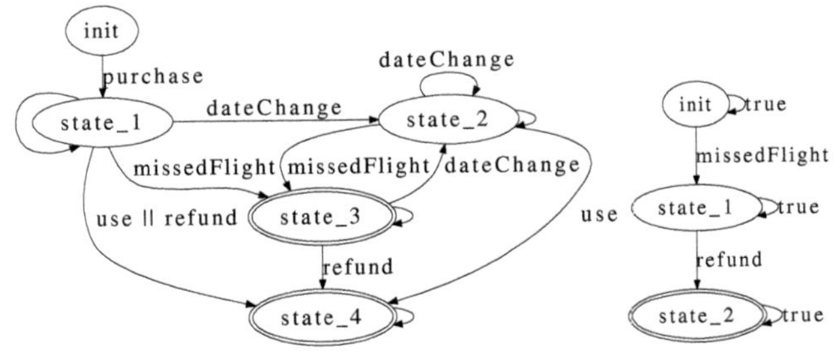

(a) (b)

Figure 1: BAs for: (a) **Ticket A** of Example 2 (no refund after a date change AND unlimited date changes, (b) a query asking for a refund after a missed flight. Double circled states are final. **For readability:** In (a), we assume that every label is a conjunction containing a literal for every event mentioned in the contract. We show only the positive ones, e.g. $refund$ is short for $refund \wedge \neg purchase \wedge \neg missedFlight \wedge \neg dateChange \wedge \neg use$. No label means that all the events are negated.

2.3 Data model

In order to reason on temporal clauses expressed in LTL, we make use of an important connection [28] between LTL and a particular kind of finite state automata, called Büchi automata (BA). Exploiting results in [28], many tools (e.g. [12]) build a BA accepting all and only the sequences that satisfy a given set of declarative LTL clauses. As we will see, this reduces our problem to searching a database of BAs representing contracts, while checking an individual contract reduces to exploring paths in its BA.

Büchi automata (BA) are similar to standard finite state automata, with the exception that they recognize infinite strings. The BA acceptance condition is that a string is accepted if the recognizing automaton traverses a final state infinitely many times. Note that the labels of our BAs are conjunctions of literals (i.e. conditions postulating the existence (positive) or absence (negated) of a single event in a snapshot, e.g. $purchase$, $\neg use$) that have to be satisfied by the current snapshot, in order for the transition to be enabled during recognition (Figure 1).

To some readers the choice of using infinite sequences might seem unnecessarily complicated. We note, however, that using infinite sequences does not reduce the expressive power of the formalism, as any finite sequence can be encoded simply appending an infinite list of dummy snapshots. Moreover, for technical reasons, infinite sequences are the standard formalization when reasoning about temporal properties [28].

We provide now an intuitive example of BAs in our context (the formal definitions can be found in §6.2.1).

EXAMPLE 6. *Let us consider the Büchi automaton in figure 1b. If we use the automaton to recognize a sequence of snapshots, it is easy to check that it will accept it if and only if this sequence contains a snapshot in which $missedFlight$ is true and in at least one snapshot after that $refund$ is true. Indeed, recall that the accepting condition is that the automaton traverses* `state_2` *infinitely many times. Since this state has a self loop with* `true` *as label, it means that once that state is reached, it will always be part of a cycle, and thus traversed infinitely many times.*

3. SYSTEM ARCHITECTURE

In §3.1 we introduce an algorithm that checks permission of a query by a contract using their BA representations. This algorithm suggests a straightforward implementation for our brokering system. At registration time, a contract LTL specification is translated to an equivalent BA representation that is the one stored. In our prototype we use an existing tool [12] to perform this stage. At query time, the query in LTL form is converted to an equivalent

BA in the same way and then checked (using the above mentioned algorithm) against all the contract BAs in the database. As we will see in §3.1, however, the permission problem has a high complexity lower bound, which makes such an approach impractical.

We expect our contract database to be fairly static and each contract to be queried multiple times. Our indexing techniques (§4 and §5) share the common idea of precomputing some auxiliary information during the registration step, in order to achieve faster online query processing. In essence, we are indexing a set of BAs for permission lookup.

3.1 Algorithm

Our algorithm uses the BA representations of a contract and a query to check if the first permits the second. From the BA accepting condition in §2.3 and Example 6, it follows immediately that, to accept a sequence, there is a path through the states of a recognizing BA that is formed by concatenating a finite simple path (*prefix*) that leads to a final state k (called *knot*) and by iterating infinitely many times through a simple *cycle* that leads back to k. These kind of paths are called *lasso paths*. They are infinite but have a finite representation, consisting of the prefix and the cycle.

A classical result [28] states that a sequence ρ satisfies a temporal property φ if and only if any BA for φ traverses a lasso path while recognizing ρ. We refer again to §6.2.1 for a formal treatment of BA in our context.

Now recall Definition 1 in §2.1. Assuming that both the contract and the query are represented by the BAs of all their allowed sequences, we provide below the intuition that the lasso path concept can be exploited for a permission checking algorithm.

EXAMPLE 7. *Let us consider the contract BA in figure 1a and the query in figure 1b. It is easy to see that the sequences that are accepted by both automata satisfy a lasso path of the form* $\{init,$ $1, ..., 1, 3, ..., 3, 4, 4, ...\ \}$ *in the contract BA, and of the form* $\{init,$ $.., init, 1, ..., 1, 2, 2, ...\ \}$ *in the query BA.*

Intuitively, we see that we can build a sequence that satisfies a lasso path for both the contract BA and the query BA (i.e. we just need to synchronize the traversal of the transitions $1 \rightarrow 3$ *in the contract BA with the* $init \rightarrow 1$ *in the query BA and* $3 \rightarrow 4$ *with* $1 \rightarrow 2$*). Note that in this process we tried to pair the labels on the mentioned transitions (evidently not all labels are 'compatible').*

The intuition in Example 7 rests on the concept of pairing a lasso path on the contract BA with another lasso path on the query BA. We can provide a more precise intuition by introducing the concept of *simultaneous lasso path*.

Definition 2. A *simultaneous lasso path* is a sequence of pairs of states $\langle s_i, q_i \rangle_{i \geq 0}$ so that:

1. $\langle s_i \rangle_{i \geq 0}$ is a lasso path in the contract BA
2. $\langle q_i \rangle_{i \geq 0}$ is a lasso path in the query BA
3. for every i, the label α_i of the ith transition of $\langle q_i \rangle_{i \geq 0}$ and the label σ_i of the ith transition of $\langle s_i \rangle_{i \geq 0}$ are *compatible*. This happens when: (i) α_i refers only to events in the contract, and (ii) α_i and σ_i do not conflict (i.e. if α_i contains *dateChange*, σ_i cannot contain $\neg$*dateChange*)

In §6.2.1 we formally treat this intuition, resulting in:

THEOREM 1. *Let C be a contract and q a query. There exists a simultaneous-lasso path in the BAs representing C and q if and only if C permits q.*

Note that simultaneous lasso paths as in Definition 2 are infinite. However, we can finitely represent them with the prefixes and cycles for both the contract and query lasso paths. Given a BA, note that there exists a finite number of simple paths that can be used as prefixes and cycles. This provides us with a finite search space for all possible lasso path representations. It follows that, using Theorem 1, we can naively solve the permission problem by generating all possible representations of lasso paths for the query and contract BAs and then checking if they are a simultaneous lasso path (i.e. they satisfy Definition 2). This naive algorithm implies decidability of the permission problem.

A better algorithm can be coded with a simple backtracking search on the two BAs. We refer to §6.2 for the complete description of the algorithm. However, the details provided in this section suffice to follow the presentation of our indexing techniques.

Complexity The backtracking search results in a LOGSPACE complexity in the size of the BAs. The size of BAs, however, is known to be worst case exponential in the size of the original clauses (i.e. contract specifications and queries) [28]. This results in a PSPACE upper bound. With a reduction from LTL satisfiability [22] we prove in [6] that the bound is tight and the problem is indeed PSPACE-complete. While this complexity implies an exponential running time, it is not an impediment to a practical implementation, for two reasons. First, the exponentiality is in the size of the query and a single contract, both of which are relatively small compared to the size of the contract database. Second, the translation from clauses to BA seldom results in an exponential blowup. Indeed, our experiments confirm that a practical implementation is feasible due to the indexing techniques described next.

4. PREFILTERING INDEX

The technique that we present in this section reduces the number of executions of the verification algorithm by pruning the number of contracts to test. At registration time, an index data structure is updated with information about the contract. At query time, the index is used to identify a set of contracts which is guaranteed to contain all contracts permitting the query. The permission algorithm can then run only on these contracts (*candidates*).

At a high level, the technique extracts a necessary condition for permission from the query BA (called *pruning condition*), it then uses the index data structure to quickly identify the set of candidate contracts satisfying that condition.

4.1 Pruning Conditions

EXAMPLE 8. *Consider the query BA in Figure 2c. Since permission is checked looking for a simultaneous lasso path, it is clear that, in order to permit this query, a contract BA must have some transitions that are compatible (as in Definition 2, point 3) with both formulas:* $dateChange$ *and* use*. Otherwise, no simultaneous lasso path can be built. While this condition is necessary, it is clearly not sufficient: the contract in Figure 2a has such transitions but does not permit the stated query.*

We now generalize the idea of Example 8. From Theorem 1 we know that we have to build a simultaneous lasso path. This means that, by definition, a lasso path has to exist in the query BA. We also know that all transitions in this query lasso path have to be 'compatible' to their simultaneous transitions in the contract BA. It follows that in the contract BA, at the very least, there has to exist one compatible label for every label in the query lasso path.

From this observation, it follows that if we find all lasso paths in the query BA, we can create a set of candidates by gathering all contracts whose BAs contain a compatible label for every label of a query lasso path. The problem is that the number of query lasso paths is exponential in the size of the query automaton. However, we never explicitly compute all lasso paths, as we can extract a more compact representation directly from the query BA.

In order to explain this, we assume access to a data structure that returns $S(\lambda)$, the set of contracts in the repository that contain a label compatible with a given query BA label λ. We will describe

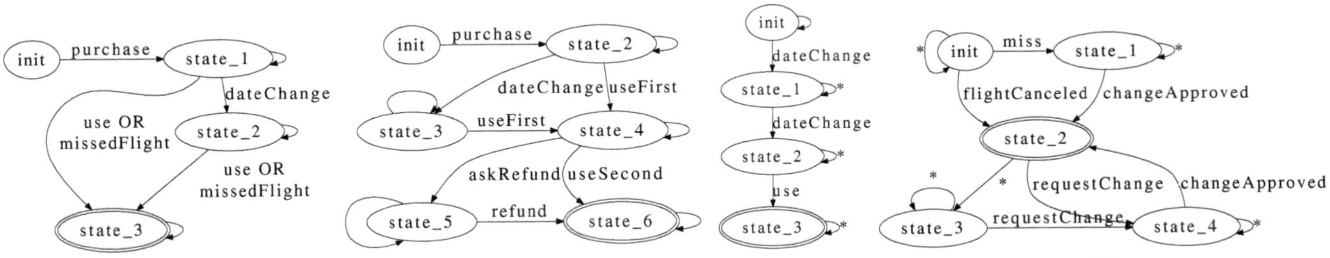

(a) (b) (c) (d)

Figure 2: Büchi automata for (a) a ticket that allows no refunds and date changes only before the scheduled departure (**Ticket C** of Example 2), (b) a round-trip ticket allowing a single change before the first flight and a refund for the second one, (c) a query asking for two date changes, (d) a query asking for tickets that can be changed indefinitely even after a flight is canceled or it is missed and already rescheduled once. Double circled states are final. **Note**: BA (a) and (b) follow the same convention as Figure 1a.

the implementation of this data structure in §4.2.

EXAMPLE 9. *Consider the query BA in Figure 2d. It only contains a single final state* `state_2`. *In order to build a lasso path knotted in* `state_2`, *we need to have both a prefix and a cycle. By visual inspection, there are only two possible prefixes that are simple paths (i.e. do not contain cycles): one with label $flightCanceled$, the other with $miss$ and $changeApproved$. We do not consider the self-loops in* `init` *and* `state_1` *(and any other cycle) because their labels are not strictly necessary to build a prefix, so we cannot exclude any contract for not having them. Knowing all the possible prefixes, it follows that all the contracts that contain labels compatible with these prefixes are in the following set:*

$S(flightCancelled) \cup (S(miss) \cap S(changeApproved))$

The idea is that this set will be smaller than the whole database. We can also prune other contracts by considering the cycles of the query lasso paths knotted in `state_2`. *Since the transition from* `state_2` *to* `state_3` *is labeled with $true$, it provides no way to prune any service. It follows that in order to go from* `state_2` *to* `state_4` *we can only force the presence of a transition compatible with $requestChange$. In order to reach back* `state_2` *we need $changeApproved$. Adding this condition to the previous one (i.e. intersecting the two sets), we know that we need to run the permission algorithm only for contracts in the following set:*

$(S(flightCancelled) \cup (S(miss) \cap S(changeApproved))) \cap (S(requestChange) \cap S(changeApproved))$ □

In Example 9 we generated a set of candidates from a condition derived from the analysis of lasso paths knotted in `state_2`. We call conditions of this kind *lasso pruning conditions*. A lasso pruning condition for a knot k selects all contracts that permit the query with a simultaneous lasso path whose query lasso is knotted in k.

It is clear that any contract permitting the query in Example 9 will permit it with a simultaneous lasso path whose query lasso is knotted in `state_2`. This is because the query BA has a single final state. In general, a query BA contains more than one final state.Since any simultaneous lasso path is enough to guarantee permission, we have to build a lasso pruning condition for every final state and then take the union of the sets retrieved by them.

Our implementation, fully described in [6], exploits a memoization scheme to compute lasso pruning conditions, that results in a linear complexity w.r.t. the query BA size.

4.2 Index data structure

In §4.1, we assumed a way to easily compute $S(\lambda)$, i.e. the set of contracts in the repository that contain a label compatible with a query BA label λ. We will now introduce the index data structure that we use to perform this operation.

At a high level, we have to find a way to identify labels that are compatible with λ, and then gather all contracts containing them. Clearly, we do not want to scan the set of all labels in the contract database. The main idea is to use the literals of λ to navigate a data structure that contains sets of contracts.

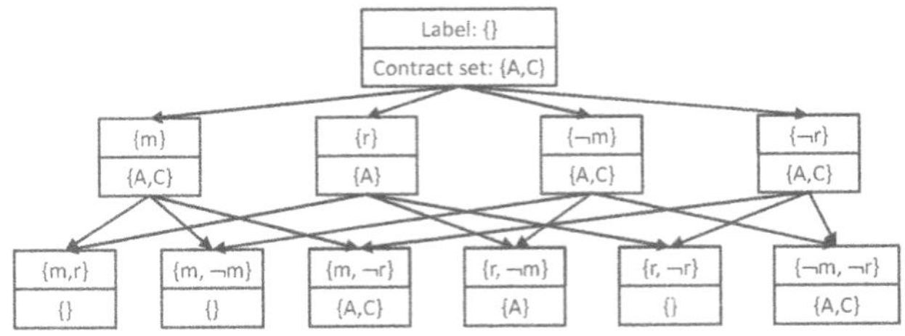

Figure 3: Prefilter index for the two contracts in Figure 1a (**Ticket A**, called A) and 2a (**Ticket C**, called C). For readability we only show nodes with labels containing events *missedFlight* (m) and *refund* (r) and the structure is limited to the first two levels.

Let us assume, for ease of presentation, that each label in contract BAs contains all events in the contract vocabulary (we shall drop this assumption shortly). This means that checking compatibility can be peformed simply by checking that the λ literals are included in the contract labels' literals. Since in the labels the order of literals is not important, the problem reduces to searching in a collection of sets for superstes of a query set. For this purpose we modify a standard TRIE [11] data structure by making it a simple directed acyclic graph (Figure 3). The root is connected with nodes labeled with single literals. Every node labeled with a literal l in this first 'level' is connected with nodes in a second level that are labeled with a set of two literals containing l, and so on. Clearly, this structure is not a tree because, for instance, a node in the second level labeled $\{a, \neg b\}$ is reachable from the node $\{a\}$ and the node $\{\neg b\}$. We, also, associate each node labeled with the set of literals l to the set of contracts whose BAs have at least one transition with a label containing l. Now, in order to retrieve $S(\lambda)$, we just navigate the graph to the node labeled with the literals in λ, and output its associated set of contracts. This lookup is linear in the number of literals in λ and independent of the number of contracts.

EXAMPLE 10. *Consider the two contracts in Figure 1a (**Ticket A**) and 2a (**Ticket C**), called A and C. For readability, we show only a partial view of the full data structure in Figure 3 (only events $missedFlight$ and $refund$, only the first two levels). Remember that the BAs in Figures 1a and 2a show only the positive literals, as noted in Figure 1a. So, for instance, both BAs have a transition labeled $missedFlight$ in the pictures, that actually stands for $missedFlight \wedge \neg refund$, considering for readability only the aforementioned events. This results in A and C being added to the nodes labeled $\{missedFlight, refund\}$, $\{missedFlight\}$ and $\{refund\}$. Note how only **Ticket A** has a label with $refund$.*

If we consider the query in Figure 1b, it is easy to see that a lasso pruning condition is $S(m) \cap S(r)$. Trivially, $S(m)$ is the set *of contracts associated with the node labeled m and evaluates to $\{A, C\}$. $S(r)$ is $\{A\}$. The whole condition selects the candidate $\{A\}$. Using the prefiltering technique, we avoid the execution of the permission checking algorithm on contract C.*

In Example 10, the transitions of contract BAs always contain all events mentioned in the contracts. This allowed us to use our previous assumption and check compatibility using containment. This is not always the case, but we present now a way to reduce compatibility to containment by introducing additional literals to the nodes' labels. First, we note that the reason our previous assumption does not work in general is because, in order to check compatibility between λ and γ, we might have to consider not only the literals in γ but also the ones cited in its contract c. This is the case, for instance, if γ is the boolean formula $refund$, in a contract that cites both $refund$ and $dateChange$. We have then that both labels, $refund \wedge dateChange$ and $refund \wedge \neg dateChange$ are compatible with γ. In order to treat compatibility checks as containment checks, we create a set for γ (called the *expansion*, $\mathcal{E}(\gamma)$) that contains all literals in γ plus all literals (both positive and negative) for any remaining event cited in its contract.

EXAMPLE 11. *Let us consider a transition label $t = p \wedge c$ from a contract that cites the events p, c and m. Given the above definition we have that its expansion $\mathcal{E}(p \wedge c) = \{p, c, m, \neg m\}$. We have that a query transition $q = p \wedge m$ is compatible with t, because $\{p, m\} \in \mathcal{E}(p \wedge c)$. And $q' = p \wedge \neg c$ and $q'' = c \wedge r$ are not, because $\{p, \neg c\} \notin \mathcal{E}(p \wedge c)$ and $\{c, r\} \notin \mathcal{E}(p \wedge c)$.*

Now, we can adopt the same strategy shown in Example 10 just by changing the contract set associated to each node. Every node labeled with a set of literals l is now associated with the set of contracts whose BAs have at least a transition with label γ *s.t.* $\mathcal{E}(\gamma)$ *contains* l.

The problem we face in the implementation and scaling of this solution is that the number of possible node labels is exponential in the size of the vocabulary. This means that the index grows exponentially in size, leading to intractability. In order to avoid this exponential blow up, we limit the size of node labels (i.e. the number of 'levels' of the data structure) to a predefined number k. We now have to deal with the lack of nodes with labels greater than k, as nothing changes when retrieving $S(\lambda)$ with $|\lambda| \leq k$. On the other hand, when we retrieve $S(\lambda)$ with $|\lambda| > k$, we can just take any set associated with a node whose label l *is contained in* the literals of λ. We call this set $S'(\lambda)$ and, by construction, $S'(\lambda)$ contains $S(\lambda)$.

This modification does not affect the soundness and completeness of the technique because pruning conditions need to evaluate to a set that just *contains* a certain set of contracts (§4.1). Since conditions use only union and intersection operators, they are monotonic. This means that the fact that the $S'()$ returned by the data structure are supersets of the required $S()$ results in a set of candidates that is a superset of the one returned if we were using the correct $S()$. Since all candidates will be checked with our permission algorithm and we are returning a superset of the original set of candidates, soundness and completeness are preserved.

5. BISIMULATION INDEX

In this section we describe an indexing technique that is based on the observation that the query usually pertains to a much smaller set of events than the full contract specification. At registration time, we precompute a set of simplified versions of every contract BA. Intuitively, these simplified versions can be thought as 'projections' of the full contract specification on a subset of events (i.e. albeit smaller, they faithfully represent the behavior of the contract with respect only to the considered events). At query time, our system retrieves the appropriate precomputed 'projection' for each candidate contract that has to be checked for permission.

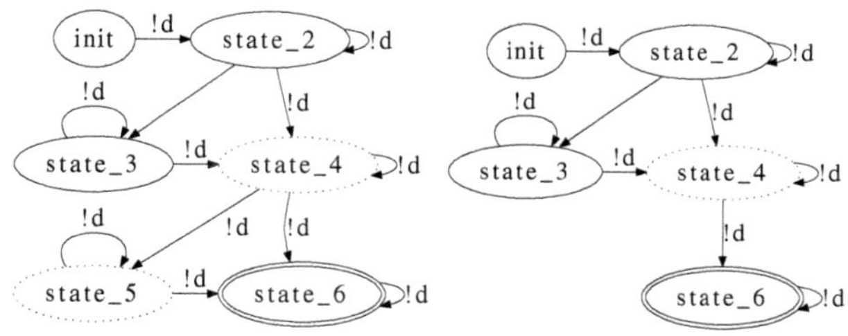

(a) (b)

Figure 4: The dotted states can be substituted with a single one, when checking permission w.r.t. query regarding only *dateChange*. For readability: *d* = *dateChange*. (a) projection of BA in Figure 2b on ¬ *dateChange*. (b) simplified version of (a).

5.1 Simplified contract automaton

We will show now how we use a simplified version in lieu of the full contract BA.First we define a notion of equivalence with respect to a query q: two contracts BA $\mathcal{A}$ and $\mathcal{B}$ are *equivalent* if they both either permit or do not permit q. From Theorem 1, it follows that this is the case if and only if we can build simultaneous lasso paths with the query BA for $\mathcal{A}$ and $\mathcal{B}$, or we fail for both.

We will now show how to simplify the transitions of a contract BA in order to obtain a *projection* BA that is equivalent to the original one w.r.t. a query. Then, we will reduce the number of states of this projection obtaining a *simplified* BA, on which to run our permission algorithm.

Let us start by simplifying the transitions. First, remember that in order to build a simultaneous lasso path we need two lasso paths (one for the contract BA, one for the query BA) whose transitions are compatible in every instant. It follows that the only information needed to find this simultaneous lasso path is if a contract label is compatible with a query label. For instance, if a query BA has transitions that contain only the labels $true$ and $dateChange$, the only information we need to derive compatibility (besides knowing all events in the contract) is the presence of $\neg dateChange$ in the contract transitions. It should be intuitive now why it is useful to introduce the concept of projection. Given a contract BA $\mathcal{A}$ and a set of literals L, we call *projection* of $\mathcal{A}$ on L (i.e. $\pi_L(\mathcal{A})$) the BA built from $\mathcal{A}$ by keeping in every label only literals in L, e.g. Figure 4a represents the projection BA on $\neg dateChange$ of the BA in Figure 2b.

In Theorem 5, §6.3, we formalize the following result:

THEOREM 2. *Given a BA $\mathcal{A}$ and a set of literals L, the projection of $\mathcal{A}$ on L is equivalent to $\mathcal{A}$ for all query BAs that refer to literals that are either negations of literals in L or pertain to events not in cited in $\mathcal{A}$.*

The use of projections alone does not improve the performance of the permission checking algorithm as the size of the projection BA is the same as the original one. Projections are, however, simpler BAs than their original counterparts in the sense that many transitions that had different labels have now the same label.

This provides the opportunity to use a standard state reduction technique [10] that produces a BA that is equivalent to the original one (i.e. it accepts the same set of strings). This classical polynomial-time technique is based on *collapsing* bisimilar states (i.e. replacing them with their bisimilarity class) and is the same used for the minimization of standard finite state automata [15]. In the case of BAs it does not produce the minimum BA (BA minimization is PSPACE-hard [23]), it does provide, however, significant reductions in the number of states of our projections. This allows us to equivalently check our query on a contract BA that is a projection of our original one but that has significatly fewer states.

EXAMPLE 12. *In Figure 4a we show a BA derived from a projection, where we have two states (`state_4` and `state_5`) that can be collapsed. Intuitively, once the recognizing BA reaches either of those states, it will accept* the exact same set of sequences, *i.e. an infinite sequence of snapshots containing* $\neg dateChange$. *Its simplification is shown in 4b.*

5.2 Using simplified BAs

The previous section details how we can equivalently use simplified projections to check permission. As we already anticipated at the beginning of the section, for every contract we precompute the projections at registration time, so that when our system has to check permission of a query, it can use the precomputed simplified projection. Clearly, the most appropriate projection is the smallest one that is still equivalent to the original BA for the current query.

Given the result in Theorem 2, it is easy to see that in order to have the smallest projection for every possible query, we need to have one projection for every subset of literals cited in the contract. The problem that immediately arises is the fact that the number of possible projections is, in the worst case, exponential in the size of the set of events of the contract. We have, however, two important observations that enable us to pursue the precomputation route.

The first observation is that we do not need to precompute all projections, as we can use *any* projection that contains all required literals for the query, albeit with a possible perfomance penalty. The second observation is that, in practice, not all subsets of literals generate distinct simplified projection BAs, e.g. in our datasets the number of distinct simplified projection BAs was $\sim 5\%$ of the number of subsets. Intuitively, removing a single event from a projection does not usually lead to a simplification of the observed behavior of the others. It follows that it is often the case that the simplifications are triggered only when whole sets of 'independent' events are excluded from the projection. Both these observations provide us great freedom in designing a system that balances runtime performance with precomputation time and storage needs.

Storage needs are quite contained, since we do not need to store a graph for every projection. Since we have the original contract BA, we can just memorize the list of bisimilar states for a particular projection. With some care in the implementation, the permission algorithm does not incur any substantial overhead.

To address precomputation time, we designed a novel algorithm that efficiently computes all simplifications in parallel. We could not use the standard bisimulation algorithm ([19]), as we would have had to run it for every subset of literals. Our algorithm avoids testing subsets that are not going to result in simplifications and reuses partial computations between different subsets. For space reasons, we relegate the description of this algorithm to [6].

In our experiments we found it feasible to precompute all projections. In the case that contract complexity grows in a way that precludes full precomputation, we can limit it to subsets of literals up to a certain size k. This would not affect the evaluation perfomance of queries with less or exactly k literals, which are the ones that mostly benefit from this technique, as the contract BAs gets significantly simplified. It would affect the evaluation performance of queries with more than k literals, which, however, mostly benefit from the complementary prefiltering index. Other possible approaches to address increasing precomputation times include the use of heuristics based on historical data and/or expected workloads to determine which simplification to precompute.

6. FORMAL TREATMENT

6.1 Permission Problem

The formal counterpart of our intuitive notion of temporal sequence is the *run*. A *run* ρ is a function $\rho(t) : \mathbb{N} \rightarrow T(\mathcal{V})$, where $\mathbb{N}$ are the natural numbers, $T(\mathcal{V})$ is the set of truth assignments for the event variables in $\mathcal{V}$, and t a particular instant. The 'tail' of the run starting at instant i is written as $\rho|_i$.

The semantics of LTL is given inductively for all boolean operators and for the temporal operators (**X**, **U**). Note that all temporal operators can be derived from **X** and **U** (e.g. $\mathbf{F}\varphi \equiv \mathit{true}\ \mathbf{U}\ \varphi$, $\mathbf{G}\varphi \equiv \neg\mathbf{F}(\neg\varphi)$, $\varphi\mathbf{B}\psi \equiv \neg(\neg\varphi\ \mathbf{U}\ \psi)$). A run ρ *satisfies* an LTL formula φ (i.e. $\rho \models \varphi$), iff, inductively:

- $\rho \models p$, with $p \in \mathcal{V}$, iff p is true in $\rho(0)$
- $\rho \models \mathbf{X}\varphi$, iff $\rho|1 \models \varphi$
- $\rho \models \phi\mathbf{U}\psi$, iff $\exists k \geq 0$ s.t. $\rho|k \models \psi$ and $\forall 0 \leq i < k(\rho|i \models \phi)$
- closure w.r.t. boolean operators ($\wedge$, $\neg$)

Remember from the discussion in §2.1 that our intuitive semantics did not take into account the behavior of events that were not explicitly cited in the contract. In particular, we wanted to avoid cases where the behavior of a variable not cited in the contract specification results in the contract permission of a query that is not intended to be supported by the contract. In order to formalize this intuition we introduce the following concepts.

Definition 3. The *projection* of a run ρ w.r.t a set of event variables V (a V-projection), is a sequence σ that assigns to the variables in V the same truth values assigned by ρ, and does not assign any truth value to other variables. A run ρ is *compatible* with a V-projection σ, if σ assigns in every instant the same truth values of ρ to all variables in V. The set of all runs compatible with a V-projection is called *projection class.*

Definition 4. Given an LTL formula φ, let V be the set of its variables. We call $P(\varphi)$ *(set of allowed projections of a contract* specified by φ) the set of V-projections of all runs satisfying φ.

Definition 5. Given an LTL formula φ, let V be the set of its variables. The contract defined by φ (referred to as $C(\varphi)$) *permits* an LTL query ψ iff there exists a V-projection $\sigma \in P(\varphi)$ s.t. *all* runs in its projection class satisfy ψ.

Intuitively, forcing the property to be true for all runs in a projection class avoids the case when a run triggers permission only due to truth assignments of variables not mentioned in the contract.

EXAMPLE 13. *Consider a query q that is satisfied by a run ρ of a contract only because of the behavior of variable v. This means that without the specific behavior of the variable v, q would not be permitted, as is the case in Example 4 for the variable 'class upgrade'. Note that in the projection class of ρ there is a run ρ' that does not exhibit the same behavior for v, as v is not part of the contract vocabulary. It follows that q is not satisfied by all runs in a projection class and thus it is not permitted by the contract.*

6.2 Checking permission

It is easily seen that Definition 5 can be rephrased to:

Definition 6. A contract $C(\varphi)$ with vocabulary V *permits* a query ψ iff the intersection of the set of runs satisfying φ with the set of runs satisfying ψ, contains a projection class w.r.t. V.

This alternative definition is more suited for the design of an algorithm as we could think of computing the intersection of the two sets, and then checking the presence of a projection class in the intersection. The first part of this algorithm is very similar to the non-empty intersection problem, extensively studied in other domains (e.g. model checking [25]). To solve this problem the theoretical tool of choice are Büchi automata (BA), which have a deeply exploited connection with LTL [28]. Using BAs, we design a new algorithm that solves the problem with a single step: scanning the intersection of the two sets of runs and, simultaneusly, checking that it includes a complete projection class.

6.2.1 Büchi automata

Formally, a Büchi automaton is a tuple $\{Q, I, \delta, F\}$, where Q is the set of states, I the initial states and F the final ones. The transition relation is $\delta \subseteq Q \times \Sigma \times Q$, where Σ is the set of disjunction-free propositional formula over $\mathcal{V}$ (e.g. Figure 1).

In order to define the semantics we introduce the concept of *path* as an infinite sequence of states $\sigma = \sigma_1, \sigma_2, \ldots$, linked by transitions in δ (i.e. $\forall i(\exists\lambda(\langle\sigma_i, \lambda, \sigma_{i+1}\rangle \in \delta))$). A path is called *lasso path* if it is formed by a finite *prefix* leading to a final state k (called *knot*) and by a *cycle*, iterated infinitely many times, leading back to k. Intuitively, a run ρ *satisfies* a path σ if at any instant i the truth assignment $\rho(i)$ satisfies the formula labeling the transition from σ_i to σ_{i+1}. Following the result in [28], the accepting condition can be stated as: a BA $\mathcal{A}$ accepts a run ρ, if ρ satisfies a lasso path of $\mathcal{A}$. We call $BA(\varphi)$ any BA that accepts all and only the runs satisfying an LTL formula φ. We assume that the transition labels of $BA(\varphi)$ contain only variables in φ.

Consider now the problem of verifying that a contract permits a property. They are both specified as LTL formulae, but our approach will handle them in form of BAs. As in §3.1, we formalize this idea by introducing the concept of *simultaneous lasso path.*

Definition 7. Given a contract defined by φ (referred to as $C(\varphi)$) and a query ψ. Let $\mathcal{A}(\varphi) = \{Q_\mathcal{A}, I_\mathcal{A}, \delta_\mathcal{A}, F_\mathcal{A}\}$ be a BA for $C(\varphi)$ and $\mathcal{B}(\psi) = \{Q_\mathcal{B}, I_\mathcal{B}, \delta_\mathcal{B}, F_\mathcal{B}\}$ a BA for ψ, we define a *simultaneous lasso path* an infinite sequence of pairs $\langle s_i, q_i\rangle_{i\geq 0}$ s.t.:

1. $\langle s_i\rangle_{i\geq 0}$ form a lasso path for $\mathcal{A}$
2. $\langle q_i\rangle_{i\geq 0}$ form a lasso path for $\mathcal{B}$
3. for every i, there exist θ_i a formula s.t. $\langle s_i, \theta_i, s_{i+1}\rangle \in \delta_\mathcal{A}$ and τ_i s.t. $\langle q_i, \tau_i, q_{i+1}\rangle \in \delta_\mathcal{B}$, and we have that $\theta_i \wedge \tau_i$ is satisfiable (i.e. they are not conflicting), and τ_i contains only variables in $C(\varphi)$. We say that θ_i and τ_i are *compatible.*

The following theorem, proved in [6], formalizes the intuition.

THEOREM 3. *Let $C(\varphi)$ be a contract with variables in V and ψ a query. There exists a simultaneous-lassopath for $C(\varphi)$ and ψ iff $C(\varphi)$ permits ψ.*

As explained in §3.1, this theorem implies that the permission problem is decidable.

6.2.2 Algorithm

Our verification algorithm looks for a simultaneous lasso path in a way inspired by the nested depth first search technique used in model checking [25], which despite solving a different problem also relies on finding lasso paths.

Recalling that a lasso path is formed by a prefix and a cycle we now define similar concepts for simultaneous lasso paths. We call *knot* any pair $\langle s_i, q_i\rangle$ s.t. it appears infinitely many times in the simultaneous lasso path and q_i is a final state for the query BA. We call prefix w.r.t. a knot k, the portion of the simultaneous lasso path from the beginning to the first appearance of k. In order to define the cycle of a simultaneous lasso path, we have to consider the fact that the sequence $\langle s_i\rangle_{i\geq 0}$ has to be a lasso path for the contract BA. This means that we need to force the existence of a contract final state in the contract BA portion of the simultaneous lasso path. More formally, let i be the instant of the first appearance of a knot k and let $j > i$ be the instant of the first appearance of a pair $\langle s_i, q_i\rangle$ where s_i is a final state for the contract BA, we call

---

Algorithm 1: Verifying that $C(\varphi)$ permits property ψ

Input: $\mathcal{A} = \{Q_\mathcal{A}, i_\mathcal{A}, \delta_\mathcal{A}, F_\mathcal{A}\}$ is the service BA,
$\mathcal{B} = \{Q_\mathcal{B}, i_\mathcal{B}, \delta_\mathcal{B}, F_\mathcal{B}\}$ is the query BA,
(w.l.o.g. they have a single initial state)
ψ, an LTL query property
Output: returns *true* if $S(\varphi)$ permits ψ

1 **begin**
2 visited = $\varnothing$
3 found = *false*
4 visit ($\langle i_\mathcal{A}, i_\mathcal{B}\rangle$)
5 **return** *found*
6 **end**
7 **procedure** visit ($\langle s, q\rangle$)
8 **begin**
9 **if** $\langle s, q\rangle \in$ *visited* **then return**
10 visited $\Leftarrow$ visited $\cup\{\langle s, q\rangle\}$
11 **if** $q \in F_\mathcal{B}$ **then**
12 visited2 $\Leftarrow \varnothing$
13 cycle_search ($\langle s, q\rangle, \langle s, q\rangle$, *false*)
14 **if** *found* **then return**
15 **foreach** $\langle s, \lambda_\mathcal{A}, s'\rangle \in \delta_\mathcal{A}$ **do**
16 **foreach** $\langle q, \lambda_\mathcal{B}, q'\rangle \in \delta_\mathcal{B}$ *s.t. compatible*($\lambda_\mathcal{A}, \lambda_\mathcal{B}$) **do**
17 visit ($\langle s', q'\rangle$)
18 **if** *found* **then return**
19 **end**
20 **procedure** cycle_search ($\langle s, q\rangle$, *start*, *foundFinal*)
21 **begin**
22 foundFinal2 $\Leftarrow$ foundFinal $\vee(s \in F_\mathcal{A})$
23 **if** $\langle s, q\rangle \in$ *visited2* **then return**
24 visited2 $\Leftarrow$ visited2 $\cup\{\langle s, q\rangle\}$
25 **foreach** $\langle s, \lambda_\mathcal{A}, s'\rangle \in \delta_\mathcal{A}$ **do**
26 **foreach** $\langle q, \lambda_\mathcal{B}, q'\rangle \in \delta_\mathcal{B}$ *s.t. compatible*($\lambda_\mathcal{A}, \lambda_\mathcal{B}$) **do**
27 **if** $\langle s', q'\rangle$ = *start* **then**
28 found $\Leftarrow$ foundFinal2
29 cycle_search ($\langle s', q'\rangle$, *start*, *foundFinal2*)
30 **if** *found* **then return**
31 visited2 $\Leftarrow$ visited2 $\setminus\{\langle s, q\rangle\}$
32 **end**

---

cycle w.r.t. a knot k, the portion of the simultaneous lasso path between i and the first subsequent appearance of k after j.

In order to verify the existence of a prefix and a cycle, we consider the initial pair, then we consider all possible prefixes using a recursive depth first search: for every pair we inspect both input BAs (contract and query), build all possible successor pairs (i.e. those satisfying condition 3 of Def. 7) and recurse on each of those.

Since we do not know in advance the length of the prefix, at every step, if the considered pair $s = \langle s_i, q_i\rangle$ is a potential knot (i.e. q_i is a final state for the query BA), we verify if there exists a cycle containing s. To do so, we start a nested search in s which looks for a path that leads back to s and that also contains a pair $\langle s_i, q_i\rangle$ in which s_i is a contract final state. A straightforward way to look for such cycles is to perform a backtracking depth first search that keeps track of paths containing a pair with a contract final state and returns true iff one of these paths lead back to s. Algorithm 1 implements the strategy we just outlined. Lines 1 through 6 initialize the sets of visited pairs for the depth first visit, and the global variable that will contain true iff a simultaneous lasso path is found. It then invokes the procedure visit which recursively generates all prefixes.

Lines 9 and 10 verify that we are visiting every pair once. Lines 11 through 14 test if the current pair is a potential knot (q_i is a final state). If this is the case, the data structure *visited2* is initialized and the procedure cycle_search is invoked. If it returns successfully, the procedure terminates. Lines 15-18 generate all possible successor pairs by inspecting the transitions in the contract BA

Table 1: LTL precedence pattern (s precedes p), from [9]

Global	$\mathbf{F}p \rightarrow (\neg p\mathbf{U}(s \vee \neg p))$
Before r	$\mathbf{F}r \rightarrow (\neg p\mathbf{U}(s \vee r))$
After q	$\mathbf{G}(\neg q) \vee \mathbf{F}(q \wedge (\neg p\mathbf{U}(s \vee \mathbf{G}(\neg p))))$
Between q and r	$\mathbf{G}((q \wedge \mathbf{F}r) \rightarrow (\neg p\mathbf{U}(s \vee r)))$

(line 15) and in the query BA (line 16). A recursive call to `visit` is then issued for each such pair. The predicate *compatible* at line 16 (and later at line 32) implements condition 3 of Definition 7.

The procedure `cycle_search` accesses the $visited2$ variable which stores the path it is currently exploring. The variable $found$-$Final2$ is true if the current path contains a pair with a contract final state. Lines 23 and 24, avoid creating paths that contain cycles.Lines 25 and 26, generate all possible successor pairs. Line 27 and 28, update the global variable $found$ if a cycle is present which contains a pair with a contract final state. If this is not the case, line 29 and 30 recursively continue to extend the current path.Line 31 backtracks to the previous explored path by removing the current pair from the $visited2$ variable. In [6], we prove the result:

THEOREM 4. *Algorithm 1 returns true iff* $C(\varphi)$ *permits* ψ.
Note that the procedure *cycle_search* can exploit a simple memoization scheme which stores for every visited pair a boolean variable, which is true if that pair can eventually lead to the original node. In this way, we can code the whole procedure as a depth first visit, never visiting any pair more than once.

6.3 Simplified contract automaton

In this section we formalize the intuition of simplified contract automata, given in the context of our bisimulation index (§5). We say that a BA $\mathcal{A}$ is *equivalent* to a BA $\mathcal{B}$ w.r.t. a query BA $\mathcal{Q}$ iff there exists a simultaneous lasso path for $\mathcal{A}$ and $\mathcal{Q}$ iff there exists one for $\mathcal{B}$ and $\mathcal{Q}$. We consider a query BA $\mathcal{Q}$, and let $L_{\mathcal{Q}}$ be the set of literals that appear in labels of $\mathcal{Q}$. $L^{n}_{\mathcal{Q}}$ is the set that contains the negation of every literal in $L_{\mathcal{Q}}$.

Definition 8. We call the *relevant* BA $\mathcal{A}^r$ of a service BA $\mathcal{A}$ w.r.t. a query BA $\mathcal{Q}$, a BA that has the same states as $\mathcal{A}$ but that for every transition $\langle s, \chi, s'\rangle \in \delta_{\mathcal{A}}$ has $\langle s, \chi', s'\rangle \in \delta_{\mathcal{A}^r}$ s.t. χ' is a conjunction of all the literals in χ that are in $L^{n}_{\mathcal{Q}}$.
The following result formalizes Theorem 2 and is proved in [6]:

THEOREM 5. *Given a contract BA $\mathcal{A}$ and a query BA $\mathcal{B}$, there exists a simultaneous lasso path for $\mathcal{A}$ and $\mathcal{B}$ iff there exists one for its relevant BA $\mathcal{A}^r$ and $\mathcal{B}$.*

As with the minimization of traditional finite state automata [15], we use the bisimulation concept to reduce the number of states.

Definition 9. Let a and b be two nodes of a BA $\mathcal{A}$. We say that $a \sim b$ (read *bisimulates*) iff: (1) if $a \in F_{\mathcal{A}}$ then $b \in F_{\mathcal{A}}$ and vice versa, and (2) for every edge $\langle a, \lambda, a'\rangle \in \delta_{\mathcal{A}}$ we have $\langle b, \lambda, b'\rangle \in \delta_{\mathcal{A}}$ with $a' = b'$ or $a' \sim b'$, and vice versa.

We create equivalence classes of BA states (called $B(\mathcal{A})$) w.r.t. bisimulation, and we use them as the states of a new BA.

Definition 10. Given a BA $\mathcal{A}$, we call $\mathcal{A}_s$ (its *simplification*) a BA s.t. (1) $Q_{\mathcal{A}_s} = B(\mathcal{A})$, (2) $I_{\mathcal{A}_s}$ is any $s \in B(\mathcal{A})$ that contains a state in $I_{\mathcal{A}}$, (3) $F_{\mathcal{A}_s}$ is any $s \in B(\mathcal{A})$ that contains only states in $F_{\mathcal{A}}$, (4) let $C(a)$ be the bisimilarity equivalence class for the state a, for every $\langle a, \lambda, a'\rangle \in \delta_{\mathcal{A}}$ we have $\langle C(a), \lambda, C(a')\rangle \in \delta_{\mathcal{A}_s}$.

The simplification of a BA is equivalent to the original one in the following sense, proved in [6]:

THEOREM 6. *For every path $\sigma = \sigma_1, \sigma_2, \ldots$ for a BA $\mathcal{A}$ there exists a path $\sigma^s = \sigma^s_1, \sigma^s_2, \ldots$ for $\mathcal{A}_s$ and vice versa, where for all i, σ^s_i is the bisimilarity class of σ_i.*

Using Theorems 5 and 6, we prove in [6] the main result that enables our bisimulation index.

THEOREM 7. *Given a service BA $\mathcal{A}$ and a query BA $\mathcal{B}$, there exists a simultaneous lasso path for $\mathcal{A}$ and $\mathcal{B}$ iff there exists one for the simplification of its relevant BA $(\mathcal{A}^r)_s$ and $\mathcal{B}$.*

7. EXPERIMENTAL EVALUATION

7.1 Prototype Architecture

Our prototype is written in Java and consists of four independent modules. The first is the data generator and produces databases of LTL formulae as described in §7.2. It also converts the formulae to BAs using the freely available library LTL2BA [12]. Its output is a text file. The second module generates the prefiltering index from a text file containing contract specifications. The third precomputes the simplified BAs from a text file containing contract specifications. The fourth module is the runtime module. It uses the prefiltering index and the simplified BAs in order to evaluate queries. It takes as input a query workload text file and outputs statistics regarding their evaluation.

We executed all code on an AMD Phenom 2.2 GHz with 4Gb of RAM and we used Sun 32bit JVM 1.6.0.10. The code does not utilize multithreading in order to isolate the technique performance from system level effects.

7.2 Contract data generation

Given the novelty of our setting, it was impossible for us to find real databases of contract specifications. Towards a realistic generation, we adopted a sophisticated generation method based on real-life usage patterns of temporal properties ([9]). The work in [9] surveys over 500 real-life specifications of temporal properties to be formally verified on finite state systems (theoretically equivalent to our contracts) and extracts recurrently appearing patterns that cover over 92% of the surveyed cases, along with their occurring frequencies. While the specifications of these systems come from different application domains (e.g. communication protocols, GUIs, distributed object systems, operating systems, databases), we contend that the sort of properties that form these specifications are very similar to the ones found in service contracts, as they are effectively describing the allowed temporal sequences of interactions between multiple actors. In [9], patterns are classified along two dimensions: required behavior and scope (i.e. temporal interval in which the behavior has to show itself). The possible scopes include *global* (the whole timeline), *before* (up to certain event), *after* (after a given event), *between* (any part of the timeline between specified event p and event q). The possible behaviors are:

Absence An event does not occur in the scope.

Existence A given event must occur within a scope. A variation can force the occurrence number to k.

Universality A given event occurs throughout the scope.

Precedence An event p must always be preceded by an event q. A variation can consider sets of events instead of p and q.

Response An event p must always be followed by an event q. A variation can consider sets of events instead of p and q.

As an example, we show in Table 1 (from [9]) the LTL expression of the precedence behavior for the cited scopes.

Contracts and queries are generated as conjunctions of clauses expressed as LTL properties. Our generator randomly generates LTL properties using the distribution reported in [9]; at each generation it substitutes the variable placeholders (e.g. p, q) with variables from the common vocabulary. Given a parameter n, it generates a contract or query specification formed by the conjunction of n properties thus generated. We refer to [6] for detailed examples of our generated contracts and queries.

Table 2 shows the statistics of our generated datasets (i.e. contract databases and query workloads). Along with the name of the dataset we report its size (i.e. number of contracts or queries) and the number of LTL properties that form each contract or query. Since we found that the actual complexity of the LTL formulae is better characterized by the statistics of their associated BAs, we

Table 2: Datasets statistics

Dataset name	size	#LTL patterns	#states avg	#states stddev	#transitions avg	#transitions stddev
Simple contracts	3000	5	31.00	34.73	628.71	1253.37
Medium contracts	1000	6	41.82	43.23	964.69	1628.66
Complex contracts	1000	7	50.85	47.5	1291.63	1904.82
Simple queries	100	1	2.31	1.41	5.2	5.4
Medium queries	100	2	5.44	4.81	23.86	33.18
Complex queries	100	3	9.6	11.11	92.84	203.42

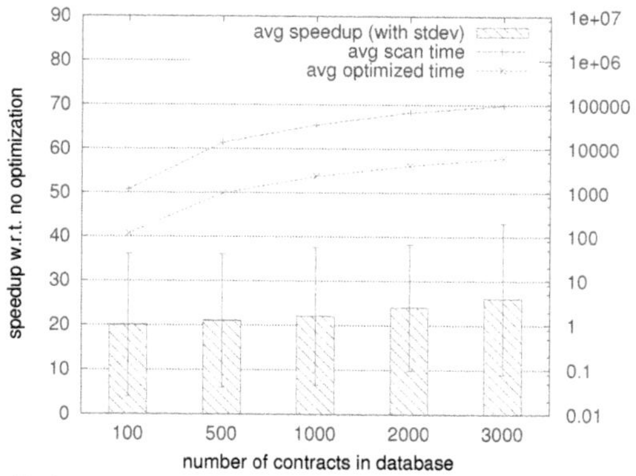

Figure 5: Average speedup and running times (unoptimized and optimized) w.r.t. database sizes (small contracts, average of all query complexities)

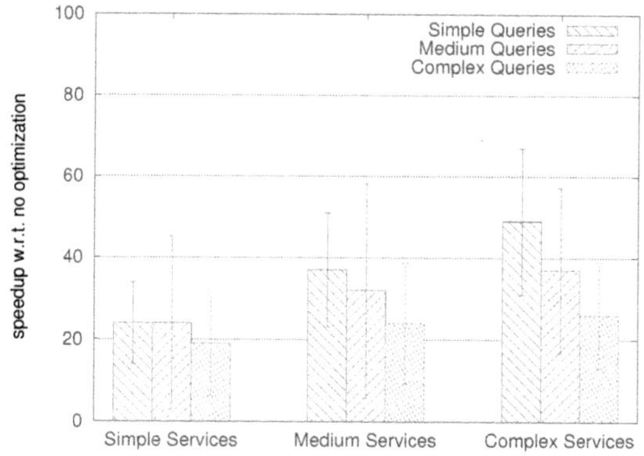

Figure 6: Average speedup w.r.t. contracts and query complexities (database size = 1000 contracts)

also report the average number of states of the BAs in the specification and its standard deviation along with the average number of transitions with its standard deviation.

7.3 Experiments

We measure the running times of query evaluation for the unoptimized system (§3) and for the system using both the prefiltering and the bisimulation techniques. The query evaluation time for the unoptimized system is the sum of the conversion time of the query from LTL to BA plus the evaluation on the contract database stored as set of contract BAs. The query evaluation time for the optimized system include the query conversion time plus the time used to evaluate the query using our precomputed data (i.e. prefilter index, simplified BAs) in addition to the contract BAs database.

A first batch of measurements aims to prove scalability w.r.t. the number of contracts in the database. We evaluate all queries (all complexity levels) on databases of sizes 100 to 3000 of simple contracts (subsets of the Simple Contract database in Table 2). For every contract database size, we record the average query evaluation time for the unoptimized and optimized systems. To some readers, these databases might seem too small for practical use. Recall, however, that a complete implementation would use relational attributes (e.g. travel date) to select the contracts that have to be checked for permission from a potentially much larger database.

A second batch of measurements aims at scalability w.r.t. complexities of both queries and contract specification. We evaluate individually every query database against contract databases of size 1000 (simple, medium, complex). For every combination of queries and contract complexities we record the query evaluation time for the unoptimized and optimized systems.

7.4 Results

First batch - Scaling w.r.t. database size. In Figure 5 the two lines at the top of the graph represent the average running time in the case of the unoptimized approach, called *scan time*, and the one of the optimized system, called *optimized time*. The times scale is on the right y axis and it is in milliseconds and logscale. The bar chart on the same picture shows the average speedup (along with standard deviation bars) achieved by the optimized system compared to the unoptimized one (the speedup scale is on the left y axis). Notice that the running times for both evaluations scale nearly linearly w.r.t. the size of the database. The unoptimized time ranges from 2sec for a small 100 contracts database to 100sec in the case of a 3000 contracts database. These times would limit the usage of our approach in interactive systems. Our optimization techniques, however, achieve an average speedup of at least 20 (scaling nicely for larger databases), reducing the average running time in the case of the 3000 contracts database to few seconds instead of minutes. Note that the speedups increase together with the size of the database, a common effect of indexing schemes. Finally, we rarely have speedups less than 10.

Second batch - Scaling w.r.t. complexity. Figure 6 reports the results for the scalabitility w.r.t. query and contract complexity. The bars represent the average speedups (along with standard deviation bars) of the optimized system compared to the unoptimized one w.r.t. complexities of both contracts in the database and queries. We explain the reduced speedup of complex queries noting that, using more variables, they cannot take advantage of the most simplified contract BAs. The bisimulation technique is also responsible for the increasing speedup w.r.t. complexities of the contracts. Usually complex contracts cite more variables and with the bisimulation technique the algorithm can ignore the behavior of all variables that are not used in the query.

Index building and size. For our optimized evaluation, each contract database required the precomputation of two data structures. The computation of the prefiltering index (§4.2) lasted less than 25 mins for our largest database of 3000 contracts. The average insertion time was around 500ms. The size is also minimal as our largest prefilter index (3000 contracts) was ~10Mb.

The computation of the simplified BAs is more expensive as we compute all possible projections. For our 3000 contract database the average insertion time of a contract is 42secs, and the total computation of our largest datasets took 11 hours on our workstation using three cores. Since the workload is completely parallel (each contract is simplified independently), scaling the number of contracts can be tackled by adding resources. Moreover, to address increase in contract complexity, we can compute only the projections with few literals, while still obtaining significant benefits. As motivated at the end of §5.2, these projections would be used by small queries, which benefit the most from this technique. The size of the simplified BAs data is on average around 80% of the database original size and in absolute terms quite contained: our largest database of 3000 contracts had a combined size (database plus simplified BAs) of 112Mb.

8. RELATED WORK

To the best of our knowledge, this is the first work that deals with the discovery of contracts based on their temporal behavior. Previous works in electronic commerce and enterprise computing have dealt with the problem of managing contracts. The field of e-contracting [2] deals with the automation of contracting practices and it is mainly tailored for the B2B case. The direction that is most relevant to the present work is the verification and monitoring of real world contracts. Contracts are usually represented using rules written in some form of temporal and/or deontic logic (i.e. stating permissions, obligations and prohibitions), [16], [18]. Both [16],[18] perform verification on contracts specified with deontic constraints. These works focus on the internal consistency of contracts, leading to the need of more expressive specification language. Queries on a *database* of contracts are never considered and we are not aware of any contract indexing scheme. Moreover, in [16] the higher order logic used to represent contracts is internally translated to Büchi Automata, opening the way to the application of our indexing techniques also for such higher order formalisms. To the best of our knowledge, our work is the first dealing with indexing of databases of Büchi Automata.

Web Service search exhibits many similarities with our problem. Web Services are complex pieces of software that expose their functionality on the web. Many works have addressed this problem. Some of them do not consider the temporal behavior, focusing on search in their annotated natural language description ([8]), hence are not applicable to our context. In [13], a method based on graph matching is proposed in order to implement behavioral similarity search of web services. This system returns approximated results, expecting a domain-knowledgeable user to read the actual specification of the returned contracts. Our system, on the other hand, implements an exact query evaluation algorithm, which avoid this. In [21], web services are modeled as directed graphs with nodes representing either actions or messages. An exact evaluation algorithm is proposed to query for graph patterns in service specifications. We contend that such a system would not be suited for our context in which both contracts and queries are inherently declarative specifications and not directly related to a procedural implementation.

The problem of querying behavioral objects is present also in the area of business process management. In [3], business processes are represented as directed graphs encoding the BPEL specification. An exact query evaluation algorithm is presented that allows to query the *structure* of the specification graphs using graph queries. The framework is extended in [7], in order to consider some behavioral semantics. The premise of this line of work differs from ours in that business processes are handled as *procedural* implementations (workflows), while in our work we manage contracts in the form of *declarative* clauses. Asking for a full workflow registration by the contract provider would significantly hinder registration into the contract database, as contracts specify only *some* key properties of the workflow. Moreover, a workflow query will likely miss all contracts whose workflows do not match its structure yet are semantically equivalent to one that does.

Finally, many techniques we used are inspired by the work done in model checking [25]. However, our permission problem is a novel variation on the standard verification of satisfiability of LTL formulae, and solving it required adapting and combining these techniques in a novel way.

9. CONCLUSIONS

We present a broker that enables providers to register service contracts and consumers to query them, in both cases based on the contracts' temporal behavior. Our novel semantics for permission of a query by a contract takes into account the fact that contracts may not mention some of the events of interest to the query. Permission does not reduce to any standard temporal decision problem, and requires an original solution. We establish the complexity of the permission problem (PSPACE-complete), and design an algorithm for checking it. We show that the theoretical worst case is not an impediment to scalable implementation, presenting two distinct and complementary indexing techniques for querying large collections of service contracts. We evaluate experimentally our implementation, showing that it scales well with both the number and the complexity of the contracts.

10. REFERENCES

[1] U. Airlines. Contract of carriage. http://www.united.com/page/article/0,6867,2671,00.html.

[2] S. Angelov and P. Grefen. The business case for b2b e-contracting. In *Proc. of the 6th Int. Conf. on Electronic Commerce*, 2004.

[3] C. Beeri, A. Eyal, S. Kamenkovich, and T. Milo. Querying business processes. In *VLDB '06*, pages 343–354. VLDB Endowment, 2006.

[4] J. Bengtsson, K. Larsen, F. Larsson, P. Pettersson, and W. Yi. Uppaal - a tool suite for automatic verification of real-time systems. In *Hybrid Systems III*. 1996.

[5] M. Brambilla, A. Deutsch, L. Sui, and V. Vianu. The role of visual tools in a web application design and verification framework : A visual notation for ltl formulae. *Int. Conf. on Web Engineering*, 2005.

[6] E. Damaggio, A. Deutsch, and D. Zhou. Querying contract databases based on temporal behavior. Technical report, 2010.

[7] D. Deutch and T. Milo. Querying structural and behavioral properties of business processes. In *Database Programming Languages*. 2007.

[8] X. Dong, A. Halevy, J. Madhavan, E. Nemes, and J. Zhang. Similarity search for web services. In *VLDB*, 2004.

[9] M. B. Dwyer, G. S. Avrunin, and J. C. Corbett. Property specification patterns for finite-state verification. In *Workshop on Formal Methods in Software Practice*, 1998.

[10] K. Fisler and M. Y. Vardi. Bisimulation minimization in an automata-theoretic verification framework. In *Formal Methods in Computer-Aided Design*, 1998.

[11] E. Fredkin. Trie memory. *Commun. ACM*, 1960.

[12] P. Gastin and D. Oddoux. Fast ltl to büchi automata translation. In *CAV*, 2001.

[13] D. Grigori, J. C. Corrales, and M. Bouzeghoub. Behavioral matchmaking for service retrieval. In *Int. Conf. on Web Services*, '06.

[14] G. J. Holzmann. The model checker spin. *IEEE Trans. Soft. Eng.*, 1997.

[15] J. E. Hopcroft. An n log n algorithm for minimizing states in a finite automaton. Technical report, Stanford, CA, USA, 1971.

[16] M. Kyas, C. Prisacariu, and G. Schneider. Runtime monitoring of electronic contracts. In *Automated Technology for Verification and Analysis*, 2008.

[17] M. R. Lowry. Software construction and analysis tools for future space missions. In *European Conf. on Theory and Practice of Software*, 2002.

[18] Z. Milosevic and R. G. Dromey. On expressing and monitoring behaviour in contracts. In *EDOC*, '02.

[19] R. Paige and R. E. Tarjan. Three partition refinement algorithms. *SIAM J. Comput.*, 1987.

[20] A. Pnueli. The temporal logic of programs. In *FOCS*, 1977.

[21] Z. Shen and J. Su. Web service discovery based on behavior signatures. In *Int. Conf. on Services Computing*, 2005.

[22] A. P. Sistla and E. M. Clarke. The complexity of propositional linear temporal logics. *J. ACM*, 1985.

[23] L. J. Stockmeyer and A. R. Meyer. Word problems requiring exponential time. In *STOC '73: ACM Symp. on Theory of Computing*.

[24] H. Strasberg. Travel terminal. http://www.travelterminal.com.

[25] M. Vardi and P. Wolper. An automata-theoretic approach to automatic program verification. In *LICS*, 1986.

[26] Wikipedia. List of passenger airlines. http://en.wikipedia.org/wiki/List_of_passenger_airlines.

[27] Wikipedia. Travel class. http://en.wikipedia.org/wiki/Travel_class.

[28] P. Wolper, M. Y. Vardi, and P. A. Sistla. Reasoning about infinite computation paths. In *FOCS*, 1983.

Neighborhood-Privacy Protected Shortest Distance Computing in Cloud

Jun Gao[†] Jeffery Yu Xu[‡] Ruoming Jin[§] Jiashuai Zhou[†] Tengjiao Wang[†] Dongqing Yang[†]
[†] Key Laboratory of High Confidence Software Technologies, EECS, Peking University
[‡] Department of systems engineering & Engineering Management, Chinese University of Hong Kong
[§] Department of Computer Science, Kent State University
{gaojun,zjiash,tjwang,dqyang}@pku.edu.cn, yu@se.cuhk.edu.hk, jin@cs.kent.edu

ABSTRACT

With the advent of cloud computing, it becomes desirable to utilize cloud computing to efficiently process complex operations on large graphs without compromising their sensitive information. This paper studies shortest distance computing in the cloud, which aims at the following goals: i) preventing outsourced graphs from neighborhood attack, ii) preserving shortest distances in outsourced graphs, iii) minimizing overhead on the client side.

The basic idea of this paper is to transform an original graph G into a link graph G_l kept locally and a set of outsourced graphs $\mathcal{G}_o$. Each outsourced graph should meet the requirement of a new security model called 1-neighborhood-d-radius. In addition, the shortest distance query can be answered using G_l and $\mathcal{G}_o$. Our objective is to minimize the space cost on the client side when both security and utility requirements are satisfied. We devise a greedy method to produce G_l and $\mathcal{G}_o$, which can exactly answer the shortest distance queries. We also develop an efficient transformation method to support approximate shortest distance answering under a given additive error bound. The final experimental results illustrate the effectiveness and efficiency of our method.

Categories and Subject Descriptors

H.2.8 [**Database management**]: Database Applications

General Terms

Algorithms

Keywords

Shortest Distance, Graph Transformation, Outsource, Privacy.

1. INTRODUCTION

Graph structured data are used in numerous applications, *e.g.*, web graphs, social networks, ontology graphs, biological and chemical pathways, transportation networks. High efficiency is essential for frequent and basic graph operations. However, even basic operations on a graph can be very time-consuming due to the complexity of structural connectivities and graph size [5]. Moreover, real graph datasets are growing rapidly in size, making the attainment of high efficiency even harder.

The paradigm shift of cloud computing offers a new approach for storage- and compute- intensive tasks [6, 10, 26, 20], allowing users to migrate their burden (*e.g.*, data maintenance and computing utilities) to an outsourced server (or cloud server). The outsourced server typically has sufficient resources to maintain very large datasets and provides quick response to users' requests with its powerful distributed and parallel architecture.

Thus, it becomes desirable (and even inevitable) to employ cloud computing to manage large graphs and process complex graph operations efficiently. The biggest problem with this approach is that client companies may be unwilling to outsource their valuable datasets. Take the outsourcing of a social network as an example. Even if its owner removes the identifier of each vertex before sending the network to the cloud server, the structural relationships can still possibly be recovered [14, 19], which will surely devalue the outsourcing.

Given this, the fundamental challenge is: *How can we utilize cloud computing to efficiently process complex operations in large graphs without compromising their sensitive information?* In this paper, we focus on computing the shortest distance between two arbitrary vertices in a large edge-weighted graph. This operation is one of the most important and widely-used graph operations [22, 7, 25, 21], yet its direct online computation is expensive on large graphs [5]. The straightforward way to process shortest distance queries using cloud computing requires outsourcing the entire graph. Thus, the solution to this problem (by avoiding outsourcing sensitive information but still utilizing the high computational power of the cloud) will not only directly benefit graph distance computation and other related operations [16], but more importantly shed light on the principles and fundamental techniques for preserving privacy in cloud computing.

1.1 Related Work

In the following, we review the current state-of-the-art techniques and point out why they cannot fully address the "privacy-in-cloud" challenge.

Privacy-Preserving Graph Publishing: Privacy protection for graph publishing has been studied recently. Most of the existing works on graph publishing focus on certain structural anonymizations, such as 1-neighborhood [2], k-degree [13], k-automorphism [17], k-isomorphism [11], cluster based vertex anonymity [9, 8], as well as many others. These techniques typically focus on using the least amount of modifications of the original graph (minimal information loss) to make it satisfy the targeted security requirement. Unfortunately, the anonymized graphs produced by these privacy protec-

SIGMOD'11, June 12–16, 2011, Athens, Greece.

tion techniques generally do not necessarily maintain the statistical and theoretical characteristics of the original graph [2, 13, 17, 11]. In particular, for any pair of vertices, there is no guarantee of the degree of similarity or preservation of shortest distances between the anonymized graph and the original graph. For example, k-isomorphism is proposed recently to partition a graph into k disjoint, isomorphic sub-graphs, which unfortunately cannot be used to compute shortest distances in the original graph [11]. In addition, most of the exiting works deal with privacy on unweighted graphs, and do not consider the impact of edge weights.

A few recent works [28, 15, 24, 18] notice the importance of preserving graph theoretical characteristics during graph publishing. Ying and Wu propose to preserve the eigenvalue of a graph, which relates to average shortest distance and other topological features, during graph transformation [28]. Liu *et al.* study edge weight perturbation by Guassian random or heuristic rules [15]. Das *et al.* propose a linear programming (LP) method to change edge weights while preserving shortest paths [24]. In both [15] and [24], the topological structure of the anonymized graph remains unchanged. Thus, even with the minimal topological knowledge, such as the vertex degree [13], some sensitive information can be re-identified. Furthermore, the greedy perturbation [15] relies on an expensive matrix operation, and the LP approach can be easily overwhelmed by the number of inequality rules (shortest path preservation conditions) [24]. For example, for a connected graph with only one thousand vertices, there are one million rules for LP, which is clearly too expensive.

Recently, differential privacy [3] has emerged as a powerful model to protect against unknown adversaries with guaranteed probabilistic accuracy. Hay, Li *et al.* perform some of the first studies to support differential privacy in analyzing networks [18, 4]. Specifically, they design an efficient method for releasing a provably private estimate of the degree distribution of a network. However, it is still an open problem on how to publish a graph with respect to the differential privacy [18], and thus it is not clear whether the techniques developed in [18] can be applied to more complicated queries, such as the shortest-path distance query.

Security Issues in Outsourced Server: Sensitive data protection and verification of query results in the outsourced server have attracted much attention recently [10, 26]. A work closely related to this paper studies the verification issue in outsourcing graphs for the shortest path discovery [20]. In their solution, the original graph data are outsourced along with verification objects, and the client side will validate the correctness of the results with the verification objects. However, they do not consider how to protect the sensitive information of the original graph.

Shortest Path Discovery: Shortest path discovery is one fundamental problem in graph theory. Dijkstra's algorithm[5] is a well-known approach to find the single-source shortest path. There are also some works to exploit pre-computed indices to speed up the running time of shortest path discovery. HEPV [23] and HiTi [25] can be viewed as multiple-level indices. The combination of the A* algorithm with the landmark index is studied in [1]. 2-HOP index [7] assigns each vertex with two vertex label sets (L_{out} and L_{in}), and finds the shortest distance between two vertices with an intersection of their label sets. In addition, the indices with different error bounds and various construction methods for approximate distance answering have also been studied in [22, 12, 21]. However, we cannot simply outsource such indices as they will also disclose sensitive information of the graph. For instance, in the 2-hop index, each vertex is very likely to record its distance to its immediate neighbors. Such information often needs to be protected [2].

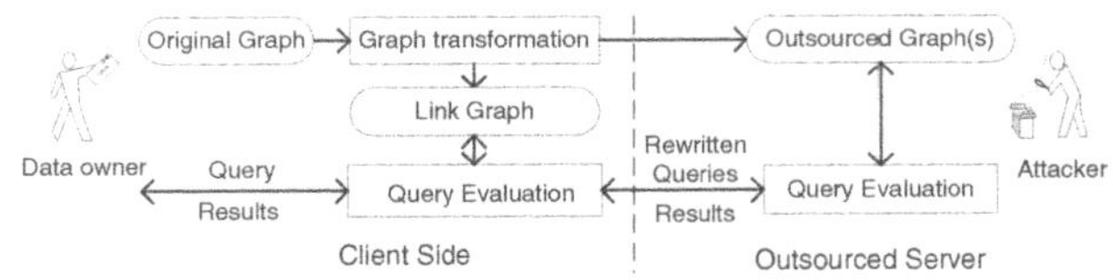

Figure 1: An Overview

1.2 Overview

Given this, our goal is to search for a computational scheme which can compute shortest distances while also protecting private information in the original graph. The key issues underlying this problem are i) what information should be protected and what can be exposed, and ii) how can we employ cloud computing while minimizing client side overhead and satisfying privacy constraints? In addition, recall that the goal in graph publishing is to generate an anonymized graph which should be similar to the original one in order to minimize information loss [2, 13, 17, 11]. Here, the information which we send to the cloud server is for computing shortest distances. Thus, it does not have to be a graph or even a sub-graph; it can be any format as long as it does not disclose the private information of the original graph. This goes back to the core problem: *what information should we protect?* Indeed, most graph publishing techniques are designed to protect specific types of private information. The most common type of attack is a neighborhood attack [2]. For example, outsiders to a social network can easily collect some users' neighborhood information. However, it generally becomes increasingly difficult for attackers to learn knowledge beyond the direct neighborhood [2]. Thus, in this paper, we focus on protecting private information against neighborhood attacks.

The overall framework of our approach is illustrated in Fig. 1. Given an original edge-weighted graph G, we represent it as two parts for both privacy protection and shortest distance computation: i) an outsourced graph(s) G_o is a high level abstraction of the original graph, which records the key information for online shortest distance answering, but does not contain sensitive neighborhood information; ii) a link graph, G_l, which includes the local private information and the relationships between vertices in G and vertices in an outsourced graph(s) G_o for shortest distance computation. The graph(s) G_o is on the cloud server and the link graph G_l is on the client side. Note that this graph representation bears a certain similarity to the 2-level index for shortest paths [23, 25]. However, the existing multiple indices such as HEPV and HiTi mainly target planar graphs, since discovering good graph separators during indexing is difficult on non-planar graphs. More importantly, the present work has a different focus: to construct an outsourced graph which eliminates the private local neighborhood knowledge and makes full use of the cloud server.

The main contributions are summarized below.

- We formulate a new graph transformation problem as minimizing the size of the link graph G_l on the client side on the condition that the privacy of outsourced graphs $\mathcal{G}_o$ is protected and shortest distances can be answered using $\mathcal{G}_o$ and G_l. We propose a new security model, named 1-neighborhood-d-radius, which hides local details in direct edges and a d-radius for each vertex to counter neighborhood attacks.

- We propose a greedy approach to generate outsourced graphs and a link graph for exact shortest distance answering with protected neighborhood privacy.

- We study how to answer approximate shortest distances in the same context with an average additive distance error bound.

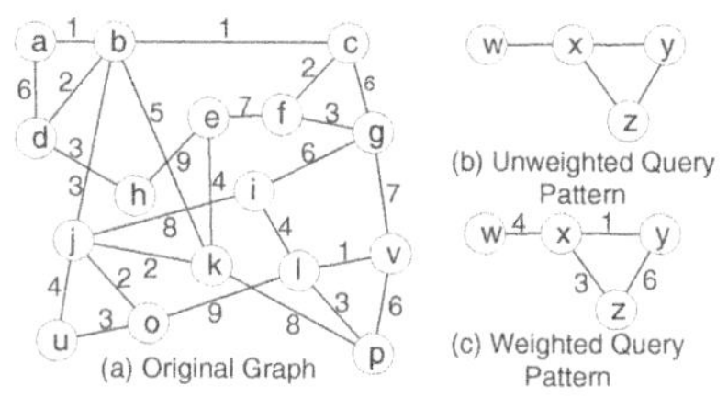

Figure 2: Sample Graph

$G(V, E)$	The original graph
$G_l(V_l, E_l)$	The link graph
$G_o(V_o, E_o)$	An outsourced graph
$\mathcal{G}_o$	Outsourced graphs
n/m	The number of vertices/edges in G
n_o	The number of vertices in G_o
n_l	The number of vertices in cluster

Table 1: Symbols

By allowing approximate shortest distance to be answered, we show that $\mathcal{G}_o$ can be constructed efficiently. We also discuss the heuristic rules used in $\mathcal{G}_o$ construction.

- We conduct extensive experiments on both real and synthetic datasets. The results show that the client side achieves significant cost saving in shortest distance computing with the aid of outsourced graphs. We confirm that our method scales well when it is used to answer approximate shortest distances within a specified error bound.

The remainder of this paper is organized as follows. In section 2, we formulate the transformation problem taking both security and utility into account. Section 3 and section 4 present methods to transform graphs with the exact and approximate distance answering respectively. Section 5 reports experimental results. Section 6 concludes the paper and discusses future works.

2. PROBLEM STATEMENT

In this section, we first define our graph-related notation and then discuss security issues for outsourced graphs and their utilization in shortest distance answering. Finally, we formulate our optimization problem.

2.1 Notation

Let $G = (V, E)$ be an edge-weighted undirected graph, where V and E are its vertex set and edge set, respectively. Each $e \in E$ takes the form of $e = (u, v)$, $u, v \in V$, and is associated with a weight denoted as $w(e)$ or $w(u, v)$ (All weights are assumed to be non-negative integers in a finite range). When the edge (u, v) does not exist, we can assume $w(u, v) = \infty$. A path is a sequence of edges $(u_0, u_1)(u_1, u_2) \dots (u_{x-1}, u_x)$, where $u_i \in V$ $(0 \leq i \leq x)$. The cost of a path p is the sum of edge weights in p, denoted as $len(p)$. A shortest distance query in graph G computes the minimal cost $\delta_G(u, v)$ of any path from u to v in G. Figure 2(a) shows a sample graph, which will be used as the running example in this paper. The character inside the circle represents the vertex's identifier, and the number annotated on the edge is its weight. The symbols used throughout the paper are listed in Table 1.

A graph pattern query can be used in re-identification over the transformed graph [14, 2, 19, 17, 11]. If an attacker has some knowledge about a fragment of the original graph, he can compose a graph pattern query to find exact matches over the transformed graph, and use the query results to infer other information. We illustrate a weighted graph pattern query in Fig. 2(c). Its result is the induced sub-graph with the vertex set $\{i, l, v, p\}$ in G, since we can build a vertex mapping from the query pattern to this sub-graph, under which the weight of each edge is the same as that of the mapped edge. Note, the result of the unweighted graph pattern in Fig. 2(b) contains 32 sub-graphs.

2.2 Protecting Neighborhood Privacy

In this work, we target at protecting the sensitive local neighborhood information. Basically, the information of how an individual vertex links to its neighbors and what are the edge weights for these links is deemed sensitive and need to be protected. In particular, we focus on 1-neighborhood attacks since it tends to be more difficult to collect information beyond that [2]. In addition, when two vertices are very close to each other (within a threshold d), even without a direct link, their relationship should also be considered important. Formally, the outsourced graph should meet the requirement of the *1-neighborhood-d-radius* graph.

DEFINITION 1. **1-Neighborhood-d-Radius Graph.** *Let $G = (V, E)$ be an original graph and $G_o = (V_o, E_o)$ an outsourced graph, $V_o \subseteq V$. For a vertex $u \in V$, its appearance in V_o can be denoted as $\overline{u}$. G_o is a 1-neighborhood-d-radius graph of G, if G_o meets the following conditions:*

1. *for any vertex pair $\overline{u}$ and $\overline{v} \in V_o$, $(u, v) \notin E$. (1-neighborhood);*
2. *for any vertex pair $\overline{u}$ and $\overline{v} \in V_o$, $\delta_G(u, v) \geq d$. (d-radius).*

For brevity, we shorten the name to d-radius graph.

Simply speaking, we do not allow any two vertices, which are adjacent or with their distance smaller than d, to appear in the same d-radius graph. Figure 3(a) shows a 2-radius graph, $G_o(V_o, E_o)$, for $G(V, E)$ in Fig. 2(a). As shown in the figure, the vertex $\overline{u}$ in V_o is an appearance of a vertex u in V. Of the 16 vertices in G, 6 appear in G_o. For any two vertices $\overline{u}$ and $\overline{v}$ in V_o, u and v are not adjacent in the original graph, and the shortest distance $\delta_G(u, v) \geq 2$. We cannot add other vertices into G_o. For example, we cannot add $\overline{a}$ since $\delta_G(a, b) = 1$ is less than $d = 2$. Notice that the edges in G_o show the connections between vertices in a global manner, and the weight associated with an edge $(\overline{u}, \overline{v})$ is the shortest distance $\delta_G(u, v)$ in the underlying original graph G.

We show differences between our method and that used in a data publishing scenario. Figure 3(b) shows a 4-isomorphism result from a recent study [11]. It builds 4 disjoint, isomorphic sub-graphs with graph splitting and structural anonymization. Given a graph pattern query as in Fig. 2(b), it can get results from the transformed graph in Fig. 3(b), but the number of matched sub-graphs is 4. Our work supports edge weights. In addition, the vertices in a d-radius graph are a proper subset of those in the original graph, and no original edges are allowed in a d-radius graph. Therefore, the direct evaluation of any pattern query cannot find meaningful results, and a subsequent re-identification is prevented. Most importantly, the operations to achieve structural anonymization in existing works [2, 13, 17, 11], including arbitrary addition/removal of edges and graph splitting, make the shortest distance computing over the transformed graph difficult or even impossible.

An interesting and important question is whether enforcing the d-radius property on each outsourced graph is too strict. For instance, can we simply remove all edges in the original graph and

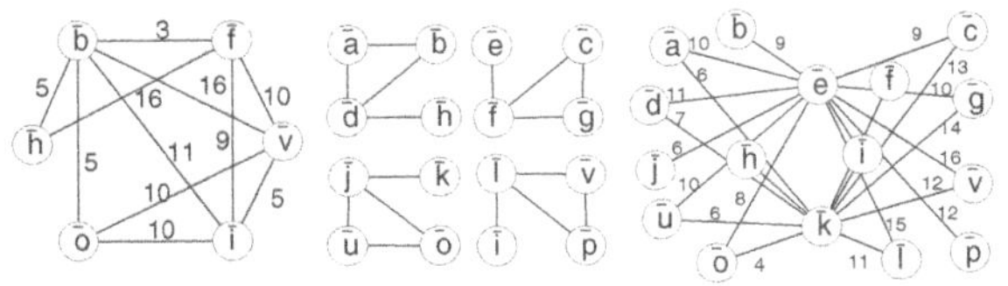

(a) 2-radius (b) 4-isomorphism (c) non 2-radius

Figure 3: Transformed Graph for Outsourcing and Publishing

then only connect those pairs of vertices whose shortest distances are no smaller than d? The answer is negative. We demonstrate a successful attack on such a graph. Suppose an outsourced graph G_o is constructed by the removal of all direct edges and addition of edges from vertex u to $\overline{v}$ if $\delta_G(u, v) \geq 2$. We show the edges related with vertices $\overline{e}$ and $\overline{k}$ in G_o in Fig.3(c). This graph is a non-2-radius graph since two adjacent vertices e and k in the original graph co-exist in the same d-radius outsourced graph, which violates the first condition of a d-radius graph. Attackers can observe that the graph is strongly connected, thus, they can know that there is a direct edge (with any weight) or a path with cost no larger than 2 between e and k in the original graph. Based on the triangle inequality over G_o, attackers can even infer that the edge weight is no smaller than 4!

2.3 Shortest Distance Computation using d-Radius Graph

We transform an original edge-weighted graph G into a set of outsourced d-radius graphs $\mathcal{G}_o = \{G_o^1, \ldots, G_o^{|\mathcal{G}_o|}\}$ which will be deployed on the cloud server, together with a link graph G_l on the client side. An edge in G_l takes the form of $(u, \overline{v})$, which maintains the relationship between vertices in G and an appearance of v in an outsourced graph. The edge can be also expressed in the form of $(u, G_o.\overline{v})$ to specify that the appearance $\overline{v}$ is in the outsourced graph G_o. The weight of an edge $(u, \overline{v})$, $w(u, \overline{v})$, in G_l is equal to $\delta_G(u, v)$. In particular, $w(u, \overline{u}) = 0$. We may use u, $\overline{u}$ and $G_o.\overline{u}$ interchangeably in the following.

Now, we give an important property to characterize the outsourced graphs $\mathcal{G}_o$ and the link graph G_l.

DEFINITION 2. **($\geq$ d)-*Shortest Distance Equivalent Graph.*** *Let $G = (V, E)$ and $G' = (V', E')$ be two graphs, $V \subseteq V'$. G' is a ($\geq$ d)-shortest distance equivalent graph of G if $\delta_G(u, v) = \delta_{G'}(u, v)$ for any vertex pair (u, v) with $\delta_G(u, v) \geq d$, $u, v \in V$.*

In order to use outsourced graphs $\mathcal{G}_o$ and the link graph $G_l = (V_l, E_l)$ to compute shortest distances, we require the union of $\mathcal{G}_o$ and G_l to be a *($\geq$ d)-shortest distance equivalent graph* of the original graph G. For graphs $G_0 = (V_0, E_0)$ and $G_1 = (V_1, E_1)$, their union result is $G = (V_0 \cup V_0, E_0 \cup E_1)$.

Given two vertices u and v in G, the outsourced graph $\mathcal{G}_o$ and the link graph $G_l = (V_l, E_l)$, the shortest distance can be computed as follows:

$$len = \min_{\substack{\overline{x}, \overline{y} \in V_o, G_o = (V_o, E_o) \in \mathcal{G}_o \\ (u, \overline{x}), (v, \overline{y}) \in E_l}} w(u, \overline{x}) + \delta_{G_o}(\overline{x}, \overline{y}) + w(\overline{y}, v)$$

$$\delta_G(u, v) = \min\{len, w\}, \text{where } w \text{ is } w(u, v) \text{ in } G_l \quad (1)$$

Notice that we only utilize the outsourced graphs and the link graph to compute the shortest distance from u to v with $\delta_G(u, v) \geq d$. For the shortest distance less than d, we can compute it in the original graph G. Thus, the complete shortest distance computing can be described as follows: *given two vertices u and v, Dijkstra's algorithm runs on the original graph to find whether u can reach v within d. If no path can be found, we begin to rewrite the distance query from u to v into multiple distance queries against the outsourced graphs $\mathcal{G}_o$. We locate $u.Edges$ for u's edges and $v.Edges$ for v's edges in the link graph G_l. For each pair of edges $e_u = (u, \overline{x}) \in u.Edges$ and $e_v = (\overline{y}, v) \in v.Edges$, if $\overline{x}$ and $\overline{y}$ are in the same outsourced graph $G_o \in \mathcal{G}_o$, a distance query from $\overline{x}$ to $\overline{y}$ is issued in G_o. We then combine the returned results from the outsourced server with the distance information ($w(u, \overline{x})$, $w(\overline{y}, v)$) in G_l to yield* len *in Equation (1). Due to the security reason or the optimization purpose, for two vertices with distance no less than d, the link graph G_l may materialize their relationship by directly linking them with an edge. Thus, the shortest distance is computed by choosing the minimum between* len *and $w(u, v)$ in G_l (if exists), as illustrated in Equation (1).*

2.4 Optimization Problem

To sum up, given a graph $G = (V, E)$ and d, the graph transformation produces outsourced graphs $\mathcal{G}_o = \{G_o^1, \ldots, G_o^{|\mathcal{G}_o|}\}$ and a local link graph G_l, which achieves the following objectives:

1. Each outsourced graph $G_o \in \mathcal{G}_o$ is a d-radius graph;
2. The union of $\mathcal{G}_o$ and G_l is a ($\geq$ d)-shortest distance equivalent graph of G;
3. The space cost of G_l and the cost of the shortest distance computation on the client side are minimized.

In the following sections, we study how to solve this problem efficiently.

3. GRAPH TRANSFORMATION WITH EXACT DISTANCE ANSWERING

In this section, we first give a naïve approach to show the problem complexity, then we give a greedy algorithm to transform a graph for exact shortest distance answering. Finally, we analyze our method.

3.1 A Naïve Approach

We observe that the two optimization targets (in Objective 3) are along the same line with one another. For instance, if we minimize the space cost of G_l, the computational cost over G_l tends to be minimized. In the following, we will focus on minimizing the space cost of G_l. In addition, as discussed above, for any pair of vertices (u, v) with distance less than d, its distance can be discovered on the original graph. Thus, only those vertex pairs whose distances are no less than d need be considered in the transformation. Formally, our graph transformation can be reduced to a problem on minimizing G_l as follows:

DEFINITION 3. ***Minimizing** G_l. Given a graph $G = (V, E)$ and d, we seek a set of d-radius graphs $\mathcal{G}_o$ from G and a link graph G_l such that for each pair of vertices (u, v) in graph $G = (V, E)$ with $\delta_G(u, v) \geq d$,*

1. *there exists an outsourced graph $G_o \in \mathcal{G}_o$, $(u, G_o.\overline{x}) \in E_l$ and $(G_o.\overline{y}, v) \in E_l$, where $\delta_G(u, v) = \delta_G(u, x) + \delta_G(x, y) + \delta_G(y, v)$;*
2. *or there exists an edge $(u, v) \in E_l$ in G_l.*

Our objective is to minimize G_l, or the number of edges in G_l.

In order to solve this problem (minimizing G_l), we may consider a straightforward brute-force approach. Basically, we can try to enumerate all candidate configurations, where each candidate configuration consists of a set of outsourced graphs and a link graph, and can answer any distance query from u to v with $\delta_G(u,v) \geq d$ (Equation (1)); then we compute the space cost of G_l in each candidate configuration. Finally, the optimal solution is the configuration (a set of outsourced graphs with a link graph) with the minimal G_l.

Now, let us look at the number of candidate configurations in the brute-force approach. We note that the vertices in an outsourced graph are actually the sub-set of the vertices in the original graph. Although not all sub-sets of vertices can produce valid d-radius graphs, the total number of different outsourced graphs (d-radius graphs) can still be $O(2^n)$ in the worst case. In addition, the maximal number of vertices in the shortest path from u to v will be $O(n)$ in the worst case, which indicates that each outsourced graph from the total $O(2^n)$ ones has the potential to be used in the distance preservation for (u,v). Based on these factors, we can observe the total number of different configurations is exponential in terms of the number of vertices in the original graph. This clearly makes the brute-force approach too expensive to be feasible.

We can also observe the relationship between the minimizing G_l problem and the set cover problem [27]. The set cover problem is described as: *given a ground set U, and a candidate family $\mathcal{S}$ consisting of the subsets of U, the goal is to find the minimal number of candidate sets, denoted as $\mathcal{C} \subseteq \mathcal{S}$, whose union is U.* We can transform an outsourced graph G_o into a candidate set S in $\mathcal{S}$ and transform a vertex pair p into an element e in the ground set U. Specifically, the candidate set S consists of all vertex pairs whose distance can be answered via G_o. Given this, we may be inclined to adopt a set-cover approach [27] to solve our problem. However, the difficulty is that in our problem, the outsourced graphs and consequently the candidate sets are not given in advance, and the vertices in an outsourced graph must satisfy the d-radius constraint. Moreover, the optimization target in our problem is to minimize the space cost of G_l, which is hard to be coded as the goal in the set cover problem.

3.2 Fast Greedy Method

The naïve solution above reveals the massive search space in achieving the optimal solution to our graph transformation problem. In this part, we design a fast greedy method to produce a reasonable graph transformation plan.

Basic Idea. The main problem with the naïve approach lies in the fact that we have to enumerate all possible outsourced graphs. To avoid producing all outsourced graphs, we wish to construct only the needed ones. Intuitively, the outsourced graph which can answer more distance queries will be constructed first, since in such a case, the edges in the link graph have higher chances to be reused and thus the space cost of the link graph can be reduced. This idea is similar to the greedy idea used in the set cover problem, which selects the sub-set with the maximal number of elements first.

We then make a heuristic restriction on edges in G_l in order to reduce the search space for the outsourced graphs. Recalling Equation (1), the shortest distance from u to v can be computed via a sub-path from $\overline{x}$ to $\overline{y}$ in an outsourced d-radius graph. Taking the sub-path from u to $\overline{x}$ as an example, we require either the distance from u to x to be less than a threshold or u to be adjacent to x in the original graph. This restriction can rule out the cases where edges in the link graph have large weights. Note that the restriction does not contradict our above intuitions. A sub-path from u to x which can be used in more distance queries always has a lower weight. For simplicity, the threshold on the maximal edge weight in the link graph has the same setting as d in d-radius graph in the following.

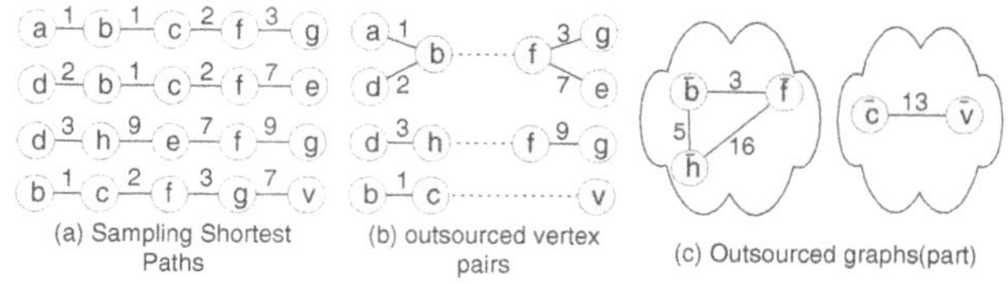

Figure 4: Outsourced Graph Generation

Under the restriction, we give the following notation on the candidate outsourced vertex pairs. The first condition is the same as Equation (1), which means the shortest distance from u to v can be answered via x and y. The second condition is the restriction on edges in the link graph. The third condition corresponds to the requirements of d-radius.

DEFINITION 4. ***Candidate Outsourced Vertex Pair.*** *Given a pair of vertices (u,v) in graph $G=(V,E)$ with $\delta_G(u,v) \geq d$ and $(u,v) \notin E$, if there exists another pair of vertices (x,y):*

1. $\delta_G(u,v) = \delta_G(u,x) + \delta_G(x,y) + \delta_G(y,v)$;
2. $\delta_G(u,x) < d$ *or* $(u,x) \in E$, $\delta_G(y,v) < d$ *or* $(y,v) \in E$;
3. $\delta_G(x,y) \geq d$ *and* $(x,y) \notin E$.

then (x,y) is the candidate outsourced vertex pair for pair (u,v).

We illustrate candidate outsourced vertex pairs for the shortest paths in Fig.4(a). Take the shortest path between vertex a and vertex g as an example. For d=2, the candidate outsourced vertex pairs include (a,f), (a,g), (b,f), and (b,g). We also note that some vertex pairs, such as (b,f) in Fig.4(b), lie on the shortest paths between multiple vertex pairs and thus can be used to answer multiple distance queries. In order to make the outsourced graph answer more distance queries, we prefer to select such vertex pairs for the outsourced graph. Also, note that $(\overline{c},\overline{v})$ cannot be put in the d-radius graph which has contained $(\overline{b},\overline{f})$, since $\delta_G(b,c) < 2$. In such a case, we have to put them into another outsourced graph.

Another problem with the naïve approach is the large intermediate space required. We need to preserve the distance for $O(n^2)$ vertex pairs in the graph transformation. On a relatively large graph, the representation of these vertex pairs alone will easily exceed the memory limit. Thus, we need to extend the greedy framework to use a pipeline approach to generate the outsourced graphs and their link graph. That is, we iteratively enumerate vertex pairs until the number of vertex pairs reaches a threshold, and then use these partial vertex pairs to guide the construction of one outsourced graph. Once the outsourced graph is constructed, the vertex pairs which have been preserved will be removed from memory. Then we load a new set of vertex pairs for the next outsourced graph, until all distances between vertex pairs have been preserved.

Greedy Graph Transformation. We present our algorithm in Algorithm 1. We initialize the shortest path set, outsourced graphs and the link graph in line 1. Then we attempt to preserve the distances of these shortest paths with newly constructed outsourced graphs. In the iteration from line 2 to line 11, when the total paths in memory exceed *MPMem* in line 5, we build a vertex sequence L with a benefit function and invoke Algorithm 2 to generate an outsourced graph according to L in line 7. *MPMem* is used to control the maximal space cost used in the graph transformation. The paths which have been preserved are removed from P in line 10.

Algorithm 1: Greedy Graph Transformation

Input: graph $G = (V, E)$, d, *MPMem* for threshold on maximal paths in memory
Output: outsourced graphs $\mathcal{G}_o$ and link graph G_l.
1 Initialize an empty shortest path set P, $\mathcal{G}_o$, and G_l;
2 **while** *there remains shortest paths not handled* **do**
3   Locate a remaining shortest path p with $len(p) \geq d$, add p into P;
4   Enumerate all candidate outsourced vertex pairs for p;
5   **if** $sizeof(P) > MPMem$ **then**
6   Build a vertex sequence L with the pair based benefit function;
7     $G_o \leftarrow OutGraph(G, d, L)$;
8     $\mathcal{G}_o \leftarrow \mathcal{G}_o \cup G_o$;
9   Build edges in G_l from vertices in G to these in G_o;
10   Remove the paths from P exactly answered by G_o;
11   Re-enumerate candidate vertex pairs in P;
12 $removed \leftarrow \infty$;
13 **while** $removed > |G_o|$ **do**
14   Generate G_o as line 6 to line 11;
15   $removed \leftarrow$ the number of removed paths by G_o;
16 For each $p \in P$, build an edge e with ending vertices of p, and add e into G_l;
17 return $\mathcal{G}_o$ and G_l.

Now we discuss the benefit function used in the greedy method. For each shortest path, we enumerate all possible candidate outsourced vertex pairs. We have two kinds of benefit functions. The first function is based on the vertex frequency. That is, we simply count the occurrences of x and y for each candidate outsourced vertex pair (x, y) separately. The second one is based on vertex pair frequency. We record the frequency of all possible vertex pairs, and sort vertex pairs in terms of their frequency. Note that L may contain duplicate vertices in such a case. Since the case that two vertices x and y have high frequencies does not imply that (x, y) can be used to compute more shortest distance queries, we use the vertex pair based benefit function in line 6. Our experimental results show that the latter function works better than the former.

As for the termination condition of the greedy method, we can continue generating new outsourced graphs and pruning path set P until P is empty. The algorithm will stop since each outsourced graph can be used to preserve at least one remaining distance. However, when the iteration from line 2 to line 11 stops, those vertex pairs whose distances can be "easily" answered by outsourced graphs have been removed. In order to reduce the transformation cost, we can terminate the construction of outsourced graphs when the number of vertices in a newly generated outsourced graph G_o is larger than the number of remaining vertex pairs whose distances can be answered via G_o. Since the remaining paths are recorded in G_l in line 16, the union of $\mathcal{G}$ and G_l is still a $(\geq d)$-shortest distance equivalent graph of the original graph.

Discovering Single Outsourced Graph. The next key problem is how to use the heuristic information collected from the greedy method to guide the construction of an outsourced graph. We now show that each d-radius graph can be easily constructed from a distance aware cluster cover.

DEFINITION 5. ***Distance Aware Cluster Cover.*** *Let $G = (V, E)$ be an original graph. A cluster cover $\mathcal{C}$ is a set of clusters, each cluster $C_d(x) \in \mathcal{C}$ having a center $x \in V$. A distance aware cluster cover meets the following requirements:*

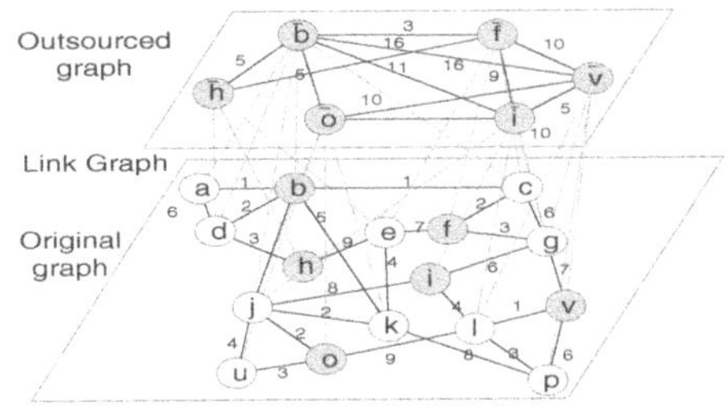

Figure 5: Link Graph and One Outsourced Graph

1. *For any vertex $u \in V$, u belongs to at least one cluster $C_d(x)$ where u is directly connected to x or $\delta_G(u, x) < d$;*
2. *For any two clusters $C_d(x)$ and $C_d(y)$, $\delta_G(x, y) \geq d$ and $(x, y) \notin E$.*

Intuitively, the centers of clusters can be used as the outsourced vertices in a d-radius graph. For example, the vertices in Fig.3(a) are the cluster centers in a cluster cover. For a vertex u in a cluster $C_d(x)$, we build an edge from u to its cluster center x, and such an edge is actually in the link graph G_l. Given a graph G, d, and a vertex sequence L which encodes the heuristic knowledge, an outsourced graph can be constructed efficiently with Algorithm 2.

Algorithm 2: $OutGraph(G, d, L)$

Input: graph $G = (V, E)$, d, a vertex sequence L.
Output: Outsourced Graph $G_o = (V_o, E_o)$.
1 Initialize empty $G_o = (V_o, E_o)$;
2 **while** *there exists uncovered vertex in L* **do**
3   Pick the top uncovered vertex x from L as a cluster center, and $V_o \leftarrow V_o \cup \{x\}$;
4   Create a cluster $C_d(x)$ containing 1-neighbor of x and vertex u with $\delta_G(u, x) < d$ with Dijkstra's search, and mark them *covered*;
5 For any two cluster centers x and y, build the necessary edge between them;
6 Return G_o.

In Algorithm 2, we select the first uncovered vertex from L as the cluster center and build its cluster, since L is sorted in terms of node benefit and the vertices closer to the head of L have higher benefits. The cluster centers will be the vertices in the outsourced graph G_o. The other vertices in a cluster can be discovered with Dijkstra's algorithm and are labeled as *covered* so they will not be selected as cluster centers. Notice that this strategy also ensures that the minimal distance between cluster centers is no smaller than d. In line 5, we build edges between any two vertices in the outsourced graph. The edge weight equals their shortest distance in the original graph discovered by Dijkstra's algorithm. Given three vertices x, y, and z, if $\delta_G(x, y) + \delta_G(y, z) = \delta_G(x, z)$, the edge from x to z need not be constructed.

Figure 5 shows one outsourced graph and its link graph produced by Algorithm 1 on the graph (Fig.2(a)). The outsourced graph is the same as Fig.3(a). It can be constructed by Algorithm 2. Lines with red color are the edges in the link graph G_l. In order to make the figure clear, we omit the weight of these edges.

3.3 Analysis of Graph Transformation

In this part, we analyze the time cost and correctness of the graph transformation algorithm, the impact of d, and the overhead distribution between the cloud server and client side. We use the following symbols. The meanings of n_o, n_l, n, m are given in Table 1. x is the total number of outsourced graphs, which is related to d and the graph's features. b is the maximal number of edges to an outsourced graph for every vertex.

The time cost of graph transformation in Algorithm 1 includes the enumeration of all shortest paths, the sorting of candidate outsourced vertex pairs, and the generation of all outsourced graphs. The enumeration of all shortest paths requires $O(n(m+n\log n))$. Since we need to sort at most $O(n^2)$ candidate outsourced vertex pairs in the benefit computation before the construction of each of x outsourced graphs, the total sorting cost is $O(xn^2\log n)$. The single outsourced graph generation in Algorithm 2 includes the vertex selection cost and edge building cost. The vertex selection requires $O(n_o n_l^2)$, since there are $O(n_o)$ clusters and each requires $O(n_l^2)$ for local shortest path discovery. In the edge building for an outsourced graph, we need $O(n_o)$ times shortest distance discovery in the original graph in the worst case. Thus, a single outsourced graph construction takes $O(n_o(m+n\log n)+n_o n_l^2)$=$O(n_o(m+n\log n))$. With all factors considered, the total time cost of graph transformation in Algorithm 1 is $O(n(m+n\log n)+xn^2\log n+xn_o(m+n\log n))$. A minor extension to Algorithm 1 is to cache the computed shortest distances which can be used in the edge building in outsourced graphs. In this way, the time complexity can be reduced to $O(n(m+n\log n)+xn^2\log n)$.

Now, we show that Equation (1) can yield correct shortest distances over the union of $\mathcal{G}_o$ and G_l produced by Algorithm 1. Algorithm 1 has enumerated all shortest paths P with their distances no smaller than d. From the construction rules, we know that a shortest path $p \in P$ can be removed from P only when p can be exactly answered by one outsourced graph in $\mathcal{G}_o$ or p is stored in the link graph G_l. Therefore, the union of $\mathcal{G}_o$ and G_l from Algorithm 1 is a ($\geq d$)-shortest distance equivalent graph of the original graph. At the same time, Equation (1) enumerates all possible paths from u to v using $\mathcal{G}_o$ and G_l. Therefore, Equation (1) can produce the correct results.

From above discussion, we can notice that d is a key factor to adjust the security strength and overhead on the client side. A larger d leads to fewer outsourced vertices, which indicates more information is hidden in a "coarser" outsourced graph. At the same time, a larger d results in more vertices in one cluster in the cluster cover, which shows that the client side requires more space cost to store the link graph and more time cost in the local path searching. In addition, since a single "coarser" outsourced graph preserves fewer shortest distances than a "finer" one, it needs more outsourced graphs along with the link graph to meet the requirement of ($\geq d$)-shortest distance equivalent graph, which also results in a higher graph transformation time cost.

	Client Side	Cloud Server
Space	$O(m+xn_o n_l)$	$O(xn_o^2)$
Query Time	$O(n_l^2+xb^2)$	$O(xb^2n_o^2)$

Table 2: Overhead Distribution with Graph Outsourcing

We discuss the overhead distribution after graphs are outsourced in Table 2. As for the space cost, the client side needs $O(m+xn_o n_l)$ to store the original graph and the link graph, while the cloud server requires $O(xn_o^2)$ space to store all outsourced graphs. As for the time cost of shortest distance query answering, the client side needs time $O(n_l^2)$ for the local search and time $O(xb^2)$ for result merging with Equation (1). The cloud server takes $O(xb^2n_o^2)$ time to compute the rewritten queries. Note that the cloud server can build indices [21, 1, 7] and perform parallel processing over x graphs to lower the query evaluation cost significantly. Compared with $O(m+n\log n)$ time cost without graph outsourcing, the client side saves much time cost with the aid of the cloud server. The final experimental results also show the effectiveness of graph outsourcing.

4. GRAPH TRANSFORMATION WITH APPROXIMATE DISTANCE ANSWERING

In this section, we relax the 2-nd objective on ($\geq d$) equivalent shortest distance graph to handle large graphs. We first propose a method to transform graph with approximate distance answering, and then discuss heuristic methods in the outsourced graph construction.

4.1 Average Additive Error Guided Graph Transformation

Although the graph transformation method discussed above can answer shortest distances exactly, the transformation requires enumerating all shortest paths and computing the edges inside outsourced graphs, which makes the method unsuitable for large graphs.

Graph transformation with approximate distance answering on large graphs thus becomes an important research problem, since approximate shortest distances are good enough in many applications [22, 12, 21]. This then raises the issue that how many outsourced graphs are needed to achieve good distance values, if we use random vertex sequences for Algorithm 2.

The quality of the approximate distance from u to v can be measured by $\alpha\delta_G(u,v)+\beta$ [22], where α is the multiplicative error, and β is the additive error. There are many studies on approximate distance answering. A pre-computed data structure is proposed to achieve α in $[1, 2k-1]$, where k can adjust the space and time cost in pre-computation [22]. Kleinberg *et al.* achieve $\alpha = 1+\phi$ and $\beta = 0$, given enough random beacons and the triangle inequality rule [12].

In this part, we attempt to achieve $\alpha = 1$ and a given average additive error $\overline{\beta}$ for all shortest distance queries. For any distance query $q \in Q$ from u to v, a path p_q is discovered for q using $\mathcal{G}_o$ and G_l. Average additive error $\overline{\beta}$ can be defined as $\frac{\sum_{q\in Q}\beta_q}{|Q|}$, where β_q = $len(p_q)-\delta_G(u,v)$. The rationale of averaged addition error is to get acceptable results with a limited number of outsourced graphs. The average additive error can be useful when a large number of shortest distance queries are evaluated in graph analysis. In addition, since our outsourced graph is generated randomly, the worst case of additive error can be lowered along with the average one simultaneously with a high possibility.

We present our graph transformation method in Algorithm 3 to achieve the given additive error $\overline{\beta}$. The basic idea is to repeatedly construct randomized outsourced graphs until the estimated additive error avg is less than $\overline{\beta}$. The estimated additive error avg is initialized in line 2 and is adjusted after a new outsourced graph is constructed in the iteration from line 3 to line 10.

In line 4, we build an outsourced graph with Algorithm 2. Since the exact edge weight computation between outsourced vertices takes $O(n_o)$ times Dijkstra's search, where n_o is the number of vertices in an outsourced graph, we relax the exact edge building as follows. We select l vertices from n_o total outsourced vertices, and we build the full shortest path trees for these l vertices in the original graph with Dijkstra's algorithm. The shortest path tree can ensure that the path in the tree is also the shortest path in the original graph. Then, we build edges for any two outsourced vertices $\overline{x}$

Algorithm 3: Average Additive Error Guided Outsourced Graph Construction

Input: Graph G, d, additive error threshold $\overline{\beta}$, s for the number of sampling queries, l for the number of full shortest path trees.

Output: Outsourced Graphs $\mathcal{G}_o$.

1 Initialize three empty query lists Q_0, Q_1 and Q_2 with length s;
2 $avg \leftarrow \infty$;
3 **while** $avg > \overline{\beta}$ **do**
4 $G_o \leftarrow OutGraph(G, d, L)$, where edge building is based on l shortest path trees, and L is a random vertex sequence;
5 $\mathcal{G}_o \leftarrow \mathcal{G}_o \cup \{G_o\}$;
6 Collect the average number n_o of vertices in G_o and the average number n_l of vertices in cluster;
7 Remove queries from Q_0 and Q_1 which do not meet the requirement of Q_0 and Q_1;
8 Add new queries into Q_0 and Q_1 until # of queries is s;
9 Evaluate queries over G with Dijkstra's algorithm and Equation (1) to obtain l_0, l_1 and l_2;
10 $avg \leftarrow pct(Q_0)l_0 + pct(Q_1)l_1 + pct(Q_2)l_2$;
11 Return $\mathcal{G}_o$.

and $\overline{y}$ when $\overline{x}$ is the lowest ancestor of $\overline{y}$ in the shortest path tree. We observe that our relaxed edge building method is similar to that of the landmark index [21]. However, the landmark index only records relationships from vertices to the root of the shortest path tree. Hence, the outsourced graph with this relaxed edge building strategy can yield results more precisely than the landmark index when using the same number of shortest path trees.

When outsourced graphs $\mathcal{G}_o$ are generated randomly and the relaxed edge building strategy is used, the result of Equation (1) may be not the shortest distance. Given two vertices u and v, the additive error of distance computed by Equation (1) comes from the error in the shortest distance between cluster centers in the outsourced graph (due to relaxed edge building strategy) and the deviation of their cluster centers from their shortest path.

The next key problem is how to estimate the average additive error avg from existing outsourced graphs. In order to compute avg more precisely, we put a shortest distance query from u to v into one of 4 categories, namely Q_l, Q_0, Q_1, and Q_2, according to the relationships of the current outsourced graphs $\mathcal{G}_o$ with u and v. Then avg can be calculated with the proportion and average additive error of each category. Specifically, if the shortest distance $\delta_G(u, v)$ is smaller than d, q belongs to Q_l. q can be answered exactly with local Dijkstra's search in the original graph. If neither u nor v has been outsourced into any $G_o \in \mathcal{G}_o$, q is in Q_0, as illustrated in Fig.6(a). Even if the outsourced graph returns the correct distance between x and y, where x is the cluster center for u and y is the cluster center for v, the maximal additive error for a query in Q_0 is $4d_m$, where $d_m = max(d, w_{max})$, and w_{max} is the maximal edge weight. If either u or v has been selected into an outsourced $G_o \in \mathcal{G}_o$, q belongs to Q_1, as illustrated in Fig.6(b). Suppose that the outsourced graph returns the correct distance, the maximal additive error for a query in Q_1 is $2d_m$. If both u and v are selected in one $G_o \in \mathcal{G}_o$, q is in Q_2, as illustrated in Fig.6(c). The additive error of q now comes from the error in the distance computation in outsourced graphs. From the above discussion, we know that the additive error for a query in Q_l is 0, and the average additive error for queries in Q_0 is larger than that for queries in Q_1, which is larger than that for queries in Q_2.

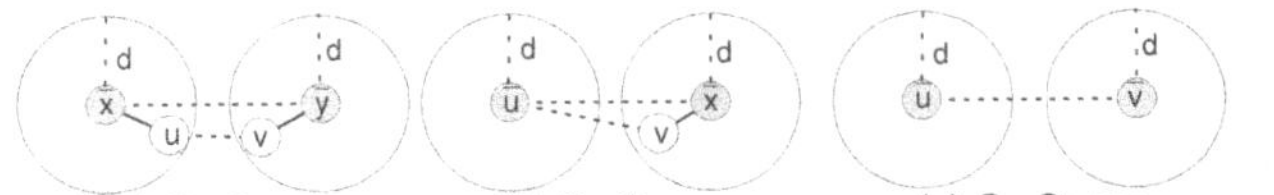

(a) Q0 Query (b) Q1 Query (c) Q2 Query

Figure 6: Query Categories

The proportion of each query category can be computed with two statistics. The average number of vertices in a cluster, n_l, and the average number of vertices in an outsourced graph, n_o, are collected in line 6 in Algorithm 3. Suppose that the total number of outsourced graphs is x. The proportion $pct(Q_l)$ for Q_l is $\frac{n_l}{|V|}$. The increase of x does not affect $pct(Q_l)$. The proportion $pct(Q_0)$ for Q_0 is $(1-\frac{n_0}{|V|})^{2x}(1-\frac{n_l}{|V|})$. A vertex is not selected as the cluster center for outsourcing under the probability $(1-\frac{n_0}{|V|})$. $pct(Q_0)$ reveals the probability that neither of two vertices is selected after x times. As the number of outsourced graphs increases, $pct(Q_0)$ decreases dramatically. The proportion $pct(Q_2)$ for Q_2 is $(1-(1-\frac{n_0}{|V|}^2)^x)(1-\frac{n_l}{|V|})$, where $(1-\frac{n_0}{|V|}^2)$ is the probability that two vertices are not selected as cluster centers simultaneously. $pct(Q_2)$ increases with the increase of the number of outsourced graphs. With three of the four proportions defined, the proportion for Q_1 is simply the remainder: $pct(Q_1)$=1-$pct(Q_l)$-$pct(Q_0)$-$pct(Q_2)$.

Now, we compute l_0, l_1, and l_2, which are the average additive errors for queries in Q_0, Q_1, and Q_2 respectively. It is not a trivial task, since these values are related to the local structure inside the cluster and the global structure between clusters. We can know that these additive distance errors decrease monotonically with more outsourced graphs. In this paper, we employ a sampling method to estimate these additive distance errors. That is, we randomly build three query lists for query categories Q_0, Q_1, and Q_2. These query lists are initialized in line 1, and the queries in the list for Q_0 and Q_1 may be adjusted after a new outsourced graph is generated in line 7 and line 8. l_0, l_1, l_2 are then computed as the average difference between the exact shortest distances from Dijkstra's algorithm and the distance with Equation (1) for all queries in corresponding query categories.

Finally, the average additive error can be computed in line 10 with

$$pct(Q_0)l_0 + pct(Q_1)l_1 + pct(Q_2)l_2, \qquad (2)$$

where l_0, l_1, and l_2 are averaged additive errors for queries in Q_0, Q_1, and Q_2 respectively. We do not mention the query category Q_l since the additive error for the query in Q_l is 0. One may wonder why we cannot produce the average additive error directly from the sampling queries. This is because the proportions of query categories are changed with more outsourced graphs. In addition, $l_2 < l_1, l_1 < l_0$. Thus, Equation (2) can estimate the additive error more precisely.

The time cost of the client side in Algorithm 3 mainly consists of the evaluation cost of sampling queries and the generation cost of outsourced graphs. Let n, m, n_l, n_o have the meanings illustrated in Table 1. l is the number of full shortest path trees constructed for each outsourced graph. x is the number of outsourced graphs, which is related with d, the additive error bound $\overline{\beta}$, and the graph's features. s is the number of sampling queries. The evaluation of sampling queries takes $O(xs(m + n\log n))$ time cost in the worst case, and the outsourced graph generation takes $O(x(l(m+n\log n)+n_o n_l^2))$ time cost, where $O(l(m+n\log n))$ is the cost for l times Dijkstra's algorithm in edge building, and

$O(n_o n_l^2)$ is the cost in outsourced vertex selection. Then the time complexity in Algorithm 3 is $O(x(t(m+n\log n)+n_o n_l^2))$, where $t = max(s,l)$.

4.2 Heuristic Construction Rules

Algorithm 3 achieves the desired additive error with outsourced graphs constructed randomly. Another extension is to introduce heuristic rules in the outsourced graph construction. From Equation (1), it is feasible for outsourced graphs to produce more precise results when they contain more shared shortest sub-paths. Existing work on landmark indices also shows that the heuristic rules work better than the random ones [21].

The basic idea behind the heuristic construction is to make it more probable for a vertex to be selected as a cluster center if it is located on more shortest paths. Thus more shortest distance queries can be answered via outsourced graphs generally. In our paper, we design two heuristic rules. The degree based outsourced graph construction attempts to select vertices with the higher degree as the cluster centers; the cluster based method selects the vertex x with the largest number of vertices in cluster $C_d(x)$ each time. In order to make the outsourced graph construction in Algorithm 2 be aware of these heuristic values, we sort the vertices in sequence L with the heuristic values, since the vertices nearer to the top of L have more chances to be outsourced in Algorithm 2.

The duplication of vertices in different outsourced graphs is another important concern in the heuristic construction method. The same vertex sequence will produce the same outsourced graph using Algorithm 2. In order to avoid constructing duplicate graphs, we make an extension to the outsourced graph construction method in Algorithm 2 with an introduction of a percentage $k(0 < k < 1)$ and a function $f(x)$, where x is the number of outsourced graphs, $f(1) = k$ and $f(i) < f(i+1)$. In the first outsourced graph construction, rather than always choosing the vertex with the maximal benefit value among the uncovered ones in vertex sequence L, we select a vertex randomly from uncovered vertices with top-k benefit values. In the following x-th outsourced graph generation, k is enlarged by $f(x)$ such as $f(x+1) = 2f(x)$ until $k \geq 1$. Thus after multiple rounds of outsourced graph construction, the heuristic values have been extensively exploited, and the outsourced graph construction retreats to the random method, which focuses on the distribution of the outsourced vertices in outsourced graphs.

5. EXPERIMENTAL RESULTS

In this section, we implement the graph transformation with the exact and approximate distance answering, and conduct extensive experiments on both real and synthetic datasets.

5.1 Experimental Setup

Measures. We focus on the following measures related to the graph transformation: the transformation time cost, the space cost of the link graph $|G_l|$ (the number of edges in G_l), and the average additive error achieved by outsourced graphs. In addition, in order to show the effectiveness of graph outsourcing in shortest distance computing, we define a local overhead ratio $r_l = t_l/t_f$, where t_l is the time cost to discover the shortest distance with Equation (1) on the client side, and t_f is the time cost used by Dijkstra's algorithm on the client side.

Implementation Details and Competitors. We implement our methods in Java with JDK 1.6. The maximal runtime memory of JVM is set to 1.55GB. All experiments are carried out on 1.8 GHz AMD processor running Windows Server 2003. The shortest distance computation in the outsourced server is simulated in the same machine. When one outsourced graph is constructed, we store it into a relational database so we can support multiple outsourced graphs. The time cost in accessing the relational database is not included in the time reported.

In addition, we implement the edge anonymization method with all-pair shortest path preserving (denoted as *LP*) in the technical report version for [24]. As discussed above, *LP* only anonymizes edge weights, and then the transformed graph cannot counter the structural attack. Here, we want to compare their work in terms of the graph transformation time cost, the space cost and the local overhead ratio. Just as in [24], we also use LPsolver 5.5 [1] to solve the rules generated.

Datasets. We use five graph datasets to test our methods, including three real graphs named *Gnut08*, *DBLP* and *Bay*, and two synthetic graphs named *Random* and *Power*.

Gnut08[2] is a directed gnutella P2P network. *DBLP* is extracted from a recent snapshot of DBLP dataset[3]. We select the records after 2004. *Bay* dataset[4] describes the road network in the San Francisco Bay Area. The edge weights in *Gnut08* and *DBLP* graph are assigned randomly in the range [1,100]. Each edge weight in Bay is divided by 30 so that the average edge weight 54 in Bay is similar to that of the other graphs.

Dataset	# of Vertices	# of Edges
Gnut08	6,301	20,777
DBLP5k	5,000	20,663
DBLP200k	200,000	847,433
Bay	321,270	400,086
Random$x$*kN*y*d*	1k-100k	yk-100yk
Power$x$*kN*y*d*	50k-200k	50yk-200yk

Table 3: Statistics of Graph Datasets

The *Random* dataset of graphs are generated as follows. Let n and m be the number of vertices and edges respectively, we randomly select the source and target vertex for m times among n vertices. The *Power* graph set is generated using *Barabasi Graph Generator v1.4*[5]. It can create graphs in which the distribution of outdegrees obeys a power law. The weights of edges in *Random* and *Power* graph are assigned randomly in [1,100].

Some statistics about these graphs are summarized in Table 3. Our synthetic graphs have the suffix x*N*y*d*, where x is the number of vertices and y is the average degree. For example, *Random100kN3d* represents a *Random* graph with 100k vertices and an average degree of 3.

5.2 Graph Transformation with Exact Answer

In this section, we study the impact of different factors on the measures of graph transformation with exact shortest distance answering. Specifically, we are interested in: i) What is the impact of d on the transformation overhead, the size of the link graph and local overhead ratio? ii) We have discussed two benefit functions. Can the vertex-pair based function *ByPair* reduce the overhead compared to the vertex based function *ByVertex*? iii) Does the threshold *MPMem* on maximal paths in memory in Algorithm 1 impact on the effectiveness of the greedy method?

[1] http://lpsolve.sourceforge.net/5.5/

[2] http://snap.stanford.edu/data/p2p-Gnutella08.html

[3] http://dblp.uni-trier.de/xml/

[4] http://www.dis.uniroma1.it/ challenge9/data/

[5] http://www.cs.ucr.edu/ ddreier/barabasi.html

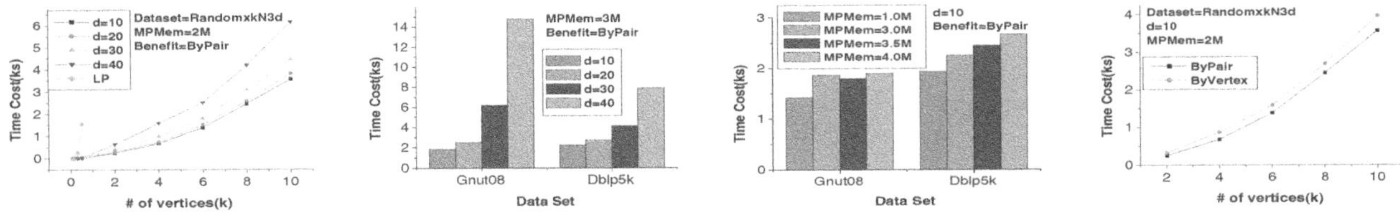

(a) Transformation Time vs. d (b) Transformation Time vs. d (c) Transformation Time vs. memory limitation (d) Transformation Time vs. benefit functions

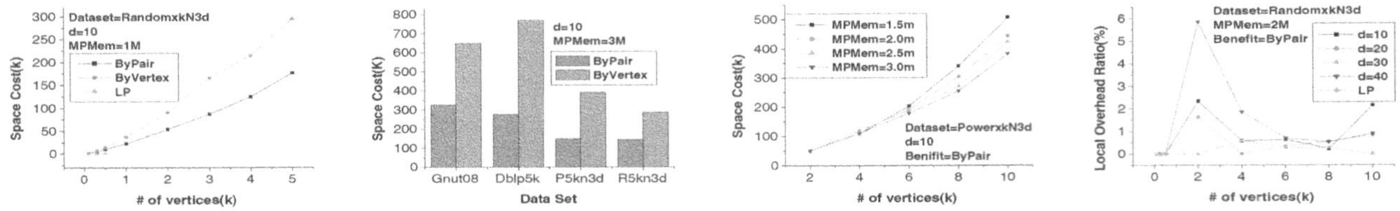

(e) $|G_l|$ vs. graph scale (f) $|G_l|$ vs. benefit functions (g) $|G_l|$ vs. memory limitation (h) Local Overhead Ratio vs. d

Figure 7: Experimental Results on Graph Transformation with Exact Answers

Transformation Time Cost. Figure 7(a) and Figure 7(b) show the transformation time cost with respect to d on *Random* graphs and real data respectively. *RandomxkN3d* is used in Fig.7(a), where x is the number of vertices in X-axis. We observe that the time cost of graph transformation also increases with the increase of d. The main reason lies in the fact that when d is larger, there are fewer vertices in each d-radius outsourced graph, and thus more outsourced graphs are required to achieve ($\geq d$)-shortest distance equivalent graph. We also find *LP* method does not scale well. *LP* produces $O(rn^2)$ rules for a graph to achieve all-pairs shortest path preservation, where r is the average degree, and n is the number of vertices. For example, a *Random* graph with only 600 vertices and average degree 3 generates 1,071,608 rules. LPSolver cannot handle this many rules and terminates. On smaller graphs with the number of vertices less than 500, we also notice that the time used by *LP* rises rapidly.

Figure 7(c) studies the impact of the threshold *MPMem* (maximal paths in memory) on the transformation time cost over two real graphs. Our algorithm introduces *MPMem* to control the total intermediate space used in the greedy method. Intuitively, the greedy method can produce more reasonable outsourced graphs based on more shortest paths with a larger *MPMem*. In addition, when the number of shortest paths exceeds *MPMem*, another new outsourced graph has to be generated inevitably. Thus, the increase of *MPMem* will reduce the graph transformation time cost in general. We also notice that when *MPMem* is large enough, its increase is not effective any more, since all computed shortest paths can be put into the memory in such a case.

Figure 7(d) compares the effects of the two benefit functions, *ByVertex* and *ByPair*, on the transformation time cost on *Random* graphs. As discussed before, the case that two vertices x and y have a higher frequency does not indicate that the vertex pair (x, y) can answer more shortest distances. Thus, *ByPair* method is a more reasonable function which can produce fewer outsourced graphs and then lower the transformation time cost, as shown in Fig.7(d). We also notice that the reduction of transformation time with the *ByPair* function is not significant. This is because we need to enumerate all shortest paths in two cases, which dominates the entire time cost.

Size of Link Graph. Figure 7(e) summarizes the space cost of the link graph on *Random* graphs, for various graph sizes. Obviously, a larger original graph results in a larger link graph. We also obtain the size of the link graph generated by *LP*. Actually, the *LP* method needs to record the anonymized edge weight for each edge in space cost $O(m)$, where m is number of edges. Although *LP* consumes less space cost than our method, the main drawback of *LP* lies in its scalability. We cannot run it on a large graph. Figure 7(f) presents the impact of different benefit functions on the space cost of the link graph across real graphs, *Power* graphs (*P*) and *Random* graphs (*R*). All datasets clearly show the effectiveness of the *ByPair* function. The space cost of link graphs with *ByPair* is nearly 1/3 to 1/2 that of the link graph with *ByVertex*. As explained above, *ByPair* is a more effective benefit function than *ByVertex* to produce fewer outsourced graphs. Figure 7(g) shows the space cost of link graph on *Power* graphs varying *MPMem* from 1.5M (M is for million) to 3M. It also verifies our earlier claim. When *MPMem* is sufficient to store shortest paths, such as in graphs with fewer than 6k vertices, the adjustment of *MPMem* is not effective. When the graph is larger and only a smaller proportion of all paths can be loaded into memory, *MPMem* is more useful in reducing the space cost of the link graph.

Local Overhead Ratio. Figure 7(h) illustrates the local overhead ratio for various d values on the *Random* graph set. We randomly generate 100 shortest distance queries, and compute the average local overhead ratio. As shown in the figure, the local overhead ratio is lower than 0.06 in all test cases. In other words, the outsourced server carries out the bulk of the computational work for shortest distance discovery. The client side handles the local shortest distance search for distances smaller than d and the merging of results in Equation (1). Therefore, the decrease of d can further reduce the time cost on the client side. We believe the curve in the figure is due to the randomization in the time recording, since all local time cost is nearly zero. As for the *LP* method, it takes $O(l)$ time cost to recover the shortest distance, where l is the total edges in the shortest path. The time cost of *LP* over small graphs is also nearly zero.

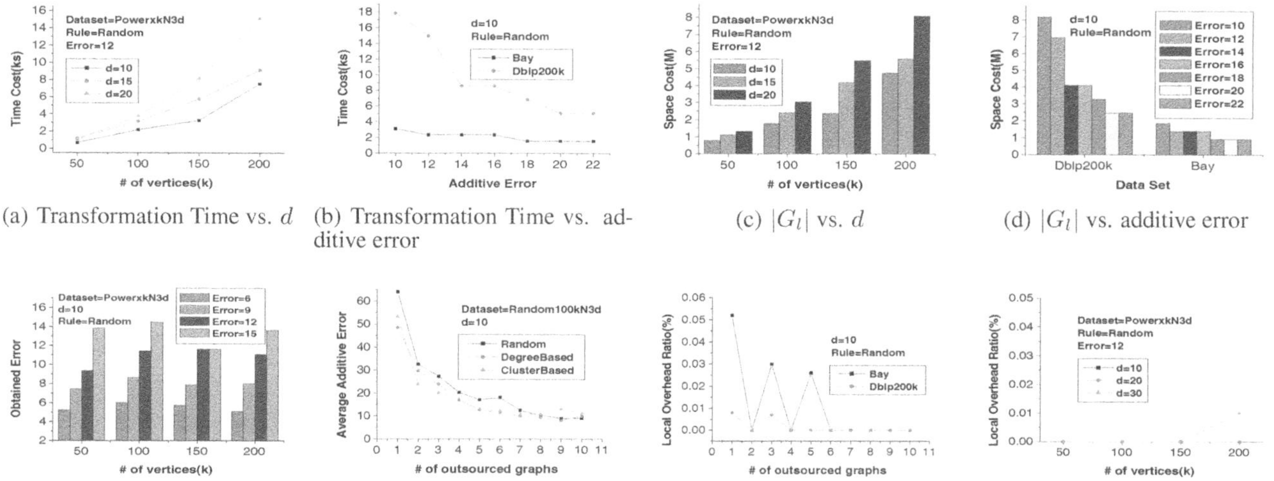

(a) Transformation Time vs. d (b) Transformation Time vs. additive error (c) $|G_l|$ vs. d (d) $|G_l|$ vs. additive error

(e) Additive Error vs. additive error (f) Additive Error vs. construction Rules (g) Local Overhead Ratio Vs. Additive Error (h) Local Overhead Ratio vs. d

Figure 8: Experimental Results on Graph Transformation with Approximate Answers

5.3 Graph Transformation with Approximate Answer

In this section, we study the impact of different factors on the measures of graph transformation with approximate shortest distance answering. Specifically, we are interested in: i) What is the impact of d on the transformation overhead and local overhead ratio? ii) Can the given additive error bound be achieved with our method? iii) What is the impact of different heuristic construction rules on the additive error? In all experiments, the number of full shortest path trees in each outsourced graph is set to 50, and the number of sampling queries for each category is 20.

Transformation Time Cost. Figure 8(a) illustrates the transformation time cost across the *Power* graph set, varying d from 10 to 20, when the average additive error $\overline{\beta}$ is set to 12. Outsourced graphs are generated in a random way (denoted by *Random*). A larger d indicates each outsourced graph preserves fewer shortest paths. In order to meet the requirement of the given additive error, more outsourced graphs are needed, which leads to more transformation time.

Figure 8(b) presents the impact of different additive errors on the transformation time cost across two real datasets. We still use the random method to construct outsourced graphs. From Fig.8(b), we can see that a larger additive error leads to less transformation time cost, since in such a case, fewer outsourced graphs are needed.

Size of Link Graph. Figure 8(c) summarizes the size of the link graph for various d on the *Power* graphs with the given average additive error 12. It is no surprise that the size of the link graph goes up with the increase of d. As we have explained in the transformation time cost, a larger d corresponds to more outsourced graphs and then more edges in the link graph to outsourced graphs. Figure 8(d) illustrates the space cost on the real datasets with different additive errors. It clearly shows that the increase of additive error results in a decrease in the size of the link graph. The reason is similar to the explanation we gave along with Fig.8(b). A larger additive error reduces the number of the outsourced graphs used, indicating fewer edges in the link graph.

Additive Error. Figure 8(e) studies whether we can achieve the additive error as expected. After we generate the outsourced graphs with Algorithm 3, we evaluate 100 shortest path queries with Equation (1) and Dijkstra's algorithm, and test whether their average additive error is the same as that specified. We observe that the two values (in X and Y axis) are very close. In other words, our graph transformation method can achieve the specified additive error quite well, which also illustrates the effectiveness of the average additive error estimation strategy in Algorithm 3.

Figure 8(f) compares the average additive errors on the same number of outsourced graphs constructed with different heuristic rules over *Random* graphs. We implement the degree based (denoted by *DegreeBased*) and the cluster based (denoted by *ClusterBased*) method for constructing outsourced graphs. The average additive errors are obtained with 100 queries on outsourced graphs. The results in Fig.8(f) show that among all heuristic construction rules, the cluster based method can produce outsourced graphs with the lowest additive error when the number of outsourced graphs is relatively small, for example, less than 4. When more outsourced graphs are generated, three construction methods produce the similar answers, since the distribution of outsourced vertices is more important in such a case.

Local Overhead Ratio. Figure 8(g) and Figure 8(h) illustrate the local overhead ratio on the real datasets and *Power* graphs. We obtain the local overhead ratio as that in Fig.7(h). In all cases, the local time cost used in shortest distance answering is nearly zero. By combining the results in Fig.7(h), we can know that the local overhead ratio scales very well in terms of the graph size. As shown in Table 2, the client side requires $O(n_l^2 + xb^2)$ time cost for shortest distance computation, while n_l, x and b are nearly constant with respect to the graph size. At the same time, the graph size has a significant impact on Dijkstra's algorithm in the distance discovery. Therefore, the local overhead ratio declines sharply with the increase of graph size.

5.4 Summary

To sum up, from the experimental results, we can draw the following conclusions: i) The increase of d, although strengthening security of outsourced graphs, drives up the transformation time cost, the space cost of the link graph and overhead of the query answering on the client side; ii) Our graph transformation with exact distance answering scales much better than the existing method. Our graph transformation with approximate distance answering achieves the given additive error quite well and can handle large graphs. iii) In all test cases, the local overhead ratio is very low and even goes down with the increase of graph size. Such results illustrate the effectiveness of graph outsourcing.

6. CONCLUSION AND FUTURE WORKS

In this paper, we study how to utilize cloud computing to efficiently compute shortest distance in large graphs without compromising their sensitive information. We define a new security model called 1-neighborhood-d-radius. Our purpose is to reduce the space cost and shortest distance evaluation cost on the client side while satisfying both security and utility requirements. We devise a greedy method to transform graphs with exact shortest distance answering, and develop a fast transformation method to support approximate distance answering within the given average additive error bound.

This work can be extended in several interesting directions. First, we will study how other graph queries such as reachability query can be computed in the cloud within our framework. In general, our framework can be useful for graph operations which can be divided into the global search and local search, in which the global search takes the most of the computational cost, and the local search result can be merged into the global one. Second, we will investigate stronger security standards over outsourced graphs. For instance, we can add noise on the edge weight or node degree on the condition that the shortest paths can be preserved in the outsourced graph. Third, incremental graph outsourcing is desirable for dynamic graphs. At the same time, incremental outsourcing should not lead to information leakage in outsourced graphs.

ACKNOWLEDGMENTS

We would like to thank the anonymous reviewers for their helpful comments. We would like to thank Victor E. Lee for helping with the paper revision. The NSFC supported Gao via 60873062 and 61073018, and supported Jin via 61003167. The research grants Council of the Hong Kong SAR supported Yu via 419008 and 419109. The NSF supported Jin via IIS-0953950. National science and technology major program supported Wang via 2010ZX01042-001-003-05 and 2010ZX01042-002-002-02

7. REFERENCES

[1] A.V.Goldberg and C.Harrelson. Computing the shortest path: search meets graph theory. In *SODA*, pages 156–165, 2005.

[2] B.Zhou and J.Pei. Preserving privacy in social networks against neighborhood attacks. In *ICDE*, pages 506–515, 2008.

[3] C.Dwork, F.McSherry, K.Nissim, and A.Smith. Calibrating noise to sensitivity in private data analysis. In *TCC*, 2006.

[4] C.Li, M.Hay, V.Rastogi, G.Miklau, and A.McGrego. Optimizing linear counting queries under differential privacy. In *PODS*, pages 123–134, 2010.

[5] E.W. Dijkstra. A note on two problems in connexion with graphs. *Numerische Mathematik*, pages 269–271, 1959.

[6] D.J.Abadi. Data management in the cloud: Limitations and opportunities. *IEEE Data Eng. Bull. (DEBU)*, 32(1):3-12, 2009.

[7] E.Cohen, E.Halperin, H.Kaplan, and U.Zwick. Reachability and distance queries via 2-hop labels. In *SODA*, pages 937–946, 2002.

[8] G.Cormode, D.Srivastava, S.Bhagat, and B.Krishnamurthy. Class-based graph anonymization for social network data. *PVLDB*, 2(1):766-777, 2009.

[9] G.Cormode, D.Srivastava, T.Yu, and Q.Zhang. Anonymizing bipartite graph data using safe groupings. *PVLDB*, 1(1):833-844, 2008.

[10] H.Hacigümüs, B.R.Iyer, and S.Mehrotra. Providing database as a service. In *ICDE*, pages 29–40, 2002.

[11] J.Cheng, A.W.Fu, and J.Liu. K-isomorphism: privacy preserving network publication against structural attacks. In *SIGMOD*, pages 459–470, 2010.

[12] J.M.Kleinberg, A.Slivkins, and T.Wexler. Triangulation and embedding using small sets of beacons. *J. ACM (JACM)*, 56(6), 2009.

[13] K.Liu and E.Terzi. Towards identity anonymization on graphs. In *SIGMOD*, pages 93–106, 2008.

[14] L.Backstrom, C.Dwork, and J.M.Kleinberg. Wherefore art thou r3579x?: anonymized social networks, hidden patterns, and structural steganography. In *WWW*, pages 181–190, 2007.

[15] L.Liu, J.Wang, J.Liu, and J.Zhang. Privacy preservation in social networks with sensitive edge weights. In *SDM*, pages 954–965, 2009.

[16] L.Zou, L.Chen, and M. TamerÖzsu. Distancejoin: Pattern match query in a large graph database. *PVLDB*, 2(1):886-897, 2009.

[17] L.Zou, L.Chen, and M. TamerÖzsu. K-automorphism: A general framework for privacy preserving network publication. *PVLDB*, 2(1):946-957, 2009.

[18] M.Hay, C.Li, G.Miklau, and D.Jensen. Accurate estimation of the degree distribution of private networks. In *ICDM*, pages 169–178, 2009.

[19] M.Hay, G.Miklau, D.Jensen, D.F.Towsley, and P.Weis. Resisting structural re-identification in anonymized social networks. *PVLDB*, 1(1):102-114, 2008.

[20] M.L.Yiu, Y.Lin, and K.Mouratidis. Efficient verification of shortest path search via authenticated hints.. In *ICDE*, pages 237–248, 2010.

[21] M.Potamias, F.Bonchi, and C.Castillo. Fast shortest path distance estimation in large networks. In *CIKM*, pages 867–876, 2009.

[22] M.Thorup and U.Zwick. Approximate distance oracles. In *STOC*, pages 183–192, 2001.

[23] N.Jing, Y.Huang, and E.A.Rundensteiner. Hierarchical encoded path views for path query processing: An optimal model and its performance evaluation. *TKDE*, 10(3):409–432, 1998.

[24] S.Das, M.Egecioglu, and A.E.Abbadi. Anonymizing weighted social network graphs. In *ICDE*, pages 904–907, 2010.

[25] S.Jung and S.Pramanik. An efficient path computation model for hierarchically structured topographical road maps. *TKDE*, 14(5):1029-1046, 2002.

[26] S.Nath, H.Yu, and H.Chan. Secure outsourced aggregation via one-way chain. In *SIGMOD*, pages 31–44, 2009.

[27] V.Chvatal. A greedy heuristic for the set-covering problem. *Mathematics of Operations Research*, 4(3):233-235, 1979.

[28] X.Ying and X.Wu. Randomizing social networks: a spectrum preserving approach. In *SDM*, pages 739–750, 2008.

On k-skip Shortest Paths

Yufei Tao† Cheng Sheng† Jian Pei‡

†Department of Computer Science and Engineering
Chinese University of Hong Kong
New Territories, Hong Kong
{taoyf, csheng}@cse.cuhk.edu.hk

‡School of Computing Science
Simon Fraser University
Burnaby, BC Canada
jpei@cs.sfu.ca

ABSTRACT

Given two vertices s, t in a graph, let P be the shortest path (SP) from s to t, and $P^\star$ a subset of the vertices in P. $P^\star$ is a *k-skip shortest path* from s to t, if it includes at least a vertex out of every k consecutive vertices in P. In general, $P^\star$ succinctly describes P by sampling the vertices in P with a rate of at least $1/k$. This makes $P^\star$ a natural substitute in scenarios where reporting every single vertex of P is unnecessary or even undesired.

This paper studies k-skip SP computation in the context of *spatial network databases (SNDB)*. Our technique has two properties crucial for real-time query processing in SNDB. First, our solution is able to answer k-skip queries *significantly faster* than finding the original SPs in their entirety. Second, the previous objective is achieved with a structure that occupies *less space* than storing the underlying road network. The proposed algorithms are the outcome of a careful theoretical analysis that reveals valuable insight into the characteristics of the k-skip SP problem. Their efficiency has been confirmed by extensive experiments with real data.

Categories and Subject Descriptors

H3.3 [**Information search and retrieval**]: Search process

General Terms

Algorithms

Keywords

k-skip, shortest path, road network

1. INTRODUCTION

Finding *shortest paths (SP)* in a graph is a classic problem in computer science. Formally, let $G = (V, E)$ be a graph where V is a set of vertices and E a set of edges. Each edge carries a non-negative weight. Define the *length* of a path P, represented as $\|P\|$, to be the total weight of the edges in P. Given two vertices $s, t \in V$, a *SP query* returns the path from s to t with the minimum length.

SIGMOD'11, June 12–16, 2011, Athens, Greece.

The SP problem has received considerable attention from the research community in the past few years (see the recent work [4, 24, 27] and the references therein), due to its profound importance in *Spatial Network Databases (SNDB)*. An SNDB manages geometric entities positioned in an underlying *road network*, and supports efficient data retrieval with predicates on network distances, and optionally also on spatial properties (a representative system is Google Maps). A standard modeling of a road network is a graph where each vertex corresponds to a junction and each edge represents a road segment. An edge's weight is often set to the length of the corresponding road segment or the average time for a vehicle to pass through the segment.

Traditionally, a SP query retrieves *every vertex* on the shortest path P, which is sometimes unnecessarily detailed in practice. Consider, for example, that a person leaves home for a retreat destination. Typically, the SP would first wind through her/his neighborhood R_1, continue onto a set of highways R_2, and eventually enter the neighborhood R_3 of the destination. The region, in which fine-detailed directions are imperative, is R_3. In R_1 and R_2, it is often sufficient to guide the user at a *coarse* level, in a manner similar to putting *sign-posts* along the way, for example, by naming some streets to be passed, and the highways to be taken in succession.

In fact, even the computation of turn-by-turn driving directions does not always demand all the vertices on P. This is because P may contain vertices at which *no turning is needed.* To illustrate, assume that P stays on the *Main Street* in an urban area for one kilometer, during which the street intersects another street every 100 meters. Each of those 10 intersections is a vertex in P, but only the first and last of them are enough to generate the instructions for turning into and away from the Main Street, respectively. The situation is similar if P involves a long highway, in which the vertices between the points where P enters and leaves the highway respectively can be ignored.

In this paper, we are interested in computing a *subset*, say $P^\star$, of the vertices in P. Instead of an arbitrary subset, however, we demand that P^* be *k-skip shortest path*, namely, it should contain *at least one* vertex out of every *k consecutive* vertices in P. Figure 1 shows an example with $k = 4$, where P consists of all the (black and white) vertices while $P^\star$ only the black ones. Note that there can be more than one black vertex in every 4 consecutive vertices in P, but it is impossible to have none.

$P^\star$ succinctly describes P by sampling its vertices with a rate of at least $1/k$. Such a sample set can replace P in answering queries like: what are the highways (alternatively, neighborhoods or cities) that P needs to go through? $P^\star$ is equally useful in discovering the gas stations (similarly, attractions or hotels) along P, because

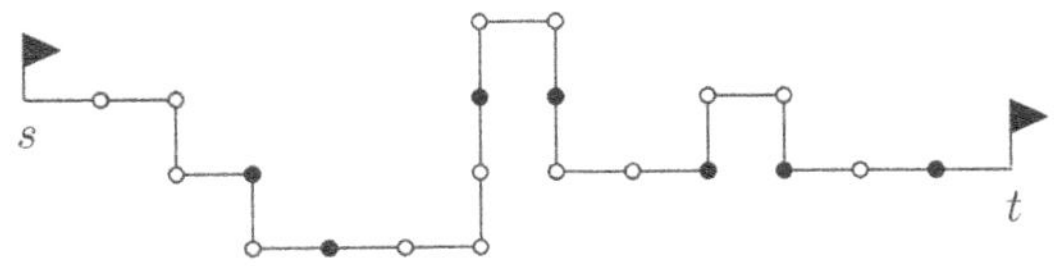

Figure 1: The black vertices constitute a 4-skip shortest path

it is often sufficient to find the stations close to the vertices in $P^\star$, as opposed to all the vertices of P. This is the idea of [18] in approaching the *continuous nearest neighbor* problem. Moreover, $P^\star$ is also adequate for estimating various statistics about P, as in the query: find the percentage of dessert coverage in the route from Los Angeles to Las Vegas. Finally, $P^\star$ is exactly what is needed to plot the original P in a digital map with a decreased resolution. For example, at Google Maps, only a subset of the vertices on a path need to be displayed according to the current zooming level.

For traditional mapping purposes, $P^\star$ has two notable advantages over P. First, it is (much) smaller in size, and hence, requires less bandwidth to transmit. This is a precious feature in mobile computing that will especially be appreciated by users charged by the amount of Internet usage. Second, using a clever algorithm, $P^\star$ can be faster to compute because, intuitively, fewer vertices need to be retrieved than P. Such an efficiency gain provides valuable opportunities for in-car navigation devices and routing websites such as Google Maps to support a great variety of on-route services in shorter time.

The concept of k-skip SP comes with a *zoom-in* operation. Given consecutive vertices u, v on $P^\star$, the operation finds the missing vertices on P from u to v. As there are at most $k-1$ missing vertices, for small k a zoom-in incurs negligible time, because it only needs to compute a *very short* path. This adds a nice *pay-as-you-go* feature in applying k-skip SP. First, a driver can request the least zoom-in's to complete the part of the route outside her/his knowledge. This allows her/him to pay for the most useful information only. Second, an algorithm preparing turn-by-turn directions can zoom-in only when necessary (i.e., a turning may exist between two adjacent vertices $P^\star$), thus saving the cost of locating the skipped vertices.

Contributions. Somewhat surprisingly, the notion of k-skip SP, or in general the idea of sampling (the vertices in) a SP, has not been mentioned previously to the best of our knowledge, let alone any algorithm dealing with the problem of k-skip SP computation. We fill the gap with a systematic study of this problem. In particular, our objectives are twofold:

1. Resolve a k-skip query *significantly faster* than calculating the original SP in entirety.
2. Achieve the previous purpose with a data structure that occupies *less space* than storing the input graph $G = (V, E)$ itself. This permits the structure to reside in memory even for the largest road network, as is crucial for real-time query processing in SNDB.

The first contribution of this paper is to formally establish the fact that, only a small subset $V^\star$ of the vertices in G need to be considered to attack the k-skip problem. In other words, the other vertices in $V \backslash V^\star$ are never needed to form any k-skip SP. Referring to $V^\star$ as a *k-skip cover*, we show that there always exists a $V^\star$ with size roughly proportional to $|V|/k$. This theoretical finding is of independent interest because it is not limited to road networks, but *actually holds for general graphs*.

Our second contribution is a full set of algorithms required to process k-skip SP queries within a stringent time limit. Specifically, these algorithms settle three sub-problems: (i) find a small $V^\star$ in time *linear* to the complexity of G, (ii) construct from $V^\star$ a space-economical structure, and (iii) answer a k-skip query by accessing only a small portion of the structure. We thoroughly evaluated these algorithms with extensive experiments on real data, including the massive road network of the US which has about 24 million vertices and 58 million edges. Our results prove that the proposed technique very well satisfy both requirements mentioned earlier in all settings.

Roadmap. The next section reviews the literature of SP computation. Section 3 formally defines the target problem, and gives an overview of our solutions. Section 4 elaborates the theoretical results on k-skip covers, and the algorithms for constructing the proposed structure. Section 5 clarifies how to answer a k-skip query and perform a zoom-in efficiently. Section 6 contains the experimental results, while Section 7 concludes the paper with directions for future work.

2. RELATED WORK

There is an extremely rich literature on the SP problem. In Section 2.1, we clarify the details of the *reach* algorithm, which is the state of the art for SP computation in road networks. Section 2.2 surveys the other recent progress in the database and theory communities.

2.1 *Dijkstra* and *reach*

To facilitate discussion, given two vertices u, v in the input graph $G = (V, E)$, we denote by $SP(u, v)$ the SP from u to v. The length of $SP(u, v)$, i.e., $\|SP(u, v)\|$, is called the *distance* between u and v. If (u, v) is an edge in G, we represent its weight as $\ell(u, v)$. In case G is directed, (u, v) is an edge from u to v, and (v, u) means the opposite. To avoid unnecessary distraction, our examples use undirected graphs, but all the notations in our description are carefully written so that they are also correct for directed graphs.

Dijkstra. Let us first review the *Dijkstra*'s algorithm [5], which is the foundation of the *reach* method described shortly. *Dijkstra* finds $SP(s, t)$ by exploring the vertices in ascending order of their distances to the source s. At any time, each vertex $u \in V$ has a status chosen from {`unseen`, `labeled`, `scanned`}. Furthermore, u is associated with a label $l(u)$ equal to the distance of the SP from s to u found *so far* (i.e., an even shorter path may be discovered later). On this path, the vertex immediately preceding u is kept in $pred(u)$, referred to as the *predecessor* of u.

At the beginning of *Dijkstra*, all vertices $u \in V$ have status `unseen`, $l(u) = \infty$ and $pred(u) = \emptyset$. The only exception is s, whose status is `labeled`, with $l(s) = 0$ and $pred(u) = \emptyset$. At all times, the vertices of status `labeled` are managed by a min-heap Q, using their labels as the sorting key. In each iteration, the algorithm (i) de-heaps the vertex $u \in Q$ with the minimum $l(u)$, (ii) *relaxes* all edges (u, v) such that the status of v is *not* `scanned`, and (iii) changes the status of u to `scanned`. Specifically, relaxation of (u, v) involves the following steps:

relax (u, v)
1. **if** the status of v is `unseen` **then**
2. $\quad l(v) \leftarrow l(u) + \ell(u, v)$
3. $\quad$ the status of $v \leftarrow$ `labeled`
4. **else if** $l(v) > l(u) + \ell(u, v)$ **then**

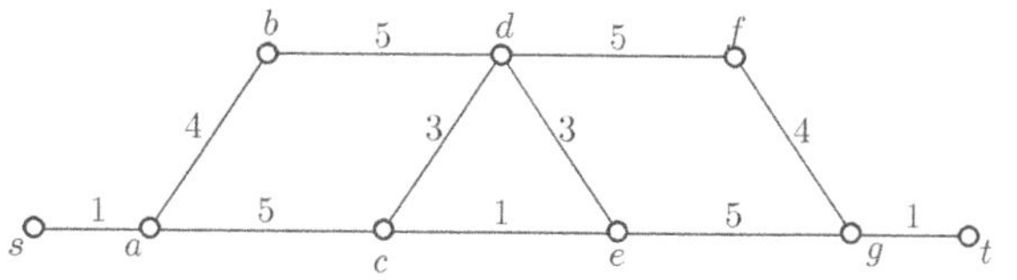

(a) The input graph

a	b	c	d	e	f	g	s	t
1	0	6	5	6	0	1	0	0

(b) Global reaches of the vertices

Figure 2: Illustration of *reach*

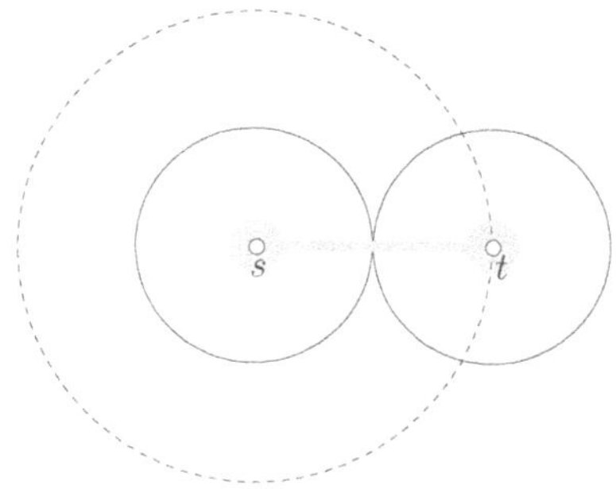

Figure 3: Comparison of *Dijkstra*, *bi-directional*, and *reach*

```
    l(v) ← l(u) + ℓ(u, v)
    pred(v) ← u
```

The present $l(u)$ is guaranteed to be $\|SP(s,u)\|$. The algorithm terminates as soon as t, the destination, is selected by an iteration.

To illustrate, assume that we want to compute $SP(s,t)$ in Figure 2a. In the first iteration, *Dijkstra* scans s and relaxes (s,a), after which $Q = \{a\}$ and $l(a) = 1$. The next iteration de-heaps a and relaxes $(a,b), (a,c)$. Note that (a,s) is not relaxed because the status of s has become `scanned`. Now Q contains b, c with labels $5, 6$, respectively. The algorithm then scans b and relaxes (b,d), which labels d with 10. This is followed by de-heaping c, and relaxing $(c,d), (c,e)$. Note that the relaxation of (c,d) decreases $l(d)$ to 9. The rest of the algorithm proceeds in the same manner. By tracing the execution, one can verify that, at termination, all the vertices except t have already been scanned.

Dijkstra can be implemented in $O(m + n\log n)$ time [3], where n, m are the number of vertices and edges, respectively (i.e., $n = |V|, m = |E|$). In a road network, each vertex has an $O(1)$ degree, so the time complexity is essentially $O(n \log n)$.

Bi-directional. *Dijkstra* starts a graph traversal from s and gradually approaches t; call this a *forward* search. Immediately by symmetry, the SP problem can also be solved by a *backward* search from t to s (if G is directed, the *backward* search implicitly reverses the direction of each edge). The *bi-directional* algorithm [10, 20] achieves better efficiency by performing both searches synchronously, the effect of which is essentially to explore the vertices $u \in V$ in ascending order of $r_{s,t}(u)$, where

$$r_{s,t}(u) = \min\{\|SP(s,u)\|, \|SP(u,t)\|\}. \tag{1}$$

In fact, if u is closer to s (than to t), then it will first be touched in the forward search; otherwise, the backward search will find it first. The forward/backward search proceeds as in the standard *Dijkstra*'s algorithm (as if the other search did not exist). Let Q_f (Q_b) be the heap of the forward (backward) direction. Synchronization is carried out by advancing in each iteration the direction that has a smaller label at the top of the heap.

Bi-directional monitors the distance λ of the shortest s-to-t path found *so far*. λ is set to ∞ initially, and may be updated when the forward search (the backward case is symmetric) de-heaps a vertex u whose status in the backward direction is `labeled`[1]. Specifically, at this time, the algorithm computes $\lambda' = l_f(u) + l_b(u)$, where $l_f(u)$ and $l_b(u)$ are the labels of u in the forward and backward search, respectively. λ is reduced to λ' if $\lambda > \lambda'$, since it implies the existence of a shorter s-to-t path that concatenates $SP(s,u)$, (u,v), and $SP(v,t)$, where v is the current predecessor of u in the backward search. The algorithm terminates when either direction de-heaps a vertex already scanned in the other direction.

[1]This status cannot be `scanned`; otherwise, the algorithm would have terminated right after u was de-heaped by the forward search, as will be clear shortly.

Let us demonstrate *bi-directional* on the graph in Figure 2a. After three iterations of each direction, which are the same as in *Dijkstra*, the forward (backward) search has scanned s, a, b (t, g, f), such that Q_f (Q_b) contains vertices c, d (e, d) with labels 6, 10, respectively. Currently, $\lambda = \infty$. Next, the forward search de-heaps $c \in Q_f$ and relaxes edges (c,d), (c,e), after which $l_f(e) = 7, l_f(d) = 9$. Similarly, the backward search then de-heaps $e \in Q_b$. As the status of e in the forward direction is `labeled`, the algorithm updates λ to $l_f(e) + l_b(e) = 7 + 6 = 13$, before it relaxes $(e,c), (e,d)$. The forward search continues by de-heaping $e \in Q_f$, which, however, has been scanned in the backward search. The algorithm therefore terminates, without de-heaping d in either direction.

Reach. Intuitively, if λ is the length of $SP(s,t)$, *Dijkstra* searches a ball that centers at s, and has radius λ, shown as the dashed circle in Figure 3. *Bi-directional*, on the other hand, explores two balls with radius $\lambda/2$ that center at s, t respectively (the two solid circles in Figure 3). The *reach* algorithm, which is the current state of the art, dramatically shrinks the search area to a small dumb-bell shape, as illustrated by the shaded region in Figure 3.

Let us start the explanation with the notion of *local reach*. Let u be a vertex on $SP(s,t)$. The *local reach of u in $SP(s,t)$* equals $r_{s,t}(u)$ as calculated in Equation 1. Note that this notion relies on a particular SP. Any vertex $v \notin SP(s,t)$ has no local reach defined in $SP(s,t)$. Now we extend the definition to *global reach*:

DEFINITION 1 (GLOBAL REACH [12]). *The **global reach**, denoted as $r(u)$, of a vertex u is the maximum local reach of u in all the shortest paths that pass u. Formally:*

$$r(u) = \max_{s,t|u \in SP(s,t)} r_{s,t}(u). \tag{2}$$

The reach $r(u)$ can be understood intuitively as follows. If u is on $SP(s,t)$, then *either s or t* must have distance at most $r(u)$ to u. In other words, in case neither s nor t is within distance $r(u)$ from u, u can be safely pruned in computing $SP(s,t)$.

Consider, for instance, vertex c in Figure 2a. To decide its global reach $r(c)$, first collect the set S of all the SPs that pass c, namely, $S = \{SP(s,t), SP(s,g), ..., SP(a,e), ...\}$. We then calculate the local reach of c in each SP of S. For example, its local reach in $SP(a,e)$ is $\min\{\|SP(a,c)\|, \|SP(c,e)\|\} = 1$. The final $r(c)$

equals the maximum of all the local reaches, which can be verified to be 6 (as is its local reach in $SP(s,t)$). Figure 2b shows the global reaches of all the vertices.

In computing $SP(s,t)$, the *reach* algorithm [10, 12] proceeds in the same way as *bi-directional*, but may prune a vertex in relaxing an edge (u,v). Without loss of generality, suppose that the relaxation takes place in the forward search (the backward case is symmetric). This implies that the forward search just scanned u, but has never scanned v (otherwise the edge would not have been relaxed). The pruning of *reach* takes place as follows:

RULE 1. *Vertex v is pruned if both of the following hold:*

1. v has status `labeled` *or* `unseen` *in the backward direction*

2. $r(v) < l_f(u)$

where $l_f(u)$ is the label of u in the forward search.

In general, *reach* can be understood as the execution of *bi-directional* on the vertices that survive pruning. In Figure 2, for example, *reach* finds $SP(s,t)$ by scanning only s, a, c, e, g, t. As in *bi-directional*, *reach* first scans s (t) in the forward (backward) direction, after which Q_f (Q_b) includes a (g) with label 1. Next, the forward search de-heaps a from Q_f, and relaxes $(a,b), (a,c)$. The relaxation of (a,b) prunes b by Rule 1 because $r(b) = 0 < l_f(a) = 1$. The backward search then eliminates f in a similar fashion. The rest of the algorithm proceeds as in *bi-directional*. Vertex d does not need to be scanned for the reason explained earlier for *bi-directional*.

The space consumption of *reach* is very economical because, except G itself, only *one extra value* needs to be stored for each vertex. However, it can be expensive to calculate the exact reach of every vertex. Fortunately, there are fast algorithms [10, 12] to obtain approximate reaches that are guaranteed to *upper bound* their original values. Pruning remains the same except that $r(u)$ should be replaced by its upper bound. The outstanding efficiency of this algorithm on road networks has been theoretically justified [1].

2.2 More results on SP computation

The $A^\star$ algorithm [13] is a classic SP solution that captures *Dijkstra* as a special case. The effectiveness of $A^\star$ relies on a method to calculate, typically in constant time, a lower bound of $\|SP(u,v)\|$ for any two vertices u, v. Apparently, 0 can be a trivial lower bound, but in that case $A^\star$ degenerates into *Dijkstra*. In general, the tighter the lower bounds are, the faster $A^\star$ is than *Dijkstra*.

Motivated by this, Agrawal and Jagadish [2] proposed to precompute the distances between each vertex and a special set of vertices called *landmarks*. In answering a SP query, those distances are deployed to derive lower bounds based on triangle inequality. This idea is also the basis of the *ALT* algorithm developed by Goldberg and Harrelson [9], which has lower query time (than [2]) at the tradeoff of consuming more space. The experiments of [10] indicate that *ALT* is slower than the *reach* method described in Section 2.1. Note, however, that *ALT* and *reach* are compatible, in the sense that their heuristics can be applied at the same time to maximize efficiency [10].

Sanders and Schultes [8, 25, 26] presented a *highway hierarchy (HH)* technique, whose rationale is to identify some edges that mimic the role of highways in reality. In computing a SP, the algorithm of *HH* modifies *Dijkstra* so that the search can skip as many non-highway edges as possible, and thus, terminate earlier. Based on the empirical evaluation of [10, 25], *HH* has comparable performance with respect to *reach*.

The *separator* technique is another popular approach [15, 16, 17] to preprocess a graph G for efficient SP retrieval. The idea is to divide the vertices of G into several components, and for each component, extract a set of *boundary vertices* such that the SP between two vertices in different components must go through a boundary vertex. Query efficiency benefits from the fact that, most computation of a SP can be restricted only to the boundary vertices. According to [25], however, separator-based methods are not as efficient as *HH* on road networks. Another disadvantage is that these methods often have expensive space consumption. For example, the space of [15] is at the order of $n^{1.5}$ (where n is the number of vertices), which is prohibitive for massive graphs.

In [28], Wagner et al. described a *geometric container* technique, which associates each edge (u,v) in G with a geometric region. The region covers all the vertices t such that the SP from u to t goes through v. In running *Dijkstra*, such regions can be used to prune many vertices that do not appear in the SP. Lauther [19] integrated a similar idea with the *bi-directional* algorithm discussed in Section 2.1. Samet et al. [24] proposed to break the geometric regions into smaller disjoint pieces that can be indexed by a quad-tree. Their solution lowers the cost of SP calculation (compared to [19, 28]), but entails $O(n^{1.5})$ space. A common shortcoming of [19, 24, 28] is that their preprocessing essentially determines the SPs between all pairs of vertices. The all-SP problem is notoriously difficult. Even on planar graphs, the fastest solution requires $O(n^2)$ time [7], which is practically intractable for large n.

Recently, Sankaranarayanan et al. [27] proposed a *path oracle* that is constructed from *well-separated pair decomposition*, and can be used to accelerate SP retrieval. Such an oracle consumes $O(s^2 n)$ space in 2-d space, where s is shown to be around 12 for practical data. Xiao et al. [30] showed that SP queries can be accelerated by exploiting symmetry in the data graph. Their approach, however, is limited to the case where all edges have a unit weight. Wei [29] developed an alternative solution by resorting to *tree decomposition* [23]. Rice and Tsotras [22] studied the shortest path problem with label restrictions. Some other work considers how to *estimate* shortest path distances, e.g., [11, 21].

We emphasize that all the works aforementioned calculate traditional, complete, SPs. The concept of k-skip SP has not appeared previously, and is formalized in the next section for the first time in the literature.

3. K-SKIP SHORTEST PATHS

For simplicity, we assume that the data graph $G = (V, E)$ is undirected, and will discuss directed graphs only when the extension is not straightforward. The following definition formalizes k-skip SP:

DEFINITION 2 (k-SKIP SHORTEST PATH). *Let $SP(s,t)$ be the shortest path from source s to destination t. Label the vertices in $SP(s,t)$ in the order they appear: $v_1, v_2, ..., v_l$ (i.e., $v_1 = s, v_l = t$), where l is the total number of vertices in the path. If $l \geq k$, let $P^\star$ be an ordered subset of $\{v_1, ..., v_l\}$, where the ordering respects that in $SP(s,t)$. $P^\star$ is a **k-skip shortest path** from s to t if*

$$P^\star \cap \{v_i, ..., v_{i+k-1}\} \neq \emptyset \quad (3)$$

for every $1 \leq i \leq l - k + 1$.

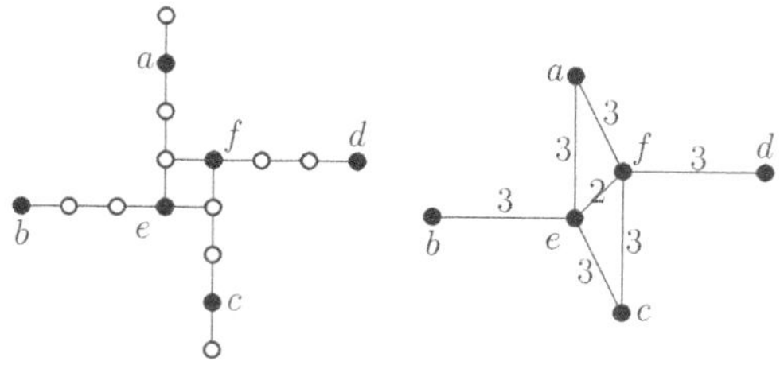

(a) Black vertices constitute a 3-skip cover

(b) 3-skip graph

Figure 4: Preprocessing for 3-skip SP computation

Even for fixed s and t, there can be multiple $P^\star$ satisfying the above condition. In other words, k-skip SPs are *not* unique, although all of them have to be subsets of $SP(s,t)$. Our objective is to preprocess G into a space-economical structure such that, given any s,t at run time, we can find a k-skip SP between any s and t efficiently.

The first step of our preprocessing is to eliminate the redundant vertices in G. The intuition is that, since most vertices in a SP need *not* be reported under the k-skip definition, certain vertices would end up being *never* returned. For example, consider the graph G in Figure 4a where all edges have a unit weight. Observe that, for $k=3$, any SP with 3 vertices must contain at least one black vertex. In other words, it suffices to form k-skip SPs using *just* the black vertices, whereas the other (white) vertices can be discarded.

We refer to the set of black vertices in the above example as a *3-skip cover*. The next definition generalizes the notion to *k-skip cover*, which contains a subset of the vertices that need to be considered for k-skip SPs.

DEFINITION 3 (k-SKIP COVER). *Let $V^\star$ be a subset of the vertices in G. $V^\star$ is a **k-skip cover** if it has the property that, for arbitrary $s,t \in V$ such that $SP(s,t)$ has at least k vertices,*

$$V^\star \cap SP(s,t)$$

is a k-skip SP from s to t, after ordering the vertices of $V^\star \cap SP(s,t)$ appropriately.

As will be clear in Section 5, the efficiency of our k-skip SP algorithm crucially depends on the fact that, it does not need to process the vertices of $V \setminus V^\star$. Hence, the minimization of $|V^\star|$ is essential, but it turns out to be rather challenging on an arbitrarily complex G. In fact, it is non-trivial even if one simply wants to know *whether* a small $V^\star$ always exists. These issues will be resolved in the next section.

We want to capture the adjacency of the vertices in $V^\star$ as far as k-skip SPs are concerned. For example, the black vertex a in Figure 4a can be consecutive only to e and f in a 3-skip SP (observe that e and f have blocked all the possible ways that can lead a to any other black vertex). We represent this by generating two "super-edges" that link a to e,f respectively. After this, the original edges (of G) incident on a can be ignored in computing any k-skip SP beginning from a.

Let us formalize the rationales behind the preceding paragraph in the next two definitions.

DEFINITION 4 (k-SKIP NEIGHBOR). *Let u,v be two vertices in a k-skip cover $V^\star$. We say that v is a **k-skip neighbor** of u if $SP(u,v)$ (namely, the shortest path from u to v in G) does not pass any other vertex in $V^\star$.*

It is easy to see that the SP from u to any of its k-skip neighbor v can have at most k edges. In an undirected G, the relation implied by the above definition is symmetric, i.e., u is a k-skip neighbor of v if and only if v is a k-skip neighbor of u. This is not necessarily true for directed graphs. In any case, let $N_k(u)$ be the set of all k-skip neighbors of u. For instance, in Figure 4a, $N_3(a)=\{e,f\}$.

DEFINITION 5 (k-SKIP GRAPH). *A **k-skip graph** of G is a graph $G^\star=(V^\star,E^\star)$, where*

- *$V^\star$ is a k-skip cover of G;*
- *for every vertex $u \in V^\star$, $E^\star$ has an edge (u,v) for each k-skip neighbor v of u, namely, $v \in N_k(u)$.*

The weight of $(u,v) \in E^\star$ is $\|SP(u,v)\|$.

We call each edge $(u,v) \in E^\star$ a *super-edge*. Figure 4b demonstrates the 3-skip graph $G^\star$ of the graph G in Figure 4a. The weight of (a,e) in $G^\star$ equals 3, which is the distance of a and e in G.

As shown later, finding a k-skip SP on the original graph G can be reduced to computing a (traditional) SP on a k-skip graph $G^\star$. In the next section, we will delve into the properties of $G^\star$, and give a method to construct it efficiently. Then, the reduction and the accompanied algorithms will be elaborated in Section 5.

4. K-SKIP GRAPH

The effectiveness of our pre-computed structure, namely a k-skip graph $G^\star=(V^\star,E^\star)$, relies on the size of the k-skip cover $V^\star$. No performance gain would be possible if a small $V^\star$ could not be guaranteed. Fortunately, we will show that such a good $V^\star$ always exists (Section 4.1). Sections 4.2 and 4.3 then elaborate the algorithms for building $G^\star$.

4.1 Size of k-skip cover

This subsection will establish:

THEOREM 1. *Let $G=(V,E)$ be a graph with $n=|V|$ vertices. For any $1 \le k \le n$, G has a k-skip cover $V^\star$ of size $O(\frac{n}{k}\log\frac{n}{k})$.*

Note that the above result applies to *all* graphs, that is, regardless of whether they are directed, planar, etc.

Our proof leverages the theory of *Vapnik-Chervonenkis (VC) dimension*, which quantifies how decomposable a search problem is. Specifically, let $\mathcal{D}$ be a dataset and $\mathcal{Q}$ be a set of queries that can be issued on $\mathcal{D}$. Given a query $q \in \mathcal{Q}$, define $q(\mathcal{D})$ to be the result of q on $\mathcal{D}$. A *shatterable* set $S \subseteq \mathcal{D}$ is such that, for any $S' \subseteq S$, there is always a query $q \in \mathcal{Q}$ with $q(\mathcal{D}) \cap S = S'$. In other words, any subset $S' \subseteq S$ needs to have the property that, a query $q \in \mathcal{Q}$ retrieves *all* the items of S', and *nothing* from $S \setminus S'$ (the result of q, however, may also include items from $\mathcal{D} \setminus S$). The VC dimension of $(\mathcal{D},\mathcal{Q})$ is the size of the largest shatterable subset of $\mathcal{D}$. Note that the VC dimension is *not* defined on a dataset, but instead, on a *pair* of a dataset and a query set.

Now let us analyze the VC dimension of the SP problem. Here, we have an input graph $G=(V,E)$. The $\mathcal{D}$ mentioned earlier corresponds to V. A SP query $q_{s,t}$ is uniquely defined by a source vertex s and a destination vertex t. Hence, the result $q_{s,t}(V)$ of $q_{s,t}$ is $SP(s,t)$. Let Q be the union of all the possible SP queries, namely, $Q=\bigcup_{s,t\in V} q_{s,t}$ (thus, $|Q|=n^2$). Next, we give a crucial lemma:

LEMMA 1. *For any graph G, the VC dimension of (V, Q) is 2.*

PROOF. Assume for contradiction that the VC dimension d of (V, Q) is at least 3 (note that d must be an integer). Hence, there is a shatterable set S with size d, which belongs to the SP returned by a query $q \in Q$. Let $u_1, u_2, ..., u_d$ be the vertices of S ordered by their appearance on the SP. Hence, u_2 is on the SP from u_1 to u_d. In this case, however, $S' = \{u_1, u_d\}$ cannot be in any SP that does not contain u_2, contradicting the fact that S is shatterable.

It remains to verify that the VC dimension can be 2. We omit the details as this is trivial. □

The rest of the proof (for Theorem 1) concerns *ϵ-net*. Let $\mathcal{D}, \mathcal{Q}$ be as defined earlier in our introduction to VC dimension. A set $S \subseteq D$ is an *ϵ-net* of $(\mathcal{D}, \mathcal{Q})$ if $S \cap q(\mathcal{D}) \neq \emptyset$ for any q satisfying $|q(\mathcal{D})| \geq \epsilon|\mathcal{D}|$. In other words, if q retrieves no less than $\epsilon|\mathcal{D}|$ items, at least one of these items must appear in S. The lemma below draws the correspondence between ϵ-net and k-skip cover:

LEMMA 2. *A $(\frac{k}{n})$-net $V^\star$ of (V, Q) is a k-skip cover of G.*

PROOF. Let Q' be the set of queries $q \in Q$ such that the SP $q(V)$ returned by q has *exactly* k vertices. By the definition of (k/n)-net, for each $q' \in Q'$, $V^\star \cap q'(V) \neq \emptyset$. Now consider a query $q \in Q \setminus Q'$ whose result $q(V)$ has more than k vertices. Clearly, any sub-path of $q(V)$ including k vertices is the result $q'(v)$ of some $q' \in Q'$, from which $V^\star$ contains at least a vertex. Therefore, $V^\star$ is a k-skip cover. □

The *ϵ-net theorem* [14] dictates that any $(\mathcal{D}, \mathcal{Q})$ with VC dimension d has an ϵ-net of size $O(\frac{d}{\epsilon}\log\frac{1}{\epsilon})$. This, combined with Lemmas 1 and 2, gives Theorem 1.

Remark 1. Effectively, the proof of the ϵ-net theorem [14] shows that a random subset of $\mathcal{D}$ with size $O(\frac{d}{\epsilon}\log\frac{1}{\epsilon})$ is an ϵ-net with high probability. Hence, we can find a k-skip cover $V^\star$ by simply taking $O(\frac{n}{k}\log\frac{n}{k})$ vertices from V randomly.

Remark 2. There is a trivial lower bound of n/k on the size of a k-skip cover. Hence, the upper bound in Theorem 1 is asymptotically tight, up to only a logarithmic factor.

4.2 Computing a k-skip cover

As mentioned in the previous subsection, a k-skip cover $V^\star$ can be obtained by taking $O(\frac{n}{k}\log\frac{n}{k})$ random vertices from V. It is well-known that randomized techniques generally work much better in practice than predicted by theory. Therefore, the $V^\star$ of a real graph would be much smaller, rendering a sample set of size $O(\frac{n}{k}\log\frac{n}{k})$ most probably unnecessarily large. Of course, we could artificially reduce the number of samples, but a good sample size appears to be difficult to decide. A large size gives only marginal improvement, whereas a small size has the risk that the sample set may no longer be a k-skip cover.

We propose an *adaptive sampling (AS)* algorithm to resolve the above issue. Before explaining the algorithm, we need a few more definitions. Let the *λ-hop neighbor set* of a vertex $u \in V$, denoted as $V_\lambda(u)$, be the set of all vertices $v \in V$ that can be reached from u by crossing *at most* λ edges. Each $v \in V_\lambda(u)$ is called a *λ-hop neighbor* of u. For example, assume an input graph G as shown in Figure 5a, where all edges, except those explicitly labeled, have weight 1. The 2-hop neighbor set $V_2(u)$ of u contains all the vertices in the shaded diamond. Note that $V_2(u)$ is decided *without* taking the edge weights into account.

Denote by $G_\lambda(u)$ the graph induced by $V_\lambda(u)$, which is referred to as the *λ-hop vicinity* of u. That is, $G_\lambda(u)$ includes *all and only* the edges in G that are between the vertices of $V_\lambda(u)$. For instance, in Figure 5a, the edges of $G_2(u)$ are those that fall *entirely* in the diamond.

By computing the SPs *inside* $G_\lambda(u)$ from u to all the other vertices in $V_\lambda(u)$ (that is, each SP uses only the edges of $G_\lambda(u)$), one obtains a *λ-hop shortest path tree* $T_\lambda(u)$ rooted at u. For every vertex v in $G_\lambda(u)$, the u-to-v path in $T_\lambda(u)$ is the SP from u to v *inside* $G_\lambda(u)$. Figure 5b demonstrates the 2-hop SP tree $T_2(u)$ of u. It is worth noting the difference between a SP inside the tree and a SP in the whole graph. For example, the u-to-c path in $T_2(u)$ has length 5. Although this is the shortest when only the edges of $G_2(u)$ are considered, there is an even shorter path $u \to f \to e \to d \to c$ which uses two edges $(e, d), (d, c)$ outside the 2-vicinity of u.

We now arrive at the most crucial concept underlying the *AS* algorithm. Let $V^\star$ be a subset of the vertices in G. We say that a λ-hop SP tree $T_\lambda(u)$ is *covered by* $V^\star$, if every u-to-v path in $T_\lambda(u)$ having at least λ edges goes through at least one vertex in $V^\star$, where v is a vertex in $T_\lambda(u)$. In Figure 5a, for example, let $V^\star$ be the set of black vertices. Then, the $T_2(u)$ in Figure 5b is *not* covered because the path u-to-b has 2 edges but passes no black vertex.

The next lemma gives an important property:

LEMMA 3. *$V^\star$ is a k-skip cover if it covers the $T_{k-1}(u)$ of all $u \in V$.*

PROOF. Assume for contradiction that a $V^\star$ fulfilling the if-condition of the lemma is not a k-skip cover. It follows that there exist two vertices $u, v \in V$ such that $SP(u, v)$ has k vertices none of which is in $V^\star$. Since $SP(u, v)$ has $k-1$ edges, by the construction of $T_{k-1}(u)$, we know (i) all the vertices on $SP(u, v)$ are in $T_{k-1}(u)$, and (ii) the u-to-v path in $T_{k-1}(u)$ is exactly $SP(u, v)$. This means, however, that $T_{k-1}(u)$ has not been covered by $V^\star$, thus reaching a contradiction. □

We are ready to clarify the *AS* algorithm:

---

adaptive-sampling
1. $V^\star = \emptyset$
2. randomly permutate the vertices of V
3. **for** each vertex $u \in V$
4.   **if** $T_{k-1}(u)$ is not covered by $V^\star$ **then**
5.   add u to $V^\star$

The correctness of the algorithm follows from Lemma 3, and the fact that, if $T_{k-1}(u)$ has not been covered by $V^\star$ yet, including u itself to $V^\star$ immediately makes $T_{k-1}(u)$ covered. For instance, as shown earlier, the $T_2(u)$ in Figure 5b is not covered, but it will be, once u is added to $V^\star$.

Heuristic. We can further reduce the size of $V^\star$ by first sorting the vertices of V in descending order of their degrees, and then, randomly permute the vertices with an identical degree. This increases the chance of sampling a vertex with a higher degree, which is beneficial because such a vertex tends to lie on more SPs, and therefore, have stronger covering power.

Time complexity. We close the subsection by analyzing the execution time of the algorithm, assuming that each vertex has an $O(1)$ degree, which is true in road networks. The randomization at Line 1 can be implemented in $O(n)$ time [6] where $n = |V|$ (the sorting in the high-degree-favoring heuristic can be done in $O(n)$

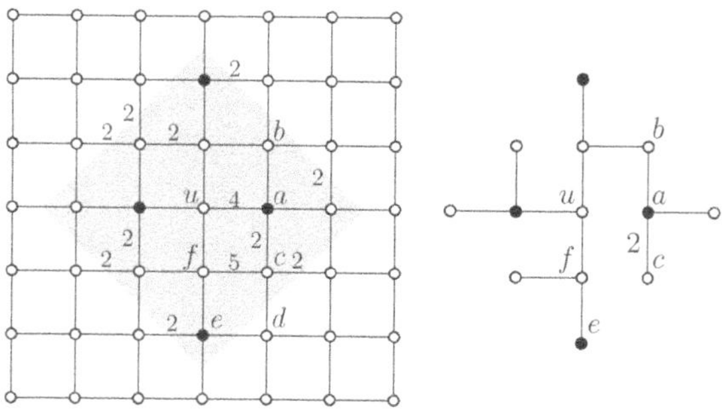

(a) 2-hop vicinity of u and its (b) 2-hop SP tree of u

Figure 5: Deciding whether to sample u into a 3-skip cover

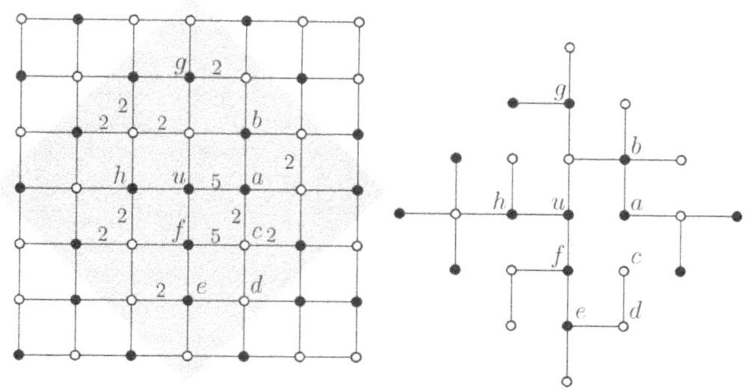

(a) 3-hop vicinity of u (b) 3-hop SP tree of u

Figure 6: Deciding $M_3(u)$

time when there are only a constant number of possible degrees). The λ-hop vicinity of a node u can be found by a standard *breath first traversal (BFT)* initiated at u, which terminates in $O(\sigma_\lambda(u))$ time where $\sigma_\lambda(u)$ is the number of λ-hop neighbors of u, i.e., $\sigma_\lambda(u) = |V_\lambda(u)|$. Then, the λ-hop SP tree $T_\lambda(u)$ can be extracted from $G_\lambda(u)$ using the *Dijkstra*'s algorithm in $O(\sigma_\lambda(u) \log \sigma_\lambda(u))$ time. Checking whether $T_\lambda(u)$ is covered by $V^\star$ demands a single traversal of $T_\lambda(u)$ in $O(\sigma_\lambda(u))$ time. Hence, the total cost of the algorithm is $O(n\bar{\sigma}_{k-1} \log \bar{\sigma}_{k-1})$, where $\bar{\sigma}_{k-1}$ is the average number of $(k-1)$-hop neighbors of the vertices in V.

The value of $\bar{\sigma}_{k-1}$ depends on the structure of the road network, but not the number n of the vertices. For example, consider two simple road networks that are a 100×100 and 1000×1000 grid, respectively. Although the second grid has 100 times more vertices, the two grids have the same $\bar{\sigma}_{k-1} = \Theta(k^2)$. Hence, when k is far smaller than n, $O(n\bar{\sigma}_{k-1} \log \bar{\sigma}_{k-1})$ grows linearly with n.

4.3 Computing a k-skip graph

Recall that the goal of our preprocessing is to produce a k-skip graph $G^\star = (V^\star, E^\star)$. $V^\star$ is simply a k-skip cover, whose derivation has been clarified in Section 4.2. Next we complete the puzzle by explaining the derivation of $E^\star$. Our discussion concentrates on the subproblem that, given a vertex $u \in V^\star$, how to calculate the set $N_k(u)$ of its k-skip neighbors (Definition 4). Once this is done, it is trivial to obtain $E^\star$ according to Definition 5, because we only need to add to $E^\star$ a super-edge from each u to every vertex $v \in N_k(u)$.

We will call each vertex of $V^\star$ a *sample* from now on, due to the sampling nature of the *AS* algorithm. A naive approach to acquire $N_k(u)$ is to first find the SP from u to every other sample $v \in V^\star$, and then add v to $N_k(u)$ if the path passes no other sample. However, since $|V^\star| \geq n/k$ (see Remark 2 of Section 4.1), doing so for all $u \in V^\star$ would incur $\Omega(n^2/k)$ time, which is prohibitive for large n. We circumvent the performance pitfall by aiming at a *superset* $M_k(u)$ of $N_k(u)$. As will be clear shortly, despite that $M_k(u)$ may result in a $G^\star$ with more edges, it has the advantage of being computable in significantly less time, thus allowing our technique to support gigantic graphs.

$M_k(u)$ can be conveniently defined by recycling the notations of the previous subsection. Let us first have the k-hop SP tree $T_k(u)$ of u (*as opposed to* the $T_{k-1}(u)$ in the *AS* algorithm). Then, $M_k(u)$ includes all the samples $v \neq u$ in $T_k(u)$ such that the u-to-v path in $T_k(u)$ does not pass any other sample. For illustration, Figure 6a shows a 3-skip cover $V^\star$ (the black vertices) on the data graph of Figure 5a. To determine $M_3(u)$, we first extract the 3-hop SP tree $T_3(u)$ as in Figure 6b. Then, it becomes clear that $M_3(u) = \{b, f, g, h\}$. Note that a, for example, is not in $M_3(u)$ due to the presence of b that blocks the path from u to a.

The lemma below establishes the relationship of $M_k(u)$ and $N_k(u)$.

LEMMA 4. $N_k(u) \subseteq M_k(u)$.

PROOF. By Definition 4, the fact $v \in N_k(u)$ implies that (i) $SP(u, v)$ does not pass any other sample, and (ii) $SP(u, v)$ has no more than k edges. Property (ii) indicates that all the vertices of $SP(u, v)$ must be in the k-hop vicinity of u, and hence, are present in $T_k(u)$. It follows that the u-to-v path in $T_k(u)$ is exactly $SP(u, v)$. Property (i) further shows that the path cannot contain any other sample. Therefore, by the construction of $M_k(u)$, we know $v \in M_k(u)$. □

We call $M_k(u)$ a *super neighbor set* of u. After acquiring it, we create a super-edge (u, v) in $E^\star$ from u to each vertex $v \in M_k(u)$, and set its weight to the length of the u-to-v path in $T_k(u)$. In other words, the super-edge represents a path in the original graph. The final $E^\star$ is complete after carrying out the above procedure for all the vertices $u \in V$.

Time complexity. After $T_k(u)$ is ready, $M_k(u)$ can be easily obtained by a single traversal of $T_k(u)$ in $O(\sigma_k(u))$ time, where $\sigma_k(u)$ is the number of the k-hop neighbors of u (i.e., the number of vertices in $T_k(u)$). A straightforward adaptation of the analysis in Section 4.2 shows that the cost of processing all $u \in V^\star$ is $O(n\bar{\sigma}_k \log \bar{\sigma}_k)$, where $\bar{\sigma}_k$ is the average number of k-hop neighbors size of the vertices in V. For k far lower than n, $O(n\bar{\sigma}_k \log \bar{\sigma}_k)$ is linear in n, due to the reasons explained at the end of Section 4.2.

5. QUERY ALGORITHM

Given vertices s, t in the data graph G, next we will explain how to obtain a k-skip SP from s to t using the k-skip graph $G^\star$ precomputed. Section 5.1 first gives an overview of our algorithm. A part of the algorithm needs to retrieve a traditional SP from $G^\star$, for which Section 5.2 presents an improved version of the *reach* method. Finally, Section 5.3 will discuss how to perform a zoom-in operation efficiently.

5.1 High-level description

Recall that the vertex set of $G^\star$ is a k-skip cover $V^\star$. The task of k-skip SP calculation is simple when both s and t are samples, namely, they belong to $V^\star$. In this case, we only need to find the

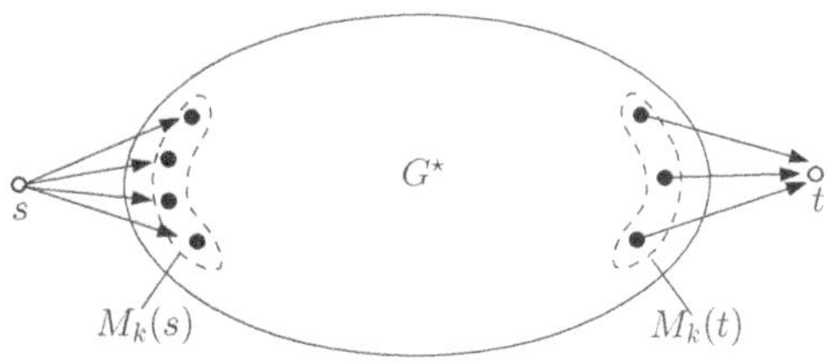

Figure 7: In-place sampling of s and t

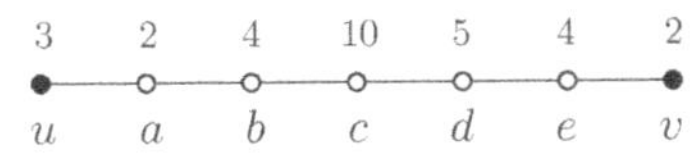

Figure 8: Super reach calculation

SP from s to t in $G^\star$, that is, traveling only on the super-edges. By the definition of $G^\star$, this SP is guaranteed to be a k-skip SP in the original graph G.

Let us focus on the situation where neither s nor t is a sample. Our solution is to sample them into $G^\star$ *right away*, so that the case can be converted to the previous scenario where s and t are samples. The inclusion of s, t as samples is *temporary*; after query processing, they will be removed from $G^\star$, whose size therefore does not change.

Incorporation of s, t in $G^\star$ involves two steps. First, s and t are inserted in $V^\star$. Second, some super-edges are created to reflect the appearance of s, t, in the same way the existing super-edges are computed. That is, given s (similarly for t), we first obtain the super neighbor set $M_k(s)$ of s, and then add to $E^\star$ a super-edge from s to each $u \in M_k(s)$, all exactly as described in Section 4.3. This process is illustrated in Figure 7. The analysis of Section 4.3 shows that, the above strategy runs in $O(\sigma_s(k) \log \sigma_s(k) + \sigma_t(k) \log \sigma_t(k))$ time. Remember that $\sigma_s(k)$, the number of k-hop neighbors of s, is low when k is small (similarly for $\sigma_t(k)$). Hence, sampling-in-place s and t incurs insignificant overhead.

Let $G^\star_{s,t}$ be the resulting $G^\star$ with the new super-edges, and $SP^\star(s,t)$ be the SP from s to t on $G^\star$. The rest of our algorithm returns directly $SP^\star(s,t)$, whose correctness is shown in the lemma below:

LEMMA 5. *$SP^\star(s,t)$ is a k-skip SP of $SP(s,t)$.*

PROOF. Let u be the first sample (counting also t) when we walk from s along $SP(s,t)$. By the definition of k-skip SP, $SP(s,u)$ has at most k edges, all of which appear in the k-hop SP tree of s. Hence, $u \in M_k(s)$ (otherwise, there would be another sample on $SP(s,u)$, contradicting the choice of u), which means (s,u) is a super-edge in $G^\star_{s,t}$.

Let v be the last sample (counting also s) on $SP(s,t)$ before we arrive at t. A similar argument shows that (v,t) is also a super-edge. The correctness of the lemma then follows from the fact that every super-edge has a weight equal to the length of the path it represents. □

Remark on directed graphs. Let S be the set of super-edges on t newly computed for $G^\star_{s,t}$. In the above, we computed S by first finding the super neighbor set $M_k(t)$ of t, and then inserting a super-edge (u,t) for each $u \in M_k(t)$. If G is directed, the derivation of S is slightly different, in the sense that we need to first *reverse* the directions of the edges in G, before proceeding as described earlier. Intuitively, $M_k(t)$ should contain the samples that can reach t "directly" (without passing another sample). Reversing directions allows us to apply the same algorithm in Section 4.2 to extract $M_k(t)$, originally designed to find samples reachable *from* t directly. The reversing incurs no additional execution time, because a direction change can take place only when the relevant edge is touched by the algorithm.

5.2 *Reach**

Now that we have converted k-skip SP computation to finding $SP^\star(s,t)$ on $G^\star$ (in case s,t are not samples, simply treat $G^\star_{s,t}$ as $G^\star$), many SP algorithms such as *Dijkstra*, *bi-directional*, and *reach*, can be plugged in to obtain $SP^\star(s,t)$. However, as those methods are not designed for our context, they may be improved by taking into account the characteristics of $G^\star$. Next, we achieve the purpose for *reach*.

As discussed in Section 2.1, *reach* prunes a vertex v in relaxing an edge (u,v), if the global reach $r(v)$ of v is small, compared to the distance that the algorithm has traveled in the forward/backward search (see Rule 1). On a k-skip graph, using only $r(v)$ for pruning may miss plenty of pruning opportunities. The reason is that, a super-edge (u,v) implicitly captures a path in the original graph, and hence, can be pruned as long as *any vertex* on that path has a low global reach. Motivated by this, we formulate a new notion:

DEFINITION 6 (SUPER REACH). *Let (u,v) be a super-edge in $G^\star$, and P be the path in G that (u,v) represents. The* ***super reach*** *of (u,v), denoted as $sr(u,v)$, equals the minimum $h(w)$ of all the vertices $w \in P$, where*

$$h(w) = r(w) - \min\{\|P_1\|, \|P_2\|\} \tag{4}$$

where $r(w)$ is the global reach of w, and P_1 (P_2) is the path on P from u to w (w to v).

To illustrate, assume that the path P captured by a super-edge (u,v) is as shown in Figure 8. The number above each vertex is its global reach (e.g., $r(u) = 3$); and suppose for simplicity all the edges have weight 1. To decide, for example, $h(b)$, we first observe $\|P_1\| = 2$ and $\|P_2\| = 4$, and then calculate by Equation 4 $h(b) = 4 - \min\{2,4\} = 2$. After $S = \{h(u), h(a), ..., h(e), h(v)\}$ is ready, the super reach $sr(u,v)$ can be determined as the minimum of S, i.e., $h(a) = 1$.

Apparently, $sr(u,v)$ can be computed in time linear to the number of vertices in P, i.e., at most k. Also, preserving all the super reaches entails small space, as only one extra value per super edge is stored. Next, we propose a new rule to enhance the pruning power of *reach*.

RULE 2. *When the forward search is about to relax a super edge (u,v), prune the edge if $sr(u,v) < l_f(u)$, where $l_f(u)$ is the label of u. A similar rule applies to the backward search.*

More precisely, pruning the super-edge (u,v) means that (i) the relaxation is not performed, and (ii) v is not en-heaped at this time (it is possible for v to get en-heaped due to another later relaxation though). Also note that the pruning happens *regardless of the status of v in the other direction* (unlike Rule 1 which requires v to have status `labeled` or `unseen` in the opposite search). This turns out to be a valuable property that permits the development of a crucial heuristic for maximizing efficiency, as discussed shortly.

Our algorithm, named *reach**, for SP computation over $G^\star$ is identical to *bi-directional* (see Section 2.1), except that Rule 2 is checked prior to every edge relaxation in an attempt to avoid the relaxation. The following theorem establishes the correctness of the algorithm.

THEOREM 2. *Reach* finds a SP on $G^\star$ correctly.*

PROOF. If the forward or backward search applies Rule 2 to prune a super-edge on $SP^\star(s,t)$, we say that a *blow* occurs. The lemma is obvious if no blow ever happens, so the subsequent discussion considers that there was at least one blow. Our argument proceeds in two steps. First, we will show that there can be only one blow during the execution of *reach**. This implies that every super-edge in $SP^\star(s,t)$ must be eventually relaxed in *at least one* direction, since two blows are needed to eliminate a super-edge from both directions. Equipped with these facts, we will prove the lemma in the second step.

Step 1. Without loss of generality, assume that the first blow occurred in the forward search, and eliminated super-edge $(u,v) \in SP^\star(s,t)$. It is easy to see that, when the blow happened, (i) the forward direction had scanned all the vertices in $SP^\star(s,u)$, and (ii) $sr(u,v) < l_f(u)$ (by Rule 2), where $l_f(u)$ equals $\|SP^\star(s,u)\| = \|SP(s,u)\|$. Thus,

$$sr(u,v) < \|SP(s,u)\|. \tag{5}$$

Let P be the path in G that (u,v) represents, and w be the vertex in P that minimizes $h(w)$ (see Equation 4), i.e., $sr(u,v) = r(w) - \min\{\|SP(u,w)\|, \|SP(w,v)\|\}$. Hence,

$$r(w) - \|SP(u,w)\| \leq sr(u,v) \tag{6}$$
$$r(w) - \|SP(w,v)\| \leq sr(u,v). \tag{7}$$

Inequalities 5 and 6 lead to $r(w) < \|SP(s,u)\| + \|SP(u,w)\| = \|SP(s,w)\|$. By definition, $r(w)$ is at least $\min\{\|SP(s,w)\|, \|SP(w,t)\|\}$. So we know $r(w) \geq \|SP(w,t)\|$ which, together with Inequality 7, gives:

$$sr(u,v) \geq \|SP(w,t)\| - \|SP(w,v)\| = \|SP(v,t)\|. \tag{8}$$

Inequalities 5 and 8 indicate $\|SP(s,u)\| > \|SP(v,t)\|$. Due to (i) the way *bi-directional* synchronizes the two directions and (ii) the choice of (u,v), the backward search must have scanned all the vertices on $SP(v,t)$ before the blow happened.

If there was a second blow, either the forward search needed to de-heap a vertex in $SP(v,t)$, or the reverse search needed to de-heap a vertex in $SP(s,u)$. But both events would have terminated the algorithm immediately, because *bi-direction* ends when the forward/backward search de-heaps a vertex already scanned in the other direction. Therefore, no second blow could have occurred.

Step 2. The analysis of Step 1 shows that, at the moment the blow took place, the status of v was `scanned` in the backward search. This means that, u had a status of `labeled` in the backward direction. Consequently, when the forward search de-heaped u (right before the blow), as in *bi-directional*, *reach** updated λ, which records the length of the SP found so far, to $l_f(u) + l_b(u) = \|SP^\star(s,u)\| + \|SP^\star(u,t)\| = \|SP^\star(s,t)\|$. In other words, *reach** found the correct SP successfully. □

After the forward (or backward) search de-heaps a vertex u, our current *reach** attempts to prune each out-going super-edge at u with Rule 2. Hence, the rule has to be applied numerous times if many super-edges out of u can be eliminated. This can harm the efficiency because each vertex in $G^\star$ may have a large degree (unlike G, where each vertex's degree is bounded), the result of which is that we may end up applying the rule a huge number of times during the entire algorithm.

The next heuristic allows us to significantly reduce the cost, while still eliminating as many super-edges as before, with *no* increase in the space assumption at all. The idea is to store the outgoing super-edges of each vertex u in $G^\star$ in *descending* order of their super reaches. After de-heaping u in the algorithm, we attempt to prune those edges in the sorted order. The benefit is that once an edge has been eliminated by Rule 2, we can assert that all the remaining edges can be pruned as well, because all of them must have *lower* super reaches (than the one pruned), and therefore, will satisfy Rule 2 for sure.

The above heuristic is made possible by the fact that, to prune an edge (u,v), Rule 2 does *not* require checking the status of v (in the search opposite to the one where the pruning happens). If this was not the case, the heuristic would virtually promise no performance gain as checking the status of v takes nearly the same amount of time as applying Rule 2 on (u,v).

Remark. It is worth pointing out that, the mechanism behind *reach**, namely the integration of *bi-directional* and the no-status-checking pruning strategy of Rule 2, actually extends the algorithmic paradigm for SP computation as illustrated in Section 2.1. In retrospect, *reach** is an immediate benefit of this extension.

5.3 Zoom-in

As mentioned in Section 1, the concept of k-skip SP is naturally accompanied by a *zoom-in* operator. Given consecutive vertices u, v on a k-skip $SP^\star(s,t)$, the operator finds all the vertices between u and v on the full $SP(s,t)$. A naive way to zoom-in is to run *Dijkstra* to extract the SP from u to v. A faster solution applies *bi-directional*. In fact, one can do even better using *reach*. However, simply executing *reach* afresh to compute $SP(u,v)$ is not likely to outperform *bi-directional* much. This is because the pruning of *reach* (i.e., Rule 1 in Section 2.1) is effective only if the vertex u de-heaped in the, for example, forward search has a large label $l_f(u)$. This requires the forward search to have come a long way from the source, a situation that will not happen between u and v, because they are at most k vertices apart on their SP.

There is a simple remedy to significantly boost the efficiency. The main idea is to *pretend* as if we were running *reach* to compute $SP(s,t)$ (as opposed to $SP(u,v)$), and that the algorithm had just come to u and v in the forward and backward searches, respectively. We "continue" the forward direction by setting $l_f(u) = \min\{\|SP(s,u)\|, \|SP(v,t)\|\}$, and making u the only vertex in the heap Q_f (which implies giving u the status `labeled`). Note that both $\|SP(s,u)\|$ and $\|SP(v,t)\|$ are available in the k-skip $SP^\star(s,t)$ already calculated. Similarly, the backward direction is also continued by setting $l_b(v) = l_f(u)$ and creating a heap Q_b with only v inside. We then start a normal iteration and proceed as in *reach*.

6. EXPERIMENTS

In this section, we empirically evaluate the performance of the proposed solutions. Our experimentation used four spatial networks[2] whose specifications are summarized in Table 1. Specifically, NY, BAY, CA-NV, and USA contain the road networks in New York city, San Francisco Bay area, California and Nevada combined, and the entire US, respectively. The weight of an edge

[2]All datasets can be downloaded from *http://www.dis.uniroma1.it/~challenge9/download.shtml*.

dataset	num. of vertices	num. of edges
NY	264,346	733,846
BAY	321,270	800,172
CA-NV	1,890,815	4,657,742
USA	23,947,347	58,333,344

Table 1: Dataset specifications

	k						
dataset	4	6	8	10	12	14	16
NY	51%	38%	31%	26%	22%	20%	18%
BAY	46%	33%	26%	22%	18%	16%	14%
CA-NV	46%	33%	21%	19%	16%	16%	15%
USA	45%	32%	25%	21%	18%	16%	15%

(a) Vertex ratio

dataset	4	6	8	10	12	14	16
NY	72%	65%	61%	58%	56%	53%	52%
BAY	66%	57%	52%	48%	45%	43%	42%
CA-NV	63%	54%	49%	45%	43%	41%	40%
USA	61%	51%	47%	44%	41%	39%	38%

(b) Edge ratio

Table 2: Sizes of k-skip graphs

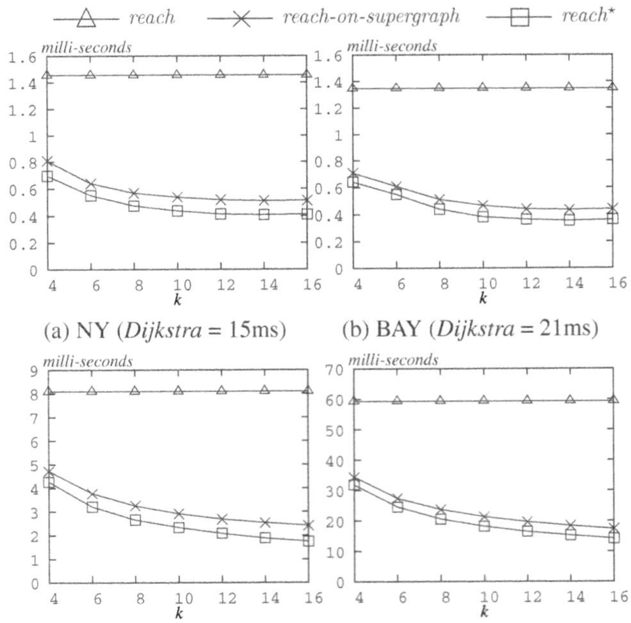

(a) NY (*Dijkstra* = 15ms) (b) BAY (*Dijkstra* = 21ms)

(c) CA-NV (*Dijkstra* = 168ms) (d) USA (*Dijkstra* = 3300ms)

Figure 9: Cost of k-skip and traditional SP queries

equals the travel time on the corresponding road segment. All of our results were obtained on a computer equipped with an Intel Core 2 DUO 3.0Ghz CPU and 2 Giga bytes memory, running Fedora Linux 13.

Size of the pre-computed structure. Our technique has the feature of demanding only a structure with *sub-linear* size, i.e., a k-skip graph $G^\star = (V^\star, E^\star)$ occupies *less space* than the underlying road network $G = (V, E)$. The first set of experiments demonstrates this by proving that $G^\star$ has fewer vertices and edges than G. Equivalently, if we define the *vertex ratio* to be $|V^\star|/|V|$ and the *edge ratio* to be $|E^\star|/|E|$, the goal is to show that both ratios are below 1 by a comfortable margin. Moreover, remember that $V^\star$ is a k-skip cover (Definition 3). Hence, the vertex ratio also reflects the effectiveness of the *AS* algorithm in Section 4.2.

Table 2a presents the vertex ratios of each dataset as k varies from 4 to 16. Interestingly, we noticed that the ratio roughly equals $2/k$ in all cases, that is, *AS* finds a k-skip cover with size about $2|V|/k$. In the same style, Table 2b shows the corresponding edge ratios, which are also much lower than 1, and decrease with the increase of k. A general observation is that, both ratios tend to be smaller (i.e., greater size reduction) when the underlying network is sparser (NY is the densest among all the datasets).

Query characteristics. Ideally, a k-skip SP query should be answered much faster than its traditional counterpart (that retrieves the whole path). Next, we compare the *reach** algorithm developed in Section 5.2 against *reach*, which is the state of the art for the (traditional) SP problem, as reviewed in Section 2.1. We also examined a method *reach-on-supergraph* that can be regarded as a compromise of the two algorithms. As mentioned in Section 5.2, any SP algorithm can be applied to produce a k-skip SP by finding a SP on the k-skip graph $G^\star$. Following this rationale, *reach-on-supergraph* is a k-skip solution that simply employs *reach* on $G^\star$. As a reference, we also report the performance of *Dijkstra*.

The cost of each method is measured as its average response time in processing a *workload* of 1000 queries whose source and destination are both randomly selected from the vertices of the original network G. Figures 9a-9d plot the costs of alternative solutions as a function of k for the four datasets, respectively. The overhead of *Dijkstra* is given separately beside the dataset name, because it is substantially slower than all other competitors.

Both k-skip algorithms *reach** and *reach-on-supergraph* outperform *reach* significantly. Furthermore, their performance gains over *reach* become increasingly obvious as k grows larger (*reach* is irrelevant to k as it always reports the entire SP). This, therefore, validates k-skip graph as an effective methodology to attack the k-skip SP problem. Between the two k-skip algorithms, the consistent superiority of *reach** ascertains the necessity of designing a new algorithm that is able to leverage the characteristics of k-skip graphs. Remember that *reach** gleans its performance advantages at very little space overhead, because only one extra value needs to be stored for each edge in $G^\star$.

For the subsequent discussion, we define the *SP-cardinality* of query as the number of vertices in its complete SP. Figure 9 does not shed much light on each method's behavior in handling queries with different SP-cardinalities. Figure 10 remedies the drawback with a detailed version of the results for $k = 10$ (*Dijkstra* is omitted due to its poor efficiency). To obtain Figure 10a, we first decided the range ρ of the SP-cardinalities of all the queries in a workload. Then, for each algorithm, we measured its average cost in answering the queries whose SP-cardinalities were among the first 10% of ρ, second 10%, ..., and the last 10%, respectively. The collection of these 10 values correspond to the dots on a curve in Figure 10a. The other diagrams in Figure 10 were acquired in the same manner. The relative performance of all algorithms remains stable throughout the whole spectrum of SP-cardinality. The bell-shape of each curve is a characteristic of the *reach* algorithm (and hence, also its variant *reach**).

The next experiment studies the number of vertices in a k-skip SP. We present the number as a percentage of the query's SP-cardinality (e.g., 50% means that the k-skip path contains half of the vertices in the entire SP), which is referred to as the *output percentage*. For each dataset, Table 3 reports the average output percentages of a workload under different values of k. As expected,

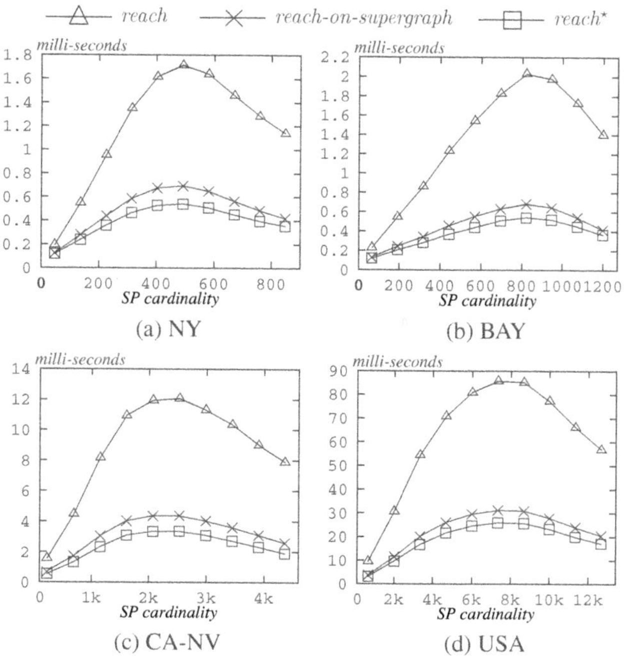

Figure 10: Query cost vs. the number of vertices in the complete SP ($k = 10$)

	k						
dataset	**4**	**6**	**8**	**10**	**12**	**14**	**16**
NY	55%	41%	34%	29%	27%	24%	22%
BAY	52%	36%	29%	25%	22%	20%	18%
CA-NV	52%	36%	29%	25%	22%	21%	19%
USA	51%	35%	28%	24%	22%	20%	19%

Table 3: Number of vertices in a k-skip SP (in percentage of the SP-cardinality)

the percentage decreases as k increases. It is not hard to observe a strong correlation between the output percentages and the vertex ratios in Table 2.

We proceed to assess the efficiency of the *zoom-in* algorithm in Section 5.3. The k-skip SP P^* of a query naturally defines $l - 1$ possible zoom-in operations if P^* has l vertices. For each road network and a particular k, we randomly performed 10% of all the zoom-in's determined by 50,000 queries with random sources and destinations, and gauged their average time. Figure 11 illustrates the results of all datasets. Note that the y-axis is in μ-seconds (1μs $= 10^{-6}$ sec). In general, for $k \leq 16$, the cost of a zoom-in is at the order of 10μs, and is thus negligible in practice.

Pre-computation overhead. The last set of experiments examines the time of constructing a k-skip graph G^*. Given an input graph G with all vertices' reaches already computed (the time of reach computation has been thoroughly evaluated in [10, 12]), the cost of building G^* has two components: the time of (i) finding a k-skip cover V^* (Section 4.2), and (ii) determining the super-edges of G^* (Section 4.3). For each road network, Figure 12 reports the overhead of these components as a function of k. The overall pre-processing time is dominated by the cost of (i) because it has to process all vertices in G, whereas (ii) only needs to process the vertices of G^*. Consulting the specifications in Table 1, we observe that the pre-processing overhead increases linearly with the number of edges in the original graph. For example, for the same k, the

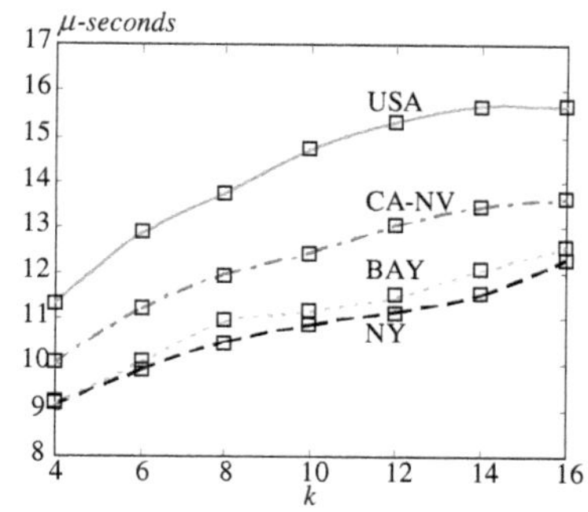

Figure 11: Zoom-in time vs. k

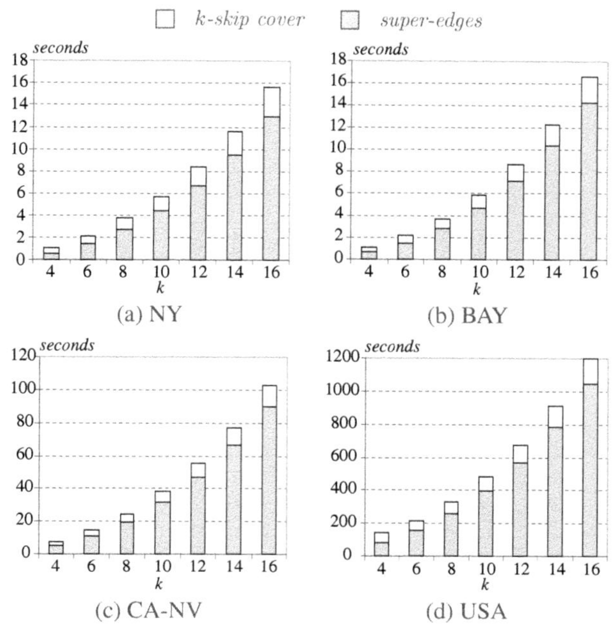

Figure 12: Pre-processing cost vs. k

overhead on USA is about 12 times that of CA-NV, where 12 is roughly the ratio between the numbers of edges in USA and CA-NV.

7. CONCLUSIONS

This paper introduced a novel concept called *k-skip shortest path*, which is a subset of the vertices in a traditional SP P, subject to the constraint that the subset must include at least one vertex in every k consecutive vertices of P. We carried out a systematic study on the problem of k-skip SP computation, where the goal is to pre-process a road network into a structure of economical size such that a k-skip query on the original network can be processed significantly faster than finding the entire SP. We settled the problem with a new methodology that constructs a *k-skip graph* from a set of selected vertices of G constituting a *k-skip cover*. The efficiency of the proposed technique has been verified with extensive experiments.

Our work also points to several promising directions for future research on the k-skip SP problem. One, for example, is to design a deterministic algorithm for finding the *minimum* k-skip cover, which does not appear to be trivial at all even for $k = 2$. Another interesting problem is to prove (possibly by resorting to the *highway dimension* [1]) a theoretical upper bound on the number of super-edges in a k-skip graph, which will immediately lead to a bound on the overall space consumption of our technique. Finally, it is certainly an important direction to explore the semantics of k-skip SP as well as the corresponding algorithms on other types of graphs, such as social networks.

Acknowledgements

Yufei Tao and Cheng Sheng were supported by grants GRF 4173/08, GRF 4169/09, and GRF 4166/10 from HKRGC. Jian Pei was supported by NSERC Discovery grants, NSERC Discovery Accelerator Supplement grants, and NRAS Research Team Program. We thank the anonymous reviewers for their constructive suggestions on improving the paper.

8. REFERENCES

[1] I. Abraham, A. Fiat, A. V. Goldberg, and R. F. F. Werneck. Highway dimension, shortest paths, and provably efficient algorithms. In *Proceedings of the Annual ACM-SIAM Symposium on Discrete Algorithms (SODA)*, pages 782–793, 2010.

[2] R. Agrawal and H. V. Jagadish. Algorithms for searching massive graphs. *IEEE Transactions on Knowledge and Data Engineering (TKDE)*, 6(2):225–238, 1994.

[3] T. H. Cormen, C. E. Leiserson, R. L. Rivest, and C. Stein. *Introduction to Algorithms, Second Edition*. The MIT Press, 2001.

[4] K. Deng, X. Zhou, H. T. Shen, S. W. Sadiq, and X. Li. Instance optimal query processing in spatial networks. *The VLDB Journal*, 18(3):675–693, 2009.

[5] E. W. Dijkstra. A note on two problems in connexion with graphs. *Numerische Mathematik*, 1:269–271, 1959.

[6] R. Durstenfeld. Algorithm 235: Random permutation. *Communications of the ACM (CACM)*, 7(7):420, 1964.

[7] G. N. Frederickson. Fast algorithms for shortest paths in planar graphs, with applications. *SIAM Journal of Computing*, 16(6):1004–1022, 1987.

[8] R. Geisberger, P. Sanders, D. Schultes, and D. Delling. Contraction hierarchies: Faster and simpler hierarchical routing in road networks. In *Proceedings of Workshop on Experimental Algorithms (WEA)*, pages 319–333, 2008.

[9] A. V. Goldberg and C. Harrelson. Computing the shortest path: A^* search meets graph theory. In *Proceedings of the Annual ACM-SIAM Symposium on Discrete Algorithms (SODA)*, pages 156–165, 2005.

[10] A. V. Goldberg, H. Kaplan, and R. F. Werneck. Reach for A^*: Shortest path algorithms with preprocessing. In *Proceedings of Workshop on Algorithm Engineering and Experiments (ALENEX)*, pages 38–51, 2006.

[11] A. Gubichev, S. J. Bedathur, S. Seufert, and G. Weikum. Fast and accurate estimation of shortest paths in large graphs. In *Proceedings of Conference on Information and Knowledge Management (CIKM)*, pages 499–508, 2010.

[12] R. J. Gutman. Reach-based routing: A new approach to shortest path algorithms optimized for road networks. In *Proceedings of Workshop on Algorithm Engineering and Experiments (ALENEX)*, pages 100–111, 2004.

[13] P. E. Hart, N. J. Nilsson, and B. Raphael. A formal basis for the heuristic determination of minimum cost paths. *IEEE Trans. Systems Science and Cybernetics*, 4(2):100–107, 1968.

[14] D. Haussler and E. Welzl. Epsilon-nets and simplex range queries. *Discrete & Computational Geometry*, 2:127–151, 1987.

[15] D. A. Hutchinson, A. Maheshwari, and N. Zeh. An external memory data structure for shortest path queries. *Discrete Applied Mathematics*, 126(1):55–82, 2003.

[16] N. Jing, Y.-W. Huang, and E. A. Rundensteiner. Hierarchical encoded path views for path query processing: An optimal model and its performance evaluation. *IEEE Transactions on Knowledge and Data Engineering (TKDE)*, 10(3):409–432, 1998.

[17] S. Jung and S. Pramanik. An efficient path computation model for hierarchically structured topographical road maps. *IEEE Transactions on Knowledge and Data Engineering (TKDE)*, 14(5):1029–1046, 2002.

[18] M. R. Kolahdouzan and C. Shahabi. Alternative solutions for continuous k nearest neighbor queries in spatial network databases. *GeoInformatica*, 9(4):321–341, 2005.

[19] U. Lauther. An extremely fast, exact algorithm for finding shortest paths in static networks with geographical background. *Geoinformation und Mobilität - von der Forschung zur praktischen Anwendung*, 22:219–230, 2004.

[20] T. A. J. Nicholson. Finding the shortest route between two points in a network. *The Computer Journal*, 9:275–280, 1966.

[21] M. Potamias, F. Bonchi, C. Castillo, and A. Gionis. Fast shortest path distance estimation in large networks. In *Proceedings of Conference on Information and Knowledge Management (CIKM)*, pages 867–876, 2009.

[22] M. N. Rice and V. J. Tsotras. Graph indexing of road networks for shortest path queries with label restrictions. *Proceedings of the VLDB Endowment (PVLDB)*, 4(2):69–80, 2010.

[23] N. Robertson and P. D. Seymour. Graph minors. iii. planar tree-width. *Journal of Combinatorial Theory, Series B*, 36(1):49–64, 1984.

[24] H. Samet, J. Sankaranarayanan, and H. Alborzi. Scalable network distance browsing in spatial databases. In *Proceedings of ACM Management of Data (SIGMOD)*, pages 43–54, 2008.

[25] P. Sanders and D. Schultes. Highway hierarchies hasten exact shortest path queries. In *Proceedings of European Symposium on Algorithms (ESA)*, pages 568–579, 2005.

[26] P. Sanders and D. Schultes. Engineering highway hierarchies. In *Proceedings of European Symposium on Algorithms (ESA)*, pages 804–816, 2006.

[27] J. Sankaranarayanan, H. Samet, and H. Alborzi. Path oracles for spatial networks. *Proceedings of the VLDB Endowment (PVLDB)*, 2(1):1210–1221, 2009.

[28] D. Wagner, T. Willhalm, and C. D. Zaroliagis. Geometric containers for efficient shortest-path computation. *ACM Journal of Experimental Algorithmics*, 10, 2005.

[29] F. Wei. Tedi: Efficient shortest path query answering on graphs. In *Proceedings of ACM Management of Data (SIGMOD)*, pages 99–110, 2010.

[30] Y. Xiao, W. Wu, J. Pei, W. Wang, and Z. He. Efficiently indexing shortest paths by exploiting symmetry in graphs. In *Proceedings of Extending Database Technology (EDBT)*, pages 493–504, 2009.

Finding Shortest Path on Land Surface

Lian Liu Raymond Chi-Wing Wong
The Hong Kong University of Science and Technology
Kowloon, Hong Kong
{lyanliu,raywong}@cse.ust.hk

ABSTRACT

Finding shortest paths is a fundamental operator in spatial databases. Recently, terrain datasets have attracted a lot of attention from both industry and academia. There are some interesting issues to be studied in terrain datasets which cannot be found in a traditional two-dimensional space. In this paper, we study one of the issues called a slope constraint which exists in terrain datasets. In this paper, we propose a problem of finding shortest paths with the slope constraint. Then, we show that this new problem is more general than the traditional problem of finding shortest paths without considering the slope constraint. Since finding shortest paths with the slope constraint is costly, we propose a new framework called surface simplification so that we can compute shortest paths with the slope constraint efficiently. Under this framework, the surface is "simplified" such that the complexity of finding shortest paths on this simplified surface is lower. We conducted experiments to show that the surface simplification is very efficient and effective not only for the new problem with the slope constraint but also the traditional problem without the slope constraint.

Categories and Subject Descriptors

H.2.8 [**Database Applications**]: Spatial databases and GIS; I.3.5 [**Computational Geometry and Object Modeling**]: Geometric algorithms, languages, and systems

General Terms

Algorithms, Design, Experimentation, Performance, Measurement

Keywords

shortest path, spatial databases, terrain, land surface, surface simplification, triangular irregular network (TIN) model

1. INTRODUCTION

Recently, terrain datasets have attracted a lot of attention from both industry and academia [27]. In industry, Microsoft and Google launched tools to display maps with terrain in "Bing Maps for Enterprise" (previously called "Microsoft Virtual Earth") in Sept 2009 and "Google Earth" in 2005, respectively. In academia, the database community [7, 6, 23, 27] has started to pay attention to studying how to perform some spatial queries over terrain datasets. One example is *surface kNN (skNN) queries*. Given a source point s and a set Q of pre-defined points on the surface, a surface kNN query returns a set Q' containing k objects which are nearest to s. That is, for each point q_i in Q' and each point q_j in $Q - Q'$, $|s, q_i| \leq |s, q_j|$. Note that, in the context of terrain, $|s, q|$ corresponds to the length of the shortest *surface path* between s and q instead of the *Euclidean distance* between s and q. Figure 1 shows a terrain in Bearhead area in Washington State where s and t are two points on the surface. In this figure, p_e is a straight line between s and t whose length corresponds to the Euclidean distance between s and t, and p_s corresponds to the shortest *surface path* between s and t. For clarity, in the following, when we write *paths* (or *shortest paths*), we mean *surface paths* (or *shortest surface paths*).

There are some interesting issues to be studied in terrain datasets which cannot be found in a traditional two-dimensional space. In this paper, we study one of the issues called a *slope* constraint which exists in terrain datasets. Consider Figure 2 where s and t are two points on the surface. Path p_1 corresponds to the shortest path from s to t. Note that p_1 involves a *steep* route from s to the top of the mountain and it is difficult for people to travel via a steep route. However, path p_2 and path p_3 are smoother and do not involve any steep route. We say that these two paths satisfy the *slope* requirement. We define a *slope parameter* $\theta_m \in [0, \pi/2]$ to denote whether a path is steep. Intuitively, if θ_m is set to 0, then the path must be flat without any inclination. If θ_m is $\pi/2$, then the path can have any inclination. Different applications have different values of θ_m. For example, the steepest road in UK (which is in Ffordd Penllech, Harlech) has a slope of 0.331 (in radian) (i.e., 19.0^o) and the steepest non-rack railway in Portugal has a slope of 0.13 (in radian) (i.e., 7.69^o) [18]. Informally speaking, given a slope parameter θ_m, a path p is said to satisfy the slope requirement if the *slope* of path p is at most θ_m. We will give a formal definition for the slope of a path later in Section 3. We also call the path satisfying the slope requirement the *gentle path*. In Figure 2, path p_2 and path p_3 are gentle but path p_1 is not.

In the following, we study the following problem. Given a source point s and a destination point t on the surface, we want to find the shortest gentle path from s to t on the surface. We call this problem *finding shortest gentle paths (FSGP)*. Note that problem FSGP is more general than the *traditional problem* of finding shortest path on the surface adopted in the literature [1, 7, 6, 23, 27] (which does not consider any slope requirement). This is because, when θ_m is set to $\pi/2$, there is no slope requirement. Then, problem FSGP becomes the traditional problem.

SIGMOD'11, June 12–16, 2011, Athens, Greece.

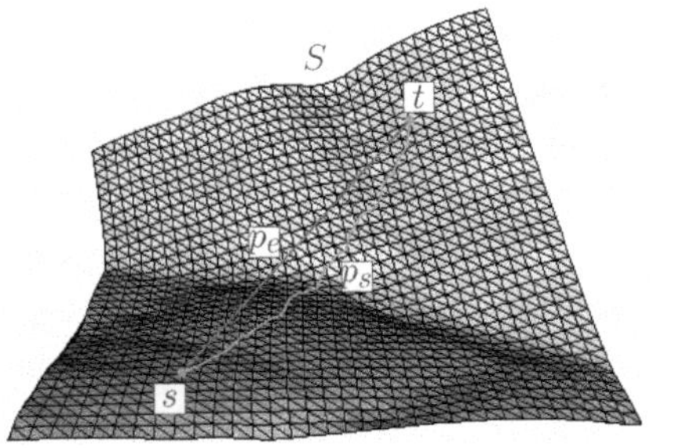

Figure 1: Terrain illustrating a surface path

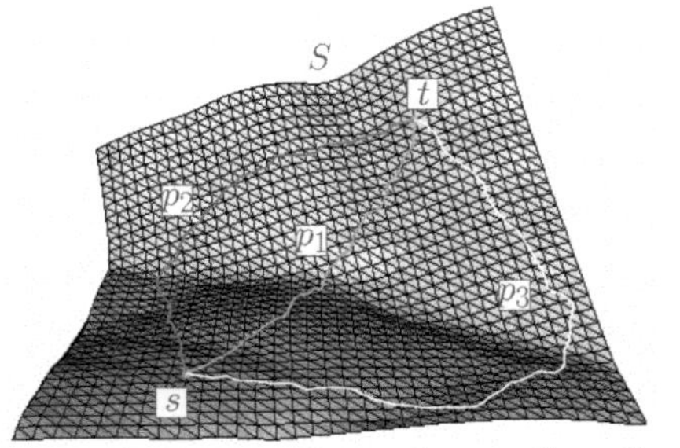

Figure 2: Terrain illustrating gentle paths

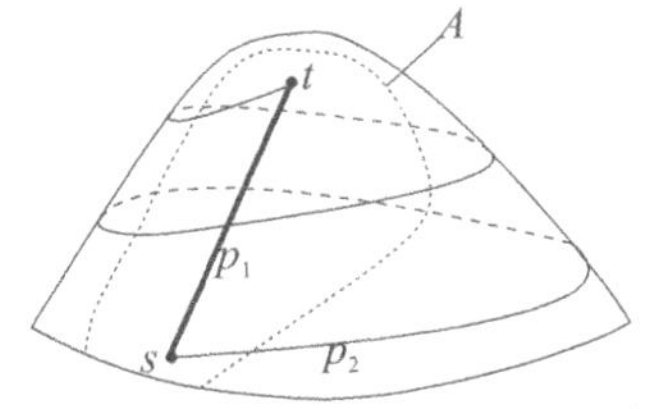

Figure 3: Terrain showing the challenge for problem FSGP

Problem FSGP is more challenging than the traditional problem. Consider Figure 3 where s and t are two points on the surface and A is an area on the surface. Path p_1 is the traditional shortest path from s to t. Path p_2 is the shortest gentle path from s to t. Informally speaking, due to the slope requirement, a gentle path passes through area A multiple times. However, a traditional path passes through A once only. Obviously, the length of the gentle path p_2 is much larger than the length of the traditional path p_1. Thus, problem FSGP is at least as hard as the traditional problem.

Obviously, one can adapt some existing algorithms in the literature or design new algorithms (e.g., breadth-first search algorithm) for problem FSGP. However, it is expected that the computation costs of these algorithms are *high* as illustrated in Figure 3. Let the algorithm which finds the shortest gentle path from s to t on a surface S be $\mathcal{A}(s, t|S)$. In our experiment on the real terrain dataset of Bearhead area in Washington State, if we set $\theta_m = 0.3$, we found that an algorithm for problem FSGP took about 3 days to find the shortest gentle path of length about 1.0km. Even if we do not consider the slope requirement (i.e., $\theta_m = \pi/2$), then the best-known algorithm [1] for the (traditional) problem ran for about 3 days to find the shortest path of length about 7.0km. In many applications, time is a critical factor. One example is some emergency situations (e.g., natural disaster). Quick evacuations in a natural disaster are needed as in the Australian fires in Feb 2009 and the Californian fires in Oct 2007. Besides, in a large-scale natural disaster such as the earthquake in China in May 2008, distributing relief supplies and rescuing are time-critical. Some other applications are military planning and robot path planning [25].

Motivated by the above observation that the computation cost for problem FSGP is high, instead of developing a new algorithm for problem FSGP, in this paper, we propose a new framework called *surface simplification* over a terrain. In the literature [7, 6, 23, 27], the surface of a terrain is usually represented by the Triangular Irregular Network (TIN) model. The TIN model involves a number of non-overlapping triangles which are arranged in a three-dimensional space. Figure 4a shows an example of the terrain in Figure 3 represented by the TIN model. Note that for illustration purpose, Figure 4a involves a *limited* number of triangles. If the number of triangles used in the model is larger, then the surface of the terrain represented by this model becomes smoother. Under the *surface simplification* framework, given the original surface S, we *simplify* or *approximate* S (Figure 4a), and generate a simplified surface $\widetilde{S}$ (Figure 4b) such that the number of triangles on the simplified surface $\widetilde{S}$ is smaller than that on the original surface S. We run an algorithm $\mathcal{A}$ for problem FSGP to find the shortest gentle path $\widetilde{p}$ on this simplified surface $\widetilde{S}$, as shown in Figure 4b. Then, we *map* this path $\widetilde{p}$ on $\widetilde{S}$ to a path p on S as shown in Figure 4c. We call this step *Path Mapping*.

Surface simplification has its advantage to speed up the computation of finding shortest gentle paths. Intuitively, since it minimizes the number of triangles on the surface, the algorithm for problem FSGP can run in a shorter period of time. Although it can speed up the computation, there are the following two challenges.

Firstly, the mapped path p on S may not satisfy the slope requirement. For example, the mapped path p in Figure 4c does not meet the slope requirement. Consider the triangle f_1. The path p in f_1 is quite steep. In order to address this issue, in this paper, we study how to construct a mapped path p on S which can satisfy the slope requirement given a gentle path $\widetilde{p}$ found on a given simplified surface $\widetilde{S}$.

Secondly, even though the mapped path p on S satisfies the slope requirement, p may be extremely long compared with the shortest gentle path p_o (or the *optimal path*) found on the original surface S. Clearly, surface simplification loses some surface information and thus the length of the mapped (gentle) path on S is larger than that of the optimal path. This motivates us to introduce an additional requirement, the *distance requirement*, in addition to the slope requirement. Let $|p|$ be the length of a path p on S. The distance requirement specifies that, given a *distance error parameter* $\epsilon \geq 0$, the length of the (mapped) path p found should be bounded by ϵ. That is, $|p| \leq (1 + \epsilon)|p_o|$ where p_o is the optimal path on S. In this paper, we study how to simplify the surface such that, given *any* source point s and *any* destination point t on surface S, the mapped (gentle) path from s to t satisfies the distance requirement.

Surface simplification speeds up the computation with the distance guarantee. If we set $\epsilon = 0.1$ and $\theta_m = 0.3$, experiments shows that the total time to find a gentle path p between two randomly chosen vertices under the surface simplification model is 2.94 seconds. However, the time to find the shortest gentle path p_o on the original surface is 12.65 seconds. Thus, the speedup in execution time is about 4.3 times if we sacrifice the length by a factor of at most 10% only. Surface simplification is very useful not only for problem FSGP but also the traditional problem. If we set $\theta_m = \pi/2$, problem FSGP becomes the traditional problem. In this case, if we set $\epsilon = 0.1$, we have the speedup in execution time by 1,320,000 times even if we sacrifice the length by a factor of at most 10% only.

Our contributions are summarized as follows. (1) To the best of our knowledge, we are the first to study how to find a shortest path which satisfies both the slope requirement and the distance requirement. (2) To the best of our knowledge, we are the first to propose a novel idea to simplify the surface of a terrain such that the length of the path found is bounded (regardless of whether there is a slope requirement). The surface simplification has its advantages to speed up the computation of finding shortest gentle paths because it minimizes the total number of triangles on the surface. (3) We present a systematic performance study using both real and synthetic datasets to verify the effectiveness and the efficiency of our surface simplification framework.

The rest of the paper is organized as follows. Section 2 reviews

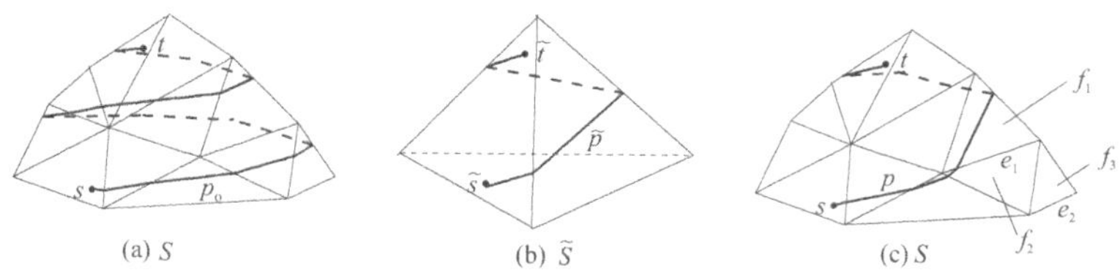

(a) S (b) $\widetilde{S}$ (c) S

Figure 4: Surface simplification

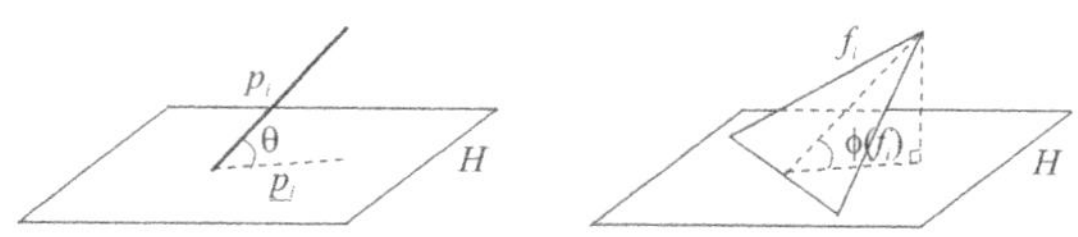

(a) Slope of a line (b) Slope of a face

Figure 5: Slope

the previous work. Section 3 formulates the problem FSGP. Section 4 and Section 5 describe the proposed algorithms. Section 7 evaluates the proposed techniques through extensive experiments with real datasets. Section 8 concludes the paper.

2. RELATED WORK

We classify the related works into two categories, finding shortest paths and surface simplification.

2.1 Finding Shortest Paths

Finding shortest paths has been extensively studied in two-dimensional spatial databases [8, 20]. Dijkstra's algorithm [8] is the well-known algorithm for finding shortest paths. Some other algorithms are the Bellman-Ford algorithm, the A* search algorithm and the Floyd-Warshall algorithm.

Finding shortest paths is a fundamental operator in a lot of spatial queries like k nearest neighbor searches. Some studies like [2, 17, 21] propose nearest neighbor searches in two-dimensional spaces.

Finding shortest paths on the surface of a terrain has also been studied by [16, 1]. [16] extends the idea of Dijkstra's algorithm and solves the problem of finding shortest paths on the surface in $O(n^2 \log n)$ time where n is the total number of triangles in the TIN model. [1] discovers a spatial property called *one-angle-one-split* and makes use of this property to design an efficient algorithm which improves the running time to $O(n^2)$ time.

In the context of terrain, finding shortest paths is also involved in other spatial queries [5, 6, 23, 27]. One example is surface kNN (skNN) queries which were first studied by [5, 6]. [5, 6] propose a filter and refinement strategy for this kind of queries. However, as pointed out by [23], the results returned by this strategy [5, 6] are not guaranteed to be correct. Motivated by this observation, [23] proposes an approach based on the Voronoi diagram for the skNN queries and guarantees that the results returned are correct. Another example of spatial queries related to finding shortest paths is the continuous skNN queries which were proposed recently by [27]. [27] studies to find the k nearest neighbors when the objects on the surface are moving.

However, most of the existing works, including the studies which propose to find shortest paths on the surface of a terrain, do not consider the *slope* requirement which appears in a terrain.

Some studies [13, 15, 11, 26] propose *approximation* algorithms for finding shortest paths. However, since they are originally designed for the traditional problem of finding shortest paths and thus do not meet the slope requirement, it is not easy to adapt their proposed algorithms to our problem.

2.2 Surface Simplification

Surface simplification, a fundamental technique in the literature of computer graphics, is widely used in multi-resolution modeling. It was first proposed to accelerate the rendering speed of complex 3D models. In the multi-resolution model, an object can be represented in different levels of details (LOD). Surface simplification is a special case of multi-resolution modeling. There are several methods for surface simplification in the literature of graphics. One is *vertex decimation* [22, 24]. Under vertex decimation, a vertex v is selected for removal as shown in Figure 6a. After this vertex is removed, all of its incident edges are removed and a new polygon is formed as shown in Figure 6b. The resulting polygon is *triangulated* as shown in Figure 6c such that the polygon is partitioned into a number of triangles. *Triangulation* is a process which partitions a given polygon into a number of triangles. There are a lot of methods for triangulation. In this paper, we adopt the method proposed by [9]. Other surface simplification methods include *edge contraction* [10], *vertex clustering* [19] and *simplification envelopes* [3].

Note that the focus of this paper is different from the above studies about surface simplification. Our focus is to simplify the surface such that the mapped path on the original surface satisfies both the slope requirement and the distance requirement. However, the focus of the above studies is to simplify the surface of an object such that the simplified surface "looks" similar to the original surface.

3. PROBLEM DEFINITION

3.1 Notation

Each point q in the three-dimensional space has an x-coordinate, a y-coordinate and a z-coordinate, denoted by $q.x$, $q.y$ and $q.z$, respectively. $q.z$ corresponds to the *elevation* of point q.

A *terrain* is the graph of a continuous function that assigns every point on a horizontal plane to an elevation [4]. In the literature [7, 6, 23, 27], the surface of a terrain is usually represented by the *Triangular Irregular Network (TIN) model* consisting of a number of disjoint *triangles*. Each triangle is represented by three corners called *vertices* and three lines connecting these three corners called *edges*. In the literature, a triangle is also referred to as a *face*. In the following, we use term "triangle" and term "face" interchangeably. Note that each vertex is also a point in a three-dimensional space. If an edge is located at the boundary of a terrain, it is *owned* by only one triangle. For example, in Figure 4c, edge e_2 at the boundary is owned by face f_3 only. Otherwise, it is *shared* by two triangles. For example, in Figure 4c, face f_1 and face f_2 share an edge e_1. Figure 4a shows an example of the terrain in Figure 3 represented by the TIN model. Let S be the surface of the terrain represented by the TIN model. Let H be a (virtual) horizontal plane located at the sea level of the terrain. We define the z-coordinate of each point on plane H to be 0.

Consider Figure 7a showing a terrain with a horizontal plane H. In the following, we follow the convention that the points on the horizontal plane H are denoted by *cross* points and symbolized by *underlined* variables while the points on the surface of a terrain are denoted by *dot* points and symbolized by *non-underlined* variables. For example, the cross point $\underline{s}$ is on the plane H and the dot point s is on surface S. Following the terrain model [4], we assume that any vertical line must intersect with the surface at only one point.

Given a source point s and a destination point t on the surface, a *path* p from s to t is defined to be a sequence of *line segments* on the surface which starts from s and ends at t. Each line segment can also be regarded as a path. For example, in Figure 7a, p' is the path from point s to point t on the surface. Path p' is a sequence of 4

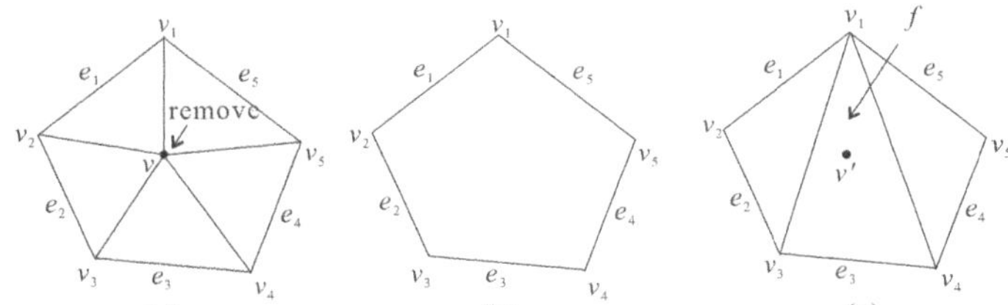

(a) (b) (c)

Figure 6: Vertex decimation

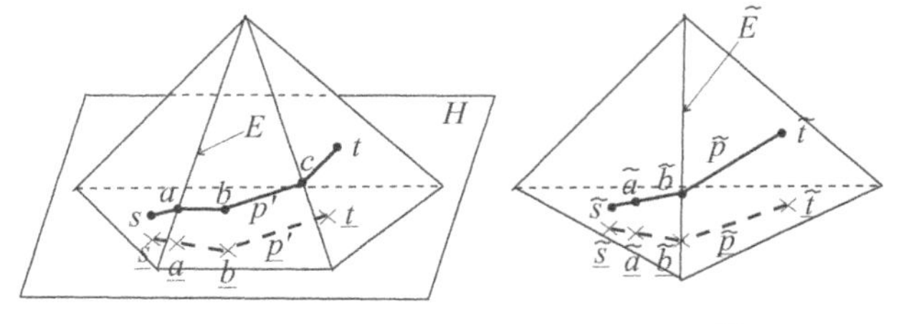

(a) S (b) $\widetilde{S}$

Figure 7: A terrain

line segments, namely (1) the segment from s to a, (2) the segment from a to b, (3) the segment from b to c and (4) the segment from c to t. The *length* of a line segment p_i from a point a to another point b, denoted by $|p_i|$, is defined to be the Euclidean distance between a and b. The *length* of path p, denoted by $|p|$, is defined to be the sum of the lengths of all line segments of p.

Given a point q on the surface, the *shadow* of q, denoted by $\underline{q}$, is defined to be a point on the plane H such that $\underline{q}.x = q.x$, $\underline{q}.y = q.y$ and $\underline{q}.z = 0$. Given a path p on the surface, the *shadow* of p, denoted by $\underline{p}$, is defined to be the shortest path on plane H covering the shadow of any point along p. For example, in Figure 7a, point $\underline{s}$ is the shadow of point s and the line segment from $\underline{s}$ to $\underline{a}$ is the shadow of the line segment from s to a. Given a face f, the *shadow* of f is defined to be the minimal region on plane H covering the shadow of any point on face f.

Consider a line segment p_i on the surface. We define the *slope* of p_i to be the acute angle (in radians) between p_i and the shadow of p_i. Figure 5a shows that the slope of line segment p_i is equal to θ. The *slope* of a path p is defined to be the greatest possible slope of a line segment of a path. The *slope* of a face f_i, denoted by $\phi(f_i)$, is defined to be the angle (in radians) (or formally the dihedral angle) between the plane covering face f_i and the horizontal plane H. Figure 5b shows that the slope of face f_i is equal to $\phi(f_i)$.

3.2 Finding Gentle Path

As described in Section 1, we propose the *slope requirement* to capture the steepness of a path by introducing a slope parameter $\theta_m \in [0, \pi/2]$. For the sake of illustration, in the following, we assume that $\theta_m > 0$. That is, θ_m is not equal to 0. This assumption avoids complicated and uninteresting discussions. If this assumption does not hold, we can set θ_m to be a very small positive value close to 0. With this parameter, we study problem FSGP. Let the algorithm which finds the shortest gentle path from s to t on a surface S for this problem be $\mathcal{A}(s, t|S)$.

A natural question may be raised for problem FSGP: *Does there exist a gentle path from a given source point s to a given destination point t on the surface?* For the sake of clarity, we first assume that there exists a gentle path from any source point to any destination point. In Section 6, we will describe how we relax this assumption.

In this paper, we propose a framework called *surface simplification* which simplifies the original surface S (Figure 4a) to surface $\widetilde{S}$ (Figure 4b) such that the number of faces on $\widetilde{S}$ is smaller than that on S. Figure 8a shows an overview of the surface simplification. In Section 5, we will study this process.

Figure 8b shows an overview to find the shortest gentle path from a source point s to a destination point t on surface S by using the simplified surface $\widetilde{S}$. We first construct a point $\widetilde{s}$ and another point $\widetilde{t}$ on the simplified surface $\widetilde{S}$ by setting $\widetilde{s}$ ($\widetilde{t}$) to be a point on $\widetilde{S}$ with the same shadow as s (t). For example, in Figure 7a, s and t are the source point and the destination point, respectively. We construct $\widetilde{s}$ and $\widetilde{t}$ on $\widetilde{S}$ with the same shadow as s and t, respectively, as shown in Figure 7b. Then, we run algorithm $\mathcal{A}(\widetilde{s}, \widetilde{t}|\widetilde{S})$ to find the shortest gentle path $\widetilde{p}$ from $\widetilde{s}$ to $\widetilde{t}$ on this simplified surface $\widetilde{S}$ (Step I). Then, we *map* this path $\widetilde{p}$ on $\widetilde{S}$ to a path p on S (Step II) such that this mapped path satisfies the slope requirement. In Section 4, we will study how to perform this path mapping.

Since the mapped path may introduce errors, we consider the *distance requirement* in this paper by introducing a distance error parameter $\epsilon \geq 0$.

PROBLEM 1 (SURFACE SIMPLIFICATION). *Given the original surface S of a terrain, generate a new surface $\widetilde{S}$ such that (1) the total number of faces on $\widetilde{S}$ is minimized and (2) for* any *source point s and* any *destination point t on S, the mapped path on the original surface S satisfies both the slope requirement and the distance requirement.*

Note that Step I used in the step of finding shortest gentle paths involves algorithm $\mathcal{A}$. Our contribution is the proposal of surface simplification over the terrain dataset with the guarantee of both the slope requirement and the distance requirement. Any algorithm $\mathcal{A}$ which finds the shortest gentle path (or the optimal path) (e.g., a breadth-first search algorithm and a best-first search algorithm) can also be used in our framework. In our experiment, we adopt the breadth-first search strategy for algorithm $\mathcal{A}$. A brief description of this algorithm can be found in Section 7.

For the sake of illustration, we follow the notation convention that all notations used in the simplified surface are symbolized with $\sim$ which appears at the top of the notations (e.g., point $\widetilde{s}$ and path $\widetilde{p}$ on the simplified surface $\widetilde{S}$ in Figure 7b) while all notations used in the original surface are not (e.g., point s and path p' on the original surface S in Figure 7a).

In the following, we first describe Step II in Section 4. Then, in Section 5, we describe how we perform surface simplification.

4. PATH MAPPING

4.1 Algorithm

Let $\widetilde{p}$ be the shortest gentle path on the simplified surface $\widetilde{S}$ found in Step I (See Figure 8b). In this section, we study Step II (i.e., how to map $\widetilde{p}$ on $\widetilde{S}$ to a path p on S).

The major idea of path mapping is based on the *common shadow* of the path $\widetilde{p}$ found on $\widetilde{S}$ and the mapped path p to be found on S. Intuitively, after we find $\widetilde{p}$ on $\widetilde{S}$, we generate the shadow of $\widetilde{p}$. Then, we generate a temporary path p' on the original surface S which has the same shadow as $\widetilde{p}$. We call p' the *pseudo path* of $\widetilde{p}$. Since path p' may violate the slope requirement, we perform an additional step called *path adjusting* to adjust path p' to path p (on surface S) such that p satisfies the slope requirement.

Specifically, we propose a three-step algorithm called algorithm *Path Mapping* to map a path $\widetilde{p}$ found on $\widetilde{S}$ to a path p on S. We

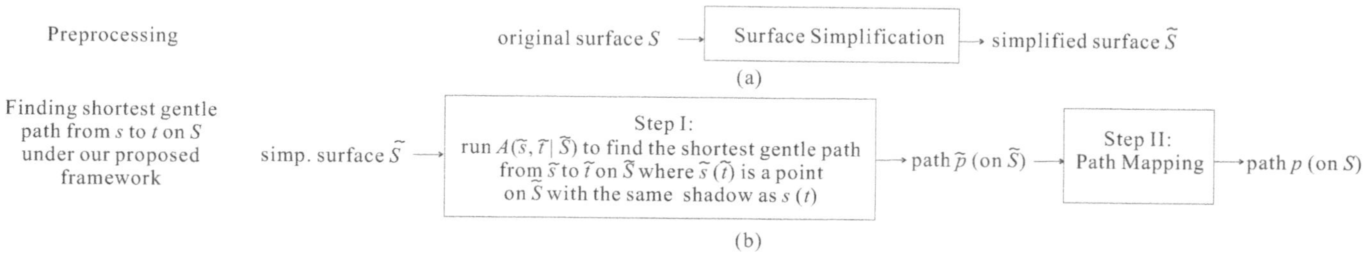

Figure 8: An overview of our proposed framework

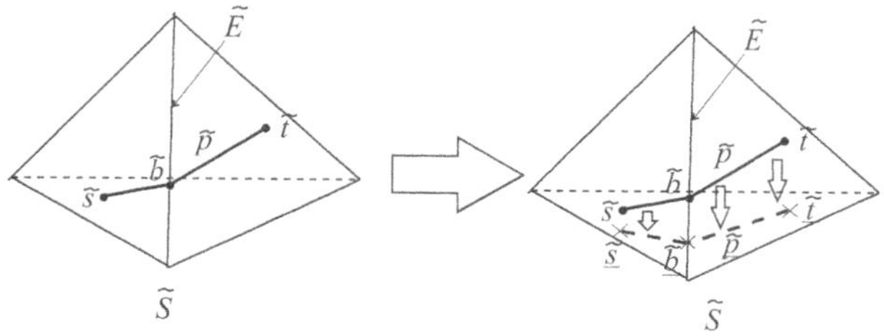

Figure 9: Shadowing

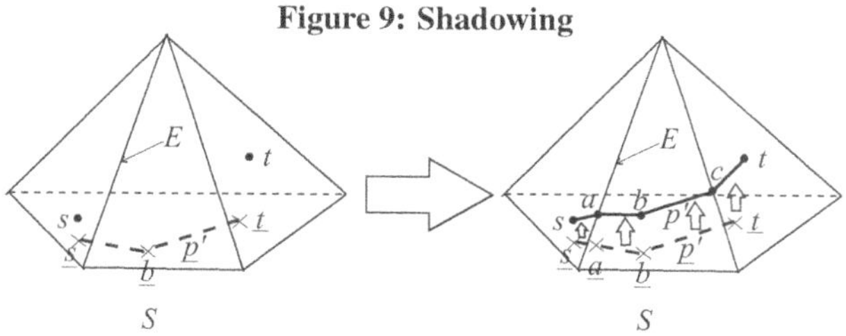

Figure 10: Segmentation

denote the relationship between $\widetilde{p}$ and p by a path mapping function PM such that

$$p = PM(\widetilde{p}) \tag{1}$$

Step 1 (Shadowing): We find the shadow of $\widetilde{p}$. For example, Figure 9 shows the shortest gentle path $\widetilde{p}$ from $\widetilde{s}$ to $\widetilde{t}$ on $\widetilde{S}$ which involves (1) the line segment from $\widetilde{s}$ to $\widetilde{b}$ and (2) the line segment from $\widetilde{b}$ to $\widetilde{t}$. The shadow of $\widetilde{p}$ is $\underline{\widetilde{p}}$ which involves (1) the line segment from $\underline{\widetilde{s}}$ to $\underline{\widetilde{b}}$ and (2) the line segment from $\underline{\widetilde{b}}$ to $\underline{\widetilde{t}}$. Note that $\widetilde{b}$ is a point connecting two line segments of path $\widetilde{p}$ on the surface. The reason why $\widetilde{b}$ appears in path $\widetilde{p}$ is that path $\widetilde{p}$ passes through edge $\widetilde{E}$ via point $\widetilde{b}$. Thus, this leads to the existence of a *shadow* point $\underline{\widetilde{b}}$ on the *shadow* path $\underline{\widetilde{p}}$.

Step 2 (Segmentation): We generate a pseudo path p' on the original surface S which has the same shadow as $\widetilde{p}$. For instance, shadow $\underline{p'}$ shown in Figure 10 (for S) is the same as shadow $\underline{\widetilde{p}}$ shown in Figure 9 (for $\widetilde{S}$). Note that shadow $\underline{p'}$ involves (1) the line segment from $\underline{s}$ to $\underline{b}$ and (2) the line segment from $\underline{b}$ to $\underline{t}$. Path p' shown in Figure 10 is the pseudo path. Although the shadow involves a *single* line segment from $\underline{s}$ to $\underline{b}$, we have to divide this line into two *segments*, namely (1) the segment from $\underline{s}$ to $\underline{a}$ and (2) the segment from $\underline{a}$ to $\underline{b}$, due to the existence of edge E. Thus, in Step 2, in addition to creating path p' with the same shadow as $\widetilde{p}$, we have to divide p' into a number of line segments such that each line segment does not pass across any edge on the original surface. After Step 2, we obtain p' which involves k line segments, namely $p'_1, p'_2, ..., p'_k$. For example, in Figure 10, we have 4 line segments of p' and thus k is equal to 4.

Step 3 (Path Adjusting): After we obtain a pseudo path p' from Step 2, we perform a step called *path adjusting* and generate path p such that p satisfies the slope requirement. Assume that the final path p contains k continuous (sub-)paths $p_1, p_2, ..., p_k$. For each line segment p'_i of p' (obtained in Step 2) with the source point a and the destination point b where $i \in [1, k]$, if it satisfies the slope requirement, we set p_i to be p'_i. Otherwise, we execute algorithm $\mathcal{A}(a, b|S)$ to find the shortest gentle path from a to b on the original surface S and assign it to p_i. The combination of the resulting (sub-)paths $p_1, p_2, ..., p_k$ is called the *adjusted path* of path p', which is the path in the output.

Intuitively, each line segment (or path) violating the slope requirement will be adjusted accordingly such that the final adjusted (sub-)path satisfies the slope requirement. Thus, we give the following theorem.

THEOREM 1 (SLOPE REQUIREMENT). *Let $\widetilde{p}$ be the shortest gentle path on the simplified surface $\widetilde{S}$. The path p on the original surface S mapped from $\widetilde{p}$ by algorithm* Path Mapping *satisfies the slope requirement.*

4.2 Theoretical Analysis

In the following, we focus on analyzing the distance bound of a path segment instead of the distance bound of the whole path. This is because once the distance bound of a path segment is found, the distance bound of the whole path also holds.

4.2.1 Distance Analysis for a Particular Path Segment

Consider a path $\widetilde{p}$ from $\widetilde{s}$ to $\widetilde{t}$ on surface $\widetilde{S}$ returned by $\mathcal{A}(\widetilde{s}, \widetilde{t}|\widetilde{S})$ (in Step I).

In the previous section, we learned that we can perform *Path Mapping* to map a path $\widetilde{p}$ to a pseudo-path p' (by Step 1 and Step 2) and then adjust p' to the final path p (by Step 3). In our algorithm, according to Step 3, we generate k sub-paths in the final path p, namely $p_1, p_2, ..., p_k$. In the example shown in Figure 7a, k is equal to 4. Let the correspondence pseudo-path line segments on S be $p'_1, p'_2, ..., p'_k$. For example, in Figure 7a, the line from a to b is an example of a line segment p'_i of p'. In order to perform analysis for the distance requirement, we also find the corresponding line segment $\widetilde{p}_i$ of $\widetilde{p}$ which has the same shadow as line segment p'_i of p' for $i \in [1, k]$. For instance, in Figure 7b, the line from $\widetilde{a}$ to $\widetilde{b}$ is an example of a line segment $\widetilde{p}_i$ of $\widetilde{p}$ which has the same shadow as p'_i.

In the following, we want to analyze the ratio of $|p_i|$ to $|\widetilde{p}_i|$ (i.e., $|p_i|/|\widetilde{p}_i|$) for each $i \in [1, k]$ when we map a *given* gentle line segment $\widetilde{p}_i$ to p_i. We call this ratio the *mapping ratio of a particular gentle path* $\widetilde{p}_i$.

Note that p_i is generated from $\widetilde{p}_i$ via a pseudo-path line segment p'_i. Thus, in the following, we calculate the mapping ratio with $|p'_i|$. Specifically, we have

$$\frac{|p_i|}{|\widetilde{p}_i|} = \frac{|p_i|}{|p'_i|} \times \frac{|p'_i|}{|\widetilde{p}_i|} \tag{2}$$

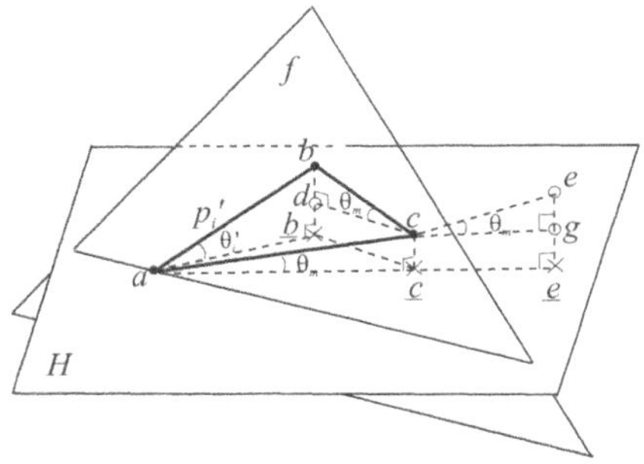

Figure 11: Illustration of the proof of Lemma 2

In the following, we will derive $\frac{|p'_i|}{|\widetilde{p}_i|}$ from Step 1 and Step 2, and derive $\frac{|p_i|}{|p'_i|}$ from Step 3.

Consider Step 1 and Step 2. After Step 2, we obtain a pseudo-path p' on S which has already been segmented. Consider a line segment p'_i of p'.

Suppose p'_i is on face f and $\widetilde{p}_i$ is on face $\widetilde{f}$. Since p'_i and $\widetilde{p}_i$ have the same shadow, we derive that face f and face $\widetilde{f}$ have an *overlapping* shadow X.

Let the slope of p'_i and the slope of $\widetilde{p}_i$ be θ'_i and $\widetilde{\theta}_i$, respectively. Define the relationship between θ'_i and $\widetilde{\theta}_i$ by function AM such that

$$\theta'_i = AM(\widetilde{\theta}_i) \tag{3}$$

We have the following lemma.

LEMMA 1 (DISTANCE BOUND). *Let $\widetilde{p}_i$ be a line segment of path $\widetilde{p}$. Let p'_i be a line segment of the pseudo path of $\widetilde{p}$. Let θ'_i and $\widetilde{\theta}_i$ be the slope of p'_i and the slope of $\widetilde{p}_i$, respectively. We have $\frac{|p'_i|}{|\widetilde{p}_i|} = \frac{\cos\widetilde{\theta}_i}{\cos\theta'_i}$.*

Proof: Since line segment p'_i is a line, the shadow of p'_i is also a line. Consider Figure 5a where p_i is set to p'_i. It is easy to verify that the length of the shadow of p'_i is $|p'_i|\cos\theta'_i$. Similarly, the length of the shadow of $\widetilde{p}_i$ is $|\widetilde{p}_i|\cos\widetilde{\theta}_i$. Since p'_i and $\widetilde{p}_i$ has the same shadow, we have the following equation: $|p'_i|\cos\theta'_i = |\widetilde{p}_i|\cos\widetilde{\theta}_i$. By changing the subject to $\frac{|p'_i|}{|\widetilde{p}_i|}$, we have $\frac{|p'_i|}{|\widetilde{p}_i|} = \frac{\cos\widetilde{\theta}_i}{\cos\theta'_i}$. □

Consider Step 3. For each line segment p'_i, we perform a path adjusting step and create a (sub-)path p_i (which satisfies the slope requirement). We have the following lemma.

LEMMA 2 (DISTANCE BOUND). *Let p'_i be a line segment of the pseudo path. Let p_i be the adjusted path of p'_i. Let θ'_i be the slope of p'_i. We have $\frac{|p_i|}{|p'_i|} \leq \frac{\sin(\max\{\theta'_i,\theta_m\})}{\sin\theta_m}$.*

Proof: Consider two cases. *Case 1: $\theta'_i \leq \theta_m$.* According to Step 3 (Path Adjusting), since p'_i satisfies the slope requirement, p_i is equal to p'_i. Thus, $|p_i| = |p'_i|$ and $\frac{|p_i|}{|p'_i|} = 1 \leq \frac{\sin(\max\{\theta'_i,\theta_m\})}{\sin\theta_m}$.

Case 2: $\theta'_i > \theta_m$. Consider a line segment p'_i from a to b on face f as shown in Figure 11. Since $\theta'_i > \theta_m$, according to Step 3, we need to execute algorithm $\mathcal{A}$ to find the shortest gentle path p_i from a to b. Consider two sub-cases. *Case (a):* There exists two line segments on face f, namely the line segment from a to c, and the line segment from c to b (as shown in Figure 11), such that the slopes of both segments are equal to θ_m. Let the Euclidean distance between a point a and another point b be $d(a, b)$. Note that each of these two line segments can be regarded as a sub-path whose length (equal to $d(a, c) + d(b, c)$) is at least the length of the adjusted path p_i because the adjusted path p_i is the optimal gentle path from a to b. Thus, we have

$$|p_i| \leq d(a,c) + d(b,c) \tag{4}$$

Without loss of generality, we assume that a is on the plane H such that H crosses face f into two parts. Consider the upper part of face f. Let l_1 be the line segment from a to c. We construct a virtual point e by prolonging line segment l_1 starting at c such that $d(c, e) = d(b, c)$. Thus, we construct a virtual line connecting c and e. Since we prolong l_1 whose slope is θ_m, the slope of this virtual line is also equal to θ_m. It is easy to verify that the trapezoid with points $b, \underline{b}, \underline{c}$ and c is equivalent to the trapezoid with points $e, \underline{e}, \underline{c}$ and c. Thus, we have $d(b, \underline{b}) = d(e, \underline{e})$. Consider the triangle with points a, b and $\underline{b}$. We have

$$\sin\theta'_i = \frac{d(b,\underline{b})}{d(a,b)} = \frac{d(b,\underline{b})}{|p'_i|} \tag{5}$$

Consider the triangle with points a, e and $\underline{e}$. We have the following equation: $\sin\theta_m = \frac{d(e,\underline{e})}{d(a,e)}$. Since $d(e, \underline{e}) = d(b, \underline{b})$ and $d(a, e) = d(a, c) + d(c, e)$ and $d(c, e) = d(b, c)$, we re-write the equation as follows.

$$\sin\theta_m = \frac{d(b,\underline{b})}{d(a,c)+d(b,c)}$$

By Equation (4) and Equation (5), we have the following inequality: $\sin\theta_m \leq \frac{|p'_i|\sin\theta'_i}{|p_i|}$. By changing the subject to $\frac{|p_i|}{|p'_i|}$, we have

$$\frac{|p_i|}{|p'_i|} \leq \frac{\sin\theta'_i}{\sin\theta_m} = \frac{\sin(\max\{\theta'_i,\theta_m\})}{\sin\theta_m}$$

Case (b): There does not exist two line segments on face f, namely the line segment from a to c, and the line segment from c to b (as shown in Figure 11), such that the slopes of both segments are equal to θ_m.

We know that Case (b) should not happen (and thus Case (a) happen) if face f has an *extremely large* area (with respect to a pseudo-path p'_i with a short length). Case (b) occurs when face f has a *limited* area (with respect to a pseudo-path p'_i with a long length). In Case (b), we can transform Case (b) to Case (a) easily by chopping line segment p'_i into a number of sub-paths $p'_{i,1}, p'_{i,2}, ..., p'_{i,l}$ (with shorter lengths) such that, for each $p'_{i,j}$ where $j \in [1, l]$, there exists two line segments for $p'_{i,j}$ on face f such that the slopes of both segments are equal to θ_m. For each $p'_{i,l}$ where $j \in [1, l]$, we can find the correspondence mapped path $p_{i,l}$ (by using similar derivations from Case (a)). Thus, it is easy to verify that $\frac{|p_i|}{|p'_i|} \leq \frac{\sin(\max\{\theta'_i,\theta_m\})}{\sin\theta_m}$. □

By Lemma 1 and Lemma 2, we re-write Equation (2) as follows.

$$\frac{|p_i|}{|\widetilde{p}_i|} \leq \frac{\sin(\max\{\theta'_i,\theta_m\})}{\sin\theta_m} \times \frac{\cos\widetilde{\theta}_i}{\cos\theta'_i}$$

Note that p_i is on face f and $\widetilde{p}_i$ is on face $\widetilde{f}$. The right hand side of the above inequality corresponds to the upper bound of the mapping ratio of a single gentle path segment. We denote it by $MRS(< p_i, f >, < \widetilde{p}_i, \widetilde{f} >)$. That is,

$$MRS(< p_i, f >, < \widetilde{p}_i, \widetilde{f} >) = \frac{\sin(\max\{\theta'_i,\theta_m\})}{\sin\theta_m} \times \frac{\cos\widetilde{\theta}_i}{\cos\theta'_i} \tag{6}$$

where p_i is a mapped path of $\widetilde{p}_i$.

4.2.2 Distance Analysis for Arbitrary Path Segment

Note that X is a region on plane H. Let $GP(\widetilde{f}, X)$ be a set of all possible gentle paths on face $\widetilde{f}$ which shadows are inside X. Note that, from Equation (1), we have $p_i = PM(\widetilde{p}_i)$. The greatest possible mapping ratio of an *arbitrary* gentle path (segment), denoted by $MR(f, \widetilde{f})$, is equal to

$$\max_{\substack{\forall \widetilde{p}_i \in GP(\widetilde{f}, X) \\ \text{where } p_i = PM(\widetilde{p}_i)}} MRS(< p_i, f >, < \widetilde{p}_i, \widetilde{f} >) \tag{7}$$

The above term $MR(f, \widetilde{f})$ can be regarded as the greatest possible mapping ratio of an arbitrary gentle path $\widetilde{p}_i$ when we map a gentle path (segment) $\widetilde{p}_i$ on a *simplified* face $\widetilde{f}$ to a path p_i on an *original* face f. This above term can be in fact expressed in terms of the coordinates of all the vertices of f and $\widetilde{f}$. Details can be found in [14].

In general, the above term can be *generalized* as follows. Consider two different surfaces S and S' each of which represents the same terrain (in the above derivation, S is the original surface and S' is the simplified surface). Given a face f on S and another face f' on S' with an overlapping shadow X, $MR(f, f')$ can be regarded as the greatest possible mapping ratio of an arbitrary gentle path p' when we map a gentle path (segment) p' on face f' to a path p on face f. With this reasoning, in addition to $MR(f, \widetilde{f})$, we can also define $MR(\widetilde{f}, f)$ similarly (i.e., the greatest possible ratio of an arbitrary gentle path p_i when we map a gentle path (segment) p_i on an *original* face f to a path $\widetilde{p}_i$ on a *simplified* face $\widetilde{f}$).

With the above definition of $MR(f, f')$, we have the following lemma.

LEMMA 3 (DIST. BOUND FOR ARBITRARY PATH SEGMENT). *Let S and S' be two different surfaces each of which represents the same terrain. Let f be a face on S and f' be another face f' on S' such that f and f' have an overlapping shadow X. Suppose that p' is the shortest gentle path (segment) on f'. If algorithm* Path Mapping *maps p' on face f' to a sub-path p on face f, then we have $\frac{|p|}{|p'|} \leq MR(f, f')$.*

5. SURFACE SIMPLIFIER

In this section, we present an algorithm called *Surface Simplifier* to simplify surface S to surface $\widetilde{S}$ such that *any* mapped path p found by algorithm *Path Mapping* satisfies the distance requirement (in addition to the slope requirement).

Let p be the mapped path on surface S (obtained in Step II in Figure 8b). Let p_o be the optimal path (i.e., the shortest gentle path) on surface S. The distance requirement specifies that, given a distance error parameter $\epsilon \geq 0$, we have $|p| \leq (1 + \epsilon)|p_o|$ or $\frac{|p|}{|p_o|} \leq 1 + \epsilon$. We define the *distance error ratio* of path p, denoted by $ER(p)$, to be $\frac{|p|}{|p_o|}$. Note that $ER(p) \geq 1$ since $|p| \geq |p_o|$. If p is the optimal path, then $ER(p) = 1$.

Obviously, if surface $\widetilde{S}$ is exactly the same as the original surface S, then any mapped path p found must be optimal and thus $ER(p) = 1$. This is because the mapped path p on S is exactly the same as the path $\widetilde{p}$ found on $\widetilde{S}$ which is considered as the shortest gentle path on $\widetilde{S}$.

However, if surface $\widetilde{S}$ is different from the original surface S, then it is likely that a mapped path p found is not optimal and thus $ER(p) > 1$. Besides, intuitively, if the "difference" between S and $\widetilde{S}$ is greater, then it is more likely that $ER(p)$ is greater where p is a mapped path. In order to satisfy the distance requirement, we want that the "difference" between S and $\widetilde{S}$ should not be too large.

The "difference" between S and $\widetilde{S}$ is denoted by $\triangle(S, \widetilde{S})$. In Section 5.1, we will describe an exact formula for $\triangle(S, \widetilde{S})$ such that the following property holds.

PROPERTY 1 (SURFACE BOUND). *Let S be the original surface and $\widetilde{S}$ be the simplified surface. If $\triangle(S, \widetilde{S}) \leq 1 + \epsilon$, then for any mapped path p, $ER(p) \leq 1 + \epsilon$.*

5.1 Formula for $\triangle(S, \widetilde{S})$

Let $\mathcal{CS}(S, \widetilde{S})$ be a set of all possible pairs $(f, \widetilde{f})$ where f is a face on S and $\widetilde{f}$ is a face on $\widetilde{S}$ such that f and $\widetilde{f}$ have an overlapping shadow. We define λ and λ' as follows.

$$\lambda = \max_{(f,\widetilde{f}) \in \mathcal{CS}(S,\widetilde{S})} MR(f, \widetilde{f}) \tag{8}$$

$$\lambda' = \max_{(f,\widetilde{f}) \in \mathcal{CS}(S,\widetilde{S})} MR(\widetilde{f}, f) \tag{9}$$

With the notations λ and λ', we define $\triangle(S, \widetilde{S})$ as follows.

DEFINITION 1. $\triangle(S, \widetilde{S}) = \lambda \times \lambda'$

With this definition, we have the following lemma for the correctness of Property 1.

LEMMA 4. *Let S be the original surface and $\widetilde{S}$ be the simplified surface. If $\triangle(S, \widetilde{S}) \leq 1 + \epsilon$, then for any mapped path p, $ER(p) \leq 1 + \epsilon$.*

Proof: Let $\widetilde{p}$ be a path found in Step I and p be a path found in Step II. Since $\widetilde{p}$ is returned by $\mathcal{A}(\widetilde{s}, \widetilde{t}|\widetilde{S})$, $\widetilde{p}$ is the shortest gentle path from $\widetilde{s}$ to $\widetilde{t}$ on $\widetilde{S}$. We have the following inequality. For any gentle path $\widetilde{g}$ from $\widetilde{s}$ to $\widetilde{t}$ on $\widetilde{S}$,

$$|\widetilde{g}| \geq |\widetilde{p}| \tag{10}$$

We adopt the notations used in Section 4.2.1 here. Specifically, in algorithm *Path Mapping*, according to Step 3, we generate k sub-paths in the final path p, namely $p_1, p_2, ..., p_k$. Let the correspondence pseudo-path line segments on S be $p'_1, p'_2, ..., p'_k$. All of these line segments form a pseudo-path p'. Besides, let $\widetilde{p}_i$ be the correspondence line segment of $\widetilde{p}$ which has the same shadow as line segment p'_i of p' for $i \in [1, k]$.

Consider a sub-path p_i and a line segment $\widetilde{p}_i$ where $i \in [1, k]$. Suppose that p_i is on face f and $\widetilde{p}_i$ is on face $\widetilde{f}$. By Lemma 3, we have

$$\frac{|p_i|}{|\widetilde{p}_i|} \leq MR(f, \widetilde{f})$$

Since each line segment $\widetilde{p}_i$ of $\widetilde{p}$ has the above inequality with the sub-path p_i of p where $i \in [1, k]$, by some simple derivations, it is easy to verify the following.

$$\frac{|p|}{|\widetilde{p}|} \leq \max_{(f,\widetilde{f}) \in \mathcal{CS}(S,\widetilde{S})} MR(f, \widetilde{f}) \tag{11}$$

With Equation (8), we have

$$\frac{|p|}{|\widetilde{p}|} \leq \lambda \tag{12}$$

Let p_o be the optimal path on S (i.e., the shortest gentle path on S). Consider that we apply algorithm *Path Mapping* to map p_o on the original surface S to generate a path $\widetilde{p}_o$ on the simplified surface $\widetilde{S}$. Similar to the derivation for Inequality (11), by Lemma 3, we have

$$\frac{|\widetilde{p}_o|}{|p_o|} \leq \max_{(f,\widetilde{f}) \in \mathcal{CS}(S,\widetilde{S})} MR(\widetilde{f}, f)$$

Thus, with Equation (9), we have

$$\frac{|\widetilde{p}_o|}{|p_o|} \leq \lambda' \tag{13}$$

Note that $\widetilde{p}_o$ on $\widetilde{S}$ generated by algorithm *Path Mapping* is a *gentle* path on $\widetilde{S}$ (by Theorem 1). Thus, from Inequality (10), we have the following inequality: $|\widetilde{p}_o| \geq |\widetilde{p}|$. With this inequality, we re-write Inequality (12) as: $\frac{|p|}{|\widetilde{p}_o|} \leq \lambda$. With Inequality (13), we re-write this inequality as: $\frac{|p|}{|p_o|} \leq \lambda \times \lambda'$. Since $ER(p) = \frac{|p|}{|p_o|}$, we have

$$ER(p) \leq \lambda \times \lambda' \quad (14)$$

Note that, from the condition of Property 1, we have $\triangle(S, \widetilde{S}) \leq 1 + \epsilon$. By Definition 1, we derive that $\lambda \times \lambda' \leq 1 + \epsilon$. Thus, Inequality (14) can be re-written as: $ER(p) \leq 1 + \epsilon$. □

5.2 Algorithm Simplifier

In this section, we describe an algorithm called *Surface Simplifier* which adopts one of the methods for surface simplification discussed in Section 2.2. Any existing methods about surface simplification reducing the number of faces in the literature of graphics can also be adopted in our algorithm provided that the simplified surface $\widetilde{S}$ is generated such that (1) $\triangle(S, \widetilde{S}) \leq 1 + \epsilon$ and (2) the shadow of the boundary of S is the same as the shadow of the boundary of $\widetilde{S}$.

In this paper, we use the techniques described in [22, 24] for surface simplification. Specifically, in [22, 24], surface simplification involves a number of iterations. Initially, we create a new surface $\widetilde{S}$ which is equal to the original surface S. It is being updated over iterations and finally represents the simplified surface we want. For each iteration, we select a vertex to be removed from $\widetilde{S}$ (See Figure 6a) such that $\widetilde{S}$ will be updated after vertex decimation (See Figure 6c) and the distance requirement is satisfied for this updated $\widetilde{S}$. We continue the above step until we cannot find any vertex to be removed such that the distance requirement is satisfied.

It is easy to verify the following theorem.

THEOREM 2. *Algorithm Surface Simplifier generates surface $\widetilde{S}$ such that $\triangle(S, \widetilde{S}) \leq 1 + \epsilon$.*

In our implementation, we design an efficient method for our algorithm *Surface Simplifier* which takes $O(|V| \log |V|)$ time where $|V|$ is the total number of vertices on the original surface. For the sake of space, we give this method in [14].

6. DISCUSSION

In Section 3, we assume that there exists a gentle path from any source point to any destination point. In this section, we relax this assumption. We will introduce a term *reachable* for a point q to describe whether q is reachable or not. In this section, we will show that if both the source point s and the destination point t are reachable, then there exists a gentle path from s to t.

6.1 Reachability

Given two distinct points q and q' on a surface, q is said to be *reachable from* q' if and only if there exists a gentle path from q' to q. q is said to be *unreachable from* q' if q is not reachable from q'.

Given a point q on a surface, q is said to be *reachable* if and only if there exists another point q' on the surface such that q is reachable from q'. q is said to be *unreachable* if q is not reachable.

Given a vertex q, a face f is said to be *adjacent* to q if one of the corners of f is q.

LEMMA 5 (UNREACHABILITY). *A point q on a surface is unreachable if and only if q is a vertex and q is unreachable from any point on all of the faces adjacent to q.*

Proof: Firstly, we want to prove that, if q is a vertex and q is unreachable from any point on all of the faces adjacent to q, then q is unreachable. We prove by contradiction. Suppose that q is reachable. That is, there exists another point q' on the surface such that q is reachable from q'. Consider two cases. *Case 1:* q' is on one of the faces adjacent to q. This leads to a contradiction.

Case 2: q' is not on all of the faces adjacent to q. Since q is reachable from q', there exists a gentle path from q' to q. Let F be the set of all faces adjacent to q. We know that path p must pass through one of the faces in F, says f. Let q'' be a point along path p on face f. Thus, q is reachable from q'' (which is on one of the faces adjacent to q). This leads to a contradiction.

Secondly, we want to prove that, if q is unreachable, then q is a vertex and q is unreachable from any point on all of the faces adjacent to q. We prove by contradiction. Consider two cases. *Case 1:* q is a vertex and there exists another point q' on one of the faces adjacent to q such that q is reachable from q'. Thus, q is reachable, which leads to a contradiction. *Case 2:* q is not a vertex. That is, q is a non-vertex point on a face f. There exists another point q' on f such that $q'.z = q.z$. Thus, q is reachable from q. So, q is reachable, which leads to a contradiction. □

The above lemma suggests that all unreachable points come from vertices on the surface. Thus, we just need to check whether each *vertex* (instead of all possible points on the surface) is unreachable or not. How to check whether a vertex is unreachable or not efficiently will be discussed in Section 6.2.

LEMMA 6 (SOURCE/DESTINATION REACHABILITY). *If a source point s and a destination point t are reachable, then t is reachable from s.*

Proof: From the proof of Lemma 5, it is easy to verify that, if a vertex q on face f is reachable, for any point q' on f, q is reachable from q'. For the sake of space, we omit the proof here. There exists a sequence of adjacent faces, namely $f_1, f_2, ..., f_l$, such that s is on face f_1, t is on face f_l and, for each $i \in [1, l-1]$, face f_i is adjacent to face f_{i+1}. Let e_i be the edge shared by face f_i and face f_{i+1} for $i \in [1, l-1]$. By the first claim in this proof, we know that there exists a non-vertex point t_1 on edge e_1 such that t_1 is reachable from s. Similarly, we know that there exists a non-vertex point t_2 on edge e_2 such that t_2 is reachable from t_1. In general, there exists a non-vertex point t_i on edge e_i such that t_i is reachable from t_{i-1} for $i \in [2, l-1]$. At the final step, similarly, we know that t is reachable from t_{l-1} (by the first claim in the proof). Since t_1 is reachable from s, t_i is reachable from t_{i-1} where $i \in [2, l-1]$, and t is reachable from t_{l-1}, we conclude that t is reachable from s. □

6.2 Algorithm

In this general setting, algorithm *Surface Simplifier* will be changed as follows. The basic idea of the change is based on the following two properties. *Property 1:* For each vertex on S which is unreachable, the algorithm still keeps the original vertex v on $\widetilde{S}$. *Property 2:* Whenever the algorithm generates $\widetilde{S}$, it makes sure that it does not introduce any new vertex which is unreachable.

Intuitively, if all vertices are unreachable, then we cannot simplify the surface. If there are only rare unreachable vertices, then we can simplify the surface aggressively.

Since algorithm *Surface Simplifier* maintains Property 1 and Property 2, it is easy to verify that there exists a gentle path on S if and only if there exists a corresponding gentle path on $\widetilde{S}$. Thus, algorithm *Path Mapping* is kept intact in this problem setting.

Efficiency: In algorithm *Surface Simplifier*, we have to check whether a vertex is unreachable or not. The following lemma helps us to perform this checking step efficiently.

Let V be a set of vertices on a surface S. Consider that v is in V. Let $N(v, V)$ be a set of vertices in $V/\{v\}$ each of which shares an edge with v. For example, in Figure 6a, $N(v, V)$ is equal to $\{v_1, v_2, v_3, v_4, v_5\}$.

LEMMA 7 (REACHABILITY). *Consider a vertex v and a surface S. Let V be a set of vertices on S. Let $Y = N(v, V)$. v is reachable if one of the following conditions holds.* Condition (1): *there exists two vertices in Y, namely v_i and v_j, such that $v_i.z \geq v.z$ and $v_j.z \leq v.z$, or* Condition (2): *there exists an edge e with an endpoint equal to v such that the slope of e is at most θ_m.*

Proof: Consider the first condition. Since there exists two vertices v_i and v_j such that $v_i.z \geq v.z$ and $v_j.z \leq v.z$, we deduce that there exists a face f adjacent to v such that f has two corners/vertices, namely v_a and v_b, where $v_a, z \geq v.z$ and $v_b.z \leq v.z$. Thus, there exists a point q on face f where $q.z = v.z$ such that v is reachable from q.

Consider the second condition. Since the edge has its slope at most θ_m, there exists a point q on this edge such that v is reachable from q. □

With the above lemma, if one of the two conditions is satisfied, we are sure that a vertex is *reachable*. Otherwise, it can be either reachable or unreachable. In our implementation, we can remove any vertex which falls in the former case (i.e., it is found to be reachable by this lemma). But, we keep each vertex which falls in the latter case. This implementation does not violate Property 1 and Property 2. We found that only 0.22% of vertices fall in the latter case in our experiment where θ_m is set to 0.3.

The efficiency of checking whether a vertex is reachable can be improved by using this lemma. For each vertex v, we check Condition (1) and Condition (2) in the lemma. If one of the conditions holds, then v is reachable. It is easy to see that performing the checking step with Condition (1) can be done in $O(|Y|)$ time and performing the checking step with Condition (2) can be done in $O(|Y|)$ time.

7. EMPIRICAL STUDY

In this paper, we used two real terrain datasets adopted in previous studies [7, 6, 23, 27]. (1) *Eagle Peak (EP) area in Wyoming State:* This dataset covers an area around 10.7km×14km, and (2) *Bearhead (BH) area in Washington State:* This dataset covers an area around 9.7km×13.7km. Both datasets can be downloaded from http://data.geocomm.com. For each real dataset, we ranodmly selected 10% of the terrain to conduct our experiments. The total numbers of faces in the EP dataset and in the BH dataset are 284,130 and 302,634, respectively. We also created synthetic datasets as follows. Each synthetic dataset contains a terrain bounded by a 10km×10km square horizontal plane. On this horizontal plane, we randomly pick four points as the centers of the mountains. Then, the elevation of all points with respect to the center of each mountain is modeled by a 2-dimensional Gaussian distribution denoted by mean m and standard derivation σ. The mean m of each distribution (corresponding to the elevation of the center of the mountain) is randomly generated from 0 to 10000. The standard derivation σ is an input parameter. Since each point belongs to four mountains with different elevations, we take the greatest elevation among the four distributions as the final elevation of the point. The datasets generated contain 600,000-1,000,000 faces. The default values of θ_m, ϵ, the total number of faces on the surface and σ are 0.3, 0.1, 600,000 and 0.1, respectively.

All programs were written in C/C++ and executed on CentOS linux platform on a 2xQuad Core 3GHz server with 32GB RAM. Our proposed algorithm returns a path denoted by p which satisfies the distance requirement and the slope requirement. We implemented a simple breadth-first algorithm $\mathcal{A}$ for finding shortest gentle paths (FSGP) on a given terrain, whose basic idea is as follows: Note that there may be multiple shortest gentle paths (SGP) in this problem. We proved that one of them must pass through a *simple face sequence*. A *face sequence* is a sequence of faces while a *simple face sequence* is a face sequence which contains no duplicate faces. So, starting from the face that contains source s, we generate all possible simple face sequences in a breadth-first manner until destination t is reached. In order to speed up, those unnecessary face sequences that are impossible to be used for finding SGP are pruned. In each simple face sequence, the length of the SGP can be represented by a *function* of the coordinates of s, t and all the vertices of the triangles in this face sequence. We can also specify a set of *slope constraints* along all faces in the face sequence in a similar way by using the coordinates of these vertices and θ_m. Then, we took the advantage of any existing optimization tool such as MATLAB, ALGLIB, OOL and IOptLib to find the minimum value of this function subject to the constraints. For each unpruned simple face sequence, we obtain the corresponding SGP. Finally, among all SGP's obtained from all unpruned face sequences, we select the shortest one as the final SGP. The detailed description of the algorithm can be found in [14]. Besides, we compared our proposed algorithm with the baseline algorithm that finds the shortest gentle path denoted by p_o on the original surface S.

Note that one may think out an algorithm based on the shortest traditional path on S as follows. Specifically, this algorithm finds the shortest traditional path on S (without considering the slope constraint) and perform a path adjusting step (described in Section 4) such that the final adjusted path satisfies the slope requirement. However, it is possible that the final adjusted path does not satisfy the distance requirement. We denote the final adjusted path by p_c.

All experiments were conducted 100 times by randomly generating 100 queries where each query involves a random source point and a random destination point. We took the average for the results.

For real datasets, we study the performance of algorithms with the following two parameters, namely (1) θ_m and (2) ϵ.

We evaluate our algorithms in terms of five measurements. (1) *Preprocessing time:* Preprocessing time corresponds to the execution time to run algorithm *Surface Simplifier*, (2)*Number of faces:* We measured the number of faces on the original surface and the number of faces (remained) on the simplified surface. (3) *Memory consumption:* Memory consumption corresponds to the storage size to store all faces on a surface (which can be derived from the number of faces measured above). (4) *Path finding time:* Path finding time of our proposed algorithm under surface simplification which finds path p corresponds to the execution time to run Step I and Step II. Path finding time of each of the baseline algorithms corresponds to the execution time of the correspondence whole algorithm. (5) *Path length:* The length of p, p_o and p_c are all measured.

7.1 Real Datasets

We conducted experiments on two real datasets, Eagle Peak and Bearhead. The results for Eagle Peak can be found in Figure 12, Figure 13, Figure 14, Figure 15 and Figure 16.

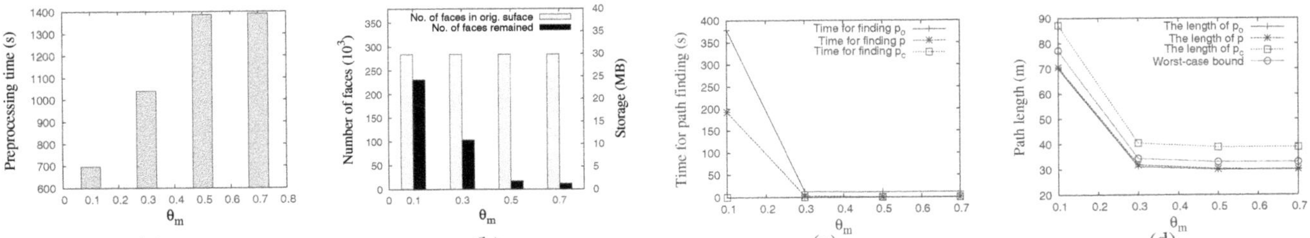

(a) (b) (c) (d)

Figure 12: Effect of θ_m (Eagle Peak where $\epsilon = 0.1$)

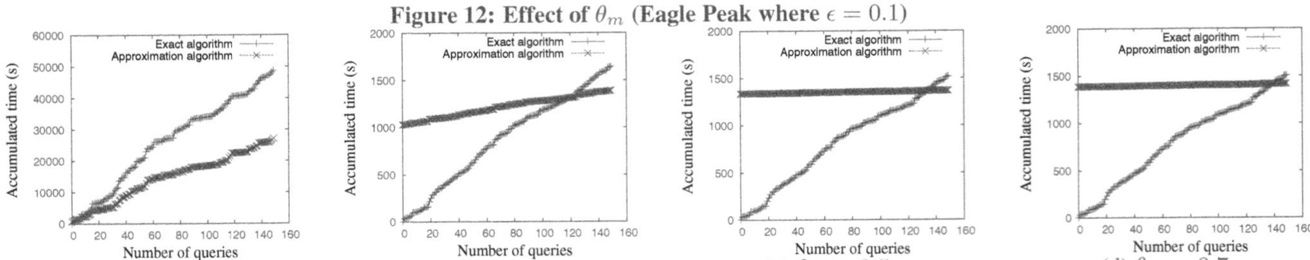

(a) $\theta_m = 0.1$ (b) $\theta_m = 0.3$ (c) $\theta_m = 0.5$ (d) $\theta_m = 0.7$

Figure 13: Comparison between the exact algorithm and the approximation algorithm (Eagle Peak where $\epsilon = 0.1$)

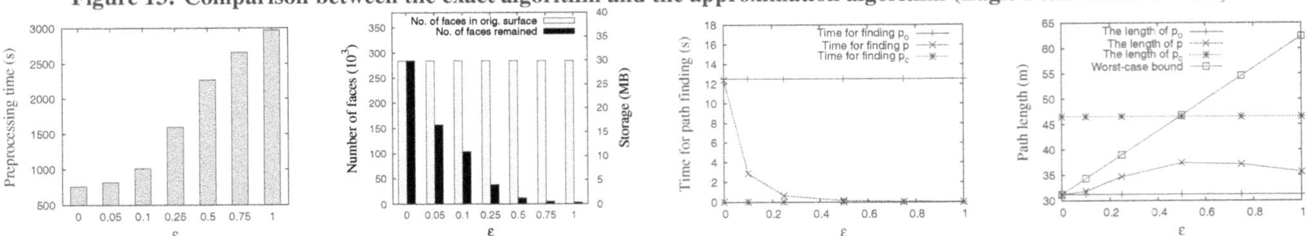

(a) (b) (c) (d)

Figure 14: Effect of ϵ (Eagle Peak where $\theta_m = 0.3$)

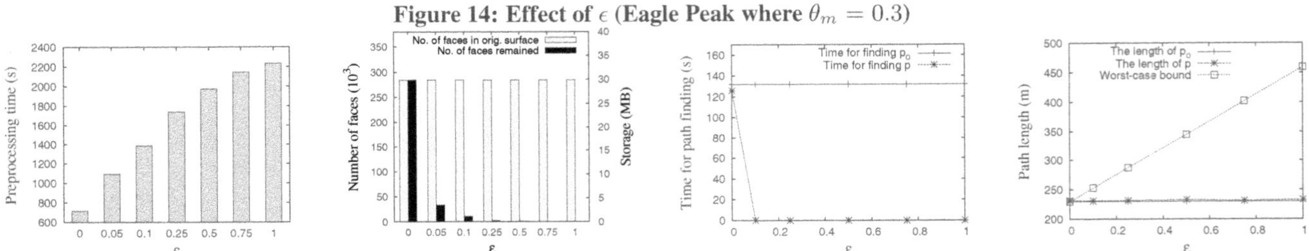

(a) (b) (c) (d)

Figure 15: Effect of ϵ (Eagle Peak where $\theta_m = \pi/2$)

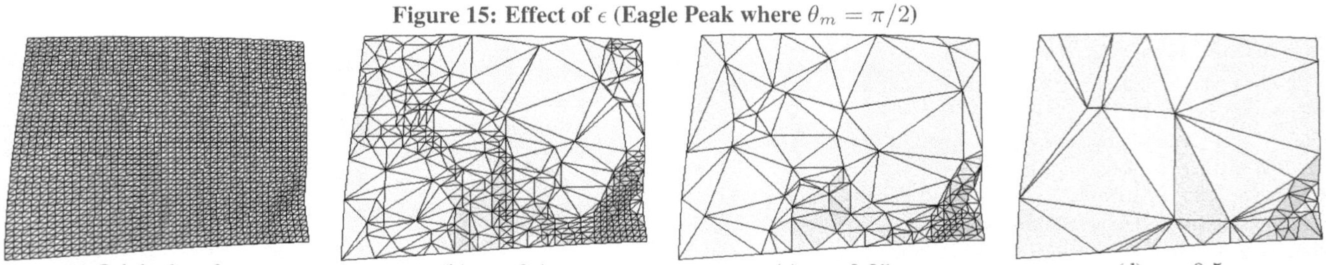

(a) Original surface (b) $\epsilon = 0.1$ (c) $\epsilon = 0.25$ (d) $\epsilon = 0.5$

Figure 16: Results of surface simplification (Eagle Peak where $\theta_m = 0.3$)

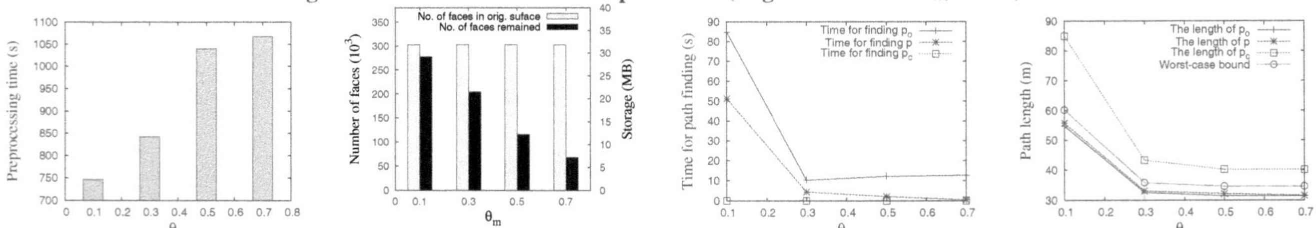

(a) (b) (c) (d)

Figure 17: Effect of θ_m (Bearhead where $\epsilon = 0.1$)

7.1.1 Effect of θ_m

In Figure 12a, when θ_m increases, the preprocessing time increases. This is because, when θ_m is larger, intuitively, the slope requirement is weaker and thus we can remove more vertices in algorithm *Surface Simplifier*. If there are more vertices removed, then the time to simplify the surface (in the preprocessing step) is larger. In Figure 12b, the number of vertices remained (and thus the memory consumption of the surface) decreases when θ_m increases. In Figure 12c, when θ_m increases, the time for finding p decreases. Since θ_m is larger, the total number of faces remained is smaller. Thus, the time for finding p is shorter. Besides, the time for finding p_o is much longer than the time for finding p. In particular, if $\epsilon = 0.1$ and $\theta_m = 0.3$, on average, our proposed algorithm which finds p takes 2.94s but the optimal algorithm which finds p_o needs 12.64s. Thus, the speedup is 4.3 times. If θ_m is set to 0.1, the speedup is 1.6 times. The time for finding p_c is shorter than the time for finding p_o and the time for finding p. Note that path p_c does not have any guarantee on the distance requirement (which will be described later). Besides, when θ_m is set to 0.3, we analyzed that the proportion of path segments (obtained after segmentation) which undergo the process of path adjusting is 26.5%. This suggests that it is not quite frequent to execute path adjusting in Step II. In Figure 12d, we denote an additional curve called "Worst-case bound" to denote the greatest theoretical error bound according to the length of p_o. This value is equal to $(1+\epsilon)|p_o|$. In this figure, the length of p_o decreases when θ_m increases. Besides, the length of p is smaller than the worst-case bound but the length of p_c is larger than the worst-case bound. In particular, if $\epsilon = 0.1$ and $\theta_m = 0.3$, the ratio of the length of p to the length of p_o is 1.02 but the ratio of the length of p_c to the length of p_o is 1.30.

In our proposed framework, we need to simplify a surface as a preprocessing step. In order to study how this preprocessing step benefits our algorithm for finding a gentle path over the simplified surface, we did the following experiments. In this experiment, we compare two algorithms, namely an *approximation algorithm* and an *exact algorithm*. The *approximation algorithm* corresponds to the algorithm for finding p while the *exact algorithm* corresponds to the algorithm finding p_o. We define the *accumulated time* of an algorithm as follows. Consider a query workload Q containing x queries where x is a non-negative integer. The accumulated time of an approximation algorithm is defined to be the sum of the preprocessing time and the total time of finding all (approximate) gentle paths among all queries in Q by the approximation algorithm. The accumulated time of an exact algorithm is defined to be the total time of finding all (exact) gentle paths among all queries in Q by the exact algorithm. Figure 13a shows that the accumulated times of the two algorithms increase with the number of queries in Q when $\theta_m = 0.1$ and $\epsilon = 0.1$. When Q contains fewer than 10 queries, the accumulated time of the exact algorithm is smaller than that of the approximation algorithm. However, when there are more than 10 queries in Q, the accumulated time of the exact algorithm is greater than that of the approximation algorithm. In other words, the approximation algorithm needs only 10 queries to compensate the preprocessing cost. We conducted other experiments when $\theta_m = 0.3, 0.5$ and 0.7, which can be found in Figure 13b, Figure 13c and Figure 13d, respectively. We find that 130 queries, 140 queries and 160 queries are needed to compensate the preprocessing cost when $\theta_m = 0.3, 0.5$ and 0.7, respectively.

7.1.2 Effect of ϵ

Figure 14a shows that the preprocessing time increases with ϵ. This is because the number of faces removed increases with ϵ and thus algorithm *Surface Simplifier* needs more time to simplify the surface. In Figure 14b, the number of faces removed increases with ϵ. In Figure 14c, the time to find path p decreases when ϵ increases. This is because the total number of faces remained is smaller if ϵ is larger. For example, when $\epsilon = 0.1$, the time to find path p is 2.87s but the time to find path p_o is about 12.517s. The speedup of finding path p (compared with finding path p_o) is about 4.4 times. When $\epsilon = 1.0$, the speedup is nearly to 240.8 times. We conclude that when ϵ increases, the speedup increases. In Figure 14d, similarly, the length of p is smaller than the worst-case bound. Note that the worst-case bound increases linearly with ϵ but the length of p does not increase linearly with ϵ.

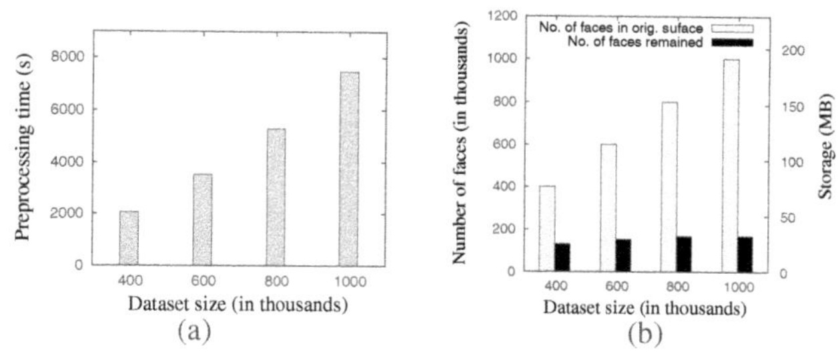

Figure 18: Effect of dataset size (Synthetic datasets)

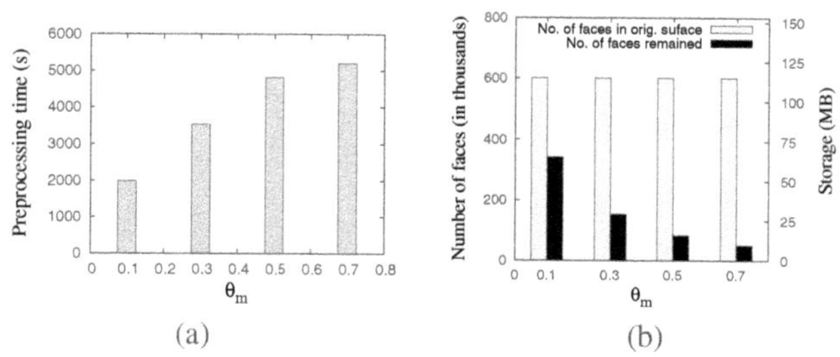

Figure 19: Effect of θ_m (Synthetic datasets)

7.1.3 Effect for Traditional Problem

We studied our proposed framework, surface simplification, for the traditional problem which does not consider any slope constraint (Figure 15). In this experiment, we adopt the implementation of Chen and Han's algorithm [12] (which is originally designed for the traditional problem) for algorithm $\mathcal{A}$ in our proposed framework. The results are also similar to Figure 14 but the preprocessing time and the time for finding p (p_o) are shorter. In particular, our proposed algorithm to find path p takes 0.0001s with 10% distance error guarantee. However, the optimal algorithm takes more than 132 seconds to find p_o. The speedup is 1,320,000 times.

7.1.4 Effect on Surface Simplification

Figure 16 shows the results of our surface simplification on the real dataset, Eagle Peak, where $\theta_m = 0.3$. For the sake of illustration, we only focus on a portion of this dataset with dimension 420m x 420m, which is shown in Figure 16a. Figures 16b, c and d show the simplified surface when we set ϵ to 0.1, 0.25 and 0.5, respectively. The number of triangles on the simplified surfaces decreases when ϵ increases.

We also did the experiments for Bearhead to study how θ_m and ϵ affect the performance of the algorithms and study how the proposed algorithm works well for the traditional problem. The results are also similar to those obtained from Eagle Peak. For the sake of space, we just show the results for parameter θ_m in Figure 17.

7.2 Synthetic Datasets

We also conducted experiments with synthetic datasets. In addi-

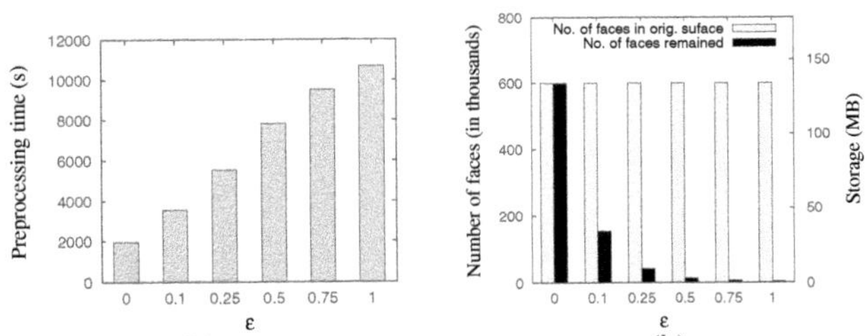

(a) (b)

Figure 20: Effect of ϵ (Synthetic datasets)

tion to the two parameters studied in real datasets (i.e., θ_m and ϵ), *dataset size* is also used to study the performance of the proposed algorithm over synthetic datasets where dataset size corresponds to the total number of faces on the surface.

7.2.1 Effect of Dataset Size

In Figure 18a, the preprocessing time increases with the dataset size. Figure 18b shows that, when the dataset size increases, the number of remaining faces keeps nearly unchanged. This is because when the dataset size is large, the number of vertices on a given fixed surface will be larger. However, since the surface generated by the synthetic data generator is nearly the same when the dataset size is larger, after surface simplification, it is likely that the given surface contains nearly the same number of faces (when the dataset size increases).

7.2.2 Effect of θ_m and ϵ

Figures 19 and 20 shows the results when we vary θ_m and ϵ, respectively. The trends for the effect of θ_m and ϵ on the synthetic datasets are similar to the trends on the real datasets.

Conclusion: Our proposed algorithm runs efficiently if we sacrifice the length of the path a little bit. The larger θ_m (ϵ) is, the faster our algorithm runs. In particular, if $\epsilon = 0.1$ and $\theta_m = 0.3$, our proposed algorithm runs 4.3 times faster than the optimal algorithm which finds the optimal path on S if the path found by our algorithm is at most 10% longer than the optimal path. If we set $\theta_m = \pi/2$, our proposed problem becomes the traditional problem. Our proposed algorithm runs 1,320,000 times faster than the optimal algorithm with 10% distance guarantee.

8. CONCLUSION

We study a fundamental operator in spatial databases, finding shortest paths on the surface of a terrain. In this problem, we consider the slope requirement such that the path is not too steep. Since solving this problem is more challenging than solving the traditional problem, we propose a new framework called surface simplification. Under this framework, we can compute shortest gentle paths efficiently. We conducted the experiments to show that our proposed framework is very efficient and effective not only for problem FSGP but also for the traditional problem.

There are a lot of promising research directions. Firstly, it is interesting to consider other popular spatial queries such as k nearest neighbors queries and range queries on the surface with the slope constraint. Secondly, another interesting direction is to study the real time spatial queries such as continuous k nearest neighbors in our problem setting, which have been studied extensively recently.

Acknowledgements: We are grateful to the anonymous reviewers for their constructive comments on this paper. The research is supported by HKRGC GRF 621309 and Direct Allocation Grant DAG11EG05G.

9. REFERENCES

[1] J. Chen and Y. Han. Shortest paths on a polyhedron. In *SCG '90: Proceedings of the sixth annual symposium on Computational geometry*, pages 360–369, New York, NY, USA, 1990. ACM.

[2] H.-J. Cho and C.-W. Chung. An efficient and scalable approach to cnn queries in a road network. In *VLDB*, 2005.

[3] J. Cohen, A. Varshney, D. Manocha, G. Turk, H. Weber, P. Agarwal, F. Brooks, and W. Wright. Simplification envelopes. In *SIGGRAPH*, 1996.

[4] M. de Berg, O. Cheong, M. van Kreveld, and M. Overmars. *Computational Geometry: Algorithms and Applications*. Springer, Berlin, 3rd ed. edition, 2008.

[5] K. Deng and X. Zhou. Expansion-based algorithms for finding single pair shortest path on surface. In *W2GIS*, pages 151–166, 2004.

[6] K. Deng, X. Zhou, H. T. Shen, Q. Liu, K. Xu, and X. Lin. A multi-resolution surface distance model for k-nn query processing. *The VLDB Journal*, 17(5):1101–1119, 2008.

[7] K. Deng, X. Zhou, H. T. Shen, K. Xu, and X. Lin. Surface k-nn query processing. In *ICDE*, 2006.

[8] E. W. Dijkstra. A note on two problems in connexion with graphs. *Numerische Mathematik*, 1(1):269–271, December 1959.

[9] S. Fortune. A sweepline algorithm for voronoi diagrams. In *Algorithmica 2(2)*, 1987.

[10] M. Garland and P. S. Heckbert. Surface simplification using quadric error metrics. In *SIGGRAPH*, 1997.

[11] T. Kanai and H. Suzuki. Approximate shortest path on polyhedral surface based on selective refinement of the discrete graph and its applications. In *GMP*, 2000.

[12] B. Kaneva and J.O'Rourke. An implementation of chen & han's shortest paths algorithm. In *the 12th Canadian Conference on Computational Geometry*, 2000.

[13] M. A. Lanthier, A. Maheshwari, and J.-R. Sack. Approximating weighted shortest paths on polyhedral surfaces. In *Proc. 13th ACM Symp. on Computational Geometry*, 1997.

[14] L. Liu and R. C.-W. Wong. Finding shortest gentle path (technical report). In *http://www.cse.ust.hk/~raywong/paper/findingShortestGentlePath-technical.pdf*, 2011.

[15] C. S. Mata and J. S. B. Mitchell. A new algorithm for computing shortest paths in weighted planar subdivisions. In *Proc. 13th ACM Symp. on Computational Geometry*, 1997.

[16] J. S. B. Mitchell, D. M. Mount, and C. H. Papadimitriou. The discrete geodesic problem. *SIAM J. Comput.*, 16(4):647–668, 1987.

[17] D. Papadias, J. Zhang, N. Mamoulis, and Y. Tao. Query processing in spatial network databases. In *VLDB*, 2003.

[18] G. W. Records. *Guinness: World Records 2010*. Guinness, 2009.

[19] J. Rossignac and P. Borrel. Multi-resolution 3d approximations for rendering complex scenes. In *In Geometric Modeling in Computer Graphics*, pages 455–465, 1993.

[20] H. Samet. *Foundations of Multidimensional and Metric Data Structures*. Morgan Kaufmann Publishers Inc., 2005.

[21] H. Samet, J. Sankaranarayanan, and H. Alborzi. Scalable network distance browsing in spatial databases. In *SIGMOD*, 2008.

[22] W. J. Schroeder, J. A. Zarge, and W. E. Lorensen. Decimation of triangle meshes. In *SIGGRAPH*, 1992.

[23] C. Shahabi, L.-A. Tang, and S. Xing. Indexing land surface for efficient knn query. *PVLDB*, 1(1):1020–1031, 2008.

[24] M. Soucy and D. Laurendeau. Multiresolution surface modeling based on hierarchical triangulation. *Computer Vision and Image Understanding*, 63:1–14, 1996.

[25] P. Tompkins, T. Stentz, and W. Whittataker. Mission planning for the sun-synchronous navigation field experiment. In *IEEE International Conference on Robotics and Automation*, 2002.

[26] K. R. Varadarajan and P. K. Agarwal. Approximating shortest paths on a nonconvex polyhedron. *SIAM J. Comput.*, 30(4):1321–1340, 2000.

[27] S. Xing, C. Shahabi, and B. Pan. Continuous monitoring of nearest neighbors on land surface. *PVLDB*, 2(1):1114–1125, 2009.

WHAM: A High-throughput Sequence Alignment Method

Yinan Li Allison Terrell Jignesh M. Patel

University of Wisconsin–Madison

{yinan, aterrell, jignesh}@cs.wisc.edu

ABSTRACT

Over the last decade the cost of producing genomic sequences has dropped dramatically due to the current so called "next-gen" sequencing methods. However, these next-gen sequencing methods are critically dependent on fast and sophisticated data processing methods for aligning a set of query sequences to a reference genome using rich string matching models. The focus of this work is on the design, development and evaluation of a data processing system for this crucial "short read alignment" problem. Our system, called WHAM, employs novel hash-based indexing methods and bitwise operations for sequence alignments. It allows richer match models than existing methods and it is significantly faster than the existing state-of-the-art method. In addition, its relative speedup over the existing method is poised to increase in the future in which read sequence lengths will increase.

The WHAM code is available at http://www.cs.wisc.edu/wham/.

Categories and Subject Descriptors

H.3.3 [**Information Storage and Retrieval**]: Information search and retrieval—*search process*; H.2.4 [**Database Management**]: Systems—*textual databases*

General Terms

Algorithms, performance

Keywords

Sequence alignment, approximate string matching, bit-parallelism

1. INTRODUCTION

Last summer marked the 10th anniversary of the sequencing of the first human genome [1, 21]. This key scientific discovery has been a turning point for modern life sciences and has dramatically changed the way in which researchers approach nearly every aspect of biomedical sciences, ranging from deciphering basic cellular mechanisms to drug discovery and drug design for personalized medicine. A crucial part of this first human genome assembly was using advanced data processing methods to assemble the entire genome from vast sets of data items, each of which described only a small portion (called a "read") of the genome. The human genome project delivered its first draft ahead of schedule, primarily because of the use of advanced data processing methods.

Existing sequencing technology has come a long way from the technology of 10 years ago, both in terms of speed (with which they can read parts of the genome) and the cost of reading each of the 3 billion "bases" that make up the whole human genome. As a consequence, while the first human genome took a few billion dollars to assemble, today with the help of next-generation sequencing machines an entire genome can be read for a few thousand dollars.

Interestingly, data processing techniques are an even more crucial aspect of assembling genomes today. The pressing problem now with the next-generation of sequencing is the so called "next-generation gap" – namely, the data processing cost associated with genomic analysis is now the dominating cost of producing a genome sequence [15]. A key component of this data processing task is the alignment of short sequence reads [15]. The focus of this paper is on the design and evaluation of a novel data processing system for speeding up this alignment task by an order of magnitude and more, while accommodating flexible match models. Our system is called WHAM – an acronym for **W**isconsin's **H**igh-throughput **A**lignment **M**ethod. WHAM employs novel database-style indexing, optimization and query processing techniques.

At its heart, the short sequence read alignment problem is similar to the common substring matching problem in data processing systems. At a high-level, the next-gen sequencing works as follows: First the (DNA) sample to be sequenced is broken (by treating with restriction enzymes or using mechanical force) into a number of short pieces. These pieces are then cut into equal-length fragments called "reads". The bases/characters in each fragment are read by the sequencing machine. From the computational perspective the set of reads/fragments can be modeled as a set of strings/sequences. The subsequent data processing task involves aligning each read sequence against some scaffolding/reference genome sequence.

For example, when assembling the genome for a specific individual to look for variations that cause specific diseases, the reference genome is often the publicly available human genome. Thus, from the string matching perspective, one can view the computation task as matching a set of equal-length short strings (reads) against a large reference string (the entire genome), using some string matching model, as described below.

When a read is compared to the reference genome, it is either deemed as a valid or an invalid alignment. The validity of an alignment is measured in terms of mismatches and gaps. A mismatch occurs when a base on the reference genome and a base on the read are aligned, but aren't the same base. A gap occurs when a base is aligned with an empty space. Either or both of these alignments may be the "right answer" when aligning a read if it is advanta-

SIGMOD'11, June12–16, 2011, Athens, Greece.

geous to do so, such as when it allows many other base pairs in the set of reads to be aligned with the reference genome sequence. Often, aligners use two mismatches and no gaps as the definition of a valid alignment, but these models are likely to get more sophisticated in the future [15].

Previous methods for sequencing reads include Maq [12], SOAP [13], and Bowtie [6]. These techniques employ a compact index that works well for aligning so called "short reads", namely reads that are typically around 30-50 characters long. In particular, Bowtie – the leading state-of-the-art method – has focused on utilizing the properties of Burrows-Wheeler Transforms (BWT) [7] to index the reference sequence. A BWT-based index has a small memory footprint, making Bowtie feasible on computers with only 2GB of memory. However, memory is quickly becoming cheaper (while the genome size is constant), making it unnecessary to place such tight memory restrictions on the alignment software. In addition, BWT-based methods use a prefix matching technique that requires only a few iterations to produce a valid alignment. While this technique works well with short reads, its performance degrades rapidly as the read length increases. Unfortunately, impending technological advances with the next-generation sequencing machines are expected to push up the read lengths to produce what are called "long reads", and loosely refer to read strings that are many factors longer than the "short reads". This trend implies that the existing BWT-based aligners will likely become computationally infeasible in the near future. In addition, sequence aligners of the future will also need to accomodate more errors in the match models (for long reads) [9, 15], and the performance of existing methods rapidly deteoriates when using these richer match models.

Our WHAM method addresses the short-comings of the existing methods. It uses a novel hash-based index built on the reference genome that accommodates complex string matching models that are natural for read alignments. This hash index is optimized for space and speed, and to work efficiently with long reads. The hash index quickly finds potential hits for each read. This list of potential hits may contain some false positives that have to be checked using a precise test. This test for an actual hit is essentially a complex string matching function, which is computationally expensive. Another novel aspect of WHAM is the use of bitwise operations to perform this string matching test efficiently. Finally, WHAM uses a novel architecture that incorporates an optimizer (to optimize the indices that are built) and a compressor to reduce the size of the input data, providing a complete data processing and management module that fits into existing computational pipelines for high-throughput genomic sequencing.

We have compared WHAM using a number of real datasets against the leading and commonly used read alignment method – Bowtie. Our results show that WHAM is often orders of magnitude faster than Bowtie, and allows for richer match models. The relative speedup of WHAM over Bowtie increases as the read length as well as the number of errors increases, which bodes well for the future in which we expect to see longer reads that need to be matched with more relaxed/richer match models.

The remainder of this paper is organized as follows: The WHAM method is described in Section 2. Results from an extensive empirical evaluation are presented in Section 3. Section 4 discusses related work, and Section 5 contains our concluding remarks.

2. METHOD

2.1 Problem Statement

A sequence is a series of characters. For genomes, each character is either a nucleic acid represented by the symbols A, G, C, or T, or an unknown character, named N. The unknown character symbol, N, indicates that there is either uncertainty about which nucleotide belongs there, or that there is a repetitive region in the genome and all nucleotides in that region are turned into Ns (since for the genome sequencing task, it does not make biological sense to match reads to these known repetitive "junk" regions).

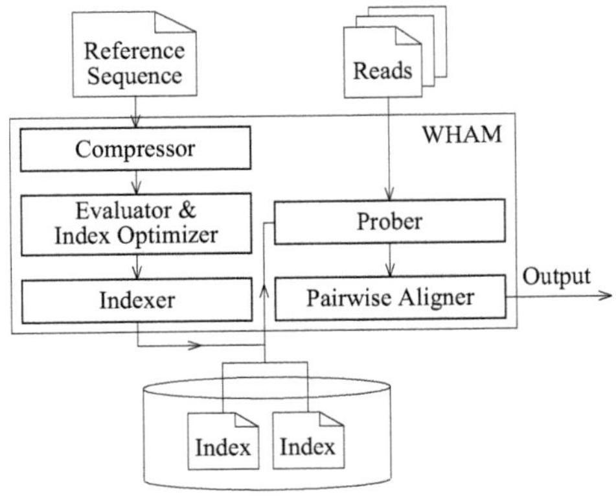

Figure 1: Architecture of WHAM

WHAM takes as input a set of query sequences of equal length, a database of reference sequence(s), and an error model. The error model specifies *alignment constraints* on three types of errors that are commonly used for read alignment. These three types of errors are: *substitutions*, which change characters in a sequence, *insertions* and *deletions*, which add or remove characters respectively. WHAM finds **all** (it is not a heuristic) valid alignments that satisfy the constraint on the number of errors in the set of query sequences. A valid alignment is formally defined as follows:

DEFINITION 1. *Given an error model specifying* s *substitutions,* i *insertions, and* d *deletions, a* valid alignment *for a given query sequence* Q *is all the subsequences in the reference sequence* R *that can be aligned by applying up to* s *substitutions,* i *insertions, and* d *deletions between* Q *and each matched subsequence in* R.

The following example demonstrates alignments between two query sequences and a reference sequence. Suppose we allow 1 substitution, 1 insertion, and 1 deletion. The first query sequence can be aligned with 1 substitution (shown as the underlined character) and 1 insertion (shown as a dash in the query sequence), while the second query sequence can be aligned with 1 substitution and 1 deletion (shown as a dash in the reference sequence). Both alignments satisfy the alignment constraint.

Reference Sequence	ATGGCCACAGAAGTT-GCGA
Query Sequence 1	G<u>A</u>CCACA-AAGTT
Query Sequence 2	ACAG<u>T</u>AGTTAGC

The error model is sometimes aggregated to a generic k-error model which implies that the total number of substitutions, insertions and deletions is no more than k in the alignment.

2.2 System Architecture

Figure 1 shows the architecture of the WHAM system. WHAM provides an interface to ingest a set of reads as they come off the alignment machine and manages the computation associated with matching the reads to a specified reference genome. WHAM typically sits as a module in a larger computational pipeline. The WHAM system builds various indices (as described below) and also keeps track of various data management needs such as storing the indices on disk, tracking the usage, reporting to the overall workflow management system, etc. In this paper, we only focus on the components related to the sequence matching parts.

The *indexer* is responsible for building indices on the reference genome. At any given time, WHAM may have stored indices for multiple genomes (e.g. human, mouse, rat, etc.). These indices persist on disk, and are built only once when the reference genome sequence is loaded into WHAM. When the WHAM module is invoked, a single reference genome is specified (e.g. human) and the entire index for that reference genome is loaded into main memory. Note that in current next-gen sequence assembly, when analyzing multiple read sets, often the reference genome remains the same, so this index can stay loaded in main memory across multiple runs.

While the indices persist on disk, the indices are optimized for access in main memory. Since main memory capacities are increasing quickly and since WHAM builds indices on the reference genome (which is of a constant length), this design choice leverages the technological trend that makes it practical and economical to fit the entire genome index in main memory. The WHAM indexing method is described in Section 2.3.

The indexer relies on an indexing configuration setting that specifies the parameters that affect the index performance. This index configuration is generated by the *index optimizer* by comparing various indexing schemes whose costs are computed by the *evaluator* based on an analytical model (described in Section 2.7). The *prober* takes as input a set of query sequences (reads), and uses the same indexing configuration to break up each query sequence, and probes the indices (on the reference genome) to find potentially matching reference subsequences. The *pairwise aligner* is then performed to verify that the reference subsequence actually aligns to the query sequence under the alignment constraint (Section 2.5).

WHAM also employs a *compressor* to remove all unnecessary characters in the reference sequence before building an index.

2.3 Indexing Method

The WHAM indexing method is motivated by the observation that the inexact alignment between two sequences can be solved by the exact alignments on the fragments of sequences [19].

2.3.1 Indexing Schemes

We first introduce a basic indexing scheme based on the following observation: If two sequences, R and Q, match within k errors and $k+1$ non-overlapping fragments are taken from R, then the matching sequence Q contains at least one fragment that will match exactly with one fragment in R. This property is evident, since k errors cannot be placed into the $k+1$ non-overlapping fragments.

Using this observation, given the length l of the query sequences, all l-character subsequences in the reference sequence R are split into $k+1$ uniform-sized fragments of length $\lfloor \frac{l}{k+1} \rfloor$. A hash index is built on all the fragments. To align a query sequence, we break down the query sequence Q into fragments in an analogous way, and search against the fragments on the hash index to find the potential matching subsequences in R.

A problem with this indexing scheme is that the index keys (fragments) may be short and may have relatively low diversity, resulting in long chains in the hash index, which in turn degrades performance. For example, suppose a 36bps[1] query sequence is to be aligned within 2 errors. Three fragments are taken from the sequence, each of length 12bps. Now, for the moment assume that each character has only four possible values – `A`, `G`, `C`, and `T` – (so ignore `N`s for this example), then the 12bps fragment has a maximum of $4^{12} = 16,777,216$ possible values. However, the reference human genome sequence contains around 3 billion characters. When loading these 3 billion 12bps fragments into a hash index, each hash bucket in the index contains on average around 170 entries. When a probe is performed on the hash index, each of these entries needs to be scanned and verified one by one, which degrades the search performance significantly.

To address this problem, we extend the basic indexing scheme to a more general one based on Lemma 1 by relaxing the limit on the number of fragments.

LEMMA 1. *If two sequences, R and Q, match within k errors and $f(f > k)$ non-overlapping fragments are taken from R, then the matching sequence Q contains at least $f - k$ fragments which match exactly with fragments in R.*

We omit a detailed proof of Lemma 1 (in the interest of space), but it is easy to see that if more than k fragments contain errors, then the complete match must have more than k errors.

Based on Lemma 1, indices are built on $f - k$ fragments of all l-character subsequences of R, rather than on one fragment, where l is the length of the query sequences. In particular, each subsequence in the reference genome is split into f non-overlapping fragments of length $\lfloor \frac{l}{f} \rfloor$, from which we select $f - k$ fragments. A selected (unselected) fragment is called an *indexed (unindexed) fragment*. An unindexed segment between two indexed fragments is called an *interval*. For each selection, we concatenate the $f - k$ selected fragments into a *concatenation*. All concatenations are of the same length $(f - k) \cdot \lfloor \frac{l}{f} \rfloor$, and are inserted into hash indices. To search using these indices, we break the query sequence Q, into fragments in an analogous way (see Section 2.3.3 below for details). Note that the extended indexing scheme is identical to the simple indexing scheme, when $f = k + 1$.

Taking the 36bps example again, if four fragments are taken from the sequence, the concatenations contain two fragments, and are 18bps long. There are $4^{18} = 68,719,476,736$ possible values for 18bps concatenations, many more than the characters in the whole human genome sequence. Consequently, the hash collision issue is dramatically mitigated.

2.3.2 Building Indices

The *indexer* component in WHAM is responsible for building indices on all concatenations of fragments for all subsequences of length l in the reference genome R. The goal of the indexer is a) to separate the concatenations into several hash indices to reduce the collisions in the bucket for each hash index, and b) to remove all duplicated concatenations to reduce the space cost.

We observe that the concatenations can be categorized into a few groups based on the intervals between the indexed fragments. The concatenations in a group are matched with others by sliding the concatenations. As an example, Figure 2 illustrates the categorization on six concatenations of choosing two indexed fragments from four fragments. The indexed fragments are represented by rectangles, whereas the unindexed fragments are represented by lines. Among these concatenations, concatenation 1, 3, and 6 contain two contiguous indexed fragments, and are categorized into group I. In concatenation 2 and 5, there is an unindexed fragment between the two indexed fragments. These concatenations belong to group II. Concatenation 4 contains a two fragment gap between the two indexed fragments, and is categorized into group III.

To achieve the first goal (i.e. to separate concatenations into several hash indices), the indexer separately loads the concatenations of all subsequences in R into various hash indices on the basis of groups. The number of hash indices (groups) that is required follows from Lemma 2.

LEMMA 2. *If f-fragment query sequences are aligned within k errors, then C_k^{f-1} indices are required for the alignments.*

[1]The term "bps" is commonly used in genomics and refers to base pairs. The bps is essentially the sequence length.

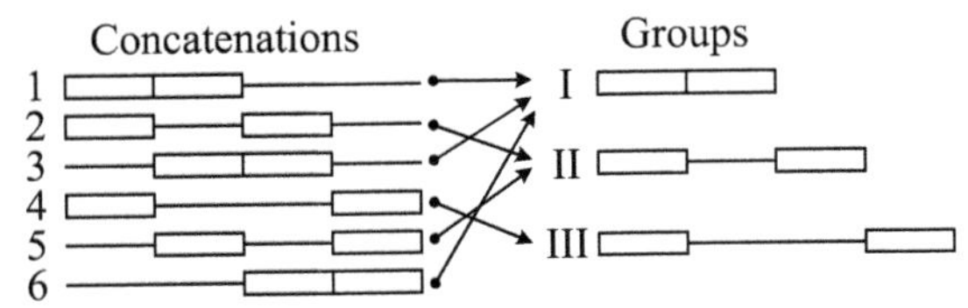

Figure 2: Categorization of six concatenations ($f = 4, k = 2$)

PROOF. The number of indices is equal to the number of groups. One way to count the number of groups is to count the number of ways to select k unindexed fragments from f fragments so that the first fragment is an indexed fragment, because other selections in the group can be matched to this kind of selection by sliding the sequence. The number of these selections corresponds to the number of ways to select k unindexed fragments from $f - 1$ fragments (the first fragment is fixed to be an indexed fragment). This is given by the formula C_k^{f-1}. □

To achieve the second goal (i.e. to reduce the indexing space), only one representative concatenation in each group is loaded into the hash index, for each subsequence in R. Other concatenations in the group will be loaded (as a representative concatenation) when sliding the subsequence, because a concatenation is identical to other concatenations in the same group when sliding the subsequence by one or a few fragments.

To build the indices, we slide a l-character window along the reference sequence R (an analysis of various sliding window schemes may be found in [8]). The C_k^{f-1} concatenations associated with the C_k^{f-1} groups are extracted from the subsequence in the window and separately loaded into C_k^{f-1} hash indices. The number of entries in each hash table roughly equals the number of characters in the reference sequence.

EXAMPLE 2.1. *Figure 3 illustrates the process of building indices on a sample sequence for alignments with two errors. Suppose that the query sequences contain 12 characters and are split into 4 fragments, each of length 3 characters. Thus, the indices are built on concatenations of length 6. For each subsequence in the reference sequence, we generate three concatenations that consist of two indexed fragments with zero, one, and two unindexed fragments in the interval, respectively. The three concatenations are then inserted into the three indices as the index keys.*

The space complexity of each hash index is $O(n)$, where n is the number of characters in the reference sequence R. The number of hash indices that are built for a reference sequence is dictated by Lemma 2.

2.3.3 Searching Indices

The *prober* (see Figure 1) is responsible for searching the query sequences (reads) against the indices. First, we describe the search procedure of the prober for alignments with only substitutions, and then (in the next paragraph) extend it to support indels (insertions or deletions). To align a query sequence Q, it is split and concatenated in an analogous way as the subsequences in R. All C_k^f concatenations are assembled with $f - k$ fragments in various combinations. Next, we search each concatenation on its associated indices. Then, the positions of the matched concatenations in R are retrieved. With these positions, we extract l-character subsequences from R as "candidate" occurrences, which are then checked using the technique described in Section 2.5.

Next, we extend our technique to support indels. First, all the C_k^f concatenations used for alignments with only substitutions are generated. Then, for each concatenation, we extend it to a set of

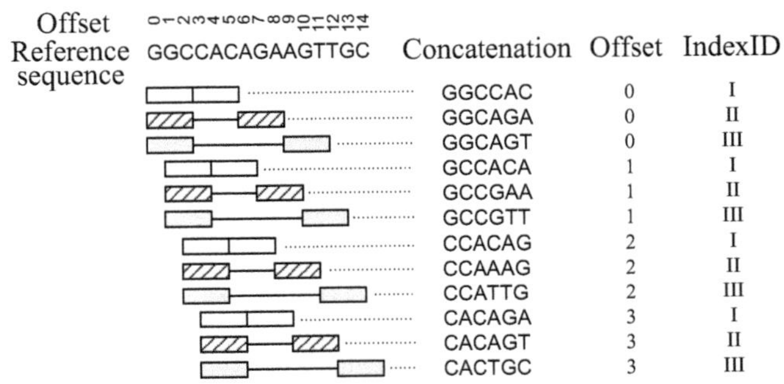

Figure 3: Building three hash indices ($f = 4, k = 2$)

new concatenations that are used to align the query sequence with indels. The basic idea is to slide some indexed fragments by a few characters. More specifically, if the error model specifies i insertions and d deletions, we place up to i insertions and up to d deletions in all intervals in the query sequence. The concatenations are then assembled with indexed fragments whose offsets are recalculated based on the number of indels in the intervals. The probes are performed on all possible placements of indels in all intervals.

The numbers of probes is formally given by Lemma 3.

LEMMA 3. *If f-fragment query sequences are aligned within k errors including i insertions and d deletions, then the number of probes for each query sequence is given by:*

$$N_{probe} = \sum_{h=0}^{k} (C_{h-1}^{k-1} + 2C_h^{k-1} + C_{h+1}^{k-1}) C_h^{f-k-1} C_i^{i+h} C_d^{d+h}$$

In particular, when $i = d = 0$, the number of probes is C_k^f.

PROOF. We have two main tasks to accomplish. The first task is to count how many ways can one select k unindexed fragments from f fragments to compose h intervals (the unindexed segments between indexed segments). Let $F(f, k, h)$ be the number of selections. The second task is to count the number of probes on each selection with h intervals, denoted as $G(h, i, d)$. Thus, we sum the products of $F(f, k, h)$ and $G(h, i, d)$ to compute the total number of probes, obtaining

$$N_{probe} = \sum_{h=0}^{k} F(f, k, h) \cdot G(h, i, d). \qquad (1)$$

First, we count the number of selections with h intervals. A selection can be viewed as interleaved segments between interval and indexed segments. Given a selection with h intervals, there are four possible arrangements of h intervals, $h + 1$ indexed segments, and (0, 1 or 2) unindexed segments at the ends, as shown in the following figure:

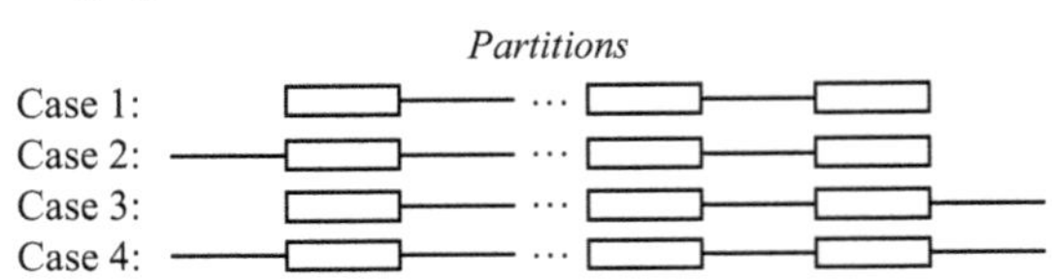

In case 1, these kind of selections have h intervals and $h + 1$ indexed segments. The number of selections is equal to the number of ways to partition k unindexed fragments into h intervals, and partition $f - k$ indexed fragments into $h + 1$ indexed segments. The formula for the number of partitioning n elements into s non-empty sets is given by C_{s-1}^{n-1}. Thus, there are C_{h-1}^{k-1} and C_h^{f-k-1} ways to partition unindexed fragments and indexed fragments, respectively. By the multiplication principle, there are $C_{h-1}^{k-1} C_h^{f-k-1}$ partitions in this case. Similarly, in case 2 and case 3, we need to partition k unindexed fragments into $h+1$ sets (h intervals and one unindexed segment at one end), and partition $f-k$ indexed fragment into $h+1$ indexed segments. There are $C_h^{k-1}C_h^{f-k-1}$ partitions in case 2 or case 3. In case 4, we need to partition k unindexed fragments into $h+2$ sets (h intervals and two unindexed segments at the both ends). The number of partitions is given by $C_{h+1}^{k-1}C_h^{f-k-1}$. By applying the addition principle to cases 1-4, we have

$$F(f,k,h) = (C_{h-1}^{k-1} + 2C_h^{k-1} + C_{h+1}^{k-1})C_h^{f-k-1}. \quad (2)$$

Next, we count the number of probes on a selection with h intervals. Consider the following correspondence. We put up to i insertions and up to d deletions into h intervals. The number of placements is equal to the number of probes, because we need to perform one lookup for each placement. One way to solve the problem is to add a "virtual" interval where all the unselected indels are placed. Thus the task is to decide how to partition i insertions into $h+1$ intervals, and partition d deletions into $h+1$ intervals. Given the formula C_n^{n+s-1} on the number of ways to partition n elements into s sets, there are C_i^{i+h} and C_d^{d+h} ways to partition i insertions and d deletions, respectively. By applying the multiplication principle, we have $C_i^{i+h}C_d^{d+h}$ different kinds of partitions on the combinations of insertions and deletions, obtaining

$$G(h,i,d) = C_i^{i+h}C_d^{d+h}. \quad (3)$$

Finally, we complete the derivation by substituting Equation 2 and 3 into Equation 1. □

EXAMPLE 2.2. *We align a query sequence GACCACAAAGTT with one substitution and one insertion to the sample sequence shown in Figure 3. The query sequence is split into 4 fragments as GAC | CAC | AAA | GTT. Then, we concatenate two of the four fragments into concatenations: (1) GAC | CAC, (2) GAC | AAA, (3) CAC | AAA, (4) GAC | GTT, (5) CAC | GTT, (6) AAA | GTT. In addition, we generate concatenations that are used to find alignments with one insertion. Since the concatenations 2, 4, and 5 have an interval between the two indexed fragments, we move the window of the second indexed fragment one character left to apply the insertion, and then get three more concatenations (7) GAC | CAA, (8) GAC | AGT, and (9) CAC | AGT. Following the relationship between the concatenations and groups as shown in Figure 2, we probe concatenation 1, 3, and 6 on index I, concatenation 2, 5, 7, and 9 on index II, 4 and 8 on index III. The concatenation (9) CAC | AGT in index II is found and the subsequence in R with 13 characters GGCCACAGAAGTT is returned.*

2.4 Hash Index Structure

WHAM uses tailored compact hash tables to index all concatenations generated by the *indexer* (see Figure 1). Hash indices are designed as static cache-efficient structures. The hash buckets are 32-bit integer arrays. For each slot in a bucket, the most significant bit (MSB) is used as a collision bit. If only one concatenation is hashed into a slot, then the collision bit of the slot is set to 0. The remaining 31 bits represent the positions of the concatenations in the reference sequence R[2]. Otherwise, if several concatenations are hashed into the same slot, then the collision bit is set to 1. The remaining 31 bits point to an array that contains the positions of all concatenations hashed into that slot. The MSB of the last entry in the overflow list is set to 1 to indicate the end of the slot's list.

[2]The offsets in the compressed reference sequence can be represented by 31-bit integers in most cases. See Section 2.6 for details. We also support 32-bit offsets by storing the MSBs of buckets and overflow entries in separate bit vectors.

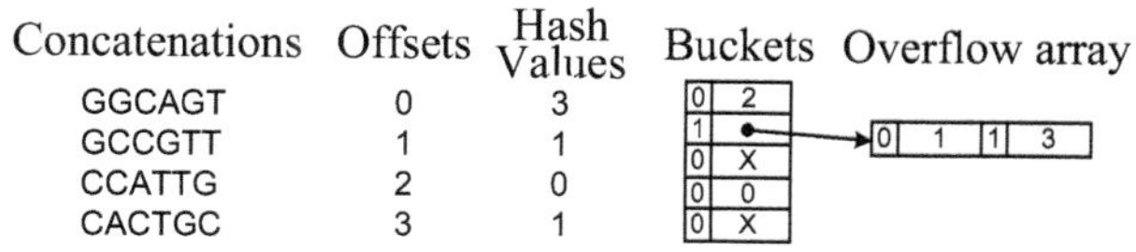

Figure 4: Hash table of index III shown in Example 2.1

EXAMPLE 2.3. *Figure 4 illustrates the hash table for Index III shown in Example 2.1 (Figure 3). The offsets of the four concatenations in the reference sequence are numbered from 0 to 3. In the bucket slots 0 and 3, only one concatenation is hashed into the slot. As a result, the concatenation positions are directly stored in the slots with* `collision bit = 0`. *In the bucket slot 1, we maintain a pointer to the starting position of the slot's overflow list in the overflow array, with* `collision bit = 1`. *Slots 2 and 4 are empty.*

Both space and time cost are taken into consideration in the design of the hash index. The design of the overflow array makes effective use of CPU caching, since the overflow entries are stored in sequential memory positions. In addition, to save space the design doesn't use next pointers that are required by linked lists. The collision bits save both time and space spent on the overflow list when a bucket slot contains only one concatenation. Moreover, the hash table only stores the positions of concatenations in the reference sequence R, rather than the actual concatenations, to save space, because the size of concatenations is typically a few times larger than that of the positions.

2.5 Pairwise Alignments

WHAM relies on the *pairwise aligner* (see Figure 1) to examine if the query sequence Q can be aligned to a potential matched subsequence in the reference sequence R within s substitutions, i insertions, and d deletions. Conventional pairwise alignment techniques are based on the Needleman-Wunsch dynamic programming method and take $O(l^2)$ time to compute the optimal alignment [16]. This alignment step can quickly become the bottleneck. WHAM uses an alternative technique that stores the sequences in a compact binary representation and leverages the ability of modern processors to compute bitwise operations fast. These two aspects are described next.

WHAM uses three bits to represent each base/symbol. The symbols `A`, `C`, `G`, `T`, and `N` are encoded as 000, 001, 010, 011, and 100 respectively. For example, the sequence `GACT` is encoded as the binary string $= (010000001011)_2$.

A sequence in WHAM is packed into a binary representation that can be fit into one or a few computer words. The proposed bitwise-based techniques (described below) manipulate a sequence as a whole, rather than manipulating the characters one by one. As a result, the alignment cost is not related to the length of sequences if they can fit into a word, but scales with the number of errors.

For ease of presentation, below we first introduce the alignment algorithms using a binary domain (each bit in a binary string is viewed as a base – so first consider a domain with only two symbols), and then extend our technique for the general case with larger number of symbols in the domain (approximately 5 in our case).

In Section 2.5.1, we first introduce three basic bitwise manipulations, that leverage the ability of modern processors to compute bitwise operations fast. Based on these manipulations, the bitwise-based alignment techniques to handle substitutions, insertions, and deletions on binary string are presented in Section 2.5.2, 2.5.3, and 2.5.4, respectively. Then, in Section 2.5.5 we describe the method for combining all three kinds of errors. In Section 2.5.6, the methods are extended to the general case when the domains have more than two symbols.

2.5.1 *Basic Bitwise Manipulations*

Given the basic bitwise operations, e.g. AND (&), OR (|), XOR ($\oplus$), and SHIFT ($\ll$, $\gg$), some of the combinations of these basic operations produce important bitwise manipulation techniques that we use in this paper. In particular, we have three bitwise manipulations that provide a fast way to find and manipulate the rightmost 1 bit [10]. The notations **R**, **S**, and **RS** are used to denote the three manipulations, respectively.

$x\&(x-1)$: remove the rightmost 1 in x. **[R]**

$x|-x$: smear the rightmost 1 to the left in x. **[S]**

$x \oplus -x$: remove and smear the rightmost 1 in x. **[RS]**

EXAMPLE 2.4. *The example demonstrates how the three bitwise operations apply on a binary sequence x.*

$$
\begin{aligned}
x &= (10001111010111001 0000)_2 \\
x\&(x-1) &= (10001111010111000000)_2 & \textbf{[R]} \\
x|-x &= (11111111111111110000)_2 & \textbf{[S]} \\
x \oplus -x &= (11111111111111100000)_2 & \textbf{[RS]}
\end{aligned}
$$

2.5.2 *Alignments with Substitutions*

A bitwise alignment with substitutions is used to check whether two binary sequences can be aligned with up to s substitutions. The idea is that we first apply a bitwise XOR operation to identify the mismatched bits in the two given binary sequences, and then count the number of 1s in the resulting binary sequence, using the bitwise technique **R** (described above). After performing $u = x \oplus y$, we continue removing the rightmost 1 of u for s iterations. If the resulting binary sequence only contains 0-bits, the original u contains up to s ones. This implementation executes s bitwise AND operations and s subtraction instructions. The complexity of this step is $O(s)$, because s steps are taken to remove s possible substitutions before checking equality of the two strings.

EXAMPLE 2.5. *An example of an alignment with at most 2 substitutions between x and y is shown below.*

$$
\begin{aligned}
x &= (10\underline{0}0111101 0\underline{1}110010110)_2 \\
y &= (10101111010011001 0110)_2 \\
u = x \oplus y &= (00100000000100000000)_2 \\
u = u\&(u-1) &= (00100000000000000000)_2 & \textbf{[R]} \\
u = u\&(u-1) &= (00000000000000000000)_2 & \textbf{[R]} \\
(u = 0) &= \texttt{true}
\end{aligned}
$$

2.5.3 *Alignments with Insertions*

A bitwise alignment with i insertions is used to determine whether a binary sequence y can be matched to x by adding at most i gaps. This algorithm is based on the following greedy algorithm: we treat the rightmost i mismatches as insertions, and then examine whether the remaining prefix of x is the same as that of y.

Table 1 demonstrates the first steps of the bitwise alignment algorithm with up to i insertions. First, a bitwise XOR operation is applied between right-aligned x and y, e.g. $u_0 = x \oplus y$. Suppose that the rightmost 1 in u_0 is at position a_0, then the binary sequence u_0 can be represented by $(*^{n-a_0-1}10^{a_0})_2$[3], where $*$ is an arbitrary value in $\{0,1\}$. Since the a_0-th bits in x and y are mismatched, a_0 can be treated as an insertion position, if x and y can be aligned with only insertions.

Table 1: Identifying the first two insertion positions ($*$ is an arbitrary binary value)

		(2nd insert)		(1st insert)	
Index	...	a_1	...	a_0	... 0
		+1 −1		+1 −1	
$u_0 = x \oplus y$	...	$*$ $*$ $*$	...	$*$ 1 0	... 0
$u_1 = (x \ll 1) \oplus y$	...	$*$ 1 0	...	0 $*$ $*$	... $*$
$m_0 = u_0 \oplus -u_0$	...	1 1 1	...	1 0 0	... 0
$u_1 = u_1 \& m_0$	...	$*$ 1 0	...	0 0 0	... 0

In the next step, we need to find the second insertion position. Since the subsequence of x on the left of the first insertion position must be shifted one character left to be aligned with y, we compute $u_1 = (x \ll 1) \oplus y$. In u_1, all bits between the first and second insertion position are 0s, whereas the bits at other positions are arbitrary binary values. If the second insertion is at position a_1, then u_1 can be represented by $(*^{n-a_1-1}10^{a_1-a_0-1}*^{a_0+1})_2$. Next, we generate a mask $m_0 = u_0 \oplus -u_0$ by removing and smearing the rightmost 1 to the left of u_0 (apply **RS**), which is of the form of $(1^{n-a_0-1}0^{a_0+1})_2$. The mask m_0 is applied on u_1 to clear all bits to the right of the first insertion position. Then, u_1 can be represented by $(*^{n-a_1-1}10^{a_1})_2$. Thus, the position of the rightmost 1 in u_1 is the second insertion position. Continuing this for i iterations, we will find all the i insertion positions.

Finally, we get a bit-difference sequence u_i between the two sequences for all bits on the left of all i insertion positions. If and only if all bits in u_i are 0s, then x can be aligned to y with i insertions.

The algorithm can also examine alignments with less than i insertions. To verify this claim, suppose that x can be aligned to y with $i'(i' < i)$ insertions. After executing the first i' iterations, we get $u_{i'} = (...000)_2$. In the next iteration, we have

$$
\begin{aligned}
m_{i'} &= u_{i'} \oplus -u_{i'} = (\ldots 000)_2 \\
u_{i'+1} &= (x \ll k) \oplus y = (\ldots ***)_2 \\
u_{i'+1} &= u_{i'+1} \& m_{i'} = (\ldots 000)_2
\end{aligned}
$$

Continuing this computation, by $i - i'$ iterations, we have $u_{i'+1} = u_{i'+2} = \cdots = u_i = (\ldots 000)_2$. According to $u_i = (\ldots 000)_2$, the algorithm identifies an alignment with at most i insertions.

The pseudocode for this technique is shown in Algorithm 1. The complexity of this algorithm is $O(i)$, because we take i steps to remove the effects of all possible insertions before checking equality of the two strings.

EXAMPLE 2.6. *This example demonstrates how we can use 12 bitwise operations to align two binary strings x and y with at most two insertions.*

$$
\begin{aligned}
x &= \quad (100011110101110010110)_2 \\
y &= (100011110\underline{1}10111\underline{0}0010110)_2 \\
u_0 = x \oplus y &= (101011001011100100000000)_2 \\
u_1 = (x \ll 1) \oplus y &= (110010001100000000111010)_2 \\
m_0 = u_0 \oplus -u_0 &= (111111111111111100000000)_2 & \textbf{[RS]} \\
u_1 = u_1 \& m_0 &= (110010001100000000000000)_2 \\
u_2 = (x \ll 2) \oplus y &= (000000000011001010011 10)_2 \\
m_1 = u_1 \oplus -u_1 &= (111111111000000000000000)_2 & \textbf{[RS]} \\
u_2 = u_2 \& m_1 &= (000000000000000000000000)_2 \\
(u_2 = 0) &= \texttt{true}
\end{aligned}
$$

[3]We use exponentiation to denote bit repetition, e.g. $(1^4 0^2)_2 = (111100)_2$.

Algorithm 1 Sequence alignment within i insertions

$u_0 \leftarrow x \oplus y$;
for $k \leftarrow 1...i$ **do**
  $m_{k-1} \leftarrow u_{k-1} \oplus -u_{k-1}$; // remove and smear the rightmost 1
  $u_k \leftarrow (x \ll k) \oplus y$;
  $u_k \leftarrow u_k \& m_{k-1}$;
return $u_i = 0$;

Algorithm 2 Sequence alignment within s substitutions, i insertions, and d deletions

1: **for** each permutation $o_{s+i+d-1}, o_{s+i+d-2}, \ldots, o_1, o_0$ with s substitutions (0), i insertions (+1) and d deletions (-1) **do**
2:   $m = (111111...)_2$;
3:   $u = x \oplus y$;
4:   **for** $k \leftarrow 0 \ldots s+i+d-1$ **do**
5:     **if** $o_k = 0$ **then**
6:       $u \leftarrow u \& (u-1)$; // remove the rightmost 1
7:     **else**
8:       **if** $o_k = +1$ **then**
9:         $m \leftarrow u \oplus -u$; // remove and smear the rightmost 1
10:       **else**
11:         $m \leftarrow u| - u$; // smear the rightmost 1 to the left
12:       $u \leftarrow (x \ll (o_0 + o_1 + ... + o_k)) \oplus y$;
13:       $u \leftarrow u \& m$
14:   **if** $u = 0$ **then**
15:     **return true**;
16: **return false**;

2.5.4 *Alignments with Deletions*

The algorithm for a bitwise alignment with d deletions is similar to that of alignments with d insertions, except for two differences. First, we replace all left shifts by right shifts. Given the property $x \ll (-k) = x \gg k$, we use $x \ll -k$ to represent shifting x right by k bits. Second, the mask m_{k-1} is generated by the bitwise technique **S** instead of the bitwise technique **RS**. We smear the rightmost 1 to the left, but do not remove the rightmost 1 because this position is not skipped by an insertion.

2.5.5 *Alignments with all the Three Types of Errors*

The final algorithm to align within s substitutions, i insertions and d deletions simply enumerates all possible orders of these three types of errors, and then verifies each permutation. Algorithm 2 shows the pseudocode. In the outer loop, all permutations with s substitutions, i insertions and d deletions are enumerated. We use -1, 0, +1 to denote a deletion, a substitution, and an insertion, respectively. A permutation represents the order of the error types that occurred in an alignment. For example, $o_3o_2o_1o_0 = -1, 0, +1, 0$ implies an alignment with four errors, which are a substitution, an insertion, another substitution, and a deletion, in right-to-left order.

For each permutation $o_{s+i+d-1}o_{s+i+d-2} \ldots o_1o_0$, we examine whether the two given sequences can be aligned with the constraints on the number and the order of error types. In the beginning, the current binary sequence u is initialized as the bit-difference sequence between the right-aligned x and y (Line 4). In the inner loop, we clear all the errors in the permutation from right to left. In iteration k, we manipulate the sequence u according to the error type indicated by o_k. If the error is supposed to be a substitution, then we remove the rightmost 1 in u (Line 6). Thus, the substitution is cleared so that we can continue identifying the next error by finding the next rightmost 1. Otherwise, we first generate a mask m by removing and smearing the rightmost 1 in u if the error is an insertion (Line 9), or by smearing the rightmost 1 in u if the error is a deletion (Line 11). Next, we update $u \leftarrow (x \ll (o_0 + o_1 + ... + o_k)) \oplus y$, and use the mask m on u to clear the rightmost bits that have arbitrary values (Line 13). As a result, the rightmost 1 in the updated u implies the next error position. Continuing this for $s + i + d$ iterations, if the resulting sequence u contains only 0s, we produce a successful alignment.

The algorithm also examines alignments with fewer than the constrained number of errors. Suppose that x can be aligned to y with $s'(s' \leq s)$ substitutions, $i'(i' \leq i)$ insertions, and $d'(d' \leq d)$ deletions. Then, there exists a permutation R such that $P = o_{s+i+d}o_{s+i+d-1} \ldots o_{s'+i'+d'+2}o_{s'+i'+d'+1}P'$, where P' is a permutation of s' substitutions, i' insertions, and d' deletions that can produce an alignment between x and y. After $(s'+i'+d')$ iterations of permutation P', we get $u = (\ldots 000)_2$. Regardless of whether the next error is a substitution ($u = u\&(u-1) = (\ldots 000)_2$), an insertion ($u = (\ldots * **)_2 \& (u\& - u) = (\ldots 000)_2$), or a deletion ($u = (\ldots * **)_2 \& (u \oplus -u) = (\ldots 000)_2$), we get $u = (\ldots 000)_2$ in the end of the next iteration. Continuing this step for $s+i+d-s'-i'-d'$ iterations, we have $u = (\ldots 000)_2$, and return true for this alignment.

The time complexity of this algorithm is $O(\frac{(s+i+d)!}{s!i!d!}(s+i+d))$, where $\frac{(s+i+d)!}{s!i!d!}$ is the number of permutations, and $s+i+d$ is the number of steps for processing each permutation. Recall that the complexity of the Needleman-Wunsch algorithm is $O(l^2)$, where l is the length of sequences. Given the fact that sequence aligner typically chooses 2 or 3 errors ($k = s+i+d$) for a sequence with 50$\sim$100 characters ($l = 50 \sim 100$), our method is much faster than the Needleman-Wunsch algorithm.

EXAMPLE 2.7. *This example shows the steps for an alignment with at most one substitution and one deletion between sequences x and y. This alignment requires a total of 16 bitwise instructions.*

$$x = (100011110101010010110)_2$$
$$y = (10101111010110010110)_2$$
$$u_0 = x \oplus y = (110110001111100000000)_2$$
$$u_1 = (x \ll -1) \oplus y = (00100000000011011101)_2$$

Case $-1, 0$:

$$v_1 = u_0 \& (u_0 - 1) = (110110001111000000000)_2 \quad [\mathbf{R}]$$
$$m_1 = v_1 | - v_1 = (111111111111000000000)_2 \quad [\mathbf{S}]$$
$$w_0 = u_1 \& m_1 = (001000000000000000000)_2$$

Case $0, -1$:

$$m_1 = u_0 | - u_0 = (111111111111100000000)_2 \quad [\mathbf{S}]$$
$$v_1 = u_1 \& m_1 = (001000000000000000000)_2$$
$$w_1 = v_1 \& (v_1 - 1) = (000000000000000000000)_2 \quad [\mathbf{R}]$$
$$(w_0 = 0)|(w_1 = 0) = \texttt{true}$$

2.5.6 *Alignments on the Genome Domain*

We extend our bitwise techniques presented above to support alignments on sequences with more than two base types in the domain. Suppose that each character in the domain can be represented by D bits (in our case, $D = 3$ to to encode the symbols A, C, G, T, and N). As we mentioned before, the techniques described in previous sections cannot be directly applied on the encoded binary strings of genome sequences. For example, given two sequences GACT $= (010000001011)_2$ and GAGT $= (010000010011)_2$, there are two different bits between the two sequences, because: $(010000001011)_2 \oplus (010000010011)_2 = (000000011000)_2$. With this test, it seems that the sequences match with two errors. However, the sequences can actually be aligned with one character error (C$\rightarrow$G).

All our bitwise alignment algorithms discussed in the previous sections (see Sections 2.5.2-2.5.5) begin with one or a few bitwise XOR operations (in the form of $v = (x \gg i) \oplus y$) to identity the different bits between the two sequences. To support alignments on the domain, we add one additional step

$$v = (v \gg D-1|...|v \gg 1|v)\&\mu, \text{ where } \mu = (...0^{D-1}10^{D-1}1)_2,$$

immediately after each of these operations to compute a character-difference sequence based on the bit-difference sequence. An OR operation is performed on the D bits representing the same character, to reflect that if any pair of bits is different, then the characters are different. We then mask it by μ to generate a binary sequence in the form: $(...0^{D-1}v_2 0^{D-1}v_1 0^{D-1}v_0)_2$, where v_i indicates the inequality between the i-th characters in the two sequences. For example, if we apply this formula on the bit-difference sequence $(000000011000)_2$ in the example shown above ($D = 3$), the resulting sequence is $(000000001000)_2$.

EXAMPLE 2.8. *This example demonstrates an alignment with at most one substitution and one deletion between x and y. The procedure is similar to that of example 2.7, except for the two added lines (shown as underlined).*

$$
\begin{aligned}
x &= \text{GCTCGAC} \\
y &= \quad \text{GATCAC} \\
x &= (010001011001010000001)_2 \\
y &= (\quad 010000011001000001)_2 \\
u_0 = x \oplus y &= (010011011010011000000)_2 \\
\underline{u_0 = (u_0 \gg 2|u_0 \gg 1|u_0)\&\mu} &= (001001001001001000000)_2 \\
u_1 = (x \ll -3) \oplus y &= (\quad 000001000000010001)_2 \\
\underline{u_1 = (u_1 \gg 2|u_1 \gg 1|u_1)\&\mu} &= (\quad 000001000000001001)_2 \\
\textit{Case } -1, 0&: \\
v_1 = u_0\&(u_0 - 1) &= (001001001001000000000)_2 \\
m_1 = v_1| - v_1 &= (111111111111000000000)_2 \\
w_0 = u_1\&m_1 &= (000000001000000000000)_2 \\
\textit{Case } 0, -1&: \\
m_1 = u_0| - u_0 &= (111111111111111000000)_2 \\
v_1 = u_1\&m_1 &= (000000001000000000000)_2 \\
w_1 = v_1\&(v_1 - 1) &= (000000000000000000000)_2 \\
(w_0 = 0)|(w_1 = 0) &= \texttt{true}
\end{aligned}
$$

2.6 Compressing Genome Sequences

Some areas of any typical genome are filled with Ns (recall from Section 2.1, the symbol N represent unknown or a repetitive region). For example, within the repeat-masked human genome, about 50.5% of the 3 billion nucleotides are Ns, because entire repetitive regions are masked out as Ns. These Ns can represent any of the nucleotides – A, C, G or T, and are always treated as an error in alignments. This property provides an opportunity to compress the genome sequence by removing unnecessary Ns, and is exploited by the compressor component shown in Figure 1.

A naive way of compression is to directly remove all Ns in the reference sequence. However, this method introduces errors when a query sequence can be aligned to the portions to the immediate left and right of a series of Ns in the reference sequence. The following example shows a wrong alignment on the naive compressed sequence. Query sequence 1 cannot be aligned to the reference sequence, but it can be aligned to the naive compressed sequence.

Reference Seq.	GGCCACAGAANNNNNNTACTACG
Naive Compressed Seq.	GGCCACAGAATACTACG
Query Seq. 1	CCACAGAATACT

To guarantee the correctness of alignments, WHAM uses an accurate compression method to remove unnecessary characters. The length of the compressed sequence is comparable to the naive compressed sequence, but the aligner generates the exact same alignments on the compressed sequence as on the original sequence.

Suppose the alignment constraint is k errors. Then, the portion in the original sequence that consists of at least $k+1$ consecutive Ns is called *N-series*. WHAM cuts all N-series into $k+1$ Ns.

Taking the above example again, if we allow 2 errors, then the N-series that consists of 6 Ns is cut to a shorter series with 3 Ns. As shown below, query sequence 1, which cannot be aligned to the original sequence within 2 errors, also cannot be aligned to the compressed sequence within 2 errors (the best alignment is with 3 substitutes, shown by the underlined characters).

Reference Seq.	GGCCACAGAANNNNNNTACTACG
WHAM Compressed Seq.	GGCCACAGAANNNTACTACG
Query Seq. 1	CCACAGAATACT

The position of a matched portion in the compressed sequence needs to be mapped to the position in the original sequence when WHAM outputs results. This can be done by building an index on all position pairs of N-series in the original and the compressed sequences. To obtain the original position of a matched portion, we search against the index using its position in the compressed sequence as a search key to find the rightmost N-series that is to the left of the matched portion. The original position is then calculated based on the distance to the N-series and the original position of the N-series. In our implementation, we employ a cache-efficient B-tree [18] to index the position mapping.

2.7 Analytical Model and Index Optimizer

In this section, we present an analytical model of WHAM's alignment performance. This model is used by the index optimizer shown in Figure 1 to pick an ideal number of fragments (such that performance when probing is maximized).

WHAM's indexing technique is based on a hashing method that is known to have low memory reference locality, which implies that the total execution time is likely to be dominated by the CPU cache stall time. Therefore, we use the number of cache misses as the metric in our model. The model relies on the input parameters including the length of query sequence l, the number of fragments f, the number of errors k, and outputs the estimated number of cache misses for each alignment.

Total alignment cost, M_{align} is simply $N_{probe} \cdot M_{probe}$, where N_{probe} is the number of probes, and has been derived in Lemma 3.

Next, we analyze the cost of a probe on a hash index, M_{probe}. The random variable X is used to represent the number of records that are hashed into a particular bucket slot. When searching records in a hash table, cache misses can be incurred as it accesses the bucket table, the overflow list, as well as the reference sequences in the database. If $X = 0$, the bucket slot is empty, and we only need to access one slot in the bucket table (1 cache miss). When $X = 1$, an extra cache miss is incurred when reading the sequence from the reference sequence following the pointer stored in the bucket slot. When $X = i (i > 1)$, we first access the bucket (1 cache miss), and then scan the overflow list ($\lceil \frac{i}{B} \rceil$ cache misses, where B is the block size of the CPU cache, also known as the cache line size). For each entry in the overflow list, we go to the reference sequence (R) to verify the alignment (i cache misses). By taking the three cases into consideration, the number of cache misses for a probe is

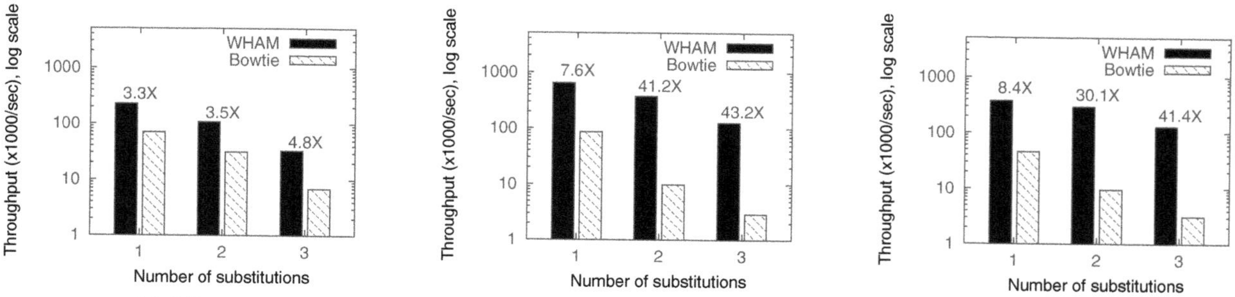

(a) 36bps (b) 60bps (c) 74bps

Figure 5: Throughput comparison between WHAM and Bowtie varying the number of substitutions

given as follows:

$$M_{probe} = P(X = 0) + 2 \cdot P(X = 1) + \sum_{i=2}^{n} (1 + \lceil \frac{i}{B} \rceil + i) \cdot P(X = i)$$

In a hash table, n records occupy b buckets. We assume that the records have uniform distribution on their range, and the hash function is a perfect hash function. If a record is hashed into a particular hash bucket with a probability of $1/b$, and all n records are hashed, then the number of records in each hash bucket can be modeled as a binomial distribution with parameters n and $\frac{1}{b}$, i.e. $X \sim B(n, \frac{1}{b})$. The probability mass function of X is:

$$P(X = i) = C_i^n (\frac{1}{b})^i (1 - \frac{1}{b})^{n-i}$$

The number of occupied buckets, b, depends on the length of concatenations $q = (f - k) \cdot \lfloor \frac{l}{f} \rfloor$. Since the sequence consists of four possible bases for each character, the maximum number of occupied buckets is 4^q. Given the total number of buckets N_{bucket} in the hash table, the number of occupied buckets is:

$$b = \min(4^q, N_{bucket}), \quad \text{where } q = (f - k) \cdot \lfloor \frac{l}{f} \rfloor$$

Using the model presented above, we have implemented an *index optimizer* (see Figure 1) that uses an analytical model *evaluator* to compute the impact of each possible f value on the performance when matching the read set. The *optimizer* (see Figure 1) enumerates the candidate f values, and determines a suitable f value that minimizes the estimated matching cost for a target read length and the error model.

3. EVALUATION

We ran our experiments on a machine with dual 2.67GHz Intel Xeon 6-core CPUs, and 24GB of DDR3 main memory, running Scientific Linux 5 (kernel 2.6.9). Each processor has 12MB of L3 cache shared by all cores on that processor. In addition, each core has a private 32KB L1 instruction and a 32KB L1 data cache, and 256KB of L2 cache. Each processor also employs a two-level hardware TLB. All algorithms were implemented in C++, and compiled using g++ 3.4.6 with optimization flags (O3 and finline-functions).

We chose three sets of *real* query sequences as workloads. These workloads have varying read lengths of 36bps, 60bps, and 74bps, providing for a wide range of read lengths corresponding to what the current next-gen sequencing machines provide today. The 36bps and 74bps workloads come from NCBI, and were chosen because their lengths are similar to the datasets used in the Bowtie paper [6], and the 60bps workload is from our collaborators. Each workload contains about 3 million reads.

Our reference genome (on which we build indices) is the repeat-masked human genome NCBI build 36. We also tested WHAM on the non-masked human genome. After filtering out junk regions that appear more than 100 times in the genome, the performance is similar to that on the masked genome.

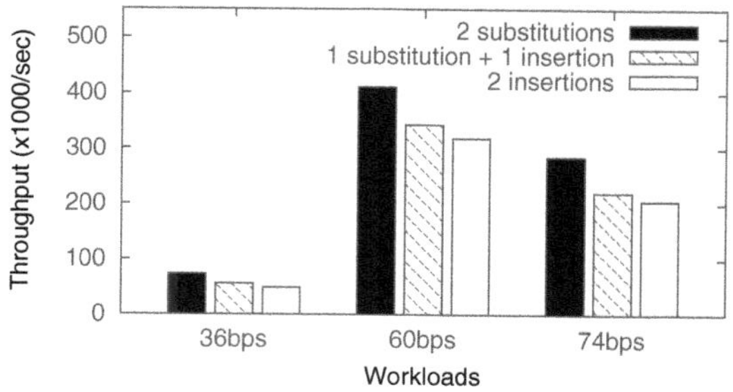

Figure 6: WHAM throughput varying the number of insertions (the number of errors is fixed at two)

The WHAM index optimizer (see Section 2.7) recommended the number of fragments for each workload, and then computed the number of indices based on Lemma 2 for each workload. Table 2 summarizes the parameters used for the three workloads. The number of fragments plays a key role in the performance of WHAM. For example, if we use 3 fragments to align a 36bps workload with 2 errors, it is one order of magnitude slower than using the recommended value. All values that we used in the experiments are recommended by the *index optimizer*, whose accuracy is evaluated in Section 3.3.

Table 2: Number of fragments and indices for the workloads

	Number of fragments			Number of indices		
	1 err	2 err	3 err	1 err	2 err	3 err
36bps	3	4	6	2	3	10
60bps	2	3	5	1	1	4
74bps	2	3	4	1	1	1

Each WHAM index is about 8.9GB in size and takes about 20 minutes to build. Loading a prebuilt WHAM index from disk takes less than two minutes. The number of indices for each workload is listed in Table 2. If the total size of indices exceeds the memory size, then WHAM loads indices and performs alignments on the loaded indices one after another.

In the evaluation below, we compare WHAM to Bowtie [6]. Bowtie also builds an index on the reference genome, and the Bowtie index is about 1.5GB and takes about 3 hours to build. We have also compared WHAM with RBSA [17], a string matching method that accommodates a broader class of error models compared to WHAM. However, our experiment results show that WHAM is several orders of magnitudes faster than RBSA. In addition, RBSA has a much larger memory footprint than WHAM making it infea-

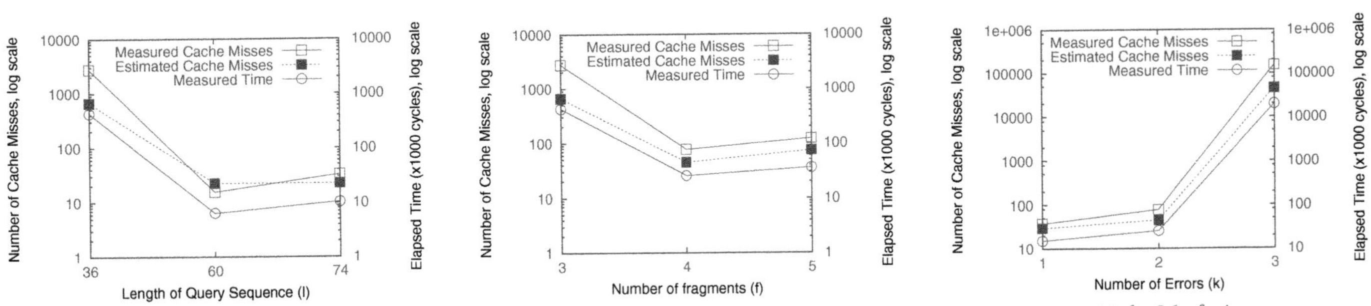

(a) f =3, k=2 (b) l =36, k=2 (c) l =36, f=4

Figure 7: Analytical Model Validation

sible to use on our machines for the whole human genome. Consequently, we do not consider RBSA further in this paper.

Since index construction and loading is a one-time cost, in the performance comparison, we do not include these costs for either Bowtie or WHAM.

3.1 Comparison between WHAM and Bowtie

We first compare the throughput of WHAM with that of Bowtie (version 0.12.3), the leading state-of-the-art method that is widely deployed in production settings today. We used the 64-bit version of Bowtie running with the -a flag, indicating that it should report all valid matches. Since Bowtie does not support indels, we only compare the throughput with varying number of substitutions.

Figure 5 shows the results on the three datasets. The speedup of WHAM over Bowtie is also marked on the top of the bars in the graph. As can be observed from Figure 5, WHAM is uniformly better, with speedup of 3X to 5X for the 36bps workload, and 8X to 43X for the 60bps and 74bps workloads. The speedup difference between the short (36bps) and the long (60bps and 74bps) query sequences is due to the hash collisions. When the query sequence is short, many of the concatenations (keys) are the same, which results in many collisions in the hash tables. Consequently, throughput drops significantly as either WHAM suffers from scanning the long overflow array on a hash probe, or it breaks the query sequences into more fragments, and thus increases the number of probes.

For the short query sequence (36bps), the throughput of both WHAM and Bowtie degrades as the number of substitutions increases (see Figure 5 (a)). The speedup of WHAM over Bowtie is relatively steady, within a small range from 3.3X to 4.8X. This means that the throughput of WHAM decreases as fast as that of Bowtie when allowing for more substitutions. This behavior is due to the combinations of two effects. First, WHAM performs more probes on the hash table as the number of allowed errors increases. Second, and more importantly, the concatenations become shorter and cause significant collisions in the hash tables when allowing for more errors. As a result, the overflow arrays become longer, and the hash probes become more expensive.

For longer query sequences, the speedup of WHAM over Bowtie increases as the number of substitutions increases. For the 60bps workload (Figure 5 (b)), WHAM is 7.6X, 41.2X, and 43.2X faster with 1, 2, and 3 substitutions respectively. For the 74bps workload (Figure 5 (c)), the speedup is 8.4X, 30.1X, and 41.4X with 1, 2, and 3 substitutions respectively. (Since the 60bps and the 74bps datasets are different workloads, the reader should not read too much into variations in performance for the specific number of substitutions across these two datasets.) For the longer query sequences, the indexed fragments in WHAM are long enough to mitigate the hash collision issue. WHAM's throughput degradation is almost always due to the increasing number of probes on the hash table and the number of errors increases. As a result, the throughput of WHAM degrades slower than that of Bowtie as the number of errors in the match model increases.

3.2 Effect of Indels

WHAM also supports indels as well as the combinations of substitutions and indels. In this experiment, we fix the number of errors at two, and vary the number of insertions (the number of substitutions is two minus the number of insertions). Since Bowtie does not support indels, we cannot make a comparison with Bowtie.

Figure 6 shows the throughput for the three combinations of substitutions and insertions. The throughput degrades as the number of insertions increases across the three datasets. This is due to two effects. First, supporting more insertions introduces more probes on the hash indices. Second, the bitwise alignments with insertions are typically more complex than those with only substitutions, and as a result, the cost of the bitwise alignment method increases with increasing indels in the model.

3.3 Model Validation

Finally, we evaluate the accuracy of our analytical model by comparing the estimated and measured performance with various parameters. Figure 7 demonstrates the measured and estimated number of cache misses, as well as the measured elapsed time, varying the parameters l, k, f. The number of cache misses is obtained by enabling the hardware performance-monitoring counters (RDPMC instruction), and only the number for the lowest level data cache is reported.

In each experiment, we fix two parameters and vary the third one. Figure 7(a) shows the measured and estimated performance on each of our three workloads. Figure 7(b) plots the performance when f varies from 3 to 5. Figure 7(c) illustrates the performance when varying the value of k from 1 to 3.

As shown in Figure 7, our estimates show a trend similar to the measured values. The gap between the measured and estimated cache misses is mainly due to the different alignment ratio in the datasets. Note that an invalid query sequence is more likely to access the bucket that has a short overflow list or an empty bucket, whereas a valid query sequence is more likely to access the "hot" bucket. Thus, more cache misses occur in the dataset with a high alignment ratio. For example, the 60bps dataset has a low alignment ratio, whereas the 74bps dataset has a high alignment ratio. As shown in Figure 7(a), our analytical model overestimates on the 60bps dataset, and underestimates on the 74bps dataset.

Furthermore, the estimated best f values match the measured best values. As shown in Figure 7(b), the analytical model accurately estimates that the best performance is achieved when partitioning the query sequence into 4 fragments. We used our ana-

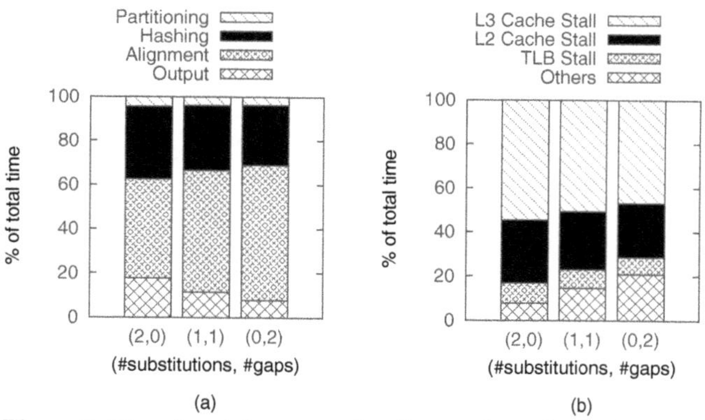

Figure 8: Time breakdown varying the number of substitutions for the 60bps workload

lytical model in our index optimizer to recommend the f value in all our experiments, and the resulting recommended index settings are shown in Table 2. By comparing WHAM's histogram in Figure 5 and the best throughput among all partitioning schemes (the results are omitted here in the interest of space), we observe that the analytical model used in the index optimizer captures the best parameters for all settings in our experiments.

3.4 Time breakdown

To better understand the performance characteristics of WHAM, next we examine the detailed time breakdown for 1) the different phases in WHAM, and 2) the different processor stall times when running WHAM.

The time breakdown for the different phases of WHAM is shown in Figure 8 (a). This time breakdown is for the 60bps workload and for three error models: 2 substitutions, 1 substitution and 1 insertion, and 2 insertions. The time breakdown for the other workloads and error models are similar to the one shown in Figure 8 (a), and we omit these other results in the interest of space.

In Figure 8 (a), the four main phases include: (a) the partitioning phase to partition the short reads into fragments and to combine these fragments into concatenations if necessary, (b) the hashing phase to perform lookups on the hash table, and to scan the corresponding overflow array, (c) the alignment phase to perform bitwise alignment between a pair of sequences, and (d) the output phase to write the results to a file. The partition phase is the fastest phase, and only accounts for about 4% of total time. The hashing time is significant (about 30%) across all three settings, due to cache misses (stalls) when accessing hash entries. Alignment is the most expensive phase. It varies from 45% to 60% of the total time. The alignments with more deletions execute more instructions and are more expensive. The output phase accounts for 8%–18% of the total time, depending on the number of successful alignments.

Figure 8 (b) illustrates the time breakdown for different processor stall times. We used the processor hardware performance counters to measure the number of L3 cache misses, L2 cache misses, and TLB misses. Since these resource stalls can overlap with useful computation in modern processors, there is no real way to measure the overlap between a stall and an instruction executing in the instruction stream, as the overlapped time depends on the degree of instruction-level parallelism. We crudely (over) estimate the stall time as the number of measured misses multiplied by the cycles for each stall. The "other" time in this figure is computed by subtracting the L2, the L3, and the TLB stall times from the total time. All results are with a single threaded execution of WHAM. Multi-threaded results are presented below in Section 3.5.

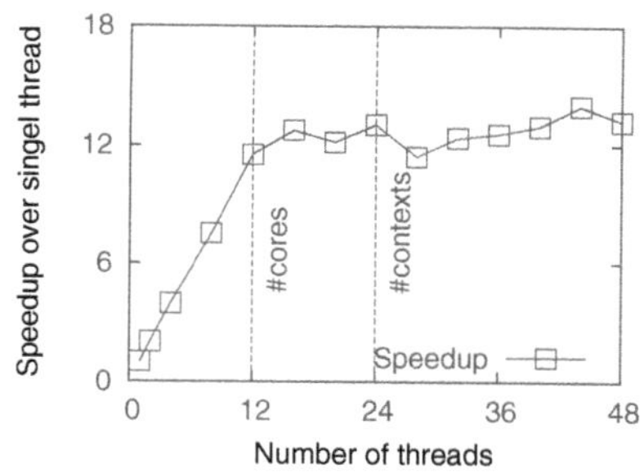

Figure 9: WHAM throughput varying number of threads

As shown in Figure 8 (b), the L3 and the L2 cache stall times account for about 50-60%, and 25-30% of the total time respectively, and are the dominating stall costs in WHAM. This empirically verifies the assumption in Section 2.7 that cache stall time is the performance bottleneck. When we allow more gaps, the "other" time increases, mainly due to more instructions involved in computing pairwise alignments.

3.5 Performance on Multi-Core CPUs

All the previous results are with WHAM running in a single thread. We have also implemented a multi-threaded version of WHAM, and examined its performance on a multi-core processor. In this setting, the batched short reads are evenly distributed across all running threads. Each thread independently lookups the shared hash indices and performs the pairwise alignment in parallel. Figure 9 illustrates the throughput speedup of the multi-threaded execution over the single threaded execution with varying number of threads.

As shown in the figure, the throughput has a linear speedup as long as the number of threads does not exceed twelve, which is the total number of physical cores in our test machine. The linear speedup indicates that, although the cache stall time dominates the execution time of a single thread execution, it does not become the performance bottleneck when using multiple cores, as memory access requests from different threads can be issued and processed in parallel. The architecture of the machine that we are using provides a higher bandwidth between the main memory and the CPU caches than what WHAM demands. However, the speedup has only a slight increase when the number of threads exceeds twelve, which means that WHAM does not benefit from Hyper-Threading. The throughput fluctuates when the number of threads is more than the number of physical cores, due to the cost of context switching when scheduling the threads across the processing cores.

3.6 Summary

The main conclusions from these experiments are that, (a) the analytical model which is at the heart of the index optimizing component of WHAM is accurate, (b) WHAM is often more than an order of magnitude faster than Bowtie on long read workloads, (c) WHAM performs much better on long read sequences than short ones, which bodes extremely well for the future in which read lengths are expected to increase, (d) WHAM supports indels with low overhead, and (e) WHAM exhibits a linear speedup as the number of threads increases to match the number of processing cores.

4. RELATED WORK

A number of commonly used alignment algorithms employ the dynamic programming technique, including the Needleman-Wunsch algorithm [16] (for global alignment) and the Smith-Waterman algorithm [20] (for local alignment).

Several q-gram based methods have been developed for approximate string matching in large sequence databases [2, 11, 14, 23]. A q-gram is a substring of length q. These q-gram based methods are based on counting the number of q-grams that are shared between the query and the reference sequences. Although these q-gram based methods and WHAM find approximately matched sequences by performing exact searches on subsequences, the key differences stem from the fact that q-gram based methods count the number of shared subsequences, whereas WHAM uses subsequences as seeds to find valid matching sequences. Another difference is that the q-grams are overlapping subsequences, whereas in WHAM fragments are non-overlapping subsequences.

Bit manipulation methods such as the Shift-Or algorithm [5] and its extended variant [22] have been used to efficiently search for a query sequence in a reference sequence. Unlike the Shift-Or algorithm and its variants, WHAM's bitwise alignment algorithms are used to globally align the two sequences along their entire lengths, with an arbitrary number of mismatches and gaps.

BLAST [3] is a popular heuristic tool to compute local alignments for long query sequences. However, a major limitation of BLAST is that there is no guarantee that the optimal local alignment will be reported (since it uses a heuristic technique). More recently, a reference-based method, called RBSA [17], was proposed for large queries and accurate results. In RBSA, query sequences are aligned to a group of references with precomputed alignment scores, instead of being aligned to the original reference sequence directly. These methods that support long query sequences and arbitrary error models are more general than WHAM, but are not as efficient for aligning short reads against genomes.

Previous methods for sequencing short reads include Maq [12], SOAP [13], and Bowtie [6]. In particular, Bowtie has focused on utilizing the properties of the Burrows-Wheeler Transforms (BWT) [7] to index the reference sequence. A BWT-based index can be viewed as a suffix tree variant, and has a small memory footprint, making Bowtie feasible on computers with only 2GB of memory. Our technique differs significantly from Bowtie and other suffix-tree based indexes, as we build hash indexes on subsequences of the reference sequence. Although a hash structure does not inherently allow for the same ease of discovering strings with different numbers of mismatches, it does take advantage of current memory sizes to produce an overall faster alignment method.

The WHAM indexing schemes are also related to PartEnum algorithm [4] proposed for set similarity joins, which uses binary vectors to represent sets, and computes the Hamming distance between the binary vectors. WHAM and PartEnum use a similar idea: partitioning, and enumeration on partitions of vectors. However, WHAM differs from PartEnum in a few key ways. First, PartEnum is designed for set similarity joins based on Hamming distance, whereas our method is used for biological sequence alignments based on edit distance. Second, WHAM builds hash-based indexes on the basis of categories of concatenations for large reference sequences. WHAM selects indexing schemes that trade off between the number of lookups on indexes and the performance of each lookup, to achieve optimal overall performance.

5. CONCLUSION AND FUTURE WORK

With the advances in sequencing technology, there is an urgent need for a fast read alignment method that can deal with longer reads and accommodate rich error models. This paper proposes a method called WHAM that addresses this need. WHAM employs novel hash-based indexing and bitwise operations for pairwise alignments. Our extensive experimental studies using real datasets show that, compared to the existing leading read alignment method, WHAM is often faster by an order-of-magnitude (or more) and can accommodate richer error models. In addition, WHAM also leverages multi-core architectures very effectively. For future work, we plan to extend WHAM to work in distributed data processing environments.

Acknowledgments

We would like to thank Ron Steward and Victor Ruotti for various discussion on the topic of next-gen sequence alignment. We would also like to thank Spyros Blanas and the reviewers of this paper for valuable feedback on an earlier draft of this paper. This work was supported in part by a grant from the National Science Foundation under grant DBI-0926269.

6. REFERENCES

[1] White House Press Release. Retrieved 2006-07-22. http://www.ornl.gov/sci/techresources/Human-Genome/project/clinton1.shtml.

[2] M.-S. K. 0002, K.-Y. Whang, J.-G. Lee, and M.-J. Lee. n-gram/2l: A space and time efficient two-level n-gram inverted index structure. In *VLDB*, pages 325–336, 2005.

[3] S. Altschul, W. Gish, W. Miller, E. Myers, and D. Lipman. Basic local alignment search tool. *Journal of Molecular Biology*, 215:403–410, 1990.

[4] A. Arasu, V. Ganti, and R. Kaushik. Efficient exact set-similarity joins. In *VLDB*, pages 918–929, 2006.

[5] R. A. Baeza-Yates and G. H. Gonnet. A new approach to text searching. *Commun. ACM*, 35(10):74–82, 1992.

[6] L. Ben, T. Cole, P. Mihai, and S. Steven. Ultrafast and memory-efficient alignment of short dna sequences to the human genome. *Genome Biology*, 10(3):R25, 2009.

[7] M. Burrows and D. Wheeler. A block-sorting lossless data compression algorithm. *Digital SRC Research Report*, 1994.

[8] T. Han, S. Ko, and J. Kang. Efficient Subsequence Matching Using the Longest Common Subsequence with a Dual Match Index. *Machine Learning and Data Mining in Pattern Recognition*, pages 585–600, 2007.

[9] E. Karakoc, Z. Ozsoyoglu, S. Sahinalp, M. Tasan, and X. Zhang. Novel approaches to biomolecular sequence indexing. *Data Engineering*, 1001:40, 2004.

[10] D. E. Knuth. *The Art of Computer Programming, Volume 4A: Combinatorial Algorithms, Part 1*. Addison-Wesley Professional, Jan. 2011.

[11] C. Li, B. Wang, and X. Yang. Vgram: Improving performance of approximate queries on string collections using variable-length grams. In *VLDB*, pages 303–314, 2007.

[12] H. Li, J. Ruan, and R. Durbin. Mapping short DNA sequencing reads and calling variants using mapping quality scores. *Genome research*, 18(11):1851, 2008.

[13] R. Li, Y. Li, K. Kristiansen, and J. Wang. SOAP: short oligonucleotide alignment program. *Bioinformatics*, 24(5):713, 2008.

[14] W. Litwin, R. Mokadem, P. Rigaux, and T. J. E. Schwarz. Fast ngram-based string search over data encoded using algebraic signatures. In *VLDB*, pages 207–218, 2007.

[15] J. D. McPherson. Next-generation gap. *Nature Methods*, 6(11s):S2–S5, October 2009.

[16] S. B. Needleman and C. D. Wunsch. A general method applicable to the search for similarities in the amino acid sequence of two proteins. *Journal of Molecular Biology*, 48:443–453, 1970.

[17] P. Papapetrou, V. Athitsos, G. Kollios, and D. Gunopulos. Reference-based alignment in large sequence databases. *PVLDB*, 2(1):205–216, 2009.

[18] J. Rao and K. A. Ross. Cache conscious indexing for decision-support in main memory. In *VLDB*, pages 78–89, 1999.

[19] R. L. Rivest. Partial-match retrieval algorithms. *SIAM J. Comput.*, 5(1):19–50, 1976.

[20] T. F. Smith and M. S. Waterman. Identification of common molecular subsequences. *Journal of Molecular Biology*, 147:195–197, 1981.

[21] Venter, et al. The Sequence of the Human Genome. *Science*, 291(5507):1304–1351, 2001.

[22] S. Wu and U. Manber. Fast text searching allowing errors. *Commun. ACM*, 35(10):83–91, 1992.

[23] X. Yang, B. Wang, and C. Li. Cost-based variable-length-gram selection for string collections to support approximate queries efficiently. In *SIGMOD Conference*, pages 353–364, 2008.

A New Approach for Processing Ranked Subsequence Matching Based on Ranked Union

Wook-Shin Han
Kyungpook National University, Korea
wshan@knu.ac.kr

Jinsoo Lee
Kyungpook National University, Korea
jslee@www-db.knu.ac.kr

Yang-Sae Moon
Kangwon National University, Korea
ysmoon@kangwoon.ac.kr

Seung-won Hwang
POSTECH, Korea
swhwang@postech.ac.kr

Hwanjo Yu
POSTECH, Korea
hwanjoyu@postech.ac.kr

ABSTRACT

Ranked subsequence matching finds top-k subsequences most similar to a given query sequence from data sequences. Recently, Han et al. [12] proposed a solution (referred to here as HLMJ) to this problem by using the concept of the minimum distance matching window pair (MDMWP) and a global priority queue. By using the concept of MDMWP, HLMJ can prune many unnecessary accesses to data subsequences using a lower bound distance. However, we notice that HLMJ may incur serious performance overhead for important types of queries. In this paper, we propose a novel systematic framework to solve this problem by viewing ranked subsequence matching as *ranked union*. Specifically, we propose a notion of the *matching subsequence equivalence class* (MSEQ) and a novel lower bound called the *MSEQ-distance*. To completely eliminate the performance problem of HLMJ, we also propose a *cost-aware density-based scheduling* technique, where we consider both the density and cost of the priority queue. Extensive experimental results with many real datasets show that the proposed algorithm outperforms HLMJ and the adapted PSM [22], a state-of-the-art index-based merge algorithm supporting non-monotonic distance functions, by up to two to three orders of magnitude, respectively.

Categories and Subject Descriptors

H.3.1 [**Information storage and retrieval**]: Content Analysis and Indexing—*Indexing methods*; H.3.3 [**Information storage and retrieval**]: Information Search and Retrieval—*Search process*

General Terms

Algorithm, Performance

Keywords

Time-series data, Ranked subsequence matching, Ranked union

1. INTRODUCTION

Time-series data are of growing importance in data mining and data warehousing [14, 19]. A time-series is a sequence of real numbers representing values at specific points in time. Typical examples include music data, stock prices and network traffic data. The time-series data stored in a database are called data sequences.

Various similarity models have been studied in similar sequence matching (finding data sequences from a database which are similar to a given query sequence). In this paper, we use the similarity model based on the dynamic time warping (DTW) distance [4]. The DTW distance is one of the most robust and widely used measures for various applications such as query by humming [24], image searching [3], and speech recognition [18].

In this paper, we study ranked subsequence matching, identifying top-k subsequences in the database that are similar to a query sequence by using DTW. The state-of-the-art solution to this problem is by Han et al. [12] (referred to here as HLMJ). However, we notice that HLMJ may incur serious performance overhead for important types of queries. We briefly illustrate HLMJ below to depict the problems which motivate our solution.

In the index building process, HLMJ divides each data sequence into disjoint windows, transforms each window into a lower-dimensional data point (say, an f-dimensional point), and stores it as a leaf entry in the R*-tree. In the ranked subsequence matching process, HLMJ first divides a query sequence into sliding windows and transforms each *query* window into an f-dimensional query point. HLMJ maintains a global priority queue to store pairs of f-dimensional query and data points with their distances. Next, HLMJ pops a query/data point pair from the priority queue where their distance is the minimum, then computes a lower bound distance using those points. If this lower bound distance is greater than the DTW distance between the query sequence and the top k-th data subsequence obtained thus far, that pair is pruned. Otherwise the corresponding data subsequence for the data point is accessed to compute the DTW distance. HLMJ repeats this process until it finds top-k subsequences. Figure 1 illustrates how HLMJ works. A data sequence S is divided into disjoint windows (s_1, s_2, $\cdots$), and these windows are transformed into 2D points and stored in the R*-tree. In query processing, HLMJ divides a query sequence Q into eight sliding windows ($q_1 \sim q_8$) and transforms these windows into 2D points. After that, HLMJ pops a pair (q_1, s_5) from the global priority queue, retrieves a data subsequence for s_5, and computes the DTW distance.

As a lower bound distance for pruning, HLMJ exploits the minimum-distance matching-window pair (MDMWP) distance. The MDMWP for a query sequence and a data subsequence is a matching window pair, where the distance between the two windows in the pair is the minimum among all matching window pairs. If there are r matching windows pairs for a query sequence and a data sub-

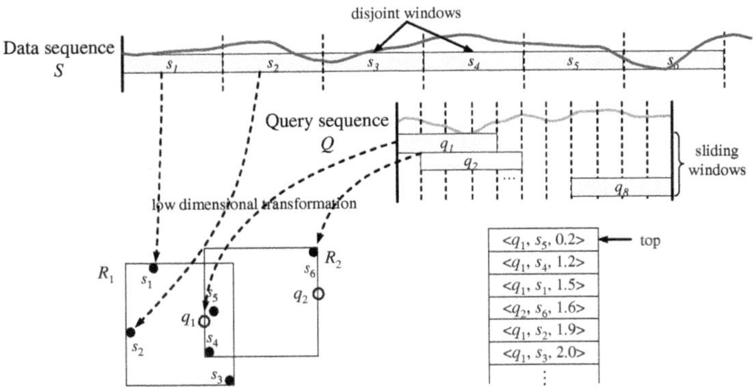

Figure 1: An example of HLMJ.

sequence, and (q_m, r_m) is the MDMWP, then the MDMWP distance is $\sqrt[p]{r \times d(q_m, s_m)^p}$ [12]. In Figure 1 for example, after popping the next entry (q_1, s_4) from the global priority queue, HLMJ computes the MDMWP distance for this entry. Since the popped entry is (q_1, s_4), the other matching window pair becomes (q_5, s_5), and thus, its distance must be ≥ 1.2 according to the definition of MDMWP. Thus, the MDMWP distance for this pair is $\sqrt[p]{d(q_1, s_5)^p \times 2} = \sqrt[p]{1.2^p \times 2}$. If $p = 2$, the MDMWP distance is nearly 1.7. Assume that the DTW distance computed for the first entry (q_1, s_5), i.e, the DTW distance between the query sequence and the top first data subsequence obtained thus far, is 1.5. Thus, if we want to find only the top-1 data subsequence, the entry (q_1, s_4) is pruned without accessing its corresponding data subsequence since its lower bound distance is greater than 1.5.

However, in HLMJ using MDMWP-based scheduling and a global priority queue, we observe the following serious performance degradation, which occurs in real datasets as we will see in Section 6. Figure 2 illustrates one such example, where a query point q_5 is placed in a sparse region while q_1 is placed in a dense region. In the global queue, all matching pairs MP_1 of q_1 and the data points in the dense region are placed in the upper part of the queue whereas such pairs for q_5 and the data points in the sparse region are placed below MP_1. Since it pops iteratively from the top of queue, HLMJ cannot reach MP_5 until it finishes the processing of all pairs in the entire MP_1. Meanwhile, accessing MP_5 first is highly effective in quickly increasing a lower bound. For example, when $\langle q_1, s_4 \rangle$ is popped, its MDMWP distance is $\sqrt[p]{d(q_1, s_4)^p \times 2}$. Instead, if we first access $\langle q_5, s_1 \rangle$, its lower bound can grow up to $\sqrt[p]{d(q_1, s_4)^p + d(q_5, s_1)^p}$ such that $d(q_5, s_1) \gg d(q_1, s_4) \simeq 0$, since the matching window pairs for q_1 and q_5 are s_4 and s_1, respectively. However, since there can be as many query points as there are sliding windows, it is non-trivial to extend HLMJ to 1) optimize the access order of query points and 2) derive a tight lower bound. Furthermore, since it is highly likely to grow very slowly as well, the MDMWP-distance can be of little use for pruning in this example. In the worst case, even if the selectivity of a query is very low, the algorithm might end up accessing too many candidates, incurring even higher cost than sequential scan.

Alternatively, one may consider applying a general ranked retrieval algorithm, such as TA-family algorithms [5, 6, 9, 20]. However, unlike these algorithms which assume that ranking functions are monotonic, the scoring function DTW and its lower bound function LB_{PAA} [24] are non-monotonic. Furthermore, only *lower bound distances* are computed at the index level since lower-dimensional data points are stored in the R*-tree. Thus, the corresponding data subsequences must be accessed additionally to calculate exact

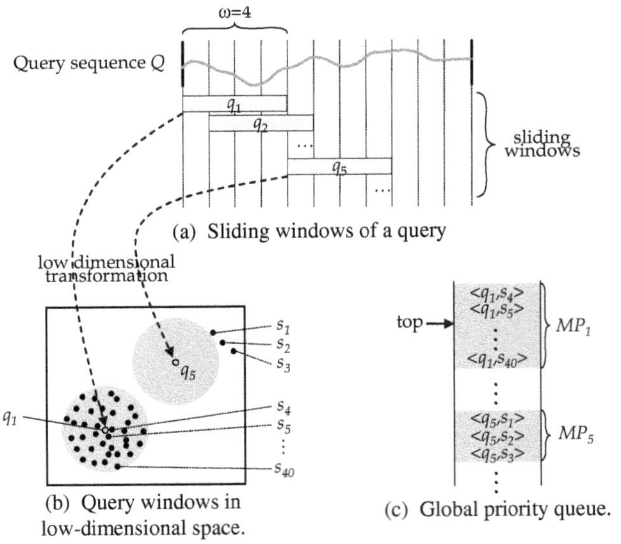

Figure 2: Example of the MDMWP-based scheduling problem.

distances. More recently, algorithms for supporting non-monotonic ranking functions have been studied [22]. We adopt the best algorithm of [22] as another baseline approach. However, as we will see in Experiment 6, this method suffers from bad performance whenever the number of disjoint query windows > 3.

In this paper, we propose the first systematic framework which viewes a ranked subsequence matching query as a ranked union query over ω ranked subqueries, where ω is the size of a sliding window, and ranked union merges the results from the subqueries and returns top-k results. Specifically, we propose the novel notion of *matching subsequence equivalence class* (MSEQ), with which we partition the query points into ω MSEQs so that each MSEQ consists of only disjoint query windows. If we regard each query point as an f-dimensional attribute, then each equivalence class $MSEQ_i$ corresponds to a ranked subquery having $|MSEQ_i|$ f-dimensional attributes. Instead of maintaining one global queue, we allocate a priority queue for each query point, so that each f-dimensional attribute has a dynamically generated and sorted list. This novel interpretation enables us to carefully control the scheduling order for the consumption of the priority queues for each subquery, i.e., sophisticated scheduling over the priority queues.

This interpretation, however, presents several challenging questions. 1) How can we derive a lower bound for ranked union? 2) What is the optimal access order for selecting subqueries? 3) If a certain subquery is selected, which priority queue should be processed? More specifically, how can we avoid the MDMWP-based scheduling problem? To answer the first two questions, we propose an execution model for ranked union and derive a new lower bound called MSEQ-distance under this execution model. We propose a cost-aware, density-based scheduling to approach the third question. This way, query points having relatively lower density can be processed quickly. The reason we consider cost-awareness is that it would be better to select a priority queue PQ_1 if the disk I/O cost of accessing the subsequences corresponding to the entries of PQ_1 is much lower than other priority queues.

Our contributions are as follows: 1) We propose the first framework to view ranked subsequence matching as ranked union using (a) a novel notion of matching subsequence equivalence class (MSEQ) and (b) a new lower bound distance, the MSEQ-distance; This can also be viewed as a generalized framework for ranked subsequence matching. 2) By doing so, we show that the state-of-the-art solution, HLMJ using MDMWP-based scheduling with a global priority queue [12] may lead to severe performance degradation. 3) To remedy this problem, we propose a cost-aware density-based scheduling technique. 4) Extensive experimental results with many real datasets show that the proposed algorithm outperforms (a) HLMJ and (b) the adapted PSM [22], a state-of-the-art index-based merge algorithm supporting non-monotonic distance functions, by up to two to three orders of magnitude.

The rest of this paper is organized as follows. Section 2 reviews DTW and HLMJ. Section 3 presents translation of the ranked subsequence matching query into the ranked union query. In Section 4, we present a cost-aware density-based scheduling method that avoids the MDMWP-based scheduling problem by minimizing the cost of accessing entries from priority queues. Section 5 presents an overview of related work, and Section 6 presents the results of performance evaluations. Section 7 summarizes and concludes the paper.

2. BACKGROUND

Table 1: Summary of notation.

Symbols	Definitions
S_{sid}	A sequence whose identifier is *sid*
$Len(S)$	Length of sequence S
$S[i]$	The i-th entry of sequence S ($1 \le i \le Len(S)$)
$S[i:j]$	A subsequence including entries from the i-th one to the j-th
ω	Length of the sliding/disjoint window
s_i	The i-th disjoint window of sequence S
$\langle\rangle$	empty sequence
$Rest(S)$	A subsequence of S, including entries from the second

We first define the DTW distance, which is recursively defined as follows. Given two sequences S and Q of the same length, there exist three cases in computing the minimal cost of possible matches of postfixes of S and Q: 1) matching postfixes of S and Q (=$DTW_\rho(Rest(S), Rest(Q))$); 2) matching Q with the postfix of S (=$DTW_\rho(Rest(S), Q)$); or 3) matching S with the postfix of Q (=$DTW_\rho(S, Rest(Q))$) [1].

$$DTW_\rho(S,Q) = \sqrt[p]{D(S[1],Q[1]) + min\begin{cases} DTW_\rho(Rest(S),Rest(Q))^p \\ DTW_\rho(Rest(S),Q)^p \\ DTW_\rho(S,Rest(Q))^p \end{cases}}$$

$$DTW_\rho(\langle\rangle,\langle\rangle) = 0, DTW_\rho(S,\langle\rangle) = DTW_\rho(\langle\rangle,Q) = \infty$$
$$D(S[i],Q[j]) = \begin{cases} |S[i]-Q[j]|^p & \text{if } |i-j| \le \rho \\ \infty & \text{otherwise} \end{cases} \quad (1)$$

Given two sequences S and Q of the same length, DTW enables "nonlinear" alignments between S and Q. Figure 3(a) illustrates the strength of DTW. Specifically, in Figure 3(b), a cell (i,j) in the matrix represents an alignment between a query point $Q[i]$ and a data point $S[j]$. The goal is to find such a path with minimal warping cost, i.e., the *warping path*. Here, the warping path consists of dark cells in the matrix. In order to prevent pathological warpings where a small portion of one sequence matches with a large portion of another sequence [13], we limit the scope of the warping path using the *warping width* ρ [1, 12, 13, 24], which is known as the Sakoe-Chiba band constraint, where matrix entry (i,j) becomes ∞ if $|i-j| > \rho$. Thus, only shaded cells in the matrix in Figure 3(b) are computed. Note that, the DTW distance becomes the L_p distance when $\rho = 0$.

In computing DTW_ρ, an element $S[i]$ can match one of $Q[i-\rho : i+\rho]$. Thus, for each element in Q, we store the maximum and the

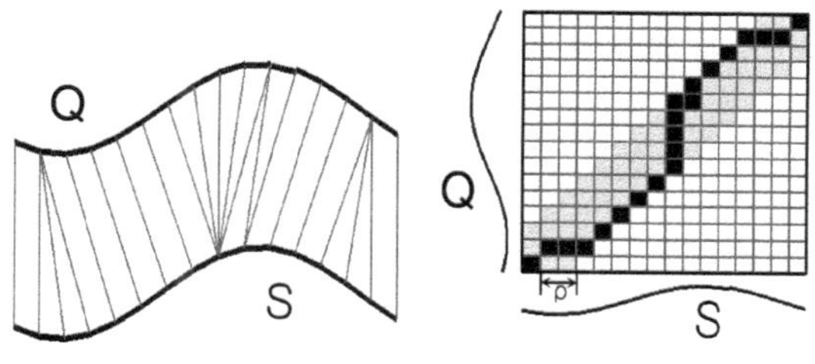

(a) DTW alignments. (b) Matrix for DTW.

Figure 3: Illustration of DTW.

minimum values from $Q[i-\rho : i+\rho]$ and thus compute a lower bound distance using pairwise computation without using expensive dynamic programming. Since we have two values for each query element $Q[i]$, these sequences are called *envelopes* [13]. Figure 4 illustrates the lower and upper envelopes of Q. The shaded area shows the lower-bound distance between Q and S. The concepts of the *query envelope* and the *lower bound distance* are formally described in subsequent paragraphs.

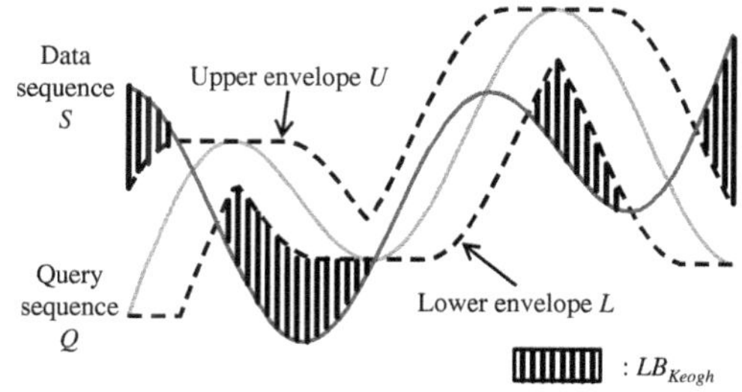

Figure 4: Example of envelopes and LB_{Keogh}.

We now define the notion of query envelope [24], which can be formally defined as below:

Definition 1. *The query envelope of a query Q, $\mathbb{E}(Q)$ consists of the upper and lower envelopes of Q and represents the region defined between the upper envelope U and the lower envelope L. The i-th element $(L[i], U[i])$ in $\mathbb{E}(Q)$ is defined as follows:*

$$L[i] = \min_{-\rho \le r \le \rho}(Q[i+r]), \quad U[i] = \max_{-\rho \le r \le \rho}(Q[i+r]) \quad \square$$

The tightest lower bound of DTW, between a query envelope $\mathbb{E}(Q)$ and a data sequence S, is known as LB_{Keogh} [13] below.

$$LB_{Keogh}(\mathbb{E}(Q), S) = \sqrt[p]{\sum_{i=1}^{N}\begin{cases} |S[i]-U[i]|^p & \text{if } S[i] > U[i] \\ |S[i]-L[i]|^p & \text{if } S[i] < L[i] \\ 0 & \text{otherwise} \end{cases}}$$

We now discuss piecewise aggregate approximation (PAA) [13, 23], a technique to reduce the dimensionality of a data sequence S of length N down to f ($f \ll N$), by dividing the sequence of length N into f equal sized segments then storing the mean values. We notate PAA of such S, $\mathcal{P}(S)$, as a time-series $[\overline{S[1]}, ..., \overline{S[f]}]$ of length f, where

$$\overline{S[i]} = \frac{f}{N} \sum_{j=\frac{N}{f}(i-1)+1}^{\frac{N}{f}i} S[j].$$

Similarly, the PAA of the query envelope $\mathbb{E}(Q)$ can be computed, by applying PAA to the upper and lower query envelopes. That is, the i ($1 \le i \le f$)-th element $(\overline{L[i]}, \overline{U[i]})$ in $\mathcal{P}(\mathbb{E}(Q))$ is:

$$\overline{L[i]} = \frac{f}{N} \sum_{j=\frac{N}{f}(i-1)+1}^{\frac{N}{f}i} L[j], \quad \overline{U[i]} = \frac{f}{N} \sum_{j=\frac{N}{f}(i-1)+1}^{\frac{N}{f}i} U[j].$$

As a lower bound that can be used at the index level, LB_{PAA} [24] is defined as Eq. (2), which is the distance between the query envelope $\mathcal{P}(\mathbb{E}(Q))$ and the PAA of the data sequence $\mathcal{P}(S)$. Figure 5 illustrates the PAAs of a query envelope and the a data sequence and LB_{PAA}.

$$\sqrt[p]{\sum_{i=1}^{f} \frac{N}{f} \begin{cases} |\overline{S[i]} - \overline{U[i]}|^p & \text{if } \overline{S[i]} > \overline{U[i]} \\ |\overline{S[i]} - \overline{L[i]}|^p & \text{if } \overline{S[i]} < \overline{L[i]} \\ 0 & \text{otherwise} \end{cases}} \quad (2)$$

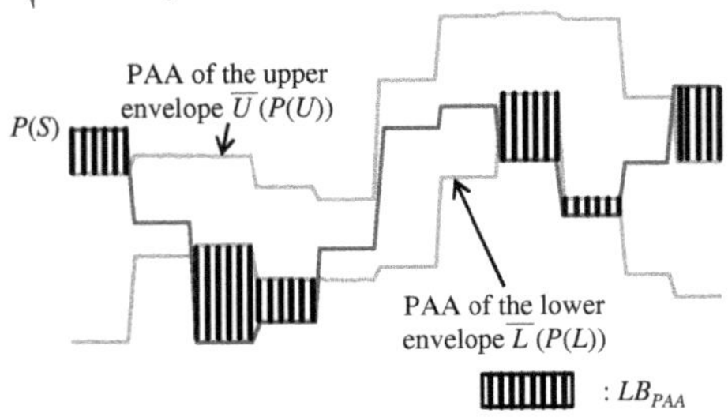

Figure 5: Illustration of LB_{PAA}

To guarantee no false dismissal under DTW, we have the following lemma [24].

Lemma 1. *Given two sequences Q and S of the same length and a warping width ρ, the following equation holds:*

$$DTW_\rho(Q, S) \geq LB_{Keogh}(\mathbb{E}(Q), S) \geq LB_{PAA}(\mathcal{P}(\mathbb{E}(Q)), \mathcal{P}(S))$$

Now, we define the MDMWP-distance in Definition 2 which can be used for pruning during ranked subsequence matching, and Lemma 2 shows the lower boundness of the MDMWP-distance.

Definition 2. [12] *Given a query envelope $\mathbb{E}(Q)$ and a data subsequence $S[i:j]$, if MDMWP of $\mathcal{P}(\mathbb{E}(Q))$ and $\mathcal{P}(S[i:j])$ is $(\mathcal{P}(\mathbb{E}(q_m)), \mathcal{P}(s_m))$, then the MDMWP-distance of $\mathcal{P}(\mathbb{E}(Q))$ and $\mathcal{P}(S[i:j])$ is defined as $\sqrt[p]{r} \times LB_{PAA}(\mathcal{P}(\mathbb{E}(q_m)), \mathcal{P}(s_m))$ where $r = \lfloor (Len(Q)+1)/\omega \rfloor - 1$. That is, r is the minimum number of disjoint windows in $S[i:j]$ regardless of the starting offset i.* □

Lemma 2. [12] *Given a query envelope $\mathbb{E}(Q)$ and a data subsequence $S[i:j]$, the following Eq. (3) holds:*

$$DTW_\rho(Q, S[i:j]) \geq MDMWP\text{–}distance(\mathcal{P}(\mathbb{E}(Q)), \mathcal{P}(S[i:j])) \quad (3)$$

3. RANKED UNION QUERY PROCESSING FRAMEWORK

We propose a systematic framework for ranked union. We first give a formal definition of our problem below. As in [12], in order to match data subsequences of length $l \neq |Q|$, one can scale Q with reasonable scale factors.

Problem Definition 1. [12] *Given n data sequences S_1, ..., S_n of variable lengths, a query sequence Q, a number k, and a warping width ρ, find k-nearest data subsequences for Q by using DTW_ρ.*

We first give an insight into our framework. We notice that we can partition sliding query windows into several groups since 1) query windows in the same group match the same corresponding subsequences, and 2) query windows in different groups do not. Consider the sliding windows in Figure 6. Sliding windows $\mathcal{P}(\mathbb{E}(q_2))$ and $\mathcal{P}(\mathbb{E}(q_6))$ match the same corresponding data subsequences, but $\mathcal{P}(\mathbb{E}(q_1))$ and $\mathcal{P}(\mathbb{E}(q_2))$ do not match. That is, if $\mathcal{P}(\mathbb{E}(q_2))$ matches a disjoint window $S[i+1:i+4]$, $\mathcal{P}(\mathbb{E}(q_6))$ matches a disjoint window $S[i+5:i+8]$. Both match the same subsequence $S[i:i+10]$. For each group, we can find top-k matching data subsequences for the query windows in this group. Thus, if we select top-k results from the results of all groups, these results become the answer to the ranked subsequence matching. Furthermore, if we can derive a lower bound for each group during execution, we can provide a tighter lower bound than MDMWP. We present formal concepts in the next subsections where such the group is formalized using the concept of the equivalence class, since any two windows in the same group are equivalent to each other in that both match the same data subsequence.

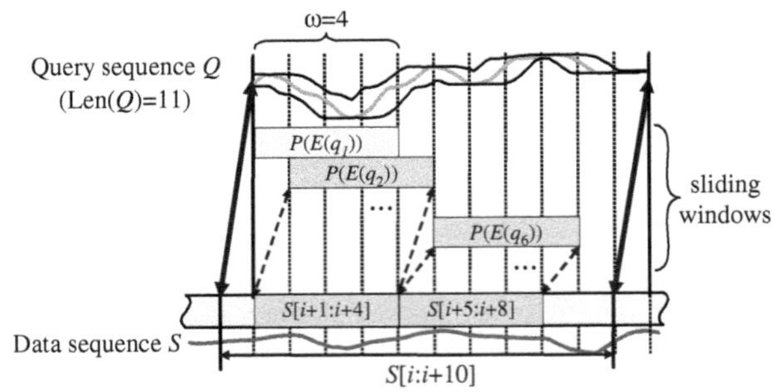

Figure 6: Matching window pairs and their corresponding data subsequences.

3.1 Translating into Ranked Union Queries

Our framework uses the windowing scheme proposed from Dual-Match [17]– This scheme divides data sequences into disjoint windows of the same size ω. Data windows are then transformed into lower-dimensional data points and indexed to an R*-tree. To support DTW, we first construct the query envelope $\mathbb{E}(Q)$ for a query sequence Q, divide the query envelope into sliding windows $\mathbb{E}(q_i)$ of size ω, and transform each query window $\mathbb{E}(q_i)$ into a lower-dimensional window $\mathcal{P}(\mathbb{E}(q_i))$. In the remainder of this paper, we will use the terms "window," "enveloped window," and "point" interchangeably unless necessary for clarity.

Our framework views a ranked subsequence matching query as a ranked union query of subqueries, where each subquery contains only disjoint windows. This enables us to formally analyze the performance issues of HLMJ and develop new techniques for solving these performance issues. Definition 3 provides a formal definition of the ranked union query.

Definition 3. *Given a query sequence Q, a ranked union query over ranked subsequence subqueries merges results from all subqueries and returns k-nearest data subsequences for Q.* □

Definition 4. *Let QS be the set of all sliding windows for a query envelope $\mathcal{P}(\mathbb{E}(Q))$. Let $\cong$ be an equivalence relation over QS such that $\mathcal{P}(\mathbb{E}(Q[i:i+\omega-1])) \cong \mathcal{P}(\mathbb{E}(Q[j:j+\omega-1]))$ if and only if $|i-j|$ **mod** $\omega = 0$.* □

The equivalence class of $\mathcal{P}(\mathbb{E}(Q[i:i+\omega-1]))$ is a set of query windows which are equivalent to (i.e., $\cong$) $\mathcal{P}(\mathbb{E}(Q[i:i+\omega-1]))$. This class is called a *matching subsequence equivalence class (MSEQ)* since all windows in an MSEQ match the same data subsequences. For convenience of notation, we use $MSEQ_i$ $(1 \leq i \leq \omega)$ to denote the equivalence class of $\mathcal{P}(\mathbb{E}(Q[i:i+\omega-1]))$. $MSEQ_{i,j}$ denotes a query window $\mathcal{P}(\mathbb{E}(Q[(i+(j-1)\times\omega):(i+(j-1)\times\omega)+\omega-1]))$. Consider a query sequence Q in Figure 2. The length of the query sequence is 11, and ω is set to 4. The equivalence class of $\mathcal{P}(\mathbb{E}(Q[1:\omega]))$, denoted as $[\mathcal{P}(\mathbb{E}(Q[1:\omega]))]_{\cong}$, consists of two windows, $\{\mathcal{P}(\mathbb{E}(Q[1:\omega])), \mathcal{P}(\mathbb{E}(Q[5:\omega]))\}$. In this example, there exist four equivalence classes under $\cong$, and each class has two windows.

In the proposed framework, we try to evaluate a ranked subsequence matching query using the corresponding ranked union query. To do this, we need to show that both queries produce the same result, that is, their query results are equivalent to each other. The following lemma shows this equivalence.

Lemma 3. *The evaluation result of a ranked subsequence matching query using sliding windows of size ω is equivalent to that of the ranked union query over ω ranked subsequence matching subqueries, where each subquery corresponds to an MSEQ.*

PROOF: To evaluate a ranked subsequence matching query correctly, we need to find k-nearest data subsequences by considering all possible data subsequences. Also, to guarantee that a ranked union query of Definition 3 produces the same result by the ranked subsequence matching query, we need to show that the results of subqueries of MSEQs cover all possible data subsequences. We thus prove every data subsequence is a result of one subquery (i.e., an MSEQ) of the ranked union query.

We prove it using Figure 7. We first denote the nth sliding window of a query Q by q_n and the mth disjoint window of a data sequence S by s_m. As illustrated in Figure 7, suppose that the jth query window $MSEQ_{i,j}$ of $MSEQ_i$ matches with the mth data disjoint window s_m. We note here that $MSEQ_{i,j}$ corresponds to the $swn(i,j)^{th}$ sliding window $q_{swn(i,j)}$, where $swn(i,j) = (j-1) \times \omega + i$, and swn stands for sliding window number. Then, the starting offset of the subsequence corresponding to this matching window pair is smaller by $swn(i,j)$ compared to the offset of s_m. That is, the start offset of the matching data subsequence is $(m\text{-}1)\times\omega\text{-}(swn(i,j)\text{-}1)\text{+}1$, and the subsequence itself is $S[(m\text{-}1)\times\omega\text{-}(swn(i,j)\text{-}1)\text{+}1\text{:}(m\text{-}1)\times\omega\text{-}(swn(i,j)\text{-}1)\text{+}Len(Q)]$. According to Definition 4, we have ω MSEQs, i.e., $1 \leq i \leq \omega$. Thus, every subsequence of S with $Len(Q)$ is a result of $MSEQ_i$ $(1 \leq i \leq \omega)$. This completes the proof. □

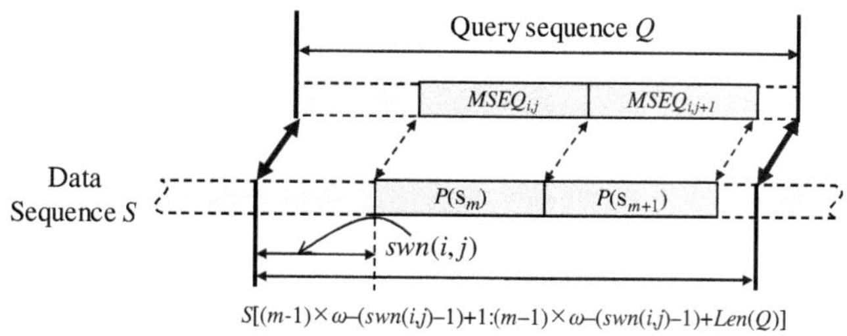

Figure 7: Matching window pairs.

3.2 Processing of Ranked Union Query

With our problem translated into a ranked union query problem, we now discuss an efficient execution model.

3.2.1 Extended Iterator Model

To process a ranked union query, we generate a query execution plan (QEP) using physical operators. Algorithms for executing such a plan can be constructed using the iterator model [8] commonly used in query processors of commercial DBMSs. In the iterator model, the operators composing the QEP receive a tuple from the child operators, which is then passed on to their parent operator if necessary. To obtain one tuple at a time from each operator, the operator provides the $GetNext()$ function as the interface. Each operator also provides the $Start()$ and $End()$ functions to initialize and finalize the operator. In our framework, a subsequence is modeled as a tuple.

In processing a ranked query, the scheduling order for consuming the priority queues from child nodes significantly affects the overall performance. Thus, we need to carefully control the scheduling of the priority queue selection, which motivates us to extend the iterator model. For such optimization, whenever each operator consumes an entry from a priority queue, it returns a lower bound as a "scheduling hint" even when no subsequence is ready to be returned. This enables finer granular scheduling.

Definition 5. *Each operator in the* ***extended iterator model*** *returns a pair of* $\langle status, obj \rangle$*. Status is one of the following values:*

- *TUPLE: obj contains the next result tuple.*
- *LB: The next result tuple is yet to be found, and obj contains the lower bound of the next result tuple instead.*
- *EOR: all tuples of the child operator are consumed.* □

3.2.2 Execution Model of Ranked Union

Our execution model provides two novel operators which follow the extended iterator model: 1) multi-way ranked union operator denoted as $\cup_r$ and 2) ranked subsequence matching subquery operator denoted as Φ. $\cup_r$ merges the results from ω subqueries and returns top-k subsequences. $\cup_r$ maintains the current top-k subsequences obtained thus far along with the current lower bounds for the subqueries. Thus, $\cup_r$ stops the processing of subqueries whenever the distance of the top k-th subsequence obtained so far $\leq$ all the current lower bounds of the subqueries. Φ_i (corresponding to the i-th subquery) allocates a priority queue $PQ_{i,j}$ for each query window $MSEQ_{i,j}$ in $MSEQ_i$, which maintains matching pairs of $MSEQ_{i,j}$ with data points or MBRs in distance order.

Figure 8 shows an example of how the ranked subsequence query Q in Figure 2 is executed using ranked union. Since there are four MSEQs for Q, $\cup_r$ has four child operators, each of which corresponds to an MSEQ. Φ_1 has two priority queues, $PQ_{1,1}$ and $PQ_{1,2}$. $\cup_r$ selects one child operator Φ_i, and Φ_i then selects a priority queue $PQ_{i,j}$ to find a matching window pair of $MSEQ_{i,j}$ with a data point or an MBR. If the matching window pair contains a data point, Φ_i computes a lower bound distance called the MSEQ-distance. If this lower bound distance is greater than the DTW distance between the query sequence and the top k-th data subsequence obtained thus far, that pair is pruned. Otherwise the corresponding data subsequence for the data point is accessed to compute the DTW distance. We repeatedly call $\cup_r$ until it finds top-k subsequences.

More specifically, the main algorithm invokes $\cup_r.GetNext()$ to retrieve top-k subsequences one at a time. $\cup_r.GetNext()$ chooses one of the subqueries and invokes $\Phi_i.GetNext()$. In $\Phi_i.GetNext()$, we choose one of its priority queues, based on a scheduling strategy we will discuss later. Entries in the chosen queue are then consumed to return either a new tuple or a new lower bound.

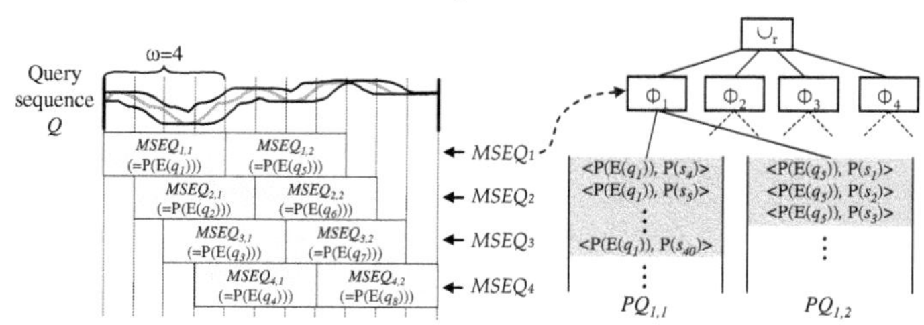

(a) MESQs of a query (b) Operator tree composed of $\cup_r$ and Φ_is.

Figure 8: Illustration of the execution model.

Our execution model, together with the concept of the MSEQ, enables us to significantly prune the index search space of ranked union. Since $PQ_{i,j}$ of Φ_i maintains all matching pairs to be popped in the order of distances, we can then compute a lower bound of the distance between the query sequence and the corresponding subsequence in advance. To further illustrate this concept, we provide Definition 6 and Lemma 4.

Definition 6. *Suppose that the current top entry of a priority queue* $PQ_{i,j}$ *of* Φ_i *contains a matching pair of* $MSEQ_{i,j}$ *and* obj_j. *MINDIST is a lower bounding distance between an MBR and a transformed window [12]. Then, the MSEQ-distance between* $MSEQ_{i,j}$ *and* obj_j *is* $\sqrt[p]{\sum_{j=1}^{|MSEQ_i|}\mathcal{D}(MSEQ_{i,j}, obj_j)^p}$,

$$\text{where } \mathcal{D} = \begin{cases} \text{MINDIST} & \text{, if } obj_j \text{ is an MBR} \\ LB_{PAA} & \text{, if } obj_j \text{ is a leaf entry.} \end{cases}$$

Lemma 4. *Suppose a matching pair* mp *is to be popped from a priority queue* $PQ_{i,j}$ *of* Φ_i *such that* mp *contains a leaf entry, and its corresponding subsequence* $S[a:b]$ *has not been retrieved yet. Then,* $DTW_\rho(Q, S[a:b]) \geq$ *MSEQ-distance*(mp).

PROOF: By Lemma 2, we have the following inequality.

$$DTW_\rho(Q,S) \geq LB_{PAA}(\mathcal{P}(\mathbb{E}(Q)), \mathcal{P}(S[a:b]))$$

Since the data subsequence $S[a:b]$ matches $MSEQ_i$, $S[a:b]$ must include $|MSEQ_i|$ disjoint windows, (possibly null) subsequences s_h (at the head), and s_t (at the tail). Thus, $S[a:b]$ can be represented as $s_h s_1 ... s_{|MSEQ_i|} s_t$. Similarly, $\mathbb{E}(Q)$ can be represented as $\mathbb{E}(q_h q_i ... q_{(i+|MSEQ_i|-1)} q_t)$. Thus, we have

$$LB_{PAA}(\mathcal{P}(\mathbb{E}(Q)), \mathcal{P}(S[a:b])) =$$
$$LB_{PAA}(\mathcal{P}(\mathbb{E}(q_h q_i ... q_{(i+|MSEQ_i|-1)} q_t)), \mathcal{P}(s_h s_1 ... s_{|MSEQ_i|} s_t))$$

Here, if we omit the two matching subsequence pairs, $(\mathbb{E}(q_h), s_h)$ and $(\mathbb{E}(q_t), s_t)$, from the above equation, we have the following inequality, since LB_{PAA} is a monotonic increasing function of the sequence length:

$$\geq LB_{PAA}(\mathcal{P}(\mathbb{E}(q_i \ldots q_{(i+|MSEQ_i|-1)})), \mathcal{P}(s_1 \ldots s_{|MSEQ_i|}))$$

$$= \sqrt[p]{\sum_{k=1}^{|MSEQ_i|} LB_{PAA}(MSEQ_{i,k}, \mathcal{P}(s_k))^p}$$

Since $S[a:b]$ has not been retrieved yet, the distance of the top entry of $PQ_{i,k}$, ($= \mathcal{D}(MSEQ_{i,k}, obj_k)$) $\leq LB_{PAA}(MSEQ_{i,k}, \mathcal{P}(s_k))$, where $k \neq j$. Then, the following equations hold:

$$\geq \sqrt[p]{\sum_{k=1}^{|MSEQi|} \begin{cases} \mathcal{D}(MSEQ_{i,k}, obj_k))^p & \text{, if } k \neq j \\ LB_{PAA}(mp)^p & \text{, if } k = j \end{cases}}$$

$= \text{MSEQ-distance}(mp)$ □

The following Lemma 5 shows that the MSEQ-distance is at least as tight as the MDMWP-distance when MDMWP-based scheduling is used for our ranked union framework.

Lemma 5. *Suppose that MDMWP-based scheduling is used, and that a matching pair* $(MSEQ_{i,j}, \mathcal{P}(s_k))$ *is to be popped from a priority queue* $PQ_{i,j}$ *of* Φ_i *where its corresponding subsequence* $S[a:b]$ *has not been retrieved yet. Then, MSEQ-distance* $(MSEQ_{i,j}, \mathcal{P}(s_k)) \geq$ *MDMWP-distance*$(MSEQ_{i,j}, \mathcal{P}(s_k))$.

PROOF: The MDMWP-distance of a matching pair $(MSEQ_{i,j}, \mathcal{P}(s_k))$ is defined as $\sqrt[p]{\lfloor (Len(Q)+1)/\omega \rfloor - 1} \times LB_{PAA}(MSEQ_{i,j}, \mathcal{P}(s_k))$. First, $|MSEQ_i| \geq \lfloor (Len(Q)+1)/\omega \rfloor - 1$. Next, since MDMWP-based scheduling is used, $LB_{PAA}(MSEQ_{i,j}, \mathcal{P}(s_k))$ is less than or equal to the distance of the current top entry in $PQ_{i,k}$. Thus, MSEQ-distance$(MSEQ_{i,j}, \mathcal{P}(s_k)) \geq$ MDMWP-distance$(MSEQ_{i,j}, \mathcal{P}(s_k))$. □

Now, we explain how to select one of the subqueries of Φ_i. To minimize the cost of the ranked union execution model, any unnecessary $\Phi_i.GetNext()$ invocations must be avoided. We have the following Lemma 6 for this purpose.

Lemma 6. *Let* CLB_i *be a current lower bound for* Φ_i. *To minimize the total number of* $\Phi.GetNext()$ *invocations,* $\cup_r$ *must choose* Φ_j *such that* $j = \arg\min_{i=1}^{\omega}(CLB_i)$.

PROOF: Let δ_{cur} represent the DTW$_\rho$ distance between the query sequence and the top k-th data subsequence obtained so far. Until δ_{cur} converges to the distance between the query sequence and the actual top-kth subsequence, the termination condition $\min_{i=1}^{\omega} CLB_i \geq \delta_{cur}$ does not hold. This condition cannot be reached without selecting Φ_j such that $j = \arg\min_{i=1}^{\omega}(CLB_i)$. □

Algorithm for $\cup_r.Start()$: $\cup_r$ maintains three global variables: δ_{cur}, $candMinQ_{\cup_r}$, and $CLBs$. δ_{cur} represents the DTW distance between Q and the top k-th subsequence obtained so far. $candMinQ_{\cup_r}$ is implemented as a minimum priority queue whose entry is a candidate subsequence. $CLBs$ is a set of current lower bounds of subqueries. Initially, since there is no candidate obtained so far, δ_{cur} is set to ∞, $candMinQ_{\cup_r}$ is set to empty, and each CLB_i is set to zero. We then call $Start()$ of each child Φ_i of $\cup_r$.
Algorithm for $\Phi_i.Start()$: In order to find the nearest leaf entries (i.e., f-dimensional points) for each window $MSEQ_{i,j}$, Φ_i allocates a minimum priority queue $PQ_{i,j}$ for each query window in Φ_i. An entry in $PQ_{i,j}$ is in the form of a triple $\langle MSEQ_{i,j}, obj, dist \rangle$. Here, $MSEQ_{i,j}$ and obj are a matching pair where obj is either a subsequence, a leaf entry, a leaf node, or a non-leaf node; $dist$ is the distance between the matching pair. Φ_i also maintains a local minimum priority queue $candMinQ_{\Phi_i}$ to store top-k candidates for Φ_i. $\Phi_i.Start()$ pushes each pair of $MSEQ_{i,j}$ and the root node MBR annotated with their MINDIST distances.
Algorithm for $\cup_r.GetNext()$: If the distance of the top entry in $candMinQ_{\cup_r} \leq$ all CLB_i ($1 \leq i \leq \omega$), we return a subsequence as a tuple by popping the top entry of $candMinQ_{\cup_r}$. Next, we select a subquery Φ_i according to Lemma 6. Then, we invoke $\Phi_i.GetNext()$. If Φ_i generates a subsequence (i.e., $status$ is equal to TUPLE), we update the lower bound of $CLB_i.dist$ with $obj.dist$ and push the subsequence into the $candMinQ_{\cup_r}$ if $obj.dist \leq \delta_{cur}$. If Φ_i generates a new lower bound, we update the lower bound of $CLB_i.dist$ with $obj.dist$. If Φ_i returns EOR, we remove CLB_i from $CLBs$ since Φ_i will return no more candidates. (A detailed algorithm is in the Appendix in [11]).
Algorithm for $\Phi_i.GetNext()$: We denote as MSEQ-dist$_{\text{next}}$, the MSEQ-distance for the entry to be popped next from a $PQ_{i,j}$ in Φ_i, i.e, the lower bound distance for the entry to be popped next. If $candMinQ_{\Phi_i}$.Top()$.dist$ (=the distance of the top entry of $candMinQ_{\Phi_i}$) $> \delta_{cur}$ and so is MSEQ-dist$_{\text{next}}$, we can guarantee that Φ_i does not contribute in generating top-k candidates. If $candMinQ_{\Phi_i}$.Top()$.dist \leq$ MSEQ-dist$_{\text{next}}$, we pop an entry from $candMinQ_{\Phi_i}$ and return it as a tuple; otherwise, we pop an entry from one of the priority queues using $SelectPriorityQueue()$. Here, an entry contains either a node or a leaf entry. We then perform one of the following actions depending on the type of the pair:

- *matching pair with a leaf/non-leaf node*: Retrieve the entries in the node and push the pairs of these entries along with the query windows annotated with their MSEQ-dist distances into the priority queue. Here, pairs whose MSEQ-dist $> \delta_{cur}$ are prunned.
- *matching pair with a leaf entry*: Retrieve the matching subsequence and compute the LB_{Keogh} and DTW$_\rho$ distances. If both distances $\leq \delta_{cur}$, push back to the priority queue.

Lastly, we compute MSEQ-dist$_{\text{next}}$ and return a new lower bound value to $\cup_r$. (A detailed algorithm is in the Appendix in [11]).
Example: Figure 9 illustrates how our rank union framework operates using an example, where a data sequence S of length 27 and a query sequence Q of length 11 are divided into disjoint and sliding windows of size $\omega = 4$. Suppose that k is set to 1. As illustrated in Figure 9(a), S is divided into six disjoint windows $\{s_1, \cdots, s_6\}$,

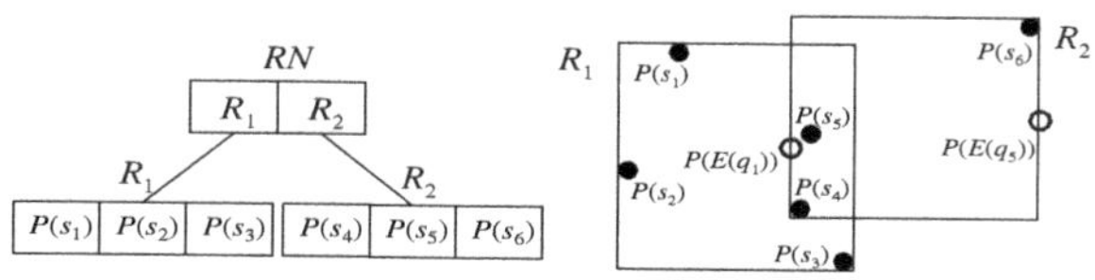

(a) An R*-tree and its search space.

matching pair	dist.	matching pair	dist.
$<P(E(q_1)), RN>$	0.0	$<P(E(q_5)), RN>$	0.0
$<P(E(q_1)), R_1>$	0.0	$<P(E(q_5)), R_1>$	3.0
$<P(E(q_1)), R_2>$	0.0	$<P(E(q_5)), R_2>$	0.0
$<P(E(q_1)), P(s_1)>$	1.5	$<P(E(q_5)), P(s_1)>$	4.6
$<P(E(q_1)), P(s_2)>$	1.9	$<P(E(q_5)), P(s_2)>$	4.8
$<P(E(q_1)), P(s_3)>$	2.0	$<P(E(q_5)), P(s_3)>$	3.6
$<P(E(q_1)), P(s_4)>$	1.2	$<P(E(q_5)), P(s_4)>$	3.4
$<P(E(q_1)), P(s_5)>$	0.2	$<P(E(q_5)), P(s_5)>$	3.3
$<P(E(q_1)), P(s_6)>$	3.9	$<P(E(q_5)), P(s_6)>$	1.6

MINDIST (rows 1–3); LB_{PAA} (rows 4–9)

(b) Matching pair distances.

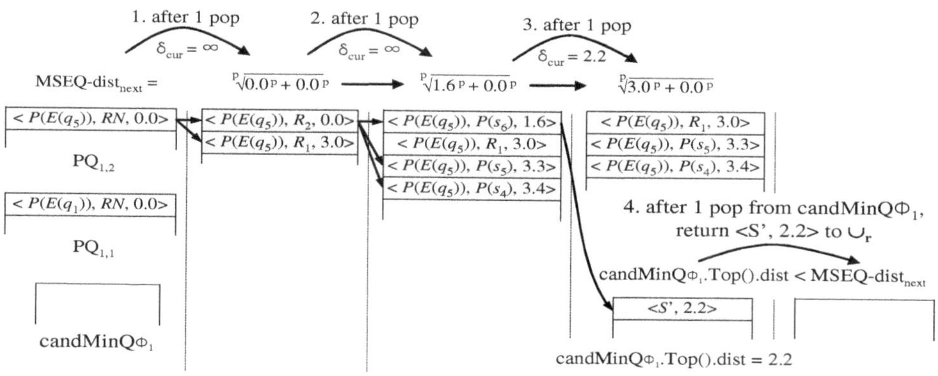

(c) Changes to $PQ_{1,j}$ and candMinQΦ_1 over time.

Figure 9: An example of the ranked union framework.

and each window of size 4 is transformed into a lower-dimensional data point (say, a 2D point). The points are indexed in an R*-tree with two MBRs– MBR R_1 with $\{\mathcal{P}(s_1), \mathcal{P}(s_2), \mathcal{P}(s_3)\}$ and MBR R_2 with $\{\mathcal{P}(s_4), \mathcal{P}(s_5), \mathcal{P}(s_6)\}$. The root node RN consists of these two MBRs. Figure 9(c) describes the changes in $PQ_{1,j}$ and $candMinQ_{\Phi_1}$ over time. We illustrate two query points, q_1 and q_5, and assume $SelectPriorityQueue()$ always chooses $PQ_{1,2}$. Since $\omega = 4$, $MSEQ_{1,1} = \mathcal{P}(\mathbb{E}(q_1))$ and $MSEQ_{1,2} = \mathcal{P}(\mathbb{E}(q_5))$, as shown in Figure 8. Note that the ranked union framework can terminate the processing much earlier than HLMJ, i.e., after only 4 pops as opposed to 12 pops required by HLMJ!

• initial state: $PQ_{1,1}$ and $PQ_{1,2}$ are initialized with the pairs of RN with $\mathcal{P}(\mathbb{E}(q_1))$ and $\mathcal{P}(\mathbb{E}(q_5))$, annotated with their MINDISTs. That is, $\langle \mathcal{P}(\mathbb{E}(q_1)), RN, 0.0\rangle$ and $\langle \mathcal{P}(\mathbb{E}(q_5)), RN, 0.0\rangle$ are inserted into $PQ_{1,1}$ and $PQ_{1,2}$. Initially, $candMinQ_{\Phi_1}$ is empty.

• after 1 pop: After $\langle \mathcal{P}(\mathbb{E}(q_5)), RN, 0.0\rangle$ is popped, it is expanded into $\mathcal{P}(\mathbb{E}(q_5)) \times \{R_1, R_2\}$, which are inserted back into $PQ_{1,2}$.

• after 2 more pops: After $\langle \mathcal{P}(\mathbb{E}(q_5)), R_2, 0.0\rangle$ is popped, it is expanded into $\{\mathcal{P}(\mathbb{E}(q_5))\}\} \times \{\{\mathcal{P}(s_4), \mathcal{P}(s_5), \mathcal{P}(s_6)\}$, which are inserted back into $PQ_{1,2}$. Next, $\langle \mathcal{P}(\mathbb{E}(q_5)), \mathcal{P}(s_6), 1.6\rangle$ is popped. Since $\mathcal{P}(s_6)$ is a leaf entry, we retrieve the corresponding subsequence S' from the database, which then is inserted into $candMinQ_{\Phi_1}$.

• after 1 more pop: Since $candMinQ_{\Phi_1}$.Top().$dist <$ MSEQ-dist$_{next}$ (i.e., $2.2 < \sqrt[p]{3^p}$), we pop an entry from $candMinQ_{\Phi_1}$ and return it to $\cup_r$ as a tuple. □

Now, we explain how to select a priority queue using $SelectPriorityQueue()$. Although DTW and LB_{PAA} distances themselves are not monotonic, our proposed translation to the ranked union framework enables the adoption of scheduling strategies developed for ranking queries, such as the scheduling heuristics of [10]. We thus adopt one such strategy for choosing a priority queue $PQ_{i,j}$ where the difference in the distances between the last top entry and the current top entry is the maximum.

Meanwhile, implementing MDMWP-based scheduling may incur serious performance degradation when some query points are placed in dense regions while other points are placed in sparse regions, as explained in Section 1. This observation motivates us to develop a density-based scheduling method, which we describe in the next section.

4. COST-AWARE DENSITY-BASED SCHEDULING WITH SELECTIVE EXPANSION

We propose a novel priority queue selection strategy called RU-COST, exploiting cost-aware scheduling with selective expansion. This method avoids the MDMWP-based scheduling problem by minimizing the cost of accessing entries from priority queues. Unlike scheduling problems explored for TA-family algorithms, this problem poses two additional challenges: 1) the list for each query window is dynamically generated; and 2) the cost of generating one leaf entry from the priority queue varies significantly, depending on how many MBRs must be expanded to reach the leaf entry.

Intuitively, a good scheduling algorithm will identify a queue whose top-h leaf entries are sparsely populated near the query point, as noted in Section 1. For example, consider the ranked union execution framework in Figure 8. Clearly, selecting $PQ_{1,2}$ rather than $PQ_{1,1}$ would quickly grow the MSEQ-distance for Φ_1. However, if the disk I/O cost of accessing the corresponding data subsequences for the top-h leaf entries in $PQ_{1,1}$ is much cheaper than that of $PQ_{1,2}$, selecting $PQ_{1,1}$ would seem to be more beneficial. To solve this challenging problem, We propose a novel concept of cost-aware density. We formally define this concept in Definition 7.

Definition 7. *Let the most recently popped leaf entry from $PQ_{i,j}$ be le_p. Let the next top-h leaf entries to be popped from $PQ_{i,j}$ be $le_1, le_2, \cdots, le_h$. Then, the cost-aware density $CDens(PQ_{i,j})$ is defined as follows. NUM_IO returns the number of I/Os when accessing the subsequences corresponding to $le_1, le_2, \cdots, le_h$.*

$$\frac{\alpha \times NUM\_IO(le_1, le_2, \cdots, le_h) + \beta \times h}{LB_{PAA}(MSEQ_{i,j}, le_h) - LB_{PAA}(MSEQ_{i,j}, le_p)},$$

where α and β are user-specified constant values.

Note that, the denominator of $CDens(PQ_{i,j})$ (or "volume" in the density) is the difference in LB_{PAA} between the last popped entry le_p and the top h^{th} entry le_h, as leaf entries are sorted in one-dimensional distance space using LB_{PAA}. The numerator of $CDens(PQ_{i,j})$ (or "mass" in the density) is the cost for leaf entries, which is a combination of the cost of disk I/Os NUM_IO and the cost of computing distances. As disk I/Os are dominant in performance of ranked union, we set α to 1 and β to 0. Finding more accurate values of α and β will be our future work. Note also that, when there is a need to choose among queues with zero density, we choose the one with the smallest denominator. For efficient computation of NUM_IO, we allocate a bitmap for pages, where each bit is set to 1 when the corresponding page is in the buffer. Thus, we can accurately count entries whose corresponding subsequences are not in the buffer. The memory overhead for the bitmap is marginal, as it requires only 8KBytes for a 256MBytes database.

However, two challenges still remain: First is the question of the optimal lookahead h. If h is too small, the estimated value cannot reflect the overall density. Meanwhile, if it is too large, scheduling does not adapt well to changes in densities, leading to suboptimal performance. To address this challenge, we considered an adaptive approach setting $h = 1$ and increasing it dynamically. However, in our extensive experiments with many real datasets, if h is set to the blocking factor of index pages, the overall performance is very stable regardless of datasets. We therefore set h as the blocking factor.

The second challenge is how to efficiently compute $CDens(PQ_{i,j})$. One naive way is to obtain the next top-h leaf entries from all priority queues of Φ_i and compute exact densities. However, this may impose serious performance overhead if a query point is placed in a dense region, in which case, all index pages in the dense region need to be accessed to obtain the top-h leaf entries.

To address the second challenge, we propose a novel *selective expansion* technique of priority queues, which consists of two steps: 1) we select one priority queue as a pivot and obtain the top-h leaf entries from this pivot queue only to compute its exact density $CDens(PQ_{i,pivot})$. 2) For the remaining queues, we selectively expand them, by choosing only the queue $PQ_{i,j}$ such that LB_{CDens} $(PQ_{i,j}) < CDens(PQ_{i,pivot})$; that is, we stop expanding priority queues whose $LB_{CDens} \geq$ the $CDens$ of the pivot priority queue. After expanding MBRs in $PQ_{i,j}$, if $CDens(PQ_{i,j}) < CDens(PQ_{i,pivot})$, $PQ_{i,j}$ becomes the pivot. We iterate this selective expansion process until $CDens(PQ_{i,pivot}) \leq LB_{CDens}$ $(PQ_{i,j})$ or $CDens(PQ_{i,j})$ for any $j \neq pivot$.

Now, we define $LB_{CDens}(PQ_{i,j})$ in the following definition.

Definition 8. *Let the most recently popped leaf entry from $PQ_{i,j}$ be le_p. Let $le'_1, le'_2, \cdots, le'_{m-1}, MBR_1, \cdots, le'_m, \cdots, le'_h$ be the entries in the priority queue ordered by their distances where le'_h is the top-h^{th} leaf entry in the priority queue. Then, $LB_{CDens}(PQ_{i,j})$ is defined as following :*

$$\frac{\alpha \times NUM\_IO(le'_1, le'_2, \cdots, le'_{m-1}) + \beta \times h}{LB_{PAA}(MSEQ_{i,j}, le'_h) - LB_{PAA}(MSEQ_{i,j}, le_p)}$$

Lemma 7. $LB_{CDens}(PQ_{i,j}) \leq CDens(PQ_{i,j})$

PROOF: Let le_p denote the last popped leaf entry from $PQ_{i,j}$ and $le_1, \cdots, le_h$ denote the real top-h leaf entries in order of distance. When le'_h is the hth leaf entry in the current queue, and its preceding entries are $le'_1, \cdots, le'_{m-1}, MBR_1, \cdots, le'_m, \cdots$, since MBR_1 must be extended to find real top-h leaf entries, $LB_{PAA}(MSEQ_{i,j}, le_h) \leq LB_{PAA}(MSEQ_{i,j}, le'_h)$. However, as such expansion cannot affect the ordering of the preceding entries $le'_1, \cdots, le'_{m-1}$, we can conclude that $(le_1, \cdots, le_{m-1})$ are equivalent to $(le'_1, \cdots, le'_{m-1})$. That is, $NUM\_IO(le_1, \cdots, le_h) \geq NUM\_IO(le'_1, \cdots, le'_{m-1})$. Therefore, we can conclude that $LB_{CDens}(PQ_{i,j}) \leq CDens(PQ_{i,j})$. □

For this selective expansion to be effective, we must avoid selecting an initial pivot with a very high density. To efficiently approximate density for pivot selection, we first access a set of leaf-node MBRs by accessing only the parent non-leaf nodes of the leaf nodes. For each query window $\mathcal{P}(\mathbb{E}(q))$, we can then determine the distance range $[d_1, d_2]$ for each leaf-node MBR by computing MINDIST and MAXDIST. Here, MINDIST and MAXDIST are the minimum and maximum distances between an MBR and a query window, respectively. For simplicity, we assume that the distances between leaf entries and the query envelope are uniformly distributed in the range $[d_1, d_2]$. After computing the distance range for each leaf MBR, we merge all distance ranges into a global range. Thus, we can estimate the distance range of the top-h entries of the priority queue using this global range.

Figure 10 illustrates how our proposed selective expansion technique works to find real top-4 leaf entries (i.e., $h = 4$). In the figure, the distances of the last popped leaf entries le_p from $PQ_{i,1}$ and $PQ_{i,2}$ are 4.0 and 3.0 respectively. Leaf entries incurring I/O costs are shaded. The first step of the selective expansion technique is to find a pivot queue, from which we find top-4 entries. In this figure, $PQ_{i,1}$ is chosen, and four leaf entries $(le_1, \cdots, le_4)$ are accessed. In this case, based on Definition 7, $CDens(PQ_{i,1})$ is computed as $\frac{2}{9.0-4.0}$ (when $\alpha = 1$ and $\beta = 0$). In the second step, we compute $LB_{CDens}(PQ_{i,j})$ to selectively expand another queue $PQ_{i,2}$. Observe from this example that $PQ_{i,2}$ has entries $(le'_1, le'_2, MBR_1, MBR_2, \cdots, le'_3, le'_4)$ with distance values $(3.1, 3.2, 3.3, 3.4, \cdots, 7.0, 9.0)$. In this queue, $LB_{CDens}(PQ_{i,2})$, stated in Definition 8, is computed as $\frac{2}{9.0-3.0}$. Since $CDens(PQ_{i,1}) > LB_{CDens}(PQ_{i,2})$, we expand MBR_1, after which a leaf entry with distance 3.3 is inserted into the queue. This updates the queue entries to $(le'_1, le'_2, le'_3, MBR_2, \cdots, le'_4)$ with distances $(3.1, 3.2, 3.3, 3.4, \cdots, 7.0)$ and also updates $LB_{CDens}(PQ_{i,2})$ to $\frac{2}{7.0-3.0}$. As $CDens(PQ_{i,1}) < LB_{CDens}(PQ_{i,2})$, we can stop expanding $PQ_{i,2}$.

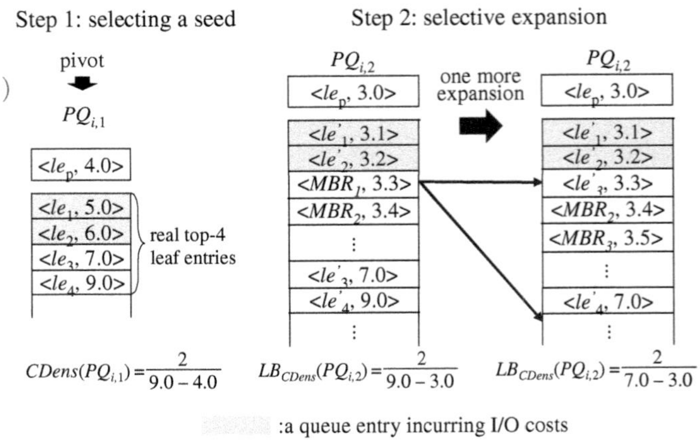

Figure 10: An example of the selective expansion technique.

5. RELATED WORK

Range subsequence matching and its solution under the Euclidean distance were first proposed by Faloutsos et al. [7] (FRM). FRM exploits the window construction mechanism of dividing data sequences into sliding windows and a query sequence into disjoint windows. FRM uses an R*-tree with the lower-dimensional transformation to store the sliding windows of data sequences and to find candidate subsequences from the disjoint windows of a query sequence. DualMatch [17] and GeneralMatch [16], improve this subsequence matching performance by using window construction methods which differ that of FRM. DualMatch divides the data sequences into disjoint windows and the query sequence into sliding windows; GeneralMatch generalizes the sliding and disjoint windows. The approach proposed here is quite different from these solutions: 1) we deal with the *ranked* subsequence matching rather than the *range* subsequence matching; and 2) we use the DTW distance.

Regarding the DTW distance, [21] proposed a range subsequence matching solution based on FRM. However, their method cannot be used for the ranked subsequence matching due to a loose lower bound and dimensionality curse on long queries [12]. [1] proposed a technique called *anticipatory DTW* to speed up DTW calculations by progressively computing DTW matrix cells. This technique is orthogonal to index-based ranked subsequence matching [1]. [2] proposed an *approximate* subsequence matching using embedding. Unlike our solution, this approximate method allows false dismissals, which cannot be used for many important time-series applications, such as electrocardiogram and gas pipeline inspection. [12] proposed an *exact* solution by introducing two tight lower bounds, the *mdmwp-distance* and the *window-group distance*. If the data points are uniformly distributed in the indexing space, this solution works well; if not, however, it shows bad performance due to the MDMWP-scheduling problem.

Top-k processing in other applications has been actively studied lately.Pioneering algorithms for the efficient processing of such queries are known as TA-family algorithms [6], followed by more algorithms [5, 9, 20] which consider a wide range of access scenarios. However, these algorithms cannot be readily applied to our proposed problem, as they assume the ranking function is monotonic over attribute values.

Using rank-awareness, Li et al. [15] extended the original semantics of relational operators including the union operator. However, our framework is significantly different from this framework: 1) they assume the ranking function is monotonic; 2) as opposed to their ranked union operator which first obtains top-k results for each *relational subquery* and then returns global top-k results (coarse-level scheduling), our ranked union framework provides a tailored execution model for *subsequence matching subqueries* by exploiting finer granular scheduling; 3) For fast subsequence matching, our framework presents a novel subsequence matching operator Φ and its lower bound MSEQ-distance. Thus, our underlying processing mechanism is completely different from their framework which is based on relational operators.

More recently, state-of-the art algorithms for supporting non-monotonic ranking functions have been studied [22]. These algorithms support non-monotonic functions using an index-merge framework with B+-trees or R*-trees. Thus, they can be adapted to ranked subsequence matching using R*-trees. To join multiple indexes efficiently, they first enumerate candidate join states progressively by increasing order of their lower bound scores from the root nodes of the indexes. For each join state, they check the state, whether it can produce the join results, by computing the join signature. If the join state cannot produce the join results, they stop enumerating the join states further. However, as we will see in Section 6, computing join signatures requires prohibitive bloom filter calls if the number of joins is larger than four (i.e., the number of query windows > 4 in our target problem). More specifically, if there are n joining indexes whose fan-outs are f, in the worst case, we need to invoke bloom filters f^n times to compute all valid join signatures from one join state.

6. PERFORMANCE EVALUATION

We evaluate the performance of the state-of-the-art algorithms against our ranked union algorithms. The algorithms considered are as follows: (1) SeqScan, a sequential scan algorithm, (2) HLMJ, (3) PSM, a top-k subsequence matching solution adopted from the recent index-based merge algorithm [22], (4) RU, the ranked union with the default scheduling strategy, and (5) RU-COST, the ranked union with the cost-aware density-based scheduling strategy.

Our main objective is to show that our algorithms 1) *consistently* outperform the competing algorithms even for query sets having no dense windows and 2) *significantly* outperform the competing algorithms for query set having dense windows.

6.1 Experiment Setup

We use five real and synthetic data sets as shown in Table 2. Each data set consists of a long data sequence and has the same effect as one consisting of multiple data sequences [7, 16]. (Refer to the Appendix in [11] for the detailed explanation on data sets.) We use the number of candidates, the number of page accesses, and the wall clock time as the performance metrics. Table 3 summarizes parameters and their values. We generate query sequences from the data sequence by taking subsequences of length $Len(Q)$ starting from random offsets as in [7, 12, 16]. Regarding the query types of the PIPE data set, refer to the Appendix in [11]. We measure the three performance metrics using all query sequences, and use their averages.

Table 2: Data sets used.

Data set	UCR	PIPE	WALK	STOCK	MUSIC
Size($\times 1,000$)	1,056	24,307	1,000	328	2,373

Table 3: Experimental parameters and their values.

Parameter	Default	Range
k	25	$5 \sim 50$
Buffer size	5%	$1\% \sim 10\%$
Len(Q)	384	256, 384, 512
ω(window size)	64	32, 64, 128

We conduct all the experiments on a Linux server with Xeon Quad Core 1.6GHz CPU and 8 Gbytes RAM. We use LRU as the buffer replacement algorithm, and set the page size to 4 KBytes. For each query sequence, we set the warping width to 5% of the query length. We also performed experiments for varying both the number of PAA features and the warping width, but the performance trends are similar, and thus we omit the results for brevity.

6.2 Experiments and Results

Experiment 1) (effect of k) Figure 11 shows the experimental results for UCR. We use the same query set consisting of 20 sequences that are used in [12]. We call this query set *UCR-REGULAR*. Note that PSM does not finish with reasonable times due to excessive bloom filter calls if $Len(Q) > 256$. Thus, we can show the performance results of PSM in Experiment 6 when the $Len(Q) = 256$. In addition, we can use the deferred retrieval mechanism [12] for HLMJ, RU, and RU-COST. This mechanism delays a set of subsequence retrieval requests, groups the requests by their corresponding subsequences, and enables batch retrieval, thereby avoiding excessive random disk I/Os. Thus, for each of these three algorithms, we experiment with two different versions: one uses the deferred retrieval mechanism (denoted as "(D)"); the other does not. In the deferred retrieval mechanism we allocate memory of only 0.5% of the database size for storing the delayed requests.

As shown in Figure 11(a), our RU-COST consistently reduces the number of candidates by up to 1.8 times compared with HLMJ. This indicates that 1) the MSEQ-distance is tighter than the lower

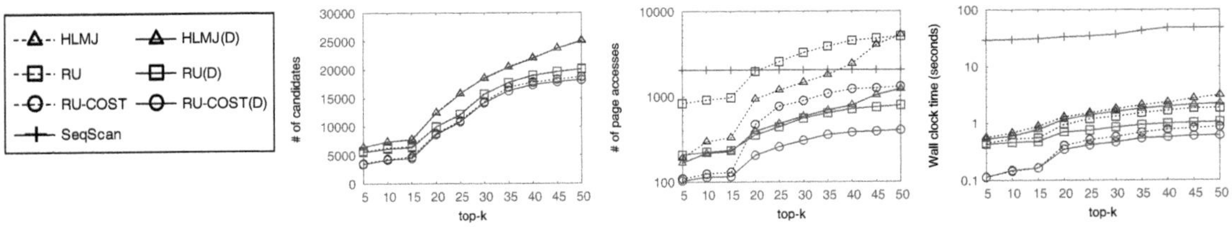

(a) Number of candidates. (b) Number of page accesses. (c) Wall clock time.

Figure 11: Experimental results with UCR-REGULAR by varying k.

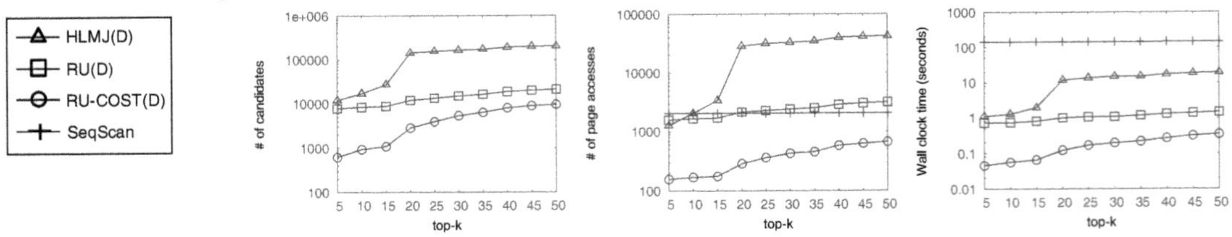

(a) Number of candidates. (b) Number of page accesses. (c) Wall clock time.

Figure 12: Experimental results with UCR-DENSE by varying k.

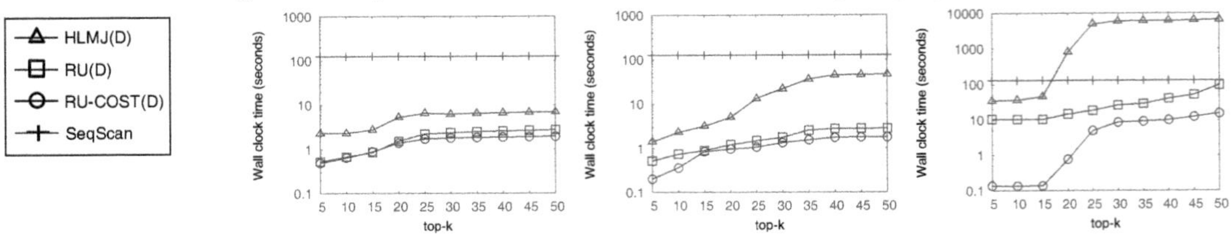

(a) PIPE-BEND. (b) PIPE-VALVE. (c) PIPE-TEE.

Figure 13: Wall clock time for different query types on PIPE by varying k.

bound of HLMJ, and 2) cost-aware density scheduling is more efficient than MDMWP-scheduling. In particular, RU-COST outperforms RU by up to 1.6 times in the number of candidates. This means that RU-COST increases the lower bound more rapidly even for *UCR-REGULAR* having no very dense windows.

In terms of the number of page accesses, RU-COST(D) provides significant reduction compared with other algorithms as shown in Figure 11(b). This outcome is due to two causes: (1) RU-COST shows the best result in reducing the number of candidates; (2) the deferred retrieval mechanism groups many random accesses into a series of sequential accesses. The first reason explains why RU-COST(D) can reduce the number of page accesses by up to 3.0 and 2.0 times compared with HLMJ(D) and RU(D), respectively, in Figure 11(b). The second reason explains why RU-COST(D) outperforms RU-COST as well as RU and HLMJ.

As shown in 11(c), RU-COST(D) reduces the wall clock time by up to 3.8, 4.7, 260 times compared with RU(D), HLMJ(D), and SeqScan. In subsequence matching, the wall clock time is determined by two major factors: 1) the time for accessing disk pages and 2) the time for computing distances between query and candidate sequences. This explains why Figure 11(c) looks like a merged version of Figures 11(a) and 11(b). In Figures 11(a) and 11(b), RU-COST(D) shows the best result in terms of both candidates and page accesses, and therefore it consistently outperforms any other algorithms in the wall clock time of Figure 11(c).

As in Figures 11(b) and 11(c), a deferred algorithm is always superior to its corresponding non-deferred algorithm. Thus, hereafter we consider only the deferred algorithms. For brevity, we omit the non-deferred algorithms from the experimental graphs.

Experiment 2) (effect of the data point density) In this experiment, we show that our ranked union approach clearly overcomes the MDMWP-based scheduling problem of HLMJ. As shown in Figure 2, this problem occurs by the density difference of data points. For this experiment, we construct another query set consisting of 20 query sequences from UCR, called *UCR-DENSE*, where each query sequence consists of two types of query points: one in the dense region, and the other in the sparse region. Thus, UCR-DENSE incurs the MDMWP-based scheduling problem.

Figure 12 shows the experimental results for UCR with UCR-DENSE. Comparing Figure 12(a) with Figure 11(a), the differences between algorithms are much larger in UCR-DENSE. In particular, the difference between RU-COST(D) and HLMJ(D) in UCR-DENSE is much larger than that in UCR-REGULAR. In Figure 12(a), RU-COST(D) reduces the number of candidates by up to 50.4 times compared with HLMJ(D). This significant reduction means that our ranked union approach resolves the MDMWP-based scheduling problem. Due to this reduction, the difference in the number of page accesses becomes large, and accordingly, the difference in the wall clock time also becomes large.

For a clearer comparison of RU-COST(D) and HLMJ(D), we use PIPE which contains lots of dense regions. Figure 13 shows the wall clock time for three representative queries sequences, *PIPE-BEND*, *PIPE-VALVE*, and *PIPE-TEE*. These query sequences are eventually mapped into dense and sparse regions in a mixed way and incur the MDMWP-based scheduling problem. Compared with HLMJ(D) and RU(D), RU-COST(D) significantly improves the performance by up to 980.9 and 78.3 times! In particular, the improvement is remarkable in PIPE-TEE and PIPE-VALVE (see Figures 13(b) and 13(c)). This is because a query sequence of PIPE-TEE or PIPE-VALUE contains many irregular patterns, i.e., its sliding windows are mapped into both sparse and dense regions, incurring the MDMWP-based scheduling problem.

Experiment 3) (effect of the buffer size) Figure 14 shows the wall clock time for UCR by varying the buffer size. As the query set, we use UCR-REGULAR in Figure 14(a) and UCR-DENSE in Fig-

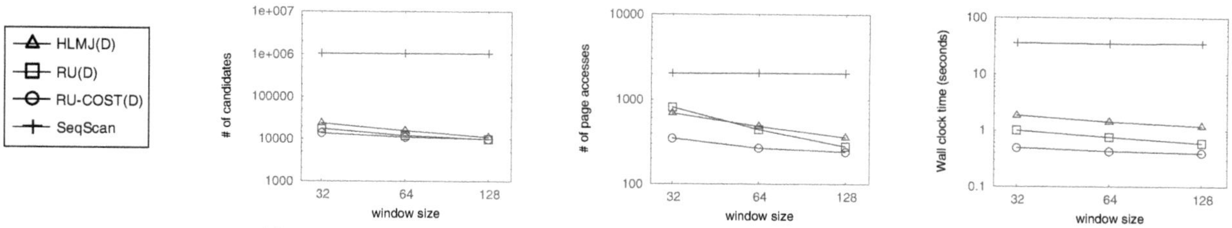

(a) Number of candidates. (b) Number of page accesses. (c) Wall clock time.

Figure 15: Experimental results for UCR with UCR-REGULAR by varying the window size.

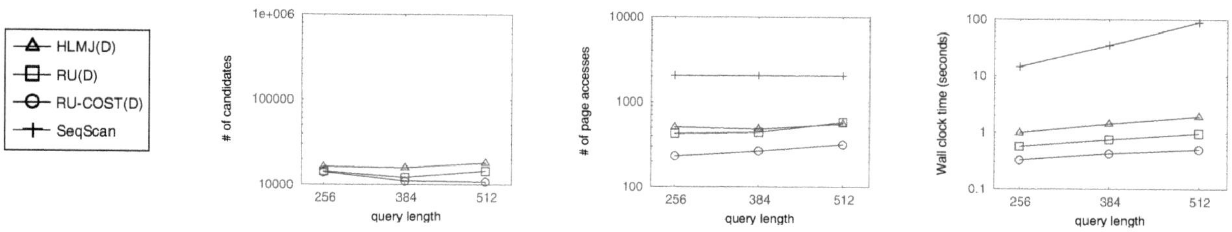

(a) Number of candidates. (b) Number of page accesses. (c) Wall clock time.

Figure 16: Experimental results for UCR with UCR-REGULAR by varying the query length.

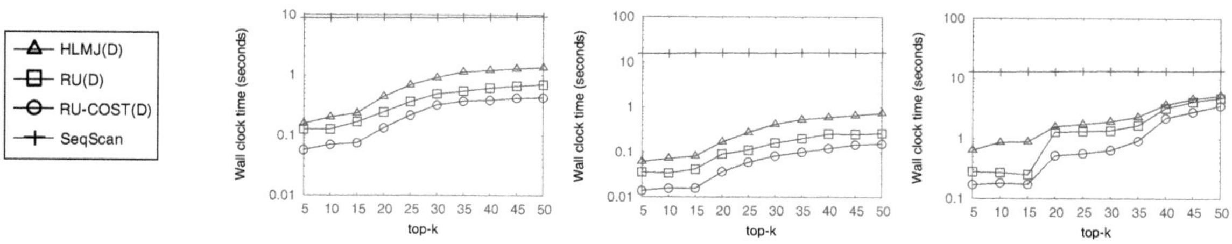

(a) WALK. (b) STOCK. (c) MUSIC.

Figure 17: Wall clock time for WALK, STOCK, and MUSIC by varying k.

ure 14(b). Like the previous experimental results, RU-COST(D) shows the best result by enlarging the lower bound aggressively.

As shown in Figure 14, SeqScan shows the constant time for all buffer sizes since it just accesses all subsequences with a small size buffer sequentially. In contrast, the wall clock time of other buffer-based algorithms slightly decreases as the buffer size increases. This is obvious since, as the buffer size increases, the buffer hit-ratio in accessing candidate subsequences increases. Note that there is a considerable performance degradation in the wall clock time for UCR-DENSE. This is because SeqScan exploits LB_{Keogh} before DTW computations, and LB_{Keogh} is much more effective in UCR-REGULAR than in UCR-DENSE. We also note that the buffer size incurs only a small performance difference in all of the buffer-based algorithms. This is because all these algorithms use the deferred retrieval mechanism which accumulates many random subsequence requests in the group subsequence access list being rescheduled to a sequential scan [12]. In general, the small buffer size is very crucial for both large (hundreds of gigabytes to terabytes) time-series data and multi-user environment. As we can see in Figure 14, our RU-COST(D) and RU(D) require only a small buffer size, and accordingly, we can say that our algorithms have the most desirable characteristic in the large database and multi-user environment.

Experiment 4) (Effect of Window Size and Query Length) Figure 15 shows the experimental results for UCR with UCR-REGULAR by varying the window size. The experimental results of Figure 15 are summarized as follows. Like the previous experiments, SeqScan shows constant values in all three measures, since it fully scans the entire database and considers all possible subsequences, regardless of the window size. On the other hand, the results of the other three algorithms are changed according to the win-

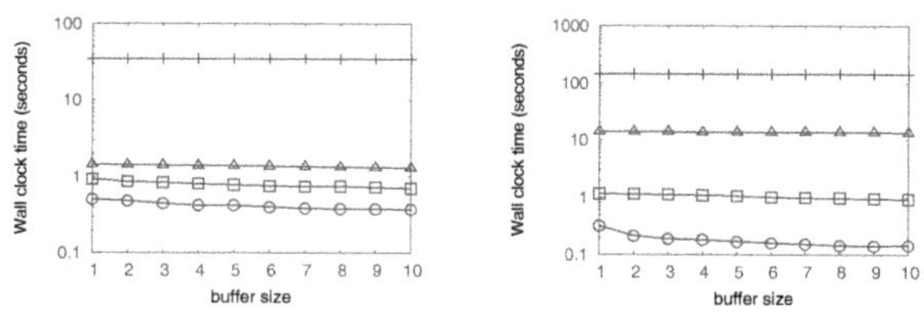

(a) UCR-REGULAR. (b) UCR-DENSE.

Figure 14: Wall clock time by varying the buffer size.

dow size, since they use window construction mechanism [7, 12, 16] of subsequence matching. We note that, as the window size increases, all three measures of these three algorithms decrease. This decreasing trend is well explained by the *window size effect* [17, 16]. That is, the larger window incurs the smaller number of candidates, and accordingly, the larger window causes the smaller number of page accesses and the shorter wall clock time. RU-COST(D) still outperforms the other three algorithms, regardless of the window size. Compared with SeqScan, HLMJ(D), and RU(D), the last RU-COST(D) improves matching performance by up to 90.6 times, 3.8 times, and 2.1 times for UCR-REGULAR; and 846.8 times, 80.2 times, and 11.6 times for UCR-DENSE (The figures of the results for UCR with UCR-DENSE are omitted due to space limit).

Figure 16 shows the experimental results by varying the query length. The experimental results of Figure 16 are summarized as follows. In the case of SeqScan, the number of candidates and the number of page accesses change only very slightly according to the query length. Its wall clock time, however, increases according to the query length, since the longer length requires more operations in computing the DTW distance. With other algorithms including RU-COST(D), the number of candidates slightly increases according to the query length. This increasing trend is also explained by the window size effect. That is, as the query length increases, the relative size of the corresponding window decreases, and thus, the more candidates occur due to the window size effect. Due to the increase in the number of candidates, the number of page accesses and the wall clock time also increase for the larger query length. Like the previous experimental results, RU-COST(D) significantly improves matching performance compared with other algorithms.

Experiment 5) (Effect of Different Data Sets) Figures 17(a), 17(b), and 17(c) show the wall clock time for WALK, STOCK, and MUSIC, respectively. (We omit the results for candidates and page accesses since their trends are very similar to that of UCR with UCR-REGULAR.) As shown in the figures, RU-COST(D) shows the best performance, and we can say that our ranked union approach always outperforms the previous algorithms, regardless of the data set. Because the results in the figures show such a similar tendency as that of UCR with UCR-REGULAR (compare Figure 17 with Figure 11(c)), we omit the detailed explanation of the performance results.

Experiment 6) (Comparison with PSM(D)) Figure 18 shows the wall clock times of PSM(D) and RU-COST(D) for UCR by varying k when the query size is 256. Figures 18(a) and 18(b) show performance results for UCR-REGULAR and UCR-DENSE, respectively. RU-COST(D) significantly outperforms PSM(D) by up to 62.5 and 135.7 times for UCR-REGULAR and UCR-DENSE, respectively. Since PSM exploits all windows using index-merge at the index level, there are no drastic performance differences for either query set. Note that we implemented the best version of PSM.

PSM maintains join signatures using the bloom filter [22], and computing join signatures requires a lot of bloom filter calls. Thus, it cannot support more than four-way joins with reasonable times due to excessive bloom filter calls. In our experiment, we observe that, on average, more than 4 billion bloom filter calls are performed to compute the join signatures.

We also performed experiments with k=25 and the query length=320. RU-COST(D) outperforms PSM(D) by up to 2440.5 times and 5352.1 times for UCR-REGULAR and UCR-DENSE, respectively.

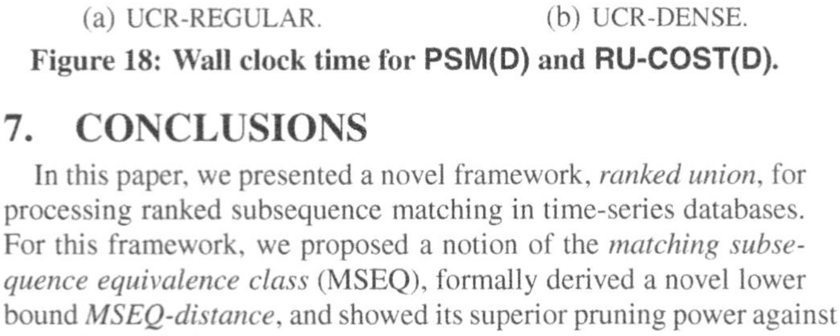

(a) UCR-REGULAR. (b) UCR-DENSE.

Figure 18: Wall clock time for PSM(D) and RU-COST(D).

7. CONCLUSIONS

In this paper, we presented a novel framework, *ranked union*, for processing ranked subsequence matching in time-series databases. For this framework, we proposed a notion of the *matching subsequence equivalence class* (MSEQ), formally derived a novel lower bound *MSEQ-distance*, and showed its superior pruning power against the MDMWP-distance. After that, we proposed a novel execution model for ranked union along with two novel operators: 1) multi-way ranked union operator and 2) ranked subsequence matching subquery operator. We then enhanced the basic ranked union with a novel priority queue selection strategy RU-COST. By exploiting both a novel concept of the *cost-aware density* and the *selective expansion* technique with another lower bound, LB_{CDens}, for the cost-aware density, RU-COST can completely eliminate the MDMWP-scheduling problem with immaterial overhead. We also showed the lower boundness of LB_{CDens}. Through extensive experiments on both real and synthetic datasets, we showed that our ranked union solutions outperform the state-of-the-art algorithms by up to two to three orders of magnitude.

8. ACKNOWLEDGMENTS

This paper is based on research supported by the R&D program of MKE/KEIT (KI10033545). This paper is also supported in part by MEST/KOSEF (R11-2008-007-03003-0).

9. REFERENCES

[1] I. Assent, M. Wichterich, R. Krieger, H. Kremer, and T. Seidl. Anticipatory dtw for efficient similarity search in time series databases. *PVLDB*, 2(1):826–837, 2009.

[2] V. Athitsos, P. Papapetrou, M. Potamias, G. Kollios, and D. Gunopulos. Approximate embedding-based subsequence matching of time series. In *SIGMOD Conference*, pages 365–378, 2008.

[3] I. Bartolini and M. Patella. Warp: Accurate retrieval of shapes using phase of fourier descriptors and time warping distance. *IEEE PAMI.*, 27(1):142–147, 2005.

[4] D. J. Berndt and J. Clifford. Finding patterns in time series: a dynamic programming approach. pages 229–248, 1996.

[5] N. Bruno, L. Gravano, and A. Marian. Evaluating top-k queries over web-accessible databases. In *ICDE 2002*, 2002.

[6] R. Fagin, A. Lote, and M. Naor. Optimal aggregation algorithms for middleware. In *PODS*, 2001.

[7] C. Faloutsos, M. Ranganathan, and Y. Manolopoulos. Fast subsequence matching in time-series databases. In *SIGMOD*, 1994.

[8] G. Graefe. Query evaluation techniques for large databases. *ACM Comput. Surv.*, 25(2):73–170, 1993.

[9] U. Güntzer, W.-T. Balke, and W. Kießling. Optimizing multi-feature queries in image databases. In *VLDB*, 2000.

[10] U. Güntzer, W.-T. Balke, and W. Kießling. Towards efficient multi-feature queries in heterogeneous environments. In *ITCC*, pages 622–628, 2001.

[11] W. Han, J. Lee, Y. Moon, S. Hwang, and H. Yu. A new approach for processing ranked subsequence matching based on ranked union. http://www-db.knu.ac.kr/rankedunion/runion-tr.pdf, 2011.

[12] W. Han, J. Lee, Y. Moon, and H. Jiang. Ranked subsequence matching in time-series database. In *VLDB*, 2007.

[13] E. Keogh. Exact indexing of dynamic time warping. In *VLDB*, 2002.

[14] E. Keogh. A decade of progress in indexing and mining large time series databases. In *VLDB*, 2006.

[15] C. Li, K. C.-C. Chang, I. F. Ilyas, and S. Song. Ranksql: Query algebra and optimization for relational top-k queries. In *SIGMOD Conference*, pages 131–142, 2005.

[16] Y. Moon, K. Whang, and W. Han. General match: a subsequence matching method in time-series databases based on generalized windows. In *SIGMOD*, 2002.

[17] Y.-S. Moon, K.-Y. Whang, and W.-K. Loh. Duality-based subsequence matching in time-series databases. In *ICDE*, 2001.

[18] L. Rabiner and B.-H. Juang. *Fundamentals of speech recognition*. Prentice-Hall, Inc., 1993.

[19] D. Rafiei and A. O. Mendelzon. Querying time series data based on similarity. *TKDE*, 12(5):675–693, 2000.

[20] S. won Hwang and K. C.-C. Chang. Optimizing top-k queries for middleware access: A unified cost-based approach. *ACM Trans. Database Syst.*, 32(1):5, 2007.

[21] T. S. F. Wong and M. H. Wong. Efficient subsequence matching for sequences databases under time warping. *IDEAS*, 2003.

[22] D. Xin, J. Han, and K. C.-C. Chang. Progressive and selective merge: computing top-k with ad-hoc ranking functions. In *SIGMOD*, 2007.

[23] B.-K. Yi and C. Faloutsos. Fast time sequence indexing for arbitrary lp norms. In *VLDB*, 2000.

[24] Y. Zhu and D. Shasha. Warping indexes with envelope transforms for query by humming. In *SIGMOD*, 2003.

Interaction between Record Matching and Data Repairing

Wenfei Fan [1,2] Jianzhong Li [2] Shuai Ma [3] Nan Tang [1] Wenyuan Yu [1]
[1] University of Edinburgh [2] Harbin Institute of Technology [3] Beihang University
{wenfei@inf., ntang@inf., wenyuan.yu@}ed.ac.uk lijzh@hit.edu.cn mashuai@act.buaa.edu.cn

Abstract

Central to a data cleaning system are record matching and data repairing. Matching aims to identify tuples that refer to the same real-world object, and repairing is to make a database consistent by fixing errors in the data by using constraints. These are treated as separate processes in current data cleaning systems, based on heuristic solutions. This paper studies a new problem, namely, the interaction between record matching and data repairing. We show that repairing can effectively help us identify matches, and vice versa. To capture the interaction, we propose a uniform framework that seamlessly unifies repairing and matching operations, to clean a database based on integrity constraints, matching rules and master data. We give a full treatment of fundamental problems associated with data cleaning via matching and repairing, including the static analyses of constraints and rules taken together, and the complexity, termination and determinism analyses of data cleaning. We show that these problems are hard, ranging from NP- or coNP-complete, to PSPACE-complete. Nevertheless, we propose efficient algorithms to clean data via both matching and repairing. The algorithms find *deterministic fixes* and *reliable fixes* based on confidence and entropy analysis, respectively, which are more accurate than possible fixes generated by heuristics. We experimentally verify that our techniques significantly improve the accuracy of record matching and data repairing taken as separate processes, using real-life data.

Categories and Subject Descriptors

H.2 [**Database Management**]: General—*integrity*

General Terms

Theory, Algorithms, Experimentation

Keywords

conditional functional dependency, matching dependency, data cleaning

1. Introduction

It has long been recognized that data residing in a database is often dirty [31]. Dirty data inflicts a daunting cost: it costs US businesses 600 billion dollars each year [15]. With this comes the need for data cleaning systems. As an example, data cleaning tools deliver "an overall business value of more than 600 million GBP" each year at BT [30]. In light of this, the market for data cleaning systems is growing at 17% annually, which substantially outpaces the 7% average of other IT segments [21].

There are two central issues about data cleaning:

- *Recording matching* is to identify tuples that refer to the same real-world entity [16, 25].
- *Data repairing* is to find another database (a candidate repair) that is consistent and minimally differs from the original data, by fixing errors in the data [4, 20].

Most data cleaning systems in the market support record matching, and some also provide the functionality of data repairing. These systems treat matching and repairing as separate and independent processes. However, the two processes typically interact with each other: repairing helps us identify matches and vice versa, as illustrated below.

Example 1.1: Consider two databases D_m and D from a UK bank: D_m maintains customer information collected when credit cards are issued, and is treated as *clean master data* [27]; D consists of transaction records of credit cards, which may be dirty. The databases are specified by schemas:

$$\mathsf{card}(\mathsf{FN}, \mathsf{LN}, \mathsf{St}, \mathsf{city}, \mathsf{AC}, \mathsf{zip}, \mathsf{tel}, \mathsf{dob}, \mathsf{gd}),$$
$$\mathsf{tran}(\mathsf{FN}, \mathsf{LN}, \mathsf{St}, \mathsf{city}, \mathsf{AC}, \mathsf{post}, \mathsf{phn}, \mathsf{gd}, \mathsf{item}, \mathsf{when}, \mathsf{where}).$$

Here a card tuple specifies a UK credit card holder identified by first name (FN), last name (LN), address (street (St), city, zip code), area code (AC), phone (tel), date of birth (dob) and gender (gd). A tran tuple is a record of a purchased item paid by a credit card at place where and time when, by a UK customer who is identified by name (FN, LN), address (St, city, post code), AC, phone (phn) and gender (gd). Example instances of card and tran are shown in Figures 1(a) and 1(b), which are fractions of D_m and D, respectively (the cf rows in Fig. 1(b) will be discussed later).

Following [17, 18], we use conditional functional dependencies (CFDs [17]) φ_1–φ_4 to specify the consistency of tran data D, and a matching dependency (MD [18]) ψ as a rule for matching tuples across D and master card data D_m:

$$\varphi_1\text{: } \mathsf{tran}([\mathsf{AC} = 131] \rightarrow [\mathsf{city} = \text{Edi}]),$$
$$\varphi_2\text{: } \mathsf{tran}([\mathsf{AC} = 020] \rightarrow [\mathsf{city} = \text{Ldn}]),$$
$$\varphi_3\text{: } \mathsf{tran}([\mathsf{city}, \mathsf{phn}] \rightarrow [\mathsf{St}, \mathsf{AC}, \mathsf{post}]),$$
$$\varphi_4\text{: } \mathsf{tran}([\mathsf{FN} = \text{Bob}] \rightarrow [\mathsf{FN} = \text{Robert}]),$$
$$\psi\text{: } \mathsf{tran}[\mathsf{LN}, \mathsf{city}, \mathsf{St}, \mathsf{post}] = \mathsf{card}[\mathsf{LN}, \mathsf{city}, \mathsf{St}, \mathsf{zip}] \wedge \mathsf{tran}[\mathsf{FN}] \approx \mathsf{card}[\mathsf{FN}] \rightarrow \mathsf{tran}[\mathsf{FN}, \mathsf{phn}] \rightleftharpoons \mathsf{card}[\mathsf{FN}, \mathsf{tel}],$$

where (1) CFD φ_1 (resp. φ_2) asserts that if the area code is 131 (resp. 020), the city must be Edi (resp. Ldn); (2) CFD φ_3 is a traditional functional dependency (FD) asserting that city and phone number uniquely determine street, area code

	FN	LN	St	city	AC	zip	tel	dob	gd
s_1:	Mark	Smith	10 Oak St	Edi	131	EH8 9LE	3256778	10/10/1987	Male
s_2:	Robert	Brady	5 Wren St	Ldn	020	WC1H 9SE	3887644	12/08/1975	Male

(a) Master data D_m: An instance of schema card

	FN	LN	St	city	AC	post	phn	gd	item	when	where
t_1:	M.	Smith	10 Oak St	Ldn	131	EH8 9LE	9999999	Male	watch, 350 GBP	11am 28/08/2010	UK
cf	(0.9)	(1.0)	(0.9)	(0.5)	(0.9)	(0.9)	(0.0)	(0.8)	(1.0)	(1.0)	(1.0)
t_2:	Max	Smith	Po Box 25	Edi	131	EH8 9AB	3256778	Male	DVD, 800 INR	8pm 28/09/2010	India
cf	(0.7)	(1.0)	(0.5)	(0.9)	(0.7)	(0.6)	(0.8)	(0.8)	(1.0)	(1.0)	(1.0)
t_3:	Bob	Brady	5 Wren St	Edi	020	WC1H 9SE	3887834	Male	iPhone, 599 GBP	6pm 06/11/2009	UK
cf	(0.6)	(1.0)	(0.9)	(0.2)	(0.9)	(0.8)	(0.9)	(0.8)	(1.0)	(1.0)	(1.0)
t_4:	Robert	Brady	null	Ldn	020	WC1E 7HX	3887644	Male	necklace, 2,100 USD	1pm 06/11/2009	USA
cf	(0.7)	(1.0)	(0.0)	(0.5)	(0.7)	(0.3)	(0.7)	(0.8)	(1.0)	(1.0)	(1.0)

(b) Database D: An instance of schema tran

Figure 1: Example master data and database

and postal code; (3) CFD φ_4 is a data standardization rule: if the first name is Bob, then it should be "normalized" as Robert; and (4) MD ψ assures that for any tuple in D and any tuple in D_m, if they have the same last name and address, and moreover, if their first names are *similar*, then their phone and FN attributes can be identified.

Consider tuples t_3 and t_4 in D. The bank suspects that the two refer to the same person. If so, then these transaction records show that the same person made purchases in the UK and in the US at about the same time (taking into account the 5-hour time difference between the two countries). This indicates that a fraud has likely been committed.

Observe that t_3 and t_4 are quite different in their FN, city, St, post and Phn attributes. No rule allows us to identify the two directly. Nonetheless, they can indeed be matched by a sequence of *interleaved* matching and repairing operations:

(a) get a repair t'_3 of t_3 such that t'_3[city] = Ldn via CFD φ_2, and t'_3[FN]=Robert by normalization with φ_4;
(b) match t'_3 with s_2 of D_m, to which ψ can be applied;
(c) as a result of the matching operation, get a repair t''_3 of t_3 by correcting t''_3[phn] with the master data s_2[tel];
(d) find a repair t'_4 of t_4 via the FD φ_3: since t''_3 and t_4 agree on their city and phn attributes, φ_3 can be applied. This allows us to enrich t_4[St] and fix t_4[post] by taking corresponding values from t''_3, which have been confirmed correct with the master data in step (c).

At this point t''_3 and t'_4 agree on every attribute in connection with personal information. It is now evident enough that they indeed refer to the same person; hence a fraud.

Observe that not only repairing helps matching (*e.g.*, from step (a) to (b)), but matching also helps us repair the data (*e.g.*, step (d) is doable only after the matching in (b)). □

This example tells us the following. (1) When taken together, record matching and data repairing perform much better than being treated as separate processes. (2) To make practical use of their interaction, matching and repairing operations should be *interleaved*. It does not help much to execute these processes consecutively one after another.

There has been a host of work on record matching (*e.g.*, [3, 5, 7, 18, 24, 36]; see [16, 25] for surveys) as well as on data repairing (*e.g.*, [4, 6, 9, 19, 20, 28, 38]). However, the problem of interleaving record matching and data repairing to improve the accuracy has not been well addressed.

Contributions. We approach this problem by *unifying* record matching and data repairing, and to provide a data cleaning solution that stresses accuracy.

(1) We investigate a new problem, stated as follows.

Given a database D, master data D_m, and data quality rules consisting of CFDs Σ and matching rules Γ, the *data cleaning problem* is to find a repair D_r of D such that (a) D_r is *consistent* (*i.e.*, satisfying the CFDs Σ), (b) no more tuples in D_r can be *matched* to master tuples in D_m by rules of Γ, and (c) D_r minimally differs from the original data D.

As opposed to record matching and data repairing, the data cleaning problem aims to fix errors in the data by unifying matching and repairing, and by leveraging master data. Here *master data* (*a.k.a.* reference data) is a single repository of high-quality data that provides various applications with a synchronized, consistent view of its core business entities [27]. It is being widely used in industry, supported by, *e.g.*, IBM, SAP, Microsoft and Oracle. To identify tuples from D and D_m, we use matching rules that are an extension of MDs [18] by supporting negative rules (*e.g.*, a male and female may not refer to the same person) [3, 36].

(2) We propose a uniform framework for data cleaning. We treat both CFDs and MDs as *cleaning rules*, which tell us how to fix errors. This yields a rule-based logical framework, which allows us to seamlessly interleave repairing and matching operations. To assure the accuracy of fixes, we make use of (a) the *confidence* placed by the user in the accuracy of the data, (b) *entropy* measuring the certainty of data, by the self-information of the data itself [11, 33], and (c) master data [27]. We distinguish three classes of fixes: (i) *deterministic* fixes for the unique solution to correct an error; (ii) *reliable* fixes for those derived using entropy; and (iii) *possible* fixes for those generated by heuristics. The former two are more accurate than possible fixes.

(3) We investigate fundamental problems associated with data cleaning via both matching and repairing. We show the following. (a) When CFDs and matching rules are taken together, the classical decision problems for dependencies, namely, the consistency and implication analyses, are NP-complete and coNP-complete, respectively. These problems have the same complexity as their counterparts for CFDs [17], *i.e.*, adding matching rules does not incur extra complexity. (b) The data cleaning problem is NP-complete. Worse still, it is approximation-hard, *i.e.*, it is beyond reach in practice to find a polynomial-time (PTIME) algorithm with a constant approximation ratio [34] unless P = NP. (c) It is more challenging to decide whether a data cleaning process terminates and whether it yields deterministic fixes: these problems are both PSPACE-complete.

(4) In light of the inherent complexity, we propose a three-phase solution consisting of three algorithms. (a) One algorithm identifies *deterministic fixes* that are accurate, based on confidence analysis and master data. (b) When confi-

dence is low or unavailable, we provide another algorithm to compute *reliable fixes* by employing information entropy, inferring evidence from data itself to improve accuracy. (c) To fix the remaining errors, we extend the heuristic based method [9] to find a consistent repair of the dirty data. These methods are complementary to each other, and can be used either alone or together.

(5) We experimentally evaluate the quality and scalability of our data cleaning methods with both matching and repairing, using real-life datasets (DBLP and hospital data from US Dept. of Health & Human Services). We find that our methods substantially outperform matching and repairing taken as separate processes in the accuracy of fixes, up to 15% and 30%, respectively. Moreover, deterministic fixes and reliable fixes are far more accurate than fixes generated by heuristic methods. Despite the high complexity of the cleaning problem, we also find that our algorithms scale reasonably well with the size of the data.

We contend that a unified process for repairing and matching is both important and feasible in practice, and that it should logically become part of data cleaning systems.

While master data is desirable in the process, it is not a must. Indeed, in its absence, our approach can be adapted by interleaving (a) record matching in a single data table with MDs, as described in [18], and (b) data repairing with CFDs. While deterministic fixes may have lower accuracy, reliable and heuristic fixes would not degrade substantially.

Organization. Section 2 reviews CFDs and extends MDs. Section 3 introduces the framework for data cleaning. Section 4 studies the fundamental problems for data cleaning. Algorithms for finding deterministic and reliable fixes are provided in Sections 5 and 6, respectively. Section 7 reports our experimental study, followed by open issues in Section 8.

Related work. Record matching is also known as record linkage, entity resolution, and duplicate detection [3,5,7,13, 18,22,24,35,36] (see [16,25] for surveys). Matching rules are studied in [18,24] (positive) and [3,36] (negative). Data repairing was first studied in [4,20]. A variety of constraints have been used to specify data consistency in data repairing, *e.g.*,FDs [37], FDs and INDs [6], and CFDs [9,17]. We employ CFDs, and extend MDs of [18] with negative rules.

The consistency and implication problems have been studied for CFDs [17] and MDs [18]. We study these problems for MDs and CFDs put together. It is known that data repairing is NP-complete [6,9]. We show that data cleaning via repairing and matching is NP-complete and approximation-hard. We also study the termination and determinism analyses of data cleaning, which are not considered in [6,9].

Several repairing algorithms have been proposed [6,9,19, 20,28,38]. Heuristic methods are developed in [6,9,20], based on FDs and INDs [6], CFDs [17], and edit rules [20]. The methods of [6,9] employ confidence placed by users to guide a repairing process. Statistical inference is studied in [28] to derive missing values. To ensure the accuracy of repairs generated, [28,38] require to consult users. In contrast to the previous work, we (a) unify repairing and matching, (b) use confidence just to derive deterministic fixes, and (c) leverage master data and entropy to improve the accuracy. Closer to our work is [19], also based on master data. It differs from our work in the following. (i) While [19] aims to fix a *single* tuple via matching with editing rules (derived from MDs), we repair a *database* via *both* matching (MDs) and repairing (CFDs), a task far more challenging. (ii) While [19] only relies on confidence to warrant the accuracy, we use entropy analysis when the confidence is either low or unavailable.

There have also been efforts to interleave merging and matching operations [13,22,35,36]. Among these, (1) [22] proposes to use uniqueness constraints to cluster objects from multiple data sources, and employs machine learning techniques to discover the true values of the objects; it differs from this work in the set of constraints used; and (2) [13,35,36] investigate record matching in the presence of error data, and advocate the need for data repairing to match records. The merge/fusion operations adopted there are more restrictive than updates (value modifications) suggested by cleaning rules of this work. Furthermore, when no matches are found, no merge or fusion can be conducted, whereas this work may still repair data with CFDs.

There has also been a host of work on ETL tools (see [25] for a survey), which support data transformations, and can be employed to merge and fix data [29], although they are typically not based on a constraint theory. These are essentially complementary to data repairing and this work.

Information entropy measures the degree of uncertainty [11]: the less the entropy is, the more certain the data is. It has proved effective in, *e.g.*, database design, schema matching, data anonymization and data clustering [33]. We make a first effort to use it in data cleaning: we mark a fix reliable if its entropy is below a predefined threshold.

2. Data Quality Rules

Below we first review CFDs [17], which specify the consistency of data for data repairing. We then extend MDs [18] to match tuples across (a possibly dirty) database D and master data D_m. Both CFDs and MDs can be automatically discovered from data via profiling algorithms (*e.g.*, [8,32]).

2.1 Conditional Functional Dependencies

Following [17], we define *conditional functional dependencies* (CFDs) on a relation schema R as follows.

A CFD φ defined on schema R is a pair $R(X \rightarrow Y,\ t_p)$, where (1) $X \rightarrow Y$ is a standard FD on R, referred to as *the FD embedded in* φ; and (2) t_p is a *pattern tuple* with attributes in X and Y, where for each A in $X \cup Y$, $t_p[A]$ is either a constant in the domain $\mathsf{dom}(A)$ of attribute A, or an unnamed variable '_' that draws values from $\mathsf{dom}(A)$.

We separate the X and Y attributes in t_p with '$\|$', and refer to X and Y as the LHS and RHS of φ, respectively.

Example 2.1: Recall the CFDs φ_1, φ_3 and φ_4 given in Example 1. These can be formally expressed as follows.

φ_1: $\mathsf{tran}([\mathsf{AC}] \rightarrow [\mathsf{city}],\ t_{p_1} = (131 \parallel \text{Edi}))$,
φ_3: $\mathsf{tran}([\mathsf{city}, \mathsf{phn}] \rightarrow [\mathsf{St}, \mathsf{AC}, \mathsf{post}],\ t_{p_3} = (\_, \_ \parallel \_, \_, \_))$
φ_4: $\mathsf{tran}([\mathsf{FN}] \rightarrow [\mathsf{FN}],\ t_{p_4} = (\text{Bob} \parallel \text{Robert}))$

Note that FDs are a special case of CFDs in which pattern tuples consist of only wildcards, *e.g.*, φ_3 given above. □

To give the formal semantics of CFDs, we use an operator $\asymp$ defined on constants and '_': $v_1 \asymp v_2$ if either $v_1 = v_2$, or one of v_1, v_2 is '_'. The operator $\asymp$ naturally extends to tuples, *e.g.*, (131, Edi) $\asymp$ (_, Edi) but (020, Ldn) $\not\asymp$ (_, Edi).

Consider an instance D of R. We say that D *satisfies* the CFD φ, denoted by $D \models \varphi$, iff for *all* tuples t_1, t_2 in D, if $t_1[X] = t_2[X] \asymp t_p[X]$, then $t_1[Y] = t_2[Y] \asymp t_p[Y]$.

Example 2.2: Recall the tran instance D of Fig. 1(b) and the CFDs of Example 2.1. Observe that $D \not\models \varphi_1$ since tuple

$t_1[\mathsf{AC}] = t_{p_1}[\mathsf{AC}]$, but $t_1[\mathsf{city}] \neq t_{p_1}[\mathsf{city}]$, *i.e.*, the single tuple t_1 violates φ_1. Similarly, $D \not\models \varphi_4$, as t_3 does not satisfy φ_4. Intuitively, φ_4 says that no tuple t can have $t[\mathsf{FN}] =$ Bob (it has to be changed to Robert). In contrast, $D \models \varphi_3$: there exist no distinct tuples in D that agree on city and phn. □

We say that an instance D of R *satisfies* a set Σ of CFDs, denoted by $D \models \Sigma$, if $D \models \varphi$ for each $\varphi \in \Sigma$.

2.2 Positive and Negative Matching Dependencies

Following [18,24], we define matching dependencies (MDs) in terms of a set Υ of similarity predicates, *e.g.*, q-grams, Jaro distance or edit distance (see *e.g.*, [16] for a survey).

We define positive MDs and negative MDs across a data relation schema R and a master relation schema R_m.

Positive MDs. A positive MD ψ on (R, R_m) is defined as:

$\bigwedge_{j\in[1,k]}(R[A_j] \approx_j R_m[B_j]) \rightarrow \bigwedge_{i\in[1,h]}(R[E_i] \rightleftharpoons R_m[F_i])$,

where (1) for each $j \in [1,k]$, A_j and B_j are attributes of R and R_m, respectively, with the same domain; similarly for E_i and F_i ($i \in [1,h]$); and (2) $\approx_j$ is a similarity predicate in Υ that is defined in the domain of $R[A_j]$ and $R_m[B_j]$. We refer to $\bigwedge_{j\in[1,k]}(R[A_j] \approx_j R_m[B_j])$ and $\bigwedge_{i\in[1,h]}(R[E_i] \rightleftharpoons R_m[F_i])$ as the LHS (premise) and RHS of ψ, respectively.

Note that MDs were originally defined on one or more unreliable data sources (see [18] for a detailed discussion of their dynamic semantics). In contrast, we focus on matching tuples across a dirty source D and a master relation D_m. To cope with this, we refine the semantics of MDs as follows.

For a tuple $t \in D$ and a tuple $s \in D_m$, if for each $j \in [1,k]$, $t[A_j]$ and $s[B_j]$ are similar, *i.e.*, $t[A_j] \approx_j s[B_j]$, then $t[E_i]$ is *changed* to $s[F_i]$, the clean master data, for each $i \in [1,h]$.

We say that an instance D of R *satisfies* the MD ψ *w.r.t. master data* D_m, denoted by $(D, D_m) \models \psi$, iff for *all* tuples t in D and *all* tuples s in D_m, if $t[A_j] \approx_j s[B_j]$ for $j \in [1,k]$, then $t[E_i] = s[F_i]$ for all $i \in [1,h]$.

Intuitively, $(D, D_m) \models \psi$ if no more tuples from D can be matched (and hence updated) with master tuples in D_m.

Example 2.3: Recall MD ψ given in Example 1.1. Consider an instance D_1 of tran consisting of a single tuple t_1', where $t_1'[\mathsf{city}] =$ Ldn and $t_1'[A] = t_1[A]$ for all the other attributes, for t_1 given in Fig. 1(b). Then $(D_1, D_m) \not\models \psi$, since $t_1'[\mathsf{FN}, \mathsf{phn}] \neq s_1[\mathsf{FN}, \mathsf{tel}]$ while $(t_1'[\mathsf{LN}, \mathsf{city}, \mathsf{St}, \mathsf{post}\,] = s_1[\mathsf{LN}, \mathsf{city}, \mathsf{St}, \mathsf{Zip}]$ and $t_1'[\mathsf{FN}] \approx s_1[\mathsf{FN}]$. This suggests that we correct $t_1'[\mathsf{FN}, \mathsf{phn}]$ using the master data $s_1[\mathsf{FN}, \mathsf{tel}]$. □

Negative MDs. Along the same lines as [3,36], we define a negative MD ψ^- as follows:

$\bigwedge_{j\in[1,k]}(R[A_j] \neq R_m[B_j]) \rightarrow \bigvee_{i\in[1,h]}(R[E_i] \not\rightleftharpoons R_m[F_i])$.

It states that for any tuple $t \in D$ and any tuple $s \in D_m$, if $t[A_j] \neq s[B_j]$ ($j \in [1,k]$), then t and s may not be identified.

Example 2.4: A negative MD defined on (tran, card) is:

ψ_1^-: $\mathsf{tran}[\mathsf{gd}] \neq \mathsf{card}[\mathsf{gd}] \rightarrow \bigvee_{i\in[1,7]}(\mathsf{tran}[A_i] \not\rightleftharpoons \mathsf{card}[B_i])$,

where (A_i, B_i) ranges over (FN, FN), (LN, LN), (St, St), (AC, AC), (city, city), (post, zip) and (phn, tel). It says that a male and a female may not refer to the same person. □

We say that an instance D of R *satisfies* the negative MD ψ^- *w.r.t. master data* D_m, denoted by $(D, D_m) \models \psi^-$, if for *all* tuples t in D and *all* tuples s in D_m, if $t[A_j] \neq s[B_j]$ for all $j \in [1,k]$, then there exists $i \in [1,h]$ such that $t[E_i] \neq s[F_i]$.

An instance D of R *satisfies* a set Γ of (positive, negative) MDs *w.r.t. master data* D_m, denoted by $(D, D_m) \models \Gamma$, if $(D, D_m) \models \psi$ for all $\psi \in \Gamma$.

Normalized CFDs and MDs. Given a CFD (resp. MD) ξ, we use LHS(ξ) and RHS(ξ) to denote the LHS and RHS of ξ, respectively. It is called *normalized* if $|\text{RHS}(\xi)| = 1$, *i.e.*, its right-hand side consists of a single attribute (resp. attribute pair). As shown by [17,18], every CFD ξ (resp. MD) can be expressed as an equivalent set S_ξ of CFDs (resp. MDs), such that the cardinality of S_ξ is bounded by the size of RHS(ξ).

For instance, CFDs φ_1, φ_2 and φ_4 of Example 1.1 are normalized. While φ_3 is not normalized, it can be converted to an equivalent set of CFDs of the form $([\mathsf{city}, \mathsf{phn}] \rightarrow A_i, t_{p_i})$, where A_i ranges over St, AC and post, and t_{p_i} consists of wildcards only; similarly for MD ψ.

We consider normalized CFDs (MDs) only in the sequel.

3. A Uniform Framework for Data Cleaning

We propose a rule-based framework for data cleaning. It treats CFDs and MDs uniformly as *cleaning rules*, which tell us how to fix errors, and seamlessly interleaves matching and repairing operations (Section 3.1). Using cleaning rules we introduce a tri-level data cleaning solution, which generates fixes with various levels of accuracy, depending on the information available about the data (Section 3.2).

Consider a (possibly dirty) relation D of schema R, a master relation D_m of schema R_m, and a set $\Theta = \Sigma \cup \Gamma$, where Σ is a set of CFDs on R, and Γ is a set of MDs on (R, R_m).

3.1 A Rule-based Logical Framework

We first state the data cleaning problem, and then define cleaning rules derived from CFDs and MDs.

Data cleaning. Following [4], we state the *data cleaning problem*, referred to as DCP, as follows. It takes D, D_m and Θ as input, and computes a *repair* D_r of D, *i.e.*, another database such that (a) $D_r \models \Sigma$, (b) $(D_r, D_m) \models \Gamma$, and (c) $\mathsf{cost}(D_r, D)$ is minimum. Intuitively, (a) D_r should be *consistent*, (b) no more tuples in D_r can be *matched* to master data, and (c) D_r is accurate and is close to the original data D. Following [9], we define $\mathsf{cost}(D_r, D)$ as:

$$\sum_{t\in D}\sum_{A\in\mathsf{attr}(R)} t(A).\mathsf{cf} * \frac{\mathsf{dis}_A(t[A], t'[A])}{\mathsf{max}(|t[A]|, |t'[A]|)}$$

where (a) tuple $t' \in D_r$ is the repair of tuple $t \in D$, (b) $\mathsf{dis}_A(v, v')$ is the distance between values $v, v' \in \mathsf{dom}(A)$; the smaller the distance is, the closer the two values are to each other; (c) $|t[A]|$ denotes the size of $t[A]$; and (d) $t[A].\mathsf{cf}$ is the *confidence* placed by the user in the accuracy of the attribute $t[A]$ (see the cf rows in Fig. 1(b)).

This quality metric says that *the higher the confidence* of the attribute $t[A]$ is and *the more distant* v' is from v, the more costly the change is. Thus, *the smaller* $\mathsf{cost}(D_r, D)$ is, *the more accurate and closer to* the original data D_r is. We use $\mathsf{dis}(v, v')/\mathsf{max}(|v|, |v'|)$ to measure the similarity of v and v' to ensure that longer strings with 1-character difference are closer than shorter strings with 1-character difference.

As remarked in [9], confidence can be derived via provenance analysis, which can be reinforced by recent work on determining the reliability of data sources (*e.g.*, [14]).

Cleaning rules. A variety of integrity constraints have been studied for data repairing (*e.g.*, [6,9,17,37]). As observed by [19], while there constraints help us determine whether data is dirty or not, *i.e.*, whether errors are present in the data, they do not tell us how to correct the errors.

To make better practical use of constraints in data cleaning, we define *cleaning rules*, which tell us what attributes should be updated and to what value they should be changed. From each MD in Γ and each CFD in Σ, we derive a cleaning rule as follows, based on fuzzy logic [26].

(1) MDs. Consider an MD $\psi = \bigwedge_{j\in[1,k]}(R[A_j] \approx_j R_m[B_j]) \rightarrow (R[E] \rightleftharpoons R_m[F])$. The *cleaning rule* derived from ψ, denoted by γ_ψ, *applies* a master tuple $s \in D_m$ to a tuple $t \in D$ if $t[A_j] \approx_j s[B_j]$ for each $j \in [1, k]$. It *updates* t by letting (a) $t[E] := s[F]$ and (b) $t[C].\mathsf{cf} := d$ for each $C \in E$, where d is the minimum $t[A_j].\mathsf{cf}$ for all $j \in [1, k]$ if $\approx_j$ is '='.

That is, γ_ψ corrects $t[E]$ with clean master value $s[F]$, and infers the new confidence of $t[E]$ following fuzzy logic [26].

(2) Constant CFDs. Consider a CFD $\varphi_c = R(X \rightarrow A, t_{p_1})$, where $t_{p_1}[A]$ is a *constant*. The *cleaning rule* derived from φ_c *applies to* a tuple $t \in D$ if $t[X] \asymp t_{p_1}[X]$ but $t[A] \neq t_{p_1}[A]$. It *updates* t by letting (a) $t[A] := t_{p_1}[A]$, and (b) $t[A].\mathsf{cf} = d$, where d is the minimum $t[A'].\mathsf{cf}$ for all $A' \in X$. That is, the rule corrects $t[A]$ with the constant in the CFD.

(3) Variable CFDs. Consider a CFD $\varphi_v = (Y \rightarrow B, t_{p_2})$, where $t_{p_2}[B]$ is a wildcard '_'. The *cleaning rule* derived from φ_v is used to *apply* a tuple $t_2 \in D$ to another tuple $t_1 \in D$, where $t_1[Y] = t_2[Y] \asymp t_{p_2}[Y]$ but $t_1[B] \neq t_2[B]$. It *updates* t_1 by letting (a) $t_1[B] := t_2[B]$, and (b) $t_1[B].\mathsf{cf}$ be the minimum $t_1[B'].\mathsf{cf}$ and $t_2[B'].\mathsf{cf}$ for all $B' \in Y$.

While cleaning rules derived from MDs are similar to editing rules of [19], rules derived from (constant or variables) CFDs are not studied in [19]. We use confidence information and infer new confidences based on fuzzy logic [26].

Embedding negative MDs. Recall negative MDs from Section 2.2. The example below tells us that negative MDs can be converted to equivalent positive MDs. As a result, there is no need to treat them separately.

Example 3.1: Consider MD ψ in Example 1.1 and negative MD ψ^- in Example 2.4. We define ψ' by incorporating the premise (gd) of ψ^- into the premise of ψ:

ψ': $\mathsf{tran}[\mathsf{LN}, \mathsf{city}, \mathsf{St}, \mathsf{post}, \mathsf{gd}] = \mathsf{card}[\mathsf{LN}, \mathsf{city}, \mathsf{St}, \mathsf{zip}, \mathsf{gd}] \wedge$
$\mathsf{tran}[\mathsf{FN}] \approx \mathsf{card}[\mathsf{FN}] \rightarrow \mathsf{tran}[\mathsf{FN}, \mathsf{phn}] \rightleftharpoons \mathsf{card}[\mathsf{FN}, \mathsf{tel}]$.

Then no tuples with different genders can be identified as the same person, which is precisely what ψ^- is to enforce. In other words, the positive MD ψ' is equivalent to the positive MD ψ and the negative MD ψ^-. □

Indeed, it suffices to consider only positive MDs.

Proposition 3.1: *Given a set Γ_m^+ of positive MDs and a set Γ_m^- of negative MDs, there exists an algorithm that computes a set Γ_m of positive MDs in $O(|\Gamma_m^+||\Gamma_m^-|)$ time such that Γ_m is equivalent to $\Gamma_m^+ \cup \Gamma_m^-$.* □

A uniform framework. By treating both CFDs and MDs as cleaning rules, one can uniformly interleave matching and repairing operations, to facilitate their interactions.

Example 3.2: As shown in Example 1.1, to clean tuples t_3 and t_4 of Fig. 1(b), one needs to interleave matching and repairing operations. These can be readily done by using cleaning rules derived from φ_2, φ_4, ψ and φ_3. Indeed, the cleaning process described in Example 1.1 is actually carried out by applying these rules. There is no need to distinguish between matching and repairing in the cleaning process. □

3.2 A Tri-level Data Cleaning Solution

Based on cleaning rules, we develop a data cleaning system UniClean. It takes as input a dirty relation D, a master

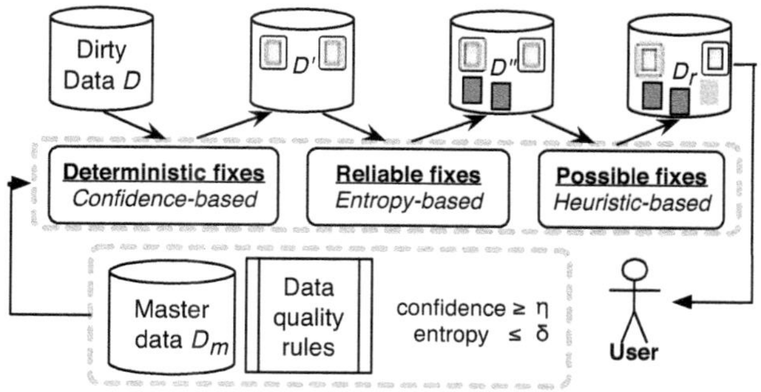

Figure 2: Framework Overview

relation D_m, a set of cleaning rules derived from Θ, as well as thresholds $\eta, \delta \in [0, 1]$ set by the users for confidence and entropy, respectively. It generates a repair D_r of D with a small $\mathsf{cost}(D_r, D)$, such that $D_r \models \Sigma$ and $(D_r, D_m) \models \Gamma$.

As opposed to previous repairing systems [6, 9, 19, 20, 28, 38], UniClean generates fixes by unifying matching and repairing, via cleaning rules. Further, it stresses the accuracy by distinguishing these fixes with three levels of accuracy. Indeed, various fixes are found by three algorithms executed one after another, as shown in Fig. 2 and illustrated below.

(1) Deterministic fixes based on confidences. The first algorithm identifies erroneous attributes $t[A]$ to which there exists a unique fix, referred to as a *deterministic fix*, when some attributes of t are accurate. It fixes those errors based on confidence: it uses a cleaning rule to update $t[A]$ *only if* certain attributes of t have confidence above the threshold η. It is evident that such fixes are accurate up to η.

(2) Reliable fixes based on entropy. For attributes with *low or unavailable confidence*, we correct them based on the relative certainty of the data, measured by entropy. Entropy has proved effective in data transmission [23] and compression [39], among other things. We use entropy to clean data: we apply a cleaning rule γ to update an erroneous attribute $t[A]$ only if the entropy of γ for certain attributes of t is below the threshold δ. Fixes generated via entropy are accurate to a certain degree, and are marked as *reliable fixes*.

(3) Possible fixes. Not all errors can be fixed in the first two phases. For the remaining errors, we adopt heuristic methods to generate fixes, referred to as *possible fixes*. To this end we extend the method of [9], by supporting cleaning rules derived from both CFDs and MDs. It can be verified that the heuristic method always finds a repair D_r of D such that $D_r \models \Sigma$, $(D_r, D_m) \models \Gamma$, while keeping all the deterministic fixes produced earlier *unchanged* (a proof can be found in the full version of the paper).

At the end of the process, fixes are marked with three distinct signs, indicating deterministic, reliable and possible, respectively. We shall present methods based on confidence and entropy in Sections 5 and 6, respectively. Due to the space constraints, we omit the algorithm for possible fixes, but encourage the reader to consult [9] for details.

4. Fundamental Problems for Data Cleaning

We now investigate fundamental problems associated with data cleaning. We first study the consistency and implication problems for CFDs and MDs taken together, from which cleaning rules are derived. We then establish the complexity bounds of the data cleaning problem as well as its termination and determinism analyses. These problems are not only of theoretical interest, but are also important to the development of data cleaning algorithms. The main conclusion of this section is that data cleaning via matching and repairing is inherently difficult: all these problems are intractable.

Consider a relation D, a master data D_m, and a set $\Theta = \Sigma \cup \Gamma$ of CFDs and MDs, as stated in Section 3.

4.1 Reasoning about Data Quality Rules

There are two classical problems for data quality rules.

The *consistency problem* is to determine, given D_m and $\Theta = \Sigma \cup \Gamma$, whether there exists a nonempty instance D of R such that $D \models \Sigma$ and $(D, D_m) \models \Gamma$.

Intuitively, this is to determine whether the rules in Θ are dirty themselves. The practical need for the consistency analysis is evident: it does not make sense to derive cleaning rules from Θ before Θ is assured consistent itself.

We say that Θ *implies* another CFD (resp. MD) ξ, denoted by $\Sigma \models \xi$, if for any instance D of R, whenever $D \models \Sigma$ and $(D, D_m) \models \Gamma$, then $D \models \xi$ (resp. $(D, D_m) \models \xi$).

The *implication problem* is to determine, given D_m, Σ and another CFD (or MD) ξ, whether $\Sigma \models \xi$.

Intuitively, the implication analysis helps us find and remove redundant rules from Σ, *i.e.,* those that are a logical consequence of other rules in Σ, to improve performance.

These problems have been studied for CFDs and MDs separately. It is known that the consistency problem for MDs is trivial: any set of MDs is consistent [18]. In contrast, there exist CFDs that are inconsistent, and the consistency analysis of CFDs is NP-complete [17]. It is also known that the implication problem for MDs and CFDs is in quadratic time [18] and coNP-complete [17], respectively.

We show that these problems for CFDs and MDs put together have the same complexity as their CFDs counterparts. That is, adding MDs to CFDs does not make our lives harder.

Theorem 4.1: *For CFDs and MDs put together, the consistency problem is NP-complete, and the implication problem is coNP-complete (when ξ is either a CFD or an MD).* □

Proof: The upper bounds are verified by establishing a small model property. The lower bounds follow from the intractability for their CFD counterparts, a special case. □

In the rest of the paper we consider only collections Σ of CFDs and MDs that are consistent.

4.2 Analyzing the Data Cleaning Problem

Recall the data cleaning problem (DCP) from Section 3.

Complexity bounds. One wants to know how costly it is to compute a repair D_r. Below we show that it is intractable to decide whether there exists D_r with $\mathsf{cost}(D_r, D)$ below a predefine bound. Worse still, it is infeasible in practice to find PTIME approximation algorithm with performance guarantee. Indeed, the problem is not even in APX, the class of problems that allow PTIME approximation algorithms with approximation ratio bounded by a constant.

Theorem 4.2: *(a) The data cleaning problem (DCP) is NP-complete. (b) Unless P = NP, for any constant ϵ, there exists no* PTIME *ϵ-approximation algorithm for DCP.* □

Proof: (a) The upper bound is verified by giving an NP algorithm. The lower bound is by reduction from 3SAT [34]. (b) This is verified by reduction from 3SAT, using gap techniques [34]. Given any constant ϵ, we show that there exists an algorithm with approximation ratio ϵ for DCP iff there is a PTIME algorithm for deciding 3SAT. □

Symbols	Semantics
$\Theta = \Sigma \cup \Gamma$	A set Σ of CFDs and a set Γ of MDs
η, δ_1, δ_2	Confidence threshold, update threshold, and entropy threshold, respectively
ρ	Selection operator in relational algebra
π	Projection operator in relational algebra
$\Delta(\bar{y})$	The set $\{t \mid t \in D, t[Y] = \bar{y}\}$ for each $\bar{y}$ in $\pi_Y(\rho_{Y \asymp t_p[Y]} D)$ *w.r.t.* CFD $(Y \rightarrow B,\ t_p)$

Table 1: Summary of notations

It is known that data repairing alone is NP-complete [9]. Theorem 4.2 tells us that when matching with MDs is incorporated, the problem is intractable and approximation-hard.

Termination and determinism analyses. There are two natural questions about rule-based data cleaning methods such as the one proposed in Section 3. (a) The *termination problem* is to determine whether a rule-based process stops. That is, it reaches a *fixpoint*, such that no cleaning rules can be further applied. (b) The *determinism problem* asks whether all terminating cleaning processes end up with the same repair, *i.e.,* all of them reach a *unique* fixpoint.

The need for studying these problems is evident. A rule-based process is often *non-deterministic*: multiple rules can be applied at the same time. We want to know whether the output of the process is independent of the order of the rules applied. Worse, it is known that even for repairing only, a rule-based method may lead to an *infinite* process [9].

Example 4.1: Consider the CFD $\varphi_1 = \mathsf{tran}([\mathsf{AC}] \rightarrow [\mathsf{city}],\ t_{p_1} = (131 \parallel \text{Edi}))$ given in Example 2.1, and another CFD $\varphi_5 = \mathsf{tran}([\mathsf{post}] \rightarrow [\mathsf{city}],\ t_{p_5} = (\text{EH8 9AB} \parallel \text{Ldn}))$. Consider D_1 consisting of a single tuple t_2 given in Fig. 1. Then a repairing process for D_1 with φ_1 and φ_5 may fail to terminate: it changes $t_2[\mathsf{city}]$ to Edi and Ldn back and forth. □

No matter how important, it is beyond reach in practice to find efficient solutions to these two problems.

Theorem 4.3: *The termination and determinism problems are both PSPACE-complete for rule-based data cleaning.* □

Proof: We verify the lower bound of these problems by reduction from the halting problem for linear bound automata, which is PSPACE-complete [2]. We show the upper bound by providing an algorithm for each of the two problems, which uses polynomial space in the size of input. □

5. Deterministic Fixes with Data Confidence

As shown in Fig. 2, system UniClean first identifies deterministic fixes based on confidence analysis and master data. In this section we define deterministic fixes (Section 5.1), and present an efficient algorithm to find them (Section 5.2).

In Table 1 we summarize some notations to be used in this Section and Section 6, for the ease of reference.

5.1 Deterministic Fixes

We define deterministic fixes *w.r.t.* a *confidence threshold* η determined by domain experts. When η is high enough, *e.g.,* if it is close to 1, an attribute $t[A]$ is assured correct if $t[A].\mathsf{cf} \geq \eta$. We refer to such attributes as *asserted* attributes. Recall from Section 3 the definition of cleaning rules derived from MDs and CFDs. In the first phase of UniClean, we apply a cleaning rule γ to tuples in a database D only when the attributes in the premise (*i.e.,* LHS) of γ are all asserted. We say that a fix is *deterministic w.r.t.* γ and η if it is generated as follows, based on how γ is derived.

(1) *From an MD* $\psi = \bigwedge_{j \in [1,k]} (R[A_j] \approx_j R_m[B_j]) \rightarrow (R[E]$

$\rightleftharpoons R_m[F]$). Suppose that γ applies a tuple $s \in D_m$ to a tuple $t \in D$, and generates a fix $t[E] := s[F]$ (see Section 3.1). Then the fix is *deterministic* if $t[A_j]$.cf $\geq \eta$ for all $j \in [1, k]$ and moreover, $t[E]$.cf $< \eta$. That is, $t[E]$ is changed to the master value $s[F]$ only if (a) all the premise attributes $t[A_j]$'s are asserted, and (b) $t[E]$ is not yet asserted.

(2) From a constant CFD $\varphi_c = R(X \rightarrow A,\ t_{p_1})$. Suppose that γ applies to a tuple $t \in D$ and changes $t[A]$ to the constant $t_{p_1}[A]$ in φ_c. Then the fix is *deterministic* if $t[A_i]$.cf $\geq \eta$ for all $A_i \in X$ and $t[A]$.cf $< \eta$.

(3) From a variable CFD $\varphi_v = (Y \rightarrow B,\ t_p)$. For each $\bar{y}$ in $\pi_Y(\rho_{Y \asymp t_p[Y]} D)$, we define $\Delta(\bar{y})$ to be the set $\{t \mid t \in D, t[Y] = \bar{y}\}$, where π and ρ are the projection and selection operators, respectively, in relational algebra [1]. That is, for all t_1, t_2 in $\Delta(\bar{y})$, $t_1[Y] = t_2[Y] = \bar{y} \asymp t_p[Y]$.

Suppose that γ applies a tuple t_2 in $\Delta(\bar{y})$ to another t_1 in $\Delta(\bar{y})$ for some $\bar{y}$, and changes $t_1[B]$ to $t_2[B]$. Then the fix is *deterministic* if (a) for all $B_i \in Y$, $t_1[B_i]$.cf $\geq \eta$ and $t_2[B_i]$.cf $\geq \eta$, (b) $t_2[B]$.cf $\geq \eta$, and moreover, (c) t_2 is the only tuple in $\Delta(\bar{y})$ with $t_2[B]$.cf $\geq \eta$ (hence $t_1[B]$.cf $< \eta$). That is, all the premise attributes of γ are asserted, and $t_2[B]$ is the only value of B-attribute in $\Delta(\bar{y})$ that is assumed correct, while $t_1[B]$ is suspected erroneous.

As observed by [19], when data quality rules and asserted attributes are assured correct, the fixes generated are unique (called "certain" in [19]). While [19] only considers MDs, the observation remains intact for CFDs and MDs.

Note that when an attribute $t[A]$ is updated by a deterministic fix, its confidence $t[A]$.cf is upgraded to be the minimum of the confidences of the premise attributes (see Section 3.1). As a result, $t[A]$ also becomes asserted, since all premise attributes have confidence values above η. In turn $t[A]$ can be used to generate deterministic fixes for other attributes in the cleaning process. In other words, the process for finding deterministic fixes in a database D is *recursive*.

Nevertheless, in the rest of the section we show that deterministic fixes can be found in PTIME, stated as follows.

Theorem 5.1: *Given master data D_m and a set Θ of CFDs and MDs, all deterministic fixes in a relation D can be found in $O(|D||D_m|\mathsf{size}(\Theta))$ time, where $\mathsf{size}(\Theta)$ is Θ's length.* □

5.2 Confidence-based Data Cleaning

We next present the algorithm, followed by the indexing structures and procedures that it employs.

Algorithm. The algorithm, denoted by cRepair, is shown in Fig. 3. It takes as input CFDs Σ, MDs Γ, master data D_m, dirty data D, and a confidence threshold η. It returns a partially cleaned repair D' with deterministic fixes marked.

Algorithm cRepair first initializes variables and indexing structures (lines 1–6). It then recursively computes deterministic fixes (lines 7–15), by invoking procedures vCFDInfer (line 12), cCFDInfer (line 13), or MDInfer (line 14), for rules derived from variable CFDs, constant CFDs, or MDs, respectively. It checks each tuple at most once *w.r.t.* each rule, makes more attributes asserted at each step, and uses these attributes to identify more deterministic fixes. It terminates when no more deterministic fixes can be found (line 15). Finally, a partially cleaned database D' is returned in which all deterministic fixes are marked (line 16).

Indexing structures. The algorithm uses the following indexing structures, to improve performance.

```
Algorithm cRepair
Input: CFDs Σ, MDs Γ, master data D_m, dirty data D, and
       confidence threshold η.
Output: A partial repair D' of D with deterministic fixes.
1.  D' := D;   H_ξ := ∅ for each variable CFD ξ ∈ Σ;
2.  for each t ∈ D' do
3.     Q[t] := ∅;  P[t] := ∅;
4.     count[t, ξ] :=0 for each ξ ∈ Σ ∪ Γ;
5.     for each attribute A ∈ attr(Σ ∪ Γ) do
6.        if t[A].cf ≥ η then update(t, A);
7.  repeat
8.    for each tuple t ∈ D' do
9.      while Q[t] is not empty do
10.        ξ := Q[t].pop();
11.        case ξ of
12.        (1) variable CFD: D' := vCFDInfer(t, ξ, η);
13.        (2) constant CFD: D' := cCFDInfer(t, ξ, η);
14.        (3) MD:           D' := MDInfer(t, η, D_m, ξ);
15. until Q[t'] is empty for any t' ∈ D';
16. return D'.
```

Figure 3: Algorithm cRepair

Hash tables. We maintain a hash table for each variable CFD $\varphi = R(Y \rightarrow B,\ t_p)$, denoted as H_φ. Given a $\bar{y} \in \rho_{Y \asymp t_p[Y]}(D)$ as the key, it returns a pair (list, val) as the value, *i.e.*, $\mathsf{H}(\bar{y})$ = (list, val), where (a) list consists of all the tuples t in $\Delta(\bar{y})$ such that $t[B_i]$.cf $\geq \eta$ for each attribute $B_i \in Y$, and (b) val is $t[B]$ if it is the only item in $\Delta(\bar{y})$ with $t[B]$.cf $\geq \eta$; otherwise, val is nil. Notably, there exist no two t_1, t_2 in $\Delta(\bar{y})$ such that $t_1[B] \neq t_2[B]$, $t_1[B]$.cf $\geq \eta$ and $t_2[B]$.cf $\geq \eta$, if the confidence placed by the users is correct.

Queues. We maintain for each tuple t a queue of rules that can be applied to t, denoted as $\mathsf{Q}[t]$. More specifically, $\mathsf{Q}[t]$ contains all rules $\xi \in \Theta$, where $t[C]$.cf $\geq \eta$ for all attributes C in LHS(ξ). That is, the premise of ξ is asserted in t.

Hash sets. For each tuple $t \in D$, $\mathsf{P}[t]$ stores the set of variable CFDs $\varphi \in \mathsf{Q}[t]$ such that $\mathsf{H}_\varphi(t[\text{LHS}(\varphi)])$.val = nil, *i.e.*, no B attribute in $\Delta(t[\text{LHS}(\varphi)])$ has a high enough confidence.

Counters. For each tuple $t \in D$ and each rule $\xi \in \Theta$, count$[t, \xi]$ maintains the number of current values of the attributes $C \in \text{LHS}(\xi)$ such that $t[C]$.cf $\geq \eta$.

Procedures. We now present the procedures of cRepair.

update. Given a new deterministic fix for $t[A]$, it propagates the change, to find other deterministic fixes with $t[A]$. (a) For each rule ξ, if $A \in \text{LHS}(\xi)$, count$[t, \xi]$ is increased by 1 as one more attribute becomes asserted. (b) If all attributes in LHS(ξ) are asserted, ξ is inserted into the queue $\mathsf{Q}[t]$. (c) For a variable CFD $\xi' \in \mathsf{P}[t]$, if RHS(ξ') is A and $\mathsf{H}_{\xi'}(t[\text{LHS}(\xi')])$.val = nil, the newly asserted $t[A]$ makes it possible for tuples in $\mathsf{H}_{\xi'}(t[\text{LHS}(\xi')])$.list to have a deterministic fix. Thus ξ' is removed from $\mathsf{P}[t]$ and added to $\mathsf{Q}[t]$.

vCFDInfer. Given a tuple t, a variable CFD ξ and the confidence threshold η, it finds a deterministic fix for t by applying ξ if it exists. If the tuple t and the pattern tuple $t_{(p,\xi)}$ match on their LHS(ξ) attributes, it does the following.

(a) If $t[\text{RHS}(\xi)]$.cf $\geq \eta$ and if no B-attribute value in $\mathsf{H}_\xi(t[\text{LHS}(\xi)])$.list is asserted, it takes $t[\text{RHS}(\xi)]$ as the B value in the set, and propagates the change via update.

(b) If $t[\text{RHS}(\xi)] < \eta$ but there is an asserted B-attribute value val in $\mathsf{H}_\xi(t[\text{LHS}(\xi)])$.list, it makes a deterministic fix by $t[\text{RHS}(\xi)]$:= val, and propagates the change via update.

(c) If $t[\text{RHS}(\xi)] < \eta$ and there is no asserted B-attribute in $\mathsf{H}_\xi(t[\text{LHS}(\xi)])$.list, no deterministic fix can be made yet, and t is added to $\mathsf{H}_\xi(t[\text{LHS}(\xi)])$.list and $\mathsf{P}[t]$, for later checking.

cCFDInfer *and* MDInfer. The first one takes as input a tuple t, a constant CFD ξ and the threshold η. The second one takes as input t, η, master data D_m and an MD ξ. They find deterministic fixes by applying the rules derived from ξ, as described earlier. The changes made are propagated by invoking procedure update(t, RHS(ξ)).

Example 5.1: Consider master data D_m and relation D of Fig. 1. Assume Θ consists of rules ξ_1, ξ_2 and ξ_3 derived from CFDs φ_1, φ_3 and MD ψ of Example 1.1, respectively. Let the threshold η be 0.8. Using Θ and D_m, cRepair finds deterministic fixes for $t_1, t_2 \in D$ *w.r.t.* η as follows.

(1) After initialization (lines 1–6), we have: (a) $\mathsf{H}_{\xi_2} = \emptyset$; (b) $\mathsf{Q}[t_1] = \{\xi_1\}$, $\mathsf{Q}[t_2] = \{\xi_2\}$; (c) $\mathsf{P}[t_1] = \mathsf{P}[t_2] = \emptyset$; and (d) $\mathsf{count}[t_1, \xi_1] = 1$, $\mathsf{count}[t_1, \xi_2] = 0$, $\mathsf{count}[t_1, \xi_3] = 3$, $\mathsf{count}[t_2, \xi_1] = 0$, $\mathsf{count}[t_2, \xi_2] = 2$, and $\mathsf{count}[t_2, \xi_3] = 2$.

(2) After $\xi_2 \in \mathsf{Q}[t_2]$ is checked (line 12), we have $\mathsf{Q}[t_2] = \emptyset$, $\mathsf{P}[t_2] = \{\xi_2\}$, and $\mathsf{H}_{\xi_2}(t_2[\mathsf{city}, \mathsf{phn}]) = (\{t_2\}, \mathsf{nil})$.

(3) After $\xi_1 \in \mathsf{Q}[t_1]$ is applied (line 13), $\mathsf{Q}[t_1] = \{\xi_3\}$, $\mathsf{count}[t_1, \xi_2] = 1$ and $\mathsf{count}[t_1, \xi_3] = 4$. This step finds a deterministic fix $t_1[\mathsf{city}]$:= Edi. It upgrades $t_1[\mathsf{city}]$.cf:=0.8.

(4) When $\xi_3 \in \mathsf{Q}[t_1]$ is used (line 14), it makes a deterministic fix $t_1[\mathsf{phn}] := s_1[\mathsf{tel}]$, and lets $t_1[\mathsf{phn}].\mathsf{cf} = 0.8$. Now we have $\mathsf{Q}[t_1] = \{\xi_2\}$ and $\mathsf{count}[t_1, \xi_2] = 2$.

(5) When $\xi_2 \in \mathsf{Q}[t_1]$ is used (line 14), it finds a deterministic fix by letting $t_2[\mathsf{St}] = t_1[\mathsf{St}]$:= 10 Oak St, and $t_2[\mathsf{St}].\mathsf{cf}$:= 0.8. Now we obtain $\mathsf{Q}[t_1] = \emptyset$ and $\mathsf{P}[t_2] = \emptyset$.

(6) Finally, the process terminates since $\mathsf{Q}[t_1] = \mathsf{Q}[t_2] = \emptyset$.

Similarly, for tuples $t_3, t_4 \in D$, cRepair finds a deterministic fix by letting $t_3[\mathsf{city}]$:= Ldn and $t_3[\mathsf{city}].\mathsf{cf}$:= 0.8. □

Suffix trees for similarity checking of MDs. For cleaning rules derived from MDs, we need to conduct *similarity checking*, to which traditional indexing techniques are not directly applicable. To cope with this, we develop a technique based on suffix trees [12]. The measure of similarity adopted is the length of the *longest common substring* of two strings. Generalized suffix trees are built for the blocking process with all the strings in the active domain. When querying the k-most similar strings of v of length $|v|$, we can extract the subtree T of suffix tree that only contains branches related to v, containing at most $|v|^2$ nodes. We traverse T to find the k-most similar strings. In this way, we can identify k similar values from D_m in $O(k|v|^2)$ time, which reduces the search space from $|D_m|$ to a constant number k of tuples. Our experimental study verifies that the technique significantly improves the performance.

Complexity. Each tuple t in D is examined at most twice for each CFD in Σ, and is checked at most $|D_m|$ times for each MD, each tuple. Hence cRepair is in $O(|D||D_m|\mathsf{size}(\Sigma \cup \Gamma))$ time. With the optimization methods above, the time complexity of cRepair is reduced to $O(|D|\mathsf{size}(\Sigma \cup \Gamma))$.

6. Reliable Fixes with Information Entropy

Deterministic fixes may not exist for some attributes, *e.g.*, when their confidences are low or unreliable. To find accurate fixes for these attributes, UniClean looks for evidence from data itself *instead of confidence*, using entropy to measure the degree of certainty. Below we first define entropy for data cleaning (Section 6.1), and present an algorithm to find reliable fixes using entropy (Section 6.2). We then present an indexing structure underlining the algorithm (Section 6.3).

Algorithm eRepair

Input: CFDs Σ, MDs Γ, master data D_m, dirty data D,
  update threshold δ_1, entropy threshold δ_2.
Output: A partial repair D' of D with reliable fixes.

```
O := the order of Σ ∪ Γ, sorted via their dependency graph;
D' := D;
repeat
    for (i = 1; i ≤ |Σ ∪ Γ|; i++) do
        ξ := the i-th rule in O;
        case ξ of
        (1) variable CFD: D' := vCFDReslove(D', ξ, δ1, δ2);
        (2) constant CFD: D' := cCFDReslove(D', ξ, δ1);
        (3) MD:           D' := MDReslove(D', Dm, ξ, δ1);
until there are no changes in D';
return D'.
```

Figure 4: Algorithm eRepair

6.1 Measuring Certainty with Entropy

We start with an overview of the standard information entropy, and then define entropy for resolving conflicts.

Entropy. The entropy of a discrete random variable $\mathcal{X}$ with possible values $\{x_1, \ldots, x_n\}$ is defined as [11, 33]:

$$\mathcal{H}(\mathcal{X}) = \Sigma_{i=1}^{n}(p_i * \log 1/p_i),$$

where p_i is the probability of x_i for $i \in [1, n]$. The entropy measures the degree of the certainty of the value of $\mathcal{X}$: when $\mathcal{H}(\mathcal{X})$ is sufficiently small, it is highly accurate that the value of $\mathcal{X}$ is the x_j having the largest probability p_j. The less $\mathcal{H}(\mathcal{X})$ is, the more accurate the prediction is.

Entropy for variable CFDs. We use entropy to resolve data conflicts. Consider a CFD $\varphi = R(Y \to B, t_p)$ defined on a relation D, where $t_p[B]$ is a wildcard. Note that a deterministic fix may not exist when, *e.g.*, there are t_1, t_2 in $\Delta(\bar{y})$ (see Table 1) such that $t_1[B] \neq t_2[B]$ but both have high confidence. Indeed, using the cleaning rule derived from φ, one may either let $t_1[B] := t_2[B]$ by applying t_2 to t_1, or let $t_2[B] := t_1[B]$ by applying t_1 to t_2.

To find an accurate fix, we define the entropy of φ for $Y = \bar{y}$, denoted by $\mathcal{H}(\varphi|Y = \bar{y})$, as

$$\mathcal{H}(\varphi|Y = \bar{y}) = \Sigma_{i=1}^{k}\left(\frac{\mathsf{cnt}_{YB}(\bar{y}, b_i)}{|\Delta(\bar{y})|} * \log_k \frac{|\Delta(\bar{y})|}{\mathsf{cnt}_{YB}(\bar{y}, b_i)}\right),$$

where (a) $k = |\pi_B(\Delta(\bar{y}))|$, the number of distinct B values in $\Delta(\bar{y})$, (b) for each $i \in [1, k]$, $b_i \in \pi_B(\Delta(\bar{y}))$, (c) $\mathsf{cnt}_{YB}(\bar{y}, b_i)$ denotes the number of tuples $t \in \Delta(\bar{y})$ with $t[B] = b_i$, and (d) $|\Delta(\bar{y})|$ is the number of tuples in $\Delta(\bar{y})$.

Intuitively, we treat $\mathcal{X}(\varphi|Y = \bar{y})$ as a random variable for the value of the B attribute in $\Delta(\bar{y})$, with a set $\pi_B(\Delta(\bar{y}))$ of possible values. The probability for b_i to be the value is $p_i = \frac{\mathsf{cnt}_{YB}(\bar{y}, b_i)}{|\Delta(\bar{y})|}$. When $\mathcal{H}(\varphi|Y = \bar{y})$ is small enough, it is highly accurate to resolve the conflict by letting $t[B] = b_j$ for all $t \in \Delta(\bar{y})$, where b_j is the one with the highest probability, *i.e.*, $\mathsf{cnt}_{YB}(\bar{y}, b_j)$ is maximum among all $b_i \in \pi_B(\Delta(\bar{y}))$.

In particular, $\mathcal{H}(\varphi|Y = \bar{y}) = 1$ when $\mathsf{cnt}_{YB}(\bar{y}, b_i) = \mathsf{cnt}_{BA}(\bar{y}, b_j)$ for all distinct $b_i, b_j \in \pi_B(\Delta(\bar{y}))$. If $\mathcal{H}(\varphi|Y = \bar{y}) = 0$ for all $\bar{y} \in \pi_Y(\rho_{Y \asymp t_p[Y]} D)$, then $D \models \varphi$.

6.2 Entropy-based Data Cleaning

We first describe an algorithm based on entropy, followed by its main procedures and auxiliary structures.

Algorithm. The algorithm, referred to as eRepair, is shown in Fig. 4. Given a set Σ of CFDs, a set Γ of MDs, a master relation D_m, dirty data D, and two thresholds δ_1 and δ_2 for *update frequency* and *entropy*, respectively, it finds reliable fixes for D and returns a (partially cleaned) database D' in which reliable fixes are marked. The deterministic fixes found earlier by cRepair remain unchanged in the process.

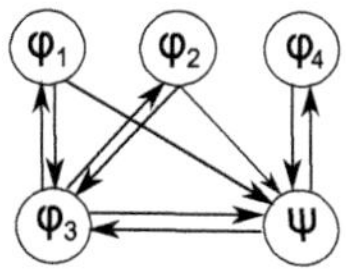

Figure 5: Example dependency graph

In a nutshell, algorithm eRepair first sorts cleaning rules derived from the CFDs and MDs, such that rules with relatively bigger impact are applied early. Following the order, it then applies the rules one by one, until no more reliable fixes can be found. More specifically, it first finds an order $\mathcal{O}$ on the rules in $\Sigma \cup \Gamma$ (line 1). It then repeatedly applies the rules in the order $\mathcal{O}$ to resolve conflicts in D (lines 3–10), by invoking procedures vCFDReslove (line 7), cCFDReslove (line 8) or MDReslove (line 9), based on the types of the rules (lines 5-6). It terminates when either no more rules can be applied or all data values have been changed more than δ_1 times, *i.e.,* when there is no enough information to make reliable fixes (line 10). A partially cleaned database is returned with reliable fixes being marked (line 11).

Procedures. We next present the procedures of eRepair.

Sorting cleaning rules. To avoid unnecessary computation, we sort $\Sigma \cup \Gamma$ based on its *dependency graph* $G = (V, E)$. Each rule of $\Sigma \cup \Gamma$ is a node in V, and there is an edge from a rule ξ_1 to another ξ_2 if ξ_2 can be applied after the application of ξ_1. There exists an edge $(u, v) \in E$ from node u to node v if $\text{RHS}(\xi_u) \cap \text{LHS}(\xi_v) \neq \emptyset$. Intuitively, edge (u, v) indicates that whether ξ_v can be applied depends on the outcome of applying ξ_u. Hence, ξ_u should be applied before ξ_v. For instance, the dependency graph of the CFDs and MDs given in Example 1.1 is shown in Fig. 5.

Based on G, we sort the rules as follows. (1) Find strongly connected components (SCCs) in G, in linear time [10]. (2) By treating each SCC as a single node, we convert G into a DAG. (3) Find a topological order on the nodes in the DAG. That is, a rule ξ_1 is applied before another ξ_2 if the application of ξ_1 affects the application of ξ_2. (4) Finally, the nodes in each SCC are further sorted based on the ratio of its out-degree to in-degree, in a decreasing order. The higher the ratio is, the more effects it has on other nodes.

Example 6.1: The dependency graph G in Fig. 5 is an SCC. The ratios of out-degree to in-degree of the nodes φ_1, φ_2, φ_3, φ_4 and ψ are $\frac{2}{1}$, $\frac{2}{1}$, $\frac{1}{1}$, $\frac{3}{3}$ and $\frac{2}{4}$, respectively. Hence the order $\mathcal{O}$ of these rules is $\varphi_1 > \varphi_2 > \varphi_3 > \varphi_4 > \psi$, where those nodes with the same ratio are sorted randomly. □

vCFDReslove. It applies the cleaning rule derived from a variable CFD $\xi = R(Y \to B, t_p)$. For each set $\Delta(\bar{y})$ with $\bar{y}$ in $\pi_Y(\rho_{Y \asymp t_p[Y]} D)$, if $\mathcal{H}(\xi | Y = \bar{y})$ is smaller than the entropy threshold δ_2, it picks the value $b \in \pi_B(\Delta(\bar{y}))$ that has the maximum $\text{cnt}_{YB}(\bar{y}, b)$. Then for each tuple $t \in \Delta(\bar{y})$, if $t[B]$ has been changed less than δ_1 times, *i.e.,* when $t[B]$ is not often changed by rules that may not converge on its value, $t[B]$ is changed to b. As remarked earlier, when the entropy $\mathcal{H}(\xi | Y = \bar{y})$ is small enough, it is highly accurate to resolve the conflicts in $\pi_B(\Delta(\bar{y}))$ by assigning b as their value.

cCFDReslove. It applies the rule derived from a constant CFD $\xi = R(X \to A, t_{p_1})$. For each tuple $t \in D$, if (a) $t[X] \asymp t_{p_1}[X]$, (b) $t[A] \neq t_{p_1}[A]$, and (c) $t[A]$ has been changed less than δ_1 times, then $t[A]$ is changed to the constant $t_{p_1}[A]$.

MDReslove. It applies the cleaning rule derived from an MD $\xi = \bigwedge_{j \in [1,k]} (R[A_j] \approx_j R_m[B_j]) \to R[E] \rightleftharpoons R_m[F]$. For each tuple $t \in D$, if there exists a master tuple $s \in D_m$ such that (a) $t[A_j] \approx_j s[B_j]$ for $j \in [1, k]$, (b) $t[E] \neq s[F]$, and (c) $t[E]$ has been changed less than δ_1 times, then it assigns the master value $s[F]$ to $t[E]$.

	A	B	C	E	F	H
t_1:	a_1	b_1	c_1	e_1	f_1	h_1
t_2:	a_1	b_1	c_1	e_1	f_2	h_2
t_3:	a_1	b_1	c_1	e_1	f_3	h_3
t_4:	a_1	b_1	c_1	e_2	f_1	h_3
t_5:	a_2	b_2	c_2	e_1	f_2	h_4
t_6:	a_2	b_2	c_2	e_2	f_1	h_4
t_7:	a_2	b_2	c_3	e_3	f_3	h_5
t_8:	a_2	b_2	c_4	e_3	f_3	h_6

Figure 6: Example relation of schema R

These procedures do not change those data values that are marked deterministic fixes by algorithm cRepair.

Example 6.2: Consider an instance of schema $R(\mathsf{ABCEFH})$ shown in Fig. 6, and a variable CFD $\phi = R(\mathsf{ABC} \to \mathsf{E}, t_{p_1})$, where t_{p_1} consists of wildcards only, *i.e.,* ϕ is an FD. Observe that (a) $\mathcal{H}(\phi | ABC = (a_1, b_1, c_1)) \approx 0.8$, (b) $\mathcal{H}(\phi | ABC = (a_2, b_2, c_2))$ is 1, and (c) $\mathcal{H}(\phi | ABC = (a_2, b_2, c_3))$ and $\mathcal{H}(\phi | ABC = (a_2, b_2, c_4))$ are both 0.

From these we can see the following. (1) For $\Delta(ABC = (a_2, b_2, c_3))$ and $\Delta(ABC = (a_2, b_2, c_4))$, the entropy is 0; hence these sets of tuples do not violate ϕ, *i.e.,* there is no need to fix these tuples. (2) The fix based on $\mathcal{H}(\phi | ABC = (a_1, b_1, c_1))$ is relatively accurate, but not those based on $\mathcal{H}(\phi | ABC = (a_2, b_2, c_2))$. Hence algorithm eRepair will only change $t_4[E]$ to e_1, and marks it as a reliable fix. □

Complexity. The outer loop (lines 3–10) in algorithm eRepair runs in $O(\delta_1 |D|)$ time. Each inner loop (lines 4–9) takes $O(|D||\Sigma| + k|D|\text{size}(\Gamma))$ time using the optimization techniques of Section 5, where k is a constant. Thus, the algorithm takes $O(\delta_1 |D|^2 |\Sigma| + \delta_1 k |D|^2 \text{size}(\Gamma))$ time.

6.3 Resolving Conflicts with a 2-in-1 Structure

We can efficiently identify tuples that match the LHS of constant CFDs by building an index on the LHS attributes in the database D. We can also efficiently find tuples that match the LHS of MDs by leveraging the suffix tree structure developed in Section 5. However, for variable CFDs, two issues still remain: (a) detecting violations and (b) computing entropy. These are rather costly and have to be recomputed when data is updated in the cleaning process. To do these we develop a 2-in-1 structure, which can be easily maintained.

Let Σ_V be the set of variables CFDs in Σ, and $\text{attr}(\Sigma_V)$ be the set of attributes appearing in Σ_V. For each CFD $\varphi = R(Y \to B,\ t_p)$ in Σ_V, we build a structure consisting of a *hash table* and an *AVL tree* [10] T as follows.

Hash table HTab. Recall $\Delta(\bar{y}) = \{t \mid t \in D,\ t[Y] = \bar{y}\}$ for $\bar{y} \in \pi_Y(\rho_{Y \asymp t_p[Y]} D)$ described earlier. For each $\Delta(\bar{y})$, we insert an entry (key, val) into HTab, where key $= \bar{y}$, and val is a pointer linking to a node $\mathsf{u} = (\epsilon, l, r, o)$, where (a) $\mathsf{u}.\epsilon = \mathcal{H}(\varphi | Y = \bar{y})$, (b) $\mathsf{u}.l$ is the value-count pair $(\bar{y}, |\Delta(\bar{y})|)$, (c) $\mathsf{u}.r$ is the set $\{(b, \text{cnt}_{YB}(\bar{y}, b)) \mid b \in \pi_B(\Delta(\bar{y}))\}$, and (d) $\mathsf{u}.o$ is the set of (partial) tuple IDs $\{t.id \mid t \in \Delta(\bar{y})\}$.

AVL tree T. For each $\bar{y} \in \pi_Y(\rho_{Y \asymp t_p[Y]} D)$ with entropy $\mathcal{H}(\varphi | Y = \bar{y}) \neq 0$, we create a node $\mathsf{v} = \text{HTab}(\bar{y})$ in T, a pointer to the node u for $\Delta(\bar{y})$ in HTab. For each node v in T, its left child $\mathsf{v}_l.\epsilon \leq \mathsf{v}.\epsilon$ and its right child $\mathsf{v}_r.\epsilon \geq \mathsf{v}.\epsilon$.

Note that both the number $|\text{HTab}|$ of entries in the hash table HTab and the number $|T|$ of nodes in the AVL tree T are bounded by the number $|D|$ of tuples in D.

Example 6.3: Consider the relation in Fig. 6 and the vari-

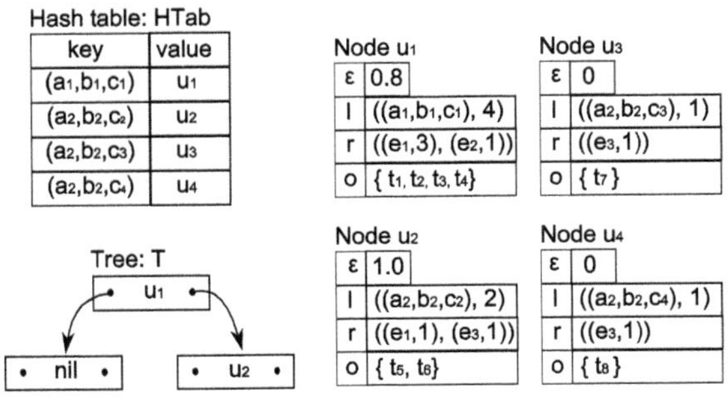

Figure 7: Example data structure for variable CFDs

able CFD ϕ given in Example 6.2. The hash table HTab and the AVL tree T for ϕ are shown in Fig. 7. □

We next show how to use and maintain the structures.

(1) Lookup cost. For the CFD φ, it takes (a) $O(\log |T|)$ time to identify the set $\Delta(\bar{y})$ of tuples with minimum entropy $\mathcal{H}(\varphi|Y = \bar{y})$ in the AVL tree T, and (b) $O(1)$ time to check whether two tuples in D satisfy φ via the hash table HTab.

(2) Update cost. The initialization of both the hash table HTab and the AVL tree T can be done by scanning the database D once, and it takes $O(|D| \log |D||\Sigma_V|)$ time.

After resolving some conflicts, the structures need to be maintained accordingly. Consider a set $\Delta(\bar{y})$ of dirty tuples. When a reliable fix is found for $\Delta(\bar{y})$ based on $\mathcal{H}(\varphi|Y = \bar{y})$, we do the following: (a) remove a node from tree T, which takes $O(\log |T|)$ time, where $|T| \leq |D|$; and (b) update the hash tables and trees for all other CFDs, which takes $O(|\Delta(\bar{y})||\Sigma_V| + |\Delta(\bar{y})| \log |D|)$ time in total.

(3) Space cost. The structures take $O(|D|\mathsf{size}(\Sigma_V)$ space for all CFDs in Σ_V in total, where $\mathsf{size}(\Sigma_V)$ is the size of Σ_V.

Putting these together, the structures are efficient in both time and space, and are easy to maintain.

7. Experimental Study

We next present an experimental study of UniClean, which unifies matching and repairing. Using real-life data, we evaluated (1) the effectiveness of our data cleaning algorithms, (2) the accuracy of deterministic fixes and reliable fixes, and (3) the scalability of our algorithms with the size of data.

Experimental Setting. We used two real-life data sets.

(1) HOSP *data* was taken from US Department of Health & Human Services[1]. It has 100K records with 19 attributes. We designed 23 CFDs and 3 MDs for HOSP, 26 in total.

(2) DBLP *data* was extracted from DBLP Bibliography[2]. It consists of 400K tuples, each with 12 attributes. We designed 7 CFDs and 3 MDs for DBLP, 10 in total.

(3) Master data for both datasets was carefully selected from the same data sources so that they were guaranteed to be correct and consistent *w.r.t.* the designed rules.

(4) Dirty datasets were produced by introducing noises to data from the two sources, controlled by four parameters: (a) $|D|$: the data size; (b) noi%: the *noise rate*, which is the ratio of the number of erroneous attributes to the total number of attributes in D; (c) dup%: the *duplicate rate*, *i.e.*,, the percentage of tuples in D that can find a match in the master data; and (d) asr%: the *asserted rate*. For each attribute A, we randomly picked asr% of tuples t from the data and set $t[A].\mathrm{cf} = 1$, while letting $t'[A].\mathrm{cf} = 0$ for the other tuples t'. The default value for asr% is 40%.

Algorithms. We implemented the following algorithms, all in Python: (a) algorithms cRepair, eRepair and hRepair (an extension of algorithm in [9]) in UniClean; (b) the sorted neighborhood method of [24], denoted by SortN, for record matching based on MDs only; and (c) the heuristic repairing algorithm of [9], denoted by quaid, based on CFDs only. We use Uni to denote cleaning based on both CFDs and MDs (matching and repairing), and Uni(CFD) to denote cleaning using CFDs (repairing) only.

We used edit distance for similarity test, defined as the minimum number of single-character insertions, deletions and substitutions needed to convert a value from v to v'.

Quality measuring. We adopted *precision, recall* and *F-measure*, which are commonly used in information retrieval, where F-measure $= 2 \cdot (\text{precision} \cdot \text{recall})/(\text{precision} + \text{recall})$.

For record matching, (a) precision is the ratio of *true matches* (true positives) correctly found by an algorithm to all the duplicates found, and (b) recall is the ratio of true matches correctly found to all the matches between a dataset and master data. For data repairing, (a) precision is the ratio of attributes correctly updated to the number of all the attributes updated, and (b) recall is the ratio of attributes corrected to the number of all erroneous attributes.

All experiments were conducted on a Linux machine with a 3.0GHz Intel CPU and 4GB of Memory. Each experiment was run more than 5 times, and the average is reported here.

Experimental Results. We conducted five sets of experiments: (a) in the first two sets of experiments, we compared the effectiveness of our cleaning methods with both matching and repairing against its counterpart with only matching or only repairing; (b) we evaluated the accuracy of deterministic fixes, reliable fixes and possible fixes in the third set of experiments; (c) we evaluated the impact of the duplicate rate and asserted rate on the percentage of deterministic fixes found by our algorithm cRepair in the fourth set of experiments; and (d) the last set of experiments tested the scalability of Uni with both the size of dirty data and the size of master data. In all the experiments, we set the threshold for entropy and confidence to be 0.8 and 1.0, respectively. We used dirty datasets and master data consisting of 60K tuples each. We now report our findings.

Exp-1: Matching helps repairing. In the first set of experiments we show that matching indeed helps repairing. We compare the quality (F-measure) of fixes generated by Uni, Uni(CFD) and quaid. Fixing the duplicate rate dup% = 40%, we varied the noise rate noi% from 2% to 10%. Observe that dup% is only related to matching via MDs. To favor Uni(CFD) and quaid, which use CFDs only, we focused on the impact of various noise rates.

The results on HOSP data and DBLP data are reported in Figures 8(a) and 8(b), respectively, which tell us the following. (1) Uni clearly outperforms Uni(CFD) and quaid by up to 15% and 30%, respectively. This verifies that matching indeed helps repairing. (2) The F-measure decreases when noi% increases for all three approaches. However, Uni with matching is less sensitive to noi%, which is another benefit of unifying repairing with matching. (3) Even only with CFDs, our system Uni(CFD) still outperforms quaid, as expected. This is because quaid only generates possible fixes

[1]http://www.hospitalcompare.hhs.gov/

[2]http://www.informatik.uni-trier.de/~ley/db/

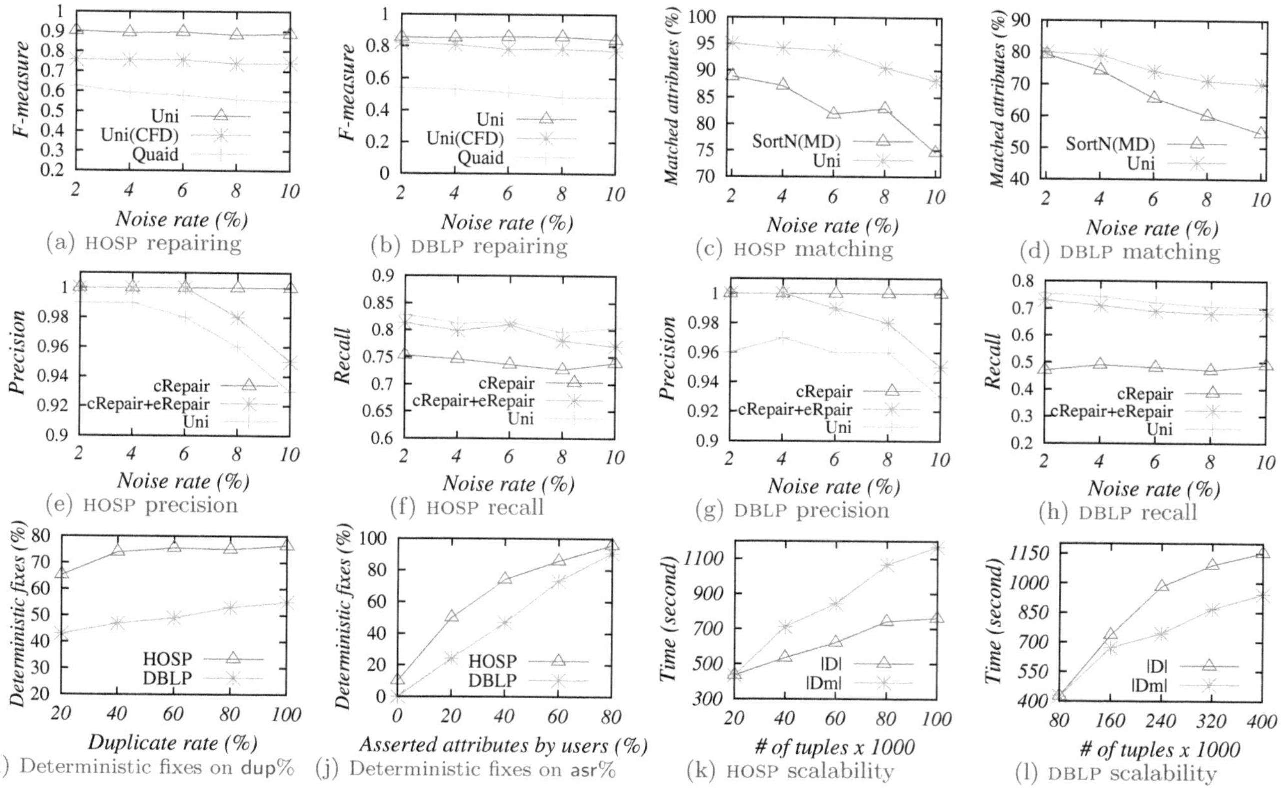

(a) HOSP repairing (b) DBLP repairing (c) HOSP matching (d) DBLP matching (e) HOSP precision (f) HOSP recall (g) DBLP precision (h) DBLP recall (i) Deterministic fixes on dup% (j) Deterministic fixes on asr% (k) HOSP scalability (l) DBLP scalability

Figure 8: Experimental results

with heuristic, while Uni(CFD) finds both deterministic fixes and reliable fixes. This also verifies that deterministic and reliable fixes are more accurate than possible fixes.

Exp-2: Repairing helps matching. In the second set of experiment, we show that repairing indeed helps matching. We evaluate the quality (F-measure) of matches found by (a) Uni and (b) SortN using MDs, denoted by SortN(MD). We used the same setting as in Exp-1. We also conducted experiments by varying the duplicate rate, but found that its impact is very small; hence we do not report it here.

The results are reported in Figures 8(c) and 8(d) for HOSP data and DBLP data, respectively. We find the following. (a) Uni outperforms SortN(MD) by up to 15%, verifying that repairing indeed helps matching. (b) The F-measure decreases when the noise rate increases for both approaches. However, Uni with repairing is less sensitive to noi%, which is consistent with our observation in the last experiments.

Exp-3: Accuracy of deterministic and reliable fixes. In this set of experiments we evaluate the accuracy (precision and recall) of (a) deterministic fixes generated in the first phase of UniClean, denoted by cRepair, (b) deterministic fixes and reliable fixes generated in the first two phases of UniClean, denoted by cRepair + eRepair, and (c) all fixes generated by Uni. Fixing dup% = 40%, we varied noi% from 2% to 10%. The results are reported in Figures 8(e)–8(h).

The results tell us the following: (a) Deterministic fixes have the highest precision, and are insensitive to the noise rate. However, their recall is low, since cRepair is "picky": it only generates fixes with asserted attributes. (b) Fixes generated by Uni have the lowest precision, but the highest recall, as expected. Further, their precision is quite sensitive to noi%. This is because the last step of UniClean is by heuristics, which generates possible fixes. (c) The precision and recall of deterministic fixes and reliable fixes by cRepair + eRepair are in the between, as expected. Further, their precision is also sensitive to noi%. From these we can see that the precision of reliable fixes and possible fixes is sensitive to noi%, but not their recall. Moreover, when noi% is less than 4%, their precision is rather indifferent to noi%.

Exp-4: Impact of dup% and asr% on deterministic fixes. In this set of experiments we evaluated the percentage of deterministic fixes found by algorithm cRepair.

Fixing the asserted rate asr% = 40%, we varied the duplicate rate dup% from 20% to 100%. Figure 8(i) shows the results. We find that the larger dup% is, the more deterministic fixes are found, as expected.

Fixing dup% = 40%, we varied asr% from 0% to 80%. The results are shown in Fig. 8(j), which tell us that the number of deterministic fixes found by cRepair highly depends on asr%. This is because to find deterministic fixes, cleaning rules are only applied to asserted attributes.

Exp-5: Scalability. The last experiments evaluated the scalability of Uni with the size $|D|$ of dirty data and the size $|D_m|$ of master data. We fixed noi% = 6% and dup% = 40% in these experiments. The results are reported in Figures 8(k) and 8(l) for HOSP and DBLP data, respectively.

Figure 8(k) shows two curves for HOSP data: one by fixing $|D_m|$ = 60K and varying $|D|$ from $20K$ to $100K$, and the other by fixing $|D|$ = 60K and varying $|D_m|$ from $20K$ to $100K$. The results show that Uni scales reasonably well with both $|D|$ and $|D_m|$. In fact Uni scales much better than quaid [9]: quaid took more than 10 hours when $|D|$ is 80K, while it took Uni about 11 minutes. These results verify the effectiveness of our indexing structures and optimization techniques developed for Uni. The results are consistent for DBLP data, as shown in Fig. 8(l).

Summary. From the experimental results on real-life data, we find the following. (a) Data cleaning by unifying matching and repairing substantially improves the quality of fixes: it outperforms matching and repairing taken as independent processes by up to 30% and 15%, respectively. (b) Deterministic fixes and reliable fixes are highly accurate. For example, when the noise rate is no more than 4%, their precision is close to 100%. The precision decreases slowly when increasing noise rate. These tell us that it is feasible to find accurate fixes for real-life applications. (c) Candidate repairs generated by system UniClean are of high-quality: their precision is about 96%. (d) Our data cleaning methods scale reasonably well with the size of data and the size of master data. It is more than 50 times faster than quaid a data repairing tool using CFDs only.

8. Conclusion

We have taken a first step toward unifying record matching and data repairing, an important issue that has been overlooked by and large. We have proposed a uniform framework for interleaving matching and repairing operations, based on cleaning rules derived from CFDs and MDs. We have established the complexity bounds of several fundamental problems for data cleaning with both matching and repairing. We have also proposed deterministic fixes and reliable fixes, and effective methods to find these fixes based on confidence and entropy. Our experimental results have verified that our techniques substantially improve the quality of fixes generated by repairing and matching taken separately.

We are currently experimenting with larger datasets and exploring optimization techniques to improve the efficiency of our algorithms. We are also studying cleaning of multiple relations of which the consistency is specified by constraints across relations, *e.g.,* (conditional) inclusion dependencies.

Acknowledgments. Fan is supported in part by the RSE-NSFC Joint Project Scheme and an IBM scalable data analytics for a smarter planet innovation award. Li is supported in part by NGFR 973 grant 2006CB303000 and NSFC grant 60533110. Shuai is supported in part by NGFR 973 grant 2011CB302602 and NSFC grants 90818028 and 60903149.

9. References

[1] S. Abiteboul, R. Hull, and V. Vianu. *Foundations of Databases.* Addison-Wesley, 1995.

[2] A. Aiken, D. Kozen, M. Y. Vardi, and E. L. Wimmers. The complexity of set constraints. In *CSL*, 1993.

[3] A. Arasu, C. Re, and D. Suciu. Large-scale deduplication with constraints using Dedupalog. In *ICDE*, 2009.

[4] M. Arenas, L. E. Bertossi, and J. Chomicki. Consistent query answers in inconsistent databases. *TPLP*, 3(4-5), 2003.

[5] G. Beskales, M. A. Soliman, I. F. Ilyas, and S. Ben-David. Modeling and querying possible repairs in duplicate detection. In *VLDB*, 2009.

[6] P. Bohannon, W. Fan, M. Flaster, and R. Rastogi. A cost-based model and effective heuristic for repairing constraints by value modification. In *SIGMOD*, 2005.

[7] S. Chaudhuri, K. Ganjam, V. Ganti, and R. Motwani. Robust and efficient fuzzy match for online data cleaning. In *SIGMOD*, 2003.

[8] F. Chiang and R. Miller. Discovering data quality rules. In *VLDB*, 2008.

[9] G. Cong, W. Fan, F. Geerts, X. Jia, and S. Ma. Improving data quality: Consistency and accuracy. In *VLDB*, 2007.

[10] T. H. Cormen, C. E. Leiserson, R. L. Rivest, and C. Stein. *Introduction to Algorithms.* The MIT Press, 2001.

[11] T. M. Cover and J. A. Thomas. *Elements of Information Theory.* Wiley-Interscience, 1991.

[12] T. de Vries, H. Ke, S. Chawla, and P. Christen. Robust record linkage blocking using suffix arrays. In *CIKM*, 2009.

[13] X. Dong, A. Y. Halevy, and J. Madhavan. Reference reconciliation in complex information spaces. In *SIGMOD Conference*, 2005.

[14] X. L. Dong, L. Berti-Equille, Y. Hu, and D. Srivastava. Global detection of complex copying relationships between sources. In *VLDB*, 2010.

[15] W. W. Eckerson. Data Quality and the Bottom Line: Achieving Business Success through a Commitment to High Quality Data. In *The Data Warehousing Institute*, 2002.

[16] A. K. Elmagarmid, P. G. Ipeirotis, and V. S. Verykios. Duplicate record detection: A survey. *TKDE*, 19(1):1–16, 2007.

[17] W. Fan, F. Geerts, X. Jia, and A. Kementsietsidis. Conditional functional dependencies for capturing data inconsistencies. *TODS*, 33(1), 2008.

[18] W. Fan, X. Jia, J. Li, and S. Ma. Reasoning about record matching rules. In *VLDB*, 2009.

[19] W. Fan, J. Li, S. Ma, N. Tang, and W. Yu. Towards certain fixes with editing rules and master data. In *VLDB*, 2010.

[20] I. Fellegi and D. Holt. A systematic approach to automatic edit and imputation. *J. American Statistical Association*, 71(353):17–35, 1976.

[21] Gartner. Forecast: Data quality tools, worldwide, 2006-2011. Technical report, Gartner, 2007.

[22] S. Guo, X. Dong, D. Srivastava, and R. Zajac. Record linkage with uniqueness constraints and erroneous values. *PVLDB*, 3(1), 2010.

[23] R. W. Hamming. Error detecting and error correcting codes. *Bell System Technical Journal*, 29(2):147–160, 1950.

[24] M. A. Hernandez and S. Stolfo. Real-World Data is Dirty: Data Cleansing and the Merge/Purge Problem. *Data Mining and Knowledge Discovery*, 2(1):9–37, 1998.

[25] T. N. Herzog, F. J. Scheuren, and W. E. Winkler. *Data Quality and Record Linkage Techniques.* Springer, 2009.

[26] G. J. Klir and T. A. Folger. *Fuzzy sets, uncertainty, and information.* Englewood Cliffs, N.J: Prentice Hall, 1988.

[27] D. Loshin. *Master Data Management.* Knowledge Integrity, Inc., 2009.

[28] C. Mayfield, J. Neville, and S. Prabhakar. ERACER: a database approach for statistical inference and data cleaning. In *SIGMOD*, 2010.

[29] F. Naumann, A. Bilke, J. Bleiholder, and M. Weis. Data fusion in three steps: Resolving schema, tuple, and value inconsistencies. *IEEE Data Eng. Bull.*, 29(2), 2006.

[30] B. Otto and K. Weber. From health checks to the seven sisters: The data quality journey at BT, Sept. 2009. BT TR-BE HSG/CC CDQ/8.

[31] T. Redman. The impact of poor data quality on the typical enterprise. *Commun. ACM*, 2:79–82, 1998.

[32] S. Song and L. Chen. Discovering matching dependencies. In *CIKM*, 2009.

[33] D. Srivastava and S. Venkatasubramanian. Information theory for data management. In *SIGMOD*, 2010.

[34] I. Wegener and R. Pruim. *Complexity Theory: Exploring the Limits of Efficient Algorithms.* Springer, 2005.

[35] M. Weis and F. Naumann. Dogmatix tracks down duplicates in XML. In *SIGMOD*, 2005.

[36] S. E. Whang, O. Benjelloun, and H. Garcia-Molina. Generic entity resolution with negative rules. *VLDB J.*, 18(6), 2009.

[37] J. Wijsen. Database repairing using updates. *TODS*, 30(3):722–768, 2005.

[38] M. Yakout, A. K. Elmagarmid, J. Neville, and M. Ouzzani. GDR: a system for guided data repair. In *SIGMOD*, 2010.

[39] J. Ziv and A. Lempel. Compression of individual sequences via variable-rate coding. *IEEE TIT*, 24(5), 1978.

We Challenge You to Certify Your Updates

Su Chen
National Univ of Singapore
chensu@comp.nus.edu.sg

Xin Luna Dong
AT&T Labs–Research
lunadong@research.att.com

Laks V.S. Lakshmanan
Univ of British Columbia
laks@cs.ubc.ca

Divesh Srivastava
AT&T Labs–Research
divesh@research.att.com

ABSTRACT

Correctness of data residing in a database is vital. While integrity constraint enforcement can often ensure data consistency, it is inadequate to protect against updates that involve careless, unintentional errors, e.g., whether a specified update to an employee's record was for the intended employee. We propose a novel approach that is complementary to existing integrity enforcement techniques, to guard against such erroneous updates.

Our approach is based on (a) updaters providing an *update certificate* with each database update, and (b) the database system verifying the correctness of the update certificate provided before performing the update. We formalize a certificate as a (challenge, response) pair, and characterize good certificates as those that are easy for updaters to provide and, when correct, give the system enough confidence that the update was indeed intended. We present algorithms that efficiently enumerate good challenges, without exhaustively exploring the search space of all challenges. We experimentally demonstrate that (i) databases have many good challenges, (ii) these challenges can be efficiently identified, (iii) certificates can be quickly verified for correctness, (iv) under natural models of an updater's knowledge of the database, update certificates catch a high percentage of the erroneous updates without imposing undue burden on the updaters performing correct updates, and (v) our techniques are robust across a wide range of challenge parameter settings.

Categories and Subject Descriptors: H.2.7 [**Database Management**]: Database Administration—*Security, integrity, and protection*

General Terms: Algorithms, Design, Experimentation

1. INTRODUCTION

Correctness of data residing in a database is of utmost importance for applications that rely on the data to make critical decisions. Much work has been done on analyzing and mining the data in a database in order to detect potential duplicates, likely errors and statistical outliers (see, e.g., [4, 3]). In this paper, we are interested in a complementary problem: starting with a correct database state, how do we minimize, if not prevent, the possibility that errors creep into the database as the data gets updated?

Ensuring correctness is not easy since databases are continuously being modified by human updaters (typically using an application) to reflect changes in reality. Consider, for example, databases supporting Project Management. Here, information about projects (such as the status of different parts of the projects, their current priorities, resource needs, and funding sources) and participants (such as roles of employees in different projects, individual project timelines, reporting of billable hours) need to be continuously updated over time; such updates are typically made by project administrators. Other such examples include Human Resources databases which contain dynamically changing information about employees (such as their compensation, disability and sick leave, and job functions) and organizations (such as management reporting structures), Inventory databases which contain continuously updated information about organizational assets, and so on.

Erroneous updates do happen in these databases, as many of us may have experienced, often with significant cost because of the difficulty of correcting the errors in the database and rolling back the decisions made due to these errors. For example, switching funding sources between projects in a Project Management database, or reporting a disability leave for the wrong employee in a Human Resources database, can create a lot of problems. In these scenarios, *it would be desirable to guard against such erroneous updates, even if it requires additional effort on the part of the database system, the application developers, and the updaters.*

A variety of classical techniques ranging from schema normalization to integrity constraint enforcement have been proposed to address this problem [14]. These existing techniques require the database designer to anticipate all possible errors and specify integrity constraints that must hold on all instances of the database schema, and which would detect (and reject) erroneous updates. However, a large variety of errors cannot be anticipated and arise due to carelessness on the part of updaters and by the inability of the database system to detect those updates as erroneous. The following example illustrates the idea.

EXAMPLE 1 (COMPLEX, BULK UPDATE). Consider the Corporate database shown in Fig. 1, which is a simplified Project Management and Human Resources database. The tables represent departments, employees, projects, and the association of employees with projects. An updater (for example, a project administrator) intends to make Dolores Quintana the Admin of all the projects whose responsible department is located in NJ, starting from 1985-02-01, but in the update, incorrectly specifies `location` as NY instead of NJ, `empId` as 000030 instead of 000130, and `stDate` as 1985-01-02 instead of 1985-02-01. For concreteness, we show below the SQL update issued by the application with which the updater interacted.

```
U1: update PROJ_EMP
    set empId = '000030', stDate = '1985-01-02'
    where job = 'Admin' and projId in (
       select PROJ.projId  from PROJ, DEPT
       where PROJ.deptId = DEPT.deptId and
          DEPT.location = 'NY' )
```


SIGMOD'11, June 12–16, 2011, Athens, Greece.

DEPT			
deptId	deptName	mgrId	location
A00	Services	000010	NJ
B01	Planning	NULL	NY
C01	Information	000030	NJ

PROJ_EMP			
empId	projId	job	stDate
000010	AD3100	Leader	1982-01-01
000010	MA2100	Leader	1982-02-01
000020	PL2100	Leader	1983-01-01
000030	IF1000	Leader	1983-06-01
000110	MA2100	Admin	1984-01-01
000130	IF1000	Admin	1984-07-01
000140	PL2100	Admin	1985-10-01
000140	IF2000	Admin	1985-03-01

EMP					
empId	name	workDept	phone	sex	salary
000010	Christine Haas	A00	3978	F	52750
000020	Michael Thompson	B01	3476	M	41250
000030	Sally Kwan	C01	4738	F	38250
000110	Vincenzo Lucchessi	A00	3490	M	46500
000120	Sean OConnell	A00	2167	M	29250
000130	Dolores Quintana	C01	4578	F	23800
000140	Heather Nicholls	C01	4578	F	28420

PROJ				
projId	projName	deptId	stDate	enDate
AD3100	Admin Services	A00	1981-01-01	1988-02-01
IF1000	Query Services	C01	1981-03-01	1987-02-01
IF2000	User Education	B01	1980-01-01	1986-02-01
MA2100	Line Automation	A00	1979-01-01	1986-03-01
PL2100	Line Planning	B01	1979-05-15	1987-09-15

Figure 1: Schema and Sample Data of a Corporate Database

Note that since valid `empId`, `stDate` and `location` values are specified in the update, integrity constraint checks may not be able to detect this erroneous update. Notice, all of the natural FDs applicable to the schema of Fig. 1 would be satisfied by this update. As a result, unintended records in the `PROJ_EMP` table are (incorrectly) updated, while the intended records are left untouched. □

The above example illustrates that catching erroneous updates to databases remains a challenging problem. In fact, almost all known classes of integrity constraints are unable to capture such updates as erroneous. One exception is the class of conditional functional dependencies (CFDs) proposed recently [6]. CFDs (with a slight extension) can assert value associations of the form "if job is Admin, then `empId` must start with 0001", thus capturing update U1 as erroneous. However, this requires the database designer to anticipate all possible correct future states of the database, and assert them as CFDs, which is not a particularly practical solution.

In this paper, we propose a novel approach to guard against erroneous updates that are "innocent mistakes" (as opposed to malicious ones). Our approach is based on (a) the updater providing, through an application, the database update and an "update certificate" that is relevant to the database update, and (b) the database system verifying the correctness of the update certificate provided before performing the update. An update certificate consists of a (challenge, response) pair, where the "challenge" intuitively asks the updater to provide additional information that is relevant to the specified database update, and the updater provides this information in the "response" to demonstrate that the updater indeed intended to make the specified update; in the absence of malice, this is evidence of correctness. The system verifies, as part of the update transaction, whether the response provided by the updater matches the challenge; if not, the specified update is rejected as being unintended. The following example illustrates the idea.

EXAMPLE 2 (CERTIFICATE CHALLENGES AND RESPONSES). Challenges for the update U1 above could include "Q1: What is the name of the employee with `empId` 000030?", "Q2: What is the day of the week of `stDate` 1985-01-02?" and "Q3: What is the name of an employee who works for a department located in NY?" If the updater responds "Dolores Quintana" to challenge Q1, or "Friday" to challenge Q2, or "Christine Haas" to challenge Q3, all of which match the *intended update* but not the *specified update* U1, the database system could reject U1 as unintended, thereby preventing any disastrous decision that might be made as a consequence of the erroneous update. □

1.1 Pragmatics of Certificates

For update certificates to be effective in guarding against erroneous updates, it requires additional effort on the part of the database system, updaters, and application developers. Our preceding discussion described the additional effort that would be incurred by the updaters (providing the certificate) and the database system (verifying the correctness of the update certificate).

A critical role also needs to be played by the applications that mediate between the updaters and the database system: that of taking the updaters' certificates and presenting them to the database system. A developer of such an application would need to pick one or more reasonable challenges for each type of update (such as U1) supported by the application, and bake them into the application. An updater using the application can choose any of the challenges relevant to the specified update and provide responses, as evidence that the updater indeed intended to make the specified update.

Note that updates need not be interactive for the certificate mechanism to be feasible. Since the challenges supported by the application are determined offline, a non-interactive updater can pass (i) the id of the chosen challenge, and (ii) the response to the challenge, as input to the application. This approach can also be used in conjunction with "batch" updates, where multiple update statements can be issued (along with their certificates) by the updater. The update transaction generated by the application would include the updates and their certificates for the system to verify.

It is important to emphasize that while the use of certificates adds some overhead to the update process, both for the updater and for the database system, and requires application developers to incorporate certificates into their applications, these overheads are significantly outweighed by the benefits of certificates in reducing errors in databases as the data gets updated. Such errors incur a significant cost for restoring the database to a correct state and rolling back the decisions made based on the incorrect state.

We next discuss various alternatives to update certificates and motivate our design choice of using certificates.

1.2 Alternatives to Certificates

Our main goal is to detect and prevent updates that might lead to innocent unintended errors. One of the simplest mechanisms for doing this, inspired by the approach taken by Unix to confirm that a user intended to delete a file, is asking the updater "Are you sure?" Another option, inspired by the practice used by most online secure systems for users to confirm a modified password, is to ask the updater to repeat their update specification. A third option is to show the updater a sample of the records that are about to be updated and let the updater visually inspect the changes before deciding if this is the correct update.

All these approaches have the significant disadvantage that they are not suitable for updaters who use non-interactive applications to update databases. The first two approaches have the added disadvantage that updaters can easily answer "Yes" to the "Are you sure?" question, or use "cut and paste" as a quick way of repeating their update specification. Two recent studies, one on the (poor) security practices of users in dealing with online bank accounts [11], and the other on user practices in (not) reading and understanding end user license agreements [9], suggest that updaters are very likely to do so. Thus, such simplistic methods are unlikely to be effective to ensure correctness of updates.

What we need is a method that proves to be effective in catching erroneous updates while not imposing an undue burden on updaters. By the first objective, we mean that the percentage of erroneous updates let through should be very small. By the second objective, we mean that under natural models of an updater's knowledge of the data, the need for update certificates should not prevent most of their correct updates from going through easily.

We next spell out desiderata for update certificates, and argue that picking challenges in a principled manner is important to reducing errors in databases as the data gets updated.

1.3 Desiderata and Contributions

For update certificates to be useful in detecting erroneous updates, the most critical issue is the *design of certificate challenges* that are relevant to updates.

Database System Desiderata: Consider a challenge "Q4: What is the sex of the employee with `empId` 000030?" While Q4 is relevant to Update U1, the updater's (correct) response of "F" would not have helped the system detect the erroneous update, since both Sally Kwan and Dolores Quintana are female. Intuitively, from the database system's viewpoint, a challenge is not desirable if there are many unintended updates for which a correct response to the challenge is the same as that for the intended update.

Updater Desiderata: Suppose that the updater is asked "Q5: What is the phone number of an employee who works for a project whose responsible department is located in NY?" Such a challenge is too complex, so reduces understandability and increases the risk of a wrong response *even when the updater knows the correct response to the challenge*. Similarly, if the *only* challenges available were "Q6: What are the salary and the sex of the employee with `empId` 000030?" and "Q7: What are the salary and the phone number of the employee with `empId` 000030?", then an updater who does not know an employee's salary would be unable to choose either challenge and provide a correct response *even when she performs a correct update*. Thus, from the updater's viewpoint, it is desirable that challenges be easy to use, without undue expectation that she is familiar with every aspect of the data she updates.

We effectively address the desiderata important to updaters and to the database system and make the following contributions:

- First, we formalize an update certificate as a *(challenge, response)* pair. We identify properties that make for "good" challenges: high *discriminating power*, low *description complexity*, and high *diversity* (Sec. 2). Intuitively, the first property permits the database system to have high confidence that the specified update was intended, the second makes sure the challenges are easy to understand, while the third ensures that every updater can respond to some challenge.
- Second, we formulate two optimization problems for finding good challenges: (i) minimize description complexity of the challenges that meet specified discriminating power and diversity thresholds, and (ii) maximize diversity of the challenges that meet specified discriminating power and description complexity thresholds. We develop efficient algorithms to optimally solve these problems (Sec. 3).
- Finally, we experimentally evaluate our techniques on benchmark databases and demonstrate that (i) databases often have many good challenges, (ii) such challenges can be efficiently identified, (iii) responses provided by updaters can be quickly verified for correctness, (iv) under natural models of an updater's knowledge of the database, update certificates enjoy good precision and recall: they catch most erroneous updates without imposing undue burden on updaters performing correct updates, and (v) our techniques are robust across a wide range of challenge parameter settings (Sec. 4).

2. CERTIFICATES: PROPERTIES

Databases allow insertions, deletions and modifications of records, tables and table spaces. We focus on *record modifications*, which allow the values of specified attributes in a set of records of a specified table to be modified to specified values. For example, Update U1 is of this form. These updates present the most challenges, and their solutions can be adapted for other updates.

2.1 Certificates

An *update certificate* consists of a *challenge* presented to the updater and a *response* by the updater. We propose certificates for both the update condition (to ensure that the intended set of records are being updated) and for the updated values (to ensure that the modified values are the intended ones).

DEFINITION 2.1 (UPDATE CERTIFICATE). Consider update condition or updated value γ of the form `attr=val`.[1] An *update certificate* C_γ for γ is a (challenge, response) pair (Q_γ, R_γ), where (i) challenge Q_γ is a SQL query, whose `where` clause condition $Cond(Q_\gamma)$ implies γ,[2] and (ii) response R_γ is the answer provided by the updater to Q_γ. An *update certificate* $\mathbf{C}_U$ for a record modification update U is a set of certificates C_γ, one for each update condition and updated value γ in the update U. □

DEFINITION 2.2 (VALID CERTIFICATE). Given a database instance D, a certificate $C_\gamma = (Q_\gamma, R_\gamma)$ is said to be *valid* if R_γ is in the answer set of Q_γ on D. A certificate $\mathbf{C}_U$ is said to be *valid* if each $C_\gamma \in \mathbf{C}_U$ is valid. □

Ex. 2 presented challenges (Q1–Q3) associated with the certificates for update U1. Example certificates for U1 might be the pairs (Q1, Dolores Quintana), (Q2, Friday) and (Q3, Christine Haas), respectively, none of which is valid. However, certificates (Q1, Sally Kwan), (Q2, Tuesday), and (Q3, Michael Thompson) are valid.

We next present three properties that we consider important for guarding against erroneous updates: *discriminating power*, *description complexity* and *diversity*. These properties formalize the desiderata for certificates by the database system and by the updater.

2.2 Discriminating Power

Should all specified updates with valid certificates (e.g., (Q4, F)) be considered as intended by the updater, and accepted by the system? The notion of *discriminating power*, discussed below, quantifies the confidence provided by a valid certificate that the specified update was indeed intended.

[1] For the purpose of certificates, an updated value `attr=val` can be treated exactly like an update condition `attr=val`.

[2] This property ensures that the challenge is *relevant* to the update.

We first need the notions of a *challenge template* and a *CR-table*. Consider a challenge Q_γ. The *challenge template* Q_γ^T is the parameterized query obtained from Q_γ by replacing γ in its `where` clause by γ^T, obtained by replacing `val` in γ by a parameter `$val`. For example, the challenge template $Q1^T$ would be "`select name from EMP where empId = $val`".[3]

A challenge template Q_γ^T is associated with a *CR-table* $T_{Q_\gamma^T}(V, R)$, which contains answers R to challenges V that can be obtained from Q_γ^T. If materialized, the CR-table can be used to quickly validate an updater's response to any challenge. For example, the projection of table EMP on attributes `(empId, name)` would be the CR-table for challenge template $Q1^T$, and the projection of the join DEPT $\bowtie_{deptId=workDept}$ EMP on attributes `(location, name)` would be the CR-table for challenge template $Q3^T$.

We are finally ready to define the notion of discriminating power. Consider an update condition or updated value γ, and a valid certificate $C_\gamma = (Q_\gamma, R_\gamma)$ for γ. This certificate could be considered as a "lucky guess" if the updater had intended to specify a different update condition/value $\gamma_j \neq \gamma$, but response R_γ is also a valid response for Q_{γ_j}. Intuitively, the discriminating power of a valid certificate is the probability that the provided certificate is *not a lucky guess*. More formally, we have the following definition.

DEFINITION 2.3 (DISCRIMINATING POWER). Consider a database instance D, an update condition or updated value γ : `attr = val`, a valid certificate $C_\gamma = (Q_\gamma, R_\gamma)$ for γ, and the CR-table $T_{Q_\gamma^T}(V, R)$ for the challenge template Q_γ^T.

The *discriminating power* (DP) of C_γ is defined as:

$$DP(C_\gamma) = 1 - \frac{|\{T_{Q_\gamma^T}.V \mid T_{Q_\gamma^T}.V \neq \texttt{val} \ \& \ T_{Q_\gamma^T}.R = R_\gamma\}|}{|\{T_{Q_\gamma^T}.V \mid T_{Q_\gamma^T}.V \neq \texttt{val}\}|}$$

We define the minimum (resp. average) discriminating power of a challenge template Q_γ^T, denoted minDP(Q_γ^T) (resp., avgDP(Q_γ^T)) as the minimum (resp., average) DP over all possible *valid responses* in the CR-table $T_{Q_\gamma^T}$.[4] □

For example, the DP of certificate (Q4, F) is 3/6, and the minDP and avgDP of $Q4^T$ are 3/6 and 7/12, respectively.

Since valid certificates with low DP are not useful as evidence of the updater's intention, applications should use only challenges that yield certificates with a high discriminating power. Only then can the system have high confidence that the specified update will not make the database dirty.

2.3 Description Complexity

If providing certificates were to place an undue burden on updaters, then certificates may not be used despite their obvious benefits. Hence, it should be *easy* for updaters to provide certificates.

In practice, we expect that a challenge to be presented in natural language. To keep the natural language question simple, we require two properties of individual challenges. First, the challenge must be a chain join query, with the updated table at one end of the chain; such queries can be translated to natural language much more easily than challenges containing arbitrary joins. For example, this property holds for challenge Q3. Second, no challenge presented to an updater should be too verbose since that would reduce understandability. The two components that contribute to this verbosity

[3]Our techniques can be extended to handle non-equality update conditions. For example, if γ was "`stDate > 1984-01-01`", the challenge template could include "`stDate > $val`".

[4]Note that, given a CR-table $T_{Q_\gamma^T}$ for challenge template Q_γ^T, the discriminating power depends only on the response R_γ.

DM for {Q11, Q21, Q31}	D	D⋈E	D⋈P
Q11	1	0	0
Q21	0.05	1	0
Q31	0.05	0	1

DM for {Q11, Q21, Q22}	D	D⋈E
Q11	1	0
Q21	0.05	1
Q22	0.05	1

Figure 2: Diversity Matrices for Sets of Challenges

are the length of the chain join (i.e., the number of tables, which is #joins + 1) and the number of response values the updater is asked to provide. This intuition is captured by the following requirement.

DEFINITION 2.4 (DESCRIPTION COMPLEXITY). We define the *description complexity* of challenge Q_γ as follows.

$$DC(Q_\gamma) = w_1 * (\#\text{joins} + 1) + w_2 * \#\text{select-clause-attrs} \quad (1)$$

In the absence of other information, we set $w_1 = w_2 = 1$.

The *description complexity*, or size, of a challenge template Q_γ^T is defined to be the same as that of the challenge Q_γ. □

For example, $DC(\texttt{Q1}) = 2$ and $DC(\texttt{Q3}) = 3$. This captures the complexity of expressing these challenges in natural language.

2.4 Diversity

It is important to realize that an updater may not be familiar with every aspect of the data she updates. Hence, the application should present an updater with a set of sufficiently *diverse* challenges, with the hope that there will be at least one challenge whose response would be correctly known to the updater.

We propose an information theoretic notion of diversity based on the chain joins present in a set of challenges, that captures the following key intuitions: (i) the more the number of distinct chain joins, the higher the diversity; (ii) the smaller the similarities between the distinct chain joins, the higher the diversity; and (iii) the more uniform the distribution of distinct chain joins, the higher the diversity. For example, the set of challenge templates $Q6^T$ ("what are the salary and sex of an employee with `empId` \$e?") and $Q7^T$ ("what are the salary and phone number of an employee with empId \$e?") is not very diverse. This is because they both involve the same table (chain join prefix).

The above intuitions can be precisely captured using the information theoretic concept of entropy, as follows.

DEFINITION 2.5 (DIVERSITY). Consider a set of challenges $\mathcal{Q}_\gamma = \{Qi_\gamma \mid 1 \leq i \leq k\}$. Let $\{J_\ell \mid 1 \leq \ell \leq m\}$ denote the set of chain joins and their prefixes that are present in $\mathcal{Q}_\gamma$, and let α denote an arbitrary constant in $(0, \frac{1}{km})$.[5] The *diversity matrix* of $\mathcal{Q}_\gamma$ is a $k \times m$ matrix whose entries are defined as follows.

$$\begin{aligned} DM(Qi_\gamma, J_\ell) &= 1, \text{if } J_\ell \text{ is } Qi_\gamma\text{'s chain join,} \\ &= \alpha, \text{if } J_\ell \text{ is a proper prefix of } Qi_\gamma\text{'s chain join,} \\ &= 0, \text{otherwise} \end{aligned}$$

Given the diversity matrix DM, the *diversity* of the set of challenges $\mathcal{Q}_\gamma$, denoted $DV(\mathcal{Q}_\gamma)$, is defined as the entropy $H(X)$ $(= \Sigma_{\ell=1}^{m} p(X = \ell) * \log_2(1/p(X = \ell)))$ of the random variable X, where

$$p(X = \ell) = \frac{\Sigma_{i=1}^{k} DM(Qi_\gamma, J_\ell)}{\Sigma_{j=1}^{m} \Sigma_{i=1}^{k} DM(Qi_\gamma, J_j)}, 1 \leq \ell \leq m$$

The diversity of a set of challenge templates $\{Qi_\gamma^T, 1 \leq i \leq k\}$ is defined to be the same as that of $\mathcal{Q}_\gamma$.[6] □

[5]$\alpha < \frac{1}{km}$ is important for Lemma 3.1.

[6]Diversity can be naturally extended to incorporate response attributes.

EXAMPLE 3 (DIVERSITY). Consider condition `location = NY` of Update U1, and the following space of possible challenges, abbreviated using (chain-join, response attributes), where each ⋈ denotes a (primary key, foreign key) left-outer-join:

- Q11: (DEPT, (deptName))
- Q21: (DEPT ⋈ EMP, (name))
- Q22: (DEPT ⋈ EMP, (phone))
- Q31: (DEPT ⋈ PROJ, (projName))

The diversity matrices for two sets of challenges S_1 = {Q11, Q21, Q31} and S_2 ={Q11, Q21, Q22} are shown in Fig. 2, for $\alpha = 0.05$. Based on the diversity matrix, the diversity for S_1, $DV(S_1)$ is 1.58, while for S_2, $DV(S_2)$ is 0.94. Note, S_1 and S_2 have the same cardinality and description complexity, but S_2 has two challenges, Q21 and Q22, with the same chain join while challenges in S_1 have no chain joins in common. □

3. FINDING CHALLENGE TEMPLATES

The database system needs to identify a set of good challenge templates for every database column that may be updated or on which an update condition may be specified and publish these templates. The application developer can consult these published templates, pick one or more reasonable challenges for each type of update supported by the application, and bake them into the application that is used by the updater to perform updates. For identifying good challenge templates, we formulate two optimization problems in Sec. 3.1, and subsequently develop efficient algorithms to solve these problems in Sec. 3.2 and Sec. 3.3.

3.1 Optimization Problems

Sec. 2 identified the properties that make for a set of good challenges: high discriminating power, low description complexity, and high diversity, which naturally extend to challenge templates as well. While desirable, it is unfortunately impossible to simultaneously optimize for all these properties. For example, it may be possible to find a set of k challenge templates from the updated table and they have a low description complexity; however, their diversity will be 0. If, instead, we find a set of k challenges with different and long chain joins, they are likely to have high diversity but larger description complexity. We thus formulate two constrained optimization problems that trade off the two ease-of-use concerns, while requiring high enough discriminating power.

Problem MinimizeDC: Given an update column `attr`, threshold values $\tau_{minDP}, \tau_{avgDP}$ and τ_{DV}, find a set of k update-relevant challenge templates $\mathcal{Q} = \{Qi^T \mid 1 \leq i \leq k\}$ that minimizes $\max(\{DC(Qi^T) \mid 1 \leq i \leq k\})$, while satisfying

1. $minDP(Qi^T) \geq \tau_{minDP}, 1 \leq i \leq k$,
2. $avgDP(Qi^T) \geq \tau_{avgDP}, 1 \leq i \leq k$,
3. $DV(\mathcal{Q}) \geq \tau_{DV}$, and
4. there does not exist any other challenge template Q^T, such that $minDP(Q^T) \geq \tau_{minDP}, avgDP(Q^T) \geq \tau_{avgDP}$, Q^T's join path is a prefix of that of Q_i^T and its attributes form a subset of those of $Q_i^T, 1 \leq i \leq k$.

Problem MaximizeDV: Given an update column `attr`, threshold values $\tau_{minDP}, \tau_{avgDP}$ and τ_{DC}, find a set of k update-relevant challenge templates $\mathcal{Q} = \{Qi^T \mid 1 \leq i \leq k\}$ that maximizes $DV(\mathcal{Q})$, while satisfying

1. $minDP(Qi^T) \geq \tau_{minDP}, 1 \leq i \leq k$,
2. $avgDP(Qi^T) \geq \tau_{avgDP}, 1 \leq i \leq k$,
3. $DC(Qi^T) \leq \tau_{DC}, 1 \leq i \leq k$, and
4. there does not exist any other challenge template Q^T, such that $minDP(Q^T) \geq \tau_{minDP}, avgDP(Q^T) \geq \tau_{avgDP}$, Q^T's join path is a prefix of that of Q_i^T and its attributes form a subset of those of $Q_i^T, 1 \leq i \leq k$.

We use both $minDP$ and $avgDP$ in our problem definitions since they provide complementary ways to characterize the discriminating power of challenge templates. For example, a medium value of τ_{minDP} and a high value of τ_{avgDP} ensure that challenge templates can be identified even if some instances of the challenge template don't have a high DP, while guaranteeing that none of the challenge template instances have a low DP. This is not possible using just $minDP$ or $avgDP$. The last condition in the definition of the two problems precludes a challenge template when a less complex one would work.

We experimentally show that our techniques are robust across a wide range of threshold values $\tau_{minDP}, \tau_{avgDP}, \tau_{DV}$ and τ_{DC}; this makes choosing of threshold values quite easy.

3.2 Minimizing Description Complexity

In this section, we present an algorithm called MINIMIZEDC for solving Problem MinimizeDC. We first give an overview (Sec. 3.2.1) and then explain it in greater detail (Sec. 3.2.2 and 3.2.3).

3.2.1 *Overview of Algorithm* MINIMIZEDC

Virtually, there is a chain-join tree where the root corresponds to the updated table (no join), each node at level-k corresponds to a join path with $k - 1$ joins, and its parent corresponds to its immediate join path prefix (see Fig. 3). To minimize description complexity, we shall explore the tree *top-down*.

Algorithm MINIMIZEDC dynamically generates the join tree in a breadth-first fashion; for each node, it maintains a *set* of lists $\{L_n\}$, $n > 0$, where L_n is a list of challenge templates with description complexity n (size-n) and with the join represented by the node. For example, the node PROJ_EMP0 represents all challenge templates sharing the join EMP $\bowtie_{empId=empId}$ PROJ_EMP. Algorithm MINIMIZEDC starts with the root of the join tree and the n-th round proceeds in three steps:

1. *Examine size-n candidate templates.* For each node N where $L_n \neq \emptyset$ and each template Q^T in $N.L_n$, (1) check if Q^T has enough discriminating power; if so, remove it from $N.L_n$, and (2) check if adding Q^T to the result set $\mathcal{Q}$ violates the diversity threshold; if not, add it to $\mathcal{Q}$. Return when $\mathcal{Q}$ contains k templates.
2. *Generate size-$(n+1)$ candidate templates by adding one more attribute, and store them in L_{n+1} for each node.* This step invokes APRIORIGEN, which we explain later.
3. *Extend all chain-join paths one step further and generate 1-attribute challenge templates for each new node.* Note that when we extend a path, we exclude the join condition that is the same as the last one in the chain join (so no loop join).

Optimizing diversity constraint checking: For each candidate template that has enough discriminating power, we need to check if adding it to $\mathcal{Q}$ does not violate the diversity constraint. However, repeated entropy computation is expensive; the following sufficient condition allows us to "translate" the global minimum threshold on diversity, τ_{DV}, to a "local threshold" on the maximum number of challenges that have the same join, which is easier to check.

LEMMA 3.1. *Let $\mathcal{Q}$ be a set of k challenge templates, and τ_{DV} be a threshold on diversity. If at most $k_l = \lceil k/2^{\tau_{DV}} \rceil$ templates in $\mathcal{Q}$ share the same chain join, then $DV(\mathcal{Q}) \geq \tau_{DV}$.*

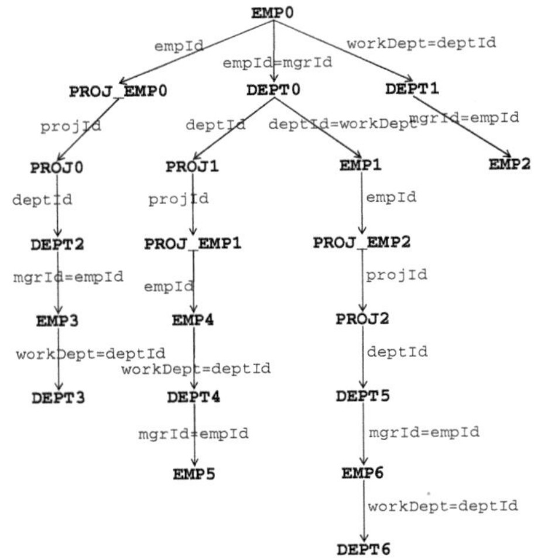

Figure 3: Chain-join tree in Ex. 4.

Proof Sketch: Recall the definition of diversity from Def 2.5. The nature of entries in the diversity matrix guarantees that with k challenge templates, the sum of all the entries in the diversity matrix will be in the closed-open interval $[k, k+1)$, since $\alpha < 1/km$. Since diversity of a set of challenge templates is computed using entropy, if $\ell \leq k$ chain joins are used by the k challenge templates in $\mathcal{Q}$, we know that $DV(\mathcal{Q}) < \log_2(\ell+1)$. Hence, the global minimum threshold on diversity, τ_{DV}, implies that at least $2^{\tau_{DV}}$ chain joins need to be used in $\mathcal{Q}$, with no more than $\lceil k/2^{\tau_{DV}} \rceil$ challenge templates that share the same chain join. Thus, ensuring this *local threshold* of $k_l = \lceil k/2^{\tau_{DV}} \rceil$ challenge templates would guarantee that $DV(\mathcal{Q}) \geq \tau_{DV}$. □

Algorithm APRIORIGEN: A key task of MINIMIZEDC is to generate candidate size-$(n+1)$ challenge templates for a node N_k. This task is non-trivial because we do not want to generate templates with a discriminating *sub-template* (i.e., with a subset of its attributes). However, checking if there exists such a sub-template can be very expensive. Inspired by the *A Priori* algorithm [1], our solution is based on two intuitions. First, we start from non-discriminating size-n challenge templates (in $N_k.L_n$) and check if any pair can be merged into a size-$(n+1)$ template. Second, for each generated template, rather than checking all of its sub-templates (exponential number), we check only those with one less attribute (linear number); such a template should be in some list $L_k, k < n$. For example, with 3-attribute templates $\{abc, abd, aef\}$ as input, the only pair that can be merged is abc and abd, resulting in a template with attributes $abcd$, which should be discarded as its size-3 sub-template acd is not included in the input set.

EXAMPLE 4. Consider an extended schema of that in Fig. 1:

```
DEPT(deptId, deptName, mgrId, location)
EMP(empId, name, workDept, phone, job, sex,
    birthdate, salary, bonus)
PROJ(projId, projName, deptId, stDate, enDate)
PROJ_EMP(empId, projId, job, stDate, enDate)
```

Fig. 3 shows the chain-join tree. The root is the table to be updated, i.e., EMP. Each node is named by the last table in the chain join plus a unique number to differentiate nodes with the same table. An edge represents a left outer join from a parent node to a child node on the attribute (or join predicate) labeled on the edge. For example, DEPT0 identifies the result table of the chain join EMP left-outer-join DEPT on empId=mgrId.

The first column of Tbl. 1 lists the top-20 challenge templates for EMP.empId returned by MINIMIZEDC (in the order they are found) with parameters $k_l = 10$ and $\tau_{DC} = 10$. For example, entry (EMP0.sex, DEPT0.deptId) represents a challenge template with join EMP left-outer-join DEPT, asking for "the employee's sex and the Id of the department she manages".

MINIMIZEDC starts with the root node EMP0. The first round inserts eight candidate templates (each corresponding to an attribute other than empId in EMP) to EMP0.L_2, and inserts three nodes PROJ_EMP0, DEPT0, DEPT1 to the join tree.

In the second round, the algorithm checks templates in EMP0.L_2 (Step 1). Assume it finds that 4 of them, each with one attribute name, phone, birthdate, or salary, have enough DP; accordingly, it removes them from EMP0.L_2 and adds them into $\mathcal{Q}$ as they also satisfy the diversity constraint. After this process, there are 4 attributes left in EMP0.L_2. The algorithm then invokes APRIORIGEN and generates 6 size-3 templates from them and puts the results into EMP0.L_3 (Step 2). Finally, it adds size-3 templates for nodes PROJ_EMP0, DEPT0, DEPT1 and four more nodes PROJ0, PROJ1, EMP1, EMP2 to the join tree (Step 3).

In the third round, the algorithm starts with node EMP0. It turns out that all of the 6 templates in EMP0.L_3 have enough DP and adding them into $\mathcal{Q}$ does not violate the diversity constraints. At this point, 10 templates are found. Then, the algorithm continues until 20 templates are found in the fourth round. □

We next explain Algorithms MINIMIZEDC and APRIORIGEN.

3.2.2 *Algorithm* MINIMIZEDC

Algorithm MINIMIZEDC is a breadth-first algorithm. In the n-th iteration, it examines candidate templates with description complexity n (size-n) (lines 6-13), then generates size-$(n+1)$ candidate templates by adding one more attribute (lines 14-17) or extending all chain joins one step further (lines 18-30).

MINIMIZEDC maintains the following data structures:

- *List*: a list of nodes, each corresponding to a node in the chain-join tree and of the form of $(parent, T, \langle attr1, attr2\rangle, level, \{L_k\})$, where $parent$ corresponds to the parent node in the join tree, T is the last table in the join path, $\langle attr1, attr2\rangle$ store the join attributes,[7] $level$ is the size of the join path, and L_k is a list of size-k challenge templates;
- *Queue*: a queue of nodes as in *List*, except that $\{L_k\} = \emptyset$. The nodes in *List* and in *Queue* never overlap;
- $\mathcal{Q}$: the set of already generated challenge templates;
- DM: the diversity matrix for templates in $\mathcal{Q}$.

The search starts with $n = 1$ and puts the root of the chain-join tree into *Queue* (lines 1-4). At the beginning of the n-th round, *List* contains all nodes that contain some size-n challenge templates [8]. The algorithm checks whether those challenge templates can be added to the result set $\mathcal{Q}$ or not. Specifically, for each such challenge template Qj^T (lines 6-7), we first check if Qj^T has enough discriminating power (line 8). If it does, we further check if adding Qj^T into the result set violates the diversity threshold (line 9). If not, Qj^T is added to the result set (line 10), and the algorithm returns once there are exactly k challenge templates in $\mathcal{Q}$ (lines 11-12). Once Qj^T has enough discriminating power, we remove it from the list L_n of the corresponding node N_i (line 13); as a result, after checking all size-n challenge templates, only the non-discriminating ones are left in the corresponding $N_i.L_n$; they will be used in generating size-$(n+1)$ challenges.

[7] Extension to the multi-attribute join attribute case is straightforward.

[8] In the first round, *List* is empty because a template is at least size-2.

Algorithm 1: MINIMIZEDC($attr, T, k, \tau_{DP}, k_l$)

Input : update column $attr$ from table T,
k, # of challenge templates to find,
τ_{DP}, discriminating power threshold
k_l, local diversity threshold
Output : a set $\mathcal{Q}$ of k challenge templates

1 $\mathcal{Q} \leftarrow \emptyset$; $DM \leftarrow \emptyset$; $Queue \leftarrow \emptyset$; $List \leftarrow \emptyset$;
2 $n \leftarrow 1$;
3 $root \leftarrow$ Node(*null, T, null, 1,* $\emptyset$); // *root of the join tree*
4 $Queue$.enqueue($root$);
5 **while** $Queue \neq \emptyset$ *or* $List \neq \emptyset$ **do**
  // *P1. Check size-n challenge templates*
6   **foreach** *node* $N_i \in List$ **do**
7   **foreach** *challenge template* $Qj^T \in N_i.L_n$ **do**
8   **if** compute-dp(Qj^T) $\geq \tau_{DP}$ **then**
9   **if** check-diversity(Qj^T, DM, τ_{DP}) **then**
10          $\mathcal{Q} \leftarrow \mathcal{Q} \cup \{Qj^T\}$;
11   **if** $|\mathcal{Q}| = k$ **then**
12   **return** $\mathcal{Q}$;
13        $N_i.L_n \leftarrow N_i.L_n - Qj^T$;
  // *P2. Generate size-$(n+1)$ templates from size-n templates*
14 **foreach** *node* $N_i \in List$ **do**
15   AprioriGen(N_i, n); // *Generate size-$(n+1)$ templates*
16   **if** $N_i.L_{n+1} = \emptyset$ **then**
17      $List \leftarrow List - N_i$;
  // *P3. Extend join paths, generate size-$(n+1)$ templates*
18 $Queue$.enqueue(*separator*);
19 **while** $true$ **do**
20    $N \leftarrow Queue$.dequeue();
21   **if** $N = separator$ **then**
22   **break**;
23   **foreach** *attribute* $A_j \in N.T$ **do**
24      $Q^T \leftarrow$ gen-challenge(A_j, N);
25      $N.L_{n+1} \leftarrow N.L_{n+1} + Q^T$;
26   **if** $N.L_{n+1} \neq \emptyset$ **then**
27      $List \leftarrow List + N$;
28   **foreach** *join from* $N.T.A_s$ *to* $T_i.A_t$ **do**
29      $N_{child} \leftarrow$ Node($N, T_i, \langle N.T.A_s, T_i.A_t \rangle, n, \emptyset$);
30      $Queue$.enqueue(N_{child});
31 $n \leftarrow n + 1$;

After checking all size-n challenge templates, the second part of a round generates size-$(n+1)$ challenge templates by adding one more attribute using Algorithm APRIORIGEN for all nodes in $List$ (lines 14-17). If L_{n+1} for a node N_i is empty, meaning that there is no size-$(n+1)$ challenge template of this node, we remove N_i from the node list $List$ (lines 16-17).

Then, the third part of a round (lines 18-30) generates size-$(n+1)$ challenge templates by extending all chain join paths one step further. Specifically, $Queue$ contains all nodes with chain joins of size n at the beginning of the n-th round; 1-attribute challenge templates of such nodes are size-$(n+1)$ challenge templates. Therefore, the algorithm generates 1-attribute challenge templates of each node in $Queue$ and puts them into the list L_{n+1} of the node (lines 23-25). If there are size-$(n+1)$ challenge templates in L_{n+1}, the corresponding node is added to the node list $List$ (lines 26-27).

As the algorithm explores the chain-join tree in a breadth-first manner, while visiting a node at the nth level, it puts all its children (with one more join) into $Queue$ (lines 28-30). The use of a $separator$ in $Queue$ helps to separate nodes on different levels, and knowing when the search is complete with all nodes on a given level. Finally, after checking all size-n challenge templates and generating all size-$(n+1)$ challenge templates, the round ends up with all nodes that have at least one size-$(n+1)$ challenge template in $List$ and all nodes on the $(n+1)^{th}$-level of the join tree in the queue $Queue$.

Algorithm 2: AprioriGen(N_k, n)

Input : N_k is a node in the join tree,
n is current size of challenge templates.
Output : N_k where $N_k.L_{n+1}$ is updated.

1 $N_k.L_{n+1} \leftarrow \emptyset$; // *$N_k$ is the kth node in $List$*
2 $\mathcal{Q}_{ex} \leftarrow \emptyset$; // *challenge templates generated, but not in $N_k.L_{n+1}$*
  // *P1: generate size-$(n+1)$ challenge templates of N_k*
3 **for** $i \leftarrow 1$ *to* $|N_k.L_n| - 1$ **do**
4   **for** $j \leftarrow i$ *to* $|N_k.L_n|$ **do**
5     $Qi^T \leftarrow i$-th challenge template in $N_k.L_n$;
6     $Qj^T \leftarrow j$-th challenge template in $N_k.L_n$;
7     $m \leftarrow$ #attributes in Qi^T ;
8   **if** Qi^T *and* Qj^T *have* $(m-1)$ *attributes in common* **then**
9       $Q^T \leftarrow$ merge(Qi^T, Qj^T);
10   **if** $Q^T \in \mathcal{Q}_{ex}$ *or* $Q^T \in N_k.L_{n+1}$ **then**
11   **continue**;
12   **foreach** *challenge template* $Q^{T'}$ *with any m attributes of* Q^T, $Q^{T'} \neq Qi^T$ *and* $Q^{T'} \neq Qj^T$ **do**
13        $N \leftarrow$ the join path of $Q^{T'}$;
14        $p \leftarrow$ 1+#joins in the join path of N;
15   **if** $Q^{T'} \notin N.L_{m+p}$ **then**
16          $\mathcal{Q}_{ex} \leftarrow \mathcal{Q}_{ex} \cup \{Q^T\}$;
17   **break**;
18   **if** $Q^T \notin \mathcal{Q}_{ex}$ **then**
19        $N_k.L_{n+1} \leftarrow N_k.L_{n+1} + Q^T$;
  // *P2: add new basis (2-attribute challenge templates) on a cross node basis if necessary*
20 **if** $N_k.level = n - 1$ **then**
21   $N_p \leftarrow N_k.parent$;
22   **while** $N_p \neq null$ **do**
23   **foreach** $Qi^T \in N_k.L_n$ **do**
24   **foreach** $Qj^T \in N_p.L_{N_p.level+1}$ **do**
25         $Q^T \leftarrow$ merge(Qi^T, Qj^T);
26         $N_k.L_{n+1} \leftarrow N_k.L_{n+1} + Q^T$;
27     $N_p \leftarrow N_p.parent$;

3.2.3 *Algorithm* APRIORIGEN

Algorithm APRIORIGEN maintains a list $\mathcal{Q}_{ex}$, storing challenge templates that have been generated but not inserted in $N_k.L_{n+1}$.

In the first part of the algorithm (line 3-19), we first check every pair of challenges in $N_k.L_n$, merge them for a new challenge template only if they share $m-1$ common attributes, where m is the number of attributes in a template in $N_k.L_n$ (lines 3-9). Then, it checks if the result Q^T should be added to $N_k.L_{n+1}$ (lines 10-18). First, if the template has been generated before (so either in $N_k.L_{n+1}$ or in $\mathcal{Q}_{ex}$), there is no need to consider it again (lines 10-11). Second, if a sub-template of Q^T has enough DP, we should discard it. We check every m-attribute sub-template $Q^{T'}$ of Q^T other than Qi^T or Qj^T (line 12). Note that it is possible that none of these m attributes are from table $N_k.T$, so the involved join path can be shorter; if we assume the join path has size p, the size of $Q^{T'}$ is $m + p (\leq n)$. Thus, $Q^{T'}$ should be in list L_{m+p} of the corresponding node if it does not have enough DP (lines 15-17).

If $N_k.L_n$ contains only 1-attribute challenge templates (line 20), we go to the second part of the algorithm (line 20-27) and generate across-table 2-attribute templates. We iteratively examine each ancestor node N_p of N_k. For each pair of a non-discriminating attribute in N_p and a non-discriminating attribute in N_k, we merge them and add the result template into $N_k.L_{n+1}$ (line 21-27). Note that since N_p has size $N_p.level$, its 1-attribute non-discriminating templates should be stored in $N_p.L_{N_p.level+1}$.

Based on Lemma 3.1, we can prove the following result.

THEOREM 3.2. *Algorithm* MINIMIZEDC *solves the Problem MinimizeDC.* □

3.2.4 *Enhancing Diversity of* MINIMIZEDC

MINIMIZEDC proceeds breadth-first, and if $\lceil k/2^{\tau_{DV}} \rceil$ challenge templates that satisfy the DP thresholds are available from a node in the chain join tree, it picks exactly that many *before moving to the next node*. The diversity of the challenge templates produced can be further boosted by greedily maximizing the diversity at each step, using a round-robin strategy for choosing discriminating challenge templates. The resulting algorithm, MINIMIZEDCHIGHDV, has the same optimality properties as MINIMIZEDC, but tries to produce more diverse challenge templates.

A second variant of MINIMIZEDC can obtain an even higher diversity in the set of returned challenge templates, at the cost of having slightly larger challenge templates. The key idea is that, instead of checking *all* size-n challenge templates in the join tree before moving to size-$(n+1)$ challenge templates, one can proceed in a more "local" fashion. Once a node N's size-n challenge templates have all been checked, one can check the size-$(n+1)$ challenge templates of N's children nodes in the join tree, together with the size-n challenges of other nodes (e.g., sibling nodes of N). The resulting algorithm, REDUCEDDCHIGHERDV, can return challenge templates with even higher diversity than MINIMIZEDCHIGHDV, but these may have a higher description complexity.

3.3 Maximizing Diversity

Problem MaximizeDV sets thresholds on discriminating power and description complexity, and seeks a set of k challenge templates that maximizes diversity. Recall from Def. 2.5 that challenges with longer chain joins yield a higher diversity; hence, we'll explore the join tree *bottom-up*. As a result, MAXIMIZEDV may return challenge templates with higher description complexity than those returned by previous algorithms. Algorithm MAXIMIZEDV (pseudo-code omitted for lack of space) proceeds in four steps:

1. Statically identify the chain-join tree that can yield challenge templates of size τ_{DC}.
2. Iteratively choose an unmarked node whose descendants are all marked and that maximizes the diversity, generate one template from this node, and mark the node as considered.
3. When all nodes are marked, unmark all nodes.
4. Repeat Steps 2-3 until we generate k challenge templates.

THEOREM 3.3. *Algorithm* MAXIMIZEDV *solves the Problem MaximizeDV.*

Proof Sketch: Let S_g and S_o be any sets of k challenge templates found by the greedy algorithm and present in any optimal solution respectively. Let Q be any template present in S_g but not in S_o. We will show $\exists P \in S_o - S_g$: replacing P by Q in S_o cannot decrease its diversity. By repeated application of this argument, it follows that S_g must be optimal.

Table 1: Top-20 challenge templates returned by MINIMIZEDC **and** MAXIMIZEDV **for column** `EMP.empId`.

MINIMIZEDC	MAXIMIZEDV
EMP0.name	EMP0.workDept, DEPT6.deptId
EMP0.phoneno	EMP0.workDept, EMP5.empId
EMP0.birthdate	DEPT2.location, DEPT3.deptId
EMP0.salary	EMP0.workDept, EMP6.empId
EMP0.job, EMP0.workDept	EMP0.workDept, DEPT4.deptId
EMP0.sex, EMP0.workDept	EMP0.job, EMP2.empId
EMP0.bonus, EMP0.workDept	DEPT2.location, EMP3.empId
EMP0.job, EMP0.sex	EMP0.workDept, DEPT3.deptId
EMP0.bonus, EMP0.job	EMP0.workDept, EMP4.empId
EMP0.bonus, EMP0.sex	DEPT2.deptId
PROJ_EMP0.projId	EMP0.workDept, PROJ2.projId
PROJ_EMP0.job	EMP0.job, DEPT1.deptId
PROJ_EMP0.stdate	EMP0.workDept, PROJ_EMP1.empId
PROJ_EMP0.endate	PROJ0.projId
EMP0.workDept, DEPT0.deptId	EMP0.workDept, PROJ_EMP2.projId
EMP0.job, DEPT0.deptId	EMP0.workDept, PROJ1.projId
EMP0.sex, DEPT0.deptId	PROJ_EMP0.projId
EMP0.bonus, DEPT0.deptId	EMP0.workDept, EMP1.empId
EMP0.workDept, DEPT0.deptname	EMP0.workDept, DEPT0.deptId
EMP0.job, DEPT0.deptname	EMP0.name

There are three cases to consider. Suppose $S_o - S_g$ contains a template P corresponding to an ancestor of Q. Then replacing P by Q will increase the diversity. Suppose $S_o - S_g$ contains a proper descendant of Q. By construction, Algorithm MAXIMIZEDV does not consider ancestors before it considers descendants, so this case cannot arise. So suppose no template in $S_o - S_g$ is an ancestor or descendant of Q. Consider replacing any template P in $S_o - S_g$ by Q. Since Q does not share a prefix with any template in $S_o - S_g$ and MAXIMIZEDV chooses Q to maximize the diversity of the solution it builds, it can be shown that replacing *any* template in $S_o - S_g$ by Q cannot decrease the diversity. □

EXAMPLE 5. Comparing with the challenges found by MINIMIZEDC in Ex. 4, Tbl. 1 also shows the top-20 challenge templates returned by MAXIMIZEDV. We observe obvious differences in the returned results. MINIMIZEDC first exhausts size-n templates from one node. MAXIMIZEDV, on the contrary, generates exactly the static tree as shown in Fig. 3, and proceeds from the bottom of the tree. It first picks leaf node DEPT6 as it has the longest join path. Then, it picks EMP5 and then DEPT3. At this time, the candidate nodes to choose from include EMP3, DEPT4, EMP6, EMP2, each from one branch. It picks EMP6 next as choosing it maximizes the diversity. As there are 20 nodes in the tree, the 20-th returned template is from the root node. □

4. EXPERIMENTAL EVALUATION

We implemented the four algorithms in Sec. 3, namely, MINIMIZEDC, MINIMIZEDCHIGHDV, MAXIMIZEDV, REDUCEDDCHIGHERDV. Tbl. 2 shows the input parameters and their settings; unless otherwise specified, we used default values. We experimented on two sets of data: the Corporate database–a sample database provided by IBM DB2i [5] with size about 20KB (schemas shown in Ex. 4), and the TPC-H data [13]. All algorithms were implemented in Java. All experiments were conducted on a PC with a 2.33GHz Core2 Duo processor, 3.25GB RAM and 200G SATA Disk, running Windows XP Pro SP3. MySQL (v.5.0.67) was used as the back-end database.

In Sec. 4.1, we demonstrate the effectiveness and usability of the certificates mechanism via a simulation study; Sec. 4.2 presents efficiency results for verifying certificates at run-time; finally in Sec. 4.3, we report results that show the efficiency of challenge-identification algorithms.

Table 2: Input parameters, their value ranges, and default values (underlined).

Parameter	Value
k, desired number of challenge templates	10, <u>20</u>, 50, 100, 200
τ_{minDP}, threshold on minimum DP	0, 0.2, <u>0.4</u>, 0.6, 0.8
τ_{avgDP}, threshold on average DP	0, 0.2, 0.4, 0.6, 0.8 <u>0.90</u>, 0.92, 0.94, 0.96, 0.98
τ_{DC}, threshold on description complexity	2, 4, <u>5</u>, 6, 8, 10
k_l, maximum number of challenge templates with the same chain join	2, 4, 6, 8, <u>10</u>
k_a, maximum number of challenge templates with the same response attribute	2, 4, 6, 8, <u>10</u>
df, probability decreasing factor	0.1, 0.3, <u>0.5</u>, 0.7, 0.9
τ_p, probability threshold	0.1, 0.3, 0.5, 0.7, <u>0.8</u>, 0.9

4.1 Simulation Study

We perform a simulation study on the Corporate database to show that, under natural models of an updater's knowledge of a database, update certificates catch a high percentage of erroneous updates without imposing an undue burden on updaters; similar results are observed using TPC-H.

Data preparation: First, we describe how we generate the updates and updaters for the simulation study, and then present the two models that characterize different types of updaters.

Generating updates: We consider simple record modifications of the form "`UPDATE T SET attr=val' WHERE attr=val`". The updated table `T` and updated attribute `attr` are randomly selected from the database. Different values `val` and `val'` are randomly chosen from $\mathcal{V}_{\texttt{attr}}$, the set of all values of `T.attr` and other attributes linked to `T.attr` via foreign key relationships. Also, each update is associated with its intended value, $\texttt{val}_i \in \mathcal{V}_{\texttt{attr}}$. For a correct update, $\texttt{val}=\texttt{val}_i$; for an incorrect update, $\texttt{val}\neq\texttt{val}_i$.

Updater models: It is natural to consider updaters who only know information about the records they update, and joinable records from other tables. Among such updaters, we categorize them in our study into *local-schema-aware* and *global-schema-aware*, depending on whether the extent of an updater's knowledge about a joinable record depends on the length of its join path from the updated table or not. The *local-schema-aware* model characterizes updaters whose knowledge of the database is centered around the updated table: the longer the chain join needed to reach a joinable record, the less likely the updater is to know about it. In contrast, the *global-schema-aware* model characterizes updaters whose knowledge of joinable records is not correlated with their distance from the updated table. Further, different updaters may know about different subsets of attributes in the schema.

We generate updater knowledge in a probabilistic manner. In the two updater models, we utilize the same join tree as used by the challenge-identification algorithms (e.g., Fig.3), to assign probability values to nodes and attributes in the join tree, denoted $P(N_{ij})$ and $P(N_{ij}.attr_k)$, respectively, where N_{ij} is the jth node on level i, and contains attribute $attr_k$. N_0 denotes the updated table (the root of the join tree) and $N_0.attr$ is the updated attribute. For a given parameter *df* (decreasing factor), the probabilities are assigned as follows.

1. $P(N_0) = P(N_0.attr) = 1.0$, in both updater models.
2. $\forall N_{ij}$ that is a child of $N(i > 0)$, $P(N_{ij})$ is uniformly drawn from the range $[df^i, P(N)]$, in the local-schema-aware model. $P(N_{ij}) = 1.0$ in the global-schema-aware model.
3. $\forall attr_k \in N_{ij}$, $P(N_{ij}.attr_k)$ is uniformly drawn from the range $[df^{i+1}, P(N_{ij})]$, in the local-schema-aware model. $P(N_{ij}.attr_k)$ is uniformly drawn from the range $[df, P(N_{ij})]$ in the global-schema-aware model.

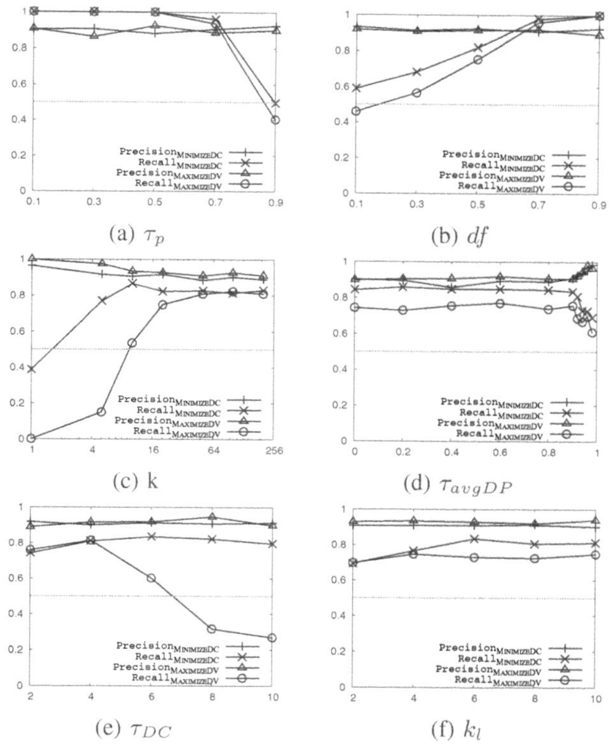

Figure 4: Local-schema aware: effect of various parameters

In both models, *an updater is able to answer a challenge only if she knows every attribute in the select clause of the challenge with a probability higher than a specific threshold parameter* τ_p.

Metrics: We use precision and recall of update verification as the performance metrics in the simulation study. *Precision* is defined as the fraction of the verified updates that are correct; this captures the effectiveness of update certificates in preventing unintended updates. *Recall* is defined as the fraction of correct updates that are verified; this captures the issue of ease of use of update certificates, as a correct update is not verified only if an updater's knowledge is insufficient to answer any presented challenge.

In our simulation study, we use average precision and recall for 1,000 updates consisting of half correct and half incorrect updates. Tbl. 2 lists the parameter values used in the simulation study. We show the results of MINIMIZEDC and MAXIMIZEDV – the other results are sandwiched between these two.

Results with Local-Schema-Aware Model: Fig. 4 shows the results of our simulation study on the Corporate data with the local-schema-aware model. The dotted lines show the precision (0.5) without using any update certificates. By applying the update certificates, the precision stays above 0.9 for both MINIMIZEDC and MAXIMIZEDV, across the entire range of parameters. This demonstrates that the certificate mechanism is very effective in reducing unintended updates. Hence, we focus the rest of the discussion on recall, which is a measure of ease of use of the certificates.

We observe in Fig. 4 that MAXIMIZEDV generally results in lower recall than MINIMIZEDC, especially when τ_{DC} is large. Recall from Sec. 3.3 that MAXIMIZEDV favors challenge templates with longer chain joins and results in challenge templates with higher description complexity. In the local-schema-aware model, updaters have lower ability to respond to challenges with long joins. However, with suitable parameter values, MAXIMIZEDV can get similar recall to that of MINIMIZEDC.

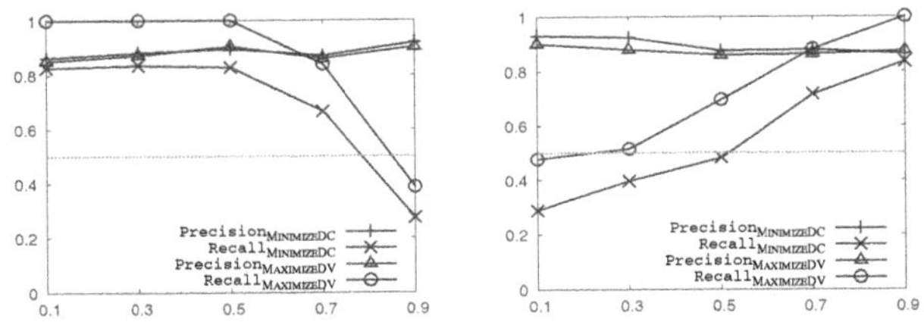

(a) probability threshold τ_p (b) decreasing factor df

Figure 5: Global-schema-aware: effect of various parameters

Probability threshold τ_p: Fig. 4(a) shows the results when we vary τ_p. Given a fixed probability of knowing an attribute, an updater's ability to answer challenges involving the attribute, and hence the recall, decreases with a higher τ_p. It is notable that even with a high threshold $\tau_p = 0.7$, about 95% of correct updates are verified.

Decreasing factor df: Fig. 4(b) shows the results as we vary df. With a smaller df, the probability of knowing a node in the join tree decreases faster with the depth of the node. Therefore, the recall increases significantly with larger df. When $df = 0.7$, the recalls are higher than 0.95. When $df = 0.5$ (the default value used), the recalls are about 0.8 and 0.7 for MINIMIZEDC and MAXIMIZEDV respectively; this models an updater with very limited knowledge, since the probability of knowing an attribute after one and two joins can be as low as 0.25 and 0.125, respectively; it is chosen to stress-test the ease of use issue.

Number of challenges k: Fig. 4(c) shows the results as we vary k. When $k = 1$, the recall of MINIMIZEDC is about 0.4, which is the probability of knowing an attribute in the updated table (for $df = 0.5$ and $\tau_p = 0.8$). For MAXIMIZEDV, the recall is close to 0 since the only challenge involves a chain join which is too long (for $\tau_{DC} = 5$) to be known by the updater. With larger k, the recall increases quickly as many challenges are provided to the updater.

Average DP τ_{avgDP}: Fig. 4(d) shows the results as we vary τ_{avgDP}. When $\tau_{avgDP} < 0.9$, it does not affect the recall much; when $\tau_{avgDP} \geq 0.9$, the challenges become more complex, reducing the recall. Our simulation study also shows that τ_{minDP} has a similar effect as $\tau_{avgDP} \in [0.9, 1.0]$ (figure omitted).

Description complexity τ_{DC}: Fig. 4(e) shows the results when we vary τ_{DC}. When $\tau_{DC} = 2$, the choices of challenge templates are quite limited and almost the same for both algorithms. Therefore, both MINIMIZEDC and MAXIMIZEDV have low recall and high precision. When $\tau_{DC} \geq 6$, the recall of MAXIMIZEDV decreases significantly, since larger τ_{DC} allows complex challenges with longer joins in MAXIMIZEDV.

Join-level diversity k_l: Fig. 4(f) shows the results when we vary k_l. With the smallest k_l, there are at most 2 challenges available from the same node, so the average complexity of the challenges is high and the recall is low. With a higher k_l, more challenges are available from each node, so the diversity is lower, but we get a higher recall because the challenges contain fewer joins and the average complexity of the challenges is lower. The attribute-level diversity k_a has a similar effect as k_l; hence we omit the figure.

Results with Global-Schema-Aware Model: To highlight a key difference between the updater models, Fig. 5 shows results for join-challenges under the global-schema-aware model, when only a few challenges ($k = 5$) are provided. With the global-schema-aware model, the precision and recall show similar trends as a function of the various parameters, *except that* MAXIMIZEDV *consistently outperforms* MINIMIZEDC. For reasons of space, we only show results for τ_p and df.

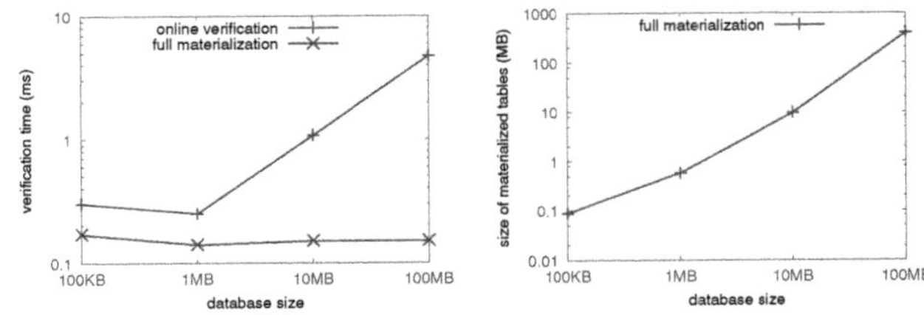

(a) verification time (b) size of materialized tables

Figure 6: Verification overhead w. no and full materialization

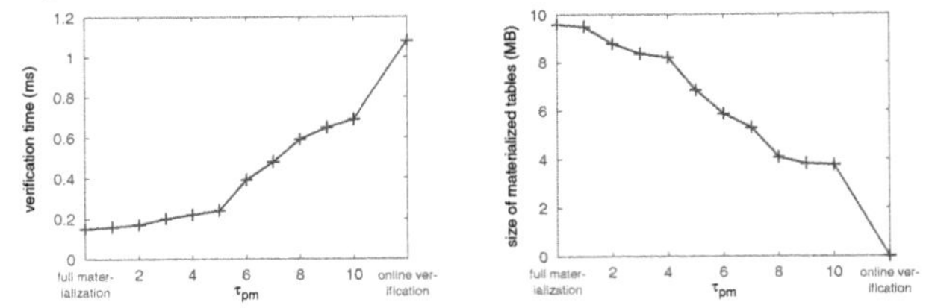

(a) verification time (b) size of materialized tables

Figure 7: Verification overhead w. partial materialization.

With a more global knowledge of the schema, MAXIMIZEDV shows the added advantage of diversity, providing challenges involving different attributes and tables, giving more choice to the updaters. An updater who does not know a particular table will not be prevented from submitting her update with challenges from other tables. Note that the lower recalls in Fig. 5 compared to Fig. 4 are due to the smaller value of k used for the results of Fig. 5.

4.2 Certificate Verification

Certificate verification is an added computational cost incurred by the database system when supporting update certificates. For this reason, the efficiency and overhead of verifying certificates is an important consideration, which we investigate next.

We consider three methods: *online verification*, executing the challenge query on original tables; *full materialization*, materializing the CR-tables (see Sec. 2.2) and verifying using the materialized tables; and *partial materialization*, materializing only "critical" (which we define shortly) CR-tables, verifying on the materialized tables when such tables exist and on original tables otherwise. We take the union of the challenge templates returned by the four algorithms for each attribute in TPC-H and report (1) the average space for storing the materialized tables for all templates for an attribute, and (2) the average time for verifying on each possible update value using each template. In our implementation, we build indexes only for key and foreign-key columns; we store each materialized CR-table as a "covering index", which takes about the same space as the normal table but accelerates access to data.

Full vs no materialization: Fig. 6 shows the time and space for online verification and with full materialization on TPC-H data of different sizes. We see that without materialization, verification time increases linearly with the database size; on a 100MB database, it took 4.75ms on average. The maximum verification time (not shown) takes 2-8 times as much as the average time.

On the other hand, when we materialize all CR-tables, the average verification time is less than 0.2ms for all databases with various sizes, and the maximum verification time is less than 3 times the average, which is much faster than online verification. However, the space required for storing all materialized CR-tables for one update column grows with the size of the database, and can take as much space as the original database.

Partial materialization: As a trade-off between time and space,

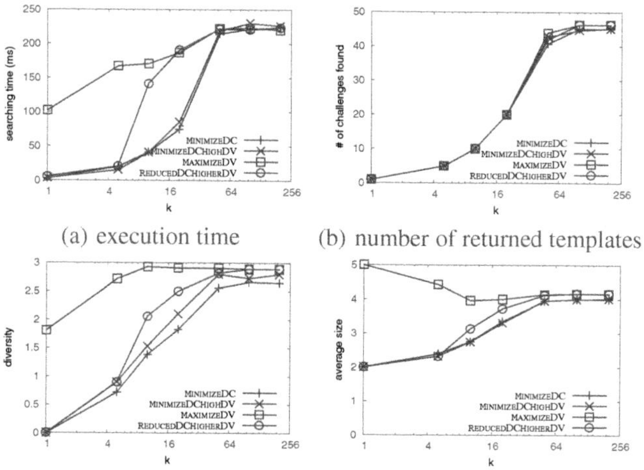

(a) execution time (b) number of returned templates

(c) diversity $DV(\mathcal{Q})$ (d) average size $avgDC(\mathcal{Q})$

Figure 8: Results of various algorithms on Corporate.

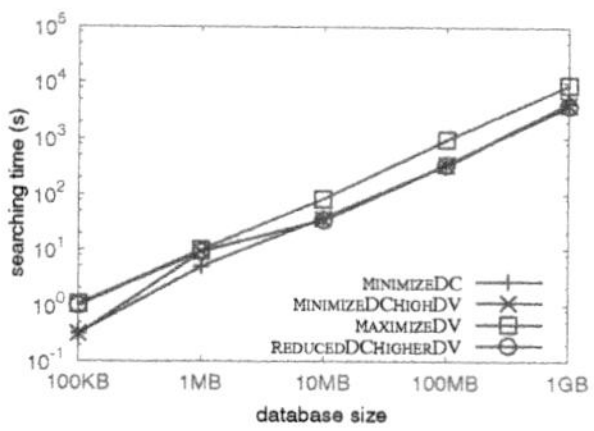

Figure 9: Effect of size

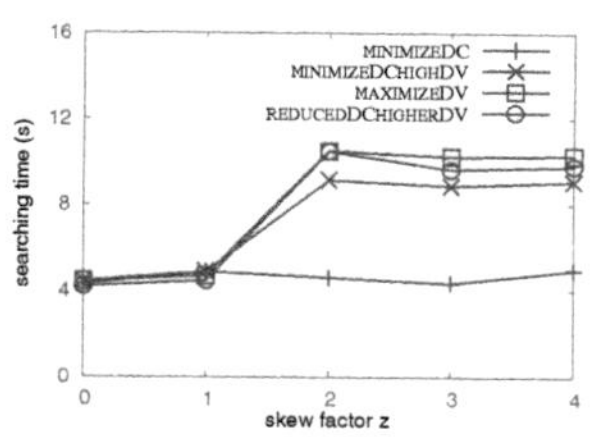

Figure 10: Effect of skew

we can materialize only some of the CR-tables. Selecting views for materialization to accelerate query answering has been well studied in the literature [10]. Here we explore a simple strategy, where we materialize a CR-table T if $\frac{\text{verification time on original tables}}{\text{verification time on materialized } T} \geq \tau_{pm}$, where τ_{pm} is a given threshold.

Fig. 7 shows the time and space cost on a 10MB TPC-H database as we varied τ_{pm} (we skip the results for 100MB TPC-H database as it shows similar trends). When $\tau_{pm} = 0$, we materialize all CR-tables; when $\tau_{pm} = 12$, we materialize no table as there does not exist any CR-table that can improve the efficiency by 12 times. As expected, the larger is τ_{pm}, the higher is the time cost for certificate verification and the lower is the space cost for CR-table materialization. As an example, when $\tau_{pm} = 5$, we can reduce the time by 78% compared with online verification, and reduce the space by 29% compared with full materialization.

4.3 Identifying Challenge Templates

In this section, we show that databases have many good challenges, and our algorithms can identify them efficiently.

Results on Corporate data: We first examine results of various algorithms on the Corporate database. Fig. 8 shows the execution time, the average number of returned challenge templates, their average size and diversity as we vary k. We have the following observations (they hold when we vary the other parameters as well).

- The algorithms run fast: even when we require top-200 templates, with the default setting, all algorithms finish in 0.25 seconds. MINIMIZEDC and MINIMIZEDCHIGHDV typically have the same running time, as they explore the same set of nodes in the join tree. When k is small, REDUCEDDCHIGHERDV is similar to MINIMIZEDC and MINIMIZEDCHIGHDV. When $k \geq 20$, REDUCEDDCHIGHERDV and MAXIMIZEDV often have similar running times: even though they explore the join tree in different directions, they end up checking most of the nodes in the join tree. The former two algorithms typically run faster than the latter two, as the latter two obtain higher diversity at the cost of exploring more complex challenge templates.
- For diversity of the results, in decreasing order the four algorithms are ranked as MAXIMIZEDV, REDUCEDDCHIGHERDV, MINIMIZEDCHIGHDV, MINIMIZEDC, consistent with our intuitions.
- For complexity of the results, in increasing order the algorithms are ranked as MINIMIZEDC/MINIMIZEDCHIGHDV (same size for these two algorithms), REDUCEDDCHIGHERDV, MAXIMIZEDV, also consistent with our intuitions.

As k increases, typically the execution time, the number of returned templates, their diversity and average size all increase. This is because the higher the k, the more challenges returned (so often higher diversity), the larger search space to explore (so higher execution time), and the less flexibility of discarding a template to reduce complexity (so higher average size). The only exception is that when k is increased from 1 to 10, the average size of MAXIMIZEDV's results decreases. This is because to maximize diversity, MAXIMIZEDV starts with nodes with longer join paths; when k is increased from 1 to 10, MAXIMIZEDV is able to add templates with shorter joins (see Ex. 5), but when k is increased further, MAXIMIZEDV has to select templates from the same nodes to meet the requirement, so the average size goes up slightly again. Finally, note that measures for different algorithms converge when $k = 200$, as there are not enough results (on average 45.3 templates are returned) so all methods explore the full search space.

Results on TPC-H data: We next experiment on TPC-H and investigate the effect of data size and skew on our algorithms. We examine each update attribute in table CUSTOMER (which has many attributes and can form both (key, foreign key) join and (foreign key, key) join with other tables) and report average results.

We first generate uniform data and vary the size of the data from 100K to 1G. Fig. 9 reports the execution time. We have the following observations. (1) The efficiency of most of our algorithms is acceptable, since challenge identification is performed offline: on 1G data, MINIMIZEDC, MINIMIZEDCHIGHDV and REDUCEDDCHIGHERDV on average terminated in about 60 minutes, and MAXIMIZEDV terminated in about 150 minutes; in addition, the execution time increases linearly with the size of the data. MAXIMIZEDV takes longer time because it checks DP for certificate templates with more joins. (2) Unlike on Corporate data, the execution time of REDUCEDDCHIGHERDV is close to that of MINIMIZEDC and MINIMIZEDCHIGHDV in most cases. This is because each table in TPC-H has a large number of attributes and the data are uniform, leading to more 1-attribute template results and so REDUCEDDCHIGHERDV does not need to go deep in the join tree. (3) The Corporate database has a much lower execution cost than the smallest TPC-H data, showing that schema complexity affects the join-tree structure and the number of templates, and hence the execution time. We also measured the diversity and average size of the returned results (not shown), and observed that the results are quite stable, conforming to our intuition that, with uniformly distributed data, size should not affect result diversity and complexity.

We next generate 1M data with various skews using the tool in [13]. We vary the skew factor z (the Zipfan distribution) of our data from 0 (uniform) to 4 and report the results in Fig. 10. When z increases from 1 to 2, there is a jump in execution time for various methods. Intuitively, when the data is more skewed, the $minDP$ and $avgDP$ of a challenge template drops; when $z = 2$, they drop to a level that cannot meet the DP thresholds, so we have to explore more complex challenges. Note that MINIMIZEDC is not affected much because it favors certificates with more attributes than those with longer chain joins, which can take shorter time for DP checking; however, if we increase k or τ_{DC}, the execution time of MINIMIZEDC would be closer to other methods. We also measured the diversity and average size of the returned results (not shown), and observed that the result complexity increases slightly when z increases from 1 to 2 (for the same reason as discussed above), but the result diversity remains stable.

4.4 Summary of Experimental Evaluation

We summarize our experimental results as follows.

- The use of update certificates successfully prevents most unintended updates, across a range of values for the DP parameters. Further, for moderate values of the complexity and diversity parameters, updaters can respond to at least one of the provided challenges, addressing the ease of use concern.
- Verifying certificates on the database is in general quite efficient, and we can further reduce the time cost by partially materializing the CR-tables.
- The challenge-identification algorithms have acceptable efficiency considering that the algorithms are executed offline.
- We have the following algorithm recommendations. When most updaters are local-schema-aware and complexity of the returned challenges is important, use MINIMIZEDCHIGHDV as it minimizes the average complexity, obtains higher diversity than MINIMIZEDC, and is almost as cheap as MINIMIZEDC. When most updaters are global-schema-aware and diversity of the returned challenges is important, use MAXIMIZEDV. To balance complexity and diversity, for a mixed workload of users use REDUCEDDCHIGHERDV.

5. RELATED WORK

Challenge-response techniques are widely used in practice for user identification; e.g., when a user needs to reset her password, she may be asked to provide her mother's maiden name. Such *user identification* is complementary to our problem of database update validation, and there has been no study of a formal notion of discriminating power of the challenges presented to the user.

Our DP measure to assess discriminating power is similar to frequency based measures (e.g., tf/idf) from Information Retrieval [12]. A key difference is that tf/idf is based on the occurrence frequency of a value, while DP is based on the frequency of a response value in the answer to all possible challenge queries. These two measures can be very different in practice.

Integrity constraints are quite powerful and useful to capture a class of erroneous updates [14]. For example, functional dependencies (FDs) and inclusion dependencies (IDs) can be used to ensure database consistency. Recent work has explored conditional variants of FDs and IDs to allow for more flexibility in having the constraint hold on a portion of the database, and also make assertions [6]. While these can achieve consistency under updates at a finer granularity, it is not practical to specify out of existence, every conceivable update error due to innocent mistakes, whether one uses CFDs or some other constraints, as illustrated by Ex. 1. In a similar spirit, the notion of matching dependencies (MDs) has been recently introduced [7, 2] as a means for capturing semantics of records in unreliable relations and in particular to help with record matching; the motivation for MDs is orthogonal to our work.

Finally, the notion of diversity has gained prominence in many areas such as recommender systems and query answering. [8] studies diversity from an axiomatic perspective and contains pointers to other works on diversity. Our notion of diversity is in the context of challenges, which are queries. To our knowledge, there has been no prior work on diversifying SQL query *expressions*.

6. CONCLUSIONS AND FUTURE WORK

The problem of ensuring that updates do not introduce errors into a database is an old and vexing problem, and existing techniques based on integrity constraints are inadequate to detect a large variety of errors that arise due to carelessness on the part of updaters. In this paper, we advocate the use of *update certificates*, a novel approach to detect erroneous updates that are unintended mistakes. We characterize good certificates as those with high *discriminating power*, low *description complexity*, and high *diversity*. We present algorithms to analyze databases and identify good challenges, and experimentally show that databases tend to have many good update certificates, these can be efficiently identified and verified, and are very effective in catching erroneous updates.

Our paper establishes the foundations of a novel approach to address the problem of erroneous updates in databases, but many interesting questions remain. A challenging problem is how to reduce the effort of updaters for multiple updates in an update transaction, without sacrificing the ability to detect erroneous updates. Another problem is to efficiently revise challenge templates as the database instance evolves in response to updates. Understanding how our techniques can work with conditional integrity constraints to comprehensively address the critical problem of erroneous updates is also an interesting direction of future work.

Acknowledgements

We would like to thank the anonymous reviewers for their many suggestions, which helped improve the quality of our paper.

7. REFERENCES

[1] R. Agrawal and R. Srikant. Fast algorithms for mining association rules in large databases. In *VLDB*, pages 487–499, 1994.

[2] O. Benjelloun, H. Garcia-Molina, D. Menestrina, Q. Su, S. E. Whang, and J. Widom. Swoosh: a generic approach to entity resolution. *VLDB J.*, 18(1):255–276, 2009.

[3] L. Berti-Equille and T. Dasu. New directions in data quality mining. In *KDD*, 2009.

[4] T. Dasu and T. Johnson. *Exploratory data mining and data cleaning*. John Wiley, 2003.

[5] Ibm db2 for i. http://www-03.ibm.com/systems/i/software/db2/sqldata.html.

[6] W. Fan. Dependencies revisited for improving data quality. In *PODS*, 2008.

[7] W. Fan, X. Jia, J. Li, and S. Ma. Reasoning about record matching rules. *PVLDB*, 2009.

[8] S. Gollapudi and A. Sharma. An axiomatic approach for result diversification. In *WWW*, 2009.

[9] N. Good, J. Grossklags, D. K. Mulligan, and J. A. Konstan. Noticing notice: a large-scale experiment on the timing of software license agreements. In *CHI*, 2007.

[10] H. Gupta and I. S. Mumick. Selection of views to materialize in a data warehouse. *TKDE*, 17(1):24–43, 2005.

[11] M. Mannan and P. C. van Oorschot. Security and usability: The gap in real-world online banking. In *New Security Paradigms Workshop (NSPW)*, Sept.18-21 2007.

[12] G. Salton and M. J. McGill. *Introduction to modern information retrieval*. McGraw-Hill, New York, 1983.

[13] Tools for controlling data skew of TPC-H data from Microsoft Research. ftp://ftp.research.microsoft.com/users/viveknar/TPCDSkew/.

[14] J. D. Ullman. *Principles of Database and Knowledge-Base Systems, Volumes I and II*. Computer Science Press, 1989.

Labeling Recursive Workflow Executions On-the-Fly

Zhuowei Bao
Department of Computer and Information Science
University of Pennsylvania
Philadelphia, PA 19104, USA
zhuowei@cis.upenn.edu

Susan B. Davidson
Department of Computer and Information Science
University of Pennsylvania
Philadelphia, PA 19104, USA
susan@cis.upenn.edu

Tova Milo
School of Computer Science
Tel Aviv University
Tel Aviv, Israel
milo@post.tau.ac.il

ABSTRACT

This paper presents a compact labeling scheme for answering reachability queries over workflow executions. In contrast to previous work, our scheme allows nodes (processes and data) in the execution graph to be labeled *on-the-fly*, i.e., in a dynamic fashion. In this way, reachability queries can be answered as soon as the relevant data is produced. We first show that, in general, for workflows that contain recursion, dynamic labeling of executions requires long (linear-size) labels. Fortunately, most real-life scientific workflows are *linear recursive*, and for this natural class we show that dynamic, yet compact (logarithmic-size) labeling is possible. Moreover, our scheme labels the executions in linear time, and answers any reachability query in constant time. We also show that linear recursive workflows are, in some sense, the largest class of workflows that allow compact, dynamic labeling schemes. Interestingly, the empirical evaluation, performed over both real and synthetic workflows, shows that our proposed dynamic scheme *outperforms the state-of-the-art static scheme* for large executions, and creates labels that are shorter by a factor of almost 3.

Categories and Subject Descriptors

H.2.8 [**Database Management**]: Database Applications—*scientific databases*

General Terms

Algorithms, Performance, Theory

1. INTRODUCTION

Scientific workflow systems are now becoming "provenance aware" by automatically recording data and module dependency during execution (*e.g.*, Taverna [12], VisTrails [6] and Kepler [4]). By using such information, provenance queries such as "Was data item A (or Module M) used to produce data item B, either directly or indirectly?" are enabled. Answering such queries entails evaluating reachability queries over large, graph-structured data, which can be expensive.

Reachability labels are an important tool for efficiently processing reachability queries on large graphs. The main idea is to assign each vertex a label such that, using only the label of any two vertices, we can quickly decide if one can reach the other. However, the effectiveness of this approach crucially depends on the ability to develop *compact* and *efficient* labeling schemes that take small storage space and allow fast query processing. More precisely, we say that a labeling scheme is *compact* if it uses logarithmic-size labels ($O(\log n)$ bits for any graph with n vertices), and *efficient* if it answers any reachability query in constant time [1]. This is indeed the best one can hope for, as even assigning unique ids for n vertices requires labels of $\log n$ bits.

An important observation in the context of workflow systems is that the execution graph (or *run*) from which provenance information is obtained is not arbitrary, but is derived from a workflow *specification*. Workflow specifications are commonly modeled as directed graphs whose vertices denote modules and whose edges denote data flow; furthermore, they are typically fairly small graphs (10s of vertices). A specification can be executed many times, using different data inputs or parameter settings, and generating multiple runs. A run is modeled as a directed, acyclic graph (DAG) in which vertices represent module executions and whose edges carry the data output by the source and input by the sink. Workflow runs can be much larger (1000s of vertices) and structurally more complex than the specification due to repeated execution of sub-workflows, *e.g.*, sequentially (*loops*), in parallel (*forked* executions) or through *recursion*.

Much research has been devoted recently to develop compact and efficient labeling schemes for workflow runs [5, 11] and graphs in general [22, 14, 15, 13, 1, 7]. A significant shortcoming, however, of the existing schemes is that they all need to examine the entire graph before labeling is performed. This may not be realistic in our setting since scientific workflows can take a long time to execute and users may want to ask provenance queries over partial executions. Labeling must therefore be done on-the-fly. That is, we must label modules as soon as they are executed and data as soon as it is produced, and cannot modify the labels subsequently.

Our goal is thus to develop a *dynamic* labeling scheme for workflow runs. Dynamic labeling has been previously considered in the context of XML *trees* [8, 18, 21], but workflow runs can have an arbitrarily more complex *DAG structure* [2]. Although there have been efficient dynamic algorithms [17, 9] for maintaining the transitive closure of DAGs, they ba-

[1]We follow the standard assumption that any operation on two words ($\log n$ bits) can be done in constant time [5].

[2]In particular, they are more general than series-parallel graphs.

sically produce a linear-size index per vertex, which is unacceptable for large graphs. Nevertheless, we will show in this paper that the knowledge of the specification can be exploited to obtain a compact (logarithmic size) and efficient (constant query time) dynamic labeling scheme for runs.

Prior Work. Reachability labeling has been studied for different classes of graphs in both static and dynamic settings. The main goal is to bound the maximum length of labels. Clearly, the more general the class of graphs is, the more difficult it is to obtain compact labeling schemes; dynamic labeling is also harder than static labeling. The maximum label lengths for different classes of graphs are summarized in Figure 1, and the main results of this paper are shaded.

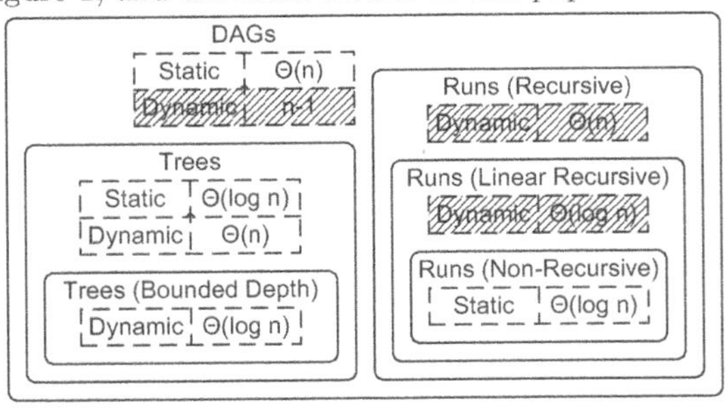

Figure 1: A Comparison of Maximum Label Length

Static. **(Trees)** The earliest work for labeling static trees [20] proposed an *interval-based* scheme that uses labels of $2\log n$ bits, where n is the number of nodes in the tree. Considerable effort [3, 16, 10] was devoted to reduce the constant factor (2). The best known scheme [3] uses labels of $\log n + O(\sqrt{\log n})$ bits, which is still separated from the known lower bound of $\log n + \Omega(\log\log n)$ bits [2]. Motivated by the fact that XML trees are not deep, recent work [10] developed a scheme that uses labels of $\log n + 2\log d + O(1)$ bits, where d is the depth of the tree.

(Workflow Runs) Workflow runs are modeled as DAGs derived from a given specification. [5] proposed a compact static scheme for labeling runs that uses labels of $3\log n + O(1)$ bits. However, it can only be applied to non-recursive workflows (with only loops and forks). [11] also proposed a static scheme for labeling runs by transforming the graph into a tree and then applying the interval-based scheme. Since the size of the new tree can be exponential in the size of the original graph, it results in linear-size labels.

(General DAGs) In contrast to the above results, compact labeling is impossible for general directed acyclic graphs (DAGs), since a known lower bound on the maximum label length is $\Omega(n)$ bits. This triggered several alternative approaches for efficiently answering reachability queries over large DAGs: Chain Decomposition [13], Tree Cover [1] and 2-Hop [7]. Other recent work includes Path-Tree [15] and 3-Hop [14] that combine the previous three approaches, and GRAIL [22] that is based on randomized interval labeling.

Dynamic. **(Trees)** The dynamic problem is harder than the static case; it was shown in [8] that labeling dynamic trees requires labels of $\Omega(n)$ bits. [8] also proposed a *prefix-based* scheme, which provides a matching upper bound of $O(n)$ bits, and if the depth of the dynamic tree is bounded by a constant, it produces labels of $O(\log n)$ bits. Other variant prefix-based schemes with similar bounds were also studied. *e.g.*, ORDPATH [18], implemented in Microsoft SQL Server, supports frequent inserts in XML documents, and DDE [21] is tailored for both static and dynamic XML documents.

(Workflow Runs and General DAGs) To our knowledge, the present work is the first to study dynamic labeling of workflow runs (and more generally of DAGs). The main contributions of this paper are summarized as follows.

- We propose a formal model, based on graph grammars, that captures a rich class of workflows with recursion, loops and forks. Based on this model we define *execution-based* and *derivation-based* dynamic labeling problems for workflow runs (Section 2).
- To get a handle on the difficulty of the two problems, we first provide tight lower and upper bounds of $\Theta(n)$ bits on the maximum label length. As a side effect, we also give tight bounds of $n-1$ bits for the general problem of labeling dynamic DAGs (Section 3).
- Nevertheless, we identify a common class of workflows with linear recursion, and show that dynamic, yet compact ($O(\log n)$ bits) labeling is possible for linear recursive workflows. Moreover, our scheme labels a dynamic run in linear time, and answers any reachability query in constant time (Sections 4 and 5).
- We also show that linear recursive workflows are, in some sense, the largest class of workflows that allow compact dynamic labeling schemes (Section 6).
- Finally, we empirically evaluate the proposed dynamic labeling scheme over both real and synthetic workflows. Interestingly, our dynamic scheme creates even shorter labels for large runs than the state-of-the-art static scheme [5] by a factor of almost 3 (Section 7).

2. MODEL AND PROBLEM STATEMENT

We start with notations and basic definitions over graphs in Section 2.1. An informal description of our workflow model is given in Section 2.2, followed by a formalization based on graph grammars in Section 2.3. Finally, Section 2.4 formulates the dynamic workflow labeling problems.

2.1 Preliminaries

Throughout the paper, the term *graphs* refers to directed acyclic graphs with no self-loops or multi-edges. Every vertex of a graph can be associated with two kinds of labels. The one, given in the graph, denotes a module name, and the other, created by our algorithm, is used for answering reachability queries. To distinguish the two labels, we will refer to the former as vertex *name*, and the latter as *reachability label* or simply *label*. We denote by $\mathtt{Name}(v)$ the name of a vertex v. Given two vertices v and v' of a graph g, let (v, v') denote an edge from v to v', and $v \rightsquigarrow_g v'$ denote that there is a path from v to v' in g. A graph g is said to be a *two-terminal graph* if it has a single source, denoted by $s(g)$, and a single target sink, denoted by $t(g)$. Given a finite set Σ of names, the set of all two-terminal graphs whose vertices are labeled by names chosen from Σ is denoted by $\mathcal{G}_\Sigma$.

Next, we introduce four graph operations, namely *series composition*, *parallel composition*, *vertex insertion* and *vertex replacement*. The first two operations are used to formalize loop and fork executions in Section 2.3. The last two operations are used to formalize execution-based and derivation-based dynamic workflow runs in Section 2.4.

Definition 1. A *series composition* of two-terminal graphs $g_1, g_2, \ldots, g_n$ forms a new two-terminal graph, denoted as $S(g_1, g_2, \ldots, g_n)$, by taking the union of their vertex sets and edges sets, and adding $(t(g_i), s(g_{i+1}))$ for all $1 \le i \le n-1$.

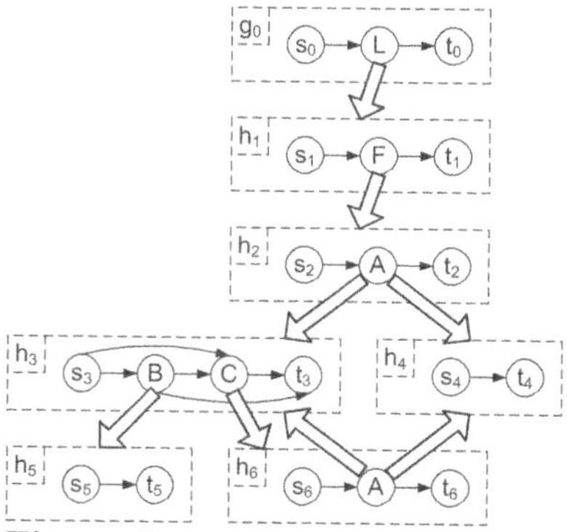

Figure 2: Workflow specification (running example)

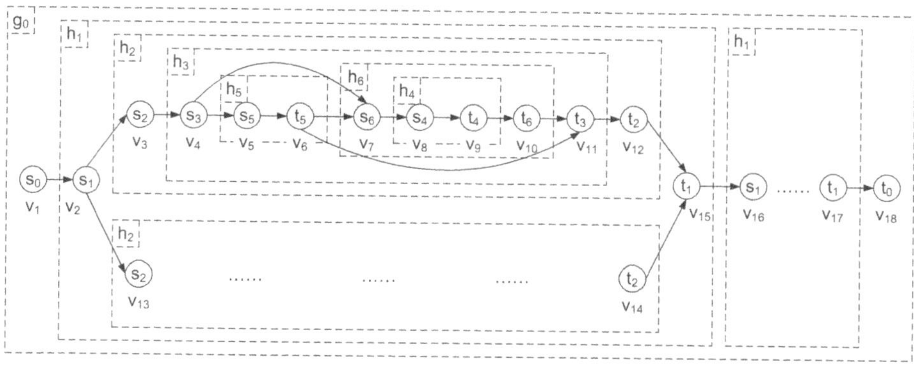

Figure 3: Workflow run (running example)

Definition 2. A *parallel composition* of two-terminal graphs $g_1, g_2, \ldots, g_n$ forms a new graph, denoted as $P(g_1, g_2, \ldots, g_n)$, by simply taking the union of their vertex sets and edge sets.

Definition 3. An *insertion* of a vertex v to a graph g, with respect to a subset C of vertices of g, forms a new graph, denoted as $g + (v, C)$, by adding v and (v', v) for all $v' \in C$.

Definition 4. A *replacement* of a vertex u of a graph g with another graph h forms a new graph, denoted as $g[u/h]$, by deleting u and all edges incident to u, and adding h and (v, s) for all predecessors v of u and all sources s of h and (t, v) for all successors v of u and all sinks t of h.

2.2 Workflow Model

Our workflow model has two components: *workflow specification* and *workflow run*. A workflow specification describes the design of a workflow, and a workflow run describes a particular execution of the given specification.

Workflow Specification. A workflow specification defines the control and data flow between a set of modules by means of a DAG. In this graph, each vertex represents a module, which takes a set of data items as input and produces a set of data items as output, and is labeled with a module name. Each directed edge represents the data flow between two modules. Each workflow has a single source, which sends out all initial data and starts the execution, and a single sink, which collects all final results and stops the execution.

The modules are either *atomic* or *composite*. Atomic modules are treated as "black boxes", since their internal structure is hidden. In contrast, composite modules, treated as "white boxes", are known to be implemented by other sub-workflows. Intuitively, we can open a white box by replacing the composite module with the corresponding sub-workflow. Some composite modules are allowed to be repeatedly executed *in series* or *in parallel*. We call them *loop* and *fork* modules respectively. Note that a composite module can be implemented by a sub-workflow that contains other composite modules (including itself). This may lead to *recursion*.

Example 1. Our running example of a workflow specification is shown in Figure 2, where the uppercase letters (*i.e.*, L, F, A, B, C) are the names of composite modules, and the lowercase letters (*i.e.*, $s_0, \ldots, s_6, t_0, \ldots, t_6$) are the names of atomic modules. In particular, L and F are the names of loop and fork modules respectively; g_0 is a start graph. The thick arrows describe the possible implementations of each composite module (*e.g.*, A has two possible implementations h_3 and h_4). Also observe that A and C form a recursion.

Workflow Run. A workflow specification is repeatedly executed using different data input and parameter settings. A valid workflow run begins with the start graph, and selects one possible implementation to execute for each composite module (*"or" semantics*). For a loop or fork module, the selected implementation is repeatedly executed one or more times in series or in parallel, respectively. Moreover, it must execute all the modules in the start graph and the selected implementation graphs (*"and" semantics*). Since all composite modules are expanded during the execution, the resulting workflow run consists only of atomic modules.

Example 2. One possible run derived from the specification in Figure 2 is shown in Figure 3, where $v_1, \ldots, v_{18}$ are unique identifiers for atomic modules. In this run, h_1 (the implementation of a loop module) is replicated twice in series. In the first copy of h_1, h_2 (the implementation of a fork module) is replicated twice in parallel. For purposes of illustration, we show only the detailed execution for one copy of h_2. Observe that, due to the recursion over A and C, h_3 and h_6 may be repeatedly executed until h_4 is selected.

2.3 Workflow Grammar

We next present a formalization of our workflow model based on graph grammars. A graph grammar is similar in spirit to the well-known string grammars, such as context-free grammars. It defines a set of graph-based productions (*i.e.*, rules), and uses them to generate a set of graphs as its language. More precisely, we consider graph grammars based on vertex replacement, that is, every production defined by the grammar replaces a single vertex (*i.e.*, the head of the rule) with a graph (*i.e.*, the body of the rule). Our idea is to map every specification to a graph grammar in such a way that the set of possible runs, derived from this specification, corresponds to exactly its graph language. To capture loop and fork executions, our grammar may have an infinite (but controlled) number of productions.

Definition 5. A *workflow specification* is defined as a system $S = (\Sigma, \Delta, \Delta_{\mathcal{L}}, \Delta_{\mathcal{F}}, \mathcal{I}, g_0)$, where

- Σ is a finite nonempty set of names;
- Δ is a nonempty subset of Σ, called the set of *atomic names*, and $\Sigma \setminus \Delta$ is called the set of *composite names*;
- $\Delta_{\mathcal{L}}$ and $\Delta_{\mathcal{F}}$ are two disjoint subsets of $\Sigma \setminus \Delta$, called the sets of *loop names* and *fork names* respectively;
- $\mathcal{I}$ is a finite set of pairs (A, h), where $h \in \mathcal{G}_\Sigma$ is called an *implementation graph* of $A \in \Sigma \setminus \Delta$; and
- $g_0 \in \mathcal{G}_\Sigma$ is called a *start graph*.

A vertex labeled with an atomic name is said to be an *atomic vertex*. Similarly, we can define *composite vertex*, *loop vertex* and *fork vertex*. In the rest of this paper, we loosely follow the convention that v, v' and v_i are used for atomic vertices; and u, u' and u_i for composite vertices.

Example 3. The specification in Figure 2 is written as $(\Sigma, \Delta, \Delta_{\mathcal{L}}, \Delta_{\mathcal{F}}, \mathcal{I}, g_0)$, where $\Sigma = \{s_0, \ldots, s_6, t_0, \ldots, t_6, L, F, A, B, C\}$, $\Delta = \{s_0, \ldots, s_6, t_0, \ldots, t_6\}$, $\Delta_{\mathcal{L}} = \{L\}$, $\Delta_{\mathcal{F}} = \{F\}$ and $\mathcal{I} = \{(L, h_1), (F, h_2), (A, h_3), (A, h_4), (B, h_5), (C, h_6)\}$.

Definition 6. Given a workflow specification $S = (\Sigma, \Delta, \Delta_{\mathcal{L}}, \Delta_{\mathcal{F}}, \mathcal{I}, g_0)$, the *workflow grammar* of S is defined as a system $G = (\Sigma, \Delta, g_0, \mathcal{P})$, where Σ, Δ and g_0 are as in S, and $\mathcal{P}$ is the possibly infinite set of productions below.

$$\begin{aligned}\mathcal{P} = \{A := h \mid (A, h) \in \mathcal{I}\} \\ \cup \{A := S(\underbrace{h, h, \ldots, h}_{i\text{'s } h}) \mid (A, h) \in \mathcal{I}, A \in \Delta_{\mathcal{L}}, i > 1\} \\ \cup \{A := P(\underbrace{h, h, \ldots, h}_{i\text{'s } h}) \mid (A, h) \in \mathcal{I}, A \in \Delta_{\mathcal{F}}, i > 1\}\end{aligned}$$

Example 4. The specification in Figure 2 is captured by a workflow grammar $(\Sigma, \Delta, g_0, \mathcal{P})$, where Σ and Δ are as in Example 3, and g_0 and $\mathcal{P}$ are shown in Figure 4.

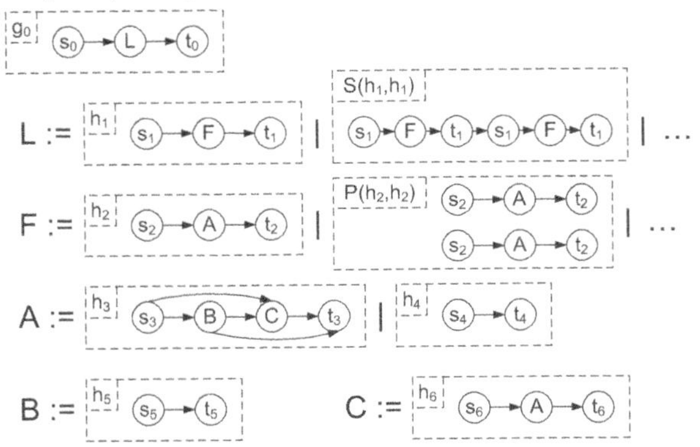

Figure 4: Workflow grammar (running example)

Let $G = (\Sigma, \Delta, g_0, \mathcal{P})$ be a workflow grammar. We say that a graph g_2 *is directly derived from* a graph g_1 (with respect to G), denoted by $g_1 \Rightarrow_G g_2$, if there is a production $A := h \in \mathcal{P}$ such that $g_2 = g_1[u/h]$, where u is a composite vertex of g_1 with $\texttt{Name}(u) = A$. Let $\Rightarrow_G^*$ be the reflexive and transitive closure of $\Rightarrow_G$, then g_2 *is derived from* g_1 (with respect to G), if $g_1 \Rightarrow_G^* g_2$. The *graph language* of G, denoted by $L(G)$, is defined as the set of all two-terminal graphs which can be derived from the start graph and consist only of atomic vertices. Formally,

$$L(G) = \{\, g \in \mathcal{G}_\Delta \mid g_0 \Rightarrow_G^* g \,\}$$

Definition 7. Given a workflow specification S, the set of *workflow runs*, with respect to S, is defined as $L(G)$, where G is the workflow grammar of S.

Example 5. The workflow run in Figure 3 can be derived from the start graph using the workflow grammar in Figure 4. A graph derivation is sketched in Figure 5, where $u_1, \ldots, u_8$ are unique identifiers for composite vertices.

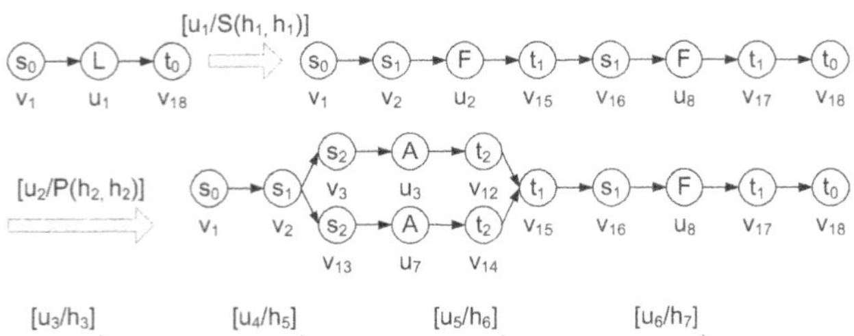

Figure 5: Graph derivation (running example)

2.4 Dynamic Workflow Labeling Problems

The classical (static) graph reachability labeling problem is defined as follows. Given a graph g, assign each vertex of g a *reachability label* such that, using only the labels of any two vertices of g, we can decide if one can reach the other.

This paper studies the problem of labeling *dynamic* workflow runs. It differs from the above problem in two aspects. Firstly, the input graph is a workflow run derived from a given specification. Formally, $g \in L(G)$, where G is a given workflow grammar. Secondly, rather than taking the entire graph as input, we get a sequence of "updates" that leads to a graph $g \in L(G)$. We do not know the update sequence in advance, but receive them online. We must label all new vertices introduced by one update before the next update is applied, and cannot modify their reachability labels subsequently. Moreover, these labels can be used to determine reachability in any intermediate graph.

Based on different models of updates, we introduce two related dynamic workflow labeling problems. The first one describes the real life setting where run steps are reported and logged one by one, and the second one is used as an auxiliary tool for exploring the structure of workflow runs.

Execution-Based Problem. The first problem defines the update as a *vertex insertion*. Recall from Definition 3 that every insertion creates a new vertex along with a set of directed edges from existing vertices to this vertex. We begin with an empty graph $g_\emptyset$, and get a sequence of insertions that leads to a graph $g \in L(G)$, called a *graph execution*.

Definition 8. An *execution-based* dynamic reachability labeling scheme for a workflow grammar G is a pair (ϕ, π), where ϕ is a labeling function and π is a binary predicate. The input is an execution of a graph $g \in L(G)$, denoted by

$$g_\emptyset \overset{+(v_1,C_1)}{\Longrightarrow} g_1 \overset{+(v_2,C_2)}{\Longrightarrow} g_2 \overset{(v_3,C_3)}{\Longrightarrow} \cdots \overset{+(v_n,C_n)}{\Longrightarrow} g_n = g$$

where $g_\emptyset$ is an empty graph and $g_i = g_{i-1} + (v_i, C_i)$, for all $1 \le i \le n$. In the ith step of the graph execution, ϕ assigns a reachability label $\phi(v_i)$ for the new vertex v_i. Note that by that time we can see only the first i insertions. ϕ and π are such that for any execution of a graph $g \in L(G)$, any intermediate graph g_i $(1 \le i \le n)$ and any two vertices v and v' of g_i, $\pi(\phi(v), \phi(v')) = \texttt{true}$ if and only if $v \leadsto_{g_i} v'$.

Derivation-Based Problem. The other problem defines the update as a *vertex replacement*. Recall from Definition 4 that every replacement substitutes an existing vertex for a new subgraph. We begin with the start graph g_0 (defined by the given workflow), and get a sequence of replacements that leads to a graph $g \in L(G)$, called a *graph derivation*.

Definition 9. A *derivation-based* dynamic reachability labeling scheme for a workflow grammar G is a pair (ϕ, π), where ϕ is a labeling function and π is a binary predicate. The input is a derivation of a graph $g \in L(G)$, denoted by

$$g_0 \overset{[u_1/h_1]}{\Longrightarrow} g_1 \overset{[u_2/h_2]}{\Longrightarrow} g_2 \overset{[u_3/h_3]}{\Longrightarrow} \cdots \overset{[u_k/h_k]}{\Longrightarrow} g_k = g$$

where g_0 is the start graph and $g_i = g_{i-1}[u_i/h_i]$, for all $1 \le i \le k$. Initially, ϕ assigns a reachability label $\phi(v)$ for each vertex v of g_0. In the ith step of the graph derivation, ϕ assigns a reachability label $\phi(v)$ for each vertex v of h_i. Again, by that time we can see only the first i replacements. ϕ and π are such that for any derivation of a graph $g \in L(G)$, any intermediate graph g_i $(0 \le i \le k)$ and any two vertices v and v' of g_i, $\pi(\phi(v), \phi(v')) = \texttt{true}$ if and only if $v \leadsto_{g_i} v'$.

At a first glance, the above two problems differ significantly from each other. The former receives and labels vertices one by one, while the latter by group. On the one hand, the execution-based model is more realistic, since it captures how runs advance; atomic modules of a workflow are executed in some topological ordering, due to data dependencies. On the other hand, the derivation-based model is more informative, since each step of a graph derivation describes exactly how a composite module is executed (*e.g.*, which sub-workflow is used or how many times a loop is repeated). However, our study in this paper reveals a tight relation between the two problems. We will show in Section 5.3 that a derivation-based scheme can be converted to an execution-based scheme, which creates the same reachability labels. A further study in Section 6 shows that in general, the execution-based problem allows shorter labels.

3. COMPACTNESS RESULTS

The effectiveness of reachability labeling crucially depends on the ability to design a compact labeling scheme that allows fast query processing. As mentioned before, a labeling scheme is said to be *compact* if it creates labels of $O(\log n)$ bits for any input graph with n vertices. Clearly, a compact labeling scheme creates the shortest possible labels up to a constant factor. In Section 5, we present a compact dynamic labeling scheme for a restricted class of workflows. Unfortunately, it is impossible to design a compact one for arbitrary workflows. In this section, we provide matching lower and upper bounds of $\Theta(n)$ bits on the maximum label length for both execution-based and derivation-based problems.

3.1 Lower Bounds

To establish the lower bounds, we first show in Theorem 1 that for some fixed workflow grammar, any possible dynamic labeling scheme requires linear-size reachability labels.

THEOREM 1. *There is a workflow grammar G such that for any execution-based (resp. derivation-based) dynamic labeling scheme (ϕ, π) for G, there is an execution (resp. derivation) of a graph $g \in L(G)$ with n vertices such that ϕ assigns a reachability label of $\Omega(n)$ bits for some vertex of g.*

PROOF. We first consider the execution-based problem. Let G be the workflow grammar shown in Figure 6, where A is a composite name and all the others are atomic names. Given an execution-based dynamic labeling scheme $D = (\phi, \pi)$ for G, for all $k \geq 0$, we define $L_k(G)$ to be the set of all graphs $g \in L(G)$ that are derived from g_0 by applying the production $A := h_1$ k times; and $S(D, k)$ to be the set of all reachability labels $\phi(v)$ that are assigned to a vertex v with $\mathtt{Name}(v) = a$ of a graph $g \in L_k(G)$. Finally, $N(k)$ is the minimum of $|S(D, k)|$ over all possible schemes D.

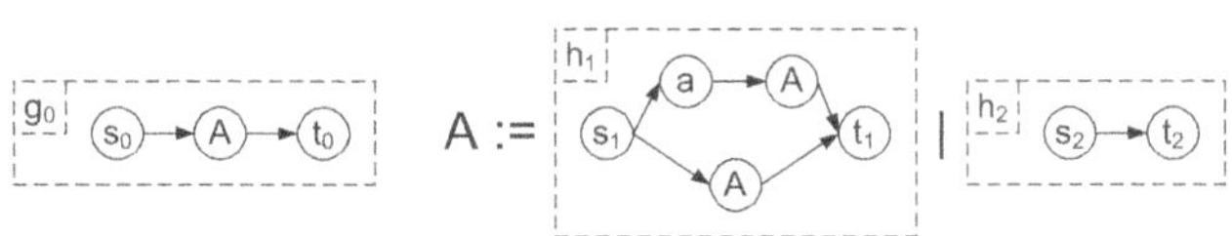

Figure 6: A workflow grammar that requires linear-size reachability labels (proof of Theorem 1).

We first prove that $N(k+1) \geq 2N(k) + 1$, for all $k \geq 0$. Given a dynamic labeling scheme $D = (\phi, \pi)$ for G, the input is an execution of a graph $g \in L_{k+1}(G)$. Suppose that the first three vertices v_1, v_2, v_3 are already inserted to g, as shown in Figure 7. Consider the label domains that are reserved for two upcoming subgraphs g_1 and g_2 independently.

We define S_1 and S_2 to be the sets of labels $\phi(v)$ that are reserved for all upcoming vertices v with $\mathtt{Name}(v) = a$ of g_1 and g_2 respectively. Let $\phi(v_3) = l$, then $\forall l' \in S_1, \pi(l, l') = \mathtt{true}$, but $\forall l' \in S_2, \pi(l, l') = \mathtt{false}$. Thus, $S_1 \cap S_2 = \emptyset$ and $l \notin S_1 \cup S_2$. Since both g_1 and g_2 can be an arbitrary graph that is derived from A by applying the production $A := h_1$ k times, $|S(D, k+1)| \geq |S_1| + |S_2| + 1 \geq 2N(k) + 1$. This holds for all possible schemes D, hence $N(k+1) \geq 2N(k) + 1$.

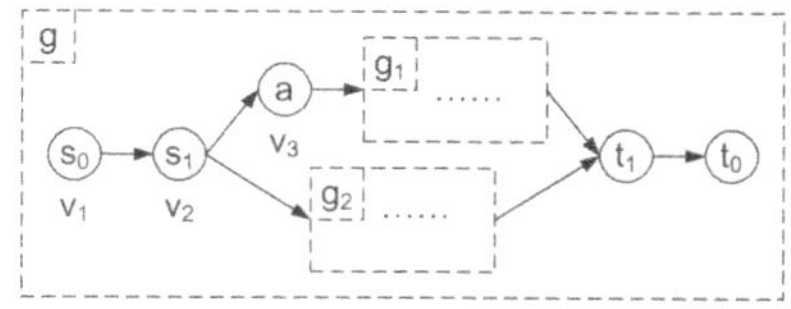

Figure 7: A graph $g \in L_{k+1}(G)$ that is derived from g_0 by applying the production $A := h_1$ $k+1$ times.

Since $N(0) = 0$ and $N(1) = 1$, we can prove by induction that $N(k) > 2^{k/2}$ for all $k \geq 2$. Therefore, we must assign a reachability label of at least $k/2$ bits for some vertex of a graph $g \in L_k(G)$. Finally, observe that g is derived from g_0 by applying the production $A := h_1$ k times and the other production $A := h_2$ $k+1$ times. Let n be the number of vertices of g, then $n = 3 + 4k + (k+1) = 5k + 4$. So $k/2 = (n-4)/10 = \Omega(n)$. The theorem follows.

We can use a similar proof for the derivation-based problem. The only modification is that, rather than inserting three vertices, we apply only one step of a graph derivation to obtain the intermediate graph shown in Figure 7. □

3.2 Matching Upper Bounds

To match the above lower bounds, we first present a simple execution-based dynamic labeling scheme (ϕ, π), which uses linear-size reachability labels. Given an execution of a graph g with n vertices, let v_i be the ith vertex to be inserted, then $\phi(v_i)$ is a binary string of $i-1$ bits. It simply encodes the reachability with respect to the previous $i-1$ vertices already inserted to the graph. Formally, for all $1 \leq i \leq n$ and $1 \leq j \leq i-1$, let $\phi(v_i)[j]$ be the jth bit of $\phi(v_i)$, then

$$\phi(v_i)[j] = \begin{cases} 1 & \text{if } v_j \rightsquigarrow_g v_i \\ 0 & \text{otherwise} \end{cases}$$

To decide if $v \rightsquigarrow_g v'$, we first compute the index of v and v' by the length of $\phi(v)$ and $\phi(v')$. Let $i = |\phi(v)| + 1$ and $i' = |\phi(v')| + 1$. Then $v \rightsquigarrow_g v'$ can be decided by

$$\pi(\phi(v), \phi(v')) = \begin{cases} \mathtt{true} & \text{if } i < i' \text{ and } \phi(v')[i] = 1 \\ \mathtt{false} & \text{otherwise} \end{cases}$$

The maximum length of labels used by this scheme is $n-1$ bits, which matches the lower bound of $\Omega(n)$ bits in Theorem 1. In fact, this scheme can be used to label executions of arbitrary DAGs. It was shown in [8] that even labeling dynamic trees with n nodes requires labels of $n-1$ bits. Hence, we provide as a side benefit tight lower and upper bounds of $n-1$ bits on the maximum label length for the general problem of labeling (execution-based) dynamic DAGs.

However, the above execution-based scheme does not work for the derivation-based problem, because a graph derivation may not introduce new vertices in a topological ordering. In Section 5.2, we will present a compact derivation-based dynamic labeling scheme, which creates logarithmic-size reachability labels for a restricted class of workflows. If we use that scheme to label arbitrary workflows, it guarantees linear-size labels. Details are deferred to Section 6.

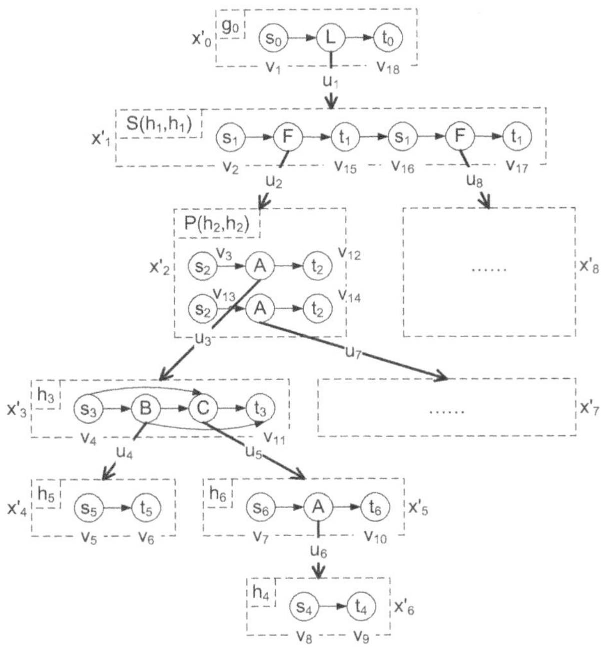

Figure 8: Canonical parse tree (running example)

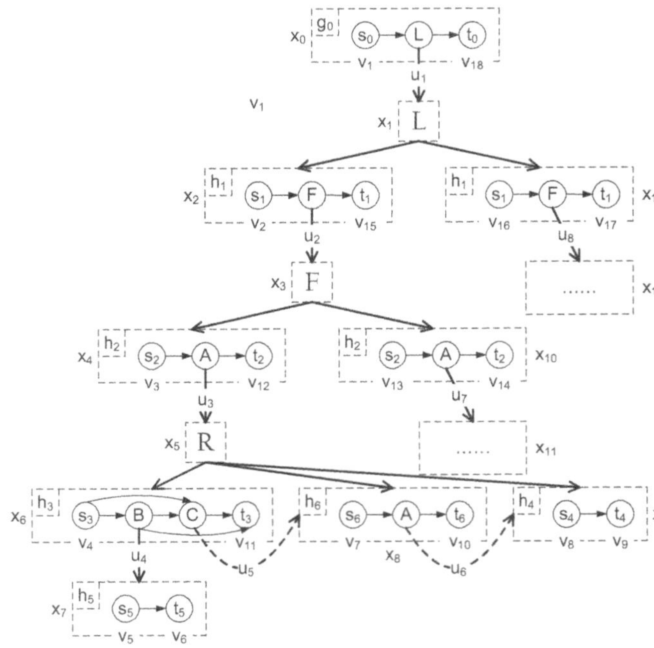

Figure 9: Explicit parse tree (running example)

4. QUERYING DYNAMIC WORKFLOWS WITH LINEAR RECURSION

Linear-size reachability labels do not scale to large graphs. As demonstrated in the proof of Theorem 1, such large labels are required when workflows have unrestricted recursion. Luckily, workflows that one encounters in practice typically have a more restricted, linear form of recursion (to be formally defined below), which does allow for compact dynamic labeling. Indeed, we will see in Section 6 that the class of linear recursive workflows is the largest for which compact derivation-based dynamic labeling is possible.

The rest of this section is organized as follows. Section 4.1 defines the class of linear recursive workflows. To develop the labeling schemes, we first introduce a tree representation for linear recursive workflows, called the *explicit parse tree*, in Section 4.2, and then describe how to efficiently answer reachability queries using explicit parse trees in Section 4.3. Due to space constraints, we omit the proofs in this section.

4.1 Linear Recursive Workflows

Let $G = (\Sigma, \Delta, g_0, \mathcal{P})$ be a workflow grammar. We say that a name A *directly induces* a name B (in G), denoted by $A \mapsto_G B$, if there is a production $A := h \in \mathcal{P}$ such that h has a vertex v with $\texttt{Name}(v) = B$. Let $\mapsto_G^*$ be the reflexive and transitive closure of $\mapsto_G$. We say that A *induces* B (in G), if $A \mapsto_G^* B$. Given a production $A := h \in \mathcal{P}$, a vertex u of h is said to be *recursive*, if $\texttt{Name}(u)$ induces A.

Example 6. Consider the workflow grammar in Figure 4. A directly induces B and C, due to the presence of $A := h_3$. Moreover, in this production, the vertex labeled with C is recursive, since C directly induces A by $C := h_6$.

Definition 10. A workflow grammar is said to be *linear recursive*, if any production has at most one recursive vertex.

Example 7. It can be verified that the workflow grammar in Figure 4 is linear recursive. Observe that $A := h_3$ has only one recursive vertex (labeled with C). In contrast, the workflow grammar in Figure 6 is not linear recursive, since $A := h_1$ has two recursive vertices (both labeled with A).

4.2 Explicit Parse Tree

We start by considering an arbitrary workflow grammar G. The derivation of a graph $g \in L(G)$ can be naturally captured by a *canonical parse tree* t, whose nodes represent nested subgraphs and edges represent composite vertices created during the graph derivation. The root of t corresponds to the start graph g_0. A subgraph h_1 is the parent of a subgraph h_2 if the graph derivation replaces a composite vertex v of h_1 with h_2, and the edge from h_1 to h_2 represents v.

Example 8. The canonical parse tree for the graph in Figure 3 is shown in Figure 8, whose nodes (denoted by dashed boxes) and edges (denoted by bold lines) are annotated with nested subgraphs and composite vertices that they represent. Note that $x'_0, \ldots, x'_8$ are unique identifiers for nodes of the tree; $u_1, \ldots, u_8$ and $v_1, \ldots, v_{18}$ are unique identifiers for composite and atomic vertices of the graph respectively. Consider the edge (x'_0, x'_1) annotated with u_1. It implies that the production $L := S(h_1, h_1)$ is applied to replace the loop vertex u_1 of g_0 with a series composition of two h_1's.

For linear recursive workflow grammars, we can convert a canonical parse tree to an *explicit parse tree* by inserting three kinds of special nodes: $\mathcal{L}$ (loop) nodes, $\mathcal{F}$ (fork) nodes and $\mathcal{R}$ (recursive) nodes. The children of an $\mathcal{L}$ or an $\mathcal{F}$ node represent one or more copies of the same loop or fork subgraph, which are combined in series or in parallel respectively; and the children of a $\mathcal{R}$ node represent a sequence of nested subgraphs, which form a linear recursion.

Example 9. The explicit parse tree for the graph in Figure 3 is shown in Figure 9, where $x_0, \ldots, x_{13}$ are unique identifiers for nodes of the new tree. Comparing with the canonical parse tree in Figure 8, we can see that x'_1 is split into two nodes x_2 and x_{12} rooted at a special $\mathcal{L}$ node x_1. Moreover, x'_3, x'_5, x'_6 are moved to be the children x_6, x_8, x_9 of a special $\mathcal{R}$ node x_5. Note that x_6, x_8, x_9 are linked by dashed edges annotated with recursive vertices u_5 and u_6.

It is important to note that the canonical parse tree for graphs generated by a fixed grammar may have unbounded depth due to recursion. However, in the explicit parse tree, the sequence of nested subgraphs in a linear recursion are flattened to be the children of a $\mathcal{R}$ node. Hence, for linear recursive grammars, the depth of the explicit parse tree is bounded by a constant that depends only on the grammar.

LEMMA 4.1. *Given a linear recursive workflow grammar $G = (\Sigma, \Delta, g_0, \mathcal{P})$, let t be an explicit parse tree for a graph $g \in L(G)$ and d be the depth of t, then $d \leq 2|\Sigma \setminus \Delta|$.*

4.3 Answering Reachability Queries

Let t be an explicit parse tree for a graph g. To avoid confusion, we use x and y to refer to nodes of t and u and v to vertices of g. Note that in this section, we abuse the notation slightly by using u and v to refer to both composite and atomic vertices of g. $\texttt{Annt}(x)$ denotes the subgraph annotated on a non-special node x, and $\texttt{Annt}(x, y)$ denotes the composite vertex annotated on an edge (x, y). Recall that a graph g_2 is said to be derived from a graph g_1 if g_2 can be obtained from g_1 by applying a sequence of productions. We extend this notion to vertices as follows: A vertex v *is directly derived from* a vertex u, denoted by $u \Rightarrow v$, if a production $\texttt{Name}(u) := h$ is applied to replace u with a graph h, and v is a vertex of h. Let $\Rightarrow^*$ be the reflexive and transitive closure of $\Rightarrow$, then v *is derived from* u, if $u \Rightarrow^* v$.

To efficiently answer reachability queries using explicit parse trees, we introduce the notions of *context* and *origin*.

Definition 11. A non-special node x of t is said to be the *context* of a vertex v of g, if v is a vertex of $\texttt{Annt}(x)$.

Definition 12. A vertex u of g is said to be the *origin* of a vertex v of g *with respect to* a non-special node y of t, if v is derived from u, and y is the context of u.

Note that the context and origin are always unique and can be defined for both atomic and composite vertices.

Example 10. Consider the explicit parse tree in Figure 9. The context of v_5 (bottom left) is x_7, since v_5 is an atomic vertex of $\texttt{Annt}(x_7)$. The origin of v_5 with respect to x_2 (top left) is u_2, since u_2 is a composite vertex of $\texttt{Annt}(x_2)$ from which v_5 is derived. Similarly, the origin of v_8 (bottom right) with respect to x_6 (bottom left) is u_5 (on the dashed edge).

The main idea is as follows. To decide if v can reach v' in g, we find the *least common ancestor* of their context x and x' in t, denoted by $\texttt{LCA}(x, x')$. If $\texttt{LCA}(x, x')$ is a special $\mathcal{L}$ or $\mathcal{F}$ node, we can immediately answer "yes" or "no" by showing that v and v' belong to two distinct copies of the same loop (reachable) or fork (unreachable); otherwise (if $\texttt{LCA}(x, x')$ is a special $\mathcal{R}$ node or a non-special node), we show that the original query for v and v' over g can be reduced to a simple query for their origins u and u' with respect to a small subgraph h. The details are given in Lemma 4.2.

LEMMA 4.2. *Let t be an explicit parse tree for a graph g. Given any two vertices v and v' of g, let x (resp. x') be the context of v (resp. v') in t, then*

- *if $\texttt{LCA}(x, x')$ is a special node, let y (resp. y') be a child of $\texttt{LCA}(x, x')$ who is an ancestor of x (resp. x'). Assume w.l.o.g. that y is on the left of y'.*
  - *if $\texttt{LCA}(x, x')$ is an $\mathcal{L}$ node, then $v \leadsto_g v'$;*
  - *if $\texttt{LCA}(x, x')$ is an $\mathcal{F}$ node, then $v \not\leadsto_g v'$, $v' \not\leadsto_g v$;*
  - *if $\texttt{LCA}(x, x')$ is a $\mathcal{R}$ node, let u (resp. u') be the origin of v (resp. v') with respect to y (note that $u' = \texttt{Annt}(y, z)$, where z is the right sibling of y), and $h = \texttt{Annt}(y)$, then $v \leadsto_g v'$ iff $u \leadsto_h u'$.*
- *if $\texttt{LCA}(x, x')$ is a non-special node, let u (resp. u') be the origin of v (resp. v') with respect to $\texttt{LCA}(x, x')$, and $h = \texttt{Annt}(\texttt{LCA}(x, x'))$, then $v \leadsto_g v'$ iff $u \leadsto_h u'$.*

Example 11. We demonstrate the above four rules using the running example. First, consider v_5 and v_{16} (top right) in Figure 9. The least common ancestor of their context x_7 and x_{12} is an $\mathcal{L}$ node x_1. By Lemma 4.2, $v_5 \leadsto_g v_{16}$, which is confirmed by Figure 3. Similarly, consider v_5 and v_{13} (middle right). The least common ancestor of their context x_7 and x_{10} is an $\mathcal{F}$ node x_3. Hence, $v_5 \not\leadsto_g v_{13}$ and $v_{13} \not\leadsto_g v_5$. Next, consider v_5 and v_8. The least common ancestor of their context x_7 and x_9 is a $\mathcal{R}$ node x_5 (note that the dashed edges are ignored). Moreover, u_4 and u_5 are the origin of v_5 and v_8 with respect to x_6 (note that u_5 is annotated on the dashed edge (x_6, x_8)). Since $u_4 \leadsto_{h_3} u_5$, by Lemma 4.2, $v_5 \leadsto_g v_8$. Finally, consider v_5 and v_{11} (bottom left). The least common ancestor of their context x_7 and x_6 is a non-special node x_6. u_4 and v_{11} are the origin of v_5 and v_{11} with respect to x_6. Hence, $u_4 \leadsto_{h_3} v_{11}$ implies that $v_5 \leadsto_g v_{11}$.

5. LABELING DYNAMIC WORKFLOWS WITH LINEAR RECURSION

Our dynamic schemes are built upon a skeleton-based labeling framework [5]. As a preprocessing step, we label the workflow specification using any static reachability scheme, and then extend the reachability labels on the specification, called the *skeleton labels*, to label workflow runs on-the-fly.

We start by discussing how to label the specification in Section 5.1. Section 5.2 presents a compact derivation-based dynamic labeling scheme for linear recursive workflows; we sketch how to adapt it to an execution-based scheme in Section 5.3. Finally, Section 5.4 proves the correctness and analyze the quality of our proposed dynamic schemes.

5.1 Labeling Workflow Specifications

Given a workflow specification $S = (\Sigma, \Delta, \Delta_{\mathcal{L}}, \Delta_{\mathcal{F}}, \mathcal{I}, g_0)$, we want to label the start graph and all implementation graphs in S. Formally, the set of graphs to be labeled is

$$\mathcal{G}(S) = \{g_0\} \cup \{h \mid (A, h) \in \mathcal{I}\}$$

It is important to note that all graphs in $\mathcal{G}(S)$ are small compared with runs derived from the specification. In practice, the largest real-life workflow that we have collected has fewer than 30 vertices, while a realistic run may repeatedly execute a loop or fork module (sub-workflow) hundreds of times. Therefore, we claim that any static scheme is scalable to label the specification. Our experiments in Section 7 show that even linear-size skeleton labels, created by the scheme described in Section 3.2, take negligible storage overhead.

5.2 Derivation-Based Dynamic Scheme

Given a labeled specification, we next explain the design of reachability labels for its runs. Let G be a linear recursive workflow grammar, and t be an explicit parse tree for a graph $g \in L(G)$. Recall from Lemma 4.2 that to decide if v can reach v' in g we only need to (1) find the least common ancestor $\texttt{LCA}(x, x')$ of their context x and x' in t; and (2) (if $\texttt{LCA}(x, x')$ is a special $\mathcal{R}$ node or a non-special node) answer an equivalent query for their origin u and u' with respect to a small subgraph h. To encode Step (1), we use a prefix-based scheme [16] [3] to label t. To encode Step (2), we enrich a prefix-based label with skeleton labels as well as other necessary information (*e.g.*, node types).

[3] In a prefixed-based scheme, every node of a tree is assigned an index i, if it is the ith child of its parent. The prefix-based label for a node consists of the indexes of all its ancestors.

The formal description of a reachability label is given below. We use (ϕ_G, π_G) to denote the static labeling scheme for the specification, and (ϕ_g, π_g) to denote our proposed dynamic labeling scheme for runs. Recall that ϕ_G and ϕ_g are labeling functions, and π_G and π_g are reachability predicates. To label a vertex v of g, we consider a path in t

$$x_0 \xrightarrow{u_0} x_1 \xrightarrow{u_1} x_2 \xrightarrow{u_2} \dots \xrightarrow{u_{k-1}} x_k$$

where x_0 is the root of t, x_k is the context of v, and for all $0 \leq i \leq k-1$, x_i is the parent of x_{i+1} and $u_i = \mathtt{Annt}(x_i, x_{i+1})$ is the composite vertex annotated on the edge (x_i, x_{i+1}). Note that $u_i = \mathtt{null}$ if x_i is a special node, otherwise, u_i is the origin of v with respect to x_i. To unify the notation, let $u_k = v$. Then $\phi_g(v)$ consists of a list of entries

$$\phi_g(v) = \{\mathtt{Entry}(x_0, u_0), \mathtt{Entry}(x_1, u_1), \dots, \mathtt{Entry}(x_k, u_k)\}$$

where $\mathtt{Entry}(x_i, u_i) = (\mathit{index}, \mathit{type}, \mathit{skl}, \mathit{rec}_1, \mathit{rec}_2)$ is a tuple obtained from a pair (x_i, u_i) by Algorithm 1.

The details of Algorithm 1 are explained as follows. The *index* of x is a positive integer i if x is the ith child of its parent (Line 1). Note that the index of the root of t is set to zero. The *type* of x is either $\mathcal{L}$ (loop) or $\mathcal{F}$ (fork) or $\mathcal{R}$ (recursive) or $\mathcal{N}$ (non-special) (Line 2). If x is a non-special node, then $\mathtt{Annt}(x)$ is already labeled by (ϕ_G, π_G). So the *skeleton label* assigned to u is given by $\phi_G(u)$ (Line 5) [4]. Finally, if $\mathtt{Annt}(x)$ has one recursive vertex (note that the parent of x must be a special $\mathcal{R}$ node), then the *recursion flags* for u are two booleans, indicating if u can reach the recursive vertex w in $\mathtt{Annt}(x)$ or vice versa. Note that they are computed by comparing the skeleton labels (Line 9 and 10). For other cases, *skl*, rec_1 and rec_2 are set to **null**.

Algorithm 1 *Entry Construction*

Input: (x, u) is a pair of a node of t and a vertex of g
(ϕ_G, π_G) is a static scheme for labeling specification
Output: $\mathtt{Entry}(x, u)$ is an entry for (x, u)

1: $\mathit{index} \leftarrow$ the index of x
2: $\mathit{type} \leftarrow$ the type of x
3: $\mathit{skl}, \mathit{rec}_1, \mathit{rec}_2 \leftarrow$ **null**
4: **if** x is a non-special node **then**
5: $\quad\mathit{skl} \leftarrow \phi_G(u)$
6: $\quad$**if** $\mathtt{Annt}(x)$ has one recursive vertex **then**
7: $\quad\quad$/* the parent of x must be a special $\mathcal{R}$ node */
8: $\quad\quad w \leftarrow$ the recursive vertex of $\mathtt{Annt}(x)$
9: $\quad\quad \mathit{rec}_1 \leftarrow \pi_G(\phi_G(u), \phi_G(w))$
10: $\quad\quad \mathit{rec}_2 \leftarrow \pi_G(\phi_G(w), \phi_G(u))$
11: $\quad$**end if**
12: **end if**
13: **return** $(\mathit{index}, \mathit{type}, \mathit{skl}, \mathit{rec}_1, \mathit{rec}_2)$

Example 12. We label the running example using the explicit parse tree in Figure 9. For example,

$$\begin{aligned}\phi_g(v_5) = \{&\mathtt{Entry}(x_0, u_1), \mathtt{Entry}(x_1, \mathtt{null}), \mathtt{Entry}(x_2, u_2),\\ &\mathtt{Entry}(x_3, \mathtt{null}), \mathtt{Entry}(x_4, u_3), \mathtt{Entry}(x_5, \mathtt{null}),\\ &\mathtt{Entry}(x_6, u_4), \mathtt{Entry}(x_7, v_5)\}\end{aligned}$$

where

$$\begin{aligned}\mathtt{Entry}(x_0, u_1) &= (0, \mathcal{N}, \phi_G(u_1), \mathtt{null}, \mathtt{null})\\ \mathtt{Entry}(x_1, \mathtt{null}) &= (1, \mathcal{L}, \mathtt{null}, \mathtt{null}, \mathtt{null})\\ &\dots\dots\\ \mathtt{Entry}(x_6, u_4) &= (1, \mathcal{N}, \phi_G(u_4), \mathtt{true}, \mathtt{false})\\ \mathtt{Entry}(x_7, v_5) &= (1, \mathcal{N}, \phi_G(v_5), \mathtt{null}, \mathtt{null})\end{aligned}$$

[4] Since the skeleton labels are shared by multiple runs, *skl* is implemented as a pointer to the label, rather than the label itself.

Since u_5 is the recursive vertex of h_3, by Algorithm 1,

$$\begin{aligned}\mathtt{Entry}(x_6, u_4).\mathit{rec}_1 &= \pi_G(\phi_G(u_4), \phi_G(u_5)) = \mathtt{true}\\ \mathtt{Entry}(x_6, u_4).\mathit{rec}_2 &= \pi_G(\phi_G(u_5), \phi_G(u_4)) = \mathtt{false}\end{aligned}$$

Similarly,

$$\phi_g(v_{16}) = \{\mathtt{Entry}(x_0, u_1), \mathtt{Entry}(x_1, \mathtt{null}), \mathtt{Entry}(x_{12}, v_{16})\}$$

where the first two entries are defined above, and

$$\mathtt{Entry}(x_{12}, v_{16}) = (2, \mathcal{N}, \phi_G(v_{16}), \mathtt{null}, \mathtt{null})$$

The above reachability labels can be generated on-the-fly during a graph derivation. The dynamic labeling algorithm ϕ_g is sketched as follows. First, we build the explicit parse tree in a top-down fashion. During this process, we also perform the following labeling. For a non-special node x, we create a label $\phi_g(v)$ for each vertex v of $\mathtt{Annt}(x)$. For a special node x, we also create a temporary label, denoted by $\phi_g(x)$. To obtain a new label for a node x, we take its parent's label, and append the new entry built by Algorithm 1.

To decide if $v \rightsquigarrow_g v'$, we compare $\phi_g(v)$ and $\phi_g(v')$ using the binary predicate π_g described in Algorithm 2, where $\phi_g(v)[i]$ denotes the ith entry of $\phi_g(v)$.

Algorithm 2 *Binary Predicate* π_g

Input: $\phi_g(v)$ is a reachability label for v
$\phi_g(v')$ is a reachability label for v'
π_G is a binary predicate for skeleton labels
Output: $\pi_g(\phi_g(v), \phi_g(v')) = \mathtt{true}$ iff $v \rightsquigarrow_g v'$

$i \leftarrow \min\{j \mid \phi_g(v)[j].\mathit{index} = \phi_g(v')[j].\mathit{index}$
$\quad$ and $\phi_g(v)[j+1].\mathit{index} \neq \phi_g(v')[j+1].\mathit{index}\}$
if $\phi_g(v)[i].\mathit{type} = \mathcal{L}$ **then**
$\quad$**return** $\phi_g(v)[i+1].\mathit{index} < \phi_g(v')[i+1].\mathit{index}$
else if $\phi_g(v)[i].\mathit{type} = \mathcal{F}$ **then**
$\quad$**return false**
else if $\phi_g(v)[i].\mathit{type} = \mathcal{R}$ **then**
$\quad$**if** $\phi_g(v)[i+1].\mathit{index} < \phi_g(v')[i+1].\mathit{index}$ **then**
$\quad\quad$**return** $\phi_g(v)[i+1].\mathit{rec}_1$
$\quad$**else**
$\quad\quad$**return** $\phi_g(v')[i+1].\mathit{rec}_2$
$\quad$**end if**
else $\{\phi_g(v)[i].\mathit{type} = \mathcal{N}\}$
$\quad$**return** $\pi_G(\phi_g(v)[i].\mathit{skl}, \phi_g(v')[i].\mathit{skl})$
end if

Example 13. Returning to the running example, consider v_5 and v_{16} in Figure 9. Since $\phi_g(v_5)$ and $\phi_g(v_{16})$, shown in Example 12, share the first two common entries, moreover,

$$\phi_g(v_5)[2].\mathit{type} = \mathcal{L} \tag{1}$$

$$\phi_g(v_5)[3].\mathit{index} = 1 < \phi_g(v_{16})[3].\mathit{index} = 2 \tag{2}$$

by Algorithm 2, $\pi_g(\phi_g(v_5), \phi_g(v_{16})) = \mathtt{true}$. Note that (1) implies that the least common ancestor of their context x_7 and x_{12} is a special $\mathcal{L}$ node, and (2) implies that x_2 is on the left of x_{12}. By Lemma 4.2, $v_5 \rightsquigarrow_g v_{16}$. The other cases $((v_5, v_{13}), (v_5, v_8)$ and $(v_5, v_{11}))$ can be verified similarly.

5.3 Execution-Based Dynamic Scheme

The above derivation-based scheme can be converted to an execution-based scheme, which creates exactly the same reachability labels. The main challenge is how to dynamically build the explicit parse tree and figure out the context of a newly inserted vertex, given only an execution of a graph. This is done by checking if the new vertex is a source or sink of a sub-workflow. If it is a source, we can infer one new step of the graph derivation, and update the explicit parse tree as before; otherwise, the context of this new vertex can be determined by any of its immediate predecessors. If it is a sink, we know that the current step of the graph derivation is completed. Note that some restrictions are required in order to avoid ambiguity of graph derivation, *e.g.*, unique names of source and sink of distinct sub-workflows. This can be achieved in practice by simple renaming. The details are deferred to the full version of this paper.

5.4 Correctness and Quality Analysis

THEOREM 2. **(Correctness)** *Let (ϕ_g, π_g) be our dynamic labeling scheme for a linear recursive workflow grammar G. For any graph $g \in L(G)$ and any two vertices v and v' of g, $\pi_g(\phi_g(v), \phi_g(v')) =$* `true` *if and only if $v \rightsquigarrow_g v'$.*

PROOF. (Sketch) This theorem can be proved by verifying all the steps of Algorithm 2 using Lemma 4.2. □

The quality of a labeling scheme (ϕ, π) is measured by *label length*, *construction time* (*i.e.*, the time to compute ϕ) and *query time* (*i.e.*, the time to evaluate π). Among them, label length is the main factor. Since the derivation-based and execution-based schemes create same labels, they differ only in the construction time. All parameters for quality analysis are listed in Table 1, where G is a linear recursive grammar, t is an explicit parse tree for a graph $g \in L(G)$ and h is a subgraph of g. The size of a graph refers to the number of vertices. Note that for a fixed G, n_G and t_G are constants. By Lemma 4.1, d_t is also bounded by a constant.

Table 1: Parameters for Quality Analysis

n_g	the size of g	n_h	the size of h
n_t	the size of t	d_t	the depth of t
θ_t	the max outdegree of a node of t		
n_G	the max size of a specification graph		
t_G	the time to compare skeleton labels		

THEOREM 3. **(Quality Analysis)** *Let G be a linear recursive workflow grammar. For any graph $g \in L(G)$, our dynamic labeling scheme (ϕ_g, π_g) guarantees*

1. *logarithmic label length: for any vertex v of g,*
$$|\phi_g(v)| = O(\log n_g) \text{ bits}$$
2. *linear total construction time: computing $\phi_g(v)$ for each vertex v of g takes a total of $O(n_g)$ time.*
   - *2a (execution-based) for any vertex insertion, $g_i = g_{i-1} + (v, C)$, computing $\phi_g(v)$ takes $O(1)$ time.*
   - *2b (derivation-based) for any vertex replacement, $g_i = g_{i-1}[u/h]$, computing $\phi_g(v)$ for each vertex v of h takes a total of $O(n_h)$ time.*
3. *constant query time: for any two vertices v and v' of g, computing $\pi_g(\phi_g(v), \phi_g(v'))$ takes $O(1)$ time.*

PROOF. (Sketch) We prove the logarithmic label length. Let $\phi_g(v)[i]$ be the ith entry of $\phi_g(v)$. By Algorithm 1,

$$|\phi_g(v)[i]| \leq \log \theta_t + 2 + \log n_G + 1 + 1 \text{ bits}$$

Recall that we use only a pointer to each skeleton label, rather than the label itself. So it takes only $\log n_G$ bits. Since $\phi_g(v)$ has at most d_t entries, and $\theta_t \leq n_t \leq n_g$,

$$|\phi_g(v)| \leq d_t * (\log \theta_t + \log n_G + 4) = O(\log n_g) \text{ bits}$$

The total construction time is $O(n_g * t_G) = O(n_g)$, and query time is $O(d_t) + t_G = O(1)$ (proofs are omitted). □

6. LABELING DYNAMIC WORKFLOWS WITH NONLINEAR RECURSION

Although our dynamic labeling scheme is for linear recursive workflows, it can be adapted to label nonlinear recursive workflows. The only modification is to create a simplified explicit parse tree without special $\mathcal{R}$ nodes by treating all vertices in a non-recursive way. A further optimization can be achieved by compressing at most one recursive vertex using a special $\mathcal{R}$ node, while treating other recursive vertices (if they exist) in a non-recursive way. However, the depth of the modified explicit parse tree is no longer bounded by a constant, but is proportional to the depth of recursion. This dynamic scheme may therefore create linear-size reachability labels, matching the lower bound in Theorem 1.

The remaining question is whether any nonlinear recursive workflow allows compact dynamic labeling. Theorem 4 shows that the answer is "no" for the derivation-based problem. It gives a stronger result than Theorem 1, showing that there is no compact derivation-based dynamic labeling scheme for *any given* nonlinear recursive workflow. Combining Theorems 3 and 4, we conclude that linear recursive workflows are the largest class of workflows that allow compact derivation-based dynamic labeling schemes.

THEOREM 4. *For any nonlinear recursive workflow grammar G and any derivation-based dynamic labeling scheme (ϕ, π) for G, there is a derivation of a graph $g \in L(G)$ with n vertices such that ϕ assigns a reachability label of $\Omega(n)$ bits for some vertex of g.*

PROOF. Since G is nonlinear recursive, by Definition 10, there is a production $A := h$ with at least two recursive vertices. By applying a sequence of productions, we can obtain from $A := h$ a new production $A := h'$ with two recursive vertices u_1 and u_2 both named A.

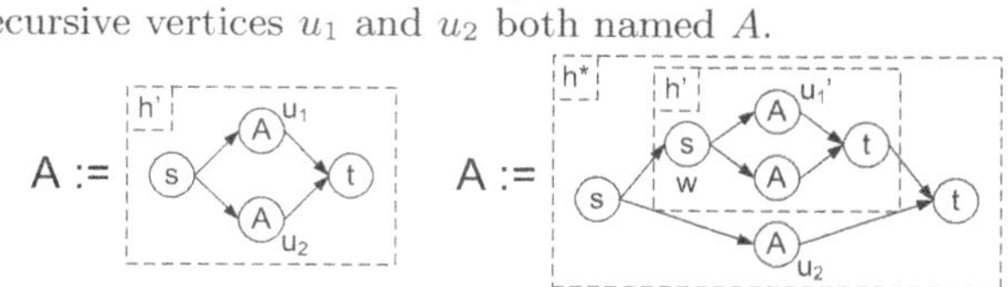

Figure 10: A new production $A := h^*$ constructed from $A := h'$ with two parallel recursive vertices u_1 and u_2.

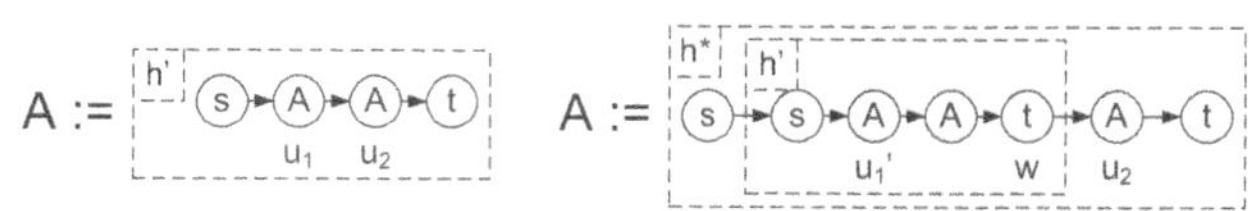

Figure 11: A new production $A := h^*$ constructed from $A := h'$ with two series recursive vertices u_1 and u_2.

Next, we want to find a *differential vertex* w that reaches exactly one of u_1 and u_2. Consider two cases. (1) If u_1 and u_2 are not reachable from each other in h' (see Figure 10), then we replace u_1 with a new copy of h', and obtain a new production $A := h^*$. Let u_1' be the new copy of u_1, and w be the source of the new copy of h', then w reaches exactly one of u_1' and u_2; and (2) If one of u_1 and u_2 can reach the other in h' (let $u_1 \rightsquigarrow_{h'} u_2$, see Figure 11), then again we replace u_1 with a new copy of h', and obtain a new production $A := h^*$. Let u_1' be the new copy of u_1, and w be the sink of the new copy of h', then w reaches exactly one of u_1' and u_2.

Recall the production $A := h_1$ in Figure 6, where the vertex named a reaches exactly one of the two vertices named A. Using the new production $A := h^*$, we can prove the theorem using the technique of Theorem 1. □

We next turn to the execution-based problem. To apply the same proof, we need to ensure that the differential vertex w precedes both recursive vertices u_1 and u_2 in the given insertion sequence, so that $\phi(w)$ can divide all reachability labels that will be later assigned to the subgraphs derived from u_1 and u_2 into two disjoint sets. *E.g.*, the proof of Theorem 1 relies on the fact that the differential vertex (named a) precedes two recursive vertices (named A) in the given insertion sequence (see Figure 6). Unfortunately, Case (2) in the proof of Theorem 4 (see Figure 11) violates the above condition. The following example inspired by Case (2) shows that some nonlinear recursive workflow indeed allows compact execution-based dynamic labeling schemes.

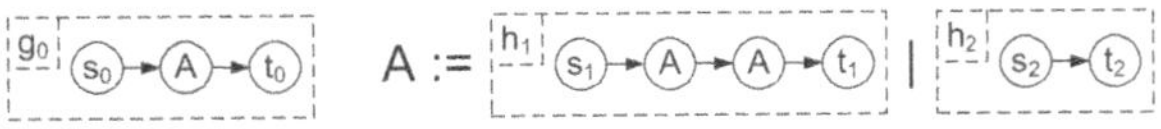

Figure 12: A nonlinear recursive workflow grammar that allows a compact execution-based dynamic scheme.

Example 14. Consider the workflow grammar G shown in Figure 12. Since any graph $g \in L(G)$ is a simple path, we simply label the ith vertex by an index of i. This naive dynamic scheme creates logarithmic-size reachability labels.

However, Case (1) (see Figure 10) respects the condition. We thus get a similar result to Theorem 4 for a subclass of nonlinear workflows, called the *parallel recursive workflows*.

Definition 13. A workflow grammar is said to be *parallel recursive*, if there is a production with two recursive vertices that are not reachable from each other (in parallel).

THEOREM 5. *For any parallel recursive workflow grammar G and any execution-based dynamic labeling scheme (ϕ, π) for G, there is an execution of a graph $g \in L(G)$ with n vertices such that ϕ assigns a reachability label of $\Omega(n)$ bits for some vertex of g.*

PROOF. (Sketch) We follow the same proof as Theorem 4. The correctness follows from Definition 13, which ensures that the new production $A := h^*$ must fall into Case (1). □

This paper leaves open the problem of whether non-parallel recursive workflows (with only series recursive vertices) allow compact execution-based dynamic labeling schemes.

7. EXPERIMENTAL EVALUATION

We empirically evaluated the proposed dynamic labeling scheme in terms of label length, construction time, query time and preprocessing overhead. We performed three sets of experiments: The first uses a collected, real-life scientific workflow (Section 7.2). The second measures a variety of synthetic workflows with different characteristics (Section 7.3). The last compares our dynamic scheme against the state-of-the-art static scheme [5] (Section 7.4).

7.1 Experimental Setup

All labeling schemes are implemented in Java 6. Our experiments were performed on a local PC with Intel Pentium 2.80GHz CPU and 2GB memory running Windows XP.

Real-Life and Synthetic Datasets. The real-life workflow, called *BioAID*, was taken from the myExperiment workflow repository [19]. To focus on the specific factors that affect the labeling performance, we also created a family of synthetic workflows using the simple topology shown in Figure 13. Due to the lack of realistic workflow runs, we simulate the execution by repeating loops, forks and recursion a random number of times. For each specification, we vary the size of runs from $1K$ to $32K$ by a factor of 2, and randomly select one derivation and one execution for each run as dynamic inputs. All data are stored in XML files.

Labeling Methodology. We compare two schemes for labeling workflow runs: (1) the one presented in this paper, which is denoted by `DRL`, for (D)ynamic scheme for (R)ecursive workflows; and (2) the state-of-the-art *static* scheme [5], which is also skeleton-based, and is denoted by `SKL`, for (SK)eleton-based scheme. To obtain skeleton labels (for both schemes), we apply two simple schemes for labeling the specification: (1) `TCL` denotes the one given in Section 3.2. It precomputes the (T)ransitive (C)losure for all vertices, and can be used to label either a static graph or an execution-based dynamic graph; and (2) `BFS` does not perform any labeling, but answers a reachability query by a (B)readth (F)irst (S)earch over the graph. Since a skeleton-based scheme for labeling runs is parameterized by the scheme for labeling the specification, we denote by `DRL(TCL)` and `DRL(BFS)` (resp. `SKL(TCL)` and `SKL(BFS)`) the corresponding combinations of the two.

Evaluation Methodology. The result for label length and construction time is an average over 10^3 sample runs, and the one for query time is an average over 10^5 sample queries.

7.2 Labeling Real-Life Workflows

In the first set of experiments, we evaluate `DRL` using *BioAID*. It consists of 11 sub-workflows with an average size of 10.5 and a nesting depth [5] of 2. There are 2 loop modules, 4 fork modules and one linear recursion of length 2. Note that the derivation-based and execution-based dynamic schemes differ only in the construction time, and the scheme used to label the specification affects only the query time and the preprocessing overhead.

Figure 14 reports the maximum and average label length. As expected, both increase logarithmically with the size of the run (note that the x-axis is log scale). The average length is always shorter than the maximum length by a small constant (about 6 bits). More interestingly, both lines are almost parallel to the asymptotic line $f(n) = \log(n) + 13$. Hence, they are bounded by $c \log(n) + O(1)$, where c is a small constant factor close to 1.

Figure 15 reports the total construction time for both derivation-based and execution-based schemes. Observe that they increase linearly with the size of the run. On average, we label a new vertex on the fly in less than 5 μs, which is comparable to the time of updating the graph itself (about 6 μs). Moreover, the derivation-based scheme is faster than the execution-based scheme. This is because the latter needs to find the context and origin of the newly inserted vertex.

Figure 16 reports the query time for `DRL(TCL)` and `DRL(BFS)`. Recall that `TCL` allows constant query time, but uses linear-size labels; in contrast, `BFS` does not use any labels, but has linear query time. However, since the specification graphs are small and fixed, `DRL` answers reachability queries in almost constant time, when combined with either (Figure 16). But `DRL(TCL)` is slightly faster than `DRL(BFS)` by about 2 μs. We also measured the preprocessing overhead for `DRL(TCL)`, and found that the overhead is negligible: the skeleton labels take totally 650 bits and are built in less than 0.05 ms.

[5] In a recursive workflow, the *nesting depth* of sub-workflows refers to the length of the longest path of sub-workflows, starting from the start graph, that implement distinct composite modules. *E.g.*, the nesting depth of sub-workflows in Figure 13 is d.

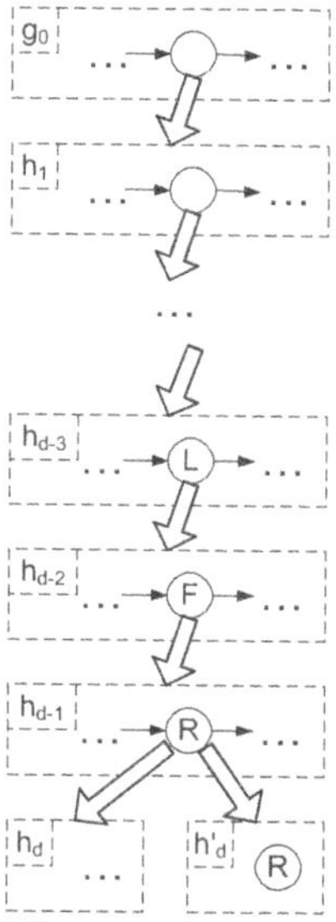

Figure 13: Synthetic Workflow

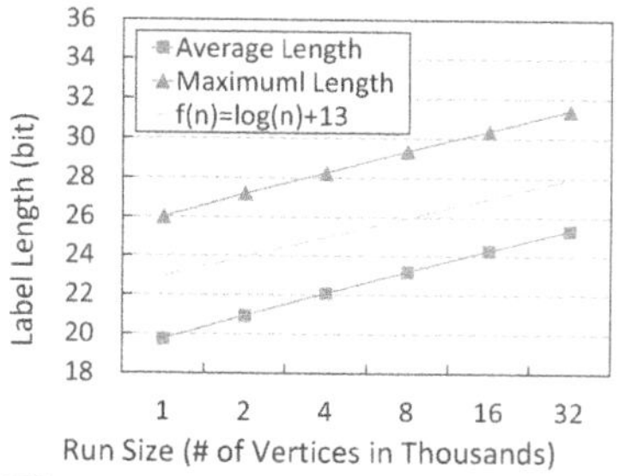

Figure 14: BioAID(Label Length)

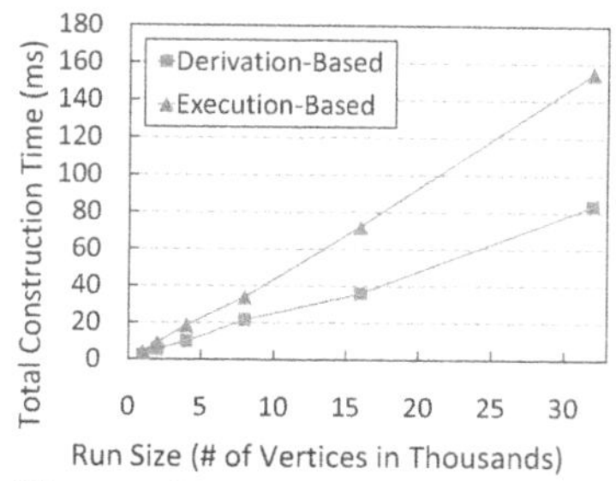

Figure 15: BioAID(Constr. Time)

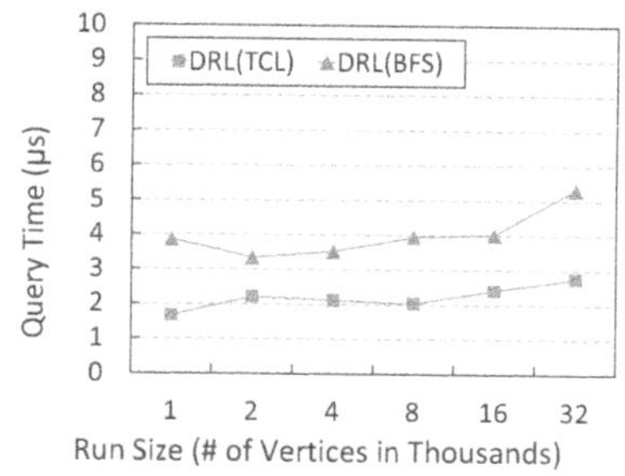

Figure 16: BioAID(Query Time)

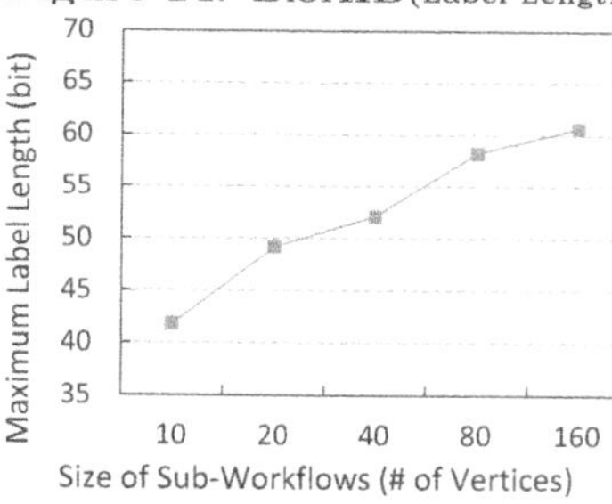

Figure 17: Varying Size

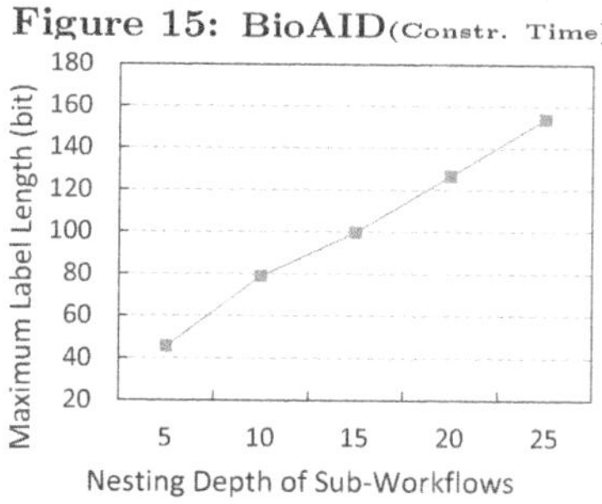

Figure 18: Varying Depth

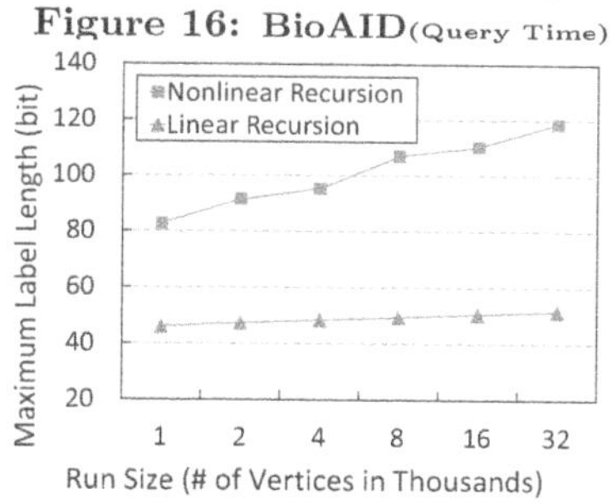

Figure 19: Nonlinear Workflows

Conclusions: Theorem 3 is experimentally validated. DRL is scalable for large dynamic runs, even when combined with simple skeleton schemes like TCL and BFS. Due to the small size of the specification graphs, the benefit of using more sophisticated schemes to label the specification is limited.

7.3 Labeling Synthetic Workflows

In the second set of experiments, we evaluate DRL for a variety of synthetic workflows created from the specification in Figure 13. It consists of a chain of nested sub-workflows with one loop module L, one fork module F and one recursive module R. Note that the recursive sub-workflow h'_d may in general contain several R modules. All sub-workflows are random two-terminal graphs of some fixed size. The parameters are: (a) the size of sub-workflows; (b) the nesting depth of sub-workflows; and (c) if the workflow is linear recursive (*i.e.*, if h'_d has more than one R modules). Due to space constraints, we report only the main factor, label length.

First, we generate a set of linear recursive workflows by varying the size of sub-workflows from 10 to 160 by a factor of 2, and fixing the nesting depth of sub-workflows to be 5. Figure 17 reports the maximum label length for dynamic runs with $5K$ vertices. As we can see, the maximum label length increases almost logarithmically with the size of sub-workflows. To explain the result, recall that a tighter upper bound of label length, given in the proof of Theorem 3, is

$$|\phi_g(v)| \leq d_t * (\log \theta_t + \log n_G + 4) \quad (3)$$

where all parameters for quality analysis are defined in Table 1. In this experiment, d_t is fixed, and n_G increases by a factor of 2. We now estimate θ_t. Since $n_G * n_t$ is roughly the size of the run (a fixed constant of $5K$), n_t decreases by a factor of 2. Note that t is a balanced tree with fixed depth. In general, θ_t decreases much more slowly than n_t. It follows that the increase of $\log n_G$ dominates the decrease of $\log \theta_t$ in (3). This confirms the result in Figure 17.

Next, we generate a set of linear recursive workflows by varying the nesting depth of sub-workflows from 5 to 25 by a constant of 5, and fixing the size of sub-workflows to be 20. Figure 18 reports the maximum label length for dynamic runs with $5K$ vertices. Observe that the maximum label length increases linearly with the nesting depth of sub-workflows. This is again confirmed by (3), where n_G and θ_t are fixed, and d_t is proportional to the nesting depth.

Finally, we generate a nonlinear recursive workflow with two R modules in h'_d (see Figure 13) and a linear recursive one with only one R module in h'_d. For both workflows, the size of sub-workflows is 20, and the nesting depth is 5. Figure 19 reports the maximum label length. Not surprisingly, the nonlinear recursive workflow produces longer labels than the linear recursive one. Although DRL creates linear-size labels for nonlinear recursive workflows in the worst case, Figure 19 shows that it performs reasonably well in practice: the maximum label length for a run with $32K$ vertices is less than 120 bits. Note that if we use TCL to label the run dynamically, it gives a label of exactly $32K - 1$ bits.

Conclusions: The main factor that affects the performance of DRL is the nesting depth of sub-workflows. However, we observe from our experience that most real-life workflows are linear recursive, and have a nesting depth of less than 5. DRL is also effective to label nonlinear recursive workflows.

7.4 DRL (Dynamic) vs SKL (Static)

In the last set of experiments, we compare DRL and SKL. The limitations of SKL are: (1) SKL is a static scheme, which takes the entire run graph as input; (2) SKL supports only non-recursive workflows (with loops and forks); and (3) SKL entails skeleton labels over a global specification graph, in which all composite modules are replaced with corresponding sub-workflows. We show only results for the real-life workflow. To achieve a fair comparison, we remove the recursion. The results for synthetic workflows are similar.

Figure 20 reports the maximum label length. Observe that DRL creates shorter labels than SKL when the run size is larger than $1.5K$. This is because DRL uses a prefix-based scheme [16] to label the explicit parse tree, while SKL uses an interval-based scheme [20]. The former performs better on balanced trees with relatively high degrees and low depth. This is exactly the case when the run becomes large. More precisely, the upper bound of the label length for SKL is

$$|\phi_g(v)| \leq 3 * \log n_t + O(\log n_G) \quad (4)$$

where $n_t = O(n_g)$ and $n_G = O(1)$. So the logarithmic label length for SKL has a factor of 3. Recall from Figure 14 that

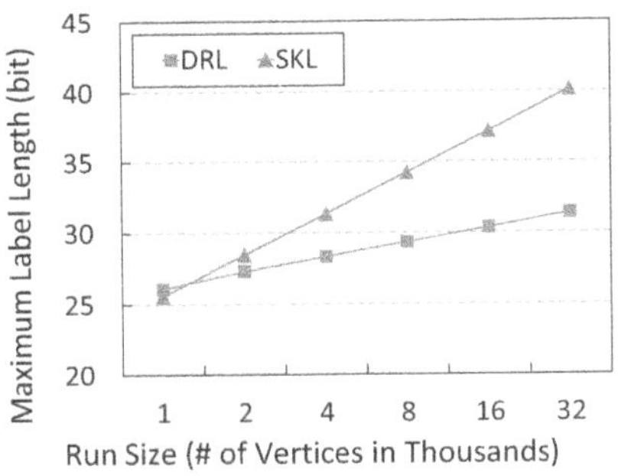

Figure 20: DRL vs SKL(Label Length)

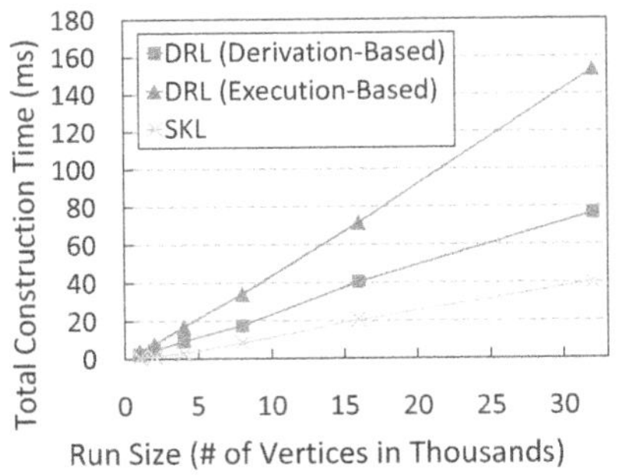

Figure 21: DRL vs SKL(Constr. Time)

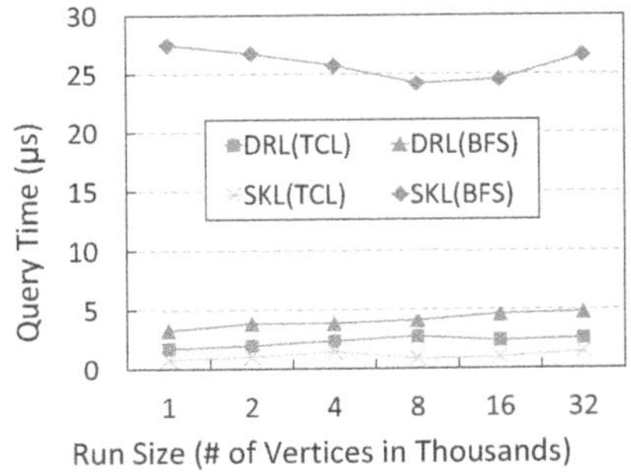

Figure 22: DRL vs SKL(Query Time)

the factor for DRL is close to 1. Hence, for large runs, DRL creates shorter labels than SKL by a factor of almost 3. This is confirmed by the slopes of the two lines in Figure 20.

Figure 21 reports the total construction time. Since SKL builds simpler (but larger) labels than DRL consisting only of three indexes and one skeleton label, SKL is faster than derivation-based and execution-based DRL by a factor of 2 and 4 respectively. However, unlike DRL, SKL cannot start labeling until the entire run is completed.

Figure 22 reports the query time for all four combinations. BFS performs a linear-time graph search over the specification. Consequently, when combined with BFS, the cost of comparing skeleton labels is the dominant factor. Note that SKL searches over a global specification graph with 106 vertices, while DRL searches over an individual sub-workflow with only 10.5 vertices on average. Hence, SKL(BFS) is slower than DRL(BFS) by one order of magnitude. In contrast, when combined with TCL, the cost of comparing skeleton labels is negligible. Given that SKL enables simple decoding which compares only three indexes and one skeleton label, SKL(TCL) is slightly faster than DRL(TCL). However, such efficiency is traded by high preprocessing overhead reported in Table 2.

Table 2: Overhead of Labeling Specification

	Total Space (bit)	Construction Time (ms)
DRL(TCL)	650	0.04375
SKL(TCL)	5565	0.16328

Conclusions: DRL creates shorter labels than SKL, and is more robust to the scheme for labeling the specification.

8. CONCLUSIONS

This paper studies derivation-based and execution-based dynamic reachability labeling problems for recursive workflows with loops and forks. We provide tight lower and upper bounds of $\Theta(n)$ bits on the maximum label length, and present a compact dynamic labeling scheme for linear recursive workflows which uses labels of $\log(n)$ bits. The evaluation, performed over both real and synthetic workflows, shows that our dynamic scheme creates shorter labels than the start-of-the-art static scheme [5] by a factor of almost 3.

This paper also shows an interesting characterization: A workflow allows a compact derivation-based dynamic scheme if and only if it is linear recursive. However, finding an execution-based characterization is still an open problem.

9. ACKNOWLEDGMENTS

We thank the anonymous reviewers for their helpful comments. This work was supported in part by the US National Science Foundation grants IIS-0803524 and IIS-0629846, by the Israel Science Foundation, by the US-Israel Binational Science Foundation, and by the EU grant MANCOOSI.

10. REFERENCES

[1] R. Agrawal, A. Borgida, and H. V. Jagadish. Efficient management of transitive relationships in large data and knowledge bases. In *SIGMOD Conference*, pages 253–262, 1989.

[2] S. Alstrup, P. Bille, and T. Rauhe. Labeling schemes for small distances in trees. In *SODA*, pages 689–698, 2003.

[3] S. Alstrup and T. Rauhe. Improved labeling scheme for ancestor queries. In *SODA*, pages 947–953, 2002.

[4] I. Altintas, C. Berkley, E. Jaeger, M. B. Jones, B. Ludäscher, and S. Mock. Kepler: An extensible system for design and execution of scientific workflows. In *SSDBM*, pages 423–424, 2004.

[5] Z. Bao, S. B. Davidson, S. Khanna, and S. Roy. An optimal labeling scheme for workflow provenance using skeleton labels. In *SIGMOD Conference*, pages 711–722, 2010.

[6] S. P. Callahan, J. Freire, E. Santos, C. E. Scheidegger, C. T. Silva, and H. T. Vo. Vistrails: visualization meets data management. In *SIGMOD Conference*, pages 745–747, 2006.

[7] E. Cohen, E. Halperin, H. Kaplan, and U. Zwick. Reachability and distance queries via 2-hop labels. In *SODA*, pages 937–946, 2002.

[8] E. Cohen, H. Kaplan, and T. Milo. Labeling dynamic xml trees. In *PODS*, pages 271–281, 2002.

[9] C. Demetrescu and G. F. Italiano. Fully dynamic transitive closure: Breaking through the $o(n^2)$ barrier. In *FOCS*, pages 381–389, 2000.

[10] P. Fraigniaud and A. Korman. Compact ancestry labeling schemes for xml trees. In *SODA*, pages 458–466, 2010.

[11] T. Heinis and G. Alonso. Efficient lineage tracking for scientific workflows. In *SIGMOD Conference*, pages 1007–1018, 2008.

[12] D. Hull, K. Wolstencroft, R. Stevens, C. A. Goble, M. R. Pocock, P. Li, and T. Oinn. Taverna: a tool for building and running workflows of services. *Nucleic Acids Research*, 34(Web-Server-Issue):729–732, 2006.

[13] H. V. Jagadish. A compression technique to materialize transitive closure. *ACM Trans. Database Syst.*, 15(4):558–598, 1990.

[14] R. Jin, Y. Xiang, N. Ruan, and D. Fuhry. 3-hop: a high-compression indexing scheme for reachability query. In *SIGMOD Conference*, pages 813–826, 2009.

[15] R. Jin, Y. Xiang, N. Ruan, and H. Wang. Efficiently answering reachability queries on very large directed graphs. In *SIGMOD Conference*, pages 595–608, 2008.

[16] H. Kaplan, T. Milo, and R. Shabo. A comparison of labeling schemes for ancestor queries. In *SODA*, pages 954–963, 2002.

[17] V. King and G. Sagert. A fully dynamic algorithm for maintaining the transitive closure. In *STOC*, pages 492–498, 1999.

[18] P. E. O'Neil, E. J. O'Neil, S. Pal, I. Cseri, G. Schaller, and N. Westbury. Ordpaths: Insert-friendly xml node labels. In *SIGMOD Conference*, pages 903–908, 2004.

[19] D. D. Roure, C. A. Goble, and R. Stevens. The design and realisation of the $my_{experiment}$ virtual research environment for social sharing of workflows. *Future Generation Comp. Syst.*, 25(5):561–567, 2009.

[20] N. Santoro and R. Khatib. Labelling and implicit routing in networks. *Comput. J.*, 28(1):5–8, 1985.

[21] L. Xu, T. W. Ling, H. Wu, and Z. Bao. Dde: from dewey to a fully dynamic xml labeling scheme. In *SIGMOD Conference*, pages 719–730, 2009.

[22] H. Yildirim, V. Chaoji, and M. J. Zaki. Grail: Scalable reachability index for large graphs. *PVLDB*, 3(1):276–284, 2010.

Tracing Data Errors with View-Conditioned Causality*

Alexandra Meliou† Wolfgang Gatterbauer† Suman Nath§ Dan Suciu†
†University of Washington,
Seattle, WA, USA
{ameli,gatter,suciu}@cs.washington.edu
§Microsoft Research,
Redmond, WA, USA
Suman.Nath@microsoft.com

ABSTRACT

A surprising query result is often an indication of errors in the query or the underlying data. Recent work suggests using causal reasoning to find explanations for the surprising result. In practice, however, one often has *multiple queries* and/or *multiple answers*, some of which may be considered correct and others unexpected. In this paper, we focus on determining the causes of a set of unexpected results, possibly conditioned on some prior knowledge of the correctness of another set of results. We call this problem *View-Conditioned Causality.* We adapt the definitions of causality and responsibility for the case of multiple answers/views and provide a non-trivial algorithm that reduces the problem of finding causes and their responsibility to a satisfiability problem that can be solved with existing tools. We evaluate both the accuracy and effectiveness of our approach on a real dataset of user-generated mobile device tracking data, and demonstrate that it can identify causes of error more effectively than static Boolean influence and alternative notions of causality.

Categories and Subject Descriptors. E.0 Data General
General Terms. Algorithms
Keywords. causality, view-conditioning, error tracing

1. INTRODUCTION

Data transformations from a source to a target dataset are ubiquitous today and can be found in data integration [26], data exchange [25, 3], and ETL tools [31]. Users often detect *errors in the target data.* For example, a user may detect that an item in a target data instance is incorrect: the tuple should not be there, or some of its attribute values are erroneous; she would like to find out which of the many input tuples that contributed to the incorrect output is faulty. It is critical that the error be *traced and corrected in the source data,* because once an error is identified, one can prevent it from propagating to multiple items in the target data. This can be viewed as a form of "post-factum" data cleaning: while in standard data cleaning one corrects errors before the data is transformed and integrated, in our setting the errors are detected only *after the data has been transformed.*

In this paper, we show how to extend the concept of causality [28] to *trace errors in a source dataset that caused incorrect results in a target dataset.* We showcase our motivation through a practical example.

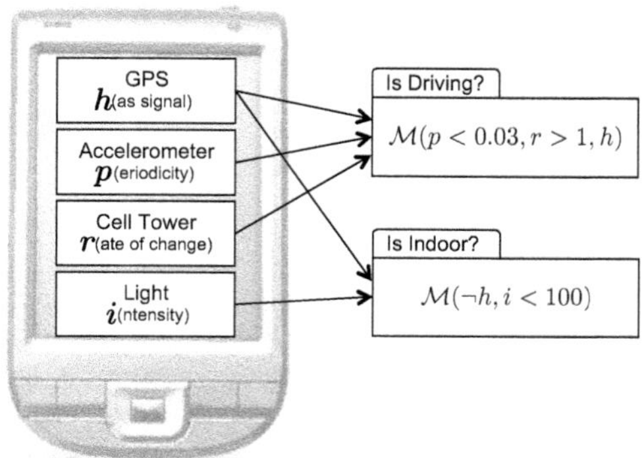

Figure 1: Two simple classifiers based on sensory input from a cell phone. The inputs to the classifiers are either Boolean variables (e.g. h), or scalar values to which an appropriate threshold is applied (e.g. i). Symbol $\mathcal{M}$ denotes a strict majority function.

Example 1 (Recommendation System). *Consider a new generation smart phone. It has multiple sensors (e.g. GPS, accelerometer, light, and cell tower signal). Based on these sensors, a set of classifiers can predict the owner's current activities (e.g. walking, driving, working, being with family, or being in a business meeting). Using the knowledge of the user's current activities allows the system to serve the user with useful targeted recommendations. For example, if the user is away from their car around lunch time, the application will suggest restaurants within walking distance.*

This is an example of data transformation: the source data (input) are the sensors, the target data (output) are the activities. Inaccuracies in the sensor data are a common occurrence: sensors have innate imprecisions (e.g., the GPS may miscalculate the current location), or some sensors may become inhibited (e.g., if the user places the cell-phone in the glove compartment while driving, then the light sensor's reading is incorrect). As a consequence, an inferred activity may be wrong. The application can often detect such errors from user feedback or based on the user's subsequent actions and reactions to the provided recommendations. But

*This work was partially funded by NSF IIS-0911036, IIS-0915054, and IIS-0713576.

SIGMOD'11, June 12–16, 2011, Athens, Greece.

the main challenge is to actually identify the responsible sensor(s). For example, in Fig. 1 the "is-driving" activity depends on 3 sensors: if "is-driving" is wrong, which of the three sensors is erroneous? With this knowledge, the system could inhibit the reading from that sensor and therefore improve the other classifiers.

The first step towards tracing errors in the source data is to compute the lineage of each item in the target data. Data lineage, or provenance, has been extensively studied recently [10, 16, 5]. But as Example 1 shows, examining the lineage of an erroneous result is not sufficient to identify the cause of the problem: all three sensor inputs are part of the lineage, and without further context, it is not possible to determine which specific sensor is erroneous.

In this work, we identify erroneous inputs by building upon a long history of work on *causality theory*. Albeit related to lineage, causality is a more refined notion. The lineage of an erroneous output reflects causal dependencies between the input and output data, and causal reasoning can use this information to return the possible causes ranked by their *degree of responsibility*. Causality has been studied extensively in philosophy, AI, and cognitive science. We base our discussion on the established definitions of *actual causes* and *responsibility* first developed by Halpern, Pearl and Chockler [11, 17], and our previous work that adapted these definitions to a database context, targeting query result explanations [28].

In error tracing, however, we face a richer context than in traditional causality theory. In addition to the erroneous output item, we also have access to several output items that we know are correct. In fact, there may even be more than one erroneous output item. Accounting for this richer context leads to much better error tracing.

EXAMPLE 2 (RECOMMENDATION SYSTEM - CONTINUED). *A modern smart phone typically has 10-12 sensors, and could have up to 20-30 classifiers, predicting a variety of activities. Based on the user's response to recommendations, the system can typically derive that multiple predictions are correct or incorrect. Suppose, for example, that the system knows that 3 predictions are wrong and 2 are correct. Now the system has more information than just knowing that one classifier is wrong. The challenge is to find the most likely input sensor that could have caused the 3 faulty predictions, while at the same time allowing the 2 correct predictions. Thus,* conditioned *on the two correct outputs, we seek the most responsible sensor(s) that explain the faulty classifiers.*

For example, assume the two simple classifiers of Fig. 1: if both are incorrect, then intuitively, the GPS becomes the most likely culprit; if the "is-driving" classification is wrong and "is-indoor" is correct, then we know that the GPS input has to be correct.

In this paper, we propose *View-Conditioned Causality*, a novel concept that allows us to trace errors in transformed target data, such as query results or views, back to the input base data. Our main contributions are as follows:

(1) We propose a new definition of view-conditioned causality and its associated notion of responsibility. In order to use causality for error tracing, we refine existing notions of causality/responsibility by conditioning on all knowledge of correct or incorrect results.

(2) Computing causality and responsibility is known to be hard in general [14]. Previously, we have studied the complexity of causality and responsibility for conjunctive queries [28]. Despite some tractable cases, computing the responsibility remains hard, in general. To date, no practical algorithms exist to compute causes or responsibilities for all cases. In order to compute causality and responsibility in practice, we propose a novel algorithm for translating the view-conditioned causality and responsibility problems into a SAT and a weighted MAX-SAT problem respectively, for which very effective tools exist [2, 4]. In the case of causality, our algorithm produces a Boolean expression Φ_{SAT} that is satisfiable iff a given input variable is a view-conditioned cause. In the case of responsibility, our algorithm also produces, in addition to the "hard" constraint Φ_{SAT}, several "soft" clauses: the larger the number of soft clauses that cannot be satisfied, the lower the responsibility.

(3) The formula Φ_{SAT} needs to be converted to CNF in order to be processed by general (Max)SAT solvers, and this has the potential of an exponential blow-up. Our third contribution describes an optimized conversion to CNF that results in exponentially smaller CNF expressions.

(4) Finally, we perform an experimental validation of our techniques on real data from an actual application analogous to Example 1. Our experiments verify the quality of our approach in identifying erroneous inputs, and evaluate its performance. We show that view-conditioned causality retains an average precision very close to 1, outperforming other techniques such as counterfactual causality and Boolean influence, by 60% and 75% respectively at certain instances. Our optimized algorithm for the CNF conversion is shown to produce SAT problems orders of magnitude smaller than the naive approach, while the SAT solvers were able to process even the larger generated problem instances in a few seconds. We further demonstrate interesting insights on how responsibility of features can function as a meaningful quantifier of classifier quality and robustness: classifiers that use features with low responsibility can be easily corrected by eliminating faulty inputs, whereas classifiers whose features are all of high responsibility (i.e. they are all likely sources of failure), cannot achieve good correction rates.

The structure of this paper follows its main contributions:

- We propose view-conditioned causality and responsibility as a solution for tracing errors from views and transformations to source data (Sect. 3).
- We demonstrate a non-trivial algorithm that reduces the problems of computing causes and responsibility to the satisfiability of Boolean expressions which can be solved with existing tools (Sect. 4).
- We propose an optimized conversion algorithm of the resulting Boolean expressions into CNF, in order to be fed into a SAT or MaxSAT solver (Sect. 5).
- We illustrate the effectiveness of using our techniques for tracking errors in a real world classifier-based recommendation system (Sect. 6).

2. BACKGROUND AND RELATED WORK

Causality is an active area of research, mostly in AI and philosophy. One of the basic notions in causality theory is *counterfactual causality* [29, 27]. An input variable is counterfactual if a change in its value reverses the value of the output variable. Counterfactuals are a very intuitive notion, but very limited in their applicability as they don't support disjunctive causes: If Z occurs when X_1 or X_2 occurs, neither of X_1 or X_2 are counterfactual causes for Z.

Halpern and Pearl [17] extended counterfactuals by introducing *actual causes* which rely upon a graph structure called a *causal network*, and added the notion of *permissive contingencies*. The causal network is defined by *structural equations*, which describe how variables relate to each other; for example $Z = X_1 \vee X_2$ is a structural equation linking inputs X_1 and X_2 to output Z. Contingencies are based on the notion of *intervention*: what becomes counterfactual if part of the input changes. For example, if X_1 and X_2 are both `true`, neither of them is counterfactual for Y. However, if the input changes in a certain way, for instance X_2 is `false`, then X_1 becomes counterfactual. One says that X_1 *is an actual cause of Z under the contingency $X_2 =$* `false`. Such contingencies can be viewed as alternative possible worlds or variable assignments. Roughly, a variable X is an actual cause if there exists a contingency (a value assignment for the other variables) that makes X counterfactual.

The notion of *responsibility* was first defined in [11] as a measure of the degree of causality: the responsibility is inverse proportional to the size of the smallest contingency set. This is a key notion for our setting, because responsibility allows us to rank causes. Ranking is critical in complex queries with large lineages, and in the case of error tracing it serves as a comparison metric of the likelihood of the various error sources. However, determining causes and responsibility was shown to be NP-hard in general [14].

Very recently, we extended the notions of causality and responsibility to database queries [28]. Here the input variables are tuples in the input database, the output variables are the answer tuples returned by the query, and the causal network is given by the *lineage expression*. An input tuple is a *counterfactual cause* for an output tuple if its removal from the input causes the output to disappear. An input tuple is an *actual cause* for an output tuple if there exists a set of tuples in the input (the contingency) such that, after removing them, the input tuple becomes a counterfactual cause. The complexity of causality and responsibility were analyzed as a function of the query (query complexity). These results are unrelated to our work, since we analyze directly the lineage expression and do not consider query complexity. Neither the general work on causality, nor its adaptation to database queries have studied the problem of tracing errors from output data to input data.

Our work relates to prior work on data provenance, in the sense that our input is a provenance expression. There, approaches are mainly classified into three categories: how-, why-, and where- provenance [6, 10, 13, 16]. Also, recent work has focused on the problem of explaining missing query results, i.e. why a certain tuple does not appear as an answer. The work in this field is divided into data-focused [22, 20, 19] where explanations are given as base tuples, and query-focused [8, 33] where explanations are based on query predicates. The ability to *rank causes* clearly distinguishes causality from the provenance and missing answers work, and makes it more appropriate for tracking errors. In independent work, Cheney [9] also discusses the analogy between provenance and causality, and describes defining causal semantics for provenance graphs.

An interesting, and related work is the view side-effects problem on tuple deletion and annotation propagation [7]. This problem involves finding a subset of tuples in the database whose deletion will eliminate a given tuple t from the view, with the minimum number of side-effects (other tuple eliminations) in the view. An analogous definition of the problem exist for tuple insertion and updates, and all are shown to be hard, in general. Very recent work [12] studies the "side-effect free" version of this problem, where zero side-effects are enforced, and the aim is to minimize the subset of tuples selected from the database. Here, the same hardness results hold as in the general version of the problem. Note that these problems differ from computing responsibility, where we need to find the minimum set of input tuples that make a given tuple counterfactual. Also, the view side-effects problem is in PTIME for queries that do not contain joins together with projection or union. In contrast, we showed the hardness criterion for computing responsibilities to be entirely different [28], and even queries that only contain joins can be NP-hard.

3. VIEW CONDITIONING

Formal setup. We use capital letters for variables (e.g. X), small letters for value assignments (e.g. x), and bold letters for sets of variables or assignments (e.g. $\boldsymbol{X}$ or $\boldsymbol{x}$). We denote Boolean values interchangeably with `true` and `false` or `T` and `F`, respectively. We consider a set of n *input variables* (also called parameters) $\boldsymbol{X} = \{X_1, \ldots, X_n\}$, and a set of observed *output variables* $\boldsymbol{Z} = \{Z_1, \ldots, Z_m\}$. Each input variable X_i takes values from a discrete or continuous domain, e.g. reals, integers, Booleans. Each output variable Z_j is Boolean. We denote $\boldsymbol{\Phi} = \{\Phi_1, \ldots, \Phi_m\}$ a transformation from the input variables to the output variables. Each Φ_j is called a *lineage expression*, and is a Boolean expression over the input variables, defined as follows. Call a *threshold predicate* a predicate of the form X_i `op` t, where X_i is an input variable, `op` is one of $<, \leq, =, \neq \geq, >$, and t is a constant threshold value. Then Φ_j is any Boolean expression over threshold predicates. Thus, the transformation $\boldsymbol{\Phi}$ takes an input vector $\boldsymbol{x}$ of values, and computes the output vector $\boldsymbol{z}$, where each $z_j = \Phi_j(\boldsymbol{x})$. We write $\boldsymbol{x} \models \boldsymbol{z}$, to denote that $\boldsymbol{z}$ are the output values of the view transformations given input values $\boldsymbol{x}$. In addition to the input and output vectors, we further assume to know the correct values for the output $\boldsymbol{Z}$ and denote this *ground truth* as $\hat{\boldsymbol{z}} = \{\hat{z}_1, \ldots, \hat{z}_m\}$. If $z_i = \hat{z}_i$ then variable Z_i is correct, otherwise it is incorrect.

For a simple illustration, consider a simple classifier that computes $Z = (X_1 > 10) \wedge (X_2 < 3)$. Given two input values x_1, x_2 the classifier returns the output `T` or `F`, in an obvious way. Classifier systems are more complex types of transformations. For a more traditional transformation example, consider a select-project-join query. Each input tuple corresponds to a Boolean variable X_i, and each output tuple is a Boolean variable Z_j. The formula Φ_j is the standard lineage expression giving the dependency of Z_j as a function of the input tuples [16].

Note that our discussion will focus on classifier systems, but our results can be invariably used for other transformation types like conjunctive queries as well. Even though data sizes are much larger in query scenarios than sensor based applications, the lineage of each output tuple is actually bound by the query size. Moreover, we only need to keep as relevant variables those that participate in the lineage of erroneous outputs, thus greatly reducing the problem size. Finally, the SAT solver component is not prohibitive to this end, as modern SAT solvers can solve problems having millions of variables and clauses in less than 10 minutes of run time (cf. [1]).

3.1 The Problem: Tracing Data Errors

By comparing the output values $\boldsymbol{z}$ to the ground truth $\hat{\boldsymbol{z}}$, we can detect errors in the output. This means that there is an error in the input data $\boldsymbol{X}$, but we don't know which one, and only know which output is erroneous. Thus, while we may learn the ground truth for the output values, we don't know the ground truth for the input variables. For example, in Example 1 it is not possible to know whether a sensor is inhibited by looking at its measurements, but it is quite possible to determine that a classifier was incorrect, by examining the user's actions. Our goal is to trace the output errors back to the input data, and this justifies the following problem:

> ***Error tracing problem:*** *Given input values $\boldsymbol{x}$ for the input variables $\boldsymbol{X}$, a set of transformations $\boldsymbol{\Phi}$ computing the values $\boldsymbol{z}$ of the output variables $\boldsymbol{Z}$, and given a ground truth $\hat{\boldsymbol{z}}$ for the output variables, detect the sources of error in the input data.*

Clearly, if $\boldsymbol{z} = \hat{\boldsymbol{z}}$ then there are no errors. We will assume that $\boldsymbol{z} \neq \hat{\boldsymbol{z}}$ for the rest of the paper. In our problem setting, the ground truth includes values for all output variables $\boldsymbol{Z}$. In practice that is often not the case: we know the ground truth for some, but not all output variables. In that case we simply restrict the output variables to those for which the ground truth is known. Thus, in the rest of this paper we will assume that the ground truth is known for all the output variables $\boldsymbol{Z}$.

3.2 Our Approach: View-Conditioned Causality

We define here counterfactual causes, and actual causes for a *set* of output values, which we call *view-conditioned causality*. Then, we explain how this can be applied to tracing errors. As a first attempt we may try to say that an input X_i is a *view-conditioned counterfactual cause* (or VCC cause, in short), if a change in the value x_i "corrects" the output $\boldsymbol{z}$ to the ground truth output $\hat{\boldsymbol{z}}$; we say in this case that X_i is a VCC cause of $\boldsymbol{z}|\hat{\boldsymbol{z}}$, and read that "$\boldsymbol{z}$ is conditioned on $\hat{\boldsymbol{z}}$". However, this is a tall order. The problem is that we are requiring that X_i, alone, can correct simultaneously *all* erroneous output values, while keeping unchanged *all* correct output values. Instead, our definition considers an entire set of input variables to be a counterfactual cause:

DEFINITION 3 (VCC CAUSE). *Consider input values $\boldsymbol{x}$ for the input variables $\boldsymbol{X}$, a transformation $\boldsymbol{\Phi}$ computing the output values $\boldsymbol{z}$, and a ground truth $\hat{\boldsymbol{z}}$. A set $\boldsymbol{X}_c \subseteq \boldsymbol{X}$ is a* view-conditioned counterfactual cause *of $\boldsymbol{z}|\hat{\boldsymbol{z}}$, if there exist values $\hat{x}_i$ for each $X_i \in \boldsymbol{X}_c$, such that the following two conditions hold:*

- *$\boldsymbol{x} \models \boldsymbol{z}$ and*

$$\{\{X_i = x_i \mid X_i \notin \boldsymbol{X}_c\} \cup \{X_i = \hat{x}_i \mid X_i \in (\boldsymbol{X} \setminus \boldsymbol{X}_c)\}\} \models \hat{\boldsymbol{z}}$$

- *$\boldsymbol{X}_c$ is minimal, i.e. no subset of $\boldsymbol{X}_c$ is a VCC cause.*

Intuitively, a VCC cause is a minimal set of input variables for which there exists a changed assignment that results in output $\hat{\boldsymbol{z}}$.

EXAMPLE 4 (VCC CAUSES). *Consider the views $\boldsymbol{Z}$ given in Fig. 2b over the inputs $\boldsymbol{X}$, where X_1 and X_3 take values from the integer domain, while X_2 is Boolean. Based on the input values from Fig. 2a, the observed output values are $\boldsymbol{z} = \{z_1, z_2, z_3\} = \{\mathtt{T}, \mathtt{T}, \mathtt{F}\}$. Assume that the ground truth is $\hat{\boldsymbol{z}} = \{\underline{\mathtt{F}}, \mathtt{T}, \underline{\mathtt{T}}\}$, where the erroneous results are underlined. Suppose first that we restrict the output variable to Z_1 (thus, ignore Z_2, Z_3). Both X_1 and X_2 are counterfactual causes of Z_1: changing the value of X_1 (e.g. $X_1 = 12$), or the value of X_2 from* T *to* F*, would make Z_1* F*. However, if we take into account all three output variables, then X_2 is* not *a VCC cause of $\boldsymbol{z}|\hat{\boldsymbol{z}}$: if X_2 is switched to* F*, Z_1 would be "corrected" but Z_2 would also become* F*, which would contradict the ground truth $\hat{\boldsymbol{z}}$. In this example, there is a unique VCC cause of $\boldsymbol{z}|\hat{\boldsymbol{z}}$, which is the set of inputs $\{X_1, X_3\}$: switching their values to 12 and 4, respectively, sets all views to the desired output $\hat{\boldsymbol{z}}$.*

$\boldsymbol{X}$	$\boldsymbol{x}$
X_1	5
X_2	T
X_3	2

(a)

$\boldsymbol{Z}$	$\boldsymbol{\Phi}$	$\boldsymbol{z}$
Z_1	$(X_1 < 10) \wedge X_2$	T
Z_2	$(X_3 > 0) \wedge X_2$	T
Z_3	$(X_3 > 3)$	F

(b)

Figure 2: (a): Value assignments for inputs $\boldsymbol{X}$. (b): The values of outputs $\boldsymbol{Z}$ are based on simple transformations (also called lineages) $\boldsymbol{\Phi}$ of the inputs $\boldsymbol{X}$.

Actual causes in view-conditioned causality are defined in a similar manner based on contingency sets.

DEFINITION 5 (VC CAUSE). *Consider input values $\boldsymbol{x}$ for the input variables $\boldsymbol{X}$, a transformation $\boldsymbol{\Phi}$ computing the output values $\boldsymbol{z}$, and a ground truth $\hat{\boldsymbol{z}}$. A variable $X_i \in \boldsymbol{X}$ is a* view-conditioned cause *(VC cause) of $\boldsymbol{z}|\hat{\boldsymbol{z}}$, if there exists a set $\Gamma \subset \boldsymbol{X}$ called the* contingency *of X_i, such that $\{X_i\} \cup \Gamma$ is a VCC cause of $\boldsymbol{z}|\hat{\boldsymbol{z}}$.*

Note that every variable X_i in a VCC cause $\boldsymbol{X}_c$ of $\boldsymbol{z}|\hat{\boldsymbol{z}}$ is an VC cause with contingency $\boldsymbol{X}_c \setminus \{X_i\}$. Also, every VCC cause is a VC cause with an empty contingency set. Therefore, in Example 4, X_1 is a VC cause of $\boldsymbol{z}|\hat{\boldsymbol{z}}$ with contingency X_3, and X_3 is a VC cause with contingency X_1. Hence, even though in our example only sets of input variables are VCC causes, there are also individual input values which are VC causes.

Finally, we define the notion of responsibility, which measures the degree of causality.

DEFINITION 6 (RESPONSIBILITY). *Let $\boldsymbol{X}$ be a set of inputs to a set of views $\boldsymbol{Z}$, and assume $\boldsymbol{z}$ and $\hat{\boldsymbol{z}}$ to be the actual and ground truth values of those views, respectively. If $X_i \subseteq \boldsymbol{X}$ is a VC cause of $\boldsymbol{z}|\hat{\boldsymbol{z}}$, then its responsibility is defined as*

$$\rho_{X_i} = \frac{1}{1 + \min_\Gamma |\Gamma|}$$

where Γ is a contingency for X_i.

The responsibility is a function of the minimal number of input variables that need to be modified together with X_i in order to achieve the output $\hat{\boldsymbol{z}}$ for the views. If X_i is counterfactual, then its contingency set is empty, and therefore $\rho_{X_i} = 1$. If X_i is not a cause, by convention $\rho_{X_i} = 0$.

> ***Our approach to the error tracing problem:*** *Given $\boldsymbol{x}, \boldsymbol{X}, \boldsymbol{\Phi}, \hat{\boldsymbol{z}}$, we will compute all causes X_i, and rank them by their responsibility ρ_{X_i}. This ranking is a good indicator for tracing the errors in the input data.*

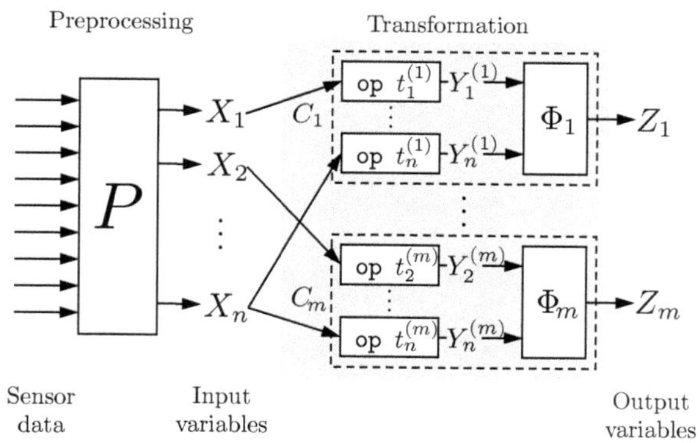

Figure 3: Structure of a classifier system.

We end this section by comparing our definition of causality and responsibility to prior work [17, 28]. In the prior definition, there is only one output variable, and this allows the definition of a counterfactual cause to be restricted to a single input variable. As we have seen, in error tracing applications we need to consider multiple output variables (some correct and some incorrect), and here the simple definition of counterfactual cause no longer works (as we saw in Example 4). Our new Def. 3 is an important extension to sets of counterfactual causes. On the other hand, this extension allows us to simplify (somewhat) the definition of an actual cause, in that the contingency set Γ is simply part of a counterfactual cause.

EXAMPLE 7. *Continuing our running example, we show it can be modeled in our formalism. Our application is a classification system with several sensor signals, and several classifiers determining user activities and status based on the sensor data. Sensor measurements can be in general vectors of values, like a time sequence of a signal. Before this data can be useful for the classification, it often undergoes some initial mathematical transformation to compute several useful metrics of the input signals (e.g. frequency, signal strength etc). We are not interested in the raw signal, but rather these computed metrics that serve as inputs to the classifiers. These represent our input* $\boldsymbol{x} = \{x_1, \ldots, x_n\}$. *There are m classifiers* $\{C_1, \ldots, C_m\}$, *producing a set of outputs* $\boldsymbol{Z} = \{Z_1, \ldots, Z_m\}$. *As an example,* $\boldsymbol{Z}$ *may represent a classification of the user's current activities (walking, driving, in a meeting).*

An abstraction of the architecture of the system is shown in Fig. 3. The classifier inputs $\boldsymbol{x}$ *are continuous values, or Boolean values. Each classifier* C_j *uses a subset of the transformed values* $\boldsymbol{x}_j \subseteq \boldsymbol{x}$ *to compute a classification result* Z_j. *Within each classifier* C_j, *each variable* $x_i \in \boldsymbol{x}_j$ *is compared against one or more predetermined thresholds, resulting in a Boolean variable* $Y_i^{(j)}$. *These thresholds are usually selected using machine learning techniques over some training data. In general,* $Y_i^{(j)} = (x_i \text{ op } t_i)$, *where op is one of* $\{<, >, \leq, \geq\}$, *and* t_i *is a threshold value. The final output* Z_j *of the classifier is determined by a Boolean function* $\Phi_j(\boldsymbol{Y}_j)$.

4. REDUCTION TO SAT AND MAXSAT

Computing the causality and responsibility are known to be NP-hard [14], and the same holds for view-conditioned-causality. Our approach for tracing errors to the data source is to reduce the causality/responsibility problem to the SAT problem, and to partial weighted MaxSAT problem respectively. This is an intensively studied research area (an extensive survey is in [4]) and there exist several highly optimized tools both for SAT and weighted MaxSAT. In this section we describe an algorithm for reducing the causality/responsibility problem to the SAT/MaxSAT problem. In the next section we show how to convert the resulting Boolean expressions into CNF, so we can feed them directly into some of these tools.

The algorithm consists of the following steps

1. Map from input variables with continuous domain to Boolean variables called *partitioned* variables.
2. Construct the constraint expression Ψ that captures the correlations between the partitioned variables.
3. For each input X_i, construct a Boolean expression Φ_{SAT} that is satisfiable iff X_i is a VC cause. Φ_{SAT} is a hard constraint.
4. Construct "soft" constraints to account for the contingency set: the more soft constraints are violated while satisfying Φ_{SAT} the larger the contingency set.

4.1 Mapping to Boolean Variables

Recall that while all the outputs $\boldsymbol{Z}$ are Boolean variables, some of the inputs $\boldsymbol{X}$ can be numerical values, and the Boolean expressions $\boldsymbol{\Phi}$ are over threshold predicates over these inputs, e.g., $\Phi_3 = (X_1 < 2.5) \vee (X_6 > 20)$. Since we need to map all inputs to Boolean variables, a first attempt is to create one Boolean variable for each threshold predicate, call it a *threshold variable*. An example threshold variable is $Y_1^{(3)} \equiv (X_1 < 2.5)$, where the subscript 1 refers to the input variable X_1, and the superscript (3) refers to the classifier Φ_3. But threshold variables are not independent, and this prevents us from using them in our translation.

EXAMPLE 8 (BOOLEAN MAPPING). *Assume 3 classifications over 6 inputs:*

$$\begin{aligned}
\Phi_1 &= \big((X_1 > 10) \wedge (X_2 < 7)\big) \vee \big((X_5 > 10) \wedge (X_3 > 20)\big)\\
&= \big(Y_1^{(1)} \wedge Y_2^{(1)}\big) \vee \big(Y_5^{(1)} \wedge Y_3^{(1)}\big)\\
\Phi_2 &= \big((X_1 < 4) \wedge (X_4 < 5)\big)\\
&= \big(Y_1^{(2)} \wedge Y_4^{(2)}\big)\\
\Phi_3 &= (X_1 < 2.5) \vee (X_6 > 20)\\
&= Y_1^{(3)} \vee Y_6^{(3)}
\end{aligned}$$

The three threshold variables $Y_1^{(1)}$, $Y_1^{(2)}$ *and* $Y_1^{(3)}$ *for the input* X_1 *are dependent in different ways:* $Y_1^{(1)}$ *cannot be true together with* $Y_1^{(2)}$ *or* $Y_1^{(3)}$, *whereas there exist values of* X_1 *for which* $Y_1^{(2)}$ *and* $Y_1^{(3)}$ *can both be true.*

Therefore, we take a different approach. For a given variable X_i, let $\{t_1, \ldots, t_{T_i}\}$ be the set of all thresholds that appear in threshold predicates associated with variable X_i across all transformations. We define a set of $2T_i + 1$ Boolean *partition variables* $\boldsymbol{X}_{[i]} = \{X_{[i,1]}, \ldots, X_{[i,2T_i+1]}\}$ as follows:

$$\begin{aligned}
X_{[i,1]} &\equiv (X_i < t_1) && \\
X_{[i,2j]} &\equiv (X_i = t_j) && 1 \leq j \leq T_i\\
X_{[i,2j+1]} &\equiv (t_j < X_i < t_{j+1}) && 1 \leq j < T_i\\
X_{[i,2T_i+1]} &\equiv (X_i > t_{T_i}) &&
\end{aligned}$$

Denote $\boldsymbol{X}_{[]}$ the set of all partition variables, $\boldsymbol{X}_{[]} = \bigcup_i \boldsymbol{X}_{[i]}$. Then, we rewrite each threshold predicate as a disjunction of these variables, and we rewrite each Boolean expression Φ_j in terms of the partitioned variables, denoting $\Phi_j^{[]}$ the rewritten expression; when it is clear from the context, we drop the superscript $[]$ and use Φ_j also for the translated expression. Note that the use of partition variables only linearly increases the number of variables with the number of thresholds per variable, with two new variables created for every threshold.

EXAMPLE 9 (EXAMPLE 8 CONTINUED). *The partition variables of X_1 are given as:*

$$X_{[1,1]} \equiv (X_1 < 2.5) \qquad X_{[1,5]} \equiv (4 < X_1 < 10)$$
$$X_{[1,2]} \equiv (X_1 = 2.5) \qquad X_{[1,6]} \equiv (X_1 = 10)$$
$$X_{[1,3]} \equiv (2.5 < X_1 < 4) \qquad X_{[1,7]} \equiv (X_1 > 10)$$
$$X_{[1,4]} \equiv (X_1 = 4)$$

The partition variables divide the domain of X_1 into non-overlapping ranges, and therefore exactly one of them is true for any given value x_1. The rewritten threshold predicates are:

$$Y_1^{(1)} \equiv X_{[1,7]}$$
$$Y_1^{(2)} \equiv X_{[1,1]} \vee X_{[1,2]} \vee X_{[1,3]}$$
$$Y_1^{(3)} \equiv X_{[1,1]}$$

Thus, each $\Phi_j^{[]}$ now depends on the new partition variables.

Every value assignment $\boldsymbol{x}$ of $\boldsymbol{X}$ defines a unique Boolean assignment $\theta_{\boldsymbol{x}}$ of $\boldsymbol{X}_{[]}$, such that $X_{[i,j]}$ is true in $\theta_{\boldsymbol{x}}$ iff the value $X_i = x_i$ satisfies the partition predicate corresponding to the variable $X_{[i,j]}$. Then, one can check that, for every j, $\boldsymbol{x} \models \Phi_j$ iff $\theta_{\boldsymbol{x}} \models \Phi_j^{[]}$.

If the input variable X_i is already a Boolean variable, it does not need to be re-written with this process, but for consistency of notation we map it to the partition variables $X_{[i,1]} = X_i$, and $X_{[i,2]} = \neg X_i$.

4.2 The Partition Variable Constraint Ψ

The Boolean variables $\boldsymbol{X}_{[i]}$ are subject to the constraint that exactly one of these variables is true. This is captured by the following formula:

$$\Psi_i = \left(\bigvee_j X_{[i,j]}\right)\left(\bigwedge_{j<l} (\neg X_{[i,j]} \vee \neg X_{[i,l]})\right)$$

Ψ_i is a conjunction of $2(T_i + 1)$ clauses, where T_i is the number of thresholds associated with variable X_i. Taking the conjunction over all input variables, we obtain the following constraint expression Ψ:

$$\Psi = \bigwedge_i \Psi_i \tag{1}$$

We have the following:

LEMMA 10. *For any assignment θ, $\theta \models \Psi$ iff there exists values $\boldsymbol{x}$ such that $\theta_{\boldsymbol{x}} = \theta$.*

The proof is straightforward and omitted. The lemma says that any assignment satisfying the constraint Ψ corresponds to some values $\boldsymbol{x}$. Note that these values are not necessarily uniquely defined: in Example 9 if θ says that $X_{1,3}$ is true, then we know that $2.5 < X_1 < 4$, without knowing the actual value of x_1.

4.3 The Hard Constraint Φ_{SAT}

Given the observed output values $\boldsymbol{z}$ and the ground truth output values $\hat{\boldsymbol{z}}$, we define here two Boolean expressions, called VC-expressions, which state that the outputs are $\boldsymbol{z}$, or that the outputs are $\hat{\boldsymbol{z}}$ respectively:

$$\Phi^{[]} = \left(\bigwedge_{i.z_i=\mathtt{T}} \Phi_i^{[]}\right) \wedge \left(\bigwedge_{i.z_i=\mathtt{F}} \neg\Phi_i^{[]}\right) \tag{2}$$

$$\hat{\Phi}^{[]} = \left(\bigwedge_{i.\hat{z}_i=\mathtt{T}} \Phi_i^{[]}\right) \wedge \left(\bigwedge_{i.\hat{z}_i=\mathtt{F}} \neg\Phi_i^{[]}\right) \tag{3}$$

The superscript $[]$ is intended to remind us that these expressions are over the partition variables $\boldsymbol{X}_{[]}$; we will drop the superscript from here on, unless it is needed to clarify the context. The expression Φ checks if the output is the "observed output" $\boldsymbol{z}$. The expression $\hat{\Phi}$ checks if the output is the "ground truth" $\hat{\boldsymbol{z}}$. If at least one error is detected in the output ($\boldsymbol{z} \neq \hat{\boldsymbol{z}}$) then Φ and $\hat{\Phi}$ cannot be satisfied simultaneously.

EXAMPLE 11 (EXAMPLE 9 CONTINUED). *Assume the observed output is $\boldsymbol{z} = \{z_1, z_2, z_3\} = \{\mathtt{T}, \mathtt{T}, \mathtt{F}\}$ and the ground truth is $\hat{\boldsymbol{z}} = \{\underline{\mathtt{F}}, \mathtt{T}, \underline{\mathtt{T}}\}$. Then (we drop superscripts $[]$):*

$$\Phi = \Phi_1 \wedge \Phi_2 \wedge \neg\Phi_3$$
$$\hat{\Phi} = \neg\Phi_1 \wedge \Phi_2 \wedge \Phi_3$$

We give next a technical definition, which measures the distance between two assignments:

DEFINITION 12 (CONSTRAINED DISTANCE). *The distance between two assignments $\theta \models \Psi$ and $\hat{\theta} \models \Psi$ of $\boldsymbol{X}_{[]}$ under constraint Ψ is*

$$d(\theta, \hat{\theta}) = \frac{1}{2} h(\theta, \hat{\theta})$$

where $h(\theta, \hat{\theta})$ is the hamming distance between the two Boolean vectors $\theta(\boldsymbol{X}_{[]})$ and $\hat{\theta}(\boldsymbol{X}_{[]})$

If we have two input values $\boldsymbol{x}$ and $\hat{\boldsymbol{x}}$ that differ in exactly one variable X_i, then their corresponding assignments $\theta_{\boldsymbol{x}}$ and $\theta_{\hat{\boldsymbol{x}}}$ will differ in exactly two variables, hence, by our definition, $d(\theta_{\boldsymbol{x}}, \theta_{\hat{\boldsymbol{x}}}) = 1$.

The crux of our translation is captured by the next definition and theorem. They map the notion of VC-causes of $\boldsymbol{z}|\hat{\boldsymbol{z}}$ into the a problem of "causes for Ψ, Φ, $\hat{\Phi}$".

DEFINITION 13. *Consider the Boolean expressions Ψ, Φ, $\hat{\Phi}$ given by (Eq. 1), (Eq. 2), and (Eq. 3), and let θ be an assignment of the partition variables $\boldsymbol{X}_{[]}$. Assume the following:*

- *$\theta \models \Psi$ (it satisfies the constraints)*
- *$\theta \models \Phi$ (it generates the "observed" output)*

A variable $X_{[i,j]}$ is a cause *for Ψ, Φ, $\hat{\Phi}$ if there exist two assignments θ^Γ and $\hat{\theta}$ such that:*

- *$\theta^\Gamma \models \Psi$ and $\hat{\theta} \models \Psi$ (both satisfy the constraint)*
- *$\hat{\theta}(X_{ij}) \neq \theta^\Gamma(X_{ij}) = \theta(X_{ij})$ and $d(\theta^\Gamma, \hat{\theta}) = 1$ (they differ in only one input variable)*
- *$\theta^\Gamma \not\models \hat{\Phi}$ and $\hat{\theta} \models \hat{\Phi}$ (θ^Γ does not yet generate the ground truth, but $\hat{\theta}$ does generate the ground truth)*

We call the set $\Gamma = \{X_{[u,v]} \mid \theta^\Gamma(X_{[u,v]}) \neq \theta(X_{[u,v]})\}$ *a contingency of* $X_{[i,j]}$, *and* θ^Γ *is the contingent assignment.*

THEOREM 14 (VC CAUSE EQUIVALENCE). $X_{[i,j]}$, *with* $\theta(X_{[i,j]}) = \mathtt{T}$, *is a cause of* Ψ, Φ, $\hat{\Phi}$ *iff* X_i *is a VC-cause of* $\boldsymbol{z}|\hat{\boldsymbol{z}}$.

The proof is in the appendix. Thus, we reduce the problem of computing VC-causes of $\boldsymbol{z}|\hat{\boldsymbol{z}}$ to the problem of computing causes for Ψ, Φ, $\hat{\Phi}$. We reduce the latter to the satisfiability problem.

Given a variable $X_{[i,j]}$, we will construct a Boolean formula that is satisfiable if and only if $X_{[i,j]}$ is a cause of Ψ, Φ, $\hat{\Phi}$. We denote with $\hat{\Phi}\left[\theta(X_{[i,j]})\right]$ the Boolean expression that results from $\hat{\Phi}$ after assigning $X_{[i,j]}$ to its value under θ, whereas $\hat{\Phi}\left[\neg\theta(X_{[i,j]})\right]$ denotes the expression that we get by assigning to it its negation. Similarly, $\hat{\Phi}\left[\theta(\boldsymbol{X}_{[i]})\right]$ denotes the expression that results from assigning to $\hat{\Phi}$ all variables in $\boldsymbol{X}_{[i]}$ to their values under θ.

If $X_{[i,j]}$ is a cause of Ψ, Φ, $\hat{\Phi}$, then there must exist an assignment that makes the following formula `true`:

$$\Phi_{\text{SAT}} = \neg\hat{\Phi}\left[\theta(\boldsymbol{X}_{[i]})\right] \wedge \hat{\Phi}\left[\neg\theta(X_{[i,j]})\right] \wedge \Psi\left[\neg\theta(X_{[i,j]})\right] \quad (4)$$

In the above formula, $\hat{\Phi}$ denotes the Boolean formula from Eq. 3, while Ψ is the constraint expression, as defined in Sect. 4.2. The first term ($\neg\hat{\Phi}\left[\theta(X_{[i]})\right]$) ensures the requirement that $\theta^\Gamma \not\models \hat{\Phi}$: when $\boldsymbol{X}_{[i]}$ is set to its original values the assignment does not satisfy $\hat{\Phi}$. The second term ($\hat{\Phi}\left[\neg\theta(X_{[i,j]})\right]$) ensures that $\hat{\theta} \models \hat{\Phi}$: when X_i switches values (since $X_{[i,j]}$ is forced to its negation) the assignment should satisfy $\hat{\Phi}$. Finally, the third term enforces the constraint over the partition variables, under the assumption that the value of X_i should change.

We can state now our main result for the reduction from causality to SAT:

THEOREM 15. X_i *is a VC-cause of* $\boldsymbol{z}|\hat{\boldsymbol{z}}$ *iff* Φ_{SAT} *given by (Eq. 4) is satisfiable.*

Note that we cannot yet use a standard SAT solver to solve the satisfiability of Eq. 4, because these require the expression to be translated into CNF. Translating Eq. 4 into CNF is a non-trivial task that can result in an exponential increase in size, and we address it in Sect. 5. First we show how to extend this construction to compute the responsibility.

4.4 Computing Responsibility

We can now define responsibility:

DEFINITION 16. *Fix the Boolean expressions* Ψ, Φ, $\hat{\Phi}$ *over variables* $\boldsymbol{X}_{[]}$. *The responsibility of* $X_{[i,j]}$ *is:*

$$\rho = \frac{1}{1 + \min_{\theta^\Gamma} d(\theta, \theta^\Gamma)}$$

where θ^Γ *is a contingent assignment of* $X_{[i,j]}$.

Like causality, we can also determine the responsibility of the input variables $\boldsymbol{X}$ over the Boolean partition variables $\boldsymbol{X}_{[]}$.

THEOREM 17 (RESPONSIBILITY EQUIVALENCE). *A variable* $X_{[i,j]}$, *with* $\theta(X_{[i,j]}) = \mathtt{T}$ *is a cause for* Ψ, Φ, $\hat{\Phi}$ *and has responsibility* ρ *if and only if* X_i *is a VC cause of* $\boldsymbol{z}|\hat{\boldsymbol{z}}$ *with responsibility* ρ.

Computing the responsibility of a cause is a harder problem, as it requires finding the minimum size contingency set Γ. Following Def. 13, that corresponds to determining the assignment $\hat{\theta}$ that differs the least from the original assignment θ, which satisfies Φ_{SAT}.

We will solve the responsibility problem by creating an instance of a partial weighted MaxSAT problem [15]. In partial weight MaxSAT each clause is given a weight, with a maximum weight identifying *hard constraints*, which are the clauses that are required to be satisfied. A solution to the problem finds an assignment that satisfies all the hard constraints, and maximizes the weight of the satisfied soft constraints.

In our case, Φ_{SAT} (Eq. 4) defines hard constraints: all of its clauses should be satisfied for a variable to be a cause. In addition we ask the solver to find an assignment that is as close as possible to θ. We do this by adding the following formula:

$$\Phi_\theta = \bigwedge_{\theta(X_{[i,j]})=\mathtt{T}} X_{[i,j]} \bigwedge_{\theta(X_{[i,j]})=\mathtt{F}} \neg X_{[i,j]} \quad (5)$$

Φ_θ represents in a Boolean expression the given assignment θ. Note that Φ_θ is already written in CNF, and each clause consists of exactly one variable $X_{[i,j]}$, possibly negated. We assign to each clause a weight of 1, thus asking the solver to violate as few clauses as possible. The only assignment that makes Φ_θ true is θ. For any other assignment $\hat{\theta}$, the number of clauses in Φ_θ that are false is precisely $d(\theta, \hat{\theta})$. Thus, a partial weighted MaxSAT solution will find the assignment that satisfies the hard constraints Φ_{SAT}, and differs the least from the assignment θ. We state this formally:

THEOREM 18. *Consider the MaxSAT problem consisting of the hard constraint* Φ_{SAT} *and the soft clauses in* Φ_θ, *and let* t *be the minimum number of clauses in* Φ_θ *that are false under any assignment. Then, the responsibility of* X_i *for* $\boldsymbol{z}|\hat{\boldsymbol{z}}$ *is* $\rho = 1/(1 + \frac{t}{2})$.

Note that t is divided by 2 in the responsibility computation due to the constraint over the partition variables: a distance of 2 in an assignment in the partition space corresponds to a single variable change in the input space.

5. CONVERSION INTO CNF

In the previous section, we described how the problem of determining view-conditioned causes and their responsibilities can be translated into a general satisfiability problem. While satisfiability is well known to be hard in general, there are highly optimized tools available that can solve satisfiability for CNF expressions [18]. Hence, we need to convert our general expression Φ_{SAT} in Eq. 4 into CNF before testing causality and responsibility for individual variables. The time complexity of CNF conversion is linear [30], but it can introduce exponential blow-ups in the size of the expression. The problem comes from the necessity to negate, at several steps, CNF formulas, but then reformulate the result as CNF. The standard way to do push the negation into the literals by applying De Morgan's laws and distributivity. There are more sophisticated conversion algorithms that can be employed (e.g. [30]), but the optimization that we propose here is orthogonal to those, and can be used in conjunction with other conversion methods. In our problem, there are two critical points in the conversion, that is expressing $\hat{\Phi}$ as CNF, and that of expressing its negation $\neg\hat{\Phi}$.

In this section we present an optimization that exploits the constraints of the Boolean partition variables in order to reduce the size of the converted CNF expression. Algorithm 1 provides a conversion that completely solves the problem for $\hat{\Phi}$ ($\hat{\Phi}$ is constructed in a way that ensures it is already in CNF) and ameliorates the size increase for $\neg\hat{\Phi}$. The algorithm exploits the fact that a threshold predicate $Y_i^{(j)}$ can either be written in the standard form given in Sect. 4, or alternatively in what we call its *dual form*. For this section, we assume that the initial classifiers are given in CNF, but the proposed optimization can be beneficial even when that is not the case. Assume we have the following $m = 2$ classifiers over $n = 3$ inputs:

$$\Phi_1 = (X_1 < 6) \wedge (X_2 \leq 8)$$
$$\Phi_2 = (X_1 < 5) \wedge (X_3 \geq 7)$$

Then the threshold predicate $Y_1^{(1)} = (X_1 < 6)$ over the partitioned variables can be expressed with either of the following two forms:

$$Y_1^{(1)} \equiv X_{[1,1]} \vee X_{[1,2]} \vee X_{[1,3]}$$
$$Y_{1D}^{(1)} \equiv \bar{X}_{[1,4]} \wedge \bar{X}_{[1,5]}$$

Here we use the optional subscript D to indicate the dual form and write $\bar{X}_i$ as short form for $\neg X_i$. When constructing Φ_{SAT}, Algorithm 1 chooses at each step an equivalent expression that minimizes the total number of clauses in the resulting CNF: Line 2 to line 4 encode the conversion for $\hat{\Phi}$ and add clauses for Φ_j or $\neg\Phi_{jD}$, depending on whether $\hat{z}_j$ is true or false, respectively. Here, again the subscript D indicates that $\neg\Phi_{jD}$ is calculated starting from the duals $Y_{iD}^{(j)}$ instead of the standard form, and becomes only one clause. For example,

$$\neg\Phi_{1D} = \left(X_{[1,4]} \vee X_{[1,5]} \vee X_{[2,3]}\right)$$

whereas starting from the standard form would result in

$$\begin{aligned}\neg\Phi_1 = &\left(\bar{X}_{[1,1]} \vee \bar{X}_{[2,1]}\right) \wedge \left(\bar{X}_{[1,1]} \vee \bar{X}_{[2,2]}\right) \wedge \\ &\left(\bar{X}_{[1,2]} \vee \bar{X}_{[2,1]}\right) \wedge \left(\bar{X}_{[1,2]} \vee \bar{X}_{[2,2]}\right) \wedge \\ &\left(\bar{X}_{[1,3]} \vee \bar{X}_{[2,1]}\right) \wedge \left(\bar{X}_{[1,3]} \vee \bar{X}_{[2,2]}\right)\end{aligned}$$

Denoting with f the number of ground truth values F, $\hat{\Phi}$ is converted into $\mathcal{O}((m-f)n)$ clauses as follows:

$$\hat{\Phi} = \underbrace{\neg\Phi_{1D} \wedge \ldots \wedge \neg\Phi_{fD}}_{f \text{ clauses}} \wedge \underbrace{\Phi_{f+1} \wedge \ldots \wedge \Phi_m}_{\mathcal{O}((m-f)n) \text{ clauses}}$$

whereas the naive conversion would lead into $\mathcal{O}(fk^n)$ clauses.

This difference becomes even more pronounced for converting $\neg\hat{\Phi}$, where an exponential blow-up is unavoidable. Here, Line 5 to line 11 first construct the following formula:

$$\neg\hat{\Phi} = \underbrace{\Phi_1 \vee \ldots \vee \Phi_f}_{\substack{\beta:\ f \text{ conjuncts} \\ \text{with } n \text{ clauses}}} \vee \underbrace{\neg\Phi_{f+1D} \vee \ldots \vee \neg\Phi_{mD}}_{\alpha:\ 1 \text{ clause}}$$

Converting this formula to CNF results in $\mathcal{O}(n^f)$ clauses, and this exponential size increase cannot be avoided. In contrast, the naive conversion would even lead to a double exponential number of clauses.

Finally, line 12 to line 14 adds the constraint expression Ψ by adding $\mathcal{O}(mk^2)$ clauses, where k is the maximum number of partitions for any input variable.

Algorithm: `CNF conversion of a VC causality problem`
Input: Partitioned variables $\boldsymbol{X}_{[]}$, ground truth $\hat{\boldsymbol{z}}$
Boolean expressions Φ_j and $\neg\Phi_{jD}$ for all j
Output: General Φ_{SAT} in CNF

1 Let Φ_{SAT} be a conjunction of disjunctions (CNF)
2 `//Add clauses for` $\hat{\Phi}$
3 $\forall j \in [m]$ with $\hat{z}_j = \texttt{T}$: add Φ_j to Φ_{SAT}
4 $\forall j \in [m]$ with $\hat{z}_j = \texttt{F}$: add $\neg\Phi_{jD}$ to Φ_{SAT}
5 `//Add clauses for` $\neg\hat{\Phi}$
6 Let $\boldsymbol{\alpha}$ be a disjunction of literals
7 $\forall j \in [m]$ with $\hat{z}_j = \texttt{T}$: add $\neg\Phi_{jD}$ to $\boldsymbol{\alpha}$
8 Let $\boldsymbol{\beta}$ be a disjunction of conjuncts
9 $\forall j \in [m]$ with $\hat{z}_j = \texttt{F}$: add Φ_j to $\boldsymbol{\beta}$
10 Convert $\gamma \leftarrow \boldsymbol{\alpha} \vee \boldsymbol{\beta}$ from DNF into CNF with De Morgan
11 Add $\boldsymbol{\gamma}$ to Φ_{SAT}
12 `//Add clauses for` Ψ
13 $\forall i \in [n]$: add $\left(\bigvee_{k\in[k_i]} X_{[i,k]}\right)$ to Φ_{SAT}
14 $\forall i \in [n], j < l \in [k_i]$: add $\left(\bar{X}_{[i,j]} \vee \bar{X}_{[i,l]}\right)$ to Φ_{SAT}

Algorithm 1 converts the problem of finding VC causes into solving a general CNF formula. The actual evaluation later replaces some clauses with actual values for variables.

6. EXPERIMENTAL EVALUATION

We validate our approach by using a real data set collected from a practical application that operates along the lines of our classification example. The application, called CARE (Context-Aware Recommendation Engine), collects various sensor data from a user's smartphone, uses it to infer the current context (e.g., whether the user is walking or driving), and provides various context-aware services. For example, CARE allows a user to search for restaurants. If CARE thinks that the user is walking alone, it will show search results or ads of restaurants within the user's walking distance from the current location. On the other hand, if it believes that the user is driving with their family, it will provide a list of family restaurants within driving distance.[1]

CARE relies on (i) a set of extractors equivalent of the pre-processing layer of Fig. 3, which extract useful features from sensor data (e.g., user's speed from GPS data) and (ii) a set of classifiers that infer the user's current context based on the values of the features. These features are used as our input variables, and all the classifier outputs comprise our views. Assuming correctness of the classifier functions, errors in the classification can still occur due to various factors, such as innate unreliability of some of the sensory input, or even unpredictable user behavior (e.g., the user is outdoors with the phone in their pocket, resulting in invalid light sensor data). CARE receives feedback on the correctness of the classifier outputs either directly from user input, or indirectly through the user response to the context-based recommendations. In cases of errors, it is important for CARE to *determine which input is responsible for the errors*, and thus ignore the corresponding classifiers in the recommendation process.

For the experiments in this section, we collect data using CARE's data collection software. We use the software on Android-based HTC Desire smartphones. When instructed, the software collects data from various phone sensors such as accelerometer, GPS, microphone, light sensor, and cell

[1]In addition to the current inferred context, CARE also uses user preferences and historical data in making such recommendations.

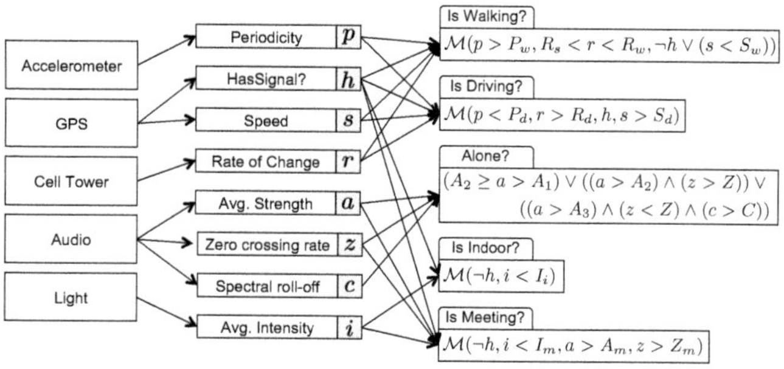

Figure 4: Structure of our classifier system based on sensory input from a mobile device.

phone signal strength. During data collection, the software also asks the user to annotate the data with the true context (e.g., walking or not) and validity of various sensor inputs (e.g., a light sensor input is invalid if the phone is inside a bag). The data and annotations are then used to build one machine learning classifier (i.e. a decision tree) for each context of interest. The resulting classifiers with five target contexts are shown in Fig. 4.

The dataset used in the experiments in this section was collected from three individuals, who carried our instrumented smartphones over a period of three weeks and collected data during their daily activities. The dataset contains in total 801 different contexts, spanning a time range of over 149 hours in a three-week period. Each of the contexts in the dataset has its start and end times, associated data from all sensors, its true label, the label given by classifiers, and the validity of each sensor input. Thus, for each case of misclassification, we use the sensor validity as the ground truth for causality against which we validate our approach.

Implementation. Our satisfiability reduction algorithm was implemented in Java.[2] For every instance of the input data, our algorithm constructs the appropriate data files in standard DIMACS CNF and WCNF format [21]. We use the `minisat` [32] and `MiniMaxSat` [18] solvers, to solve the SAT and partial weighted MaxSAT instances, respectively.

6.1 Effectiveness

In our experiments we want to validate the quality of information of the view-conditioned responsibility ranking over possible sources of error. We ran our algorithms over the test data collected through the CARE system, and each test case took only a couple of seconds to complete. We first evaluate the effectiveness of our approach compared to other schemes using average precision as the metric of comparison [23]. *Average precision* (AP) quantifies the accuracy of a ranking in identifying points of relevance. Given the ground truth on the validity of the sensory input, an average precision of 1 means that the faulty sensors were indeed ranked first in the ranking of most likely errors.

We compare view-conditioned causality against three other techniques that can be used to produce error rankings: (*i*) Boolean variable influence, (*ii*) view-conditioned counterfactuals, and (*iii*) causality without conditioning. *Boolean influence* produces a *static ranking* of the input parameters for each classifier. The influence of a variable X_i in formula Φ is defined as the probability that Φ remains undetermined when values are assigned to all variables except X_i [24]. For example, in the simple formula $\Phi = A \vee (B \wedge C)$, the influence of A is 0.75, whereas the influence of B is 0.25. Note that influence quantifies the importance of a variable within a function over all possible assignments. On the other hand, causality-based schemes quantify this importance based on the actual assignment. Intuitively, we expect schemes that take into account the current state of the world to be more accurate in error identification.

Figure 5a shows the results of this first set of experiments. The horizontal axis shows the number of faults in the input parameters, starting from a single parameter failing, and going up to 7 (recall from Fig. 4 that the classifiers operate over 8 parameters in total). Causality-based schemes are depicted with solid lines. Also depicted are random average precision and the worst case average precision for each fault range.[3] Note that view-conditioned causes are always a better predictor for errors than view-conditioned counterfactuals or causes without conditioning. And this difference gets more pronounced with the number of faults. Also note that that the precision of counterfactual causes follows that of random ranking from a point on. It is normal because as the number of faults increases, we stop having any counterfactual causes at all.

The dip observed across all schemes at the instances with 2 faults is due to the lack of granularity in the ground truth of sensor validity. Our ground truth is restricted to the level of the sensors (e.g. GPS), rather than the individual parameters (e.g. h). So when the GPS is considered faulty, the features h and s are both deemed incorrect. However, with this few errors, only one or two classifiers are wrong, and they are likely to only include h (not s). The result is that s is not really a cause (it is not part of the classifiers that failed), but because it is always considered to fail with h in the ground truth, it is reflected as loss in precision.

In Figure 5b we studied the next step: how well can we correct errors in the classifiers, once the likely input errors are identified. The graph displays the portion of errors in the particular classifier that can be corrected if the top ranked view-conditioned cause is omitted from the calculation of the classifier result. This involves a modification in the classifier function. For example, the driving classification is a strict majority function between 4 predicates; if feature p is omitted, then it becomes a strict majority among the other three predicates. An interesting observation in our experiments is that certain classifiers can achieve better correction ratios than others. For example, omitting features r or s corrects more than 85% of the errors of the driving classification, whereas omitting parameter s corrects the walking classifier by only 25%. This behavior may seem random or surprising at first, but in fact it highlights a very important insight that causality brings into error correction. This can be understood from Fig. 5c, which focuses on three of the classifiers (walking, driving, and meeting) to explain the reasons for this difference in corrections: Note that the driving classification, as seen in Fig. 4, uses 4 features (p, r, s and h), two of which (r and s) are counterfactual ($\rho = 1$ in Fig. 5c), whereas the other two have zero responsibility. This is very

[2]In practice, the algorithm would be running on the phone itself. If the implementation is heavy weight, it can run on the Cloud and the phone can communicate with it when needed.

[3]Random AP is the expected AP when a list of k relevant and n total items is randomly sorted. Worst case AP is when those k are sorted last in the list of n total items.

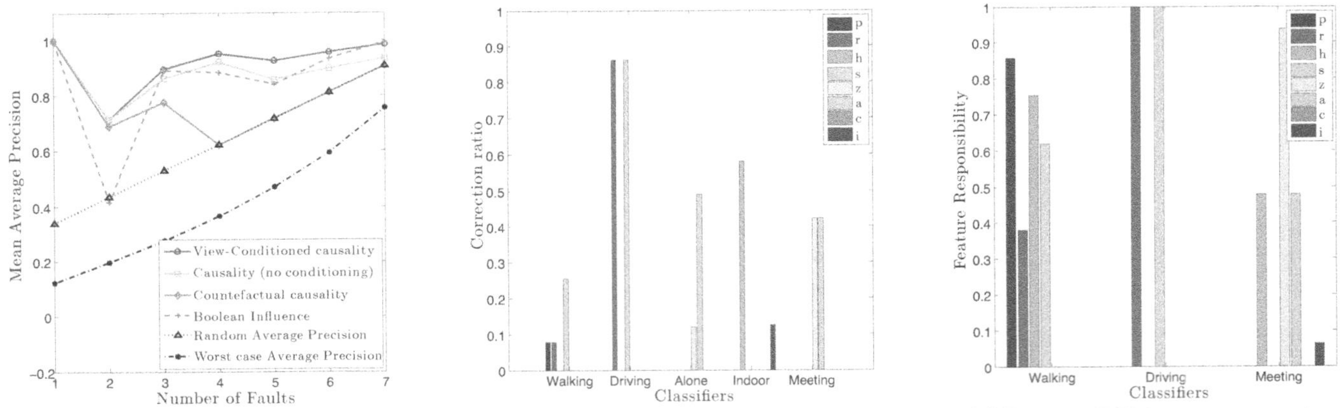

(a) Mean average precision (AP) (b) Ratio of Corrections (c) Responsibilities per parameter

Figure 5: (a): Mean average precision across different approaches: View-conditioned causality outperforms the static and simpler causality schemes. (b): Portion of errors that get corrected when the parameter with the highest responsibility is omitted from the computation. (c): Comparison among the responsibility rankings for different classifiers. (b & c): The ratio of correction actually depends on whether there exist variables *reliable* for the classifier (compare walking and driving).

important, as it means that the parameters h and p are very unlikely to cause errors in the driving classification, and are thus reliable predictors for it. Thus, when omitting r or s from the classifier function, the result becomes much more reliable. On the other hand, the walking classifier does not have reliable features, as all of them have fairly high responsibility across our test cases. When all features of a classifier have high responsibility, it means that all of them are likely causes of error. Without a single reliable predictor, it is less likely that we can achieve corrections by simply removing a parameter and not changing the classifier function otherwise. The meeting classifier stands on a middle ground: it has one reliable predicate (based on parameter i), but still contains 3 unreliable ones resulting in less gain compared to the driving classification. Hence, using responsibility to determine the reliability of features is very important in this application, as it can *quantify the quality of a classifier*, and implies possible ways to improve it. For example, in the driving classification, the vast difference between the reliable and unreliable features is an indication that parameters r and s should be disregarded in this classifier altogether, whereas the absence of reliable predicates for walking likely means that the learned models need to be improved.

6.2 Scalability

In our second set of experiments we study how our approach performs for bigger problem sizes. We generate synthetic data with a similar structure to the one in CARE. We randomly generate classifier functions as a conjunction over ranges of the different parameters, and randomly assign classification failures with a probability of about 10%, following the failure rate that we observed in the real data. In the context of an application like the CARE system we do not expect to have more than 15-20 parameters/features and 20-30 classifiers. Yet in this evaluation, we generate instances from 5 to 70 parameters, and from 5 to 60 classifiers.

Figure 6a and Fig. 6d show the execution time of our CNF conversion algorithm 1, which takes as input the classification formulas, variable assignments and observed errors, and produces instances of SAT and partial weighted MaxSAT. Note that the vertical axis of these graphs is in log scale. As discussed in Sect. 5, conversion of the computed formulas into CNF is required in order to be solved by standard satisfiability tools. As the problem size grows with more variables or classifiers, thus generating larger formulas, our algorithm is more likely to suffer the effects of exponential growth during the necessary CNF conversion. Note however that this conversion is not an inherent part of our reduction from view-conditioned causality to SAT, which is polynomial in size, but rather a complication imposed by the CNF requirement of currently available SAT solvers. In spite of the CNF conversion step, the runtime of our algorithm remains feasible with average runtime of around one minute for the larger problem sizes, and around one second for sizes of parameters and classifiers what an application along the lines of CARE would actually need or have available.

Figure 6b and 6e show that our optimized conversion produces CNF formulas of at least an order of magnitude smaller than a naive conversion. Smaller expression sizes are desirable, as on expectation they are likely to improve both the runtime of our own conversion algorithm, and the execution times of the SAT solvers.

Through these experiments, we also verify the rationale of our initial premise, which was to reduce view-conditioned causality to a satisfiability problem in order to be able to use existing efficient tools to solve it. Even though satisfiability is hard in general, current tools can very efficiently handle a large space of problems. Figure 6c and 6f demonstrate the execution times of the SAT solver (`minisat`) and partial weighted MaxSAT solver (`MiniMaxSat`), which remain highly competitive. In our problem structure, it seems that the solvers are barely affected by the number of classifications with their runtime kept well below a second. When increasing the number of parameters, the `minisat` runtime remains fairly stable. The runtime of `MiniMaxSat` does increase, but is still under 7sec for our larger problem size.

7. CONCLUSIONS

In this paper we considered data transformations that map a source database to a target database, and studied the problem of tracing errors detected in the target data

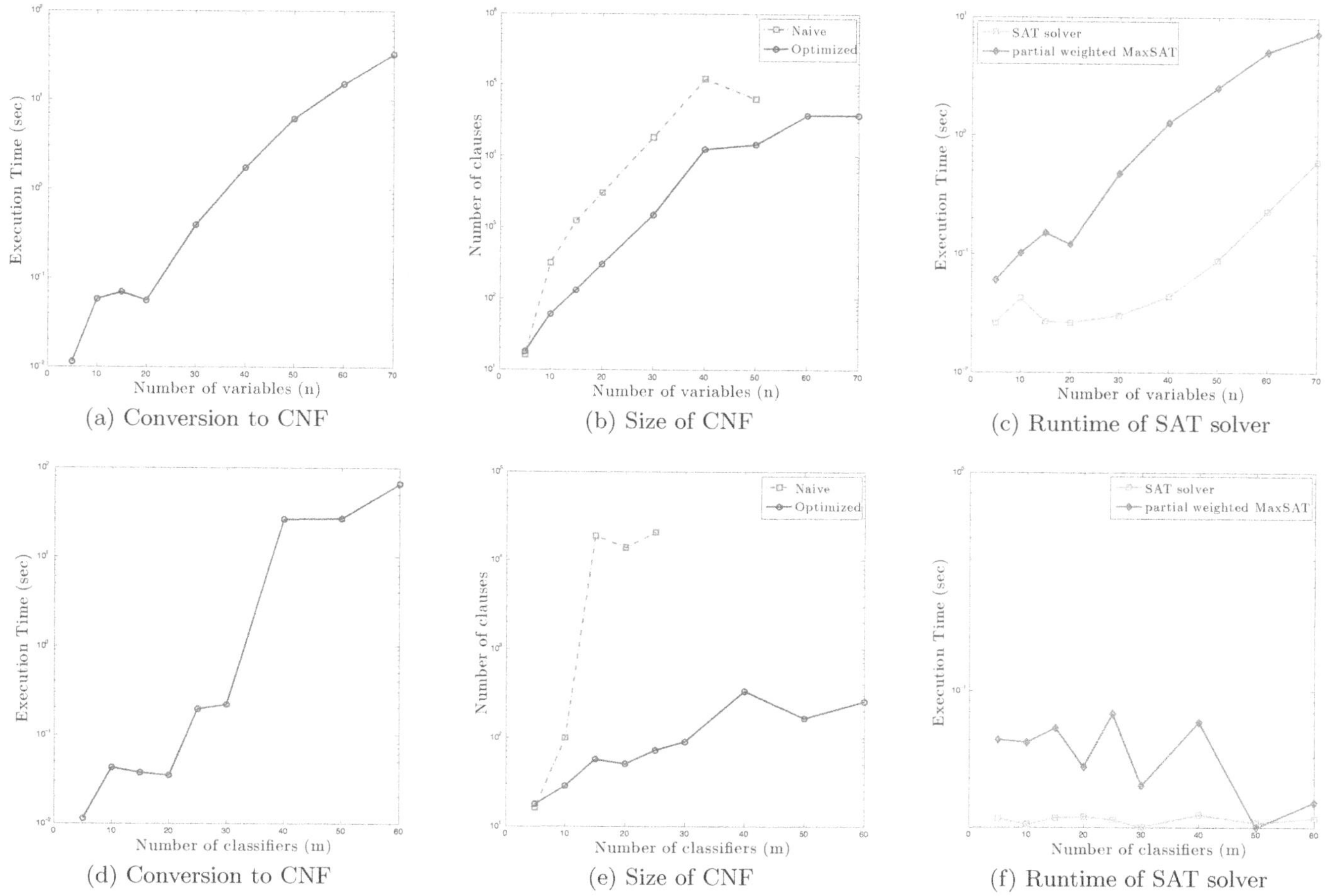

(a) Conversion to CNF (b) Size of CNF (c) Runtime of SAT solver

(d) Conversion to CNF (e) Size of CNF (f) Runtime of SAT solver

Figure 6: Scalability when varying the number n of input variables (a-c), and the number m of classifiers (d-f), averaged over $N = 10$ random input problems. As expected, the runtime of converting a view-conditioned causality problem to a CNF satisfiability problem is exponential in n (a) and m (d). However, the size of the CNF produced by our optimized conversion is considerably smaller than a naive conversion (b,e). The runtime of the SAT solvers is exponential in n (c), but for the structure of the formulas in our setting it does not seem to be affected by m (f).

back to the source data. Our source data is described by a set of numerical or Boolean variables, the target data is given by a set of Boolean variables, and the transformation is given by a set of Boolean expressions. We proposed *view-conditioned* causality and responsibility as a solution to trace errors from transformations to source data. Next, we described an algorithm that reduces the view-conditioned responsibility problem to general satisfiability, which can be solved with existing tools. We also illustrated the effectiveness of using our techniques for tracking, and even correcting errors in a real application.

We believe that the data-level transformations studied in this paper can be improved in future work by considering the query that generated the transformations. By taking into account the query expression it may be possible to extend our algorithm for view-conditioned responsibility to handle larger scale transformations, as found in data integration and ETL tools.

8. REFERENCES

[1] http://www.satcompetition.org/.

[2] T. Alsinet, F. Manyà, and J. Planes. Improved exact solvers for weighted Max-SAT. In *SAT*, pp. 371–377, 2005.

[3] P. A. Bernstein and S. Melnik. Model management 2.0: manipulating richer mappings. In *SIGMOD*, pp. 1–12, 2007.

[4] A. Biere, M. Heule, H. van Maaren, and T. Walsh, editors. *Handbook of Satisfiability*, vol. 185 of *Frontiers in Artificial Intelligence and Applications*. IOS Press, 2009.

[5] P. Buneman, J. Cheney, W. C. Tan, and S. Vansummeren. Curated databases. In *PODS*, pp. 1–12, 2008.

[6] P. Buneman, S. Khanna, and W. C. Tan. Why and where: A characterization of data provenance. In *ICDT*, pp. 316–330, 2001.

[7] P. Buneman, S. Khanna, and W. C. Tan. On propagation of deletions and annotations through views. In *PODS*, pp. 150–158, 2002.

[8] A. Chapman and H. V. Jagadish. Why not? In *SIGMOD*, pp. 523–534, 2009.

[9] J. Cheney. Causality and the semantics of provenance. In *DCM*, pp. 63–74, 2010.

[10] J. Cheney, L. Chiticariu, and W. C. Tan. Provenance in databases: Why, how, and where. *Foundations and Trends in Databases*, 1(4):379–474, 2009.

[11] H. Chockler and J. Y. Halpern. Responsibility and blame: A structural-model approach. *J. Artif. Intell. Res. (JAIR)*, 22:93–115, 2004.

[12] G. Cong, W. Fan, F. Geerts, and J. Luo. On the

complexity of view update and its applications to annotation propagation. *TKDE*, 2011.

[13] Y. Cui, J. Widom, and J. L. Wiener. Tracing the lineage of view data in a warehousing environment. *ACM Trans. Database Syst.*, 25(2):179–227, 2000.

[14] T. Eiter and T. Lukasiewicz. Complexity results for structure-based causality. *Artif. Intell.*, 142(1):53–89, 2002. (Conference version in *IJCAI*, 2002).

[15] Z. Fu and S. Malik. On solving the partial Max-SAT problem. In *SAT*, pp. 252–265, 2006.

[16] T. J. Green, G. Karvounarakis, and V. Tannen. Provenance semirings. In *PODS*, pp. 31–40, 2007.

[17] J. Y. Halpern and J. Pearl. Causes and explanations: A structural-model approach. Part I: Causes. *Brit. J. Phil. Sci.*, 56:843–887, 2005. (Conference version in *UAI*, 2001).

[18] F. Heras, J. Larrosa, and A. Oliveras. MINIMAXSAT: an efficient weighted Max-SAT solver. *J. Artif. Int. Res.*, 31(1):1–32, 2008.

[19] M. Herschel and M. A. Hernández. Explaining missing answers to SPJUA queries. *PVLDB*, 3(1):185–196, 2010.

[20] M. Herschel, M. A. Hernández, and W. C. Tan. Artemis: A system for analyzing missing answers. *PVLDB*, 2(2):1550–1553, 2009.

[21] H. H. Hoos and T. Stützle. SATLIB: An online resource for research on SAT. pp. 283–292. IOS Press, 2000.

[22] J. Huang, T. Chen, A. Doan, and J. F. Naughton. On the provenance of non-answers to queries over extracted data. *PVLDB*, 1(1):736–747, 2008.

[23] K. Järvelin and J. Kekäläinen. IR evaluation methods for retrieving highly relevant documents. In *SIGIR*, pp. 41–48, 2000.

[24] J. Kahn, G. Kalai, and N. Linial. The influence of variables on Boolean functions (extended abstract). In *FOCS*, pp. 68–80, 1988.

[25] P. G. Kolaitis. Schema mappings, data exchange, and metadata management. In *PODS*, pp. 61–75, 2005.

[26] M. Lenzerini. Data integration: A theoretical perspective. In *PODS*, pp. 233–246, 2002.

[27] D. Lewis. Causation. *The Journal of Philosophy*, 70(17):556–567, 1973.

[28] A. Meliou, W. Gatterbauer, K. F. Moore, and D. Suciu. The complexity of causality and responsibility for query answers and non-answers. *PVLDB*, 4(1):34–45, 2010.

[29] P. Menzies. Counterfactual theories of causation. Stanford Encylopedia of Philosophy, 2008.

[30] D. Sheridan. The optimality of a fast CNF conversion and its use with SAT. In *SAT*, 2004.

[31] A. Simitsis, P. Vassiliadis, and T. K. Sellis. Optimizing ETL processes in data warehouses. In *ICDE*, pp. 564–575, 2005.

[32] N. Sorensson and N. Een. Minisat v1.13 – a SAT solver with conflict-clause minimization. In *SAT 2005 competition*, 2005.

[33] Q. T. Tran and C.-Y. Chan. How to conquer why-not questions. In *SIGMOD*, pp. 15–26, 2010.

APPENDIX

A. PROOFS

PROOF (THEOREM 14). Let $X_{[i,j]}$ be a VC cause of $\boldsymbol{z}|\hat{\boldsymbol{z}}$ with responsibility ρ. Then $\exists \theta^\Gamma$ as per the conditions of Def. 13. Assign $\Gamma' = \{X_{[u,v]} \,|\, \theta^\Gamma(X_{[u,v]}) \neq \theta(X_{[u,v]})\}$. Γ' contains exactly those variables $X_{[u,v]}$ that changed their assignment between θ and θ^Γ. Since $\theta^\Gamma \models \Psi$, for each $X_{[u,v_1]} \in \Gamma'$ there exists a second $X_{[u,v_2]} \in \Gamma'$ corresponding to the same variable X_u. Let Γ be the set $\{X_u \,|\, \boldsymbol{X}_{[u]} \cap \Gamma' \neq \emptyset\}$. Then $|\Gamma| = \frac{|\Gamma'|}{2} = d(\theta, \theta^\Gamma)$. Since $\theta^\Gamma \not\models \hat{\Phi}$, we know that Γ is not counterfactual for $\boldsymbol{z}|\hat{\boldsymbol{z}}$. But $\hat{\theta} \models \hat{\Phi}$, which means that $X_i \cup \Gamma$ is counterfactual, and therefore X_i is a cause with contingency Γ. We will now prove the reverse. Let X_i be a cause of $\boldsymbol{z}|\hat{\boldsymbol{z}}$. Then there exists set Γ such that $X_i \cup \Gamma$ is counterfactual for $\boldsymbol{z}|\hat{\boldsymbol{z}}$. That means that there exist values $\hat{x}_u$ for each $X_u \in \Gamma$, different from the original values, and $\hat{x}_i \neq x_i$, that switch the output to $\hat{\boldsymbol{z}}$. Also, $X_i \cup \Gamma$ is minimal, which means that none of the value changes are redundant. Therefore, each value change $x_u \rightarrow \hat{x}_u$ results in value changes for two partition variables $X_{[u,v_1]}$ and $X_{[u,v_2]}$. Let θ^Γ be the assignment of the partition variables after we apply all the value changes $x_u \rightarrow \hat{x}_u$. Since Γ is not counterfactual, we know that $\theta^\Gamma \not\models \hat{\Phi}$. Let $\hat{\theta}$ be the Boolean assignment after we apply the value change $x_i \rightarrow \hat{x}_i$ to θ^Γ, which results in two changes in the partition variables $\boldsymbol{X}_{[i]}$: $X_{[i,j]}$ switching from Tto F, and some other variable in $X_{[i]}$ switching from Fto T. Since $X_i \cup \Gamma$ is counterfactual for $\boldsymbol{z}|\hat{\boldsymbol{z}}$, we know that $\hat{\theta} \models \hat{\Phi}$. So, $X_{[i,j]}$ is a VC cause for $\boldsymbol{z}|\hat{\boldsymbol{z}}$. □

PROOF (THEOREM 15). Let X_i be a VC cause. Then, from Theorem 14 variable $X_{[i,j]}$ is a VC cause and there exists assignment $\theta^\Gamma \models \Psi$, such that $\theta^\Gamma \not\models \hat{\Phi}$, and $\hat{\theta} = \theta^\Gamma \cup \{X_[i,j] = \texttt{F}\} \models \hat{\Phi}$. But that means that θ^Γ satisfies Φ_{SAT}. Now let $\theta^\Gamma \models \Phi_{\text{SAT}}$. Then $\theta^\Gamma \models \neg\hat{\Phi}\left[\theta(\boldsymbol{X}_{[i]})\right] \Rightarrow \theta \not\models \hat{\Phi}, \theta \models \Psi$, and $\theta \models \hat{\Phi}\left[\neg\theta(X_{[i,j]})\right] \Rightarrow \theta^\Gamma \cup \{X_[i,j] = \texttt{F}\} \models \hat{\Phi}$. But then θ^Γ is a contingent assignment for $X_{[i,j]}$, and therefore X_i is a cause. □

PROOF (THEOREM 17). The result is straightforward from the proof of Theorem 14: we have $|\Gamma| = \frac{|\Gamma'|}{2} = d(\theta, \theta^\Gamma)$, which means the responsibility ρ is the same. □

PROOF (THEOREM 18). Let θ^Γ be the assignment that is the solution to the partial weighted MaxSAT. Then θ^Γ violates the minimum number of clauses (since all soft constraints have the same weight). If θ is the original assignment, t is the number of clauses that θ^Γ violates, then $d(\theta, \theta^\Gamma) = \frac{t}{2}$. □

B. NOMENCLATURE

$\boldsymbol{X}$	Set of input parameters: $\boldsymbol{X} = (X_1, \ldots, X_n)$
$\boldsymbol{x}$	Actual value assignment for input parameters: $\boldsymbol{x} = (x_1, \ldots, x_n)$ with $x_i \in D_i$ and D_i its domain
n	Number of input variables
$\boldsymbol{X}_{[n]}$	Boolean partitions of input variable X_n: $\boldsymbol{X}_{[n]} = (X_{[n,1]}, \ldots, X_{[n,k_n]})$
$\boldsymbol{x}_{[n]}$	Actual value assignment for partitions of input variable X_n: $\boldsymbol{x}_{[n]} = (x_{[n,1]}, \ldots, x_{[n,k_n]})$ with $x_{[n,i]} \in \{\texttt{T}, \texttt{F}\}$ and exactly one $x_{[n,j]}$ true, the rest are false
k_n	Number of partitions for input variable X_n
$\boldsymbol{X}_{[]}$	Set of all partitioned input variables: $\boldsymbol{X}_{[]} = (X_{[1,1]}, \ldots, X_{[1,k_1]}, X_{[2,1]}, \ldots X_{n,1}, \ldots X_{[n,k_n]})$
$\boldsymbol{Z}$	Set of Boolean output variables: $\boldsymbol{Z} = (Z_1, \ldots, Z_m)$
$\boldsymbol{z}$	Observed values of classifiers: $\boldsymbol{z} = \{z_1, \ldots, z_m\}$
$\hat{\boldsymbol{z}}$	Actual ground truth for outputs: $\hat{\boldsymbol{z}} = \{\hat{z}_1, \ldots, \hat{z}_m\}$
m	Number of output variables (classifiers)
Φ_m	Boolean expression for classifier C_m
$\boldsymbol{Y}^{(m)}$	Set of threshold predicates for classifier C_m, e.g. $Y_n^{(m)} \equiv (X_n > t_n^{(m)})$
t_i	One of several thresholds for variable X_i
T_i	Number of threshold values for variable X_i
θ	Boolean assignment of $\boldsymbol{X}_{[]}$

Hybrid In-Database Inference for Declarative Information Extraction

Daisy Zhe Wang
University of California, Berkeley

Michael J. Franklin
University of California, Berkeley

Minos Garofalakis
Technical University of Crete

Joseph M. Hellerstein
University of California, Berkeley

Michael L. Wick
University of Massachusetts, Amherst

ABSTRACT

In the database community, work on information extraction (IE) has centered on two themes: how to effectively manage IE tasks, and how to manage the uncertainties that arise in the IE process in a scalable manner. Recent work has proposed a probabilistic database (PDB) based declarative IE system that supports a leading statistical IE model, and an associated inference algorithm to answer top-k-style queries over the probabilistic IE outcome. Still, the broader problem of effectively supporting general probabilistic inference inside a PDB-based declarative IE system remains open. In this paper, we explore the in-database implementations of a wide variety of inference algorithms suited to IE, including two Markov chain Monte Carlo algorithms, the Viterbi and the sum-product algorithms. We describe the rules for choosing appropriate inference algorithms based on the model, the query and the text, considering the trade-off between accuracy and runtime. Based on these rules, we describe a hybrid approach to optimize the execution of a single probabilistic IE query to employ different inference algorithms appropriate for different records. We show that our techniques can achieve up to 10-fold speedups compared to the non-hybrid solutions proposed in the literature.

Categories and Subject Descriptors

H.2.4 [**Database Management**]: Systems—*Textual databases, Query Processing*; G.3 [**Mathematics of Computing**]: Probability and statistics—*Probabilistic algorithms (including Monte Carlo)*

General Terms

Algorithms, Performance, Management, Design

Keywords

Probabilistic Database, Probabilistic Graphical Models, Information Extraction, Conditional Random Fields, Viterbi, Markov chain Monte Carlo Algorithms, Query Optimization

1 Introduction

For most organizations, textual data is an important natural resource to fuel data analysis. Information extraction (IE) techniques parse raw text and extract structured objects that can be integrated into databases for querying. In the past few years, declarative information extraction systems [1, 2, 3, 4] have been proposed to effectively manage IE tasks. The results of IE extraction are inherently uncertain, and queries over those results should take that uncertainty into account in a principled manner. Research in probabilistic databases (PDBs) has been exploring scalable tools to reason about these uncertainties in the context of structured query languages and query processing [5, 6, 7, 8, 9, 10, 11, 12].

Our recent work [4, 13] has proposed a PDB system that natively supports a leading statistical IE model (conditional random fields (CRFs)), and an associated inference algorithm (Viterbi). It shows that the in-database implementation of the inference algorithms enables: (1) probabilistic relational queries that returns top-k results over the probabilistic IE outcome; (2) a tight integration between the relational and inference operators, which leads to significant speed-up by performing query-driven inference.

While this work is an important step towards building a probabilistic declarative IE system, the approach is limited by the capabilities of the Viterbi algorithm, which can only handle top-k-style queries over a limited class of CRF models: linear chain models, which do a poor job capturing features like repeated terms. Different inference algorithms are needed to deal with non-linear CRF models, such as skip-chain CRF models, complex IE queries that induce cyclic models over the linear-chain CRFs, and marginal inference queries that produce richer probabilistic outputs than top-k. The broader problem of effectively supporting general probabilistic inference inside a PDB-based declarative IE system remains open.

In this paper, we first explore the in-database implementation of a number of inference algorithms suited to a broad variety of models and outputs: two variations of the general sampling-based Markov chain Monte Carlo (MCMC) inference algorithm—Gibbs Sampling and MCMC Metropolis-Hastings (MCMC-MH)—in addition to the Viterbi and the sum-product algorithms. We compare the applicability of these four inference algorithms and study the data and the model parameters that affect the accuracy and runtime of those algorithms. Based on those parameters, we develop a set of rules for choosing an inference algorithm based on the characteristics of the model and the data.

More importantly, we study the integration of relational query processing and statistical inference algorithms, and demonstrate that, for SQL queries over probabilistic extraction results, the proper choice of IE inference algorithm is not only model-dependent, but also query- and text-dependent. Such dependencies arise when relational queries are applied to the CRF model, inducing additional variables, edges and cycles; and when the model is instantiated over different text, resulting in model instances with drastically different characteristics.

To achieve good accuracy and runtime performance, it is imperative for a PDB system to use a hybrid approach to IE even within a single query, employing different algorithms for different records. In the context of our CRF-based PDB system, we describe query processing steps and an algorithm to generate query plans that apply hybrid inference for probabilistic IE queries.

Finally, we describe example queries and experiment results showing that such hybrid inference techniques can improve the runtime of the query processing by taking advantage of the appropriate inference methods for different combinations of query, text, and CRF model parameters.

Our key contributions can be summarized as follows:

- We show the efficient implementation of two MCMC inference algorithms, in addition to the Viterbi and the sum-product algorithms, and we identify a set of parameters and rules for choosing different inference algorithms over models and datasets with different characteristics;
- We describe query processing steps and an algorithm to generate query plans that employ hybrid inference over different text within the same query, where the selection of the inference algorithm is based on all three factors of data, model, and query;
- Last, we evaluate our approaches and algorithms using three real-life datasets: DBLP, NYTimes, and Twitter. The results show that our hybrid inference techniques can achieve up to 10-fold speedups compared to the non-hybrid solutions proposed in the literature.

Based on our experience in implementing different inference algorithms, we also present four design guidelines for implementing statistical methods in the database in the Appendix.

2 Related Work

In the past few years, declarative information extraction systems [1, 2, 3, 4, 13] have been proposed to effectively manage information extraction (IE) tasks. The earlier efforts in declarative IE [1, 2, 3] lack a unified framework supporting both a declarative interface as well as the state-of-the-art probabilistic IE models. Ways to handle uncertainties in IE have been considered in [14, 15]. A probabilistic declarative IE system has been proposed in [4, 13], but it only supports the Viterbi algorithm, which is unable to handle complex models that arise naturally from advanced features and relational operators.

In the past decade, there has been a groundswell of work on Probabilistic Database Systems (PDBS) [5, 6, 7, 8, 9, 10, 11, 12]. As shown in previous work [8, 10, 12], Graphical Modeling techniques can provide robust statistical models that capture complex correlation patterns among variables, while, at the same time, addressing some computational efficiency and scalability issues as well. In addition, [8] showed that other approaches to represent and handle uncertainty in database [5, 6], can be unified under the framework of Graphical Models, which express uncertainties and dependencies through the use of random variables and joint probability distribution. However, there is no work addressing the problem of effectively supporting and optimizing different probabilistic inference algorithms in a single PDB, especially in the IE setting.

3 Background

This section covers our definition of a probabilistic database, the conditional random fields (CRF) model and the different types of inference algorithms over CRF models in the context of information extraction. We also introduce a template for the types of IE queries studied in this paper.

3.1 Probabilistic Database

As we described in [10], a *probabilistic database* $\mathcal{DB}^p$consists of two key components: (1) a collection of incomplete relations $\mathcal{R}$ with missing or uncertain data, and (2) a probability distribution F on all possible database instances, which we call *possible worlds*, and denote by *pwd*($\mathcal{DB}^p$). An incomplete relation $R \in \mathcal{R}$ is defined over a schema $A^d \cup A^p$ comprising a (non-empty) subset A^d of deterministic attributes (that includes all candidate and foreign key attributes in R), and a subset A^p of probabilistic attributes. Deterministic attributes have no uncertainty associated with any of their values. A *probabilistic attribute* $\mathcal{A}^p$ may contains missing or uncertain values. The probabilistic distribution F of these missing or uncertain values is represented by a probabilistic graphical model, such as Baysian Networks or Markov Random Fields. Each possible database instance is a possible completion of the missing and uncertain data in $\mathcal{R}$.

3.2 Conditional Random Fields

The linear-chain CRF [16, 17], similar to the hidden markov model, is a leading probabilistic model for solving IE tasks. In the context of IE, a CRF model encodes the probability distribution over a set of *label* random variables (RVs) $\mathbf{Y}$, given the value of a set of *token* RVs $\mathbf{X}$. We denote an assignment to $\mathbf{X}$ by $\mathbf{x}$ and to $\mathbf{Y}$ by $\mathbf{y}$. In a linear-chain CRF model, label y_i is correlated only with label y_{i-1} and token x_i. Such correlations are represented by the feature functions $\{f_k(y_i, y_{i-1}, x_i)\}_{k=1}^{K}$.

EXAMPLE 1. *Figure 1(a) shows an example CRF model over an address string* $\mathbf{x}$ *'2181 Shattuck North Berkeley CA USA'. Observed (known) variables are shaded nodes in the graph. Hidden (unknown) variables are unshaded. Edges in the graph denote statistical correlations. The possible labels are* $Y = \{$*apt.num, streetnum, streetname, city, state, country*$\}$*. Two possible feature functions of this CRF are:*

$$\begin{aligned} f_1(y_i, y_{i-1}, x_i) &= [x_i \text{ appears in a city list}] \cdot [y_i = \text{city}] \\ f_2(y_i, y_{i-1}, x_i) &= [x_i \text{ is an integer}] \cdot [y_i = \text{apt.num}] \\ &\quad \cdot [y_{i-1} = \text{streetname}] \end{aligned}$$

A segmentation $\mathbf{y} = \{y_1, ..., y_T\}$ is one possible way to tag each token in $\mathbf{x}$ of length T with one of the labels in Y. Figure 1(d) shows two possible segmentations of $\mathbf{x}$ and their probabilities.

DEFINITION 3.1. *Let* $\{f_k(y_i, y_{i-1}, x_i)\}_{k=1}^{K}$ *be a set of real-valued feature functions, and* $\Lambda = \{\lambda_k\} \in R^K$ *be a vector of real-valued parameters, a CRF model defines the probability distribution of segmentations* $\mathbf{y}$ *given a specific token sequence* $\mathbf{x}$*:*

$$p(\mathbf{y} \mid \mathbf{x}) = \frac{1}{Z(\mathbf{x})} exp\{\sum_{i=1}^{T} \sum_{k=1}^{K} \lambda_k f_k(y_i, y_{i-1}, x_i)\}, \quad (1)$$

where $Z(\mathbf{x})$ *is a standard normalization function that guarantees the probability distribution sums to 1 over all possible extractions.* □

3.3 Relational Representation of Text and CRF

We implement IE algorithms over the CRF model within a database using the relational representations of text and the CRF-based distribution in the token table TOKENTBL and the factor table MR respectively.

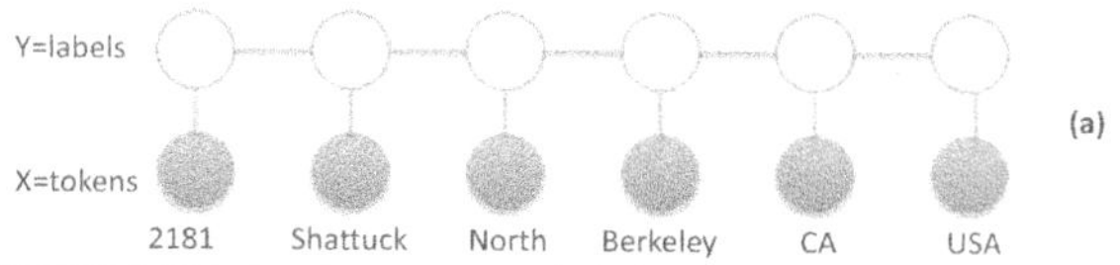

(b)

id	docID	pos	token	label
1	1	0	2181	
2	1	1	Shattuck	
3	1	2	North	
4	1	3	Berkeley	
5	1	4	CA	
6	1	5	USA	

(c)

token	prevLabel	label	score
2181 (DIGIT)	null	street num	22
2181 (DIGIT)	null	street name	5
...	..	..	
Berkeley	street	street name	10
Berkeley	street	city	25
..	..	..	

(d)

x	2181	Shattuck	North	Berkeley	CA	USA	
y1	street num	street name	city	city	state	country	(0.6)
y2	street num	street name	street name	city	state	country	(0.1)

Figure 1: (a) Example CRF model; (b) Example TOKENTBL table; (c) Example MR table; (d) Two possible segmentations $\mathbf{y}_1, \mathbf{y}_2$.

Token Table: The token table TOKENTBL, as shown in Figure 1(b), is an incomplete relation R in $\mathcal{DB}^p$, which stores a set of documents or text-strings $\mathcal{D}$ as a relation in a database, in a manner akin to the inverted files commonly used in information retrieval.

TOKENTBL (id, docID, pos, token, label^p)

TOKENTBL contains one probabilistic attribute—label^p, and the main goal of IE is to perform inference on label^p. As shown in the schema above, each tuple in TOKENTBL records a unique occurrence of a token, which is identified by the text-string ID (docID) and the position (pos) the token is taken from. The id field is simply a row identifier for the token in TOKENTBL.

Factor Table: The probability distribution F over all possible "worlds" of TOKENTBL can be computed from the MR. The MR is a materialization of the *factor tables* in the CRF model for all the tokens in the corpus $\mathcal{D}$. The factor tables $\phi[y_i, y_{i-1} \mid x_i]$, as shown in Figure 1(c), represent the correlation between x_i, y_i, and y_{i-1}, and are computed by the weighted sum of a set of feature functions in the CRF model: $\phi[y_i, y_{i-1} \mid x_i] = \sum_{k=1}^{K} \lambda_k f_k(y_i, y_{i-1}, x_i)$. As in the following schema, each unique token string x_i is associated with an array, which contains a set of scores ordered by {prevLabel, label}.

MR (token, score ARRAY[])

3.4 Inference Queries over a CRF Model

There are two types of inference queries over the CRF model [17].

- **Top-k Inference**: The top-k inference computes the label sequence $\mathbf{y}$ (i.e., extraction) with the top-k highest probabilities given a token sequence $\mathbf{x}$ from a text-string d. Constrained top-k inference [18] is a special case, where the top-k extractions are computed, conditioned on a subset of the token labels, that are provided as evidence.
- **Marginal Inference**: Marginal inference computes a marginal probability $p(y_t, y_{t+1}, ..., y_{t+k} | \mathbf{x}, \mathbf{s})$ over a single label or a sub-sequence of labels conditioned on the set of evidence $\mathbf{s} = \{s_1, ..., s_T\}$, where s_i is either NULL (i.e., no evidence) or the evidence label for y_i.

Many inference algorithms are known that can answer the above inference queries over the CRF models, varying in their effectiveness for different CRF characteristics (e.g., shape of the graph). In the next sections, three inference algorithms will be described: Viterbi, sum-product, Markov chain Monte Carlo (MCMC) methods.

3.5 Viterbi Algorithm

Viterbi, a special case of the Max-Product algorithm [19, 20] can compute top-k inference for linear-chain CRF models. Viterbi is a dynamic programming algorithm that computes a two dimensional V matrix, where each cell $V(i, y)$ stores a ranked list of partial label sequences (i.e., paths) up to position i ending with label y and ordered by *score*. Based on Equation (1), the recurrence to compute the top-1 segmentation is as follows:

$$V(i,y) = \begin{cases} \max_{y'}(V(i-1,y') \\ \quad + \sum_{k=1}^{K} \lambda_k f_k(y, y', x_i)), & \text{if } \ i \geqslant 0 \\ 0, & \text{if } \ i = -1. \end{cases} \quad (2)$$

The top-1 extraction y^*can be backtracked from the maximum entry in $V(T, y_T)$, where T is the length of the token sequence $\mathbf{x}$. The complexity of the Viterbi algorithm is $O(T \cdot |Y|^2)$, where $|Y|$ is the number of possible labels.

The constrained top-k inference can be computed by a variant of the Viterbi algorithm which restricts the chosen labels $\mathbf{y}$ to conform with the evidence $\mathbf{s}$.

3.6 Sum-Product Algorithm

Sum-product (i.e., belief propagation) is a message passing algorithm for performing inference on graphical models, such as CRF [19]. The simplest form of the algorithm is for tree-shaped models, in which case the algorithm computes exact marginal distributions.

The algorithm works by passing real-valued functions called messages along the edges between the nodes. These contain the "influence" that one variable exerts on another. A message from a variable node y_v to its "parent" variable node y_u in a tree-shaped model is computed by summing the product of the messages from all the "child" variables of y_v in $C(y_v)$ and the feature function $f(y_u, y_v)$ between y_v and y_u over variable y_v:

$$\mu_{y_v \to y_u}(y_u) = \sum_{y_v} f(y_u, y_v) \prod_{y_u^* \in C(y_v)} \mu_{y_u^* \to y_v}(y_v). \quad (3)$$

Before starting, the algorithm first designates one node as the root; any non-root node which is connected to only one other node is called a leaf. In the first step, messages are passed inwards: starting at the leaves, each node passes a message along the edge towards the root node. This continues until the root has obtained messages from all of its adjoining nodes. The marginal of the root note can be computed at the end of the first step.

The second step involves passing the messages back out: starting at the root, messages are passed in the reverse direction, until all leaves have received their messages. Like Viterbi, the complexity of the sum-product algorithm is also $O(T \cdot |Y|^2)$.

Variants of the sum-product algorithm for cyclic models require either an intractable junction-tree step, or a variational approximation such as loopy belief propagation (BP). In this paper, we do not study these variants further as they are either intractable (junction tree), or can fail to converge (loopy BP) on models with long-distance dependencies such as those we discussed in this paper.

3.7 MCMC Inference Algorithms

Markov chain Monte Carlo (MCMC) methods are a class of randomized algorithms for estimating intractable probability distributions over large state spaces by constructing a Markov chain sampling process that converges to the desired distribution. Relative to other sampling methods, the main benefits of MCMC methods are that they (1) replace a difficult sampling procedure from a high-dimensional target distribution $\pi(w)$ that we wish to sample with an easy sampling procedure from a low-dimensional local distribution $q(\cdot|w)$, and (2) sidestep the $\#P$-hard computational problem of computing a normalization factor. We call $q(\cdot|w)$ a "pro-

```
GIBBS (N)
1   w0 ← INIT(); w ← w0; // initialize
2   for idx = 1, ..., N do
3       i ← idx%n; // propose variable to sample next
4       w' ∼ π(wi | w−i) // generate sample
5       return next w' // return a new sample
6       w ← w'; // update current world
7   endfor
```

Figure 2: Pseudo-code for Gibbs sampling algorithm over a model with n variables.

posal distribution", which—conditioned on a previous state w—probabilistically produces a new world w' with probability $q(w'|w)$. In essence, we use the proposal distribution to control a random walk among points in the target distribution. We review two MCMC methods we will adapt to our context in this paper: Gibbs sampling and Metropolis-Hastings (MCMC-MH).

3.7.1 Gibbs Sampling

Let $w = (w_1, w_2, ..., w_n)$ be a set of n random variables, distributed according to $\pi(w)$. The proposal distribution of a specific variable w_i is its marginal distribution $q(\cdot|w) = \pi(w_i|w_{-i})$ conditioned on w_{-i}, which are the current values of the rest of the variables.

The Gibbs sampling algorithm (i.e., Gibbs sampler) first generates the initial world w_0, for example, randomly. Next, samples are drawn for each variable $w_i \in w$ in turn, from the distribution $\pi(w_i|w_{-i})$. Figure 2 shows the pseudo-code for the Gibbs sampler that returns N samples. In Line 4, $\sim$ means a new sample w' is drawn according to the proposal distribution $\pi(w_i|w_{-i})$.

3.7.2 Metropolis-Hastings (MCMC-MH)

Like Gibbs, the MCMC-MH algorithm first generates an initial world w_0 (e.g., randomly). Next, samples are drawn from the proposal distribution $w' \sim q(w_i|w)$, where a variable w_i is randomly picked from all variables, and $q(w_i|w)$ is a uniform distribution over all possible values. Different proposal distribution $q(w_i|w)$ can be used, which results in different convergence rates. Lastly, each resulting sample is either accepted or rejected according to a Bernoulli distribution given by parameter α:

$$\alpha(w', w) = \min(1, \frac{\pi(w')q(w|w')}{\pi(w)q(w'|w)}) \tag{4}$$

The acceptance probability is determined by the product of two ratios: the model probability ratio $\pi(w')/\pi(w)$, which captures the relative likelihood of the two worlds; and the proposal distribution ratio $q(w|w')/q(w'|w)$, which eliminates the bias introduced by the proposal distribution.

3.8 Query Template

Over the CRF-based IE from text, the queries we consider are probabilistic queries, which inference over the probabilistic attribute $\texttt{label}^p$ in the TOKENTBL table. Each TOKENTBL is associated with a specific CRF model stored in the MR table. Such CRF-based IE is captured by a sub-query with logic that produces the IE results from the base probabilistic TOKENTBL tables. The sub-query consists of a relational part Q_{re} over the probabilistic token tables TOKENTBL and the underlying CRF models, followed by an inference operator Q_{inf}. A canonical "query template" captures the logic for the "SQL+IE" sub-query in Figure 3. It supports SPJ queries, aggregate conditions and two types of inference operators, `Top-k` and `Marginal`, over the probabilistic TOKENTBL tables.

The relational part of a "SQL+IE" query Q_{re} first specifies, in the `FROM` clause, the TOKENTBL table(s) over which the query and extraction is performed.

```
SELECT   Top-k(T1.docID,[T1.pos|exist]) |
         [Marginal(T1.docID,[T1.pos|exist])] |
         [Top-k(T1.docID, T2.docID,[T1.pos|T2.pos|exist])] |
         [Marginal(T1.docID,T2.docID,[T1.pos|T2.pos|exist])]
FROM     TokenTbl1 T1[, TokenTbl2 T2]
WHERE    T1.label = 'bar1' [and T1.token = 'foo1']
         [and T1.docID = X] [and T1.pos = Y]
         [and T1.label = T2.label] [and T1.token = T2.token]
         [and T1.docID = T2.docID]
GROUP BY T1.docID[, T2.docID]
HAVING   [aggregate condition]
```

Figure 3: The "SQL+IE" query template.

The `WHERE` clause lists a number of possible selection as well as join conditions over the TOKENTBL tables. These conditions when involve $\texttt{label}^p$ are probabilistic conditions, and deterministic otherwise. For example, a probabilistic condition `label='person'` specifies the entity types we are looking for is `'person'`, while a deterministic condition `token='Bill'` specifies the name of the entity we are looking for is `'Bill'`. We can also specify a join condition `T1.token=T2.token` and `T1.label=T2.label` that two documents need to contain the same entity name with the same entity type.

In the `GROUP BY` and the `HAVING` clause, we can specify conditions on an entire text "document". An example of such aggregate condition over a bibliography document can be that all `title` tokens are in front of all the `author` tokens. Following the Possible World Semantics [5], the execution of these relational operators involve modification to the original graphical models as will be shown in Section 4.1.

The inference part Q_{inf}, of a "SQL+IE" query, takes the $docID$, the *pos*, and the CRF model resulting from Q_{re} as input. The inference operation is specified in the `SELECT` clause, which can be either a `Top-k` or a `Marginal` inference. The inference can be computed over different random variables in the CRF model: (1) a sequence of tokens (e.g., a document) specified by `docID`; or (2) a token at a specific location specified by `docID` and `pos`; or (3) the "existence" (`exist`) of the result tuple. The "existence" of the result tuple becomes probabilistic with a selection or join over a probabilistic attribute, where `exist` variables are added to the model [10].

For example, the inference `Marginal(T1.docID,T1.pos)`, for each position `(T1.docID,T1.pos)` computed from Q_{re}, returns the distribution of the `label` variable at that position. The inference `Marginal(T1.docID,exist)` computes the marginal distribution of `exist` variable for each result tuple. We can also specify an inference following a join query. For example, the inference `Top-k(T1.docID,T2.docID)`, for each document pair `(T1.docID,T2.docID)`, returns the `top-k` highest probability joint extractions that satisfy the join constraint.

4 In-Database MCMC Inference

In this section, we first describe IE models that are cyclic (e.g., the skip-chain CRF model) and review the way that simple relational queries can often induce cyclic models—even over text that is itself modeled by simple linear-chain CRFs. Such cyclic models call for an efficient general-purpose inference algorithm such as an MCMC algorithm. Next, we describe our efficient in-database implementation of the Gibbs sampler and MCMC-MH. Finally, we discuss query-driven sampling techniques that push the query constraints into the MCMC sampling process.

4.1 Cycles from IE Models and Queries

In many IE tasks, good accuracy can only be achieved using non-linear CRF models like skip-chain CRF models, which model the

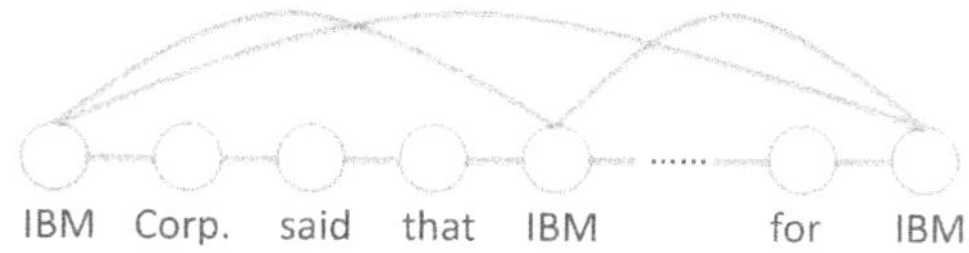

Figure 4: A skip-chain CRF model that includes skip-edges between non-consecutive tokens with the same string (e.g.,"IBM").

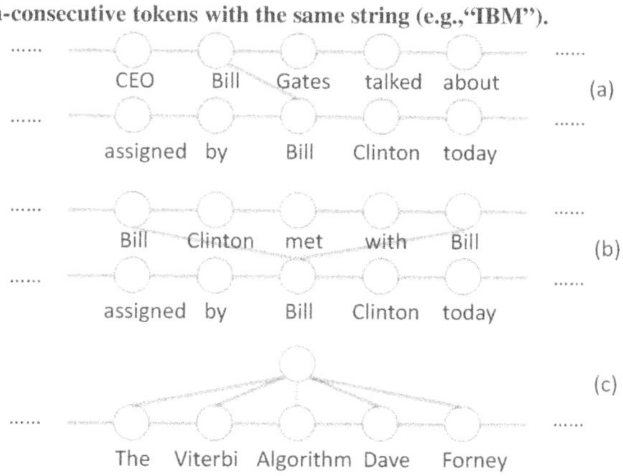

Figure 5: (a) and (b) are example CRF models after applying a join query over two different pairs of documents. (c) is the resulting CRF model from a query with an aggregate condition.

correlation not only between the labels of two consecutive tokens as in linear-chain CRF, but also between those of non-consecutive tokens. For example, a correlation can be modeled between the labels of two tokens in a sentence that have the same string. Such a skip-chain CRF model can be seen in Figure 4, where the correlation between non-consecutive labels (i.e., skip-chain edges) form cycles in the CRF model.

In simple probabilistic databases with independent base tuples, the "safe plans" [5] give rise to tree-structured graphical models [8], where the exact inference is tractable. However, in a CRF-based IE setting, an inverted-file representation of text in TOKENTBL inherently has cross-tuple correlations. Thus, even queries with "safe plans" over the simple linear-chain CRF model, result in cyclic models and intractable inference problems.

For example, the following query computes the marginal inference `Marginal(T1.docID,T2.docID,exist)`, which returns pairs of `docID`s and the probabilities of the existence (`exist`) of their join results. The join query is performed between each document pair on having the same token strings labeled as 'person'. The join query over the base TOKENTBL tables adds cross-edges to the pair of linear-chain CRF models underlying each document pair. Figure 5(a),(b) shows two examples of the resulting CRF model after the join query over two different pairs of documents. As we can see, the CRF model in (a) is tree-shaped, and the one in (b) is cyclic.

```
Q1: [Probabilistic Join Marginal]
SELECT   Marginal(T1.docID,T2.docID,exist)
FROM     TokenTbl1 T1, TokenTbl2 T2
WHERE    T1.label = T2.label and T1.token = T2.token
              and T1.label = 'person';
```

Another example is a simple query to compute the top-k extraction conditioned on an aggregate constraint over the label sequence of each document (e.g., all "title" tokens are in front of "author" tokens). This query induces a cyclic model as shown in Figure 5(c).

```
Q2: [Aggregate Constraint Top-k]
SELECT   Top-k(T1.docID)
FROM     TokenTbl1 T1
GROUP BY docID
HAVING   [aggregate constraint] = true;
```

```
CREATE FUNCTION Gibbs (int) RETURN VOID AS
$$
-- compute the initial world: genInitWorld()
insert into MHSamples
select setval('world_id',1) as worldId, docId, pos, token,
          trunc(random()*num_label+1) as label
from tokentbl;

-- generate N sample proposals: genProposals()
insert into Proposals
with X as (
  select foo.id, foo.docID, (tmp\%bar.doc_len) as pos
  from (
      select id, ((id-1)/($1/numDoc)+1) as docID,
        ((id-1)\%($1/numDoc)) as tmp
      from generate_series(1,$1) id) foo, doc_id_tbl bar
      where foo.doc_id = bar.doc_id
  )
select X.id,S.docId,S.pos,S.token, null as label,
  null::integer[] as prevWorld, null::integer[] as factors
from X, tokentbl S
where X.docID = S.docID and X.pos = S.pos;

-- fetch context: initial world and factor tables
update proposals S1
  set prev_world = (select * from getInitialWorld(S1.docId))
  from proposals S2
  where S1.docId <> S2.docId and S1.id = S2.id+1;
update proposals S1
  set factors = (select * from getFactors(S1.docId))
  from proposals S2
  where S1.docId <> S2.docId and S1.id = S2.id+1;

-- generate samples: genSamples()
insert into MHSamples
select worldId, docId, pos, token, label
from (
    select nextval('world_id') worldId, docId, pos, token, label,
             getalpha_agg((docId,pos,label,prev_world,factors)
             ::getalpha_io) over (order by id) alpha
    from (select * from proposals order by id) foo) foo;
$$
LANGUAGE SQL;
```

Figure 6: The SQL implementation of Gibbs sampler takes input N – the number of samples to generate.

Next, we describe general inference algorithms for such cyclic models.

4.2 SQL Implementation of MCMC Algorithms

Both the Gibbs sampler and the MCMC-MH algorithm are iterative algorithms, which contain three main steps: 1) initialization, 2) generating proposals, and 3) generating samples. They differ in their proposal and sample generation functions.

We initially implemented the MCMC algorithms in the SQL procedure language provided by PostgreSQL—PL/pgSQL—using iterations and three User Defined Functions (UDF's):

- GENINITWORLD() to compute the initialized world (line 1 for Gibbs in Figure 2);
- GENPROPOSAL() to generate one sample proposal (line 3 for Gibbs in Figure 2);
- GENSAMPLE() to compute the corresponding sample for a given proposal (line 4 for Gibbs in Figure 2).

However, this implementation ran hundreds of times slower than the Scala/Java implementation described in [12]. This is mainly because calling UDF's iteratively a million times in a PL/pgSQL function is similar to running a SQL query a million times. A more efficient way is to "decorrelate", and run a single query over a million tuples. The database execution path is optimized for this approach. With this basic intuition, we re-implemented the MCMC algorithms, where the iterative procedures are translated into set operations in SQL.

The efficient implementation of the Gibbs sampler is shown in Figure 6, which uses the feature of *window functions* introduced in PostgreSQL 8.4. MCMC-MH can be implemented efficiently in a similar way with some simple adaptations.

This implementation achieves similar (within a factor of 1.5) runtime compared to the Scala/Java implementation of the MCMC algorithms, as shown in the results in Section 7.1.

4.3 Query-Driven MCMC Sampling

Previous work [4] has developed query-driven techniques to integrate probabilistic selection and join conditions into the Viterbi algorithm over the linear-chain CRF model. However, the kind of constraint that Viterbi can handle is limited and specific to the Viterbi and potentially the sum-product algorithm. In this section, we explore query-driven techniques for the sampling-based MCMC inference algorithms. Query-driven sampling is needed to compute inference conditioned on the query constraints. Such query constraints can be highly selective, where most samples generated by the vanilla MCMC methods do not "qualify" (i.e., satisfy the constraints). Thus, we need to adapt the MCMC methods by pushing the query constraints into the sampling process. Note that our adapted, query-driven MCMC methods still converge to the target distribution as long as the proposal function can reach every "qualified" world in a finite number of steps.

There are three types of query constraints: (1) selection constraints; (2) join constraints; and (3) aggregate constraints. Both (1) and (2) were studied for Viterbi in [4]. The following query contains an example selection constraint, which is to find the top-k highest likelihood extraction that contains a 'person' entity 'Bill'.

```
Q3: [Selection Constraint Top-k]
SELECT   Top-k(T1.docID)
FROM     TokenTbl1 T1
WHERE    token = 'Bill' and label = 'person'
```

An example of a join constraint can be found in $Q1$ in Section 4.1, and an example of an aggregate constraint can be found in $Q2$ in the same Section.

The naive way to answer those conditional queries using *MCMC* methods is to: first, generate a set of samples using Gibbs sampling or MCMC-MH regardless of the query constraint; second, filter out the samples that do not satisfy the query constraint; last, compute the query over the remaining "qualified" samples.

In contrast, our query-driven sampling approach pushes the query constraints into the MCMC sampling process by restricting the worlds generated by GENINITWORLD(), GENPROPOSALS() and GENSAMPLES() functions, so that all the samples generated satisfy the query constraint. One of the advantages of the MCMC algorithms is that the proposal and sample generation functions can naturally deal with the deterministic constraints, which might induce cliques with high tree-width in the graphical model. Such cliques can easily "blow up" the complexity of known inference algorithms [19]. We exploit this property of MCMC to develop query-driven sampling techniques for different types of queries.

The query-driven GENINITWORLD() function generates an initial world that satisfies the constraint. The first "qualified" sample can either be specified according to the query or generated from random samples.

The query-driven GENPROPOSAL() and GENSAMPLES() functions are called iteratively to generate new samples that satisfy the constraint. The next "qualified" jump (i.e., new sample) can be generated by restricted jumps according to the query constraints or from random jumps.

5 Choosing Inference Algorithms

Different inference algorithms over the probabilistic graphical models have been developed in a diverse range of communities (e.g., natural language processing, machine learning, etc). The characteristics of these inference algorithms (e.g., applicability, accuracy, convergence rate, runtimes) over different model structures have since been studied to help modeling experts select an appropriate inference algorithm for a specific problem [19].

In this section, we first compare the characteristics of the four inference algorithms we have developed over the CRF model. Next we introduce parameters that capture important properties of the model and data. Using these parameters, we then describe a set of rules to choose among different inference algorithms.

5.1 Comparison between Inference Algorithms

We have implemented four inference algorithms over the CRF model for IE applications: (1) Viterbi, (2) sum-product, and two sampling-based MCMC methods: (3) Gibbs Sampling and (4) MCMC Metropolis Hastings (MCMC-MH). In Table 1, we show the applicability of these algorithms to different inference tasks (e.g. top-k, or marginal) on models with different structures (e.g., linear-chain, tree-shaped, cyclic).

As we can see, Viterbi, Gibbs and MCMC-MH can all compute top-k queries over the linear-chain CRF models; sum-product, Gibbs and MCMC-MH can all compute marginal queries over the linear-chain and tree-shaped models; while only MCMC algorithms can compute queries over cyclic models. Although there are heuristic adaptations of the sum-product algorithm for cyclic models, past literature found MCMC methods to be more effective in handling complicated cyclic models with long-distance dependencies and deterministic constraints [21, 22]. In terms of handling query constraints, Viterbi and sum-product algorithms can only handle selection constraints, Gibbs sampling can handle selection constraints and aggregate constraints that do not break the distribution into disconnected regions. On the other hand, MCMC-MH can handle arbitrary constraints in the "SQL+IE" queries.

5.2 Parameters

Next, we introduce a list of parameters that affect the applicability, accuracy and runtime of the four inference algorithms that we have just described:

1. **Data Size:** the size of the data is measured by the total number of tokens in information extraction;
2. **Structure of Grounded Models:** the structural properties of the model instantiations over data:
   (a) shape of the model (i.e., linear-chain, tree-shaped, cyclic),
   (b) maximum size of the clique,
   (c) maximum length of the loops (e.g., skip-chain in linear CRF)
3. **Correlation Strength:** the relative strength of transitional correlation between different label variables;
4. **Label Space:** the number of possible labels.

The data size affects the runtime for all the inference algorithms. The runtime of Viterbi and sum-product algorithms is linear to the data size. The MCMC algorithms are iterative optimizations that can be stopped at any time, but the number of samples needed to converge depend linearly on the size of the data.

The structure of the grounded model can be quantified with three parameters: shape of the model, maximum size of the clique and the maximum length of the loops. The first parameter determines the applicability of the models, and is also the most important factor

inference algorithm	Top-k Chain	Tree	Cyclic	Marginal Chain	Tree	Cyclic	Constraints Some	Arbitrary
Viterbi	✓						✓	
sum-product				✓	✓		✓	
MCMC-Gibbs	✓	✓	✓	✓	✓	✓	✓	
MCMC-MH	✓	✓	✓	✓	✓	✓		✓

Table 1: Applicability of different inference algorithms for different queries (e.g., top-k, marginal) over different model structures (e.g., linear-chain, tree-shaped, cyclic), and in handling query constraints.

in the accuracy and the runtime of the inference algorithms over the model. Although not studied in this paper, the maximum clique size and the length of the loops play an important role in the runtime of several known inference algorithms (including, for example, the junction tree and the loopy belief propagation algorithms) [19].

The correlation strength is the relative strength of the transition correlation between different label variables over the state correlation between tokens with their corresponding labels. The correlation strength does not influence the accuracy or the runtime of the Viterbi or the sum-product algorithm. However, it is a significant factor in the accuracy and runtime of the MCMC methods, especially the Gibbs algorithm. Weaker correlation strengths result in faster convergence for the Gibbs sampler. At the extreme, zero transition correlation results in complete label independence, rendering consecutive Gibbs samples independently, which would converge very quickly.

The size of the label space of the model is also an important factor of the runtime of all the inference algorithms. The runtime of the Viterbi and sum-product algorithms is quadratic in the size of the label space, while the runtime of the Gibbs algorithm is linear in the label space because each sampling step requires enumerating all possible labels.

5.3 Rules for Choosing Inference Algorithms

Among the parameters described in the previous section, we focus on (1) the shape of the model, (2) the correlation strength, and (3) the label space into consideration, because the rest are less influential in the four inference algorithms we study in this paper. The data size is important for optimizing the extraction order in the join over top-k queries as described in [4]. However, since the complexity of the inference algorithms we study in this paper are all linear in the size of the data, it is not an important factor for choosing inference algorithms.

Based on analysis in the last section on the parameters, the following are the rules to choose an inference algorithm for different data and model characteristics, quantified by the three parameters, and the query:

- For cyclic models:
  - If cycles are induced by query constraints, choose query-driven MCMC-MH over Gibbs Sampling;
  - Otherwise, choose Gibbs Sampling over MCMC-MH. As shown in our experiments in Sections 7.3-7.4, the Gibbs Sampler converges much faster than the random walk MCMC-MH for computing both top-k extractions and marginal distribution;
- For acyclic models:
  - For models with small label space, choose Viterbi over MCMC methods for top-k and sum-product over MCMC methods for marginal queries;
  - For models with strong correlations, choose Viterbi and sum-product over MCMC methods;
  - For models with both large label space and weak correlations, choose Gibbs Sampling over MCMC-MH, Viterbi, and sum-product.

For a typical IE application, the label space is small (e.g., 10), and the correlation strength is fairly strong. For example, `title` tokens are usually followed by the `author` tokens in a bibliography string. Moreover, strong correlation exists with any multi-token entity names (e.g., a `person` token is likely to be followed by another `person` token). Thus, the above rules translate in most cases in IE to: choose Viterbi and sum-product over MCMC methods for acyclic models for top-k and marginal queries respectively; choose Gibbs Sampling for cyclic models unless the cycles are induced by query constraints, in which case choose query-driven MCMC-MH. In this paper, we use heuristic rules to decide the threshold for a "small" label space and for a "strong" correlation for a data set. Developing a cost-based optimizer to make such choices based on the data and model is one of our future directions.

6 Hybrid Inference

Typically, for a given model and dataset, a single inference algorithm is chosen based on the characteristics of the model. In this section, we first show that in the context of SQL queries over probabilistic IE results, the proper choice of IE inference algorithm is not only model-dependent, but also query- and text-dependent. Thus, to achieve good accuracy and runtime performance, it is imperative for a PDB system to use a hybrid approach to IE even within a single query, employing different inference algorithms for different records.

We describe the query processing steps that employ hybrid inference for different documents within a single query. Then we describe an algorithm, which, given the input of a "SQL+IE" query, generates a query plan that applies the hybrid inference. Finally, we show the query plans with hybrid inference generated from three example "SQL+IE" queries to take advantage of the appropriate IE inference algorithms for different combinations of query, text and CRF models.

6.1 Query Processing Steps

In the context of SQL queries over probabilistic IE results, the proper choice of the IE inference algorithm is not only dependent on the model, but also dependent on the query and the text.

First of all, the relational sub-query Q_{re} augments the original model with additional random variables, cross-edges and factor tables, making the model structure more complex, as we explained in Section 4.1. The characteristics of the model may change after applying the query over the model. For example, a linear-chain CRF model may become a cyclic CRF model, after the join query in `Q1` or the query with aggregate constraint in `Q2`.

Secondly, when the resulting CRF model is instantiated (i.e., grounded) over a document, it could result in a grounded CRF model with drastically different model characteristics. For example, the CRF model, resulting from a join query over a linear-chain CRF model, when instantiated over different documents, can result in either a cyclic or a tree-shaped model, as we have shown in Figure 5(a) and (b).

The applicability, accuracy and runtime of different inference algorithms vary significantly over models with different characteristics, which can result from different data for the same query and

```
HYBRID-INFERENCE-PLAN-GENERATOR (Q)
1   apply Q_re over the base CRF models → CRF*
2   apply deterministic selections in Q over base TOKENTBLs → {T_i}
3   apply deterministic joins in Q over {T_i} → T
4   apply model instantiation over T using CRF* → groundCRFs
5   apply split operation to groundCRFs → linearCRFs, treeCRFs, cyclicCRFs
6   if Q_inf is Marginal then
7       apply sum-product to (linearCRFs + treeCRFs) → res2
8       apply Gibbs to (cyclicCRFs) → res3
9   else if Q_inf is Top-k then
10      apply Viterbi to (linearCRFs) → res1
11      if Q_re contains aggregate constraint but no join then
12          apply Viterbi to (cyclicCRFs + treeCRFs) → res
13          apply aggregate constraint in Q over res → res1
14          apply query-driven MCMC-MH to (res − res1).T → res3
15      else
16          apply Gibbs to (cyclicCRFs + treeCRFs) → res3
17  endif endif
18  if Q_inf is Top-k then
19      apply union of res1 and res3
20  else if Q_inf is Marginal then
21      apply union of res2 and res3
22  endif
```

Figure 7: Pseudo-code for the hybrid inference query plan generation algorithm.

model. As a result, to achieve good accuracy and runtime, we apply different inference algorithms (i.e., hybrid inference) for different documents within a single query. The choice of the inference algorithm over a document is based on the characteristics of its grounded model, and rules for choosing inference algorithms we described in Section 5.3.

The main steps in query processing with hybrid inference are as follows:

1. **Apply Query over Model:** Apply the relational part of the query Q_{re} over the underlying CRF model;
2. **Instantiate Model over Data:** Instantiate the resulting model from the previous step over the text, and compute the important characteristics of the grounded models;
3. **Partition Data:** Partition the data according to the properties of grounded models from the previous step. In this paper, we only partition the data according to the shape of the grounded model. More complicated partitioning techniques, such as one based on the size of the maximum clique can be considered for future work;
4. **Choose Inference:** Choose the inference algorithms to apply according to the rules in Section 5.3 over the different data partitions based on the characteristics of the grounded models;
5. **Execute Inference:** Execute the chosen inference algorithm over each data partition, and return the union of the results from all partitions.

6.2 Query Plan Generation Algorithm

We envision that the query parser takes in a "SQL+IE" query and outputs, along with others non-hybrid plans, a query plan which applies hybrid inference over different documents.

The algorithm in Figure 7 generates a hybrid inference query plan for an input "SQL+IE" query Q, consisting of the relation part Q_{re}, and the subsequent inference operator Q_{inf}. In Line 1, the relational operators in Q_{re} are applied to the CRF models underlying the base TOKENTBL tables, resulting in a new CRF model CRF^*. In Lines 2 to 3, selection and join conditions on the deterministic attributes (e.g., docID, pos, token) are applied to the base TOKENTBL tables, resulting in a set of tuples T, each of which represents a document or a document pair. In Line 4, the model instantiation is applied over T using CRF^* to generate a set of "ground" models `groundCRFs`. In Line 5, a split operation is performed to partition the `groundCRFs` according to their model structures into `linearCRFs`, `treeCRFs` and `cyclicCRFs`.

Lines 6 to 19 capture the rules for choosing inference algorithms we described in Section 5.3. Finally, a union is applied over the result sets from different inference algorithms for the same query.

Lines 11 to 14 deals with a special set of queries, which compute the top-k results over a simple query with aggregate conditions that induce cycles over the base linear-chain CRFs. The intuition is that it is always beneficial to apply the Viterbi algorithm over the base linear-chain CRFs as a fast filtering step before applying the MCMC methods. In Line 12, it first computes the top-k extractions `res` without the aggregate constraint using Viterbi. In Line 13, it applies the constraint to the top-k extractions in `res`, which results in a set of top-k extractions that satisfy the constraints in `res1`. In Line 14, the query-driven MCMC-MH is applied to the documents in T with extractions that do not satisfy the constraint: `(res-res1).T`. An example of this special case is described in Section 6.3.3.

Complexity: The complexity of generating the hybrid plan depends on the complexity of the operation on Line 5 in Figure 7, where the `groundCRFs` are split into subsets of `linearCRFs`, `treeCRFs` and `cyclicCRFs`. The split is performed by traversing the ground CRFs to determine their structural properties, which is linear to the size of the ground CRF $O(N)$, where N is the number of random variables. The complexity of choosing the appropriate inference (lines 6 to 21) is $O(1)$.

On the other hand, the complexity of Viterbi, sum-product algorithms over `linearCRFs` and `treeCRFs` is $O(N)$ with a much larger constant, because of the complex computation (i.e., sum, product) over $|Y| \times |Y|$ matrices, where $|Y|$ is the number of possible labels. The complexity of exact inference algorithm over `cyclicCRFs` is NP-hard. Thus the cost of generating the hybrid plan is negligible from the cost of the inference algorithms.

6.3 Example Query Plans

In this section, we describe three example queries and show the query plans with hybrid inference generated from the algorithm in Figure 7, which take advantage of the appropriate inference algorithms for different combinations of query, text and CRF models.

6.3.1 Skip-Chain CRF

In this query, we want to compute the marginal distribution or the top-k extraction over an underlying skip-chain CRF model as shown in Figure 4. The query is simply:

```
Q4: [Skip-Chain Model]
SELECT  [Top-k(T1.docID) | Marginal(T1.pos|exist)]
FROM    TokenTbl T1
```

As described in [12], the MCMC methods are normally used to perform inference over the skip-chain CRF model for all the documents, like the query plan in Figure 8(b). The Viterbi algorithm fails to apply because the skip-chain model contains skip-edges, which make the CRF model cyclic.

However, the existence of such skip-edges in the grounded models, instantiated from the documents, is dependant on the text! There exist documents, like the one shown in Figure 4, in which one string appears multiple times. Those documents result in cyclic CRF models. But, there also exist documents, in which only unique tokens are used except for "stop-words", such as "for", "a". Those documents result in linear-chain CRF models.

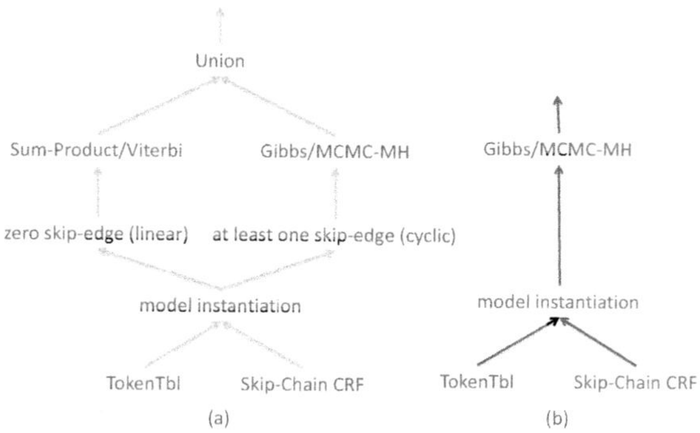

Figure 8: The query plan for an inference, either top-k or marginal, over a skip-chain CRF model.

The query plan generated with hybrid inference is shown in Figure 8(a). After the model instantiation, the ground CRF model is inspected: if no skip-edge exists (i.e., no duplicate strings exist in a document), then the Viterbi or the sum-product algorithm is applied; otherwise, the Gibbs algorithm is applied to the cyclic ground CRFs. Compared to the non-hybrid query plan, the query plan with hybrid inference is more efficient by applying more efficient inference algorithms (e.g., Viterbi, sum-product) over the subset of the documents, where the skip-chain CRF model does not induce cyclic graphs. The speedup depends on the performance of Viterbi/sum-product compared to Gibbs Sampling, and on the percentage of such documents that instantiate a skip-chain CRF model into a grounded linear-chain CRF models.

6.3.2 Join over Linear-chain CRF

In this example, we use the join query `Q1` described in Section 4.1, which computes the marginal probability of the existence of a join result. The join query is performed between each document pair on having tokens with the same strings labeled as 'person'.

Such a join query over the underlying linear-chain CRF models induces cross-edges and cycles in the resulting CRF model. A typical non-hybrid query plan, shown in Figure 9 with black edges, perform MCMC inference over all the documents.

However, as we see in Figure 5(a) and (b), depending on the text, the joint CRF model can be instantiated into either a cyclic graph or a tree-shaped graph. The red edge in Figure 9 shows the query plan with hybrid inference for the join query `Q1`. As we can see, instead of performing MCMC methods unilaterally across all "joinable" document pairs (i.e., contain at least 1 pair of common tokens), the sum-product algorithm is used over the document pairs that contain only 1 pair of common tokens. Compared to the non-hybrid query plan, the hybrid inference reduces the runtime by applying the more efficient inference (i.e., sum-product) when possible. The speedup depends on the performance of sum-product compared to the MCMC methods, and the percentage of the "joinable" document pairs that only share one pair of common tokens that are not "stop-words".

6.3.3 Aggregate Constraints

In this example, we use `Q2`, the query with an aggregate constraint, described in Section 4.1. As shown in Figure 5(c), the aggregate constraints can induce a big clique including all the label variables in each document. In other words, regardless of the text, based on the model and the query, each document is instantiated into a cyclic graph with high tree-width.

Again, typically, for such a high tree-width cyclic model, MCMC-MH algorithms are used over all the documents to compute the top-

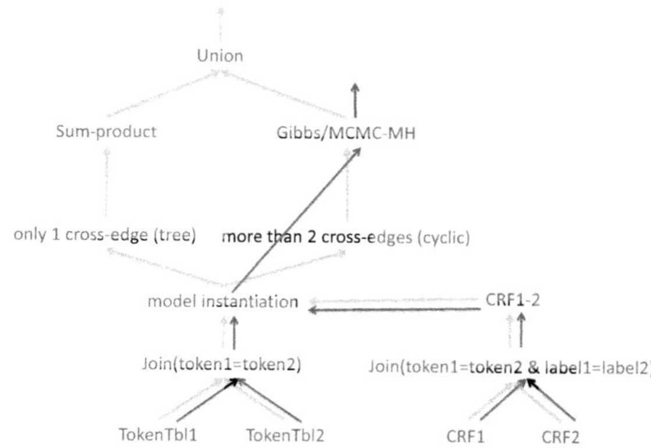

Figure 9: The query plan for the probabilistic join query followed by marginal inference.

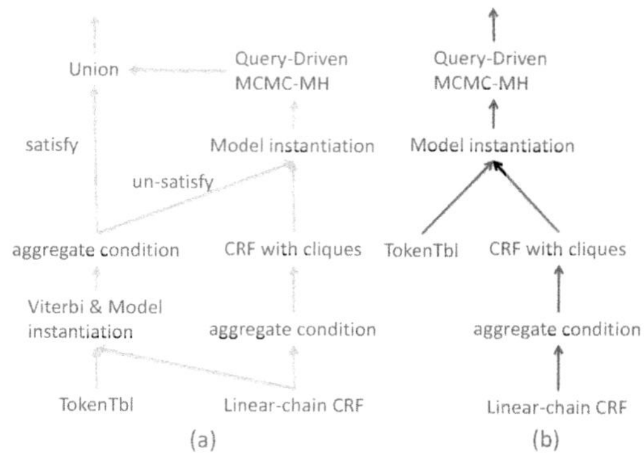

Figure 10: The query plan for the aggregate selection query followed by a top-k inference.

k extractions that satisfy the constraint. Such a non-hybrid query plan is shown in Figure 10(b).

However, this query falls into the special case described in the query plan generation algorithm in Section 6.2 for hybrid inference. The query is to return the top-k extractions over the cyclic graph induced by an aggregate constraint over a linear-chain CRF model. Thus, the resulting query plan is shown in Figure 10(a).

In the query plan with hybrid inference, the Viterbi algorithm runs first to compute the top-k extraction without the constraint. Then, the results are run through the aggregate: those that satisfy the constraint are returned as part of the results, and those that do not satisfy the constraint are fed into the query-driven MCMC-MH algorithm.

7 Evaluation

So far, we have described the implementation of the MCMC algorithms, and the query plans for the hybrid inference algorithms. We now present the results of a set of experiments aimed to (1) evaluate the efficiency of the SQL implementation of the MCMC methods and the effectiveness of the query-driven sampling techniques; (2) compare the accuracy and runtime of the four inference algorithms: Viterbi, sum-product, Gibbs and MCMC-MH, for the two IE tasks—top-k and marginal; and (3) analyze three real-life text datasets to quantify the potential speedup of a query plan with hybrid inference compared to one with non-hybrid inference.

Setup and Dataset: We implemented the four inference algorithms: Viterbi, sum-product, Gibbs and MCMC-MH in PostgreSQL 8.4.1. We conducted the experiments reported here on a 2.4 GHz Intel Pentium 4 Linux system with 1GB RAM.

For evaluating the efficiency of the in-database implementation of the MCMC methods, and for comparing the accuracy and run-

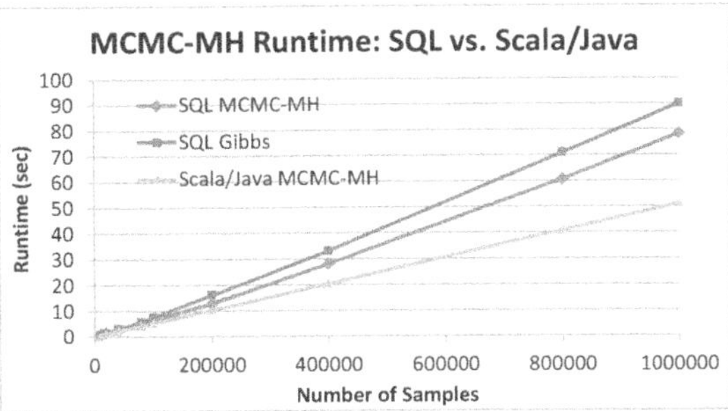

Figure 11: Runtime comparison of the SQL and Java/Scala implementations of MCMC-MH and Gibbss algorithms over DBLP.

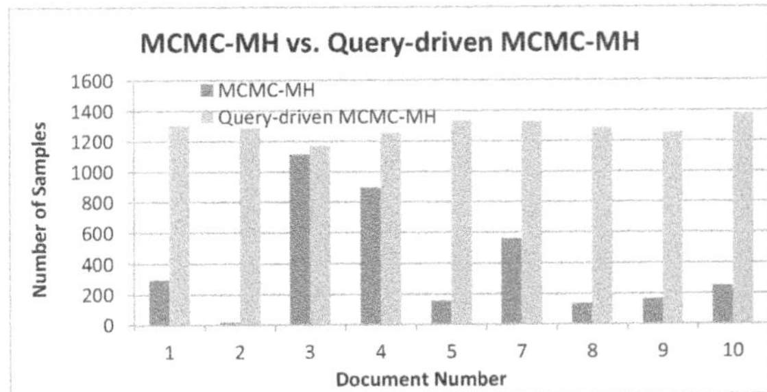

Figure 12: The number of qualified samples generated by the query-driven MCMC-MH and the vanilla MCMC-MH algorithm in 1 second for different documents in DBLP.

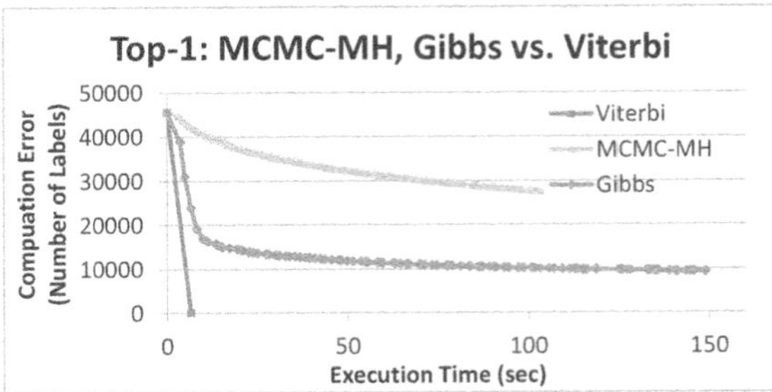

Figure 13: Runtime-Accuracy graph comparing Gibbs, MCMC-MH and Viterbi over linear-chain CRF for top-1 inference on DBLP.

time of the inference algorithms, we use the DBLP dataset [23] and a CRF model with 10 labels and features similar to those in [18]. The DBLP database contains more than 700,000 papers with attributes, such as conference, year, etc. We generate bibliography strings from DBLP by concatenating all the attribute values of each paper record. We also have similar results for the same experiments over NYTimes dataset, which we include in our technical report.

For quantifying the speedup of query plans with hybrid inference, we examine the New York Times (NYTimes) dataset, and the Twitter dataset in addition to the DBLP dataset. The NYTimes dataset contains ten-million tokens from 1,788 New York Times articles from the year 2004. The Twitter dataset contains around 200,000 tokens from over 40,000 tweets obtained in January 2010. We label both corpora with 9 labels, including person, location, etc.

7.1 MCMC SQL Implementation

In this experiment, we compare the runtime of the in-database implementation of the MCMC algorithms, including Gibbs Sampling and MCMC-MH, with the runtime of the Scala/Java (with Scala 2.7.7 and Java 1.5) implementation of MCMC-MH described in [12] over linear-chain CRF models. The runtime of Scala/Java implementation is measured on a different machine with better configurations (2.66GHz CPU Mac OSX 10.6.4 with $8G$ RAM).

As we can see in Figure 11, the runtime of the MCMC algorithms grow linearly with the number of samples for both the SQL and the Java/Scala implementations. While the Scala/Java implementation of MCMC-MH can generate 1 million samples in around 51 seconds, it takes about 78 seconds for the SQL implementation of the MCMC-MH, and about 89 seconds for that of the Gibbs Sampling. This experiment shows that the in-database implementations of the MCMC sampling algorithms achieve comparable (within a factor of 1.5) runtimes to the Java/Scala implementation.

7.2 Query-Driven MCMC-MH

In this experiment, we evaluate the effectiveness of the query-driven MCMC-MH algorithm described in Section 4.3 with the vanilla MCMC-MH in generating samples that satisfy the query constraint. The query we use is `Q2` described in Section 4.1, which computes the top-1 extractions that satisfy the aggregate constraint that all `title` tokens are in front of the `author` tokens.

We run the query-driven MCMC-MH and the vanilla MCMC-MH algorithm over a randomly picked 10 documents from the DBLP dataset. Figure 12 shows the number of "qualified" samples that are generated by each algorithm in 1 second. As we can see, the query-driven MCMC-MH generates more "qualified" samples, roughly 1200 for all the documents, and for half of the documents the query-driven MCMC-MH generates more than 10 times more qualified samples than vanilla MCMC-MH.

7.3 MCMC vs. Viterbi on Top-k Inference

This experiment compares the runtime and the accuracy of the Gibbs, the MCMC-MH and the Viterbi algorithms in computing top-1 inference over linear-chain CRF models. The inference is performed over 45,000 tokens in 1000 bibliography strings from the DBLP dataset. We measure the "computation error" as the number of labels different from the exact top-1 labelings according to the model [1]. The Viterbi algorithm only takes 6.1 seconds to complete the exact inference over these documents, achieving zero computation error.

For the MCMC algorithms, we measure the computation error and runtime for every $10k$ more samples, starting from $10k$ to 1 million samples over all documents. As we can see in Figure 13, the computation error of the Gibbs algorithm drops to 22% from 45,000 to 10,000 when $500k$ samples are generated. This takes around 75 seconds, more than 12 times longer than the runtime of the Viterbi algorithm. The MCMC-MH converges much slower than the Gibbs Sampling. As more samples are generated, the top-1 extractions generated from the MCMC algorithms get closer and closer to the exact top-1, however very slowly. Thus, Viterbi beats the MCMC methods by far in computing top-1 extractions with linear-chain CRF models: more than 10 times faster with more than 20% fewer computation errors.

7.4 MCMC vs. Sum-Product on Marginal Inference

This experiment compares the runtime and the accuracy of the Gibbs, MCMC-MH and the sum-product algorithms over tree-shaped graphical models induced by a join query similar to `Q1`, described in Section 4.1. The query computes the marginal probability of the existence of a join result for each document pair in DBLP, joining on the same 'publisher'. The query is performed over a set of 10,000 pairs of documents from DBLP, where the two documents in each pair have exactly one token in common.

[1]The top-1 extractions with zero computation error may still contain mistakes, which are caused by inaccurate models.

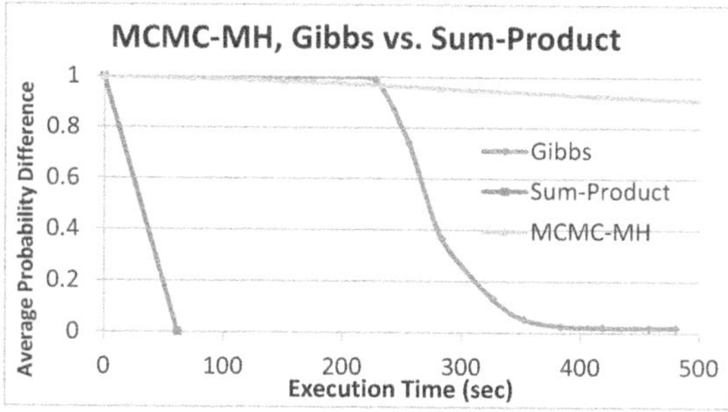

Figure 14: Runtime-Accuracy graph comparing Gibbs, MCMC-MH and sum-product over tree-shaped models for marginal inference on DBLP.

Data Corpora	Skip-chain CRF	Probabilistic Join	Aggregate Constraint
NYTimes	×5.0	×4.5	×10.0
Twitter	×5.0	×2.6	N/A
DBLP	×1.0	×1.0	N/A

Table 2: Speed-ups achieved by hybrid inference for different queries.

The sum-product algorithm over these 10,000 tree-shaped graphical models takes about 60 seconds. As an exact algorithm, the sum-product algorithm achieves zero computation error. We measure the "computation error" as the difference between the marginal probabilities of join computed from the MCMC-MH algorithms and the sum-product algorithm, averaging over all document pairs.

For the MCMC algorithms, we measure the computation error and runtime for every $200k$ more samples, starting from $200k$ to 2 million samples over all document pairs. As we can see in Figure 14, the probability difference between Gibbs and sum-product converges to zero quickly: at 400 second, the probability difference is dropped to 0.01. The MCMC-MH on the other hand, converges much slower than the Gibbs.

This experiment shows that MCMC algorithms performs relatively better in computing marginal distributions than in computing top-1 extractions. However, sum-product algorithm still outperforms MCMC algorithms in computing marginal probabilities over tree-shaped models: more than 6 times faster with about 1% less computation error.

7.5 Exploring Model Parameters

In this experiment, we explore how different correlation strengths, one of the parameters we discussed in Section 5.2, affect the runtime and the accuracy of the inference algorithms. As we explained earlier, the correlation strength does not affect the accuracy or the runtime of the Viterbi algorithm. On the other hand, weaker correlation between different random variables in the CRF model leads to faster convergence for the MCMC algorithms. The setup of this experiment is the same as in Section 7.3.

In Figure 15, we show the runtime-accuracy graph of the Viterbi and the Gibbs algorithm to compute the top-1 extractions over models with different correlation strengths. We synthetically generated models with correlation strengths of 1, 0.5, 0.2 and 0.001 by dividing the original scores in the transition factors by 1, 2, 5 and 1000 respectively. As we can see, the weaker correlation strengths lead to faster convergence for the Gibbs algorithm. When correlation strength is 0.001 the computation error reduces to zero in less than twice that of the Viterbi runtime.

The correlation strength of the CRF model depends on the dataset on which the CRF model is learned. The model we learned over NYTimes and DBLP dataset both contains strong correlation strength.

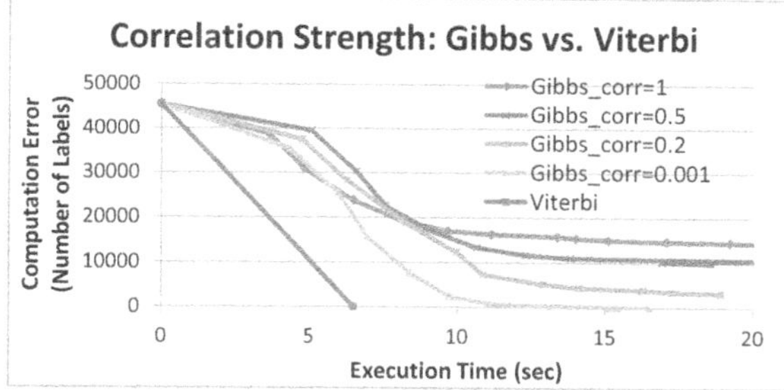

Figure 15: Runtime-Accuracy graph comparing Gibbs and Viterbi over models with different correlation strengths on DBLP.

7.6 Hybrid Inference for Skip-chain CRF

In this and the next two sections, we describe the results, in terms of runtime speed-ups, comparing the query plan generated by hybrid inference with a non-hybrid solution. Table 2 summarizes the results of hybrid inference for different queries over different models.

The query we use in this experiment is `Q4` over the skip-chain CRF model, described in Section 6.3.1. Given that the Viterbi is more than 10 times more efficient than Gibbs with zero computation error, as we showed in Section 7.3, the speed-up enabled by the hybrid inference for `Q4` is determined by the percentage of the documents that do not contain duplicate non-"stop-word" tokens.

For NYTimes dataset, we use the sentence breaking function in NLTK toolkit [24], and the full-text stop-word list from MySQL [25]. Over all sentences, only about 10.3% contain duplicate non-"stop-word" tokens. Thus, the optimizer will use the Viterbi algorithm for 89.7% of the sentences, while using the Gibbs algorithm for the rest. This hybrid inference plan can achieve a 5-fold speedup compared to the non-hybrid solution, where the Gibbs algorithm is used over all the documents.

We did the same analysis on the Twitter dataset. The number sentences that contains non-"stop-word" duplicate tokens is 10.0%, which leads to a similar 5-fold speedup. On the other hand, for DBLP dataset, the number of documents that contains non-"stop-word" duplicates is as high as 96.9%, leading to a 3% speedup.

7.7 Hybrid Inference for Probabilistic Join

The query used in this experiment is the join query `Q1`, described in Section 6.3.2. Given that the sum-product is more than 6 times more efficient than Gibbs with zero computation error, as we showed in Section 7.4, the speed-up enabled by the hybrid inference for `Q1` is determined by the percentage of the "joinable" document pairs that share only one pair of common non-"stop-word" tokens.

For the NYTimes dataset, about 6.0% "joinable" sentence pairs share more than one pair of non-"stop-word" common tokens. Thus, the sum-product algorithm can be applied to the other 93.6% of the sentences, achieving a 4.5 times speedup compared to the non-hybrid approach of running Gibbs over the joint CRF model of all the document pairs.

For the Twitter datset, around 25.6% "joinable" sentence pairs share more than one pair of tokens. This is much lower than NYTimes dataset mainly because tweets contain a lot of common shorthands. Thus the speedup is around 2.6 times. For DBLP dataset, on the other hand, the speedup is little due to the high percentage of document pairs contain more than one pair of common words.

7.8 Hybrid Inference for Aggregate Constraint

The query used in this experiment is `Q2` with an aggregate constraint described in Section 6.3.3. We performed this query over the DBLP dataset. Out of all the top-1 extractions of the 10,000 bibliography strings, only 25 of them do not satisfy the aggregate constraint that all `title` tokens are in front of all `author` tokens. Thus, although the aggregate constraint in the query induce a big clique in the CRF model, which calls for MCMC algorithms, the MCMC is not needed for most of the cases. To perform `Q2` over DBLP, MCMC only needs to be performed over 25 out of 10,000 documents, which leads to a 10-fold speedup.

Summary: The results in Section 7.1 and Section 7.2 show that MCMC algorithms can be implemented in database, achieving comparable runtimes to the Scala/Java implementation. The query-driven sampling techniques can effectively generate more samples that satisfy query constraints for conditional queries. Section 7.3 and Section 7.4 show that the Viterbi and sum-product algorithms are by far more efficient and more accurate than the MCMC algorithms over linear-chain and tree-shaped models in IE. Lastly, based on the text analysis over NYTimes, Twitter and DBLP datasets, we conclude that the query plans with hybrid inference can achieve up to 10-fold speed-up compared to the non-hybrid solutions.

8 Conclusion

In this work, we show the in-database implementations of two MCMC-based inference algorithms. The in-database implementations enable efficient probabilistic query processing with a tight integration of the inference and relational operators. This work also demonstrates the feasibility and potential of using a query optimizer to support a declarative query language for different inference operations over probabilistic graphical models. Results from three real-life datasets demonstrate that hybrid inference can achieve up to 10-fold speed-up compared to the non-hybrid solutions. As future work, we intend to explore the development of a cost-based optimizer that can balance the efficiency and accuracy in answering probabilistic queries. In addition, we intend to support other text analysis tasks, such as entity resolution, and learning algorithms.

Acknowledgements: This work was supported by AMPLab founding sponsors Google and SAP, and RADLab sponsors Amazon Web Services, Cloudera, Huawei, IBM, Intel, Microsoft, NEC, NetApp, and VMWare, NSF grants 0722077 and 0803690, and the European Commission under FP7-PEOPLE-2009-RG-249217 (HeisenData).

9 Appendix

Having implemented a number of inference algorithms in the database, including Viterbi dynamic programming for linear-chain CRF, sum-product belief propagation, and the MCMC methods described above, we have developed a set of design guidelines for implementing statistical methods in the database:

- *Avoid using iterative programming patterns in PL/pgSQL and other database extension languages.* This is easily overlooked, since many machine learning inference techniques are described as iterative methods. Database architectures are optimized for running a single query over lots of data, rather than iteratively running a little query over small amounts of data. The passing of "iterative state" is achieved in a single query expression via recursive queries in Viterbi and sum-product, and window aggregate functions in MCMC-MH and Gibbs.
- *Use efficient representations for factor tables.* Tables and rows are heavy-weight representations for cells in a factor table. Array data types (which are now standard in many relational database systems) provide better memory locality, faster look-up and more efficient operations.
- *Drive the data-flow via a few SQL queries, and use user-defined functions (and aggregates) to do inner-loop arithmetic.* This design style enables the database optimizer to choose an efficient data-flow, while preserving programmer control over fine-grained efficiency issues.
- *Keep running state in memory, and update using user-defined functions and aggregates.* This is typically far more efficient than storing algorithm state in the database and updating using SQL.

10 References

[1] F. Reiss, S. Raghavan, R. Krishnamurthy, H. Zhu, and S. Vaithyanathan, "An Algebraic Approach to Rule-Based Information Extraction," in *ICDE*, 2008.

[2] W. Shen, A. Doan, J. Naughton, and R. Ramakrishnan, "Declarative Information Extraction Using Datalog with Embedded Extraction Predicates," in VLDB, 2007.

[3] A. Doan, R. Ramakrishnan, F. Chen, P. DeRose, Y. Lee, R. McCann, M. Sayyadian, and W. Shen, "Community information management," 2006.

[4] D. Wang, M. Franklin, M. Garofalakis, and J. Hellerstein, "Querying Probabilistic Information Extraction," in *PVLDB*, 2010.

[5] N. Dalvi and D. Suciu, "Efficient Query Evaluation on Probabilistic Databases," in *VLDB*, 2004.

[6] O. Benjelloun, A. Sarma, A. Halevy, and J. Widom, "ULDB: Databases with Uncertainty and Lineage," in *VLDB*, 2006.

[7] A. Deshpande and S. Madden, "MauveDB: Supporting Model-based User Views in Database Systems," in *SIGMOD*, 2006.

[8] P. Sen and A. Deshpande, "Representing and Querying Correlated Tuples in Probabilistic Databases," in *ICDE*, 2007.

[9] L. Antova, T. Jansen, C. Koch, and D. Olteanu, "Fast and Simple Relational Processing of Uncertain Data," in *ICDE*, 2008.

[10] D. Wang, E. Michelakis, M. Garofalakis, and J. Hellerstein, "BayesStore: Managing Large, Uncertain Data Repositories with Probabilistic Graphical Models," in *VLDB*, 2008.

[11] R. Jampani, L. Perez, M. Wu, F. Xu, C. Jermaine, and P. Haas, "MCDB: A Monte Carlo Approach to Managing Uncertain Data," in *SIGMOD*, 2008.

[12] M. Wick, A. McCallum, and G. Miklau, "Scalable Probabilistic Databases with Factor Graphs and MCMC," in *VLDB2010*, 2010.

[13] D. Wang, E. Michelakis, M. Franklin, M. Garofalakis, and J. Hellerstein, "Probabilistic Declarative Information Extraction," in *ICDE*, 2010.

[14] E. Michelakis, P. Haas, R. Krishnamurthy, and S. Vaithyanathan, "Uncertainty Management in Rule-based Information Extraction Systems," in *Proceedings of the SIGMOD*, 2009.

[15] W. Shen, P. DeRose, R. McCann, A. Doan, and R. Ramakrishnan, "Toward best-effort information extraction," in SIGMOD, 2008.

[16] J. Lafferty, A. McCallum, and F. Pereira, "Conditional Random Fields: Probabilistic Models for Segmenting and Labeling Sequence Data," in *ICML*, 2001.

[17] C. Sutton and A. McCallum, "Introduction to Conditional Random Fields for Relational Learning," in *Introduction to Statistical Relational Learning*, 2008.

[18] T. Kristjansson, A. Culotta, P. Viola, and A. McCallum, "Interactive Information Extraction with Constrained Conditional Random Fields," in *AAAI'04*, 2004.

[19] D. Koller and N. Friedman, "Probabilistic Graphical Models: Principles and Techniques," in *PVLDB*, 2009.

[20] G. D. Forney, "The Viterbi Algorithm," *IEEE*, vol. 61, no. 3, pp. 268–278, March 1973.

[21] B. Milch, B. Marthi, and S. Russell, "BLOG: Relational modeling with unknown objects," Ph.D. dissertation, University of California, Berkeley, 2006.

[22] A. McCallum, K. Schultz, and S. Singh, "Factorie:probabilistic programming via imperatively defined factor graphs," in *NIPS*, 2009.

[23] "DBLP dataset, http://kdl.cs.umass.edu/data/dblp/dblp-info.html."

[24] "NLTK toolkit. http://www.nltk.org/."

[25] "MySQL full-text stop-words. http://dev.mysql.com/doc/refman/5.1/en/fulltext-stopwords.html."

Faerie: Efficient Filtering Algorithms for Approximate Dictionary-based Entity Extraction

Guoliang Li Dong Deng Jianhua Feng
Department of Computer Science and Technology, Tsinghua University, Beijing 100084, China.
liguoliang@tsinghua.edu.cn; buaasoftdavid@gmail.com; fengjh@tsinghua.edu.cn

ABSTRACT

Dictionary-based entity extraction identifies predefined entities (e.g., person names or locations) from a document. A recent trend for improving extraction recall is to support *approximate* entity extraction, which finds all substrings in the document that approximately match entities in a given dictionary. Existing methods to address this problem support either token-based similarity (e.g., Jaccard Similarity) or character-based dissimilarity (e.g., Edit Distance). It calls for a unified method to support various similarity/dissimilarity functions, since a unified method can reduce the programming efforts, hardware requirements, and the manpower. In addition, many substrings in the document have overlaps, and we have an opportunity to utilize the shared computation across the overlaps to avoid unnecessary redundant computation. In this paper, we propose a unified framework to support many similarity/dissimilarity functions, such as jaccard similarity, cosine similarity, dice similarity, edit similarity, and edit distance. We devise efficient filtering algorithms to utilize the shared computation and develop effective pruning techniques to improve the performance. The experimental results show that our method achieves high performance and outperforms state-of-the-art studies.

Categories and Subject Descriptors: H.2 [Database Management]: Database applications; H.3.3 [Information Search and Retrieval]

General Terms: Algorithms, Experimentation, Performance

Keywords: Approximate Entity Extraction; Unified Framework; Filtering Algorithms; Pruning Techniques

1. INTRODUCTION

Dictionary-based entity extraction identifies all the substrings from a document that match the predefined entities in a given dictionary. For example, consider a document "*An Efficient Filter for Approximate Membership Checking. Venkaee shga Kamunshik kabarati, Dong Xin, Surauijt ChadhuriSIGMOD*", and a dictionary with two entities "**Surajit Chaudhuri**" and "**Dong Xin**". Dictionary-based entity extraction finds the predefined entity "**Dong Xin**" from the document. This problem has many real applications in the fields of information retrieval, molecular biology, bioinformatics, and natural language processing.

However, the document may contain typographical or orthographical errors and the same entity may have different representations [22]. For example, the substring "*Surauijt Chadhuri*" in the above document has typographical errors. The traditional (exact) entity extraction cannot find this substring from the document, since the substring does not *exactly* match the predefined entity "**Surajit Chaudhuri**". Approximate entity extraction is a recent trend to address this problem, which finds all substrings from the document that *approximately* match the predefined entities.

To improve extraction recall, we study the problem of approximate dictionary-based entity extraction, which, given a dictionary of entities and a document, finds all substrings from the document *similar* to some entities in the dictionary. Many similarity/dissimilarity functions have been proposed to quantify the similarity between two strings, such as jaccard similarity, cosine similarity, dice similarity, edit similarity, and edit distance. For instance, in the above example, suppose we use edit distance and the threshold is 3. Approximate entity extraction can find the substring "*Surauijt Chadhuri*" which is similar to entity "**Surajit Chaudhuri**".

Although there have been some recent studies on approximate entity extraction [22, 4], they support either token-based similarity (e.g., Jaccard Similarity) or character-based dissimilarity (e.g., Edit Distance). It calls for a unified method to support different similarity/dissimilarity functions, since the unified method can reduce not only the programming efforts, but also the hardware requirements and the manpower needed to maintain the codes for different functions.

In addition, we have an observation that many substrings in the document have overlaps. For example, consider the above document, many substrings (e.g., "*Surauijt Chadhuri*", "*urauijt ChadhuriSIG*", "*rauijt ChadhuriSIGMOD*") have overlaps (e.g., "*Chadhuri*"). We have an opportunity to utilize this feature to avoid the redundant computation across overlaps of different substrings. For example, we can share the computation on "*Chadhuri*" for different substrings.

To remedy the above problems, we propose a unified framework to support various similarity/dissimilarity functions.

*This work is partly supported by the National Natural Science Foundation of China under Grant No. 61003004, the National Grand Fundamental Research 973 Program of China under Grant No. 2011CB302206, and National S&T Major Project of China under Grant No. 2011ZX01042-001-002.

To avoid redundant computation across overlaps, we develop efficient filtering algorithms for approximate dictionary-based entity extraction, called "Faerie". To summarize, we make the following contributions.

- We propose a unified framework to support many similarity/dissimilarity functions, such as jaccard similarity, cosine similarity, dice similarity, edit similarity, and edit distance.
- We devise efficient filtering algorithms, which can utilize the shared computation across the overlaps of multiple substrings of the document.
- We develop effective pruning techniques and devise efficient algorithms to improve the performance.
- We have implemented our method, and the experimental results show that our method achieves high performance and outperforms state-of-the-art approaches.

The remainder of this paper is organized as follows. We propose a unified framework to support various similarity functions in Section 2. Section 3 introduces a heap-based filtering algorithm to utilize shared computation. We develop pruning techniques in Section 4 and introduce our algorithm Faerie in Section 5. We conduct extensive experimental studies in Section 6. Related works are provided in Section 7. Finally, we conclude the paper in Section 8.

2. A UNIFIED FRAMEWORK

We first formulate the problem of approximate (dictionary-based) entity extraction (Section 2.1), and then introduce a unified method to support various similarity/dissimilarity functions (Section 2.2). Finally we introduce a concept of "valid substrings" to prune unnecessary substrings (Section 2.3).

2.1 Problem Formulation

DEFINITION 1 (APPROXIMATE ENTITY EXTRACTION). *Given a dictionary of entities $E = \{e_1, e_2, \ldots, e_n\}$, a document D, a similarity function, and a threshold, it finds all* "**similar**" *pairs $\langle s, e_i \rangle$ with respect to the given function and threshold, where s is a substring of D and $e_i \in E$.*

This paper focuses on token-based similarity, character-based similarity, and character-based dissimilarity.

Token-based Similarity: It includes Jaccard Similarity, Cosine Similarity, and Dice Similarity. The token-based similarity takes a string as a set of tokens. Let JAC, COS, and DICE respectively denote the jaccard similarity, cosine similarity, and dice similarity. Given two strings r and s, let $|r|$ denote the number of tokens in r. $\text{JAC}(r,s) = \frac{|r \cap s|}{|r \cup s|}$, $\text{COS}(r,s) = \frac{|r \cap s|}{\sqrt{|r| \cdot |s|}}$, and $\text{DICE}(r,s) = \frac{2|r \cap s|}{|r|+|s|}$. For example, JAC("`sigmod 2011 conference`", "`sigmod 2011`") $= \frac{2}{3}$, COS("`sigmod 2011 conference`", "`sigmod 2011`") $= \frac{2}{\sqrt{6}}$, and DICE("`sigmod 2011 conference`", "`sigmod 2011`") $= \frac{4}{5}$.

Charater-based Dissimilarity: It includes Edit Distance. The charater-based dissimilarity takes a string as a sequence of characters. The edit distance between two strings r and s, denoted by $\text{ED}(r,s)$, is the minimum number of single-character edit operations (i.e., insertion, deletion, and substitution) needed to transform string r to string s. For example, ED("`surajit`", "`surauijt`") $= 2$.

Table 1: A dictionary of entities and a document.

(a) Dictionary E

ID	Entity e	len(e)	$\lvert e \rvert$ (# of q-grams with $q = 2$)
1	`kaushik ch`	10	9
2	`chakrabarti`	11	10
3	`chaudhuri`	9	8
4	`venkatesh`	9	8
5	`surajit ch`	10	9

(b) Document D

an efficient filter for approximate membership checking. venkaee shga kamunshik kabarati, dong xin, surauijt chadhurisigmod.

Charater-based Similarity: It includes Edit Similarity. The edit similarity between two strings r and s is defined as $\text{EDS}(r,s) = 1 - \frac{\text{ED}(r,s)}{\max\left(\text{len}(r), \text{len}(s)\right)}$, where len($s$) denotes the length of s. For instance, EDS("`surajit`", "`surauijt`") $= 1 - \frac{2}{8} = \frac{3}{4}$.

In this paper two strings are said to be *similar*, if their (jaccard, cosine, dice, edit) similarity is no smaller than a given similarity threshold δ, or their edit distance is no larger than a given edit-distance threshold τ. For instance, consider the document D and dictionary E in Table 1. Suppose the edit-distance threshold $\tau = 2$. $\langle$"*venkaee sh*", "`venkatesh`"$\rangle$, $\langle$"*surauijt ch*", "`surajit ch`"$\rangle$, and $\langle$"*chadhuri*", "`chaudhuri`"$\rangle$ are three example results. Especially, although the substring "*chadhurisigmod*" in the document misses a space between "*chadhuri*" and "*sigmod*" (a typographical error), our method still can find "*chadhuri*" (similar to entity "`chaudhuri`").

It has been shown that approximate entity extraction can improve recall [22]. For example, the recall can increase from 65.4% to 71.4% when performing protein name recognition. In this paper, we emphasize on improving the performance. We focus on extracting textual entities. We assume the thresholds (δ and τ) are pre-defined and take the selection of such thresholds as a future work.

2.2 A Unified Method

In this section, we propose a unified framework to support various similarity/dissimilarity functions.

We model both the entity and document as a set of tokens. Especially for edit distance and edit similarity, we take q-grams of an entity as tokens. A q-gram of a string s is a substring of s with length q. The q-gram set of s, denoted by $G(s)$, is the set of all of s's q-grams. For example, the 2-gram set of "`surajit_ch`" is {`su`, `ur`, `ra`, `aj`, `ji`, `it`, `t_`, `_c`, `ch`}. If the context is clear, we use token to denote token/gram; for edit distance and edit similarity, we use e to denote $G(e)$, $e \cap s$ to denote $G(r) \cap G(s)$, and $|e|$ to denote $|G(e)|$ (i.e., $|e| = \text{len}(e) - q + 1$).

Given an entity e and a substring s, we transform different similarities/dissimilarities to the *overlap similarity* ($|e \cap s|$) and use the *overlap similarity* as a unified filtering condition: if e and s are similar, then $|e \cap s|$ must be not smaller than a threshold $T > 0$, where T can be computed as follows.

- Jaccard Similarity: $T = \lceil (|e| + |s|) * \frac{\delta}{1+\delta} \rceil$.
- Cosine Similarity: $T = \lceil \sqrt{|e| \cdot |s|} * \delta \rceil$.
- Dice Similarity: $T = \lceil (|e| + |s|) * \frac{\delta}{2} \rceil$.
- Edit Distance: $T = \max(|e|, |s|) - \tau * q$.
- Edit Similarity:

  $T = \lceil \max(|e|, |s|) - (\max(|e|, |s|) + q - 1) * (1 - \delta) * q \rceil$.

The correctness of these thresholds is stated in Lemma 1.

LEMMA 1. *Given an entity e and a substring s, we have*[1],

- Jaccard Similarity : *If* $\text{JAC}(e,s) \geq \delta$, $|e \cap s| \geq \lceil (|e|+|s|) * \frac{\delta}{1+\delta} \rceil$.
- Cosine Similarity : *If* $\cos(e,s) \geq \delta$, $|e \cap s| \geq \lceil \sqrt{|e| \cdot |s|} * \delta \rceil$.
- Dice Similarity : *If* $\text{DICE}(e,s) \geq \delta$, $|e \cap s| \geq \lceil (|e|+|s|) * \frac{\delta}{2} \rceil$.
- Edit Distance : *If* $\text{ED}(e,s) \leq \tau$, $|e \cap s| \geq \max(|e|,|s|) - \tau * q$.
- Edit Similarity : *If* $\text{EDS}(e,s) \geq \delta$,

  $|e \cap s| \geq \lceil \max(|e|,|s|) - (\max(|e|,|s|)+q-1)*(1-\delta)*q \rceil$.

In this way, we can transform various similarities/dissimilarities to the overlap similarity, and develop a unified filtering condition: if $|e \cap s| < T$, we prune the pair $\langle s, e \rangle$.

Note that given any similarity function and a threshold, if we can deduce a lower bound for the overlap similarity of two strings, our method can apply to this function. Specially, the five similarity/distance functions we studied are commonly used in information extraction and record linkage [22, 4].

2.3 Valid Substrings

We have an observation that some substrings in D will not have any similar entities. For instance, consider the dictionary and document in Table 1. Suppose we use edit distance and $\tau = 1$. Consider substring "*surauijt chadhurisigmod*" with length 23. As the lengths of entities in the dictionary are between 9 and 11, the substring cannot be similar to any entity. Next we discuss how to prune such substrings.

Given an entity e and a substring s, if s is similar to e, the number of tokens in s ($|s|$) should be in a range $[\bot_e, \top_e]$, that is $\bot_e \leq |s| \leq \top_e$, where $\bot_e$ and $\top_e$ are respectively the lower and upper bound of $|s|$, computed as below:

- Jaccard Similarity: $\bot_e = \lceil |e| * \delta \rceil$ and $\top_e = \lfloor \frac{|e|}{\delta} \rfloor$.
- Cosine Similarity: $\bot_e = \lceil |e| * \delta^2 \rceil$ and $\top_e = \lfloor \frac{|e|}{\delta^2} \rfloor$.
- Dice Similarity: $\bot_e = \lceil |e| * \frac{\delta}{2-\delta} \rceil$ and $\top_e = \lfloor |e| * \frac{2-\delta}{\delta} \rfloor$.
- Edit Distance: $\bot_e = |e| - \tau$ and $\top_e = |e| + \tau$.
- Edit Similarity: $\bot_e = \lceil (|e|+q-1)*\delta - (q-1) \rceil$ and $\top_e = \lfloor \frac{|e|+q-1}{\delta} - (q-1) \rfloor$.

where δ is the similarity threshold and τ is the edit-distance threshold. The correctness of the bounds is stated in Lemma 2.

LEMMA 2. *Given an entity e, for any substring s, we have*

- Jaccard Similarity : *if* $\text{JAC}(e,s) \geq \delta$, $\lceil |e| * \delta \rceil \leq |s| \leq \lfloor \frac{|e|}{\delta} \rfloor$.
- Cosine Similarity : *if* $\cos(e,s) \geq \delta$, $\lceil |e| * \delta^2 \rceil \leq |s| \leq \lfloor \frac{|e|}{\delta^2} \rfloor$.
- Dice Similarity : *if* $\text{DICE}(e,s) \geq \delta$, $\lceil |e| * \frac{\delta}{2-\delta} \rceil \leq |s| \leq \lfloor |e| * \frac{2-\delta}{\delta} \rfloor$.
- Edit Distance : *if* $\text{ED}(e,s) \leq \tau$, $|e| - \tau \leq |s| \leq |e| + \tau$.
- Edit Similarity : *if* $\text{EDS}(e,s) \geq \delta$,

$$\lceil (|e|+q-1)*\delta - (q-1) \rceil \leq |s| \leq \lfloor \frac{|e|+q-1}{\delta} - (q-1) \rfloor.$$

Based on Lemma 2, given an entity e, only those substrings with token numbers between $\bot_e$ and $\top_e$ could be similar to entity e, and others can be pruned. Especially, let $\bot_E = \min\{\bot_e | e \in E\}$ and $\top_E = \max\{\top_e | e \in E\}$. Obviously the substrings in D with token numbers between $\bot_E$ and $\top_E$ may have a similar entity in the dictionary E, and others can be pruned. Based on this observation, we introduce the concept of "valid substring."

[1]In this paper, we omit the proof due to space constraints.

DEFINITION 2 (VALID SUBSTRING). *Given a dictionary E and a document D, a substring s in D is a valid substring for an entity* $e \in E$ *if* $\bot_e \leq |s| \leq \top_e$. *A substring s in D is a valid substring for dictionary E if* $\bot_E \leq |s| \leq \top_E$.

For instance, consider the dictionary and document in Table 1. Suppose we use edit similarity, and $\delta = 0.8$ and $q = 2$. Consider entity e_5 = "`surajit ch`", $\bot_{e_5} = \lceil (|e_5| + q - 1) * \delta - (q-1) \rceil = 7$ and $\top_{e_5} = \lfloor \frac{|e_5|+q-1}{\delta} - (q-1) \rfloor = 11$. Only the valid substrings with token numbers between 7 and 11 could be similar to entity e_5. As $\bot_E = 7$ and $\top_E = 12$, only the valid substrings with token numbers between 7 and 12 could have similar entities in the dictionary, and all other substrings (e.g., "*surauijt chadhurisigmod*") can be pruned.

We employ a filter-and-verify framework to address the problem of approximate entity extraction. In the filter step, we generate *the candidate pairs* of a valid substring in document D and an entity in dictionary E, whose overlap similarity is no smaller than a threshold T; and in the verify step, we verify the candidate pairs to get the final results, by computing the real similarity/disimilarity. In this paper, we focus on the filter step.

3. HEAP-BASED FILTERING ALGORITHMS

In this section, we propose heap-based filtering algorithms to utilize the shared computation across overlaps. We first introduce an inverted index structure (Section 3.1), and then devise a multi-heap-based algorithm (Section 3.2) and a single-heap-based algorithm (Section 3.3).

3.1 An Inverted Index Structure

A valid substring is similar to an entity only if they share enough common tokens. To efficiently count the number of their common tokens, we use the inverted index structure. We build an inverted index for all entities, where entries are tokens (for jaccard similarity, cosine similarity, and dice similarity) or q-grams (for edit similarity and edit distance), and each entry has an inverted list that keeps the ids of entities that contain the corresponding token/gram, sorted in ascending order. For example, Figure 1 gives the inverted list for entities in Table 1 using q-grams with $q = 2$.

ka→1→4	k_→1	***ra→2→5***	ud→3	en→4	aj→5
au→1→3	***_c→1→5***	ab→2	dh→3	nk→4	ji→5
us→1	***ch→1→2→3→5***	ba→2	hu→3	at→4	it→5
sh→1→4	ha→2→3	ar→2	***ur→3→5***	te→4	***t_→5***
hi→1	ak→2	rt→2	ri→3	es→4	
ik→1	kr→2	ti→2	ve→4	***su→5***	

Figure 1: Inverted indexes for entities in Table 1.

For each valid substring s in D, we first get its tokens and the corresponding inverted lists. Then for each entity in these inverted lists, we count its *occurrence number* in the inverted lists, i.e., the number of inverted lists that contain the entity. Obviously, the occurrence number of entity e is exactly $|e \cap s|$[2]. For each entity e with occurrence number no smaller than T ($|e \cap s| \geq T$), $\langle s, e \rangle$ is a candidate pair.

For example, consider a valid substring "*surauijt ch*". We first generate its token set {`su`, `ur`, `ra`, `au`, `ui`, `ij`, `jt`, `t_`, `_c`, `ch`} and get the inverted lists (the italic ones in Figure 1). Suppose we use edit distance and $\tau = 2$. For entity e_5, $T = \max(|e_5|, |s|) - \tau * q = 6$. As e_5's occurrence number is 6, ⟨"*surauijt ch*", e_5="`surajit ch`"⟩ is a candidate pair.

[2]In this paper, we take e and s as multisets, since there may exist duplicate tokens in entities and substrings of the document. Even if they are taken as sets, we can also use our method for extraction.

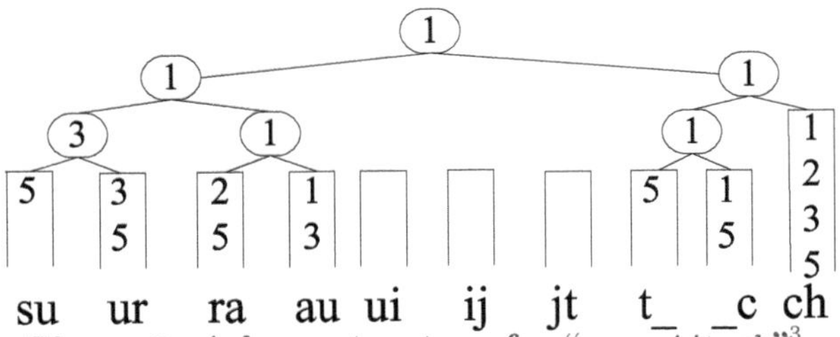

Figure 2: A heap structure for "surauijt ch"[3].

For simplicity, given an entity e and a valid substring s, we use e's occurrence number in s (or s's inverted lists) to denote e's occurrence number in the inverted lists of tokens in s. To efficiently count the occurrence numbers, we propose heap-based filtering algorithms in the following sections.

3.2 Multi-Heap based Method

In this section, we propose a multi-heap based method to count the occurrence numbers.

We first enumerate the valid substrings in D (with token number between $\perp_E$ and $\top_E$). Then for each valid substring, we generate its tokens and construct a min-heap on top of the non-empty inverted lists of its tokens. Initially we use the first entity of every inverted list to construct the min-heap. For the top entity on the heap, we count its occurrence number on the heap (i.e., the number of inverted lists that contain the entity). If the number is not smaller than T, the pair of this valid substring and the entity is a candidate pair. Next, we pop the top entity, add the next entity of the inverted list from which the top entity is selected into the heap, adjust the heap, and count the occurrence number of the new top entity. Iteratively we find all candidate pairs.

For example, consider a valid substring "*surauijt ch*". We first generate its token set and construct a min-heap on top of the first entities of every inverted list (Figure 2). Next we iteratively adjust the heap and get the entities {1, 1, 1, 2, 2, 3, 3, 3, 5, 5, 5, 5, 5, 5} in ascending order. We count the occurrence numbers of each entry. For example, the occurrence numbers of e_1, e_2, e_3, and e_5 are respectively 3, 2, 3, and 6. Suppose we use edit distance and $\tau = 2$. For entity e_5, $T = \max(|e_5|, |s|) - \tau * q = 6$. The pair of the substring and entity e_5 is a candidate pair. Finally, we verify the candidate pair and get the final result.

Complexity: For a valid substring with l tokens, its corresponding heap contains at most l non-empty inverted lists. Thus the space complexity of the heap is $\mathcal{O}(l)$. As we can construct heaps one by one, the space complexity is the space of the maximum heap, i.e., $\mathcal{O}(\top_E)$ (Table 2(a)).

The time complexity for constructing a heap of a valid substring with l tokens is $\mathcal{O}(l)$. As there are $|D|-l+1$ valid substrings with l tokens, the heap construction complexity for such valid substrings is $\mathcal{O}\big((|D|-l+1)*l\big)$, and the total heap construction complexity is $\mathcal{O}\big(\sum_{l=\perp_E}^{\top_E}(|D|-l+1)*l\big)$ (Table 2(b)). In addition, for each entity, we need to adjust the heap containing the entity. Consider such heap with l inverted lists. The time complexity of adjusting the heap once is $\mathcal{O}(log(l))$. There are l such heaps that contain the entity (Figure 3). Thus for each entity, the time complexity of adjusting the heaps is $\mathcal{O}\big(\sum_{l=\perp_E}^{\top_E} log(l)*l\big)$. Suppose N is the total numbers of entities in inverted lists of tokens in D. The total time complexity of adjusting the heaps is $\mathcal{O}\big(\sum_{l=\perp_E}^{\top_E} log(l)*l*N\big)$ (Table 2(b)).

[3]For ease of presentation, we use a loser tree to represent a heap structure in our examples.

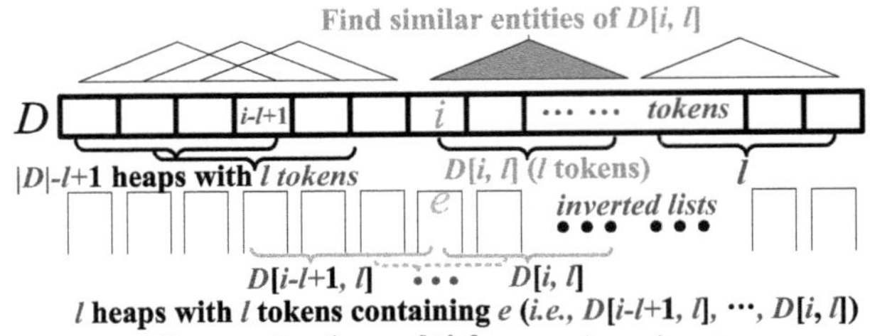

Figure 3: A multi-heap structure.

Table 2: Complexity of multi-heap based methods.

(a) Space Complexity

Maximum Heap	$\mathcal{O}(\top_E)$

(b) Time Complexity

Heap Construction	$\mathcal{O}\big(\sum_{l=\perp_E}^{\top_E}(\lvert D\rvert-l+1)*l\big)$
Heap Adjustment	$\mathcal{O}\big(\sum_{l=\perp_E}^{\top_E} log(l)*l*N\big)$

The multi-heap based method needs to access inverted lists multiple times and does large numbers of heap-adjustment operations. To address this issue, we propose a new method which accesses every inverted list only once in Section 3.3.

3.3 Single-Heap based Method

In this section, we propose a single-heap-based method. We first tokenize the document D and get a list of tokens. For each token, we retrieve the corresponding inverted list. We use $token[i]$ to denote the i-th token, and $\mathcal{IL}[i]$ to denote the inverted list of the i-th token. We construct a single min-heap on top of non-empty inverted lists of all tokens in D, denoted by H, and use the heap to find candidate pairs.

For ease of presentation, we use a two-dimensional array $V[1\cdots|D|][\perp_E\cdots\top_E]$ to count an entity's occurrence numbers in every valid substring's inverted lists. Formally, let $D[i,l]$ denote a valid substring of D with l tokens starting with the i-th token. Given an entity e, we use $V[i][l]$ to count e's *occurrence number* in $D[i,l]$'s inverted lists, i.e., $V[i][l] = |e \cap D[i,l]|$. We compute $V[i][l]$ as follows. $V[i][l]$ is initialized as 0 for $1 \le i \le |D|$ and $\perp_E \le l \le \top_E$.

For the top entity e on the heap selected from the i-th inverted list, we increase the values of *relevant entries* in the array by 1 as follows. Without loss of generality, firstly consider the heap with l tokens. Obviously only $D[i-l+1,l],\ldots,D[i,l]$ contain the i-th inverted list (Figure 4), thus $V[i-l+1][l],\ldots,V[i][l]$ are relevant entries. Similarly for $\perp_E \le l \le \top_E$, $V[i-l+1][l],\ldots,V[i][l]$ are relevant entries. We increase the value of each relevant entry by 1. If $V[i][l] \ge T$, $\langle D[i,l], e\rangle$ is a candidate pair. Then, we pop the top entity, add the next entity in $\mathcal{IL}[i]$ into the heap, adjust the heap and get the next entity, and count the occurrence number of the new entity. We repeat the above steps, and iteratively we can find all candidate pairs.

Actually, for entity e, only the valid substrings with token numbers between $\perp_e$ and $\top_e$ could be similar to entity e.[4] Thus we only need to maintain array $V[1\cdots|D|][\perp_e\cdots\top_e]$.

Next, we give a running example to walk through the single-heap-based method. For example, in our running example, consider a document "*venkaee shga kamunshi*", we construct a single heap on top of the document as shown in Figure 5. Suppose we use edit distance and $\tau = 2$. $\perp_E = 6$ and $\top_E = 12$. For the entity e_4 selected from the first token, we only need to increase its occurrence numbers in valid

[4]Note that, we can get entity e's token number $|e|$ using a hash map, which keeps the pair of an entity and its token number, thus we can get the token number of an entity in $\mathcal{O}(1)$ time complexity.

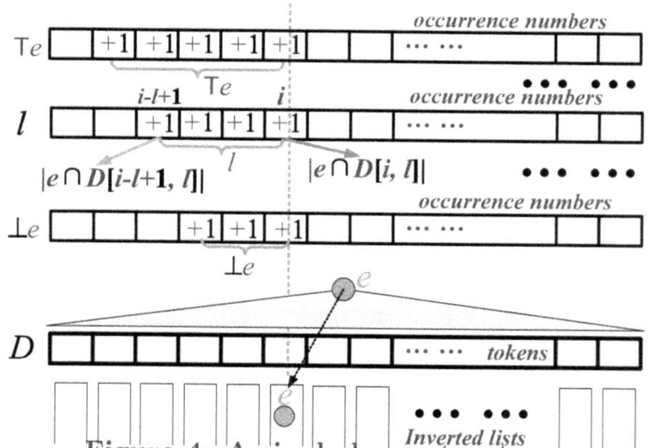

Figure 4: A single-heap structure.

Table 3: Complexity of single-heap based methods.

(a) Space Complexity

Single Heap	$\mathcal{O}(\|D\|)$
Counting Occurrence Numbers	$\mathcal{O}(\|D\| - \bot_E + 1\|)$

(b) Time Complexity

Heap Construction	$\mathcal{O}(\|D\|)$
Heap Adjustment	$\mathcal{O}(log(\|D\|) * N)$
Counting Occurrence Numbers	$\mathcal{O}(N * \max\{\sum_{l=\bot_e}^{\top_e} l \| e \in E\})$

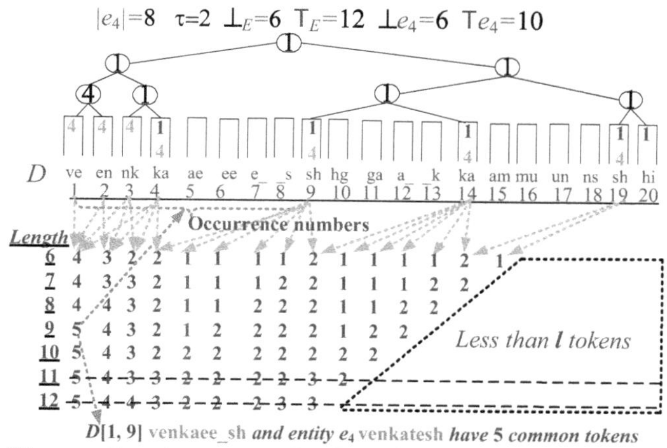

Figure 5: An example for the single-heap-based method on a document "venkaee shga kamunshi".

substrings $D[1, l]$ for $\bot_E \leq l \leq \top_E$, i.e., $D[1, 6], \ldots, D[1, 12]$. We increase the values of $V[1][6], \ldots, V[1][12]$ by 1. For the next entity e_4 selected from the second token, we increase its occurrence numbers in valid substrings $D[1, l], D[2, l]$ for $\bot_E \leq l \leq \top_E$. Similarly, we can count all occurrence numbers. For instance, the occurrence number of entity e_4 ("venkatesh") in $D[1, 9]$ is 5. As the occurrence number is no smaller than $T = \max(|e_4|, |D[1, 9]|) - \tau * q = 9 - 2 * 2 = 5$, the pair of $D[1, 9]$ ("venkaee sh") and entity e_4 ("venkatesh") is a candidate pair. Actually as $\bot_{e_4} = 6$ and $\top_{e_4} = 10$, we only need to consider the entries in $V[1 \cdots 20][6 \cdots 10]$.

Complexity: The space complexity of the single heap is $\mathcal{O}(|D|)$ (Table 3(a)). To count the occurrence numbers of an entity, we do not need to maintain the array and propose an alternative method. We first pop all entities with the same id from the heap (with $|D|$ space to store them). Suppose the entity is e. Then we increase e's occurrence numbers in $V[1 \cdots |D| - l + 1][l]$ by varying l from $\bot_e$ to $\top_e$. In this way, we only need to maintain a one-dimensional array. Thus the space complexity for counting the occurrence number is $\mathcal{O}(\max\{|D| - \bot_e + 1 | e \in E\}) = \mathcal{O}(|D| - \bot_E + 1)$ (Table 3(a)).

The time complexity of heap construction is $\mathcal{O}(|D|)$ (Table 3(b)). To compute the occurrence numbers of each entity, we need to adjust the heap, and the total time complexity of adjusting the heap is $\mathcal{O}(log(|D|) * N)$, where N is the total number of entities in every inverted list. In addition, for each entity, we need to increase its occurrence numbers. For entity e, there are $\sum_{l=\bot_e}^{\top_e} l$ entries needed to be increased by 1 (Figure 4), and the maximum number of such entries (for any entity) is $\max\{\sum_{l=\bot_e}^{\top_e} l | e \in E\}$. Thus the total time complexity is $\mathcal{O}(N * \max\{\sum_{l=\bot_e}^{\top_e} l | e \in E\})$ (Table 3(b)).

Note that the single-heap-based method has used the shared computation across the overlaps (tokens) of different valid substring, since it only needs to scan each inverted list once. It has much lower time complexity than multi-heap-based method, and achieves much higher performance (Section 6).

4. IMPROVING THE SINGLE-HEAP-BASED METHOD

In this section, we propose effective techniques to improve the performance of the single-heap-based method. Li et al. [18] have studied efficient heap-merge algorithms to find similar entities for a *single* substring. In this paper, we propose effective algorithms to simultaneously find similar entities for *multiple* substrings (with large number of overlaps), which are orthogonal to the heap-merge algorithms.

4.1 Pruning Techniques

In this section, we propose several pruning techniques by estimating the lower bounds of $|e \cap s|$.

Lazy-Count Pruning: For each top entity on the heap, we will not count its occurrence numbers for every valid string immediately. Instead, we count the numbers in a lazy manner. We first count its occurrence number in the heap, and if the number is small enough, we can prune the entity.

Formally, given an entity e, we use a sorted position list $P_e = [p_1, \cdots, p_m]$ to keep its occurrences in the heap (in ascending order). Each element in P_e is the position of the corresponding token whose inverted list contains entity e. We can easily get the position list using the heap structure. Then we count e's occurrence number in the heap, i.e., the number of elements in P_e ($|P_e|$). If the number is smaller than a threshold, denoted as T_l, we prune the entity; otherwise we count its occurrence number in its valid substrings with token numbers between $\bot_e$ and $\top_e$ (Section 3.3). For example, in Figure 5, $P_{e_1} = [4, 9, 14, 19, 20]$ and $|P_{e_1}| = 5$.

Next we discuss how to compute the threshold T_l. Recall the threshold T for the overlap similarity (Section 2.2). T depends on both $|e|$ and $|s|$. To derive a lower bound of T which only depends on $|e|$, we use $\bot_e$ to replace $|s|$ and the new bound T_l is computed as below.

- Jaccard Similarity: $T_l = \lceil |e| * \delta \rceil$.
- Cosine Similarity: $T_l = \lceil |e| * \delta^2 \rceil$.
- Dice Similarity: $T_l = \lceil |e| * \frac{\delta}{2-\delta} \rceil$.
- Edit Distance: $T_l = |e| - \tau * q$.
- Edit Similarity: $T_l = \lceil |e| - ((|e| + q - 1) * \frac{(1-\delta)}{\delta} * q) \rceil$.

Obviously $T_l \leq T$. If $|P_e| < T_l \leq T$, e cannot be similar to any substring, and thus we can prune e (Section 2.2). For instance, in Figure 5, consider e_1. Suppose $\tau = 1$. $|e_1| = 9$. $T_l = |e_1| - \tau * q = 9 - 2 = 7$. As $|P_{e_1}| = 5 < T_l$, e_1 can be pruned. The correctness is stated in Lemma 3.

LEMMA 3. *Given an entity e on the single heap, if its occurrence number in the heap ($|P_e|$) is smaller than T_l, e will not be similar to any valid substring.*

Bucket-Count Pruning: Consider an entity e. If a valid substring s is similar to e, s must have at most $\top_e$ tokens and shares at least T_l tokens with e. In other words, if s is similar to e, they must have no larger than $\top_e - T_l$ mismatched tokens. We can use this property for effective pruning.

Formally, given two neighbor elements in P_e, p_i and p_{i+1}, any substring containing both the two tokens (TOKEN$[p_i]$ and TOKEN$[p_{i+1}]$) has at least $p_{i+1} - p_i - 1$ mismatched tokens. If $p_{i+1} - p_i - 1 > \top_e - T_l$, any substrings containing both the two tokens cannot be similar to e. Thus we do not need to count e's occurrence numbers for any substrings.

To use this feature, we partition the elements in P_e into different buckets. If the number of elements in a bucket is smaller than T_l, we can prune all the elements in the bucket (lazy-count pruning); otherwise we use the elements in the bucket to count e's occurrence number for valid substrings with token numbers between $\bot_e$ and $\top_e$ (Section 3.3).

Next we introduce how to do the partition. Initially, we create a bucket b_1 and put the first element p_1 into the bucket. Then we consider the next element p_2. If $p_2 - p_1 - 1 > \top_e - T_l$, we create a new bucket b_2 and put p_2 into bucket b_2; otherwise, we put p_2 into bucket b_1. Iteratively we can partition all elements into different buckets.

We give a tighter bound for different similarity functions. For example, consider edit distance. We can use $p_{i+1} - p_i - 1 > \tau * q$ for pruning, since there exists at least $\tau * q + 1$ mismatched tokens between p_i and p_{i+1}, which need at least $\tau + 1$ single-character edit operations to destroy these $\tau * q + 1$ mismatched tokens. Similarly for edit similarity, we can use $p_{i+1} - p_i - 1 > \lfloor \frac{(|e|+q-1)}{\delta} * (1-\delta) * q \rfloor$ for pruning.

For example, in Figure 5, suppose we use edit distance and $\tau = 1$. Consider $P_{e_4} = [1, 2, 3, 4, 9, 14, 19]$. $T_l = |e_4| - \tau * q = 8 - 1 * 2 = 6$. Obviously, e_4 can pass the lazy-count pruning as $|P_{e_4}| \geq T_l$. Next we check whether it can pass the bucket-count pruning. We first partition P_{e_4} into different buckets. Initially, we create a bucket b_1 and put p_1 into the bucket. Next for $p_2 = 2$, as $p_2 - p_1 - 1 \leq \tau * q = 2$, we put p_2 into bucket b_1. Similarly $p_3 = 3$ and $p_4 = 4$ are added into b_1. For $p_5 = 9$, as $p_5 - p_4 - 1 > \tau * q$, we create a new bucket b_2 and add p_5 into bucket b_2. We repeat theses steps and finally get $b_1 = [1, 2, 3, 4]$, $b_2 = [9]$, $b_3 = [14]$, and $b_4 = [19]$. As the size of each bucket is smaller than T_l, we can directly prune the elements in each bucket. Thus, we do not need to count the occurrence number of e_4 in any valid substrings.

Moreover, we can generalize this idea: Given two elements p_i and p_j $(i < j)$, if $p_j - p_i - (j - i) > \top_e - T_l$, any substrings containing both the two tokens (TOKEN$[p_i]$ and TOKEN$[p_j]$) cannot be similar to entity e. Next we will introduce how to use this property to do further pruning.

Batch-Count Pruning: We have an observation that we do not need to enumerate each element in the position list P_e to count the occurrence numbers for every valid substring. Instead, we check sublists of P_e and test whether the sublists can produce candidate pairs. If so, we find candidate pairs in the sublists; otherwise we prune the sublists.

Formally, if a valid substring s is similar to entity e, they must share *enough* common tokens ($|e \cap s| \geq T_l$). In other words, we only need to check the sublist with no smaller than T_l elements. Consider a sublist $P_e[i \cdots j]$ with $|P_e[i \cdots j]| = j - i + 1 \geq T_l$. Let $D[p_i \cdots p_j]$ denote the substring exactly containing tokens $token[p_i], token[p_{i+1}], \cdots, token[p_j]$ (Figure 6). If $|D[p_i \cdots p_j]| = p_j - p_i + 1 > \top_e$, any valid substring containing all tokens in $D[p_i \cdots p_j]$ has larger than $\top_e$ tokens. Thus we can prune $P_e[i \cdots j]$. On the contrary, $D[p_i \cdots p_j]$ may be similar to e if $\bot_e \leq |D[p_i \cdots p_j]| \leq \top_e$. This pruning technique is much power than the mismatch-based pruning, since if $p_j - p_i - (j - i) > \top_e - T_l$, then $p_j - p_i + 1 > \top_e$; on the contrary if $p_j - p_i + 1 > \top_e$, $p_j - p_i - (j - i) > \top_e - T_l$ may not hold. In addition, as $|P_e[i \cdots j]| \leq |D[p_i \cdots p_j]|$, $|P_e[i \cdots j]|$ should be not larger than $\top_e$, thus $T_l \leq |P_e[i \cdots j]| \leq \top_e$.

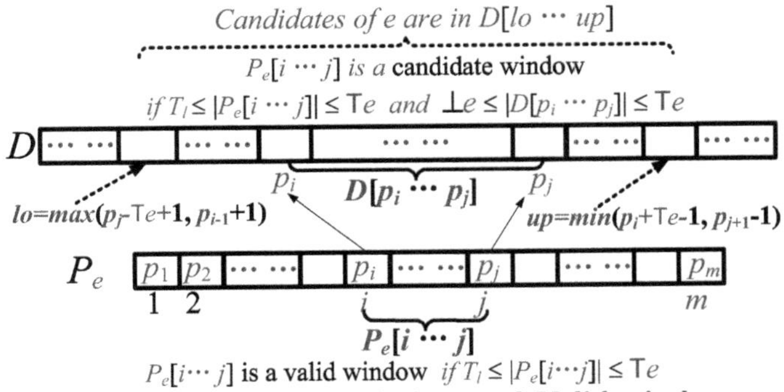

Figure 6: Candidate window and Valid window.

Based on this observation, we can first generate sublists of P_e with sizes (number of elements) between T_l and $\top_e$, i.e., $T_l \leq |P_e[i \cdots j]| \leq \top_e$. Then for each such list $P_e[i \cdots j]$, if $|D[p_i \cdots p_j]| > \top_e$, we prune the sublist; otherwise if $\bot_e \leq |D[p_i \cdots p_j]| \leq \top_e$, we find *candidates* of entity e (a substring s is a candidate of e if $|e \cap s| \geq T$ and $\bot_e \leq |s| \leq \top_e$). For each candidate s of entity e, $\langle s, e \rangle$ is a candidate pair.

Next we discuss how to find candidates of e based on P_e. For ease of presentation, we first introduce two concepts.

DEFINITION 3 (VALID WINDOW AND CANDIDATE WINDOW). *Consider an entity e and its position list $P_e = [p_1 \cdots p_m]$. A sublist $P_e[i \cdots j]$ is called a window of P_e for $1 \leq i \leq j \leq m$. $P_e[i \cdots j]$ is called a valid window, if $T_l \leq |P_e[i \cdots j]| \leq \top_e$. $P_e[i \cdots j]$ is called a candidate window, if $P_e[i \cdots j]$ is a valid window and $\bot_e \leq |D[p_i \cdots p_j]| \leq \top_e$.*

The valid window restricts the length of a window. The candidate window restricts the number of tokens of a valid substring. If a valid substring is a candidate of entity e, it must contain a candidate window (Figure 6). For example, consider the document and entities in Table 1. $P_{e_4} = [10, 17, 33, 34, 43, 58, 59, 60, 61, 66, 71, 76, 81, 86]$. Suppose we use edit distance and $\tau = 2$. $|e_4| = 8$, $T_l = |e_4| - \tau * q = 4$. $\bot_{e_4} = |e_4| - \tau = 6$ and $\top_{e_4} = |e_4| + \tau = 10$. $P_{e_4}[1 \cdots 4] = [10, 17, 33, 34]$, $P_{e_4}[1 \cdots 5] = [10, 17, 33, 34, 43]$, and $P_{e_4}[6 \cdots 9] = [58, 59, 60, 61]$ are three valid windows. $P_{e_4}[1 \cdots 4]$ is not a candidate window as $p_4 - p_1 + 1 = 34 - 10 + 1 > \top_{e_4}$. The reason is that $D[p_1 \cdots p_4]$ contains more than $\top_{e_4}$ tokens and any substring containing $P_{e_4}[1 \cdots 4]$ must have more than $\top_{e_4}$ tokens. Although $p_9 - p_6 + 1 \leq \top_{e_4}$, $P_{e_4}[6 \cdots 9]$ is not a candidate window as $p_9 - p_6 + 1 < \bot_{e_4}$.

Notice that we can optimize the pruning condition for jaccard similarity, cosine similarity, and dice similarity, since they depend on $|e \cap s|$. Given a valid window $P_e[i \cdots j]$, let $s = D[p_i \cdots p_j]$. $|P_e[i \cdots j]| \geq |e \cap s|$[5]. Take jaccard similarity as an example. If s and e are similar, $\frac{|e \cap s|}{|e \cup s|} \geq \delta$. $|D[p_i \cdots p_j]| = |s| \leq |e \cup s| \leq \frac{|e \cap s|}{\delta} \leq \frac{\min(|e|, |P_e[i \cdots j]|)}{\delta}$. Thus we give a tighter bound of $|D[p_i \cdots p_j]|$. For jaccard similarity, $\bot_e \leq |D[p_i \cdots p_j]| \leq \frac{\min(|e|, |P_e[i \cdots j]|)}{\delta}$; for dice similarity,

[5]As $D[p_i \cdots p_j]$ may contain duplicate tokens, $|P_e[i \cdots j]| \geq |e \cap s|$ and $|P_e[i \cdots j]|$ may also be larger than $|e|$.

$\perp_e \leq |D[p_i \cdots p_j]| \leq \min(|e|, |P_e[i,j]|) * \frac{2-\delta}{\delta}$; for cosine similarity, $\perp_e \leq |D[p_i \cdots p_j]| \leq \frac{\min(|e|,|P_e[i \cdots j]|)}{\delta^2}$.

Now we introduce how to find candidates of e from candidate windows $P_e[i \cdots j]$. The substrings that contain all tokens in $D[p_i \cdots p_j]$ may be candidates of e. We can find these substrings as follows. As these substrings must contain $token[p_i]$, the "maximum start position" of such substrings is p_i and the "maximum end position" is $\mathsf{up}{=}p_i + \top_e - 1$. Similarly, as these substrings must contain $token[p_j]$, the "minimum start position" is $\mathsf{lo} = p_j - \top_e + 1$ and the "minimum end position" is p_j. Thus we only need to find candidates among substrings $D[p_{start} \cdots p_{end}]$ where $\mathsf{lo} \leq p_{start} \leq p_i$, $p_j \leq p_{end} \leq \mathsf{up}$. Substring $s = D[p_{start} \cdots p_{end}]$ is a candidate of e if $\perp_e \leq |s| = p_{end} - p_{start} + 1 \leq \top_e$ and $|e \cap s| \geq T$. (Here we use threshold T as $s = D[p_{start} \cdots p_{end}]$ is known.)

However this method may generate duplicate candidates. For example, suppose $p_j - \top_e + 1 < p_{i-1} + 1$. $D[p_{i-1}, \top_e] = D[p_{i-1} \cdots (p_{i-1} + \top_e - 1)]$ could be a candidate generated from $P_e[i \cdots j]$. In this case, as $\perp_e \leq p_j - p_i + 1 \leq p_j - p_{i-1} + 1 \leq \top_e$ and $T_l \leq |P_e[i \cdots j]| \leq |P_e[i-1 \cdots j]| = p_j - p_{i-1} + 1 \leq \top_e$, $P_e[(i-1) \cdots j]$ is also a candidate window. Thus $P_e[(i-1) \cdots j]$ also generates the candidate $D[p_{i-1}, \top_e]$. For $P_e[i \cdots j]$, to avoid generating duplicates with $P_e[i-1 \cdots j]$ and $P_e[i \cdots j+1]$, we will not extend $P_e[i \cdots j]$ to positions smaller than $p_{i-1}+1$ and larger than $p_{j+1} - 1$, and set $\mathsf{lo} = \max(p_j - \top_e + 1, p_{i-1}+1)$, $\mathsf{up} = \min(p_i + \top_e - 1, p_{j+1} - 1)$. In this way, our method will not generate duplicate candidates.

In summary, to find all candidates for an entity, we first get the entity's position list, and then generate the valid windows and candidate windows. Next we identify its candidates from candidate windows. Finally the pair of each candidate and the entity is a candidate pair. The correctness and completeness of our method is formalized as below.

THEOREM 1 (CORRECTNESS AND COMPLEXNESS). *Our method finds the candidate pairs completely and correctly.*

4.2 Finding Candidate Windows Efficiently

Given an entity e, as there are larger numbers of valid windows ($\sum_{l=T_l}^{\top_e} |P_e| - l + 1$), it could be expensive to enumerate the valid windows for finding all candidate windows. To improve the performance, this section proposes efficient methods to find candidate windows.

Span and Shift based method: For ease of presentation, we first introduce a concept "possible candidate windows." A valid window $P_e[i \cdots j]$ is called a *possible candidate window* if $p_j - p_i + 1 \leq \top_e$. Based on this concept, we introduce two operations: span and shift. Given a current valid window $P_e[i \cdots j]$, we use the two operations to generate new valid windows as follows (Figure 7).

- span: If $p_j - p_i + 1 \leq \top_e$, for $k \geq j$, $P_e[i \cdots k]$ may be a possible candidate window. We span it to generate all possible candidate windows starting with i: $P_e[i \cdots (j+1)]$, $\ldots$, $P_e[i \cdots x]$, where x satisfies $p_x - p_i + 1 \leq \top_e$ and $p_{x+1} - p_i + 1 > \top_e$. For $j \leq k \leq x$, if $p_k - p_i + 1 \geq \perp_e$, $P_e[i \cdots k]$ is a candidate window. On the contrary, if $p_j - p_i + 1 > \top_e$, for $k \geq j$, as $p_k - p_i + 1 \geq p_j - p_i + 1 > \top_e$, $P_e[i \cdots k]$ cannot be a candidate window. Thus we do not need to span $P_e[i \cdots j]$.
- shift: We shift to a new valid window $P_e[(i+1) \cdots (j+1)]$.

We use the two operations to find candidate windows as follows. Initially, we get the first valid window $P_e[1 \cdots T_l]$. We do span and shift operations on $P_e[1 \cdots T_l]$. For the new valid windows generated from the span operation, we check whether they are candidate windows; for the new valid window generated from the shift operation, we do span and shift operations on it. Iteratively we can find all candidate windows from $P_e[1 \cdots T_l]$. We give an example to show how our method works. For e_4("`venkatesh`"), $P_{e_4} = [10, 17, 33, 34, 43, 58, 59, 60, 61, 66, 71, 76, 81, 86]$. Suppose $\tau{=}2$. $|e_4| = 8$, $T_l = |e_4| - \tau * q = 4$, $\perp_{e_4} = |e_4| - \tau = 6$, $\top_{e_4} = |e_4| + \tau = 10$. The first valid window is $P_{e_4}[1 \cdots 4] = [10, 17, 33, 34]$. As $p_4 - p_1 + 1 = 34 - 10 + 1 > \top_{e_4}$, we do not need to do span operation. We do a shift operation and get the next window $P_{e_4}[2 \cdots 5]$. As $p_5 - p_2 + 1 = 43 - 17 + 1 > \top_{e_4}$, we do another shift operation. When we shift to valid window $P_{e_4}[6 \cdots 9]$, as $p_9 - p_6 + 1 = 61 - 58 + 1 < \perp_{e_4}$, $P_{e_4}[6 \cdots 9]$ is not a candidate window. We do a span operation. As $p_{10} - p_6 + 1 = 9 \leq \top_{e_4}$ and $p_{11} - p_6 + 1 = 14 > \top_{e_4}$, $x = 10$. We get a valid window $P_{e_4}[6 \cdots 10]$, which is a candidate window. Next we shift to $P_{e_4}[7 \cdots 10]$. Iteratively we find all candidate windows: $P_{e_4}[6 \cdots 10]$ and $P_{e_4}[7 \cdots 10]$ (Figure 8).

Given a valid window $P_e[i \cdots j]$, if $p_j - p_i + 1 > \top_e$, the shift operations can prune the valid windows starting with i, e.g., $P_e[i \cdots k]$ for $j < k \leq i + \top_e - 1$. However this method still scans large numbers of candidate windows. To further improve performance, we propose a binary-search-based method which can skip many more valid windows.

Binary Span and Shift based method: The basic idea is as follows. Given a valid window $P_e[i \cdots j]$, if $p_j - p_i + 1 > \top_e$, we will not shift to $P_e[(i+1) \cdots (j+1)]$. Instead we want to directly shift to the *first possible candidate window* after i, denoted by $P_e[mid \cdots (mid + j - i)]$, where mid satisfies $p_{mid+j-i} - p_{mid} + 1 \leq \top_e$ and for any $i \leq mid' < mid$, $p_{mid'+j-i} - p_{mid'} + 1 > \top_e$. Similarly, if $p_j - p_i + 1 \leq \top_e$, we will not iteratively span it to $P_e[i \cdots (j+1)], P_e[i \cdots (j+2)], \ldots, P_e[i \cdots x]$. Instead, we want to directly span to the *last possible candidate window* starting with i, denoted by $P_e[i \cdots x]$, where x satisfies $p_x - p_i + 1 \leq \top_e$ and for any $x' > x$, $p_{x'} - p_i + 1 > \top_e$.

If the function $F(x) = p_x - p_i + 1$ for span and $F'(mid) = p_{mid+j-i} - p_{mid} + 1$ for shift are monotonic, we can use a binary-search method to find x and mid efficiently.

For the span operation, obviously $F(x) = p_x - p_i + 1$ is monotonic as $F(x+1) - F(x) = p_{x+1} - p_x > 0$. Next we give the lower bound and upper bound of the search range. Obviously $x \geq j$. In addition, as $p_i + j \leq p_{i+j}$, we have $p_x \leq p_i + \top_e - 1 \leq p_{i+\top_e-1}$ and $x \leq i + \top_e - 1$. Thus we find x by doing a binary search between j and $i + \top_e - 1$.

However $F'(mid) = p_{mid+j-i} - p_{mid} + 1$ is not monotonic. We have an observation that $F''(mid) = (p_j + (mid - i)) - p_{mid} + 1$ is monotonic, since $F''(mid-1) - F''(mid) = p_{mid} - p_{mid-1} - 1 \geq 0$. More importantly for $i \leq mid \leq j$, $F''(mid) < F'(mid)$ as $(p_j + (mid - i)) \leq p_{mid+j-i}$. Thus if $F''(mid-1) > \top_e$, $F'(mid-1) > \top_e$ and $P_e[(mid-1) \cdots (mid-1+j-i)]$ cannot be a candidate window. If $F''(mid) \leq \top_e$, $P_e[(mid) \cdots (mid+j-i)]$ could be a candidate window. In this way, we can find mid by doing a binary search between i and j such that $F''(mid-1) > \top_e$ and $F''(mid) \leq \top_e$. If $F'(mid) \leq \top_e$, we have found the last possible candidate window; otherwise, we continue to find mid' between $mid+1$ and $mid+1+j-i$. Iteratively, we can find the last possible candidate window.

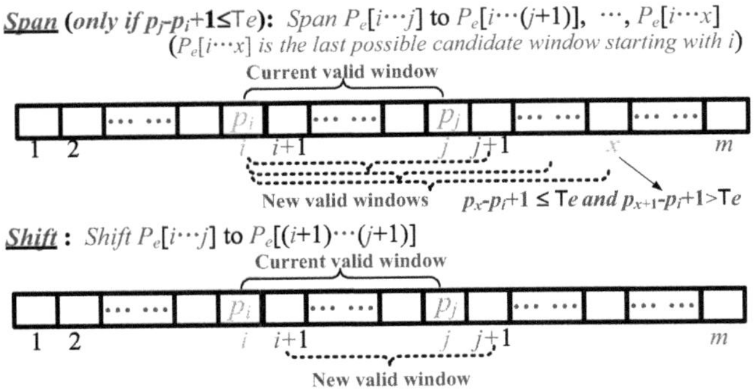

Figure 7: span and shift operations.

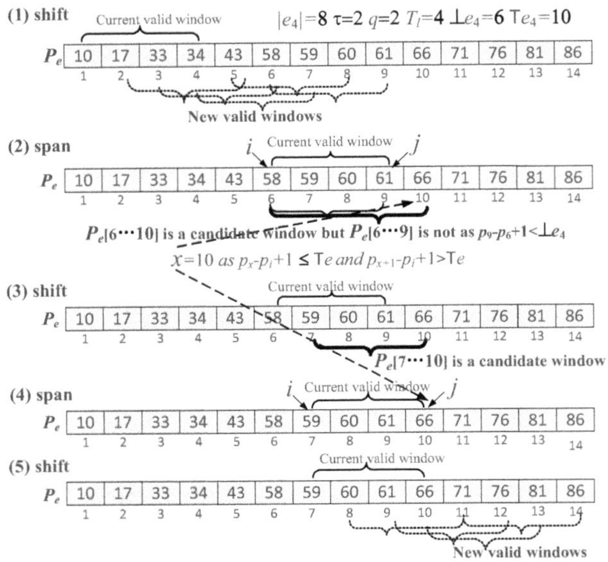

Figure 8: An example for span and shift operations.

Thus given a valid window $P_e[i \cdots j]$, we use binary span and shift operations to find candidate windows (Figure 9).

- Binary span: If $p_j - p_i + 1 \leq \top_e$, we first find x by doing a binary search between j and $i + \top_e - 1$, where x satisfies $p_x - p_i + 1 \leq \top_e$ and $p_{x+1} - p_i + 1 > \top_e$, and then directly span to $P_e[i \cdots x]$.
- Binary shift: If $p_j - p_i + 1 > \top_e$, we find mid by doing a binary search between i and j where mid satisfies $(p_j + (mid - i)) - p_{mid} + 1 \leq \top_e$ and $(p_j + (mid - 1 - i)) - p_{mid-1} + 1 > \top_e$. If $p_{mid+j-i} - p_{mid} + 1 > \top_e$, we iteratively do the binary shift operation between $mid + 1$ and $mid + 1 + j - i$.
  On the contrary, if $p_j - p_i + 1 \leq \top_e$, we shift to a new valid window $P_e[(i+1) \cdots (j+1)]$.

Given a valid window $P_e[i \cdots j]$, the binary shift can skip unnecessary valid windows (non-candidate windows), such as $P_e[(i+1) \cdots (j+1)]$, ..., $P_e[(mid-1) \cdots (mid-1+j-i)]$, as proved in Lemma 4. For example, consider the position list in Figure 10. Suppose $\tau = 2$. $T_l = 4, |e_4| = 8, \top_{e_4} = 10$. Consider the first valid window $P_{e_4}[1 \cdots 4]$. The shift operation shifts it to $P_{e_4}[2 \cdots 5]$, $P_{e_4}[3 \cdots 6]$, $\cdots$, $P_{e_4}[6 \cdots 9]$, and checks whether they are candidate windows. The binary shift operation can directly shift it to $P_{e_4}[3 \cdots 6]$ and then to $P_{e_4}[6 \cdots 9]$. Thus it skips many valid windows.

Lemma 4. *Given a valid window $P_e[i \cdots j]$ with $p_j - p_i + 1 > \top_e$, if $(p_j + (mid - i)) - p_{mid} + 1 \leq \top_e$ and $(p_j + (mid - 1) - i) - p_{mid-1} + 1 > \top_e$, $P_e[(i+1) \cdots (j+1)]$, ..., $P_e[(mid-1) \cdots ((mid-1) + j - i)]$ are not candidate windows.*

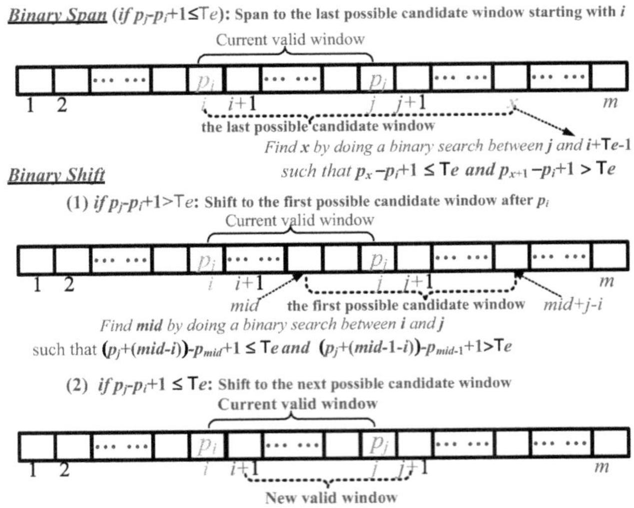

Figure 9: span and shift in a binary-search way.

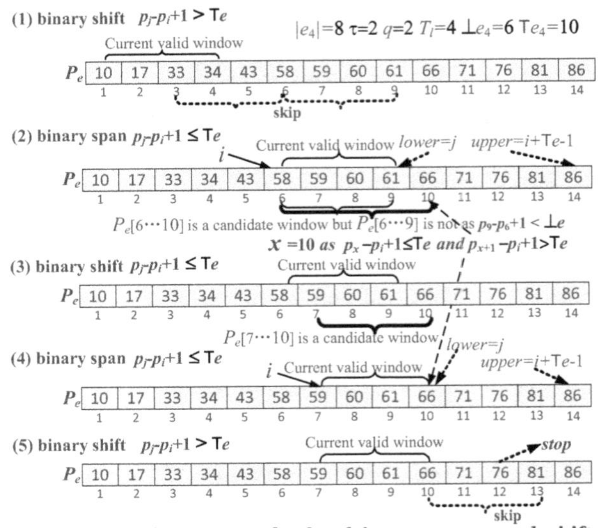

Figure 10: An example for binary span and shift.

The binary span operation can directly span to $P_e[i \cdots x]$ and has two advantages. Firstly, in many applications, users want to identify the best similar pairs (sharing common tokens as many as possible), and the binary span can efficiently find such substrings. Secondly, we do not need to find candidates of e for $P_e[i \cdots (j+1)], \ldots, P_e[i \cdots x]$ one by one. Instead since there may be many candidates between $lo = p_j - \top_e + 1$ and $up = p_{i+x-j} + \top_e - 1$, we find them in a batch manner. We group the candidates based on their token numbers. Entities in the same group have the same number of tokens. Consider the group with g tokens, suppose T_g is the threshold computed using $|e|$ and g. If $|P_e[i \cdots x]| < T_g$, we prune all candidates in the group.

We can use the two binary operations to replace the shift and span operations in order to skip valid windows. We give an algorithm to find candidate windows using the two operations as illustrated in Figure 11. It first initializes the first valid window (line 2-line 4). Then it uses the two binary operations to extend the valid window until reaching the last valid window (line 3). If its token number is no larger than $\top_e$, we do a binary span operation by calling its subroutine BinarySpan (line 6) and do a shift operation (line 7); otherwise calling its subroutine BinaryShift (line 8). BinarySpan does a binary search to find the last possible candidate window starting with p_i (lines 3-6). Then it retrieves the

```
Algorithm 1: Find Candidate Windows
 Input: e: An entity; P_e: Position list of e on the heap;
        T_l: Threshold; ⊤_e: The upper bound of token numbers;
1 begin
2   i = 1;
3   while i ≤ |P_e| − T_l + 1 do
4     j = i + T_l − 1;
5     if p_j − p_i + 1 ≤ ⊤_e then
6       BinarySpan(i, j);
7       i = i + 1; /* shift to the next window */
8     else i = BinaryShift(i, j);
9 end
```

```
Procedure BinarySpan(i, j)
 Input: i: the start point; j: the end point;
1 begin
2   lower = j; upper = i + ⊤_e − 1 ;
3   while lower ≤ upper do
4     mid = ⌈(upper + lower)/2⌉;
5     if p_mid − p_i + 1 > ⊤_e then upper = mid − 1;
6     else lower = mid + 1;
7   mid = upper ;
8   Find candidate windows in D[i ··· mid];
9 end
```

```
Procedure BinaryShift(i, j)
 Input: i: the start point; j: the end point
 Output: i: the new start point;
1 begin
2   lower = i; upper = j;
3   while lower ≤ upper do
4     mid = ⌈(lower + upper)/2⌉;
5     if (p_j + (mid − i)) − p_mid + 1 > ⊤_e then
6       lower = mid + 1;
7     else upper = mid − 1;
8   i = lower; j = i + T_l − 1;
9   if p_j − p_i + 1 > ⊤_e then i = BinaryShift (i, j);
10  else return i;
11 end
```

Figure 11: Algorithm: Find candidate windows

candidate windows (line 8). BinaryShift does a binary search to find the first possible candidate window after p_i. Iteratively our method finds all candidate windows. Figure 10 illustrates an example to walk through our algorithm.

5. THE Faerie ALGORITHM

In this section, we propose a single-heap-based algorithm, called Faerie, to efficiently find all answers.

We first construct an inverted index for all entities in the given dictionary E. Then for the document D, we get its tokens and corresponding inverted lists. Next we construct a single heap on top of inverted lists of tokens. We use the heap to generate entities in ascending order. For each entity e, we get its position list P_e. If $|P_e| < T_l$, we prune e based on lazy-count pruning; otherwise we use the two binary operations to find candidate windows. Then based on the candidate windows, we generate candidate pairs. Finally, we verify the candidate pairs and get the final results. Figure 12 gives the pseudo-code of the Faerie algorithm.

The Faerie algorithm first constructs an inverted index for predefined entities (line 2), and then tokenizes the document, gets inverted lists (line 3), and constructs a heap (line 4). Faerie uses $\langle e_i, p_i \rangle$ to denote the top element of the heap, where e_i is the current minimal entity and p_i is the position of the inverted list from which e_i is selected. Faerie constructs a position list P_e to keep all the positions of inverted lists in the heap that contain e (line 6). Then for each top element $\langle e_i, p_i \rangle$ on the heap, if $e_i = e$, we add p_i

```
Algorithm 2: Faerie Algorithm
 Input: A dictionary of entities E = {e_1, e_2, ..., e_n};
        A document D;
        A similarity function and a threshold;
 Output: {⟨s, e⟩| s and e are similar for the function and
         threshold}, where s is a substring of D and e ∈ E.
1 begin
2   Tokenize entities in E and construct an inverted index;
3   Tokenize D and get inverted lists of tokens in D;
4   Construct a heap H on top of inverted lists of D;
5   e is the top element of H; /* keep the current entity*/
6   Initialize a position list P_e = φ;
7   while (⟨e_i, p_i⟩ = H.top)! = φ do
8     if e_i == e then
9       P_e ∪ = {p_i}; /* e_i is the new top entity. */
10    else
11      Derive the threshold T_l for entity e;
12      if |P_e| ≥ T_l then
13        Find candidate windows using Algorithm 1;
14        Get candidates using candidate windows;
15      e = e_i; P_e = {p_i}; // update the current entity
16    Adjust the heap;
17  Verify candidate pairs;
18 end
```

Figure 12: The Faerie Algorithm.

into P_e (line 8-line 9), where e is the last popped entity from the heap; otherwise Faerie checks the position list as follows. Faerie derives a threshold T_l for entity e based on the similarity function and threshold. If $|P_e| \geq T_l$, there may exist candidate pairs. Faerie generates candidate windows based on Algorithm 1 (line 13), and finds candidate pairs based on candidate windows (line 14). Faerie adjusts the heap to generate candidates for the next entity (line 16). Finally Faerie verifies the candidates to get final results (line 17).

Next we give a running example to walk through our algorithm. Consider the entities and document in Table 1. We fist construct a single min-heap (Figure 5). Then we adjust the heap to generate the position list for each entity. Consider the position list for entity e_4 ("**venkatesh**") in Figure 10. Suppose $\tau = 2$. $|e_4| = 8$, $\perp_E = 6$, $\top_E = 12$, $\perp_{e_4} = 6$, $\top_{e_4} = 10$, $T_l = 4$. We use the binary shift and span operations to get candidate windows ($P_e[6 \cdots 10]$ and $P_e[7 \cdots 10]$), and then generate candidate pairs based on the candidate windows (e.g., $\langle D[58, 9]$="*venkaee sh*", e_4="**venkatesh**"$\rangle$). Finally we verify the candidates to get the final answers.

6. EXPERIMENTS

We have implemented our proposed techniques. The objective of the experiments is to measure the performance, and in this section we report experimental results.

Experimental Setting: We compared our algorithms with state-of-the-art methods NGPP [22] (the best for edit distance) and ISH [4] (the best for jaccard similarity and edit similarity). We downloaded the binary codes of NGPP [22] from "Similarity Joins" project website[6] and implemented ISH by ourselves. We reported the best performance of the two existing methods. The algorithms were implemented in C++ and compiled using GCC 4.2.4 with -O3 flag. All the experiments were run on a Ubuntu machine with an Intel Core 2 Quad X5450 3.0GHz processor and 4 GB memory.

Datasets: We used three real datasets, DBLP[7], PubMed[8], and ACM WebPage[9]. DBLP is a computer-science publi-

[6] http://www.cse.unsw.edu.au/~weiw/project/simjoin.html
[7] http://www.informatik.uni-trier.de/~ley/db
[8] http://www.ncbi.nlm.nih.gov/pubmed
[9] http://portal.acm.org

cation dataset. We selected 100,000 author names as entities and 10,000 papers as documents. PubMed is a medical-publication dataset. We selected 100,000 paper titles as entities and 10,000 publication records as documents. WebPage is a set of web pages. We crawled 100,000 titles as entities and 1,000 web pages as documents (thousands of tokens). Table 4 gives the dataset statistics (len denotes the average length and token denotes the average token number). We did not consider different attributes in the entities and documents. Each entity in the dictionary is just a string.

Table 4: Datasets.

Datasets	Cardinality	len	tokens	Details
DBLP Dict	100,000	21.1	2.77	Author
DBLP Docs	10,000	123.3	16.99	Papers
PubMed Dict	100,000	52.96	6.98	Title
PubMed Docs	10,000	235.8	33.6	Papers
WebPage Dict	100,000	66.89	8.5	Title
WebPage Docs	1,000	8949	1268	Web Pages

6.1 Multi-Heap vs Single Heap

In this section, we compared the multi-heap-based method with the single-heap-based method (without using pruning techniques in Section 4). We tested the performance of the two methods for different similarity functions on the three datasets. Figure 13 shows the experimental results.

We see that the single-heap-based method outperforms the multi-heap-based method by 1-2 orders of magnitude, and even 3 orders of magnitude in some cases. For example, on DBLP dataset with edit-distance threshold $\tau = 3$, the multi-heap-based method took more than 10,000 seconds and the single-heap-based method took about 180 seconds. On PubMed dataset with EDS similarity threshold $\delta = 0.9$, the multi-heap-based method took more than 14,000 seconds and the single-heap-based method took only 600 seconds. There are two reasons that the single-heap-based method is better than the multi-heap-based method. Firstly, the multi-heap-based method scans each inverted list of the document many times and the single-heap-based method only scans them once. Secondly the multi-heap-based method constructs larger numbers of heaps and does larger numbers of heap adjustment than the single-heap-based method. As the single-heap-based method outperforms the multi-heap-based method, we focus on the single-heap-based method in the remainder of the experimental comparison.

6.2 Effectiveness of Pruning Techniques

In this section, we tested the effectiveness of our pruning techniques. We first evaluated the number of candidates by applying different pruning techniques to our algorithm (lazy-count pruning, bucket-count pruning, and binary span and shift pruning. As batch-count pruning is a special case of binary span and shift pruning, we only show the results for binary span and shift pruning.). In the paper, the number of candidates refers to the number of non-zero values in the occurrence arrays, which need to be verified. Figure 14 gives the results. In the figure, we tested edit distance on DBLP dataset, jaccard similarity on WebPage dataset, and edit similarity on PubMed dataset. Note that in the figures, the results are in 10^x formate. For example if there are 100 million candidates, the number in the figure is 8 ($10^8 = 100M$). In the paper, our method used parameters of $q = 16, 8, 5, 4, 3$ for $\tau = 0, 1, 2, 3, 4$ respectively for edit distance on DBLP and $q = 26, 11, 7, 5, 4$ for $\delta = 1, 0.95, 0.9, 0.85, 0.8$ edit similarity on PubMed.

We observe that our proposed pruning techniques can prune large numbers of candidates. For example, on the DBLP dataset, for $\tau = 3$, the method without any pruning techniques involved 11 billion candidates, and the lazy-count pruning reduced the number to 860 million. The bucket-count pruning further reduced the number to 600 million. The binary span and shift pruning had only 200 million candidates. On the WebPage dataset, for $\delta = 0.9$, the binary span and shift pruning reduced the number of candidates from 10 billion to 35. On the PubMed dataset, for $\delta = 0.85$, the binary span and shift pruning reduced the number of candidates from 180 billion to 120 million. The main reason is that we compute an upper bound of the overlap of an entity and a substring, and if the bound is smaller than the overlap threshold, we prune the substring. If for any substring, the bound of an entity is smaller than the threshold, we prune the entity. This confirms the superiority of our pruning techniques.

Then we evaluated the performance benefit of the pruning techniques. Figure 15 shows the results. We observe that the pruning techniques can improve the performance. For instance, on the DBLP dataset, for $\tau = 3$, the elapsed time of the method without any pruning technique was 180 seconds, and the lazy-count pruning decreased the time to 43 seconds. The binary span and shift pruning reduced the time to 25 second. On PubMed dataset, for $\delta = 0.9$, the pruning techniques can improve the time from 600 seconds to 8 seconds. This shows that our pruning techniques can improve the performance. In the remainder of this paper, we compared the single-heap-based method using the binary span and shift pruning with existing methods.

6.3 Comparison with State-of-the-art Methods

In this section, we compared our algorithm Faerie with state-of-the-art methods NGPP [22] (which only supports edit distance) and ISH [4] (which supports edit similarity and jaccard similarity). We tuned the parameters of NGPP and ISH (e.g., prefix length of NGPP) to make them achieve the best performance. Figure 16 shows the results. We see that Faerie achieved the highest performance. Especially Faerie outperformed ISH by 1-2 orders of magnitude for edit similarity and jaccard similarity. For example, on the PubMed with edit-similarity threshold $\delta = 0.9$, the elapsed time of ISH was 1000 seconds. Faerie reduced the time to 8 seconds. This is because Faerie used the shared computation across overlapped tokens. In addition, our pruning techniques can prune large numbers of unnecessary valid substrings and reduce the number of candidates. Although NGPP achieved high performance for smaller edit-distance thresholds, it is inefficient for larger edit-distance thresholds. The reason is that it needs to enumerate neighbors of entities and an entity has larger numbers of neighbors for larger thresholds. On jaccard similarity, as each entity has a smaller number of tokens (the average number is 8) and the thresholds T_l and $\top_e$ for different thresholds are nearly the same ($T_l = 8$ for δ=1 and $T_l = 10$ for δ=0.8), Faerie varied a little for different jaccard-similarity thresholds.

In addition, we compared index sizes of difference algorithms. Note that NGPP had different index sizes for different edit-distance threshold τ, as NGPP uses τ to generate neighborhoods. The larger the edit-distance threshold, the larger indexes are involved for the neighborhoods of an entity, since an entity has larger numbers of neighbors for larger thresholds. On DBLP dataset, for $\tau = 3$, NGPP con-

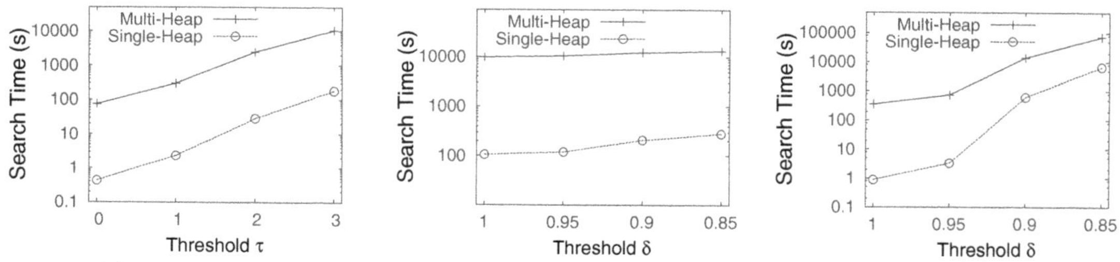

(a) ED (DBLP) (b) JAC (WebPage) (c) EDS (PubMed)

Figure 13: Performance comparison of multi-heap-based methods and single-heap-based methods.

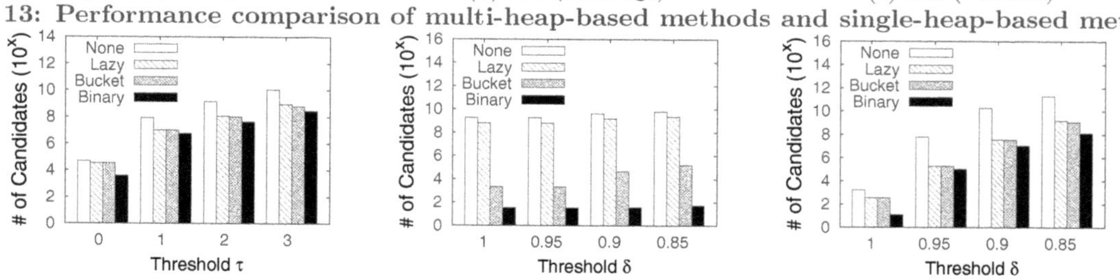

(a) ED (DBLP) (b) JAC (WebPage) (c) EDS (PubMed)

Figure 14: Number of candidates with different pruning techniques.

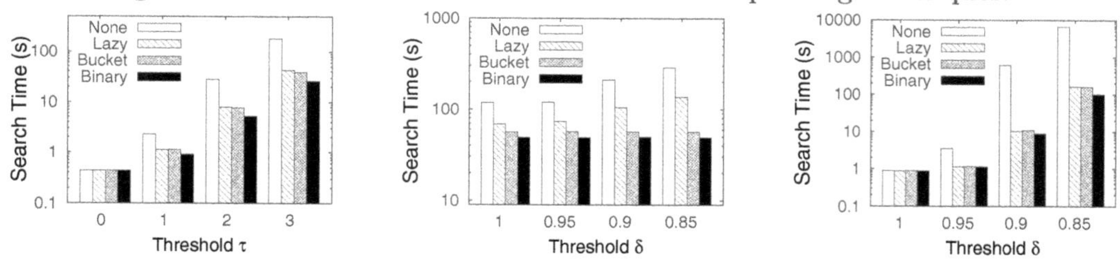

(a) ED (DBLP) (b) JAC (WebPage) (c) EDS (PubMed)

Figure 15: Performance comparison with different pruning techniques.

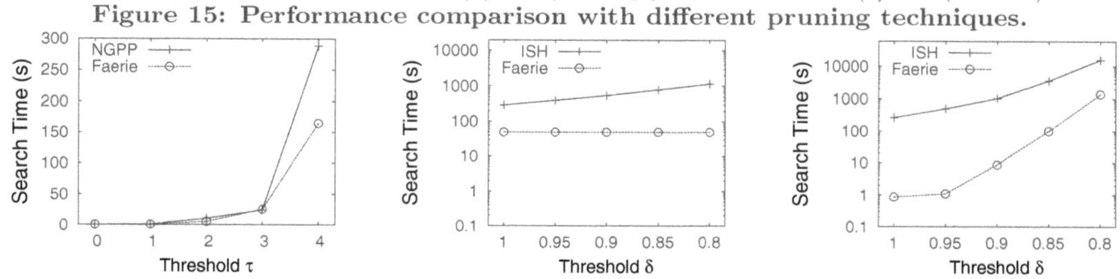

(a) ED (DBLP) (b) JAC (WebPage) (c) EDS (PubMed)

Figure 16: Comparison with existing methods.

sumed about 43 MB index size. The index size of Faerie was only 7 MB ($q = 4$). This result consists with that in [22]: the q-gram-based method has smaller index sizes than the neighborhood-based method (NGPP). On WebPage, ISH involved about 18 MB index size for jaccard-similarity threshold $\delta = 0.9$ (its parameter $k = 3$) and Faerie only used 4 MB.

6.4 Scalability with Dictionary Sizes

This section evaluates the scalability of our proposed method on various similarity functions. We varied the number of entities in the dictionary and identified similar pairs from the document collection in Table 4. Figure 17 shows the results for the five similarity functions. We observe that our method scaled well as the dictionary size increased. For example, on DBLP, for $\tau = 3$, Faerie took 6 seconds for 20, 000 entities and 25 seconds for 100, 000 entities. On WebPage, as each entity has a smaller number of tokens, Faerie varied a little for different thresholds. On PubMed, we evaluated edit similarity, dice similarity, cosine similarity, using q-grams. For edit similarity, when $\delta = 0.85$, Faerie took 9 seconds for 20, 000 entities and 48 seconds for 100, 000 entities.

In addition, we also evaluated the index sizes as the dictionary size increased. Table 5 shows the results. We see that the index sizes of our method were very small and scaled well as the number of entities increased.

Table 5: Scalability of index sizes.

(a) DBLP ($q = 5$)

# of Entities	20k	40k	60k	80k	100k
Inverted Index (MB)	1.6	3.22	4.9	6.5	8.2
Heap+Array (KB)	4.5	4.5	4.5	4.5	4.5

(b) WebPage

# of Entities	20k	40k	60k	80k	100k
Inverted Index (MB)	0.8	1.63	2.45	3.3	4.2
Heap+Array (KB)	38	38	38	38	38

(c) PubMed ($q = 7$)

# of Entities	20k	40k	60k	80k	100k
Inverted Index (MB)	4.5	9.2	14.1	18.3	22.8
Heap+Array (KB)	7.2	7.2	7.2	7.2	7.2

7. RELATED WORKS

There have been some recent studies on approximate entity extraction [22, 9, 20, 1, 4, 5]. Wang et al. [22] proposed neighborhood-generation-based methods for approximate entity extraction with edit-distance thresholds. They

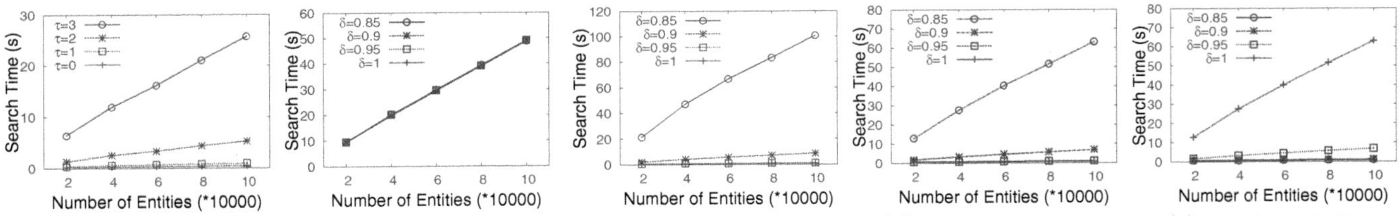

(a) ED (DBLP) (b) JAC (WebPage) (c) EDS (PubMed) (d) DICE (PubMed) (e) COS (PubMed)

Figure 17: Scalability of performance for various similarity functions on different datasets.

first partition strings into different partitions, and guarantee that two strings are similar only if there exist two partitions of the two strings, which have an edit distance no larger than 1. Then they generate neighborhoods of each partition by deleting one character from the partitions, and the edit distance between two partitions is not larger than 1 only if they have a common neighbor. However this method cannot support the token-based similarity. Chakrabarti et al. [4] proposed an inverted signature-based hash-table for membership checking. They first selected top-weighted tokens as signatures and encoded the dictionary as a 0-1 matrix. Then they built a matrix for the document and used the matrix to find candidates. Lu et al. [20] proposed signature-based inverted lists to improve [4] by using a tighter threshold. However this method cannot support edit distance. In addition, Agrawal et al. [1] proposed to use inverted lists for ad-hoc entity extraction. Chandel et al. [5] studied the problem of batch top-k search for dictionary-based exact entity recognition. Chaudhuri et al. [9] proposed to expand a reference dictionary of entities by mining large document collections.

Many studies have been proposed to address the approximate-string-search problem [4, 14, 2, 8, 6, 11, 18, 19, 15, 25, 12] and the similarity-join problem [10, 2, 3, 7, 21, 23, 24]. Although we can extend them to solve our problem, they are very inefficient, since they need to enumerate all valid substrings in the document and cannot use the shared computation across overlaps of substrings. Existing works (NGPP[22] and ISH[4]) have proved that the extraction-based methods outperform similarity-join-based methods for the approximate entity-extraction problem, and thus we only compare with state-of-the-art methods NGPP[22] and ISH[4].

In addition, there have been many studies on estimating selectivity for approximate string queries [13, 16, 17].

8. CONCLUSION

In this paper, we have studied the problem of approximate entity extraction. We proposed a unified framework to support various similarity functions. We devised heap-based filtering algorithms to efficiently extract similar entities from a document. We developed a single-heap-based algorithm which can utilize the shared computation across overlaps of substrings by constructing a single heap on top of inverted lists of tokens in the document and scanning every inverted list only once. We proposed several pruning techniques to prune large numbers of unnecessary candidate pairs. We devised binary-search-based techniques to improve the performance. We have implemented our method, and tested our method on several real datasets. The experimental results show that our method achieves high performance and outperforms state-of-the-art studies.

Acknowledgement

The authors thank Professor Wei Wang, Professor Chen Li, and the three anonymous reviewers for their comments and suggestions that definitely help us improve the paper.

9. REFERENCES

[1] S. Agrawal, K. Chakrabarti, S. Chaudhuri, and V. Ganti. Scalable ad-hoc entity extraction from text collections. *PVLDB*, 1(1):945–957, 2008.

[2] A. Arasu, V. Ganti, and R. Kaushik. Efficient exact set-similarity joins. In *VLDB*, pages 918–929, 2006.

[3] R. J. Bayardo, Y. Ma, and R. Srikant. Scaling up all pairs similarity search. In *WWW*, pages 131–140, 2007.

[4] K. Chakrabarti, S. Chaudhuri, V. Ganti, and D. Xin. An efficient filter for approximate membership checking. In *SIGMOD Conference*, pages 805–818, 2008.

[5] A. Chandel, P. C. Nagesh, and S. Sarawagi. Efficient batch top-k search for dictionary-based entity recognition. In *ICDE*, page 28, 2006.

[6] S. Chaudhuri, K. Ganjam, V. Ganti, and R. Motwani. Robust and efficient fuzzy match for online data cleaning. In *SIGMOD Conference*, pages 313–324, 2003.

[7] S. Chaudhuri, V. Ganti, and R. Kaushik. A primitive operator for similarity joins in data cleaning. In *ICDE*, pages 5–16, 2006.

[8] S. Chaudhuri, V. Ganti, and R. Motwani. Robust identification of fuzzy duplicates. In *ICDE*, pages 865–876, 2005.

[9] S. Chaudhuri, V. Ganti, and D. Xin. Mining document collections to facilitate accurate approximate entity matching. *PVLDB*, 2(1):395–406, 2009.

[10] L. Gravano, P. G. Ipeirotis, H. V. Jagadish, N. Koudas, S. Muthukrishnan, and D. Srivastava. Approximate string joins in a database (almost) for free. In *VLDB*, pages 491–500, 2001.

[11] M. Hadjieleftheriou, A. Chandel, N. Koudas, and D. Srivastava. Fast indexes and algorithms for set similarity selection queries. In *ICDE*, pages 267–276, 2008.

[12] M. Hadjieleftheriou, N. Koudas, and D. Srivastava. Incremental maintenance of length normalized indexes for approximate string matching. In *SIGMOD Conference*, pages 429–440, 2009.

[13] M. Hadjieleftheriou, X. Yu, N. Koudas, and D. Srivastava. Hashed samples: selectivity estimators for set similarity selection queries. *PVLDB*, 1(1):201–212, 2008.

[14] M.-S. Kim, K.-Y. Whang, J.-G. Lee, and M.-J. Lee. n-gram/2l: A space and time efficient two-level n-gram inverted index structure. In *VLDB*, pages 325–336, 2005.

[15] N. Koudas, C. Li, A. K. H. Tung, and R. Vernica. Relaxing join and selection queries. In *VLDB*, pages 199–210, 2006.

[16] H. Lee, R. T. Ng, and K. Shim. Extending q-grams to estimate selectivity of string matching with low edit distance. In *VLDB*, pages 195–206, 2007.

[17] H. Lee, R. T. Ng, and K. Shim. Power-law based estimation of set similarity join size. *PVLDB*, 2(1):658–669, 2009.

[18] C. Li, J. Lu, and Y. Lu. Efficient merging and filtering algorithms for approximate string searches. In *ICDE*, pages 257–266, 2008.

[19] C. Li, B. Wang, and X. Yang. Vgram: Improving performance of approximate queries on string collections using variable-length grams. In *VLDB*, pages 303–314, 2007.

[20] J. Lu, J. Han, and X. Meng. Efficient algorithms for approximate member extraction using signature-based inverted lists. In *CIKM*, pages 315–324, 2009.

[21] S. Sarawagi and A. Kirpal. Efficient set joins on similarity predicates. In *SIGMOD Conference*, pages 743–754, 2004.

[22] W. Wang, C. Xiao, X. Lin, and C. Zhang. Efficient approximate entity extraction with edit distance constraints. In *SIGMOD Conference*, 2009.

[23] C. Xiao, W. Wang, and X. Lin. Ed-join: an efficient algorithm for similarity joins with edit distance constraints. *PVLDB*, 1(1):933–944, 2008.

[24] C. Xiao, W. Wang, X. Lin, and H. Shang. Top-k set similarity joins. In *ICDE*, pages 916–927, 2009.

[25] C. Xiao, W. Wang, X. Lin, and J. X. Yu. Efficient similarity joins for near duplicate detection. In *WWW*, 2008.

Joint Unsupervised Structure Discovery and Information Extraction

Eli Cortez[1] Daniel Oliveira[1] Altigran S. da Silva[1]

Edleno S. de Moura[1] Alberto H. F. Laender[2]

[1]Departamento de Ciência da Computação
Universidade Federal do Amazonas
Manaus, AM, Brazil
{eccv,dpo,alti,edleno}@dcc.ufam.edu.br

[2]Departamento de Ciência da Computação
Universidade Federal de Minas Gerais
Belo Horizonte - MG - Brazil
laender@dcc.ufmg.br

ABSTRACT

In this paper we present JUDIE (Joint Unsupervised Structure Discovery and Information Extraction), a new method for automatically extracting semi-structured data records in the form of continuous text (e.g., bibliographic citations, postal addresses, classified ads, etc.) and having no explicit delimiters between them. While in state-of-the-art Information Extraction methods the structure of the data records is manually supplied the by user as a training step, JUDIE is capable of detecting the structure of each individual record being extracted without any user assistance. This is accomplished by a novel Structure Discovery algorithm that, given a sequence of labels representing attributes assigned to potential values, groups these labels into individual records by looking for frequent patterns of label repetitions among the given sequence. We also show how to integrate this algorithm in the information extraction process by means of successive refinement steps that alternate information extraction and structure discovery. Through an extensively experimental evaluation with different datasets in distinct domains, we compare JUDIE with state-of-the-art information extraction methods and conclude that, even without any user intervention, it is able to achieve high quality results on the tasks of discovering the structure of the records and extracting information from them.

Categories and Subject Descriptors

H.2 [**Database Management**]: Miscellaneous

General Terms

Algorithms, Performance, Experimentation

Keywords

Data Management, Information Extraction, Text Segmentation

SIGMOD'11, June 12–16, 2011, Athens, Greece.

1. INTRODUCTION

Information Extraction by Text Segmentation (IETS) is a widely applied technique to extract attribute values occurring in implicit semistructured data records in the form of continuous text, such as product descriptions, bibliographic citations, postal addresses, classified ads, etc. Current IETS methods rely on probabilistic graph-based models [10, 17] in which nodes (states) represent attributes and edges (transitions) represent the likely structures of the data records. When properly trained, such models are able to accurately predict a sequence of labels to be assigned to a sequence of text segments corresponding to attribute values.

The learning process thus consists in capturing content-related (or state) features, which characterize the domain of the attributes (e.g., typical values, terms composing them, their format, etc.), and structure-related (or transition) features (e.g., the positioning and sequencing of attribute values, etc.), which characterize the structure of the records within the source text. In recent years, the effort for training such models has been drastically reduced [1, 5, 14] or even eliminated [8]. This is mostly due to the use of pre-existing data sources such as reference tables, knowledge bases, etc., from which content-related features can be automatically learned. These features are, thus, source-independent. Structure-related features, however, are source-dependent. In most cases, they can be learned from user-provided training [1, 14] or can be automatically induced from the input texts in an on-demand way [8].

An important limitation in all previous IETS methods proposed in the literature is that they rely on the user to implicitly provide the likely structures of the records found on the source. This is true even for the most recent methods that apply some form of unsupervised learning [1, 5, 8, 14]. In most cases, the information on the likely structures is provided in the training phase, through sample records labeled by a user [1, 14]. The generated model is then able to extract information from one record at a time, what requires the user to separate each individual record prior to providing them as input for the extraction process. In other cases [5, 8], although the structure-related features can be automatically learned from the unlabeled input records, i.e., no explicit training is required, these records must still be provided one by one.

This requirement implies into several shortcomings for situations in which many implicit records are available in a single textual document (e.g., a list of references in a research article, or products in an inventory list) or a user is not available for separating the records (e.g., an extractor coupled with a crawler or when processing a stream of documents). Although straightforward methods could be applied to simple cases in which the set of attributes is fixed for all records, dealing with semi-structured records such as heterogeneous bibliographic references, classified adds, etc., is much more complex. In the case of HTML pages, sometimes it is possible to automatically identify record boundaries and, thus, separate records by using heuristics based on the tags and paths inside the page [6,7]. However, this is not the most common scenario on the Web and other on-line sources of textual documents, such as social networks or RSS messages.

1/2 cup butter 2 eggs 4 cups white sugar 1/2 cup milk 1 1/2 cups applesauce 2 tablespoons dark rum 2 cups all-purpose flour 1/4 cup cocoa powder 2 teaspoons baking soda ground cinnamon 1/8 teaspoon salt 1 cup raisins 6 chopped pecans 1/4 cup dark rum

Quantity	*Unit*	*Ingredient*
1/2	*cup*	*butter*
2		*eggs*
4	*cups*	*white sugar*
1/2	*cup*	*milk*
1 1/2	*cups*	*applesauce*
2	*tablespoons*	*dark rum*
2	*cups*	*all-purpose flour*
1/4	*cup*	*cocoa powder*
2	*teaspoons*	*baking soda*
		ground cinnamon
1/8	*teaspoon*	*salt*
1	*cup*	*raisins*
6		*chopped pecans*
1/4	*cup*	*dark rum*

Figure 1: Chocolate Cake recipe (top) and structured data extracted from it (bottom).

As an example, consider the Chocolate Cake recipe available in a pure text message illustrated in Figure 1. To provide a proper input to current IETS methods, a user would have to scan the message and manually separate each record containing the specification of an ingredient in the recipe. Notice the cases in which attributes "Quantity" and "Unit" are missing in the input message. Automatically processing several of such messages with current IETS methods is unfeasible, even if they come from the same source.

In this paper we present JUDIE (Joint Unsupervised structure Discovery and Information Extraction), a new method for IETS that addresses the problem of automatically extracting several implicit records and their attribute values from a single text input. Unlike previous methods in the literature, ours is capable of detecting the structure of each individual record being extracted without any user intervention. The table in Figure 1 illustrates the output of our method when the text on the top is given as input.

To uncover the structure of the input records, we use a novel algorithm that, given a sequence of labels representing attribute values, groups these labels into individual records by looking for frequent patterns of label repetitions, or *cycles*, among the given sequence. The *Structure Discover (SD)* algorithm is, thus, our first contribution in this paper.

Our second contribution is the way we integrate this algorithm in the information extraction process. This is accomplished by successive refinement steps that alternate information extraction and structure discovery. Following, we briefly describe how our method executes this process.

Given an input text with a set of implicit data records in textual format, such as the one illustrated in Figure 1, the first step of our method performs an initial labeling of the candidate values identified in this input with attribute names. As at this point there is no information on the structure of the data records, we resort only to content-related features for this labeling. Thus, this step, called *Structure-free Labeling*, generates a sequence of labels in which some candidate values may be missing or have received a wrong label. Despite being imprecise, this sequence of labels is accurate enough to allow the generation of an approximate description of the structure of the records in the input text (as demonstrated in our experiments). This is accomplished in the second step of our method, called *Structure Sketching*, by using the SD algorithm. The output of this step is a set of labeled values grouped into records that already bear a structure close to the correct one. Thus, from these records it is possible to learn structure-related source-dependent features. These features can now be used to revise the *Structure-free Labeling* from the first step. This *Structure-aware Labeling* is the third step of our method. As demonstrated by our experiments, the results produced by this step are more precise than those obtained by the *Structure-free Labeling*, since now content-related and structure-related features are taken into consideration. Our method then takes advantage of this more precise sequence of labels to revise the structure of the records. This new sequence is given as input to the SD algorithm. This is the fourth and final step of our method. It is called *Structure Refinement*. We notice that all of these steps are completely unsupervised.

The remainder of this paper is organized as follows. Section 2 discusses related work. Section 3 describes our method, while Section 4 focuses on the features used by our method. Section 5 presents a detailed description of the Structure Discovery algorithm. Section 6 reports the results of an empirical evaluation we have performed with several sources and different domains. Finally, Section 7 presents conclusions and discusses future work.

2. RELATED WORK

Since the pioneering work of Soderland [19], the problem of extracting information from textual inputs containing implicit data records has received considerable attention in the literature. This problem is also known as *Information Extraction by Text Segmentation (IETS)* and the most successful methods that deal with it rely on machine learning techniques. In general, these methods are supervised [10,12,13,16], in the sense they require hand-labeled examples (training data) that are provided by an expert user. In order to alleviate this need, unsupervised methods have been proposed, for which training data is created from pre-existing data sources [1,5,8,14].

However, existing IETS methods do not address the problem of automatically discovering the structure of implicit records. Usually, they consider that such structure is either inferred from given examples or provided in advance by the user. In this sense, JUDIE is a novel approach to automatically extracting several implicit records and their attribute values from a single text input, since it performs the extraction process while dealing with text inputs containing data records with different structures. This task is not accomplished by any previously mentioned method. For instance, ONDUX [8] and U-CRF [5] require direct user intervention to delimit each record within the text input as well as to define the structure of the records to be extracted. It is important to stress that the record structure plays a very important role in this context, since both U-CRF and ONDUX rely on structural features (positioning and sequencing) to perform the extraction task.

The task of structure discovery was studied earlier in the literature. For example, in [6] and [7], the authors propose methods to automatically find the structure of data records available in HTML pages. Notice that our context and the input texts we deal with are different from those treated by such methods. In our scenario, we do not rely on the existence of HTML tags and record delimiters, but only on the actual text that contains attribute values that might compose a record. This provides more flexibility and robustness to our method, since HTML markup is not always available and, even when it is available, there is no guarantee that it is consistently used, which is an important requirement for those methods. This is particularly true on today's Web in which the extensive use of automatic layout generators and style-sheets may result in HTML structures that are hard to handle automatically.

Indeed, the development of unsupervised methods for information extraction is motivated by the increasing number of textual documents that are made available on the Web, not only in HTML format, but also as plain text. Thus, new information extraction methods should not only work at Web scale, but also be free, or at least highly independent, from any user assistance [4]. We believe that our method, JUDIE, is a step towards fulfilling these requirements, since it does not require any specific information from the user, neither to help discovering the structure of the target records, nor to extract any piece of information included in the input text.

3. METHOD DESCRIPTION

In this section, we present our method by describing the main four steps that comprise it. For that, we use a running example illustrated in Figures 2(a) to (f). We consider that the unstructured sequence of tokens corresponding to a list of items of a chocolate cake recipe, shown in Figure 2(a), is given as input. Our method then carries out the task of simultaneously extracting the components of each item, i.e., Quantity (**Q**), Unity (**U**) and Ingredient (**I**), and structuring them into records. The final output is illustrated in Figure 2(f). The four steps that comprise our method are described next.

3.1 Structure-free Labeling

Given an unstructured input text containing a set of implicit data records in textual format, such as the one illustrated in Figure 2(a), the first step of our method consists of initially labeling potential values identified in this input with attribute names. As at this point there is no information on the structure of the data records, we resort only to content-related features for this labeling. Thus, we call this step *Structure-free Labeling*.

All content-related features we use can be computed from a preexisting dataset. Consider an attribute A and let v_A be a set of typical values for this attribute. Then, for any segment of tokens $x_i, \ldots, x_j$ from the input text, we can compute the value of a feature function $g^k(x_i, \ldots, x_j, A)$. Intuitively, g^k returns a real number that measures how well a hypothetical value formed by tokens in the text segment $x_i, \ldots, x_j$ follows some property of the values in the domain of A [17]. Obviously, the accuracy of such functions often depends on how representative v_A is with respect to the values in the domain of A.

A very important aspect we exploit in our method is that it is possible to compute g^k for a segment of tokens $x_i, \ldots, x_j$ independently of the input text in which it occurs. Thus, we say that g^k is *domain-dependent*, meaning that it is *source-independent*. Using domain-dependent features is a common trend in recent work on information extraction. While in most cases they are used only with textual attributes for computing string similarity [1,3,5,14] or vocabulary affinity [8], here we investigate other possibilities.

In Section 4.1 we present the details of the content-related features we use in our method. In the following, we describe how these features are used to process the structure-free labeling.

From now on, we assume that all datasets are representative of their attributes for the purpose of computing the features we use. Also, for a given extraction task that involves attributes $A_1, \ldots, A_n$, we say that datasets $v_{A_1}, \ldots, v_{A_n}$ form a knowledge base KB. Given a data source on a certain domain that includes values associated with attributes, building such a knowledge base is a simple process that consists in creating attribute-value pairs. Examples of such data sources are relations, reference tables, ontologies, etc.

Processing the Structure-free Labeling

The targets of the structure-free labeling are sequences of tokens in the input text that are likely to represent attribute values. We call them *candidate values* and they are defined as follows.

Let $I = t_1, t_2, \ldots, t_n$ be the set of tokens occurring in an input text, such that no token contains white space. Consider a knowledge base KB representing attributes $A_1, \ldots, A_m$. A *likely value* in I is the largest sequence of tokens $s = t_i, t_{i+1}, \ldots, t_{i+k}$ ($1 \leq i \leq n, k \geq 0$) from I that occurs as a value, or part of a value, of some attribute A_j. In the input text I, all likely values and all individual tokens that do not belong to any likely values are called *candidate values*.

Figure 2(b) illustrates the candidate values found in the input text of Figure 2(a). Notice that candidate values such as "raising flour" and "Melted butter" can only be likely values. In the knowledge base we use in our experiments for the Cooking Recipes domain, values such as "Milk" and "Salt" are represented. Thus, the corresponding candidate values, in spite of being formed by a single token, are also likely values. On the other hand, "Tbsp" is not present in that knowledge base. Thus, it is an isolated token taken as a candidate value.

Given a candidate value s, the decision on what label must be assigned to it takes into account different domain-dependent features g^k evaluated by feature functions of the form $g^k(s, A)$. To combine these features, we assume that they represent the probability of the candidate value s to occur as a value of the attribute A domain, according to KB. If we assume that these features exploit different properties of the attribute A domain, we can say they are independent, what allows us to combine them by means of the Bayesian disjunctive operator or, also known as *Noisy-OR-Gate* [15], which is defined as:

$$or(p_1, \ldots, p_n) = 1 - ((1 - p_1) \times \ldots \times (1 - p_n))$$

where each p_i is a probability.

Thus, our final equation is:

$$\ell(s, A) = 1 - \left((1 - g^1(s, A)) \times \ldots \times (1 - g^n(s, A))\right) \quad (1)$$

Informally, by using the disjunctive operator we assume that any of the features is likely to determine the labeling (i.e., significantly increase its final probability), regardless of other factors [15]. By doing so, we avoid having to fine-tune relative weights for individual factors. As we shall see, this hypothesis is confirmed in our experiments.

Function $\ell(s, A)$ is computed for each candidate value s in the input text for all attributes A of the same data type (i.e., text or numeric). Thus, s is labeled with a label representing the attribute that yielded the highest score according to this function.

The results of applying the structure-free labeling over the input sequence of Figure 2(a) is illustrated in Figure 2(c), in which capital letters represent labels assigned to candidate values, each label representing an attribute as follows: **Q** for Quantity, **U** for Unity and **I** for Ingredient. Notice that one of the candidate values is marked with a "?", meaning that no label could be assigned to it. This occurs when no feature used in Equation 1 gives a value greater than zero. This exemplifies one of the anticipated limitations of the structure-free labeling, which we discuss below.

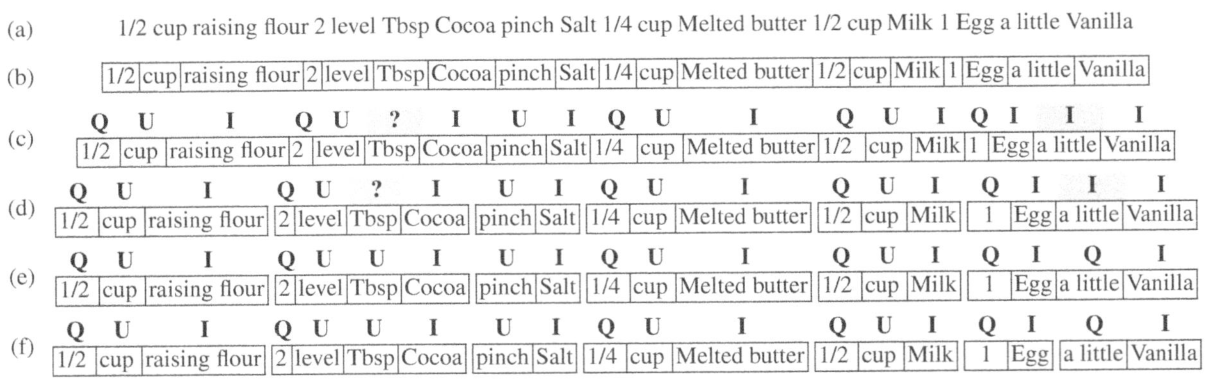

Figure 2: Running example with illustrations of the main steps that comprise our proposed method.

Limitations of the Structure-free Labeling

The use of very effective domain-dependent features yields a highly precise label assignment in the structure-free labeling step. This claim is supported by the results of extensive experiments we report in this paper, involving more than 30 distinct attributes on five distinct datasets.

In spite of that, using such features may represent a problem in two important cases: (1) two (or more) attributes in the same knowledge base are similar with respect to the property being evaluated by the feature function; (2) the property being evaluated is under-represented within the known values of some attribute in the knowledge base. In the first case, wrong labels can be assigned to some segment, i.e., a *label misassignment* occurs. In the second case, there is no support for "safely" assigning a label to that segment, i.e., a *label fault* occurs.

In Figure 2(a) we exemplify these two cases by shadowing the labels assigned to two of the candidate values. For the candidate value "Tbsp", the "?" indicates a label fault, while for the candidate value "a little" the shadowed "I" indicates a label misassignment. In this second case, the correct label would be "Q".

For dealing with such cases, state-of-the-art information extraction methods rely on features that also consider the context in which the segment being evaluated occurs within the input text. These features are derived from the structure of the record used as training data [1, 3, 5, 8, 10, 12, 14].

In our case, it is not possible to use these structure-related features simply because our input text bears no structure. However, imprecise as is, this sequence of labels generated by the structure-free labeling is accurate enough to allow the generation of an approximate description of the structure of the records in the input text. This is accomplished by the second step of our method, called *Structure Sketching*, which we describe next.

3.2 Structure Sketching

The goal of the structure sketching step is to organize the labeled candidate values into records, effectively inducing a structure on the unstructured text input. As this step takes as input the labels generated in the structure-free labeling step, in which imprecisions are expected, we consider this structure as a first approximation. The output of this step is a set of labeled values grouped into records that already bear a structure close to the correct one. In our method, this step plays an important role: with the structure of the input text uncovered, we can evaluate structural features and improve the initial labeling from the first step.

The structure sketching step uses a novel algorithm called *Structure Discover (SD)*, which is one of the main contributions of this paper. Let $\ell_1, \ell_2, \ldots, \ell_n$ be a sequence of labels generated by the structure-free labeling step, in which each label was assigned to a candidate value. The SD algorithm is used to identify in this sequence common subsequences of labels that are frequently repeated in the input text, which we call *cycles*. When a cycle that covers all the input text is found, it can be used to group labels in subsequences according to it. Each of these subsequences corresponds to a record grouping values from distinct attributes. These subsequences are called *candidate records*. We postpone a detailed discussion of the SD algorithm to Section 5.

The result of applying the SD algorithm on the labeled sequence of Figure 2(c) is shown in Figure 2(d). Notice that now candidate values are grouped into distinct subsequences, that is, into candidate records. In this example, the cycle found is a simple sequence of the attributes Quantity, Unit and Ingredient.

As this example illustrates, the algorithm is able to deal with irregularities in the candidate records, such as missing or repeated attribute values. Dealing with irregularities is important not only to address natural irregularities often found in real cases, but also to make the process robust to errors caused by the labeling process. In this particular example, while a candidate value of attribute Quantity is indeed missing in the third candidate record, the sequence of three candidate values for attribute Ingredient in the last candidate record is caused by an error in the structure-free labeling step.

As our experimental results indicate, in spite of these and others irregularities (e.g., candidate records with distinct orderings of attribute occurrence), the SD algorithm is able to discover a plausible structure for the input sequence of labels. Again, we refer the reader to Section 5 for details on the SD algorithm.

With a plausible structure already uncovered by the SD algorithm, it is now possible to compute structure-related features in conjunction with content-related features to improve the initial labeling of the candidate values. This procedure is explained next.

3.3 Structure-aware Labeling

Consider a candidate record $R = s_1, \ldots, s_r$, where each $s_i (1 \leq i \leq r)$ is a candidate value. Also, consider an attribute A and let ℓ_A be a label used for this attribute. Then, for any candidate value s_i, we can compute the value of a feature function $f^k(s_i, A, R)$. Function f^k returns a real number that measures the likelihood of a segment labeled ℓ_A to occur in the same place as s_i in R. Thus, the value of f^k is related to the structure of R.

Differently from the content-based features used so far, which are only domain-dependent, structure-based features such as f^k depend on the particular organization of the candidate values within the input text. This means that these features are *source-dependent*.

Like other information extraction methods (e.g., [5, 8, 14]), our method uses two structure-related features. The first considers the absolute position of the segment and the second considers its relative position, i.e., its occurrence between segment s_{i-1} (if any, i.e., when $i > 0$) and segment s_{i+1} (if any, i.e., when $i < r$).

For computing such features, it is common to build a graph model that represents the likelihood of attribute transitions within the input text (or any other input text from the same source). In this paper, we adopt the same approach as in [8]. More specifically, we built a probabilistic HMM-like graph model that we call PSM (Positioning and Sequencing Model). This model and the source-dependent features computed based on it are described in Section 4.2.

With the structure-related features in hand, we can use them to improve the initial structure-free labeling, as we describe next.

Processing the Structure-aware Labeling

Given a candidate value s, the decision on which label to assign to it can now consider the structure-related features f^j in addition to the content-related features g^k. As these features are also independent from the content-related ones, since they depend on the source, we again resort to the Bayesian Noisy-OR-Gate [15] to combine all features as follows:

$$\ell(s,R,A) = 1 - \big((1-g^1(s,A)) \times \ldots \times (1-g^n(s,A)) \times (1-f^1(s,A,R)) \times \ldots \times (1-f^m(s,A,R))\big) \quad (2)$$

Function $\ell(s,R,A)$ is computed for each candidate segment s of all candidate records R in the input text for all attributes A of the same data type (i.e., text or numeric). Thus, s is labeled with a label representing the attribute that yielded the highest score according to ℓ.

The result of applying the structure-free labeling over the candidate records of Figure 2(d) is illustrated in Figure 2(e). Notice that with the addition of the structure-related features, the candidate value "Tbsp" is now correctly labeled as **U** for Unity (this term is indeed used in place of "tablespoon"). For the same reason, candidate value "a little" is now correctly labeled as **Q** for Quantity.

As this example suggests, in general, combining structure-related and content-related features produce more precise results than the initial structure-free labeling. This trend is clearly indicated by our experiments.

Our method then takes advantage of this more precise sequence of labels to also revise the structure of the records. This new sequence is given as input to the SD algorithm. This is the fourth and final step of our method.

3.4 Structure Refinement

This last step of our method simply consists in applying again the SD algorithm. This time, however, it takes as input the labels generated by the structure-aware labeling. As the labeling produced by this step is more precise, the result is a more accurate structure. This is also indicated by our experimental results.

To illustrate it, notice that in Figure 2(f) the last candidate record from Figure 2(g) has now been split in two different records by the SD algorithm. Again, we refer the reader to Section 5 for details on the SD algorithm.

4. FEATURES USED

In this section, we described the features we use in our method. We begin by presenting the content-related, domain-dependent features and then we present the structure-related, source-dependent features.

4.1 Content-related Features

Attribute Vocabulary. These features exploit the common vocabulary often shared by values of textual attributes (e.g., neighborhood and street names, author names, recipe ingredients, etc.). To capture this property, we resort to a function called *AF* (Attribute Frequency) [9], which estimates the similarity between a given value and the set of values of an attribute. In our case, the function AF is used to estimate the similarity between the content of a candidate value s and the values of an attribute A represented in the knowledge base KB. Function AF is defined as follows:

$$AF(s,A) = \frac{\sum_{t \in T(A) \cap T(s)} fitness(t,A)}{|T(s)|} \quad (3)$$

In Equation 3, $T(A)$ is the set of all terms found in the values of attribute A represented in KB and $T(s)$ is the set of terms found in the candidate value s. The function $fitness(t,A)$ evaluates how typical a term t is among the values of attribute A. It is computed as follows:

$$fitness(t,A) = \frac{f(t,A)}{N(t)} \times \frac{f(t,A)}{f_{max}(A)} \quad (4)$$

where $f(t,A)$ is the number of distinct values of A that contain the term t, $f_{max}(A)$ is the highest frequency of any term among the values of A, and $N(t)$ is the total number of occurrences of the term t in all attributes represented in KB.

The first fraction in Equation 4 expresses the likelihood of term t to be part of a value of A according to KB. This fraction is multiplied by a normalization factor in the second fraction. This prevents attributes with many values in KB from dominating and is also useful for making the term frequency comparable among all attributes.

We notice that although we could have used any other similarity function, for instance, based on the vector space model, experiments reported in the literature [9] have shown that AF is very effective for dealing with small portions of texts such as the ones typically found in candidate values.

It is also worth mentioning that we use inverted indexes over the knowledge base to speed up the computation of this feature.

Attribute Value Range. For the case of numeric candidate values (e.g., page numbers, year, phone number, price, quantity, etc.) textual similarity functions such as AF do not work properly. Thus, for dealing with these candidate values a proper feature function is needed. We assume, as proposed in [11], that the values of numeric attributes follow a Gaussian distribution. Based on this assumption, we measure the similarity between a numeric value v_s present in a candidate value s and the set of values v_A of an attribute A in KB, by evaluating how close v_s is from the mean value of v_A according to its probability density function. For that, we use the function *NM* (Numeric Matching), defined in Equation 5, normalized by the maximum probability density of v_A, which is reached when a given value is equal to the average[1].

$$NM(s,A) = e^{-\frac{v_s - \mu}{2\sigma^2}} \quad (5)$$

where σ and μ are, respectively, the standard deviation and the average of values in v_A, and v_s is the numeric value of s.

Notice that when v_s is close to the average of values in v_A, $NM(s,A)$ is close to 1. As v_s assumes values far from the average, the similarity tends to zero.

[1] The maximum probability density of v_A is $1/\sqrt{2\pi\sigma^2}$.

In many cases, numeric values in the input texts may include special characters (e.g., prices and phone numbers). Thus, prior to the application of the NM function, these characters are removed and the remaining numbers are concatenated. We call this process *Normalization*. For instance, the string "412-638-7273" is normalized to form a numeric value 4126387273 that can be applied to the function NM. Normalization is also performed over numeric values that occur in KB.

Attribute Value Format. Another property we exploit as a content-related feature is the common format often used to represent values of some attributes. Let v_A be the set of values available for an attribute A in KB. We automatically learn a sequence Markov model m_A that captures the format style of the values in v_A. This model is similar to the inner HMM used in [12] and is also applied to capture the format of values as a state feature.

For that, we first tokenize each value of v_A on white-spaces. Using a taxonomy proposed in [12], we encode this value as a sequence of *symbol masks* or simply *masks*. A mask is a character class identifier, possibly followed by a quantifier. For example, the value "Rivers inc." of the Company attribute is encoded as "[A-Z][a-z]+ [a-z]+.", where mask [A-Z] represents a string that starts with an uppercase letter, mask [a-z]+ represents a sequence of one or more lowercase letters, etc. This process is repeated for all known values of a given attribute.

Then, the model m_A is generated based on these masks, so that each node n corresponds to a mask that represents the values of v_A. An edge e between nodes n_i and n_j is built if n_i is followed by n_j in the masks. Thus, each value in v_A can be described by a path in m_A.

To express the likelihood of sequences of masks in the model, we define the *weight* of an edge $\langle n_x, n_y \rangle$ as:

$$w(n_x, n_y) = \frac{\text{\# of pairs } \langle n_x, n_y \rangle \text{ in } m_A}{\text{\# of pairs } \langle n_x, n_z \rangle, \forall n_z \in m_A}$$

Now, let s be a candidate value. We can encode s using the symbol taxonomy as above. This results in a sequence of masks. We evaluate how similar a candidate value s is to the values in v_A with respect to their formats by computing

$$format(s, A) = \frac{\sum_{\langle n_x, n_y \rangle \in path(s)} w(n_x, n_y)}{|path(s)|} \tag{6}$$

where $path(s)$ represents a path formed by the sequence of masks generated for s in m_A. Notice that, if no path matching for this sequence is found in m_a, $format(s, A) = 0$.

Intuitively, $format(s, A)$ evaluates how likely are the sequences of symbols forming a given candidate value s with respect to the sequences of symbols typically occurring as values of some attribute A. By using such feature, we capture specific formatting properties of URLs, e-mails, telephone numbers, etc.

Notice that the model m_A is learned from the set of values v_A only. Thus, differently from [12], no manual training is needed.

4.2 Structure-related Features

State-of-the-art information extraction methods (e.g., [5, 8, 14]) usually use two types of structure-related feature. The first type considers the absolute position of the text segment or token to be evaluated and the second one considers its relative position, i.e., its occurrence between other segments or tokens in the input text. For computing such features, it is common to build a graph model that represents the likelihood of transitions within the input text (or other input texts from the same source).

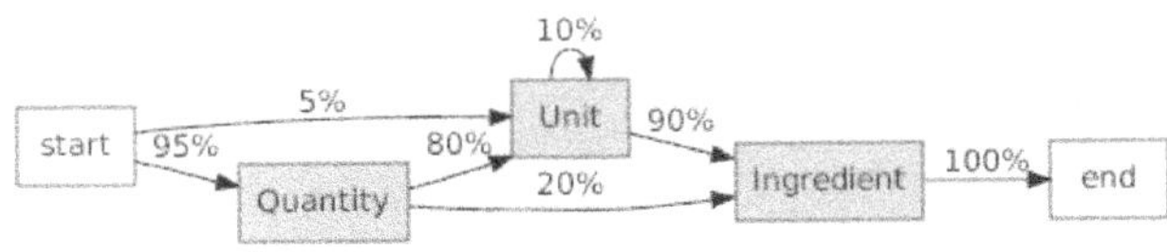

Figure 3: Example of a PSM

In most CRF-based methods, this model is built from training data, which consists of a set of delimited records manually labeled taken from the same input text [14]. In [5] and [8], the model is built in an unsupervised way during the extraction process itself. While in [5] a fixed order, learned from a sample, is assumed for the attributes in the input text, in [8] the model is built using all records available in the input text and no fixed order is assumed. Thus, in our work we adopt the same approach as in [8]. More specifically, we built a probabilistic HMM-like graph model called PSM (*Positioning and Sequencing Model*).

In our case, a PSM consists of: (1) a set of states $L = \{begin, \ell_1, \ell_2, \ldots, \ell_n, end\}$ where each state ℓ_i corresponds to a label assigned to a candidate value in the structure-free labeling step; (2) a matrix T that stores the probability of observing a transition from state ℓ_i to state ℓ_j; and (3) a matrix P that stores the probability of observing a label ℓ_i in the set of candidate labels that occupies the k-th position in a candidate record.

Matrix T, which stores the transition probabilities, is built using the ratio of the number of transitions made from state ℓ_i to state ℓ_j in a candidate record to the total number of transitions made from state ℓ_i in all known candidate records. Thus, each element $t_{i,j}$ in T is defined as:

$$t_{i,j} = \frac{\text{\# of transitions from } \ell_i \text{ to } \ell_j}{\text{Total \# of transitions out of } \ell_i} \tag{7}$$

Matrix P, which stores the position probabilities, is built using the ratio of the number of times a label ℓ_i is observed in position k in a candidate record to the total number of labels observed in candidate values that occupy position k in all known candidate records. Thus, each element $p_{i,k}$ in P is defined as:

$$p_{i,k} = \frac{\text{\# of observations of } \ell_i \text{ in } k}{\text{Total \# of candidate values in } k} \tag{8}$$

By using Equations 7 and 8, matrices T and P are built to maximize the probabilities of the sequencing and the positioning observed for the attribute values, according to the labeled blocks in the output of the matching step. This follows the Maximum Likelihood approach, commonly used for training graphical models [12, 17].

In practice, building matrices T and P involve performing a single pass over the input text which, at this point, has already been processed in the Structure Sketching step. Notice that candidate values left unmatched are discarded when building these matrices. Obviously, possible mismatched candidate values will be used to build the PSM, generating spurious transitions. However, as the number of mismatches resulting from the Structure-free Labeling step is rather small, as demonstrated in our experiments, they do not compromise the overall correctness of the model.

Figure 3 shows an example of the PSM built for an input text with cooking recipes. As we can see, the graph represents not only information on the sequencing of labels assigned to candidate values, but also on the positioning of candidate values in the input text. For instance, in this example, input texts are more likely to begin with blocks labeled Quantity than with blocks labeled Unit. Also, there is a high probability that blocks labeled Ingredient occur after blocks labeled Unit.

Let s_k be a candidate value in a candidate record $R = \ldots, s_k, \ldots$ for which a label ℓ_i corresponding to an attribute A_i is to be assigned. Also, suppose that in R the candidate value next to s_k is labeled with ℓ_j corresponding to an attribute A_j. Then, using Equations 7 an 8, we can compute the two structure-related features we consider, i.e, the *sequencing feature* and the *positioning feature*, respectively as:

$$seq(s_k, A_i, R) = t_{i,j} \text{ and } pos(s_k, A_i, R) = p_{i,k} \qquad (9)$$

5. THE SD ALGORITHM

In this section, we present a detailed description of the Structure Discovery (SD) algorithm. As discussed in Section 3, this algorithm plays an important role in our method: to uncover the structure of the implicit records from the input text. Besides the ultimate goal of structuring the data extracted in the final step (Structure Refinement), this algorithm is also used to induce structure-related features that improve the quality of the extraction in an intermediate step (Structure Sketching). In both steps, the SD algorithm takes as input a sequence of labels assigned to candidate values generated in the preceding steps and generates the structure of each record available in the input text. Following, we present preliminary concepts related to the algorithm and describe its main steps.

The main intuition behind the algorithm is that it is possible to identify patterns of sequences by looking for cycles into a graph that models the ordering of labels in the labeled input text. This graph, called *Adjacency Graph*, is defined below.

Adjacency Graph. Consider the sequence $s_1, s_2, \ldots, s_n$ of candidate values in the input text, such that s_i is labeled with ℓ_i. The ordered list $L = \langle \ell_1, \ell_2, \ldots, \ell_n \rangle$ is called an *Adjacency List*. An *Adjacency Graph* is a digraph $G = \langle V, E \rangle$ in which V is the set of all distinct labels in L, plus two special labels *begin* and *end*, and E is the set of all pairs $\langle \ell_i, \ell_j \rangle$ in E for all i, j such that $j = i + 1$ $(1 \leq i \leq n - 1)$, plus two special edges $\langle begin, \ell_1 \rangle$ and $\langle \ell_n, end \rangle$.

Title Conference Year Author Author Title Conference Year Author Title Conference Year ... Author Title Journal Issue Year Author Title Journal Issue Year Author Author Journal Issue Year Title Year ... Author Title Conference Year Author Author Author Title Journal Issue Year

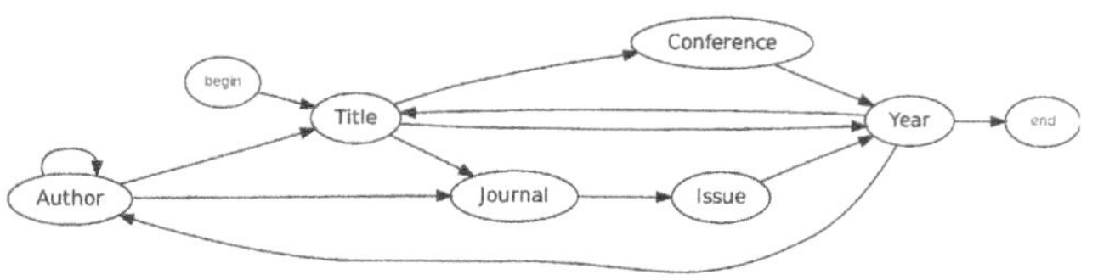

Figure 4: An Adjacency List and an Adjacency Graph for an input text with bibliographic data.

Figure 4 illustrates portions of an Adjacency List built from a sample unstructured text containing a number of implicit bibliographic data records. This sample is a simplified version of a real bibliographic data source such as *CORA* (a dataset we have used in our experiments) represented by some of the attributes involved (e.g., no volume or page information is represented). This sample, however, exemplifies some of the problems faced when processing real textual inputs.

Figure 4 also illustrates an Adjacency Graph built from this Adjacency List. In this graph, nodes corresponding to attributes are represented by ellipses identified by their respective labels in the adjacency list. Nodes *begin* and *end* are considered as if they occurred only once in this list, respectively, before and after the sequence of candidate values $s_1, \ldots, s_n$. Their role is simply to serve as references for the graph processing algorithms used by our method.

The two long paths ⟨Author,Title,Conference,Year⟩ and ⟨Author, Title,Journal,Issue,Year⟩ correspond, respectively, to publications in conferences and journals. Notice, however, that some edges indicate the occurrence of implicit records with missing attributes. This is the case of the edge ⟨Author,Journal⟩ that indicates a missing value for Title. Also notice that ⟨Year,Author⟩ and ⟨Year,Title⟩ intuitively indicate records ending with an Year candidate value leading to another record that may begin with either Author or Title. Indeed, the first implicit record in the input text begins with a Title candidate value.

The occurrence of implicit records with missing attributes is a very common issue in most real cases. This situation occurs either due to errors in the labeling process, specially in the case of the structure-free labeling, or because the implicit record indeed has no value for some attributes.

An important aspect the SD algorithm exploits in the adjacency graph is the occurrence of cycles. A cycle is a sequence of adjacent nodes $\langle \ell_i, \ldots, \ell_{i+k}, \ell_i \rangle$. For convenience, we use the notation $[\ell_i, \ldots, \ell_{i+k}]$, omitting the last node, which is always equal to the first one.

The different configurations of implicit records, i.e., the set of attributes composing them and the order in which their candidate values appear, can be detected by looking for cycles in the adjacency graph. This is the case of cycles [Author,Title,Conference,Year], [Author,Title,Journal,Issue,Year] and [Title,Conference,Year] in Figure 4.

Two important issues arise when using the adjacency graph to analyze the possible record structures in the input text: (1) in which order the labels in the cycle occur in the input text and (2) which cycles correspond to actual implicit records in the input text. To deal with both issues, we verify the correspondence between cycles and the sequence of labels in the adjacency list. For the definitions below, let G be an adjacency graph generated from an adjacency list L.

Coincident Cycles. Two cycles c_a and c_b are said to be *coincident*, meaning that they represent the same cycle in G, if they include the same edges in the same order, but beginning and ending at a different node in the cycle.

Cycle Instances and Viable Cycles. Let $c = [\ell_i, \ldots, \ell_{i+k}]$ be a cycle in G. Any sequence $\ell_i, \ldots, \ell_{i+k}$ in L is said to be an *instance* of c. The cycle c is said to be *viable* if there is at least one instance of c in L.

Dominant Cycles. Let $\{c_1, \ldots, c_n\}$ be a set of coincident cycles. The viable cycle c_i for which the order of labels is the most frequent in L is called the *dominant cycle*.

To exemplify these concepts, cycles c_a = [Author,Title,Conference,Year] and c_b = [Title,Conference,Year,Author] are coincident in the adjacency graph of Figure 4. By looking into the adjacency list, we find that c_b is the dominant cycle.

These concepts are used by the SD algorithm (Algorithm 1). This algorithm works by first identifying all dominant cycles in the adjacency graph and then processing each of these cycles in the order of their sizes, the largest cycles being processed first. Notice that nodes *begin* and *end* never participate in any cycle, since they are both connected to the graph by a single edge.

In Lines 2 and 3, the Adjacency List and the Adjacency Graph are created. Next, in Lines 4 and 5, the algorithm detects all single cycles in the graph in order to remove all sequences of a same label

Algorithm 1: Structure Discovery Algorithm

```
   input : I: input text with labeled candidate values
   output: L: sequence of records that structure I
1  begin
2      L ← adjlist(I);
3      G ← adjgraph(L);
4      foreach single cycle [ℓ, ℓ] in G do
5          Replace all sequences ℓ, ..., ℓ by one single element ℓ+ in L
6      G ← adjgraph(L);
7      C ← dominant_cycles(G);
8      i ← 0;
9      while C ≠ ∅ do
10         dc_i ← next(C);
11         for each instance ℓ_1, ..., ℓ_k of dc_i in L do
12             Replace ℓ_1, ..., ℓ_k by r_i in L;
13         i++;
14 end
```

from the adjacency list. Such sequences usually represent multi-valued attributes (e.g., lists) that must be considered as a single component in the records being identified. Thus, these sequences are replaced by a single label $\ell+$ in the adjacency list.

In Line 6, a new Adjacency Graph is generated for reflecting the removal of theses sequences. If we consider the graph in Figure 4, the only effect will be the removal of the cycle involving Author.

In Line 7, the algorithm extracts all dominant cycles from G. Next, these dominant cycles are used to structure their instances in the input text. This is carried out by the loop in Lines 9 to 13. In Line 10, the function $next$ selects and removes the largest dominant cycles from C and, in Lines 11 and 12, the instances of the cycles in the adjacency list L are replaced by an indication that a record has been formed with each of these instances. Thus, in our algorithm, records are taken as cycle instances whose boundaries are determined by matching cycles derived from the graph to the adjacency list (Line 11).

We notice the importance of processing larger cycles first. Considering the graph in Figure 4, if the cycle $c_b =$ [Title,Conference, Year] was processed before $c_a =$ [Author,Title,Conference,Year], part of each instance of c_b would be taken as a instance of c_a. This process continues while there are cycles unprocessed in C.

For the Adjacency List and the Adjacency Graph of Figure 4, the sequence of dominant cycles that would be processed is the following: [Author,Title,Journal,Issue,Year], [Author,Title,Conference, Year], [Author,Journal,Issue,Year], [Title,Conference,Year] and [Title,Year].

6. EXPERIMENTAL EVALUATION

In this section, we describe the experiments we have performed to evaluate JUDIE using five distinct datasets. First, we describe the experimental setup and the metrics used to assess JUDIE's performance. Then, we report on the quality of the extraction results for each dataset.

6.1 Setup

The datasets employed in our experiments and the data sources used to generate the knowledge bases for JUDIE are summarized in Table 1. We notice that some of these datasets are the same employed in the evaluation of other information extraction methods. We also recall that our method takes as input sets of records without any explicit delimiters between them, as illustrated in Figure 1.

The dataset of the *Cooking Recipes* domain was previously used in [2]. In order to build the knowledge base for this domain, we have collected structured recipes from FreeBase[2]. For the *Product Offers* domain, the dataset is formed by unstructured strings containing lists of product offers from 25 Brazilian e-commerce stores. Data for building the respective knowledge base has been taken from Nhemu[3], a Brazilian price comparison website. For the *Postal Adresses* domain, both the dataset and the data source used to build the knowledge base have been obtained from *Bigbook*, a dataset available in the RISE repository[4] and that has been previously used in [5] and [8].

For the *Bibliography* domain, the dataset is part of the Cora Collection[5] and is composed of a large diversity of bibliographic citations in distinct styles and formats. It includes citations to journal articles, conference papers, books, technical reports, etc. The data source for building the knowledge base, PersonalBib, is also a dataset of bibliographic citations that has been used in [14]. Finally, for the *Classified Ads* domain we have taken the dataset previously used in [8]. This dataset is composed of unstructured strings containing ads from Brazilian newspaper websites. For building the knowledge base, we have collected data from a database available on the website of a major Brazilian newspaper.

For all performed experiments, we evaluated the extraction results for each individual attribute (attribute-level) and for each record type as whole (record-level). As evaluation metrics, we have used the well known precision, recall and F-measure as defined next.

Let B_i be a reference set and S_i be a test set to be compared with B_i. We define precision (P_i), recall (R_i) and F-measure (F_i) respectively as:

$$P_i = \frac{|B_i \cap S_i|}{|S_i|},\; R_i = \frac{|B_i \cap S_i|}{|B_i|} \text{ and } F_i = \frac{2(R_i.P_i)}{(R_i + P_i)}$$

In order to present attribute-level results, we calculate precision, recall and F-measure according to the above equations by considering B_i as the set of terms that compose the values of a given attribute a_i and S_i the set of terms assigned to a_i by our method. Likewise, for record-level results, we calculate precision, recall and F-measure by considering each record set B_i as the set of field values in a given structured record C_i and S_i the set of field values extracted for C_i by our method.

6.2 General Quality Results

In this section, we analyze the general quality of the extraction task performed by JUDIE on the datasets described in Table 1. For each domain, we have run the extraction task five times, each time selecting different data samples for the data extraction task and for building the respective knowledge bases. For all performed extractions, we report the average F-measure obtained for all runs. We also notice that there is no intersection between the knowledge bases and the corresponding datasets we use in our experiments.

Tables 2(a)–(e) present attribute-level F-measure values that assess the extraction quality in each dataset. Column "C1" refers to results obtained after the Structure-free Labeling and Structure Sketching steps, which correspond to what we call Phase 1, and Column "C2" refers to results obtained after the Structure-aware Labeling and Structure Discovery steps, which correspond to what we call Phase 2. Column "G" presents the gain in quality achieved from Phase 1 to Phase 2.

Each of these columns assesses a distinct aspect of our method. Results in column "C1" assess how well the content-related source-independent features alone have been able to assign correct labels

[2] http://www.freebase.com

[3] http://www.nhemu.com

[4] http://www.isi.edu/info-agents/RISE

[5] http://www.cs.umass.edu/~mccallum/data

Domain	Dataset	Text Inputs	Attributes	Source	Attributes	Records
Cooking Recipes	*Recipes*	500	3	*FreeBase.com*	3	100
Product Offers	*Products*	10000	3	*Nhemu.com*	3	5000
Postal Addresses	*BigBook*	2000	5	*BigBook*	5	2000
Bibliography	*CORA*	500	3 to 7	*PersonalBib*	7	395
Classified Ads	*WebAds*	500	5 to 18	*Folha On-line*	18	125

Table 1: Domains, datasets and KB data sources used in the experiments.

	Phase 1			Phase 2		
Attribute	FI/NM	FO	C1	S+P	C2	G %
Quantity	0.81	0.69	0.89	0.78	0.96	7.1
Unit	0.86	0.46	0.91	0.82	0.94	3.9
Ingredient	0.84	0.74	0.91	0.76	0.96	4.9
Average	0.84	0.63	0.90	0.79	0.95	5.3

(a) Recipes

	Phase 1			Phase 2		
Attribute	FI/NM	FO	C1	S+P	C2	G %
Name	0.77	0.37	0.85	0.69	0.90	5.3
Brand	0.74	0.52	0.83	0.71	0.92	10.5
Price	0.89	0.92	0.93	0.88	0.95	1.9
Average	0.80	0.60	0.87	0.76	0.92	5.8

(b) Products

	Phase 1			Phase 2		
Attribute	FI/NM	FO	C1	S+P	C2	G %
Name	0.79	0.48	0.94	0.63	0.97	2.6
Street	0.82	0.40	0.95	0.75	0.97	2.6
City	0.92	0.39	0.94	0.84	0.97	2.8
State	0.89	0.63	0.96	0.88	0.97	1.3
Phone	0.94	0.93	0.95	0.89	0.97	2.3
Average	0.87	0.57	0.95	0.80	0.97	2.3

(c) BigBook

	Phase 1			Phase 2		
Attribute	FI/NM	FO	C1	S+P	C2	G %
Author	0.79	0.60	0.83	0.65	0.88	5.9
Title	0.60	0.52	0.70	0.48	0.79	13.8
Booktitle	0.82	0.46	0.81	0.67	0.86	6.2
Journal	0.69	0.53	0.72	0.62	0.84	16.9
Volume	0.84	0.88	0.88	0.72	0.90	2.9
Pages	0.79	0.80	0.83	0.73	0.86	3.9
Date	0.72	0.76	0.79	0.69	0.87	9.5
Average	0.75	0.65	0.79	0.65	0.86	8.1

(d) CORA

	Phase 1			Phase 2		
Attribute	FI/NM	FO	C1	S+P	C2	G %
Bedroom	0.75	0.36	0.79	0.48	0.82	3.8
Living	0.81	0.46	0.85	0.69	0.89	5.6
Phone	0.79	0.84	0.80	0.62	0.87	8.8
Price	0.85	0.85	0.86	0.66	0.92	7.2
Kitchen	0.80	0.29	0.79	0.73	0.83	4.9
Bathroom	0.73	0.59	0.75	0.69	0.77	2.9
Suite	0.85	0.45	0.87	0.60	0.89	2.4
Pantry	0.79	0.50	0.77	0.66	0.80	3.7
Garage	0.78	0.52	0.79	0.73	0.84	6.6
Pool	0.77	0.63	0.78	0.78	0.82	5.2
Others	0.70	0.44	0.72	0.68	0.73	1.6
Average	0.78	0.54	0.80	0.67	0.84	4.8

(e) WebAds

Table 2: Attribute-level results for each dataset.

to the input text, while results in column "C2" also account for the use of structure-related source-dependent features learned from the input text itself.

To provide a perspective on the contribution of each feature to the overall extraction quality, we also present F-measure values obtained when each type of feature is individually used. The cases considered are: (1) either the *fitness* function for textual attributes (Eq. 4) or the *NM* function for numeric attributes (Eq. 5) is used (Column "FI/NM"); (2) only the *format* function (Eq. 6) is used (Column "FO"); and (3) only the *pos* and *seq* (Eq. 9) functions are used (Column "S+P'). We recall that "C1" results are obtained by combining in Phase 1 functions *fitness* (or *NM*) and *format* by using Eq. 1, and that "C2" results are obtained by combining in Phase 2 functions *fitness* (or *NM*), *format*, *pos* and *seq* by using Eq. 2.

As anticipated, we observe that the attribute-level results obtained in Phase 1 by combining features are already acceptable and, more importantly, are sufficient to yield a reasonable approximation of the records' structure. Furthermore, the *fitness* and *MN* functions are, in general, more accurate than the *format* function. However, their combination, as proposed in our method, leads to better results in all cases.

Phase 2 results are higher in all cases. While in most cases the gain is under 6%, there are interesting cases in which this gain is above 10%. For example, Title and Journal are attributes that present a large content overlap in the Bibliography dataset. Due to this problem, the percentage of labels incorrectly assigned to values of Title and Journal in Phase 1 was 25% and 16% respectively. In Phase 2, the majority of these misassignments were corrected. A large gain was also observed in the case of attribute Brand from the Products dataset. Because brand names are formed by terms usually not available in the knowledge base, more than 12% of values of this attribute were left unmatched in Phase 1. The structure-related features used in Phase 2 helped to recover these errors.

The behavior of our method when dealing with numeric attributes deserves specific comments. Considering the eight numeric attributes from the five distinct datasets used in our experiments, the *NM* function yielded an average attribute-level F-measure of 0.83 when used alone. This result is close to that obtained for the non-numeric attributes using the *fitness* function. For instance, with phone numbers, using only the *NM* function we obtained F-measure values of 0.94 and 0.79 for the BigBook and WebAds datasets, respectively. Moreover, the *format* function is also used with these attributes, but, in this case, unlikely to what happens with the *NM* function, values are not normalized (see Section 4.1). When used alone, this function also yielded an average F-measure of 0.83. Finally, the structure-based features helped to improve these results. When combined with the other two features, an average F-measure of 0.91 was obtained. As we can see, our method achieves equally good results with both numeric and textual attributes.

Dataset	Phase 1	Phase 2	Gain %
Recipes	0.79	0.90	13.2
Products	0.82	0.88	7.2
BigBook	0.86	0.93	8.8
CORA	0.69	0.83	19.3
WebAds	0.70	0.77	9.7

Table 3: General record-level results for each dataset.

Table 3 presents, for each dataset, record-level F-measure results obtained in Phase 1 and Phase 2. While results in Phase 1 are also acceptable (most of them above 0.7), improvements in labeling achieved in Phase 2 had a very positive effect. Indeed, in Phase 2 record-level F-measure has achieved results above 0.8 for four out of five datasets and, in all cases, gains have been above 7%. Notice, for instance, the case of the CORA dataset, in which the gain is higher than 19%, reflecting the improvements obtained by the structure-aware labeling step. As we can notice, adding the structure-related features (only possible in Phase 2) also leads to significant improvements regarding record-level results.

6.3 Impact of the Knowledge Base

In [8] the authors present an experiment to evaluate how dependent on the composition of the knowledge base is the quality of the extraction results.

In the case of JUDIE such study is even more important for the following reasons: (1) the extraction process entirely relies on the initial Structure-free Labeling step, which is solely based on content-related features learned from the knowledge base; (2) while in our closest competitor, ONDUX [8], the knowledge base is used only for matching, JUDIE also deploys a format feature based on its values. Thus, in JUDIE the knowledge base plays a crucial role, as we show in this experimental evaluation.

Here we compare JUDIE with ONDUX and U-CRF. These two methods are the current state-of-the-art unsupervised IETS methods. U-CRF was developed by adapting the publicly available implementation of CRF by Sunita Sarawagi[6] according to [5] and using additional features described in [10] (e.g., dictionary features, word score functions, transition features, etc.). As required by U-CRF, a batch of input strings is used to infer the order of the attribute values. Based on the information provided in [5], this batch is built using a sample of 10% of these strings.

As in [8], this experiment was performed using the *BigBook* dataset from the RISE repository. The knowledge base for ONDUX and JUDIE and the reference table for U-CRF were built by using sets of records already extracted. Once again, we notice that there is no intersection between these records and the corresponding datasets used in this experiment. Recall that while ONDUX and U-CRF received the input in a record-by-record basis, JUDIE received a single input text containing all 2000 records with no explicit delimiters between them.

The experiment consisted of varying the number of known terms common to the knowledge base (or reference table in the case of U-CRF) and the input test records from 50 to 1000 terms and evaluating the extraction quality in terms of average attribute-level F-measure. The results are presented in Figure 5(a).

The first important observation regarding this graph is that JUDIE is, as expected, more dependent on the knowledge base than ONDUX and U-CRF. Indeed, only when the number of shared terms approaches 1000, it reaches the same quality level as the baselines. This occurs because in both ONDUX and U-CRF the structure-related and content-related features are independent, while in JUDIE, as previously explained, content-related features are used to induce structured-based features through successive refinement steps.

Indeed, if content-based features are not enough, the induction of structure-based features fails. This can be observed in Figure 5(a), where the attribute-level F-measure values obtained with less than 250 common terms are very low. For this level of term intersection, the results of JUDIE's Phase 1, i.e., before any refinement, are better than the results of its Phase 2, in which structure-based features are also considered.

In spite of this limitation, JUDIE achieves results comparable to the state-of-the-art baselines for a task considerably harder, that is, extracting information while simultaneously uncovering its underlying structure. As already explained, this underlying structure is assumed as provided in the baseline methods. In Section 6.5, we present a detailed comparison between JUDIE and these baselines using other datasets.

6.4 Impact of Structure Diversity

In this section we study how our method deals with different types of structure observed in the implicit records found in the input text. For this we consider two different scenarios, structure diversity in different sources and within a single source. These two scenarios are discussed in the following.

6.4.1 *Structure Diversity in Different Sources*

To discuss the first scenario we use the Classified Ads domain, for which the knowledge base was build using data from one source and the input texts came from other five distinct sources. In the experiments reported below, each source corresponds to a different input text. Here, our goal is to demonstrate that the content-related features learned from data taken from one source can be used to induce the structure-related features for several related input texts from other distinct sources in the same domain.

In Figure 5(b) we show the attribute-level and record-level F-measure values obtained for each different source given as input to JUDIE. In all cases, the values are above 0.7 and for two cases they are above 0.8. This indicates that our method is source-independent, since it was able to correctly uncover the structure of implicit records in each source while also achieving good extraction level quality. This occurs despite of the differences in structure of the implicit records in each source.

6.4.2 *Structure Diversity within a Single Source*

For discussing the second scenario we use the Bibliography domain in which the knowledge base was built from the PersonalBib dataset [14] and single input texts came from the CORA collection. In this case we aim at showing how our method deals with a heterogeneous dataset in terms of structure.

By examining the distribution of citation styles among the 500 implicit records available in the CORA dataset, a total of 33 distinct styles were identified, but only six of them account for more than 90% of the citations[7].

For these experiments, we generated different input texts containing 100 to 500 implicit records randomly selected from the CORA dataset. We then process each of these input texts separately with JUDIE using the knowledge base described above. The process was repeated 10 times for each input text size.

To characterize the diversity of each input text we have used the Shannon Index [18], which is frequently used to measure diversity in categorical datasets. This index is defined as: $H = -\sum_{i=1}^{S} p_i ln(p_i)$, where S is the total number of styles (33 in this case) and p_i is the relative frequency of each style i found in the input text. As the H index does not return values between 0 and 1, we normalize H values obtained for each input text by the maximum possible value for H. This value occurs when the input contains all citations available in the CORA dataset, that is, when all 33 different citation styles are present in the input text[8]. Thus, the closer the

[6] http://crf.sourceforge.net/

[7] A citation style characterized by the set of attributes composing the record and their ordering.

[8] $H = 2.23671$ for the input containing 500 records.

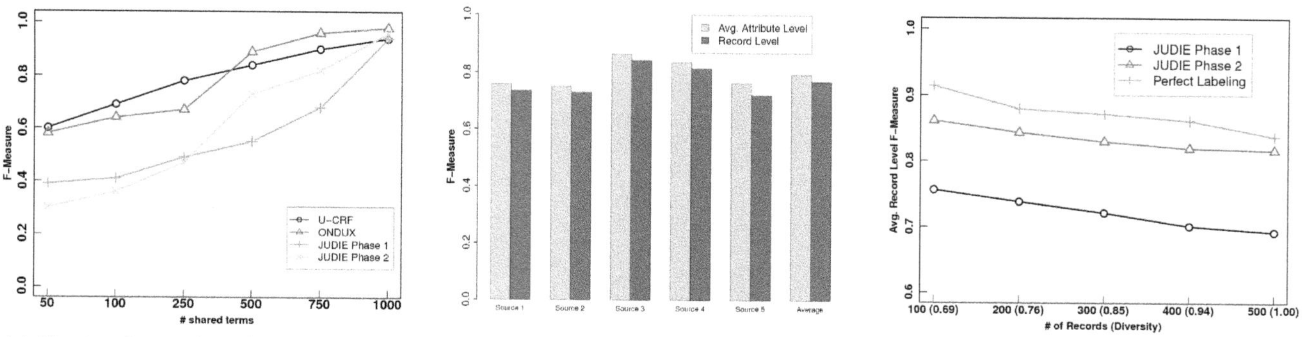

(a) Varying the number of shared terms. (b) Results for distinct Ads sources. (c) Results varying diversity.

Figure 5: Results obtained by our method varying distinct aspects in the input texts.

normalized H value is to 1, the greater is the diversity of the input text.

The results obtained are presented in Figure 5(c) in terms of the average record-level F-measure, considering Phases 1 and 2 of JUDIE. As a baseline, we use the record-level F-measure we would obtain if the labeling of attribute values was perfect in the input texts. In the X-axis, we present the number of records and the diversity of each input text in terms of the normalized H index.

This figure shows that our SD algorithm deals very well with structure diversity if the labels are correctly assigned, as it can be seen by comparing the curves representing JUDIE Phase 1 and the perfect labeling. As we can also observe, the improvements on the quality of the labeling provided by adding the structure-related features in Phase 2 impacts positively on the quality of the structure discovery. Indeed, record-level F-measure values obtained in Phase 2 are close to those obtained with the perfect labeling.

6.5 Comparison with Previous Work

In this section we present a comparison between the results obtained by JUDIE with those obtained by two state-of-the-art IETS methods, namely ONDUX [8] and U-CRF [5].

This comparison is made by reproducing in Tables 4(a) to (c) the attribute-level results obtained for three datasets, which were reported in [8] for the two methods, along with the results we obtain by running JUDIE over the same datasets.

While ONDUX was first presented and fully described in that paper, U-CRF was used there as a baseline. The details on its implementation are summarized in Section 6.3. In all cases, we have used the same sources for generating the knowledge bases and the input texts. We recall again that among the three methods, JUDIE is the only one that is able to both discover the structure and extract information automatically.

As a general observation, in spite of the fact the JUDIE faces a harder task, its performance was very close to that of ONDUX. In most cases, ONDUX outperformed JUDIE, but there are a few cases in which JUDIE performed better than ONDUX. These cases are explained mainly by the use of the format feature in JUDIE. Such feature is not considered in ONDUX.

In comparison with U-CRF, JUDIE performed worse on the BigBook dataset, but better on the CORA and WebAds datasets. This was expected, since these datasets are much more irregular in terms of structure than the first one.

6.6 Performance Issues

In Table 5 we present the running times of the experiments executed with JUDIE. For the datasets we used to run comparative experiments with our baselines ONDUX and U-CRF, we also include the running times of these systems. As the number of implicit input records is different for each dataset, we present both the total running time and the average running time by record.

Before discussing the results, we notice that JUDIE running times depend on two main factors: the number of implicit input records and the diversity in the structure of these records. Regarding the first factor, in all steps the input is scanned once. Thus, there is a linear influence of this factor. As for the second factor, having more

Attribute	JUDIE	ONDUX	U-CRF
Name	0.967	0.996 (2.97%)	0.995 (2.86%)
Street	0.970	0.995 (2.58%)	0.993 (2.37%)
City	0.971	0.995 (2.43%)	0.990 (1.92%)
State	0.971	1.000 (2.95%)	0.999 (2.84%)
Phone	0.975	1.000 (2.57%)	0.988 (1.34%)
Average	0.971	0.997 (2.70%)	0.993 (2.27%)

(a) BigBook

Attribute	JUDIE	ONDUX	U-CRF
Author	0.881	0.922 (4.65%)	0.876 (-0.57%)
Title	0.794	0.792 (-0.25%)	0.694 (-12.59%)
Booktitle	0.855	0.892 (4.33%)	0.560 (-34.50%)
Journal	0.843	0.908 (7.71%)	0.553 (-34.40%)
Volume	0.901	0.958 (6.33%)	0.430 (-52.28%)
Pages	0.861	0.849 (-1.39%)	0.503 (-41.58%)
Date	0.865	0.895 (3.47%)	0.488 (-43.58%)
Average	0.857	0.888 (3.60%)	0.586 (-31.60%)

(b) CORA

Attribute	JUDIE	ONDUX	U-CRF
Bedroom	0.818	0.861 (5.25%)	0.791 (-3.30%)
Living	0.893	0.905 (1.34%)	0.724 (-18.93%)
Phone	0.873	0.926 (6.12%)	0.754 (-13.59%)
Price	0.923	0.936 (1.41%)	0.786 (-14.84%)
Kitchen	0.830	0.849 (2.29%)	0.788 (-5.06%)
Bathroom	0.773	0.792 (2.51%)	0.810 (4.84%)
Suite	0.894	0.881 (-1.50%)	0.900 (0.62%)
Pantry	0.800	0.796 (-0.55%)	0.687 (-14.17%)
Garage	0.844	0.816 (-3.28%)	0.714 (-15.37%)
Pool	0.818	0.780 (-4.66%)	0.683 (-16.52%)
Other	0.732	0.796 (8.68%)	0.719 (-1.84%)
Average	0.836	0.849 (1.52%)	0.760 (-9.16%)

(c) WebAds

Table 4: Comparison of results.

Datasets	Total (secs.)			Avg. per record (msecs.)		
	JUDIE	ONDUX	U-CRF	JUDIE	ONDUX	U-CRF
Recipes	37.5	-	-	75.1	-	-
Products	69.2	-	-	6.9	-	-
BigBook	50.2	14.1	297.1	25.1	7.1	148.5
CORA	74.4	10.7	185.9	148.8	21.4	371.8
WebAds	59.2	8.0	2701.9	118.5	16.0	5403.7

Table 5: JUDIE running times in comparison with baselines.

diverse records in terms of structure implies that a larger number of edges will occur in the Adjacency Graph and in the PSM. Thus, processing these graphs has higher costs for more heterogeneous structures. This explain why the average running times per record are higher for CORA and WebAds, which, as discussed in Section 6.4, are the more diverse datasets in our experiments.

Nevertheless, these running times are in the same order of magnitude as those of ONDUX and are, in general, smaller than those of U-CRF. ONDUX is faster since it executes fewer steps and does not include a structure discovery step. U-CRF has a worst performance due to costly inference steps, particularly when dealing with diverse structures, and due to the use of a larger number of features than ONDUX and JUDIE.

7. CONCLUSIONS AND FUTURE WORK

In this paper, we have presented JUDIE a novel method for extracting semi-structured data records in the form of continuous text (e.g., bibliographic citations, postal addresses, classified ads, etc.) with no explicit delimiters between them. Differently from state-of-the-art IETS methods, in which the structure of the data records is manually supplied by an expert user in a training step, JUDIE is capable of detecting the structure of each individual record being extracted without any user assistance. For this, we propose a novel Structure Discovery algorithm that, given a sequence of labels representing attributes assigned to potential values, groups these labels into individual records by looking for frequent patterns of label repetitions among the given sequence. We have also shown how to integrate this algorithm in the information extraction process by means of successive refinement steps that alternate information extraction and structure discovery.

By means of a thoroughly experimental evaluation, we have studied different aspects regarding our method and compared it with state-of-the-art IETS methods. Results indicate that our method performs quite well when compared with such methods, even without any user intervention.

As future work , we intend to investigate techniques for automating the generation of knowledge bases usually required by unsupervised IETS methods. In addition, since JUDIE currently does not handle nested structures, we also plan to address this issue by generalizing the SD algorithm to deal with nested cycles.

Acknowledgements

This work is partially supported by INWeb (MCT/CNPq grant 57.3871/2008-6), by project MinGroup (CNPq grant 575553/2008-1), by UOL Bolsa Pesquisa program (grant 20090213165000), and by the authors' individual grants and scholarships from CNPq, CAPES, FAPEMIG and FAPEAM.

8. REFERENCES

[1] E. Agichtein and V. Ganti. Mining Reference Tables for Automatic Text Segmentation. In *Proc. 10th ACM SIGKDD Intl. Conf. on Knowl. Discov. and Data Mining*, pages 20–29, 2004.

[2] L. Barbosa and J. Freire. Using Latent-structure to Detect Objects on the Web. In *Proc. of the 13th Intl. Workshop on the Web and Databases*, pages 1–6, 2010.

[3] W. Cohen and S. Sarawagi. Exploiting Dictionaries in Named Entity Extraction: Combining Semi-Markov Extraction Processes and Data Integration Methods. In *Proc. 10th ACM SIGKDD Intl. Conf. on Knowl. Discov. and Data Mining*, pages 89–98, 2004.

[4] A. Doan et. al. Information Extraction Challenges in Managing Unstructured Data. *SIGMOD Record*, 37(4):14–20, 2008.

[5] C. Zhao et. al. Exploiting Structured Reference Data for Unsupervised Text Segmentation with Conditional Random Fields. In *Proc. SIAM Intl. Conf. on Data Mining*, pages 420–431, 2008.

[6] D. Buttler et. al. A Fully Automated Object Extraction System for the World Wide Web. In *Proc. of the 21st Intl. Conf. on Dist. Comp. Syst.*, pages 361–370, 2001.

[7] D. W. Embley et. al. Conceptual-model-based data extraction from multiple-record web pages. *Data Knowl. Eng.*, 31(3):227–251, 1999.

[8] E. Cortez et. al. ONDUX: On-Demand Unsupervised Learning for Information Extraction. In *Proc. ACM SIGMOD Intl. Conf. on Management of Data*, pages 807–818, 2010.

[9] F. Mesquita et. al. LABRADOR: Efficiently publishing relational databases on the web by using keyword-based query interfaces. *Inform. Proc. and Management*, 43(4):983–1004, 2007.

[10] J. D. Lafferty et. al. Conditional Random Fields: Probabilistic Models for Segmenting and Labeling Sequence Data. In *Proc. 8th Intl. Conf. on Mach. Learning*, pages 282–289, 2001.

[11] S. Agrawal et. al. Automated Ranking of Database Query Results. In *Proc. of the First Biennial Conf. on Innov. Data Syst. Research*, 2003.

[12] V. Borkar et. al. Automatic Segmentation of Text into Structured Records. In *Proc. ACM SIGMOD Intl. Conf. on Management of Data*, pages 175–186, 2001.

[13] D. Freitag and A. McCallum. Information Extraction with HMM Structures Learned by Stochastic Optimization. In *Proc. of the 17th Nat. Conf. on Art. Intell. and 12th Conf. on Innov. Appl. of Art. Intell.*, pages 584–589, 2000.

[14] I. R. Mansuri and S. Sarawagi. Integrating Unstructured Data into Relational Databases. In *Proc. 22nd Intl. Conf. on Data Engineering*, page 29, 2006.

[15] J. Pearl and G. Shafer. *Probabilistic reasoning in intelligent systems: networks of plausible inference*. Morgan Kaufmann, 1988.

[16] F. Peng and A. McCallum. Information extraction from research papers using conditional random fields. *Inform. Proc. and Management*, 42(4):963–979, 2006.

[17] S. Sarawagi. Information extraction. *Foundations and Trends in Databases*, 1(3):261–377, 2008.

[18] C. E. Shannon. A mathematical theory of communication. *ACM SIGMOBILE Mobile Comp. and Comm. Rev.*, 5(1):3–55, 2001.

[19] S. Soderland. Learning information extraction rules for semi-structured and free text. *Mach. Learn.*, 34:233–272, 1999.

Attribute Domain Discovery for Hidden Web Databases

Xin Jin
George Washington University
Washington, DC 20052, USA
xjin@gwu.edu

Nan Zhang*
George Washington University
Washington, DC 20052, USA
nzhang10@gwu.edu

Gautam Das†
University of Texas at Arlington
Arlington, TX 76019, USA
gdas@uta.edu

ABSTRACT

Many web databases are hidden behind restrictive form-like interfaces which may or may not provide domain information for an attribute. When attribute domains are not available, domain discovery becomes a critical challenge facing the application of a broad range of existing techniques on third-party analytical and mash-up applications over hidden databases. In this paper, we consider the problem of domain discovery over a hidden database through its web interface. We prove that for any database schema, an achievability guarantee on domain discovery can be made based solely upon the interface design. We also develop novel techniques which provide effective guarantees on the comprehensiveness of domain discovery. We present theoretical analysis and extensive experiments to illustrate the effectiveness of our approach.

Categories and Subject Descriptors

H.2.7 [**Database Administration**]; H.3.5 [**Online Information Services**]: Web-based services

General Terms

Algorithms, Measurement, Performance

Keywords

Hidden Web Database, Domain Discovery

1. INTRODUCTION

The Attribute Domain Discovery Problem: In this paper, we develop novel techniques to discover the attribute domains, i.e., the set of possible values for each attribute, from hidden web databases, by external users. Hidden databases, as a large portion of the deep web, are hidden behind restrictive form-like interfaces which allow a user to form a search query by specifying the desired values for one or a few attributes; and the system responds by returning a small number of tuples satisfying the user-specified search condition. A typical example of a hidden database is the award search database of the US National Science Foundation (NSF)[1], which allows users to search for NSF-award projects featuring user-specified values on up to 20 attributes.

Each attribute specifiable by users through the form-like interface is represented by an input control on the interface. For certain types of controls, e.g., drop-down menus and radio buttons, the attribute domain can be readily retrieved by external users from source code of the interface (e.g., an HTML file). In the NSF example, attributes such as NSF organization and Award Instrument belong to this category. For other controls, especially text-boxes (without features such as autocompletion), no domain information is provided. Attributes such as Program Manager belong to this category.

The focus of this paper is to develop domain discovery techniques, *restricted to accessing the database only via the proprietary form interface*, that external users can employ to unveil possible attribute values that appear in tuples of the hidden databases. An important design goal is to develop techniques that unveil all (or most) attribute values by issuing only a small number of queries, and to provide analytical guarantees on the coverage and query cost of our methods.

We emphasize that in this paper, we do not consider approaches to the domain discovery problem that rely on external knowledge sources or domain experts to provide the required domain values. We argue that while the use of external knowledge sources may have applicability in very general scenarios (e.g., the use of a USPS data source to list all values of an attribute such as zipcode), these approaches will not work in more focused applications such as the Program Manager attribute on the NSF award search database. Our emphasis is to develop automated domain discovery algorithms that can power a a variety of third-party applications only using the public interfaces of these databases, and without requiring any further collaborations or agreements with the database owners.

Applications: Domain discovery from hidden databases belongs to the area of information extraction and deep web analytics (see tutorials in [6, 11] and survey in [18]). To the best of our knowledge, the only prior work that tackles our specific problem of discovering attribute domains of hidden databases is [20]. This problem has a broad range of applications. First and foremost, it serves as a *critical prerequisite* for data analytics over hidden databases, because all existing aggregate estimation [8] and sampling [7, 9, 10] techniques for hidden databases require prior knowledge of the attribute

*Partially supported by NSF grants 0852673, 0852674, 0915834 and a GWU Research Enhancement Fund.

†Partially supported by NSF grants 0812601, 0915834, 1018865, a NHARP grant from the Texas Higher Education Coordinating Board, and grants from Microsoft Research and Nokia Research.

[1] *http://www.nsf.gov/awardsearch/tab.do?dispatch=4*

domains. In addition, the attribute domains being discovered can be of direct interest to third-party web mashup applications. For example, such an application may use the discovered attribute domains to add autocompletion feature to text-boxes in the original form-like interface, so as to improve the usability of the interface. The discovered domains may also be used to identify mapping between attributes in different hidden databases to facilitate the creation of mashup.

Challenges: The main challenges to effective attribute domain discovery are the restrictions on input and output interfaces of hidden databases. Normally, input interfaces are restricted to issuing only *search* queries with conjunctive selection conditions - which means that queries like SELECT UNIQUE(Program Manager) FROM D cannot be directly issued, eliminating the chance of directly discovering the domain of Program Manager through the interface.

The output interface is usually limited by a top-k constraint - i.e., if more than k tuples match the user-specified condition, then only k of them are preferentially selected by a scoring function and returned to the user. This restriction eliminates the possibility of trivially solving the problem by issuing the single query SELECT * FROM D and then discovering all attribute domains from the returned results.

The existing technique for attribute domain discovery is based on *crawling* the database [20]. A simple instantiation of crawling is to start with SELECT * FROM D, then use domain values returned in the query answer to construct future queries, and repeat this process until all queries that can be constructed have been issued. One can see that no algorithm can beat the comprehensiveness of attribute domain discovery achieved by crawling. But crawling requires an extremely large number of queries to complete, and since most hidden databases enforce a limit on the number of queries one can issue over a period of time (e.g., $1,000$ per IP address per day), or even charge per query, often the crawling process has to be terminated prematurely. Due to this reason, such techniques cannot provide any guarantees on the comprehensiveness of discovered attribute domains.

A seemingly promising way to address the query cost problem of crawling is to instead perform *sampling* - i.e., one first draws representative samples from the hidden database, and then discover attribute domains from the sample tuples to achieve statistical guarantees on the comprehensiveness of domain discovery. Sampling of hidden databases is an intensively studied problem in recent years [7, 9, 10]. Nonetheless, a key obstacle here is a "chicken-and-egg" problem - i.e., all existing sampling algorithms for hidden databases require the attribute domains to be known in the first place, preventing them from being applied to hidden databases with unknown attribute domains!

Outline of Technical Results: In this paper we initiate a study of query-efficient attribute domain discovery over hidden databases. We consider two types of output interfaces commonly offered by hidden databases: COUNT and ALERT. For a user-specified query, a COUNT interface returns not only the top-k tuples, but also the number of tuples matching the query in the database (which can be greater than k). ALERT interface, on the other hand, only *alerts* the user with an *overflow flag* when more than k tuples match the query, indicating that not all tuples which match the query can be returned. The NSF award database features an ALERT interface.

For COUNT interface, we start by studying the feasibility of developing deterministic algorithms for attribute domain discovery. Our main results are two achievability conditions - lower bounds on k and query cost, respectively - which a deterministic algorithm must satisfy to guarantee the discovery of all attribute domains. Unfortunately, neither condition is achievable in practice for a generic hidden database. Nonetheless, a promising lead we find from the study is that efficient and complete attribute domain discovery is indeed possible for a special type of (perhaps unrealistic) databases in which each attributes has only two domain values. For this special case, we develop B-COUNT-DISCOVER, a deterministic algorithm based on the key idea of constructing a series of *nested search spaces* for unknown domain values, and prove that the algorithm guarantees the discovery of all attribute domains with only $O(m^2)$ queries, where m is the number of attributes, as long as $k \geq 2$.

Our main observation from B-COUNT-DISCOVER is an understanding of why it cannot be extended to generic hidden databases containing attributes with arbitrary-sized domains - we find the main reason to be the large number of queries required by a deterministic algorithm to decide how to construct the nested search space. To address this, we consider the design of randomized algorithms which allows query-efficient randomization of the nested-space construction process. To this end, we develop RANDOM-COUNT-DISCOVER, a Monte Carlo algorithm which only requires a small amount of queries to discover a large number of domain values.

For ALERT interface, we similarly prove the infeasibility of developing a query-efficient deterministic algorithm which guarantees complete attribute domain discovery. Our main result here is then an extension of RANDOM-COUNT-DISCOVER to RANDOM-ALERT-DISCOVER, a Monte Carlo algorithm which achieves similar performance to RANDOM-COUNT-DISCOVER by estimating COUNTs of queries based on historic query answers, and using estimated COUNTs to bootstrap RANDOM-COUNT-DISCOVER to discover domain values.

In summary, the main contributions of this paper are as follows:

- We initiate the study of attribute domain discovery over a hidden database through its restrictive web interface.
- We derive the achievability conditions for complete attribute domain discovery on k and the query cost. These conditions indicate the infeasibility of designing a query-efficient deterministic algorithm which guarantees the discovery of all attribute domains.
- We propose two randomized algorithms, RANDOM-COUNT-DISCOVER and RANDOM-ALERT-DISCOVER, for COUNT and ALERT interfaces, respectively. Both algorithms require only a small amount of queries to develop a large number of domain values.
- We provide a thorough theoretical analysis and experimental studies that demonstrate the effectiveness of our proposed algorithms over the real-world NSF award search database and a local patient discharge dataset.

Paper Organization: In Section 2 we introduce preliminaries and discuss simple but ineffective crawling algorithms for attribute domain discovery over hidden databases. Sections 3 and 4 are devoted to the development of deterministic and randomized algorithms for COUNT interfaces, respectively. In Section 5 we extend the results to ALERT interfaces. Section 6 contains a detailed experimental evaluation of our proposed approaches. Section 7 discusses related work, followed by conclusion in Section 8.

2. PRELIMINARIES

2.1 Model of Hidden Databases

Consider a hidden database table D with n tuples. Let there be m attributes $A_1, \ldots, A_m$ which can be specified through the input interface, and V_i be the domain of A_i. We assume each tuple to be unique, and each value in V_i ($i \in [1, m]$) to occur in at least one tuple in the database, because otherwise V_i can never be completely discovered from the database. Consider a prototypical interface which allows user to query D by specifying values for a subset of attributes - i.e., to issue queries q of the form:

SELECT * FROM D WHERE $A_{i_1} = v_{i_1} \& \cdots \& A_{i_s} = v_{i_s}$,

where $v_{i_j} \in V_{i_j}$. Let $Sel(q)$ be the set of tuples in D which satisfy q. Since the interface is restricted to return up to k tuples, a overly broad query (i.e., $|Sel(q)| > k$) will *overflow* and return only the top-k tuples in $Sel(q)$ selected according to a scoring function. In addition, a COUNT interface will return $|Sel(q)|$, the number of tuples satisfying q, while an ALERT interface will return an overflow flag indicating that not all tuples which satisfy q can be returned.

When a query does not overflow, COUNT and ALERT interfaces return the exact same information to the user. In particular, if the query is too specific to return any tuple, we say that an *underflow* occurs. If there is neither overflow nor underflow (i.e., $|Sel(q)| \in [1, k]$), then $Sel(q)$ will be returned in its entirety and we have a *valid* query result. For each tuple returned by an overflowing or valid query, the values of all its attributes are displayed, enabling the discovery of domain values of an attribute with unknown domain.

Running Example: We consider a running example of the above-mentioned NSF award search database with $k = 50$. There are 9 attributes, award amount, instrument, PI state, field, program manager, NSF organization, PI organization, City, and ZIP code, with domain sizes 5, 8, 58, 49, 654, 58, 3110, 1093, 1995, respectively (these are the estimates we generated by running our domain discovery algorithms to be presented in the paper for an extended period of time. We do not have the ground truth for all attributes. But they can be safely considered as lower bounds on domain sizes).

2.2 Problem Definition

We consider the problem of attribute domain discovery - i.e., the discovery of $V_1, \ldots, V_m$ through the restrictive interface. Since many hidden databases impose limits on the number of queries one can issue through their interfaces over a period of time, the performance of a domain discovery algorithm should be measured by not only the *comprehensiveness* of discovered domain values, but also the *query cost*, i.e., the number of queries issued through the interface of hidden database for domain discovery.

While the metric for query cost is straightforward, to measure the comprehensiveness of discovered domain values we consider the following two metrics.

- *Coverage*, i.e., the total number of domain values discovered for one or a set of attributes.
- *Recall*, i.e., the number of tuples in the database for which all attribute values (of $A_1, \ldots, A_m$) have been discovered.

Note that while the two metrics are positively correlated (e.g., a recall of n indicates a coverage of $|V_i|$ for each A_i), they may be preferred in different applications. For example, if the objective of domain discovery is to unveil the metadata, e.g., to discover the list of program managers from the NSF award database, then coverage is a more important metric. If the objective is to enable data analytics over the hidden database, then recall is more important as it guarantees how many tuples will be covered by the subsequent aggregate estimation and sampling algorithms.

Given the measures for comprehensiveness and query cost, we define the problem of attribute domain discovery as follows:

Problem Statement: *How to maximize the coverage and recall of attribute domain discovery while minimizing the query cost through COUNT and ALERT interfaces, respectively.*

2.3 Crawling-Based Algorithms

In this subsection, we consider depth-first search (DFS) and breadth-first search (BFS), two simple crawling-based algorithm for attribute domain discovery, and point out their problems in terms of the tradeoff between coverage/recall and query cost. Both algorithms start with SELECT * FROM D to learn the first few domain values, but then take different methods to construct the subsequent queries.

DFS: With DFS, one constructs the next query by finding an attribute that is not specified in the previous one, and then adding to the previous query a conjunctive condition defined by the attribute and one of its already discovered domain values. Such a process continues, with DFS learning all domain values from tuples returned by each issued query, until either the query returns underflows/valid or no discovered domain value is available for constructing the next query, at which time the algorithm backtracks by removing the last-added condition and adding a new one based on another discovered domain value. We refer to the algorithm as DFS because it keeps increasing the number of predicates included in the query if possible.

A main problem of DFS, however, is poor coverage and recall when a large number of attributes are strongly correlated with the first few attributes appended to SELECT * FROM D. For example, consider the case where $A_1 = v_1$ is first appended to the SELECT * query, and $A_1 \rightarrow A_m$ forms a functional dependency. Since DFS with a small query budget is likely to explore only queries with predicate $A_1 = v_1$, the domain values of A_m which are corresponding to the other values of A_1 will not be discovered.

BFS: With BFS, one first exhausts all 1-predicate queries that can be constructed from discovered domain values, before moving forward to construct and issue 2-predicate queries, etc. The main problem of BFS arises when a large number of domain values are strongly correlated with the scoring function used to select the top-k tuples, because BFS with a small query budget is likely to issue only overflowing queries. For example, consider a total order of values for A_m and suppose that tuples with "larger" A_m receives higher scores. Then, BFS will likely to only discover the larger values of A_m.

3. DETERMINISTIC ALGORITHMS FOR COUNT INTERFACES

In this section, we analyze the achievability conditions for attribute domain discovery over a top-k-COUNT interface, and also develop deterministic algorithms which guarantee the discovery of all attribute domains when the achievability conditions are met. The purpose of introducing deterministic algorithms is to use them as the basis for our design of more efficient randomized algorithms in the next section.

3.1 Discover Binary Domains

We start with a simple case where each attribute has only two possible values, both unknown to the third-party analyzer[2]. An example of such an attribute is transmission for an auto database which has two values, "manual" and "automatic". While hardly any practical database consists solely of binary attributes, the results in this subsection are illustrative when considering extensions to handle arbitrary attribute domains, as we shall show in the next subsection.

3.1.1 *Achievability of Domain Discovery*

[2]The third-party analyzer may or may not know the binary nature of all attributes - our results apply either way.

Before devising concrete attribute domain discovery algorithms, we first consider the problem of achievability - i.e., whether it is at all possible for the third-party analyzer to discover all attribute domains from the top-k interface. There are two sub-problems: (1) whether complete attribute domain discovery is possible when the analyzer can afford an unlimited query cost, and (2) if the first answer is yes, then what is the minimum number of queries required by a deterministic algorithm to accomplish attribute domain discovery in the worst case?

Our main results, as shown by the following three theorems, can be summarized as follows: The answer to the first question is a lower bound on k - i.e., no algorithm without knowledge of the scoring function can guarantee complete discovery over any hidden database if $k = 1$, while complete discovery is always possible for any combination of database and scoring function when $k \geq 2$. For the second question, if $k \geq 2$, a deterministic algorithm require (at least) $\Omega(m^2/\log m)$ queries to discover all attribute domains in the worst case, where m is the number of attributes, unless $k \geq n$, in which case SELECT * FROM D returns all tuples in the database.

THEOREM 3.1. *If $k = 1$, then for any given binary database, there exists a scoring function such that no algorithm can discover the domains of all attributes.*

PROOF. This impossibility proof is simple - Let the tuple returned by SELECT * FROM D be $t = [0_1, \ldots, 0_n]$. Assign the highest score to t. One can see that no algorithm can discover any domain value other than $\{0_1, \ldots, 0_n\}$. $\square$

THEOREM 3.2. *For any given number of attributes m, there exists a binary database and a scoring function such that no deterministic algorithm can complete attribute domain discovery without incurring a worst-case query cost of $\Omega(m^2/\log m)$, even if $k \geq 2$.*

PROOF. For the sake of simplicity, we consider the case where m is even. The case where m is odd can be proved in analogy. We construct a set of $2^{m^2/4}$ database instances $D_1, \ldots, D_{2^{m^2/4}}$ as follows: Each instance D_i consists of $2^{m/2}+m/2$ tuples $t_1, \ldots, t_{2^{m/2}+m/2}$. We consider the first $2^{m/2}$ tuples first - for these tuples (i.e., with $i \in [1, 2^{m/2}]$), if $j \in [1, m/2]$, $t_i[A_j] = 0_j$ (resp. 1_j) iff the j-th most significant bit of the binary representation of $i-1$ is 0 (resp. 1); if $j \in [m/2+1, m]$, then there is always $t_i[A_j] = 0_j$.

For the latter $m/2$ tuples, their values of $A_{m/2+1}, \ldots, A_m$ are set such that $t_i[A_j] = 1_j$ iff $i = 2^{m/2} - m/2 + j$, and $t_i[A_j] = 0_j$ otherwise. For the values of $A_1, \ldots, A_{m/2}$ of these tuples, they are set such that each database instance has a different combination of the $m/2$ tuples. Note that for each tuple, there are $2^{m/2}$ possible choices. Thus, we can construct $(2^{m/2})^{m/2} = 2^{m^2/4}$ different database instances. The scoring function for each instance is designed with only one condition: each tuple which satisfies $t_i[A_j] = 0_j$ for all $j \in [m/2+1, m]$ has a higher score than all tuples which do not satisfy this condition.

There are two important observations one can make from the above construction when $k = 2$. First, each database instance requires a different sequence of queries to unveil all domain values. The reason for this is because the only way to unveil 1_j for $j \in [m/2+1, m]$ is to issue a query that contains at least $m/2$ predicates corresponding to the values of $A_1, \ldots, A_{m/2}$ for tuple $t_{2^{m/2}-m/2+j}$, respectively. Since each database instance has a different combination of values for $t_{2^{m/2}+1}, \ldots, t_{2^{m/2}+m/2}$, each instance requires a different sequence of queries for complete attribute domain discovery.

The second important observation is that the ability for any query to distinguish between the $2^{m^2/4}$ database instances is limited. Note that if only the returned tuples are concerned, then almost all queries (except those that unveil one of 1_j for $j \in [m/2+1, m]$) return the exact same tuples when $k = 2$. The more powerful distinguishing factor is COUNT. Nonetheless, the COUNT of any query has only $m/2$ different answers for all database instances, because after all these instances differ by at most $m/2$ tuples.

Since we focus on deterministic algorithms, it is impossible for an algorithm to receive the same answer for all previous queries but then issue a different query in the next step for two database instances. Thus, in order for the algorithm to have a different sequence of queries for each database instance, the query cost is at least $\log_{m/2} 2^{m^2/4}$, i.e., $\Omega(m^2/\log m)$. $\square$

Given the achievability conditions shown in the above two theorems, we now show the existence of a deterministic algorithm that is capable of discovering all attribute domains when the achievability conditions are met, and achieves a near-optimal query cost (within a factor of $\log m$ where m is the number of attributes).

THEOREM 3.3. *If $k \geq 2$, there exists a deterministic algorithm which guarantees complete attribute domain discovery for all binary databases and all scoring functions with a query cost of $O(m^2)$.*

The following deterministic algorithm, B-COUNT-DISCOVER, serves as the proof. One can see from this theorem that for databases with only binary domains, the problem of attribute domain discovery can indeed by solved with a small query cost as long as $k \geq 2$.

3.1.2 B-COUNT-DISCOVER

B-COUNT-DISCOVER starts by issuing query q_1: SELECT * FROM D. Without loss of generality, let $t : [0_1, \ldots, 0_m]$ be a tuple returned by q_1. Since $k \geq 2$, there must be another tuple returned by q_1 which differs from t on at least one attribute value. Again without loss of generality, let such an attribute be A_1 - i.e., the analyzer learns from the answer to q_1 at least the following $m+1$ values: $\{0_1, \ldots, 0_m, 1_1\}$. The objective of B-COUNT-DISCOVER then becomes to unveil $1_2, \ldots, 1_m$.

To discover any of these values, say 1_m, we essentially need to find a tuple with $A_m = 1_m$. Initially, the *search space* - i.e., the set of possible tuple values in the database featuring $A_m = 1_m$ - is very large. In particular, the initial space $\mathcal{S}_1(1_m)$ is formed by all possible value combinations for $A_1, \ldots, A_{m-1}$ (and $A_m = 1_m$) and thus of size 2^{m-1}. Our main idea of B-COUNT-DISCOVER is to shrink the search space by leveraging COUNT information provided by the interface. In particular, we construct a series of *nested spaces* $\mathcal{S}_1(1_m), \mathcal{S}_2(1_m), \ldots$, each half the size of the preceding one, while ensuring that every $\mathcal{S}_i(1_m)$ contains at least one tuple in the database with $A_m = 1_m$. Then, even in the worst-case scenario, we can unveil 1_m when the search space is shrinked to size 1 - by simply issuing an $(m-1)$-predicate query with $A_1, \ldots, A_{m-1}$ specified according to the value left in the search space.

To understand how the nested spaces are constructed, consider the following three queries.

q_2. SELECT * FROM D WHERE $A_m = 0_m$
q_3. SELECT * FROM D WHERE $A_1 = 0_1$
q_4. SELECT * FROM D WHERE $A_1 = 0_1$ AND $A_m = 0_m$

Let $C(q_i)$ be the COUNT returned alongside query q_i. We can compute from the query answers C_1 : COUNT($A_1 = 0_1$ AND $A_m = 1_m$) and C_2 : COUNT($A_1 = 1_1$ AND $A_m = 1_m$) as

$$C_1 = C(q_3) - C(q_4), \tag{1}$$

$$C_2 = C(q_1) - C(q_2) - (C(q_3) - C(q_4)). \tag{2}$$

Note that either C_1 or C_2 (or both) must be greater than 0 if 1_m occurs in the database. Suppose that $C_1 > 0$. We can now shrink our search space by half to size 2^{m-2} - by constructing $\mathcal{S}_2(1_m) \subset \mathcal{S}_1(1_m)$ with only values in $\mathcal{S}_1(1_m)$ which satisfy $A_1 = 0_1$. One can see that, since $C_1 > 0$, at least one value in $\mathcal{S}_2(1_m)$ appears in the database and has $A_m = 1_m$.

The shrinking process continues from here. To see how, note that since $C_1 > 0$, q_3 either returns a tuple with $A_m = 1_m$ or overflows. If q_3 overflows without returning 1_m, there must exist another attribute (in $A_2, \ldots, A_{m-1}$) which has both values appearing in the k tuples returned for q_3. Without loss of generality, let the attribute be A_2. We now issue the following two queries.

q_5. SELECT * FROM D WHERE $A_1 = 0_1$ AND $A_2 = 0_2$

q_6. SELECT * FROM D WHERE $A_1 = 0_1$ AND $A_2 = 0_2$ AND $A_m = 0_m$

Similar to the last step, we compute C_3 : COUNT($A_1 = 0_1$ AND $A_2 = 0_2$ AND $A_m = 1_m$) and C_4 : COUNT($A_1 = 0_1$ AND $A_2 = 1_2$ AND $A_m = 1_m$) as

$$C_3 = C(q_5) - C(q_6), \tag{3}$$

$$C_4 = C(q_3) - C(q_4) - (C(q_5) - C(q_6)). \tag{4}$$

Again, at least one of C_3 and C_4 must be greater than 0 because $C_1 > 0$. Suppose that $C_4 > 0$. We can then further shrink our search space to size 2^{m-3} by constructing $\mathcal{S}_3(1_m) \subset \mathcal{S}_2(1_m)$ with only values in $\mathcal{S}_2(1_m)$ which satisfies $A_2 = 1_2$. Once again, at least one value in $\mathcal{S}_3(1_m)$ appears in the database and has $A_m = 1_m$ because $C_4 > 0$. Note that before the next shrinking step, we might need to issue

q_7. SELECT * FROM D WHERE $A_1 = 0_1$ AND $A_2 = 1_2$

in order to discover the complete domain of another attribute (in $A_3, \ldots, A_{m-1}$), so that we can continue the shrinking process. Note that similar to the discovery of A_2's domain from q_3, this discovery is guaranteed by q_7 because it either returns a tuple with $A_m = 1_m$ (which accomplishes our task) or overflows, in which case at least one attribute unspecified in q_7 must have different values appear in the $k \geq 2$ tuples returned by q_7.

One can see that eventually, we can always discover 1_m after issuing at most $3m$ queries, because the search space would then become $\mathcal{S}_m(1_m)$ of size 1. Thus, B-COUNT-DISCOVER requires a query cost of $O(m^2)$. This concludes the proof of Theorem 3.3.

3.2 Discover Arbitrary Domains

We now extend our results for binary domains to arbitrary domains. We start by showing that the originally practical achievability conditions for binary domains, i.e., lower bounds on k and query cost, now become unrealistic for arbitrary domains. Then, we illustrate the fundamental reason for such a change which motivates our design of randomized algorithms in the next section.

3.2.1 *Achievability of Attribute Domain Discovery*

For arbitrary domains, the achievability condition for attribute domain discovery imposes a much large lower bound on k, as indicated by the following theorem. Recall that $|V_i|$ is the domain size of A_i.

THEOREM 3.4. *If $k < 1+\prod_{i=1}^{m}(|V_i|-1)$, then no deterministic algorithm can guarantee the discovery of all attribute domains for all database instance/scoring function combinations.*

PROOF. Arbitrarily pick one attribute value v_i from each V_i ($i \in [1, m]$), respectively. Consider a database D formed by $1 + \prod_{i=1}^{m}(|V_i| - 1)$ tuples. $\prod_{i=1}^{m}(|V_i| - 1)$ of them are the Cartesian product of $V_i \backslash \{v_i\}$ for all $i \in [1, m]$. The one additional tuple is $t : [v_1, \ldots, v_m]$. Suppose that t has the lowest score. One can see that no algorithm can discover any of $v_1, \ldots, v_m$ if t is not returned by SELECT * FROM D. Thus, no algorithm can guarantee complete attribute domain discovery when $k < 1+\prod_{i=1}^{m}(|V_i|-1)$. □

One can see from Theorem 3.4 that the binary-case result, Theorem 3.1, is indeed a special case when $|V_1| = \cdots = |V_m| = 2$. Another observation from Theorem 3.4 is that the lower bound on k has now become hardly reachable because real-world database often features a number of attributes with large domains.

> Running Example: The NSF award search database requires $k \geq 1 + \prod_{i=1}^{m}(|V_i| - 1) = 1.93 \times 10^{19}$ to guarantee complete attribute domain discovery.

What reinforces this impracticability result is the following theorem. Note that since the achievability condition on k is now infeasible, it makes little practical sense for us to assume $k \geq 1 + \prod_{i=1}^{n}(|V_i| - 1)$, as in the binary case, when deriving the lower bound on query cost. As such, we consider the following question: for a given value of k, is it possible for a deterministic algorithm to use a small number of queries to discover all domain values that *can* be discovered from such a top-k interface (given unlimited query cost)? The following lower bound on k shows that the answer to this question is also no for hidden databases with arbitrary domains.

THEOREM 3.5. *For given k and m, there exists a database and a scoring function such that no deterministic algorithm can complete the discovery of all domain values that can be discovered from the top-k COUNT interface without incurring a worst-case query cost of*

$$\Omega\left(\frac{m^2 \cdot |V_{\max}| \cdot \log |V_{\max}|}{k \cdot \log(m \cdot |V_{\min}|)}\right) \tag{5}$$

where $|V_{\max}|$ and $|V_{\min}|$ are the maximum and minimum values in $|V_1|, \ldots, |V_m|$, respectively.

The proof of this theorem follows in analogy to Theorem 3.2. We do not include it due to the space limitation. One can see that the binary-case lower bound on query cost, Theorem 3.2, is indeed a special case of Theorem 3.5 when $|V| = 2$ and $k = 2$. Another observation from Theorem 3.5 is that this arbitrary-domain lower bound on query cost, just like the lower bound on k, is hardly achievable in practice, especially when the hidden database contains one or a few attributes (e.g., ZIP code) with large domains.

> Running Example: With the setting of our NSF award search example, $m^2 \cdot |V_{\max}| \cdot \log |V_{\max}|/(k \cdot \log(m \cdot |V_{\min}|)) = 1.06 \times 10^4$. While the bound may differ by a constant factor, 10^4 is at least an order of magnitude larger than what one would desire for attribute domain discovery (e.g., in our experimental results).

Although the achievability conditions for both k and query cost are unrealistic for arbitrary domains, in the following we still extend B-COUNT-DISCOVER to COUNT-DISCOVER, a deterministic algorithm that is capable of discovering all attribute domains. Of course, the extended algorithm has to follow the achievability conditions and therefore cannot provide meaningful worst-case performance. Our main purpose of studying it is to identify which part of the extension causes the significant increase on query cost. Theorem 3.6 summarizes the query cost of COUNT-DISCOVER.

THEOREM 3.6. *For an m-attribute database with $k \geq 1 + \prod_{i=1}^{n}(|V_i| - 1)$, there exists an algorithm which requires at most*

$$\sum_{i=1}^{m}\left((2|V_{d_i}| - 1) \cdot \sum_{j=1}^{m-i+1}\left(\frac{|V_{d_j}| \cdot (|V_{d_j}| - 1)}{2}\right)\right) \tag{6}$$

queries to discover all attribute domains, where $d_1, \ldots, d_m$ is the permutation of $1, \ldots, m$ which satisfies $|V_{d_1}| \geq \cdots \geq |V_{d_m}|$.

Running Example: With NSF award search example, the worst-case query cost of COUNT-DISCOVER is 1.07×10^{11}, orders of magnitude larger than what one can afford.

Similar to the binary case, we explain the proof of this theorem in the description of COUNT-DISCOVER. Note yet again that the binary-case result, Theorem 3.3, is a special case of Theorem 3.6 when $|V_i| = 2$ for all $i \in [1, m]$. Nonetheless, unlike in the binary case where B-COUNT-DISCOVER has a query cost within a factor of $O(\log m)$ from optimal, the query cost of COUNT-DISCOVER is further away from the lower bound in Theorem 3.5. In particular, observe from Theorem 3.6 the worst-case query cost of COUNT-DISCOVER is $\Omega(|V_{d_1}|^2 + |V_{d_m}|^3)$, a factor of $O(|V_{d_1}| + |V_{d_m}|^2)$ from optimal. We did not pursue to close this gap for two reasons: First, since the lower bound itself is infeasible in practice, even an optimal algorithm would not be practical anyway. Second, our purpose of introducing COUNT-DISCOVER is not to promote its practical usage, but to use the comparison between B-COUNT-DISCOVER and COUNT-DISCOVER to illustrate the main obstacle facing the discovery of arbitrary attribute domains, which motivates our design of efficient (and thus practical) randomized algorithms.

3.2.2 *COUNT-DISCOVER*

We now extend B-COUNT-DISCOVER to arbitrary domains, given the condition that $k \geq 1 + \prod_{i=1}^{n}(|V_i| - 1)$. Note that this lower bound on k guarantees that SELECT * FROM D must reveal the complete domain for at least one attribute, assumed to be A_1 without loss of generality. In addition, it must reveal at least one domain value for the remaining $m - 1$ attributes, assumed to be $0_2, \ldots, 0_m$. As such, the objective of COUNT-DISCOVER is to unveil $1_i, \ldots, (|V_i|)_i$ for all $i \in [2, m]$.

Like in the binary case, we consider the discovery of an arbitrary attribute domain, say V_m, by constructing a series of nested spaces that are guaranteed to contain at least one tuple in D which has its value of A_m yet to be discovered. Consider the worst-case scenario where the only value of V_m revealed by SELECT * FROM D is 0_m. The starting search space $\mathcal{S}_1(V_m)$ then has a size of $(|V_m| - 1) \cdot \prod_{i=1}^{m-1} |V_i|$. Since we already know the complete domain of A_1, the next step is to find one value in V_1 which can be used to construct the next nested space - which must guarantee the appearance of at least one value in $1_m, \ldots, (|V_i|)_m$.

In the binary case, we only need to determine whether 0_1 can be used because if it cannot, then 1_1 can always be used because A_1 has only these two possible values. In particular, the judgement for 0_1 can be done with just two queries - WHERE $A_1 = 0_1$ and WHERE $A_1 = 0_1$ and $A_m = 0_m$ - because we can then infer the COUNT of tuples that satisfy $A_1 = 0_1$ and $A_m = 1_m$. Note that for arbitrary domains, we can still determine whether 0_1 can be used with the two exact same queries, because they now reveal the COUNT of tuples that satisfy $A_1 = 0_1$ and have their values of A_m yet to be discovered. Nonetheless, since the domain of A_1 is much larger (than binary), we must continue testing other values of A_1 if 0_1 cannot be used. In the worst-case scenario, we may not be able to find the next search space until testing $|V_1| - 1$ possible values of A_1. Thus, at this step, the query cost for arbitrary domain becomes $|V_1| - 1$ times as large as that for binary domain.

Let $w_1 \in V_1$ be the value we find and use to construct the next nested search space. We can now construct the next nested space $\mathcal{S}_2(V_m)$ by only including value combinations in $\mathcal{S}_1(V_m)$ which satisfy $A_1 = w_1$. One can see that the size of search space now becomes $(|V_m| - 1) \cdot \prod_{i=2}^{m-1} |V_i|$. COUNT-DISCOVER continues the shrinking process in the same way as the binary case - i.e., by issuing query q: SELECT * FROM D WHERE $A_1 = w_1$ (if it has not already been issued). One can see that either q returns a yet-to-be-discovered value in V_m, or it overflows, in which case we can always find the complete domain of an attribute in $A_2, \ldots, A_{m-1}$ from the k tuples returned by q because $k \geq 1 + \prod_{i=1}^{n}(|V_i| - 1)$. As such, eventually we can always unveil one value in V_m that has not yet been discovered. Nonetheless, since we do not maintain in the search space *all* yet-to-be-discovered value in V_m, the entire shrinking process may have to be repeated multiple times to unveil the entire V_m. Theorem 3.6 can be derived accordingly.

A key observation from the design of COUNT-DISCOVER is that the significant increase on query cost (from the binary case) is not because the shrinking of search spaces becomes less powerful - indeed, ALERT-DISCOVER still needs only m nested spaces $\mathcal{S}_1(V_m), \ldots, \mathcal{S}_m(V_m)$ to reach size 1. The increase on query cost is largely due to the cost of determining how to construct the next nested space (i.e. by filtering the current one) - a task previously accomplished by just two queries now requires many more. In the next section, we shall show that randomizing such nested-space construction process is our key idea for building efficient randomized algorithms for discovering arbitrary attribute domains.

4. RANDOMIZED ALGORITHMS FOR COUNT INTERFACES

In the last section, we developed a query-efficient algorithm for discovering binary domains, but found its extension to arbitrary domains to be extremely inefficient. We also found the main reason behind this obstacle to be the increased cost of determining how to construct the nested search spaces - in particular, for a given search space and an attribute A_i, how to select a domain value v of A_i such that $A_i = v$ can be used to filter the current search space while maintaining at least one tuple with yet-to-be-discovered domain value(s) in the filtered space.

Now that any deterministic construction of nested spaces is provably expensive due to the achievability conditions we derived in the last section, our main idea in this section is to *randomize* nested-space construction, so as to spend a small number of queries for search space construction while maintaining yet-to-be-discovered domain value(s) in the constructed space with high probability. In the following, we first describe our randomized process of nested-space construction and the performance (i.e., recall and coverage) guarantee it is able to achieve, and then combine this process with COUNT-DISCOVER to form RANDOM-COUNT-DISCOVER, our randomized (Monte Carlo) algorithm for attribute domain discovery which can unveil attribute domains (though not necessarily completely) no matter if the achievability conditions are met.

4.1 Randomize Nested-Space Construction

Recall that the main obstacle for nested-space construction is to find a predicate $A_i = v$ that can be used to filter the current search space. In the worst-case scenario, one may have to find $m - 1$ such conditions to discover a domain value for an attribute say A_j - this occurs when the complete domains of all attributes but A_j have been discovered. For the purpose of discussing the randomization of nested-space construction, we consider a worst-case scenario where the complete domains of $A_1, \ldots, A_{m-1}$ have been discovered, and our objective now is to discover the domain of A_m. As a side note - this problem is actually interesting in its own right because it captures the scenario where A_m is a textbox attribute (with unknown domain) on the hidden database interface, while a large number of other attributes (i.e., $A_1, \ldots, A_{m-1}$) have domains provided by the interface (e.g., through options in drop-down menus). We shall shown in the experiments section that our algorithms can effectively discover the domain of A_m in this scenario.

RANDOM-SPACE: A simple idea to randomize the construction of nested spaces is to choose v uniformly at random from the domain of A_i. With this idea, every round (i.e., search-space shrinking process) of our RANDOM-SPACE algorithm starts with SELECT * FROM D as the first query. Then, if no new domain value of A_m is discovered from the query answer, it randomly chooses v_1 from V_1 and then uses $A_1 = v_1$ to filter the search space (i.e., by issuing query SELECT * FROM D WHERE $A_1 = v_1$). More generally, if RANDOM-SPACE fails to discover a new domain value of A_m from the first $b-1$ queries issued in the current round, then it constructs the b-query by adding a conjunctive condition $A_b = v_b$, where v_b is chosen uniformly at random from V_b, to the selection condition of the $(b-1)$-th query.

Each round of RANDOM-SPACE requires at most m queries, and may lead to two possible outcomes: One is a new domain value being discovered. The other is that RANDOM-SPACE reaches a valid or underflowing query *without* discovering any new domain value. Note that while this outcome never occurs for COUNT-DISCOVER, it might occur for RANDOM-SPACE because of the random construction of nested spaces. RANDOM-SPACE may be executed for multiple rounds to discover more domain values.

One can see that the randomization used by RANDOM-SPACE guarantees a positive probability for each domain value to be discovered. Nonetheless, the main problem of it occurs when the distribution of tuples in the database is severally skewed - e.g., when almost all tuples have the same values for A_1, A_2, etc. In this case, a large number of queries may be wasted on a small number of tuples, rendering it unlikely for RANDOM-SPACE to unveil many domain values.

RANDOM-COUNT-SPACE: The main problem of RANDOM-SPACE can be solved by leveraging the COUNT information provided by the interface. In particular, RANDOM-COUNT-SPACE constructs the nested spaces in a similar fashion to RANDOM-SPACE, with the only exception that the value v in selection condition $A_i = v$ is no longer drawn uniformly at random from V_i. Instead, RANDOM-COUNT-SPACE first retrieves the COUNT of all $|V_i|$ possible queries that define the next search space (each corresponding to a different value of v). Then, it selects v in proportional to its corresponding COUNT. The construction of nested search spaces continues until either finding a new domain value or reaching a valid query. Note that since we now leverage COUNT information, an underflowing query will never be selected to construct the next search space.

An important property of RANDOM-COUNT-SPACE is that if we continue the search-space shrinking process until reaching a valid query, then the valid query returns each tuple in the database with roughly equal probability (precisely equal if $k = 1$, varies at most k times otherwise). This property explains why RANDOM-COUNT-SPACE solves the above-mentioned problem of RANDOM-SPACE. Nonetheless, RANDOM-COUNT-SPACE also has its own problem. In particular, if A_m is strongly correlated with A_1, A_2, etc (e.g., $A_1, A_2 \rightarrow A_m$ forms a functional dependency), and all but a few tuples have the same value of A_m, then RANDOM-COUNT-SPACE may spend too many queries retrieving tuples featuring the "popular" value of A_m (because the spaces it constructs most likely follow the "popular" value combination of A_1 and A_2), but fails to retrieve the other values. Interestingly, one can see that RANDOM-SPACE can handle this case pretty well, motivating our idea of mixing the two randomization approaches.

HYBRID-SPACE: We now consider a hybrid of RANDOM- and RANDOM-COUNT-SPACE to avoid the problems of both. In particular, HYBRID-SPACE starts with RANDOM-SPACE. It is repeated executed until none of the last $r_1 + 1$ times returns any new domain value, where r_1 is a small number (e.g., 0 to 5), the setting of which shall be discussed in the next subsection and in the experiments. At this time, we switch to RANDOM-COUNT-SPACE.

One round of RANDOM-COUNT-SPACE is performed. If it unveils a new domain value, then the *entire* process of HYBRID-SPACE is restarted by going back to the beginning of RANDOM-SPACE. If no new value is discovered, we repeat RANDOM-COUNT-SPACE for up to r_2 other rounds or until a new domain value is discovered, whichever happens first. Similar to r_1, we shall discuss the setting of r_2 in the next subsection and in the experiments. If a new domain value is discovered, then the entire HYBRID-SPACE is restarted. Otherwise, If $r_2 + 1$ consecutive rounds of RANDOM-COUNT-SPACE fails to return any new domain value, we terminate HYBRID-SPACE. Algorithm 1 depicts the pseudocode for HYBRID-SPACE. Note that the input parameter in the pseudocode is designed for integration into RANDOM-COUNT-DISCOVER.

Algorithm 1 HYBRID-SPACE

```
1: Input parameter: q0, set to SELECT * FROM D by default
2: repeat
3:     //Perform one round of RANDOM-SPACE
4:     q ← q0
5:     while q overflows AND returns no new domain value do
6:         Select A_i not specified in q. Select v uniformly at random from the discovered domain of A_i
7:         q ← (q AND A_i = v). Issue q to learn new values.
8:     end while
9: until the last r1 + 1 rounds return no new domain value
10: repeat
11:     //Perform one round of RANDOM-COUNT-SPACE
12:     q ← q0
13:     while q overflows AND returns no new domain value do
14:         Select A_i not specified in q. For each discovered v ∈ V_i, Query c(v) ← COUNT of (q AND A_i = v)
15:         Select v with probability proportional to c(v)
16:         q ← (q AND A_i = v). Issue q to learn new values.
17:     end while
18:     if q returns a new domain value then Goto 2.
19: until the last r2 + 1 rounds return no new domain value
```

4.2 HYBRID-SPACE Performance Guarantee

An important feature of HYBRID-SPACE is the performance guarantee it provides *independent* of the underlying data distribution. To illustrate such a guarantee, we consider an example where $A_1, \ldots, A_{m-1}$ each has a domain of size 10. Let there be k = 50, n = 1,000,000 tuples and $m = 10$ attributes in the database (note that n is readily available from the interface). Consider a parameter setting of $r_1 = r_2 = 0$. The following derivation shows how HYBRID-SPACE guarantees either a coverage of 46 values or a median recall of 500,000 tuples with only 4,036 queries.

Case 1: First consider the case where HYBRID-SPACE did not terminate before $4,036$ queries were issued. Let w_{B} and w_{T} be the number of rounds RANDOM- and RANDOM-COUNT-SPACE were performed, respectively. Since $r_1 = 0$, the number of discovered domain values is at least $w_{\mathrm{B}} - 1$. Since $A_1, \ldots, A_{m-1}$ each has 10 domain values, an RANDOM-COUNT-SPACE shrinking process issues at most $9(m-1)$ queries. Thus, the $w_{\mathrm{B}} + w_{\mathrm{T}}$ finished rounds consume at least $4036 - (9(m-1)-1) = 4046 - 9m$ queries because the final unfinished round could have issued at most $9(m-1) - 1$ queries. As such,

$$c \cdot w_{\mathrm{B}} + 9(m-1) \cdot w_{\mathrm{T}} \geq 4046 - 9m. \quad (7)$$

where c is the average number of queries issued by a round of

RANDOM-SPACE during the execution. Since $r_2 = 0$, $w_B \geq w_T$. Thus, $(c + 9(m-1)) \cdot w_B \geq 4046 - 9m$. If HYBRID-SPACE did not discover at least 46 values, then $w_B \leq 46$ and therefore $c \geq (3956/46) - 9(m-1) = 5$.

A key step now is to prove that $c \geq 5$ indicates an absolute recall of at least $500,000$. This is enabled by the following theorem which illustrates a positive correlation between the *absolute recall* γ and the *average query cost* c (per round) of RANDOM-SPACE.

THEOREM 4.1. *There is $\gamma \geq k \cdot 10^{c-1}$ with probability close to 1 when the number of rounds is sufficiently large.*

PROOF. Let there be a total of s rounds of RANDOM-SPACE performed. Consider the i-th round ($i \in [1, s]$). Let γ_i be the absolute recall of discovered domain values before the round begins. Given the discovered values, let Ω_i be the set of queries which may be the second-to-last query issued by this i-th round. One can see that each query in Ω_i must overflow and have all returned tuples featuring the already discovered domain values. Thus, we have $\gamma_i \geq k \cdot |\Omega_i|$, where $|\Omega_i|$ is the number of queries in Ω_i.

For each $q \in \Omega_i$, let $p(q)$ and $h(q)$ be the probability for q to be chosen in this round of RANDOM-SPACE and the number of predicates in v, respectively. Since each attribute in $A_1, \ldots, A_{m-1}$ has 10 possible values, we have $p(q) \leq 1/10^{h(q)}$. Thus,

$$E_{q \in \Omega_i}(k \cdot 10^{h(q)}) = \sum_{q \in \Omega_i} \frac{k \cdot 10^{h(q)}}{10^{h(q)}} = k \cdot |\Omega_i| \leq \gamma_i \quad (8)$$

where the expected value is taken over the randomness of nested space construction in RANDOM-SPACE.

Note that $k \cdot 2^x$ is a convex function of x. According to Jensen's inequality, $E_{q \in \Omega_i}(k \cdot 10^{h(q)}) \geq k \cdot 10^{E_{q \in \Omega_i}(h(q))}$. Also note that for any i, $\gamma_i \leq \gamma$. Thus, $k \cdot 10^{E_{q \in \Omega_i}(h(q))} \leq \gamma_i \leq \gamma$.

When s, the total number of rounds of RANDOM-SPACE, is sufficiently large, according to the central limit theorem, the probability of $E_{q \in \Omega_i}(h(q)) < c - 1$ for every $i \in [1, s]$ tends to 0. Thus, the probability of $\gamma \geq k \cdot 10^{c-1}$ tends to 1 when the number of drill-downs is sufficiently large. □

According to the theorem, $c \geq 5$ indicates an absolute recall of at least $k \cdot 10^{5-1} = 500000$.

Case 2: Now consider the other case where HYBRID-SPACE terminates *before* 4,036 queries were issued. This indicates that the last round of RANDOM-COUNT-SPACE returns no new domain value. Let the absolute recall be $\alpha \cdot n$. With each round of RANDOM-COUNT-SPACE, the probability for the $(1 - \alpha) \cdot n$ "unrecalled" tuples to be retrieved is $1 - \alpha$. Thus, with Bayes' theorem, the posterior probability for $\alpha < 50\%$ given the empty discovery of the last round of RANDOM-COUNT-SPACE is

$$\Pr\{\alpha < 50\% | \text{empty discovery}\} < \frac{1/2 \cdot 1/2}{\int_0^1 p \, dp} = 1/2. \quad (9)$$

That is, the median absolute recall is at least 500000. In summary of both cases, HYBRID-SPACE either discovers at least 46 values, or has a median absolute recall of 500000.

Generic Performance Guarantee: More generally, we have the following algorithm:

THEOREM 4.2. *For a query budget of d over a top-k interface, HYBRID-SPACE achieves either an absolute coverage of m_0 values, or a median absolute recall of at least*

$$\min\left(k \cdot \prod_{i=1}^{\sigma} |V_i|, \sqrt[r_2+2]{\frac{1}{2(r_2+2)}} \cdot n\right) \quad (10)$$

where

$$\sigma = \frac{d - \sum_{i=1}^{m-1} |V_i| + 1}{m_0 \cdot (r_1 + 1)} - \frac{r_2 + 1}{r_1 + 1} \cdot \sum_{i=1}^{m-1} |V_i|. \quad (11)$$

We do not include the proof due to the space limitation. One can see from the theorem that a suggest setting for r_1 and r_2 is $r_1 = r_2 = 0$, as it maximizes the lower bound derived in (10). We shall verify this suggested setting in the experiments.

> Running Example: To discover the domain of Instrument from the NSF award search database based on pre-known domains of award amount, PI state, NSF organization, and field, HYBRID-SPACE requires at most 1563 queries to guarantee either the complete discovery of all domain values, or an absolute recall of $\min(4.12 \times 10^7, n/2)$.

4.3 RANDOM-COUNT-DISCOVER

We now integrate HYBRID-SPACE into COUNT-DISCOVER to produce RANDOM-COUNT-DISCOVER, our randomized (Monte Carlo) algorithm for discovering attribute domains. RANDOM-COUNT-DISCOVER starts with SELECT * FROM D, and uses the domain values discovered from the returned results to bootstrap HYBRID-SPACE. After that, RANDOM-COUNT-DISCOVER executes HYBRID-SPACE for multiple rounds, using the domain values discovered from previous rounds to bootstrap the next round.

In particular, at any time, RANDOM-COUNT-DISCOVER maintains a set of domain values that have been discovered but not used in the current round of HYBRID-SPACE. Let it be $V \subseteq \cup_{i=1}^{m} V_i$. At the start, V is empty. After every round of HYBRID-SPACE, the new domain values discovered are added to V. Then, in the next round of HYBRID-SPACE, we randomly select an attribute with domain values in V, say A_j and $\{v_{j1}, \ldots, v_{jh}\} = V \cap V_j$, and start the search-space construction process with a selection condition of $A_j = v$ where $v \in \{v_{j1}, \ldots, v_{jh}\}$. We then remove v from V. RANDOM-COUNT-DISCOVER terminates when V is empty or the query budget is exhausted.

Algorithm 2 RANDOM-COUNT-DISCOVER

$q_0 \leftarrow$ SELECT * FROM D, $V \leftarrow \phi$.
repeat
  Execute HYBRID-SPACE(q_0)
  $V \leftarrow$ domain values discovered by HYBRID-SPACE
  Arbitrarily select j and v such that $v \in V \cap V_j$
  $q_0 \leftarrow$ SELECT * FROM D WHERE $A_j = v$
  $V \leftarrow V \backslash v$
until $V = \phi$ or the query budget is exhausted

5. ATTRIBUTE DOMAIN DISCOVERY FOR ALERT INTERFACES

We now extend our results to ALERT interfaces which does not offer COUNT. Since the information provided by an ALERT interface is a proper subset of that provided by the corresponding COUNT interface, the results in §3.2 already shows the impracticability of deterministic algorithms. Our results in this section further shows that ALERT interfaces require an even higher lower bound on query cost. To efficiently discover attribute domains, we develop RANDOM-ALERT-DISCOVER, a randomized algorithm which extends RANDOM-COUNT-DISCOVER by augmenting a query answer returned by an ALERT interface with an approximate COUNT estimated from historic query answers.

5.1 Achievability for Deterministic Algorithms

For ALERT interfaces, the achievability condition for k is exactly the same as the one for COUNT interfaces - which is shown in Theorem 3.4 - as one can easily verify that the proof of Theorem 3.4 does not use any COUNT returned by the interface. For the condition on query cost, however, the lower bound is significantly higher for ALERT interfaces, as shown by the following theorem.

THEOREM 5.1. *For given k and m, there exists a database and a scoring function such that no deterministic algorithm can complete the discovery of all domain values that can be discovered from the top-k ALERT interface without incurring a worst-case query cost of $\prod_{i=h+1}^{m}|V_{d_i}|$, where $d_1, \ldots, d_m$ is the permutation of $1, \ldots, m$ which satisfies $|V_{d_1}| \geq \cdots \geq |V_{d_m}|$, and h is the minimum value which satisfies $k \leq 1 + \prod_{i=1}^{h}(|V_{d_i}| - 1)$.*

PROOF. We prove by induction. In particular, we start with constructing a database instance D_1, and then show that for any $b < \prod_{i=h+1}^{m}|V_{d_i}|$, if a deterministic algorithm uses exactly b queries $q_1, \ldots, q_b$ to discover all attribute domains from D_1, then there must exist another database instance D_2 which (1) provides the exact same query answers for $q_1, \ldots, q_{b-1}$, such that the deterministic algorithm will always issue q_b next, and (2) ensures that $q_1, \ldots, q_b$ cannot discover all attribute domains. One can see that if this is proved, then any deterministic algorithm which discovers all attribute domains must has a query cost of at least $\prod_{i=h+1}^{m}|V_{d_i}|$.

We construct D_1 with $1+k\cdot\prod_{i=h+1}^{m}|V_{d_i}|$ tuples $t_1, \ldots, t_{2^{m-1}}$ in the following manner. First, for each A_{d_i} $(i \in [1, h])$, we arbitrarily choose a domain value $v_i \in A_{d_i}$. Then, For each value combination of $V_{d_{h+1}}, \ldots, V_{d_m}$, we include k other tuples with $A_{d_{h+1}}, \ldots, A_{d_m}$ defined by the value combination and $A_{d_i} \neq v_{d_i}$ for all $i \in [1, h]$. It is always possible to find such k tuples because of our assumption that $k \leq 1 + \prod_{i=1}^{h}(|V_{d_i}| - 1)$. The one additional tuple in D_1 is t which satisfies $A_{d_i} = v_{d_i}$ for all $i \in [1, h]$ and has an arbitrary value combination for $A_{d_{h+1}}, \ldots, A_{d_m}$. The scoring function is designed such that t has the lowest score.

Note that the deterministic algorithm must unveil t with the first b queries. Without loss of generality, we assume that the b-th query returns t. An important observation here is that t can only be unveiled by a query which has no predicate for $A_{d_1}, \ldots, A_{d_h}$ (because $v_1, \ldots, v_h$ could not have been discovered before t is unveiled) and one predicate for each of $A_{d_{h+1}}, \ldots, A_{d_m}$ (because of k). If $b < \prod_{i=h+1}^{m}|V_{d_i}|$, there must exist at least one value combination of $A_{d_{h+1}}, \ldots, A_{d_m}$ which has not yet been (fully) specified by any issued query. We then construct D_2 by changing the values of $A_{d_{h+1}}, \ldots, A_{d_m}$ of t to this not-yet-specified combination. One can see that the answers of $q_1, \ldots, q_{b-1}$ over D_2 is exactly the same as D_1. Nonetheless, q_b no longer returns t, mandating a query cost of at least $b+1$ for attribute domain discovery over D_2. □

Running Example: With the NSF award search example, the lower bound on worst-case query cost over a top-50 ALERT interface is 9.40×10^{15}, orders of magnitude larger than even the upper bound for COUNT interface.

THEOREM 5.2. *For given k and m-attribute, there exists an algorithm which requires at most $h - 1 + \prod_{i=1}^{h-1}|V_{d_i}|$ queries to discover the domains of at least h (out of the m) attributes, where $d_1, \ldots, d_m$ is the permutation of $1, \ldots, m$ which satisfies $|V_{d_1}| \geq \cdots \geq |V_{d_m}|$.*

The following description of ALERT-DISCOVER serves as the proof for this theorem.

5.1.1 ALERT-DISCOVER

The deterministic COUNT-DISCOVER is capable of shrinking the search space significantly at each step because it can infer the COUNT of a domain value yet to be discovered from COUNTs returned by other queries. ALERT interfaces do not provide such luxury. In particular, for the discovery of V_m, there is no direct way to check whether an unknown domain value in V_m occurs in tuples satisfying an overflowing query such as q_3: SELECT * FROM D WHERE $A_1 = 0_1$, unless q_3 returns the domain value in its top-k result.

Despite of the lack of COUNT information, we can still shrink the search space with an ALERT interface, though the shrinking may not be as significant as in COUNT-DISCOVER. For example, if the above-mentioned q_3 turns out to be valid or underflowing without returning any unknown domain value in V_m, we can safely remove from the search space $\mathcal{S}_1(V_m)$ all values which satisfy q_3 - a reduction of size $\prod_{i=2}^{m-1}|V_i|$ - while still ensuring that the reduced search space contains at least one tuple in the database which has an unknown value of V_m.

ALERT-DISCOVER, our deterministic algorithm for ALERT interfaces, exactly follows this strategy to construct a series of nested spaces $\mathcal{S}_1(V_m)$, $\mathcal{S}_2(V_m)$, ..., for the discovery of V_m. To decide which query to issue next, ALERT-DISCOVER uses the following simple rule: Suppose that the complete domains of h attributes have been discovered, say $A_1, \ldots, A_h$ without loss of generality (note that $h = 1$ at the start of the algorithm). The next query ALERT-DISCOVER issues is an h-predicate query with one conjunctive condition for each attribute A_i $(i \in [1, h])$. The value v_i specified for A_i in the query is determined as follows: First, the value combination $\langle v_1, \ldots, v_h\rangle$ must lead to a query that cannot be answered based solely upon the historic query answers - i.e., no previously issued query is formed by a subset of $A_1 = v_1, \ldots, A_h = v_h$ and returns valid or underflow. Within the value combinations which satisfy this condition, we select the highest-ordered one according to an arbitrary global order. The above process is repeated until all domains are discovered.

To understand how such a query-issuing plan leads to the shrinking of nested search spaces, consider the three possible outcomes of an above-constructed query q - underflow, valid, or overflow. If q underflows or is valid, then we can construct the next search space by removing from the current one all value combinations that satisfy q - a reduction of size $\prod_{i=h+1}^{m-1}|V_i|$ where h is the number of predicates in q. On the other hand, if q overflows, then we can always discover the complete domain of at least one additional attribute because $k \geq 1 + \prod_{i=1}^{n}(|V_i| - 1)$. One can see that if ALERT-DISCOVER has issued at least m queries with the second outcome, then it must have discovered the domains for all m attributes. The first outcome, on the other hand, guarantees the reduction of search space. Theorem 5.2 follows accordingly.

5.2 RANDOM-ALERT-DISCOVER

A simple approach to enable aggregate estimation is to directly integrate RANDOM-COUNT-DISCOVER with HD-UNBIASED-AGG, the existing aggregate estimator for hidden databases [8]. Intuitively, since RANDOM-COUNT-DISCOVER starts with RANDOM-SPACE, one can use queries answers received by RANDOM-SPACE to estimate each COUNT value required by the subsequent execution of RANDOM-COUNT-SPACE. The estimations will become more accurate over time after more queries are issued by RANDOM-SPACE or RANDOM-COUNT-SPACE).

Nonetheless, such a direct integration has a key problem: The existing HD-UNBIASED-AGG can only generate a COUNT estimation from a *valid* query answer. Most queries issued by RANDOM-COUNT-SPACE, however, are likely to overflow as the shrinking of search space only continues (i.e., with "narrower", and possibly valid, queries being issued) if no new domain value can be discovered from the previously issued overflowing queries - an unlikely event especially at the beginning of RANDOM-COUNT-DISCOVER. As a result, the integration with HD-UNBIASED-AGG faces a dilemma: either uses only a few valid queries and suffers a high estimation variance, or issues a large number of extra queries to "narrow down" the queries issued by RANDOM-COUNT-SPACE (by adding conjunctive conditions to the queries) to valid ones. Either way, the large number of overflowing queries issued by RANDOM-COUNT-SPACE would be wasted.

To address this problem, we propose a step-by-step estimation process which can generate COUNT estimations based the the results of all historic queries, including the overflowing ones. For the ease of understanding, we consider an example of estimating SELECT COUNT(*) FROM D WHERE $A_1 = v_1$, denoted by COUNT(v_1). Handling of other COUNT queries immediately follows. Consider one round of RANDOM-SPACE or RANDOM-COUNT-SPACE during which b queries $q_1, \ldots, q_b$ are issued in order. Recall that q_1 is SELECT * FROM D. q_b may be overflowing, valid or underflowing. Without loss of generality, let $A_1, \ldots, A_{i-1}$ be the attributes involved in the selection conditions of q_i ($i \in [2, b]$). Let p_i be the *transition probability* from q_i to q_{i+1} - i.e., the probability for q_{i+1} to be selected (out of all possible values of A_i) after q_i is issued. For example, $p_i = 1/|V_i|$ for RANDOM-SPACE, and may differ (based on the currently estimated COUNTs) for RANDOM-COUNT-SPACE. We estimate COUNT(v_1) from all b queries with the following two steps:

- We first choose i.i.d. uniformly at random $v_i \in V_i$ for each $i \in [b, m-1]$, and then construct and issue a (conjunctive) query q_F formed by appending conditions ($A_b = v_b$) AND $\cdots$ AND ($A_{m-1} = v_{m-1}$) to q_c.
- We then return the following estimation of COUNT(v_1):

$$\omega = \left(\sum_{i=1}^{b} \frac{S_{v_1}(\beta_i)}{\prod_{j=1}^{i-1} p_j}\right) + \frac{S_{v_1}(\beta_F) \cdot \prod_{j=b}^{m} |V_j|}{\prod_{j=1}^{b-1} p_j} \tag{12}$$

where $\beta_i = \{t | t \in q_i, t \notin (q_1 \cup \cdots \cup q_{i-1})\}$, $\beta_F = \{t | t \in q_F, t \notin (q_1 \cup \cdots \cup q_c)\}$, and $S_{v_1}(\cdot)$ stands for the result of applying COUNT(v_1) over a set of tuples. Note that here q_i stands for the set of tuples returned by query q_i. We assume $\prod_{j=1}^{i-1} p_j = 1$ when $i = 1$, and $S_{v_1}(\phi) = 0$.

One can see that each query in $q_1, \ldots, q_b$ contributes an additive component to the final estimation ω - e.g., q_i contributes $S_{v_1}(\beta_i)/\prod_{j=1}^{i-1} p_j$, which is essentially an estimated COUNT of tuples that sastify $A_1 = v_1$, can be returned by a query with predicates on $A_1, \ldots, A_i$, but cannot be returned by a query with predicates only on $A_1, \ldots, A_{i-1}$. This is why we call the idea "step-by-step estimation". In terms of query cost, step-by-step estimation reuses all queries issued by RANDOM-SPACE or RANDOM-COUNT-SPACE. In addition, it issues at most one additional query q_F per round (of search-space shrinking). It is easy to verify that the proof of unbiasedness for HD-UNBIASED-AGG [8] remains valid with step-by-step estimation.

6. EXPERIMENTAL RESULTS

6.1 Experimental Setup

1) Hardware and Platform: All our experiments were performed on a 2.6GHz Intel Core 2 Duo machine with 2GB RAM and Windows XP OS. All algorithms were implemented in C++.

2) Dataset: We conducted our experiments on two real-world datasets. One is the NSF award search database which has been used as a running example throughout the paper. We tested our algorithms over the real-world web interface of NSF award search by issuing queries through the "search all fields" option of NSF award search, available at *http://www.nsf.gov/awardsearch/tab.do?dispatch=4*. Since this interface uses HTTP GET to specify query selection conditions, we issue search queries through the interface by appending search conditions to the URL. Since NSF award search returns up to 50 awards on a returned page, we set $k = 50$, but also tested cases where k varies from 10 to 40 by truncating the returned results. As mentioned in §2.1, NSF award search is an ALERT interface. We conducted experiments with all 9 attributes listed in §2.1, with objective being the discovery of domain values for these attributes.

While experiments over the NSF award search database demonstrates the practical impact of our approach, to more thoroughly evaluate its effectiveness we need access to certain *ground truth*, e.g., the total number of tuples in the database or the total number of domain values to be discovered, which we do not have over NSF award search. Thus, we also conducted experiments over a local hidden database built from a Texas inpatient discharge dataset published by the Texas Department of Health [22]. There are 707, 735 tuples and 260 attributes. We used all tuples but randomly chose 23 attributes with domain size ranging from 2 to 19028, in order to better simulate the number of attributes commonly available from a hidden database. We constructed the top-k interface with $k = 100$ and a random scoring function, but also tested cases where k varies from 100 to 400. We considered both COUNT and ALERT interfaces for this database.

3) Algorithms: We tested seven algorithms: the crawling-based DFS and BFS (as baseline), our main algorithms RANDOM-COUNT-SPACE and RANDOM-ALERT-SPACE, a main component of them HYBRID-SPACE, as well as stand-alone RANDOM-SPACE and RANDOM-COUNT-SPACE. The only parameters required are r_1 and r_2 for HYBRID-SPACE, which is in turn used by RANDOM-COUNT-SPACE and RANDOM-ALERT-SPACE. We set $r_1 = r_2 = 0$ by default but also tested other values which justified our default settings. To test HYBRID-SPACE and the standalone RANDOM- and RANDOM-COUNT-SPACE, we considered the case where all attribute domains except the largest one have been completely discovered, and set the goal to be the discovery of the largest domain with 19028 values.

3) Performance Measures: For query cost, we focused on the number of queries issued through the web interface of the hidden database. For estimation accuracy, we tested both measures discussed in §2.2: absolute recall and coverage. For the local hidden database, we also tested the relative recall, i.e., absolute recall divided by the total number of tuples in the database, and relative coverage, i.e., absolute coverage for an attribute domain divided by its domain size (ground truths that we only have access to over the local database), to provide an intuitive demonstrate of the effectiveness of our algorithms.

6.2 Experimental Results

We compared the performance of RANDOM-ALERT-DISCOVER, DFS and BFS over the NSF award search database when no attribute domain is pre-known. Figures 1 and 2 depict the change of recall and coverage with query cost, respectively. Note that in Figure 2, we present both the coverage for attribute Program Manager and the SUM of coverage for all attributes. One can see from the figures that RANDOM-ALERT-DISCOVER provides a significantly higher recall and coverage than both baseline algorithms.

We also tested the NSF award search database with varying k, the only parameter we can control over its interface. Figures 3 and 4 depict the change of recall with k when 100 queries were issued. One can see that as suggested by intuition, the larger k is, the more

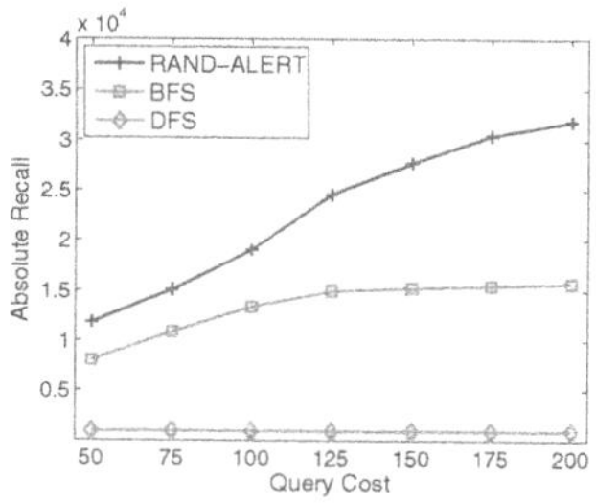

Figure 1: Recall vs query cost

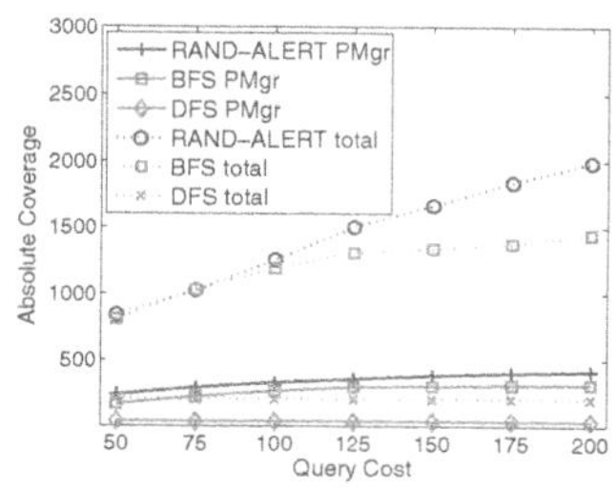

Figure 2: Coverage vs query cost

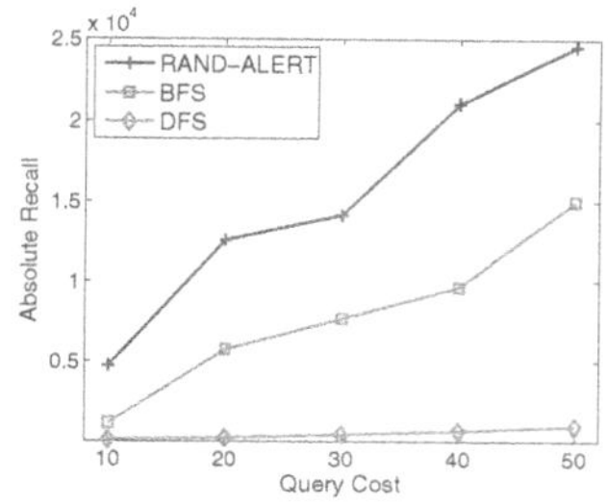

Figure 3: Recall vs k

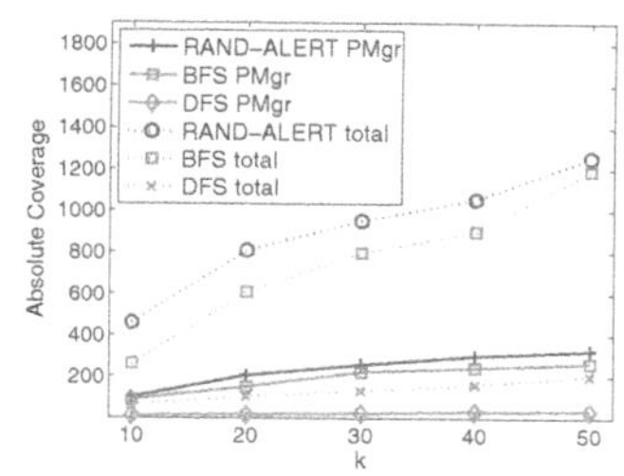

Figure 4: Coverage vs k

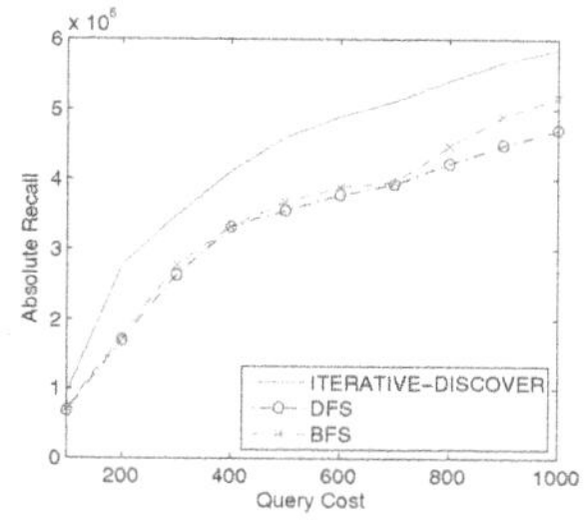

Figure 5: Recall vs query cost

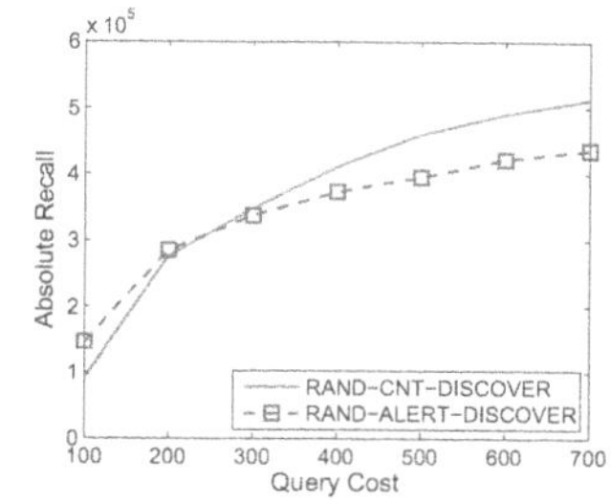

Figure 6: ALERT vs COUNT

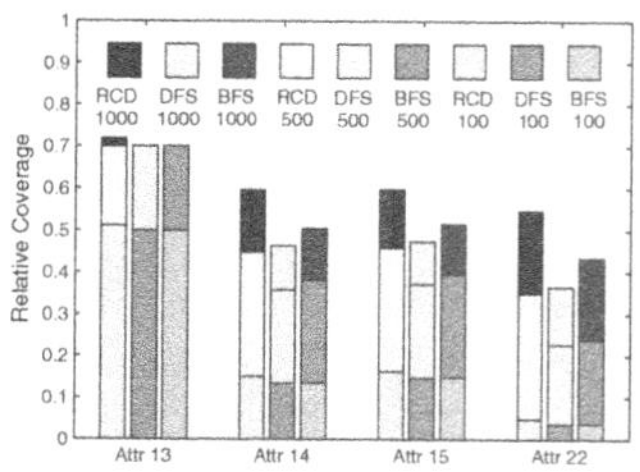

Figure 7: Relative coverage

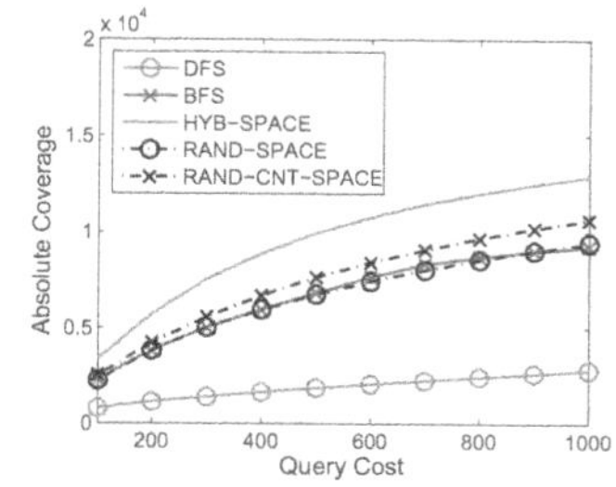

Figure 8: HYB-SPACE coverage

recall all three algorithms will achieve. In addition, RANDOM-ALERT-DISCOVER significantly outperforms DFS and BFS for all settings of k.

To provide a more thorough evaluation of the algorithms, we turned our attention to the local hidden database. We compared the tradeoff between recall and query cost for RANDOM-COUNT-DISCOVER, DFS and BFS. The results are shown in Figure 5. We also compared the performance of RANDOM-COUNT-DISCOVER with RANDOM-ALERT-DISCOVER, with results shown in Figure 6. One can see that RANDOM-COUNT-DISCOVER significantly outperforms DFS and BFS, while the difference between recall of RANDOM-COUNT-DISCOVER and RANDOM-ALERT-DISCOVER is not significant.

An interesting (and somewhat counter-intuitive) observation here is that when the query cost is small (e.g., 100), RANDOM-ALERT-DISCOVER even *outperforms* RANDOM-COUNT-DISCOVER. This is because RANDOM-ALERT-DISCOVER leverages previously issued queries estimate the COUNT of each discovered domain value (to decide which to use in the shrinking of search space), instead of actually querying the COUNTs as in RANDOM-COUNT-DISCOVER. This leads to a significant saving of query cost in the beginning. But when more queries are issued, many of the saved queries may be (randomly) selected for shrinking search space and issued anyway. As such, the advantage provided by precise COUNTs becomes more evident and helps increase the recall.

To further demonstrate the coverage achieved by RANDOM-COUNT-DISCOVER, we evaluated the relative coverage for all attributes and present in Figure 7 the four attributes with the *minimum* (i.e., worst) relative coverage when 100, 500 and 1000 queries have been issued. One can see that even for these worst-case attributes, RANDOM-COUNT-DISCOVER can still unveil more than half of the domain values for every attribute with a query cost of only 1000. In addition, RANDOM-COUNT-DISCOVER outperforms both DFS and BFS on all four attributes.

Since HYBRID-SPACE is the key component of both RANDOM-COUNT-DISCOVER and RANDOM-ALERT-DISCOVER, we compared experiments on HYBRID-SPACE alone with the aforementioned experimental setup to justify our design of mixing RANDOM-SPACE with RANDOM-COUNT-SPACE. In particular, we compared the performance of HYBRID-SPACE, DFS, BFS, as well as RANDOM-SPACE and RANDOM-COUNT-SPACE. Figures 8 and 9 depict the absolute coverage and recall achieved by all 5 algorithms, respectively. One can see that HYBRID-SPACE significantly outperforms all other approaches on both measures.

We also tested the five algorithms with varying database size n. Figures 10 and 11 depict the relative recall and absolute coverage for a query cost of 100, respectively. Note that while the relative recall naturally decreases for a larger database, the absolute coverage actually increases. Also, our approach consistently outperforms the others over all database sizes, again justifying the mixing of RANDOM- and RANDOM-COUNT-SPACE.

We also studied how the parameters r_1 and r_2 of HYBRID-SPACE affects its performance. Figure 12 shows the change of absolute recall when r_1 and r_2 varies from 0 to 4 (absolute coverage shows a similar trend). One can see that while r_2 does not appear to have a significant impact on the completeness of attribute domain discovery, r_1 should be set as small as possible - justifying our default setting of $r_1 = 0$.

7. RELATED WORK

Information Integration and Extraction for Hidden databases: A significant body of research has been done on information integration and extraction over deep web data sources such as hidden databases - see tutorials in [6, 11]. Nonetheless, to the best of our knowledge, the only prior work which directly tackles the attribute domain discovery problem is [20]. In particular, it proposes a crawling-based technique, the disadvantage of which has been extensively discussed in §2.3. Much other work though is related but orthogonal to attribute domain discovery. Since there is no space to enumerate all related papers, we only list a few examples closely related to this paper. Parsing and understanding web query interfaces has been extensively studied (e.g., [12,23]). The mapping of

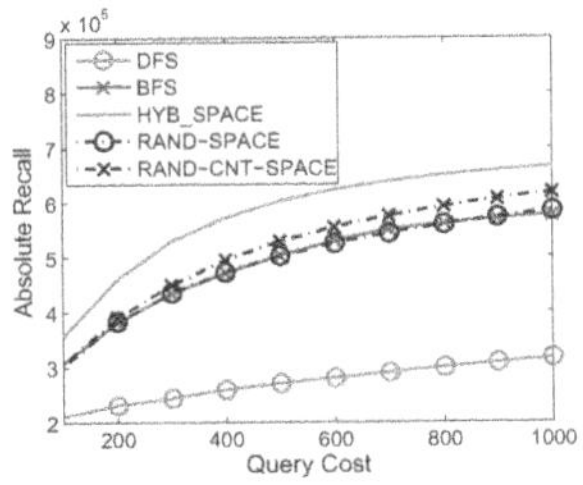

Figure 9: HYB-SPACE recall

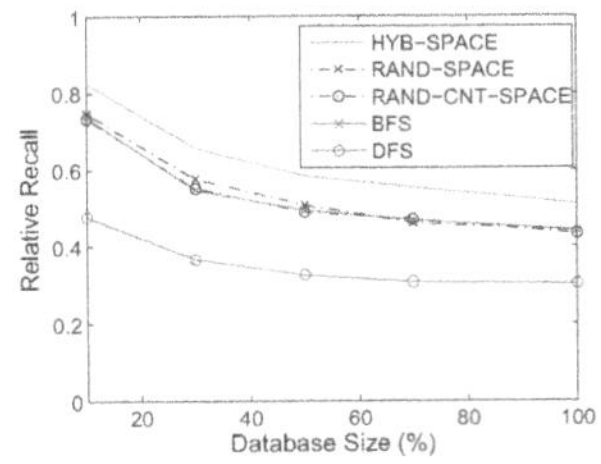

Figure 10: Recall vs DB size

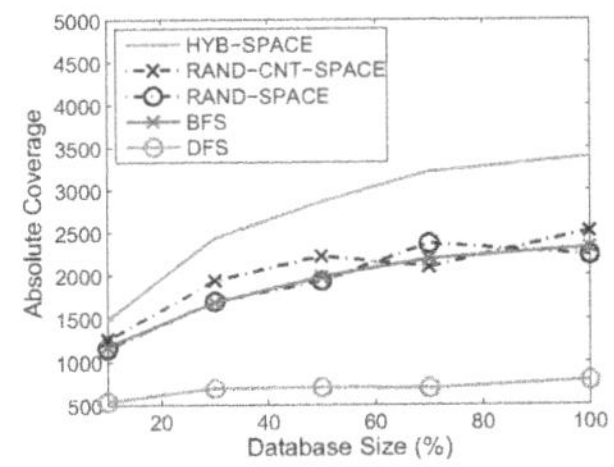

Figure 11: Coverage vs DB size

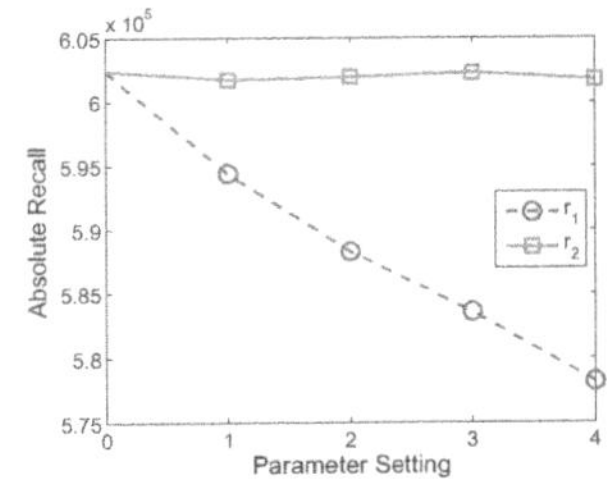

Figure 12: Varying r_1, r_2

attributes across different web interfaces has also been addressed (e.g., [15]). Also related is the work on integrating query interfaces for multiple web databases in the same topic-area (e.g., [13, 14]). Our paper provides results orthogonal to these existing techniques as it represents the first formal study on attribute domain discovery over hidden databases.

Data Analytics over Hidden Databases: There has been prior work on crawling, sampling, and aggregate estimation over the hidden web, specifically over text [2, 3] and structured [20] hidden databases and search engines [1, 19, 21]. In particular, sampling-based methods were used for generating content summaries [5, 16, 17], processing top-k queries [4], etc. Prior work (see [8] and references therein) considered sampling and aggregate estimation over structured hidden databases. A key difference between these techniques and this paper is that the prior techniques assume full knowledge of all attribute domains, while this paper aims to integrate domain discovery with aggregate estimation. As we demonstrated in §6, our integrated approach significantly outperforms the direct application of previous techniques [8] after domain discovery.

8. CONCLUSION

In this paper we have initiated a formal study of the discovery of attribute domains through the web interface of a hidden database. We investigated the achievability of deterministic algorithms for both COUNT and ALERT interfaces, and proposed query-efficient randomized algorithms for attribute domain discovery based on the idea of constructing nested search spaces. We provided theoretical analysis and extensive experimental studies over real-world datasets to illustrate the effectiveness of our approach.

9. REFERENCES

[1] Z. Bar-Yossef and M. Gurevich. Efficient search engine measurements. In *WWW*, 2007.

[2] Z. Bar-Yossef and M. Gurevich. Mining search engine query logs via suggestion sampling. In *VLDB*, 2008.

[3] K. Bharat and A. Broder. A technique for measuring the relative size and overlap of public web search engines. In *WWW*, 1998.

[4] N. Bruno, L. Gravano, and A. Marian. Evaluating top-k queries over web-accessible databases. In *ICDE*, 2002.

[5] J. Callan and M. Connell. Query-based sampling of text databases. *ACM TOIS*, 19(2):97–130, 2001.

[6] K. Chang and J. Cho. Accessing the web: From search to integration. In *Tutorial, SIGMOD*, 2006.

[7] A. Dasgupta, G. Das, and H. Mannila. A random walk approach to sampling hidden databases. In *SIGMOD*, 2007.

[8] A. Dasgupta, X. Jin, B. Jewell, N. Zhang, and G. Das. Unbiased estimation of size and other aggregates over hidden web databases. In *SIGMOD*, 2010.

[9] A. Dasgupta, N. Zhang, and G. Das. Leveraging count information in sampling hidden databases. In *ICDE*, 2009.

[10] A. Dasgupta, N. Zhang, and G. Das. Turbo-charging hidden database samplers with overflowing queries and skew reduction. In *EDBT*, 2010.

[11] A. Doan, R. Ramakrishnan, and S. Vaithyanathan. Managing information extraction. In *Tutorial, SIGMOD*, 2006.

[12] E. Dragut, T. Kabisch, C. Yu, and U. Leser. A hierarchical approach to model web query interfaces for web source integration. In *VLDB*, 2009.

[13] E. Dragut, C. Yu, and W. Meng. Meaningful labeling of integrated query interfaces. In *VLDB*, 2006.

[14] B. He and K. Chang. Statistical schema matching across web query interfaces. In *SIGMOD*, 2003.

[15] B. He, K. Chang, and J. Han. Discovering complex matchings across web query interfaces: A correlation mining approach. In *KDD*, 2004.

[16] Y.-L. Hedley, M. Younas, A. E. James, and M. Sanderson. Sampling, information extraction and summarisation of hidden web databases. *Data and Knowledge Engineering*, 59(2):213–230, 2006.

[17] P. Ipeirotis and L. Gravano. Distributed search over the hidden web: Hierarchical database sampling and selection. In *VLDB*, 2002.

[18] R. Khare, Y. An, and I.-Y. Song. Understanding deep web search interfaces: A survey. *SIGMOD Record*, 39(1), 2010.

[19] K. Liu, C. Yu, and W. Meng. Discovering the representative of a search engine. In *CIKM*, 2002.

[20] S. Raghavan and H. Garcia-Molina. Crawling the hidden web. In *VLDB*, 2001.

[21] M. Shokouhi, J. Zobel, F. Scholer, and S. Tahaghoghi. Capturing collection size for distributed non-cooperative retrieval. In *SIGIR*, 2006.

[22] Texas Department of State Health Services. User manual of Texas hospital inpatient discharge public use data file, 2008. *http://www.dshs.state.tx.us/thcic/Hospitals/HospitalData.shtm.*

[23] Z. Zhang, B. He, and K. Chang. Understanding web query interfaces: best-effort parsing with hidden syntax. In *SIGMOD*, 2004.

Keyword Search over Relational Databases: A Metadata Approach

Sonia Bergamaschi
University of Modena and Reggio Emilia, Italy
sonia.bergamaschi@unimore.it

Elton Domnori
University of Modena and Reggio Emilia, Italy
elton.domnori@unimore.it

Francesco Guerra
University of Modena and Reggio Emilia, Italy
francesco.guerra@unimore.it

Raquel Trillo Lado
University of Zaragoza, Spain
raqueltl@unizar.es

Yannis Velegrakis
University of Trento, Italy
velgias@disi.unitn.eu

ABSTRACT

Keyword queries offer a convenient alternative to traditional SQL in querying relational databases with large, often unknown, schemas and instances. The challenge in answering such queries is to discover their intended semantics, construct the SQL queries that describe them and used them to retrieve the respective tuples. Existing approaches typically rely on indices built a-priori on the database content. This seriously limits their applicability if a-priori access to the database content is not possible. Examples include the on-line databases accessed through web interface, or the sources in information integration systems that operate behind wrappers with specific query capabilities. Furthermore, existing literature has not studied to its full extend the inter-dependencies across the ways the different keywords are mapped into the database values and schema elements. In this work, we describe a novel technique for translating keyword queries into SQL based on the Munkres (a.k.a. Hungarian) algorithm. Our approach not only tackles the above two limitations, but it offers significant improvements in the identification of the semantically meaningful SQL queries that describe the intended keyword query semantics. We provide details of the technique implementation and an extensive experimental evaluation.

Categories and Subject Descriptors

H.3.3 [**Information Storage and Retrieval**]: Information Search and Retrieval—*Search process; Retrieval models; Query formulation*

General Terms

Algorithms, Experimentation, Performance

Keywords

Semantic Keyword Search, Intensional Knowledge, Relational Databases, Metadata

SIGMOD'11, June 12–16, 2011, Athens, Greece.

1. INTRODUCTION

The more the relational data complexity is increasing and the user base is shifting towards the less technically skilled, the more the keyword searching is becoming an attractive alternative to traditional SQL queries, mainly due to its simplicity. Unfortunately, this simplicity comes with the price of inherent ambiguity. Thus, the challenge of answering a keyword query over a relational database is to discover the database structures that contain the keywords and explore how these structures are inter-connected to form an answer. The discovered structures, alongside their inter-connections, are actually representing in relational terms the semantic interpretation of the keyword query.

Numerous studies and tools can already be found in the scientific literature. They include DISCOVER [16], DBXplorer [2], BANKS [1], SPARK [22], SQAK [31], and many others [21, 29, 27, 33, 34, 38]. Generally, these works consider the database as a network of interconnected tuples, they detect those containing the keywords in the query, they generate connected components based on how these tuples are associated, and they return these connected tuples as an answer to the query. To do so, specialized structures that index the database content [2] are used. By using these indices, they may directly retrieve the tuples of interest, or they may instead construct the queries expressions that retrieve these tuples when evaluated. This is the basic idea followed by the modern commercial database management systems supporting full-text search over their relational database.

Unfortunately, existing techniques suffer from two main limitations. The first is that they require a-priori access to the data instance in order to build the indices that will locate the tuples related to the given keywords at run time. This seriously limits their applicability if such access is not possible. Examples of such situations include databases on the hidden web and sources located behind wrappers in data integration systems [19] that typically expose only their schema information and lack notification mechanisms for their data updates. The second limitation is that no considerable attention has been paid to the inter-dependencies among the query keywords. The likelihood that a specific data structure represent the same semantics as a keyword in a user query does not only depend on the relationship between the keyword and the data structure, but also on the data to which the other keywords in the query are mapped. This is because despite the fact that a keyword query is a flat list of keywords, the meaning of each keyword is not independent of the meaning of the others, but they all collectively represent the intended concepts the user had in mind posing the query. Furthermore, not all the keywords represent instance values. Many are used as meta-data specification of the adjacent keywords. Although there are already keyword based approaches on relational data that take into consideration metadata [21][31], they provide only partial solutions to the problem, and they only use the metadata as a way to improve their technique.

In this work, we propose a novel technique for answering keyword queries over relational databases. The queries are translated into a number of SQL queries that capture the possible semantics of the keyword query. The generated SQL queries can be evaluated on the database, and their results serve as the answer to the keyword query. One of the novelties of the technique is that it is not based on an a-priori access to the database instances. Moreover, our approach exploits the relative positions of the keywords in the query alongside auxiliary external knowledge in order to make a more educated guess of the semantics that most likely represent those of the keyword query, and then rank them accordingly. The strategy can not only be easily incorporated to many relational database management systems, but it can also be used as an enhancement of existing keyword searching techniques that utilize the database instance, offering them significant improvements over effectiveness and efficiency.

An advantage of our approach is that it can be used to assist users browsing databases with large unknown schemas. It is often the case that users formulate keyword queries without some specific semantics in mind but in an exploratory manner, mainly when they are neither fully aware of the type of information that is stored in a database, nor of the way this information is stored. The possible interpretations of a keyword query according to the schema and domain information of the database will be generated by our approach. In contrast to other keyword searching techniques on relational data that return sets of linked tuples, we can return the interpretations expressed in SQL. The study of these queries can reveal tables, attributes and join paths, providing the user with enough information to understand the kind of data that is stored in the database and the way this data is structured.

Our key contributions are as follows: (i) we formally define the problem of keyword querying over relational databases that lack a-priori access to the database instance; (ii) we introduce the notion of a weight as a measure of the likelihood that the semantics of a keyword are represented by a database structure, i.e., a table, an attribute, or a value. We further distinguish the weights to intrinsic and contextual, to emphasize that this likelihood does not depend only on the meaning of the keyword semantics when the keyword is considered in isolation (intrinsic), but also on the way the semantics of the remaining, especially the neighbouring, keywords are represented in the data (contextual). (iii) we extend and exploit the Hungarian (a.k.a., Munkres) algorithm [7] to develop a technique for the systematic computation of the contextual weights that leads into to the generation and ranking of the different interpretations of a keyword query in terms of SQL; finally, (iv) we experimentally evaluate our approach on real application scenarios.

The remainder of the paper is structured as follows: Section 2 provides a motivating example and Section 3 formally defines the problem. Section 4 describes our technique. Sections 5 - 7 provides details on our technical contributions, i.e. the computation of the intrinsic weights, the contextualization and the selection of the best mappings. The relationship of our approach to the related work is discussed in Section 8 and Section 9 describes our experimental evaluation and discusses our findings. Finally some conclusions are presented in Section 10.

2. MOTIVATING EXAMPLE

Consider the database illustrated in Figure 1, containing information about academic researchers, departments, publications, and publication databases, all modeled by the respective tables. The tables `Affiliated` and `Author` materialize many-to-many relationships between `Person-Department` and `Person-Publication`, respectively. Let "`Date Database`" be a keyword query posed over this database. To answer this query we need to understand the meaning of each keyword and build an SQL query that offers an interpretation of the keyword query semantics in terms of the relational database.

The first problem of this translation is to decide *what* role each keyword plays in the query, i.e., it represents a value or describes some meta-information (specification) about another keyword or the element of interest. In the above query, the keyword `Date` may represent the value of a name, and the keyword `Database` the value of a research area. In that case, a possible interpretation of the keyword query is information about a person called `Date` that has done work in the `Database` area. If the intended meaning of the keyword query was instead to find the online databases containing `Date`'s publications, then the keyword `Database` is actually representing meta-information about the element of interest.

Knowing *what* kind of information each keyword represents, the next critical step is to decide *which* part of the database actually models the intended keyword meaning. Consider the keyword query "`Director Watson Address`" and assume that the first and last keyword represent meta information while the second represents a value. The intended information of the keyword `Director` is most probably the one modeled by the attribute with the respective name. It is not clear, however, whether the keyword `Address` refers to the homonym attribute in the table `Person` or to the one in the table `Department`. Choosing one over another leads to completely different interpretations of the keyword query. Furthermore, the keyword `Watson`, even though we know it is a value, might be the name of a director, the name of a street, or even a value of some other attribute.

Deciding *which* database structures model the meaning of the different keywords in the query is not enough. It is also important to decide *how* these structures relate to each other. In relational databases, such relationships are expressed either through the table-attribute-value hierarchy or through join paths, i.e., chains of key/foreign key relationships. Between two database structures there may be multiple different join paths. Each such path leads to a different interpretation of the query keywords. For instance, consider the keyword query "`email CS`", and assume that the keyword `email` corresponds to attribute `Email` and keyword `CS` to a value of the attribute `DName`. Between `DName` and `Email`, there are two different paths, one that goes through the table `Affiliated` and one through the `Director`. If the semantics of the keyword query were to find emails of the CS affiliated persons, then the database query describing this semantics is one that uses the first path. If instead the semantics were to find the email of the CS department director, the query is one that uses the second path.

Finding the different semantic interpretations of a keyword query is a combinatorial problem which can be solved by an exhaustive enumeration of the different ways that mappings can be associated to database structures and values. The challenging task is to develop a mechanism that is able to significantly reduce the possible associations that most likely represent the intended keyword semantics. One way to do this is to exploit syntactic knowledge or other forms of auxiliary information. For instance, a keyword "`(320)463-1463`" is more likely to represent a phone number due to its format, while a keyword `Everest`, given the publicly available geo-name knowledge, is very likely to represent the mount Everest. Similarly, the keyword "`article`" is likely to cor-

Person

Name	Area	Phone	Address	Email
Watson	Database	(320) 4631234	30 Bloor	watson@aaa.bb
Lenzerini	Database	(390) 6987654	Ariosto 25	lenzerini@bbb.cc
Date	Database	(817) 1937842	107 GACB	date@ccc.dd
Hunt	Inf. Systems	(343) 2920812	17 Helix	Hunt@ddd.ee

Affiliated

Professor	Department
Watson	x123
Lenzerini	cs34
Date	cs34
Hunt	m111

Department

id	DName	Address	Director
x123	CS	25 Blicker	Watson
cs34	IE	15 Tribeca	Hunt
ee67	EE	5 Charles	Date
m111	ME	2 Cottle	Hunt

Author

Name	Publication
Lenzerini	Data Integration
Date	Foundation Matters

Publication

Title	Year	Resource
Data Integration	2002	ACM DL
Foundation Matters	2002	DBLP

Database

Name	Address
DBLP	http://www.informatik.uni-trier.de
ACM DL	http://portal.acm.org/dl.cfm

Figure 1: A fraction of a database schema with its data.

respond to the table `Publication`, based on some lexical database knowledge like WordNet[1].

The quest for the database structure that a keyword corresponds should not be an isolated task. Keywords are not independent entities, but it should be seen in the *context* of the presence of the other keywords in the query. To illustrate this fact, consider the keyword query "`Name Date Database`". A possible interpretation of the query is that the user is looking for the person called Date who works in the area of databases. This means that keywords `Name` and `Date` may correspond to the attribute `Name` of the table `Person` and one of its values, respectively, while the keyword `Database` to one of the values of the attribute `Area`. Consider now the query "`Name Date Database DBLP`". In this case, a possible interpretation is that the user is looking for data items related to Date in the DBLP database, hence, the meaning of the keyword `Database` is represented by the table `Database` and not by some value of the `Area` attribute.

A natural and challenging question that comes to mind is which of the different semantic interpretations of a query should be considered as the correct one. It is a well-known and documented fact that keyword queries are under-specified queries [18]. As such, any of the possible interpretations may be correct, and all have to be considered. However, based on some known patterns of human behavior [18], we know that the order of keywords is important and that correlated keywords are typically close. This means that certain interpretations of a keyword query are actually more likely than others. Thus, instead of returning a flat list of possible interpretations to the user, one can return a ranked list based on the likelihood that they represent the intended keyword semantics.

3. PROBLEM STATEMENT

A database D is a collection of relational tables. A relational table is denoted as $R(A_1, A_2, \ldots, A_n)$, where R is the name of the table and $A_1, A_2, \ldots, A_n$ its attributes. The *vocabulary* of the database D, denoted as V_D, is the set $V_D=\{X \mid \exists R(A_1, A_2, \ldots, A_n)\in D$, s.t. $X=R \vee X=A_k \vee X=Dom(A_k)$ with $1\leq k\leq n\}$. In other words, the vocabulary of a database is the set of all its relation names, their attributes and their respective domains. A *database term* is a member of its vocabulary.

A keyword query q is an ordered list of keywords $\{k_1, k_2, \ldots, k_n\}$. Each keyword is a specification about the element of interest. The specification may have been modeled in the database as a relational table, an attribute, or a value of an attribute. A configuration is a mapping function that describes a specification for each query keyword in terms of database terms.

DEFINITION 3.1. *A* configuration *C of a keyword query q on a database D is an injective mapping from the keywords in q to database terms in the vocabulary of D.*

[1]wordnet.princeton.edu

We have made the natural assumption that each keyword cannot have more than one meaning in the same configuration, i.e., it can be mapped to only one database term. Furthermore, we have assumed that no two keywords can be mapped into the same database term based on the fact that overspecified queries is only a small fraction of the queries that are typically met in practice [18]. However, our technique can be extended to work without this assumption with only minor modifications. We have also made the natural assumption that every keyword plays some role in the query, i.e., there are no unjustified keywords.

Answering a keyword query over a database D means finding a set of SQL queries, with each of these queries using all the database elements that belong to the range[2] of a specific configuration. Such an SQL query is referred to as an *interpretation* of the keyword query, since it provides a possible meaning of the keyword query in terms of the database vocabulary. In the current work, we consider only select-project-join (SPJ) interpretations, that are typically the queries of interest in similar works [2, 16]. Nevertheless, interpretations involving aggregations [31] are also in our list of future extensions.

DEFINITION 3.2. *An* interpretation *of a keyword query $q=\{k_1, k_2, \ldots, k_n\}$ on a database D using a configuration C is an SQL query:* select $A_1, A_2, \ldots, A_j$
from R_1 JOIN R_2 JOIN ... JOIN R_n
where $A'_1=v_1$ AND $A'_2=v_2$ AND ... AND $A'_m=v_m$
such that $\forall k\in q$ one of the following is true:

- $C(k)\in\{R_1, R_2, \ldots, R_n\}$
- $C(k)\in\{A_1, A_2, \ldots, A_j\}$
- $C(k)=dom(A'_i)\in\{dom(A'_1), dom(A'_2), \ldots, dom(A'_j)\}$ *and* $\langle A'_i, k\rangle \in \{\langle A'_1, v_1\rangle, \langle A'_2, v_2\rangle, \ldots, \langle A'_m, v_m\rangle\}$

To eliminate redundancies, we require any use of a database term in an interpretation to be justified either by belonging to the range of the configuration, or by participating in a join path connecting two database terms that belong in the range of the configuration. Note that even with that restriction, due to the multiple join paths in a database D, it is still possible to have multiple interpretations of a given keyword query q and a configuration C of it. We will use the notation $\mathcal{I}(q, C, D)$ to refer to the set of these interpretations. and $\mathcal{I}(q, D)$ for the union of all these sets for all the possible configurations of the query q.

EXAMPLE 3.1. *Consider the keyword query "email CS" over the database of Figure 1, and a configuration that maps* `email` *to* `Email` *and* CS *to* DName. *At least two different interpretations can be generated from this. One is the:*

select *Email*
from *Person P* JOIN *Affiliated A* ON *(P.name=A.professor)*
JOIN *Department D* ON *(A.Department=D.id)*
where *D.DName='CS'* AND *D.id=A.Department*
AND *A.Professor=P.Name*

[2]Since a configuration is a function, we can talk about its range.

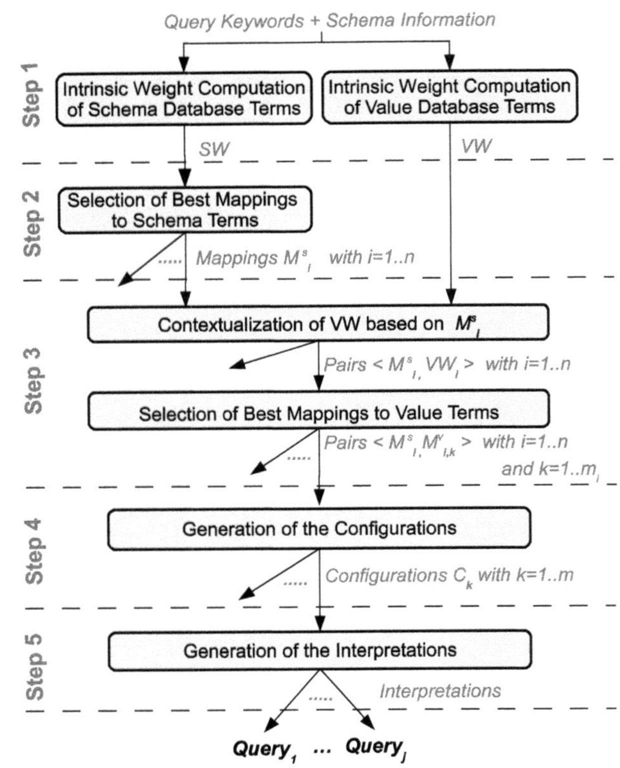

Figure 2: Overview of the keyword query translation process

and the other is the:

select *Email*
from *Person P* JOIN *Department D* ON *(P.person=D.Director)*
where *D.DName='CS'* AND *D.Director=P.Name*

DEFINITION 3.3. *An* answer *to a keyword query q over a relational database D is the set* $ans(q) = \{t \mid t \in eval^D(q') \wedge q' \in \mathcal{I}(q, D)\}$, *where* $eval^D(q')$ *denotes the evaluation of the relational query q' on the database D.*

Note that since there is no restriction on the number of attributes in the select clause of an answer, the answer set of a keyword query will naturally be heterogeneous.

Since each keyword in a query can be mapped to a relation name, an attribute name or an attribute domain, there are $2*\Sigma_{i=1}^{|D|}|R_i| + |D|$ different configurations, with $|R_i|$ denoting the *arity* of the relation R_i and $|D|$ the number of tables in the database. Based on this, and on the fact that no two keywords can be mapped to the same database term, for N keywords, there are $\frac{|V_D|!}{(|V_D|-N)!}$ possible configurations. Of course, not all the interpretations generated by these configurations are equally *meaningful*. Some are more likely to represent the intended keyword query semantics. In the following sections we will show how different kinds of meta-information and inter-dependencies between the mappings of keywords to database terms can be exploited in order to effectively and efficiently identify these interpretations and present them first. Our work is based on the natural assumption that the intended semantics of the keyword query can be expressed as a query over the relational database. If those semantics cannot be expressed, no answer can be provided.

4. FROM KEYWORDS TO QUERIES

The generation of interpretations that most likely describe the intended semantics of a keyword query is based on semantically

	R_1	...	R_n	A_1^{R}	...	$A_{n_1}^{R_1}$	...	$A_{n_n}^{R_n}$	$A_1^{R_1}$	...	$A_{n_1}^{R_1}$	...	$A_{n_n}^{R_n}$
$keyword_1$													
$keyword_2$													
...													
$keyword_k$													

Figure 3: Weight table with its SW (light) and VW (dark) parts

meaningful configurations, i.e. sets of mappings between each keyword and a database term. We introduce the notion of *weight* that offers a quantitative measure of the relativeness of a keyword to a database term, i.e., the likelihood that the semantics of the database term are the intended semantics of the keyword in the query. The sum of the weights of the keyword-database term pairs can form a score serving as a quantitative measure of the likelihood of the configuration to lead to an interpretation that accurately describes the intended keyword query semantics. The range and full semantics of the score cannot be fully specified in advance. They depend on the method used to compute the similarity. This is not a problem as long as the same method is used to compute the scores for all the keywords. This is the same approach followed in schema matching [28] where a score is used to measure the likelihood that an element of a schema corresponds to an element of another.

The naive approach for selecting the best configurations, and, as a consequence, generating the most prominent interpretations of a keyword query, is the computation of the score of each possible configuration and then selecting those that have the highest scores. Of course, we would like to avoid an exhaustive enumeration of all the possible configurations, and compute only those that give high scores. The problem of computing the mapping with the maximum score without an exhaustive computation of the scores of all the possible mappings is known in the literature as the problem of *Bipartite Weighted Assignments* [9]. Unfortunately, solutions to this problem suffer from two main limitations. First, apart from the mutual exclusiveness, they do not consider any other interdependencies that may exist between the mappings. Second, they typically provide only the best mapping, instead of a ranked list based on the scores.

To cope with the first limitation, we introduce two different kinds of weights: the *intrinsic*, and the *contextual* weights. Given a mapping of a keyword to a database term, its intrinsic weight measures the likelihood that the semantics of the keyword is that of the database term if considered in isolation from the mappings of all the other keywords in the query. The computation of an intrinsic weight is based on syntactic, semantic and structural factors such as attribute and relation names, or other auxiliary external sources, such as vocabularies, ontologies, domains, common syntactic patterns, etc. On the other hand, a contextual weight is used to measure the same likelihood but considering the mappings of the remaining query keywords. This is motivated by the fact that the assignment of a keyword to a database term may increase or decrease the likelihood that another keyword corresponds to a certain database term. This is again based on observations that humans tend to write queries in which related keywords are close to each other [18]. As an example, for the keyword query "Watson Area Database" expressed on the database in Figure 1, since the keyword "Database" is right next to keyword Area, mapping the keyword Area to the attribute **Area** of the table **Person** makes more likely the fact that the keyword Database is an area value, i.e., should be mapped to the domain of the attribute **Area**. At the same time, it decreases its relativeness to the table **Database**. A similar idea has already been exploited in the context of schema matching [24] with many interesting results. To cope with the second limitation, we have developed a novel algo-

	P	D	P.Na	P.Ar	P.Ph	P.Ad	P.Em	D.Id	D.Dn	D.Ad	D.Di	P.Na	P.Ar	P.Ph	P.Ad	P.Em	D.Id	D.Dn	D.Ad	D.Di
workers	68	0	0	0	0	0	0	0	0	0	0	1	1	0	1	0	1	1	1	1
department	0	100	0	0	0	0	0	0	0	0	0	1	1	0	1	0	1	1	1	1
CS	0	0	0	0	0	0	0	0	0	0	0	1	1	0	1	0	1	1	1	1

Figure 4: Intrinsic Weight SW (light gray) and VW (dark gray) matrix.

rithm for computing the best mappings. The algorithm is based on and extends the Hungarian (a.k.a., Munkres) algorithm [7] and will be described in detail in Section 7.

A visual illustration of the individual steps in the keyword query translation task is depicted in Figure 2. A special data structure, called *weight matrix*, plays a central role in these steps. The *weight matrix* is a two-dimensional array with a row for each keyword in the keyword query, and a column for each database term. The value of a cell $[i, j]$ represents the weight associated to the mapping between the keyword i and the database term j. Figure 3 provides an abstract illustration of a weight matrix. An R_i and $A_j^{R_i}$ columns correspond to the relation R_i and the attribute A_j of R_i, respectively, while a column with an underline attribute name $\underline{A_j^{R_i}}$ represents the data values in the column A_j of table R_i may have, i.e., its domain. Two parts (i.e., sub-matrices) can be distinguished in the weight matrix. One corresponds to the database terms related to schema elements, i.e., relational tables and attributes, and the other one corresponds to attribute values, i.e., the domains of the attributes. We refer to database terms related to schema elements as *schema database terms*, and to those related to domains of the attributes as *value database terms*. In Figure 3, these two sub-matrices are illustrated with different shades of gray. We refer to the weights in the first sub-matrix as *schema weights*, and to those of the second as *value weights*. We also use the notation SW and VW to refer either to the respective sub-matrix, or to their values. The details of the individual steps of Figure 2 are provided next.

Intrinsic Weight Computation. The first step of the process is the intrinsic weight computation. The output is the populated SW and VW sub-matrices. The computation is achieved by the exploitation and combination of a number of similarity techniques based on structural and lexical knowledge extracted from the data source, and on external knowledge, such as ontologies, vocabularies, domain terminologies, etc. Note that the knowledge extracted from the data source is basically the meta-information that the source makes public, typically, the schema structure and constraints. In the absence of any other external information, a simple string comparison based on tree-edit distance can be used for populating the SW sub-matrix. For the VW sub-matrix the notion of *Semantic Distance* [11] can always be used in the absence of anything else. As it happens in similar situations [28], measuring the success of such a task is not easy since there is no single correct answer. In general, the more meta-information has been used, the better. However, even in the case that the current step is skipped, the process can continue with the weight matrix where all the intrinsic values have the same default value. The computation of the intrinsic weights is detailed in Section 5.

Selection of the Best Mappings to Schema Terms. The intrinsic weights provide a first indication of the similarities of the keywords to database terms. To generate the prominent mappings, we need on top of that to take into consideration the inter-dependencies between the mappings of the different keywords. We consider first the prominent mappings of keywords to schema terms. For that we work on the SW sub-matrix. Based on the intrinsic weights, a series of mappings M_1^S,M_2^S, ..., M_n^S, of keywords to schema terms are generated. The mappings are those that achieve the highest overall score, i.e., the sum of the weights of the individual keyword mappings. The mappings are partial, i.e., not all the keywords are mapped to some schema term. Those that remain unmapped will play the role of an actual data value and will be considered in a subsequent step for mapping to value database terms. The selection of the keywords to remain unmapped is based on the weight matrix and some cut-off threshold. Those with a similarity below the threshold remain unmapped. For each of the mappings M_i^S, the weights of its SW matrix are adjusted to take into consideration the context generated by the mapping of the neighborhing keywords. It is based on the observation that users form queries in which keywords referring to the same or related concepts are adjacent [18, 33]. The generation of the mappings and the adjustment of the weights in SW are performed by our extension of the Hungarian algorithm that is described in detail in Section 7. The output of such a step is an updated weight matrix SW_i and, naturally, an updated score for each mapping M_i^S. Given the updated scores, some mappings may be rejected. The selection is based on a threshold. There is no golden value to set the threshold value. It depends on the expectations from the keyword query answering systems. The higher its value, the less the interpretations generated at the end, but with higher confidence. In contrast, the lower the threshold value, the more the mappings with lower confidence.

Contextualization of VW and selection of the Best Mappings to Value Terms. For each partial mapping M_i^S of keyword to schema terms generated in the previous step, the mappings of the remaining unmapped keywords to value terms needs to be decided. This is done in two phases. First, the intrinsic weights of the VW sub-matrix that were generated in Step 1 are updated to reflect the added value provided by the mappings in M_i^S of some of the keywords to schema database terms. This is called the process of contextualization of the VW sub-matrix. It is based on the documented observation that users form queries in which keywords specifying metadata information about a concept are adjacent or at least neighboring [18, 33]. Thus, when a keyword is mapped to a schema term, it becomes more likely that an adjacent keyword should be mapped to a value in the domain of that schema term. The contextualization process increases the weights of the respective values terms to reflect exactly that. For example, in the keyword query "`Name Alexandria`" assume that the keyword `Alexandria` was found during the first step to be equally likely the name of a person or of a city. If in Step 2 the keyword `Name` has been mapped to the attribute `Name` of the table `Person`, the confidence that `Alexandria` is actually the name of a person is increased, thus, the weight between that keyword and the value database term representing the domain of attribute `Name` should be increased, accordingly. In the second phase, given an updated VW_i sub-matrix, the most prominent mappings of the remaining unmapped keywords to value database terms are generated. The mappings are generated by using again the adapted technique of the Hungarian algorithm (ref. Section 7). The result is a series of partial mappings M_{ik}^V, with k=1..m_i, where i identifies the mapping M_i^S on which the computation of the updated matrix VW_i was based. Given one such mapping M_{ik}^V the value weights are further updated to reflect the mappings of the adjacent keywords to value database terms, in a way similar to the one done in Step 2 for the SW sub-matrix. The outcome modifies the total score of each mapping M_{ik}^{V}, and based on that score the mappings are ranked.

Generation of the Configurations. As a fourth step, each pair of a mapping M_{ik}^{V} together with its associated mapping M_{i}^{S} is a total mapping of the keywords to database terms, forming a configuration C_{ik}. The score of the configuration is the sum of the scores of the two mappings, or alternatively the sum of the weights in the weight matrix of the elements $[i, j]$ where i is a keyword and j is the database term to which it is mapped through M_{ik}^{V} or M_{i}^{S}.

Generation of the Interpretations. Having computed the best configurations, the interpretations of the keyword query, i.e., the SQL queries, can be generated. The score of each such query is the score of the respective configuration. Recall, however, that a configuration is simply a mapping of the keywords to database terms. The presence of different join paths among these terms results in multiple interpretations. Different strategies can be used to further rank the selections. One popular option is the length of the join path [17] but other heuristics found in the literature [16] can also be used. It is also possible that a same interpretation be obtained with different configurations. A post-processing analysis and the application of data-fusion techniques [6] can be used to deal with this issue. However, this is not the main focus of the current work and we will not elaborate further on it. We adopt a greedy approach that computes a query for every alternative join path. In particular, we construct a graph in which each node corresponds to a database term. An edge connects two terms if they are structurally related, i.e., through a table-attribute-domain value relationship, or semantically, i.e., through a referential integrity constraint. Given a configuration we mark all terms that are part of the range of the configuration as "marked". Then we run a breath-first traversal (that favors shorter paths) to find paths that connect the disconnected components of the graph (if possible). The final SQL query is then constructed using the "marked" database terms, and in particular, the tables for its `from` clause, the conditions modeled by the edges for its `where` clause and the remaining attributes for its `select` clause. Then the process is repeated to find a different interpretation, that will be based on a different join path. The final order of the generated interpretations is determined by the way the different paths are discovered and the cost of the configuration on which each interpretation is based.

It is important to note here that if the thresholds used in the above steps are all brought down to zero, then our technique is able to generate all the possible interpretations that can be defined on a database, even the most unlikely. In that sense, our technique is complete. The thresholds serve only to exclude from the results any interpretation that is not likely to represent the semantics of the keyword query, while the weights are used to provide the basis for a ranking metric.

5. INTRINSIC WEIGHT COMPUTATION

To compute the intrinsic weights, we need to compute the relevance between every query keyword and every database term. Some fundamental information that can be used towards this directions, and that is typically available, is the schema information. It may include the table and attribute names, the domains of the attributes, and very often referential and integrity constraints, such as keys and foreign keys. Syntactic descriptions of the contents of an attribute (e.g., regular expressions) can also lead to a better matching of keywords to database terms since they offer indications on whether a keyword can serve as a value for an attribute or not. There are already many works that offer typical syntax for common attributes such as phone numbers, addresses, etc. [28], and have been used extensively and successfully in other areas. If access to the catalog tables is possible, assertion statements can offer an alternative source of syntactic information. In the same spirit, relevant values [5], i.e., clusters of the attribute domains, are also valuable auxiliary information. Furthermore, there is today a large volume of grammatical and semantic information that is publicly available on the Internet and can be used as a service. Examples include the popular WordNet and the many community specific ontologies.

Algorithm 1: Intrinsic SW Matrix Computation

Input: Q: Keyword Query
T: Schema Database Terms
Output: SW matrix

ComputeISW(Q,T)
$SW \leftarrow [0, 0, \ldots, 0]$
$\Sigma \leftarrow$ { Synonyms(w,t), Hyponyms(w,t), Hypernyms(w,t), StringSimilarity(w,t) ... }
foreach $w \in Q$
  foreach $e \in T$
    $sim \leftarrow 0$;
    foreach $m \in \Sigma$
      if $m(w, e) > sim$
        $sim \leftarrow m(w, e)$
    if $ssim \leq threshold$
      $sim \leftarrow 0$;
  $SW[w, c] = ssim * 100$

5.1 Weights for Schema Database Terms

Finding matches between the flat list of keywords and the schema terms looks like the situation of schema matching [28] in which one of the schemas is the flat universal relation [23]. We follow a similar approach in which we employ a number of different similarity measurement techniques and consider the one that offers the best result. One of these techniques is the string similarity [12]. For the string similarity we further employ a number of different similarity metrics such as the Jaccard, the Hamming, the Levenshtein, etc., in order to cover a broad spectrum of situations that may occur. Since string similarity may fail in cases of highly heterogeneous schemas that lack a common vocabulary, we also measure the relativeness of a keyword to schema database term based on their semantic relationship. For that we employ public ontologies, such as SUMO[3], or semantic dictionaries such as WordNet, that can provide synonyms, hypernyms, hyponyms, or other terms related to a given word.

Algorithm 1 describes the computation procedure of the intrinsic schema weight matrix SW. The set Σ represents the similarity methods we employ. We have a number of default methods that represent the state of the art in the area, but additional methods can be included. Each such method takes as input two strings and returns their respective similarity in a range between 0 and 1. We trust the method that gives the highest similarity. If a similarity between a keyword and a schema term is found below a specific threshold (that is set by the application) then the similarity is set explicitly to 0. As a result, at the end of the procedure there might be rows in the matrix SW containing only zeros. These rows represent keywords that are not similar enough to any of the schema database terms, thus, they will be considered later as candidates for mapping to value database terms, i.e., domains of the schema attributes. The fact that their rows in the SW matrix are 0 instead of

[3]www.ontologyportal.org

some low value, makes the similarities of the keyword to the value database terms that will be computed in a later step to be the dominating factor determining the guess on the role a specific keyword can play.

EXAMPLE 5.1. *Consider the keyword query "workers department CS" posed on the database of Figure 1. Figure 4 illustrates a fraction of the weight matrix containing the intrinsic weights for the database terms derived from the tables* `Person` *and* `Department`. *Instead of the full names of tables and attributes, only the first letter of the tables and the first two letters of the attributes are used. The schema weights SW are the light gray colored part of the matrix. Note that the keyword* `CS` *has not been mapped to any of the schema terms since all the values of its row in SW are 0.*

5.2 Weights for Value Database Terms

For computing the intrinsic value weights, we mainly exploit domain information, and base our decision on whether a keyword belongs to the domain of an attribute or not. Furthermore, we have adapted the notion of *Semantic Distance* [11] that is based on results retrieved by a search engine in order to evaluate the relatedness of two concepts. In particular, we define the *semantic relatedness* $SR(x,y)$ of two terms x and y as: $SR(x,y){=}e^{-2NXD(x,y)}$ where $NXD(x,y){=}\{max\{logf(x),logf(y)\}-logf(x,y)\}/\{logN-min\{logf(x),logf(y)\}\}$ with $f(x)$ denoting the number of web documents containing x, and $f(x,y)$ the number of documents containing both x and y, as these numbers are reported by specific search engines such as Google, Yahoo!, Cuil, Excite!, etc. The number N represents the number of documents indexed by the corresponding search engine. For our purpose, we compute the semantic relatedness of every keyword - attribute domain pair and this gives us an indication of the similarity degree between the keyword and the attribute domain. Information about possible values that an attribute can accept is also an important factor. The information is based on the explicit enumeration of values, as in the *Relevant Values* approach [5]. When a keyword is found among (or is similar to) the valid values that an attribute can get, the keyword receives a high weight. Additional comparison techniques include semantic measures based on external knowledge bases.

EXAMPLE 5.2. *For the keyword query introduced in Example 5.1, the intrinsic value weights are indicated in the VW part of Figure 4 i.e., the dark gray-colored part. These weights have been computed by using domain knowledge and regular expressions. Note that these are the value weights, thus, the similarity is not between the keyword and the name of the attribute, but concerns the compatibility of the keyword with the attribute domain.*

6. CONTEXTUALIZATION

The process of contextualization, as previously explained, exploits the interdependencies across mappings of different keywords. There are three different forms of contextualization that we consider. The first one increases the confidence of a keyword corresponding to an attribute (respectively, relation), if an adjacent keyword is mapped to the relation it belongs (respectively, one of the attributes of the relation). This is based on the generally observed behavior that users may sometimes provide more than one specification for a concept in a keyword query. For instance, they may use the keyword `Person` before the keyword `Name` to specify that they refer to the name of a person. The second form of contextualization is similar to the first, but applies on the value weights

Algorithm 2: Contextualizing Value Weight Sub-Matrix VW

Input: M : Partial keyword assignment to schema database terms
Q : Keyword Query
SW : Schema intriscic weight sub-matrix
VW : Value intrinsic weight sub-matrix
Output: Updated VW sub-matrix

```
COMPUTECVW(SW,VW,M)
foreach k ∈ Q
  t ← x: ∃ (k,x) ∈ M
  if t = null
    continue
  if t is a relation R
    foreach attribute A of R
      foreach k' ∈ T(k)∪P(k)
        VW[k', R.A] ← VW[k', R.A] + Δw
  else if t is an attribute A of a relation R
    foreach attribute A' of R with A'≠A
      foreach k' ∈ T(k)∪P(k)
        VW[k', R.A] ← VW[k', R.A] + Δw
    foreach attribute A' of R' s.t. ∃ join path from A' to A
      foreach k' ∈ T(k)∪P(k)
        VW[k', R.A] ← VW[k', R.A] + Δw
```

instead of the schema weights. The third and most important contextualization form is the one that updates the confidence of certain keywords corresponding to value database terms based on the mappings of other keywords to schema terms. The process consists of three phases and takes as input the value weight matrix VW and a partial mapping of keywords to schema database terms, and returns an updated matrix VW. Let K be the ordered list of keywords in a query, M_i^S a partial mapping of keywords in K to schema terms, and K^S the subset of K containing the keywords for which M_i^S is defined, i.e., those that are mapped to some schema terms. We define the notion of *free trailing keywords* of a keyword k, denoted as $T(k)$, to be the maximum set $k_1, k_2, \dots k_m$, of consecutive keywords in K that are between two keywords k_s and k_e in the query and for which $k_s{=}k$, M_i^S is defined for k_s and k_e and undefined for every k_i with $i{=}1..m$. The notion of *free preceding keywords* of a keyword k, denoted as $P(k)$, is defined accordingly, with k playing the role of k_e.

As an initialization step, all the weights in the rows of VW corresponding to keywords already mapped to database terms are set to zero. This is done to guarantee that in the three phases that are described next, none of these keywords will be mapped to a value term. In the first phase of the contextualization, for every keyword k mapped to a relation R through M_i^S, the weights of the trailing and preceding keywords $T(k)$ and $P(k)$ for terms representing the domains of the attributes of the relation R are increased by a constant value Δw. The rational of this action is that queries typically contain keywords that are generic descriptions for the values they provide. For instance, "`Person Bill`", "`Department CS`", etc., which means that consecutive keywords may correspond to a relation and a value of one of that relation's attributes. During the second phase, for every keyword k mapped to an attribute A through M_i^S, the weights of the trailing and preceding keywords $T(k)$ and $P(k)$ with the database terms representing domains of attributes in the same relation as A are also increased by a constant value Δw. The rational of this rule is that consecutive keywords may represent value specifications and related values. An example is the query "`Name Bill Databases`" intended to ask about the person Bill who works in the area of databases. In the third phase, if a keyword k is mapped to an attribute A, the weights of the trailing and preceding keywords related to domains of attributes

	P.Na	P.Ar	P.Ph	P.Ad	P.Em	D.Id	D.Dn	D.Ad	D.Di
workers	0	0	0	0	0	0	0	0	0
department	0	0	0	0	0	0	0	0	0
CS	30	18	0	18	0	50	75	50	50

Figure 5: Contextualized Value Weights VW

related to A through some join path are increased by the constant value Δw. The rational is that users use keywords referring to concepts that are semantically related, even if these concepts have been modeled in the database in different tables. An example of this situation is the keyword query "`Phone Tribeca`". If `phone` is mapped to the attribute `Phone` of the relation `Person`, then the keyword `Tribeca` most likely represents the address of the department, which is stored in a separate table, and then the keyword query is about finding the phone number of the department that is on Tribeca street. Note that the weight increase Δw can also be a percentage, instead of a constant, but our experimentations have showed no significant differences. The three phases described above are illustrated in pseudocode in Algorithm 2.

EXAMPLE 6.1. *Figure 5 illustrates the VW sub-matrix after the value weights of Figure 4 have been contextualized based on the mapping that maps the keyword* `person` *into* `workers` *and* `department` *to* `department`. *Note that the lines for keywords* `person` *and* `department` *are 0, a result of the initialization step.*

7. SELECTION OF THE BEST MAPPINGS

Given a weight matrix, computing the best possible mapping of keywords to database terms is known as the *assignment problem* [9]. Unfortunately, the traditional solutions return the first best mapping while we would like them all in descending order, or at least the top-k. Furthermore, we need a solution that, during the computation of the best mappings, takes into consideration inter-dependencies of the different assignments, i.e., the contextualization process. For this reason, we have adapted the popular systematic Hungarian, a.k.a. Munkres, algorithm [7] in order not to stop after the generation of the best mapping but to continue to the generation of the second best, the third, etc. Furthermore, some of its internal steps have been modified so that the weight matrix is dynamically updated every time that a mapping of a keyword to a database term is decided during the computation.

The execution of the algorithm consists of a series of iterative steps that generate a mapping with a maximum score. Once done, the weight matrix is modified accordingly to exclude the mapping that was generated and the process continues to compute the mapping with the second largest score, etc. More specifically, the maximum weight of each row is first identified and characterized as *maximum*. If the characterized as maximum weights are all located in different columns, then a mapping is generated by associating for each of the characterized as maximum weights the keyword and the database term that correspond to its respective row and column. On the other hand, if there is a column containing more than one weight characterized as maximum, all maximums in the column except the one with the maximum value loose their characterization as maximum. This last action means that some of the rows are left without some characterized weight. The values of the weights in these rows are then updated according to a number of contextual rules mentioned in Section 4. This is the effect of the mapped keywords to those that have remained unmapped.

In the sequel, for each row with no characterized weight, the one with the maximum value that belongs to a column corresponding to a database term different from the previous one is selected and characterized as *maximum*. If this leads to a matrix that has each characterized weight in a different column, then a mapping is generated as above or the process of un-characterizing some of the values as previously described is repeated.

Algorithm 3: Keyword to db term mapping selection

Input: $I(i_{ij})$ where $I \equiv SW$ or $I \equiv VW$
Output: $M^I = \{M_1^I, \ldots, M_z^I\}$: Mappings generated by I

MAPPING(I, W_{MAX})
$tempM = \bigcup i_{pt} \leftarrow HUNGARIAN_{Ext} * (I)$
$W \leftarrow \sum i_{pt}$
$M^I \leftarrow tempM$
if $(W > c * W_{MAX})$
  $W_{MAX} \leftarrow W$
while $(W > c * W_{MAX})$
  foreach $i_{pt} \in tempM$
    $i_{pt} \in I \leftarrow -100$
    $Mapping(I, W_{MAX})$

Once a mapping of all the keywords has been formed, it is included in the set of mappings that will be returned by the algorithm. Then, the algorithm needs to be repeated to generate additional mappings. To avoid recomputing the same assignments, the algorithm is re-executed cyclically with a new matrix as input. The new matrix is the old one modified to exclude mappings that have already been considered in previous runs of the algorithm. This is done by setting the values of the respective weights to a large negative number, forcing the algorithm to never select them again. This whole process is repeated until the scores of the mappings that the algorithm generates fall below some specific threshold. By construction, the most prominent mapping is the one that is first reported by this task.

The original Hungarian algorithm for rectangular matrices has an $O(n^2 * m)$ complexity [7], where n is the number of keywords and m is the number of databases terms. Extending the algorithm to consider dynamic weights as described above brings the complexity to $O(n^3 * m^2)$ which is due to the fact that a mapping may affect any other mapping, thus, in the worst case, $(n-1)*(m-1)$ weight updates may take place. Nevertheless, this worst case rarely happens since only a subset of the matrix is updated in each iteration, and, due to the threshold, not all the possible updates are evaluated.

Algorithm 3 depicts the overall process of computing the set of most prominent mappings of a set of keywords to database terms, given a weight matrix. The expression $HUNGARIAN_{ext}$ refers to our extended version of the Hungarian algorithm.

EXAMPLE 7.1. *Figure 6 illustrates a VW matrix similar to the one of Figure 5, but with additional keywords to better demonstrate the steps described in this section. The initial version of the matrix is the one composed of the first 7 lines. The lines of the keywords workers and department will remain unchanged since the keywords are mapped to schema terms, and for this reason they are omitted from the subsequent versions. The weights in white cells are those characterized as maximum. Each one is the largest weight in its row. Note that for column* <u>`P.N`</u> *there are more than one weight characterized as maximum. From those, only the largest one is kept, in our case the 46. This leaves the row of keyword* `Hopkins` *with no weight characterized as maximum. The result is the second VW matrix illustrated in Figure 6. The three characterized weights suggest a mapping for the keywords* `CS`, `Mary` *and* `Summerhill`.

	P.N	P.A	P.P	P.Ad	P.E	D.I	D.D	D.A	D.Di
workers	0	0	0	0	0	0	0	0	0
department	0	0	0	0	0	0	0	0	0
CS	30	18	0	18	0	50	75	50	50
Hopkins	45	30	0	35	10	32	40	35	39
Mary	46	20	0	5	7	20	25	30	40
Summerhill	10	7	0	34	22	20	10	32	15

CS	30	18	0	18	0	50	75	50	50
Hopkins	45	30	0	35	10	32	40	35	39
Mary	46	20	0	5	7	20	25	30	40
Summerhill	10	7	0	34	22	20	10	32	15

CS	30	18	0	18	0	50	75	50	50
Hopkins	49	34	0	39	14	34	42	37	41
Mary	50	24	0	9	11	22	27	32	42
Summerhill	14	11	0	38	26	22	12	34	17

CS	30	18	0	18	0	50	75	50	50
Hopkins	49	34	0	39	14	34	42	37	41
Mary	50	24	0	9	11	22	27	32	42
Summerhill	14	11	0	38	26	22	12	34	17

Figure 6: Weight matrix during best mapping computation

Given these mappings, the weights are adjusted to reflect the interdependencies according to the contextual rules. For instance, the mapping of `CS` *to the database term* D.D*, triggers an increase in the weights of the database terms on the attributes in the same table. The result of firing the contextual rules is the third matrix in Figure 6. In the updated matrix, the highest value is 49, which is in the column* P.N*, but cannot be chosen since the keyword* `Mary` *is already mapped to it. The same applies for the second and third largest weights in the row, which are 42 and 39, respectively. The fourth largest weight, 37, is in a column of a database term that no keyword is mapped to, and it is becoming characterized as maximum. The final outcome is the fourth matrix of Figure 6 and, based on this, the mappings of keywords* `CS`*,*`Hopkins`*,* `Mary` *and* `Summerhill` *to the database terms* D.D*,* D.Di*,* P.N *and* P.Ad*, respectively, which is added to the mapping results generated by the algorithm. After that, the mapping is again considered for generating a new input for the algorithm. Four new matrices are derived from it, each one having one of the weights that was in a white cell in the last matrix reduced. For each obtained matrix, the whole process starts again from the beginning.*

8. RELATED WORK

The popularity of keyword searching is constantly increasing. It has been the successful retrieval model in IR for text databases [30] and the web [8] for more than a decade. It has also been adopted by the data management community in the context of XML [13, 20, 32]. To answer a keyword query over XML data, the appearances of the query keywords are first identified within the documents (possibly through some free-text search) and then combined together into Meaningful Lowest Common Ancestor Structures (MLCAS). A score is computed based on this structure and according to this score the respective XML documents containing the MLCAS are ranked and returned to the user. XML benefits from the fact that its basic information model is the "document", which is the same as in IR, thus, many IR techniques can be easily employed in the XML context. On the other hand, keyword search in relational databases is particularly challenging [31], first because the database instances are way larger, and second because the basic model is fundamentally different making hard the identification of the information units that are to be returned. Nevertheless, keyword search over relational data is particularly appealing, and there are already many interesting proposals in the scientific literature [36, 10]. DISCOVER [16] and DBXplorer [2] have been among the first such systems. The typical approach is to build a special index on the contents of the database and then to use that index to identify the appearances of the query keywords in the attribute values. Many approaches use inverted indexes [1, 16, 29] for that purpose, while others, like DBXplore, use symbol tables. A symbol table is an index consisting of a set of triples ⟨*value, attribute, relation*⟩, used to map every value to its schema information. Once the keywords are located, the different ways by which their respective tuples are connected are discovered, forming the so-called "joining network" of tuples or tuple trees, that often become the information unit returned to the user. The joining networks are constructed either directly from the instances, or by building query expressions and evaluating them [16]. DISCOVER is interested in finding total and minimal joining networks. A joining network is total if each keyword query is contained in at least one tuple of the network, and minimal if the removal of any tuple makes the network no longer total. More recent approaches [27], are oriented towards reducing the number of tuples that need to be considered in order to improve previous techniques. BANKS [1] follows a similar approach but employs the Steiner tree algorithm to discover how the tuples are associated. SQAK [31] is another system that is based on the same generic principles but focuses on the discovery of aggregate SQL expressions that describe the intended keyword query semantics. Since the set of possible answers may be large, and since the results are already ranked, the above systems typically return the top-k results.

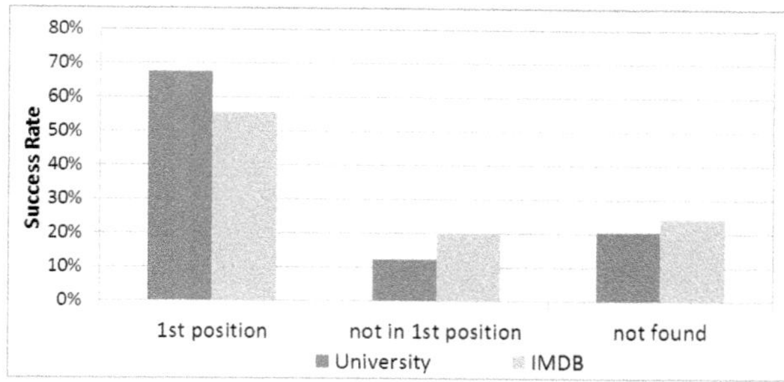

Figure 7: Success in finding the intended query semantics

As happened in all the above approaches, we are also trying to identify the possible semantics (i.e., expected answers) to the ambiguous keywords queries, and rank the results. We return the top-k but by bringing the thresholds down to their extreme values we can provide the whole set if needed. Our fundamental difference is that we do not assume a-priori access to the database instance, as our approach do not need pre-build and exploit any index. Unavoidably, we are based on schema and meta-data, i.e., intensional information, which makes our work applicable to scenarios where the above techniques cannot work. Nevertheless, our approach should not be seen as an alternative to the above methods. Since we operate on different information, i.e., the meta-data, our work can be used to enhance these techniques by providing a better exploitation of the meta-information and the relationships among the keywords. The idea of using schema information and keyword semantics has been considered in one of the approaches [21], but this is only limited to word semantics based on WordNet. We go further by combining not only additional semantic similarity techniques, similar to those used in schema matching [28], but also on syntactic and structural information. Data behavior has also been considered [31]. All these works are complementary.

Another distinction of our approach is on the relationship among

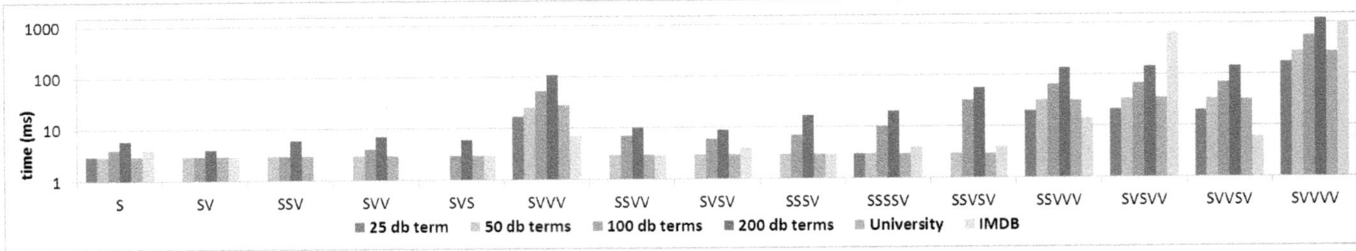

Figure 8: Time performance for different database sizes and different kinds of queries

the keywords. Existing approaches compute the relationship among the keywords by considering the relationships of the data values in the database instance. We believe that the keyword query should be the one driving the translation and not the data. Our approach takes into consideration in a systematic way the position of the keywords in the query itself and the inter-dependencies between the matchings of the keywords to the database structure. Furthermore, we map keywords to schema elements that will form the SQL query, instead of mapping them to the tuples themselves [31]. This allows us, without performing any query evaluation, to present these queries to the user and communicate the considered semantics. Of course, this is an optional step, but in highly heterogeneous environments, this is the norm for matching and mapping techniques [26].

A related field is query relaxation [3], but the main difference is that queries are expected to provide some form of structure specification while keyword queries, which are our interest, are completely flat. The same applies for approximate query answering techniques [14, 15, 20]. The latter may not map all the parts of the query, an assumption that for the moment we also have. Keyword search has also been considered by the Semantic Web community for RDF and linked data [33, 34, 37, 38]. The research issues and the approaches are similar to the keyword search in relational systems, but in the context of the triple-based RDF data.

Our effort can also find applications in the field of graphical tools that assist the user in formulating queries [25]. By finding the different interpretations of a keyword query, we could detect related schema structures, make suggestions and guide the user in the query formulation. Furthermore, in cases of exploratory searches, the user can use the generated interpretations as a way to explore an (unknown) data source and understand better its semantics.

9. EVALUATION

We implemented the proposed technique into the Keymantic system [4] and we run numerous experiments for studying its efficiency and effectiveness. The experiments were performed on a 32bit Centrino Duo vPro Windows machine with 3GB of RAM. Our work is intended for applications that heavily depend on the user semantics, thus, generating synthetic dataset was not an effective alternative. We instead selected for our experiments two real data sets. The first was a university database containing information about courses, professors, students, publications, employees and other academic issues. The second database was a fraction of the popular IMDB service that is publicly available from the respective web site (www.imdb.com). 29 real users were asked to provide a set of keyword queries for these databases alongside a natural language explanation of what they were looking for. The users had no access to schema information, they neither were technical experts. Only a verbal high level explanation of what the database contents were about had been provided to them. A database expert translated each natural language explanation of what the user was looking as it had been provided by her, into SQL. Since many queries were vague, high level and of exploratory nature, some of these queries were translated into more than one SQL query. The answer expected for each keyword query was the result of evaluating the SQL queries that the expert had created, and this was used as a reference to evaluate the results returned by our implementation. We used a total of 99 and 44 queries for the university and the IMDB database, respectively. It is important to note that evaluating a keyword search technique for relational databases is a challenging task, mainly due to the lack of standards [35]. The task is becoming more challenging in our case since existing techniques have different assumptions and goals, making sometimes unfair any direct comparison among them. One of the reasons is that most of these techniques assume the availability of the instance.

[The importance of Schema Information] Despite the existence of many keyword search techniques, few exploit schema information. We would like to study whether our claim that, a significant number of keywords in keyword queries correspond, not to the data, but to meta-data (schema) information, is true. For that, we studied the SQL answers to the keywords queries of our evaluation dataset, and found that 58% of the keywords were actually referring to schema terms.

[Effectiveness] To measure the effectiveness of our technique we tested whether the queries that generate the intended answers (as specified by the users and created by the expert) were among those our algorithm generates. We also measured how many times the expected results appear in the first place. In case a keyword query had an answer generated by more than one SQL query, we considered in the counting multiple copies of the keyword query each one with only one of these SQL queries. The threshold we used, i.e., the parameter c in Algorithm 3, definitely played an important role. When it was brought to zero, every expected answer to a keyword query was included in the result. The percentage of keyword queries that returned the expected answer in the first position was not much different from the one in the case of a threshold with some default value, thus, the results we report here are for that default value. The results are graphically illustrated in Figure 7. The "1st position" refers to the percentage of the keyword queries in which we found the expected interpretation in the first position. The "not in 1st position" indicates the percentage of the queries in which our algorithm did generated the expected interpretation but did not return it in the first position. Finally, the "not found" indicates the percentage in which the expected interpretation was not returned at all in the results produced by our algorithm. In the IMDB scenario, we obtained worst results than in the university scenario. This was mainly due to the fact that the IMDB schema consists of many nested tables with the same structure, i.e., same name and very similar data-types.

[Efficiency] To measure the efficiency of our system, we studied

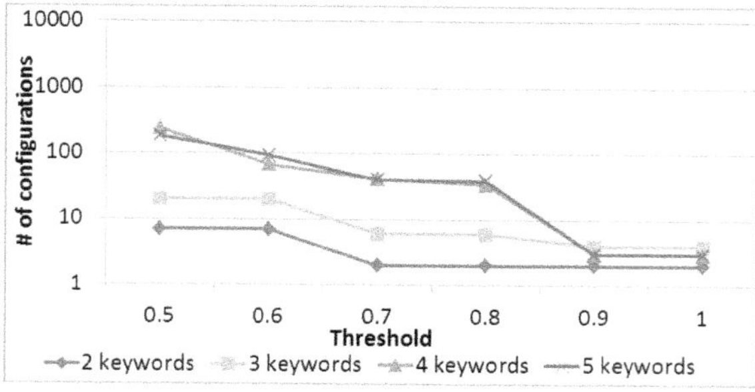

(a) Generated configurations for the University database

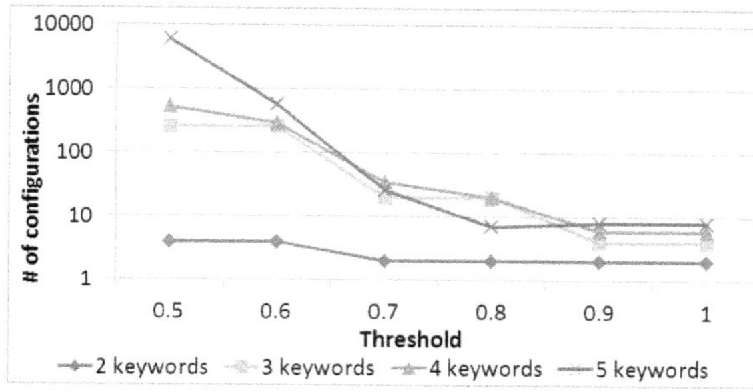

(b) Generated configurations for the IMDB database

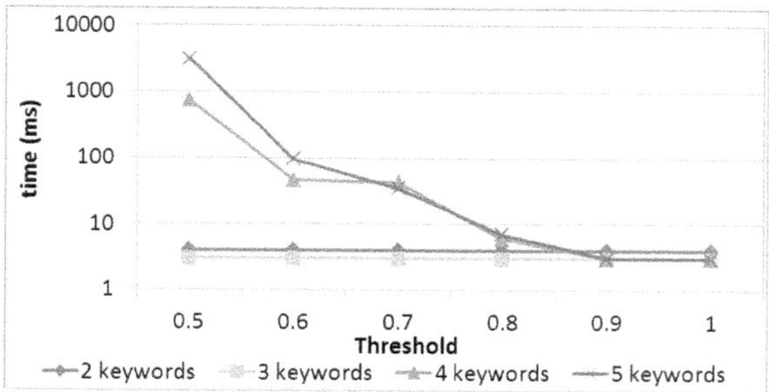

(c) Time performance for the University database

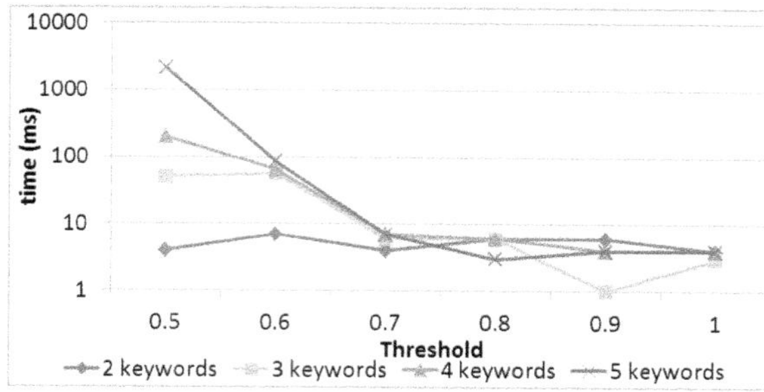

(d) Time performance for the IMDB database

Figure 9: Experimental results using different thresholds

its time performance with respect to two different parameters: the queries and the size of the database. For the former, we considered queries that differ not only on the number of keywords, but also on their type, i.e., whether the keywords correspond to schema or value terms. For the latter, since our approach assumes no access to the instance, the variation in size was considered in terms of the size of the schema. We created fractions of different sizes from our original evaluation database. Our performance measurements are illustrated in Figure 8. Each query is characterized by a string. Each character of the string corresponds to a keyword in the query and can be S, if the respective keyword is intended to be a schema term, or V, if it is intended to be a value term. For instance, the string SVS represents a keyword query in which the first and last keyword represent schema terms while the middle a value. As expected, the response time increases with the number of keywords, but when there is a prevalence of keywords mapped to schema terms this increase is not dramatic. The interesting result is the increase in time due to the increase of the number of keywords representing value terms. In general, this increase should have been factorial (ref. Section 3), but the experiments showed no such increase, which is because the metadata and the auxiliary information alongside the contextual rules are significantly restricting the number of possible mappings of keywords to database terms. Only in the last case, where there was one keyword referring to a schema element and four keywords referring to data values, the response time increased. The comparison between the IMDB database and the university database showed no significant difference, which means that the nesting level of the database schema did not really affect the time performance. In the experiments above, we did not report the time needed to actually evaluate the interpretations, i.e., queries, to avoid having the query engine performance blurring the results. We did measured, however, the performance as well as the overall time needed to answer a keyword query. We noticed that the overall time was highly related to the number of results retrieved and the number of join operations required. It ranged from some tenths of a second for selective queries involving one table to a few minutes for general queries. For example, in the IMDB scenario, the keyword query `"film"` took 1.9 sec and retrieved 166936 records, while the query `"actor film 2007"` took 1 min and 40 sec and retrieved about 2.7 million tuples.

[Algorithm Configuration] To evaluate the effect of the threshold value in the behavior of our system, we have experimented with the same keyword query but with different threshold values. As expected, a selective, i.e., high, threshold reduces the number of results and the response time. Figure 9 provides an insight on the dependencies between these two factors. A study of the results allows us to observe that different number of configurations can be obtained for the same threshold value. The reason of this discrepancy is mainly due to the different keyword queries with which the scenarios were evaluated and the different schemas of their respective databases. In particular, the university database is composed of few tables with a large number of attributes and the IMDB database contains many related tables with few attributes.

[Qualitative comparison to other approaches] Our approach is the first to operate under the assumption that there is no prior access to the relational database instance. Under such a condition, existing works will return no results since they will have no way to determine where the keywords appear. Even works that take schema information into account [21] do so as an optimization step after they find the appearance of some keywords in the database instance. Thus, a direct comparison in terms of effectiveness and efficiency would be unfair. Nevertheless, to realize a qualitative comparison, we run some experiments using two popular systems for keyword searching in relational databases, DBXplorer [2] and DISCOVER [16], alongside our system. For DISCOVER, we had exactly the same results as in DBXplorer, thus, we report only the former. The first experiment we run was with DBXplorer assuming that the relational database was not allowing access to its instance so that DBXplorer could not create its index. As such, all the queries we executed returned zero results. Then, we allowed such access, and repeated the experiment. We run the same queries against our system, naturally assuming no access to the instances. The number of queries generated by our system was larger than the one generated by DBXplorer. This was expected since our system was using no information about the existing data values and was making more generic guesses of possible semantically meaningful queries. We also tried what happens if our system did have information about the instance values. This allowed it to identify and eliminate the queries generated by mappings of certain keywords to value terms that were leading to zero results. The number of queries generated by our system was less than the number of queries generated by DBXplorer since in our case some queries that were not very likely to occur semantically were eliminated by the threshold (the parameter c in Algorithm 3). We obtained the same number of queries if the threshold was set to zero.

10. CONCLUSION

We have presented a novel framework for keyword search in relational databases. In contrast to traditional keyword search techniques that require access to the actual data stored in the database in order to build an index, our technique uses intensional knowledge. This allows our approach to be used in a wide range of applications, including, besides databases on the web, information integration systems, where building and maintaining specialized indexes is not a feasible option, because the only service offered by the source is to access the data through wrappers, predefined queries or web forms. For the challenging task of interpreting the keyword queries, we have extended the Hungarian algorithm in order to find the SQL queries the most likely describe the meaning of the keyword queries. We have implemented and evaluated the technique and reported our findings.

REFERENCES

[1] B. Aditya, G. Bhalotia, S. Chakrabarti, A. Hulgeri, C. Nakhe, Parag, and S. Sudarshan. Banks: Browsing and keyword searching in relational databases. In *VLDB*, pages 1083–1086, 2002.

[2] S. Agrawal, S. Chaudhuri, and G. Das. Dbxplorer: A system for keyword-based search over relational databases. In *ICDE*, pages 5–16. IEEE Computer Society, 2002.

[3] S. Amer-Yahia, L. V. S. Lakshmanan, and S. Pandit. FleXPath: Flexible structure and full-text querying for XML. In *SIGMOD*, pages 83–94. ACM, 2004.

[4] S. Bergamaschi, E. Domnori, F. Guerra, M. Orsini, R. T. Lado, and Y. Velegrakis. Keymantic: Semantic keyword-based searching in data integration systems. *PVLDB*, 3(2):1637–1640, 2010.

[5] S. Bergamaschi, C. Sartori, F. Guerra, and M. Orsini. Extracting relevant attribute values for improved search. *IEEE Internet Computing*, 11(5):26–35, 2007.

[6] J. Bleiholder and F. Naumann. Data fusion. *ACM Comput. Surv.*, 41(1), 2008.

[7] F. Bourgeois and J.-C. Lassalle. An extension of the Munkres algorithm for the assignment problem to rectangular matrices. *Communications of ACM*, 14(12):802–804, 1971.

[8] S. Brin and L. Page. The anatomy of a large-scale hypertextual web search engine. *Computer Networks*, 30(1-7):107–117, 1998.

[9] R. Burkard, M. Dell'Amico, and S. Martello. *Assignment Problems*. SIAM Society for Industrial and Applied Mathematics, 2009.

[10] S. Chakrabarti, S. Sarawagi, and S. Sudarshan. Enhancing search with structure. *IEEE Data Eng. Bull.*, 33(1):3–24, 2010.

[11] R. Cilibrasi and P. M. B. Vitányi. The google similarity distance. *IEEE TKDE*, 19(3):370–383, 2007.

[12] W. W. Cohen, P. D. Ravikumar, and S. E. Fienberg. A comparison of string distance metrics for name-matching tasks. In *IIWeb*, 2003.

[13] D. Florescu, D. Kossmann, and I. Manolescu. Integrating keyword search into xml query processing. In *BDA*, 2000.

[14] S. Guha, H. V. Jagadish, N. Koudas, D. Srivastava, and T. Yu. Approximate XML joins. In *SIGMOD*, pages 287–298, 2002.

[15] S. Helmer. Measuring the Structural Similarity of Semistructured Documents Using Entropy. In *VLDB*, pages 1022–1032. ACM, 2007.

[16] V. Hristidis and Y. Papakonstantinou. Discover: Keyword search in relational databases. In *VLDB*, pages 670–681, 2002.

[17] Y. Kotidis, A. Marian, and D. Srivastava. Circumventing Data Quality Problems Using Multiple Join Paths. In *CleanDB*, 2006.

[18] R. Kumar and A. Tomkins. A Characterization of Online Search Behavior. *IEEE Data Engineering Bulletin*, 32(2):3–11, 2009.

[19] M. Lenzerini. Data integration: A theoretical perspective. In *PODS*, pages 233–246. ACM, 2002.

[20] Y. Li, C. Yu, and H. V. Jagadish. Schema-free XQuery. In *VLDB*, pages 72–83, 2004.

[21] F. Liu, C. T. Yu, W. Meng, and A. Chowdhury. Effective keyword search in relational databases. In *SIGMOD*, pages 563–574, 2006.

[22] Y. Luo, X. Lin, W. Wang, and X. Zhou. Spark: top-k keyword query in relational databases. In *SIGMOD*, pages 115–126. ACM, 2007.

[23] D. Maier, J. D. Ullman, and M. Y. Vardi. On the Foundations of the Universal Relation Model. *ACM Trans. Database Syst.*, 9(2):283–308, June 1984.

[24] S. Melnik, H. Garcia-Molina, and E. Rahm. Similarity flooding: A versatile graph matching algorithm and its application to schema matching. In *ICDE*, pages 117–128. IEEE Computer Society, 2002.

[25] A. Nandi and H. V. Jagadish. Assisted querying using instant-response interfaces. In *SIGMOD*, pages 1156–1158. ACM, 2007.

[26] L. Popa, Y. Velegrakis, R. J. Miller, M. A. Hernandez, and R. Fagin. Translating web data. In *VLDB*, pages 598–609, 2002.

[27] L. Qin, J. X. Yu, and L. Chang. Keyword search in databases: the power of rdbms. In *SIGMOD*, pages 681–694. ACM, 2009.

[28] E. Rahm and P. A. Bernstein. A survey of approaches to automatic schema matching. *VLDB Journal*, 10(4):334–350, 2001.

[29] A. Simitsis, G. Koutrika, and Y. E. Ioannidis. Précis: from unstructured keywords as queries to structured databases as answers. *VLDB Journal*, 17(1):117–149, 2008.

[30] A. Singhal, C. Buckley, and M. Mitra. Pivoted document length normalization. In *SIGIR*, pages 21–29, 1996.

[31] S. Tata and G. M. Lohman. SQAK: doing more with keywords. In *SIGMOD*, pages 889–902. ACM, 2008.

[32] M. Theobald, H. Bast, D. Majumdar, R. Schenkel, and G. Weikum. TopX: efficient and versatile top-k query processing for semistructured data. *VLDB Journal*, 17(1):81–115, 2008.

[33] T. Tran, H. Wang, S. Rudolph, and P. Cimiano. Top-k exploration of query candidates for efficient keyword search on graph-shaped (rdf) data. In *ICDE*, pages 405–416. IEEE Computer Society, 2009.

[34] V. S. Uren, Y. Lei, and E. Motta. Semsearch: Refining semantic search. In *ESWC*, pages 874–878. LNCS Springer, 2008.

[35] W. Webber. Evaluating the effectiveness of keyword search. *IEEE Data Engineering Bulletin*, 33(1):55–60, 2010.

[36] J. X. Yu, L. Qin, and L. Chang. *Keyword Search in Databases*. Synthesis Lectures on Data Management. Morgan & Claypool Publishers, 2010.

[37] G. Zenz, X. Zhou, E. Minack, W. Siberski, and W. Nejdl. From keywords to semantic queries-incremental query construction on the semantic web. *Journal of Web Semantics*, 7(3):166–176, 2009.

[38] Q. Zhou, C. Wang, M. Xiong, H. Wang, and Y. Yu. Spark: Adapting keyword query to semantic search. In *ISWC*, pages 694–707, 2007.

Sharing Work in Keyword Search over Databases

Marie Jacob
University of Pennsylvania
Philadelphia, PA, USA
majacob@cis.upenn.edu

Zachary Ives
University of Pennsylvania
Philadelphia, PA, USA
zives@cis.upenn.edu

ABSTRACT

An important means of allowing non-expert end-users to pose ad hoc queries — whether over single databases or data integration systems — is through keyword search. Given a set of keywords, the query processor finds matches across different tuples and tables. It computes and executes a set of relational sub-queries whose results are combined to produce the k highest ranking answers.

Work on keyword search primarily focuses on single-database, single-query settings: each query is answered in isolation, despite possible overlap between queries posed by different users or at different times; and the number of relevant tables is assumed to be small, meaning that sub-queries can be processed without using cost-based methods to combine work. As we apply keyword search to support ad hoc data integration queries over scientific or other databases on the Web, we must *reuse and combine* computation. In this paper, we propose an architecture that continuously receives sets of ranked keyword queries, and seeks to reuse work across these queries. We extend multiple query optimization and continuous query techniques, and develop a new query plan scheduling module we call the ATC (based on its analogy to an air traffic controller). The ATC manages the flow of tuples among a multitude of pipelined operators, minimizing the work needed to return the top-k answers for all queries. We also develop techniques to manage the sharing and reuse of state as queries complete and input data streams are exhausted. We show the effectiveness of our techniques in handling queries over real and synthetic data sets.

Categories and Subject Descriptors

H.2.4 [**Database Management**]: Systems—*Query Processing*

General Terms

Performance, Management, Algorithms

Keywords

Keyword search, top-k queries, multiple query optimization

1. INTRODUCTION

In recent years, there has been increasing acknowledgment that database technologies must be made more accessible to end-users.

SIGMOD'11, June 12–16, 2011, Athens, Greece.

One promising approach is that of providing keyword search interfaces over tables or XML trees [1, 2, 11, 12, 13, 18, 27, 33]: here, keyword searches get reformulated into sets of database-style join queries, whose answers are merged and ranked according to some distance, cost, or relevance metric. Keyword search interfaces are especially appealing for settings where users must pose novel (ad hoc) queries over large numbers of tables that they do not fully understand: this occurs, for instance, in scientific communities where many interrelated public databases, rather than a single global data warehouse, exist. A specific example is the life sciences, where individual databases may have more than 350 tables [21], and multiple such databases may have relevant data that can be pieced together to answer a scientist's exploratory query.

Anecdotally, scientists often pose *sequences* of related queries, iteratively refining their search for a particular relationship; and they may refer back to previous queries[1]. Moreover, certain core concepts (e.g., proteins) will appear in many queries.

Unfortunately, while a substantial body of research has been conducted on keyword search over databases, such work has been directed at settings in which a *single database* is answering a *single user's query* in isolation. Techniques have been developed to use precomputed indices to quickly winnow down the number of database subqueries that must be posed to return the top query answers [9, 13], to find promising join "paths" linking the matching tables [1, 2, 11, 12, 13, 18, 27, 33], and to efficiently compute and merge top-k results [7, 28]. These techniques assume that limited numbers of join subqueries are necessary to obtain top-k answers, and that few relations appear in multiple join subqueries. In the data integration setting, it is much more common that *multiple* source relations have highly relevant answers for each keyword; we must consider ways of computing all combinations of these relations, thus computing a set of queries with high mutual overlap (see, e.g., [33]). Moreover, as mentioned previously, we may wish to exploit the fact that queries posed across time may overlap.

In this paper we focus on scaling keyword search interfaces to data integration scenarios with commonly-used sources, by exploiting the overlap among the join subqueries that partially answer a *single* keyword search, and also the overlap among *different* keyword searches performed over time and even across users. We show that through cost-based computation of common subexpressions, clever caching, and pruning of the query optimization search space, we can handle large numbers of queries and relevant sources — while still delivering top-k results quickly.

We assume a very general model of ranked query processing, in which the score of a query result may include a *static* compo-

[1]See, e.g., Protein Data Bank, `pdbbeta.rcsb.org/robohelp/site_navigation/reengeneered_site_features.htm`, for a system that supports query reuse.

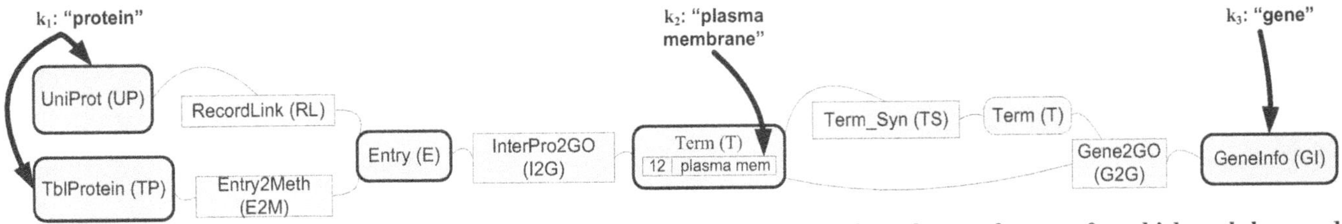

Figure 1: Example of a set of relations from multiple bioinformatics databases, plus a keyword query, for which each keyword ($k_1 \ldots k_3$) may match a table either based on its name, or based on an inverted index of its content.

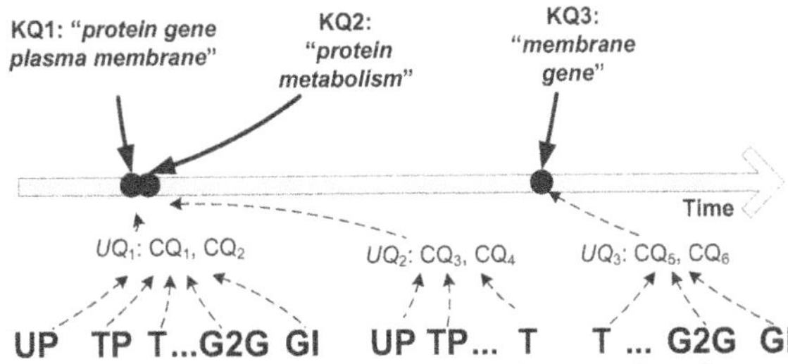

Figure 2: Timeline showing user queries posed to the system. Note the overlap between tables that they access.

nent (based on the formulation of the query and/or properties of the source relations) as well as a *dynamic* one (based on specific attribute values from the source tuples). We even allow for the fact that different users may have different scoring functions, possibly taking into account context or user preference [3, 20, 31, 33]. We assume that keyword searches are posed over time — sometimes concurrently, sometimes in sequence. When queries are posed concurrently, we perform cost-based multiple query optimization over the query batch. When they are posed over time, we reuse results computed by the earlier queries (resembling a continuous query model [4]). See Figures 1 and 2 for an example database schema and a visualization of queries posed over time (we describe details in Section 2). Our approach takes advantage of several properties: (1) top-k queries generally create a limited amount of intermediate state [16], as they only run until the desired number of results are processed; (2) it is often possible to compute bounds on the range of scores for tuples from any query, by considering the query's static score component [33] and information about score attribute maxima; (3) top-k queries should support fully pipelined execution so each subquery only reads the amount of data necessary to produce top-scoring answers; (4) even subqueries that use different scoring functions will read from the source relations in the same order — they will just read at different relative rates from the sources.

Our work is implemented as part of the Q System [32, 33], which enables customization of ranking functions for each user. It could alternatively be used with the Kite data integration system [27] or with other keyword search in database schemes [2, 11, 13]. We make the following contributions:

- A new top-k query processing architecture that keeps in-memory state and existing query plan structures from one query execution to the next, enabling effective result reuse and recomputation over time.
- An optimizer that combines cost-based and heuristic search, in order to find common subexpressions across and within top-k queries, and which supports the reuse of existing subexpressions from past query executions.
- A fully pipelined, *adaptive* top-k query execution scheme for answering multiple queries, consisting of a query plan graph of m-joins (STeM eddies) [24, 34] and rank-merge [7] operators, supervised by a novel ATC controller.
- A query state manager that can *graft* and *prune* elements in an executing query plan, and which manages the reuse and eviction of state.
- A comprehensive set of experiments over synthetic and real datasets, demonstrating the performance gains of our approach.

We provide a problem definition in Section 2, then outline our approach in Section 3. Section 4 explains how multiple queries can be executed simultaneously. We describe how we optimize batches of queries for simultaneous execution in Section 5, then how we handle further queries over time in Section 6. We experimentally validate the performance of our system in Section 7, we describe related work in Section 8, and we conclude and describe future work in Section 9.

2. PROBLEM DEFINITION

Our goal in the Q System is to provide high performance to a user base that continuously poses keyword queries over remote (and possibly local) database instances — where the resulting top-k SQL queries overlap in the relations they access, both with other concurrent queries and with other queries to be posed in the future. Intuitively, the goal is to create and maintain a small set of pipelined *query plan graphs* consisting of query processing operators — where each operator may produce sub-results that get fed to one *or more* downstream operators, ultimately depositing results into *ranking queues* that return the top-k answers. In general, we expect the plans' in-memory state to be small, if the queries have a high overlap with one another and can share work. Moreover, top-k queries tend to only fetch a small number of the highest-scoring tuples from their relations. Once execution of a batch of queries completes, we do not discard the query plan graph and its state — rather, we take subsequent queries and attempt to *graft* them onto the existing graph, reusing existing plan state and operators as appropriate. Only if we run out of resources (in particular, memory) do we *prune* plan state and operators.

2.1 Keyword Search in Data Integration

We introduce some notation and review the basics of keyword search over databases, with an emphasis on databases that may be remotely stored and in need of integration, as in [27, 33].

EXAMPLE 1. *Suppose we are running a portal for biologists to pose ad hoc queries. Perhaps we have a known schema graph, such as the one shown in Figure 1. The sources UniProt, ProSite and InterPro correspond to protein databases; GeneOntology, NCBI Entrez correspond to gene information, and OMIM stores information about genetic diseases. These tables are bridged by record linking tables (shown as orange squared rectangles). Edges in the graph represent foreign keys, hyperlinks, and potential join relationships.*

A biologist may pose the keyword query KQ_1*: "protein 'plasma membrane' gene." A keyword search system would find matches between each keyword and data/metadata of each relation (as shown*

Table 1: Conjunctive queries CQ_1, CQ_2 from user query UQ_1, answering keyword query KQ_1.

CQ_1	*q(prot, gene, typ, dis):-TP(id, prot, . . .), E2M(ent, id, . . .), I2G(ent, gid1)*, **T**(*gid1*, 'plasma membrane', *score*), **TS**(*gid1, gid2, score*), *G2G(gid2, gild), GI(gild, gene, . . .)*
CQ_2	*q(nam, gene, typ, dis):-UP(ac, nam, . . .)*, **RL**(*ac, nam, ent, prot, score*), *I2G(ent, gid1)*, **T**(*gid1*, 'plasma membrane', *score*), *G2G(gid1, gild), GI(gild, gene, . . .)*

Table 2: Conjunctive queries CQ_3, CQ_4 from user query UQ_2, answering keyword query KQ_2, posed at the same time as KQ_1.

CQ_3	*q(prot, typ):-TP(id, prot, . . .), E2M(ent, id, . . .), I2G(ent, gid1), T(gid1*, 'metabolism', *score)*
CQ_4	*q(nam, typ):-UP(ac, nam, . . .)*, **RL**(*ac, nam, ent, prot, score*), *I2G(ent, gid1)*, **T**(*gid1*, 'metabolism', *score*)

in Figure 1). In some cases, the match might be exact while in other cases, it might be approximate. The goal of the keyword search system is find a set of trees that contain relations matched to all keywords. Each subgraph is then mapped to a conjunctive query which is then evaluated. Table 1 shows conjunctive queries CQ_1 and CQ_2 corresponding to our example. The answers to KQ_1 may include results from these and other conjunctive queries; together these form the user query UQ_1. □

Keyword searches are inherently uncertain during the matching process, and systems will typically score the answers according to some score function C that maps a tuple answer to a real score value. Many scoring models have been proposed, with most usually taking into account a static component (such as query size), as well as a dynamic component (such as keyword-to-tuple score matches). We describe three different models/systems that we believe are representative of the state of the art:

DISCOVER: The systems in [12, 13] enumerate ordered conjunctive queries (called *candidate networks*) for a particular keyword search, and rank tuples based on the size of the query that produced the tuple, as well as standard IR scores that are derived from a particular DBMS. Under their ranking model, a sample score function C for CQ_1 would be $C(t) = \frac{1}{size(CQ_1)}$ or $C(t) = \frac{\sum_{t_i} score(t_i)}{size(CQ_1)}$, where t is a tuple of CQ_1 and t_i belongs to the derivation of t.

Q System: The model in the Q System [32, 33] is similar to that of DISCOVER, in that conjunctive queries are found over a schema graph. Each edge in the graph is annotated with a cost that represents how useful the edge is. Additionally, each relation may be annotated with a cost that denotes how authoritative it is. These edge and node costs are learned and may be different across user queries. For a result tuple t of CQ_1, the scoring function C would be $C(t) = \frac{1}{2^c}$, where $c = (\sum_e c_e) + (\sum_i cost(t_i))$, c_e is a cost for each edge in the subgraph and $cost$ is a function that maps a tuple to a cost value.

BANKS, BLINKS: Unlike the previous systems, query execution in BANKS [2] and BLINKS [11] involves traversing a *data* graph (where nodes are tuples and edges are key/foreign key relationships between tuples), in order to enumerate the top-k list. Nodes and edges in the graph are annotated with scores and weights, with the ranking function forming a monotonic combination of both.

The challenge for keyword search systems lies in efficiently returning the top-k answers, *without* exhaustively computing every answer satisfying the query conditions. If we know the potential range bounds of scores for the conjunctive queries, we may be able to eliminate some queries from consideration, because they will not return top-scoring answers. If we fetch tuples from the various relations in decreasing order of their score, we may likewise be able to stop once we have returned enough answers. These concepts have formed the cornerstones of work on top-k query processing, ranging from keyword search systems [2, 11, 13, 18, 19, 33] to generic rank-merging algorithms [7] to custom rank-join algorithms [5, 9, 12, 15, 16, 23, 28] and ranked query optimization strategies [22]. Our goal is to build on the foundations of all these works, to address (for any of the three scoring models) two tasks that can arise from the keyword search scenario of Figure 2.

2.2 Task 1: Handling overlapping queries

EXAMPLE 2. *Concurrently with the first biologist, a second biologist may simultaneously pose a second keyword query KQ_2 to the system: "protein metabolism." Two example conjunctive queries are shown in Table 2. Observe that these queries not only overlap with each other — but they are also subexpressions of CQ_1 and CQ_2, respectively. Note, however, that KQ_2 was posed by a different user, and so a* different scoring function *might be associated with this query (our Q System supports custom ranking functions for each user [33]).*

This overlap in concurrently posed queries provides an opportunity for doing *shared computation*, which has only been explored to a limited extent in the keyword search context. The works of [2, 11] investigate this to some degree, where sharing computation essentially amounts to discovering join paths from a single (keyword-matched) tuple to other tuples in a data graph. They thus employ graph searching algorithms, assuming that the relationships between tuples are already known, and that the cost of joining two tuples (i.e., traversing a link) is negligible. We address a more general case, where tuples are stored in remote databases on the Internet, which can be accessed in streaming fashion or *probed* (remotely queried for matches) using some join key.

Our **first set of contributions** in this paper is a new scheme for simultaneously producing results for multiple pipelined, ranked queries within a middleware layer for data integration. We emphasize pushing down subqueries, whose results get streamed to the middleware, where they are joined with one another, and with sources that must be remotely probed. It is important to *simultaneously* (in interleaved fashion) support answering of *multiple* conjunctive queries: Such queries might be ones whose results are being merged in rank order to form top-k answers, as with queries CQ_1 and CQ_2 in our previous example; or they might be returning results to *different* users whose queries are posed simultaneously. In our context, this requires fully *pipelined* execution of joins. To share work across query plans, we support *graph-structured* rather than tree-structured query plans, where a given query subexpression may produce answers whose results must be fed into multiple "downstream" operators belonging to different queries.

2.3 Task 2: Handling dynamic changes

Our interest is not only in efficiently executing sets of queries posed concurrently, but also in handling the *dynamic* operation of the system: over time new users pose new queries, and existing users *refine* their keyword queries by posing related queries with further or fewer keywords. Recall the scenario of Figure 2.

Table 3: Two conjunctive queries CQ_5, CQ_6 from user query UQ_3, corresponding to the first user's second keyword query, KQ_3.

CQ_5	*q(gene, typ, dis)*:-**T**(*gid*, 'plasma membrane', *score*), *G2G*(*gid, gild*), *GI*(*gild, gene, . . .*)
CQ_6	*q(gene, typ, dis)*:-**T**(*gid1*, 'plasma membrane'), **TS**(*gid1, gid2, conf*), *G2G*(*gid2, gild*), *GI*(*gild, gene, . . .*)

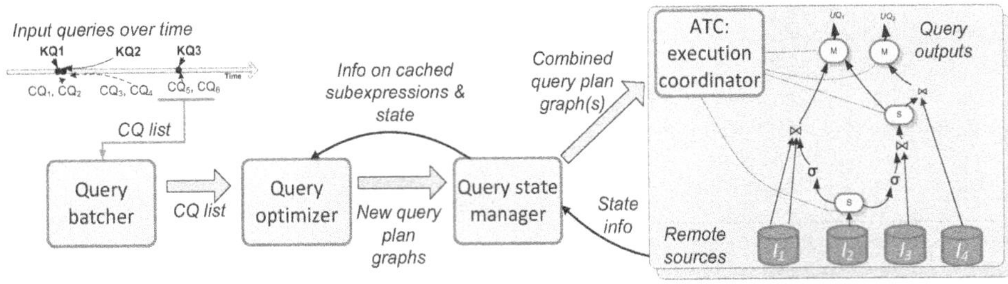

Figure 3: Query processing components of the Q System. Sets of CQs from the query generator are batched, optimized to exploit state from prior executions, and *grafted* into running query plan graphs for execution by the ATC.

EXAMPLE 3. *Suppose the first user, upon getting the results for* KQ_1*, decides to* revise *or refine his or her query, in this case to see what other genes are related to the plasma membrane. This results in a new keyword query* KQ_3*, "membrane gene". The resulting user query* UQ_3 *includes conjunctive queries* CQ_5 *and* CQ_6 *in Table 3. Observe that both of these queries are subexpressions of the original* CQ_1*, omitting the protein-related relations.* □

Perhaps our system has completed execution of the query UQ_1 from the first example; but if we retain its state (and portions of its query plan) in memory, we might be able to *reuse* portions of the state and plan to answer UQ_3. Our **second set of contributions** focus on retaining a query plan graph and reusing it from one query execution step to the next, with appropriate "grafting" of new operators into the existing plan, and "pruning" of operators and state as necessary to fit within a memory budget.

3. APPROACH AND ARCHITECTURE

Our presentation focuses on the modules *after* keyword terms have been converted to ranked lists of candidate conjunctive queries (candidate networks): we assume a set of conjunctive queries for each search, generated using any of the methods cited in Section 2.1[2].

Formally, each *keyword query* KQ_j is converted to the union of a set of conjunctive queries: we refer to this set as UQ_j. Each conjunctive query CQ_i within UQ_j is paired with a monotonic *score function* C_i, which maps result tuples to real-valued scores, following any of the cost models of Section 2.1. We assume the existence of a function $\mathbf{U}(C_i)$ that allows us to compute the upper bound on the score of any tuple returned by CQ_i. Finally, we assume the conjunctive queries return results in nonincreasing order relative to **U**. We assume the source relations referenced in the queries are typically SQL DBMSs, able to return results in nonincreasing score order; we refer to such sources as *streaming sources*. In addition to streaming sources, we expect other Web-based sources that can be *probed* with specific tuple values to return join results [10, 25]. We refer to these as *random access sources*. We now describe how our implementation, within the Q System, processes these queries.

Refer to Figure 3 for a diagram of the query processing architecture of the Q System, which functions as a middleware layer over remote data sources. Users pose keyword queries KQ_j that get converted into conjunctive queries and associated scoring functions: these are passed along to the **query batcher** as lists of triples $[(UQ_j, CQ_i, C_i)|CQ_i \in UQ_j]$, in nonincreasing order of the maximum score they return, i.e., their bound $\mathbf{U}(CQ_i)$. The batcher typically waits for these conjunctive queries to collect over a small time interval before it passes them along to the next stage. Following our example, the list of triples after keyword queries KQ_1 and KQ_2 would be $[(UQ_1, CQ_1, C_1), (UQ_1, CQ_2, C_2), (UQ_2, CQ_3, C_3), (UQ_2, CQ_4, C_4)]$.

The **query optimizer** takes a set of conjunctive queries from the batcher, and performs several forms of multiple query optimization over them. It first checks with the **query state manager** to determine if previous queries have been executed and their runtime state has been preserved: if this is the case, it determines what query expressions can be reused from in-memory buffers. Then it finds an efficient plans for computing the complete set of batched queries (which may involve reusing *or* recomputing existing expressions, sharing computation across multiple conjunctive queries in the batch, or pushing down portions of the query to the remote data sources). For example, the optimizer may note the high similarity in the new conjunctive queries of UQ_3 to those of UQ_1 and UQ_2, and it may reuse tuples that have already been read in for some of the common relations. The result of this optimization is one or more *query plan graphs*, which form the core of our query processor. We discuss query plan graphs and operators in the next section. Briefly, each plan graph may share subexpressions across queries by pipelining results through a *split* operator; each conjunctive query joins multiple relations using an *m-join* operator; conjunctive queries' results are merged into the top-k answers to a user query via a *rank-merge* operator. Execution of these operators is coordinated by a module called the **ATC**, named after an air traffic controller, as it routes tuples to different destination operators.

The **query state (QS) manager** is responsible for managing the set of query plan graphs that occupy the CPU and memory. Given a new set of query plan graphs, its first task is to *merge* them with any plan graphs that currently exist in memory. For each user query, it *incrementally* takes the highest-scoring conjunctive queries (which come in nonincreasing order of maximum-scoring contribution to the results) and identifies which subexpressions overlap with existing plans; it then *grafts* the new subgraphs into place (using *split* operators) and notifies the execution system. As execution progresses and the maximum score of the next result drops, further conjunctive queries can be activated. Additionally, after producing some answers, certain queries may no longer be able to contribute to top-k results: the QS manager deactivates (*prunes*) these for efficiency. Even if a query subexpression gets pruned from execution, its state is retained for possible reuse, until the system runs out of cache space and needs to evict it. Finally, the QS manager maintains cardinality information about intermediate results in the query plan graph, such that the query optimizer can determine what can be reused in subsequent executions.

[2]BANKS and BLINKS enumerate tuples instead of queries, but one could abstract their data graph into a schema graph.

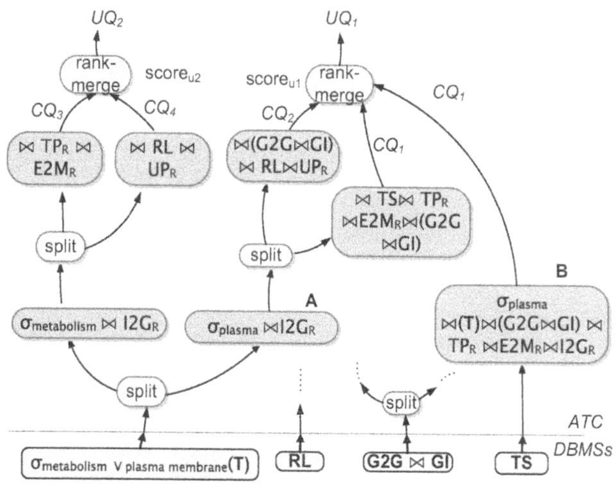

Figure 4: Partial query plan graph demonstrating *split*, *rank-merge* and *m-join* operators.

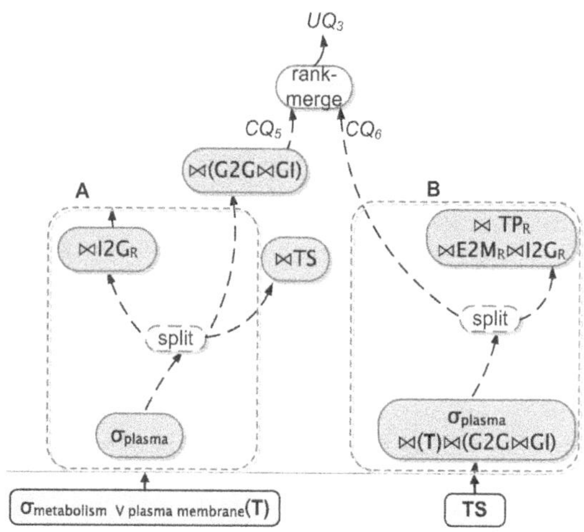

Figure 5: Grafting new segments within the marked modules from Figure 4 by using new split operators.

We now describe our simultaneous query execution process in more detail, deferring a discussion of optimizing query batches to Section 5 and of reusing results to Section 6.

4. QUERY PLAN GRAPH

Unlike in a traditional iterator-based query processor, our goal here is to fully pipeline and multiplex the execution of *multiple queries simultaneously*. In addition, we seek to preserve an important aspect of top-k query processing work [5, 7, 9, 15, 23, 28]: the streaming sources (each with data sorted in nonincreasing order of score) are read in a context-sensitive way according to their score upper bounds, and query processing ends once the k top-scoring answers are known. Both these aspects warrant an *adaptive* set of techniques that focus on reading the most promising tuples and executing all queries that use these tuples. To accomplish this, we use a novel coordinator called the **ATC**, which manages and routes tuples to different destination operators, using a *query plan graph* as a base instructor. In this section, we define the query plan graph and how it operates in more detail, starting with the operators and then discussing the ATC.

4.1 Query operators

The query plan graph represents operators as nodes and dataflows

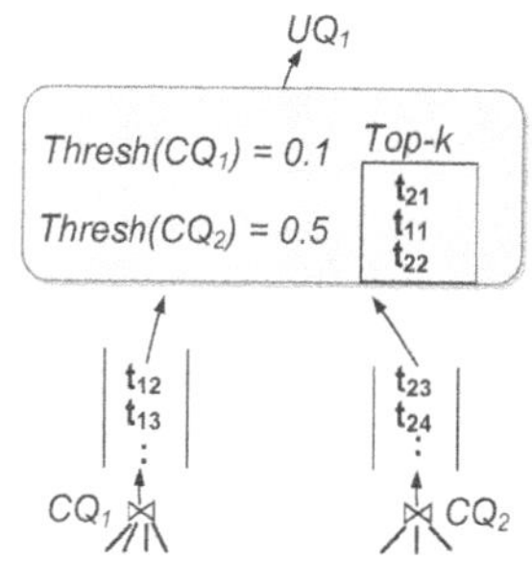

Figure 6: Query output streams and a rank merge operator.

as edges. As discussed previously, the main node types include the *split* operator, the *multi-way join* operator (m-join), and the *rank-merge* operator. Refer to Figure 4, which shows a detailed excerpt of a query plan graph for our running example.

Split operator (for subexpression sharing). Our example scenario shows how different conjunctive queries may have overlapping subexpressions whose computation might be performed once, then fed into multiple query plans. Figure 4 shows how the pipelined *split* operator is used to feed the output of a shared expression to multiple downstream m-joins or rank-merge operators.

M-way joins (for query computation). In producing ranked results, the choice of which input to read next is dependent on the relative scores of the inputs. A traditional binary join plan enforces a particular order of processing: $(R \bowtie S) \bowtie T$ will always produce RS subresults that get joined with T. A much more flexible scheme, which in different contexts is called the *m-join* [34] or the *STeM eddy* [24], is to generalize the pipelined hash join to support m-way joins. Here, each input has an associated *access module* [6][3] — against which other tuples may be probed to compute join results. As tuples are read from a streaming input, they are inserted into the access module, then probed against the other access modules according to a *probe sequence*. We also exploit the fact that this probe sequence can be adjusted at runtime based on monitored values for the various join selectivities, using techniques proposed in [24] — in particular, we monitor the number of tuples output from each probe into the hash table or access module, and update selectivities after a certain number of tuples have been read. This results in an adaptive form of optimization within the multi-way join that can use a *different* ordering for each input relation.

Rank-merge operator (for top-k). The results of a single user query must *merge* the outputs of multiple conjunctive queries, i.e., the outputs of multiple m-joins. The Q System generates query plans in a way that ensures the streaming sources are returned in nonincreasing order of score, and that the m-joins produce their results in nonincreasing order of score. We define an m-way *rank-merge* operator (Figure 6) that receives tuples from each query CQ_i, and uses each score function C_i to computes the threshold for the next value to be returned by CQ_i. It maintains a priority queue of the k highest scoring tuples seen from all conjunctive queries; from this, it outputs the highest-scoring tuple above all thresholds, and reads a tuple from the output stream that will drop the score threshold the most (generally, the stream with the highest threshold). This basic operation follows the the ideas of the Threshold Algorithm and No-random-access Algorithm of [7].

To illustrate the ideas above, we define $\mathcal{Q}$ as the current set of conjunctive queries given to the query batcher. We define an *input*

[3]For a streaming source, the access module is simply the associated hash table; for a random access source, the module is a wrapper for probing the remote site using the join key.

assignment as a pair ($\mathcal{I}$,**I**), where $\mathcal{I}$ is a set consisting of the logical subexpressions that will be computed outside the middleware (by the streaming and random access sources). The results of each input in $\mathcal{I}$ will be fed into (possibly multiple) queries in $\mathcal{Q}$. We use a map **I**: $\mathcal{I} \rightarrow$ P($\mathcal{Q}$), where P($\mathcal{Q}$) are all subsets of $\mathcal{Q}$, to relate the inputs to the corresponding queries: for any input J in $\mathcal{I}$, **I**[J] refers to the queries that will use J in their query plans.

EXAMPLE 4. *Refer to the query plan graph of Figure 4. The input assignment* $\mathcal{I} = \{\sigma(T), RL, G2G \bowtie GI, TS, TP_R, E2M_R, UP_R, I2G_R\}$ *with the subscripts by R denoting random access sources. The corresponding queries for input* $\sigma(T)$ *is* $\mathbf{I}[\sigma(T)] = \{CQ_1, CQ_2, CQ_3, CQ_4\}$. *Once a tuple from the stream of* $\sigma(T)$ *is read, it is split into two different paths that lead to two different m-join operators, and ultimately along paths that lead to join results for all "its" queries. There are probes into the hash tables created for* RL, $G2G \bowtie GI$ *and* TS, *as well as the random access sources of* TP_R, $E2M_R$, UP_R *and* $I2G_R$. *Likewise, a tuple read from the streaming source* TS *is sent to the m-join operator that will create results for* CQ_1.

4.2 Coordinating Simultaneous Execution

Each rank-merge operator requests result tuples from its constituent conjunctive queries, which in turn indirectly request tuples from input streaming sources in $\mathcal{I}$. Given that different user queries have different score functions for their queries, their associated rank-merge operators may prioritize different input expressions. Yet the input expressions are often shared across queries, leading to contention.

To solve these issues, we exploit the fact that the m-join operator is in some sense *push-based*: given the arrival of a new tuple from any of its streaming sources, it stores and probes this tuple according to an optimized probe sequence. We can "holistically" choose an input to read, and ensure that its tuples are propagated through split operators to *all* conjunctive queries' m-join operators, which will pipeline the results downstream. The choice of *which* source should be read next — across all conjunctive queries — is dependent on the state of the thresholds in each rank-merge operator. The **ATC module** has the task of "looking across" the set of rank-merge operators' thresholds, and using this information to choose the next source to fetch from. We explored a variety of scheduling schemes, and found that a round-robin scheme worked best. Here we look at each rank-merge operator in every round, and we read from its preferred stream before moving on to the next query. This scheme has the same outcome as a voting strategy where the input stream with the highest number of tuple requests gets read the most. It also prevents starvation of sources, which might otherwise be neglected if only a few operators requested tuples from them.

5. QUERY PLAN GENERATION

We now consider how to choose the most efficient query plan graph for answering an *initial* batch of conjunctive queries $\mathcal{Q}$, forming one or more user queries. Section 6 discusses how we implement the dynamic behavior of the Q System over time.

The initial query optimization problem can be considered one of top-k multiple query optimization. Recall from our previous discussion that data originates from either a streaming or random access source. Our goal is to generate a query plan graph for the entire set of queries in $\mathcal{Q}$, which takes advantage of the query processing capabilities of the underlying remote data sources (if they support SQL), accommodates any restrictions on data access (via Web forms), and exploits overlap among the conjunctive queries.

Our system adopts a two-stage approach to generate a query plan graph. In the first stage, it does a cost-based exploration of possible strategies for *pushing query operations into the streaming data sources*: push-down can reduce the overall amount of computation to be performed *and* create common subexpressions used by multiple conjunctive queries. In the second stage, for the remainder of the query, the optimizer performs a heuristics-based *factorization* of the query plan graph into select-project-join subexpressions that are shared by multiple conjunctive queries, and generates a query plan graph with split, m-way join, and rank-merge operators. The next two sections describe each of these stages in turn.

5.1 Pushing Down Common Subexpressions

The optimizer's first task is to factor out from the set of queries an input assignment $\mathcal{I}$, to be executed at the remote DBMS sites. The results of each $J \in \mathcal{I}$ will be shared among multiple conjunctive queries, namely those queries in the set **I**[J].

Our goal is to find subexpressions large enough to source more than one conjunctive query, yet avoid forcing the optimizer to create a bad plan that requires streaming in too many tuples or executing expensive joins. This requires a form of multi-query optimization that is known to be intractable if done in exhaustive fashion: optimization of a single query already results in a number of plans exponential in the number of joins, and a full-blown dynamic programming enumeration of plans with shared subexpressions would compound this by the number of different ways of sharing subexpressions. Hence our optimizer, like other modern multi-query optimizers [35], employs a set of pruning heuristics in looking for opportunities to combine and push down subexpressions.

5.1.1 Pruning Heuristics

Consider queries as shared subexpressions. We estimate the overall cardinality for each query that can be pushed-down. If a query produces few results, we do not consider its subexpressions — unless those subexpressions are shared by a different (larger) set of conjunctive queries.

Only stream relations that have scoring attributes. Not all relations may have attributes contributing to the scoring function. For any relation R with no score-related attributes, if R is read as a stream, then generally it must be read entirely before a terminating condition can be reached (each tuple in R contributes equally to the score, so there is no change in the query threshold). Hence, we treat R as a source to be probed against, rather than to be streamed, *unless* its estimated cardinality is less than a threshold $\tau(R)$ [4].

Filter subexpressions by estimated utility. We consider subexpressions we deem to be "useful": those that are shared by a minimum number of conjunctive queries, or that have low cardinality. Conversely, if we know that certain subexpressions are expensive to compute at the source (for example, non key-key or key-foreign key joins), then these are pruned away. We always designate base relations from streaming sources as useful.

Do not consider overlapping pushed-down subexpressions. If a subexpression has not been pruned according to one of the heuristics above, then we consider it as a candidate only if for every query CQ, it is a subexpression of CQ, or it does not overlap with CQ. Intuitively, we would like to avoid overlapping subexpressions pushed down to the base sources, as this requires streaming in a base relation more than once.

We expect the set of subexpressions predicted to be useful to change over time, as better statistics are learned about base data

[4] $\tau(R)$ is set offline according to the relative cost of probing the source vs. streaming its tuples.

Algorithm 1 BestPlan($\mathcal{Q}$, ($\mathcal{S}$, **S**), ($\mathcal{A}$, **A**)):
Input $\rightarrow$ Query set $\mathcal{Q}$, Candidates ($\mathcal{S}$, **S**), partial inputs ($\mathcal{A}$, **A**)
Output $\rightarrow$ A plan P with the input assignment ($\mathcal{I}$, **I**), $\mathcal{A} \subseteq \mathcal{I}$

1: **if** $\exists$ cached plan P' for inputs $\mathcal{A}$ **then**
2:    return P
3: **end if**
4: **if** $|\mathcal{S}| = 0$ **then**
5:    ($\mathcal{I}$, **I**)$\leftarrow$ ($\mathcal{A}$, **A**)
6:    construct a plan P with inputs ($\mathcal{I}$, **I**)
7:    $C \leftarrow$ calculate cost of P
8:    return (P, C)
9: **end if**
10: $(bestCost, bestPlan)$ $\leftarrow$dummy plan with cost ∞
11: **for** each input J in $\mathcal{S}$ **do**
12:    ($\mathcal{S}'$, **S'**)$\leftarrow$ $(\emptyset, \emptyset)$
13:    **for** each input $J' \neq J$ in $\mathcal{S}$ **do**
14:       **if** J and J' share a common relation **and** **S**[J'] - **S**[J] is not empty **then**
15:          add J' to $\mathcal{S}'$ with **S'**[J'] = **S**[J'] - **S**[J]
16:       **end if**
17:    **end for**
18:    ($\mathcal{A}'$, **A'**)$\leftarrow$ ($\mathcal{A} \cup \{J\}$, **A**) ; **A'**[J] $\leftarrow$ **S**[J]
19:    $(P, C) \leftarrow BestPlan(\mathcal{Q}$, ($\mathcal{S}'$, **S'**), ($\mathcal{A}'$, **A'**))
20:    **if** $C < bestCost$ **then**
21:       $(bestPlan, bestCost)$ $\leftarrow$$(P, C)$
22:    **end if**
23: **end for**
24: cache $bestPlan$ for $\mathcal{A}$
25: **return** $bestPlan$

sources during dynamic operation (as described in the next section). The search process that we describe below is flexible enough to accept any combination of subexpressions and queries, and is guaranteed to find a *valid* combination of subexpressions (see below), so long as we include all base relations from streaming sources as useful subexpressions.

DEFINITION 1. *We consider the input assignment* ($\mathcal{I}$, **I**) *to be valid if for each query* $CQ_i \in \mathcal{Q}$ *and each relation* R *in* CQ_i, *there exists exactly one input* $J \in \mathcal{I}$, *such that* J *is a subexpression of* CQ_i, *involving* R, *and* $CQ_i \in$ **I**[J].

5.1.2 Cost-Based Enumeration

We next enumerate the set of possible subexpressions satisfying the pruning heuristics. For efficiency, we employ a memoization structure called an AND-OR graph, commonly used in multi-query optimization [26]. The AND-OR representation of subexpressions is a directed acyclic graph that consists of alternating levels of two types of nodes: "OR" nodes that encode equivalent subexpressions, and "AND" nodes that encode selection and join operations.

The optimizer enumerates an AND-OR graph representing all subexpressions of all queries in $\mathcal{Q}$, except those pruned according to our heuristics above. We convert this set of subexpressions into a *candidate input assignment* ($\mathcal{S}$, **S**), where each candidate in $\mathcal{S}$ is an input expression to consider evaluating outside the ATC.

Given these candidates, our goal is now to find the input assignment ($\mathcal{I}$, **I**) such that $\mathcal{I} \subseteq \mathcal{S}$ for which the cost of computing all the queries in $\mathcal{Q}$ is minimum. Algorithm 1 shows our search procedure, which uses memoization and top-down search similar to the Volcano model [8]. Our input to the algorithm is a query set $\mathcal{Q}$, the candidates ($\mathcal{S}$, **S**) and and the input assignment ($\mathcal{A}$, **A**) that constitutes a partial plan. $\mathcal{A}$ is initially the empty set, and candidates from $\mathcal{S}$ are continually moved to $\mathcal{A}$ so that a valid input assignment can be found. At the end of each recursive step, $BestPlan$ returns a query plan P with inputs ($\mathcal{I}$, **I**) such that $\mathcal{A} \subseteq \mathcal{I}$ (i.e., P is the best plan that uses all inputs/subexpressions of $\mathcal{A}$).

After initially calling $BestPlan(\mathcal{Q}$, ($\mathcal{S}$, **S**), $(\emptyset, \emptyset)$), we iterate over each candidate (lines 10-22) in $\mathcal{S}$ and find the best plan that uses that candidate along with others in $\mathcal{A}$. At each point $BestPlan$ chooses to use an expression J, it creates a modified candidate assignment ($\mathcal{S}'$,**S'**) in order to ensure queries using J will not also use overlapping expressions. Note that moving candidates from $\mathcal{S}$ to $\mathcal{A}$ ensures $\mathcal{S}$ decreases in size each time a recursive call is made. This, along with our step for adjusting the remaining candidates in $\mathcal{S}$ ensures that we will generate a valid plan.

PROPOSITION 1. *The plan* P *with input assignment* ($\mathcal{I}$, **I**) *returned by BestPlan is a valid plan for the query set* $\mathcal{Q}$ *and the set of streaming data sources. (Proof appears in the technical report [17].)*

EXAMPLE 5. *Consider our running example again when* KQ_1 *and* KQ_2 *are posed. The query set is* $\mathcal{Q} = \{CQ_1, CQ_2, CQ_3, CQ_4\}$. *In order to build the candidate input assignment* ($\mathcal{S}$, **S**), *the optimizer decides that a set of useful subexpressions* [5] *may be* $G2G \bowtie GI$, $G2G \bowtie GI \bowtie T$ *and* $TP \bowtie E2M$, *with* **S**$[G2G \bowtie GI] = \{CQ_1, CQ_2\}$, **S**$[G2G \bowtie GI \bowtie T] = \{CQ_2\}$, *and* **S**$[TP \bowtie E2M] = \{CQ_1\}$. *After calling BestPlan(*$\mathcal{Q}$*, (*$\mathcal{S}$*,* **S**), $(\emptyset, \emptyset)$*), the optimizer finds the best plan using each of these subexpressions. In order to find the best plan using* $G2G \bowtie GI \bowtie T$, *it will call BestPlan(*$\mathcal{Q}$*, (*$\mathcal{S}'$*,* **S'**), ($\mathcal{A}'$, **A'**)), *where* $\mathcal{A}' = \{G2G \bowtie GI \bowtie T\}$ *and* **A'**$[G2G \bowtie GI \bowtie T] = \{CQ_2\}$; $\mathcal{S}' = \{G2G \bowtie GI, TP \bowtie E2M\}$ *and* **S'**$[G2G \bowtie GI] = \{CQ_1\}$.

5.2 Factorization of Query Plan Graph

Once the set of expressions to be pushed to the sources, $\mathcal{I}$, is determined by $BestPlan$, we are faced with the challenge of determining join and selection orderings within the middleware portion of the query plan graph P. Our approach is to first *factor* the query plan graph into different connected components with different amounts of sharing, and then to defer decisions about join ordering *within* each component to runtime, by computing all joins within that component using a single m-join that uses monitored selectivities to choose a sequence for probing. Our ultimate plan graph will look like the one of Figure 4, where each *split* or *rank-merge* represents the boundary between connected components.

To construct this query plan graph, we build up query expressions in iterative fashion. Start with a *frontier set* consisting of the streaming inputs in $\mathcal{I}$. For each E in this set, suppose E is a common subexpression for the set of conjunctive queries **I**$[E]$.

- If possible, find the most selective join or selection operation o common to all queries in **I**$[E]$, which can be applied to E. Replace E in the frontier set with $o(E)$ and iterate.
- Otherwise, insert a *split* operator over E, then choose a set of operators into which it feeds, using the following iterative process. Let $Rm =$ **I**$[E]$ and remove E from the frontier set. Choose the join or selection operation o_x such that $o_x(E)$ is common to the maximal number of queries in Rm (breaking ties by picking the most selective such operator). Add $o_x(E)$ to the frontier set. Now eliminate from Rm those queries that include $o_x(E)$, and repeat, until Rm is empty.

We repeat until the frontier set contains all expressions in $\mathcal{Q}$: we now have a complete query plan graph. Note that the problem presented here is another form of multi-query optimization — finding the best ordering of joins and selections in order to compute all queries, which is NP-hard in the number of joins involved. Instead, the greedy heuristic above is targeted at creating as few factored components as possible. This way, we defer as many decisions about operation ordering to the eddy modules. Changing orderings *between* factored components is an interesting challenge that for future work.

[5]We omit base relations for simplicity.

6. INCREMENTAL ATC MODIFICATION

We now discuss the *dynamic* aspects of our implementation — specifically, how state is maintained for reuse and removed to assist with newly arriving queries. When a batch of queries is first posed, these queries must be optimized given an existing query plan graph and its state; we discuss this in Section 6.1. To execute the resulting query, we must modify an existing query plan graph, and then notify the ATC about the new operators, as discussed in Section 6.2. Finally, under resource constraints we may need to discard some state from memory (Section 6.3).

6.1 Optimizing New Queries

As new queries arrive over time, they are likely to overlap with queries previously executed by the ATC. The optimizer must be able to determine whether it should reuse in-memory state (e.g., the hash tables within join operators) of prior query execution runs.

Updated cost estimates. The optimizer must be modified to properly estimate the costs of reusing existing tuples. After it receives a new batch of queries, the optimizer builds the new candidate assignment ($\mathcal{S}$, $\mathbf{S}$) as in Section 5. For each subexpression $J \in \mathcal{S}$, if J represents a streaming source, it queries the QS manager about whether J is in memory (i.e., whether it has been used for a previous set of queries) and if so, the number of results that have been streamed in. Since the costing of plans is based on the number of tuples to be read from the source, the optimizer then adjusts the estimate of using J in a plan to account for any source tuples already read in. It next prevents J from being evicted, by requesting that the QS Manager "pin" J down. Finally, it runs the $BestPlan$ algorithm with the updated cost estimates.

Preventing over-sharing of results. One trade-off that may arise is due to the limited amount of concurrency in the ATC: in very large query plan graphs, any given query UQ_j may only depend on a small percentage of the overall graph. This can result in a phenomenon like thrashing in a multithreaded system: much of the ATC's resource budget gets spent on computing subresults for queries *other* than UQ_j. To improve concurrency, we can generate *multiple* query plan graphs, each with their own ATC. We accomplish this by *clustering* user queries in a simple hierarchical fashion. Given the initial set of conjunctive queries, we identify the most frequently occurring source relations in the workload. We build an initial cluster for each source by adding the set of user queries that reference the source, more than T_m times (where T_m is a configurable threshold). Then we repeatedly merge clusters whose Jaccard similarity (i.e., ratio of overlap) exceeds a second threshold T_c, until it is no longer possible to merge. The resulting set of clusters defines the sets of user queries to separately group, optimize, and execute.

6.2 Grafting New Query Plan Graphs

The optimizer passes a new query plan graph to the QS manager, to *graft* it onto the existing query plan graph. This is done by individually merging each path in the new query plan graph, as sketched below. For each node n in a path, iterating from source (leaf) to rank-merge operator, assign a *mapping* $m(n)$ from n to a query operator as follows.

1. If a query operator in the existing query plan matches n, let $m(n)$ be that operator.
2. If n's parent operator n' matches $m(n)$'s parent operator, then repeat the above step for n'.
3. Stop at any node n whose parent node n_p has no match in the existing query plan graph, then (if necessary) inject a split operator between $m(n)$ and its parent in the existing graph. Create a new operator for n_p, let $m(n_p)$ be this operator, and connect one of the outputs of the split operator to $m(n_p)$.

For any unmatched node n in the new graph, create a new operator for $m(n)$.

In order to prevent race conditions, we create the new query plan graph segments first, then suspend execution of the original graph and lock it from concurrent modification. Next we ensure that for each n in the new graph and its parent n_p, ensure that $m(n)$ feeds data to $m(n_p)$. Finally, the new conjunctive queries are registered with downstream rank-merge operators and the main ATC, so that thresholds are maintained. Whenever a new query reuses an old stream, the threshold is initialized to the current score upper bound of that stream. Execution may now resume.

EXAMPLE 6. *Consider again, our running example, when KQ_3 is posed (some time after KQ_1 and KQ_2). The optimizer decides that a plan for these queries is $\mathcal{I} = \{G2G \bowtie GI, TS, T\}$, with $\mathbf{I}[G2G \bowtie GI] = \{CQ_5, CQ_6\}$, $\mathbf{I}[TS] = \{CQ_6\}$, $\mathbf{I}[T] = \{CQ_5, CQ_6\}$. As the first step, a new rank merge operator is created for UQ_3. Then, the new plan graph created for CQ_5 and CQ_6 is merged with the original graph in Figure 4. We show a part of the merging process for the inputs T and TS in Figure 5. Observe two new split operators are added in order to route intermediate tuples of $\sigma(T)$ and $\sigma(T) \bowtie (G2G \bowtie GI)$ to new destination operators.*

Reusing state. A major complexity is that a new conjunctive query CQ_i may make use of data from input streams that have already been read. In such an event, simply reading further from the streams is insufficient; we must first re-process the earlier parts of the streams, which are buffered within the query plan graph's state.

A naive approach is simply to find the various streams' tuples buffered in the hash tables of existing m-joins, and to simply iterate over these tuples and join them. Not only would this require us to suspend normal query processing until the new join was complete — but in fact such an approach is score-unaware and would emit tuples in a way that do not conform to the downstream rank-merge operator's requirement that each conjunctive query's tuples be generated in nonincreasing score order.

The problem is that we need to re-process the tuples according to their original order; we accomplish this with a more sophisticated approach. We modify the hash tables to also embed a *linked list*: each time we add a tuple to the hash table, we update the *last*-added tuple to include a *next* pointer to the newly added tuple. Given the initial pointer to the first tuple added, we can visit the set of tuples in the order they were received from the input stream. Every time the QS manager provides a new set of queries to the ATC, it increments a counter called the *epoch* (a logical timestamp). Then, for each CQ_i that references input streams that have already been read, we create an additional new query CQ_i^e, to compute all the missing tuples for CQ_i. This query takes as its inputs the contents of the appropriate linked lists as recorded *before* epoch e, in order to avoid the introduction of duplicate results. Internally, we keep track of the association between tuples and epochs by storing each epoch's tuples in a separate *partition* within the m-join hash tables. Note that once CQ_i^e's plan is created, it is just another conjunctive query, and the linked lists from the hash tables are treated as another input in $\mathcal{I}$. The new query is registered with the rank-merge operator which takes into account the upper bounds for the linked lists just as another ranked input, in order to maintain correct thresholds.

Algorithm 2 shows the steps to recover missing tuples: RecoverState is called when the QS Manager discovers that the streaming sources for CQ_i have been read before its arrival. Lines 2-5 show steps to partition the hash table for each streaming input J that be-

Algorithm 2 RecoverState(CQ_i, ($\mathcal{I}$,**I**)):
Input $\rightarrow$ Conjunctive query CQ_i, Current assignment ($\mathcal{I}$, **I**)

1: e $\leftarrow$ current epoch
2: **for** each input $J \in \mathcal{I}$ s.t. J is a stream and $CQ_i \in \mathbf{I}[J]$ **do**
3:    create a new hash table H_J^e where new tuples will be indexed
4: **end for**
5: $CQ_i^e \leftarrow CQ_i, C_i^e \leftarrow C_i$
6: Choose a streaming input J s.t. $CQ_i \in \mathbf{I}[J]$
7: Let J_e be a streaming source which is the linked list of tuples from hash tables H_J^l where $l < e$
8: add J_e as a streaming source to $\mathcal{I}$ with $\mathbf{I}[J_e] = \{CQ_i^e\}$
9: **for** each $J' \in \mathcal{I}$ s.t. $J' \neq J$ and $CQ_i \in \mathbf{I}[J']$ **do**
10:    **if** J' is a streaming input **then**
11:       add J'_e as a random access source to $\mathcal{I}$ with $\mathbf{I}[J'_e] = \{CQ_i^e\}$
12:    **else**
13:       $\mathbf{I}[J'] = \mathbf{I}[J'] \cup \{CQ_i^e\}$
14:    **end if**
15: **end for**
16: Add the new query CQ_i^e with updated assignment ($\mathcal{I}$,**I**)

longs to $\mathbf{I}[J]$. Note that the tuples that arrived before epoch e are exactly those tuples that need to be joined for recovering the missing tuples of CQ_i — these results are represented by the query CQ_i^e which is created in line 5. Now, since CQ_i^e requires a set of inputs, we reuse exactly the set of inputs for CQ_i, but we choose one streaming input J that will be the streaming source for CQ_i^e, (lines 6-8). Every other input J' is treated as a random access source (since tuples from J'_e are already indexed in a hash table). Lines 9-15 add the new query and modify the input assignment to $\mathcal{I}$.

6.3 Query Termination and Discarding State

Once a conjunctive query has completed, or can longer contribute to top-k output (its threshold is lower than the kth tuple in the ranking queue of the downstream rank-merge operator), it gets unlinked from the query plan graph and deactivated. We simply traverse the graph *backwards* starting from the query node, removing nodes and edges until we reach a split operator. The split operator can only be removed if it does not route tuples along another path. If the split gets removed, we repeat the removal process recursively.

A natural question is when we remove the state for a query that is terminated. In a conventional OLAP query processing setting, one would expect that our basic approach — keep everything around in memory as a large cache for re-use — may be impractical due to large intermediate result sizes. In our setting, we expect memory and resource problems to be very infrequent on a modern machine, as ranking queries tend to read only (quite small) prefixes of relations, and most machines have multiple GB of RAM. Nonetheless, for completeness we develop strategies for cache replacement. Two types of objects are considered "cacheable": the contents of ranking queues that hold pending tuples to be output to the user, and hash tables corresponding to specific query subexpressions. Such items can be fully evicted if unreferenced by running or pending queries; or flushed to disk otherwise.

We experimented with a variety of potential cache replacement policies. The most obvious policy is least-recently-used (LRU), but we also considered factors such as result size and recomputation cost. We found that LRU, with size as a tie-breaker, worked quite well in practice. Since the results were not particularly informative, we omit them from the experiments section.

7. EXPERIMENTAL ANALYSIS

Our Q System implementation comprises approximately 50,000 lines of Java code and runs as a middleware layer over remote SQL databases. Evaluation was done using Java 6 JDK 1.60_04 on a dual-processor, dual-core Xeon 5140 machine with 8GB RAM and Windows Server 2003, using JDBC to connect to MySQL databases running on an identically configured machine. We briefly describe our experimental setup and methodology.

UQ	1	2	3	4	5	6	7	8
Queries	12.75	4.5	11	13.5	8.5	6	13.75	8.75

UQ	9	10	11	12	13	14	15
Queries	3.75	5.75	13.75	3.25	12.5	13	7.75

Table 4: Average number of conjunctive queries executed to return top-50 results over synthetic datasets

To create conjunctive queries from keyword searches, we used the Q System's query generator algorithm of [33]. We used both synthetic and real-world data sets.

Synthetic workload. Our synthetic dataset made use of the Genomics Unified Schema [21] (GUS), which has 358 relations. We created 4 simulated database instances by populating the relations in schema with 20,000-100,000 randomly generated tuples apiece. Each synonym/relationship table in the schemas was extended with an additional attribute representing a similarity score. Scores, join keys, and coefficients on the score functions for the various user queries were drawn from a Zipfian distribution. We stored these instances in MySQL, indexed by join keys and score attributes.

We generated a suite of 15 user queries by choosing pairs of keywords from a list of common biological terms, using a Zipf distribution on the keywords[6]. Each such query yielded a maximum of 20 conjunctive queries over GUS. For each relation matching a search term, we also added a synthetic score attribute, simulating an IR-style keyword similarity score.

Real-data workload. We also conducted tests over real data from the biological datasets Pfam (`http://pfam.sanger.ac.uk/`), a collection of protein families with multiple relationship tables to protein sequences, and Interpro (`http://www.ebi.ac.uk/interpro/`), another integrated database of protein families and sequence information. The former database contains a mapping table that relates Pfam families to Interpro entries. We created 15 keyword queries using the same methodology as in our synthetic case, using keywords that matched to sequence, family, and publication data.

Delays. To simulate wide-area delays over our local-area network, we added random delays for each tuple read from a data stream and each join probe performed against a remote DBMS. Delays were chosen from a Poisson distribution with an average of 2 milliseconds. Keyword search queries were posed within 6 seconds of one another. All graphs include averaged values taken over three different runs over each database instance (12 runs in total), and we include 95% confidence intervals.

Overview of experiments. Our experiments seek to answer the following questions: What are the performance implications of (1) shared subexpressions and (2) state reuse? (3) Given state reuse, is shared subexpression computation even necessary? (4) How does the time to perform multiple query optimization affect overall performance? (5) Do our results, done over synthetic data, generalize to real-world data?

7.1 Benefits of Sharing

We first study the impact of sharing and result reuse. Each user query in our query workload gets expanded into a set of conjunctive queries: refer to Table 4 to see how many conjunctive queries were

[6]Keyword queries can be found in `https://dbappserv.cis.upenn.edu/home/?q=node/132`

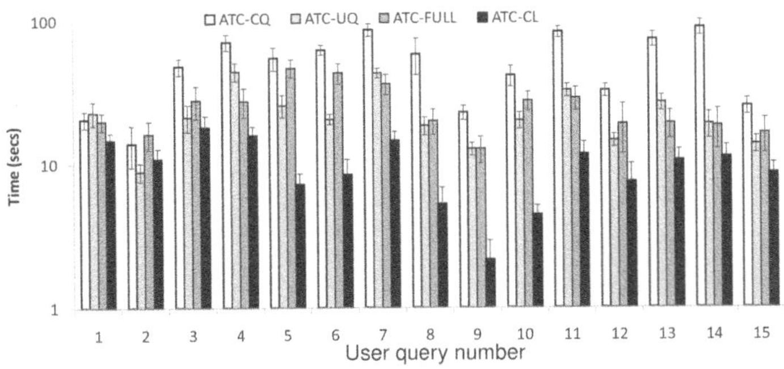

Figure 7: Running times to return the top-50 results for each user query.

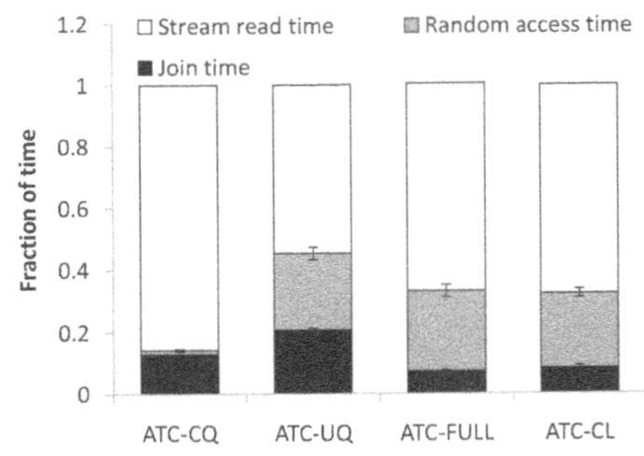

Figure 8: Breakdown of execution time.

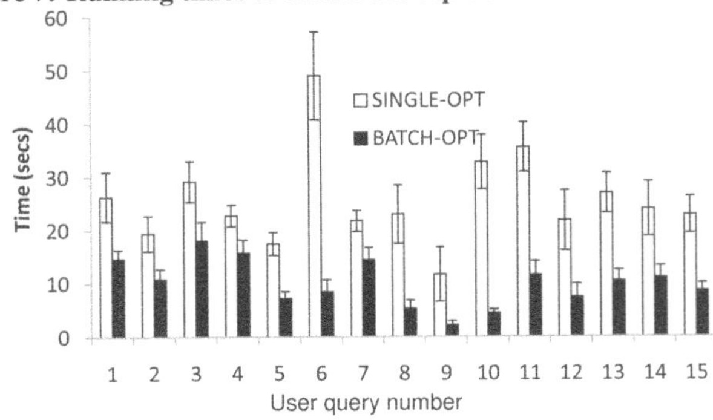

Figure 9: Running times: individually versus batch-optimized queries.

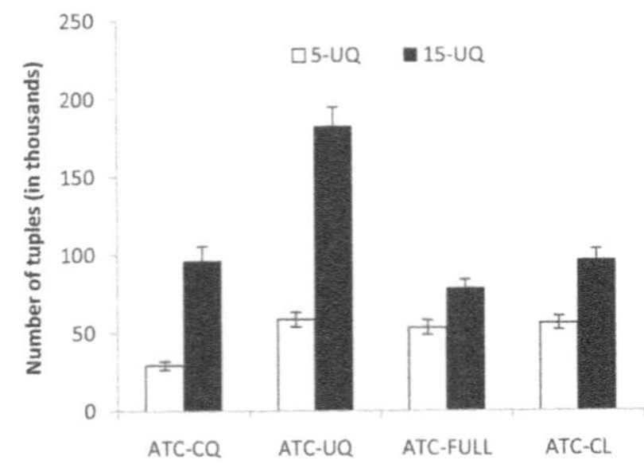

Figure 10: Total work done, 5 vs. 15 UQs

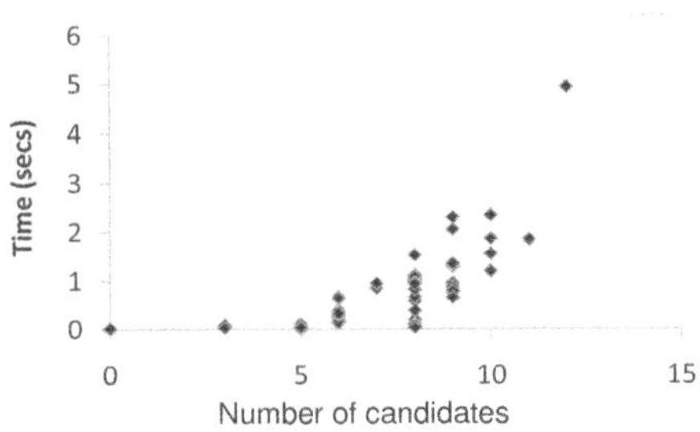

Figure 11: Optimization times vs. candidate inputs.

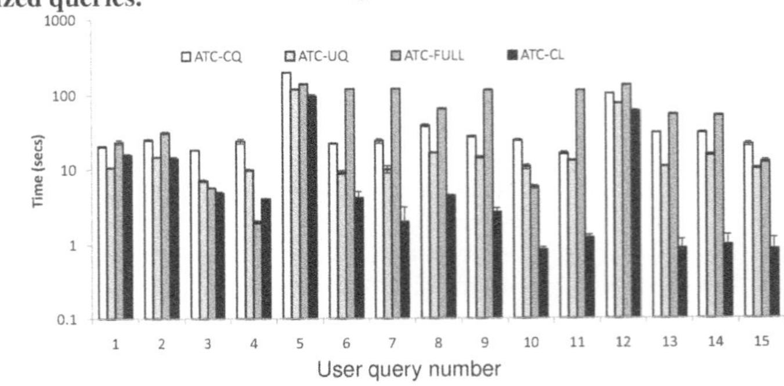

Figure 12: Execution times over the Pfam/Interpro dataset.

required to return the top-50 results for each user query, averaged across the four different synthetic data sets. Recall that the QS manager and ATC coordinate in order to ensure that additional CQs are executed only as necessary to return relevant results. In our experiments, we never needed more than 20 CQs per user query.

We studied several different optimization and QS manager configurations:

- As a baseline, we *separately* optimize each user query and *disable sharing* across conjunctive subexpressions; we refer to this method as **ATC-CQ** since the ATC executes conjunctive queries as separate m-joins whose results are merged.
- We enable subexpression sharing *within* a given user query, but disable it *across* queries. We refer to this as **ATC-UQ**.
- We use and update a *single* query plan graph to execute all user queries received at any point in time; this process automatically reuses existing state. This is strategy **ATC-FULL**.
- We manually clustered the user queries to create *multiple* query plan graphs when different sets of queries had significantly different inputs (see Section 6.1 for a way of doing this automatically). We call this **ATC-CL**.

In all configurations, the sequence of queries is user posed over time, with random delays of up to 6 seconds. Our query batcher is set to group queries into batches of size 5. Figure 7 shows the resulting execution times for each user query. We see that virtually across the board, sharing within a user query (**ATC-UQ**) provides benefits versus the baseline (**ATC-CQ**). When we look at sharing *across* user queries, we see that a different issue arises. **ATC-FULL** only performs better than **ATC-UQ** in 5 out of the 15 queries: here, several different rank-merge operators are requesting tuples from different subexpressions, seeking to optimize a different goal; the resulting contention means each query suffers a delay waiting for the others. We see that the clustering method, **ATC-CL**, handles this problem well by separating the contending queries and increasing parallelism.

Overall, we see that subexpression sharing and reuse both provide significant benefits — up to 90% for Query 9. We consider whether the two kinds of sharing can be used in isolation in later experiments, but first look in more detail at a breakdown of time versus query execution operations (Figure 8). Here we divide the total time into three operations: reading tuples from the streaming sources (*Stream read time*), performing in-memory joins (*Join time*), and probing remote sources with tuples to perform a two-way semijoin (*Random access time*). **ATC-UQ**, **ATC-FULL** and **ATC-CL** spend much less time reading tuples from the base streams than **ATC-CQ**, as they optimize by sharing and reusing tuples. On the other hand, they spend much more time probing against remote sources: we attribute this to the fact that probes are commonly used against relation sources that have no scoring attributes, and that the ATC may need to execute a fairly large number of probes in order to maintain the full set of results required to properly maintain the query threshold. Given that we cache tuples from random probes, we can expect the rate of probing to decrease over time.

7.2 Benefits of Subexpression Sharing

We next consider whether the process of identifying shared subexpressions — i.e., multiple query optimization — makes a useful contribution, given that in principle reuse of results from one run to the next might achieve similar behavior. To study this, we took the **ATC-CL** configuration and our query workload, and compared their running times when each query was optimized separately (batch size = 1) versus multiply (batch size = 5, as in the previous experiments). Figure 9 shows significant gains in performance for larger batch sizes, clearly indicating that it is advantageous to proactively identify opportunities for subexpression sharing.

7.3 State Reuse across Time

Assuming adequate memory and sufficient overlap among queries in the workload, we would expect that the *incremental* cost of answering newly posed queries should go down over time, if we can reuse subexpressions. Figure 10 shows that this is indeed the case for our query workload: it plots the total amount of work done (measured as the total number of input tuples consumed) in answering the first 5 queries of the workload, versus the full set of 15 queries. We see for the cases where tuples are not reused (**ATC-CQ** and **ATC-UQ**) that executing 15 queries takes approximately three times the amount of work as executing 5 queries. On the other hand, for **ATC-FULL** the complete suite requires only about 75% more work, and for **ATC-CL** about twice the amount of work. (Recall that **ATC-CL** shares less than **ATC-FULL**, which reduces contention and thus running time, but actually does slightly more work as measured by intermediate result production.)

7.4 Optimizer Running Times

While our previous timings included query optimization as a component, we now focus on the actual cost of performing multiple query optimization. In general multiple query optimization costs are determined by the number of unique query atoms (source relations), and in this case the main portion of the search is the number of candidate expressions considered for push-down into the source relations. We measured the amount of time spent optimizing the 15 user queries, batched in groups of 5. Figure 11 shows the results for a single run (other runs showed similar trends), where we plot the number of candidate subexpressions for a set of queries, against the time taken to generate a plan. Not surprisingly, the distribution follows an exponential curve as the number of candidates increase.

7.5 Generalization to Real Data

Finally, we investigated whether our conclusions transfer to queries over real rather than synthetic datasets. Given our combined Pfam-Interpro dataset, we used MySQL's text search capability to match pairs of two-keyword phrases against database tuples, capturing MySQL's similarity score as well as the tuples. Additionally, we included one additional score attribute, namely the age (year) of publication. Each user query here resulted in 4 conjunctive queries; we posed the user queries in sequence with random delays of up to 6 seconds. Figure 12 shows the execution times of all queries using our various configurations, for $k = 50$ results.

As with the synthetic data, **ATC-UQ** tends to provide a minor improvement over **ATC-CQ** (with a best case of 77% better for UQ_5). **ATC-FULL**, on the other hand, showed few gains — this was because the real dataset resulted in significantly larger amounts of data, hence more computation time and more contention delay in our middleware layer. The **ATC-CL** confugration clustered the user queries into three query plan graphs (queries 3 and 12 in one plan graph; query 5 in another; and the remaining queries in the final graph). This less-contentious arrangement provided significant improvement, especially in queries 7 through 15, with a maximum performance gain of 97% over **ATC-CQ** and 90% over **ATC-UQ**. All told, the results over real data are very consistent with those over synthetic data.

Our overall conclusion from the experiments is that our techniques for subexpression sharing, and for threshold-based selection of input tuples via the ATC, provide significant performance benefits. Our studies show that clustering user queries together can also alleviate the problem of contention occurring due to a high rate of incoming user queries. We plan to further investigate techniques for eliminating contention and I/O bottlenecks, including selective use of multithreading over portions of the same query plan graph.

8. RELATED WORK

This paper addresses a distributed, data integration-centric application of keyword search over databases [2, 11, 13, 18, 27, 33], with concurrent and ongoing sequences of user query requests. Our approach adopts a fairly general model and ranking scheme; it can be directly incorporated into any of the existing systems that generate queries before executing them [11, 13, 27]. Some other systems like [2, 11, 18] tend to interleave query generation with tuple retrieval and intermediate result creation, and there our techniques for performing multiple query optimization are somewhat more difficult to fit architecturally.

Our goal, through the ATC and query plan graph, is to support efficient top-k query answering [9, 23], but across multiple queries simultaneously (and allowing for reuse). The problem of developing efficient algorithms for executing these queries includes the Fagin et al. threshold and no-random-access algorithms [7] and work on (pairwise) rank joins [15, 28]. Our multiway join is essentially a STeM eddy [24], which uses adaptivity to determine an order of join evaluation. It also resembles the m-join [34], with the distinction that the control logic is separated into the ATC, rather than into the operator.

The problem of optimizing individual top-k queries was considered in [16, 29], and we leverage their cost estimation techniques. So far as we know, multiple query optimization has only been studied in the unranked context [26, 30, 35]. The related problem of view selection and materialization for ranked queries, as well as merging of ranked union queries, is studied in [14].

In many ways, our work resembles the continuous query execution model considered in NiagaraCQ [4] and other related systems, where the goal was to optimize an initial set of queries and produce a continuous query plan; then to leverage the existing plans for executing subsequent queries. Our context is quite different, in that the queries are not truly continuous, so certain query subexpressions truly become irrelevant and may be evicted; and the top-k setting changes the query execution mode.

9. CONCLUSIONS AND FUTURE WORK

This paper has addressed the issue of improving keyword search performance for data-integrating queries, through sharing and reusing subexpressions, as well as adaptive query processing techniques. Our contributions were:

- A new top-k query processing architecture that keeps in-memory state and existing query plan structures from one query execution to the next, enabling effective result reuse and recomputation over time.

- An optimizer that combines cost-based and heuristic search, in order to find common subexpressions across and within top-k queries, and which supports the reuse of existing subexpressions from past query executions.
- A fully pipelined, *adaptive* top-k query execution scheme for answering multiple queries, consisting of a query plan graph of m-joins (STeM eddies) and rank-merge operators, supervised by a novel ATC controller.
- A query state manager that can *graft* and *prune* elements in an executing query plan, and which manages the reuse and eviction of state.
- A comprehensive set of experiments over synthetic and real datasets, demonstrating the performance gains of our approach.

As future work, we plan to study opportunities to strategically exploit threads to limit contention among different queries; to extend our query processor to consider more complex queries that include aggregation; and to consider the problem of incremental maintenance of views defined over multiple queries.

Acknowledgments

This work was funded in part by NSF grants IIS-0447972, 0713267, and 1050448, and DARPA grant HRO1107-1-0029. We also thank the reviewers for their helpful feedback.

References

[1] S. Agrawal, S. Chaudhuri, and G. Das. DBXplorer: A system for keyword-based search over relational databases. In *ICDE*, 2002.

[2] G. Bhalotia, A. Hulgeri, C. Nakhe, S. Chakrabarti, and S. Sudarshan. Keyword searching and browsing in databases using BANKS. In *ICDE*, 2002.

[3] H. Cao, D. Jiang, J. Pei, Q. He, Z. Liao, E. Chen, and H. Li. Context-aware query suggestion by mining click-through and session data. In *KDD*, New York, NY, USA, 2008.

[4] J. Chen, D. DeWitt, F. Tian, and Y. Wang. NiagaraCQ: A scalable continuous query system for Internet databases. In *SIGMOD*, 2000.

[5] W. W. Cohen. Integration of heterogeneous databases without common domains using queries based on textual similarity. In *SIGMOD*, 1998.

[6] A. Deshpande, Z. Ives, and V. Raman. Adaptive query processing. *Foundations and Trends in Databases*, 2007.

[7] R. Fagin, A. Lotem, and M. Naor. Optimal aggregation algorithms for middleware. *Journal of Computer and System Sciences*, 66(4), June 2003.

[8] G. Graefe and W. J. McKenna. The Volcano optimizer generator: Extensibility and efficient search. In *ICDE*, 1993.

[9] L. Gravano, P. G. Ipeirotis, N. Koudas, and D. Srivastava. Text joins in an RDBMS for web data integration. In *WWW*, 2003.

[10] A. Y. Halevy. Answering queries using views: A survey. *VLDB J.*, 10(4), 2001.

[11] H. He, H. Wang, J. Yang, and P. S. Yu. Blinks: ranked keyword searches on graphs. In *SIGMOD*, 2007.

[12] V. Hristidis, L. Gravano, and Y. Papakonstantinou. Efficient IR-style keyword search over relational databases. In *VLDB*, 2003.

[13] V. Hristidis and Y. Papakonstantinou. Discover: Keyword search in relational databases. In *VLDB*, 2002.

[14] V. Hristidis and Y. Papakonstantinou. Algorithms and applications for answering ranked queries using ranked views. *The VLDB Journal*, 13(1), 2004.

[15] I. F. Ilyas, W. G. Aref, and A. K. Elmagarmid. Supporting top-k join queries in relational databases. In *VLDB*, 2003.

[16] I. F. Ilyas, W. G. Aref, A. K. Elmagarmid, H. G. Elmongui, R. Shah, and J. S. Vitter. Adaptive rank-aware query optimization in relational databases. *ACM Trans. Database Syst.*, 31(4), 2006.

[17] M. Jacob and Z. Ives. Sharing work in keyword search over databases. Available from `www.cis.upenn.edu/~majacob/papers/techATC.pdf`.

[18] V. Kacholia, S. Pandit, S. Chakrabarti, S. Sudarshan, R. Desai, and H. Karambelkar. Bidirectional expansion for keyword search on graph databases. In *VLDB*, 2005.

[19] G. Kasneci, F. M. Suchanek, G. Ifrim, M. Ramanath, and G. Weikum. Naga: Searching and ranking knowledge. In *ICDE*, 2008.

[20] H. Kautz, B. Selman, and M. Shah. Referral web: combining social networks and collaborative filtering. *Commun. ACM*, 40(3), 1997.

[21] J. C. Kissinger, B. P. Brunk, J. Crabtree, M. J. Fraunholz, B. Gajria, A. J. Milgram, D. S. Pearson, J. Schug, A. Bahl, S. J. Diskin, H. Ginsburg, G. R. Grant, D. Gupta, P. Labo, L. Li, M. D. Mailman, S. K. McWeeney, P. Whetzel, C. J. Stoeckert, Jr, and D. S. Roos. The Plasmodium genome database: Designing and mining a eukaryotic genomics resource. *Nature*, 419, 2002.

[22] C. Li, K. C.-C. Chang, I. F. Ilyas, and S. Song. RankSQL: Query algebra and optimization for relational top-k queries. In *SIGMOD*, 2005.

[23] A. Marian, N. Bruno, and L. Gravano. Evaluating top-k queries over web-accessible databases. *ACM Trans. Database Syst.*, 29(2), 2004.

[24] V. Raman, A. Deshpande, and J. M. Hellerstein. Using state modules for adaptive query processing. In *ICDE*, 2003.

[25] N. Roussopoulos and H. Kang. A pipeline [sic] n-way join algorithm based on the 2-way semijoin program. *IEEE Trans. on Knowl. and Data Eng.*, 3(4), 1991.

[26] P. Roy, S. Seshadri, S. Sudarshan, and S. Bhobe. Efficient and extensible algorithms for multi query optimization. In *SIGMOD*, volume 29(2), 2000.

[27] M. Sayyadian, H. LeKhac, A. Doan, and L. Gravano. Efficient keyword search across heterogeneous relational databases. In *ICDE*, 2007.

[28] K. Schnaitter and N. Polyzotis. Evaluating rank joins with optimal cost. In *PODS*, 2008.

[29] K. Schnaitter, J. Spiegel, and N. Polyzotis. Depth estimation for ranking query optimization. In *VLDB*, 2007.

[30] T. K. Sellis. Multiple-query optimization. *TODS*, 13(1), 1988.

[31] X. Shen, B. Tan, and C. Zhai. Context-sensitive information retrieval using implicit feedback. In *SIGIR*, New York, NY, USA, 2005.

[32] P. P. Talukdar, Z. G. Ives, and F. Pereira. Automatically incorporating new sources in keyword search-based data integration. In *SIGMOD*, 2010.

[33] P. P. Talukdar, M. Jacob, M. S. Mehmood, K. Crammer, Z. G. Ives, F. Pereira, and S. Guha. Learning to create data-integrating queries. In *VLDB*, 2008.

[34] S. D. Viglas and J. F. Naughton. Rate-based query optimization for streaming information sources. In *SIGMOD*, 2002.

[35] J. Zhou, P.-Å. Larson, J. C. Freytag, and W. Lehner. Efficient exploitation of similar subexpressions for query processing. In *SIGMOD*, 2007.

Nearest Keyword Search in XML Documents

Yufei Tao Stavros Papadopoulos Cheng Sheng Kostas Stefanidis
Department of Computer Science and Engineering
Chinese University of Hong Kong
New Territories, Hong Kong
{taoyf, stavros, csheng, kstef}@cse.cuhk.edu.hk

ABSTRACT

This paper studies the *nearest keyword* (*NK*) problem on XML documents. In general, the dataset is a tree where each node is associated with one or more keywords. Given a node q and a keyword w, an NK query returns the node that is nearest to q among all the nodes associated with w. NK search is not only useful as a standalone operator but also as a building brick for important tasks such as XPath query evaluation and keyword search. We present an indexing scheme that answers NK queries efficiently, in terms of both practical and worst-case performance. The query cost is provably *logarithmic* to the number of nodes carrying the query keyword. The proposed scheme occupies space *linear* to the dataset size, and can be constructed by a fast algorithm. Extensive experimentation confirms our theoretical findings, and demonstrates the effectiveness of NK retrieval as a primitive operator in XML databases.

Categories and Subject Descriptors

H3.1 [**Content analysis and indexing**]: Indexing methods

General Terms

Theory

Keywords

Nearest keyword, XPath, keyword search, group steiner tree

1. INTRODUCTION

We consider the problem of *nearest keyword* (*NK*) search on XML documents. The dataset is a tree $\mathcal{T}$ with undirected edges. Each node is associated with one or more keywords. Define the *distance* between two nodes as the number of edges in the (unique) path linking them. Given a node q in $\mathcal{T}$ and a keyword w, an *NK query* finds the *nearest w-neighbor* of q, namely, the node having the minimum distance to q among all the nodes associated with w.

To illustrate, Figure 1 shows part of an XML document, where all nodes have been encoded with the Dewey code [34] for easy reference. An *element node* has its *type* displayed in brackets, while the other nodes are *value nodes*. Given a node q = `012000` and a keyword w = `guard`, an NK query returns node `012010`, whose distance to q is 4 (edges). It is the nearest `guard`-neighbor of q.

SIGMOD'11, June 12–16, 2011, Athens, Greece.

1.1 Motivation

NK queries can serve as the building brick to tackle some important problems in XML databases, as elaborated below. For convenience, we assign each value node to a type, whose name concatenates its parent's type and the string `Val` (e.g., node `0100` has type `tnameVal`, and so does node `0200`). Every node carries its type as a keyword. In addition, each value node has its value as another keyword. For example, node `0100` has two keywords: its type `tnameVal`, and its value `Lakers`.

XPath query evaluation. NK search gives a new methodology for efficiently solving a class of XPath queries. An example is:

> Q: *Find the names of all players that originated from Maryland, but are in a team of the west division.*

The XPath statement of Q can be expressed as a *twig pattern* [4, 15] shown in Figure 2a, where a single-lined (double-lined) edge represents parent-child (ancestor-descendent) relationship. The goal is to find *occurrences* of the pattern in the data tree, and for each occurrence, output the value at the position of `pnameVal` (signified as underlined). Figure 2b demonstrates such an occurrence in Figure 1, from which the output is the value `Blake` of node `012000`.

There are two interesting facts about the pattern Q in Figure 2a, with respect to the data of Figure 1:

- Let q be the node in an occurrence corresponding to the node `Maryland` of Q. The type of q is `fromVal`. The nearest `west`-neighbor of q must have distance exactly 6 to q. For example, q is node `012020` in Figure 2b, and its nearest `west`-neighbor is node `0110`.
- Let q be any `fromVal` node that carries the word `Maryland`, but is *not* in any occurrence, i.e., the team of q is in the east division. The nearest `west`-neighbor of q must have distance *greater than* 6 to q, noticing that the neighbor must come from a team different from that of q. For example, let q be node `022020` in Figure 1. Its nearest `west`-neighbor is node `0110`, which has distance 8 to q.

The above facts enable us to process Q via NK search as follows. We enumerate all the `fromVal` nodes that contain `Maryland`. For each such node q, find its nearest `west`-neighbor. If the neighbor retrieved has a distance greater than 6 to q, it is ignored. Otherwise, we have found an occurrence, from which the `pnameVal` should be output. The `pnameVal` node can be found with another NK query, which obtains the nearest `pnameVal`-neighbor of q.

Group steiner tree retrieval. *Keyword search* has emerged as a new paradigm of inquiring XML databases. It enables a user to

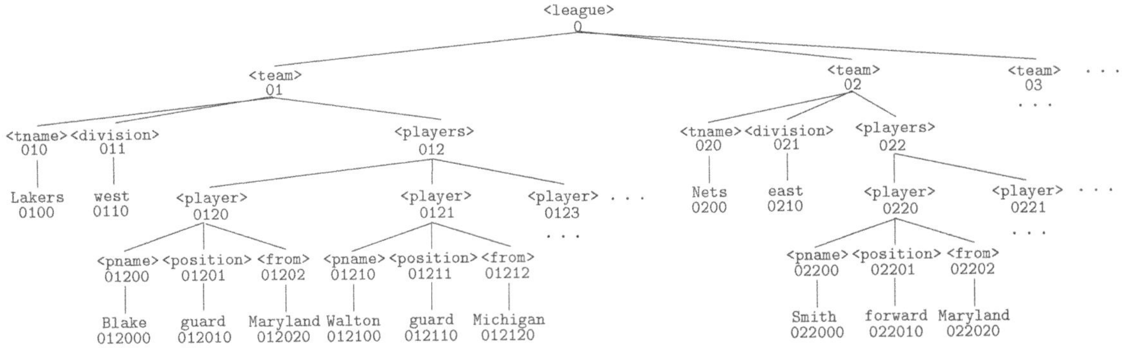

Figure 1: A sample of the NBA dataset

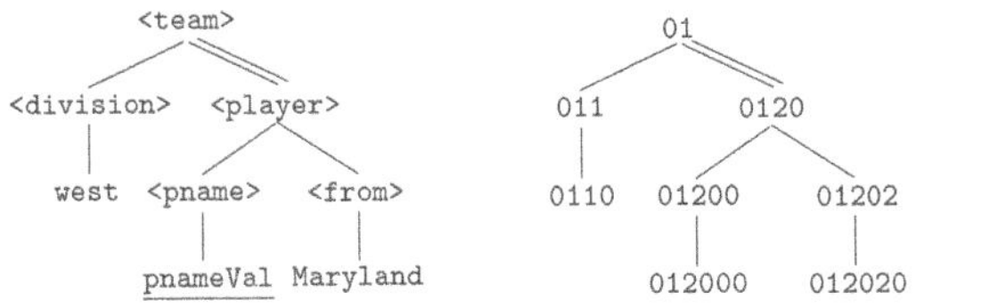

(a) Twig pattern for Q (b) An occurrence in Figure 1

Figure 2: An XPath query example

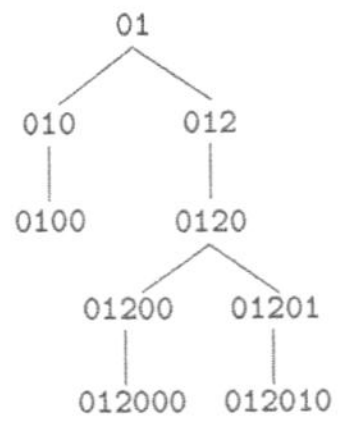

Figure 3: The group steiner tree of {Lakers, Blake, guard} in Figure 1

specify only a few keywords as the query, instead of complying with a rigorous syntax. Its advantage is that the user does not need to learn any query language like XPath, and neither does s/he need to be aware of the data schema. The disadvantage, however, is that what should be the query result becomes heavily dependent on the application backdrop. This has triggered the propositions of a variety of result semantics, among which an intuitive one is to return the *group steiner tree* (*GST*) [12, 20, 23, 25].

More specifically, given a set of query keywords $\{w_1, ..., w_l\}$, a GST is a tree that (i) contains all the query keywords in the texts of its nodes, and (ii) has the fewest edges among such trees. For example, Figure 3 presents the GST for {Lakers, Blake, guard} on the data of Figure 1. GST computation is known to be NP-hard (even if the dataset is a tree) [17]. Fortunately, as discussed later, NK queries provide an elegant way to extract a good approximate solution, namely, a tree that satisfies requirement (i), and has more edges than the GST by only a small factor.

1.2 Contributions

This paper presents the first study on the NK problem. We propose an indexing scheme that can answer any NK query in $O(\log N_w)$ time, where N_w is the number of nodes associated with the query keyword w. The scheme consumes space *linear* to the size of the dataset. Somewhat surprising is the fact that, despite the complication of the underlying theory, our access method can be implemented as merely a number of binary trees. All the results also hold in disk-oriented environments, where each binary tree is simply replaced with a B-tree. Accordingly, the query cost is $O(\log_B N_w)$ I/Os, where B is the size of a disk block.

The proposed index also leads to rigorous results on the usefulness of the NK operator. Specifically:

- We theoretically establish the fact that a large class of XPath queries can be reduced to NK search (in a way similar to how the query of Figure 2a was answered earlier). Our algorithm for processing this query class enjoys a worst-case time complexity that is *irrelevant* to the number of elements whose types appear as an internal node of Q. No previous solution is known to have this feature (as surveyed in Section 5).
- We give a fast solution to finding an approximate GST with an attractive quality guarantee (which is actually optimal if the query has only two keywords). We achieve the running time of $O(N_{min} l \log N_{max})$, plus the cost of outputting the resulting tree, where l is the number of keywords in the query, N_{min} is the number of nodes carrying the *rarest* query keyword (i.e., the one appearing the least times in the XML document), and N_{max} conversely is the number of nodes carrying the *most frequent* query keyword.

Besides confirming our theoretical findings, our experimentation also demonstrates the effectiveness of the NK operator on real XML documents. In particular, we show that XPath queries like the one in Figure 2a can be processed via NK search with performance comparable to or better than that of the existing approaches. Furthermore, for XML keyword search, our NK-based algorithm discovers high-quality approximate GSTs in real time.

Roadmap. The rest of the paper is organized as follows. Section 2 clarifies the problem definition and several technical preliminaries. Section 3 elaborates on the proposed solutions for NK search. Section 4 discusses the applications of NK queries in XPath evaluation and keyword search. Section 5 reviews the previous work related to ours. Section 6 contains extensive experimentation to evaluate the effectiveness and efficiency of our techniques. Finally, Section 7 concludes the paper with a summary of our findings.

2. PRELIMINARIES

For each node u in the data tree $\mathcal{T}$, we use $W(u)$ to represent the set of keywords associated with u. For simplicity, assume that $W(u)$ has at least one keyword. Define the *length* of a path in $\mathcal{T}$ as the number of edges it contains. Denote by $\|u, v\|$ the distance between two nodes u, v, namely, the length of the path connecting u and v. Let $U(w)$ be the set of nodes in $\mathcal{T}$ that include word w (hence, $N_w = |U(w)|$). Given a node q and a keyword w, the result of an NK query is a node $u \in U(w)$ such that

$$\|u, q\| \le \|v, q\| \quad \forall v \in U(w).$$

We denote u, the nearest w-neighbor of q, as $NN(q, w)$.

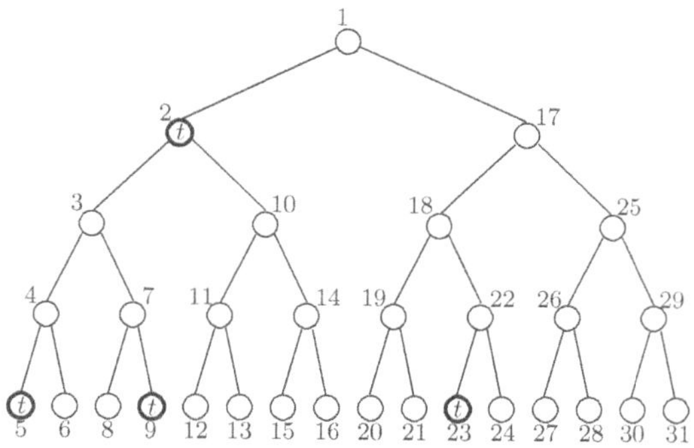

Figure 4: A running example

Figure 4 shows an example $\mathcal{T}$, where each node is labeled an integer. Sometimes we may refer to a node by its label directly, when the meaning is clear. For instance, as node 2 carries a single keyword t, we write $W(2) = \{t\}$. Similarly, as t also appears in nodes 5, 9 and 23, $U(t) = \{2, 5, 9, 23\}$. The keywords of the other nodes are omitted for clarity. Given q = node 17 and $w = t$, an NK query returns node 2, namely, $NN(17, t) = 2$.

Let N be the number of nodes in $\mathcal{T}$, and K the total number of keywords in all the nodes (counting a word twice if it appears in two nodes), i.e., $K = \sum_u |W(u)|$. Note that $\mathcal{T}$ requires $\Omega(K)$ space to store. In other words, *linear* cost should be interpreted as $O(K)$, instead of $O(N)$. We label the levels of $\mathcal{T}$ in a top-down manner, setting the root at level 0. Denote by $level(u)$ the level of a node u, which is also the number of edges on the path from the root to u. In Figure 4, all the leaf nodes are at level 4. Also, we use $sub(u)$ to represent the subtree of u.

In the sequel, we review several basic results useful in our technical discussion.

Interval encoding. For each node u of $\mathcal{T}$, define its *rank*, denoted as $rank(u)$, to be the sequence number of u in the *pre-order* traversal of $\mathcal{T}$. We associate u with an interval $R(u) = [x, y]$, where x is the rank of u, and y is the largest rank of the nodes in $sub(u)$. In Figure 4, the label of each node indicates its rank directly. As an example, the interval $R(10)$ associated with node 10 is $[10, 16]$.

The intervals defined this way have several properties commonly utilized in managing XML data:

- For any two nodes u and v, $R(u)$ contains $R(v)$ *if and only if* u is an ancestor of v. In other words, the ancestor-descendent relationship of u and v can be verified in constant time.
- The intervals of the nodes at the *same* level of $\mathcal{T}$ must be disjoint. In Figure 4, for instance, the nodes at level 2 have disjoint intervals $R(3) = [3, 9]$, $R(10) = [10, 16]$, $R(18) = [18, 24]$, and $R(25) = [25, 31]$.

The above properties allow us to solve the so-called *level-on-path* queries efficiently. Let u be an ancestor of v; given a level $\ell \in [level(u), level(v)]$, a level-on-path query finds the level-ℓ node on the path from u to v. For example, if u (v) is node 1 (15), a level-on-path query with $\ell = 2$ retrieves node 10.

LEMMA 1. *$\mathcal{T}$ can be pre-processed into a structure that occupies $O(N)$ space, such that any level-on-path query can be answered in $O(\log N)$ time. The structure can be built in $O(N \log N)$ time.*

PROOF. We manage the nodes of $\mathcal{T}$ of each level separately. Specifically, create a binary tree to index the ranks of the nodes at the same level (i.e., there are as many trees as the number of levels in $\mathcal{T}$). As each node appears in only one tree, the overall space is $O(N)$. Assume that we want to perform a level-on-path operation to find the level-ℓ node from u to v (which is a descendent of u). We find in $O(\log N)$ time the predecessor of $rank(v)$, among all the ranks indexed in the level-ℓ binary tree. The node whose rank equals that predecessor is exactly what we are looking for. □

Subtree NK search. NK search is easy if attention is restricted to the subtree of the query node. Formally, given a node q and a keyword w, a *subtree-NK query* finds the node u with the smallest distance to q, among all nodes in $sub(q)$ that are associated with w. We refer to u as the *subtree nearest w-neighbor* of q. For instance, let q be node 17 in Figure 4; the subtree-NK query with $w = t$ returns node 23. Note that the (global) nearest t-neighbor of node 17 is in fact node 2.

LEMMA 2. *$\mathcal{T}$ can be pre-processed into a structure that occupies $O(K)$ space, such that any subtree-NK query can be answered in $O(\log N_w)$ time. The structure can be built in $O(K \log K)$ time.*

PROOF. Let us first review a related result. Let S be a set of numbers in the real domain $\mathbb{R}$. Each number $x \in S$ is associated with a *weight* in $\mathbb{R}$. Given an interval I, a *range-min* query finds the number that has the minimum weight among all the numbers in $S \cap I$. We can index S with an SB-tree [36] that uses $O(|S|)$ space, and solve any range-min query in $O(\log |S|)$ time. The tree can be built in $O(|S| \log |S|)$ time.

We can convert subtree-NK search to the range-min problem. Let w be the keyword of concern. Construct S to include the ranks of the nodes in $U(w)$. Each rank is associated with a weight that equals the level of the corresponding node. Subtree-NK search with node q is equivalent to a range-min query on S with interval $R(q)$. We settle the problem with an SB-tree in $O(\log N_w)$ query time. The tree occupies $O(N_w)$ space and can be built in $O(N_w \log N_w)$ time. The SB-trees of all keywords require $O(\sum_w N_w) = O(K)$ space in total. The overall construction time is $O(\sum_w (N_w \log N_w)) = O(K \log K)$. □

Both Lemmas 1 and 2 will be needed to analyze the construction cost of the proposed structure.

Lowest common ancestor (LCA). We use $lca(u, v)$ to denote the LCA of nodes u, v in $\mathcal{T}$ (e.g., $lca(20, 26)$ is node 17 in Figure 4). In general, the distance of two nodes can be calculated in constant time, once their LCA has been identified, as can be seen from the following equation:

$$\|u, v\| = (level(u) - level(z)) + (level(v) - level(z))$$

where $z = lca(u, v)$.

LCA computation has been thoroughly studied. Harel and Tarjan [18] were the first to observe that the problem can be settled optimally in constant time using linear space. Their structure, however, is rather theoretical and difficult to implement. To remedy the drawback, several (much) simpler structures [1, 2, 13] have been developed, keeping the same space and query performance. As a corollary, we can obtain $\|u, v\|$ of any u, v in constant time.

3. NEAREST KEYWORD SEARCH

We pre-process the data tree $\mathcal{T}$ by building a separate structure for each distinct keyword w that appears in $\mathcal{T}$. This is reminiscent of the *inverted index*, which also has an *inverted list* dedicated to each w. Instead of a simple list, however, our structure for w is a binary tree constructed in a more sophisticated manner.

3.1 Overview

We concentrate on NK queries with a specific keyword w, as the structure is identical for all keywords. The term "nearest w-neighbor" will be abbreviated as *nearest neighbor (NN)*, when no ambiguity arises. Accordingly, we simplify notation $NN(u, w)$ to $NN(u)$.

A straightforward solution to answering an NK query is to perform a *breath first traversal (BFT)* starting from q. Namely, the BFT explores the nodes of $\mathcal{T}$ in ascending order of their distances to q, and stops as soon as it encounters a node associated with w. This approach is efficient only if the NN of q is close, and may end up visiting a large number of nodes otherwise.

Alternatively, we can pre-compute the NN of every node in $\mathcal{T}$. Each query can be answered in constant time, because we can simply return the (pre-computed) NN of the query node q. This approach, however, has the severe drawback that, the pre-computation incurs $\Omega(N)$ space for *every* keyword appearing in T. The number of distinct keywords can be easily $\Omega(N)$. In this case, the space complexity of the above approach is $\Omega(N^2)$, which is prohibitively large in practice.

The chief observation towards reducing the space is that, many nodes of $\mathcal{T}$ have the same NN, thus raising the hope that we could capture them collectively with much less information. Recall that each node can be uniquely identified by its rank, while the ranks of all nodes come from the *rank domain* $\mathbb{D} = [1, N]$ (e.g., $\mathbb{D} = [1, 31]$ in Figure 4). We can always partition $\mathbb{D}$ into a set $\mathcal{I}$ of disjoint intervals such that, for each interval $I \in \mathcal{I}$, the nodes with ranks in I have the same NN, which can be associated with I. Given an NK query with node q, we can solve it by identifying the (only) interval I that covers $rank(q)$, and returning the NN associated with I. This can be easily achieved by indexing $\mathcal{I}$ with a binary tree, which consumes $O(|\mathcal{I}|)$ space and has query cost $O(\log |\mathcal{I}|)$. Figure 5 illustrates the contents of a possible $\mathcal{I}$ for the data of Figure 4 when the keyword w of concern is t.

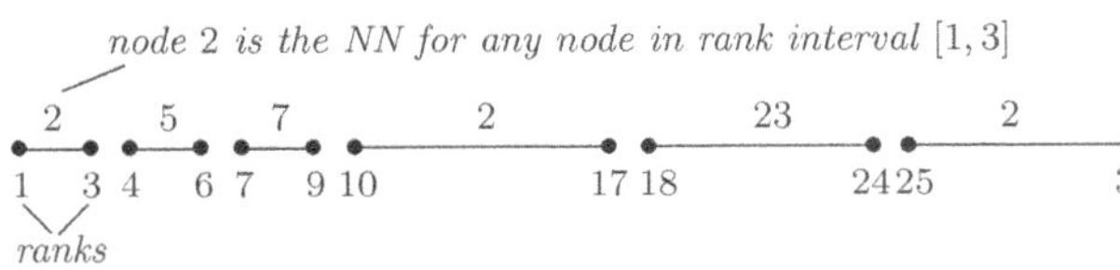

Figure 5: A tree Voronoi partition

We refer to $\mathcal{I}$ as a *tree Voronoi partition (TVP) of* w. An immediate issue is whether a small $\mathcal{I}$ *always* exists. Fortunately, we will show in Section 3.2 that there is definitely an $\mathcal{I}$ with size $O(N_w)$, where N_w is the size of $U(w)$ (i.e., the number of nodes in $\mathcal{T}$ carrying w). Furthermore, the size of $O(N_w)$ is asymptotically tight because $|\mathcal{I}|$ needs to be at least N_w – every node in $U(w)$ apparently finds itself as the NN.

Another important issue is how to compute $\mathcal{I}$ efficiently. Naively, one could first compute the NN of every node in $\mathcal{T}$, and then go over the nodes in ascending order of their ranks, merging consecutive nodes into an interval if their NNs are the same. This approach, however, entails $\Omega(N)$ time, which would render the total pre-computation cost (for all keywords) prohibitively expensive in practice. In Section 3.3, we will give a significantly faster algorithm to produce $\mathcal{I}$ in $O(N_w \log N_w)$ time.

3.2 TVP characteristics

This subsection will establish our first main result:

THEOREM 1 (TVP THEOREM). *For any keyword w appearing in $\mathcal{T}$, there is a tree Voronoi partition $\mathcal{I}$ with size less than $8N_w$, where N_w is the number of nodes in $\mathcal{T}$ associated with w.*

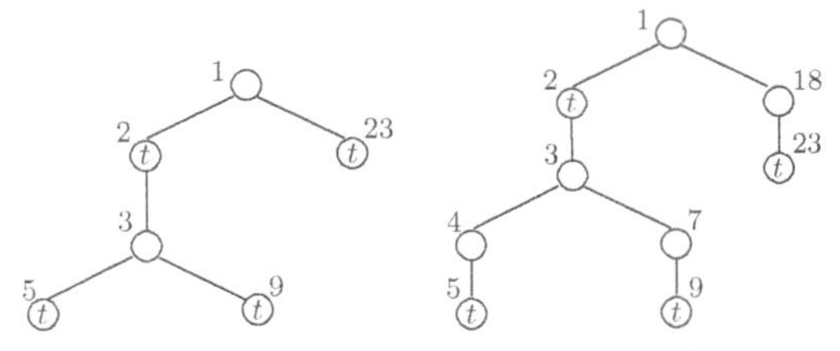

(a) $CT(t)$ (b) $ECT(t)$

Figure 6: Compact and extended compact trees

Let us start the proof by introducing the *compact tree* of w, denoted as $CT(w)$. First, all the nodes of $U(w)$ are in $CT(w)$, and termed the *data nodes*. Second, a non-data node u belongs to $\mathcal{T}$, *if and only if* there are *at least* two child nodes of u whose subtrees contain a data node. We call u a *branching node*. Consider $w = t$ in Figure 4. There are four data nodes 2, 5, 9, 23, and two branching nodes 1, 3. Node 17, for example, is not a branching node because only *one* of its child nodes (i.e., node 18) has a data node in its subtree. Let S be the set of all data and branching nodes. We form $CT(w)$ by drawing an edge from each node $u \in S$ to its lowest ancestor in S. Figure 6a shows the $CT(t)$ for the data of Figure 4. Node 5, for instance, is connected to node 3, because among all the data and branching nodes, node 3 is the lowest ancestor of node 5.

LEMMA 3. *$CT(w)$ has at most $2N_w - 1$ nodes.*

PROOF. Each branching node must have at least two child nodes in $CT(w)$. As $CT(w)$ has at most N_w leaf nodes, the total number of branching nodes cannot be more than $N_w - 1$. □

Consider any edge (u, v) in $CT(w)$. Let us walk, in the data tree $\mathcal{T}$, along the path from u to v. As we go, monitor the $NN(z)$ of the node z being visited, and count how many *changes* in $NN(z)$ there are in total. Call each of those changes an *NN-change* on (u, v). As an example, consider edge $(1, 23)$ in the $CT(t)$ of Figure 6a. Now we walk from node 1 to node 23 in the $\mathcal{T}$ of Figure 4. Along the path there is only a single NN-change, which happens as we move from node 17 to node 18 (i.e., $NN(17) = 2$, but $NN(18) = 23$). The next lemma gives an important fact:

LEMMA 4. *There can be at most one NN-change on each edge of $CT(w)$.*

PROOF. Let (u, v) be an edge of $CT(w)$. The removal of (u, v) cuts $CT(w)$ into two connected components. Let C_u (C_v) be the component including u (v). Denote by P the path from u to v in $\mathcal{T}$. Suppose that $u^\star$ ($v^\star$) is the data node in C_u (C_v) closest to u (v). We claim that, for any node z on P, $NN(z)$ must be either $u^\star$ or $v^\star$. In fact, for any node $u' \in C_u$, it holds that

$$\|z, u^\star\| = \|z, u\| + \|u, u^\star\| \leq \|z, u\| + \|u, u'\| = \|z, u'\|.$$

Similarly, for any node $v' \in C_v$, we have $\|z, v^\star\| \leq \|z, v'\|$. Therefore, except $u^\star$ and $v^\star$, no other data node in $C_u \cup C_v$ can be the NN of z.

Hence, if there were at least two NN-changes on (u, v), there would have to be three nodes z_1, z_2, z_3 on P such that z_2 was on the path from z_1 to z_3, but $NN(z_1) = NN(z_3) \neq NN(z_2)$. It is trivial to show that such a scenario cannot happen. □

Next, $CT(w)$ is augmented with the nodes where NN-changes occur. Consider any edge (u, v) of $CT(w)$ on which there is an

NN-change. Let z be the first node on the u-to-v path in $\mathcal{T}$ such that $NN(z) \neq NN(u)$. If z is different from v, we add it to $CT(w)$, breaking (u, v) into two edges (u, z) and (z, v). Denote by $ECT(w)$ the resulting tree, after applying such transformation on all edges of $CT(w)$ with NN-changes. In case $root(\mathcal{T})$ is not already in $ECT(w)$, we add it as the parent of the current root of $ECT(w)$. The final $ECT(w)$ is called the *extended compact tree* of w. Let us illustrate the transformation with edge $(1, 23)$ in the $CT(t)$ of Figure 6a (i.e., $u = 1, v = 23$). As mentioned earlier, on the path from node 1 to node 23 in Figure 4, there is an NN-change as we cross from node 17 to node 18. Hence, $z = 18$, and accordingly, $(1, 23)$ is broken into two edges $(1, 18)$ and $(18, 23)$ in the extended compact tree $ECT(t)$, as shown in Figure 6b.

We are ready to generate a tree Voronoi partition $\mathcal{I}$ of w. It suffices to invoke the following algorithm for every node u of $ECT(w)$ in turn (ordering does not matter):

```
algorithm voronoiIntv(u)
/* u is a node in ECT(w) */
1. S = {R(u)}
2. for each child node v of u in ECT(w) do
3.     I ← the (only) interval in S covering R(v)
4.     break I into intervals I_1, R(v), I_2
       /* I_1 (I_2) is the part of I to the left (right) of R(v) */
5.     remove I from S, and add I_1, I_2
6. add to 𝓘 the intervals in S, after associating them with NN(u)
```

For example, let u be node 1 in the $ECT(t)$ of Figure 6b. At Line 1, voronoiIntv sets $S = \{R(1)\} = \{[1, 31]\}$. Since node 1 has two child nodes in $ECT(t)$, the for-loop in Lines 2-5 is executed twice. The first time trims $R(2) = [2, 16]$ away from $[1, 31]$, after which $S = \{[1, 1], [17, 31]\}$. The second execution cuts $R(18) = [18, 24]$ out of $[17, 31]$, leaving $S = \{[1, 1], [17, 17], [25, 31]\}$. Line 6 adds all three intervals of S to $\mathcal{I}$, after associating them with $NN(1) = 2$, indicating that node 2 is the NN of any node (whose rank falls) in those intervals.

LEMMA 5. *Applying* voronoiIntv *to all nodes of $ECT(w)$ creates a tree Voronoi partition $\mathcal{I}$ with less than $8N_w$ intervals.*

PROOF. We start by proving that the intervals of $\mathcal{I}$ are disjoint, and their union covers the rank domain $\mathbb{D}$. Observe that the intervals inserted in $\mathcal{I}$ at Line 6 are disjoint with the $R(v)$ of any child node v of u, where u is the input to the current execution of voronoiIntv. None of those intervals can overlap with the intervals added to $\mathcal{I}$ by the execution of voronoiIntv invoked with v (which only adds intervals within $R(v)$). On the other hand, every value $x \in \mathbb{D}$ is covered by an interval in the final $\mathcal{I}$. Such an interval is inserted in $\mathcal{I}$ by running voronoiIntv with the lowest node u in $ECT(w)$ whose $R(u)$ covers x.

We proceed to show that, for each interval $I \in \mathcal{I}$, the NN associated with I is indeed the NN of all nodes in I. Consider any node u in $ECT(w)$. Denote its child nodes in $ECT(w)$ as $v_1, ..., v_f$ for some $f \geq 0$. For each $1 \leq j \leq f$, cutting $R(v_j)$ out of $R(u)$ at Line 4 effectively removes $sub(v_j)$ from $sub(u)$ (recall that $sub(.)$ represents the subtree of a node). Let $sub^{\triangle}(u)$ be the set of nodes in $sub(u)$, but not in the $sub(v_j)$ of any j. It suffices to prove that all nodes in $sub^{\triangle}(u)$ have the same NN as u. For each edge (u, v_j) of $ECT(w)$, define $P(u, v_j)$ as the path in $\mathcal{T}$ from node u to v_j, but *excluding* node v_j. Each node $z \in sub^{\triangle}(u)$ is either (i) on $P(u, v_j)$ for some j, or (ii) has an ancestor z' in $\mathcal{T}$ that is on $P(u, v_j)$ for some j. In the former case, $NN(z)$ must be $NN(u)$ by the way $ECT(w)$ is constructed. In the latter case, $NN(z) = NN(z')$, while z' is a node of case (i), implying $NN(z) = NN(u)$ as well.

It remains to bound the size of $\mathcal{I}$. By Lemma 3, $CT(w)$ has at most $2N_w - 2$ edges. As each of them may generate two edges in $ECT(w)$, the number of edges in $ECT(w)$ is at most $4N_w - 4 + 1 = 4N_w - 3$, including the (potential) extra edge due to $root(\mathcal{T})$. In voronoiIntv, each edge breaks $\mathbb{D}$ into at most 2 more intervals. Therefore, the final $|\mathcal{I}|$ is bounded above by $1 + 2(4N_w - 3) = 8N_w - 5$. □

The proof of Theorem 1 is thus completed.

3.3 Finding the minimum TVP

This subsection completes our discussion of NK search by elaborating an algorithm for computing a TVP $\mathcal{I}$ of a keyword w with the *minimum* size. In fact, the main idea of the algorithm has been mentioned in Section 3.2, as summarized below:

```
algorithm computeTVP(w)
1. build CT(w)
2. build ECT(w) from CT(w)
3. 𝓘 = ∅
4. for each node u in ECT(w) do
5.     voronoiIntv(u)
   /* at the end of the for-loop, |𝓘| < 8N_w */
6. merge consecutive intervals in 𝓘 that are associated with
   the same NN
7. return 𝓘
```

Next, we clarify the details of Lines 1 and 2, because voronoiIntv has been presented in the previous subsection.

Construction of $CT(w)$. We construct $CT(w)$ in two steps: first collect the set S of nodes in $CT(w)$, and then connect them properly to meet the definition of $CT(w)$. The first step applies the algorithm below to compute S:

```
algorithm collectCTnodes(U(w))
S = U(w)
sort the nodes of U(w) in ascending order of ranks
for each pair of consecutive nodes u, v do
    S = S ∪ lca(u, v)
```

We claim that the final S includes all the branching nodes. Let z be any branching node. By definition, it has at least two child nodes that have a data node in their subtrees, respectively. Let u_1, u_2 be the two left-most ones of those child nodes, with u_1 being the left-most one. Denote by v_1 (v_2) the data node with the largest (smallest) rank in the subtree of u_1 (u_2). By the property of pre-order ranking, v_1 and v_2 constitute a pair of consecutive data nodes in the rank domain. Hence, z will be discovered as $lca(v_1, v_2)$.

Recall that each node in $CT(w)$ should be connected to its lowest ancestor (if any) among all the nodes in $CT(w)$. We achieve the purpose using a stack J. Specifically, we process the nodes of S in ascending order of their ranks, and maintain $CT(w)$ for the nodes already seen. At each moment, J keeps the right-most root-to-leaf path of the current $CT(w)$. Nodes of the path are pushed in J in the same order they are scanned, i.e., with the leaf (root) at the top (bottom).

```
algorithm computeCTedges(w)
sort the nodes of S in ascending order of ranks
J = ∅
while S ≠ ∅ do
    u ← the first node of S; remove u from S
```

```
5.     keep popping the top node v of J as long as R(v) is
       disjoint with R(u)
6.     if J is not empty then
7.         add an edge between u and the top node of J
8.     push u in J
```

Let us illustrate the algorithm using the set of nodes in the $CT(t)$ of Figure 6a. Here, $S = \{1, 2, 3, 5, 9, 23\}$. Node 1 is the first scanned, and directly pushed to J. For node 2, Line 5 has no effect, while Lines 6-7 add an edge between nodes 1 and 2. $J = \{2, 1\}$ at this time (with node 2 at the top). Similarly, the scanning of nodes 3 and 5 create edges $(2, 3)$ and $(3, 5)$ respectively, after which $J = \{5, 3, 2, 1\}$. Next, the algorithm comes to node 9. Line 5 pops node 5 out of J because $R(5)$ is found to be disjoint with $R(7)$. Line 6 then spawns another edge $(3, 9)$ in $CT(t)$. Finally, the handling of node 23 pops nodes 9, 3, 2, and adds one more edge $(1, 23)$. The $CT(t)$ now becomes final as S has been exhausted.

Construction of $ECT(w)$. Let (u, v) be an edge in $CT(w)$, with u being an ancestor of v. Lemma 4 states that there can be at most one NN-change on (u, v). In case no NN-change exists, (u, v) is kept directly in $ECT(w)$. Otherwise, we should create two edges (u, z), (z, v) in $ECT(w)$, where z is the first node (on the u-to-v path in $\mathcal{T}$) such that $NN(u) \neq NN(z)$.

Our algorithm for building $ECT(w)$, named `computeECT`, processes the edges (u, v) of $CT(w)$ in ascending order of $level(u)$. It keeps the invariant that, at the time (u, v) is to be processed, we have already determined $NN(u)$. It is easy to see that $NN(v)$ can only be either $NN(u)$ or $NN_{sub}(v)$, where $NN_{sub}(v)$ is the subtree nearest w-neighbor of u (see Section 2). Another key to the algorithm is that, if $NN(v)$ turns out to be different from $NN(v)$, the node z splitting (u, v) can be identified by a level-on-path query. This is because the level ℓ of z can be calculated as:

$$\ell = \left\lceil \frac{\delta + level(u) + level(v)}{2} \right\rceil \quad (1)$$

where $\delta = \|v, NN(v)\| - \|u, NN(u)\|$.

```
algorithm computeECT(CT(w))
1.  sort the edges (u, v) of CT(w) in ascending order of
    level(e); E ← the sorted list
2.  find the NN of the root of CT(w) with a subtree NK query
3.  while E ≠ ∅ do
4.      (u, v) ← the first edge of E; remove it from E
5.      NN_sub(v) ← the subtree nearest w-neighbor of v
6.      NN(v) ← whichever of NN(u) and NN_sub(v) that
        is closer to v
7.      if NN(u) = NN(v) then
8.          create edge (u, v) in ECT(w)
9.      else
10.         z ← the result of a level-on-path query using
            (u, v) and ℓ (Equation 1)
11.         create edges (u, z) and (z, v) in ECT(w)
```

We demonstrate the algorithm by explaining how to derive the $ECT(t)$ in Figure 6b from the $CT(t)$ in Figure 6a. First, Line 1 arranges the edges of $CT(t)$ in the order of $E = \{(1, 2), (1, 23), (2, 3), (3, 5), (3, 9)\}$. Line 2 obtains $NN(1) = 2$. The subsequent execution examines each edge of E in turn. The first one, $(1, 2)$, is easy to handle because $NN(2) = NN(1) = 2$. Hence, $(1, 2)$ is included in $ECT(t)$ directly. Consider the second edge $(1, 23)$ of E. As $NN(23) = 23$ is different from $NN(1)$, Line 10 calculates $\ell = \lceil (-1 + 0 + 4)/2 \rceil = 2$, and issues a level-on-path query to find the level-2 node z on the path from node 1 to node 23 in the data tree of Figure 4. The z retrieved is node 18. Line 11 then adds edges $(1, 18)$ and $(18, 23)$ into $ECT(t)$. The rest of the algorithm proceeds in the same manner.

Analysis. Line 1 of `computeTVP` invokes `collectCTnodes` and `computeCTedges`, both of which terminate in $O(N_w \log N_w)$ time. The same complexity applies to at Line 2, which executes `computeECT`. Lines 4-5 essentially spend constant time on each edge of $ECT(w)$, and hence, incur only $O(N_w)$ cost. Line 6 apparently requires $O(N_w)$ time. Therefore, the overall complexity of `computeTVP` is $O(N_w \log N_w)$.

THEOREM 2. *$\mathcal{T}$ can be pre-processed into a structure that occupies $O(K)$ space, such that any NK query can be answered in $O(\log N_w)$ time, where N_w is the number of nodes in T carrying the query keyword. The structure can be built in $O(K \log K)$ time.*

PROOF. The result follows from the discussion in Section 3.1, Theorem 1, the analysis of this subsection, and the fact that (i) the total construction cost of the structures of all keywords is $O(\sum_w (N_w \log N_w)) = O(K \log K)$, and (ii) the space of all these structures is $O(\sum_w N_w) = O(\sum_u |W(u)|) = O(K)$. □

When B-trees, instead of binary trees, are deployed, the space and query complexities of our structure are $O(K/B)$ disk blocks and $O(\log_B N_w)$ I/Os, respectively, where B is the size of a block.

4. NEAREST KEYWORD SEARCH AS AN OPERATOR

In the introduction, we outlined why NK search can be deployed as a primitive operator to support other tasks efficiently. Sections 4.1 and 4.2 elaborate this for XPath query answering and group steiner tree computation, respectively.

4.1 XPath evaluation

This subsection aims at a theoretical justification that many XPath queries can be reduced to NK search. We consider queries that can be represented as a twig pattern Q as follows. Each internal node of Q gives an element type. A leaf node is designated as the *output*, indicating the information solicited (extension to multiple output nodes is trivial). Every other, non-output, leaf node carries a keyword, which imposes a predicate that must hold on each occurrence of Q in the data tree $\mathcal{T}$. See Figure 2a for an example. Without loss of generality, we assume that Q is compatible with the data schema; otherwise, it can be rejected by standard syntax checking with the DTD.

We will prescribe two conditions whose satisfaction *guarantees* the success of reducing Q to a set of NK queries. These conditions are conservative, in the sense that one may still carry out reduction even if the conditions do not hold (as shown in the experiments). We will see that the class of reducible queries can be processed by a new algorithm with an attractive worst-case performance bound.

Type-sequence condition. Let P be any path of $\mathcal{T}$ starting from $root(\mathcal{T})$. Define the *type sequence* of P as the ordering of the node types encountered as we walk along P. For instance, if P is the path from node `0` to node `010` in Figure 1, its type sequence is (`league`, `team`, `tname`).

CONDITION 1. *For each node u of the same type, the root-to-u path in $\mathcal{T}$ has the same type sequence.*

In Figure 1, for example, the path from the root to every `player` node has type sequence (`league`, `team`, `players`, `player`).

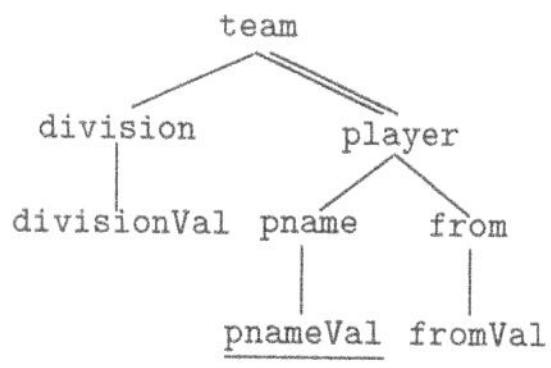

Figure 7: Type pattern of the query in Figure 2a

Anchor condition. As the next condition is more complex, we first explain the idea using an example. Consider Q to be the pattern in Figure 2a. Let us examine its *type pattern*, which is also a tree, and results from replacing each node of Q with its type, as shown in Figure 7. Denote the type pattern of Q as $type(Q)$.

Let us fix a leaf node, `fromVal`, in $type(Q)$ as the *anchor*, denoted as anc. Then, find the LCA, called a *critical LCA*, of anc and every other leaf, namely, (i) $clca_1$ = `team`, which is the LCA of anc and $leaf_1$ = `divisionVal`, and (ii) $clca_2$ = `player`, which is the LCA of anc and $leaf_2$ = `pnameVal`. Each pair $(clca_i, leaf_i)$ decides a *critical set* represented as $cset_i$, which includes all the types on the path from $clca_i$ to $leaf_i$. That is, $cset_1$ = {`team`, `division`, `divisionVal`}, and $cset_2$ = {`player`, `pname`, `pnameVal`}.

In the $\mathcal{T}$ of Figure 1, for each type-$clca_i$ node u, $sub(u)$ (i.e., the subtree of u) has *at most one* node of each type in $cset_i$. To be specific, let us inspect $clca_1$ = `team`. The subtree of a `team` node can have at most one node of type `team`, `division`, and `divisionVal`, respectively. Similarly, this is also true for $clca_2$, i.e., every `player` node can have in its subtree at most one `player`, `pname`, and `pnameVal` node, respectively. In this case, we say that Q is *unambiguous*.

Not all the choices of anc would make Q unambiguous. For example, it is not hard to see that Q is not unambiguous if `divisionVal` is selected as the anchor. The second condition requires:

CONDITION 2. *At least one choice of anchor makes Q unambiguous.*

To grasp the intuition behind the condition, consider again the strategy explained in Section 1.1 for processing the query Q of Figure 2a. Recall that we used the `fromVal` nodes carrying `Maryland` as the query nodes q for NK search. Instead, let us choose q as the `divisionVal` nodes associated with `west`. That is, for each such q, say node `0100`, the algorithm finds its nearest `Maryland`-neighbor (i.e., node `012020`) in the set of `fromVal` nodes, and then checks whether the neighbor has distance 6 to q. The answer is yes, so the presence of an occurrence has been detected. The problem, however, is that we can no longer find the output value `Blake` by identifying the nearest `pnameVal`-neighbor of q. This is because multiple `pnameVal` nodes have an *identical* (smallest) distance 6 to q and, hence, the NK search with `pnameVal` as the query word may happen to return a node (e.g., `012100`) that is not describing the same player as node `012020`.

We point out that, although the definitions and notations leading to Condition 2 were introduced with an example, they can be generalized in a straightforward manner to arbitrary Q.

Reducibility. The theorem below formally establishes the reduction from XPath evaluation to NK search.

THEOREM 3. *An XPath query can be reduced to NK search under Conditions 1 and 2.*

PROOF. As in Section 1.1, we set the type of each node u in $\mathcal{T}$ as a keyword in u. Each value node has its value as an extra keyword. An XPath query Q is processed with the following algorithm:

---

algorithm `xpath`(Q)

1. **for** each node q in $\mathcal{T}$ having type anc **do**
2. **for** each non-output leaf node u of Q **do**
3. $w \leftarrow$ the keyword of u
4. $v \leftarrow$ the result of $NN(q, w)$ among all nodes in $\mathcal{T}$ of the same type as u
/* This can be done with minor extension to our technique in Section 3. For example, one simple solution is to prefix each word with the type of the node containing it. Such a prefix is added to w, which automatically restricts the search to the nodes of the designated type. */
5. **if** $\|q, v\| \neq$ the correct value as in an occurrence **then**
6. mark q as pruned
7. **break for**
8. **if** q has not been pruned **then**
9. $w \leftarrow$ the type of the output node of Q
10. $v \leftarrow NN(q, w)$
11. **if** $\|q, v\| =$ the correct value as in an occurrence **then**
12. report the value of v

Let us refer to the type-anc node in an occurrence of Q as an *anchor node*. Denote by f be the number of leaf nodes in $type(Q)$ other than anc. Lines 2-12 of `xpath` are collectively called an *iteration*. We will prove that (a) the output value in every occurrence is reported by `xpath`, and (b) every value reported is indeed the output value of an occurrence.

Proof of statement (a). Let occ be any occurrence with q as its anchor node. Denote by u_i the type-$leaf_i$ node in occ ($1 \leq i \leq f$). Each u_i must be retrieved by the NK-query at Line 4 (or 10) in the iteration for q, and pass the if-condition at Line 5 (or 11). The iteration reports the output value of occ at Line 12.

Proof of statement (b). Under Condition 1, it suffices to consider Q with single-lined edges only, because any double-lined edge can be expanded into a set of single-lined edges without affecting the query result. Condition 1 also allows us to focus on Q (i) that has only a single node, or (ii) whose root has at least two child nodes. If $root(Q)$ has a single child, we can remove the root while still obtaining the same result.

Assume that `xpath` reports a value in an iteration with q as the anchor node. Line 4 or 10 must have fetched a type-$leaf_i$ node u_i ($1 \leq i \leq f$). Let occ be the tree that (i) is rooted at the LCA of $u_1, ..., u_f, q$, and (ii) includes (only) the edges on the path from the LCA to each of $u_1, ..., u_f, q$. The rest of the proof argues that occ is an occurrence. Towards this, we consider tree $type(occ)$, which is obtained by replacing each node of occ with its type. Our goal is to show that $type(occ)$ and $type(Q)$ are exactly the same.

Condition 1 implies that all nodes of a type must be at the same level. Given a node type z, we use $seq(z)$ to represent the type sequence of the path in the data tree $\mathcal{T}$ that goes from the root (of $\mathcal{T}$) to an arbitrary type-z node u (recall that $seq(z)$ is unique regardless of u). Also, suppose that $clca_1$, ..., $clca_f$ are in the top-down order.

As $clca_i \in seq(anc)$ for each $i \in [1, f]$, q has a (unique) type-$clca_i$ ancestor in $\mathcal{T}$, which we represent as v_i. A key observation is that u_i must be in the subtree of v_i. Otherwise, $\|q, u_i\|$ would have been at least 2 more than the correct value in an occurrence, noticing that the path from q to u_i would need to go outside $sub(v_i)$, and then eventually descend to the level where type-$leaf_i$ nodes are. From $type(Q)$, we know that $clca_i$ is the last common type in $seq(leaf_i)$ and $seq(anc)$, implying that v_i must be the LCA of u_i and q, and belong to occ. Hence, the root of occ has type $clca_1$.

Let P_Q (or P_{occ}) be the path in $type(Q)$ (or $type(occ)$) from the root to anc. The earlier analysis indicates that P_Q is identical to P_{occ}. Next we prove that $type(occ)$ and $type(Q)$ are the same in the other parts as well. Let us walk down P_Q and P_{occ} synchronously, and stop as soon as encountering a $clca_i$ (of any $i \in [1, f]$) in both paths. Let T_Q (or T_{occ}) be the subtree of $clca_i$ in $type(Q)$ (or $type(occ)$), removing the subtree rooted at z, where z is the child node of $clca_i$ that is an ancestor of anc.

Define $S = \{j \mid clca_j = clca_i\}$ (it is possible for several critical LCAs to coincide on one node). Let z be any type in the $cset_j$ of any $j \in S$. Under Condition 2, there is a unique type-z node in the subtree of v_i in $\mathcal{T}$. Therefore, each type in T_Q (T_{occ}) can appear only once. For each $leaf_j$ ($j \in S$), define a type-sequence s_j that equals the suffix of $seq(leaf_j)$ starting from $clca_i$. Regarding each type as a symbol, both T_Q and T_{occ} are in fact a trie of the same set of strings $\{s_j \mid j \in S\}$.

The above reasoning of T_Q and T_{occ} is independent of i. We thus have established the equivalence of $type(Q)$ and $type(occ)$. □

Remark 1. We outline the main ideas on how to verify Conditions 1 and 2 efficiently, while leaving the complete details to the full paper. We regard each rule of the DTD as having the form $e \rightarrow s$, where e is an element type and s a string specifying the possible child element types of e. Combine multiple rules whose left hand sides are the same type. Denoting by S the set of resulting rules, we can show that Condition 1 is satisfied if and only if every element type appears on the right hand side (RHS) of exactly one rule in S.

To check Condition 2, we resort to a *schema tree* ST, where each node is an element type e, whose child nodes are the element types in the RHS of rule $e \rightarrow s$. Recall that every element type c in s may carry a star (e.g., $e \rightarrow c^*$ means that there can be multiple instances of c below e directly). In this case, the edge (in ST) from e to c is a *star edge*; otherwise, it is a *non-star edge*. Given a query Q, ST allows us to verify Condition 2 as follows. First pick a leaf node of $type(Q)$ as the anchor anc. Perform the following for every other leaf node u: identify the LCA v of anc and u, and examine if the path from v to u in ST has a star edge. If the answer is no for all u, we assert that Q satisfies Condition 2. Otherwise, pick a different anchor and repeat the above process. If all anchors have been attempted and Q has not been confirmed to satisfy Condition 2, we conclude that it violates the condition. Clearly, the time of Condition-2 checking depends only on the schema, is irrelevant to the size of the XML document, and hence, typically accounts for only a fraction of the total query cost.

Note that Condition 1 (2) is a constraint on the data (queries). It is worth mentioning that the two conditions are satisfied by many real datasets and meaningful queries. In particular, we note that all the datasets experimented in [4, 6, 10, 34, 35] and at least one in [7, 15, 16, 20, 27, 28, 29, 30, 32, 37] satisfy Condition 1 (see also our experiments). We point out that simple *aliasing* can often be carried out to make a dataset satisfy Condition 1. For example, in the well-known *DBLP* dataset, an `author` element may be under an `article` or `inproceedings` element. To meet Condition 1, we can rename the `author` of former type as `a-author`, and that of the latter type as `i-author`.

Remark 2. Denote by $leaf_1, ..., leaf_f$ the leaf nodes of Q that are not the anchor anc. By Theorem 2, algorithm `xpath` terminates in $O(N_{anc} \sum_{i=1}^{f} \log N_{leaf_i})$ time, where N_x is the number of nodes in the data tree $\mathcal{T}$ fulfilling the *predicate* implied by the node x in $type(Q)$. For example, for the Q of Figure 2a, the execution time is $O(N_{\texttt{Maryland}}(\log N_{\texttt{west}} + \log N_{\texttt{pnameVal}}))$. In general, the time complexity of `xpath` is independent on the number of nodes in $\mathcal{T}$ whose types are *internal* nodes of $type(Q)$. This is a unique performance characteristic that is not shared by any previous solution.

4.2 Finding approximate group steiner trees

This section discusses the GST problem as motivated in Section 1. The dataset is a tree $\mathcal{T}$ as described in Section 2. A query specifies a set of keywords $QS = \{w_1, ..., w_l\}$. Recall that $U(w_i)$ is the set of nodes in $\mathcal{T}$ associated with w_i ($1 \le i \le l$). Any l nodes $u_1, ..., u_l$, where $u_i \in U(w_i)$ for each i, uniquely determines a *minimum connecting tree* (*MCT*) [20] M as follows. M has the LCA of all $u_1, ..., u_l$ as its root, and includes (all and only) the edges on the path in $\mathcal{T}$ from the LCA to every u_i. Referring to $(u_1, ..., u_l)$ as a *vector*, the GST problem is equivalent to discovering the vector that minimizes the number of edges in M. This problem is NP-hard [17].

As an example, assume $\mathcal{T}$ to be the data tree in Figure 1, and w_1 = `Lakers`, w_2 = `Blake`, w_3 = `guard` ($l = 3$). Given u_1 = node `0100`, u_2 = node `012000`, and u_3 = node `012010`, Figure 3 demonstrates the corresponding MCT M. Notice that the root of M is the LCA of u_1, u_2 and u_3.

We assume that $w_1, ..., w_m$ have been arranged in such a way that $|U(w_1)| \le ... \le |U(w_l)|$. The following algorithm extracts an MCT with a small number of edges.

---

algorithm approxGST($w_1, ..., w_l$)

1. $d_{min} \leftarrow \infty$
2. **for** each node $u_1 \in U(w_1)$ **do**
3. **for** $i \leftarrow 2$ to l **do**
4. $u_i \leftarrow NN(u_1, w_i)$
5. $d \leftarrow \sum_{i=2}^{l} \|u_1, u_i\|$
6. **if** $d < d_{min}$ **then**
7. remember $(u_1, ..., u_l)$ as the *best vector*
8. $d_{min} = d$
9. **return** the MCT M determined by the best vector

The for-loop in Lines 2-8 enumerates each node $u_1 \in U(w_1)$. Lines 3-4 find the nearest w_i-neighbor of u_1 for every other query keyword w_i. The resulting neighbors, together with u_1, determine an MCT. The key of the algorithm is to measure the quality of the tree as the sum of the distance from u_1 to each retrieved neighbor (see Line 5). The algorithm eventually returns the best tree according to this quality metric.

We say that an MCT M is a *c-approximate GST* if it has at most c times more edges than the GST. Formally, if $cost(M)$ represents the number of edges in M, it holds that $cost(M) \le c \cdot cost(M^\star)$, where $M^\star$ is the (optimal) GST.

LEMMA 6. *The output of* approxGST *is an* ($l - 1$)-*approximate GST.*

PROOF. For each $i \in [1, l]$, let $u_i^\star$ be a node in $M^\star$ associated with keyword w_i (if there are several such nodes, $u_i^\star$ can be any of them). Define $d^\star = \sum_{i=2}^{l} \|u_1^\star, u_i^\star\|$. Since every edge of $M^\star$ is included at most once in the path from $u_1^\star$ to each $u_i^\star$ ($2 \le i \le l$), it holds that:

$$d^\star \le (l-1) \cdot cost(M^\star). \quad (2)$$

Let M_{apx} be the output of approxGST. The d_{min} in the sequel refers to the final d_{min} of approxGST. Notice that $\{u_1^\star, NN(u_1^\star, w_2), ..., NN(u_1^\star, w_l)\}$ is a set $\{u_1, ..., u_l\}$ that must have been inspected at Line 5 of approxGST. In other words:

$$d_{min} \le \sum_{i=2}^{l} \|u_1^\star, NN(u_1^\star, w_i)\| \le d^\star. \quad (3)$$

where the second $\le$ is because $\|u_1^\star, NN(u_1^\star, w_i)\| \le \|u_1^\star, u_i^\star\|$.

Let $\{\hat{u}_1, ..., \hat{u}_l\}$ be the set $\{u_1, ..., u_l\}$ that determines M_{apx} at Line 7 of approxGST. Then, $d_{min} = \sum_{i=2}^{l} \|\hat{u}_1, \hat{u}_i\|$. Every edge of M_{apx} is used at least once in the union of the paths from $\hat{u}_1$ to $\hat{u}_2$, ..., $\hat{u}_l$, respectively. Hence:

$$cost(M_{apx}) \leq d_{min}. \tag{4}$$

Combining Inequalities 2-4 gives $cost(M_{apx}) \leq (l-1) \cdot cost(M^\star)$. □

By Theorem 2, the execution time of approxGST is bounded by $O(N_{min} l \log N_{max})$, plus the cost of outputting the tree, where $N_{min} = |U(w_1)|$ and $N_{max} = |U(w_l)|$.

Remark 3. Sometimes it is useful to return k MCTs with small cost, where k is a user-specified parameter. In this case, we maintain the k best vectors currently found, as opposed to only the top-1. This can be achieved with minor modification to approxGST.

5. RELATED WORK

NK search has not been studied previously. In the sequel, we review the existing work on other topics related to our discussion.

The first topic is the processing of *holistic twig joins*, where the goal is to enumerate *all* occurrences of a twig pattern. The existing algorithms can be classified as *sequential* or *indexed*. A *sequential algorithm* [4, 5, 8, 7, 15, 21, 30, 32, 37] scans synchronously the nodes, whose types appear in the query pattern, in ascending order of their ranks. The drawback of these algorithms is that they must access every such node *at least once*, even though it does not participate in any occurrence. Motivated by this, an *indexed algorithm* [4, 21] utilizes a data structure that can be used to efficiently retrieve a particular ancestor/descendent of a node. Such an ability allows the algorithm to skip many nodes not involved in any occurrence and, therefore, to terminate much earlier.

In this paper, we do not attempt to attack general holistic twig joins. Instead, our focus is to improve the efficiency of those XPath queries that can be processed with NK search. As far as these queries are concerned, our method significantly outperforms all the solutions in the sequential category because (similar to indexed algorithms) it only needs to access a small number of nodes that may form an occurrence. Regarding the indexed category, the comparison is more subtle, mainly because the algorithms of [4, 21] are heuristic in nature, and are not accompanied by any non-trivial complexity analysis. We will experimentally compare our technique against the state of the art, *TSGeneric*$^+$ [21], of that category. Noteworthily, an advantage of our algorithm xpath (Section 4.1) is that, in practice, its cost can be accurately estimated by a query optimizer. This is not possible for [4, 21], as their behavior is sensitive to the data distributions.

We note that no existing algorithm has the performance characteristic pinpointed in Remark 2. The only approach that comes close to having the characteristic is TJFast [30], which is a sequential algorithm that needs to scan the nodes matching only the leaves of the query pattern. Unfortunately, the *extended dewey codes* that TJFast relies on can be as long as the height of the XML tree. The time of reading a node is proportional to the length of its extended dewey code. The length, unfortunately, is linear to the number of ancestors of the node, which can be asymptotically identical to the total number of nodes in the tree in the worst case. It is also worth mentioning that there exist some other methods [9, 24], just like ours, that are designed for certain special classes of XPath queries.

Another related topic is keyword search in XML databases. A bulk of the existing research [6, 10, 16, 20, 27, 28, 29, 35] explores various semantics of query results that is suitable for different scenarios. In this work, we showed the applicability of NK search to the GST semantics [12, 20, 23, 25]. This choice does not imply our preference of GST; in fact, the potential application of the NK operator to the other semantics is an exciting direction for future work. As mentioned before, the GST problem on trees is NP-hard, and remains so even if the goal is changed to finding an $O(\log^{2-\epsilon} n)$-approximate solution for arbitrarily small $\epsilon > 0$ [17], where n is the number of nodes in the data tree. The best known approximation ratio achievable in polynomial time is $O(\log n \log l)$ [14], where l is the number of query keywords (and can be as large as n). The algorithm of [14], which is based on linear programming, is highly theoretical and not appropriate for practical implementation.

In the database area, research on GST computation (e.g., [3, 12, 19, 20, 22, 25]) is largely motivated by the observation that the value of l can often be regarded as a constant in reality. In this case, the $l-1$ approximation ratio guaranteed by our solution (Lemma 6) can be (much) lower than $O(\log n \log l)$. A small l also considerably shrinks the search space for discovering the GST. This fact is leveraged in [20] to enumerate all the MCTs (defined in Section 4.2), and thereby, eventually come across the GST (which is also an MCT). While the method of [20] works on trees only, the approaches reviewed below apply to general graphs[1]. Algorithms for computing approximate GSTs (faster than extracting the GST with [20]) are presented in [3, 22]. Somewhat surprisingly, there is a dynamic-programming algorithm [12] for finding the *exact* GST, in even less time than the approximate methods of [3, 22].

The above approaches do not rely on pre-computation, whereas the BLINKS system [19] leverages a sophisticated access method constructed in advance to produce l-approximate GSTs efficiently. The most serious drawback of BLINKS, however, is that it occupies $\Omega(n^{4/3})$ space[2], where n is the number of nodes in the graph. For n at the order of millions, $\Omega(n^{4/3})$ amounts to duplicating the database 100 times, which is too expensive in many environments. Furthermore, the query algorithm of BLINKS is ad-hoc and has no interesting worst-case performance bound. Note that our result in Lemma 6 in fact dominates the performance of BLINKS, i.e., we guarantee a slightly better approximation ratio, with a *linear* space access method and worst-case efficient query time. It should be noted, however, that the improvement is made possible by utilizing properties of a tree (recall that BLINKS deals with general graphs). The work of [23, 25] considers the *steiner tree* problem, which is a special case of the GST problem where there can be only a single node in the data tree associated with each query keyword. Note that, while the steiner tree problem is NP-hard on graphs, it is not on trees, as is clear from the way that MCT is built from a vector in Section 4.2.

Finally, in the special case where only one distinct keyword exists, NK retrieval is similar to *nearest neighbor search on spatial networks*. In that problem, the data consist of a graph G and a set S of points, each located at a node of G. Given a node q of G, a query returns the point in S that has the smallest shortest-path distance to q. This problem has been well studied in various settings with different performance goals (see [11, 26, 31, 33] and the references therein). The existing solutions (i) perform Dijkstra-like expansion from the query point (e.g., [11]), (ii) pre-compute the answer for each node of G (e.g., [31]), or (iii) rely on specialized structures that leverage properties of spatial data (e.g., [26, 33]). In our con-

[1]Given a set of keywords, the GST in a graph is the minimum tree (i) whose nodes and edges come from the underlying graph, and (ii) that has the minimum number of edges among all trees satisfying (i). When the graph is a tree, this definition degenerates into the one in Section 4.2.

[2]This can be derived from Theorem 3 of [19] by observing that, $\sum_b N_b^2 + BP \geq n^2/B + B^2$, which is $\Omega(n^{4/3})$.

text, solutions of (i) degenerate into the BFT approach explained in Section 3.1, those of (ii) incur prohibitive space when the number of keywords is large, whereas those of (iii) are simply inapplicable to XML data.

6. EXPERIMENTS

This section empirically evaluates the performance of the proposed techniques. We used two real XML documents:

- *NBA*, which contains all the teams and players of the leagues during 1946-2004.
- *DBLP*, which includes all the conference papers during 1959-2010 collected by the DBLP website.

Figure 8a (8b) shows the part of the *NBA* (*DBLP*) schema that is relevant to the queries in our experiments. An asterisk indicates that the corresponding node can have an arbitrary number of siblings of the same type. For example, an `NBA` node can have multiple child nodes of type `league`. Table 1 lists the main statistics about each dataset.

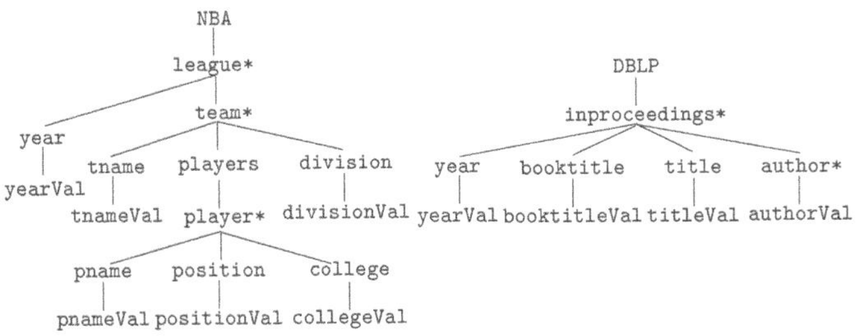

(a) (b)

Figure 8: Schemas of *NBA* and *DBLP* relevant to our queries

	NBA	*DBLP*
num. of nodes	135,940	17,501,788
num. of keywords	223,500	48,191,004
num. of distinct keywords	8,302	2,893,195

Table 1: Dataset statistics

We will first explore the characteristics of NK search, and then assess the usefulness of the NK operator in XPath evaluation and GST computation, respectively. Our experiments were performed on a computer that was running Linux, and equipped with an Intel DUO CPU at 3.0Ghz and 4 GB of memory. All the data were memory resident.

Performance of NK search. In our indexing scheme, named *TVP*, we followed the convention mentioned in Section 1.1 to associate nodes with keywords. Specifically, every node had its type as a keyword. Furthermore, if u is a value node, each word w in the value of u was taken as another keyword of u, after w was prefixed with the type of u (see Remark 1 of Section 4.1). The name of a person/team was always regarded as a single word. For instance, if u has type `pnameVal` and a value `Kobe Bryant`, then it carries a (prefixed) keyword `pnameVal:Kobe-Bryant`. Table 2 shows the space consumption of *TVP* and the raw dataset, while Table 3 gives the construction time of *TVP*.

The next experiment compares the query efficiency of *TVP* and the *BFT* algorithm described in Section 3.1. For this purpose, we report their performance on the (realistic) queries in Figure 9, each of which can be handled by a single NK operator. Queries denoted with a first letter N (D) were designed for *NBA* (*DBLP*). For each

	NBA	*DBLP*
TVP	3.8	972
raw dataset	2.4	807

Table 2: Space (mega bytes)

NBA	*DBLP*
< 1 second	< 2.5 minutes

Table 3: Construction cost of *TVP*

$NQ1$: Find the team of Shaquille O'Neal in 2000.
q = the `pnameVal` node with value Shaquille-O'Neal in the league 2000; w = `tnameVal`

$NQ2$: Were Shaquiile O'Neal and Kobe Briant in the same team in year 2000?
q = same as $NQ1$; w = `pnameVal:Kobe-Bryant`*; distance (of a positive answer) = 6*

$NQ3$: Same as $NQ2$ but in 2002.
q = same as $NQ1$ but in 2002; w and distance as in $NQ2$

$DQ1$: Find the conference name of "Holistic Twig Joins: Optimal XML Pattern Matching".
q = the `ptitleVal` node of the paper; w = `booktitleVal`

$DQ2$: Is Nicolas Bruno an author of the paper in $DQ1$?
q = same as $DQ1$; w = `authorVal:Nicolas-Bruno`*; distance = 4*

$DQ3$: Same as $DQ2$ but with respect to Jim Gray.
q and distance same as $DQ2$; w = `authorVal:Jim-Gray`

Figure 9: Query set for examining NK efficiency

query, Figure 9 clarifies the node q and keyword w of the corresponding NK operator. For a boolean query, the figure also points out the distance (to q) that the nearest w-neighbor should have in order to return a positive answer. For instance, the answer for $NQ2$ is "yes" if and only if the retrieved neighbor has distance 6 to q.

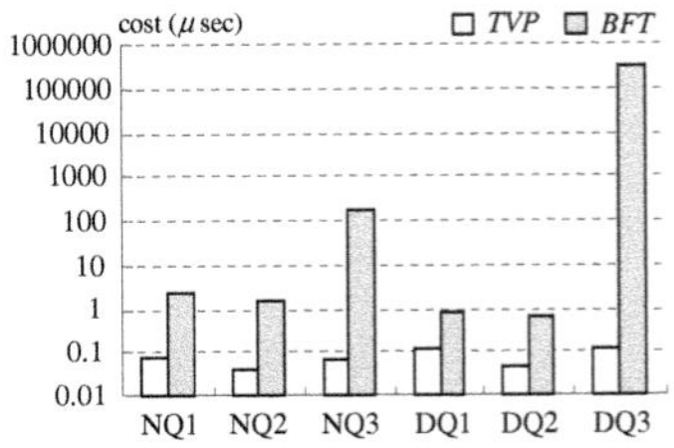

Figure 10: Cost of NK search

Figure 10 illustrates the cost of *TVP* and *BFT* for each query. Note that the vertical axis is in logarithmic scale, and has the unit of μ-second (= 10^{-6} second). *BFT* is especially slow for the boolean queries $NQ3$ and $DQ3$ with answers "no". This is expected because, for these queries, the retrieved neighbor has a large distance to the query node.

XPath evaluation. We proceed to assess the efficiency of the NK operator in answering XPath queries. Our technique integrated the proposed access method *TVP* with the `xpath` algorithm developed in Section 4.1. As discussed in Section 5, the existing algorithms for holistic twig joins can be classified into the *sequential* and *indexed* categories, with the solutions in the latter category significantly faster than those of the former. Therefore, we chose to compare *TVP* against the state-of-the-art indexed algorithm *TSGeneric*$^+$ [21].

Figures 11a and 11b explain the meaning and twig patterns of the queries examined, respectively. The box in each pattern signifies the anchor node chosen by `xpath`. Observe that $NQ7$ and $DQ7$ *violate* the anchor condition (i.e., Condition 2) in Section 4.2. Nevertheless, they are still reducible to NK search and, in fact, can be answered directly by the `xpath` algorithm *with no modification.*

For fairness, our implementation of *TSGeneric*$^+$ utilizes an inverted index to filter all the nodes that do not satisfy the keyword conditions. For example, for $NQ4$, only the `collegeVal` nodes

$NQ4$: Find the names of all players from Duke University.

$NQ5$: Find the names of all centers from the west division.

$NQ6$: Find the names of all players that came from Boston College but were in a team of the west division in year 1999.

$NQ7$: Find the teams where Hakeem Olajuwon and Charles Barkley were teammates.

$DQ4$: Find the titles of all papers by Jim Gray.

$DQ5$: Find the titles of the SIGMOD papers by Nick Koudas.

$DQ6$: Find the conferences of the papers by Divesh Srivastava that contained "XML" in the titles.

$DQ7$: Find the titles of the SIGMOD papers co-authored by Hector Garcia-Molina and Jennifer Widom.

(a) Query description

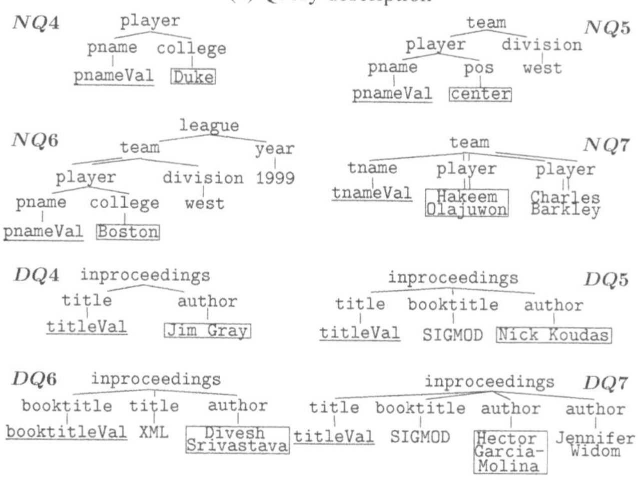

(b) Twig patterns

Figure 11: Query set for examining XPath efficiency

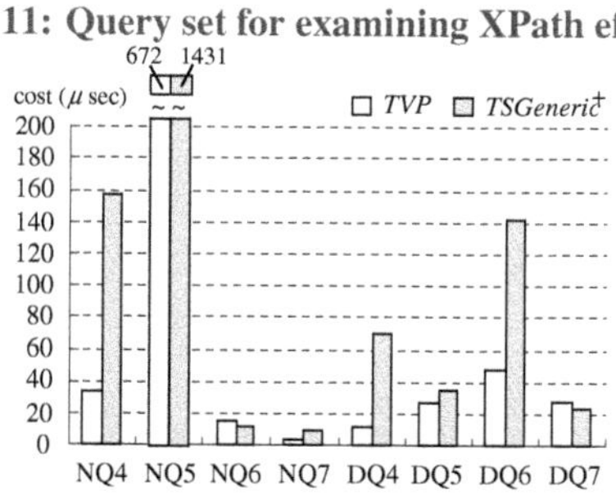

Figure 12: Cost of XPath queries

whose values are equal to `Duke` are considered, as opposed to all the `collegeVal` nodes (as proposed in [21]). This optimization reduces the average overhead of the original *TSGeneric*$^+$ by at least an order of magnitude. Figure 12 demonstrates the execution time of *TVP* and *TSGeneric*$^+$ for all queries. *TVP* lost narrowly in two out of the eight queries, but was at least twice faster in four queries.

GST computation. The final set of experiments investigate the efficiency and effectiveness of the NK operator in keyword search. Our approach combined the *TVP* indexing scheme with the `approxGST` algorithm in Section 4.2. We compared the approach against the dynamic programming algorithm of [12] (as reviewed in Section 5), hereafter denoted by *DP*. Recall that *DP* returns the *exact* GST. We evaluated the two methods only with *NBA*, as the excessive memory requirements of *DP* rendered it infeasible to run experiments with *DBLP* on our hardware. As the XML schema is irrelevant to keyword search, the *TVP* built here does not require the keyword prefixing explained earlier. In other words, each element node (as before) is associated with its type, whereas each

$NQ8$: {`Shaquille-O'Neal`, `Anfernee-Hardaway`}

$NQ9$: {`Shaquille-O'Neal`, `Anfernee-Hardaway`, `Orlando-Magic`}

$NQ10$: {`Shaquille-O'Neal`, `Anfernee-Hardaway`, `Orlando-Magic`, `2000`}

Figure 13: Query set for keyword search evaluation

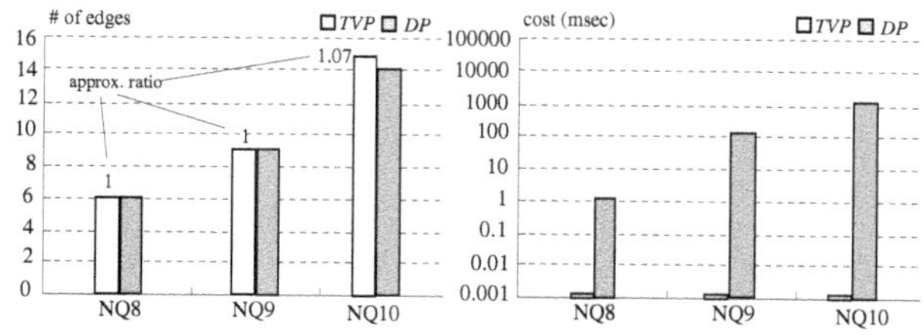

(a) Number of edges (b) CPU time

Figure 14: Quality and efficiency of GST computation

value node is simply associated with the words in its value. Figure 13 illustrates the queries executed.

Figure 14a depicts, for each query, the number of edges in the trees output by *TVP* and *DP*, respectively. It also indicates the approximation ratio of *TVP*. Notice that *TVP* returns the exact GST for $NQ8$ and $NQ9$, whereas its result for $NQ10$ has one more edge than the optimal solution. This shows that, in practice, the actual approximation ratio of *TVP* is much better than predicted by theory (Lemma 6). Figure 14b plots the CPU time of the two methods. *TVP* outperforms *DP* by two to five orders of magnitude. Moreover, unlike *DP* whose cost surges with the number of query words, the overhead of *TVP* is only slightly affected.

To better capture the usefulness of *TVP* in keyword search, Figure 15 presents the trees returned by *TVP* in the previous experiment. The result of $NQ8$ essentially states that `Shaquille-O'Neal` and `Anfernee-Hardaway` played for the same team at least once in their career. The tree of $NQ9$ implies that the above players were once teammates in `Orlando-Magic`. Finally, the $NQ10$ result indicates that `Shaquille-O'Neal` and `Anfernee-Hardaway` belonged to different teams in `2000`, neither of which was `Orlando-Magic`.

We conclude our experiments by comparing *TVP* and *DP* in searching for the top-k GSTs of $NQ9$ with $k > 1$. *TVP* now modifies `approxGST` as discussed in Remark 3. Note that *both TVP* and *DP* are approximate, namely, *DP* guarantees returning the top-1 GST, but such optimality is not ensured for $k > 1$. Figure 16a plots the result quality (in the number of tree edges) as a function of k. The two algorithms output trees with identical sizes when

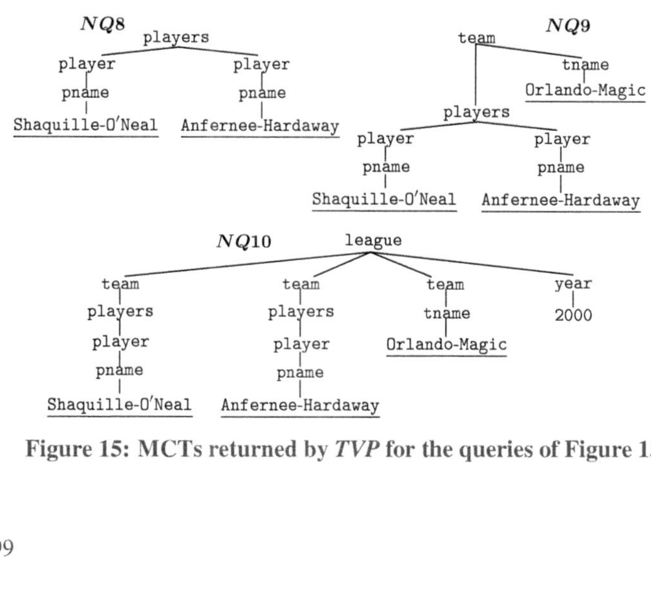

Figure 15: MCTs returned by *TVP* for the queries of Figure 13

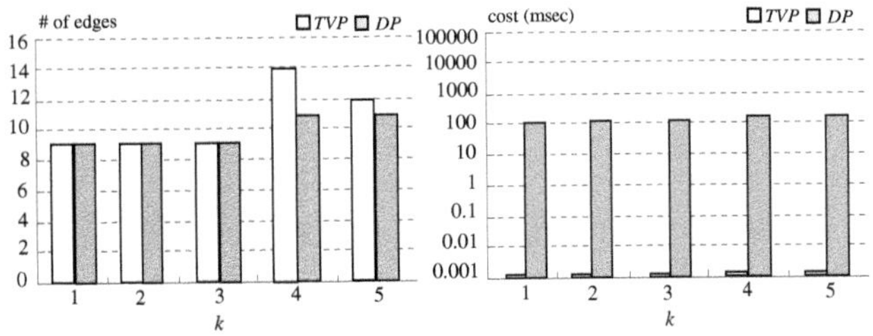

(a) Number of edges (b) CPU time

Figure 16: Quality and efficiency of top-k GST computation

$k \in [1, 3]$, whereas *DP* offers slightly smaller trees for $k \in [4, 5]$. Figure 16b gives their CPU cost. The overhead for both methods gradually elevates with k. *TVP* constantly outperforms *DP* by more than four orders of magnitude.

7. CONCLUSIONS

This paper proposed the problem of NK search on XML documents. Given a node q and a keyword w, an NK query returns the node in the XML tree that has the shortest distance to q, among all nodes associated with w. We solved the problem with a novel technique called tree Voronoi partition that gives rise to an indexing scheme with rigorous worst-case performance guarantees. Specifically, our scheme consumes linear space, and answers every NK query in time logarithmic to how many nodes carry the query keyword. We also demonstrated, both theoretically and experimentally, the usefulness of the NK operator in supporting several important tasks in XML databases. In particular, our technique results in (i) a new methodology for solving a wide class of XPath queries that is both asymptotically and practically efficient, and (ii) a fast algorithm for finding an approximate GST with bounded quality.

Acknowledgements

This work was supported by grants GRF 4173/08, GRF 4169/09, and GRF 4166/10 from HKRGC. We thank the anonymous reviewers for their constructive suggestions on improving the paper.

8. REFERENCES

[1] S. Alstrup, C. Gavoille, H. Kaplan, and T. Rauhe. Nearest common ancestors: a survey and a new distributed algorithm. In *SPAA*, pages 258–264, 2002.

[2] O. Berkman and U. Vishkin. Recursive star-tree parallel data structure. *SIAM J. of Comp.*, 22(2):221–242, 1993.

[3] G. Bhalotia, A. Hulgeri, C. Nakhe, S. Chakrabarti, and S. Sudarshan. Keyword searching and browsing in databases using BANKS. In *ICDE*, pages 431–440, 2002.

[4] N. Bruno, N. Koudas, and D. Srivastava. Holistic twig joins: Optimal XML pattern matching. In *SIGMOD*, pages 310–321, 2002.

[5] L. Chen, A. Gupta, and M. E. Kurul. Stack-based algorithms for pattern matching on dags. In *VLDB*, pages 493–504, 2005.

[6] L. J. Chen and Y. Papakonstantinou. Supporting top-k keyword search in XML databases. In *ICDE*, pages 689–700, 2010.

[7] S. Chen, H.-G. Li, J. Tatemura, W.-P. Hsiung, D. Agrawal, and K. S. Candan. Twig^{2}stack: Bottom-up processing of generalized-tree-pattern queries over XML documents. In *VLDB*, pages 283–294, 2006.

[8] T. Chen, J. Lu, and T. W. Ling. On boosting holism in XML twig pattern matching using structural indexing techniques. In *SIGMOD*, pages 455–466, 2005.

[9] Y. Chen, S. B. Davidson, and Y. Zheng. Blas: An efficient XPath processing system. In *SIGMOD*, pages 47–58, 2004.

[10] S. Cohen, J. Mamou, Y. Kanza, and Y. Sagiv. Xsearch: A semantic search engine for XML. In *VLDB*, pages 45–56, 2003.

[11] K. Deng, X. Zhou, H. T. Shen, S. W. Sadiq, and X. Li. Instance optimal query processing in spatial networks. *VLDB J.*, 18(3):675–693, 2009.

[12] B. Ding, J. X. Yu, S. Wang, L. Qin, X. Zhang, and X. Lin. Finding top-k min-cost connected trees in databases. In *ICDE*, pages 836–845, 2007.

[13] J. Fischer and V. Heun. Theoretical and practical improvements on the RMQ-problem, with applications to LCA and LCE. In *Annual Symp. on Combinatorial Pattern Matching*, pages 36–48, 2006.

[14] N. Garg, G. Konjevod, and R. Ravi. A polylogarithmic approximation algorithm for the group steiner tree problem. *J. Algorithms*, 37(1):66–84, 2000.

[15] N. Grimsmo, T. A. Bjørklund, and M. L. Hetland. Fast optimal twig joins. *PVLDB*, 3(1):894–905, 2010.

[16] L. Guo, F. Shao, C. Botev, and J. Shanmugasundaram. XRANK: Ranked keyword search over XML documents. In *SIGMOD*, pages 16–27, 2003.

[17] E. Halperin and R. Krauthgamer. Polylogarithmic inapproximability. In *STOC*, pages 585–594, 2003.

[18] D. Harel and R. E. Tarjan. Fast algorithms for finding nearest common ancestors. *SIAM J. of Comp.*, 13(2):338–355, 1984.

[19] H. He, H. Wang, J. Yang, and P. S. Yu. BLINKS: ranked keyword searches on graphs. In *SIGMOD*, pages 305–316, 2007.

[20] V. Hristidis, N. Koudas, Y. Papakonstantinou, and D. Srivastava. Keyword proximity search in XML trees. *TKDE*, 18(4):525–539, 2006.

[21] H. Jiang, W. Wang, H. Lu, and J. X. Yu. Holistic twig joins on indexed XML documents. In *VLDB*, pages 273–284, 2003.

[22] V. Kacholia, S. Pandit, S. Chakrabarti, S. Sudarshan, R. Desai, and H. Karambelkar. Bidirectional expansion for keyword search on graph databases. In *VLDB*, pages 505–516, 2005.

[23] G. Kasneci, M. Ramanath, M. Sozio, F. M. Suchanek, and G. Weikum. STAR: Steiner-tree approximation in relationship graphs. In *ICDE*, pages 868–879, 2009.

[24] R. Kaushik, R. Krishnamurthy, J. F. Naughton, and R. Ramakrishnan. On the integration of structure indexes and inverted lists. In *SIGMOD*, pages 779–790, 2004.

[25] B. Kimelfeld and Y. Sagiv. Finding and approximating top-k answers in keyword proximity search. In *PODS*, pages 173–182, 2006.

[26] M. R. Kolahdouzan and C. Shahabi. Voronoi-based k nearest neighbor search for spatial network databases. In *VLDB*, pages 840–851, 2004.

[27] Y. Li, C. Yu, and H. V. Jagadish. Enabling schema-free XQuery with meaningful query focus. *VLDB J.*, 17(3):355–377, 2008.

[28] Z. Liu and Y. Chen. Identifying meaningful return information for XML keyword search. In *SIGMOD*, pages 329–340, 2007.

[29] Z. Liu and Y. Chen. Return specification inference and result clustering for keyword search on xml. *TODS*, 35(2), 2010.

[30] J. Lu, T. W. Ling, C. Y. Chan, and T. Chen. From region encoding to extended dewey: On efficient processing of XML twig pattern matching. In *VLDB*, pages 193–204, 2005.

[31] A. Okabe, B. Boots, K. Sugihara, and S. N. Chiu. *Spatial Tessellations, Concepts and Applications of Voronoi Diagrams*. John Wiley & Sons Ltd., 2000.

[32] P. Rao and B. Moon. Sequencing XML data and query twigs for fast pattern matching. *TODS*, 31(1):299–345, 2006.

[33] H. Samet, J. Sankaranarayanan, and H. Alborzi. Scalable network distance browsing in spatial databases. In *SIGMOD*, pages 43–54, 2008.

[34] I. Tatarinov, S. Viglas, K. S. Beyer, J. Shanmugasundaram, E. J. Shekita, and C. Zhang. Storing and querying ordered xml using a relational database system. In *SIGMOD*, pages 204–215, 2002.

[35] Y. Xu and Y. Papakonstantinou. Efficient keyword search for smallest LCAs in XML databases. In *SIGMOD*, pages 537–538, 2005.

[36] J. Yang and J. Widom. Incremental computation and maintenance of temporal aggregates. *VLDB J.*, 12(3):262–283, 2003.

[37] N. Zhang, V. Kacholia, and M. T. Ozsu. A succinct physical storage scheme for efficient evaluation of path queries in xml. In *ICDE*, pages 54–65, 2004.

Efficient and Generic Evaluation of Ranked Queries

Wen Jin
Independent Consultant
james.wenjin@gmail.com

Jignesh M Patel
University of Wisconsin–Madison
jignesh@cs.wisc.edu

ABSTRACT

An important feature of the existing methods for ranked top-k processing is to avoid searching all the objects in the underlying dataset, and limiting the number of random accesses to the data. However, the performance of these methods degrades rapidly as the number of random accesses increases. In this paper, we propose a novel and general sequential access scheme for top-k query evaluation, which outperforms existing methods. We extend this scheme to efficiently answer top-k queries in subspace and on dynamic data. We also study the "dual" form of top-k queries called "ranking" queries, which returns the rank of a specified record/object, and propose an exact as well as two approximate solutions. An extensive empirical evaluation validates the robustness and efficiency of our techniques.

Categories and Subject Descriptors

H.3.3 [**Information Storage and Retrieval**]: Information search and retrieval—*search process*; H.2.4 [**Database Management**]: Systems—*textual databases*

General Terms

Algorithms, design, performance

Keywords

Top-k queries, preference queries, ranking queries

1. INTRODUCTION

Ranked query processing has many practical applications. For example, Google returns the search results as a sequence of URLs ranked by a scoring function. As another example, Amazon lists an ordered set of products based on how closely the products match the customer's keyword query.

1.1 Top-k Queries

Existing work on ranked query processing has largely focused on the top-k query, where the result of the query is a set of k objects ordered by scores that are generated by some scoring function. Typically, k is much smaller than the number of objects (n) in the underlying input dataset. A naive way to evaluate a top-k query is to score all the objects in the dataset, and then to select the k objects with the highest scores. However, this approach is expensive as it requires a full scan of the entire dataset, and it also requires examining the score of each object.

A key technique to evaluate top-k queries is the *threshold algorithm* (TA) [9]. A number of follow-on methods have built on the TA algorithm as it addresses a common category of top-k queries, where the scoring function is a monotone function composed by using various attributes associated with the objects in the input dataset. The TA algorithm employs a set of sorted lists, with one such list per attribute. The entries in a list are [objectID, attributeValue] pairs sorted by the descending attribute values. Each sorted list can be accessed sequentially (called *sequential access*, or *sorted access*), or can be accessed by the objectID from the other lists (called *random access*). A monotone function F [1] is used to aggregate the individual attribute values. The TA algorithm has an *early termination* criteria that allows it to stop accessing the lists, if some threshold conditions are met.

However, random access to the lists is generally more expensive than sequential access [17]. Consequently, the performance of the TA algorithm degrades rapidly when the lists are long, and hence have to be disk-resident. To address this issue, methods try to either reduce the random accesses or to remove the random accesses.

The number of random accesses can be *reduced* by scheduling these accesses only when needed [3–6, 15, 19, 21]. This approach requires extra computation to make I/O scheduling changes, but still provides no guarantee on the total number of random accesses.

Some of the random accesses can be *removed* by one of two methods: (a) Maintaining lower and upper bounds of scores in a buffer during sequential access, and pruning objects that are guaranteed to not be part of the top-k result [11, 12, 20, 23, 24]. Note that these techniques cannot use small bounded buffer sizes, as the worst case space requirement is $O(n)$, and the computation cost could be high. (b) The other method is to materialize views of the top-k results with different preference vectors [8, 14], or pre-computing convex/skyline layers [7, 13, 29]. These methods rely on expensive convex/skyline computation, and also require significant extra storage space. Furthermore, most of these methods are generally restricted to linear scoring functions.

[1] F is monotone if $F(a_1, \cdots, a_m) \leq F(a'_1, \cdots, a'_m)$ whenever $a_i \leq a'_i$ for every i.

SIGMOD'11, June 12–16, 2011, Athens, Greece.

List1	List2	List3
(t_5,29)	(t_4,24)	(t_4,27)
(t_4,27)	(t_0,22)	(t_5,24)
(t_2,23)	(t_2,20)	(t_7,24)
(t_6,22)	(t_5,19)	(t_8,20)
(t_1,21)	(t_3,17)	(t_6,17)
(t_3,19)	(t_7,16)	(t_9,16)
(t_7,18)	(t_9,16)	(t_1,9)
(t_0,16)	(t_8,12)	(t_0,5)
(t_8, 7)	(t_1, 6)	(t_3,4)
(t_9, 1)	(t_6, 3)	(t_2,2)
...	...	...

Table 1: Different sorted lists

List1	List2	List3
(t_5, 29)^1	(t_4, 24)^2	(t_4, 27)
(t_4, 27)	(t_0, 22)^3	(t_5, 24)
(t_2, 23)^4	(t_2, 20)	(t_7, 24)^5
(t_6, 22)^6	(t_5, 19)	(t_8, 20)^7
(t_1, 21)^8	(t_3, 17)^9	(t_6, 17)
(t_3, 19)	(t_7, 16)	(t_9,16)^{10}
(t_7, 18)	(t_9, 16)	(t_1, 9)
(t_0, 16)	(t_8, 12)	(t_0, 5)
(t_8, 7)	(t_1, 6)	(t_3, 4)
(t_9, 1)	(t_6, 3)	(t_2, 2)
...	...	...

Table 2: The order of accessing objects

Similar issues arise when evaluating top-k queries in subspaces. Although the TA-based methods can handle subspace top-k queries, they still incur random access during the query execution. Many existing methods process top-k queries in full space and subspaces separately, which requires rebuilding subspace views or indices on the requested subspaces. Some methods [25,26] can work with both the entire space or a subspace using the same index structure, but performance generally degrades as the dimensionality increases.

Unlike top-k queries which returns the top ranked objects, users sometimes request *ranking* query to a dataset by identifying an object of interest (e.g. the grade record for a student), and asking *what is the rank of that object*. This is a "dual" form of top-k queries. Such queries potentially require more computation than top-k queries as a user can ask for the rank of any arbitrary record. There is no existing work that examines this type of query.

1.2 Our Contributions

The main contributions of this paper are as follows: First, we propose a novel sequential access scheme to evaluate top-k queries based on the TA algorithm. The objects in the sorted lists used by TA are transformed into a table R' so that their sequential access order in the lists is maintained. The score computation of an object using sorted lists via both sequential and random accesses can now be reduced to only one sequential access to the tuple in R'. The *early termination* property is nicely held in R', thereby avoiding any unnecessary further accesses to the table. Our proposed technique is general and can be used with any threshold-based top-k method that builds off the TA algorithm.

Second, we extend the proposed sequential access scheme to answer top-k queries in subspaces, and on dynamic data involving batch updates.

Third, we propose the ranking query operation, and develop efficient algorithms to evaluate this operation using the same data structure that is used to evaluate top-k queries.

Finally, we evaluate our methods using both synthetic and real datasets, and also test our approach on a commercial DBMS. Extensive experimental evaluation demonstrates the robustness and efficiency of our proposed methods.

The remainder of this paper is organized as follows: Section 2 covers related work. Section 3 introduces our new top-k method. Extensions to this method to cover dynamic top-k queries and ranking queries is presented in Sections 4 and 5 respectively. Empirical results are reported in Section 6, and Section 7 contains our concluding remarks.

Round	SA	RA	Δ	Top-2 (Score)
1	t_5, t_4, t_4	t_5(2), t_4(1)	80	(t_4,78), (t_5,72)
2	t_4, t_0, t_5	t_0(2)	73	(t_4,78), (t_5,72)
3	t_2, t_2, t_7	t_2(1), t_7(2)	67 (stop)	(t_4,78), (t_5,72)
Subtotal	9	8		

Table 3: TA and Random Accesses, $F = a_1 + a_2 + a_3$

2. BACKGROUND AND RELATED WORK

In this section, we briefly summarize the related work on top-k queries. We begin by reviewing the TA algorithm.

2.1 Revisiting the TA algorithm

Given the sorted lists $L_1, \ldots, L_m$ for attributes $a_1, \cdots, a_m$ respectively, belonging to objects in a dataset on which we want to compute the top-k results, using a m-dimensional monotone scoring function $F(a_1, \cdots, a_m)$, the TA algorithm runs as follows:

(1) Access the sorted lists in parallel. As an object t is encountered under the sorted access in some list, use random access to probe the other lists and retrieve the remaining attribute values of that object t. Compute the overall score of object t. If this score is one of the k highest seen so far, then remember the object t and its score.

(2) Let s_i^L be the value of the last object seen under sorted access in L_i. Define the threshold value Δ as $F(s_1^L, \cdots, s_m^L)$. If the score of the current kth best object is worse than Δ, continue with step 1. Otherwise, return the current top-k objects as the answer.

As an example, given the sorted lists in Table 1, to answer a top-2 query on $F = a_1 + a_2 + a_3$, the TA algorithm first sequentially accesses the first row in each list, i.e. t_5, t_4, t_4 in L_1, L_2, and L_3 respectively, which incurs two random accesses for t_5 in L_2 and L_3 and one random access for t_4 in L_1 to compute their scores (72 and 78 for t_5 and t_4, respectively). To determine the termination condition, the threshold value is also computed using the values in the current row, which is 29+24+27=80. Since $72 < 80$, the access to the lists continues. Table 3 shows the steps in the execution of the TA algorithm, and the overall number of random (RA) and sequential (SA) accesses that are incurred by the TA algorithm.

Since the TA algorithm exploits the structural property that the objects' values in each attribute list is sorted, *early termination* is possible when accessing the sorted lists. However, even with early termination, TA has no limit on the number of random accesses that can be incurred. When the sequential access to the sorted lists reaches the depth of d, there are up to $m \cdot d$ sequential accesses and $m \cdot d \cdot (m-1)$ random accesses, as each sequential access leads up to $m-1$ random accesses.

2.2 Removing Random Access

Various recent efforts aim to remove the random accesses in top-k query evaluation by using extra storage space or using expensive convex/skyline computation. Many of these methods are also restricted to linear scoring functions.

The first category of these methods are the extensions to the TA algorithm, which includes J^* [23], LARA [20], NRA [9] and Stream-Combine [11]. The basic idea behind these methods is to maintain lower bound and upper bound scores of the objects in a buffer during the sequential accesses, and objects that cannot be in the top-k results are pruned using these bounds. However, the buffer size used in these methods is not bounded, which can result in space requirement for the buffer that is of the same magnitude as n (the number of objects in the input dataset). Recently, Pang et al. [24] provide an estimate for the portion of each list that has to be scanned, and devise a corresponding pruning mechanism, but their method is still a sorted list-based method: the cost of accessing multiple lists to collect scores and maintaining candidates could be high. Bansal et al. [2] study top-k query based on a linear monotone scoring function in the presence of hierarchies, and proposed a NRA-style solution with bounded buffer size. Their solution produces an approximate answer with a precision guarantee. Gurský et al. [12] improve the efficiency of NRA, but usually still cannot avoid the large bookkeeping cost.

The second category of methods employ a *layer-based* approach to compute convex hull or skyline layers, and read at most k layers to answer a top-k query, where each layer is potentially a large set [7, 13, 28]. These methods rely on expensive convex/skyline computation and are typically restricted to linear scoring functions. Some recent method, such as the Traveler [29] algorithm (which supports monotone scoring functions), can speed up the top-k evaluation based on dominant relationship, but it incurs a high overhead when the dimensionality increases.

The third category of methods employ a *view-based* approach by precomputing and materializing the top-k results with different preference/score vectors [8, 14]. A given top-k query is answered by reading tuples from the views with score vectors most similar to the given query. These methods usually work with linear scoring functions, and require extra storage space for the views. When the dimensionality increases, the number of views (hence the storage space) has to increase quickly to achieve a certain level of performance.

Some recent top-k query methods, including [25, 26], use index structures (i.e. R-tree and B-tree) to speed up the evaluation. These methods are also restricted by some limitations of these indexes. For example, the pruning technique in [25] is based on the "hierarchical containment property" of MBRs in an R-tree index. When the dimensionality increases, the MBRs become sparse and overlap each other, and the pruning process becomes less effective. The technique in [26] can answer top-k query on a subset of attributes. This technique requires expensive pre-computation (computational geometry and cluster analysis) to find a few useful reference points ("anchors"), and it maintains the L_∞ distance between every tuple and its closest reference point in a B-tree. Ilyas et al. [16, 18] introduce a rank-aware query optimization framework that integrates rank-join operators into relational query engines and propose a probabilistic model for estimating the cost of a rank-join operator.

2.3 Reducing Random Access

Instead of removing random access that are incurred during top-k processing, some methods, such as [1, 3–6, 15, 19, 21, 27], employ a strategy of sequential accesses with scheduled random accesses. These methods help improve the performance of top-k query evaluation, but in most cases, these methods add extra scheduling costs that has to be incurred during runtime (instead of the preprocessing stage). In addition, these methods have no limit on the number (or the cost) of random accesses.

The CA algorithm [9] builds on the TA algorithm and assumes that the random access in each list has the same cost. It defines a ratio between the random access cost c_r and the sequential access cost c_s to control the number of random accesses. One random access is only performed periodically after every $\lfloor c_r/c_s \rfloor$ sequential accesses. The work in [4, 21] assumes that different lists support random access at different costs, and obtains an initial candidate set by using sequential access. It then chooses the best candidates by using controlled random accesses.

Compared to the round-robin style of list accesses in the TA algorithm, several algorithms select a different order of lists to access. In [19], the algorithm chooses the next list to access such that the overall cost is minimized. The algorithm in [27] adapts to feature value distribution and minimizes the number of objects to be accessed. Bruno et al. [5] study the issue of adapting TA to database management systems, where the relational optimizer can take advantage of different strategies to efficiently evaluate queries. The *Minimal Probing* (*MPO*) algorithm [6, 15] considers a top-k query with a scoring function F that is defined on a set of predicates on different lists, and is an algorithm that aims to minimize the predicate evaluation cost.

The work in [1, 3] aims to find an earlier termination criteria when performing sequential accessing in the TA algorithm, thereby decreasing the corresponding number of random accesses. The scheduling methods in [3] are based on the knapsack optimization for sequential accesses and a cost model for random accesses. The work in [1] takes into account the previously seen positions in the lists and avoids re-accessing data items via sorted and random accesses.

3. A SEQUENTIAL ACCESS SCHEME

For the discussion below, assume that there are m sorted lists of n objects, with each list corresponding to an attribute a_i $(1 \leq i \leq m)$. We denote objects aligned at the same sequential position from each list as a *row*.

3.1 Motivation

As discussed in Section 2, an interesting and useful property of the TA algorithm is the *early termination* technique when accessing the sorted lists. However, when there are multiple sorted lists, it is either inevitable that random access is needed to compute the overall score of an object, or that the book-keeping (to bound the score) is very high and the required buffer size is very large [17].

Intuitively, the most natural way to avoid random accesses is to have the entire object with all the attribute values ready when computing the scores. There are two straightforward solutions to achieve this goal. (1) For any [objectID, attributeValue] pair in a sorted list, add other attribute values of this object. This augmentation incurs no additional random access for computing the scores of objects, and it also supports the early termination feature. But, this technique has a large storage space requirement ($O(n \cdot m^2)$), and hence is not practical; (2) Collect attribute values of each object from different lists into a tuple, adding these tuples to a table and answering any top-k query with this table. This transformation results in no random access under the table structure, which is more compact ($O(n \cdot m)$ space) than the sorted lists ($O(2 \cdot n \cdot m)$), but it loses the nice property of *early termination*, and needs to examine every tuple to find the k best objects.

tupleID	a_1	a_2	a_3	Indicator
t_5	29	19	24	1
t_4	27	24	27	2
t_0	16	22	5	2
t_2	23	20	2	1
t_7	18	16	24	3
t_6	22	3	17	1
t_8	7	12	20	3
t_1	21	6	9	1
t_3	19	17	4	2
t_9	1	16	16	3
...				...

Table 4: Preprocessing sorted lists into a table R'

Based on the above discussion, the ideal case is to abandon the disadvantages of both solutions and combine their advantages: i.e., design a solution that *reduces the random accesses, is space efficient and allows early termination.* We achieve this goal by designing a table that is transformed from the original sorted lists such that the search for the top-k answers does not need to scan the whole table. Below we describe this transformation and how it can be used to answer top-k queries.

3.2 Preprocessing Sorted Lists

By carefully studying how the TA algorithm works, we have invented a novel solution that satisfies the requirements stated above. Our solution is reusable and generic: once the preprocessing is finished, the original lists can be dropped, and the transformed table, R', can be used as an input for any subsequent top-k queries with any arbitrary monotone scoring function.

The following method is employed during the preprocessing step to transform the sorted lists into a table R': First, for any input object, all the attribute values that are scattered in different sorted lists are collected as a tuple in the transformed table. Second, the order of the tuples in R' matches the order in which they are visited for the first time using the TA algorithm. Third, we add one more attribute to each tuple to indicate the list number from which each tuple is first seen, and we call this attribute the *indicator* attribute. Hence the format of a tuple t in R' is defined as:

DEFINITION 1. **(Format of the Tuple in the Transformed Table R')** *Given an input object t with entry pairs $[t\_id, t(a_1)]$, ..., $[t\_id, t(a_m)]$ in L_1, ..., L_m respectively, where $t(a_i)$ $(1 \leq i \leq m)$ denotes the ith attribute value of t, its corresponding tuple format in R' is $(t\_id, t(a_1), \ldots, t(a_m), I)$. This tuple format is simply denoted as (t, I), where I is the indicator $(1 \leq I \leq m)$ to show the sorted list number from which t originated.*

For example, $(t_5, 1), (t_4, 2)$ in Table 4 denote two tuples and their *indicators*.

Algorithm 1 shows the pseudocode for creating the transformed table. Step 9 outputs the tuple t together with the sorted list number it comes from. This preprocessing step only needs to be performed once for all the objects. After obtaining R', the original lists can be dropped.

Without loss of generality, we choose the access order using the ascending list number, hence from the list L_1 (leftmost) to the list L_m (rightmost).

Algorithm 1 Preprocessing Sorted Lists

```
1: INPUT: SL = {L1, ..., Lm}
2: OUTPUT: table R'
3: Set row pos = 1
4: while access of SL is not finished do
5:    Move to row pos
6:    for i = 1 To m do
7:       Access current row object t in list Li
8:       if t has not been seen so far then
9:          Add (t, i) to R'
10:      end if
11:      pos = pos + 1
12:   end for
13: end while
14: return R'
```

As an example, given the sorted lists in Table 1, the tuples being collected are in the order shown with the superscript numbers (of the entries) in Table 2: $t_5 \rightarrow t_4 \rightarrow t_0 \rightarrow t_2 \rightarrow t_7 \rightarrow t_6 \rightarrow t_8 \rightarrow t_1 \rightarrow t_3 \rightarrow t_9$. By running Algorithm 1, we obtain the following tuples in R': (t_5,1), (t_4,2), (t_0,2), (t_2,1), (t_7,3), (t_6,1), (t_8,3), (t_1,1), (t_3,2), (t_9,3), as shown in Table 4.

Algorithm 1 can be implemented in $O(mn \log n)$ time as follows:

(1) Collect object IDs (together with their *indicator attributes*) by traversing the sorted lists row-by-row (with the same distinct sequential execution path as in the TA algorithm). The collected object IDs are in the same order as they appear in R'. Each time an object is encountered, we need to check whether it has already appeared before. This check is facilitated by using a bit array (with the assumption that the object ID is in the range of [0, n-1]). Whenever an object is seen, the corresponding bit is set to 1, if the bit is not set already. It takes the same constant time to check whether an object has already been seen via its corresponding bit. This step takes $O(n \cdot m)$ time. Lets assume that the list containing the collected object IDs is L.

(2) Next, sort each list (originally ordered by values) by the object IDs. This step results in the object IDs from each list having the same order of 0, 1, 2, ..., n-1. The same row from each list corresponds to exactly one object. This step takes $O(m \cdot n \cdot \log(n))$ time.

(3) Next, for each object ID in the list L, retrieve the object from the sorted objects produced in the previous step, and add the object with its *indicator* to R'. This step takes $O(n \log(n))$ time.

Overall, the time complexity of Algorithm 1 is $O(mn \log(n))$ (when typically $m << n$, the complexity is $O(n \log(n))$).

The *indicator* attribute for each tuple requires a modest amount of additional space – for example, with 1 additional byte of storage per input object, we can cover up to 256 attributes. The total space requirement of R' is $O(n \cdot m + n)$, which is more space-efficient than the original sorted lists.

3.3 Evaluating Top-k Queries

Next, we explore some useful properties of the transformed table R'. For the discussion below, let r'_i denote the ith tuple/object in R'.

DEFINITION 2. **(Distinct Batch Group (DBG))** *A distinct batch group is a group of consecutive tuples (t_i, I_i) in R' such that all the values of I_i are distinct in the group; i.e. no two objects in a DBG are originally from the same sorted list.*

As an example, in Table 4, $\{t_5, t_4\}$, $\{t_0, t_2, t_7\}$, $\{t_6, t_8\}$, $\{t_1, t_3, t_9\}$ (which are marked in different gray backgrounds) are four DBGs. However, $\{t_5, t_4, t_0\}$ is not a DBG since both t_4 and t_0 come from the second list.

LEMMA 1. *A DBG contains at most m tuples.*

PROOF. Tuples in a DBG are chosen from at most m sorted lists, and their list numbers have to be distinct according to Definition 2, leading to at most m tuples located contiguously in R' for a DBG. □

The DBGs for R' are constructed by starting from the first tuple, and it is easy to see that the transformed table R' is composed of a set of contiguous DBGs. To differentiate from other tables without such groups, R' is also called *DBG-Table* or *D-Table*. When a DBG contains less than m tuples, we call the list numbers not shown in this DBG as *missing indicators*.

Some partial orders in the original sorted lists are kept amongst the DBGs, as illustrated below.

LEMMA 2. *Given DBGs G_i, G_j in R', if $(t, I) \in G_i$, $(t', I) \in G_j$ and $i < j$ (i.e. G_i appears before G_j), then $t(a_I) \geq t'(a_I)$. Here I is the indicator value for t and t'.*

PROOF. The tuples t and t' are originally from the same sorted list as they have the same *indicator* attribute value I, and also the tuple t appears before the tuple t' in the sorted list due to $i < j$, hence the proof. □

For example, of the four DBGs in Table 4, $t_5(a_1) = 29$, $t_2(a_1) = 23$, $t_6(a_1) = 22$ and $t_1(a_1) = 21$ have the values indicated by the first attribute in descending order.

The sequential access of R' saves the extra cost of random accesses in the original sorted lists, as illustrated by the following lemma.

LEMMA 3. *The sequential access from r'_1 to r'_i in R' covers both the sequential and random accesses in the original sorted lists from the first access of r'_1 to the first access of r'_i.*

PROOF. This property can be easily derived from the construction process of R'. Sequentially accessing r'_1 to r'_i means that we have traversed all the rows in the original sorted lists till the row where r'_i first appears, just as TA's parallel access does. The TA algorithm incurs random access when an object is first seen to collect data from other lists to compute scores. In contrast, R' already has all the attribute values available for an object, so no random access is required. Meanwhile, the visited objects $r'_1, \ldots, r'_i$ cover all the distinguished objects that the TA algorithm visits. □

For example, the sequential accesses to objects t_5 to t_7 in Table 4 actually covers all the random and sequential accesses for the first three rows in Table 2.

Our top-k processing uses DBG as the basic unit for evaluating tuples. Each time a DBG from R' is picked, (at most m) tuples in this DBG are accessed, their scores are computed and compared with the score of the current kth best tuple to see if any better candidate exists. The algorithm does needs a method to detect the termination condition for the sequential access of R', for which it uses a threshold element that is defined as follows:

Algorithm 2 Sequential Top-k Algorithm (STA)

INPUT: *D-table* R', F, k
OUTPUT: k objects with highest $F(a_1, \ldots, a_m)$
Set position *pos* of R' to 1; Heap $h = \emptyset$
Initialize a distinct batch group G (with empty objects)
Initialize threshold element T with empty dimension attributes
while true **do**
  Get the current tuple $r'_{pos++} = (t, I)$ from R'
  Compute score of t and add/replace objects in h
  if $G \cup r'_{pos}$ is within a DBG **then**
    $G = G \cup r'_{pos}$
    Update $T_I = t(a_I)$
  else
    if $\exists i (1 \leq i \leq m)$, T_i is empty **then**
      $T_i = \max(\{t(a_i) | \ t \in G\})$
    end if
    Compute threshold value by $F(T)$
    if $F(T) <$ kth value in h **then**
      Break;
    end if
    Clear G; $G = G \cup r'_{pos}$
  end if
end while
OUTPUT objects in h

DEFINITION 3. **(Threshold Element)** *Threshold element T is a m-dimensional virtual tuple that can be used as a stopping condition by comparing with the temporary top-k tuples' scores during the access of R'. The ith attribute of T and the score of T is denoted as T_i and $F(T)$ respectively.*

The attribute values of the threshold element T are obtained following each DBG's sequential visit, and its score $F(T)$ is computed as well. The process to compute T is as follows: (1) Initially, for any tuple (t, I) in the first DBG G, fill in T_I with $t(a_I)$, and fill T_j $(j \neq I)$ with the maximum value of the jth attribute for $t \in G$ if none of the tuples in G has indicator value of j. For example, T for DBG $\{t_5, t_4\}$ in Table 4 is (29, 24, 27), the maximum value of the third attribute from $\{t_5, t_4\}$ is adopted for T_3. (2) In subsequent accesses, T is updated with the next DBG G' by only filling T_I with $t(a_I)$ for $(t, I) \in G'$. If there exists no such t for a specific *indicator* I, then T_I keeps its previous value. For example, T at DBG $\{t_0, t_2, t_7\}$ is (23, 22, 24), while at DBG $\{t_6, t_8\}$ it is updated to (**22**, 22, **20**). This is because t_6's *indicator* is 1, t_8's *indicator* value is 3, so T_1=$t_6(1) = 22$, T_3=$t_8(3) = 20$, and T_2 is still 22.

LEMMA 4. *The score of the threshold element decreases monotonically after each update.*

PROOF. Given two DBGs G and G', G' is the DBG next to G in R'. Based on Lemma 1, each DBG has at most m tuples. Hence: (1) We first assume G has m tuples. When accessing G, the threshold element T is updated by $T_I = t(a_I)$ for $(t, I) \in G$. If G' has m tuples, then when accessing G', T is updated by $T_I = t'(a_I)$ for $(t', I) \in G'$. Based on Lemma 2, $t(a_I) \geq t'(a_I)$ $(1 \leq I \leq m)$, T_I at G is no less than T_I at G', so $F(T)$ at G is no less than $F(T)$ at G'. If G' has m' $(m' < m)$ tuples, then when accessing G', T is updated by $T_I = t'(a_I)$ for $(t', I) \in G'$, $I \in \{m'$ *indicators* of $G\}$, and the values of T_J $(J \neq I)$ do not change (same as T_J at G). Since T_I at G is still no less than T_I at G', $F(T)$ at G is no less than $F(T)$ at G'. (2) If G has m'' tuples $(m'' < m)$. In this case, when accessing G, T_J $(J \notin \{m''$

Round	SA	RA	Δ	Top-2
1	t_5, t_4	0	80	(t_5,72), (t_4,78)
2	t_0, t_2, t_7	0	69	(t_5,72), (t_4,78)
Subtotal	5	0		

Table 5: Top-k in R', $F = a_1 + a_2 + a_3$

indicators in G}) is the same as T_J for the previous DBG G", which is no less than T_J at G'; for the other case of T_I ($I \in \{m''$ *indicators* in $G\}$), T is updated by $T_I = t(a_I)$ for $(t, I) \in G$, clearly, T_I is no less than T_I at G', so the claim still holds. □

The algorithm to answer a top-k query, called **STA**, is shown in Algorithm 2. This algorithm sequentially accesses tuples in R' (step 7) and computes scores (step 8) and the threshold score accordingly (step 16). Threshold element T is updated dynamically (steps 11 and 14) during the sequential access and the scores decrease monotonically (as illustrated by Lemma 4). For some DBG, there might exist *missing indicator* say i, and this means that a certain object that is in the original sort list i has been seen in other lists earlier according to Algorithm 1, and hence is collected by other preceding DBGs in R', which we have already visited so far in the algorithm. So inheriting the ith attribute value from the DBG seen before is the right choice. The process stops when the score of the kth best object in the heap (which only maintains top k scores so far) is found to be better than the current threshold (step 17).

To illustrate the process with an example, we show the steps in answering a top-2 query in Table 5. The first DBG of $\{t_5, t_4\}$ produces a threshold of 80 and the second DBG of $\{t_0, t_2, t_7\}$ produces 69, which makes the process stop with only 5 sequential accesses.

THEOREM 1. *Algorithm 2 correctly finds top-k answers.*

PROOF. First, we show that when the algorithm stops, any object after the last visited object in R' cannot be a top-k object. Assume that the last visited object in the algorithm is r'_d and the corresponding threshold element T has the values of $T_1, \ldots, T_m$. (1) For any object r'_j ($j > d$), the ith ($1 \leq i \leq m$) attribute value of r'_j is smaller than that of T if the ith attribute of T is filled using the indicator attribute value from an object r'_l ($l \leq d$). This conclusion can be derived since r'_j is first seen after r'_l when referring to the original parallel access process of TA, so r'_j cannot have its ith value greater than r'_l (otherwise, it should be at a position before r'_l in R'). (2) For any object $r'_j (j > d)$, if the value of T_i is not from any indicator attribute in a DBG, we know that this value must be from an object r'_l appearing before r'_j in the original sort list i, but the order of the lists' access in Algorithm 1 makes r'_l bear another sorted list number other than i as the indicator. From the two points above, we know that r'_j cannot have a score greater than the threshold element, hence it is not greater than the current kth object in the heap. On the other hand, for any object appearing before r'_d, we have a heap that guarantees that the top-k results are picked correctly. □

3.4 Evaluating Subspace Top-k Queries

The *D-table* structure works well for answering a top-k query on the full attribute space. Interestingly, it can also be adapted to answer top-k queries on *any* arbitrary (small) subset s of attributes. We now describe a new subspace-based top-k algorithm, which we call **SUBTA**, to evaluate top-k queries in any arbitrary subspace of the original m-dimensional attribute space.

Algorithm 3 Subspace Top-k Algorithm (SUBTA)

```
INPUT: D-table R', F, k, subspace s
OUTPUT: k objects of highest F(a_1, ..a_i, ..a_|s|), i ∈ s
Set position pos of R' to 1; Heap h = ∅
Initialize a DBG G in s (with empty objects)
Initialize threshold element T in s with empty attributes
while true do
  Get the current tuple r'_{pos++} = (t, I) from R'
  Compute score of t in s and add/replace objects in h
  if (I ∈ s) && (G ∪ r'_pos is within a DBG in s) then
    G = G ∪ r'_pos
    Update T_I = t(a_I)
  else
    if I ∈ s then
      if ∃j(j ∈ s), T_j is not assigned an indicator attribute value then
        T_j = max(T_j, max ({t(a_j)| t ∈ G }))
      end if
      Compute threshold value F(T)
      if F(T) < kth value in h then
        Break;
      end if
      Clear G; G = G ∪ r'_pos; CONTINUE
    end if
    Update T_j = max(T_j, t(a_j)) for j ∈ s
  end if
end while
OUTPUT objects in h
```

The SUBTA algorithm follows a similar procedure as Algorithm 2, with a change in the construction of the *threshold element*, which now turns into a subspace tuple. DBGs and F are also considered in subspace s. Instead of only accessing tuples with the indicators in s, other tuples in the DBG are evaluated as well, so as to pick the highest attribute value for the threshold. The pseudocode for SUBTA is shown in Algorithm 3.

Consider a top-2 query of subspace $s = \{a_1, a_2\}$ with $F = a_1 + a_2$ on R' in Table 4. The first DBG of $\{t_5, t_4\}$ produces a threshold of 53. The second DBG of $\{t_0, t_2, t_7\}$ produces a threshold of 45, which makes the process stops with only 5 sequential accesses, as shown in Table 6.

Round	SA	RA	Δ	Top-2
1	t_5, t_4	0	53	(t_4,51), (t_5,48)
2	t_0, t_2, t_7	0	45	(t_4,51), (t_5,48)
Subtotal	5	0		

Table 6: Subspace Top-k in R', $F = a_1 + a_2$

In contrast, when using the TA algorithm to process the same top-2 query for subspace $\{a_1, a_2\}$ as above on the sorted lists in Table 1, it is easy to see that 5 sequential accesses and 4 random accesses are required.

THEOREM 2. *Algorithm 3 correctly finds top-k answers for subspace s.*

PROOF. The proof is derived from the fact that the process presented in the algorithm can be mapped to the execution structure of the TA algorithm on a subspace. First, Algorithm 3 follows the same tuple access order as the TA algorithm. For the objects in R' that carry the indicators in the subspace s, they are accessed sequentially as from the original sorted lists (steps 9-11). For the objects seen by the TA method in the original sorted lists of s, but not seen in R' as carrying the indicators in s, these objects must have been visited by Algorithm 3 using indicators not in s (due to their high ranked values on those dimensions). This case is covered in steps 14-15 and step 23, where the threshold element values are updated. So the threshold computation (step 17) of Algorithm 3 does not miss any object in the sorted lists produced from s. This guarantees that there is no tuple after the stop position that can get into the top-k rank, just like in the TA algorithm. Second, all the tuples before the stop condition have been verified to qualify as a top-k result (step 8). Hence the proof. □

3.5 Discussions

Threshold algorithm typically works on separate sorted lists instead of the relational table on which the top-k query is being posed. The major challenge when working with a relational table is organizing the data in a certain order that satisfies the requirement of threshold algorithm. Our proposal solves this problem with the D-table structure that can completely replace the storage of the original table, but at the same time serves as a useful index structure. Our proposed technique can also be applied to other preference query types such as the skyline or ranking query methods.

The D-table can be used to progressively answer skyline queries since it provides a nice property of identifying skyline objects: if a tuple u appears after another tuple v in R', then u can not dominate v. The skyline evaluation can be performed with a sequential access of the D-table: if any existing skyline object dominates the threshold element of the current DBG, then the process stops. Interestingly, a similar technique like **SUBTA** can be easily adapted to subspace skyline computation as well.

The D-table can also be used to evaluate *ranking* queries. A naive solution requires scanning the entire dataset. Using D-table we can sequentially access DBGs to find out the number of objects ranking before the queried object. For details, please refer to Section 5.

4. PROCESSING BATCH UPDATES

Updates to a database often come in batches. In this section, we describe how our methods can be adapted to handle batch updates. Under this scenario, each batch is organized as a D-table. If continual small ad-hoc updates are detected (which results in very small D-tables), these small D-tables can be merged quickly into one larger D-table at runtime.

4.1 Top-k Queries on Batched D-Tables

As mentioned above, each input batch is organized into a D-table. If there are $v-1$ D-tables at a certain time, then the next incoming batch is put into the v-th D-table. To evaluate a top-k query, the top-k query is run on each of the D-tables $R'_1, \ldots, R'_v$, and the results are merged. To quickly find top-k objects among multiple D-tables, the key point is to access all the input tables in a selective way instead of a round-robin fashion, so as to avoid unnecessary data

Algorithm 4 Sequential Top-k Algorithm on Multiple R' Tables (STAM)

1: **INPUT:** *D-table* $R'_1, \ldots, R'_w$, F, k
2: **OUTPUT:** k objects with highest $F(a_1, \ldots, a_m)$
3: Initialize threshold elements T_i empty for each input R'_i
4: $firstRound = true$; heap $h = \emptyset$
5: Add each R'_i to table name list S
6: **while** true **do**
7:   **for** each R'_i from S **do**
8:     **if** $h.size() == k$ && $F(T_i) <$ kth value in h **then**
9:       Remove R'_i from S;
10:     **end if**
11:     **if** !firstRound && $F(T_i)! = \max\{F(T_j), T_j \in S\}$ **then**
12:       CONTINUE;
13:     **end if**
14:     Get next DBG G from R'_i
15:     Add/Update tuples from G to h, and maintain the top k scored tuples
16:     Update T_i with tuples from G
17:   **end for**
18:   $firstRound = false$
19:   **if** $S.size() == 0$ **then**
20:     break;
21:   **end if**
22: **end while**
23: OUTPUT objects in h

accesses. We propose a new method called **STAM** for this task. The pseudocode for STAM is shown in Algorithm 4.

The basic idea behind the STAM algorithm is to choose an input table that has the most potential to provide tuples with high scores for processing each time. This potential can be measured by the threshold value of the current DBG being accessed.

Algorithm 4 selects one table with the best DBG threshold each time (steps 11-14), then sequentially accesses the tuples in the corresponding DBG, and finally computes the scores and the new threshold values (steps 15-16). It stops accessing a table whenever its current DBG's threshold score is smaller than the kth best scores seen so far (steps 8-9). The whole process stops when all the tables meet the early termination condition during the execution (steps 19-20).

To handle deletions, the tuples being deleted can be temporarily marked as such, and they are skipped during the query evaluation. The top-k results are the correct results that reflect these deletions. The physical deletions can be executed when the D-tables are scheduled for maintenance.

4.2 Maintenance of D-Table

As described above, the STAM algorithm supports top-k queries on multiple D-tables that are present as a result of batch updates. However, when a large number of D-tables accumulate, it is preferable to merge these D-tables into a single table. A straightforward way is to collect all the data in the D-tables, build sorted lists, and apply Algorithm 1.

This straightforward way does not utilize any tuple order information kept in the D-tables. With the ordered tuples, sorted lists can be restored from each D-table incrementally by accessing each DBG and merging them at the same time. The merge operation is carried out by picking the proper tuples from the sorted lists and outputting them to the merged D-table. More specifically, each dimension from the sorted lists built so far is iterated over and compared. The higher value in a dimension indicates that the corresponding tuple should be selected and outputted. The smaller value is left

Algorithm 5 Approximate Ranking Algorithm I (ARA1)

1: **INPUT:** table R, F, q, ϵ, δ
2: **OUTPUT:** $aRank(q)$
3: Initialize $N = 0$; $X = 0$
4: Compute the score $F(q)$.
5: **while** R not finish accessing **do**
6:   Sequential access next tuple p
7:   N++
8:   Compute score $F(p)$
9:   Compare $F(q)$ with $F(p)$
10:   **if** $F(p) > F(q)$ **then**
11:     X++
12:   **end if**
13:   **if** $N \geq \frac{3\ln(2/\delta)}{\epsilon^2}$ **then**
14:     break;
15:   **end if**
16: **end while**
17: $aRank(q) = \frac{X}{N} \cdot n$
18: return $aRank(q)$

Algorithm 6 Approximate Ranking Algorithm II (ARA2)

INPUT: D-table R', F, q, ϵ, δ
OUTPUT: $aRank(q)$
$aRank(q) = 1; N = \min\{n, \frac{3\ln(2/\delta)}{\epsilon^2}\}; Count = 0; T = \emptyset$
while R' not finish accessing **do**
  Sequential access R' to find next DBG G
  Update T for G; Compute score $F(T)$
  for $p \in G$ **do**
    if $F(p) > F(q)$ **then**
      $aRank(q)$++
    end if
    if $F(T) < F(q)$ **then**
      return $aRank(q)$;
    end if
    $Count$++
    if $Count \geq N$ **then**
      return $\frac{aRank(q)}{N} \cdot n$
    end if
  end for
end while

for comparison in the next round. The whole process continues until all the tuples are outputted. Using this merging process, the tuple indicators in the final merged D-table could be different from those in the original D-tables.

Alternatively, we can keep the indicators of tuples intact as long as the merged table satisfies the partial order property described in Lemma 2. During the merging, we only compare those tuples with the same indicator from the D-tables, and output the larger ones to the merged table each time. This method avoids the extra effort of recovering the sorted lists and can be more cost-effective.

5. EXTENSION ON RANKING QUERY

As mentioned in Section 1, *ranking queries* can be viewed as the "dual" form of top-k queries, since they find the rank of a specified query object. The *ranking query* operation is defined as follows: Given a dataset R of n objects, a query object $q \in R$, and a monotone scoring function F, a ranking query returns the rank of q: $Rank(q) = |\{t|F(t) > F(q), t \in R, t \neq q\}|$. If multiple objects in R have the same F-score as q, then they all have the same rank as q.

5.1 Exact Algorithm

In this section, we present an (exact) ranking algorithm that uses our new sequential access scheme to answer *ranking queries*. This algorithm is called **SRA** (Sequential Ranking Algorithm), and can be derived from **STA** with the following modification: during the sequential access of the DBGs, the scores of the tuples within the scanned DBG are compared with the score of the queried tuple, instead of the kth score in the heap. The number of tuples with higher score than the queried tuple is counted. The scan stops when the threshold score becomes smaller than the query tuple's score, and the count value is outputted as the rank. In the interest of space, we omit the pseudocode for the **SRA** algorithm.

For the ranking query of t_4 in the sample dataset shown in Table 4, SRA returns the rank of 1 with only 5 sequential accesses, compared to 10 accesses by the naive solution (which simply scans the entire dataset and computes the final rank).

5.2 Approximate Algorithms

Besides the exact solution for *ranking queries*, we also provide two approximate solutions. The use of approximation is similar to quantile statistics in database systems, which retrieves the ϕN-th ($\phi \in [0, 1]$) smallest F-value of the objects for a continuous function F.

The problem definition for the approximate rank query operation is as follows: Given a dataset R, a query object $q \in R$, a monotone scoring function F, a precision threshold ϵ and a probability threshold δ, $0 \leq \epsilon \leq 1$, $0 \leq \delta \leq 1$, $aRank(q)$ is the approximate rank of q such that: $\Pr[|aRank(q) - Rank(q)| \leq \epsilon \cdot Rank(q)] > 1 - \delta$.

Note that the notion of $aRank(q)$ provides the user the (ϵ, δ)-approximation [22] to rank the query tuple. Smaller ϵ and δ values implies a more precise rank of q, and generally higher computational costs.

The first algorithm, called **ARA1** is shown in Algorithm 5. This algorithm is based on the (ϵ, δ)-approximation scheme, and returns an approximate rank of the input tuple by sampling N tuples. In this algorithm, sampling N tuples uniformly at random from a table R is equivalent to sequentially choosing N tuples from R. Here, N is a parameter associated with ϵ and δ. The sampled tuples are examined (steps 6–9) and those with higher scores than q's are counted (steps 10–12). After examining the N samples, the algorithm outputs the count multiplied by n/N (steps 17–18).

THEOREM 3. *Algorithm 5 correctly finds the (ϵ, δ)-approximation of $Rank(q)$ for R with i.i.d.*

PROOF. Suppose that the rank of q is $Rank(q)$. Let X_i be 1 if $F(p) > F(q)$ for the ith tuple p in R, and 0 otherwise. Then $X = \sum_{i=1}^{N} X_i$. Since $\Pr[X_i = 1] = \frac{Rank(q)}{n}$, $\Pr[X] = N \cdot \frac{Rank(q)}{n}$. Hence, by linearity of expectations, $E[aRank(q)] = \frac{E[X]}{N} \cdot n = \frac{N \cdot \frac{Rank(q)}{n}}{N} \cdot n = Rank(q)$. Based on Theorem 10.1 in [22]: $X_1, \ldots, X_s$ be independent and identically distributed (i.i.d.) indicator random variables, with $\mu = E[X_i]$. If $s \geq \frac{3\ln(2/\delta)}{\epsilon^2 \cdot \mu}$, then $\Pr\left(\left|\frac{1}{s}\sum_{i=1}^{s} X_i - \mu\right| \geq \epsilon\mu\right) \leq \delta$, we conclude that X/N gives an (ϵ, δ)-approximation of $Rank(q)/n$, so Algorithm 5 outputs an (ϵ, δ)-approximation of $Rank(q)$, when $N \geq \frac{3\ln(2/\delta)}{\epsilon^2} \cdot \frac{n}{Rank(q)} \geq \frac{3\ln(2/\delta)}{\epsilon^2}$. □

The second approximate algorithm, called **ARA2**, is shown in Algorithm 6. This algorithm is a hybrid of the exact sequential ranking technique and the sampling technique, and thus combines the strengths of both.The idea behind the ARA2 algorithm is that if we can find the *exact rank* by examining less than N tuples, then we output this rank, otherwise we just output the approximate rank. Under the same input ϵ, δ, Algorithm 6 accesses at most the same number of tuples as Algorithm 5 but can often achieve better results than Algorithm 5 since it contains exact rank computation during the first N tuples.

6. EXPERIMENTAL EVALUATION

In this section, we present results from an extensive empirical evaluation of our proposed methods.

For top-k query processing, we compare our method STA with a few state-of-the-art TA/TA-based algorithms including TA [9], 3P-NRA [12] (an improved version of the NRA algorithm), BPA [1], IO-Topk (KSR-Last-Ben scheme) [3] and TBB [24]. We chose these methods since they are all generic algorithms and work with any monotone scoring function. We also compare our method with a most recent layer-based approach PL-Index [13] since it outperforms other existing layer/view based methods, despite its restriction to linear scoring functions. We further compare our SUBTA algorithm with the SUB-TOPK [26] algorithm for subspace top-k query evaluation.

The top-k query evaluation method STAM for batch updates is also compared with the methods listed above, but we assume that all the data is available as a single input to the other methods, as these other methods do not have any specific method for batch updates. The ranking query evaluation method SRA is compared with the naive full-scan based solution, and the algorithms ARA1 and ARA2.

All the above methods are implemented in C++ and the experiments are performed on a 3.0 GHz Intel Pentium D machine with 2GB RAM, running Windows Vista, and a 250 GB SATA Seagate disk. All reported results here are from cold runs that start with the data originally on the disk. Sorted lists and transformed D-tables are stored in the file system for the experiments.

6.1 Evaluation Criteria

In order to make a consistent comparison with previous work on TA-based algorithms, we follow the same evaluation criteria in [1,3,9,10], which adopts an execution cost function $C = a_s + c_r/c_s \cdot a_r$, where c_s and c_r are the costs of a single sorted access and random access respectively, and a_s and a_r are the number of sorted access and random access respectively. The ratio c_r/c_s changes depending on different ways in which the data is stored and accessed. The cost C essentially represents the I/O cost in terms of the number of sorted access by converting random access into the equivalent number of sorted access. We also measure the raw query response time since it reflects the overall performance from which we can observe some interesting aspects of the algorithms (e.g. I/O bound or computation intensive). For the PL-Index method, we measure and compare with its actual response time, as this method does not organize data as sorted lists per attribute. We use a weighted sum score functions in all the experiments.

6.2 Test Data

We use two categories of datasets: (a) Synthetic datasets are generated to explore the effect of different parameters such as cardinality, dimensionality and data distributions (uniform and correlated). The cardinality of synthetic datasets varies from 200,000 to 5,000,000, and the dimensionality varies from 4 to 16; (b) The real Forest CoverType dataset is from UCI (archive.ics.uci.edu/ml). This dataset contains 581,012 objects with 54 attributes, including 10 quantitative attributes and 44 binary attributes. We randomly select 6 quantitative attributes as the ranking attributes (and values for these attributes are used as sorted lists in the experiment). The default testing parameter settings for these datasets are shown in Table 7.

Parameter	Default Setting
#objects in the synthetic input dataset	500,000
#dimensions	6
Data distribution	Uniform
k (for top-k query)	50
Ratio c_r/c_s	100

Table 7: Default parameter settings

Method	Response Time (secs)	Execution Cost (C)	# Distinct Objects Accessed
TA	7.78	24,905,114	245,858
3P-NRA	11.25	2,996,820	500,000
BPA	8.2	24,903,095	285,838
IO-Topk	7.3	2,705,500	472,273
TBB	6.3	2,966,300	480,821
STA	0.09	245,862	245,862

Table 8: Results under the default setting

To investigate the real effect of our proposed sequential access scheme, a commercial DBMS is also used to store the transformed *D-table* R', and an Index Organized Table (IOT) in the DBMS is used to store the whole tuple set (indexed by tuple id) for supporting native SQL top-k query. ODBC is used to connect and access the data stored in the DBMS.

6.3 Evaluating Top-k Queries

6.3.1 Test Results under the Default Setting

We use the default parameters in Table 7 to test STA and the other TA-based algorithms. As shown in Table 8, STA outperforms other TA-based algorithms by 1-2 order of magnitude. The number of distinct objects that STA visits is almost the same as that of TA, but it does not incur any random access during top-k query processing. So the STA algorithm outperforms the TA algorithm by roughly c_r/c_s times.

The TBB and the IO-Topk algorithms follow next with similar performance for both the response time and the execution cost. The BPA and the TA algorithms come after them in both of these two aspects. The 3P-NRA algorithm, which does not have any random access, is CPU intensive due to the large amount of book-keeping and score bounds checks that it has to incur, and hence has poor run time.

6.3.2 Scalability Testing

In this section, we evaluate the impact of various factors, including the value of k, input cardinality, number of dimensions, and data distribution, on the execution cost C and the

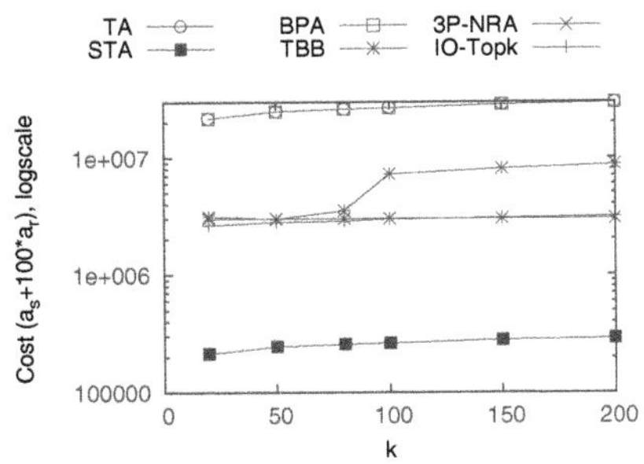

Figure 1: Top-k query evaluation cost for varying k (synthetic uniform dataset)

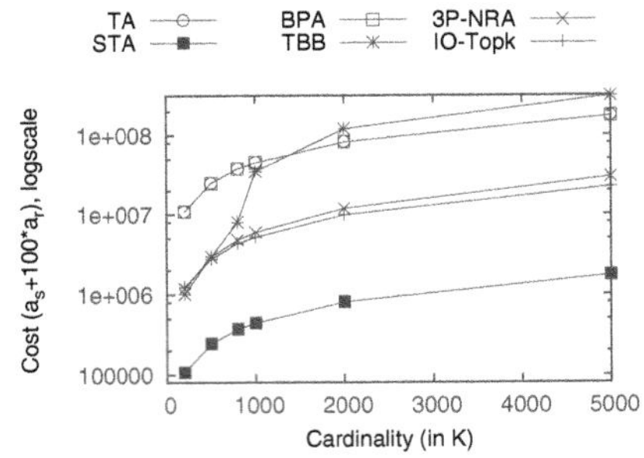

Figure 2: Top-k query evaluation cost for varying input cardinalities (synthetic uniform dataset)

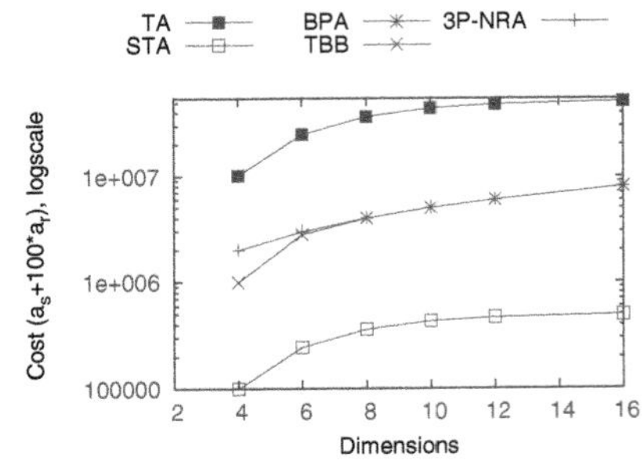

Figure 3: Top-k query evaluation cost for varying dimensionality (synthetic uniform dataset)

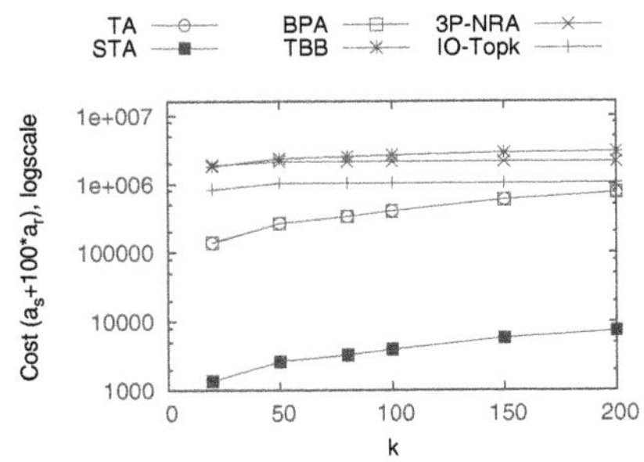

Figure 4: Top-k query evaluation cost for varying k (synthetic correlated dataset)

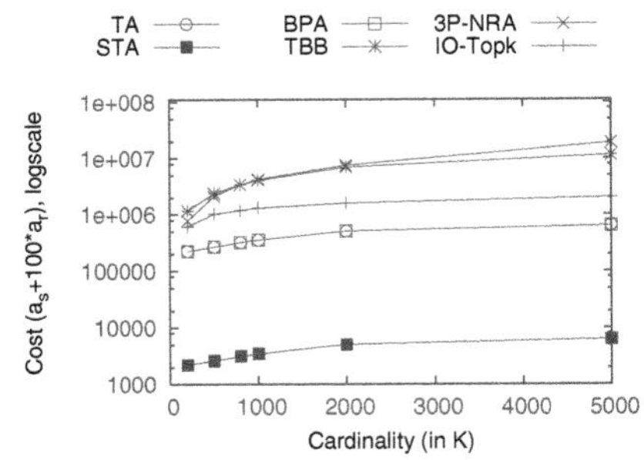

Figure 5: Top-k query evaluation cost for varying input cardinalities (synthetic correlated dataset)

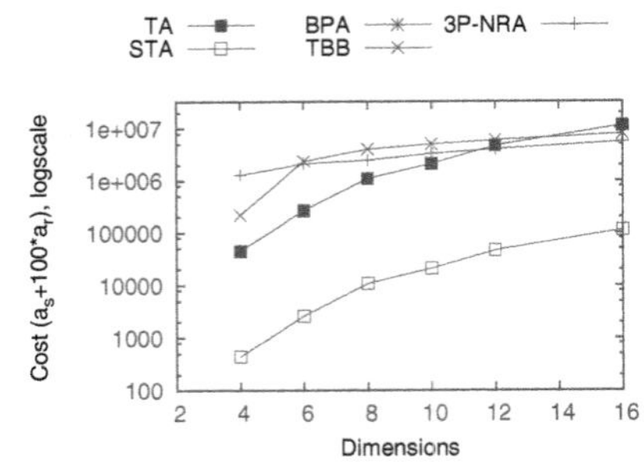

Figure 6: Top-k query evaluation cost for varying dimensionality (synthetic correlated dataset)

actual response time. While we have exhaustively examined the impact of these factors on both execution cost C and the actual response time, in the interest of space we only present some representative results.

Execution Cost on Uniform Data: We first study the effect of k on the execution cost. Figure 1 shows the execution costs (C) of the top-k query when k changes from 20 to 200, while the other parameters are set as in Table 7. As can be seen, the execution costs of all the methods increase as the value of k increases. In general, the IO-Topk, 3P-NRA and TBB algorithms outperform the TA and BPA algorithms by a big ratio, but the STA algorithm again far outperforms all the other methods.

Next, we change the cardinality of the uniform dataset from 200,000 to 5,000,000, with the other parameters set as in Table 7. As shown in Figure 2, when the cardinality increases, the overall cost increases as the values become more distributed. Similar to the results presented in Figure 1, the STA algorithm outperforms the other algorithms.

Next, we vary the dimensionality from 4 to 16, with the other parameters using the default setting. These results are shown in Figure 3. In this figure, we do not show the results for the IO-Topk algorithm, as its execution costs are much higher than the other methods. From Figure 3, we observe that the STA algorithm is 1 to 2 order of magnitude more efficient than the other methods.

Execution Cost on Correlated Data: We also conduct the experiments above with correlated datasets. Figure 4 shows the result of the test with respect to different k values. We observe that the cost under this distribution is smaller than with the corresponding uniform dataset, since sequential access typically stops earlier with the correlated data. Compared to Figure 1, in most cases the query cost with the correlated dataset is more sensitive to the value of k, especially when k gets larger. Again, the STA algorithm is far more efficient than the other methods.

Figure 5 shows the results with varying input cardinalities, which exhibits a similar behavior (to the uniform case) in terms of comparing the STA algorithm with the other methods. However, the more flattened curve in Figure 5 indicates that cardinality has a lower impact on the cost in the correlated dataset than in the uniform dataset.

The results with increasing dimensionality from 4 to 16 on the correlated dataset are shown in Figure 6. Again, the results for the IO-Topk algorithm are omitted as it has much higher costs. From this figure, it is clear that the STA algorithm incurs a far smaller cost than the other methods, and also scales well with increasing number of dimensions.

Response Time on Uniform Data: In this experiment, we examine the impact on the actual response time as we change the cardinality of the uniform dataset from 200,000 to 5,000,000. From Figure 7, we observe that the response time increases as the input cardinality increases. The STA algorithm is still 1-2 orders of magnitude faster than the remaining TA-based methods as it avoids random I/O accesses during top-k query processing.

Response Time of STA vs SQL on Uniform Data: Many commercial DBMSs now natively support SQL top-k queries. In this experiment we compare this native implementation with the STA algorithm, on the uniform dataset with input cardinalities varying from 200,000 to 5,000,000. The SQL top-k query is:

```
SELECT * FROM (SELECT ID, rank()
OVER (ORDER BY (col1+col2+col3+col4+col5+col6)) DESC rnk
FROM TAB1) WHERE rnk <= 50
```

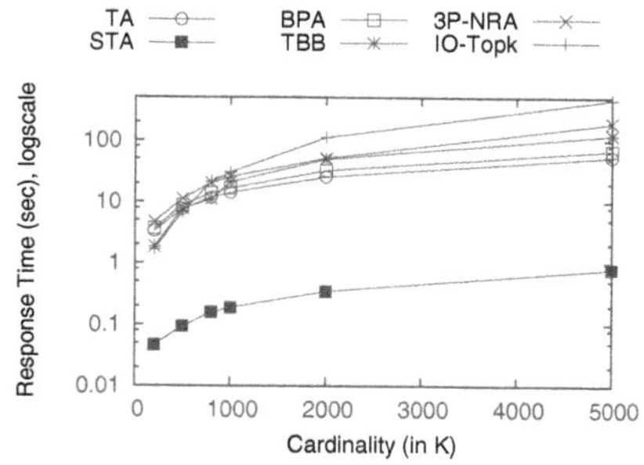

Figure 7: Top-k query evaluation time for varying input cardinalities (synthetic uniform dataset)

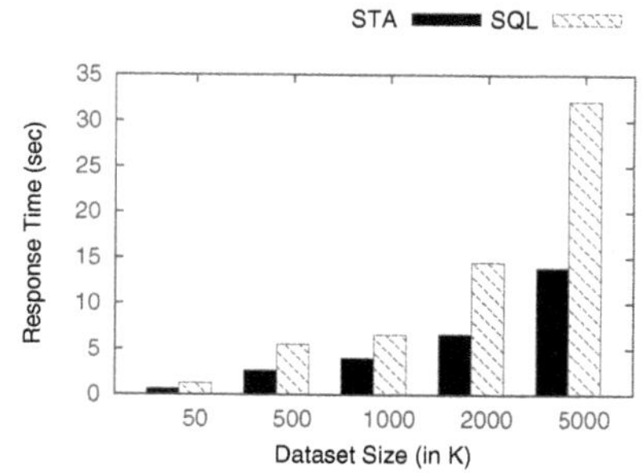

Figure 8: SQL vs STA (synthetic uniform dataset)

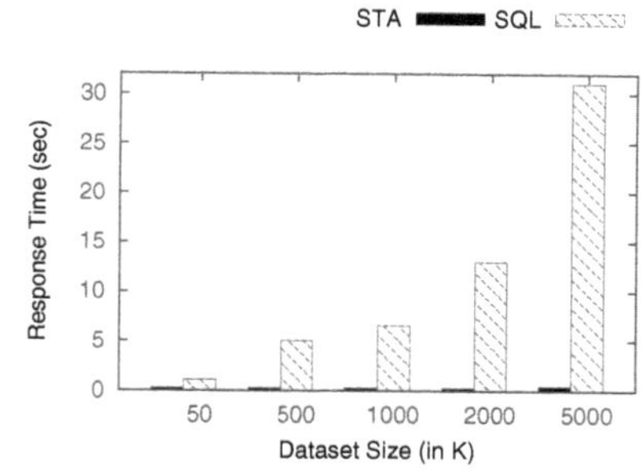

Figure 9: SQL vs STA (synthetic correlated dataset)

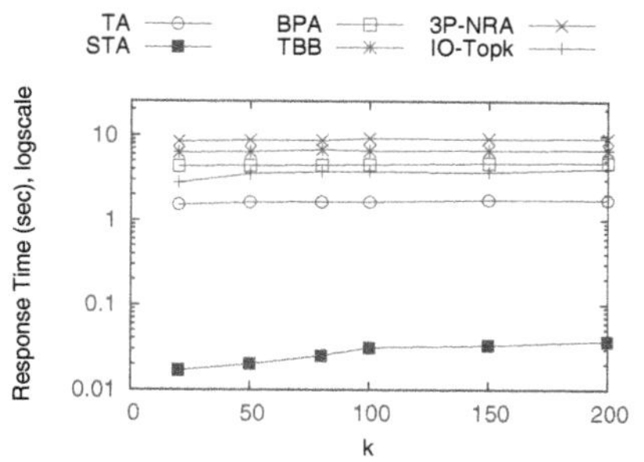

Figure 10: Top-k query evaluation time for varying k (real dataset)

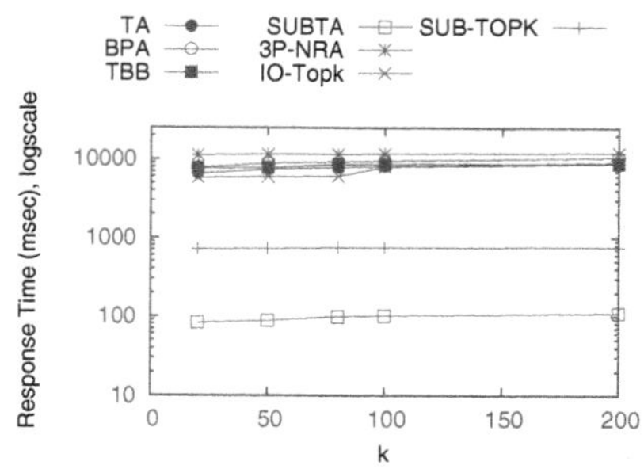

Figure 11: Top-k subspace-query evaluation time for varying k (synthetic uniform dataset)

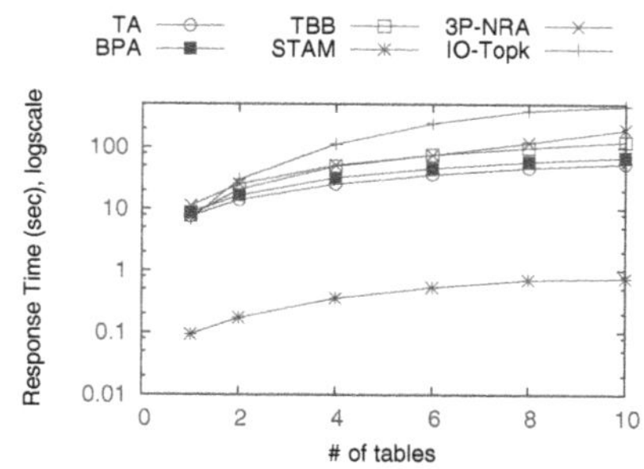

Figure 12: Top-k query evaluation time vs # of tables (synthetic uniform dataset)

The results of this experiment are shown in Figure 8. As can be seen in this figure, the STA method far outperforms the native SQL implementation, even though the STA method is going through the relatively slow ODBC interface to connect and access data in the DBMS.

Response Time of STA vs SQL on Correlated Data: The previous test was also carried out on the correlated dataset (with the same cardinality settings as the uniform dataset). These results, plotted in Figure 9, show that the STA method has a higher relative performance gain (compared to the uniform dataset), as it can stop much earlier on correlated data compared to the uniform dataset.

Response Time on the Real Data: Figure 10 shows the actual response time on the real dataset, when varying the parameter k. Similar to the synthetic dataset case, the STA method is again far more efficient than the other TA-based methods.

Response Time of Subspace Top-k on Uniform Data: To test the performance of our proposed method SUBTA, we use the synthetic uniform dataset, then randomly pick 10 different subspaces of attributes (with dimensionality from 2 to 6, amongst $2^5 = 32$ subspaces), and finally measured the average response time. The results, shown in Figure 11, demonstrate that the SUBTA method is faster than the other methods. The reason for this higher performance is that in the case of subspace query, even though sometimes SUBTA might (sequentially) access more tuples than the other methods, these additional accesses are compensated by the larger cost savings from not using any random I/O accesses during the top-k query processing.

Response Time of Dynamic Top-k on Uniform Data: Next, we test the performance of top-k queries when there are batch updates in the form of D-Tables. In this test, to test the performance of the STAM method, we start with the initial table of size 500,000, with 6 dimensions, and incrementally add one more D-table each time of the same size. For the tests with the other methods, we simply use the combined data from the multiple D-Tables as the input. The results for the uniform dataset are shown in Figure 12. From this figure, we can see that the STAM method clearly outperforms the other methods. By comparing with Figure 7, we observe that the performance of the STAM method is very similar to the STA method for the case where all the data is organized in one (bigger) D-Table.

6.3.3 Comparison with the Layer-based Method

We also compared the STA method with the layer-based PL-Index method by varying the cardinality from 100,000 to 1,000,000, while keeping other parameters at their default values. As shown in Figure 13, both methods have similar performance when the cardinality is 100,000, but the PL-Index method is significantly slower when the cardinality increases. This behavior is because the PL-Index method consists of (sub)layered convex skyline – when the cardinality of the dataset increases, more objects become skylines (and the number increases more significantly when the dimensionality grows), therefore the (sub)layer size (index size) increases, and the time spent searching for qualified top-k candidates in the index increases as well.

We have also compared the preprocessing time of both methods for varying cardinalities. Figure 14 shows that the PL-Index method incurs a higher preprocessing cost than the STA method, since it incurs expensive costs ($O(n^2)$) to compute both the convex hull and the skylines [13].

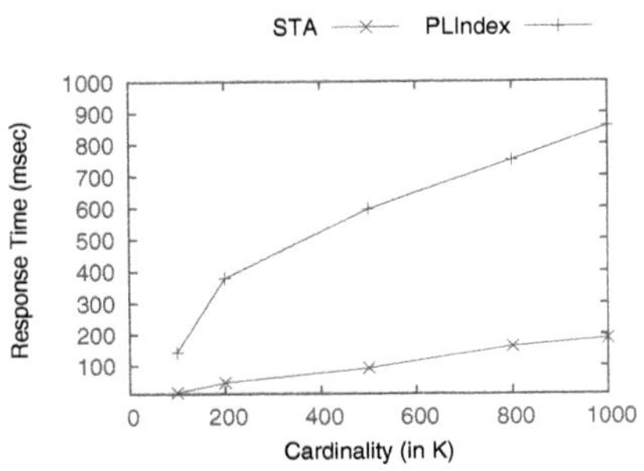

Figure 13: Top-k query evaluation for varying input cardinalities (synthetic uniform dataset)

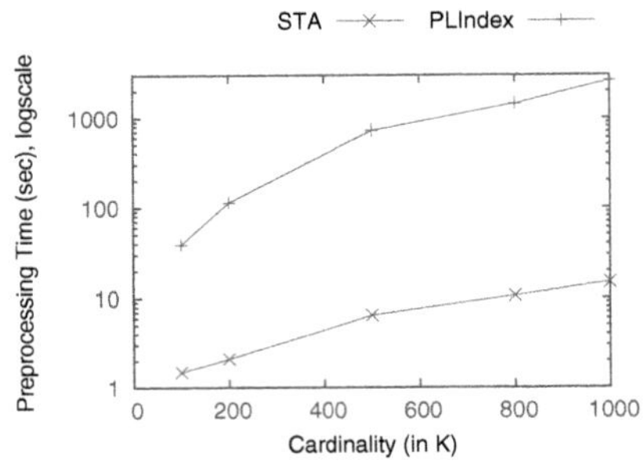

Figure 14: Preprocessing time for varying input cardinalities (synthetic uniform dataset)

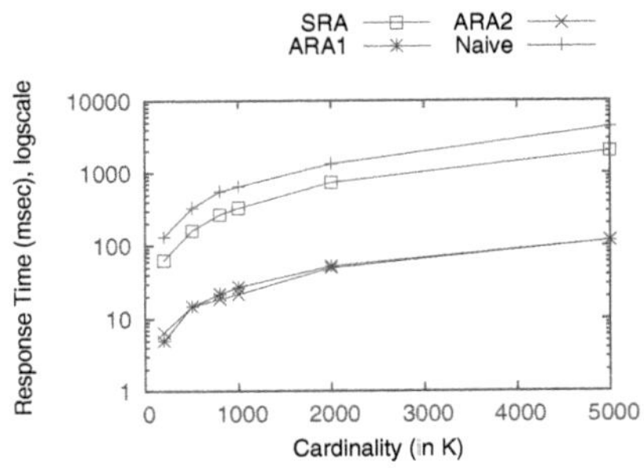

Figure 15: Ranking query evaluation for varying input cardinalities (synthetic uniform dataset)

6.4 Evaluating Ranking Queries

To evaluate the ranking query algorithms, we randomly pick a group of 10 objects (using object IDs) and measure the average response time with the ranking algorithms proposed in Section 5. These results, shown in Figure 15, demonstrate that the ARA2 and ARA1 algorithms run far faster than the other methods, and that the SRA method is about twice as fast as the Naive method when the input cardinality varies. This experiment validates the robustness of the ranking evaluation using our sequential access scheme.

7. CONCLUSIONS AND FUTURE WORK

In this paper, we have presented a novel and generic sequential access scheme for evaluating top-k queries. Our techniques not only discard random accesses in a simple way, but also allow for *early termination* when evaluating top-k queries. We have developed efficient methods to answer top-k queries in subspace and top-k queries on dynamic data using the proposed sequential access scheme. We also study *ranking* query, which finds the *rank* of a specified input tuple, and present both exact and approximate algorithms to evaluate ranking queries. A comprehensive set of experiments on both real and synthetic datasets demonstrate the significant performance improvement and scalability of the proposed techniques. Future work includes designing fast algorithms for updates to the D-tables, and adapting the methods to multi-core systems.

Acknowledgments

This work was supported in part by the National Science Foundation under grant IIS-0929988.

8. REFERENCES

[1] R. Akbarinia, E. Pacitti, and P. Valduriez. Best position algorithms for top-k queries. In *VLDB*, 2007.

[2] N. Bansal, S. Guha, and N. Koudas. Ad-hoc aggregations of ranked lists in the presence of hierarchies. In *SIGMOD*, 2008.

[3] H. Bast, D. Majumdar, R. Schenkel, M. Theobald, and G. Weikum. Iotopk: Index-access optimized top-k query processing. In *VLDB*, 2006.

[4] N. Bruno, L. Gravano, and A. Marian. Evaluating top-k queries over web-accessible databases. In *ICDE*, 2002.

[5] N. Bruno and H. Wang. The threshold algorithm:from middleware systems to relational engine. *IEEE Trans.Knowl.Data Eng.*, 19(4), 2007.

[6] K. C. C. Chang and S. W. Hwang. Minimal probing: supporting expensive predicates for top-k queries. In *SIGMOD*, 2002.

[7] Y. Chang, L. Bergman, V. Castelli, C.Li, M.Lo, and J.Smith. The onion technique:indexing for linear optimization queries. In *SIGMOD*, 2000.

[8] G. Das, D. Gunopulos, N. Koudas, and D. Tsirogiannis. Answering top-k queries using views. In *VLDB*, 2006.

[9] R. Fagin, A. Lotem, and M. Naor. Optimal aggregation algorithms for middleware. In *PODS*, 2001.

[10] R. Fagin, A. Lotem, and M. Naor. Optimal aggregation algorithms for middleware. *J. Comput. Syst. Sci.*, 66(4), 2003.

[11] U. Güntzer, W. T. Balke, and W. Kießling. Towards efficient multi-feature queries in heterogeneous environments. In *ITCC*, 2001.

[12] P. Gurský and P. Vojtás. On top-ksearch with no random access using small memory. In *ADBIS*, 2008.

[13] J. S. Heo, K. Y. Whang, M. S. Kim, Y. Kim, and I. Song. The partitioned-layer index:answering monotone top-k queries using the convex skyline and partitioning merging technique. *Inf. Sci.*, 179(19), 2009.

[14] V. Hristidis and Y. Papakonstantinou. Algorithms and applications for answering ranked queries using ranked views. *VLDB J.*, 13(1), 2004.

[15] S. W. Hwang and K. C. C. Chang. Optimizing top-k queries for middleware access: A unified cost-based approach. *ACM Trans. Database Syst.*, 32(1), 2007.

[16] I. F. Ilyas and W. G. Aref. Rank-aware query processing and optimization. In *ICDE*, 2005.

[17] I. F. Ilyas, G. Beskales, and M. A. Soliman. A survey of top-query processing techniques in relational database systems. *ACM Comput. Surv.*, 40(4), 2008.

[18] I. F. Ilyas, R. Shah, W. G. Aref, J. S. Vitter, and A. K. Elmagarmid. Rank-aware query optimization. In *SIGMOD*, 2004.

[19] C. Lang, Y. Chang, and J. Smith. Making the threshold algorithm access cost aware. *IEEE Trans. Knowl.Data Eng.*, 16(10), 2004.

[20] N. Mamoulis, K. H. Cheng, M. L. Yiu, and D. W. Cheung. Efficient aggregation of ranked inputs. In *SIGMOD*, 2006.

[21] A. Marian, N. Bruno, and L. Gravano. Evaluating top- queries over web-accessible databases. *ACM Trans. Database Syst.*, 29(2), 2004.

[22] M. Mitzenmacher and E. Upfal. *Probability and Computing: Randomized Algorithms and Probabilistic Analysis.* Cambridge University Press, New York, NY, USA, 2005.

[23] A. Natsev, Y. C. Chang, J. R. Smith, C. S. Li, and J. S. Vitter. Supporting incremental join queries on ranked inputs. In *VLDB*, 2001.

[24] H. H. Pang, X. H. Ding, and B. H. Zheng. Efficient processing of exact top- queries over disk-resident sorted lists. *VLDB J.*, 19(3), 2010.

[25] Y. F. Tao, V. Hristidis, D. Papadias, and Y. Papakonstantinou. Branch-and-bound processing of ranked queries. *Inf. Syst.*, 32(3), 2007.

[26] Y. F. Tao, X. K. Xiao, and J. Pei. Efficient skyline and top-k retrieval in subspaces. *IEEE Trans. Knowl. Data Eng.*, 19(8), 2007.

[27] U. üntzer, W. T. Balke, and W. Kießling. Optimizing multi-feature queries for image databases. In *VLDB*, 2000.

[28] D. Xin, C. Chen, and J. W. Han. Towards robust indexing for ranked queries. In *VLDB*, 2006.

[29] L. Zou and L. C. 0002. Dominant graph: An efficient indexing structure to answer top-k queries. In *ICDE*, 2008.

Changing Flights in Mid-air: A Model for Safely Modifying Continuous Queries

Kyumars Sheykh Esmaili, Tahmineh Sanamrad, Peter M. Fischer, Nesime Tatbul
Systems Group, ETH Zurich, Switzerland
{kyumarss, sanamrat, petfisch, tatbul}@inf.ethz.ch

ABSTRACT

Continuous queries can run for unpredictably long periods of time. During their lifetime, these queries may need to be adapted either due to changes in application semantics (e.g., the implementation of a new alert detection policy), or due to changes in the system's behavior (e.g., adapting performance to a changing load). While in previous works query modification has been implicitly utilized to serve specific purposes (e.g., load management), to date no research has been done that defines a general-purpose, reliable, and efficiently implementable model for modifying continuous queries at run-time. In this paper, we introduce a punctuation-based framework that can formally express arbitrary lifecycle operations on the basis of input-output mappings and basic control elements such as start or stop of queries. On top of this foundation, we derive all possible query change methods, each providing different levels of correctness guarantees and performance. We further show how these models can be efficiently realized in a state-of-the-art stream processing engine; we also provide experimental results demonstrating the key performance tradeoffs of the change methods.

Categories and Subject Descriptors

H.2.4 [**Database Management**]: Systems - Query Processing; H.2.4 [**Database Management**]: Systems - Transaction Processing

General Terms

Reliability, Verification

Keywords

Continuous Query, Stream Processing, Query Lifecycle, Query Modification

1. INTRODUCTION

With the proliferation of dynamically generated data and the need for its continuous monitoring to the end, we have witnessed the emergence of data stream processing as a new data management paradigm. Stream processing has proven to have a wide spectrum of practical applications with varying requirements such as real-time financial analysis, network traffic monitoring, sensor-based tracking. As a result, a significant number of academic (e.g., Borealis [6], STREAM [21], TelegraphCQ [12]) and commercial (e.g., StreamBase [4], Truviso [5], IBM InfoSphere Streams [1], MS StreamInsight [7]) stream processing engines (SPE) have been built to meet these needs.

In SPEs, continuous queries over infinitely long data streams can run for unpredictably long time periods. During their lifetime, these queries may need to be modified either due to changes in application semantics, or due to changes in the system's behavior, as we illustrate with a few examples in the next part.

1.1 Selected Use Cases

1. Security Monitoring:

Consider a bank that applies the following security policy for its ATM machines (adapted from real-world policies we observed in the compliance research project MASTER [2]): Block a customer card upon 3 failed logins at the same ATM location within a time window of 10 minutes. This policy can be implemented as a continuous count query on a 10-minute window over a stream of failed login events. Now suppose that, due to a change in regulations, the bank would like to change the window in this query to 15 minutes. If this change happens while a user has already tried 2 failed logins within 5 minutes, it is not obvious how the system should behave. A naive approach would be to replace the query with the new one immediately, discarding any existing state. In this case, the user would be able to try up to 3 more logins in the next 15 minutes in addition to the 2 failed ones in the past 5 minutes (leading to a total of 5 tries over 20 minutes, not matching any policy!). A more cautious approach would be to defer the query replacement until a time there is no incomplete query state left, but in more complex monitoring use cases such as stock trading, such times typically do not exist. (Sections 3.3.3 and 3.3.4 show solutions).

2. Sensor Networking: Consider a network of temperature and smoke sensors deployed over a forest in order to detect and monitor wildfires. Again, continuous queries can be defined over these sensor readings in order to signal unusual increases in sensor values. Whenever such activity is reported for a certain region of the forest, the firefighters want to replace the currently running query with a more specific query so that the possible fire can be located with a higher degree of certainty. However, in sensor-based applications, there is already an inherent level of uncertainty and loss, and it is also critical for the new query to take effect as fast as possible. Therefore, for this application a naive, but more responsive approach is better (leading to the solution in Section 3.3.1).

In the above two use cases, the application semantics necessitates query modification, albeit with different requirements. There are also cases where the modification is triggered by the system itself.

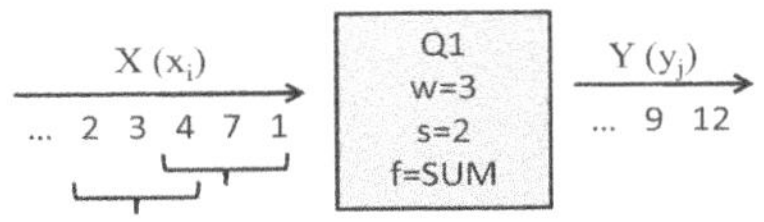

Figure 1: Running example - Q1: window size 3 slide 2 tuples.

3. Adaptive Load Management: SPEs need to deal with resource overload, e.g., caused by fluctuating arrival rates. The most common technique is load shedding, e.g., by inserting/removing load-reducing drop operators into/from selected parts of a running query plan [22]. This yields a "cheaper" version of the query, while the quality of the results becomes lower. A drawback of load shedding is that it takes the control away from the query writer and introduces non-deterministic behavior. In an alternative strategy, several versions of the same query are defined by the application in advance, each tailored for a different load level (see the military use case in [6]). As the system load changes due to fluctuations in input rates, the system is expected to switch adaptively between different query versions. It is crucial that the switch across different query versions happens seamlessly and efficiently, with as little additional system overhead as possible.

The above examples show the importance and diversity of query modification capability in SPEs. Each requires a different tradeoff between correctness parameters and performance, and provides different information to exploit. What is needed is a general-purpose, reliable, and efficiently implementable model for modifying continuous queries at run-time.

Since these use cases cover specific areas of the problem space, we now introduce a running example that will be used throughout the paper. $Q1$ uses a tuple-based sliding window of size 3 and slide 2, applying a sum operation on the window (Figure 1). Without limiting generality, we are using windows as a representative of operators whose semantics exhibit non-trivial behavior on change.

1.2 Our Contribution

In this paper, we introduce a punctuation-based framework for correctly modeling and efficiently implementing on-the-fly modifications over continuous queries. Our framework provides a set of basic control elements for starting and stopping queries, over which various advanced change variants can be defined, each providing different levels of correctness and performance. *Correctness* is defined through two types of criteria, *Safety* and *Liveness* [18]. Our model allows choosing different change variants for different use cases as well as defining new ones as needed. We further show how our model can be realized in a state-of-the-art stream processing engine ([3]) with few code changes and provide experimental results, demonstrating the key tradeoffs across different change variants.

The rest of this paper is outlined as follows. Section 2 introduces the basic framework and methodology on which our modification model is built. The description of the model itself follows in Section 3. In Section 4, we describe how our model can be refined onto real-life SPEs and provide an architecture and implementation on a state-of-the-art SPE in Section 5. Results of our performance study are provided in Section 6, giving guidelines about when to use which method. After a summary of related work in Section 7, we conclude the paper in Section 8 with directions for future work.

2. FRAMEWORK AND METHODOLOGY

Query modification can best be rooted in a general framework that tackles the boundary conditions (e.g., start, stop) of continuous queries. In order to achieve generality, precision, and deterministic behavior, this framework should not rely on semantics of specific operators, timing, or state, which are all notoriously hard to reason about (e.g., see [6] for an approach that encounters timing issues). Instead, we focus on describing input and output streams, annotating these with *punctuations* [24] which we call *Control Element*. With this approach, semantics and execution of queries are abstracted into their data dependencies. We define a minimal set of basic control elements (including their impact on output and their interaction) and derive complex control elements out of them. Within the scope of this work, we primarily focus on queries with a single input and output stream, a restriction which we plan to remove in future work. In this section, we will first introduce the foundations of our model, then the basic control elements, their interaction, and finally our methodology to model complex control elements in a generic manner. Section 3 will describe the complete execution of this methodology for *query modification*.

2.1 Foundations

To build our formal framework, we will first provide clear definitions for data streams and continuous queries. Moreover, we introduce a set of mapping functions, which provide the basis for all following definitions.

2.1.1 *Streams*

A stream S is an unbounded sequence of *stream elements*, where each stream element has a *tuple* part and a *position*. The *position* assures the total order among the stream elements.

Given our approach of inserting control elements into the stream, there are two types of stream elements:

- *Data Elements*, which carry regular data values.
- *Control Elements*, which carry control metadata.

Control Elements do not directly take part in query processing and therefore do not contribute to the query result. However, they convey important information to our framework regarding how the query should behave if encountering them. *Control Elements* are punctuated into the input stream either by the user or by the system itself, depending on the use case. The order among data elements can be relaxed to a partial order (for models that process elements in groups, such as STREAM [21]), only control elements need to have a total order among them and with data elements. For clarity of presentation, we assume total order among all *stream elements* in the rest of the paper.

2.1.2 *Continuous Queries*

A continuous query is a query that is issued once but runs forever. It takes a stream X as input and produces a stream Y as output. At any point in time t, the answer to a continuous query Q is based on the elements of its input stream X seen up to t, and this answer is updated as new stream elements continue to arrive on X, following the monotonicity definition in [19]. In our model, each continuous query Q is defined by a unique *query identifier* and a *query expression*. As a convention, we use the notation of x_i to indicate input stream elements and y_j to indicate output stream elements, where x and y correspond to the tuple parts, and i and j correspond to the positions ($i, j \in \mathbb{N}$), respectively.

2.1.3 *Query Mapping Functions*

We use the notion of *mapping functions* as an abstraction of the details of the query expression. Mapping functions are defined on of a pair of streams (input and output stream) and establish a relationship between a single element in one stream to a set of elements in the other. We specify two mapping functions, which capture the data dependencies established by the query expression of a given continuous query Q:

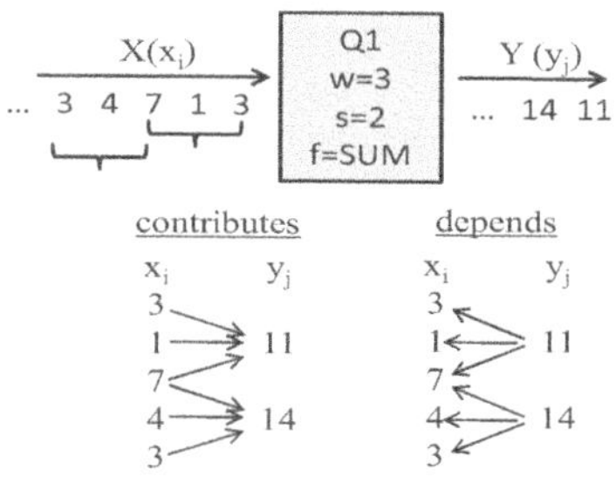

Figure 2: Mapping Functions of Q1

- *depends*(y_j), $E \longmapsto \{E\}$: Given an output data element y_j, returns the set of all input data elements that y_j depends on.

  $depends(y_j) = \{x_i | x_i \in X \text{ where } Q(X) = y_j\}$

- *contributes*(x_i), $E \longmapsto \{E\}$: Given an input data element x_i, returns the set of all output data elements which x_i has contributed to.

  $contributes(x_i) = \{y_j | x_i \in depends(y_j)\}$

We illustrate the query mapping functions in Figure 2, on query $Q1$ of our running example. Note that the mapping functions are not only driven by the query expression, but also the *starting position*, which is their reference point in the streams. For example, in Figure 2, a mapping starting at the input element 1 instead of 3 would not give the sequence (14,11) as a result, but one starting with 12. As we will show in the next section, this will play an important role when defining lifecycle operations. In Section 4 we will describee how mapping functions work for individual operators, and how, in turn, they can be composed for the mapping function of a complete query.

2.2 Basic Control Elements

We establish a minimal set of basic control elements, which define basic lifecycle behavior and serve as building blocks for complex control elements.

2.2.1 Start

Upon encountering a start control element, a query Q will start producing output, otherwise the arriving inputs will be ignored.

- *Fresh Start (FStart)*: We denote this control element x_{fstart} (and short **F** in figures where no details are needed), where $fstart$ is its position in the stream. Upon receiving an x_{fstart}, query Q will be started, i.e., the input data elements having a greater position than $fstart$ will contribute to the output. More formally:

  $Y_{fstart} = \{y_j \in Y \mid \forall x_i \in depends(y_j),\ i > fstart\}$

  Y_{fstart} is the output after receiving the x_{fstart} control element.

  Figure 3 illustrates *Fresh Start* applied on $Q1$. It is important to note that a *Fresh Start* element restarts the *starting position* of the underlying query mapping functions (*depends*(y_j) and *contributes*(x_i)). As an example, applying *Fresh Start* after 1 instead of 3 in Figure 3 would shift the input sets of all windows by one position. For completeness, we also investigated start control elements that keep the mapping function as if the output had just been surpressed, e.g. for a pause/resume operation.

  We will not cover them in this paper for the following reasons: 1) Such start methods are not necessary to describe query modification, since a modification will establish a new mapping function. 2) Maintaining a mapping function incurs an overhead which can approach the cost of query exececution (e.g., for a complex pattern query), making it infeasible for all but restricted cases. Details can be found in [15].

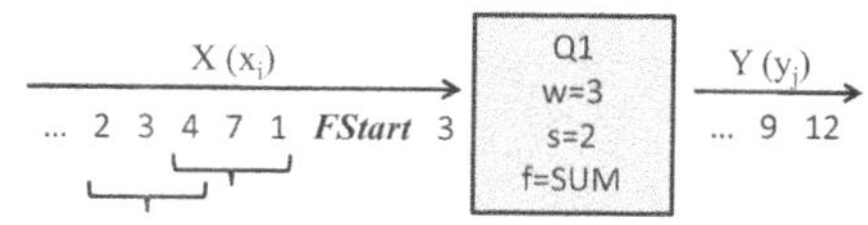

Figure 3: *Fresh Start* on Q1

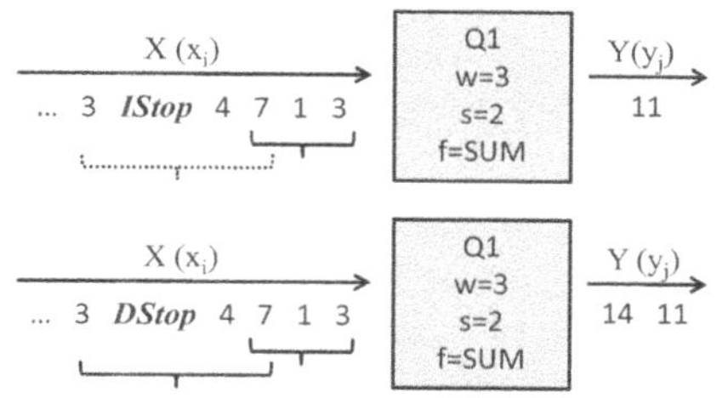

Figure 4: *Immediate Stop* vs. *Drain Stop* on Q1

2.2.2 Stop

Upon encountering a stop control element, a query Q will eventually stop producing output. We define two kinds of stop elements:

- *Immediate Stop (IStop*: We denote this control element with x_{istop} (short **I**)), where $istop$ is its position in the stream. Upon receiving an x_{istop}, a query Q will be immediately stopped, i.e., the input data elements having a position greater than $istop$ will no longer contribute to the output. More formally:

  $Y_{istop} = \{y_j \in Y \mid \forall x_i \in depends(y_j),\ i < istop\}$

- *Drain Stop (DStop)*: We denote this control element with x_{dstop} (short **D**), where $dstop$ is its position in the stream. Upon receiving an x_{dstop}, a query Q will be gradually stopped, i.e., Q will continue to produce output which has dependencies on input data elements appearing before $dstop$ and completing its partially produced output elements. More formally:

  $Y_{dstop} = \{y_j \in Y \mid \exists x_i \in depends(y_j),\ i < dstop\}$

Figure 4 illustrates *Immediate Stop* and *Drain Stop* applied on $Q1$, showing that IStop discards the uncompleted window, whereas DStop finishes uncompleted windows, but does not open new ones and stops when there aren't any windows left. As we will show later in the paper, both stop elements not only provide relevant semantics, but are also efficiently implementable on existing data stream systems.

2.3 Interaction of Basic Control Elements

An important aspect to completely define the semantics of query lifecycle is to cover the interaction of multiple control elements, both for the single query cases as well as for the interaction of multiple queries and expressions, which can be derived from the single query case. The interaction should maintain two design decisions established so far: (1) Control elements should become effective at the position they are specified, as defined in Section 2.2. (2) The order of control elements determines which control element is effective, superseding older ones.

We have chosen to use an interaction diagram, which can trivially be turned into an automaton by defining the start and end states for a specific operation. Figure 5 gives the states and the transitions, which correspond to the basic control elements. Initially, a query is in *Stopped* state, in which the *starting position* of the mapping function has not been set up. Using *FStart* (F), the mapping function is set up and the query transitions into the *Running* state, in which output is produced, as seen on Figure 3 for $Q1$. An *IStop* (I)

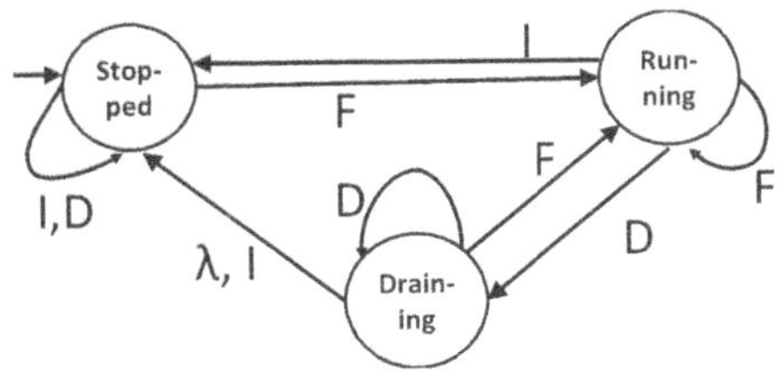

Figure 5: Lifecycle Interaction Diagram - Single Query

directly changes to the *Stopped* state, while an additional *Draining* state is needed for *DStop* (D) in which the pending output is produced. The transition from *Draining* to *Stopped* is not driven by any control element and is also no ϵ-transition, but depends on data elements (which we call λ). All these transitions can be seen in the handling of the values (3,4,7) in Figure 4: after the arrival of the *IStop* element, all following input can be ignored due to the immediate change to the stopped state. For *DStop*, the Draining state is kept until the arrival of 3, which closes the window and triggers the transition to *Stopped*. Conceptually, the λ transition is similar to the notion of Timed Automata [8], yet not based on time, but on the progress of the underlying mapping function. Applying *FStart* in any state will re-initialize the mapping function and lead to the *Running* state, while applying *IStop* when *Draining* immediately stops the query. Applying *DStop* while *Draining* has no effect, since neither extends nor restricts the output defined by the previous drain. To sum up, all this behavior is consistent with our design so far, and allows the specification of complex operations.

2.4 Creating Complex Control Elements

While the basic control elements can already support many use cases, the real benefit of this approach is that it provides a solid foundation to establish complex control and a modification model. In order to do so, we propose the following methodology:

1. Formally define the new operation (e.g., *Query Modification*) on top of our mapping functions. This leads to new complex control element(s) (e.g., *Change*), and some small extensions to our basic foundations (e.g., adding a *query version number* to the query definition that originally consists of an identifier and an expression (as defined in Section 2.1.2)).
2. Define the required/desirable behavior of the new operation, through what we call *Correctness Criteria* (e.g., safety, liveness).
3. Derive the possible options for this complex control element by the combination of the interaction diagrams of the individual queries, yielding a new interaction diagram with the powerset of the states. Choose start and end states, and sequences of transitions that connect them. Parameters influencing the number of options are (1) the types of basic control elements considered, (2) the number of control elements allowed, (3) their order, and (4) the distance between two basic control elements (e.g., directly following, data-driven, time-driven).
4. Evaluate the behavior of variants against the *Correctness Criteria*.

Using this formalism, we can establish that all possible options within the control element framework are covered. The next section will show how we apply the above methodology to define *query modification* operation.

We chose to show *query modification* as it is the most challenging and the least explored lifecycle operation. It adds a new set of semantics to describe how results should behave in the transition phase, which cannot be easily described by looking at one query. *Query Migration*, *Query Pause-Resume*, or *Query Re-Optimization* are much more constrained in this respect, can be more easily supported, and have also received much more attention in previous work. We therefore discuss them in our technical report [15].

2.5 Discussion

We have strived to build our model on as few fundamental assumptions as possible: The mapping functions and two classes of basic control elements: *start* and *stop*. The mapping functions ensure that our model can be applied on any SPE, as long as its operations are monotonic (i.e., new input does not change old results). The specific semantics of operators, their composition and the execution model can all be catered for. Our choice of basic control elements and their variants reflects the fundamental operations one can perform on mapping functions. Intuitively, they provide all that is needed and we can exhaustively derive all variants of stop/start and complex elements from there. They also cover all the lifecycle operations we have studied so far. At this time, it appears premature to establish a formal proof of their completeness with respect to all possible lifecycle operations, since it is not even clear what all lifecycle operations might be - we consider this a topic for future work.

3. QUERY MODIFICATION

Having introduced our basic query management framework and methodology in the previous section, we now show how *Query Modification* can be modeled. In *Query Modification* there are two versions of a query Q, namely Q^{old} and Q^{new}, and we would like to switch from the former to the latter. Following the first step in our methodology, we will first express the *Query Modification* operation by a new complex control element, which we call *Change* (Section 3.1). Secondly, we will define *Correctness* criteria for *Query Modification* (Section 3.2). In our basic framework, *Change* can be translated into a combination of a *Stop Control Element*, which targets Q^{old}, and a *Start Control Element*, which targets Q^{new}. However, as we will explain, there can be different variations of this combination, which we derive by interaction diagram composition, and analyze them in Section 3.3. This is complemented by an analysis of interaction of complex and basic control elements in Section 3.4. Finally, we will conclude this section by showing that our approach is as good as possible in terms of *Correctness* rules (Section 3.5).

3.1 Definition of Query Modification

In *Query Modification*, there are two versions of a query Q, old (Q^{old}) and new (Q^{new}), which are applied on a single input stream. The change control element is formalized by extending the query definition to include query versions (*old* and *new*). Accordingly, we will also use two pairs of query mapping functions: $depends_{old}(y_j^{old})$ and $contributes_{old}(x_i)$ for Q^{old}, and $depends_{new}(y_j^{new})$ and $contributes_{new}(x_i)$ for Q^{new}, respectively. In case of *Change* we will have three output streams: Output stream of Q^{old}, output stream of Q^{new}, and *Change* output stream, denoted by Y^{old}, Y^{new}, Y^{chg} respectively. A change control element defines how the Y^{chg} is built from Y^{old} and Y^{new}.

As a running example throughout the rest of this section, we want to *Change* $Q1^{old}$ (introduced earlier in Figure 2) into $Q1^{new}$, which is another continuous aggregation with a tuple-based sliding window of size 2 and slide 2, applying a sum over each window.

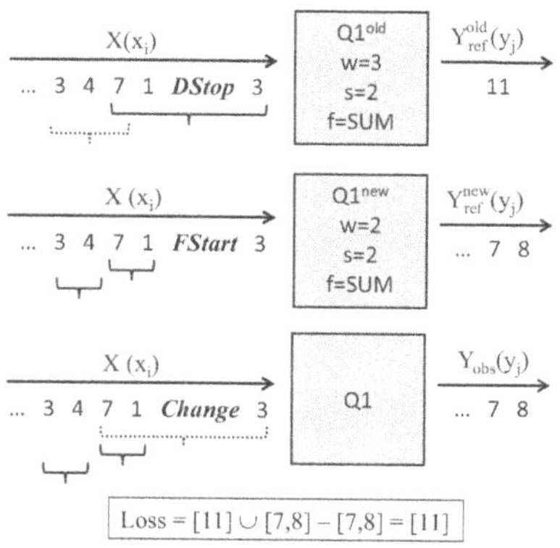

Figure 6: A lossy *Change* on Q1

3.2 Correctness of Query Modification

Inspired by the approaches in system design and verification [18], we defined two general classes of *Correctness* criteria for *Query Modification*: *Safety* and *Liveness*.

3.2.1 Safety Criteria

A safety property expresses that *"something bad will not happen"* during a given execution [18]. We identified *Loss*, *Disorder*, and *Duplicates* as possible safety problems.

1. **Loss**: A common undesirable consequence of changing a continuous query is losing some of the output elements. We formalize this concept as the set difference between *tuples* of the reference output stream (Y_{ref}) and those of the observed output stream (Y_{obs}):
   $Loss = [Y_{ref}] - [Y_{obs}]$
   where Y_{ref} is the *ideal* output stream generated by a given query Q consuming the change control element, and Y_{obs} is the output stream that Q actually generates. Intuitively, an ideal or lossless *Change* for a query Q should not lose any incomplete contributions from Q^{old}, and at the same time, it should include all contributions from Q^{new}. Note that in *Loss*, only the existence of *tuples* is considered. Their positions, which contain the order information, are captured as a separate safety issue later (hence, [ ] denoting a bag of tuples instead of a sequence).
   As an example, assume that we want to switch from $Q1^{old}$ to $Q1^{new}$ by enforcing an IStop on $Q1^{old}$ and an FStart on $Q1^{new}$ (i.e., Change = IStop + FStart). As shown in Figure 6, this leads to a lossy *Change* since it produces one fewer output (11) than then the reference stream. This reference stream would be modeled by a change using DStop + FStart.
2. **Disorder**: Order is a core property of data streams. Therefore, disorder is another critical threat to safety in continuous query execution. We identified two levels of order violation for *Change*:

   (a) **Query-Level Disorder**: In an execution that preserves query-level order, no output stream element from Q^{old} should appear after an output stream element of Q^{new}.

   (b) **Stream-Level Disorder**: In an execution that preserves stream-level order, output stream elements follow the order that is imposed by the query semantics and the structure of the input streams.

   Figure 7 depicts the difference between these two. Note that to be able to illustrate the difference better, just in this example, we used w=4 for $Q1^{old}$ instead of w=3. The upper part of the figure shows that the output appears in the same

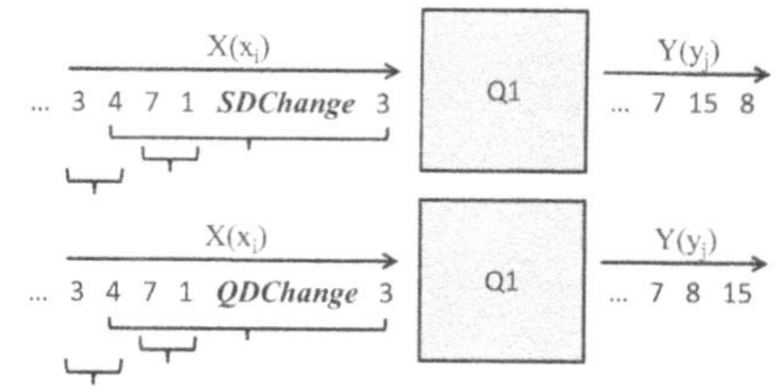

Figure 7: Query- vs. Stream-level Disorder on Q1

   order as the windows are closing, and the lower part shows that the output appears according to the order of query versions, meaning that the output of the Q^{old} will be seen first and then the output of the Q^{new} will show up.
3. **Duplicates**: In case of *Change*, it is possible that the same exact input elements contribute to both the outputs of Q^{old} and Q^{new}. These outputs are considered duplicates, since they have the exact same dependency sets.

A complete formalization of the above can be found in technical report [15].

3.2.2 Liveness Criteria

A *Liveness* property expresses that *"something good must eventually happen"* during a given execution [18]. We identified two complementary *Liveness* criteria for *Query Modification*:

1. **Termination of the Old Query**: The system should guarantee that Q^{old} will eventually terminate, producing no more output and freeing up its occupied resources. As an example, *DStop* without any restrictions on the semantics of the query expression may lead to termination problems (e.g., closing condition of a semantic window never being satisfied).
2. **Progress of the New Query**: The system should guarantee that Q^{new} will eventually progress, starting to consume and process input. Note that *Progress* is not necessarily a property that is observable in terms of the query output, since certain query semantics may prohibit the generation of output (e.g., a selection query whose condition is never satisfied).

3.3 Change Control Elements

We will now derive the *Change* options by combining our basic control elements (Start and Stop) in different ways (i.e., Step 3 in our methodology). The key idea is to build a common interaction diagram for both query versions from the interaction diagram of a single query, as presented in Figure 5. On this common interaction diagram, we can determine and evaluate the possible options to perform the change. The resulting interaction diagram is shown in Figure 8, on which each of the states is labeled with the state for each of the queries (e.g., RS means Q^{old} is **R**unning and Q^{new} is **S**topped), and transitions are the combination of the individual query version's transitions (e.g., *IStop* for Q^{old} on RS will lead to SS). As outlined before, we want to stop Q^{old} and start Q^{new}, so our goal is to go from RS to SR. Table 1 shows the options to do so on the left-hand side. We also model the distance between executing these steps, in order to allow data operations during the change (e.g., waiting for completion of a drain). In total, there are 8 options, of which one can be discarded (IStop-FStart with waiting), since it does not provide any meaningful guarantees by adding a distance when no activity is ongoing. Some of these options are equivalent, since (1)they are executed next to each other with no data operations in between, (2) changing the order of two control elements does lead to the same target state, e.g., for both cases of *IChange*.

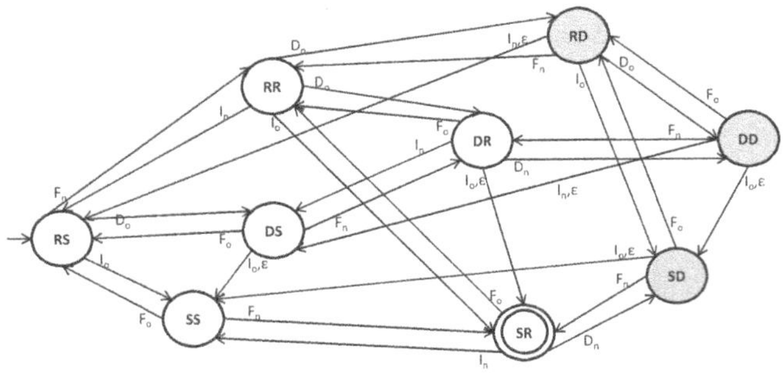

Figure 8: Lifecycle Interaction Diagram - Two Queries

Stop Type	Order	Distance	Change Option
IStop	I F	direct	IChange
IStop	I F	waiting	n/a
IStop	F I	direct	IChange
IStop	F I	at first result	GIChange
DStop	D F	direct	DChange
DStop	D F	drain completion	DDChange
DStop	F D	direct	DChange
DStop	F D	at first result	GDChange

Table 1: Change Variation Derivation

As a result, we get 5 variants of change, which we will now discuss in terms of their correctness, performance, and use cases.

3.3.1 *Immediate Change (IChange)*

In some applications, a *Change* should be performed as early as possible, disregarding any partial results of Q^{old}.

Formally speaking, this is expressed with an IChange control element, depicted as $x_{ichange}$, composed of an *IStop* for Q^{old}, followed directly by an *FStart* for Q^{new}, or vice versa. Thus, the output stream is defined as:

$$Y^{ichg} = Y^{new}_{fstart} \mid\mid Y^{old}_{istop}$$
$$= \left\{ y^{new}_j \in Y^{new} \mid \forall x_i \in depends_{new}(y^{new}_j),\ i > ichange \right\}$$
$$\mid\mid \left\{ y^{old}_j \in Y^{old} \mid \forall x_i \in depends_{old}(y^{old}_j),\ i < ichange \right\}$$

Note that (1) || is the *append* operator, which concatenates two streams, and (2) each input element contributes exclusively to the output element of Q^{old} or Q^{new}.

Figure 9 shows an example of using IChange control element.

In terms of safety, IChange can cause *Loss*, since the partial results of Q^{old} are discarded. It produces the outputs in the correct order (both stream- and query-level), and does not generate any duplicate output elements (see Figure 10(a)). Moreover, in terms of liveness, IChange guarantees both the termination of Q^{old} as well as the progress of Q^{new} (see Figure 10(b)) [1]. With respect to the use cases introduced in Section 1, *Sensor Networking* is a candidate for IChange, since loss is tolerable while the immediate progress of the new query (in case of an emergency) and preserving the energy-saving requirements of the sensors need to be guaranteed. Given that IChange does not require *DStop* nor any other kind of complex change coordination, its behavior corresponds to what a typical SPE would do.

3.3.2 *Delayed Drain Change (DDChange)*

An alternative approach for *Change* is to ensure that Q^{old} is drained, and only then Q^{new} is started. We call the corresponding control element DDChange, denoted as $x_{ddchange}$. Formally

[1]Please see the technical report [15] for formal proof of these guarantees.

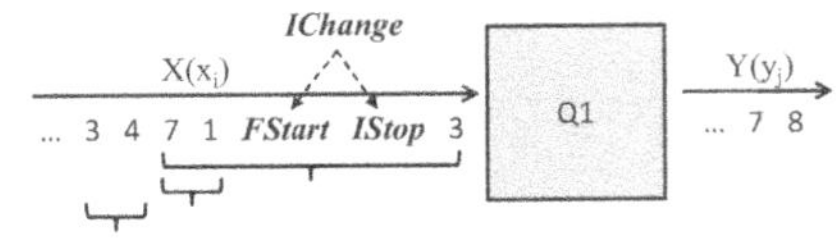

Figure 9: Immediate Change on Q1

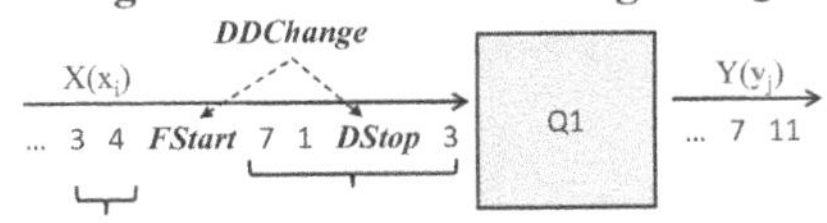

Figure 11: Delayed Drain Change on Q1

speaking, it is composed of a *DStop* for Q^{old}, followed by an *FStart* for Q^{new} in a statically-incomputable distance . Thus, the output stream is defined as:

$$Y^{ddchg} = Y^{new}_{fstart} \mid\mid Y^{old}_{dstop}$$
$$= \left\{ y^{new}_j \in Y^{new} \mid \forall x_i \in depends_{new}(y^{new}_j),\ i > ? \right\}$$
$$\mid\mid \left\{ y^{old}_j \in Y^{old} \mid \exists x_i \in depends_{old}(y^{old}_j),\ i < ddchange \right\}$$

where $'?'$ denotes the fact that the real position of the FStart element which will be inserted is not known in advance. Therefore the *starting position* of the mapping function for Q^{new} is different to that of all the other change cases (which are all initialized at the position of change), so that output after the change may also be different. Figure 11 shows an example of using DDChange control element.

In terms of safety, DDChange exhibits a behavior similar to that of IChange; it also holds the exclusive contribution property.

3.3.3 *Drain Change (DChange)*

Both *Change* variants presented above can induce *Loss*, which is not desirable in many streaming scenarios. This *Loss* is caused by the input elements that are no longer picked up by Q^{old} and have not yet considered by Q^{new}, since Q^{new} is only started when Q^{old} has been completed. Next, we introduce Drain Change, which is composed of a *DStop* for Q^{old} followed directly by an *FStart* for Q^{new}, or vice versa. Figure 12 shows an example of using a DChange control element.

In contrast to previous *Change* variations, merging the output streams of the old and the new queries is not straightforward in *Drain Change*, due to the fact that we have overlapping output elements. Hence, we distinguish between two variants of DChange, $x_{qdchange}$ and $x_{sdchange}$: QDChange, a Query-level order preserving *Drain Change* and SDChange, a Stream-level order preserving *Drain Change* . In QDChange is the output stream is defined as:

$$Y^{qdchg} = Y^{new}_{fstart} \mid\mid Y^{old}_{dstop}$$
$$= \left\{ y^{new}_j \in Y^{new} \mid \forall x_i \in depends_{new}(y^{new}_j),\ i > dchange \right\}$$
$$\mid\mid \left\{ y^{old}_j \in Y^{old} \mid \exists x_i \in depends_{old}(y^{old}_j),\ i < dchange \right\}$$

while the output stream in SDChange is defined as:

$$Y^{ddchg} = Y^{new}_{fstart} \mid\mid\mid Y^{old}_{dstop}$$
$$= \left\{ y^{new}_j \in Y^{new} \mid \forall x_i \in depends_{new}(y^{new}_j),\ i > dchange \right\}$$
$$\mid\mid\mid \left\{ y^{old}_j \in Y^{old} \mid \exists x_i \in depends_{old}(y^{old}_j),\ i < dchange \right\}$$

in which ||| is the *interleave* operator. It interleaves the output elements from the new and the old queries based on their relative dependencies on the input elements.

Going back to Figure 7, the *Change* element at the top is behaving like a SDChange element, while the one at the bottom acts like an QDChange element.

In terms of safety, both DChange variants are lossless and free of duplicates, but neither of them can provide both order guarantees at the same time. As will bed discussed further in Section 3.5, this is not caused by the design of our *Query Modification* model, but

Change \ Safety	No Loss	No Query-Level Disorder	No Stream-Level Disorder	No Duplicates
IChange	✗	✓	✓	✓
DDChange	✗	✓	✓	✓
QDChange	✓	✓	✗	✓
SDChange	✓	✗	✓	✓
GIChange	✗	✓	✓	✓
GDChange	✓	✗	✓	✗

(a) Safety guarantees

Change \ Liveness	Progress	Termination
IChange	✓	✓
DDChange	✗	✗
QDChange	✓	✗
SDChange	✓	✗
GIChange	✓	✗
GDChange	✓	✗

(b) Liveness guarantees

Figure 10: *Correctness* guarantees of Change variants

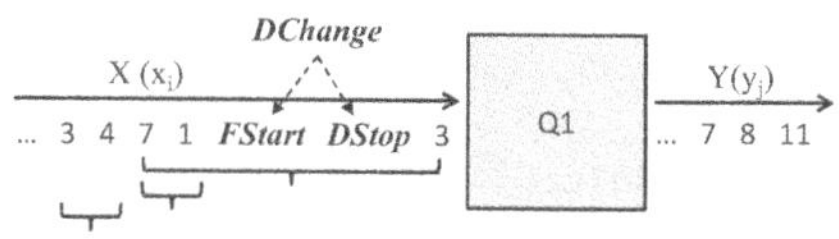

Figure 12: Drain Change on Q1 (QDChange)

is rather an inherent problem of *Query Modification*. In terms of liveness, both DChange variants guarantee the progress of Q^{new}, but not the termination of Q^{old}. The *DChange* variants provide a good match to the requirements of the *Security Monitoring* use case, since they avoid *Loss* and end the execution of Q^{new} by draining.

3.3.4 *Graceful Change (GChange)*

The approaches discussed so far did not cater for performance, in particular responsiveness, which measures the time elapsed between the last output of Q^{old} to the first output of Q^{new}. By keeping Q^{old} running (instead of draining or stopping it) until the first output of Q^{new} is produced, the responsiveness can be significantly improved. We call this change method *Graceful Change* (GChange).

We further distinguish between two variants of GChange: *Graceful Immediate Change* (GIChange) and *Graceful Drain Change* (GDChange). In GIChange, *Loss* can occur, but no *Duplicates* and *Disorder*; whereas in GDChange, *Duplicates* and query-level *Disorder* can occur, but no *Loss*. Q^{new} will make progress, since it starts immediately, but the termination Q^{old} is not guaranteed, since it depends on the existence of output of Q^{new}, which is not guaranteed. A typical good use of GChange is when Q^{new} has a low output rate (e.g., very large window size and very small window slide, very low selectivity, etc.). As shown in Section 6, GChange can indeed outperform other *Change* approaches in terms of responsiveness.

3.4 Interaction of Control Elements Revisited

So far we have defined the semantics of a *single* complex control element by a translation to several basic control elements and their interaction. In the next step, we need to cater for the interaction of *multiple* complex control elements or of a complex control element with a basic control element on the whole query. In particular, since changes (apart from IChange) do not complete immediately, such overlapping actions need to be properly defined. An examples of such a case would be an IStop on a query that currently performs a DDChange, as the user decides that results are no longer needed. In this scenario, one would expect no more output after an IStop, but the naive application of the DDChange translation means to perform a FStart after draining, which would start the query again.

Similar to the interaction of basic control elements, we therefore want to ensure that (1) control elements become effective at their specified position, and (2) the order of control elements determines that the latest control element is effective. The interaction diagram for two queries (Figure 8) does not provide a direct answer, since it only specifies the behavior of two query versions, no global operations. Yet it already contains the necessary foundations to define our extended semantics:

For a basic control element appearing during a change, we can translate IStop and DStop by applying them on both versions, thus achieving stop semantics. In turn, FStart can be translated into an IStop for Q^{old} and an FStart for Q^{new}. This ensures a start of Q^{new} with correct *starting index*, albeit with possible *Loss* on Q^{old}, since the change is turned into an IChange. A change applied after a basic control element will in any case lead to a running query, since our definition of change requires lifeness. If the query is already started or stopped, the implementation is obvious, for a draining query we can again rely on the interaction rules of basic control elements, since the stop of Q^{old} will not extend the drain period of the stop on the whole query.

For complex control elements following other complex control elements, we can build an interaction diagram for three (or more) query versions using the same rules as we built one for two query versions in Section 3.3. In the case of 3 query versions, Q^{new} of the first change is Q^{old} of the second. We then translate the actions that are applied to Q^{old} (on the two-version case) onto the first two queries. Due to space limitations and the general similarity to the two-version change, the complete correctness analysis for multiple overlapping changes is presented in our technical report [15].

As a result, we are getting a weak transactional model for change: ensuring that we always complete a change is only possible for IChange, while other change models do not provide this guarantee. In our opinion, this is actually a desirable behavior, as it allows more flexibility. In addition, stronger transactional models require giving up strict definitions of position impact and sequential order of Control Elements.

3.5 Correctness Rules for Change

In addition to covering the design space for change implementation, we investigated the correctness guarantee space. We have observed some common patterns, which we were able to compile into a set of rules. These rules help us determine that we indeed provide the strongest possible guarantees. For space reasons, we are present the actual rules in the paper, while their proofs can be found in the technical report [15].

- **LDD rule**: In the general case, a *Change* policy can ensure at most two out of three of the following guarantees: No **L**oss, No Stream-level **D**isorder, No Query-level **D**isorder.
- **LD rule**: When Q^{new} has a larger depends-set than Q^{old}, Disorder at stream level cannot occur. In this case, No **L**oss and No **D**isorder can both be guaranteed.
- **LT rule**: No **L**ossless *Change* policy can guarantee **T**ermination.

These rules show us that we have indeed covered all possible options for change when considering strong guarantees (at least two out of LDD and no duplicates, as well as termination where possible). This can be seen by comparing Table 10 with the set of all possible combinations of correctness guarantees. Other, new options will only reduce guarantees, and these reductions are typically not useful (e.g., having no order at all, or one kind of disorder with loss). Thus we have shown that our methods to express change cover the relevant problem space and cannot be improved further for the general case.

4. REFINEMENT AND MODEL MAPPING

So far, we have investigated our model for lifecycle and change using a black-box mapping function that covers a single query with a single input and a single output. To make our model applicable in practice, we need to perform several steps: (1) Refine the mapping functions and control elements to the level of operators, and determine how control elements need to be implemented on operators and their compositions. In turn, this also allows us to work with the compositions of queries. (2) Investigate how real-life SPEs can be adapted to support the lifecycle and change model established in this work.

4.1 Operator Composition

Since operators provide the building blocks for complete queries, we now need to decrease our abstraction level to that of operators, analyze each operator and then compose them in order to achieve mapping functions and control element processing for complete queries. In a first step, we do this by generalizing our query mapping functions (Section 2.1) to operators instead of queries, and showing how to build a query mapping function from the operator mapping functions. In a second step, we determine how control elements need to be handled on this composition in order to achieve the same semantics as with a single black-box mapping function, thus completing the refinement.

Conceptually, mapping functions apply to operators in the same way as they apply to entire queries, defining on which input data item an output items depends and vice versa. We can thus complement our definition of mapping for an operators OP.

- *depends(y_j)*: Given an output data element y_j, returns the set of all input data elements that y_j depends on.
  $dependsOP(y_j) = \{x_i | x_i \in X \text{ where } OP(X) = y_j\}$
- *contributes(x_i)*: Given an input data element x_i, returns the set of all output data elements which x_i has contributed to.
  $contributesOP(x_i) = \{y_j | x_i \in dependsOP(y_j)\}$

Queries are composed of these operators, forming a query plan. In this composition, mapping functions are transitive, since the output items of one operator form the input items for the next. We can formalize this composition as follows, focusing on depends (cotributes can be expressed in an analogous way):

Given a query Q with $dependsQ()$ and operators $OP1, OP2, ...$ with $dependsOP1(), ...$, we prove: For $Q = OP1$, the single operator determines the results for the full query, thus $dependsQ() = dependsOP1(),$.

For a sequential composition, $Q = OP1 || OP2$, we can see that $dependsQ(yj) = dependsOP1(dependsOP2(yj))$, since the transitive function composition holds.

Since operators are the basic building parts of queries, their mapping functions can be derived from their formal definitions. Instead of analyzing each operator individually, we can categorize them in two classes, each with different results for our analysis:

- *Stateless* operators (e.g., selection, projection) perform their computation on one tuple at a time. More formally, for a stateless operator *op*, each output stream element y_j depends on exactly one tuple:
  $\forall y_j \in Y, |depends(y_j)| = 1$
- *Stateful* operators (e.g., window-based operators, pattern matching) perform their computation possibly on multiple tuples at a time. More formally, for a stateful operator *op*, some (if not all) output stream elements y_j depend on more than one tuple:
  $\exists y_j \in Y, |depends(y_j)| > 1$

Given this method to derive the mapping functions from formal operator specification and the composition rules for mapping functions, we now can determine the overall mapping functions of sequential query plans. More complex operators and query plans such as trees or DAGs follow the same approach, but need extensions on the definition of the mapping functions and the composition.

4.2 Control Elements on Composition

In the previous section, we have defined how query mapping functions can be composed out of operator mapping functions, thus defining how output is computed. To complete this composition, we need to determine the semantics in the presence of control elements. More specifically, the following need to be investigated, showing how each control element needs to be applied on a composition to achieve the same semantics as on the black-box query mapping function.

$$Y_{IS} = Q(X_{IS})$$
$$Y_{IS} = OP2(OP1(X_{IS}))$$
$$Y_{FS} = Q(X_{FS})$$
$$Y_{FS} = OP2(OP1(X_{FS}))$$
$$Y_{DS} = Q(X_{DS})$$
$$Y_{DS} \neq OP2(OP1(X_{DS}))$$

Applying *FStart* and *IStop* on the first operator of the composition achieves the desired semantics, since (1) the control element is defined on the input stream, (2) the first operator determines the contributions to the following operators and (3) *FStart* and *IStop* affect the output immediately. Due to the lack of space, we are not showing the full proof here. For *DStop*, this useful property does not generally hold, since the output elements which are drained cannot be determined by considering the first operator alone, unless all operators but the first are stateless. As example for such a problematic drain consider nested windows, in which draining on the first window operator will not permit the second to produce meaningful results any more. The proof for this can be found in [15]. Instead, we need a more complex coordination among operators, since the first and intermediate operators do not have enough knowledge to handle the control elements, and therefore need to delegate this task to their following operators. This delegation ends when a *dominant* operator is reached, which will determine the drain output elements. On linear plans, the last stateful operator dominates the query output, and previous stateful operators (we call them subordinate) are to be kept producing output until the dominant operator has determined all input for draining.

If there is a dominant function, the precise mapping functions of the subordinate operators are not needed any more. Therefore, we can also support user-defined functions without knowing the detailed mapping function, as long as it is monotonic. For more general query plans, a dominant operator can be constructed using techniques similar to those proposed in the literature for load-shedding on multiple aggregates [23].

4.3 Our Framework on SPE models

The query modification framework that we have introduced in this paper has been designed to be general, abstract, and conservative in terms of its assumptions, thus making it applicable in the context of a broad range of SPEs and their query models. In practice, individual SPEs often provide more restricted models, and

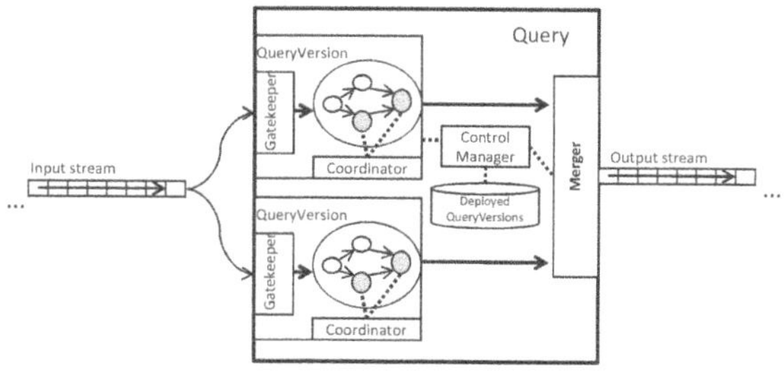

Figure 13: Query Modification architecture

therefore, our framework can be specialized for the SPE at hand. By doing so, stronger correctness guarantees and more efficient implementations can be achieved. For example, systems providing only count- and time-based windows (e.g., Borealis [6]) do, by definition, always fulfill Termination and Progress criteria. Similarly, for certain SPEs, the query mapping functions stay fixed over a Stop/Start cycle, since time-based windows are opened based on a pre-defined time domain, and are not influenced by the index position of the Start control element. Thus no issues deriving from initializing a mapping functions come up.

Our approach reaches its limitations when (1) non-monotonic operators are present, and (2) the output data elements are computed in a non-deterministic way (e.g. affected by system time). It can still be implemented, but the guarantees it can provide are inherently weaker.

5. IMPLEMENTATION

5.1 General Architecture

Up to this point, we have discussed query lifecycle, in particular query modification on the level of formal models. Since our goal for this work has been to provide a complete picture of query lifecycle, we studied ways to implement our proposed semantics. Many approaches have been studied for efficient specific lifecycle operation in databases and SPEs, of whic we will provide an overview in Section 7. Since these options typically solve a specific problem and make several assumptions in order to achieve good performance, we instead chose to develop generic architectural extensions that require only minimal changes to the SPE's data and query models, while allowing the implementation of the necessary control and change logic on top of its already existing architecture. We then show how to incorporate this architecture into existing stream processing engines. At a later stage, more optimizations can be incorporated into this architecture.

For an SPE architecture to support query modification, we must ensure that the system can keep track of multiple versions of a given query, and execute them in a coordinated way during the change period, while taking the chosen change policy and its correctness guarantees into account.To achieve this, we propose the architectural extensions shown in Figure 13. Let us now describe each of the new components in this figure.

Query Versions: An SPE will keep track of each individual *Query*, which in turn consists of a set of *Query Versions*. *Query Versions* are stored in a *Query Version Repository*, possibly in an already validated/compiled/optimized form, so as to avoid potential errors and minimize overhead during the actual query modification period. These versions can be added or removed from the repository when not required. Each *Query Version* uses its own *Gatekeeper* and *Coordinator*, and the whole repository shares a common *ControlManager* and a *Merger*.

Gatekeeper: An important aspect of our framework is the implementation of the basic control elements (i.e., FStart, IStop, DStop), since complex control elements can then be built on top of these. As shown in the previous section, *FStart* and *IStop* can be implemented by just affecting the first operator in the plan. Instead of modifying each operator to support these semantics, we place a special operator with an identity mapping function and the control logic in front of the plan, which we call *Gatekeeper*. Therefore, we do not need to change any operator, greatly simplifying the integration. Since we need to control each *Query Version* independently, there is a *Gatekeeper* for each.

Drainable Operators: *DStop*, on the other hand, requires a slightly more invasive approach for stateful operators: Stateful operators in the query plan (e.g., windowing, pattern matching, joins) need to be extended with the ability to perform draining (i.e., completing the processing of the already started windows, but not initiating new ones), yet this facility needs only to be enabled on the dominant operator. For a given windowing operator implementation, only minimal extensions are necessary, since it is already computing the contributing elements when building the windows. For example, for our MXQuery implementation, the draining extension required only about 10 LOC to be added to the windowing operator.

Coordinator: Instead of extending all operators to propagate the information necessary for a *DStop* to the dominant operator, we externalize this logic into a separate component, called *Coordinator*. It interacts with the dominant operator and the gatekeeper, passing on the relevant information and controlling the execution flow.

Control Manager: Control Manager is responsible for interpreting the control elements. If the queries are known in advance, optimizations can be performed by this component, such as identifying common subexpressions, minimizing the state to be changed.

Merger: Merger combines the output of both query versions into a single stream. The key task of the Merger is to establish the correct delivery order over the two streams. For IChange, DDChange, and QDChange, this is straight-forward, since all output of Q^{old} will be produced before that of Q^{new}. For SDChange and GChange, additional order-related metadata (e.g., starting index) needs to be known for each stream element. This component can be seen as the implementation of the *Append* (||), and *Interleave* (|||) operators.

5.2 SPE-specific Implementation

We implemented our architecture on MXQuery [10] and also studied how an implementation on top of Borealis [6] could be done. Given the differences in the data model, operator semantics and execution strategies, this should provide a good coverage of the SPEs space. *MXQuery* is an implementation of XQuery 3.0, which has few implicit assumptions on the data model (sequences of semi-structured items), expressive predicate-based windows and a set of fully composable, Turing-complete expressions. It uses a classical DBMS-style pull model, which requires explicit threading for parallel query execution, yet simplifies output control and merging, since the output is always explicitly requested, and the end of available output is explicitly indicated. Determining the relative *depends* set for two items out of different versions (as needed by the ||| (Interleave) operation, and thus the Merger) is conceptually difficult, given the flexible data model, the data creation operations and the large number of operators. Due to the lazy execution strategy of MXQuery (which ensures that only required data is read from the input), observing the Gatekeeper before requesting the next element gives this information in a very lightweight way, thus not requiring to change the data model and instrument the operators.

Borealis uses relational tuples in combination with a small number of streaming operators, most prominent count- and time-based windows. Push-based operators are connected by queues and manually composed to form a query network. A scheduler can decide how to prioritize certain operators. This form of coupling simplifies parallel execution, but makes it harder to determine when all output for a given input has been produced, so that a switch can be performed. This limitation can be overcome by instructing the scheduler to prefer operators which are connected to closed or draining Gatekeeper. When operators cannot process any more, the scheduler can detect this, and indicate it to the Merger. Computing the *depends* set for the ||| operation is simple, since aggregates on windows will assign the maximum contributing timestamp to the produced tuple, which correspond to the order-by-end semantics of the window model.

6. EXPERIMENTS

Our experiments were performed on a system with an Intel Core2 Duo, 2.66 Ghz, 4 GB RAM, running Windows 7, Java 6 (both 32 bit). We ran two sets of experiments on top of MXQuery [10]: (1) A synthetic data/query set to perform a sensitivity analysis for stateful operators. (2) A Linear Road Benchmark [9] implementation to study the impact of change on complex queries under strict time constraints.

6.1 Sensitivity Analysis for Stateful Operators

Our sensitivity analyis focuses on the behavior of stateful operators, since stateless operators will have a negligible effect on change performance. MXQuery uses a predicate-based window operator which can conveniently be used to express complex windows constructs, including count- and application time-based windows [10]. We study the impact of *window size*, and *window slide* on *performance*, *correctness criteria*, and *cost*. Both versions of our query compute a sum over count-based windows, since this provides a clear way to define the workload and the expected results. The input data consists of a sequence of 2000 XML elements containing an integer payload, which are fed to the system as fast as it could consume it. The change control element is inserted after 1000 data items, ensuring that the system has reached a steady state in terms of open windows and also has enough input to complete the change. All measurements were repeated 100 times. For performance we took the averages, for correctness we checked across all these runs that we always saw the same results. Since standard deviation on all results was small, we do not report it explicitly.

6.1.1 Response Time

In the first experiment, we vary the window size of Q^{new} between 10 and 100 elements, while keeping that of the Q^{old} at 50. Both queries are using a slide of 1, providing a significant overlap amount the windows. As Figure 14 shows, the different impact of window size on the response times (time between the last element of Q^{old} and the first element of Q^{new}) is quite profound for the various methods: For *IChange* and *DChange*, the response time is linear to the size of the new window (from 1.7 msec at WS=10 to 22.6 msec at WS=100), as processing of Q^{new} only starts when Q^{old} has ended, and the processing time is proportional to the number of input items in a window. For *QDChange*, the response time is 0.2msec for window sizes of Q^{new} that are smaller than or equal to 50, since the output of Q^{new} would have been produced earlier, and needs to be held up until Q^{old} finishes. Once Q^{new} has window sizes bigger than that of Q^{old}, the same trend as for IChange is visible, because now the size of the new window dominates. The additional cost of synchronization between Q^{old} and Q^{new} causes response times to increase somewhat faster. For *SDChange*, smaller windows of Q^{new} mean that the output of Q^{new} needs to be produced before the output of Q^{old}, yielding a negative response time for the smaller values, e.g. -7 msec for WS=10. As the window size of Q^{new} increases, the response time increases, showing values similar to *QDChange* for WS greater than 50. *GIChange* shows "perfect" response times (3 microseconds), since Q^{old} is kept producing until Q^{new} can produce output, then it is terminated immediately. *GDChange* uses the same approach, but drains Q^{old}, thus showing a "negative" response time of around 10 msec, slightly more than cost of producing windows of Q^{old}, as the two queries run in parallel and need to be coordinated.

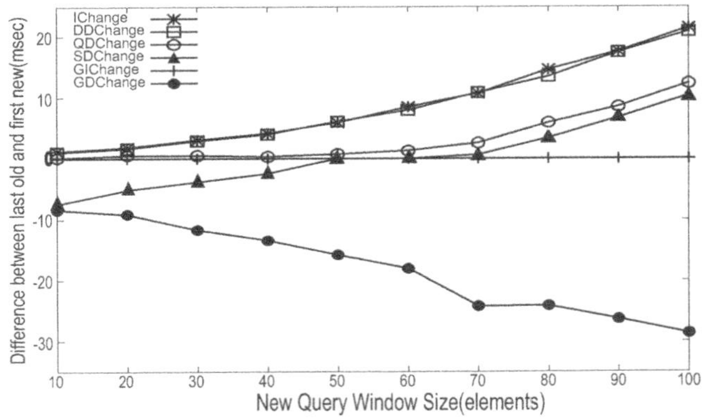

Figure 14: Responsiveness on Window Size, Slide=1

6.1.2 Correctness

We measure correctness by creating the reference streams according to the definition in Section 3.2.1 and compare the outputs against it. Figure 15(a) shows that there is constant loss (49 expected elements) for *IChange* and *DDChange*, corresponding to the loss of a complete Q^{old} window until Q^{new} picks up. *QDChange*, *SDChange*, and *GDChange* do not show any loss, since the draining of Q^{old} and the starting of Q^{new} are balanced to avoid this. *GIChange* has loss proportional to the size difference of the new window and old window, since Q^{old} receives an *IStop* as soon as the first output of Q^{new} is available, discarding the last window of Q^{old}. For disorder (Figures 15(b) and(c)) we also see the expected results: *IChange*, *DDChange*, and *GIChange* never cause any disorder, since no overlapping results are produced. *QDChange* produces results out of stream order if the window size of Q^{new} is smaller. The number of errors is proportional to the difference in window size (e.g., 39 at WS=10), since as many "smaller" windows are produced (due to the slide of 1) before the completion of Q^{old} and need to be delayed to maintain query order. In turn, *SDChange* shows the same behavior in respect to items out of query order, while *GDChange* has has a number proportional to the window size of Q^{old}, as it drains it after the start of Q^{new}. We only see duplicates (i.e, exact same input to a pair of results from both versions) when the window of size of Q^{new} is the same as that of Q^{old} and the change method is *GDChange*. Nonetheless it should be noted that both *GIChange* and *GDChange* produce additional results (with different inputs), both by the overlap of mapping functions and the output produced by Q^{old} while "waiting" for output from Q^{new} (which is not part of the reference stream).

6.1.3 Cost

The different change methods also have a different runtime overhead. In our measurements, we focused on the CPU cost, since the actual memory overhead depends on how an SPE supports the sharing of items, queues, etc. For all methods, we measured the CPU time of the main thread over the whole experiment execution as well as the use of any helper threads required to perform parallel query execution. The cost of the main thread is almost the same for all methods, thus we just show the results for the helper thread in

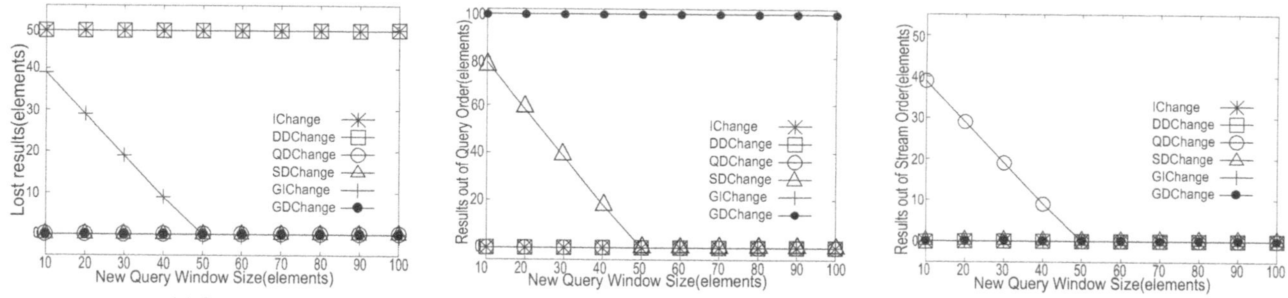

(a) Loss (b) Query Order (c) Stream Order

Figure 15: Correctness results for different changes

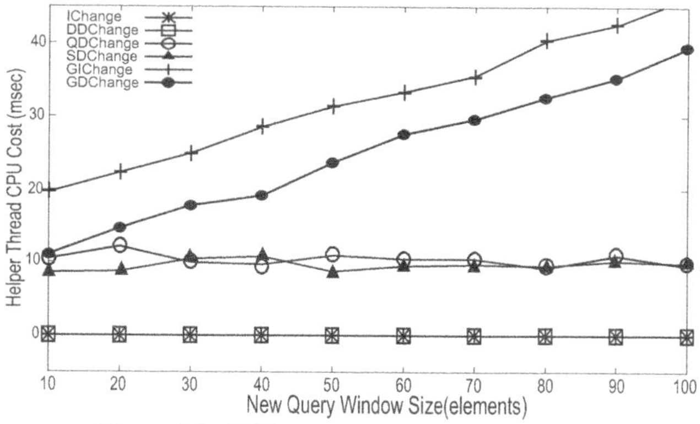

Figure 16: CPU cost on Window Size, Slide=1

Figure 16, measured in milliseconds of CPU time. Since *IChange* and *DDChange* do not execute both versions in parallel, there is obviously no cost for them. *SDChange* and *QDChange* always produce the reference output, so the relative cost stays the same. For *GIChange* and *GDChange*, additional output of Q^{old} is produced while waiting for output of Q^{new}, therefore we see a higher cost in general and an increase with the window size of Q^{new}. In our implementation, *GIChange* is slightly more expensive, since it computes output that might be discarded, while *GDChange* avoids that.

6.2 Other Experiment Results

We also performed tests with different slides and different relative positions of the change elements. The results showed the expected results. The bigger the slide and thus the smaller the overlap, the fewer correctness problems occur. If there are only tumbling windows, placing the change at the window change resulted in error-free results for all methods.

Multiple changes performed in decreasing distance did not influence each other as long as draining areas of earlier query versions did not overlap with the start of later versions. As soon as this overlap started, we would observe both additional overhead (due to a higher number of version executed in parallel) as well as duplicates and disorder.

Finally, we also tested the different change methods on the Linear Road Benchmark [9] workload, in particular on the Accident Segment query. There are several differences compared to the synthetic workload: (1) The query is significantly more complex, using multiple nested windows with predicates, grouping inside windows and parallel aggregation. (2) Data arrives using a specific timing (3) Results are expected within 5 seconds. Yet the observed results closely mirrored what we had seen on the synthetic data, with a slightly bigger impact on the arrival timing and window slide on the delays. In addition, our architecture extensions did not create a significant overhead when no change was happening.

Important	Irrelevant	Method
Runtime Resources, Implementation Overhead	Loss, Response Time	IChange
Loss, Query Order	Response Time	QDChange
Loss, Stream Order	Response Time	SDChange
Response Time, Duplicates	Runtime Resources, Implementation Overhead, Loss	GIChange
Response Time, Loss	Runtime Resources, Implementation Overhead, Duplicates, Order	GDChange

Table 2: Change Method Decision Matrix

6.3 Summary and Guidelines

The results of the conceptual as well as the experimental analysis give a fairly clear answer to when to use which change method, given that there cannot be a single winner which fulfills all criteria. We have summarized the tradeoffs in Table 2. Generally speaking, achieving zero loss and low response time incur additional implementation complexity and runtime overhead. So if neither of them is required, using *IChange* is viable in environments like sensor networks (due to limited resources) or complex query processors (due to the implementation effort). When loss must be avoided, but response time is less critical, *QDChange* and *SDChange* are the most suitable. The order that is expected during the change then determines which of them to use. Finally, Graceful Changes address Response Time, trading it off with higher resource usage. Among them, *GIChange* should be chosen if loss is tolerable, while *GDChange* should be preferred if it is not tolerable. *DDChange* is suitable only in very rare circumstances, since it does not provide stronger guarantees than IChange and requires drain support, In addition, it does not always guarantee the same results as the other change methods on Q^{new}, since the *start position* of the new mapping function is set at the end of the drain area, and not at the change element position as in all other approaches.

7. RELATED WORK

The basic vision for dynamic modification of continuous queries (CQ) was first put forth by the Borealis project [6]. The Borealis approach, however, is much more restricted: It focuses on specific operators (such as windows) with specific changes (slide or size) instead of allowing arbitrary changes on queries. No formal semantics of change are given, and the architecture ties its strategies to system time and execution speed. To our knowledge, this approach has never been implemented.

The use of control elements has been inspired by the punctuation-based stream processing work of Tucker et al. [24], yet with different semantics. In that work, data streams are annotated with punctuations to mark the end of a subset of data in the stream, which are then exploited for optimizations.

Query modification shares a lot of challenges and solutions with other lifecycle problems in CQ, namely failure handling [16] and plan migration [26, 25]. The guarantees defined by these approaches are a subset of ours, e.g. Hwang et al. [16] omit order and liveness. A fundamental difference is that all of these approaches try to maintain a semantically unchanged query over changes of the infrastructure or execution plan, and change is driven by the system. In our context, change can also be triggered by the application, and therefore, we do not make assumptions about the timing and semantics of the new query.

In a similar spirit, the extensive work on adaptive query processing [14] targets a subset of the problem we are solving: No matter how the actual query execution is modified, the semantics of the query stay the same, and no errors are allowed to occur during the adaptation. Our formal framework can describe the behavior of such a system quite well, e.g. using stop and start to mark the boundaries of an adaptation. In terms of implementation, many approaches have been been studied on how to optimize this adaptation. In particular, reductions of resource consumption and improvements on transition time were studied. Many of these ideas might be relevant for our work and could be incorporated in our implementation. This will further improve performance on top of our conservative approach, which avoids re-engineering of existing SPEs.

Application-driven CQ changes are proposed by Lindeberg et al. [20], who investigate changing window sizes in order to improve results of a health monitoring use case. In contrast to our model, this model is very restricted in terms of the allowed query modifications (size change for tumbling windows) and use cases (heart attack prediction), and provides no formal correctness guarantees.

Finally, our work also relates to stopping and restarting of long-running in data warehouses [17, 11, 13]. In this case, some queries are intentionally terminated and later restarted to deal with resource contention. The restart should reuse some of the old state for efficiency reasons. Stopping and restarting the same query constitutes a special case in our more general framework. Furthermore, streaming has different semantic requirements than traditional warehouses, e.g., ordered data delivery.

8. CONCLUSION

In this work, we have presented a punctuation-based framework for correct and efficient modification of continuous queries over data streams. By representing query semantics with dependency functions, we were able to establish a general model where complex CQ lifecycle operations can be created out of the basic operations like start and stop. Moreover, our work builds on a powerful methodology that allows us to easily extend our framework even further to implement other query lifecycle operations beyond modification. We have also shown that an implementation of this framework is possible on typical SPEs, without requiring much effort or fundamental changes on the existing implementation.

Benchmark results on our prototype implementation clearly reveal the practical aspects and significant performance/correctness tradeoffs among our query modification techniques.

For future work, we foresee three directions: 1) Extending our modification model to queries with operators that accept multiple input streams (i.e., join and union); 2) Optimizing change performance by exploiting query knowledge (e.g., by identifying common subexpressions across versions to minimize change cost); 3) Utilizing our methodology for other query lifecycle operations and settings, such as query migration.

Acknowledgements.
The work published in this article was partially funded by the MASTER project (FP7-216917) under the EU 7th Research Framework Programme Information and Communication Technologies Objective . We would like to thank to Donald Kossmann for the discussions on early versions of this work. In addition, we want to thank Simonetta Zysset and Eva Ruiz for their invaluable services of proofreading.

9. REFERENCES

[1] IBM InfoSphere Streams. `http://www-01.ibm.com/software/data/infosphere/streams/`.
[2] Master: Managing Assurance, Security and Trust for sERvices. `http://www.master-fp7.eu/`.
[3] MXQuery: A Light-weight, Full-featured XQuery Engine. `http://mxquery.org/?page_id=2`.
[4] StreamBase Systems, Inc. `http://www.streambase.com/`.
[5] Truviso, Inc. `http://www.truviso.com/`.
[6] D. Abadi et al. The Design of the Borealis Stream Processing Engine. In *CIDR Conference*, 2005.
[7] M. H. Ali et al. Microsoft CEP Server and Online Behavioral Targeting. *PVLDB*, 2(2), 2009.
[8] R. Alur and D. L. Dill. A theory of timed automata. *Theoretical Computer Science*, 126(2), 1994.
[9] A. Arasu et al. Linear Road: A Stream Data Management Benchmark. In *VLDB Conference*, 2004.
[10] I. Botan et al. Extending XQuery with Window Functions. In *VLDB Conference*, 2007.
[11] B. Chandramouli et al. Query Suspend and Resume. In *ACM SIGMOD Conference*, 2007.
[12] S. Chandrasekaran et al. TelegraphCQ: Continuous Dataflow Processing for an Uncertain World. In *CIDR Conference*, 2003.
[13] S. Chaudhuri et al. Stop-and-Restart Style Execution for Long Running Decision Support Queries. In *VLDB Conference*, 2007.
[14] A. Deshpande, Z. Ives, and V. Raman. Adaptive Query Processing. *Found. Trends databases*, 1:1–140, January 2007.
[15] K. S. Esmaili, T. Sanamrad, P. M. Fischer, and N. Tatbul. Changing Flights in Mid-air: A Model for Safely Modifying Continuous Queries. Technical Report 722, ETH Zurich, 2011. ftp://ftp.inf.ethz.ch/pub/publications/tech-reports/7xx/722.pdf.
[16] J.-H. Hwang et al. High-Availability Algorithms for Distributed Stream Processing. In *IEEE ICDE Conference*, 2005.
[17] W. J. Labio et al. Efficient Resumption of Interrupted Warehouse Loads. In *ACM SIGMOD Conference*, 2000.
[18] L. Lamport. Proving the Correctness of Multiprocess Programs. *IEEE TSE Journal*, 3(2), 1977.
[19] Y. Law, H. Wang, and C. Zaniolo. Query languages and data models for database sequences and data streams. In *VLDB*, 2004.
[20] M. Lindeberg et al. Adaptive-sized Windows to Improve Real-time Health Monitoring: A Case Study on Heart Attack Prediction. In *ACM MIR Conference*, 2010.
[21] R. Motwani et al. Query Processing, Approximation, and Resource Management in a Data Stream Management System. In *CIDR Conference*, 2003.
[22] N. Tatbul et al. Load Shedding in a Data Stream Manager. In *VLDB Conference*, 2003.
[23] N. Tatbul and S. Zdonik. Window-aware Load Shedding for Aggregation Queries over Data Streams. In *VLDB Conference*, 2006.
[24] P. A. Tucker et al. Exploiting Punctuation Semantics in Continuous Data Streams. *IEEE TKDE Journal*, 15(3), 2003.
[25] Y. Yang et al. HybMig: A Hybrid Approach to Dynamic Plan Migration for Continuous Queries. *IEEE TKDE Journal*, 19(3), 2007.
[26] Y. Zhu et al. Dynamic Plan Migration for Continuous Queries over Data Streams. In *ACM SIGMOD Conference*, 2004.

How Soccer Players Would do Stream Joins

Jens Teubner
Systems Group, Dept. of Computer Science
ETH Zurich, Switzerland
jens.teubner@inf.ethz.ch

Rene Mueller
IBM Almaden Research Center
San Jose, CA, USA
muellerr@us.ibm.com

ABSTRACT

In spite of the omnipresence of parallel (multi-core) systems, the predominant strategy to evaluate *window-based stream joins* is still strictly sequential, mostly just straightforward along the definition of the operation semantics.

In this work we present *handshake join*, a way of describing and executing window-based stream joins that is highly amenable to parallelized execution. Handshake join naturally leverages available hardware parallelism, which we demonstrate with an implementation on a modern *multi-core system* and on top of *field-programmable gate arrays (FPGAs)*, an emerging technology that has shown distinctive advantages for high-throughput data processing.

On the practical side, we provide a join implementation that substantially outperforms CellJoin (the fastest published result) and that will directly turn any degree of parallelism into higher throughput or larger supported window sizes. On the semantic side, our work gives a new intuition of window semantics, which we believe could inspire other stream processing algorithms or ongoing standardization efforts for stream query languages.

Categories and Subject Descriptors

H.2.4 [**Database Management**]: Query Processing

General Terms

Algorithms

Keywords

stream joins, parallelism, data flow

1. INTRODUCTION

One of the key challenges in building database implementations has always been an efficient support for *joins*. The problem is exacerbated in *streaming databases*, which do not have the option to pre-compute access structures and which have to adhere to *window semantics* in addition to value-based join predicates.

SIGMOD'11, June 12–16, 2011, Athens, Greece.

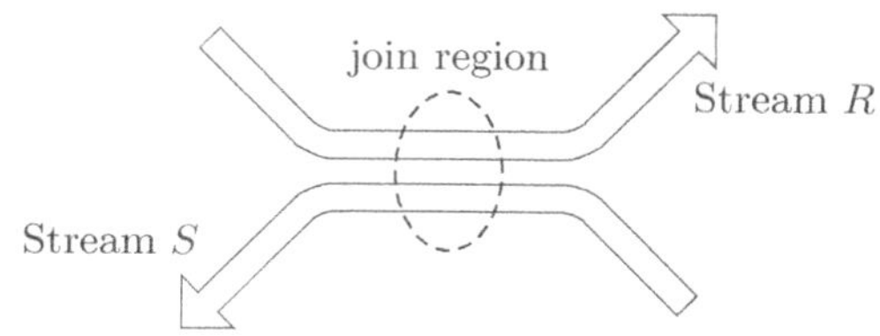

Figure 1: Handshake join idea.

In this work we present *handshake join*, a stream join implementation that naturally supports *hardware acceleration* to achieve unprecedented data throughput. Handshake join is particularly attractive for platforms that support very high degrees of parallelism, such as *multi-core CPUs*, *field-programmable gate arrays (FPGAs)*, or *massively parallel processor arrays (MPPAs)* [5]. FPGAs were recently proposed as an escape to the inherent limitations of classical CPU-based system architectures [23, 24].

The intuition behind handshake join is illustrated in Figure 1. We let the two input streams flow by in opposing directions—like soccer players that walk by each other to shake hands before a match. As we detail in the remainder of this report, this view on the join problem has interesting advantages with respect to parallel execution and scalability.

Our main contribution is a stream join algorithm that, by adding compute cores, can trivially be scaled up to handle larger join windows, higher throughput rates, or more compute-intensive join predicates (handshake join can deal with *any* join predicate, including non-equi-joins). As a side effect, our work provides a new look on the semantics of stream joins. This aspect of our work might be inspiring for ongoing efforts toward a standard language and semantics for stream processors [4, 16]. Likewise, we think that the design principles of handshake join, mainly its data flow-oriented mode of execution, could have interesting applications outside the particular stream processing problem. As such, our work can help cut the multi-core knot that hardware makers have given us.

We first recap the semantics of stream joins in Section 2, along with typical implementation techniques in software. Section 3 introduces handshake join. Section 4 discusses how handshake join could be implemented in computing systems, which we realize with a prototype implementation on top of a modern multi-core CPU (Section 5) and with a massively parallel implementation for FPGAs (Section 6). In Section 7 we relate our work to others', before we wrap up in Section 8.

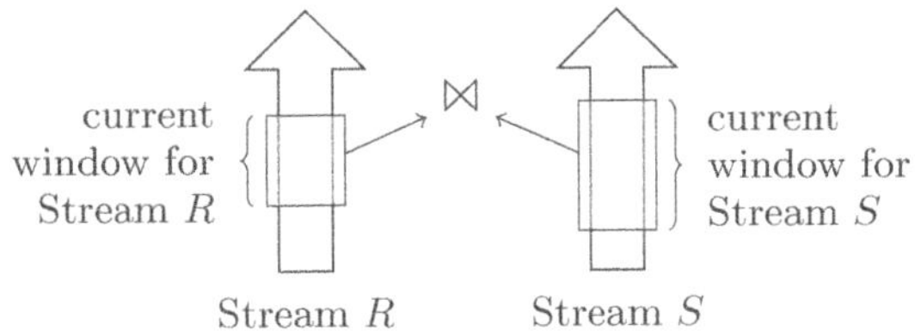

Figure 2: Window join (figure adopted from [17]).

2. STREAM JOINS

It is the very nature of stream processing engines to deal with unbounded, "infinite", input data. These data arrive by means of a stream and have to be processed immediately, in real time.

2.1 Windowing

Infinite input data causes obvious semantic problems when some of the classical database operators—most notably joins and aggregates—are to be evaluated over data streams. This has lead to the notion of *windows* in the streaming community. By looking at a finite subset of the input data (a window), all algebraic operations become semantically sound again.

Figure 2 (adopted from [17]) illustrates this for the case of a join operation. The join is always evaluated only over finite subsets taken from both input streams. Windows over different input data can span different numbers of tuples, as indicated by the window sizes in Figure 2.

Various ways have been proposed to define suitable window boundaries depending on application needs. In this work we focus on *sliding windows* which, at any point in time, cover all tuples from some earlier point in time up to the most recent tuple. Usually, sliding windows are either time-based, *i.e.*, they cover all tuples within the last τ time units, or tuple-based, *i.e.*, they cover the last w tuples in arrival order. Handshake join will deal with both types of window specification equally well.

2.2 Sliding-Window Joins

The exact semantics of window-based joins (precisely which stream tuple could be paired with which?) in existing work was largely based on how the functionality was implemented. For instance, windowing semantics is implicit in the three-step procedure devised by Kang *et al.* [17]. The procedure is performed for each tuple r that arrives from input stream R:

1. *Scan* stream S's window to find tuples matching r.
2. *Insert* new tuple r into window for stream R.
3. *Invalidate* all expired tuples in stream R's window.

Tuples s that arrive from input stream S are handled symmetrically. Sometimes, a transient access structure is built over both open windows, which accelerates Step 1 at the cost of some maintenance effort in Steps 2 and 3.

The three-step procedure carries an implicit semantics for window-based stream joins:

Semantics of Window-Based Stream Joins. *For $r \in R$ and $s \in S$, the tuple $\langle r, s\rangle$ appears in the join result $R \bowtie_p S$ iff (t_i denote tuple arrival timestamps, T_i denote window sizes)*

(a) r arrives after s ($t_r > t_s$) and s is in the current S-window at the moment when r arrives (i.e., $t_r < t_s + T_S$) or

(b) r arrives earlier than s ($t_s > t_r$) and r is still in the R-window when s arrives ($t_s < t_r + T_R$)

and r and s pass the join predicate p.

A problem of the three-step procedure is that it is not well suited to exploit the increasing degree of *parallelism* that modern system architectures support.

Optimal use of many-core systems demands *local* availability of data at the respective compute core, because systems increasingly exhibit *non-uniform memory access (NUMA)* characteristics, where the cost of memory access increases with the distance of an item in memory to the processing core that requests it. Such non-uniformity is contrary to the nature of the join problem, where *any* input tuple might have to be paired with *any* tuple from the opposite stream to form a result tuple.

Gedik *et al.* [10] discuss *partitioning* and *replication* as a possible solution. Thereby, either the in-memory representation of the two windows is partitioned over the available compute resources or arriving tuples are partitioned over cores. Local data availability then needs to be established explicitly by replicating the corresponding other piece of data (input tuples or the full in-memory windows).

Partitioning and replication are both rather expensive operations. The latter involves data movement which—in addition to the necessary CPU work—may quickly overload the memory subsystem as the number of CPU cores increases. A dedicated coordinator core has to *re-partition* the dataset every k input tuples (where k is a small configuration parameter), at a cost that grows linearly with the number of processing cores n [10]. Such cost may still be acceptable for the eight cores of the Cell processor, but will be hard to bear on upcoming systems with large n.

In this work, by contrast, we aim for a work distribution scheme that remains scalable even when the number of processing cores grows very large (we tested with hundreds of cores).

3. HANDSHAKE JOIN

In the most generic case, the three-step procedure of Kang *et al.* [17] corresponds to a *nested loops-style* join evaluation. To evaluate a stream join $R \bowtie_p S$, the scan phase first *enumerates* all combinations $\langle r, s\rangle$ of input tuples $r \in R$ and $s \in S$ that satisfy the window constraint. Then, the resulting tuple pairs are *filtered* according to the join predicate p and added to the join result. Only for certain join predicates (such as equality or range conditions), specialized in-memory access structures, typically hash tables or tree indices, can help reduce the number of pairs to enumerate.

3.1 Soccer Players

The enumeration of join candidates may be difficult to distribute efficiently over a large number of processing cores. Traditional approaches (including CellJoin) assume a central coordinator that partitions and replicates data as needed over the available cores. But it is easy to see that this will quickly become a bottleneck as the numbers of cores increase. The aim of our work is to scale out to very high degrees of parallelism, which renders any enumeration scheme unusable that depends on centralized coordination.

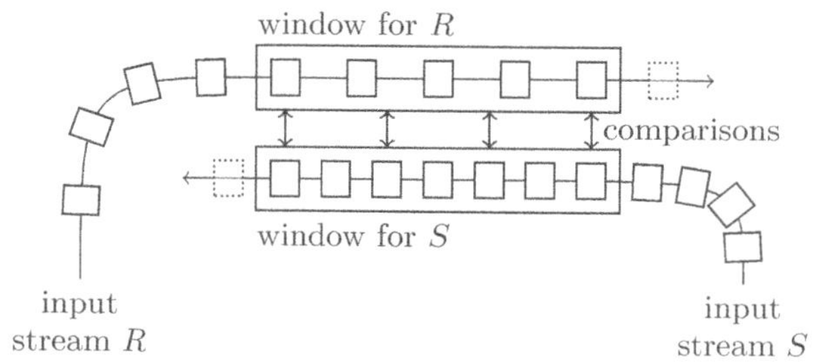

Figure 3: Handshake join sketch. Streams flow by each other in opposite directions; comparisons (and result generation) happens in parallel as the streams pass by.

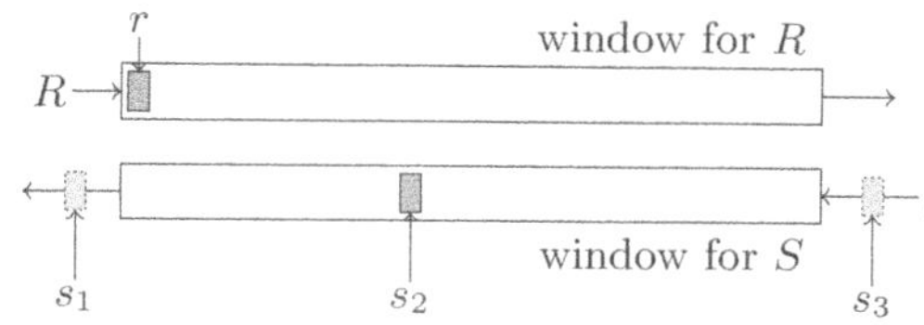

Figure 4: Handshake join semantics.

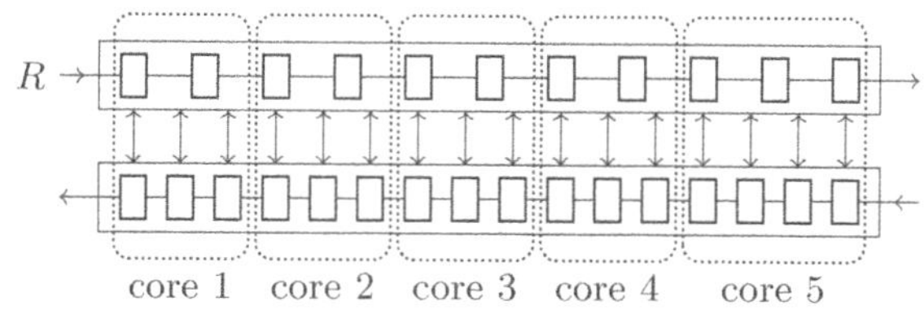

Figure 5: Parallelized handshake join evaluation. Each compute core processes one segment of both windows and performs all comparisons locally.

It turns out that we can learn from soccer players here. Soccer players know very well how all pairs of players from two opposing teams can be enumerated without any external coordination. Before the beginning of every game, it is custom to shake hands with all players from the opposing team. Players do so by *walking by* each other in opposite directions and by *shaking hands* with every player that they encounter.

3.2 Stream Joins and Handshaking

The handshake procedure used in sports games inspired the design of *handshake join*, whose idea we illustrated in Figure 3 (this particular illustration assumes tuple-based windows).

Tuples from the two input streams R and S, marked as rectangular boxes □, are pushed through respective join windows. When entering the window, each tuple pushes all existing window content one step to the side, such that always the oldest tuple "falls out" of the window and expires (we detail later how to implement such behavior). Both join windows are lined up next to each other in such a way that window contents are pushed through in opposing directions, much like the players in soccer (cf. Figure 3).

Whenever two stream tuples $r \in R$ and $s \in S$ encounter each other (in a moment we will discuss what that means and how it can be implemented), they "shake hands", *i.e.*, the join condition is evaluated over r and s, and a result tuple $\langle r, s \rangle$ appended to the join result if the condition is met. Many "handshakes" take place at the same time, work that we will parallelize over available compute resources.

We next look at handshake join and its characteristics from the abstract side. In Sections 4–6 we then discuss techniques to implement handshake join on different types of actual hardware, including multi-core systems and FPGAs.

3.3 Semantics

To understand the semantics of handshake join, consider the situation at moment t_r when tuple r enters its join window (illustrated in Figure 4).

A tuple from S can now relate to r in either of the following three ways (indicated in Figure 4 as s_1 through s_3):

(1) Tuple s_1 is so old that it already left the join window for input stream S, *i.e.*, $t_r > t_{s_1} + T_S$. Thus, r will not see s_1 and no attempt will be made to join r and s_1.

(2) Tuple s_2 is somewhere in the join window of S when r enters the arena, *i.e.*, s_2 is older than r ($t_r > t_{s_2}$), but still within the S-window (that is, $t_r < t_{s_2} + T_S$).

As r and s_2 move along their join windows, the two tuples are guaranteed to meet eventually, and $\langle r, s_2 \rangle$ will be added to the join result if they pass the join predicate.

(3) Tuple s_3 has not arrived yet (*i.e.*, $t_r < t_{s_3}$). Whether or not a join $r \bowtie s_3$ will be attempted depends on s_3's time of arrival and on the window specification for stream R. Once s_3 arrives, both factors will determine whether r takes a role that is symmetric to cases *(1)* or *(2)* above.

Cases *(1)* and *(2)* are the ones where r arrives after s, and a join will be attempted when $t_r < t_s + T_S$. Hence, these cases coincide with part *(a)* of the classical definition of stream join semantics (Section 2.2). Case *(3)* is the situation where r arrives earlier than s. It follows by symmetry that this case yields the same output tuples as covered by part *(b)* in Section 2.2.

In summary, handshake join produces the exact same output tuples that the classical three-step procedure would, and we can use handshake join as a safe replacement for existing stream join implementations.

Handshake join typically produces its output in a different *tuple order*. A certain degree of local disorder is prevalent in real applications already (and stream processors may explicitly be prepared to deal with it [18]). If necessary, it can be corrected with standard techniques such as *punctuations* [21].

Even though our view at window-based stream join differs significantly problem's classical treatment, handshake join still yields the same output semantics. On the one hand side, this may provide new insights into ongoing work on defining standards and abstract specifications for stream processors [4, 16]. On the other hand, handshake join opens opportunities for effective *parallelization* on modern hardware. Next, we will demonstrate how to exploit the latter.

3.4 Parallelization

Figure 5 illustrates how handshake join can be parallelized over available compute resources. Each processing unit (or "core") is assigned one *segment* of the two join windows. Tuple data is held in local memory (if applicable on a particular architecture), and all tuple comparisons are performed locally.

Data Flow vs. Control Flow. This parallel evaluation became possible because we converted the original *control flow* problem (or its procedural three-step description) into a *data flow* representation. Rather than synchronizing join execution from a centralized coordinator, processing units are now driven by the flow of stream tuples that are passed on directly between neighboring cores. Processing units can observe locally when new data has arrived and can decide autonomously when to pass on tuples to their neighbor.

The advantages of data flow-style processing have been known for a long time. Their use in shared-nothing systems was investigated, *e.g.*, by Teeuw and Blanken [28]. Modern computing architectures increasingly tend toward shared-nothing setups. Recently, we demonstrated how data flow-oriented approaches can thus be advantageous to compute distributed joins [9] or to solve the frequent item problem on FPGAs [29].

Communication Pattern. In addition, we have established a particularly simple *communication pattern*. Processing units only interact with their immediate neighbors, which may ease inter-core routing and avoid communication bottlenecks. In particular, handshake join is a good fit for architectures that use *point-to-point* links between processing cores—a design pattern that can be seen in an increasing number of multi-core platforms (examples include HyperTransport links; the QuickPath interconnect used in Intel Nehalem systems; the messaging primitives in Intel's SCC prototype [14]; or Tilera's iMesh architecture with current support for up to 100 cores).

Scalability. Both properties together, the representation as a data flow problem and the point-to-point communication pattern along a linear chain of processing units, ensure scalability to large numbers of processing units. Additional cores can either be used to support larger window sizes without negative impact on performance, or to reduce the workload per core, which will improve throughput for high-volume data inputs.

Soccer Players. We note that the same properties are what make the handshake procedure in soccer effective. Most importantly, soccer players organize themselves using only local interaction.

In addition, the soccer analogy exhibits the same *locality* property that is beneficial for us. While soccer players emphasize locality for the limited length of their arms, in handshake join we benefit from an efficient use of hardware with NUMA-style memory characteristics.

3.5 Encountering Tuples

We yet have to define what exactly it means that stream tuples in the two windows "encounter" each other and which pairs of stream elements need to be compared at any one time. Note that, depending on the relative window size configuration, stream items might never line up in opposing positions exactly. Both our previous handshake join illustrations were examples of such window size configurations (only every second R-tuple lines up exactly with every third S-tuple in Figure 5, for instance).

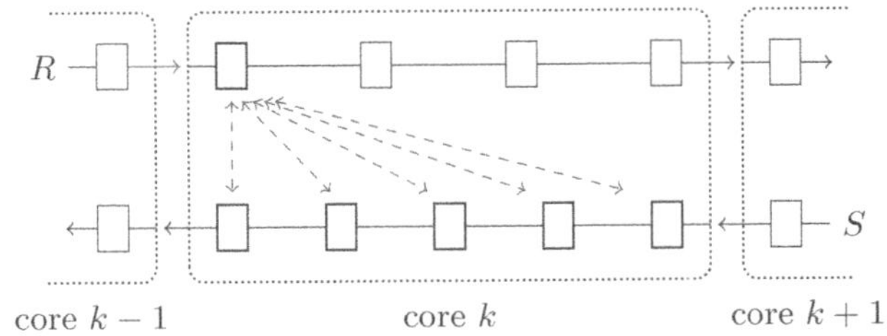

(a) Tuple from stream R entered segment.

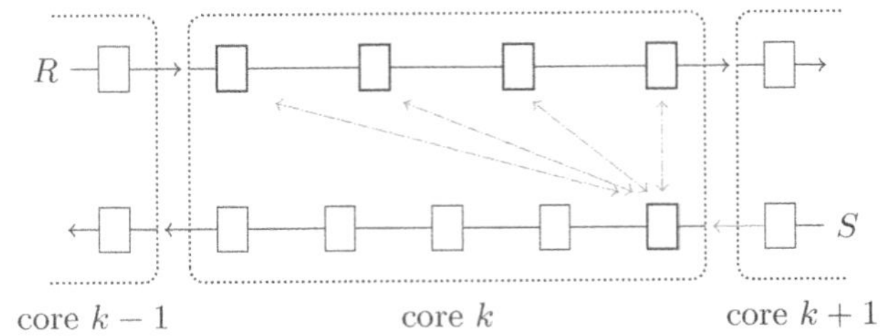

(b) Tuple from stream S entered segment.

Figure 6: Immediate scan strategy. A tuple entering from stream R or S will trigger immediate comparisons ⤢ or ⤡ in the segment of processing core k (respectively).

For proper window join semantics, the only assumption we made in Section 3.3 was that an item that enters either window will encounter all current items in the other window *eventually*. That is, there must not be a situation where two stream items can pass each other without being considered as a candidate pair. Thus, any local processing strategy that prevents this from happening will do to achieve correct overall window semantics.

Immediate Scan Strategy. One particular strategy (which we will call *immediate scan strategy*) that can be used to process a segment k is illustrated in Figure 6. In this illustration, we assume that every tuple $r \in R$ is compared to all S-tuples in the segment immediately when r enters the segment. Figure 6(a) shows all tuple comparisons that need to be performed when a new R-tuple is shifted into the segment.

Likewise, when a new tuple $s \in S$ enters the segment, it is immediately compared to all R-tuples that are already in the segment, as illustrated in Figure 6(b). The strategy will operate correctly *regardless* of how window sizes relate to each other.

The latter property is interesting when it comes to the distribution of load within a handshake join configuration. In particular, it means that segment borders can be chosen arbitrarily, which can be used to very flexibly balance load between the involved processing cores. Our software implementation (details in Sections 4 and 5) autonomously re-balances segment boundaries to achieve an even load distribution over all participating cores.

Other Strategies. Observe that *locally* on each processing core, immediate scanning is essentially identical to the three-step procedure of Kang *et al.* [17]. The difference is that the procedure is used only as part of an overall join execution. Further, we allow the processing cores some flexibility to arrange with their neighbors on the precise segmentation (*i.e.*, on the local window size). In a sense, the algorithm of Kang *et al.* is only one particular instance of handshake join that runs with a single processing unit and uses the immediate scan strategy.

One consequence is that we can plug in any (semantically equivalent) stream join implementation to act as a local processing core. This includes algorithms that use additional access structures or advanced join algorithms (as they might apply for certain join predicates; handshake join is agnostic to that). Handshake join then becomes a mechanism to distribute and parallelize the execution of an existing algorithm over many cores.

3.6 Handshake Join and its Alternatives

Among existing approaches to parallelize the execution of stream joins in a multi-core environment, CellJoin [10] clearly has been most successful. In essence, CellJoin treats stream joins as a *scheduling* and *placement* problem. A central coordinator assigns workload chunks ("basic windows" of input data) to individual cores for processing. Thereby, CellJoin assumes that all chunks have to be fetched from a global memory beforehand.

The nature of a nested loops-style join evaluation makes such a strategy difficult to scale. During join processing, every pair of tuples has to be co-located on some core at least once.[1] The *movement of data* is thus much more inherent to the join problem than the placement of CPU work or data.

This is why we address the problem from a *data flow perspective* instead. While the handshake join strategy does not necessarily reduce the aggregate amount of moved data, it leads to a much more regular and organized communication pattern. In particular, there is no hot spot that could become a bottleneck if the system is scaled up. In Section 5, we illustrate the communication pattern for a concrete piece of hardware and show how handshake join leads to linear scaling even for very large core counts.

4. REALIZING HANDSHAKE JOIN

Our discussion so far was primarily based on a high-level intuition of how tuples flow between segments in a handshake join setup. We now map the handshake join intuition onto communication primitives that can be used to implement handshake join on actual hardware, including commodity CPUs or FPGAs.[2]

4.1 Lock Step Forwarding

In Section 3, we assumed that a newly arriving tuple would synchronously push all tuples of the same stream through the respective window. Essentially, this implies an atomic operation over all participating processing cores. For instance, upon a new tuple arrival, all cores must simultaneously forward their oldest tuple to the respective left/right-next neighbor.

Obviously, an implementation of such lock step processing would obliterate a key idea behind handshake join, namely high parallelism without centralized coordination. This problem arises at least for commodity hardware, such as multi-core CPU systems. It turns out that lock step processing is still a viable route for FPGA-based implementations, as we shall see in Section 6.2.

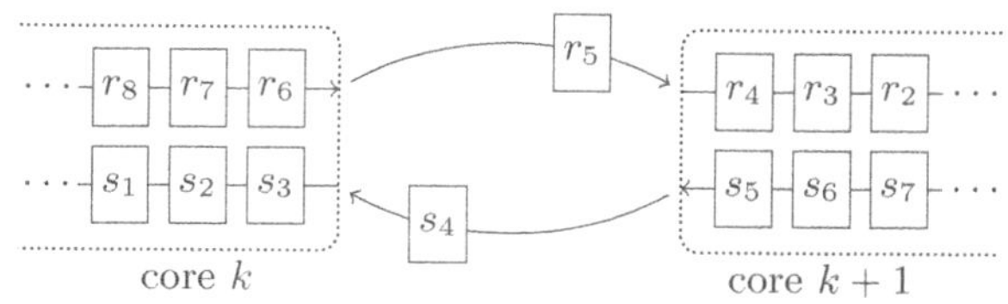

Figure 7: Missed-join pair problem. Tuples sent via message queues might miss each other while on the communication channels.

4.2 Asynchronous Message Queues

Handshake join can also be run in an *asynchronous communication* mode. We will now demonstrate how to implement handshake join based on *message passing* between neighboring cores, a communication mode that is known for its scalability advantages with increasing core counts [3].

In particular, one pair of *FIFO queues* (indicated as arrows ⇝ below) between any two neighboring processing cores is sufficient to support data propagation along the chain of cores in either direction:

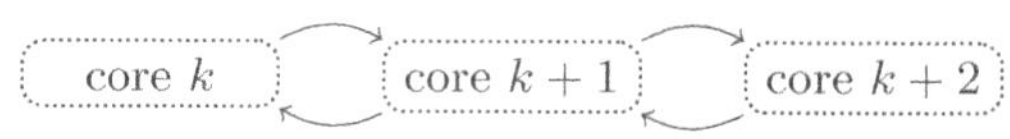

FIFO queues can be tuned for high efficiency and provide fully asynchronous access. In particular, no performance-limiting locks or other atomic synchronization primitives are necessary to implement point-to-point message queues. Some architectures even provide explicit messaging primitives in hardware [14].

Though supportive of increased parallelism, asynchronous communication between cores can bear an important risk. As illustrated in Figure 7, tuples from opposing streams might *miss* each other if they both happen to be in the communication channel at the same time (in Figure 7, tuples r_5 and s_4 are both in transit between the neighboring cores k and $k+1$; thus, no comparison is attempted between tuples r_5 and s_4).

Two-Phase Forwarding. To avoid the missing of join candidates, we have to make sure that in such cases, the two in-flight tuples will still meet on exactly one of the two neighboring cores, say the right one, C_{right}. To this end, we use an *asymmetric* core synchronization protocol. C_{right} (and only C_{right}) will keep around copies of sent data for short moments of time. These copies will be used to join tuples on C_{right} that would otherwise have missed each other in-flight.

More specifically, we introduce *two-phase forwarding* on the right core. Whenever the right core C_{right} places a tuple s_i into its left send queue, it still keeps a copy of s_i in the local join window, but marks it as *forwarded.* This is illustrated in Figure 8(a): tuple s_4 was sent to C_{left} and marked as forwarded on C_{right} (indicated using a dashed box).

The forwarded tuple remains available for joining on C_{right} until the second phase of tuple forwarding, which is initiated by an *acknowledgment message* from C_{left} (indicated as a diamond-shaped message in Figure 8). In the example, s_4 is still kept around on C_{right} to partner with r_5.

[1]CellJoin first *replicates* all new input tuples to every core. That is, all data is moved to every core at least once.

[2]We currently experiment with graphics processors (GPUs) as another promising platform to implement handshake join.

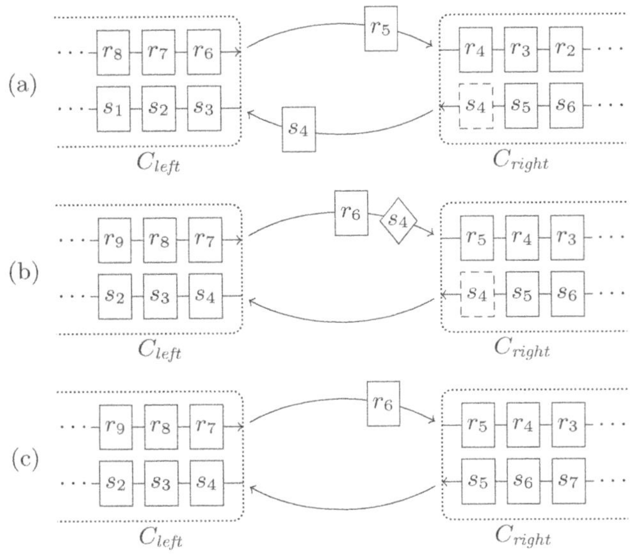

Figure 8: Two-phase tuple forwarding (on right core). Tuples are kept in C_{right}-local join window and removed only after an acknowledgment message from C_{left}.

Figure 8(b) shows the state after C_{left} and C_{right} have processed the data on their message queues. s_4 was joined with $r_6, r_7, \ldots$ on C_{left} and r_5 saw $s_4, s_3, \ldots$ on C_{right}. C_{left} further indicated its reception of s_4 with the acknowledgment message ⟨s_4⟩, then forwarded another tuple r_6 to its right neighbor.

Message ⟨s_4⟩ notifies C_{right} that any tuple sent afterward will already have seen s_4. Thus, C_{right} removes the tuple from its local join window (cf. Figure 8(c)) before accepting the next tuple r_6. This way, each necessary tuple pairing is performed exactly once (on some core).

FIFO Queues. Note that tuple data and acknowledge messages must be sent over the same message channels. In the example of Figure 8, correct semantics is only guaranteed if the acknowledgment for s_4 is received and processed by the right core *in-between* the two tuples r_5 and r_6.

Figure 9 describes an implementation of handshake join based on asynchronous message passing. This code is run on every participating core. Procedure `handshake_join ()` selects one of the two incoming message queues and invokes a `process_... ()` handler to process the message.

The `process_... ()` handlers essentially implement the three-step procedure of Kang *et al.* [17]. In addition, acknowledgment messages are placed in the queues whenever a new input tuple was accepted. The removal of tuples from the two windows is asymmetric. S-tuples are marked forwarded after sending (line 26) and removed when the acknowledgment was seen (line 15). R-tuples, by contrast, are removed from their window immediately after sending (line 29).

Our illustrations in Figure 8 suggested an explicit tuple reference in each acknowledgment message. In practice, this information is redundant, since an acknowledgment will always reference the oldest tuple in the predecessor core. This is reflected in line 15 of Figure 9, which does not actually inspect the content of the acknowledgment message.

```
1  Procedure: handshake_join ()
2  while true do
3      if message waiting in leftRecvQueue then
4          process_left () ;
5      if message waiting in rightRecvQueue then
6          process_right () ;
7      forward_tuples () ;

8  Procedure: process_left ()
9  msg ← message from leftRecvQueue ;
10 if msg contains a new tuple then
11     r_i ← extract tuple from msg ;
12     scan S-window to find tuples that match r_i ;
13     insert r_i into R-window ;
14 else
       /* msg is an acknowledgment message        */
15     remove oldest tuple from S-window ;

16 Procedure: process_right ()
17 msg ← message from rightRecvQueue ;
18 if msg contains a new tuple then
19     s_i ← extract tuple from msg ;
20     scan R-window to find tuples that match s_i ;
21     insert s_i into S-window ;
22     place acknowledgment for s_i in rightSendQueue ;

23 Procedure: forward_tuples ()
24 if S-window is larger than that of left neighbor then
25     place oldest non-forwarded s_i into leftSendQueue ;
26     mark s_i as forwarded ;
27 if R-window is larger than that of our right neighbor
   then
28     place oldest r_i into rightSendQueue ;
29     remove r_i from R-window ;
```

Figure 9: Handshake join with asynchronous message passing (ran on each core).

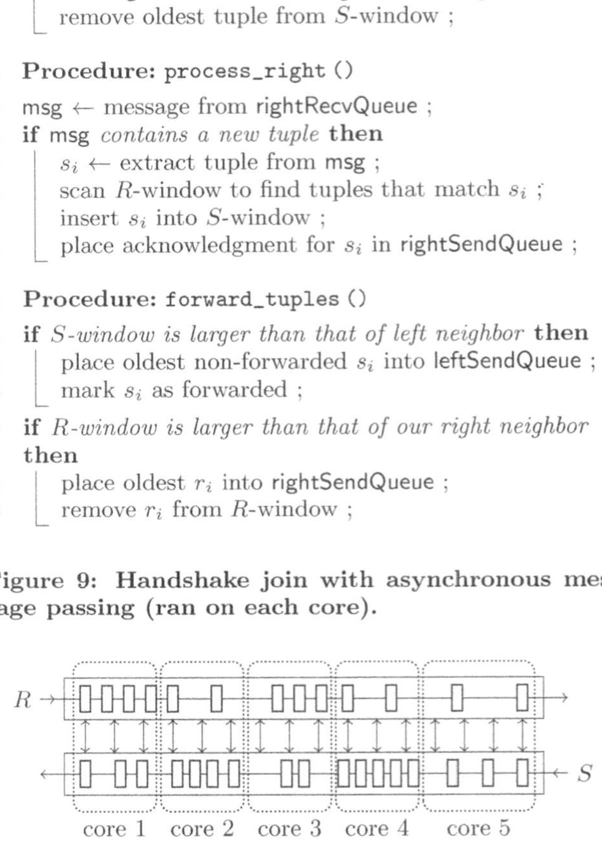

Figure 10: Data items need not be distributed evenly over processing cores for a correct join result.

4.3 Autonomic Load Balancing

We expect the highest join throughput when all available processing cores run just at the maximum load they can sustain without becoming a bottleneck in the system. To this end, load should be *balanced* over compute resources in a flexible manner and—to maintain scalability—without a need for centralized control.

The handshake join code in Figure 9 includes such an *autonomic load balancing* scheme, realized by the tuple forward-

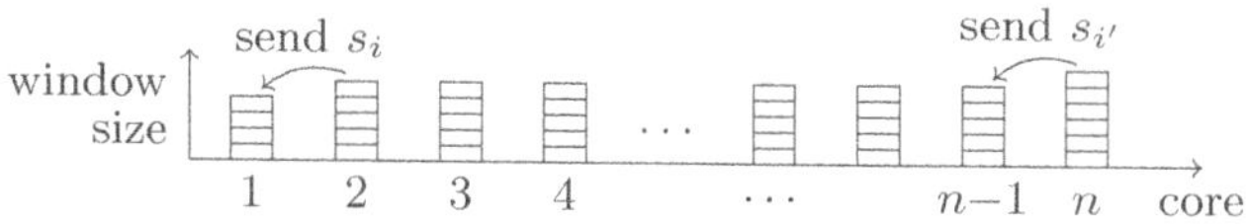

Figure 11: Tuple forwarding based on local window sizes; results in autonomous load balancing.

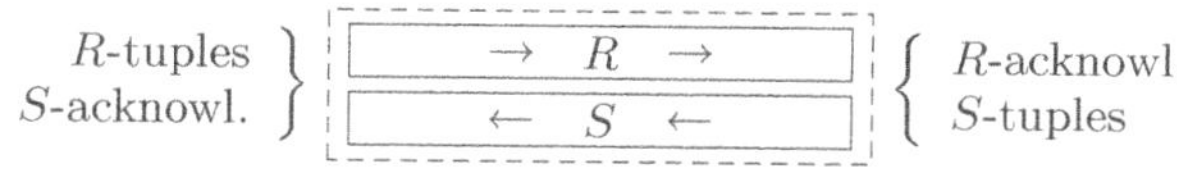

Figure 12: A driver sends tuple data and acknowledgments to opposite ends of the pipeline to realize a given window configuration.

```
Procedure: process_right ()
else
    /* msg is an acknowledgment message                    */
    remove oldest tuple from R-window ;

Procedure: forward_tuples ()
if R-window is larger than that of our right neighbor
then
    place oldest r_i into rightSendQueue ;
    mark r_i as forwarded ;
```

Figure 13: Rightmost core runs a slightly different code to handle tuple removal via acknowledgment messages.

ing procedure `forward_tuples ()`. This scheme is based on the insight that the produced join output is *not* affected by the exact distribution of tuples over processing segments. In fact, the join output would still be correct even when the distribution was very skewed, as illustrated in Figure 10.

This gives us the freedom to forward data (*i.e.*, forward work) at an arbitrary time and we use *load* to guide the forwarding mechanism. Procedure `forward_tuples ()` implements this in a fairly simple manner, which in practice we found sufficient to achieve good load balancing even when the number of cores becomes large or when input data becomes bursty.

The idea is illustrated in Figure 11 for stream S. All processing cores have mostly even-sized local S-windows. New data is pushed in on the right end, which increases the load on core n. Tuple expiration (discussed below) removes tuples from core 1. Cores n and 2 will observe the local imbalances and send S tuples toward their left. Like water in a pipe, tuples will be pushed through the handshake join window, evenly distributed over all processing cores.

The strategy works well in homogeneous environments like ours, where load is directly proportional to window sizes. To tune handshake join for different environments, such as cloud infrastructures or virtualized hardware, all necessary code changes remain local to `forward_tuples ()`.

4.4 Synchronization at Pipeline Ends

Observe that the algorithm in Figure 9 did not explicitly mention the desired window configuration, neither the window type (tuple- or time-based) nor any window size. Instead, handshake join assumes that tuple insertion and removal are signaled by an outside driver process that knows about the precise window configuration.

Since the exact flow of tuples through the handshake join pipeline is immaterial to the join result (see above), these signals only have to be sent to the two *ends* of the processing pipeline. That is, for each input stream the driver process feeds data into one end of the pipeline and takes out expired tuples at the opposite end.

The mechanism to realize tuple insertion and removal by the driver process uses the same acknowledgment messages that helped us avoid the missed-join pair problem above. Earlier we reacted to acknowledgments by removing "forwarded" tuples from the join window. As illustrated in Figure 12, the driver process now takes advantage of this reaction and simply sends acknowledgment messages to trigger the removal of tuples at the far end of each stream window.

The generation of acknowledgment messages is straightforward to implement in the driver process. Depending on the window configuration, the driver either has to count tuples (tuple-based windows) or it must keep a list of the tuples in each window and monitor timestamps accordingly.

In Figure 9, we constructed two-phase forwarding in an asymmetric way and ignored acknowledgment messages for R (this was to make sure that in-flight tuples will be processed on C_{right} only). Messages from the driver process, by contrast, must be interpreted in a symmetric way (the join problem itself is symmetric). To this end, the *right-most* code in any handshake join setup runs a slightly different code that is symmetric to both input streams. Figure 13 lists the necessary changes, based on the `handshake_join ()` code in Figure 9.

To make handshake join sound at both ends of the pipeline, we further assume that window sizes are 0 for non-existent "neighbors." This helps to "pull" data from both input streams toward the respective pipeline end.

Explicit signals that trigger tuple removal have interesting uses also outside handshake join. In fact, they have become a common implementation technique for stream processors, referred to as *− elements* (Stanford STREAM, [2]), *negative tuples* (Nile, [11]), or *deletion messages* (Borealis, [1]) depending on the system. These systems will readily provide all necessary functionality to plug in handshake join seamlessly.

5. HANDSHAKE JOIN IN SOFTWARE

Handshake join can effectively leverage the parallelism of modern multi-core CPUs. To back up this claim, we evaluated the behavior of handshake join on a recent 2.2 GHz AMD Opteron 6174 "Magny Cours" machine. The machine contains 48 real x86-64 cores, distributed over 8 NUMA regions. The system was running Ubuntu Linux, kernel version 2.6.32.

5.1 Non-Uniform Memory Access

The eight NUMA regions are connected through a set of point-to-point HyperTransport links, indicated as dashed lines in Figure 14 (refer to [6] for details). Observe that HyperTransport links do *not* form a fully connected mesh. Rather, two CPU cores can be up to two HyperTransport hops apart (*e.g.*, a core in NUMA region 0 and a core in

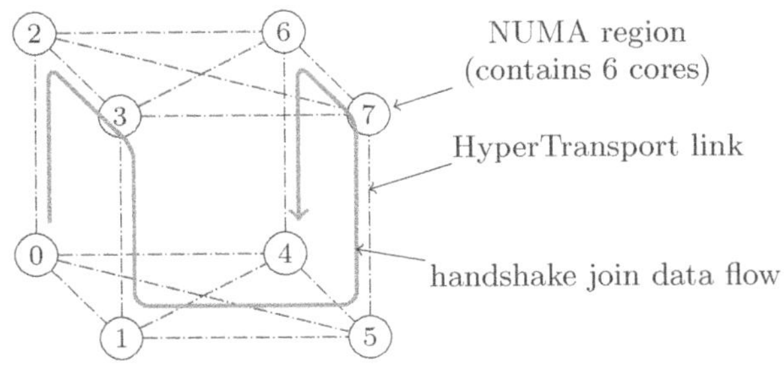

Figure 14: AMD "Magny Cours" architecture (8 dies × 6 cores). Handshake join pipeline laid out along point-to-point HyperTransport links.

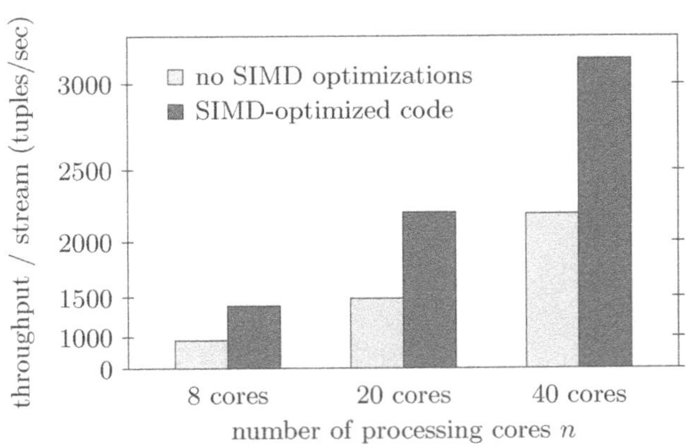

Figure 15: Effect of SIMD optimization. Use of SIMD compiler intrinsics yields a two-fold performance improvement (15 min windows).

NUMA region 3). Similar topologies have become prevalent in modern many-core systems.

Handshake join is well prepared to support a system of this kind. As indicated by the arrow in Figure 14, the data flow of the algorithm can be laid out over the available CPU cores such that only short-distance communication is needed and no congestion occurs on any link or at any NUMA site.

Our prototype implementation[3] uses the **libnuma** library to obtain a data flow as shown in Figure 14 and an asynchronous FIFO implementation similar to that of [3] (within NUMA regions as well as across).

5.2 Experimental Setup

For easy comparison with existing work we used the same benchmark setup that was also used to evaluate CellJoin [10]. Two streams $R = \langle \mathsf{x} : \mathsf{int}, \mathsf{y} : \mathsf{float}, \mathsf{z} : \mathsf{char}[20] \rangle$ and $S = \langle \mathsf{a} : \mathsf{int}, \mathsf{b} : \mathsf{float}, \mathsf{c} : \mathsf{double}, \mathsf{d} : \mathsf{bool} \rangle$ are joined via the two-dimensional band join

$$\texttt{WHERE } r.\mathsf{x} \texttt{ BETWEEN } s.\mathsf{a} - 10 \texttt{ AND } s.\mathsf{a} + 10$$
$$\texttt{AND } r.\mathsf{y} \texttt{ BETWEEN } s.\mathsf{b} - 10. \texttt{ AND } s.\mathsf{b} + 10. \;.$$

The join attributes contain uniformly distributed random data from the interval 1–10,000, which results in a join hit rate of $1 : 250,000$. As in [10], we ran all experiments with symmetric data rates, that is $|R| = |S|$.[4]

We implemented handshake join processing cores as Linux threads. Two additional threads asynchronously generate input data (driver process) and collect join results.

5.3 SIMD Optimization

Like most modern general-purpose processors, the AMD Opteron provides a number of *vector* (or *SIMD*) *instructions*, using which the computational density of each CPU core can be increased substantially. In handshake join, the *scan step* is a candidate for SIMD optimization. The majority of the CPU work is spent in this phase.

With the 128 bit-wide SIMD registers of our machine, up to four value comparisons can be performed within a single CPU instruction. The idea has a catch, however. In x86-64 architectures, SIMD instructions operate largely *outside* the main CPU execution unit and have only limited functionality. Most importantly, there are no *branching primitives* that operate on SIMD registers and it is relatively expensive to *move data* between SIMD registers and general-purpose registers (*e.g.*, to perform branching there).

Therefore, we modified our code to evaluate full join predicates *eagerly* using bit-wise SIMD operations (effectively the full predicate is evaluated even when one band condition was early found to fail). The positive effect on this strategy on branch (mis)prediction was already investigated by Ross [26]. Here we additionally benefit from a reduction of data movement between register sets; only the final predicate result is moved to general-purpose registers after SIMD-only evaluation.

As shown in Figure 15, vectorization using SIMD instruction yields significant performance advantages. The SIMD-optimized implementation can sustain more than double the load of the non-optimized code.

In CellJoin, Gedik *et al.* [10] used similar techniques to leverage the SIMD capabilities of the Cell SPE processors (also with substantial performance improvements). The additional low-level optimizations in [10] (loop unrolling and instruction scheduling) should be applicable to handshake join, too. Unfortunately, such optimizations make code highly processor dependent, while our current code only uses back-end-independent intrinsics to guide an optimizing C compiler (gcc).

5.4 Scalability

The main benefit of handshake join is massive scalability to arbitrary core counts. To verify this scalability, we ran handshake join instances with 4 to 44 processing cores (we left four CPU cores available for the driver and collector threads as well as for the operating system). For each configuration, we determined the maximum throughput that the system could sustain without dropping any data.

Figure 16 illustrates the throughput we determined for window sizes of ten and fifteen minutes (the y-axis uses a quadratic scale, since the workload grows with the square of the input data rate). The result confirms the scalability advantages of handshake join with respect to core counts and input data rates. Somewhat harder to see in Figure 16 is that, alternatively, additional cores can be used to support larger join windows while maintaining throughput.

[3]Source code can be downloaded via **http://people.inf.ethz.ch/jteubner/publications/soccer-players/**.

[4]Workload and output data rates grow with $|R| \times |S|$ or *quadratically* with the reported stream rate.

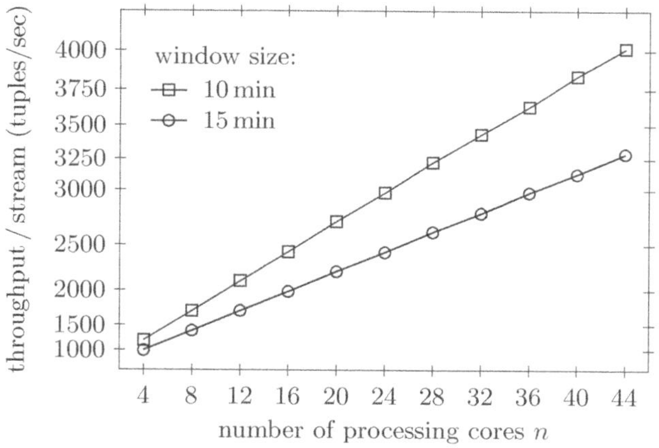

Figure 16: Handshake join scalability on multi-core CPU (AMD Opteron "Magny Cours"; immediate scan strategy). y-axis uses quadratic scale.

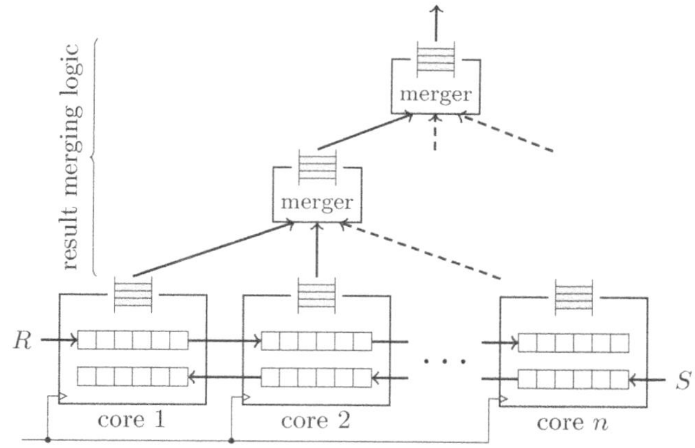

Figure 17: FPGA Implementation of Handshake Join for Tuple-based Windows.

Comparison to CellJoin. The scalability evaluation for CellJoin is limited to the eight SPEs available on the Cell processor. For 15-minute windows, Gedik *et al.* [10] report a sustained throughput of at most 750 tuples/sec when using the Cell PPE unit *plus* all eight SPEs and their "SIMD-noopt" implementation (which is best comparable to our code; with low-level optimizations, Gedik *et al.* pushed throughput up to 1000 tuples/sec). With eight CPU cores, handshake join sustained a load of 1400 tuples/sec—a 2–3.5-fold advantage considering the quadratic workload increase with throughput.

We note that the workload of this benchmark (consisting of band joins) favors an architecture like Cell. The task is very compute-intensive (including single-precision floating-point operations toward which the Cell processor has been optimized) and amenable to SIMD optimizations. On such workloads, the Cell should benefit more from its higher clock speed (3.2 GHz vs. 2.2 GHz) than the Opteron can take advantage of its super-scalar design.

For the workload sizes at hand, both join algorithms have to fetch all data from main memory during the scan phase (in 15 minutes, a stream rate of 1000 tuples/sec accumulates to around 40 MB—too large for any on-chip cache). Thereby, CellJoin inherently depends on a high-bandwidth centralized memory (25.6 GB/s for that matter). Handshake join, by contrast, keeps all memory accesses local to the respective NUMA region and thus achieves high aggregate bandwidth even when the local bandwidth is more modest (21.3 GB/s with DDR3-1333 memory).

6. HANDSHAKE JOIN ON FPGAS

48 CPU cores clearly do not mark the end of the multi-core race. To see how handshake join would scale to very large core numbers, we used *field-programmable gate arrays (FPGAs)* as an emulation platform, where the only limit to parallelism is the available chip space. FPGAs themselves are an interesting technology for database acceleration [23, 24, 29], but our main focus here is to demonstrate scalability to many cores (in particular, we favor simplicity over performance if that helps us instantiate more processing cores on the chip).

6.1 FPGA Basics

In essence, an FPGA is a programmable logic chip which provides a pool of digital logic elements that can be configured and connected in arbitrary ways. Most importantly the FPGA provides *configurable logic* in terms of *lookup tables* (LUTs) and *flip-flop registers* that each represent a single bit of fast distributed *storage*. Finally, a configurable *interconnect network* can be used to combine lookup tables and flip-flop registers into complex logic circuits.

Current FPGA chips provide chip space to instantiate up to a few hundred simple join cores. The cores contain local storage for the respective window segments of R and S and implement the join logic. In this paper we implement simple nested loops-style processing. To keep join cores as simple as possible, we only look at *tuple-based* windows that fit into on-chip memory (flip-flop registers).

6.2 Implementation Overview

Figure 17 illustrates the high-level view of our handshake join implementation on an FPGA. The windows of the R and S streams are partitioned among n cores. The cores are driven by a common clock signal that is distributed over the entire chip. The clock signal allows us to realize *lock-step forwarding* at negligible cost, which avoids the need for FIFO queues and reduces the complexity of the implementation. Effectively, the windows represent large shift registers, which are directly supported by the underlying hardware.

Following the basic handshake join algorithm (Figure 9) for each core we need to provide a hardware implementation of the segment for the R and S windows, a digital circuit for the join predicate, and scheduling logic for the tuples and the window partitions. The figure shows the two shift registers (labeled 'R window' and 'S window', respectively) that hold the tuple data. When a new tuple is received from either stream, the tuple is inserted in the respective shift register and the key is compared against all keys in the opposite window (using a standard nested-loops implementation).

Result Collection. As illustrated in the top half of Figure 17, each join core will send its share of the join *result* into a FIFO queue (indicated as ▤). A merging network will merge all sub-results into the final join output at the top of Figure 17.

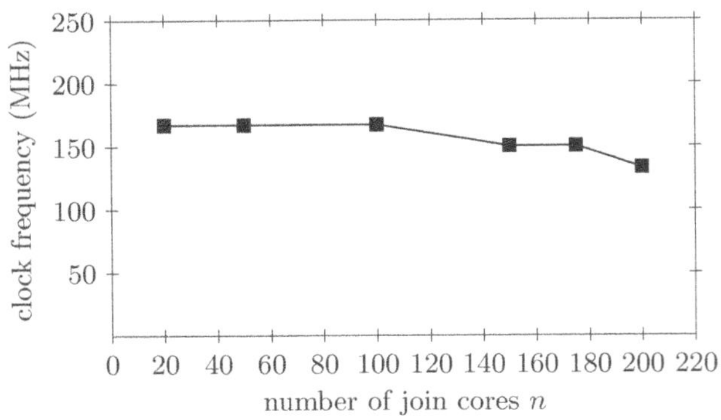

Figure 18: Scalability of FPGA Handshake join with a constant segment size of 8 tuples per window and core.

6.3 Experimental Setup

We stick to a simple stream format where join keys and payload are all 32-bit integers. We assume an equi-join and return 96 bit-wide result tuples (32-bit key plus 2×32 bits of payload).

Again our main interest is in measuring the *scalability* of handshake join. To this end, we instantiate up to 200 join cores on a Virtex-6 XC6VLX760T FPGA chip. Each of the join cores can hold eight tuples per input stream (*i.e.*, with $n = 100$ cores the overall window size will be $100 \times 8 = 800$ tuples per stream). For each configuration we determine the *maximum clock frequency* at which the resulting circuit can be operated.

In hardware design, clock frequency is an excellent indicator for scalability. In many circuit designs, the clock frequency has to be reduced according to a n^{-k} law as the circuit size is increased (larger circuit areas generally lead to longer signal paths). Only highly scalable designs allow a constant clock frequency over a large range of circuit sizes ($k \approx 0$).

6.4 Scalability and Performance

As shown in Figure 18, clock frequencies for our design remain largely unaffected by the core count (the absolute value of $150 \sim 170$ MHz is not relevant for this assessment). This confirms the good scalability properties of handshake join.

Even on the right end of Figure 18, the drop in clock frequency is not very significant. On this end our design occupies more than 96 % of the available chip area. This means we are operating our chip already far beyond its maximum recommended resource consumption of 70–80 % [8]. The fact that our circuit can still sustain high frequencies is another indication for good scalability.

By contrast, earlier work on FPGA-based stream join processing suffered a significant drop in clock speeds for the window sizes we consider, even though their system operated over only 4 bit-wide tuples [25].

6.5 Parallelism and Power Considerations

Handshake join allows to losslessly trade individual core performance for parallelism. This opens up interesting opportunities for system designers. Here we show how the flexibility of handshake join can be used to minimize the *power consumption* of an application system. More specifically, we try to find the most power-efficient handshake join configuration that satisfies a given throughput demand (which comes from the application requirements).

Table 1: Power consumption and circuit size for two windows of size 100 and a throughput of 500 ktuples/sec implemented using different numbers of cores and clock rates.

cores	clock (MHz)	power (mW) dynamic	static	total	LUTs
1	50	100	4398	4498	1.54 %
2	25	64	4396	4459	1.59 %
5	10	62	4395	4447	2.01 %
10	5	68	4306	4464	2.78 %

Table 2: Power consumption weighted by area.

cores	clock (MHz)	weighted (mW) dynamic	static	total
1	50	100	68	168
2	25	64	69	133
5	10	62	88	150
10	5	68	120	188

Again we use our FPGA framework to illustrate the concept. Assume the system has to provide a throughput of 500 ktuples/sec with a window size of 100 tuples. Configurations with 1, 2, 5, and 10 join cores can guarantee this throughput if operated at clock frequencies of 50, 25, 10, or 5 MHz, respectively. For the same throughput, however, the four configurations will require different amounts of electrical power.

Table 1 shows how core counts and clock frequencies affect the power consumption of our FPGA chip. The total power consumption of a chip results from two components: *dynamic power losses* are a result of the switching transistors (charge transfers due to parasitic capacities and short-circuit currents in CMOS technology), while *static power losses* are caused by leaking currents due to the high chip integration density.

Dynamic losses directly depend on the clock frequency of the circuit; leakage is proportional to the chip area. This can be seen in Table 1, where the dynamic component strongly decreases with the clock frequency (even though the number of cores grows). The static component, by contrast, is barely affected by the circuit configuration.

Also apparent in Table 1 is that the total power consumption is strongly dominated by the static part. This is a sole artifact of the FPGA technology that we use for this evaluation (and not indicative of the situation in custom silicon chips). In FPGAs, static losses occur on the entire chip space, even though our design occupies only 1.5 %–2.8 % of the available lookup tables (last column in Table 1). For a fair comparison with custom silicon devices, Kuon and Rose [20] suggest to weight the static FPGA power consumption by the used chip area.

Table 2 shows the weighted power consumption for our four chip configurations. Clearly, among the configurations that we looked at, the one that uses two cores is the most power-efficient. In terms of absolute numbers, this result may be different for other architectures, in particular for realistic multi-core machines. But the ability to tune a system in this way is a general consequence of handshake join's scalability properties, with potentially significant power savings in real-world scenarios.

7. RELATED WORK

The handshake join mechanism is largely orthogonal to a number of (very effective) techniques to accelerate stream processing. As motivated in Section 3.5, handshake join could, for instance, be used to coordinate multiple instances of *double-pipelined hash join* [15, 30] or window joins that use indexes [12]. If handshake join alone is not sufficient to sustain load, load shedding [27] or distribution [1] might be appropriate countermeasures.

Handshake join's data flow is similar to the *join arrays* proposed by Kung and Lohman [19]. Inspired by the then-new concept of *systolic arrays* in VLSI designs, their proposed VLSI join implementation uses an array of bit comparison components, through which data is shifted in opposing directions.

The model of Kung and Lohman can also be found in *cyclo-join* [9], our own work on join processing of static data in distributed environments. In *cyclo-join*, fragments of two input relations are placed on network hosts in a *ring topology*. For join processing, one relation is rotated along this ring, such that tuples encounter each other much like in handshake join. A key difference is that handshake join properly deals with *streaming* joins, even though the semantics of such joins is highly dynamic by nature.

The only work we could find on stream joins using FPGAs is the *M3Join* of Qian *et al.* [25], which essentially implements the join step as a single parallel lookup. This approach is known to be severely limited by on-chip routing bottlenecks [29], which causes the sudden and significant performance drop observed by Qian *et al.* for larger join windows [25]. The pipelining mechanism of handshake join, by contrast, does not suffer from these limitations.

A potential application of handshake join outside the context of stream processing might be a parallel version of *Diag-Join* [13]. Diag-Join exploits time-of-creation clustering in data warehouse systems and uses a sliding window-like processing mode. The main bottleneck there is usually throughput, which could be improved by parallelizing with handshake join.

8. SUMMARY

The multi-core train is running at full throttle and the available *hardware parallelism* is still going to increase. Handshake join provides a mechanism to leverage this parallelism and turn it into *increased throughput* for stream processing engines. In particular, we demonstrated how *window-based stream joins* can be parallelized over very large numbers of cores with negligible coordination overhead. Our prototype implementation reaches throughput rates that significantly exceed those of CellJoin, the best published result to date [10]. Alternatively, the scalability of handshake join can be used to optimize system designs with respect to their power consumption.

Key to the scalability of handshake join is to avoid any coordination by a centralized entity. Instead, handshake join only relies on local core-to-core communication (*e.g.*, using local message queues) to achieve the necessary core synchronization. This mode of parallelization is consistent with folklore knowledge about *systolic arrays*, but also with recent research results that aim at many-core systems [3].

The principles of handshake join are not bound to the assumption of a single multi-core machine. Rather, it should be straightforward to extend the scope of handshake join to *distributed stream processors* in networks of commodity systems (such as the *Borealis* [1] research prototype) or to support massively-parallel multi-FPGA setups (such as the BEE3 multi-FPGA system [7] or the *Cube* 512-FPGA cluster [22]). As mentioned before, we already demonstrated the former case for static input data with *cyclo-join* [9]. In ongoing work we investigate the use of graphics processors (GPUs) to run handshake join.

Acknowledgements

This work was supported by an *Ambizione* grant of the Swiss National Science Foundation under the grant number 126405 and by the Enterprise Computing Center (ECC) of ETH Zurich (`http://www.ecc.ethz.ch/`).

9. REFERENCES

[1] D. J. Abadi, Y. Ahmad, M. Balazinska, U. Çetintemel, M. Cherniack, J.-H. Hwang, W. Lindner, A. S. Maskey, A. Rasin, E. Ryvkina, N. Tatbul, and S. Zdonik. The Design of the Borealis Stream Processing Engine. In *Proc. of the 2nd Biennial Conference on Innovative Data Systems Research (CIDR)*, Asilomar, CA, USA, 2005.

[2] A. Arasu, B. Babcock, S. Babu, J. Cieslewicz, M. Datar, K. Ito, R. Motwani, U. Srivastava, and J. Widom. STREAM: The Stanford Data Stream Management System. `http://infolab.stanford.edu/~usriv/papers/streambook.pdf`.

[3] A. Baumann, P. Barham, P.-E. Dagand, T. Harris, R. Isaacs, S. Peter, T. Roscoe, A. Schüpbach, and A. Singhania. The Multikernel: A new OS architecture for scalable multicore systems. In *Proc. of the 22nd ACM Symposium on Operating Systems Principles (SOSP)*, Big Sky, MT, USA, 2009.

[4] I. Botan, R. Derakhshan, N. Dindar, L. Haas, R. J. Miller, and N. Tatbul. SECRET: A Model for Analysis of the Execution Semantics of Stream Processing Systems. *Proc. of the VLDB Endowment*, 3(1), 2010.

[5] M. Butts. Synchronization Through Communication in a Massively Parallel Processor Array. *IEEE Micro*, 27(5):32–40, 2007.

[6] P. Conway, N. Kalyanasundharam, G. Donley, K. Lepak, and B. Hughes. Cache Hierarchy and Memory Subsystem of the AMD Opteron Processor. *IEEE Micro*, 30(2):16–29, 2010.

[7] J. Davis, C. Thacker, and C. Chang. BEE3: Revitalizing Computer Architecture Research. Technical Report MSR-TR-2009-45, Microsoft Research, 2009.

[8] A. DeHon. Balancing Interconnect and Computation in a Reconfigurable Computing Array (or, why you

don't really want 100 % LUT utilization). In *Proc. of the Int'l Symposium on Field Programmable Gate Arrays (FPGA)*, Monterey, CA, USA, 1999.

[9] P. Frey, R. Gonçalves, M. Kersten, and J. Teubner. A Spinning Join That Does Not Get Dizzy. In *Proc. of the 30th Int'l Conference on Distributed Computing Systems (ICDCS)*, Genoa, Italy, 2010.

[10] B. Gedik, P. S. Yu, and R. Bordawekar. CellJoin: A Parallel Stream Join Operator for the Cell Processor. *The VLDB Journal*, 18(2):501–519, 2009.

[11] T. M. Ghanem, M. A. Hammad, M. F. Mokbel, W. G. Aref, and A. K. Elmagarmid. Incremental Evaluation of Sliding-Window Queries over Data Streams. *IEEE Trans. on Knowledge and Data Engineering (TKDE)*, 19(1):57–72, 2007.

[12] L. Golab, S. Garg, and T. Öszu. On Indexing Sliding Windows over Online Data Streams. In *Proc. of the 9th Int'l Conference on Extending Database Technology (EDBT)*, Crete, Greece, 2004.

[13] S. Helmer, T. Westmann, and G. Moerkotte. Diag-Join: An Opportunistic Join Algorithm for 1:N Relationships. In *Proc. of the 24th Int'l Conference on Very Large Databases (VLDB)*, New York, NY, USA, 1998.

[14] J. Howard, S. Dighe, Y. Hoskote, S. Vangal, D. Finan, G. Ruhl, D. Jenkins, H. Wilson, N. Borkar, G. Schrom, F. Pailet, S. Jain, T. Jacob, S. Yada, S. Marella, P. Salihundam, V. Erraguntla, M. Konow, M. Riepen, G. Droege, J. Lindemann, M. Gries, T. Apel, K. Henriss, T. Lund-Larsen, S. Steibl, S. Borkar, V. De, R. v. d. Wijngaart, and T. Mattson. A 48-Core IA-32 Message-Passing Processor with DVFS in 45nm CMOS. In *2010 IEEE International Solid-State Circuits Conference*, San Francisco, CA, USA, February 2010.

[15] Z. Ives, D. Florescu, M. Friedman, A. Levy, and D. S. Weld. An Adaptive Query Execution System for Data Integration. In *Proc. of the Int'l Conference on Management of Data (SIGMOD)*, Philadelphia, PA, USA, 1999.

[16] N. Jain, S. Mishra, A. Srinivasan, J. Gehrke, J. Widom, H. Balakrishnan, U. Çetintemel, M. Cherniack, R. Tibbetts, and S. Zdonik. Towards a Streaming SQL Standard. *Proc. of the VLDB Endowment*, 1(2), 2008.

[17] J. Kang, J. F. Naughton, and S. D. Viglas. Evaluating Window Joins over Unbounded Streams. In *Proc. of the 19th Int'l Conference on Data Engineering (ICDE)*, Bangalore, India, 2003.

[18] S. Krishnamurthy, M. J. Franklin, J. Davis, D. Farina, P. Golovko, A. Li, and N. Thombre. Continuous Analytics Over Discontinuous Streams. In *Proc. of the Int'l Conference on Management of Data (SIGMOD)*, Indidanapolis, IN, USA, 2010.

[19] H. T. Kung and P. L. Lohman. Systolic (VLSI) Arrays for Relational Database Operations. In *Proc. of the Int'l Conference on Management of Data (SIGMOD)*, Santa Monica, CA, USA, 1980.

[20] I. Kuon and J. Rose. Measuring the gap between FPGAs and ASICs. In *Proc. of the 14th Int'l Symposium on Field-Programmable Gate Arrays (FPGA)*, Monterey, CA, USA, 2006.

[21] J. Li, D. Maier, K. Tufte, V. Papadimos, and P. A. Tucker. Semantics and Evaluation Techniques for Window Aggregates in Data Streams. In *Proc. of the Int'l Conference on Management of Data (SIGMOD)*, Baltimore, MD, USA, 2005.

[22] O. Mencer, K. H. Tsoi, S. Craimer, T. Todman, W. Luk, M. Y. Wong, and P. H. W. Leong. CUBE: A 512-FPGA Cluster. In *Proc. of the Southern Programmable Logic Conference (SPL)*, São Carlos, Brazil, 2009.

[23] A. Mitra, M. R. Vieira, P. Bakalov, V. J. Tsotras, and W. A. Najjar. Boosting XML Filtering Through a Scalable FPGA-Based Architecture. In *Proc. of the 4th Biennial Conference on Innovative Data Systems Research (CIDR)*, Asilomar, CA, USA, 2009.

[24] Netezza Corp. `http://www.netezza.com/`.

[25] J.-B. Qian, H.-B. Xu, Y.-S. Dong, X.-J. Liu, and Y.-L. Wang. FPGA Acceleration Window Joins Over Multiple Data Streams. *Journal of Circuits, Systems, and Computers*, 14(4):813–830, 2005.

[26] K. A. Ross. Selection Conditions in Main Memory. *ACM Trans. on Database Systems (TODS)*, 29:132–161, 2004.

[27] N. Tatbul, U. Çetintemel, S. Zdonik, M. Cherniack, and M. Stonebraker. Load Shedding in a Data Stream Manager. In *Proc. of the 29th Int'l Conference on Very Large Databases (VLDB)*, Berlin, Germany, 2003.

[28] W. B. Teeuw and H. M. Blanken. Control Versus Data Flow in Parallel Database Machines. *IEEE Trans. on Parallel and Distributed Systems (TPDS)*, 4(11):1265–1279, 1993.

[29] J. Teubner, R. Mueller, and G. Alonso. FPGA Acceleration for the Frequent Item Problem. In *Proc. of the 26th Int'l Conference on Data Engineering (ICDE)*, Long Beach, CA, USA, 2010.

[30] A. Wilschut and P. Apers. Dataflow Query Execution in a Parallel Main-Memory Environment. In *Proc. of the 1st Int'l Conference on Parallel and Distributed Information Systems (PDIS)*, Miami Beach, FL, USA, 1991.

BE-Tree: An Index Structure to Efficiently Match Boolean Expressions over High-dimensional Discrete Space

Mohammad Sadoghi
Department of Computer Science
University of Toronto, Canada
mo@cs.toronto.edu

Hans-Arno Jacobsen
Dept. of Electrical and Computer Engineering
University of Toronto, Canada
jacobsen@eecg.toronto.edu

ABSTRACT

BE-Tree is a novel dynamic tree data structure designed to efficiently index Boolean expressions over a high-dimensional discrete space. BE-Tree copes with both high-dimensionality and expressiveness of Boolean expressions by introducing a novel two-phase space-cutting technique that specifically utilizes the discrete and finite domain properties of the space. Furthermore, BE-Tree employs self-adjustment policies to dynamically adapt the tree as the workload changes. We conduct a comprehensive evaluation to demonstrate the superiority of BE-Tree in comparison with state-of-the-art index structures designed for matching Boolean expressions.

Categories and Subject Descriptors

H.3.3 [**Information Search and Retrieval**]: Information filtering

General Terms

Algorithms, Design, Measurement, Experimentation, Performance

Keywords

Boolean expressions, Data Structure, Algorithm, Publish/Subscribe, and Complex Event Processing

1. INTRODUCTION

The efficient indexing of Boolean expressions is a common problem at the center of a number of data management applications. For example, for event processing and publish/subscribe, Boolean expressions represent events and subscriber interests [2, 13, 6, 26], for online advertising and information filtering, Boolean expressions represent advertiser profiles and filters [26, 14], for algorithmic trading, they represent market events and investment strategies [25], and for approximate string matching, they represent string patterns using q-grams [8]. In all scenarios, key challenges are the scaling to millions of expressions and to sub-second matching latency. We use a data management scenario for co-spaces as in-depth example. Co-spaces are an emerging concept to model the co-existence of physical and virtual worlds touted by the Claremont Report as an area of rising interest for database researchers [1].

SIGMOD'11, June 12–16, 2011, Athens, Greece.

Consider, for example, a mobile shopping application, where a shopper enters a physical mall and her mobile device submits her shopping preferences (i.e., subscriptions) to the virtual mall database: [$genre =$ classics, $era \in \{1920s, 1940s\}$, $price$ BETWEEN $[20, 40]$, $ranking < 5$, $format \notin$ {paperback}]. Now, assume a new promotion (i.e., an event) matches the shopper's interests and the item detail is pushed to her mobile device. An example of a matching item is as follows: [$genre =$ classics, $title =$ *'The Sun Also Rises'*, *author* = Hemingway, $era = 1920s$, $price = 26$, $ranking = 2$, $format$ = hardcover]. In the example, both the shopper's interest and the promotional item are defined over multiple attributes (i.e., dimensions in space) such as *genre* and *price* in which each attribute has a discrete and finite domain. Furthermore, each attribute of interest is constrained to a set of values with an operator. The triple consisting of attribute, operator, and set of values is referred to as a *Boolean predicate*. A conjunction of Boolean predicates, which here represents both the shopper's interest and the promotional item, is a *Boolean expression*.

There are four major challenges to efficiently index Boolean expressions. First, the index must scale to millions of Boolean expressions defined over a high-dimensional space and afford efficient lookup (i.e., expression matching.) Second, the index must support predicates with an expressive set of operators. Third, the index must enable dynamic insertion and deletion of expressions. Lastly, the index must adapt to changing workload patterns and expression schemata.

However, existing techniques are inadequate to satisfy these four requirements. For instance, techniques used in expert and rule-based systems support expressive predicate languages [15], but are unable to scale to millions of expressions. Recent work addresses the scalability limitation, but either restricts the predicate expressiveness [13] or assumes a static environment in which the index is constructed offline [2, 26, 14]. Our goal is to address scalability, expressiveness, dynamic construction, and adaptation by proposing a novel, self-adjusting index structure that is specifically geared towards high-dimensionality over discrete and finite domains. To achieve these goals, we propose **BE**-Tree a novel tree structure to efficiently index and match large sets of **B**oolean **E**xpressions defined over an expressive predicate language in a high-dimensional space. BE-Tree is dynamically constructed through a novel two-phase space-cutting technique that exploits the discrete and finite structure of both the subscription and event space. Another distinct feature of BE-Tree is a novel self-adjusting mechanism that adapts as subscription and event workloads change.

We make the following five contributions in this paper:

1. Unify subscription and event language to enable a more expressive matching semantics (Sec. 3),
2. propose a novel data structure, BE-Tree, that supports an extensive set of operators and dynamic expression schemata,

gracefully scales to millions of subscriptions, thousands of dimensions, and dozens of predicates per subscription and event (Sec. 4),

3. develop a novel self-adjusting mechanism for BE-Tree that continuously adapts to both subscription and event workload changes (Sec. 5),
4. present the first comprehensive evaluation framework that benchmarks state-of-the-art matching algorithms, including SCAN [27], SIFT [27], Gryphon [2], Propagation [13], and k-index [26] (Sec. 7), and
5. present a novel approach to leverage real-world high-dimensional datasets for evaluation (Sec. 7).

2. RELATED WORK

Problems related to indexing Boolean expressions have been studied in many contexts: Expert systems [15], active databases [19, 10], trigger processing [18, 7], publish/subscribe matching [27, 2, 13, 6, 5, 26, 14], XPath/XML matching (e.g.,[11, 23]), and stream processing (e.g., [12, 9]). Indexing in multi-dimensional space has also been extensively studied (e.g., [17, 3, 4].)

The work on expert systems, active databases, and trigger processing [15, 19, 10, 18, 7] as well as certain publish/subscribe (pub/sub) systems (e.g., [5]) focus on language expressiveness and not on scaling to thousands of dimensions and millions of expressions. In addition, most XPath/XML matchings are based on a completely different language from what BE-Tree supports and is not in the scope of this work (e.g., [11]). These approaches are therefore not directly applicable, and our review concentrates on pub/sub matching algorithms [27, 2, 13, 6, 22, 20, 21, 26, 14].

Two main categories of matching algorithms have been proposed: counting-based [27, 13, 26] and tree-based [2, 6, 21] approaches. These approaches can further be classified as either key-based, in which for each expression a set of predicates are chosen as identifier [13], or as non-key based [27, 6, 26]. Counting-based methods aim to minimize the number of predicate evaluations by constructing an inverted index over all unique predicates. The two most efficient counting-based algorithms are Propagation [13], a key-based method, and the k-index [26], a non-key-based method. Likewise, tree-based methods are designed to reduce predicate evaluations and to recursively divide the search space by eliminating subscriptions on encountering unsatisfiable predicates. The most prominent tree-based method, Gryphon, is a static, non-key based algorithm [2]. Our BE-Tree is a novel tree-based approach, which also employs keys, that we show to outperform existing work [27, 2, 13, 26].

The latest advancement of counting-based algorithms is k-index [26], which gracefully scales to thousands of dimensions and supports equality predicates ($\in$) and non-equality predicates ($\notin$). k-index partitions subscriptions based on their number of predicates to prune subscriptions with too few matching predicates; however, k-index is static and does not support dynamic insertion and deletion. What distinguishes our BE-Tree from k-index is that BE-Tree is fully dynamic, naturally supports richer predicate operators (e.g. range operators), and adapts to workload changes.

Another emerging area of research is to improve language expressiveness. For example, the subscription languages in [6, 14] support matching complex Boolean expression, while k-index supports either Conjunctive Normal Form or Disjunctive Normal Form [26]. Most important, the latest technique that supports matching complex Boolean expressions relies on existing matching algorithm to match the low-level conjunctive expressions [14]; thus, it dovetails well with BE-Tree. Finally, there is a paradigm shift, manifest in what is referred to as symmetric pub/sub, in which event producers are also able to impose filtering conditions on event subscribers [22, 20], which substantially improves the expressive power of the event language. This new paradigm is also supported by our BE-Tree and proposed matching semantics [24].

Finally, matching in high-dimensional space diverges from classical database indexing in four crucial ways. First, BE-Tree has to cope with data of much higher dimensionality (order of thousands), that is orders of magnitude larger than capabilities of existing high-dimensional indexing structures [17, 3]. Second, Expressions indexed by BE-Tree impose restrictions only on a small subspace and are fully defined everywhere else. As a result, there is a high degree of overlap among expressions which renders current indexing techniques inapplicable. For instance, X-Tree [3], often the most suitable index for high-dimensional data, degenerates to a sequential scan when all expressions overlap. Third, classical high-dimensional indexing focuses on utilizing disk space and reducing random accesses, as opposed to directly optimizing the matching process (lookup time); disk is assumed as storage medium and disk I/O is the bottleneck. BE-Tree, on the other hand, is a main memory structure. Forth, BE-Tree aims to support discrete, finite domains, while many high-dimensional indexing structures are designed for continuous unbounded domains that are unable to benefit from the finite and discrete domain properties.

3. EXPRESSION MATCHING MODEL

Expression Language Traditionally, pub/sub matching algorithms take as input a set of subscriptions (a conjunction of Boolean predicates) and an event (an assignment of a value to each attribute), and return the subset of subscriptions satisfied by the event. Unlike most existing work, we model both subscriptions and events as Boolean expression. This generalization gives rise to more expressive matching semantics while still encompassing the traditional pub/sub matching problem. Each Boolean expression is a conjunction of Boolean predicates. A predicate is a triple, consisting of an attribute uniquely representing a dimension in n-dimensional space, an operator, and a set of values, denoted by $P^{\texttt{attr,opt,val}}(x)$, or more concisely as $P(x)$. A predicate either accepts or rejects an input x such that $P^{\texttt{attr,opt,val}}(x) : x \longrightarrow \{\texttt{True}, \texttt{False}\}$, where $x \in \texttt{Dom}(P^{\texttt{attr}})$ and $P^{\texttt{attr}}$ is the predicate's attribute. Formally, a Boolean expression *be* is defined over an n-dimensional space as follows:

$$be = \{P_1^{\texttt{attr,opt,val}}(x) \wedge \cdots \wedge P_k^{\texttt{attr,opt,val}}(x)\},$$
$$where\ k \leq n;\ \ i, j \leq k,\ P_i^{\texttt{attr}} = P_j^{\texttt{attr}}\ \ iff\ \ i = j$$

We support an expressive set of operators for the most common data types: relational operators ($<, \leq, =, \neq, \geq, >$), set operators ($\in, \notin$), and the SQL BETWEEN operator.

Matching Semantics Our unique formulation of subscriptions and events as expressions enables us to support a wide range of matching semantics. We start with the classical pub/sub matching problem: *Given an event e and a set of subscriptions, find all subscriptions s_i satisfied by e.* We refer to this problem as *stabbing subscription*[1] $\texttt{SQ}(e)$, and specify the problem as follows:

$$\texttt{SQ}(e) = \{s_i |\ \forall P_q^{\texttt{attr,opt,val}}(x) \in s_i,\ \exists P_o^{\texttt{attr,opt,val}}(x) \in e,$$
$$P_q^{\texttt{attr}} = P_o^{\texttt{attr}}, \exists x \in \texttt{Dom}(P_q^{\texttt{attr}}),\ P_q(x) \wedge P_o(x)\}$$

A complete list of matching semantics supported by BE-Tree is presented in the extended paper [24], our supported semantics also includes the symmetric pub/sub matching [22, 20].

[1]This is a generalization of stabbing query, which determines which of a collection of intervals overlap a query point.

4. BE-TREE ORGANIZATION

BE-Tree dynamically indexes large sets of expressions (i.e., subscriptions) and efficiently determines which of these expressions match an input expression (i.e., event). BE-Tree supports Boolean expressions with an expressive set of operators defined over a high-dimensional space. The main challenge in indexing a high-dimensional space is to effectively cut the space in order to prune the search at lookup time. BE-Tree copes with this challenge—the curse of dimensionality—through a novel two-phase space-cutting technique that significantly reduces the complexity and the level of uncertainty of choosing an effective criterion to recursively cut the space and to identify highly dense subspaces. The two-phases BE-Tree employs are: (1) *space partitioning* which is the global structuring to determine the best splitting $\texttt{attr}_i$, i.e., the ith dimension (Sec. 4.2) and (2) *space clustering* which is the local structuring for each partition to determine the best grouping of expressions with respect to the expressions' range of values for $\texttt{attr}_i$ (Sec. 4.3).

This two-phase approach, the space partitioning followed by the space clustering, introduces new challenges such as how to determine the right balance between the space partitioning and clustering, and how to develop a robust principle to alternate between both. These new challenges are addressed in BE-Tree by exploiting the underlying discrete and finite domain properties of the space. We begin by discussing the structure and the dynamics of BE-Tree before presenting the main design principles behind BE-Tree. All these are prerequisites to the actual, but much simpler, expression matching with BE-Tree, described in Sec. 6.

4.1 BE-Tree Structure

BE-Tree is an n-ary tree structure in which a leaf node contains a set of expressions and an internal node contains partial predicate information (e.g., an attribute and a range of values) about the expressions in its descendant leaf nodes. We distinguish among three classes of nodes: a partition node (p-node) which maintains the space partitioning information (an attribute), a cluster node (c-node) which maintains the space clustering information (a range of values), and a leaf node (l-node) which stores the actual expressions. Moreover, p-nodes and c-nodes are organized in a special directory structure for fast space pruning. Thus, a set of p-nodes are organized in a *partition directory* (p-directory), and a set of c-nodes are organized in a *cluster directory* (c-directory.) Before giving a detailed account of each node type and the BE-Tree dynamics, we outline the structural properties of BE-Tree as shown in Fig. 1, and give an example showing the overall dynamics of BE-Tree.

Example *Initially,* BE-Tree *has an empty root node which consists of a c-node that points only to an l-node. Upon arrival, new expressions (subscriptions) are inserted into the root's l-node, and once the size of the l-node exceeds the leaf capacity—a tunable system parameter—the space partitioning phase is triggered and a new* $\texttt{attr}_i$ *for splitting the l-node is chosen. The new* $\texttt{attr}_i$ *results in the creation of a new p-node. The* $\texttt{attr}_i$ *is chosen based on statistics gathered from expressions (subscriptions) in the overflowing l-node. The selected attribute is passed on to the space clustering phase that divides the domain of the* $\texttt{attr}_i$ *into a set of intervals, in which each range of values is assigned to a new c-node, and all the expressions having a predicate on* $\texttt{attr}_i$*, in the overflowing l-node, are distributed across these newly created c-nodes based on the c-nodes' range of permitted values. In brief,* BE-Tree *recursively partitions and clusters the space, which together recursively identify and refine dense subspaces, in order to maintain the size of each l-node below a threshold.*

Strictly speaking, in BE-Tree, each p-node is assigned an $\texttt{attr}_i$ such that all the expressions in its descendant l-nodes must have a

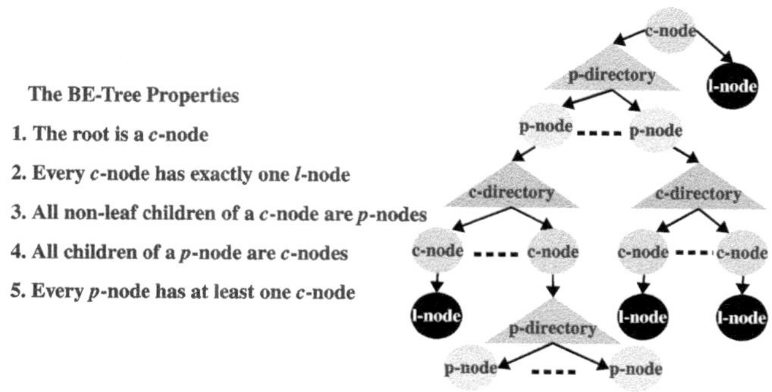

Figure 1: The BE-Tree data structure.

predicate defined over $\texttt{attr}_i$. Similarly, each c-node is associated with a predicate $P_i^{\texttt{attr},\texttt{opt},\texttt{val}}(x)$ (i.e., a range of permitted values), and all the expressions in its descendant l-nodes must have a predicate $P_j^{\texttt{attr},\texttt{opt},\texttt{val}}(x)$ such that

$$(P_i^{\texttt{attr}} = P_j^{\texttt{attr}}) \wedge (\forall x \in \texttt{Dom}(P_j^{\texttt{attr}}),\ P_j(x) \rightarrow P_i(x)).$$

Provided that each c-node is denoted by a predicate $P_j(x)$, we can assign each l-node a key $\texttt{key}_j$ defined as a conjunction of all c-nodes' predicate along the path from the root to the l_j-node.

In what follows, in order to uniquely identify a node, a unique id is assigned to each node. For example, in order to refer to the jth l-node, we write l_j-node. In addition, we adopt the following notation: $\texttt{max}_{cap}$ (maximum leaf capacity), $\texttt{min}_{size}$ (minimum partition size), $\texttt{max}^j_{cap}$ (l_j-node maximum capacity), $\texttt{rank}_{\texttt{window}}$ (window for updating the rank), and θ (l-node recycling threshold).

4.2 Space Partitioning

In BE-Tree, space partitioning, conceptually a global adjusting mechanism, is the first phase of our space-cutting technique. The space partitioning is triggered after an l_j-node overflows and uses a scoring function (cf. Sec. 5) to rank each candidate $\texttt{attr}_i$ in order to determine the best attribute for partitioning. Thus, the highest ranking attribute, appearing in at least $\texttt{min}_{size}$ number of expressions, implying that the attribute has a sufficient discriminating power, is chosen for the space partitioning phase. Essentially, this process identifies the next highest ranking dimension, only as the need arises, to segregate expressions into smaller groups based on a high-ranking attribute in order to prune the search space more effectively while coping with the curse of dimensionality.

Upon successful selection of an $\texttt{attr}_i$ for space partitioning, a new p-node for $\texttt{attr}_i$ is added to the parent of the overflowing l_j-node, and the set of expressions in the l_j-node is divided based on whether or not they have a predicate defined on $\texttt{attr}_i$. The partitioning procedure is repeatedly applied to the l_j-node to keep its size below $\texttt{max}^j_{cap}$.

The need for $\texttt{min}_{size}$ is to avoid ineffective partitioning. For instance, if none of the expressions in an l_j-node have a predicate on a common attribute, then there is no computational incentive to form a partition. Therefore, a natural problem that might arise in the space partitioning for any given l_j-node is the handling of scenarios for which no candidate attribute exists with size larger than $\texttt{min}_{size}$. For such cases, we introduce the notion of an extended l_j-node in which the size of the l_j-node, $\texttt{max}^j_{cap}$, is increased by a constant factor $\texttt{max}_{cap}$ such that $\texttt{max}^j_{cap} = \texttt{max}^j_{cap} + \texttt{max}_{cap}$. Thus, in order to support dynamic expansion and contraction of the leaf node size, after every successful partitioning, the l_i-node capacity is re-evaluated as follows:

$$\texttt{max}^j_{cap} = \begin{cases} \left\lceil \frac{|l_j\text{-node}|}{\texttt{max}_{cap}} \right\rceil \times \texttt{max}_{cap}, & \text{if } |l_j\text{-node}| > 0 \\ \texttt{max}_{cap}, & \text{otherwise} \end{cases}$$

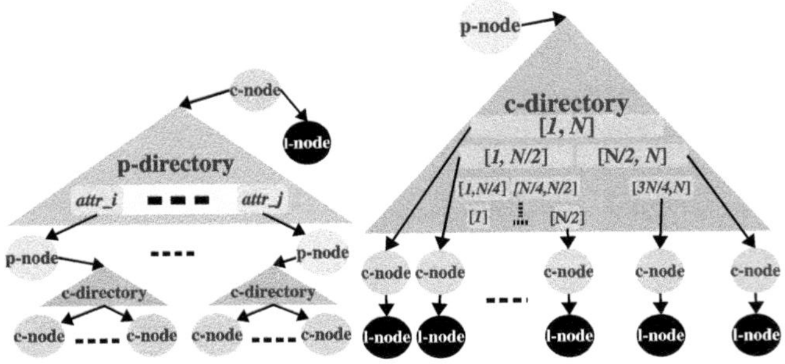

(a) Partition directory (b) Clustering directory

Figure 2: The BE-Tree directories.

Another subtle point in the space partitioning is how to guide the attribute selection such that (1) it guarantees that subsequent space partitioning on lower levels of BE-Tree do not ineffectively cycle over a single $\mathtt{attr}_i$ (2) it enables dynamic insertions and deletions without performance deterioration. To achieve these properties, we must ensure that in any path from the root to a leaf node, each $\mathtt{attr}_i$ is selected at most once and that a deterministic clustering is employed after each partitioning (cf. Sec. 4.3). Moreover, we show in Sec. 4.3, the attribute selection restriction is not a limitation; in fact, we prove that it is sufficient to pick each $\mathtt{attr}_i$ at most once yet fully exploiting the domain of $attr_i$ because when $\mathtt{attr}_i$ is selected, then reselecting it at a lower level of the tree provides no additional benefit.

Moreover, it is evident that the number of partitions for each c-node grows linearly in the dimensionality of space. Since each edge from a c-node leading to a p-node is uniquely identified by a single attribute, we can employ a hash table over all edges leaving the node, potentially scaling BE-Tree to thousands of dimensions. The inner working of the partition directory is shown in Fig. 2a.

Finally, as the split operator is required to eliminate overflowing l-nodes, similarly, a merge operator is necessary to eliminate underflowing l-nodes. If an l-node is underflowing, then its contents are either merged with its grandparent's l-node or reinserted into BE-Tree. The latter approach is preferred because it provides an opportunity to avoid deterioration of BE-Tree. In any case, if an l-node is empty and its c-node has no other children, then the l-node is removed. This node removal naturally propagates upward removing any non-leaf nodes with no outgoing edges.

4.3 Space Clustering

Our proposed space partitioning reduces the problem of high-dimensional indexing into one-dimensional interval indexing. Interval indexing is addressed in our space clustering phase, conceptually a local adjusting mechanism. The key insight of our space clustering, and ultimately of our BE-Tree, is a deterministic clustering policy to group overlapping expressions (into regions) and a deterministic policy to alternate between the space partitioning and the space clustering. The absence of a predictable policy gives rise to the dilemma of whether to further pursue the space clustering or to switch back to the space partitioning. Besides, once a region is partitioned, that region can no longer be split without running into the cascading split problem [16]. Thus, a deterministic clustering policy that is influenced by the insertion sequence is either prone to ineffective regions that do not take advantage of the dimension selectivity to effectively prune the search space or prone to suffer from substantial performance overhead due to the cascading split problem. Therefore, to achieve determinism in our space clustering, while supporting dynamic insertion and deletion, our structure must be independent of insertion sequence.

Clustering Directory Organization To address these challenges, we propose a novel grid-based approach, with unique splitting and merging policies, to build the clustering directory in BE-Tree. The clustering directory is a hierarchical structure that organizes the space into sets of expressions by recursively cutting the space in halves. A key feature of this grid-based clustering is a novel forced split rule that (1) avoids the cascading split problem and that (2) enables deterministic clustering and partition-clustering alteration strategies that are independent of the insertion sequence. To describe the dynamics of our clustering directory, first, we formally define few concepts.

A *bucket* represents an interval boundary (range of values) over $attr_i$, and an expression is assigned to a bucket over $attr_i$ only if the set of values defined by the expression's predicate on $attr_i$ is covered by that bucket; for brevity, we say an expression is assigned to a bucket if the expression is enclosed by that bucket. Furthermore, a bucket has a minimal interval boundary which is a best-effort-smallest interval that encloses all of its expressions. Each bucket is associated with exactly one c-node in BE-Tree, which is responsible for storing and maintaining information about the bucket's assigned expressions. We further distinguish among four types of buckets: An *open bucket* that is a bucket with a not yet partitioned c-node; a *leaf bucket* that is a bucket that has no children (a bucket that has not been split); an *atomic bucket* that is a single-valued bucket that cannot further be split, an indivisible bucket; and a *home bucket* that is the smallest possible bucket that encloses an expression. Furthermore, an atomic bucket is also a leaf bucket, but the reverse is not necessarily true.

Essentially the clustering directory is constructed based on the following three rules to avoid the cascading split problem and to achieve the deterministic properties of BE-Tree: (1) an expression is always inserted into the smallest bucket that encloses it (*insertion rule*), (2) a non-atomic bucket (i.e., a multi-valued, divisible bucket) is always split before its c-node switches back to the space partitioning (*forced split rule*), and (3) an underflowing leaf bucket is merged with its parent only if the parent is an open bucket (*merge rule*).

The cascading split problem is avoided, first, due to the forced split rule because a bucket is always split before it is partitioned and, second, due to the insertion and merge rules because both current and future expressions are always placed in the smallest bucket that encloses them. Therefore, the partitioned c-node always remains the home bucket to all of its expressions. As a result, there is no benefit or need to further split a bucket that is the home to all of its expressions. This home bucket's uniqueness property is achieved through a rigorous splitting policy that deterministically cuts the space in half independent of the insertion sequence such that each expression could uniquely be associated to a *home bucket*.

The deterministic clustering is achieved through a grid-based organization of space in which each overflowing bucket is split in halves. The deterministic partition-clustering alteration is also achieved through the forced split rule which always enforces the split of non-atomic buckets before initiating the space partitioning. Thus, the space partitioning is always applied to expressions that are residing in their home bucket such that if the space clustering is further pursed, these expressions are unaffected by it.

In short, the deterministic and no split cascading properties of BE-Tree are obtained by satisfying the below specified BE-Tree invariance. A complete proof of BE-Tree's invariance is presented in the technical report [24]. Most importantly, these desired properties are possible only due to the existence of an atomic bucket, which itself is possible only due to the underlying discrete domain property.

INVARIANCE. *Every expression always resides in the smallest bucket that encloses it, and the c-node of a non-atomic leaf bucket is never partitioned.*

Subsequently, we present our unique clustering directory structure. We also propose a predicate transformation, which converts our expressive set of operators into an interval boundary that is compatible with our clustering directory.

Space Clustering Structure The main guiding principles of the BE-Tree space clustering are the insertion and the forced split rules. Both are used to dynamically construct BE-Tree as follows. The clustering directory starts with an empty top-level bucket which spans the entire domain for $\texttt{attr}_i$. Once the leaf node associated to the top-level bucket overflows, the bucket is split in half resulting in the creation of two new child buckets; each child bucket is also assigned a new c-node and l-node. Subsequently, expressions in the overflowed leaf node that are enclosed by either of the two child buckets are moved accordingly. This process is recursively applied until either an atomic bucket is reached or every bucket's c-node has its l_j-node below $\texttt{max}^j_{cap}$. Finally, an overflowing non-leaf or an atomic bucket is handled by switching to the partitioning mode. A snapshot of the clustering directory is shown in Fig. 2b.

In summary, the two-phase space-cutting begins with the space partitioning followed by a sequence of space clusterings until a safe point (no split cascading), i.e., a non-leaf or an atomic bucket, is reached at which point a fresh instance of the two-phase space-cutting, starting with the space partitioning, begins. Also, as explained in Sec. 4.2, each attribute is selected at most once in any path along the root of BE-Tree to a leaf node because switching back to the space partitioning occurs only at a safe point, in which the overflowing leaf node, which is subjected to partitioning, is associated with a home bucket, and a further clustering is no longer beneficial. In other words, once an attribute is chosen, before switching to the partitioning mode, the space clustering strategy will exploit the entire space to fully leverage the dimension selectivity independent of the insertion sequence.

The clustering directory supports indexing one-dimensional intervals. However, our predicate language supports a richer set of predicates. In Table 1, we show the conversion of predicates with different types of operators into one-dimensional intervals, where v_{min} and v_{max} are the smallest and the largest possible values in the domain, and $\{v_1, \cdots, v_k\}$ is sorted in ascending order. All predicates transformations are simple algebraic conversions except for the $(\neq, \notin, \in)$ operators. A predicate $P_j^{(attr_i, \neq, v_1)}(x)$ implies that every value in the domain of $attr_i$ is acceptable except for v_1. Therefore, under the uniform distribution assumption, the predicate $P_j(x)$ is satisfied with a high probability by an event expression having a predicate on $attr_i$. This observation supports the transformation of the $\neq$ operator into a one-dimensional interval $[v_{min}, v_{max}]$. This transformation results in an early pruning of expressions with a predicate on $\texttt{attr}_i$ during the matching of an event that does not have any predicate defined on $\texttt{attr}_i$. This pruning strategy is especially effective because the number of predicates per expression is on the order of tens while the number of space dimensions is on the order of thousands. Likewise, the $\notin$ operator is a generalization of the $\neq$ operator, which filters out a set of values from the domain instead of a single value. Thus, by converting $\notin$ to an interval that spans the entire domain, again, we are imposing a filtering strategy to effectively reduce the search space. Finally, applying a similar conversion to the $\in$ operator results in a further improved filtering strategy compared with the $(\neq, \notin)$ conversion because, now, the assigned interval is bounded by the minimum and the maximum values in the predicate with the $\in$ operator.

BE-Tree Operations The BE-Tree matching follows a typical tree traversal operation in which starting from the root multiple paths of a tree may be traversed until all relevant l-nodes are reached; the matching pseudocode is given in Sec. 6. In contrast, for insertion, the tree traversal follows exactly one path, which is explained in-depth in Sec. 6. The deletion algorithm is conceptually similar to the matching algorithm and is omitted for brevity.

Table 1: Transformations

Predicates	Interval-based
$i < v_1$	$[v_{min}, v_1 - 1]$
$i \leq v_1$	$[v_{min}, v_1]$
$i = v_1$	$[v_1, v_1]$
$i \neq v_1$	$[v_{min}, v_{max}]$
$i > v_1$	$[v_1 + 1, v_{max}]$
$i \geq v_1$	$[v_1, v_{max}]$
$i \in \{v_1, \cdots, v_k\}$	$[v_1, v_k]$
$i \notin \{v_1, \cdots, v_k\}$	$[v_{min}, v_{max}]$
i BETWEEN v_1, v_2	$[v_1, v_2]$

BE-Tree Complexity The height of BE-Tree is bounded by $O(k \log N)$, where k is the maximum number of predicates per expression and N is the domain cardinality. Thus, the height of BE-Tree, unlike for other tree-based matching structures such as Gryphon [2], does not grow in the number of subscriptions avoiding memory- and performance-detrimental tree degeneration; the complete proof is presented in the technical report [24].

5. BE-TREE SELF-ADJUSTMENT

BE-Tree self-adjustment is based on a novel cost-based ranking function and adaptation policies that utilize this ranking function.

Cost-based Ranking Function We present a novel ranking objective that directly reduces the matching cost as opposed to a ranking that is founded solely on popularity measures and, consequently, biased towards either the least or the most popular key [13], such ranking is a deviation from the actual index objective. Thus, we propose a ranking objective to directly reduce the matching cost based on the notion of *false candidates: the retrieved expressions (subscriptions) that are not matched by an input expression (events).*

We formalize the index objective based on the matching cost as follows. The matching cost is defined as the total number of predicate evaluations broken down into *minimizing false candidate computations* and *minimizing true candidate computations*. The false candidate computation is the total number of predicate evaluations until an unsatisfied predicate is reached which discards the prior computations along the search path, therefore, penalizing multiple search paths of the tree that are discarded eventually. Also, the false candidate computation tracks the total number of predicates evaluated for each unsatisfied expression; therefore, penalizing keys that produce many false candidates. The true candidate computation is the number of predicate evaluations before reporting a set of expressions as matched, namely, promoting the evaluation of the common predicate exactly once.

We define a ranking model for each node in BE-Tree using our proposed matching cost. For an improved ranking accuracy, we also introduce the notion of *covered* and *subsumed* predicates. The covered predicates are defined as all predicates $P_l(x)$ in each l_j-node's expressions such that there exists a $P_i(x) \in \texttt{key}_j$ and $P_i^{\texttt{attr}} = P_l^{\texttt{attr}}$ because by the definition of the leaf node's key, all the $P_l(x)$ must be covered by $P_i(x)$. However, if $P_i(x)$ and $P_l(x)$ are also equivalent, i.e., $\forall x \in \texttt{Dom}(P_i^{\texttt{attr}})\ P_i(x) \leftrightarrow P_l(x)$, then $P_l(x)$ is considered subsumed and not covered. Thus, subsumed predicates are preferred because the covered predicates are approximate and must be re-evaluated at the leaf level for each expression. The ranking model assigns a rank to each node n_i using the function $Rank(n_i)$ which is a combination of the $Loss(n_i)$ and $Gain(l_j)$ functions. $Loss(n_i)$ computes for each node the false candidates generated over a window of m events. $Gain(l_j)$ is defined for each l_j-node, and it is the combination of the number of

Algorithm 1 `MatchBETree`($event$, $cnode$, $matchedSub$)

```
1: matchedSub ← CheckSub(cnode.lnode)
   {Iterate through event's predicates}
2: for i ← 1 to NumOfPred(event) do
3:     attr ← event.pred[i].attr
       {Check the c-node's p-directory (hashtable) for attr}
4:     pnode ← SearchPDir(attr, cnode.pdir)
       {If attr exists in the p-directory}
5:     if pnode ≠ NULL then
6:         SearchCDir(event, pnode.cdir, matchedSub)
```

subsumed and covered predicates for each of its expressions. Formally, $Rank(n_i)$, $Loss(n_i)$, and $Gain(l_j)$ are defined as follows:

$$Rank(n_i) = \begin{cases} \beta Gain(n_i) - \gamma Loss(n_i) & \text{if } n_i \text{ is a } l\text{-node} \\ (\sum_{n_j \in des(n_i)} Rank(n_j)) - \gamma Loss(n_i) & \text{otherwise,} \end{cases}$$

where $0 \leq \beta, \gamma \leq 1$, and $des(n_i)$ returns n_i's immediate descendants

$$Loss(n_i) = \sum_{e' \in window_m(n_i)} \frac{\#\,\texttt{discarded pred eval for}\ e'}{|window_m(n_i)|}$$

$$Gain(l_j) = \alpha_s Gain_s(l_j) + \alpha_c Gain_c(l_j),\ 0 \leq \alpha_s, \alpha_c \leq 1$$

$$Gain_s(l_j) = \#\,\texttt{subsumed pred},\ \ Gain_c(l_j) = \#\,\texttt{covered pred}$$

The proposed ranking model is simply generalized for splitting an overflowing node l_j-node using a new $\mathtt{attr}_i$, and it is given by

$$Rank(l_i) = \beta Gain(l_i) - \gamma Loss(l_i),\ \ where\ 0 \leq \beta, \gamma \leq 1,$$

where $Gain(l_i)$ is approximated by the number of expressions that have a predicate on $\mathtt{attr}_i$ and $Loss(l_i)$ is estimated by constructing a histogram in which $Loss(l_i)$ is the average bucket size in the histogram. Essentially, the average bucket size estimates the selectivity of $\mathtt{attr}_i$, meaning, in the worst case the number of false candidates is equal to the average bucket size. Alternatively, in an optimistic approach $Loss(l_i)$ is initially set to zero to eliminate any histogram construction and to rely on the matching feedback mechanism for adjusting the ranking if necessary. This optimistic approach initially estimates the popularity of $\mathtt{attr}_i$ as opposed to selectivity of $\mathtt{attr}_i$. Based on our experimental evaluation, the optimistic approach results in an improved matching and insertion time. Similarly, based on our empirical evidence, this model can be further simplified by setting all parameters β, γ, α_s, and α_c to 1; hence, eliminating them. This simplification is possible because nearly in all our experiments the rate of false candidate was sufficiently low such that altering the values of these parameters had no influence on the overall BE-Tree's matching rate.

Adaptation Policies In BE-Tree, we also consider three strategies to utilize our ranking function and to further avoid tree degeneration: recycling l-node, reinserting Boolean expression, and exploration vs. exploitation [24]; in the interest of space we only discuss the first property. Recycling l-node is another BE-Tree's self-adjusting policy that monitors each node over a window, $\mathtt{rank}_{\mathtt{window}}$, of the number of insertion, deletion, and matching operations. If at the end of each node's window, the rank of a node drops below the threshold, θ, then the entire contents of that node, including all of its descendant leaf nodes (if any), are removed and re-inserted into BE-Tree.

6. BE-TREE IMPLEMENTATION

Matching Pseudocode Event matching consists of two routines: (1) MatchBETree (Alg. 1) which checks subscriptions in a leaf node and traverses through BE-Tree's p-directory and (2) SearchCDir (Alg. 2) which traverses through BE-Tree's c-directory.

Algorithm 2 `SearchCDir`($event$, $cdir$, $matchedSub$)

```
1: MatchBETree(event, cdir.cnode, matchedSub)
2: if IsEnclosed(event, cdir.lChild) then
3:     SearchCDir(event, cdir.lChild, matchedSub)
4: if IsEnclosed(event, cdir.rChild) then
5:     SearchCDir(event, cdir.rChild, matchedSub)
```

Algorithm 3 `InsertBETree`(sub, $cnode$, $cdir$)

```
1: {Find attr with max score not yet used for partitioning}
2: if cnode.pdir ≠ NULL then
3:     for i = 1 to NumOfPred(sub) do
4:         if !IsUsed(sub.pred[i]) then
5:             attr ← sub.pred[i].attr
6:             pnode ← SearchPDir(attr, cnode.pdir)
7:             if pnode ≠ NULL then
8:                 foundPartition = true;
9:                 if maxScore < pnode.score then
10:                    maxPnode ← pnode
11:                    maxScore ← pnode.score
   {if no partitioning found then insert into the l-node}
12: if !foundPartition then
13:     Insert(sub, cnode.lnode)
        {if c-node is the root then partition; otherwise cluster}
14:     if isRoot(cnode) then
15:         SpacePartitioning(cnode)
16:     else
17:         SpaceClustering(cdir)
18: else
19:     maxCdir ← InsertCDir(sub, maxPnode.cdir)
20:     InsertBETree(sub, maxCdir.cnode, maxCdir)
21:     UpdatePartitionScore(maxPnode)
```

Algorithm 4 `InsertCDir`(sub, $cdir$)

```
1: if IsLeaf(cdir) then
2:     return cdir
3: else
4:     if IsEnclosed(sub, cdir.lChild) then
5:         return InsertCDir(sub, cdir.lChild)
6:     else if IsEnclosed(sub, cdir.rChild) then
7:         return InsertCDir(sub, cdir.rChild)
8:     return cdir
```

MatchBETree algorithm takes as inputs: an event, a c-node (BE-Tree's root initially), and a list to store the matched subscriptions. The algorithm, first, checks all subscriptions in the c-node's leaf to find the matching subscriptions (Line 1). Second, for every $\mathtt{attr}_i$ in the event's predicates, it searches the c-node's p-directory (Line 4). Lastly, the algorithm calls SearchCDir on all relevant p-nodes. (Line 6).

SearchCDir takes as inputs: an event, c-directory, and a list to store the matched subscriptions. The algorithm is as follows: it calls MatchBETree on the c-node of the current c-directory (Line 1), and it recursively calls SearchCDir on the bucket's left child if the left child encloses the event (Line 3), and on the bucket's right child if the right child encloses the event (Line 5).

Insertion Pseudocode Unlike matching, insertion is rather involved because it also manages the overall dynamics of BE-Tree, i.e., the space partitioning and the space clustering. To insert, BE-Tree's root and a subscription is passed to InsertBETree (Alg. 3) that attempts to find the most effective l-node that encloses the subscription. Basically, the insertion is done recursively in two stages. Initially, the p-directory is searched for every unused $\mathtt{attr}_i$ in the subscription, and the $\mathtt{attr}_{max}$ with highest p-node score is selected (Lines 2-11); an unused $\mathtt{attr}_i$ is one that has not been selected at a higher level of BE-Tree by InsertBETree. Alternatively,

Algorithm 5 SpacePartitioning(*cnode*)

```
1: lnode ← cnode.lnode
2: while IsOverflowed(lnode) do
3:     attr ← GetNextHighestScoreUnusedAttr(lnode)
       {Create new partition for the next highest score attr}
4:     pnode ← CreatePDir(attr, cnode.pdir)
       {Move all the subscriptions with predicate on attr}
5:     for sub ∈ lnode do
6:         if sub has attr then
7:             cdir ← InsertCDir(sub, pnode.cdir)
8:             Move(sub, lnode, cdir.cnode.lnode)
9:     SpaceClustering(pnode.cdir)
10: UpdateClusterCapacity(lnode)
```

Algorithm 6 SpaceClustering(*cdir*)

```
1: lnode ← cdir.cnode.lnode
2: if !isOverflowed(lnode) then
3:     return
4: if !IsLeaf(cdir) or IsAtomic(cdir) then
5:     SpacePartitioning(cdir.cnode)
6: else
7:     cdir.lChild ← [cdir.startBound, cdir.endBound/2]
8:     cdir.rChild ← [cdir.endBound/2, cdir.endBound]
9:     for sub ∈ lnode do
10:        if IsEnclosed(sub, cdir.lChild) then
11:            Move(sub, lnode, cdir.lChild.cnode.lnode)
12:        else if IsEnclosed(sub, cdir.rChild) then
13:            Move(sub, lnode, cdir.rChild.cnode.lnode)
14:    SpacePartitioning(cdir.cnode)
15:    SpaceClustering(cdir.lChild)
16:    SpaceClustering(cdir.rChild)
17: UpdateClusterCapacity(lnode)
```

if no such $\mathtt{attr}_{max}$ is found, then the subscription is inserted into the l-node of the current c-node (Line 13). However, if an $\mathtt{attr}_{max}$ is found, then the subscription is pushed down to its corresponding p-node (Line 19).

On the one hand, when $\mathtt{attr}_{max}$ is found (Line 19), the c-directory of the corresponding p-node is searched for the smallest possible c-node that encloses the subscription, the search is done through InsertCDir (Alg. 4). Upon choosing the smallest c-node, the subscription advances to the next level of BE-Tree, and the routine InsertBETree is recursively called on the new c-node. On the other hand, when no $\mathtt{attr}_{max}$ is found (Line 13), the l-node at the current level is declared as the best l-node to hold the new subscription so that InsertBETree's recursion reaches the base case and terminates; however, after the insertion into the l-node, the node may overflow, which, in turn, triggers the BE-Tree's two-phase space-cutting technique: partitioning and clustering.

In particular, if the chosen l-node is at the root level, in which no partitioning or clustering has yet taken place, then the space partitioning is invoked first (Line 15) because the space clustering is feasible only after the space is partitioned; otherwise, the space clustering is invoked (Line 17).

SpacePartitioning (Alg. 5) proceeds as follows. It uses a scoring function (e.g., selectivity or popularity) to find an unused attribute with the highest ranking, $\mathtt{attr}_{max}$, that appears in predicates of the overflowing subscription set (Line 3); consequently, a new p-node is created for the $\mathtt{attr}_{max}$. Next, the algorithm iterates over all the subscriptions in the overflowing l-node, and moves all subscriptions having a predicate defined over $\mathtt{attr}_{max}$ into the c-directory of the $\mathtt{attr}_{max}$'s p-node (Lines 5-8). Lastly, the space clustering is called on the c-directory to resolve any potential overflows resulting from moving subscriptions (Line 9); the entire process is repeated until the l-node is no longer overflowing.

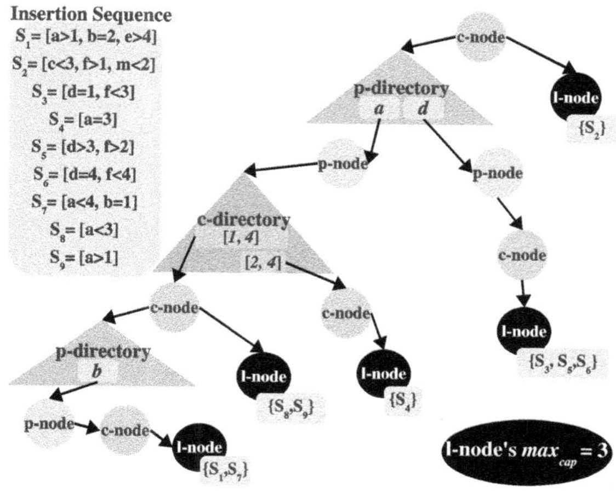

Figure 3: An Insertion Example

SpaceClustering (Alg. 6) is always invoked after the space is partitioned in order to resolve any overflowing l-node by recursively cutting the space in half, and only if the space clustering is unfeasible, then it switches back to the space partitioning. The space clustering is unfeasible when an overflowing l-node is associated to a c-directory bucket that is either a non-leaf bucket, in which further splitting does not reduce the l-node size, or an atomic bucket, in which further splitting is not possible (Line 4). If the space clustering is feasible, then the algorithm splits the current bucket directory in half and moves subscriptions accordingly (Lines 7-13). Next the algorithm recursively calls SpacePartitioning on the current bucket (Line 14) and calls SpaceClustering on the current bucket's left and right child (Lines 15-16).

Next we present an example to further elucidate the insertion algorithm. The final BE-Tree is shown in Fig 3.

Example *Initially,* BE-Tree *is empty. After inserting S_1-S_4, the root's l-node overflows, and based on* InsertBETree *(Line 15), the root is partitioned, and the attribute $[a]$ is selected as $attr_{max}$, and S_1 and S_4 are pushed down to the next level of* BE-Tree. *After inserting S_5-S_6, another overflow occurs at the root, which results in selecting $[d]$ as $attr_{max}$, and, similarly, S_3, S_5, and S_6 are pushed down the tree. After inserting S_7-S_8, both having predicates defined on $[a]$, they are directed toward the l-node containing S_1 and S_4 along the root's p-node with value $[a]$. Consequently, this node will overflow, and based on* InsertBETree *(Line 17), the l-node is clustered. Finally, the insertion of S_9 will overflow the top-level (non-leaf) c-directory, reachable through the root's p-node with value $[a]$; thereby, triggering the space partitioning and selecting $[b]$ as the next $attr_{max}$ through* SpaceClustering *(Line 5).*

7. EVALUATIONS

We present a comprehensive evaluation of BE-Tree using both synthetic and real datasets. The experiments were ran on an Intel 2.66 MHz Quad-core machine with 4GB of memory running Ubuntu 10.04. All algorithms are implemented in C and compiled using gcc 4.4.3 with optimizations set to $O3$.

We compare BE-Tree with several popular matching algorithms over a variety of controlled experimental conditions: *workload distribution, workload size, space dimensionality, average subscription and event size, dimension cardinality, predicate selectivity, dimension selectivity, subscription expressiveness,* and *event matching probability*.

We also ran experiments to determine optimal choices for BE-Tree internal parameters, cf. Sec. 7.3.1. The values used throughout our experiments are: $\mathtt{max}_{cap}$ ranging from 5-160, $\mathtt{min}_{size} = 3$,

Table 2:

(a) Levels of Expressiveness

Op Class	Operators
Min	$(=)$
Low	$(=, \in)$
Med	$(<, \leq, =, \geq, >, \in,$ BETWEEN)
High	$(<, \leq, =, \neq, \geq, >, \in, \notin,$ BETWEEN)

(b) $P_j^{(i,=,v_*)}$ Inferred Pred

$i \neq v_1$ where $v_1 \neq v_*$
$i < v_1$ where $v_1 \geq v_*$
$i > v_1$ where $v_1 \leq v_*$
$i \in \{v_1, \cdots, v_k\} \cup \{v_*\}$
$i \notin \{v_1, \cdots, v_k\} - \{v_*\}$
i BETWEEN v_1, v_2 where $v_1 \leq v_*$ and $v_2 \geq v_*$

$\texttt{rank}_{\texttt{window}}$ for each node is 10% of expressions in the node's subtree, and $\theta = 0$.

7.1 Datasets

Synthetic Dataset One of the key challenges in generating synthetic datasets with high-dimensions is the inability to control the matching probability. With no control mechanism, the matching probability would be virtually zero. To address this concern, we developed a novel workload generation framework, *BEGen*[2]. The workloads are generated in two steps: (1) a set of base expressions with only equality predicates are generated, in which a predicate's attribute is chosen based on either a uniform or a Zipf distribution; (2) for each base expression e_B, we generate a set of derived expressions, e_i, such that

$$\forall P_q(x) \in e_i,\ \exists P_o(x) \in e_B,\ P_q^{\text{attr}} = P_o^{\text{attr}}, \forall x\ P_o(x) \rightarrow P_q(x).$$

Moreover, each predicate in a base expression is kept with probability $\Pr_{pred}$ in its derived expressions, and each predicate in derived expressions is transformed with probability $\Pr_{trans}$ using one of the inferred predicate rules given in Table 2(b). In our synthetic experiments, base expressions model events, and derived expressions model subscriptions. In addition, the probability $\Pr_{pred}$ and $\Pr_{trans}$ are chosen such that with a high probability, we avoid generating any duplicate subscriptions. Thus, if the average number of predicates per event is x and the average number of predicates per subscriptions is y, we choose x and y such that $\binom{x}{y}$ is large enough such that duplicate subscriptions are unlikely. For example, by tuning the number of generated base expressions, we can control the matching probability for a given subscription workload. For instance, to generate a workload size of $1,000$ with matching probability 1%, we generate 100 base expressions and 10 derived expressions for each base expression.

In our evaluation, we assign up to 6 values for $(\in, \notin)$, and on average, we use a predicate range size of 12% of the domain size for the BETWEEN operator, and we randomly pick a value for the remaining operators. The value of each parameter in our synthetic workload is summarized in Table 3 (columns 1-8), in which each column corresponds to a different workload profile while each row corresponds to the actual value of the workload parameters. Lastly, Table 2(a) captures our four levels of operator expressiveness.

Real Dataset In the absence of a standard benchmark for evaluating matching algorithms with real data, as part of our *BEGen* framework, we propose a novel generation of real workloads from public domain data. We focus on data extracted from the DBLP repository. In particular, we use the proceeding titles and author names as two sources of data extracted from DBLP. We, first, employ a de-duplication technique to eliminate duplicate entries and to convert the data into a set of q-grams. This conversion is based on tokenization of a string into a set of q-grams (sequence of q consecutive characters). For example, a 3-gram tokenization of "string" is given by {'str', 'tri', 'rin','ing'}. Second, we use a novel transformation to convert each string from a collection of q-grams into a Boolean expression. Therefore, we model the collection of q-grams {'str', 'tri', 'rin', 'ing'} by a set of equality predicates as follows: ['*st*' = 'r', '*tr*' = 'i','*ri*'='n', and '*in*'='g']. Our 3-grams-based transformation results in Boolean expressions in a space of 677 dimensions. For the real datasets, we also carry out experiments in which we control the degree of matching probability using the profile generation technique that was used for the synthetic datasets. Table 3 (last 4 columns) summarizes various workloads generated using the real data sets.

[2]http://msrg.org/datasets/BEGen

7.2 Matching Algorithms

The algorithms in our comparison studies are (1) SCAN (a sequential scan of the subscriptions), (2) SIFT (the counting algorithm [27] enhanced with the enumeration technique of [26] to support range operators), (3) k-ind (the conjunction algorithm implemented over k-index [26]), (4) GR (the Gryphon algorithm [2]), (5) P (the Propagation algorithm [13], in which subscriptions are clustered based on their most selective attribute), (6a) BE (our fully dynamic version of BE-Tree in which the index is constructed by individually inserting each subscription, and (6b) BE-B (our batching version of BE-Tree in which all subscriptions are known in advance resulting in a better initial statistics to guide the space partitioning at the root level). Unlike the construction of our dynamic BE-Tree, we have constructed k-index, Gryphon, and Propagation using a static workload in which all subscriptions are known in advance. In addition, we have implemented the specialized Gryphon algorithm that supports only equality predicates and the generic Gryphon algorithm that supports arbitrary predicates [2] including all optimizations proposed in [2].

In our experiments, we distinguish between four levels of predicate expressiveness because not all algorithms can naturally support our expressive set of operators. In particular, SIFT [27] and k-index [26] naturally support only a weak semantics for operators $\notin$ and $\neq$ in which subscription predicates with inequality on $attr_i$ are also matched by an input event that does not define any predicate on $attr_i$. The common alternative semantic is to consider a subscription as matched only if an event provides a value for all subscription predicates with inequality (strong semantics). To support inequality operators with the strong semantics, a default value must be added to both subscriptions' inequality predicate and the unspecified attributes in the event [26]. This scheme results in an unacceptable performance as space dimensionality increases for the strong semantics. Thus, we do not consider SIFT and k-index for the inequality (strong semantics) experiments. Similarly, Propagation does not support inequality predicates as access predicates and relies on a post processing step to resolve inequalities. Thus, we do not consider Propagation in the inequality experiments either.

7.3 Experiment Results

In our micro experiments, we study the BE-Tree parameters and their relation to the overall performance of BE-Tree. Most importantly, we establish that the maximum l-node capacity is the main parameter of BE-Tree and provide a systematic guideline on how to adjust it. We then shift gears to focus on macro experiments in which an extensive evaluation and comparison of BE-Tree with other related approaches are conducted. Finally, we illustrate the effectiveness of BE-Tree's self-adjustment under changing workloads.

7.3.1 Micro Experiments

Primary Parameter The most important parameter of BE-Tree is the maximum l-node capacity size, $\texttt{max}_{cap}$, which triggers our two-phase space-cutting technique. In Fig. 4, for various workloads with different matching probability, the effect of varying the

Table 3: Synthetic and Real Workload Properties

	Workload Size	Number of Dimensions	Dimension Cardinality	Predicate Selectivity	Dimension Selectivity	Sub/Event Size	% Equality Pred	Match Prob	DBLP (Author)	DBLP (Title)	Match Prob (Author)	Match Prob (Title)
Size	100K-1M	1M	100K	100K	100K	100K	1M	1M	100-760K	50-250K	400k	150
Number of Dim	400	50-1400	400	400	400	400	400	400	677	677	677	677
Cardinality	48	48	48-150K	48	2-10	48	48	48	26	26	26	26
Avg. Sub Size	7	7	7	7	7	5-66	7	7	8	35	8	30
Avg. Event Size	15	15	15	15	15	13-81	15	15	8	35	16	43
Pred Avg. Range Size %	12	12	12	6-50	—	12	12	12	—	—	12	12
% Equality Pred	0.3	0.3	0.3	0.3	1.0	0.3	0.2-1.0	0.3	1.0	1.0	0.3	0.3
Op Class	Med	Med	Med	Med	Min	Med	Med	Lo-Hi	Min	Min	Lo-Hi	Lo-Hi
Match Prob %	1	1	1	1	—	1	1	0.01-9	—	—	0.01-9	0.01-9

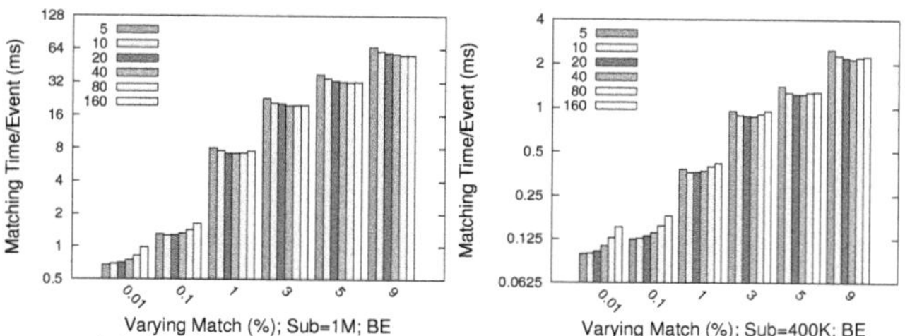

(a) Unif: Med Exp (b) Author: Med Exp

Figure 4: Varying the l-node Capacities

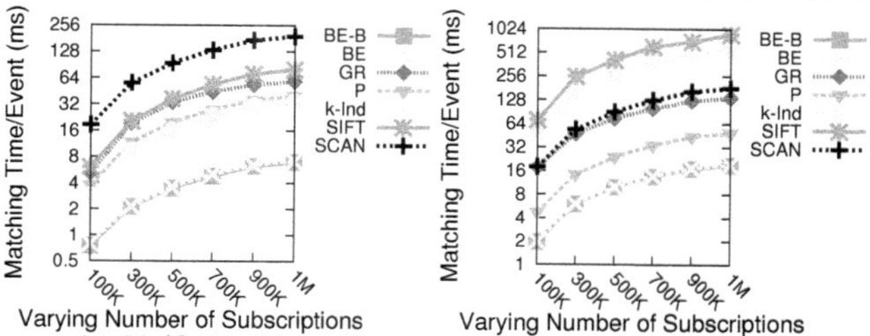

(a) Unif: Workload Size (b) Zipf: Workload Size

Figure 5: Varying Workload Size

l-node capacity is shown. Although, there is a correlation between the optimal value of maximum l-node capacity and the degree of the matching probability, the effect is not significant. Thus, we conclude that BE-Tree is not highly sensitive to the maximum l-node capacity parameter. The results of varying l-node capacities are summarized in Table 4, which we use as a guiding principle throughout our evaluation for choosing the optimal value with respect to the degree of matching probability. Another important factor is that the l-node capacity is a tunable parameter which can be dynamically adjusted (increased or decreased) based on the matching feedback to tune future executions of the two-phase space-cutting technique.

Table 4: Guiding principles for adjusting $\mathtt{max}_{cap}$

	$\mathtt{max}_{cap}$
Match Prob $< 1\%$	5
$1\% \leq$ Match Prob $< 10\%$	20
Match Prob $\geq 10\%$	160

BE-Tree Construction The construction time of the dynamic BE-Tree, for the largest workload of up to one million subscriptions, was under 5 seconds in our experiments. For the main datasets, the BE-Tree's average construction time and index size are summarized in Table 5.

Table 5: BE-Tree Construction Time & Size

Data Sets	Construction Time (second)	Index Size (MB)
Unif (1M)	4.75	84
Zipf (1M)	4.27	82
Author (760K)	4.46	74
Title (250K)	2.48	37

7.3.2 Macro Experiments

Effect of Workload Distribution The major distinguishing factor among matching algorithms is the workload distribution, which clearly sets apart key vs. non-key based methods. Both k-index and SIFT (non-key-based methods) are highly sensitive to the distribution of the workload whereas BE-Tree and Propagation (key-based methods) are robust with respect to the distribution. The effects of the distribution are shown in Fig. 5-11 in which the graphs on the left column correspond to a uniform distribution (for choosing predicates' attributes) while the graphs on the right column correspond to a Zipf distribution. The general trend is that under uniform distribution BE-Tree, k-index, Propagation, Gryphon, SIFT all outperform SCAN that benefits only from sequential memory access. However, under Zipf distribution both k-index and SIFT are outperformed by SCAN in some cases. The poor matching time is attributed to few popular attributes that are common among all subscriptions. Therefore, for every event about 80-90% of subscriptions have at least one satisfied predicate which translates into a large number of random memory accesses to increment subscription counters in SIFT and to sort and scan through k-index hashtable buckets (refereed to as the posting list in [26]). Overall, the BE-Tree matching time is at least four times better than the next best algorithm (k-index) for uniform distribution and at least two and half times better (Propagation) for Zipf distribution.

Effect of Workload Size Next, we consider the matching time as we increase the number of subscriptions processed. Fig. 5a,b illustrate the effect on matching time as the number of subscriptions increases in which all algorithms scale linearly with respect to the number of matched subscriptions. In these experiments, BE-Tree exhibits an 80% better matching time as compared to the next best algorithm for the uniform workload and a 63% better matching time for the Zipf workload.

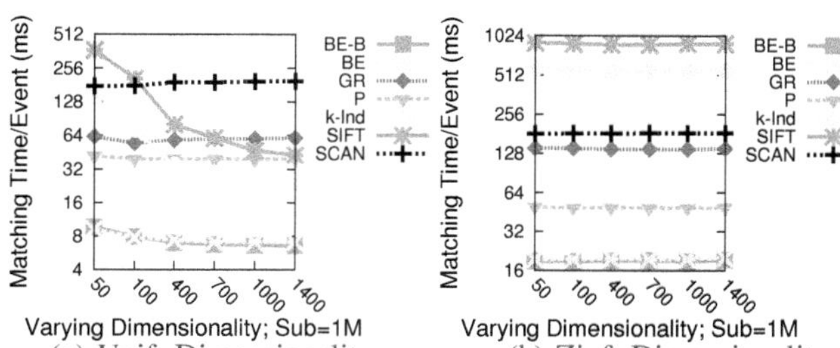

(a) Unif: Dimensionality (b) Zipf: Dimensionality

Figure 6: Varying Space Dimensionality

Effect of Dimensionality Unlike the workload size, the effect of space dimensionality is more subtle; all algorithms with exception of k-index and SIFT are unaffected as the dimensionality varies, Fig. 6a,b. Both k-index and SIFT substantially suffer in lower dimensionality for the uniform workload in which subscriptions tend to share many common predicates, which results in high overlap among subscriptions. Therefore, k-index and SIFT are sensitive to degree of overlap among subscriptions and achieve peak matching time when subscriptions are distributed into a set of disjoint subspaces. For instance, when dimension is set to $d = 50$, BE-Tree improves over k-index by 93% and for $d = 1400$, BE-Tree improves over k-index by 75% in which k-index is the second best algorithm for such high dimensionality. However, for the Zipf workload, Fig. 6b, k-index and SIFT matching time does not improve as the dimensionality increases because of the existence of few popular dimensions, resulting in a large overlap among subscriptions. Thus, BE-Tree improves over k-index by 97%.

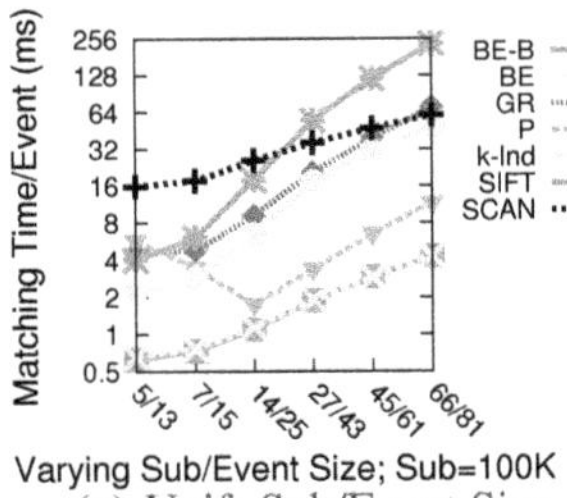

(a) Unif: Sub/Event Size

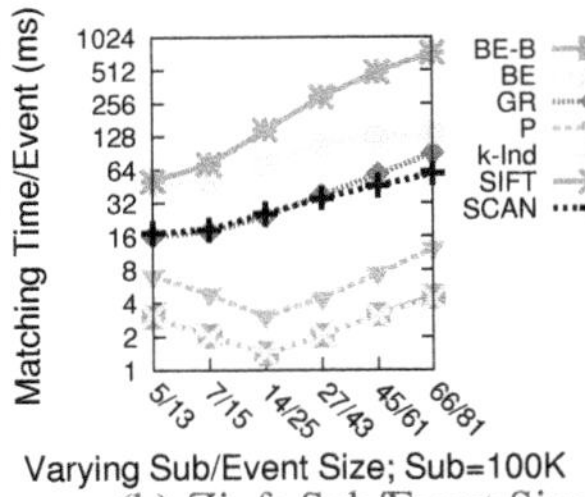

(b) Zipf: Sub/Event Size

Figure 7: Varying Subscription/Event Size

Effect of Subscription/Event Size Another key workload characteristic is the average number of predicates per subscription and event, Fig. 7a,b. In particular, both k-index and SIFT are highly sensitive to the number of predicates: in addition to increasing the overlap among subscriptions, for k-index it also translates into a longer sorting time and for SIFT it translates into a larger number of retrieving and scanning hashtable buckets. The Propagation algorithm starts with a lower matching time because subscriptions have fewer predicates and the chances of finding an equality access predicate with high selectivity is lower, as subscriptions are not evenly distributed in space. As a result, the Propagation algorithm reaches its optimal performance when average subscription size reaches 14, and no noticeable benefit is gained as the subscription size further increases, instead the response time gradually decreases due to an increase in computation cost for checking each predicate. In general, BE-Tree gracefully scales as the number of predicates increases because of its multi-layer structure and improves over the next best algorithm by 63% for the uniform and by 65% for the Zipf workload.

Effect of Dimension Cardinality The importance of increasing the dimension cardinality is twofold: the matching rate and the memory requirement. The matching rate of most algorithms scales gracefully as the dimension cardinality increases, e.g., BE-Tree and Propagation (Fig. 8). In short, BE-Tree improves over Propagation's matching time by 66% for the uniform workload and improves over Propagation's matching time by 59% for the Zipf workload, Fig. 8a,b, respectively.

However, unlike in BE-Tree, the memory footprint of k-index and SIFT blows up exponentially as we increase the dimension cardinality, while keeping constant the ratio of predicate range size with respect to cardinality. Both approaches rely on the enumeration technique to resolve range predicates. For example, in order to cope with the operator BETWEEN $[v_1, v_2]$, the enumeration essentially transforms the value of $v_2 - v_1$ from a decimal to a unary representation—an exponential transformation. Therefore, we were unable to run k-index and SIFT on workloads with cardinality of 6K and beyond. For instance, the workload with a 6K cardinality has on average a predicate range size of 150 which in turn replaces a single range predicate with 150 equality predicates.

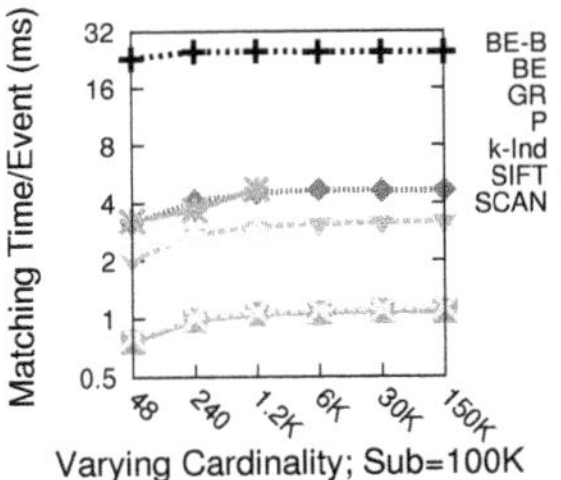

(a) Unif: Dim Cardinality

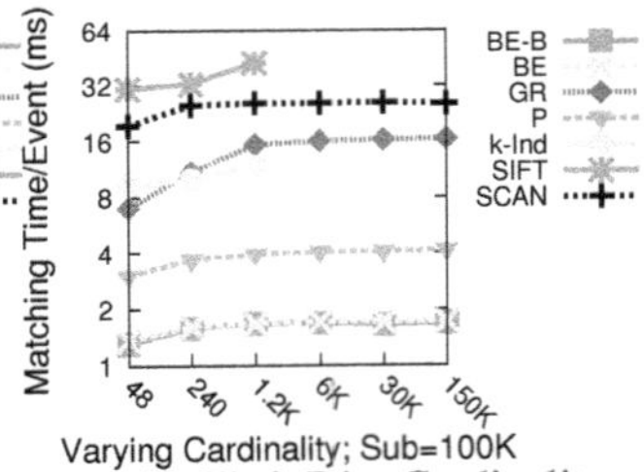

(b) Zipf: Dim Cardinality

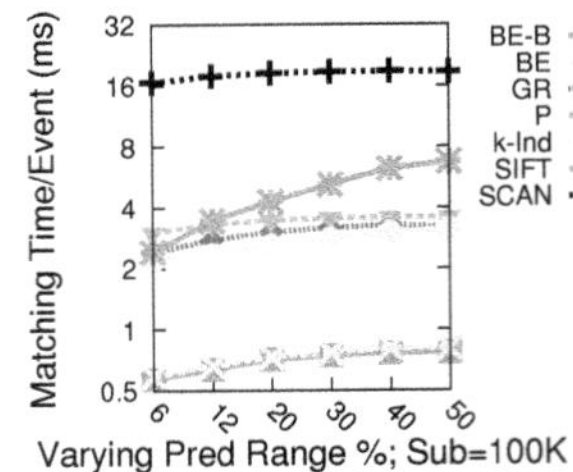

(c) Unif: Pred Range Ratio

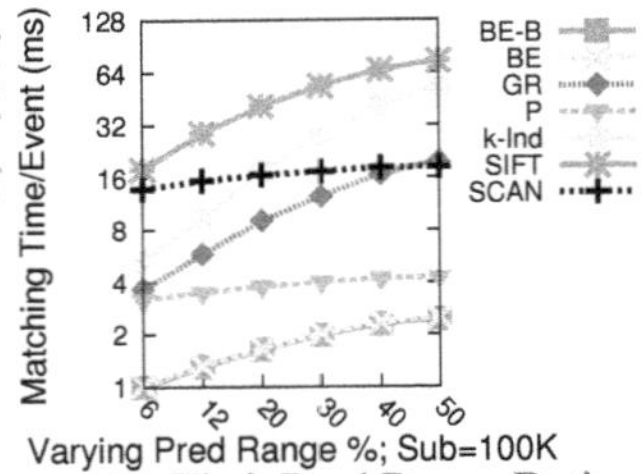

(d) Zipf: Pred Range Ratio

Figure 8: Varying Cardinality & Pred Range/Cardinality Ratio

To further analyze the role of predicate range sizes, we devise another experiment that varies the predicate range size while fixing the cardinality.

Effect of Predicate Selectivity In fact, the ratio of predicate range size with respect to the dimension cardinality is inversely proportional to the predicate selectivity. The predicate selectivity has a small influence on Propagation, which relies solely on selective equality predicates, while it has a huge influence on k-index and SIFT, which do not utilize the predicate selectivity information. Therefore, as shown in Fig. 8c,d, as the ratio of the predicate range size increases (selectivity decreases), the search space pruning mechanism of k-index and SIFT suffer due to the increased number of false candidates.

In general, a low selective predicate causes a less effective pruning of the search space, and BE-Tree compensate for the low selectivity with a deeper tree structure that provides a greater opportunity to prune the search space by using both highly selective predicates (equality) and low selective predicates (range operators). As a result, BE-Tree improves over the next best algorithms by 76% and 43% for the uniform and the Zipf workloads, respectively (cf. Fig. 8c,d.)

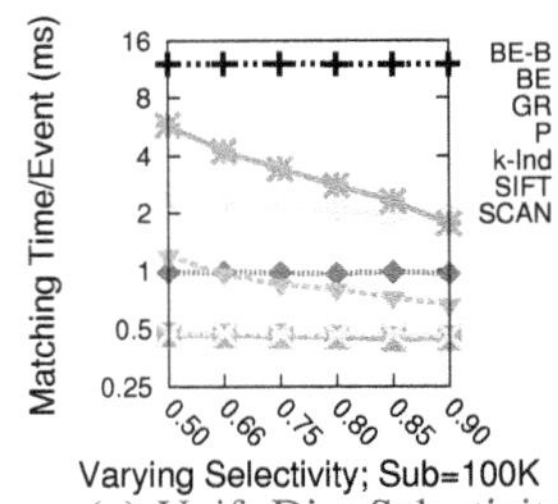

(a) Unif: Dim Selectivity

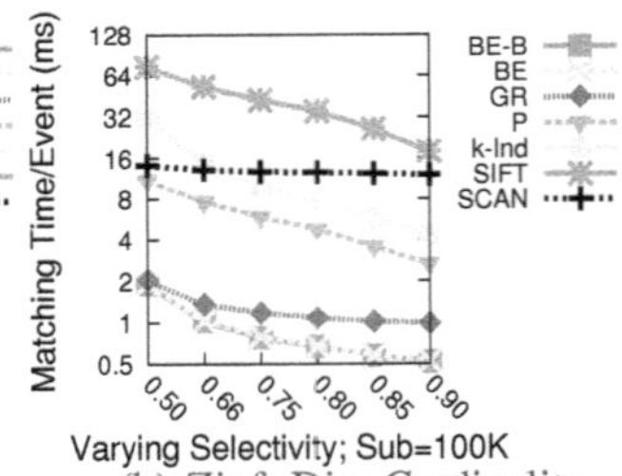

(b) Zipf: Dim Cardinality

Figure 9: Varying Dimension Selectivity

Effect of Dimension Selectivity A notable workload characteristic is dimension selectivity of the space, which could have a direct influence on the ability of the matching algorithm to effectively prune the search space. The result of our dimension selectivity is captured in Fig. 9. For a uniform workload the robustness of BE-Tree and Gryphon is evident because as the dimension selectivity varies only a negligible increase in matching time of at most 1% is observed while for Propagation and k-index a significant increase in matching time of upto 80% and 27% is observed, respectively. The importance of dimension selectivity is further magnified for a

Zipf workload (cf. Fig. 9b) in which a few dimensions are dominant. Therefore, for low selectivity a substantial overhead is incurred due to a larger number of false candidates. For instance, as we decrease selectivity from 0.9 to 0.5, the response time is increased by 411% and 650% for Propagation and k-index, respectively. Therefore, low selectivity results in a less effective pruning of the search space, and BE-Tree prunes the search space more effectively by employing a multi-layer tree structure.

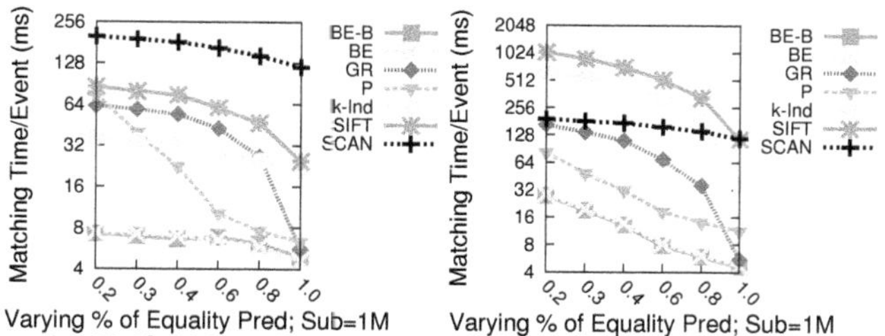

(a) Unif: % Equality Pred (b) Zif: % Equality Pred

Figure 10: Varying % of Equality Predicates

Effect of Percentage of Equality Predicates In this experiment, we study the effects of ratio of equality vs. non-equality predicates for each subscription. The general trend is that the matching times for all algorithms improve as the percentage of subscription equality predicates increases because the overlap among subscriptions is reduced, Fig. 10a,b. Most notably, when subscriptions consist only of equality predicates, the specialized Gryphon (for equality predicates) results in a substantial performance gain, being the best algorithm after BE-Tree, compared with the generic Gryphon. The Propagation algorithm also improves significantly when subscriptions are restricted to only equality predicates because there is a better chance to find more effective access predicates. However, among all algorithms, Gryphon and Propagation, are the most highly sensitive to the percentage of equality predicates. As the percentage of equality predicate decreases, their performance substantially deteriorates. For instance, for the uniform workload, Fig. 10a, BE-Tree improves over Gryphon matching time by 88% when subscriptions only have few equality predicates and by 20% when subscriptions only have equality predicates.

Effect of Percentage of Matching Probability As the matching probability increases, the number of candidate subscriptions and the event matching time also increases. Therefore, we studied the effects of varying matching probability under both uniform and Zipf workload based on different levels of predicate expressiveness. Under a uniform workload with low and medium expressiveness, while keeping the matching probability below 1%, k-index outperforms both Propagation and SIFT, while BE-Tree improves over k-index by 97%. However, as the matching probability goes beyond 3%, the Propagation algorithm begins to outperform both k-index and SIFT, while BE-Tree improves over Propagation by up to 33%, even as the matching probability reaches 9%, Fig. 11a,c. As the matching probability goes beyond 35%, the success of BE-Tree continues as BE-Tree becomes marginally the better algorithm followed by Propagation and SCAN (omitted in the interest of space [24].) In general, an increase in matching probability results in an increase in the number of candidate matches. Therefore, SIFT is forced to scan large hashtable buckets, using random access, to increment subscription counters for each of the satisfied predicates. Similarly, k-index is forced to scan large buckets (i.e., posting lists) with a reduced chance of pruning and an increased application of sorting to advance through each bucket. For the Zipf distribution, Propagation remains the next best algorithm after BE-Tree, Fig. 11b,d. Furthermore, in the experiments where the highest

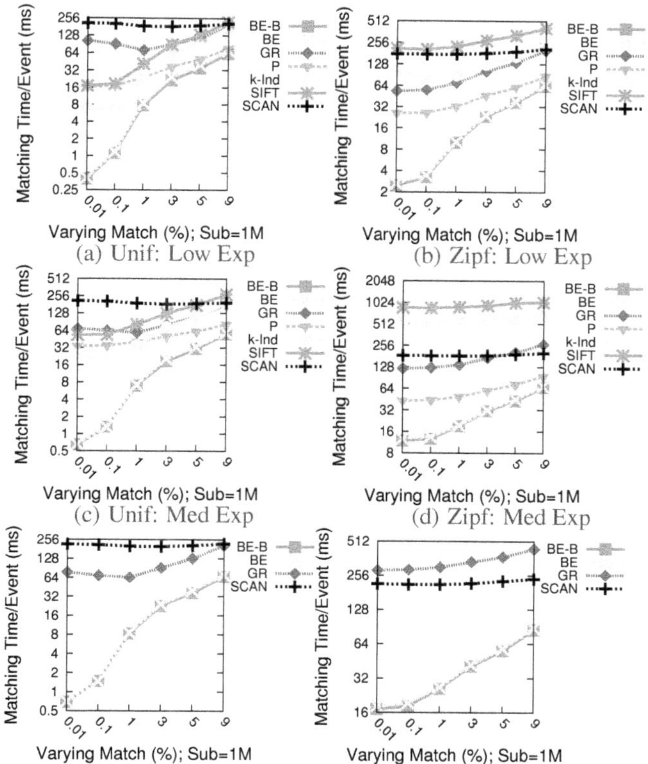

(a) Unif: Low Exp (b) Zipf: Low Exp
(c) Unif: Med Exp (d) Zipf: Med Exp
(e) Unif: High Exp (f) Zipf: High Exp

Figure 11: Varying Matching Probability

level of expressiveness was used, BE-Tree dominates both Gryphon and SCAN by orders of magnitude, Fig. 11e,f.

Real Datasets In our synthetic experiments in which the percentage of equality predicates was varied, BE-Tree and Gryphon were the top performing algorithms followed by Propagation and k-index. Similar trends are also observed for real datasets. In particular, for the author dataset, Fig. 12a, with an average of 8 predicates per subscriptions, BE-Tree improves over Gryphon by 37% while substantially improving over Propagation by over 98%. For the title dataset with much larger number of predicates per subscriptions, that is at around 35 predicates per subscriptions, the gap between BE-Tree and the other algorithms further widens. This is due to the novel scoring that exploits interrelationships within dimensions and the multi-layer structure of BE-Tree that effectively utilizes most of the subscription predicates to reduce the search space. Therefore, as demonstrated in Fig. 12b, BE-Tree improves over Gryphon by 51% and significantly improves over Propagation by more than 99%, up to three orders of magnitude. Moreover, we have conducted the matching probability experiments with varying degree of expressiveness which produced similar results as for the synthetic dataset, not included due to lack of space (cf. available in a technical report [24]).

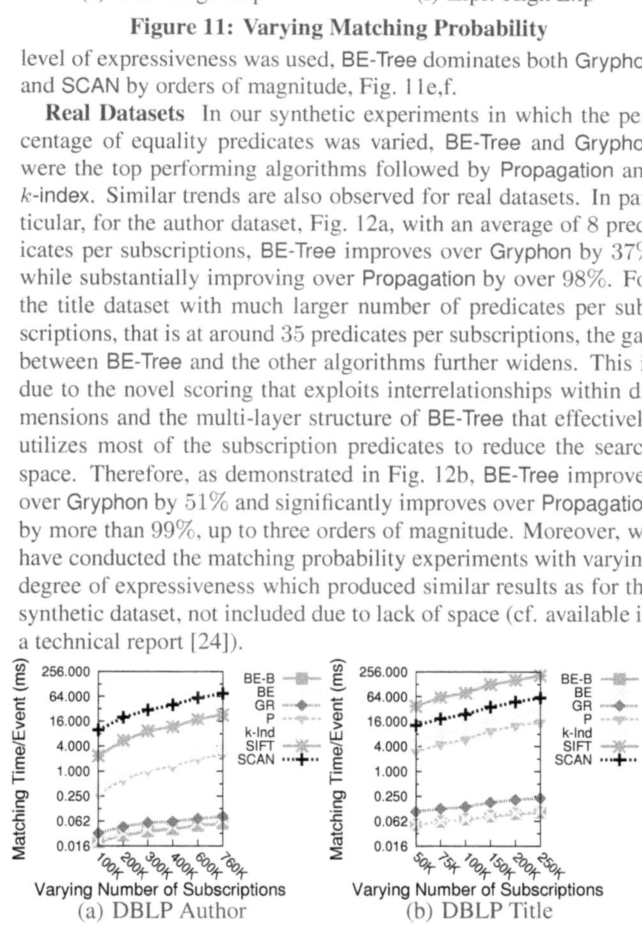

(a) DBLP Author (b) DBLP Title

Figure 12: Varying the workload size

Adapting to Subscription Changes In our last experiment, we

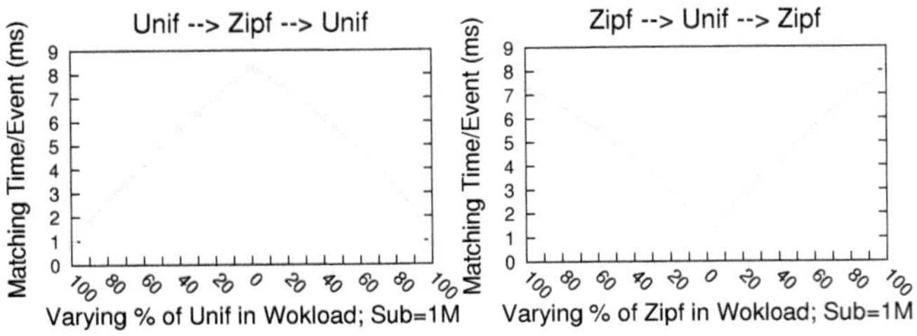

Figure 13: Dynamic Workload

studied the self-adjusting mechanism of BE-Tree. The experiment setup is as follow. First, we fixed the event workload in which half of the events are generated using a uniform while the other half using a Zipf distribution. Second, we generated uniform and Zipf subscription workloads with 0.1% matching probability. In each experiment, we start by individually inserting each subscription from workload X into BE-Tree, then we individually remove each subscription from BE-Tree and individually insert subscriptions from the workload Y until BE-Tree contains only subscriptions from workload Y, then we reverse this process until we gradually switch back to the original workload X. After a fixed number of deletions and insertions, we run our event workload, and record the matching time. The objective is to illustrate that BE-Tree adapts to workload changes and the performance of BE-Tree does not significantly deteriorate even in extreme situations in which the distribution rapidly and dramatically changes. In the first experiment, while transitioning from uniform to Zipf and back again, the matching time at the end of the transition approaches the original performance, Fig. 13a. A similar adaptation was observed when we transitioned from Zipf to uniform and back again, Fig. 13b.

8. CONCLUSIONS

In this work, we presented BE-Tree, a novel index structure to efficiently index and match **B**oolean **E**xpressions defined over a high-dimensional discrete space. We introduced a novel two-phase space-cutting technique to cope with the curse of dimensionality underlying the subscription and event space, which underlies many application domains, and we developed a cost model and self-adjustment policies that enable BE-Tree to actively adapt to workload changes. Moreover, we demonstrated that BE-Tree is a generic index for Boolean expressions that supports predicates with expressive operators.

To summarize our evaluation, let us consider three main workload categories: (1) workloads with uniform distribution and a low-to-high degree of expressiveness, (2) workloads with Zipf distribution and a low-to-high degree of expressiveness, and (3) real-world and synthetic workloads with minimum degree of expressiveness (equality predicates only). From best to worst performing algorithms, in the first category (uniform) we have: BE-Tree, k-index [26], Propagation [13], and SIFT [27]. In the second category (Zipf) we have: BE-Tree, Propagation, k-index, and SIFT. Lastly, in the third category we have: BE-Tree, Gryphon [2], Propagation, and k-index. The general trends are that non-key based algorithms, i.e., k-index and SIFT, do poorly on workloads that consist of few popular dimensions (i.e., low dimensional space and Zipf distribution) because of the significant increase in the number of false candidates that have to be considered. Also, Gryphon and Propagation are highly sensitive to the degree of expressiveness of subscriptions. Finally, BE-Tree dominated in every category.

9. REFERENCES

[1] R. Agrawal, A. Ailamaki, P. A. Bernstein, et al. The Claremont report on database research. *SIGMOD Rec.'08*.

[2] M. K. Aguilera, R. E. Strom, D. C. Sturman, M. Astley, and T. D. Chandra. Matching events in a content-based subscription system. In *PODC'99*.

[3] S. Berchtold, D. A. Keim, and H.-P. Kriegel. The X-tree: An index structure for high-dimensional data. In *VLDB'96*.

[4] K. S. Beyer, J. Goldstein, R. Ramakrishnan, and U. Shaft. When is "nearest neighbor" meaningful? In *ICDT'99*.

[5] L. Brenna, A. Demers, J. Gehrke, M. Hong, J. Ossher, B. Panda, M. Riedewald, M. Thatte, and W. White. Cayuga: high-performance event processing engine. *SIGMOD'07*.

[6] A. Campailla, S. Chaki, E. Clarke, S. Jha, and H. Veith. Efficient filtering in publish-subscribe systems using binary decision diagrams. In *ICSE'01*.

[7] S. Ceri, R. Cochrane, and J. Widom. Practical applications of triggers and constraints: Success and lingering issues (10-year award). In *VLDB'00*.

[8] A. Chandel, O. Hassanzadeh, N. Koudas, M. Sadoghi, and D. Srivastava. Benchmarking declarative approximate selection predicates. In *SIGMOD'07*.

[9] B. Chandramouli, J. Goldstein, and D. Maier. High-performance dynamic pattern matching over disordered streams. *PVLDB'10*.

[10] U. Dayal, E. N. Hanson, and J. Widom. Active database systems. In *Modern Database Systems'95*.

[11] Y. Diao, M. Altinel, M. J. Franklin, H. Zhang, and P. Fischer. Path sharing and predicate evaluation for high-performance XML filtering. *ACM TODS'03*.

[12] N. Dindar, B. Güç, P. Lau, A. Ozal, M. Soner, and N. Tatbul. Dejavu: declarative pattern matching over live and archived streams of events. In *SIGMOD'09*.

[13] F. Fabret, H.-A. Jacobsen, F. Llirbat, J. Pereira, K. A. Ross, and D. Shasha. Filtering algorithms and implementation for fast pub/sub systems. *SIGMOD'01*.

[14] M. Fontoura, S. Sadanandan, J. Shanmugasundaram, S. Vassilvitski, E. Vee, S. Venkatesan, and J. Zien. Efficiently evaluating complex Boolean expressions. In *SIGMOD'10*.

[15] C. L. Forgy. Rete: A fast algorithm for the many pattern/ many object pattern match problem. *AI'82*.

[16] M. Freeston. A general solution of n-dimensional B-tree problem. *SIGMOD'95*.

[17] A. Guttman. R-tree dynamic index structure for spatial searching. *SIGMOD'84*.

[18] E. N. Hanson, C. Carnes, L. Huang, M. Konyala, L. Noronha, S. Parthasarathy, J. Park, and A. Vernon. Scalable trigger processing. In *ICDE'99*.

[19] E. N. Hanson, M. Chaabouni, C.-H. Kim, and Y.-W. Wang. A predicate matching algorithm for database rule systems. In *SIGMOD'90*.

[20] H. Leung and H.-A. Jacobsen. Efficient matching for state-persistent publish/subscribe systems. In *CASCON'03*.

[21] G. Li, S. Hou, and H.-A. Jacobsen. A unified approach to routing, covering and merging in publish/subscribe systems based on modified binary decision diagrams. In *ICDCS'03*.

[22] W. Rjaibi, K. R. Dittrich, and D. Jaepel. Event matching in symmetric subscription systems. In *CASCON'02*.

[23] M. Sadoghi, I. Burcea, and H.-A. Jacobsen. GPX-Matcher: A generic Boolean predicate-based XPath expression matcher. In *EDBT'11*.

[24] M. Sadoghi and H.-A. Jacobsen. Indexing Boolean expression over high-dimensional space. *Technical Report CSRG-608, University of Toronto, 2010*.

[25] M. Sadoghi, H.-A. Jacobsen, M. Labrecque, W. Shum, and H. Singh. Efficient event processing through reconfigurable hardware for algorithmic trading. *PVLDB'10*.

[26] S. Whang, C. Brower, J. Shanmugasundaram, S. Vassilvitskii, E. Vee, R. Yerneni, and H. Garcia-Molina. Indexing Boolean expressions. In *VLDB'09*.

[27] T. Yan and H. Garcia-Molina. Index structures for selective dissemination of information under the Boolean model. *ACM TODS'94*.

TI: An Efficient Indexing Mechanism for Real-Time Search on Tweets *

Chun Chen‡
‡College of Computer Science
Zhejiang University, P.R. China
chenc@zju.edu.cn

Feng Li§ Beng Chin Ooi§ Sai Wu§
§School of Computing
National University of Singapore, Singapore
{li-feng, ooibc, wusai}@comp.nus.edu.sg

ABSTRACT

Real-time search dictates that new contents be made available for search immediately following their creation. From the database perspective, this requirement may be quite easily met by creating an up-to-date index for the contents and measuring search quality by the time gap between insertion time and availability of the index. This approach, however, poses new challenges for micro-blogging systems where thousands of concurrent users may upload their micro-blogs or tweets simultaneously. Due to the high update and query loads, conventional approaches would either fail to index the huge amount of newly created contents in real time or fall short of providing a scalable indexing service.

In this paper, we propose a tweet index called the *TI* (Tweet Index), an adaptive indexing scheme for microblogging systems such as Twitter. The intuition of the *TI* is to index the tweets that may appear as a search result with high probability and delay indexing some other tweets. This strategy significantly reduces the indexing cost without compromising the quality of the search results. In the *TI*, we also devise a new ranking scheme by combining the relationship between the users and tweets. We group tweets into topics and update the ranking of a topic dynamically. The experiments on a real Twitter dataset confirm the efficiency of the *TI*.

Categories and Subject Descriptors

H.2.4 [**Database Management**]: Systems

General Terms

Algorithms, Design

Keywords

Real-time Search, Index, Ranking

*In Twitter, tweet refers to the microblog published by users. In this paper, we use it as a common phrase for microblogs.

SIGMOD'11, June 12–16, 2011, Athens, Greece.

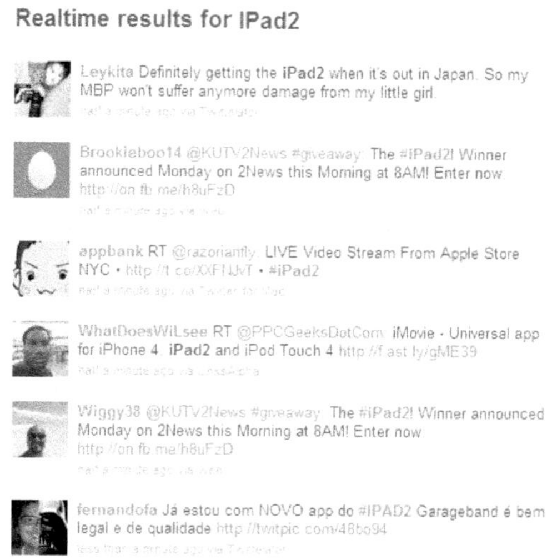

Figure 1: Example of Twitter Search on 3/11/2011

1. INTRODUCTION

The increasing popularity of social networking systems changes the form of information sharing. Instead of issuing a query to a search engine, the users log into their social networking accounts and retrieve news, URLs and comments shared by their friends. This is in part caused by the failure of conventional search engines in providing real-time search service for social networking systems. For example, it is difficult to search a new blog or tweet uploaded a few minutes ago using a conventional search engine. The problem is further amplified in the microblogging systems such as Twitter due to unprecedented amount of tweets or microblogs being posted each day. For example, Tumblr (http://www.tumblr.com) estimated that there were more than 2 million posts and fifteen thousands new users every day[1]; and based on a latest report from Twitter[2], it handled more than 50 million tweets per day.

Providing real-time search service is indeed very challenging in large-scale microblogging systems. In such a system, thousands of new updates need to be processed per second. To make every update searchable, we need to index its effect in real time and provide effective and efficient keyword-based retrieval at the same time. The objectives are therefore con-

[1]http://staff.tumblr.com/post/434982975/a-billion-hits
[2]http://thenextweb.com/socialmedia/2010/02/22/twitter-statistics-full-picture/

tradictory since maintenance of up-to-date index will cause severe contention for locks on the index pages.

Another problem of real-time search is the lack of effective ranking functions. Figure 1 illustrates an example on the search results of Twitter for the keyword "IPad2". The query was submitted a few minutes later after IPad2's sale starts. The user is perhaps looking for the reviews and comments about the IPad2, or he is trying to find out the length of queue at the apple stores around his neighborhood. However, most search results are advertisements and most of the returned tweets do not even provide any useful information. This is because the current Twitter search engine sorts the results based on time, and therefore, the latest tweets have the higher rankings. Recall that one key factor of Google's early success is its PageRank [14] algorithm. Without proper ranking functions, the search results are meaningless. However, defining a ranking function for real-time search is not trivial, and the function must have the following two desiderata:

1. The ranking function must consider both the timestamp of the data and the similarity between the data and the query. As an example, for a given query submitted to Twitter, we do not want to get tweets posted many weeks ago, even though they may contain the keywords of the query. On the other hand, newer tweets with less information are not preferred either. Hence, the ranking function is composed of two independent factors, time and similarity.
2. The ranking function should be cost-efficient. As we want to support real-time search using a ranking function partially based on time, we have to compute the rankings during query time. Thus, the computation of the ranking function should not incur high overhead.

In this paper, we propose the Tweet Index (*TI*), a novel indexing and ranking mechanism for enabling real-time search in microblogging systems such as Twitter. The *TI* is designed based on the observation that most tweets will not appear in the search results. Therefore, we can significantly reduce the indexing cost by delaying indexing less useful tweets. In essence, the *TI* classifies the tweets into two types, *distinguished* tweets and *noisy* tweets. The *TI* consists of two indexing schemes: a real-time indexing scheme for distinguished tweets and a background batch indexing scheme for noisy tweets. Given a new tweet, *TI* analyzes its contents and determines its type. If it is a distinguished tweet, we will index it immediately. Otherwise, it is grouped with other noisy tweets and periodically, the batch indexing scheme is invoked to index all the noisy tweets in one go. The design principle of the *TI* is similar in spirit to the partial indexing scheme [20, 18], and is also related to the view selection problem [1]. To the best of our knowledge, this is the first proposal that addresses the index issues for the real-time search.

In the *TI*, the ranking function plays the major role in deciding whether the tweets are distinguished tweets or noisy tweets and in retrieving meaningful answers. We therefore propose a new ranking function by combining the user graph and tweet graph. In social networks, each user can be considered as a node and different nodes are connected together via the friend links. The user graph denotes the relationship among the users. Naturally, a popular user will have more friends and his/her blogs/tweets also attract wider readership. Therefore, we run a PageRank algorithm for the user graph to compute the ranking for each user. Besides the user graph, the tweets also form a graph, as some tweets are exchanged between people and some tweets reply to the other tweets. We group tweets into topics based on their relationship, and we measure the popularity of the topics based on their statistics. Finally, our proposed ranking function is composed of the user's PageRank, the popularity of topics, the TF (Term Frequency) and the timestamp. The IDF (Inverse Document Frequency) is not used in the *TI*, since the length of a microblog is fairly small and often capped at certain length (e.g. in Twitter, it is capped at 140 characters).

We evaluate the *TI* by using a real Twitter dataset collected for a user group within the last three years. The experiments examine the performance of our indexing scheme and the effect on the quality of query results. We also compare our ranking function with the other relevant ranking functions.

The rest of the paper is organized as follows. In Section 2, we review the previous work in social network search and the corresponding database techniques. In Section 3, we introduce the overview architecture of *TI*. And the details of the *TI*'s indexing scheme and ranking function are discussed in Section 4 and Section 5, respectively. We evaluate the performance of the proposed schemes in Section 6. And the paper is concluded in Section 7.

2. RELATED WORK

2.1 Partial Indexing and View Materialization

In database systems, indexes are created to facilitate efficient query processing. However, existing indexes designed for similarity and KNN search such as iDistance [28] could not be directly applied to tweet indexing, since they have not been designed for very high insertion load. Instead of indexing the whole dataset, a partial index was proposed for indexing the records that may be queried with high probability. The idea of partial indexing was first proposed in [20], where the advantages of a partial index are analyzed. In [18], a statistical model is built to monitor the query distribution and the partial index is created adaptively. Partial indexing technique is also adopted in the distributed environment. In PIER [13], only rare items are indexed in the DHT (Distributed Hash Table), while the popular items are searched via flooding. In PISCES [25], a just-in-time indexing scheme that can be dynamically tuned to follow query patterns was proposed to facilitate query processing in a peer-to-peer based data management system on BATON [9].

View materialization shares some similar principles with the partial indexing technique. [3] and [27] discuss how to adaptively materialize the views in multi-dimensional databases and data warehouse systems. Cost models were proposed in [1] and [5] to automatically select views for materialization. In [19], the adaptive view materialization strategy is applied to reduce the overhead of stream feeding systems. The proposed *TI* adopts a similar design philosophy with the above work. In the *TI*, only data that are deemed essential for the queries are indexed in real-time, while the remaining data are processed in bulk and batch mode.

2.2 Microblog Search

Google and Twitter have released their real-time search engines recently. Google designs its web crawler to adap-

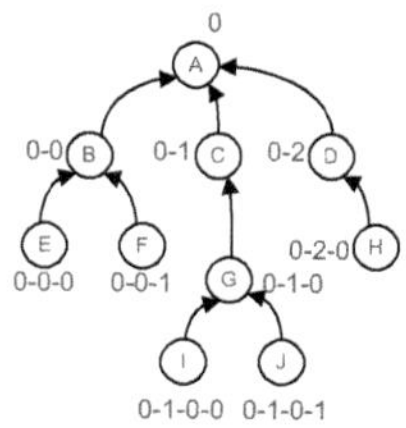

Figure 2: Tree Structure of Tweets

tively crawl the microblogs, while Twitter relies on an existing technique, such as Lucene[3], to provide the search service. Both of them treat a query as a continuous query and update the results in real time. However, the ranking function only considers the time dimension, and as a result, the results are sorted by time. By studying the users' behavior in the microblogging systems [11], more sophisticated ranking schemes, such as [23] and [15], were proposed. However, most ranking schemes are too complex and therefore too expensive and time consuming. They are precomputed in an offline manner. To address this problem, in [16], noisy tweets are pruned and similar tweets are clustered together. Ranking is computed for the tweets of the same cluster so that the computation cost can be significantly reduced.

In the *TI*, we also group tweets into some topics by examining their relationships captured in a tree structure. In particular, tweets replying to the same tweet or belonging to the same thread are organized as a tree. Similar schemes were adopted for forum search [17, 26]. To reduce the ranking cost, *TI* maintains the popular topics in memory and modifies the structure of an inverted index. Compared to the previous work, *TI*'s ranking function is more efficient and incurs less overhead.

3. SYSTEM OVERVIEW

3.1 Social Graphs

As the *TI* is proposed to support efficient search in microblogging systems, we first review the features of social networks that influence the design of the index.

In social networks, users are connected together by friend links (in Twitter, it's following/follower link). Typically, a popular and famous user will have more friends than an ordinary or low-profile user. Here, we define a user graph $G_u = (U, E)$, where U is set of users in the system and E is the friend links between them.

Apart from the user graph, we have another graph that is induced by the relationship of microblogs or tweets. Figure 2 shows a tree structure of tweets, where each node denotes a tweet and the directed edge indicates that one tweet replies to or retweets another tweet. For example, tweet B replies to tweet A and thus A is the parent node of B in the tree. The tweet that does not reply to others becomes the root of the tree. In this paper, we use a tweet tree to represent a discussion topic. When searching, tweets in the same topic can be grouped together and returned. We do not explicitly maintain the tweet tree, as it may incur too much overhead. Instead, we assign each tweet a tree encoding ID, which is similar to the Dewey Order ID [22] in XML search. Given tweet t_i, we sort its child nodes by their timestamps (the time that the tweet is inserted into the system). Suppose the encoding of t_i is "x" and tweet t_j is t_i's kth child, t_j's encoding is "x"+"-"+"k", where + indicates the string concatenation. With the help of tree encoding, we can easily reconstruct the tree structure.

[3]http://lucene.apache.org

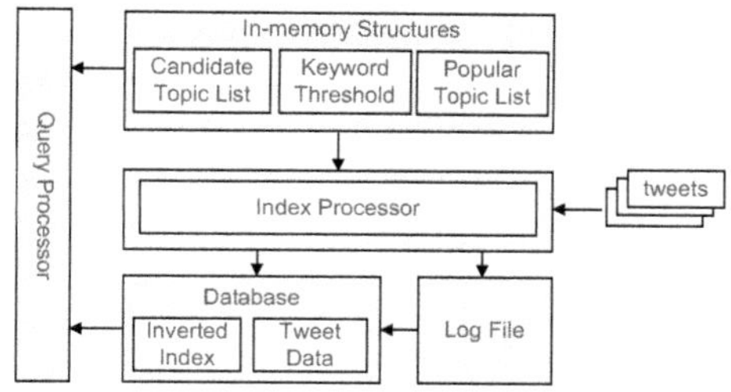

Figure 3: Architecture of *TI*

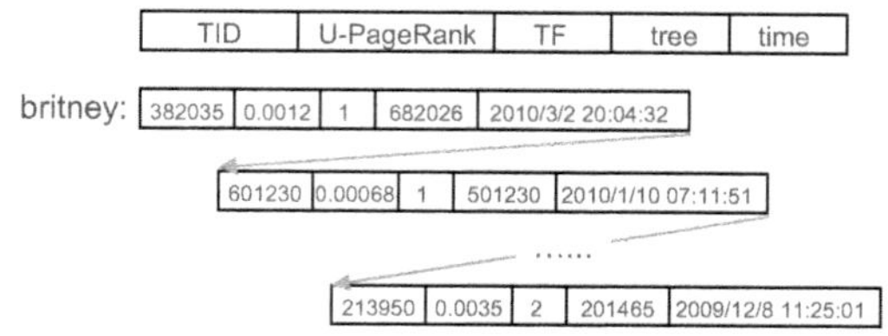

Figure 4: Structure of Inverted Index

3.2 Design of the TI

The *TI* provides its search via an inverted index. When a new tweet is inserted into the microblogging system, the indexing process determines whether it should be indexed or not. To facilitate the fast index maintenance and search process, some statistics are maintained in memory. Figure 3 shows the architecture of the *TI*.

In the *TI*'s database, we keep an inverted index for the tweet data. Given a keyword, the inverted index returns a tweet list, T. T consists of a set of tweet IDs and tweets in T are sorted by their timestamps (the time when a tweet is inserted into the system). Figure 4 shows the index structure of the inverted index. For each record in the index, we keep its tweet ID, TID (inherited from the status ID provided by Twitter), to identify different tweets. Then, for the ranking purpose, we keep the U-PageRank of a tweet (to be defined in Section 5), the TF (Term Frequency) value, the tree ID and the timestamp of the tweet. Tree ID is the TID of the root node in a tweet tree. Records of the same keyword are maintained as a list and the latest record is inserted into the head of the list. As a result, the records are sorted by their timestamps in the list.

To facilitate our ranking scheme, we also keep the metadata of a tweet. We define a tweet table as follows.

Table 1 Example of Tweet Table

TID	RID	tree	time	count	coding	UID	pointer
26476	76732	25742	...	0	0-0-0	...	null
57380	76732	25742	...	0	0-0-1	...	null
26980	null	26980	...	1	0	...	1022

Based on a tweet's content, we know whether the tweet replies/re-tweets another tweet. We maintain the ID of the replied tweet as RID, and it can be used to retrieve the parent tweet. If a tweet belongs to an existing tree, we keep the root ID of the tree, which can be obtained from its parent tweet. Otherwise, we create a single node tree by using the tweet itself as the root. We also keep the timestamp of each tweet and the *count* attribute denotes the number of tweets that reply to this tweet. To enable efficient reconstruction of the tree, the encoding is stored with each tweet. The author ID UID of a tweet is defined as the foreign key in the tweet table. Finally, if a tweet is not indexed and written back to the log file, we keep a pointer to its offset in the log file. To support efficient retrieval via tweet ID and user ID, we build a B$^+$-tree index for TID and UID in the database.

Besides the tweet table, the TI keeps a log file for recording the unindexed tweets. The TI selectively indexes the inserted tweets, the distinguished tweets. The noisy tweets are appended to the log file and periodically, a background batch indexing process will scan the log file to index the noisy tweets.

To support the TI's indexing and ranking algorithm, we keep some useful information in the memory, such as keyword threshold, candidate topic list and popular topic list. Keyword threshold records the statistics of recent popular queries. The candidate topic list maintains the information about recent topics, while popular topic list represents the hotly discussed topics. Based on above information, we can quickly classify a tweet as a distinguished or noisy tweet and adopt different indexing scheme accordingly. Moreover, based on our in-memory structures, we rank the tweets in the querying time by combining the time, popularity and similarity.

4. CONTENT-BASED INDEXING SCHEME

The basic idea of the TI's indexing scheme is to index the tweets based on their contents and their rankings with respect to existing queries. Intuitively, it streams a new tweet into an existing set of popular queries, and based on its ranking, determines if it should be indexed in real-time or in batch periodically. To improve the quality of search results, our ranking function considers the user's pagerank, the popularity of a topic and the similarity between queries and tweets. Figure 5 shows the data flow in TI's index processor. In this section, we present how we classify the tweets and apply the adaptive tweet indexing strategy. The details of ranking function $\mathcal{F}$ will be discussed in next section.

4.1 Tweet Classification

The first challenge in the design of TI's indexing strategy on the measurement of the importance of a tweet. Limited by its size, a tweet itself does not provide too much information. Therefore, we apply a query-based classification approach. We assume that users are only interested in the top-K results. This assumption can easily be verified by the statistics of search engines [8] where 62% of the users click a result in the first page and more than 90% of the users stop their browsing after three pages of results.

In particular, the problem can be formalized as follows.

DEFINITION 1. Tweet Classification
Given a tweet t and a user's query set $\mathcal{Q}$, t is said to be a distinguished tweet, if $\exists q_i \in \mathcal{Q}$ and t is a top-K result for q_i based on the ranking function $\mathcal{F}$. Otherwise, t is a noisy tweet.

To answer top-K queries in query set $\mathcal{Q}$, we just need to index the distinguished tweets, while the noisy tweets can be indexed periodically. In this way, we avoid high real-time update costs.

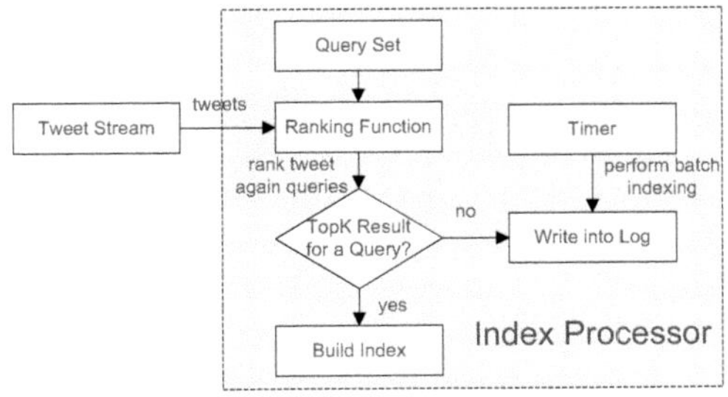

Figure 5: Data Flow of Index Processor

Obviously, for a different query set $\mathcal{Q}$, the classification result will be different. Ideally, when all possible queries are considered, the classification will provide an accurate result for every query. However, the maintenance cost may neutralize the benefit of partial indexing. Fortunately, it has been confirmed that, like any social phenomenon, the search engine queries [2] and social networking queries [21] do in fact follow the well known Zipf's distribution. In other words, the top 20% queries represent 80% of the user requests. Therefore, only popular queries are maintained in $\mathcal{Q}$ to reduce maintenance cost. In particular, suppose the nth query appears with a probability of

$$p(n) = \frac{\beta}{n^{\alpha}} \tag{1}$$

where α and β are parameters that describe the Zipf's distribution. Let s be the number of submitted queries per second. The expected time interval of the nth query is

$$t(n) = \frac{1}{p(n)s} \tag{2}$$

That is, after $t(n)$ seconds, the nth query will be submitted to the system with high probability. Suppose we perform our batch indexing every t' seconds. We will keep the nth query in $\mathcal{Q}$, only if $t(n) < t'$. The intuition of this strategy is that for infrequent queries, we do not need to update the index frequently.

To estimate the query distribution, we keep a query log in disks. When a new unseen query arrives at the system, we assume it is an infrequent query and do not insert it into $\mathcal{Q}$. $\mathcal{Q}$ is updated during at the next batch indexing process. We search the query log to build a query histogram and simulate the distribution using Zipf's law. Based on Equation 2, popular queries are inserted into $\mathcal{Q}$.

After having defined the classification problem, a naive method can be designed directly from the definition. Suppose the tweet set is $\mathcal{T}$. Given a query $q_i \in \mathcal{Q}$, we use $\mathcal{F}(q_i, t_j)$ to denote the rank of a tweet $t_j \in \mathcal{T}$. To simplify the discussion, we define dominant set as:

DEFINITION 2. Dominant Set
Given a tweet t, a query q and a tweet set $\mathcal{T}$, t's dominant set in relation to q is defined as the tweets that have higher ranks than t, namely

$$ds(q,t) = \{t_i | t_i \in \mathcal{T} \wedge \mathcal{F}(q, t_i) > \mathcal{F}(q,t)\}$$

A straightforward approach would compute t's dominant set for all queries in $\mathcal{Q}$. Algorithm 1 illustrates the idea. If

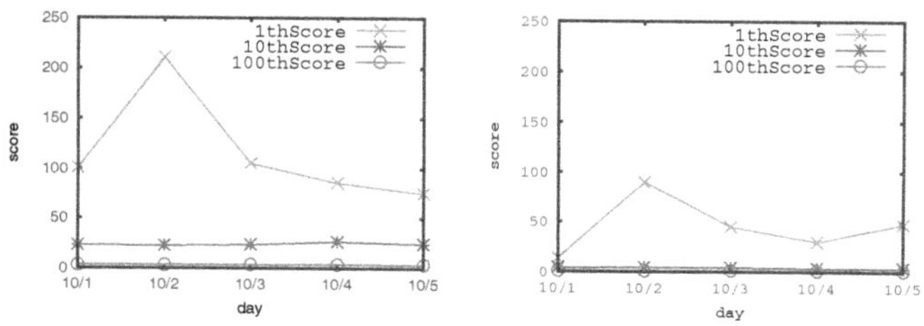

(a) Query "Coupon" (b) Query "Database"

Figure 6: Statistics of Keyword Ranking

there exists a query q_i satisfying $|ds(q_i, t)| < K$, we classify t as a distinguished tweet (line 3-4). Otherwise, it is a noisy tweet. Algorithm 1 suffers from two performance problems. First, to compute the dominant set, we need a full scan of the tweet set. Second, given a tweet t, we test it against every query in $\mathcal{Q}$. To address the above problems, two optimization approaches adopted.

Algorithm 1 NaiveClassifier(Tweet t, QuerySet $\mathcal{Q}$)

```
1: for ∀q_i ∈ Q do
2:     ds(q_i, t)=getDominantSet(Q, t)
3:     if ds(q_i, t).size< K then
4:         return distinguished tweet
5: return noisy tweet
```

4.1.1 *Optimization 1: Top-K Threshold*

The first optimization is to employ the query statistics to speed up the dominant set computation. Figure 6 shows the statistics of top-K query results in our Twitter dataset. The x-axis denotes the date of the ranking and the y-axis is the ranking score computed by our ranking function $\mathcal{F}$. The naive approach is invoked to compute the scores of pair (t_i, q_j), where t_i denotes an existing tweet by that specific day and q_j is a query in $\mathcal{Q}$. In Figure 6(a) and 6(b), we present the results for the query "coupon" and "database" respectively. Other queries share the same property. In particular, in the figures, we compare the scores of top 1 tweet, the top 10th tweet and the 100th tweet (our threshold). We find that although the score of top 1 tweet varies a lot with time, the scores of the top 10th and 100th tweet are quite stable. This is because in natural language, the words follow Zipf's distribution [12], where each word tends to appear in the text with certain frequency. Given a query, the expected number of hot tweets remains stable over time. We have the following theorem.

THEOREM 1. *Suppose each keyword appears in the tweets with a fixed probability and the tweets are inserted into the system with a stable rate. If query q_i has m results ($m >> K$), the variance of top-K score for q_i decreases for a larger K.*

PROOF. Suppose we have n tweets and there are m tweets ($m > K$) containing the search keyword. We try to estimate the Kth score of m resultant tweets, assuming they are randomly distributed in the tweet dataset. We sort the tweets by their ranks and have a list $\{t_1, t_2, ..., t_n\}$. The Kth tweet appears in the position x with probability of

$$p(x) = \frac{\binom{x-1}{K-1}\binom{n-x}{m-K}}{\binom{n}{k}}$$

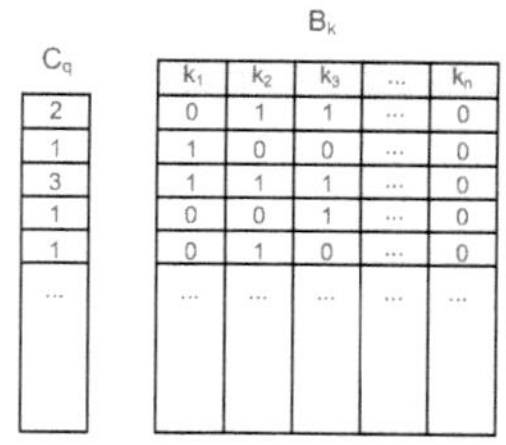

Figure 7: Matrix Index

And the expectation of top-K score is

$$E(K) = \sum_{i=k}^{n} p(i)score(i)$$

where $score(i)$ denotes the score of the ith tweet. The problem can be transformed into an order statistic problem. Based on the estimated bounds in [4], when m is sufficiently large, we get a more closer bound for $E(K)$ for a larger K. □

The above observation motivates our classification scheme. We keep a top-K threshold for each query $q \in \mathcal{Q}$, which is called threshold table T_θ. Given a query q, $T_\theta(q)$ returns the threshold for the top K tweets.

LEMMA 1. *For a tweet t, if $\mathcal{F}(q_i, t) < T_\theta(q_i)$, the size of t's dominant set is larger than K at the moment.*

PROOF. If $\mathcal{F}(q_i, t) < T_\theta(q_i)$, t's score is smaller than current Kth result. Therefore, more than K tweets have higher ranks than t. □

THEOREM 2. *For a tweet t, if $\mathcal{F}(q_i, t) < T_\theta(q_i)$ for all $q_i \in \mathcal{Q}$ and $\mathcal{F}(q_i, t)$ decreases with time, t is a noisy tweet.*

PROOF. If $\mathcal{F}(q_i, t)$ decreases with time, the tweet will never be a top-K result for a query. Thus, it is a noisy tweet. □

In Theorem 2, we require $\mathcal{F}(q_i, t)$ to be monotonically decreasing with time. In fact, in our ranking function, to catch the hotly discussed topics and discussion trend, $\mathcal{F}(q_i, t)$ may increase for a small number of hot tweets. We shall discuss how to handle such case in Section 5.2.

T_θ can be constructed and updated by Algorithm 2. Initially, T_θ's values are set to 0 for all queries. After a query is processed, we update its threshold based on the query result.

Algorithm 2 UpdateThreshold(T_θ, Query q)

```
Result R= getTopResult(K, q)
if R.size= K then
    Score s = R[K].score
    T_θ(q) = s
else
    T_θ(q) = 0
```

4.1.2 *Optimization 2: Matrix Index for Queries*

In Algorithm 1, computing the dominant set for every query in $\mathcal{Q}$ is time consuming. Therefore, our second optimization is to avoid unnecessary dominant set computation. We consider both queries and tweets as a bag of words. To simplify our discussion, we define the candidate query set as:

Definition 3. Candidate Query

For a tweet $t = \{k_1, k_2, ..., k_n\}$ and a query $q = \{k'_1, k'_2, ..., k'_m\}$, q is a candidate query for t, i.f.f.

$$\forall k_i \in t \rightarrow \exists k'_j \in q \wedge k'_j = k_i$$

Instead of checking every query for an incoming tweet t, we just need to compute the dominant set for t's candidate queries. To facilitate the discovery of candidate queries, we propose a matrix index.

Figure 7 illustrates the index structure. B_k is a $m \times n$ matrix index (m is the size of $\mathcal{Q}$ and n is the number of unique keywords in $\mathcal{Q}$) and C_q is the counter vector for queries. Each row in B_k refers to a query and each column in B_k denotes a keyword. If the jth keyword appears in the ith query, we set $B_k[i][j]$ to 1. Otherwise, it is set to 0. C_q keeps the number of keywords in a query. The ith query has $C_q[i]$ keywords. Given a tweet t, we define its vector as $V_t = (v_1, v_2, ..., v_n)$, where $v_i = 1$ if t contains the ith keyword. Otherwise, $v_i = 0$. To find all candidate queries, we compute an evaluation vector as

$$V_e = V_t \times B_k^T \tag{3}$$

where B_k^T is the transpose of B_k. If $V_e[i] = C_q[i]$, then the ith query is a candidate query for tweet t. By applying the matrix index, we transform the discovery process of candidate queries into matrix computation. Because B_k is a sparse matrix, Equation 3 can be computed efficiently, which is shown in our optimized classification algorithm.

4.1.3 Optimized Classifier

Algorithm 3 Classifier(Tweet t, QuerySet $\mathcal{Q}$)

1: Array *count*=0
2: V_t=getTweetVector(t)
3: **for** $j = 0$ to n **do**
4:   **if** $V_t[j] == 1$ **then**
5:     **for** i=0 to m **do**
6:       **if** $B[i][j] == 1$ **then**
7:         *count*(j)++
8:         **if** *count*[j] == $C_q(j)$ **then**
9:           **if** t's ranking is larger than $T_\theta(j)$ **then**
10:             return distinguished tweet
11: return noisy tweet

Algorithm 3 shows our tweet classification algorithm. It is an evolution from Algorithm 1 by combining two optimization approaches. Given a tweet t, we first create a temporary counter for recording the queries that have been processed (line 1). Then we scan each column of matrix index (line 3-10). Once we detect the keyword is contained by a query (line 6), we will increase the count of the query in the temporary counter. If the counter indicates that all keywords of the queries have been seen (line 8), we will test the tweet's score against the query's threshold (line 8). If larger than the threshold, t is classified as the distinguished tweet.

In Algorithm 3, we use a temporary counter to simplify the matrix computation. As an example, in Figure 7, suppose a tweet t contains k_1, k_2 and k_3 as the keywords. We will start scanning the columns of the three keywords. By scanning the first column, we know that query q_1 and q_2 contain k_1. And after comparing with the value in counter C_q, we know q_1 is a candidate query, as it only has 1 keyword. Hence, we can compare its threshold with the score of the tweet.

We now discuss the complexity analysis of the above algorithm. Suppose we have m queries and n keywords. We need m bytes for the counter vector C_q and $\frac{nm}{8}$ bytes for the matrix index B_k. The top-K threshold is an array of floats. Therefore, its takes $4m$ bytes. Algorithm 3 incurs a storage overhead of

$$S = 5m + \frac{nm}{8} \tag{4}$$

As an example, when $m = 100000$ and $n = 5000$, we need approximately 60 MB memory. Suppose the average number of tweet's keywords is x, Algorithm 3 scans x columns of B_k. During scanning, instead of testing each bit one by one, we test the whole word. In a W-bit system, the time complexity is $\frac{xm}{W}$.

To further optimize the classification algorithm, we adopt compression technique. For each column in B_k, most bits are 0, as only a few queries contain the keyword. Therefore, we apply WAH (Word Aligned Hybrid) encoding [24] to compress the index.

4.2 Implementation of Indexes

For each incoming tweet, we will classify it as a distinguished or noisy tweet, and insert it into the index or log file for batch update. We shall present both indexing schemes in this subsection.

4.2.1 Real-Time Indexing

A new tweet that is identified as a distinguished tweet is indexed immediately. The indexing process entails the following steps,

1. If the tweet belongs to an existing tweet tree, we retrieve its parent tweet (2-3 I/Os via the index on TID) to get the root ID and generate the corresponding encoding. Then, we update the *count* number in the parent tweet. This incurs one I/O since the parent tweet has already been retrieved and cached in memory.
2. The tweet is subsequently inserted into the tweet data table, which incurs 1 I/O for the insertion and 2-3 I/Os for the index update.
3. Lastly, the tweet is inserted into the inverted index, which incurs a few I/Os depending on the number of keywords in the tweet. This is the dominant component of the indexing cost.

The first step is used to maintain the tree structure of tweets, which may incur one or two database operations. This cost can be saved, if the ranking function does not consider the effect of the tree structure. However, even in our case where the tree structure is used, this is not a major cost. Based on the statistics of [7], less than 23% of the tweets get replies, for which we need to maintain the tree structures. Furthermore, most of the tweets get replies in a relatively short period, and thus, caching the recent tweet records can significantly reduce the cost.

The main overhead of the indexing process is the cost of updating the inverted index. For a given tweet which has n keywords, we need to update the inverted list of each keyword.

4.2.2 Batch Indexing

When a noisy tweet is submitted to the microblogging system, instead of indexing it in the inverted index, we append it to the log file. The operation is straightforward, and it incurs one I/O. The only update is to insert a new tweet tuple in the tweet data table with the cost of 2-3 I/Os. Hence, batch indexing is very efficient compared to the real-time indexing.

Periodically, the batch indexing process scans the log file and indexes the tweets in an offline manner. To reduce the cost of building the inverted index, we build an in-memory inverted index. We maintain a list for each encountered keyword in memory, and the list denotes the tweets that contain the keyword. If the memory is full, we combine the in-memory inverted index with the disk based index. In this manner, we can significantly reduce the I/Os, as the updates to an inverted list of a keyword can be performed in groups.

5. RANKING FUNCTION

In the *TI*, the indexing scheme is independent of the ranking function. The user can therefore define different ranking functions. In this section, we propose a computational efficient and effective ranking function tailored for the social networking systems by exploiting the features of user behaviors. Our proposed ranking function used is composed of the user's PageRank, popularity of the topic, the timestamp and the similarity between the query and the tweet.

5.1 User's PageRank

To capture the relationships between social networking users, we have a user graph $G_u = (U, E)$ where U denotes all the available users and E describe the links between them. In a system such as Twitter, there are two links defined for a user, the *followers* and *following*. Given a user u, its *followers* is a set of users, who follow u's tweets, while its *following* is another set of users that u currently follows. We use $f(u)$ and $f^{-1}(u)$ to denote the *followers* and *following* set of user u, respectively.

For ease of discussion, we consider G_u as a complete graph, where a user's *follower* or *following* must be another user in G_u. In a complete graph, the *following* link is analogical to the *follower* link. Therefore, in the remaining discussion, we only consider the *following* link. We build a matrix M_f to record the *following* links between users. As shown in Figure 8, if u_i follows u_j, we set $M_f[i][j]$ to 1. To compute PageRank, we also define a weight vector $V = (w_1, w_2, ..., w_n)$, where w_i is the weight of user u_i. Currently, w_i is set to 1 for all users, by assuming that every user is equally important initially. We then compute the user's PageRank as follows:

$$P_u = VM_f^x \tag{5}$$

x keeps increasing, until M_f^x converges. $P_u[i]$ denotes the PageRank value of user u_i. We normalize it as $P_u[i] = \frac{P_u[i]}{\sum_{1 \le i \le n} P_u[i]}$.

The PageRank values are stored in a user table, which is defined as *(UID, Name, PageRank)*, where *UID* is the ID of the user. We also have a follower and following table for capturing the friend links. In the ranking function, the tweet inherits the PageRank from its author. In particular, we define the tweet's U-PageRank as

DEFINITION 4. *U-PageRank*
Suppose the tweet t's author is u, t's U-PageRank is defined as u's PageRank value.

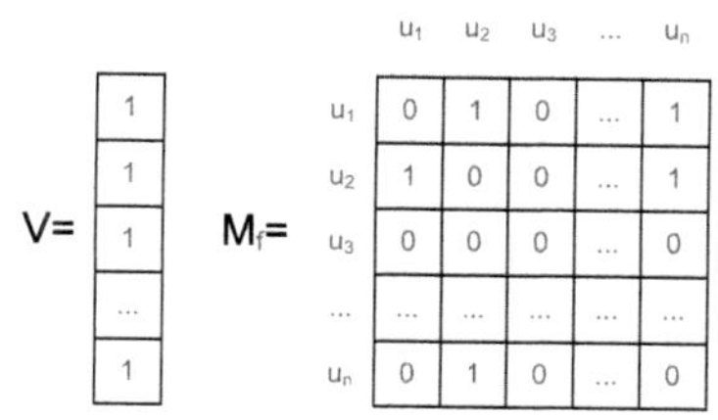

Figure 8: Following Matrix

A higher PageRank value indicates that the user has more friends and his tweets are probably more attractive than others. Therefore, we can use U-PageRank to decide whether a tweet is important for the users. In [23], an extended PageRank algorithm is also applied to rank Twitter data.

Computing the user's PageRank is costly. However, the active users in a system tend to be stable over time. Hence, the PageRank is computed in an offline manner. We can periodically, say every ten days, recompute the PageRank values. When a new user joins the system before the next computation, we set its PageRank value to 0.

5.2 Popularity of Topics

In Twitter, users retweet tweets of other people to broadcast the tweets to their friends. They also express their own ideas when replying to other's tweets. In the *TI*, tweets are grouped into a tree by the retweet/reply links. We define a tweet tree as a discussion topic or thread. To help users retrieve the popular topics, our ranking function is designed to favor the tweet trees with many discussions. This strategy is also adopted by the news group search [26] and community search [17]. In particular, given a tweet tree $\mathcal{T}$, we define its popularity as:

$$Pop(\mathcal{T}) = \sum_{\forall t_i \in \mathcal{T}} t_i.UPageRank \tag{6}$$

As a result, the popularity of a tree is equal to the sum of U-PageRank values of all tweets in the tree. For a single node tree, the popularity of the tree is equal to the root's U-PageRank.

The tree's popularity can be computed fairly easily by joining the tweet table and user table. For example, the following query can be used for its computation.

```
SELECT SUM(U.PageRank) as Popularity, tree
FROM tweet T, user U
WHERE T.UID = U.UID
GROUP BY T.tree
```

However, processing such queries is costly, especially for a large-scale Twitter dataset. If we can reduce the number of records that need to be processed, we can effectively speed up the above query.

It is observed that more than 70% of tweets do not get any response (be replied or retweeted) [7]. For a majority of tweets, we do not need to compute the tree popularity, as the single node tree's popularity is equal to the root's U-PageRank, which can be directly obtained from the inverted index. Figure 9 verifies our assumption. It shows the changes of popularity values (without normalization). Most tweet trees exhibit the same behavior. When a tweet is published, it probably does not attract the interest of other users right away. As a result, in the first few hours, it has a low popularity. However, if the tweet discusses a popular topic,

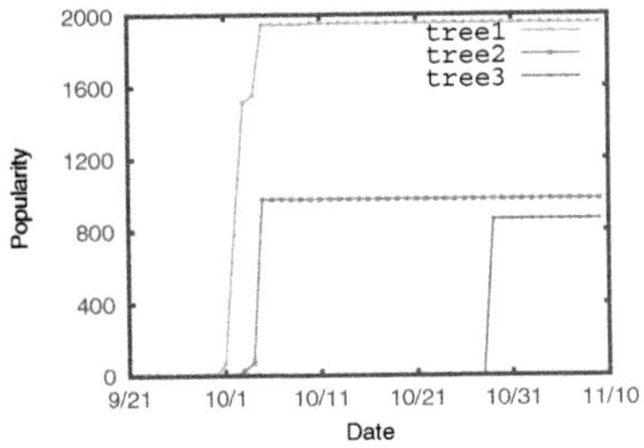

Figure 9: Popularity of Topics

it will gain continuous concern afterwards. The popularity of the corresponding tweet tree increases significantly, until the topic becomes stale some days later. Then, there will be no new tweets in this tree and the popularity remains stable after that.

We call a tweet topic that is being hotly discussed an *Active Tweet Tree*, which is defined as following:

DEFINITION 5. *Active Tweet Tree*
A tweet tree T is an active tweet tree, if the number of tree nodes keeps on increasing continuously.

For example, in Figure 9, tree 1 is an active tweet tree for tweets posted from October 1st to October 3rd. Instead of computing the popularities of all tweet trees, we just compute the popularities of active trees and maintain them in memory. By doing so, we can update the popularities of active trees efficiently when new tweets are submitted. To process the queries, we can look up the popularities kept in memory to rank the tweets.

Algorithm 4 isActiveTree(Tweet t)

1: ID rid = getRootID(t)
2: **if** rid is not null **then**
3: **if** L_t.containsKey(rid) **then**
4: $L_t(rid)$.popularity += t.UPageRank
5: $L_t(rid)$.timestamp = t.timestamp
6: **if** t.timestamp-$L_c(rid)$.timestamp> θ **then**
7: $L_c(rid)$.count = 1
8: **else**
9: $L_c(rid)$.count++
10: **if** $L_c(rid)$.count> γ **then**
11: L_t.insert(rid, getPopularity(rid), t.timestamp)
12: **if** some tweets in the tree are not indexed **then**
13: create index for the tweets on the fly
14: $L_c(rid)$.timestamp = t.timestamp

In Algorithm 4, we outline the steps entailed in maintaining the active tree in memory. Initially, all the trees are assumed to be inactive trees. We keep two lists, a candidate tree list L_c and an active tree list L_t, and use hash tables to implement the lists. When a new tweet joins a tweet tree t, we use t's root ID to find its corresponding bucket in L_t and L_c. If t belongs to an active tree, we increase the tree's popularity and reset its timestamp (line 3-5). Otherwise, we retrieve t's record in L_c and compare the timestamp (line 6). If $t.timestamp - L_c(t.rid) > \theta$, we reset the counter to 1 (line 7). Otherwise, we update the timestamp and increase the value of counter by 1 (line 9). If the counter is larger than γ, we promote t as the active tree (line 10). In function *getPopularity*(rid), we compute the popularity by issuing the query:

SELECT SUM(U.PageRank) as Popularity
FROM tweet T, user U
WHERE T.UID = U.UID AND T.tree= rid

To efficiently process the above query, we build B$^+$-tree indexes on attribute $T.UID$, $U.UID$ and $T.tree$. Recall that in Theorem 2, we require the ranking function to be decreasing with time. But for an active tree, its popularity may increase with time. Therefore, in line 12 and 13, we index all the tweets which are not yet indexed in the active tree, This can be done efficiently by following the pointers in the tweet table.

The active tree will be discarded, if it does not obtain any new tweet in more than δ time. In fact, in our ranking function, the popularity of a tree remains steady after a certain time. That is, after δ days, the rank of an inactive tree becomes too small and does not affect the top-K results. In that case, we remove it from L_t. The parameters θ, γ and δ are used to control the accuracy and memory overhead, which can be tuned based on statistics. In our experiment, θ, γ and δ are set to 8 hours, 3 tweets and 10 days respectively.

5.3 Time-based Ranking Function

The final part of our ranking function is the similarity between a query q and a tweet t. By using the bag-of-words model, we transform q and t into vectors. Their similarity is estimated as

$$sim(q,t) = \frac{q \times t}{|q||t|} \quad (7)$$

The general ranking function combines all the factors and are computed as

$$\mathcal{F}(q,t) = \frac{w_1 \times t.UPageRank + w_2 \times sim(q,t)}{q.timestamp - t.timestamp} + \frac{w_3 \times tree.popularity}{q.timestamp - tree.timestamp} \quad (8)$$

where q.timestamp denotes the time when the query is submitted, $tree$.timestamp is the timestamp of the tree that t belongs to (computed as the timestamp of the root node). In Equation 8, *UPageRank*, $sim(q,t)$ and *popularity* are normalized into the same domain, [0, 1]. w_1, w_2 and w_3 are used to control the importances of different factors. Currently, w_1, w_2 and w_3 are set to 1, as we treat all factors equally important. If a tweet does not belong to a popular tree, we discard the second term in above formula, as in that case, the popularity should not contribute to its ranking. In our definition, a tweet's ranking is affected by its timestamp. An older tweet is less important than a newly inserted one. When searching, we prefer to the latest tweets with high similarity.

5.4 Adaptive Index Search

To process a query, the inverted index is employed to retrieve the result tweets based on the scores derived from the ranking function. In our ranking function, the PageRank value, the timestamp and the similarity can be computed based on the information in the inverted index, while the popularity can be obtained by querying the active tree list in memory. Hence, the ranking function is computationally efficient as it does not incur a significant overhead.

Nevertheless, the main problem that affects the search performance is the size of inverted index. Suppose the inverted index for keyword k_i is $\mathcal{I}_i$. The size of $\mathcal{I}_i$ will keep

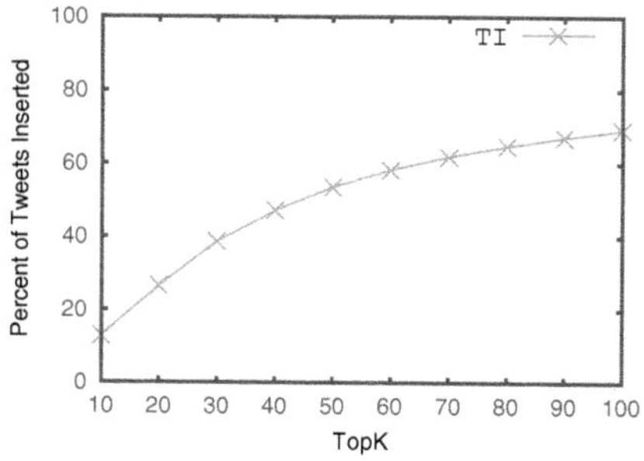

Figure 10: Number of Indexed Tweets in Real-Time

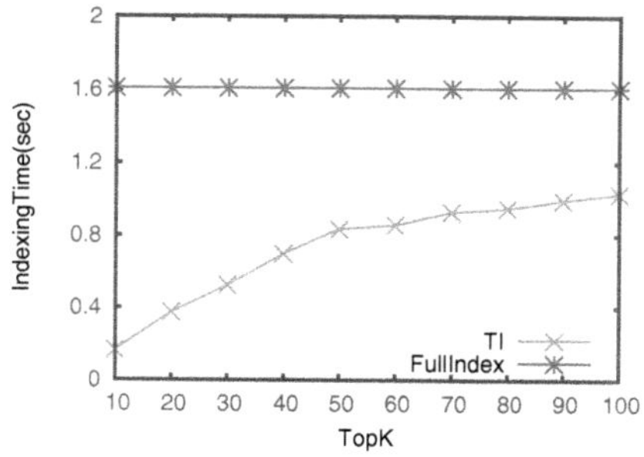

Figure 11: Indexing Cost (per 10,000 tweets)

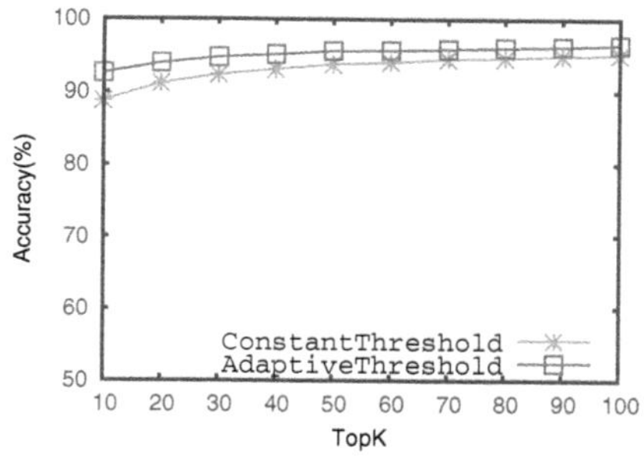

Figure 12: Accuracy of Adaptive Indexing

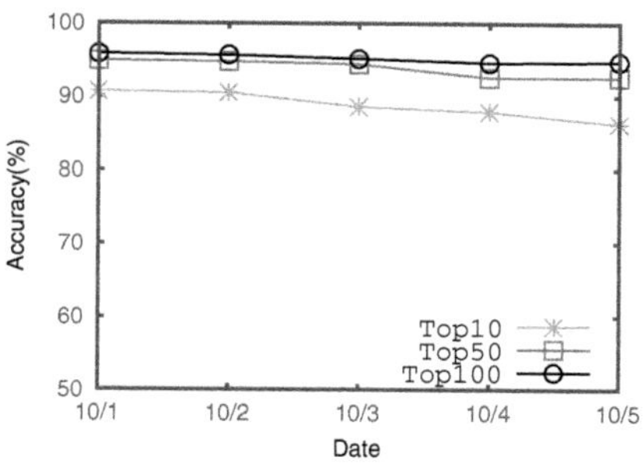

Figure 13: Accuracy by Time (constant threshold)

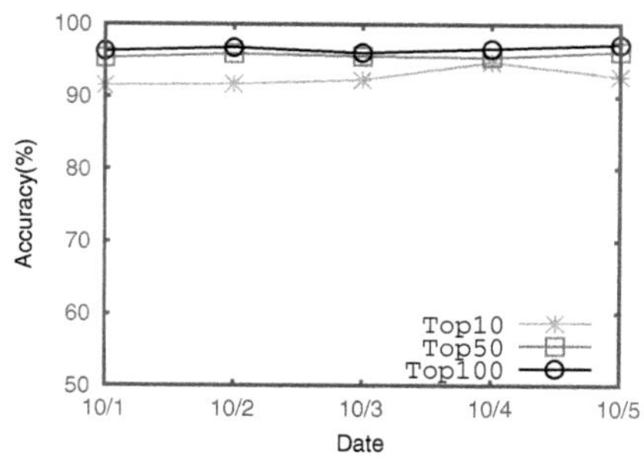

Figure 14: Accuracy by Time (adaptive threshold)

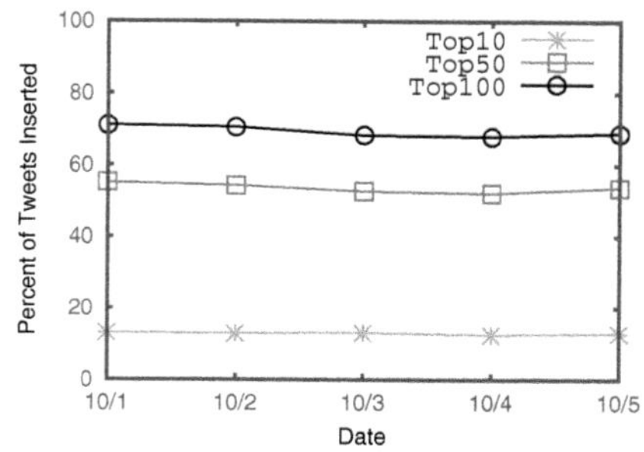

Figure 15: Effect of Adaptive Threshold

increasing, as more tweets are inserted.To address this problem, we propose an adaptive index searching scheme. The maximal possible score of a tweet at timestamp ts is estimated as:

$$score = \frac{w_1 \times UPageRank_{max} + w_2 + w_3 \times popularity_{max}}{q.timestamp - ts}$$

$UPageRank_{max}$ denotes the maximal user PageRank. We set similarity to 1. And $popularity_{max}$ is estimated by current active tree set. Let S_{tree} denote the active trees that have a timestamp before ts. If no such tree exists, $popularity_{max}$ is set to 0. Otherwise, $popularity_{max}$ equals to the maximal popularity in S_{tree}.

Let $T_\theta(q)$ be the top-K threshold for query q. Instead of reading the whole inverted index blindly, we iteratively read a block of the index. If the last entry in the block has a timestamp ts and based on the above equation, the maximal score before ts is smaller than $T_\theta(q)$, we will stop reading the index, since the remaining tweets will not contribute the the search results. This strategy effectively reduces the index search cost.

6. EXPERIMENTAL EVALUATION

In this section, we shall evaluate the performance of the *TI* indexing scheme and the effectiveness of the propose ranking functions. In the experiments, we use a Twitter dataset collected for three years [6] from October 2006 to November 2009. 500 random users are selected from Twitter as the seeds, including politicians, musicians, environmentalists and techies. Following the friend links, more users are discovered and added into the social graph. The total number of involved users is about 465K. For each user, the tweets are crawled every 24 hours. There are more than 25 million of tweets in the dataset.

In the experiments, we start from September 26 2009 and simulate users' behavior for ten days. The first five days are used to warm up the system (e.g. building the top-K threshold, learning the popularities of topics). The remaining five days are used to measure the performance. We collect keywords from the first five days' tweets. After removing the keywords in the stop-list and the infrequent words (frequency less than 10), we have less than 5K keywords left. Queries in real-time search engine follows a skewed distribution [10]. Therefore, in the experiments, queries are generated by randomly combining the keywords, and the number of keywords in queries follows Zipf's distribution. Approximately, 60% are 1-word queries; 30% are 2-word queries; and 10% are queries with more than two keywords. The queries are submitted to the system at random timestamps, while the tweets are inserted into the system based on their recorded timestamps. Each experiment is repeated for ten times and the average result is reported.

6.1 Effects of Adaptive Indexing

In the first set of experiments, we study how the adaptive indexing scheme affects the performance. In Figure 10, we show the percentage of tweets that are indexed in real-time. When only top-10 results are required, we can prune more than 80% of tweets (by using batch indexing scheme). As more results are returned to users, more tweets need to be indexed to be searchable. Because only a portion of tweets need to be indexed in real-time, the indexing cost is significantly reduced. Figure 11 compares the indexing time of *TI* and full indexing scheme. In *TI*, the cost of indexing is proportional to the number of indexed tweets. Therefore, when more tweets are required in the results, *TI* will incur higher indexing overhead.

To evaluate whether the adaptive indexing scheme reduces

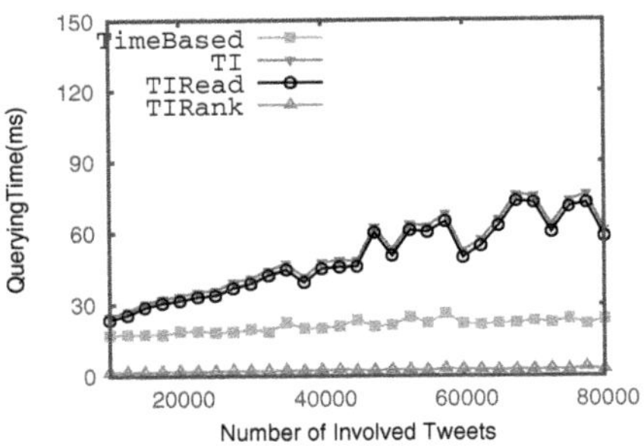

Figure 16: Performance of Query Processing

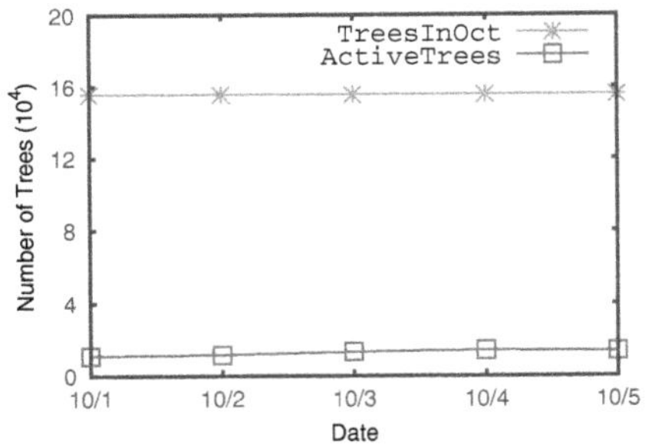

Figure 17: Popular Tree in Memory

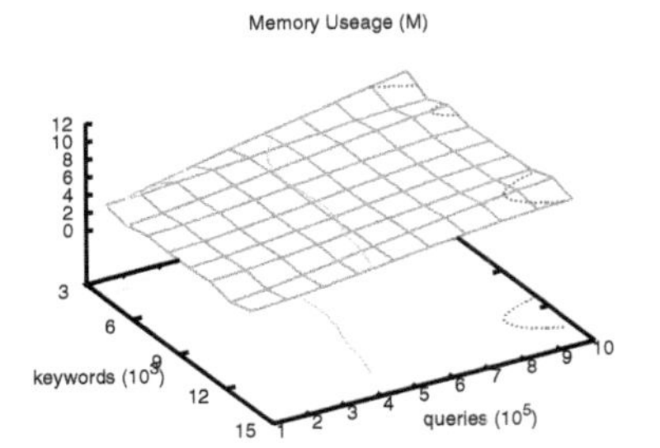

Figure 18: Size of In-memory Index

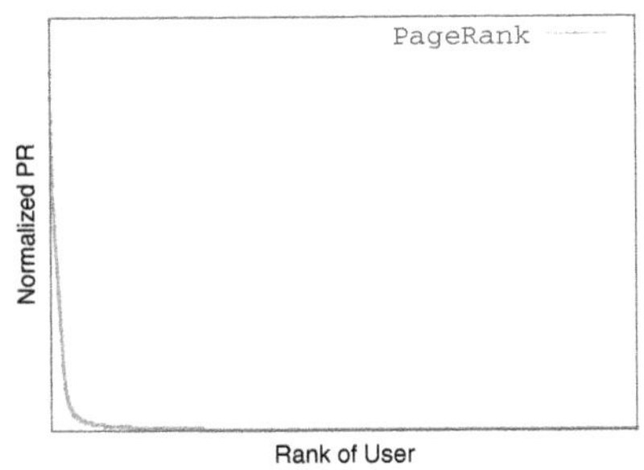

Figure 19: Distribution of PageRank

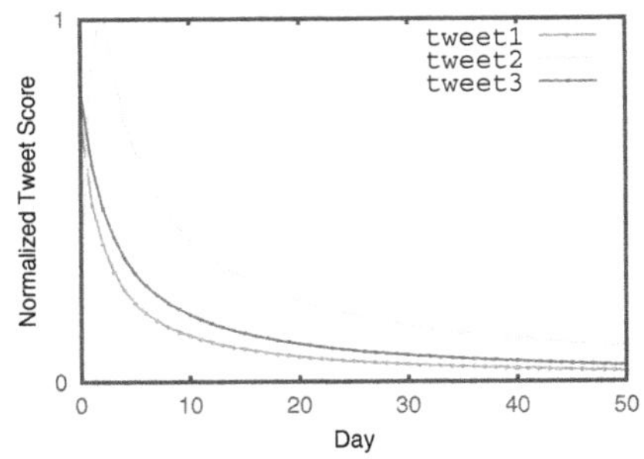

Figure 20: Popularity of Tweets by Time

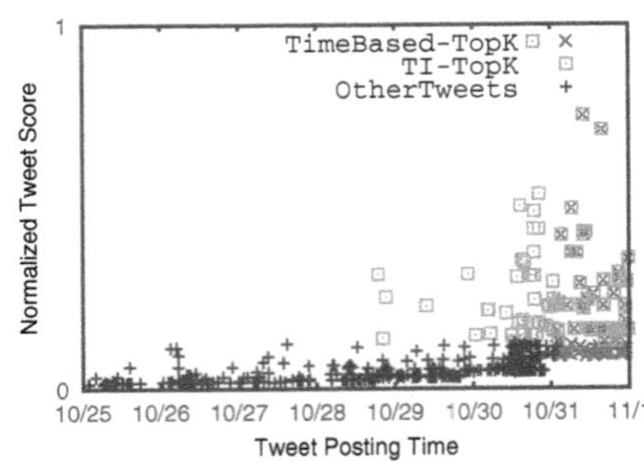

Figure 21: Distribution of Results

the quality of results, we compute the query accuracy as $accuracy = \frac{R \bigcap R'}{|R|}$, where R denotes the result set returned by full indexing scheme (all tweets are inserted in real-time), R' denotes the result set returned by TI, $R \bigcap R'$ represents the number of tweets in both result sets. Figure 12 shows the accuracy of TI's results. For comparison, we use two strategies. In *Constant Threshold*, we do not update the top-K threshold when processing queries. On the contrary, in *Adaptive Threshold*, we use Algorithm 2 to update the threshold adaptively. As shown in Figure 12, the accuracy of *Constant Threshold* is just slightly worse than *Adaptive Threshold*. The result verifies our observation made in Figure 6, where the top-K threshold remains stable in a period of time. The accuracy of both strategies decreases as K decreases. This can also be observed in Figure 6. When K is small, the top-K threshold changes more significantly. An extreme case is when $K = 1$. Thus, the TI may wrongly delay indexing some high ranking tweets. This problem can be fixed by setting a lower bound, e.g. 20, for K. Although user only requests for top 1 result, we always maintain the threshold for top 20 results.

In Figure 13 and Figure 14, we show the changes of accuracy by dates. The accuracy of *Constant Threshold* degrades, because it never updates its threshold values. However the quality of the results is still acceptable. For *Adaptive Threshold*, as the threshold is updated by the queries, we always get results with high accuracy. In Figure 15, we show the percentage of indexed tweets in *Adaptive Threshold* by dates. We can observe from the figure that the *Adaptive Threshold* scheme does lead to a stable performance, independent of K. As the *Adaptive Threshold* exploits the query results to update its threshold, which is almost free, we will always use *Adaptive Threshold* strategy in the TI indexing scheme.

6.2 Query Performance

To provide better search results, TI adopts a sophisticated ranking function. In this experiment, we study whether the ranking function leads to a better query performance. For comparison purposes, we implement a tweet search, which only ranks tweets via their timestamps. Such ranking strategy has been adopted by Twitter and Google's real-time search. As we sort the tweets in the inverted index by their timestamps, for a single keyword query, we just need to read the first K entries from the index, which is quite efficient. For a multi-keyword query, we iteratively read a block of the index for all keywords, and we stop when K results are obtained; otherwise, more blocks are searched.

Figure 16 shows the query performance of the TI and time-based ranking schemes. TI's costs are decomposed into two parts, the ranking cost $TIRank$ and the index search cost $TIRead$. We group queries by their total number of involved tweets. In Figure 16, the x-axis ranges from 0 to 80000, indicating that some popular queries get about 80000 hits in our dataset. Since the size of the inverted index for a keyword k_i is proportional to the number of tweets containing k_i, the index search cost increases as more tweets are involved. This is verified by the results. We have adopted some optimization approaches, such as the adaptive index search outlined in Section 5.4, in order to reduce the cost. As shown in Figure 16, $TIRead$ increases linearly with the number of involved tweets. We can further reduce the search cost by distributing the inverted index over a set of compute nodes and applying the parallel search. We will study the problem in our future work. On the contrary, the time-based ranking scheme only retrieves some top tweets, and hence, incurs less overhead. However, it achieves the efficiency by sacrificing the quality of results. Without a reasonable ranking scheme, the query results are less useful.

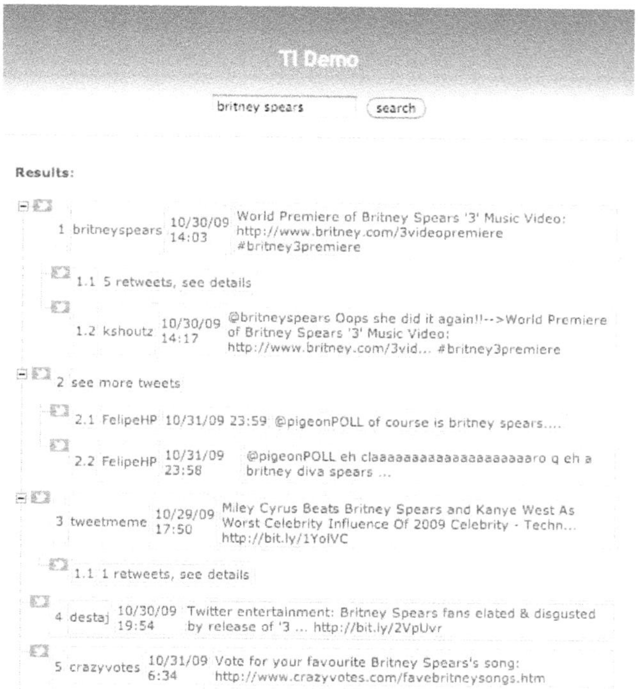

Figure 22: Search Result Ranked by *TI*

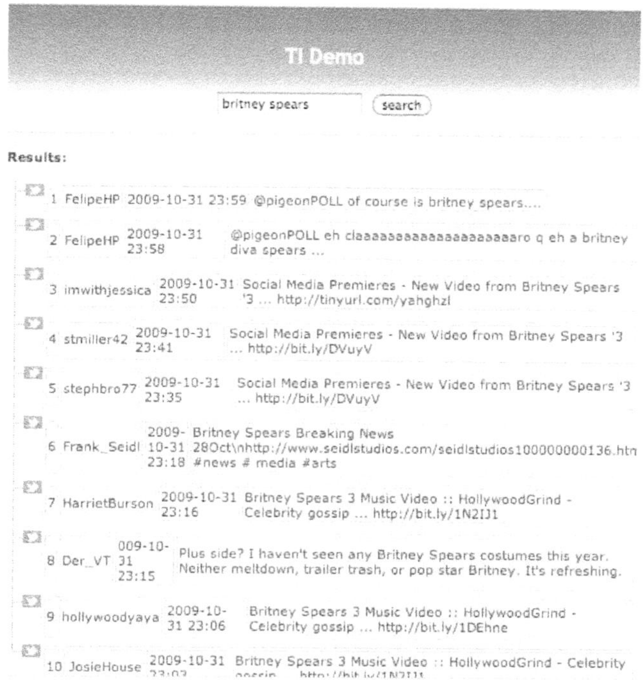

Figure 23: Search Result Ranked by Time

6.3 Memory Overhead

In this experiment, we evaluate the memory overhead in our system. We have maintained some memory structures to support adaptive indexing and efficient ranking. One structure is the active trees. Figure 17 shows the number of active trees. For comparison, we also show the number of total trees generated in October,2009, where less than ten percent of the trees, approximately 13000 trees, are identified as active trees. Moreover, we observe that the number of active trees does not increase with time. In conclusion, the memory requirement is well controlled and is not high.

Another memory structure is the matrix index. Given n keywords and m queries, we need $\frac{nm}{8}$ bytes to maintain the index. To reduce the overhead, we adopt WAH encoding to compress the matrix index. Figure 18 shows how the size of in-memory index changes for different n and m. We change the number of keywords from 3000 to 15000 and the number of queries from 100000 to 1 million. The maximal memory usage is only 12 MB, which indicates that the matrix index is very cost-efficient and we can maintain a much larger one for holding most keywords and queries. Another interesting observation is that the memory use does not necessarily increase even when more keywords and queries are used. This is because more keywords and queries lead to more 0s and 1s in the matrix index, which improves the compression performance of the WAH.

6.4 Ranking Comparison

In the ranking function, we have three components, the similarity between query and tweets, the PageRank of authors and the popularity of topics. Figure 19 shows the distribution of users' PageRanks in our dataset. It is not surprising that the PageRank value follows a highly skewed distribution, resembling that of Zipf's or power law distribution. Figure 20 shows the effects of time over the score of tweets. In the figure, X-axis represents the elapsed time, where 0 indicates the starting time of the tweets. Y-axis is a score computed by Equation 8. In our ranking function, the score is inversely proportional to time. Thus, the score of a specific tweet will decrease with time. However, a few popular tweets receive many replies within a short period of time after they are posted, contributing to a sudden rise in its score. Figure 21 illustrates the ranking scores over the post time of tweets. In the figure, the X-axis is the posting time of tweets, while the Y-axis is the score computed by removing the denominators in Equation 8. We use "Britney Spears" as our query. Based on observation of the results, time-based ranking scheme retrieves all recent queries as its top results, while our approach considers both time and other factors, which provides better results.

We show a demo result in Figure 22 and Figure 23. The search is processed by assuming the time is at *Nov 1, 2009 00:00:00*, when the last tweets in our dataset were crawled (some tweets after Nov 1 are considered as noisy and pruned). For each result, we show its ranking, author, timestamp and content. In Figure 22, we show the result of *TI*, where tweets are ordered by our ranking function. The first three tweets form a group, as they belong to the same tweet tree. The first tweet is posted by the official account of Britney Spears to publish a new video link. The second one represents 5 retweets. We aggregate them together, for all tweets have the same content. The third tweet is a reply to the first tweet, which shows the song name of the shared video. By grouping tweets via their tree structures, we provide a better visualization result.

In Figure 23, we show the result of time-based ranking, where tweets are strictly sorted by their timestamps. As a matter of fact, most results in Figure 23 also appear in Figure 22. And many results in Figure 23 are duplicates. This is because when a hot tweet is published, many users will retweet it within a short time after that. Another problem of the time-based results is the lack of tree structures. Both the first and second tweets are replies to another tweet, but the time-based scoring function shows them individually, while the *TI* scheme groups them together, presenting the results more meaningfully.

7. CONCLUSION

The quest for real-time indexing has recently become more pressing due to the inability of search engines in indexing and retrieving the huge amount of social networking data as soon as they are produced. The problem is further exacerbated by the increasing popularity of microblogging systems where millions of tweets are produced each day. In this paper, we have proposed the Tweet Index (*TI*), a new indexing and ranking scheme for supporting real-time search in microblogging systems. The *TI* adopts an adaptive indexing scheme to reduce the update cost. To this end, a new tweet is indexed only if it may appear in the top-K results of some cached queries with high probability. Otherwise, it is grouped with other unimportant tweets, and a batch indexing scheme is used to reduce the indexing latency. We have also proposed a cost-efficient and effective ranking function, by taking the users' PageRank, the popularity of topics, the similarity between the data and the query, and the time into consideration. To evaluate the performance of the *TI* indexing scheme and ranking function, we have conducted an extensive experimental study using a real dataset from Twitter. The experimental results show that the *TI* is efficient in handling tweets as they are produced and is able to achieve high query effectiveness and efficiency at the same time.

8. ACKNOWLEDGEMENTS

The work of Chun Chen was in part supported by National Natural Science Foundation of China (Grant No. 61070155). The work of Feng Li, Beng Chin Ooi and Sai Wu was in part supported by Singapore MDA grant R-252-000-376-279.

9. REFERENCES

[1] S. Agrawal, S. Chaudhuri, and V. R. Narasayya. Automated selection of materialized views and indexes in sql databases. In *VLDB*, pages 496–505, 2000.

[2] L. Backstrom, J. Kleinberg, R. Kumar, and J. Novak. Spatial variation in search engine queries. In *WWW*, pages 357–366, 2008.

[3] E. Baralis, S. Paraboschi, and E. Teniente. Materialized views selection in a multidimensional database. In *VLDB*, pages 156–165, 1997.

[4] D. Bertsimas, K. Natarajan, and C.-P. Teo. Tight bounds on expected order statistics. *Probab. Eng. Inf. Sci.*, 20(4):667–686, 2006.

[5] R. Chirkova, C. Li, and J. Li. Answering queries using materialized views with minimum size. *The VLDB Journal*, 15(3):191–210, 2006.

[6] M. D. Choudhury, Y.-R. Lin, H. Sundaram, K. S. Candan, L. Xie, and A. Kelliher. How does the sampling strategy impact the discovery of information diffusion in social media? In *ICWSM*, 2010.

[7] S. Inc. Replies and retweets on twitter. 2010.

[8] iProspect. iprospect search engine user behavior study.

[9] H. V. Jagadish, B. C. Ooi, and Q. H. Vu. Baton: a balanced tree structure for peer-to-peer networks. In *VLDB*, pages 661–672, 2005.

[10] B. J. Jansen, G. Campbell, and M. Gregg. Real time search user behavior. In *CHI*, pages 3961–3966, 2010.

[11] A. Java, X. Song, T. Finin, and B. Tseng. Why we twitter: understanding microblogging usage and communities. In *WebKDD*, pages 56–65, 2007.

[12] W. Li. Random texts exhibit zipf's-law-like word frequency distribution. *IEEE Transactions on Information Theory*, pages 1842–1845, 1992.

[13] B. T. Loo, J. M. Hellerstein, R. Huebsch, S. Shenker, and I. Stoica. Enhancing p2p file-sharing with an internet-scale query processor. In *VLDB*, pages 432–443, 2004.

[14] L. Page, S. Brin, R. Motwani, and T. Winograd. The pagerank citation ranking: Bringing order to the web. In *Technical Report, Stanford University*, 1998.

[15] T. Sakaki, M. Okazaki, and Y. Matsuo. Earthquake shakes twitter users: real-time event detection by social sensors. In *WWW*, pages 851–860, 2010.

[16] J. Sankaranarayanan, H. Samet, B. E. Teitler, M. D. Lieberman, and J. Sperling. Twitterstand: news in tweets. In *GIS*, pages 42–51, 2009.

[17] J. Seo, W. B. Croft, and D. A. Smith. Online community search using thread structure. In *CIKM*, pages 1907–1910, 2009.

[18] P. Seshadri and A. N. Swami. Generalized partial indexes. In *ICDE*, pages 420–427, 1995.

[19] A. Silberstein, J. Terrace, B. F. Cooper, and R. Ramakrishnan. Feeding frenzy: selectively materializing users' event feeds. In *SIGMOD*, pages 831–842, 2010.

[20] M. Stonebraker. The case for partial indexes. *SIGMOD Rec.*, 18(4):4–11, 1989.

[21] A. Sun, M. Hu, and E.-P. Lim. Searching blogs and news: a study on popular queries. In *SIGIR*, pages 729–730, 2008.

[22] I. Tatarinov, S. D. Viglas, K. Beyer, J. Shanmugasundaram, E. Shekita, and C. Zhang. Storing and querying ordered xml using a relational database system. In *SIGMOD*, pages 204–215, 2002.

[23] J. Weng, E.-P. Lim, J. Jiang, and Q. He. Twitterrank: finding topic-sensitive influential twitterers. In *WSDM*, pages 261–270, 2010.

[24] K. Wu, E. J. Otoo, and A. Shoshani. Compressing bitmap indexes for faster search operations. In *SSDBM*, pages 99–108, 2002.

[25] S. Wu, J. Li, B. C. Ooi, and K.-L. Tan. Just-in-time query retrieval over partially indexed data on structured p2p overlays. In *SIGMOD*, pages 279–290, 2008.

[26] W. Xi, J. Lind, and E. Brill. Learning effective ranking functions for newsgroup search. In *SIGIR*, pages 394–401, 2004.

[27] J. Yang, K. Karlapalem, and Q. Li. Algorithms for materialized view design in data warehousing environment. In *VLDB*, pages 136–145, 1997.

[28] C. Yu, B. C. Ooi, K.-L. Tan, and H. V. Jagadish. Indexing the distance: An efficient method to knn processing. In *VLDB*, pages 421–430, 2001.

More Efficient Datalog Queries: Subsumptive Tabling Beats Magic Sets*

K. Tuncay Tekle
LogicBlox, Inc.
Atlanta, GA
tuncay@cs.sunysb.edu

Yanhong A. Liu
Department of Computer Science
State University of New York at Stony Brook
liu@cs.sunysb.edu

ABSTRACT

Given a set of Datalog rules, facts, and a query, answers to the query can be inferred bottom-up starting with the facts or top-down starting with the query. The dominant strategies to improve the performance of answering queries are reusing answers to subqueries for top-down methods, and transforming rules based on demand from the query, such as the well-known magic sets transformation, for bottom-up methods. However, the performance of these strategies vary drastically, and the most effective method remained unknown.

This paper describes precise time and space complexity analysis for efficient implementation of Datalog queries using subsumptive tabling, a top-down evaluation method with more reuse of answers than the dominant tabling strategy, and shows that subsumptive tabling beats bottom-up evaluation of rules after magic sets transformation in both time and space complexities. It also describes subsumptive demand transformation, a novel method for transforming the rules so that bottom-up evaluation of the transformed rules mimics subsumptive tabling; we show that the time complexity of bottom-up evaluation after this transformation is equal to the the time complexity of top-down evaluation with subsumptive tabling. The paper further describes subsumption optimization, an optimization to increase the use of subsumption in subsumptive methods, and shows its application in the derivation of a well-known demand-driven pointer analysis algorithm. We support our analyses and comparisons through experiments with applications in ontology queries and program analysis.

*This work was supported in part by NSF under grants CCF-0964196 and CCF-0613913 and by ONR under grant N000140910651. This work was carried out in part while the first author was a Ph.D. student at the State University of New York at Stony Brook.

SIGMOD'11, June 12–16, 2011, Athens, Greece.

Categories and Subject Descriptors

D.3.2 [**Programming Languages**]: Language Classifications—*constraint and logic languages*; D.3.4 [**Programming Languages**]: Processors—*Optimization*;
F.2.2 [**Analysis of Algorithms and Problems Complexity**]: Nonnumerical Algorithms and Problems—*Computations on discrete structures*;
H.2.3 [**Information Systems**]: Database Management—*Query languages*; H.2.4 [**Information Systems**]: Systems—*Query processing, Rule-based databases*

General Terms

Languages, Performance

Keywords

Complexity analysis, Datalog, demand-driven evaluation, program transformation, optimization, tabling

1. INTRODUCTION

Datalog [5] is a logic language for deductive databases [1], program analysis [30], security [9], networking [17], and many other applications [14, 10, 24, 26].

Given a set of Datalog rules, facts, and a query, answers to the query can be inferred using bottom-up evaluation starting with the facts or top-down evaluation starting with the query. The dominant strategies for efficient evaluations are top-down evaluation with *variant tabling* [25] to memoize and reuse answers to subqueries, and bottom-up evaluation with the *magic set transformation* (MST) [3] so that evaluation of the transformed rules are driven by demand from the query.

For a subquery encountered during top-down evaluation with variant tabling, only answers from identical subqueries are reused. However, there may exist another subquery already encountered that *subsumes* the current subquery, i.e., whose answers are guaranteed to contain all answers to the current subquery. Using this, top-down evaluation can be coupled with a tabling strategy, called *subsumptive tabling* [21], that performs more reuse of previously inferred answers.

The performance of Datalog engines is difficult to understand due to the multitude of factors involved. For example, the performance of different tabling strategies vary drastically [21], and bottom-up evaluation after MST may be much slower than the bottom-up evaluation of the original rules [23]. Choosing the best evaluation method for a given set of rules requires precise characterization of the time and space complexities of each evaluation method.

Despite extensive research on optimization of Datalog rules [7, 22, 18, 13], given a set of rules and a query, no transformations that yield better time complexity than MST are known. *Demand transformation* [27] is similar to MST, with better space complexity in program size, but the same time complexity. There exists no transformation such that the bottom-up evaluation of transformed rules achieves the performance of subsumptive tabling.

This work describes precise time and space complexity analysis for efficiently answering Datalog queries using subsumptive tabling, and precise relationships between top-down evaluations with variant and subsumptive tabling, and their relationship to bottom-up evaluation after MST. We give complexity analyses for top-down evaluation with subsumptive tabling by determining the binding patterns of arguments for queries, and the subqueries that are guaranteed to reuse answers from subsuming subqueries, and then extending the analysis for variant tabling [27] to subsumptive tabling. We show that top-down evaluation using subsumptive tabling is equal to or better than using variant tabling in both time and space complexities. Using this result and the relationship between top-down evaluation with variant tabling and bottom-up evaluation after MST as shown in [27], we show that subsumptive tabling is equal to or better than MST in both time and space complexities. Then, we characterize a class of Datalog rules for which subsumptive tabling is guaranteed to be better than variant tabling in both time and space complexities.

Additionally, we describe a transformation, called *subsumptive demand transformation* (SDT), such that bottom-up evaluation of the rules produced by SDT achieves the performance of subsumptive tabling. We modify bottom-up evaluation slightly, and couple it with SDT to obtain *subsumptive bottom-up evaluation*. We show that the time and space complexities of subsumptive bottom-up evaluation and subsumptive tabling are equal for rules with no more than two hypotheses each and no singleton variables; and that the time complexity of subsumptive bottom-up evaluation may be better than subsumptive tabling for other rules. We also show that using SDT is equal to or better than using MST. We show that for rules for which subsumptive tabling outperforms variant tabling, SDT outperforms MST.

Building on our analyses, we devise a transformation, called *subsumption optimization*, for making sure that a query that subsumes another in subsumptive tabling is performed first when it is better to do so in time complexity. Using this method, we show how to systematically derive Heintze and Tardieu's demand-driven pointer analysis [11] from the definition of Andersen's pointer analysis.

We show experimental results on an illustrative set of Datalog rules, rules for Andersen's pointer analysis [2], and rules for ontology queries from OpenRuleBench [15]. We first confirm our complexity analyses, and then confirm when subsumptive tabling and SDT are necessary for efficient evaluation of queries.

The rest of the paper is organized as follows. Section 2 defines Datalog, evaluation methods, and terminologies. Section 3 presents complexity analysis of subsumptive tabling, and the relationships with variant tabling and magic sets. Section 4 describes subsumptive demand transformation, and its relationship with the other methods. Section 5 presents subsumption optimization and its application to pointer analysis. Section 6 presents experimental results. Section 7 discusses related work and concludes.

2. DATALOG AND EVALUATION METHODS

Datalog is a language for defining rules, facts, and queries, where rules can be used with facts to answer queries. A Datalog rule is of the form:

$$p(a_1, ..., a_k) :- p_1(a_{11}, ..., a_{1k_1}), ..., p_h(a_{h1}, ..., a_{hk_h}).$$

where h is a finite natural number, each p_i (respectively p) is a predicate of finite number k_i (respectively k) arguments, each a_{ij} and a_i is either a constant or a variable, and each variable in the arguments of p must also be in the arguments of some p_i.

A predicate with arguments is called an *atom*. If the right side of a rule is empty, then the atom on the left must have only constant arguments, and is called a *fact*; we indicate a fact with an ending dot. If the left side of a rule is empty, then each atom on the right side is called a *query*; we indicate a query with an ending question mark. For the rest of the paper, "rule" refers only to the case where both sides of the rule are not empty, where each atom on the right is called a *hypothesis*, and the atom on the left is called the *conclusion*.

The meaning of a set of rules, facts, and queries is the set of facts that are given or can be inferred using the rules and that match the queries. We will consider the case of one query, because a set of queries is equivalent to one query by adding a rule whose hypotheses are the set of queries and whose conclusion is the one query.

Tabling for top-down evaluation. Top-down evaluation starts with a given query, generates subqueries from hypotheses of rules whose conclusions match the query, considering rules in the order given and considering hypotheses from left to right, and generates repeatedly until the subqueries match given facts. This may lead to repeated subqueries or, when recursive rules exist, infinite recursion. To address this problem, *tabling* memoizes answers to subqueries, and reuses them when possible.

Variant tabling [6] is the dominant tabling strategy. It stores and reuses the answers to *variants* of previously encountered subqueries, where a subquery is a variant of another if they are equal modulo variable renaming.

Subsumptive tabling [21] reuses more answers by considering previous subqueries that *subsume* a new query, not only previous queries that are variants of the new query. A subquery q_1 *subsumes* subquery q_2 if there is a substitution θ of variables such that $\theta(q_1) = q_2$.

Precise complexity analysis for variant tabling has been studied recently [27]. We describe precise complexity analysis for subsumptive tabling in Section 3.

Demand-driven transformations for bottom-up evaluation. Bottom-up evaluation starts with given facts, infers new facts from conclusions of rules whose hypotheses match existing facts, and does so repeatedly until all facts are inferred. In this work, by *bottom-up evaluation*, we refer to the optimal bottom-up evaluation method of Liu and Stoller [16] that can be systematically analyzed for time and space complexities.

Bottom-up evaluation infers all facts that can possibly be inferred without taking the given query into account, and thus may take asymptotically more time than necessary. To take the query into account, a source-level transformation, like the well-known magic set transformation (MST) [3], is performed. *Demand transformation* [27] is such a transformation that results in rules with the same time complexity and better space complexity in program size by improving the annotations used in MST. It transforms a set of rules and a query into a new set of rules, such that the set of facts that can be inferred from the new set of rules contains only facts that would be inferred during a top-down evaluation of the original rules with variant tabling. We call this transformation *variant demand transformation* in this paper.

There exists no transformation analogous to subsumptive tabling for bottom-up evaluation. We develop the first such transformation, called *subsumptive demand transformation*, in Section 4.

Terminology. We refer to the different evaluation methods described above as follows:

- *v-topdown*: Top-down evaluation with variant tabling
- *s-topdown*: Top-down evaluation with subsumptive tabling
- *v-bottomup*: Bottom-up evaluation after variant demand transformation
- *s-bottomup*: Bottom-up evaluation after subsumptive demand transformation

The asymptotic time complexities of the above methods are denoted $T_{v-topdn}$, $T_{s-topdn}$, $T_{v-botup}$, $T_{s-botup}$. Similarly, asymptotic space complexities are denoted with S and the corresponding subscripts. For space complexities, we do not consider the stack space used by top-down evaluation. Bottom-up evaluation does not use stack space. For both time and space, the denoted complexities are in data size. We assume that program size, including the number of rules, the number of hypotheses in rules, and the number of arguments of predicates, is constant.

A singleton variable in a Datalog rule is a variable that occurs in one hypothesis and not in other hypotheses or the conclusion. Any set of Datalog rules can be transformed easily into rules that have at most two hypotheses and no singleton variables. We say that rules in this form are in *minimal form*.

An *IDB (intensional database) predicate* is a predicate defined by rules. An *IDB hypothesis* is a hypothesis whose predicate is an IDB predicate.

In examples, we use letters from `p` to `z` for variables, `c` for constants, and `a` for either constant or variable arguments of predicates.

For complexity calculation, we use the following notations.

- `#p`: the number of facts of predicate `p` (given or inferred), called the *size of* `p`.
- `#p.`$i_1,...,i_n/j_1,...,j_m$: the maximum number of combinations of values for the $i_1,...,i_n$th arguments of the facts of predicate `p`, given a fixed combination of values for the $j_1,...,j_m$th arguments.
- `#p.i`: the *actual* number of values of the ith argument of predicate `p`.
- `dom(p.i)`: the size of the domain of the `i`th argument of predicate `p`, i.e., the number of all possible values of that argument of `p`.

Running example. We define a predicate of being *related* as a running example. A person x is related to a person y if x is in an immediate family with y, or if there is a person u in an immediate family with another person v, u is related to x, and v is related to y. This relation can be defined in Datalog using the following two rules:

```
rel(x,y) :- imm(x,y).                          (1)
rel(x,y) :- imm(u,v), rel(u,x), rel(v,y).  (2)
```

For example, given these two rules and a query `rel(x,y)?`, a subquery `rel(c,x)?` for some constant `c` will be generated from the second hypothesis of the second rule. In variant tabling, this subquery will be used to generate more subqueries. In subsumptive tabling, since the given query subsumes this subquery, the answers to the subquery will be looked up in the table entry for the given query.

3. COMPLEXITY ANALYSIS OF SUBSUMPTIVE TABLING FOR TOP-DOWN EVALUATION

For analyzing the time and space complexities of top-down evaluation with subsumptive tabling, we make the following assumptions:

- *Depth-first scheduling* is used. This selects the next subqueries to evaluate in a depth-first manner. For v-topdown, the selection of the scheduling strategy does not change the complexities, since each distinct subquery is guaranteed to be processed, regardless of when. But, for s-topdown, the order of evaluation of subqueries may change whether a subquery is processed or not, since a subsuming one may have been encountered before in an order, and may not have been encountered in another. We show complexity analyses for depth-first scheduling, and then describe the changes necessary for other dominant scheduling strategies.
- *No early completion* is used. This uses all relevant rules to infer answers to a subquery the first time it is evaluated, even when it is a subquery whose arguments are all bound and has been evaluated to be true.
- All IDB predicates are tabled. This allows for the best asymptotic time complexity.
- All predicates are perfectly indexed. So, it takes constant time to retrieve a fact of a predicate given fixed values for some of its arguments. Not using perfect indices would increase asymptotic complexity by the cost of retrieving facts in the absence of perfect indices. Mainstream implementations of tabling, such as XSB [6] and YAP [8], support perfect indexing.

In this section, we show the calculation of time and space complexities for s-topdown, that it is equal to or better than v-topdown, and that it is equal to or better than MST for rules in a certain minimal form, and we identify a class of rules for which s-topdown is guaranteed to outperform v-topdown and MST.

3.1 Subsumptive binding annotation and complexity analyses

The time complexity of s-topdown is the sum of the number of facts that match the hypotheses in the body of each rule for each subquery that is not looked up in the table. The space complexity is the number of facts stored in the table entries. These are impossible to determine statically, since it is not possible to determine whether a subquery will be looked up or evaluated.

We give a method for obtaining an upper bound on the complexities that is as close as possible to the actual complexities. For easier and more precise calculation of the complexities, we first generate a query and rules annotated with the patterns of argument bindings based on the given query, but whose evaluation using s-topdown is otherwise the same as the given query and rules. Then, we calculate the complexity of evaluating the annotated query and rules.

To annotate a set of rules with respect to a query, we first determine the patterns of argument bindings during the evaluation of the query, called *subsumptive demand patterns*, and then generate an annotated rule for each pattern determined. This method is a generalization of the binding annotation method shown in [27] that is used for v-topdown.

Subsumptive demand patterns. For each subquery, we determine whether it is *guaranteed to be evaluated* during s-topdown, where a subquery is guaranteed to be evaluated if it will be evaluated during s-topdown regardless of what facts are given or inferred. Given a set of rules and a query, each subquery `p(a1,...,ak)` encountered during s-topdown yields an *s-demand pattern* $\langle \mathtt{p}, n, r, g, s\rangle$, where the subquery is the nth hypothesis of rule r, s is a string, called the *pattern string*, of length k whose ith character is 'b' if $\mathtt{a}_i$ is bound, and 'f' otherwise, and g is a boolean value indicating whether this subquery is guaranteed to be evaluated. For an atom `p(a1,...,ak)` and a pattern string `s` of length k, we say that $\mathtt{a}_i$ is *bound by* `s` if the ith character of `s` is 'b'.

An s-demand pattern d is said to subsume another s-demand pattern d_2 if d is guaranteed to be evaluated and any subquery with the pattern d subsumes subqueries with the pattern d_2. Formally, an s-demand pattern $\langle \mathtt{p}, n, r, g, s\rangle$ subsumes an s-demand pattern $\langle \mathtt{p}_2, n_2, r_2, g_2, s_2\rangle$ if g is `true`, and either (i) s contains no 'b's, or (ii) for each j such that the jth character of s is 'b', the jth character of s_2 is 'b', and the hypotheses of r to the left of its nth hypothesis is a subset of the hypotheses of r_2 to the left of its n_2th hypothesis.

S-demand patterns are computed iteratively as follows until no new s-demand patterns can be added. The s-demand pattern of the given query `p(a1,...,ak)` is $\langle \mathtt{p}, 1, \_, \mathtt{true}, s\rangle$, where 1 and _ indicate that the given query can be regarded as the first (and only) hypothesis of a non-existing rule, and the ith character of s is 'b' if $\mathtt{a}_i$ is a constant, and 'f' otherwise. For each computed s-demand pattern $\langle \mathtt{p}, n, r, g, s\rangle$, for each rule r_2 that defines `p`, and for each jth hypothesis h of r_2 whose predicate is an IDB predicate, say, `q`, add an s-demand pattern $\langle \mathtt{q}, j, r_2, g_2, s_2\rangle$, if this s-demand pattern is not subsumed by an s-demand pattern already computed, where g_2 is `true` iff (i) g is `true`, (ii) j is 1, and (iii) the ith character of s_2 is 'b' if the ith argument of h is a constant, appears in a hypothesis to the left of h in r, or is an argument of the conclusion of r bound by s; and 'f' otherwise.

After s-demand patterns are computed, we take the projection of the first and last element of each pattern to obtain a set of predicate-annotation pairs, and use s-demand patterns to refer to only these pairs.

Annotation. For each s-demand pattern $\langle \mathtt{p}, \mathtt{s}\rangle$ computed, and for each rule r that defines `p`, we generate an annotated rule that obeys the pattern string `s`, where the conclusion is annotated with `s`, and each hypothesis is annotated with the pattern string obtained as described above.

Formally, for each s-demand pattern $\langle \mathtt{p}, \mathtt{s}\rangle$, and each rule of the form

```
p(...)  :- h1(...),...,hn(...).
```

we generate the rule

```
p_s(...)  :- h1_s1(...),...,hn_sn(...).
```

where for each $1 \le k \le n$, the ith character of $\mathtt{s}_k$ is 'b' if the ith argument of $\mathtt{h}_k$ is a constant, appears in a hypothesis to the left of $\mathtt{h}_k$, or is an argument of the conclusion bound by `s`, and 'f' otherwise.

For the given query `p(...)?`, the annotated query `p_s(...)?` is generated, where the ith character of `s` is 'b' if the ith argument of the given query is a constant; and 'f' otherwise.

Example. For the rules in the running example and the query `rel(x,y)?`, we show the difference between the annotated rules for v-topdown and s-topdown. For s-topdown, the computed set of s-demand patterns is $\{\langle \mathtt{rel}, \text{'ff'}\rangle\}$, since the given query with both arguments free subsumes all other subsequent subqueries for `rel`, and hence the query `rel_ff(x,y)?` and the following two annotated rules are generated.

```
rel_ff(x,y) :- imm(x,y).                          (1a)
rel_ff(x,y) :- imm(u,v), rel_bf(u,x),             (2a)
               rel_bf(v,y).
```

For v-topdown, since subsumption is not used, the set of demand patterns would be $\{\langle \mathtt{rel}, \text{'ff'}\rangle, \langle \mathtt{rel}, \text{'bf'}\rangle, \langle \mathtt{rel}, \text{'bb'}\rangle\}$, and annotation results in the same annotated query, the two annotated rules above, plus the four annotated rules below:

```
rel_bf(x,y) :- imm(x,y).                          (1b)
rel_bf(x,y) :- imm(u,v), rel_bb(u,x),             (2b)
               rel_bf(v,y).
rel_bb(x,y) :- imm(x,y).                          (1c)
rel_bb(x,y) :- imm(u,v), rel_bb(u,x),             (2c)
               rel_bb(v,y).
```

To the best of our knowledge, subsumptive binding annotation is the first annotation method that considers subsuming queries, and is distinct from previous methods used for v-topdown [27] and predicate splitting [28].

Other scheduling strategies. For local scheduling, batched scheduling, or other scheduling strategies, the method for obtaining the demand patterns need to be modified. The idea is that for each scheduling strategy, one needs to determine a heuristic that identifies subqueries guaranteed to be evaluated. For example, for local scheduling, which retrieves all answers from a subquery before continuing to other hypotheses, a subquery is guaranteed to be evaluated if it is the first hypothesis of a rule whose conclusion is guaranteed to be evaluated. For batched scheduling, which retrieves one answer from a subquery and then continues to other hypothesis, only the given query and the first hypothesis of the first rule that defines the given query is guaranteed to be evaluated.

Using these heuristics, the demand pattern identification method can be modified to obtain the relevant demand patterns, and the same annotation method can be used afterwards.

Time and space complexity analyses. After subsumptive binding annotation, we use the method in [27] on the annotated rules for computing time and space complexities.

The time complexity is the sum of asymptotic complexities incurred by all annotated rules. For an annotated rule, the asymptotic time complexity it incurs is the product of: (1) *local complexity*—the number of different values that the free variables in the rule can take, and (2) *number of invocations*—the number of different values that the bound arguments of the conclusion can take.

The local complexity of a rule is the product of complexity factors incurred by all hypotheses of the rule. Each hypothesis, say `p_s(a1,...,an)`, of r incurs the complexity factor$O($`#p.f1,...,fk/b1,...,bl`$)$, where $\mathtt{f}_i$ is the index of the ith 'f' in s, and $\mathtt{b}_i$ is the index of the ith 'b' in s.

The number of invocations of a rule is the sum of all values possibly taken by its bound arguments in all possible subqueries. This is calculated by considering the hypotheses in all rules that have the same annotation as the conclusion of the rule being analyzed. For each hypothesis in each rule whose annotation is the same as the conclusion of the analyzed rule, we determine how many values the bound arguments take by finding out which argument of which hypotheses bind those arguments.

For the running example, the local complexity of (2a) is $O(\texttt{\#imm} \times \texttt{\#rel.2/1} \times \texttt{\#rel.2/1})$, and the number of invocations is $O(1)$ because there are no bound arguments, based on the annotation of the conclusion being 'ff'. Therefore, the time complexity incurred by (2a) is $O(\texttt{\#imm} \times (\texttt{\#rel.2/1})^2)$.

The space complexity of s-topdown is bound by the number of facts stored. This is the sum, over all s-demand patterns, of the product of (i) the number of distinct table entries for an annotation and (ii) the number of facts for each table entry.

The number of distinct table entries is the number of values that the bound arguments in the conclusion take for an annotated predicate. It can be calculated using the method for calculating the number of invocations in time complexity, where the annotated predicate being analyzed for space complexity is considered as the predicate of the conclusion of the rule being analyzed in the method for calculating the number of invocations.

The number of facts for each table entry is the number of values that the free arguments in the conclusion take for rules defining that annotated predicate. Each free argument in the conclusion is bound by one or more hypotheses, and the number of values it can take is the minimum of the number of values that argument can take in the hypotheses it appears in. The number of facts is calculated as product of the number of values that each free argument in the conclusion can take.

For the running example, the only s-demand pattern is ⟨rel,'ff'⟩, therefore there is $O(1)$ table entries, and the number of facts for that table entry is $O(\texttt{\#rel})$. Hence, the space complexity is $O(\texttt{\#rel})$.

3.2 Subsumptive beats variant and magic sets

We show that s-topdown always beats v-topdown, and therefore beats the magic set transformation (MST) for a form of Datalog rules, which all Datalog rules can be reduced to.

The following lemma shows that the check for subsuming used in s-topdown is more expensive than the check for being variant in v-topdown.

Lemma 1. *Let q be an IDB subquery of k arguments. The first time q is encountered in top-down evaluation, the time complexity of table lookup for q is $O(k)$ in variant tabling, and $O(2^k)$ in subsumptive tabling.*

Proof. In variant tabling, the evaluation looks up whether there is a previous table entry with the same label up to variable renaming, and create it if not. This lookup can be trivially done in $O(k)$ time. Table entry creation can also be done in $O(k)$ time.

In subsumptive tabling, the evaluation needs to look up for every possible subsuming query, whether there is a table with that label. If the query has b bound arguments, there are 2^b queries that subsume q, and b is $O(k)$, therefore table lookup takes $O(2^k)$ time. Table entry creation can be done in $O(k)$ time. Therefore, the total time complexity is $O(2^k)$. □

However, the difference is asymptotic only in the number of arguments, which is considered a constant because it affects only program complexity. This paper considers only data complexity, which is standard practice for data-intensive applications.

We show that the time complexity of s-topdown is no worse than the time complexity of v-topdown. For the theorems below, the time and space complexities are compared for a set of rules and a given query.

Theorem 2 (Subsumptive beats variant in time). $T_{s-topdn} \leq T_{v-topdn}$.

Proof. A subquery generated during s-topdown is guaranteed to be generated during v-topdown, since they follow the same algorithm, except that s-topdown may avoid generating some subqueries. Therefore, the facts inferred during s-topdown is a subset, not necessarily proper, of the facts inferred during v-topdown. Table lookup is more costly in s-topdown as shown in Lemma 1, but it does not affect data complexity. We obtain $T_{s-topdn} \leq T_{v-topdn}$. □

Using a similar argument, we show that s-topdown uses no more space than v-topdown asymptotically.

Theorem 3 (Subsumptive beats variant in space). $S_{s-topdn} \leq S_{v-topdn}$.

Proof. As described in the last proof, the subqueries generated during s-topdown is a subset of the subqueries generated during v-topdown. Therefore, the number of tables created during s-topdown is no more than during v-topdown, and the number of answers stored in tables that exist in both are equal since they both should compute the same answers. Therefore, $S_{s-topdn} \leq S_{v-topdn}$. □

We have established that s-topdown is at worst equal to v-topdown. The following theorem shows that it can in fact be better in both time and space complexities.

Theorem 4 (Subsumptive properly beats variant). *There exists a set of rules and a query for which* $T_{s-topdn} < T_{v-topdn}$ *and* $S_{s-topdn} < S_{v-topdn}$.

Proof. We prove this theorem using the running example. Recall that subsumptive binding annotation of the rules for the query with both arguments free results in rules `(1a)` and `(2a)`, whereas annotation for v-topdown results in the same two rules plus four extra rules.

We have shown that the time complexity incurred by `(2a)` is $O(\texttt{\#imm} \times (\texttt{\#rel.2/1})^2)$. However, for v-topdown, consider annotated rules `(2b)` and `(2c)`, copied below:

```
rel_bf(x,y) :- imm(u,v), rel_bb(u,x), rel_bf(v,y).
rel_bb(x,y) :- imm(u,v), rel_bb(u,x), rel_bb(v,y).
```

The local complexity for `(2c)` is $O(\texttt{\#imm})$, however, there are at least $O((\texttt{\#imm.2})^2)$ invocations to `(2c)` due to the last hypothesis of `(2c)`. Therefore, the time complexity of v-topdown is at least $O(\texttt{\#imm} \times (\texttt{\#imm.2})^2)$.

Now, notice that values for the second argument of `rel` always come from the second argument of `imm`, therefore $O(\texttt{\#imm.2})$ may asymptotically be larger than $O(\texttt{\#rel.2})$, hence $O(\texttt{\#rel.2/1})$, but not vice versa. Therefore, $O(\texttt{\#imm} \times (\texttt{\#rel.2/1})^2)$ is asymptotically smaller than $O(\texttt{\#imm} \times (\texttt{\#imm.2})^2)$. Therefore, we have proven our theorem for time complexity.

For space complexity, we have shown that the space complexity of these two rules for s-topdown is $O(\texttt{\#rel})$, which is optimal since it is only as large as the output. For v-topdown, there are $O((\texttt{\#imm.2})^2)$ table entries created for `rel_bb`, which is asymptotically larger than $O(\texttt{\#rel})$ in the worst case. Therefore, we have proven our theorem for space complexity as well. □

Using Theorems 1-3 and theorems about v-topdown in [27], we establish that s-topdown beats MST for Datalog rules in *minimal form*. First, we recall the following theorem from [27].

Theorem 5 (Variant vs. MST for minimal form). *For rules in minimal form,* $T_{v-botup} = T_{v-topdn}$ *and* $S_{v-topdn} \leq S_{v-botup}$.

Combining Theorem 5 with Theorems 2 and 3, we obtain that for rules in minimal form, s-topdown beats v-bottomup.

Corollary 6 (Subsumptive beats magic sets for minimal form). *For rules in minimal form,* $T_{s-topdn} \leq T_{v-botup}$ *and* $S_{s-topdn} \leq S_{v-botup}$.

Finally, we give a class of rules for which the time complexity of s-topdown is better than v-topdown and v-bottomup. The main property of this class is that there are asymptotically more subsumed subqueries than answers to such subqueries in s-topdown.

Theorem 7 (A class of rules for which subsumptive properly beats variant). *Let P be a set of Datalog rules and a query. If there is a rule r in P such that (i) during s-topdown evaluation, r will be used to infer answers for a query q, and the subqueries generated by a hypothesis in r are properly subsumed by q, (ii) the pattern string of those subqueries used for the conclusion of r do not bind any variables of the first hypothesis of r, (iii) the number of facts that match those subqueries is asymptotically smaller than the number of those subqueries. Then,* $T_{s-topdn} < T_{v-topdn}$ *for P.*

Proof. We analyze a set of rules and a query that satisfy the given properties. Let Q be the set of subqueries generated as described in (i), and q be the subsuming query. r is guaranteed to match all subqueries in Q, since it matches q that subsumes them. Therefore, in v-topdown, r would be used to infer answers to each subquery in Q, but in s-topdown evaluation, subqueries in Q are discarded since a subsuming query q has already been generated.

Note that each subquery in Q contains at least one more bound argument than q, since q properly subsumes subqueries in Q. Due to (ii), that bound argument does not filter any facts of the first hypothesis of r for queries in Q during v-topdown. Therefore, the complexity of v-topdown includes the product of the number of subqueries in Q and the size of the predicate of the first hypothesis of r. The complexity of s-topdown does not include this complexity since the subqueries in Q are subsumed, and due to q, it includes (as v-topdown), the product of the *answers* to subqueries in Q and the size of the predicate of the first hypothesis. If (iii) is satisfied, then the latter is asymptotically smaller than the former. Therefore, $T_{s-topdn} < T_{v-topdn}$ for P. □

4. SUBSUMPTIVE DEMAND TRANSFORMATION FOR BOTTOM-UP EVALUATION

We have shown that s-topdown beats v-topdown and the analogous transformation MST for bottom-up evaluation. However, there has been no transformation analogous to subsumptive tabling for bottom-up evaluation. In this section, we develop *subsumptive demand transformation* (SDT) for which bottom-up evaluation of the resulting rules has no worse performance than s-topdown, and compare SDT with subsumptive tabling and MST.

4.1 Subsumptive demand transformation

Subsumptive demand transformation transforms a set of rules and a query into a new set of rules, such that the set of facts that can be inferred from the new set of rules contains only facts that would be inferred during v-topdown of the original rules. It adds new rules that define needed facts for each hypothesis in each rule, adds hypotheses to the original rules to restrict computation to infer only needed facts, and adds negated hypotheses to the rules that define needed facts to make use of subsumption. For each s-demand pattern $\langle \texttt{p}, \texttt{s} \rangle$, and for each rule

```
p(...)  :- h1,..., hn.
```

it generates

```
p(...)  :- d_p_s(a1,...,ak), h1,..., hn.
```

where `d_p_s` is a new predicate, called *demand predicate*, and $\texttt{a}_1,\ldots,\texttt{a}_k$ are arguments of the conclusion that are bound by s. The added hypotheses restrict the rules to infer only facts necessary. The demand predicates are defined as follows. For the given query, p(a_1,...,a_k)?, the following fact is generated

```
d_p_s(a_b1,...,a_bl).
```

where a_{b1},...,a_{bl} are the constant arguments of the query, and s is the pattern string of the query. For each rule r generated, c :- h_0,..., h_n., and for each h_i of an IDB predicate p, the following rule is generated

```
d_p_s(a1,...,ak) :- h0,..., h(i-1),
                    not d_p_s1(...), ...
```

where a_1,...,a_k are the bound arguments of h_i, s is the pattern string of h_i, and there is a negated hypothesis not d_p_s_j(...) for each pattern string s_j that *properly subsumes* s, over those arguments among a_1,...,a_k that are bound by s_i. A pattern string s_1 of length n properly subsumes a pattern string s_2 of length n iff s_1 and s_2 are different, and for each i less than n, the ith character of s_1 is either 'f' or the same as the ith character of s_2. The negated hypotheses ensure that no demand has been inferred that would correspond to a subsuming query in s-topdown.

For the rules in the running example, and the query rel(c,y)?, the s-demand patterns are ⟨rel,'bf'⟩ and ⟨rel,'bb'⟩, and subsumptive demand transformation results in the following rules:

```
rel(x,y) :- d_rel_bf(x), imm(x,y).           (1bf)
rel(x,y) :- d_rel_bf(x), imm(u,v),
            rel(u,x), rel(v,y).               (2bf)
rel(x,y) :- d_rel_bb(x,y), imm(x,y).         (1bb)
rel(x,y) :- d_rel_bb(x,y), imm(u,v),         (2bb)
            rel(u,x), rel(v,y).
d_rel_bf(c).                                  (Q)
d_rel_bb(u,x) :- d_rel_bf(x), imm(u,v),      (2bf.3)
                 not d_rel_bf(u),
                 not d_rel_fb(x),
                 not d_rel_ff.
d_rel_bf(v) :- d_rel_bf(x), imm(u,v),        (2bf.4)
               rel(u,x),
               not d_rel_ff.
d_rel_bb(u,x) :- d_rel_bb(x,y), imm(u,v).    (2bb.3)
                 not d_rel_bf(u),
                 not d_rel_fb(x),
                 not d_rel_ff.
d_rel_bb(u,x) :- d_rel_bb(x,y), imm(u,v),    (2bb.4)
                 rel(u,x).
                 not d_rel_bf(u),
                 not d_rel_fb(x),
                 not d_rel_ff.
```

where each rule (Ns) is generated from rule (N) for the pattern string s, the fact (Q) is generated from the given query, and each rule (Ns.M) captures the demand due to the Mth hypothesis of rule (Ns).

Finally, each resulting rule is split into rules of two hypotheses from left to right. This transformation coupled with the bottom-up evaluation provides an implementation method with the same time complexity as and better space complexity than v-bottomup.

This transformation follows the same method as variant demand transformation, except that it uses subsumptive demand patterns and inserts the negated hypotheses for subsumption of demand facts.

Handling negation. SDT introduces negated hypotheses to rules, and negation in Datalog may be interpreted under several different semantics. To match the behavior of subsumptive tabling, we use *inflationary semantics* [12] for negation in bottom-up evaluation. It is a temporal semantics. It checks whether a fact exists at the time when the negation is encountered. In other words, when there exists a substitution of variables in the rule such that all non-negated hypotheses of the rule are facts, then the negated hypotheses under that substitution are checked whether any of them has currently been inferred as a fact. If none has been inferred as a fact, the rule is used to infer the conclusion under the substitution as a fact. We call bottom-up evaluation extended with inflationary semantics *inflationary bottom-up evaluation.*

During inflationary bottom-up evaluation, a fact may be considered false at one point, and true at a later point. We show that the implementation of the rules obtained by SDT with inflationary semantics infers the same facts of the given predicates as the rules obtained by variant demand transformation, therefore SDT preserves correctness.

Theorem 8. *Let P be a set of Datalog rules and a query, P_v be the rules obtained by variant demand transformation from P, and P_s be the rules obtained by subsumptive demand transformation from P. Then, for each predicate p in P, the bottom-up evaluation of P_v and inflationary bottom-up evaluation of P_s infer the same facts of p.*

Proof. The rules that define given predicates are the same in P_v and P_s; only rules that define demand predicates from SDT have additional negated hypotheses. Suppose a fact d of a demand predicate is inferred in bottom-up evaluation of P_v and not in the bottom-up evaluation of P_s, and that d is used to infer a fact f of a given predicate. Then, for the rule used to infer d in P_v, during bottom-up evaluation of P_s, all positive hypotheses were satisfied, but at least one of the negated hypothesis was not satisfied due to a fact d'. By definition of the rule, d' is a demand fact that corresponds to a query subsuming the query corresponding to d, therefore there exists a rule that infers f using d'. Hence, the evaluation of P_v does not infer more facts for given predicates than the evaluation of P_s.

For the other direction, since the evaluation is monotonic, the evaluation of P_s cannot infer more facts than the evaluation of P_v. □

Scheduling in bottom-up. We have shown that the order of subqueries are important for s-topdown as discussed in Section 3. Analogously, the order of demand facts inferred and considered is important in s-bottomup. In inflationary bottom-up evaluation, facts are processed in an undefined order. We modify that by considering facts for the demand predicates first, and in the order they are inferred. If no demand facts are left, then we consider facts for given predicates. We call this evaluation method *demand-first inflationary bottom-up evaluation.*

By considering demand facts first and in order, demand-first inflationary bottom-up evaluation mimics s-topdown. The only difference that remains is the retrieval order of facts of given predicates. We have not defined such an order for s-topdown either, and in practice, different systems may opt for different orders. From now on, we assume that a particular retrieval order is used for facts of given predicates, and the same order is used during demand-first inflationary bottom-up evaluation.

For P being a set of rules and a query, we call the demand-first inflationary bottom-up evaluation of the rules resulting from SDT of P, *s-bottomup* of P.

4.2 Relationship to subsumptive tabling and MST

By using the analogy in the inferred demand facts and encountered subqueries, we first show that s-bottomup beats s-topdown in time complexity.

Theorem 9 (S-bottomup beats s-topdown in time). $T_{s-botup} \leq T_{s-topdn}$.

Proof. Let P be a set of rules and a query. Let P_a be the set of rules and query after subsumptive binding annotation of P, and P_s be the set of rules obtained by SDT of P.

For a rule r in P_a of the form `p(...) :- body.`, the complexity incurred by r for $T_{s-topdn}$ is $i \times l$, where i is *the number of invocations* of r, and l is *the local complexity*, which is the product of the sizes of hypotheses.

For each such rule r, there is a rule r' in P_s of the form `p(...) :- d(...), body, negated_hypos.`, where `d(...)` is the new demand hypothesis. In s-bottomup, facts of `d` in r' are obtained from all queries of `p`, in s-topdown, whose s-demand pattern is captured by `d`. S-bottomup ceases to infer new facts for `d` in the same asymptotic time as it would take for s-topdown to reach a subquery subsuming the query corresponding to the demand of `d`, since the scheduling for s-bottomup is analogous to s-topdown. Therefore, `#d` $= i$. For $T_{s-botup}$, the complexity incurred by a rule is the number of times the rule fires. Therefore, the complexity incurred by r' has an upper bound `#d`$\times l = i \times l$. Note that the negated hypotheses do not incur additional time complexity since they require constant-time lookups in the set of facts inferred.

The only rules in P_s that do not correspond to a rule in P_a are the rules that infer facts of the demand predicates. The additional complexity incurred for $T_{s-botup}$ by each such rule is already dominated by a component of the complexity in $T_{s-topdn}$, because this complexity equals the number of invocations for the rule that the demand hypothesis would be added to, and the number of invocations is used as a factor in a summand of $T_{s-topdn}$.

Hence, $T_{s-botup} \leq T_{s-topdn}$. □

For space complexity, the result is the opposite.

Theorem 10 (S-topdown beats s-bottomup in space). $S_{s-topdn} \leq S_{s-botup}$.

Proof. S-topdown and s-bottomup infer the same set of facts for IDB predicates in the given rules. $S_{s-topdn}$ consists of the space used by these facts in the tables. $S_{s-botup}$ also contains the size of predicates introduced when the rules are split to contain at most two hypotheses. Therefore, $S_{s-topdn} \leq S_{s-botup}$. □

We show that s-bottomup and s-topdown have the same time complexity for rules in minimal form. This is as in the case between v-topdown and v-bottomup [27]. For this purpose, we reuse the lemma from [27] below.

Lemma 11. *In bottom-up evaluation, if all variables in the hypotheses of a rule r are also in the conclusion of r, then the number of facts inferred using r equals the number of firings of r.*

Theorem 12 (S-bottomup equals s-topdown for minimal form). *For rules in minimal form, $T_{s-botup} = T_{s-topdn}$.*

Proof. Let P be a set of rules and a query. Let P_a be the set of rules and query after subsumptive binding annotation of P, and P_s be the set of rules obtained by SDT of P. Each rule r in P_a is of one of two forms:

(i) r has one hypothesis, and so has the form `c :- h.` In P_s, there is a rule r' corresponding to r, and is of the form `c :- d, h.`, where `d` is the new demand hypothesis. The complexity incurred by r' to $T_{s-botup}$ and by r to $T_{s-topdn}$ are both dominated by the size of the predicate of `h`, since `h` contains all variables in `d`.

(ii) r has two hypotheses, and so has the form `c :- h1, h2.` In P_s, there is a rule r' corresponding to r, and is of the form `c :- d, h1, h2.`, where `d` is the demand hypothesis added. As before, the complexity incurred by r to $T_{s-topdn}$, denoted $T_{s-topdn}(r)$, equals the product of the sizes of the predicates `d`, `h1`, and `h2`, and the number of facts of `d` and the number of invocations to the rule is the same as argued in Theorem 9. However, bottom-up computation can decompose the rules to possibly improve performance. In this case, it would obtain the following two rules: `new :- d, h1.` and `c :- new, h2.` The complexity of the first rule is less than $T_{s-topdn}(r)$. The variables of `d` must appear in `new`, because they appear in `c`, and the variables of `h1` must appear in `new` because there are no singleton variables in the rule. Then, by the lemma above, the size of the predicate of `new` equals the running time of the rule that generates it, and hence the complexity incurred by the second rule obtained from r' equals $T_{s-topdn}(r)$.

Therefore, for each complexity summand incurred by rules in P_a for $T_{s-topdn}$, there is a rule in P_s that incurs the same complexity summand for $T_{s-botup}$. Combining this with Theorem 9, which states that $T_{s-botup} \leq T_{s-topdn}$, we obtain $T_{s-botup} = T_{s-topdn}$. □

To compare s-bottomup and v-bottomup, note that Theorem 8 implies that s-bottomup beats v-bottomup in space complexity, because both infer the same facts for the given predicates per Theorem 8 and s-bottomup may infer fewer facts for demand predicates.

For time complexity, s-bottomup beats v-bottomup due to Theorem 12 and Corollary 6, and is asymptotically faster for the class of rules and queries described in Theorem 7 due to the aforementioned results. Therefore, we obtain the following corollary.

Corollary 13. $T_{s-botup} \leq T_{v-botup}$ *and* $S_{s-botup} \leq S_{v-botup}$.

For the rules described in Theorem 7, $T_{s-botup} < T_{v-botup}$ and $S_{s-botup} < S_{v-botup}$.

5. SUBSUMPTION OPTIMIZATION

We have shown that s-topdown beats v-topdown, and s-bottomup beats v-bottomup. However, there are cases when the subsumptive methods are not effective because subqueries that subsume others appear later during evaluation, and the complexity may have been reduced if they had appeared earlier. In this section, we show a transformation method to ensure that subqueries that subsume others for s-topdown and s-bottomup are processed first. We first show the effectiveness of the method for s-topdown, and then show that it works for s-bottomup as well. We call this transformation *subsumption optimization*.

The method first identifies demand patterns that should be subsumed, and then transforms the rules so that any subquery with such a demand pattern is subsumed during s-topdown.

(i) Identification of demand patterns to subsume. For a set s of demand patterns of a predicate determined for the given rules and query, the method generates all sets of subsuming demand patterns, and generates annotated rules for each such set. Then, for each set of the resulting rules, we compare the time complexity of the resulting annotated rules with the original annotated rules. If it can be proven that the asymptotic time complexity of the resulting rules due to a set s_2 of subsuming demand patterns is lower than the original annotated rules, then we say that the demand patterns in s should be subsumed by the demand patterns in s_2.

For rules (1) and (2) in the running example, and the query `rel(c,y)?`, the demand patterns are ⟨`rel`,'`bf`'⟩ and ⟨`rel`,'`bb`'⟩. The rules obtained by subsumptive binding annotation are:

```
rel_bf(x,y) :- imm(x,y).
rel_bf(x,y) :- imm(u,v), rel_bb(u,x), rel_bf(v,y).
rel_bb(x,y) :- imm(x,y).
rel_bb(x,y) :- imm(u,v), rel_bb(u,x), rel_bb(v,y).
```

It would be asymptotically better in time complexity if the calls to `rel_bb` were subsumed by previously encountered `rel_bf` subqueries. The intuition is that if the outdegree of the `rel` relation is not constant, then asymptotically many more queries to `rel_bb` may be made than the ones that would be relevant due to the last rule. Therefore, the call with pattern ⟨`rel`,'`bb`'⟩ should be subsumed by the call with pattern ⟨`rel`,'`bf`'⟩.

(ii) Transformation. For each s-demand pattern ⟨`p`, `s`⟩ for calls that should be subsumed by calls with pattern ⟨`p`, `s2`⟩, for each hypothesis $\texttt{p}(\texttt{a}_1, \ldots, \texttt{a}_n)$ whose pattern string is `s` in a rule, we generate the following rule:

$\texttt{q}(\texttt{a}_{b1}, \ldots, \texttt{a}_{bk})$:- $\texttt{p}(\texttt{a}_1, \ldots, \texttt{a}_n)$.

where `q` is a fresh predicate name, and $\texttt{a}_{b1}, \ldots, \texttt{a}_{bk}$ are those arguments among $\texttt{a}_1, \ldots, \texttt{a}_n$ that are bound by `s2`. Then, before this hypothesis in r, we insert $\texttt{q}(\texttt{a}_{b1}, \ldots, \texttt{a}_{bk})$ as a hypothesis. After this transformation, a subquery that subsumes the subquery by the original ith hypothesis $\texttt{p}(\texttt{a}_1, \ldots, \texttt{a}_n)$ will be guaranteed to be made first during s-topdown, so all subqueries with the demand pattern ⟨`p`, `s`⟩ will be avoided.

For the second rule in the running example, the second hypothesis is the only hypothesis whose pattern string '`bb`' should be avoided. Thus, this rule is transformed into the following two rules.

```
new(u) :-  rel(u,x).
rel_bf(x,y) :- imm(u,v), new(u), rel(u,x), rel(v,y).
```

We prove that subsumption optimization preserves the semantics of the original set of rules.

Theorem 14. *Let P be a set of Datalog rules and a query. For each given predicate of P, s-topdown of P and s-topdown of the rules resulting from subsumption optimization infer the same facts.*

Proof. The rules after subsumption optimization are more restricted due to added hypotheses, so s-topdown of those rules cannot infer more facts than s-topdown of P. However, they cannot infer fewer either, since the added hypotheses are defined by rules whose hypothesis subsume existing hypotheses, therefore they cannot be false while all other hypotheses are true. Hence, s-topdown of P and s-topdown of the rules after subsumption optimization infer the same facts for given predicates. □

We show that this transformation achieves the same effect for s-bottomup, by showing that the introduced hypotheses and rules ensure that demand facts cannot be inferred for demand patterns that the optimization determines to subsume.

Theorem 15. *Let P be a set of Datalog rules and a query. The s-bottomup of P after subsumption optimization does not infer any fact for the demand predicates that correspond to the demand patterns that the optimization determines to subsume.*

Proof. For any hypothesis h with a demand pattern that the optimization determines to subsume, the transformation introduces a new hypothesis to its left. For that hypothesis to be true, the demand fact that corresponds to a subsuming demand pattern must be inferred by construction of the transformation. Thus, when all of the hypotheses to the left of h is true, a demand fact corresponding to a demand pattern subsuming the demand pattern for h must have been inferred. Therefore, no fact can be inferred for demand predicates of demand patterns that the optimization determines to subsume. □

Application to demand-driven pointer analysis. We show that by applying subsumption optimization to the specification of Andersen's pointer analysis for C [2], we automatically derive Heintze and Tardieu's algorithm for demand-driven pointer analysis [11], and our complexity analysis can be used to obtain precise time and space complexities.

Given a C program, statements in a program relevant to pointer analysis can be reduced to four kinds, which can be represented directly as Datalog facts:

- `p = &q` is represented by `bare_addr(p,q)`.
- `p = q` is represented by `bare_bare(p,q)`.
- `p = *q` is represented by `bare_star(p,q)`.
- `*p = q` is represented by `star_bare(p,q)`.

Andersen's pointer analysis can be specified directly using four Datalog rules, where `pt(p,q)` denotes `p` points to `q`:

```
pt(p,q) :- bare_addr(p,q).                          (A1)
pt(p,q) :- bare_bare(p,r), pt(r,q).                 (A2)
pt(p,q) :- bare_star(p,s), pt(s,r), pt(r,q).        (A3)
pt(p,q) :- star_bare(r,s), pt(r,p), pt(s,q).        (A4)
```

Given a query `pt(c,q)?`, the s-demand patterns are ⟨`pt`,'`bf`'⟩ and ⟨`pt`,'`bb`'⟩. Subsumptive binding annotation yields:

```
pt_bf(p,q) :- bare_addr_bf(p,q).
pt_bf(p,q) :- bare_bare_bf(p,r), pt_bf(r,q).
pt_bf(p,q) :- bare_star_bf(p,s), pt_bf(s,r),
              pt_bf(r,q).
pt_bf(p,q) :- star_bare_ff(r,s), pt_bb(r,p),
              pt_bf(s,q).

pt_bb(p,q) :- bare_addr_bb(p,q).
pt_bb(p,q) :- bare_bare_bf(p,r), pt_bb(r,q).
pt_bb(p,q) :- bare_star_bf(p,s), pt_bf(s,r),
              pt_bb(r,q).
pt_bb(p,q) :- star_bare_ff(r,s), pt_bb(r,p),
              pt_bb(s,q).
```

Our complexity analysis can be used to show that asymptotically more queries to `pt_bb` may be made than the ones that would be relevant due to the last two rules generated. The number of calls to `pt_bb` may be as many as v^2 where v is the number of variables in the C program. However, the `pt` relation may not be as dense as $O(v^2)$. Due to this fact, the complexity of the last rule defining `pt_bb` is $O(\texttt{\#star\_bare\_ff} \times v^2)$. This is greater than the complexity of the last rule defining `pt_bf`, which is $O(\texttt{\#star\_bare\_ff} \times \texttt{\#pt.2/1} \times v)$. Therefore, ⟨`pt`,'`bb`'⟩ should be subsumed by ⟨`pt`,'`bf`'⟩ so that the last four rules are not generated. Subsumption optimization results in the rules `(A1)`, `(A2)`, `(A3)`, and the following two rules due to `(A4)`:

```
new(r) :- pt(r,p).
pt(p,q) :- star_bare(r,s), new(r), pt(r,p), pt(s,q).
```

S-bottomup of the resulting rules corresponds precisely to Heintze and Tardieu's algorithm, and performing precise complexity analysis gives the explanation for when and why the algorithm is efficient.

6. EXPERIMENTS

We support our complexity analyses and comparisons by experiments. For s-topdown and v-topdown, we use XSB [6]. For v-bottomup and s-bottomup, we use the implementation method of [16] modified with the described extensions when necessary to generate Python code from the rules.

We instantiate the complexity parameters in predicted complexities with their values computed from the data. We use *space units* to mean the number of unique table inserts for v- and s-topdown, and the number of facts inferred plus the number of elements in auxiliary maps [16] for v- and s-bottomup. We use *returns* to mean the number of facts returned from rule invocations for tabled top-down evaluation, and *firings* to mean the number of firings for demand-driven bottom-up evaluation.

In our benchmarks, predicates have two arguments. For experiments, we first fix `#p` and `#p.1/2` for each input predicate `p`, and generate a set of data such that the size of each predicate is maximal, i.e., the worst-case behavior is exhibited. Then, we increase `#p` and `#p.1/2` to generate the next set of data, and repeat.

We first show experimental results for the running example and the demand-driven pointer analysis problem.

For a query with both arguments free for the running example, we confirm the asymptotic time and space complexities analyzed. The left plot in Figure 1 for the running example shows that s-topdown and s-bottomup are asymptotically faster than v-topdown and v-bottomup, respectively, as predicated by Theorems 2 and 4, and by Corollary 13, respectively. It also shows that s-bottomup is asymptotically faster than s-topdown, due to splitting of rules into two hypotheses each, as predicated by Theorem 9.

The right plot in Figure 1 for the running example shows that the space usage of v- and s-topdown is much smaller than v-bottomup and s-bottomup, respectively. This is because s-bottomup infers facts for demand predicates and the predicates introduced for splitting rules, and maintains auxiliary maps. Demand predicates are avoided in top-down evaluation by backtracking, which uses stack space that this paper does not consider. Predicates introduced for splitting rules allow s-bottomup to be faster than s-topdown as shown in Theorem 9. Auxiliary maps are avoided in s-topdown by separate indexing mechanisms (such as tries in XSB), whose space is not counted separately in this paper. The plot also shows that the space usage of s-topdown and s-bottomup is smaller than v-topdown and v-bottomup, respectively, due to fewer facts being inferred, as shown in Theorems 3 and 4, and in Corollary 13, respectively

For demand-driven pointer analysis, and a query with the first argument bound, we apply subsumption optimization to the rules and confirm the asymptotic improvement in time complexity against s-bottomup, and show the difference in space usage. Figure 2 for demand-driven pointer analysis confirms that subsumption optimization improves time complexity and reduces space usage.

We also performed experiments on a well-known benchmark in semantic web [15] that has 961 rules and 654 facts; and we also performed the pointer analysis on real data from a C program with 2430 facts. Both queries run out of memory in XSB when v-topdown is used on a machine with 4 GB of RAM, but when s-topdown is used, the ontology query runs in 12 seconds, and the pointer analysis runs in under 0.1 seconds.

Finally, to compare our results with existing SQL database implementations, we converted the rules of the running example into SQL queries and performed experiments on MSSQL, one of the few SQL databases that support recursion. The running example timed out (more than 10 minutes) on all of our data points except for the smallest two. The variant and subsumptive demand transformations cannot be used on SQL databases because no mainstream SQL database implementation supports mutual recursion, and demand transformations result in mutually recursive rules.

7. RELATED WORK AND CONCLUSION

Datalog has been extensively studied [5, 1]. Variant tabling was introduced in the 1980s [25], and has been widely studied. It has been implemented in top-down evaluation engines such as XSB [6] and YAP [8]. Subsumptive tabling was introduced ten years later [21], but has not been studied widely, and has only been implemented in XSB.

The time and space complexity of variant tabling for Datalog was given an imprecise upper bound in [29], and a method for precise calculation of the time and space complexities of variant tabling for Datalog is given in [27]. There is no prior work on complexity analysis of subsumptive tabling to the best of our knowledge. Our work builds on [27] to present the first method for precise calculation of worst-case time and space complexities of subsumptive tabling, and establishes that it beats variant tabling.

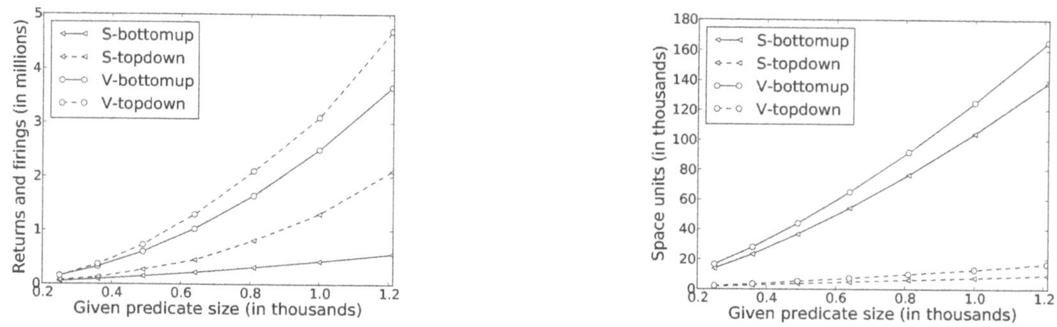

Figure 1: Firings/returns and space units for v-topdown, v-bottomup, s-topdown, and s-bottomup for the running example.

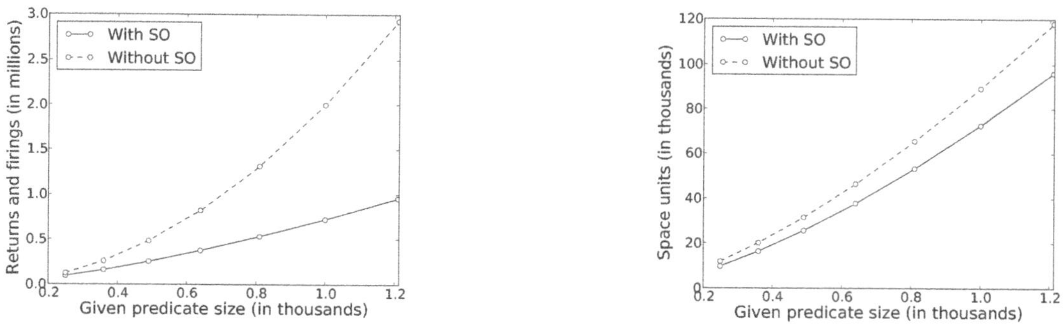

Figure 2: Firings/returns and space units for s-bottomup with and without subsumption optimization (SO) for the pointer analysis benchmark.

For bottom-up evaluation, transformations for demand-driven evaluation have been studied, including the well-known magic-set transformation (MST) [3] and the recent demand transformation [27] that our work extends. It has been shown that both of these transformations are equivalent to variant tabling both operationally [4] and in terms of complexities [27]. We show that subsumptive tabling beats MST, and then give the first transformation, subsumptive demand transformation, so that bottom-up evaluation of resulting rules is similar to subsumptive tabling. We show that the complexity of the resulting rules from this new transformation beats subsumptive tabling and MST in time complexity.

The relationship between top-down and bottom-up evaluation has been studied in a variety of contexts with different flavors of rules [20, 28, 19, 4]. Our work is the first to establish precise relationships between variant and subsumptive tabling, and MST and the new subsumptive demand transformation.

By characterizing improvement using complexity analysis, we also introduce a new transformation, subsumption optimization, to reuse as many facts as possible. We have shown that our methods can be used to systematically derive a well-known demand-driven pointer analysis algorithm [11].

Additionally, we have implemented our method and confirmed our analysis results through experiments on well-studied benchmarks.

8. REFERENCES

[1] S. Abiteboul, R. Hull, and V. Vianu. *Foundations of Databases*. Addison-Wesley, 1995.

[2] L. O. Andersen. Program analysis and specialization for the C programming language. Technical report, DIKU, Department of Computer Science, University of Copenhagen, 1994.

[3] C. Beeri and R. Ramakrishnan. On the power of magic. *J. Logic Programming*, 10(1/2/3&4):255–299, 1991.

[4] F. Bry. Query evaluation in deductive databases: Bottom-up and top-down reconciled. *Data Knowledge Engineering*, 5:289–312, 1990.

[5] S. Ceri, G. Gottlob, and L. Tanca. *Logic Programming and Databases*. Springer, 1990.

[6] W. Chen and D. S. Warren. Tabled evaluation with delaying for general logic programs. *J. ACM*, 43(1):20–74, 1996.

[7] S. S. Cosmadakis, H. Gaifman, P. C. Kanellakis, and M. Y. Vardi. Decidable optimization problems for database logic programs (preliminary report). In *Proc. of the 20th Annual ACM Symp. on Theory of Computing*, pages 477–490, 1988.

[8] A. F. da Silva and V. S. Costa. The design of the YAP compiler: An optimizing compiler for logic programming languages. *J. of Universal Computer Science*, 12(7):764–787, 2006.

[9] J. DeTreville. Binder, a logic-based security language.

In *Proc. of the 2002 IEEE Symp. on Security and Privacy (S&P)*, pages 105–113, 2002.

[10] E. Hajiyev, M. Verbaere, and O. de Moor. *CodeQuest: Scalable source code queries with Datalog*. In *Proc. of the 20th European Conf. on Object-Oriented Programming (ECOOP)*, pages 2–27, 2006.

[11] N. Heintze and O. Tardieu. Demand-driven pointer analysis. In *Proc. of the 2001 ACM SIGPLAN Conf. on Programming Language Design and Implementation (PLDI)*, pages 24–34, 2001.

[12] P. G. Kolaitis and C. H. Papadimitriou. Why not negation by fixpoint? *J. Comput. Syst. Sci.*, 43(1):125–144, 1991.

[13] A. Y. Levy and Y. Sagiv. Semantic query optimization in Datalog programs. In *Proc. of the 14th ACM SIGACT-SIGMOD-SIGART Symp. on Principles of Database Systems (PODS)*, pages 163–173, 1995.

[14] N. Li and J. C. Mitchell. Datalog with constraints: A foundation for trust management languages. In *Proc. of the 5th Intl. Symp. on Practical Aspects of Declarative Languages (PADL)*, pages 58–73, 2003.

[15] S. Liang, P. Fodor, H. Wan, and M. Kifer. OpenRuleBench: An analysis of the performance of rule engines. In *Proc. of the 18th Intl. Conf. on World Wide Web (WWW)*, pages 601–610, 2009.

[16] Y. A. Liu and S. D. Stoller. From Datalog rules to efficient programs with time and space guarantees. *ACM Trans. Programming Languages and Systems*, 31(6):21:1–21:38, August 2009.

[17] B. T. Loo, T. Condie, M. N. Garofalakis, D. E. Gay, J. M. Hellerstein, P. Maniatis, R. Ramakrishnan, T. Roscoe, and I. Stoica. Declarative networking. *Communications of the ACM*, 52(11):87–95, 2009.

[18] R. Ramakrishnan. Magic templates: A spellbinding approach to logic programs. In *Proc. of the 5th Intl. Conf. and Symp. on Logic Programming*, pages 140–159, 1988.

[19] R. Ramakrishnan and S. Sudarshan. Top-down versus bottom-up revisited. In *Proc. of of the 1991 Intl. Symp. on Logic Programming (ISLP)*, pages 321–336, 1991.

[20] R. Ramakrishnan and J. D. Ullman. A survey of deductive database systems. *J. Logic Programming*, 23(2):125–149, 1995.

[21] P. Rao, C. R. Ramakrishnan, and I. V. Ramakrishnan. A thread in time saves tabling time. In *Proc. of the 1996 Joint Intl. Conf. and Symp. on Logic Programming*, pages 112–126, 1996.

[22] Y. Sagiv. Optimizing Datalog programs. In *Foundations of Deductive Databases and Logic Programming*, pages 659–698. Morgan Kaufmann, 1988.

[23] D. Sereni, P. Avgustinov, and O. de Moor. Adding magic to an optimising Datalog compiler. In *Proc. of the ACM SIGMOD Intl. Conf. on Management of Data (SIGMOD)*, pages 553–566, 2008.

[24] W. Shen, A. Doan, J. F. Naughton, and R. Ramakrishnan. Declarative information extraction using Datalog with embedded extraction predicates. In *Proc. of the 33rd Intl. Conf. on Very Large Data Bases (VLDB)*, pages 1033–1044, 2007.

[25] H. Tamaki and T. Sato. OLD resolution with tabulation. In *Proc. of the 3rd Intl. Conf. on Logic Programming (ICLP)*, pages 84–98, 1986.

[26] K. T. Tekle, M. Gorbovitski, and Y. A. Liu. Graph queries through Datalog optimizations. In *Proc. of the 12th Intl. ACM SIGPLAN Conf. on Principles and Practice of Declarative Programming (PPDP)*, pages 25–34, 2010.

[27] K. T. Tekle and Y. A. Liu. Precise complexity analysis for efficient Datalog queries. In *Proc. of the 12th Intl. ACM SIGPLAN Conf. on Principles and Practice of Declarative Programming (PPDP)*, pages 35–44, 2010.

[28] J. D. Ullman. Bottom-up beats top-down for Datalog. In *Proc. of the 8th ACM SIGACT-SIGMOD-SIGART Symp. on Principles of Database Systems (PODS)*, pages 140–149, 1989.

[29] D. S. Warren. Programming in tabled Prolog. Available at http://www.cs.sunysb.edu/~warren/xsbbook/, 1999.

[30] J. Whaley, D. Avots, M. Carbin, and M. S. Lam. Using Datalog with binary decision diagrams for program analysis. In *Proc. of the 3rd Asian Symp. on Programming Languages and Systems (APLAS)*, pages 97–118, 2005.

Author Index

www.ingramcontent.com/pod-product-compliance
Ingram Content Group UK Ltd.
Pitfield, Milton Keynes, MK11 3LW, UK
UKHW051240300926
15471UKWH00015B/1219

9 781450 312608